THE MISSISSIPPI ENCYCLOPEDIA

The MISSISSIPPI ENCYCLOPEDIA

Senior Editors

**Ted Ownby and
Charles Reagan Wilson**

Associate Editors

**Ann J. Abadie, Odie Lindsey,
and James G. Thomas, Jr.**

Sponsored by the Center for the Study of Southern Culture
at the University of Mississippi

University Press of Mississippi / Jackson

The Mississippi Encyclopedia was produced through a major grant from the Phil Hardin Foundation and generous gifts from Lynn and Stewart Gammill and other supporters of the Center for the Study of Southern Culture.

www.upress.state.ms.us

The University Press of Mississippi is a member of the Association of American University Presses.

First printing 2017

∞

Library of Congress Cataloging-in-Publication Data

Names: Ownby, Ted, editor. | Wilson, Charles Reagan, editor. | University of Mississippi. Center for the Study of Southern Culture, sponsoring body.
Title: The Mississippi encyclopedia / Ted Ownby and Charles Reagan Wilson, senior editors ; Ann J. Abadie, Odie Lindsey, and James G. Thomas, Jr., associate editors ; sponsored by the Center for the Study of Southern Culture at the University of Mississippi.
Description: Jackson : University Press of Mississippi, [2017] | Includes bibliographical references and index.
Identifiers: LCCN 2016043630 (print) | LCCN 2016044817 (ebook) | ISBN 9781628466928 (cloth : alk. paper) | ISBN 9781496811615 (mobi) | ISBN 9781496811578 (epub single) | ISBN 9781496811585 (epub institutional) | ISBN 9781496811592 (pdf single) | ISBN 9781496811608 (pdf institutional)
Subjects: LCSH: Mississippi—Encyclopedias.
Classification: LCC F342 .M464 2017 (print) | LCC F342 (ebook) | DDC 976.2003—dc23
LC record available at https://lccn.loc.gov/2016043630

British Library Cataloging-in-Publication Data available

PREFACE

The first time the editors gave a public talk about *The Mississippi Encyclopedia*, the first question was, "Will all of it be negative?" The answer was a polite no, but the question said something about the expectations some readers may have. Mississippi has appeared last on so many lists of state attributes that many residents and others might well wonder whether a heavy academic book on the state is likely to be a tome full of bad news. Others have assumed that such a book should be a celebration of the state and what its people have accomplished.

This book is in fact neither a criticism nor a celebration, though its publication does occur as part of Mississippi's bicentennial celebration. As an encyclopedia, it does not have a thesis, and it has no starting point except to begin with A and continue through Z. *The Mississippi Encyclopedia* attempts above all to be a scholarly work about life in the state, past and present. Through its choices of subjects, we hope to present not just problems but also the stories of people who addressed the problems. Instead of celebrating, the book presents a wide variety of experiences and perspectives. The authors and editors have worked to display the diversity of the state, its people, its politics, its religions, its economy, its arts, and its geography and the dramatic ways all of these facets of life have changed over time. We have relied on and embodied the best recent scholarship and sought to present material that is clear and readable to scholars and nonscholars alike. In addition, many of the entries concern individuals or topics that had not previously been the subject of scholarly work, especially in relation to Mississippi, and we are delighted to have brought them some of the attention they deserve.

Many people have also asked how we went about organizing and writing a book of this length. The answer is that we relied on the expertise developed by the Center for the Study of Southern Culture, which has extensive experience with encyclopedia projects—most notably, the *Encyclopedia of Southern Culture* (University of North Carolina Press, 1989) and its update, *The New Encyclopedia of Southern Culture* (24 vols., University of North Carolina Press, 2006–13). Both of those projects offered models of scholarly, authoritative, inclusive, thorough, and well-written encyclopedias.

The first lesson of encyclopedia work is to rely on experts for suggestions about what to include and who should write those entries. In this case, those authorities included scholars who study Mississippi, many—though not all—of whom live and/or work in the state. The editors of *The Mississippi Encyclopedia* asked thirty leaders in their fields to serve as subject editors on the topics of agriculture, archaeology, architecture, the civil rights movement, the Civil War, contemporary issues, drama, education, ethnicity, environment, fiction, folklife, foodways, geography, government and public policy, industry and industrial workers, law, medicine, music, myths and representations, Native Americans, nonfiction, poetry, politics, the press, religion, social and economic history, sports, visual arts, and women. The subject editors suggested possible entries in those fields and in many cases wrote overview entries. Further suggestions came from numerous other sources, including authors, editors, colleagues, and friends. After the topics had been chosen, managing editors Andrea Driver and subsequently Odie Lindsey worked with the editors and associate editors to communicate with the authors and coordinate the nuts and bolts of the volume. Ultimately, more than six hundred authors contributed nearly fifteen hundred entries. Each of those entries was then reviewed by editors Ann Abadie, Charles Reagan Wilson, Ted Ownby, Odie Lindsey, and James G. Thomas, Jr.

If there are perspectives that mark this work as being distinctive to the Center for the Study of Southern Culture, they are an inclusive approach to the choice of people and topics, attention to cultural expression and cultural meaning, and scholarly concern for the present as well as the past. This project has been an ongoing part of life at the Center for more than a decade, and graduate students in the Southern Studies program contributed numerous entries, checked material, conducted research, and made suggestions.

County histories posed an intriguing challenge. Members of the project staff—primarily Southern Studies graduate students working under the close supervision of the editors—wrote histories of each Mississippi county. We sought to provide similar information for all counties and, using the US census as a starting point, to emphasize how populations and economies have changed.

The entries on Mississippi's governors began as articles David Sansing wrote for *Mississippi History Now*. We use those articles with the kind permission of the Mississippi Department of Archives and History.

James G. Thomas, Jr., associate director for publications at the Center and previously managing editor of *The New Encyclopedia of Southern Culture*, gathered illustrations and helped manage the final few years of the project. He and Becca Walton, the Center's associate director for projects, have contributed in numerous ways.

The University of Mississippi Law School and its dean, Samuel Davis, helped with the writing of law-related entries, and the university's History Department and its chairs, Robert Haws and Joe Ward, helped arrange to have some of their graduate students write entries.

Of course, this encyclopedia, like all such volumes, is far from perfect. The book could have covered many topics more thoroughly, and it could have included entries on many topics that have been left out. In addition, Mississippi is a living entity. Its people continue to change and create—to write new books, to make new music, to pass new laws, to modify their views. Some people pass from the scene, while others arrive to make new contributions. Thus, in some sense, the book is already outdated. But it nonetheless constitutes a valuable resource—a starting point for learning about the state and the people and institutions who have made it what it is today. We trust that other projects will extend this knowledge as Mississippi moves into its third century of statehood. In particular, we hope to create an online version of *The Mississippi Encyclopedia* and to provide updated and expanded material through that venue.

ACKNOWLEDGMENTS

The project began with suggestions from Seetha Srinivasan at the University Press of Mississippi. Former University of Mississippi chancellor Robert Khayat and his chief of staff, Andy Mullins, energetically supported the idea, and Charles Reagan Wilson, Ann Abadie, and Ted Ownby of the Center for the Study of Southern Culture became involved in 2003. Dean Glenn Hopkins of the university's College of Liberal Arts and chancellor Dan Jones have also backed the project.

At the University Press of Mississippi, Press former director Leila Salisbury supported the project with great enthusiasm, and Craig Gill has set high standards and offered encouragement for more than a decade, first as the press's assistant director and editor in chief and now as its director. On the editorial side, Anne Stascavage, Katie Keene, and Shane Gong Stewart have made significant contributions, and copyeditor Ellen Goldlust caught last-minute errors and improved awkward sentences. Margaret Gaffney and Rebecca Lauck Cleary joined the process to help with proofreading.

The project began with an appropriation from the Mississippi legislature. Grants from the National Endowment for the Humanities, the Mississippi Humanities Council, and the Mississippi Department of Archives and History helped sustain the project, as did funding from the University of Mississippi's College of Liberal Arts. We have benefited greatly from the assistance of Mississippi Department of Archives and History directors Elbert Hilliard, Hank Holmes, and Katie Blount and Mississippi Humanities Council directors Barbara Carpenter and Stuart Rockoff. We are also grateful for the ideas we received from discussions about *The Mississippi Encyclopedia* at meetings of the Mississippi Historical Society and the Mississippi Library Association.

Members of the Advisory Committee of the Center for the Study of Southern Culture have supported the project both financially and in other ways. Thanks especially to Lynn and Stewart Gammill for their generous support for the project. We extend our gratitude to the Henry Brevard Family, Michelle Hyver Oakes, and John Sewell as well. Other Center friends who provided support include Nancy Ashley, Elizabeth Hollingsworth, Mary Lucia Holloway, Toni James, Albert and Eugenia Lamar, Keith Dockery McLean, Carol Puckett, Jack Rice, Elaine Scott, and Gerald Walton. At the Center, Sarah Dixon Pegues took care of financial issues.

We thank the family, friends, and students who have for years listened to us talk, think, and worry about this project. Above all, we express our gratitude to the authors and editors who have contributed to this encyclopedia.

THE MISSISSIPPI ENCYCLOPEDIA

A

Abdul-Rauf, Mahmoud (Chris Jackson)

(b. 1969) Athlete

From the late 1980s through the mid-1990s, Gulfport native Mahmoud Abdul-Rauf (born Chris Jackson) was one of the most recognizable figures in American basketball. As a senior guard at Gulfport High School in 1987–88, Jackson averaged 29.9 points and 5.7 assists. His play earned him spots on the Parade and McDonald's All-American basketball teams in 1988, and Gatorade honored Jackson as the Mississippi State Player of the Year.

Upon graduating from Gulfport High, Jackson took his skills across the Mississippi state line and enrolled at Louisiana State University (LSU), where he became an instant star. In the 1988–89 season, he averaged 30 points per game and scored a total of 965 points, both records for a freshman playing NCAA Division I basketball. Jackson was the consensus pick for numerous Freshman of the Year awards, was selected the Southeastern Conference (SEC) Player of the Year, and was named to several all-American teams. *Sports Illustrated* caught the buzz surrounding the sharpshooting freshman and put Jackson on the cover of its 20 February 1989 issue. The headline read, "He's a Pistol," a reference to LSU basketball legend "Pistol" Pete Maravich. Jackson's outstanding performances brought back memories of the late 1960s and early 1970s, when Maravich dazzled fans with his prolific scoring and creative ball handling. In his sophomore year, Jackson averaged 28 points per game and once again was the SEC Player of the Year and a first-team all-American. In the NCAA Tournament, Jackson and the Tigers suffered a disappointing second-round loss to Georgia Tech. Following the end of the 1989–90 season Jackson withdrew from LSU and put his name in the National Basketball Association (NBA) draft. Despite playing only two years of college ball, Jackson left LSU in sixth place on the list of the school's all-time leading scorers.

The Denver Nuggets drafted Jackson, and in 1991 he became a Muslim and changed his name. He played in the NBA for eleven years and had a solid career, although he failed to duplicate his feats from college. Abdul-Rauf scored 8,553 total points, won the league's Most Improved Player award in 1993, and earned a place as one of the league's best free-throw shooters during the 1990s. In 1996 Abdul-Rauf violated league rules by refusing to stand for the US national anthem, claiming that his faith prohibited him from taking part in any kind of "nationalistic ritualism." He also commented that the American flag and the national anthem were symbols of the long US history of racial oppression. Abdul-Rauf's controversial stance received national attention from both the news and sports media. The combination of public anger at his statements and a one-game suspension from the NBA prompted Abdul-Rauf to seek a compromise with the league. He agreed to stand for the anthem but bowed his head in silent prayer rather than looking at the flag.

In 2001 Abdul-Rauf retired from the NBA, continuing his career in various European and Japanese leagues. For a time, he spent the off-seasons serving as an imam at a mosque in Gulfport. In December 2012 his hometown held a public ceremony honoring him and presented him with a key to the city. He currently lives in Atlanta.

Chuck Westmoreland
Delta State University

Ken Denlinger, *Washington Post* (14 March 1996); A. J. Giardina, WLOX TV website, www.wlox.com; Kelly B. Koenig, *Washington Law Quarterly* (Spring 1998); LSU Sports website, www.lsusports.net.

Academies, Private, Antebellum

Private academies were the primary form of education in Mississippi for the first sixty years of the nineteenth century. *Academy* referred to any type of secondary education, including what are also known as seminaries, institutes, classical schools, colleges, and universities. While some academies received limited financial support from the state, most were privately owned, were controlled by self-perpetuating boards of trustees, and offered flexible and varied curricula. These institutions took on students of both sexes and appealed primarily to the wealthy, although some institutions offered scholarships for poor students or those intending to enter the ministry.

The creation of academies in Mississippi followed settlement patterns that often divided people by region within the territory and later the state. While the Ker School at Natchez was the first academy on record (1801), in 1802 Gov. William C. C. Claiborne spoke of the need to found a "seminary of learning." Shortly thereafter, the territorial legislature passed an act establishing a college, leading to the chartering of

Jefferson College the same year. Nine academies opened in the Mississippi Territory from 1802 to 1817, seven of them located within the Natchez District, primarily because much of the territory's wealth and population were concentrated in this political, commercial, and intellectual center. The rest of the territory was more sparsely populated and poorly developed and lacked the means to create educational institutions.

After statehood in December 1817, the Mississippi academy movement grew rapidly, with six new academies in operation by 1820. Among them was the Elizabeth Female Academy, which opened its doors in 1818 and was the first female-only school incorporated by a territory or a state and the first institution to achieve college status in the Gulf States. Throughout the 1820s, the academy movement garnered new strength, with thirteen additional institutions chartered by the legislature and seventeen others established or operated without legislative recognition. Although Natchez remained the state's educational center, the number of schools expanded in the central, eastern, and northern parts of the state; the coastal sections, however, lagged behind. By the prosperous early 1830s, when settlement increased and the state developed, fifty-seven new academies were chartered and an additional twenty-two were established. A delayed reaction to the economic depression of the late 1830s led to a slight decline in the number of academies established in the 1840s, but the late 1840s and 1850s realized a revival of interest in education owing to a healthier economy, a growing population, and the rise of new educational centers in the state, such as Holly Springs, which boasted four institutions with a total of between four hundred and five hundred students.

Considerable variation existed because no centralized system of control existed and most academies were privately owned by individuals, stock companies, or religious denominations. In most cases, a board of trustees elected the principal and assistants, created rules and regulations, determined salaries, and prescribed the curricula. Teachers planned courses of study, enforced rules, and conducted day-to-day operations. Many teachers were college graduates, and in 1821 the legislature required that they be qualified to teach Latin and Greek in addition to all common school subjects. Small schools often had one or two teachers, while larger schools could employ five to ten instructors, but turnover remained high as teachers moved into more profitable positions. All institutions had boards of visitors, often appointed by the trustees, who examined students, observed and evaluated the facilities, and then made public reports. Most academies were boarding schools in which the students paid extra fees for room, meals, and laundry. Departments of study and classrooms were frequently housed in a single building, with separate dormitories constructed for the students.

Most academies struggled financially and sought to obtain money by hosting lotteries, through loans or grants from the state, and via private donations from individuals or organizations. The major source of revenue, however, was tuition fees, which averaged between twenty and thirty dollars per student per term (between twenty and twenty-two weeks).

Academy rules and regulations also varied, but most established specific study hours, dress codes, and mealtimes. Academy officials often imposed strict discipline, filling parental roles. Corporal punishment was acceptable for boys when serious situations required it but was seldom employed in girls' schools, where demerits constituted the major form of punishment. Academies sought to develop students' moral and intellectual capabilities, generally beginning and ending each day with organized prayer.

By 1860 Mississippi had fifty-two chartered female academies. Coeducational academies had separate departments for the sexes and were characterized by close supervision and a "lock door and a ceiled partition" between the two departments. Most academies had three levels of work—elementary, secondary, and collegiate—but focused on the secondary level. Some institutions had only age requirements for admission, while others stipulated reading levels, and still others had more in-depth entrance examinations. The curricula combined classical, literary, and scientific subjects. Students took courses in Latin and Greek language and literature, English language, rhetoric, history, engineering, and mathematics. Quarterly, semiannual, and annual examinations were public events to which community residents were invited, providing good publicity for the schools. While the state legislature allowed some academies to confer degrees, most granted diplomas or certificates of completion.

Mary Clingerman Yaran
Washington, D.C.

Edgar W. Knight, *Public Education in the South* (1922); David Sansing, *Making Haste Slowly: The Troubled History of Higher Education in Mississippi* (1990); Herbert Glenn Stampley, "The Academy Movement in Mississippi during the Nineteenth Century" (master's thesis, University of Mississippi, 1950).

Ace Records

Although widely regarded as a New Orleans product, 1950s rhythm and blues powerhouse record label Ace Records was based in Jackson. Established in 1955 by former Specialty Records producer and salesman Johnny Vincent (born John Vincent Imbragulio in Hattiesburg in 1927), who was responsible for Savoy recordings of Earl King, Huey Smith,

Huey "Piano" Smith's hit single, "Rockin' Pneumonia" (1957), on the Ace Records label (*Living Blues* Collection, Department of Archives and Special Collections, J. D. Williams Library, University of Mississippi)

and John Lee Hooker, Ace grew out of Vincent's previous label, Champion. The earliest Ace recordings, including the first Ace hit, King's "Lonely, Lonely Nights," took place in the Trumpet Records studio in Jackson. However, most of Ace's success came from the New Orleans studio of Cosimo Matassa. Arthur "Big Boy" Crudup, Lightnin' Hopkins, Eddie Bo, Joe Tex, Bobby Marchan, James Booker, and a young Dr. John all recorded for Matassa and Vincent. Dr. John also served as engineer and producer on some Ace releases. Vincent enjoyed several early successes with Ace. Huey "Piano" Smith's recording of "Rockin' Pneumonia and the Boogie Woogie Flu" rose as high as No. 52 on the Billboard pop chart and No. 9 on the Billboard R&B chart. In 1958 Smith's "Don't You Just Know It" peaked at No. 9 and No. 4 on the pop and R&B charts, respectively. Although sales in the relatively limited R&B and blues markets were brisk, Vincent wanted more for himself and his label. To achieve this success, Ace needed a star who could appeal to the much wider white pop audience.

Ace's greatest success came with crossover hits from Jimmy Clanton and Frankie Ford. Clanton embodied Vincent's ideal of the clean-cut, all-American teen idol the label needed to gain a piece of the US pop charts dominated in the late 1950s by teen idols such as Elvis Presley, Pat Boone, and Frankie Avalon. Clanton's biggest hit, "Just a Dream," scored Ace Records's only No. 1 hit when it reached the top of the Billboard R&B chart in July 1957 and the No. 4 position on the pop chart in April 1958. Ford's "Sea Cruise," actually a Huey Smith recording with Ford's dubbed vocals, made it to No. 14 on the pop charts in February 1959. From 1957 through 1963 Ace placed nineteen singles on the Billboard Top 100 pop chart. Jimmy Clanton was featured on eleven of these.

In 1964 Vincent entered into a disastrous distribution deal with Vee-Jay Records. Although Vee-Jay appeared to be a strong company, it went bankrupt in early 1965. At that time it owed Ace Records as much as one million dollars. This collapse dealt a severe blow to Ace, for, like many independent record companies, it operated on a very slim profit margin. This financial setback, coupled with changing musical tastes after the British invasion, ended Ace's run on the pop charts. Despite these difficulties, Ace continued to operate in the Jackson area as a regional label that featured soul-blues artists until Vincent's death in 2000.

Ricky Stevens
Coldwater, Mississippi

Charlie Gillett, *The Sound of the City: The Rise of Rock and Roll* (2nd ed. 1996); Mississippi Blues Trail website, www.msbluestrail.org.

Ackia, Battle of

The Battle of Ackia, 26 May 1736, ended the first major expedition of the Chickasaw War (1732–43). It was fought about seven miles northwest of Tupelo. Ackia (Oekya) was a fortified Chickasaw village in a seventy-five-square-mile area containing some eleven such villages collectively called Ackia.

When the Chickasaw defeated Maj. Pierre Dartaguiette Diron's force on 25 March, his captured orders informed them of Gov. Jean-Baptiste Le Moyne, Sieur de Bienville's approach with possibly fifteen hundred whites, blacks, and Indians (mostly Choctaw). Accordingly, between four hundred and five hundred Chickasaw hastened south and hid in the rolling plains around the adjacent villages of Oekya, Tchoukafala, and Apeony. The Ministry of Marine had ordered Bienville to attack any Natchez refugees found in Ackia. But on 26 May, ignorant of Dartaguiette's defeat, tired of waiting, and fearing desertions, Bienville—pressured by Choctaw chiefs Red Shoe and Alibamon Mingo—decided to attack Oekya immediately. Ironically, Oekya's chief, Imayatabé le Borgne, was the strongest French partisan of the Chickasaw. A Chickasaw delegation approached with a calumet to negotiate, presumably about surrendering the refugees. A group of Choctaw fired, killed two emissaries, and took their scalps to Bienville.

Oekya, with Tchoukafa and Apeony in a triangular formation on a hilltop, was well defended and double stockaded. One village flew an English flag, indicating the presence of English advisers. The assault began at two o'clock in the afternoon with 160 Regulars and 60 Swiss. It made significant progress but then was caught in a murderous crossfire from the concealed Chickasaw nearby. Lacking artillery (which had failed to arrive from France) and with casualties mounting, Bienville was forced to break off. The Choctaw, hitherto "waiting for the outcome" (according to Bienville), fired several volleys and then helped the wounded during the retreat, beginning on 27 May, to Fort Tombecbé. The engagement lasted about three hours. Bienville praised the Chickasaw marksmanship. He reported between sixty and seventy French and twenty-two Choctaw killed or wounded, but these figures probably were underestimates. Casualties among the officers were especially heavy, significantly hampering future operations.

David S. Newhall
Centre College

Patricia Galloway, *Journal of Mississippi History* (September 1982); Arrel M. Gibson, *The Chickasaws* (1971); John Brice Harris, *From Old Mobile to Fort Assumption* (1959); Mary Ann Wells, *Native Land: Mississippi 1540–1798* (1994); Joe Wilkins, *Proceedings of the Twelfth Meeting of the French Colonial Historical Society, Ste. Geneviève, May 1986*, ed. Philip P. Boucher and Serge Courville (1989); Patricia Dillon Woods, *French-Indian Relations on the Southern Frontier* (1980).

Adams, John

(1825–1864) Confederate General

Confederate general John Adams was born on 1 July 1825 in Nashville, Tennessee. Adams entered West Point in 1841 and graduated in June 1846. Commissioned second lieutenant in the First Dragoons, he saw action in the Mexican War and won a brevet to first lieutenant for gallantry in combat. From 1850 to 1856 Adams moved frequently, serving in various outposts. While in Minnesota he married Georgia McDougal, the daughter of an army surgeon. They went on to have four sons and two daughters.

Promoted to captain in 1856, he spent the next two years on recruiting duty. Stationed in California when the Civil War began, he resigned his commission in late May 1861 and made his way down south. After receiving an appointment as a captain of cavalry in the Confederate service, he commanded the post at Memphis and served in western Kentucky before being ordered to Jackson, Mississippi. Adams won promotion to colonel in 1862 and led a cavalry brigade in field operations until the late summer of 1862, when he was placed in command at Columbus, the site of a Confederate arsenal. In early 1863 he went back to Jackson to command the Fourth Military District.

Following the death of Gen. Lloyd Tilghman in mid-May 1863, Adams was promoted to brigadier and placed in command of Tilghman's old brigade, which consisted of six Mississippi infantry regiments. He led this unit through the Vicksburg Campaign, where he served under Gen. Joseph E. Johnston as part of the force that maneuvered between Vicksburg and Jackson. Following the fall of Vicksburg, Adams and his command served under Gen. Leonidas Polk, primarily in Mississippi, before moving with Polk's corps to Resaca, Georgia, in May 1864. Adams's brigade served with distinction throughout the Atlanta Campaign and then was in the vanguard of Gen. John Bell Hood's force that attempted unsuccessfully to draw the Federals away from Atlanta. After capturing a large number of prisoners at Dalton, Georgia, Adams and his brigade accompanied Hood on his ill-fated invasion of Tennessee.

At Franklin, Tennessee, on 30 November 1864, Adams led his troops in a desperate charge that decimated his brigade. His unit suffered more than 450 casualties, and Adams himself was among the many officers who fell. Although several versions exist of his last moments, it is clear that Adams had spurred his horse too near the Federal breastworks when he was shot down. The horse struggled to its feet, plunged forward, and died astride the Union parapet. Mortally wounded, Adams died shortly after being brought inside the Federal works.

Christopher Losson
St. Joseph, Missouri

"Gen. John Adams at Franklin," *Confederate Veteran* (June 1897); Terry Jones, in *The Confederate General*, ed. William C. Davis (1991); Christopher Losson, "Jacob Dolson Cox: A Military Biography" (PhD dissertation, University of Mississippi, 1993); James D. Porter, in *Confederate Military History: Tennessee*, ed. Clement A. Evans (1899); Ezra Warner, *Generals in Gray: Lives of the Confederate Commanders* (1959).

Adams, Victoria Gray

(1926–2006) Activist

Victoria Almeter Jackson was born on 5 November 1926 to Mack and Annie Mae Ott Jackson, in Palmer's Crossing, Hattiesburg's historically black community. She graduated from the Depriest Consolidated Schools in Palmer's Crossing and attended Jackson State College (now Jackson State University), Wilberforce University, and Tuskegee Institute (now Tuskegee University). Adams served as a campus minister at Virginia State University and a guest lecturer at colleges and universities throughout the United States.

She began her four decades as a civil rights advocate in Hattiesburg by attempting to enable African Americans to register to vote. She operated freedom schools in the Hattiesburg area to teach literacy classes that empowered and enabled African Americans to pass the voter registration test. In 1964 her commitment to civil and political justice was tested when she ran for the US Senate, challenging incumbent Democrat John C. Stennis. Her candidacy represented a bold move at a time when most of Mississippi's African Americans were disfranchised. That same year Adams gained even more notoriety when she and cofounders of the Mississippi Freedom Democratic Party (MFDP) Fannie Lou Hamer and Annie Devine challenged the legitimacy of the Mississippi delegation—all of whose members were white men—to the Democratic National Convention in Atlantic City, New Jersey. The national party offered a compromise under which two MFDP members would be seated along with the Regular Democrats, but the MFDP rejected the deal. Though the attempt to unseat the Regular Democrats failed, the MFDP personalized and highlighted the racial and political tension in Mississippi. In 1968 Adams and her MFDP cofounders became the first African American women seated as guests on the US Senate floor.

Adams's papers, which chronicle her life as a civil rights pioneer, are held in the University Archives at the University of Southern Mississippi in Hattiesburg. The Office of Campus Ministry at Virginia State University, where Adams served as chaplain, holds records relating to her life there. In the documentary *Standing on My Sisters' Shoulders*, Adams shares the story of her struggle in the civil rights movement.

Adams died on 12 August 2006 at her son's Baltimore home after a lengthy illness. Her motto was "Life shrinks or expands in direct proportion to the courage with which we live."

Annie Payton
Mississippi Valley State University

Joyce Ladner, *Crisis* (November–December 2006); Vicky Crawford, *Cross Currents* (Summer 2007); *Victoria Gray Adams (1926–2006)*, University of Southern Mississippi University Archives website, www.lib.usm.edu /spcol/collections/uarchives.

Adams, William Wirt
(1819–1888) Confederate General

William Wirt Adams, the older brother of fellow Confederate general Daniel W. Adams, was born in Frankfort, Kentucky, on 22 March 1819. He was the son of George Adams, who moved the family to Natchez when Wirt, as he was called, was six years old. George Adams, a federal district judge, later sent his son to be educated at St. Joseph's Academy in Bardstown, Kentucky. Wirt subsequently went west and served briefly in the army of the Republic of Texas in 1839. Later that year he returned to Mississippi after his father died. He was a sugar planter in Louisiana for several years but married Sallie Huger Mayrant of Jackson in 1850 and settled in Mississippi, where he became a successful banker and planter. Adams was elected to the state legislature from Issaquena County in 1858 and 1860.

After Mississippi's secession he went as a commissioner to Louisiana, soliciting that state's cooperation. In February 1861 Confederate president Jefferson Davis offered Adams a cabinet position as postmaster general. Adams declined, citing pressing business interests, but settled his banking affairs and began organizing a cavalry regiment. Mustered into Confederate service in August 1861 as the First Mississippi Cavalry, the regiment consisted of companies from Alabama, Louisiana, and Mississippi. Adams served as colonel of the unit, which went to Kentucky in late 1861. It formed part of the rear guard for Gen. Albert Sidney Johnston's force as it retreated south after the fall of Fort Henry and Fort Donelson in early 1862. The regiment fought at Shiloh and then operated independently in West Tennessee and Mississippi. It captured a Federal battery at Britton's Lane, near Denmark, Tennessee, in September 1862, helped secure Earl Van Dorn's line of retreat after the Battle of Corinth the next month, and captured a trainload of Union troops near Burnsville.

Adams's regiment then operated in Washington County, where it kept abreast of Federal movements and endeavored to protect the region from enemy incursions. Sent south of Vicksburg in the spring of 1862, Adams unsuccessfully pursued a Federal cavalry force that was marauding through the state under Col. Benjamin Grierson, although the regiment's resistance did force Grierson to divert away from Natchez. During the Vicksburg Campaign Adams's men fought at Raymond and protected the retreat of Brig. Gen. John Gregg's infantry. Adams and his cavalry harassed Union forces operating against Vicksburg and skirmished with Federal troops near Jackson after Vicksburg fell. His services in the Vicksburg Campaign brought Adams a promotion to brigadier general on 25 September 1863. Later that year his command operated near Natchez and was involved in engagements at Port Hudson and Baton Rouge. The brigade clashed with Federal troops during William Tecumseh Sherman's campaign against Meridian in February 1864 but could not prevent the city's capture and destruction. Adams's men met a Union expedition up the Yazoo River in mid-April and captured the gunboat USS *Petrel*, removing eight naval guns before burning the vessel. Over the next several months his command skirmished with various enemy forces in Mississippi.

Late in the war Adams's brigade was attached to Lt. Gen. Nathan Bedford Forrest's cavalry, serving with it until the end of hostilities. Adams ultimately surrendered and was paroled near Gainesville, Alabama, on 12 May 1865.

After the war Adams resided in both Vicksburg and Jackson. He was appointed state revenue agent in 1880 and was later named postmaster of Jackson by Grover Cleveland. Adams's life ended abruptly in Jackson on 1 May 1888, when he encountered John Martin, a hostile newspaper editor, on the street: the two men drew pistols and fatally wounded each other.

Christopher Losson
St. Joseph, Missouri

John H. Eicher and David J. Eicher, *Civil War High Commands* (2001); *Goodspeed's Biographical and Historical Memoirs of Mississippi*, vol. 1 (1891); Dunbar Rowland, *Mississippi: Comprising Sketches of Counties, Towns, Events, Institutions, and Persons, Arranged in Cyclopedic Form*, vol. 1 (1907).

Adams County

Bordering the Mississippi River in the southwestern part of the state, Adams County, the first county organized in the Mississippi Territory, has played a crucial role for three centuries. From its importance in Native American history and its role as Fort Rosalie in the colonial period to its prominence as a center of Mississippi economic and political life in the early 1800s, from Natchez as an urban center in the middle of cotton wealth to cultural tourism in the mid-twentieth century and a major civil rights boycott in the 1960s, the region has been central to Mississippi's history and identity.

An ancient home of mound-building people, the area that became Adams County was by the early 1700s home to a confederation of Indian groups that included the Natchez. Beginning in 1716, when French colonists established the Natchez District and built Fort Rosalie as a central governmental and military post, the Natchez and French came into contact and then conflict. French leaders first brought African slaves to the area in the 1720s. French economic interests included trading with the Natchez for deerskins and trying to grow tobacco, both for sale to European markets. In 1729 the Natchez attacked Fort Rosalie, killing more than 200 of the fort's 750 residents and undermining some of the French interest in the area. War between the French (and their Choctaw allies) and the Natchez from 1729 to 1733 led to the enslaving of a number of the Natchez. Beginning in the 1730s, the Natchez began to break up into different groups,

with some of them leaving the area and some forming alliances with the English.

The successive European claims to the Mississippi River Valley meant that Natchez had multiple influences and complex demography from early in its history. The French and Africans and various Native American groups had a presence in the county in the 1730s, followed by English and then Spanish colonists. The Spanish period from the 1760s to the 1790s left a major mark on Adams County. Spanish governor Manuel Gayoso de Lemos had authority in Natchez territory from 1789 to 1798, when the region came under US control. Gayoso encouraged agricultural experimentation, planned a set of avenues for the city of Natchez, and welcomed many of the groups that gave Natchez its distinctive character.

Cotton, slavery, and trade on the Mississippi River revolutionized life in the early national period. Tobacco and especially cattle were key to the area's economy in the late 1700s, and population increased dramatically after farmers in the Natchez area first grew cotton successfully in the 1790s. Natchez developed one of Mississippi's first slave markets at the Forks of the Road, and it often held several hundred slaves at a time.

In the late colonial and early national periods, Natchez was Mississippi's center for government, education, science, and religion, as well as for slave trading and the wealth generated by plantation agriculture and commerce. Founded in 1799 in the Mississippi Territory, Adams County was named for the nation's second president. From the first territorial census in 1792 through 1840, Adams County had the highest population in Mississippi, with slaves accounting for between 42 and 52 percent of residents. As a meeting place, Adams County became crucial to movement on the Mississippi River and as the end point of the Natchez Trace. The area called Natchez Under-the-Hill became a temporary home for many steamboat workers, travelers, and gamblers.

The Natchez District was home to Mississippi's first territorial government, and many the members of Mississippi's political elite resided in the area. George Poindexter moved to Adams County in 1802 and became territorial attorney general in 1803, representative to the General Assembly in 1806, and the state's second governor in 1820. William Bayard Shields arrived in Adams County in 1803 and served in a series of positions dealing with land, banking, and the law, becoming the state's first chief justice in 1817. Conflict between Natchez elites and other Mississippi voters and political voices began in the 1790s and continued through the movement of the capital to Jackson in 1820.

With the French and then the Spanish presence, Natchez in the 1700s was the home of Mississippi's first small group of Catholic settlers. All of the Protestant groups that ultimately grew to dominate much of Mississippi church life set up establishments in early Adams County. Baptists came to the area in 1799, and Tobias Gibson formed the first Methodist church in Washington in 1799. In 1807 James Smylie helped start the first Presbyterian group in Mississippi outside Washington. In addition, Jewish services were held in Natchez beginning around 1800.

From 1800 to 1820 Adams County's population grew from 4,660 to 12,076, with its slave population far outnumbering whites or free blacks. In 1820 the county's population consisted of 4,005 whites, 118 free blacks, and 7,953 slaves. With the growing cosmopolitan center of Natchez and the remarkably profitable large cotton plantations surrounding it, Adams County possessed a unique combination of urbanity and large-scale plantation slavery. For example, Adams County had far more people employed in manufacturing and commerce than any other county, and most of Mississippi's planters who owned more than 250 slaves lived in Natchez. Adams County was one of the nation's wealthiest areas and various commercial enterprises were established as a result. Publisher Andrew Marschalk, sometimes called the Father of Mississippi Journalism, started several newspapers in the area, including the *Mississippi Gazette*, which he founded in Natchez in 1802. The state's first bank, the Bank of Mississippi, opened in Natchez in 1809, and Mississippi's first academy, the Ker School, opened in Natchez in 1801. The territory's first college, Jefferson College, opened in Washington in 1802, and Elizabeth Female Academy opened there in 1818.

Architecture marked and continues to distinguish Natchez. The combination of wealth, ambition, cosmopolitan tastes, and skilled craftspeople shows in numerous homes built in the early and mid-1800s, many of them large brick buildings with distinctive names. The styles shifted from Federal to Greek Revival to Italianate, often with unique artistic touches.

In the 1830s and 1840s Adams County's importance within the state had begun to wane a bit, but it remained the county with the most residents, including the most slaves. In 1840 the county had 4,910 free whites, 283 free blacks, and 14,241 slaves. The most famous free African American in the county was William Johnson, known as the Barber of Natchez, who owned multiple businesses and left a diary detailing life in the city. Adams County trailed only Warren County in number of commercial and manufacturing workers in the state. A sprawling sawmill operation owned by Andrew Brown was one of the largest businesses in Mississippi, which helped rank Adams County among the leaders in the lumber industry.

On the eve of the Civil War, Adams County remained home to both slave plantations and city dwellers, but while many areas of the state had seen dramatic population growth, Adams County stagnated in the prewar years. With 5,648 free whites, 225 free blacks (by far the state's largest such population), and 14,292 slaves in 1860, the population had hardly changed since 1840. What had been the richest place in Mississippi, with the biggest houses, the wealthiest people, and the most productive cotton plantations (with the highest numbers of slaves), now ranked in the middle of the state's counties in the value and productivity of farm property—seventh in cotton production, thirtieth in corn production, and twenty-seventh in value of livestock. Fourteen counties had larger populations.

With a population of 6,612, Natchez nevertheless remained Mississippi's largest city in 1860. Whereas foreign-born immigrants were rare in most of Mississippi, Natchez had 767 foreign-born men and 475 women, the state's largest immigrant population. Many of the foreign-born were Irish workers.

Adams County stood as a striking exception to the Methodist and Baptist domination of the state's religion. In 1860 census takers counted just six churches in Adams—two Presbyterian churches, one Episcopal, one Baptist, one Methodist, and one Catholic. However, these churches were larger than most of the state's other congregations.

Among the many notable individuals in antebellum Natchez were Varina Howell, who married Jefferson Davis in 1845 and eventually became the only First Lady of the Confederate States of America, and Elizabeth Taylor Greenfield, who was born a slave and became a popular opera singer in both the United States and England. Natchez native John F. H. Claiborne was a political figure and newspaperman who became an important postbellum historian of Mississippi.

After the Civil War and emancipation, Adams County retained a large African American majority. The county was briefly a center for African American politics, with Natchez minister and educator Hiram Rhoades Revels serving briefly as Mississippi's first African American senator in 1870–71. Revels later became the first president of Alcorn College. John Roy Lynch, who like Revels arrived in Natchez during the Civil War, became the Speaker of the Mississippi House of Representatives and then a member of the US Congress from 1873 to 1877.

Although Adams County had many of the largest plantations in the antebellum period, its farming people worked on some of the smallest farms in the state after the war. Only four counties had average farm sizes smaller than Adams County's 104 acres. The transformation of large plantations into small farms was accompanied by a dramatic increase in sharecropping. About two-thirds of the county's farmers—the highest percentage in the state in 1880—worked for shares.

Postbellum Adams County nevertheless remained one of the state's leading centers for manufacturing and a destination for immigrant workers. In 1880 Adams County manufacturers employed 417 workers, the second-highest number in the state, and the county's 619 foreign-born men and women (most of them from Ireland, Germany, England, and Italy) gave it the state's largest nonnative population.

By 1900 the average farm size in Adams County had dropped to 55 acres, as the increasing use of sharecropping and especially tenancy divided land into even smaller units. The county's population of 30,111 included more than

24,000 African Americans, and only 6 percent of the African Americans who farmed were landowners. Natchez remained one of the state's larger cities, and Adams County continued to have substantial numbers of foreign-born residents (443) and industrial workers (811).

In the early twentieth century Adams County in many ways remained unique by Mississippi standards, and religion was one of the clearest manifestations of that uniqueness. In 1916 Adams ranked very low in the number of Southern Baptists (420) but third in the number of Episcopalians (463) and fourth in the number of Catholics (2,533). African Americans comprised the majority of Adams's churchgoers. The largest group in the county was the National Baptist Convention (3,800 members), while the African Methodist Episcopal Church had a sizable membership.

Early twentieth-century Adams County was home to a number of notable and creative individuals. Residing in Natchez were editor and Prohibition leader Harriet B. Kells, prolific adventure novelist Prentiss Ingraham, and writer Alice Walworth Graham, who set some of her romance novels on the area's plantations.

Two of Mississippi's most important efforts to preserve particular visions of the state's history started in Natchez. In the 1930s Natchez women led by Katherine Grafton Miller began marketing their city as a destination for tourists who wanted to experience antebellum homes and their history. In the same decade Roane Byrnes Fleming began work that eventually led to the creation of the Natchez Trace Parkway, offering both natural beauty and historic travel.

At the time of the Great Depression, Adams County retained a largely agricultural economy, but 12,608 of its 23,564 residents lived in Natchez, making it one of only three Mississippi counties in which a majority of the population lived in urban areas. African Americans made up about two-thirds of the county's population, while the remainder featured greater ethnic diversity than existed in much of the rest of Mississippi, with a substantial number of immigrants, especially from Italy. Businesses in Adams County employed about 800 industrial workers, many of them in sawmills and a creamery. Tenants operated 80 percent of the county's farms, which concentrated on growing cotton.

By 1960 Adams County's population had grown to 37,730, with whites achieving a slim majority (50.5 percent) for the first time as a consequence of African American out-migration as well as an increase in the white population. Agricultural labor had declined to one of the lowest percentages in the state, and a majority of workers were employed in manufacturing. Over the next two decades, Adams County experienced an 82 percent increase in manufacturing jobs, and it ranked seventh in the state in per capita income and second in retail sales. Adams was home to Armstrong Tire and Rubber, one of the larger factories that moved to Mississippi as part of the Balance Agriculture with Industry plan. The county also had the highest value of mineral production in the state, mostly petroleum from its thirty-four proven oil wells.

In the 1950s and 1960s Adams County played a significant role in both civil rights activism and opposition to civil rights. The county's chapter of the National Association for the Advancement of Colored People (NAACP) demanded desegregated schools immediately after the 1954 *Brown v. Board of Education* decision. Ten years later, shortly after local NAACP president George Metcalfe attended a Natchez school board meeting to ask for the desegregation of schools, he was injured in a car bombing and activists in several groups, including the Student Nonviolent Coordinating Committee (SNCC), responded with a long boycott of white-owned stores. The Americans for the Preservation of the White Race formed in 1963 in a gas station outside Natchez, and the city's Ku Klux Klan was among the strongest and most active in the state, with members responsible for several murders, including that of Wharlest Jackson, a black man whose truck was bombed after he was promoted over two white men at a factory in 1967. Because of the constant threat of violence, black men in Natchez welcomed a chapter of the Deacons of Defense and Justice, a militant organization that pledged to protect the black community by using violence if necessary. SNCC, the Congress of Racial Equality, and the Mississippi Freedom Democratic Party did not attempt mass mobilization in Natchez until they had undertaken efforts in the rest of the state.

Like many of the state's Mississippi River counties, Adams County's 2010 population had decreased by about 15 percent over the previous half century, reaching 32,297, most of them African Americans. The county also featured a small but significant Latino minority, about 6.5 percent of the population. With historical attractions, pilgrimage tours, museums, and festivals, Adams County is one of Mississippi's leaders in the arts and cultural tourism.

Mississippi Encyclopedia Staff
Oxford, Mississippi

Mississippi State Planning Commission, *Progress Report on State Planning in Mississippi* (1938); *Mississippi Statistical Abstract*, Mississippi State University (1952–2010); Charles Sydnor and Claude Bennett, *Mississippi History* (1939); University of Virginia Library, Historical Census Browser website, http://mapserver.lib.virginia.edu; E. Nolan Waller and Dani A. Smith, *Growth Profiles of Mississippi's Counties, 1960–1980* (1985).

AFL-CIO in Mississippi

The Mississippi AFL-CIO (American Federation of Labor–Congress of Industrial Organizations) is the political arm of AFL-CIO affiliated unions and their members located within the Magnolia State. The Mississippi AFL-CIO lobbies state agencies, endorses candidates for statewide office, and educates and mobilizes its members in support of such liberal goals as union security, progressive taxes, improved public services, and civil rights. But low union density within the state has required the Mississippi AFL-CIO to reach beyond its official membership in efforts to be politically effective. The Mississippi AFL-CIO has encouraged voter registration and voting among its members and has funded and organized registration and voting drives among such progressive allies as African Americans not in the union. It has defined its constituency as extending beyond its official membership to advance liberal candidates and policies in a state that has often has been hostile to them.

The Mississippi AFL-CIO was originally named the Mississippi Labor Council, AFL-CIO and was founded in June 1957. (The name changed to its current one in 1962.) The organization was formed as a result of the merger of the Mississippi State Industrial Union Council, which was affiliated with the CIO, and the larger Mississippi State Federation of Labor, which represented AFL local unions statewide. Although relations between the two state organizations had been antagonistic and competitive, they agreed to combine their political resources to defend themselves from the antilabor politicians who dominated the state government in Jackson. The first president of the organization was Ray S. Bryant, a Hattiesburg firefighter. In 1959 he was succeeded by another former AFL member, Claude Ramsay, who had served previously as president of Paperworkers Local 103 at the Moss Point International Paper plant on the Gulf Coast. Ramsey remained the organization's president for the next twenty-six years; in 1962, the group changed its name to the Mississippi AFL-CIO. Ramsey worked tirelessly for black equality, the national Democratic Party, and labor unions in a state whose leaders reviled all three.

In 1961 the state council increased dues and passed a long-term eighteen-point legislative initiative, the Program of Progress, designed to increase the group's political muscle. But Ramsey believed that given labor's low membership in the state, the success of labor's new legislative program depended more on black enfranchisement than anything the state council could do for itself. Consequently, the Mississippi AFL-CIO allied with civil rights groups in the 1960s—and paid dearly for doing so. Local unions and their members who supported segregation repudiated Mississippi AFL-CIO endorsements and disaffiliated from it. Membership fell from twenty-six thousand in 1960 to sixteen thousand in 1966. Less than 50 percent of the statewide AFL-CIO membership was affiliated with the Mississippi AFL-CIO. The state organization survived financially only because of subsidies it received from the national group.

As the turmoil over civil rights that rocked the state in the 1960s subsided, the Mississippi AFL-CIO regained its footing. Membership in the state federation increased from its nadir in the 1960s to about twenty-seven thousand in 2000. The building trades, which had always had a powerful voice within the state federation, were now joined by public employee unions as influential affiliates. In addition, the Mississippi AFL-CIO's courageous stand on civil rights gave it credibility with emergent African American leaders. But electoral and legislative success continued to elude the state federation. Even though the Democratic Party no longer dominated state politics, antilabor conservatives remained in control, having switched to the state's resurgent Republican Party. Moreover, the organizing environment has shown little improvement.

As of 2000, union density in Mississippi had declined to just 5.5 percent of the nonagricultural workforce, the fourth-lowest total among the states, and even many unionized workers were not members of the Mississippi AFL-CIO. More than half of the state's AFL-CIO membership in the twenty-first century has remained unaffiliated with the state federation.

Alan Draper
St. Lawrence University

Alan Draper, *Conflict of Interests: Organized Labor and the Civil Rights Movement in the South, 1954–1968* (1994); Robert S. McElvaine, in *Southern Workers and Their Unions, 1880–1975*, ed. Merl E. Reed, Leslie S. Hough, and Gary M. Fink (1981); Donald C. Mosley, in *A History of Mississippi*, vol. 2, ed. Richard Aubrey McLemore (1973).

African Methodist Episcopal Church

The African Methodist Episcopal Church (AME Church) originated as the Free African Society, established by Rev. Richard Allen in Philadelphia, Pennsylvania, in 1787. Formally reorganized into the African Methodist Episcopal Church in 1816, the church sought to provide persons of African descent the opportunity to worship without the racial discrimination that had become common in the white-dominated Methodist Church.

The name African Methodist Episcopal represents both the history and the functioning of the church, but membership is not and never has been restricted solely to those of African descent; rather, the AME Church has always welcomed all people, regardless of their racial background. *Methodist* refers to the church's roots in and connection to the original Methodist Church, while *Episcopal* refers to the church's internal governing system.

The AME Church motto is "God Our Father, Christ Our Redeemer, Man Our Brother," acknowledging not only the belief in the Holy Trinity but also the idea that the church's mission is to spread the Gospel and to minister to the needs of fellow humans. The bedrock of the church's beliefs is the Apostles' Creed, which lists the key fundamentals of church doctrine.

In the first decades after its formal organization, the AME Church spread over a wide geographic area confined largely but not entirely to the North. During the 1850s congregations formed in the slave states of Kentucky, Missouri, Louisiana, and South Carolina as a consequence of the work of Theophilus G. Steward, an AME minister in South Carolina who issued the message, "I Seek My Brethren," which urged his parishioners to reach out to free blacks. This missionary effort eventually extended beyond the United States into Africa, South America, and Europe.

During the Civil War, AME Church missionaries began to penetrate the Deep South in the wake of the Union Army. In 1864 Bishop James A. Shorter led a group of missionaries—A. H. Dixon, James C. Embry, Adam Jackson, Henry A. Jackson, John Miller, Edward A. Scott, and Thomas W. Stringer—into Mississippi to establish congregations. Shorter also oversaw the establishment of the first AME congregations in Tennessee and Texas.

Establishing AME congregations in the former Confederacy proved difficult, particularly in Mississippi. Missionaries sent there endured extreme ridicule, not only from whites who resented their presence but also from many newly freed slaves who saw these outsiders as promoting foreign religious and educational ideas. Nevertheless, the missionaries had some success, and in May 1868 Mississippi's AME congregations were represented at the denomination's Thirteenth General Conference in Washington, D.C. Some AME ministers, most notably US senator Hiram Rhoades Revels, became leaders in postemancipation Mississippi. By 1916 the AME Church had 498 congregations and more than 26,000 members in the state. It was especially popular in the Mississippi Delta, with the largest number of members in Washington, Sunflower, and Yazoo Counties.

Today the AME Church has an estimated worldwide membership of about 2.5 million, with congregations in more than thirty nations. It publishes the *Christian Recorder*, which features church news and events. The church also operates various universities and theological seminaries throughout the southern United States.

Adam E. Maroney
Prescott, Arizona

James T. Campbell, *Songs of Zion: The African Methodist Episcopal Church in the United States and South Africa* (1995); Bishop Cornal Garnett Henning Sr., *The Doctrine and Discipline of the African Methodist Episcopal Church, 2000–2004* (2001); Charles Spencer Smith, *A History of the African Methodist Episcopal Church, 1856–1922* (1922); Richard R. Wright Jr., *Centennial Encyclopedia of the African Methodist Episcopal Church, 1816–1916* (1916).

Agricultural Adjustment Administration

In 1933, the first year of the Franklin Roosevelt administration, the New Deal dramatically changed the nature of Mississippi agriculture by setting up the Agricultural Adjustment Administration (AAA), a large federal agency that had the job of raising agricultural prices, stabilizing agricultural expenses to help farm owners keep from losing their land to debt, and possibly improving the conditions of agricultural workers. The AAA addressed the problem of low cotton prices by setting up a subsidy program to encourage farmers to decrease production so prices would increase and expenses would decrease.

The program was voluntary and dramatic. Planters plowed up more than ten million acres of cotton in 1933. Cotton prices responded quickly, rising from 6.5 cents a pound in 1932 to 10.17 cents a year later and increasing slightly more over the next few years.

The primary controversy involved how the program should deal with sharecroppers and renters. AAA leaders disagreed about whether the subsidies should go to agricultural laborers. US secretary of agriculture Henry Wallace hoped the crop subsidies would be divided evenly so that cutting production would not further harm tenants, who were already facing severe poverty. Other officials—most notably, Oscar G. Johnston, the Mississippian who was president of the massive Delta and Pine Land Company and the financial director of the AAA cotton programs, and Cully Cobb, the Mississippian who ran the agency's Cotton Section—believed that the program needed to focus on stabilizing the agricultural system rather than on addressing the problems of laborers. Arguments continued, with the side that wanted to guarantee payments to laborers losing most battles. Officials tried to clarify payment programs in 1934 and 1935, but AAA lawyers (including Alger Hiss) who pushed for fair treatment of agricultural workers were fired in 1935.

The subsidy programs allowed plantation owners to fire some workers and reclassify others, and Agriculture Department officials failed to recognize that most of Mississippi's African Americans lacked the power to challenge the system through formal complaints. The AAA almost always sent checks to landlords, allowing them to decide how to split the money. The largest planting operations received the largest checks: Delta and Pine Land, for example, received more than three hundred thousand dollars between 1933 and 1935.

AAA policies, therefore, ultimately permitted farm owners to keep their land while laborers either lost their jobs or had to shift from sharecropping to more occasional wage labor. Many laborers were evicted or moved on to other work.

Ted Ownby
University of Mississippi

James C. Cobb, *The Most Southern Place on Earth: The Mississippi Delta and the Roots of Regional Identity* (1992); Pete Daniel, *Breaking the Land: The Transformation of Cotton, Tobacco, and Rice Cultures since 1880* (1985); Jack Temple Kirby, *Rural Worlds Lost: The American South, 1920–1960* (1987); Bruce J. Schulman, *From Cotton Belt to Sunbelt: Federal Policy, Economic Development, and the Transformation of the South* (1994); Jeannie Whayne, *A New Plantation South: Land, Labor, and Federal Favor in Twentieth-Century Arkansas* (1996).

Agricultural Cooperatives

Cooperatives are business organizations that differ from sole proprietorships, partnerships, and investor-owned corporations along three distinct organizational lines: (1) democratic control by their members, (2) member ownership, and (3) benefits that include savings, profits, and patronage refunds for doing business with the cooperative. Community-based agricultural cooperatives represent a distinctive form of the cooperative business with a unique history.

Community-based agricultural cooperatives resemble traditional producer and consumer cooperatives but tend to be organized on more local and geographically specific levels. In addition, they typically have broader social agendas, given their roots in the civil rights movement, community organizing, and grassroots development. Across the southern United States this agenda often involves activism concerning the plight of black farmers. Operating on cooperative principles, some of these organizations are classified as nonprofits, given their mission of working for the survival and improved quality of life for farmers traditionally underserved by mainstream private businesses and government agencies.

Originally referred to as "poor people's cooperatives," community-based agricultural cooperatives started in the 1880s, when small-scale farmers and sharecroppers were marginalized by competition with larger producers, high costs for production inputs, depressed commodity prices, and the crop lien system, whereby farmers mortgaged their crops to merchants for supplies. Although many southern cooperatives (including some chapters of the populist-oriented Farmers' Alliance) primarily served whites, the Colored Farmers' Alliance and Cooperative Union promoted the interests of independent farmers, sharecroppers, and general farm laborers, black and white.

Social and economic concerns were even more central to the Southern Tenant Farmers' Union, organized in Arkansas after laborers were pushed off the land in response to the Agricultural Adjustment Act (AAA), a federal New Deal policy intended to limit overproduction. The Tenant Farmers' Union was involved in establishment of Mississippi's interracial Delta Community Farm in 1936. Cooperative organizers and progressive policymakers rallied for services, and one outcome was the 1937 creation of the US Department of Agriculture's Farm Security Administration (FSA), which eventually helped displaced farmers by creating resettlement communities and developing cooperative businesses. The FSA assisted more than one hundred black families in chartering a cooperative in the community of Mileston by 1941, and over the years the Mileston Farmers' Cooperative's projects included affordable housing, a grocery store, an equipment repair shop, and a cotton gin.

The civil rights movement gave another great push to the development of community-based agricultural cooperatives, resulting in what Ray Marshall and Lamond Godwin have termed the "New Poor People's Cooperatives." Independent black landowning farmers proved crucial to the movement in rural areas because of their relative economic autonomy. Furthermore, as advances occurred in voting rights and public accommodations, many organizers turned their attention to issues of economic justice. Agricultural and consumer cooperatives as well as their financial counterparts, credit unions, sprung up across the South. A wide array of national and Mississippi civil rights organizations contributed to the movement, and well-known grassroots leaders were part of the effort. In Ruleville, Fannie Lou Hamer led the establishment of Freedom Farm, and the nearby North Bolivar County Farm Cooperative was established with the involvement of L. C. Dorsey. Many of the cooperative organizers were also instrumental in developing the Delta Health Center.

The movement gained ground in the mid- to late 1960s as local organizations created broader collaborative networks. The Southern Cooperative Development Program was established in 1967 through the Southern Consumers' Education Foundation, which sought to establish and promote cooperatives among low-income residents across the South. Leaders from twenty-two community-based cooperatives, including those focused on agriculture, met in 1967 to address their common concerns and to discuss strategies for overcoming the challenge of limited access to financial resources and the opposition from reactionary whites who feared black power and saw collective agricultural efforts as socialist enterprises. The meeting resulted in the establishment of an umbrella organization, the Federation of Southern Cooperatives, to meet their common needs; it later merged with a land security organization to become the Federation of Southern Cooperatives/Land Assistance Fund. Drawing funds from membership dues, service fees, grants, and contracts, the federation provided training in cooperative development, technical assistance, research, and advocacy.

Using membership data reported by the federation in 1969, Marshall and Godwin estimate that it had eighty affiliated cooperatives in fourteen states, with seventeen in Mississippi serving nearly five thousand members. The federation's state-level affiliate, the Mississippi Association of Cooperatives, was founded in 1972 with a primary focus on assisting limited-resource and black farmers, their families, and their communities. Over the years, it has worked with a variety of cooperatives across the state, among them the Beat Four Farm Cooperative (Macon), the Indian Springs Farmers Association (Petal), the Sweet Potato Growers Association (Mound Bayou), and the Winston County Self-Help Cooperative (Louisville). Contemporary efforts include helping cooperatives to organize and operate farmers markets, grow and sell alternative products, and market specialty products such as fair-trade watermelon destined for East Coast markets.

John J. Green and
Eleanor M. Green
University of Mississippi

Emily Weaver
Delta State University

Delta Black Farmers Oral History Collection and the Jerry Dallas Delta Cooperative Farm Collection, Charles W. Capps Jr. Archives and Museum, Delta State University; Federation of Southern Cooperatives/Land Assistance Fund, *Twenty-Fifth Anniversary Annual Report* (1992); John J. Green, "Community-Based Cooperatives and Networks: Participatory Social Movement Assessment of Four Organizations" (PhD dissertation, University of Missouri at Columbia, 2002); Ray Marshall and Lamond Godwin, *Cooperatives and Rural Poverty in the South* (1971); Kay Mills, *This Little Light of Mine: The Life of Fannie Lou Hamer* (1994); Bruce J. Reynolds, *Black Farmers in America, 1865–2000: The Pursuit of Independent Farming and the Role of Cooperatives* (2003); Al Ulmer, *Cooperatives and Poor People in the South* (1969).

Agricultural Extension and the Smith-Lever Act

Mississippi was one of several states where the efforts of agricultural reformers led to the passage of the Smith-Lever Act of 1914, which established a federal program for agricultural extension work. Educator Seaman Knapp of Iowa conceived the idea of starting farms that would literally demonstrate new agricultural techniques and the benefits farmers would gain from them. Knapp encouraged Mississippi and other states to start demonstration services, funded first by the General Education Board of the Rockefeller Foundation and then by the US Department of Agriculture.

The emphasis on teaching distinguished agricultural extension work from agricultural experiment stations, which had originated after the 1888 Hatch Act at Mississippi Agricultural and Mechanical College (now Mississippi State University) in Oktibbeha County. Stations then followed in Newton, Marshall, and Washington Counties.

Beginning in 1905, Mississippi agricultural extension agents focused on staple crops, particularly cotton, but within five years had moved on to a wide range of innovations. By 1911 at least fifteen hundred Mississippi farmers were enrolled in extension programs in fifty counties. William H. Smith, the superintendent of schools in Holmes County, started the first boys' corn club in the state (and possibly the country), followed shortly by a home study club for girls. Pig clubs, poultry clubs, and tomato clubs began to meet within the next few years.

Despite opposition from some white Mississippians, the federal government's plan for agricultural extension work included African Americans. The first Negro Extension agent was J. A. Booker, working in Mound Bayou and other parts of the Delta. The Smith-Lever Act, first proposed in 1911, took advantage of this sort of club-building enthusiasm by offering a permanent structure and some federal funds. The bill the US Congress passed in 1914 required agricultural colleges to work with the US Department of Agriculture and provided ten thousand dollars to each participating state with the promise of steady increases to be matched by local and state governments.

One of the first beneficiaries of the Smith-Lever Act was Mississippi Agricultural and Mechanical College, which became the center for extension work and energetically took on the goal of teaching farmers and rural residents about innovations in agriculture and farm life.

The Extension Service quickly became a force, following national trends and having agents provide instruction in new techniques on demonstration farms and in demonstration homes. By the 1930s at least one agent worked in each of the state's counties, often providing both agricultural and home demonstrations. In 1937 the Extension Service employed 131 agricultural demonstration workers and 115 home demonstration workers, 61 of whom worked for the Negro Extension service.

The Extension Department tried to combine practical and sometimes scientific advice for farmers with more specific suggestions about architecture, community life, and finance, with early bulletins featuring articles on such topics as "Growing Hogs in Mississippi," "Dairy Barn Construction," "Grasses and Forage Plants," "Practical Spraying for Practical Orchardists," "Helps for Mississippi Poultry Raisers," "Spraying in Mississippi," "The Mississippi Community Congress," "Catalog for Farm Building Plans," "The Terrace in Mississippi," and "Farm Plans for Using Borrowed Capital." Subsequent bulletins dealt a great deal with cotton and agricultural diversity and by the 1920s with canning and sewing.

The Extension Service continues to have its home at Mississippi State University and issues bulletins through the outreach program MSUCares. Reports have become shorter, with more illustrations and fewer scientific discussions.

Recent topics reflect a growing interest in landscaping, intensified concerns about conservation, and Mississippi's growing multiculturalism ("4-H Te Necesita"), as well as a continuing focus on using the latest scientific knowledge to expand agricultural production. A recent director's letter emphasizes both continuity and novelty: "Our goal has always been to improve the quality of life for every Mississippian," though extension work now involves "cell phones, distance learning, video conferencing, sophisticated computer networks, [and] digital imaging diagnostics."

Ted Ownby
University of Mississippi

Annual Reports of Cooperative Extension Work in Agriculture and Home Economics (1916–20, 2000–2010); Roy Vernon Scott, *The Reluctant Farmer: The Rise of Agricultural Extension to 1914* (1971).

Agricultural High Schools

In the early years of the twentieth century, white Mississippians pursued educational improvements that included school consolidation, new colleges for teachers, and a county-based system of agricultural high schools. The second session of the 1908 state legislature provided matching funds for counties that hired teachers and erected classrooms and dormitories to instruct young Mississippians of both sexes in agriculture and domestic science. By 1911 seventeen of the state's eighty-one counties had agricultural high schools, a number that had grown to forty-nine two years later.

Before the school consolidation movement mushroomed in the 1920s alongside the construction of state and county roads, few rural Mississippi children attended high school. State educators, civic-minded farm families, and other self-proclaimed progressives intended agricultural high schools to fill the void of educational opportunity among Mississippi's rural white youth.

In their enthusiasm for new rural schools, education boosters and their supporters in the state legislature got off to a false start. The 1908 law established agricultural high schools for white children only; the measure generated legal challenges, and in 1909 the Mississippi Supreme Court rejected it. After the legislature rewrote the law to nominally provide separate agricultural high schools for the state's African American youth, the number of schools rose until 1919. Mississippians eventually founded only one agricultural high school for African Americans, in Coahoma County.

Yalobusha County Agricultural High School, Oakland, ca. 1906 (Ann Rayburn Paper Americana Collection, Department of Archives and Special Collections, J. D. Williams Library, University of Mississippi [rayburn_ann_26_04_002])

State educators intended the schools' agriculture and domestic science curricula to prepare students for success as farmers and homemakers. Boys practiced fieldwork, animal husbandry, and farm management. Girls studied home economics, gardening, sanitation, and caregiving. The agricultural high schools showcased Mississippians' desire to revitalize their homes, farms, and rural industries by harnessing scientific progress and modern business methods.

The decline of the state's agricultural high schools mirrored their rapid rise. After the initial local enthusiasm that established the institutions, rural school consolidation steadily siphoned off support. By the 1920s most Mississippi taxpayers were no longer willing to support the schools and voted many down in county referendums. Some schools closed when the state board of education refused to fund them. A few survived as two-year community colleges, while others reorganized to provide conventional high school curricula in a process known in the 1930s as superconsolidation. Today, only a handful of the state's secondary schools retain the title of "agricultural high school," and only Forrest County Agricultural High School maintains an agricultural curriculum.

David Hargrove
Gibson Memorial Library,
Winterset, Iowa

James D. Anderson, *The Education of Blacks in the South, 1860–1935* (1988); Joseph A. Bailey, *Seaman A. Knapp: Schoolmaster of American Agriculture* (1948); Ronald K. Goodenow and Arthur O. White, eds., *Education and the Rise of the New South* (1981); William A. Link, *A Hard Country and a Lonely Place: Schooling, Society, and Reform in Rural Virginia, 1870–1920* (1986); Roy V. Scott, *Eugene Beverly Ferris and Agricultural Science in the Lower South* (1991); Wayne J. Urban, *Essays in Twentieth-Century Southern Education: Exceptionalism and Its Limits* (1999).

Agricultural Stabilization and Conservation Service

The Agricultural Stabilization and Conservation Service (ASCS) administered federal farm subsidies, loans, and conservation programs via offices in each of Mississippi's eighty-two counties from 1961 to 1994. The ASCS was part of the US Department of Agriculture (USDA). Officially created in June 1961, the ASCS traced its heritage to the Agriculture Adjustment Administration of the 1930s. Despite being a federal agency, local control over policy represented a central tenet of the ASCS. Local farmers elected three "county committeemen" to serve three-year terms; the members of these committees selected directors to manage the day-to-day affairs of each county ASCS office. The US secretary of agriculture appointed a state ASCS committee of five farmers, and this committee oversaw statewide operations and appointed the state director with an office in Jackson.

The ASCS sought to control cotton surpluses via allotments—a specific number of acres that each farmer could plant in cotton. Farmers who exceeded their allotments received marketing penalties. These allotments were a vital issue in Mississippi, which had a total of 1,546,280 acres of cotton allotments in 1963. Mississippi's ASCS employees and committee members encouraged farmers who were not going to use their entire allotment to release surplus acreage, which could then be offered to farmers who sought additional acres. In 1962 the ASCS newsletter chastised Mississippi's farmers for keeping 78,000 acres of unused cotton allotments while other growers had requested an additional 346,713 acres. County offices attempted to find ways to maximize the usage of cotton allotments. In 1969, for example, the Leflore County ASCS held a "Cotton Transfer Referendum" that asked farmers to vote on the sale or lease of allotments outside of the county for 1970. The USDA abandoned cotton allotments under the Food and Agricultural Act of 1977. Under the new program, the ASCS utilized the national crop averages to set target prices for cotton, while ASCS aid became tied to market price rather than acreage allotment.

The Mississippi ASCS also managed USDA experimental programs. In 1963, Mississippi and thirteen other states piloted the Cropland Conversion Program authorized by the Agriculture Act of 1962. Under this program, farmers would set aside regularly used cropland for pastures, forests, wildlife habitats, or recreational facilities in exchange for payments of approximately thirty-seven dollars an acre. In the first year, only the counties of Itawamba, Lee, Tippah, and Union were eligible for the program, and they set aside 7,348 acres. In 1964–65 the USDA authorized the Mississippi ASCS to conduct the program only in Montgomery and Union Counties, where 1,376 acres were set aside.

Among the other programs administered by the Mississippi ASCS were the Feed Grain Program, Appalachian Land Stabilization and Conservation Program, Acreage Allotment and Marketing Quota Programs, Farm Storage and Drying Equipment Loan Program, Upland Cotton Program, and Agriculture Conservation Program. The state committee not only issued annual reports that detailed county-by-county crop yields, acreage, and dollars in federal assistance but also published the *Mississippi ASCS Newsletter*, which provided the state's farmers with information regarding agriculture politics in Washington, deadlines for farm subsidies, and personnel decisions within the ASCS. Mississippi county ASCS offices also published newsletters detailing local ASCS votes, committee information, and farm program deadlines.

As in broader elections, African American farmers initially had difficulty voting in local ASCS elections, but in the wake of the Voting Rights Act of 1965, black participation very slowly increased. In 1976 only 3 African Americans (including 1 Mississippian) numbered among the 984 elected ASCS county committee members nationwide. That year showed some improvement, with 7 African Americans elected as alternate members of Mississippi's county committees; nevertheless, the limited black participation on county committees and in crucial ASCS county office jobs remained a central point of contention for the remainder of the agency's existence.

US secretary of agriculture Mike Espy, a Mississippi native, reorganized the USDA in 1994, and the ASCS and other farm-related agencies merged into the newly created Farm Service Agency.

Ryan L. Fletcher
University of Mississippi

ASCS Annual Reports for Mississippi, 1963–79; Clyde Farnsworth, *New York Times* (28 April 1962, 6 May 1962); Valerie Grim, *Agricultural History* (Spring 1996); *Leflore County ASCS Newsletter* (1969); *Mississippi ASCS Newsletter* (1962–63); Wayne D. Rasmussen and Gladys L. Baker, *The Department of Agriculture* (1972).

Agriculture

As read from the bottom up and the top down, the history of agriculture in Mississippi tells some of the most revealing stories about the state's social, political, cultural, and economic history. In this narrative, rural and farm people position themselves at the heart of the southern agricultural experience. Agriculture in Mississippi is a story of many

A 1937 model cotton picker, Stoneville (Library of Congress, Washington, D.C. [LC-USZ62-63140])

Advertisement for fertilizer dispersed by crop-dusting airplanes, Mississippi Delta, October 1939 (Photograph by Marion Post Wolcott, Library of Congress, Washington, D.C. [LC-USF34-052399-D])

cotton, vegetable crops, and livestock. This movement created opportunities for farming interests in Mississippi, which, like the rest of the South, came to depend increasingly on slave labor to maximize production.

Between 1798 and 1865 agricultural slave labor became entrenched in the Magnolia State. Indeed, after 1820 field labor evolved as the most contested issue in social and political conversations involving agricultural production. Planters shaped and controlled Mississippi's social, political, and economic life through the ownership of land, rural merchandising, and a style of farm and plantation management that oppressed all farm laborers, slave or free, black or white, often resulting in resentment and various forms of retaliation.

Scholars of nineteenth- and twentieth-century agriculture have analyzed Old South and New South agricultural production. The two eras share a common plantation organization, agricultural management, and company formation. Old South descriptions emphasize life among blacks in slave communities, organization of the labor force on large slave plantations and small farms, and the advantages and disadvantages of life as a farmworker in these two very different environments. Planters and other investors considered resources in land and in human property investments in farming and a foundation for Mississippi's agricultural politics. Descriptions of New South postbellum agriculture discuss farm production in similar but often ambiguous ways. The state political apparatus reestablished a system in which former slave owners continued to control farm production as the owners of free labor. Examples include the institution of Black Codes in the immediate postemancipation years, the establishment of the convict lease system, the failure of free wage work in the farm economy, the evolution of tenancy and sharecropping, the appearance of crop liens and peonage, conflicts between former slaves and former masters over land, and the efforts of poor whites to earn a living on the land. In time, farm families across the state had difficulty competing with planters in the Delta, where New South plantation companies such as Delta and Pine Land became some of the largest businesses in the country.

Although New South plantation owners and managers believed they had a business structure in place sufficient to make profits, they also had to admit that southern farms in the late nineteenth and early twentieth centuries produced low yields, suffered from debt, and were embattled over labor. Government intervention was required to pull southern agriculture and Mississippi farmers out of a credit-debt cycle and marginal farming. An understanding of farming history beginning in the 1930s requires an analysis of farm-related federal policies. The members of the planter class— many of them descendants of slave owners—often exerted great power over federal intervention into state politics and agricultural production, manipulating New Deal politics and using the Agricultural Adjustment Act and the Farm Credit Administration to maintain control over labor. By using federal social programs to benefit selected workers, planters

tales, especially of the powerful and how they ruled the countryside and of the common folk and how they attempted to resist oppression. This history reveals the experiences of those who held positions, power, and land in abundance and who appropriated farm labor through various forms of intimidation to maintain control. It is also the history of those low-wage workers responsible for making farms and agriculture-related industries profitable for the powerful few. Mississippi's agriculture has for centuries been competitive, productive, violent, and disruptive, with fierce competition between Native Americans, black Americans, and white farmers. Conflict over and on the land occurred especially between plantation owners, relatively large farmers, and small family farm producers, each working to control farm politics, farm labor, and farm production.

The question of land domination led to Indian Removal, one of the greatest pushes in American history. In the 1820s and 1830s the US government entered into a number of treaties that restricted Native Americans to reservations and made their former lands available for the production of found ways to keep government funding for themselves and avoid paying for services their laborers needed. For example, plantations manipulated parity payments to their advantage to begin the transition to capital-intensive farming, while Mississippi's state- and national-level politicians shaped farm subsidy programs so that they benefited powerful supporters, such as Delta planters. Few if any policies supported small farmers and agricultural laborers, whose living conditions worsened as their earning power diminished.

Cotton monoculture persisted in Mississippi's farm economy until the late 1940s and early 1950s, with nearly all of the state's arable land devoted to the cultivation of hand-planted and -picked cotton. Developments in science and technology along with changing production needs and demands enabled the mechanization of agriculture and profoundly affected farm production, although the process was slow in the Magnolia State. Tractors began to replace low-grade plows and planters pulled by mules and other draft animals in the 1930s, while the cotton picker appeared during the following decade. Throughout this period yields remained low, labor remained oppressed, and poor sharecroppers and wage workers remained locked in a cycle of debt and lawlessness. Mississippi's farm economy diversified beginning around the time of World War II, adding other staples, including corn, soybeans, rice, and ultimately wheat, which enabled crops to be grown year-round.

Among the many representations of rural and farm life in the early twentieth century were images that indicated that farm communities were experiencing alarming stress and humiliating poverty. Rural families and communities were seen as underdeveloped, backward, and ignorant. Mississippi benefited from several farm-related federal educational programs, including land-grant colleges for whites in the 1870s and for blacks in the 1890s. Services provided by agents at agricultural experiment stations beginning in 1898 helped improve farming methods and conditions, beginning the transition to scientifically based agricultural production. The state also improved farm and rural life by using programs of the Cooperative Extension Service, created in 1914 by the Smith-Lever Act. Home visits, farm demonstrations, and community club work taught rural dwellers better practices for farming, home economics, and home management. Demonstration work created opportunities for social and cultural uplift among children, women, limited-resource farmers, and blacks and whites in plantation communities. These educational programs also helped large planters and plantation owners by minimizing the cost of providing for and monitoring the labor of those whose work they controlled.

The rural poor experienced limited benefits from federal housing and resettlement programs during and after the New Deal. For example, because food was available but not affordable, the need for agricultural commodities and, later, food stamps swelled. Despite the obvious need for assistance, agricultural employers opposed any reforms that might weaken their control over low-wage labor, stymieing federally funded rural housing, health, and food programs.

Because federal intervention into land acquisition and farm production pitted blacks against whites and the poor against the wealthy, many movements and individual acts of resistance evolved from people and families who struggled to achieve agency and inclusion in democratic societies. Such efforts resulted in the establishment of such organizations as the Farmers' Alliance, the Colored Farmers' Alliance, the Farmers' Union, the Grange, and the Southern Tenant Farmers' Union as well as in the creation of agrarian movements such as Populism.

Poor farm families and laborers also used other strategies to minimize their exploitation at the hands of white planters and to challenge the rural elite. Such efforts included the formation of cooperatives as well as migration away from agriculture and/or away from Mississippi. By leaving the state's fields, laborers and small farm producers freed themselves from the cycles of debt and imprisonment that the rural elite had used to shackle these workers to the land.

Members of the planter class responded with a variety of strategies to maintain control of Mississippi's land, labor, and wages in the face of these agrarian movements and social and political organizing. These responses included peonage; crop liens; convict labor; encouraging immigration, especially by Italian and Chinese workers; levee camp construction; and establishing Indian reservations. Planters and farmers also organized political and social groups, such as the Deer Creek Association and the Farm Bureau, chambers of commerce, and the Delta Council. These efforts have largely succeeded, and Mississippi's agriculture remains largely controlled by the privileged, who continue to define the roles played by many others in agriculture.

Valerie Grim

Indiana University

Sharon D. Wright Austen, *The Transformation of Plantation Politics: Black Politics, Concentrated Poverty, and Social Capital in the Mississippi Delta* (2006); John M. Barry, *Rising Tide: The Great Mississippi Flood of 1927 and How It Changed America* (1998); James E. Bell, *The Evolution of the Mississippi Delta: From Exploited Labor and Mules to Mechanization and Agribusiness* (2008); Bradley Bond, *Mississippi: A Documentary History* (2003); James C. Cobb, *The Most Southern Place on Earth: The Mississippi Delta and the Roots of Regional Identity* (1992); Pete Daniel, *Dispossession: Discrimination against African American Farmers in the Age of Civil Rights* (2013); James T. Graves, *From the Old South to the New, a Delayed Transition: Mississippi Cotton Growers and the Agricultural Adjustment Act, 1933–1936* (2003); David J. Libby, *Slavery and Frontier Mississippi, 1720–1835* (2004); Richard A. McLemore, *A History of Mississippi*, 2 vols. (1973); John H. Moore, *Agriculture in Antebellum Mississippi* (1958); George S. Pabis, *Daily Life along the Mississippi* (2007); Ronald E. Seavoy, *The American Peasantry: Southern Agricultural Labor and Its Legacy, 1850–1995: A Study in Political Economy* (1998); Star R. Spurlock, *Costs and Returns for Cotton, Rice, and Soybeans in the Delta Area of Mississippi* (1996); William B. Taylor, *Down on Parchman Farm: The Great Prison in the Mississippi Delta* (1999); Herbert Weaver, *Mississippi Farmers, 1850–*

1860 (1968); Nan E. Woodruff, *American Congo: The African American Freedom Struggle in the Delta* (2003); Clyde A. Woods, *Development Arrested: The Blues and Plantation Power in the Mississippi Delta* (1998).

Agriculture and Commerce, Commissioner of

Agriculture has long been and remains the dominant force in Mississippi's economy, accounting for almost eight billion dollars annually and directly or indirectly employing about 29 percent of the state's workforce. Agriculture constitutes the state's single-largest industry.

To promote and regulate the business of agriculture, the Mississippi legislature created the Department of Agriculture and Commerce in 1906. Every four years Mississippi voters choose a commissioner of agriculture and commerce, one of eight statewide elected officials. The commissioner's duties range from food and sanitation inspection to the certification of gasoline pumps. He or she is responsible for promoting Mississippi's agricultural products to expand their share of the retail market as well as for preventing and investigating agriculture and livestock theft. Two of the commissioner's most visible roles are as manager of the Mississippi Farmers Market and of the Mississippi Agriculture and Forestry Museum in Jackson; the latter receives approximately 130,000 visitors annually.

In the more than a century since the position's creation, only seven people have served as commissioner of agriculture and commerce: Henry Edward Blakeslee (1906–16), Peter Parley Garner (1916–28), J. C. Holton (1928–40), Silas Edward Corley (1940–68), Jim Buck Ross (1968–96), Lester Spell Jr. (1996–2012), and Cindy Hyde-Smith (2012–present).

Brian Wilson
University of Mississippi

Dana B. Brammer and John W. Winkle, eds., *A Contemporary Analysis of Mississippi's Constitutional Government: Proceedings of a Forum, May 2–3, 1986* (1986); Dale Krane and Stephen D. Shaffer, *Mississippi Government and Politics: Modernizers versus Traditionalists* (1992); Mississippi Department of Agriculture and Commerce, *2010 Annual Report* (2011); Mississippi Department of Agriculture and Commerce website, www.mdac.ms.gov; *Mississippi Official and Statistical Register* (2009); Joseph Parker, *Politics in Mississippi* (1993).

Air Quality

Mississippi is fortunate to have an abundant supply of clean air, historically meeting all federal air quality standards. The Mississippi Department of Environmental Quality (MDEQ) is responsible for protecting the state's air as part of its mission to protect the health and safety of Mississippians by conserving and improving the environment and fostering wise economic growth through research and responsible regulation.

Under the Clean Air Act, the US Environmental Protection Agency (EPA) establishes primary air quality standards to protect public health and secondary standards to protect public welfare—including protecting ecosystems, plants, and animals. The EPA has set national air quality standards for six principal air pollutants: ground-level ozone, particulate matter, nitrogen dioxide, sulfur dioxide, carbon monoxide, and lead. MDEQ monitors all of these pollutants except lead and carbon monoxide, which are so low in the state that the EPA and MDEQ have determined that they no longer need to be monitored.

The data collected in 2010 at various monitoring sites show that Mississippi is meeting all the ambient air quality standards. Also, the monitoring data for hazardous air pollutants indicate that the numbers are well below the required thresholds.

However, new, more stringent federal standards are raising additional questions. Recent data trends and air-monitoring data indicate that DeSoto County and the coastal counties have numbers that are very close to the ozone standard. Therefore, MDEQ has initiated a voluntary ozone precursor air pollution control program in partnership with local government and business leaders to prevent future nonattainment designations from the EPA. MDEQ continues to operate a network of sophisticated continuous air analyzers and twenty-four-hour samplers to measure ambient air pollution.

Maya Rao
Mississippi Department of
Environmental Quality

Mississippi Department of Environmental Quality website, www.deq.state.ms.us; US Environmental Protection Agency website, www.epa.gov.

Alcohol and Drug Abuse

In 2005 Mississippi had 13,953 drug abuse violation arrests, 912 of them involving youth under the age of eighteen. Additional 2004–5 National Surveys on Drug Use and Health results indicate that roughly 68,000 Mississippi citizens (2.9 percent) reported illicit drug dependence or abuse within the past year, and approximately 23,000 (8.82 percent) twelve- to seventeen-year-olds reported using an illicit drug in the past month. Approximately 63,000 Mississippi citizens (2.68 percent) reported needing but not receiving treatment for illicit drug use within the past year. The director of the Office of National Drug Control Policy is authorized to designate areas within the United States that exhibit serious drug trafficking problems that harm other areas of the country as "high-intensity drug trafficking areas." As of 2015, eight Mississippi counties—Forrest, Hancock, Harrison, Hinds, Jackson, Lafayette, Madison, and Rankin—bear that designation, meaning that they participate in a program to coordinate drug control efforts among local, state, and federal law enforcement agencies and receive equipment, technology, and additional federal resources to help combat drug trafficking.

Reports from the US Drug Enforcement Administration acknowledge that Mississippi is one of several southern river and gulf port states that are experiencing significant problems with the movement of illegal drugs. Drug trafficking patterns indicate that the interstate highway system is the preferred method of transporting illegal drugs into and through the state.

A variety of illegal drugs are being abused in Mississippi. Cocaine, specifically solid, smokable crack, is the predominant drug threat in Mississippi because of its availability and its high addiction rate. Cocaine is distributed and abused in both the state's metropolitan and rural areas and is associated with more incidents of violent crime than any other drug in Mississippi.

Methamphetamine poses the second-most-serious drug threat in Mississippi as a consequence of its increasing availability, low cost, rapid growth of abuse, and threat to human life and the environment. The state's law enforcement officers now frequently encounter methamphetamine labs, which manufacture the drug using the chemical anhydrous ammonia and cold pills, mostly in rural communities. During 2006 the Drug Enforcement Administration and state and local authorities reported 134 methamphetamine lab seizures.

Marijuana is the most frequently abused and abundantly available drug in Mississippi, regularly sold and used by citizens from all ethnic and socioeconomic groups. The marijuana being distributed and used in the state comes primarily from Mexico. According to 2004–5 National Surveys on Drug

Church with a "Vote against Liquor" sign in foreground Myrtle (Photograph by David Wharton)

Use and Health data, approximately 113,000 Mississippi citizens aged twelve or older reported using marijuana during the preceding month.

Club drugs are available in small quantities throughout Mississippi, especially around university towns. MDMA (also known as Ecstasy) has become the most prevalent and popular of the club drugs, primarily among middle- to upper-class young adult whites. The drugs GHB and ketamine are not currently known to be widely available or popular in Mississippi.

As of 2015, heroin was on the rise at an alarming rate, and in 2014 Mississippi had more heroin cases than any year in the previous decade. The drug has become a larger threat because of the increasing demand and relatively low cost.

Diverted pharmaceuticals are a popular means for obtaining drugs illegally. Law enforcement officials report that OxyContin abuse remains a threat in Mississippi, and it is currently the pharmaceutical drug of concern. Prescription forgeries, doctor shopping, and Internet pharmacies all aid in the diversion process. Clinics in neighboring states continue to be a source for the abuse of methadone by Mississippi residents.

Mississippi's alcohol statistics are also alarming. In 2005 underage drinking cost the state's citizens $534 million in medical care, work loss, and pain and suffering. This figure translates to $1,747 per year for each youth in the state—forty-first among the states. Underage drinking is widespread: approximately 135,000 Mississippi youth drink each year. In 2005 underage drinkers consumed 12.7 percent of all alcohol sold—$143 million. Underage drinkers accounted for 2.3 percent of Mississippi's 2003 arrests for driving under the influence, a statistic that remained unchanged through 2005. That year, the costs of underage drinking were estimated at violence, $222.4 million; traffic crashes, $199.3 million; high-risk sex (among those aged fourteen to twenty), $53.3 million; property crime, $27.6 million; injury, $13.2 million; poisonings and psychoses, $3.0 million; fetal alcohol syndrome (among mothers aged fifteen to twenty), 10.6 million; and alcohol treatment, $5.2 million.

Mississippi ranks among the worst states in the country for alcohol-related behaviors, driving under the influence, and deaths of underage drinkers. The state's adult males are twice as likely as females to be heavy drinkers (4.9 percent to 2.3 percent on the Behavioral Risk Factor Surveillance System). Treatment data from the Mississippi Department of Mental Health show that in 2005, 22.3 percent of adult patients received treatment for alcohol as their primary problem, and 23.7 percent received treatment for alcohol as a secondary problem. Patients reported alcohol as their drug of choice 36.4 percent of the time. The 2005 Mississippi Smart Track Survey showed that alcohol was the most frequently abused substance among high school students and that 10.3 percent of ninth, tenth, and eleventh graders had been suspended or expelled as a result of an alcohol-related incident. These statistics strongly indicate that Mississippi could benefit from investing more dollars in the prevention of drug and alcohol problems as opposed to the higher costs associated with alcohol and other drug treatment.

Charline R. McCord

Clinton, Mississippi

2008 Mississippi State Factsheet, Drug Enforcement Administration website, www.usdoj.gov/dea/; International Institute for Alcohol Awareness website, www.iiaaonline.org; Mississippi Department of Education and Mississippi Department of Mental Health, Mississippi's Health Data Source website, www.snapshots.ms.gov; National Institute on Alcohol Abuse and Alcoholism website, http://nationalsubstanceabuseindex.org; Office of National Drug Control Policy website, www.whitehouse.gov /ondcp; Substance Abuse and Mental Health Services Administration, Office of Applied Studies website, www.oas.samhsa.gov.

Alcorn, James Lusk

(1816–1894) Twenty-Eighth Governor, 1870–1871

James L. Alcorn was Mississippi's first elected Republican governor and the namesake of Alcorn County and Alcorn State University. Alcorn had previously served in the state legislatures of Kentucky and Mississippi and had risen to the rank of general in the Confederate military service during the Civil War.

Alcorn was born near Golconda, Illinois, on 4 November 1816. At a very early age he moved to Kentucky with his family. He graduated from Cumberland College and then served as deputy sheriff in Livingston County from 1839 to 1844 and in the Kentucky House of Representatives in 1843 before moving to Mississippi to establish a law practice at Delta, in Panola County. While practicing law and accumulating large landholdings and numerous slaves, Alcorn served in the Mississippi legislature. He also represented his county in the state constitutional conventions of 1851 and 1861. Perhaps his most important contribution to his adopted state prior to the Civil War was his authorship of the bill creating the levee board and his service as its first president.

A member of the Whig Party, Alcorn opposed secession in 1861, but like most Mississippi Whigs, he served in the Confederate Army and supported the Confederacy. After the war Alcorn advocated full civil rights for former slaves, including the rights to vote, to hold public office, and to testify in court. Alcorn became a leader in Mississippi's newly established Republican Party and won its nomination for governor. Following his election in 1869 and Mississippi's readmission to the Union, Alcorn was inaugurated on 10 March 1870. In Reconstruction parlance, Alcorn was a scalawag, a white southerner who became a Republican after the Civil War.

During his administration the Mississippi legislature established a state system of public education and founded Alcorn University, the first land-grant college for blacks in the United States. The legislature also granted new business corporations certain tax exemptions and other benefits to make Mississippi more attractive to railroads and other industry. Alcorn's administration worked to improve public education but did not resolve issues of segregation and unequal funding in education.

Alcorn resigned in November 1871 to accept an appointment to the US Senate. Two years later he again ran for governor but lost to Adelbert Ames. Following the expiration of his Senate term in 1877, Alcorn returned to Eagle's Nest, his plantation home in Coahoma County.

Alcorn's last act of public service came when he became a delegate to the convention that drafted Mississippi's 1890 constitution, the third such gathering in which he participated. On 19 December 1894 he died at Eagle's Nest.

David G. Sansing

University of Mississippi

Biographical Directory of the United States Congress (1950); Eric Foner, *Reconstruction: America's Unfinished Revolution, 1865–1877* (1988); William C. Harris, *The Day of the Carpetbagger: Republican Reconstruction in Mississippi* (1979); *Mississippi Official and Statistical Register* (1912); Lillian A. Pereyra, *James L. Alcorn: Persistent Whig* (1966); Dunbar Rowland, *Encyclopedia of Mississippi History*, vol. 1 (1907).

Alcorn County

Waldron Street, Corinth, seat of Alcorn County, ca. 1908 (Ann Rayburn Paper Americana Collection, Department of Archives and Special Collections, J. D. Williams Library, University of Mississippi [rayburn_ann_23_134_001])

Located along the Tennessee border in northeastern Mississippi, Alcorn County is named for James L. Alcorn, Mississippi's twenty-eighth governor. The county was carved out of Tishomingo County in 1870, when it was originally home to 10,431 residents, roughly 75 percent of them white. Corinth, which eventually became Alcorn's county seat, emerged in the 1850s as an important railroad center, making it a strategic site during the Civil War.

Two major battles occurred in Corinth, the first in May 1862, after the Battle of Shiloh, and the second in the fall of that year, when fighting broke out between forces helmed by Ulysses S. Grant and those led by Earl Van Dorn. The latter battle left more than eight hundred soldiers dead and the city under Union control. Corinth was also home to a Union camp for escaped slaves and served as a major hospital center for the Confederate wounded. Corinth National Cemetery houses the remains of Civil War soldiers from fifteen states. During Reconstruction some of the earliest known Ku Klux Klan activity took place in what is now Alcorn County.

By 1880 the county's population had increased to 14,272, with whites now comprising only 69 percent of the total. As in most of northeastern Mississippi, Alcorn County's farms were relatively small and mostly cultivated by their owners. In 1880 Alcorn ranked high among Mississippi counties in livestock and tobacco production, while corn and wheat output remained average and cotton production low. Although Alcorn had sixty-five manufacturing firms at this time, most were fairly small, and the county's industrial sector employed only 130 men and 9 women. Whitfield Manufacturing was Alcorn's first textile factory.

Alcorn has a unique early history with regard to women in academia. Born in 1850 in what became Alcorn, Modena Lowrey Berry had an extraordinary career as an administrator at Tippah County's Blue Mountain College from 1873 to 1934. Her father, educator and Confederate general Mark Perrin Lowrey, had helped establish Blue Mountain in 1873. Corona College, one of the South's first higher education institutions open to women, opened in Corinth in 1857.

In the early twentieth century Alcorn experienced significant growth. By 1910 the county's population had reached 18,159. Despite the predominance of small farms, Alcorn ranked among the top third of Mississippi's counties in average farm size. Most of Alcorn's agricultural lots were plantations that had been subdivided into farms averaging about one hundred acres each. During this era more than half of Alcorn's white farmers could claim ownership of their land, while only a small percentage of black farmers were landholders. By 1900 Alcorn County had sixty-six manufacturing establishments, employing 455 men, 126 women, and 17 children. The 1916 religious census showed that the largest denominations in Alcorn were the Methodist Episcopal Church, South; the Southern Baptist Convention; and the Missionary Baptists. The Colored Methodist Episcopal Church and the Churches of Christ had significant congregations as well.

Corinth and its surrounding areas have been home to a number of notable individuals. Authors Thomas Hal Phillips and Etheridge Knight were born there in 1922 and 1931, respectively. Phillips set many of his novels in southern locations. *The Bitterweed Path*, his first book, dealt more directly with homosexuality than most fiction of the era. Knight suffused his work with African American vernacular, eventually becoming an important figure in the Black Arts movement of the 1970s. Corinth also produced two notable figures associated with aviation. Born in 1909, cartoonist Russell Keaton drew the *Flyin' Jenny* comic strip from 1939 to 1945. And popular stunt pilot Roscoe Turner, for whom Alcorn's airport is named, was born outside Corinth in 1895.

By 1930 the county's population had grown to 23,653. While a high percentage of Alcorn's land was still cultivated, average farm size had decreased to roughly fifty acres per lot. Corinth was a growing town of 5,500 people, and the county had more than 700 people working in industry. In 1934 Alcorn County became the home of the nation's first rural electrical cooperative. Corinth's Depression-era residents are reputed to have developed the "slugburger," a five-cent hamburger made affordable through the addition of cheaper, nonmeat ingredients. Corinth now hosts the annual Slugburger Festival.

In 1960 Alcorn had a population of 25,282, 87 percent of them white. The county's farmers continued to focus on corn, ranking seventh in the state in its production. Alcorn's manufacturing and agricultural workforces were almost equal in size, both employing more than 2,000 people. Women working in garment factories comprised a substantial proportion of the county's labor pool. Twenty years later, however, the county experienced a significant labor shift: by 1980

Alcorn's industrial sector employed 6,860 people, the fourth-highest number of industrial workers in the state, while fewer than 200 people worked full time in agriculture.

Alcorn's population increased by about 47 percent between 1960 and 2010, reaching 37,057 in that year. Like many of northeastern Mississippi's counties, Alcorn's population was predominantly white, with small but significant African American and Latino minorities.

Mississippi Encyclopedia Staff
University of Mississippi

Mississippi State Planning Commission, *Progress Report on State Planning in Mississippi* (1938); *Mississippi Statistical Abstract*, Mississippi State University (1952–2010); Charles Sydnor and Claude Bennett, *Mississippi History* (1939); University of Virginia Library, Historical Census Browser website, http://mapserver.lib.virginia.edu; E. Nolan Waller and Dani A. Smith, *Growth Profiles of Mississippi's Counties, 1960–1980* (1985).

Alcorn State University

Founded in 1871, Alcorn State University is the oldest historically black land-grant institution in the United States and the second-oldest state-supported university in Mississippi. Alcorn is located in rural southwestern Mississippi, in Claiborne County, forty-five miles south of Vicksburg and forty miles north of Natchez. It was founded on a site originally occupied by Oakland College, a school for white youth established by Presbyterians in 1828 and closed as a result of the Civil War. The state purchased the abandoned Oakland College campus in 1871 for forty thousand dollars, named the new school after Gov. James L. Alcorn, and designated it for the education of black youth. Alcorn University's first president was Hiram Rhoades Revels, the first black senator in US history.

The school initially had three major components: a four-year college course, a two-year preparatory course, and a three-year graded course. Subjects offered were English, Latin, and mathematics as well as those included in the Industrial Department—agriculture, carpeting, blacksmithing, shoemaking, printing, painting, nurse training, sewing, domestic science, and laundering. Room and board was five dollars a month. The institution, like other African American schools during these years, was more like a trade school than a college. It was at first exclusively for black males, but women were admitted in 1895.

In 1878 Alcorn University became Alcorn Agricultural and Mechanical College, and on the basis of the federal government's 1862 Morrell Act, it was named a land-grant college. The Mississippi legislature's goals for the institution clearly emphasized training rather than education: "The establishment and maintenance of a first class institution at which the youth of the state of Mississippi may acquire a common school education and a scientific and practical knowledge of agriculture, horticulture, and the mechanical arts, also in the proper growth and call of stock, without, however, excluding scientific and classic studies, including military tactics."

In 1974, House Bill 298, signed by Gov. William L. Waller, gave all state-supported colleges university status, and Alcorn Agricultural and Mechanical College became Alcorn State University. By continually expanding, Alcorn has overcome the difficulties faced by a predominantly black school in a society that emphasizes white supremacy. The initial emphasis on preparing youth for service in both general and applied knowledge areas was accomplished despite lukewarm support. By the early 1990s, however, Alcorn had grown into a more diversified university. It has expanded its educational services to meet the needs of the community at large, a concept known today as the "communiversity." The school provides an undergraduate education that enables students to continue their work in graduate and professional schools, engage in teaching, and enter other professions. The athletic program, which once encompassed only football, basketball, and baseball, now includes track, tennis, volleyball, and golf.

As Mississippi has come to recognize the importance of educating all of its citizens in the post-civil-rights world, Alcorn has gained in status and size. From eight faculty members in 1871, Alcorn has now grown to more than five hundred faculty and staff. The student body has increased from 179 male students to nearly 4,000 students—men and women, whites and blacks, and from all over the world. While early graduates of Alcorn had limited horizons, more recent graduates have gone on to success as doctors, lawyers, dentists, teachers, principals, superintendents, managers, business owners, and many other occupations. The university has had sixteen presidents, with Walter Washington (1969–94) serving as the longest-tenured president at any US institution of higher education. Alcorn State is now fully accredited, with seven divisions and degree programs in more than fifty areas. The facilities have grown from three buildings to more than eighty, while graduating classes have grown from three members to more than five hundred per year. The more than twenty thousand alumni include educators Cleopatra Thompson, S. E. Johnson, and Ruby Stutts Lyells; civil rights activists Medgar Evers and Myrlie Evers-Williams; and NFL star Steve McNair. *Roots* author Alex Haley studied at Alcorn as a teenager, and Memphis business leader Joseph Edison Walker and journalist Horace R. Cayton were early graduates. Alcorn State is now a true university, having long discarded its trade school status and image.

Josephine M. Posey
Alcorn State University

D. Milan Davis, *Pushing Forward Okolona: Okolona Industrial School* (1938); Guy Merlerson Dunham, *Centennial History of Alcorn A&M College* (1971); Josephine M. Posey, *Against Great Odds: The History of Alcorn State University* (1994); Tammy Wayne Rogers, *Journal of Mississippi History* (May 1974); George A. Sewell, *Crisis* (April 1972).

Alexander, Margaret Walker

(1915–1998) Author

Margaret Walker Alexander, 1976 (William R. Ferris Collection, Southern Folklife Collection, Wilson Library, University of North Carolina at Chapel Hill)

Margaret Walker Alexander, a poet, novelist, biographer, and essayist, was groomed from birth for a literary life. She entered the world on 7 July 1915 in Birmingham, Alabama, joining an educated and gifted family: her grandfather, father, and mother all received college degrees and expected the same of their children. She finished elementary school by the age of eleven and graduated from high school by fourteen to attend the University of New Orleans. She received a bachelor's degree from Northwestern University before attending the University of Iowa for graduate school, receiving a master's in 1940 and a doctorate in 1965. She and her husband, Firnist James Alexander, had four children.

Alexander belonged to an illustrious group of African Americans writing in the 1940s. Her college poetry was published in W. E. B. Du Bois's *Crisis*, and she was the first African American writer to win the Yale Series of Younger Poets competition. Her true literary career began, however, with the publication of her first book of poetry, *For My People* (1942). In her first published poem, "Why I Write," which appeared in *Crisis* when she was just nineteen, Walker made clear the connection between her life as a poet and the voices of African Americans. The poem begins, "I want to write / I want to write the songs of my people / I want to hear them singing melodies in the dark." "For My People," her best-known, most-loved, and most-often-recited poem, is a work *for* African Americans: she writes of their beauty, wisdom, music, religion, anger, frustration, certainties and uncertainties, hopes, and determinations. The poem opens, "For my people everywhere singing their slave songs repeatedly: their dirges and their ditties and their blues and jubilees," and ends with a flourish that recalls biblical language: "Let a new earth rise. Let another world be born. Let a bloody peace be written in the sky. Let a second generation full of courage issue forth; let a people loving freedom come to growth. Let a beauty full of healing and a strength of final clenching be the pulsing in our spirits and our blood. Let the martial songs be written, let the dirges disappear. Let a race of men now rise and take control."

Alexander's most critically acclaimed work is her only novel, *Jubilee* (1966). *Jubilee* won the Houghton Mifflin Literary Fellowship Award and breathed new life into her career, igniting new academic interest in her poetry. *Jubilee* follows Alexander's great-grandmother from slavery to her new life after Reconstruction, developing a major theme in her work: black people's ability to overcome obstacles. Alexander believed that she was a social activist, fighting for the rights of African Americans. "I'm always looking back in order to understand what's happening today, and what may happen tomorrow," Alexander said in an interview. "If we understand yesterday, then we know what's happening tomorrow."

Alexander's other literary endeavors include *Prophets for a New Day* (1970), *October Journey* (1973), and *A Poetic Equation: Conversations between Nikki Giovanni and Margaret Walker* (1974). She also published two collections of essays, *How I Wrote Jubilee and Other Essays of Life and Literature* (1990) and *On Being Female, Black, and Free: Essays by Margaret Walker, 1932–1992* (1997). In *Richard Wright: Daemonic Genius* (1988), Alexander offers a biography of her famous friend and literary contemporary.

Alexander also dedicated herself to education, serving as a professor of English at Jackson State University for thirty years before retiring in 1979. Alexander played an integral part in building the university's humanities and honors programs, but her most lasting effort was the Institute for the Study of the History, Life, and Culture of Black People, which she founded in 1968 and which was later renamed the Margaret Walker Alexander National Research Center. Her work is the subject of a lively and growing body of scholarship. She died in Chicago on 30 November 1998 at the age of eighty-three.

Lisa Sloan
University of Mississippi

Carolyn J. Brown, *Song of My Life: A Biography of Margaret Walker* (2014); Hazel Carby, in *Slavery and the Literary Imagination*, ed. Deborah E. McDowell and Arnold Rampersad (1989); Joanne V. Gabbin, *Callaloo* (1999); Maryemma Graham, *African American Review* (Summer 1993); Maryemma Graham, ed., *Fields Watered with Blood: Critical Essays on Margaret Walker* (2001); Maryemma Graham, *The House Where My Soul Lives: The Life of Margaret Walker* (forthcoming); Robert A. Harris, in *Mississippi Women: Their Histories, Their Lives*, ed. Martha H. Swain, Elizabeth Anne Payne, Marjorie Julian Spruill, and Susan Ditto (2003); *The Journal of Blacks in Higher Education* (Spring 1999).

Allain, William A.

(1928–2013) Fifty-Ninth Governor, 1984–1988

William Allain was born on 14 February 1928 in the Adams County community of Washington. He was educated at the University of Notre Dame and the University of Mississippi, where he earned a law degree in 1950. Allain served in the US infantry for three years during the Korean War, spending significant time in combat. He practiced law in Natchez from his discharge in 1953 until 1962, when he was appointed assistant state attorney general.

In 1983, while serving as Mississippi's attorney general, Allain filed a suit asking the state supreme court to separate the functions of the executive and legislative branches of state government, especially in the budgetary process. Members of the legislature commonly served on boards, commissions, and agencies in the executive branch, but Allain asserted that Mississippi's 1890 constitution required a separation of powers and that legislative officials could not serve in the executive branch. The Mississippi Supreme Court ruled in favor of the attorney general and ordered the two branches to remain separate. That ruling strengthened the executive branch of state government, especially the office of governor, which is considered one of the weakest chief executives in the nation. The court's mandate was carried out in the Administrative Reorganization Act of 1984.

From 1962 to 1975 Allain represented the State of Mississippi in cases before state courts, the federal district court, the federal circuit court of appeals, and the US Supreme Court. In 1979 he was elected state attorney general, a post in which he built a strong reputation as a consumer advocate. Two of his most notable achievements were the prevention of a utility rate increase and the exclusion of Mississippi as a nuclear waste site. In his successful 1983 campaign for governor, Allain, a Democrat, carried seventy-four of the state's eighty-two counties.

Shortly after his inauguration as governor on 10 January 1984, Allain appointed a 250-member commission to study the state's 1890 constitution. After a thorough review, the commission drafted a new constitution, and Allain recommended its adoption. The state legislature, however, took no action on the proposal.

A constitutional amendment restructuring the state board of education, part of the Education Reform Act of 1982, was implemented during Governor Allain's administration. That amendment provided for an appointed superintendent of education and a nine-member board of education.

As governor, Allain continued to work to remove members of the legislature from boards that were part of the executive branch. Though unpopular with many legislators, who feared that the law gave too much power to the governor, Allain's proposal was passed by the legislature in 1984.

In 1985 Allain appointed Reuben Anderson to the Mississippi Supreme Court, making him the state's first African American justice.

A constitutional amendment allowing the governor to succeed himself was passed near the end of Allain's term, with his strong endorsement. Allain considered running for reelection but eventually decided not to seek a second term.

After leaving office in January 1988, Allain resumed the practice of law in Jackson. He died there on 2 December 2013.

David G. Sansing
University of Mississippi

William Allain Subject File, Mississippi Department of Archives and History; *Mississippi Official and Statistical Register* (1984–88); Jere Nash and Andy Taggart, *Mississippi Politics: The Struggle for Power, 1976–2006* (2006).

Allen, Jere

(b. 1944) Painter

Jere Hardy Allen, an internationally known figurative painter who has been called the Mississippi Rembrandt, was born on 15 August 1944 in Selma, Alabama. Early on, inspired by landscapes and wildlife paintings made by his great-grandmother, Annie Bell Rives Hardy, he decided he, too, wanted to be an artist and began drawing constantly. He was often a challenge to his teachers, including one who scolded him in front of his classmates for drawing a nude during school—in fifth grade. Undaunted, Allen kept drawing and completed high school, and after working at a television station in Montgomery, Alabama, and joining the US Marine Corps Reserve, he decided to attend the Ringling School of Art and Design in Sarasota, Florida. He received his bachelor's of fine arts from Ringling in 1970, earned a master's of fine arts from the University of Tennessee in

1972, and became an instructor at Carson-Newman College before joining the art faculty at the University of Mississippi in 1975. He taught painting and drawing there until his retirement in 2000 and continues to work tirelessly on his own creations and to maintain an active exhibition schedule. His wife, Joe Ann, a ceramicist and a master gardener, and their son, Jeffrey, a painter of still lifes, share Allen's Oxford studio.

Allen paints primarily in oil, using dramatic, electric colors and most often creating figures against backgrounds of black or red. His canvases, which range in size from 6 inches by 4 inches to 144 inches by 125 inches, tend to be large because, he says, "I prefer to react to the people in my paintings who are in a scale that approximates my own." His works are often inspired by myths and symbols but also represent political and social realities. Some compositions include animals, which Allen describes as psychopomps, mythical spiritual guides to the human figures in the paintings.

"Allen paints in the tradition of the nineteenth-century portrait artist, but with an expressionistic flair," observes art historian Peter J. Baldaia, who comments on "the evocative and haunting elegance" of Allen's work and notes that "his paintings present what the artist calls 'notions,' images that rise up from his subconscious and are usually explored in a series of a dozen or more works." Art historian Patti Carr Black describes Allen's work as "coolly sensual, presenting the figure more as a universal symbol than as a narrative device." In 2007 Allen started painting with layers and layers of white, and his exhibitions of new works in 2008 and 2011 surprised admirers by showing figures appearing on white rather than black or red backgrounds.

Allen received a Group Studies Abroad Fulbright Grant to Costa Rica in 1979 as well as the 1993 Visual Art Award of the Mississippi Institute of Arts and Letters. In 2003 his work, along with that of Robert Rauschenberg, Roy Lichtenstein, Wolf Kahn, and others, toured Southeast Asia as part of the Washington-based Meridian International Center's exhibition *Outward Bound: American Art at the Brink of the Twenty-First Century*. Allen's paintings have also been shown in forty states and in Canada and Europe. His work is in permanent collections at the Meridian Museum of Art, the Fine Arts Museum of the South in Mobile, the Huntsville Museum of Art in Alabama, the Tennessee Art League in Nashville, the Coos Art Museum in Oregon, the Robert I. Kahn Gallery in Houston, and others.

Ann J. Abadie
University of Mississippi

Peter J. Baldaia, in *Resource Library Magazine* (2000); Patty Carr Black, *Art in Mississippi, 1720–1980* (1998); Wil Cook, in *Oxford Town* (2011); Charlotte Flemes, *Jere Allen: Bilder aus Amerika* (1989); Lawrence Wells, in *Art and Antiques* (November 1999).

Allison, Mose
(b. 1927) Jazz and Blues Musician

Mose Allison has enjoyed a prolific and critically acclaimed musical career that defies easy definitions or labels. He has charted his own course, creating a unique sound that reflects his Delta roots and his introspective nature, and along the way he has accumulated a legion of followers and influenced a range of artists, from the groundbreaking punk band the Clash to such venerated acts as the Rolling Stones and Hot Tuna. Allison's music continues to evolve but retains the blues aesthetic that evokes the unique region of his childhood.

Allison was born on 11 November 1927 in the small Mississippi Delta town of Tippo. The Allison family was close-knit and well respected in the community. Allison's father, Mose Allison Sr., an accomplished stride-style piano player, became an early advocate of land rights for African Americans in the racially segregated Delta. Allison's mother, Maxine Collins Allison, played the ukulele and traveled. His early childhood home featured sawdust-covered floors and ragtime music. The blues of the Mississippi Delta profoundly influenced Allison's approach to music, and taking that sound as an artistic aesthetic, he renders the blues in his own unique style. His music has always enjoyed a particular popularity in England, where he has achieved cult status with his mellow, blues-inflected jazz. Evidence of the esteem with which he is held is seen by the legion of Allison cover songs emerging from British artists.

Allison began formal piano lessons at the age of five, and by grade school he was an accomplished songwriter and piano and trumpet player. After graduating from high school, he enrolled as a chemical engineering major at the University of Mississippi, where he joined the popular jazz band the Mississippians. Following a stint in the US Army, Allison briefly returned to the University of Mississippi before heading to Louisiana State University to earn a degree in philosophy and literature. Following graduation, Allison married St. Louis native Audre Mae Schwartz and embarked on an extended tour of the South. In the fall of 1956 Allison moved to New York to try his hand in America's premier jazz city. New York offered him the opportunity to associate with legendary jazz saxophonists such as Stan Getz and Lester Young, and he found an artistic home in now-legendary jam sessions in a 34th Street apartment that featured provocative jazz musicians such as Zoot Sims and Buddy Jones. The apartment served as an oasis of artistic freedom for southern expatriates.

Allison's multidecade career has included recordings on several significant music labels, among them Prestige, Columbia, and Atlantic Records. His debut recording session with Prestige Records in 1957, *Back Country Suite*, harkens back to his roots, evoking the warm pastoral setting of his youth. Allison's lyric capabilities match his prowess on piano; he sings in a candid and conversational idiom, lacing his lyrics with biting wit and introspective observation. Refusing to compromise his music for mass-market audiences, Allison remains true to his vision and philosophy. His accolades include a 1987 Grammy nomination for Best Jazz Vocalist and a 2002 Grammy nomination for *Mose Chronicles, Live in London*, vol. 1. He also appears in the major motion picture *The Score*, starring Robert De Niro. Allison tours extensively, delighting fans by playing in smaller venues and with local musicians.

In 2013 Mose Allison was named a National Endowment for the Arts Jazz Master, "the nation's highest honor in jazz." When not on tour or in the studio, Allison lives with his family in New York.

Catherine Riggs
Lawrence, Kansas

Mose Allison website, www.moseallison.com; Wayne Enstice and Paul Ruban, *Jazz Spoken Here: Conversations with Twenty-Two Musicians* (1992); Patti Jones, *One Man's Blues* (1995); National Endowment for the Arts website, www.arts.gov; Paul Zollo, *Songwriters on Songwriting* (1997).

Alworth, Lance

(b. 1940) Athlete

Nicknamed Bambi for his leaping and catching abilities, Lance Alworth was one of the greatest wide receivers in the history of college and professional football. He is a member of the College Football Hall of Fame and was the first player from the American Football League (AFL) inducted into the Pro Football Hall of Fame.

Born in Houston, Texas, on 3 August 1940, Lance Dwight Alworth moved with his family to Lincoln County, Mississippi, as a child, and grew up in Hog Chain, which he once described as having "about 80 people." There, he was befriended by an older boy, Harold Lofton, who wore football jersey number 19 at Brookhaven High School. Alworth often visited Lofton at his family's dry goods store and later wore the number 19 with the San Diego Chargers of the AFL.

Alworth played football, baseball, and basketball and ran track in high school and teamed with future University of Mississippi star Ralph "Catfish" Smith to help Brookhaven win the Big Eight Basketball Tournament. He almost ended up with Smith at the University of Mississippi, but the university had a policy against recruiting married football players, and Alworth was already married to his high school sweetheart. "Ole Miss actually offered me a baseball scholarship with the idea that I would come out for football, too," said Alworth, "but I didn't want to be the first player to get around the policy that way."

Instead, Alworth went to the University of Arkansas, where he led the Razorbacks to three straight Southwest Conference football championships from 1959 to 1961. Although he did not catch many passes in college, Alworth's sprinter speed, athletic grace, and tremendous leaping ability caught the attention of professional scouts. He signed with the Chargers immediately after his last college game in 1962.

Alworth and the Chargers made the fledgling AFL entertaining and fun to watch. According to Kansas City Chiefs owner Lamar Hunt, Alworth "made it look like a wide-open game because he always was wide open." In his eight AFL seasons, Alworth led the league in receiving yards and catches three times and was named to the all-AFL team seven straight years. He was the league's most valuable player in 1963 as the Chargers won the AFL Championship. After a trade to the Dallas Cowboys in 1971, Alworth helped the team to a victory in Super Bowl VI, scoring the first touchdown. Alworth played two seasons for Dallas and retired after the 1972 season.

Alworth caught 543 passes over his professional career, recording 87 touchdowns and 10,266 yards. He led the league in pass receiving three times and still holds the record for most games (five) with more than 200 yards receiving. At one point he owned the league record for most games (96) with at least one pass reception. Alworth also showed the versatility he had first displayed at Brookhaven High School, rushing for 129 yards, returning 29 punts for 309 yards, and gaining 216 yards on 10 kickoff returns.

In addition to the college and professional football halls of fame, Alworth is a member of the AFL all-time team, the NFL seventy-fifth anniversary team, and the San Diego Chargers Hall of Fame. The Chargers retired his number 19 jersey in 2005.

Brad Schultz
University of Mississippi

Grant Hall, *Northwest Arkansas Morning News* (24 December 2006); Jerry Magee, *Pro Football Weekly* (24 November 2006); Pro Football Reference website, www.pro-football-reference.com.

American Missionary Association

The Confederate shelling of Fort Sumter had barely penetrated northern consciousness when the American Missionary Association (AMA) exulted that the war had opened a grand field for missionary labor. Organized as a nonsectarian antislavery society in 1846, it quickly focused on establishing schools and churches for southern blacks. It sent a missionary to escaped Virginia slaves in September 1861, and its teachers tracked the Union Army so closely that booming cannons sometimes interrupted classes.

In late 1862 approaching Confederates forced Rose Kinney to flee Corinth, where she was teaching children of black refugees, but by May 1863 nine AMA teachers were providing relief and instruction there. In 1864 Lizzie Welsh began a class at Natchez under a large magnolia tree, and Fannie Campbell lived in a tent while teaching black soldiers in Vicksburg. "I have taught in the North," Campbell wrote, "and have *never* seen such zeal on the part of pupils, nor such advancement."

The AMA quickly increased its presence in Mississippi after the war. It supported twenty-four teachers in eight schools in 1866, numbers that grew to eleven schools and thirty-three teachers in 1868 and thirteen and forty-five the following year. AMA institutions were coeducational, open to all races, and staffed by both black and white teachers. African Americans in Natchez joyously welcomed northern black teachers Blanche V. Harris and Pauline Freeman in 1865. Although the association's attempts to establish churches were mostly unsuccessful, its teachers often emphasized religion in schools. In June 1863 G. M. Carruthers opened his Corinth school with Scripture reading, prayer, and religious songs. Harris proudly reported from Vicksburg that "a deep seriousness seems to have settled over my whole school and many with streaming eyes" are asking "what shall I do to be saved?" Nearly all of the AMA schools established temperance societies.

The AMA concluded that blacks must be empowered by being trained to teach their own. By 1869 Columbus's Union Academy was educating youth to teach in elementary schools, and in 1871 Tougaloo College established a normal department for teacher training. Its graduates subsequently earned widespread praise from public school officials.

African Americans eagerly accepted AMA teachers, but whites were less enthusiastic. Many at first opposed black education, and even supporters were often hostile to the AMA's interracial faculties and to its advocacy of suffrage and equal rights for former slaves. Whites frequently refused to rent to teachers and insulted, ostracized, and occasionally molested them. When Mary Close went to Brandon in early 1866, whites refused to board or acknowledge her. Close moved in with a mulatto woman and opened both a day and a night school, but white boys disrupted her classes by throwing rocks through the windows. In Grenada, a white citizen backed by a mob choked, struck, and viciously beat AMA agent J. P. Bardwell with a cane. In 1871 the Ku Klux Klan closed or destroyed numerous black schools, including AMA institutions, and forced teachers of both races to abandon their students. As late as 1875, armed men seized and roughly handled the Union Academy principal in Columbus.

Although AMA officials believed that the state should be responsible for the education of all its citizens and turned its students over to public schools as soon as they were available, it operated a few primary and secondary institutions until the 1930s. In 1892 the AMA opened Mound Bayou Normal Institute on land donated in part by Isaiah T. Montgomery, the only black man to attend the 1890 Mississippi constitutional convention, which effectively disfranchised African Americans. The Mound Bayou school had 226 students and six teachers in 1914, and the association continued to operate it until 1918, when it was transferred to the Episcopal Diocese of Mississippi. Although the AMA favored coeducation, two of its elementary schools, Girls' Industrial School (later Almeda Gardner Industrial School) in Moorhead and Mount Herman Seminary near Clinton, were for females. The AMA opened the former in 1892 in a virtual forest, with the aim of providing elementary, industrial, and character training to females aged seven to fifteen. An elderly black neighbor called the school the House of Principle. In 1902 a boarding department for those living beyond walking distance housed sixty young women. Sarah A. Dickey, the founder and principal of Mount Herman Seminary, which had five teachers, eighty-one students, and dormitory space for forty-five boarders, deeded the school to the AMA in 1905. Both schools closed when adequate public schools became available, which in the case of Almeda Gardner was not until 1930.

The AMA trained thousands of black students in primary and secondary schools, but its most significant contribution to Mississippi was Tougaloo College, chartered in 1871. Tougaloo initially emphasized normal, elementary, secondary, and industrial education. Thirteen students graduated from the normal and high school departments in 1897. It awarded its first bachelor's degree in 1901 and grew steadily thereafter. In 1945 Tougaloo had a college enrollment of 217, with 36 graduates. As late as 1950 it was the only college in the state where black youth could acquire a liberal arts education. Tougaloo College played an active role in the civil rights movement and remains a significant institution for African Americans.

Joe M. Richardson
Florida State University

Lura Beam, *He Called Them by the Lightning: A Teacher's Odyssey in the Negro South* (1967); Augustus Field Beard, *A Crusade of Brotherhood* (1909); Fred L. Brownlee, *New Day Ascending* (1946); Clarice T. Campbell and Oscar A. Rogers, *Mississippi: The View from Tougaloo* (1979); Harlan Paul Douglass, *Christian Reconstruction in the South* (1909); Helen Griffith, *Dauntless in Mississippi: The Life of Sara A. Dickey, 1838–1904* (1966); Joe M. Richardson, *Christian Reconstruction: The American Missionary Association and Southern Blacks, 1861–1890* (1986); Joe M. Richardson and Maxine D. Jones, *Education for Liberation: The American Missionary Association and African Americans, 1890 to the Civil Rights Movement* (2009); Randy Sparks, *Journal of Mississippi History* (February 1992); Vernon Lane Wharton, *The Negro in Mississippi, 1865–1890* (1947).

Americans for the Preservation of the White Race

Started in May 1963 by nine white men at a gas station outside Natchez, Americans for the Preservation of the White Race (APWR) was one of several new Mississippi organizations that formed to oppose the civil rights movement. The first issue of the group's newspaper, *American Patriot*, included a policy statement asserting, "Americans for the Preservation of the White Race, Inc., is an organization dedicated to keeping the White Man White and the Black Man Black like GOD intended." Led by its first president, charter member Rowland N. Scott of Natchez, the group had more than twenty chapters by 1964, primarily in central and southwestern Mississippi and in Louisiana. The short-lived group attracted working-class and some middle-class whites who were not only horrified by the civil rights movement but also concerned about what they saw as the moderation of some of the state's leaders in business, education, and government.

The APWR and many other massive resistance groups claimed not to represent extremists or supporters of violence. Like the Citizens' Councils, the APWR hosted talks by right-wing leaders: speakers at APWR meetings in 1963–64 included former governor Ross Barnett, Judge Tom Brady, Maj. Gen. Edwin Walker, and several state legislators and ministers. The group's language varied between calls for American patriotism and angry denunciations of opponents of white supremacy. A newsletter argued in 1964 that "the only thing extreme about the organization is that we advocate 'extreme conservatism,' which the whole country needs a dose of." Group leaders officially rejected violence, but some members belonged to the Ku Klux Klan and announced that they had armed themselves in preparation for the Mississippi Summer Project in 1964. Some members at the state fair in 1967 sold booklets explaining how to construct homemade bombs and raised money to help defend the men accused of murdering activist Vernon Dahmer.

As historian Joseph Crespino argues, the APWR was one of the groups, like the Ku Klux Klan, that Mississippi leaders, even those in the Citizens' Council and government agencies such as the Mississippi State Sovereignty Commission, feared as a consequence of the potential for violence and bad publicity. While many white leaders were taking slow and small steps in the mid-1960s to avoid inflaming tensions or encouraging the federal government to take new action against injustices in Mississippi, the APWR took a hard line. Members condemned Erle Johnston, head of the Sovereignty Commission, for saying that the APWR "stirred whites against whites."

Above all, the APWR used economic pressure against white business leaders who supported some forms of desegregation. The group's leaders organized a boycott against Carthage merchants who did business with a black-owned grocery popular among civil rights activists. More dramatically, the APWR organized a "buy-in" campaign to counter a sustained civil rights boycott of stores in downtown Natchez and then fumed when some business leaders agreed to the boycotters' demands. In early December 1964 the group asked white shoppers throughout the region to shop in downtown Natchez but denounced twenty-three businessmen who had signed an agreement ending the boycott. The APWR later took the same approach to oppose civil rights efforts in Fayette and Edwards.

The APWR remains a fairly mysterious group. The fact that the Mississippi State Sovereignty Commission amassed files on the organization shows that people in a very conservative state government considered the APWR's tactics a threat to social order. The group was in decline by 1965 and seems to have disappeared by 1968.

Ted Ownby
University of Mississippi

Joseph Crespino, *In Search of Another Country: Mississippi and the Conservative Counterrevolution* (2007); Mississippi State Sovereignty Commission files on the Americans for the Preservation of the White Race, Mississippi Department of Archives and History.

Ames, Adelbert

(1835–1933) Twenty-Seventh and Thirtieth Governor, 1868–1870, 1874–1876

When Gov. Benjamin G. Humphreys was removed from office on 15 June 1868, Pres. Andrew Johnson appointed Adelbert Ames provisional governor of Mississippi. At the time of his appointment, Ames was also the governor of the Fourth Military District, which had been established under federal Reconstruction policy and included Arkansas and Mississippi. Ames continued as both military and provisional governor until the reestablishment of civil authority on 10 March 1870.

Ames, born in Rockland, Maine, on 31 October 1835, had been a highly decorated Union officer. He won a Congressional Medal of Honor at the First Battle of Bull Run and a battlefield promotion at Gettysburg. After he left the governor's office, he and his wife, Blanche, the daughter of Gen. Benjamin Butler, established a family residence in Natchez. Ames was called a carpetbagger, a term of contempt that referred to northerners who held office in the South after the Civil War.

Adelbert Ames, ca. 1860–75 (Brady-Handy Photograph Collection, Library of Congress, Washington, D.C. [LC-BH83-2263])

Because Ames was a highly vocal advocate of black suffrage, he became enormously popular among Mississippi's former slaves and emerged quickly as the leader of the Radical wing of the state's Republican Party. As military governor, Ames garnered praise as well as great criticism for dismissing numerous state and local officials for having supported the Confederacy. He wrote to William Tecumseh Sherman that disputes in Reconstruction-era Mississippi occurred not between different parties "but between loyal men and a class of men who are disloyal," and he governed in ways that limited the power of those he considered disloyal. James L. Alcorn, a former Whig leader and wealthy Delta planter, was the leader of the moderate faction of the state's newly established Republican Party.

After Mississippi was readmitted to the Union in 1870, the legislature appointed Ames to the US Senate. In 1873, while still a senator, Ames ran for governor against Mississippi's other senator, Alcorn, who had also served as governor in 1870–71. In the gubernatorial election most of the state's black leaders supported Ames and most of the white leaders backed Alcorn. Ames won, and several blacks were elected to statewide office, including Lt. Gov. Alexander K. Davis.

During Ames's second administration, the state was torn by racial discord and political bitterness. When the legislature raised property taxes, a taxpayers' convention assembled in Jackson in 1875 in protest. During the following summer, racial disturbances occurred in several cities, with the most serious taking place in Vicksburg.

The fall elections of 1875 saw more violent disturbances, and Ames called out the state militia to maintain order. His actions incited more unrest, and widespread violence, fraud, and voter intimidation occurred during the election. Ames called for federal intervention to combat the violence,

but Pres. Ulysses S. Grant declined. The Democratic Party secured a large majority in the state legislature and regained control of most county governments.

The legislature convened in January 1876 and brought impeachment charges against Ames and several other Republican officials, including Davis. In most cases, especially those of Ames and Davis, the charges were politically motivated. When it became apparent that Ames would be convicted and removed from office, his lawyers arranged a compromise with the state legislature. Ames resigned on 29 March 1876, and the charges were dropped. Davis was removed from office through impeachment.

Ames subsequently returned to Lowell, Massachusetts, and remained there until his death at age ninety-eight on 12 April 1933.

David G. Sansing
University of Mississippi

Blanche Ames, *Adelbert Ames, 1835–1933* (1964); *Biographical Directory of the United States Congress* (1950); Eric Foner, *Reconstruction: America's Unfinished Revolution, 1863–1877* (1998); William C. Harris, *The Day of the Carpetbagger: Republican Reconstruction in Mississippi* (1979); *Mississippi Official and Statistical Register* (1912); Dunbar Rowland, *Encyclopedia of Mississippi History*, vol. 2 (1907).

Amite County

Named for the Amite River, which the French had named for the word *amitié* (friendship) in hopes or celebration of good relations with the native Choctaws, Amite County is located in southern Mississippi on the Louisiana border. Amite was one of the earliest counties established in the Mississippi Territory—one of just eleven counties in existence in 1810. Notable geographic features of Amite County include the West and East Forks of the Amite River as well as several tributary creeks. The Homochitto National Forest includes some of northern Amite. Towns include Liberty, the county seat; Centreville; Crosby; Gloster; Gillsburg; and Smithdale.

In 1820 Amite was Mississippi's third-largest county, with 6,853 people, among them 2,833 slaves. Like most of the territory not located on the Mississippi River or the Gulf of Mexico, Amite was an agricultural county, with just 35 people employed in commerce or manufacturing. Slavery remained important to Amite's economy through the antebellum period, and by 1840 60 percent of the county's 9,511 residents were enslaved; on the eve of the Civil War, that number peaked at 64 percent. Amite farmers produced cotton, corn, rice (ranking third among the state's counties), orchard products (fifth), and sweet potatoes (sixth). Substantial numbers of livestock were also raised. The county's thirty-two manufacturing establishments employed eighty-three men, mostly in lumber work and blacksmithing.

In 1853 Douglas Hancock Cooper, an Amite County planter and political figure, became the US agent to the Choctaw Nation. Cooper later worked to persuade Native American nations to support the Confederacy during the Civil War. North Carolina native James Smylie became an important leader among Amite's Presbyterians as well as a large slave owner and a prominent church-based defender of slavery.

As in much of Mississippi, the majority of Amite County residents were Baptists. According to the religious census of 1860, Amite had twenty-two churches—eleven Baptist, eight Methodist, and three Presbyterian. The 1916 religious census similarly identified Amite as a Baptist county, with Missionary Baptists and Southern Baptists making up more than two-thirds of all church members. Most of the county's other congregations were Colored Methodist Episcopal, Presbyterian, or Methodist.

Amite County's population increased after the Civil War, reaching 14,000 by 1880. African Americans made up 61 percent of the population. The county remained rural and agricultural, with just 56 people employed in manufacturing. About half the county's 1,620 farmers owned their land. Amite County's voters gave considerable support to Populist candidates in the late 1800s.

Agriculture remained Amite's primary industry through the early twentieth century. In 1900, 68 percent of white farmers owned land, compared to just 18 percent of African American farmers, most of whom labored as tenants and sharecroppers. Manufacturing had increased, and the county's 69 factories employed 143 workers, almost all of them male. By 1930 86 percent of Amite's population lived on farms, substantially higher than the 67 percent figure for the state as a whole. As in past decades, African Americans made up slightly more than half of the county's population, most of them working as tenant farmers.

During World War II, Amite County became home to the US Army's Camp Van Dorn, where soldiers trained for combat in Europe. The camp housed more than fifty thousand troops and was the site of significant confrontations between white and African American soldiers.

Amite was the site of important civil rights activism, especially in the early years of the organized movement. During the 1950s E. W. Steptoe, the head of the county's chapter of the National Association for the Advancement of Colored People (NAACP), organized potential voters and started a newsletter, making his group one of the state's largest. Amite County farmer Herbert Lee, who joined the NAACP in 1953, was killed in antiactivist violence in 1961. Anne Moody's memoir, *Coming of Age in Mississippi* (1968), describes growing up in Centreville under Jim Crow. Will Campbell's memoir, *Brother to a Dragonfly* (1977), chronicles rural Amite County

during the Great Depression and Campbell's role as one of the few white religious activists in the civil rights movement.

In 1960 Amite was home to 15,573 people, 54 percent of them African Americans; other than a very small Native American population, all of the rest were white. Amite ranked fifth in the state in the number of cattle and was noteworthy for its petroleum and gas production. The county was about average in the amount of corn, soybeans, and wheat produced but fell far below the state average in the production of cotton and the amount of commercial timberland. The leading industrial employer was the timber industry. As the population declined in the 1960s and 1970s, the number of people engaged in farming dropped dramatically, from 1,940 in 1960 to 200 two decades later.

Amite's population has continued to decrease, falling to 13,599 in 2000 and 13,131 in 2010, when 41 percent of the residents were African American and 58 percent were white.

Amite County was the home of storytelling comedian Jerry Clower, who used local language and characters in his work. Artist George Williams, a self-taught woodcarver, and the Williams Brothers, gospel music producers, also have roots in Amite.

Mississippi Encyclopedia Staff
Oxford, Mississippi

Mississippi State Planning Commission, *Progress Report on State Planning in Mississippi* (1938); *Mississippi Statistical Abstract*, Mississippi State University (1952–2010); Charles Sydnor and Claude Bennett, *Mississippi History* (1939); University of Virginia Library, Historical Census Browser website, http://mapserver.lib.virginia.edu; E. Nolan Waller and Dani A. Smith, *Growth Profiles of Mississippi's Counties, 1960–1980* (1985).

Amphibians

The name *amphibian* derives from the Greek word *amphibios*, which means "living a double life." Most amphibians spend their early lives in water and then move onto land as adults. Nearly all amphibians share numerous anatomical, physiological, and molecular features. Most are quadrupedal (four-footed), anamniote (no amniotic sac) vertebrates that have glandular skins and utilize cutaneous (skin) respiration in addition to lung and/or gill respiration. Scales, claws, feathers, and hair are absent. Skeletal features include two occipital condyles and no more than one sacral vertebra. Their eggs lack shells, and most species have aquatic larvae that metamorphose into terrestrial adults. The amphibians in Mississippi are frogs and salamanders.

Spring peeper (*Pseudacris crucifer*) (Courtesy Edmund D. Keiser)

Frogs are tailless except as larvae and usually have long hind legs, short front legs, large eyes, and smooth or warty moist skins. Most features defining frogs are skeletal and include nine or fewer presacral vertebrae, presence of a bony urostyle, and fused lower limb elements. The aquatic larvae are called tadpoles. Mississippi has thirty native species of frogs belonging to five families and two introduced species representing a sixth family.

The best-known and most exploited amphibian food species in the southern United States is the bullfrog (*Lithobates catesbeianus*). In southern Mississippi the similar pig frog (*Lithobates grylio*) is prized for the same reason. While bullfrog hunting has declined in Mississippi in recent years, it remains a popular sport in the Delta, Pearl River, and other areas of the state with swamps and freshwater marshes. Fried frog legs, a particularly southern treat, are served in restaurants throughout the South (although most restaurants serve commercially raised frogs, and the ones imported from other countries may not even be bullfrogs).

Mississippi populations of gopher frogs (*Lithobates sevosus*) have nearly disappeared in recent years and are considered endangered within the state. Other frog species—crawfish frogs (*Lithobates areolatus*), ornate chorus frogs (*Pseudacris ornata*), mountain chorus frogs (*Pseudacris brachyphona*), and Gulf Coast toads (*Oolotis nebulifer*)—are also rare and should have protected status. Some frogs have declined in some areas of the state but not in others. For example, American toads (*Anaxyrus americanus*) and upland chorus frogs (*Pseudacris feriarum*) have become considerably less abundant in North Mississippi in recent years.

Southern folklore sometimes mentions rains of frogs and toads and claims of toads causing warts. Neither is true. Frogs also do not have a venomous bite. If the skin secretions of some Mississippi frogs come into contact with moist membranes of human nasal passages or mouth, however, repeated sneezing and respiratory discomfort can result.

When biologists discuss frog larvae, they frequently refer to the works of Ronald Altig, a professor emeritus at Mississippi State University and a resident of Starkville who is a world-renowned frog authority. He has published more than one hundred papers on amphibians.

Salamanders resemble lizards in body shape but have glandular, usually moist, skins and lack scales and claws. Most have four limbs, body trunks with costal grooves, and long tails. Eardrums and middle ear cavities are absent, and many skull bones typical of vertebrates have been lost. Mississippi has thirty species representing seven families.

Mississippi populations of green salamanders (*Aneides aeneus*), spring salamanders (*Gyrinophilus porphyriticus*), and cave salamanders (*Eurycea lucifuga*) have endangered status. The tiger salamander (*Ambystoma tigrinum*) has nearly disappeared in recent years. Other Mississippi species are of special concern because they have limited ranges and habitats that, if altered by human activity, would result in their speedy elimination. These include eastern hellbenders (*Cryptobranchus alleganiensis*), Catahoula salamanders (*Plethodon ainsworthi*), and the one-toed amphiuma (*Amphiuma pholeter*).

Bear Creek in extreme northeastern Mississippi harbors a large, grotesque, aquatic salamander that is one of the two bulkiest species in the world. Its unsightly appearance results from its numerous wrinkled and fleshy skin folds. Larger individuals approach thirty inches in total length. This is the eastern hellbender (*Cryptobranchus alleghaniensis*). Somewhat similar, though smaller and less grotesque, are the aquatic mudpuppies (genus *Necturus*), the largest of three Mississippi salamander species that reach nearly a foot in total length. Mudpuppies occur in many Mississippi streams. Fisherman catching hellbenders and mudpuppies often call them "devil dogs" or "water dogs" and erroneously believe that they have poisonous bites.

The two largest salamanders in the United States can be found in Mississippi. Residents often refer to them as eels or Congo eels, although they are neither from the Congo nor eels. The two-toed amphiuma (*Amphiuma means*) of southern Mississippi has been known to reach forty-five inches in total length; the three-toed amphiuma (*Amphiuma tridactylum*) is nearly as long and is found statewide. Both are aquatic with eel-like bodies and four tiny legs. Their bites are painful but not poisonous.

Mississippi's Catahoula salamander (*Plethodon ainsworthi*) occurs in no other state. The state name identifies the common and scientific names of the Mississippi slimy salamander (*Plethodon mississippi*).

Amphibians are extremely important in food chains necessary for the continuing survival of higher vertebrates, including humans. Nevertheless, many world populations of amphibians appear to be rapidly declining and are believed to be on the verge of extinction.

Edmund D. Keiser
University of Mississippi

R. D. Bartlett and Patricia P. Bartlett, *Guide and Reference to the Amphibians of Eastern and Central North America (North of Mexico)* (2006); J. William Cliburn, *A Key to the Amphibians and Reptiles of Mississippi* (1976); William Duellman and Linda Trueb, *Biology of Amphibians* (1986); Edmund D. Keiser, *Salamanders of the University of Mississippi Field Station* (1999); Edmund D. Keiser, *Frogs of the University of Mississippi Field Station* (2008); Ren Lohoefner and Ronald Altig, *Mississippi Herpetology* (1983).

Walter Anderson, *Goldenrod on Horn Island*, ca. 1965, watercolor on paper, 8½″ × 11′ (Courtesy Walter Anderson Museum of Art)

Anderson, Walter Inglis
(1903–1965) Artist

Walter Anderson was born in New Orleans on 29 September 1903, the second son of George Walter Anderson, a grain merchant, and Annette McConnell Anderson, an artist who taught him a love of art, music, and literature. He grew up valuing the importance of art in everyday life and developed what would become a lifelong interest in mythology. He attended grade school in New Orleans, went to boarding school in New York, and was later trained at the Parsons Institute of Design in New York (1922–23) and the Pennsylvania Academy of Fine Arts (1924–28). He received a scholarship that enabled him to study and travel in Europe. He read broadly in history, natural science, poetry, art history, folklore, philosophy, classical and modern literature, and epic narratives of journeying.

Anderson returned to Mississippi, working with his brother on earthenware at Shearwater Pottery in Ocean Springs. He married Agnes Grinstead Anderson in 1933, and they raised four children. His developing interest in murals coincided with his work on Works Progress Administration mural projects in Ocean Springs during the 1930s. The late 1930s saw the onset of mental illness, for which he was hospitalized for three years. After his release, he and his family moved to the estate of his wife's family, Oldfields Plantation, in Gautier. While there, Anderson, a voracious reader, created nearly ten thousand pen-and-ink drawings to illustrate page after page of books as he read them, and he made watercolors, tempera paintings, and block prints illustrating his favorite literary works, from *Don Quixote, Paradise Lost*, and Pope's *Iliad* to *Legends of Charlemagne, Rime of the Ancient Mariner*, and *The Magic Carpet*. Anderson also made block prints for *An Alphabet*, a book he created for his own children. "There are many artists who explored a story but few who fused with it," said the former curator of exhibitions at the Walter Anderson Museum of Art in Ocean Springs. "The book to Anderson was a way of life, part of the quest to find realization and meaning. It was the distillation of the timeless epics that gave him the grasp of the significance of the moment. Great books and great art are about insight, and Anderson gives us insight into both."

Anderson had long been interested in nature, but at Oldfields natural scenes began to appear in his watercolors and tempera paintings and in the large linoleum block prints he created. In 1947 he secluded himself in a cottage at Shearwater, where he wrote, painted, decorated pottery for the family business, and carved. He rowed the twelve miles to Horn Island, one of the barrier islands off the Mississippi Coast, an unspoiled natural landscape that became his home for long stretches of time during the last decade and a half of his life. "So much depends on the dominant mode on shore," he wrote, "that it was necessary for me to go to sea to find the conditional. Everything seems conditional on the islands." Anderson's paintings and drawings captured the numerous species of flora and fauna in this pristine environment, as he illustrated birds, insects, animals, flowers, trees, shrubs, and any other natural life he saw while exploring the wild underbrush and coastal lagoons. He used the term *realization* to suggest his hope of becoming at one with the natural species he observed. On one occasion, he tied himself to a tree during a hurricane to experience the fury of nature. He documented everything he saw, from the life of a spotted frog to the near extinction of the brown pelican as a consequence of the pesticide DDT. Anderson kept ninety journals and logs recording what he experienced, writings mostly for himself that drew from his broad artistic and philosophical knowledge.

Walter Anderson died of lung cancer in New Orleans in 1965. In honor of the centennial of his birth in 2003, the Smithsonian Institution mounted a major exhibition of his work. The Walter Anderson Museum was established in Ocean Springs in 1991. Much of Anderson's work is there, but many of his watercolors, paintings, and ceramics were housed at his family compound at Shearwater until they were damaged or destroyed when Hurricane Katrina hit the

Mississippi Coast in 2005. Conservators have sought to save and restore his work.

Charles Reagan Wilson
University of Mississippi

Ellen Douglas, with the illustrations of Walter Anderson, *The Magic Carpet and Other Tales* (1987); Christopher Mauer, *Fortune's Favorite Child: The Uneasy Life of Walter Anderson* (2003); Mary Anderson Pickard and Patricia Pinson, eds., *Form and Fantasy: The Block Prints of Walter Anderson* (2007); Patricia Pinson, ed., *The Art of Walter Anderson* (2003); Redding S. Sugg Jr., ed., *The Horn Island Logs of Walter Anderson* (2006); Redding S. Sugg Jr., ed., *Illustrations of Epic and Voyage by Walter Anderson* (2006); *Walter Anderson and World Literature,* 2009 exhibition, online subject guide, University of Mississippi Libraries website, www.olemiss.edu/depts/general_library/.

Andrews, Dana

(1909–1992) Actor

Remembered for the diffident and handsome average-Joe characters he often played, Dana Andrews was one of Hollywood's leading men during the 1940s. Born in Collins on New Year's Day 1909, he was one of thirteen children of a Baptist minister. During his youth, Andrews and his family moved several times before finally settling down in Texas, where he attended Sam Houston State Teachers College.

In 1931 he left his job as an accountant in Austin and hitchhiked to Los Angeles, hoping to find work as an actor or singer in Hollywood. He got a job at a filling station in the suburb of Van Nuys, making enough money to pay for acting and singing lessons. He soon began performing at the small but prestigious Pasadena Playhouse, and he met Janet Murray and married her in 1932. Before her unexpected death in 1935, the couple had one son, David.

In 1938 a talent scout noticed Andrews, leading Samuel Goldwyn Productions to offer him a small contract and several bit parts over the next few years, including a supporting role in William Wyler's *The Westerner* (1940). In 1941, Twentieth Century Fox took notice of the promising supporting actor and bought half of Andrews's contract and cast him in small roles in *Tobacco Road* (1941) and *The Ox-Bow Incident* (1943).

He began to take on leading parts in a slew of war pictures and romance films, almost always playing the same signature character: a laconic and brooding yet sensitive figure trying to ignore some unspoken internal hardship. One of his most memorable roles was as brusque detective Mark McPherson in the film noir masterpiece *Laura* (1944).

Andrews was fairly successful and well known during the war era, starring in some of the decade's most celebrated films, among them *A Walk in the Sun* (1945), *The Best Years of Our Lives* (Best Picture of 1946), and *Boomerang* (1947). During this time, Andrews met and married Mary Todd; they had three children before their divorce in 1968.

Andrews's success, however, was short-lived. While he appeared in many more movies and a handful of TV shows, none measured up to his earlier films. Heavy drinking contributed to his problems, and following a brief theater run in the 1950s, he retired from acting in the 1960s. He worked in real estate and toured the country, giving lectures for Alcoholics Anonymous. In 1963 Andrews was elected president of the Screen Actors Guild, focusing his efforts on combating the degradation of the acting profession, particularly the way in which actresses were forced to do nude scenes to get roles. In 1972 he became one the first actors to do public service announcements on the dangers of alcoholism.

He lived the latter half of his life in a modest house in Studio City, California. In his last years, Andrews suffered from Alzheimer's disease, and he died of pneumonia on 17 December 1992.

Katherine Treppendahl
University of Virginia

Jim Beaver, Internet Movie Database website, www.imdb.com; Tom and Sara Pendergast, eds., *International Dictionary of Films and Filmmakers,* vol. 3, *Actors and Actresses* (2000); Reel Classics: The Classic Movie Site website, www.reelclassics.com (2006).

Appellate Courts

Mississippi has had a different court system under each of its four constitutions. Frequently changed were the method of judicial selection, the number of judges, and even the names of the courts. Harder to discern but perhaps more important are the changes in the kinds of cases that have dominated the dockets of the courts and the judicial philosophies that have controlled them.

The 1817 Mississippi Constitution provided that the "judicial power of this state shall be vested in one supreme court, and such superior and inferior courts of law and equity as the Legislature may, from time to time, direct and establish." The legislature determined that there would be four superior (trial) court districts, each with one judge. A fifth district was added in 1822. The legislature authorized the superior court judges to sit twice a year in Natchez as the

A

supreme court. Any two superior court judges could resolve an appeal, though the judge who had presided over a trial was ineligible.

The judges were elected by the legislature and served for life, though few remained that long. Twenty superior court judges served during the fourteen years that this court system existed, with an average service of a little more than three years. The first judge elected was William Bayard Shields, who quickly resigned because he was appointed as a federal judge.

In 1824 the supreme court boldly declared a state statute unconstitutional. The legislature at its next session ordered the judges to appear and explain why they should not be removed from office. Though an investigation occurred, the court continued.

The 1832 constitution made Mississippi the first state where voters elected all judges. The new constitution created the High Court of Errors and Appeals with three justices. The first justices, elected in May 1833, were William L. Sharkey, who became chief justice, and associate justices Daniel Wright and Cotesworth Pinckney Smith. After staggered-length initial terms, all had six-year terms. In 1839 the entire state was divided into northern, central, and southern districts, a basic configuration that persists today.

A 1836 constitutional amendment required the high court to sit in Jackson. The newly constructed Capitol opened in 1839, and the court had its own courtroom in the center of the building. Many suits involved land, banks, bonds, and railroads. Numerous cases from 1830 to 1860 involved slavery.

Among the most important cases the high court decided concerned the state's 1838 purchase of a substantial amount of stock in a new state bank. Bonds, backed by the credit of the state, were sold to fund the purchase. The bank failed, and in 1842 the legislature repudiated the bonds. In an 1852 decision, *State v. Johnson*, the court ruled that the bonds remained a valid debt of the state.

During the disruptions of the Civil War, only nineteen cases were decided, but the court began meeting more regularly by November 1865. An October 1866 case, *Ex parte Lewis*, received nationwide attention. Lewis, a black Union soldier from Maryland who remained in Mississippi at the end of the war, had kept his gun, violating an 1865 state statute declaring that blacks could not possess firearms. However, that statute violated the 1866 federal Civil Rights Act. Lewis petitioned Mississippi chief justice Alexander Hamilton Handy for release from jail, but Handy issued a lengthy opinion finding the state statute valid and the Civil Rights Act unconstitutional. The US military commander ignored the *Lewis* ruling. The state courts were further thwarted when civilians were tried in military courts. In October 1867 all three high court justices resigned to protest military rule, and the US Army commander named three new judges. Three decades later, the court in *Lusby v. Kansas City Railroad* invalidated all decisions issued during the two years when military commanders appointed the judges.

The 1869 Constitution replaced the elected high court with an appointed supreme court. The governor nominated justices, and the Senate confirmed them for nine-year terms. The new court had to address the effects of secession and defeat, ruling on agreements to pay debts in Confederate money and the validity of state laws passed during the war. Taxation and regulation of large corporations, including railroads, were also new and recurring controversies. Significant post-Reconstruction justices included J. A. P. Campbell (1876–94), Tim Cooper (1881–96), Thomas Woods (1889–1900), and Albert Whitfield (1894–1910).

The 1890 constitution did not change the number of Supreme Court justices or their method of selection. It did authorize onerous limits on suffrage with the goal of disfranchising African Americans. In 1896 the court upheld these limits in *Dixon v. State*. Another new provision barred leasing convicts for farmwork or other labor. Politically powerful landowners found a way around the law, and their subterfuge was sustained in *Henry v. State* (1906).

In 1903, with the opening of the new Mississippi State Capitol, the court moved to ornate new chambers in that building and remained there until 1973, when the Carroll Gartin Justice Building opened. A second building by that name built behind the first one opened in 2008 for the supreme court and the court of appeals.

A 1916 constitutional amendment doubled the size of the court to six justices and made the judgeships elective. Among the important justices of the first half of the twentieth century were Sydney Smith (1909–48), Eugene O. Sykes (1916–25), George Ethridge (1917–41), and Virgil Griffith (1929–49). These justices faced new issues dealing with automobiles, Prohibition, and the validity of various relief measures during the Great Depression.

One of the biggest political controversies the court faced was in a 1922 decision, *Aetna Insurance Co. v. Robertson*. The state revenue agent brought suit against many national insurance companies under the state antitrust laws, and the trial court returned a judgment in the state's favor equal to half of that year's budget. On appeal, Chief Justice Smith set aside the judgment because the alleged violations had been unchallenged for more than a decade.

In *Brown v. State* (1935), Justice Griffith wrote one of the most noteworthy dissents in the court's history when Chief Justice Smith cited errors by the defense attorney to sustain the admission of confessions beaten out of three black men accused of murder. A year later, the US Supreme Court agreed with Griffith and reversed the decision.

The civil rights struggle came to the fore by the late 1940s. While desegregation cases were brought in federal court, the state court faced civil rights issues in criminal appeals. Willie McGee, a black man, was sentenced to death for the 1945 rape of a white woman. Bella Abzug, a New York attorney and later a member of the US House of Representatives, came to Mississippi to defend him. The Mississippi Supreme Court reversed his first two convictions but affirmed a third conviction in 1949. The defense had offered evidence that the woman had been engaged in an affair with the defendant. Justice Harvey McGehee was quoted as saying that such a suggestion was insulting.

In 1952 the Supreme Court was increased from six justices to nine. Leadership was provided by McGehee (1937–64; chief justice, 1949–64), Percy Lee (1950–66; chief justice 1964–66), William N. Ethridge (1952–71; chief justice, 1966–71), Robert Gillespie (1954–77; chief justice, 1971–77), and Neville Patterson (1964–86; chief justice 1977–86).

The court followed the directions of the Warren Court on expanded rights for criminal defendants. A personal injury lawsuit revolution began, from product liability to other claims.

Chief Justice Patterson oversaw significant changes to the administration of the court system. The court entered a May 1981 order claiming sole power to adopt rules of procedure for all the state courts. Almost all other states and the federal courts recognize the legislative branch's right to a substantial role in the process.

A further reordering of power among the branches occurred in *Alexander v. State ex rel. Allain* (1983). In an opinion written by Chief Justice Patterson with the aid of Justice James L. Robertson, the court found that legislators' historic practice of serving on executive branch boards violated the separation of powers.

Beginning in the mid-1990s, court elections centered on whether Mississippi had become a haven for frivolous personal injury suits. Justice Chuck McRae, an advocate for plaintiffs, clashed publicly with business-oriented justices and was defeated in 2002. What many observers perceived as a plaintiff-oriented court in the 1990s has changed so much that it is now often considered precisely the opposite. Chief Justice Jim Smith was defeated in 2008, perhaps because of such perceptions.

Among the trailblazers on the Supreme Court was Billy Ethridge, wheelchair-bound from childhood polio, who was appointed to the court in 1952. Lenore Prather was appointed the first female justice in 1982 and became the first female chief justice sixteen years later. The first African American, Reuben Anderson, was appointed in 1985. The first Republican to serve in the twentieth century, Jim Smith, elected in 1992, was also the last, since judicial elections became nonpartisan two years later.

Leslie H. Southwick
US Court of Appeals for the Fifth Circuit

Frank E. Everett Jr., in *History of Mississippi* (1973); Meredith Lang, *Defender of the Faith: The High Court of Mississippi, 1817–1875* (1977); Dunbar Rowland, *Courts, Judges, and Lawyers of Mississippi, 1798–1935* (1935); Herbert Shapiro, *White Violence and Black Response: From Reconstruction to Montgomery* (1988); John Ray Skates Jr., *A History of the Mississippi Supreme Court, 1817–1948* (1973); Leslie H. Southwick, *Mississippi Law Journal* (Winter 2002), *Mississippi Law Journal* (Spring 1996), *Mississippi College Law Review* (Fall 1997).

Archaeology

Archaeologists have been studying Mississippi since 1902, when Charles Peabody from Harvard University's Peabody Museum conducted excavations at the Oliver Mound site in Sunflower County. He uncovered a remarkable array of late prehistoric artifacts there and established a pattern of archaeologists from eastern institutions spending extended field seasons in the state exploring the rich cultural resources, focusing primarily on the Delta. Through the 1950s and 1960s, archaeologists documented hundreds of sites and, more important, established the cultural chronology for the region. After about 1970 one of the major sources of external funding was cultural resources management (CRM) contracts. A suite of federal laws required that archaeological sites be studied in advance of any projected impact on those sites as a result of a federally funded project. Perhaps the most notable of the CRM projects conducted in Mississippi was associated with the construction of the Tennessee-Tombigbee Waterway in the northeastern part of the state. Thousands of previously unrecorded archaeological sites were discovered, and archaeologists excavated many of them. Not only did we learn a great deal about an area that was poorly understood, the archaeological research funded by this and other CRM projects represented a shift in focus. While the archaeologists of the first half of the twentieth century concentrated on establishing a chronology for the artifacts and sites they were studying, CRM archaeologists explained the archaeological record in terms of environmental adaptation, technology, raw material exchange, and social organization, among many other concerns. As a result, the prehistory of the state is now understood as a complex and regionally diverse network of settlements that changed through time in ways that depended on evolving subsistence bases, changing environments, and contacts with contemporary peoples from throughout the South.

The prehistory of the South is generally understood in terms of four major stages. The earliest of these, the Paleo-Indian period, is poorly represented in Mississippi. Paleo-Indian sites in other states have demonstrated that these early hunters took advantage of large, late Pleistocene animals such as mammoths and a now extinct species of bison. Analysis of these sites indicates that Paleo-Indians were largely nomadic, following the big game they were exploiting. Spear

A

points from this period are usually made from the best raw material available within a fairly large area, indicating that during their seasonal migration, Paleo-Indians made a point of stopping where the finest stone was available and replenishing their tool kits. This high-grade stone was transformed into some of the most finely crafted spear points that have been found in Mississippi. Not only are Paleo-Indian points extremely symmetrical and carefully flaked, they characteristically have a single large flake taken from each face of the tool, beginning at the base and running up to three-quarters of the way to the point. The flutes or grooves are thought to have made hafting the point on a shaft more secure. The argument for this innovation is that since the hunting strategy focused on a few large and likely difficult-to-kill animals, the Paleo-Indians increased their chances of success by maximizing their technology. Although rare, Paleo-Indian spear points are found in surface collections from Mississippi. A large number of these points are made from the high-grade bedrock cherts from extreme northwestern Mississippi. Since no examples have been excavated in the state, there are no dates for this period in Mississippi, but it is generally dated to between 13000 and 8000 BC.

The Archaic period accounts for the next sixty-five centuries, the longest of any of the prehistoric periods. It is broken into the Early, Middle, and Late Archaic. We are fortunate to have data from the excavation of the Hester, a stratigraphic site near Aberdeen in northeastern Mississippi that spans all of the Early and most of the Middle Archaic periods. This prehistoric campsite was located on a terrace of the Tombigbee River where, over the centuries, flood deposits alternated with periods of occupation so that several feet of deposition preserved the prehistoric sequence, with Early Archaic artifacts at the bottom and Middle Archaic tools at the top. Careful excavation of this site documented a series of different styles of spear points. During the first half of the twentieth century, prior to the excavation of stratified sites such as Hester, these styles of points were thought to represent different and possibly contemporaneous tools with a separate tool for certain kinds of game or tasks, somewhat like a prehistoric golf bag with drivers, irons, and putters. A better analogy would be the way that automobile designs have evolved over time. Some developments reflect changes in technology, but the large majority—the kinds that allow viewers to differentiate a 1959 Cadillac from one made in 1969 or 1979—fall into the general area of style. However, some distinctive technological features allow archaeologists to identify Early Archaic spear points. Most are corner notched—that is, they are roughly triangular, with notches at the two basal corners—apparently to facilitate their attachment to hafts. The bases of Early Archaic spear points are usually ground to dull the sharp edges made while flaking the tool. This style is generally interpreted as a way to improve hafting. Finally, when viewed in cross section, Early Archaic points are not roughly symmetrical, like most spear points, but are more like parallelograms with beveling on alternate edges. This trait indicates that they were regularly resharpened while still hafted and must have been used as knives as well as spear points. Microscopic analyses of the traces of wear preserved on the edges of these points confirm that they were used for a number of tasks. The Early Archaic lasted for several centuries (8000–5000 BC). Studies of animal and plant remains recovered from sites dating to this period indicate that hunting, primarily white-tailed deer, was a major activity, while wild plants were exploited for seeds, fruit, and nuts. These Early Archaic hunters were nomadic, moving from resource to resource on a seasonal basis, though across a smaller range than their Paleo-Indian ancestors. Local resources were used almost exclusively for manufacturing their stone tools.

The Middle Archaic (5000–3000 BC) is marked by a change in the style of spear point. Basal-notched and corner-removed forms predominate. Beveling and basal grinding are rare. Other, more significant changes also occurred. For the first time in Mississippi we have evidence for long-term and intensive settlement in some locations. The best examples are the midden mounds of the Upper Tombigbee River Valley near Amory in northeastern Mississippi. These sites are located in low-lying areas of the floodplain, often surrounded by swamps. Excavation has shown these to have been low elevations in the swamp that were reoccupied for hundreds of years. The result is a rich organic deposit where the earth is dark brown or black as a result of the midden (trash) left at these sites. These deposits are often as much as six feet deep and are well stratified, with a few Early Archaic artifacts in the bottommost layers and a few late prehistoric artifacts in the top levels. The majority of the artifacts date to the Middle Archaic. One of the most interesting developments during the late Middle Archaic is the introduction of well-constructed, medium-sized, corner-removed points that were not made from locally available gravel. These points, called Benton after the county in Tennessee where they were first described, are made from a high-quality blue-gray bedrock chert from the Fort Payne formation located more than eighty miles to the northeast near Muscle Shoals in the Tennessee River Valley. These spear points were brought to the midden mound sites as nearly complete blanks to be finished, used, and discarded there. Archaeologists excavating the large mounds of shell along the banks of the Tennessee River that mark the location of Middle Archaic campsites found levels containing finished Benton points, blanks, and so much flaking debris that these were dubbed the workshop levels. Another set of artifacts, oversized Benton points, also were made from Fort Payne chert and deposited in the midden mounds. They are four or five times as long as the standard forms, with even longer bipointed "spear points." The bipointed forms and oversized Benton points were almost certainly not actually used as spear points because they are much too long and thin and would have shattered on impact. Instead, they might have been used in ritual and were certainly used to mark status, since they have been found in burials. In addition, middens include what appear to have been burned clay floors with isolated post holes. So far, none of the midden mound excavations has uncovered a pattern of post holes that outline a structure, but they are still the first evidence of structures to have been recorded in Mississippi.

Other, more spectacular finds indicate that technology and by implication social organization had become more complex during the Middle Archaic. Ground-stone tools have long been recognized as a marker of the Middle Archaic. The characteristic ground-stone artifact of this period is the banner stone. These are symmetrical cylinders of stone three to five inches long and two to three inches in diameter. They are sometimes square or rectangular in cross section and often have flattened panels or "wings" on either side. They were made from quartzite and other extremely hard stone. Examples broken during manufacture and discarded show that they were shaped by pecking and grinding. The final step was to drill a hole about an inch in diameter following the long axis of the cylinder. This was done using a drill made of cane with sand as an abrasive. Hundreds of hours were invested in the manufacture of these objects, and some are quite fantastic. They have been found in burial context with sufficient preservation so that a characteristic bone hook is found in line with the hole and twelve or more inches away from it, indicating that these were spear thrower weights. Spear throwers were wooden shafts with hooks on the end that fit into sockets in the bases of spears. They extended the arm, allowing the hunter to exert more force. The banner stones counterbalanced the weight of the shaft of the spear. The hunter could watch for game with the spear ready to throw.

Another kind of ground-stone artifact has recently been associated with the late Middle Archaic as the result of research done in Mississippi. Small, tubular beads, one or two inches long and less than half an inch in diameter, were made using a technology similar to that used to make banner stones. While the majority of these beads are simple tubes, many are formed in the shape of stylized insects and animals. These beads are found throughout the state, but one of the largest collections of them was recovered from the plowed fields of the Denton site near the town of Lambert in northwestern Mississippi. Other ground-stone effigy forms without holes drilled for suspension were found at Denton. Benton-like spear points made from Fort Payne chert have also been found at Denton, although it is more than 180 miles from the source area. The Denton site also has a small earthen mound that was originally related to the small number of pieces of broken pottery found at the site and dating to a much later period of time. Middle Archaic Indians were not previously thought to have lived in large enough groups or have the social organization required to build mounds. A number of discoveries in Louisiana dating back to the 1990s have proven that those assumptions were false. Several late Middle Archaic mound sites just across

the Mississippi River have been positively dated using spear point types, soil analysis, and radiocarbon dating. Some contain ground-stone beads and the tools used to make them. A small mound in Lincoln County in southwestern Mississippi has recently been dated to this period. Although it was once argued that the social organization implied by mound construction was possible only with advent of horticulture, no evidence suggests that the Middle Archaic Indians who built these mounds had access to any cultivated plants. These discoveries have forced archaeologists to reassess their understanding of the Middle Archaic.

In fact, the archaeological record of Mississippi and the rest of the Southeast can be characterized in terms of periods of cultural florescence where raw material obtained from outside the immediate area was transformed into elaborate and nonutilitarian artifacts that were likely used to mark differential status. In addition, mounds were constructed to define sacred spaces and to demonstrate the power of a few elite members of the culture to mobilize labor. These periods of florescence are often punctuated by several centuries when mounds and special classes of artifacts are absent or rare. The Late Archaic (3000–1500 BC) in Mississippi is, as far as we know, one such period. The same utilitarian tools are made with a whole new set of spear point shapes. Ample evidence indicates that natives lived well, and in fact, the state has more Late Archaic sites than Early or Middle Archaic sites, suggesting that the population continued to grow. However, earthworks, long-distance exchange, and specialized tools do not appear again until the very end of the Late Archaic. The extensive and elaborate earthworks at the Poverty Point site, a short distance across the Mississippi River from Vicksburg, have been known since the 1960s to date to the terminal Late Archaic. Until recently, this complex of concentric ridges arranged in a hexagonal pattern around a central plaza large enough to hold a couple of football fields confounded archaeologists as a unique and too early expression of monumental architecture. In addition, the site complex includes three large mounds and evidence for considerable fill in the plaza as well as a large number of artifacts made from raw material derived from distant sources. With the discovery of the Middle Archaic mounds, Poverty Point is no longer considered so unusual, but we still do not understand how nomadic hunters and gatherers generated the surplus resources to build these large earthworks. Moreover, recent remote sensing surveys of the plaza at Poverty Point have revealed large circular structures, too big to be houses, that may have been ritual post enclosures. Several sites in Mississippi were contemporaneous with Poverty Point and contain similar assemblages of artifacts made from exotic raw materials. The best known of these is the Jaketown site near Belzoni in the Delta. Recent work there has uncovered what may have been earthworks buried by more than ten feet of river deposits.

One diagnostic artifact of the Poverty Point period is fired clay balls about the size of plums. These Poverty Point objects, as they are called, come in a variety of shapes and appear to have served as cooking stones in the stone-poor environment of the Mississippi Alluvial Valley. A pit was dug and lined with Poverty Point objects, and then a fire was built. Once the fire had burned down and the Poverty Point objects were red hot, food was placed in the pit to cook. The use of fired clay at Poverty Point anticipates ceramics, a technology that was important during the subsequent occupation of Mississippi. Fragments of broken pottery are the predominant artifact at most prehistoric sites dating to the Woodland and Mississippian periods. In fact, ceramics are generally used to mark the beginning of the Woodland period (1500 BC–AD 1000). During this time there is increasing evidence for long-term, sometimes permanent settlement. Group size appears to have grown, since some Woodland sites are quite large. Hunting of deer and other land mammals continues to have been important, but analyses of the faunal remains from Woodland sites show that in addition to nuts and wild plants, the Woodland Indians domesticated sunflowers and other indigenous seed-bearing plants. This early agriculture no doubt explains the changes in settlement patterns and site type that characterize the Woodland period. The period is usually broken into three segments, Early Woodland (1500–200 BC), Middle Woodland (200 BC–AD 500), and Late Woodland (AD 500–1000). While archaeologists usually distinguish these phases on the basis of changes in the way the Indians decorated pots, other aspects of the archaeological record are more interesting.

The characteristic earthwork of the Woodland period is the burial mound. These mounds vary a good deal in internal structure, occasionally containing a central burial that was placed in a pit dug into the original land surface and covered with logs before the earth was mounded over it. At times the burials were placed in the mound, and the mound grew as burials were added. Occasionally both customs were followed, with the central tomb followed by several stages of construction with accompanying burials. There are clearly not enough mounds to accommodate the entire population, indicating that the mounds must have been reserved for elite members of society. The often-elaborate artifacts buried in the mounds support this argument. In addition to the introduction of horticulture and ceramics, the Woodland marks the beginnings of differential status as expressed in the archaeological record. Some of the most elaborate grave goods are found in mounds dating to the Middle Woodland period. The Bynum Mound, located near Houston in east-central Mississippi, is a good example. Ceramic vessels with elaborate incised images of stylized birds were included in the central tomb, along with greenstone adzes and cremated burials. Other Middle Woodland burial mounds contain pan pipes made from cold-hammered copper and shell cups made from marine shell. Stone tools were often made from midwestern raw materials, and there is a similarity between the way that Middle Woodland ceramics were decorated in Mississippi and contemporaneous ceramics from the Midwest. The similarities exist primarily in the ceramics from the burial mounds.

Woodland burial mounds are generally semihemispherical and fairly small. Topped mounds that are rectangular in plan view are usually called temple mounds and associated with the subsequent Mississippian period. Over the past two decades, a number of flat-topped mounds have been discovered that do not date to the Mississippian period and were not temple mounds. Mound B at the Batesville Mound site is a good example of a Woodland period platform mound. Although the mound is flat on top, no evidence indicates that a structure was ever built on its summit. One of the early stages of mound construction is full of the locally available gravel that had been heated and then cooled so quickly that it exploded. This fractured rock was likely used in cooking—a good deal of cooking. This stage of the mound appears to have been made up of the residue of large, likely ceremonial feasts. This mound dates to the Early Woodland. An even larger Woodland period flat-topped mound was erected near what is now the city of Ingomar just south of New Albany.

The most dramatic shift in settlement occurred with the introduction of corn-based agriculture at the beginning of the Mississippian period (AD 1000–1700). The period is named after the river and the vast floodplain of the Mississippi River, which was densely populated from St. Louis to the Gulf of Mexico during this period.

Mississippi contains a substantial number of Mississippian period sites. In contrast, the uplands of the state—areas that were well used by Archaic and Woodland Indians—were sparsely settled during the Mississippian period. Mississippian populations targeted the natural levees of the major rivers. These were the highest ground and less likely to flood and had prime agricultural soil.

The typical larger Mississippian site consists of one or more platform mounds arranged around a central plaza with associated conical burial mounds. The platform mounds are often imposing structures. The main mound at the Winterville Mounds located near Greenville is more than fifty-five feet high. Excavations in these mounds show that the mounds served as platforms for some of the largest structures on the site. Excavation in the main mound at the Parchman Place Mounds near Coahoma in the Delta exposed six burned floors, stacked one above the other, representing mound-top structures that were intentionally burned and immediately buried. Some sort of renewal ceremony as well as an expression of social power in terms of mobilized labor and mound construction is implied. There can be no doubt that Mississippian social structure was hierarchical, with powerful elites living at major mound centers in structures located atop temple mounds. When the elites died, they were buried in central locations within the mound centers, often accompanied by elaborately constructed and decorated artifacts. The major mound sites were surrounded by small mound sites (often single mounds) that in turn were surrounded by smaller village sites without mounds. Intense rivalry likely occurred between sites on the different levels, with rapid shifts in power as sets of leaders had more or less success in attracting followers. Ample evidence documents warfare at least during the early part of this period—iconography, burials containing arrowheads, trophy skulls, and fortified villages. Power centers rose and fell in cycles that sometimes lasted little more than a century. A major task for the next couple of decades in Mississippian archaeology will be working out the local histories of the distribution of power as expressed by the construction and abandonment of Mississippian mound centers.

The corn and beans that formed the economic basis for Mississippian society were clearly derived from Mesoamerica, and archaeologists have been quick to point out the superficial similarities between the temple mounds–plaza arrangement of Aztec and Mayan sites and the mound architecture of the Mississippian ceremonial centers. Given what we now know about the indigenous Woodland period development of flat-topped mounds, the mound tradition may well have grown at least in part from local antecedents. While similarities can be seen between Mesoamerican and Mississippian iconography, recent analyses based on native North American myths have made a persuasive argument for a rich indigenous belief system with only general similarities to those of Mexico and Guatemala. Moreover, plazas, while certainly present on Mississippian sites, are not an invariable element. In fact, one of the major discoveries of the past two decades of archaeology focusing on Mississippian sites is that a remarkable degree of variation exists in terms of site organization, symbolism, and complexity. For example, the Mississippian culture in the northern half of the Delta rests on a local, relatively conservative Woodland base. The transition into the Mississippian period was initiated at least in part through contact with major northern Mississippian centers such as Cahokia near St. Louis in west-central Illinois. Although the southern half of the Delta shows evidence of northern influence, the local Woodland tradition was expressed in terms of larger mound sites and represents a culture that is common to the South and along the Gulf Coast.

Given the regional diversity and the unstable nature of centralized power that we have come to recognize, it should come as no surprise that the Europeans recorded much different cultures in different parts of the state. De Soto and his party encountered the Chickasaw living in villages without mounds scattered throughout the Black Prairie of eastern Mississippi, somewhere in the vicinity of Columbus or West Point. Although medium-sized Mississippian mound centers had been located on the terraces of the Tombigbee River, they appear to have been abandoned prior to the de Soto expedition. After leaving the Black Prairie, de Soto crossed the north-central hills of North Mississippi as quickly as possible because there were no villages that the Spaniards could plunder for food. The Delta, conversely, was populous, and de Soto met with native leaders who lived in substantial structures built on large mounds. The Delta was abandoned by the late seventeenth century, when French explorers returned to the region, likely as a result of the political and economic disruption caused by the European-sponsored trade in Indian slaves. The Fatherland site to the south in Natchez was, however, the home of the Great Sun, the paramount leader of the Natchez who lived on one of the mounds until conflict with the French forced the Natchez to leave their homeland in the early eighteenth century.

Mississippi's archaeological record provides the opportunity to better understand the relationship between humans and their environment as well as the way that different forms of social and economic organization relate to one another. Remarkable parallels connect our culture and that of the native Mississippians. Almost every major city in the Delta, for example, was built on the remains of a Mississippian site. The main street in Clarksdale once split to go on either side of a mound too large to easily dismantle. The same factors that made the location favorable for European settlement were also important prehistorically. The city of Tupelo has completely encompassed the location of the major eighteenth-century Chickasaw villages. The Fatherland site is located within the Natchez city limits. And although undeniable similarities exist, so do stark differences. As we learn more about the archaeological record, we learn more about ourselves. After all, the Indians lived in Mississippi for more than fifteen thousand years, and only a small fraction of that period of time is accessible through historic documents.

Jay K. Johnson
University of Mississippi

David G. Anderson and Robert C. Mainfort Jr., eds., *The Woodland Southeast* (2002); Judith A. Bense, *Archaeology of the Southeastern United States: Paleoindian to World War I* (1994); Judith A. Bense, ed., *The Midden Mound Project* (1987); Jeffrey P. Brain, in *Mississippian Settlement Patterns*, ed. Bruce D. Smith (1978); Samuel O. Brookes, *The Hester Site: An Early Archaic Occupation in Monroe County, Mississippi* (1979); John L. Cotter and John M. Corbett, *Archeology of the Bynum Mounds, Mississippi* (1951); Charles Hudson, *Knights of Spain, Warriors of the Sun: Hernando de Soto and the South's Ancient Chiefdoms* (1997); Jay K. Johnson, in *Histories of Southeastern Archaeology*, ed. Shannon Tushingham, Jane Hill, and Charles. H. McNutt (2002); Vernon J. Knight Jr., James A. Brown, and George E. Lankford, *Southeastern Archaeology* (Winter 2001); Bonnie G. McEwan, ed., *Indians of the Greater Southeast: Historical Archaeology and Ethnohistory* (2000); Samuel O. McGahey, in *The Paleoindian and Early Archaic Southeast*, ed. David G. Anderson and Kenneth E. Sassaman (1996); Robert S. Neitzel, *Archaeology of the Fatherland Site: The Grand Village of the Natchez* (1965); Robert S. Neitzel, *The Grand Village of the Natchez Revisited: Excavations at the Fatherland Site, Adams County, Mississippi, 1972* (1983); Philip Phillips, James A. Ford, and James B. Griffin, *Archaeological Survey in the Lower Mississippi Alluvial Valley, 1940–1947* (1951); Joe Saunders et al., *Science* (September 1997).

Archaic Period

The Mississippi Archaic follows the end of the Paleo-Indian period (13000–8000 BC) and the Pleistocene epoch (1.8 MYA–8,000 BC) and is generally divided into three distinct subperiods: Early (8000–5000 BC), Middle (5000–3000 BC), and Late (3000–1500 BC). At the beginning of the Mississippi Archaic period, North America was quickly changing from a heavily glaciated continent populated by megafauna like mammoths, mastodons, and saber-toothed tigers to a warmer, more stable ecosystem populated by smaller mammals. Globally, the end of the Pleistocene marks the change from the European Paleolithic to the Neolithic. Known as the Epipaleolithic transition, this is when humans are thought to have first developed agriculture.

In Mississippi the beginning of the Archaic period marks the extinction of the large mammals and the development of increasingly stationary human societies. Rather than moving from place to place utilizing readily available resources, humans began settling down and exploiting seasonally available foodstuffs. This is partly the result of a climactic phenomenon starting in the Middle Archaic known as the Hypsithermal interval, which resulted in the gradual warming of what became the southeastern United States. This warming altered the environment and made it more amenable to less mobile lifestyles. Rising sea levels, a result of increasing temperatures, caused river systems to meander, forming oxbows and backwater swamps ideal for the proliferation of edible aquatic foods. Evidence for this change is seen in increasingly thick middens (trash pits) at Middle Archaic archaeological sites formed from large amounts of shellfish and edible marine resources. Other distinctive elements of the Mississippi Archaic are the development of ground-stone tool technology, the invention of fiber-tempered pottery at the end of the period, and longer-term occupations of seasonal habitation sites. This period also saw a general growth, florescence, and disappearance of regional trade networks.

While the Early Archaic in Mississippi is not very well understood, scholars believe that this period is marked by the continuation of generalized pre-Archaic hunting and gathering adaptations. That humans lived in small bands and maintained highly mobile lifestyles is evident from the absence of expansive village/settlement sites discovered dating to this period as well as from the dearth of any significant well-formed middens. Without repeated or long-term settlement in one area, trash cannot accumulate to indicate human settlement. One distinctive change in projectile point technology is the shift from Clovis-style points, which are large bifacially worked spear points with a centralized groove, to side-notched and stemmed projectile points. Distinctive point types for the Early Archaic are Big Sandy, Cache River, Hardin, and Jude; other common stone tools are manos, pitted cobbles, scrapers, and hafted scrapers.

Post-Pleistocene changes in human lifestyles began in earnest during the Middle Archaic period. As a result of gradually warming environments during the Hypsithermal, aquatic species became more prevalent and hardy and therefore more reliable as a source of calories. Consequently, semipermanent settlement patterns tied to aquatic environs become de rigueur in Mississippi during this time. Seasonal base camps associated with wet and dry seasons are thought to have been utilized; during times of low water (summer), floodplain settlements were preferred, and during the high-water seasons (fall and winter), upland base camps were preferred. In addition to changes in settlement patterns, stone-tool utilization was also shifting. One of the most distinctive technologies to emerge at this time was ground-stone tools. With the inception of this method of manufacturing, axes and blades no longer had the jagged, flaked appearance common to older indigenous weapons and tools. Rather, these objects approached an aesthetic that mirrors our modern concern for balancing form with function. Such ground-stone objects were often made into celts (one-sided and blunt-ended axes), grooved axes, atlatl weights, pendants, grinding stones, and most impressively, a variety of bead forms. The Middle Archaic lapidary (bead-making) industry produced significant numbers of zoomorphic (animal-shaped) stone objects. Artisans at Mississippi's Denton and Loosa Yokena sites crafted elaborate symbolic reproductions of turtles, locusts, owls, and other creatures. These animal-shaped beads are thought to have had a ceremonial or ritual function and have been found at these sites in conjuction with bead blanks, raw materials, and unfinished pieces. These beads were often made of jasper, nonlocal greenstone, local cherts and quartzites, sandstone, and other exotic materials. The large-scale production of beads at these manufacturing sites shows that while local resources were being used with greater frequency, an elaborate prestige-goods trading network was developing and spanned as far north as the Great Lakes and as far south as the Gulf Coast. This long-distance trading network can also be inferred from the high quantity of nonlocal and exotic materials recovered from Middle Archaic burials.

By the Late Archaic period, the warming trend brought by the Hypsithermal event had ended and was subsequently replaced by cooler, moister weather similar to contemporary weather patterns. Shorelines stabilized, and the shape of Mississippi's modern-day coastline was established. Streams began flowing swiftly, thereby eroding creek bottoms and exposing more local lithic resources; as a result, local stone materials were used with greater frequency. With the increasing abundance of local resources, humans chose to settle down in one place for longer periods of time. In addition, human populations are thought to have increased during this period as a result of increasing sedentism and the serial utilization of particular food crops. As people lived in one place for longer periods of time, certain plant species experienced increased human consumption and redistribution, thereby possibly marking the beginnings of plant domestication in Mississippi. The Late Archaic period is also marked by the development of ceramic pottery in the Upper Tombigbee Basin. Called the Wheeler series, this type of pottery appears infrequently during the end of the Late Archaic and continues into the overlapping Gulf Formational period. Wheeler pottery is fiber tempered and mostly undecorated, although some has punctations and stamped design motifs; common vessel forms are flat-bottomed bowls and beakers.

Jayur Mehta
Tulane University

David Anderson, *The Paleoindian and Early Archaic Southeast* (1996); Judith Bense, *Archaeology of the Southeastern United States: Paleoindian to World War I* (1994); Philip Phillips, James A. Ford, and James B. Griffin, *Archaeological Survey in the Lower Mississippi Alluvial Valley, 1940–1947* (1951).

Archer, Chalmers, Jr.
(1938–2014) Author and Educator

Born in Mississippi and educated in the South, Chalmers Archer Jr. was a teacher, lecturer, columnist, and author whose work influenced education for African American students and shed light on the important experiences of black Mississippians in the twentieth century.

Son of Chalmers Archer, a farmer, and Eva Rutherford Archer, an educator, Chalmers Archer Jr. was born on 21 April 1938 in the small Delta town of Tchula. Archer and his five younger siblings spent their childhood on the land that his father rented from a white family, farming and enjoying the natural setting. Aside from the richness of the landscape, however, the rural Mississippi Delta offered little in the way of comforts to the Archer family. Archer came of age surrounded by the threat of white violence and reprisal for political organization and witnessed the inequities in education, medical care, and economic opportunity that plagued his community. His memoir chronicles many of these experiences as well as the community's unique relationship to land and cultural practices, including herbal healing, inherited from the older generations.

Archer served in the US Army for more than a decade in the 1950s and 1960s, working as a medic in Korea and later joining the newly formed Special Forces and becoming a captain. He subsequently returned to Mississippi and

earned an associate's degree from Saints Junior College in Lexington. He then received bachelor's and master's degrees from Alabama's Tuskegee Institute in 1972 and 1974 and earned a doctorate in counseling and psychology from Auburn University in 1979.

Archer worked in educational administration while in school, assisting the president and registrar at Saints and serving as a career counselor, as an assistant dean of admissions, and ultimately as an assistant professor in education at Tuskegee. In 1983 he moved to Virginia and became a professor at Northern Virginia Community College, remaining there until his retirement in 2000.

In addition to his long career in education, Archer authored two books detailing his life experiences, *Green Berets in the Vanguard: Inside Special Forces, 1953–1963* (1992) and *Growing Up Black in Rural Mississippi: Memories of a Family, Heritage of a Place* (2001). Archer frequently visited Tchula and his family's farm and stayed connected to his home state by contributing a weekly column to the *Jackson Advocate*. He died in Manassas, Virginia, on 24 February 2014.

Frances Abbott
Digital Public Library of America,
Boston, Massachusetts

Adam Bernstein, *Washington Post* (6 March 2014); The HistoryMakers website, www.thehistorymakers.com; Thomson Gale Contemporary Authors Series.

Armstrong Tire and Rubber Company

Armstrong Tire and Rubber became Mississippi's first tire manufacturer when it opened a plant in Natchez in 1939 as part of the Balance Agriculture with Industry (BAWI) program. The city's voters approved a three-hundred-thousand-dollar bond issue to build the new factory and agreed that Armstrong would pay no rent for five years and then pay just thirty-six hundred dollars a year for the next forty-five years. Natchez also exempted Armstrong Tire and Rubber from local taxes.

The company initially hired about two hundred employees, a number that grew to nearly a thousand a decade later and surpassed a thousand by the 1960s. Armstrong at first hired white men almost exclusively, especially for skilled jobs, but by the 1960s about four hundred employees were African Americans. In some ways, Armstrong was a BAWI success story, attracting numerous workers displaced by changes in agriculture and paying most of them higher wages than they had received in farmwork or at other industrial jobs. Workers organized a chapter of the United Rubber, Cork, Linoleum, and Plastic Workers of the Congress of Industrial Organizations in 1945.

The Armstrong Tire and Rubber plant—and especially its parking lot—became the site of violence against civil rights workers in the 1960s. On 27 August 1965 George Metcalfe, president of the local chapter of the National Association for the Advancement of Colored People (NAACP) and an Armstrong employee, was the victim of a car bombing in the parking lot just a few days after he had petitioned the Natchez School Board to begin desegregating the schools. The attack on Metcalfe inspired extensive civil rights protests. Two years later, Wharlest Jackson, also an Armstrong employee and the former treasurer of the NAACP, was killed in a car bombing. Arguing that Jackson's murderers had targeted him because he had just been promoted to a skilled job once considered for whites only, members of the NAACP called on the company to fire all employees who were members of the Ku Klux Klan. The company offered a reward for information about the murderer, but no one was ever charged.

Armstrong Tire and Rubber began to decrease its Natchez workforce in the 1980s and finally decided to close the plant in 1986. A group of city residents bought the factory and renamed it the Fidelity Tire Company. Titan International, with headquarters in Illinois, bought the factory in 1998, but a major labor strike soon began, followed by lawsuits over worker safety and violations of the Clean Water Act, leading Titan to close the plant in 2001.

Ted Ownby
University of Mississippi

James C. Cobb, *The Selling of the South: The Southern Crusade for Industrial Development, 1936–1990* (1993); Jack E. Davis, *Race against Time: Culture and Separation in Natchez since 1930* (2001); *Water Log: Legal Reporter of the Mississippi-Alabama Sea Grant Consortium*, Mississippi-Alabama Sea Grant Consortium website, www.masgc.org.

Art

Visual arts have been a mark of the area now called Mississippi for at least six thousand years. Before the Egyptian pyramids were built, an artist in South Mississippi was carving river rock into forms representing animals of the region. A vast amount of other archeological material has been recovered across the state—vessels decorated with abstract designs, carved stone, decorative ceramic pipes and discs,

ceramics in the shape of animals—but extensive investigation needs to be undertaken before a clearer picture can emerge of Mississippi's prehistoric past, its cultures, and the contributions of artists. Only a small fraction of the state has been thoroughly studied. The largest group of ceramics so far uncovered were made during the Mississippian era (AD 1000–1700) and came from the Yazoo River Basin.

By the time the French arrived to colonize the area in 1699, regional tribes—most notably the Biloxi, Natchez, Tunica, Choctaw, and Chickasaw—were producing decorative pottery with distinctive designs and colors. The Choctaw and Chickasaw were producing intricate basketry made of swamp cane dyed with natural substances. During the eighteenth century the Choctaw produced elaborate beadwork sashes and other wearable pieces, worked in silver, and created clothing styles based on European patterns with appliquéd color strips. At the same time, a few of the first European settlers created drawings, decorative maps, and watercolor sketches of the natives and terrain. Most early European settlers in Mississippi had little time to create art, however. The daily struggle of clearing and cultivating land or managing herds of cattle or fishing or building boats occupied the energy of the men, while the women were busy fulfilling household needs. As soon as towns became established, however, itinerant artists began arriving from the East and Midwest. Coming down the Mississippi and Tombigbee Rivers, they offered primarily portraiture in oil or pencil or silhouettes in paper. The area's flora and fauna also attracted traveling artists intent on recording the new country and new species. One of the first professional artists to live in the state was John James Audubon, whose interest in birds brought him down the Mississippi River in 1820. In 1822 he brought his family from Kentucky to live in Natchez, where he taught drawing and dancing and tried to make a living with his painting. A close brush with yellow fever convinced him to move on, but Audubon documented a number of Mississippi's birds and left portrait sketches and a beautiful cityscape of Natchez.

As the state prospered and expanded, more painters arrived and stayed for extended periods to complete multiple portraits in a community or family. Some of the earliest traveling portraitists in Mississippi were William Edward West, Matthew Jouett, James Reid Lambdin, and George Caleb Bingham. The first native artist was James Tooley Jr., who was born in Natchez in 1816 and earned a national reputation for portrait miniatures, including the portrait of his teacher in Philadelphia, Thomas Sully.

By the 1840s Mississippi began to attract artists who wanted to make their homes there. Thomas Cantwell Healey settled in Port Gibson, William Carroll Saunders and John Randolph Saunders took residence in Columbus, Louis Joseph Bahin moved to Natchez, and Charles Weigand came to Jackson. Still, itinerant artists continued to pour into the prospering state until the Civil War. In addition to painters, the state supported other creators of the visual arts. Edwin

Lyon of Natchez was a professional sculptor working in wax, plaster, and marble. Louis Emile Gustave Profilet and George Macpherson of Natchez and Jacob Faser of Macon were prominent silversmiths.

The earliest woman artist to gain recognition was Fannie McMurtry of Natchez, a landscape painter who worked in the 1850s. From earliest settlement, a varied and extensive array of visual arts was created by women whose names were known only to their families. Homes were embellished with quilting, embroidery, and other textile arts; decorative fire boards and painted ceramics; and reverse paintings on glass, stencil, and tinsel paintings. Experienced slave artisans were assigned to create decorative wrought iron tracery and railings, while female slaves had to learn the patterns of European needlework.

A new form of visual art was introduced to Mississippi in 1842 when a traveling daguerreotype artist opened up shop in a Jackson hotel. The first resident photographer in Jackson was probably Erich von Seutter, who moved there prior to the Civil War. At the University of Mississippi, chemistry professor Edward Boynton experimented with photography before the Civil War forced him to leave for his home in Vermont. The first renowned photographer with a portrait studio was Henry Gurney, who opened a shop in Natchez the 1850s. In 1870 Gurney hired a young assistant, Henry C. Norman, who became Mississippi's first art photographer. Norman and his brother, Earl, documented the life and people of Natchez with extraordinary sensitivity and skill. Upriver, H. J. Herrick and J. Mack Moore captured life in Vicksburg, while Aberdeen-based F. S. McKnight covered the northeastern corner of the state. John C. Coovert of Greenville worked in the Delta.

The Civil War and its aftermath disrupted the production of visual arts, but emancipation permitted the aesthetics of African American tradition to emerge. String quilts and other African techniques suppressed in the slave culture were recovered and showed up in textiles created primarily by African American women.

Out of the stymied atmosphere of poverty and Reconstruction, an exceptional artist began his career in his hometown. George Ohr opened Biloxi Art and Novelty Pottery in 1879 and showed his work at the 1885 World's Exposition in New Orleans. At the 1904 St. Louis Exposition he won an award as the most original art potter and was cited in a national ceramics journal as "one of the most interesting potters in the United States." Except for his "souvenir" pieces, his work did not sell well, however. In the Victorian era, Ohr's inventive glazes were considered garish. Moreover, his delicate, thin-walled pots were twisted, dented, ruffled, and folded into exotic forms. When he closed his shop in 1909, he packed up several thousand pieces, and they remained stored until 1968, when they were sold on the New York market. Art pottery collectors enthusiastically paid thousands of dollars for Ohr's pots, and art historians reevaluated his importance. Biloxi's Ohr-O'Keefe Museum of Art, designed by Frank Gehry, opened in 2010.

Another Gulf Coast pottery destined to become nationally known opened in 1928 when Peter Anderson founded Shearwater Pottery in Ocean Springs. The workshops and showroom, rebuilt after Hurricane Katrina, are still largely staffed by talented family members under the leadership of Peter Anderson's son, Jim. Pup and Lee McCarty founded an important Mississippi Delta pottery in 1954. The Merigold pottery is distinctive in its use of earth tones of nutmeg and jade. The colorful patterns and stylish pieces of the Gail Pittman Pottery of Madison have made it the state's leading production pottery and exporter.

Mississippi has a wealth of outdoor sculpture, primarily created in the first half of the twentieth century to commemorate the loss of life in the Civil War. The largest collection of Civil War sculptures can be seen at the Vicksburg National Military Park, where some of the nation's top sculptors are represented. More mundane Confederate monuments have been erected in the centers of some forty communities as well as in cemeteries wholly or partially devoted to that purpose. Major public pieces in the capital city of Jackson include *Soldiers of World War I* at the War Memorial Building and Belle Kinney's elegant bronze memorial, *Women of the Confederacy*, at the new Capitol. Virtually every college and university campus has bronze or stone sculptures, and many cemeteries contain beautiful artwork, the most impressive of which is Malvina Hoffman's sculpture, *The Patriot*, which marks LeRoy Percy's grave in Greenville.

Stained glass, which became popular in nineteenth-century America through the technology of LaFarge and Tiffany, can be found throughout the state, primarily in religious structures and houses. Ventress Hall at the University of Mississippi features a secular Tiffany window depicting the organization of the University Greys, an infantry company of students who became part of the Confederate Army. Today the most esteemed artist and purveyor of stained glass windows and objets d'art is Andrew Young, who founded Pearl River Studio in Jackson in 1975 and whose work can be seen in homes, churches, and public buildings throughout the state.

Folk art in its purest sense of communal art passed down through generations has been mainly the province of the Choctaw Indians of Philadelphia and of African American quilters, woodcarvers, and textile artists. *Visionary, self-taught*, and *outsider art* are contemporary terms for painting and sculpture created by untutored but intuitive artists working outside a communal tradition. Mississippi has a plethora of such expressive artists working with materials ranging from conventional oil and watercolor to tempera paints and crayons, corrugated tin, clay laced with putty, sequins, bottles, and other found objects. The first folk artist to gain national attention was Theora Hamblett of Oxford, who had art training and worked with memory and vision painting. New York's Museum of Modern Art purchased one of her "vision" paintings in 1954. Other well-known folk artists include Mary T. Smith, Earl Simmons, Luster Willis, Willie Barton, and James "Son" Thomas. The research of Vicksburg native William Ferris first brought folk art and outsider art to the attention of a wide audience in Mississippi. Roland Freeman did important documentation of African American quilting.

Mainstream visual arts, however, have focused on traditional painting and printmaking. Some of the state's best-known twentieth-century artists include Walter Anderson, Marie Hull, William Hollingsworth, John McCrady, Dusti Bongé, Karl Wolfe, Mildred Wolfe, Caroline Compton, Lawrence Jones, Mary Katherine Loyocano, Malcolm Norwood, William Dunlap, Lynn Green Root, Mary Ann Ross, Ke Francis, Wyatt Waters, Marshall Bouldin III, Sammy Britt, Glennray Tutor, Emmitt Thames, Alan Flattman, George Thurmond, Bebe Wolfe, John Gaddis, Elizabeth Johnson, and Mary Ann Ross. In other media were Ethel Mohamed (needlework); Elizabeth Robinson, Susan Ford, and Andrew Young (glass); Fletcher Cox (wood); Bill Beckwith, Kim Sessums, and Sam Gore (bronze); George Berry and Sulton Rogers (woodcarving); Obie Clark, Emmett Collier, and Springwood Pottery (ceramics); and Elayne Goodman (constructions).

The twentieth century brought national fame to two Mississippi photographers. Before Eudora Welty became a writer, she was an avid photographer. Her images of life in Mississippi during the Depression era earned her a reputation as one of America's most perceptive photographers. Mississippi's major contemporary photographer is William Eggleston, called the Father of Color Photography. Eggleston emphasized color relationships and composition almost abstract in its realization. Today, among the outstanding photographers at work in the state are Lyle Bongé, Maude Schuyler Clay, Langdon Clay, Jane Rule Burdine, Kim Rushing, Kay Holloway, Gretchen Haien, Jack Spencer, Robert Hubbard, David Rae Morris, Birney Imes III, and Eyd Kazery.

In twenty-first-century Mississippi, many visual artists make their living as painters, printmakers, ceramists, glassmakers, sculptors, woodcarvers, fabric artists, and furniture makers. Some of the best-known artists working today include Randy Hayes, Charles Carraway, Ellen Langford, Lea Barton, Jere H. Allen, Ron Dale, Duncan Baird, Collier Parker, Richard Kelso, Jason Bouldin, Baxter Knowlton, Ron Lindsey, Joseph Pearson, Martha Ferris, Norma Bordeaux, Sandy McNeal, Anthony Difatta, Cleta Ellington, Kathleen Vernell (ceramics), Billy and Marianne Wynn (glass), and Mary Ott Davidson (bronze).

Mississippi has taken giant steps to provide venues for the visual arts. The Lauren Rogers Museum in Laurel, established in 1923, is the state's oldest art museum. The Gulf Coast Art Association, started in 1926, provided juried shows that traveled to communities along the coast and to Mobile but had no permanent gallery. The Mississippi Art Association in Jackson obtained its first gallery in 1926 (now the Jackson Municipal Art Gallery) and in 1978 spearheaded the creation of the Mississippi Museum of Art, now in its second home. The Mississippi Museum of Art has, in effect, created a statewide museum network with its Affiliates program, which includes most of Mississippi's visual arts venues. Among the other venues for visual arts are the Ethel Wright Mohamed Stitchery Museum in Belzoni, the Ohr-O'Keefe Museum of Art in Biloxi, the Smith Robertson Museum in Jackson, and the Cedars in Jackson as well as university museums and commercial art galleries and artists' studio galleries across the state. The Craftsmen's Guild of Mississippi, established in 1973, opened a new facility near the Natchez Trace in Ridgeland in 2007. It houses the organization's administrative offices, but its main function is to exhibit and market members' work.

Art festivals also showcase the work of Mississippi visual artists. Some of the most prominent are the annual Chimneyville Crafts Festival in Jackson, sponsored by the Craftsmen's Guild of Mississippi; the Gumtree Festival in Tupelo; the Peter Anderson Memorial Arts, Crafts, and Foods Festival in Ocean Springs; the George Ohr Fall Festival of Arts in Biloxi; and events at the Mississippi Museum of Art, which has a permanent exhibition and programs featuring Mississippi art. The annual Choctaw Indian Fair features art and crafts by the Mississippi Band of Choctaws, who continue their basketry, beadwork, and dress traditions.

Visual artists are honored each year through the Mississippi Institute of Arts and Letters awards and frequently through the Governor's Awards for Excellence in the Arts. With the support of the Mississippi Arts Commission and state and local governments as well as an increased interest in promoting visual arts in the school systems, the future is promising for visual arts in Mississippi.

Patti Carr Black
Jackson, Mississippi

Patti Carr Black, *Art in Mississippi: 1720–1980* (1998); Patti Carr Black, *The Mississippi Story*, ed. Robin C. Dietrick (2007).

Art Colonies

Alongside museums and galleries, art colonies thrive in Mississippi. The Mississippi and Tougaloo art colonies are formal examples of such organizations, while the area of the Gulf Coast from Bay St. Louis to Biloxi is also frequently described as a colony.

Founded in 1948, the Mississippi Art Colony is one of the oldest artist-run organizations in the United States. Past and present members include Marie Hull, Lallah Perry, Andrew Bucci, Richard Zoellner, and the "Summit Three"—Bess Dawson, Halcyone Barnes, and Ruth Holmes. Membership requires an invitation from existing members.

Originally known as the Allison's Wells Art Colony, the organization formed and met at the Allison's Wells Hotel in Allison's Wells, where the hosts were hotel owners John and Hosford Fontaine. When a fire destroyed the hotel in 1962, the group relocated to Stafford Springs, near Heidelberg. The colony moved to the Pinehurst Hotel in Laurel Springs in 1970 but decided to return to a rural location three years later. Since 1973 colony members have gathered at Camp Henry Jacobs in Utica.

Colony members currently meet for a five-day workshop every April and October. There, in addition to peer critique, members receive the tutelage of an invited regional or nationally recognized artist-instructor. After formal talks and a critique, the instructor judges artwork to be included in the Colony Travel Show, which is displayed at various public locations in Mississippi. In 1998, as part of the colony's fiftieth anniversary, longtime patron and teacher Hugh Williams curated a traveling exhibition featured at museums and galleries around the state. The colony's records from 1954 to 1991 are held at the Smithsonian Archives of American Art.

The annual Tougaloo Art Colony was founded in 1997, the first such arts organization at a historically black college or university. (Tougaloo College, which hosts the colony, was founded in 1868 and holds a noted collection of African American art.) Participants produce work under the guidance of established artists and art instructors from around the Southeast and beyond. Unlike the Mississippi Art Colony, with its single-instructor format, the Tougaloo Art Colony enlists six to seven artist-instructors "selected for their outstanding achievement [and] teaching influence, and who represent a variety of artistic media, geographic regions, and ethnic backgrounds." Since its inception, the colony has grown from a student body of fifteen to seventy-five or more. An annual Thursday night "Hot Art Exhibit" is open to the public, features artwork from both students and instructors, and in part benefits scholarship, art supply, and textbook funds for the Tougaloo Art Department. In 2009 the colony added a three-day children's art camp.

The Mississippi Gulf Coast is often considered an art colony unto itself. Working artists flourish in Ocean Springs, Bay St. Louis, Biloxi, and other cities, while the area as a whole is noted for its galleries, museums, public art spaces, and art festivals. From the generations-old Shearwater Pottery to the recently completed Ohr-O'Keefe Museum, the Gulf Coast gives visitors ample opportunities to interact with creative culture and enterprise.

The prevalence of art and artists along the Gulf Coast has resulted in part from the migration and/or vacationing of wealthy patrons from beyond the state who brought their creative interests with them. Along with the Northeast, New Orleans has had a particularly strong influence on the area. Beginning in the early twentieth century, noted New Orleans artists such as William Steen, Charles and Ethel Hutson, and William Posey Silva first visited and then relocated to the region, inspired by the bounty of natural subject matter. In addition, many artists from the region have influenced the art world, including Walter Anderson, Richmond Barthé, Dusti Bongé, and George Ohr, among others. Another contributor to the arts colony designation may have to do with the coast's history of greater social permissiveness than has existed other areas of the state. To some extent, rigid social codes were eased on the coast as a consequence of its status as a vacation area, the influx of visitors from beyond the South, the proximity to New Orleans, and the established gambling and resort industry. In this environment, the perceived progressiveness often associated with artists was at least somewhat more welcomed if not encouraged.

Odie Lindsey
Nashville, Tennessee

Patti Carr Black, *Art in Mississippi, 1720–1980* (1998); Patti Carr Black, *American Masters of the Mississippi Gulf Coast: George Ohr, Dusti Bongé, Walter Anderson, Richmond Barthé* (2008); Mississippi Art Colony website, www.msartcolony.org; Smithsonian Archives of American Art website, http://www.aaa.si.edu/collections/collection/missart.htm; Norma Watkins, *The Last Resort: Taking the Mississippi Cure* (2011).

Art Deco Architecture

The world first encountered the Art Deco style at the 1925 Exposition Internationale des Arts Decoratifs et Industriels Modernes in Paris. Art Deco has many facets, especially in the United States, where it arrived later and thus merged with industrial and streamlined elements and manifestations such as those introduced during the 1939 World's Fair in New York City. This combination formed a pastiche of Art Deco: Zig-Zag Moderne, PWA Moderne, Federalist Deco, Streamlining Moderne, Industrial Moderne, Miami Deco, and other expressions of the style, mixed with obvious elements of Bauhaus and International Modernism. The proper terminology for the eclectic subcategories of Art Deco remains quite fluid.

Art Deco in Mississippi cannot be divorced from the Works Public Administration (WPA), created in the 1930s as part of New Deal efforts to alleviate unemployment. The architectural branch of the WPA, the Public Works Administration (PWA), stimulated the economy by building civic structures. The lack of funding in Mississippi meant that even after Art Deco went out of style, the state's WPA/PWA treasures were not torn down and replaced, and they have garnered a new appreciation since the late twentieth century.

Almost all aspects of Art Deco architecture exist in Mississippi. The elegant, high style of Art Deco (the closest to the 1925 exposition) is found in the Mary Buie Museum (1939) by Steven and Johnson on the Oxford campus of the University of Mississippi and Meridian's Threefoot Building (1939) by Lindsley and Fort. The Oxford City Hall by Canizaro (1938, destroyed 1976) was a fine example of Streamline Moderne, with its recessed entrance, ribbon windows, metal capping, and facade clock.

To keep costs low, Art Deco often bore minimal ornamentation: even mass-produced sculptural panels were expensive. However, some of Mississippi's Art Deco buildings contain sculptural elements. Senatobia High School has design elements (frozen fountain imagery, transportation imagery, and bombastic human figures) that reference the Zig-Zag Moderne, Miami Deco, and Streamlining/Streamlining Moderne aspects of Art Deco, and Tupelo's Church Street School (1938) by N. W. Overstreet has similar design elements. Clarksdale's Civic Auditorium (1939, dedicated 1943, according to the two building plaques) by Malvaney has a large relief sculptural panel that contains a personification of Mississippi holding a Deco skyscraper, signifying a revitalized future through the PWA, while at her feet lie symbols of the past—a Native American Indian war bonnet, a conquistador helmet, and a bale of cotton.

Because of the expense of ornamentation, many architects, designers, and builders used what was on hand—primarily red brick—in creative ways, such as fabricating Deco wave designs or combining it with small quantities of the more expensive white stone (for example, Milam Junior High by Bem Price [1939]). Though no longer extant, Booneville High School (1937) by Steven and Johnson was a showpiece of value engineering through brick placement in banding and wave motifs, glass block, cantilevered awnings, and the use of faux masonry and a few precious prefabricated Deco stylized floral medallions.

Art Deco architecture in Mississippi gradually moved toward extinction until the mid-1990s, when public consciousness of historic preservation came to encompass the buildings of the 1930s and 1940s. Two exceptional examples of PWA Art Deco building rehabilitation are in New Albany—the Union County Jail, now an office building, and the New Albany Post Office, now the headquarters for the Union County Development Association. An example of preservation from the private arena is the domestic architecture of the Parkhaven neighborhood in Hattiesburg, an eclectic mix of architectural styles connected to Art Deco. Current residents are working to preserve it.

Karyn Larlee Ott
Brevard Community College

Victor Arwas, *Art Deco* (1992); Patricia Bayer, *Art Deco Architecture* (1992); Tom Dewey II, *Art Nouveau, Art Deco, and Modernism: A Guide to the Styles* (1983); Michael W. Fazio, *Overstreet and Overstreet, a Legacy in Architecture* (1993); Karyn Larlee Ott, "Civic Art Deco Architecture in North Mississippi" (master's thesis, University of Mississippi, 1994); Richard Striner, *Winterthur Portfolio* (Spring 1990); Elayne H. Varian, *American Art Deco Architecture* (1975); Eva Weber, *Art Deco in America* (1985); Valerie Wells, *Mississippi Magazine* (1 May 2002).

Art, Folk

Folk art encompasses several genres found in Mississippi: traditional crafts and decorations, including woodcarving, basketry, ceramics, and quilting; the art of common folks; self-taught, outsider, visionary, and vernacular art. The American art world's attention was drawn to folk art when Berthe Kroll Goldsmith and Holger Cahill opened the American Folk Art Gallery in 1931 in New York City. Folk art forms exhibited there were promoted as ancestors of modern art. During a revival of interest in folk art in the 1970s, traditional ethnic arts were linked to non-Western cultures, especially those from Africa. During the same decade outsider art was defined as the product of artists outside a Western aesthetic. Visionary art emerged as the product of individuals' dreams and visions, and folk architecture forms such as shotgun and dogtrot houses were labeled vernacular art. Many artists combined several genres.

Pottery and basketry were important crafts among indigenous groups of the Southeast, including the Mississippian culture Natchez Chiefdom and the Choctaw, who still practice split-cane basketry, one of the oldest indigenous crafts. A common pattern consists of a cross inside a diamond. The most frequently used pattern is a five/five herringbone. Commonly used colors, some of which may be symbolic, include yellow, red, purple, brown, and black. Basket forms include the winnowing basket, tray or catch basket, sieve, pack basket, hamper, carrying or burden basket, triangular basket, elbow basket, and lunch basket. The Choctaw, Europeans, and African Americans wove white oak and pine-needle baskets.

By the early nineteenth century, quilts had become primary bed coverings. European and African American craftspersons made whole-cloth, broderie perse, appliqué, and pieced quilts. Among the many patterns used were Whig Rose, Whig's Defeat, Martha Washington's Flower Garden, Star of Bethlehem, Feathered Star, Princess Feather, Tulip, Pomegranate, Drunkard's Path, Irish Chain, Pinwheel, Log Cabin, and Nine Patch. Some patterns made symbolic references, while others were merely decorative. Essie Emaline Epting Myers and Pecolia Warner were among the many outstanding Mississippi quilters.

Art scholar Patti Carr Black has called walking canes the most widespread sculptural form produced by Mississippi woodcarvers. Snakes, frogs, alligators, turtles, and humans are frequent subjects. Carvers include Victor "Hickory Stick Vic" Bobb from Vicksburg, Leon Rucker from Jefferson County, and Luster Willis from near Crystal Springs.

Elijah Pierce, from near Baldwyn, was one of Mississippi's most renowned folk sculptors. Recognized as a National Heritage Fellow, he established an art gallery in his barber's shop (now a National Historic Site) in Columbus, Ohio. Pierce carved walking canes, freestanding sculpture, and elaborate painted biblical reliefs. *Book of Wood* depicts the life of Jesus and was used along with other carved reliefs to illustrate Pierce's sermons. The Columbus Museum of Art holds a major collection of his works.

George Williams of Amite County carved human figures and miniature heads as good luck charms. Sulton Rogers, from Lafayette County, whittled what he called "futures"—images from dreams. A skilled carpenter, Rogers created a stream of haints—corpses in coffins, snakes, vampires, and fanged and deformed figures. Beginning as a child, James "Son" Thomas, a blues musician from Leland, made animals from clay, but his signature form became the human skull.

A number of Mississippi artists were inspired by dreams, visions, and memories. Theora Hamblett, from Paris, painted all three. Her vision paintings were often populated with deceased relatives and acquaintances and filled with revelations and messages. More numerous were her paintings of childhood memories, landscapes, and more than two hundred children's games. Ethel Wright Mohamed, from near Eupora, stitched narratives and family memories in thread.

William Beecher, from Bay St. Louis, produced what French artist Jean Dubuffet called Art Brut (raw art), original and uncorrupted by cultural conditioning, the art of the alienated, the insane, and the self-taught. Beecher was committed to a mental institution in 1940 and began painting memories in vivid colors after being transferred to a geriatric hospital thirty-one years later. Self-taught painters Henry Speller, from Rolling Fork, and his wife, Georgia, from Aberdeen, produced erotic drawings and paintings while living in Memphis. M. B. Mayfield, who was born in Ecru, sculpted and painted Mississippi genre using discarded materials and plant juices.

The folk art environment is particularly suited to the Mississippi context. Rev. H. D. Dennis (born near Mayersville) began transforming his wife's business, Margaret's Grocery and Market near Vicksburg, following their marriage in 1984 and by 1990 had converted it into a showpiece of biblical and Masonic symbolism. Inside were replicas of the Ark of the Covenant and the tablets of the Ten Commandments. Window shutters outside were painted with compasses, squares, all-seeing eyes, and the letter *G*. When Steve Tuminello photographed the environment in 1991, the sidewalk leading to the doorway was painted with compasses and squares and a red-and-white checkerboard pavement,

perhaps a reference to Masonic tracing boards. The sidewalk passed through an arched gateway that supported the store sign and a cutout double-headed eagle, "Margaret's Grocery and Market, The Home of the Double-Headed Eagle." The pillars of the gateway were inscribed with the letters *J* and *B*, which are standard in tracing-board designs.

The Kosciusko front yard of L. V. Hull, born in McAdams, is an assemblage of painted shoes, car tires, bed frames, toys, television monitors, signs, collectibles, bottles, planters, flowers, and shrubs. Inside, painted furniture, Christmas tree ornaments, beaded bottles, biblical inscriptions, jewelry, and cigarette lighter assemblages create an environment that a child once described as "Santa's Workshop." Determined to keep busy and avoid idleness, Hull has created a yard and house that invite passersby to enter and commune with the artist.

The home/workshop/art gallery/café of Earl Wayne Simmons, born in Warren County, was a living environment before it burned in 2002. With no building codes to restrain him, Simmons began constructing walls around salvaged windows. Over twenty-three years he assembled thirty-two rooms of various sizes, with stairs winding in and out among multiple levels. Handmade painted signs advertised snacks, beverages, and cigarettes. A large sculpture made of Kool cigarette packs greeted visitors on the lawn. Simmons furnished his "saloon" by building jukeboxes that played eight-track tapes. The jukeboxes became a signature form that attracted commissions from the House of Blues nightclubs.

Mary T. Smith, from Copiah County, built an environment of painted slogans, script, self-portraits, family and neighbors' portraits, scarecrows, and assemblages on her one-acre lot alongside a main highway into Hazlehurst. Her signature paintings, made on scavenged tin and often of Jesus and the Holy Trinity, hung on her fence and outbuildings. Debilitated by poor hearing and inarticulate speech from childhood, Smith used paintings to communicate.

Shotgun and dogtrot houses were common forms of Mississippi vernacular architecture. Scholar John Michael Vlach has traced the shotgun—a long, narrow house with rooms connected directly to one another (no hallways) and doors aligned in a row—back through New Orleans to Haiti and to West Africa. The dogtrot house (also called dog-run or double log cabin) evolved from the single-room log cabin built by settlers. As the need for space increased, two log cabins would be joined under one roof with a breezeway for ventilation between them.

Whether producing baskets, woodcarvings, memory drawings, vision paintings, environments, or vernacular architecture, Mississippi artists occupy a significant niche in the major genres created by the common folk.

Betty J. Crouther
University of Mississippi

Paul Arnett and William Arnett, eds., *Souls Grown Deep: African American Vernacular Art* (2001); Jim Barnett, *The Natchez Indians* (1998); Patti Carr Black, *Art in Mississippi, 1720–1980* (1998); William Ferris, *Local Color: A Sense of Place in Folk Art* (1982); Marshall Gettys, ed., *Basketry of Southeastern Indians* (1984); Theora Hamblett, *Dreams and Visions* (1975); Mary Elizabeth Johnson, *Mississippi Quilts* (2001); John Michael Vlach, *The Afro-American Tradition in Decorative Arts* (1978).

Art, Visionary

Visionary art is conventionally defined as art with spiritual or mystical themes. It suggests a wider vision of awareness or portrays experiences based on such awareness. In Mississippi, where evangelical Christianity dominates, much of the visionary art is specifically religious in nature.

Both trained and self-taught artists produce visionary works, but the majority comes from the untrained folk art or intuitive genres. The first visionary artist in Mississippi to gain national recognition was Oxford's Theora Hamblett. A schoolteacher and poultry farmer, she took art classes at the University of Mississippi in her fifties and began painting. She became famous statewide as a "primitive" artist who painted memories of her childhood, dreams, and "divine revelations." "There are people who call my visions weird," she said, "but to me they are very real and very true to life." The Museum of Modern Art bought one of her canvases in 1954, pegging her art as visionary and changing the painting's title from *The Golden Gate* to the more explicit *The Vision*.

Mary Tillman Smith of Hazlehurst was always explicit in her religious influence, explaining that she painted bold enamel portraits on corrugated tin or weathered boards "to please the Lord." She frequently incorporated biblical exhortations and prayers into her designs.

Woodcarvers in the folk tradition often include religious references in their work. Both George Williams of Amite County and Sulton Rogers of Oxford have produced crucifixion scenes as well as portraits of devils. Willie Barton produced a variety of angels.

Exact assignment of artistic style as visionary art is sometimes difficult when other influences are present. For example, surrealism and fantastic realism might feature dreams, fantasies, otherworldliness, the grotesque or drug experiences. Woodcarvers Willie Barton of Union and Joe Williams of Jackson produced fanciful dragons, and Lynn Green Root included hands in many of her paintings to express a spiritual dimension.

Mississippi has also traditionally had visionary environments: structures or sculpture areas created by visionary artists. The most famous example is *Margaret's Grocery* north of Vicksburg. Rev. H. D. Dennis promised his wife-to-be, "Margaret, marry me and I'll build you a palace." He began in 1980, turning a simple community store into an ever-evolving monument to wife, God, and humanity. Bright reds, whites, blues, and yellows adorned the walls, pillars, and archways at the entrance to the structure. In addition, the building featured icons of Christianity and Freemasonry and hand-lettered signs proclaiming, "This is the Church of Christ, The only one He Build," and "All is welcome, Jews and Gentiles, here at Margaret's Gro. & Mkt and Bible Class." Of the fifty-foot tower overlooking a gravel parking lot, Dennis said, "God keeps telling me to keep going higher." Since Dennis's death in 2012, however, *Margaret's Grocery* has fallen into ruins.

It is not clear that Loy Allen Bowlin of McComb, who called himself the Rhinestone Cowboy, had a mystical impetus in his work, but he called his creation his "beautiful holy jewel home." Working on poster boards in mosaics of dazzling colors and designs, he created an overwhelming environment with glittery sequins and rhinestones covering every inch of the walls and ceilings in his four-room house and his 1967 Cadillac.

One example of yard art that had a mystical beginning has now entered the realm of popular decorative art. African Americans originally created bottle trees to catch evil spirits. Today they are found in not only in the yards of rural cabins but also on urban lawns and patios. Far beyond the Milk of Magnesia bottles of the early twentieth century, today's bottle tree may sport imported champagne or hand-blown bottles.

Patti Carr Black

Jackson, Mississippi

Patti Carr Black, *Art in Mississippi, 1720–1980* (1998); Theora Hamblett, *Theora Hamblett's Paintings* (1975); Alice Rae Yelen, ed., *Passionate Visions of the American South: Self-Taught Artists from 1940 to the Present* (1993).

Assemblies of God

Organized in Hot Springs, Arkansas, in 1914, the Assemblies of God (AG) is one of the largest Christian denominations in the United States. The American South and Mississippi were early centers of strength. Today the AG ranks as the leading denomination of Pentecostalism and the global charismatic movement. In 2013 it claimed 12,792 churches and 3,127,857 adherents in the United States, part of a worldwide following of more than 67,000,000. The Mississippi

District alone included 170 churches and 16,570 adherents. That number does not include members in the church's Southeastern Spanish District, which stretches from Mississippi to North Carolina.

Certain doctrines and practices distinguish the AG and other Pentecostal groups from non-Pentecostal churches. Like others in this spirit-centered movement, many members of the AG speak in tongues (glossolalia), which they believe is a sign of Spirit baptism, or the infilling of the Holy Ghost. They also practice faith healing and believe in a variety of signs and wonders. (Pentecostals largely fashion their religious lives on the New Testament book of Acts and hence are often described as restorationists.) Pentecostals and charismatics have pioneered free church worship, including chorus singing, multimedia presentations, and lively congregational participation. Moreover, they are deeply committed to missions.

Many first-generation AG enthusiasts had once associated with other holiness and Pentecostal groups. Holiness believers in the South—many of whom championed sanctification, a religious work that liberates individuals from the grip of sin—organized loosely in holiness associations. Regardless of affiliation, all were united by their belief in the imminent return of Jesus, their interest in healing, and their openness to new religious experiences.

Much of the AG's membership was once linked to Charles Fox Parham's Apostolic Faith organization, which spread through Kansas, Texas, Arkansas, and Missouri. In 1901 students at Parham's Bible school and healing home in Topeka, Kansas, spoke in tongues, in much the same way, they believed, as the apostles experienced in the second chapter of Acts. They interpreted this charism as a manifestation of the Spirit and preparation for foreign missions. One of Parham's students, William J. Seymour, an African American preacher from Louisiana, took the apostolic message to Los Angeles in 1906 and organized the now famous Azusa Street Revival—marked by emotional worship and interracialism—which spread the Pentecostal message of tongues speech and the Second Coming of Jesus across the United States.

Mississippi native Charles Harrison Mason, black holiness leader of the Church of God in Christ (COGIC), was one of many southern pilgrims to the West Coast meeting. He, like others, returned convinced that what he saw and heard was the second Pentecost he had anticipated. In 1907 two white southern holiness ministers, H. G. Rodgers and M. M. Pinson, attended Pentecostal services at Mason's church in Memphis. After observing others worship, both spoke in tongues. They conducted a series of revivals and established white Pentecostalism and later the AG in Mississippi. Congregations in Alabama and Mississippi looked to the two men for spiritual guidance. Pinson ushered Elmer E. Van Ness and William George Mizelle into the Pentecostal fold. As a result, the holiness camp meetings that Mizelle and Van Ness operated in DeSoto and Hurley, Mississippi, became crucial to the spread of Pentecostalism in the state.

Mason formed ties with other white seekers in the region as well. In 1911 he allowed white Pentecostals in Arkansas, Texas, Alabama, and Mississippi to join the COGIC, which was already an incorporated denomination. White ordained ministers could then receive reduced train fares and other benefits of official organization. When this group of whites united with other, like-minded adherents in 1914, forming the AG, they hoped to stem the tide of religious fanaticism, put an end to financial scandals, and organize around key doctrinal and governmental principles. At the 1914 General Council, the denomination endorsed the Neshoba Holiness School, near Union, Mississippi, operated by a recent convert to Pentecostalism, Reuben Benjamin Chisolm.

Theological and personal controversies quickly erupted among Pentecostals. Disciples wrangled over the Trinity. The AG anathematized nontrinitarian, Oneness Pentecostals. The faithful fought with one another over the role of traveling, healing evangelists. And members of the AG later disagreed over the ethics of military service, the place and ordination of African Americans in a nearly all-white church, and the role of women in the ministry. The church now ranks as one of the most conservative denominations in the United States on a wide range of issues—evolutionary science, abortion, feminism, homosexuality, environmentalism, and theology.

At the same time the AG in Mississippi and elsewhere has distinguished itself for its innovative use of latest technology and its sophisticated organizational strategies. AG churches have been unencumbered by much of the formalism and tradition that shaped so many mainline churches. Hence, the denomination has pioneered the use of print, TV, radio, and the Internet to spread its Pentecostal Gospel. It is little wonder that such musical trailblazers as Elvis Presley and Jerry Lee Lewis credited AG church music with inspiring them.

In the mid-twentieth century Mississippi natives such as Edgar W. Bethany and James E. Hamill emerged as influential AG leaders. (Bethany's daughter, Jan Crouch, and her husband, Paul, established Trinity Broadcasting Network, a Pentecostal TV empire.) Since 2009 Rev. Bob Wilburn has served as the Mississippi District superintendent. The church's state headquarters is in Jackson. Though churches are scattered throughout Mississippi, the denomination is weakest in the Delta.

Members of the Mississippi District sponsor several outreach programs, including Convoy of Hope, which distributes food and clothing and offers medical assistance to the needy. The district also supports approximately ten foreign missionaries and ten domestic missionaries. The AG also assists a gospel radio station, WEEZ-AM 890, in Laurel. The church operates two camp meeting sites in the state, one in Kosciusko, in the center of Mississippi, and another outside of Jackson.

Nearly one hundred years after its founding, the AG continues to grow rapidly and draw converts from all classes and, more than ever, races. As of 2013, about 11 percent of those in the denomination's Mississippi District are African American and about 4.5 percent are Latino; eight churches are majority-black, and four more are majority-Latino.

Randall J. Stephens
Northumbria University

Assemblies of God website, ag.org; Edith Blumhofer, *Assemblies of God: A Chapter in the Story of American Pentecostalism* (1989); Edith Blumhofer, *Restoring the Faith: The Assemblies of God, Pentecostalism, and American Culture* (1993); Gary Don McElhany, "The South Aflame: A History of the Assemblies of God in the Gulf Region" (PhD dissertation, Mississippi State University, 1996); William W. Menzies, *Anointed to Serve: The Story of the Assemblies of God* (1971); Randall J. Stephens, *The Fire Spreads: Holiness and Pentecostalism in the American South* (2007); Vinson Synan, *The Holiness-Pentecostal Tradition: Charismatic Movements in the Twentieth Century* (1997); Grant Wacker, *Heaven Below: Early Pentecostals and American Culture* (2001).

Association of Southern Women for the Prevention of Lynching, Mississippi Council

Women from eight southern states met in Atlanta in 1930 to form the Association of Southern Women for the Prevention of Lynching (ASWPL). Three of the original twenty-six leaders came from Mississippi—Bessie Alford of McComb, Ethel Featherstun Stevens of Jackson, and Mrs. Ernest Moore of Clarksdale. The organization grew out of efforts by the Commission on Interracial Cooperation to oppose violence and to encourage greater communication between whites and African Americans. Most members, including Alford and Stevens, belonged to the Woman's Missionary Society of the Methodist Episcopal Church, South, a group that was working to extend its reach into issues of labor, violence, education, and race relations, especially after women gained the right to vote in 1920.

Jessie Daniel Ames, the ASWPL's founder and president, encouraged several Mississippians to form a chapter of the organization. Stevens, Moore, and ten other women, most of them from Clarksdale and Jackson, met in 1931 to form the North Mississippi ASWPL. Alford helped form the South Mississippi chapter, which published its mission that "as a group of Mississippi women," they were "joining our own protest to the protest of other Southern women who feel a peculiar abhorrence to mob violence." A 1931 lynching tested the new group's determination, but the executive committee published a statement in Jackson newspapers that condemned as inaccurate and hypocritical the reason supporters of lynching typically gave for the practice: the protection of white women against the violence of African American men. "Mississippi women know, in their souls, that the heart, the life, and the sacred honor of our men are pledged to our protection; but we plead with all our heart that we may find that protection behind justice, swift, clear-eyed, and calm, and not behind lynching, that howling, cowardly creature of the jungle."

For a short time, Mississippians helped lead the way in advancing the organization. Alford, Stevens, and others in the state developed rules and objectives for organizing into chapters and attracting new members. In 1931 Mississippi had more women (560) in more counties (44) in the ASWPL than did any other state. By the mid-1930s, the group had about 12,000 members.

Members of the group tended to operate by alerting sheriffs and other government officials about potential lynchings. Alford, the group's first state chair, tried to cover several South Mississippi counties, listening for news of potential violence and passing the news along to sheriffs; equally important, she encouraged women in all parts of the state to report acts of violence to the organization. After a 1934 Clarksdale lynching, she wrote to the sheriff to demand "that you & other officers use your authority and official power to identify the ringleaders of this mob and see that they are punished according to *our* law!"

Some women could not join the ASWPL because of opposition from their husbands or other men in their families or communities, and some remained quiet about their activities. Many felt frustrated that their church organizations and other women's groups chose not to take stronger stances against lynching. Alford and the group's second chair, Montie Greer of Potts Camp, wrote to the state's senators and governor for assistance in opposing lynching.

Some past and present critics of the organization have noted that the ASWPL never admitted African American members and that some leaders seemed at least as concerned that white male atrocities were committed in the name of chivalry as they were that lynching victims died tragic deaths outside the law. National leaders such as Ames never called for a federal antilynching law, primarily because they said such a law could never cover the range of violence in the South, but that refusal put the group at odds with many other reform groups.

The ASWPL adopted a new practice in the late 1930s with a series of educational initiatives they called antilynching institutes. The institutes continued until the ASWPL disbanded in 1942 when its parent group, the Commission on Interracial Cooperation, became part of the Southern Regional Council.

Ted Ownby
University of Mississippi

Jacquelyn Dowd Hall, *Revolt against Chivalry: Jessie Daniel Ames and the Women's Campaign against Lynching* (1993); Caroline Beverly Herring, "The Mississippi Council of the Association of Southern Women for the Prevention of Lynching" (master's thesis, University of Mississippi, 1998).

Atkins, Ace

(b. 1970) Writer

Though he was born William Ellis Atkins on 28 June 1970 in Troy, Alabama, no one has ever called the author anything but "Ace." Before he had reached age thirty, Atkins had been nominated for a Pulitzer Prize and published two critically acclaimed crime novels featuring the only fictional detective with a doctorate in southern studies from the University of Mississippi.

After the first of Atkins's crime novels, *Crossroad Blues* (1998), was published, Kinky Friedman wrote, "If Raymond Chandler came from the South, his name would be Ace Atkins." Indeed, *Crossroad Blues* and Atkins's subsequent three novels—*Leavin' Trunk Blues* (2000), *Dark End of the Street* (2002), and *Dirty South* (2004)—can be enjoyed simply as traditional detective novels, written with a keen eye for detail in language that is by turns brutal and lyrical. They are southern noir spiced with humor and unexpected plot twists involving indelible characters that are often eccentric (Cracker, an albino; the oddly endearing Elvis-wannabe hit man introduced in *Crossroad Blues*) and sometimes despicable (sociopath Stagger Lee; butcher-knife-wielding Annie in *Leavin' Trunk*).

However, lovers of the blues and Elvis Presley—as Atkins is—can appreciate his first four novels on another level. A James Bond fan from his youth, Atkins acknowledges that Ian Fleming's novels "were one of the reasons I became a writer" and admires Chandler, Ernest Hemingway, and Dashiell Hammett. However, Atkins also cites the influence of blues legends Robert Johnson and Muddy Waters on his work. Atkins describes his novels as "a cross-pollination of hard-boiled detective stories with southern music."

His protagonist, Nick Travers, teaches blues history at Tulane and hangs out in the blues bar owned by his best friends, JoJo Jackson and his blues-singing wife, Loretta (who appear in all the novels). Travers's investigations take him to the Mississippi Delta in search of nine lost Robert Johnson recordings and to Chicago's South Side to help out an imprisoned blues singer who, like so many other Mississippi blacks, had migrated north. In Memphis and at the Tunica casinos, Travers encounters the Dixie Mafia and a forgotten and supposedly dead soul singer. The final novel returns to Louisiana and involves a teenage Dirty South rapper from the notorious Calliope housing project. Readers who go along for the ride end up sharing Atkins's fascination with the blues, whether or not they started out that way.

Travers is also an ex-pro football player, reflecting Atkins's own background. His father, Billy Atkins, was an All-Pro football player and later coach with the Buffalo Bills, and Ace played defensive end on Auburn's undefeated 1993 football team.

In 2006 Atkins left the popular Nick Travers series behind and began exploring real-life crime with the publication of *White Shadow*, based on the 1955 murder of Tampa, Florida, crime boss Charlie Wall. The book grew out of Atkins's five years as a crime reporter with the *Tampa Tribune* and his earlier year with the *St. Petersburg Times*. In 2000 he earned Pulitzer Prize and Livingston Prize nominations for his seven-part series, "Tampa Confidential," on the 1956 slaying of socialite Edy Parkhill, the wife of Charlie Wall's attorney. While conducting his voluminous research for the series, Atkins received the two-thousand-page file on Wall's bludgeoning death.

Wall's story and images of vibrant and violent 1950s Tampa stayed with Atkins when he left the *Tribune* in 2001 to move to Oxford and write full-time. *White Shadow* represented the culmination of five years of work that involved revisiting court and police records, interviewing surviving observers of the 1950s scene, and even a trip to Cuba. Since the crime officially remains unsolved, Atkins wrote the story as fiction. However, he used the real names of many of those involved and made it plain who he thinks was guilty.

Based on the critical and commercial success of *White Shadow*, Atkins's subsequent historical fiction novels—*Wicked City* (2008), *Devil's Garden* (2009), and *Infamous* (2010)—also blended dedicated research, true crime, and reimagined characters. Among other true-to-life twists, the protagonist of *Devil's Garden* is none other than noir icon and Atkins influence Dashiell Hammett, who worked as a Pinkerton detective before moving on to create characters such as Sam Spade.

Atkins returned to contemporary fiction with *The Ranger* (2011), which introduces Quinn Colson, an army veteran who returns from deployment to his hometown of Jericho, Mississippi. The series reflects the developmental rigor and complexities of the historical fiction novels while continuing a slight dialog with Mississippi culture, a theme that began with the Nick Travers books. Character names in the Colson series—Quinn, Caddy, and Jason—wink at Faulkner's literary landscape redeployed in modern age noir.

In 2010, the Robert Parker estate selected Atkins to write new crime novels featuring the late writer's fabled Boston detective, Spenser. In 2014, the ever-prolific Atkins published both the Spenser series title *Cheap Shot* and his fourth Quinn Colson novel, *The Forsaken*.

Ace Atkins lives in rural Lafayette County with his family and an ever-changing pack of rescued canines.

Jan Humber Robertson
Oxford, Mississippi

Ace Atkins website, www.aceatkins.com; Zac Bissonnette, *Boston Globe* (12 May 2013); Susan Clifford Braun, *Library Journal* (January 2009); Dick Lochte, *Los Angeles Times* (1 July 2006); Kevin Walker, *Tampa Tribune* (7 May 2006).

Attala County

Attala is a hilly county located in the very heart of the state and bordered on the west by the Big Black River. Founded on 23 December 1833, Attala comprises land relinquished to the United States by the Choctaw Nation under the 1830 Treaty of Dancing Rabbit Creek. The county derives its name from Chateaubriand's 1801 novel, *Atala*, which depicts a romance between a white settler and a member of Mississippi's Natchez tribe. The county seat is Kosciusko, and notable towns and communities include Ethel, McCool, and Sallis.

In its first census, in 1840, Attala County reported 3,221 free people and 1,082 slaves. The economy was largely agricultural, though a small manufacturing sector employed locals at cotton gins, blacksmith shops, and lumber mills. By 1860 the county ranked twenty-ninth in the state in cotton production, twenty-fifth in the value of livestock, and nineteenth in production of corn. Despite its diminutive population, antebellum Attala County had a significant number of churches, the majority of which hosted Baptist and Methodist congregations.

At the turn of the century, the county's population had risen to 26,248, with white residents continuing to slightly outnumber African Americans. Farmers still dominated the workforce, with the majority of white farmers (63 percent) owning their own land; by contrast, more than 75 percent of black farmers worked as sharecroppers. Attala was also home to a large number of manufacturing establishments, although industrial development still had little to offer the county's population in terms of employment opportunity. By 1930, however, Attala County's manufacturing labor force had topped eleven hundred.

Attala's religious community continued to thrive during the early twentieth century. Indeed, the county's Magnolia Bible College was the site of the first radio performance by the Blackwood Brothers, a quartet that eventually became a powerful force in American gospel music.

In 1960 the county's main agricultural products included corn, cotton, soybeans, and cattle, and Attala's timber industry had begun to produce substantial economic benefits. Yet a population decline in the county during the 1960s and 1970s contributed to diminishing agricultural production. In 1960 more than twenty-six hundred people made their living by farming, a number that dropped to two hundred by 1980.

A varied and impressive group of Mississippians have called Attala County home, including *National Geographic* writer Carolyn Bennett Patterson, artist L. V. Hull, folklorist Arthur Palmer Hudson, basketball star and Delta State University coach Margaret Wade, and blues musician Charlie Musselwhite. Celebrated author and civil rights activist James Meredith was born in Kosciusko in 1933. Meredith initiated the process of desegregation at the University of Mississippi, becoming the first African American student to attend the college in 1962. Actress and television personality Oprah Winfrey was born in Kosciusko in 1954 and remained there under the care of her grandmother until age six.

Between 1960 and 2010, Attala County's population declined slightly from 21,355 to 19,564. Like other central Mississippi counties in the early twenty-first century, Attala County was mostly (56 percent) white.

Mississippi Encyclopedia Staff
University of Mississippi

Mississippi State Planning Commission, *Progress Report on State Planning in Mississippi* (1938); *Mississippi Statistical Abstract*, Mississippi State University (1952–2010); Charles Sydnor and Claude Bennett, *Mississippi History* (1939); University of Virginia Library, Historical Census Browser website, http://mapserver.lib.virginia.edu; E. Nolan Waller and Dani A. Smith, *Growth Profiles of Mississippi's Counties, 1960–1980* (1985).

Attaway, William Alexander
(1911–1986) Author

William Attaway was born in Greenville, Mississippi, on 11 November 1911 but spent most of his life outside the South. He moved north to Chicago with his family by the time he was six, and his most important work was shaped by his experience as an African American in the Great Migration and the Great Depression.

As a young man, Atttaway attended the University of Illinois and spent two years as a hobo, riding the rails across the United States. After graduating from college, he moved to New York and worked as an actor under the tutelage of his sister, Ruth, a successful Broadway actress. He later became a member of group of writers associated with the Harlem Renaissance.

In 1939 Attaway published his first novel, *Let Me Breathe Thunder*, the story of a group of hobo migrant farmworkers. Attaway's most important work, *Blood on the Forge* (1941), also deals with the issue of migration and the rootlessness of African Americans who moved to the North in the early twentieth century in search of opportunity and to escape the suffocating and violent experience of living in the South. *Blood on the Forge* follows the lives of three brothers who move from the hills of Kentucky to the Allegheny Valley at the end of World War I. This novel is considered the greatest treatment not only of African American migration but also of turn-of-the-century labor strife in America and the disintegration of folk cultures in the wake of modern industrialism. However, *Blood on the Forge* was largely ignored in its day, perhaps because of the publication of Richard Wright's *Native Son* one year earlier.

Attaway never wrote another novel. He became a songwriter for calypso singer Harry Belafonte and penned most of Belafonte's biggest hits. Attaway was also the first African American to break into television and film writing. As a consequence of his success with shows such as *Wide Wide World* and *The Colgate Hour*, Attaway was able to bring African American culture to the small screen with 1964's *Hundred Years of Laughter*. After living in Barbados for many years, Attaway returned to California to continue his career as a screenwriter. He died there of cancer in June 1986.

Courtney Chartier
Martin Luther King Jr. Collection,
Robert W. Woodruff Library

James P. Drapher, *Black Literature Criticism*, vol. 1 (1992); James B. Lloyd, ed., *Lives of Mississippi Authors, 1817–1967* (1981).

Audubon, John James, in Mississippi

John James Audubon spent approximately three years in Mississippi in the early 1820s, visiting, teaching, drawing, and painting, and he did some of his finest work in the state. Many of the most famous images from his great 1838 work *Birds of America* came from his time in Mississippi. Audubon was born on 26 April 1785 in Saint-Domingue (now Haiti) to Jean Audubon, a French naval officer who owned a sugar plantation and refinery there, and Jeanne Rabin, a French maidservant who died shortly after the boy's birth. In 1803 Jean sent his son to the young United States to manage one of his investments, Mill Grove Plantation near Philadelphia, and to protect him from the military draft.

In 1820, after several years working at various pursuits, Audubon decided to travel down the Mississippi River, collecting and drawing as many bird species as possible to be published in a book.

Audubon's fascination with birds began when he was a toddler, when he imagined birds as playmates, preferring them to every other wild or domesticated creature. Sensitive to his son's interests and imagination, Jean Audubon guided the boy toward a more pragmatic path, taking him on walks to observe birds and teaching him about their silhouettes in flight, seasonal migrations, nests, foods, and habitat. Jean also encouraged his son to study illustrated books about birds and caught birds for the boy to draw. By the time of Audubon's trip to the Lower Mississippi area, he had been diligently collecting, drawing, and recording birds in his journal in his adopted country for nearly a decade and a half. Audubon simultaneously taught himself ornithology. Many early bird painters did likewise, and in America he befriended the best—Charles Willson Peale, probably William Bartram, and Scotsman Alexander Wilson, whose nine-volume *American Ornithology* (1808–14) became the standard resource until the publication of Audubon's masterpiece.

Through 1823 Audubon studied bird life along the banks of the Mississippi and Yazoo Rivers. In his journal he wrote that he was stunned by the Yazoo—"a beautiful stream of transparent water covered with thousands of geese and ducks and filled with fish." Audubon and an associate followed and chased swift black cormorants, one of which was killed and which Audubon drew. On Christmas Day 1820, the owner of the flatboat they used shot a great-footed hawk (peregrine falcon), possibly near Petit Gulf. Audubon finished his drawing of the bird the next day while held up on the river. Years earlier, Audubon had developed a method of pinning a shot bird in an accurate lifelike pose to a wooden board for drawing with his handmade version of a physiognotrace (an instrument designed to draw a creature's physical features).

When he was not pursuing, studying, drawing, and painting birds, Audubon worked in Natchez and New Orleans drawing portraits, giving drawing lessons, and occasionally teaching additional subjects, such as cotillion dancing and French. Casting about for more portrait work in Natchez, he befriended Benjamin Wailes, a young self-taught naturalist who brought Audubon the nest of an orchard oriole from the Wailes Plantation on the Natchez Trace. Benjamin and his brother, Edmund, soon were hunting with Audubon, and the friendship translated into black chalk portraits of the brothers as well as their parents, Levin and Eleanor. Levin Wailes was subsequently responsible for Audubon's appointment as a drawing instructor at the Elizabeth Female Academy in nearby Washington, Mississippi, but Audubon contracted yellow fever, recovered, and secured another teaching position, this time at a new academy in Natchez.

From mid-March through May 1822 Audubon completed fourteen bird drawings, including his discovery and painting of the willow flycatcher, his dramatic composition of two chuck-will's-widows hissing at a coral snake coiled around a branch between them, and the delicate watercolor of two tiny Carolina chickadees camouflaged amid a rattan vine (supplejack) dated 3 May 1822. Audubon's compilation of bird images from the Lower Mississippi River area was probably the most crucial to his entire collection and book project, even though he spent much of the next fifteen years adding drawings of other birds obtained from the Florida Keys to Labrador. Furthermore, an important marker of Audubon's southern Mississippi–Louisiana trip came during the winter of 1826 when visiting his wife at Beech Woods. Audubon went on a hunting trip into a Mississippi cane thicket, shot a male wild turkey weighing at least twenty-two pounds, and spent days drawing it. This watercolor joined the three-hundred-plus others that Audubon took to England in May of that year, forming the basis of his mammoth book project. *The Birds of America* consisted of four enormous double-elephant folio volumes, printed on paper measuring 39¼ × 26⅓ inches and weighing 80 pounds each. Each volume required two men to lift it. The 435 pages of engraved, hand-colored etchings with aquatint bird species contained a total of 1,065 bird images, life-size at eye level and in natural positions and habitat. The first image of Audubon's landmark publication is the *American Wild Turkey*, with cane stalks behind it, made to seem even larger than its page by slightly cropping the tail feathers. This image became Audubon's most famous, and it may well have been collected in Mississippi. Audubon's obsession, *The Birds of America*, became the standard by which all later efforts have been measured.

Thomas Dewey II
University of Mississippi

Patti Carr Black, *Art in Mississippi 1720–1980* (1998); Duff Hart-Davis, *Audubon's Elephant: The Story of John James Audubon's Epic Struggle to Publish "The Birds of America"* (2003); Douglas Lewis, *Southern Quarterly* 29 (1990–91); Linda Dungan Partridge, "From Nature: John James Audubon's Drawings and Watercolors, 1805–1826" (PhD dissertation, University of Delaware, 1992); Jessie Poesch, *The Art of the Old South* (1983); Richard Rhodes, *John James Audubon: The Making of an American* (2004).

Autobiography

Mississippians have written some of the world's most powerful autobiographies. Reasons for the popularity of autobiography are numerous. Many Mississippians write autobiographies either to praise their family's past or to figure out their complicated, love-hate relationships with their home state, community, and sometimes family. Some write autobiographies to deal with what they see as misconceptions about Mississippi. Some write to inspire change, using their lives as examples of problems and attempts to overcome them. Some write autobiographies because the traditions of autobiographical writing are so strong that they feel they have to continue or respond to them.

One popular genre for Mississippi autobiographers has been the pastoral. Many autobiographers have written to describe the positive features of a rural life that has changed, primarily for the worse. Most famously, William Alexander

William Alexander Percy's seminal memoir, *Lanterns on the Levee* (1941) (Courtesy Louisiana State University Press)

Percy's *Lanterns on the Levee* (1941) lovingly details what he considered the nearly permanent values he associated with an agricultural upper class: respect for leisure and good manners, love of nature and art, love and respect for family tradition, and a sense of obligation to the rest of society, especially African American farm laborers.

Many less famous Mississippians have written pastoral autobiographies to describe memories of rural family and community life, the special skills necessary to live near nature, and the unique pleasures of farming, gardening, hunting, and fishing. Some, like S. G. Thigpen's *Work and Play in Grandpa's Day* (1969), take a straightforward approach to remembering the good old days. Many others complicate something they see as positive about rural life and how it changed. David Cohn's *Where I Was Born and Raised* (1947), based in part on his earlier work, *God Shakes Creation* (1935), repeats some of the themes of Percy's autobiography, with its depiction of the power and beauty of nature in the Mississippi Delta and the paternalism of the planter class. Mary Hamilton's *Trials of the Earth*, completed in 1933 and published in 1992, tells a compelling story of a family struggling to find work, health, and security while moving around the Mississippi Delta and working in logging camps. Hamilton's narrative is not a conventional pastoral, in that she does not look back longingly toward the peaceful past. However, she has a pastoral ideal in the ways she always hopes that each new move might lead the family to settle down and farm.

More recently, some African American autobiographers, among them Chalmers Archer Jr. and especially Clifton Taulbert, have detailed the particular strengths rural families and communities showed in protecting each other, looking after everyone's children, and developing black-run institutions. Taulbert's first memoir, *Once upon a Time When We Were Colored* (1989), portrays a strong and creative community life of a sort the author thinks no longer exists.

A second type of autobiography crucial to Mississippi writers is the story of the outsider. Richard Wright's *Black Boy: A Record of Childhood and Youth* (1945) is probably the best example of the outsider autobiography, a genre in which the author writes to describe life as someone who is misunderstood and mistreated. Wright's work dramatizes his alienation from a society that tries to limit his behavior and demands that he not ask difficult questions. *Black Boy* explores the quandary of wanting to tell the truth but knowing that it is often necessary to play roles demanded by Jim Crow and recognizing the consequences of playing those roles poorly. The book also details physical hunger; Wright's distrust of most southern institutions, especially those run by whites but also those controlled by African Americans; and his decision to move north. Much of the book discusses his frustration with life in Chicago and New York.

Many Mississippians have written to describe their lives as outsiders. Noel Polk's *Outside the Southern Myth* (1997),

Kevin Sessums's *Mississippi Sissy* (2007), and Edward Cohen's *Peddler's Grandson: Growing Up Jewish in Mississippi* (1999) position these authors' stories as those of people who do not fit into what some part of society expects of them—Polk because he grew up in the Piney Woods, Sessums because he is gay, and Cohen because he is Jewish in an overwhelmingly Christian state. A literal outsider, born in the Midwest, Anthony Walton wrote *Mississippi: An American Journey* (1996) to describe his attempt to come to terms with the state and its history. Walton drove around Mississippi, talking to people and reading about the state, in an effort both to confront the difficulties of his immediate ancestors and to understand the strength they showed in surviving segregation and violence. Walton memorably describes *Mississippi* as "perhaps the most loaded proper noun in American English." James Silver, creator of another powerful phrase, "Mississippi: The Closed Society," tells the story of leaving the state amid controversy in *Running Scared in Mississippi* (1984).

Willie Morris was Mississippi's most prolific memoirist, publishing *North toward Home* in 1967 and spending much of the rest of his life writing about the themes it raised. Did he love home or hate it? *North toward Home* explores his mixed feelings—his love for the fun and security of small-town life in Yazoo City as well as his growing hatred for racism and cruelty and the difficulty of asking questions. Morris wrote several other memoirs, one dealing with his work in the publishing world in New York—where he also felt like an outsider—and another describing his return to Mississippi in the 1980s.

The civil rights movement has been so important to Mississippians that it inspired a relatively new genre, the civil rights narrative. Anne Moody's *Coming of Age in Mississippi* (1968) continues Richard Wright's outsider approach but takes a new direction with her involvement in activism in Jackson and Canton. Much of the book details her anger about segregation and rural poverty and sometimes her frustration with most African Americans. But initially at Tougaloo College and later in a series of mid-1960s protests, she found some of the sense of purpose and community she sought. The book ends with memorable uncertainty.

Will Campbell's *Brother to a Dragonfly* (1977) is engaging autobiography that combines the author's love for his troubled brother with the distance his own activism creates between him and the white Mississippians he knew in his Pike County youth. Combining pastoral themes with alienation and the excitement of the civil rights movement, Campbell dramatizes his fear that Christian activists may become so full of righteousness and moral certainty that they will forget their own religious principles.

Among the many other important autobiographies related to civil rights issues, several recent works stand out as especially revealing. *From the Mississippi Delta* (1997), by playwright Endesha Ida Mae Holland, portrays the civil rights movement as a virtual conversion experience, giving her hope and inspiration to change her life, especially by pursuing her creative interests, after early years filled with poverty and pain. *Civil Rights Childhood* (1999) blends the memories of Jordana Shakoor with excerpts from a journal kept from her father, Cleveland Jordan, a Greenwood activist. National Association for the Advancement of Colored People leaders Aaron Henry and Charles Evers tell the stories of their long commitments to changing Mississippi in *Aaron Henry: The Fire Ever Burning* (2000) and *Have No Fear* (1997), respectively.

Another powerful genre, less unique to Mississippi, is the creative autobiography, in which writers or musicians describe the course of their creative lives. Eudora Welty's *One Writer's Beginnings* (1983) is perhaps the best example of such a work by a Mississippi author. Welty describes how her Jackson upbringing may have influenced her writing, particularly in the ways she loved to listen to people talk and then tried to re-create that conversation in her work. Elizabeth Spencer's *Landscapes of the Heart* (1998) traces the influences on her life as a writer, combining stories specific to Mississippi with stories reaching far beyond the state. Autobiographies by B. B. King (*The Blues All Around Me*, 1996) and David "Honeyboy" Edwards (*The World Don't Owe Me Nothing*, 1997) describe the relationship between life in the Mississippi Delta and playing the blues.

Like the creative autobiography, the story of people in politics and political crusades is not distinctive to Mississippi, but the state has produced several political works of note. *Crusade for Justice: The Autobiography of Ida B. Wells* (1970) describes the author's early years in Mississippi and her work as an opponent of lynching and a supporter of African American organizing, while Belle Kearney's *A Slaveholder's Daughter* (1900) tells of how the author became involved in crusades for temperance and women's rights. Mary Craig Kimbrough Sinclair intriguingly chose *Southern Belle* (1957) as the title of her autobiography about life with her husband, writer and socialist activist Upton Sinclair. John Roy Lynch's *Reminiscences of an Active Life* (1970), Frank Smith's *Congressman from Mississippi* (1964), Erle Johnston's *Politics Mississippi Style* (1993), and Trent Lott's *Herding Cats: A Life in Politics* (2005) all detail various moments in the state's politics, often with an attempt to assert or defend the author's place in history.

Ted Ownby
University of Mississippi

William Andrews, ed., *African American Autobiography: A Collection of Critical Essays* (1993); J. Bill Berry, ed., *Located Lives: Place and Idea in Southern Autobiography* (1990); Will Brantley, *Feminine Sense in Southern Memoir* (1993); Joanne Braxton, *Black Women Writing Autobiography: A Tradition within a Tradition* (1989); David Dudley, *My Father's Shadow: Intergenerational Conflict in African American Autobiography* (1991); V. P. Franklin, *Living Our Stories, Telling Our Truths: Autobiography and the Making of the African-American Intellectual Tradition* (1995).

Autry, James A.
(b. 1933) Poet

Poet James Autry grew up in rural Benton County, between Hickory Flat and Ashland, the son and grandson of Baptist ministers. His mother painted. After graduating from the University of Mississippi with a bachelor's degree in journalism in 1955, Autry served four years as a fighter pilot with the US Air Force in France. He then began a successful career in the magazine industry, ultimately becoming editor in chief and president of the Meredith Corporation's Magazine Group, which published *Better Homes and Gardens*, *Ladies' Home Journal*, and *Successful Farming*.

Autry has authored thirteen books, among them two books of poetry published by Yoknapatawpha Press, *Nights under a Tin Roof* (1983) and *Life after Mississippi* (1989). His poems have generally been characterized as both elegiac and vernacular encounters with rural life and the encroaching values of a culture caught in the modernity of urbanism, mechanism, and distance from traditional rituals. Many of his subsequent nonfiction works focus on the search for meaning and ethics in the world of commerce and business while drawing strength from the poetic form. For example, *Real Power* (1998, with poet and translator Stephen Mitchell) draws inspiration from the morals set by the ancient philosophy of the Tao Te Ching in the pursuit of the power in the business community. Other books include *Love and Profit* (1992) as well as *Life and Work* (1994); *Confessions of an Accidental Businessman*, a memoir (1996); *Spirit of Retirement* (2002); *The Servant Leader* (2004); *The Book of Hard Choices* (2006, with Peter Roy); *Looking around for God* (2007); *Choosing Gratitude: Learning to Love the Life You Have* (2012); *Choosing Gratitude 365 Days a Year: Your Daily Guide to Grateful Living* (2012, with Sally J. Pederson); *On Paying Attention: New and Selected Poems* (2015). Autry's poetry was the topic of a 1991 special issue of the *Kentucky Poetry Review*, and he was a featured poet in Bill Moyers's PBS special series *The Power of the Word* (1994). He again appeared with Moyers on PBS in 2012, discussing his home state and reading the poem "Leaving Mississippi." In addition to being named a distinguished alumnus of the University of Mississippi, Autry has received an honorary doctorate of literature from William Jewel College and the Missouri Medal of Honor for distinguished service in journalism from the University of Missouri at Columbia.

Married to Sally Joanne Pederson, a writer, editor, and former lieutenant governor of Iowa, Autry is the father of three sons and currently resides in Des Moines, Iowa.

Richie Caldwell
Dallas, Texas

James A. Autry website, www.jamesaautry.com; Bill Moyers and James Haba, eds., *The Language of Life: A Festival of Poets* (1995).

Aviation

After the Wright Brothers first soared above the Outer Banks of North Carolina in December 1903, most Mississippians were impressed but saw little immediate need for such a lofty invention as the airplane. However, World War I sparked the imagination of many young Mississippians, including William Faulkner, Samuel Kaye, Samuel Reeves Keesler, and Roscoe Turner. Captain Sam Kaye became a war ace, while Keesler lost his life after a crash landing behind German lines. Turner returned home and began a colorful career as a barnstormer, speed racer, airline executive, and Hollywood insider. Faulkner's aviation adventures became a collection of tall tales.

The earliest recorded airport in Mississippi was Payne Field at West Point. During World War I, the US Army established an advanced aviation school there to train American pilots to fly over the battlefields of France. The school had a fleet of 125 Curtiss JN-4 airplanes and trained more than fifteen hundred pilots between May 1916 and March 1920.

During the 1920s aviators across Mississippi began to establish flying clubs. They usually found a suitable pasture, built some tin-shack hangars, and obtained a couple of World War I–surplus airplanes. Because of the poor conditions of the landing strips, airports had only daylight operations. The planes had water-cooled engines that produced ninety horsepower of thrust. On weekend afternoons curious folks could drive to their local airfields and watch small, colorful planes bump their way down the pastures before leaping into the air. To help raise money to improve airfields and maintain planes, enthusiasts promoted sightseeing flights and short trips. Such flights became the first opportunity for aerial adventures for the many Mississippians who mustered up the courage to climb into the noisy open-cockpit airplanes.

Mississippians turned to agricultural aviation during the 1920s to fight the infestation of the boll weevil. Farmers had previously tried to eradicate the pests by using mules to dust cotton fields with calcium arsenate, a highly toxic poison that literally took the hide off the sides of the valued farmed animals. As early as 1909 the Delta Laboratory in Tallulah, Louisiana, was trying to develop practical dusting techniques to eradicate the boll weevil and other crop pests. C. E. Woolman, an entomologist, farm agent, and aviation enthusiast, became convinced that airplanes would be more efficient than mules to control both the Mexican boll weevil

and the sphinx moth. In 1922 Delta Labs began employing World War I–surplus Curtiss Jenny (JN-6H) airplanes with specially designed spraying hoppers to begin an airborne assault on the boll weevil. On 31 August, Lt. L. C. Simon of the Army Air Service flew a demonstration crop-dusting flight over the Delta-Pineland Plantation near Scott.

The pioneering crop-dusting work in Louisiana and Mississippi drew the attention of George B. Post, vice president of New York's Huff-Daland Airplane Company. After visiting Delta Labs, he went home and by early 1923 had developed the Huff-Daland Duster. In 1924 crop dusting along the Lower Mississippi River Valley became a booming enterprise. The first commercial aerial application of insecticide in the United States occurred at the Robertshaw Plantation near Heatherton in September 1924. Mississippi's flourishing crop-dusting operations soon included J. O. Dockery, Clarksdale; E. O. Champion, Oxford; Self and Company, Quitman; Champion Air Service, Marks; and Dixie Dusting and the Finklea Brothers' Dawn Patrol in Leland.

Mississippi's first modern airport was Davis Field in Jackson, which opened in February 1928 and cost $53,300 to build. The first commercial flight by Woolman's Delta Air Service departed from Davis Field on its western route to Texas. This airport was subsequently renamed Hawkins Field, and the Army Air Corps trained pilots there during World War II. During the Great Depression the Works Project Administration helped to build modern airport facilities in Biloxi, Columbus, Greenwood, Gulfport, Meridian, and Tupelo.

Aviation in Mississippi boomed as war clouds descended across Western Europe. On 27 September 1939 the Mississippi National Guard at Meridian's Key Field organized the 153rd Observation Squadron. The unit's main task was aerial photography and documenting government war projects across the state. Numerous pilots trained in Mississippi during World War II. Primary civilian pilot schools were established at the Columbus Army Air Field, and flight classes began during February 1942. By 1945 more than seventy-seven hundred pilots had trained at this facility. Mississippi also had pilot training facilities in Biloxi, Clarksdale, Greenville, Greenwood, Grenada, Gulfport, Indianola, Jackson, Laurel, Madison, Meridian, Natchez, and Pascagoula.

During the late 1940s and early 1950s Mississippi secured federal funding to modernize many of the former army airfields into commercial airports. By the early 1960s scheduled airline service existed in sixteen communities around the state. Other Mississippi towns built industrial parks near their airports to attract new manufacturing and service industries.

By the twenty-first century, Mississippi boasted eighty-eight airports plus four military airfields. New aviation facilities include Pine Belt Regional Airport near Hattiesburg, Trent Lott International Airport near Pascagoula, and a recent forty-million-dollar airport at Tunica.

David L. Weatherford
Northwest Florida State College

Mabry I. Anderson, *Low and Slow: An Insider's History of Agricultural Aviation, with Many Rare and Vintage Photographs* (1986); David W. Lewis, *Delta: A History of an Airline* (1979); Mississippi Department of Transportation website, www.gomdot.com; National Agricultural Aviation Museum website, www.msagmuseum.org.

Morris W. H. (Bill) Collins Speaker Series, Mississippi State University, website, http://lib.msstate.edu/collins/speakers/aycock; Thomas A. Wicker, interview with Judge Sharion Aycock.

Aycock, Sharion

(b. 1955) Judge

The first female judge to sit on the federal bench in Mississippi, Sharion Marie Harp Aycock was born to Darrell and Mary Ruth Harp on 19 December 1955 in Tupelo. She was raised in Tremont, where she graduated from high school in 1973. Aycock attended Mississippi State University, earning a bachelor of arts degree in economics in 1977. Encouraged by one of her professors, Aycock pursued her juris doctorate degree at Mississippi College School of Law, graduating second in the Class of 1980.

Aycock took a position at the A. T. Cleveland Law Office in Fulton, remaining there until 1983. She subsequently opened her own practice, Sharion H. Richardson, P.A., in Fulton, representing clients including the Itawamba County Board of Supervisors, Itawamba County School District, Town of Tremont, City of Fulton, and the Northeast Mississippi Natural Gas District. In addition, she served as the Itawamba County prosecuting attorney from 1984 to 1992 and received gubernatorial appointments to the Mississippi Home Corporation Board, the Mississippi State Personnel Board, and the Governor's Commission on Youth and Children. In 2000 she became the first woman elected president of the Mississippi Bar Foundation, and two years later she became the first woman elected as a circuit judge for the First Circuit Court District (covering Alcorn, Itawamba, Lee, Monroe, Pontotoc, Prentiss, and Tishomingo Counties).

In March 2007, at the request of Mississippi's US senators, Thad Cochran and Trent Lott, Pres. George W. Bush nominated Aycock to replace US District Court judge Glen H. Davidson of Aberdeen. The US Senate unanimously confirmed her nomination on 4 October 2007 and she was sworn in on 26 October.

In May 2008 Aycock received honorary doctor of laws degree from the Mississippi College School of Law and delivered the school's commencement address. She was also recognized as Mississippi State University's 2008 Woman of the Year and as the Mississippi Trailblazer of the Year. She is married to William R. "Randy" Aycock.

Thomas A. Wicker

Jackson, Mississippi

Ayers v. Fordice

In 1975 Jake Ayers Sr., a civil rights veteran from Glen Allan and parent of a student at historically black Jackson State University, filed suit in federal district court claiming that the State of Mississippi had not provided adequate resources to its historically black institutions of higher education. The Ayers suit, based on the Equal Protection Clause of the Fourteenth Amendment and on Title VI of the Civil Rights Act of 1964, eventually became a class-action lawsuit with the United States and Bennie Thompson, later a member of the US Congress, intervening as plaintiffs. The case originally was known as *Ayers v. Waller* since Bill Waller was Mississippi governor when it was filed. It was renamed *Ayers v. Fordice* in 1991 and later *Ayers v. Musgrove*. Attorney Ike Madison first represented the plaintiffs but later turned the case over to Alvin Chambliss.

Mississippi has three publicly funded historically black colleges and universities, Jackson State University, Alcorn State University, and Mississippi Valley State University. Before the desegregation of the University of Mississippi in 1962, black Mississippians who sought public in-state education could attend only the black schools. The state legislature unequally appropriated tax dollars so that these schools were severely underfunded, resulting in gross inequities in the available educational opportunities. Ayers's lawsuit sought to correct these inequities.

The federal district court ruled in 1987 that by adopting race-neutral policies in admissions and other areas, Mississippi had satisfied its duty to correct the de jure segregated state university system. The 5th Circuit Court of Appeals upheld the lower court's decision in 1990. In 1992, however, the US Supreme Court found that both the district and appellate courts had applied an incorrect legal standard. The Supreme Court ruled that the Equal Protection Clause and Title VI required Mississippi to abolish any policy or practice that could be traced to de jure segregation, that continued to promote segregation, and that could be eliminated. Returning the case to district court, the Supreme Court made clear that the issue was eliminating effects of prior state-enforced segregation, not mandating equality among the state's public institutions.

In 1995, using the Supreme Court's standard, the district court found vestiges of segregation in Mississippi's higher education system. In 2002, nearly three decades after the lawsuit's inception, the state and a majority of plaintiffs reached an agreement to award the three historically black institutions $503 million over seventeen years. The settlement included funds for new programs, new facilities, and large endowments if each of the schools achieved a 10 percent nonblack student enrollment for three consecutive years. Some plaintiffs, including Lillie Ayers, the widow of Jake Ayers, who had died in 1986, appealed the settlement because they felt that the financial enhancements were not enough to compete with the state's white institutions and that the condition of increased nonblack enrollment would be difficult to meet and was not relevant to the original intent of the suit. In 2004, however, the US Supreme Court refused to hear an appeal of the settlement.

Crystal R. Sanders
Penn State University

Cynthia Jackson and Eleanor F. Nunn, *Historically Black Colleges and Universities: A Reference Handbook* (2001); Avery Sheldon, *Academic Questions* (September 2009).

B

Babbitt, Milton
(1916–2011) Composer

Milton Byron Babbitt was one of the world's leading intellectual forces in contemporary music in the late twentieth and early twenty-first centuries. His pioneering work on the RCA Mark II synthesizer at the Columbia-Princeton Electronic Music Center established his international reputation in the late 1950s, and he was a vital and creative composer until his death at age ninety-four. Babbitt's many honors include a special Pulitzer citation for his life's work in 1986 and a three-hundred-thousand-dollar MacArthur Fellowship in 1986. He earned diplomas from New York and Princeton Universities and received honorary degrees from numerous other institutions of higher education. He was a fellow of the American Academy of Arts and Sciences and a member of the American Academy of Arts and Letters.

Babbitt grew up in Jackson in the Belhaven neighborhood, a friend of writer Eudora Welty from an early age. Proud of his Mississippi roots, he insisted that his biographical information in liner notes and record jackets note that he was "educated in the public schools of Jackson, Mississippi." His family had moved to Mississippi from Philadelphia, Pennsylvania, after his father accepted an invitation from Welty's father to work at the Lamar Life Insurance firm. Babbitt's father was an actuary, a position that sparked Babbitt's later interest in mathematics. Babbitt gave his first public performance at age five on the violin. A Jackson newspaper called him a "whiz kid" and noted that he had perfect pitch and could add up his family's grocery bills in his head. Soon thereafter he learned saxophone and clarinet, and he became a great fan of jazz cornet player Bix Beiderbecke. At age ten Babbitt was sitting in on clarinet when touring professional jazz bands from New Orleans came through Jackson. He began writing songs in the popular style of the day at age seven, and at thirteen he won a songwriting contest in his hometown.

After graduating from Central High School at age fifteen, he enrolled at the University of Pennsylvania to study mathematics and philosophy. He quickly discovered that he was more interested in composing and transferred to New York University, where he earned a bachelor's degree in music. He subsequently studied with composer Roger Sessions at Princeton, earning a master of fine arts degree in 1942. He also worked as a music critic and wrote articles on the subject for various publications. In addition, he served on Princeton's mathematics faculty from 1942 to 1945 and did highly classified mathematical research in Washington, D.C., for the US government. In 1948 he moved from Princeton's mathematics faculty to the school's music faculty, and in 1965 he was named the William Shubael Conant Professor of Music. He continued to teach at Princeton until 1982; in 1973 he also joined the faculty of New York's Juilliard School. Babbitt also gave courses at the Rubin Academy in Jerusalem, the University of Wisconsin, New York University, and Harvard University, where he held the Fromm Foundation Visiting Professorship.

As a music theorist, Babbitt made significant contributions. His influence on the understanding and development of serial composition was second only to that of Arnold Schoenberg, its creator. According to Joseph N. Straus, "Virtually all modern work in 12-tone theory stems from the writing and teaching of Milton Babbitt." Babbitt coined many terms now widely in use in music theory, and his writings appeared in all of the most respected international music journals, including *Perspectives of New Music, Journal of Music Theory, Musical Quarterly*, and *The Score*. In 2003 Princeton University Press published *The Collected Essays of Milton Babbitt*.

First and foremost, however, Babbitt was a composer. Every college music history textbook in current use devotes significant space to his work. He was one of the first to identify the possibilities of electronic music, and he used his training in mathematics to create unique and beautifully rigorous musical structures. He described himself as a "maximalist," seeking to make each piece "literally as much as possible." He discovered new ways to connect pitches, dynamics, and rhythms, and he was the first to pursue the "integral serialism" that influenced Pierre Boulez, Luigi Nono, and other European composers in the 1950s. Babbitt wrote many pieces for multiple combinations of instruments and voice as well as orchestral works, including two piano concertos. Frequently demanding, his works have been performed and recorded by world-class performers.

Lynn Raley
Millsaps College

Elaine Barkin, in *The New Grove Dictionary of Music and Musicians*, ed. Stanley Sadie (2000); Donald Jay Grout and Claude V. Palisca, *A History of Western Music* (2001); Allan Kozinn, *New York Times* (29 January 2011); Andrew Mead, *An Introduction to the Music of Milton Babbitt* (1994); Robert P. Morgan, *Twentieth-Century Music* (1991); Lynn Raley, interview with Milton Babbitt (2003); John Rockwell, *All American Music* (1983); Joseph N. Straus, *Introduction to Post-Tonal Theory* (1999).

Baggett, William Carter

(b. 1946) Painter, Printmaker, Muralist

Born on 12 January 1946 in Montgomery, Alabama, William Carter Baggett grew up and attended public schools in Nashville, Tennessee, before earning a bachelor's degree in art from Auburn University in 1968 and a master of fine arts degree from the school five years later. He taught in the art and design programs at the University of Mississippi (1973–76), Auburn University (1976–86), and the University of Southern Mississippi (1986–2010) prior to retiring and returning to his studio endeavors on a full-time basis.

Baggett worked primarily in watercolors and printmaking in the 1970s. Many of his works from this period were inspired by William Faulkner's real and imaginary counties, Lafayette and Yoknapatawpha, and were exhibited during annual Faulkner and Yoknapatawpha conferences in Oxford. Baggett began using egg tempera in his paintings in the 1980s, continued his interest in printmaking, and became known as a master in color lithography. Baggett's early work is usually labeled representational and figurative, realistic and traditional, but as art historian and critic Renata Karlin explains, "he employs the structural world of forms, landscapes, figures, and buildings to seduce the viewer to enter the pictorial space" and then see beyond the surface. "Painting to Baggett is a way of seeing and about the role of pictorial elements of in his words 'creating a situation; where everything is posed and becomes significant.'"

From 1992 through 2005 Baggett dedicated most of his creative time to designing and painting monumental murals for public spaces in Mississippi and Alabama. *The Spirit That Builds* (1995, alkyd oil on sandblasted stainless steel, 10 feet by 167 feet) depicts the history of South Mississippi in a circular panorama hanging thirty feet above the main desk of the Hattiesburg, Petal, and Forrest County Library. *Sharing Life* (1999, alkyd enamel on stainless steel, 22 feet by 11 feet) at the University of Mississippi Medical Center in Jackson celebrates the diverse roles of women. *Alma Mater* (2003, oil on canvas, 36 feet by 18 feet), displayed in the Jule Collins Smith Museum of Fine Art at Auburn University, evokes daily life on the campus and in the community.

In 2006 Baggett returned to the small rectangular panels he previously used for watercolors and egg tempera paintings but continued using alkyd oil pigments adopted for his murals. *The Intelligent Eye—Reality Re-Seen*, an exhibition of thirty oils painted between 2006 and 2010, previewed in Hattiesburg in September 2010 before beginning a tour of museums across the United States.

Baggett's paintings and prints are included in collections throughout the United States, Europe, and Japan. He has worked with French and American art publishers to execute fifteen original print editions in ateliers in Paris and New York. The US Information Agency has placed his prints in US embassy collections throughout the world. He currently maintains studios in Mississippi and Maine, where he continues to paint "reconfigured" landscapes and figurative images.

Ann J. Abadie
University of Mississippi

William Baggett website, www.williambaggett.com; Patti Carr Black, *Art in Mississippi, 1720–1980* (1998); Renata Karlin, ed., *The Intelligent Eye—Reality Re-Seen: Recent Paintings by William Baggett* (2010).

Bailey, Thomas Lowry

(1888–1946) Forty-Eighth Governor, 1944–1946

Before his election to the state's highest office, Thomas L. Bailey served twenty-four years in the Mississippi House of Representatives, including twelve years as Speaker of the House. Bailey, Walter Sillers, Joseph George, and Walter Kennedy comprised the "Big Four," chairing key committees in the House and controlling the flow of legislation during their time in power.

Bailey was born in Webster County on 6 January 1888. After a short stint teaching in the state's public school system, he opened a law practice at Meridian in 1913. A Democrat, he represented Lauderdale County in the state legislature from 1916 to 1940, coauthoring Mississippi's homestead exemption law and strongly supporting pension benefits for senior citizens. He was also an early supporter of the Balance Agriculture with Industry program, and after his election as governor he championed industrial expansion in the state.

Though Bailey's administration was cut short by his death as a result of a stroke on 2 November 1946, his tenure included a series of positive and enduring accomplishments. He established the Agricultural and Industrial Board to promote industrial growth and the Mississippi Marketing Commission to assist farmers in the sale and distribution of their goods. To facilitate the transportation of goods throughout rural parts of the state, Bailey promoted the development of a secondary highway system known as the farm-to-market roads.

The Board of Trustees of the State Institutions of Higher Learning was established during his first year in office, creating Mississippi's first nonpolitical college board. His administration also saw establishment of the University of Mississippi Medical Center in Jackson and of the African

American Mississippi Vocational College (now Mississippi Valley State University) in Itta Bena.

More than 237,000 Mississippians (one out of every nine) served in the armed forces during World War II, and Bailey predicted that their experiences would dramatically change both the state and the wider South. In his last address to the legislature he urged lawmakers to think beyond the next biennium and instead to plan for the next twenty-five years.

After the governor's death his widow, Nellah Massey Bailey (1893–1956), entered politics. Her election as tax collector in 1947 made her Mississippi's first woman to hold a statewide office. She won reelection in 1951 and 1955.

Thomas Bailey Drive, a segment of I-59 around Meridian, honors the former governor.

David G. Sansing
University of Mississippi

Jackson Clarion-Ledger (3 November 1946); *Jackson Daily News* (25 August 1943, 3 November 1946); *Mississippi Official and Statistical Register* (1924–28).

Balance Agriculture with Industry Program

In 1936 the Mississippi legislature established the nation's first state-sponsored economic development plan, Balance Agriculture with Industry (BAWI). An initiative of Gov. Hugh L. White, the BAWI program attempted to minimize the effects of the Great Depression by coupling low taxes, cheap land, and low wages with tax abatements and other subsidies and incentives to entice northern industries to expand or relocate in the South.

While cities and counties throughout the nation had established a variety of programs to attract business to their areas, BAWI was the first organized statewide endeavor of this kind. BAWI targeted companies for recruitment after the state industrial commission had researched them for suitability. The primary criteria for suitability were a low risk of business failure and a high number of jobs created. After a company was selected, the State Industrial Commission issued a certificate to the pertinent locality stating that the recruitment of the firm was a public necessity because of poor economic conditions. The certificate legally authorized the company to receive public funds provided that voters in the locality ratified the subsidy arrangement via a bond election. Proceeds from bonds bought land, erected factory buildings, and leased the buildings to the manufacturing concern. Under the leasing contract, approved by the State

Industrial Commission, the company might pay as little as one dollar per year for use of the facilities. The operating tenant installed its own machinery (which was exempt from taxation) and guaranteed a specific number of jobs.

Before the legislature terminated BAWI in 1940, the program brought twelve companies to Mississippi, the best-known of which was Ingalls Shipbuilding. The others included four hosiery plants, three shirt factories, a chenille concern, a woolen-goods mill, a plywood plant, and a rubber and tire plant. Various economic development activities have continued in Mississippi and elsewhere, with most states using industrial development bonds of some sort by the 1960s. Evaluating BAWI's effectiveness has proven difficult: although statistics show a rise in Mississippi manufacturing jobs after the legislation passed, other southern states without such programs enjoyed greater growth rates during the same period.

Some critics have faulted BAWI and similar programs for institutionalizing low wages, poor working conditions, antiunion tendencies, and poor environmental policies. Considering BAWI to be corporate welfare, these critics have argued that companies established through industrial recruiting programs attract a greater number of uneducated, unskilled workers to the target area, keeping wages depressed. Others have argued that Mississippi's use of its lower-wage structure successfully drew industry from the Rust Belt and the Frost Belt and that other southern states followed Mississippi in developing such programs.

BAWI is still cited in current economic development debates. Mississippi House Speaker pro tempore Robert Clark expressed concern about Mississippi workforce skills after Hyundai's 2002 decision not to locate a one-billion-dollar plant in the state. According to Clark, when BAWI was passed, "out-of-state firms were attracted to the non-unionized, cheap labor force. But now, that work is moving into cheaper markets."

The debates continue. The 1988 Mississippi Economic Development Plan indicated that some individuals cited BAWI as the basis for the state's enduring economic problems, creating what became a sustained tradition of low wages and low income. The 1988 plan characterized BAWI as a short-run marketing strategy and stressed the long-run economic development of fundamental resources such as existing manufacturing. However, the Advantage Mississippi initiative passed by special legislative session in 2000 returned to the mechanism of a business assistance fund involving a two-level (local and state) approval process, very much in the tradition of BAWI.

Landy Carien Johnson
Assumption College

John E. Anderson and Robert W. Wassmer, *Bidding for Business: The Efficacy of Local Economic Development Incentives* (2000); James C. Cobb, *The Selling of the South: The Southern Crusade for Industrial Development,*

1936–1990 (1993); Osha Gray Davidson, *Broken Heartland: The Rise of the Rural Ghetto* (1990); Julie Goodman, *Jackson Clarion-Ledger* (26 March 2002); E. J. Hopkins, *Mississippi's BAWI Plan: An Experiment in Industrial Subsidization* (1944).

Baldwin, Joseph Glover

(1815–1864) Author

Joseph Glover Baldwin, an attorney, historian, legislator, and judge, is known principally as the humorist who wrote *The Flush Times of Alabama and Mississippi* (1853), a memoir of his early days as a frontier lawyer.

Baldwin was born in Friendly Grove Factory, Virginia, on 15 January 1815, to Eliza Cook Baldwin and Joseph Clarke Baldwin. After his education at the Staunton Academy, he tried his hand at journalism, editing two small-town papers in the Shenandoah Valley while studying law with his uncle, Briscoe G. Baldwin, to whom Joseph Baldwin later dedicated his first book. In 1836, Baldwin left economically depressed Virginia ("urged by hunger and the request of friends," he later recalled) and sought out new opportunities in the West. Arriving in De Kalb, Mississippi, he was admitted to the state bar (by a circuit court judge who asked him "not a single legal question") and quickly emerged as one of the state's leading attorneys. In 1837 he moved the short distance to Gainesville, Alabama, where he married Sidney Gaylord White in 1840; they had seven children, of whom only three—Alexander, Joseph, and John—reached adulthood. Baldwin continued to prosper at the bar and became active in Alabama politics, serving in the state House of Representatives and as a delegate at the Whig Party's national convention in 1848. He eventually ran for a seat in the U.S. Congress, losing narrowly.

By 1851 Baldwin had begun work on the memoir that became his best-known book. It emphasized the rawness of the southwestern frontier of the 1830s and the comic ineptitude or outright fraudulence of most of its lawyers and judges but presented them with tolerant good humor. Published in 1853, *The Flush Times of Alabama and Mississippi* garnered good reviews and sales. It is regarded today as a major contribution to the important literary subgenre known as southwestern humor, which flourished from the 1830s through the 1860s. In 1855 Baldwin published his only other book, *Party Leaders*, a collection of serious historical essays about notable moments in American politics.

By this time Baldwin had moved to San Francisco, where he again prospered at the bar, eventually winning election to the California Supreme Court. After a visit to the East during the Civil War (he met Pres. Abraham Lincoln, who expressed admiration for *The Flush Times of Alabama and Mississippi*),

Baldwin began work on a sequel, *The Flush Times of California*. This work remained unfinished when Baldwin died of tetanus on 30 September 1864 in San Francisco.

John M. Grammer
University of the South

John M. Grammer, *Pastoral and Politics in the Old South* (1996).

Baldwin, William Edwin

(1827–1864) Confederate General

Born on 28 July 1827 in Statesburg, South Carolina, William Edwin Baldwin moved to Columbus, Mississippi, at a young age. He later worked at a book and stationery store in Columbus and joined the local militia, serving as a lieutenant. On 27–30 May 1861 the 14th Mississippi Infantry Regiment was organized at Corinth, and Baldwin was elected the unit's colonel on 5 June. The regiment remained in Corinth until August 1861, when it moved into Tennessee.

In late October 1861 Baldwin took command of a brigade that included the 14th, 20th, and 26th Mississippi as well as the 26th Tennessee. After spending the winter months in Kentucky, the 14th Mississippi received orders to head to Fort Donelson, Tennessee, prior to the rest of the brigade. While Baldwin arrived before the battle on 15 February 1862, he did not see his unit, which fought and lost one hundred men. Baldwin and the rest of the brigade were captured by Union forces after Ulysses S. Grant secured victory. While the rank and file were sent to Chicago's Camp Douglas Prison, Baldwin and other officers journeyed to Fort Warren in Boston.

After his exchange on 15 August 1862, Baldwin earned an official promotion to brigadier general on 19 September, commanding the 14th, 20th, 23rd, and 26th Mississippi as well as the 8th Kentucky and 15th Alabama. Baldwin's brigade engaged Union troops under Grant at Coffeeville, Mississippi, on 5 December. While the battle constituted only a minor engagement, the Confederates created confusion for the advance guard of the Union Army and captured military items that included horses and guns. Baldwin's soldiers advanced to Vicksburg and participated in the battle at Port Gibson on 1 May 1863 as well as in the fighting at Champion Hill, and his units led the rear guard when Confederate general John C. Pemberton withdrew into Vicksburg later in the month. Baldwin and his brigade, which now included the 17th and 31st Louisiana, the 4th and 46th Mississippi, and Tobin's Tennessee Battery, continued to serve under Maj. Gen. Martin Luther Smith. The soldiers endured the Siege of Vicksburg until the city surrendered on 4 July 1863. Baldwin was again captured; he was exchanged for Union commander Jacob B. Sweitzer on 13 October. Although he moved with his brigade into Georgia in the fall, Baldwin was subsequently reassigned to Mobile, Alabama, to assist in the protection of the city against Union troops.

On 19 February 1864 Baldwin, who had a broken stirrup, was thrown from his horse while riding near Dog River Factory, Alabama, and he died that evening from a broken neck. He was buried at Columbus's Friendship Cemetery, and a memorial was erected in his honor several years later.

Brian Craig Miller
Mission College

John Eicher and David Eicher, *Civil War High Commands* (2001); Ezra J. Warner, *Generals in Gray: Lives of the Confederate Commanders* (1996).

Angela Ball (University of Southern Mississippi Photo Services)

Ball, Angela
(b. 1952) Poet

Poet Angela Ball was born in 1952 in Athens, Ohio, and went on to earn a bachelor's degree from Ohio University, a master of fine arts degree from the University of Iowa, and a doctorate from the University of Denver. Her first chapbook of poems, *Recombinant Lives*, appeared in 1987, followed by *Kneeling between Parked Cars* (1990), *Quartet* (1995), *Possession* (1995), and *The Museum of the Revolution: 58 Exhibits* (1999). Ball then took time off before returning in 2006 with a Pitt Poetry Series collection, *Night Clerk at the Hotel of Both Worlds*, which won the 2006 Donald Hall Prize in poetry. Her poem "Jazz" appeared in the 2001 edition of *The Best American Poetry*, while her "Specs for Hephestos" was included in the 2008 volume.

Ball currently serves as poetry editor of the *Mississippi Review* and as a professor of English at the Center for Writers at the University of Southern Mississippi in Hattiesburg. When asked about her activities, she answered, "On a typical Sunday morning, you might find me cycling past pine trees—riding my road bicycle on Longleaf Trace. I usually ride from Hattiesburg to Sumrall and back, a distance of 30 miles. The trail used to carry trains. It's a well-read text: its bumps and cracks, parts of it filmed over with shadows, parts a sunbed for the occasional copperhead or black snake—trails and traveler in one. My average speed is about 16 miles per hour. In an ideal world, it would be 18 to 20."

In a 2008 interview Ball discussed how she relates her poetry to poetic tradition: "One of the huge perks about making art is that it doesn't necessarily matter whether you are dead or alive after you've finished—if the art is good enough it becomes a permanent part of the conversation, louder in one part of the room, softer in another, in a rhythm like that of fireflies igniting in a meadow."

Ball's talent has won her many other awards and grants, including fellowships from the Mississippi Arts Commission and the National Endowment for the Arts, a Sotheby's International Poetry Award (Duncan Lawrie Prize), the Long Poem Prize from the *Malahat Review*, and an invitation to corepresent the United States at the Poetry International Festival held in the Netherlands in 1989. Her poems have appeared in the *New Yorker*, *Ploughshares*, the *New Republic*, the *Colorado Review*, *Grand Street*, the *Kenyon Review*, and *Poetry*, among many other journals.

Jamie C. Dakin
Center for Reproductive Rights

Southeast Review website, www.southeastreview.org; University of Southern Mississippi, Department of English website, www.usm.edu/English.

Banking

American banking has a history full of intriguing and sometimes shocking episodes. This holds true even for Mississippi, a state not known for its financial leadership. Several events in the development of Mississippi banking since the early nineteenth century bear an eerie resemblance to modern banking crises such as the subprime

Merchants and Planters Bank, Tchula, November 1939 (Photograph by Marion Post Wolcott, Library of Congress, Washington, D.C. [LC-USF34-052284-D])

mortgage meltdown. Others reflect a somewhat sophisticated approach to banking.

The rise of cotton production and cotton profits around Natchez in the late eighteenth and early nineteenth centuries resulted in substantial accumulations of cash receipts and expenditures. Demand quickly arose for banking services more local than those available in New Orleans. In response, Mississippi's territorial legislature chartered the Bank of Mississippi in Natchez in 1809, several years before Mississippi became a state. In 1830 the state legislature chartered a second bank, the Planters Bank, to serve as the state's fiscal agent. This action violated the legislature's pledge not to charter another bank while the charter of the Bank of Mississippi was in effect, and that bank went out of business in 1832. The Planters Bank also had several branches, a phenomenon that did not reappear in the United States until the late twentieth century. The state's third bank, the Agricultural Bank, was chartered in 1833.

When the Bank of the United States, the country's first central bank, considered locating a branch in Mississippi, Gov. Gerard Brandon opposed the idea, instead urging the chartering of state banks. Nevertheless, the Bank of the United States opened a Natchez branch that provided local planters and merchants with a substantial volume of currency. Pres. Andrew Jackson opposed the Bank of the United States, and its charter expired in 1836, leaving the nation

without a central bank until the founding of the Federal Reserve System in 1913. Mississippi thus had just two banks, the Planters and the Agricultural, which were inadequate to finance the cotton crop, much less anything else. Reversing its heretofore rather conservative practices, the state began chartering banks in large numbers.

During the 1830s, speculation in land, slaves, and railroads flourished in Mississippi, although the volume of currency and bank capital did not expand nearly as quickly. In 1836 Jackson issued the "specie circular," announcing that the federal government would accept only specie (gold or silver coin) in the purchases of public lands. This order hastened the Panic of 1837. To meet the increased demands for specie, the Mississippi legislature chartered the Union Bank, with state-issued bonds providing the capital, a move that violated Mississippi's constitution. Bad management and reckless lending practices drove the Union Bank (and the state's other financial institutions) toward insolvency. Gov. Alexander G. McNutt urged that the state repudiate the bond issue behind the Union Bank in 1840; his successor, Gov. Tilghman Tucker, was elected in 1841 on a platform that urged repudiation, and the legislature complied the following year. The Union Bank collapsed, as did most banking in Mississippi. The state's credit suffered both nationally and internationally. Although a few private banks survived, cotton factors and brokers undertook most banking.

The National Bank Acts of 1863 and 1864 did little to improve banking in Mississippi after the Civil War because they required high amounts of initial capital before a national charter could be obtained. Local merchants who received funds from northern banks and financial houses undertook a large share of banking in postbellum Mississippi. Planters and tenants used the cotton crop to obtain credit, with local merchants receiving liens against crops. Vicksburg had Mississippi's first nationally chartered bank in 1865, but it failed three years later. Not until 1883 did the state gain another nationally chartered bank, although a few private and state banks were established in the interim. The Mississippi Bankers Association formed in 1889 to promote sound banking practices. For a variety of reasons, the number of banks in the state began expanding rapidly, growing from thirty in 1889 to more than three hundred by 1910; the number of national banks grew more slowly during this period as a consequence of higher capital requirements. Some contemporary observers viewed this expansion as reckless, mirroring some of the developments in antebellum times. Members of the Mississippi Bankers Association regularly urged the institution of stricter controls on banking.

The Federal Reserve Act of 1913 compelled all national banks to join the system or lose their national charter and encouraged state banks to join the system. Four years passed before the first Mississippi bank, the Union Bank of Pike County at Summit, joined. Officials of most state-chartered banks felt that the costs of Federal Reserve membership were too high.

Even though Federal Reserve membership was not particularly appealing to Mississippi's banks, the state instituted legislation to raise banking standards. The Banking Law of 1914 established the State Banking Department and mandated that it examine banks at least twice a year, a significant change from the earlier practice of at best sporadic examinations. The law also established a guarantee fund for deposits, a service provided by the Federal Deposit Insurance Corporation today. While the fund could withstand normal economic conditions, it could not weather the recession of 1921–22 and the subsequent weak agricultural economy. By 1929 the fund was running a deficit and bankers were calling for the law's repeal.

The Great Depression devastated Mississippi's banking industry. In 1929, the state had 334 banks, 115 of which failed in 1930–31. Excessive previous expansion was one of many reasons cited for this massive contraction of banking. The guarantee fund was suspended as a result of the damage caused by the Depression. The combined efforts of the Federal Deposit Insurance Corporation and the Reconstruction Finance Corporation after Franklin Roosevelt's 1933 Bank Holiday turned banking around in Mississippi, and by 1934 some observers claimed that the industry was as sound as it had ever been. Weak banks had been weeded out and the remaining banks strengthened.

The Banking Act of 1934 reformed Mississippi's banking laws along the lines of those of federal legislation and explicitly authorized branch banking, which was more widespread in the Magnolia State than in most other parts of the country until the 1980s. In Mississippi today, as in most other parts of the nation, large regional banks operate alongside small, local institutions.

Jon Moen
University of Mississippi

James Thomas Brown, *A Story of Banking in Mississippi* (1961); Harvey Lewis, Nolan Waller, and Don Moak, *Commercial Banking in Mississippi: 1940 to 1980* (1983); William P. McMullan Jr., "History of Banking in Mississippi" (master's thesis, the Wharton School, University of Pennsylvania, 1949).

Banks, Charles

(1873–1923) Businessperson

Charles Banks was the second of four children born to former slaves Daniel A. Banks, a Clarksdale, Mississippi, farmer, and his wife, Sallie Ann, a housekeeper and cook. Charles was born on the property of John and Eliza Clark, members

Charles Banks in the library of his home in Mound Bayou, 1915 (New York Public Library [Image ID: 1230989])

of the town's most prominent white family and namesake. Charles received his early education in the Coahoma County school system before enrolling at Rust University (now Rust College) in Holly Springs from 1887 to 1890, though he apparently left without graduating. Around the same time, he opened a Banks and Bro., a Clarksdale mercantile business that became so successful that some observers believed it a credit to all people in Clarksdale. According to one Banks contemporary, "He always liked the jingle and clink of the dollars of commerce and their sound is as pleasing to [his] ears as the rhapsody of a Beethoven sonata."

In 1893, at the age of twenty, Banks married Trenna Ophelia Booze of Natchez, who had attended Natchez Baptist College and then worked as a schoolteacher. Her peers considered her highly refined and intelligent, and she became a leader among the Magnolia State's black women.

In 1900 Charles Banks traveled to Boston to attend the first meeting of the National Negro Business League, where he met Booker T. Washington, the organization's founder. Three years later, inspired by the stories of business success he heard at the meeting, Banks moved about twenty miles from Clarksdale to Mound Bayou, an all-black town founded by Isaiah T. Montgomery and his cousins, Benjamin T. Green and Joshua P. T. Montgomery, in 1887. Reportedly the country's largest all-black town, Mound Bayou became a beacon of hope for blacks all over the state. It was self-sufficient, with its own drugstores, restaurants, post office, newspaper, cotton oil mill, physicians, attorneys, and undertakers. Banks then founded the Bank of Mound Bayou and soon surpassed Isaiah Montgomery as the town's leading citizen. Unlike many African Americans who moved away from the Deep South, Banks stayed in Mississippi during the height of Jim Crow terror.

Elected third vice president of the National Negro Business League in 1903, Banks rose to the position of first vice president in 1907, second in command only to Washington. Banks founded the Mississippi Negro Business League in 1905 (the first and reputedly the strongest state affiliate of the national organization); assisted in starting up dozens of black-owned businesses; and formed alliances with professionals, farmers, educators, and ministers. By 1910 he was considered Mississippi's most powerful black leader.

Banks also promoted several of Washington's forays into Mississippi and acted as the educator's eyes and ears in the state. In return for Banks's assistance, Washington provided political patronage and ensured that Banks had access to media, white philanthropy, and expertise from other members of the Tuskegee machine.

Banks used his influence (along with Washington's endorsement) to induce steel magnate Andrew Carnegie to establish a Carnegie Library in Mound Bayou. Banks also worked to secure white largesse from numerous other philanthropic sources, including the General Education Board, the Rosenwald Fund, and the Jeanes Fund. Although Banks believed in the philosophy of industrial education, he supported normal school training just as vigorously. He secured funds for Benjamin F. Ousley's Mound Bayou Normal and Industrial Institute, one of the best normal schools in the Delta.

Although he never ran for elected office, Banks continuously involved himself in national, state, and local politics. In 1890 he received an appointment as census enumerator for his Clarksdale district. A decade later US secretary of the interior Ethan A. Hitchcock appointed Banks as census supervisor for the Third District of Mississippi. Banks served as a member of the state executive committee for the Republican Party and in 1904 represented the Third District as a delegate to the Republican National Convention; he also served as a delegate at large to the Republican conventions of 1908 and 1912. Banks personally met with Pres. Theodore Roosevelt and Pres. William H. Taft on several occasions in Washington, D.C.

Banks was active in numerous fraternal, religious, civic, and educational organizations and institutions. He served as a trustee at Ohio's Wilberforce College and for fifteen years was a delegate to the General Conference of the African Methodist Episcopal Church. He also participated with the Knights of Pythias, the Masons, the Odd Fellows, the Negro Bankers Association of Mississippi, and the National Negro Bankers Association.

But Banks concentrated most of his efforts on business and economic development. In *My Larger Education* (1911), Washington described Banks as "the most influential businessman in the United States." Although Mississippi had twelve black-owned financial institutions, Washington called Banks "the state's leading Negro Banker." By 1911 he served as director of two insurance companies; general manager of the Mound Bayou Cotton Oil Mill; and owner of a cotton brokerage company, a blacksmith shop, and a laundry. He also formed a partnership with the local black undertaker, John W. Francis, that dealt in land speculation, building supplies, lumber sales, and other mercantile ventures. By 1912 Banks had an estimated net worth of one hundred thousand

dollars, and he wrote that he provided hundreds of jobs for black people in and around Mound Bayou.

The Bank of Mound Bayou remained one of Banks's favorite business ventures, and as the primary source of loans for the town, the bank gave him a tremendous amount of power. In addition, the establishment of the Bank of Mound Bayou forced white bankers to offer more competitive interest rates and to offer better treatment to their black customers.

Banks's most ambitious business venture was the Mound Bayou Oil Mill and Manufacturing Company. The plant was capitalized at one hundred thousand dollars, "the largest thing of the kind ever undertaken by Negro people." It manufactured cotton meal, cotton oil, fertilizing substances, and other by-products from cottonseed. The mill generated $12,600 during its first season of operations, but the plant's lessee, Benjamin B. Harvey, a white businessman from Memphis, reneged on his contract with Banks and stole money from the mill. After a court battle that lasted several years, Banks emerged victorious, but since the mill had been out of operation during that time, its financial woes continued and even worsened. Nevertheless, Banks eventually got the oil mill out of debt and back to making a profit.

These endeavors earned Banks the nickname the "Wizard of Mound Bayou." "The most public-spirited citizen in the history of Mississippi," Banks died from food poisoning in Memphis, Tennessee, on 18 October 1923.

David H. Jackson Jr.
Florida A&M University

Louis R. Harlan, *Booker T. Washington: The Wizard of Tuskegee, 1901–1915* (1983); Janet Sharp Hermann, *The Pursuit of a Dream* (1981); David H. Jackson Jr., *A Chief Lieutenant of the Tuskegee Machine: Charles Banks of Mississippi* (2002); David H. Jackson Jr., *Journal of Mississippi History* (Winter 2000); Neil R. McMillen, *Dark Journey: Black Mississippians in the Age of Jim Crow* (1989).

Banner, David (Levell Crump)

(b. 1973) Musician

David Banner's projects, from *Mississippi: The Album* to his Jackson-based organization, Heal the Hood, reflect a long-standing dedication to his home state. The son of Zeno and Carolyn Crump, Levell Crump grew up in the Queens neighborhood of Jackson. After graduating from Provine High School, Crump earned a business degree at Southern University, where he served as student government association president. He enrolled in the master of education program at the University of Maryland but left prior to graduation to focus on his music career.

Though hip-hop is one of the most prevalent popular music styles in Mississippi, rappers and producers frequently showcase their talent in informal spaces such as clubs, house parties, and impromptu gatherings and through demo recordings submitted to local radio. Crump borrowed the stage name David Banner from the Incredible Hulk comic book and embarked on a career that followed this pattern. Starting with a ten-dollar keyboard in elementary school, he began rapping at school events, experimenting with the production of beats and other musical compositions and honing his ability to translate complex social circumstance into taut lyrics. By his teenage years, Banner found selling demo recordings in the parking lot at Kroger more lucrative than his job bagging groceries inside.

In the late 1990s Banner earned regional acclaim after Jackson station WJMI began playing his songs, and in 1999 he signed a recording contract as part of the duo Crooked Lettaz. A solo album soon followed, and Banner also produced hits for several established rappers. This momentum led to a reported ten-million-dollar deal with Universal Records and the release of *Mississippi: The Album* in 2003.

Mississippi reached No. 1 on the *Billboard* R&B/hip-hop chart, establishing Banner as a leading figure in the genre. It was followed by *MTA2: Baptized in Dirty Water* (2004), *Certified* (2005), and *The Greatest Story Ever Told* (2008). Ten years into his major-label career, Banner had accumulated more than one hundred recording credits. As performer or producer he has recorded alongside rap's most successful artists, including Snoop Dogg, Wyclef Jean, and Lil Wayne. Banner had a role in a 2006 film, *Black Snake Moan*, and served as executive producer of an Old South–skewering cartoon, *That Crook'd 'Sipp*, for the Cartoon Network.

Banner's lyrics, though at times misogynistic, violent, and acutely profane, have added to the debate about the negative impact of certain hip-hop themes. While hit songs such as "Like a Pimp" substantiate this concern, others focus on complex struggles within Mississippi's African American community. In "Cadillac on 22's" Banner details everyday social pressures yet also targets structural issues: the lyric "Lord, they hung Andre Jones," for example, both memorializes an individual and references the spate of suicides of young black men in Mississippi prisons in the 1990s, a suspicious series of events that resulted in an investigation by the US Justice Department. As for the debate about violent and sexist hip-hop lyrics, Banner testified during a 2007 congressional hearing that hip-hop "is only a reflection of what is taking place in our society. Hip-hop is sick because America is sick."

Banner has worked to translate commercial success into community-based improvement. His Heal the Hood nonprofit organization has raised money, goods, and awareness for victims of Hurricane Katrina, provided schoolbooks and

college scholarships to students in need, and hosted toy drives. Of these efforts, Banner notes, "I just thank God I have an opportunity to make kids where I'm from feel like they're somebody." In part because of his personal response to Katrina—suspending his career, deploying his tour buses as rescue vehicles—the National Black Caucus honored him in 2006 with a Visionary Award for humanitarian efforts.

Banner released the studio albums *Death of a Pop Star* in 2010 and *Sex, Drugs, and Video Games* in 2012. The latter represented a return of sorts to his days of nontraditional distribution; Banner enacted what he termed a "2M1" movement, with the goal of selling two million records directly to consumers for one-dollar each via Internet download. As concept, the 2M1 model represented for Banner a grassroots opportunity to involve black consumers in black business and creative industries without corporate oversight.

Banner addresses the contradiction between his lyrics and his community-based efforts the same way many of his blues and country forebears have: by pointing out the divide between Saturday night and Sunday morning. As for his love of his home state, problems and all, he explains that he named his first album *Mississippi* in part to point out some frequently overlooked good points: "Every time they acknowledge me, they're gonna have to acknowledge my state."

Jennifer Gunter
University of South Carolina

Odie Lindsey
Nashville, Tennessee

Davey D., *Southern Shift* website, www.thesouthernshift.com; *Jackson Clarion-Ledger* (16 June 2003); *New York Times* (21 February 1993, 15 April 1993, 26 September 2007); Tamara Palmer, *Country Fried Soul: Adventures in Dirty South Hip Hop* (2005).

Barbecue

Mississippi barbecue has a few elements found in other states. The earliest extant commercial establishments, among them Abe's in Clarksdale, date from the 1920s, when good roads and inexpensive cars catalyzed American automobile culture. Mississippi barbecue is ethnically diverse—Abe's was and is Lebanese-owned, while Old Timer's in Richland has a Greek proprietor.

Community barbecues have a long tradition in the state and may be more central to the history of Mississippi barbecue than commercial establishments are. In Panola,

Exterior wall of Abe's Barbecue, Clarksdale, ca. 2006 (Photograph by James G. Thomas, Jr.)

Lafayette, and Tate Counties, goat barbecue has been a part of summer picnics and reunions for generations. The state's oldest public barbecue event is almost certainly the Turner family's Labor Day picnic in Gravel Springs, the small community that produced musicians Fred McDowell, Othar Turner, Napoleon Strickland, and the Hemphill family.

On picnic weekends, goats are slaughtered and dressed, parboiled in big cast-iron laundry kettles over open fires, and then smoked briefly over charcoal. Music and dancing are led by bands of homemade cane fifes and drums that form circles with crowds dancing around them. Once found in African American communities across the South, this music remains a living tradition only in this place, and the picnics are more of a celebration of music than of the barbecue, beer, and pickled boiled eggs that fuel the revelers.

Mississippi's commercial barbecue establishments follow three identifiable patterns. Many proprietors, like Deke Baskin in Oxford and Randy Lepard of Lep's in Pontotoc, began cooking in a welded trailer rig. A trailer rig may be the easiest way to move from home barbecue to commercial—when Greenwood's Leroy "Spooney" Kenter hauled his cooker from his backyard to his front yard, he started a small neighborhood business.

The second kind of place has a traditional pit, the underrecognized hallmark of what many consider honest barbecue. The stable gentle heat and smoke that can be achieved in a block pit accomplishes slow cooking like nothing else. Both Old Timer's in Richland and Leatha's in Hattiesburg feature waist-high cinder-block pits set in tin-roof sheds.

More recently, some places have changed over to electric ovens designed to cook a load of pork shoulders while burning no more than a stick or two of wood. Critics contend that this approach diminishes the traditional scene. Rodney Beasley at Beasley's Best Bar-B-Q, who cooks over hickory and pecan on a rig he welded himself, says that electric and gas cookers "don't put the flavor into the meat."

Mississippi barbecue is defined by family relationships. At Leatha's in Hattiesburg, Leatha Jackson's daughters take orders and declare that they have the best barbecue there is. At Westside, Mr. Reaves and sons make the barbecue and Mrs. Reaves bakes the cakes. The Shed in Ocean Springs—one of several new barbecue places that have opened on the Gulf Coast since Katrina—grew out of a family's campground business and now has a huge outdoor party area where blues music goes along with ribs and shoulder and a sweet, mild sauce that may be the one constant of Mississippi barbecue.

Tom Freeland
Oxford, Mississippi

Southern Foodways Alliance, Southern BBQ Trail website, www.southern bbqtrail.com.

Barber, Red
(1908–1992) Sports Announcer

Walter Lanier "Red" Barber, one of the most recognizable voices in baseball history, announced games for the Cincinnati Reds, Brooklyn Dodgers, and New York Yankees for thirty-three summers. His southern accent, baseball expertise, and unique blend of folksy colloquialisms and impeccable grammar and syntax made Barber a radio icon and cherished personality. From the time of his retirement from the broadcasting booth until his death, Barber remained famous and beloved for his writings, public appearances, and commentary on National Public Radio.

Born in Columbus, Mississippi, on 17 February 1908 to a locomotive engineer and a schoolteacher, Barber received his middle name in homage to a distant relative, famed poet Sidney Lanier. Barber lived in Mississippi until 1918, when his father took a job with the Atlantic Coast Line and moved the family to Florida. After high school Barber worked as a janitor to pay his tuition at the University of Florida. In Gainesville, Barber did his first radio work, fell in love with broadcasting, and dropped out of school to run the campus station.

In 1934 Powel Crosley Jr. hired Barber to broadcast Cincinnati Reds' games. Barber's first game as Cincinnati's announcer was the first big-league game he ever attended. The highlight of Barber's five summers with the Reds came on 24 May 1935, when he announced the first night game in Major League history. In 1938 Barber left Cincinnati for the Brooklyn Dodgers, beginning the period during which he made his most famous calls and became the preeminent announcer in baseball. Barber's distinct language and witticisms made him a legend. In Barber's world, a base runner would set off a "rhubarb" by "swinging the gate" on a shortstop, a third baseman would mishandle a ball "slicker than oiled okra," a slugger would smile "as big as a slice of watermelon" after hitting a home run, and a high-scoring game would turn into a "ring-tailed, double-jointed doozy."

Barber's run with the Dodgers nearly ended in 1945. When Branch Rickey informed him that the organization intended to sign Jackie Robinson to a Minor League contract, Barber, who had absorbed the Jim Crow South's rigid racial orthodoxy, threatened to quit. After talking to his wife, Lylah, and imbibing several martinis, Barber considered the financial and professional recklessness of quitting and opted to stay on as Brooklyn's announcer. When Robinson broke Major League Baseball's color barrier in 1947, Barber was in the broadcast booth.

He left the club six years later when Walter O'Malley took over and asked Barber to adjust his announcing style to portray the Dodgers more positively. Barber then signed with the New York Yankees, remaining the team's announcer until he retired from the broadcast booth in 1966. Barber's most famous moment with the Yankees came in 1961, when Roger Maris hit his sixty-first home run to break Babe Ruth's single-season record.

After retirement Barber wrote books and articles about a wide range of subjects and dedicated himself to service as a lay preacher in the Episcopal Church. Barber's sermons and writings often invoked figures from the sports world: in *Walk in the Spirit* Barber used the lives of Jackie Robinson, Ben Hogan, Roy Campanella, and Roger Bannister to praise moral and religious values such as hard work, moderation, patience, and self-sacrifice. Barber's evolved views on race relations, which condemned the segregation of his younger years as ugly and outdated but regarded blacks as dangerously militant and fatally pessimistic, reflected these values. From 1981 until his death on 10 October 1992 in Tallahassee, Florida, Barber appeared every Friday on the National Public Radio's *Morning Edition*, showcasing his gifts for storytelling and conversation.

Thomas John Carey
University of Mississippi

Red Barber, *The Broadcasters* (1970); Red Barber, *Show Me the Way to Go Home* (1971); Bob Edwards, *Fridays with Red: A Radio Friendship* (1993); *New York Times* (23 October 1992).

Barbour, Haley

(b. 1947) Sixty-Third Governor, 2004–2012

Haley Barbour made his name in national Republican politics and was a successful Washington, D.C., lobbyist before returning to his native Mississippi and unseating one-term Democratic governor Ronnie Musgrove in 2003.

Haley Reeves Barbour was born 22 October 1947 in Yazoo City, a small Delta town about twenty-five miles northwest of Jackson. His father, an attorney, died when Haley was young, and he and his brothers were raised by their mother. After starring at high school baseball in the 1960s, he attended the University of Mississippi, leaving a few credits short of earning an undergraduate degree.

Barbour began his political career in 1968 as a staffer for Republican Richard Nixon's presidential campaign. Barbour subsequently returned to the University of Mississippi and earned a law degree in 1972 before becoming the southeastern coordinator for Republican Gerald Ford's unsuccessful 1976 presidential campaign. Barbour ran for the US Senate in 1982 but was defeated by the Mississippian who had held the seat for more than thirty years, Democrat John C. Stennis.

Barbour served as Pres. Ronald Reagan's White House political director in 1985 and chaired the Republican National Committee from 1993 to 1997. In November 1994, under Barbour's leadership, Republicans won control of both chambers of Congress for the first time in forty years. In 2000 Barbour headed Texas governor George W. Bush's presidential campaign advisory committee.

Barbour was one of the founders of Barbour Griffith and Rogers, a high-profile Washington lobbying firm whose client list included a wide range of corporate interests, among them Microsoft to tobacco and utility companies.

In the 2003 Mississippi governor's race, Barbour easily defeated Jackson attorney Mitch Tyner in the primary before turning his attention to Musgrove in the general election. The Republican candidate relentlessly criticized the incumbent governor's signature achievement—persuading Nissan to build Mississippi's first automotive manufacturing plant, which opened about five months before the gubernatorial election. Barbour went on to defeat Musgrove, receiving 53 percent of the overall vote.

During his first year as governor Barbour was sharply criticized by advocates for the poor when he persuaded lawmakers to cut millions of dollars from the Medicaid budget. Barbour said the proudest achievements of his first term were improving the state budget, enacting limits on civil lawsuits, and persuading Toyota to build an auto manufacturing plant in the Northeast Mississippi town of Blue Springs. However, his first term was most strongly defined by Hurricane Katrina, which left a wide swath of destruction across South Mississippi when it struck in August 2005. Barbour persuaded federal officials to give Mississippi billions of dollars for storm recovery, and he easily won a second term in November 2007, receiving 57 percent of the vote.

Barbour continues to be a force in Republican politics, and in 2015 he published, with Jere Nash, *America's Greatest Storm: Leading through Hurricane Katrina*.

Emily Wagster Pettus
Jackson, Mississippi

Haley Barbour, *America's Great Storm: Leading through Hurricane Katrina* (2015); Mississippi Secretary of State, 2003 Election Results, *Mississippi Official Statistical Register* (2004–8); Emily Wagster Pettus, Associated Press (31 October 2003, 3 November 2007).

Barbour, William Henry, Jr.

(b. 1941) Judge

William Henry Barbour Jr. has served as a US District Court judge for the Southern District of Mississippi since 1983. He was born in Yazoo City on 4 February 1941 and received a bachelor's degree from Princeton University in 1963 and a law degree from the University of Mississippi School of Law in 1966. Barbour also studied at the New York University School of Law. He practiced with the Yazoo City law firm of Henry, Barbour, and DeCell until 1983; in addition, he held the position of youth counselor at the Yazoo City Court from 1971 to 1982. On 15 March 1983 Pres. Ronald Reagan named Barbour to succeed William H. Cox as a US district judge. Barbour served as chief judge from 1989 to 1996 and assumed senior status in 2006.

One of Barbour's most notable rulings occurred in *Chrissy F. v. Mississippi Department of Public Welfare* (1991), which involved a chancery court that had granted custody of a six-year-old girl to her father even though he had been accused of sexually abusing her. Barbour ruled that both the chancery judge and the youth court referee had violated the girl's constitutional rights of access to courts as well as her procedural due process rights. Children's rights activists welcomed the decision because of its potential to increase federal courts' protection of children. The US Court of Appeals for the Fifth Circuit reversed Judge Barbour's ruling on the ground of lack of subject matter jurisdiction but affirmed the decision in all other respects.

In another well-known case, 1998's *ACLU v. Fordice*, Barbour ordered Mississippi to unseal the files of the defunct State Sovereignty Commission, a state agency created in 1956 to maintain racial segregation. The Mississippi legislature had officially dissolved the commission in 1977 but had also sealed the agency's files until 2027. When the American Civil Liberties Union challenged that provision, Barbour held that the files should be unsealed but that interested parties named in the files had privacy rights that had to be protected. Barbour allowed affected persons time to protect their privacy rights before requiring the state to open the files.

In 2003 Barbour presided over *United States v. Avants*, which involved the 1966 slaying of sixty-seven-year-old black sharecropper Ben Chester White. Prosecutors argued that Ernest Avants and two other Klansmen had killed White to lure the Reverend Dr. Martin Luther King Jr. to Natchez, where they intended to assassinate the civil rights leader. Avants was convicted of aiding and abetting a premeditated murder thirty-seven years earlier and died in prison in 2004.

Natalya Seay
Washington, D.C.

Almanac of the Federal Judiciary, vol. 1 (2008); Rick Bragg, *New York Times* (26 January 2003); Jonathan M. Moses, *Wall Street Journal* (10 December 1991); *The American Bench: Judges of the Nation* (18th ed., 2008).

Barksdale, Ethelbert

(1824–1893) Politician and Editor

Ethelbert Barksdale was the father of Mississippi secession and its most vocal proponent. He was a longtime newspaperman as well as politician, a vocational combination that was common under the journalistic standards of the nineteenth-century South.

Barksdale was a dominant character from a prominent family. Born in Rutherford County, Tennessee, Ethelbert Barksdale moved to Mississippi during his childhood. His younger but better-known brother, William, became a congressman and later a Confederate general before being killed at Gettysburg on 3 July 1863. At age twenty, Ethelbert began his newspaper career as editor of the *Yazoo City Democrat*. In 1850 he moved to Jackson and bought controlling interest in the *Mississippian*, which until the secession crisis was a mouthpiece for the Democratic Party. The combination of politics and journalism suited Barksdale, who served as a delegate to the 1860 Democratic National Convention in Charleston.

The convention was already divided by the time the first gavel fell. The protection of slavery in US territories was the controversy embodied in conflicting interpretations of the Democratic Platform of 1856. Southern Democrats interpreted that platform as protecting territorial slavery, while northern Democrats believed it supported the right of the territory to determine for itself whether slavery would be allowed. The latter position became embodied by the buzzword "popular sovereignty," which Illinois senator Stephen A. Douglas helped popularize as offering the best chance of compromise between North and South. The southern delegations went to Charleston anxious to defend the proposition that slavery was legal in all territories and therefore that slaveholders could move freely among territories with their slaves.

Barksdale was head of the Mississippi convention delegation and was selected to present the viewpoints of all southern delegations. He was prominent at the convention from the beginning, and a fellow journalist observed, "He is full of fire and prone to fly off the handle . . . there is a dangerous glitter in his eye." In his major address to the convention, Barksdale asked that Democrats take a stand that only the states could decide on the legality of slavery in a territory while it remained a territory.

When the convention failed to adopt the majority platform committee report, which Barksdale had articulated, choosing instead the minority popular sovereignty platform of the Douglasites, Mississippi and six other southern delegations walked out. The remaining delegates nominated Douglas for president, and the southern delegations met in Baltimore and nominated John C. Breckinridge of Kentucky. Barksdale returned to Jackson determined to convince Mississippians to support Breckinridge and if necessary to secede, writing editorials to that effect. As early as 27 June Barksdale was writing about disunion and blaming the North for sectional disputes. But Breckinridge did not support disunion; he challenged his enemies to "point out an act, to disclose an utterance, to reveal a thought of mine hostile to the Constitution and the union of the States." The election of Abraham Lincoln left no doubt in Barksdale's mind as to what course Mississippi should take.

After serving in the Confederate Congress, Barksdale was elected to serve in the US House of Representatives in 1882 and 1884. He served on the platform committees for the Democratic Party in 1868, 1870, 1872, and 1880. But for all of Barksdale's political successes, he recorded many failures as well. His 1877 and 1881 efforts to become Mississippi's governor failed to earn him the nomination, and he was defeated in bids for the US House in 1890 and for the US Senate in 1892. Fellow newspaperman R. H. Henry, who owned and edited the *Jackson Clarion-Ledger*, wrote that Barksdale "made more editors and public men mad than any other politician in the state, and rarely was there a reconcilement."

At his death in Yazoo City on 17 February 1893, the *Clarion-Ledger* reported neither the controversy surrounding his life nor the role he played in leading Mississippi into the Civil War. Instead, the state's leading newspaper emphasized that Barksdale had served as its editor, concluding, "Love of Mississippi and Democracy . . . was his ruling motive—was the most deeply rooted sentiment in the heart that is now stilled."

Nancy McKenzie Dupont
University of Mississippi

John A. Barksdale, *Barksdale Family History and Genealogy* (1940); Reuben Davis, *Recollections of Mississippi and Mississippians* (1890); Frank C. Heck, *Journal of Southern History* (1955); R. H. Henry, *Editors I Have Known since the Civil War* (1922); *Jackson Daily Clarion-Ledger* (17 February 1893); Christopher J. Olsen, *Political Culture and Secession in Mississippi: Masculinity, Honor, and the Antiparty Tradition, 1830–1860* (2000); Owen Peterson, *Journal of Mississippi History* 14 (1952); David M. Potter, *The Impending Crisis, 1848–1861* (1976).

Barksdale, Rhesa Hawkins
(b. 1944) Judge

Rhesa Hawkins Barksdale has served as circuit judge on the US Court of Appeals for the Fifth Circuit since 1990. He was born on 8 August 1944 in Jackson and went on to earn a bachelor's degree from the US Military Academy at West Point, New York, in 1966. As a company commander in Vietnam, Barksdale was decorated for bravery in combat, receiving the Purple Heart, Bronze Star, Silver Star, and Cross of Gallantry with Silver Star. He left the army in 1970 and earned a law degree from the University of Mississippi School of Law two years later.

Barksdale spent a year as a law clerk for US Supreme Court justice Byron R. White before entering private practice with the Jackson firm of Butler, Snow, O'Mara, Stevens, and Cannada; he remained there until 1990, becoming a partner. Barksdale also taught law at the University of Mississippi School of Law and Mississippi College School of Law. He chaired the Mississippi Vietnam Veterans Leadership Program from 1982 to 1985. On 17 November 1989 Pres. George Bush appointed Barksdale to succeed Alvin R. Rubin on the US Court of Appeals for the Fifth Circuit, and he took his oath of office on 12 March 1990.

In a 1991 decision, *Murray v. City of Austin*, the court held that the depiction of the Christian cross on the insignia of the City of Austin, Texas, was not a violation of the Establishment Clause of the US Constitution. Barksdale, writing for the panel, held that the inclusion of the Christian cross on the city's coat of arms neither inhibited nor advanced religion because the insignia did not have any proselytizing effect and did not endorse religion.

In 2000 Judge Barksdale wrote for the panel in *Burdine v. Jackson*. Calvin Jerold Burdine had petitioned for habeas corpus on the grounds that his attorney had provided ineffective counsel by repeatedly falling asleep during Burdine's trial for capital murder, which resulted in his conviction and death sentence. The US District Court granted relief, and the government appealed the court's order. On appeal, the US Court of Appeals for the Fifth Circuit found that the presumption of prejudice for purposes of ineffective assistance claim was a new rule and that could not be applied retroactively to benefit Burdine. The court also found that the attorney's behavior did not warrant a presumption of prejudice for Burdine's claim of ineffective counsel. On rehearing en banc, the majority of the Fifth Circuit affirmed the district court's grant of habeas corpus relief. Barksdale and four other judges dissented.

In 2004 Judge Barksdale wrote the opinion affirming the conviction of Ernest Avants for murdering sixty-seven-year-old Ben Chester White in 1966. Thirty-seven years after the crime occurred, prosecutors brought Avants to trial on charges that he and two other Klansmen had killed White to lure Martin Luther King Jr. to Natchez, where they intended to assassinate the civil rights leader. A jury convicted Avants, now seventy-two, of aiding and abetting a premeditated murder. Avants appealed, arguing that the government had intentionally delayed indicting him to gain a tactical advantage. Writing for the court, Barksdale affirmed the district court's finding that the government's delay in bringing the indictment was not motivated by bad faith.

Natalya Seay
Washington, D.C.

Almanac of the Federal Judiciary, vol. 2 (2008); *The American Bench: Judges of the Nation* (2008); *Biographical Directory of the Federal Judiciary, 1789–2000* (2001).

Barksdale, William

(1821–1863) Politician

William Barksdale was an important political figure in antebellum Mississippi. He was born on 21 August 1821, near Smyrna, Rutherford County, Tennessee. His parents were descended from prominent southerners whose civil and patriotic achievements inspired William, an ambitious and intelligent youth. Barksdale attended public school in Rutherford County and later pursued a partial course of classical study at the University of Nashville. In 1837, at age sixteen, he emigrated with his brothers to Mississippi and settled in the recently formed county of Lowndes, where he first mastered the intricacies of frontier law and then established a successful legal practice in Columbus. He prospered, investing his capital in land and slaves and acquiring more of the latter through his 1849 marriage to Narcissa Saunders of Louisiana. By 1860 he owned thirty-six slaves and a plantation valued at ten thousand dollars. In 1844, not content as a lawyer-planter, he purchased half of a local newspaper, the *Columbus Democrat*, and became its coeditor. He immersed himself in local and state politics and began to consider running for office. That endeavor was interrupted by the outbreak of armed conflict with Mexico. A captain, he served as assistant commissary of the 2nd Mississippi Infantry Regiment.

In response to the 1851 secession crisis Barksdale aligned himself with the moderate faction of the Democratic Party, which tried to guide the state to accept the Compromise of 1850. That effort, coupled with his recent military service, contributed substantially to his initial success as a candidate. In November 1852, after several months of intense campaigning, he was elected as a states' rights Democrat to the US House of Representatives, winning reelection three times and serving until 1861. The most controversial issue before the national assembly was the question of expanding slavery in federal territory, and as a representative from one of the South's largest slaveholding states, Barksdale was frequently called on to defend southern rights and institutions. He was a firm advocate of low tariffs, the institution of slavery, and a social order based on the concept of white supremacy.

He was especially adamant when confronted with legislative proposals that might deprive his region of its proper share of the spoils of the Mexican War. He also had a penchant for dueling and fisticuffs that left him open to severe criticism and eventually caused some northern congressmen to regard him as a fire-eating secessionist. His adverse experiences at the center of the political maelstrom in Washington left him equally embittered and distrustful of his northern counterparts. Nevertheless, Barksdale remained more moderate in his views of important issues than some of his more radical contemporaries and did not sanction disunion as the best safeguard of southern institutions until after the election of Republican Abraham Lincoln as president in 1860.

During the Civil War, Barksdale commanded a brigade of Mississippi infantry in the Army of Northern Virginia. On the eve of hostilities, he was appointed quartermaster general of the Army of Mississippi but soon entrained for the front lines in Northern Virginia as a colonel of the 13th Mississippi Infantry Regiment, which he personally led into combat at First Manassas. On 12 August 1862 he was promoted to the rank of brigadier general and assigned command of the 13th, 17th, 18th, and 21st Mississippi Infantry Regiments. His record as a brigade commander was characterized by conspicuous personal gallantry on the battlefield, especially at Antietam and Fredericksburg. Altogether, he participated in six major campaigns in the eastern theater but remained unscathed until the summer of 1863. During the fighting on the second day of the Battle of Gettysburg, Barksdale was mortally wounded while leading his now famous brigade in resolute attack against a formidable enemy near the Peach Orchard and died the following day, 3 July 1863.

James W. McKee Jr.
East Tennessee State University

John A. Barksdale, *Barksdale Family History and Genealogy* (1940); Douglas S. Freeman, *Lee's Lieutenants* (1942); W. L. Lipscomb, *A History of Columbus, Mississippi, during the Nineteenth Century* (1909); Harry W. Pfanz, *Gettysburg: The Second Day* (1987).

Barnard, Frederick A. P.

(1809–1889) Educator and Scientist

Frederick Augustus Porter Barnard was born 5 May 1809 in Sheffield, Massachusetts. He graduated second in the Class of 1828 with honors at Yale. He began teaching at Connecticut's Hartford Grammar School, and in his spare time he played piano and flute and learned seven languages. By 1832 Barnard had determined that pedagogy was not a good career choice because of his acute hearing impairment. He spent the next six years working at the New York State Institute, a school for the deaf and mute. In 1837, after returning from a research trip to Yale, Barnard met Basil Manly, president of the University of Alabama, who offered Barnard the school's chair of mathematics and natural philosophy. He accepted.

Barnard spent the next decade and a half there, conducting scientific researching and publishing, before moving on in 1854 to hold the chair of mathematics at the University of Mississippi. Soon after moving to Oxford, Barnard entered the Episcopal priesthood. When Augustus B. Longstreet resigned as the university's president, the religious factions among the school's leaders scrambled to select his successor, and in 1856 the Episcopalians, who held a majority on the board, appointed Barnard to the position.

Barnard worked tirelessly to place the university in the top tier of American institutions. His outgoing nature, support of the school's literary societies, and efforts to construct a recreational gymnasium won him the admiration of the students. He also advocated the creation of departments of medicine, law, agriculture, science, classics, and political history. Barnard used the legislature's 1856 appropriations for the university to build an observatory for the world's largest telescope and laboratories for barometry, geology, and chemistry, facilities considered "the most perfect" in America. Although several of his proposed reforms did not materialize, the school added a chair in English literature, expanded the administration, achieved better disciplinary control over students, and instituted an emphasis on grammar and composition during the freshman and junior years.

Despite his successes, Barnard also faced a stream of problems, including disputes with professors and lack of funds for a respectable library. In 1861, when the Civil War erupted, Barnard resigned. Even though he owned slaves, Barnard never accepted the legitimacy of slavery and opposed secession. In December 1861 he moved back to the Northeast, and in May 1864 Barnard accepted the presidency of the small Columbia College (now Columbia University) and shaped it into a first-rate university. While in New York, he helped found the National Academy of Sciences and championed coeducation. Barnard remained at Columbia until his death in 1889, at which time the University of Mississippi faculty

Frederick A. P. Barnard (Collection of the Center for the Study of Southern Culture)

paid him tribute: "We hear of his death with regretful sorrow, recognizing the fact that the University of Mississippi has lost a friend, the cause of education, a strong support, and science, a vigorous advocate."

William P. Hustwit
Birmingham Southern University

"Autobiographical Sketch of Dr. F. A. P. Barnard," *PMHS* (1912); Frederick A. P. Barnard, *Letter to the Honorable Board of Trustees of the University of Mississippi* (1858); William J. Chute, *Damn Yankee! The First Career of Frederick A. P. Barnard* (1978); John Fulton, *Memoirs of Frederick A. P. Barnard* (1896); John Wesley Johnson, "Sketches of Judge A. B. Longstreet and Dr. F. A. P. Barnard" *Publication of the Mississippi Historical Society*, 12 (1912); Robert Mellown and Gene Byrd, *Alabama Heritage* (Spring 2000); Ronald L. Numbers and Janet S. Numbers, *Journal of Southern History* (May 1982); David G. Sansing, *The University of Mississippi: A Sesquicentennial History* (1998).

B

Barnes, Walter

(1905–1940) Musician

Walter "Brother" Barnes was a popular bandleader from the late 1920s until his death. A clarinetist, conductor, and tour organizer and advertiser, he fronted the Royal Creolians and then the Kings of Swing. A native of Vicksburg, Barnes spent most of his early years in Chicago, where he learned to please both white and black audiences. A diminutive, smooth, smiling showman, Barnes led his swing bands dressed in a tuxedo. He is perhaps best known for popularizing long tours by bands of African American musicians and for his horrific death.

In the late 1920s Barnes became a popular figure as the bandleader at Chicago's version of the Cotton Club. He benefited from having Al Capone as a sponsor: Capone told Chicago radio stations to play Barnes's music, making him one of the first African Americans to receive substantial airplay. He and the thirteen-piece Royal Creolians recorded several singles in 1928 and 1929.

In the 1930s Barnes turned primarily to African American audiences, barnstorming through the South on the sort of tours that became known as the Chitlin' Circuit. Part of Barnes's influence and knowledge came from his role on the *Chicago Defender*, the most important African American newspaper and a connection between the cosmopolitan, urban world and the rural and small-town South. After first writing columns about bands playing in Chicago, especially the African American Bronzeville neighborhood, Barnes turned to producing stories about southern places to play and about the bands, like his, that played there. As historian Preston Lauterbach writes, "Though he began as Chicago orchestra columnist and self-publicist, Barnes rapidly became central dirt dispatcher for traveling black jazz bands." Barnes and his wife, Dorothy, who also wrote for the *Defender*, became proprietors of the Walter Barnes Music Corporation. Barnes's last band, the Kings of Swing, left Chicago in the fall of 1936 for a six-month bus tour stretching from Oklahoma to southern Florida.

In April 1940 Barnes and most of the other members of the Kings of Swing died in a fire that killed more than two hundred people at the Natchez Rhythm Club. Crowds had packed the club, but management closed all but one of the doors to guarantee that only paying customers entered. According to reports in the *Defender* and legends associated with the tragedy, Barnes and his musicians continued to play during the fire in an effort to calm the panicking patrons.

Ted Ownby
University of Mississippi

Davarian L. Baldwin, *Chicago's New Negroes: Modernity, The Great Migration, and Black Urban Life* (2007); Preston Lauterbach, *The Chitlin' Circuit and the Road to Rock 'n' Roll* (2011); Michael Rugel, *American Blues Scene* website, www.americanbluesscene.com.

Barnett, Ross Robert

(1898–1987) Fifty-Third Governor, 1960–1964

The office of governor is the only public office Ross Barnett ever held and the only political office for which he ever campaigned. He is also one of only two Mississippians who ran for the office four times. He ran and lost in 1951 and 1955, he was elected in 1959, and he ran again unsuccessfully in 1967.

Born at Standing Pine in Leake County on 22 January 1898 (the last Mississippi governor born in the nineteenth century), Barnett graduated from Mississippi College in 1922 before earning a law degree from the University of Mississippi in 1926 and opening a law practice in Jackson. He went on to become one of Mississippi's most successful trial lawyers.

During Barnett's administration the state of Mississippi was celebrating the centennial of the Civil War. It was also responding to the great changes brought on by the civil rights movement. Barnett, who made his first speech as governor-elect at a Citizens' Council meeting, vowed to maintain segregation in the state's public schools, even pledging to go to jail before he would allow any integration. In announcing his candidacy in 1959, Barnett had said, "I am a vigorous segregationist. I will work to maintain our heritage, our customs, constitutional government, rights of the states, segregation of the races, and industrial and agricultural development." Barnett spoke widely inside and outside

Ross Barnett at a football game in Jackson, 1962 (Library of Congress, Washington, D.C. [LC-USZ62-111240])

Mississippi on his support for state control on issues of education and voting.

In 1962 the US Supreme Court directed the University of Mississippi to admit African American James H. Meredith. Barnett took numerous steps to slow or directly oppose Meredith's admission and condemned John F. Kennedy's presidential administration, vowing to never "surrender to the evil and illegal forces of tyranny." Opponents of the university's integration clashed violently with federal troops, leading to the deaths of two people on the night of 30 September 1962. Nevertheless, Meredith ultimately enrolled, the first step in the eventual elimination of state-sponsored racial segregation in Mississippi's public schools and universities.

Several significant economic developments also occurred during Barnett's administration. A series of amendments to the worker's compensation law and the enactment of a right-to-work law made Mississippi more attractive to outside industry, and more than forty thousand new jobs were created during his four years in office. Barnett's industrial development program also included the construction of industrial parks throughout the state and the establishment of the Youth Affairs Department under the Agricultural and Industrial Board. His administration made it easier for localities to use industrial revenue boards to attract new business, and he was especially proud of persuading Standard Oil to locate refining operations on the Gulf Coast.

Barnett resumed his law practice after leaving office in 1964 but continued an active interest in state politics. In 1967 he ran for governor but was eliminated in the first primary. He was one of Mississippi's last popular stump speakers and remained a favorite at the Neshoba County Fair until his death on 6 November 1987. While a reservoir in Hinds County and a lake in Smith County bear his name, he is most remembered for his role in the unsuccessful resistance to the desegregation of the University of Mississippi.

David G. Sansing
University of Mississippi

Ross Barnett Subject File, Mississippi Department of Archives and History; Joseph Crespino, *In Search of Another Country: Mississippi and the Conservative Counterrevolution* (2009); Erle Johnston, *I Rolled with Ross!* (1980); David G. Sansing, *The University of Mississippi: A Sesquicentennial History* (1999).

Barq's Root Beer

Though many observers think of New Orleans as the home of Barq's Root Beer, the popular soft drink got its start in

Biloxi in 1898, when New Orleans native Edward Charles Edmond Barq invented the soft drink with a bite. A trained chemist, Barq worked on Louisiana sugar plantations in the winters and spent his summers in Biloxi, bottling artesian water and concocting "soda pop flavors." Barq's Root Beer was first bottled by the Biloxi Artesian Bottling Works and began to be distributed nationally in 1906.

In the 1930s, Barq chose to bottle the beverage in twelve-ounce bottles rather than the standard six- and eight-ounce bottles, and franchises began to spread, first to Mobile, Alabama, and then to New Orleans. According to one source, "By 1937, 62 bottling plants had been established in 22 states." In 1976 businessman John Koerner and attorney John Oudt purchased the company from the Barq family and moved its headquarters to New Orleans. The Coca-Cola Company purchased Barq's in 1995. Slogans for the soft drink include "Barq's Has Bite," "Famous Ole Tyme Root Beer since 1898," and "It's Good."

Margaret T. McGehee
Oxford College of Emory
University

Bill Lockhart, "Barq's Bottling Co. and Double Cola Bottling Co.," *Password* 49 (2004); Allan Petretti, *Petretti's Soda Pop Collectibles Price Guide: The Encyclopedia of Soda Pop Collectibles* (3rd ed., 2003); "Third Generation Root Beer Maker Dies in Biloxi," *Associated Press* (13 June 2003).

Barry, Marion
(1936–2014) Activist and Politician

Mississippi native Marion Barry was an early leader in the Student Nonviolent Coordinating Committee and later became a political leader in Washington, D.C. Born in Itta Bena on 6 March 1936 to Marion and Mattie Barry, Barry moved with his mother and sister to Memphis, Tennessee, at a young age. He graduated from the city's Booker T. Washington High School in 1954 before earning a bachelor's degree in chemistry from LeMoyne College (now LeMoyne-Owen College). Barry then moved to Nashville, Tennessee, to attend Fisk University, where he participated in one of James Lawson's workshops on nonviolent direct action and became involved in the sit-in movement that ultimately desegregated the city's lunch counters.

In 1960 Barry was one of the cofounders of the Student Nonviolent Coordinating Committee (SNCC) and was elected its first chair. In that role, he represented SNCC at the 1960 Democratic National Convention, urging the Platform Committee to adopt a strong stance on the issues of segregation, fair employment, voting rights, white violence, and police misconduct. Later that year, after securing funds for SNCC and attending workshops on voter registration at the Highlander Folk School in Monteagle, Tennessee, Barry moved to McComb, Mississippi, to conduct workshops on nonviolent direct action and to organize the Pike County Nonviolent Movement. He encouraged McComb students to stage sit-ins and to protest the expulsion of their classmates, Brenda Travis and Ike Lewis, in retaliation for their civil rights activities.

Barry went on to participate in the Jackson Nonviolent Movement, before resigning as SNCC's chair to pursue a doctorate at the University of Tennessee in Knoxville. He maintained his ties to the organization, however, and led demonstrations to protest segregation in Knoxville and worked to garner support for the Mississippi Freedom Democratic Party's challenge to the state's all-white delegation to the 1964 Democratic National Convention.

Barry subsequently moved to New York to manage a SNCC office before heading to Washington, D.C., in 1965 to spearhead the group's efforts there. He helped to organize the White House Conference on Civil Rights and founded and directed the Free D.C. Movement, which sought self-government for the District. Barry resigned from SNCC but continued to work as an organizer, directing an anti-poverty group, Pride, Inc. After Congress granted the District the power to hold its own elections, Barry served on the city's first board of education and on the city council for several terms. In 1979, voters elected Barry the District's second mayor, and he remained in that office until 1990, when he was convicted of a misdemeanor drug charge. In 1992 Barry was again elected to the city council, and in 1995 he again became mayor, serving until 1999. From 2005 until his death, he represented Ward 8 on the city council.

When Barry died on 23 November 2014 after years of health problems, he was celebrated as an innovative political figure with great popularity among African American voters in Washington, D.C., but was also remembered for his personal failings. The *Boston Globe*, for example, called him a "charismatic yet confounding politician."

Amy Schmidt
Lyon College

Clayborne Carson, *In Struggle: SNCC and the Black Awakening of the 1960s* (1981); John Dittmer, *Local People: The Struggle for Civil Rights in Mississippi* (1994); Ernest M. Limbo, in *The Human Rights Tradition in the Civil Rights Movement*, ed. Susan Glisson (2006); Charles M. Payne, *I've Got the Light of Freedom: The Organizing Tradition and the Mississippi Freedom Struggle* (1995); David Stout, *Boston Globe* (24 November 2014); *Washington Post* (23 November 2014); Howard Zinn, *SNCC: The New Abolitionists* (2002).

Barthé, Richmond
(1901–1989) Sculptor

A sculptor often associated with the Harlem Renaissance, Richmond Barthé focused on the human form and on capturing both everyday and iconic members of the African American community. His sculptures are often noted for their sense of fluid motion and sensuality.

James Richmond Barthé was born in Bay St. Louis on 28 January 1901. His father died soon thereafter, and his mother, Marie Clementine Robateau Barthé, supported the family by sewing. While at work she often gave paper and pencil to the toddler to occupy him, and she raised her son a devout Catholic. Spirituality, race, and sexuality influenced his later art.

During his grade school years Barthé's family, teacher, and priest all began to take note of his advanced drawing and painting talent, yet his Creole descent meant that Barthé was barred from pursuing formal art education. At age fourteen Barthé took a job as houseboy with a prominent white family in New Orleans. There, noted figures such as writer and editor Lyle Saxon encouraged the boy's art and lobbied art schools on his behalf, to no avail. Determined to help, his patrons secured his admission to the School of the Art Institute of Chicago in 1924.

Barthé's painted portraits soon earned him notice from important collectors. During his senior year, he took a sculpture class to better understand perspective, and he subsequently pursued that medium. In 1928 his sculptures were included in the Chicago Art League's Negro in Art Week, which led to his first professional commissions and to the promise of a solo exhibition.

Barthé moved to New York City in 1929 and quickly became part of the well-established Harlem Renaissance scene. In 1930 he won a Julius Rosenwald Fellowship, and in 1933–34 his work was shown at both the Chicago World's Fair and New York's Whitney Museum. The latter purchased several of his works and helped establish his reputation as the country's leading African American sculptor. Barthé remained in New York for nearly two decades, during which time the Metropolitan Museum of Art and other museums acquired his work and he won Guggenheim Fellowships in 1941 and 1942. Barthé's subjects were people who represented the everyday African American experience as well as noted celebrities such as Josephine Baker, George Washington Carver, John Gielgud, and Paul Robeson. His patrons and friends also included Eleanor Roosevelt, Carl Van Vechten, and Langston Hughes.

Barthé's sculptures frequently focus on the human form in motion, and he applied classical influence to representations of African American life. Barthé broadened the formal art world's tendency to depict African Americans as agricultural laborers. For example, with *The Negro Mother* he used the classical pietà form to depict an African American mother holding the body of her lynched son. His sculpting of African American male nudes bestowed the classical ideal on bodies that had been excluded from such consideration. His most famous bronze, *The Boxer*, is a lean, graceful representation of Cuban boxer Kid Chocolate in midswing.

Barthé's sculptures also reflected his personal experience. As the creations of a gay black man with strong religious convictions, *The Negro Mother* and other works not only engaged his spirituality but represented the pain associated with his life. *The Boxer* served as sensual representation of a black male frozen in a complex, perpetual fight. Scholars note that Barthé was at times torn between images and expectations. For example, his mostly white clientele often considered him a race man because of his subjects, while some of his African American counterparts labeled him an Uncle Tom because of his clientele.

Barthé left New York in the 1940s and completed several commissions, including the Toussaint-Louverture Monument and General Dessalines Monument for the Haitian government, before spending almost twenty years in Jamaica and several years in Europe. During Mississippi's Freedom Summer of 1964 Barthé was invited back to Bay St. Louis, which held a public celebration in his honor and at which the town's white mayor gave him the key to the city.

In 1977 the University of Southern Mississippi bought two of Barthé's artworks, and he was honored by the governor of Mississippi. He died in Pasadena, California, on 5 March 1989: the street where he lived was renamed Barthé Drive. His work continues to be exhibited in and beyond Mississippi.

Odie Lindsey
Nashville, Tennessee

Patti Carr Black, *American Masters of the Mississippi Gulf Coast: George Ohr, Dusti Bongé, Walter Anderson, Richmond Barthé* (2009); Margaret Rose Vendryes, *Barthé: A Life in Sculpture* (2008).

Barthelme, Frederick

(b. 1943) Author

Frederick Barthelme is a writer, educator, editor, and artist. He may be best known for his fiction and is critically acclaimed as a master of literary minimalism, a title that causes him discomfort. The American South provides the setting both for his fiction and for much of his professional life as writer and professor at the University of Southern Mississippi.

Barthelme was born 10 October 1943 in Houston to Donald Barthelme, an accomplished modernist architect, and Helen Bechtold Barthelme, a teacher. He is one of seven children from a literary family: two of his brothers, Donald and Steven, are also respected writers. Barthelme attended Tulane University in 1961–62 and the University of Houston from 1962 to 1967, pausing in 1965–66 to study painting at the Museum of Fine Arts in Houston.

While building a painting career, Barthelme worked as an architectural draftsman, an exhibit installer, assistant to the director of the Kornblee Gallery in New York City, and creative director and senior writer at several Houston advertising firms. During this period, several galleries, including the Museum of Modern Art in New York, featured his artwork.

Barthelme subsequently decided to switch artistic direction because, as he later stated, he "didn't want to carry big pieces of lumber through the streets of New York" for the rest of his life. He changed from working with found objects to viewing books as "containers" rather than as literary entertainment, a transition evident in his first two books. He enrolled at Johns Hopkins University and earned a master's degree from the Writing Seminars in 1977. His short story "The Storyteller" earned the Eliot Coleman Award for prose in 1976–77.

In 1977 he became director of the Center for Writers at the University of Southern Mississippi, a position he held until 2010. During that time he also edited the *Mississippi Review*, a quarterly publication that includes poetry, fiction, and creative nonfiction and became widely recognized as a top-tier literary journal. In 2004 Barthelme was nominated for the PEN/Faulkner Award for his novel *Elroy Nights*, and in 2010 he won the Mississippi Institute of Arts and Letters award for fiction. He currently serves as a coeditor of the online journal *New World Writing*.

Barthelme's publications include the collections of stories *Rangoon* (1970), *Moon Deluxe* (1983), *Chroma* (1987), and *The Law of Averages: New and Selected Stories* (2000). He has written the novels *War and War* (1971), *Second Marriage* (1984), *Tracer* (1985), *Two against One* (1988), *Natural Selection* (1990), *The Brothers* (1993), *Painted Desert* (1995), *Bob the Gambler* (1997), *Elroy Nights* (2003), *Waveland* (2009), and *There Must Be Some Mistake* (2014). In 1999 Frederick and Steven Barthelme published a memoir, *Double Down: Reflections on Gambling and Loss*. Frederick has also authored the screenplays *Second Marriage* (1985) and *Tracer* (1986), and his work has appeared in numerous periodicals.

Characterized by *Los Angeles Times* reviewer Daniel Akst as the "bard of suburban disconnectedness," Barthelme belongs to what has become known as the minimalist movement of writing. His books and short stories portray a world that critics call the New South, defined by shopping malls, drive-through windows, neon signs, and brand names. Through economical use of language and dialogue and of vivid description peppered with buzzwords of contemporary American culture, Barthelme captures modern life in suburban America.

Frances Abbott
Digital Public Library of America,
Boston

Frederick Barthelme website, www.frederickbarthelme.com; *Contemporary Literary Criticism*, vol. 36 (1986); *Dictionary of Literary Biography Yearbook: 1985* (1986); John C. Hughes, *Frederick Barthelme* (2004); John C. Hughes, *The Novels and Short Stories of Frederick Barthelme: A Literary Critical Analysis* (2005).

Barton, Lea

(b. 1956) Artist

Lea Barton is the daughter of Henry Ray Smith and Barbara Ann Gregory Smith and was born on 23 February 1956 in Yazoo City. Barton received a bachelor's degree in liberal studies from Millsaps College in Jackson (1996) and a master of fine arts degree from the Pratt Institute in Brooklyn, New York (1998). She maintains a studio in Flora, Mississippi, where she creates mixed-media collage paintings and works on paper exploring themes related to the history, traditions, politics, and culture of the Deep South. Since 1996 Barton has exhibited her art in institutional collections across the United States, and in 2008 she held her first solo exhibition at Denise Bibro Fine Art in New York City.

After a brief initial exploration of abstraction while at Pratt, Barton's works began to incorporate imagery and text drawn from the culture of the South and particularly her native Mississippi. Historical and contemporary photographs, quotes from southern writers, text from roadside signs, advertising illustrations, newspaper articles, and comic strips appeared along with similar appropriated material in her collage compositions, first as works on paper, then later in larger format on canvas. Barton's strategy of juxtaposing seemingly unrelated elements to create a new, unified narrative soon became the hallmark of her art.

Barton is particularly interested in the stereotypical identity and role of the southern woman and how her traditional characteristics are evolving into new ones. Barton often includes her own image in her collages, either as self-portrait or female archetype. Other southern types also populate her works—for example, the southern belle, the debutant, and the evangelical churchgoer. By enlisting her friends and neighbors as models, she infuses her art with a sense of both familiarity and universal appeal.

René Paul Barilleaux
McNay Art Museum, San Antonio,
Texas

René Paul Barilleaux, Correspondence with Lea Barton.

Baseball, Minor League, in Jackson

Jackson's professional baseball history goes back more than a century, to 1904, when the first team came into existence. Until the early 1950s, teams played home games at the grandstand on the fairgrounds. Between 1953 and 1974, however, the city lacked a squad; thereafter, teams began playing at Smith-Wills Stadium, and since 2005 a Minor League team has played at Trustmark Park in Pearl.

The Greenville Cotton Pickers, Natchez Indians, and Vicksburg Hill Climbers were the first professional teams organized in the state of Mississippi. All began play in 1902, the inaugural year of the Class D Cotton States League and the beginning of the modern era of Minor League baseball. In 1904 the Jackson Senators began life in the Class D Delta League. The league folded after only one year, and the next year the Jackson team was known as the Blind Tigers, an apparent reference to sponsorship by a group of bootleggers operating on Rankin County's Gold Coast. That year the team affiliated with the Cotton States League, remaining there through 1931. In 1905 play was suspended because of a yellow fever epidemic. From 1906 to 1908 the team played as the Senators, and they were league champs in 1908. That same year the legislature approved statewide Prohibition, initiating a tradition of brown-bagging alcohol in the first-base bleachers while the third-base bleachers were reserved for families.

The Cotton States League did not play in 1909, and in 1910 the team returned as the Tigers. They became the Drummers in 1911, the Senators again in 1912, and in 1913 the Lawmakers. World War I brought a temporary halt to Minor League baseball in the South, and when the sport resumed in 1921, the Jackson team was known as the Red Sox. Its moniker changed back to the Senators four years later, and the team won league championships in 1927, 1928, and 1931. The squad moved to the Class B Southeastern League in 1932 and to the Class C Dixie League the following year. In 1934–35 the team was known as the Mississippians. It became the Senators again in 1936 and rejoined the now Class C Cotton States League; in 1937 the team moved back to the Class B Southeastern League, remaining there until 1950. The team was a farm club of the Detroit Tigers in 1936, of the New York Yankees in 1937–38, of the Boston Braves from 1946 to 1950, and again of the Detroit Tigers in 1953.

In 1946 independent oilman Emmett A. Vaughey Jr. purchased and reorganized the Jackson Baseball Club, serving as its president for three years. In 1948 Vaughey sponsored a promotion in which children in Jackson orphanages could write a short essay on "Why I would like to meet Babe Ruth." A boy from the Baptist Orphanage won the contest and, chaperoned by sportswriter Purser Hewitt of the *Jackson Clarion-Ledger*, traveled to New York and he met the Babe and received an autographed baseball.

The 1950 season was shortened by the conflict in Korea. The Southeastern League ceased to exist at the end of the season, and no professional teams played in Jackson in 1951 or 1952. The year 1953 brought a return to the Class C Cotton States League, which attempted to exclude the Hot Springs Bathers during the season after the team signed an African American player, Jim Tugerson. Several teams refused to take the field and consequently forfeited games. The Jackson franchise collapsed following a 3 August 1953 tornado that blew the roof off the grandstand, necessitating a move to nearby Yazoo City for the remainder of the season. The Senators' owner, president, and manager, Willis Hudlin, told the *Clarion-Ledger*, "Unless there is a new park, Jackson will be without baseball in 'fifty-four. Not only for 'fifty-four but probably for years to come. With a new park, there is a chance for affiliation with the Southern Association." The following day J. M. Dean, executive secretary of the Mississippi State Fair, sounded the death knell: "There will be no attempt to restore the grandstand to accommodate baseball." Whether for purely economic reasons or in a further attempt to stem the tide of integration, Jackson remained without professional baseball for twenty-one years.

In 1974 the New York Mets brought their AA farm club to Jackson to coincide with construction of Smith-Wills Stadium. The Jackson Mets remained until 1990, and a year after their departure, the Houston Astros moved their AA Texas League affiliate to Jackson. After a fan vote the team was named the Jackson Generals, in honor of General Andrew Jackson. The Generals won championships in 1993 and 1996 before moving to Round Rock, Texas, after the 1999 season.

The Jackson Senators were reincarnated and played in the Central League from 2002 to 2004, winning the championship in 2003. The Senators folded in 2005 when the Atlanta Braves moved their AA farm club from Greenville, South Carolina, to the newly constructed Trustmark Park in Pearl. For the past decade, the Mississippi Braves have played in the South Division of the Southern League.

Bill Patrick
Jackson, Mississippi

Lloyd Johnson and Miles Wolff, eds., *The Encyclopedia of Minor League Baseball* (1997); John D. McCain, *The Story of Jackson*, 2 vols. (1953); James A. Riley, *The Biographical Encyclopedia of the Negro Baseball Leagues* (1994); Rick Wolff, ed., *The Baseball Encyclopedia* (1993).

Basketball

Like most other sports played in Mississippi, basketball sometimes seems a minor sport compared to football. Since the mid-twentieth century basketball has been known as a city game, and Mississippi's relative lack of urban centers, along with football's powerful hold on the state's sporting culture, has made basketball less clearly identified with the state. Mississippi lacks the kind of intense basketball culture found in such rural states as Indiana, North Carolina, Kansas, and Kentucky. Still, basketball has a significant place in the state's sports history.

For many years Mississippi basketball displayed a tendency toward informality or at least local eccentricity. For example, Nick Revon made all-state junior college teams playing for Hinds Junior College in 1948 and 1949 even though he was still in high school. A few years later James "Babe" McCarthy made a jump rare in major-college sports when he went from coaching Tupelo Junior High in 1953–54 to coaching Mississippi State University (MSU) the following year. McCarthy went on to a successful career coaching in the American Basketball Association. Teams used the irregularities associated with limited finances to their advantage. For years the Jackson State University Tiger basketball teams played in a gym known as the Snake Pit, a venue so hot and crowded that the home team always had a profound advantage.

Many of the state's successful coaches have retained their positions for decades. Charles Rugg coached basketball at Belhaven College from 1963 to 1995; Orsmond Jordan Jr. coached at Murrah High in Jackson from 1970 to 1994; between 1950 and 1989, Bert Jenkins coached for eleven years at Gulfport Junior High and twenty-eight years at Gulfport High School; Bonner Arnold coached at Northeast Mississippi Junior College from 1948 to 1974; and Dave Whitney coached at Alcorn State from 1969 to 1988 and again from 1996 to 2003. All are members of the Mississippi Sports Hall of Fame.

Mississippi's women basketball players have in many ways been more prominent than the men despite the paltry attention given to women's sports between the 1920s to the 1970s. In 1999, *Sports Illustrated* published lists of the fifty greatest athletes in the history of each state: the first four basketball figures in Mississippi were Coach Margaret Wade of Delta State and high school, college, Olympic, and professional star players Lusia Harris-Stewart, Ruthie Bolton-Holiefield, and Jennifer Gillom. Mississippi's women's basketball teams have achieved far greater glory than their male counterparts. Delta State won national championships as a member of Association for Intercollegiate Athletics for Women in 1975, 1976, and 1977 and at the Division II level of the National Collegiate Athletic Association (NCAA) in 1989, 1990, and 1992. Mississippi University for Women also won the Association for Intercollegiate Athletics for Women's national title in 1971, while Rust College's women's team took the NCAA Division III championship in 1984 and the women of Phillips Junior College in Gulfport recorded National Small College Athletic Association championships in 1985 and 1986. For their part, the state's men have won only a single national championship—the Bearcats of Rust College won the National Small College Athletic Association championship in 1977. The pinnacle of men's basketball success came in 1996, when MSU's team reached the NCAA Final Four and lost in the semifinal game. In addition, the University of Southern Mississippi's men's team won the National Invitational Tournament in 1987. The University of Mississippi men are the only squad in the Southeastern Conference never to have won a regular season championship.

Racial segregation in sports persisted longer in Mississippi than in most other southern states, as leaders first refused to allow teams from the state to play against integrated teams and held out even longer before allowing African American players on the state's once all-white teams. The unwritten policy of refusing to play teams with African Americans came about in 1955, when Mississippi's legislators and educational leaders reached a "gentlemen's agreement" after Jones County Junior College played an integrated California team in the Junior Rose Bowl.

The policy meant that even though MSU's men's basketball teams won Southeastern Conference championships in 1959, 1961, and 1962, they did not participate in the NCAA's national tournament. The Bulldogs (as they became known in 1961) again took the conference title in 1963, and in the wake of the crisis over desegregation at the University of Mississippi, MSU coach Babe McCarthy and school president Dean W. Colvard quietly pushed to accept the invitation to the NCAA tournament. Legislators and members of Mississippi's Board of Trustees of the State Institutions of Higher Learning were divided on the issue, and Gov. Ross Barnett chose not to become involved, but state senator Billy Mitts and former state senator B. W. Lawson filed a last-minute lawsuit in Hinds County Court that resulted in a judge's order forbidding the team from leaving the state. An odd comedy ensued in which McCarthy and other coaches left the state earlier than planned to avoid sheriffs who might be enforcing the injunction. To avoid having players arrested, the starters and other important players hid in a dorm while freshmen, some reserves, and the trainer went to the airport. The entire team ultimately participated in the tournament, losing to the racially integrated Loyola of Chicago team, 61–51. Not long thereafter, state officials quietly did away with the prohibition on competition against integrated teams.

The awkward and contested desegregation of public schools meant that Mississippi's traditionally white universities and colleges began recruiting African American players only in the late 1960s and early 1970s. In the fall of 1968 Wilbert Jordan Jr. became the first African American to play for a previously all-white team when he joined the freshman squad at the University of Southern Mississippi.

A debate about the greatest basketball player from Mississippi would likely include Lusia Harris-Stewart (Delta State); Bailey Howell, Red Stroud, and Erik Dampier (Mississippi State); Gerald Glass, Country Graham, John Stroud, and Peggy Gillom (University of Mississippi); Purvis Short and Lindsey Hunter (Jackson State University); Clarence Weatherspoon, Nick Revon, and Wendell Ladner (Southern Miss); Dot Easterwood Murphy (Mississippi University for Women); Lorenzen Wright (University of Memphis); Antonio McDyess and Mo Williams (University of Alabama); Ruthie Bolton-Holiefield (Auburn University); Mahmoud Abdul-Rauf (Chris Jackson) (Louisiana State); Sam Lacey (New Mexico State); Spencer Haywood (University of Detroit); and Monta Ellis and Al Jefferson, who went from Mississippi high schools to successful careers in the National Basketball Association (NBA).

The epicenter of Mississippi basketball would certainly be Jackson and the surrounding area. An incomplete but still representative survey of sixty recent NBA players with Mississippi roots shows that at least sixteen attended high school in Jackson, including four at Murrah High, four at Jim Hill High, and three at Lanier High. The Jackson Coliseum, known as the Big House, is the home of the annual Mississippi High School Athletic Association basketball tournament, an intense competition with boys' and girls' teams playing in six divisions.

Ted Ownby
University of Mississippi

Basketball-Reference.com website, www.basketball-reference.com; Chris Dortch, *String Music: Inside the Rise of SEC Basketball* (2002); J. Russell Henderson, in *The Sporting World of the Modern South*, ed. Patrick Miller (2002); Charles Martin, *Benching Jim Crow: The Rise and Fall of the Color Line in Southern College Sports, 1890–1980* (2010); Mississippi Sports Hall of Fame and Museum website, www.msfame.com.

Bass, Rick

(b. 1958) Writer

The son of a geologist, Rick Bass seemed in the process of following in his father's footsteps, graduating with a degree in geology from Utah State University in 1979 and subsequently moving to Mississippi to work as a petroleum geologist in charge of prospecting for new wells. But shortly after finishing college he began to write magazine articles about hunting and fishing, work that led to the publication of his first two books of essays, *The Deer Pasture* (1985) and *Wild to the Heart* (1987). Bass has subsequently published more than a dozen works of fiction and nonfiction.

In 1987 Bass moved with his family to the Yaak Valley in the northwest corner of Montana to dedicate himself to writing full time. Two years later he published a memoir of his time as a geologist in Mississippi, *Oil Notes*, and his first collection of stories, *The Watch*, which won the 1988 PEN/Nelson Algren Award. The title story, set in the piney woods and swamps of central Mississippi, also won a 1989 O. Henry Award. The central theme of the collection is the passage of time and people's relation to it. Concerns regarding humans and their temporal, physical, and spiritual connections to the natural world have become the defining characteristic of Bass's work. Bass has called Montana the state of his "rebirth," and in his writings the wilderness is often the source of a revitalizing power. In works such as *Winter: Notes from Montana* (1991), *In the Loyal Mountains* (1995), *The Sky, the Stars, the Wilderness* (1997), *The Hermit's Story, The Diezmo* (2005), and *Why I Came West: A Memoir* (2008), Bass explores the nature and potential of this power, and he has earned a reputation as significant writer and activist.

A founding member of the Yaak Valley Forest Council, which works for conservation and restoration in the area, Bass continues to live and work in northwestern Montana.

Jacob Sullins
Georgia Highlands College

Bonnie Lyons and Bill Oliver, eds., *Passion and Craft* (1998); O. Alan Weltzien, ed., *Literary Art and Activism of Rick Bass* (2001).

Bates, Gladys Noel

(1920–2010) Educator and Activist

Gladys Noel was born on 26 March 1920 in McComb. Her father, railway postal clerk Andrew Jackson Noel, was a civil rights activist and the son of former slaves once owned by Edmond F. Noel, who went on to serve as Mississippi's governor. Her mother, Susie Hallie Davis Noel, was also the daughter of freed slaves.

Noel and her four siblings were raised on Pearl Street in Jackson, where she attended Jim Hill School, Lanier High School, and Alcorn Preparatory School and was involved in the African Methodist Episcopal Church. She attended Alcorn A&M, where she met and married John Milton Bates, a football coach. Marriage cost Bates his position at Alcorn, forcing the couple to relocate to secure a teaching position for him and to enable her to enroll at Tougaloo College, where she served as class president and secretary for three years on her way to receiving a bachelor's degree in biology in 1942. Gladys Bates later earned a master's degree from West Virginia University and studied at the University of Colorado and the University of Denver. Bates taught home economics at Buffalo Creek School in Kosciusko, Mississippi, learning more from her students than she taught them: her parents had refused to teach their daughters skills that would lead them to be domestic servants. She also worked as a matron at Mary Porter Academy in North Carolina and then became a science teacher at Smith Robertson Junior High School in Jackson.

In 1948 Bates became a plaintiff in one of Mississippi's first education-related civil rights cases. With the aid of Constance Baker Motley and Robert L. Carter of the National Association for the Advancement of Colored People's Legal Defense Fund, Meridian attorney James A. Burns sued the Jackson Separate School District seeking equal salaries for black and white teachers. The suit led to violence against the Bates family: opponents fired shots into their home on Deerpark Street, burned the house, and left crosses burning nearby. Both Bates and her husband lost their positions with the Jackson schools as a result of the filing: because she no longer had standing to sue, Richard Jess Brown, an automotive science and technology teacher at Lanier High School, became a party to the suit.

Over the ensuing decade, Bates raised her two children, Kathryn and John M. Bates Jr., and worked for the Mississippi Association of Teachers in Colored Schools, while her husband took various jobs. In 1960 they relocated to Denver and continued their activism and careers as educators, receiving numerous awards for their work. The Colorado Education Association's human relations award is named in their honor, and in 2009, Jackson opened the Gladys Noel Bates Elementary School. She died on 15 October 2010.

Catherine M. Jannik
Georgia Institute of Technology
Library and Information Center,
Atlanta

Townsend Davis, *Weary Feet, Rested Souls: A Guided History of the Civil Rights Movement* (1998); Catherine M. Jannik, "Gladys Noel Bates: Educator and Activist" (master's thesis, University of Southern Mississippi, 1999); "Oral History with Gladys Noel Bates" (1998), Center for Oral History and Cultural Heritage, University of Southern Mississippi, http://www.lib.usm.edu/legacy/spcol/coh/cohbatesg.html.

Beadle, Samuel Alfred

(1857–1932) Author

Samuel Alfred Beadle was born into slavery in Georgia on 17 August 1857 and was brought to Rankin County, Mississippi, by his mother at the end of the Civil War. Little is known about Beadle's life before he completed undergraduate work at Atlanta University and at Jackson's Tougaloo College. While in Jackson, Beadle met and married Aurelia Thomas.

Beadle received some legal training as he read for the bar in the offices of Patrick Henry and Anselm J. McLaurin in Brandon. In 1884 Beadle was admitted to the Mississippi bar after a grueling examination from both white and African American lawyers. The rules of racial segregation prevented him from appearing in the courtrooms of many Jackson judges, but he nevertheless maintained a successful civil practice for more than forty years with his partner, fellow African American lawyer Perry Howard. One of their most significant clients was a prominent Jewish cotton merchant firm J. B. Hart and Company. Beadle and Howard also represented several local banking institutions and fraternal organizations, including the Gideons and the Odd Fellows.

Beadle began his career as an author by composing verses for his friends' amusement. His first published work, *Sketches from a Life in Dixie* (1899), consisted of seven stories and fifty-three poems. Seven of these works comment directly on the oppressive realities of racism and institutionalized segregation in the American South. One of the most effective pieces, "Lines," is a poem that deals with assaults endured by African American soldiers as they passed through the South on their way to America's war with Spain in 1898. Another poem, "Strike for Equal Rights," stresses that African American "citizen-fighters" must possess moral fortitude and personally represent the values of freedom for which they are fighting on the military stage.

Beadle's second work, *Adam Shuffler* (1901) is another collection of short prose pieces commenting on African American life in the South; some of the stories explore regional African American dialect. The poems in his final volume, *Lyrics from the Underworld* (1912), won critical acclaim for both their style and their thematic elements. The author's preface explains that the book's title is a direct commentary on his frustration about his treatment as a second-class citizen in his native land. The collection also includes many early photographs by Beadle's son, Richard H. Beadle, who for half a century was one of Mississippi's only black photographers.

In 1930 Beadle moved to Chicago, where he practiced law until his death.

Cale Nicholson
Little Rock, Arkansas

James B. Lloyd, ed., *Lives of Mississippi Authors, 1817–1967* (1981); Randy Patterson, *POMPA: Publications of the Mississippi Philological Association* (1992).

Beauty Pageants

Mississippians have invested considerable time and effort in creating a beauty pageant tradition and have excelled in competition with women from other states. European festivals that crowned women as symbols of May Day and other ritual occasions were the predecessors of modern American beauty pageants, and in the colonial era this custom took root in the South more than among the New England Puritans. The ideology of the Old South included a prominent role for the beautiful white woman, whose chaste, idealized image undergirded the white-dominated society. The identification of whiteness, beauty, and women survived into the twentieth century. W. J. Cash called the southern woman "the shield-bearing Athena gleaming whitely in the clouds." In short, southern culture placed white women on a pedestal and invested great meaning in their symbolic role, with the mythic southern belle figure the cultural icon that beauty contests came to honor and that empowered young women who embraced it.

Schools for young southern white women throughout the nineteenth century included contests for selection of attractive, popular queens, and by the early twentieth century agricultural, state, and county fairs were including beauty competitions among women. Commercial beauty pageants emerged in northern resort communities about the same time, and southern coastal resorts began sponsoring such contests shortly thereafter. The most famous national beauty pageant, the Miss America contest, began in 1921. Mississippians who have won that crown are Mary Ann Mobley (1959), Lynda Lee Mead (1960), Cheryl Prewitt (1980), and Susan Akin (1985). Between 1968 and 1988, Mississippi surpassed any other state in consecutive preliminary winners in the Miss America contest, in contestants placing in the top five, and in winners of the swimsuit competition. The 1988 Mrs. World was from Mississippi, as was that year's Miss Teen USA. The University of Mississippi has made the beauty queen a part of campus lore, as the university has had three Miss Americas (Mobley, Mead, and Akin). In 2007 Miss Arkansas, Miss Illinois, and Miss Tennessee were all University of Mississippi students.

Southern society barred African American women from beauty pageants until the end of Jim Crow segregation in the 1960s, thus excluding many Mississippians from competition. Black ideals of beauty were long apparent through

Jasmine Murray, Miss Mississippi 2014 (Courtesy Matt Boyd)

an extensive network of cosmetics, beauty salons, and cultural meanings associated with shades of skin color. The civil rights movement strengthened pride in a specifically black ideal of beauty. Popularized in the 1960s, the phrase "black is beautiful" reflected an empowered ideal of dark skin as a more general reflection of pride in black culture. Beauty pageants became a fixture at historically black colleges and in black communities across the South, and black women soon began competing in community-wide beauty contests. Toni Seawright, a Mississippi University for Women student, became the first black Miss Mississippi in 1988, and she went on to place in the top five at the Miss America Pageant. In 2007 Alcorn State student Kimberly Morgan became the second black Miss Mississippi, and seven years later, Jasmine Murray of Columbus became the third.

Mississippi has developed an infrastructure to nurture beauty queens. For example, America's Model Miss is a Caledonia-based business that sponsors the Miss Southern Babes State Pageant, aimed specifically at Mississippi girls. Its website notes that "Our home is in Mississippi, and this Pageant is for all the Beautiful Mississippi Girls!" Competition occurs in age divisions ranging from newborns to teenagers, with such categories as sportswear, denimwear, photogenic, beauty optionals ("prettiest eyes, best smile, prettiest hair, and fashion"), and most beautiful face. Another company sponsored the First Butterfly Beauties Pageant in 2006 and Mississippi's Little Princess Pageant, held in Hattiesburg in March 2007. December 2007 saw competition for Miss Teen Mississippi Magnolia State Pageant, Miss Mississippi Magnolia State, and Mrs. Mississippi Wife of the Year—all held in Vicksburg. The Dixie Diamond Pageant is held each fall for girls across all age ranges—from children to young women. Winners in all these contests typically receive scholarship money and clothes. A *Jackson Clarion-Ledger* reporter visiting the 2007 state fair noted the presence of six beauty queens: Miss Mississippi State Fair, Teen Miss Mississippi State Fair, Little Miss Mississippi State Fair, Tiny Miss Mississippi State Fair, Preteen Miss Mississippi State Fair, and

Baby Miss Mississippi State Fair. Miss Hospitality was also among the feted women in attendance.

One of the reasons for the success of the state's beauty queens in national contests is the stability and preparation associated with pageants. Mississippi has been a leader in advanced training to prepare the state pageant winner for the Miss America contest. The Briggs Hopson family has long held the license to produce the state pageant, which has been held in Vicksburg since 1958, generating a reported economic impact of $1.6 million in 2015. The Hopsons work with the winner for more than a month before the Miss America pageant. Other trainers across the state assist contestants in countless beauty pageants with tutoring in image, pageant techniques, sharpening of talent, and general self-improvement.

Beauty contest winners become Mississippi celebrities. Pageants from hundreds of festivals provide opportunities for achievement in local communities. Beth Henley's 1980 play, *The Miss Firecracker Contest*, and the 1989 film version, *Miss Firecracker*, dramatize the compelling quality of such contests for participants. Beauty queens make personal appearances, travel extensively, earn scholarship money, and have their photos on calendars. The pageants remain popular rituals for the performance of what Elizabeth Bronwyn Boyd calls a "fairly specific, regional understanding of gender." Even in a changing Mississippi, new citizens adapt to the state's cultural ways. For example, in June 2004 the India Association of Mississippi sponsored the first Miss India Mississippi Beauty Pageant. Contestants performed Indian dance, music, martial arts, and theater for the talent segment. One trainer coached young Indian women in Punjabi costumes—golden turbans and embroidered vests—as they adapted rap dance moves to a song from a Bollywood movie. The president of the association, Hitesh Desai, told the crowd in Jackson that the "pageant is a step for us and it's big, y'all."

Charles Reagan Wilson
University of Mississippi

Elizabeth Bronwyn Boyd, "Southern Beauty: Performing Femininity in an American Region" (PhD dissertation, University of Texas at Austin, 2000); Elizabeth Bronwyn Boyd, *Voices: A Journal of Oral Tradition* (January 1998); La Raye Brown, *Jackson Clarion-Ledger* (8 July 2007); Anne Goodwyn Jones, *Tomorrow Is Another Day: The Woman Writer in the South, 1859–1936* (1981); Tara McPherson, *Reconstructing Dixie: Race, Gender, and Nostalgia in the Imagined South* (2003); Jay Paris, *Mississippi Magazine* (July–August 1988); Cheryl Prewitt with Kathryn Slattery, *A Bright-Shining Place* (1981).

Beauty Parlors and Barbershops

Women and men in all regions of America frequent beauty parlors and barbershops. In the South the shops not only took on the gendered aspects evident throughout the rest of the country but also represented the racial divisions unique to the region. Not merely businesses that catered to beauty and grooming needs of southerners, beauty parlors and barbershops became important cultural institutions where people of different classes and occupations interacted. In a region where beauty is valued, both white and black women looked forward to their hair appointments so they could not only appear their best but also converse with friends and neighbors. In addition, hair salons were one of the public spaces outside of church where African Americans escaped the glare of white eyes and could share news, conduct business, and discuss any number of subjects. Beauty parlors and barbershops developed along separate racial lines.

For Mississippians eager to improve their status by owning businesses, cutting and styling hair became one of the most accessible avenues to entrepreneurship because of the small capital investment required. In the antebellum South in particular, barbering offered African American men a rare path to prosperity. In addition to the low startup costs, barbering fit neatly into the concept of servility and deference that whites expected in the racial hierarchy. William Johnson of Mississippi, known as the Barber of Natchez, owned three barbershops and a plantation and at his death in 1851 left an estate valued at twenty-five thousand dollars. After the Civil War other avenues opened for African Americans, and the percentage of black business owners who were barbers dropped from 10 percent to less than 2 percent. By the early twentieth century, the black barbershop began to resemble the modern institution—a rare black public space where men could openly discuss issues and share information that might be dangerous outside the protective wall of the racially segregated barbershop. Black barbershops would have been one of the only places to discuss, read, or purchase the *Chicago Defender*, for example.

The beauty industry enabled former slave and onetime Vicksburg resident Madame C. J. Walker to become one of the first black women millionaires. Walker employed twenty thousand people to sell her beauty products. The black beauty culture stressed greater opportunities through self-help and personal hygiene, emphasizing clean scalps and bodies and the societal opportunities available through self-improvement and beauty. Beauty entrepreneurs were often community leaders and worked to oppose lynching, obtain benefits for World War I veterans, and gain greater African American equality and civil rights in other areas.

White women also found career opportunities as beauticians. Before World War I beauty shops were frequented

Segregated beauty parlor (Bern and Franke Keating Collection, Department of Archives and Special Collections, J. D. Williams Library, University of Mississippi)

primarily by elite women. The advent of bobbed hair, however, changed the beauty culture. Instead of simply shampooing and styling their hair, women of all classes wanted their hair cut in a style that needed regular maintenance. Many white women also operated informal salons in their kitchens, fixing hair for friends and neighbors. By the early twentieth century beauty organizations began to professionalize hair styling by instituting training requirements and requiring licenses and state agencies to inspect and regulate practitioners. During the New Deal, the National Recovery Act set codes, hours, and wages and targeted kitchen beauticians who charged less and often mixed their own products. The trade journals for white and black beauticians demonstrated different attitudes toward the beauty culture. Whereas white trade publications stressed technical developments, African American not only covered new technologies but also featured articles on female entrepreneurs, neighborhood shops, and political struggles.

Mississippi beauty and barbershops occupy an enduring place in both southern society and culture. Eudora Welty set "Petrified Man" in a beauty shop, and William Faulkner used a barbershop as a backdrop in "Dry September."

Minoa D. Uffelman
Austin Peay University

Melissa Victoria Harris-Lacewell, *Barbershops, Bibles, and BET: Everyday Talk and Black Political Thought* (2004); Craig Marbery, *Cuttin' Up: Wit and Wisdom from Black Barbershops* (2005); Julie A. Willett, *Permanent Waves: The Making of the American Beauty Shop* (2000).

Beauvoir

Beauvoir, French for "Beautiful View," was home to Confederate president Jefferson Davis for the final twelve years of his life, from 1877 to 1889. James Brown, a planter from Madison County, constructed the Louisiana plantation–style mansion in 1852 on the Gulf Coast shoreline between Biloxi and Gulfport. The elevated, nine-room home faced the water and featured decor imported from Europe. Sarah A. Dorsey, who owned plantations in Mississippi and Arkansas and who gave the mansion its name, acquired the home in 1873. A school friend of Jefferson Davis's wife, Varina Howell Davis, Dorsey invited Jefferson Davis to visit Beauvoir in 1877 when he was looking for a quiet place to write his memoirs. Davis rented a cottage on the grounds and two years later bought the home from Dorsey for fifty-five hundred dollars. While at Beauvoir, Davis wrote *The Rise and Fall of the Confederate Government* and *A Short History of the Confederate States of America*.

When Davis died, the house passed to his daughter, Varina "Winnie" Davis; she died in 1898, and the mansion then passed to her mother, Varina Howell Davis. In failing health and with insufficient income to maintain the mansion, Varina Howell Davis nevertheless rejected a lucrative offer from a commercial developer and instead sold the property in 1903 to the Mississippi Division of the Sons of Confederate Veterans for ten thousand dollars. The agreement called for the State of Mississippi to operate Beauvoir as a home for Confederate veterans, their wives, and their orphans as long as such a need existed. In 1924 the state constructed a hospital for veterans east of the main building. Housing more than two thousand veterans and their widows, Soldiers' Home functioned from 1904 to 1957, when the state transferred the final two Confederate widows to another facility.

In 1940 state legislation authorized the conversion of Beauvoir into a Jefferson Davis shrine, and it was restored and opened to visitors the following year. A Davis family museum now occupies the mansion's ground floor. The property also includes two cottages; the hospital, which houses a Confederate museum; a replica of one of the twelve barracks that housed veterans; a superintendent's home; the gardens; and a Confederate cemetery containing the graves of 771 veterans and their wives and the Confederate Tomb of the Unknown Soldier, dedicated in 1981. While Jefferson Davis is buried in Richmond, Virginia, his father, Samuel, a Revolutionary War veteran, is interred at Beauvoir. In 1998 a presidential library and museum opened.

In 1969 Hurricane Camille destroyed many artifacts and severely damaged the house. Thirty-six years later, Hurricane Katrina wreaked further havoc, leaving paintings and artifacts in disarray. Beauvoir reopened in 2008 under the operation of the Mississippi Division of the Sons of Confederate Veterans.

Lisa K. Speer
Arkansas History Commission

Beauvoir website, www.beauvoir.org; Richard R. Flowers, in *Down South with the Dixie Press*, ed. Charles L. Sullivan (2006); Michael Thomason, *Gulf Coast Historical Review* (1985).

Beckwith, Bill
(b. 1952) Sculptor

William Norwood Beckwith was born in Greenville, Mississippi, in 1952 and educated in the public schools of that city, long known as an arts mecca because of its many writers and artists as well as the influence of planter, attorney, poet, and arts patron William Alexander Percy. As a memorial to his father, US senator LeRoy Percy, Will Percy commissioned *Patriot*, a bronze statue of a medieval knight in armor created in 1930 by Malvina Hoffman, an internationally acclaimed sculptor who had studied with Auguste Rodin in Paris. Percy later sent his protégé, Leon Z. Koury, the son of Greenville grocers who had immigrated from Syria, to study with Hoffman in New York. After returning to Greenville in 1961, Koury worked as a sculptor and a painter and was a leader in the local arts scene for three decades.

Beckwith became an apprentice in Koury's studio in 1966 and studied with him for four years before moving to Oxford to earn bachelor of fine arts and master of fine arts degrees in sculpture at the University of Mississippi. There, under the guidance of art professor Charles M. Gross, Beckwith became "as hooked on casting bronze as an addict is to heroin. If you have ever poured molten metal or held the sun in your hand, you understand the power and the energy. I was hooked bad." For his senior thesis in 1974, he built a complete foundry behind Koury's studio in Greenville; the project won Beckwith an award as the best student artist on campus. The building became Vulcan Studios and Foundry, Mississippi's first commercial fine arts bronze foundry, and the enterprise enabled Beckwith to cast for other sculptors as a way of financing his own work. Vulcan moved to Greenwood in 1976 and to Taylor, a small village south of Oxford, six years later.

Beckwith operated the foundry until 1986, when he stopped casting for other sculptors and began working only on his own projects. He has shown his bronzes in numerous single and group exhibitions, including shows at the Frank Marino Gallery and Splashlight Studios in New York, the 1984 World's Fair in New Orleans, and the National Museum of American Art, Smithsonian Institution, in Washington, D.C. His commissioned work includes several life-size or larger monuments, among them *William Faulkner*, Oxford; *George Merrick*, Coral Gables, Florida; *Chief Piomingo, Chickasaw* and *Elvis Presley*, Tupelo; *B. B. King*, Indianola; *Jefferson Davis*, Biloxi; and *Flag Bearer, Mississippi 11th*, Gettysburg National Military Park, Pennsylvania. Beckwith has sculpted portrait busts of Jim Henson, Eudora Welty, Tennessee Williams, Richard Wright, Herman Melville, L. Q. C. Lamar, Margaret Wade, and numerous others. He received an artist's fellowship from the Mississippi Museum of Art in 1989, and the Village of Taylor was recognized with a Governor's Award for Excellence in the Arts in 2001. In 2014, Beckwith received the Noel Polk Lifetime Achievement Award from the Mississippi Institute of Arts and Letters. He currently works out of a studio in Taylor and teaches part-time at the University of Mississippi.

Ann J. Abadie
University of Mississippi

William N. Beckwith website, www.williamnbeckwith.com; Patti Carr Black, *Art in Mississippi, 1720–1980* (1998); Patti Carr Black, *The Mississippi Story* (2007); Hank Burdine, *Delta Magazine* (September–October 2009); Barbara Shissler Nosanow, *More Than Land or Sky: Art from Appalachia* (1981); Arthur Williams, *The Sculpture Reference* (2005); Arthur Williams, *Sculpture, Technique, Form, Content* (1989).

Beittel, Adam
(1898–1988) Educator and Activist

Adam Daniel Beittel was a distinguished educator and administrator who played a key role in the struggle for civil rights in Mississippi. Born in Lancaster, Pennsylvania, on 19 December 1898, Beittel graduated from the University of Findlay in 1922 and earned a doctorate from the University of Chicago in 1929. After serving in numerous teaching and administrative positions, Beittel became the president of Tougaloo College, near Jackson, Mississippi, on 1 September 1960. That post became the greatest professional and personal challenge in his long and illustrious career. Tougaloo, a private institution governed by a board of trustees in New York, had long demonstrated a commitment to civil and human rights that earned the school the enmity of Mississippi's white power structure, and Beittel assumed his post with no intention of changing the controversial culture or climate of the often embattled college.

Beittel arrived in Jackson just months after black collegians in North Carolina had begun an assault on Jim Crow via direct action protests—sit-ins. The movement quickly spread to other black colleges across the South, and on 27 March 1961 nine Tougaloo students entered the downtown branch of the Jackson Public Library to protest its policies regarding segregation. Their actions placed Tougaloo squarely in the crosshairs of Mississippi's white supremacist culture, but Beittel backed the students and refused to expel them. Over the next three years, Beittel's administration encouraged Tougaloo students to pursue both academic achievement and active involvement in the growing civil rights movement.

In response, the State of Mississippi repeatedly tried and failed to strip Tougaloo of its accreditation. In 1964, however, Brown University and Tougaloo College entered into an academic partnership, and representatives of the Rhode Island school criticized Beittel's work and described him as an obstacle to the partnership's future success. Some Brown faculty members who served as Tougaloo College trustees discussed Beittel with the Mississippi State Sovereignty Commission.

Tougaloo's board of trustees decided to replace Beittel with the school's first black president, George Owens, who had previously served as its business manager. During Owens's inauguration, the president of Brown University, Barnaby Keeney, noted that the true academic environment was no place for the promotion of social activism, a thinly veiled attack on Tougaloo's traditions and on Beittel's administration. Beittel later relocated to California, where he died on 26 July 1988.

Jelani M. Favors
Duke University

Adam Daniel Beittel Papers, Tougaloo College Archives; Clarice T. Campbell and Oscar Allen Rogers, *Mississippi: The View from Tougaloo* (1979); John Dittmer, *Local People: The Struggle for Civil Rights in Mississippi* (1994); Erle Johnston, *Mississippi's Defiant Years, 1955–1973* (1990).

Belhaven University

In 1894 Lewis T. Fitzhugh founded Belhaven College for Young Ladies in Jackson, Mississippi. The college was housed

Belhaven University (Courtesy Belhaven University)

in the former residence of Col. Jones Hamilton, located on Boyd Street, and took its name from Hamilton's ancestral home in Scotland. On 7 February 1895, just seven months after it opened, the college burned to the ground. A new, larger structure was erected on the same site and opened in the fall of 1896. Fire struck again in 1910, resulting in a total loss. The college then moved a few blocks north to its present location on Peachtree Street, where it occupied a new three-story brick structure on a fifty-five-acre campus. A third major fire on 9 August 1927 destroyed the central portion of the building, although the north and south wings were salvaged. Covered in stucco and painted white, they became the present Fitzhugh and Preston Halls.

The name and ownership of the college changed several times during its early years. James Rhea Preston purchased the college from Fitzhugh's heirs in 1904 and operated it until 1911, when he donated the "name and goodwill" to the Central Mississippi Presbytery of the Presbyterian Church. From 1911 to 1917 the college was known as Belhaven Collegiate and Industrial Institute.

Guy Tillman Gillespie served as president between 1921 and 1954 but struggled to gain accreditation for the college. Inadequate library holdings, low faculty salaries, and lack of endowment were the three shortcomings cited by the Southern Association of Colleges and Schools as reasons for withholding accreditation until 1946.

Following World War II, costs escalated as enrollment declined from a peak of 310 full-time students in 1945 to a low of 140 in 1953. Threatened with the possible loss of its newly earned accreditation, the college underwent a major transformation that included the retirement of Gillespie, who did not favor either coeducation or intercollegiate sports, and his replacement by Robert McFerran Crowe, who served as Belhaven's president from 1954 to 1960. Crowe not only opened the college to men and added athletic programs but worked to raise the faculty's professional standards and to strengthen the academic program. In 1958 the board of trustees assumed governance of the college from

the Presbyterian Church; the board received ownership of the college in 1972.

Since the mid-1980s, under the leadership of presidents Newton Wilson (1986–95) and Roger Parrott (1995–), Belhaven has undergone an ambitious program of modernization and expansion. Graduate programs have been introduced and satellite campuses opened in Memphis and Orlando. In 2010 Belhaven College became Belhaven University. The school's mission remains offering a blend of Christian faith, liberal arts, and career preparation on a campus that encourages racial and cultural diversity.

Notable Belhaven graduates have included artist Marie Hull and author Elizabeth Spencer. Eudora Welty lived most of her life in her family's home across the street from the campus.

Paul R. Waibel
Belhaven University

James F. Gordon Jr., *A History of Belhaven College, 1894 to 1981* (1983); Paul R. Waibel, *Belhaven College* (2000).

Bell, Charles G.
(1916–2010) Writer and Educator

In a time when academic specialization is the rule, Charles G. Bell's career as a physicist, poet, novelist, philosopher, historian, art and music historian, and professor was a dramatic exception. From the Mississippi Delta to Europe and finally to the Santa Fe desert, Bell's journey of learning and teaching helped to create an eclectic and impressive body of work.

Bell was born on Halloween night 1916 in Greenville, Mississippi. His parents, Percy Bell and Nona Archer Bell, encouraged their son's intellectual development from the start. Indeed, Bell claimed that he could not remember learning to read. He excelled in school and survived the great flood of 1927. The river as much as the land was instrumental to his development. He often referenced his "Tom and Huck" childhood and acknowledged that the racial politics of his childhood informed his writing.

Bell's voracious reading was the start of a lifetime of learning. He earned a bachelor's degree in physics from the University of Virginia in 1936. He then won a 1938–39 Rhodes Scholarship to the University of Oxford in England, earning two bachelor's degrees and a master's degree. During that time, Bell's younger brother, a University of the South student, committed suicide; Bell returned home for a semester, and the tragedy shaped his future writing. After completing his formal education, Bell lectured at many colleges and universities, and during World War II he did physics research at Princeton. Bell also received a Rockefeller fellowship, a Ford Foundation fellowship, and a Fulbright fellowship.

Bell's collections of poetry are *Songs for a New America* (1953), *Delta Return* (1956), and *Five Chambered Heart* (1986). His poems, especially those in *Delta Return*, are often recognizably the work of a southern male but also transcend the regional label. His novels, *The Married Land* (1962) and *The Half Gods* (1968), similarly come from the perspective of a man from the South but explore universal themes. Bell also made *The Spirit of Rome* (1964), a film for *Encyclopedia Britannica*. He published an autobiography, *Millennial Harvest* (2007), at age ninety.

Bell's masterwork, *Symbolic History through Sight and Sound*, is a sixty-hour video cultural history of the world that brings alive history, art, music, politics, philosophy, and literature using thousands of images of art and architecture. Bell gave the dates of the project as 1970–1990, but his academic career suggests that he may have begun the endeavor as a child in his father's library.

Bell befriended such luminaries as Albert Einstein, Walker Percy, John Berryman, William Carlos Williams, and scores of other famous and lesser-known people. In addition to his poetry collections and novels, he published numerous essays, poems, and stories in popular and academic periodicals. Bell spent nearly four decades living in Santa Fe and was tutor emeritus at St. John's College. Through his career, however, traces of "the Yazoo and Mississippi flood plain of [his] Huck-Finn-and-Tarzan-of-the-Apes origin" remained. Near the end of his life, he moved to Maine to live with one of his daughters, and he died on Christmas Day 2010.

Ben Gilstrap
University of Mississippi

Contemporary Authors New Revision Series, vol. 2 (1981); Mississippi Writers and Musicians website, www.mswritersandmusicians.com.

Bell, James "Cool Papa"
(1903–1991) Athlete

James "Cool Papa" Bell was by all accounts the fastest and one of the best baseball players in the Negro Leagues. Born in Starkville, Mississippi, in 1903, Bell grew up on a farm not far from Mississippi State College. He learned to play baseball in Mississippi but never played in an organized league until he left the state. He moved to St. Louis in 1920, looking both for work and for a chance to play baseball for

pay, and never again lived in Mississippi. His first job was in a St. Louis meatpacking house, and he soon was playing semipro and then professional baseball for the city's African American teams.

Bell was especially famous for his speed and his calm under pressure. He received the nicknames "Cool" and later "Cool Papa" in the early 1920s in recognition of his demeanor when facing the biggest stars in the Negro Leagues. Two stories about Bell's speed have become so common that commentators sometimes use them as general descriptions about any fast baseball player. According to teammate Satchel Paige, Bell could turn out the light and be in bed before the room got dark. Another story says that Bell was hit by his own batted ball as he rounded second base.

Bell had a long and impressive career as a centerfielder, hitter, and base stealer. Between 1922 and 1946 he played for the St. Louis Stars, the Pittsburgh Crawfords, the Detroit Wolves, the Kansas City Monarchs, the Chicago American Giants, the Memphis Red Sox, and the Homestead Grays. In 1937 he left the Negro Leagues to play for a team Cuban dictator Rafael Trujillo owned in Santo Domingo; he also played in Mexico. He returned to the Negro Leagues in 1942, played until 1946, and then served as a player-coach until 1950. Negro League statistics are spotty, but Bell consistently hit in the mid-.300s and led his leagues in stolen bases. He was the leadoff hitter in the Negro League's East-West all-star games from 1933 to 1936 and from 1942 to 1944.

On one occasion when Bell and his Negro League teammates were traveling through Mississippi, the team bus stopped at a diner in Picayune, but the restaurant's African American owner encouraged them to keep driving so that local authorities would not put the players to work on plantations. Bell spent much of his later life as a custodian and night watchman at St. Louis's City Hall. He lived long enough to see baseball fans pay tribute to his skills. He was elected to the Baseball Hall of Fame in Cooperstown in 1974, and at least two cities, St. Louis and Jackson, Mississippi, named streets for him. He died in March 1991, only a few weeks after his wife, Clara Bell.

Ted Ownby
University of Mississippi

Dick Clark and Larry Lester, eds., *The Negro Leagues Book* (1994); Donald Honig, *A Donald Honig Reader* (1988); William F. McNeil, *Cool Papas and Double Duties: The All-Time Greats of the Negro Leagues* (2001); Robert Peterson, *Only the Ball Was White: A History of Legendary Black Players and All-Black Professional Teams* (1992); Arthur Shaffer and Charles Korr, interview with Cool Papa Bell, Black Community Leaders Project, Western Historical Manuscript Collection, University of Missouri–St. Louis.

Bellamann, Katherine
(1877–1956) Writer

A novelist and poet in her own right, Katherine Jones Bellamann's many artistic accomplishments were often overshadowed by those of her husband, Henry Bellamann, a poet and novelist best known for his 1940 novel, *Kings Row*. Katherine was very proud of her unique creative association with her husband and described it vividly in her foreword to *Parris Mitchell of Kings Row*, her husband's unfinished sequel to *Kings Row*, which she completed in 1948, after his death. The combined papers and manuscripts of Henry and Katherine Bellamann, housed in the University of Mississippi's Department of Archives and Special Collections, testify that the work of the two writers was closely entwined: they often shared notebooks and sometimes even single pages. Because Henry Bellamann was the more famous writer, it is easy to lose sight of the fact that Katherine Bellamann published two novels of her own, one seventeen years before *Parris Mitchell of Kings Row* and the other several years later.

Born Katherine Jones in Carthage, Mississippi, on 7 October 1877, she was teaching at Grayson College in Texas when she married Henry Bellamann in 1907. The two took teaching posts at Chicora College in Greenville, South Carolina. When the college moved to Columbia, they went, too, and over the next decade they entertained such eminent people as Carl Sandburg, Amy Lowell, and Charles Ives. In 1924 Henry Bellamann began teaching at Juilliard in New York; Katherine joined him a year later.

Katherine Bellamann's literary efforts were not limited to novels. Her sketchbooks reveal that throughout her life she wrote hundreds of poems, some of which were published in journals and in two small volumes in 1956 and 1958 (posthumously). Many of Bellamann's verses can be classified as romantic southern nature poems, and she experimented with sonnets.

During the last years of her life, she devoted herself almost exclusively to poetry and became actively involved with several poetry societies and journals. After her husband died in 1945, she returned to Jackson and lived there until her death on 8 November 1956. She was buried with her husband in New York City.

Brenda Ayres
Liberty University

Leslie Campbell Rampey
Middle Georgia College

Harry McBrayer Bayne, "A Critical Study of Henry Bellamann's Life and Work" (PhD dissertation, University of Mississippi, 1990); Henry and Katherine Bellamann Collection, Department of Archives and Special Collections, J. D. Williams Library, University of Mississippi; Leslie Jean Campbell, "Henry Bellamann's *Kings Row*: A Reevaluation of a Forgotten Best-Seller" (master's thesis, University of Mississippi, 1978); Jay Miles Karr, introduction, *Parris Mitchell of Kings Row* (1986); James B. Lloyd, *Lives of Mississippi Authors, 1817–1967* (1981); Mississippi Writers and Musicians Project website, www.mswritersandmusicians.com.

B

Bender, William Albert
(1886–1957) Educator and Activist

In 1934 Rev. William Albert Bender began serving as chaplain at Tougaloo College near Jackson, and he was serving in that capacity in 1946 when he voted in the first statewide election since the US Supreme Court outlawed all-white primaries in 1944. Though local newspapers warned African Americans not to vote, and Theodore Bilbo, one of the candidates, urged white voters to prevent blacks from doing so, Bender persuaded two Tougaloo students to drive him to Ridgeland to cast his ballot. He was a registered voter, but when he arrived at the polls, he was stopped first by three white men and then by the deputy sheriff, who drew his pistol. Bender was ultimately denied his vote, and shortly after the incident, a cross was burned on the Tougaloo campus.

After returning to Jackson, Bender filed a complaint with the US Attorney General's Office, and a US Senate committee began investigating the election, employing Bender as a key witness to link Bilbo's campaign speeches to the intimidation of black voters. While under investigation, Bilbo agreed to take a leave of absence for his health, and he died before he could rejoin the Senate.

In addition to leading one of the first open and organized challenges to the State of Mississippi's discrimination and denial of civil rights, Bender was a leader of Jackson's chapter of the National Association for the Advancement of Colored People and was instrumental in the organization's suit to equalize the salaries of public schoolteachers. Because of Bender's accomplishments in Jackson, one of the organization's attorneys, Thurgood Marshall, recommended him to serve as the first president of the group's Mississippi State Conference, responsible for coordinating statewide efforts and initiating new chapters.

Amy Schmidt
Lyon College

John Dittmer, *Local People: The Struggle for Civil Rights in Mississippi* (1994); Charles M. Payne, *I've Got the Light of Freedom: The Organizing Tradition and the Mississippi Freedom Struggle* (1995); Mississippi Digital Library Website, Tougaloo College Digital Collection, www.msdiglib.org.

Bennett, Lerone, Jr.

(b. 1928) Activist and Author

Born in Clarksdale, Mississippi, in 1928, Lerone Bennett Jr. has since the 1960s been one of the most prolific authors describing African American history and its place in contemporary struggles for justice. He is most famous as a senior editor and executive editor at *Ebony* magazine and as the author of numerous books on history and civil rights.

After graduating from Morehouse College in Atlanta, Bennett went to work as a journalist first at the *Atlanta Daily World*, then at *Jet*, and then at *Ebony*, where he served as a contributor and editor from 1953 to 2005. The Chicago publication has long been a central institution for African Americans, and Bennett wrote countless essays that connected contemporary issues with African American history.

Bennett's historical essays in *Ebony* became the basis for his first book, *Before the Mayflower: A History of the Negro in America, 1618–1962* (1962), published by John H. Johnson, who was also the publisher of *Ebony*. With a title that emphasized the fact that African Americans' presence in North America predated the Pilgrims, Bennett wrote to show "the depth of involvement of Negroes in the American experience." His books stress the continuity of African American struggle; many of his writings take a broad historical view that shows the deep roots of self-determination and protest. History mattered in whatever he discussed: as he wrote in *The Challenge of Blackness* (1972), "History is everything; it is everywhere." In *Confrontation: Black and White* (1965), he emphasized that fighting back defined African American history, and he did the same with his choice of subjects in *Wade in the Water: Great Moments in Black History* (1979)— Richard Allen, Nat Turner, Frederick Douglass, Harriet Tubman, African American Civil War soldiers, political leaders in Reconstruction South Carolina, Jack Johnson, Marcus Garvey, A. Philip Randolph, the *Brown* decision, the Montgomery Bus Boycott, the Greensboro sit-ins, and the March on Washington. Bennett made clear the political implications of his work. When the term *Black Power* became a point of controversy in the mid-1960s, Bennett situated it as part of a long legacy by titling his 1967 history of southern Reconstruction *Black Power USA*.

As an author and activist, Bennett has been involved in many struggles. He taught for a year at Northwestern University in the early days of its Black Studies Program, and he has served on numerous boards and in consulting positions. But he is surely most notable for his willingness to lead and write about confrontation. Like many activists who use the phrase *Black Power*, he criticizes white Americans who take the roles of heroes of liberalism. In *The Negro Mood* (1964) Bennett took to task whites who wished blacks well but did not address issues of power. In "Have We Overcome?," a 1978 talk at the University of Mississippi, Bennett argued that the civil rights movement had not overcome injustice. Despite its many successes, the struggle for freedom had taught four lessons: reform is a long and hard process, reformers have to force change from their oppressors, real change relies on "a fundamental transformation of institutional structures," and "the problem of race in Mississippi, and in America, is a white problem." His 2000 book about Abraham Lincoln pictured the president as a white supremacist not particularly interested in African American freedom and clearly opposed to African American equality. Subsequent discussions of the issue of reparations as "back pay" returned Bennett in his chosen position as a leader of confrontation.

Ted Ownby
University of Mississippi

Lerone Bennett Jr., *Forced into Glory: Abraham Lincoln's White Dream* (2000); Lerone Bennett Jr., *The Shaping of Black America* (1975), in *Have We Overcome?*, ed. Michael Namorato (1978).

Benton, Samuel

(1820–1864) Confederate General

Confederate general Samuel Benton, a nephew of Senator Thomas Hart Benton of Missouri, was born on 18 October 1820, probably in Williamson County, Tennessee. After a brief interval as a schoolteacher, Benton migrated to Holly Springs, Mississippi, where he became a prominent lawyer and politician. He represented Marshall County at the 1861 secession convention and voted for disunion.

His political status probably helped him win the captaincy of Company D, the Jeff Davis Rifles, in the 9th Infantry Regiment early in the war, and he was appointed colonel of the 37th Mississippi Infantry Regiment when it was organized in April 1862. The regiment was reorganized in early 1862 and renamed the 34th Mississippi. It participated in the 1862 Kentucky Campaign and fought valiantly at the Battle of Perryville on 8 October, reputedly suffering a 50 percent casualty rate. In late 1862 the command was transferred to a brigade led by Gen. Edward C. Walthall. At Chickamauga the regiment was heavily engaged, but Benton was apparently absent from his command, and a major led the unit.

Benton was back in charge at Lookout Mountain, where on 24 November 1863 the 34th Mississippi lost 4 wounded and 231 missing, most of them captured after they were assigned picket duty at the foot of the western slope and were overwhelmed by a rapid Union advance. By the time the Atlanta Campaign opened, the regiment was severely reduced in numbers, but at Resaca it lost 15 more men out of the 198 in action. The unit participated in the incessant maneuvering and skirmishing that marked the campaign, and when Walthall was promoted to divisional command, Benton took charge of the brigade.

At the Battle of Atlanta on 22 July 1864, Benton was leading his command when he was struck over the heart by a shell and sustained a wound to his right foot that resulted in amputation. Although Benton was commissioned a brigadier general effective 26 July 1864, he never knew of the promotion, dying in the hospital at Griffin, Georgia, on 28 July.

Christopher Losson
St. Joseph, Missouri

Samuel Benton subject file, Mississippi Department of Archives and History; Charles E. Hooker, *Confederate Military History: Mississippi*, ed. Clement A. Evans (1899; Kenneth W. Noe, *Perryville: This Grand Havoc of Battle* (2001)); Dunbar Rowland, *Military History of Mississippi, 1803–1898*, taken from *The Official and Statistical Register of the State of Mississippi, 1908* (1988).

Benton County

Bordering Tennessee in north-central Mississippi, Benton County was organized during Reconstruction from sections of neighboring Marshall and Tippah Counties. Founded on 15 July 1870, the county comprises land formerly belonging to the Chickasaw Nation and relinquished to the United States in the 1834 Treaty of Pontotoc. According to various sources, locals declared Sen. Thomas H. Benton of Missouri to be the county's official namesake to conceal their true allegiance to Confederate general Samuel Benton of Holly Springs. Ashland, Benton's county seat, is named after the home of Henry Clay, a Kentucky legislator and an antebellum secretary of state.

In its first census in 1880, Benton County reported a population of 11,023 people, divided almost evenly between African Americans and whites. Sharecroppers and tenants cultivated the majority of the county's farms, concentrating production on grain, livestock, and tobacco rather than cotton. By 1900, 57 percent of the county's 1,550 white farmers owned their land, while only one-tenth of Benton's African American farming community could claim ownership.

As in much of Mississippi, Baptists made up a majority of churchgoers in Benton. The 1916 religious census reported that the National Baptist Convention and the Southern Baptist Convention were the county's two largest groups, with the Methodist Episcopal Church, South, and the Colored Methodist Episcopal Church also significant.

The decline in Benton County's population during the first decades of the twentieth century paralleled diminishing farm ownership. Only about a third of the county's farmers owned their own land in 1930. Four years later Benton County became one of the first counties to receive electric power from the Tennessee Valley Authority.

By 1960 Benton's agricultural production largely consisted of corn, cotton, soybeans, wheat, and oats. The county had also developed small but substantial timber and textile manufacturing industries. County population was 7,723 that year. During the decades that followed, the number of people making their living in agriculture dropped sharply.

Benton County is the home of poet James A. Autry, who was born between Ashland and Hickory Flat in 1933, the son and grandson of Baptist ministers. Autry's work has often contrasted rural Mississippi life with the modern world.

From 2000 to 2010 Benton's population grew from 8,026 to 8,729. Like most counties in north-central Mississippi, Benton County had a white majority (61 percent of residents, compared to 37 percent who were African American), and its population had grown over the previous half century (by 1,005 people, or about 13 percent).

Mississippi Encyclopedia Staff
University of Mississippi

Mississippi State Planning Commission, *Progress Report on State Planning in Mississippi* (1938); *Mississippi Statistical Abstract*, Mississippi State University (1952–2010); Charles Sydnor and Claude Bennett, *Mississippi History* (1939); University of Virginia Library, Historical Census Browser website, http://mapserver.lib.virginia.edu; E. Nolan Waller and Dani A. Smith, *Growth Profiles of Mississippi's Counties, 1960–1980* (1985).

Berry, D. C.
(b. 1942) Poet

Poet David Chapman Berry Jr. was born on 23 July 1942 in Vicksburg, Mississippi, the only son of David C. Berry and Annette Hays Berry. The family, which also included daughter Betty, born in 1946, moved to Greenville, where his father ran several service stations. Berry graduated from Greenville High School in 1960 and moved on to study science and English at Delta State University in Cleveland.

While commuting to Delta State, Berry worked in the emergency room at Greenville's General Hospital.

After graduating from Delta State in 1965 and turning down medical school, Berry and his wife, Terri Stoutenborough, whom he had met and married that summer, moved to Flint, Michigan, where he was a member of the management staff at General Motors. In the summer of 1966, Berry was drafted by the US Army and served for three years in the Medical Corps, attaining the rank of captain. Berry spent much of that time in Vietnam, where he wrote the poems for his first collection, *Saigon Cemetery* (1972).

Berry subsequently returned to school and in 1973 received a doctorate in English from the University of Tennessee, writing a dissertation on the poetry of James Dickey. After his divorce from Stoutenborough, Berry and his second wife, Anne, had one child, David Berry III. That union also ended, and in 1985 Berry married Sarah Adele Rawls from Columbia, Mississippi; their son, Hays, was born the following year.

An Episcopalian, Berry began writing poetry in the ninth grade out of boredom while in church, motivated by his early interest in "the sound of language as an art form." Boredom and mental conflicts, he stated in an interview, led him to write poetry while in Vietnam. Though Berry says he was in no danger in Vietnam, George Garrett, in his foreword to *Saigon Cemetery*, praises Berry's consistency in "telling the truth" about the war. *Divorce Boxing* (1998) contains satiric poems that reflect Berry's two failed marriages as well as writings that examine the death of his father and his mother's cancer.

Berry has described the purpose of his poetry as to "celebrate, to *realize*, to discover" the things around him, especially in his native Mississippi: "I want to use common things and common sounds to discover the uncommon insight." Widely published in little magazines, literary journals, and anthologies of Mississippi writers, Berry is often asked for his advice to students who want to learn to write poetry: "Read, write, and erase."

Berry taught at the Center for Writers at the University of Southern Mississippi in Hattiesburg for twenty-seven years. He has served as editor of the *Mississippi Review* and has received numerous teaching and writing awards and grants, including recognition from the Mississippi Arts Commission, the Mississippi Institute of Arts and Letters, the *Florida Review*, and the Southern Federation of State Arts Agencies. Now a resident of Oxford, he created the Elvis Meets Einstein Award Fund in 2012 to provide income each year for two students in the master of fine arts program in the English department at the University of Mississippi.

Gary Kerley
Gainesville, Georgia

Dorothy Abbott, ed., *Mississippi Writers: Reflections of Childhood and Youth* (1988); D. C. Berry, *Divorce Boxing* (1998); D. C. Berry, *Hamlet Off Stage* (2009); D. C. Berry, *Jawbone* (1978); D. C. Berry, *Saigon Cemetery* (1972); Hal May and James G. Lesniek, eds., *Contemporary Authors: New Revision Series*, vol. 27 (1989); Noel Polk and James R. Scafidel, eds., *An Anthology of Mississippi Writers* (1979); Colleen Marie Ryor, *Adirondack Review* (Summer 2003).

Berry, Modena Lowrey

(1850–1942) Educator

Born at Farmington in present-day Alcorn County on 16 November 1850, Modena Lowrey was the oldest of eleven children of Gen. Mark Perrin Lowrey and Sarah Holmes Lowrey. Only ten years old when the Civil War began, she held her ground when Union soldiers came looking for her father, telling them rather confidently, "He's in the army killing Yankees." After a few more questions, the soldiers left, convinced that she could only have been so emphatic if what she said were the truth. Neither Modena nor the soldiers realized that her father was hiding in the attic of the house, watching from a window.

Her education was piecemeal, much of it coming from reading the King James Version of the Bible, but she graduated from Stonewall College in Ripley. She attended the Baptist Female Seminary at Pontotoc, where she later taught for several years. She spent most of her summers at Lake Chautauqua, New York, attending lectures. In the fall of 1873 she helped her father establish the Blue Mountain Female Institute (later renamed Blue Mountain College).

In 1876 Modena married Rev. William Edwin Berry, who joined the faculty of Blue Mountain College and served as

Modena Lowrey Berry (Courtesy Blue Mountain College)

professor of Greek and Latin and business manager until his death in 1919. The couple had three children.

"Mother Berry," as the women at the college affectionately called her, served as Blue Mountain's principal and vice president from 1873 to 1934. She continued to advise and show her genuine concern for the students until her death. Her college "daughters" honored her on two special occasions, her eightieth and ninetieth birthdays in 1930 and 1940, noting, "She loved life. She loved laughter. She loved humanity." She served the college and the students she loved throughout the presidencies of her father, two of her brothers, and a nephew.

On Berry's ninetieth birthday, Pres. Franklin D. Roosevelt sent a letter in honor of her achievements, and the college presented a pageant, "A Harvest of Light," involving more than one hundred women. The college also dedicated the Modena Lowrey Berry Auditorium to honor her work, faith, commitment, and vision.

Modena Lowrey Berry died at home in Blue Mountain on 31 January 1942 at the age of ninety-one. The state legislature passed a resolution requesting that the board of trustees of the Mississippi Department of Archives and History place a painting of her in the Mississippi Hall of Fame in Jackson, making her the second woman so honored. Gen. Mark Perrin Lowrey's portrait also hangs there: they are the only father-daughter combination in the state's Hall of Fame.

Thomas D. Cockrell
Northeast Mississippi
Community College

Modena Lowrey Berry Papers, Archives of the National Alumnae Association of Blue Mountain College, Blue Mountain, Mississippi; David E. Guyton, *Mother Berry of Blue Mountain* (1942); *Jackson Daily News* (16 November 1940); *Memphis Commercial Appeal* (1 February 1942); *Southern Sentinel* (5 February 1942); Robbie Neal Sumrall, *A Light on a Hill: A History of Blue Mountain College* (1947); *Tupelo Daily News* (16 November 1940).

Best, Willie
(1913–1962) Actor

Born on 27 May 1913 in Sunflower, William Best was an African American actor in television and film. Lauded for his comedic talent, Best had minor roles in more than one hundred movies, including such notable films as *Cabin in the Sky*, *Ghost Breakers*, and *High Sierra*. Best received screen credit for many of his performances, an uncommon honor for an actor of his status. Bob Hope, who appeared with Best in *Ghost Breakers*, declared him "the best actor I know."

Best purportedly traveled to Hollywood from Mississippi as a chauffeur and later signed a contract with RKO studios. He made his first on-screen appearance as Charcoal in Harold Lloyd's 1930 film *Feet First*. Best was occasionally billed as Sleep 'n' Eat in the early years of his career, and in 1940 the *New York Times* described him as "a slightly accelerated Stepin Fetchit." Much like Fetchit, Best was typecast as a cringing, ignorant caricature of racist African American stereotypes, a fact that earned him opprobrium from civil rights activists. Though the film industry claimed that Best enjoyed playing these roles, in a 1934 interview, the actor said, "I often think about these roles I have to play. Most of them are pretty broad. Sometimes I tell the director and he cuts out the real bad parts." Best continued, "But what's an actor going to do? Either you do it or get out."

In 2000 Spike Lee invoked Sleep 'n' Eat in the movie *Bamboozled*, a minstrel satire criticizing contemporary representations of African Americans. Excerpts from Best's work were also included in Melvin Van Peebles 1998 documentary *Classified X*, which lambasted historical portrayals of African Americans in cinema.

Although a 1951 arrest for possession of narcotics severed his relationship with the film industry, Best continued acting into the mid-1950s, landing regular roles on several of Hal Roach's television series, including *The Stu Erwin Show* and *My Little Margie*. Best died of cancer in 1962 at the Motion Picture Home Hospital in Woodland Hills, California.

Kathryn Radishofski
Columbia University

Thomas Cripps, *Slow Fade to Black: The Negro in American Film, 1900–1942* (1977); Bosley Crowther, *New York Times* (July 1940); Hal Erickson, Internet Movie Database website, www.imdb.com.

Bevel, James
(1936–2008) Civil Rights Activist

James Bevel was born 19 October 1936 in Itta Bena, Mississippi. After graduating from high school, Bevel served a stint in the military before moving to Nashville to attend American Baptist Theological Seminary. While living in Nashville, he joined the Southern Christian Leadership Conference and attended workshops at the Highlander Folk School in Monteagle, Tennessee, where he and other civil rights activists learned techniques for organizing communities. In addition to the Highlander workshops, Bevel attended James Lawson's workshops on nonviolent direct action and employed those strategies in a series of sit-ins that desegregated Nashville's lunch counters.

During the summer of 1961 Bevel and other Nashville activists joined the Freedom Rides after the initial participants encountered the violence of white mobs and were injured. Arrested in Jackson, Mississippi, Bevel and others were jailed; at the end of the summer, when local and county jails were overflowing with several hundred Freedom Riders, Gov. Ross Barnett moved Bevel's group to Parchman State Penitentiary. After his release from Parchman, Bevel began working full time for the newly formed Student Nonviolent Coordinating Committee (SNCC). Bevel and several other veterans of the Freedom Rides set up a SNCC office in Jackson to help coordinate the group's Mississippi Project for voting rights.

Bevel, however, was part of a SNCC faction that focused more on desegregation than on voter registration, and he led a campaign urging students to participate in nonviolent direct action protests. With Bevel's encouragement, students from Jackson State and Tougaloo College formed the Jackson Nonviolent Movement. After encouraging the students to stage a sit-in, Bevel was arrested and later convicted of contributing to the delinquency of minors. Such consequences, however, failed to deter Bevel, and in 1962 he organized a boycott of the city's segregated buses. That year he married Diane Nash, another veteran of the Nashville sit-ins who was in Jackson working for SNCC. Though the couple later divorced, they worked on social justice projects together for a number of years.

Shortly after marrying, Bevel and Nash left Jackson for Cleveland, Mississippi, where they lived with Amzie Moore, setting up citizenship classes for voter registration, leading workshops on nonviolent direct action, and sending letters to prominent whites urging them to support the movement. Using Cleveland as a base for his work throughout the Delta, Bevel regularly spoke at mass meetings about voter registration, educational and economic issues, and nonviolent direct action. Bevel also organized efforts for desegregation and voter registration in Clarksdale and McComb, and in Greenwood he coordinated voter registration efforts with food and clothing distribution centers. Bevel also worked with Fannie Lou Hamer to form the Mississippi Freedom Democratic Party, which challenged Mississippi's delegation to the Democratic National Convention in 1964.

By the mid-1960s Bevel extended his civil rights activities beyond Mississippi. In Alabama, he organized the Children's March in Birmingham as well as the 1965 march from Selma to Montgomery. In 1963 he coordinated efforts for the March on Washington, and in 1966 he began working for the Chicago freedom movement to improve housing. Before leaving the Southern Christian Leadership Council in 1969, Bevel helped with the 1968 Memphis sanitation workers' strike. In the 1980s he founded Students for Education and Economic Development, and in 1992 he helped organize the Million Man March. Bevel served for many years as pastor of the Hebraic-Christian-Islamic Assembly in Chicago. In 2008 Bevel was convicted of unlawful fornication and sentenced to fifteen years in prison. Seven months later, freed on bail in preparation for appeal, he died of cancer.

Amy Schmidt
Lyon College

Raymond Arsenault, *Freedom Riders: 1961 and the Struggle for Racial Justice* (2006); Clayborne Carson, *In Struggle: SNCC and the Black Awakening of the 1960s* (1981); John Dittmer, *Local People: The Struggle for Civil Rights in Mississippi* (1994); Ernest M. Limbo, in *The Human Rights Tradition in the Civil Rights Movement*, ed. Susan M. Glisson (2006); Charles M. Payne, *I've Got the Light of Freedom: The Organizing Tradition and the Mississippi Freedom Struggle* (1995); Jennifer A. Stollman, in *The Human Rights Tradition in the Civil Rights Movement*, ed. Susan M. Glisson (2006); Howard Zinn, *SNCC: The New Abolitionists* (2002).

Biedenharn, Joseph

(1866–1952) Businessperson

Born on 13 December 1866 in Vicksburg, Joseph Biedenharn was the eldest of twelve children born to Herman Biedenharn, a German immigrant, and Louisa Wilhelmine Lundberg Biedenharn, a native of Denmark. Herman Biedenharn and his brother, Henry, founded a retail confectionary business in Vicksburg, and Joseph grew up working in the store.

In 1888, at the age of twenty-two, Joseph Biedenharn inherited the confectionary business and renamed it Biedenharn Candy Company. The operation remained a family affair, with his seven younger brothers working in the store. Joseph married Anna Schlottman the following year. The business expanded, and in 1890 Biedenharn Candy Company started serving its customers a new fountain drink, Coca-Cola. Herman Biedenharn had imparted some lasting wisdom: "Son, go into the nickel business. Everybody's got a nickel. People will spend a nickel, but they will hold on to a dime." Sales of five-cent glasses of Coca-Cola took off.

Coca-Cola's rise in popularity had in many ways paralleled the Biedenharns' progress in Vicksburg. Created in 1886 by chemist Dr. J. S. Pemberton of Atlanta, the product was originally available only at a single Atlanta soda fountain. Asa Candler, a wholesale druggist in the city, bought into the fledgling Coca-Cola Company, added the new soda to his product line, and used creative marketing strategies and a sales force of mobile representatives to boost the drink's popularity. Joseph Biedenharn already sold carbonated soda to local vendors and decided to become a wholesaler, providing Coca-Cola syrup to soda vendors in Mississippi.

At the time, Coca-Cola could be purchased only at soda fountain counters, where the syrup was mixed with carbonated soda, but in Biedenharn's words, "I wanted to bring Coca-Cola to the country people outside the limits of the fountain. Even in the cities, the fountains were often limited in number and scattered here and there. I could see that many townsfolk wanted Coca-Cola, but it was not easily available." In 1894 Biedenharn's operation on Washington Street in Vicksburg became the first Coca-Cola bottler. After sending the first twelve bottles to Candler, Biedenharn set out in a horse and buggy and sold bottled Coca-Cola to the people of rural Mississippi for seventy cents per case. All seven of Biedenharn's brothers followed his lead, establishing additional Coca-Cola bottling plants in Mississippi, Texas, Arkansas, and Louisiana.

In 1913 Joe and Anna Biedenharn and their three children moved to Monroe, Louisiana, where he continued bottling operations and expanded into other successful businesses. In 1944, commemorating fifty years of bottling Coca-Cola, company president Harrison Jones honored Biedenharn, and his portrait was hung in the halls of the Atlanta headquarters. Bidenharn died in 1952. The family's former home in Louisiana is now open to the public as the Biedenharn Museum and Gardens. In 1979 the Biedenharn family reacquired the building on Washington Street in Vicksburg where Coca-Cola was first bottled, and the Vicksburg Foundation for Historic Preservation now owns it and operates it as the Biedenharn Coca-Cola Museum.

Chris Colbeck

University of Mississippi

Correspondence with Nancy Bell, Vicksburg Foundation for Historic Preservation, Biedenharn Coca-Cola Museum; Emy-Lou Biedenharn, *Biedenharn Heritage 1852–1952* (1962); Biedenharn Museum and Gardens website, www.bmuseum.org; Coca-Cola Company website, www.the coca-colacompany.com; Dennis Seid, *Northeast Mississippi Daily Journal* (9 September 2007); Pat Watters, *Coca-Cola: An Illustrated History* (1978).

Bienville, Jean-Baptiste Le Moyne, Sieur de

(1680–1768) Governor of French Louisiana

Jean-Baptiste Le Moyne, Sieur de Bienville was a high official and then governor of Louisiana, including present Mississippi, during the French regime (1699–1763) and was the colony's dominant political personality until 1743.

He was baptized on 23 February 1680 in Montreal, the eighth son of Charles Le Moyne, Sieur de Longueuil, and Catherine Thierry/Primot. In 1692 Jean-Baptiste inherited the Bienville title after the death of his brother, François. He served in the navy (1692–97) during the War of the League of Augsburg and then accompanied an elder brother, Pierre Le Moyne, Sieur d'Iberville, on his 1688–89 expedition to rediscover the mouth of the Mississippi and found a colony. Iberville left Ensign Sauvolle in charge at Biloxi (in present Ocean Springs), with Bienville second in command.

When Sauvolle's died on 22 August 1701 Bienville became the principal military commander as king's lieutenant (1701–13), commandant (1713–17), and commandant general (1717–25), but he never became governor because of quarrels among Louisiana's governing elite and suspicions directed at the Le Moyne family after Iberville's death. Accused of maladministration, Bienville was recalled to France for "consultation," leaving in the late summer of 1725. He was shelved despite a convincing defense but eventually returned triumphantly in February 1733, having finally received the title of royal governor when the Company of the Indies surrendered its concession. After requesting relief, he departed on 17 August 1743. He died in Paris on 7 March 1767, anguished by the cession of "his" colony to Spain following the French and Indian War.

Bienville resided primarily at Biloxi until about 1722. He founded Mobile (1711) and New Orleans (1717), which became the capital in 1722. He played prominent or decisive roles in building several forts in or near Mississippi: Fort Maurepas (1699) in present Ocean City; Fort Louis (1702) on the Mobile at Twenty-Seven Mile Bluff, later moved to the mouth of the river (1711); Fort Rosalie (1716) at Natchez; Fort St. Pierre (1719), about nine miles from the mouth of the Yazoo at Vicksburg; and Fort Tombecbé (1736) at Jones Bluff on the Tombigbee near Epes, Alabama, thirty miles northeast of Meridian, Mississippi.

Bienville's services often involved relations with the Native Americans. He had known some of them from childhood and possessed a remarkable talent for learning their languages and customs. They visited him freely and stayed at his home. (He never married.) He sent young men to live among them to become translators and keep him informed. Many Native Americans esteemed him, mourned his absence after 1725, and celebrated his return in 1733. Nevertheless, he did not hesitate to compel their respect by employing tactics he had seen them use. For example, after the Natchez murdered four Canadian voyageurs in 1716, he enticed nineteen chiefs and warriors to negotiate, suddenly took them hostage, and threatened to raise an Indian coalition to annihilate their tribe. The Indians ultimately surrendered the seven killers, four of whom were among those Bienville had captured. The tribe quietly accepted his behavior and helped him to construct Fort Rosalie, as he had demanded.

Bienville knew that French influence among the Indians depended on increasing their reliance on Western goods, but France seldom could supply sufficient goods. He won over or suppressed some minor tribes but never brokered a permanent peace between the Choctaw and Chickasaw. By the 1720s the French were fully committed to the Choctaw, while the Chickasaw were persistently drawn to the English traders. In 1723 Bienville even recommended that Louisiana's security could be ensured by inciting intertribal warfare to eliminate the Indians. The context, however, suggests that he was playing a subtle game with the Company of the Indies' administration rather than conveying his personal views.

After his 1733 return, he reluctantly decided to end the Chickasaw conflict by destroying the tribe or forcing its members to leave the region. Two hugely expensive campaigns during the Chickasaw War (1732–43) failed dismally. Bienville negotiated a fragile peace with the wearied Chickasaw and resigned, aging, ailing, and exhausted by his exertions.

Typifying minor noblemen and the milieu of colonial Louisiana, Bienville routinely quarreled with rival civil and military authorities and yearned for promotions and the higher social status and the wealth they promised, but he inspired wide respect and affection for his determination, cunning, and inexhaustible resourcefulness.

David S. Newhall
Centre College

Dictionary of American Biography (1929); *Dictionary of Canadian Biography* (1974); W. J. Eccles, *France in America* (1972); Marcel Giraud, *Histoire de la Louisiane Française* (5 vols., 1953–87); John Brite Harris, *From Old Mobile to Fort Assumption* (1959); Patricia Dillon Woods, *French-Indian Relations on the Southern Frontier* (1980).

Big Black River Bridge, Battle of

The 17 May 1863 Battle of Big Black River Bridge, part of the Vicksburg Campaign, resulted from a Confederate Army attempt to slow Union pursuit as the Southerners retreated following their defeat at the Battle of Champion Hill. A division of Lt. Gen. John C. Pemberton's Southern army had become separated from the main body. Pemberton ordered the units headed by Maj. Gen. John S. Bowen and Brig. Gen. John Vaughn to hold the bridge over the Big Black River, less than twenty miles from Vicksburg, to allow time for the missing division to reunite with the army. Unbeknownst to Pemberton, however, the troops he was waiting for had been cut off by the enemy and were headed away from the river.

The Confederate line of entrenchments at the Big Black River Bridge was about a mile long and ran north to south inside a horseshoe-shaped curve on the east side of the river. Flanked by swampy terrain, it was fronted by relatively flat, open ground. Confederate manpower along the line was estimated at about four thousand, with nearly twenty pieces of artillery. To the rear of the fortifications were two bridges over the river: the Vicksburg and Jackson Railroad bridge, and a makeshift bridge formed by mooring the steamer *Dot* crossways in the river and removing its machinery.

Union troops under the command of Maj. Gen. John A. McClernand appeared on the edge of the fields in front of the Confederate works on the morning of 17 May 1863. An artillery engagement ensued, followed by a brisk exchange of musketry by sharpshooters from both sides. Not until the afternoon, however, did Brig. Gen. Mike Lawler's Iowa, Wisconsin, and Indiana troops attempt an attack. The Federals formed near the fortifications on the Confederate left while hidden from sight by a slight rise in the terrain known at the time as a "meander scar." At the command, US forces charged across the short span of open ground to the Confederate line, overrunning the entire southern position in less than three minutes.

The Confederates quickly abandoned their lines in a disorganized retreat to the bridges over the Big Black. In the confusion, some soldiers drowned as they tried to swim across. Only the foresight of army engineer Samuel Lockett prevented the catastrophe for Pemberton's army from being even worse: he had prepared the bridges to be burned in just such an emergency. Their destruction temporarily halted the Federals, giving the Southerners the time they needed to retreat to the Vicksburg lines.

The Union Army achieved total victory at Big Black River Bridge. For the relatively small cost of approximately 275 casualties, Federal forces inflicted heavy losses on the Confederates, including capturing more than 1,700 prisoners, 18 cannons, vast quantities of ammunition and small arms, and five battle flags. The battle left the Confederate Army weakened and effectively bottled up inside the Vicksburg lines, cut off from supply.

Mike Bunn
Historic Chattahoochee
Commission

Michael Ballard, *Pemberton: The General Who Lost Vicksburg* (1991); Leonard Fullenkamp, Stephen Bowman, and Jay Luvaas, eds., *Guide to the Vicksburg Campaign* (1998); Terrence Winschel, *Triumph and Defeat: The Vicksburg Campaign* (1999); Terrence Winschel, *Vicksburg: Fall of the Confederate Gibraltar* (1999).

Biggers, Neal B., Jr.

(b. 1935) Judge

Neal Brooks Biggers Jr. is senior US District Court judge for the Northern District of Mississippi. Biggers was born on 1 July 1935 in Corinth. He received his bachelor of arts degree from Millsaps College in 1956 and then joined the US Navy, serving until 1960. Biggers graduated cum laude from the University of Mississippi School of Law in 1963.

From 1963 to 1968 Biggers practiced law in the private sector. In 1964 he also served as a prosecuting attorney of Alcorn County. He was elected district attorney for the 1st Judicial District of Mississippi in 1968 and served until 1975. In 1974 he worked as an assistant instructor at the University of Mississippi. From 1975 to 1984 Biggers served as circuit judge for the 1st Judicial District of Mississippi.

In 1984 Pres. Ronald Reagan appointed Biggers to succeed William C. Keady as US District Court judge. Biggers took the oath of office on 28 March 1984 and served as chief judge from 1998 to 2000, when he took senior status.

In 1987 Biggers presided over the case that some call the *Brown v. Board of Education* of higher education. In 1975 a black Mississippi Delta sharecropper, Jake Ayers, filed a suit on behalf of his son, Jake Jr., against the State of Mississippi. Ayers claimed that the state had failed to desegregate its universities and sought more money and better programs for historically black universities. In *Ayers v. Musgrove* Biggers ruled that Mississippi had done enough to end segregation in the state: the US 5th Circuit Court of Appeals affirmed the decision, but the US Supreme Court overturned Biggers's ruling. The case was sent back to Biggers with instructions to consider new desegregation proposals. A second trial was held in 1994, at the conclusion of which Biggers issued a remedial decree requiring the state to upgrade its historically black universities, adopt uniform admission standards, and provide programs at historically black colleges that would attract white students. More appeals followed, and settlement talks finally began in 2000. The case was settled in 2002, when Judge Biggers approved a $503-million settlement the state legislature agreed to fund.

In 1996 Biggers ruled in a school prayer case that the Pontotoc County School District had violated the First Amendment rights of the Lisa Herdahl family, which protested school prayers and religious instruction in school. The school's religious practices included daily prayers by students over the intercom, classroom prayers before lunch, Bible classes, and a voluntary morning prayer in the school gym. Biggers ruled that prayer sessions in the gym were permissible but found the other religious practices illegal. "The Bill of Rights was created to protect the minority from tyranny," Biggers wrote in his opinion.

Natalya Seay
Washington, D.C.

Almanac of the Federal Judiciary, vol. 2 (2008); *Ayers v. Musgrove*, 2002 US Dist. LEXIS 1973 (2002); *Biographical Directory of the Federal Judiciary, 1789–2000* (2001); *Herdahl v. Pontotoc County School District*, 933 F. Supp. 582 (1996); *The American Bench: Judges of the Nation* (2008).

B

Bilbo, Theodore Gilmore

(1877–1947) Thirty-Ninth and Forty-Third Governor, 1916–1920, 1928–1932

Although he was only five feet, two inches tall, Theodore G. Bilbo, in life as in legend, was a towering figure who stalked across the pages of Mississippi history. Between 1907 and 1947 "the Man," as he was called by friends and foes alike, occupied a prominent place in Mississippi politics.

Born at Juniper Grove in Pearl River County on 13 October 1877, Bilbo entered public school at age fifteen and graduated from high school four years later. Following a short teaching career, he attended Peabody College and Vanderbilt Law School, though he did not graduate from either institution. After losing a 1903 bid for circuit clerk to a "one-armed Confederate veteran," Bilbo went on to win election as a state senator (1908–12), lieutenant governor (1912–16), governor (1916–20, 1928–32), and US senator (1935–47). His long career was punctuated by other defeats as well—unsuccessful campaigns for US Congress in 1918 and 1932 and for governor in 1923. Governor Bilbo's wife, Linda Gaddy Bedgood Bilbo, made several campaign speeches for him in 1915 and may have been the first woman to actively participate in a statewide political race.

Theodore G. Bilbo, 6 May 1939 (Photograph by Harris and Ewing, Library of Congress, Washington, D.C. [LC-H22-D-6520])

A combative individual, Bilbo made many enemies. He often insulted his political foes and responded to challenges with anger and bitterness. Bilbo faced scandals and controversies throughout his political career, including charges of bribery in 1910 and 1913 and of misappropriation of funds in the 1920s and 1940s.

Bilbo described himself as the representative of hardworking ordinary people and denounced the influence of both traditional planter elites and newer corporate elites. He wore a red necktie in reference to charges that he and his supporters were rednecks. He was a strong proponent of maintaining racial segregation and other forms of privilege for white Mississippians.

In Governor Bilbo's second inaugural address, on 17 January 1928, he recommended moving the University of Mississippi from Oxford to Jackson and constructing a new, fifteen-million-dollar university campus. He also advocated a thorough reorganization of Mississippi's other public institutions of higher learning, including the establishment of a commissioner of higher education. After those recommendations were defeated, Bilbo persuaded the college board to dismiss two college presidents and about fifty-three faculty members. (Critics have greatly exaggerated the number of presidents and faculty Bilbo dismissed.) Though Bilbo has been accused of attempting to punish his enemies and reward his friends, he was actually seeking to upgrade the state's colleges. Nevertheless, several agencies withdrew accreditation from Mississippi's institutions of higher learning for two years.

Bilbo also advocated a wide range of other political and economic reforms intended to improve the quality of life for Mississippi's poor white farmers and workers, who formed his base of support. Bilbo's flamboyant and often racially inflammatory campaign rhetoric and his personal involvement in higher education earned him a reputation as a demagogue.

After his second term as governor ended in 1932, Bilbo ran unsuccessfully for the US Congress. Two years later he was elected to the US Senate, winning reelection in 1940 and 1946. During his early years in the Senate Bilbo strongly supported the New Deal.

However, he gained notoriety for his aggressive opposition to all civil rights legislation. In the 1930s he supported movements to encourage African Americans to move to Africa, and he introduced a bill to prohibit racial intermarriage in Washington, D.C. He opposed antilynching legislation and conducted long filibusters against the Fair Employment Practices Committee and efforts to repeal the poll tax. In 1947 Bilbo published his only book, *Take Your Choice, Separation or Mongrelization*, a rambling defense of racial segregation.

After Bilbo's 1946 reelection, a group of black World War II veterans challenged the validity of his election on the grounds that African Americans had not been allowed to vote. Before the Senate could rule on that challenge or on new corruption charges, Bilbo died at his mansion, Dream House, near Poplarville on 21 August 1947.

David G. Sansing
University of Mississippi

Biographical Directory of the United States Congress (1950); A. Wigfall Green, *The Man Bilbo* (1963); Jerry A. Hendrix, in *The Oratory of Southern Demagogues*, ed. Cal M. Logue and Howard Dorgan (1981); *Mississippi Official and Statistical Register* (1917); Chester Morgan, *Redneck Liberal: Theodore G. Bilbo and the New Deal* (1985); David G. Sansing, *Making Haste Slowly: The Troubled History of Higher Education in Mississippi* (1990).

Billington, Johnnie
(1935–2013) Blues Teacher and Musician

Although he played guitar and sang, Johnnie Billington was best known as a teacher with the Delta Blues Education Program. He was born in Crowder, in Quitman County, Mississippi, in 1935, and as a young man he listened regularly to the *King Biscuit Time* radio program, broadcast on KFFA out of Helena, Arkansas. The show exposed Billington to blues music performed by Aleck Miller (Sonny Boy Williamson II), Joe "Pinetop" Perkins, Robert Jr. Lockwood, and others. At age nine, Billington received a guitar from his father and began learning the blues. He made his first semiprofessional music money playing as a solo act for a juke joint. He briefly moved to Arizona before heading north to Chicago, where he performed with Elmore James, Muddy Waters, Earl Hooker, and others for more than twenty years.

Billington moved back to Mississippi in 1977 and set up shop as an auto mechanic in Clarksdale. He soon discovered his passion for teaching. Encouraged by the generosity James and Waters had shown him by allowing him up onto stage with them, Billington wanted to inspire and teach the youth of the Mississippi Delta. He taught hundreds of children to play the blues and to appreciate the Delta's cultural heritage. For students without an aptitude for music, Billington taught auto repair. As the number of students seeking his guidance grew, "Mr. Johnnie," as they affectionately called him, moved from teaching out of his home to holding classes at Clarksdale's Delta Blues Museum; he also conducted workshops in Florida and Massachusetts.

In 1992 Billington helped create the Delta Blues Education Program to "bring together the children and master musicians of the Mississippi Delta for the continuation of the Delta Blues tradition." His student group, usually known as Johnnie Billington's Kids, performed at blues festivals around the state. Among his students who have gone on to form their own blues bands are Arthniece "Gas Man" Jones and the Stone Gas Band. Billington's efforts earned him awards from several blues organizations as well as the Governor's Award for Excellence in the Arts in 1999. Until his death in 2013 he performed with his group, J. B. and the Midnighters, though his work appeared on only a few sound recordings. He saw his mission as more than a means of teaching children, including seven of his own, to play music: he sought to instill good values and inspire hope.

Greg Johnson
University of Mississippi

Delta Blues Education Program website, www.bluesed.org; Edward Komara, in *Encyclopedia of the Blues*, ed. Edward Komara (2006); Mississippi Folklife and Folk Artist Directory website, http://www.arts.state.ms.us/folklife/; Leonard Watkins, *Blues and Rhythm* (April 1996).

Biloxi schooner (Courtesy Biloxi Historical Society)

Biloxi Schooner

The heyday of the Biloxi schooner lasted just four decades, bookended by a hurricane and the rise of gas-powered boats. The schooner's emergence coincided with the expansion of the Biloxi seafood industry at the end of the nineteenth century. Commercial fishing operations utilized recently completed inland railroad networks, particularly the one linking New Orleans and Mobile. Seafood packaging also benefited from new technologies of canning and refrigeration to extend their markets inland.

Fishermen began turning to the schooner out of practical necessity and to keep up with increasing demand, particularly for oysters. As an oyster vessel, Biloxi schooners replaced catboats, which were single- or double-sail flatbottom boats. Catboats were smaller and lacked the sail power to pull sizable oyster dredges and shrimp seines. The new schooners made up for these shortcomings, as they were broad enough to accommodate large crews, shallow enough to navigate inland waterways and Biloxi's back bay, and powerful enough to haul in hundreds of barrels of seafood. They differed from the ubiquitous cargo schooners, which used higher freeboards to carry passengers, mail, timber, and other goods. The primary impetus for transitioning over to the Biloxi schooner came in 1893, when a hurricane devastated most of the fishing fleet and provided the opportunity for fishermen to switch over to the new boat design.

Biloxi's boat builders constructed the schooners out of indigenous lumber from nearby forests. Builders used cypress from Louisiana for the boat's frame and planking and longleaf yellow pine from Mississippi forests for the boat's keel, masts, and spars. Completed Biloxi schooners ranged in length from twenty-nine feet to sixty-seven feet and maintained three working sails. Fishermen outfitted oyster schooners with winches, dredges, and dredge tables. Schooners harvesting white shrimp deployed seines that were usually about a quarter-mile long.

While Biloxi schooners served as the workhorse for the city's fishing fleet, they also provided recreation. Each of the six major companies sent a schooner to compete in the Annual Biloxi Schooner Race, a fifteen-mile competition beginning and ending in the west end of Biloxi Channel. This race ended in 1938, by which time most schooners had converted to motor power, but the Biloxi Maritime and Seafood Industry Museum revived the tradition in the 1990s using replicas.

Mississippi lifted its ban on the use of motor-powered dredges in 1933, ending the golden age of the Biloxi schooner. Before converting to total motor power, fishermen used motors in place of the topsail, fisherman sail, and flying jib. Converted Biloxi schooners continued to serve the industry for decades, with the last known schooner wrecked by Hurricane Elena in 1985.

Carter Dalton Lyon
St. Mary's Episcopal School,
Memphis, Tennessee

Val Husley, *Maritime Biloxi* (2000); Aimée Schmidt, *Mississippi Folklife* (Winter–Spring 1995).

Birds and Bird Migration

Mississippi's diverse natural environment provides habitat for an abundance of birdlife. The state's central geographical location, with the Mississippi River on the west and the Gulf of Mexico to the south, attracts a great number of seasonal visitors as well as occasional vagrants from the western states and the Caribbean. In the fall, the so-called Mississippi Flyway gathers migrating birds from a vast area in the northern United States and Canada and funnels them along the Lower Mississippi River onto their wintering grounds in the southern United States and Latin America. Several species of birds cover much of this great flyway twice every year. Well-watered, with forested bottomland areas, and uninterrupted by mountain ranges, the Mississippi Flyway is one of the four main migration routes for North American birds and of utmost importance for many Arctic species of geese, ducks, and shorebirds.

Altogether some four hundred species of birds from fifty different families have been observed in Mississippi. While no full bird species are endemic to Mississippi, the state serves as breeding ground for many rare birds, among them the brown pelican, bald eagle, Swainson's warbler, and Bachman's sparrow. A true state specialty is the Mississippi sandhill crane, a nonmigratory subspecies of the sandhill crane, with its sole population found in a small area of the Pascagoula watershed in Jackson County.

While much of Mississippi's woodlands have been heavily modified for the purposes of agriculture and commercial tree growing, forests still dominate the state's landscape. Different forest types support different species of birds. The most abundant and diverse bird populations are typically found in the remaining hardwood forests of the Delta and Loess Bluffs, but pine forests also support distinctive fauna. Found only in the southern United States, the endangered red-cockaded woodpecker depends on fire-sustained, open pine forest for habitat and cannot survive in contemporary, young, and heavily managed pine plantations.

Some species of birds today considered critically endangered or even extinct previously numbered among Mississippi's wildlife, including the passenger pigeon, Carolina parakeet, Bachman's warbler, and ivory-billed woodpecker. The disappearance of these species can often be traced to persecution and the destruction of their habitat by humans. Many Mississippi birds continue to experience population declines because of the loss of forest habitat on both their breeding and wintering grounds, while severely disturbed beach and coastal habitat has been cited as a major problem for species such as the least tern and piping and snowy plovers. The Mississippi sandhill crane and wood stork have suffered greatly from the draining of southern wetlands, which has destroyed much of their feeding grounds and preferred habitat.

Early settlers in Mississippi as well as Native Americans were intimately familiar with many birds and their habits, but the scientific study of the birds found in the state remains a rather recent phenomenon. While such great American naturalists as William Bartram, Alexander Wilson, and John James Audubon visited the Mississippi region in the late eighteenth and early nineteenth centuries, systematic study of the state's birds really began only during the twentieth century. The Mississippi Ornithological Society was founded in 1955 and has published its bulletin, *The Mississippi Kite*, since 1965.

Recreational observation and study of birds—"bird-watching" or "birding"—have become an increasingly popular pastime in the United States, and Mississippi is no exception. Several birders' organizations are now active in the state, including chapters of the National Audubon Society. Chapter members typically participate in breeding bird surveys and the traditional Christmas Bird Count. Mississippi's public lands offer excellent birding opportunities. For example, the state's numerous national wildlife refuges feature nature trails that offer easy access to prime bird habitat and usually provide a seasonal species checklist for the serious birder. While the greatest abundance and variety of bird species are encountered in such protected areas, it is possible to observe many birds even without leaving one's home, especially if bird feeders and nest boxes have been placed on the property. Species such as Mississippi's state bird, the mockingbird, as well as the mourning dove, American robin, blue jay, Carolina wren, northern cardinal, and numerous others can also be encountered in habitats significantly altered by humans.

Mikko Saikku
University of Helsinki

Audubon Mississippi website, www.ms.audubon.org; Mississippi Ornithological Society website, www.missbird.org; David Allen Sibley, *The Sibley Field Guide to Birds of Eastern North America* (2003); William H. Turcotte and David L. Watts, *Birds of Mississippi* (1999).

Black Bears

The role of the black bear in Mississippi has changed dramatically over time. Native Americans used bears for subsistence, killing them when needed to provide food and clothing. The arrival of European explorers saw the trading of bear products for items such as guns and fabrics. As humans inhabited more land, they came to see bears as a threat and a nuisance to crops and livestock and started killing at every opportunity. In the Delta region of the state, bear hunting became a sport, attracting people from all over the United States and Europe. Hunting bears from horseback with the aid of dogs gave rise to some of the greatest bear hunting legends in North America as well as the world's most popular children's toy—the teddy bear.

Mississippi is currently home to two subspecies of black bears. The American black bear (*Ursus americanus americanus*), which occurs in the northern half of Mississippi, was once distributed throughout most of eastern North America, the Great Plains, and Canada. The Louisiana black bear (*Ursus americanus luteolus*), which occurs in the southern half of the state, once ranged throughout eastern Texas, Louisiana, southern Arkansas, and southern Mississippi.

Generally speaking, black bears are found in three areas within the state: the Gulf Coast, the Loess Bluffs of Southwest Mississippi, and the Mississippi River Delta. It is believed that the majority of bears found in Mississippi are males that have dispersed from populations in other states at some point during their lives. In recent years, however, females have been documented with greater frequency.

Black bears in Mississippi are generally black with brown muzzles. Some bears exhibit a white patch of hair or "blaze" on their chest. Bears can grow to six feet in length and stand three feet tall at the shoulder. Average body weights are 150 to 350 pounds for adult males and 120 to 250 pounds for adult females, although larger bears have been documented in the state.

Black bear habitat consists of escape cover, dispersal corridors, den sites, and a diversity of natural foods. Bears are highly adaptable but prefer large, remote blocks of bottomland hardwood forests, although they have been found to thrive in smaller, fragmented habitats, particularly in agricultural areas. Most bear sightings in Mississippi occur in forested areas close to rivers or streams.

Range sizes for black bears can vary depending on habitat quality and time of year. The range for an adult male bear in Mississippi has been found to be up to one hundred thousand acres, while the range for an adult female can be up to thirty-two thousand acres. Range sizes typically increase during the summer mating season and during fall, when bears are foraging heavily to build fat reserves.

Although classified as carnivores, black bears are not active predators. Up to 90 percent of a black bear's diet is composed of plant materials, including acorns, berries, grasses, and agricultural crops. The majority of protein in a bear's diet comes from insects and carrion.

Black bears do not truly hibernate but rather go into a deep sleep that can begin in November and last until May. During this period, bears exhibit reductions in body temperature, metabolism, and heart rate but can be easily aroused if disturbed. Bears typically make their dens in hollow cypress or oak trees or in ground dens beneath fallen logs or logging debris.

Females generally breed for the first time at three years of age and will give birth every other year in optimal habitat conditions. Cubs are born in winter dens during January, with litter sizes ranging from one to five. Cubs weigh only eight ounces at birth but will weigh four to five pounds when they emerge from the den in April. Cubs will stay with their mothers for eighteen months before dispersing.

Mississippi black bears are normally very shy and secretive animals and are not aggressive toward humans. Contrary to popular belief, female bears are not typically aggressive in defense of their young. Although there has never been a documented attack on a person by a bear in Mississippi, black bears are wild animals and should always be treated with respect.

Brad W. Young
Mississippi Wildlife Federation

J. F. Benson, "Ecology and Conservation of Louisiana Black Bears in the Tensas River Basin and Reintroduced Populations" (master's thesis, Louisiana State University, 2005); M. R. Pelton, in *Ecology and Management of Large Mammals in North America*, ed. Stephen Demarais and Paul R. Krausman; C. C. Shropshire, "History, Status, and Habitat Components of Black Bears in Mississippi" (PhD dissertation, Mississippi State University, 1996); Brad Young, "Conservation and Management of Black Bears in Mississippi," Mississippi Department of Wildlife, Fisheries, and Parks (2006).

Black Belt/Prairie

The Mississippi Black Belt is part of a larger region, stretching from Virginia south to the Carolinas and west through the Deep South, defined by a majority African American population and a long history of cotton production. In 1936 sociologist Arthur Raper identified two hundred counties with majority-black populations from Virginia to Texas. Most of Mississippi's counties are part of this broad region. The Mississippi Black Belt/Prairie, however, consists of parts of six counties (Chickasaw, Clay, Lowndes, Monroe, Noxubee, and Oktibbeha) along the state's eastern boundary with Alabama, linked geologically and in many ways culturally to the larger Alabama Black Belt/Prairie that runs through central and eastern Alabama. The prairie is a crescent-shaped land feature about twenty-five miles wide, stretching from eastern south-central Alabama into northeastern Mississippi and ending in McNairy County in southern Tennessee. The fertile black soil lies atop decomposed limestone known as the Selma Chalk, the remnants of a prehistoric ocean floor. The prairie runs through ten Mississippi counties, but the ones closest to the Tennessee line are defined more by the northeastern hills than the prairie. The Black Belt/Prairie has interconnecting waterways that have promoted transportation, including connections to the port of Mobile, facilitating the marketing of the region's agricultural goods. The Tombigbee River runs north-south and is the major waterway, with its tributaries the Tibbee, Line Houlka, Sun, Chewah, and Chuquatonchee Creeks providing ample water to the area. The Noxubee River and the Buttchatchee River are also notable waterways in the region.

The original inhabitants of the region were Native Americans in the Tombigbee River Valley. Archaeologists trace Paleo-Indian activity at the Hester Site, near Amory, to ten thousand years ago. The Bynum Mound and Village near Houston are other archaeological locations in the region that document early Native American activity. These early peoples settled along the river, hunting, gathering, and trading throughout the Southeast. Between 6500 and 2500 BC Indians settled in small migratory groups in the Black Prairie areas of the Tombigbee, developing cultures similar to those of other tribes in the Gulf Coast plain. By 2000 BC sites existed where the Eutaw Hills and Black Prairie converged. The Mississippian era (around AD 1500) saw corn and beans become standard dietary and farming items in the fertile valley. When settlements became too dense, the Black Prairie became depopulated. The British and French arrived and competed with the region's Chickasaw and Choctaw. Indian names continue to mark the Black Belt/Prairie landscape. The town of Okolona takes its name from the Indian word for "much bent," and Oktibbeha is a Chickasaw term meaning "ice there in creek." Historian Dunbar Rowland observed in the 1925 that one Black Belt/Prairie county, Noxubee, was "rich in the dim remains of Indian civilization."

The Treaty of Dancing Rabbit (1830) and the Treaty of Pontotoc (1832) opened Native American lands to white settlement, and the plantation system, with labor supplied by slaves, subsequently took root. In 1840 Chickasaw County had 2,148 free whites and 806 slaves, but by 1860 slaves accounted for 55 percent of the population. In Monroe County slaves comprised 60 percent of the 1860 population; in Lowndes County that number was 71 percent.

By 1860 the Black Belt/Prairie had become a major agricultural producer, raising corn, sweet potatoes, and fruit, but cotton was far and away the major crop. The presence of prairie grasses led the area to become a center for raising cattle, mules, and horses. Columbus developed into a prominent cultural center, with a distinctive architectural form, the Black Belt house—a Greek Revival house with more attenuated proportions and refined ornamentation than similar houses in other parts of the antebellum South. Slender columns defined the Black Belt house, which was typically a frame house rather than brick. Waverly, one of the area's most spectacular antebellum houses, has been described as an "architectural extravaganza of elaborate ornamentation."

Political leaders from the Black Belt/Prairie generally supported secession, and the area was the scene of raids and small skirmishes during the Civil War. Federal troops tried but failed to destroy the Mobile and Ohio Railroad lines in Chickasaw County. Columbus was home to Briarfield Arsenal, which produced gunpowder, handguns, and cannons. Gen. Nathan Bedford Forrest repelled several Union Army attempts to capture Columbus, resulting in the survival of many antebellum homes (and consequently an annual spring historic home pilgrimage in the twentieth century). When Union forces captured Jackson, the state government moved to Columbus. Both Union and Confederate casualties were brought to Columbus after the Battle of Shiloh, and thousands of soldiers are buried in the town's Friendship Cemetery. Columbus's women decorated Union and Confederate graves on 25 April 1866, which is often seen as the progenitor of Memorial Day. Okolona's cemetery provides a final resting place for almost one thousand Confederate soldiers killed in Union raids in the region.

Reconstruction was divisive and violent in the Black Belt/Prairie. African American political leaders emerged, but the Ku Klux Klan was active, helping to end postwar reforms. Agricultural reformers had some strength in the region in the 1890s: among that group was Populist editor and politician Frank Burkitt, a Chickasaw County native. Railroads had come to the region before the war, but postwar rail companies expanded, including the Gulf, Mobile, and Northern; the Illinois Central; the Southern; and the Mobile and Ohio. All connected the region to outlying markets for its predominantly agricultural products.

The post–Civil War years saw the decline of the antebellum plantation system and the rise of tenant farming in the Black Belt/Prairie, as in other parts of the South. The region had low rates of farm ownership through the end of the tenant system in the mid-twentieth century, and freed slaves and their descendants formed the bulk of sharecroppers. Census records show the continuing dominance of African Americans in the region. Clay County's 1880 population, for example, was 70 percent black, while African Americans accounted for 85 percent of Noxubee County's population ten years later. Leading crops through the late nineteenth century were cotton, livestock, corn, wheat, hay, and tobacco, with the region among the state's most productive agricultural areas.

Educational institutions subsequently emerged to promote cultural and economic development. The Agricultural and Mechanical College of the State of Mississippi (now Mississippi State University) opened in 1878 in Starkville (another leading cultural center of the Black Belt/Prairie). This land-grant college made key contributions to the farming industry in the region as well as in the rest of the state. The school began operating agricultural experiment stations in 1888, and its research and outreach activities promoted the modernization of agriculture in the early twentieth century. The Industrial Institute and College (now Mississippi University for Women) opened in 1884 in Columbus and represented the nation's first state-supported college for women. Mary Holmes Seminary, a Presbyterian Church institution for African American women, opened in 1895 in Jackson, but after the school burned three years later, a new campus was constructed in West Point.

In the early twentieth century dairy farming and cattle raising became increasingly prominent. Fruit production also expanded: Chickasaw County boasted ten thousand fruit-bearing trees in 1919. By the 1930s many of the region's counties were diversifying economically. Bryan Foods began operating in Clay County in 1936 and became one of the region's most important industries. The Carter No. 1 Well near Amory had opened gas production in the Black Belt/Prairie in 1926. *Mississippi: The Guide to the Magnolia State* (1938) described the region as a mostly treeless landscape with rolling plateaus, "spotted with silos and cheese factories, cottonmills, dairy barns, and condensaries." "For miles," the volume said, "little is visible except herds of cattle and meadows of alfalfa and corn." If the Delta in this era presented scenes of white cotton fields, the guide's writers observed a different image in the Black Belt/Prairie, where "at harvest time when the grain turns gold the landscape is a monotone—a vast stretch of gold spreading to the horizon." The guide identified economic diversity in the meatpacking plants, garment factories, dairy product enterprises, and the activities of the Tennessee Valley Authority. Still, the Great Depression and World War II led to loss of population in the region, including many African Americans. By 1960 two-thirds of Monroe County's population was white, and although Noxubee County's overall population had decreased, it remained 72 percent African American. By 1960 less than one-third of the Clay County workforce was involved in agriculture, a trend seen in other parts of the region as well. Small manufacturing companies provided more jobs than ever, although the textile and furniture plants that provided many post–World War II jobs had closed by the turn of the twenty-first century. The Black Belt/Prairie towns nonetheless grew in population between 1960 and 2010. The white proportion of the population increased to just over half the population by 2010.

One of the most important recent developments in the Black Belt/Prairie was the 1984 opening of the Tennessee-Tombigbee Waterway, a project initiated in 1972 and costing $1.992 billion. This 234-mile waterway begins on Pickwick Lake on the Tennessee River and flows south to the Black Warrior–Tombigbee navigation system at Demopolis, Alabama, before traveling another 217 miles to Mobile Bay. Coal and timber are the most important commodities shipped, with a 2009 Troy University study suggesting a forty-three-million-dollar national economic impact since 1996, much of it in the Black Belt/Prairie. The waterway constituted the largest earth-moving project in world history and was controversial because of its cost.

Columbus Air Force Base has also brought economic vitality to the region, not only by training pilots but also by attracting aviation and aerospace businesses to the area, many of them served by the Golden Triangle Regional Airport, situated in Lowndes County between Columbus, Starkville, and West Point.

The Black Belt/Prairie identity is nurtured through stories in the region's main communication sources, including WCBI television in Columbus and newspapers that include the *Columbus Commercial Dispatch*, the *West Point Daily Times Leader*, and the *Starkville Daily News*.

The Black Belt/Prairie has produced a thriving and nationally noted culture. Blues performers Bukka White (Chickasaw County) and Chester "Howlin' Wolf" (Clay County) were born in the area in the early twentieth century: West Point has a museum dedicated to Wolf and since 1995 has hosted the Howlin' Wolf Festival. Pop singer Bobbie Gentry was born in Chickasaw County, which figures in her song lyrics. Prominent late-twentieth-century African American journalist William Raspberry was from Okolona, and poet T. R. Hummer was born in Macon in 1950. Sports announcer Red Barber made his fame as an announcer for the Brooklyn Dodgers, but he was from Columbus and loved to tell stories about growing up there. Photographer Birney Imes has documented life in the region from the late twentieth century to the early twenty-first. While the region's soils remain rich and agriculture is still important, much of the prairie land that originally characterized the region has been lost to agriculture, with less than 1 percent of open prairie habitat remaining. The region's economic development, diversification, and population growth define it for the twenty-first century.

Charles Reagan Wilson

University of Mississippi

Federal Writers' Project of the Works Progress Administration, *Mississippi: The WPA Guide to the Magnolia State* (1938); Joe MacGown, Richard Brown, and JoVonn Hill, Mississippi Entomological Museum website, http://mississippientomologicalmuseum.org.msstate.edu; Arthur F. Raper, *Preface to Peasantry* (1936); Dunbar Rowland, *History of Mississippi: The Heart of the South* (1925); University of Virginia Library, Historical Census Browser website, http://mapserver.lib.virginia.edu; Ronald C. Wimberley and Libby V. Morris, *The Southern Black Belt: A National Perspective* (1997).

Black Codes

Black Codes were southern state laws that harshly restricted the rights of African Americans in 1865–66. These laws represented the former Confederate states' first official response to slave emancipation after rejoining the Union. The legislation recognized African Americans' freedom in part by stating that people could no longer be legally classified as property, but they denied former slaves the same rights as white men. In fact, the legislators believed that African Americans should be governed by a separate set of laws—by a *black* code—to firmly set aside freedpeople's claims to citizenship. Northerners and southerners alike interpreted these laws as a defiant rejection of full African American freedom by an unredeemed southern political elite. The US Congress responded by stripping each state of its sovereignty (except for Tennessee), placing it under military rule, and initiating what became known as Radical Reconstruction.

Mississippi was the first southern state to form a new government after the Confederacy's defeat and the first to write Black Codes. All eyes were on Mississippi, and state legislators aware of their leadership position decided to take a stand. Ignoring Pres. Andrew Johnson's plea for moderation, the Committee on Emancipation and Freedmen wrote laws that its members warned might "seem rigid and stringent." Yet the Black Codes were enacted with remarkable speed in November 1865. Emboldened, the other southern states quickly followed.

The Black Codes fell under three different sections of state law: civil rights, apprenticeship, and vagrancy. All three sections worked to limit freedpeople's mobility, labor, and autonomy. In Mississippi, the revised civil rights statutes acknowledged the abolition of slavery by granting African Americans access to the courts. This action shifted African Americans' legal status from property to personhood. Yet the Black Codes denied freedpeople the right to serve as witnesses against white people. African Americans, in other words, were not equal to white southerners under the law.

After establishing freedpeople's access to the courts, the Black Codes turned to questions of marriage. The law granted marriage rights to African Americans as long as they married within the race. Any person, white or black, who married a member of another race faced life imprisonment. Legislators anticipated that this law would be difficult to interpret since race could often be unclear. In a tortuously complex passage, the marriage statute defined black people as "those who . . . are of pure negro blood, and those descended from a negro to the third generation, inclusive though one ancestor in each generation may have been a white person."

The civil rights section of the Black Codes also restricted African American rights to property, freedom of movement, and employment. African Americans could not rent or lease land except in towns and cities. African American citydwellers had to carry written evidence of their employment and residence. Finally, African Americans who worked for employers longer than one month had to sign written labor contracts. These restrictions undermined independent farming by blacks, limited their movement in and out of the cities, and forced them to commit to long-term employment. Each of these mandates undercut a central principle of free labor—the ability to move and change jobs.

African Americans' labor contracts also differed from those of white Mississippians. Former slaves who violated their labor contracts by moving off the plantation before their time of service was finished would forfeit all wages previously earned. Furthermore, the Black Codes granted all white southerners the power to enforce this law, with the legislature promising cash rewards to white people who seized and arrested African Americans who had deserted their jobs.

The Vagrancy Acts put teeth into the Black Codes' labor regulations. Any African American without a written labor contract two weeks after New Year's Day could be jailed as a vagrant. This policy left vulnerable to arrest anyone who was self-employed, in the process of moving, or working a short-term job that did not require a formal written contract. Moreover, vagrants had no right to trial by jury. This section of the Black Codes caught national public attention. Many Americans considered a jury trial an ancient right, and newspapers declared that Mississippi lawmakers had made freedom a farce by refusing African Americans this right.

A freedperson found guilty of vagrancy would be jailed. To keep jails from bursting at the seams, state legislators gave sheriffs the right to "hire out" imprisoned African Americans. The people who "hired" vagrants would pay the sheriffs, not the workers, sidestepping the issue of wages. To help finance this system, the state imposed a tax on all African Americans—and declared anyone unable to pay the tax a vagrant.

These laws reflected tremendous planter-class anxiety regarding the maintenance of control over land and labor. With the Vagrancy Law and the laws regulating contracts, planters attempted to guarantee themselves a large labor pool to continue production of cash crops. More pointedly, they wanted these workers cheap. The Vagrancy Law promised convict labor, and the civil rights statutes provided loopholes to avoid paying wages altogether.

The Apprenticeship Law followed the same logic, requiring each county court semiannually to record the names of all African American children under the age of eighteen whose parents "have not the means" to support them. Such boys would be apprenticed to a master until they reached age twenty-one, while girls would be apprenticed until they turned eighteen. The Black Codes required masters to provide apprentices with food, clothing, medical attention, and reading lessons (for children under the age of fifteen) but permitted "the master or mistress . . . to inflict . . . moderate corporeal chastisement."

African Americans vigorously protested the Apprenticeship Laws and sued to get their children back. Apprenticeship was a painful reminder of slavery when children "belonged to masters," were valued for their labor, and could be taken from family at will. Children also sued for their freedom.

Anticipating protests about this curtailment of basic freedoms, legislators attempted to keep African Americans from meeting in public. The Black Codes included acts prohibiting freedpeople from "assembling themselves together, either in the day or night," preaching without a license, making seditious speeches, disturbing the peace, using insulting language and gestures, and carrying weapons. Any gathering, large or small, carried a threat in the eyes of law.

The protests did come, and they came from all directions. Usually sympathetic Mississippi newspapers condemned the legislators' rashness, outraged northerners claimed that the South refused to accept defeat, and eventually the US Congress disbanded the Mississippi legislature and returned the state to military rule. The Black Codes unwittingly helped turn the tide of public opinion in favor of African American citizenship and the right to vote.

Nancy Bercaw

Smithsonian National Museum
of African American History
and Culture

Laura Edwards, *Agricultural History* (Spring 1998); Noralee Frankel, *Freedom's Women: Black Women and Families in Civil War Era Mississippi* (1999); James Wilford Garner, *Reconstruction in Mississippi* (1901); William C. Harris, *Presidential Reconstruction in Mississippi* (1967); Christopher Waldrep, *Roots of Disorder: Race and Criminal Justice in the American South, 1817–80* (1998); Karen L. Zipf, *Journal of Women's History* (Spring 2000).

Black Power

Black Power became a national phenomenon shortly after James Meredith began a one-man march from Memphis, Tennessee, to Jackson, Mississippi, on 5 June 1966. Although Meredith had been the first black student to enter the University of Mississippi, his announcement that he would undertake a "March against Fear" attracted little attention. On the first day of the march, however, an unidentified sniper shot him in the leg. In response, nationally known civil rights leaders banded together and continued the march while Meredith recovered. These leaders attracted not only the media but also scores of black Mississippi residents who participated in the march and in voter registration rallies across the state.

Although a number of movement leaders participated, the combination of Martin Luther King Jr. and Stokely Carmichael (later Kwame Ture) primarily attracted the national media and propagated the Black Power philosophy. This new approach to civil rights advocated independence from white authority through cultural pride and economic and political strategies. But the media tended to focus on a more controversial component, the promotion of self-defense in the face of violence. This new notion of empowerment represented

a dramatic change from the nonviolent philosophy that had previously surrounded much of the movement.

Carmichael, chair of the Student Nonviolent Coordinating Committee (SNCC), had already considered the slogan and believed that it would arouse emotion and encourage more movement participation among black citizens. But Black Power was far more than a slogan. It was a new approach to winning civil rights that would influence the nation's social and racial convictions for years to come. The concept became the centerpiece of a campaign that instilled cultural pride and promoted the idea that blacks should resist the horrific circumstances that often led to poverty, illiteracy, entrapment, and fear.

Black Power transcended organizational structure. But since Carmichael headed SNCC, that organization became a central source for communicating the Black Power message. Carmichael and others had first discussed and used the Black Power ideas (although not the phrase) while working to register voters in Lowndes County, Alabama, in the summer of 1965. Although the slogan did not appear for another year, the powerful and iconic Black Panther political symbol first emerged as a tactic to encourage voter registration in Lowndes County.

The phrase *Black Power* was a condensed version of an older slogan, *Black Power for Black People*, which had previously been used by African and African American activists, poets, and writers. Carmichael, however, is credited with introducing the shorter version and using it to propel a new stage of the civil rights movement that officially began during Meredith's march through Mississippi.

During parts of the march, Carmichael walked alongside King, who discussed nonviolence as a strategy. Carmichael, however, suggested alternatives that essentially included self-empowerment and self-defense rather than acquiescence to violence. The media were captivated.

When Carmichael arrived in Greenville, Mississippi, he was arrested for refusing to dismantle tents set up for an evening rally. After spending several hours in jail, he returned to the rally site and proclaimed to the crowd, "What we are going to start saying now is Black Power." The crowd responded passionately, and the Black Power philosophy became a central and defining component of the movement.

Almost instantly, Carmichael became the Black Power spokesperson, and he was well equipped for the job. He was handsome, articulate, intelligent, and ideally suited for the increasingly available and exciting medium of television. Ironically, Carmichael's popularity with the media encouraged his resignation from SNCC the following year. The group's workers wanted a broader focus, while the media seemed content to focus on one dynamic man with a dynamic message.

SNCC's new chair, H. Rap Brown, was far more radical than Carmichael and frequently suggested that violence should be used in the fight for civil rights. Consequently, Black Power and SNCC became increasingly associated with violence. Many former supporters deserted the group, which largely dissolved in 1968.

Black Power was not exclusive to SNCC, and many groups and individuals adopted the philosophy throughout the late 1960s and early 1970s. The Black Panther Party, based in Oakland, California, was the most notable organization, but because it received a good deal of criticism for activities associated with violence, the Black Power movement lost momentum. When the group split in 1972, the Black Power movement began to fade. Nevertheless, Black Power continued to instill community and cultural pride in black America and had a lasting effect.

Vanessa Murphree
University of Southern
Mississippi

Clayborne Carson, *In Struggle: SNCC and the Black Awakening of the 1960s* (1981); James Forman, *The Making of Black Revolutionaries* (1985); Charles V. Hamilton and Stokely Carmichael (Kwame Ture), *Black Power: The Politics of Liberation* (1992); Peniel E. Joseph, *Waiting 'til the Midnight Hour: A Narrative History of Black Power in America* (2006); William L. VanDeburg, *New Day in Babylon: The Black Power Movement and American Culture, 1965–1975* (1992).

Blackwell, Unita

(b. 1933) Activist and Political Leader

Civil rights activist Unita Blackwell has had a fascinating life at the intersection of local politics and national and international affairs dealing with race and poverty as well as a perhaps surprising degree of celebrity. Born in Lula in Coahoma County in 1933, Unita Brown started working in the cotton fields when she was six. She married Jeremiah Blackwell when she was nineteen, and the young couple moved into a small, tin-roofed shotgun house in Mayersville, Issaquena County.

Not well educated, Blackwell said she "went back to school" in 1964 when local resident Henry Sias introduced her to Robert Moses and she began working with Student Nonviolent Coordinating Committee activists. Her activism began when she saw her son, Jeremiah Jr., going to the same sort of poor school she had attended and said, "No, not again." On behalf of her son she helped file a 1965 lawsuit to desegregate the Rolling Fork schools, later recalling, "I wanted my child to have decent books. Now that I think back, I wasn't so interested in going to school with white people. I just wanted my son, all black children, to get a good education." She was on the original board of directors of the Child Development Group of Mississippi and worked with the Mississippi Action for Community Education.

Blackwell was part of the small group of African Americans in Mayersville who tried to register to vote. After being rebuffed she worked for voting rights in the Delta, went to Atlantic City as part of the contingent of Mississippi Freedom Democratic Party activists at the 1964 Democratic National Convention, and returned home to become involved in and sometimes even to create local politics, though at first she "had to learn what a board of supervisors was, what a precinct was." She estimates she has been arrested about seventy times, and she participated in the 1966 sit-in at the Greenville Air Force Base.

Blackwell became part of the first generation of black Mississippians since Reconstruction to hold political office. Mayersville, with a population of under four hundred, was unincorporated before Blackwell saw that incorporation would help in applying for government grants. In 1976, after she and others arranged the town's incorporation, she was elected the mayor, the first African American female to hold that office in Mississippi. During her tenure, she undertook programs to build a sewer system, pave streets, and use the resources of the federal government and private groups such as the Ford Foundation to improve housing for poor residents. The town's public housing project for the elderly is called Unita Blackwell Estates.

She served as mayor until 1993, when she did not run for reelection, instead running for the US congressional seat ultimately won by Mike Espy. She ran again for mayor in 1997, winning by three votes; her 2001 reelection bid failed by nine votes.

Blackwell has traveled widely, visiting China more than a dozen times as part of various projects, most of them involving the training of mayors in poor and rural communities. From 1967 to 1975 she served as housing coordinator for the National Council of Negro Women. She traveled as a delegate to the International Women's Year Conference in Houston in 1977 and to numerous Democratic National Conventions. In addition, she served on the board or as an officer of the World Conference of Mayors and the National Conference of Black Mayors (a group that made her its first female president in 1990) as well as on advisory councils for women and children.

Without a college degree, Blackwell was admitted into the graduate program in regional planning at the University of Massachusetts at Amherst and received her master's degree in 1983. Nine years later she received a John D. and Catherine T. MacArthur Foundation "genius" award for her work in community organizing.

Popular with journalists and on lecture circuits, Blackwell has emerged as an inspiration to many people. In 2006 she authored a memoir, *Barefootin': Life Lessons from the Road to Freedom*, with JoAnne Prichard Morris. That memoir concentrates on Blackwell's early life and activist years, family life, religious perspective, and work to fight poverty, violence, and injustice. She began the book with her first effort to register to vote, referred to her involvement as "growing up all over again," and ended with encouragement to all people to understand that "your spirit is in your feet, and your feet can run free."

Ted Ownby
University of Mississippi

Unita Blackwell File, Mississippi Department of Archives and History; Unita Blackwell, with JoAnne Prichard Morris, *Barefootin': Life Lessons from the Road to Freedom* (2006); John Dittmer, *Local People: The Struggle for Civil Rights in Mississippi* (1995).

Blackwood Brothers
Gospel Music Singers

The Blackwood Brothers are one of the most famous quartets in the history of gospel music. The group was formed in 1934 by brothers Roy Blackwood (1900–1971), singing second tenor; Doyle Blackwood (1911–74), singing bass; and James Blackwood (1919–2002), singing baritone; along with Roy Blackwood's oldest son, R. W. Blackwood (1921–54), singing first tenor. Sons of sharecroppers Carrie and Emmett Blackwood, the three brothers were born and raised in rural Choctaw County, Mississippi. Devout Christians, Carrie and Emmett helped develop their sons' devotion to Christ with daily readings from their family Bible that always concluded with song and prayer. The quartet's first official performance was on their local radio station, WHEF, in Kosciusko. Initially scheduled to perform for fifteen minutes, their airtime was extended a full hour longer and won the boys a weekly show. Along with their radio appearances, the quartet built a fan base by touring throughout the Southeast and performing at churches and schools. During the pre–World War II era the quartet hosted radio shows on WJDX in Jackson, Mississippi, and KWKH in Shreveport, Louisiana.

In 1952 the Blackwood Brothers signed a contract with RCA/Victor, making them one of the first gospel quartets signed by a major record label. When their first album, *Favorite Gospel Songs and Spirituals*, was recorded in January 1952, members included Dan Huskey, singing first tenor; James Blackwood, singing second tenor; R. W. Blackwood, singing baritone; and Bill Lyles, singing bass, with Jackie Marshall playing piano. The Blackwood Quartet gained further success in 1954 when they appeared on a national television show, *Arthur Godfrey's Talent Scouts*, winning first place with a rendition of "The Man Upstairs." At the pinnacle of their career, they were one of RCA's Top 10 sellers and were considered the most famous quartet in gospel music. On 30 June 1954, two weeks after appearing on Godfrey's show, however, R. W. Blackwood and Bill Lyles died in a plane crash in Clanton, Alabama.

The Blackwood Brothers returned to Clanton on 5 August. Cecil Blackwood (1934–2000) replaced R. W., and renowned gospel songwriter J. D. Sumner replaced Lyles. In 1956 the Blackwood Brothers established the National Quartet Convention, an annual gathering of gospel musicians that has continued to the present day. The Blackwood Brothers introduced the first customized tour bus, designed and built by Cecil Blackwood and Sumner. During the 1950s the Blackwood Brothers befriended a young admirer from Tupelo, Elvis Presley, who became so close to them that he asked them to sing at his mother's funeral in 1958.

With various lineups, the Blackwood Brothers stayed at the top of gospel music well into the 1960s and 1970s. Cecil Blackwood's death in 2000 prompted James Blackwood to decide that the group's name should be laid to rest as well. However, Jimmy Blackwood, James's son and member of the Blackwood Brothers Quartet from 1969 to 1986, resuscitated the name after James's death in 2002.

Jacques de Marché
Little Rock, Arkansas

Paul Davis, *The Legacy of the Blackwood Brothers: Authorized Biographies of Cecil Blackwood and James Blackwood* (2000).

Blessing of the Fleet

The seafood industry has long been part of the Mississippi Gulf Coast. Seafood harvesting and processing were thriving businesses in the late nineteenth and early twentieth centuries, so much so that Biloxi was known as the Seafood Capital of the World. Croatian and Slavonian immigrants and Cajuns from Southwest Louisiana built the early industry. In the late 1970s and early 1980s, Vietnamese refugees entered the business, first in the packing plants and later owning and operating their own boats.

Though the seafood industry has waned over the years, it remains economically and culturally significant. The most visible and public celebration of this industry and its traditions is the annual Blessing of the Fleet, an event that continues a European Catholic tradition and reflects the faith of most of those who immigrated to Mississippi to work in the business.

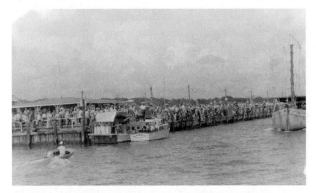

Blessing of the Fleet, Biloxi, ca. 1962 (Courtesy Biloxi Historical Society)

Both Biloxi and Pass Christian hold annual blessings in late spring or early summer, prior to the opening of Mississippi's shrimp season. Biloxi held its first blessing in 1929, with Pass Christian following eight years later and repeating the blessing intermittently in subsequent years. In both cities, fishermen and their families and the greater public participate in the events.

Biloxi holds its blessing on the first weekend in May. The celebration begins on Saturday morning with a race between the *Mikey Sekul* and the *Glenn L. Swetman*, reproductions of the old Biloxi schooners. In the afternoon, St. Michael Catholic Church, the main sponsor of the fleet blessing, holds a special mass. This church has historically been known as the fishermen's church, and it features a clam-shaped roof and stained glass images of fishermen. The evening's activities include the Seafood Festival, which features food and music and culminates in the crowning of the Shrimp King and Queen. The king is usually an older man honored for his experience on the water, while the queen is chosen after a pageant and essay contest in which the competitors are high-school-aged girls with family ties to the industry. The winner receives a cash scholarship for college from a local bank.

Shrimp boats and pleasure craft take to the water on Sunday morning. The event begins with the ceremonial dropping of a wreath into the water in memory of those fishermen who have died, a sobering reminder that the sea can be dangerous. The bishop of the Diocese of Biloxi stands aboard the "blessing boat" and sprinkles the boats with holy water as they pass by. In Pass Christian either a Catholic or Episcopal priest or both stand on the breakwater overlooking the harbor entrance and bless the boats as they pass below. Both working shrimp boats and pleasure craft may receive a blessing, but only the shrimp boats are eligible for judging in the decoration contest. Decorations—particularly colorful plastic bunting—cover the boats from bow to stern. Some also fly the American flag, the Mississippi state flag, or the Confederate battle flag. Religious items such as crucifixes, portraits of Jesus, and rosary beads made of

flotation devices adorn some boats. Vessels are divided into three classes according to size and are scored on originality, appearance, and adherence to the annual theme. Prizes include such items as diesel fuel, a haul-out, an engine tune-up, and coolers.

Despite the changes in the seafood industry brought on by such factors as the introduction of dockside gambling, increased competition from international markets, and the devastating effects of Hurricane Katrina, Mississippi's Gulf Coast still embraces this part of its heritage. Though fewer residents rely on the industry for their livelihood, the Blessing of the Fleet remains an important tradition and a public celebration of a proud community.

Aimée Schmidt
Decatur, Georgia

Val Husley, *Maritime Biloxi* (2000); Trent Lott, *Biloxi, Mississippi's Blessing of the Fleet*, Library of Congress American Folklife Center, Local Legacies Project website, www.loc.gov/folklife/roots.

Block, Sam

(1939–2003) Civil Rights Activist

Born in Cleveland, Mississippi, in 1939 to Samuel Theodore Block Sr., a construction worker, and Alma Block, a domestic, Sam Block left Mississippi to attend college in St. Louis. After graduating, he served in the US Air Force before returning to Cleveland in 1961 to work at his uncle's gas station and to attend Mississippi Vocational College (now Mississippi Valley State University). In 1962 Block lost his job at the gas station for arguing with a white customer, and Amzie Moore invited him to help set up citizenship classes for the Southern Christian Leadership Conference. After Block attended workshops on nonviolent direct action and voter registration at the Highlander Folk School in Monteagle, Tennessee, the Student Nonviolent Coordinating Committee (SNCC) hired him as a field secretary and sent him to Greenwood, where he worked with Willie Peacock, Laurence Guyot, and Hollis Watkins.

During Block's efforts to register voters and to organize mass meetings in Greenwood, he encountered violence from local whites and intimidation from the police. Block and other SNCC workers were shot at, and their offices were vandalized and burned. Whites also threatened members of the local African American community, further hindering SNCC's organizing efforts. While Block initially held meetings at the local Elks Hall, the owners denied him access to the building after discovering that he was teaching freedom songs. Local residents hesitated to rent Block a room, and for a time, he lived in Cleveland and commuted to Greenwood. Eventually, however, several local churches allowed Block to hold mass meetings in their buildings, and Block gained the support of established and prominent community leaders, who rented him an office and raised money to purchase a car for the SNCC workers. In addition, multiple members of the community ultimately became willing to board the workers, enabling Block frequently to change his housing arrangements and thus providing him some protection from the movement's enemies.

To gain the trust of the Greenwood community, Block frequented local hangouts and listened as residents discussed their problems. Locals soon began to help Block with canvassing and voter registration classes. The Board of County Supervisors retaliated in 1962 by cutting off supplies of surplus food to the black community, but Block and the other workers organized centers to distribute food donated from outside the state. SNCC's food drive not only proved to be a useful organizing tool but also alerted outsiders to the Delta's pervasive poverty. White intimidation continued, and in 1963 several black-owned businesses were burned. Block publicly commented on the intimidation, and police arrested him for disturbing the peace. The court fined Block five hundred dollars and sentenced him to six months in jail. Shortly after his arrest, however, nearly 150 blacks tried to register to vote in protest.

In 1963 Block opened a library in Greenwood that was better than any other available to African Americans in the Delta, and he participated in a mock election organized by the Council of Federated Organizations as part of the Freedom Vote initiative. Before leaving Greenwood to register voters in Holmes and Humphreys Counties, Block helped organize the Greenwood Voters League, which not only continues to function but is one of the most visible and influential groups in the Delta.

After leaving SNCC, Block moved to California, and he was residing in Culver City at the time of his death on 13 April 2003.

Amy Schmidt
Lyon College

Raymond Arsenault, *Freedom Riders: 1961 and the Struggle for Racial Justice* (2006); Clayborne Carson, *In Struggle: SNCC and the Black Awakening of the 1960s* (1981); Civil Rights Movement Veterans website, www.crmvet.org; John Dittmer, *Local People: The Struggle for Civil Rights in Mississippi* (1994); Charles M. Payne, *I've Got the Light of Freedom: The Organizing Tradition and the Mississippi Freedom Struggle* (1995); Howard Zinn, *SNCC: The New Abolitionists* (1964).

Blue Mountain College

In 1869, at a time when little was being done for young women, two men discussed the idea of establishing an institution of higher learning for females in rural Northeast Mississippi. Gen. Mark Perrin Lowrey and J. B. Gambrell decided that Lowrey was the logical man to take on such a task. The general secured a property on a hillside in the southern part of Tippah County and established Blue Mountain Female Institute. It opened for its first session in 1873 with fifty students and four faculty members. The general served as president and professor of history and ethics. In 1876 the general's oldest daughter, Modena, married the Rev. William E. Berry, who bought a half interest in the school. The school also changed its name to Blue Mountain College. The next year, the institution received a charter from the State of Mississippi to maintain "a school of high grade for the education of girls and young women."

Lawrence Tyndale Lowrey Administration Building, Blue Mountain College (Courtesy Blue Mountain College)

By the 1882–83 session, enrollment reached 148 students, and the faculty had grown to 10 members. Lowrey died suddenly in Middleton, Tennessee, on 27 February 1885 but his will expressed his desire for the property to remain within the family and used in the interest of female education. His wishes were followed, with two of his sons and a grandson occupying the president's office for the next seventy-five years. Under their leadership the small liberal arts college expanded, became affiliated with the Mississippi Baptist Convention in 1919, and gained accreditation by the Southern Association of Colleges and Schools in 1927. A program for men training for church-related vocations began in 1957. Through these years, Blue Mountain College stood as a symbol of spiritual and intellectual growth in rural Northeast Mississippi and provided an education for thousands of young women and hundreds of young men, especially in teacher education.

On 1 January 2006, during the presidency of Bettye Coward, the college opened its doors to men on an equal basis with women. The school's mission statement recognizes the desire for students to gain "intellectual integrity, academic excellence, and Christian character." To pursue that goal, the college continues to expand its general four-year curriculum in liberal arts and pre-professional and professional programs and added a graduate program in elementary education in 2007. Since 2012 Dr. Barbara Childers McMillin has served as the college's president. Notable alumni include artist Dusti Bongé, travel writer Carolyn Bennett Patterson, and former Mississippi State College president George Duke Humphrey.

Thomas D. Cockrell
Northeast Mississippi
Community College

Blue Mountain College Catalog (2002–3); Blue Mountain College Papers, Archives of the National Alumnae Association of Blue Mountain College, Blue Mountain, Mississippi; Blue Mountain College website, www.bmc.edu; Robbie Neal Sumrall, *A Light on a Hill: A History of Blue Mountain College* (1947); Jane H. Talbert, *Faithful Daughters* (2000).

Blues

Mississippi—particularly the Delta region—is often called the Birthplace of the Blues, a designation that derives from the oppressive sociopolitical conditions that shaped the music's development, the historic overrepresentation of Mississippi natives among blues recording artists, and the great influence of musical styles that derive from Mississippi. There is scant evidence, however, to support the music's genesis here rather than in other areas of the South, largely as a consequence of the paucity of historical documentation of African American vernacular cultural expressions.

The term *Delta blues* is widely used to describe music characterized by the percussive use of the guitar, the employment of the slide or "bottleneck" in guitar playing, minimal harmonic development, a harsh vocal approach, and a general quality of intensity. Many leading blues scholars refrain from using the term *Delta blues*, however, because its "typical" traits also characterize styles found in other parts of the South.

Musically, blues is typified by the twelve-bar chord progression (though other lengths are common); in practice this means that a song segment extends over twelve musical measures and employs specific patterns of the tonic, dominant, and subdominant chords. A notable characteristic of the blues (as well as other types of music based on the pentatonic scale) is the "blue note," which is expressed in the diatonic scale as flattened thirds, fifths, and sevenths.

The blues most likely emerged in a recognizable form in the 1880s or 1890s, around the same time that both jazz and ragtime were born. While many researchers speculate that blues first emerged in the Mississippi Delta, by the early 1900s the music was rapidly gaining popularity across the South from Virginia to Texas. Some of the earliest accounts of the blues were in Mississippi. Harvard archaeologist Charles Peabody documented blues lyrics during a 1901–2 excavation of Indian mounds near Clarksdale, and W. C. Handy—dubbed the Father of the Blues because of his pioneering song publishing work—recalled first encountering the blues around 1903 at the train station in Tutwiler, describing it as "the weirdest music I ever heard." The unnamed musician played his guitar using a knife for a slide and sang about where the "Southern crosses the Dog," a reference to a railway crossing in Moorhead.

Distinctive local styles emerged in both rural and urban areas of the South. Although no African American recorded the blues until 1920, these styles spread earlier via itinerant musicians, the vaudeville circuit, the sheet music of professional songwriters such as Handy, and traveling tent shows such as the Port Gibson–based Rabbit's Foot Minstrels that brought sophisticated entertainment to rural areas such as the Delta. From 1920 to 1925 the vast majority of blues recordings were of women who worked on the vaudeville circuit, very few of whom were Mississippi natives. In the latter part of the decade labels increasingly documented "down-home" blues styles via mobile recording units and field agents in the South; the process captured many regional styles, including the rich traditions of Mississippi musicians. Over subsequent decades the blues changed dramatically, the result of its mass mediation via phonograph and radio, migration and urbanization, electrification, and broad changes in cultural taste.

It is impossible to explain exactly why the Mississippi Delta became such an influential center for blues, but it is evident why the area was ripe for innovations in secular culture. The Delta was settled largely in the decades following the Civil War, and the workers recruited for land-clearing projects and the resultant plantation system were largely African Americans from more established areas of Mississippi and other southeastern states. Consequently, older folk traditions had less traction in the Delta, and the preponderance of African Americans in Delta counties meant that less cross-racial musical interchange occurred there than in other areas. Although the string band music that flourished among both blacks and whites in the 1800s remained popular in the Delta into the 1930s via groups such as the Mississippi Sheiks, the relative "blackness" of Delta blues appears to reflect the area's unique demographic makeup. In an early 1940s study of the Clarksdale region, John Work III noted the Delta's relative lack of religiosity—the pervasiveness of religious authority across social life—compared to more settled areas. Under such conditions, secular music flourished, particularly as many plantation owners either encouraged or tolerated juke joints and other informal music gatherings. Documentary evidence also suggests that itinerant gamblers, musicians, and sex workers were well aware of the pay schedules of plantations, levee camps, and logging camps. Larger cities such as Greenville and Clarksdale also offered more formal venues in addition to good locations for soliciting tips.

The most important early center for blues in the state surrounded the Drew area beginning in the 1910s and revolved around Charley Patton (1891–1934), a native of Edwards who has been called the Father of the Delta Blues. Patton influenced many local artists as well as bluesmen from other parts of the state, including Howlin' Wolf (Chester Arthur Burnett) from White Station and Booker White from Houston. Patton's colleague Eddie "Son" House, known for his conflict between the blues and religion, was also very influential and served as the mentor to both Robert Johnson, who modernized the Delta style by incorporating sounds he heard by artists from other areas via phonograph records, and Muddy Waters (McKinley Morganfield) from Rolling Fork. Waters played a major role in electrifying and popularizing Delta blues after moving to Chicago, as did fellow Delta natives including Jimmy Reed, John Lee Hooker, Elmore James, and Sonny Boy Williamson II. James and Williamson made their first recordings in 1951 for Jackson's Trumpet Records, one of the few labels in the state at the time.

Most other important early artists came from the Jackson area and areas bordering the Delta. These include Crystal Springs's Tommy Johnson, the most important bluesman in the Jackson area; Skip James from Bentonia; and Mississippi John Hurt from Avalon. For social reasons, female musicians were relatively scarce in rural blues traditions; notable exceptions in Mississippi included Memphis Minnie, long associated with Walls, and Geechie Wiley, about whom little is known. Compared to more urbanized areas of the South, Mississippi spawned relatively few piano players, though notable exceptions include Albert "Sunnyland Slim"

Luandrew, Little Johnny Jones, Joe Willie "Pinetop" Perkins, and Waters's longtime sideman, Otis Spann.

Acoustic country blues styles declined in popularity beginning in the 1930s, particularly after electric amplification became commonplace. The influence of radio and records dampened the relative role of oral tradition, and in the 1940s–50s artists such as B. B. King and Little Milton Campbell developed popular styles that were based largely on jump blues traditions from the Southwest. They were better able to adapt to changes in the African American market than those who played in a straight Delta blues style, scoring national hits into the 1970s. By the mid-1950s most of the younger influential artists native to Mississippi had moved north, but blues remained popular locally, particularly in Clarksdale, Greenville, and Jackson, with a vibrant juke joint and nightclub network throughout the state. In the 1960s the music of this circuit began to turn more and more toward soul, and by the latter 1970s and early 1980s the music became popularly known as soul blues, a genre with a largely southern and almost exclusively African American base. Jackson's Malaco Records became the dominant label in this field in the early 1980s, continuing in this role into the twenty-first century; stars on its roster include Mississippi natives and/or residents including Little Milton, Denise LaSalle, Tyrone Davis, Bobby Rush, Willie Clayton, and Dorothy Moore.

Folklorists including Herbert Halpert, John Lomax, and Alan Lomax began documenting folk traditions in Mississippi in late 1930s. A new wave of folkloric activity was sparked by Alan Lomax's 1959 return visit, which resulted in the discovery of Mississippi Fred McDowell in Como. Many early Mississippi blues artists subsequently were "rediscovered" and brought to the festival-coffeehouse circuit, including Son House, Mississippi John Hurt, Booker White, and Skip James. By the mid-1960s the largely white "blues revival" audience on both sides of the Atlantic had embraced the electrified down-home blues of Mississippians, including Waters, Hooker, and Williamson, whose music was at the base of much popular music in the late 1960s and beyond. Beginning in the early 1980s, labels such as Earwig and Rooster Blues began documenting and popularizing the music of contemporary down-home artists in Mississippi, such as the Jelly Roll Kings, and in the 1990s the Oxford-based Fat Possum label successfully reached out to alternative rock audiences through recordings and later modern remixes of North Mississippi hill country artists David "Junior" Kimbrough and R. L. Burnside.

Blues-related tourism has grown considerably since 1978, when the Delta Blues Festival was founded in Greenville, and many other annual events now draw thousands of international visitors and highlight the state's contemporary blues talents. The Delta Blues Museum in Clarksdale opened in 1979, and the University of Mississippi began actively documenting the blues in 1983 via its acquisition of *Living Blues* magazine and the founding the following year of the Blues

Archive. In 2008 the B. B. King Museum and Delta Interpretive Center, budgeted at more than ten million dollars, opened in Indianola. Most promotion of blues initially came from grassroots activists, but the state and local tourist bureaus gradually began marketing blues more actively as they recognized the economic potential of using the music to promote cultural tourism. In 2003 the state created the Mississippi Blues Commission, which three years later initiated the Mississippi Blues Trail, comprised of more than 170 historic markers around the state, to encourage tourism and recognize the state's historically overlooked blues heritage.

Scott Barretta

Greenwood, Mississippi

Blues Archive, University of Mississippi Libraries, website, http://www .olemiss.edu/depts/general_library/archives/blues/; David "Honeyboy" Edwards, *The World Don't Owe Me Nothing: The Life and Times of Delta Bluesman David "Honeyboy" Edwards* (1997); David Evans, *Big Road Blues: Tradition and Creativity in Folk Blues* (1982); William Ferris, *Give My Poor Heart Ease: Voices of the Mississippi Delta* (2009); Ted Gioia, *Delta Blues* (2008); Alan Lomax, *The Land Where the Blues Began* (1993); Paul Oliver, *The Story of the Blues* (1969); Robert Palmer, *Deep Blues: A Musical and Cultural History of the Mississippi Delta* (1981); Elijah Wald, *Escaping the Delta: Robert Johnson and the Invention of the Blues* (2004); John Wesley Work, Lewis Wade Jones, and Samuel C. Adams Jr., *Lost Delta Found: Rediscovering the Fisk University–Library of Congress Coahoma County Study, 1941–1942*, ed. Robert Gordon and Bruce Nemerov (2005).

Blues Festivals

The first US blues festivals emerged not in Mississippi but in Michigan, Wisconsin, Illinois, and California during the mid- to late 1960s. Not until 1978 did Mississippi stage its first such event, the Mississippi Delta Blues and Heritage Festival (MDBHF) in Freedom Village, located near the port city of Greenville. Organized by Mississippi Action for Community Education (MACE), the MDBHF is recognized as the first major blues festival in the South and the second-oldest ongoing blues festival in the United States. During the early years of the festival, the MDBHF featured local Delta blues musicians such as James "Son" Thomas playing traditional "down-home" Delta blues music in front of a few thousand spectators. Nearly forty years later the festival has grown significantly to include local blues musicians and international stars as well as a variety of blues styles from Delta blues to soul blues (or southern soul music). The MDBHF and many of the state's other blues festivals also feature a number of gospel performers. Depending on the size of the event, a blues festival may include as many as three stages—typically an acoustic or heritage stage, a gospel stage, and a main stage.

Festival organizers argue that blues festivals preserve and promote the music, honor local musicians' contributions to the development of the art form, provide financial assistance to destitute musicians, and insert a much-needed economic boost into the local communities. MACE claims that the MDBHF pumps approximately three million dollars per year into the local economy. Attendance at blues festivals ranges from approximately twenty-five thousand to fewer than one hundred, although these figures are often unreliable: attendance figures for the 2006 MDBHF, for example, have been reported as twenty thousand and as fifty-five hundred. Although audience members typically possess a degree of ethnic and racial diversity, an increasing number of tourists, primarily white baby boomers, are attending the festivals, and whites have largely replaced the music's traditional African American audience. To attract tourists, promoters market Mississippi and particularly the Delta region as the legitimate home of the blues and make frequent claims regarding the festivals' "authenticity." For example, the Sunflower River Blues and Gospel Festival, held annually in August in Clarksdale, has long claimed to be "America's purest blues festival." Conversely, some festivals, including the Cotton Capital Blues Festival in Greenwood and the Tri-State Blues Festival in Southaven, feature almost exclusively soul blues artists to attract members of the local African American population. Soul blues, a subgenre that blends the blues with R&B and soul, is the most popular form of blues within the African American community. Some blues festivals are free to the public (Sunflower River Blues and Gospel Festival), while other events charge an admission fee typically ranging from three dollars (Rosedale Heritage and Blues Festival) to twenty dollars (MDBHF). Virtually all of the festivals rely on financial support from local and state governments, corporate sponsors, local businesses, and private citizens, among other contributors.

Until recently, Mississippi's blues festival season lasted approximately five months, from mid-May to mid-October, and included only a handful of events, mostly located in the Delta region. Yet, reflecting increasing interest in capturing blues tourism as an alternative source of revenue, the blues festival season now lasts almost ten months, from February to November, with new events staged in virtually every part of the state. At present, approximately fifty different blues festivals are held annually in Mississippi.

Stephen A. King

Eastern Illinois University

Stephen A. King, *I'm Feeling the Blues Right Now: Blues Tourism and the Mississippi Delta* (2011); Mississippi Action for Community Education website, www.deltamace.org; Jim O'Neal, in *Nothing but the Blues: The Music and the Musicians*, ed. Lawrence Cohn (1993).

Board of Trustees, Mississippi Institutions of Higher Learning

Kerry Brian Melear
University of Mississippi

Board of Trustees, Mississippi Institutions of Higher Learning, *Policies and Bylaws* (2008); James Allen Cabaniss, *A History of the University of Mississippi* (1949); Miss. Code Ann., sec. 37–4-3 (1986); Miss. Const., Art. VIII, sec. 213-A (1943); David G. Sansing, *Making Haste Slowly: The Troubled History of Higher Education in Mississippi* (1990); John W. Winkle, *The Mississippi State Constitution: A Reference Guide* (1993).

The Board of Trustees of the Mississippi Institutions of Higher Learning is the coordinating agency for Mississippi's eight publicly funded universities—Alcorn State, Delta State, Jackson State, Mississippi State, Mississippi University for Women, Mississippi Valley State, the University of Mississippi, and the University of Southern Mississippi. It provides organization and oversight of the university system across policy, financial, legal, and other administrative concerns.

Conceived as an entity that would shield the state's public institutions from the political influence that plagued its predecessors, the board held its first meeting on 18 May 1944. Past boards had also sought to mitigate the pernicious and consistent influence of Mississippi politics, but they had met with little success. The final act of political intervention leading to the creation of the present board occurred soon after the 1939 gubernatorial election, when Gov. Paul B. Johnson Sr. dismissed a number of faculty members and administrators at State Teachers College in Hattiesburg (now the University of Southern Mississippi). In response to this political intrusion into academia, the regional educational accrediting agency, the Southern Association of Colleges and Schools, placed the college on probation and threatened to rescind accreditation for the state's other institutions of higher learning as well. The association also cautioned that it would remain watchful for further political intrusions into higher education in the state.

In response to this threat, a small group of Mississippians urged Johnson to consider creating a constitutional board of trustees that would insulate the universities from political influence. A paramount concern was that any change in the structure of a constitutionally created board would require amendment of the state's constitution rather than simply legislation. The governor agreed, and the necessary constitutional amendment was introduced during the 1942 legislative session. It passed both houses of the Mississippi legislature and was ratified in 1943, becoming Article 8, sec. 213-A of the Mississippi Constitution. The constitutional language empowered the new board to elect the various institutional presidents and contract with faculty members and administrators as well as to terminate their employment "at any time for malfeasance, inefficiency, or contumacious conduct, but never for political reasons."

The board is now comprised of one member from each congressional district, one member from each Mississippi Supreme Court district, and two members from the state at large. The board's headquarters is located at the Education and Research Center of Mississippi in Jackson.

Bobwhite Quail

Colinus virginianus, better known to Mississippians as the bobwhite quail, has long been regarded among the most popular game birds of the eastern United States. Hailing from the family *Odontophoridae*, the eastern bobwhite quail occupies an important role in Mississippi's social, cultural, and environmental history.

The bobwhite quail is a farm bird that flourishes in early successional habitat—the mix of vegetation that grows just after soil disturbances in heavily worked landscapes. Field edges, hedgerows, old fields, and open woodlands—all central ecological components of Mississippi's agricultural landscape before World War II—offered the birds plentiful food and effective cover from predators, thus making ideal quail ground. Quail were undoubtedly widespread across Mississippi during the antebellum era, but the negotiation of tenantry and sharecropping after the Civil War led to an exponential increase in quail populations throughout the South. As sharecroppers spread across the countryside in the late nineteenth century, a new spatial mosaic created a fragmentary landscape that greatly increased quail habitat. In addition, the annual southern custom of using fire to clear forests of dense undergrowth maintained ground cover that was perfect for both quail and quail hunting. Around the same time, breech-loading shotguns and new hunting dog breeds made shooting quail a more practical endeavor. As a result, Mississippi and the South became a national center for game bird hunting. Northern hunters filled the southern countryside during the winter and by the turn of the twentieth century created a highly stylized hunt with accoutrements such as hunting wagons, specially groomed horses, and a bevy of dog handlers and servants attending to every need.

Southerners themselves, however, were more likely to hit the fields and woods on foot with at most one or two dogs. Mississippians tended to engage the bobwhite quail in two distinct ways during the first half of the twentieth century. For rural dwellers struggling to make a living from the land, quail supplemented incomes and diets. Tenants and small landowners shot or trapped quail, eating some themselves and selling others in urban markets. Some even found a good meal during the late spring by raiding quail nests for eggs. Beyond household or market use, Mississippians also found good sport in quail hunting. Many in the landowning classes took to boasting about their land's quail production, and a large bag at the end of the day was a source of significant pride. Statewide bag limits in the early 1930s reined in some of the revelry, but enforcement was weak early on, and locals continued to hunt for many years despite state conservation laws.

The heavy hunting pressure in the first half of the twentieth century did not do in the bobwhite quail, however. Rather, New Deal farm programs and the increasing mechanization of southern agriculture after World War II brought about substantial agricultural change. Tenants and sharecroppers left the land, fields grew in size, modern methods of cultivation encouraged farmers to till fields clean and plow up hedgerows, and bobwhite quail populations declined accordingly. Quail, then, are no longer a byproduct of agricultural production; the few places in Mississippi with shootable numbers of wild quail today are those managed specifically for the bird. Nonetheless, the bobwhite quail remains an important symbol of Mississippi's agrarian past.

Albert G. Way
Kennesaw State University

Jack Temple Kirby, *Rural Worlds Lost: The American South, 1920–1960* (1987); Stuart Marks, *Southern Hunting in Black and White: Nature, History, and Rituals in a Carolina Community* (1991); Wiley Prewitt, "The Best of All Breathing: Hunting and Environmental Change in Mississippi, 1890–1980" (master's thesis, University of Mississippi, 1991).

Bogan, Lucille
(1897–1948) Musician

Lucille Bogan was among the first classic blues singers to be recorded and to have a strong influence on many later blues artists. She was born Lucille Anderson on 1 April 1897 in Amory, Mississippi. Her family moved to Birmingham, Alabama, when she was very young. She married Nazareth Lee Bogan in 1914 and gave birth to a son, Nazareth Bogan Jr., the following year. She moved to Chicago in the late 1920s and to New York in the early 1930s, probably moved back to Birmingham in the mid-1930s, and spent her later years in Los Angeles.

She was first recorded in Atlanta by the OKeh label in 1923, making her the first blues singer recorded outside the record industry centers of Chicago and New York. She went on to record for Paramount (1927), Brunswick (1928–30), Banner (1933–35), and the American Record Company (1934–35). After 1933 Bogan began recording under the name Bessie Jackson, probably in an attempt to get around recording contracts. Bogan ultimately recorded almost one hundred songs.

Bogan's style helped define the classic blues sound of the 1920s, though her first recordings were, like those of many early female blues singers, more from the vaudeville tradition than blues. She was also very much influenced by singer Viola McCoy, whose songs Bogan covered early in her career. Her songs often dealt with highly sexual themes as well as gambling and alcoholism. Titles such as "Coffee Grindin' Blues," "Tricks Ain't Walking No More," and "Stew Meat Blues" often contain thinly veiled double meanings. Other song titles are more direct: "Cravin' Whiskey Blues," "Drinking Blues," and "Sloppy Drunk Blues." Songs such as "B[ull]. D[yke]. Woman's Blues" address lesbianism; the song's opening line states "Comin' a time, B.D. womens ain't gonna need no men."

Her songs have been performed by many blues artists. "Sloppy Drunk Blues" was recorded by Walter Davis, Leroy Carr, John Lee "Sonny Boy" Williamson, and Jimmy Rogers. "Black Angel Blues" was recorded by Tampa Red, Robert Nighthawk, B. B. King, Buddy Guy, and others.

Bogan died of coronary sclerosis in Los Angeles on 10 August 1948.

Greg Johnson
University of Mississippi

Robert Dixon, John Godrich, and Howard Rye, *Blues and Gospel Records, 1890–1943* (1997); Bob Eagle, *Living Blues* (Autumn 1979); Sheldon Harris, *Blues Who's Who* (1981); Guido Van Rijn, *Encyclopedia of the Blues* (2006).

Bolivar County

With the Mississippi River and Arkansas border forming its western edge, Bolivar County lies in the heart of the Delta. The county was established on 9 February 1836 from lands ceded to United States by the Choctaw Nation in 1830. The county is named for Simón Bolívar, a Spanish general celebrated for his contributions to independence movements in Central and South America. Bolivar possesses two county seats, Cleveland and Rosedale.

In its early years, Bolivar County had an almost entirely agricultural economy. In its first census in 1840, 838 people worked in agriculture, while only 5 were employed in manufacturing and commerce. In that year the county's population consisted of 384 free whites, 1 free black, and 971 slaves. By 1860 Bolivar's 9,078 slaves constituted 87 percent of the population, the fourth-highest ratio of slaves to free people in Mississippi.

Delta farmland was astonishingly valuable: on the eve of the Civil War Bolivar County had the second-highest land value in Mississippi. Despite its small population, the county ranked fourteenth in the state in cotton production. However, Bolivar ranked much lower in corn production (thirty-first) and in the value of its livestock (twenty-ninth). In 1860 Bolivar County employed only one person, a carriage maker, in manufacturing.

Postbellum Bolivar had a relatively small number of farms, but they, like many agricultural establishments in the Delta, were among the state's largest. Bolivar's nonagricultural economic sector remained relatively undeveloped, as the county's twenty manufacturing firms employed only fifty-one men in 1880.

In 1887 Isaiah T. Montgomery, Joshua P. T. Montgomery, and Benjamin T. Green formed the town of Mound Bayou. An experiment in African American self-determination, Mound Bayou featured black mayors, banks, businesses, consumers, schools, and eventually a hospital. With much discussion about using Booker T. Washington's Tuskegee model, Mound Bayou earned the nickname the Jewel of the Delta.

Mound Bayou made Bolivar County a favored destination for African Americans interested in finding work, land, and a thriving African American economy and society. By 1880 Bolivar County was home to 15,958 African Americans and 2,694 whites. Leading Reconstruction-era politician Blanche Bruce, a former slave from Virginia, held several political positions and ran a newspaper in Bolivar County before serving as one of Mississippi's US senators from 1875 to 1881.

The rush into the Delta continued in the late nineteenth century, and by 1900 Bolivar County had more than thirty-five thousand people, more than thirty-one thousand of them African Americans. But only 12 percent of Bolivar's black farmers owned their own land, compared to 44 percent of the county's white farmers. The partitioning of plantation farmland and shrinking lot acreage in Bolivar reflected a dramatic trend throughout the Mississippi Delta in the late 1800s. In 1880 the average farm in Bolivar was 311 acres, far larger than the state average. By 1900, with owners dividing land among growing numbers of tenants and sharecroppers, the county's average farm size of 44 acres was among the lowest in the state.

The presence of Mound Bayou eventually helped to stimulate the development of small manufacturing firms. By the turn of the century, Bolivar County's 117 manufacturing firms employed 383 workers, all of them male. Bolivar was also home to a small but significant portion of the Mississippi Delta's growing immigrant population. In 1900 this population comprised 311 people and included some of the most sizable Italian (135 people) and Chinese (31 people) groups in the state.

With a small free population and a heavy concentration on agriculture, residents in antebellum Bolivar County did relatively little to develop a religious infrastructure. In 1860 the county had only five churches, all of them Methodist. By 1916, however, Bolivar was home to more than sixteen thousand Missionary Baptists, the largest concentration of the state's leading religious denomination and more than two-thirds of Bolivar's church members. The African Methodist Episcopal Church; the Methodist Episcopal Church, South; the Catholic Church; and the Colored Methodist Episcopal Church also had large memberships.

From 1900 to 1930 Bolivar County witnessed one of the most dramatic population increases in the state, doubling from around 35,000 to more than 71,000, all but 3,240 of whom lived in what were considered rural areas. As the Great Depression set in, Bolivar had the second-largest population and fourth-highest population density among Mississippi counties. Bolivar continued to maintain a significant African American majority. The county was also home to 314 Italians and 766 Russians, an uncommonly diverse population for rural Mississippi. Bolivar had more than thirteen thousand farms, but only 8.6 percent of farmers owned their land.

With the simultaneous presence of Mound Bayou and a large African American majority, it is no surprise that Bolivar County was the site of creative efforts both to organize African Americans and to address issues specific to residents of the Mississippi Delta. During the 1920s Bolivar County was home to seventeen chapters of the Universal Negro Improvement Association (UNIA), one of the highest concentrations of such groups in the country. Founded by Marcus Garvey, the UNIA held up the goal of self-determination for all people of African descent. UNIA leader Adam Newson of Merigold was one of the state's most prominent organizers. In 1936 the Southern Tenant Farmers' Union and a group of activists working from a range of Christian, socialist, and integrationist perspectives established the Delta Cooperative Farm near Hillhouse. To address the area's lack of medical care, the Alpha Kappa Alpha sorority created the Mississippi Health Project in the 1930s.

Activist Amzie Moore moved to Bolivar County in 1935 and lived and worked there for the rest of his life. Moore provided an important link between early organizational efforts and the civil rights protests of the 1960s. Doctor and business leader T. R. M. Howard moved to Mound Bayou in the 1940s and in 1951 organized the Regional Council of Negro Leadership, one of Mississippi's first homegrown civil rights organizations. Sam Block, an activist who worked a great deal in Greenwood, was born in Cleveland in 1939. The short-lived Mississippi Freedom Labor Union began among Bolivar's cotton farmers in 1965.

Several important musicians and artists hail from Bolivar County, which is divided by the famed blues thoroughfare Highway 61. Henry Townsend grew up in Shelby, David "Honeyboy" Edwards was born in Shaw, and Jimmy Reid is also from Bolivar. In 1954 Pup and Lee McCarty started McCarty Pottery, a unique and lasting effort to create art from Mississippi mud. Milburne Crowe founded the Mound Bayou Historical Society to gather information and to share the area's unique story. Editor and author Charles East was born in Shelby in 1924, and author Jack Butler was born in Alligator in 1944.

Delta State Teachers College was created by the legislature in 1924 and opened in Cleveland the following year. Although the school was located in a largely black county, it admitted only white students. In 1955 the school expanded, becoming Delta State College and developing a larger set of institutional goals; by 1974 it had become a university. The school began admitting African American students in 1967 and has subsequently worked in numerous ways to serve its larger community. Delta State's notable sports figures include basketball star Lusia Harris and baseball coach Dave "Boo" Ferris, and the teams have been known as the Statesmen, Lady Statesmen, and more recently the Fighting Okra.

The Sillers family held considerable power in and beyond Bolivar County. Walter Sillers Jr., the son of a powerful state legislator, helped organize the Delta Council, a cotton planters' organization that helped influence national agricultural policy for generations. Sillers served in the Mississippi House of Representatives for fifty years, representing cotton growers and opposing the state's political system and efforts to integrate schools. His sister, Florence Sillers Ogden, wrote a conservative column in the Delta for years and helped organize the Women for Constitutional Government in Jackson in 1962.

In the mid-twentieth century, Bolivar County's substantial population began to decline. In 1960 the county was home to 54,464 people, more than two-thirds of them African Americans. Bolivar was among the top five counties in Mississippi in the percentage of people with less than five years of schooling (37 percent). Although the county's agricultural workforce declined by 89 percent from 1960 to 1980, Bolivar still had the most agricultural laborers of any county in the state throughout the 1980s. During this era Bolivar ranked second in cotton production and first in wheat and rice; in fact, almost half of the state's rice came from Bolivar. Conversely, the county had relatively little livestock and low corn production. By Mississippi standards, Bolivar maintained a large international community, with more than a thousand people born outside the United States. About half of the county's immigrants were from Italy, while the majority of the others hailed from China and Mexico.

In 2010 Bolivar County's population of 34,145 remained predominantly African American. As in many Mississippi Delta counties, Bolivar's population had declined since 1960, losing 20,319 people (37 percent) over the previous half century.

Mississippi Encyclopedia Staff
University of Mississippi

Bolivar County, Mississippi Genealogy and History Network website, bolivar.msghn.org; Mississippi State Planning Commission, *Progress Report on State Planning in Mississippi* (1938); *Mississippi Statistical Abstract*, Mississippi State University (1952–2010); Charles Sydnor and Claude Bennett, *Mississippi History* (1939); University of Virginia Library, Historical Census Browser website, mapserver.lib.virginia.edu; E. Nolan Waller and Dani A. Smith, *Growth Profiles of Mississippi's Counties, 1960–1980* (1985).

Boll Weevil

The boll weevil, a small grayish-brown beetle dependent on cotton plants for its food and reproduction, first entered the United States from Mexico around 1892. By early 1907 it stood poised to enter Mississippi's rich farmlands. The pest had already destroyed an estimated four hundred million bales worth of cotton in Texas, Louisiana, Oklahoma, and Arkansas, an amount valued at more than $230 million. While the insect had been present in the United States for fifteen years, it had stymied efforts to curb its damage and check its advance. Congress had allocated thousands of dollars for research and farmer education, and the infested states had built up their agriculture departments and land-grant colleges in hopes of finding a solution. Though the boll weevil caused significant damage elsewhere, no state depended on cotton the way Mississippi did.

During its first year in Mississippi the weevil destroyed less than 1 percent of the state's cotton, but by 1913 it was present throughout the state and destroyed more than a third of the crop. In the decade that followed, the average crop loss caused by the weevil was 26 percent—substantial but not enough to convince farmers to halt all cotton production in the state. In fact, farmers in the Delta were happy to discover that the productive power of the region's soil allowed their crops to ripen and be picked by late fall, when weevil populations were highest, thus limiting the pest's damage. In other areas of the state, however, farmers fought the boll weevil on less productive land and with already slim profit margins. State and federal extension agents and researchers at Mississippi A&M (now Mississippi State University) had

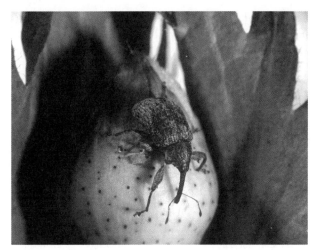

Cotton boll weevil (US Department of Agriculture, K2742-6)

the state to keep up with the technology and costs of successfully battling the insect.

In the 1980s and 1990s researchers at Mississippi State perfected a weevil trap that worked by using a synthetic pheromone to attract the bugs and snare them in containers. These bright green traps soon appeared on sticks at the edges of cotton fields throughout the South. This invention allowed farmers and extension agents to monitor weevil populations and target pesticide applications·to places that had demonstrated an outbreak. In 1978 an effort to eradicate the boll weevil from the South using this method began in North Carolina and slowly spread west across the region. Mississippi farmers rallied behind the cry "Boll Weevil Free by 2003," and the state essentially met that goal. Though the weevil has not been completely eradicated, it no longer poses the major threat that it did for almost a century.

James C. Giesen
Mississippi State University

Pete Daniel, *Breaking the Land: The Transformation of Cotton, Tobacco, and Rice Cultures since 1880* (1985); James C. Giesen, *Boll Weevil Blues: Cotton, Myth, and Power in the American South* (2011); Robert Higgs, *Agricultural History* (April 1976); Kathryn McKee, "Sherwood Bonner and the Postbellum Legacy of Southwestern Humor," in *Beyond Southern Frontier Humor: Prospects and Possibilities*, ed. Piacentino (2013).

developed some basic battle strategies that included planting specific seed varieties, clearing brush from the edges of fields, and applying pesticides at various times during the growing season. Many Mississippi farmers balked at these complicated and costly instructions.

Even prior to the weevil's arrival in the state, Mississippi musicians and artists had begun to depict it in their songs and stories. Charley Patton, a blues progenitor, first learned to play guitar the same year that the weevil arrived at the Dockery Plantation, where he lived. His "Mississippi Boweavil Blues" was the first commercially recorded song about the bug. Other musicians followed suit, producing hundreds of variations of boll weevil songs in the blues, country, and folk genres. In many versions, the weevil is presented as a kind of trickster, a character who fools with landowners and delights sharecroppers. In reality, however, the pest hurt those at the bottom of the agricultural labor system more profoundly than those at the top. When landowners wanted to spread poison on their cotton to fight the weevil, for example, they passed this cost along to the laborers, for whom the debt became another escalating number on the record books at the country store.

Following World War II, technical developments in airplanes and synthetic chemical pesticides made fighting the pest easier but more costly. Crop dusters could be hired to spread the poisons—first calcium arsenate and later DDT and malathion—if the farmer could afford it. By the 1950s mechanized planters and harvesters enabled farmers to more closely control the timing of cotton planting, which limited weevil damage. Seed research conducted at both Mississippi State University's research farms and private businesses like the Delta and Pine Land Company resulted in fast-maturing cotton varieties that allowed farmers to limit the amount of time the crop spent in the field with the weevils. These advances curbed the extent of boll weevil damage but also made it increasingly difficult for small farmers in

Bolton, Ruthie
(b. 1967) Athlete

Former Auburn University basketball star Ruthie Bolton is one of the pioneers of women's professional basketball. Bolton played guard on three conference championship teams at Auburn, played on several European professional teams, and became one of the first stars in the Women's National Basketball Association (WNBA) in the United States. She played eight years with the Sacramento Monarchs and was a member of two US Olympic gold medal teams.

Alice Ruth Bolton and her twin brother, Ray, were born in McLain, Mississippi, on 25 May 1967; their parents, Rev. Linwood Bolton and Leola Bolton, had eighteen other children. Raised in rural Mississippi, Ruthie and her siblings shared chores, sports, and their Baptist faith. At McLain High School, Ruthie played basketball in the shadow of her older sister, Mae Ola, who was recruited to Auburn in 1984.

In 1986 Ruthie followed her sister to Auburn, where they and teammates Vickie Orr and Carolyn Jones enjoyed great success. Auburn's record during Bolton's four years at the school was 119–13: the team won three Southeastern Conference (SEC) championships and played in the National Collegiate Athletic Association (NCAA) Tournament every year, making two trips to the Final Four. Bolton achieved numerous honors, including second team all-SEC in 1989, all–Final Four in 1988, and all-Academic SEC in 1988 and 1989. She graduated in 1989 with a degree in exercise physiology and was commissioned a second lieutenant in the US Army Reserve, serving until 2000. At Auburn, Bolton shares the record for games played and is among the Top 10 on the career lists for assists and steals. Bolton scored a total of 1,176 points, putting her in twenty-fourth place on the Auburn career scoring list. In February 2001 Auburn retired Bolton's jersey along with those of Orr and Jones.

Bolton married Mark Holifield in 1991; they had no children prior their 2002 divorce. In 2014, Bolton publicly declared that she had been the victim of domestic violence during that marriage.

Bolton began her professional basketball career in Europe because the United States had no women's league at that time. She played in Sweden in 1991, Hungary in 1992 (where she was the first American woman to play professionally), Italy from 1993 until 1995, and Turkey in 1996. In 1995–96 Bolton played on the US women's national team that achieved a perfect 60–0 record. She was also a key player on the US team that won the world championship in 1998. Perhaps her greatest recognition, however, came from her role as a member of the 1996 and 2000 US Olympic teams, both of which won gold medals. In 1996 she set an Olympic record for the most three-pointers in a game.

Capitalizing on the success of the women's Olympic team, the American Basketball League (ABL) and the WNBA introduced professional women's basketball to the United States in 1996 and 1997, respectively. (The ABL folded in 1998.) Bolton joined the Sacramento Monarchs, one of the WNBA's eight teams. She was Sacramento's first marquee player, a two-time all-star (1997, 2001) and first team all-WNBA (1997, 1999). After a career-threatening knee injury in 1998, repaired by Olympic speed skater turned orthopedic surgeon Eric Heiden, Bolton returned to the Monarchs in 1999, starting in all but one game. After the 2000 season, Bolton's playing time and productivity declined as she became a role player off the bench. She retired after an eight-year WNBA career during which she averaged ten points per game. She remained in her adopted hometown of Sacramento, where she conducted basketball clinics, speaking engagements, and community work as the team's fan and team relations manager. The Monarchs retired her No. 6 jersey in 2005.

From 2004 to 2007 Bolton served as head women's basketball coach at William Jessup University in Rocklin, California. After stepping down as head coach she assumed the post of associate head coach. In 2013 Bolton took the job of head coach of the varsity girls' basketball team at Vacaville Christian High School in Vacaville, California. She has

also released a gospel music CD, developed a line of clothing under the label RUWEAR, and started the nonprofit Ruthie Bolton Foundation to help motivate teens and student athletes in the Sacramento area. In June 2011 Bolton was inducted into the Women's Basketball Hall of Fame in Knoxville, Tennessee. She has remarried and has two children.

Boyd Childress
Auburn University

2014–15 Auburn Women's Basketball Record Book; Boyd Childress, *Encyclopedia of Alabama*, www.encyclopediaofalabama.org; Cynthia Hubert, *Sacramento Bee* (28 July 2004); William Jessup University official athletic website, www.jessupathletics.com; Alison Roberts, *Sacramento Bee* (7 January 2006); Michelle Smith, espnW.com (10 October 2014). Adapted with permission from the online *Encyclopedia of Alabama*.

Bongé, Dusti (Eunice Lyle Swetman)
(1903–1993) Artist

Born Eunice Lyle Swetman, Dusti Bongé was an artist best known for her intuitive abstract paintings, which first came to public attention in a solo exhibition at the Betty Parsons Gallery in New York City in 1956. Her work went through several stylistic evolutions, beginning with local scenes and moving through abstract surrealism, abstract expressionism, and ultimately delicate abstract paintings on small joss paper she bought at a Vietnamese market.

A native of Biloxi, Swetman was first interested in the theater. After graduating from Blue Mountain College, she moved north to study drama at the Lyceum in Chicago. She enjoyed limited success on the stage there, with a traveling company, and then later in New York. She took Dusti as her stage name and retained it for the rest of her life. She met her future husband, Archie Bongé, in Chicago. They married in Biloxi in 1926 and settled in New York City. Bongé, a native of Nebraska, had attended the University of Nebraska and the Pennsylvania Academy (with Mississippi artist Walter Anderson) and was receiving critical acclaim for his realistic paintings and illustrations. Their son, Lyle, was born in 1929, and the family moved to Mississippi six years later, thinking that the rural South would be a better place for him to grow up and would provide Archie with more time to paint. However, Archie Bongé died in 1936.

He had encouraged Dusti's artwork and invited her to accompany him on his frequent excursions to draw and paint local scenes, especially the charming vernacular buildings and the waterfront that characterized Biloxi before it was ravaged by Hurricane Camille in 1969 and Hurricane Katrina in 2005. After Archie's death Dusti found solace in his studio and began painting and drawing seriously. Her early work owes much to her husband's local scenes and experimentation with modernist geometry and color. She continued to produce brightly colored Cubist-inspired depictions of local scenes, and after a period of surrealist experimentation from 1945 to 1955, she embraced the approach of color-field and gesture painting that dominated American art of the period. Her association with the Betty Parsons Gallery lasted from 1956 to 1972. Her work has been widely exhibited, with significant collections at the Ogden Museum of Southern Art in New Orleans; Alabama's Mobile Museum of Art; the Lauren Rogers Museum of Art in Laurel, Mississippi; and the Mississippi Museum of Art in Jackson.

Her work, along with that of Archie and photographs by Lyle, who trained at Black Mountain College in North Carolina, has been preserved and promoted by the Dusti Bongé Foundation in Biloxi since 1995.

Julian Brunt
Biloxi, Mississippi

David Houston
New Orleans, Louisiana

Patti Carr Black, *American Masters of the Mississippi Gulf Coast: George Ohr, Dusti Bongé, Walter Anderson, and Richmond Barthé* (2008); Dusti Bongé Art Foundation website, www.dustibonge.org.

Bonner, Sherwood (Katharine Sherwood Bonner McDowell)

(1849–1883) Author

Born on 26 February 1849 in Holly Springs, Mississippi, writer Katharine Sherwood Bonner was the eldest of three surviving children of the five born to physician Charles Bonner and Mary Wilson Bonner. Kate was educated at a local academy except for a brief term in 1863 at Hamner Hall, an Episcopal boarding school in Montgomery, Alabama. She witnessed the Civil War firsthand when Holly Springs was occupied by Federal troops: Gen. Ulysses S. Grant and his officers commandeered local residences, including Cedarhurst, the Bonner home. In 1865 Mary Bonner died, leaving fourteen-year-old Kate and younger siblings Ruth and Sam to be cared for by their father; his sister, Martha; and the family's black "Grandmammy" to several generations, Molly Wilson.

On Valentine's Day 1871 Kate married a persistent beau, Edward McDowell. Their only child, Lilian, was born the following December. They soon moved to Texas, where Edward had relatives, but by the fall of 1873, Kate and Lilian had returned. Leaving the baby with disapproving relatives, Kate went on alone to Boston. Secretarial positions with a series of prominent Bostonians—editor Nahum Capen, reformer Dr. Dio Lewis, and renowned poet Henry Wadsworth Longfellow—provided her entrée to the city's highest social and literary circles. In Longfellow, Kate found a lifelong friend and literary patron.

She took Sherwood Bonner as her pen name and discovered a marketable voice with a series of southern-slanted reports about Boston written for the *Memphis Avalanche* in 1874–75. She gained notoriety with "The Radical Club," a satiric poem that appeared in the *Boston Times*; she subsequently financed an 1876 European tour with travel columns prominently featured in Boston and Memphis newspapers. Over the next few years, she placed short fiction, nonfiction, and poetry in respected periodicals, including *Harper's Monthly*. In particular, her five "Grandmammy Tales," affectionate memoirs featuring Wilson's character and voice, helped to launch the nationally popular genre of black-dialect fiction. Other stories in the raucous tradition of Mark Twain built her a substantial reputation as an atypical female humorist. Several biographical sketches hint at emerging feminist themes, and two evocative historical essays describe wartime events in Holly Springs and the 1878 yellow fever epidemic there that claimed the lives of Bonner's father and brother.

In 1878 Harper Brothers published Bonner's unconventional Reconstruction novel, *Like unto Like*, set in Yariba, a fictional blend of Holly Springs and Huntsville, Alabama. *The Valcours*, a lighthearted novella with a tomboy heroine, was serialized in *Lippincott's* in 1881. She continued to mine the profitable vein of local-color fiction with four Tennessee mountain stories as well as four later tales that represent the first published fiction to depict realistic characters and dialects of southern Illinois. After Bonner finally obtained an Illinois divorce from Edward McDowell, her daughter and her aunt, Martha Bonner, returned with her to Boston.

When Bonner's health declined, she returned to Holly Springs and a diagnosis of advanced breast cancer. She died at home on Salem Street on 22 July 1883 and is buried, at her request, in an unmarked grave in the local cemetery.

Sherwood Bonner's literary reputation remains linked to her local-color and black-dialect fiction, which is collected in *Dialect Tales* (1883) and *Suwanee River Tales* (1884). Her travel letters, essays, and representative short fiction are reprinted in *A Sherwood Bonner Sampler, 1869–1884*.

Anne R. Gowdy
University of Mississippi

Anne R. Gowdy, ed., *A Sherwood Bonner Sampler, 1869–1884* (2000); Hubert McAlexander, *The Prodigal Daughter* (1981).

Book Publishing

Mississippi has long been home to important and popular writers, but until recently it has not been a central location for publishing books. Today, led by University Press of Mississippi, several book publishers make Mississippi their home—and often the subject of their published volumes.

In the 1800s and early 1900s authors with manuscripts to publish either sent them out of the state or arranged to have newspaper printers publish the books. By the middle of the twentieth century, however, many institutions arranged to publish a few books. For example, the Mississippi Poetry Society published some volumes beginning in the 1940s, and the Mississippi Historical Society did the same some years later. In Greenville in 1947, Hodding Carter, Kenneth Haxton, and Ben Wasson started Levee Press, a limited-edition operation that published four impressive volumes—William Faulkner's *Notes on a Horsethief*; Eudora Welty's *Music from Spain*; William Alexander Percy's poetry collection, *Of Silence and Stars*; and Shelby Foote's *The Merchant of Bristol*.

A major change took place in 1970 with the founding of the state's only not-for-profit publisher, University Press of Mississippi (UPM). Originally located on the campus of the University of Southern Mississippi under the direction of Robert Cecil Cook, UPM subsequently moved to its present location in Jackson. Sponsored by the state's eight public universities, UPM is a successful academic press that brings to market more than eighty new books each year in print and electronic editions. The press has published over two thousand books and has distributed more than 2.8 million copies worldwide. UPM is known for publishing books of the highest distinction and acquires, edits, promotes, and distributes books on southern history (especially Mississippi and Louisiana), African American studies, music, folklore, comics studies, popular culture, civil rights studies, Caribbean studies, diaspora studies, media studies, literary studies, and art and photography. The press is well known for its collected conversations with literary figures (Literary Conversations Series); film and television personalities (Conversations with Filmmakers, Television Conversations); and comic artists (Conversations with Comic Artists). In addition, the press is noted for several of its other series: the American Made Music Series, the Hollywood Legends Series, the Margaret Walker Alexander Series in African American Studies, and Willie Morris Books in Memoir and Biography. UPM also publishes volumes in collaboration with other state entities—for example, the Mississippi Historical Society's Heritage of Mississippi Series and volumes based on the University of Mississippi's Faulkner and Yoknapatawpha Conference and the Chancellor Porter L. Fortune Symposium in Southern History. For over forty years, University Press of Mississippi has maintained its high publishing standards and continues to bring national and worldwide recognition to the state.

Former UPM director Barney McKee and his wife, Gwen, started Quail Ridge Press in Brandon in 1978. Quail Ridge issues books on southern cultural topics, especially food, and describes itself as "preserving America's food heritage." Quail Ridge publishes the "Best of the Best" cookbooks—for example, *Best of the Best from Louisiana* and *Best of the Best from the Great Plains*. Gwen McKee, sometimes known as the Cookbook Lady, and Barbara Moseley are responsible for gathering recipes for many of the volumes. Quail Ridge Press also publishes Phil Hardwick's series of mysteries set in Mississippi, children's books including *Mississippi Alphabet* by Laurie Parker, and travel and political books.

Yoknapatawpha Press, named for William Faulkner's fictional county and based in his hometown of Oxford, was founded in 1975 by local clothier and historian Howard Duvall, whose first publications were reprints of John Faulkner's novels *Men Working* and *Dollar Cotton*; his memoir, *My Brother Bill*; and a facsimile of William Faulkner's *The Marionettes*. William Faulkner's niece, Dean Faulkner Wells, and her husband, Lawrence Wells, became Duvall's partners in 1976; edited and copublished a photobiography, *William Faulkner: The Cofield Collection*; and bought out Duvall in 1979. Since then, they have published some thirty titles, among them facsimiles of William Faulkner's *Mississippi Poems* and *Helen: A Courtship*; reprints of Willie Morris's *North towards Home*, *Good Ole Boy: A Delta Childhood*, and *Terrains of the Heart and Other Essays on Home*; two illustrated books of poems by James A. Autry; children's books by Dean Wells; and books she has edited. Larry Wells has continued to operate Yoknapatawpha Press since the death of his wife in July 2012.

Wilbur O. Colom and his wife, Dorothy Colom, of Columbus and James W. Parkinson of California combined to found Genesis Press in 1993. The Coloms' daughter, Niani Colom-Omotesa, works as associate publisher at the Columbus press, which is "the largest privately owned African American book publisher in the country." Genesis has become one of the major publishers of African American popular fiction, especially fiction by women, and its authors come from around the world. The press currently has nine imprints—Black Coral for women's literature, Indigo for romance fiction, Indigo after Dark for romantic and erotic fiction, Indigo Love Spectrum for fiction that features romance among multiethnic people, Indigo Vibe for young adult readers, Mount Blue for Christian material, Obsidian for mystery and science fiction, Sage for inspirational works, and Kiswahili, which republishes works of world literature.

Dogwood Press, a small but traditional publishing house headquartered in Brandon, began in 2002 when Editor in Chief Joe Lee released his first suspense novel, *On the Record*, and began seeking out strong southern voices for publication. Derringer Award–winning short story writer John Floyd was published for the first time by Dogwood Press in 2006, and since then the company has published five additional authors and more than twenty titles. Dogwood Press is primarily known for suspense fiction and southern humor, but it does consider some nonfiction projects for publication.

The Nautilus Publishing Company was founded in Oxford, Mississippi, in 1994 by Neil White. Nautilus publishes regional nonfiction books with a focus on memoir, education, history, sports, business, trivia, and photography. Nautilus authors include University of Mississippi Chancellor Emeritus Robert Khayat, musician Marty Stuart, College Football Playoff Executive Director Bill Hancock, historian David Sansing, radio host Jim Dees, sports columnist Rick Cleveland, psychologist Ken Sufka, noted physician Neil Spector, entrepreneur Jay Martin, investment advisor Scott Reed, and law professor Debbie Bell. Nautilus has been awarded the gold IPPY award for best book marketing by an independent press (twice), and silver IPPYs in the categories of memoir, music, and textbook publishing. Nautilus founder Neil White is also the bestselling author of *In the Sanctuary of Outcasts*.

A major factor in the sustainability of these Mississippi publishers is the presence of many vibrant independent booksellers across the state. Mississippi boasts two of the cardinal independent bookstores in the South if not the nation—Lemuria in Jackson and Square Books in Oxford. Both of these stores have helped launch and/or shape the careers of major writers nationwide while serving hometown communities. Richard Howorth, cofounder of Square Books, has served as president of the American Booksellers Association, and John Evans, owner of Lemuria, is a founding force of the Mississippi Book Festival. Independent stores primarily selling new books in Mississippi include Bay Books (Bay St. Louis), Southern Bound Books (Biloxi), Bay Window Books (Brandon), Cotton Row Bookstore (Cleveland), Pentimento (Clinton), Turnrow Book Co. (Greenwood), Main Street Books (Hattsieburg), Turning Pages Books & More (Natchez), Pass Christian Books (Pass Christian), The Book Mart & Café (Starkville), Sage Books (Starkville), Reed's Gumtree Books (Tupelo), and Lorelei Books (Vicksburg).

Established as a nonprofit organization in 2013, the inaugural Mississippi Book Festival was held on the lawn of the State Capitol in August 2015 and attracted more than 3,700 enthusiastic attendees. The second annual festival, held August 20, 2016, attracted 6,200 attendees and featured over 150 authors participating in thirty-two official panels and interviews. Known as Mississippi's Literary Lawn Party, the festival has quickly become a nationally recognized premier event that attracts book lovers, writers, and publishers from Mississippi, the region, and across the country. Free and open to the public, the festival hosts author panel discussions and interviews, book signings, live music, local food, young adult and children's activities, and exhibitors from across the state. The mission of the festival is to recognize authors and the books they produce, to celebrate writing, reading, and our literary heritage, and to connect readers with contemporary authors.

Ted Ownby
University of Mississippi

Charles Chappell, *Mississippi Quarterly* (Spring 1995); *Faulkner Newsletter and Yoknapatawpha Review*, University of Mississippi Libraries, Archives and Special Collections website, www.olemiss.edu/depts/general_library/archives/; University Press of Mississippi website, www.upress.state.ms.us; Joe Lee, Dogwood Press, www.dogwoodpress.com; Neil White, Nautilus Publishing Company, www.nautiluspublishing.com; Jere Nash, Mississippi Book Festival, www.msbookfestival.com.

Borinski, Ernst
(1901–1983) Scholar and Activist

A lifelong advocate for human and civil rights, Ernst Borinski fled Nazi Germany for the United States, where he worked to promote social change.

Borinski was born on 26 November 1901 to a Jewish merchant and his wife in Kattowitz (Katowice), a little town near the border between Germany and Poland. Known to those closest to him as "Bobo," Borinski was educated as a lawyer and became a magistrate for the town of Kelbra. In 1938, after Adolf Hitler had come to power and begun to institute his "New Order," Borinski decided that Jews should leave while they could. Borinski gave all his money to "ze conductor of ze train and told him, I am going to take a sleeping pill now. You are to vake me vhen ve have crossed ze border." He could not convince the members of his family to come along, and all of them except for one brother perished in the Holocaust.

After serving as an interpreter in the US Army's North African Campaign during World War II and becoming a US citizen in Canastelles, Algeria, while in the field of battle, Borinski returned to the United States and earned a master's degree in sociology at the University of Chicago (1946). In 1953 he completed his doctoral dissertation, "Sociology of Judge-Made Law in Civil Rights Cases," at the University of Pittsburgh.

In 1947 Borinski accepted a position at the all-black Tougaloo College in Jackson and he taught there for the remainder of his life. He inspired generations of students, among them Jerry Ward, now professor emeritus at Dillard University, and Joyce A. Ladner, a sociologist and former interim president of Howard University. Borinski encouraged numerous events—meetings, lectures, and German language classes—that cut across racial lines, and his social science lab was an oasis of journals, newspapers, and other related publications that ultimately led to an African study group that included students from nearby Millsaps College despite the dangers faced by participants in integrated activities.

Borinski was also a music lover, and at the conclusion of his annual birthday fete at his home on 23 November 1977, he announced his desire to establish in Mississippi an "academy" of music lovers devoted to the cultivation and practice of early music. The following year, he announced the establishment of the Mississippi Academy of Ancient Music (MA'AM). With the help of Richard McGinnis, who purchased a building in Edwards, Borinski provided a permanent home for the academy. MA'AM held its first public concert on 22 February 1981. In 1978 Max Christopher Garriott honored Borinski's birthday by commissioning a thirteen-movement, half-hour-long ode, "Welcome, All Ye Colleagues of Collegiate Climes." Borinski attended every MA'AM concert until his death and insisted that the concerts must continue even when he was no longer around to attend.

Annie Payton
Mississippi Valley State University

Rosellen Brown, *Life* (April 1995); Janne Patterson, in *The Voice of the American Civil Liberties Union/Mississippi* (Fall 1983); Mississippi Academy of Ancient Music, *Ernst Borinski Memorial Concert: Brief History and Synopsis of the Music for the Borinski Birthday Parties*, Tougaloo College Archives.

"Born of Conviction" Statement

The 2 January 1963 issue of the *Mississippi Methodist Advocate* contained a statement, "Born of Conviction," signed by twenty-eight pastors of the white Methodist Mississippi Conference, which represented the southern half of the state. In response to "the grave crises precipitated by racial discord within our state in recent months," especially the 1962 University of Mississippi riot, the statement offered an expression of conscience and commitment from "Christian ministers and . . . native Mississippians." Because of the silence of the bishop and other top Conference leaders on

these matters, the signers felt compelled to speak publicly. The emphasis on native Mississippians was designed to prevent the statement's dismissal as the words of "outside agitators." Most of the signers were young—half were under thirty and three-quarters were under thirty-six.

The statement (1) called for freedom of the pulpit so that ministers might speak against injustice without fear of reprisal; (2) quoted passages from the 1960 *Methodist Discipline*, the denomination's law book, including "all men are brothers" and "no discrimination because of race, color, or creed"; (3) expressed support for the state's public schools and unalterable opposition to their closing "or to the diversion of tax funds to the support of private or sectarian schools"; and (4) affirmed the signers' "unflinching opposition to Communism," refuting the common contention that anyone who challenged the status quo must be a communist.

The state's daily newspapers carried front-page stories on the statement and responses to it for several days. Public expressions of support came from the Conference's lay leader, Dr. J. P. Stafford of Cary; an associate conference lay leader, Francis B. Stevens of Jackson; Dr. W. B. Selah, pastor of Jackson's Galloway Memorial Methodist Church; twenty-three Methodist ministers of the Tupelo District of the white North Mississippi Conference; and a small number of newspaper editors. However, the overwhelming response from editors, political leaders, church members, and others was negative. The segregationist Mississippi Association of Methodist Ministers and Laymen issued a lengthy statement opposing "Born of Conviction." Bishop Marvin Franklin declined comment, and on 16 January he and his cabinet (six district superintendents) issued a statement in the *Advocate* that made no mention of "Born of Conviction" and assured white Methodists that "integration is not forced on any part of our Church."

Two signers were almost immediately ousted by their congregations with the cooperation of their district superintendents, and a third felt forced out of his position because of violence against his property and further threats. All of the participants received many expressions of support, but most also received telephoned threats and hate mail, and several were shunned or accosted by some members of their congregations. Officials told a few of the pastors that their current churches wanted them moved and that no other church in the Conference would accept them. Some churches passed resolutions stating that they did not want any of the twenty-eight appointed as their pastor. Nevertheless, ten of the twenty-eight were reappointed to their churches in May 1963.

By that summer, eleven signers had transferred to other Methodist annual conferences, and five more followed over the next year. In all, nineteen transferred out of the Mississippi Conference (most outside the South), and another signer spent much of his subsequent career outside the state. Only eight remained in the ministry in the Mississippi Conference for the rest of their careers; two others returned to the North Mississippi Conference a few years later.

In his description of Mississippi's "Closed Society" in the early 1960s, James Silver argued that "a never-ceasing propagation of the 'true faith' [white supremacy and segregation] must go on relentlessly, with a constantly reiterated demand for loyalty to the united front, requiring that nonconformists and dissenters from the code be silenced, or in a crisis, driven from the community." "Born of Conviction" and the widespread publicity surrounding it resulted in one important crack in that "united front" and called into question the "orthodox" belief that all white Christians supported the maintenance of segregation at whatever cost.

Joseph T. Reiff

Emory and Henry College

Paul Hendrickson, *Sons of Mississippi: A Story of Race and Its Legacy* (2003); Peter C. Murray, *Methodists and the Crucible of Race, 1930–1975* (2004); Joseph T. Reiff, *Born of Conviction: White Methodists and Mississippi's Closed Society* (2015); James W. Silver, *Mississippi: The Closed Society* (1966); Jim L. Waits, *Concern* (1 March 1963).

Borroum's Drug Store

Borroum's Drug Store, located at 604 East Waldron Street on the square in Corinth, Mississippi, is a landmark in the northeastern part of the state. Borroum's has existed for nearly a century and a half and continues to serve as a site of tourism and a resource for local living history as well as to minister to the medical needs of Corinth residents.

The store was established in 1865 by Andrew Jackson Borroum, a doctor who had obtained his degree from Louisiana Medical School and served as an assistant surgeon in Company C of the 34th Mississippi Infantry in the Civil War. Convinced by a friend to settle in Corinth, Borroum began practicing and then opened a drugstore. He moved it to its present location in 1916.

The store has remained in the hands of family members and is presently owned and operated by the founder's great-granddaughter, Camille Borroum Mitchell, one of the first two female students to obtain pharmacy degrees from the University of Mississippi. Early in her involvement with the store, Mitchell recognized the importance of making it a tourist destination as well as a drugstore and added a museum that included old medicine bottles, antique fixtures, photographs of the early days of Corinth, family relics from the Civil War, and an arrowhead collection compiled by her father, James Lannes Borroum. The store also features a working 1926 cash register, Mitchell's portraits of the store's former owners, and a functioning antique soda

fountain and Art Deco–style bar. The store has been featured on numerous television programs and in such magazines as *Mississippi Farm Country* and *Southern Living*. Along with tourists, customers continue to come to buy both prescription and over-the-counter drugs and to have sodas, phosphates, and malts at the soda fountain, making Borroum's Drug Store an intriguing combination of a historical artifact and living organism unique and important to the texture of Corinth and North Mississippi.

Taylor Hagood

Florida Atlantic University

Borroum's Drug Store website, http://www.borroumsdrugstore.com/; Elmo Howell, in *Mississippi Scenes: Notes on Literature and History* (1992); Scott Jones, *Southern Living* (June 2003); "Solve the Mystery," *Mississippi Farm Country: Publication of the Mississippi Farm Bureau Federation* (July–August 2002).

Boswell, George

(1919–1995) Folklorist

George Worley Boswell was born in Nashville, Tennessee, in 1919, when the South was already well into an economic decline that would virtually cripple the United States a decade later. Boswell maintained a lifelong interest in folksinging, and two aunts who made their living teaching piano may have planted the musical seed in the young boy. As a child Boswell enjoyed Nashville's Grand Ole Opry, one of the twentieth century's most important musical venues.

Boswell learned to read and write music at David Lipscomb Junior College, then entered Vanderbilt University, where he earned a bachelor's degree in English and studied under Donald Davidson, whom Boswell credited as instrumental to his understanding of British ballads. In 1939 Boswell earned a master's degree from the George Peabody College for Teachers. He taught high school for a short period and was drafted into the army, where he served in the Signal Corps. After World War II, Boswell returned to Peabody and earned a doctorate. In 1950–51 he took a teaching position at Austin Peay State College, finished his dissertation, and married Emily Hall.

Boswell published numerous literary essays, but his greatest contribution to scholarship was his enormous collection of folk songs from Middle Tennessee and his numerous scholarly essays on southern folklore. He began collecting songs in 1948 and had collected more than twelve hundred by the end of his career. He and J. Russell Weaver published a seminal monograph, *Fundamentals of Folk Literature*, in

1962. His journal articles include "The Kinds of Folksongs," "Otherwise Unknown or Rare Ballads from the Tennessee Archives," "A Shiloh Cante Fable," "Three Tennessee Folksongs," "Pitch: Musical and Verbal in Folksong," "Mississippi Folk Names of Plants," "Folk Recipes of the South," and dozens of others pertaining to virtually every aspect of folk culture in Mississippi and Tennessee. He also contributed essays to the book *Folksongs of Mississippi and Their Background*.

Boswell spent the majority of his career teaching literature at the University of Mississippi. Blending his love of folklore with his duties as a professor, Boswell was among the first generation of professional scholars to view folklore as real literature that was interesting for its literary merits in addition to its anthropological and sociological value. Boswell also encouraged his students to participate in gathering local folk songs—as many as four hundred of the songs in Boswell's monumental collection came from his graduate and undergraduate students. Boswell also published two short pieces inspired by his students, "Ole Miss Jokes and Anecdotes" and "Irony in Campus Speech."

As a literary scholar working in Oxford, Boswell perhaps inevitably devoted a considerable portion of his career to the study of William Faulkner. Boswell explored folkways in the Nobel Prize winner's fiction and published journal articles including "The Legendary Background in Faulkner's Work," "Folkways in Faulkner," "Epic, Drama, and Faulkner's Fiction," "Superstition and Belief in Faulkner," and the curious "Pet Peeves of William Faulkner." Boswell also published literary essays on folklore in Sir Walter Scott and J. R. R. Tolkien's fiction.

Boswell died on 2 March 1995 at his home in Tupelo.

Ben Gilstrap
University of Mississippi

George Boswell Collection, Department of Archives and Special Collections, J. D. Williams Library, University of Mississippi; George W. Boswell and Russell Weaver, *Fundamentals of Folk Literature* (1962); Charles K. Wolfe, ed., *Folk Songs of Middle Tennessee: The George Boswell Collection* (1997).

Bottle Trees

Bottle trees, an American Deep South custom, have their beginnings on African soil. They are a Kongo-derived tradition dating back to around the ninth century and were introduced to America as early as the seventeenth century as a consequence of the Atlantic slave trade. While the exact origin of bottle trees is unknown, the most probable beginning is in African graveyards as a funereal ritual. Using various glass objects, including bottles, to decorate the burial sites of the dead is a long-standing tradition. Bottles were laid either in a symmetrical pattern on the site or randomly around the borders of the site, thus creating a horizontal bottle tree. If a tree draped over the grave, colorful bottles were hung from the tree's limbs. The grave decorations protected the dead person's talents from escaping into a space of nothingness.

This tradition carried over into the American South, where many African American graves have such decorations. Bottle trees also have long stood in the yards of African Americans, and the kaleidoscopic wonders eventually made their way into yards of Euro-Americans. The belief is that sunlight dancing through the colored bottles will lure evil spirits into the bottles, entrapping them and protecting the home. Tradition states that the sound created when the wind blows through the necks of the bottles is the evil spirits howling or moaning. In addition to capturing evil spirits, bottle trees are believed to protect homes from thieves or other intruders. Sometimes the bottles house dirt from someone's grave.

Although many types of trees are used in making bottle trees, the most widely used is the cedar, which is resistant to decay and favored for its heavenward-stretching limbs. Colored bottles are hung on the ends of the limbs, creating a magical delight when the sunlight plays among the bottles. Blue bottles, though scarce, are favored and prized for their increased ability to ward off evil and keep fever from one's home.

Mississippi is one of three states located in an area known as bottle tree territory. No wonder, then, that bottle trees have been spotted in many Mississippi communities, including Oxford, Pontotoc, Sarepta, and Madison. One of the earliest pictorial depictions of a bottle tree in the United States was provided by Mississippi author and photographer Eudora Welty in a Depression-era photo taken in Simpson County. The Mississippi bottle tree shows up in other artwork. James W. Bailey, a Mississippi-born photographer, created "wind painting," a distinctive naturalistic art practice inspired by the bottle tree. The bottle tree constitutes an essential image in Welty's 1943 short story, "Livvie." The trees show up in *The Celestial Jukebox* (2005), by former Oxonian and Rowan Oak curator Cynthia Shearer. In addition, Kentucky artist Henry Dorsey modeled his art on the bottle tree after traveling through Mississippi.

The popularity of bottle trees has waned along with the belief that they serve as a talisman against evil spirits. Nonetheless, they persist because people enjoy their artistic appeal.

Susan R. Barclay
University of Central Arkansas

Francis Edward Abernethy, ed., *Folk Art in Texas* (1985); H. Carrington Bolton, *Journal of American Folklore* (July–September 1891); William Ferris, ed., *Afro-American Folk Art and Crafts* (1983); Dan R. Goddard, *San-Antonio Express-News* (October 2006); Richard Graham, in *Corners of Texas: Publications of the Texas Folklore Society*, ed. Francis Edward Abernathy (1993); Ellen Orr, *Mississippi Folklore Register* (1969); Robert Farris Thompson, *Flash of the Spirit: African and Afro-American Art and Philosophy* (1983).

B

Bouldin, Jason

(b. 1965) Painter

Jason Bouldin, the youngest of four sons of portrait artist Marshall Bouldin III and physician Mary Ellen Stribling Bouldin, grew up on a cotton farm near Clarksdale. The family home sits in a pecan grove, which also shelters the studio where Marshall Bouldin III worked for more than half a century. "Since I was a boy, my brothers and I all painted little projects in the studio," Jason said. "Dad encouraged us to be around the studio; he never barred us from coming in. It was always a creative place to be. I learned as much by osmosis—just being around my father and in this space—as I did from my more formal instruction."

Bouldin attended the University of Mississippi, where he studied science, and received a bachelor of fine arts degree from Harvard University in 1989. After a two-year apprenticeship with his father, he began his professional career as a portrait painter in 1991. Since then, he has painted more than two hundred commissioned portraits, among them public works hanging in such varied locations as the US Department of Agriculture, the Judiciary Committee Room of the US House of Representatives, Harvard University, Tulane University Law School, the Mississippi State Capitol, Willcox House (London, England), and more than a dozen US federal courthouses. He has also painted portraits of former governor William Winter for the lobby of the William F. Winter Archives and History Building, Elise Winter for the First Ladies Gallery of the Old Capitol Museum, and Medgar Evers and Myrlie Evers-Williams for the Mississippi Museum of Art. The Evers paintings were unveiled in 2013 on the fiftieth anniversary of the civil rights leader's assassination in Jackson.

Bouldin has attained national and international recognition for his portraits. He received first place for portraiture in *Artist's Magazine*'s annual art competition in 1999 and won the Portrait Society of America's Grand Prize in 2002; his portraits have been selected nine times for the Royal Society of Portrait Painters Annual Exhibition in London, England.

Although he works primarily as a portrait artist, Bouldin also enjoys painting landscape and still life studies and has garnered prizes for works in those genres as well. He is also popular as a teacher of plein air classes, which he has presented at sites ranging from Atlanta's Piedmont Park to a cow pasture in Madison County.

Bouldin lives in Oxford with his wife, Alicia, and son, William. He remodeled the house next door to theirs and, with the help of two master craftsmen, turned it into his ideal studio, complete with a kitchen and a bedroom for guests, clients, and friends.

Ann J. Abadie
University of Mississippi

ArtistsNetwork website, www.artistsnetwork.com; Patti Carr Black, *The Mississippi Story*, ed. Robin C. Dietrick (2007); Jerry Mitchell, in *Journey to Justice* (11 June 2013).

Bouldin, Marshall, III

(1923–2012) Painter

Marshall Bouldin III was Mississippi's most prolific portrait artist, with more than eight hundred commissions during his lifetime. He was born to Laurenze Cooper Bouldin and Marshall Jones Bouldin Jr. in their Dundee, Mississippi, home on 6 September 1923. Marshall III and his sister, Helen, enjoyed a quiet childhood in the Mississippi Delta, and he expressed himself through drawing and painting, steadily improving his skills. By the time he graduated from Clarksdale High School in 1941, Bouldin had decided to pursue a career as a professional illustrator.

Bouldin received a scholarship to enroll in the Art Institute of Chicago in 1941. While he had hoped for formal training in art techniques, he was met with unstructured learning that allowed students to experiment with their own emerging styles. Bouldin believed that the best lessons he learned at the Art Institute were those he taught himself by studying works by master artists. He left the school after less than two years.

Unable to join the military because of a partial paralysis he incurred at birth, Bouldin contributed to the war effort through his work in a Nashville, Tennessee, aircraft factory beginning in 1943. He created isometric assembly plans from blueprints, always pondering his goal of becoming an illustrator. In 1945 Bouldin left Nashville for Chicago, where he had secured an apprenticeship with a group of magazine illustrators. Bouldin subsequently served another apprenticeship in Westport, Connecticut, from 1946 to 1950, producing covers and illustrations for *Outdoor Life*, *American Magazine*, *Collier's*, and other magazines.

Despite having achieved his childhood dream, Bouldin was unhappy with his career. Inspired by a Van Gogh exhibition at New York's Metropolitan Museum of Art, Bouldin decided that he could paint "for fun." He returned to Mississippi in 1950 and spent his time working on the family farm. Over the next decade, he painted in his spare time, teaching himself the fundamentals first by copying masterworks and later by creating original artwork, the bulk of which falls into the category of genre painting. Bouldin's first portrait work featured farmhands who worked for the family in the early 1950s.

After returning to his home state, Bouldin met Mary Ellen "Mel" Stribling, whom he married in 1954. The two were quite a couple, breaking any sort of stereotypes of Delta inhabitants in the mid-twentieth century. While Marshall pursued his artwork full time, Mel became a successful Memphis obstetrician and gynecologist, flying herself to and from work each day in her own Cessna aircraft. She also served as Coahoma County's health officer for more than thirty years.

In the mid-1950s Bouldin was offered his first commission by someone who had seen one of his farmhand paintings. Bouldin was still unsure about his skills as a portrait artist, so he asked the client for some time to hone his skills. At about the same time, Mel Bouldin had been issued a box of human bones as part of her medical studies. The artist began to carefully study and draw the bones, and after about nine months of exploration, he had created a detailed anatomy book that he consulted for the rest of his career. Bouldin then studied the color wheel and experimented with mixing various colors and making swatches, creating another large book of reference materials. After about two years of intense study and experimentation, Bouldin accepted the commission, receiving one hundred dollars for a painting of his late grandfather, Marshall Bouldin, who had founded the Delta Grocery and Cotton Company in 1903.

Not only did Bouldin approach each painting with detailed knowledge of color and human form, he was careful to get to know each subject before picking up a brush. A typical commission began with multiple interviews, sketches, photographs, and even video. Bouldin searched for the essence of his subject—personality, mannerisms, expressions—and believed that capturing this essence created a portrait that was truer to its subject than one that simply illustrated someone's likeness. Bouldin created portraits of hundreds of people, from his relatives to members of the broader Delta and Mississippi community to world-famous subjects. His most notable portraits include Julie and Tricia Nixon, Sen. Thad Cochran, Speaker of the House Jim Wright, Sen. John C. Stennis, Gov. William Winter, astronaut Ronald E. McNair, Gen. Louis Wilson, and a posthumous painting of author William Faulkner.

Bouldin's artwork can be found in collections across the country, including in the White House and in the halls of Congress. He was the only American to exhibit at the Royal Society of British Artists in 1987, 1988, and 1989, and three of his paintings were included in the 1990 show. Bouldin received the Governor's Award for Excellence in the Arts in 1997 and the Mississippi Institute of Arts and Letters Lifetime Achievement Award in 2009. Bouldin attributed his success as an artist to his hard work and a religious faith he strengthened through worship at First Presbyterian Church in Clarksdale. He and his wife raised four sons: Marshall IV, Jamie, Mahlon, and Jason, who spent two years as an apprentice with his father and is an accomplished portrait painter in his own right.

Marshall Bouldin III died in Memphis in November 2012.

Robin C. Dietrick
Mississippi Museum of Art

Patti Carr Black, *Art in Mississippi* (1998); Robin C. Dietrick, ed., *A Painter's Odyssey: The Art of Marshall Bouldin III* (2008); Paul Vitello, *New York Times* (15 November 2012).

Bowman, Sister Thea
(1937–1990) Religious Leader and Activist

A religious leader, scholar, and activist, Sister Thea Bowman was a unique voice in African American Catholicism. The granddaughter of slaves, Thea (originally named Bertha) was born in 1937 to physician Theon Edward Bowman and teacher Mary Esther Bowman in Yazoo City and raised in nearby Canton. Faced with inadequate public education, she transferred in 1949 to Canton's Holy Child Jesus Catholic School, administered by the Franciscan Sisters of Perpetual Adoration. Bowman later recalled that only two dozen of the school's 180 students were Catholic; the vast majority were Baptist, Methodists, and holiness. Her experience at the school led her to "accept the Catholic faith because of the day-to-day lived witness of Catholic Christians who first loved me." Bowman's educational experience also prompted her lifelong mission to advance the cause of education both as a secular means of personal improvement and as a religious tool of evangelization.

Bowman traveled to La Crosse, Wisconsin, in 1953 to enter the community of Franciscan Sisters of Perpetual Adoration. She joined their ranks in 1956 and took the name *Thea*, meaning "of God." Bowman then took a position teaching at Blessed Sacrament School in La Crosse. She returned home to Canton in 1961 to teach English and music at Holy Child Jesus School. From 1968 to 1972 Bowman studied English at Catholic University of America. Bowman then toured

Europe and returned to La Crosse in 1972 to teach and serve as head of the English department at Viterbo College.

Bowman frequently wrote and spoke on the importance of pluralism and multiculturalism within the church, calling on church leaders to "abandon the Catholic ghetto mentality" that isolated the church from dialogue with other cultures and religions. In 1978 Bowman returned to Mississippi to care for her parents and to take a position with the Diocese of Jackson as director of the Office of Intercultural Awareness. She fought for the inclusion of "black expression" in Catholic preaching and liturgy. Bowman assisted in the founding of the Institute of Black Catholic Studies at Xavier University in New Orleans in 1980 and served on its faculty through 1989. She aggressively campaigned for the incorporation of African American hymns into Catholic worship. Bowman noted that African American Catholics in the 1940s "had to leave behind us the music that was an expression of the spirituality of our home, community, and upbringing." Vatican II increased the opportunity for expression of that heritage. In 1987 Bowman authored the introduction to *Lead Me, Guide Me: The African American Catholic Hymnal*. She wrote that African American hymns were "shared by black American Christians across time, geographic, socioeconomic, and denominational lines." The following year, she recorded an album of African American spirituals, *Sister Thea: Songs of My People*.

Bowman addressed the annual conference of United States bishops on 17 June 1989 at Seton Hall University, delivering a powerful speech on "Being a Black Catholic." She warned the bishops that African Americans remained "victims within the church of paternalism." According to Bowman, the absence of black leadership inside the church coupled with paternalism fostered a "mission mentality" whereby African Americans did not feel called to or responsible for taking action within the church. She implored the bishops to maintain Catholic educational programs as the "primary instrument of evangelization within the black community." In an appeal for unity, Bowman beseeched the church to be "truly Catholic . . . overcome the poverty, overcome the loneliness, overcome the alienation, and build together a new holy city."

Starting in 1974, Bowman regularly attended and spoke at the Faulkner and Yoknapatawpha Conference sponsored by the University of Mississippi. She challenged the scholars who attended these conferences to think differently about the relationship between Faulkner and African Americans. Fittingly enough, Bowman's final presentation to the 1989 conference was "Faulkner and Religion."

In 1984 Bowman was diagnosed with breast cancer. The cancer subsequently spread to her bones and confined her to a wheelchair. Days prior to her death, she proclaimed, "This Holy Week when Jesus gave his life for love, let us truly love one another." Bowman died on 30 March 1990.

Bowman was the subject of a *60 Minutes* interview in 1987 and received numerous honorary degrees and awards for advancing the cause of women, promoting peace and justice, and supporting black Catholic education. Schools, clinics, a retirement home, a retreat house, and a theater have been named for her, and educational scholarships are given in her name. Her canonization is under way.

Ryan L. Fletcher
University of Mississippi

Joseph A. Brown, *A Retreat with Thea Bowman and Bede Abram: Leaning on the Lord* (1997); Celestine Cepress, ed., *Sister Thea Bowman, Shooting Star: Selected Writings and Speeches* (1993); Lisa Neumann Howorth and the Center for the Study of Southern Culture, *"Are You Walkin' with Me?": Sister Thea Bowman, William Faulkner, and African American Culture* (DVD 1990).

Boycotts, Civil Rights

Boycotts consist of withholding business or involvement as a form of protest. Mississippians frequently used boycotts as political tools in the civil rights movement to challenge particular forms of discrimination. Boycotts were ways of forcing issues by making situations difficult and potentially unbearable for the targeted people or businesses. Civil rights activists frequently used the phrase *selective buying* to make clear that they were giving their business only to people who treated them with respect or who had clearly rejected Jim Crow practices.

Boycotts often began after a dramatic incident—an act of violence or insult. The murder of George Lee in Belzoni, the attempted murder of George Metcalfe in Natchez, and the murder of Martin Luther King Jr. in Memphis all led

Demonstrators protest during a boycott of local businesses, Grenada, 14 July 1966 (Mississippi State Sovereignty Commission Records, Mississippi Department of Archives and History [9-37-0-2-9-1-1])

immediately to boycotts. In Clarksdale the decision to prohibit African American musicians from marching in a parade sparked a boycott. Some boycotts began as parts of broad strategies to force change, while others addressed very specific issues.

The boycotts of white-owned businesses often involved grievances regarding issues outside the stores. Boycotters addressed school segregation, violence, hiring practices, the makeup of local government agencies, and other matters. In some cases boycotters demanded greater access to government. Boycotts also dramatized issues involving the stores themselves, such as the refusal to allow African Americans to eat in restaurants or to try on clothing before purchasing it. "Don't Shop Where You Can't Eat" was a common demand. Other boycotts involved what activists called "courtesy titles"—that is, African Americans' right to be called "Mr.," "Mrs.," or "Miss" rather than by their first names. And some involved demands that stores hire African Americans in positions other than the most menial.

Boycotts are intriguing forms of protest, because unlike strikes, marches, pickets, or other forms of direct action, they consist of *not* doing something: authorities have difficulty arresting people for staying out of stores. By *not* shopping, boycotters could also uphold an ideal of self-control, saying that some ideals outweighed the need for certain goods or conveniences such as riding a bus. Women were especially important in boycotts, in part because they were often the primary shoppers in their households. Ministers often made the point that boycotting was an expression of high moral principle, sometimes encouraging people to avoid spending money on new clothing for Easter or Christmas when higher goals were at stake.

Activists grew quite ready to boycott, especially after the tactic proved effective. Charles Evers led boycotts in Natchez and Fayette and showed he was ready to use force against African Americans who continued to patronize the boycotted stores. The 1965–66 Natchez boycott ended with a complete victory for Evers and his fellow activists: according to Evers, "Everything we asked for we have gotten concessions on, and then some."

White Mississippians who opposed the civil rights movement responded to the boycotts in a variety of ways. Sometimes they tried to ignore the boycotts, hoping the protesters would run out of energy and nerve. Increasingly, however, authorities tried to make boycotts illegal. Boycotters in Jackson, Clarksdale, Natchez, and Greenwood faced arrest for "conspiring to commit acts injurious to public trade." In 1966 Mississippi senator James O. Eastland suggested that the federal government should make boycotting illegal, and in 1968 the Mississippi legislature passed a law prohibiting certain types of boycotts. Business leaders in Port Gibson and Vicksburg sued activists, including the National Association for the Advancement of Colored People, for money supposedly lost because of the boycotts.

Some white Mississippians used organized boycotts against groups they felt were becoming too friendly to the goals of the civil rights movement. Americans for the Preservation of the White Race, a small group organized in Natchez in 1963, condemned and sometimes boycotted businesses, especially national chain stores without strong Mississippi ties, that changed their traditionally discriminatory practices.

Prominent civil rights boycotts in Mississippi included Belzoni, 1955; Jackson, 1960, 1962–63; Clarksdale, 1961; Canton, 1964; Issaquena County, 1964; Sharkey County, 1964; Natchez, 1965–66; Greenwood, 1965, 1968; Edwards, 1966; Grenada, 1966; Port Gibson, 1966; Fayette, 1966; Indianola, 1968; Rosedale, 1970; Vicksburg, 1972; Holly Springs and Byhalia, 1974.

Ted Ownby
University of Mississippi

Emilye Crosby, *A Little Taste of Freedom: The Black Freedom Struggle in Claiborne County, Mississippi* (2005); John Dittmer, *Local People: The Struggle for Civil Rights in Mississippi* (1994); Laura Lynn McKnight, "Lessons in Freedom: Race, Education, and Progress in a Mississippi Delta Community since 1965" (master's thesis, University of Mississippi, 1996); Ted Ownby, *American Dreams in Mississippi: Consumers, Poverty, and Culture, 1830–1998* (1999); Charles M. Payne, *I've Got the Light of Freedom: The Organizing Tradition and the Mississippi Freedom Struggle* (2007); Michael Vinson Williams, *Medgar Evers: Mississippi Martyr* (2011).

Boyd, Dennis "Oil Can"
(b. 1959) Athlete

Dennis Ray "Oil Can" Boyd gained fame in the 1980s as an eccentric pitcher for the Boston Red Sox. Boyd was born in Meridian, Mississippi, on 6 October 1959 to Willie James and Sweetie Boyd. He attributes his passion for baseball to his father, a former pitcher in the Negro Leagues. Boyd received his nickname after he was caught at a young age drinking home-brewed whiskey out of an oil can. According to Boyd, when he was young, Jackie Robinson "gave me pride" and underscored the notion "that it was only ignorance that was pushing racism." Boyd reveres his teenage baseball years in Mississippi even more than his professional career: "Playing with my friends, that was the best times for the Can."

He attended Jackson State University until the Boston Red Sox took him in the sixteenth round of the 1980 amateur draft. He made his Major League debut with Boston on 13 September 1982, giving up two earned runs over five innings and taking the loss. He split the next season between the Minor and Major Leagues before sticking with Boston in 1984, when he posted a 12–12 record and a 4.37 earned run average (ERA). The following year, he had his first winning season with a record of 15–13 and an ERA of 3.70. Tensions with the Red Sox organization and city itself plagued Boyd's tenure with the team. Race lurked behind many of these issues. Ellis Burks, another Mississippi-born African American player with the Red Sox, recalled that Boyd warned him to avoid South Boston because of racial violence over forced busing. In addition, Boyd's unconventional personality and drug use caused the team to conduct psychiatric evaluations of him. Boyd resented his treatment, and after an adultery scandal involving teammate Wade Boggs, Boyd scoffed, "Who needs the psychiatrist now?"

The 1986 season represented a watershed for Boyd. He won eleven games through July but did not make the American League all-star team. He exploded in anger and received a three-game suspension and medical evaluation. He returned to pitch the pennant-winning game against Toronto. Boyd started Game 3 of the 1986 World Series against the New York Mets, giving up six runs in seven innings of work and taking the loss. The Red Sox then opted not to start Boyd in the decisive Game 7 even though it was his turn in the rotation. The Red Sox placed Boyd on the disabled list five times between 1987 and 1989 because of blood clots in his right arm. After the 1989 season, he became a free agent and signed with the Montreal Expos, for whom he pitched in 1990 and 1991. Midway through the 1991 season the Expos traded Boyd to the Texas Rangers, who released him at the end of the season, ending his career. In his ten years in the Major Leagues, Boyd posted a 78–77 record and a 4.04 ERA.

In 2007 Boyd headlined the Oil Can Boyd Traveling All-Stars, whose roster included some other big baseball names—Marquis Grissom, Delino DeShields, Sam Horn, Kenny Ryan, Chris Howard, Bill Lee, Mike Smith, and Derek Bell. The team played exhibition games and took part in various promotions designed to increase African Americans' participation in baseball. Central to that goal was sharing the inspired history of the Negro Leagues with young athletes.

In his 2012 autobiography Boyd admitted to using marijuana and cocaine during his high school, college, and professional career, including smoking crack cocaine every day during the 1986 season. He also discussed racial issues and other on- and off-field details from his career. Boyd and his family live in East Providence, Rhode Island, and spend time in Mississippi. He has a daughter, Tala, and son, Dennis. He continues to pitch in two divisions of the Men's Senior Baseball League.

Ryan Fletcher
University of Mississippi

Baseball Almanac website, www.baseball-almanac.com; Dennis "Oil Can" Boyd with Mike Shalin, *They Call Me Oil Can: Baseball, Drugs, and Life on the Edge* (2012); Howard Bryant, *Shut Out: A Story of Race and Baseball in Boston* (2002); Terry Nau, *Pawtucket Times* (27 April 2007); "'Oil Can' Boyd Discusses Drug Use," espn.go.com (2 May 2012); Mike Shatzkin, ed., *The Ballplayers: Baseball's Ultimate Biographical Reference* (1989); Dan Shaughnessy, *Boston Globe* (17 May 2005).

Brady, Thomas P.
(1903–1973) Judge

Thomas Pickens Brady (pronounced *Braddy*) emerged as a prominent segregationist after the publication of his 1955 book *Black Monday*. Born in 1903 and raised in Brookhaven, Mississippi, Brady earned a bachelor of arts degree from Yale in 1927 and a bachelor of laws degree from the University of Mississippi Law School three years later. Brady returned to Brookhaven and practiced law in his father's firm. Brady worked on Paul Johnson's campaign for the governor's office and became active in the state's Democratic Party in the 1930s. He served as a States' Rights Party delegate at the 1948 Democratic Convention and denounced much of Harry Truman's Fair Deal and civil rights agenda. In 1950 Brady's tireless political energy secured him a seat as circuit court judge in Mississippi's 14th Judicial District.

When the US Supreme Court handed down its decision in *Brown v. Board of Education* (1954), Brady found the ruling contemptible and expressed his views in *Black Monday*. The work, which became a handbook for segregationists, developed from Brady's speeches and writings and his ardent belief that *Brown* represented a usurpation of states' rights by the federal government. *Black Monday*, a combination of legal arguments and specious anthropological ideas, called for the popular election of Supreme Court justices, a youth education program on ethnology and communist infiltration, the elimination of the National Association for the Advancement of Colored People, the abolition of public schools, and the creation of a forty-ninth state for African Americans. Brady also argued that the separation of the races preserved an orderly society and that a disregard for southern mores would create racial turmoil. He urged white citizens to prevent racial amalgamation. *Black Monday* won accolades from segregationists and other conservatives and raised money for the White Citizens' Council. Brady was an architect of that group, helping to write its charter and bylaws and traveling the country as its spokesperson. He viewed the Council as a peaceful organization that could stop a race war and serve as the core of a new grassroots conservative party to thwart the encroachment of socialism and the disregard for law at the federal level.

Thomas P. Brady, 1954 (McCain Library and Archives, University of Southern Mississippi)

Brady represented Mississippi as a delegate at several Democratic conventions. In 1963, he filled a vacancy on the Mississippi Supreme Court, remaining on the bench for the rest of his life. Despite his strong rhetoric and prejudiced views, Brady firmly denounced violence and honored his oath to follow the Constitution and laws of the United States. Despite his personal views, Brady ruled in *Bolton v. City of Greenville* (1965), for example, that African Americans could use a traditionally segregated public park. One year later, Brady reversed the conviction of an African American because blacks had been excluded from the jury that indicted him. In January 1973 Brady died of heart failure.

William P. Hustwit
Birmingham Southern University

Numan V. Bartley, *The Rise of Massive Resistance: Race and Politics in the South during the 1950s* (1969); Tom P. Brady, *Black Monday* (1955); Daniel M. Hoehler, "Thomas P. Brady: A Passion for Order" (master's thesis, University of Mississippi, 1998); "Interview with the Honorable Thomas P. Brady: Associate Justice, Mississippi Supreme Court" (1972), Center for Oral History and Cultural Heritage, University of Southern Mississippi, http://digilib.usm.edu/cdm/compoundobject/collection/coh/id/9309/rec/1; Neil R. McMillen, *The Citizens' Council: Organized Resistance to the Second Reconstruction, 1954–1964* (1971).

Bramlett, Delaney
(1939–2008) Musician

Delaine Alvin "Delaney" Bramlett was born 1 July 1939 in Pontotoc County, Mississippi, where he grew up picking cotton with his mother, Iva "Mamo" Bramlett, and older brother, Johnny. They lived in a log cabin that had no electricity or indoor plumbing, and the three of them made a total of a dollar a day working in the fields. Mamo Bramlett was musically inclined and saw to it that Santa Claus brought Delaney the guitar that she taught him how to play. A musical grounding of blues and church music influenced Bramlett's records and songwriting, and his music, in turn, influenced artists such as Eric Clapton and Duane Allman.

In 1959 Bramlett moved to Los Angeles and joined the US Navy. In September 1964, after his discharge, he joined the Shindogs, the house band for the ABC television show *Shindig!*, which featured the hottest pop singers and bands of the day. Bramlett made several important musical connections with other regular members of the Shindogs, among them Billy Preston, Leon Russell, and James Burton.

In 1967 Bramlett met Bonnie Lynn O'Farrell, a native of Alton, Illinois, who was a vocal prodigy. O'Farrell sang with Albert King by the time she was fourteen, and at the age of fifteen she joined the Ike and Tina Turner Revue as the first white Ikette. (She supposedly performed wearing a black wig and darkened her skin using Man Tan.) O'Farrell moved to Hollywood when she was twenty-three, and she and Bramlett fell in love, began singing together as Delaney and Bonnie, and married in 1967.

In 1968 Delaney and Bonnie commenced their friendship with Eric Clapton. Clapton had seen them perform in Los Angeles and later invited them to open for his band, Blind Faith, on a tour that included a performance before one hundred thousand fans in London's Hyde Park. After Blind Faith dissolved, Clapton joined Delaney and Bonnie and Friends. The group was named "and Friends" because of the constantly shifting personnel. In addition to Clapton, other notables who regularly played with Delaney and Bonnie included Duane Allman, George Harrison, Gram Parsons, Bobby Keys, King Curtis, Leon Russell, Rita Coolidge, Carl Radle, Bobby Whitlock, Jim Gordon, Jim Keltner, and Dave Mason. At the height of his fame Jimi Hendrix briefly toured with Delaney and Bonnie when his band was off the road for a few weeks.

Between 1969 and 1972, seven Delaney and Bonnie albums were released. Their best-known songs include "When the Battle Is Over," "Never Ending Song of Love," and "Let It Rain," which became a hit for Clapton.

Delaney and Bonnie had three daughters, Michele, Suzanne, and Bekka, but their relationship was tempestuous, and they divorced in 1972. Both kept performing, and Delaney kept writing songs. In 2005 he married actress/photographer Susan Lanier, and three years later he released a well-received album, *A New Kind of Blues*. He died of surgical complications on 27 December 2008 in Los Angeles, his longtime home.

Richard Holland
Austin, Texas

Rob Bowman, *Soulsville U.S.A.: The Story of Stax Records* (1997); Eric Clapton, *Clapton: The Autobiography* (2007); Jac Holzman and Gavan Daws, *Follow the Music: The Life and High Times of Electra Records in the Great Years of American Pop Culture* (1998); *Swampland* website, www .swampland.com; Jerry Wexler and David Ritz, *Rhythm and the Blues* (1993).

Brandon, Gerard Chittocque

(1788–1850) Fourth and Sixth Governor,
1825–1826, 1826–1832

Gerard C. Brandon was the first native Mississippian elected the state's governor. He also held the state's top office longer than any other governor before the Civil War and served as governor twice before being elected to the post. As lieutenant governor he assumed the governorship in 1825 after the death of Walter Leake and again in 1826 when David Holmes resigned because of failing health. In 1827, while completing Holmes's term, Brandon was elected governor; he won reelection two years later.

Brandon was born at Selma Plantation in Adams County in September 1788 and was educated at the College of New Jersey (now Princeton University) and the College of William and Mary. He practiced law in Washington, Mississippi's territorial capital, and was a successful planter in Adams County. A veteran of the War of 1812, Brandon served as a delegate to the state constitutional convention of 1817 and helped draft Mississippi's first constitution. He also served in the state legislature and was elected Speaker of the House in 1822.

Brandon was the chief executive of Mississippi at the beginning of a prosperous era known as the Flush Times. The period was also called the "Era of the Common Man" because the right to vote and the right to hold office were extended to all white males, even those who did not own any property.

Two major Indian land cessions finalized during his administration, the Treaty of Dancing Rabbit Creek (1831) and the Treaty of Pontotoc Creek (1832), made several million acres of good cotton land available for settlement, and Mississippi soon became the heartland of the Cotton Kingdom. The rapid development of the newly acquired territory required a road system into the interior parts of the state, and Brandon promoted the construction of roads, bridges, and turnpikes as well as the development of water transportation to facilitate that settlement. Brandon also oversaw the beginning of a transportation revolution in 1831 when the state chartered its first railroad.

After the acquisition of the Indian lands, the Mississippi legislature created several new counties in North Mississippi.

The addition of those new counties and the extension of suffrage to all white males, along with other social and political changes, made Mississippi's 1817 constitution outdated. In 1831 the people voted by a margin of four to one in favor of a new constitution. The next year a convention assembled in Jackson and drafted a much more democratic constitution. Brandon, whose term as governor had just expired, represented Adams County at that convention. It was his last act of public service. For the remainder of his life, Brandon lived on his Columbian Springs Plantation in Adams County, where he died on 28 March 1850. Brandon, the seat of Rankin County, is named in his honor.

David G. Sansing
University of Mississippi

Mississippi Official and Statistical Register (1912); Dunbar Rowland, *Encyclopedia of Mississippi History*, vol. 1 (1907).

Brandon, William Lindsay

(1802–1890) Confederate General

Confederate general William Lindsay Brandon was born in October 1802 near Washington in Adams County, Mississippi. He was the youngest son of a Revolutionary War veteran and the brother of Gerard C. Brandon, a multiterm governor of Mississippi. William Brandon resettled in Wilkinson County in 1824 and carved out a plantation he named Arcole. He was educated at Virginia's Washington College (now Washington and Lee University) and at the College of New Jersey (now Princeton University) before returning to Mississippi. Brandon and his first wife, Ann Davis Brandon, had two children, but both she and the children died at an early age. Brandon then married Ann Eliza Ratliff in 1833, and three of their four sons lived to adulthood.

Brandon was a planter with keen interests in hunting and medicine. He served one term in the state legislature and became a major general in the state militia. Brandon raised a company of volunteers after Mississippi seceded, was elected the unit's captain, and accompanied it to Virginia. When his company became a portion of the 21st Mississippi Infantry, Brandon was promoted to major and then lieutenant colonel. At the Battle of Malvern Hill on 1 July 1862 he suffered a severe wound to the ankle that resulted in the amputation of his right leg. Doctors doubted whether he would survive, but after a long recuperation in Richmond, Virginia, he felt well enough to leave the hospital. One visitor who anticipated finding Brandon on his deathbed was astonished at his fighting spirit and confidence, which may have hastened his recovery. Finding a suitable artificial leg proved troublesome, and he was unable to mount or dismount a horse without assistance. Brandon rejoined his regiment on crutches and participated in the Gettysburg and Chickamauga Campaigns. He was appointed colonel of the regiment upon the ascension of Benjamin G. Humphreys to brigade command after Gettysburg. Brandon's advanced age, the poor fit of his artificial leg, and recurring illness prevented him from properly attending to his field duties, and he evidently tendered his resignation in October 1863, although he reportedly served in the Knoxville Campaign later that year and returned to Virginia with his command.

The Confederate government was unwilling to dispense entirely with Brandon's services, and on 18 June 1864 he was appointed brigadier general and assumed command of Mississippi's Reserve Corps and Conscription Bureau, headquartered at Enterprise. He found himself frustrated by this assignment, which involved rounding up deserters and resulted in squabbles with Gov. Charles Clark over placing state troops into Confederate service. Brandon remained at this post until just prior to the end of the war. He was paroled at Meridian on 10 May 1865 and returned to his plantation, spending the remainder of his life attempting to rebuild his fortunes. Although biographical sketches universally state that he died on 8 October 1890, his tombstone in the family plot at Arcole lists 8 August 1890, and obituaries support the latter date.

Christopher Losson

St. Joseph, Missouri

Harold A. Cross, *They Sleep beneath the Mockingbird: Mississippi Burial Sites and Biographies of Confederate Generals* (1994); Gary Gallagher, in *The Confederate General*, ed. William C. Davis (1991); *Goodspeed's Biographical and Historical Memoirs of Mississippi* (1891); Jack D. Welsh, *Medical Histories of Confederate Generals* (1995).

Brantley, William Felix

(1830–1870) Confederate General

Born in Alabama in 1830, William Felix Brantley moved to Mississippi with his family at an early age. He became an attorney and represented Choctaw County as a delegate to the Mississippi Secession Convention. Brantley voted in favor of secession and subsequently volunteered for service in the Confederate Army. Brantley captained a local company, the Wigfall Rifles, which became Company D of the 15th Mississippi Infantry. Wounded at Shiloh, he later served

as an officer in the 29th Mississippi Infantry and eventually rose to the rank of brigadier general. Brantley was wounded again at Murfreesboro but returned to lead regiments at Chickamauga and Chattanooga. He took part in the Atlanta Campaign, accompanied John Bell Hood on his ill-fated invasion of Tennessee, and finally surrendered with Joseph E. Johnston at Durham Station, North Carolina, in 1865.

At the war Brantley returned home to Greensboro in Choctaw County to find the life he had known shattered. Both his wife and his mother had died during the war years, and he was ruined financially. He settled back into civilian life and worked to reestablish his once-thriving legal practice. He soon resumed his involvement in local politics, but he did not live to see the end of Reconstruction. In what became one of the region's most legendary crimes, the former general was shot and killed in an ambush on 2 November 1871 as he traveled by carriage from Winona to Greensboro. Although there were a number of suspects, including political enemies and members of a family with whom the Brantleys had a long-standing feud, authorities never solved the crime.

Ben Wynne

University of North Georgia

William T. Blain, *Journal of Mississippi History* (November 1975).

Brewer, Earl Leroy

(1869–1942) Thirty-Eighth Governor, 1912–1916

Gov. Earl Brewer's inauguration in 1912 was an unusually festive occasion and attracted the largest crowd in the state's history up to that time. Railroad companies offered reduced rates and thousands of people came to Jackson from all over the state. There was an enormous parade and a public reception at the new Capitol, followed by a gala inaugural ball at the Stag Club. First Lady Minnie Marian Block Brewer's Parisian gown, which was a bright shade of yellow chiffon and satin, elicited considerable comment.

Earl Brewer, the first graduate of the University of Mississippi Law School to be elected governor, was born in Carroll County on 11 August 1869. After completing the school's regular two-year law course in less than one year, Brewer opened a law office in Water Valley in 1892. One of his most famous clients was the widow of legendary railroad worker Casey Jones, whom Brewer represented in her out-of-court settlement with the Illinois Central Railroad.

Earl Leroy Brewer (Milton McFarland Painter Sr. Collection, Archives and Records Services Division, Mississippi Department of Archives and History, PI/1988.0006/Box 557 Folder 1])

Brewer represented Yalobusha County in the State Senate from 1896 to 1900 and in 1902 was appointed district attorney for the 11th Judicial District. After receiving that appointment he moved to Clarksdale. Brewer ran for governor in 1907 but was narrowly defeated in a runoff election.

Brewer again ran for governor four years later and holds the distinction of being the state's only Democratic gubernatorial candidate to run unopposed in the primary since the enactment of the primary law. In the general election Brewer easily defeated Socialist candidate S. W. Rose, who received only 2,049 votes.

Shortly after Brewer took office the legislature passed House Concurrent Resolution No. 65 authorizing the use of trusties from the State Penitentiary to work as domestic servants in the Governor's Mansion. That system continued for many years and proved highly satisfactory. The rate of recidivism among participating inmates was extremely low.

While in office Brewer continued to promote the progressive reforms of his immediate predecessors. During his administration the constitutional amendment establishing an elective judiciary was implemented, a consolidated Board of Trustees for the Mississippi Institutions of Higher Learning was created, several banking laws were passed, and the Bureau of Vital Statistics was established.

After he left office in January 1916, Brewer continued his law practice in Clarksdale. In 1924 he ran for the US Senate but was defeated by Sen. Pat Harrison. Brewer then retired from public life, and he died on 10 March 1942.

David G. Sansing
University of Mississippi

Jackson Daily News (14 January 1912); *Mississippi Official and Statistical Register* (1917); C. P. J. Mooney, *The Mid-South and Its Builders* (1920); WPA Source Papers, Coahoma County.

Brewer, Minnie Elizabeth
(1898–1978) Publisher

Minnie Elizabeth Brewer was born on 28 July 1898 in Water Valley, Mississippi, to Earl Leroy and Minnie Marian Block Brewer. When she was three years old, the family moved to Clarksdale after her father's appointment as district attorney for the 11th Judicial District. The family lived in Clarksdale until Earl Brewer's inauguration as governor in 1912. At fourteen, Minnie was sent to Hollins preparatory school in Virginia, and the next year she enrolled in Hollins College as an "irregular" student, a status she retained throughout her college career. She studied briefly at the University of Virginia, Millsaps College, and the University of Wisconsin but never earned a degree because she would take only courses that interested her—primarily English and writing courses. "Why would I want to know about bugs?" she asked.

With the coming of World War I, Brewer joined the ranks of young women who volunteered to patrol the shores of the eastern United States to look for enemy ships. She was not happy sleeping among the sand dunes, however, and her father got her out of her commitment. She went home and contributed to the war effort by knitting scarves for the soldiers.

By this time the Brewers were back in Clarksdale, where Earl Brewer had built a house replicating the governor's mansion and made a fortune in cotton and land speculation. Minnie went on a two-month grand tour of Europe in 1920 with a group from Hollins College. Back in Clarksdale she lived the life of a flapper, with hosts of suitors and at least three broken engagements.

In April 1922 Brewer went to Baltimore for the third annual convention of the National League of Women Voters, the organization that replaced the National American Woman Suffrage Association after the passage of the Nineteenth Amendment in 1920. More than one thousand women were in attendance, including prominent suffrage leaders such as Carrie Chapman Catt and Emmeline Pankhurst. Women were pinning their hopes for progressive social change on their newly won right to vote.

Brewer went home from Baltimore determined to start a political newspaper to educate the women of Mississippi as voting citizens. With her father's encouragement and money, the first issue of the *Woman Voter* appeared on 3 August 1922. The paper was published for two years, carrying news from women's organizations and nuts-and-bolts articles on the workings of government by such political women as Nellie Nugent Somerville and her daughter, Lucy. While the newspaper and the woman's vote did not spark the revolution for which Brewer had hoped, women's votes played an important factor in the election of Henry Whitfield, former president of Mississippi State College for Women, as the state's governor.

At one point Brewer moved the headquarters of the *Woman Voter* from Clarksdale to Jackson, and while she claimed that the paper was distributed into every county in the state, still it did not pay its way. In January 1924 Minnie decided to leave the paper in the hands of Joe Howorth, a young Jackson lawyer, and to accompany her younger sister, Claudia, to the University of Wisconsin. She wanted to strengthen her skills as a journalist and to prepare for the Democratic National Convention in June, to which she was a delegate. In April 1924 the *Woman Voter* ceased publication, primarily because of Earl Brewer's financial ruin. Minnie and Claudia had to return to Clarksdale in January 1925 and go to work.

Until 1939, Minnie worked in a dress shop, ran a boardinghouse, and became increasingly eccentric. In the spring of that year, her father had her committed to the Hospital for the Insane at Whitfield, where she lived for nearly forty years. Her initial diagnosis was "psychosis due to syphilitic meningo encephalitis" although "she lacks some of the symptoms." If she had contracted syphilis from a World War I soldier, as one report indicated, and the condition had gone untreated until 1939, it seems unlikely she would have lived until 1978. An unconfirmed report indicated that she was among the patients smuggling out letters about the living conditions at Whitfield, an action that sparked a legislative investigation and brought about improvements in patient care.

Whatever the facts of her last forty years, Minnie Brewer was a pioneering feminist whose newspaper is a valuable resource for those interested in Mississippi's history.

Dorothy Shawhan
Delta State University

Brewer-Howorth Correspondence, Somerville-Howorth Papers, Schlesinger Library on the History of Women in America, Radcliffe College; Brewer Papers, Clarksdale Public Library; Earl L. Brewer and Family Papers, Mississippi Department of Archives and History; Vinton M. Prince Jr., *Southern Studies* (Winter 1980); Dorothy Shawhan, in *Mississippi Women: Their Histories, Their Lives*, ed. Martha H. Swain, Elizabeth Anne Payne, Marjorie Julian Spruill, and Susan Ditto (2003).

Brice's Cross Roads, Battle of

By 1864 much of Confederate Mississippi had been overrun by Federal troops. Jackson, the state capital, had been occupied, and Vicksburg, the vital port city on the Mississippi River, had fallen. As a result, military movements in the state were driven in large part by activities taking place elsewhere. During the summer of 1864 William Tecumseh Sherman was moving on Atlanta from the north, meeting limited resistance from an outnumbered Confederate Army under the command of Joseph E. Johnston. Sherman pushed Johnston back, but not without concerns regarding the Union general's ever-lengthening supply lines. Sherman was particularly worried that his supply lines between Nashville and Chattanooga were vulnerable to attack from Confederate cavalry under Nathan Bedford Forrest. While he had never studied military science, Forrest was recognized by both sides as perhaps the most effective cavalry commander the war produced. Some referred to him as the Wizard of the Saddle, while Sherman called him "the very devil."

Sherman's fears were well-founded. Desperate to stop Sherman's advance, the Confederate high command realized that Union supply lines in Middle Tennessee might be vulnerable. As a result, Gen. Stephen D. Lee ordered Forrest out of Mississippi toward Nashville with instructions to destroy railroad lines and disrupt communication between the Union-controlled Tennessee capital and Sherman's army. Forrest left Tupelo on 1 June with three thousand cavalry and two artillery batteries. At the same time, Union general Samuel Sturgis left Memphis and moved southeast into Mississippi with eight thousand infantry and cavalry in hopes of keeping Forrest occupied. Lee ordered Forrest back to meet the threat, and the two forces clashed several days later at Brice's Cross Roads, near Baldwyn in Northeast Mississippi.

On 10 June 1864 a bloody, daylong battle ensued there in the summer heat. Though outnumbered, the Confederates soundly defeated the Federals, forcing them into a disorderly retreat. By the end of the day Sturgis had lost more than 2,200 men, while the Confederates had suffered only 492 casualties. In Forrest's words, the Federals had been "beaten, defeated, routed, [and] destroyed." Sturgis shouldered the blame for the defeat, and his career as a Civil War commander effectively ended that day. For Forrest, the Battle of Brice's Cross Roads was the high point of a unique military career, and he emerged from the clash as a hero if not a living legend. Despite the Confederate success, however, Sherman's supply lines remained intact, and Atlanta fell later in the year.

Sturgis remained in the army until his retirement in 1888. Forrest survived the war to great glory, and in 1867, while living in North Mississippi, he became grand wizard of the Ku Klux Klan, a position he held for two years. He later settled in Memphis.

Ben Wynne
Gainesville State College

Edwin C. Bearss, *Forrest at Brice's Cross Roads and in North Mississippi* (1979); John Allan Wyeth, *That Devil Forrest* (1989).

Brickell, Herschel
(1889–1952) Columnist and Editor

Henry Herschel Brickell, a columnist and editor and US State Department official in Colombia, was born on 13 September 1889 in Senatobia, Mississippi. The son of Henry Hampton Brickell and Lula Johns Harrison Brickell, he grew up in Yazoo City, where he developed an insatiable appetite for reading. He enrolled at the University of Mississippi in 1906 and quickly became involved in campus literary activities. In 1910, after repeatedly failing mathematics, Brickell left without graduating and began a career in journalism, working for a series of southern newspapers. For several months in 1916 he served as a battalion sergeant major in the Alabama National Guard along the Mexican border, where Pancho Villa's raids were threatening American citizens. After returning to Mississippi, Brickell became editor of the *Jackson Daily News*. In 1918 he married Norma Long of Jackson, and the following year the couple moved to New York so that Herschel could pursue greater journalistic opportunities.

His first assignment in New York was at the copy desk of the *Evening Post*. From 1919 to 1923 he penned articles and editorials and carved out a niche reviewing new books by southern authors. In 1923 he launched his pioneering daily column, "Books on Our Table." Over the next three decades Brickell contributed reviews and essays to the *New York Times*, *New York Herald Tribune*, *Saturday Review of Literature*, *Atlantic Monthly*, and a host of other major publications, firmly establishing himself as one of the country's most influential book critics. In 1928 he left the *Post* to join Henry Holt and Company, where as editor he sought out new literary talent. As a result of many trips to Europe in the 1920s and 1930s, he developed strong feelings of kinship with Spain and became enamored of all things Spanish. A great admirer of Cervantes, Brickell wrote the introduction to the Modern Library edition of *Don Quixote* (1930). To memorialize his friend Federico García Lorca, he led the effort to get Lorca's *Poet in New York* (1940) published in the United States. In 1934 Brickell returned to the *Post* for a second stint, this time as literary editor, and remained there until 1938. He also authored "The Literary Landscape," a regular feature in the *North American Review* from 1927 to 1935, and in the 1940s he contributed annual essays on American literature to the *Britannica Book of the Year*.

Brickell's other literary activities included lecturing at writers' workshops such as the prestigious Bread Loaf Conference in Vermont. At these gatherings he established close ties with seasoned writers as well as newcomers. His *Writers on Writing* (1949), an edited volume, grew out of these workshops. Because he devoted so much time to developing the talents of others, he neglected his own work. He received two prestigious awards in 1939—one from the Julius Rosenwald Foundation to research the history of Natchez and the other a Guggenheim Fellowship to write a book on Spain— but failed to complete either project. Brickell is perhaps best remembered for his editorship of the O. Henry Memorial Award Prize Stories series from 1941 to 1951. In these annual collections of the best short stories published in American magazines he introduced the wider reading public to an impressive list of young fiction writers, among them Eudora Welty, Truman Capote, J. D. Salinger, and Ray Bradbury.

In 1940 Brickell began serving on the editorial staff of the Latin American edition of *Reader's Digest*, and the following year he took a job with the State Department as senior cultural relations officer assigned to the US embassy in Bogotá, Colombia. While there he wrote, delivered lectures on US literature and history, met prominent literary figures, and helped establish libraries. After returning to the United States in 1944 he remained in government service, using his position as head of the State Department's cultural relations program in Latin America to promote hemispheric cooperation and understanding. He made subsequent trips to Latin America in the early 1950s under the auspices of the State Department and the American Council on Education.

Brickell collected his Colombian lectures in *Literatura norteamericana contemporánea* (1943), *Cosecha colombiana* (1944), and *Panorama de la historia de los Estados Unidos* (1945). During this period he teamed with Carleton Beals, Bryce Oliver, and Samuel Guy Inman to produce *What the South Americans Think of Us* (1945) and collaborated with Carlos Videla on a translation of Ricardo Rojas's biographical study, *San Martín: Knight of the Andes* (1945). He also coedited (with Dudley G. Poore and Harry R. Warfel) a short story collection, *Cuentistas norteamericanos* (1946).

Overworked and suffering from lingering ill health, he committed suicide at his home in Ridgefield, Connecticut, on 29 May 1952.

Melvin S. Arrington Jr.
University of Mississippi

Melvin S. Arrington Jr., *Chasqui* (1994); Melvin S. Arrington Jr., *Southern Quarterly* (Summer 1989); Herschel Brickell Collection, Department of Archives and Special Collections, J. D. Williams Library, University of Mississippi; Grace Leake, *Holland's* (February 1938); Omie Wall Parker, "Herschel Brickell: An Estimate of His Works as Critic, Writer, and Lecturer" (master's thesis, Mississippi College, 1961).

Brocks-Shedd, Virgia
(1943–1992) Poet and Librarian

Virgia Brocks-Shedd was born in Carpenter, Mississippi, in 1943. Her family moved to the community of Bel Pine when the Carpenter sawmill closed. At age thirteen Brocks-Shedd became a boarding student at the Piney Woods Country Life School, twenty-four miles south of Jackson, where she lived and studied until 1961. At Piney Woods, Brocks-Shedd became an avid reader and noted *The Negro Caravan* and biographies of Ethel Waters and Eartha Kitt as particularly influential. At sixteen she read Norman Vincent Peale's *The Power of Positive Thinking* and was inspired to follow her dreams of being a poet.

Brocks-Shedd heard Margaret Walker Alexander read her poetry to the students at Piney Woods and later studied under Alexander at Jackson State University, where Brocks-Shedd earned a bachelor's degree in 1964. Brocks-Shedd then attended Atlanta University and earned a master of library science degree in 1965.

Upon graduation Brocks-Shedd was hired by Tougaloo College in Jackson, where she worked her way up from assistant librarian to the position of director of library services at L. Zenobia Coleman Library. Through her role in the library, Brocks-Shedd spread her love of literature to Tougaloo students by introducing them to local poets including Alexander, Coleman, Ernestine Lipscomb, and Lelia Rhodes.

Brocks-Shedd used her writing to pass along her love of reading and books. The chapbook *Mississippi Woods* (1980) includes poems by fellow Mississippi poets Melvin Turner, Hampton Williams, and Henry Wilbanks. *Mississippi Earthworks* (1982) was published in conjunction with the Jackson Writers/Actors Guild. The following year she published a chapbook composed of two longer poems, "Southern Roads/City Pavement" and "We Must Rise!" The cycle "Southern Roads/City Pavement" also appeared in a 1997 anthology, *Trouble the Water: 250 Years of African-American Poetry.* Her poetry and articles appeared in several Jackson publications, including the Tougaloo College literary magazine, *Pound; Close-Up; Hoo-Doo II/III;* the *Jackson Advocate;* and the *Northside Reporter.*

As her career progressed Brocks-Shedd became active in the movement to integrate the Mississippi Library Association and held distinguished posts in the library associations throughout the state. She was a founding member of the Society of Mississippi Archivists and of the African American Librarians Caucus of Mississippi. As an active member of the American Library Association she was a charter member of the Black Caucus of the American Library Association. In 1989 she became the first African American appointed head of the Mississippi Library Commission.

Throughout her career Brocks-Shedd fought for the inclusion of African American works in Mississippi libraries, which she saw as essential to understanding the black experience in the South.

Brocks-Shedd died on 4 December 1992 after battling pancreatic cancer. In 1993 the Piney Woods Country Life School established the Virgia Brocks-Shedd Memorial Fund for Student Scholarships and Literary Achievement. Since 1994 the Mississippi Library Association Black Caucus Roundtable has awarded the Virgia Brocks-Shedd Scholarship to a minority student at the University of Southern Mississippi's School of Library and Information Science.

Cale Nicholson
Little Rock, Arkansas

Virgia Brocks-Shedd, *Mississippi Earthworks* (1982); Virgia Brocks-Shedd, *Mississippi Woods* (1980); Clarence W. Hunter, *Mississippi Libraries* (Fall 1992); *Mississippi Libraries* (Spring 1993); Mississippi Library Association website, www.misslib.org.

Brooks, Owen H.
(1928–2014) Activist

The career of Owen H. Brooks dramatizes some of the main directions the Mississippi civil rights movement took during and after the late 1960s. Brooks, the son of West Indian immigrants, grew up in Massachusetts, where he received a degree from Northeastern University. In 1965 he went to Bolivar County to work for the Delta Ministry, a project the National Council of Churches had established the preceding year. Brooks took on a number of jobs in the Delta, sometimes as a director, sometimes as a coworker. His activism sometimes illustrated the tensions between native Mississippians and newcomers to the state and as well as among various strategies within the movement.

In the mid- and late 1960s Brooks worked with the Poor People's Campaign, helped organize some new groups and bring existing groups together for meetings, offered technical support to a range of activist groups, and encouraged African American political organizing and striking agricultural workers. He was appointed acting director of the Delta Ministry in 1966 and became director later in the decade.

He faced the challenge of trying to keep up both funding and other support for activist organizations at a time when national attention was turning away from Mississippi. Brooks believed the Delta Ministry should have a centralized program for African American economic development and political mobilization, whereas some Mississippi-born

African Americans believed that the ministry should work more within individual communities, with dispersed leadership and different strategies. In his calls for centralized authority, Brooks clashed with Mississippi natives Amzie Moore, Aaron Henry, and Sarah Johnson, who called Brooks a male chauvinist. Brooks used the language of Black Power and called for African American economic independence and separate political institutions and for new organizations distinct from older groups. He was the Mississippi distributor of the Black Manifesto, an ambitious 1969 statement about the need for reparations for African Americans.

With some allies but many opponents and with little funding from the National Council of Churches, Brooks, in the words of historian Mark Newman, "continued the Ministry, often as little more than a one-man operation," during the early 1970s. Brooks concentrated much of his work on grant writing and forms of technical assistance that encouraged African Americans to use money from federal government programs. He also worked with Robert Clark, the state's first African American state legislator, and concentrated much of his attention on Mound Bayou. Brooks kept up his efforts at organizing local communities to gain access to the political and economic resources of national organizations into the 1980s and 1990s. As the project field director of the Delta Oral History Project, Brooks organized and led a team of interviewers who canvassed several Mississippi Delta counties asking activists how they interpreted the degree and direction of change since the civil rights movement. He died in Jackson on 27 July 2014.

Ted Ownby
University of Mississippi

Bruce Hilton, *The Delta Ministry* (1969); *Jackson Clarion-Ledger* (1 August 2014); Mississippi State Sovereignty Commission files for Owen Brooks, Mississippi Department of Archives and History, Sovereignty Commission Online website, http://mdah.state.ms.us/arrec/digital_archives /sovcom/; Mark Newman, *Divine Agitators: The Delta Ministry and Civil Rights in Mississippi* (2004); Kim Lacy Rogers, *Life and Death in the Delta: African American Narratives of Violence, Resilience, and Social Change* (2006).

Broonzy, Big Bill
(1898–1958) Blues Musician

Big Bill Broonzy wrote and recorded hundreds of blues songs. He started out recording for Paramount, scoring his first success with "Big Bill Blues" in 1927, and later recorded on some of the most influential labels of his time, including OKeh, Bluebird, Vocalion, Columbia, Chess, and Folkways.

Broonzy performed or recorded with an impressive array of blues greats, including Tampa Red, Memphis Minnie, Washboard Sam, Sleepy John Estes, Memphis Slim, John Lee, Sonny Boy Williamson, and Georgia Tom Dorsey.

William Lee Conely Broonzy was born in Scott, Mississippi, on 26 June 1898. His parents, Frank and Nettie, were sharecroppers who eked out a living from the Delta soil by growing cotton. Seeking an improvement in their situation, the family moved to Arkansas, where Big Bill spent much of his youth and began playing the fiddle. In 1914 he married and began sharecropping on his own. He considered entering the Baptist ministry and played fiddle for various gatherings in Arkansas and Mississippi. The US Army drafted him during World War I, eventually sending him overseas, where he saw no action but did a lot of hard labor.

After his discharge and return to Mississippi, he decided to leave the South because of both racism and the breakup of his marriage. In 1920 Broonzy traveled to Chicago, where he fell under the tutelage of such bluesmen as Papa Charlie Jackson and Blind Blake. Until this time, Broonzy played in the songster mode, spinning out reels and waltzes on his fiddle. Switching to the guitar, he learned the rudiments of the blues. Before long, Broonzy could fingerpick or flat-pick the blues with equal dexterity. His newfound abilities brought him to the attention of Paramount, and his recording career began.

Over the next two decades Broonzy wrote, performed, and recorded numerous blues songs. He often used an urban blues style that showed both jazz and pop influences closer to the music of cosmopolitan players such as Blind Blake and Lonnie Johnson rather than the Delta style of Robert Johnson or Charley Patton. Legendary producer John Hammond tapped Broonzy for the first historic Spirituals to Swing concert at Carnegie Hall in 1938. For the concert, Broonzy was encouraged to play in a down-home mode and was introduced as an Arkansas sharecropper, to boost his authenticity. This exposure was not enough to ensure his continued success in the 1940s, when musical tastes drifted toward the propulsive electrified blues of Muddy Waters and Elmore James or toward rhythm and blues performers such as Louis Jordan and Charles Brown.

In the 1940s and 1950s Broonzy fell back on playing solo on his acoustic guitar and drawing on older down-home-style blues songs, some of which he had to relearn from recordings. This style and material especially appealed to the burgeoning leftist folk scene in New York and Chicago. His resulting popularity with this audience put him into contact with such performers as Woody Guthrie, Pete Seeger, and Josh White. In part owing to the progressive nature of the folk scene, protest songs also became part of his act. "When Will I Get to Be Called a Man" and "Black, Brown, and White Blues" are unrepentant attacks on racism in Jim Crow America. Broonzy's career had a resurgence in the 1950s when he toured Western Europe, one of the first American bluesmen to do so. He found fame once again in Paris and

London, but his new success was cut short because of failing health, and he died of cancer on 15 August 1958.

Mark Allan Jackson
Middle Tennessee State University

William Broonzy, *Big Bill Blues* (1955); Alan Lomax, *The Land Where the Blues Began* (1993); Paul Oliver, *The Story of the Blues* (1997); Jeff Place and Anthony Seeger, *Trouble in Mind* (2000), liner notes; Bob Riesman, *I Feel So Good: The Life and Times of Big Bill Broonzy* (2011).

Brown, Albert Gallatin

(1813–1880) Fourteenth Governor, 1844–1848

Albert Gallatin Brown was Mississippi's youngest and perhaps most popular antebellum governor. Following his reelection in 1845 by a very large majority and the completion of his second term, Brown was elected to the US House of Representatives, where he served until his appointment to the US Senate in 1854.

Brown was born in Chester District, South Carolina, on 31 May 1813 and moved with his family to Copiah County, Mississippi, in 1823. Brown attended Jefferson College and Mississippi College and then read law with Ephraim G. Peyton. After serving two terms in the state legislature, the twenty-four-year-old Brown was elected to Congress. Five years later he was elected circuit judge as a Democrat in a predominantly Whig district. In 1843, when he was thirty-one years of age, he was elected governor.

Brown was a strong advocate of public education and tried and failed to establish a statewide system of free schools. He had more success, however, with his effort to establish a state university. In 1844 Brown signed the charter establishing the University of Mississippi at Oxford, and the school opened four years later.

After his election to the Senate, Brown became one of the most ardent defenders of states' rights and one of the South's first advocates of secession. After Abraham Lincoln became president, Brown stated, "The Union is dead and nothing now remains to be done but to bury the rotten carcass." After Mississippi seceded and joined the Confederate States of America, Brown resigned his US Senate seat and organized a military company, Brown's Rifles. He was stationed briefly in Virginia before being elected one of Mississippi's two Confederate senators, and he served until the end of the Civil War.

After the fall of Vicksburg on 4 July 1863, Brown and other leaders who realized that the Confederacy would not win the war advocated an immediate settlement and a negotiated peace treaty. Neither Mississippi nor the Confederate States of America accepted that suggestion. When the war finally ended two years later, Brown advised the people of Mississippi to accept the consequences of military defeat and the emancipation of the former slaves.

Brown retired from public life after the Civil War and spent his last years practicing law. He died at his home in Terry, Hinds County, on 12 June 1880.

David G. Sansing
University of Mississippi

Biographical Directory of the United States Congress (1950); *Mississippi Official and Statistical Register* (1912); James B. Ranck, *Albert Gallatin Brown: Radical Southern Nationalist* (1937); Dunbar Rowland, *Encyclopedia of Mississippi History*, vol. 2 (1907).

Brown, Andrew

(1793–1871) Industrialist

One of the leading businessmen in antebellum Natchez, Andrew Brown was born in Crail, Scotland, and educated as an architect at the University of Edinburgh between 1807 and 1810. Brown's father, Andrew Bailie Brown, was a member of the municipal government in Crail but was not prosperous. The younger Brown came to America in the early 1820s and settled for a short time in Pittsburgh. He later moved to Natchez, where he first worked as a builder and then in 1828 bought a sawmill from Peter Little. The mill, located at Natchez-under-the-Hill, was a small, single-blade establishment but soon grew, and by 1860 it and its related operations had become the largest business in the Old Southwest. By the start of the Civil War the Brown sawmill produced three million linear feet of lumber annually, and a subsidiary in New Orleans constituted that city's largest woodworking factory.

By 1835 Brown was operating the sawmill and working as a building contractor. The sawmill employed seventeen slaves (some owned and some hired) and one white worker. Sometime early in the decade, wealthy Natchez doctor and cotton planter Stephen Duncan became a silent partner in the firm. The 1830s was a prosperous time in Natchez, and Brown's position as the principal manufacturer of lumber helped him quickly become wealthy.

In 1817, Brown married Elizabeth Key, a neighbor's daughter. Their son, Andrew Brown Jr., was born in 1818. Andrew Jr. joined his father's firm in 1840 and became a full partner in 1843 when he bought out Duncan's share of the company for more than thirty-six thousand dollars. The name of the firm became Andrew Brown and Son. The younger Brown founded and operated the New Orleans branch of the company's business until his death from yellow fever in 1848.

In 1837 the elder Brown became a director of the Mississippi Rail Road Company, headed by Duncan. Brown also owned a Mississippi River steamboat, the *Hail Columbia*, as well as many acres of timberland in the Yazoo River Valley. Brown was elected as a selectman in Natchez in 1837. He was a member of the Whig Party and served in a group aimed at preventing the practice of dueling.

Brown was known for his unusual treatment of his slaves. In spite of the provisions of the Mississippi slave code, most of Brown's slaves were literate; some were allowed to carry guns, were trusted with large sums of money, and were paid salaries; some traveled as part of their work in the lumber industry; and some were allowed to buy their freedom and that of their family members.

Brown's elegant home, Magnolia Vale, was built beneath the bluff in Natchez in the 1830s at a cost of more than sixty thousand dollars and stood for more than one hundred years before being destroyed by fire. In 1839 he hosted a party for five hundred people at his home.

Brown died in 1871. His personal and business papers are housed in Archives and Special Collections in the J. D. Williams Library at the University of Mississippi.

Dale L. Flesher
University of Mississippi

Biographical and Historical Memoirs of Mississippi (1891); Andrew Brown and Son–R. F. Learned Lumber Company/Lumber Archives, Department of Archives and Special Collections, J. D. Williams Library, University of Mississippi; Dale L. Flesher and Tonya K. Flesher, *Accounting and Business Research* (1979); Rufus F. Learned Collection, Lumber Archives, Department of Archives and Special Collections, J. D. Williams Library, University of Mississippi; John Hebron Moore, *Andrew Brown and Cyprus Lumbering in the Old Southwest* (1967).

Brown, R. Jess
(1912–1989)

Carsie A. Hall
(1908–1989)

Jack H. Young Sr.
(1908–1975)
Civil Rights Attorneys

Attorneys R. Jess Brown, Carsie A. Hall, and Jack H. Young Sr. took on the enormous task of handling most of the significant civil rights cases in Mississippi in the 1950s and 1960s, and they paved the way for other black lawyers in the state. Overcoming the structural barriers that discouraged African Americans from practicing law in the state, the three attorneys helped dismantle legalized segregation by representing hundreds of litigants and defendants who challenged Mississippi's Jim Crow laws.

Prior to 1962, most of Mississippi's white lawyers were reluctant to handle civil rights cases, and the state's only accredited law school was closed to African Americans. Aspiring black attorneys had to leave the state to study law and then return to pass the Mississippi bar exam, from which the white graduates of the University of Mississippi Law School were exempt. As late as 1965 only a handful of the state's twenty-two hundred lawyers were African Americans.

Jack Harvey Young was born in Jackson on 9 March 1908. He attended Jim Hill Elementary School, where he was a schoolmate of author Richard Wright, and Smith-Robinson School. Since the city had no public high school that admitted black students, Young enrolled in the high school department of Jackson College in 1923. There he met Carsie A. Hall. One of their professors, A. A. Latting, encouraged them to pursue law. Young graduated from Jackson College in 1931 and Hall a year later. Both men worked full time for the Jackson Post Office until the late 1940s, when they persuaded a former Mississippian, Sidney R. Redmund, to guide their study of the law. When in town from his practice in St. Louis, Redmund tutored Young and Hall and lent them his law books and notes from Harvard Law School. Young passed the Mississippi bar exam in 1951, while Hall did so the following year. Hall recalled that when he went to take the exam, he had to enter the Heidelberg Hotel through the rear entrance and ascend to the examining room in the freight elevator.

Richard Jess Brown was born in Coffeeville, Kansas, on 2 September 1912 and spent most of his childhood in Muskogee, Oklahoma. He graduated from Illinois State University and received a master of education degree from the University of Indiana in 1942. In the late 1940s Brown came to Mississippi and taught industrial arts at Alcorn College, Lanier High School, and Campbell College. In 1948 he signed on as a coplaintiff with Gladys Noel Bates in her suit against the Jackson School Board seeking equalization of teacher's salaries. Like Bates, Brown lost his teaching position. He then decided to become an attorney. He attended Texas Southern Law School before returning to Mississippi in 1953, when he passed the state bar exam.

Young, Hall, and Brown subsequently worked to curb the state's renewed efforts to disenfranchise black voters, provided criminal defense throughout the state, and worked to develop support systems for other black lawyers. In 1956, two years after the *Brown v. Board of Education* decision, Mississippi adopted new rules to tighten the already stringent voter registration process, requiring applicants not only to read a section of the Mississippi Constitution but also to provide a "reasonable" interpretation of it. In addition, applicants needed to register at the county courthouse rather than in local election precincts or other satellite offices. Officials in several counties also purged the voter rolls and required people to reregister, another strategy for removing black voters. After Jefferson Davis County registrars disqualified more than a thousand black voters in 1958, Brown, funded in part by the National Association for the Advancement of Colored People (NAACP), filed a federal suit to challenge the state's rules. During this time Hall became president of the Jackson Chapter of the NAACP.

Numerous black defendants employed the three attorneys in criminal cases, many of them involving alleged black-on-white crimes. Brown defended Mack Parker, who was accused of raping a white woman near Poplarville. With the victim unable to identify her assailant, prosecutors built their case around forced confessions from some of Parker's acquaintances. Before the trial a white mob seized Parker from jail and shot him, disposing of his body in the Pearl River. The Federal Bureau of Investigation looked into Parker's lynching, but a local grand jury never returned an indictment. Brown also led the defense of Clyde Kennard, who was trying to enroll at Mississippi Southern College (now the University of Southern Mississippi) when police arrested him for possession of liquor, which someone had planted in his car. Brown, Young, and Hall also encouraged the work of other black attorneys: they were among the eight founding members of the Magnolia Bar Association, an African American group formed in 1955.

With the spread of the sit-in phase of the civil rights movement in the early 1960s, Brown, Hall, and Young labored to free activists from jail and defend them in courts throughout Mississippi. In 1961 the NAACP Legal Defense Fund contracted with the three attorneys to handle civil rights cases in the state. For the next several years, the men sometimes worked in tandem with William Kunstler and other out-of-state lawyers and with outside legal groups such as the Lawyers' Committee for Civil Rights under Law and the Lawyers' Constitutional Defense Committee. In March 1961 Young defended nine Tougaloo students and NAACP Youth Council members after Jackson police arrested them for their sit-in at the whites-only downtown public library. Two months after the Tougaloo Nine trial, Brown, Hall, and Young became involved in the defense of the more than three hundred Freedom Riders whom police arrested in Jackson, cases that dragged on for years. Brown joined a bevy of NAACP attorneys as the local counsel representing James Meredith in his ultimately successful fight to gain admission to the University of Mississippi in 1962. In 1963 the three attorneys defended the more than six hundred African Americans, most of them under the age of eighteen, who participated in the Jackson movement demonstrations. In late 1963 and early 1964 Brown provided the local counsel for the dozens of men and women whom police arrested for attempting to desegregate white churches in Jackson. During the Freedom Summer of 1964 the three crisscrossed the state to defend activists in jail.

For the rest of their legal careers, Brown, Hall, and Young strove to ensure that their clients received equal treatment before the law and often tackled cases involving alleged black-on-white crimes. Brown became counsel for the American Civil Liberties Union and helped reverse many convictions by proving discrimination in jury selection.

Carter Dalton Lyon
St. Mary's Episcopal School,
Memphis, Tennessee

Crisis (December 1976); John Dittmer, *Local People: The Struggle for Civil Rights in Mississippi* (1994); Worth Long, *Southern Changes* (December 1983); George Alexander Sewell and Margaret L. Dwight, eds., *Mississippi Black History Makers* (1984); Grace Simmons, *Jackson Clarion-Ledger* (2 January 1990); US Commission on Civil Rights, *Justice in Jackson, Mississippi: Hearings Held in Jackson, Miss., February 16–20, 1965*, vol. 2 (1971).

Brown, Larry
(1951–2004) Author

Writer William Larry Brown was born 9 July 1951 in Oxford, Mississippi. His mother, Leona Barlow Brown, was a postmaster and store owner, and his father, Knox Brown, was a World War II veteran and sharecropper. Brown spent his childhood years near Potlockney, in southeastern Lafayette County, and in Memphis, Tennessee, where the family lived from 1954 to 1964. After graduating from high school in August 1969, he enlisted in the US Marines in 1970 and served stateside for two years. In 1973 he joined the Oxford Fire Department as a firefighter, and the following year he married the former Mary Annie Coleman, a secretary. They had four children, one of whom died in infancy. Brown attained the rank of captain in 1986 and retired from the fire department four years later to pursue his writing career full time.

In 1980 Brown began his apprenticeship as a writer of fiction. He published his first short story in *Easyriders* magazine in 1982, the same year he enrolled in a creative writing course at the University of Mississippi under Greenville novelist Ellen Douglas. His first book, the critically acclaimed story collection *Facing the Music*, appeared in 1988. It was followed by the novels *Dirty Work* (1989), *Joe* (1991), *Father and Son* (1996), *Fay* (2000), and *The Rabbit Factory* (2003); a second story collection, *Big Bad Love* (1990); a memoir of his firefighting days, *On Fire* (1993); a book of essays, *Billy Ray's Farm: Essays from a Place Called Tula* (2001); and the

Larry Brown (Photograph © Tom Rankin)

posthumous, incomplete novel *A Miracle of Catfish* (2007). Material from *Big Bad Love* was adapted into a 2001 film coproduced by Arliss Howard and Debra Winger.

Brown's work received numerous literary honors, including the Mississippi Institute of Arts and Letters Award for Literature, the University of North Carolina's Thomas Wolfe Prize, and the Lila Wallace–Reader's Digest Award. Both *Joe* and *Father and Son* received the Southern Book Critics Circle Award for Fiction. He held teaching positions at the Bread Loaf Writers' Conference in Middlebury, Vermont, at Bowling Green State University, at Lynchburg College, at the University of Montana, and at the University of Mississippi.

Like his great Lafayette County precursor William Faulkner, Brown wrote with a sharp and loving eye for the rural environments of North Mississippi—the small, scruffy farms, the muddy rivers and streams, the forests of hardwood and pine hanging on against the depredations of the timber industry, the beautiful vagaries of weather and light and season—and for the rhythms and sensory details of working life in the fields, woods, and shops of the hill country. Stylistically, his work has been compared with the "minimalism" of contemporaries such as Raymond Carver and Richard Ford. Though in early stories he experimented with stream-of-consciousness techniques and cut-and-paste exercises in narrative fragmentation, his signature style is a lean, muscular prose that settles easily and comfortably into the speaking and thinking rhythms of his rough-hewn characters.

Brown's stories and novels bear thematic affinities with the so-called grit lit of Georgia's Harry Crews and Alabama's Tom Franklin. They focus on the often-violent lives of working-class men and women, victims of tough luck and tougher love who face difficult questions of moral responsibility and personal honor as they grapple with deteriorating marriages, alcohol abuse, the legacy of prison, or the horrors of war. Brown's rural South is an angry and often dangerous world in which old habits die hard, old wounds are slow to heal, and old scores wait to be settled. The poverty

his characters suffer is often desperate, bitter, and real, yet some find sustenance in fishing, riding the backroads, the occasional wild night in Oxford or Tupelo, or the simple pleasures of cigarettes and cold beer. Ordinary companionship and conversation count for much in Brown's fiction, as does endurance; his most memorable characters, such as young Gary Jones of *Joe* and the title character of *Fay*, find ways to persevere in a world that asks far more of them than it promises in return.

On the morning of 24 November 2004, Brown died of a heart attack at his home in Tula. His remains were laid to rest there, on the family land he wrote about and loved.

Jay Watson
University of Mississippi

Robert A. Beuka, in *Dictionary of Literary Biography*, ed. Patrick Meanor and Richard E. Lee (2001); Jean W. Cash, in *Dictionary of Literary Biography*, ed. Lisa Abney and Suzanne Disheroon-Green (2004); Jean W. Cash, *Larry Brown: A Writer's Life* (2011); Jean W. Cash and Keith Perry, eds., *Larry Brown and the Blue-Collar South* (2008); Lucy Schultze, *Oxford Eagle* (25–26 November 2004).

Brown, Little Willie

(1900–1952) Blues Musician

Blues musician Willie Lee Brown was born on 6 August 1900 near Clarksdale. The son of sharecroppers whose identities are unknown, Brown, a noteworthy guitarist, is best known for his association with the legendary Mississippi bluesman Charley Patton. Brown traversed the Mississippi countryside and beyond, playing music at a wide array of venues ranging from fish fries to formal studio recordings. Friends and acquaintances called Brown, who was small in stature, Little Willie Brown or simply Little Bill to distinguish him from the physically larger Mississippi blues guitarist known as Big Willie Brown. Many of Patton's acquaintances who were still living in the 1960s recalled the larger Brown because of his boisterous, outgoing personality; the smaller Brown had a quiet, diminutive personality. Although both men were traveling and musical partners of Patton, another legendary Mississippi bluesman, Son House, and a handful of other acquaintances recalled that Little Willie was more closely associated with Patton than was Big Willie.

Prior to World War I Brown lived and worked as a sharecropper on the Alex Peerman Plantation in rural Sunflower County. During these years he honed his skills as a guitarist and developed a distinctive playing style characterized by what fellow bluesman Willie Moore described as a "slapping of the first bass string." According to House, Brown was an excellent sideman who was reluctant to play a musical lead. Moore also recalled that Brown preferred not to sing while playing his guitar. Nonetheless, he developed a penchant for performing for his fellow sharecroppers on the plantation. Brown and Moore formed an itinerant musical duo soon after meeting and provided entertainment not only on the Peerman Plantation but also on neighboring plantations and on street corners. However, their musical career was put on hold when they were drafted into the US Army in 1918 at Camp Shelby. The war ended while they were still in basic training, and the two men set about becoming professional musicians.

The life of a professional bluesman of the time often consisted of traveling, drinking, and gambling. Both Moore and House recalled that Brown developed a love of alcohol, and he would repeatedly sing and play a tune known as "Old Cola" when drunk.

Although Brown met Patton prior to World War I, their professional relationship did not begin until the early 1920s. The two men, often in the company of Moore and House, performed at places such as the Will Dockery Plantation in Dockery and the Webb Jennings Plantation in Drew. Despite their long professional acquaintance, Brown and Patton bickered almost constantly over playing styles. Brown accompanied Patton and House to Grafton, Wisconsin, to record for Paramount Records in 1929–30. Brown chose to remain a sideman during these sessions and waxed no known solo 78s under his own name. Brown subsequently returned to his itinerant ways, eventually drifting to the Memphis area, where he performed with House, Tommy Johnson, and Memphis Minnie. Careful listening to Robert Johnson's legendary "Crossroads Blues" reveals a mention of Willie Brown, though it is not known whether Johnson was referring to Little Willie or Big Willie.

In 1941 Brown made his last known foray into music when he was recorded by Alan Lomax for the Library of Congress in Lake Cormorant, Mississippi. Brown likely chose to give up actively performing when his former musical partner, House, moved to New York in 1943. After the Library of Congress sessions, Brown returned to sharecropping near Tunica with his common-law wife, Annie Lee Brown. He died on 30 December 1952 from coronary thrombosis brought on by acute alcoholism.

Adam E. Maroney
Prescott, Arizona

Stephen Calt and Gayle Wardlaw, *King of the Delta Blues: The Life and Music of Charlie Patton* (1988); David "Honeyboy" Edwards, *The World Don't Owe Me Nothing: The Life and Times of Delta Bluesman Honeyboy Edwards* (1997); Sheldon Harris, *Blues Who's Who: A Biographical Dictionary of Blues Singers* (1981); Gayle Dean Wardlaw, *Chasin' That Devil's Music: Searching for the Blues* (1998).

Brown, Willie
(b. 1940) Athlete

Pro Football Hall of Fame cornerback William Ferdie Brown was born on 2 December 1940 in Yazoo City, Mississippi. He attended Grambling College and excelled on defense. No team in either the National Football League (NFL) or American Football League (AFL) drafted him; he signed with the AFL's Houston Oilers as a free agent in 1963. The Oilers cut Willie before the end of training camp, but he signed with the Denver Broncos for the 1963 season. Brown became the starting cornerback for the Broncos midway through his rookie season. The 6'1", 195-pound linebacker quickly established himself as a standout at his position, earning AFL all-star honors in 1964 and 1965. Brown also earned outstanding defensive player honors at the 1965 AFL All-Star Game.

The Broncos traded Brown to the Oakland Raiders prior to the 1967 season. Brown's skills and aggressive leadership of the talented Raider defense helped Oakland achieve a record of 125–35–7 over his twelve-year tenure. The Raiders played in three AFL championship games and six AFC championship games with Brown at cornerback and earned trips to Super Bowls II and XI. Brown intercepted 54 passes during his pro career, returning them for a total of 472 yards and 2 touchdowns, including a memorable pick-six during Super Bowl XI against the Minnesota Vikings. The Raiders led 26–7 midway, through the fourth quarter when Viking QB Fran Tarkenton threw a pass intended for wide receiver Sammy White. Brown intercepted Tarkenton's pass and ran 75 yards down the sideline for a touchdown. The Raiders prevailed 32–14, earning their first NFL championship.

Over his sixteen seasons in the AFL and NFL, Brown stood out as the premier cornerback of his time. He earned all-league honors seven times, three in the AFL and four in the NFL. He played in five AFL all-star games, was named all-AFC four times, and started in four NFL Pro Bowls. Brown retired as a player in 1978 but remained with the Raider organization as a defensive backfield coach through 1988 and subsequently as the director of squad development. He was elected to the Pro Football Hall of Fame in 1984 and is also a member of the Louisiana Sports, Grambling State, Southwestern Athletic Conference, Mississippi Sports, Black Sports, Bay Area Sports, and Black College Football Halls of Fame.

Dave Ray
University of Mississippi

John Lombardo, *Raiders Forever: Stars of the NFL's Most Colorful Team Recall Their Glory Days* (2000); Pro Football Hall of Fame website, www.profootballhof.com.

Brown v. Board of Education

In the decade after World War II, African Americans in Mississippi achieved some small measure of success in their fight for civil rights. Thousands of African Americans, especially in the state's urban areas, registered to vote. Mississippi also initiated a school equalization program in 1946, in part the result of black complaints; the program did not eliminate the gap between white and black schools but did improve black school facilities and black teacher salaries. This era of slow, piecemeal change, however, came to an abrupt end following the US Supreme Court's *Brown* decision, issued on 17 May 1954, and the *Brown* implementation decree, issued on 31 May 1955. Indeed, white opposition to incipient black strivings for civil rights became more intense and firmly institutionalized following the landmark decision, which declared that separate schools were inherently unequal and, by extension, challenged the entire Jim Crow structure that governed social relations in the South. The court's mandate for school desegregation "with all deliberate speed" created a vague timetable that ultimately encouraged white delay and resistance.

Mississippi whites' response to *Brown* included outrage and defiance as well as some efforts to get black Mississippians to disavow the ruling. US representative John Bell Williams called the day the decision was announced "Black Monday," and US senator James O. Eastland claimed that the South would not obey the court order and urged resistance to the decree. Mississippi governor Hugh White and other state officials met with black leaders in July 1954 and offered to expand the existing equalization program—to make separate black schools truly equal to white ones—in exchange for a pledge that the members of the black delegation would not press for an end to racial segregation. African American leaders rejected this deal, instead offering solid support for *Brown*. Gov. White then joined the rising chorus of white Mississippians who resolved to resist the federal assault on segregation through any means necessary.

Over the ensuing months, the state legislature adopted an official policy of "massive resistance" to all attacks on the racial status quo. After the failed meeting with black leaders, the governor called the Mississippi legislature into special session to pass a constitutional amendment allowing the state to abolish the public schools in any district where segregated schooling was threatened. Voters ratified the amendment in December 1954. In an effort to halt voter registration attempts, the legislature passed and voters approved another constitutional amendment that required all registrants not only to be able to read the state constitution but also to be able to offer a "reasonable" interpretation of a part of the document, a vague standard that individual registrars could use to avoid allowing African Americans to

register. At the same time, many Mississippi counties conducted reregistration campaigns to purge the voter rolls and force blacks to reapply under the new, tougher standards. In 1956 the state legislature also passed a resolution promising to "interpose" the sovereignty of the State of Mississippi between any federal court decree requiring school integration and any local school district subject to such an order. That year the state also created the Sovereignty Commission, initially funded with a $250,000 appropriation, to enforce segregation and disfranchisement through a network of spies and informers.

In addition to official state government actions, individual white Mississippians joined the effort to resist the *Brown* decision. Sunflower County plantation owner Robert B. Patterson spearheaded the creation of the White Citizens' Councils, which soon spread throughout the state and the region. The groups comprised white elites who utilized their prestige and financial power to intimidate black supporters of civil rights through such strategies as firing black employees known to be members of civil rights groups, refusing to make loans to black business officials or farmers who supported civil rights activity, and evicting black renters involved in the freedom struggle. The Council claimed that it did not advocate violence and tried to distance itself from the Ku Klux Klan, but the Council's activities ultimately created an atmosphere in which Klan-style racial violence could thrive. In 1955 three outspoken black leaders were murdered in Mississippi: Rev. George Lee, Gus Courts, and Lamar Smith. That same bloody year, fourteen-year-old Emmett Till, a Chicago youth visiting his Mississippi relatives, was murdered by Roy Bryant and J. W. Milam, who were later acquitted by an all-white, male jury. A handful of whites—among them newspaper journalists Hodding Carter of Greenville, Bill Minor of Jackson, and Oliver Emmerich of McComb—publicly opposed the Citizens' Council, but most other white moderates were effectively silenced by a climate that demanded absolute conformity to white supremacy.

Black Mississippians tried to exercise their rights under the *Brown* decision, but their efforts were swiftly and absolutely rebuffed. Early efforts to expand voter registration and desegregate the state's public schools met the full force of white massive resistance. For example, after the Walthall County branch of the National Association for the Advancement of Colored People submitted a school desegregation petition in August 1954, local authorities responded by closing the county's black schools for two weeks and firing school employees thought to be involved in the effort. African Americans made similar attempts to desegregate schools in the summer of 1955 in Vicksburg, Jackson, Natchez, Clarksdale, and Yazoo City. In all these locales, whites responded by publishing the names of the signers in the local paper, an action that subjected the black activists to economic pressure and verbal intimidation. With the power of the state government and the ire of mobilized white citizens arrayed against them, and with white moderates providing only token dissent from the white party line, Mississippi's African Americans were forced to mute their struggle for black civil rights until the early 1960s. Those who did not faced violence and even death.

Charles C. Bolton
University of North Carolina
at Greensboro

Brown v. Board of Education of Topeka, 347 US 483 (1954), 347 US 294 (1955); Charles C. Bolton, *The Hardest Deal of All: The Battle over School Integration in Mississippi, 1870–1980* (2005); John Dittmer, *Local People: The Struggle for Civil Rights in Mississippi* (1994); Neil R. McMillen, *The Citizens' Council: Organized Resistance to the Second Reconstruction, 1954–1964* (1971).

Brown v. Mississippi

Brown v. Mississippi (1936) was a landmark US Supreme Court decision issued at a time when the Court was most noted for its opposition to some of Pres. Franklin D. Roosevelt's New Deal legislation. The Court was so set in its opposition to progressive reform that the justices were known collectively as the Nine Old Men.

Brown v. Mississippi, for which Chief Justice Charles Evans Hughes wrote the unanimous opinion, was important for at least two reasons. First, the facts of the case were shocking, calling into question the legitimacy of a legal process that would allow confessions coerced by violence. Second, the case marked the first time that the US Supreme Court reversed state court convictions that rested on coerced confessions.

The crime and the trial took place in Kemper County, Mississippi. Raymond Stewart, a white planter, died from a brutal beating on 30 March 1934. The three defendants, all black, were arrested shortly thereafter. One, Yank Ellington, was taken that night to the scene of the crime and alternately interrogated and hanged by a rope from a tree limb. One of his interrogators was a deputy sheriff, and the rope marks remained visible at his trial. He was then tied to a tree and whipped. Still refusing to confess, he was released. A day or two later he was picked up and whipped again until he confessed.

The other two men, Ed Brown and Henry Shields, were taken into custody on the night of 1 April. The same deputy came to their jail cell, where each was laid across a chair and whipped viciously with the buckle end of a strap. The beatings continued until they confessed.

The defendants were indicted on 4 April and arraigned later that day. Their trial began on 5 April and concluded on 6 April. They were found guilty and sentenced to death. Thus, in the course of one week the crime was discovered and the defendants were arrested, indicted, tried, and sentenced to hang.

John A. Clark, L. P. Spinks, J. H. Daws, and D. P. Davis were appointed to represent the defendants. Spinks was sick and unable to attend the trial, leaving the defense to the other three men, with Clark in the lead. The prosecutor was district attorney John C. Stennis. After the trial, the judge refused to pay Clark and the others the customary twenty-five-dollar fee for representing indigent defendants because he feared the public reaction if he authorized the payment.

Following the guilty verdicts, Clark appealed to the Mississippi Supreme Court. Daws refused to take part in the appeal, and Davis's involvement consisted only of allowing his name to be used. On 7 January 1935 the court affirmed the convictions, with Chief Justice Sydney M. Smith writing the opinion. The court held that the defendants' confessions were properly admitted into evidence at the trial. Justice Anderson dissented. Appalled that the trial court had allowed the confessions into evidence, he said, "In some quarters there appears to be very little regard for that provision of the Bill of Rights guaranteeing persons charged with crime from being forced to give evidence against themselves. The pincers, the rack, the hose, the third degree, or their equivalent, are still in use."

At this point, Clark suffered a mental and physical collapse. His wife, Matilda, called on a family friend, former governor Earl Brewer, who had a private practice in Jackson, to seek further review from the court. Brewer, largely at his own expense, took a suggestion of error (similar to today's petition for rehearing) to the court. The suggestion of error was overruled on 29 April 1935, slightly over a year after the trial. Execution was set for 6 June. Justice Griffith dissented, joined by Justice Anderson. Justice Griffith said, "The transcript reads more like pages torn from some medieval account than a record made within the confines of a modern civilization which aspires to an enlightened constitutional government."

Clark made a serious mistake in the direct appeal from the convictions. He failed to allege a violation of federal constitutional law at the trial, which would have secured the possibility of review by the US Supreme Court. Realizing this flaw, Brewer included a federal constitutional claim in his suggestion of error, so that the Mississippi Supreme Court's overruling of the suggestion of error opened the way for review by the US Supreme Court.

The Supreme Court granted the petition for writ of certiorari. Brewer argued the case for the petitioners, and William D. Conn and William H. Maynard argued the case for the state. Brewer urged that the defendants had been denied due process of law under the Fourteenth Amendment. Describing the trial as a "pretense," the Court's ruling condemned the prosecutor and the trial court for allowing confessions known to have been extracted by torture and brutality to be offered and received into evidence. The Court said that a state was free to govern its own procedures unless in doing so it "offends some principle of justice so rooted in the traditions and conscience of our people as to be ranked as fundamental." The state might even abolish jury trial, the Court said, but it might not "substitute trial by ordeal." Further, "the rack and torture chamber may not be substituted for the witness stand." "It would be difficult," the Court said, "to conceive of methods more revolting to the sense of justice than those taken to procure the confessions of these petitioners, and the use of the confessions thus obtained as the basis for conviction and sentence was a clear denial of due process."

Following the Supreme Court's reversal of the convictions and remand to the state courts, Stennis threatened to retry the case. Eventually, an agreement was reached whereby the defendants would plead no contest to a charge of manslaughter. Because of time already served, Brown effectively received a sentence of 7.5 years, Shields received 2.5 years, and Ellington received 6 months.

The personal and professional consequences for the major lawyers in the case were considerable. Clark not only bore the effects of his physical collapse but also paid a heavy political price. At the time of the trial he was serving as floor leader in the State Senate. He lost his reelection bid in the 1935 summer primaries and died five years later. Stennis was elected a circuit court judge in 1937 and served until 1947, when he was elected to the US Senate to fill the unexpired term of Theodore H. Bilbo. Stennis served for nearly forty-two years, one of the longest tenures in history.

Brown v. Mississippi was a watershed decision. The Nine Old Men had rendered a decision so progressive that it remains one of the US Supreme Court's most important rulings.

Samuel Marion Davis
University of Mississippi

Brown v. Mississippi, 297 US 278 (1936); Morgan Cloud, *Texas Law Review* (1996); Richard C. Cortner, *A "Scottsboro" Case in Mississippi: The Supreme Court and Brown v. Mississippi* (1986); James W. Ely, *Law and History Review* (Spring 1991).

Brown-Wright, Flonzie (Goodloe)
(b. 1942) Activist

In 1968 twenty-six-year-old Flonzie Brown Goodloe won a close victory in the race to become Madison County election commissioner, thereby becoming the first African American woman to hold elective office in Mississippi since Reconstruction. Just five years earlier, she had been denied the right to vote.

Flonzie Brown was born in 1942 in Farmhaven to Little T. Dawson Brown and Frank Brown Sr. and grew up in Canton. She attended Holy Child Jesus School along with Thea Bowman, who later became a noted Catholic activist, and the Canton public schools. She enrolled at Tougaloo College, moved to California, married and had three children, divorced, and returned to Mississippi in 1962.

At that time, she recalled, "Canton was a hot spot" in the civil rights movement. Goodloe grew interested in the movement while working at a restaurant where attorneys R. Jess Brown, Jack Young, and Carsie Hall ate and committed herself to voting rights work after the June 1963 murder of Medgar Evers. She attempted to register to vote, was rejected for not knowing the meaning of *habeas corpus*, took a month to study the US Constitution, and passed the test. She worked for a Head Start program and helped teach classes for the National Association for the Advancement of Colored People.

In 1968 African American voters made up a small minority in Madison County. Activist Annie Devine suggested that Goodloe, with her knowledge of voting rules and commitment to fairness, run for the election commission, and she defeated the white incumbent, 3,613 to 3,391. She remained in office for four years.

During that time, Goodloe also served as vice president of the Institute of Politics at Millsaps College, teaching "grass-roots organizing and campaign management" to newly enfranchised African American voters and would-be officeholders. She also ran campaigns. She subsequently married William Wright and in 1994 she published a memoir, *Looking Back to Move Ahead*. In February 2016 Canton renamed the courtroom in its City Hall in her honor.

Ted Ownby
University of Mississippi

Flonzie Brown-Wright, *Looking Back to Move Ahead* (1994); *Jackson Free Press* website, www.jacksonfreepress.com; Shanderia K. Posey, Mississippi Link website (25 February 2016), themississippilink.com; Veterans of the Civil Rights Movement website, www.crmvet.org.

Browne, Jill Conner
(b. 1952) Author

Known for her memorable comic prose, Tupelo native Jill Conner Browne is most famous for her Sweet Potato Queens series, which has garnered national attention and brought new interest into the genre of wry, coquettish southern humor. Though Browne has no formal training or postsecondary education, she has always had a knack for writing that has been instrumental in building the Sweet Potato Queens into a multimedia franchise.

Browne first pursued her writing career through the underground paper *Diddy Wah Diddy*, founded by Jackson locals Malcolm White and Paul Canzoneri. Using the pen name Betty Fulton, she wrote a variety of humorous articles for both *Diddy Wah Diddy* and the *Mississippi Business Journal*. Browne expanded her career when she began a fitness and humor column in the *Jackson Clarion-Ledger*, writing under the byline J. C. Browne. Browne's work was also published in *Roy Blount's Book of Southern Humor* (1994). When the *Mississippi Business Journal* changed editorial direction, Browne's column was not considered suitable for the new image. As a single mother with a young daughter, she started looking for a new avenue of income "out of utter desperation." That desperation led to the Sweet Potato Queens series.

Browne approached editor JoAnne Prichard Morris with the idea of publishing a collection of short stories. Though she later abandoned that project, Browne had also suggested the idea of the *Sweet Potato Queens Book of Love* during their initial meeting. Browne's idea was to provide romantic "advice" from the perspective of the Sweet Potato Queens, the alter egos she and her friends assumed for Mal's St. Paddy's Day Parade in downtown Jackson. Nine months later, Morris was working with the Crown Division of Random House and pitched the idea of Browne's book. "When people ask me 'How do you get a book published?'" Browne said, "I can only speak from my own personal experience, which is that you go home and wait for them to call you."

Morris and her husband, writer Willie Morris, helped craft the prose and character of Browne's first book. Browne said her most memorable advice from Willie Morris was to "be as raucous and funny and wild as you want to be, but the essence of your writing is sweetness—you have to bring them back to that."

The Sweet Potato Queens' Book of Love (1999) met instant success across the United States. Because the *New York Times* classified it as a "self-help" book, determining how the book ranked among other releases proved difficult, but more than 250,000 copies were sold in the first months after publication, and multiple editions were printed to satisfy market demand. The follow-up release, *God Save the Sweet Potato Queens* (2001), also classified as "self-help," met a similar fate. Browne titled the third book of the series *The Sweet Potato Queens' Big-Ass Cookbook and Financial Planner* (2003) so that it could be classified only as nonfiction and not part of any specific genre. As a result, it reached the top of the *New York Times* Best Seller List. The franchise has continued to grow with the successful releases of *The Sweet Potato Queens' Field Guide to Men: Every Man I Love Is Either Married, Gay, or Dead* (2004), *The Sweet Potato*

Queens' Wedding Planner/Divorce Guide (2005), *The Sweet Potato Queens' First Big-Ass Novel* (2007), *American Thighs: The Sweet Potato Queens' Guide to Preserving Your Assets* (2008), and *Fat Is the New 30: The Sweet Potato Queens' Guide to Coping with (the Crappy Parts of) Life* (2012) as well as music releases and associated merchandise.

The Sweet Potato Queens Book of Love has been translated into Japanese and German, and Browne has appeared on ABC's *Good Morning America* and National Public Radio's *Michael Feldman's Whad'Ya Know?* When she is not writing, she tours the country for book signings and meets some of the legions of fans who have formed their own "queenly" clubs. For them, Mal's St. Paddy's Day Parade is an annual pilgrimage to revel in all things feminine, coquettish, and hilarious.

Jill Clark
University of Mississippi

Jill Clark, interview with Jill Conner Browne (28 October 2003); Sweet Potato Queens website, www.sweetpotatoqueens.com.

Bruce, Blanche K.

(1841–1898) Politician

Blanche Kelso Bruce, a Reconstruction-era senator from Mississippi, was born a slave in Virginia in 1841. He went to Missouri as the servant of his owner's son, gained training as a printer, escaped to Kansas during the Civil War, and subsequently attended Oberlin College. He set up a school for African Americans in Missouri and in 1868 moved to Mississippi, where he entered politics as a Republican and quickly gained both popularity and wealth in Bolivar County. At one point in the early 1870s, Bruce simultaneously held the influential positions of school superintendent, sheriff, and tax collector. He grew wealthy investing in real estate, owned a large and successful plantation, and started and operated a newspaper, the *Floreyville Star*.

Bruce used his popularity to run for the US Senate in 1874. He condemned efforts by the Democratic Party to overturn African American voting rights, writing with other Republican politicians that if the Democrats returned to office, "the colored man will at once sink back to the status he held in 1865—free in name but not in fact." In the Senate, Bruce supported efforts to improve education for African Americans, investigated the failure of the once-promising Freedman's Bank, and criticized his colleagues for refusing to seat P. B. S. Pinchback, whom Louisiana voters had elected to represent them. Bruce worked closely with powerful

B

Blanche K. Bruce, ca. 1865–80 (Library of Congress, Washington, D.C. [LC-BH832-30088])

senators such as New York's Roscoe Conkling, and in 1879 Bruce and wife, Josephine, a native of Cleveland, Ohio, named their son Roscoe Conkling Bruce.

Mississippi voters turned Bruce out of office in 1880 in favor of a Democrat who supported white supremacy. Bruce moved to Washington, D.C., and received several appointed positions in the federal government. He was also popular as a speaker. Bruce and his family were part of what historian Willard Gatewood has called "Aristocrats of Color," wealthy and powerful African Americans at the center of Washington social life. After Bruce died in 1898, Josephine Bruce moved to Alabama to take a position as principal of Tuskegee Institute. Both Roscoe Conkling Bruce and his son attended Harvard University.

Ted Ownby
University of Mississippi

Eric Foner, *A Short History of Reconstruction* (1990); John Hope Franklin and Alfred A. Moss Jr., *From Slavery to Freedom: A History of African Americans* (7th ed., 1947); Willard B. Gatewood, *Aristocrats of Color: The Black Elite, 1880–1920* (1990); William C. Harris, *The Day of the Carpetbagger: Republican Reconstruction in Mississippi* (1979); Melvin Urofsky, *Journal of Mississippi History* (May 1967).

Brunini, Joseph

(1909–1996) Religious Leader

A longtime Catholic bishop active in many aspects of Mississippi life throughout the twentieth century, Joseph Bernard Brunini was born on 24 July 1909, the sixth child of John Brunini and Blanche Stein Brunini of Vicksburg. The Brunini family was a tightly knit group, with the father in full charge. A successful lawyer, he did legal work for the diocese gratis. Strong willed and very vocal, he decided that his sons would all go to Georgetown and his daughters would attend Trinity College. Joseph was seen as the child who would succeed his father in the law firm. Ironically, however, Joseph found his vocation at Georgetown.

Brunini's education was a typical Catholic one. He attended St. Aloysius in Vicksburg before moving on to Georgetown, where he edited the school newspaper. During this time Brunini realized he wanted to enter the priesthood and, with the help of his sister, Blanche, told his father during one of his Christmas holidays. John Brunini consulted with Bishop Richard Gerow, who helped decide that Joseph should attend the Pontifical North American College in Rome, where he studied for four years. He was ordained a priest on 5 December 1933 by Cardinal Francesco Marchetti-Selvaggiani. Bishop Gerow wanted Brunini to study canon law in Rome rather than going directly into parish work. Having been away from his family for so long, Brunini compromised by agreeing to study canon law at Catholic University of America.

With his doctorate in hand, Brunini was assigned temporarily to Brookhaven, Mississippi, in 1937. In 1941 he was moved to the cathedral parish in Natchez, where he stayed as rector, chancellor, and eventually monsignor. Bishop Gerow frequently relied on Brunini's advice, and he helped Gerow move the chancery from Natchez to Jackson in 1949. Gerow then appointed Brunini as the pastor of St. Peter's, vicar general of the diocese, and auxiliary bishop in 1956.

Gerow, also a native Mississippian, was happy with Brunini's promotion. Brunini took as his coat of arms and motto "God and Neighbor." Having grown up around Gerow, he naturally saw Gerow as his "spiritual godfather." They worked well together while Brunini also pursued his own tasks such as his work with hospitals. When Bishop Gerow could not attend Vatican II, Brunini took his place and was there for all the council meetings. On 11 July 1966, Pope Paul VI appointed Brunini as apostolic administrator of the diocese without the right of succession. Shortly thereafter, Brunini became the eighth bishop of Natchez-Jackson.

A simple man who loved people, Brunini was down-to-earth and loved to have a good meal surrounded by people who were laughing and talking. Yet underneath this exterior was a man would decide on a course of action and then convince others to do as he wanted, giving them a lot of freedom and responsibility. Under his leadership, Natchez-Jackson grew. He actively recruited priests and religious, appointing Father David O'Connor as his liaison in Ireland for vocations. He constantly communicated with his people, allowed his priests to develop intellectually, brought Spring Hill College into the diocese to offer courses and degrees, and encouraged lay groups to take on more responsibility. He endorsed and attended the annual Mississippi conventions, changed the name of the diocesan newspaper, and wrote a weekly column, "One Who Serves." He updated Catholic Charities, closed the orphanages, and implemented the changes called for by Vatican II. He also had his diocese adopt a mission in Saltillo, Mexico.

Within his diocese, Brunini changed the rules for priests staying in a parish, set up a Catholic Foundation for gifts, reorganized the chancery after the devastation caused by Hurricane Camille, and was the first bishop in America to have a black auxiliary bishop—Joseph Howze. With Rome's approval, Brunini divided his diocese into the Diocese of Biloxi and the Diocese of Jackson, taking the smaller of the two and giving Howze the larger one on the Gulf Coast.

Outside his diocese, he worked with his fellow bishops on numerous committees, was active politically with the Catholic Committee on Appalachia, the Three Rivers Ministry, and STAR (Systematic Training and Redevelopment, an antipoverty program). He had the diocese apply for federal grants to help provide better housing for senior citizens.

Brunini really became a church reformer on the issue of school integration. Troubled by Mississippi's Jim Crow history and sensing that the time was right for action, Brunini worked with Gerow to begin integrating the state's Catholic schools before the public schools started the process. In a 1969 "Christmas message," Brunini let the world know that things were changing. Between 1967 and 1984 he made sure that the Diocese of Jackson integrated, despite severe criticisms from his own school superintendent. If any sign or action of discrimination occurred, he acted quickly to stop it and punish those responsible. He was one of the founders and first chairs of the Mississippi Religious Leadership Conference. He and a new superintendent, Msgr. Paul Canonici, established guidelines for school integration in 1974. And he continually supported St. Augustine's seminary for African American priests, ordained black priests, and supported civil rights movements such as the Greenwood movement and Pax Christi. His actions changed the makeup and sense of the diocese.

Joseph Bernard Brunini died on 7 January 1996.

Michael V. Namorato
University of Mississippi

Joseph B. Brunini, "Memoirs of a Southern Bishop" (Catholic Diocese of Jackson Archives); *Mississippi Today*, special edition (1997); Michael V. Namorato, *The Catholic Church in Mississippi, 1911–1984* (1998); Michael V. Namorato, interviews with Joseph B. Brunini (1987–88).

Bryant, C. C.
(1917–2007) Activist

Curtis Conway Bryant was born in Walthall County on 15 January 1917 and lived most of his life in McComb. He worked for the Illinois Central Railroad from 1940 to 1979, led some unionization efforts among railroad workers, and owned a popular barbershop. In 1954 Bryant was elected president of the Pike County chapter of the National Association for the Advancement of Colored People (NAACP), and he led that organization through a challenging period in the 1950s–60s.

Bryant is particularly noteworthy because he provided a link between local civil rights activists and the national movement. After reading an article about the Student Nonviolent Coordinating Committee (SNCC) in *Jet* magazine, Bryant asked Robert Moses and other young activists to visit McComb in 1961. Moses stayed at the Bryants' home when he arrived to begin a new stage of activism in southern Mississippi. Bryant's barbershop was a popular meeting place where visitors could find African American periodicals and NAACP literature. Bryant and the NAACP welcomed the energy and effort of SNCC workers in helping African Americans attempt to register to vote, and he helped introduce the young activists to numerous people in the area. But Bryant and the NAACP were less comfortable with SNCC methods after the murder of local minister Herbert Lee and a student protest divided parts of the African American community. At that point, according to historian John Dittmer, Bryant was "the man in the middle," opposed to direct action strategies and especially to the use of children in protests.

In 1964 Bryant was again in the middle of civil rights activism. Members of the Ku Klux Klan bombed his business and several of the homes and churches of civil rights workers. Bryant fired back at the bombers and made clear that he would protect himself. Later that year, Bryant was part of a group that successfully tested the Civil Rights Act by asking for and receiving service at the restaurant of a previously whites-only McComb hotel.

Bryant headed the Pike County NAACP for more than thirty years. His NAACP work earned him numerous awards, including the Aaron Henry Award. He and his wife, Emogen, had two children and numerous grandchildren. After Bryant died in 2007, supervisors in Pike County and McComb proclaimed his birthday C. C. Bryant Day, and the street where he lived has been renamed in his honor.

Ted Ownby
University of Mississippi

Raymond Arsenault, *Freedom Riders: 1961 and the Struggle for Racial Justice* (2006); Clayborne Carson, *In Struggle: SNCC and the Black Awakening of the 1960s* (1981); John Dittmer, *Local People: The Struggle for Civil Rights in Mississippi* (1994); "Oral History with C. C. Bryant" (1995), Center for Oral History and Cultural Heritage, University of Southern Mississippi, digilib.usm.edu/cdm/ref/collection/coh/id/16249; Charles M. Payne, *I've Got the Light of Freedom: The Organizing Tradition and the Mississippi Freedom Struggle* (1995); Judith Barlow Roberts, "C. C. Bryant: A Race Man Is What They Call Him" (master's thesis, University of Mississippi, 2012).

Bryant, Phil

(b. 1954) Sixty-Third Governor, 2012–

Born in the Mississippi Delta town of Moorhead, Phil Bryant worked as an arson insurance investigator and Hinds County deputy sheriff before running for an open seat on the Rankin County Board of Supervisors in 1988. He lost in the Republican primary but tried again for elective office three years later, when he won a seat in the Mississippi House of Representatives. He served for five years before Gov. Kirk Fordice appointed Bryant to fill the remaining three years of Steve Patterson's term as state auditor. Bryant was reelected to the post in 1999 and 2003 before winning the lieutenant governorship in 2007.

Four years later, Bryant became governor, taking about 61 percent of the vote against Hattiesburg mayor Johnny Dupree, the first black major-party nominee for governor in Mississippi history. Bryant campaigned as a populist conservative, promising to create jobs and lower taxes while opposing abortion, gay rights, illegal immigration, and gun restrictions. In 2014 he announced Opportunity Mississippi, a program designed to bring "performance-based budgeting" to state government agencies.

His economic development efforts and large financial incentives recorded a few high-profile successes, such as Yokohama Tire Corporation, but the net number of new jobs remained relatively small as the state struggled to recover from the 2009 recession. Bryant also faced a rash of high-profile public corruption cases. Among those accused were two cabinet officers he appointed to run the Department of Marine Resources and Department of Corrections.

Bryant embraced his reputation as the nation's first Tea Party governor by spending considerable energy opposing Pres. Barack Obama's policies. For example, Bryant refused to expand Medicaid in Mississippi under the Affordable Care Act, and his administration joined dozens of other states suing to overturn deferment of immigration law enforcement by executive order. Bryant also publicly vowed to block resettlement of Syrian civil war refugees in the state. Bryant led the opposition that defeated Initiative 42, a proposed state constitutional amendment regarding public school funding, and fought efforts to remove Confederate symbols from the state flag. In 2016 he added to his conservative record, designating April as Confederate Heritage Month and signing the Religious Liberty Accommodations Act, which protected people who had religious objections to serving gay, lesbian, and transgendered individuals, and the Church Protection Act, which created a process under which designated church members could undergo gun training to allow them to carry holstered weapons in church.

In 2015 Bryant easily won a second term as governor, taking 66 percent of the vote against Democrat Robert Gray, a surprise nominee and truck driver who ran a low-budget campaign.

Mississippi Encyclopedia Staff
University of Mississippi

Governor Phil Bryant website, www.governorbryant.com; *Mississippi Official and Statistical Register* (2014).

Bucci, Andrew

(1922–2014) Painter

The calligraphic gestures and soft colors that compose many of Andrew Bucci's paintings won the artist widespread recognition within and beyond Mississippi. Born in Vicksburg on 12 January 1922, Bucci studied art as a teenager, though his high school did not offer formal classes. Beginning at age seventeen he spent summers painting under longtime mentor and revered painter Marie Hull and earned a degree in architectural engineering from Louisiana State University. During World War II Bucci served as a meteorologist, training at New York University before being sent to Europe, where he also studied at the Académie Julian in Paris. After the war he resumed his work under Hull and had his first show at Allison's Art Colony (now the Mississippi Art Colony) in 1947. That year he also enrolled at the Art Institute of Chicago, where he received a bachelor of fine arts degree in 1952 and a master of fine arts degree in 1954.

Bucci's career with the US Weather Bureau took him to Washington, D.C., for several decades. He often exhibited with the Society of Washington Artists and served as president of the Washington Watercolor Society.

Bucci was one of the first Mississippi artists to use a nonobjective approach to his landscapes. His work is lyrical and inventive, embracing expressionism and its variations. His signature style is calligraphic, with flowing structural lines and delicate colors. While sometimes grouped with the abstract expressionists, Bucci created figures and landscapes that at times may be defined as gesture-based (meaning that they result from quick movements of the brush and convey a sense of motion). The oil painting *Fox Fire* (1976), included in a 2007 Mississippi Museum of Art exhibition, *The Mississippi Story*, shows many of his characteristic attributes: soft colors, gestural strokes, an Asian aspect. (Fox fire is the luminescence of decaying wood, perhaps a memory of Bucci's childhood on the Mississippi River.) Bucci's watercolors from the 1960s, influenced by Japanese woodblock prints, have been described as "subtle and translucent as haiku poems."

B

In contrast to Hull's vibrant use of color and energetic abstraction, Bucci's paintings are frequently softer and more formal—refined in their employ of watercolor and oil. Following Bucci's studies at the Art Institute of Chicago, Hull took on more of a mentee role, learning from her erstwhile pupil the formal techniques he had picked up. In 2010 the University of Mississippi Museum presented the exhibition *Teacher and Student: The Abstract Works of Marie Hull and Andrew Bucci.*

Bucci's paintings have been viewed throughout the South and East for more than half a century and included in shows at the Pennsylvania Academy of Fine Arts, the Smithsonian Institution, and the Corcoran Gallery of Art in Washington, D.C., among others. In 2009 Bucci received the Governor's Excellence in the Arts Lifetime Achievement Award; three years later, the Mississippi Institute of Arts and Letters also presented him with a Lifetime Achievement Award. Several of Bucci's works and his papers are housed at the Smithsonian Institution's Archives of American Art. His paintings are included in the collections of the Ogden Museum of Southern Art, Lauren Rogers Museum of Art, Arkansas Art Center, Memphis Brooks Museum of Art, Florence Art Gallery in South Carolina, Delta State University, Hinds Junior College, and Mississippi University for Women.

He moved back to Vicksburg shortly before his death on 16 November 2014.

Patti Carr Black
Jackson, Mississippi

Patti Carr Black, *Art in Mississippi, 1720–1980* (1998); Patti Carr Black, *The Mississippi Story* (2007); Andrew Bucci, Smithsonian Archives of American Art website, www.aaa.si.edu/; Sherry Lucas, *Jackson Clarion-Ledger* (18 November 2014).

Buffett, Jimmy
(b. 1946) Musician

Singer, songwriter, author, and one-man genre James William Buffett was born on 25 December 1946 in Pascagoula, Mississippi. Buffett attended Auburn University before graduating from the University of Southern Mississippi with a degree in journalism in 1969. While in college he worked as a singer in New Orleans. After graduating he moved to Nashville, Tennessee, to pursue a career in the music business. He worked as a reporter for *Billboard* magazine before landing a recording contract with Barnaby Records. Buffett's first album, *Down to Earth*, sold poorly in its 1970 release, and the master tapes for his second album, *High Cumberland Jubilee*, were "lost" but mysteriously reappeared as Buffett's career began to soar in the mid-1970s.

A trip to Florida landed Jimmy Buffett in Key West, a city that proved an important catalyst for his musical development. On his next three albums, *A White Sport Coat and a Pink Crustacean* (1973), *Living and Dying in 3/4 Time* (1974), and *A1A* (1974), all released on the Dunhill label, Buffett introduced the tropical- and travel-oriented themes that captured the collective imagination of legions of Buffett fans, known affectionately as Parrot Heads. Songs such as "Tin Cup Chalice" and "Cuban Crime of Passion" still remain on Buffett's touring set lists forty years after they were originally penned, a testament to both his songwriting and the loyalty of his fans. Of equal importance from this period are the still-popular reflective and poignant songs such as "He Went to Paris," "A Pirate Looks at Forty," and "Come Monday."

Surprisingly, in a recording career spanning more than forty years, Buffett has had only one Top 10 hit as a solo artist: "Margaritaville" from the 1977 album *Changes in Latitudes, Changes in Attitudes.* Although his early country-oriented album for Barnaby faired poorly, Buffett has subsequently found significant success in that genre. A 2003 duet with Alan Jackson, "It's Five O'Clock Somewhere," gave Buffett his first No. 1 hit, while his 2004 album of country duets, *License to Chill*, gave him his first chart-topping album. The duet with Jackson held the No. 1 spot on the country charts for eight weeks and earned the Country Music Association's 2003 Vocal Event of the Year award. In 2011 another duet, "Knee Deep," with the Zac Brown Band, went to No. 1 on the country charts.

Buffett has described his music as being "90 percent autobiographical." With clever song and book titles (and subtitles) such as "Fictional Facts and Factional Fictions," "That's My Story and I'm Sticking to It," and "Semi-True Story," one wonders where the autobiography ends and the fiction begins. His song "Jamaica Mistaica," for example, relates an incident in which the Negril, Jamaica, police mistakenly opened fire on Buffett's seaplane. Buffett's gift for storytelling has helped him make the transition into a successful author. Buffett has written two children's books; a collection of short stories called *Tales from Margaritaville*; the novels *Where Is Joe Merchant?*, *A Salty Piece of Land*, and *Swine Not? A Novel Pig Tale*; and a memoir, *A Pirate Looks at Fifty.* Buffett is one of only a handful of authors to have had No. 1 *New York Times* best sellers in both fiction and nonfiction.

The tropical themes of Buffett's music play a significant role in these works as well as in his two restaurant chains, Margaritaville Café and Cheeseburger in Paradise. In addition to establishments in Key West, New Orleans, Orlando, and Las Vegas, the singer has also offered up a tropical atmosphere to establishments in such unlikely places as Downers Grove, Illinois;, Middleton, Wisconsin; Myrtle Beach, South Carolina; Omaha, Nebraska; Indianapolis, Indiana and Fredericksburg, Virginia. International locations in Mexico (Cancun) and Jamaica (Montego Bay, Negril, and Ocho Rios) round out his club offerings. In 2016 Buffett opened Margaritaville Resort Biloxi.

To his fans, the essence of Jimmy Buffett is adventure, exotic locales, and a nonstop tropical beach party. This lifestyle, which he terms "island escapism," proves a continual source of entertainment for his fans. Buffett has been known to stand on stage and tell fans that he is spending their money foolishly. They don't seem to mind as long as the music and the stories keep coming.

Kevin Herrera
University of Mississippi

Donald Clarke, ed., *The Penguin Encyclopedia of Popular Music* (1998); Brock Helander, *The Rock Who's Who* (1996); Colin Larkin, ed., *The Encyclopedia of Popular Music* (1998); William Ruhlmann, Alabama Music Hall of Fame website, www.alamhof.org.

Bungalows

The bungalow is one of the most successful vernacular housing styles in twentieth-century America. In Mississippi as well as the rest of the country, bungalows were built in large numbers and reflect all different climates, owner aesthetics, and income levels. The word *bungalow* comes from the Hindu word *bangla* and historically referred to dwellings of light construction with verandas for English officials in colonial India. The American vernacular bungalow, also known as the California bungalow, first appeared in trade literature in 1904.

By the 1920s bungalows had gained tremendous popularity, and they remained popular through the 1930s. Most vernacular bungalows are long and low—1 or 1.5 stories. Other common characteristics include a prominent front gable or hip roof, overhanging eaves, large front porch encompassed by the main roof, and an open interior floor plan. The length of the house is usually greater than the width. The bungalow's simple, unassuming design was further accentuated by the use of natural materials and colors that were supposed to blend into the building's surroundings.

Compared to the overly detailed Victorian styles that preceded it, the bungalow was simple and appealed to middle-class America. It was often linked to the Arts and Crafts movement, which indulged the growing US middle class and its large demand for affordable yet attractive suburban houses. Constructed in the Craftsman style or with some Craftsman-style detailing, many bungalows incorporated such features as exposed rafter ends, enormous stone or brick exterior chimneys, local natural materials, and open floor plans.

Perhaps the best-known example of a bungalow in Mississippi was the Louis Sullivan bungalow in Ocean Springs, a vacation house for Chicago School architect Louis Sullivan. It was listed on the National Register of Historic Places for its connection with Sullivan and another famous architect, Frank Lloyd Wright, both of whom claimed to have designed the structure in the early 1890s. It was destroyed in 2005 by Hurricane Katrina. While the high-style Louis Sullivan bungalow is not typical of Mississippi's bungalows, it exhibited the spacious interiors, overhanging eaves, and open verandas of the more abundant vernacular bungalows.

Bungalows largely fell out of vogue after the 1930s but continued to be built sparingly into the 1940s and 1950s in rural settings. Extant examples are found throughout Mississippi on urban and suburban blocks and in rural communities.

Summer J. Chandler
Austin, Texas

Rachel Carley, *The Visual Dictionary of American Domestic Architecture* (1994); Jan Jennings and Herbert Gottfried, *American Vernacular Interior Architecture, 1870–1940* (1993); Library of Congress, Prints and Photographs Reading Room website, www.loc.gov/rr/print; James C. Massey and Shirley Maxwell, *House Styles in America* (1996); Mary Ann Smith, *Gustav Stickley: The Craftsman* (1983).

Burkitt, Benjamin Franklin

(1843–1914) Political Leader

Frank Burkitt was one of the most important advocates of small-farmer interests in Mississippi during the late nineteenth and early twentieth centuries. Benjamin Franklin Burkitt was born in Lawrenceburg, Tennessee, on 15 July 1843 to lawyer Henry L. Burkitt and Louisa Burkitt. By 1860 he was working as a clerk for a merchant in nearby Waynesboro. During the Civil War, Burkitt enlisted in Company I of the 9th Tennessee Cavalry, serving through the war and ending up a captain. Burkitt subsequently taught school in northern Alabama before moving to Chickasaw County early in the 1870s. He acquired the *Okolona Chickasaw Messenger* and commenced a career as an outspoken newspaper editor. Like most Mississippi whites, Burkitt opposed the Republican state government, and his editorials advocated aggressive efforts to overturn Republican power. During the pivotal 1875 campaign during which Democrats emerged triumphant, he helped lead conservative efforts in Chickasaw.

After Reconstruction, Burkitt's views began to diverge from those of most elite whites. After joining the state Grange, a farmers' organization, he emerged as arguably the leading advocate of small-farmer interests. Having championed the formation of a state agricultural college, he was named one of the original trustees of Mississippi Agricultural and Mechanical College (now Mississippi State University). By the time of his election to the state House of Representatives in 1886, however, Burkitt had grown disenchanted with the college, which he viewed as a wasteful expenditure that served wealthy students and drained money from the common schools. Such views formed the centerpiece of *The Wool Hat*, a widely distributed pamphlet in which Burkitt glorified small farmers, railed against the elite, and argued for retrenchment of state expenses.

Embracing the Farmers' Alliance movement, Burkitt, often wearing a Confederate uniform and wool hat, traveled the state in the late 1880s and early 1890s as the organization's state lecturer. He pushed for a new state constitution to redress the political imbalances he perceived at the root of Bourbon power. Elected to the 1890 constitutional convention, he served on the franchise committee and worked to alter apportionment to favor white-majority counties. He was one of the few delegates to vote against the constitution because its disfranchising provisions, aimed at African Americans, targeted poor whites as well. In an impassioned speech he exploited pro-Confederate sympathies: "This constitution deprives many poor men of the right to vote, one of whom was my comrade in the army. . . . My right arm shall fall palsied at my side before I put my signature to such a document."

For the next two years Burkitt continued to work for agrarian interests within the Democratic Party. While remaining committed to retrenchment of the state government, he embraced the Alliance's most radical national goals, including the subtreasury plan, government regulation of railroads, and an income tax. In 1891 he led the state Farmers' Alliance in a failed effort to replace Sen. James Z. George with Ethelbert Barksdale, a Democrat more sympathetic to Alliance-supported initiatives. The following year he forfeited a slot as a Democratic presidential elector after the party nominated Grover Cleveland for president. Leading many of his supporters into the People's (Populist) Party, Burkitt ran a competitive but unsuccessful campaign for Congress and then threw his efforts into building up the Populist cause.

From the outset, Mississippi Populists faced insurmountable obstacles. Although the racial views of Burkitt and other Populists did not differ substantively from those of Democrats, the latter made partisan and racial orthodoxy virtually synonymous. Burkitt did not flinch from Democratic attacks and continued to defend the interests of the state's poor, whether they were white or black. However, by disfranchising almost all of the African American electorate and many poor whites as well, the Constitution of 1890

minimized potential Populist growth. Burkitt fought gamely to overcome such problems, but his race for governor in 1895 underscored the party's weakness, and he received less than 30 percent of the total vote and carried only Choctaw County.

Like many Populists, Burkitt later returned to the Democratic Party. Early in the twentieth century, as Mississippi's agrarian interests gained new strength behind the leadership of James K. Vardaman, Burkitt remained a powerful advocate. In 1907 he returned to the state House of Representatives, where he became one of Vardaman's chief allies. Elected to the State Senate in 1911, Burkitt chaired the joint committee on contingent funds prior to his death in December 1914.

William Bland Whitley
Thomas Jefferson Papers,
Princeton, New Jersey

John K. Bettersworth, *People's College: A History of Mississippi State* (1953); Stephen Cresswell, *Multiparty Politics in Mississippi* (1995); Albert D. Kirwan, *Revolt of the Rednecks: Mississippi Politics, 1876–1925* (1951); Thomas Adams Upchurch, *Journal of Mississippi History* (Fall 2003).

Burnett, Charles
(b. 1944) Filmmaker

While perhaps not a well-known name in mainstream media, Charles Burnett has written and directed critically acclaimed films that create intimate and realistic portraits of contemporary African American life.

Burnett was born in Vicksburg, Mississippi, on 13 April 1944. Shortly thereafter, his family moved to Los Angeles. In the 1960s he studied electronics at Los Angeles Community College before receiving a master of fine arts degree in 1973 from the film school at the University of California at Los Angeles. His thesis project, *Killer of Sheep* (released in 1977), is recognized as one of the most poetic and insightful movies concerning contemporary African American life. Shot on 16mm film over a series of weekends and using a cast of nonprofessional actors, *Killer of Sheep* tells the story of a blue-collar worker in south-central Los Angeles. The visually austere film details this ordinary workman's everyday interactions with his family and neighbors. What makes *Killer of Sheep* distinctive is the way in which Burnett refuses to sensationalize either his plot or his characters, a pointed response to Hollywood's stereotypical depictions of African Americans in the 1960s and 1970s. Instead, this film, like his subsequent films, strives to depict life realistically and personally. His characters are neither heroes nor villains, and the circumstances they encounter are neither purely tragic nor simply comic. While some critics describe Burnett's works as plotless, those who praise his films point out the way in which he draws attention to the beauty and significance of life's quotidian rhythms. In 1990 the Library of Congress selected *Killer of Sheep* as one of the second group of twenty-five films to be included in the National Film Registry. Despite its many accolades, licensing concerns and poor distribution relegated the movie to obscurity until 2007, when it was fully restored and blown up to 35mm. Its rerelease brought international acclaim.

Burnett's next project, *My Brother's Wedding* (1983), concentrates on generational differences and class tensions within the family sphere, once again providing a refreshingly realistic depiction of human relationships. While appreciated by movie critics, Burnett's second film, like his first, never found a wide public audience.

In 1988 Burnett received a John D. and Catherine T. MacArthur Foundation "genius" award, and he soon began work on his next feature film, *To Sleep with Anger* (1990). Starring Danny Glover, *To Sleep with Anger* tells the story of a black middle-class family as it deals with issues of race and cultural identity. The movie is deeply concerned with the ties between past and present and the bonds between individual and family. In contrast to the neorealism of *Killer of Sheep*, *To Sleep with Anger* is more akin to a parable. Burnett's film again received praise within artistic circles, winning three Independent Spirit Awards in 1991 (Best Director and Best Screenplay for Burnett and Best Actor for Glover), though the public paid it little attention.

Over the next few years Burnett continued to work in film and television to address important issues in modern society, particularly those concerning the African American community. Some of his more notable projects during this time were *The Glass Shield* (1995), a Hallmark Hall of Fame made-for-television film; *Night John* (1996); and *The Wedding* (1998), a TV miniseries produced by Oprah Winfrey. Burnett's recent work includes the 2003 documentary, *Nat Turner: A Troublesome Property*, and *Namibia: The Struggle for Liberation* (2007), a feature film about Namibia's fight for independence from apartheid-era South Africa.

Katherine Treppendahl
University of Virginia

Manohla Dargis, *New York Times* (30 March 2007); Tom and Sara Pendergast, eds., *International Dictionary of Films and Filmmakers*, vol. 4, *Directors* (2000).

Burnside, R. L.
(1926–2005) Blues Musician

In the early 1990s R. L. Burnside became an unlikely star of the blues world, largely the result of a unique marketing strategy employed by his label, Oxford-based Fat Possum Records. He was born on 23 November 1926 in Harmontown, Mississippi, north of Oxford, and from age seven to seventeen lived in Coldwater with his mother and maternal grandparents. His given name appears to have been R. L.; his friends often called him Rule or Rural. He began playing guitar as a young man after receiving an instrument from his brother-in-law. His major influence was the Como-based bluesman Mississippi Fred McDowell, who popularized the distinctive North Mississippi style of blues during the 1960s blues revival. Other local influences were Ranie Burnette and Son Hibler.

Shortly after World War II Burnside moved to Chicago, where he often saw performances by Muddy Waters, whose slide guitar technique Burnside adopted. He found Chicago too rough for his taste and soon moved back to Mississippi, where he met his wife, Alice Mae, with whom he was married for more than fifty years. For much of his adult life Burnside was a cotton sharecropper, drove farm machinery, and worked with commercial fishing; he played music mostly on the weekends.

During the 1950s he served briefly at the Parchman Penitentiary. In a 1994 account he suggested that his prison sentence was associated with transporting stolen goods; he later said it was for manslaughter committed in self-defense, and he often joked, "I didn't mean to kill him. I just shot him in the head. His dying was between him and his God." Burnside was famously good-natured and a master storyteller: several of his "toasts" were captured on record.

In 1967–68 folklorist George Mitchell, who was documenting the distinctive musical styles of North Mississippi, recorded Burnside as well other local artists, including Jessie Mae (Hemphill) Brooks, Joe Callicot, and Othar Turner. Six of Mitchell's recordings of Burnside, including repertoire staples "Poor Black Mattie," "Goin' Down South," and "Long Haired Doney," appeared on the 1969 Arhoolie compilation album *Mississippi Delta Blues*, vol. 2.

In the wake of the Arhoolie release Burnside began appearing at music festivals, but over the next several decades he received relatively little attention in blues circles aside from occasional small tours performed mostly locally and appearances at juke joints run by fellow Marshall County bluesman David "Junior" Kimbrough and in the company of guitarist and Nesbit native Kenny Brown.

In the late 1970s and early 1980s Burnside recorded two acoustic albums for the Dutch Swingmaster label and a single with the electric Sound Machine band—which included his sons, Joseph and Daniel, and son-in-law, Calvin Jackson—for folklorist David Evans's High Water label. Two full CDs of the High Water recordings, *Sound Machine Groove* and *Raw Electric*, were issued many years later.

In the early 1990s Peter Lee, former editor of *Living Blues* magazine, and Mathew Johnson formed the Oxford-based Fat Possum Records, whose first release was the 1992 Burnside CD *Bad Luck City*. Burnside's live band sound was more accurately captured on the 1994 Fat Possum CD *Too Bad Jim*, which was recorded at Junior Kimbrough's juke joint in Chulahoma. Music scholar and critic Robert Palmer produced both CDs and narrated the 1993 documentary *Deep Blues*, which helped bring broader attention to Burnside, Kimbrough, and other North Mississippi musicians.

Burnside's first two Fat Possum CDs were well received by critics but sold poorly. On the 1996 CD *A Ass Pocket of Whiskey* Fat Possum embarked on a new marketing strategy by teaming Burnside with the alternative band Jon Spencer and the Blues Explosion and various outside producers who utilized modern technologies such as sampling and looping. The album—and Fat Possum's marketing of Burnside and other acts as primitives with chaotic lifestyles—introduced Burnside to alternative rock circles. At the same time he began appearing as a headliner at international blues festivals, performing with Kenny Brown on second guitar and his young grandson, Cedric Burnside, on drums.

Fat Possum also utilized the remix approach on the CDs *Mr. Wizard* (1997) and *Come on In* (1998); a remixed version of the blues standard *Rollin' and Tumblin'* from the latter was featured often in the opening credits of *The Sopranos*. The various studio innovations were not reflected in Burnside's live sound, which was captured on the Fat Possum CD *Burnside on Burnside* (2001). *Wish I Was in Heaven Sitting Down* (2000) and *Bothered Mind* (2004) mixed Burnside's "regular" sound and the remixes of outside producers.

In the early 2000s Burnside began suffering from various health problems that kept him from touring regularly. He died on 1 September 2005 and was buried in Harmontown. Many family members, including his sons, Duwayne and Garry; grandson, Cedric; and his "adopted" son, Kenny Brown, have carried on his legacy through recordings and live performances.

Scott Barretta
Greenwood, Mississippi

David Evans, *Sound Machine Groove* (1997); Tom Freeland, *Living Blues* (November–December 2005); Michael Pettengell, *Living Blues* (October 1994).

Butler, Jack
(b. 1944) Author

Best known as a fiction writer, Jack Armand Butler Jr. is also a poet, essayist, and food columnist. He was born in the small Mississippi Delta town of Alligator on 8 May 1944 to Jack Butler, a Southern Baptist minister, and Dorothy Niland Butler, a homemaker.

The writer's early childhood was spent in New Orleans, where his father attended New Orleans Baptist Theological Seminary. Butler attended high school in Clinton, lettering in track and becoming interested in writing, before enrolling at Central Missouri State College (now the University of Central Missouri). He received bachelor's degrees in mathematics and English in 1966 but spent 1964 at Mississippi College, where he ran on the cross country and track teams, acted in plays, and wrote poetry and fiction for the college literary magazine, *Arrowhead*. As a young child, Butler was, in his words, a "preacher boy," speaking frequently from the pulpit, an experience that strongly influenced his life, although he moved away from that vocation after a brief experience as a pastor of a small church in Sedalia, Missouri, in 1966.

In 1968 Butler entered the creative writing program at the University of Arkansas. Over the next decade he held a series of jobs, including writer in residence for the Joint Educational Consortium in Arkadelphia, Arkansas, and instructor of English at the University of Arkansas. He completed his master of fine arts degree in 1979 and worked in public relations and as an actuarial analyst before returning to the academic world as an assistant dean at Hendrix College in Conway, Arkansas. In 1993 he moved to Santa Fe, New Mexico, and served as associate professor of creative writing and the codirector of the creative writing program at the College of Santa Fe. He retired in 2004.

Butler's poetry has been published in numerous journals and magazines, including *Atlantic Monthly*, *New Yorker*, *Poetry*, *Southern Poetry Review*, and *Mississippi Review*, and his work has been included in several anthologies. Butler has published two collections of poems, *West of Hollywood: Poems from a Hermitage* (1981) and *The Kid Who Wanted to Be a Spaceman* (1982). He acknowledges the influence of Robert Frost and W. B. Yeats and, unlike most contemporary poets, primarily writes formal poetry rather than free verse.

Butler has always written fiction as well. He won first prize for fiction from the *Black Warrior Review* in 1978 for the story "Without Any Ears" and in 1981 for "A Country Girl." He has published a collection of stories, *Hawk Gumbo and Other Stories* (1982), and a novel, *Jujitsu for Christ* (1986), that was widely praised and republished in 1988 as part of the Penguin Contemporary Fiction series. Set primarily in and around Jackson in the 1960s, the novel uses the integration of the University of Mississippi and related civil rights events to develop an antiracist satire. *Nightshade* (1989), a science fiction novel, reflects Butler's long-held interest in that genre. Another novel, *Living in Little Rock with Miss Little Rock* (1993), was nominated for the Pulitzer Prize and for the PEN/Faulkner award.

Butler's next work, *Jack's Skillet: Plain Talk and Some Recipes from a Guy in the Kitchen* (1997), followed a series of successful food columns and revealed anew the wide diversity of his interests and talents. In 1998 he returned to the science fiction genre with the publication of *Dreamer*. Most recently, he has published *Practicing Zen without a License* (2011) and *Broken Hallelujah: New and Selected Poems* (2013).

Butler has two daughters, Lynnika and Sarah, and now lives in Eureka, California, where he writes and paints.

Verbie Lovorn Prevost
University of Tennessee
at Chattanooga

"Jack Butler" *Contemporary Authors*, new rev. ser., vol. 53 (1997); Jack Butler website, authorjackbutler.wordpress.com; Ashby Bland Crowder, *Mississippi Quarterly* (Winter 1992).

Byington, Cyrus
(1793–1868) Missionary and Translator

Cyrus Byington, a missionary to the Choctaw and an important linguist and translator, was born on 11 March 1793 in Stockbridge, Massachusetts, one of nine children in a poor but respectable farm family. Although his early education was limited by his family's circumstances, he later studied Latin and Greek and read law with Joseph Woodbridge. He was admitted to the bar in 1814 and practiced for several years in Stockbridge and Sheffield. Stockbridge was the site of a mission to the Housatonic Indians, part of the Mohican tribe. It had also been the home of Jonathan Edwards, whose sermons sparked the Great Awakening of American religious sensibility in 1739–40. In this milieu of religious sentiment, Byington felt called to the ministry, and in 1816 he enrolled at Andover Theological Seminary, where he studied Hebrew and theology. He was licensed to preach in September 1819.

Andover was the training ground for clergy of the Congregational Church as well as the site of the founding of the American Board of Commissioners for Foreign Missions in 1810. The Presbyterian Church joined the Congregational Church to expand the board in 1812, and Byington decided to train as a missionary. He originally hoped to be assigned to the Armenians in Turkey when he graduated, but there were no openings, and he spent time preaching in various churches in Massachusetts.

Byington's place in history came with his assignment to the Choctaw Mission in Mississippi. In 1819 the US government had embarked on its formal policy of "civilizing" Indians, supporting the activities of "benevolent societies" to teach them to read, write, and live like their white neighbors. The American Board established its first mission to the Choctaw in 1818 and drew on funding from the federal "Civilization Act" for support. Byington joined the Choctaw mission in Mississippi on 1 May 1821 at Eliot, the first station, established in 1818. He assumed leadership of the station when Cyrus Kingsbury, the founder of the Choctaw Mission, went on to establish a new station at Mayhew.

The missionaries found themselves in a cultural setting totally foreign to their New England cultural and religious milieu. The most obvious obstacle to their efforts at conversion was language. If they were to preach the Word of God, how could they communicate to their incipient parishioners? The Board of Commissioners had originally adopted a policy of translating the Bible into the languages of its potential converts but soon abandoned it in the face of the difficulty of learning those languages. Nevertheless, Byington and fellow missionaries Alfred Wright and Loring S. Williams attempted to learn Choctaw with the assistance of David Folsom, son of a white father and a Choctaw mother who was fluent in Choctaw and English. Byington's earlier studies of Hebrew and Greek prepared him for the task, although the structure of the Choctaw language differs substantially from the languages that he had studied.

In 1823 Byington moved from Eliot to a mission school, Ai-ik-hun-nah, located near Folsom's home, to concentrate on studying Choctaw. By the spring of 1824 he was confident enough to preach his first sermon in the language and within six months was able to write his own sermons in it. By the fall of 1825 he and Wright had compiled a Choctaw spelling book, which became the first book published in the Choctaw language (1825). By 1827 Byington and Wright, with the assistance of Folsom's son, Israel, had translated portions of the New Testament into Choctaw, and a second edition of the spelling book and a Choctaw reader were also ready for publication.

Byington's work focused on a crucial issue for the missionaries. Should they teach boarding school students to speak English to instruct them in Christian principles, or should they translate the Bible into Choctaw and speak to potential converts in their own language? Byington's preaching and his translation and publication of texts in Choctaw for use in mission schools put him firmly on the translation side.

The work of the Choctaw mission was threatened in the 1820s by the federal government's policy of removing Indians to the West. The change from a policy of civilizing Indians to removing them from contact with white civilization meant that to continue the work of conversion, the missionaries needed to move west. Byington joined with other missionaries of the American Board in denouncing the injustice of the Indian Removal policy, but in 1830 Pres. Andrew Jackson pushed the Indian Removal Act through Congress. Choctaw leaders signed the Treaty of Dancing Rabbit Creek in September 1830, and large contingents of the tribe, including many of the American Board's converts, moved to Indian Territory during the fall and winter of 1831–32.

Byington remained behind in Mississippi to close out the affairs of his mission station, Yok-Nok-Chaya. In 1834 he sent his family to Ohio while he undertook a rigorous journey to locate a site for a new mission in the Indian Territory. He found a site near the Red River in what is now Oklahoma, where he established a new station named Stockbridge. He and his wife established a school and a church, and he continued his work translating biblical texts into Choctaw.

The national crisis over slavery beginning in the 1840s confronted the missionaries of the American Board with another painful decision. Should they follow the American Board's hard-line position against slavery? Many of the Choctaw that they served were slave owners, and Byington and his fellow missionaries finally broke with the board in 1859 to continue their mission.

Byington remained in the Choctaw Nation during the Civil War, but his declining health led him to give up his post and move to his daughter's home in Belpre, Ohio, in 1866. He continued work on his translations and oversaw their publication. He died on 31 December 1868. His grammar of the Choctaw language was published in 1870, and his dictionary of the language was finally published by the Smithsonian Institution in 1915.

Clara Sue Kidwell
University of North Carolina
at Chapel Hill

Louis Coleman, *Cyrus Byington: Missionary and Choctaw Linguist* (1996); Arminta Spalding, "Cyrus Byington, Missionary to the Choctaws" (PhD dissertation, University of Oklahoma, 1976).

Byrnes, Roane Fleming
(1890–1970) Preservation Leader

Roane Fleming Byrnes was instrumental in the creation and development of the Natchez Trace Parkway. Born in Natchez on 11 August 1890 to James Stockman Fleming and Anna Metcalfe Fleming, Roane Fleming had all the family lines to classify her as a member of southern aristocracy and to qualify her for admission to the Colonial Dames of America, Daughters of the American Revolution, Order of the First Families of Mississippi, and the United Daughters of the Confederacy. In 1917 she married Charles Ferriday Byrnes, a Natchez lawyer.

For almost twenty years Roane Byrnes pursued the goal of becoming a writer but published only two children's stories. However, her carefully honed writing skills served her well in her other pursuits. A charter member of the Natchez Garden Club, organized in 1929, Byrnes led efforts to restore the historic Connelly's Tavern on Ellicott's Hill and played a significant role in establishing the Natchez Pilgrimage. In 1935 she was elected president of the Natchez Trace Association and immediately threw herself into efforts to establish the Natchez Trace Parkway, the project that became a major focus for the rest of her life.

Byrnes worked with the members of Mississippi's congressional delegation to attract support in Washington, D.C., for parkway appropriations and with the Mississippi legislature to get rights-of-way funds. When Pres. Franklin D. Roosevelt signed the 1938 bill making the Natchez Trace Parkway a permanent part of the National Park Service, Byrnes received the pen he used.

But Byrnes's work had only barely begun. She spent the remainder of her life writing hundreds of letters and dozens of articles emphasizing the parkway's importance, lobbied state and national legislators for appropriations, and led members of the Natchez Trace Association in their efforts to keep the public informed and the project on track. On 9 November 1951 the first segment of the Natchez Trace Parkway opened—a sixty-four-mile section extending from Jackson to Kosciusko. The parkway continued to face major obstacles, including lack of adequate funding at both federal and state levels and difficulty obtaining rights-of-way. Each time a problem arose, Byrnes provided leadership that helped to ensure the project's continuation.

In 1968 Byrnes traveled over approximately three hundred miles of completed parkway, and a *National Geographic* article brought national attention to the Natchez Trace Parkway and emphasized Byrnes's role in its development. Natchez mayor John Nosser acknowledged her contributions by naming her Mother of the Natchez Trace, while the Mississippi legislature proclaimed her Queen of the Natchez

Trace and parkway officials designated her the first Honorary Post Rider.

In her later years, Byrnes often proclaimed, "I want to ride on the Natchez Trace all the way before I have to ride on the golden streets." Although she never realized that dream, by the time of her death on 3 October 1970, the Natchez Trace Parkway had become a major US park system, with more than ten million visitors every year.

Verbie Lovorn Prevost
University of Tennessee
at Chattanooga

Roane Fleming Byrnes Collection, Department of Archives and Special Collections, J. D. Williams Library, University of Mississippi; Natchez Trace Association Papers, Natchez Trace Parkway Headquarters, Tupelo; Verbie Lovorn Prevost, "Roane Fleming Byrnes: A Critical Biography" (PhD dissertation, University of Mississippi, 1974).

B

C

Cain, Mary Dawson
(1904–1984) Journalist

Mary Dawson Cain was born near Burke, Louisiana, and spent most of her life in Pike County, Mississippi. From 1936 to 1984, she served as owner and editor of the *Summit Sun*, the weekly newspaper of the small Southwest Mississippi community. Cain distinguished herself as a foe of big government and an advocate of states' rights, battles she fought in her newspaper, in the courts, on the campaign trail, and as a leader in various conservative organizations. Cain used her newspaper as a mouthpiece to critique the federal government. She was a vocal opponent of Prohibition, the New Deal, civil rights, and other programs that expanded federal government powers over the states. She was active in organizations and movements that supported her worldview, including the Women's Organization for National Prohibition Reform and the Dixiecrat splinter party. In addition, in the wake of the integration of the University of Mississippi Cain became a founding member of Women for Constitutional Government and served as the group's state and national president.

Cain made history as the first woman to run for governor of Mississippi, though both her 1951 and 1955 bids failed. Her platform called for reduced federal influence in the state. Her prominence as a public figure led to her appointment to the speakers' bureaus of the Citizens' Council and the Mississippi State Sovereignty Commission, and on several occasions, she lectured around the country on the topic of states' rights. During the turbulent decades of the civil rights movement, Cain argued against integration. She nevertheless believed herself to be a friend of the African American community. Her newspaper regularly featured a column devoted to news of Summit's African American community and incorporated photographs and courtesy titles (e.g., Mr., Mrs.), an unusual practice for a white-owned southern newspaper in this period.

She is perhaps best known nationally for her refusal to pay self-employment taxes in 1951, the first year that the Social Security Administration implemented the tax. An ardent opponent of personal income taxes, Cain argued that the self-employment tax was unconstitutional. The Internal Revenue Department (IRD) then seized and padlocked her newspaper office, but she took a hacksaw to the padlock and mailed it back to the IRD with a defiant note inviting legal action. This episode earned her national press attention and the nickname Hacksaw Mary. The IRD responded with a civil suit. The case eventually made its way to the 5th Circuit Court of Appeals and the US Supreme Court, which refused to hear it. In an effort to avoid paying future self-employment taxes, she sold her newspaper for one dollar to a relative. Cain reportedly never paid the back taxes owed to the IRD.

Lisa K. Speer
Arkansas History Commission

Lisa K. Speer, "'Contrary Mary': The Life of Mary Dawson Cain" (PhD dissertation, University of Mississippi, 1998).

Caldwell, Charles
(?–1875) Politician

A former slave who rose to become the leading Republican in Hinds County and one of the county's state senators during Reconstruction, Charles Caldwell embodied the radical changes that swept through Mississippi in the aftermath of the Civil War. His assassination in the wake of the 1875 Redemption campaign exemplified the closing of many of Reconstruction's opportunities.

Caldwell was born in Hinds County of a slave mother and a white father. By the time of the Civil War, Caldwell had become a blacksmith, a relatively privileged position that afforded him more flexibility than most slaves had and left him well positioned to take full advantage of emancipation.

In the immediate postwar period, Caldwell assumed a leadership position among African Americans in the area of Clinton, twelve miles west of Jackson. Rewarded for his talents and persuasiveness, he was elected as one of sixteen African American members of the 1868 constitutional convention, which set out to dismantle the antebellum social and political order. Caldwell took an active if largely silent role in the convention, generally voting with the Radical majority. Shortly after the convention's adjournment, an event involving Caldwell signaled the coming of a new order. Fired on by the possibly deranged son of a highly respected white judge, Caldwell returned fire, killing the young man. He was tried for murder and acquitted, underscoring the legal rights that Reconstruction granted to freedpeople.

With the inauguration of Republican power in the state, Caldwell became a member of Hinds County's board of supervisors, a powerful position with tax and allocation powers. He forfeited this seat in 1871 to become a state senator, an office he held until his death. Like most African American politicians, Caldwell aligned himself with the Radical faction of the Republican Party, but he does not appear to have been dogmatic. Still, he remained a Republican stalwart, frequently offering advice and strategy on how best to preserve his party's dominant position.

Caldwell played a crucial role in the climactic 1875 campaign that effectively ended Reconstruction in Mississippi. When the violent tenor of the Democrats' efforts became clear, Radical governor Adelbert Ames called up the state militia, placing Caldwell in charge of the two companies based in Jackson. Caldwell marched his men from Jackson to Edwards Depot and delivered arms to another company there. The incident provoked fears of a race war among the state's white population, and Ames was forced to broker an agreement that disbanded the militia in exchange for Democratic pledges to campaign peacefully. In a letter to Ames, Caldwell and another leading Hinds County Republican sharply questioned Democrats' willingness to adhere to the agreement: "So far as the democracy in a large portion of this county are concerned, the peace agreement is held in utter contempt, and only serves as a cover for the very wrongs upon the freedom of the elective franchise which it was intended to prevent." Ames either ignored such reports or felt he could do no more to help the Republican cause.

Deprived of any military support, Caldwell still managed to provide a forceful example for other Republicans in Clinton. On Election Day, when some of his Republican colleagues expressed a desire to heed the Democrats' warnings not to vote, Caldwell insisted that surrender was not an option. "No; we are going to stay right here," one ally quoted him. "You must just come right along, and keep your mouth shut. I don't care what they say to you, don't you say a word." Although Caldwell lost his Senate seat that day, he proved that no amount of Democratic intimidation would shake him from his political resolve.

Caldwell's powerful resistance to the Democrats helps explain his assassination a month and a half after the election. Invited to have a drink with a friend in the basement of a Clinton grocery store, Caldwell was ambushed and shot several times. He died after his last request was granted: he was carried out into the street so that all could see that he remained defiant.

Caldwell and other local leaders represented perhaps better than anyone else the opportunities that existed under Reconstruction for freedpeople to develop a potent and responsible class of leaders. That so many influential blacks met the same end as Caldwell illuminates the violence on which Democratic power ultimately rested.

William Bland Whitley
Thomas Jefferson Papers,
Princeton, New Jersey

Herbert Aptheker, *To Be Free: Studies in American Negro History* (1969); Charles Hillman Brough, in *Publications of the Mississippi Historical Society*, vol. 6, ed. Franklin L. Riley (1901); William C. Harris, *The Day of the Carpetbagger: Republican Reconstruction in Mississippi* (1979); *Mississippi in 1875: Report of the Select Committee to Inquire into the Mississippi Election of 1875, with the Testimony and Documentary Evidence* (1876).

Calhoun County

Located in north-central Mississippi on land historically populated by Choctaw and Chickasaw peoples, Calhoun County was founded in 1852 and named for South Carolina political leader John C. Calhoun. Notable geographic features in Calhoun County include the Skuna and Yalobusha Rivers. Calhoun is also home to a ceremonial site from the late Woodland period. The county seat is Pittsboro. Other towns in Calhoun County include Bruce, Calhoun City, Derma, and Vardaman.

In its first census in 1860, Calhoun was home to more than nine thousand people. Slaves made up 19 percent of the population—the second-lowest percentage in Mississippi. As in many counties with more free people than slaves, corn was a more important commodity than cotton and other cash crops. Sixty-five men worked in industry—mostly in the lumber industry and small blacksmith shops. Calhoun County had thirty-six churches, sixteen of them Baptist, fourteen Methodist, and six Presbyterian.

By 1880 the population of Calhoun County had grown to 13,492, with African Americans accounting for one quarter of the residents. Calhoun had only thirty-eight industrial workers, and more than 75 percent of the county's farmers owned their own land. By 1900 the population increased by more than two thousand, yet landownership had declined dramatically: 57 percent of the county's white famers owned their land, as did just 24 percent of African American farmers.

The 1916 religious census found that members of the Southern Baptist Convention made up more than half of Calhoun's churchgoers, with the Methodist Episcopal Church, South; Colored Methodist Episcopal Church; and the National Baptist Convention as the next-largest groups. Calhoun County hosted the state's first Sacred Harp singing convention in 1878. Born in Calhoun County in 1898, Zelma Wells Price became a state legislator from Washington County with a particular interest in opposing the sale of alcohol.

Calhoun County's overall population changed very little between 1900 and 1930, though African Americans dropped to one-fifth of all residents. By 1930 Calhoun had seventy-one manufacturing establishments, and they employed 528 people. Agriculture remained the primary employer, and corn was the most important crop.

By 1960 Calhoun had a population of almost sixteen thousand people, 73 percent of them white. Calhoun's farmers grew the second-highest amount of corn in the state and had the seventh-highest number of hogs. The county's production of other agricultural crops and timber was about average for the state. Along with its timber industry, Calhoun had a growing furniture industry that employed 763 people.

Vardaman has become a central place for the growing and marketing of sweet potatoes. Now called the Sweet Potato Capital of the World, the town hosts the annual Sweet Potato Festival.

Calhoun County was the home of the forty-second and forty-seventh governor of Mississippi, Dennis Murphree. Maj. Gen. Fox Conner, chief of operations for the American Expeditionary Force during World War I and a mentor to George C. Marshall and Dwight D. Eisenhower, was also born in Calhoun County. Ann Downing, an important southern gospel musician, was born in Pittsboro in 1945 and learned to sing in area churches and singing schools. Laurie Parker, author of *Everywhere in Mississippi* and other works about the state, was born in Bruce in 1963.

Other notable people from Calhoun County include National Football League players Frederick L. Thomas, Armegis Spearman, Cornelius Wortham, and M. D. Jennings as well as Major League Baseball player Dave Parker, who was the National League's Most Valuable Player in 1978. Saxophone player and Mississippi Musicians' Hall of Fame member John "Ace" Cannon also resided in Calhoun County.

The county's population fluctuated slightly but remained relatively stable between 1960 (15,941) and 2010 (14,962). In 2010, 67 percent of Calhoun's residents were white, 28 percent were black, and 5.4 percent were Latino/Hispanic.

Mississippi Encyclopedia Staff
University of Mississippi

Mississippi State Planning Commission, *Progress Report on State Planning in Mississippi* (1938); *Mississippi Statistical Abstract*, Mississippi State University (1952–2010); Charles Sydnor and Claude Bennett, *Mississippi History* (1939); University of Virginia Library, Historical Census Browser website, http://mapserver.lib.virginia.edu; E. Nolan Waller and Dani A. Smith, *Growth Profiles of Mississippi's Counties, 1960–1980* (1985).

Cameron, Ben
(1890–1964) Judge

Benjamin Franklin Cameron Jr. sat for nine historic years on the federal appeals court that decided most of the momentous civil rights cases of the twentieth century. Born in Meridian in 1890 to Benjamin Franklin Cameron and Elizabeth Garner Cameron, Ben Cameron Jr. attended Meridian High School, the University of the South, and Cumberland University, where he received his law degree in 1914.

Cameron first considered a career as a minister, became a Latin and German professor at Virginia's Norfolk Academy, and then served as director of athletics at Cumberland University. In 1914 he returned to Meridian to practice law. For five years he served as the unpaid coach of Meridian High School's first football teams. In 1948 more than one hundred former players established the Ben Cameron Wildcat Scholarship in his honor.

Cameron enjoyed a distinguished career at the bar in Meridian. A man of religious convictions and an absolute teetotaler, Cameron was offended by Democrat Al Smith's 1928 anti-Prohibition platform and promptly realigned his politics with the Republican Party. Herbert Hoover's presidential election led to Cameron's 1929 appointment as US attorney for the Southern District of Mississippi, a position he held for four years.

Democrats disdained Cameron as a turncoat "Hoovercrat" or he might have risen to the federal bench as early as 1930. US district judge Edwin Holmes seemingly was slated for appointment to the US Court of Appeals for the Fifth Circuit, and many observers thought that Cameron would get Hoover's nod for the district court slot. But political turmoil meant that Holmes was not elevated to the Fifth Circuit until 1936, and Cameron remained in private practice.

When the GOP regained national power in 1953 after a two-decade hiatus, the Eisenhower administration keenly sought Republicans to fill judicial vacancies. An opening occurred at the Fifth Circuit in 1954 when Judge Holmes retired. Cameron, who had been US attorney in the previous GOP administration, was an obvious candidate to succeed the man he had nearly followed to the federal bench a quarter century earlier. Eisenhower supporters in Mississippi backed Cameron, and Democratic Senators James O. Eastland and John C. Stennis eventually backed him as well. President Eisenhower appointed Cameron on 18 February 1955 with the endorsement of both the American Bar Association and the National Association for the Advancement of Colored People. He took his seat on 23 March.

Judge Cameron's controversial and acrimonious tenure on the Fifth Circuit was marked by his adherence to his states' rights perspective on constitutional issues and his determined rejection of federal desegregation policy. An unabashed defender of Old South ways, Cameron was pitted against the court's progressive pro–civil rights majority, whom he dubbed the Four: Judges John Minor Wisdom, Elbert Tuttle, John Brown, and Richard Rives. Cameron famously complained that the court "rigged" outcomes by refusing to assign him to hear civil rights cases from Mississippi. On three occasions Cameron entered orders preventing James Meredith's historic enrollment at the University of Mississippi, only to be overruled each time.

Greg Snowden
Meridian, Mississippi

Jack Bass, *Unlikely Heroes* (1981); Sheldon Goldman, *Picking Federal Judges: Lower Court Selection from Roosevelt through Reagan* (1997); *Jackson Daily News* (1954–55); *Memphis Commercial Appeal* (1964); *Meridian Star* (1954–55); Frank T. Read and Lucy S. McGough, *Let Them Be Judged* (1978); R. E. Wilbourn, Speech to the Life and Career of Honorable Ben F. Cameron, Special Memorial Proceedings and Presentation of Portraits, US District Court Room, Jackson, Mississippi (24 April 1970).

Cameron, Jennie Mae Quinn

(1880–1976) Nursing Leader

Jennie Mae Quinn, a leader in the professional development of nursing in Mississippi, was born in Milford, Pennsylvania, a rural community near the Poconos. She attended Milford's public schools before graduating from the Lackawanna County Hospital Training School for Nurses in Scranton, Pennsylvania, in 1899. She recalled that her student life was characterized by twelve-hour days of practice and classes, with many hours of overtime following mine disasters in the coalfields near Scranton. For the first ten years after graduation she practiced with two intervals of hospital duty. She enrolled in the New York Registry of Nurses and began to accept calls away from home. She went to western Pennsylvania, Georgia, and Upstate New York to serve during epidemics.

In the fall of 1910 she was called to Hattiesburg to assume the responsibilities of superintendent of nurses. She arrived in Hattiesburg on 5 October 1910 at 4:58 and immediately assumed her duties. After discovering that nine students were enrolled at the hospital for nursing, she also became the director of the nursing school.

Quinn noticed immediately that nurses in Mississippi did not enjoy the collegiality and advantages that came from alumnae associations or other nursing organizations and that Mississippi lacked licensure for trained nurses, practices that had already been established in the North. She consequently began work on the Hattiesburg Association of Graduate Nurses, which organized in 1911 with her as president. Within a month she traveled to Natchez to work with a colleague from the Natchez Hospital to draft the constitution and bylaws for a state association. On 7 June 1911 a group of ten nurses met at the Natchez Hospital and approved the constitution, bylaws, and code of ethics for the Mississippi State Association of Graduate Nurses (later the Mississippi Nurses' Association), with the goal of advancing nursing standards and education. Although she was the only out-of-town participant, Quinn was elected the group's president.

Quinn led a committee of nurses and worked with state political leaders for the next three years to persuade the legislature to pass a measure that would license and recognize trained nurses. With the bill's passage, a board of nurse examiners had to be formed, and Quinn was named its president. Under her guidance, the board administered the first licensure exam in July 1916.

On 4 April 1917 Quinn married James A. Cameron, a Hattiesburg businessman. She continued to teach at the school and serve the hospital as an anesthetist and X-ray technician until she left active practice in 1925 to be at home with her family, which included a daughter, Helen. Cameron remained interested in the nursing profession and remained a popular speaker, continuing to serve nurses and nursing until her death on 7 July 1976 in Hattiesburg. The Mississippi Nurses' Association has honored Mississippi's First Lady of Nursing with a portrait that hangs in the state headquarters.

Linda Sabin
University of Louisiana at Monroe

Mississippi Nurses Association Historical Committee, *Passing the Flame: The History of the Mississippi Nurses Association, 1911–1986* (1986); Papers of Jennie Quinn Cameron, Mississippi Department of Archives and History.

Camille, Hurricane

Hurricane Camille demonstrated the US Gulf Coast's vulnerability to hurricanes and their extreme potential for destruction. Nearly five decades after it hit, Camille remains entrenched in modern myth and scientific fact as setting the standard for measuring future hurricanes. Camille was even stronger than the more recent Hurricane Katrina, with record sustained wind speeds of 172 miles per hour and gusts that are believed to have exceeded 200 miles per hour, though the storm destroyed all wind-measuring instruments. When it slammed ashore near Pass Christian on 17 August 1969, Camille brought a deadly barometric pressure of 26.84 inches and a record storm surge of 25 feet. The unofficial death toll stands at 256, 143 on the Gulf Coast and 113 in Virginia floods. Damage was estimated at $1.4 billion (in 1969 dollars).

Camille began on 5 August as a tropical wave about one hundred miles due east of the Cape Verde Islands off the coast of Africa. After taking four days to cross the Atlantic Ocean, it entered the eastern Caribbean Sea as a disorganized but powerful system, bringing rainstorms and gale-force wind gusts to Jamaica. At that point, a cool upper-level air mass descended south into the Gulf of Mexico, and on 14 August the system featured sustained winds of 65 miles per hour and became Tropical Storm Camille. As forecasters monitored the effects of the cold air mass to the north, Camille's barometric pressure continued to drop. It became a hurricane on 15 August and began to curve north-northwest toward the Florida Panhandle. The cold air mass began to disintegrate, strengthening Camille by creating a low-pressure zone that the hurricane filled. Wind gusts reached 130 miles per hour. Forecasters extended a hurricane warning to the Alabama and Mississippi coasts on 16 August as Camille turned to the northwest and entered the area of low pressure. On 17 August, the barometric pressure fell to 26.61 inches, and winds near the storm's center topped 200 miles per hour. Camille was sixty miles south of Gulfport by seven o'clock that evening and made landfall shortly before midnight near Bay St. Louis.

The immediate effects were catastrophic. Camille destroyed Pass Christian. The storm surge killed eleven parishioners gathered in a church that shattered when the hurricane hit. About two dozen people attempted to ride out the storm in the Richelieu Apartments in Pass Christian, but the structure crumbled under the power of the storm surge, and most of the people there drowned. The storm surge also lifted three massive freighters and deposited their battered hulks on the beach in Gulfport. Camille left 114 people dead and 45,000 families homeless in Harrison County alone. The storm then continued north into Tennessee and Kentucky as a tropical depression before turning east, gaining strength, and bringing record rainfall to Virginia. Pres. Richard Nixon declared Mississippi a federal disaster area and allocated $1 million in immediate aid. In December 1969 Congress designated another $180 million in aid for Camille's victims.

Camille provided valuable lessons in hurricane forecasting. It was the first major hurricane monitored with satellite imagery, and meteorologists made significant technical advancements in the storm's wake. The Saffir-Simpson scale for measuring hurricane strength was created two years later: experts declared that Camille had met the criteria for the highest rating, a Category 5.

Serious mistakes were made in the aftermath of Camille. Historian Ted Steinberg argues that the federal response to Camille was a disaster. The Department of Housing and Urban Development offered trailers to the homeless but required recipients to provide land lots, meaning that the policy excluded most poor families. The homeless received rent-free living for only ninety days. Private loan companies charged as much as 40 percent interest.

Steinberg also claims that a twenty-year lull in severe hurricanes after Camille allowed an expansion in coastal development with few restrictions from insurance companies, which vastly underestimated a severe hurricane's financial impact, but Ernest Zebrowski and Judith Howard argue that development on the Mississippi Coast stagnated because most residents could not afford to meet the improved building standards. The completion of Interstate 10 contributed to the economic decline by rerouting traffic away from the coast. Beginning in 1990, Mississippi's coastal economy benefited from the advent of legalized gambling, but the casinos had to be built over the water. The Gulf Coast became a continuous sprawl awaiting the next disaster. It arrived on 29 August 2005 in the form of Hurricane Katrina.

Karl Rohr
South Carolina Governor's School
for Science and Mathematics

Phillip D. Hearn, *Hurricane Camille: Monster Storm of the Gulf Coast* (2004); David Longshore, *Encyclopedia of Hurricanes, Typhoons, and Cyclones* (1998); *National Geographic* website, www.nationalgeographic.com; Mark Smith, *Camille, 1969: Histories of a Hurricane* (2011); Ted Steinberg, *Acts of God: The Unnatural History of Natural Disaster in America* (2000); US Army Corps of Engineers, Mobile District, *Report on Hurricane Camille 14–22 August 1969* (1970); Ernest Zebrowski and Judith A. Howard, *Category 5: The Story of Camille* (2005).

Camp Van Dorn

Camp Van Dorn was a 41,844-acre US military camp located in Amite and Wilkinson Counties, just south of Centreville in southern Mississippi. Named for Confederate general Earl Van Dorn of Mississippi, this US Army post served as a training camp for ground force division soldiers destined for the European Theater from 1942 to 1945. The camp played a critical role in preparing American troops for combat in World War II.

With war looming in the fall of 1940, officials began discussing the possibility of locating an emergency training camp in isolated Southwest Mississippi. In February 1941 Centreville mayor Lee Robinson and other local leaders appeared before a board of army officers at Camp Shelby, near Hattiesburg, stressing the advantages of the Centreville area for such a camp. The War Department expressed serious interest in the proposal, and after the attack on Pearl Harbor it bought the land and began designing the camp. By February 1942 construction had started. The Centreville area boomed economically with the influx of thousands of workers to construct the buildings, roads, and railroad spurs as well as install the telephones, electricity, and water and sewage systems. The camp was officially activated on 20 September 1942, and the first recruits arrived in November.

Camp Van Dorn operated as a small city. It could accommodate 39,114 enlisted men and 2,173 officers plus 750 personnel at the station hospital. A small detachment of German prisoners of war was also located at the camp. The cantonment area covered the western side of the base and was located in the Wilkinson County section. This area featured barracks, warehouses, a bakery, a laundry, latrines, gatehouses, guardhouses, sentry boxes, a hospital, medical and dental clinics, a bank, a bus station, a theater, a fire station, mess halls, gas chambers, grenade courts, and at least ten chapels, where many soldiers married before leaving the camp. The rest of the camp was to the east in Amite County and included various ranges and areas for training with weapons ranging from small arms to 155mm artillery. Maj. Gen. Walter Lauer remembered, "Camp Van Dorn, hastily built as the army mushroomed in every direction, was a tar paper shanty town sprawled across the red mud of Southern Mississippi."

Two major US Army infantry divisions trained at the camp. The soldiers of the 99th Infantry Division, known as the Checkerboard Division, began arriving in December 1942 and finished their advanced training by September 1943. Arriving in Belgium for combat in November 1944, the division participated in the Battle of the Bulge and other fighting in the Rhineland, Ardennes-Alsace, and Central Europe, eventually crossing the Danube. The 63rd Infantry, known as the Blood and Fire Division, arrived at the camp soon after the 99th departed. Its soldiers trained at the camp until November 1944 and then were sent to France for combat in the Rhineland, the Ardennes, and Central Europe. The first detachments went into battle toward the end of December 1944. The division played a significant role on the European front, participating in the capture of Landsberg on 30 April 1945, just over a week before Germany's final surrender.

In addition to these large infantry divisions, many nondivisional units, regiments, and battalions trained at Camp Van Dorn. Among these units was the 364th Infantry Regiment, an African American unit that reported to the camp in May 1943 for retraining after having been involved in violent incidents at its previous station in Arizona. Sixteen members of the regiment had been court-martialed, with several receiving fifty-year jail sentences. Many soldiers arrived resentful of the transfer and of the racial segregation in place at the camp and in nearby Centreville. On 30 May 1943 Private William Walker of the 364th was shot to death in Centreville by the Wilkinson County sheriff. In response one of the regiment's companies stormed a supply room to obtain guns, and the military police fired into the crowd during the disturbance. Centreville's mayor subsequently requested that the army remove the 364th from camp, but another near riot by the unit erupted at a service club dance in July. By year's end the 364th was shipped out to Alaska, where it defended key installations in the Aleutian Islands for the rest of the war. Approximately eight thousand African American troops were stationed at the camp during this period, serving in various detachments and regiments. The units were segregated from white troops, in keeping with the official army protocol of the period.

The camp was declared surplus on 1 October 1945 and officially deactivated on 31 December. By June 1947 former owners were given the opportunity to repurchase their lands from the government, which removed most of the buildings from the site. The Department of Defense lists the site as contaminated by bombs, unexploded shells, and other hazardous materials. Early in 2015 the army announced plans to clean up the site, with fieldwork expected to be completed in 2016.

During the war rumors circulated that a mass killing of more than one thousand members of the 364th had occurred at Camp Van Dorn. Pike County writer and artist Carroll Case spent more than thirteen years researching the claims, and in August 1998 he published *The Slaughter: An American Atrocity*, which alleged that a massacre had indeed taken place. The book garnered national attention and precipitated a swirl of activity and research. Congressman Bennie Thompson of Mississippi and the National Association for the Advancement of Colored People asked the Department of the Defense and the Department of the Army to determine the veracity of Case's allegations. The US Army Center of Military History undertook an investigation and released a 1999 report that concluded that there was "no documentary evidence whatsoever that any unusual or inexplicable loss of personnel occurred."

At the turn of the twenty-first century Centreville resident Mildred Field and other local historians realized the camp's significance and began an effort to establish the Camp Van Dorn World War II Museum in Centreville, which was officially dedicated on 19 March 2005. Honoring the men and women who trained at the camp, the museum displays historical artifacts and photographs that document the camp's contribution to the war effort.

Lucius M. Lampton
Magnolia, Mississippi

Glen Francis Brown and William Franklin Guyton, *Geology and Ground-Water Supply at Camp Van Dorn* (1943); Carroll Case, *The Slaughter: An American Atrocity* (1998); Greg DeHart, *Mystery of the 364th* (video, 2001); *Magnolia Gazette* (25 March, 30 December 1999); US Army, *Historical and Pictorial Review of Camp Van Dorn, Mississippi* (1944) ; US Department of the Army, *A Historical Analysis of the 364th Infantry in World War II* (1999); Debra Valine, "Meeting Informs Public of Actions to Clean Up Formerly Used Defense Site" (10 February 2015), http://www.army.mil, *The Official Homepage of the United States Army*.

Campbell, A. Boyd

(1889–1963) Business Leader

Alexander Boyd Campbell was born in Winona, Mississippi, on 10 September 1889 to William Alexander Campbell and Carrie Boyd Campbell. The Campbell family moved to a small farm in Hesterville, in Attala County, while Boyd was still a boy. There, the man who made his career and fortune catering to the needs of Mississippi's schoolchildren was educated in a one-room, one-teacher, cypress-log schoolhouse and began attending Bethel Methodist Church, another institution that remained dear to him throughout his adult life.

After graduating from high school in Kosciusko, Campbell attended Millsaps College, a Methodist school in Jackson, where he joined Kappa Alpha fraternity, helped found the student newspaper, and earned a bachelor's degree in 1910. For most of his adult life, Campbell served as treasurer for the Millsaps board of trustees, the highest position laymen could attain. In 1963 the board of trustees renamed the student union the A. Boyd Campbell Student Center in his honor.

Campbell's position as treasurer of the Millsaps board gave him the idea that would make him a very successful businessman. After noting that Mississippi's public schools had no provider of school supplies, Campbell and his neighbor, Carl White, a school supply representative, started the Mississippi School Supply Company. According to Boyd Campbell's nephew, James Campbell, "Boyd Campbell had only one son—the Mississippi School Supply Company, and that is the way it should have been. He sired it. He nurtured it in its infancy. He brought it to maturity and to greatness as a business institution." The company opened as a one-room shop on East Capitol Street in Jackson in 1919.

Campbell's business acumen earned him numerous appointments in civic organizations. In addition to helping found the Mississippi Symphony Orchestra, he served as president of the Jackson Rotary Club, the Official Board of the Galloway Memorial Church, the Andrew Jackson Council of the Boy Scouts of America, the National School Service Institute, and the Jackson Chamber of Commerce. He was a director of the First National Bank, the Mississippi Power and Light Company, and the Gulf, Mobile, and Ohio Railroad. He was a trustee of Emory University, a member of the Commission on Goals for Higher Education in the South, and a perennial chair of the US Chamber of Commerce's Committee on Education. The pinnacle of his civic achievements came in 1955, when he was elected to the first of his two consecutive terms as president of the US Chamber of Commerce. He was the first Mississippian elected to the Chamber's board of directors or to preside over it.

Campbell's personal motto was "Free enterprise is a stewardship," by which he meant "stewardship of business, the handling of individual and organized business affairs as private service for the public good." For a man making his livelihood in educational supplies during the 1950s in Jim Crow Mississippi, stewardship was a complicated matter. Whatever his personal racial views, Campbell believed that segregation was bad for business and thus bad for Mississippians. In 1956 education scholar Preston Valien noted, "A. Boyd Campbell of Mississippi, president of the U.S. Chamber of Commerce, has also expressed the belief that racial tension could result in a slow-down in the industrial development of the South." Campbell died in 1963.

Ben Gilstrap
University of Mississippi

James Boyd Campbell, *For the Public Good: The Story of Boyd Campbell and the Mississippi School Supply Company* (1963); Preston Valien, *Journal of Negro Education* (Summer 1956).

Campbell, Clarice T.

(1907–2000) Activist and Educator

Clarice T. Campbell, a self-described "outside agitator" from California, promoted civil rights while teaching at black colleges in Mississippi and South Carolina. Born in 1907 in Los Angeles, Campbell attended the University of Southern California in 1925–26 before interrupting her college education to become a wife and mother. She spent her early adulthood raising four children and working as a bookkeeper. Returning to college, she earned her undergraduate degree at the age of forty-five. She spent ten years as a schoolteacher in Pasadena, where she initiated efforts to end the busing of white students to predominantly white schools. She came to the South to take summer courses at the University of Mississippi in 1956 and the University of Alabama in 1957.

When her husband, Harold, died in 1959, Campbell took a leave of absence from the Pasadena City Schools and volunteered to teach in exchange for room and board at Rust College, a historically black Methodist-affiliated school in Holly Springs, Mississippi. Campbell, a devout Methodist, remained at Rust throughout the 1960–61 school year. She found life as the only white person on the campus of the badly underfunded school to be a challenge. Administrators resisted even such minor improvements as a ping-pong table that Campbell purchased for student recreation. The students, products of a Jim Crow educational system, were underprepared for the academic rigors of higher education. In addition, the local white community resisted her outspoken opposition to segregated restrooms, restaurants, churches, and drinking fountains. During the 1961–62 school year, Campbell taught at Claflin College in South Carolina and joined the board of directors of the Southern Conference Educational Fund, an organization that promoted school integration.

At the end of the 1963 school year, Campbell planned to join the Peace Corps to work overseas, but the murder of National Association for the Advancement of Colored People field secretary Medgar Evers in Jackson prompted her to change her mind. Instead, she moved to Mississippi to teach at historically black Tougaloo College, where she remained until 1965. During this time, Campbell worked to desegregate motels, restaurants, and churches, including her own Galloway Methodist Church. She attempted, without success, to pressure national organizations such as churches and oil companies to force their local branches to integrate. Campbell described teaching at Tougaloo as working just behind the front lines since students frequently missed classes to testify in court or serve time in jail. Passage of the Civil Rights Act of 1964 brought substantial improvements, but Campbell ended her lifelong affiliation with the Republican Party in 1968 over its civil rights stance.

Campbell believed her integrationist activities demonstrated that nothing terrible happened to anyone who stepped over the color line. Her frequently humorous letters to family and friends about life in the South during the early 1960s appeared in *Civil Rights Chronicle: Letters from the South*.

Mississippi captured Campbell's heart for reasons that she found herself unable to explain. In 1965 she began work on a doctorate in history at the University of Mississippi, earning the degree five years later with a dissertation on the history of Tougaloo. She then returned to Rust to teach and serve as the chair of the history department. After retiring in 1978, she taught part time at Mississippi Industrial College, a private liberal arts school across the street from Rust. Campbell died in 2000.

Caryn E. Neumann
Miami University at Middletown

Clarice T. Campbell, *Civil Rights Chronicle: Letters from the South* (1997); Clarice T. Campbell Papers, Tougaloo Civil Rights Archive, Brown University; Clarice T. Campbell and Oscar Allen Rogers Jr., *Mississippi: The View from Tougaloo* (1979).

Campbell, J. A. P.
(1830–1917) Judge

Josiah Abigail Patterson Campbell, a Mississippi Supreme Court justice from 1876 to 1894, was born in Lancaster District, South Carolina, on 2 March 1830. The Campbell family traces its roots to Scotland, where his ancient forbears established the House of Argyle and were numbered among the Scottish chiefs.

J. A. P. Campbell's parents were well educated. His father, Robert Bond Campbell, was a Presbyterian minister, a graduate of the Princeton Theological Seminary. His mother, Mary Adams Patterson Campbell, was the daughter of a wealthy planter, Josiah Patterson, from the Abbeville District, South Carolina. She taught all of her six children reading, writing, arithmetic, geography, and English grammar before they entered formal education. J. A. P. Campbell learned to read by the time he was four. Not content with his intellectual growth alone, his mother also instilled in him spiritual and philosophical values and a love for literature and law.

Campbell graduated from Davidson College. In 1845, at the age of fifteen, he moved with his parents from South Carolina to Madison County, Mississippi. He received a license to practice law two years later and moved to Kosciusko and established a law practice. In 1850 he married Eugenia Elizabeth Nash, daughter of the Rev. William Whitfield Nash, founder of the First Baptist Church of Kosciusko. J. A. P. and Eugenia Nash Campbell had eight children.

Campbell's law practice in Kosciusko flourished, as did his reputation. In 1851, at age twenty-one, he was elected to the state legislature. Campbell was held in high regard by his fellow legislators, who elected him Speaker of the House in 1860, on the threshold of the Civil War. He was chosen as a delegate from Mississippi to the Confederate Constitutional Convention and was one of the signers of the permanent Confederate Constitution adopted on 11 March 1861. The convention reconstituted itself as the Provisional Congress of the Confederacy, and Campbell represented Mississippi from 1861 to 1863, serving as president pro tempore in 1863. He then enlisted in the Confederate Army and served in Polk's Corps, reaching the rank of colonel.

After the war, the thirty-five-year-old Campbell was elected circuit judge for the 5th Judicial District, serving Attala, Leake, Madison, Yazoo, and Holmes Counties until 1868. In 1876, Gov. John M. Stone appointed Campbell to a seat on the Mississippi Supreme Court. He served for the next eighteen years and held the post of chief justice from 1888 to 1894. In 1878, the legislature invited Judge Campbell to draft a new code for the state, an assignment he readily accepted.

Campbell was living in Jackson when he died on 10 January 1917.

Samuel M. Davis
University of Mississippi

Michael L. Landon, *The University of Mississippi School of Law: A Sesquicentennial History* (2006); Rev. W. W. Nash Family Bible (copy in possession of the author); Dunbar Rowland, *Courts, Judges, and Lawyers of Mississippi, 1798–1935* (1935); David G. Sansing, *The University of Mississippi: A Sesquicentennial History* (1999).

Will D. Campbell (McCain Library and Archives, University of Southern Mississippi)

Campbell, Will D.

(1924–2013) Activist and Author

Will Davis Campbell was born in Amite County, Mississippi, in 1924. After he survived a childhood illness, Campbell's family marked him as a spiritual leader, and the East Fork Baptist Church ordained him as a preacher at the age of seventeen. His humble beginnings in a poor, farming family in South Mississippi, framed by an expectation of future spiritual leadership, shaped the rest of Campbell's life and directed him to challenge much of the dictates of southern culture, from white supremacy to the institutional church.

Campbell spent his early life on his family's farm and was particularly close to his older brother, Joseph, who figured significantly in Campbell's best-known and honored book, *Brother to a Dragonfly*. After a year attending Louisiana College, where he met his wife, Brenda, Campbell served as a US Army medic during World War II. He subsequently graduated from Wake Forest College, did a year of graduate work at Tulane University, and received a bachelor of divinity degree from Yale Divinity School. He then served for two years as pastor of a small Southern Baptist Church in Taylor, Louisiana, but concluded that he was meant to be a "pastor without a steeple."

In 1953 Campbell moved his family to Oxford, to serve as chaplain for the University of Mississippi. He expected to spend the rest of his religious career on the quiet campus, but larger clashes over race shaped his experiences there in ways that diverted his plan. In May 1954 the Supreme Court's *Brown v. Board of Education* decision reverberated across the South, creating hope among black civil rights activists and massive resistance to the Court's decree among most white southern politicians. In this maelstrom, Campbell's efforts to reach across racial lines in the Oxford community drew ire and eventually death threats.

In the most public incident Campbell invited Alvin Kershaw, a white Episcopal priest who had donated some of his recent winnings on a television game show to the National Association for the Advancement of Colored People, to speak during Religious Emphasis Week. University administrators demanded that Campbell withdraw the invitation, but he refused. When campus officials withdrew the invitation, Campbell crafted a silent protest, hosting sessions for the week in a campus chapel with empty chairs on stage and inviting the campus community to join him for reflection.

For his irreverent challenges to white supremacy, officials encouraged Campbell to resign. He moved to Mount Juliet, Tennessee, and became more engaged in the civil rights movement. Hired as a field officer for the National Council of Churches, Campbell traveled the South to movement hot spots, including nearby Nashville, where he befriended and worked with Rev. Kelly Miller Smith and Rev. James Lawson, who were training local students such as Diane Nash and John Lewis in the strategies of nonviolent resistance.

In 1956 Campbell was the only white pastor present when Rev. Martin Luther King Jr. founded the Southern Christian Leadership Conference in Atlanta. In 1957 Campbell helped escort the Little Rock Nine into Central High School in Arkansas. But while he was always a steadfast supporter of the civil rights movement, he also lamented the easy demonization of poor, rural, southern whites, who he believed were also victims of capitalism's exploitation of the poor. Such theological understandings of Christianity often put Campbell at odds with activists on the left, especially when he began to minister to members of the Ku Klux Klan. His most searing analysis of race and religion came after the 1965 murder of Jonathan Daniels, an Episcopal priest visiting Alabama to work for civil rights, by a local sheriff. Campbell had previously been pushed to define Christianity in ten words or less by a journalist friend. His reply, "We're all bastards but God loves us anyway," came to be challenged when Daniels was murdered. Campbell's immediate desire to condemn the sheriff gave way to a fuller understanding of compassion and grace, and that understanding guided the rest of Campbell's life and work.

Campbell refused to waver from a prophetic role in matters of race and poverty, and he assembled a network of other such prophets to sound a clarion call for truth, justice, and reconciliation. Under the auspices of the Committee of Southern Churchmen, Campbell coedited *Katallagete: Be Reconciled*, a theological journal that boasted contributors such as Walker Percy, H. Richard Niebuhr, Fannie Lou Hamer, and Thomas Merton and that described many of the themes evocative of Campbell's ministry: mistrust of institutions, faithfulness to an old-time radical Gospel, and reconciliation, not simply between humans but also of humans to God's world.

In time, editing the journal and constant travel gave way to writing books. His well-received *Brother to a Dragonfly*, a finalist for the National Book Award in 1978 and winner of the Lillian Smith Prize, preceded *Forty Acres and a Goat*, *The Glad River*, *Cecelia's Sin*, *Providence*, *The Convention*, *The Stem of Jesse*, *And Also with You*, and others.

In 2000 Pres. Bill Clinton presented Campbell with the National Humanities Medal, but his most treasured award remained his notice of ordination from the East Fork Baptist Church. The plain, typed paper rested inside and on top of his framed Yale Divinity School degree in the front room of his Mount Juliet home.

Will Campbell died in 2013 from complications related to a stroke.

Susan M. Glisson
University of Mississippi

Thomas L. Connelly, *Will Campbell and the Soul of the South* (1982); Merrill M. Hawkins Jr., *Will Campbell: Radical Prophet of the South* (1997); Lawrence Wright, *Saints and Sinners: Walker Railey, Jimmy Swaggart, Madalyn Murray O'Hair, Anton LaVey, Will Campbell, Matthew Fox* (1993).

Campbell College

Campbell College, an African Methodist Episcopal (AME) junior college, educated black college and high school students in Mississippi between 1890 and 1964. Campbell first opened in Vicksburg but moved to Jackson in 1899 in hopes of attracting more students. During the civil rights era, students at Campbell participated in direct action protests in Jackson and supported activists at nearby high schools and colleges. When the state seized Campbell and closed the school, Campbell's physical plant became part of Jackson State College (now Jackson State University).

Throughout its existence, Campbell's enrollment remained low, and the school suffered from chronic financial problems. The AME Church had established Wilberforce University (Wilberforce, Ohio) in 1856 and Allen University (Columbia, South Carolina), Morris Brown College (Atlanta), Paul Quinn College (Waco, Texas), and Edward Waters College (Jacksonville, Florida) after the Civil War, but Campbell struggled to replicate the stability of these colleges. Enrollment at Campbell never came close to the enrollment at the AME's senior colleges, and even other AME junior colleges such as Daniel Payne College (Birmingham, Alabama), Shorter College (Little Rock, Arkansas), and Kittrell College (Kittrell, North Carolina) had far more students than did Campbell.

During the Great Depression, the funding crisis at Campbell grew desperate. In 1933 the AME Church reported to the *Journal of Negro Education* that donations had slowed considerably, imperiling the church's educational fund. Campbell, younger and smaller than the other AME schools, hardly possessed the endowment or resources to insulate itself from problems in church funding. Though Campbell survived the Depression, enrollment hovered at around fifty throughout the 1940s. By 1960, Campbell enrolled forty high school students and seventy-five college students.

Despite its small size, Campbell played an important role in Jackson's civil rights movement. As an AME school, Campbell did not rely on state money and could therefore openly support the civil rights movement without jeopardizing funding. Campbell students not only participated in demonstrations and protests but also served as supporters and ambassadors of the movement. In October 1961, after students had staged a walkout at Burglund High School to show solidarity with participants in a sit-in in McComb, Campbell attracted the ire of white officials when it allowed students boycotting Burglund to enroll.

In 1961 the State of Mississippi seized the college via eminent domain. Though neighboring Jackson State had long considered purchasing Campbell's land and ultimately erected a new building on the old Campbell site, veterans of the McComb movement, most notably Hollis Watkins, believed that the state had seized Campbell in retaliation for the college's role in the Burglund High boycott. By 1964 Campbell's last students had graduated, and the college died a martyr to Mississippi's civil rights movement.

Thomas John Carey
University of Mississippi

John Dittmer, *Local People: The Struggle for Civil Rights in Mississippi* (1994); Sherman L. Greene Jr., *Journal of Negro Education* (Summer 1960); *Journal of Negro Education* (January 1933); Charles M. Payne, *I've Got the Light of Freedom: The Organizing Tradition and the Mississippi Freedom Struggle* (1995); Lelia Gaston Rhodes, *Jackson State University: The First Hundred Years, 1877–1977* (1979).

Cane Basketry

Basketry crafted from splints of native cane (*Arundinaria gigantea*) is one of the oldest signature artistic traditions among the American Indians of the Southeast. The natural range for this native grass (commonly called river cane, swamp cane, or switch cane) roughly conforms to the southeastern Indian culture area that includes the state of Mississippi. This plentiful and adaptable resource was utilized in a variety of ways, but its most enduring traditional use was for the production of split cane mats and baskets.

Ancient Mississippi artisans—typically women and young girls—cut and gathered cane along waterways and streambeds. Often traveling in groups, the artisans camped near the canebrakes for several days to harvest and process cane before returning to their villages. Cane stands were revisited from year to year, with preference given to those that produced strong, straight cane with long joints. The cane was gathered and scoured in fresh water to remove dirt and leaves. A splitter and a knife made from sharpened cane were used to split the stalks into quarters and to peel away the outer layer to form six to eight strips or splints. These cane splints were rolled into bundles and transported back to the villages, where they were stored until the cold winter months and then soaked in water and woven into baskets.

Some basketry was left unadorned, with the design formed by plaiting, most commonly the herringbone over-five-under-five weave; other basketry was decorated with interwoven splints dyed red or black. Geometric designs reflected the natural world, evoking birds' eyes, deer toes, and other zoomorphic imagery, but no names for these designs have survived to the present day. Everyday baskets used for gathering and in food processing were rarely dyed, but mats and baskets created for personal or ritual use displayed intricate and beautiful designs. Red dye was produced using puccoon (bloodroot) or sumac berries, while black dye was derived from black walnut or blackjack oak.

Basketry forms and sizes were diverse. Utilitarian baskets included fanners and sifters used to process corn and other grains, heart-shaped baskets for processing salt from briny water, elbow baskets and hampers for storage, and burden baskets for carrying small children or firewood and other bulky resources. Woven mats were used for beds and room dividers as well as to demarcate sacred spaces within mounds and in burials. Double-walled or double-woven lidded baskets were used to inter the disarticulated skeletons of social elites.

Colonial Europeans who settled alongside the Mississippi Indians came to appreciate the beauty and the utility of cane basketry, which became a highly prized commodity in the regional market economy. English naturalist Mark Catesby observed around 1740 that "baskets made by the ...

Choctaughs and *Chigasaws*, are exceeding neat and strong. . . . These are made of cane in different forms and sizes and beautifully dyed black and red with various figures; many of them are so close wrought that they will hold water."

Although cane baskets are still made in much the same fashion and form as was the case hundreds of years ago, this once-ubiquitous southeastern tradition is maintained in fewer than ten contemporary southeastern Indian communities. Among the most gifted practitioners, Mississippi Choctaw weavers maintain these ancient practices while accepting some innovation into the artistic complex. Fanners today may be decorated with splints colored with aniline dyes of fuchsia, magenta, turquoise, and teal, reflecting the aesthetics of individual weavers.

Canebrakes have been diminished by agricultural practices and by changes in the cultural landscape. Nevertheless, cane is making a comeback on tribal properties, the result of a cooperative program between the Mississippi Band of Choctaw and the US Department of Agriculture Natural Resources Conservation Service to transplant stands of cane on tribal properties. In twenty-first-century Mississippi, split-cane basketry remains a viable, living tradition and a symbol of the persistence of the Choctaw people.

Dayna Bowker Lee
Louisiana Regional Folklife
Program, Northwestern
State University

Marshall Gettys, *Basketry of Southeastern Indians* (1984); Tim Oakes, in *The Work of Tribal Hands: Southeastern Indian Split Cane Basketry*, ed. Dayna Bowker Lee and H. F. Gregory (2006); John R. Swanton, *Source Material for the Social and Ceremonial Life of the Choctaw Indians* (1931).

Cannon, Gus

(1883–1979) Blues Musician

Gus Cannon lived long enough for his style of music to go from the cutting edge of southern African American tastes to being labeled "archaic" by a latter-day scholar. Cannon was born on 12 September 1883 in Red Banks, Mississippi, the tenth child of former slaves who became sharecroppers. Perhaps they taught their youngest son the refrain that he issued on a record exactly one hundred years after the delivery of the proclamation that freed them: "Well my old mistress promised me / when she died she'd set me free / she lived so long that her head got bald / thought I'd have to kill her with a white oak maul."

Cannon initially played the banjo in a family or string orchestra and made his first instrument out of a guitar neck and a tin bread pan with a raccoon hide stretched over the open end, periodically tightened by a flame from the matches he carried. Cannon lived near Clarksdale around 1900 and worked as a cotton picker. There he heard one of the earliest slide guitarists recalled in the Delta and adapted the new style to his banjo. Like other African American musicians of this region and generation, Cannon chose the life of a traveling musician after experiences in agriculture and on the railroad and levee. Before the popularity of the phonograph and radio in the region, the medicine show spread new musical ideas across the rural landscape and was a venue of musical exchange. Traveling with various medicine shows before World War I, Cannon acquired the moniker Banjo Joe, and he recorded under that name during his first session. He also made contact with Tennessee-born harmonica player Noah Lewis and multi-instrumentalists Hosea Woods and Elijah Avery.

Unlike many blues musicians of the era who struggled to compose the four original pieces needed to earn a recording session, Cannon was a veteran musician at his first session in November 1927. That session highlighted his versatility and creativity (as well as that of his accompanist, guitarist Blind Blake) and hinted at the breadth of Cannon's repertoire. The six recordings from that session included "Jonestown Blues," named for a hamlet of cotton pickers near Clarksdale and recognized as the first "standard" blues recorded with banjo as the lead instrument. Cannon learned "Poor Boy Long Ways from Home" in the Delta around the turn of the century, but his slide banjo performance at this session was unprecedented in any recorded blues. He also lampooned Booker T. Washington's 1901 White House visit in "Can You Blame the Colored Man?"

Like many other musical Mississippians of his generation, Cannon migrated north to Memphis, possibly to enhance his musical income. He saw that jug bands were popular and profitable and formed his own, perhaps at the behest of rural music scout Ralph Peer. Cannon and Lewis formed the core of the band, with Woods, Avery, and Lewis's neighbor from Ripley, Tennessee, Ashley Thompson, taking turns playing guitar during the band's nine recording sessions. The band recorded blues, rags, and medicine show songs such as "Whoah! Mule Get up in the Alley" and "Feather Bed," which included the verse, "I remember the time just before the war / Colored man used to hunt for chips and straw / but now bless God, Ol' Marse is dead / Colored man plumb fool 'bout a feather bed." The most enduring of their twenty-nine recordings proved to be "Walk Right In." Written by Cannon in 1913, the song reached the top of the *Billboard* charts fifty years later, performed by the Rooftop Singers. Cannon had spent the three previous decades digging ditches but earned some well-deserved royalties and briefly reentered the rather dim spotlight of the American folk music revival.

This child of slaves lived to witness and participate in the emergence of blues in Mississippi, the heyday of Beale Street in Memphis, the rise and demise of the race record industry in the South, and the 1960s American blues revival. In addition, he heard three of his compositions recorded by groups of musicians sixty years his junior. Cannon's story was featured in at least two books, *Time* magazine, and the *Saturday Evening Post*, and he appeared in the first motion picture with an all-black cast, King Vidor's *Hallelujah!* (1929). Cannon died on 15 October 1979.

Preston Lauterbach
Nellysford, Virginia

William Barlow, *Looking up at Down* (1989); Samuel B. Charters, *The Country Blues* (1975); John Godrich and Robert M. W. Dixon, *Blues and Gospel Records: 1902–1943* (1969); Bengt Olsson, *Memphis Blues* (1970).

Canton Civil Rights Movement

The Canton movement for civil rights sought to address issues common to many segregated communities in the state. In addition to experiencing voter disfranchisement, many African Americans in the town lived in extreme poverty, and the community had an infant mortality rate of 42 percent, one of the highest in the state. Community activists included local residents and, beginning in 1963, workers from the Council of Federated Organizations (COFO), an umbrella group that comprised the Student Nonviolent Coordinating Committee (SNCC) and the Congress of Racial Equality (CORE), among other organizations. CORE was particularly active in Canton. Workers had a variety of aims, including voter registration, the building of a community center and library, and increased literacy.

In the early 1950s three hundred black Cantonians marched to the courthouse to register to vote; forty applicants succeeded. Throughout the decade and into the 1960s, only two hundred more of Canton's African Americans registered. Over an eight-month period beginning in 1963, COFO organized one thousand attempted registrations, only thirty of which succeeded. At this point, hundreds of people filed affidavits with the US Justice Department on the grounds of voter discrimination.

In January 1964 members of the black community began a selective buying campaign, boycotting twenty-one stores and three products (Mosby's Milk, Barq's Root Beer, and Hart's Bread) because the companies that produced them maintained unfair hiring practices. COFO said the boycott was 90 percent effective. One store owner came to a mass meeting to apologize for past discrimination. However, many community members active in the boycott faced reprisals from hostile police and an active Citizens' Council. The Canton City Council passed a law banning people from handing out leaflets without the permission of the police department, and many arrests followed when activists continued to spread the word about the boycott. Later that year the State Senate discussed making selective buying campaigns illegal.

Individual community members often faced reprisals—sometimes violent—as well. When George Washington, a black businessman, refused to serve as an informer for those trying to halt the work of activists, the gas pumps at his grocery store were removed and his meat deliveries cut off. Police officers beat two teens severely after they left a voter registration meeting in February 1964, shooting blanks near the young men's heads and threatening to kill their family members. In July 1964 white gas station attendant Price Lewis shot at a group of black teenagers who volunteered with COFO.

The workers in Madison County planned the first of three Freedom Days on 28 February 1964, when 350 African Americans marched to the courthouse to register to vote. In March almost 3,000 black schoolchildren boycotted Canton's segregated schools to protest their inadequate facilities. A second Freedom Day followed on 13 March, with a third held on 29 May and featuring CORE director James Farmer as a speaker. Following that meeting, white supremacists shot at and attempted to bomb the Freedom House.

An important element of the movement in Canton was the creation of the Child Development Group of Mississippi (CDGM) in 1965. CDGM was a Head Start program that provided preschool and medical care for children as well as jobs in impoverished areas. Despite these advances, state officials often charged CDGM with mismanagement. Many members of Canton's black community felt that the CDGM's hiring practices, controlled by Rev. James McRee and George Raymond, were unfair. The state cut funding from the Head Start programs in 1967, and CDGM was replaced by other organizations.

James Meredith's March against Fear came to Canton in July 1966, and activists met the two hundred marchers as they entered the town, taking them to a rally at the courthouse with a crowd of one thousand. The marchers had planned to camp at a black public school, but city officials forbade this action. Led by Stokely Carmichael, the crowd began to set up tents in spite of the presence of heavily armed state troopers. The troopers fired gas into the crowds, burning and blinding many of marchers, and then beat those who did not disperse.

The movement in Madison County relied on the leadership of several key persons. C. O. Chinn, a local business owner known for his fearlessness, provided his store as a space for meetings and protected other activists from violent attacks. George Raymond, a former freedom rider from New Orleans, provided much of the strategy for the Canton movement, serving as the only staff member when the first CORE office opened in the county in 1963. Anne Moody, a Tougaloo College graduate later known for her memoir, *Coming of Age in Mississippi*, spent Freedom Summer 1964 in Canton. Annie Devine, a well-respected teacher and insurance saleswoman who was intimately familiar with the workings of both Canton's black and white communities, provided essential leadership and later served as a member of the Mississippi Freedom Democratic Party's delegation to the 1964 Democratic National Convention.

Becca Walton
University of Mississippi

John Dittmer, *Local People: The Struggle for Civil Rights in Mississippi* (1994); Mississippi Department of Archives and History, Sovereignty Commission Online website, www.mdah.state.ms.us/arlib/contents/er/sovcom; Anne Moody, *Coming of Age in Mississippi* (1968); Charles Payne, *I've Got the Light of Freedom: The Organizing Tradition and the Mississippi Freedom Struggle* (1995).

Canzoneri, Robert
(1925–2010) Author

Robert Canzoneri was an author and teacher raised and educated in Mississippi. Though he left for doctoral work and teaching jobs, his experiences in the state influenced his writings in a variety of genres as he grappled with the meaning of his identity as a Mississippian, an Italian American, and a southerner in decades particularly fraught with southern political and social debate.

Canzoneri was born in San Marcos, Texas, on 21 November 1925 to Joe and Mabel Barnett Canzoneri. His mother was a cousin of former Mississippi governor Ross Barnett, while his father was originally from Sicily. His family moved to Clinton, Mississippi, and he attended the city's public schools. After graduating from high school, Canzoneri joined the US Navy and served in World War II. He subsequently returned to Mississippi and received a bachelor's degree from Mississippi College in 1948 and a master's degree from the University of Mississippi in 1951. Canzoneri also attended graduate programs at Vanderbilt University, the University of Michigan, and the University of Kentucky.

Canzoneri received a doctorate in English from Stanford University in 1965 and won the Henry H. Bellamann Foundation Award, recognizing and encouraging writers with unusual literary promise. He taught English at several colleges before settling at Ohio State University in 1968. He was married twice, first to Dorothy Mitchell, with whom he had two children, and subsequently to Candyce Barnes.

Canzoneri published nonfiction, novels, short stories, and poetry, and his work appeared in a number of literary journals. His first book, *I Do So Politely: A Voice from the South* (1965), is a work of nonfiction that responded autobiographically to the contemporary "race question" in Mississippi. Written as a free-flowing personal essay full of argument and anecdote, the book criticized Mississippi's government and societal opposition to integration following the US Supreme Court's 1954 *Brown v. Board of Education* ruling. The book used Canzoneri's childhood experiences to outline the dilemma facing Mississippians who had been taught to see the world in Christian and democratic terms and found contradictions in segregationist policy and rhetoric.

Canzoneri's next published work, *Watch Us Pass* (1968), featured poetry drawing on his experiences. His first novel, *Men with Little Hammers* (1969), offered an ironic and comic look at the hypocrisy of students and teachers on a midwestern college campus. Canzoneri followed up with *Barbed Wire and Other Stories* (1970), a collection set primarily in the South from the 1940s to the 1960s that focused on the lives of Italian immigrants and their children and drew heavily on his experiences with his extended family. He also penned *A Highly Ramified Tree* (1976), a collection of sketches covering his boyhood and featuring portraits of his Sicilian relatives in the United States and Italy. Thirteen years later, he authored an autobiographical cookbook, *Potboiler: An Amateur's Affair with la Cuisine*.

In December 1970 Canzoneri donated the manuscripts of his published and unpublished works to the University of Mississippi Department of Archives and Special Collections. He died in Westerville, Ohio, in 2010.

Frances Abbott
Digital Public Library of America,
Boston

Robert Canzoneri File, Department of Archives and Special Collections, J. D. Williams Library, University of Mississippi; James B. Lloyd, *Lives of Mississippi Authors, 1817–1967* (1981).

Capers, Charlotte
(1913–1996) Archivist and Author

As longtime friend Eudora Welty described Charlotte Capers in the foreword to *The Capers Papers*, "Charlotte does a variety of things well and enthusiastically besides write. She'd rather rise up and dance than sit down and type [but] she writes entirely too well not to take an honest satisfaction from doing it."

Early in life, Capers, a Tennessee native, moved with her parents, an Episcopal rector and his wife, to Jackson, where she lived for the rest of her life. Recognizing in high school that she wanted to be a journalist, she attended Millsaps College, took journalism courses at the University of Colorado, and graduated from the University of Mississippi with a degree in English. After brief employment with Condé Nast Publications, she took a temporary job as a secretary at the Mississippi Department of Archives and History.

She remained at the department for the next forty-five years, becoming a research assistant, acting director, and assistant director; in 1955, she became director. When she retired in 1983, the Mississippi legislature renamed the Archives and History Building in her honor.

Capers was part of a circle of Jackson friends who called themselves the Basic Eight. The group, whose most famous member was Eudora Welty, dined and traveled together, entertaining themselves and frequent guests. According to Welty biographer Suzanne Marrs, Capers was "one of the world's great raconteurs, even if the world beyond Mississippi did not know it."

As dedicated as she was to her friends and to state and local history, Capers was a versatile and energetic individual who never gave up on her writing or lost sight of her role as a public servant. She served as a planner and principal executive in the restoration of the Old Capitol Museum, the Governor's Mansion, and the Faulkner house. She held the post of editor in chief of the *Journal of Mississippi History*, wrote ninety-nine book reviews for the *New York Times Book Review*, and penned columns for the *Jackson Daily News* and *States Times*. In 1982 the University Press of Mississippi published *The Capers Papers*, a collection of essays and columns she had initially written in her "Miss Quote" column for Jackson newspapers. Miss Quote wrote short, lively pieces commenting on everyday topics—relatives, pets, cars, technology, her house and tenants, health, and trends. In Welty's words, "Most of the pieces were written to amuse, and they abundantly did so." Capers also edited archaeological surveys, inaugural papers, and memoirs, but *The Capers Papers* is her most unforgettable work.

Mary Frances Marx
Southeastern Louisiana University

Charlotte Capers, *The Capers Papers* (1982); Suzanne Marrs, *Eudora Welty: A Biography* (2005); Mississippi Department of Archives and History, www.mdah.state.ms.us.

Carloss, Helen

(1893–1948) Government Lawyer

Helen Rembert Carloss, a lawyer for the US Department of Justice, was born on 18 April 1893 in Yazoo City, Mississippi, and educated in the city's public schools. She went on to attend the Industrial Institute and College (now Mississippi University for Women), where she was vice president of her senior class and graduated in 1913. After a few years as a teacher, a profession she disliked heartily, she decided that she wanted to become a lawyer. Few women worked as attorneys at the time, so Mississippi senator John Sharp Williams advised her to move to Washington, D.C., where she became a clerk in the Division of Internal Revenue in 1918. That experience likely shaped the direction she took after she enrolled in night classes and earned a law degree from George Washington University in 1923. She joined the Department of Justice's legal staff on the recommendation of Mable Walker Willebrandt, a Tennessee native serving as a US assistant attorney general. Carloss became a specialist in estate and gift taxation and was one of the few lawyers who made up the department's new Tax Division when it was organized in 1934.

The quiet and unassuming Carloss soon became known for her brilliance as a litigator. As a special assistant to the attorney general, she became the first woman to argue a case before the US Court of Appeals, ultimately appearing in all ten of the appeals courts. Judge Learned Hand termed her "one of the best men who appears before the court." She also argued twenty-seven cases before the US Supreme Court, a record for any attorney in the Tax Division up to that time. The justices admired her arguments: according to Chief Justice Harlan Fiske Stone, it was "an intellectual treat" whenever Carloss appeared before the Court. Justice Robert Jackson spoke of her knowledge, research, and "balance of judgment," which "made you feel when she had finished that you had the whole story."

Carloss retired in 1947 because of ill health and died of cancer in 1948 at her mother's home in Yazoo City.

Martha H. Swain
Mississippi State University

Sam Olden, *Yazoo Historical Society Journal* (1983); John C. Stennis, *Congressional Record* (1949); *Washington Post* (28 March 1934); *Yazoo Herald* (30 December 1948).

Carr, Sam (Samuel Lee McCollum)

(1926–2009) Musician

Samuel Lee McCollum was born in 1926 near Marvell, Arkansas, but was soon adopted and raised by the Carr family on a farm near Dundee, Mississippi. Carr's biological father was a highly influential and innovative electric slide guitarist, Robert Lee McCollum (1909–1967), known more widely on the blues performance circuit as Robert Nighthawk. Although Carr was not raised by Nighthawk, Nighthawk's musical notoriety and landmark recordings for the Decca, Bluebird, and Chess labels had a profound impact on Carr, as they did for many other Delta musicians.

Around 1942, when Carr was sixteen years old, he moved to the bustling river town of Helena, Arkansas, to work as a doorman during his father's nightclub performances. Carr had already become an adept musician, having mastered the blues harmonica and the Jew's harp, an ancient pastoral instrument that was popular throughout rural America in the late nineteenth and early twentieth centuries.

Carr married his wife, Doris, in 1946, and after a brief and unpleasant stint in sharecropping, the young couple boarded a ferry across the Mississippi River and caught a northbound train to St. Louis, where Carr's mother lived. While there, Carr found work playing drums with various blues acts, including harmonica player Tree Top Slim, the great Sonny Boy Williamson II, and most notably Frank Frost, a guitarist, harmonica player, and singer with whom Carr developed a long-standing musical collaboration, beginning in 1956. The Carrs moved to Mississippi in the early 1960s, as did Frost, and the two bluesmen teamed up with Clarksdale's Big Jack Johnson and recorded a full-length album for legendary producer Sam Phillips's record label, Phillips International, in 1962. This effort, titled *Hey Boss Man*, now stands as a highly sought after and collectable Delta blues classic, and their recording of the song "Jelly Roll King" soon earned the trio the name the Jelly Roll Kings. They released several singles under Frost's name on the Nashville-based Jewel label in 1966, including "My Back Scratcher," which became a short-lived jukebox hit.

Throughout the 1960s and 1970s Carr made his living driving a tractor in addition to steadily playing regional club gigs with Frost, Johnson, T-Model Ford, and many others in the Greenville and Clarksdale areas. In 1978 blues enthusiast Michael Frank recorded the Jelly Roll Kings' debut LP, *Rockin' the Juke Joint Down*, for his Earwig record label, which also later released Frost's LP *Midnight Prowler* (1988) as well as Johnson's *Daddy, When's Mama Comin' Home* (1991), both of which featured Carr's fine drumming. In 1996 the Jelly Roll Kings released *Off Yonder Wall* on Fat Possum Records, and Carr was regularly brought in as session drummer for several other Fat Possum releases, including those of Asie Payton, T-Model Ford, and Paul "Wine" Jones. Carr also played on Buddy Guy's award-winning album *Sweet Tea*. Carr went on to form his own band, the Delta Jukes, with guitarist Dave Riley and harmonica player John Weston, and the trio recorded several albums, including *Working for the Blues* (2002), *Down in the Delta* (2004), and *Let the Good Times Roll* (2007). Carr earned several *Living Blues* awards and in 2007 received Mississippi's Governor's Award for Excellence in the Arts. Following a long series of health complications, Carr died on 21 September 2009.

Jake Fussell
Durham, North Carolina

Living Blues (January–February 2004).

Carroll County

Carroll County is a hilly area with fertile valleys in central Mississippi, flanked by the Big Black River along its southeastern border and originally by the Tallahatchie and Yazoo Rivers at its western periphery. The county was founded on 23 December 1833 from land ceded to the United States by the Choctaw Nation under the 1830 Treaty of Dancing Rabbit Creek. A significant percentage of the original county acreage was eventually incorporated into neighboring Leflore, Grenada, and Montgomery Counties. Carroll County and its seat, Carrollton, take their names from wealthy colonial politician Charles Carroll. In 1840 the county's population was almost evenly divided, with 5,136 whites, 1 free black, and 5,344 slaves.

By 1860 the county's slave population of 13,808—the ninth-highest in the state—was markedly larger than the county's free population of 8,227. Through the toil of this sizable slave labor force, antebellum Carroll County developed a flourishing agricultural economy and the sixth-most-valuable farmland in Mississippi. Carroll County's farms and plantations ranked eighth in the state in cotton grown, fifth in corn and sweet potatoes, third in livestock, and first in peas and beans by a wide margin. The county had twenty-three churches, divided evenly among Baptists, Methodists, and Presbyterians.

In the postbellum period, the county's population remained largely African American. Carroll County had a higher percentage of farmers who owned their farms (65 percent) than the state average in the last decades of the nineteenth cen-

tury, and those farmers tended to work larger-than-average lots of land. The county had a small manufacturing economy in 1880, with twenty-one establishments employing forty-five men, nineteen women, and eleven children.

In the early 1890s Mississippi's first chapter of the Southern Farmers' Alliance formed in Carroll County, and the journal of the state's Colored Farmers' Alliance, the *Advocate*, was published in Vaiden. Carroll County was the home of James Z. George, a Populist leader who became a main force behind the state's 1890 constitution.

By the early twentieth century, Carroll had grown to more than twenty thousand people, with African Americans still slightly outnumbering whites. Farming continued to dominate the economy. Slightly more than half of Carroll's white farmers owned their own land, while only 17 percent of African American farmers did so; the rest were either tenants or sharecroppers.

In 1916 the county's churchgoing population was divided among several Protestant groups. The National Baptist Convention and Southern Baptist Convention were the largest denominations, followed by the Methodist Episcopal Church, South; the Methodist Episcopal Church; the Colored Methodist Episcopal Church; the Presbyterian Church, and the Disciples of Christ.

In 1930 Carroll County was still extremely rural, with 90 percent of the population living on farms. Less than a quarter of the county's farmers owned their land, while Carroll had a small but growing industrial base of about 150 workers.

Carroll has been home to a good number of creative Mississippians. Willie Narmour and Shell Smith, popular string band musicians of the 1920s and 1930s, grew up there. Elizabeth Spencer, author of *The Voice at the Back Door* and *Light in the Piazza*, grew up in Carrollton, which she discusses in her memoir, *Landscapes of the Heart*.

In 1960 Carroll County was home to 11,117 people, about 58 percent of them African American. Two-thirds of the workforce was involved in production of various agricultural staples, including cotton, corn, wheat, livestock, soybeans, and timber. By 1980 the agricultural workforce had decreased to around 10 percent of the working population. The county's few manufacturing firms were largely connected to the timber and furniture industries, while a few minor mineral industries had emerged as well, producing sand and gravel. Carroll was one of the state's poorest counties, with the second-lowest per capita income and more than 10 percent of the population receiving federal aid.

Between 1960 and 2010, Carroll County's population remained relatively stable, although the white proportion of the total increased to 66 percent, a phenomenon common in many central Mississippi counties.

Mississippi Encyclopedia Staff
University of Mississippi

Mississippi State Planning Commission, *Progress Report on State Planning in Mississippi* (1938); *Mississippi Statistical Abstract*, Mississippi State University (1952–2010); Charles Sydnor and Claude Bennett, *Mississippi History* (1939); University of Virginia Library, Historical Census Browser website, http://mapserver.lib.virginia.edu; E. Nolan Waller and Dani A. Smith, *Growth Profiles of Mississippi's Counties, 1960–1980* (1985).

Carter, Betty Werlein

(1910–2000) Journalist

Betty Werlein Carter, the matriarch of the Carter family of journalists, was the wife of Pulitzer Prize–winning newspaperman Hodding Carter Jr. and the mother of Hodding Carter III and Philip Carter. She was also a journalist, publicist, and editor in her own right. For more than fifty years she helped publish the *Delta Democrat-Times*, known for its attacks on Mississippi politicians and its moderate stance during the volatile years of the civil rights movement.

Born in New Orleans, Betty Werlein was the oldest of four children. Her father, Philip, managed his family's music company, the original publisher of the Confederate song "Dixie." After her father died in 1917, her life was largely dominated by her mother, Elizabeth, and her paternal grandmother, Bettie. In 1927 she graduated from high school at McGehee's School and enrolled in Sophie Newcomb College, the women's school associated with Tulane University. She met Hodding Carter through his sister, Corinne, a classmate, and dated him for much of her college years. They married on 14 October 1931. The Carters honeymooned in Pass Christian but cut the vacation short when Gov. Theodore Bilbo called a legislative special session in Jackson, an event Hodding covered for the Associated Press. Shortly after the couple settled in the Mississippi capital, Hodding was fired over a dispute with his editor, and the Carters returned to Louisiana, where they scraped together the money to found their own newspaper. They quickly turned the *Hammond Daily Courier* into a vocal critic of Huey Long's politics. In 1936 they sold the paper and began publishing the *Delta Star* in Greenville. Two years later they purchased their competition, the *Daily Democrat-Times*, and merged the two into the *Delta Democrat-Times*.

From 1942 to 1945 Betty Carter served as a publicist, researcher, and writer for the Office of War Information in Washington, D.C. After Hodding returned from service in World War II, the couple relocated to Greenville, where they resumed control of their newspaper. Betty was extremely active in the community, serving on a variety of committees and organizations, among them the National Association of Educational Broadcasters. She also helped to create a haven for both state and national journalists at the Carter home, Feliciana, during the civil rights movement.

In addition to publishing the *Delta Democrat-Times*, the Carters coauthored several books, including *So Great a Good: A History of the Episcopal Church in Louisiana, 1805–1955* (1955) and *Doomed Road of Empire* (1963). Betty also aided Hodding in researching and editing his books and articles. The Carters suffered personal tragedy when their youngest son, Thomas, killed himself playing Russian roulette in 1964. After Hodding's death in 1972, Betty helped Hodding III and then Philip publish the *Delta Democrat-Times*, but in 1980 the family sold the newspaper to Freedom Newspapers of Santa Ana, California. Betty Werlein Carter died on 4 March 2000 and was buried in Greenville Cemetery.

Summer Hill-Vinson
University of Mississippi

Ginger Rudeseal Carter, in *The Press and Race: Mississippi Journalists Confront the Movement*, ed. David Davies (2001); Rebekah Ray, *American Journalism* (Spring 2007); Gene Roberts and Hank Klibanoff, *The Race Beat: The Press, the Civil Rights Struggle, and the Awakening of a Nation* (2006); Ann Waldron, *Hodding Carter: The Reconstruction of a Racist* (1993).

Carter, Bo (Armenter Chatmon)

(1893–1964) Blues Musician

Bo Carter was one of the early country blues artists whose music had a strong impact on the development of blues. Armenter Chatmon was born to Henderson Chatmon and Eliza Jackson on the Dupress Plantation near Bolton on 21 March 1893. In his very musical family, his parents and all twelve siblings played instruments or sang. Though known mostly for his guitar playing and singing, Bo Carter also played bass, banjo, violin, and clarinet. He first performed with several of his brothers in a string band later known as the Mississippi Sheiks. Although he often played live with the Mississippi Sheiks, Carter appeared on only a few of their recordings.

Carter is often most remembered for his double entendre, hokum-style blues from the 1930s, where titles such as "Banana in Your Fruit Basket," "Please Warm My Wiener," "My Pencil Won't Write No More," and "Don't Mash My Digger So Deep" left little lyrical ambiguity. Carter did, however, write a large number of nonbawdy songs. In 1928 Carter recorded the earliest version of the blues standard "Corrine, Corrina." Carter recorded with artists such as Walter Vincson, Charlie McCoy, and others from 1928 to 1930. In late 1930 he began a decadelong solo recording career, producing more than one hundred songs for the Bluebird and OKeh labels. Despite losing his eyesight in the 1930s, Carter continued to perform.

Although he is most often classified as a blues musician, Carter performed in a number of different styles. He often played country dance tunes and songs. Some of his songs fit a thirty-two-bar AABA structure, which is not common to blues.

Carter died in relative obscurity after suffering a brain hemorrhage in Memphis on 21 September 1964.

Greg Johnson
University of Mississippi

Steve Calt, *Bo Carter: Banana in Your Fruit Basket* (2002), liner notes; Steve Cheseborough, in *Encyclopedia of the Blues*, ed. Edward Komara (2006); Steve Douglas Cheseborough, "Mashing That Thing: Meaning and Eroticism in the Music of Bo Carter" (master's thesis, University of Mississippi, 1999).

Carter, Hodding, Jr.
(1907–1972) Journalist and Author

Hodding Carter Jr., a bold newspaper editor and publisher, spent his career challenging the most powerful interests in two Deep South states. Before he was thirty, Carter founded a small tabloid, the *Daily Courier*, in his hometown of Hammond, Louisiana, and used it to assail the politics of Huey P. Long. Following Long's assassination in 1935, a group of Mississippi Delta men recruited Carter to come to Greenville and establish the *Delta Star* to compete with an uninspiring local newspaper, the *Daily Democrat-Times*. Within two years, Carter bought out his rival and merged the two papers into the *Delta Democrat-Times*, which served as the base for his broadsides against reactionary politicians and the Citizens' Council. Carter won a Pulitzer Prize in 1946 for editorial commentary that attacked the racist Sen. Theodore G. Bilbo of Mississippi and upbraided the US government for its treatment of Japanese Americans.

His son, Hodding Carter III, wrote that the family "lived in a sporadic state of siege" during the long period when the elder Carter was a lonely white voice in opposition to Mississippi's segregationist forces. He kept an arsenal of guns to defend himself and rallied members of his family to maintain an armed vigil at his Greenville home during the 1962 fight over the integration of the University of Mississippi.

During the turbulent 1960s Carter began to break down both mentally and physically. Yet when he died in 1972, he was lionized for his fierce defense of the First Amendment,

Hodding Carter Jr. (Bern and Franke Keating Collection, Department of Archives and Special Collections, J. D. Williams Library, University of Mississippi)

for his courage in confronting influential enemies, and for championing unpopular causes.

Born in Hammond, Louisiana, on 3 February 1907, William Hodding Carter Jr. was a child prodigy who started school and was immediately placed in the fourth grade. He went on to graduate from Bowdoin College in Maine in 1927. He studied journalism at Columbia University for a year and then accepted a teaching opportunity at Tulane University, where he met his future wife, Betty Werlein, a member of a well-known New Orleans family. She acted as a valuable adviser and anchor to his newspaper operations for the rest of his life. They had three sons—Philip and Hodding III, who became prominent journalists, and Thomas, a Tulane student who died while playing Russian roulette in 1964.

Carter worked briefly for the *New Orleans Tribune* and the United Press bureau in that city before moving with his young wife to Jackson, where he took a job with the Associated Press. Within five months he was fired for "insubordination," an experience he cheerfully described in *Where Main Street Meets the River*, a 1952 memoir believed to be his favorite among the many books he wrote.

He went back to Louisiana to take on Long, who had moved from the governor's mansion to become a US senator. With a wide following at home, the man known as the Kingfish still dominated state government and represented a threat to Pres. Franklin D. Roosevelt's reelection chances. Hailed by the national magazine *Literary Digest* as "one of the most articulate" Louisiana opponents of the Long machine, Carter found a wider audience with a 1934 *New Republic* article, "Kingfish to Crawfish." Long retaliated by stripping the *Daily Courier* of advertising for the legal profession, a major source of revenue for Carter's paper.

Greenville writer David L. Cohn and planter-poet William Alexander Percy were among the men who lured Carter to the Delta. After quick success there, he received a Nieman Fellowship to Harvard in 1939 and worked for a summer at Ralph Ingersoll's famous New York daily, *PM*, before returning to Greenville. But he left again when called to serve in the US Army during World War II. While in the service, he was partially blinded after he injured his right eye in a freak accident.

The 1946 Pulitzer secured Carter's reputation and earned him the enmity of Bilbo, who declared, "No self-respecting Southern white man would accept a prize given by a bunch of nigger-loving, Yankeefied Communists for editorials advocating the mongrelization of the races."

Despite the positions Carter took against Bilbo and other ardent segregationists, the editor-publisher was not a classic liberal. His oldest son, Hodding, labeled him a "Disraeli conservative," an internationalist in a parochial setting, and a man "who could not stand to see organized power used against people." That characteristic led to Carter's famous wars against the Citizens' Council, formed in 1954 to preserve segregation in Mississippi despite the *Brown v. Board of Education* decision. After Carter criticized the group in a *Look* magazine article, the Mississippi House of Representatives voted 89–19 to censure him. He fired back with an editorial beginning, "I hereby resolve by a vote of 1 to 0 that there are 89 liars in the state legislature."

Carter wrote prolifically and attracted a cadre of outstanding young journalists to work for him in Greenville. As the civil rights era intensified and his health declined, Betty Carter quietly maintained her role as a manager of the Greenville paper, and their son, Hodding III, came home to take over the effective editorial control of the *Delta Democrat-Times* while his father returned to the Tulane faculty. Harassed by political adversaries and afflicted by blindness, grief over his son's death, and a deteriorating mind, Carter was compared in his final years to King Lear. The *Delta Democrat-Times* was sold five years after his death, but the Greenville newspaper left an indelible legacy in Mississippi.

Curtis Wilkie
University of Mississippi

Hodding Carter Jr., *Where Main Street Meets the River* (1952); David G. Davies, ed., *The Press and Race* (2001); Ann Waldron, *Hodding Carter: The Reconstruction of a Racist* (1993); Curtis Wilkie, *Dixie: A Personal Odyssey through Events That Shaped the Modern South* (2001); Curtis Wilkie, Interview with Hodding Carter III (10 May 2003).

Carter, Hodding, III

(b. 1935) Journalist

William Hodding Carter III was born on 7 April 1935 in New Orleans to Betty Werlein Carter and Hodding Carter Jr. Hodding III grew up in the Mississippi Delta city of Green-

ville, where his father served as publisher and editor of the *Delta Democrat-Times* newspaper.

Hodding III attended Phillips Exeter Academy in New Hampshire and Greenville High School, from which he graduated in 1953. He then attended Princeton University, graduating summa cum laude in 1957. He then married Margaret Ainsworth and spent two years in the US Marine Corps before returning to Greenville, where he served as a reporter/editorial writer, managing editor and editor, and associate publisher at the *Delta Democrat-Times*. During his eighteen years with his family's paper Carter was active in many side projects and garnered acclaim for his excellence in public relations and broadcasting. He won the 1961 Society of Professional Journalists' national award for editorial writing, received a 1965–66 Nieman Fellowship at Harvard University, and worked for the presidential campaigns of Lyndon Johnson and Jimmy Carter.

Hodding Carter III distinguished himself as one of the South's most intrepid journalists and organizers. In addition, he served as a board member of the Japan Society, the Center for Policy Alternatives, the George C. Marshall Foundation, the Population Resource Center, the Pew Center for Civic Journalism, the Southern Regional Council, and the International Center for Journalists. Carter was also a founding member of the American Council of Young Political Leaders, serving as the group's chair for five years, and Mississippi Action for Progress, a statewide Head Start agency that served ten thousand children. Carter was a founder of the biracial Loyalist Democrats of Mississippi during the late 1960s and served as a state delegate to the National Democratic Party Conventions in 1968, 1972, and 1976.

Carter left Mississippi in 1977 to become the spokesperson for the Department of State and the assistant secretary of state for public affairs. He is most noted for his media criticism series, *Inside Story*, for which he won four Emmy Awards and the Edward R. Murrow Award in the 1980s. Along with his involvement in a number of public affairs television shows throughout the 1980s and 1990s, Carter was a columnist for the *Wall Street Journal* and United Media/NEA and a contributor to the *New York Times*, *Washington Post*, and various other publications. He is a member of the editorial board of *Southern Cultures*, the southern studies journal of the University of North Carolina at Chapel Hill, and has written two books, *The South Strikes Back* (1970) and *The Reagan Years* (1988).

Along with his experience and success in the world of public affairs and broadcasting, Carter has also served in various capacities in universities across the nation. He served on Princeton University's board of trustees from 1983 to 1998 and as an adjunct professor at American University in Washington, D.C., and at Duke University's Sanford School of Public Policy. Beginning in 1994 Carter served as the Knight Professor of Public Affairs Journalist at the University of Maryland, College Park. He resigned from the position in 1998 to assume the presidency of the John S. and James L.

Knight Foundation, a nonprofit dedicated to advancing journalism in the digital age and promoting informed and engaged communities. Carter currently serves as University Professor of Leadership and Public Policy at the University of North Carolina at Chapel Hill.

Hodding and Margaret Carter had four children, Hodding IV, Catherine, Margaret, and Finn, before divorcing in 1978. Hodding Carter III subsequently married Patricia M. Derian, an author and former human rights official in the Jimmy Carter administration.

Eva Walton Kendrick
Birmingham, Alabama

"A Diplomat on the Podium: Hodding Carter, the New Voice of America." *Time* (10 December 1979).

Carter, Mae Bertha
(1923–1999) Activist

Mae Bertha Carter was born on 13 January 1923 to a family of cotton sharecroppers on the Smith and Wiggins Plantation in the heart of the Mississippi Delta. She married Matthew Carter in 1939 and raised their thirteen children, sharecropping on the Pemble Plantation in Sunflower County, about fourteen miles from Drew.

Matthew and Mae Bertha Carter joined the National Association for the Advancement of Colored People (NAACP) in 1955 and went to meetings in Cleveland for several years. Her children were active in the Freedom Summer in 1964, and two of her daughters went to jail for marching for voting rights. In the summer of 1965 the Carters enrolled their seven school-age children in previously all-white schools. As Mae Bertha Carter said, "I was tired of the old worn-out books and raggedy buses at the black schools, and as I told my first born, Edna, when I looked at her little hand, 'These tiny fingers won't pick cotton forever.'"

In response to their insistence on integrating the schools, the Carters' house was shot into, their credit was cut off, and they were evicted from the plantation. However, their children became the first African Americans to attend Drew's formerly all-white schools. The Carters were also plaintiffs in NAACP-backed lawsuit that led to the abolition of Mississippi's dual school system in 1970. Eight of the Carter children graduated from Drew High School, and seven went on to graduate from the University of Mississippi.

Mae Bertha Carter remained a community and civil rights activist. She worked in a local Head Start program for twenty years and continued to push for quality public

education in Drew. She was active in voter registration, served as an officer in the local NAACP, and helped elect several black candidates to state and local office.

The University of Mississippi honored Carter with its Award of Distinction in 1993, and in February 1996, Marian Wright Edelman, the NAACP attorney who represented the Carters nearly three decades earlier, presented Mae Bertha Carter with an award for moral leadership from the Children's Defense Fund. She was interviewed on National Public Radio and appeared on *CBS This Morning*, and in May 1996 she received the NAACP's Equal Justice Award.

Mae Bertha Carter died on 28 April 1999, eleven years after her husband. The University of Mississippi has honored her with a red leaf maple tree and a plaque noting that seven of her children graduated from the school.

Constance Curry
Emory University

Constance Curry, *Silver Rights* (1995); *New York Times* (6 May 1999).

Cartwright, George
(b. 1950) Jazz Composer and Musician

George Cartwright, a leading composer and performer of avant-garde music since 1979, was born in the Mississippi Delta community of Midnight (near Belzoni in Humphreys County) on 10 December 1950 to George and Elizabeth Rosa Cartwright. The Methodist Church was an early influence on his music and view of life. In high school he discovered the blues by reading in a magazine that Cream, his favorite rock band, drew inspiration from Mississippi Delta music. As a college student at Mississippi State University, from which he graduated in 1972 with a degree in sociology, he heard memorable performances by B. B. King and Big Joe Williams. A sense of vocation was mysteriously aroused when Howlin' Wolf silently tapped him on the shoulder and shook his hand between sets at the Black Elks Club in Greenville. He also studied at the University of Southern Mississippi, where Wilbur Moreland was an influential music teacher; Jackson State University; and Memphis State University. Cartwright was a conscientious objector to the Vietnam War. While in Jackson, he met free jazz drummer Alvin Fielder and in the mid-1970s joined an avant-garde ensemble, Ars Supernova, with Evan Gallagher, Bruce Golden, Mark Howell, and Jeb Stuart, all of whom stayed active as performers, and John Evans, who founded Jackson's Lemuria Bookstore.

Already familiar with piano and guitar, Cartwright took up the saxophone during his senior year in college and thereafter played tenor, soprano, and alto sax. In 1977 he studied at the Creative Music Studio in Woodstock, New York, where he was influenced by Ornette Coleman's harmolodic idea of music that is structurally open to the spontaneous contributions of all its players but also accessible to an audience. After moving to New York City in 1979 Cartwright began to work with notable musicians including Coleman, Fred Frith, Bill Laswell, and John Zorn. He founded a band, Curlew, in 1979 and became a leading figure in the Downtown New York music scene of the next two decades, with Curlew playing regularly at the Knitting Factory on Leonard Street.

Mississippians who have recorded with Cartwright include Howell, Curlew's guitarist in the mid-1980s; Golden, percussionist in Curlew since 2002 and on the solo albums *Dot* (1994) and *The Ghostly Bee* (2006); and Gallagher (organ), Randy Everett (guitar), and Tim Lee (bass) on *Dot*.

Cartwright lived in Memphis from 1993 to 1999, a sojourn reflected in Curlew's *Paradise* (1996), with baritone saxophonist Jim Spake, and in a Cartwright solo project, *The Memphis Years*. He has been based in Minnesota since 1999, performing with a trio called GloryLand PonyCat as well as with Curlew.

Representative recordings include *Meltable Snaps It* with Michael Lytle and David Moss (1986), *Integrated Variables* with Kevin Norton and Mark Dresser (1992), *Red Rope* with Michael Lytle (1998), *Black Ants Crawling* with GloryLand PonyCat (2003), and Curlew's *Live in Berlin* (1986), *Fabulous Drop* (1998), and *Mercury* (2003). A Curlew concert at the Knitting Factory was documented in the video *The Hardwood* (1992). Cartwright has written several settings for poetry by Paul Haines, including the Curlew album *A Beautiful Western Saddle* (1993) and *The Memphis Years*. Cartwright has also collaborated with artist Anne Elias, his wife, on projects combining music, poetry, and film, one of which is represented by *A Tenacious Slew* (2007).

The hallmarks of Curlew's music have been genre-crossing, whimsical geniality, high energy, and a mixture of virtuosic free playing and tightly composed "beat" tunes, often with a strong Americana flavor or southern derivation. Cartwright's saxophone playing can be beautifully warm and restrained but often fiercely attacks the boundaries of intelligible sound and technique. As a composer, he favors modular riffs, often in odd meters, and a sense of journeying within a piece through diverse yet somehow continuous phases, with plenty of vernacular references. As player, composer, and bandleader, Cartwright places a high value on surprises, though generally within a firm structure.

Steven G. Smith
Millsaps College

Allen Huotari, *All about Jazz* (March 2000); Mark Jordan, *Memphis Flyer* (10 June 1999); Robert E. Sweet, *Music Universe, Music Mind: Revisiting the Creative Music Studio, Woodstock, New York* (1996); Peter Watrous, *New York Times* (2 October 1988).

Cartwright, Samuel Adolphus

(1793–1863) Physician, Scientist, Political Advocate

Dr. Samuel Adolphus Cartwright of Natchez was the most prominent physician, surgeon, and medical scientist in antebellum Mississippi. A prolific writer, he published more than eighty articles in the national medical press on a spectrum of topics, winning many medals and prizes for his original research and contributions to medical literature. His influence extended beyond medicine, and he involved himself in state and national politics, becoming a widely known slavery advocate and publishing articles on slave physiology and health.

Born on 30 November 1793 in Fairfax County, Virginia, Cartwright was the son of Rev. John S. Cartwright. His early education focused on Latin and Greek, and by his late teenage years he had begun studying medicine. His medical education was disrupted by his enlistment in the War of 1812. Battlefield injuries left him with a mild deafness that worsened progressively over the rest of his life. After completing his military service, he resumed his studies at the University of Pennsylvania, the first US medical school. Cartwright received additional medical training in Maryland and at Kentucky's Transylvania University. He began practicing medicine in Huntsville, Alabama, and soon moved to Mississippi, practicing briefly in Monroe County in 1822. Within a year he established himself in Natchez, where he practiced for more than a quarter century and earned a reputation as the greatest medical mind in the Old Southwest.

In 1825 Cartwright married Mary Wren of Natchez. He wore many hats in the city and often spoke out regarding the period's divisive politics. Politically, he was an enthusiastic Democrat and helped establish the *Mississippi Statesman and Natchez Gazette*, Mississippi's first Jacksonian newspaper. According to a contemporary journalist, Cartwright could compose "a dissertation on Cayenne Pepper or Democracy with equal facility." He became Natchez's most prominent physician, earning a medical reputation that surpassed even that of his longtime friend, physician-historian John W. Monette. Among other prominent citizens, Cartwright's patients included his friends Jefferson Davis and Gov. John A. Quitman, whom he cared for during his final illness.

Soon after Cartwright's arrival in Natchez, the city suffered a yellow fever epidemic, and other outbreaks occurred through the 1830s. His training in Philadelphia had focused on the theories of Benjamin Rush, then considered the national authority on the disease, and Cartwright's treatment methods, coupled with his scholarly publications examining the epidemics, soon earned him wide acclaim.

As early as 1822 his medical essays began attracting national attention, praise, and prizes. In addition to essays on yellow fever, he published articles on cholera, diphtheria, syphilis, the uses of iodine, surgical removal of ovarian tumors, treatment of rectovaginal fistulas, and a "sugar-house cure of consumption." His successful treatments and observations had great influence both nationally and in Europe. In 1831, for example, Cartwright announced in the *American Journal of Medical Science* a "contrivance" to drain the "thorax of liquids, excluding at the same time the admission of air," and this essay subsequently received notice in the *London Medical Gazette*. He conducted extensive physiologic experiments on alligators, hoping to better understand human physiology, and used the results to develop theories on circulation and respiration. By 1836 his successful and lucrative medical practice allowed him to take his family on an eighteen-month European tour, which he documented in a two-volume diary. In January 1846 Cartwright was elected as first president of the Mississippi State Medical Society, organized in Jackson.

Cartwright focused his writings on the principal diseases of the southern states, and his peers recognized him as a specialist in southern diseases and medicine. His experience and research led him to conclude that the region's climate resulted in different diseases than existed in the North and that southern physicians consequently required different medical training than that provided in northern medical schools. He also stressed that blacks and whites were physiologically different and required different medical approaches. Nineteenth-century southern physicians had long discussed the role of ethnicity in medicine and health, noting decades before the Civil War that many black patients had different disease susceptibilities and medical outcomes than their white neighbors. As the nation drifted toward sectional conflict, doctors often attempted to use these ideas to provide scientific justifications for slavery and black inferiority. Cartwright revealed his racial views in an series of letters to Rev. William Winans published in 1843. Cartwright contended that the relation of master and slave was "not based upon human but Divine law" and concluded that the Bible doomed the "Ethiopian" to be a "servant of servants." Cartwright's extreme racial and prosouthern political views mingled with his medical research into what one contemporary physician-editor, Dr. John Bell of Philadelphia, derided as "States' Rights Medicine."

In the fall of 1848 Cartwright traveled to New Orleans in the midst of a cholera epidemic to study the disease at Charity Hospital and to witness autopsies on the cholera dead. Falling in love with the Crescent City, he decided to relocate his practice there and opened an office on Canal Street. The following year he published a forty-page book, *The Pathology and Treatment of Cholera; with an Appendix Containing His Latest Instructions to Planters and Heads of Families in Regard to Its Prevention and Cure*. At this time he entered his most prolific period of medical writing, publishing articles on diverse medical and surgical matters. However, his writing increasingly centered on the ethnology of disease, specifically the physiology of the "negro race" and the "Ethiopian." In December 1849 the Louisiana State Medical Society appointed Cartwright to chair a committee to study the "Diseases and Physical Peculiarities of the Negro Race." He published this report as a series of controversial articles in the *New Orleans Medical and Surgical Journal* from 1850 to 1853. He coined terms such as *drapetomania* (the "disease causing negroes to run away") and *Dysaesthesia aethiopica* (a condition causing rascality). In 1851 Cartwright was appointed professor of "diseases of the Negro" at the University of Louisiana (now Tulane University). This appointment at a respected medical school reinforced his position as a national authority on black diseases and medicine.

By the time the Civil War erupted, Cartwright's age and poor general health prevented his active service in the Confederate Army. In 1862 he advised his old friend and patient, Confederate president Jefferson Davis, that the Confederacy should utilize slaves as soldiers in place of "our tenderly bred gentlemen." On 31 December 1862 Davis asked Cartwright to serve as surgeon general of the Confederacy's Department of the West, then under the command of Gen. Joseph E. Johnston. By the end of January Cartwright had established himself in Jackson, Mississippi, and begun an extensive inspection of the medical conditions of Johnston's armies, which involved an initial three-month study of the camps and hospitals serving such posts as Vicksburg, Port Hudson, and Grand Gulf. His appointment was not without controversy, with established physician officers of higher rank resenting his broad powers and often refusing to cooperate with his inspections. Despite his frail health and near total deafness, he committed himself fully to his work. While examining camps at Vicksburg, the sixty-nine-year-old physician suddenly took ill, and he died at a private residence near Jackson on 2 May 1863.

Lucius M. Lampton
Magnolia, Mississippi

Samuel A. Cartwright, in *Cotton Is King, and Proslavery Arguments*, ed. E. N. Elliott (1860); Family Papers of Samuel A. Cartwright, Louisiana State University, Baton Rouge; Lucius M. Lampton, *Journal of the Mississippi State Medical Association* (February 2006); Mary Louise Marshall, *Louisiana State Medical Journal* 93 (1940); Ronald L. Numbers and Todd L. Savitt, eds., *Science and Medicine in the Old South* (1989); Kenneth Williams, *American National Biography* (1999).

Cassity, Turner

(1929–2009) Poet

Turner Cassity was a poet whose rigorously formal and wickedly satirical poems take aim at the hubris of human nature. Born 12 January 1929 in Jackson to Allen Cassity and Dorothy Turner Cassity, Allen Turner Cassity grew up around his family's sawmill businesses and in movie theaters, where his mother played piano during silent films. Cassity received a bachelor's degree from Millsaps College in 1951 and a master's degree from Stanford University in 1952. While at Stanford, he learned from poet-critic Yvor Winters to eschew what Winters described as the irrational emotionalism of twentieth-century imagistic free verse and to master traditional poetic forms. After serving in the US Army (1952–54), Cassity earned a master's degree in library science from Columbia University in 1956. Cassity worked at the Jackson Municipal Library (1957–58) and in South Africa at the Transvaal Provincial Library (1959–61) before beginning his long tenure at the Woodruff Library at Emory University in Atlanta (1962–91).

Cassity's poems offer an unusual combination of Winter's classical moral austerity and Wallace Stevens's playfully punning exoticism. Cassity's sardonic wit skewers the persistent folly of human judgment throughout history, from the grandest of human aspirations to conquer the globe to the latest popular culture trends. Among his greatest themes is the role of chance. In "Calvin in the Casino" in his first book, *Watchboy, What of the Night?* (1966), the theologian of divine election says of the roulette ball, "By whose autonomy one apprehends / The limits where predestination ends." In "Why Fortune Is the Empress of the World," from *Hurricane Lamp* (1986), Cassity asks, "What then is human wholly?" Regularity exists in nature, but what characterizes humanity is our reliance not on reason but our turning "to Fortune, as a mindlessness of mind," knowing that "the random that we create creates us." Combining themes of chance, religion, and history in "When in Doubt, Remain in Doubt," from *Between the Chains* (1991), he wrote that Delphi never gave "a competent response. / No oracle does, ever. That is why / Great men consult them. Oracles are doubt / Objectified, but left ambiguous, / So as to force a choice." Here "Harry Truman / Hears exotic dancers speak in tongues. / The meaning is not clear, but just may be / 'Waste not, want not,' of which one must assume / H. heard the first fourth only, as he wastes / Hiroshima and Nagasaki." The predestination that awaits all human vanity is the topic of "WTC," from *No Second Eden* (2002). Cassity's obsession with fate, the ubiquity of self-love and evil, and the ruins of great cultures zeroes in on New York City, 11 September 2001: "Against the best advice, / We put up Babel twice"; as the twin symbols of economic might fall, we realize that we never relinquished the dream of the Tower of Babel or learned its lesson, remaining "unschooled as to response."

Cassity's ten volumes of poetry are represented in *The Destructive Element: New and Selected Poems* (1998). His work garnered numerous awards, among them the Blumenthal-Leviton-Blonder Prize, the Michael Braude Award for Light Verse, and the Levinson Prize.

Turner Cassity died in Atlanta in 2009.

Richard Joines
University of North Texas

Robert L. Barth and Susan Barth, *A Bibliography of Works of Turner Cassity, 1952–1987* (1988); Leon Stokesbury, *The Made Thing: An Anthology of Contemporary Poetry* (1987).

Catalog Shopping

In the 1890s, the US Postal Service established rural free delivery, which brought packages and letters directly to previously isolated farm families. In response, businesses—most notably, Sears, Roebuck, and Company and Montgomery Ward—began mailing catalogs picturing their merchandise to potential customers across the country. The Sears, Roebuck catalog became as much a part of rural life as the Oliver turning plow and the Model T Ford.

The arrival of a new catalog was a noteworthy event. Though families might not have enough money to order all they wanted from the "wish book," particularly during the Great Depression, looking at pictures of new clothes, furniture, appliances, hardware, patent medicine, plow tools, and toys provided a form of entertainment for rural residents in the days before radio, television, and in some cases electricity.

The catalogs included necessities but were especially important in offering large and small luxuries to rural people and bringing them new styles. Farm women learned what was in fashion and could buy fabric, find a dress they liked in the catalog, cut a pattern out of newspaper, and create a garment that looked much like the one featured in the catalog.

The Sears, Roebuck catalog even offered prefabricated homes that could be ordered and then assembled on-site. Many of these houses, which ranged in price from $1,584 for a six-room home to $5,164 for a home ten-room dwelling, remain in use today.

Even outdated catalogs had many uses. The pages could be torn out and used as backing when women pieced string quilts on a sewing machine: when the colorful quilt squares were completed, the paper was torn away and they were stitched together. Children could cut not only paper dolls of all ages from the catalogs but also furniture, dishes, and cooking utensils for the doll families to "use." During the Depression, paper from discarded catalogs was substituted for toilet tissue.

Catalogs could allow African Americans to shop without going deeper into debt—and sometimes facing other indignities—at plantation stores. Shopping through the mail might have seemed impersonal but was preferable to being poorly treated.

Catalog shopping has declined substantially in recent years as a result of a number of factors. The advent of automobiles and paved roads made cities and towns more accessible, while toll-free numbers and the Internet diminished the importance of the mail-order catalog to the general public and to those who live along rural mail routes. Although catalogs continue to exist, they are rapidly moving into that area of Americana that includes the *Farmer's Almanac*, the autograph book, and movie magazines.

Ovid Vickers
East Central Mississippi
Community College

Thomas D. Clark, *Pills, Petticoats, and Plows: The Southern Country Store* (1989); Lizabeth Cohen, *Making A New Deal: Industrial Workers in Chicago, 1919–1939* (1991); James R. Grossman, *Land of Hope: Chicago, Black Southerners, and the Great Migration* (1991); Ted Ownby, *American Dreams in Mississippi: Consumers, Poverty, and Culture, 1830–1998* (1999).

Channel catfish (Photograph by Eric Engbretson, courtesy US Fish and Wildlife Service)

Catfish

The world possesses some two thousand species of catfish, of which two dozen can be found in the United States and about a dozen are native to the South. They can be roughly divided into three types: flathead, channel, and blue catfish. Flatheads and blues weighing upward of 150 pounds have been hauled out of southern waters. People in the South have been eating catfish since time immemorial. They are found in every fishable body of water—farm ponds, streams, lakes, and rivers of all sizes, including the Mississippi.

Catfish are omnivores in the true sense. They will eat practically anything, making them easy to catch with even a chicken liver or a ball of dough. They grow to eighteen inches in a year and if left alone will stay down near the bottom, living to old age and growing to huge size. In the South, Native Americans were first to exploit the fish, followed by Americans of African and European descent, who tended

to cook catfish in one way—bread it in cornmeal and fry it in hot grease in an iron skillet. Because of its omnivorous eating habits and preference for feeding close to the bottom, wild catfish has a strong flavor regardless of how it is prepared.

The time-honored method of skinning a catfish is to nail it to a board or a tree by its head, make a slit around the gills with a knife, break off the dorsal and pectoral fins with pliers, then use the pliers to grasp a loose flap of skin from the incision and peel it down toward the tail like a tight piece of clothing.

Extreme care needs to be exercised when handling catfish. The spines at the tip of a catfish's dorsal and pectoral fins have a venom gland whose secretions can put a human being in severe pain lasting between twenty minutes and a couple of days; hospitalization may be necessary if a fin breaks off in a hand.

The catfish has proven adaptable to aquaculture, and it is the largest-selling farm-raised fish in the United States. Catfish can be easily trained to come to the surface for food, and if they are fed a grain-based aquaculture diet, their flesh has a neutral flavor that takes on the taste of whatever spices are used in its preparation. The lion's share of the North American fish-buying public does not want the fish it consumes to have a strong flavor, and the blandness of farm-raised catfish has been a marketing plus.

Catfish has been a significant form of farming in Mississippi, especially in the Delta, since the late 1960s. Belzoni, the seat of Humphreys County, has sponsored an annual festival since 1976 to celebrate its status as the Catfish Capital of the World. In the late 1980s farmers began catfish production in East Mississippi's Black Prairie—mainly in Noxubee, Lowndes, and Kemper Counties, but catfish production has declined significantly in the twenty-first century.

Until the 1970s, catfish farmers sold their fish directly to restaurants, supermarket chains, and other outlets; local plants subsequently began stunning, beheading, gutting, filleting, and freezing the fish for sale through brokers. Production increased dramatically in the 1980s when automation replaced manual filleting of catfish. As the industry grew, cooperatives, most owned by a hundred or more catfish farmers, helped cut costs and increase profits. The industry has benefited owners as well as workers, especially in the Delta, which has a high poverty rate and double-digit unemployment, and where jobs on catfish farms and processing plants are coveted even though pay is low and benefits are minimal. In 2010 some six hundred union members in Mississippi Delta catfish plants defeated a contract that would have erased gains they won in a 1990 strike. The new, agreed-upon contract offers hope for improved wages and benefits in the future.

Catfish restaurants, most of them specializing in fried catfish, are common throughout Mississippi. Many of them proclaim that they serve Mississippi-raised catfish to differentiate their product from imported fish. Mississippians have long enjoyed local catfish at home as well as in restaurants, and in recent decades they have helped make it a favorite food across the country. "Even cerebral gourmands in restaurants on the Upper East Side of Manhattan and the Sunset Strip of Los Angeles have been extolling the piquant delicacies of Delta catfish," Willie Morris observed in his 2000 book, *My Mississippi*.

Mississippians' longtime enjoyment of catfish is reflected in history, folklore, literature, and music. William Faulkner, Eudora Welty, David L. Cohn, Willie Morris, and countless other Mississippi authors have written about catfish. The first extended fictional portrait of catfish farming appeared in Mississippi Delta native Steve Yarbrough's 1999 novel, *The Oxygen Man*, which tells the story of Ned Rose, who checks oxygen levels in the fish ponds surrounding Indianola. Larry Brown's posthumous novel, *A Miracle of Catfish* (2007), moves aquaculture fiction from the Delta to the hill country of North Mississippi. Central in the novel is Ursula, a forty-pound brooder who lived first in a river and then in a barn in Arkansas, where she served as "a fish factory, a maw-jawed mamaw, endlessly turning in her tank like a soul endlessly assigned to purgatory forever," before being secretly moved to pond near Oxford. There, acting "kind of like a killer whale," Ursula ate little catfish, "scoop[ed] them up in mouthfuls in the shallow end where hundreds of them had gathered to hover in dumb anticipation of nothing," and "was the nightmare fish of small boys and . . . came from the depths of sweaty dreams to suck them and their feeble cane poles from the bank or the boat dock to a soggy grave."

Ann J. Abadie
University of Mississippi

Richard Schweid
Barcelona, Spain

Joseph B. Adkins, *Progressive Populist* (15 November 2010); Catfish Institute website, uscatfish.com/news; Catfish Institute, *Southeast Farm Press* (25 February 2013); "Commercial Catfish Production," Mississippi State University website, http://msucares.com/aquaculture/catfish; Linda Crawford, *Catfish Book* (1991); John Egerton, *Southern Food: At Home, on the Road, in History* (1993); Bruce Halstead, *Poisonous and Venomous Marine Animals of the World* (1988); Terrell R. Hanson, Mississippi History Now website, www.mshistorynow.mdah.statems.us; Michael McCall, *Catfish Journal* (August 1990); *New York Times* (18 July 2008, 31 July 2012); Richard Schweid, *Catfish and the Delta* (1992); *USA Today* (22 June 2008).

Catfish Farming

Catfish farming is the raising of catfish, from eggs to food size, in large, controlled environments. Mississippi was instrumental in the birth and progress of the US farm-raised catfish industry. Mississippians began commercially producing catfish around 1965 for a variety of reasons, including crop diversification, alternative crops for marginally productive lands, and the novelty of growing fish as a crop. Before catfish were produced in ponds, Mississippians supplied their fish needs by either catching their own or buying from commercial fishermen. When wild-caught river catfish could not fill the needs, aquacultured catfish began to fill the excess demand, and over time, many buyers came to prefer the consistent quality and quantity of pond-raised catfish.

In the 1980s and 1990s the catfish industry became one of the most important agricultural activities across the South. Mississippi, Arkansas, Alabama, and Texas are home to 95 percent of all US acreage devoted to catfish production. In the early twenty-first century, the catfish industry was the largest aquaculture industry in the United States, far outstripping trout, the nation's second-largest aquaculture industry. In 2006, Mississippi produced 53 percent of all US catfish sales, and in 2015 the state's farms produced more than twice the catfish of Alabama, the next largest catfish producer.

Catfish production occurs primarily in two regions, with 85 percent of the acreage located in the Delta. The remaining 15 percent is located in the east-central area of the state. The clay content in the soil in these regions allows for good water-retaining ponds. The Delta region has abundant water supplies from shallow aquifers, while East Mississippi catfish producers rely on surface water streams to fill their ponds.

Catfish farming practices have changed over time. Production ponds have shrunk from between twenty and forty acres to between ten and fifteen acres today: management, feeding, and harvesting are easier in smaller ponds. Mechanization of catfish harvesting and loading have proven faster began developing special harvesting boats, nets, and gear, while other companies developed electric- or tractor-powered paddlewheel aerators. The CFA and the state catfish farmers associations of Mississippi, Alabama, Arkansas, and Louisiana helped to introduce these innovations to producers. An annual fish farming trade show started in Greenville to promote and sell machinery, feed, software programs, supplies, and chemicals.

In 1986 the CFA created the Catfish Institute to advertise and market US farm-raised catfish products. By 2000 the success of the industry attracted imports that directly competed with existing processor markets. In a span of eighteen months, frozen "basa" and "tra" fillets from Southeast Asia replaced nearly a quarter of the catfish fillet market previously held by US processors. The US Department of Commerce's International Trade Commission ruled that these substitute products were being sold in the United States below fair market value and levied duties (tariffs) on the major Vietnamese fish importers. To support U.S. aquaculture, in 2004 the US Congress passed the Country of Origin Labeling (COOL) legislation, which requires retailers to mark fish and shellfish products as either farm-raised or wild-caught and identify the country of origin.

The US and Mississippi farm-raised catfish industry has struggled during the last few years, with low selling prices at the wholesale and producer levels and high input costs, primarily for feed and fuel. One result has been a decrease in the amount of Mississippi land devoted to catfish production from 112,000 acres in 2001 to 92,500 acres in 2007 to 37,000 acres in 2015. This decline cost the state more than 5,000 jobs in that period, though Mississippi remains the nation's leader in catfish production.

Terry Hanson
Mississippi State University

Mississippi History Now website, http://mshistorynow.mdah.state.ms.us; Mississippi State University Extension Service website, www.msucares.com; National Agricultural Statistics Service, US Department of Agriculture website, www.nass.usda.gov; C. Tucker and J. Hargreaves, *Biology and Culture of Channel Catfish* (2004); USDA, National Agricultural Statistics Service, Catfish Production (24 July 2015); Jimmy Avery, Terry Hanson, Jim Steelby, "US Farm-Raised Catfish Industry: Production, Processing, and Import Trends" (2013).

Workers prepare to haul a basket of catfish from the sock, where fish are gathered and held overnight before being sent to market (Photograph by Stephen Ausmus, courtesy US Department of Agriculture)

than earlier labor-intensive harvesting techniques, while improvements in aeration technology have increased production. Today, most Mississippi catfish operations sell their fish directly to processing plants and no longer operate retail outlets.

In the early 1970s the Catfish Farmers of America (CFA) and the Catfish Farmers of Mississippi were organized with the help of the state's commissioner of agriculture and commerce, Jim Buck Ross. These groups worked to share ideas, solve industry problems, and present a unified voice when representation of the industry was required. CFA members were instrumental in creating local mills to make special feed for raising catfish. Mississippi State University was the first institution to conduct research on the nutritional requirements of catfish, with researchers determining protein, carbohydrate, energy, vitamin, and amino acid requirements for catfish.

During the 1980s hand filleting of catfish became automated, resulting in an enormous increase in the amount of catfish that could be processed. Service companies also

Catholicism

Catholicism came to what is now Mississippi when the area was being explored and settled by Europeans in the 1600s and 1700s. Natchez became the center of Mississippi's small but growing Catholic population, and in 1837 Pope Gregory XVI established the Diocese of Natchez. It retained that name until 1957, when it became the Diocese of Natchez-Jackson. In 1977, a new Diocese of Biloxi was created, encompassing seventeen counties in the southern part of the state. The original diocese was renamed the Diocese of Jackson, and it now encompasses the largest area of any US diocese east of the Mississippi River.

The first bishop of Natchez, John Mary Joseph Chanche (1840–52), sought to build his rather small congregation as well as a cathedral. His successor, James Oliver Van de Velde (1853–55), continued construction of the cathedral while seeking to resolve property issues and problems. Bishop William Henry Elder (1857–80) was an effective and strongwilled leader whom Union forces accused of being a traitor and forced to leave the diocese for a short time. He went on to bring religious orders to the diocese. Francis August Jannsens (1881–88) was responsible for paying off the cathedral's debts, helping African Americans, and setting up an association of priests. Thomas Heslin (1889–1911) continued his predecessors' policies of building up the diocese. During the tenure of his successor, John Edward Gunn (1911–24), the number of churches in the diocese grew from 75 to 149, reflecting the growth in the number of Catholics in the state from 17,000 to 34,000. Bishop Richard Gerow (1924–67), who served the longest as bishop of the diocese, brought the sacraments to every parish, helped establish St. Augustine's Seminary in Bay St. Louis to train African American priests, and worked to improve the diocese's financial condition. Gerow's successor, Joseph B. Brunini (1968–84), the only native Mississippian to serve as bishop in the state, was a courageous advocate of integration. He oversaw the Natchez diocese's division into the Jackson and Biloxi dioceses and subsequently remained the bishop of Jackson. William Russell Houck (1984–2003) succeeded Brunini and focused on lay ministry and lay leadership. Joseph Nunzio Latino (2003–14) devoted his time in office to social justice initiatives, lay leadership, and vocations. Since 2014, Joseph R. Kopacz has served as bishop of Jackson.

The first bishop of the Diocese of Biloxi was Joseph Lawson Howze (1977–2001), who was also the first African American bishop to head a US diocese in the twentieth century. He was followed by Thomas J. Rodi (2001–8) and Roger Morin (2009–).

In 1842 the Diocese of Natchez laid the cornerstone for St. Mary's Basilica, which is now recognized as an architectural masterpiece among the South's Catholic churches and is a Natchez landmark. It was consecrated on 19 September 1886 and remained the cathedral of the diocese until 1977, when it was replaced by Jackson's Cathedral of St. Peter the Apostle, which was dedicated in 1900. The Diocese of Biloxi's cathedral is the Cathedral of the Nativity of the Blessed Virgin Mary, which was built in 1902.

Throughout the twentieth century, immigrant Irish priests (often comprising around 20 percent of diocesan priests) were most responsible and most visible in demonstrating the Catholic presence in a highly Protestant and not always friendly state. While Mississippi today has fewer Irish clergy, their imprint remains.

Still considered a missionary area and thus receiving financial support from the church outside the state, Mississippi has relied on laity to sustain the church. Laypersons have filled the gaps left by the modern-day priest shortages, serving as apostolic administrators and at times receiving religious training through programs offered by Catholic universities and colleges such as Spring Hill and Notre Dame. Lay organizations and events such as the Knights of Columbus, the Mississippi Lay Conventions, and a host of other traditional Catholic sodalities and societies have assumed growing responsibility for the Catholic Church in the state. Nearly two hundred different religious orders have devoted time, money, and personnel to the missionary diocese of Mississippi. The Sisters of Charity and the Sisters of St. Joseph have been particularly active, as have the Sacred Heart Brothers.

Catholic Mississippi is, in many ways, in the mainstream of the Catholic Church in the American South, and like the church elsewhere, Mississippi's dioceses have confronted numerous problems. Under the direction of Bishop Brunini, Mississippi's Catholic schools integrated with very little violence in 1968–69, almost a year before the state's public schools. Mississippi's Catholics have also endeavored to become more financially independent of outside sources. Holy Family Catholic Church in Natchez, where William J. Morrissey was priest, was a center of that city's civil rights activism. Other challenges have included abuse perpetrated by priests, a few cases of which have occurred in Mississippi, and the damage caused by Hurricanes Camille and Katrina.

Mississippi Catholics still work to reach out to African Americans, Native Americans, and Hispanics in parishes, schools, hospitals, and everyday life. Whether on the coast in the Diocese of Biloxi, where large Catholic centers are clearly visible, or in the Diocese of Jackson, where parishes are smaller and more distant from one another, Mississippi Catholicism is alive and continues to grow. As of 2013, the Diocese of Jackson had 101 parishes and missions serving 52,900 Catholics (2.4 percent of the area's total population), while the Diocese of Biloxi had 53 parishes and missions and 70,630 Catholics (8.3 percent).

Michael V. Namorato
University of Mississippi

Catholic Diocese of Biloxi website, www.biloxidiocese.org; Catholic Diocese of Jackson website, jacksondiocese.org; Michael V. Namorato, *The Catholic Church in Mississippi, 1911–1984: A History* (1998); Charles E. Nolan, *The Catholic Church in Mississippi, 1865–1911* (2002); James J. Pillar, *The Catholic Church in Mississippi, 1837–1865* (1964); Randy J. Sparks,

Religion in Mississippi (2001); St. Mary Basilica Archives website, www .stmarybasilicaarchives.org.

Cattle Tick Eradication

The southern cattle tick was an arachnid that caused considerable damage to livestock in the South and carried a protozoan that caused massive cattle deaths from babesiosis when introduced to northern herds. In 1906 the federal government appropriated money to eradicate the pest by dipping all of a region's cattle, horses, and mules in a vat filled with arsenic every fourteen days during the growing season. Involvement was voluntary, with counties deciding whether to participate.

Farmers and agriculture officials in many counties rejected participation for a variety of reasons. In some counties cattle grazed freely, often in swamps, piney woods, mountains, or other marginal terrain, making it difficult to round them up every two weeks. In addition, many yeoman farmers raised livestock largely for home consumption and saw few benefits to cattle tick and babesiosis eradication. Because participation was so sparse, cleaned areas became reinfected.

For example, Simpson County, Mississippi, on the banks of the Pearl River, was a mainly white county where most of the farms were less than one hundred acres and stock ran free. The county government opposed the program, but in 1913 a local veterinarian presented the board of supervisors with a petition signed by seven hundred citizens who wanted eradication. The board agreed to institute an eradication program if the same number of people did not oppose the proposition, but at the board's next meeting, it received a petition signed by fifteen hundred people "praying the Board not to take up the work."

In 1916, therefore, Mississippi made participation mandatory, passing the country's first statewide tick eradication law. The US government had quarantined the state, and legislators and Governor Theodore Bilbo wanted to eliminate federal involvement. The law went into effect in April 1916, and on 1 December 1917 Mississippi celebrated what Bilbo described as "an epoch in our State": the federal quarantine was lifted and Mississippi was "declared free from the cattle fever tick."

In actuality, however, the state government had achieved only the appearance of success by persuading the US Bureau of Animal Industry to turn the work over to state and local officials. Thus, individual herds and regions of Mississippi counties remained infested and under state quarantine even though the federal restrictions had been removed. Consider-able infestation remained, and federal inspectors returned by 1919.

Bilbo had made a tactical error in implementing mandatory dipping, failing to realize that opposition to the program would be concentrated among poor white farmers, who also constituted his base of support. He sought to make amends by focusing on the lifting of federal quarantine and by minimizing the effects of the tick law. He ran for the US House of Representatives in 1918 against Judge Paul B. Johnson, who had consistently opposed mandatory dipping. Bilbo lost the election and later said that he had been "crucified on a cross of ticks."

Stone County protested mandatory dipping via the Mississippi Budget Law of 1923, under which each county's board of supervisors drafted a budget each September for the following year. Under Section 6 of the law, if a majority of resident taxpayers petitioned for the removal of any item, the expense had to be struck, and Stone County residents forced the removal of the money budgeted for tick eradication. The state retaliated by taking the county to court; although the state won, the victory required the court to declare Section 6 unconstitutional. Consequently, enforcement of the statewide law was achieved only by reducing grassroots power.

Other opponents of dipping fought back violently. In the early 1920s dipping virtually reached a standstill in Amite County because foes dynamited the dipping vats, and enforcement efforts led to gun battles. To control the situation, federal inspectors leased 240 acres about ten miles outside Liberty, right in the middle of the dynamited area, and established an armed camp to treat livestock. Black laborers were hired to clear the underbrush and trees but faced threats from local farmers, so most of the work fell to the range riders. Living in tents, these men erected corrals to hold the livestock and mounted machine guns on the dipping vats. They always traveled in threes, with one man armed with a rifle and watching for ambush.

The cattle tick was finally eradicated, and Mississippi was released from federal quarantine in the late 1920s. The elimination of the cattle tick and babesiosis certainly helped the state's farmers establish a more profitable dairy and beef industry. However, the need for universal compliance meant that the program infringed on individual and local rights, reducing yeoman power at the expense of the state and federal governments.

Claire Strom
Rollins College

Chester M. Morgan, *Redneck Liberal: Theodore G. Bilbo and the New Deal* (1985); Claire Strom, *Making Catfish Bait out of Government Boys: The Fight against Cattle Ticks and the Transformation of the Yeoman South* (2010); US Department of Agriculture Records, National Archives and Records Administration II, College Park, Md.

Cemeteries, Union and Confederate

At the outset of the Civil War few people could have foreseen the enormous death toll that would result from four years of conflict. Men on both sides died from battlefield wounds, disease, illness, and infection. From the earliest months of the war, the disposal of bodies presented a challenge. Some remains were claimed by relatives and interred in family burial grounds or local cemeteries. As the war wore on and the number of deaths increased, mass burials took place near battlefields, field hospitals, and encampments. Sometimes these interments were swift, haphazard affairs, occurring during cease-fires precipitated by the stench of exposed corpses. At least one such interlude occurred during the Siege of Vicksburg.

Although embalming became common in northern culture during the war as an expedient means of preserving bodies long enough to send them home, most Federal soldiers who died were buried permanently in the South. However, their remains were likely moved after the war ended—an estimated three hundred thousand Union dead were exhumed from their original resting places and reinterred in newly established national cemeteries, including the ones at Corinth, Natchez, and Vicksburg, Mississippi. Corinth National Cemetery was originally created to accommodate Union dead from battles in northeastern Mississippi, particularly Corinth and Iuka, but it eventually received remains from scattered battles and skirmishes, camp sites, and hospitals from Alabama and Tennessee as well as Mississippi. By late 1870, when the reinterment program was nearly finished, Corinth had received 5,688 remains representing 273 regiments from 15 states. Natchez National Cemetery, also begun in 1866, received the remains of more than 3,000 Union soldiers, collected initially from a fifty-mile-wide radius around Natchez in Louisiana and Mississippi. A number of these were naval personnel, including one seaman, Wilson Brown, who won

Confederate cemetery, Natchez (Photograph by David Wharton)

the Medal of Honor for heroism during the assault on Mobile Bay on 5 May 1864.

By far the largest Federal cemetery in Mississippi was established on a portion of the Vicksburg battlefield in 1865 and opened for burials the next year. Soldiers interred there had originally been buried in a variety of locales in Arkansas, Louisiana, and Mississippi; some had died during engagements at Chickasaw Bayou, Grand Gulf, Jackson, and Meridian as well as during the Siege of Vicksburg. More than 17,000 Union soldiers repose in the Vicksburg National Cemetery, but as a consequence of poor record keeping and the often-hurried burials during the war, 75 percent of them are unidentified. Two Confederates were mistakenly buried in the Vicksburg National Cemetery, while three rest in the Corinth National Cemetery.

An expanse designated as Soldiers' Rest in Vicksburg's Cedar Hill Cemetery (also known as Vicksburg City Cemetery) contains the largest single group of Confederate dead buried in Mississippi. The Confederate government employed a local undertaker, J. Q. Arnold, to bury soldiers who died of illness and wounds at Vicksburg. Although Arnold kept meticulous records, assigning each deceased soldier a grave number, his list and map of the cemetery vanished after Vicksburg fell in July 1863. A portion of his list was discovered nearly a century later, allowing the United Daughters of the Confederacy and the Veterans Administration to mark 1,600 of the graves, but approximately 3,500 remain unknown.

Elsewhere in the state, deceased soldiers hailing from not only Mississippi but virtually every state in the Confederacy are interred in an array of spots: in family plots, in church graveyards and city cemeteries, and near the sites of Civil War hospitals, camps, and battlefields. Unlike their Federal counterparts, Confederates were not typically exhumed unless relatives retrieved the remains and took them home. One exception occurred in Prentiss County, where citizens sought to find all the Confederate dead, placed them in new coffins, and laid them to rest in the Citizens' Cemetery at Booneville. In 1904 Prof. R. W. Jones of the University of Mississippi published results of a questionnaire he sent to county chancery clerks seeking information on local Confederate cemeteries and monuments. He received replies for thirty-two counties indicating considerable numbers of Confederate dead buried near what had been wartime hospitals—in Columbus, Grenada, Holly Springs, Jackson, Newton, Okolona, and Woodville and on the University of Mississippi campus. Sizable numbers of soldiers were interred in Amite, Brandon, Canton, Corinth, Hernando, Iuka, Macon, and Magnolia Counties as well as in three cemeteries in Lauderdale County. Men killed during train accidents during the war had been interred along the right of way in Newton County and at Duck Hill.

Union soldiers hurriedly buried large numbers of Confederate dead in trenches, like those constructed after several battles during the Vicksburg Campaign. By the time Jones made his inquiries, these areas had become so neglected that there was "not the slightest trace to indicate their resting place," although an August 1911 issue of *Confederate Veteran* magazine contains a photograph of a May 1910 gathering at the Confederate Cemetery in Raymond. In an era where death generally occurred at home and evoked powerful cultural expressions, the grief attendant to losing a relative in service was heightened when mourning relatives had no way to ascertain their loved ones' final resting places. One probable impetus for gathering Union dead in the newly established national cemeteries was to provide at least some reassurance to northern mourners that their deceased relative was likely in a carefully tended locale among comrades. Southern families received no such reassurance, and this calamity struck both Mississippians (whose dead often were buried in distant locales) and residents of other Confederate states whose sons lie anonymously in graves throughout Mississippi.

Christopher T. Losson
St. Joseph, Missouri

Dean W. Holt, *American Military Cemeteries: A Comprehensive Illustrated Guide to the Hallowed Grounds of the United States, Including Overseas Cemeteries* (1992); R. W. Jones, in *Publications of the Mississippi Historical Society* 8 (1904); Gary Laderman, *The Sacred Remains: American Attitudes toward Death, 1799–1883* (1996); Vicksburg National Military Park website, www.nps.gov/vick.

Center for Oral History and Cultural Heritage

The Center for Oral History was founded at the University of Southern Mississippi in 1971. This unit, primarily staffed by history professors such as Neil R. McMillen and Kenneth McCarty, began by recording the life stories of individuals who had lived through and participated in the civil rights movement. This endeavor blossomed into a larger effort that included capturing the oral histories of a wide range of Mississippians, from the famous to ordinary citizens. Though its budget and staff remained small throughout its first two decades of existence, the center demonstrated its worth by capturing and archiving the stories of Mississippi's most famous politicians, writers, and journalists as well as its unsung heroes and little-known citizens, thereby providing the public with unlimited access to these stories.

This public access has made the center the place of choice for those doing research on any number of topics related to Mississippi—the timber industry; quilt making; foodways; blues music; the lives of veterans of World Wars I and II, the Vietnam War, and both Gulf Wars and the Afghanistan War. By the early 1990s the center had evolved into a freestanding unit at the University of Southern Mississippi and changed its name to the Center for Oral History and Cultural Heritage, reflecting its new vision and mission. Under the leadership of Mississippi native and Southern Miss graduate Charles Bolton, who arrived as director in 1990, the center embarked on a number of ambitious projects. One of the most successful of these projects has been the Mississippi Oral History Program (MOHP).

With funding from the Mississippi legislature, through the Mississippi Department of Archives and History and the Mississippi Humanities Council, the Center for Oral History and Cultural Heritage created the MOHP to record the voices of Mississippians from all walks of life and to encourage communities to document their local histories. This funding provided grants to the communities, offered staff time for technical assistance, and helped support the facility where those histories are preserved and made available to the public. The MOHP captured national attention in the spring of 2001, when National Public Radio came to Mississippi to do a retrospective on thirty years of change in the state and featured the program as a positive and creative state effort. MOHP projects have been featured in numerous books and popular and scholarly articles as well as incorporated into theatrical productions, museum exhibits, film documentaries, and K–12 curricula across the state.

The MOHP has conducted projects from Lee County and Starkville in Northeast Mississippi through the Delta region and all along Mississippi's Gulf Coast. The directors of these projects then put on public programs to demonstrate how these oral histories were essential to understanding the many changes and advances that had taken place in the state. Highlighting the lives of individuals such as John C. Robinson, a Gulfport resident and former head of the Haile Selassie's Ethiopian Air Force who helped to train the Tuskegee Airmen, these projects became a staple of the center's operation.

The Center for Oral History and Cultural Heritage continued under the leadership and direction of historian Curtis Austin, a native of Yazoo City and a graduate of the University of Southern Mississippi. With resources taken from the MOHP, Austin put together a CD-ROM and timeline, *Ordinary People Living Extraordinary Lives: The Civil Rights Movement in Mississippi*, that teachers use to educate grade school students in the history of the movement. In 2003 Stephen Sloan arrived as assistant director and later codirector and helped create *Mississippi Moments*, a radio program that used MOHP interviews to tell the story of the Magnolia State through four-minute vignettes. The Center for Oral History and Cultural Heritage was later led by Louis Kyriakoudes and then codirected by Kevin Greene and Heather Stur.

By 2016 the MOHP's collection numbered in the thousands and included the Hurricane Katrina Project, Mississippi Nurses Association Project, Mississippi Supreme Court Oral History Project, John C. Stennis National Aeronautics and Space Center Project, Choctaw Band of Mississippi Indians Project, and Madison County Oral History Project. Today the MOHP serves as a national and international model of an oral history program that is responsive to a growing and constantly changing community.

Curtis J. Austin
Ohio State University

Mississippi Oral History Program, University of Southern Mississippi, website, www.usm.edu/msoralhistory/.

Barnard Observatory, the home of the Center for the Study of Southern Culture at the University of Mississippi (Photograph by James G. Thomas, Jr.)

Center for the Study of Southern Culture

Established in 1977 at the University of Mississippi with funding from the National Endowment for the Humanities (NEH), the Center for the Study of Southern Culture (CSSC) was initially proposed by history professor Robert Haws and philosophy professor Michael Harrington, who suggested creating a place where scholars would study the South's literature, history, and music with a specific focus on race relations. The university's vice chancellor for academic affairs, Art DeRosier, and chancellor, Porter L. Fortune Jr., supported the proposal, and folklorist William R. Ferris, a Vicksburg native, became the center's founding director, serving from 1978 to 1998. Charles Reagan Wilson followed Ferris, holding the position through 2007, and Ted Ownby became director the following year.

The CSSC's first program was the 1977 Eudora Welty Symposium, which featured the Mississippi author in person. An interdisciplinary program working with university departments and faculty, including anthropology and sociology, English, history, literature, art, and political science, the center offers more than sixty courses covering life, culture, and heritage in the American South. Although it began with a focus on southern US culture and history as a microcosm of the American experience, the CSSC has broadened its scope to encompass the future of southern culture, the global South, and challenges to long-held conceptions of what is southern. The CSSC found a physical home on the university campus in the historic Barnard Observatory, built in the late 1850s and renovated in 1989–91.

One of the first regional centers in the nation, the CSSC, with an NEH grant, developed a bachelor of arts program in southern studies and a master of arts program that accommodates about thirty students from around the world. Awards are presented to students for excellence in research papers on the South, with special prizes for the best master's theses and works on music and documentary media. The Gammill Gallery in Barnard Observatory displays the work of students and teachers as well as visiting collections from across the nation. Much of the center's research is housed in the Department of Special Collections and Archives at the university's J. D. Williams Library. The CSSC began the Southern Media Collection, now housed in the library's visual archive, and the Blues Archive, the largest public blues collection in the world.

The CSSC's work led to the creation of several affiliated institutions, such as the Southern Foodways Alliance, which holds its annual Southern Foodways Symposium on the university campus each fall, and the William Winter Institute for Racial Reconciliation. The center has also partnered with the university's Southern Documentary Project and has published several periodicals, most successfully *Living Blues*, a magazine devoted to blues musicians and the culture that produced them, founded in 1983. The CSSC helped establish *Highway 61*, a blues program on Mississippi Public Radio, with Ferris as the first host. Wilson and Ferris edited the *Encyclopedia of Southern Culture* (1989), which won the Dartmouth Prize from the American Library Association as the year's best reference work. From 2006 to 2013, the CSSC produced the twenty-four-volume *New Encyclopedia of Southern Culture*. Other CSSC publications include Dorothy Abbott's multivolume *Mississippi Writers* (1985–91) and the online journal *Study the South*.

The CSSC is recognized for its worldwide symposia and conferences, including a Richard Wright conference in Paris and a William Faulkner conference in Moscow. The University of Mississippi campus in Oxford hosts most conferences, however, including the Faulkner and Yoknapatawpha Conference, the Oxford Conference for the Book, the Southern Foodways Symposium, the Future of the South Conference, the Blues Today Symposium, and a weekly lecture series. Funding for the center's projects has come from the National Endowment for the Humanities, the Mississippi Arts Commission, the Mississippi Humanities Council, the Ford Foundation, the Phil Hardin Foundation, and Friends of the Center. An advisory committee has assisted the CSSC's work since its beginning.

Anna F. Kaplan
Columbia University

Marie Antoon and Tom Rieland, *The Center for the Study of Southern Culture* (film, 1984); Blues Archive, University of Mississippi Libraries, website, http://www.olemiss.edu/depts/general_library/archives/blues/; Center for the Study of Southern Culture website, www.olemiss.edu/depts/south; David Sansing, *The University of Mississippi: A Sesquicentennial History* (1999).

Chalmers, James Ronald

(1831–1898) Confederate General and Politician

James Ronald Chalmers was born in Halifax County, Virginia, on 11 January 1831. In 1839 his family moved to Holly Springs, Mississippi, where Chalmers was educated at St. Thomas Hall. Chalmers graduated from South Carolina College in 1851, then returned to Holly Springs, read law, and was admitted to the bar in 1853. He became district attorney in 1858, served as a delegate to Mississippi's secession convention, and then raised a military company when the Civil War began. Entering the Confederate Army as a captain, he was soon appointed colonel of the 9th Mississippi Infantry and first saw action near Pensacola, Florida. Promoted to brigadier general on 13 February 1862 on the recommendation of Gen. Braxton Bragg, Chalmers distinguished himself at Shiloh, where his brigade held the far right of the Confederate line on the first day of the battle.

He assumed command of cavalry operating in northern Mississippi before returning to his brigade in time to take part in Bragg's 1862 invasion of Kentucky. Chalmers led an ill-advised assault on a Union garrison near Munfordville but redeemed himself at Stones River, Tennessee, where on 31 December 1862 he led his men against a formidable Federal position. A shell fragment knocked Chalmers down and he was "borne senseless from the field," according to his divisional commander. The blow terminated Chalmers's career as an infantry officer. In March 1863 he received command of the 5th Military District, with responsibility over the northern counties of Mississippi. Chalmers organized a cavalry force and sparred with Federal detachments that made expeditions into the region.

At the beginning of 1864 Chalmers's division was assigned to Gen. Nathan Bedford Forrest's command. Relations between the two officers were occasionally strained, and Chalmers may have felt that his services merited promotion instead of a subordinate position under Forrest. Chalmers was present during the controversial April 1864 attack on a garrison of black soldiers and Tennessee Unionists at Fort Pillow, Tennessee. The high death rate among the black troops led to charges that a massacre took place, although Chalmers's role remains unclear. According to his report, the Federals refused to surrender, and many were killed while attempting to escape. Chalmers was with Forrest during a successful raid into West Tennessee as well as during John Bell Hood's invasion that culminated in disastrous battles at Franklin and Nashville. The two generals and their troops retreated to Mississippi and ended the war in Alabama, where Chalmers surrendered and was paroled in May 1865.

After the war, Chalmers moved to Friars Point, Mississippi, and married Rebecca Arthur, with whom he had one daughter. He resumed his law practice and became a controversial political figure. In 1876 he led an armed force of white men against freedmen near Friars Point and drove their leader, the sheriff, out of the county. Chalmers served two terms in the US House of Representatives but was defeated in his 1880 reelection bid by Republican John R. Lynch, an African American. Disgruntled by what he took to be lack of support from US Sen. L. Q. C. Lamar, Chalmers bolted the Democratic Party in 1882 and returned to Congress with Republican support after a campaign marked by allegations of fraud on both sides. His congressional career ended with a defeat by a Democratic opponent in 1884, after which he abandoned politics, moved to Memphis, and practiced law until his death on 9 April 1898.

Christopher Losson
St. Joseph, Missouri

Dictionary of American Biography (rev. ed., 1957–58); Jack Hurst, *Nathan Bedford Forrest: A Biography* (1993); Terry Jones, in *The Confederate General*, ed. William C. Davis, vol. 1 (1991); Thomas Jordan and J. P. Pryor, *The Campaigns of Lieut.-Gen. N. B. Forrest and of Forrest's Cavalry* (1868; reprint, 1996); *The National Cyclopedia of American Biography* (1906); Ezra Warner, *Generals in Gray: Lives of the Confederate Commanders* (1959).

Chamani, Miriam (Mary Robin Adams)

(b. 1943) Religious Leader

Priestess Miriam Chamani is one of the most prominent voodoo queens in contemporary New Orleans. She has been providing spiritual services to the New Orleans community since she moved with her husband, Priest Oswan Chamani, to New Orleans in 1990 to found the Voodoo Spiritual Temple. Since her husband's death in 1995, Miriam has overseen the New Orleans Voodoo Spiritual Temple and Cultural Center, where she provides readings, rituals, and other spiritual services. The Temple, located in the French Quarter across from the entrance to Armstrong Park, focuses on West African spiritual and herbal healing.

Born to sharecroppers in Pocahontas, Mississippi, on 8 March 1943, Mary Robin Adams took on the mantle Priestess Miriam when she began her spiritual work away from her home state. Raised deeply Baptist in post–World War II rural Mississippi, she showed an early inclination toward religiosity, as her family remembers her speaking to spirits as a child. To escape the harsh Jim Crow–era South, she left to work in New York as a domestic in 1962, only four days after graduating from high school.

After working as a housekeeper in New York for several years, Miriam moved to Chicago and began a nursing program in the fall of 1966. There, she was introduced to the Spiritual Church, which incorporated voodoo as well as Protestant, Catholic, and Native American religious components. Miriam became involved with Angel Angel All Nations Spiritual Church on Chicago's South Side, and she was ordained and served as a bishop there from 1982 to 1989.

In 1989 Miriam met Oswan Chamani, a priest of obeah, an Afro-American folk magic and belief system of his native Belize. Obeah, like voodoo, Santeria, and Shango, has roots as a form of resistance in New World African slave cultures. Miriam and Osman soon left Chicago for New Orleans and married in 1990. They performed divination readings at Marie Laveau's House of Voodoo and were involved with the New Orleans Historic Voodoo Museum before establishing the Voodoo Spiritual Temple. Temple gatherings took place in Miriam and Oswan's living room until 1994, when the Temple opened its current location on Rampart Street. Priest Oswan died in 1995, but not before he had shared with Miriam his extensive knowledge of herbs used for spiritual and physical healing, which she continues to utilize at the Voodoo Spiritual Temple.

Priestess Miriam has linked her medical training with her spiritual preparation, noting that Marie Laveau used her pharmacological knowledge of herbs both in her work nursing the sick during yellow fever outbreaks and in providing spiritual services. Priestess Miriam combines her medical knowledge, her Spiritual Church training, and the spiritual and herbal healing techniques she learned from her husband to serve those who visit the Voodoo Spiritual Temple. She holds readings and consultations at the Temple and performs rituals in the courtyard. Priestess Miriam often gives interviews with the news and entertainment media and has advised on voodoo practices for Hollywood films such as *The Skeleton Key* (2005).

Brooke Butler
New Orleans, Louisiana

Hans A. Baer, *The Black Spiritual Movement: A Religious Response to Racism* (2nd ed. 2001); Toni Costonie, *Priestess Miriam and the Voodoo Spiritual Temple: A Brief History* (2004); Toni Costonie, *A Voodoo Queen in New Orleans: The Story of Priestess Miriam and the Voodoo Spiritual Temple* (2006); Carolyn Morrow Long, *Spiritual Merchants: Religion, Magic, and Commerce* (2001); Anthony Pinn, *Varieties of African American Religious Experience* (1998).

Champion Hill, Battle of

In 1861 Abraham Lincoln stated emphatically, "Vicksburg is the key. The war can never be brought to a close until that key is in our pocket." For both the United States and the Confederacy, Vicksburg was a strategic focal point from the outset of the Civil War. Situated on a large bluff overlooking the Mississippi River, Vicksburg controlled the river. Lincoln and his generals knew that if they could wrest Vicksburg from the Confederates, they could control river traffic and effectively split the Confederacy in two. Likewise, the Confederates realized that holding Vicksburg was essential to their war effort. An attempt by the Federals to take the city in 1862 failed, but Ulysses S. Grant moved on Vicksburg again the following year. The decisive battle of the 1863 Vicksburg Campaign was fought on and around ground known as Champion Hill, a rise named for the Champion family, who were local property owners.

Grant moved twenty-three thousand Federal troops down the western bank of the Mississippi River and on 30 April 1863 crossed the river into Mississippi at Bruinsburg, well below his intended target. The Federals moved steadily northeast toward Jackson. John C. Pemberton, the Confederate general in charge of the region, had thirty thousand troops at his disposal, but they were scattered in various detachments around the state and consequently would provide little impediment to the Federals' progress. The Union won victories against Confederate commands at Port Gibson and Raymond before capturing the state capital on 14 May. With Jackson secure, the Federals turned their full attention toward Vicksburg, moving on the port city from the east. With the addition of troops who had been operating in North Mississippi under William Tecumseh Sherman, Grant had more than forty thousand men at his disposal.

Union and Confederate troops clashed in the largest and most important battle of the Vicksburg Campaign on 16 May at Champion Hill, near Edward's Station, about halfway between Jackson and Vicksburg. There Grant concentrated twenty-nine thousand men against twenty-three thousand under Pemberton. Grant's men were organized into two corps, commanded by John A. McClernand and James B. McPherson. Pemberton's command was made up of three divisions under John S. Bowen, Carter L. Stevenson, and William W. Loring. Early on 16 May Pemberton deployed his men. At about 10:30 in the morning Grant launched an all-out assault on the Confederate positions. During several hours of bitter fighting, Champion Hill changed hands three times. The outnumbered Confederates eventually lost the field and by 5:00 that evening were in full retreat, leaving behind twenty-seven cannons and hundreds of prisoners. The Confederates suffered 3,840 casualties, compared to 2,441 for the Union. While covering the Confederate retreat, Loring's division was cut off and forced to move east toward Crystal Springs. The bulk of the Confederate Army fell back to the west and eventually entered Vicksburg. Grant's troops followed and, after a forty-seven-day siege, Pemberton surrendered the city on 4 July 1863.

Ben Wynne
Gainesville State College

Edwin C. Bearss, *The Campaign for Vicksburg* (1986); Richard Wheeler, *The Siege of Vicksburg* (1978).

Chatmon Family and the Mississippi Sheiks

The Mississippi Sheiks, a loosely organized, family-based musical group, were the most renowned and commercially successful African American string band of the 1930s. Based in Jackson, the band included at least three members of the large Chatmon (sometimes spelled Chatman) clan, several of whom figured prominently in the history of Mississippi blues, including brothers Lonnie (1888–?) Armenter (1893–1964), and Sam Chatmon (1897–1983). Between 1930 and 1935 the Mississippi Sheiks recorded an extensive collection of country blues, waltzes, fox-trots, pop songs, and hokum numbers, including their most famous song, "Sitting on Top of the World" (composed by band member Walter Vincson), now considered a blues classic.

The Chatmon family hailed from the hill country around Bolton, Mississippi, roughly halfway between Jackson and Vicksburg, where their neighbors included fellow bluesmen Charley Patton and Charlie and Joe McCoy. The family patriarch, Henderson Chatmon (1850–1934), fathered at least thirteen children, most of whom learned to play musical instruments. Around World War I, seven of the nine sons formed a string band, the Chatmon Brothers, and performed for both black and white audiences at square dances and social gatherings around Bolton. Lonnie Chatmon, the group's leader, was a superb dance fiddler. Other members of the band included Armenter "Bo" Chatmon, who played clarinet and guitar, and Sam Chatmon, who played second violin. One of their neighbors, gifted singer and guitarist Walter Vincson (also known by the surnames Vinson, Vincent, and Jacobs), also performed with the band. The band played together until around 1928, when several of the brothers relocated, first to Hollandale and in the early 1930s to Jackson, then an important regional blues center.

After the breakup, Lonnie Chatmon and Vincson continued to play together, and in 1929 Ralph Lembo, a white Itta Bena record dealer, arranged their first recording session. In February 1930 Lonnie and Bo Chatmon and Vincson made their first records together for OKeh's field-recording unit in Shreveport, Louisiana. This session produced the band's biggest-selling hits, "Sitting on Top of the World" and "Stop and Listen Blues." The trio dubbed themselves the Mississippi Sheiks at Vincson's suggestion, allegedly from the title of Rudolph Valentino's 1921 blockbuster film, *The Sheik*.

Over the next five years the Mississippi Sheiks recorded more than eighty sides for a series of record labels, including OKeh, Columbia, and Bluebird. Band members simultaneously pursued solo recording careers and accompanied other blues groups at recording sessions. Lonnie Chatmon (violin) and Vincson (guitar and lead vocals) formed the core of the studio band, often accompanied by Bo Chatmon (guitar and violin) and occasionally joined by Sam Chatmon (guitar and violin) and Charlie McCoy (banjo and mandolin). Members of the band also recorded in various other combinations under such names as Walter Jacobs and the Carter Brothers, Chatman's Mississippi Hot Footers, the Mississippi Mud Steppers, the Down South Boys, and the Chatman Brothers. Outside the studio the Mississippi Sheiks performed with a large revolving ensemble of musicians, including other Chatmon brothers and various Jackson bluesmen. The band toured widely, performing throughout Mississippi, Louisiana, Tennessee, and Georgia and reportedly as far away as Illinois and New York.

The Mississippi Sheiks' recordings featured a wide range of vernacular music that borrowed heavily from both Anglo- and African American musical traditions. They recorded country blues ("West Jackson Blues"), party blues ("Driving That Thing"), hokum numbers ("She Ain't No Good"), and pop-oriented numbers ("Lonely One in This Town"). The band also cut topical numbers, such as "Jake Leg Blues," a commentary on the 1930 jake leg epidemic that paralyzed drinkers of adulterated Jamaica ginger during Prohibition. Their repertoire revealed a sophisticated familiarity with current hillbilly and race records. "Yodeling Fiddling Blues" and "Jail Bird Love Song," for example, reflect the influence of fellow Mississippian Jimmie Rodgers. Indeed, several of the band's recordings, including "The Sheik Waltz" and "The Jazz Fiddler," were issued as part of OKeh's Old Time Tunes series, which was marketed chiefly to white southern record buyers.

Although the Mississippi Sheiks' recording contract expired in 1935, several members of the band continued to make records until the advent of World War II. Bo Chatmon in particular enjoyed a distinguished career as a solo blues artist. Under the pseudonym Bo Carter, he recorded more than one hundred sides between 1928 and 1940, most of them bawdy, double-entendre party blues. In 1972, during the urban folk revival, Vincson and Sam Chatmon collaborated on an album for Rounder Records under the name the New Mississippi Sheiks and performed together at the Smithsonian Festival of American Folklife in Washington, D.C.

Although the band recorded together for only six years, the Mississippi Sheiks exerted a significant influence on American popular music, and partly as a result of Vincson and Sam Chatmon's revived professional careers, a new generation of musicians and music fans discovered their music. "Sitting on Top of the World," their biggest hit, became a Delta blues classic before World War II, and Howlin' Wolf scored an R&B hit with his electrified version of the song in 1957. Other artists who have covered this song include Cream, Bill Monroe, Bob Wills, Lonnie Johnson, Ray Charles, and the Grateful Dead. Bob Dylan also covered two Mississippi Sheiks' songs, "The World Is Going Wrong" and "I've Got Blood in My Eyes for You," on his 1993 album, *World Gone Wrong*.

Patrick Huber
Missouri University of Science
and Technology

Stephen Calt, Don Kent, and Michael Stewart, *Mississippi Sheiks: Stop and Listen* (2006), liner notes; Stephen Calt and Gayle Wardlow, *King of the Delta Blues: The Life and Music of Charlie Patton* (1988); Lawrence Cohn, *Honey Babe Let the Deal Go Down: The Best of the Mississippi Sheiks* (2004), liner notes; Chris Smith, *Mississippi Sheiks: The Complete Recorded Works in Chronological Order*, vols. 1–4 (1991), liner notes.

Chaze, Elliot

(1915–1990) Author

Lewis Elliot Chaze devoted his career in journalism to exploring issues facing Mississippians and his energy as a novelist to imagining life experiences both inside and outside the American South. Born on 15 November 1915 in Mamou, Louisiana, Elliot was the son of Lewis Ernest and Sue Grigsby Chaze. He graduated from Bolton High School in Alexandria, Louisiana, in 1932 and attended Washington and Lee University in Lexington, Virginia, from 1932 to 1934 before transferring to Tulane University in 1935. The following year, Chaze went to Oklahoma University, graduating in 1937 with a bachelor's degree in journalism.

Chaze found his first job in journalism as a news editor with the Associated Press in New Orleans from 1941 to 1943. He served in US Army as a technical sergeant with the 11th Airborne Division during World War II, remaining in Japan while American troops occupied the country. Chaze returned to the United States in 1946 and became a news editor with the Associated Press in Denver. Five years later, he returned to the South to begin a job as a reporter at the *Hattiesburg American*. Chaze remained at the newspaper for the rest of his career, earning a promotion to city editor in 1970 before retiring in 1980.

Chaze penned nine novels and a book of essays, using his writings to explore journalism, the suspense genre, crime, and the American South. Chaze's fiction pulled directly from his own diverse experiences. His first novel, *The Stainless Steel Kimono* (1947), tells the story of seven American paratroopers in Japan after the end of World War II. *The Golden Tag* (1950) narrates the life of a young journalist in New Orleans, while *Black Wings Has My Angel* (1953) depicts an armored car robbery in Colorado. A decade later, Chaze authored his fourth book, an essay collection, *Two Roofs and a Snake on the Door* (1963). During the height of Chaze's career as reporter for the *Hattiesburg American*, he wrote two novels, *Tiger in the Honeysuckle* (1965) and *Wettermark* (1969), both of which chronicle the lives of young newspaper reporters in Mississippi. His last three novels, published after his retirement from the newspaper, continue to engage material from Chaze's life. *Goodbye Goliath* (1983) portrayed the politics in a small Alabama newspaper office after the murder of a tyrannical general manager. Also in this period, Chaze published both *Mr. Yesterday* (1984) and *Little David* (1985). Chaze's writings won several awards, including the Fawcett Gold Medal Paperback Award for *Black Angel Has My Wings*. Explaining his motivation for writing, Chaze once commented, "My motivation, if there is any discernible, is probably ego and fear of mathematics, with overtones of money. Primarily I have a simple desire to shine my ass—to show off a bit."

Chaze and his wife, Mary Vincent Chaze, had five children. He died following a brief illness in Hattiesburg on 11 November 1990.

Frances Abbott
Digital Public Library of America,
Boston

James B. Lloyd, ed., *Lives of Mississippi Authors, 1817–1967* (1981).

Chicago, Black Mississippians in

Between 1910 and 1950 Chicago was the crossroads of northern urbanity. The first mass movement of black southerners to northern cities occurred during and immediately after World War I. Participants in this Great Migration left their southern homes but brought with them, as Mississippi native Richard Wright notes in his 1945 autobiography *Black Boy*, the "scars, visible and invisible," of southern boyhood. Wright was both fascinated and intimidated by his move north. "I was seized by doubt," he recalled of the moment he walked out of the railroad station in Chicago. "Should I have come here? But going back was impossible. I had fled a known terror, and perhaps I could cope with this unknown terror that lay ahead."

Wright wrote that, on the one hand, Chicago was the quintessential "self-conscious" and "known" city; on the other, it was the place where the contemporary facts of African American experience took "their starkest form [and] crudest manifestation." Wright stressed, "There is an open and raw beauty about that city that seems either to kill or endow one with the spirit of life. I felt those extremes of possibility, death and hope, while I lived half hungry and afraid in a city to which I had fled . . . to tell my story."

Most migrants were barely literate and never left such vivid recollections of their experience. Yet black southerners "recognized that their future lay in the North." "Northern fever" permeated the black South, as letters, rumors, gossip, and black newspapers carried word of higher wages and better treatment in the North. Approximately half a million black southerners chose to say farewell to the South and start life anew in northern cities during 1916–19, and nearly one million more followed in the 1920s. From the cities, towns, and farms of the Deep South, especially Mississippi, they poured into any northern city where jobs could be found.

Stepping off the trains, African American migrants flocked to Chicago's South Side neighborhoods. In 1910, 78 percent of black Chicagoans lived in a narrow strip of South Side land known as the Black Belt. From 1916 until 1948, racially restrictive covenants kept other Chicago neighborhoods white. These covenants covered large parts of the city and, in combination with zones of nonresidential use, almost wholly surrounded the African American residential districts of the period, cutting off corridors of extension.

The urban landscape, while segregated and disorienting, was exciting as well. In the early 1920s migrants headed for the Stroll District—South State Street and 35th Street. A decade later migrants headed deeper into Chicago's Black Belt to the popular Bronzeville neighborhood, whose heart was the intersection of 47th Street and South Parkway (now Martin Luther King Jr. Boulevard). The massive migration of African Americans from the South to northern cities revealed the creation of "a city within a city" in Chicago, as Bronzeville became the capital of black America. An extended walk in any direction from that intersection would have brought institutions of local black life into view—the Wabash YMCA west on 39th Street and the Provident Hospital east along 51st Street, Supreme Liberty Life Insurance on South Park at 35th, and the offices of the *Chicago Defender* and the Associated Negro Press just west along 35th. A wide variety of churches and spiritual homes could also be found, among them the Olivet Baptist Church at 31st and South Park, the Metropolitan Community Church ten blocks south, and the small but growing Second Temple of the Nation of Islam further south and west of 63rd and Cottage Grove.

Bronzeville certainly possessed many of the signs of a high quality of life. But it was also a community of stark contrasts, the "facets of its life as varied as the colors of its people's skins." These contrasts between urban achievement and profound social problems grew with continued northward migration through the Great Depression and World War II, as Bronzeville's already crowded tenement apartments absorbed wave after wave of newcomers. As migration picked up steam again between 1942 and 1944, some sixty thousand more new arrivals doubled the city's black population to 337,000, one-tenth of the total. Buildings abandoned and condemned in the 1930s were reinhabited during the war years, and the Black Belt remained, in Richard Wright's words, "an undigested lump in Chicago's melting pot."

Elizabeth Schroeder
Schlabach
Earlham College

St. Clair Drake and Horace R. Cayton, *Black Metropolis: A Study of Negro Life in a Northern City* (rev. ed. 1993); Adam Green, *Selling the Race: Culture, Community, and Black Chicago, 1940–1955* (2007); James R. Grossman, *Land of Hope: Chicago, Black Southerners, and the Great Migration* (1989); Allen H. Spear, *Black Chicago: The Making of a Negro Ghetto, 1890–1920* (1967); Maren Stange, *Bronzeville: Black Chicago in Pictures, 1941–1943* (2003); Richard Wright, *12 Million Black Voices* (rev. ed. 1992); Richard Wright, *Black Boy (American Hunger): A Record of Childhood and Youth* (rev. ed. 1991); Richard Wright, "Shame of Chicago," *Ebony* (1951).

C

The Chickasaw

Of the "Five Civilized Tribes" of the southeastern United States in the early nineteenth century—the Chickasaw, Choctaw, Creek, Cherokee, and Seminole—the Chickasaw were the smallest. Around 1700, when continuous contact with whites began, they are estimated to have numbered about 7,000 (2,000 warriors), compared with 17,500 neighboring Choctaw. Since 1670 both tribes had suffered large losses from warfare and especially foreign diseases, particularly smallpox. By 1775 their populations had declined to 2,300 Chickasaw and 13,400 Choctaw. Thereafter, with the fading of warfare and the rise of immunities to imported diseases, the populations rose steadily.

Chickasaw and Choctaw are two constituents of the Western Muskogean branch of the Muskogean language family. (As of 2015, about seventy-five people, most of them over the age of fifty-five, still spoke Chickasaw.) Hence, they are dialects with a common root. The tribes also share many cultural traits and a migration story, indicating that they separated fairly late in prehistoric times. Indeed, the English name *Chickasaw* was adopted from the Choctaw phrase *chik'asha ashachi*, meaning "they left as a tribe not a very great while ago."

Both tribes tell of a migration from "the land of the Setting Sun." According to legend, the Chickasaw wanderings from the West ended at the "Chickasaw Old Fields" near the Tennessee River in far northwestern Alabama. They subsequently relocated to new "Old Fields" in the highlands of the Tombigbee River, in Lee County, Mississippi, between Belden and Verona, just west of present Tupelo. They finally spread to the area bounded by the Tennessee and Ohio Rivers on the east and north, Okatibbee Creek (a tributary of the Tombigbee) on the south, and the Mississippi River. During relatively peaceful times they scattered in small villages, sometimes into northwestern Alabama and to at least two semipermanent settlements on the Savannah River in South Carolina and Georgia. Hunting parties ranged nearly to the Atlantic and to the Great Plains. Chickasaw raiders, much feared, struck north of the Ohio, south to the Gulf of Mexico, and west along the Red and Arkansas Rivers.

The Chickasaw generally lived in small towns containing up to two hundred households. The tribal domain was held in common ownership. Towns had common fields. Private use and even inheritance (through females) was permitted, but formal ownership was not. Towns could move but kept the same names, spreading apart during peacetime but clustering during war. A typical town contained a log-palisaded fort; grounds for councils, festivals, and sports; and religious and council buildings. In 1702 the French were told that eighteen such towns existed. The "capital," boasting more than two hundred households, was Chickafalaya, called Log

Town by the English and Old Pontotoc by early American settlers. Households customarily included a winter house (or hothouse) that was circular, twenty-five feet in diameter, and framed with pine logs and poles, with mud-plaster walls and a sunken earthen floor; one or two summer houses, which were rectangular and had two rooms, walls of loosely woven mats, and roofs of grass thatch and bark; a storage house for crops; and a hut for menstruating women.

Early European observers described Chickasaw men as physically impressive—tall and robust, with reddish-brown skin, jet-black hair, and large, dark eyes—and women as attractive. Warriors shaved the sides of their heads, leaving a tuft soaked in bear grease; old men and women wore their hair long. The Chickasaw kept their persons and dwellings exceptionally clean. Their endurance in hunting and war was legendary: they were said to chase fleeing enemies as far as three hundred miles. They exuded an air of superiority and independence. One early visitor, Bernard Romans, took a jaundiced view, however, calling the warriors haughty, cruel, "filthy in their discourse," and "corrupt in their morals."

The primary social unit was the household (or house group), consisting of matrilineally related women and their husbands, children, and unmarried brothers. A man was subject to the regulations of his wife's household, which functioned, with its own name, as an autonomous part of a clan. Like the clan, the household was led by a hereditary chief from the female line (later chosen by a council of elder men). The number of clans varied between seven and fifteen (though six remained extant in 2002), with each composed of households and usually taking totemic animal names (e.g., panther, bird, deer) derived from a clan ancestor's visionary dream. Clans were ranked and exercised ceremonial and other prerogatives. Men could marry only outside their birth clan; lineage was traced through females, who arranged or approved all marriages.

The clans were grouped into two moieties (groups), the Imosaktca and Intukwalipa. Men could not marry outside their moiety. Moieties had their own rituals and a "prophet" (priest-curer). The tribe separated secular from religious leadership. By the early nineteenth century, it had a hereditary principal chief (high minko), a member of the highest-ranking clan of the Imosaktca, the senior moiety. Anthropologists, however, are uncertain whether the tribe previously had a true principal chief. Clans and towns were essentially self-governing, with chiefs who had few coercive powers; important questions were resolved by calling a council comprised of the adult males. Clan or town chiefs with strong followings may have acted for the tribe in some diplomatic situations or called a tribal council of chiefs and elders to deliberate. Councils were more advisory than legislative; oratory and persuasion conferred authority.

Individuals enjoyed great personal freedom. Tribal laws were few, enforced by clan courts of elders. Especially strict rules dealt with homicide and adultery. In cases of murder, the victim's clan was obligated to capture and kill the perpetrator. If he escaped, his brother or one of his clan members would be killed instead; if the victim were female, a female relative was killed. Most scholars agree that only women were punished for adultery. An adulterous woman's husband could beat her and crop her hair, nose, and ears. When asked why men were not punished similarly, the Chickasaw responded that disfigured men were unfit to fight.

Like the far more numerous Iroquois in the Northeast, Chickasaw warriors were feared throughout the Southeast. James Adair (ca. 1709–ca. 1783), an English trader who lived among them and even led them in battle, called them "the readiest and quickest of all people in going to shed blood," as "brave as ever trod the ground, and faithful under great danger even unto death." They usually fought in bands of fifty or fewer from a single clan. The most common motive for offensive warfare was to avenge the death of kin. The appearance of Chickasaw dugouts, some capable of carrying more than sixty warriors, inspired undiluted dread along the Southeast's waterways. Slain enemies were scalped and captured warriors burned alive, but captives might also be enslaved to help the women in the fields or, from the late seventeenth century, sold to English traders for muskets, munitions, and manufactured articles. The whole tribe was involved only in defensive warfare. The palisaded forts in towns were particularly formidable, as the French learned during the Chickasaw Wars (1723–53).

To go to war, a famed warrior, usually a chief, would persuade a group of followers. Dances, ceremonies, and a fast would precede the warriors' departure, with further ceremonies after their return. Success required tactical knowledge, principally of surprise and ambush, and correct performance of rituals. By the eighteenth century, muskets were added to the traditional armory of bows and arrows, hatchets, spears, clubs, and stone knives. (Like most Indians, the Chickasaw found whites' method of fighting in formation in the open all but incomprehensible.) After agreeing to make peace, an opponent's delegation would be met in a town with ceremonies, dances, oratory, and the climactic smoking of a white calumet.

The Chickasaw subsisted on hunting, fishing, gathering, and, to a lesser extent than the Choctaw, agriculture. Hunting parties, sometimes with families, ranged as far as the High Plains. Hunting dwindled after 1805 because herds had declined as a consequence of the trade in furs and especially deer hides. Men subsequently turned gradually toward agriculture and raising stock. The traditional crops were corn, beans, peas, squash, pumpkins, melons, sunflowers, and tobacco, to which the eighteenth-century English added potatoes, watermelons, and "marshmallow" (perhaps okra or maypop). Berries, plums, grapes, persimmons, sassafras roots, nuts, onions, honey, and salt were gathered. Horses arrived around 1700 from English and Spanish sources. Herding and raising horses took root during the 1700s. The Chickasaw were perhaps the first southeastern Indians to use horses in warfare. The long-striding, durable Chickasaw horse began gaining fame.

Clothing was made from animal skins—especially deer but also other furs—and from cloth, which was woven from mulberry bark thread, buffalo hair, and hemp. Men wore breechclouts and deerskin shirts, while women wore hide skirts with belts or sashes. Winter brought out fur robes; hunters wore leggings and high deerskin boots. Both sexes wore moccasins only occasionally. Robes with feathers woven into them appeared on ceremonial occasions. The Chickasaw flattened the heads of both boys and girls at birth. Both wore bracelets and ear, nose, and finger rings, but tattooing and body painting were reserved for males.

Religion permeated Chickasaw culture. The correct performance of personal and public rituals was believed essential to the tribe's well-being and survival. Each household, clan, and moiety originally had a priest and shaman (healer), though after 1700 they combined into a caste of holy men. These positions were hereditary and were held by men too old to fight or hunt. They maintained each town's sacred fire, which provided coals for every dwelling. The holy men also healed, conducted rituals, and interpreted signs, dreams, and events.

The supreme being, Ababinili, the creator of life, fire, and light, was "a composite force consisting of the Four Beloved Things Above—Sun, Clouds, Clear Sky, and 'He that Lives in the Clear Sky.'" Lesser gods and good and evil spirits abounded, with a personal spirit to guide and guard each individual. Witches did evil; good spirits would aid those who observed the rituals. Festivals or rituals involving fasting and purging, feasting, dancing, and games marked the new year (at the first new moon after the spring equinox), the beginning and end of the harvest, and other occasions. The dead were buried inside the home in a sitting position facing west, with the face painted red and with personal possessions. The good would go to heaven in the west, the evil to a wandering existence in the Land of the Witches or perhaps to a void in the west between heaven and the material world.

With no written language, the Chickasaw relied on oral tradition. Monogamy prevailed, but polygamy was permitted well into the nineteenth century. Children could be betrothed. Temporary and trial marriages were allowed, as were separation and divorce. A man could marry his deceased brother's widow, and widows and widowers could remarry after prescribed mourning periods. Boys and girls were separated after age three. Mothers disciplined girls, while boys were disciplined by an "uncle," probably the mother's oldest brother or the eldest uncle of the mother's clan. Children enjoyed great freedom, disciplined by admonition and shaming rather than corporal punishment. Marriage and burial rites were simple and primarily public. A warrior killed in battle was placed on a scaffold at the site or buried, with his bones later retrieved for burial in his home.

The Chickasaw remained largely unresponsive to Christian missionaries until the 1820s and often ignored them thereafter. Baptists, Methodists, and Presbyterians made some headway, with the Presbyterians in particular encouraging education and founding the Charity Hall and Monroe schools. After 1824 the tribal council subsidized the Tokshis, Martya, and Caney Creek schools through the Presbyterians, but these schools closed by 1834 because of the impending Removal. Christianity grew apace after Removal, weakening the tribe's ties to its past. Today, most Chickasaw are Baptist or Methodist.

David S. Newhall
Centre College

W. David Baird, *The Chickasaw People* (1974); Chickasaw Nation website, www.chickasaw.net; Mary B. Davis, ed., *Native Americans in the Twentieth Century: An Encyclopedia* (1994); Arrell Morgan Gibson, *The Chickasaws* (1971); Duane Hale and Arrell Morgan Gibson, *The Chickasaw* (1991); Norman J. Heard, *Handbook of the American Frontier: Four Centuries of Indian-White Relationships*, vol. 1, *The Southeastern Woodlands* (1987); Sharon Malinowski and Anna Sheets, eds., *Gale Encyclopedia of Native American Tribes*, vol. 1 (1988); Harvey Markowitz, ed., *American Indians*, vol. 1 (1995); Daniel H. Usner Jr., *American Indians in the Lower Mississippi Valley: Social and Economic Histories* (1998); Daniel H. Usner Jr., *Indians, Settlers, and Slaves in a Frontier Economy: The Lower Mississippi Valley before 1783* (1992).

Chickasaw Bayou, Battle of

Despite several Union attempts to take it, Vicksburg remained a Confederate stronghold in 1862. In the fall and winter of that year, Gen. Ulysses S. Grant devised an overland campaign to seize the city and cut the Confederacy in two. The campaign lasted for weeks and consisted of several small engagements. One battle, fought on 29 December, occurred between Union forces under Gen. William Tecumseh Sherman and Confederate defenders at Chickasaw Bayou (also known as Chickasaw Bluffs), northeast of Vicksburg.

Grant hoped to occupy Confederate forces, including the main army under Gen. John C. Pemberton, in Northeast Mississippi near Grenada. If these forces could be lured into battle away from Vicksburg, then Sherman, moving south from Memphis with four divisions (more than thirty thousand men) could capture the city. The plan, however, began to unravel almost before it started. Grant's supply lines stretched nearly two hundred miles from North Mississippi through Tennessee and into Kentucky. Nathan Bedford Forrest and his cavalry began wreaking havoc on these lines, so Grant decided to build a new supply depot at Holly Springs, Mississippi. Soon after the depot's completion, Gen. Earl

Van Dorn led a successful raid to destroy it, capturing fifteen hundred Union troops and plundering more than two million dollars in supplies. This action, coupled with Forrest's raids in Tennessee, forced Grant to call off the plan and withdraw from Mississippi.

Sherman, however, was busy making his way south from Memphis by ship to a landing at Milliken's Bend, Louisiana, twenty miles north of Vicksburg on the Yazoo River. He had not gotten word of the cancellation of the operation, mostly owing to the disruption of telegraph lines by Confederate cavalry. Pemberton, sensing something amiss, had fourteen thousand defenders on the bluffs overlooking Sherman's position. Once Sherman and his troops disembarked from the transports, they found not solid ground conducive to marching but swamps, marshes, and bayous. In addition, Confederate troops created even more obstacles, such as felled trees, rifle pits, sharpshooters, and artillery positions. Sherman's forces needed more than two days to travel four miles and position themselves to attack the Confederates.

On 29 December 1862, after a small skirmish the day before, Sherman ordered a full frontal assault on the bluffs at Chickasaw Bayou. Though some of his subordinates doubted him, Sherman believed the operation could succeed: "We will lose 5,000 men before we take Vicksburg, and we may as well lose them here as anywhere else." After a two-hour artillery bombardment beginning at 10:00 in the morning, the infantry advanced but immediately encountered problems. One brigade became lost and maneuvered in the wrong direction, another could not make it across the bayou to get in the fight, and one unit found itself pinned down by relentless Confederate fire. After five separate attempts to take the bluffs, Sherman decided the Confederate position could not be taken.

Sherman's force suffered more than seventeen hundred total casualties, while Confederate losses amounted to fewer than two hundred. He withdrew back through the difficult terrain to the transports waiting on the river. Sherman decided against another assault further up the Yazoo River and ordered his force back to Milliken's Bend, possibly to await Grant. But at least temporarily, the Confederate victory at Chickasaw Bayou had obstructed Grant's campaign to take Vicksburg by direct assault.

Ryan S. Walters
Hattiesburg, Mississippi

Bruce Catton, *Grant Moves South, 1861–1863* (1960); Lee Kennett, *Sherman: A Soldier's Life* (2001); David G. Martin, *The Vicksburg Campaign* (1990).

Chickasaw County

Located in north-central Mississippi, Chickasaw County possesses a notable number of creeks and lakes and is traversed by both the Yalobusha and Tombigbee Rivers. Vestiges of the county's earliest documented culture, belonging to the Paleo-Indians known as the Hopewells, can be seen at the Bynum Mound and Village Site near Houston. The French and British also occupied Chickasaw lands during the seventeenth and eighteenth centuries. Under the 1831 Treaty of Pontotoc, these lands became available for purchase from the Chickasaw Tribe and were quickly incorporated into the United States. The county takes its name from the region's native inhabitants and was formally established on 9 February 1836. Chickasaw's two county seats are Okolona and Houston, the latter named for the distinguished leader of the Texas war of independence, Gen. Sam Houston.

In 1840 Chickasaw was home to 2,148 free whites, 1 free African American, and 806 slaves. Early on, the county was almost entirely agricultural, and the plantation economy was central to Chickasaw's antebellum prosperity. By 1860 the county had changed substantially. Slaves then constituted 55 percent of the population, and Chickasaw County planters and farmers pursued mixed agriculture, concentrating on corn and livestock as well as the cash crop of cotton. Following the construction of the Mobile and Ohio Railroad through Chickasaw in 1859, the county's main sphere of commercial activity shifted from Houston to Okolona. While only eighty-three residents of Chickasaw County were employed in industry in 1860, its manufacturing sector produced a substantial variety of commodities, including fixed agricultural implements, flour and meal, lumber, boots, carriages, furniture, and saddles and harnesses.

As in much of Mississippi, most of Chickasaw's antebellum congregants attended Baptist or Methodist churches. Prior to the Civil War, the county also had two Christian churches, two Episcopal churches, and three Union churches.

Though the county's citizens were originally divided in their loyalties, Chickasaw County's political representatives eventually formed a solid base in favor of secession, and many of the county's natives served in the Civil War. In addition to several attempts by federal troops to destroy the stretch of the Mobile and Ohio Railroad running through the county, a number of battles and raids took place in Chickasaw. Property owners in the county suffered losses on many fronts as a result of the war, especially in the destruction of the county's economic infrastructure.

Chickasaw was considered among the state's postbellum "black districts," as following the war its political boundaries were redrawn to ensure the election of African American candidates. Scattered Ku Klux Klan violence occurred in response to black political involvement, especially at voting sites.

The county's population struggled during the postbellum era. In 1872 Clay and Webster Counties annexed portions of Chickasaw. Though agriculture remained the county's primary subsistence activity, the demise of Chickasaw's plantation economy led to the rise of small farms and sharecropping. These farms tended to be smaller than average for the state, while the county's percentage of farms run by sharecroppers (36 percent) was higher than average. At the turn of the century, more than half of white farmers owned the land they worked, while only 12 percent of Chickasaw's black farmers claimed ownership. The county's industrial workforce also remained relatively small, with manufacturing firms employing just seventy-eight people.

Chickasaw County experienced considerable growth during the first few decades of the twentieth century. By 1900 the county's population had grown to almost twenty thousand, and in 1909 the county constructed Mississippi's first Carnegie Library in Houston. Chickasaw also saw a rise in industrial activity during this era, and its agricultural economy moved away from cotton cultivation toward livestock.

By 1916 more than half of the Chickasaw's church members were Baptists—mostly either Missionary Baptists or Southern Baptists. Smaller but still significant numbers of congregants attended the Methodist Episcopal Church, the Colored Methodist Episcopal Church, and the Presbyterian Church. Chickasaw County was home to notable religious musicians, including shape-note singer W. A. Beasley and the Pilgrim Jubilees gospel group.

Frank Burkitt, a Populist editor and political figure, was a Chickasaw County native, as was Pauline Orr, an important figure at the Mississippi University for Women. Blues musician Booker "Bukka" White was born in Houston in 1909. Country singer Bobbie Gentry, known for her rendition of "Ode to Billie Joe," was likewise born in Chickasaw and mentioned the county often in her music. Chickasaw has long been home to Sparta Opry, a live country music show. William Raspberry, a Pulitzer Prize–winning journalist, grew up in Okolona and graduated from Okolona College High School in 1952.

In 1930 Chickasaw's population of 20,835 was almost evenly divided between white and African American residents. Only about 29 percent of farmers owned their own land. Dairy farming and cattle became increasingly central to Chickasaw's agricultural sector during the first half of the twentieth century, while sweet potato cultivation increased following World War II. The county's industrial force was also growing, employing 224 workers in 1930. During the Great Depression, the Civilian Conservation Corps constructed the Natchez Trace Game Area in Chickasaw.

By 1960 Chickasaw County's population had dropped below 17,000, and almost two-thirds of residents were white. Twenty years later, only 220 people were still involved in agriculture, while more than half of the workforce, almost

5,000 people, held manufacturing positions, largely in timber and textiles.

Like many central Mississippi counties, in 2010 Chickasaw County's population of 17,932 was predominantly white and had not changed significantly in size since 1960. However, a small but significant Latino/Hispanic minority had emerged.

Mississippi Encyclopedia Staff
University of Mississippi

Chickasaw County Historical and Genealogical Society, *A History of Chickasaw County, Mississippi* (1985); Mississippi State Planning Commission, *Progress Report on State Planning in Mississippi* (1938); *Mississippi Statistical Abstract*, Mississippi State University (1952–2010); Charles Sydnor and Claude Bennett, *Mississippi History* (1939); University of Virginia Library, Historical Census Browser website, http://mapserver.lib.virginia.edu; E. Nolan Waller and Dani A. Smith, *Growth Profiles of Mississippi's Counties, 1960–1980* (1985).

Chickasaw-European Relations

Hernando de Soto's treasure-hunting expedition from mid-December 1540 to mid-June 1541 marked the first direct exposure to Europeans for the members of the Chickasaw tribe. After three months of the Spaniards' demands and impositions, the Chickasaw suddenly attacked, inflicting heavy losses in terms of men, horses, and equipment. The weakened Spaniards at last moved on, but for two centuries thereafter they left the Chickasaw strictly alone. The tribe remained out of continuous contact with Europeans until the end of the seventeenth century. (La Salle briefly encountered two of them on his 1682 expedition down the Mississippi.)

In 1698 Thomas Welch and Anthony Dodsworth arrived with packhorses from Charles Town, South Carolina, and in short order the English built a thriving commerce. A year later, Iberville landed at Biloxi and founded the French colony of Louisiana and two Englishmen led a Chickasaw raid on an Acolapissa village near the mouth of the Pearl River, taking many captives. The French knew that they now faced a grave strategic threat to their North American empire (governed from Quebec) as a consequence of the English presence on the Mississippi near the mouth of the Ohio. The Chickasaw thus occupied an area both England and France deemed crucial to control of North America.

The English pack trains brought profound, traumatic change to Chickasaw culture and destiny. Into a Late Stone Age society the English introduced guns, ammunition, and horses; machine-woven cloth and Bengal silk; metal hoes, knives, hatchets, axes, and scissors; brass wire and kettles; beads, mirrors, vermillion pigment, and "Dutch pretties"; and alcohol. In return, the Chickasaw offered deer hides (leather, buckskins); bear and buffalo furs and robes; wolf, panther, and other pelts; honey, beeswax, tallow, salt, and hickory-nut oil; and captives for the Charles Town slave market. When needed, conch shells continued as currency, but the demand had increased tremendously.

Like the Choctaw and others, the Chickasaw began to crave the traders' wares and soon considered them necessities. Without firearms, the Indians rightly concluded, their existence was at stake. Hence, the Chickasaw and others expanded their hunting range dramatically to get more deerskins for trade, leading to clashes with many tribes—Choctaw, Shawnee, Cherokee, Kickapoo, Illini, Mobile, Osage, Quapaw, and Creek—some of them French allies. Particularly after 1763, as white settlers moved west and plantation agriculture began appearing, increasing hunting ranges fueled economic rivalries, movement, conflict, pillage, and bloodshed among the tribes.

The heavy involvement by the Chickasaw in the slave trade intensified their warlike character, making them the most notorious Indian slavers of the Southeast. Enslavement of captives was an ancient Chickasaw practice. The tribe's women, who did most of the farming, had often urged their men to get more captives. Now, with English traders providing a huge market for Indian slaves, Chickasaw slaving parties ranged along the Lower Mississippi into Illinois and up the Arkansas and Red Rivers. The English paid well in goods, guns, and horses and then sold the captives at Charles Town, whence they usually were shipped to the West Indies in exchange for blacks to work on the North American plantations. The Chickasaw slave trade not only filled English pockets but also stoked the tribe's resistance to French traders and French-influenced tribes, particularly the Choctaw, and to Roman Catholic missionaries, thereby serving England's strategic interests. The French retaliated, though less effectively, by offering bounties to the Choctaw for Chickasaw scalps and captives and inciting the Choctaw to attack the pack trains.

Knowing that they needed support from the major tribes to establish Louisiana, the French tried, with modest success at times, to promote peace between the Choctaw and Chickasaw. By the 1720s, however, it was obvious the Chickasaw would never expel the English traders, with whom the French could not compete at any level—quantity, quality, or price. If the French North American empire were to defeat the English challenge, not only was Choctaw support, wavering but still holding, essential, but the Chickasaw must be destroyed. France's attempts to do so resulted in the Chickasaw Wars (1723–53), during which the tribe frustrated two hugely expensive French expeditions (1736, 1739–40). Though the Chickasaw remained unconquered, repeated French and Choctaw raids and crop burnings and devastating outbreaks of smallpox weakened the Chickasaw both in numbers and in cultural cohesion.

From the start, a smattering of English traders had lived with and married the Chickasaw. After the French and Indian War (1754–63) ended France's North American empire, increasing numbers of English joined the Chickasaw, raised mixed-blood families, and became tribal leaders because of their and their descendants' knowledge of English, writing, and business. The tribe also continued to adopt remnants of other tribes, most notably Natchez refugees after 1729. A small but persistent pro-French faction, hoping to avoid French and Choctaw depredations, unintentionally undermined tribal leaders' authority. Moreover, warriors were evolving from subsistence hunters to frontier businessmen, eagerly searching for items to pay for English goods. Trading posts gradually displaced the old council houses.

With the French gone and the Spanish weakening, the Chickasaw, like all of the southeastern Indians, found less maneuvering room between rival white powers. For the Chickasaw, subjection to the authority of another government was unprecedented. A 1763 British royal decree reserved for the Indians the vast territory from the Appalachians to the Mississippi and from the Ohio south to the thirty-first parallel. The Chickasaw supported the British against Pontiac's Rebellion (1763) and maintained claims to land along the Tennessee and Cumberland Rivers against the Shawnee and Cherokee, but relative peace prevailed. A growing group of traders, peddlers, hunters, and frontier farmers, however, strained the tribe. Unscrupulous traders cheated and stole, smuggled liquor, and wreaked havoc in the villages; hunters poached on tribal lands; transient frontiersmen squatted or "bought" land (which was illegal). Chickasaw began to own black slaves, thus beginning the transformation of the Lower Mississippi Valley into an agricultural-export economy. Continuing white-Indian marriages spawned more mixed-blood families whose power in the tribe continued to grow.

During the American Revolution (1775–83), most Chickasaw villages preferred neutrality. The British courted the chiefs, who agreed in 1777 to guard the land routes and the Mississippi River from the Ohio past the Chickasaw Bluffs. The Americans completed Fort Jefferson at the mouth of the Ohio in 1780 as a base for operations down the Mississippi by George Rogers Clark. A force of Chickasaw led by James Colbert, son of James Logan Colbert, an immigrant Scottish trader who became patriarch of a family of mixed-bloods that dominated Chickasaw political life for generations, besieged the fort and forced its abandonment in June 1781.

Spain, seeking recovery of Florida from Great Britain, joined the Americans in 1779 and captured Pensacola, Mobile, Baton Rouge, and Natchez. British refugees from West Florida fled to the Chickasaw, the sole British ally in the region, further increasing the Anglo presence among the tribe. Reinforced by refugees, Chickasaw raiders, most notably Colbert's Chickasaw Company, virtually closed the Mississippi to Spanish shipping. They also foiled Spanish attempts to capture Colbert at Chickasaw Bluffs and to use the northern Indians, especially the Kickapoo, against them. In 1782 Colbert captured the wife and children of Spain's lieutenant governor of Illinois. Yet Spanish intrigues among the southeastern Indians continued long after the revolution. For a time, the Indians again played white governments against each other: Spain versus the new United States of America. Factions among the Chickasaw—pro-Spanish (formerly pro-French), pro-British (after 1783, pro–United States), vacillators, and many self-serving mixed-bloods—disputed the tribe's future course. Three years of palavers and intrigues led to an agreement concluded by the pro-American (and largest) faction. The Treaty of Hopewell (signed by the Chickasaw on 3 January 1786) recognized US sovereignty.

Spain continued to seek control of the Lower Mississippi, principally by posing as the protector of the southeastern Indians but also by inciting the pro-Spanish Creek against the pro-American Chickasaw. In 1785 Spanish troops, supported by the pro-Spanish Chickasaw, built Fort San Fernando at Chickasaw Bluffs. Nevertheless, a majority of the Chickasaw finally supported fighting against the pro-Spanish Creek in 1793–95. (Some Chickasaw fought under Gen. Anthony Wayne at Fallen Timbers in 1794 to subdue Ohio's Indians.) In the Treaty of San Lorenzo (1795), the United States prevailed. Spain recognized American sovereignty east of the Mississippi down to the thirty-first parallel and abandoned Fort San Fernando, which became Fort Adams (1797).

David S. Newhall
Centre College

David W. Baird, *The Chickasaw People* (1974); Arrell Morgan Gibson, *The Chickasaws* (1971); Duane Hale and Arrell Morgan Gibson, *The Chickasaw* (1991); Norman J. Heard, *Handbook of the American Frontier: Four Centuries of Indian-White Relationships*, vol. 1, *The Southeastern Woodlands* (1987); Sharon Malinowski and Anna Sheets, eds., *Gale Encyclopedia of Native American Tribes*, vol. 1 (1988); Harvey Markowitz, ed., *American Indians*, vol. 1 (1995); Daniel H. Usner Jr., *American Indians in the Lower Mississippi Valley: Social and Economic Histories* (1998); Daniel H. Usner Jr., *Indians, Settlers, and Slaves in a Frontier Economy: The Lower Mississippi Valley before 1783* (1992); Mary Ann Wells, *Native Land: Mississippi, 1540–1798* (1994).

Chickasaw-US Relations

Once it assumed power over Mississippi in 1798, the United States wasted no time establishing its authority over Chickasaw lands. Congress created the Mississippi Territory north of the thirty-first parallel, and the Chickasaw agency was founded in 1801 on the Natchez Trace, which was made into a wagon trail. A trading store opened near Fort Adams in 1802 and by 1809 had become the leading seller of pelts among the fourteen existing federal stores. Spain's continuing presence in West Florida (south of the thirty-first) and west of the Mississippi still gave the Indians some leverage in Spanish-US relations. Spain's 1800 cession of Louisiana to France and France's sale of it to the United States three years later, however, left the southeastern Indians little recourse against federal authorities' increasingly aggressive policies.

The terms of the Treaty of Hopewell (1785–86) were intended "for the benefit and comfort" of the Indians and authorized the United States to manage their affairs "as it might think proper." It is quite possible that none of the signatories properly grasped the implications of such conventional phrases. The federal government believed that persuasion—encouraging agriculture and trade through treaties—and policing of the boundaries of the Indians' land would help them become "civilized" but probably overestimated the success of such policies among the Chickasaw. Immigrating frontiersmen and the territorial and later state governments increased the pressure on both the Indians and federal authorities, slowly dissolving the moral bases on which the US government had hoped to buttress its policies.

Of all the changes in Chickasaw fortunes and way of life up to the 1820s, the cession of their lands was the most dramatically symbolic. Treaties concluded in 1805, 1816, and 1818 ceded some twenty million acres to United States authority. The cessions covered lands north of the Tennessee border, in extreme western Kentucky, and in all but a fraction in northwestern Alabama, leaving the Chickasaw confined to northern Mississippi. Federal authorities negotiated with the Colbert family, who were prominent military, political, and economic leaders in the Chickasaw Nation, and then gave the chiefs gifts of cash and land. The chiefs' debts to traders made them vulnerable: for example, in 1805 they ceded a vast tract in west-central Tennessee for twenty thousand dollars, twelve thousand of which went to pay debts. If other methods failed, government agents threatened to withhold the chiefs' annuities.

Continuing loyalty to the federal government did the Chickasaw little good. Just as they had resisted Pontiac's 1763 plans to support rebellion against British authority, they also resisted Tecumseh's 1812–13 call to oppose the encroaching Americans. A total of 350 Chickasaw joined in Andrew Jackson's crushing of the Red Stick Creek at the Battle of Horseshoe Bend and the destruction of Creek fortifications in northern Alabama in 1813–14, but Jackson nevertheless brushed aside Chickasaw claims to Creek lands. He cynically summed up the events of the preceding two decades: the United States could take Indians' land by "touching their interests and feeding their greed."

The War of 1812 all but destroyed the southeastern Indians' military power. An idea broached back in 1803 by Thomas Jefferson rapidly gained support: Why not remove the now-helpless peoples to a reserved territory in the Louisiana Purchase west of the Mississippi? Alabama and Mississippi mounted a legal offensive against the Chickasaw and the other tribes and put heavy pressure on the federal government in favor of Removal. A series of laws from 1819 to 1830 abolished tribal government and put the Indians under ordinary state jurisdiction. The desperate Chickasaw council, under strong mixed-blood influence, responded in 1829 with a written code of laws protecting private property, creating a law enforcement agency staffed by one hundred mounted men, and banning whiskey sales. The federal government's failure to enforce the Indian treaties, however, doomed efforts to prevent Removal, and Congress approved the policy in 1830. For the Chickasaw, a series of conferences and treaties settled their fate. Removal began on 1 June 1837, with the first contingent crossing the Mississippi on 4 July.

In 1822 about 4,000 Chickasaw remained. Fifteen years later, the official roll at Removal listed 4,914 Chickasaw and 1,156 black slaves they owned. About 200, temporarily joined at times by others, moved west of the Mississippi to hunt and fight (most notably against the Osage between 1802 and 1821). Some others dominated trade in the Lower Arkansas and Red River Valleys, while a few settled on the St. Francis. To the east, hunting dried up after 1819, discouraging appreciable eastward emigration from the traditional northern Mississippi and northwestern Alabama lands.

Probably the most striking development before Removal was the economic and political ascendance of the so-called mixed-bloods, which had been growing since the latter 1700s. After 1819 even more whites pressed on and around the Chickasaw, with many whites marrying Chickasaw and often taking advantage of the tribe's traditional landholding practices to carve out plantations worked by African American slaves. Some of these families founded virtual dynasties—Colbert, Adair, Love, Harris, McIntosh, Jennings, Cheadle. In addition to agriculture, they raised livestock, traded, and operated gins and gristmills. They worked politically through traditional tribal institutions, exercising covert influence and acting as spokesmen and negotiators with white authorities.

The people identified as mixed-bloods owned most of the black slaves, who constituted an important element of Chickasaw society. Arrel Gibson notes that their labors in agriculture and construction enhanced Chickasaw property values, which helped them obtain better Removal terms than most of the other tribes. Moreover, English-speaking slaves became agents of Chickasaw acculturation.

Full-blood Chickasaw suffered more from the tide of change engulfing their traditional ways than did mixed-bloods. Federal improvement of the Natchez Trace and the building of feeder roads attracted even more whites to the region. As hunting declined, many Chickasaw drifted into subsistence farming, raising livestock, or simple manual labor. Villages declined or disappeared, replaced by dispersed log cabins. The old religion, ceremonies, and communal sports decayed. Cheating or underpaying by whites pushed many Indians toward hopeless poverty. Withdrawal, idleness, depression, and drunkenness became more common.

Most of the tribe understandably continued to regard missionaries as agents of white penetration and rule. Consequently, education—an invariable accompaniment of most missionaries' activities—was widely ignored. Amid the uncertainties clouding the impending Removal, the missionaries withdrew and closed their schools until 1844. However, most post-Removal Chickasaw leaders had attended the early schools, and in 1849 the Chickasaw legislature decided to appropriate money for schools, with the first such institution, the Chickasaw Manual Labor Academy, opening in 1851.

Virtually the only positive note sounded during these years was the tribe's unanimity in opposing Removal. Leaders (virtually all of them mixed-bloods) knew that Removal could not be stopped but astutely frustrated federal authorities enough to wring better terms from them than other tribes obtained. As one result, the Chickasaw became the last to leave.

The final stragglers arrived in the Indian Territory (present Oklahoma) around 1850. In 1854 the final parcel of the millions of acres they had owned was sold. After centuries of life on the banks of the Great River and in the highlands of the Tombigbee, the Chickasaw could no longer call Mississippi their home.

By the 1890 census the Chickasaw numbered 6,400. The 2000 census showed 38,351 persons claiming Chickasaw ethnicity. Of these, 22,946 resided in Oklahoma, mainly in thirteen south-central counties, but only 211 remained in Mississippi.

David S. Newhall
Centre College

David W. Baird, *The Chickasaw People* (1974); Mary B. Davis, ed., *Native Americans in the Twentieth Century: An Encyclopedia* (1994); Arrell Morgan Gibson, *The Chickasaws* (1971); Duane Hale and Arrell Morgan Gibson, *The Chickasaw* (1991); Norman J. Heard, *Handbook of the American Frontier: Four Centuries of Indian-White Relationships*, vol. 1, *The Southeastern Woodlands* (1987).

Chickasaw War

The Chickasaw War—sometimes called the Second Chickasaw War to distinguish it from much smaller conflicts in 1723–25 and 1752–53—consisted of raiding and two major expeditions by French forces and mainly Choctaw Indians against the Chickasaw in western Tennessee and northern Mississippi. It was by far French Louisiana's largest military enterprise.

The French believed almost from Louisiana's founding in 1699 that they needed the loyalty of the Choctaw, the region's largest tribe and the traditional foe of the Chickasaw. The French hoped to keep the Chickasaw friendly or at least away from the influence of English traders. By the 1720s, however, this dream was all but gone. In the early 1730s the new governor, Jean-Baptiste Le Moyne, Sieur de Bienville, faced a desperate situation. The English government was using Chickasaw-English relations to weaken France's hold on the Mississippi Valley and thus threatening its entire North American empire.

By 1731 the Chickasaw were harboring several hundred Natchez Indians whom the French had tried to destroy after their 1729 uprising. The Chickasaw also occasionally attacked Louisiana's communications with its Illinois outposts and thus with New France (Canada). Under heavy French pressure, a substantial minority of Chickasaw favored meeting the demands to surrender the Natchez refugees. At the same time, however, the Chickasaw made overtures to the Choctaw, who were increasingly unhappy with France's inability to supply European goods. The English, who could provide sufficient supplies, eagerly promoted a Chickasaw-Choctaw reconciliation—a nightmare scenario for the French, who believed that it would doom Louisiana.

The Choctaw, tempted by English traders, were becoming unreliable. Moreover, Bienville's predecessor, Étienne Boucher de Périer, had damaged Choctaw cohesion by creating too many chiefs and promising too many "presents." A disgruntled minority, led by Red Shoe, openly flirted with the English. Bienville kept the principal chiefs loyal, authorizing a series of damaging raids on the Chickasaw from 1732 on. Losing warriors and divided over the question of what to do with the Natchez refugees, the Chickasaw still refused to sue outright for peace.

On 1 December 1734 France's minister of marine, Jérôme Phélypeaux de Maurepas, conveyed Louis XV's authorization to destroy the Chickasaw and to do it soon, because peace with England might not last much longer. Still, in the summer of 1735 Bienville hoped somehow to avoid a showdown. But when news arrived that the English planned to create several settlements near the Alabama Indians, thus threatening Fort Toulouse (near present Montgomery), and when the Chickasaw attacked a bateau sent from Illinois to fetch munitions, Bienville reluctantly concluded that he must destroy the Chickasaw or force them to leave the region; otherwise, he would lose the respect of the Choctaw. Maurepas reconfirmed the king's consent in December and authorized Bienville's proposed expedition.

A force from Illinois under Maj. Pierre Dartaguiette (D'Artaguette) Diron joined Bienville's army from Mobile with plans to destroy Ackia, the major fortified-village complex of the Chickasaw. Dartaguiette, with some 140 French and 266 northern Indians, left Fort de Chartres (about forty miles below present St. Louis) on 22 February 1736 and reached the Fourth Chickasaw Bluff (part of then Prud'homme Bluffs), just north of present downtown Memphis, six days later. Dartaguiette left for Ackia on 5 March, having waited in vain for a body of French-led Indians, mainly from the Ohio Valley, who had been impeded by organizational problems. He reached the outskirts of Ackia on the 24 March. About four days earlier a dispatch from Bienville had informed him that the linkup would be postponed to late April. With supplies dwindling and his Indians advising action, Dartaguiette decided to attack Ogoula Tchetoka, a fortified village, to capture supplies. On 25 March, between four hundred and five hundred Chickasaw suddenly surrounded his attacking force. Surprised, most of Dartaguiette's Indians fled, having expected an easy victory. On the retreat, thirty-six French, including Dartaguiette, and an unknown number of Indians died. Father Antoine Sénat and eighteen soldiers were captured; Sénat and sixteen of the men were burned alive. Having captured Bienville's orders, the Chickasaw then moved south to confront him.

Plagued through 1735 into 1736 by delays of men and supplies from France and without the promised artillery, Bienville left Fort Condé (Mobile) on 1 April. He ascended the Tombigbee with six hundred men, including French and Swiss Regulars, militia, volunteers, and 140 black slaves led by free blacks. Drenched by relentless torrential rains, they rested at newly begun Fort Tombecbé (near Epes, Alabama, about thirty miles northeast of Meridian, Mississippi), where Choctaw chiefs, including Alibamon Mingo and a repentant Red Shoe, joined them. Further up the Tombigbee, they reached the Oktibbeha River, near present Amory, on 18 May and were joined by about six hundred Choctaw, substantially fewer than expected. On 24 May they reached the Ackia complex. Still unaware of Dartaguiette's defeat, Bienville attacked two days later. The Battle of Ackia marked a Chickasaw triumph. Bienville's retreat, covered by the Choctaw, reached Fort Tombecbé on 2 June and Mobile six days later. There, he learned of Dartaguiette's fate.

Although the failed campaign cost more than a million livres, the French launched another one that sought not only the same goal but also to restore France's honor and impress its uncertain Indian allies. The campaign turned into an endless chronicle of delays, administrative snarls and rivalries, and sheer bad luck, a cautionary tale of how an eighteenth-century European nation could fail when trying to wage war in a vast wilderness hundreds of miles from the sea.

Noüailles d'Aymé was appointed military commander to oversee Bienville but proved to be a mere figurehead. Once again, a force from Canada and Illinois met an expedition from the south, though this one ascended the Mississippi rather than the Tombigbee. To reduce the fortified Chickasaw villages, artillery would be shipped from France—not the requested light artillery, in short supply, but cannons and mortars weighing upward of one thousand pounds. Artillery meant building heavier boats, stockpiling heavier munitions, and finding oxen as well as horses and men to move everything over roads to be hacked through forests and swamps.

Preparations went forward in 1737–39, accompanied by some French-led Choctaw raiding. A fortified base was built in 1738 at the mouth of the St. Francis River near present Helena, Arkansas. After tardily learning that Ackia was about twice as far east of the Mississippi (about 120 miles) as they had previously thought, the French built Fort Assumption in 1739 as a forward base at Fourth Chickasaw Bluff a couple of miles south of the mouth of the Margot (present Wolf) River. Deciding he could not feed twelve hundred men for another year, Bienville declined the government's suggestion to wait until 1740. He dispatched contingents north from 24 July to 12 September 1739. After immense labor in the face of foul weather, the expedition reached Fort Assumption via the Fort St. Francis base by 8 December. Maj. Charles Le Moyne de Longueuil (Bienville's nephew) had arrived with 123 Canadians and 319 Indians gathered from Montreal, Detroit, Mackinac, and the Upper Mississippi.

But now the would-be attackers could not locate the vital Memphis-Pontotoc-Mobile Trail to Ackia. On 11 January 1740 scouts finally reported that it was only sixty miles away. Confronting winter cold and rain, rapidly shrinking supplies, rampant sickness, desertions, impatient and drunken northern Indians, and the absence of the promised Choctaw forces led by Red Shoe, and with oxen and horses dying or weakened from disease and lack of fodder, Bienville agonizingly concluded that his forces could not clear a sixty-mile road to the trail and thus would have to do without the precious artillery.

Capt. Pierre-Joseph Céloron de Blainville, bearing secret orders to negotiate, left for Ackia on 6 February with 180 volunteers and 400 Indians, including late-arriving Choctaw. They reached the Ackia complex on 22 February. After two days of skirmishing, Céloron agreed to negotiate. Disgusted, the Choctaw left. The Chickasaw, weakened from years of attacks and anticipating that the main French force would surely arrive, promised to surrender the Natchez refugees, expel the English, and burn the forts. Bienville and a Council of War decided on 15 February to end the campaign and begin to leave Fort Assumption. After a long wait at the fort, Bienville, his forces there now shrunken to five hundred, met a Chickasaw delegation on 31 March and approved Céloron's terms. He chose not to contest their latest explanation that most of the Natchez had fled but that the few still hiding would be found and surrendered. Angry, humiliated, and exhausted, Bienville and the army arrived back in New Orleans by late April. The cost of this second expedition probably exceeded the 1,000,000 livres of the first at a time when Louisiana's entire budget was set at 330,000 livres.

From 1740 through 1742 heavy raids by resurgent Choctaw forces under French sponsorship burned villages and destroyed crops. The English temporarily curtailed their activities, impressed by the magnitude of the French expeditions despite their failure. Forcing an optimistic note, Bienville reported that the Chickasaw-English threat could now be contained. With his departure in 1743—discouraged, aging, and ailing—the Chickasaw War faded to something resembling an end.

David S. Newhall
Centre College

Samuel Dorris Dickinson, *Arkansas Historical Quarterly* (1984); Michael J. Forêt, *Louisiana History* (1990); Michael J. Forêt, *Revue de Louisiane/Louisiana Review* (1982); Arrel M. Gibson, *The Chickasaws* (1971); John Brice Harris, *From Old Mobile to Fort Assumption* (1959); Mary Ann Wells, *Native Land: Mississippi, 1540–1798* (1994); Joe Wilkins, *Proceedings of the Twelfth Meeting of the French Colonial History Society, Ste. Geneviève, May 1986* (1988); Patricia Dillon Woods, *French-Indian Relations on the Southern Frontier* (1980).

Child Development Group of Mississippi

The Child Development Group of Mississippi (CDGM) was a statewide Head Start program begun during the summer of 1965 with a $1.5 million War on Poverty grant to provide poor children with school readiness, two nutritious meals each day, and basic medical services. It was the largest inaugural program in the nation, and during its first summer it employed eleven hundred working-class individuals in eighty-four centers spanning twenty-four counties and serving six thousand children. CDGM's founders included Tom Levin, a psychoanalyst from New York; Arthur Thomas, director of the Delta Ministry; and Polly Greenberg, a US Office of Economic Opportunity employee and early childhood education specialist. Board members included former Tougaloo College president Adam Beittel, Glen Allan civil rights leader Jake Ayers, Mississippi Freedom Democratic Party leader Victoria Gray Adams, and Children's Defense Fund founder Marian Wright Edelman.

CDGM was unique in that from its inception it was overwhelmingly black and was closely allied with civil rights organizations. Its employees included civil rights veteran Unita Blackwell and Roxy Meredith, the mother of James Meredith. For Meredith and many others, CDGM employment was the only option as a consequence of white reprisals for earlier civil rights participation. Because of the connection between the freedom struggle and CDGM employees, the program faced significant opposition and criticism from Mississippi's political leaders and members of the Mississippi State Sovereignty Commission, who alleged that federal dollars were subsidizing civil rights activity. In addition to the political scrutiny, CDGM employees and their supporters faced constant harassment and violence from whites who shot into and burned down Head Start centers.

Head Start was a part of Pres. Lyndon Johnson's War on Poverty authorized by the Economic Opportunity Act of 1964 and administered by the Office of Economic Opportunity. The War on Poverty was largely a response to the demands of civil rights workers for programs that fought poverty and disadvantage, so its authorizing legislation included language calling for the "maximum feasible participation" of the poor. This stipulation meant that parents and other poor members of the community such as Blackwell and Meredith would play roles in creating and administering local Head Start centers. In Mississippi, which had few public kindergartens and severely underfunded black schools, Head Start sought to provide black youngsters with the skills they needed to do well in school and to provide much-needed jobs and income for their parents.

After the summer of 1965 Head Start became a year-round program, and CDGM applied for new funds. The grant was delayed for more than five months, in large part because Sen. John C. Stennis charged the CDGM with fiscal mismanagement. During the unfunded period, more than fifty centers remained open and operated by volunteers. In February 1966 the preschool program finally received six months' worth of new funding on the condition that CDGM relocate from Mount Beulah, its headquarters since 1965, which also served as the headquarters of the Delta Ministry and the Mississippi Freedom Democratic Party. At the end of the 1966 grant, CDGM officials learned that moderate forces had created a rival Head Start program, Mississippi Action for Progress. Following a very public nationwide battle to save CDGM, the program received a third round of funding, but in January 1968 CDGM essentially dissolved. During Head Start's celebration of its twenty-fifth anniversary in Mississippi, twenty-one of the state's Head Start programs traced their existence to CDGM.

Crystal R. Sanders
Penn State University

John Dittmer, *Local People: The Struggle for Civil Rights in Mississippi* (1994); Polly Greenberg, *The Devil Has Slippery Shoes: A Biased Biography of the Child Development Group of Mississippi* (1969); Charles M. Payne, *I've Got the Light of Freedom: The Organizing Tradition and the Mississippi Freedom Struggle* (1995).

Children's Crusade

Discontentment with life in a segregated society gave impetus to youth activism in Jackson during the civil rights era. In response to the perceived need for social change, African American children between the ages of seven and eighteen combined forces with community leaders and civil rights workers to challenge Jim Crow in Mississippi's capital city.

Organized political engagement for social change was evident among Jackson youth as early as 1957, when one of two Mississippi chapters of the National Association for the Advancement of Colored People (NAACP) Youth Council was established in Jackson. The West Jackson Youth Council sought primarily to educate young people on voter rights. By 1960 the city also had a North Jackson Youth Council as well as collegiate chapters of the NAACP.

The Jackson Youth Councils became a powerful force in mobilizing the city's African American community for social change. The children encouraged African Americans in Jackson to vote; to apply for respectable jobs, especially in white-owned establishments; and to boycott segregated events and public facilities. As the Youth Councils' involvement increased, so did their membership. The Jackson movement intensified, with members of the Youth Councils conducting freedom workshops and surveys, distributing leaflets, and recruiting more members.

Between 1960 and 1962, youth activists encouraged blacks to boycott downtown Jackson businesses, particularly during the Easter and Christmas holidays, and to stay off Capitol Street. As part of this effort, college and high school students conducted house-to-house canvasses of the sixty-one thousand blacks in the Jackson area.

Jackson's Youth Councils continued their efforts to dismantle the capital city's system of segregation by attempting to integrate city parks and pools. Young people also tested the city bus lines by sitting on seats reserved for whites only. The Jackson Zoo and the Mississippi State Fair also became targets for civil rights protests.

Children's participation in the Jackson movement reached its height in the spring of 1963. In late April, Mayor Allen C. Thompson met with African American leaders and acquiesced to most of their demands, but he later denied having made any agreement. In response to officials' refusal to negotiate, youth orchestrated Jackson's first mass demonstration of the freedom struggle in late May. Demonstrations, marches, and sit-ins took place in the downtown area, and youth activism influenced other civil rights organizations to take a more active role in the Jackson movement.

On 30 May 1963 Jackson youth organized a crusade for equality. Many participants were students from Lanier, Jim Hill, Brinkley, and Holy Ghost Catholic High Schools. As they marched, the children carried American flags, chanted "We want freedom!" and sang freedom songs. Jackson city police officers, sheriff's deputies, and state highway patrolmen were on hand to arrest the young demonstrators—more than a thousand over a two-week period. The vast number of children arrested forced the conversion of the state fairgrounds into a temporary jail, which many activists referred to as a concentration camp.

In the fall of 1965 the Jackson Youth Council of the NAACP organized the Jackson Youth Movement, which continued boycotting and demonstrating. Jackson's young people remained significant agents of change in the civil rights movement until 1967.

Daphne R. Chamberlain
Tougaloo College

Daphne Rochelle Chamberlain, "'And a Child Shall Lead the Way': Children's Participation in the Jackson, Mississippi, Black Freedom Struggle, 1946–1970" (PhD dissertation, University of Mississippi, 2009); Mississippi History Now website, http://mshistorynow.mdah.state.ms.us; John Dittmer, *Local People: The Struggle for Civil Rights in Mississippi* (1995); Myrlie Evers-Williams and Manning Marable, eds., *The Autobiography of Medgar Evers: A Hero's Life and Legacy Revealed through His Writings, Letters, and Speeches* (2005); John R. Salter, *Jackson, Mississippi: An American Chronicle of Struggle and Schism* (1979).

Chinese

During the post–Civil War period, southern planters experimented with Chinese labor as an alternative to freed slaves. The experiment failed, but the Chinese immigrants remained. Many found an economic niche by opening grocery stores in black neighborhoods. The union benefited both the African Americans, who found relief from plantation-based commissaries, and the Chinese, who found new financial opportunities as merchants.

Other Chinese also came to the Mississippi Delta—some from California after having worked on the railroads, others escaping turmoil in China in the early twentieth century. As Chinese established an economic presence, family members came to join them, often to work in the grocery stores. That support system, combined with difficult political and economic conditions in China, led the number of Chinese in the Delta to grow from 183 in 1900 to 743 in 1940.

Living in the Delta was a challenge for early Chinese immigrants. Not inclined toward assimilation with the black minority and rejected by the prejudice of the white majority, the Chinese found themselves socially isolated. Many Chinese

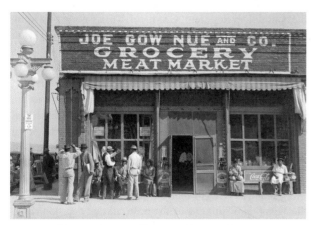

Chinese grocery store, Greenville, November 1939 (Photograph by Marion Post Wolcott, Library of Congress, Washington, D.C. [LC-USF34-052450-D])

cultivated the white community, seeking social affirmation. They began sending their children to white churches and giving money to causes and programs favored by white leaders. Some anglicized their Chinese family names.

Such efforts ultimately met with some success, and the white community gradually ceased to perceive the Chinese as nonwhite and began to grant them some degree of privilege, allowing them to frequent public places from which blacks were barred. Chinese grocers improved their stores, acknowledged Jim Crow laws, and began to have white customers. In addition to business, these efforts provided Delta Chinese with increased social mobility.

In some communities, embracing the white community had the important tangential benefit of giving the Chinese access to white public schools. The Mississippi Constitution, adopted in 1890 by conservative Democrats determined to eliminate the last vestiges of Republican Reconstruction, included a clear mandate for a dual school system for whites and blacks. Since the document did not address education for Chinese, they attended white schools in communities throughout the Delta. In 1924, however, Rosedale officials declared that Chinese children could no longer attend white schools, prompting a lawsuit. The case, *Lum v. Rice*, ultimately reached the US Supreme Court, which upheld the Mississippi Supreme Court's ruling denying Chinese students access to white public schools.

In response, Mississippi Chinese developed partnerships with local (usually Baptist) churches to establish mission schools. Chinese children attending these schools received instruction from a white teacher during the regular school day and supplemental instruction from Chinese tutors in the evenings. In return for their financial support, the churches required inclusion of religious instruction in the curriculum and received decision-making responsibility for the schools.

These schools provided an educational lifeline for Chinese living throughout the Delta, where few acceptable educational alternatives existed. Not only did Chinese children receive an education comparable to that of whites, but the refusal to send children to black schools provided further evidence that the Chinese deserved social acceptance.

World War II gave the Delta Chinese further opportunities to prove themselves. Some enlisted in the armed services, others engaged in rigorous fund-raising in support of the war effort, and all demonstrated their patriotism. The alliance between China and the United States against a common enemy, Japan, further cemented the bond between white and Chinese Mississippians. The enthusiasm with which the Delta Chinese embraced the war effort impressed their white neighbors.

After World War II, Chinese children in the Delta gradually began to attend white public schools, with the timeline for doing so dictated by the individual school districts. The significant increase in access to high-quality public education at both the K–12 and postsecondary levels proved a double-edged sword for Chinese families. The downside to improved education was a decrease in the willingness to take over the family grocery store and remain insulated from the outside world and an increase in the desire to pursue economic and educational opportunities elsewhere. The number of people of Chinese ancestry in the Delta peaked at about 1,200 in 1960 and declined to fewer than 1,000 by the 1990s. The 2010 census counted 3,695 people of Chinese ancestry in the state of Mississippi.

The Chinese have made valuable contributions to the quality of life in the Delta. People of Chinese descent have served as mayors, as leaders of civic clubs and churches, and in all facets of community life. Their stores and businesses have contributed significantly to the economy, and they have a strong record of philanthropic support for community causes, especially education. And when US president Bill Clinton proclaimed 26 October 1998 Chinese Veterans of World War II Day, longtime Delta resident Kenneth Gong was one of the White House honorees.

In 2012 the Mississippi Delta Chinese History Museum opened in the Capps Archive and Museum at Delta State University in Cleveland.

John Thornell
University of North Alabama

James C. Cobb, *The Most Southern Place on Earth: The Mississippi Delta and the Roots of Regional Identity* (1992); *Jackson Clarion-Ledger* (9 September 1944); John Jung, *Chopsticks in the Land of Cotton: Lives of Mississippi Delta Chinese Grocers* (2009); James W. Loewen, *The Mississippi Chinese: Between Black and White* (1971).

Chinn, C. O.
(1919–1999) Activist

C. O. Chinn was an integral figure in the civil rights movement in Canton, Mississippi. Known for his bravery and strength, Chinn had what scholar John Dittmer calls a "deserved reputation for courage and stubbornness." Chinn's actions demonstrated the sacrifices made by Mississippi's black civil rights leaders, as he lost much of his property and was frequently jailed, including serving time on a chain gang.

Chinn was born on 18 September 1919 to a family that owned 154 acres in Farmhaven, Madison County. He received little formal education but became a leading businessman in Canton, owning a café on Franklin Street. His wife, Minnie Lou, and their children were active in civil rights work. Minnie Lou Chinn worked to organize teenage volunteers and to distribute shipments of clothing and food to the largely impoverished community. Student Nonviolent Coordinating Committee member Anne Moody, who worked on voter registration in Canton, described the Chinns as "the one Negro family in Canton who had put their heads on the chopping block," fearless in the face of economic and violent reprisals. Flonzie Brown Wright, a friend of the family and Mississippi's first black female elected official, noted that the Chinns frequently provided shelter and protection for civil rights workers and thus "set the standards of courage for those of us who later became involved."

The Congress of Racial Equality (CORE) had an office adjacent to Chinn's café, and he provided a building for a proposed community center. The Chinn family's Club Desire (where entertainers such as James Brown performed) was also the site of twice-weekly CORE meetings. In the summer of 1963 the drive for voter registration intensified, and Chinn began working with the movement full time. According to Moody, Chinn's heightened involvement was "the luckiest thing that happened to us. . . . [H]e was a powerful man, known as 'bad-ass C. O. Chinn' to the Negroes and white alike. All of the Negroes respected him for standing up and being a man. Most of the whites feared him." Chinn spoke effectively in area churches, recruiting people to register to vote. His activities brought reprisals from Canton whites, and he was forced to close his café and was frequently arrested on spurious charges. The Mississippi State Sovereignty Commission closely followed Chinn's activities, and hundreds of documents in the commission's archive track his movements throughout the 1960s and 1970s. The files describe Chinn as Charles Evers's bodyguard on several occasions, as a leader of boycotts of stores that would not serve or hire blacks, and as the "number one troublemaker in Madison County." The files also noted Chinn's work with the Child Development Group of Mississippi, providing transportation for children attending centers in Madison County.

The day before marchers participating in James Meredith's 1966 March against Fear were scheduled to arrive in Canton, a group of whites attempted to bomb the Mississippi Freedom Democratic Party headquarters. After Chinn and others chased the carload of bombers, he was accused of shooting one of the white men in the arm and was arrested for "assault with a deadly weapon with intent to kill." He denied the charge but was found guilty at an October 1966 trial. He was granted a retrial in 1968 and was again found guilty, but the Mississippi Supreme Court reversed that decision based on "substantial errors" and prejudicial instructions from the court to the jury. In 1970, Chinn was found guilty of killing a different man, Vernon Ricks, though Chinn asserted that he had shot Ricks in self-defense. Chinn was sentenced to twenty years in the Mississippi State Penitentiary and served time before his release in the late 1970s.

Chinn continued as a community leader in Madison County, and the Headstart in Canton was named in his honor, along with Annie Devine and E. W. Garrett. Before his death on 19 July 1999 from colon cancer, Chinn saw his son, Robert, and daughter-in-law, Mamie Chinn, become judges. Alice Scott, Canton's first black mayor, cited Chinn as an inspiration, noting that "his perseverance, endurance, and his insistence in making things better helped pave the way for where I am."

Becca Walton
University of Mississippi

John Dittmer, *Local People: The Struggle for Civil Rights in Mississippi* (1994); Linda Man, *Jackson Clarion-Ledger* (23 July 1999); *Memphis Commercial Appeal* (10 April 1973); Mississippi Department of Archives and History, Sovereignty Commission Online website, http://mdah.state.ms.us/arrec/digital_archives/sovcom/; Anne Moody, *Coming of Age in Mississippi* (1968); *New York Times* (23 July 1999); Charles Payne, *I've Got the Light of Freedom: The Organizing Tradition and the Mississippi Freedom Struggle* (1995).

Choctaw and Chickasaw in Oklahoma

According to the terms of the Removal treaties signed with the Five Civilized Tribes, each tribe had complete control over its local government, judiciary, and educational system in its new nation in Indian Territory. Both the Choctaw and Chickasaw adopted constitutional governments modeled after that of the United States, with a principal chief and other executive officers, a general council, and a system of courts. All of the positions were elected, political interest was high, and the local press kept voters well informed on the issues. The Choctaw and Chickasaw also had a national schooling system. While some elite Indian families sent their children east to attend private boarding schools, most children received their education from members of their own community.

Despite their adoption of Anglo-American systems of government and education, the Choctaw and Chickasaw continued their traditional system of communal land tenure. Tribe members could hunt, fish, and cut timber anywhere outside of town limits. Cultivated land was surrounded by fences so that cattle and other livestock could freely roam the public lands. Most tribe members settled on small plots of land and engaged in subsistence farming. In addition, a group of Native Americans owned black slaves and used them to cultivate large plantations dedicated to growing cotton and foodstuffs. Chickasaw Robert Love owned and operated two Red River plantations worked by more than two hundred slaves. Robert M. Jones, a Choctaw planter, owned five Red River plantations, more than five hundred slaves, and a number of steamboats.

The Choctaw and Chickasaw adopted slave codes to control their black chattel. These laws were very strict, forbidding slaves from owning property, holding political office, or marrying Native Americans. Anyone caught harboring runaway slaves or teaching abolitionism faced severe punishment. Like white slaveholders, some Indians were cruel and physically assaulted their slaves, while others seldom resorted to violence, preferring a paternalistic approach to master-slave relations. By the time of the Civil War, then, the Choctaw and Chickasaw had developed a slaveholding elite that backed the Confederacy.

As a result of that official support for the southern states, the federal government included Indian Territory in its Reconstruction policy. In 1866 the United States forced the Indian nations to sign new treaties requiring the sale of "surplus" land to the federal government. In addition, the Native Americans had to adopt their former slaves as citizens or have them removed from their territory. The Choctaw in particular resisted the end of slavery: the Freedmen's Bureau received reports that they refused to tell their former slaves that they were now free and that some Choctaw killed their ex-slaves rather than free them. US representatives told the Choctaw Council that unless the former slaves received full citizenship rights in the Choctaw nation, they would be relocated at Choctaw expense to the "Leased District," which the United States had recently purchased. Most Choctaw initially preferred Removal, but the tribe's chief argued that relocation so close to the Choctaw nation might attract a flood of African American migrants from the Deep South. After a debate that lasted almost two decades, the tribe finally adopted its former slaves and their descendants and gave them full citizenship rights—equality before the law in civil and criminal cases, equal educational facilities,

eligibility for any political office in the nation except principal chief and district chief, and land on which to establish homesteads.

The Chickasaw proved even more resistant to granting former slaves full tribal membership. An 1866 treaty between the Chickasaw and the US government declared that the former slaves would be removed from the Chickasaw nation within two years of the treaty's ratification if the Chickasaw Council so demanded. However, US officials refused to abide by the terms of the agreement, prompting the Chickasaw to argue that the federal government had never intended to hold up its end of the bargain. The Chickasaw remained intransigent and never agreed to adopt their ex-slaves; as a result, the former Chickasaw slaves and their descendants spent more than forty years without civil rights or legal protection.

Murray Wickett
Brock University

Angie Debo, *And Still the Waters Run* (1940); Daniel F. Littlefield Jr., *The Chickasaw Freedmen: A People without a Country* (1980); Murray R. Wickett, *Contested Territory: Whites, Native Americans, and African Americans in Oklahoma, 1865–1907* (2000).

Choctaw Constitution of 1945

The current government of the Mississippi Band of Choctaw Indians derives its powers from a constitution approved in 1945. The Constitution and Bylaws of the Mississippi Band of Choctaw Indians established a governing body made up of a tribal council and a chief, vice chief, and secretary-treasurer. The tribal council consists of sixteen members elected from the eight major communities of the reservation and meets at least four times a year. The chief chairs the tribal council and serves as the chief executive and administrative officer. The constitution designates membership to those residents who are at least half Choctaw blood. Members of the tribe elect the council and the chief, while the council members select the vice chief and secretary-treasurer. The tribal council negotiates with the various levels of government, employs legal counsel, appropriates tribal funds, supervises economic affairs, and can veto any transactions involving tribal lands or other assets.

The Mississippi Band of Choctaw Indians adopted this constitution following a crucial shift in federal Indian policy during Franklin D. Roosevelt's administration. The passage of the Indian Reorganization Act (IRA) of 1934, often referred to as the Indian New Deal, reflected a new direction among federal policymakers—a shift from the assimilationist aims of the late nineteenth and early twentieth centuries in favor of policies that would foster indigenous culture and Native American self-determination. One major concern by the 1930s was the substantial loss of tribal land over the past half century. The General Allotment Act of 1887, or Dawes Act, required tribes to divide commonly held property and transfer ownership to individual Native Americans. The act opened up "surplus" tribal land to non-Indians, resulting in the loss of millions of acres nationwide. The IRA reversed this policy by ending the allotment process, extending the trust time periods, and instigating a new process whereby tribes could petition the secretary of the interior to return lands to trust status. Empowered by the IRA, the Mississippi Band of Choctaw purchased much of the tribe's current reservation lands.

The IRA also granted more sovereignty to tribal governments, though in an anglicized form. The measure encouraged tribes to adopt written constitutions and bylaws based on majority vote by tribe and subject to the approval of the Department of the Interior. Yet for the Mississippi Choctaw, this process of constructing a constitutional form of government proved difficult, taking eleven years. Two competing political organizations claimed authority over the creation of tribal government. Just a few weeks prior to the signing of the IRA, the Mississippi Choctaw Indian Federation formed in Union, elected leaders, and approved a constitution. The meeting claimed to be the largest assemblage of Native Americans in Mississippi since 1895, and membership was open to anyone with at least half Indian blood as well as to those living outside the tribe's eight main communities. But the Choctaw superintendent had already created the Tribal Business Committee, which included representatives from each of the communities and was tasked with considering the IRA and the possibility of a tribal government. While the issue of tribal government remained unresolved, the Mississippi Choctaw formed local councils and voted to allow the business committee to negotiate economic decisions with the federal government. Not until April 1945 did the Choctaw approve a tribal council and a constitution and bylaws by a 346–71 vote. The Department of the Interior approved the constitution a month later, and the Mississippi Band of Choctaw Indians became an official tribe under the IRA.

Carter Dalton Lyon
St. Mary's Episcopal School,
Memphis

Dan Cobb and Loretta Fowler, eds., *Beyond Red Power: Indian Activism in the Twentieth Century* (2007); Donald A. Grinde Jr., ed., *Native Americans: American Political History Series* (2002); Seena B. Kohl, *Holocaust and Genocide Studies* (1986); Veronica E. Velarde Tiller, ed., *Tiller's Guide to Indian Country: Economic Profiles of American Indian Reservations* (1996).

Choctaw County

Choctaw County, founded in 1833, is located in central Mississippi. The county is named for the Choctaw people. The Natchez Trace Parkway travels through Choctaw County, and the Tombigbee National Forest is partially located in the county. Waterways in the county include Besa Chitto Creek and Big Bywy Ditch. The county seat is Ackerman. Other towns include French Camp, Mathison, and Weir.

In its first census in 1840, Choctaw County had a population of 6,010, 74 percent of them free and 26 percent slaves. The vast majority of residents worked in agriculture, with only sixty-three people employed in manufacturing. While many parts of Mississippi witnessed dramatic increases in the percentage of slaves in the 1840s and 1850s, Choctaw County registered only a 1 percent increase in slaves by 1860. At the end of the antebellum period, Choctaw was home to more than fifteen thousand residents, most of whom worked on farms. As in many areas with free majorities, Choctaw emphasized corn and livestock more than cotton. With forty-three industrial establishments employing 146 workers, Choctaw had a more active industrial economy than most Mississippi counties. The Mississippi Manufacturing Company, chartered in 1848, became one of the state's first significant textile mills. Choctaw had forty free women working in establishments that turned cotton and wool into cloth. Other industrial workers were employed primarily in blacksmithing and lumber.

In the religious census of 1860, Choctaw County had seventy-three churches, the most in the state, among them thirty-six Baptist churches, twenty-seven Methodist churches, eight Presbyterian churches, and two Christian churches.

In 1880 Choctaw County had a population of 9,036, 6,537 of them white and 2,498 African American. The county's twenty-nine manufacturing establishments employed just fifty-three men and no women. Agriculture remained the primary economic concern, and about two-thirds of the 1,358 farmers owned their land. Representing the interests of smaller farmers, the Populist movement did particularly well in Choctaw County.

By 1900 Choctaw County's population had topped 13,000. Two-thirds of the 1,684 white farmers owned their farmland, about twice the rate among the 505 black farmers. The number of industrial workers increased to 102.

According to the religious census of 1916, the largest church groups in Choctaw County were Southern Baptists and Missionary Baptists, which combined to account for more than half of Choctaw's churchgoers. Other major groups included the Methodist Episcopal Church, South; the Methodist Episcopal Church; the Presbyterian Church; and the Churches of Christ. Methodists founded Wood

College in Mathiston in 1886. The Blackwood Brothers, one of the most popular quartets in gospel music, started in Ackerman in the 1930s, first singing in churches and soon performing on the radio. Other musicians of note who grew up in Choctaw County include fiddlers Hoyt Ming, Willie Narmour, and Dock Hemphill.

From 1900 to 1930 Choctaw's population declined slightly, with the county now home to 12,339 people, 8,866 of them white and 3,473 African American. Choctaw County farmers grew more corn than their counterparts elsewhere in Mississippi.

By 1960 Choctaw County's 8,423 people represented one of the state's smallest and most sparsely settled populations, and 70 percent of residents were white. More than half of the workforce still labored in agriculture, largely corn and cattle. Over the next two decades, the number of people involved in manufacturing rose from 310 to 1,310, though personal income rose only from third-lowest in the state to seventh-lowest over that period.

Notable people born or residing in Choctaw County include National Football League player Kenneth Johnson and Major League Baseball pitcher Roy Oswalt, who also played on the gold-medal-winning team during the 2000 Olympics. Choctaw County was home to another Olympian, track star Coby Miller, who earned a silver medal in the men's 4 × 100 relay in the 2004 Olympics. Cheryl Prewitt, Miss America 1980, is from Choctaw County, as are two Mississippi governors. James P. Coleman, the state's fifty-first chief executive, and Ray Mabus (fifty-ninth), who later served as US secretary of the navy and ambassador to Saudi Arabia.

Like many central Mississippi counties, Choctaw County's 2010 population remained predominantly white, and at 8,547, it had not changed significantly in size since 1960.

Mississippi Encyclopedia Staff
University of Mississippi

Mississippi State Planning Commission, *Progress Report on State Planning in Mississippi* (1938); *Mississippi Statistical Abstract*, Mississippi State University (1952–2010); Charles Sydnor and Claude Bennett, *Mississippi History* (1939); University of Virginia Library, Historical Census Browser website, http://mapserver.lib.virginia.edu; E. Nolan Waller and Dani A. Smith, *Growth Profiles of Mississippi's Counties, 1960–1980* (1985).

Choctaw Education

Today's Choctaw education has it roots in the passage of the Indian Self-Determination and Education Assistance Act of 1975. That law paved the way for tribal governments to take control of programs and services previously provided by the federal government on the Choctaw Reservation. Tribal members receive educational services from early childhood through adult education.

One of the first actions undertaken by the Indian Agency established in Mississippi in 1918 was the establishment of Bureau of Indian Affairs schools for tribe members. Elementary schools gradually were built in all Choctaw communities, but not until 1965 did a high school open in the Pearl River community to serve all of the reservation's secondary students. For the most part, these schools implemented the federal policy of assimilation, attempting to educate tribal members according to and in the ways of the dominating culture.

Now, however, six elementary schools, one middle school, and one boarding high school provide services including Choctaw culture to more than seventeen hundred Choctaw students, making it the "largest unified and locally controlled Indian school system in the country." The schools are located in Choctaw communities in a four-county area in east-central Mississippi. In addition, eight Head Start Centers provide low-income students with a wide-ranging child development program, including Choctaw language instruction. In many classrooms, tribe members serve as aides, supporting learning through a variety of means, including the use of Choctaw language. The tribal language program provides further assistance in language instruction in the classrooms as well as after school and during the summer.

Today, Choctaw education shares many of the characteristics of other Mississippi schools. The Choctaw system offers classes in history, mathematics, science, physical education, and other subjects that conform to national standards. There are also extracurricular programs such as the Beta Club, which supports superior achievement; FIRST LEGO League, which supports interactive engineering and robotics education; tutoring programs that target students who need extra assistance; and NASA science programs. In addition, the tribal schools have access to federal education programs such as Title I and Title VII.

A generation ago, most Choctaw students did not go on to receive higher education because of financial constraints or discrimination, but many students now matriculate at institutions ranging from local community colleges to first-rate universities across the country. Students receive tribal support for these endeavors as a result of the success of various economic development efforts.

The tribe operates a thriving adult education department that offers employment and training programs, vocational education, and disability services as well as summer job-training programs that provide youth with skills and opportunities to perform community service. In addition, tribal employees can participate in the Criminal Investigator Training Program at the Federal Law Enforcement Training

Center or wildlife response training from the Audubon Center, among other such opportunities.

William Brescia
University of Tennessee Health
Science Center

Rodney L. Brod, *Choctaw Education* (1979); *Choctaw Community News* (January 2008); *Indian Self-Determination and Education Assistance Act* (88 Stat. 2203), PL 93–638 (4 January 1975); Mississippi Band of Choctaw Indians website, www.choctaw.org.

Choctaw stickball (Bern and Franke Keating Collection, Department of Archives and Special Collections, J. D. Williams Library, University of Mississippi)

Choctaw Fair

The Choctaw Fair began in 1949 and has been held annually ever since in the Pearl River community, just outside Philadelphia, Mississippi. The weeklong fair is the largest community event held by the tribe and attracts members as well as non-Choctaw visitors.

The fair is an outgrowth of less formal events held during the second half of the nineteenth century and the first half of the twentieth. Tribe members from the eight Choctaw communities spread across central Mississippi gathered for several days of eating, socializing, dancing, and playing stickball. Some Choctaw trace the fair to an even more distant antecedent, the Green Corn Ceremony, a southeastern Indian sacred and social ritual thanking the Great Spirit for the corn grown that year. Today's fair formalized the events of the informal reunions and transformed selected elements of Choctaw culture into symbols of a unique tribal identity. While the sacred elements of the Green Corn Ceremony are gone, the social and cultural aspects remain. Further, the fair now serves another function: to introduce Choctaw culture to the tribe's non-Indian neighbors. The result is an eclectic event that highlights three layers of Choctaw identity—tribal, ethnic, and regional.

Displays of traditional Choctaw culture are set up on one side of the road that runs through the center of the Pearl River community. Pots of hominy simmer in large black kettles over open fires while groups perform a series of social dances in formal traditional Choctaw clothing: long embroidered dresses for the women, black pants, ribbon shirts, and black hats for the men. A chanter stands nearby, providing vocal accompaniment while dancers weave back and forth in shifting lines, performing the Snake Dance, Coon Dance, Quail Dance, Duck Dance, and other dances that recognize the intimate relationship between the Choctaw and the natural world. Other dances, among them the Stealing Partners Dance and Losing Wife Dance, are equally playful but comment on human relationships. Here the distinction between Choctaw and visitor is clear. Across the road, however, ethnic identity blurs into shared regional identity, with amusement park rides whirring, barkers shouting, and the smell of corn dogs and elephant ears permeating the air. Identical to any rural county fair, the scene helps break down stereotypes and remind visitors that the Choctaw are southerners, too, with shared cultural traditions and ideas of entertainment.

The Choctaw realize that many non-Indians consider Choctaw culture and American Indian culture synonymous and create divisions to help guide visitors. Choctaw arts and crafts appear on one side of the road, while the arts and crafts of other American Indian tribes are on the other. The Choctaw are Indian, but tribal distinctions are important: feathered headdresses and turquoise jewelry, for example, are Indian but not Choctaw.

The fair's main performance stage synthesizes all three layers of identity. Tribal identify is reified and honored in the Choctaw Princess Pageant, where young women compete in formal wear appropriate at any American prom as well as in formal Choctaw dresses with traditional handcrafted jewelry to match. Later that evening, American Indian music stars perform, followed by nationally known country music stars who draw large crowds from across the state.

For tribe members, however, the main event is the World Championship Stickball tournament, held each evening of the fair. Stickball resembles lacrosse and is played with sticks with cups at each end that allow a small leather ball to be caught and thrown at the opponent's goal, a tall, narrow post. Games are rough and often bloody; an ambulance remains on the sidelines for the more serious injuries. While stickball has traditionally been played by men, women's and youth teams now compete in their own tournaments earlier in the day.

Tom Mould
Elon University

Jesse O. McKee and Jon A. Schlenker, *The Choctaws: Cultural Evolution of a Native American Tribe* (1980); John R. Swanton, *Source Material for the Social and Ceremonial Life of the Choctaw Indians* (1931).

Choctaw Folktales

In the eighteenth and nineteenth centuries, storytelling was part of the formal education for Choctaw youth. With no written language, the Choctaw depended on a rich oral tradition to maintain a sense of history and identity. Today, storytelling continues to help tribal members construct a sense of shared identity, even though its role has become less formal, with stories shared more casually among friends and family.

For all the diversity of types of stories, the Choctaw have few native terms to distinguish one kind of story from another. The major exception is *shukha anumpa*, literally "hog talk" but translated perhaps more accurately as "hogwash." *Shukha anumpa* are stories marked by humor, often raucous and outrageous, whose explicit function is to induce laughter. But rarely are such stories confined to humor alone. Animal tales about a possum burning all the hair off its tail or a rabbit trying to carve a steak from its side reveal the dangers of imitation and of appropriating the roles or skills of another. The turtle who beats the rabbit in a race is as much an indictment on the boastful rabbit as it is a testament to the importance of family who help the turtle win. Inept hunters who try to compensate for their lack of skill through trickery end up losing respect among their peers as well as from women they are courting. Told among children, these animal stories can be moralistic; told among adults, however, they tend to critique contemporary social and cultural norms.

While many of the animal tales have clear cognates in the Indo-European narrative tradition, all of the stories have distinctly Choctaw elements. The tall tales and humorous anecdotes that are also told as *shukha anumpa* are even more specific to Choctaw social life. Particularly humorous are the Ashman stories, which describe a hapless Choctaw trying to understand a world that is changing too fast. Air-conditioning baffles him, as does the English language more generally. Anglo culture is seen at worst as incompatible with Choctaw culture and at best as perplexing, highlighting the struggles of synthesizing two cultures.

Alongside the *shukha anumpa* are a group of stories more serious in tone, often referred to as the "talk of the elders." While these stories can be humorous, laughter is not their explicit goal. Instead, they reflect the narratives that elders are expected to tell to their grandchildren—how the world was formed, how the Choctaw were created, how corn was brought to the people. These are the tribe's sacred myths. Talk of the elders also includes historical legends that document the past and pass down the names of leaders so that they are remembered. Pushmataha, for example, is said to have been born when a lightning bolt split an oak in half. This past cast in narrative is populated first by Indians and then by a steady stream of white settlers, bringing with them new technology to be embraced and new vices such as alcohol that continue to haunt the community. The historical legends are dominated by these interactions with whites and provide a means to critique contemporary social relations.

This social critique is nowhere more evident than among the prophecies that continue to be shared and interpreted anew. Stories of fulfilled prophecies tend to focus on modern conveniences cast in descriptive metaphor: prophecies of metal birds, spiderwebs covering the earth, and two-eyed monsters racing across the ground are revealed to be airplanes, telephone wires, and cars. Far more dire, however, are those prophecies that have yet to be fulfilled—prophecies dominated by cultural, economic, and geographic loss in which the future suffers in comparison to the past. Yet hope remains. The future described in these prophetic stories is not necessarily unalterable. This loss can be avoided, but one must work hard to turn the tide. And in virtually all cases, the maintenance of one's cultural identity, whether by continuing to wear traditional Choctaw clothing or speaking the language, is the key to salvation in upcoming wars.

By far the most widespread and vibrant stories involve the supernatural—both legends of supernatural beings such as *kashehotapalo* and *kashikanchak*, who once roamed the Mississippi woods, and contemporary personal encounters with supernatural beings who continue to lurk under the cloak of pine forests, murky waters, or dark of night. Virtually every tribe member has either encountered one of these supernatural beings or knows someone who has. Stories about floating lights, dark shadowy figures, and half-animal, half-human creatures are shared to interpret both nature and the significance of the encounter. Floating lights could be *hashok okwa hui'ga* (will-o'-the-wisp), *bohpoli* (little people), witches, or any of a number of mundane things such as streetlights, headlights, or swamp gas. Tales of these encounters may be told as scary stories among youth but are at least as common among adults, who recognize deep spiritual and cultural significance in interactions with supernatural beings.

Tom Mould
Elon University

Tom Mould, *Choctaw Tales* (2004).

Choctaw Indians, Mississippi Band of

The Mississippi Choctaw live in eight recognized communities throughout east-central Mississippi. Despite one of the highest blood quorum requirements of any American Indian tribe (50 percent), tribal rolls have been steadily increasing in recent years, with approximately ten thousand members today.

Two distinct myths explain how the Choctaw came to live in Mississippi. In the migration myth, two brothers, Chahta and Chikasa, traveled from the West looking for more fertile hunting grounds. Each night they planted a pole in the ground, and each morning the pole leaned in the direction the group was to travel that day. One rainy night, the two groups became separated, with Chikasa's group continuing across the swelling waters of the Pearl River while Chahta's group remained behind. In the morning, Chahta found the pole upright, indicating that they had finally reached their new home at the Nanih Waiya mound, translated variously as "leaning hill" or "mother mound." In the second myth, the Choctaw emerged from the center of the earth out of a hole in the sacred Nanih Waiya mound, following the Seminole, Cherokee, Creek, and Chickasaw, who scattered throughout the Southeast. Emerging last, the Choctaw were granted the lands of their birthplace as their home. Although the two myths differ dramatically, both describe connections to neighboring tribes and identify Nanih Waiya as the spiritual and geographical center of the Choctaw homeland, granted to the tribe by divine right. Archaeological, historical, and linguistic records support both a migration from the West and the coherent founding of a distinct tribe in the Nanih Waiya area in Winston County.

Written documents first record the name *Choctaw* at the end of the seventeenth century. At this time, the Choctaw lived in three distinct districts, with two divisions and multiple clans within each division that established social and political boundaries. As an exogamous, matrilineal community, tribe members were expected to marry outside their clan. While clan identity is no longer recognized, some tribe members, particularly in the more conservative communities of Bogue Chitto and Conehatta, continue to encourage dating and marriage outside a member's community.

With the increase in Europeans in America during the eighteenth century, the Choctaw formed alliances first with the French in wars against the British and their Indian allies, the Chickasaw, and then, after the Revolutionary War, with the new Americans against the Spanish and their Indian allies, the Creek. However, while Western histories focus on colonial powers and alliances, oral traditions within the tribe today emphasize relations with neighboring Indian tribes, in particular the cyclical conflicts with the Chickasaw and Creek over hunting grounds. The major exception is Removal, a cataclysmic policy that dominates both written and oral accounts. In the first decades of the nineteenth century, Andrew Jackson was struggling with the "Indian problem"—that is, too many autonomous Indian groups unwilling to allow unrestricted access to the lands and resources of their homelands. His solution was to remove the Indians east of the Mississippi to lands far west of it even though those lands were less agriculturally fertile and less forested and thus less suitable for the game Indians traditionally hunted. This Removal eventually became known as the Trail of Tears, and an estimated 20–25 percent of the southeastern Indians died during Removal. The Choctaw were the first of the southeastern tribes to be removed, following the signing the Treaty of Dancing Rabbit Creek in 1830. Over the next seventy years, the US government exerted consistent pressure to remove all of the Choctaw to Oklahoma, with at least one other major Removal effort at the turn of the century. According to estimates, roughly fourteen thousand of the twenty thousand Choctaw were removed to Oklahoma, with approximately twenty-five hundred dying along the way. In light of the two tribal creation myths, forced Removal from what they viewed as their divinely given lands was particularly traumatic. Today, Choctaw prophecies warn of the Third Removal, which will signal dramatic changes for Choctaw and non-Choctaw alike, perhaps a sign of the end of the world.

Each Choctaw who remained in Mississippi was promised 640 acres of land in return for agreeing to become an American citizen. However, few Choctaw ever received their land, and those who did often lost it through swindles perpetrated by unscrupulous land speculators. Most who stayed were soon driven onto undesirable swampland, where they attempted to continue farming. Eventually, they became sharecroppers on land they had once owned, entering a period of intense geographical and social isolation. As brown-skinned people in a color-conscious South that saw things in black and white, the Choctaw did not fit in. They fought aggressively to avoid being categorized as black and thus subjected to intense discrimination, but the white community refused to accept the Choctaw.

The tribe's increasingly visible and powerful role in the Mississippi economy has begun to change this isolation. The creation of an industrial park in 1979 opened an era during which the tribe enticed major businesses to build factories on Choctaw lands. As part of the effort to develop industry and factory jobs, the tribe eventually started establishing tribal businesses, including casinos that opened in 1994 and 2000. Today, the Mississippi Band of Choctaw Indians is one of the state's largest employers. Under the Indian Reorganization Act of 1934 (which permitted the organization of tribal governments) and the Indian Self-Determination and Education Assistance Act of 1975 (which permitted tribes to have greater ownership of services and programs on the reservation), the Mississippi Choctaw have reestablished an autonomous tribal government that has received federal recognition.

Despite brief periods of isolation, the Choctaw generally have been open to new ideas and new technologies, readily transforming other American Indian or Anglo rituals, clothing, weapons, and political systems to fit within their own culture. This borrowing and sharing have led to some of the most iconic symbols of Choctaw identity today, such as the black felt hats worn by the men, known in the Choctaw language as *shapo* (from the French *chapeau* [hat]), and the men's traditional ribbon shirts, which are worn by Indian tribes throughout the Southeast. Women's dresses draw from both European settlers and neighboring Indian tribes, employing the basic form worn by European missionary women in the nineteenth century but adding ribbons and beadwork to transform their clothing within a Choctaw and more broadly southeastern Indian aesthetic. Of course, European missionaries brought with them much more than clothing styles. Written records from early missionaries suggest the Choctaw had a coherent belief system that governed their views on both earthly and otherworldly matters, including sources of supernatural power, with the ultimate source being the sun. However, those belief systems were organized only loosely in terms of a single pervasive religion. Written records and oral traditions do not provide enough evidence for contemporary Choctaw interested in following a native religion to do so. By choice or by default, the majority of contemporary Choctaw are Christian.

The synthesis of multiple cultures continues today. Modern Choctaw homes are indistinguishable from the homes of their socioeconomically comparable non-Choctaw neighbors in terms of technological amenities. However, aesthetic and decorative elements articulate a distinct ethnic identity as both American Indian and Choctaw. Many homes display arts and crafts from other Indian tribes, particularly items bought on visits out west. Virtually all homes, however, have specifically Choctaw items hanging on walls, among them star quilts and stickball sticks and swamp cane baskets, which are still made from materials drawn directly from nearby forests and swamps. While tribe members continue to prepare traditional foods such as *banaha*—a mixture of corn and peas—and hominy, their dinner tables are more likely to be indistinguishable from those of their non-Indian neighbors, featuring southern staples such as cornbread, fried chicken, greens, and slow-cooked vegetables seasoned with meat.

Tom Mould
Elon University

Arthur H. DeRosier Jr., *The Removal of the Choctaw Indians* (1970); Patricia Galloway, *Choctaw Genesis: 1500–1700* (1995); Clara Sue Kidwell, *Choctaws and Missionaries in Mississippi, 1818–1918* (1995); Jesse O. McKee and Jon A. Schlenker, *The Choctaws: Cultural Evolution of a Native American Tribe* (1980); Mississippi Band of Choctaw Indians website, www.choctaw.org; Tom Mould, *Choctaw Prophecy: A Legacy of the Future* (2003); Tom Mould, *Choctaw Tales* (2004); John H. Peterson Jr., *The Mississippi Band of Choctaw Indians: Their Recent History and Current Social Relations* (1971); John R. Swanton, *Source Material for the Social and Ceremonial Life of the Choctaw Indians* (1931); Samuel Wells and Roseanna Tubby, eds., *After Removal: The Choctaw in Mississippi* (1986).

Choctaw Language

The Choctaw language belongs to the Muskogean language family, an extensive group that includes Creek (also referred to as Muskogee), Chickasaw, Mikasuki (either a dialect of or very similar to now extinct Hitchiti), Seminole (a dialect of Creek), Alabama, and Koasati. At the time of European arrival, the Muskogean language family was one of the largest in the southeastern United States in both population and geographical range.

Today, Choctaw is the traditional language of the Mississippi Band of Choctaw Indians. About 80 percent of the approximately ten thousand tribe members speak the language fluently. The language is also spoken by older members of the Oklahoma Choctaw Nation, a group forced to leave their original Mississippi homeland and follow the Trail of Tears to Indian Territory in the 1830s.

The Choctaw language was and is unique. The Mississippi Band of Choctaw Indians continued to speak Choctaw as their first language and as the vehicle of everyday communication until the late 1980s. This achievement, based in part on their social isolation and to an even greater degree on their belief that their language and their identity were inseparable, distinguished them from almost all other North American native groups. Until the early 1990s most children began kindergarten speaking primarily if not exclusively Choctaw. Today, however, some children still speak mainly Choctaw, but most perceive the language as backward and English as modern. Nonetheless, most teenagers remain bilingual to at least some extent, speaking not only English but a variety of Choctaw marked by a large number of English vocabulary borrowings and incorporating some features of English grammar.

The majority of Choctaw sounds are familiar to the English ear. The language employs only two sounds not ordinarily found in English: (1) a glottal stop /ʼ/, similar to the sound between the two syllables of English *uh oh*; and (2) a lateral fricative /ɬ/, similar to the simultaneous pronunciation of *thl*, as in the English onomatopoetic *thlunk*. Unlike English, Choctaw may also create meaning differences between words by distinguishing between long, short, nasal, and nonnasal vowels and between single and double consonants.

Choctaw base or elemental words usually consist of one to three syllables. Verb bases are routinely lengthened by the addition of particles conveying additional meaning—when the action occurred, in what manner the activity was conducted (quickly, intensely, and so forth), and who performed the action (if a pronoun).

There is no exact equivalent of the English *to be* forms. Instead, Choctaw has a special set of verbs to indicate the positional and spatial relationship of two items. These verbs indicate whether the referents are singular, dual, or plural; whether they are "existing, being somewhere"; "standing"; "sitting"; "setting on"; or "hanging from." They function similarly to the English all-purpose *is*. For example, the counterpart of the English query "Is Rose there?" (for example, in an office), utilizes the subject's probable position instead of *is*:

Rose + at   biniili + h   + ˌo?
Rose + Subject Particle   sit + Verb Particle   + Interrogative

Positional verbs and verbs referring to other attributes of the referents (shape, for example) are not uncommon in North American Native languages.

Nouns may be modified by attaching possessive pronouns at the beginning of the base word (for example, *my*) or by attaching demonstrative (*this*, *that*), locative (*here*, *there*), or emphatic particles (among other types) at the end of the base. Nouns may also be followed by separate words specifying number, color, size, or the like, functions that are similar to English adjectives.

The normal order of basic sentence constituents in Choctaw is Subject-Object(s)-Verb. (In English, the order is Subject-Verb-Object.) However, Choctaw has more freedom than English in its ability to vary word order because the subject (or subject noun phrase) always has a specific, terminal particle ({-at}). Thus, no matter where the subject noun or noun phrase appears in the sentence, its grammatical function is immediately identifiable. Complex sentences (those consisting of more than one clause) can signal, with an attachment at the end of the first clause, whether or not the subject of the second clause is the same or different from that of the first.

Today, the Mississippi Band of Choctaw Indians, recognizing the language-erosive effects of socioeconomic integration with English speakers, has initiated the Choctaw Tribal Language Program, which focuses on immersing Choctaw children in day care and Head Start programs in the Choctaw language. This approach is based on the fact that almost all Choctaw children begin day care around the age of six weeks and on the assumption that the acquisition of English is inevitable, whereas the acquisition of Choctaw is no longer certain. Regular evaluation and annual testing will ultimately determine the success of such programs, but data so far are promising.

Patricia Kwachka
University of Alaska at Fairbanks

Roseanna Thompson
Mississippi Band of Choctaw
Indians

Karen M. Booker, *Languages of the Aboriginal Southeast: An Annotated Bibliography* (1991); George Aaron Broadwell, *A Choctaw Reference Grammar* (1996); James M. Crawford, ed., *Studies in Southeastern Indian Languages* (1975); Heather Hardy and Janine Scancarelli, eds., *Native Language of the Southeastern United States* (2005); Patricia Kwachka, ed., *Perspectives on the Southeast: Linguistics, Archaeology, and Ethnohistory* (1994); Pamela Munro and Catherine Willmond, *Chickasaw, an Analytical Dictionary* (1994); T. Dale Nicklas, "Elements of Choctaw" (PhD dissertation, University of Michigan, 1972).

Choctaw Music

Today's Mississippi Choctaw listen both to the popular music repertoires common throughout the rural South—thus various forms of rock music, especially classic rock, and quite a bit of country and western—and also certain repertoires that are either specific to the tribe or in more general circulation among native peoples. The most specifically Choctaw of their musical genres are those connected with Choctaw social dance.

When wide-ranging collector of native music Frances Densmore stopped briefly in Mississippi in 1933, she collected sixty-five performances of songs from just a few men. Most of these were the songs accompanying social dances much like those of the Cherokee and other southeastern tribes. A majority of these are what the Choctaw call animal dances, such as the Duck, Tick, Snake, Bear, Terrapin, Quail, Turkey, Chicken, Rabbit in the Garden, Dog Chases Raccoon, and similar dances. Other Choctaw social dance songs—some of which Densmore collected, and most of which are known in various versions throughout the Southeast—include the Stomp Dance, Walk Dance, Stealing Partners Dance, War Dance, and Wedding Dance. Densmore found and recorded few singers because Choctaw secular expressive culture was then in decline, in part because the Baptist Church had become a unifying social force for the Mississippi Choctaw. By the 1960s little Choctaw music was performed publicly. But an Anglo-American schoolteacher, Minnie Hand, encouraged and facilitated the recording of songs from Choctaw elders. She then helped Choctaw social dance and its music to become part of the regular school curriculum.

Today, troupes of young dancers based in more than a dozen schools represent their communities at the annual Choctaw Fair, at powwows (in sets of a half dozen social dances inserted between the usual powwow dances), and so on. One or two young men in each ensemble sing with clear, relaxed voices, performing pentatonic or diatonic melodies composed of nonlexical syllables. The young men and women, wearing outfits that join older rural Anglo-American clothing styles with Native American decoration, dance in long lines, in parallel lines, or as couples, generally with restrained movements but in some dances featuring one couple at a time running around and happily shrieking.

In recent decades, the Mississippi Choctaw have joined with most of the Native American world in welcoming the powwow complex of arts and culture. On Veterans Day, for example, local Indians join with visitors from other states to put on powwows lasting several days. Choctaw and a few visiting Indians dance into a consecrated dance circle during the Grand Entry in a prescribed order, led by veterans carrying flags. While the music is the same for most dances, regalia (dance outfits) and linked dance types vary, with the men and boys divided into men's traditional dancers (among them dancers imitating hunting), fancy dancers, and grass dancers; the women and girls may be traditional dancers, fancy shawl dancers, or jingle dress dancers. Songs after the first few many be "intertribals," during which all dancers in regalia and perhaps nonoutfitted dancers dance, or may be specific to the dance type and perhaps also the age of a group of dancers. Most of the music is performed by "drums," ensembles of approximately five to twelve men who sing while playing a single large, horizontal drum. The men sing in approximate unison with tight, nasal voices and a very wide vibrato. Melodies start high, descend in terraced contours, return to near the beginning, then fall as before. This whole contour is repeated several times within a song, with each song lasting three to four minutes. The ensembles are of two types, northern (relatively high) and southern (somewhat lower), with reinforcement at the upper octave by women standing behind the drummers. The Mississippi Choctaw community includes members of both types of ensemble, and groups from elsewhere may also participate.

Chris Goertzen
University of Southern Mississippi

Frances Densmore, "Choctaw Music," *Anthropological Papers, No. 28, Bureau of American Ethnology Bulletin* (1943); Victoria Lindsay Levine, "Choctaw Indian Musical Cultures in the Twentieth Century" (PhD dissertation, University of Illinois, 1990).

Choctaw Stickball

For centuries, stickball has been an important custom of Mississippi's native Choctaw. Stickball (*ishtaboli*) is the forerunner of lacrosse and served as an early means of recreation as well as strengthened Choctaw identity. In addition, stickball was used to resolve conflict among different Choctaw communities and among neighboring Chickasaw or Creek. These games could often avert war while venting passions.

Games sometimes lasted from around nine in the morning to sundown or longer. The ballfield (*hitoka*) could vary from one hundred feet to several miles, and between twenty and seven hundred people could play at a time. Entire communities from many miles around came to watch and participate.

Players use two types of stick, the *kabocca* and *kapucha*, both carved from hickory about 2.5 feet long and ending in an oval hoop tied with buckskin thongs to make a cup. Players use only the sticks, never their hands, to move the leather ball (*towa*) to the goalposts. A team scores by hitting the other team's goalpost with the ball. In early games, the victor was the first team to reach a preselected number of points, often up to one hundred, and rules about prohibited behavior were lax, with only head butting prohibited. Play was violent and often resulted in broken bones.

The night before the game Choctaw women made their family's bets, placing some of the family's belongings on the line, while elders set up the goalposts. Players and others would gather around the team's goalpost to sing and perform the Stickball Dance all night to invoke the Great Spirit to help the team win. The players wore their game costumes, which consisted of breechclouts, beaded belts, and manes and tails that represented strong animals. Medicine men also sent smoke to the Great Spirit all night and throughout the game stood at their team's goalpost, beating a drum, chanting, clapping, and singing to influence the team's luck.

Stickball games dwindled in the early 1900s but were revived by the Choctaw Fairs starting in 1949. Stickball is currently played in four fifteen-minute quarters, and additional rules exist about play. Choctaw craftsmen still create handmade sticks and balls, and players wear traditional Choctaw patterns on their uniforms. An important part of the Choctaw Fairs, contemporary stickball preserves an ancient and significant Choctaw tradition.

Betsy Martin
Jackson, Mississippi

James H. Howard and Victoria Lindsay Levine, *Choctaw Music and Dance* (1990); Mississippi Band of Choctaw Indians website, www.choctaw.org.

Choctaw Sweat Lodges

The present-day or modern Choctaw sweat lodge is associated with traditional Choctaw practices. Choctaw sweat lodges are places of prayer and healing for participants, and Choctaw medicine men have long used a sweat bath (*hobichi*) in their healing ceremonies. During sweat lodge ceremonies, participants sit in a circle inside a round, domed structure made of willow branches covered with blankets or tarps. In the center of the circle, lava rocks, called grandfather rocks, are stacked in a pit and a fire is built around them until they become red-hot. The conductor of the ceremony pours water on the rocks, creating steam that envelops the participants. Prayers and songs, including Choctaw sweat lodge songs, traditional Choctaw spiritual songs, and songs from other tribes, are offered during ceremonies.

Individuals who conduct sweat lodges run the ceremony differently based on their training and experience. Generally, the conductor encourages participants to be themselves and to pray from their hearts. In addition, the conductor typically divides the sweat lodge ceremony into four parts. The first round often is a cleansing or purification round, with participants encouraged to pray for themselves as the water is poured on the hot lava rocks. In the second round, participants are encouraged to pray for others. The third round is usually a healing round or an honor round. During the fourth round, participants usually give thanks to the Creator.

A number of practices precede a sweat lodge ceremony. The sweat lodge grounds need to be properly cleaned before a ceremony can take place. Cleaning includes sweeping out the interior of the sweat lodge and the surrounding area to remove the old prayers and pave the way for new prayers. The fire pit is also cleaned out and a new fire is made with the lava rocks stacked inside. As the fire burns and the rocks heat, the conductor of the sweat lodge or the fireman may watch or listen to the fire for signs of spiritual intervention. As people arrive for the ceremony, there is often a lot of joking. Sometimes, coffee or drinks may be available. Before entering, participants smudge the sweat lodge—generally with smoke from burning tobacco and cedar and sometimes with sage and sweetgrass. Cedar is a traditional Choctaw purifier, while tobacco is a traditional offering to the Creator. The smudge helps prepare the ceremonial space and the individuals for spiritual intercession.

Many participants consider the sweat lodge their place of spirituality. Participants do not have to dress up or attempt to impress others at sweat lodges. Rather, participants pray and seek spiritual assistance, knowledge, and understanding. Participants often attempt to leave their bad or destructive practices at the sweat lodge and emerge as new people focused on acting positively to build healthy relationships with their families and communities.

Sweat lodges are often located in people's backyards. Sweat lodges may also be temporarily constructed at important cultural and spiritual sites, such as the top of Nanih Waiya, an earth mound of great cultural significance to the Choctaw.

Stephen Rosecan
Boston, Massachusetts

Robert C. Tubby
Mississippi Band of Choctaw
Indians

Tom Mould, *Choctaw Prophecy: A Legacy of the Future* (2003); John R. Swanton, *Source Material for the Social and Ceremonial Life of the Choctaw Indians* (1931); Stephen Rosecan, "Striving to Remake Their Lives: Spirituality, Social Relations, and Sweat Lodges among the Mississippi Choctaws," Paper Presented at the Southern Anthropological Society Meeting (April 2002).

Christian Methodist Episcopal Church (Colored Methodist Episcopal Church)

Almost immediately after emancipation, African American and white members of the Methodist Episcopal Church, South (MECS) began working to form African American Methodist organizations along with a Plan of Separation that would lead to the new denominations. In 1870, the Colored Methodist Episcopal Church (CME) was formed in Jackson, Tennessee.

The founders sought to adhere to the traditions of Methodism and made few changes to the MECS organizational structure beyond lowering the educational standards for preachers, deleting all racial designations for preachers and members, and adding rules against using church buildings for political purposes. CME leaders for years argued that they, rather than the African Methodist Episcopal Church and the African Methodist Episcopal Church, Zion, were the proper heirs to the Methodist tradition. In return, some leaders of those groups criticized the CME for its close relationships to whites in the MECS.

Mississippians were especially important during the CME's formative years. The MECS had two Colored Conferences in the state. The first, in North Mississippi, was organized in 1867 and had district offices in Grenada, Verona, Iuka, Courtland, and Holly Springs. The other, the Mississippi Conference, was organized in 1869 and covered the rest of the state, with district offices in Sunflower, Starkville,

Blackhawk, Vicksburg, Fayette, Jackson, Crystal Springs, Brookhaven, Summit, Paulding, and Burtenton. The two conferences sent five representatives, Frank Ambrose, Frank Funchess, William Jones, Nat Harris, and M. Mitchell, to the founding meeting in 1870. One early CME bishop, Elias Cottrell, a native of Old Hudsonville in Marshall County, served as a pastor in several Tennessee locations before returning to Mississippi with a particular interest in education. Another Mississippi native, John Scurlock, was the first assistant editor for the denomination's journal, the *Christian Index*.

By 1900 the CME had two Mississippi conferences, roughly continuing the geographic division the MECS had established. The state was home to about 340 CME churches with about twenty-two thousand members, second only to Georgia. Those numbers stayed roughly the same for several decades. The 1936 Religious Census counted 332 CME churches and more than twenty-six thousand members.

One of the CME's most aggressive efforts to transform the South lay in its effort to operate schools and eventually colleges throughout the region. CME leaders tried unsuccessfully to start a CME school in Sardis in 1874 but had better results in Holly Springs with Mississippi Theological and Industrial Academy (soon renamed Mississippi Industrial College), chartered in 1906 and initially headed by F. H. Rogers. Within a few years, the school had become with largest CME school in the country, with more than four hundred students from first grade through college. Construction of a large auditorium with the help of a donation from Andrew Carnegie dramatized CME leaders' great ambitions for the school, which emphasized the training of teachers until it closed in 1982.

The CME changed its name to the Christian Methodist Episcopal Church in May 1954. Membership has declined with the migration of African Americans away from Mississippi, but the denomination continues to play an important role in the state. Numerous current and former CME bishops have roots, educations, and churches in Mississippi.

Ted Ownby
University of Mississippi

Christian Methodist Episcopal Church website, thecmechurch.org; *Census of Religious Bodies*, 1906, 1936; Alicia Jackson, "The Colored Methodist Episcopal Church and Their Struggle for Reform in the New South" (PhD dissertation, University of Mississippi, 2004); Othal H. Lakey, *The History of the CME Church, Revised* (1996); William E. Montgomery, *Under Their Own Vine and Fig Tree: The African-American Church in the South, 1865–1900* (1994).

Church of Christ (Holiness)

The Church of Christ (Holiness) USA (COCHUSA) is an African American holiness denomination that began as a holiness fellowship among black Baptist churches in Mississippi, Arkansas, and Tennessee in 1896 and was led by Charles Price Jones, Charles Harrison Mason, Walter S. Pleasant, and other Baptist clergy. These leaders first met in 1895 and forged an alliance based on their common goal of introducing the doctrine of sanctification. In 1899 Jones, Mason, and others were expelled by the Baptists. From 1899 to 1906 the fellowship grew throughout the Mid-South and surrounding states. Christ Missionary and Industrial School, the denomination's leading educational institution, was organized as Christ Holiness School in 1901 in Jackson. (During the 1920s, COCHUSA also supported the Boydton Institute in Virginia.) A mission in Liberia was established in 1902.

Jones was elected in 1906 as the general overseer of the Church of God in Christ, a nondenominational holiness fellowship of more than 110 congregations in Mississippi, Alabama, Arkansas, Louisiana, Tennessee, Texas, and Missouri. Almost 50 percent of the churches were in Mississippi. The epicenter of the fellowship was Jackson's Christ Temple, Jones's pastorate and the site of the annual convocation.

In the spring of 1907 the fellowship became embroiled in a theological controversy after Mason, John A. Jeter, and David J. Young, whom Jones had sent to assess the validity of the Azusa Street Revival in Los Angeles and the emerging Pentecostal movement, returned to the South proclaiming the Pentecostal message. Although Jeter recanted his testimony, Mason and Young, joined by others, continued to advance the Pentecostal doctrine. The controversy was addressed in August 1907 with the decision to dismiss Mason from fellowship. While ten congregations followed Mason, the vast majority remained with Jones.

Various African American holiness associations subsequently joined Jones's fellowship, including the (Holiness) State Convention in Louisiana around 1907, the Virginia and North Carolina Convention in 1921, and the Nashville District of the Holiness Church in 1927. During the 1920s COCHUSA entered into discussions about merging with the predominantly white Church of the Nazarene and the Christian Church; for certain periods, COCHUSA had cooperative arrangements with the Christian and Missionary Alliance and the Pilgrim Holiness Church.

Committed to nondenominationalism, the fellowship resisted incorporation until the 1910s, after Mason incorporated the name Church of God in Christ. For most of its history, COCHUSA was led by two people: Charles Price Jones (1906–49) and Major Rudd Conic (1949–93). Bishop Maurice D. Bingham of Jackson, Mississippi, was elected Senior Bishop in 1996, a position he held until August of

2004. As of 2015 Bishop Emery Lindsay of Chicago is the Senior Bishop, and Bishop Vernon Kennebrew, from Little Rock, Arkansas, is the President.

Many COCHUSA leaders and laypeople participated in the civil rights movement, most of them on the local level. However, Fannie Lou Hamer was a prominent national civil rights activist.

In recent years COCHUSA has consisted of 167 congregations in the United States, 19 congregations in Liberia, and 9 congregations in the Dominican Republic. It also cosponsors mission projects in West Africa.

David D. Daniels III
McCormick Theological Seminary

Willenham Castilla, *Moving Forward on God's Highway: A Textbook History of the Church of Christ (Holiness) U.S.A.* (2007); Otto B. Cobbins, ed., *History of the Church of Christ (Holiness) U.S.A., 1895–1965* (1966); David D. Daniels III, "The Cultural Renewal of Slave Religion: Charles Price Jones and the Emergence of the Holiness Movement in Mississippi" (PhD dissertation, Union Theological Seminary, 1992).

Church of God in Christ

The Church of God in Christ (COGIC) was formed in 1907 by Charles Harrison Mason, who was expelled from his Baptist church in the late nineteenth century because of his views and teachings regarding salvation, sanctification, and holiness. In 1891 Mason was licensed to preach by Mount Gale Missionary Baptist Church in Preston, Arkansas. He entered Arkansas Baptist College in Little Rock in 1893 but became dissatisfied and withdrew after three months as a result of the new methods of teaching in the era of post-Reconstruction racial uplift that stressed rational preaching over emotional worship. Mason traveled for several years as an itinerant preacher throughout Arkansas and Mississippi before settling in Jackson in 1896 and joining Charles Price Jones, a fellow holiness preacher and pastor of the Mount Helms Baptist Church. Mason's messages were primarily based on the controversial doctrine of sanctification, which stressed that all men could free themselves from sin by righteous living.

In 1897 Mason established his first holiness congregation as the result of a revival he conducted in Lexington, Mississippi. As the holiness revival grew, Mason obtained the use of an abandoned cotton gin near the bank of a small creek in Lexington, turning it into the first COGIC structure; those converted during the revival became the first congregation members. Later that year, while on a trip to Little Rock,

Mason came to believe that God had revealed the name for his holiness following. According to Mason, the name Church of God in Christ was biblically supported in I Thessalonians 2:14, II Thessalonians 1:1, and Galatians 1:22.

In 1899 Mason also became associated with two other holiness ministers, J. A. Jeter of Little Rock and W. S. Pleasant of Hazlehurst, Mississippi. Mason, Jones, Jeter, and Pleasant concluded that a holiness association should be formed and met in Jackson to bring together all of the black holiness congregations in Arkansas, Tennessee, and Mississippi. Jones served as the general overseer, Mason served as overseer of Tennessee, and Jeter served as overseer of Arkansas. The three maintained this organizational structure until 1907, when a dispute over church leadership, especially involving the biblical issue of glossolalia (speaking in tongues), caused the organization to dissolve. Mason then became COGIC's first bishop.

Although headquartered in Memphis, COGIC retains deep roots in the state of Mississippi. Its first large concentration of followers resided in the state. In 1917 the Church established Saints Industrial College in Lexington to educate children from Holmes County. In 1926 Mason appointed Arenia C. Mallory as the college's president. Mallory used the school as a platform to link COGIC and Mississippi to the national racial uplift movement. Saints Industrial College served as the headquarters for the Mississippi Health Program and for literacy programs that reached throughout the state via COGIC congregations. As a result, COGIC's influence on Mississippi politics, culture, and social life can still be felt today.

Calvin White Jr.
University of Arkansas

Anthea Butler, *Women in the Church of God in Christ: Making a Sanctified World* (2007); David D. Daniels III, "The Cultural Renewal of Slave Religion: Charles Price Jones and the Emergence of the Holiness Movement in Mississippi" (PhD dissertation, Union Theological Seminary, 1992); Calvin White Jr., *The Rise to Respectability: Race, Religion, and the Church of God in Christ* (2012).

Church Property Bill

In March 1960 the Mississippi legislature passed the Church Property Bill, the collective and popular name for measures originally introduced as Senate Bill 1517 and House Bill 220. Like much legislation passed during that session, the bill was an openly segregationist measure designed to shore up Jim Crow's legal foundations and to protect segregation at its most vulnerable points. The bill offered legal provisions to help local congregations sever ties with their parent denominations. Such separations could become necessary, according to the legislation's proponents, if the denomination "changed social policy"—that is, if it "forced integration" on white churches. The measure permitted local congregations to retain ownership of church property—buildings, furnishings, and supplies—when they struck out on their own rather than returning these goods to the denomination, as both existing Mississippi church property law and many denominations required.

This bill marked the second time in the civil rights era that the legislature had sought to manipulate the law in an effort to foreclose religious critiques of segregation. A bill considered during the 1956 legislative session had proposed depriving churches of their tax-exempt status if they "practiced integration." While the earlier measure met opposition in the House and ultimately died, the 1960 incarnation fared much better.

The religious threat to segregation seemed to emanate most strongly from the Methodist Church, and many white Mississippi Methodists thought the bill was aimed directly at them and their congregations, which claimed the second-largest membership in the state. The denomination's reputation as a threat to segregation had grown in intensity and immediacy for more than a decade. Nationally, the church's official publications consistently condemned segregation, and its ministers and representatives openly advocated racial equality. Some denominational agencies, boards, and facilities had already been integrated. Leaders continued to lay plans for absorbing the all-black administrative unit, the Central Jurisdiction, into the existing white geographic jurisdictions; indeed, the segregated unit had already been dissolved in the western United States.

These developments troubled many southern Methodists. The conservative Mississippi Association of Methodist Ministers and Layman had been working since about 1950 to hold at bay the denomination's "integrationist tendencies." Since its inception, this group had held out the possibility of forming a breakaway movement in the event that the national organization insisted that local churches admit all races. The Church Property Bill, drafted by the group's leader, prominent Mississippi attorney John Satterfield, provided segregationist Methodists the necessary legal protection to effect such a separation.

While the Methodist Church came under the most fire, segregationists seemed concerned that any white denomination might provide a potential point of entry for a racially egalitarian impulse, and debate over the Church Property Bill reflected this concern. As one legislator remarked in his defense of the bill, "When integration finally comes to Mississippi it will come through the front doors of the churches, in the disguise of religion." Thus, Baptists, Presbyterians, Episcopalians, and Catholics also debated the bill's merits from their pulpits, in their official publications, and at the public hearing on it. Opponents argued that the legislation violated the principle of separation of church and state, that it would exacerbate the tendency for religious friction and divisiveness, and, perhaps most significantly, that it was utterly unnecessary since no denomination would force a practice on its members against their will. Ignoring these objections, the bill's supporters claimed that the measure was essential in defending white Mississippi churchgoers from forced integration of their sanctuaries.

The notion that religion constituted a threat to segregation sufficient to warrant preventive legislation proved a tough sell to the public. During the roughly nine weeks that the measure spent wending its way through the Mississippi legislature, public opposition ran overwhelmingly against it. Large lay organizations, Sunday school classes, church agencies, and often even entire congregations under unanimous vote registered their disapproval of the bill. By some estimates, opponents outnumbered supporters four to one.

Nevertheless, the Church Property Bill passed the Senate by a comfortable 29–10 vote and the House by an overwhelming 87–13. Gov. Ross Barnett signed the measure into law without comment. As tensions over civil rights issues grew more acute over the next several years, every white religious community in the state suffered from the divisiveness the bill's opponents had feared. The most significant fracture appeared among Mississippi Methodists in 1965, when disaffected members left their local churches in droves, and some formed the Association of Independent Methodists, with two new congregations in Jackson.

Carolyn Dupont
Eastern Kentucky University

Joseph Crespino, *In Search of Another Country: Mississippians and the Conservative Counterrevolution* (2007); W. J. Cunningham, *Agony at Galloway: One Church's Struggle with Social Change* (1980); Carolyn Renée Dupont, *Mississippi Praying: Southern White Evangelicals and the Civil Rights Movement, 1945–1975* (2013); Peter Murray, *Methodists and the Crucible of Race, 1930–1975* (2004).

Churches of Christ

In 1804 Barton W. Stone, a Presbyterian minister in Kentucky, withdrew from his church and urged his religious neighbors to embrace Christian unity based on the teachings of the "Bible alone." Five years later Alexander Campbell, an Irish Presbyterian, landed on North American shores and joined his father, Thomas, in launching a "reformation" or "restoration" of New Testament Christianity. In 1832

Stone's "Christians" and the Campbells' "Disciples" united and mushroomed across the western frontier. By the 1880s, however, the Stone-Campbell movement began dividing into two factions, and by the early twentieth century it had separated into the noninstrumental Churches of Christ and the Christian Church (Disciples of Christ), which used musical instruments in worship.

This restoration movement first touched Mississippi in 1828, when Jacob Creath Jr. became the earliest known Stone-Campbell evangelist to preach in the Magnolia State. Taking his cue from Alexander Campbell's debates and his writings in the *Christian Baptist* (1823–30), Creath insisted on baptism "for the remission of sins," so kindling the ire of neighboring Episcopalians, Methodists, and Presbyterians that they burned him in effigy. Apart from doctrinal disputes, social turmoil often accompanied religious friction as the explosive issues of black slavery and Indian Removal polarized the nation and its churches in the 1830s. In spite of this social and political upheaval, the indefatigable efforts of Creath, W. L. Matthews, D. L. Phares, Jefferson H. Johnson, and Tolbert Fanning lifted the Stone-Campbell movement to visibility in Mississippi by the 1840s.

In 1850 James A. Butler immersed one hundred people into the restoration movement in Athens, Mississippi. Four years later T. W. Caskey reported ministering to a three-hundred-member congregation in Palo Alto. Robert Usrey worked effectively with Churches of Christ in Carroll County, while B. F. Manire served a congregation in Columbus. By 1860 Mississippi had approximately 2,450 Stone-Campbell adherents. As the Civil War loomed, Caskey canvassed the state, urging fellow Mississippians to leave the Union, and when they did so, he became a chaplain for the 18th Mississippi Regiment.

Religious disputes continued after the political violence abated. Churches of Christ in Mississippi divided over the issues of using instrumental music in worship and missionary societies in evangelistic efforts. Churches of Christ, often called loyals, opposed worshipping with musical instruments and evangelizing through missionary societies; Disciples of Christ (or Christian Churches), often referred to as either progressives or digressives, endorsed both practices. By 1916 the rupture between the two groups in Mississippi left the 122 loyals with congregations of 5,994 members and the progressives with 77 churches counting 5,364 members.

A decade later Churches of Christ in Mississippi listed 125 congregations and claimed 6,968 members. From 1940 to 1982 frequent gospel meetings and debates led to the creation of some 236 new congregations in the state. Churches of Christ in Mississippi had become numerous and prosperous enough by 1976 to launch Kosciusko's Magnolia Bible College, designed to train ministers to advance the restoration cause in the Deep South and beyond. Since 1978 the college has published the *Magnolia Messenger*, a bimonthly paper intended to minister to both black and white congregations.

The presence of African Americans in Mississippi Churches of Christ predates the Civil War, as slaveholders affiliated with the Stone-Campbell movement listed slaves among their property. John G. Cathey and Alexander Cathey, white restorationists in Tate County, owned several enslaved Africans who later became charter members of the state's first black Church of Christ. Like most black Christians who founded and formed independent congregations after emancipation, African Americans in Churches of Christ prayed separately from their white counterparts but imitated the rigid doctrinal practices of their coreligionists, worshipping without musical instruments and evangelizing without missionary societies.

Black Churches of Christ in Mississippi, however, assumed little independent vitality before the evangelistic labors of two African American preachers from Tennessee, G. P. Bowser and Marshall Keeble. In 1928 Bowser helped plant a congregation in Senatobia. Three years later Keeble, supported by white Christians, established the first black Church of Christ in Jackson; he then founded a congregation in Ripley. In 1938 Keeble, again empowered by white beneficence, gathered a black church in Tupelo, and seven years later he organized a black congregation in Natchez.

Bowser and Keeble, however, were not solely responsible for the emergence and expansion of black Churches of Christ in Mississippi. C. C. Locke, a native of Senatobia and a Keeble convert, helped develop the Sycamore Street Church of Christ in Greenwood. James L. Cothron, a Keeble protégé from Georgia, indelibly marked black Churches of Christ in the Mississippi Delta, where his skillful preaching produced congregations in Greenville, Cleveland, Merigold, Ruleville, and Mound Bayou. Laboring beyond the Delta, William Whitaker, another Keeble disciple, established a congregation in Houston and strengthened fledgling churches in Tupelo, Booneville, and Laurel.

Because of the need for better trained ministers, Loyd Clay Harris, a Shongaloo, Louisiana, native, launched Greenville's School of Religious Studies in 1978. When Harris relocated to Moss Point, he carried his educational enterprise with him to strengthen black congregations across the state. Many black preachers received certificates from Harris's school before enrolling at Magnolia Bible College to further their education. In an endeavor conjoining education and fellowship, black Churches of Christ in Mississippi also host their own annual lectureship and youth conference.

Churches of Christ in Mississippi presently boast a total membership of 31,205 divided among 375 congregations. Of these communicants, 7,346 (23.5 percent) are African Americans. In certain parts of Mississippi, black and white churches have abandoned Jim Crow mandates and now collaborate in evangelizing their communities and displaying racial and spiritual unity. Despite such efforts, however, most whites and blacks in Churches of Christ still worship in separate congregations.

Edward J. Robinson
Abilene Christian University

Peter Donan, *Memoir of Jacob Creath Jr.* (1872); Don Jackson, *The Churches of Christ in Mississippi* (1985); Lynn A. McMillon, *A History of the Churches of Christ in Tate County, Mississippi, 1836–1965* (1966); Edward J. Robinson, *Show Us How You Do It: Marshall Keeble and the Rise of Black Churches of Christ in the United States, 1914–1968* (2008); Randy J. Sparks, *Religion in Mississippi* (2001).

Congress of Industrial Organizations and Operation Dixie

In May 1946 the Congress of Industrial Organizations (CIO) launched Operation Dixie, a unionization drive in the American South. Under the leadership of the CIO Southern Organizing Committee, Operation Dixie was an interracial campaign to increase labor's power in the region and close the southern wage differential. Although the campaign achieved some success and continued until 1953, it failed to affect a significant portion of the southern workforce. Historians attribute this failure to the Red Scare, the Taft-Hartley Act, and deep-seated regional racism. In spite of those difficulties, the CIO made substantive efforts throughout Mississippi. Robert Starnes, a native of Hazlehurst and a graduate of Mississippi College, was the statewide CIO director and led the campaign from Jackson. Knox Walker served as his assistant.

Starnes and Walker achieved their greatest success at the Laurel-based Masonite Corporation. The American Federation of Labor (AFL) represented the workforce, but the union contract was set to expire in June 1946, and new elections were called for 27 June. The AFL, CIO, and an independent union formed by Dick Goff competed for the workers' support. On 22 June, in the midst of the competition, the AFL called a strike, a move that CIO organizers charged was intended to win workers' allegiance rather than economic gains. Whatever the strike's motivations, the CIO won the election, receiving 812 votes to 637 for the AFL and 92 for Goff's union. With this victory, the CIO began to negotiate a new contract while the strike continued. The strike did not end until 12 August, after workers signed a new contract. The success at the Masonite Plant enabled the CIO to unionize eleven other plants in Laurel over the next two years.

A second CIO effort took place at the Stonewall Cotton Mills, where, as at Masonite, the AFL contract was about to expire. New elections were set for May 1947, and the CIO claimed that the AFL had colluded with the mill to limit workers' wages and benefits and that the CIO could bring better pay, safer working conditions, and improvements in the mill village. However, this election went to the AFL, which received 272 votes to 244 for the CIO and 96 for "no union." The CIO claimed that the election results were inconclusive, called for a runoff, and appealed to the National Labor Relations Board (NLRB). The NLRB approved a runoff, which the CIO won 261–109. The company protested that the second round of elections had been "illegally ordered and held" and demanded another vote. During an NLRB investigation into the company's claims, North Carolina's Erwin Cotton Mill Company purchased the Stonewall Mills. The NLRB rejected the protest, but the new owners refused to recognize the CIO since the election occurred prior to their acquisition of the company. A court rejected this claim, and the CIO began negotiations on a new contract.

The CIO made similar efforts to help the state's large agricultural workforce. The Food, Tobacco, Agricultural, and Allied Workers of America, a CIO-affiliated union, created organizing committees in each Delta county and staged a successful strike against the Buckeye Cotton Seed Oil Plant in Corinth. The International Woodworkers of America, another CIO-affiliated union, added 3,887 new members in Mississippi in the late 1940s, the largest increase in the lumber-producing South.

But some CIO efforts garnered less success. In September 1946 the union attempted to win over the workers at the AFL-affiliated Grenada Industrial Company. The local press opposed the CIO and claimed it was communist, while locals attacked union organizers. The CIO denied the charge of communism and defended its right to organize but nevertheless lost the election, 297-122. The AFL continued to represent the workers.

Despite this and other failures, CIO organizers in Mississippi made among the largest relative gains of any organizers in the South. According to Van Bittner, national director of Operation Dixie, the CIO achieved more success in Mississippi than in any other southern state. The union participated in approximately ninety elections between June 1946 and January 1949, winning fifty-seven, losing twenty-five, and withdrawing from eight. Those achievements, however, were not enough to overcome the regional difficulties, and the CIO discontinued Operation Dixie in Mississippi by the end of 1949.

Gregory S. Taylor
Chowan University

Barbara Griffith, *The Crisis of American Labor: Operation Dixie and the Defeat of the CIO* (1988); Michael Honey, *Mississippi Quarterly* (Winter

1991–Fall 1992); Michael Honey, *Southern Labor and Black Civil Rights* (1993); F. Ray Marshall, *Labor in the South* (1967); Eugene Roper, "CIO Organizing Committee in Mississippi, June, 1946–January, 1949" (master's thesis, University of Mississippi, 1949).

Citizens' Council (Newspaper)

The Citizens' Councils formed in the Mississippi Delta just months after the US Supreme Court handed down its landmark *Brown v. Board of Education* decision in 1954. Founder William "Tut" Patterson was determined to fight the integration of Mississippi's public schools and began to gather individuals who shared his resolve. When William J. Simmons became the organization's primary strategist for positioning the Councils in the court of public opinion, he knew that mass distribution of its message would be key. The organization had quickly outgrown its pamphlet and town-meeting-style information distribution system and needed a communication tool to help promote its ideologies beyond Mississippi's borders.

The first edition of the *Citizens' Council* was published in October 1955. The four-page newspaper-style monthly newsletter became the "official publication of the Citizens' Council," and organizers claimed distribution to all fifty states and beyond. The publication was "dedicated to the maintenance of peace, good order, and tranquility in our community and in our State and to the preservation of States' Rights." With extreme optimism, the Council printed 125,000 copies of the first issue for distribution to like-minded individuals throughout the South. Subsequent print runs dropped substantially, and Simmons estimated the average circulation at 40,000 in November 1956.

At first glance, the *Citizens' Council* could have easily been mistaken for a small-town weekly, since it featured many traditional newspaper elements (a distinct nameplate, letters to the editor, and political cartoons). However, each monthly edition featured a very focused and strategic message: supporters needed to mobilize and fight to preserve segregated classrooms in the South. Because it did not carry advertising, the publication became the mouthpiece for the Councils, offering editors complete license to espouse the organization's propaganda. Contributors promoted participation in the Citizens' Councils as a means to preserve the "southern way of life." Charts, maps, and stories detailed the organization's rapid growth and radio and television efforts.

Stories also reported incidents of violence and the supposedly negative consequences where schools had been integrated. The publication often cited survey data to substantiate these claims, including one study that found "Racial

The *Citizens' Council* was the "official publication of the Citizens' Council," which helped promote the organization's ideologies beyond Mississippi's borders (Citizens' Council Collection, Department of Archives and Special Collections, J. D. Williams Library, University of Mississippi)

Integration Has Lowered Standards of Public Education." Typical headlines read "Big City Press Conceals Face in Racial Violence" or "Council Movement Spreads as Nation Reacts to Danger."

The *Citizens' Council* filled its pages with stories from journalists across the South. Thomas Waring, editor of South Carolina's *Charleston News and Courier*, was a frequent contributor. Early issues included Waring's three-part series on the formation of the Citizens' Council and its benefits for southerners. Other contributions included editorial comment from the pages of the *Jackson Clarion-Ledger*, *Prentiss Headlight*, *Natchez Times*, and *Winston County Journal*, while Council supporters authored guest editorials.

The *Citizens' Council* maintained its four-page newspaper layout for five years. In October 1961 the format changed to a newsmagazine-style publication and the name was shortened to *The Citizen*. At this point, the content shifted to longer pieces written as features. The magazine often devoted entire issues to one specific topic, with articles contributed by prestigious members of Congress, scientists, authors, and clergy. Each issue sold for thirty-five cents; a yearly subscription cost three dollars.

Although the appearance changed, the message remained the same—organizing to resist desegregation. Attacking the credibility and patriotism of civil rights proponents, providing data to support the demise of society should integration occur, and continuing to encourage active resistance remained the publication's primary focus. In 1961, the organization reported 50,000 subscribers, but that number dropped to 23,056 the following year.

By the mid-1960s the Citizens' Councils and their publications began to promote the idea of private school education as an alternative to integrated public school systems. *The Citizen* remained in publication until 1989 with Simmons as publisher.

Laura R. Walton
Mississippi State University

Neil R. McMillen, *The Citizens' Council: Organized Resistance to the Second Reconstruction, 1954–64* (1994); Laura Richardson Walton, "Segregationist Spin: The Use of Public Relations by the Mississippi State Sovereignty Commission and the White Citizens' Council, 1954–1973" (PhD dissertation, University of Southern Mississippi, 2006).

Citizens' Councils

In July 1954, following the Supreme Court's *Brown v. Board of Education* decision, a small grassroots organization formed in Indianola, Mississippi, to mount organized resistance against integration. Representing the first of the Citizens' Councils, the Indianola branch, under the leadership of Delta planter Robert "Tut" Patterson, was the first in a wave of chapters throughout Mississippi that sought to maintain states' rights and racial integrity. The Citizens' Councils (also known as the White Citizens' Councils) soon became one of the South's most recognizable and active white resistance organizations. By October 1954 the rapid growth of individual chapters led to the formation of an umbrella organization, the Association of Citizens' Councils of Mississippi (ACC), providing access to a broader base of funding and opportunities for more diverse activities. Similar state organizations formed throughout the South, leading to the 1956 formation of the Citizens' Councils of America, a loosely organized network of white resistance groups that included the Georgia States' Rights Council, the North Carolina Patriots, the Tennessee Federation for Constitutional Government, and the Virginia Defenders of State Sovereignty

and Individual Liberties. Nevertheless, the ACC remained the most closely connected and effective organization of its kind.

The Citizens' Council primarily mobilized white business and civic leaders to commit to maintaining racial segregation in their communities through economic pressure. White employers could exercise their economic power over black employees, for example, as a way to discourage them from working for integration or voting rights. Council leaders throughout Mississippi emphasized this method over violent or illegal means, distinguishing their methods and members from those of the Ku Klux Klan and other more brutal organizations. Despite this distinction, however, the Council gained a reputation among civil rights groups for using members' economic and political positions to stifle Mississippi's civil rights movement. This reputation led many Council opponents to label the organization "the uptown Klan." Its supporters included Mississippi governor Ross Barnett, Sen. James O. Eastland, Jackson mayor Allen Thompson, and Reps. John Bell Williams and William Colmer.

The core of Council ideology encompassed firm notions of white supremacy, as evidenced by the organization's publications. Citizens' Council leaders remained fully dedicated to the preservation of segregation and denial of equal political rights for black Mississippians. Exploiting long-standing fears of a growing federal government and of communist subversion, the Council's leaders connected the organization's objectives to national concerns, concealing racist attitudes within a more complex web of conservative values. This tactic left a thriving conservative legacy in the white South long after the Council movement dissipated.

In 1956 the ACC began the Educational Fund of the Citizens' Council, receiving an official charter of incorporation from Mississippi's secretary of state on 15 December. The Educational Fund, headquartered in Greenwood, represented a fundamental function of the Citizens' Council that extended beyond local concerns, working to promote open discussion throughout the United States about "pertinent" national issues, to disseminate "facts" to all Americans, and to "improve" the US educational system. The fund advanced these objectives primarily by issuing publications and using radio and television to "tell the South's story" to the rest of the nation. ACC leaders also traveled extensively throughout the country to spread the Council's message and to connect its fight for segregation to conservative perspectives on national issues.

As part of the Educational Fund's public relations effort and under the editorship of William J. Simmons, perhaps the best known of Council spokesmen, a monthly newsletter, the *Citizens' Council*, began publication in October 1955. The newsletter evolved into a monthly magazine in October 1961 and continued publication until 1989 under the title *The Citizen*. Some chapters of the Citizens' Councils published newsletters as well. The Jackson Citizens' Council, for example, published a monthly newsletter, *Aspect*, that contained local news related to civil rights activity and to the status of the Jackson Council.

The Citizens' Council also funded *Forum*, a weekly television and radio program that aired between 1957 and 1966. Most of the episodes were recorded in Washington, D.C., and they frequently featured members of Congress, lending them legitimacy as public affairs programming and concealing their function as an arm of segregationist propaganda. Topics rarely dealt directly with race or segregation, focusing instead on issues such as foreign policy, the federal deficit, and the threat of communism. By April 1961 the Citizens' Council boasted that 383 television and radio stations aired *Forum*. The Citizens' Council's commitment to *Forum* revealed the diversity of the organization's activities and its vision of reaching out to an American rather than regional audience.

Perhaps the Council's most lasting legacy in Mississippi was its campaign to establish a series of Council schools for white children as an alternative to an integrated public school system. Dr. Medford Evans, a former professor and frequent Council spokesman, led an effort to create a "how-to" guide for starting a private school. In 1964 the Citizens' Council officially opened Council School No. 1 in a North Jackson home. By 1967, Nos. 2 and 3 had been established. The Jackson academies served as models for similar schools throughout the state, although the Council itself was not directly affiliated with most of the private academies that arose throughout the late 1960s and early 1970s.

While the Citizens' Council movement throughout the South began to weaken by the early 1960s, it remained effective in Mississippi until the end of the decade. White southerners' acceptance of integration as inevitable, coupled with shifting national priorities, contributed to a severe decline in membership. Ironically, the Council's tactic of subverting race to more nationally potent issues in its various public relations campaigns led to a less cohesive message that was easily absorbed by the national conservative wave of the late 1960s and early 1970s.

Stephanie R. Rolph
Millsaps College

Joseph Crespino, *In Search of Another Country: Mississippi and the Conservative Counterrevolution* (2007); *The Jackson Citizen* (1961–89); *Jackson Citizens' Council* (1955–61); *Citizens' Council Forum* (1957–66), Special Collections, Mitchell Memorial Library, Mississippi State University, and Mississippi Department of Archives and History; Neil R. McMillen, *The Citizens' Council: Organized Resistance to the Second Reconstruction, 1954–64* (1971).

Civil Rights Law of 1873

Passed after the Civil War, the Thirteenth Amendment abolished slavery and freed some four million slaves in the United States, leading led to the question of their legal status: they were no longer slaves, but they also were not citizens. The governments of all of the former slave states grappled with this issue, but it was especially important in Mississippi, where former slaves comprised 55 percent of the population.

Southern white Democratic leaders could not imagine former slaves as equals after generations of prohibiting them from even learning to read and write. Moreover, whites feared that blacks would vote for the Republican Party of Abraham Lincoln and the North and were concerned about losing the relatively cheap labor considered integral to the economy. The governments of Mississippi and many other former slave states reacted by adopting a series of restrictive laws known as the Black Codes that sought to prevent African Americans from gaining political power and to prevent changes in labor and social relations. Mississippi simply replaced the word *slave* with *freedman* in the criminal code and used vagrancy laws to maintain the previous rules of etiquette governing black-white social interactions.

The Radical Republican–dominated US Congress, already in a power struggle with Pres. Andrew Johnson, a southern Democrat, reacted angrily and deposed the state governments appointed by Johnson immediately after the Civil War. Congress declared Mississippi under the control of the Fourth Military District, subject to martial law, and prohibited most white southern leaders from political and civic participation, beginning what became known as Radical Reconstruction or Congressional Reconstruction. Fearing that the return of southern Democrats to national politics would help the party regain control of the federal government, Radical Republicans demanded that blacks receive not only civil liberties but also the right to vote, which had been denied to African Americans as late as 1867 in New Jersey, Ohio, and Maryland. That same year, at least ten states, including California, New Jersey, and Ohio, initially rejected the Fourteenth Amendment, which granted citizenship to blacks and former slaves.

White Mississippians who joined the new Republican Party were known derisively as scalawags; the party, which dominated Mississippi's Reconstruction-era politics, also included carpetbaggers (northerners and former Union soldiers who had moved south) and local free blacks and former slaves. The new state government began adopting a series of laws abolishing the Black Codes by guaranteeing civil liberties and voting rights and ratifying the Fourteenth Amendment. On 7 February 1873 their efforts culminated in Mississippi's adoption of the most sweeping civil rights legislation enacted to date.

The Civil Rights Law of 1873 sought to guarantee a degree of social equality beyond mere civic equality by requiring equal accommodations and prohibiting discrimination in places of public accommodation and entertainment such as inns, hotels, and theaters. It amended and expanded an 1871 law that outlawed segregation on railroads, stagecoaches, and steamboats, imposing penalties of up to one thousand dollars and three years in jail. The sweeping new law soon received its first test when George Donnell, doorkeeper of the Angelo Concert Hall in Jackson, denied admission to a black man, Hannibal C. "Ham" Carter, and Carter obtained a warrant for Donnell's arrest.

Carter was a unique plaintiff. He came from an Indiana family of free blacks, captained a regiment of the Louisiana Native Guards, and was a Republican Party activist who had been an 1872 presidential elector for Ulysses S. Grant and had served a brief stint as Mississippi's interim secretary of state. Representing Warren County in the Mississippi House of Representatives, he sponsored the bill and worked for its passage. The theater incident might have represented a deliberate test of the new law, a strategy civil rights activists pursued decades later.

Donnell allowed Carter and his companion, D. Webster, inside the hall but denied Carter's request to sit in a section reserved for whites, arguing that the value of the tickets would drop if Carter were allowed to sit there. Carter summoned the sheriff of Hinds County, who then jailed Donnell until he paid a hundred-dollar fine. A judge agreed with Donnell's treatment, so he appealed to the state's highest court. The Mississippi Supreme Court heard *Donnell v. State of Mississippi* during its April 1873 term and then unanimously upheld the law and Donnell's arrest. However, the Civil Rights Law of 1873 apparently fell into desuetude, a legal principle that renders a law invalid after a long period of nonenforcement. Although none of the amended statutes were explicitly repealed, they were not included in the 1880 Mississippi Code or in subsequent publications of state law. The 1888 Mississippi criminal statute that required all railroads to provide separate but equal accommodations for white and black travelers may have invalidated portions of the Civil Rights Law by declaring all prior conflicting statutes repealed.

Other southern states and the US Congress adopted or debated similar legislation around the time of Mississippi's enactment of the Civil Rights Law. In 1870 Radical Republican senator Charles Sumner proposed the most well known of these measures, which Congress enacted as the Civil Rights Act of 1875, known as the Force Act to its opponents. The US Supreme Court struck down the law as unconstitutional by an 8–1 majority in a series of decisions known as the Civil Rights Cases of 1883. Congress did not pass another civil rights bill until 1957. Many northern states filled the void with carbon copies of the civil rights bills adopted by Congress and the southern states in the 1870s, but these measures did not enjoy widespread popular support in either the North or the South and were not regularly enforced until after the modern civil rights movement.

Brian Wilson
University of Mississippi

Edward L. Ayers, *The Promise of the New South* (1992); Morroe Berger, *Equality by Statute: The Revolution in Civil Rights* (rev. ed. 1968); David Herbert Donald, *Charles Sumner and the Rights of Man* (1970); John Hope Franklin, ed. *Reminiscences of an Active Life: The Autobiography of John Roy Lynch* (1970); Mississippi Supreme Court, *Mississippi Reports: Cases Argued and Decided*, 48 vols. (1873); James G. Randall and David Donald, *The Civil War and Reconstruction* (2nd ed. 1961); US Commission on Civil Rights, *Freedom to the Free: Century of Emancipation, 1863–1963* (1963); Vernon Lane Wharton, *The Negro in Mississippi, 1865–1890* (1965); C. Vann Woodward, *Origins of the New South, 1877–1913* (1951).

Civil Rights Movement

The civil rights movement in Mississippi challenged generations of inequality in the state. Though it had much deeper roots, the Mississippi movement was especially active and creative in the early and mid-1960s, when the state became a center of national efforts to demand legal equality, voting rights for all citizens, and an end to racial segregation.

When the modern civil rights movement began in the mid-twentieth century, Mississippi had the highest percentage of African American residents in the United States and the lowest percentage of African American voters. Many civil rights activists argued that segregation and disfranchisement were so deeply entrenched—and perhaps so deeply interconnected with the maintenance of a large body of poorly paid workers—that if unequal laws could be eliminated in Mississippi, they could be eliminated anywhere. The effort included a variety of organizations, some of them well-known national groups—the National Association for the Advancement of Colored People (NAACP), which had a long and uneven history in Mississippi but a steady presence in Jackson; the United Negro Improvement Association, which had a short period of extraordinary popularity in the 1920s; the Congress of Racial Equality (CORE); the Student Nonviolent Coordinating Committee (SNCC); and the Southern Christian Leadership Conference. The freedom struggle also gave rise to new Mississippi groups such as the Council of Federated Organizations, the Mississippi Freedom Democratic Party (MFDP), and Womanpower Unlimited and encompassed activists from older agricultural unions and labor unions and African American institutions, such as churches, schools, and businesses.

Scholars have argued that the best way to understand the civil rights movement is to appreciate its multiple organizations, multiple goals, and even its multiple languages. Some groups sought to overturn racial segregation laws and practices and gain the right to vote and hold office, while others espoused broader goals such as self-determination, fighting poverty and violence, and overturning a range of institutionalized insults and white privilege. Mississippi contributed some of the most memorable language about the movement and its goals: the language of religious deliverance, sacrifice, and perseverance; lawyers' language about legal equality; Fannie Lou Hamer's "I Question America" speech; James Silver's book, *Mississippi: The Closed Society*; multiple uses and meanings of the term *freedom*; and the first popularization of the phrase *Black Power*.

In Mississippi, the modern civil rights movement began in the late 1940s and early 1950s. The NAACP's membership and activities increased dramatically, and the Regional Council of Negro Leadership formed in Mound Bayou in 1951. Helmed by Dr. T. R. M. Howard, the Regional Council led some of the first large political gatherings for African Americans in Mississippi. The NAACP gained popularity during World War II and through the growing success of NAACP lawsuits. In 1954 and 1955, NAACP chapters in at least six Mississippi counties demanded school desegregation in response to the *Brown v. Board of Education* decision, and the state organization appointed its first field secretary, Medgar Evers. In 1955, Regional Council vice president George Lee was murdered, and the killing of teenager Emmett Till stirred national anger about the dangers and injustices African Americans faced in the state. Massive resistance against the civil rights movement began in the mid- and late 1950s, with the rise of the Citizens' Councils, the Mississippi State Sovereignty Commission, numerous new laws about education and activism, and countless small and large groups that used violence, the law, the media, and/or economic pressure to combat civil rights activism.

The civil rights movement registered enormous gains between 1960 and 1968. In 1960 Mississippi activism embarked in at least two new important directions. On the Gulf Coast, Dr. Gilbert Mason led a small group of activists in a "wade-in" against beach segregation—possibly Mississippi's first direct-action protest. In the same year, Clarksdale's Aaron Henry became head of the state's NAACP, a position he held into the 1990s.

In 1961 three forms of direct action protest became crucial to Mississippi activism. In Jackson, nine Tougaloo College students tested segregation laws by sitting-in at a public library. CORE activists, some black and some white, challenged segregation on buses and in bus stations on a Freedom Ride through much of the state, and a Hinds County group, Womanpower Unlimited, supported Freedom Ride participants and later helped with a broader range of efforts.

The major civil rights organizations—the NAACP, CORE, SNCC, and the Southern Christian Leadership Conference—formed a new group, the Council of Federated Organizations, in 1962. In that year, SNCC moved into the Delta and organized numerous voter registration efforts. For the first time since Reconstruction, an African American candidate, Robert L. Smith, ran for US Congress. In September, after complicated legal and political efforts, James Meredith enrolled at the University of Mississippi, desegregating the institution and setting off white supremacist violence that killed two and injured dozens. Also in 1962 the NAACP and other groups started a sustained boycott against segregated institutions in Jackson, beginning with the Mississippi State Fair.

During the following year the Jackson boycott expanded into a selective-buying campaign against merchants that practiced forms of white privilege. Opponents of a sit-in at Woolworth's on Capitol Street heaped food and insults on the protesters. Evers, the boycott's best-known leader, made a televised address about the effort's goals and strategies and was assassinated the next day. Jackson also saw a campaign in which African Americans from Mississippi and whites, mostly from outside the state, went together to worship in all-white churches. Also in 1963, numerous Mississippians took part in the March on Washington, and the Council of Federated Organizations sponsored the Freedom Vote, with Aaron Henry running for governor and Edwin King running for lieutenant governor in an ingenious display of African American voting at a time when most could not officially register.

Events in 1964 drew the most national attention to the Mississippi movement and the dangers activists faced. In the spring, several communities sponsored Freedom Days, sustained efforts by African American communities to register people to vote. Victoria Gray Adams ran for the US Senate seat held by John Stennis, and the US Congress passed the Civil Rights Act of 1964. The Mississippi Summer Project, often simply called Freedom Summer, constituted an ambitious effort to bring together Mississippi activists with more than one thousand non-Mississippians to register African Americans to vote, to organize African American community centers, to teach in newly created institutions called Freedom Schools, and to publicize both the injustices and potential of life for black Mississippians. At the start of the summer young volunteers James Chaney, Michael Schwerner, and Andrew Goodman were murdered in Neshoba County, and over the next few violent, tense, frustrating, and sometimes exciting months, Mississippi activists formed the MFDP. Chaired by Lawrence Guyot, with Fannie Lou Hamer as vice chair, the MFDP challenged the acceptance of an all-white delegation from the state at the Democratic National Convention by demanding that Hamer, Adams, and Annie Devine be seated as Mississippi delegates.

In 1965 and 1966 the MFDP worked to gather information on voter discrimination, and the Child Development Group of Mississippi was formed to seek federal funding for Head Start programs. After the passage of the Voting

Rights Act of 1965, multiple new protest movements pressed for immediate results. Sustained protest efforts bringing together NAACP leaders with others in Natchez in 1965 and Port Gibson in 1966 ended with some successes. Natchez activists initiated a boycott against white merchants after a car bombing injured NAACP chapter head George Metcalfe. The protesters demanded the desegregation of schools, parks, and swimming pools; the equalization of city services; an end to police brutality; and the use of courtesy titles for African Americans patrons in white-owned establishments. The boycott ended in December, when merchants agreed to most of the demands. In Port Gibson, merchants agreed to hire more African American workers and to use courtesy titles when addressing African American customers. Resentment and opposition continued in both places, as evidenced by the murder of Wharlest Jackson in Natchez in 1967 and by an unsuccessful 1969 lawsuit, *Claiborne Hardware, et al., v. NAACP*, that challenged boycotting as an illegal activity. In 1966 James Meredith began his March against Fear, claiming that with the Civil Rights Act in place, he should be able to walk across the state. He was shot early in his march, but other activists stepped in to take his place. In the Delta, Stokely Carmichael and other members of SNCC began to use the term *Black Power*.

For the first time since Reconstruction, African Americans voted and ran for office in substantial numbers in 1967 and 1968. Twenty-two of the more than one hundred African Americans who ran for office in Mississippi in 1967 won election, including Holmes County's Robert Clark, who took a seat in the Mississippi legislature. In 1968 Flonzie Brown Goodloe became election commissioner in Madison County, the first black woman elected to office in Mississippi. In the same year, the Democratic Party welcomed African Americans to the national convention as part of the national delegation. In 1969 Charles Evers, Medgar Evers's brother, became mayor of Fayette, and in 1970, the US Supreme Court mandated that Mississippi finally desegregate its public schools. At least three expressions of African American frustration with the continuing problems of Mississippi life became clear in the late 1960s. The Republic of New Afrika, making efforts to form a separate nation of people of African descent in five southern states, including Mississippi, bought land in Bolton in 1968 and began recruiting members. A violent 1971 confrontation between Republic members and state and federal officials led to murder charges and the end of the group's influence. In 1968 a mule train of Mississippians representing the Poor People's Campaign left Marks for Washington, D.C., hoping that their trip would culminate in new national efforts to address American poverty. And the first great work of literature from the state's civil rights movement, Anne Moody's 1968 volume, *Coming of Age in Mississippi*, ended with people singing "We Shall Overcome," and Moody responding, "I WONDER. I really WONDER."

In the twenty-first century, Mississippians continue to debate how much success the civil rights movement truly had

in overturning school segregation, voter discrimination, and legal inequality. The movement set examples for sacrifice, organization, and inspiration and eliminated de jure segregation, but many issues remain unresolved—de facto segregation; ongoing issues such as poverty, poor health, and high rates of incarceration; and newer issues such as the rights of immigrants and same-sex couples. Some Mississippi conservatives emphasize the end to legal inequality, while people on the political left tend to stress problems left unresolved and to note the rise of both the Republican Party and private schools that include few if any African Americans. Mississippians also continue to discuss how best to interpret and remember the civil rights movement. Laws requiring that public schools teach about the movement, growing efforts to celebrate movement individuals and moments through statues and historic markers, and the creation of a civil rights museum in Jackson reveal the movement's central place in Mississippi's history and its relevance for contemporary life.

Ted Ownby
University of Mississippi

Emilye Crosby, *A Little Taste of Freedom: The Black Freedom Struggle in Claiborne County, Mississippi* (2005); Chris Danielson, *After Freedom Summer: How Race Realigned Mississippi Politics, 1965–1986* (2011); John Dittmer, *Local People: The Struggle for Civil Rights in Mississippi* (1994); Charles Eagles, *The Price of Defiance: James Meredith and the Integration of Ole Miss* (2009); Françoise N. Hamlin, *Crossroads at Clarksdale: The Black Freedom Struggle in the Mississippi Delta after World War II* (2012); Wesley Hogan, *Many Minds, One Heart: SNCC's Dream for a New America* (2007); Charles Marsh, *God's Long Summer: Stories of Faith and Civil Rights* (1997); Doug McAdam, *Freedom Summer* (1990); Tiyi M. Morris, *Womanpower Unlimited and the Black Freedom Struggle in Mississippi* (2015); J. Todd Moye, *Let the People Decide: Black Freedom and White Resistance Movements in Sunflower County, Mississippi, 1945–1986* (2004); Chris Myers-Asch, *The Senator and the Sharecropper: The Freedom Struggles of James O. Eastland and Fannie Lou Hamer* (2008); Mark Newman, *Divine Agitators: The Delta Ministry and Civil Rights in Mississippi* (2004); Ted Ownby, ed., *The Civil Rights Movement in Mississippi* (2013); Frank R. Parker, *Black Votes Count: Political Empowerment in Mississippi after 1965* (1990); Charles M. Payne, *I've Got the Light of Freedom: The Organizing Tradition and the Mississippi Freedom Struggle* (1995); Renee Romano and Leigh Raiford, eds., *The Civil Rights Movement and American Memory* (2006); Akinyele Umoja, *We Will Shoot Back: Armed Resistance in the Mississippi Freedom Movement* (2013).

Civil Rights Movement, Legacies of

The civil rights movement had a lasting impact on Mississippi's politics, culture, and society. And although pinpointing the impact or legacy of social movements is notoriously difficult, the civil rights movement in Mississippi has received considerable scholarly attention, with particular focus on the movement's impact on the development of leaders and organizations, changes in political participation and office-holding, shifts in school desegregation, and the development of social policies. The movement also shaped social attitudes, racial interactions, and collective memory, but those arenas are less well understood. The movement's legacy also includes the white response to the civil rights movement that further shaped Mississippi after the movement's heyday.

The Mississippi civil rights movement in the early 1960s was noteworthy for its emphasis on community organizing and the development of new local leaders and organizations, many of whom went on to become involved in later phases of the civil rights movement and other social movements. This category includes Mississippians Fannie Lou Hamer, Aaron Henry, and Hollis Watkins and leaders from outside Mississippi such as Mario Savio and Stokeley Carmichael. While the Mississippi Freedom Democratic Party and some other organizations folded, numerous other groups, among them legal advocacy organizations, community health centers, and educational programs, have continued to pursue movement goals.

The increase in black political participation is one of the most visible and widely celebrated legacies of the civil rights movement. Mississippi had the country's lowest rates of black voter registration and voting at the beginning of the 1960s, but by the end of the decade, the combination of civil rights organizing and the 1965 Voting Rights Act had led to dramatic increases in those areas. The election of black candidates to office lagged behind, however, as a consequence of a variety of vote dilution mechanisms (such as the gerrymandering of electoral districts to favor white candidates) that thwarted black candidates at the municipal, county, and state levels. Court decisions handed down during the 1970s reversed many policies that had discriminatory effects, paving the way for a new generation of black elected officials, and Mississippi has long boasted the largest number of African American elected officeholders in the United States. The political impact of black elected officials on policy has been uneven, however. Some gains have occurred in the form of more responsive and equitable policies, but political influence has been limited mainly to offices in majority-black electoral districts. As African Americans' political participation and officeholding increased, many whites in Mississippi (and elsewhere in the South) shifted their support to the Republican Party. Thus, the civil rights movement helped to undermine traditional one-party politics and the Democratic Party's long-standing dominance in Mississippi, one of the most important changes in American politics in the post–civil rights era.

Court-ordered school desegregation plans instituted beginning in the early 1960s initially generated minimal changes because they required black parents to apply to have their children attend formerly all-white schools, potentially subjecting the children and their families to harassment. The US Supreme Court's *Alexander v. Holmes* decision (1969) paved the way for widespread school desegregation over the next few years, with little of the massive resistance that had followed the 1954 *Brown v. Board of Education* decision. However, many Mississippi communities established private, white-controlled academies that not only refused to integrate but also damaged the public school systems. Initial efforts to desegregate Mississippi's colleges and universities also met fierce resistance, as in the case of James Meredith's 1962 enrollment at the University of Mississippi, which led to a full-scale riot by white students. However, the past five decades have seen significant increases at black enrollment in Mississippi's formerly all-white postsecondary institutions.

Changing attitudes and beliefs are more difficult to document, but public discourse by elected officials and community leaders has shifted away from traditional white supremacist arguments on behalf of Mississippi's segregated institutions and culture. Key leaders and events of the civil rights movement have been memorialized. Civil-rights-era crimes against movement activists have recently received new investigations, and in some cases, perpetrators have been tried, convicted, and jailed. By opening up educational and job opportunities, the civil rights movement played an important role in reducing economic inequalities, especially by creating new possibilities for the growth of black middle class. However, these and subsequent initiatives have garnered less success in reducing the broader structural economic inequities between blacks and whites, and many of the movement's larger objectives have been undermined by continued resistance to racial equality.

Kenneth T. Andrews
University of North Carolina at
Chapel Hill

Kenneth T. Andrews, *Freedom Is a Constant Struggle: The Mississippi Civil Rights Movement and Its Legacy* (2004); Joseph Crespino, *In Search of Another Country: Mississippi and the Conservative Counterrevolution* (2007); John Dittmer, *Local People: The Struggle for Civil Rights in Mississippi* (1994); Jenny Irons, *Gender and Society* (December 1998); Jenny Irons, *Mobilization* (June 2006); Doug McAdam, *Freedom Summer* (1988); J. Todd Moye, *Let the People Decide: Black Freedom and White Resistance Movements in Sunflower County, Mississippi, 1945–1986* (2004); Frank Parker, *Black Votes Count: Political Empowerment in Mississippi after 1965* (1990); Charles Payne, *I've Got the Light of Freedom: The Organizing Tradition and the Mississippi Freedom Struggle* (1995); Frederick Wirt, *"We Ain't What We Was": Civil Rights in the New South* (1997).

Civil Rights Movement, Women in

African American and white women involved in the civil rights movement never represented a homogeneous group. Different women had different tools with which to exercise their influence and effect change.

African American women stood stalwartly on the front lines of the civil right movement, but they often did not hold formal leadership positions and are consequently not always visible in photographs and other historical documentation. These women organized via their churches, in their homes, and throughout their immediate communities, taking advantage of their traditional gender roles and domestic space. In many cases, therefore, the opportunities available involved positions that supported the activities of male leaders; in other instances, however, women taught citizenship classes, attended mass meetings, and canvassed for voter registration, enhancing their ordinary activities to encompass the movement's needs.

Class also played a determining factor in black women's experiences and activism. Vera Pigee, a Clarksdale beautician loyal to the National Association for the Advancement of Colored People (NAACP), and other self-employed women could spend considerable time and resources organizing and planning, as Pigee did in her work with the group's Youth Councils and as secretary of the local branch. In contrast, Fannie Lou Hamer, a displaced sharecropper with a greater sense of urgency, found her voice in the direct-action-driven Student Nonviolent Coordinating Committee and later in the Mississippi Freedom Democratic Party. Many black women found motivation for their activities in their religious faith, putting their bodies on the line, endangering their families and friends, and suffering the same indignities and dangers as black men. Many of the women associated with the movement went on to work with poverty programs such as Head Start or ran for office: Victoria Gray Adams, for example, ran for the US Senate on the Freedom Democratic Party ticket, and Unita Blackwell of Mayersville became Mississippi's first black female mayor.

Unlike their black peers, white women in the civil rights movement rarely felt physically imperiled. Their involvement stemmed from a sense of empathy with the plight of African Americans and from a strong desire for social, legal, political, and economic justice, often cultivated by educational or religious institutions. In particular, northern white women lived and worked with African Americans during the 1964 Summer Project, with many of these volunteers returning to college in the fall. Some of these same women went on to found the women's movement shortly thereafter, as their politicization manifested itself in other struggles for equality.

White women from Mississippi also participated. Most of them came from middle-class families and joined the movement via student activities or religious institutions. Hazel Brannon Smith questioned the morality of segregation in her newspaper, the *Lexington Advertiser*, while Jean Cauthen did so via her Clarksdale radio show. Both women suffered harassment. Others, among them Barbara Barnes, the president of Young Women's Christian Association operations in Jackson, mediated institutional integration quietly, and Jane Schutt served on the state's first US Civil Rights Commission Advisory Committee until her husband's job became threatened. Such women's involvement risked their economic, social, and political standing in white society.

Françoise N. Hamlin
Brown University

Bernice McNair Barnett, *Gender and Society* (June 1993); Sally Belfrage, *Freedom Summer* (1965); Bettye Collier-Thomas and V. P. Franklin, eds., *Sisters in the Struggle: African American Women in the Civil Rights–Black Power Movement* (2001); Patricia Hill Collins, *Black Feminist Thought: Knowledge, Consciousness, and the Politics of Empowerment* (1990); Vicki Crawford, Jacqueline Rouse, and Barbara Woods, eds., *Women in the Civil Rights Movement: Trailblazers and Torchbearers, 1941–1965* (1990); Constance Curry et al., *Deep in Our Hearts: Nine White Women in the Freedom Movement* (2000); Paula Giddings, *From Where and When I Enter: The Impact of Black Women on Race and Sex in America* (1984); Debbie Z. Harwell, *Wednesdays in Mississippi: Proper Ladies Working for Radical Change, Freedom Summer 1964* (2015); Jenny Irons, *Gender and Society* (December 1988); Tiyi M. Morris, *Womanpower Unlimited and the Black Freedom Struggle in Mississippi* (2015); Lynne Olson, *Freedom's Daughters: The Unsung Heroines of the Civil Rights Movement from 1930 to 1970* (2001); Vera Pigee, *Struggle of Struggles* (1975); Belinda Robnett, *How Long? How Long? African-American Women in the Struggle for Civil Rights* (1997).

Civil War

When the Civil War began at Fort Sumter, South Carolina, in April 1861, Mississippi had already left the United States. On 9 January 1861, Mississippi had become the second state to secede, following South Carolina's lead. But Mississippi's population was not unanimous in supporting secession. African Americans—most of whom were slaves—had no say in the matter, while whites whose livelihoods were based on Mississippi River commerce, especially in port towns such as Natchez and Vicksburg, feared the effects of war on the state's economy. Many residents of the northeastern and southern areas of the state, where slavery was a minor factor, also objected to secession.

Yet secessionists had carried the day, mainly by turning slavery into an emotional issue that could be sold to most of the people as something worth fighting for. Although later observers have claimed that the war was about states' rights, the Mississippi secession convention declared, "Our position is thoroughly identified with the institution of slavery. . . . We must either submit to degradation, and to the loss of property worth four billions of money, or we must secede from the Union framed by our fathers, to secure this as well as every other species of property. For far less cause than this, our fathers separated from the Crown of England."

Like many other members of the newly formed Confederate States of America, Mississippi was ill prepared for war. Vicksburg had local guards and a few cannons, but the town did not need protecting early in the war. Untrained men occasionally fired at passenger vessels, causing no damage or casualties. Mississippi's governor, John J. Pettus, a fiery prosecessionist, attempted to get some small arms shipped to Jackson but received only a pile of metal and wood junk. Though many white Mississippians joyfully joined in the war spirit spreading across the new Confederacy, their cause ended up a pile of rubble like Pettus's guns.

In early 1862 Vicksburg became the first place in the state to come under attack by Union forces—specifically, the Union Navy. Historians have debated Vicksburg's military significance, but because both Jefferson Davis, the Mississippian who became the Confederacy's first and only president, and US president Abraham Lincoln decided that the town was important, the two sides fought furiously over it. Lincoln believed that Vicksburg was the key to Union control of the Mississippi, while Davis not only thought that the town was symbolically important but also knew that the Central Railroad of Mississippi, which ran east to Jackson from Vicksburg, constituted a vital lifeline that had to be protected.

David Farragut's navy had already taken New Orleans, Baton Rouge, and Natchez but failed in its initial attack on Vicksburg, even with the help of Charles Davis's flotilla coming down from Memphis. Although the river north of Vicksburg had been cleared of the few Confederate naval vessels that had been protecting it, Farragut and Davis realized that taking Vicksburg would require infantry support. Confederate cannons positioned at various levels along the Vicksburg bluffs put up a good fight. And the only Confederate ironclad vessel of note in the Western Theater of the war, the *Arkansas*, came down the Yazoo River north of Vicksburg, ran the gauntlet of the Union Navy, and held its own until Farragut and Davis decided to retreat until a combined operation with the army could be organized. The crippled *Arkansas* was later blown up downriver to prevent its capture by Union forces.

But US ground troops were not sent to Vicksburg, primarily as a consequence of events in Northeast Mississippi. After the Battle of Shiloh, Tennessee, in early April 1862, Gen. Henry W. Halleck led a massive force composed of three federal armies to Corinth, where two vital railroads intersected. Halleck's campaign moved very slowly: Lincoln, frustrated by George McClellan's inaction in Virginia, had cautioned the general not to risk losing a battle. Halleck's

one hundred thousand men eventually forced Confederate general P. G. T. Beauregard, with half that number, to withdraw south from Corinth. But rather than marching to Vicksburg and easily taking the town, Halleck began dividing up his army, sending forces to Tennessee and Arkansas.

Braxton Bragg, who took command of the Confederate forces at Corinth after Beauregard left under controversial circumstances, led most of his army into Tennessee, both to take pressure off North Mississippi and Memphis and to try to regain territory in the Volunteer State. Halleck ultimately was called to Washington to take command of all of Lincoln's armies, bringing Grant back into the picture in Mississippi. The scattering of the Union Army had left Grant with the challenges not only of holding the Memphis-Corinth line but also of figuring out how to take Vicksburg.

Before any action could be taken against Vicksburg, two battles cemented Grant's hold on Northeast Mississippi. At Iuka, east of Corinth, near the Alabama state line, Grant led forces to trap Sterling Price, whom Bragg had left behind. Fighting took place at Iuka primarily because Price and Grant were trying to keep each other from sending reinforcements to Tennessee—Grant to Don Carlos Buell, and Price to Bragg. Price won a tactical victory at Iuka but had to withdraw to avoid becoming trapped between Grant's two wings, one of which never got into the battle. A short time later, Confederate general Earl Van Dorn, commanding at Vicksburg, came north, joined Price, and after feinting a march into Tennessee turned and attacked Corinth in an effort to return the town and its railroads to Confederate hands. The Union forces there, under the immediate command of William S. Rosecrans, were well dug in, and after two days of hard fighting, Van Dorn retreated, his army shattered by losses, heat, and lack of food.

The Iuka-Corinth Campaign ended military action for several weeks as both sides rested and sought reinforcements for their armies. Jefferson Davis sent John C. Pemberton, a Pennsylvania-born Confederate general, to take Van Dorn's place after the disaster at Corinth.

The second phase of the Vicksburg Campaign began when Grant advanced south into North Mississippi along the Mississippi Central Railroad, which he used as his supply line. Difficult terrain, bad weather, and Pemberton's army slowed progress until Grant heard that John A. McClernand, a well-connected Illinois politician, was scheming in Washington to put together his own army to float down the Mississippi and capture Vicksburg. McClernand's plan was less ominous than Grant thought, but Grant took immediate action.

His friend William Tecumseh Sherman marched his men from Grant's front to Memphis to lead an expedition down the Mississippi ahead of McClernand. The plan fell apart when Sherman suffered a resounding defeat at Chickasaw Bayou north of Vicksburg, and Van Dorn led a cavalry raid to Holly Springs in Grant's rear, destroying tons of supplies and forcing Grant to retreat back to Tennessee. Thus, by the end of 1862, Mississippi had seen a good deal of fighting, but it would become much more severe over the next two years.

As 1863 dawned, Grant ordered a series of attempts to approach Vicksburg either from the Delta region of Northwest Mississippi or from the south. Various problems doomed his efforts, though his army's activities led to mass flooding and damage to Delta farmland, a source of supplies for Confederate forces in Vicksburg.

Finally, in April Grant marched his army down the Louisiana side of the river, while Union naval commander David Porter ran ironclads and other vessels south past Vicksburg, suffering only minor losses from the Confederate guns. Grant planned to ferry his army across the Mississippi to begin an inland campaign south of Vicksburg. Beaten back at the town of Grand Gulf, Grant had to settle for a landing further south at Bruinsburg.

The last phase of the Vicksburg Campaign had begun. After winning the Battle of Port Gibson on 1 May, Grant established a supply base at Grand Gulf, from which wagons loaded with supplies followed the Union Army inland to the northeast. Pemberton kept Grant east of the Big Black River, creating a natural barrier between Grant and Vicksburg. Grant's army then won victories at Raymond and Jackson before turning west and defeating Confederate forces at Champion Hill (the key confrontation) and the Big Black Bridge. On 17 May the Union Army began crossing the Big Black River.

On 19 and 22 May, Grant launched unsuccessful attacks against Pemberton's well-entrenched army in Vicksburg. On 23 May, Grant began siege operations, which continued until Pemberton's surrender on 4 July. A Rebel "army of relief" commanded by Joseph E. Johnston east of the Big Black did not move to relieve Pemberton until it was too late. Grant then sent Sherman to Jackson to chase away Johnston. After several days of fighting, Johnston abandoned the city. Sherman let him go. Johnston's force was no longer a threat. With Vicksburg now in Union hands, the only other Rebel obstacle on the Mississippi, at Port Hudson, Louisiana, had no choice but to surrender, and large military operations in Mississippi ceased.

In early 1864 Sherman led a march from Vicksburg to Meridian to make sure that the Confederates did not have enough men or supplies to attempt to retake Vicksburg. Sherman's men met little resistance and destroyed much of the land they crossed, much as his forces later did in Georgia. The only hitch occurred when a cavalry detachment led by Gen. William Sooy Smith encountered Nathan Bedford Forrest at West Point and was chased nearly all the way back to Memphis.

Later that summer Sherman, campaigning in Georgia, sent three expeditions from the Memphis area into Mississippi to neutralize Forrest and keep him away from the Union supply line that ran north of Chattanooga and beyond. These forays resulted in a brilliant Forrest victory at Brice's Crossroads in June and a bloody two-day fight at Harrisburg (or Tupelo) in July in which the Confederates, technically commanded by Stephen Lee but mostly Forrest's men, suffered heavy casualties. Union forces led by A. J. Smith were victorious but nevertheless marched back to Memphis because of supply problems.

Sherman immediately sent Smith back into Mississippi to find and attack Forrest. Smith marched his troops down the Mississippi Central, but Forrest, his force weakened by the Tupelo fight, chose not to stand and fight and instead made an end run to raid Memphis.

A winter 1864–65 operation led by Benjamin Grierson, who had commanded a successful raid during the Vicksburg Campaign, ended campaigning in Mississippi. Grierson's men cut a path of destruction through northeastern and central Mississippi. His troops were so effective that when John Bell Hood retreated back into Mississippi after the disastrous Franklin-Nashville Campaign, few supplies remained.

All of this military action meant that Mississippi's civilians, towns, and farmland suffered greatly. Houses were burned, especially if Union troops found them empty, as they often were because so many families had fled the state or were hiding in the woods. Towns and crops were looted and burned. Jackson suffered greatly, though both armies contributed to destruction there. Barns, fences, and other farm structures were trampled and used as firewood, as both armies sought food and warmth.

Guerrilla warfare by Confederate partisans contributed to the destruction by provoking the Union troops to retaliate. Despite the fact that such actions contributed to civilians' misery, the guerrillas remained active for most of the war. Their practice of shooting at Union vessels going down the Mississippi led to so many house burnings that the east side of the river became dotted with chimneys standing where homes had been.

Though little evidence indicates that Union soldiers directly attacked white women and children, accounts show that some slave women were raped by Northern troops. White civilians nevertheless were terrorized by the presence of the hated Yankees, who robbed gardens, stole valuables, cut up furniture and bedding, and in general wreaked havoc everywhere they went. Such examples of destruction grew more numerous as the war went on, but Union officers often attempted to control their men, a few of whom were arrested. White women's experiences led them to take a hard line against the North after the war, and they were very active in the creation of the Lost Cause movement.

Many Mississippians never accepted the war or the Confederacy, though most dissenters kept their opinions to themselves. A few Vicksburg citizens spoke up after Grant captured the city, and others in the state aided the Union cause by acting as spies or simply by sharing important military information. When most Mississippians realized that the war was lost, especially after the surrender of Vicksburg, some pro-Confederates became depressed and opposed the continuation of the fighting. They may have believed in the ideal of the Confederate cause, but they had no faith in the Confederate government's ability to protect them. They may have respected their soldiers, but they knew the odds against the Confederate Army were too great to overcome. Aside from anger at Union soldiers' mistreatment of civilians, many if not most Mississippians turned their backs on war and embraced hopes for peace in the belief that nothing could be worse than the war.

It has been said that the South lost the war and won the peace. But that peace was for whites only, and the seeds of white supremacy sown during Reconstruction crippled the state for decades to come. The effects still have not completely disappeared.

Michael B. Ballard
Mississippi State University

Michael B. Ballard, *The Civil War in Mississippi: Major Campaigns and Battles* (2011); Michael B. Ballard, *Vicksburg: The Campaign That Opened the Mississippi* (2004); Edwin C. Bearss, *Rebel Victory at Vicksburg* (1963); Peter Cozzens, *The Darkest Days of the War: The Battles of Iuka and Corinth* (1997); Nicholas Lemann, *Redemption: The Last Battle of the Civil War* (2006); William L. Shea and Terrence V. Winschel, *Vicksburg Is the Key: The Struggle for the Mississippi River* (2005); Timothy B. Smith, *Champion Hill: Decisive Battle for Vicksburg* (2004); Brian Steel Wills, *A Battle from the Start: The Life of Nathan Bedford Forrest* (1992).

Civil War Arsenals

The second state to secede from the Union, Mississippi began the Civil War lacking in the industrial capacity needed to outfit a modern military force. The largest and perhaps best-known arsenal was the Confederate Briarfield Arsenal in Columbus. Other minor works and depots were located in Vicksburg, Corinth, and Tupelo.

Columbus was an important junction of the Mobile and Ohio Railroad. The building that housed the Briarfield Arsenal was described in 1865 as a brick building some "300-feet long with two wings forming three sides of a square." Lt. Col. William R. Hunt of the Confederate Niter and Mining Corps, a Memphis native, commanded the ordnance operation, which employed more than one thousand workers between the summer of 1861 and December 1862. An 1862 Ordnance Department memo listed Columbus as fourth in the Confederacy in the production of small-arms ammunition (behind only Richmond, Virginia; Augusta, Georgia; and Atlanta). The site received some seven thousand pounds of powder from the Atlanta Powder Works. In addition to ammunition, the arsenal produced bronze six-pounder cannons. German master Jacob Faser set up shop at the arsenal

and made several custom swords for general officers along with a set of dueling pistols for Pres. Jefferson Davis.

After the April 1862 Battle of Shiloh roughly five thousand damaged muskets were sent to the arsenal for repair by a staff of fifty gunsmiths gathered from throughout the region. The manufacturing works of Leech and Rigdon of Memphis fled that city in the summer of 1862 and set up a factory across the street from the Briarfield Arsenal. The company produced iron-framed .36 caliber Colt pattern 1851 Navy revolvers along with a number of cavalry sabers and knives.

Confederate general Braxton Bragg declared in 1862 that the arsenal contained "machinery and stores we cannot replace; so that its loss would be great and irreparable." When Lt. Gen. John C. Pemberton was forced to abandon his lines in North Mississippi and fall back on Vicksburg and Jackson in November 1862, he petitioned Gen. Joseph E. Johnson for permission to move the Briarfield Arsenal away from advancing Union armies, and the machinery was moved to Selma, Alabama. There, the works remained in operation until destruction by Union lieutenant general James H. Wilson's cavalry on 6 April 1865. The Union Army captured the Columbus Arsenal buildings and used them for storage. Arson was suspected in a 1 December 1865 fire that destroyed about four thousand bales of cotton.

The strategic river fortification of Vicksburg had two cannon foundries in operation during the first half of the Civil War. The most prolific was A. B. Reading and Brother, which produced at least six bronze three-inch rifles, two twelve-pounders, and thirty-five six-pounder guns between 1861–63. Vicksburg rival A. M. Paxton produced at least fourteen Federal model 1841 bronze six-pounder guns for the Confederacy in his own works. The town's siege and eventual fall to Grant on 4 July 1863 closed both works.

Several other temporary depots operated in Mississippi during the Civil War, but none is known to have produced weapons or equipment; rather, they served as collection and distribution points. During the summer of 1862, eighty-seven hundred pounds of gunpowder from the Atlanta Powder Works were stockpiled in Tupelo, and a similar shipment of small-arms ammunition was collected in Corinth. With the evacuation of North Mississippi, these supplies were moved to prevent them from falling into Union hands.

Christopher Eger
Biloxi, Mississippi

Michael B. Ballard, *Vicksburg: The Campaign That Opened the Mississippi* (2002); Patti Carr Black, *Art in Mississippi, 1720–1980* (1998); C. L. Bragg, *Never for Want of Powder: The Confederate Powder Works in Augusta, Georgia* (2007); James C. Hazlett, *Field Artillery Weapons of the Civil War* (2004).

Civil War Centennial

In the early 1960s, Mississippi and the rest of the nation commemorated the centennial of the American Civil War. Coming in the midst of the Cold War with the Soviet Union and the acrimonious civil rights struggle at home, the occasion appeared destined to resonate with contested meanings and disputed legacies. In Mississippi it coincided with the rise to power of Ross Barnett and other massive resistance leaders, setting the stage for a potential orgy of race-driven propaganda. Indeed, Barnett used the centennial to publicize his views about the "southern way of life," emboldening support for his oppositionist stance to integration. One of the state's largest centennial events, the March 1961 celebration of Mississippi's secession from the Union, featured Barnett, costumed as a Confederate general, marching at the head of several thousand similarly dressed "Mississippi Greys" in downtown Jackson. Tens of thousands of spectators roared to the sounds of "Dixie" and cheered the University of Mississippi's half-block-long Confederate battle flag.

Yet Barnett inadvertently undercut the unifying power of the centennial in the minds of many white Mississippians by pressing forward with a largely economic agenda for the celebration. Gov. James P. Coleman, Barnett's predecessor, had envisioned a relatively conservative commemoration and looked to the state's heritage organizations and historical community to shape a respectful remembrance. Among the leaders were Charlotte Capers, head of the Department of Archives and History; Frank Everett, a Vicksburg attorney and amateur historian who chaired the Mississippi Commission on the War between the States; and William Winter, state tax collector, future governor, and like Everett a former president of the Mississippi Historical Society. Edwin Bearss, a renowned Civil War historian at the Vicksburg National Military Park, added to the decorous atmosphere. Barnett, however, unceremoniously dumped this prestigious assemblage once he came into office, stacking the commission with his friends and political associates. Only three of Coleman's original sixteen appointees survived the purge, among them Sidney Roebuck, a former chair of the state highway commission and a longtime tourism promoter, whom Barnett elevated to the position of executive director. New members included the mayors of Mississippi's two largest tourist destinations, John Holland of Vicksburg, who was elected chair of the reorganized group, and Laz Quave of Biloxi. Roebuck and Holland worked with the state's leading advertising professional, George Godwin, to develop an economic theme for the centennial that devalued its propaganda potential at home while increasing its usefulness as a marketing tool across the nation.

Barnett so prioritized economic development that Walter Lord observed, "Whatever might be said of Ross Barnett on racial matters, he was a bear on getting business, and his administration featured an all-out drive to bring new industry into the state." The economic development package that Barnett presented to the legislature included funding for the centennial, and Natchez, Vicksburg, and most of the other towns where he proposed staging large-scale events were already major tourist draws. However, leaders in Corinth, Port Gibson, Holly Springs, Columbus, and other towns sought to use the free publicity and advertising provided by the centennial to jump-start their nascent tourism industries.

White Mississippians ultimately found themselves consumed by more pressing issues such as the riot that accompanied James Meredith's enrollment at the University of Mississippi and the Cuban Missile Crisis, which occurred almost back-to-back in September–October 1962. Writing to Barnett in May 1963, Roebuck remarked that interest in state centennial events was waning as a consequence of the "turmoil created by the Kennedy Administration, with the help of the [civil rights] agitators, the Cubans, and the Russians." In the end, the centennial showed the Confederacy's diffuse legacy in Mississippi, as the state sought a way out of its crushing poverty while still clinging to old traditions.

James Matthew Reonas
Louisiana State University

John E. Bodnar, *Remaking America: Public Memory, Commemoration, and Patriotism in the Twentieth Century* (1992); Robert Cook, *Journal of Southern History* (November 2002); Robert Cook, *Troubled Commemoration: The American Civil War Centennial, 1961–1965* (2007); Michael G. Kammen, *Mystic Chords of Memory: The Transformation of Tradition in American Culture* (1991); Sally Leigh McWhite, "Echoes of the Lost Cause: Civil War Reverberations in Mississippi from 1865 to 2001" (PhD dissertation, University of Mississippi, 2002); James Matthew Reonas, "Mississippi's Civil War Centennial: Heritage and Tourism in the Emerging South" (master's thesis, Louisiana State University, 2000); US Civil War Centennial Commission, *The Civil War Centennial: A Report to the Congress* (1968).

Civil War Commemorations

Although military actions ceased after four years, the battle to shape historical interpretation of the Civil War has involved generations of Mississippians and other southerners. In the years following Appomattox, former Confederates validated their actions by promulgating a version of the past in which a utopian, agrarian South seceded to preserve the constitutional rights of states, the North's overwhelming numbers and resources triumphed despite superior Confederate military ability, and Reconstruction constituted a tragic period of corrupt administration by northern carpetbaggers, former slaves, and southern scalawags brought to a halt only when white southerners "redeemed" political control of their state governments from federal intervention. Despite the sway this depiction held with later generations of white Mississippians, alternative interpretations of this past have always existed within the state.

Even before hostilities ceased, federal forces erected a monument to commemorate the first anniversary of Grant's victory at Vicksburg. Soon after the war, the federal government created the National Cemetery System to care for fallen soldiers' remains. In Mississippi, this postbellum burial project created cemeteries on the battlefields at Vicksburg and Corinth and another at Natchez. These protected enclaves both honored the Union dead and distinguished them from their enemies, most of whom remained scattered across the countryside in shallow, unmarked graves unless family members or residents of a nearby town provided a proper burial.

Mississippi Confederate commemorative activity immediately after the war also concentrated on the dead. Annual Decoration Day ceremonies in the spring provided opportunities to place floral tributes on graves, while orators recalled the sacrifices of the fallen and defended the righteousness of their cause. Approximately sixty communities in the state possess either separate Confederate cemeteries or plots. Several "ladies' memorial associations" formed to tend the graves, sponsor Decoration Day programs, and begin planning for memorials. In 1871 Liberty raised the state's first Confederate monument, with five other communities following during Reconstruction. Before the turn of the twentieth century at least sixteen more monuments appeared on the state's landscape. The predominant focus was memorializing the dead, as evidenced by inscriptions, designs (typically Victorian motifs with funereal connotations such as obelisks and urns), and location (usually inside a cemetery or on church grounds).

Under Pres. Andrew Johnson's lenient plan for Reconstruction, white southerners resumed control of the state and began planning to preserve Mississippi's Confederate history. In August 1865 the new legislature revived an 1864 law creating a superintendent of army records to compile a list of state residents with Confederate or state military service and to identify when and where the dead had fallen. The legislature also provided funds for the Vicksburg Confederate Cemetery Association reinterment project as well as for two different Virginia groups working to remove Mississippians' remains to nearby cemeteries. In addition, the politicians ratified the creation of a new county named after Robert E. Lee (Lee County) and approved the creation of another, Davis County, in the Piney Woods region, to honor for Jefferson Davis.

By March 1867 Congressional Reconstruction brought forth federal military oversight. A Republican Party comprised of newly enfranchised freedmen and northern transplants gained power and quickly renamed Davis County and named several counties for the Union (Union County) and Republican political leaders (Alcorn, Lincoln, Sumner, and Colfax). With the end of Republican Reconstruction, Democrats changed Sumner County to Webster County and Colfax County to Clay County. In 1906 legislators created Jefferson Davis County to honor the Confederate president and Forrest County to honor Nathan Bedford Forrest.

During this period, both African American and white Union veterans enrolled in Grand Army of the Republic camps across the state. Even after white Democrats regained control of the state by 1877, the legislature made few gestures toward honoring Confederate history over the next decade.

By the late 1880s, however, veterans' associations for those who had worn the gray and auxiliary groups began forming in communities across Mississippi. The United Confederate Veterans (UCV) came into existence in 1889, and by 1900 the state division reported eighty camps. Primarily a social organization, the UCV held local, state, and regional reunions that proved popular among both members and white southern society in general. However, the UCV also evinced concern for how future generations would view Confederate soldiers' actions. The organization's history committee rated the sectional bias of textbooks and called for a "renaissance" in southern history. The UCV also lobbied for Confederate veterans' pensions and battlefield preservation.

In 1899, at the urging of the UCV, the Grand Army of the Republic, and various state legislators, the federal government created Vicksburg National Military Park, spending almost fifty-nine thousand dollars for the initial land purchase of just under thirteen hundred acres. Veterans from both sides converged on the new park to map the terrain so that their states could properly mark the historic siege. In 1909 Mississippi became the first southern state to dedicate a monument on the site. Reconciliation was the theme of this federal bastion, and both Union and Confederate memorials ignored slavery and secession, focusing instead on the heroism displayed by both forces.

As the UCV's members aged, two organizations formed to share the historical burden—the United Daughters of the Confederacy (UDC) in 1895 and the Sons of Confederate Veterans (SCV) in 1896. The SCV's major achievement in Mississippi was the purchase of Jefferson Davis's home, Beauvoir, on the Gulf Coast and its establishment as a Confederate Soldiers' Home. In 1905 the organization ceded the property to the state, which accepted responsibility for the administration and expenses of the Soldiers' Home. In 1915 Mississippi had 10 SCV camps and 107 UDC chapters and a total of 3,653 members. The women were much more active than their male counterparts, lobbying the legislature for increased appropriations for Beauvoir and for the preservation of the Governor's Mansion and the Old Capitol, organizing Decoration Day observances as well as other Confederate holidays, raising funds for scholarships, watching over history textbooks, and sponsoring an auxiliary, Children of the Confederacy. The UDC also concentrated on building Confederate monuments, playing a significant role in the construction of forty-six of the fifty-two memorials erected in the state between 1895 and the start of World War I.

After the early 1890s Confederate commemorations expanded beyond simple grief for the dead to pay tribute to soldiers who had survived as well as to women and Confederate descendants: "God of our fathers," begs the Brooksville monument, "help us to preserve for our children the priceless treasure of the true story of the Confederate soldier." Memorials also began to be erected in public locales such as courthouse grounds, serving as important daily reminders of the past. Monuments also began to include figural sculpture—most commonly the solitary sentinel but also more elaborate versions such as Yazoo City's statue of a woman presenting a banner to a Confederate soldier.

Erected on the cusp of this transition, the 1891 state Confederate monument in Jackson has features from both traditions. The original funereal impulse is apparent in the lone exterior inscription, "To the Confederate Dead of Mississippi," and in the life-sized sculpture of Jefferson Davis (who died just before the monument's construction) in the crypt-like vault at the base. However, the memorial rests on the Capitol grounds and features a solitary soldier atop the tall shaft. An engraving within the vault exults, "Truth will shine in history and blossom into song." The state's ten-thousand-dollar contribution was the largest single donation to the monument's construction.

State mandates and appropriations greatly assisted other Confederate commemorative activity as well. Textbooks with a northern bias started to receive censure with an 1890 law. Four years later, the government adopted a state flag that included the St. Andrew's Cross of the Confederate battle flag. Three Confederate-related holidays received state sanction: the birthdays of Jefferson Davis and Robert E. Lee and Confederate Memorial Day. Among many other gestures toward the boys in gray, the 1906 legislature enacted a law permitting county and city contributions toward local Confederate monuments, and over the next two decades, at least twenty counties donated large sums. The state itself supplied seventy-five hundred dollars for the Monument to Women of the Confederacy, dedicated on the grounds of the New Capitol in 1917.

During both the Spanish-American War in 1898 and World War I nearly two decades later, Mississippians and other southerners espoused a patriotic enthusiasm that did much to promote national unity. After 1910, as the number of surviving Confederate veterans dwindled, fewer communities observed Decoration Day, the momentum of monument building slowed, and membership in the SCV and UDC declined. However, the Confederate interpretation of history retained considerable influence over white Mississippians, and national allegiance did not necessarily preclude pride in a sectional identity tied closely to a secessionist past.

Mississippi's African Americans, however, retained an alternative historical view that recalled the horrors of enslavement, the joy of emancipation, and the pride of political participation during Reconstruction. Without state support and in a hostile environment, families and communities relied heavily on oral tradition to transmit their version of events. Columbus's black population held an annual emancipation celebration on 8 May that involved a parade, a church service, a barbecue, dancing, baseball, and a bonfire. In both Natchez and Vicksburg, African Americans paraded to their local national cemetery on Memorial Day, a holiday that most white southerners eschewed as a consequence of its Union origins. By the 1920s popular and scholarly accounts of black history had begun to supplement these family legends and local ceremonies.

In the early 1960s the federal Civil War Centennial Commission urged a program of national reconciliation that focused on the heroism of both sides. The Mississippi Commission on the War between the States, however, viewed the occasion as an opportunity to bolster the cause of white supremacy against the recent challenges of the civil rights movement. In addition to boosting state revenues with tourist dollars, the Mississippi Commission used the commemoration to improve the state's image in the rest of the nation and to foster regional loyalty among the state's white inhabitants. An estimated one hundred thousand people watched the 1961 Secession Day procession, in which Confederate-clad regiments from eighty-nine Mississippi communities marched through Jackson. Over the next four years, centennial speakers across the state esteemed the principles that had led their forebears into battle.

Recognizing historical parallels, segregationists had adopted the Confederate banner and anthem, "Dixie," for the States' Rights Party in 1948 and subsequently for other organizations. In the mid-1960s civil rights activists began to publicly challenge these symbols. Beginning with James Meredith's 1966 March against Fear, activists verbally condemned courthouse Confederate monuments. During the early 1970s, African American students at the University of Mississippi burned Confederate flags. By the 1980s the institution's Confederate symbols had become the focus of a decades-long dialogue, and the university has sought to discourage fans from displaying the Confederate flag at sporting events.

In 2001 Mississippi voters weighed in on the question of whether the state flag should continue to contain the Confederate symbol. Although a majority favored retaining the current flag, the contest demonstrated the resilience of an alternative interpretation that had gained adherence among a growing number of white Mississippians as well as African Americans. By the twenty-first century, the state no longer granted the traditional Confederate historical construction exclusive official endorsement. In 2000 the legislature provided $2.8 million for the development of sites significant in African American history, including the erection of a monument honoring black Union soldiers buried in the Vicksburg National Cemetery as well as grants for the Natchez slave market, a former slave/contraband camp in Corinth, and the slave quarters at the Tullis-Toledano House in Biloxi.

The issue of the state flag returned to prominence in 2015 in the wake of shootings in Charleston, South Carolina, perpetrated by a gunman who used the Confederate battle flag as a symbol of white supremacy. Several cities in the state announced they would no longer fly the state flag on city property as long as it contains the Confederate emblem, and numerous prominent Mississippians publicly called for the emblem's removal from the state flag.

Leigh McWhite
University of Mississippi

David Blight, *Race and Reunion: The Civil War in American Memory* (2001); Karen Cox, *Dixie's Daughters* (2003); Mary Ann Dazey, *Mississippi Folklore Register* (Spring 1980); Gaines M. Foster, *Ghosts of the Confederacy: Defeat, the Lost Cause, and the Emergence of the New South, 1865–1913* (1987); J. Michael Martinez, William D. Richardson, and Ron McNinch-Su, *Confederate Symbols in the Contemporary South* (2000); Sally Leigh McWhite, "Echoes of the Lost Cause: Civil War Reverberations in Mississippi from 1865 to 2001" (PhD dissertation, University of Mississippi, 2003); Jerry Mitchell, *Jackson Clarion-Ledger* (17 August 2015); Michael Alan Upton, "'Keeping the Faith with the University Greys': Ole Miss as *Lieu de Memoire*" (master's thesis, University of Mississippi, 2002).

Civil War Diaries and Memoirs

When Mississippi seceded from the Union on 9 January 1861, politicians, soldiers, women, and children began to document what would become their own personal histories of the American Civil War. In the four bloody years that followed, many Mississippians emerged as prolific writers, busily chronicling their tragic and tumultuous lives.

Most Civil War diaries were written by white southerners of middle-class status and above. Some were kept as community records to be published after the war; others were secret places that allowed individuals to explore their most intimate thoughts and feelings. Diarists had different motivations for writing their stories, and the purpose and audience profoundly shaped the construction, inclusion, and exclusion of people, places, and events.

Mississippi infantrymen frequently recorded their experiences in diaries. They documented camp life, including leisure activities such as reading, sports, and music, as well as their social activities in nearby towns or on plantations. They wrote about food, provisions, shelter, the weather, and morale. They penned poignant accounts of their experiences in battle, the death of comrades, sickness and injury, promotions, and their commanders and the enemy. William Pitt Chambers of Covington County left his post as a schoolteacher and joined the Covington Rebels, participating in the Siege of Vicksburg before being captured by Union troops. His diary, like many others, ended in May 1865 with the statement, "I am a soldier no longer."

Female diarists provided a vivid picture of the home front in wartime Mississippi. They documented secession celebrations, preparations for war, shortages of household goods, the changing nature of master-slave relations, Union occupation, and the death of loved ones and friends. Amanda Worthington, a young woman from Wayside Plantation near Lake Washington, used her diary to record her rigorous domestic regime after her family's slaves fled to Union lines. Natchez resident Elizabeth Christie Brown wrote about the difficulty of supervising "impudent" servants and of her doubts about the ultimate success of the war effort. Emma Balfour and Emilie Riley McKinley of Vicksburg recorded their experiences as occupants of a city under siege. Other accounts, such as that by schoolteacher Caroline Seabury, provide the perspective of a northerner in Mississippi during the war.

Memoirs provide yet another interpretation of the war, reflecting on the past through the powerful lens of hindsight. Many of these accounts were written in the late nineteenth century, at the height of the southern memorial movement, and were heavily influenced by the rhetoric of the Lost Cause. As a literary genre, memoirs are also influenced by mood and memory and are prone to inaccuracy. Women's memoirs, in particular, were constrained by organizations such as the United Daughters of the Confederacy, which provided writers with guidelines to promote the development of a "collective memory" of the war. In other cases, senior military men and politicians published memoirs to defend their conduct during the war. Jefferson Davis, for example, wrote *The Rise and Fall of the Confederate Government* (1881) largely to explain and justify his role as Confederate president. These documents constituted a collective attempt to vindicate and reclaim the past and to record what the Daughters described as the "true history of the South."

Giselle Roberts
La Trobe University, Melbourne,
Australia

Emma Balfour, *Vicksburg: A City under Siege: Diary of Emma Balfour, May 16, 1863–June 2, 1863*, ed. Phillip C. Weinberger (1983); Elizabeth Christie Brown Diary, Department of Archives and Special Collections, J. D. Williams Library, University of Mississippi; William Pitt Chambers Diary, McCain Library and Archives, University of Southern Mississippi; Columbus Chapter UDC, ed., *War Reminiscences of Columbus,*

Mississippi, and Elsewhere, 1861–1865 (1961); Emilie Riley McKinley, *From the Pen of a She-Rebel: The Civil War Diary of Emilie Riley McKinley*, ed. Gordon A. Cotton (2001); Caroline Seabury, *The Diary of Caroline Seabury, 1854–1863*, ed. Suzanne L. Bunkers (1991); Amanda Worthington Diary, Amanda Dougherty Worthington Papers, Southern Historical Collection, University of North Carolina at Chapel Hill.

Civil War Monuments

Memorials that honor Civil War participants exist in numerous Mississippi communities, with the vast majority erected in homage to the Confederate cause. Most monuments are found on battlefields, in cemeteries, and on courthouse lawns or public squares. The single largest site for memorials is within and near Vicksburg National Military Park. After Congress established the park in 1899, efforts to accurately mark troop positions and honor participants in both armies resulted in the erection of an astonishing array of battlefield monuments—more than 1,320 state memorials, unit monuments, markers, plaques, statues, busts, and reliefs. Among the most imposing of these monuments is the Illinois State Memorial, dedicated in October 1906. Modeled after the Roman Pantheon, the memorial contains bronze tablets bearing the names of all 36,325 Union participants from Illinois. Former Confederate states likewise commemorated their soldiers. The Mississippi State Memorial, dedicated in 1909, soars seventy-six feet into the air and is constructed of granite. Bronze figures depict the actions of Mississippi troops during the siege, while a statue of Clio is perched at the monument's front. Elsewhere, an equestrian statue of Ulysses S. Grant honors the conqueror of Vicksburg, while a dramatic Confederate memorial depicts the moment when Gen. Lloyd Tilghman received a mortal wound at Champion Hill.

While Vicksburg represents the pinnacle of Civil War memorialization efforts in Mississippi, monuments in individual communities symbolize efforts to recognize units and men from those locales as well as the Confederate experience. Immediately after the war, political turmoil and the general impoverishment of the state prevented most communities from recognizing their veterans with a monument. When monuments later began to appear, they were generally placed in cemeteries and were relatively modest obelisks. Such monuments are found in cemeteries at Baldwyn, Booneville, Brookhaven, Canton, Columbus, Crystal Springs, Hernando, Holly Springs, and Meridian. A monument at Woodville features a draped cloth reminiscent of a shroud. Placing monuments in the midst of Confederate dead conveyed the sense of loss felt by many Mississippians.

Civil War monument, Columbus: the inscription reads, "This monument is erected in honor of the soldiers of Lowndes County who nobly dared life and fortune in defense of the Southern Confederacy" (Ann Rayburn Paper Americana Collection, Department of Archives and Special Collections, J. D. Williams Library, University of Mississippi [rayburn_ann_23_27_001])

The shift toward more ornate memorials coincided with a monument-building boom between 1885 and 1915, the era when most local monuments were erected in Mississippi and in other states. An intense interest in the Civil War in this period coincided with the solidification of the Lost Cause ideology. Commercial firms vied for contracts to erect monuments, solicited business from chapters of the United Confederate Veterans (UCV) and United Daughters of the Confederacy (UDC), and extolled successes in advertisements in *Confederate Veteran* magazine. John A. Stinson of the Columbus Marble Works obtained contracts for several monuments in the state.

The monuments represented a considerable investment from individuals and groups. Raising money to erect a memorial often took years and involved numerous fundraising schemes, the vast majority of them undertaken by UDC women. These efforts constituted a socially approved outlet for women's energies and talents, and speakers at dedication ceremonies fittingly extolled these women's crucial role in the projects. By the 1880s and 1890s women played key roles in memorialization efforts and in selecting monument designs. Those designs became more elaborate, usually including a statue of a Confederate soldier, almost invariably at parade rest, atop a marble or granite pedestal. Monuments increasingly appeared in highly visible public venues such as courthouse squares. Many towns, among them Columbus and Meridian, that had previously erected monuments in cemeteries added one in the heart of the community. The Columbus monument, dedicated in 1912, features three soldiers and forms a striking adornment to the backdrop provided by the Lowndes County Courthouse. Other multifigure monuments were erected in Greenwood, Hattiesburg, Heidelberg, Laurel, West Point, and Yazoo City; those in Belzoni and Poplarville jointly commemorate Confederate men and women as well as veterans of World War I. Holly Springs placed a second monument in a more prominent part of Hillcrest Cemetery. The monument features two soldiers on either side of the monument with arms grounded. The New Capitol in Jackson has the Monument to Women of the Confederacy, which is identical to a monument in Nashville, Tennessee.

Dedication festivities eventually took on the trappings of ritual. On 29 September 1907, for example, a thirty-seven-foot-tall monument was unveiled at Brandon, in Rankin County. Surmounted by a "lifelike, beautiful, and impressive" statue of a representative "Confederate infantryman on guard," the monument is inscribed on all four sides with "appropriate expressions of sentiment in verse and prose." An "eloquent prayer" opened the ceremony, after which Major Patrick Henry, commander of the local UCV, made a brief address before acting as master of ceremonies. The "popular young Mayor of Brandon," G. O. Robinson, "extended a cordial welcome to veterans and other guests." Addresses were made by Daisy McLaurin Stevens, president of the Mississippi Division, UDC, and W. S. May and Julia Jayne Walker, representing the Brandon UDC chapter, which had labored to erect the monument. Although Gen. Robert Lowry, commander of the Mississippi Division, UCV, was absent as a consequence of the death of his son, four former Confederate officers spoke before May, Annie Henry, and Marie Collier unveiled the monument. After the singing of the "Bonnie Blue Flag" and "Dixie," a benediction concluded the exercises and the assembled crowd "adjourned to the courthouse yard and enjoyed a bountiful dinner provided by the good ladies of Brandon."

The *Confederate Veteran* reported glowingly on similar ceremonies in scores of Mississippi communities. In each case, speakers lauded both the Confederate veterans and the women who toiled so diligently to build the monuments. By 1900 time was winnowing the ranks of the Civil War generation, and monuments were perceived as a means of permanently enshrining the Confederate cause. A Confederate monument erected in 1908 in Lexington was explicitly dedicated "To the Holmes County soldiers of 1861–65 and members of Holmes County Camp, No, 398, U.C.V., in memory of their patriotism and heroism, and to commend their example to future generations." This monument also reflected unrepentant Lost Cause ideology with an inscription declaring, "The men were right who wore the gray, and right can never die." The twin themes of honoring local Confederate veterans and defending southern honor appear on the vast majority of monuments erected after 1900.

Less explicitly, the ceremonies also buttressed white supremacy. One of the state's most unusual monuments reflects the paternalism of some former Confederates toward their erstwhile slaves. In Canton, William Howcott of New Orleans dedicated a monument to the slave who accompanied him during the Civil War, Willis Howcott, "a colored boy of rare loyalty and faithfulness." The seventeen thousand African Americans from Mississippi who served the Union cause have been memorialized in a sculpture dedicated in February 2004 at Vicksburg National Military Park. The African American Monument depicts two Union soldiers and a field hand and evinces modern recognition for the thousands of men who served in US Colored Troops units during the Civil War. By extension, it also rebuffs the Lost Cause ideology reflected in the many Confederate monuments scattered across the state.

Christopher Losson
St. Joseph, Missouri

"Confederate Monument at Brandon, Miss.," *Confederate Veteran* (March 1908); "Confederate Monument at [Lexington], Miss.," *Confederate Veteran* (March 1910); Gaines M. Foster, *Ghosts of the Confederacy: Defeat, the Lost Cause, and the Emergence of the New South* (1987); Vicksburg National Military Park website, www.nps.gov/vick; Ralph W. Widener, *Confederate Monuments: Enduring Symbols of the South and the War between the States* (1982)

Civil War Soldiers, African American

With the outbreak of the Civil War on 12 April 1861 loyal citizens of the United States pursued armed conflict to preserve the Union. When former slaves and free blacks attempted to volunteer for military service, many northerners resolutely maintained that only white men could serve. Nevertheless, by war's end, approximately 180,000 black men had enlisted in the Union Army to fight for their own freedom.

Prominent abolitionists such as Frederick Douglass encouraged black men to actively participate in a fight against slavery. While the army initially turned away blacks, fleeing slaves increasingly sought refuge behind Union lines and forced the issue of African American military service to the fore. The First and Second Confiscation Acts, passed on 6 August 1861 and 17 July 1862, respectively, both provided safe haven for "contrabands" and allowed limited numbers of blacks to be used in conjunction with the army for any purpose judged "best for the public welfare." Abraham Lincoln's Emancipation Proclamation, which went into effect on 1 January 1863, allowed black men to serve in combat with the US military. Black soldiers suffered the indignities of a racist military, receiving lower pay than white soldiers and facing restrictions to fatigue duty and severe limits on promotions to the officer corps.

Under the command of Union general Lorenzo Thomas, recruitment of black Mississippians began in March 1863. As the Union forces moved through the Mississippi Valley, slaves fleeing plantations and farms joined up, initially serving in state-designated regiments. The 1st Mississippi (African Descent) participated in Ulysses S. Grant's campaign against Vicksburg, seeing action at Milliken's Bend on the Louisiana side of the Mississippi River on 7 June 1863. Although poorly trained, ill equipped, and outnumbered, black troops performed well in battle, routing Confederates under Gen. John George Walker. Military officials eventually reorganized most black soldiers into the US Colored Troops, which incorporated the Mississippi regiments. As part of Union general William Tecumseh Sherman's campaign to destroy Confederate general Nathan Bedford Forrest's cavalry in 1864, the 55th US Colored Troops under Gen. Samuel D. Sturgis engaged Forrest's men at Brice's Crossroads near Baldwyn on 10 June. Although the Confederates emerged victorious, Union officers praised the black soldiers' performance under fire.

Approximately eighteen thousand black Mississippians served in the Civil War, fighting in all theaters of operation and making significant contributions to the Union war effort. The US victory enabled black veterans to cite their service to the nation's cause in support of their claim to equal citizenship rights.

M. Keith Harris
Los Angeles, California

Dudley Taylor Cornish, *The Sable Arm: Black Troops in the Union Army, 1861–1865* (1956); James M. McPherson, *The Negro's Civil War: How American Blacks Felt and Acted during the War for the Union* (1965); Benjamin Quarles, *The Negro in the Civil War* (1953); Noah Andre Trudeau, *Like Men of War: Black Troops in the Civil War, 1862–1865* (1998).

Civilian Conservation Corps

In March 1933 Pres. Franklin D. Roosevelt signed into law a bill creating the Civilian Conservation Corps (CCC). The CCC addressed two issues that reflected glaring deficiencies in the country's management: unemployment and the nation's failure to conserve natural resources. Mississippi struggled on both fronts, and after some initial misgivings about the New Deal in general, the state warmly embraced the federal dollars the program brought.

While some states struggled to consistently fill their CCC allotments, Mississippi routinely received more than its share, largely because of the leadership of director George Sadka, who oversaw Mississippi's CCC for virtually all of its existence. Moreover, though unofficial policy entirely sought to exclude African Americans from the CCC's relief efforts, Sadka fought to have allotments benefit all Mississippians, and thirteen of the state's camps ultimately were designated for African Americans.

Between 1933 and 1942 the Mississippi CCC offered direct relief by employing approximately sixty thousand men between the ages of seventeen and twenty-four—roughly 12 percent of that population. Enrollees received thirty dollars per month, the majority of which they sent back home. The CCC spent sixty-one million dollars in Mississippi and allotted another fifteen million dollars to dependents of enrollees. CCC camps also indirectly affected nearby communities, since each camp cost approximately twenty-two thousand dollars to build and five thousand dollars per month to maintain. Local businesses and farmers supplied much of the materials and services in support of local camps.

The entrance to swinging bridge over Bear Creek, erected in 1939 in Tishomingo State Park by the Civilian Conservation Corps (Photograph by James G. Thomas, Jr.)

In addition to economic relief, the CCC considerably enhanced Mississippi's infrastructure and natural surroundings. The CCC built and maintained ten state parks: Leroy Percy, Tombigbee, Clarkco, Legion, Tishomingo, Holmes County, Roosevelt, Spring Lake (Wall Doxey), Percy Quinn, and Magnolia (now part of the Gulf Islands National Seashore). CCC enrollees ran 2,689 miles of telephone lines and constructed 2,346 miles of roads. They planted 17 million trees for erosion control and 137 million trees in reforestation. One of the most enduring legacies of the CCC, however, may be its introduction of kudzu in an effort to halt soil erosion.

Like most New Deal programs, the CCC did not fundamentally alter Mississippi's social or economic systems, nor was it designed to do so. But the CCC did significantly aid a portion of Mississippi's young male population that might otherwise have slipped through the New Deal relief net, helping thousands of families during a time of stifling depression. By pumping almost eighty million dollars into the state from 1933 to 1942, the CCC significantly boosted Mississippi's beleaguered economy. And while the CCC did not undo decades of devastating natural resource policies, it gave Mississippi a system of state parks, salvaged thousands of acres of Piney Woods timber, and saved tons of Delta topsoil. Similarly, while it did not challenge the state's entrenched segregation, it did benefit both black and white Mississippians.

Andy Harper
University of Mississippi

Justin C. Eaddy, *Journal of Mississippi History* (Summer 2003); Andrew C. Harper, "The Civilian Conservation Corps and Mississippi: A New Deal Success Story" (master's thesis, University of Southern Mississippi, 1992).

Claiborne, Craig

(1920–2000) Food Writer and Editor

Raymond Craig Claiborne was born on 4 September 1920 in Sunflower, in Sunflower County in the Mississippi Delta. His father, Lewis Edmond Claiborne, moved the family to Indianola because of financial hardships, and Kathleen Claiborne, Craig's mother, took in boarders to help make ends meet. Craig subsequently spent much time in the kitchen with his mother and the African American servants who prepared meals for the lodgers, sparking his passion for food and cooking.

After graduating from Indianola High School, Claiborne attended Mississippi State University, intending to study medicine. He later transferred to the University of Missouri and earned a degree in journalism. In the summer of 1942, less than one month after graduation, Claiborne joined the US Navy and served in World War II aboard the USS *Augusta*. After participating in the Moroccan invasion, Claiborne discovered French cuisine in Casablanca. When he returned to the United States, Claiborne briefly worked in advertising at the *Chicago Daily News* before moving to radio public relations. Bored, Claiborne used his savings to travel to France and rediscovered the cuisine. When he ran out of money, Claiborne rejoined the US Navy and served in the Korean War. After his discharge, he used the GI Bill to enroll in culinary school at L'École Hôtelière, L'École Professionnelle de la Société Suisse des Hôteliers near Lausanne, Switzerland, where the head chef of the famed Peabody Hotel in Memphis had trained.

Claiborne completed his schooling and moved back to the United States to work at *Gourmet* magazine, where he billed himself as the first restaurant critic who had culinary training. He became an editor at the magazine before realizing his dream of serving as food editor for the *New York Times*, the first male to hold that post.

Claiborne remained at the *Times* from 1957 to 1970 and 1974 to 1986, becoming recognized as one of the foremost figures in the culinary arts. He is credited with the four-star restaurant rating system that remains in use today and has been adapted for other fields. Claiborne authored and edited more than twenty cookbooks, the first of which was the *New York Times Cookbook* (1961), which sold more than three million copies. Another cookbook, *Southern Cooking* (1987), paid homage to his roots with more than three hundred recipes from across the region. Claiborne also published an autobiography, *A Feast Made for Laughter* (1982). Proud of its native son, Sunflower named two intersecting roads Claiborne Street and Craig Avenue.

Claiborne's most outlandish stunt occurred when he paid three hundred dollars at a charity auction for dinner for two at the restaurant of the winner's choice, sponsored by American Express. Claiborne took his friend and culinary collaborator, Pierre Franey, to Chez Denis in Paris, where they ran up a four-thousand-dollar bill on a meal consisting of thirty-one courses, many of which they merely tasted, and nine wines. After publishing an article on his night out, Claiborne received thousands of letters criticizing his extravagance, including one from the Vatican.

Openly gay, Claiborne never married or had any long-term partners. He died in Manhattan on 22 January 2000 at the age of seventy-nine, leaving his entire estate to the Culinary Institute of America.

Brooke Butler
New Orleans, Louisiana

Georgeanna Milam Chapman, "Craig Claiborne: A Southern-Made Man" (master's thesis, University of Mississippi, 2008); Craig Claiborne, *Craig Claiborne's Southern Cooking* (2007); Craig Claiborne, *A Feast Made for Laughter* (1982); John L. Hess and Karen Hess, *The Taste of America* (2000); Thomas McNamee, *The Man Who Changed the Way We Eat: Craig Claiborne and the Food Renaissance* (2012); Doris Witt, *Black Hunger* (1999).

Claiborne, John F. H.

(1807–1884) Political Leader and Historian

John Francis Hamtramck Claiborne, a politician, newspaper editor, and historian, was born on 24 April 1807 near Natchez, the eldest son of Ferdinand Leigh Claiborne and Magdalene Hutchins Claiborne. Claiborne's father was a veteran of the Revolutionary War who later became a general, and his uncles included governor of the Mississippi Territory William C. C. Claiborne.

After graduation from Jefferson College, Claiborne studied law in Virginia and in Natchez. His studies were interrupted several times by ill health; respiratory ailments, probably tuberculosis, affected his entire career. On 18 December 1828 he married Martha Dunbar. The couple had two daughters and one son, who was mortally wounded at the end of the Civil War.

Claiborne soon gave up practicing law to pursue his interests in politics. A supporter of Andrew Jackson, Claiborne was elected in 1828 to the Mississippi House of Representatives from Adams County and served for three terms. He played an important role in organizing the Democratic Party in the state.

Soon after moving to Madison County in 1835, Claiborne won election to the US Congress on the Democratic ticket. Intending to seek reelection, Claiborne and Samuel Gholson won a July 1837 special election and attended a special session of Congress called by Pres. Martin Van Buren. Claiborne and Gholson contended that this election replaced the regular November election, but the Whig Party disagreed and ran Seargent S. Prentiss and Thomas J. Word, who easily defeated the two Democrats. Unable to reach a decision, the House Committee on Elections ordered Mississippi to hold a new election. Bad health prevented Claiborne from campaigning, and he lost narrowly to the Whig candidates in April 1838.

Claiborne returned to Natchez in July 1841 to edit the *Mississippi Free Trader*, in which he published "Trip through the Piney Woods" and other historical sketches. His 1842 appointment by the federal government to lead an investigation of land claims by Choctaw Indians plunged Claiborne back into controversy. He worked hard to sort out the legitimate claims and to stifle the land speculators who sought to exploit the Choctaw and defraud the government. Representing a land company, Prentiss accused Claiborne of bias and challenged him to a duel. Claiborne avoided this and other duels and Congress adopted his report, but he alienated many people in Mississippi. Beginning in 1844 he assumed the editorship of a series of Democratic newspapers in New Orleans. His support for Pres. Franklin Pierce led to a federal appointment as custodian of public timber for Alabama, Mississippi, and Louisiana, and he moved near Bay St. Louis, which proved beneficial for his health.

As the nation moved into civil war, Claiborne believed that the North was infringing on southern rights but had no sympathy for secession, and he subsequently avoided all connections with the Confederacy. With a significant collection of his family's letters, Claiborne spent the last three decades of his life researching and writing Mississippi history. In 1860 he published *Life and Times of General Sam Dale* and the two-volume *Life and Correspondence of John A. Quitman*. He continued to acquire manuscript collections and pamphlets and undertook a history of Mississippi. In 1881 he published his most famous work, *Mississippi, as a Province, Territory, and State*, volume 1. Although later historians have noted factual errors and biases, Claiborne's labors were invaluable because of the documents he preserved and donated to the state as well as his firsthand observations of political events and personalities. In March 1884 Claiborne's home, Dunbarton, burned, taking with it the manuscript of volume 2 of his history of Mississippi. Devastated, Claiborne died in Natchez on 17 May 1884. As his tombstone suggests, Claiborne took pride in his public service but wished to be remembered as "Mississippi's Historian."

M. Philip Lucas
Cornell College

William B. Hamilton and Ruth K. Nuermberger, *Journal of Mississippi History* (July 1945); Franklin L. Riley, *Publications of the Mississippi Historical Society* (1903).

Claiborne County

Claiborne County lies directly east of Tensas Parish, Louisiana, between Vicksburg and Natchez. The county is bordered on the west by the Mississippi River, and the Big Black River forms its northern boundary with Warren County.

Bayou Pierre wends east across the county from its Mississippi River origins in southwestern Claiborne.

The county's lands were home to the Natchez and Choctaw Indians prior to the arrival of Europeans. The French and then the Spanish occupied the area during the eighteenth century, before it was formally annexed by the United States in 1798. Claiborne officially became the Mississippi Territory's fourth county on 27 January 1802. It is named for William C. Claiborne, the territory's second governor.

In 1810 Claiborne's population of 3,102 was almost evenly divided between slaves and whites. The potential for increased cotton production contributed to a rapid expansion of the slave population to 12,296 (the eighth-highest total in the state) by 1860, while the county's white population leveled off and actually declined slightly to less than a third of the number of slaves.

Early on, the number of people employed in commerce and manufacturing was small—less than one-tenth of the county's agricultural workforce. By 1840, however, Claiborne County ranked third in the state in the number of commercial and manufacturing laborers. The county's largest nonagricultural employers included four lumber mills and two carriage manufacturers.

The county seat, Port Gibson, became a trading hub for white settlers, helping the county relatively quickly develop large-scale cotton cultivation. Thus, the plantation economy dominated antebellum Claiborne, and the county was home to some of the largest farms in Mississippi, with its 305 farms averaging more than four hundred acres of improved land. In 1860 it ranked fourteenth in the state in cotton production but only twenty-fourth in the production of corn.

Revivalist Lorenzo Dow, one of the state's first ministers, built a cabin and began preaching near Port Gibson in 1807. The county was also home to Mississippi's third governor, Walter Leake. A decade later, Presbyterian leaders founded Oakland College, one of the state's first higher-education institutions. Later in the antebellum period, Port Gibson native and Oakland College alumnus Henry Hughes wrote *Treatise on Sociology, Theoretical and Practical*, a proslavery tome considered one the first important sociological works. Poet Irwin Russell, author of "Christmas Night in the Quarters," was born in Port Gibson in 1853. The Windsor Ruins, the columns of one of the South's largest Greek Revival mansions, still stand in Claiborne County, more than a century after a fire devastated the home.

In 1860 the county had fourteen established churches, with the Methodists and Presbyterians possessing both the largest congregations and the largest buildings. One of Mississippi's earliest synagogues was built in Port Gibson in 1859. A year earlier, architect James Jones began construction on an elaborate replacement for the original First Presbyterian Church of Port Gibson. This church, still standing, is known for its unusual steeple, which is crowned by a twelve-foot gold hand pointing skyward.

With the interests of the county's entrenched plantation majority to defend, Claiborne's white citizens staunchly supported the Confederate cause. Many residents suffered greatly during the war, enduring privation from Union raids, the loss of many soldiers, the repeated burning and bombardment of Great Gulf by US forces, and the Battle of Port Gibson, along with a number of smaller conflicts. When Union troops led by Ulysses S. Grant took Port Gibson as part of the 1863 Vicksburg Campaign, Grant proclaimed the town "too beautiful to burn."

In the postbellum period, Claiborne County's population remained stable, maintaining a substantial African American majority (77 percent of the county's 16,768 people in 1880). By 1900 Claiborne's population had topped 20,000. Significant Irish and German populations moved to the area in the late 1800s, and Syrian and Lebanese immigration began in the early 1900s. In spite of the port economy of its county seat, turn-of-the-century Claiborne County possessed only a small industrial population of about 200, and most residents still worked in agriculture. More than half of Claiborne's 671 farming families owned their farms in 1900, compared to only 7 percent of the county's 2,300 black farm families. Most African Americans were tenants or sharecroppers.

A 1916 religious census showed that about half of the church members in Claiborne County belonged to Missionary Baptist Conventions. The Methodist Episcopal Church, African Methodist Episcopal Church, Southern Baptist Convention, Presbyterians, Disciples of Christ, and Episcopalians were other religious groups of significant size.

In 1930 African Americans made up about three-quarters of Claiborne's population of 12,152. The county remained very rural, with no towns of more than 2,000 people and just 358 industrial laborers. Thirty years later the population remained almost unchanged, with about 11,000 people and African Americans still outnumbering whites three to one. However, in 1960 less than a third of its population worked in agriculture, with another third employed in manufacturing. A significant portion of Claiborne's female laborers were employed as domestic workers. During the mid-twentieth century the county's agriculture combined cotton, corn, soybeans, wheat, and livestock. Claiborne boasted the second-highest number of hogs in the state in 1960 and was the only county with more hogs than people.

In 1918 F. S. Wolcott established Port Gibson as the official home of the Rabbit's Foot Minstrels, a traveling music group that included such celebrated performers as Rufus Thomas, Ma Rainey, and Louis Jordan. Olivia Valentine Hastings, one of the greatest proponents of education in Mississippi, grew up in Claiborne County. Author Berry Morgan was born in Port Gibson in 1919 and modeled the fictional Kings Town after his hometown. Pete Brown, who in 1964 became the first African American golfer to win a Professional Golfers' Association of America event, was born in Port Gibson.

Claiborne County was the site of years of voter registration efforts, a sustained and effective civil rights boycott that ended in 1967, and leadership from Charles Evers of the National Association for the Advancement of Colored People (NAACP). The county was also the home of significant civil rights opposition. Port Gibson native John Satterfield, a leading adversary of the movement, served as Gov. Ross Barnett's lawyer and a lobbyist against civil rights legislation. A noteworthy case, *NAACP v. Claiborne Hardware Co.*, began in 1969 when white-owned businesses sued the NAACP and others for the economic harm caused by boycotts. The case spent more than eleven years winding its way through the judicial system until the US Supreme Court ruled that the First Amendment prevented states from prohibiting peaceful political activity such as boycotts.

Like most counties along the Mississippi River, Claiborne County's 2010 population was predominantly black—84 percent of its 9,604 citizens identified themselves as African American. The county's overall population had declined by roughly 11 percent (1,241 people) over the previous half century.

Mississippi Encyclopedia Staff
University of Mississippi

Emilye Crosby, *A Little Taste of Freedom: The Black Freedom Struggle in Claiborne County, Mississippi* (2005); Katy McCaleb Headley, *Claiborne County, Mississippi: The Promised Land* (1976); Mississippi State Planning Commission, *Progress Report on State Planning in Mississippi* (1938); *Mississippi Statistical Abstract*, Mississippi State University (1952–2010); Charles Sydnor and Claude Bennett, *Mississippi History* (1939); University of Virginia Library, Historical Census Browser website, http://mapserver.lib.virginia.edu; E. Nolan Waller and Dani A. Smith, *Growth Profiles of Mississippi's Counties, 1960–1980* (1985).

Clark, Charles

(1810–1877) Twenty-Fourth Governor, 1864–1865

Charles Clark has the distinction of being one of the three Mississippi governors, along with John Quitman and Theodore Bilbo, to be arrested and imprisoned. When the Civil War ended, Union authorities arrested Gen. Clark and incarcerated him briefly at Fort Pulaski in Savannah, Georgia. According to a witness, "The old soldier, when informed of the purpose of the officers, straightened his mangled limbs as best he could, and with great difficulty said, 'I denounce before high heaven and the civilized world this unparalleled act of tyranny and usurpation. I only yield obedience because I have no power to resist.'"

In 1831, Clark had moved to Jefferson County, Mississippi, from Ohio, where he was born in 1810. He taught school, practiced law, and represented Jefferson County in the state legislature for several years. During the Mexican War, Clark organized the Thomas Hinds Guards, an infantry company that became a part of the 2nd Regiment of Mississippi Volunteers. After the resignation of Reuben Davis, the regimental commander, Clark was elected colonel of the regiment.

Shortly after the war with Mexico, Clark moved to Bolivar County to become a planter. As a member of the Whig Party, Clark represented Bolivar in the state House of Representatives from 1856 to 1861. As a delegate to the constitutional convention of 1851, Clark had opposed secession, but by 1861 he had become convinced that Mississippi's interests were best served by withdrawal from the Union. He joined the Confederate military, suffering injuries at Shiloh and later at Baton Rouge.

In 1863, after the fall of Vicksburg, many Mississippians wanted to end the war and called for negotiations with the US government. But many more favored the continuation of the war, and Clark ran for governor as an antipeace candidate, winning over only token opposition. Late in the war, Clark became one of the few southern governors to support the idea of allowing African Americans to join Confederate forces. He did not, however, support rewarding such work with emancipation.

During Clark's administration the Union Army occupied Jackson and forced the state capital to move to Macon, to Columbus, and then back to Macon. After Confederate troops in Alabama and Mississippi surrendered on 6 May 1865, Clark issued a proclamation convening the state legislature for a special session and ordered all state officials to return to Jackson. When Clark arrived in occupied Jackson, he was informed by the Union military commander that he and the legislature would be placed under arrest. Most of the lawmakers fled.

After his release from Fort Pulaski, Clark returned to his home in Bolivar County and resumed the practice of law. In 1876, after the Reconstruction period had ended, he was appointed chancellor for the 4th Judicial District, and he served on the bench until his death on 17 December 1877.

David G. Sansing
University of Mississippi

William C. Harris, *Presidential Reconstruction in Mississippi* (1967); *Mississippi Official and Statistical Register* (1912); Dunbar Rowland, *Encyclopedia of Mississippi History*, vol. 1 (1907); Timothy B. Smith, *Mississippi in the Civil War: The Home Front* (2010).

Clark, Charles
(1925–2011) Judge

Charles Clark served as a judge on the US Court of Appeals for the Fifth Circuit from 1969 to 1992. His great-grandfather, Charles Clark, served as a Confederate general and as Mississippi's governor during the Civil War. Governor Clark's only son, Fred, began practicing law in 1874, and his son, Charles, did so in 1906. From 1919 to 1923 he practiced in Bolivar County with his second cousin, Walter Sillers Jr., who later became Speaker of the Mississippi House.

This Charles Clark and his second wife, Anita Massengill Tigrett Clark, had their only child, also named Charles Clark, on 12 September 1925. The elder Charles Clark died when the boy was only two, and he was raised in Cleveland, Mississippi. Anita Clark died just after her son started at Millsaps College, and Sillers became his legal guardian.

On 1 July 1943 Clark began active military duty in the US Navy's V-12 program, in which college students engaged in regular studies and in military training. He transferred from Millsaps to Tulane University before receiving his commission in July 1945 and serving on a ship in the Pacific. Clark was discharged from the navy in July 1946 and soon enrolled at the University of Mississippi School of Law, graduating in 1948. Clark married Emily Russell in 1947, and they eventually had six children.

Clark began his practice with the Jackson law firm of Wells, Wells, Newman, and Thomas before returning to active duty in the US Navy from February 1951 to December 1952, during the Korean War. On 15 July 1961 Clark formed a law firm with Vardaman S. Dunn and William Harold Cox Jr., who later became a US district judge. Clark was primarily a litigator. From 1961 to 1966 he was a part-time Mississippi special assistant attorney general, a capacity in which he represented the state college board in its legal fight against the admission of James Meredith to the University of Mississippi.

Clark appeared at numerous hearings before the Fifth Circuit. One of that court's judges who is most identified with promoting civil rights, John Minor Wisdom, said that Clark "argued vigorously, made the best of a bad case, was deferential to the Court, acted with dignity and grace, and conducted himself in every way according to the highest tradition of Anglo-American advocacy. He won my respect then and the respect of all the judges on our Court."

When Fifth Circuit judge Claude Clayton of Tupelo died in July 1969, Sen. James Eastland encouraged the selection of Clark for the vacancy. Pres. Richard Nixon nominated Clark on 7 October 1969. Clark was considered for promotion to the US Supreme Court in both 1971 and 1975, but neither Nixon nor his successor, Gerald Ford, chose to nominate the Mississippi jurist.

In 1981 Congress split the six-state, twenty-six-judge Fifth Circuit into two smaller circuits. Clark became chief judge of the new Fifth Circuit, which included Mississippi, Louisiana, and Texas, and remained in that position for eleven years.

Clark was a member of the US Judicial Conference, a committee of federal judges that serves as the principal policymaking body for the federal courts. He was chairman of its budget committee from 1981 to 1987. In January 1989 the chief justice appointed Clark to be chairman of the executive committee of the Judicial Conference.

During his twenty-two years on the Fifth Circuit, Judge Clark authored more than twenty-eight hundred opinions. He resigned from the court on 15 January 1992 and returned to private law practice in Jackson. He retired in 2009 and died on 6 March 2011.

Leslie H. Southwick
US Court of Appeals for the
Fifth Circuit

Jack Bass, *Unlikely Heroes* (1981); John W. Dean, *The Rehnquist Choice* (2001); *Jackson Clarion-Ledger* (9 March 2011); Frank T. Read and Lucy S. McGough, *Let Them Be Judged: The Judicial Integration of the Deep South* (1978); Leslie H. Southwick, *Hinds County Bar Association Newsletter* (August 2009); Florence Warfield Sillers, comp., *A History of Bolivar County, Mississippi* (1948); "A Tribute to Chief Judge Charles Clark," *Mississippi College Law Review* (Spring 1992).

Clark, Colia Liddell LaFayette
(b. 1940) Activist

Colia Liddell was born in rural Hinds County and grew up in Jackson, where she was educated in the city's segregated school system. Her family was active in the Southern Tenant Farmers' Union and other social movements. Every fall until Liddell was fifteen, her family migrated to Bentonia, in the Mississippi Delta, to pick cotton, where she and her siblings saw firsthand the mistreatment of and acts of violence against blacks. The murder of Emmett Till in August 1955 had a particularly strong influence on the girl's determination to fight for civil rights.

The Liddell family was actively involved in the Jackson movement, and Colia joined the city's chapter of the National Association for the Advancement of Colored People (NAACP) and served as special assistant to Medgar Evers, the organization's first Mississippi's field secretary. In 1961, while a student at Tougaloo College, Liddell organized and became the first president of the North Jackson Youth Council, with John Salter, a social science professor, as the youth group's adviser. Under Clark's leadership, the Youth Council played an integral role in the development of the Jackson movement, planning and initiating economic boycotts against various venues, especially on Capitol Street in downtown Jackson.

By the summer of 1962 Clark had resigned from her position with the NAACP and joined the Student Nonviolent Coordinating Committee (SNCC) under the leadership of Bob Moses, helping promote voter education among African Americans in Jackson, Hattiesburg, and the Mississippi Delta. In November 1962 she married Bernard LaFayette Jr., who had participated in the 1961 Freedom Rides and served as a SNCC field secretary.

In early 1963 the couple moved to Selma, Alabama, to organize a voter registration project in Dallas County, where blacks comprised a majority of the population but had no political power. Bernard LaFayette became director of SNCC's Black Belt Alabama Voter Registration Project, while Colia became the organization's field secretary. The LaFayettes' work helped to lay the foundation for a sustained and organized movement in Selma.

In May 1963 SNCC executive secretary James Forman chose Colia LaFayette to help organize the Birmingham movement. She and other activists met organized resistance under the authority of police commissioner Eugene "Bull" Conner: she was one of the demonstrators hit by water from fire hoses on 8 May 1963. Her involvement in the Jackson movement had taught her the importance of youth activism, and she helped recruit Birmingham high school students to participate in civil rights activism.

In 1964 LaFayette moved to Nashville, Tennessee, becoming a member of the Southern Organizing Committee. Her activism later took her to Chicago, where she and other civil rights activists took on racial discrimination and inequality in the North. In early 1978 she returned to Mississippi and served as the editor of the state's premier black publication, the *Jackson Advocate*. She later earned a master's degree at Georgia's Albany State University. She now lives in New York, where in 2010 and 2012 she ran for the US Senate on the Green Party ticket. She remains active in the struggle for human rights, working to confront issues such as American involvement in foreign wars, imperialism, capitalism, homelessness, and police brutality.

Daphne R. Chamberlain
Tougaloo College

Civil Rights Movement Veterans website, www.crmvet.org; Colia Liddell Lafayette Clark, interview with Dr. Alferdteen Harrison, Margaret Walker Alexander Center for Research and Culture, Jackson, Miss. (17 July 1974); James Forman, *The Making of Black Revolutionaries* (1985); David Halberstam, *The Children* (1998); Anthony Palmer and Colia Clark, *Socialist Organizer* (3 March 2015), socialistorganizer.org; John R. Salter, *Jackson, Mississippi: An American Chronicle of Struggle and Schism* (1979).

Clark, Kate Freeman

(1875–1957) Artist

Kate Freeman Clark was born on 3 September 1875 in Holly Springs. Her father, Edward Clark, was a Vicksburg attorney who served as an assistant to L. Q. C. Lamar; her mother was Cary Freeman Clark. After her father's death, Kate, her mother, and grandmother moved to New York City, where Kate graduated from the Gardiner School in 1891. She subsequently enrolled in drawing and painting courses at the Art Students League, receiving instruction from John Henry Twachtman, Irving Ramsey Wiles, and most importantly William Merritt Chase.

Attracted by Chase's masterly touch and dark, Munich School manner, Clark left the League in 1896 for the Chase School of Art. That summer, she attended Chase's first Shinnecock Hills Summer Art School on Long Island, the first major summer art colony of its kind. Clark became enthralled with the summer school, especially painting outside amid the landscape, a practice called "plein air" in Europe. She and many other students also became fascinated with Chase, a natural teacher full of enthusiasm. Leading by example, he encouraged his students to launch directly into a painting, responding immediately to the imagery without careful preliminary drawing or compositional mapping. His art lectures were often peppered with admonitions to which Clark gave careful thought. Clark returned to the summer school for five years, completing at least one work per day during the three- to four-month school period. Some paintings were large, while other works were painted on cigar box lids.

As winter and summer studies with Chase became a routine for Clark, her skills improved. Her landscapes reflect Chase's

Portrait of Kate Freeman Clark, painted by her mentor, William Merritt Chase, ca. 1902 (Courtesy Kate Freeman Clark Art Gallery)

preference for persistent diagonals; undramatic scenery; the earthy color schemes of the French Barbizon School; quick, confident brushwork; soft treatment of distant spaces; and genteel subject matter.

Clark began exhibiting her works at New York's National Academy of Design in 1904 and then at other prestigious venues, including Pittsburgh's Carnegie Institute; the Boston Art Club; the Buffalo Fine Arts Museum; the Concord School of Art in Washington, D.C.; and the Pennsylvania Academy of Fine Arts. She had some solo exhibitions, and one of her paintings was selected for the 1915 Panama-Pacific Exposition in San Francisco. Reserved by nature and social class, Clark hid her gender by signing works *Freeman Clark* and declined to sell her paintings. Her last exhibition occurred in 1918 in New York City.

Clark's promising career was brought to a halt by Chase's death in 1916, followed by the deaths of her grandmother in 1919 and her mother in 1923. She put all of her paintings and drawings into storage in the New York City area, returned to her family home in Holly Springs, and essentially stopped painting even though she had few responsibilities and a generous inheritance. She died on 3 March 1957, leaving money to build a facility to house and exhibit her works. The Kate Freeman Clark Art Gallery in Holly Springs contains at least one thousand oil paintings, watercolors, and drawings.

Tom Dewey II
University of Mississippi

Kathleen McLain Jenkins, in *Mississippi Women: Their Histories, Their Lives*, ed. Martha H. Swain, Elizabeth Anne Payne, Marjorie Julian Spruill, and Susan Ditto (2003); Cynthia Grant Tucker, *Kate Freeman Clark: A Painter Rediscovered* (1981).

Clark, Robert G., Jr.
(b. 1928) Politician

Robert George Clark Jr. became the first African American elected to the Mississippi state legislature in the twentieth century. He was born on 3 October 1928 in Holmes County on land acquired by his grandparents after emancipation. His grandfather had chaired the Hinds County Republican Party during Reconstruction. Clark worked as a schoolteacher in Holmes County but was fired after voicing support for desegregated schools. He eventually became an administrator at Saints Junior College in Lexington, Mississippi, where he coached football and oversaw a federal antipoverty program.

In 1967, two years after the passage of the Voting Rights Act, Clark made a bid for public office after the all-white Holmes County School Board refused to approve an adult education program. When changes to state election laws prevented him from running for county school superintendent, he decided to challenge Rep. J. P. Love, chair of the Mississippi House's Education Committee. Clark ran with eleven other black independent candidates, all members of or backed by the Mississippi Freedom Democratic Party (MFDP), though Clark never officially joined. The black slate followed the MFDP's independent course and boycotted the county Democratic primary. Clark ran an intensive campaign, and his popularity as a teacher and coach, along with his opponent's refusal to campaign for black votes, led to his narrow victory. Clark was the only one of the year's eight black legislative candidates to win, and he did so because the multimember legislative district in which he ran consisted of majority-black Yazoo and Holmes Counties, creating a voting district that was 65 percent black. Although Love challenged the election, Clark went to Jackson in 1968.

Clark remained the only black in the Mississippi legislature until 1975, and his early years were difficult. Few white House members would sit next to him at social gatherings, and on some occasions, he argued against bills he supported so that white legislators would vote for them. He supported Republican Gil Carmichael in the 1975 gubernatorial election but switched from an independent to a Democrat after Gov. Cliff Finch reconciled the Loyalist and Regular wings of the state Democratic Party in 1976. In 1975 three new black state legislators were elected from Hinds County after the courts ordered the county to adopt single-member districts. Clark did not share the legislature with a significant number of black representatives until 1979, when a statewide single-member-district plan led to the election of seventeen new black members. Clark's seniority made him the leader of the legislature's black caucus, but he sometimes drew criticism from younger and newer black legislators for his close working relationship with House Speaker C. B. Newman, an archconservative known for blocking all liberal or progressive reforms. Clark became chair of the House Education Committee in 1977 and played a key role in the passage of the Education Reform Act of 1982, arguably the high point of his legislative career. With the support of Gov. William Winter, Clark ushered through a bill that restored compulsory school attendance and provided for publicly funded kindergartens.

In 1982 Clark made a bid for the US House of Representatives in Mississippi's 2nd Congressional District, which encompassed the black-majority Mississippi Delta. He won the Democratic nomination and ran a vigorous campaign against Webb Franklin, a white Republican from Greenwood. Many white Democrats, among them Sen. John Stennis, who was running for reelection, refused to campaign for Clark, and Clark lost, taking only a small percentage of the white vote. He ran against Franklin again in 1984 but lost in the face of high Republican turnout for Ronald Reagan's reelection. Clark continued to serve in the Mississippi House and was elected Speaker Pro Tem in 1992. He retired from political life in 2003. In 2004 a government building in Jackson was renamed the Robert G. Clark Jr. Building, a first for an African American in the state. Jackson State University honors Clark with an annual Robert Clark Symposium that studies issues of contemporary public life.

Chris Danielson
Montana Tech at the University
of Montana

Will D. Campbell, *Robert G. Clark's Journey to the House: A Black Politician's Story* (2003); James C. Cobb, *The Most Southern Place on Earth: The Mississippi Delta and the Roots of Regional Identity* (1992); John Dittmer, *Local People: The Struggle for Civil Rights in Mississippi* (1994); Melany Nielson, *Even Mississippi* (1989); Frank Parker, *Black Votes Count: Political Power in Mississippi after 1965* (1990).

Clark, Thomas Dionysius

(1903–2005) Historian

In 1991 the governor of Kentucky called Tom Clark "Kentucky's greatest treasure." Clark's inspiration to become one of America's preeminent historians, however, grew from the soil of Mississippi, where he was born in Louisville, Winston County, on 14 July 1903. He was the eldest of seven children born to John Collinsworth Clark, a cotton farmer, and Sallie Bennett Clark, a schoolteacher. Tom Clark left school to work on the farm and then as a deckhand on a dredger for two years before enrolling at the Choctaw County Agricultural School. He went on to enroll at the University of Mississippi to study law. But a young history professor, Charles Sackett Sydnor, persuaded him to become a historian.

The conversion was easy. Clark's mother loved history, and he had grown up listening to the stories of former slaves, ex-Confederate soldiers, and Choctaw and was constantly reminded of the South's terrible ordeal while recovering from the Civil War. He later mused that he had not become a historian of the war because of "just the gruesomeness of it and the tragedy of the whole thing." His Mississippi upbringing awakened an abiding love of "earthy" history, notably as found in southern frontier life and the emergence of the New South from the "long, slow, and sad struggle over the years." Likewise, he turned toward social history as a consequence of his college and summer jobs: tending a golf course with William Faulkner, cutting railroad ties, growing cotton, and shoring up and mapping new Mississippi River channels.

After graduating from the University of Mississippi in 1928, he earned a master's degree from the University of Kentucky in 1929, enticed there by a small scholarship, and a doctorate from Duke University in 1932. He taught at the University of Kentucky until 1968 and chairing the history department from 1942 to 1965. He also taught and lectured at many other universities, including Harvard, Duke, North Carolina, Indiana, and Oxford. He served as president of the Southern Historical Association and the Mississippi Valley Historical Association and helped found the Organization of American Historians. An avid collector of historical documents, he fathered the Kentucky State Archives, the University of Kentucky Archives, and the Kentucky History Center and Museum.

In addition to scores of articles, Clark authored, coauthored, or edited an astonishing fifty books between 1933 and 2002, among them *A History of Kentucky* (1937); *The Kentucky* (1942); *Pills, Petticoats, and Plows: The Southern Country Store* (1944); *The Southern Country Editor* (1948); *Frontier America: The Story of the Westward Movement* (1959); *Travels in the South*, 6 vols. (1948–69); *Kentucky: Land of Contrast* (1968); and *Indiana University: Midwestern Pioneer*, 4 vols. (1970–77).

Clark married Martha Elizabeth Turner in 1933; they had a son and daughter. After her death in 1995, he married Loretta Gilliam Brock in 1998. He died on 28 June 2005.

David S. Newhall
Centre College

Roger Adelson, *Historian* (Spring 1992); John E. Kleber, ed., *Thomas D. Clark of Kentucky: An Uncommon Life in the Commonwealth* (2003); Frank Steely and H. Lew Wallace, *Filson Club History Quarterly* (1986); H. Lew Wallace, *The Kentucky Encyclopedia* (1992).

Clarke County

Traversed from north to south by the Chickasawhay River, Clarke County borders Alabama in southeastern Mississippi's Piney Woods region. The county was established in December 1833 from lands ceded to the United States by the Choctaw Nation under the 1830 Treaty of Dancing Rabbit Creek. It is named for Joshua G. Clarke, Mississippi's first state chancellor. Clarke's county seat is Quitman, and its largest towns include Pachuta, Shubuta, and Stonewall.

At the time of its first census in 1840, the county had about twice as many whites (2,077) as slaves (909). However, Clarke's reliance on slave labor subsequently intensified, and by 1860 the county had 5,695 whites and 5,076 slaves. Like most Piney Woods counties during this era, Clarke County comprised primarily small farms and ranked fairly low in the state in agricultural production. Clarke County remained distinctive in that it was the only county in the Mississippi to concentrate on tobacco cultivation. The eighty thousand pounds of tobacco grown on Clarke's farms in 1860 outstripped the entirety of the rest of the state. On the eve of the Civil War, Clark County had only six churches—three Baptist, two Methodist, and one Presbyterian—a surprisingly low ratio of churches to citizens.

Clarke County's 1880 population of 15,021 remained almost evenly split between whites and African Americans. Although the county's producers continued to concentrate on agriculture, its twenty manufacturing firms employed more workers (158) than most Mississippi counties of the era.

By 1900 two-thirds of Clarke's white farmers owned their land, compared to one-third of the county's black farmers (considerably higher than the state average of 14 percent). With the rise of textile mills in Stonewall at the end of the nineteenth century, Clarke's industrial workforce expanded to 575 (including 198 women and 120 children) in 1900. Mississippi's first (unsuccessful) attempt to drill an oil well took place near Enterprise in 1903.

As in much of Mississippi, Baptists made up about half of the county's churchgoers in the early twentieth century. The 1916 religious census showed that the National Baptist Convention and the Southern Baptist Convention had the highest memberships in the county, followed by the Methodist Episcopal Church, South; the African Methodist Episcopal Church; the Presbyterians; and the Disciples of Christ.

In 1930 Clarke County's 1,793 industrial workers ranked fifth in the state. The county's largest business, Stonewall Cotton Mill in Enterprise, employed more than 500 people. During the Great Depression, the Congress of Industrial Organizations made significant efforts to recruit Stonewall's workers.

Clarke was home to nearly 20,000 people in 1930, but the county's population declined over the next several decades, reaching 16,493 in 1960. Its racial demographics remained stable, with whites maintaining a slight majority (60 percent) over African Americans. Clarke's economic activity largely revolved around textiles and timber, and the county possessed the sixth-largest timber acreage in the state. With sixteen oil wells, petroleum also figured prominently in the county's economy.

Clarke County has left its distinctive mark on popular culture. Shubuta's Osceola McCarty attracted national attention in the 1990s for her major donation to the University of Southern Mississippi. In 2004 Women's Studies scholar Gayle Graham Yates published *Life and Death in a Small Town: Memories of Shubuta, Mississippi*, a personal memoir and history of Yates's hometown. In addition, Al Young, a distinguished novelist and 2005–8 poet laureate of California, set a poem, "Pachuta, Mississippi/A Memoir," in Clarke County.

Like many of Mississippi's eastern counties, Clarke County's 2010 population of 16,732 was predominantly (two-thirds) white. While Clarke's population had not changed significantly in size over the previous half century, the county boasted a small but growing Latino population.

Mississippi Encyclopedia Staff
University of Mississippi

Mississippi State Planning Commission, *Progress Report on State Planning in Mississippi* (1938); *Mississippi Statistical Abstract*, Mississippi State University (1952–2010); Charles Sydnor and Claude Bennett, *Mississippi History* (1939); University of Virginia Library, Historical Census Browser website, http://mapserver.lib.virginia.edu; E. Nolan Waller and Dani A. Smith, *Growth Profiles of Mississippi's Counties, 1960–1980* (1985).

Clay, Maude Schuyler
(b. 1953) Photographer

Maude Schuyler Clay is a photographer who has published three books and had multiple exhibits of images of the Mississippi Delta. Born in Greenwood, she attended the University of Mississippi and the Memphis College of Art. She has lived in Sumner with her family since the 1980s.

Clay's father was Adyn Eugene Schuyler, a lawyer who had studied in Illinois. Working in Memphis, he met Minnie Maude May, a Mississippi Delta native and a New York model, at the Memphis Cotton Carnival. Maude Schuyler, one of three children, grew up in a large Delta home and attended the University of Mississippi, the Instituto Allende in Mexico, and the Memphis Academy of Art. Her cousin William Eggleston, often called the father of modern color photography, helped inspire Maude's interest in photography and other visual arts and offered plenty of examples of personal eccentricity. She apprenticed with her cousin, "doing laboratory work and accompanying him on his roving photo shoots." Eggleston also "schooled me in the history of photography and introduced me to many of its leading contemporary participants."

Clay moved to New York in her twenties, working as a photographer and photo editor for *Vanity Fair*, *Esquire*, and other major magazines. In 1987 she and her husband, Langdon Clay, moved their growing family back into the Schuyler family home in Sumner in Tallahatchie County, in part to help her mother when her health declined and in part because she felt she belonged there. Clay worked in color photography until the 1990s, when a doctor new to Sumner asked her to photograph the area in black and white. In the late 1990s and early 2000s, she also served as the photography editor for *Oxford American*.

Clay has published three books of photography. *Delta Land*, released in 1999 by the University Press of Mississippi, consists

Maude Schuyler Clay (Courtesy Langdon Clay)

Quarterly (Winter 205); Mary Warner, Bitter Southerner website, www .bittersoutherner.com (28 January 2014).

of black and white photographs of Delta scenes and features an introduction by author Lewis Nordan. Clay described the work as "a photographic project which involves the recording and preservation of the Mississippi landscape and its rapidly disappearing indigenous structures: mule barns, field churches, cotton gins, commissaries, crossroads stores, tenant houses, cypress sheds, and railroad stations." Her second work, *Delta Dogs* (2014), documents the lives of dogs as important figures in the Delta landscape.

For an exhibit in Oxford, she described her goal and part of her process as a photographer: "I prefer to take photographs in the natural low light of early morning or late afternoon, 'in the gloaming,' as the Scots called it—the last rays of eerie, orangey light that blanket the evening before the sun disappears for the night. I use stark black and white for my landscape photographs. In that work, it is my intention to record the Mississippi Delta."

In her afterword to *Delta Land*, Clay places her work within both Mississippi's history of exploitation (slavery, agricultural labor, segregation, and the murder of Emmett Till) and Mississippi's photographic history (New Deal–era documentarians, civil rights photographers, and Eggleston). She has won the photography prize from the Mississippi Institute of Arts and Letters in 1988, 1992, 2000, 2015, and 2016, and her work has appeared in many galleries.

Her book *Mississippi History*, composed of color portraits with a foreword by Richard Ford, was published in 2015.

Ted Ownby
University of Mississippi

Michael Donahue, Go Memphis website, www.gomemphis.com (5 August 2008); Carol Ann Fitzgerald, *Oxford American* website, www.oxford american.org (11 November 2010); Southside Art Gallery, Oxford, Miss., website, www.southsideartgallery.com; James G. Thomas, Jr., *Southern*

Clay County

One of the counties organized during Reconstruction, Clay County in northeastern Mississippi was formed from parts of Chickasaw, Lowndes, Monroe, and Oktibbeha Counties. Originally named Colfax County for Schuyler Colfax, a Republican who served as vice president under Ulysses S. Grant, the county was established in May 1871. Following the end of Reconstruction and the return of Democratic ascendancy, the county was renamed after Henry Clay, secretary of state under John Quincy Adams. West Point, the county seat, was formerly a nexus of the Illinois Central, Mobile and Ohio, and Southern railways. The Tombigbee River shapes a long stretch of Clay's eastern border.

At its first census in 1880, Clay was home to 17,367 residents, with African Americans comprising 70 percent of the population. Tenants and sharecroppers did most of the farming during this era, as owners operated only 43 percent of the county's farms. Clay's early agricultural economy was mixed, with farmers concentrating on grain, cotton, and livestock. Clay's manufacturing sector remained nascent: twenty-four small companies employed only fifty-nine male workers. The county had a small foreign-born population, most of them Irish.

The average farm size in Clay County declined from 132 acres in 1880 to 70 acres in 1900. This development, a typical consequence of the increase in tenancy and sharecropping, had a far more pronounced impact on African American farmers. At the turn of the century, 62 percent of Clay County's white farmers worked their own land, while only 11 percent of African American farmers did so.

Though Clay remained largely agricultural, by 1900 the town of West Point had grown to 4,400 people. Clay County's 70 industrial establishments employed 228 workers, almost all of them men. The county's foreign-born contingent had grown to 90 people and included Russians and Germans.

In 1916 West Point's Payne Field, a training area for American troops during World War I, opened as Mississippi's first airport. The county seat also served as an educational center for women in eastern Mississippi: in 1894 the Southern Women's College moved to West Point from Oxford. A year later, the town became the site of Mary Holmes College, a Presbyterian school for African American women.

Clay County's population remained steady in the early twentieth century. In 1930 African Americans made more than two-thirds of Clay's population of 17,931. The county's agricultural production was evenly divided among cotton, corn, and grain, and tenant farmers outnumbered landowners by about two to one. Fifteen manufacturing firms employed 185 people. Among these firms was Bryan Foods, a meat products manufacturer founded in Clay County in 1936 that remains in operation, billing itself as the Flavor of the South.

Blues musician Howlin' Wolf (Chester Burnett) was born in the Clay County community of White Station in 1910. Lenore Prather, the first woman to serve as the chief justice of the Mississippi Supreme Court, was born in West Point in 1931 and began her judicial career there in 1965. Clay County hosted the state's first national golf championship in 1999 when the US Women's Open was held at West Point's Old Waverly Golf Club.

By 1960 Clay County was home to 18,933 people, 51.3 percent of them African Americans. Less than one-third of Clay's workforce was employed in agriculture, which focused largely on the production of soybeans. Agriculture continued to decline, and by 1980 only 150 workers were employed in this economic sector. The majority of nonagricultural laborers worked in food production and fabricated metal; the county's female workers were mostly employed in textiles or domestic labor.

The county's 2010 population, 20,634, remained largely unchanged over the previous half century. However, the percentage of African Americans had risen to nearly 60 percent.

Mississippi Encyclopedia Staff
University of Mississippi

Clay County, Mississippi, Genealogy and History Network website, http://clay.msghn.org; Mississippi State Planning Commission, *Progress Report on State Planning in Mississippi* (1938); *Mississippi Statistical Abstract*, Mississippi State University (1952–2010); Charles Sydnor and Claude Bennett, *Mississippi History* (1939); University of Virginia Library, Historical Census Browser website, http://mapserver.lib.virginia.edu; E. Nolan Waller and Dani A. Smith, *Growth Profiles of Mississippi's Counties, 1960–1980* (1985).

Clayton, Alexander

(1801–1889) Judge

A powerful figure in Mississippi law and politics from the 1840s through the 1860s, Alexander Mosby Clayton was a judge on the state's highest court and on the Confederate District Court. Born in Campbell County, Virginia, on 15 January 1801, Clayton was the first child of William Willis Clayton and Clarissa Mosby Clayton. After receiving some education in local schools, he spent two years at a classical school. Clayton studied under a lawyer in Lynchburg in 1822 and was admitted to the bar the following year. He practiced first in Louisa County, Virginia.

Clayton married Mary Walker Thomas in 1826. He had little professional success, so the family moved to Clarksville, Tennessee, in 1829. His practice thrived, but when his wife died on 20 July 1832, leaving an infant daughter, Mary, and perhaps a son, he moved further west. On 11 December 1832 Pres. Andrew Jackson nominated Clayton to be one of the three federal judges in the Arkansas Territory. He served until 1834, when he contracted cholera.

In 1837 Clayton moved to Mississippi, his home for the remainder of his life. He established a plantation near Lamar in Marshall County and in 1839 married Barbara A. Barker of Clarksville. They had two children, Arthur and Clara.

Clayton was elected to the state's High Court of Errors and Appeals in 1842. His opinions were thorough and largely free from political passions. All three judges on his court were delegates to the Nashville Convention in June 1850. In his 1851 reelection campaign, he was allied with Jefferson Davis's candidacy for governor. Both men were defeated.

From 1844 to 1852 Clayton served as the first president of the Board of Trustees of the University of Mississippi. He also served on the board from 1857 to 1870 and 1878 to 1889.

On 24 May 1853 Pres. Franklin Pierce gave Clayton a recess appointment as consul for the port of Havana, Cuba. Clayton arrived in Havana in July, during a yellow fever epidemic, but soon left for Washington and offered to resign. Instead, he agreed to return in a healthier season. Arriving again in Havana on 28 November, Clayton quickly dealt with a key part of his mission, determining that England and France had not entered into a secret treaty to guarantee Spain's possession of Cuba if it would free all the slaves there. Having accomplished that task and facing continued health risks, Clayton resigned and sailed for home before the year ended.

Clayton then practiced law in Holly Springs and in nearby Memphis. He served as a delegate to the 1860 Democratic National Convention in Charleston, South Carolina. He was elected to the January 1861 Mississippi secession convention, where he wrote the declaration of reasons for withdrawing from the Union. He also served as a delegate to the Montgomery convention that established the Confederacy. Clayton signed the Provisional Constitution on 11 March and became chair of the Judiciary Committee of the Provisional Congress.

On 9 May 1861 President Davis nominated Clayton to the Confederate District Court for Mississippi, and he was confirmed and served for the remainder of the Confederacy's existence. It was often impossible to hold court because of Union occupation. Despite the military's concerns, Clayton ruled that when the Confederacy lost control of an area, trading with the enemy was no longer a crime.

Around 1 April 1866 Gov. Benjamin Humphries appointed Clayton the circuit judge for the counties near his home. The Fourteenth Amendment, adopted on 4 July 1868, barred from office all prewar public officials who had supported the Confederacy. The US Army removed Clayton from his position as judge on 2 March 1869, and for the remainder of his life, he practiced law, managed his plantation, and served as a director of the Mississippi Central Railroad.

Leslie Southwick
US Court of Appeals for the
Fifth Circuit

Alexander M. Clayton, *Journal of Southern History* (August 1940); *Hispanic American Historical Review* (August 1929); Holly Springs Bar, *A Tribute to the Memory of Hon. Alexander M. Clayton* (1889); John Livingston, *Biographical Sketches of Distinguished American Lawyers* (1852); James D. Lynch, *Bench and Bar of Mississippi* (1881); Michael P. Mills, *Mississippi Law Journal* (Fall 2001); John Ray Skates Jr., *History of the Mississippi Supreme Court, 1817–1948* (1973).

Climate

Mississippi's climate is controlled by the North American land mass to the north, the state's subtropical latitude, and the Gulf of Mexico to the south. These controls produce the humid subtropical climate type, typified by mostly mild winters without extended periods of below-freezing temperatures; long, hot summers; and no routine wet or dry seasons.

Throughout much of the year prevailing southerly winds result in semitropical conditions. High humidity, combined with hot days and nights, generally produces discomfort during the warm season, with dew point temperatures routinely in the upper 70s. In the colder season the state's weather is dominated by the positions of the polar and subtropical jet streams, which control warm and cold fronts that alternately subject the state to warm tropical air and cold continental air. Cold spells seldom last more than three or four days, and the ground rarely freezes. Continental polar and Arctic air masses occasionally cause extreme cold spells, including a record low temperature of −19° F. Conversely, warm fronts regularly raise temperatures into the 80s during January and February.

Daily maximum and minimum temperatures in January average about 50° F and 30° F in the north and about 61° F and 43° F along the coast. July daily average highs are about 93° F and 90° F in the north and on the coast, respectively. July daily minimum temperatures average about 70° F

Ruins of the Meridian business district after a tornado struck, 1906 (Ann Rayburn Paper Americana Collection, Department of Archives and Special Collections, J. D. Williams Library, University of Mississippi [rayburn_ann_25_43_001])

(north) and 75° F (south). Temperatures of 90° F or higher occur an average of just fifty-five days per year on the coast, where the Gulf waters have a cooling effect. However, the number of days 90° F or higher rapidly increases inland, topping one hundred about fifty miles from the water. Temperatures of 32° F or lower occur on average about thirteen days a year on the immediate Gulf Coast and about seventy-three days per year on the Tennessee border.

Temperatures exceed 100° F each summer, with a record high for the state of 115° F. Temperatures below zero occur an average of once every five years, though below-freezing temperatures occur every winter throughout the state. Last freeze dates are quite variable, averaging from 3 April in the north to 20 February along the coast.

Mean annual precipitation ranges from about fifty inches along the northern border to about sixty-five inches along the coast and averages about fifty-six inches statewide. Irrigation is becoming increasingly common because rainfall, though abundant, does not always come when it is most needed. Mississippi commonly experiences general agricultural droughts, especially during the summer season. Stream flow and precipitation records indicate at least nine significant periods of extended drought since 1930.

Snow and other forms of winter precipitation are not as rare in Mississippi as is generally believed. Measurable snow or sleet falls on some part of the state in about 95 percent of all years. Many individual snow events of as much as twelve inches have been recorded in the northern part of the state. Ice storms occur about once every four years in the northern half of the state and about once every thirteen years in the southeastern part of the state.

Thunderstorms occur on an average of fifty to sixty days a year in the northern section of the state and seventy to eighty days a year near the coast. Tropical storms and hurricanes pose a hazard to life and property and generally come from the south. These systems weaken quickly when they pass over land, so damage in Mississippi is confined mainly to the coastal areas, while losses further inland generally result from rain damage to crops and from floods.

Mississippi also commonly experiences tornadoes. The state ranks twelfth nationally in number of reported tornadoes and eighth in number of tornadoes per ten thousand square miles. Unfortunately, the state ranks first nationally in tornado deaths per one million population. About two-thirds of the state's tornadoes occur between February and May, but they can come throughout the year.

C. L. Wax
Mississippi State University

John L. Baldwin, *Climates of the United States* (1973); James R. Fleming, *Meteorology in America, 1800–1870* (1990); Cary J. Mock, in *Hurricanes and Typhoons: Past, Present, and Future*, ed. Richard J. Murnane and Kam-biu Liu (2004); Edgar T. Thompson, *Agricultural History* (January 1941).

Jerry Clower—Live in Picayune (1975) (Courtesy James G. Thomas, Jr.)

Clower, Jerry
(1926–1998) Humorist

"If I'm lying, I'm dying" was a typical refrain Howard Gerald "Jerry" Clower used to punctuate his comedy routines inspired by growing up in the rural South. He was born on 28 September 1926 in Liberty and liked to say he "backed into show business" as a popular humorist. He was already in his early forties when MCA Records signed him. He made nearly thirty albums, spun tales as a member of the *Grand Ole Opry*, and was a frequent guest on the television variety series *Hee Haw*.

Some of the first audiences who enjoyed his homespun humor were aboard the USS *Bennington C-20*. Clower joined the US Navy when he was seventeen and served on the aircraft carrier during World War II, earning three battle stars and a presidential citation for bravery. After the war Clower attended Southwestern Mississippi Community College and Mississippi State University, where he played football. In 1947, he married Homerline Wells, his high school sweetheart, whom he said "flung a craving" on him. They went on to have four children. Clower graduated from Mississippi State in 1951 with a degree in agriculture and moved to Oxford, where he worked as an assistant county agent. Two years later he accepted a job as a fertilizer salesman for Mississippi Chemical Corporation in Yazoo City. His sales increased when he entertained farmers with stories about "coon hunting, rat killin'," and his colorful neighbors, leading to his new career. His first album, *Jerry Clower from Yazoo*

City, Mississippi Talkin' (1971) was a recording of one of his talks. It became one of his two gold records, selling more than half a million copies in just one month.

Clower was proud to be a Southern Baptist and served as a deacon at East Fork Baptist Church. His faith informed how he saw the world and, as he wrote in his autobiography, "pricked his conscience" about race relations. By 1970 he was publicly denouncing hypocrites and often asked how they could "let God run every fiber of their being except how they treat blacks." His public statements about his convictions led to verbal abuse of his children and to threats to burn down his house.

Rednecks and good old boys were staples of his comedic routines. Like other gifted southern storytellers, he drew out vowels ("JAY-reee Clower") to add color and rhythm to his stories. "You know a man is a Redneck if the front porch falls and [pause] always kills about four dogs," he'd say. He was a major influence on comedians Jeff Foxworthy and Bill Engvall. Clower's albums made eight appearances on the Billboard country list between 1971 and 1981, including *Clower Power*, which reached No. 7 in 1973. The posthumously released double-CD *Classic Clower Power* hit No. 4 among Billboard's top comedy albums for the week ending 3 June 2006.

Clower was a tenacious man with a strong will to succeed. He called this quality his "bulldog, hang-on feverishness." Known for his flashy suits and vivacious personality, he delighted audiences at military bases, association meetings, and state fairs, performing until just prior to his death in Jackson on 24 August 1998 as a result of complications from heart bypass surgery. In 1991 he said, "Ain't no feeling like that of walking away from where you've performed knowing you've pleased the audience, you've pleased the man that hired you, and you've pleased the critic." Part of Highway 49 in Yazoo City was renamed Jerry Clower Boulevard, and the city holds an annual Jerry Clower Festival.

Sally Graham
Hot Springs, Arkansas

Simon J. Bronner, in *Encyclopedia of Southern Culture*, ed. Charles Reagan Wilson and William Ferris (1989); Chet Flippo, *Billboard* (5 September 1998); Wade Jessen, *Billboard* (3 June 2006); Mississippi Writers Page website, www.olemiss.edu/mwp/.

Club Ebony

Marked by a Delta Blues Trail Marker, Club Ebony sits under the giant oak trees at 404 Hanna Street in Indianola. The building is a pale green wooden structure with a front porch that sits low on the quiet street. The club has changed little through the years. It is a place of entertainment and of memories.

In the early and mid-1900s juke joints fulfilled the need for community and fellowship. After working all week in the fields or at other jobs, people came from miles around to enjoy the social scene and to listen to the music of the Delta. Indianola's residents were divided by railroad tracks in the 1940s, but the music often reached across racial and class boundaries. In 1943 Johnny Jones opened a club to allow people to relax and work off pent-up energy. First known as the Jones Night Spot, the simple structure later became one of the oldest and most famous juke joints in the Delta, Club Ebony, a living room home away from home for many locals and musicians.

The original club had recessed lighting that gave an orange glow to the dance floor and bar, an idea Jones took from a club in France. According to local legend, the name changed from Jones Night Spot to Club Ebony around 1950 when Ruby Edwards, former mother-in-law of B. B. King, rented the club from Jones. After Jones died, Edwards purchased the building and ran the club until 1974, when Mary and Willie Shepard purchased Club Ebony. The Shepards divorced, and for the next thirty years Mary Shepard ran the club alone. She struggled to keep Club Ebony afloat and endured the hardships that came along with the business. In April 2009 King purchased Club Ebony.

Numerous local musicians and nationally and internationally known musical greats have played at Club Ebony, among them King, Bobby Rush, David Lee Durham, Howlin' Wolf, Ray Charles, Little Milton, Little Richard, Ruth Brown, Ike and Tina Turner, Jerry Butler, Lou Rawls, Jackie Wilson, Willie Clayton, Bobby Bland, Albert King, Tyrone Davis, Clarence Carter, Ted Taylor, Candy Staton, Rogers featuring Zap, the Staple Singers, McKinley Brown, Bennie Latimore, Marvin Sease, Nathaniel Kimble, Betty Swann, Ruth Davis, Brown Sugar, Jessie Robertson, O. V. Wright, John Lee Hooker, and Rufus Brown.

The rich, soulful music heard in Club Ebony continues to serve an important role in the community and the world. Along with the B. B. King Museum, Club Ebony helps mark Indianola as an important site in blues history.

Jennie Gunn, Carroll Gunn
Huebner, and John Gunn
Oxford, Mississippi

Jennie Gunn, Carroll Gunn, and John Gunn, *The Life of Mary Shepard: Queen of the Legendary Club Ebony* (2007).

Coahoma County

Coahoma County is located in the northern Delta, with the Mississippi River shaping much of the county's winding western border. Founded on 9 February 1836 from land ceded to the United States by the Choctaw Nation in 1830, the county derives its name from a Choctaw term meaning "red panther." Clarksdale, the county seat and Coahoma's largest city, is named for John Clark, a Coahoma resident and brother-in-law of Mississippi governor and senator James Alcorn.

Coahoma County remained a sparsely settled frontier until late in the antebellum period, with only 766 whites and 524 slaves in the 1840 census, numbers that grew to 1,521 and 5,083, respectively, in 1860. With slaves comprising 77 percent of Coahoma's population, the county had one of Mississippi's highest slave majorities on the eve of the Civil War. In addition, only about a quarter of the county's farmland was improved, half the statewide cultivation rate. The county ranked thirty-second among Mississippi jurisdictions in the production of cotton, forty-third in livestock, and forty-sixth in corn. Coahoma had no one employed in commerce or manufacturing. With the fourteenth-highest farm property value, however, the county had great agricultural potential.

In 1880 African Americans comprised 82 percent of the county's population of 13,568. Unlike many Delta counties, Coahoma had a substantial landowning population. The county's farmers owned more than half of Coahoma's farms, while sharecroppers accounted for less than 20 percent of the agricultural workforce. The average farm in Coahoma was 357 acres, among the largest in the state. The county

Coahoma County Courthouse, Clarksdale (Ann Rayburn Paper Americana Collection, Department of Archives and Special Collections, J. D. Williams Library, University of Mississippi [rayburn_ann_23_108_001])

remained predominantly agricultural, with only three manufacturing firms employing fifty-six men and four children.

By the turn of the century, the county showed evidence of dramatic regional transitions. Large numbers of African Americans moved to the Delta in search of land and employment, nearly doubling Coahoma's population over the last two decades of the nineteenth century and ranking the county fourth in Mississippi in population density. By 1900 the county had more than twenty-six thousand residents, the overwhelming majority of them African American. The average farm in Coahoma County had shrunk to just forty-eight acres, a startling decline in just a generation. This decline was typical of the region, where plantations were being partitioned into small farms for tenants and sharecroppers. Coahoma County had more than twenty-six hundred sharecropping households, the second-highest figure in the state, while the number of landowners had dropped: only 235 of the 3,797 African American farming households (6 percent) could claim ownership. By contrast, almost half of the county's 258 white farmers owned their land. The development of the timber industry also produced a sudden increase in industrial employment. In 1900 Coahoma's 78 manufacturing firms employed 475 workers, all of them men. Finally, the county's developing economy attracted a significant immigrant contingent. In the opening decade of the twentieth century,

Coahoma had a significant number of residents from Russia, China, Germany, Italy, Palestine, Syria, and Poland, the great majority of them male.

Though only thirteen churches, most of them Methodist, had served the county's people in 1860, by 1916 Coahoma's religious infrastructure reflected the choices of the county's black majority. More than sixteen thousand of Coahoma's twenty-one thousand congregants attended Missionary Baptist churches, and another twenty-two hundred were members of the African Methodist Episcopal Church. The Methodist Episcopal Church, South and the African Methodist Episcopal Zion Church had significant memberships. In addition, the county was home to more Catholics (314) than Southern Baptists (286).

Early twentieth-century Coahoma County was the second home of playwright Tennessee Williams, who based many of his works on scenes in and around Clarksdale. Feminist editor Minnie Brewer also grew up in Clarksdale, and scientist Elizabeth Lee Hazen was born in Rich and grew up in Lula. Charlie Conerly, a football star for the University of Mississippi and the New York Giants, was born in Clarksdale in 1921.

In 1930 Coahoma had a population of 46,237, the fifth-highest in Mississippi. As the Great Depression set in, an exceptionally large percentage of the county's land was cultivated. The county continued to suffer from low rates of landownership, as 94 percent of all farmers were tenants or sharecroppers. Like many Delta counties, Coahoma experienced a substantial influx of Mexican farm laborers during the 1920s and 1930s. Although the county continued to support a substantial industrial workforce, with 462 industrial workers, this sector had not grown over the previous three decades.

Coahoma County occupies a crucial place in the history of the blues, and Clarksdale is the site of the Delta Blues Museum as well as the annual Sunflower River Blues and Gospel Festival and the Juke Joint Festival. Muddy Waters (McKinley Morganfield) grew up in Coahoma County. Son House was born in Riverton, near Clarksdale, and John Lee Hooker was born in Vance. Willie Brown, Sam Cooke, Ike Turner, and Big Jack Johnson are just a few of the other important musicians associated with Coahoma County. Many more spent time in Clarksdale, often at the Riverside Hotel, as part of their travels, and the hotel is where Bessie Smith died. Charley Patton, Son House, Louise Johnson, and Bertha Lee Pate lived in Lula for a time. When folklorists Alan Lomax and John Work began documenting the Delta blues in the 1930s, Coahoma County was a principal locality for their study. Much-loved blues disc jockey Early Wright worked for years for Clarksdale's WROX. And according to a popular blues legend, Robert Johnson sold his soul to the devil in exchange for musical genius at the crossroads of Highway 61 and Highway 49.

Coahoma was central to other important movements in Mississippi. The county was home to the state's first African

American agricultural high school and for a time to Mississippi's only community college for African Americans. Oscar Johnston, a banker and planter who became the president of Delta Pine and Land Company and a leader in American agricultural policy in the 1930s, lived in Clarksdale. Clarksdale native Blanche Montgomery Ralston edited the *Mississippi Woman's Magazine* for the Mississippi Federation of Women's Clubs before working with Johnston and others to form the Delta Council in the 1930s.

Aaron Henry, a political organizer for the National Association for the Advancement of Colored People (NAACP) and a longtime civil rights activist, worked as a pharmacist in Clarksdale. Dr. T. R. M. Howard ran the Regional Council of Negro Leadership from Mound Bayou. Unita Blackwell, famous for her work farther south in Issaquena County, was born in Lula. Activist and author Vera Pigee worked for the NAACP in Coahoma from the 1950s through the 1970s. Author and *Ebony* editor Lerone Bennett, whose political activism manifested in such works as *Confrontation: Black and White*, *The Negro Mood*, and *Black Power USA*, grew up in Clarksdale.

Coahoma's population demographics changed little over the three decades following the Great Depression: in 1960 the county was home to 46,212 residents, 68 percent of them African American. The majority of Coahoma's workforce was employed in agriculture, focusing on cotton, wheat, oats, and soybean production. Although the number of agricultural workers had declined significantly by 1980, Coahoma still ranked fifth in the state in the number of people employed in farming. Coahoma's manufacturing sector was based largely on food processing and fabricated metal, with a significant number of laborers also involved in retail. More than a third of Coahoma's population had less than five years of schooling, and Coahoma County ranked second in the state in amount of public assistance payments received. The county also possessed Mississippi's third-largest Chinese American community.

Like many Delta counties in 2010, Coahoma County's population of 26,151 was predominantly African American (76 percent) and had declined during the second half of the twentieth century. Indeed, Coahoma County's population showed one of the greatest proportional decreases in the state during this period, shrinking by 43 percent since 1960. Though the number of total inhabitants shrank between 1960 and 2010, the county's proportion of African Americans increased, and its Latino population grew to about 300.

Mississippi Encyclopedia Staff
University of Mississippi

Coahoma County Mississippi Genealogy and History Network website, http://Coahoma.msghn.org; Mississippi State Planning Commission, *Progress Report on State Planning in Mississippi* (1938); *Mississippi Statistical Abstract*, Mississippi State University (1952–2010); Charles Sydnor and Claude Bennett, *Mississippi History* (1939); University of Virginia Library, Historical Census Browser website, http://mapserver.lib.virginia .edu; E. Nolan Waller and Dani A. Smith, *Growth Profiles of Mississippi's Counties, 1960–1980* (1985).

Coahoma County Folklore Study

Undertaken in 1941–42, this sociomusical survey of Coahoma County was the most ambitious undertaken on the subject of black folklore in Mississippi to that time. John Wesley Work III, an assistant professor of music at Fisk University, had wanted to study folk songs generated by the 23 April 1940 fire in a Natchez dance hall that killed more than two hundred patrons and most of the Royal Creolians Orchestra. Financially troubled, the historically black college could not subsidize Work's project, so in June 1940 Fisk applied for a General Education Board grant in Work's name. The application was ultimately denied, but it had cited the Library of Congress's support for the project. When the Library's Archive of American Folk Song assistant in charge, Alan Lomax, came to Fisk in May 1941, negotiations for a joint folklore project began.

The Fisk team included Charles S. Johnson, the chair of the social sciences department, and Lewis Jones, an assistant professor of social sciences. Johnson suggested conducting an in-depth, localized survey of all aspects of African American folklife in Coahoma: music, folktales, religious practices, foodways, and occupational lore. Johnson had authored such noted sociological studies as *Shadow of the Plantation*, *The Collapse of Cotton Tenancy*, and *Growing Up in the Black Belt: Negro Youth in the Rural South*. The Coahoma Study was designed to follow the model of Johnson's earlier work. Statistical surveys and questionnaires would be blended with interviews and sound and film recordings to create a complete portrait of Coahoma's black communities. The sound recordings, made by Lomax using the Library of Congress's disc recorder, are the best-known outcome of the study. The project made early recordings of the music of Muddy Waters and David "Honeyboy" Edwards, but investigators focused more on gathering sociological data than on making records. Lomax, Work, Jones, and John Ross of Fisk's drama department traveled to Clarksdale in late August 1941 for a week's preliminary fieldwork. Work and Lomax surveyed the musical landscape, while Jones and Ross explored town and plantation culture.

By the end of the first week of September, Work had returned to Nashville. Though his direct participation in the fieldwork was all but over, he did agree to transcribe and analyze the music. Scholars have made different suggestions regarding Work's absence from the field. Work was the only trained musician on the team and an African American who could give "the help of black scholars to overcome racial suspicion and to facilitate rapport with informants," as the Library of Congress guide to the Coahoma Study put it. Evidence nonetheless suggests that Lomax did not value Work's potential contributions to the gathering process, and the two men had a conflict of musical interest. Lomax was at heart a preservationist and had a history of recording older music forms, while Work was more interested in documenting the process whereby newer forms emerged to replace the old.

Jones stayed in the Delta through the cotton harvest, supervising graduate students Samuel C. Adams and Ulysses Young as they surveyed the county's rural and urban Negro communities. Their field reports were sent to Johnson in Nashville, where they were copied and sent to Lomax in Washington. In September 1941, before the fieldwork was completed, Lomax proposed a book, and in July 1942 he returned his attention to the Coahoma Study. Lomax and Jones spent a month in Mississippi; Work was there for a week.

The book as originally conceived was not completed. Copies of various parts of the manuscripts lay dormant in institutional and private files for the next sixty years. In 2005 the best copies of Jones's and Work's manuscripts, along with Adams's master's thesis, were published as *Lost Delta Found: Rediscovering the Fisk University–Library of Congress Coahoma County Study, 1941–1942* by Vanderbilt University Press. These manuscripts are rich in cultural details of life in the Mississippi Delta at a time of rapid change for its African American residents.

Bruce Nemerov
Murfreesboro, Tennessee

Alan Lomax, *The Land Where Blues Began* (2002); John Wesley Work, Lewis Wade Jones, and Samuel C. Adams Jr., *Lost Delta Found: Rediscovering the Fisk University–Library of Congress Coahoma County Study, 1941–1942*, ed. Robert Gordon and Bruce Nemerov (2005).

Cobb, Charles E., Jr.

(b. 1943) Activist and Educator

A field secretary for the Student Nonviolent Coordinating Committee (SNCC), Charlie Cobb was one of the committed student activists from outside Mississippi who came to the state to challenge the system of white supremacy. Charles E. Cobb Jr. was born in 1943, the son of a minister from Springfield, Massachusetts. As a high school student in Washington, D.C., Cobb began participating in demonstrations, and he continued his activities while a student at Howard University. He went to Mississippi in 1962 just as SNCC activists such as Lawrence Guyot and Robert Moses were planning new projects in the Delta.

In 1963, the twenty-year-old Cobb originated the idea of freedom schools as part of the 1964 Summer Project. He imagined that the schools could overcome the poor training African American students received in underfunded Mississippi public schools, teach new lessons about African American history and culture, and provide lessons in citizenship, including ways of organizing and protesting. He hoped the schools would be a way "to challenge the myths of our society, to perceive more clearly its realities, and to find alternatives, and ultimately, new directions for action." He stressed the need to make education relevant, with considerable emphasis on case studies in local communities. The schools turned out to be more popular than Cobb had imagined. Under the leadership of freedom school director Staughton Lynd, roughly forty-one schools taught approximately two thousand students in the summer of 1964.

Like many activists, Cobb experienced intimidation: he was arrested about a dozen times, and he and other activists faced gunfire in the Mississippi Delta. In 1965 Cobb worked as campaign manager when Julian Bond ran for the US House of Representatives from Georgia, and the following year Cobb helped draft SNCC's statement condemning the US war in Vietnam. He later worked as a writer, with interests in the civil rights movement and African American migration to Chicago, and has taught in Brown University's Department of Africana Studies. He has also researched the roots of his great-grandparents, one of whom helped found New Africa, a community near Clarksdale. Cobb and Moses have been involved with the Algebra Project, which teaches math skills to Mississippi children. The two men coauthored *Radical Equations: Math Literacy and Civil Rights* (2001). Cobb has also published *On the Road to Freedom: A Guided Tour of the Civil Rights Trail* (2007) and *This Nonviolent Stuff'll Get You Killed: How Guns Made the Civil Rights Movement Possible* (2014).

Ted Ownby
University of Mississippi

Charles Bolton, *The Hardest Deal of All: The Battle over School Integration in Mississippi, 1870–1980* (2005); Clayborne Carson, *In Struggle: SNCC and the Black Awakening of the 1960s* (1995); John Dittmer, *Local People: The Struggle for Civil Rights in Mississippi* (1994); Doug McAdam, *Freedom Summer* (1988); "Oral History with Mr. Charles Cobb" (1996), Mississippi Oral History Program, University of Southern Mississippi, http://digilib.usm.edu/cdm/compoundobject/collection/coh/id/15294; Charles M. Payne, *I've Got the Light of Freedom: The Organizing Tradition and the Mississippi Freedom Struggle* (2007).

Cobb, Cully

(1884–1975) Agricultural Administrator

A leading agricultural administrator and educator, Cully Cobb was born on a farm in Giles County, Tennessee, in 1884. Cobb moved to Mississippi in 1904 to attend Mississippi Agricultural and Mechanical College in Starkville (now Mississippi State University). After graduating, he began a career in agricultural education, becoming the first principal of the new agricultural high school in Chickasaw County in 1908. He gained more renown in Mississippi in 1910 as the first head of the state's Corn Clubs. With a base in Starkville, Cobb toured the state, teaching agricultural methods, especially to boys, by encouraging them to grow corn in innovative ways and to compete for prizes at county fairs. When the 1914 Smith-Lever Act provided funds to turn groups like the Corn Clubs into 4-H Clubs, Cobb helped expand their focus to include pigs, cattle, and tomatoes. Under his leadership, the state agricultural department published *Mississippi Club Boy* for its members, and Cobb became a popular speaker.

In 1919 Cobb moved to Atlanta to publish one of the South's leading agricultural magazines, *Southern Ruralist*. It printed how-to articles, discussed agricultural modernization, and called for government aid to agriculture through changes in tariff policy.

In 1933 Cobb moved to Washington, D.C., to serve as the first head of the cotton division of the New Deal's Agricultural Adjustment Administration. He administered programs that encouraged cotton farmers and planters to destroy the 1933 cotton crop and then limit production to raise prices. These programs included subsidies for farmers, and when agency leaders divided over whether local committees of southern cotton planters would fairly allocate subsidies between landowners and their workers, Cobb supported the local committees. He endured significant criticism for not siding more often or more aggressively with tenant farmers, many of whom lost their jobs and began migrating to cities in both the North and the South. Cobb argued that the Agricultural Adjustment Administration's goal was to stabilize the system of agriculture during a time of depression, not to reform it to make it more fair.

Cobb retired from the Department of Agriculture in 1937, moved back to Georgia, wrote and edited, and pursued a number of civic projects along with his wife, Lois Dowdle Cobb. The Cobbs returned to Starkville to endow the Cobb Institute of Archaeology at Mississippi State University in the early 1970s, and he died in 1975.

Ted Ownby
University of Mississippi

Pete Daniel, *Breaking the Land: The Transformation of Cotton, Tobacco, and Rice Cultures since 1880* (1985); Jack Temple Kirby, *Rural Worlds Lost: The American South, 1920–1960* (1987); Mississippi State University, Cobb Institute of Archaeology website, www.cobb.msstate.edu; Lawrence J. Nelson, *King Cotton's Advocate: Oscar G. Johnston and the New Deal* (1999); Roy V. Scott and J. G. Shoalmire, *The Public Career of Cully A. Cobb: A Study in Agricultural Leadership* (1973).

Cobb, Joseph Beckham

(1819–1858) Author and Politician

A planter, newspaper editor, and politician, Joseph Beckham Cobb published three books during his relatively short life, but he is today most remembered as the author of *Mississippi Scenes*, a collection of thirteen sketches in the style of southwestern humorists such as Johnson Jones Hooper, George Washington Harris, Thomas Bangs Thorpe, and especially Augustus Baldwin Longstreet, like Cobb a Georgia native who relocated to the Magnolia State.

Cobb was born near Lexington, Georgia, on 11 April 1819, the son of Thomas W. Cobb, a US congressman and later senator. Joseph was educated at the Willington Academy in South Carolina and the University of Georgia in Athens, where he studied law but did not complete the requirements for a degree. On 5 October 1837 he married Almira Clayton of Athens, and the following year they moved to Noxubee County.

Cobb flourished in Mississippi, first as a planter and then as a politician. He won election to the state legislature in 1841 but resigned two years later after refusing to attend a special session. In 1844 he moved to Columbus in Lowndes County and established Longwood Plantation, his home for the rest of his life.

From January 1845 to November 1846 he edited the *Columbus Whig*, advocating Unionist policies opposing the nullificationist and secessionist ideologies of Democrats. In the early 1850s he again turned to politics, first as a delegate to the Mississippi state convention to ratify the Compromise of 1850 and then as a delegate to an 1851 convention in Nashville to consider the Wilmot Proviso. In 1853 he lost a bid to serve in the US House of Representatives.

Cobb's first book, *The Creole; or, The Siege of New Orleans* (1850), is a historical novel set for the most part following Andrew Jackson's January 1815 victory against the British. The novel is a loosely organized romance whose hero, Henri La Sassuriere, was both a French marquis and one of Lafitte's pirates (or corsairs, as Cobb called them) who loses his lover first to another man and then to death.

The title of Cobb's second book, *Mississippi Scenes; or, Sketches of Southern and Western Life and Adventure, Humorous, Satirical, and Descriptive, Including the Legend of Black Creek* (1851), consciously mirrored Longstreet's *Georgia Scenes*, which had inaugurated the genre of southwestern humor when it was published in 1835. Cobb dedicated his collection to Longstreet, then serving as president of the University of Mississippi. Though many of Cobb's sketches were modeled on those by Longstreet, other influences included eighteenth-century British writers such as Joseph Addison, Richard Steele, Samuel Johnson, and American writer Washington Irving.

Like works by other southwestern humorists, *Mississippi Scenes* often offered insightful observations regarding the customs and mores of the people about whom the author was writing. Cobb's journalistic approach toward morally questionable characters and situations gave the book a much more modern sense of realism than is found in many similar works published in the antebellum South. Cobb's narrator was an urbane, reasonable gentleman who abhorred excesses and pretenses, and he objectively scrutinizes a number of common northeastern Mississippi predilections and predicaments. Country bumptiousness, credulousness, and religious enthusiasm were among the excesses noted in the six "Rambler" sketches, while the remaining seven focus on the absurdity of campaign rhetoric, a Virginia woman's steadfast patriotism during the American Revolution, and slavery. Two of the most noteworthy sketches in the book were superstitious tales patterned on those written by Irving.

Cobb's final book, *Leisure Labors; or, Miscellanies, Historical, Literary, and Political* (1858), was a collection of essays he had earlier contributed to the *American Whig Review*. Most were lengthy reviews of books, though he also conveyed a strong sense of his Whig political sympathies and his views on slavery and the slave trade. He did not oppose slavery itself, but he argued that the Constitution allowed Congress the power to limit the spread of slavery. The final essay in the book, "The True Issue between Parties in the South: Union or Disunion," staunchly rejected the growing southern movement toward secession: "I am a Southerner by birth and education—a Southerner in pride of land and in feeling—a Southerner in interest, and by every tie which can bind mortal man to his native clime; and I shall abide the destinies of the South. But I venerate the Federal Constitution. I love the Union."

These proved to be among Cobb's last published words, as he died in September 1858 at the age of thirty-nine from what cemetery records termed "dropsy of the stomach." He left to his wife and four children an estate of fifteen hundred acres and more than one hundred slaves.

John B. Padgett
Brevard College

George T. Buckley, *American Literature* (May 1938); Elmo Howell, *Mississippi Home-Places: Notes on Literature and History* (1988); Robert L. Phillips Jr., in *Lives of Mississippi Writers, 1817–1967*, ed. James B. Lloyd (1981).

Cochran, Thad
(b. 1937) Politician

The year 1978 marked the end of one era in Mississippi politics and the beginning of the next. After a thirty-seven-year tenure in the US Senate, Democrat James O. Eastland retired. His successor was Thad Cochran, who won the election for Eastland's seat with a plurality of the votes. Cochran became the first Mississippi Republican in one hundred years to be elected to a statewide office.

William Thad Cochran was born on 7 December 1937 in Pontotoc. His father, William Holmes Cochran, was a school principal, while his mother, Emma Grace Cochran, taught in Pontotoc, Tippah, and Hinds Counties. After attending public schools, Thad Cochran graduated from the University of Mississippi in 1959 with bachelor's degree in psychology. After two years in the US Navy, Cochran enrolled in the University of Mississippi Law School. He was admitted to the bar in 1965 and started practice in Jackson.

By that time, Cochran had already been involved in politics for more than a decade. In 1951 he had helped his mother deliver tabloids for the Paul B. Johnson Jr. campaign for governor. In 1967 he appeared on television for the first time to endorse Fred Thomas for Hinds County sheriff. A year later, Cochran became the executive director of Mississippi Citizens for Nixon-Agnew. Presidential candidate George Wallace won the Magnolia State in 1968, but the GOP was on the rise in the South. With the leftward turn

Thad Cochran (Courtesy Thad Cochran)

of the national Democratic Party, the strong conservative voting bloc in the region increasingly turned its allegiance to the Republicans.

In 1972 Cochran profited from this change in voting patterns. Democratic incumbent Charles Griffin of Mississippi's 4th Congressional District decided not to run for reelection, and Cochran narrowly defeated Democratic state senator Ellis Bodron for the seat. Republican Trent Lott was also elected to the House from Mississippi's Fifth District, marking what state GOP chair Clarke Reed described as "the birth of the two-party system in Mississippi."

Cochran remained in the House until 1978, when he won election to the US Senate. He has served on the Rules Committee, the Ethics Committee, and the Judiciary Committee, and he has chaired the Senate Republican Conference; the Agriculture, Nutrition, and Forestry Committee; and the powerful Appropriations Committee. As a senator, he reflected the South's changing political culture. "With his broad shoulders, silver hair, and deep, drawling voice, Thad Cochran seems a paragon of the old-fashioned Southern politician," *Time* reported in 1984. "He is not. . . . A boosterish supporter of Reaganomics, Cochran is less conservative on civil rights and funding for public education." By the standards of southern Republicanism, Cochran's voting record can be considered fairly moderate. He supported the extension of the Voting Rights Act and the creation of the Martin Luther King Jr. holiday. In 2006 Cochran backed a bill to provide for human embryonic stem cell research. Nonetheless, on most issues he has aligned himself with the conservative forces on Capitol Hill.

Although Cochran's political style differs significantly from that of his predecessor, both he and Eastland shunned the political limelight. But Cochran's unassuming appearance belies his effectiveness as a power broker. He has become an expert on farm policy and has arranged funding for numerous research and military projects in his home state. After Hurricane Katrina wrecked the Mississippi Gulf Coast in August 2005, Cochran played an important role in securing funds for the region's recovery. "He doesn't get a whole lot of play in terms of coverage," said one Republican colleague, "but he is effectively stubborn doing what needs to be done." In 2014 Cochran won reelection to a seventh term in the Senate after a tough primary fight against Tea Party favorite Chris McDaniel.

Maarten Zwiers
University of Groningen,
the Netherlands

Earl Black and Merle Black, *The Rise of Southern Republicans* (2005); Jere Nash and Andy Taggart, *Mississippi Politics: The Struggle for Power, 1976–2006* (2006); *Time* (29 October 1984, 14 April 2006).

Coe, Fred

(1914–1979) Producer and Director

Fred Coe was a stage, television, and film producer and director whose work is closely associated with the Golden Age of Television. Born on 23 December 1914 in the Delta town of Alligator, Frederick Hayden Hughs Coe was the only son of Thursa Annette Harrell, a nurse, and Frederick Hayden Hughs Coe, a railroad worker. Coe attended high school at Peabody Demonstration School in Nashville, Tennessee, before moving on to Peabody College for Teachers.

While in Nashville, Coe developed his directing and producing talents by creating the Hillsboro Players and working with the Nashville Community Playhouse. In 1938 Coe enrolled in the graduate program at the Yale School of Drama. He left academia in 1940 to manage and direct the Town Theatre in Columbia, South Carolina, turning this community theater into an experimental outpost for new works.

Coe began his television career in 1945 in New York City, quickly moving from floor manager to director to producer-director for *NBC Television Theater*. In 1948 he became the producer-director of NBC's *Philco Television Playhouse* (later the *Philco-Goodyear Television Playhouse*). This Peabody Award–winning dramatic anthology was known for its high-quality adaptations of plays, short stories, and novels as well as for its original plays written specifically for television. Among the new playwrights whose work Coe showcased were Paddy Chayefsky, Tad Mosel, Horton Foote, and Vincent Donehue. During his tenure as a television producer, Coe fought for the writer's freedom to create real human drama. He asked for extended character sketches that placed one or two people in engrossing, real-life situations. Coe explained his approach: he did not have money to pay big stars, so he would make stars out of the writers. Coe also knew that good scripts would attract good performers, and those attracted to Coe's work included Steve McQueen, Joanne Woodward, Eva Marie Saint, Grace Kelly, Jack Klugman, and Walter Matthau. Coe received the 1953 Sylvania Award for producing and directing the most popular anthology of the time, Paddy Chayefsky's *Marty*, starring Rod Steiger.

Between 1952 and 1955 Coe was the executive producer for *Mr. Peepers*, a live television series starring Wally Cox that was honored with the Peabody Award in 1953. In 1954 he took the helm of the *Producer's Showcase*, winning an Emmy as Best Producer of a Live Series. This ninety-minute anthology aired the Broadway production of *Peter Pan*, an adaptation of Robert Sherwood's *Petrified Forest*, and Thornton Wilder's *Our Town*, among other productions. Coe then left NBC for CBS, where he produced three seasons of *Playhouse 90*, including productions of *Days of Wine and Roses* (1958), *The Plot to Kill Stalin* (1958), and *For Whom the Bell Tolls* (1959).

In the late 1960s and 1970s Coe began to expand his influence, creating specials for all three major television networks. He produced the Emmy Awards on CBS in 1962 and directed *All the Way Home* (NBC, 1971), which won the Peabody Award. Coe also produced *Of Men and Women* (ABC, 1972) and produced and directed *The Adams Chronicles* (PBS, 1976), earning his fourth Peabody Award. In 1979 Coe won the highest television honor, the Emmy, for his production of NBC's *The Miracle Worker*.

Coe also produced versions of his television plays on Broadway, among them *Two for the Seesaw* (1958), *All the Way Home* (1960), and *A Thousand Clowns* (1962). His 1959 production of *The Miracle Worker* won a Tony Award, and he was responsible for award-winning productions of *Fiddler on the Roof* (1964) and *Wait until Dark* (1966).

Coe found success in the film world with productions of *The Left-Handed Gun* (1958), *The Miracle Worker* (1962), and *A Thousand Clowns* (1965). For 1966's *This Property Is Condemned*, Coe not only served as the producer but also shared screenplay credit with Francis Ford Coppola and Edith Sommer. Coe's success earned him the position of television adviser for John F. Kennedy's 1960 presidential campaign.

Coe was married twice and fathered four children. He died in Los Angeles on 29 April 1979, and in 1986 he was inducted into the Hall of Fame of the Academy of Television Arts and Sciences.

Rene E. Pulliam
University of Mississippi

William Hawes, *The American Television Drama: The Experimental Years* (1986); Gorham Kindem, ed., *The Live Television Generation of Hollywood Film Directors: Interviews with Seven Directors* (1974); Jon Krampner, *The Man in the Shadows: Fred Coe and the Golden Age of Television* (1997); Frank Sturcken, *Live Television: The Golden Age of 1946–1958 in New York* (1990); Ray Waddle, *Vanderbilt Magazine* (2006); Max Wilk, *The Golden Age of Television: Notes from the Survivors* (1977).

Cohn, David L.
(1894–1960) Author

A prolific nonfiction writer born in the Mississippi Delta, David L. Cohn was the son of a Polish-born Jewish immigrant who moved to Greenville in the 1880s to become a dry goods merchant. Cohn wrote three memoirs, the last of which, *The Mississippi Delta and the World*, was published long after his death. The changes between *God Shakes*

David Cohn (Bern and Franke Keating Collection, Department of Archives and Special Collections, J. D. Williams Library, University of Mississippi)

Creation (1935), *Where I Was Born and Raised* (1947), and *The Mississippi Delta and the World* show the ways Cohn became increasingly concerned with his place in the racial and class hierarchies of twentieth-century Mississippi. His best writing showed his attempts to understand his home region, of which he famously said, "The Mississippi Delta begins in the lobby of the Peabody Hotel in Memphis and ends on Catfish Row in Vicksburg."

God Shakes Creation is in part a memoir, with considerable discussion of Cohn's family and friends in the Greenville area; above all, however, it is a study of African American life in the Delta. He took the title from a sermon in which an African American preacher described the end of winter in the Mississippi Delta: "De seeds dey sleeps in de ground and de birds dey stops dey singing. Den God shakes creation in de spring." After describing the natural environment of the Delta and briefly discussing plantation-owning families, Cohn spends most of the book on African Americans' family and sex lives, the medical and folk practices he called "Delta Magic," crime, sharecropping, and religion. Part folkloric with long quotes, part descriptive, and part defensive, the book alternates between great respect for what he called African Americans' "joy of living" and a paternalistic sense that sharecroppers were better off in situations where they were secure and knew who was in charge. Cohn wrote of the Delta neither as a problem or a paradise, but he clearly loved the region's land, people, and complexities.

In 1948 Cohn added 150 pages to *God Shakes Creation* and titled his new book *Where I Was Born and Raised*. The title and new chapters placed Cohn more at the center of the book. He wrote as an insider, someone "born and raised" in Greenville, but he did not write as a member of a landowning elite. In addition, he wrote as an expatriate who no longer lived in the Delta. The main theme of the new chapters is that technological change and the migration of thousands of agricultural workers were creating a new Delta that Cohn found troubling. Thus, the more things changed, the more Cohn seemed to admire the way things used to be. In fact, *Where I Was Born and Raised* seems much more similar in tone than *God Shakes Creation* to the 1941 *Lanterns on the Levee* by Cohn's friend and fellow Greenville author William Alexander Percy.

In the 1940s and 1950s Cohn wrote several nonfiction books and countless magazine articles for popular audiences on an array of topics he found compelling: New Orleans architecture, the history of cotton, the effects of the Sears-Roebuck catalog, the automobile, the American military, and the Democratic Party. He also published *Love in America: An Informal Study of Manners and Morals in American Marriage* (1943). He wrote with considerable wit and a taste for social criticism. Despite his cosmopolitanism and wide travels, he never chose to condemn or work against racial segregation, usually describing it as a tragedy for the South to solve and critiquing the moral certainty of nonsouthern critics and reformers.

Cohn showed great interest in American internationalism. He urged the United States to take a more aggressive stance against world hunger, communism, and especially anti-Semitism. He was a friend and adviser to several Democratic leaders and wrote speeches for, among others, Sen. William Fulbright and Sen. Adlai Stevenson. Cohn died in Copenhagen in 1960.

Ted Ownby
University of Mississippi

James C. Cobb, *The Most Southern Place on Earth: The Mississippi Delta and the Roots of Regional Identity* (1992); David L. Cohn, *Love in America* (1943); David L. Cohn, *The Mississippi Delta and the World*, ed. James C. Cobb (1995); David L. Cohn, *This Is The Story* (1947); David L. Cohn Collection, Department of Archives and Special Collections, J. D. Williams Library, University of Mississippi.

Cohran, Kelan Philip

(b. 1927) Jazz Musician

Jazz musician and composer Kelan Philip Cohran has played and taught music, primarily in Chicago, since the 1950s. He is best known for his work as a member of Sun Ra's Arkestra and as one of the founding members of the Association for the Advancement of Creative Musicians in the mid-1960s.

Born in Oxford on 8 May 1927, Cohran moved with his family to St. Louis when he was about ten. He learned to play numerous instruments and early in his musical career played trumpet behind Sara Vaughn and Jay McShann, among others. Cohran was drafted in 1951 and studied at the Naval Conservatory of Music in Washington, D.C.

Cohran was influenced by the music of jazz composer and bandleader Sun Ra, for whom Cohran played from 1958 to 1961. He saw Sun Ra as a searcher inspired by the stars and a quest for knowledge. Self-described as a "sphereologist," Cohran has long been interested in math, astronomy, and music history as well as the relationships among them. Always an experimenter, Cohran invented a new stringed instrument, the frankiphone, which he named for his mother.

In May 1965 Cohran, Muhal Richard Abrams, Steve McCall, and Jodi Christian invited many of their jazz musician friends in Chicago to Cohran's home to form a group encouraging creative, original music. That group became the Association for the Advancement of Creative Musicians (AACM), a leading force in experimental jazz in the 1960s and 1970s. Cohran's Artistic Heritage Ensemble played the second concert organized through the new group. The AACM set professional practices, encouraged music at "a high artistic level," and embodied issues in the search for creativity among African Americans in the midst of the civil rights era. Almost all AACM participants were African American, many had roots in the American South, and many faced questions about whether they should play music rooted in history. Cohran left the new group in part out of dissatisfaction with AACM's concentration on originality: he also wanted to deal with musical heritage, including ancient music.

In 1967 Cohran established the Afro-Arts Theater in the Bronzeville section of Chicago. It became an important site for both music and African American political activism, with events by LeRoi Jones and Stokely Carmichael. Cohran formed the Zulu record label and in 1968 and 1969 recorded four albums, *On the Beach*, *Spanish Suite*, *Armageddon*, and *The Malcolm X Memorial*.

Cohran has spent much of his life teaching—at schools and colleges, in prisons, and in his own family. Cohran taught his eight sons to be musicians, and they have performed together, first as Philip Cohran and the Youth Ensemble and later as the Hypnotic Brass Ensemble.

Ted Ownby
University of Mississippi

Jason C. Bivins, *Spirits Rejoice! Jazz and American Religion* (2015); J. B. Figi, *Downbeat* (December 1984); George E. Lewis, *A Power Stronger Than Itself: The AACM and American Experimental Music* (2008); National Public Radio, "One Father, Eight Sons, Nine Shiny Brass Bells" (17 June 2012); Peter Shapiro, *The Wire* (May 2001).

Colbert, William (Chooshemataha)

(ca. 1742–1824)

Colbert, Levi (Itawamba Mingo)

(ca. 1759–1834)

Colbert, George (Tootemastubbe)

(ca. 1764–1839)
Chickasaw Leaders

George, Levi, and William Colbert served as prominent military, political, and economic leaders in the Chickasaw Nation prior to Removal. Their father, James Logan Colbert (ca. 1721–83), emigrated from Scotland and became a successful trader among the Chickasaw. Fluent in Chickasaw, he served as an interpreter at the Augusta (1763) and Mobile Indian conferences (1765 and 1771) and fought with the British and their southern Indian allies during the American Revolution. His first marriage to a Chickasaw woman resulted in a daughter and a son, William (Chooshemataha). His second Chickasaw wife gave birth to four sons, George (Tootemastubbe), Joseph, Levi (Itawamba Mingo), and Samuel. He and his third wife, a mixed-blood Chickasaw, had a son and daughter, James and Susan.

William and George Colbert began their military service during the Revolutionary War as members of their father's loyal British raiders. In 1791 William, George, and another Chickasaw chief, Piomingo, led Chickasaw forces under Gen. Arthur St. Clair against the Ohio Indians and gained the attention of Pres. George Washington. In honor of their service, Washington sent silver peace medals and military uniforms to the three Chickasaw chiefs in June 1792. George and Piomingo met with Washington in July 1794. William met with the president in August 1795 and asked for his assistance in the Chickasaw war against the Creek and for recognition as the Chickasaw war leader. Washington demurred on both requests but sought to assuage Colbert by giving him a commission as a major general for his service with St. Clair.

While George and Levi became principal speakers and chiefs, William Colbert continued to receive recognition as a political and military leader until his death on 30 May 1824. He garnered accolades for his exploits during the Creek War of 1813–14, especially at the Battle of the Holy Ground on 23 December 1813. In March 1814 William, George, Levi, and James led 230 Chickasaw into Florida, captured a number of hostile Creek, and returned with them to Fort Montgomery. William Colbert signed treaties at Chickasaw Bluffs (1801), at the Chickasaw Council House (1816), and at Chickasaw Old Town (1818). Throughout his postrevolutionary career, his first wife, Jessie Moniac, a mixed-blood Creek, was a constant companion and accompanied him on the war trail.

Described as "honest, brave & respected" and "full of animation & never dulled—possessed of wit & pleasantry," he was often impetuous, eager for a fight, and overindulgent in his consumption of alcohol. At his death in Chickasaw County, his family included his second wife, Ishtanaha, and five adult children.

George Colbert emerged as a leader among the Chickasaw through his martial exploits against the Creek and earned the rank of colonel. In October 1798 he traveled to Philadelphia with Wolf's Friend and others to meet with Pres. John Adams. One observer described George as "tall, slender and handsome with straight black hair," while another declared him "naturally the smartest man of the Colberts." Although he lacked formal education and "talked very common English," his shrewd negotiating skills and business acumen earned him leadership roles. At the Chickasaw Bluffs treaty conference in October 1801, Chinubbee, identified in the treaty as king of the Chickasaw, deferred to Colbert as the nation's chief speaker. When the Chickasaw agreed to open the Natchez Trace between Nashville and Natchez in 1801, he used his influence to route the new federal wagon road across the Tennessee River, where he and his brother, Levi, operated Colbert's Ferry until 1819. His ferry business, plantations near present-day Booneville and Tupelo, and stock raising made him wealthy, influencing his opposition to intruders and demands for land cessions.

George participated in several treaty conferences and signed the treaties at the Chickasaw Council House (1816) and at Old Town (1818). The 1816 treaty reserved a large tract of land north of the Tennessee River for "Col. George Colbert and heirs" and smaller tracts for "Major Levi Colbert" and others. The treaties provided cash payments of $150 or $100 to the Chickasaw signatories, but William, George, Levi, and James Colbert and Tishomingo also received $1,000 each. When the Chickasaw relinquished their remaining claims in Tennessee and Kentucky in 1818, the Colberts received additional cash payments and guarantees regarding their land reservations. George also signed the subsequent treaties at Franklin, Tennessee (1830), at Pontotoc Creek (1832), and in Washington, D.C. (1834), that shaped and finalized Chickasaw Removal.

George Colbert, his brothers, and their extended bicultural families became wealthy merchant-planters and slave owners with large livestock holdings and fields of cotton and corn. He married two daughters of Cherokee chief Doublehead: one died before 1818, though the second, Saleachy, moved with George to Indian Territory in 1837. He married his third wife, Tuskeahookto, in 1834. After Removal, George Colbert used his slaves to establish farming operations near Fort Towson, Indian Territory, where he died on 7 November 1839.

Levi Colbert served as principal speaker for the Chickasaw Nation during the turbulent years leading up to Removal. Thomas McKenney, commissioner of Indian affairs, described Levi as being "to the Chickasaws, what the Soul is to the body.

They move at his bidding." He placed his mark on the treaties of 1805, 1816, 1818, 1830, and 1832. In 1812 he lived and operated a stand at Buzzard Roost on the Natchez Trace, about nine miles southwest of Colbert's Ferry, and by 1817 he had moved to the west bank of the Tombigbee opposite Cotton Gin Port, where he built a gristmill and farmed and raised stock. Levi and George supported the development of schools, including Charity Hall (started by Rev. Robert Bell in 1820) and Monroe Mission (started by Rev. Thomas C. Stuart in 1822), and enrolled their children.

Although generally self-serving, the Colberts, especially Levi, promoted Chickasaw economic interests and resisted Removal. He rejected an 1826 request to exchange the Chickasaw homeland for lands in the West and refused a similar proposal during McKenney's visit in 1827, though Levi agreed to visit the West. He led an exploring party into present-day Oklahoma in 1828 and reported that the "vacant country" was not acceptable. After agreeing to the 31 August 1830 Treaty of Franklin, which provided for Removal based on finding acceptable lands in the West, Levi led a second western expedition in October 1830. His party explored eastern and southeastern Oklahoma and crossed the Red River into Mexican territory. Colbert informed Pres. Andrew Jackson that if the United States purchased the lands along the Sabine River, the Chickasaw would remove.

With their sovereignty and economy threatened by the extension of Mississippi law and the withholding of annuity payments, the Chickasaw agreed to Removal under the Treaty of Pontotoc Creek. Although illness prevented his active participation, Levi placed his mark on the 20 October 1832 treaty that provided for the Chickasaw lands to be surveyed and sold and the proceeds to be paid to the Chickasaw Nation. In October 1833 he led a third Chickasaw party to the West, holding a conference with Choctaw delegates at Fort Towson, where he offered to purchase lands for a new Chickasaw homeland. After failing to reach agreement with the Choctaw, federal officials agreed to consider amending the 1832 treaty. Unable to travel, Levi appointed his brother, George, as the principal negotiator for the Chickasaw delegation that signed the Treaty of Washington on 24 May 1834. It provided permanent reservations for the Colberts and other full-bloods and mixed-bloods and created a tribal commission to monitor and approve Chickasaw land sales. Levi Colbert died on 2 June 1834, before Chickasaw Removal began in 1837.

James P. Pate
University of Mississippi, Tupelo

James R. Atkinson, *Splendid Land, Splendid People: The Chickasaw Indians to Removal* (2004), *Journal of Mississippi History* (Spring 2004); Arrell M. Gibson, *The Chickasaws* (1971); Charles J. Kappler, ed., *Indian Affairs: Laws and Treaties* (1904–41); Don Martini, *Who Was Who among the Southern Indians: A Genealogical Notebook, 1698–1907* (1997).

Coleman, James Plemon
(1914–1991) Fifty-Second Governor, 1956–1960

Not since George Poindexter (1820–22) had Mississippi had a governor with a broader range of political experience than James Plemon Coleman. He was also one of the few twentieth-century governors elected in his first campaign for the office. At the time of his 1955 election, Coleman, who was born near Ackerman on his family farm in Choctaw County on 9 January 1914, had already served as an aide to a US congressman, a district attorney, a circuit judge, a state attorney general, and a justice of the state Supreme Court.

Coleman was elected in Mississippi's first general election after the *Brown v. Board of Education* decision, in which the US Supreme Court ruled that racial segregation in public schools was unconstitutional. Segregation was the overriding issue of the 1955 campaign, and Coleman promised to avoid integrating the schools. He also emphasized the need for a new state constitution and the need for continued industrial development. At a 1957 meeting in the Mississippi Governor's Mansion, Coleman and Gov. James E. Folsom of Alabama, along with legislators from both states, initiated plans for the Tennessee-Tombigbee Project, a vast inland waterway linking the Tennessee and Tombigbee Rivers with the Gulf of Mexico that finally opened in the early 1980s.

Coleman failed in his effort to secure a new constitution for Mississippi. Although he called the legislature into special session and urged lawmakers to write a new constitution, he could not persuade the leaders to do so. However, legislators did pass a resolution of interposition, authorizing the state to prohibit the implementation of the *Brown* decision in Mississippi, and created the Mississippi State Sovereignty Commission to carry out the resolution. Coleman considered the theory of interposition "legal poppycock," but under his leadership, the state maintained segregated schools, and he claimed that African Americans were satisfied with

James P. Coleman appears before the US Senate Constitutional Rights Subcommittee, 5 March 1957 (Library of Congress, Washington, D.C. [LC-USZ62-110823])

Mississippi's school equalization efforts, though many African American leaders publicly disagreed. Coleman worked with university leaders to obstruct and deny Clennon King's application to attend the University of Mississippi and Clyde Kennard's application to Mississippi Southern College (now the University of Southern Mississippi).

After his gubernatorial term expired, Coleman was elected to the Mississippi House of Representatives from Choctaw County, making him one of the few Mississippians to serve in all three branches of state government.

In 1965 Coleman was appointed to the US Court of Appeals for the Fifth Circuit, and he served as chief judge from 1979 to 1981. He retired from the Fifth Circuit on 31 January 1984, and he died in 1991.

In addition to his public service and legal career, Coleman was also an author and historian. He is best known for *Choctaw County Chronicles: A History of Choctaw County Mississippi, 1830–1973*. J. P. Coleman State Park near Iuka is named in his honor.

David G. Sansing
University of Mississippi

Charles C. Bolton, *The Hardest Deal of All: The Battle over School Integration in Mississippi, 1870–1980* (2005): James P. Coleman Subject File, Mississippi Department of Archives and History; David G. Sansing, *Making Haste Slowly: The Troubled History of Higher Education in Mississippi* (1990).

Collier, Holt
(ca. 1846–1936) Hunter

Holt Collier was born about 1846 on Home Hill Plantation in Jefferson County. He was enslaved by the family of Gen. Thomas Hinds, the man for whom Hinds County was named. At the age of ten Collier was transported upriver to what would become modern-day Greenville. There, on Plum Ridge Plantation, he was trained to hunt, supplying meat for the labor force. He killed his first bear soon after arriving and went on to kill more than three thousand others. By age fourteen he had become not only an accomplished marksman but also a runaway slave, serving on behalf of the Confederacy with the 9th Texas Cavalry.

After the war Collier was prosecuted for the murder of Union captain James A. King but was acquitted. Collier lived in Texas and worked as a cowboy before returning to Mississippi, where he earned substantial sums as a hunter and guide. The Mississippi Delta, at the time a swampy wilderness, was one of the most diverse ecosystems on the North American continent and contained what was considered an endless supply of game. Collier achieved so much success that by the end of the century business and political leaders sought him out as a guide.

In 1902 Pres. Theodore Roosevelt visited Mississippi in hopes of killing a black bear and chose Collier as his guide. Collier single-handedly captured a large wild black bear for Roosevelt to shoot, but the president refused to kill the tethered animal, leading to the phenomenon of the Teddy Bear. Roosevelt, who also hunted with Collier in Louisiana in 1907, is said to have called him "the greatest hunter and guide I have ever known." He also taught the young men of Washington County, among them future US senator Leroy Percy, how to hunt.

During the 1920s and 1930s Collier became a legendary figure in and around Greenville. In a gunfight at Washburn's Ferry, he outdrew notorious Louisiana outlaw Travis Elmore Sage. William Faulkner was a frequent visitor to Greenville, and he borrowed some of Collier's exploits for the fictional Sam Fathers.

Minor Ferris Buchanan
Jackson, Mississippi

Minor Ferris Buchanan, *Holt Collier: His Life, His Roosevelt Hunts, and the Origin of the Teddy Bear* (2002).

Comeback Sauce (Come-Back, Kum-Bak, Kumback, Kumbak)

There are almost as many spellings for this uniquely Jackson salad dressing/dipping sauce as there are recipes and theories for its origin. Many observers trace the oddly orange concoction, consisting of a variety of ingredients that generally include mayonnaise, tomato ketchup, Worcestershire sauce, mustard, black pepper, chili sauce, lemon, and plenty of garlic, to Alex Dennery's Rotisserie Restaurant, located on US 49 at Five Points in Jackson. Recipes for "rotisserie dressing" (or sauce) are said to have originated directly from the restaurant.

The name is obviously a reference to the idea that people who try the zesty blend will always come back for more. Many native Jacksonians and visitors alike are fond of pouring the dressing over saltine crackers as a first course while waiting for the salad to arrive. Locals enjoy this "redneck hors d'oeuvre" so much that many restaurants will not put large bottles of sauce on the table for fear that the entire bottle will be consumed before the salad arrives.

In the early days of fine dining in Jackson, Greek immigrants dominated the kitchens and counters of the city's restaurant scene. According to Mike Kountouris of the Mayflower Café, language difficulties meant that young Greek immigrants could find work only in kitchens or as busboys. Comeback dressing may have been the Greek American answer to Thousand Island, the most popular salad dressing of the mid-twentieth century in the American South.

Paper records are scarce for such ephemeral matters as family-held salad dressing recipes, but oral histories point to Five Points in Jackson as the source of the legendary spread. In 1936 Alex Dennery (born John Alexander Tounaris in Greece) supposedly was searching for a signature salad dressing for his newly remodeled property, the Rotisserie, at the intersection of Highway 49 and Livingston Road. A former drive-in movie theater, the Rotisserie occupied a unique location in southwest Jackson at the junction of five streets and featured a different entrance on each street. According to Roy Milner, a longtime employee of the Dennery family, after staff tried and failed several times to concoct what Dennery wanted, Alex took to the kitchen and began experimenting. He first made mayonnaise by combining raw egg yolks with oil and then added chili sauce, garlic, and other ingredients. Dennery's Restaurant in downtown Jackson still serves a version of the sauce, but hundreds of other variations have developed, among them the tangy Mayflower Café version, the smooth Crechale's rendition, a kicked-up version at Walker's Drive-In, and a super garlic version at my family's Hal & Mal's. But no matter where diners find this sauce, the empty bottle marks the spot where they will have to come back for more.

According to legend, writer Henry Miller so persistently demanded that Eudora Welty invite him to Jackson that she gave in and issued the invitation, though she hesitated because of Miller's reputation for extravagance. Miller arrived and announced—to Welty's dismay—that he would be staying for several days longer than she had intended. At a loss for ways to entertain her guest, Welty took him to the Rotisserie five times, each time entering the restaurant via a different door. On his final evening of copious eating and drinking, Miller noted approvingly that Jackson certainly had a large number of fine dining establishments for such a small town. The house dressing was undoubtedly one of the delights he sampled during his visits.

Malcolm White
Mississippi Arts Commission

Symphony League of Jackson, comp., *The Jackson Cookbook*, foreword by Eudora Welty (1971).

Community and Junior Colleges

Mississippi's system of community and junior colleges developed out of the state's agricultural high schools, which had been established as boarding schools in the early twentieth century. By the 1920s, however, cities and counties began to build high schools, and the agricultural boarding schools lost their role. Influenced by the idea of junior colleges developed at the University of Chicago, Julius Christian Zeller, a state senator from Yazoo City who had previously served as superintendent of Bolivar County Agricultural High School, introduced legislation in 1922 allowing agricultural high schools to offer the first two years of college classes if local leaders wished to fund them.

Mississippi's junior college movement developed out of the populist political atmosphere. In Poplarville, home of Theodore G. Bilbo, Pearl River Agricultural High School offered its first college-level courses in 1921–22, prior to the passage of Zeller's legislation. Hinds County followed in 1922–23. By 1928, twelve schools had added junior college work, and Zeller authored legislation that created a commission to oversee them and provided the first state funds for their support. The new state commission established attendance zones and other rules to prevent every agricultural high school from establishing a junior college and to prevent the colleges from competing with each other and with senior colleges.

The junior colleges established an unofficial accrediting agency made up of professors from Mississippi's colleges and universities to approve course offerings. Agricultural high school teachers became the junior college faculty. When teachers lacked the graduate work needed to qualify as college instructors, they spent summers taking courses. Faculty members continued to teach both college and high school classes and to fulfill other duties, such as imposing discipline, monitoring dining halls, and chaperoning Saturday night movies in the school auditoriums.

Students who could not afford senior colleges could attend the junior colleges and work to defray their expenses. The agricultural schools had farms attached, so students worked in the fields, cooked in the dining hall, or washed dishes in return for room and board. Most schools maintained strictly regimented schedules, ringing bells to direct students through days filled with chapel, classes, and two hours of evening study before lights out. "Social hours" allowing males and females to spend time together were closely supervised. The schools gradually developed newspapers, sports teams, debating societies, bands, and theater groups, providing students many of the same opportunities available at senior colleges. Library facilities long remained subpar, but many transfer students did well at the senior colleges.

In 1937 Meridian's city schools added grades 13 and 14, creating Mississippi's only municipal junior college and the only one that did not begin as an agricultural high school. The city later created T. J. Harris Junior College to serve black students.

The system was shaped by the Mississippi Junior College Association, made up of the presidents of the junior colleges (the former superintendents of the agricultural high schools). They weathered the Depression with help from New Deal programs, which they used to supplement scarce county and state funding. During World War II, the junior colleges developed into vocational training centers, so that when the veterans returned, the schools were positioned to serve the GI Bill students who flooded campuses. Military surplus buildings added housing and classrooms at little cost to the institutions. State appropriations for vocational training increased, and the junior colleges prospered.

Itawamba and Northeast Junior Colleges filled a vacuum in the hill area of the state when they opened in 1948. By 1950 the legislature severed junior college ties to agricultural high schools. Junior colleges for black students did not exist until 1949, when Coahoma's black agricultural high school added college courses; Utica followed suit in 1954. All of the white schools earned accreditation from the Southern Association during those years.

Significant desegregation of the traditionally white junior colleges did not occur until the mid- to late 1960s. Meridian Junior College remained part of the city's public schools and merged with T. J. Harris Junior College under a 1970 court order. A decade later the college established a board of trustees and severed its ties to the municipal school system. All of the other junior colleges gradually admitted African Americans beginning in the vocational programs, which were subject to federal funding guidelines. None of the junior colleges reported any confrontations over integration. In response to 1982 court order, Utica Junior College became a branch campus of Hinds Junior College; however, the legislature created a district for Coahoma, making it the state's only historically black junior college.

Between the 1960s and 1980s, rural schools built branches in urban centers, vocational and technical students came to outnumber students preparing to transfer to four-year colleges, and part-time commuter students became increasingly common. Reflecting these developments, all of the junior colleges except Jones County Junior College changed their names to community colleges in 1987.

As the state provided more funding than the counties, conflicts arose between the institutions' presidents and local trustees, who were appointed by the county supervisors, and state officials. Legislative investigations and reports from outside consultants resulted in a 1986 compromise: the State Board for Community and Junior Colleges replaced the old governing body comprised of the school presidents, but local trustees retained control under state regulation.

By the turn of the twenty-first century, Mississippi boasted fifteen community and junior colleges that offered job training, adult education, and traditional college courses at campuses and centers around the state as well as online via the Mississippi Virtual Community College. They have remained connected to their historical roots in the state's agricultural high schools as they have brought high-quality, low-cost educational opportunities to hundreds of thousands of Mississippians.

Dennis Mitchell
Mississippi State
University–Meridian

Ben H. Fatherree, "The Community and Junior College System in Mississippi: A Brief History of Its Origin and Development," mshistorynow.mdah.state.ms.us; Mississippi Community College Board website, http://www.sbcjc.cc.ms.us; James B. Young and James M. Ewing, *The Mississippi Public Junior College Story: The First Fifty Years, 1922–1972* (1978).

Community and Junior Colleges in Mississippi

Coahoma Community College, Clarksdale
Copiah-Lincoln Community College
    Wesson (Main Campus)
    Natchez Campus
    Magee Campus
East Central Community College, Decatur
East Mississippi Community College
    Scooba (Main Campus)
    Golden Triangle Campus, Mayhew
    Columbus Air Force Base
Hinds Community College, Raymond
Holmes Community College, Goodman
Itawamba Community College, Fulton
Jones County Junior College, Ellisville
Meridian Community College, Meridian
Mississippi Delta Community College, Moorhead
Mississippi Gulf Coast Community College
    Perkinston (Main Campus)
    Applied Technology and Development Center, Gulfport
    George County Center, Lucedale
    Jackson County Campus, Gautier
    Jefferson Davis Campus, Gulfport
    Keesler Center, Keesler Air Force Base
    West Harrison County Center, Long Beach
Northeast Mississippi Community College
    Booneville (Main Campus)
    Corinth
    New Albany
Northwest Mississippi Community College
    Senatobia (Main Campus)
    Benton-Marshall Center, Ashland
    De Soto Center, Southaven
    De Soto Center–Olive Branch Campus, Olive Branch
    Lafayette-Yalobusha Technical Center, Oxford
Pearl River Community College, Poplarville
Southwest Mississippi Community College, Summit

Community Festivals

Community festivals are recurrent seasonal public celebrations of a town's history, people, holidays, local products, and/or common interests. They are held in parks, streets, and facilities that permit gatherings of large numbers of people, often of different ages, classes, occupations, races, ethnicities, and genders. Locals, former residents, and visitors gather for the annual day or multiday events. Chambers of commerce, tourism committees, and local organizations organize and oversee the festivals. In addition, local businesses, civic/religious organizations, and community members volunteer and provide monetary or in-kind donations such as tables, chairs, tents, and facilities. Nevertheless, each festival is unique because of the people who create and attend it.

These celebrations provide social, economic, and political opportunities that are especially important to communities that no longer have thriving downtowns and growing populations. Although festivals have always been a way to bring together people to celebrate and honor facets of local life, they have become a strategy for revitalizing towns. School, family, and church reunions are frequently scheduled during festivals, and organizations, businesses, and politicians use these events for fund-raising, recruitment, advertising, and/or exposure. Moreover, locals can enjoy a change from their everyday routines as streets and parks are transformed into bustling entertainment centers. These "invented traditions" can create and foster a sense of pride, fellowship, and belonging.

Most festivals adhere to a basic structure: opening and closing events, food and drink, arts and crafts, competitions or demonstrations, and musical entertainment. Some have parades or carnivals. Most community festivals are free or charge a minimal entrance fee for patrons, while vendors pay for booth space. Volunteer labor is often essential. The festival may begin with local leaders and organizers on a central stage, an announcement on a loudspeaker, or a parade. Carnival-type and often regionally specific food is available throughout the day. Most events classified as family-oriented do not serve alcohol. Vendors offer an enormous array of homemade and manufactured items and services such as marshmallow shooters, clothing, jewelry, hand-painted picture frames, and face painting.

Despite the similarities in basic structure, community festivals can differ greatly depending on the local attraction, product, or season being celebrated. In addition to various Fourth of July, seasonal, and Mississippi River–related festivals, the state offers some more unusual gatherings. The one-day World Catfish Festival, held in Belzoni since 1975, has recently featured a 5K fun run/walk, a children's color run, and the crowning of Miss Catfish and Little Miss Catfish, along with musical entertainment and appearances by local celebrities. The Choctaw Indian Fair, a four-day event now in its seventh decade, offers attendees a chance to learn about the tribe's history and culture, including traditional Choctaw food and stickball, along with carnival rides, games, and music. The Delta's storied history as the Birthplace of the Blues has given rise to numerous celebrations of the music, among them Clarksdale's Juke Joint Festival, Sunflower River Blues and Gospel Festival, and Deep Blues Festival; Greenville's Mississippi Delta Blues and Heritage Festival, Highway 61 Blues Festival, and Mighty Mississippi Music Festival; and the Hollandale Sam Chatmon Blues Festival. Food-related festivals include the Delta Hot Tamale Festival (Greenville), the Pour Mississippi Beer and Music Festival (Cleveland), Mardi Gras Mambo-cue (Pass Christian), the Slugburger Festival (Corinth), the Natchez Food and Wine Festival, the Vardaman Sweet Potato Festival, and numerous crawfish festivals.

Tiff Graham
University of California at Los Angeles

Choctaw Indian Fair website, www.choctawindianfair.com; Deep South USA website, www.deep-south-usa.com; Alessandro Falassi, ed., *Time out of Time: Essays on the Festival* (1987); Eric Hobsbawm and Terence Ranger, *The Invention of Tradition* (1992); Mississippi Delta Tourism website, www.visitthedelta.com; Robert Jerome Smith, in *Folklore and Folklife: An Introduction*, ed. Richard M. Dorson (1972); Beverly J. Stoeltje, in *Folklore, Cultural Performances, and Popular Entertainment*, ed. Richard Bauman (1992); Rory Turner and Philip H. McArthur, in *The Emergence of Folklore in Everyday Life: A Fieldguide and Sourcebook*, ed. George H. Schoemaker (1990); World Catfish Festival website, www.belzonims.com/catfishfest.htm.

Conerly, Charlie
(1921–1996) Athlete

Charles Albert "Chunkin' Charlie" Conerly Jr., one of Mississippi's first football superstars at the national level, played quarterback for the New York Giants of the National Football League (NFL) from 1948 to 1961. He was born in Clarksdale on 19 September 1921 to Charles Albert Conerly Sr. and Winiford Fite Conerly and graduated from Clarksdale High School in 1941.

He received a football scholarship from the University of Mississippi, where he played single-wing tailback, but left the university after the 1942 season and joined the US Marines, seeing combat duty in the South Pacific. Conerly returned to the university after the war, and despite the

Rebels' miserable 2–7 record in 1946, he was selected to the all–Southeastern Conference (SEC) team. As captain during his senior year Conerly teamed with Barney Poole to lead first-year head coach John Vaught's Rebels to the 1947 SEC championship, the school's first. That season, as half of the heralded "Conerly to Poole" passing and receiving duo, he set national collegiate passing records. For his exploits, Conerly won all-SEC and all-American recognition and finished fourth in the voting for the Heisman Trophy.

Also an outstanding collegiate baseball player, he was offered a contract to play professional baseball but chose pro football instead. In 1948 he joined the New York Giants and enjoyed a record-setting first season that earned him NFL Rookie of the Year honors. In 1949 he married Perian Collier, also from Clarksdale. She became a noted sportswriter and author who chronicled her husband's NFL career in her 1963 book, *Backseat Quarterback*. During Conerly's tenure with the team, the Giants won four Eastern Division titles (1956, 1958, 1959, and 1961), and he twice earned a spot on the Pro Bowl team. In 1956 he led the Giants to the NFL championship, and two years later he was the quarterback in the Giants' sudden-death overtime loss to the Baltimore Colts. That contest, called by many commentators one of the greatest pro football games ever played, helped usher in the modern era of big-time sporting events on television. On 29 November 1959 the Giants held Charlie Conerly Day in his honor at Yankee Stadium. That year, at age thirty-eight, he won the NFL's Most Valuable Player Award. At the conclusion of the 1961 season, he retired from football, and the following year the Giants retired his uniform number, 42, the same number he had worn during his playing days at the University of Mississippi.

Conerly spent his career in New York, the NFL's largest market, where he played the glamour position, quarterback, at a time when live broadcasts of pro football games were in their infancy. Since he was such a high-profile figure, Madison Avenue turned him into a spokesman for a wide array of products, among them car batteries, men's apparel, chewing gum, life insurance, deodorant, bread, and cigarettes. Of all these endorsements, his most famous was undoubtedly his portrayal of the Marlboro Man.

A skilled passer, quiet leader, and courageous performer known for his physical and mental toughness, Conerly took terrible beatings playing behind weak lines in the early 1950s and was often blamed by Giants fans for the team's poor records. Whether he was cheered or, as was often the case during those early years at the Polo Grounds, booed, he showed little emotion on the field. Referred to by New York sportswriters as the "Old Pro," he took a low-key approach to the game, avoided the limelight, and was something of a reluctant hero. In 1966 Conerly was inducted into the College Football Hall of Fame. He is also a member of the Mississippi Sports Hall of Fame, and in 1993 Rebel football fans named him to the Ole Miss Team of the Century. Since 1996 the Conerly Trophy has been awarded annually to the state's top collegiate football player.

Following a lengthy illness, Conerly died in Memphis of congestive heart failure on 13 February 1996.

Melvin S. Arrington Jr.
University of Mississippi

Charlie Conerly with Tom Meany, *The Forward Pass* (1960); Perian Conerly, *Backseat Quarterback* (1963); Lud Duroska, ed., *Great Pro Quarterbacks* (1972); Frank Gifford with Charles Mangel, *Gifford on Courage* (1976); Booton Herndon, *Football's Greatest Quarterbacks* (1961); Mickey Herskowitz, *The Golden Age of Pro Football: NFL Football in the 1950s* (1990); William W. Sorrels and Charles Cavagnaro, *Ole Miss Rebels: Mississippi Football* (1976); John Vaught, *Rebel Coach: My Football Family* (1971).

Confederate Army, Mississippians in

The Confederate Army served a newly created government and consisted mainly of volunteers, but it was not raised from an entirely unprepared population. In 1859, responding to John Brown's raid on Harpers Ferry, southern states revived their largely dormant militia units. Mississippi appropriated funds and a few companies organized in early 1860, but militia formation lagged until Abraham Lincoln's election. Mississippians now began preparing in earnest to answer what the state's adjutant general called the "ignominious taunts of the Black Republican horde." By the time Mississippi seceded in January 1861, four thousand men had joined sixty-five militia companies.

Militia officers were expected to provide training and supervision, but militiamen were not a battle-ready army. Mississippi officials had trouble finding a reliable weapons contractor, officers had spotty knowledge of tactics, and there were limits to local reaction to the political furor of 1860–61: most companies were undermanned, others disbanded altogether, and voters frequently ignored elections for militia officers.

Apathy vanished, however, when war became a reality. The capture of Fort Sumter in April 1861 led Lincoln to call for seventy-five thousand troops, a move the South viewed as a declaration of war. Military-age men responded immediately, forming companies in villages and towns across the region. Mississippians organized two hundred companies (each of which typically had one hundred soldiers) by mid-May, reversing the state's dilemma: where finding volunteers had once been the problem, authorities were now confronted with far more enlistees than they could equip and supply. Not until the fall of 1861 did a substantial number of Mississippi units enter regular Confederate service.

A complex combination of motives influenced enlistment in the Confederate Army. Soldiers' testimony tended to personalize their purposes: Samuel Meek of Lowndes County was fighting for "my wife & child & relatives and friends & country," while Ben Harris of Copiah County wanted "to defend my helpless Brother & sister." Volunteers were nonetheless aware of the war's political issues—Meek declared that he was also fighting "against the brutal violence of a fiendish people." Newspapers such as the *Canton American Citizen* had warned about this brutishness: "The North threatens us with subjugation, confiscation, and emancipation; terms that no freeman can think of submitting to, without having lost all honor and traits of character belonging to manhood."

The editor's mention of manhood hints at the ways in which the multiple dimensions of masculinity could also stimulate enlistment. Young men often equated masculinity with military obligation: Robert Moore of Holly Springs believed that "our country calls & he that would not respond deserves not the name of man." Women also had a role in invoking masculinity. As companies prepared to leave for their camps of instruction, "patriotic ladies" customarily held flag-presentation ceremonies, reminding soldiers of their duty to defend community honor. For men unmoved by such demonstrations, women's reminders could be more pointed. A Natchez woman asked men who had not yet enlisted to "be men once more, and make every woman in the land proud of having you as protectors." A resident of Jefferson County reported that "the young ladies say they will not marry any of the boys that stay at home. They will wait for them that has gone to fight for their rights."

In addition to patriotism and manhood, Mississippians' circumstances also influenced their likelihood of enlisting. Among a sample of military-age Mississippians taken from the 1860 census, men younger than twenty-five were more likely to enlist than were older men. Having a stake in slavery was also a key reason to enlist: men who had been born in slave states or whose families had invested in slaves were considerably more likely to join the army than were other men. Conversely, a sense of geographical vulnerability seems to have discouraged enlistment. Residents along the Mississippi River and the Gulf Coast expressed apprehension about bearing the brunt of a Yankee invasion, and men from these areas were less likely to join the Confederate Army. Indeed, an 1861 military roll from a river county indicates that many military-age men had left the area as the war was beginning.

The rush to enlist that had frustrated Confederate officials in mid-1861 diminished in the fall, and by the spring of 1862 the opposite problem had emerged. Not only had volunteering tapered off, but many of those who had enlisted were nearing the end of their one-year terms (though others had signed on for three years). Faced with these problems, the Confederate Congress enacted a national draft in April 1862. One-year enlistments were extended to three years, and white men between the ages of eighteen and thirty-five were subject to conscription unless they hired substitutes or worked in exempt occupations. The age limit for regular service was later raised to forty-five, substitution was abolished, and exemptions were added for men on large plantations. The army continued to accept volunteers because officials hoped that holdouts would volunteer rather than be drafted. Across the South an estimated two hundred thousand new Confederate soldiers reported for duty in 1862, more than half of them volunteers. Mississippi had an estimated eight thousand draftees over the course of the war: there are no precise figures for men who volunteered instead, but they probably totaled several times the number of draftees.

In 1864 Confederate draft officials, drawing on county reports, estimated that sixty-seven thousand Mississippians had joined the army since the war began. A few more joined over the war's last year, and some Mississippians crossed state lines to enlist. However, identifying how many men did not serve is considerably more difficult. In 1860 Mississippi had approximately eighty-eight thousand white male residents aged between fifteen and fifty, but some of them left the state (and the South) before the Civil War. According to some reports, men hid out to avoid conscription, and local resistance to Confederate authority occasionally arose, especially in Mississippi's Piney Woods, though the overall number of evaders is unknown. A good estimate is that at least three-quarters of military-age white men in wartime Mississippi joined the Confederate Army.

Larry M. Logue
Mississippi College

John K. Bettersworth, *Confederate Mississippi: The People and Politics of a Cotton State in Wartime* (1943); Victoria E. Byum, *The Free State of Jones: Mississippi's Longest Civil War* (2001); Larry M. Logue, *Journal of Social History* (Spring 1993); Albert B. Moore, *Conscription and Conflict in the Confederacy* (1924); Dunbar Rowland, *Military History of Mississippi, 1803–1898* (1978); *The War of the Rebellion: A Compilation of the Official Records of the Union and Confederate Armies* (1880–1901); Bell Irvin Wiley, *The Life of Johnny Reb: The Common Soldier of the Confederacy* (1943).

Confederate Symbol Controversies at the University of Mississippi

Although a number of other educational institutions have utilized Confederate symbols, the University of Mississippi is the school most closely associated with these emblems.

And while protests over the use of Confederate symbols spanned the South during the late twentieth and early twenty-first centuries, the University of Mississippi has maintained the longest continuing dialogue on the issue. Opponents of these representations of the Lost Cause point out their adoption by segregationists, trace their origins to a conflict fought to preserve slavery, stress that campus symbols should represent all students, and highlight the damage these relics of the past cause to the university's reputation and recruitment efforts. Proponents, conversely, reject historical interpretations that place slavery as a central cause of the Civil War, tout the emblem either as honoring dead soldiers or as simply representing school spirit, deny any personal racism, and defend the Confederate flag, the song "Dixie," and Colonel Reb against perceived assaults on southern heritage.

The University of Mississippi and what is now the University of Southern Mississippi (USM) began using Confederate symbols in the 1930s and early 1940s. The University of Mississippi sports teams became known as the Rebels, while USM started in 1940 as the Confederates before quickly changing to the Southerners. Colonel Reb became the University of Mississippi's mascot in 1937, while USM adopted General Nat, in a reference to Nathan Bedford Forrest, in 1953. USM changed its sports team and mascot to the Golden Eagles in 1972, but change came more slowly at the University of Mississippi.

Confrontations regarding Confederate symbols at the University of Mississippi and the effort to eliminate their use began in 1970. By that time, black enrollment had increased to more than two hundred students. At three separate protests, African American students burned a rebel banner, and the Black Student Union (BSU) published a set of demands that included curtailing the use of Confederate flags on campus. A proposal by the administration to add the letters *UM* to the school flag never became a reality, and the issue faded from public consciousness until 1979, when a brief flurry of debate occurred after the senior class donated Traveler, a horse named after Robert E. Lee's steed, for the Colonel Reb mascot to ride.

The symbol conflict received national attention in 1982 when the university's first black cheerleader, John Hawkins, refused to wave the Confederate flag at football games. In addition, when the university commemorated the twentieth anniversary of James Meredith's 1962 integration of the school, he called for his alma mater to eliminate the use of all Civil War symbols. A few weeks later, twenty-nine members of the Ku Klux Klan marched through Oxford in support of the Confederate flag. While the student government passed a resolution favoring the continued use of such symbols and white students circulated supportive petitions, the BSU held a demonstration, presented the governor and the president of the board of trustees with a list of thirteen demands that included the abandonment of all Confederate symbols, and sponsored a boycott of the Red-Blue football game.

In April 1983, two days after a student rally of fifteen hundred flag proponents threatened to turn violent, Chancellor Porter L. Fortune instituted a new policy restricting official representatives of the university from wearing anything but university-registered symbols, which did not include the Confederate banner. In addition, the campus bookstore stopped selling rebel flags and merchandise with its image. But private individuals were still permitted to display the flag at university functions. The following autumn, the administration attempted unsuccessfully to introduce a new red, white, and blue flag with the words *Ole Miss*.

In 1985 Chancellor Gerald Turner requested that the school band play "Dixie" less often at sporting events, prompting a wave of columns and letters to the editor in the campus newspaper. The Confederate symbol issue subsequently resurfaced every fall with the start of football season. In 1989 the senior class fund-raiser created the "Battle M" flag (a blue block *M* with white stars on a solid red background). The mild success of this grassroots initiative encouraged the administration officially to adopt the new emblem, but the rebel standard continued to dominate in the stands.

In 1991, recognizing that the controversial symbols harmed the university's image and recruitment efforts, both the Alumni Association Board and the Faculty Senate officially requested that fans not bring these Confederate emblems to university athletic events. The administration then announced a ban on all flags larger than twelve inches by eighteen inches in an effort to sidestep concerns about freedom of speech. During the 1993 basketball season, four black band members announced their refusal to play "Dixie." The student government endorsed the song's use, while the BSU instituted an economic boycott of campus food services. Outside organizations including the Southern Heritage Foundation, the Sons of Confederate Veterans, and a Civil War reenactors group sponsored rallies in support of the campus Confederate symbols.

In 1996 the university altered the official flag to a solid red *M* on a blue background, a design that television viewers were less likely to confuse with the rebel battle standard. Many spectators nevertheless continued to favor the Confederate flag. Thus, in the fall of 1997, head football coach Tommy Tuberville asked fans to leave these banners at home, and the Associated Student Body requested that sticks be banned in the stands, another attempt to discourage spectators from bringing the flags. The administration quickly instituted the ban.

When rumors surfaced in 2002 that the administration was trying to eliminate "Dixie" from the band's repertoire, Chancellor Robert Khayat announced that the university would retain both the tune and the Colonel Reb mascot. The following year, however, the university removed Colonel Reb as an on-field mascot, and in 2009 Chancellor Dan Jones ended the university band's playing of "From Dixie with Love" so that students would not yell, "The South will rise again!" after the song ended. In 2010, the school adopted the

Rebel Bear as its official mascot, a move that remains controversial in 2015, albeit less so as time goes by.

The issue of the Confederate battle flag returned to prominence in 2015 in the wake of shootings in Charleston, South Carolina, perpetrated by a gunman who used the flag as a symbol of white supremacy. According to a statement released by interim chancellor Morris H. Stocks, "The University of Mississippi community came to the realization years ago that the Confederate battle flag did not represent many of our core values such as civility and respect for others. Since that time, we have become a stronger and better university."

Leigh McWhite
University of Mississippi

J. Michael Martinez, William D. Richardson, and Ron McNinch-Su, *Confederate Symbols in the Contemporary South* (2000); Eryn Taylor and CNN Wire, wreg.com (23 June 2015); Kevin Pierce Thornton, *South Atlantic Quarterly* (Summer 1987); *Washington Post* (21 April 1983).

Freedom Riders CORE button

Congress of Racial Equality (CORE)

The Congress of Racial Equality (CORE) was especially important in Mississippi from 1961 to 1966. CORE was formed in Chicago in 1942 to test the effectiveness of nonviolence in desegregating restaurants and other public facilities in the United States. In 1947 the group staged a journey of reconciliation to test the Supreme Court's decision outlawing segregation on interstate transportation. An interracial group of fourteen riders, including James Peck and Bayard Rustin, rode two buses through the Upper South, encountering little violence and only a few arrests.

CORE enjoyed little support in the South until the late 1950s, when the organization began cosponsoring workshops on nonviolent direct action with the Southern Christian Leadership Conference (SCLC). CORE played an instrumental role in educating and organizing students for the nascent sit-in movement, and in 1960 representatives of the group attended the Atlanta conference that established the Student Nonviolent Coordinating Committee (SNCC) as a permanent organization, with CORE's nonviolent direct action strategy and its "jail, no bail" policy greatly influencing the new group's stance.

As efforts to push for desegregation became increasingly organized, CORE members Gordon Carey and Tom Gaither recommended that the organization conduct another Freedom Ride in the summer of 1961 to test the Supreme Court's ruling that terminals for interstate travelers could not be segregated. After CORE's national council approved the project, the group's new national director, James Farmer, issued a call for volunteers on 13 March 1961. An interracial group of thirteen riders, among them John Lewis and Henry Thomas, proposed riding two buses from Washington, D.C., to New Orleans. Before the first group of riders left on 4 May, Peck and Farmer held a session on nonviolence. The group encountered little violence prior to reaching Anniston, Alabama, where a white mob set one bus on fire and beat the riders. With several riders badly injured and no drivers willing to transport them to Montgomery, CORE decided to end the ride and flew the riders to New Orleans.

After SNCC workers encouraged CORE members to continue the rides and vowed to join them, Farmer joined SNCC and SCLC leaders at a press conference to announce that the rides would continue. Because of the violence in Alabama, the Kennedy administration told Mississippi governor Ross Barnett that if he protected the riders, the federal government would not interfere when local police arrested the demonstrators. The buses safely arrived in Jackson, where the riders were arrested for breaching the peace or for refusing to obey officers. The activists received fines and suspended sentences of sixty days, but they refused to pay either their fines or bail, and most of them remained jail for thirty-nine days, the maximum time they could serve and still appeal their convictions.

CORE adopted a strategy of filling Mississippi's jails, and Gaither went to Jackson to coordinate the continuing busloads of activists. By the end of the summer, a total of 328 riders were being held in city and county jails as well as Parchman Prison. The Justice Department encouraged the Interstate Commerce Commission to prohibit separate facilities in terminals, and that policy went into effect on 1 November 1961. CORE organizers subsequently remained in Mississippi, with Gaither moving to Clarksdale to work with Aaron Henry and David Dennis working in several communities, including Jackson, Ruleville, and Hattiesburg. Other CORE workers joined SNCC in McComb, where they were beaten on several occasions for attempting to eat at the lunch counter in the Greyhound bus terminal.

With Mississippi as the focus for voter registration drives and desegregation efforts, the Council of Federated Organizations (COFO), which was formed in 1961 by black groups working for social justice, was reorganized in 1962 to include CORE and SNCC. The SCLC and National Association for the Advancement of Colored People (NAACP) also joined COFO, so the alliance allowed the young workers of CORE and SNCC to tap into the older groups' networks. COFO designated CORE (represented by Dennis) to work in Mississippi's 4th Congressional District. Because of the Kennedy administration's pressure to focus on voter registration rather than desegregation, COFO organized the Voter Education Project, which was largely funded by foundations close to the Kennedys.

CORE chose to begin its voter registration drive in Madison County and particularly the town of Canton because SNCC lacked workers in the area and the local NAACP chapter was inactive. CORE later expanded the campaign into Leake, Neshoba, Leflore, and Rankin Counties. Like SNCC, CORE sought to develop local leadership and encourage grassroots organizing. In 1963 the only staff member for the Madison County project was George Raymond, who had first come to Mississippi during the 1961 Freedom Rides, but by 1964 CORE's Madison County project was the most active in the state, with seven organizers, including Anne Moody and Rudy Lombard. Two Canton residents, Annie Devine and C. O. Chinn, were instrumental in CORE's success, donating resources and helping the workers gain community members' trust and support. Despite police intimidation and the high levels of white violence in the area, CORE workers canvassed neighborhoods, held mass meetings at local churches, and organized a boycott of white businesses.

On 28 February 1964 CORE held Madison County's first Freedom Day, during which 350 black residents tried to register to vote. With only 5 permitted to take the test, CORE and local residents scheduled two more Freedom Days. On the third day, 29 May, Farmer spoke to boost morale, but in the absence of national media, the police stopped a march to the courthouse and arrested 55 marchers. Dennis and other CORE workers remained defiant, and Dennis sent a telegram to Pres. Lyndon Johnson, chiding him for failing to protect the workers. In early June many of the 55 demonstrators arrested remained in jail, assailants shot at the freedom house, and a bomb exploded on the sidewalk outside CORE's office. Local African Americans continued to support CORE, however, and the organization recruited more summer volunteers to participate in COFO's Freedom Summer Project. Led by Raymond, workers opened ten freedom schools, continued

to promote the boycott of Canton's white merchants, and worked in the local community center. In addition, CORE worker Mike Piore organized a Farmers' League to provide information about the federal government's acreage allotment program.

After receiving news of CORE's efforts in Canton, Greenwood scheduled its first Freedom Day for 25 March 1964. The night before, workers held a mass meeting that featured Farmer as a speaker and was attended by more than 400 residents. Despite the arrests of several workers and the Klan's burning of a cross in front of SNCC's office, 200 residents of Leflore County went to register on Freedom Day. The hopeful registrants were protected by almost 100 demonstrators, including some white ministers, who formed a line around the courthouse. Police arrested no one, but only 35 blacks were allowed to take the test. The Mississippi legislature responded on 8 April by barring pickets of state buildings, an attempt to deprive the registrants of protection. Greenwood's second Freedom Day occurred on 9 April, and police arrested 46 demonstrators, charging them with violating the new law. Eight demonstrators were evicted from the plantations where they worked and lived, and opponents shot into the homes of several volunteers.

Recruited by CORE's Matt Suarez in the fall of 1963, James Chaney helped Suarez and Raymond organize Canton's first Freedom Day before moving to Meridian, where he met Michael Schwerner and his wife, Rita, New Yorkers who had recently joined the CORE staff. The Schwerners organized a community center that provided locals with reading and sewing classes, clerical training, and a library. After CORE appointed Schwerner as the project director for Mississippi's 4th District, he and Chaney began planning freedom houses, freedom schools, and community centers in Neshoba County. To announce their plans, the two workers met with residents at the Mount Zion Methodist Church in the Longdale community outside of Philadelphia. Mount Zion was later chosen as a freedom school site, but because of its support of the movement, Klansmen attacked church members as they were leaving the building on 16 June 1964 and later returned to burn the church. Chaney and Schwerner, however, continued recruiting volunteers, including Andrew Goodman, with whom they spent the night of 20 June in Meridian. The three workers attempted to drive back to Philadelphia the next day but were arrested and jailed. After their release, police stopped them and turned them over to a white mob. Klansmen executed the three men and buried them in a dam that was under construction. Their bodies were not found until 4 August. CORE's Dennis delivered the eulogy at Chaney's funeral, and the organization's national council voted to build a community center in Meridian as a memorial to the workers.

In addition to voter registration projects, CORE, along with the SCLC, SNCC, the NAACP, and the Urban League, participated in the 1963 March on Washington and in a

Freedom Walk from Chattanooga, Tennessee, to Jackson. A member of the Baltimore's CORE chapter, William Moore, initiated the walk, carrying signs protesting discrimination, but after he was murdered in Alabama, CORE and SNCC decided to jointly continue the freedom walk. Similarly in 1966, CORE, SNCC, and the SCLC continued James Meredith's March against Fear from Memphis to Jackson after Meredith was shot.

After 1966, however, CORE was largely absent from Mississippi. The preceding year, CORE and SNCC had begun to embrace black separatism and to focus on more urban areas and on the problems of unemployment, poor housing, and inadequate schools. Despite their physical absence, however, both organizations continued to affect the state because they had helped to develop local leadership.

Amy Schmidt
Lyon College

Raymond Arsenault, *Freedom Riders: 1961 and the Struggle for Racial Justice* (2006); Clayborne Carson, *In Struggle: SNCC and the Black Awakening of the 1960s* (1981); John Dittmer, *Local People: The Struggle for Civil Rights in Mississippi* (1994); Charles M. Payne, *I've Got the Light of Freedom: The Organizing Tradition and the Mississippi Freedom Struggle* (1995); Howard Zinn, *SNCC: The New Abolitionists* (2002).

Conner, Douglas L.
(1920–1998) Physician and Activist

Douglas L. Conner was a Starkville physician and civil rights organizer. The son of Jerry Conner, a lumber yard worker, and Mary Elnora Washington Conner, a custodian for the telephone company, Conner was born in Hattiesburg on 25 October 1920. When he was twelve years old, his parents divorced, apparently because of his father's alcoholism.

Conner suffered from the pervasive racial segregation of the time but believed that he was kept from despair because of his mother's insistence that he was not inferior; the black history instruction he received in school; the role modeling of Dr. Charles Smith, a black Hattiesburg physician; and his education and reading. When he graduated from Eureka High School and earned a fifty-dollar scholarship to Alcorn A&M College, he dreamed of becoming a doctor.

His four years at Alcorn were another positive experience, as was the summer of his junior year, when he worked in the Connecticut tobacco fields with Polish laborers, who, he was amazed to discover, displayed no prejudice against him. After graduating from Alcorn in 1943, he moved to Detroit and worked in a General Motors automobile plant to earn money for medical school. A year later he was drafted and entered the segregated military of World War II. While attending an integrated course for medical corpsmen at Walter Reed Army Hospital, he learned that he could hold his own with white people. On furlough before his assignment to Okinawa in 1945, Conner married Juanita Macon, the niece and ward of Starkville black leaders Robert and Sadye Wier. In the Pacific, Conner served under a physician who encouraged his dream of becoming a medical doctor and had the unusual experience of receiving more cordial treatment from the island's people of color than did the white soldiers.

After his discharge from the army, the Conners moved to Chicago, where he worked for a summer in a steel mill. In the fall of 1946 he entered Howard University Medical School in Washington, D.C., and after his graduation he served an internship at the Homer G. Phillips Hospital, St. Louis's major black health facility.

In 1951, with the encouragement of the Wiers, he began practicing medicine in Starkville. He served thousands of black patients and a handful of whites and became the acknowledged leader of the black community. He founded the Oktibbeha County chapter of the National Association for the Advancement of Colored People, served in the county and state Democratic Party, and was a prominent member of the Second Baptist Church. He led marches, endured arrest, initiated lawsuits, and in various other ways served as the driving force behind the integration of the Starkville schools, the initiation of voting rights for black people, and the hiring of black clerks in the city's downtown stores and banks.

Douglas and Juanita Conner raised two daughters, Sadye Yvonne, who became a pediatrician, and Eileen Yvette, a registered nurse. The Conners also took in a young boy, Richard Holmes, who in 1965 became the first black student at Mississippi State University and later a physician. After Douglas and Juanita divorced in 1987, he married Rhonda Taylor. He died in Starkville on 13 November 1998. Soon after his death, city leaders renamed Washington Street, the route of his many civil rights marches and the location of his office, Dr. Douglas L. Conner Drive.

John F. Marszalek
Mississippi State University

Douglas L. Conner with John F. Marszalek, *A Black Physician's Story: Bringing Hope in Mississippi* (1985).

Conner, Martin Sennet

(1891–1950) Forty-Fourth Governor, 1932–1936

During the depths of the worst depression in American history, Martin S. Conner was inaugurated as Mississippi's governor on 19 January 1932. "We assume our duties," he said, "when men are shaken with doubt and with fear, and many are wondering if our very civilization is about to crumble." Conner inherited a bankrupt treasury and a thirteen-million-dollar deficit. At forty-one, Conner was one of the state's youngest governors, but few had entered the office better trained or with more experience in public service.

Born in Hattiesburg on 31 August 1891, the son of a prosperous planter and businessman, Conner earned a bachelor's degree from the University of Mississippi and a law degree from Yale University. After opening a law office in Seminary, he won a seat in the state House of Representatives in 1916 and in his first term, at the age of twenty-five, was elected Speaker of the House. Conner was a member of the "low pressure" coalition of state legislators who believed in low taxes, balanced budgets, minimal government services, and a "pay-as-you-go" fiscal policy.

After unsuccessful campaigns in 1923 and 1927, Conner won the governorship in 1931. When he assumed office the treasury was exhausted, unemployment was at a record high, and the state's institutions of higher learning were no longer accredited. To solve the deficit problem Conner recommended reducing expenditures by cutting back on government services and on the number of state employees. To create additional revenue, he proposed a sales tax. Most of his suggestions were enacted, making Mississippi one of the first states to impose a sales tax. Conner's economic policies were effective, and by the time he left office Mississippi had accumulated a treasury surplus.

Under his leadership the legislature combined the three existing college boards and staggered board members' terms. With these reforms, Conner persuaded the various agencies to restore full accreditation for Mississippi's institutions of higher education.

To provide new jobs, Conner recommended a policy of tax incentives to attract new industry to Mississippi. That program, which was a revival of earlier efforts by Gov. Henry James Whitfield, later expanded into the Balance Agriculture with Industry plan.

Four years after leaving office, Conner was appointed to serve as the first commissioner of the Southeastern Conference, a position he held until his death on 16 September 1950.

David G. Sansing
University of Mississippi

Roger Biles, *The South and the New Deal* (2006); *Jackson Daily News* (17 September 1950); *Mississippi Official and Statistical Register* (1924–28).

Constitution of 1817

The framers of Mississippi's first charter of governance modeled the document on the content and style of the frontier constitutions of sister states Tennessee and Kentucky. As a result, the six articles of this statehood constitution contained rather standard features for its time, such as a functional division of power into separate legislative, executive, and judicial departments; a declaration of civil liberties; and nominal recognition of popular sovereignty.

Jefferson Military Academy in the town of Washington, Mississippi, hosted the summer convention of aristocratic delegates, mostly attorneys and landowners, drawn from the sparsely settled fourteen counties in the southernmost part of what would become the state. A representational imbalance gave a disproportionate advantage to the wealthy conservatives from the western Mississippi River counties, much to the dismay of the more liberal delegates from the eastern Piney Woods region. Territorial governor David Holmes presided.

Legislative representation and the right to vote were the pivotal issues facing the convention. On the first matter, compromise produced at least one seat per county in the General Assembly as well as extra seats for populous towns. The convention adopted a formula for apportionment based on the population of white male property owners in voting districts. Mississippi became the last admitted state to require real property holdings as preconditions for holding legislative office. Under this document, candidates for the State Senate, who would serve three-year terms, had to prove land assets of 800 acres, while candidates for the House, who would serve one-year terms, had to own 150 acres. Mississippi was also the last state to place restrictions on the franchise for white males. Along with standard age (twenty-one years) and residency requirements (one year in the state and six months in the county), the convention required either service in the militia or the remittance of a tax before white men could cast their ballots.

A weak executive branch, long a hallmark of Mississippi politics, originated in institutional limitations contained in the 1817 document. The elected governor (two-year renewable term) exercised veto and appointment power but no other substantive authority. Officeholders had to be thirty years of age, US citizens for two years, and Mississippi residents for five years and had to possess six hundred acres of land or property valued at two thousand dollars.

The first judiciary resembled the federal model, both in structure and in selection method. The constitution created a supreme court and such inferior tribunals of law as lawmakers deemed necessary. It further called for appointed judges (a selection method that citizens soon challenged) who served, as did their federal counterparts, during "good behavior."

Miscellaneous provisions included a ban on clergy holding high office, a Jeffersonian-style testament to education as essential to an enlightened citizenry, and—unlike all other states except Kentucky and Georgia—a statement on emancipation. The legislature could liberate slaves whose owners consented or who could prove that they had rendered distinguished service to the state.

Delegates labored through five weeks of summer, and on 15 August they voted forty-five to one in favor of the draft prepared by a special committee chaired by George Poindexter. On 10 December 1817, Mississippi became the twentieth state.

John W. Winkle III
University of Mississippi

Barbara Carpenter, ed., *Understanding Mississippi's Constitutions* (1989); George Etheridge, *Mississippi Constitutions* (1927); *Mississippi Law Journal* (April 1986); John W. Winkle III, *The Mississippi State Constitution: A Reference Guide* (1993).

Constitution of 1832

About eight years after the passage of Mississippi's 1817 constitution, sectional concerns led dissatisfied citizens to begin calling for a new constitutional convention. Voters approved a convention by an overwhelming four-to-one margin in 1831, and forty-eight delegates—again, elite businessmen, lawyers, and doctors, though only five men had participated in the earlier convention—assembled in Jackson in September 1832. Rutilius Pray presided.

Three issues topped the agenda. The first two, land expansion and a permanent location for the state capital, generated little discussion, much less controversy. Delegates first disposed of vast new properties acquired through agreements with the Choctaw (Treaty of Doak's Stand in 1820 and Treaty of Dancing Rabbit Creek in 1830) and the Chickasaw (Treaty of Pontotoc in 1832) before selecting Jackson as the permanent capital. But the third issue, the method of selection for judges, splintered the assembly into three distinct camps. The more conservative element, labeled "aristocrats" by delegate Stephen Duncan, preferred to continue having

judges appointed. The "half-hogs" promoted a mixed system, with appointment of appellate judges and election of the trial bench. The "whole-hogs" endorsed the changeover to a fully elected judiciary. The convention eventually settled on the third option, making Mississippi the first state to elect its judges.

The convention approved modest alterations in the organization of state institutions and in the service of officeholders. Minimum ages for lawmakers as well as their tenure changed. On the House side, delegates lowered the age threshold to twenty-one and increased the term of office to two years; eligibility for the Senate was raised to age thirty, while terms were increased to four years. The executive branch fared less well, losing the gubernatorial power to appoint judges and the post of lieutenant governor, and the right to unlimited succession. The assembly also restructured and detailed the judicial subsystem by creating a dual system of trial courts—circuit and chancery (divided along the lines of subject-matter jurisdiction)—which became overseen by the new High Court of Errors and Appeals.

The 1832 assembly championed participatory democracy, though it is unclear whether identifiable Jacksonian impulses inspired its delegates. The convention eliminated property ownership as a qualification for public office and no longer required militia service or tax payment as a criterion for service in the legislature. In addition, legislative apportionment was based on the total number of free white residents. The document also banned the sale of slaves as merchandise and gave Native Americans in the state the same rights as whites.

On 26 October, two months after the opening gavel, the convention approved the new constitution by a vote of thirty-six to ten. Despite the national democratic culture and the document's participatory features, it was never submitted to the people for ratification, though it remained in force until Mississippi seceded from the United States in 1861.

John W. Winkle III
University of Mississippi

Barbara Carpenter, ed., *Understanding Mississippi's Constitutions* (1989); George Etheridge, *Mississippi Constitutions* (1927); *Mississippi Law Journal* (April 1986); John W. Winkle III, *The Mississippi State Constitution: A Reference Guide* (1993).

Constitution of 1868

Mississippi's third constitution arose in the context of federally imposed martial law during Reconstruction. National officials created five provisional military districts to govern the ten states (other than Tennessee, where reforms had already taken place) of the former Confederacy until they enacted constitutional reform. Mississippi citizens, including former slaves, passed an 1867 referendum approving a convention.

The following January, the "black and tan" assembly, as opponents labeled it because of the predominance of African American and "disloyal" white delegates, opened in Jackson. By all accounts, it was a passionate and divisive gathering that featured bitter controversy and impulsive resignations. The convention ended in May, having approved a document that would be submitted to the people for ratification, the only time in the state's history that such a vote would be held. Mississippians rejected the draft constitution by a vote of 63,860 to 56,231, the only former Confederate state to fail to ratify its new constitution. White supremacist and Democratic opposition, instability among radical and moderate Republicans, and objections to a proposed bill of attainder in the document doomed its passage. The bill of attainder provision would have barred from public office any citizen, military officer, legislator, or convention delegate who had served or sympathized with the Confederate cause.

Undaunted, Pres. Ulysses S. Grant decreed that the constitution would appear on the ballot for the upcoming November general election. This time, however, voters would weigh in not on the document in its entirety but on each individual article: all were approved except for the section that restricted public service. The 1868 constitution not only abolished slavery but also extended an array of civil liberties to all citizens, including limited property rights for women. Seats in the legislature were apportioned based on the number of eligible voters in districts. The document also established free public education throughout Mississippi, though that issue later became entangled in the unremitting racial tension wrought by white supremacy. The lieutenant governorship was restored with a four-year term that matched the governor's, and the governor regained the power to appoint judges. Ratification facilitated Mississippi's return to the Union in early 1870, the first former Confederate state to do so.

John W. Winkle III
University of Mississippi

Barbara Carpenter, ed., *Understanding Mississippi's Constitutions* (1989); George Etheridge, *Mississippi Constitutions* (1927); *Mississippi Law Journal* (April 1986); John W. Winkle III, *The Mississippi State Constitution: A Reference Guide* (1993).

Constitution of 1890

The Mississippi Constitution of 1890, the state's fourth basic document, capped a turbulent century of legal and political change. Situated squarely in the context of state party politics, the charter reflected post-Reconstruction activists' goal of restoring white supremacy in the state. Democrats, who in 1875 had used fraud and intimidation to wrest control of state government from retreating Republicans, split into two factions, the Bourbons and the Rednecks. The two groups agreed on the goal of minimizing political participation by black citizens, who outnumbered whites in thirty-nine of the state's seventy-five counties, but disagreed on the preferred legal means for doing so. The Bourbons, most of them Delta plantation owners, supported formal voting limitations via educational and property ownership qualifications and poll taxes. In contrast, the Rednecks, who included more numerous poor residents from the hill regions, objected to such strategies, which would have disenfranchised poor whites as well as blacks, and sought instead to apportion legislative seats based solely on white population counts.

The Democratic factions remained at odds until early 1890, when Mississippi officials, alarmed by the possibility that Congress would pass a bill authorizing federal supervision of state and local elections, acted. Gov. John Stone approved a legislative call for an August constitutional convention. While more occupationally diverse than its predecessors, the 1890 assembly broke fundamentally along the divides of partisanship and race, with Democrats holding 134 of the 137 seats. Among the Republicans was the lone black delegate, Isaiah T. Montgomery.

For ten weeks delegates pursued the Bourbon-Redneck agenda and constructed barriers to full black participation in Mississippi governance. Like other conservative southern constitutions of the time, Mississippi's 1890 document prescribed common voting qualifications but added a cumulative poll tax and a literacy test. No citizen could vote without paying two dollars and showing valid receipts for the previous two elections. Nor could one vote without interpreting a passage from the state constitution, chosen at the discretion of a polling registrar. For statewide elections, delegates also instituted a new "county unit system" that assigned one electoral vote to the winner of the county popular vote. Much like the national Electoral College, aggregated unit votes determined the victor. The convention also fashioned a complex legislative reapportionment scheme, including floater delegates and three geographic zones, as a fail-safe in case federal courts struck down the suffrage restrictions.

The 1890 constitution also featured institutional changes that shaped Mississippi's governance for much of the twentieth century. Delegates authorized the legislature to levy taxes and to regulate private corporations. Bourbons instituted a mandatory committee system to review all proposed legislation, a tactic that worked in their political favor for decades. The office of the governor both won and lost, keeping the authority to appoint judges and gaining partial veto power over revenue bills but losing the privilege of succession. All told the document contained 15 articles and 285 sections.

The convention approved the 1890 constitution by a 129–8 vote. Neither Bourbons nor Rednecks claimed an ideological victory except in their joint efforts to reinstate white supremacy.

The *Jackson Clarion-Ledger* offered one hundred dollars in gold to anyone who truly understood the lengthy and complex document. No one has ever claimed the reward.

John W. Winkle III
University of Mississippi

Barbara Carpenter, ed., *Understanding Mississippi's Constitutions* (1989); George Etheridge, *Mississippi Constitutions* (1927); *Mississippi Law Journal* (April 1986); John W. Winkle III, *The Mississippi State Constitution: A Reference Guide* (1993).

Constitutional Development since 1890

Mississippi still operates under a constitution adopted more than 125 years ago. Unlike the nineteenth century, when Mississippians preferred holistic political reform at almost generational intervals, citizens and their elected representatives subsequently have opted for piecemeal change. Like many states, Mississippi has come to prefer amendments as the primary agents of constitutional change. Approximately 150 amendments have come before the electorate, and about 80 percent have been approved. More than 60 amendments have become law in the past third of a century alone.

A few patterns of change have emerged. The dynamic generally involves repeal rather than regeneration, as voters have used amendments to correct the errors of the past rather than to innovate. Several amendments, for example, have redressed Mississippi's legacy of racism. The framers of the 1890 constitution had intended the document to restore white supremacy, and it did so for nearly three-quarters of a century. Since the 1960s, however, voters have repealed key impediments to the full participation by blacks in the public life of the state. Literacy tests and poll taxes fell by the wayside in 1975, followed by segregated schools in 1978 and mixed-race marriages nine years later. These changes came years and sometimes decades after Congress or the

US Supreme Court had already invalidated these practices; thus, the amendments merely amounted to housekeeping. Another set of amendments repealed an array of restrictions on corporations, mainly railroads, in keeping with ongoing impulses to create a more favorable climate for economic growth and industry. A third group of measures has removed outdated provisions, such as one providing pensions for widows of Confederate veterans. Despite these efforts, however, Mississippi's constitution still contains many archaic provisions.

A few amendments have introduced new practices or institutions, particularly regarding the operations of the judicial branch. Dissatisfied with having the governor responsible for appointing judges, voters in the early twentieth century approved the election of the trial and appellate bench, and in 1995 the state moved to nonpartisan campaigns and ballots. In 1979 the electorate approved the creation of the Commission on Judicial Performance, now an active and well-respected entity that investigates charges of misconduct against sitting judges.

Some Mississippians, however, continue to argue that a comprehensive overhaul would be preferable to incremental constitutional reform. State officials, citizens, and outside observers have at various times called for constitutional conventions, and in the 1980s Gov. William Allain appointed a special study commission to consider wholesale revision. The group prepared and circulated a draft of a proposed new constitution designed to cure the inadequacies of the current document. Included in this streamlined version (thirteen articles and fifty-five sections) were new clauses on equal protection, civil rights, and an initiative procedure. None of these more drastic efforts has yet succeeded, but modernization of the 1890 constitution, whether piece by piece or wholesale, will certainly continue.

John W. Winkle III
University of Mississippi

Barbara Carpenter, ed., *Understanding Mississippi's Constitutions* (1989); George Etheridge, *Mississippi Constitutions* (1927); *Mississippi Law Journal* (April 1986); John W. Winkle III, *The Mississippi State Constitution: A Reference Guide* (1993).

Contemporary Issues

The problems that have long troubled Mississippi seem clear—high poverty rates, jobs that pay less than most American jobs, racial division and distrust, and limited government services, especially in education. While some of these problems have abated and others continue, new and renewed challenges have also arisen. Mississippi's small towns and cities have seen an influx of legal and illegal immigrants from South and Central America. These migrant communities, which exist largely in areas where poultry plants and construction jobs dominate, have created Spanish-language churches, grocery stores, and restaurants. Whole neighborhoods, some populated with aging parents whose children left their hometown communities three decades ago or more, are now inundated with Spanish-speakers, creating cultural clashes even though most of the new arrivals rise early, work hard, and build institutions. Mississippi is fast becoming one of the most culturally diverse states in the Deep South, with Latino, Asian, Native American, African American, and Anglo-American populations. This diversity presents both challenges and opportunities in areas such as the arts, health care, housing, public education, and crime.

New residents are adding stress to the state's already strained health care system. Mississippians face many chronic illnesses, and in many instances, available health care options are poor, particularly for people who lack insurance. Diseases that pose particular problems in Mississippi include diabetes, obesity, hypertension and heart disease, and childhood maladies such as autism and asthma.

In addition, many Mississippians have access only to very poor housing stock. Latinos in particular frequently must live in worn trailers or in houses without electricity and/or indoor bathrooms. Allegations of employer exploitation are also rampant in Latino communities. The new poor and the strivers among them are competing in an economy that has not generated enough well-paying jobs, especially for the unskilled or underskilled.

Child poverty is an integral part of the story for both Mississippi's old and new poor. In 2014, 33.7 percent of Mississippi's children were classified as impoverished, the highest rate in the country. And among African Americans and Hispanics, those rates are even higher—50 percent and 45 percent, respectively, in 2013. Moreover, as in much of the nation, inequality in Mississippi is increasing and with it disparities in public educational and health access and unequal educational learning and health outcomes.

Many of today's college attendees remain underprepared for the rigors of postsecondary education. That lack of preparation begins early in life and persists unless stringent reading programs and family support and discipline work in tandem with competent public school teachers. Mississippi has made some gains in the area of high school dropout rates. Whereas only 63.8 percent of students graduated on time at the end of the 2009–10 school year (the third-lowest rate in the country), that number had risen to 75.0 percent by 2011–12 (ranking the state thirty-seventh in the nation). Nevertheless, much room for improvement remains. In 2013 79 percent of Mississippi's fourth-graders enrolled in public schools were unable to read at grade level, and 74 percent measured below

grade level at math. And once again, those numbers were generally higher for African American children (89 percent for both reading and math) and Hispanic children (84 percent for reading, 73 percent for math). The state faces a persistent challenge in ensuring that children from materially impoverished families receive not only a sound education but also the benefits that can and should come from such an education.

Many of Mississippi's institutions of higher education, particularly the historically black colleges and universities (HBCUs), admit a sizable percentage of intelligent students who do not perform well on standardized tests and who have not mastered their high school curricula. In many cases, however, the schools lack the need-based scholarship funds that would allow students to immerse themselves in their studies and benefit from experiential opportunities such as study abroad and service learning. Consequently, these opportunities are not available to the students who most need them. In addition, many of these students must work while attending college, further complicating their efforts to obtain a quality education. Moreover, as the state's white colleges and universities have opened their doors to African Americans, competition for talented African American students has increased. In 2001, after twenty-five years of litigation, the state reached a settlement in a class-action lawsuit initiated by Jake Ayers over the inferior education offered at the state's three HBCUs. The state agreed to spend five hundred million dollars to improve the resources and opportunities available to students choosing to attend Mississippi's HBCUs. While some improvements have been recorded, overall state appropriations for higher education have declined, increasing the need for colleges and universities to secure external funds. Both greater scrutiny of the use of scarce resources and higher levels of resource allocation are needed to ensure the integrity of all of Mississippi's institutions of higher education—HBCUs, other four-year colleges, and community/junior colleges.

States cannot be great laboratories for democracy unless all residents are encouraged and helped to prepare themselves for robust citizenship. Reading and thinking are prerequisites for personal and collective decision making that will lead to a healthy and prosperous future. Schools, colleges, universities, parents, communities, and the corporate society must remain alert for ways to jointly facilitate promising ideas and ideals.

Competent and accountable legislative, judicial, and executive branches of government contribute immensely to Mississippi's public and civic health. The Mississippi Supreme Court has increasingly come under public and attorney scrutiny over questions of transparency and suspicions engendered by the court's recent tendency to rule against plaintiff claims.

The legislature and governor have locked horns over how to fund a responsible health care program and how best to fund the public education system. State as well as local government agencies often suffer from low levels of funding and sometimes face questions about their racial fairness. In addition, these layers of government must continue to grapple with the challenge of making cooperative federalism work in the areas of national security, responses to disaster, and protecting the general welfare of citizens.

Mary Delorse Coleman
Lesley University

Center for American Progress, Half in Ten Campaign website, www.talk poverty.org; Children's Defense Fund website, www.childrensdefense.org; Andrew P. Mullins, *Building Consensus: A History of the Passage of the Mississippi Education Reform Act of 1982* (1992); National Center for Children in Poverty website, www.nccp.org; David G. Sansing, *Making Haste Slowly: The Troubled History of Higher Education in Mississippi* (1990).

Prisoners from Mississippi State Penitentiary work in the fields (Bern and Franke Keating Collection, Department of Archives and Special Collections, J. D. Williams Library, University of Mississippi)

Convict Leasing and Chain Gangs

Bankrupt in the wake of the Civil War and faced with the difficult task of rebuilding and sustaining an infrastructure, Mississippi and other state governments turned to a familiar expedient to fund their penal institutions. In the late 1860s many southern prisons began leasing convicts to plantations and industries bereft of the cheap labor formerly supplied by slaves. As the majority of inmates were African American, this new form of compulsory labor helped to bridge the gap between the Black Codes and Jim Crow as a form of social control that embodied the common racial hierarchies in the South. Likewise, vagrancy laws criminalized the social mobility recently acquired by former slaves and produced a steady supply of bodies for the prison labor system.

Although prisoners in the convict lease system were used for a variety of arduous tasks from railroad construction to cutting timber, inmates in Mississippi worked primarily on large cotton plantations. Edward Richardson, a plantation owner who had lost his fortune in the Civil War, was perhaps the state's greatest beneficiary of prison labor. The first to have a convict contract with the state, officials paid Richardson eighteen thousand dollars a year for "care" of the prisoners. With the added income from the profits of their labor, he eventually regained his wealth, setting an inspiring precedent for the southern business community.

After reaching its acme in the 1880s, the convict leasing era wound down as a consequence of accusations that too many affluent southerners had profited from the system and of moral indignation over the treatment of convicts. Inmates were forced to work dangerous jobs that free laborers refused to take and were subject to wanton physical punishment and severe deprivation, conditions that resulted in high death rates among the prison population. Outrage was further fueled by the fact that the state did not maintain separate facilities or mandate special treatment for children, and many were leased out under the system. Publicity regarding these deplorable realities led to a public outcry that forced Mississippi to abolish convict leasing in 1890, the first state to do so.

Individual counties, however, retained the right to use prison labor, and county-run chain gangs replaced convict labor in the early 1900s. Cuffed together at the ankle in small groups, prisoners were put to work expanding and repairing transportation routes as part of the Good Roads Movement, an urbanization effort aimed at increasing accessibility in the South. Though considered a troubling part of the past today, this use of convicts was generally championed in its time, and supporters, including the US Department of Agriculture, considered it an efficient and progressive way to both build roads and control criminals.

As with the convict lease system, most of the chain gang laborers were African Americans, who were thought to require a generous measure of discipline for proper "rehabilitation." But convicts on county-run chain gangs often slept in cages and were subject to brutal corporal punishment and suffered from a host of debilitating ailments, including malnutrition, heatstroke, frostbite, contagious diseases, and shackle poisoning (infections caused by the constant rubbing of iron against the skin). Work songs helped to sustain morale and increase chances of survival, allowing prisoners to labor in a steady rhythm that could be slowed to protect the infirm or inefficient. As with the convict lease system, mounting public outrage resulted in bans on chain gangs nationwide by the mid-twentieth century.

Mississippi consolidated much of its convict labor force on Parchman Farm, a profitable and self-sustaining penal cotton plantation located on twenty thousand acres in the Yazoo Delta. Parchman was established in 1904 by Gov. James K. Vardaman, a proponent of prison reform who billed himself as a progressive and visionary but who regarded African Americans as mentally inferior and touted a paternalistic brand of racism that envisioned a pacified black population reconciled to subordinate social position.

Kathryn Radishofski
Columbia University

Jaron Browne, *Race, Poverty, and the Environment* (Spring 2010); Alex Lichtenstein, *Journal of Southern History* (February 1993); Matthew J. Mancini, *Journal of Negro History* (October 1978); David M. Oshinsky, *"Worse Than Slavery": Parchman Farm and the Ordeal of Jim Crow Justice* (1996).

Cook, Fannye
(1889–1964) Conservationist

Born in Crystal Springs, Mississippi, in 1889, Francis Addine "Fannye" Cook led a remarkable life of wildlife conservation and public service. Known to her friends and colleagues as "Miss Fannye," she found her calling in the difficult economic times and restrictive social atmosphere of 1920s Mississippi. Cook overcame a perennial shortage of state money and a general resistance to female leadership to help form a statewide game and fish conservation commission, supervise a plant and animal survey of the state, and establish a modern museum of natural science.

After earning her undergraduate degree at the Mississippi University for Women, Cook taught history and English in Wyoming and Panama. She later did graduate work in ornithology at the University of Colorado and at George Washington University and spent some time at the Smithsonian. By 1926 she had returned to Mississippi and begun working to overhaul what she recognized as an ineffective, county-based system of game and fish conservation and law enforcement.

Cook formed the Mississippi Association for the Conservation of Wildlife and used it to lobby politicians, leading citizens, and the general public on the need to reform game laws. Under the association's banner, Cook traveled throughout the state, speaking at garden clubs, civic meetings, and local fairs. She used her personal collections of mammals, birds, and aquatic life to create exhibits that illustrated the diversity of life in the state's various habitats and the need for their protection. In 1932 the legislature finally created the Game and Fish Commission, leading to the development of an organized system of wildlife conservation including state

refuges, restocking programs, licensing procedures, and effective law enforcement.

Joining the commission as a research assistant, Cook wrote bulletins and pamphlets and created more exhibits, particularly for the state fair. Though she was eminently qualified for the position of director of the commission, the times dictated that Cook stay with the educational work deemed suitable for women. In 1935 the Works Progress Administration funded a plant and animal survey sponsored by the Game and Fish Commission. Cook headed the survey, supervising the dozens of workers who collected and preserved thousands of specimens from around the state for a network of local museums, including the state museum, which opened in Jackson in 1939. The survey lasted until 1941, and its collections formed the foundation of the state museum's scientific inventory. As museum director, Cook found a permanent place to pursue her scientific scholarship and educational outreach. She produced reports on the state's mammals, birds, fish, and amphibians, basing her work in part on the survey collections. Researchers still consult her preserved collections and her writings on such topics as snakes and salamanders and fur resources.

Cook retired in 1958. After she died in 1964, the legislature officially designated the Mississippi Museum of Natural Science as the Fannye A. Cook Memorial.

Wiley C. Prewitt Jr.
Yocona, Mississippi

Fannye A. Cook, *Freshwater Fishes in Mississippi* (1959); Fannye A. Cook, *Fur Resources of Mississippi* (1945); B. E. Gandy, *The Mississippi Kite* (1 May 1965); Mississippi Museum of Natural Science website, http://museum.mdwfp.com.

Cooke, Sam
(1931–1964) Soul Singer

Sam Cooke was a gospel and rhythm and blues musician whose distinctive vocal talents defined soul music. He was born on 22 January 1931, in Clarksdale, Mississippi, the fourth child of Rev. Charles Cook and Annie May Cook. According to family legend, Sam was born with musical talent and when he had no audience, he would create one out of the sticks he found in his backyard.

About two years after Sam was born, Charles Cook, a preacher in the Church of Christ (Holiness), moved the family to Chicago, where he became pastor at the Christ Temple Church in Chicago Heights. The eight Cook children grew up in the church, and several of them formed a gospel quintet,

Sam Cooke (Courtesy Blues Archive, Department of Archives and Special Collections, J. D. Williams Library, University of Mississippi)

the Singing Children, to perform there. Sam sang tenor harmony, and though he was only six when the group formed, he often sought the lead. The children traveled frequently with their father, priming revival audiences before his sermons, until the older siblings tired of performing and the group disbanded.

In the spring of 1947 Cooke became one of two lead singers for what would be his first professional gospel quartet, the Highway QCs. His talent proved so impressive that at the age of nineteen he was offered lead vocals for the Soul Stirrers, one of the country's most renowned gospel quartets. While performing with the Soul Stirrers, Cooke developed his singular vocal style, a melismatic bending of notes that has been described as a yodel. Cooke also wrote songs for the group, and the quartet constantly recorded and toured. While the Soul Stirrers remained popular with the gospel music audience, the musical climate was changing. In December 1956, with his father's blessing, Cooke crossed the mythical line between Sunday morning and Saturday night. He recorded his first pop songs under the pseudonym Dale Cook, though few listeners were fooled by the name. Cooke left the Soul Stirrers in April 1957.

Cooke's second pop recording session, which took place on 1 June 1957, produced "You Send Me," the B-side to a rendition of George Gershwin's "Summertime." The single eventually reached No. 1 on both the pop and R&B charts, selling more than one million copies. Cooke had developed a strong business sense and took control of his publishing rights early in his solo career. In 1959 he became the first pop artist to start his own label, SAR Records, where he renewed his affiliation with the Soul Stirrers, producing many of their singles. Cooke was under contract at RCA and

released many popular recordings for that company, including million-sellers "Wonderful World," "Chain Gang," and "Twistin' the Night Away" as well as the mournful, haunting civil-rights-era record "A Change Is Gonna Come."

Cooke was known to be a ladies' man, marrying twice and fathering numerous children out of wedlock. His second wife, Barbara Campbell, was his childhood sweetheart, and after their 1959 marriage, they had three children, the youngest of whom, Vincent, accidentally drowned in June 1963. Less than two years later, on 11 December 1964, Sam Cooke was shot dead in self-defense by the manager of a Los Angeles motel where Cooke had brought a woman during an alleged kidnapping. The circumstances surrounding his death remain a mystery. Cooke's songs are still popular in movies, as recorded by other musicians, and with new generations of music fans.

Molly Boland Thompson
Vanderbilt University

Peter Guralnick, *Dream Boogie: The Triumph of Sam Cooke* (2005); Brian Ward, *Just My Soul Responding: Rhythm and Blues, Black Consciousness, and Race Relations* (1998); Daniel Wolff with S. R. Crain, Clifton White, and G. David Tenenbaum, *You Send Me: The Life and Times of Sam Cooke* (1995).

Cooper, Douglas Hancock

(1815–1879) Confederate General and Indian Agent

Douglas Hancock Cooper was born on 1 November 1815 in Amite County, Mississippi Territory, the son of a Baptist minister and physician. He attended the University of Virginia in 1832–34 but returned to Mississippi without graduating. Cooper married Martha Collins of Natchez and the couple raised seven children on their plantation. He was elected to the state legislature in 1844 and volunteered for service during the Mexican War, where he was commissioned a captain in the 1st Mississippi Rifles, commanded by Jefferson Davis. In 1853 Cooper used his ties to Davis, who had become the US secretary of war, to receive an appointment as US agent to the Choctaw Nation in Indian Territory.

This appointment profoundly shaped Cooper's life. He remained in Indian Territory for the remainder of the antebellum period, and when secession came, the proslavery Cooper sought to gain an alliance with the Five Civilized Tribes on behalf of the Confederacy. He was not entirely successful. Although perhaps thirty-five hundred Cherokee, Chickasaw, Choctaw, Creek, and Seminole Indians fought for the Confederacy, other members of the same tribes remained loyal to the United States. Cooper's recruiting success gained him a commission as colonel of the 1st Choctaw and Chickasaw Mounted Rifles, the only commander of a Confederate Indian unit who was not a Native American. Cooper led his command in several actions in Indian Territory; at Pea Ridge, Arkansas; and at Newtonia, Missouri. He was promoted to brigadier general in May 1863.

Although Cooper fought in a series of small engagements the following summer, he focused primarily on winning the post of commander of the Indian Territory with authority over all the Native American combatants. Cooper had both powerful friends and adversaries, and the latter apparently cited Cooper's fondness for alcohol when they labored to thwart his ambitions. Cooper feuded with Gens. Albert Pike (whom Cooper arrested on grounds of "treason or insanity"), William Steele, and Samuel Maxey. Even after Richmond authorities finally appointed Cooper to head Indian Territory in July 1864, Gen. Edmund Kirby Smith, who had grave doubts about Cooper's abilities, delayed making the change until 21 February 1865.

When the war ended, no Confederate authority notified Cooper, and there is no record of his having been paroled. Cooper remained in Indian Territory, where he helped the Choctaw and Chickasaw sue the federal government for failed promises dating back to the Indian Removals of the 1830s. Cooper died at Old Fort Washita in Oklahoma on 29 April 1879 and is buried in an unmarked grave in the fort cemetery.

Christopher Losson
St. Joseph, Missouri

Anne Bailey, in *The Confederate General*, ed. William C. Davis, vol. 2 (1991); John H. Eicher and David J. Eicher, *Civil War High Commands* (2001); Charles E. Hooker, *Confederate Military History: Mississippi*, ed. Clement A. Evans (1899).

Coordinating Committee for Fundamental American Freedoms

A prosegregation propaganda organization with close links to the Mississippi State Sovereignty Commission (MSSC), the Coordinating Committee for Fundamental American Freedoms (CCFAF) was founded in July 1963 and headquartered at the Carroll Arms Hotel in Washington, D.C. It was established after a month of exploratory talks in the capital between Mississippi senator James O. Eastland, MSSC

director Erle E. Johnston Jr., Yazoo City attorney John C. Satterfield, and the former executive director of the Virginia Commission on Constitutional Government, Hugh V. White Jr. The committee's explicit goal was to raise and coordinate opposition to Pres. John F. Kennedy's pending civil rights bill, but it also represented a broader ideological effort to bridge the gap between Mississippi's segregationists and national conservatives. Attempting to recast the South's sectional battle for continued segregation as part of a broader national conservative movement, the group appointed New England publisher William Loeb as its chair. Virginia newspaperman James J. Kilpatrick served as vice chair, Satterfield held the post of secretary-treasurer, and the founder of Richmond's Patrick Henry Club, John S. Synon, was hired as full-time director.

The committee disseminated reams of propaganda material (1.4 million mailings by April 1964) decrying the civil rights proposals. Notable pamphlets included *The Federal Eye Looking down Your Throat*, *Blueprint for Total Regimentation*, and *Due Process of Law or Government by Intimidation?*, which originated as a speech Satterfield delivered to the Jackson Rotary Club in November 1962. An advertisement headed "$100 Billion Blackjack" appeared in 215 newspapers published outside the South and drew on many of the traditional arguments of southern resistance to desegregation, including claims that the proposed legislation promoted socialist ideas, violated states' rights, and would create a dictatorial and "omnipotent president." Reflecting the committee's desire to rid itself of the taint of southern resistance's sectionalism, it made no clear reference to segregation and promoted the committee as a group based in the nation's capital. CCFAF outspent every other lobby group in the nation in 1964, and that expenditure brought tangible results: New York Republican Kenneth Keating, for example, claimed that the blackjack advertisement swung his mailbag from five to one in favor of the bill to five to two against.

Satterfield, a close aide to Ross Barnett during the University of Mississippi crisis of 1962, former president of the American Bar Association, and according to *Time* magazine the "most prominent segregationist lawyer in the country," was the driving force behind the CCFAF. He was also the closest link between the committee and the MSSC, whose board members agreed to pay him $2,000 per month for the first four months of CCFAF's existence. Indeed, of the $343,191 that CCFAF spent, $262,581 arrived through Sovereignty Commission coffers, and more than $200,000 of that money was donated anonymously by the New York–based racist Wickliffe Preston Draper. Once the 1964 Civil Rights Act passed, Draper offered further financial support for Satterfield's plans to develop CCFAF into a permanent organization studying state sovereignty and civil rights, but newly elected Mississippi governor Paul B. Johnson Jr. ignored Satterfield's schemes. After brief attempts to funnel the emerging "white backlash" into support for George C. Wallace's 1964 presidential campaign, CCFAF dissolved.

George Lewis
University of Leicester

Joseph Crespino, *In Search of Another Country: Mississippi and the Conservative Counterrevolution* (2007); Yasuhiro Katagiri, *The Mississippi State Sovereignty Commission: Civil Rights and States' Rights* (2001); George Lewis, *Massive Resistance: The White Response to the Civil Rights Movement* (2006); Clifford M. Lytle, *Journal of Negro History* (October 1966); James W. Silver, *Mississippi: The Closed Society* (1963).

Copeland, James
(1823–1857) Outlaw

From the late 1830s through the 1850s outlaw James Copeland and his clan terrorized settlers on the frontiers of southern Alabama, Mississippi, and Louisiana. Consequently, a tremendous crowd gathered on the banks of the Leaf River just outside the town of Augusta in Perry County on 30 October 1857 to witness his hanging for murder. Despite the solemnity of the occasion, a carnival-like atmosphere prevailed among the members of the throng, many of whom had traveled considerable distances from nearby counties. Word had spread that Copeland had dictated the details of his ignominious career to sheriff J. R. S. Pitts while awaiting execution. *The Life and Confession of the Noted Outlaw James Copeland* appeared in print the next year and created a furor among the folk of the Piney Woods.

Because of the Copeland gang's infamy, the fear it generated, and the intense interest in the names of his confederates, copies of the first edition soon disappeared. Rumors began to circulate that members of the clan had taken an oath to steal all copies, a myth that persisted in rural South Mississippi as late as the 1970s. Indeed, no copies of the first edition have ever surfaced despite decades of diligent searching by historians, archivists, and booksellers. In 1874 Pitts published a second edition containing a new introduction and an expanded appendix. In 1909 his son, A. S. Pitts, published a third edition, and in 1980 the University Press of Mississippi published a facsimile of the 1909 edition.

Copeland was born in Jackson County on 18 January 1823. His father, a veteran of the War of 1812, settled in the Pascagoula River Valley approximately ten miles from the Alabama line. At age twelve Copeland stole a pocketknife from a neighbor in whose garden he had picked some collard greens. A few years later Copeland was indicted after stealing some pigs from the same neighbor, although the senior Copeland had hired an attorney to represent his son. Fearing the boy's conviction, his mother sought advice from an unsavory character from Mobile, Gale H. Wages, who recommended that the Copelands destroy the evidence by burning the Jackson County Courthouse. They did so. Smitten with the style and swagger of Wages, Copeland followed him to Mobile for initiation into his "clan." While at one time that group bore both their names, it eventually became known simply as the Copeland Clan. As he faced the gallows, Copeland blamed his life of crime on his mother because she had failed to punish him for stealing the pocketknife and had introduced him to Wages.

Though South Alabama and Mississippi remained their favorite haunt, these outlaws roamed and engaged in crime as far east as the Chattahoochee River, as far west as San Antonio, and as far north as the Wabash River. While they specialized in stealing livestock and slaves, their activities encompassed arson, hijacking flatboats, murder, and counterfeiting. One clan member, Charles McGrath, masqueraded as a Methodist preacher, attracting huge crowds to his "revivals" while his confederates robbed worshipers' homes.

Most of the Copeland Clan's crime involved violence, frequently including deadly force, but their favorite technique for stealing slaves was treachery. After gaining the confidence of unsuspecting slaves, sometimes at slave revivals, gang members would promise to lead them to freedom; the slaves would run away, only to be sold at distant slave auctions. In one particularly despicable case, Copeland enticed a slave girl to run away with him, impregnated her, and then sold her at a New Orleans slave market.

The Life and Confession of the Noted Outlaw James Copeland provides a rare window through which one can observe the economic and social lives of the plain folk of the Old Southwest, with frequent references to timber-related industries, religion, narcotics, and, above all, frontier violence.

John D. W. Guice
University of Southern Mississippi

J. R. S. Pitts, *Life and Confession of the Noted Outlaw James Copeland* (1980).

Copiah County

Copiah County is located in central Mississippi, just south of Hinds County. The Pearl River forms its eastern boundary, and several tributaries of Bayou Pierre traverse its northwestern region. Copiah County was established on 21 January 1823 from land ceded to the United States by the Choctaw Tribe and takes its name from a Choctaw word meaning "calling panther." Hazlehurst, Copiah's county seat, was named for local railroad engineer George Hazlehurst. Other sizable towns include Crystal Springs and Wesson. In the late nineteenth century the mineral springs at Brown Wells attracted visitors seeking its reputed medicinal benefits, and Lake Chautauqua was a popular recreational and religious destination in Copiah.

In 1830 Copiah County had far more free people (5,247) than slaves (1,754). By 1860, however, the county's 7,965 slaves slightly outnumbered the free population of 7,433. Twenty years later, Copiah County's population had grown dramatically to 27,552, making it one of the larger counties in the state. African Americans continued to outnumber whites by a small margin, and most of the county's population lived on farms.

Both railroad construction and the rise of manufacturing in the county contributed to Copiah's increasing prosperity after the Civil War, an unusual combination for Mississippi. Industrialist James Wesson established a mill village, with several large and impressive buildings, in an attempt to re-create his earlier successes in Bankston and in his native state of Georgia. In 1880 Copiah County firms had more than one million dollars invested in manufacturing, by far the largest such investment in any Mississippi county and almost a quarter of the state's total industrial assets. The county's 659 nonagricultural workers also topped the state, and its 232 women employed in manufacturing comprised more than half of the state's female industrial workforce.

Copiah's population continued to grow in the early twentieth century, exceeding thirty-four thousand in 1900, and the county remained central to the state's industrial economy. Its 137 industrial establishments and 1,287 industrial workers (roughly half of them women and children) ranked among the highest in Mississippi. Nevertheless, most of Copiah's citizens worked on farms. The distinction between the county's white and black farmers was clear: 61 percent of white farmers owned their land, compared to 18 percent of African American farmers.

Like many parts of Mississippi, Copiah was a Baptist county. In 1916 more than 9,000 of the county's 13,800 church members identified as congregants of either the Southern Baptist Convention or the Missionary Baptists. Other denominations with significant membership included the Methodists and Presbyterians. Hazlehurst was the home of W. S. Pleasant, an early leader of the Church of God in Christ.

Blues legend Robert Johnson was born in Copiah County in 1911, although he is frequently more associated with the Mississippi Delta. Tommy Johnson and his blues-playing brothers likewise grew up in Copiah. Susie Powell started several of Mississippi's first canning clubs in Copiah County in 1911.

In 1930, 92 percent of Copiah's African American farmers and 58 percent of white farmers were tenants. The county's population was almost evenly split between white and black residents. Copiah retained its larger-than-average industrial workforce, which was now supported by four canneries, a cottonseed oil mill, and several sawmills.

By 1960 Copiah County's population had decreased to 27,051, with African Americans comprising 52 percent of the total. The number of agricultural laborers subsequently declined by nearly 90 percent, from 2,120 workers in 1960 to 270 in 1980. However, Copiah's economy continued to rely on livestock, and in 1980 the county had the state's fourth-largest cattle population. Copiah also contained a significant amount of commercial forest acreage, and almost half of its manufacturing workforce was involved in lumber or furniture production. Manufacturing, primarily work in textiles, employed the largest number of women.

Celebrated Copiah County natives include civil rights activist A. M. E. Logan, who was born in Myles; artists Mary T. Smith and Luster Willis; and Judge Burnita Shelton Matthews. Jackson-born playwright Beth Henley set her play and movie *Crimes of the Heart* in Hazlehurst. The county is also home to Copiah-Lincoln Junior College, founded in 1928 in Wesson. Copiah is well known as the Tomato Capital of the World, and it holds annual festivities to celebrate this agricultural heritage.

Copiah County's population has increased only slightly since 1960, reaching 29,449 in 2010. African Americans continued to make up slightly more than half the population, and a small Latino/Hispanic minority had emerged.

Mississippi Encyclopedia Staff
University of Mississippi

Copiah County, Mississippi Genealogy and History website, www.copiah.msgenweb.org; Mississippi State Planning Commission, *Progress Report on State Planning in Mississippi* (1938); *Mississippi Statistical Abstract*, Mississippi State University (1952–2010); Charles Sydnor and Claude Bennett, *Mississippi History* (1939); University of Virginia Library, Historical Census Browser website, http://mapserver.lib.virginia.edu; E. Nolan Waller and Dani A. Smith, *Growth Profiles of Mississippi's Counties, 1960–1980* (1985).

Cora, Cat

(b. 1968) Chef

Jackson native Catherine "Cat" Cora is a popular chef who has worked in television, written cookbooks, and opened restaurants in California, Florida, and Singapore. *Cat Cora's Kitchen: Favorite Meals for Family and Friends*, the first of

Cat Cora

her three books cowritten with Ann Krueger Spivack, begins by saying that kitchens introduce chefs to a life of cooking. The first kitchen in Cora's life "was my parents' kitchen in Jackson, Mississippi, and the second was the kitchen of my aunt Demetra and uncle Yiorgios on Skopelos, one of the Aegean Islands in Greece."

Cora attended the University of Southern Mississippi before moving to New York to study at the Culinary Institute of America. She then worked at restaurants in France and New York before moving to Northern California. *Cat Cora's Kitchen*, published in 2004, begins with meals she learned during her Mississippi youth, moves to meals rooted in her Greek family background, and ends with meals from her California home and restaurants. *Cooking from the Hip* (2007) offers instructions for meals that are fast and "phenomenal," with emphasis on the pleasure of cooking and eating as a group. Her 2010 book, *Classics with a Twist*, reads more like a traditional cookbook, with instructions divided into categories for appetizers, side dishes, main dishes, and desserts.

Cora often describes southern cooking in terms of its parallels with cooking and eating in other parts of the world. A pork dish comes from "my close-to-home and around-the-world menu." "Greens, too," she claims, "conjure up images of the South, but this recipe comes to Jackson via Skopelos." And lemon-roasted chicken with beans and potatoes, a meal she learned to make in Jackson, can be found in different combinations "in New York and California, Europe and South America, and just about every place in between." With such a broad approach, Cora has situated southern food as part of a wide range of influences and possibilities.

Cora is best known for serving modern meals with Greek and more broadly Mediterranean influences. Cora provides memorable details about growing up Greek in Mississippi. She describes Jackson's Elite restaurant and its owners, Pete and Jimmy Zouboukos, as well as Celebration Sundays in Greek American church halls.

Since 1999 Cora has appeared as a chef or host on several television shows, including *Melting Pot*, *Kitchen Accomplished*, *Celebrity Cooking Showdown*, *Date Plate*, *Simplify Your Life*, *My Country, My Kitchen: Greece*, and *Around the World in 80 Plates*. Her skills generated special attention when in 2005 she became the first—and to date only—woman named an Iron Chef on *Iron Chef America*, a Food Network adaptation of a Japanese show in which prominent chefs compete using various cooking styles and ingredients. Cora has won more than twenty competitions on *Iron Chef America*.

In response to the 2004 Indian Ocean tsunami, Cora started Chefs for Humanity, and she remains the group's president. The organization provides food relief to people in disasters, addresses hunger issues, and assists with nutrition education, and Cora has traveled throughout the world to publicize and work to find solutions for hunger and its causes. In 2012 she was elected to the American Academy of Chefs Culinary Hall of Fame.

Cat Cora is married to Jennifer Cora, and they have four children.

Ted Ownby
University of Mississippi

Chefs for Humanity website, www.chefsforhumanity.org; Cat Cora official website, www.catcora.com; Culinary Hall of Fame website, www.culinaryhalloffame.com.

Corinth, Battle of

Corinth, a town and important rail junction in Northeast Mississippi, was the scene of much military activity during the Civil War, including a siege in the spring of 1862 following the Battle of Shiloh and a bloody battle in October of the same year. The latter engagement resulted in more than seven thousand casualties and a Confederate repulse, leaving northern Mississippi largely in Union hands.

The Mobile and Ohio and the Memphis and Charleston Railroads, which intersected at Corinth, were constructed during the 1850s. The rail lines made the small town a strategic location during the opening years of the Civil War. After Shiloh, Confederate forces under P. G. T. Beauregard defended Corinth against the slow-moving Union forces of Henry W. Halleck, who eventually occupied the town in late May 1862.

In the fall of 1862 Corinth again became the target of military operations as the Confederacy launched a strike into Northeast Mississippi as part of a larger offensive that also included Robert E. Lee's invasion of Maryland and Braxton Bragg's and Edmund Kirby Smith's movement into Kentucky. In Mississippi, small southern armies under

Battle of Corinth, 3–4 October 1862, lithograph ca. 1891 (Kurz and Allison, Library of Congress, Washington, D.C. [LC-DIG-pga-01847])

Sterling Price and Earl Van Dorn focused first on Iuka and ultimately Corinth. On 14 September, Price's Army of the West, in an effort to prevent Union troops from reinforcing those opposing Bragg in Tennessee, occupied Iuka, which had been evacuated by Federal forces under William S. Rosecrans. Ulysses S. Grant quickly ordered Rosecrans and Edward Ord to retake the town and drive off Price. On 19 September a spirited engagement between Rosecrans and Price took place near Iuka, after which Price withdrew from the town.

In the aftermath of the fighting at Iuka, Price met with Earl Van Dorn, commander of a separate small Confederate force operating in northern Mississippi, and discussed a joint attack on either Bolivar, Tennessee, or Corinth. The two generals settled on Corinth, believing that Rosecrans, who had moved his forces to that location, was vulnerable to attack. The Confederates would make a feint against Bolivar before moving their combined force of twenty-two thousand, commanded by Van Dorn and now called the Army of West Tennessee, against Corinth. Rosecrans strengthened three lines of inner and outer defensive works, one of which had been constructed by Confederate troops during their earlier defense of the town.

This outer line, known as the Beauregard Line, was located about 2.5 miles north of the town, while a shorter group of artillery positions called the Halleck Line had been erected 1 mile closer to Corinth. Finally, the Federals constructed the College Hill Line of five artillery batteries and supporting earthworks closest to the town. The Union general positioned his twenty-three-thousand-man force, organized into four divisions, under generals Thomas McKean, Thomas Davies, Charles Hamilton, and David Stanley. On 29–30 September Van Dorn's forces moved northward from Ripley toward Pocahontas, Tennessee; they then turned eastward to Chewalla before marching southeast toward Corinth. On the morning of 3 October they launched their initial assault against the town's outer defenses.

One of Van Dorn's divisions, commanded by Mansfield Lovell, took its position on the Confederate right, while Price's forces under Dabney Maury and Louis Hebert occupied the left. During the first day's fighting the Federals conducted a fighting withdrawal southward toward Corinth and the protection of the College Hill Line. In particular, Davies's division inflicted heavy casualties on the attackers, though the Rebels ultimately captured the Union position at the White House. By late afternoon the Southern forces were threatening the last Union line, but Van Dorn and Price delayed a final assault until the following morning.

Before dawn on 4 October, Confederate artillery began bombarding the Union-held town, with Federal cannons soon responding. The Confederate left, now commanded by Gen. Martin Green after Hebert had gone down with an illness, assaulted and captured Battery Powell, driving the exhausted Union defenders back into the streets of Corinth, with heavy fighting taking place near the railroad junction and the Tishomingo Hotel. Despite being reinforced by a brigade from Maury's division, Green's troops eventually fell victim to Union infantry and artillery fire and withdrew. While the defenders fought to stop Green's advance, they also faced an assault by the remainder of Maury's division, which focused on Battery Robinett, one of the main positions of the College Hill Line held by Union troops under Stanley. Despite heavy musket and artillery fire, elements of John Moore's Confederate Brigade, especially the 42nd Alabama, the 35th Mississippi, and the 2nd Texas, managed to reach the battery and briefly occupy part of it until a counterattack killed or captured most of those Confederates who had advanced that far. Col. William P. Rogers of the 2nd Texas fell dead while leading a small group of his men in the vanguard of the attack. The failure to hold Robinett ended the major fighting, and Van Dorn quickly determined to withdraw. Lovell's division, which had not become engaged in the second day's fighting, covered the Confederate retreat. Southern casualties in the two-day battle numbered 4,838, including 505 killed. The Federals had 2,520 casualties, including 355 dead.

In the battle's aftermath, Grant, the area commander, moved to consolidate various forces in an unsuccessful effort to pursue Van Dorn's defeated army. Van Dorn was relieved of his command and replaced by John C. Pemberton. Criticism of Van Dorn's leadership during the campaign led him to ask for a court of inquiry, which eventually found him innocent of all charges. Corinth remained in Union hands for the rest of the war, though the region was the scene of a number of skirmishes and other military activity.

David J. Coles
Longwood College

Monroe F. Cockrell, *The Lost Account of the Battle of Corinth and the Court Martial of Gen. Van Dorn* (2003); Peter Cozzens, *The Darkest Days of the War: The Battles of Iuka and Corinth* (1997); Earl J. Hess, *Banners to the Breeze: The Kentucky Campaign, Corinth, and Stones River* (2000).

Corn

Corn, though never closely identified with Mississippi, has played an important role throughout the state's history, first as the crop crucial to Choctaw and Chickasaw agriculture and religious ritual, then as part of nineteenth-century southerners' efforts to feed themselves, and more recently as a major cash crop in the twentieth and twenty-first centuries. Mississippi has never been one of the nation's leading producers of corn—in 2013 it ranked seventeenth in the nation—but the crop's varied history shows how agriculture has changed over the years. Corn was a central feature of Native American life in Mississippi, and it set the stage for a diet and economy in which grits and cornbread have played major parts for generations. The issue of how to prepare corn—with beans, as hoecake, as grits, on the cob, as moonshine, and eventually in other products—became central to southern foodways.

Historians have long discussed corn and hogs as the key to yeoman farmers' efforts to pursue household independence and, perhaps at least for men, some degree of leisure. It would be incorrect to suggest that small farmers produced corn and other subsistence crops and large plantations produced cotton and other cash crops. Mississippi's plantation counties produced large amounts of corn in addition to their primary cotton crop; however, many smaller farming areas, especially those in the northern part of the state, produced far more corn than cotton.

Slaves also produced substantial quantities of corn, but the experience of work in corn differed in significant ways for free people and slaves. Both enslaved people and landowning farmers produced corn in part to feed themselves and in part to feed livestock. Farm families celebrated successful corn harvests with community or multifamily corn-shucking parties that ran late into the night. For slaves, pulling leaves for fodder to be used for livestock, as historian John Hebron Moore writes, "was regarded as especially unpleasant, as it was performed in periods of high temperatures and humidity, and slaveowners believed that fodder pulling imperiled the health of slaves more than any other regular summer labor."

Corn production declined dramatically after the Civil War as landowners focused even more strongly on cotton and its greater financial rewards. Mississippi's corn production fell from a record high of more than twenty-nine million bushels in 1860 to just fifteen million bushels in 1870 and remained there for the rest of the decade. Historians debate the relative importance of market forces and of efforts to control land and labor in the growth of cotton production, but people who were in debt and/or working as tenants and sharecroppers clearly grew the state's leading cash crop at the expense of corn and other subsistence crops. By 1900, however, corn production had begun a resurgence, with farm owners growing far more corn than did tenants. In that year, according to the agricultural census, farm owners grew an average of 281 bushels of corn per farm, while renters averaged 213 bushels of corn and sharecroppers just 178 bushels. Many farmers and the state government continued to discuss corn as part of traditional farm life. In the early twentieth century, for example, Mississippi leaders sought to encourage farmers to stay on the land through strategies that included the creation of Corn Clubs, which sought to teach schoolboys not only how to generate high yields but also the language of household independence.

In the mid- and late twentieth century, corn became a crop for large-scale commercial agriculture, farmed with large-scale technology and government support. As corn became part of all sorts of popular consumer products during and after World War II, it changed from a crop produced by smaller farmers throughout the state to a commercial crop produced primarily in certain areas. In the twenty-first century most of the state's corn is grown in the Mississippi Delta, with Washington and Leflore Counties as the leading corn producers, followed by Bolivar, Sunflower, Tallahatchie, and Sharkey. Corn is also grown in the prairie counties and to a lesser degree other parts of the northern half of the state, but relatively few farmers grow corn south of Hinds County. Mississippi's corn production increased dramatically beginning in the 1990s and by the second decade of the twenty-first century approached one hundred million bushels per year.

Ted Ownby
University of Mississippi

Corn, Washington County, June 1937 (Photograph by Dorothea Lange, Library of Congress, Washington, D.C. [LC-USF34-017065-C])

Betty Fussell, *The Story of Corn: The Myths and History, the Culture and Agriculture, the Art and Science of America's Quintessential Crop* (1994); Thomas L. Gregory and Fred L. Shore, *Mississippi Cotton and Corn*

Statistics (2009); Sam Bowers Hilliard, *Hog Meat and Hoecake: Food Supply in the Old South, 1840–1860* (1972); Mississippi State University, MSU Cares website, http://msuccares.com; Mississippi State University, Division of Agriculture, Forestry, and Veterinary Medicine, *Mississippi Agriculture, Forestry, and Natural Resources Factbook* (2012); Frederick Douglas Opie, *Hog and Hominy: Soul Food from Africa to America* (2010); US Agricultural Census (1860).

Cotton, James "Superharp"

(b. 1935) Blues Musician

James "Superharp" Cotton is one of the most influential postwar blues harmonica players. During his sixty-five-year career he has recorded and performed with blues legends Sonny Boy Williamson II, Howlin' Wolf, and Muddy Waters, among others. He became a star in his own right as a bandleader in the 1970s and has worked with blues-based rock and roll musicians such as Paul Butterfield, Mike Bloomfield, and Carlos Santana.

Cotton was born on 1 July 1935 near Tunica. He first learned how to make his harmonica sound like a train and a cackling hen by imitating his mother's playing on her harmonica. As a young boy, Cotton was inspired by Sonny Boy Williamson II's harmonica playing, which he heard on the *King Biscuit Time* radio show on KFFA in Helena, Arkansas. By the time Cotton was nine, his uncle took him to Helena to meet Williamson, who was so impressed that he invited the boy to move into his home and study under him for the next six years.

In 1950 Cotton and Williamson moved north to West Memphis, Arkansas. He began playing shows with area musicians Joe Willie Wilkins and Willie Nix. In 1952, following in Williamson's footsteps, Cotton received his own radio show on KWEM. As his reputation grew, Cotton met Howlin' Wolf, who enlisted the teenager to sit in on gigs around the Memphis area as well as on early Wolf recordings with Sam Phillips at Sun Studio. Cotton recorded two singles at Sun, 1953's "Straighten Up, Baby," on which he played drums instead of harmonica, and "Cotton Crop Blues" the next year.

Cotton first met Muddy Waters later in 1954 while driving a gravel truck in West Memphis. Waters hired Cotton to replace harmonica player Junior Wells, who had abandoned Muddy's band in midtour. After Cotton finished the tour, he moved to Chicago and rented a room in Waters's house. While Cotton became a regular in Waters's band at gigs, Chess Records insisted that Little Walter play on most of Waters's recordings until 1958. Cotton's first studio recording with Waters was "All Aboard." The track called for two harmonicas, and Cotton provided the train sounds. Later that year, Cotton also played on recordings of "She's Nineteen Years Old" and "Close to You." Cotton also urged Waters to record what would become one of the bluesman's signature tracks, "Got My Mojo Working," and Cotton played on the tune's definitive recording at the 1960 Newport Jazz Festival. Cotton stayed with Waters until 1966 and eventually became his bandleader. During the mid-1960s Cotton served as a bridge between blues musicians and the burgeoning folk community.

In 1966 the James Cotton Blues Band set out on its first tour. The first gig was recorded and released in 1998 as *Late Night Blues* on Justin Time Records. Cotton's first full-length record was released in 1967 on Verve Records, and he soon recorded for Sam Charters on the Vanguard label's *Chicago/The Blues/Today* series. At this time Cotton's band included guitarist Luther Tucker and drummer Sam Lay. The James Cotton Blues Band released four more albums in the late 1960s and opened for Janis Joplin on two tours. In the 1970s Cotton's profile rose as a crossover artist. He continued to play for both rock and blues audiences and signed a managing contract with Albert Grossman, who also managed Bob Dylan. In 1974 Cotton released *100% Cotton*; subsequent records were produced by Todd Rundgren, Mike Bloomfield, and Allen Toussaint. Cotton was reunited with Waters on his 1977 comeback album, *Hard Again*, produced by Johnny Winter. The album won a Grammy, and Cotton joined Waters on a successful world tour.

Cotton was nominated for solo Grammy Awards for 1984's *Live from Chicago: Mr. Superharp Himself*, 1987's *Take Me Back*, and 1988's *James Cotton Live*. Recovering from a bout of throat cancer in 1994, Cotton won his first solo Grammy with 1996's *Deep in the Blues*, released on Verve. During the late 1990s Cotton and his band toured the United States, Canada, Europe, Japan, and South America. He continues to record and released the Grammy-nominated *Giant* in 2010, *Cotton Mouth Man* (2013), and *The Alligator Years* (2014).

Cale Nicholson
Little Rock, Arkansas

Vladimir Bogdanov, Chris Woodstra, and Stephen Thomas Erlewine, eds., *All Music Guide to the Blues: The Definitive Guide to the Blues* (2003); James Cotton website, jamescottonsuperharp.com; Robert Gordon, *Can't Be Satisfied: The Life and Times of Muddy Waters* (2002); Edward Komara, ed., *Encyclopedia of the Blues*, vol. 1 (2006); Helen Doob Lazar, *Living Blues* (August 1987); Sandra Tooze, *Muddy Waters: The Mojo Man* (1997).

Cotton

Cotton was first grown in what is now Mississippi in 1795 in the Spanish-ruled Natchez District as an alternative to tobacco and indigo. Cotton cultivation in the Mississippi Valley previously had been either unsuccessful or unproductive. Despite Eli Whitney's inventing the modern cotton gin in 1794, cotton remained a marginal crop in the early 1800s, largely because the strains initially used—Creole seed and then Tennessee green seed—provided only mediocre yields. Mississippi growers began using the more productive Mexican seed around 1820, and within a decade Dr. Rush Nutt had developed Petit Gulf cotton, a Mexican–Tennessee green hybrid, on his Rodney plantation. This seed produced the white gold that helped to make Mississippi the nation's top cotton-producing state.

With the high profitability of cotton during the antebellum period came enormous population growth in Mississippi. In 1800 the white population of the Mississippi Territory (the modern states of both Mississippi and Alabama) numbered just over 5,000; sixty years later, Mississippi alone had more than 350,000 white residents. The slave population increased even more—from 3,500 at the turn of the century to 440,000 on the eve of the Civil War. The state reached an important benchmark in 1830, when the number of slaves first surpassed the number of whites. South Carolina is the only other state that ever had a similar demographic.

During the antebellum period cotton production spread east from the river valleys along Mississippi's western border. Cotton became a primary endeavor of settlers throughout the state except along the coast. While regions such as the Pine Belt quickly proved unfavorable for cotton cultivation, the crop's profitability encouraged settlers to try. The

Picking cotton on plantation outside Clarksdale, October 1939 (Photograph by Marion Post Wolcott, Library of Congress, Washington, D.C. [LC-USF33-030626-M3])

Delta was the last region of the state populated by whites and enslaved blacks, as its impenetrable thickets and cane-brakes hindered widespread settlement until after the Civil War. Ironically, however, it proved to be some of the world's most productive cotton land.

The Civil War devastated Mississippi's cotton growers. Many farms and plantations lay in physical ruin, and the loss of the slave labor force was even more overwhelming. Without cheap labor, wide-scale cotton cultivation was impossible.

This issue was resolved with the development of the sharecropping system, under which former slaves entered into annual lease contracts with landowners. Poor whites soon began to find themselves in much the same situation when debts resulted in the loss of their small farms. Sharecropping further increased Mississippi's economic dependence on cotton agriculture. Landlords often demanded that sharecroppers grow almost nothing except cotton.

During the first decade of the twentieth century Mississippi's cotton growers faced a new and potentially devastating problem—the boll weevil. Mississippi agricultural scientists made preemptive efforts to attempt to curtail boll weevil infestation. The Delta Branch Experiment Station was established at Stoneville in Washington County for the sole purpose of developing a way to stop the weevil. The experiment station was run by the Mississippi Agricultural Extension Service, one of the most visible creations of the progressive era in rural Mississippi.

During World War I Mississippi cotton growers experienced a boom in international demand as well as prices. Farmers sought to grow as much cotton as possible. With the end of the war, however, cotton prices dropped precipitously and did not increase significantly until 1933. In spite of the poor market and mounting debts, Mississippi farmers continued to focus on growing cotton. By the end of the 1920s, the state's cotton economy was on the brink of collapse. Nevertheless, the highest recorded acreage planted to cotton was in 1930, at 4.163 million acres.

Pres. Franklin Roosevelt took office in 1933 and immediately acted to remedy the agricultural crisis. His most significant move was the creation of the Agricultural Adjustment Administration, which stabilized prices by paying farmers not to grow cotton. However, the program also resulted in the eviction of thousands of sharecroppers because landowners had no need for laborers to work fields that were not planted.

The changes in cotton production that developed out of the Great Depression and New Deal accelerated during World War II. The war brought tremendous demands for virtually all products, including cotton. Many former sharecroppers and agricultural laborers left Mississippi and sought employment in northern factories. At the same time, cotton was in high demand. This dichotomy resulted in perhaps the greatest advancement in cotton agricultural technology since Whitney's cotton gin: the first effective mechanical cotton picker, developed by International Harvester in 1947. Within two decades virtually all of Mississippi's cotton sharecroppers were gone.

During the second half of the twentieth century many Mississippi planters and farmers moved away from cotton production and toward other row crops such as soybeans and corn as well as highly commercialized catfish and poultry operations. Cotton has recently ranked third, behind poultry and forestry, among Mississippi's leading forms of agriculture. Today, approximately 1.1 million acres are planted to cotton in Mississippi, depending on a number of factors, including weather, price, and commodity markets.

J. Toby Graves
Copiah-Lincoln Community
College

James C. Cobb, *The Most Southern Place on Earth: The Mississippi Delta and the Roots of Regional Identity* (1992); Pete Daniel, *Breaking the Land: The Transformation of Cotton, Tobacco, and Rice Cultures since 1880* (1985); Gilbert Fite, *Cotton Fields No More* (1984); James Toby Graves, "From the Old South to the New, a Delayed Transition: Mississippi Cotton Growers and the Agricultural Adjustment Administration, 1933–1936" (master's thesis, University of Southern Mississippi, 2003); Jack Temple Kirby, *Rural Worlds Lost: The American South, 1920–1960* (1987); Richard A. McLemore, ed., *A History of Mississippi* (1973).

Cotton Gins

In 1794 Eli Whitney patented the modern cotton gin, a machine capable of separating the rough, green seeds from the fiber of short-staple cotton. Before the development of Whitney's invention, hand-cranked roller gins separated the smooth, black seeds in long-staple cotton, a variety of the crop that only grew in certain coastal regions. Short-staple cotton could grow in almost all of the South, however, and Whitney's gin made the commercial production of the crop feasible. Land-hungry men from the South Atlantic states began to pour west to plant cotton, and as the crop assumed the leading role in Mississippi's economy, developments in picking, ginning, and distribution both shaped and reflected the pace of agricultural labor in the state.

Most antebellum cotton plantations had their own gins, but they were less common on smaller farms. Operating a gin house required purchasing the gin stand, the running gear, and the balling press and then erecting a two-story wooden building to house the machinery. Slaves, who hand-separated trash and foreign matter from the fiber and carried the baskets of cotton to the lint room, and horses or mules, which powered the running gear, provided the labor

Modern gin and dryer with tractor, Hopson Plantation, near Clarksdale, October 1939 (Photograph by Marion Post Wolcott, Library of Congress, Washington, D.C. [LC-USF34-052214-D])

to operate the gins. To maximize efficiency, planters often had slaves attend to ginning on rainy days when fieldwork was not possible.

After the Civil War, new labor patterns moved ginning off plantations. Tenant-labor arrangements such as sharecropping provided workers with more freedom than they had enjoyed under slavery, and planters struggled to bring croppers together to operate the labor-intensive gins. New technology also made plantation gins obsolete. In the 1880s the ginning system, which used steam power to automate the ginning and balling processes, increased the efficiency and quality of public gins. By the early twentieth century, large, public facilities that not only ginned cotton but also sold seeds to cottonseed oil firms, populated nearly every town and county in the state's cotton belt.

In addition to playing a role in Mississippi's agricultural economy, public gins also performed a social function in rural communities. Trips to the gin provided farmers living in the far reaches of Mississippi's counties with breaks in the tedium and solitude of toiling on small, isolated tracts of land. During the busiest times of the year, mule-drawn wagons jammed the roads leading to gins. The same gins served black and white farmers, and gin operators made no efforts to serve whites before blacks. While waiting in line to gin their cotton, farmers of both races came together to discuss pests, weather patterns, and prices. As shared public spaces, therefore, gins offered brief respites from the stifling confines of Mississippi's racial caste system.

After World War II, planters began to convert to mechanized harvesting, a process that forced large numbers of Mississippians off the land and increased the size and capacity of farms and gins. As mechanical pickers decreased the demand for farm labor, field hands began to seek nonagricultural employment. Blacks poured out of Mississippi's rural areas, heading for the state's towns and cities or leaving the South altogether. The mechanical revolution occurred with startling quickness in the Delta, where in the 1950s the number of farms decreased by one-third, the size of farms tripled, and the rural farm population decreased by

54 percent. Gins reflected this pattern, as the condensed harvest season of the mechanical era necessitated expansive, modern facilities that could process larger amounts of cotton in shorter intervals of time. By the 1960s the county gin of the past, where small farmers smoked or chewed tobacco and chatted while waiting in line, had become obsolete. Cotton gins today are large, high-tech operations with small, skilled crews.

Thomas John Carey
University of Mississippi

Charles S. Aiken, *Geographical Review* (April 1973); James C. Cobb, *The Most Southern Place on Earth: The Mississippi Delta and the Roots of Regional Identity* (1992); Pete Daniel, *Breaking the Land: The Transformation of Cotton, Tobacco, and Rice Cultures since 1880* (1985); Gavin Wright, *Old South, New South: Revolutions in the Southern Economy since the Civil War* (1986).

Cottrell, Elias

(1853–1937) Religious Leader

A bishop in the Colored Methodist Episcopal (CME) Church, Elias Cottrell cofounded Mississippi Industrial College in Holly Springs in 1906 and later served as the school's trustee, general manager, and treasurer. Cottrell was born a slave on 31 January 1853 and grew up in Old Hudsonville, a few miles outside of Holly Springs. His parents were Daniel Cottrell and Ann Mull Cottrell. At the age of four, Cottrell was sold and separated from his mother and siblings. After the Civil War Daniel Cottrell educated his son, who went on to take theological courses at Central Tennessee College (later Walden University) in Nashville, Tennessee.

In 1880 Cottrell married Catherine Davis of Nashville, and they had one child. After his wife's death in 1912 he named a campus building, Catherine Hall, after her. In 1917 he remarried, and his second wife, Alice, who was more than forty years his junior, bore him four more children. He was licensed to preach in the CME Church in 1875, ordained as a deacon in 1877, and named an elder in 1878. In 1894 he was elected as the denomination's bishop. While in Tennessee, he served as a pastor of Mother Liberty in Jackson, Caper Chapel in Nashville, and Collins Chapel in Memphis. In 1895 he received an honorary degree from Rust College.

Before his election as bishop, Cottrell served as the denomination's educating agent, book agent, and fraternal messenger to the Methodist Episcopal Church, South. Before establishing Mississippi Industrial College, he worked with several of the denomination's educational endeavors, including

Haygood Industrial School in Pine Bluff, Arkansas; Texas College in Tyler; and Miles College in Birmingham, Alabama. Cottrell also served as treasurer of the Mississippi chapter of the Negro Business League, and he was a well-known Republican. Cottrell died of a heart ailment on 6 December 1937.

Alicia Jackson
Covenant College

John Cade, *Holsey the Incomparable* (1969); G. P. Hamilton, *Beacon Lights of the Race* (1912); Alicia Jackson, "The Colored Methodist Episcopal Church and Their Struggle for Autonomy and Reform in the New South" (PhD dissertation, University of Mississippi, 2004); Othal H. Lakey, *The History of the CME Church, Revised* (1996); Frank Lincoln Mather, ed., *Who's Who of the Colored Race*, vol. 1 (1915); C. H. Phillips, *The History of the Colored Methodist Episcopal Church in America* (3rd ed. 1925); Olga Pruitt, *It Happened Here: True Stories of Holly Springs* (1950); US Census (1920, 1930).

Council of Federated Organizations (COFO)

The Council of Federated Organizations (COFO) was an umbrella organization formed in 1962 to unite civil rights groups throughout Mississippi. Its members included the National Association for the Advancement of Colored People (NAACP), the Congress of Racial Equality (CORE), the Student Nonviolent Coordinating Committee (SNCC), and the Southern Christian Leadership Conference (SCLC). COFO constituted one of the first attempts to unify civic groups in a statewide coalition. The NAACP's Aaron Henry, CORE's David Dennis, and SNCC's Bob Moses founded and led COFO.

COFO became a major proponent of black voting. In 1963 the group organized the Freedom Ballot for Governor, a mock election intended to give blacks experience at the ballot box and to communicate to all levels of government that African Americans desired to vote and would exercise that right if given the opportunity. The campaign's platform demanded school desegregation and the protection of voting rights. The group chose Henry as candidate for governor and Ed King, a white minister, as Henry's running mate. COFO held rallies across the state and employed one hundred white college students to assist the campaign. Blacks cast more than eighty-three thousand ballots despite white intimidation, debunking the contention that African Americans did not desire suffrage. While the vote had no legal standing, the campaign further united black Mississippians in their quest for civil rights.

COFO subsequently expanded its operations and organized the massive 1964 Freedom Summer voter registration project. Building on the success of using white student-activists during the Freedom Vote, Moses and Dennis invited hundreds of northern white college students to participate in Freedom Summer, a strategy that created considerable controversy but also generated media coverage. The students and thousands of local blacks attended freedom schools, where they received training in voter registration techniques and nonviolence. COFO experienced a major setback when volunteers James Chaney, Michael Schwerner, and Andrew Goodman disappeared just before Freedom Summer began and were later found murdered by the Ku Klux Klan. White and black COFO volunteers nevertheless canvassed the state to register blacks to vote, participating in rallies, attending freedom schools, and living in black communities. The murders of Chaney, Schwerner, and Goodman as well as other violent reprisals by Mississippi whites hampered the project, and only a small number of blacks registered.

COFO also founded the Mississippi Freedom Democratic Party (MFDP) in 1964 in hopes of allowing African Americans to participate in the state's party system, which excluded them. MFDP members attempted to attend state political functions but were barred by whites. The group also endeavored to join forces with the national Democratic Party but found efforts there stymied as well. At the 1964 Democratic National Convention, Pres. Lyndon Johnson feared alienating white southerners and proposed allowing only two of the MFDP's forty-four delegates to be seated. The MFDP refused the compromise, which demonstrated to many observers the superficiality of Democratic support for civil rights. Four years later the MFDP group combined forces with other organizations to form the Mississippi Loyal Democrats, and all of the delegates were seated at the party's national convention.

COFO's most important accomplishments, Freedom Summer and the MFDP, helped highlight voting issues in Mississippi and in the South. The federal government took an increased interest in black voting, and Johnson confirmed COFO's success by signing the Voting Rights Act into law in August 1965. COFO ultimately proved short-lived. In July 1965 the group dissolved after deciding that the MFDP had assumed many of COFO's responsibilities.

Brian D. Behnken
Iowa State University

John Dittmer, *Local People: The Struggle for Civil Rights in Mississippi* (1994); Doug McAdam, *Freedom Summer* (1988); Charles M. Payne, *I've Got the Light of Freedom: The Organizing Tradition and the Mississippi Freedom Struggle* (1995); "Mississippi: Is This America?," *Eyes on the Prize: America's Civil Rights Years* (PBS Video, 1986).

Country Music Oprys

The country music opry is a localized music performance tradition that has proliferated in Mississippi and throughout the southeastern United States since the 1980s. Although they vary in content and style from community to community, most opry shows in Mississippi are reoccurring public programs that feature amateur musicians performing a mixture of country, bluegrass, and gospel music for a local audience. The format for the shows is based on historic live country music radio shows, most prominently Nashville's *Grand Ole Opry*.

While country music opry shows are not unique to Mississippi, they have taken hold as a popular form of entertainment in rural areas of the state. They are presented in a wide range of facilities, from local armory buildings and community centers to unused machine equipment sheds. They take place almost exclusively on Friday or Saturday evenings and are held at different intervals—weekly, monthly, or at specific times of the year.

Most opry musicians and audience members are older Anglo-Americans based in rural areas. Much of the music performed at the shows is country songs from the 1950s through the mid-1970s. Many shows also include some gospel music (primarily southern gospel) and bluegrass. The music of early rock and roll performers (Elvis Presley and Carl Perkins) and old-time southern fiddle tunes are occasionally heard at opry shows.

Most of the musicians who perform at local opry shows are amateurs from the surrounding area, and many are life-long musicians. Some have played professionally in the past. The instrumentation used at the shows varies. Those that present country music from the 1950s and 1960s use electric guitars, drums, and electronic keyboards. The shows more focused on bluegrass and old-time string band music generally rely on acoustic instruments.

Most audience members come from the local community, although some shows draw individuals from outside the region. Opry shows in Mississippi are promoted as "family friendly" events and almost always prohibit alcohol. Most shows do not charge admission, but many ask audience members for donations to help pay for utilities and other expenses. Organizers frequently make income by selling food and soft drinks.

Opry shows are found throughout Mississippi, but they are most common in northeastern Mississippi and the Piney Woods region in the southern part of the state. Since most opry-type shows are produced by small groups of individuals, new ones frequently start and existing ones often become inactive.

One of northern Mississippi's longest-running shows is the Sparta Opry, held every weekend since the late 1980s in the tiny community of Sparta in southern Chickasaw County. Some more recently started shows include the Barnyard Opry outside Brandon and the Mississippi Opry, presented monthly at the community center in Pearl. While some Mississippi opry shows have websites, the most reliable source of information is the calendar listings in small-town weekly newspapers.

Larry Morrisey
Mississippi Arts Commission

Reita Jackson, *Mississippi Magazine* (January–February 2007); Robbie Ward, *Northeast Mississippi Daily Journal* (27 March 2005).

County Government

Once described as "the 'dark continent' of the state's political system," Mississippi's counties have experienced considerable change since the 1980s. In the wake of Operation Pretense and the Mississippi legislature's subsequent passage of the County Government Reorganization Act of 1988, officials have made considerable progress in modernizing and professionalizing the county as a unit of local government.

Counties have existed as organizational units in what is now Mississippi since 1799, eighteen years before statehood. All four of Mississippi's constitutions (1817, 1832, 1869, and 1890) have mentioned counties, placed the county's governing authority in the judicial branch of government, and established functions for the governing authority that were executive or legislative in nature. Although constitutional bodies, counties are creatures of the state and possess the powers and functions granted by the Mississippi Constitution and the statutes adopted by the state legislature.

Since 1918 Mississippi has been divided into eighty-two counties, each of which is subdivided into five districts (traditionally called beats), which are to be as equal as possible in population. County government is headquartered at municipalities designated as county seats. Seventy-two counties have one county seat, while the remainder have two county seats because the county is divided into two court districts. Each county seat maintains a county courthouse.

Prior to 1988, counties operated under a beat system of organization and road and bridge management, with each of the county's five supervisors independently managing roads and bridges in his or her beat and allocating money as he or she saw fit subject to the limitations of state law and the approval of the entire board of supervisors. County revenues for roads and bridges were usually divided equally among the beats, without regard to road mileage or conditions.

Between 1984 and 1987, the FBI, with the cooperation of state auditor Ray Mabus, conducted Operation Pretense, a sting operation involving purchasing activities in twenty-six counties. Seventy-one public officials, including fifty-five county supervisors, were ultimately convicted on felony charges. The Mississippi legislature responded to this corruption by passing the County Government Reorganization Act of 1988, which required all counties to move to a unit system of centralized road administration unless exempted by a majority of the qualified electors of the county. Under a unit system, the administration of roads (planning, funding, construction, purchase of equipment and supplies, employment, and so forth) is conducted on the basis of the needs of the county as a whole, without regard to district boundaries. A unit system requires the appointment of a county administrator and a road manager. At present, forty-four counties operate under the unit system, with the remainder using beat or district systems. In addition, the legislation required all counties to adopt a centralized system for purchasing, receiving, and inventory control and general personnel administration.

Each county's governing authority consists of a five-member board of supervisors, each of whom is elected from a district. No professional qualifications exist for the position of supervisor, and there is no limit on the number of terms a supervisor may serve. State statutes provide a process to fill vacancies, and the constitution and statutes list nine reasons for a supervisor's removal from office. The annual salary of a supervisor is fixed by statute based on the total assessed valuation of property in the county for the preceding tax year. The board of supervisors elects one member as president and one member as vice president. Regular meetings are held every month, and the board is attended by the county sheriff or deputy sheriff and the chancery clerk or deputy chancery clerk to execute and process the board's orders.

The board of supervisors has powers in the areas of general administration (meetings, budget, appropriation of funds, elections, and managing county property), law enforcement and courts (funding the employees, facilities, and programs of the sheriff, the court system, and the county jail), health and public welfare (zoning, planning, construction, subdivision regulation, solid waste collection and disposal, fire protection, emergency management, homeland security, public welfare, and physical and mental health), taxation, recreation and soil and water conservation, public works (roads, bridges, drainage, and public buildings), industrial development, and intergovernmental cooperation. Thus, the board of supervisors must guide and establish policy for the complex multimillion-dollar enterprise of county government.

County government also requires other elected and appointed officials. Elected officials serve four-year terms concurrent with those of the members of the board of supervisors and include the chancery clerk, the circuit clerk, the sheriff, the coroner, the constables, the justice court judges, and the tax assessor and/or collector. The major appointed county officials include the board attorney, the county administrator, the county engineer, and the road manager.

The chancery clerk serves as the clerk of the chancery court, the clerk of the board of supervisors, the recorder and preserver of all land records, and the bookkeeper. The circuit clerk serves as the clerk of the circuit court; has certain administrative duties in the election process, including voter registration; and issues marriage licenses. The sheriff is the county's chief law enforcement officer. Justice court judges have jurisdiction over limited civil and criminal actions and receive assistance from the constables in executing criminal judgments. Depending on qualifications, the county coroner serves as either the county medical examiner or the county medical examiner investigator and is responsible for investigating deaths.

The attorney for the board of supervisors performs a wide range of legal duties. The county administrator is charged by statute with performing twenty specific administrative duties. The county engineer has a full range of typical engineering responsibilities, and the road manager oversees the construction and maintenance of roads and bridges.

Administration of justice at the county level is handled by the justice courts (found in all eighty-two counties), the county courts (nineteen counties), and two general-jurisdiction trial courts—the circuit courts (twenty-two districts covering the state) and the chancery courts (twenty districts covering the state). The justice courts have jurisdiction over small-claims civil cases, misdemeanor criminal cases, and traffic offenses occurring outside a municipality. County courts have jurisdiction over eminent domain proceedings and juvenile matters, share jurisdiction with the circuit and chancery courts in some civil matters and noncapital felony cases transferred from circuit court, and have concurrent jurisdiction with justice courts, both civil and criminal. Chancery courts have responsibility for land records as well as jurisdiction over juvenile matters in counties that lack county courts, equity disputes, domestic matters, guardianships, sanity hearings, wills, and challenges to the constitutionality of state laws. Circuit courts hear major felony cases, major civil lawsuits, and appeals from lower courts and certain administrative boards and commissions.

Mac McLaurin
Mississippi State University

James R. Crockett, *Operation Pretense: The FBI's Sting on County Corruption in Mississippi* (2003); Robert B. Highsaw and Charles N. Fortenberry, *Government and Administration of Mississippi* (1954); Gokhan R. Karahan, Laura Razzolini, and William F. Shughart, in *Economics of Governance* (August 2006); Dale Krane and Stephen D. Shaffer, *Mississippi Government and Politics: Modernizers versus Traditionalists* (1992); Mississippi State University, Center for Governmental Training and Technology, *County Government in Mississippi* (2004).

Courthouse Squares

One of the most identifiable public spaces in Mississippi is the courthouse square. Courthouse squares are defined as places located at the center of the original town plan and designated as the location for the county courthouse.

The idea for a centrally located courthouse square apparently originated with Scots-Irish immigrants, many of whom were familiar with a central square with a prominent public building from some early seventeenth-century towns the English had laid out in Northern Ireland.

Complicating the origins of this town form as it developed in Mississippi was the political significance the Mississippi legislature gave it in the mid-1830s. After the Choctaw and Chickasaw land cessions of the early 1830s, the legislature granted full power to the boards of police (the forerunners of today's boards of supervisors) to locate the "seats of justice of several of these new counties at the geographical center or the most convenient point within five miles thereof." Although not all courthouse squares were mandated in this fashion, the idea certainly worked well and was imitated throughout the state. The centralized location of the seat of government was one of the most concrete examples of Jacksonian democracy. Courthouse squares were theoretically located equidistant from citizens in all parts of the county, just as many southern states had placed their capitals in geographically central locations to improve access for all citizens.

Courthouse squares are not as ubiquitous or as similar as many people believe. They can generally be classified into four common types:

Block square: The center square of a nine-block grid is the location of the courthouse. The streets bordering the square

Oxford courthouse square (Martin J. Dain Collection, Department of Archives and Special Collections, J. D. Williams Library, University of Mississippi)

intersect at right angles. This is the most common type of central courthouse square in Mississippi. Included in this type are Canton, Carrollton, Houston, Kosciusko, Philadelphia, and Ripley.

Philadelphia or Lancaster square: The center square is superimposed over the intersection of two roads, with the corner area from each surrounding square taken to form the center square. Each street intersects the central square at the midpoint of a side. Mississippi currently has no squares that follow this pattern.

Harrisonburg square: The center square has streets intersecting the midpoint on two flanking sides, with no intersecting streets on the other two sides. In Mississippi, Charleston and Oxford follow this layout.

Four-block square: The center square has streets intersecting each of its sides as well as intersecting streets at each corner, meaning that a total of twelve streets enter the square. Hernando and Lexington are two Mississippi examples of this type.

The square in Holly Springs is a combination of the Harrisonburg and four-block square plans. The square in Holly Springs is more of a rectangle, with roughly twice the space of the better-known Oxford square.

A few county seats have open squares but no courthouse. Some of these, such as Grenada, Calhoun City, and Bruce, have never had courthouses. The open square in Pontotoc resulted from the demolition of the nineteenth-century courthouse, which stood on the square until the 1916 construction of the present courthouse, which faces onto the square. A similar fate befell Brandon in the 1920s, when its 1850s Greek Revival courthouse burned and a newer, larger building was constructed facing the now open square.

The courthouse in Natchez is located on the original plaza laid out by the Spanish in the 1790s. As originally designed in typical Spanish Colonial fashion, the plaza was an open area onto which public buildings, most notably the church, would face. However, this arrangement did not last long, and the courthouse was constructed in the middle of the plaza around 1820, thus Americanizing the Spanish plan.

Woodville's square is really a long rectangle that includes the square with the courthouse and a smaller area with the town hall (originally the location of the market house) to the north across Main Street. To the south of the courthouse was a small monument park.

In addition, the courthouse occupies an entire city block in many county seats, but this block was never the town's center square. The land often was donated to the county after the town was established or was purchased by the county when it needed a site for a new courthouse arose. Corinth, for example, was designated as the second district seat of old Tishomingo County in 1859, five years after the town was laid out at the intersection of the Mobile and Ohio and Memphis and Charleston Railroads. That arrangement persisted, with Jacinto as the first judicial district seat, until the county was subdivided in 1870 into Alcorn County, Prentiss

County, and a smaller Tishomingo County. Corinth then became the seat of Alcorn County. Other railroad towns laid out on a grid include Tupelo, Cleveland, and Meridian.

Todd Sanders
Mississippi Department of
Archives and History

Dell Upton and John Michael Vlach, *Common Places: Readings in American Vernacular Architecture* (1986); Mississippi Department of Archives and History, Historic Preservation Division website, http://mdah.state.ms.us/hpres/index.php.

Courtney, Ezra
(1775?–1855) Religious Leader

Ezra Courtney was an important Baptist frontier missionary and theologian, yet certainty about his life continues to elude historians. Courtney's tombstone and most scholarly accounts say that he was born in 1775 in the Darlington District of South Carolina, but other sources suggest that he was born in 1771 in Pennsylvania. Courtney must have heard the call early in life because records from the Bethel Black River Church in Burnt County, South Carolina, list him as working for the church by 1790. Soon thereafter, he married Elizabet Dearmond, and on 25 August 1792 their first child, Sarah, was born.

Courtney moved to Amite County, Mississippi, around the turn of the nineteenth century. Just to the south lay West Florida, where Spanish Catholics had established a powerful presence. Early evangelical Protestant orators on the frontier commonly faced arrest, a situation in which Courtney found himself after ministering to a group nine miles west of Baton Rouge, Louisiana. A Spanish government official interceded on Courtney's behalf, however, and the young minister avoided incarceration.

Courtney established several churches in South Mississippi and Louisiana. In 1806 he helped found the Mississippi Baptist Association, which covered what is now southwestern Mississippi and southeastern Louisiana. He went on to serve as the association's moderator for eight consecutive terms.

Courtney played a fundamental role in developing the frontier Baptist theological worldview. He opposed the antimission sentiments of American and English Baptists, who had been reluctant to support William Carey's work in India, and rallied support for the mission system. When some Baptists began to espouse Campbellite doctrine, practices Courtney considered heterodox, he outspokenly criticized their ideas. Glenn Lee, an early Baptist historian, described

Courtney as "a vigorous and faithful Calvinist, unrelenting in his stance."

Courtney's faith was rooted in the salvation of the individual soul, an ideology that became synonymous with southern evangelical faith later in the nineteenth century. He taught the depravity of man, election, ministerial calling, and salvation by grace solely for the elect. He eventually drafted the Mississippi Baptist Association's Articles of Faith, which are clearly indebted to the theological view of the Calvinistic reformers but also demonstrate Baptist ecclesiastical influences. Courtney and other early Mississippi Baptists ascribed to the five soteriological statements of the Synod of Dort, as the Articles of Faith demonstrate.

The last years of Courtney's life, like his youth, remain murky. As late as 1832 he was still defending and spreading his style of theology, which would become orthodox, mainstream, evangelical theology. He died in 1855.

Ben Gilstrap
University of Mississippi

David Benedict, *A General History of the Baptist Denomination in America and Other Parts of the World* (1848); Jessie Laney Boyd, *Popular History of the Baptists in Mississippi* (1930); *Founders Journal* (Summer 2001); Rev. John G. Jones, *A Concise History of the Introduction of Protestantism into Mississippi and the Southwest* (1866); Joe B. Nessum, *Founders Journal* (Winter 1993).

Courts, Gus

(ca. 1889–1969) Activist

Gus Courts, a Belzoni grocer, helped organize the Humphreys County chapter of the National Association for the Advancement of Colored People (NAACP) and in parts of 1954–55 served as that chapter's president. He was part of an older generation of black activists who worked for change in the years before and immediately after the 1954 *Brown* decision, and his stubborn personality saw him through many difficult situations during that time. Even as the Delta's African American community demanded civil rights following World War II, white intransigence met black activism with a swift and sometimes deadly resolve that helped define much of Courts's later life.

In the postwar years, Courts established connections with a promising network of Delta civil rights workers. He participated in the Regional Council of Negro Leadership, a group designed to promote school equality in the Delta, which linked him to such other activists as Amzie Moore and Aaron Henry. Courts's sister, Laura McGhee, and her

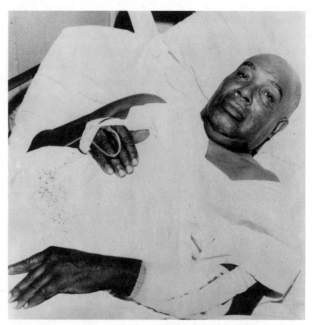

Gus Courts in the hospital in Mound Bayou after being shot, 26 November 1955 (Library of Congress, Washington, D.C. [LC-USZ62-123834])

sons became important activists in neighboring Leflore County, and his close friend Rev. George W. Lee, a Belzoni preacher, print shop owner, and fellow grocer, also organized for the NAACP. In 1953 Lee and Courts founded the organization's Belzoni chapter, and over the next two years, they registered a handful of Humphreys County black voters, a significant feat in a county where no African American had voted since Reconstruction. When the local sheriff refused to allow African Americans to pay their poll taxes, Lee and Courts sued. Their civil rights activities brought an upsurge in violence and threats toward the black community, and in April 1955 white supremacists killed Lee in a drive-by shooting. Courts reacted by taking twenty-two more African Americans to register to vote.

As a small businessman, Courts had a degree of economic independence, but he nevertheless faced intense pressure to give up his activism and reveal the names of other NAACP members. The white business community used all its resources to ruin Courts's store—bankers refused him credit, wholesalers denied him service, his landlord tripled the rent, a local gas station refused to sell him fuel, and whites warned blacks not to shop at his grocery. Courts remained in business by purchasing supplies from Memphis and Jackson, but his sales eventually plummeted.

The year 1955 brought a series of reprisals across the South as a result of anger over the *Brown* ruling. Six months after Lee's murder, white gunmen shot the sixty-five-year-old Courts in front of his store. Courts suffered serious arm and abdominal injuries, but despite losing significant amounts of blood, he sought treatment at the black hospital in Mound Bayou, eighty miles from Belzoni, rather than at the local hospital.

Belzoni police did not seriously investigate the crime, instead blaming the black community, and his shooting received little national attention because it came shortly after the trial and acquittal of the men accused of killing Emmett Till the preceding August. The shooting forced Courts to seek financial assistance from the NAACP, and he and his wife later left Mississippi and started a business in Chicago.

Courts's movement career coincided with an outpouring of black protest in the Delta and a retrogression toward overt violence to thwart civil rights enthusiasm. Despite the attacks on the Delta's older black leadership, African American resistance persisted and formed the basis for future projects.

William P. Hustwit
Birmingham Southern University

Townsend Davis, *Weary Feet, Rested Souls* (1997); John Dittmer, *Local People: The Struggle for Civil Rights in Mississippi* (1994); *Jet* (8 May 1969); Charles Payne, *I've Got the Light of Freedom: The Organizing Tradition and the Mississippi Freedom Struggle* (1995).

Covington County

Covington County lies in southern Mississippi's Piney Woods region, with the Okatoma River running north–south through it. Covington County was long inhabited by Native Americans prior to the arrival of Europeans. Covington was established from parts of Lawrence and Wayne Counties on 5 January 1819. Many of its early settlers came from North Carolina. The county is named for congressman and Revolutionary War hero Leonard Covington of Maryland, who was stationed in Mississippi Territory during the war and played a central role in negotiations with the Creek Indians. Williamsburg served as Covington's county seat from 1824 to 1906, when the seat was moved to Collins.

In the 1820 census Covington had 1,824 whites and 406 slaves. Forty years later the county was home to 2,845 whites and 1,564 slaves, much smaller population growth than occurred in many other parts of Mississippi. The enslaved percentage of the county's population was also much lower than that in many of the state's other counties.

While much of Mississippi intensified cotton cultivation in the late antebellum period, Covington, like other Piney Woods counties, decreased production of the staple. Though the county ranked among the bottom ten in cotton, corn, and livestock, it placed among the state's top rice producers. A small number of Covington's men worked in manufacturing during this era, most of them in lumber mills.

Covington County's population showed little growth early in the postbellum period: as late as 1880 the county had only six thousand people. Growth subsequently picked up, and the population more than doubled by 1900, topping thirteen thousand, including forty-six hundred African Americans. With the newly constructed Gulf and Ship Island Railroad and a growing lumber industry, the county's population continued to grow during the first decades of the twentieth century.

As in most of the Piney Woods region, few of Covington's farmers were tenants or sharecroppers. In 1900, 86 percent of all white farmers and 59 percent of black farmers owned their land, far above the state averages. With slightly larger-than-average farms, agriculture was Covington's central economic activity during this era. In 1880 the county's twelve manufacturing firms employed a mere eighteen people. However, the county's industrial production, especially in lumber, increased in the late 1800s, and two decades later the county had forty-two companies employing almost three hundred men. Collins was one of many South Mississippi towns that began as a lumber camp.

While in 1860 the county was home to six Baptist, six Methodist, and four Presbyterian churches, by 1916 about two-thirds of the county's church congregants were members of either the Southern Baptist or Missionary Baptist conventions. Others belonged to the Methodist Episcopal Church, South; the Presbyterian Church US; or the Colored Methodist Episcopal Church.

Covington County's population growth slowed after the first decade of the twentieth century. In 1930 the county was home to 15,028 people, about two-thirds of them white. Though the county's racial profile remained stable over the next three decades, its population began to decline, reaching 13,637 in 1960. That year also marked the beginning of a declining reliance on agriculture, though manufacturing was slow to take its place. In 1980 Covington still ranked in the bottom half of the state in industrial employment.

Covington County can claim actors, athletes, and at least one important writer among its natives. Dana Andrews, a major film star during the 1940s, was born in 1909 in Collins. Gerald McRaney, who has often portrayed southern characters in television and film and is perhaps best known for his starring role in the television sitcom *Major Dad*, was born in Collins in 1947. Alcorn State University and Tennessee Titans quarterback Steve McNair was born in Mount Olive in 1973. And author Ralph Eubanks described his childhood in Mount Olive in his memoir, *Ever Is a Long Time: A Journey into Mississippi's Dark Past*.

Like many southern Mississippi counties, Covington's 2010 population was predominantly white and had increased in size since 1960, growing by about 43 percent to 19,568.

Mississippi Encyclopedia Staff
University of Mississippi

Gwen Keys Hitt, *Covington Crossroads: A History of Covington County, Mississippi* (1985); Mississippi State Planning Commission, *Progress Report on State Planning in Mississippi* (1938); *Mississippi Statistical Abstract*, Mississippi State University (1952–2010); Charles Sydnor and Claude Bennett, *Mississippi History* (1939); University of Virginia Library, Historical Census Browser website, http://mapserver.lib.virginia.edu; E. Nolan Waller and Dani A. Smith, *Growth Profiles of Mississippi's Counties, 1960–1980* (1985).

Cox, Minnie Geddings

(1869–1933) Postmistress and Businessperson

Minnie M. Geddings was born in Lexington, Mississippi, in 1869 to former slaves William and Mary (or Elizabeth) Geddings. Few details survive about Cox's early life in Holmes County. She worked in her parents' restaurant, and they saved enough money to send her to Fisk University in Nashville. She left Fisk's Normal School around 1888 and returned to Mississippi. She earned a first-grade teaching certificate, the highest-level certificate available in the state at that time. She moved to Indianola to teach in the local segregated public school. On 30 October 1889 she married Wayne Wellington Cox, then principal of the Colored School in Indianola. The couple had one daughter, Ethyl.

In 1891 Pres. Benjamin Harrison sought advice about patronage positions from black Republicans in Mississippi. Wayne Cox suggested his wife, Minnie, for the Holmes County postmistress position, and she became the first black woman to hold the post in Mississippi. Wayne Cox later claimed that he suggested his wife so that the position would not go to a black man from outside of Sunflower County.

Minnie Cox remained postmistress until 1902, when white supremacists angered by her power and position demanded that she resign. James K. Vardaman heard of the controversy and criticized Indianola for "tolerating a negro wench as postmaster." However, Pres. Theodore Roosevelt refused to accept her resignation on the principle that the federal government had the power to decide who should be a federal employee. Roosevelt closed the Indianola post office but kept Cox on the federal payroll until her term ended in 1904.

Cox had long been involved in real estate and business transactions. Even prior to her marriage, she had sold two improved properties in Indianola. Contemporaries praised Wayne Cox's large plantation on the outskirts of Indianola, but his wife owned most of the land. In 1891 she sold a downtown lot with a small building to the Atlanta-based Southern Home Building and Loan Association.

In October 1904 Wayne Cox chartered the Delta Penny Savings Bank, the state's second black-owned bank. The bank opened for business in early 1905 and soon became one of the Delta's most successful banks, black or white. In 1914 it became Mississippi's first black-owned bank approved to guarantee deposits. In an ironic twist, many of the whites who had once vigorously opposed Cox deposited funds in her bank. A contemporary observer noted that it was "a curious circumstance" that the same whites who had objected to Cox as postmistress were perfectly comfortable with her husband as a bank president.

After Wayne Cox's death in 1916 his widow became vice president of Delta Penny and secretary-treasurer of Mississippi Life, the most powerful position in the company. She moved Mississippi Life's headquarters to Memphis in August 1920 before selling the company to Standard Life, a black-owned Georgia insurance company, in 1923.

The sale of Mississippi Life, majority ownership of Delta Penny Savings Bank, and land and property holdings made Cox one of the richest black women in the United States. In 1925 she married George Hamilton and moved to Rockford, Illinois, though she returned to Indianola at least once a year to take care of her business matters. In 1928 the Delta Penny failed. Minnie Cox Hamilton died in Rockford in 1933 and is buried in the Little Rock Cemetery in Indianola next to Wayne Cox.

Mississippi writer Steve Yarbrough fictionalized Cox's life in his 2001 novel *Visible Spirits*.

Shennette Garrett-Scott
University of Mississippi

Chancery Clerk Records, Sunflower County, Indianola, Mississippi; Minnie Cox, Subject File, Mississippi Department of Archives and History, Jackson; Marie M. Hemphill, *Fevers, Floods, and Faith: A History of Sunflower County, Mississippi, 1844–1976* (1980); Steven J. Niven, in *African American National Biography*, ed. Henry Louis Gates Jr. and Evelyn Brooks Higginbotham (2008); David M. Tucker, *Lieutenant Lee of Beale Street* (1971); David M. Tucker, "W. W. Cox," *Beacon Lights of the Race*, ed. Green Polonius Hamilton (1911); Steve Yarbrough, *Visible Spirits* (2001).

Cox, William Harold

(1901–1988) Judge

Judge William Harold Cox presided over the 1967 trial of the men accused of the 1964 murders of three civil rights workers that became a turning point in the struggle for racial equality in the South. Born in Indianola on 23 June 1901, Cox attended the University of Mississippi, where he roomed with future US senator James Eastland before receiving bachelor's and law degrees in 1924. Cox practiced corporate and civil law until Pres. John F. Kennedy nominated him to serve as US district court judge for the Southern District of Mississippi. The US Senate confirmed him on 27 June 1961 and he took his oath of office three days later. Cox served as chief judge from 1962 to 1971 and took senior status on 4 October 1982.

Cox became known for his rulings that slowed down the federal government's attempts to integrate the South, though those rulings were repeatedly overruled on appeal. In 1964 he called a group of black witnesses "a bunch of chimpanzees," a statement that caused Sen. Jacob Javits of New York and Rep. Peter Rodino of New Jersey to attempt to impeach the judge.

On 21 June 1964 Neshoba County deputy sheriff Cecil Ray Price arrested civil rights workers Michael Schwerner, James Chaney, and Andrew Goodman just outside Philadelphia, Mississippi, on speeding charges. They paid a fine and were released later that night but subsequently disappeared. Their bodies were found buried in a Neshoba County dam the following August. Price had handed the three men over to members of the Ku Klux Klan, who shot and killed the workers. Since the chances of getting justice in the state courts of Mississippi were virtually nonexistent, a federal grand jury indicted eighteen men implicated in the killings on charges related to nineteenth-century civil rights statutes. Judge Cox dismissed the felony indictments on the grounds that murder did not fall within the federal court's jurisdiction, though he allowed misdemeanor charges to stand against Price, Sheriff Lawrence Rainey, and patrolman Richard Willis because they were the only suspects who allegedly acted "under color of law," a requirement for federal jurisdiction.

The US Supreme Court unanimously reversed Cox's ruling and reinstated the indictments against all of the defendants. Judge Cox then presided over their October 1967 trial before an all-white jury of five men and seven women. Defense attorneys assumed that Cox was their ally, but he "conducted the trial with scrupulous fairness." When a defense attorney asked a witness whether Schwerner sought "to get young male Negroes to sign a pledge to rape a white woman once a week during the hot summer of 1964," Cox said that he considered such a question "highly improper" and that he would not "allow farce to be made of this trial." After the jury found seven of the defendants guilty, Cox sentenced them to between three and ten years in jail. Cox declared a mistrial for the rest of the defendants, including Edgar Ray Killen, who in 2005 was convicted of planning and directing the murders. Judge Cox died in 1988.

Natalya Seay
Washington, D.C.

Biographical Directory of the Federal Judiciary, 1789–2000 (2001); Federal Judicial Center website, www.fjc.gov; *United States v. Price* (1966).

Crane, Florence Hedleston
(1888–1973) Artist

An artist, teacher, and missionary to Korea, Florence Hedleston Crane was born in Paint Lick, Kentucky, to Dr. Wynn David Hedleston, a Presbyterian minister and professor of philosophy at the University of Mississippi, and Lillian Andrus Hedleston. Florence Hedleston attended the University of Mississippi (1904–8), majoring in botany. She was a lover of nature all her life and began at an early age to paint images of wild and cultivated flowers. Her early watercolor illustrations of flowers and landscapes show a keen eye and careful attention to the natural form. She received first prize in painting in her category at the 1903 St. Louis World's Fair.

In 1913 in Yazoo City Hedleston married John Curtis Crane, an ordained minister and a missionary of the Presbyterian Church, US. She traveled with him to Suncheon, Korea, and taught at the mission's school for girls. She organized classes in the industrial department, manufacturing silk and other products. The entire process of silk making was done at the school, from the raising of the silkworms to the weaving of thread into cloth. The combination of her knowledge of botany and her artistic skills proved invaluable, as she and her students drew and painted designs for the textiles.

Crane also painted watercolors capturing the details of the life around her. She recorded all types of Korean dress and painted hundreds of landscapes and watercolors of exotic flora and fauna. She also collected the folk legends associated with the flowers she was painting. In 1931 her work appeared in an artistic and literary book, *Flowers and Folklore from Far Korea*, printed by Sanseido Press in Tokyo. The bookplates in the first edition were created using seven-tone wood blocks.

The Cranes lived in Korea during turbulent times. They had five children, two of whom died in infancy and are buried in Korea. In 1940 Curtis Crane became a prisoner of war, though he escaped shortly before Pearl Harbor. From 1942 to 1946 the Cranes lived in Pascagoula, where he served as the minister of the First Presbyterian Church. They returned to Korea as missionaries in 1946, 1949, and 1954.

During her career Crane's paintings were exhibited in Seoul, Pyeng Yang, New York, and New Orleans as well as on the Gulf Coast. At the time of her death in Old Hickory, Tennessee, in 1973, she left hundreds of landscapes and more than a thousand paintings of flowers.

Deborah Freeland
Oxford, Mississippi

Florence Hedleston Crane, *Flowers and Folklore from Far Korea* (1931); Choon Bok Lim, *The Korean Mission of the Crane Family* (1999); Mayumi Morishita, "Florence Hedleston Crane: A Mississippi Woman Painting in Korea" (master's thesis, University of Mississippi, 2005); David G. Sansing, *The University of Mississippi: A Sesquicentennial History* (1999).

Creek War

The Creek War was a part of the larger War of 1812 fought between a faction of the Creek tribe and US forces in 1813–14. It resulted in the defeat of the Creek nation and paved the way for the division of the Mississippi Territory into the states of Mississippi and Alabama. The war originated in Creek uneasiness regarding increasing Anglo influence in tribal life. The Creek, a loose confederation of Indians who lived in areas that are now part of Alabama and Georgia, were especially concerned about the construction of a federal road that ran through much of their homeland and facilitated an influx of white migration. Many Creek reluctantly accepted the changes as inevitable and attempted to adopt Anglo-American ways for economic survival. A minority, however, determined to resist white settlement and maintain the traditional Creek way of life at any cost.

In the fall of 1811 Tecumseh, a Native American leader from the Great Lakes region who claimed Creek ancestry, seized on this instability during a prolonged visit to the Southeast. In impassioned speeches to several Indian nations, he appealed to his kinfolk to rise up and cast out the white intruders and resist assimilation into their culture. Although other tribes in the region, including the Choctaw and Chickasaw, rejected his message, Tecumseh found a receptive audience among the Upper Creek, who lived along the Coosa and Tallapoosa Rivers in what is now Alabama. His fiery oratory sparked a civil war between Creek who sought peace and cooperation with Anglo-Americans and those openly hostile to them, who became known as the Red Sticks because of the color of their war clubs. The Creek civil war eventually grew to involve conflict with US troops.

Fighting between Anglo-Americans and Red Sticks first broke out in July 1813 at the Battle of Burnt Corn Creek. A Red Stick victory, the battle revealed the complicated international nature of the conflict and its relationship to the larger War of 1812. The battle was actually a surprise attack by Mississippi territorial militia on a group of Red Sticks returning from Spanish-held Pensacola, where they had gone to obtain arms and ammunition for use in the fight against the Anglo-Americans. Anglo-American settlers had long believed that the Spanish intended to instigate the Creek to violence against them, and this chain of events seemed to confirm such suspicions. Complicating matters, the United States and Great Britain were already at war. The powerful British, allied with the Spanish, were rumored to be planning to solicit the Creek to assist in a campaign against the United States along the Gulf Coast. However, the British did not begin serious recruitment of Red Sticks in the region until after US forces had defeated British soldiers. Had the British moved earlier, they might have prolonged or even altered the outcome of the Creek War.

The event most responsible for the escalation of the conflict was the Red Stick attack on Fort Mims in Alabama. One of several hastily constructed fortifications north of Mobile, Fort Mims housed dozens of frontier families and a small garrison of troops who had gathered there in anticipation of a confrontation. In a bold, surprise attack on 30 August 1813, Red Stick Creek killed more than 250 residents of the fort before burning it to the ground. Reports of the "massacre" shocked the nation and persuaded thousands of men to volunteer to avenge those killed.

Within weeks, militia from the Mississippi Territory, Tennessee, and Georgia were organized to restore order in the region. A large number of Creek, Choctaw, and Cherokee friendly to United States volunteered for service against the Red Sticks. These troops, eventually accompanied by reinforcements from the US Army, converged on hostile Creek territory from multiple directions. By burning villages and destroying crops as well as defeating warriors in battle, US forces sought to weaken the Red Sticks' resistance and bring about their surrender.

Almost all of the fighting occurred within the Mississippi Territory. Lasting from July 1813 to March 1814, the war featured several loosely coordinated offenses facilitated by the construction of a series of forts. US forces won several significant victories at such Red Stick strongholds as Autossee and the Holy Ground but generally failed to follow up with sustained campaigns as a consequence of severe shortages in supplies, inadequate transportation and communication, and the short-term enlistments of many of the troops.

The campaigning of Andrew Jackson and his Tennessee troops ultimately broke the power of the Red Sticks as a military force and simultaneously brought Old Hickory to national prominence. By holding together his army under adverse conditions and winning sweeping victories at Tallushatchee, Talladega, and elsewhere, Jackson became a national hero. His efforts culminated in victory at the Battle of Horseshoe Bend, the largest and last major engagement of the war. Jackson led his men in defeating one of the Red Sticks' largest fighting forces, killing more Native Americans than died in any other battle in American history. Shortly after this defeat, the devastated Creek nation was forced to sign the Treaty of Fort Jackson, surrendering more than twenty-three million acres of land to the United States, including territory that belonged to portions of the tribe that had fought alongside the US forces. A few months later, Jackson captured Pensacola and prevented the British from using the town as a base for their Gulf Coast campaign. On 8 January 1815 he won one of the new nation's most important military victories in the final battle of the War of 1812 by defeating the British at New Orleans.

The Creek War had far-reaching effects on both the region and the nation. Thousands of white settlers and their slaves soon moved onto former Creek lands. This rise in population led in part to Mississippi's 1817 statehood and to Alabama statehood two years later. Just as significantly, the war set the precedent for the eventual removal of all southeastern tribes from their native lands and helped propel Jackson to the presidency.

Mike Bunn
Historic Chattahoochee
Commission

Clay Williams
Mississippi Department of
Archives and History

Mike Bunn and Clay Williams, *Battle for the Southern Frontier: The Creek War and the War of 1812* (2008); Sean Michael O'Brien, *In Bitterness and in Tears: Andrew Jackson's Destruction of the Creeks and Seminoles* (2003); Frank L. Owsley Jr., *Struggle for the Gulf Borderlands: The Creek War and the Battle of New Orleans, 1812–1815* (1981); Robert V. Remini, *Andrew Jackson and His Indian Wars* (2001); George Stiggins, *Creek Indian History: A Historical Narrative of the Geneaology, Traditions, and Downfall of the Ispacoga of Creek Tribe of Indians* (1989); Gregory A. Waselkov, *A Conquering Spirit: Fort Mims and the Redstick War of 1813–1814* (2006).

Creekmore, Hubert

(1907–1966) Author

Hiram Hubert Creekmore was born on 16 January 1907 in Water Valley, Mississippi. He earned fame as a poet, although he was also a novelist, translator, editor, critic, publisher, pianist, composer, and gardener. He graduated from the University of Mississippi in 1927, went to work for the Mississippi Highway Department in Jackson, and then became an editor with the Federal Writers' Project. In 1940 he earned a master's degree from Columbia University, where his thesis focused on the metrics in the works of Ezra Pound. Creekmore's startling documentary style frequently caused his work to be compared to Pound's.

Creekmore was a frequent contributor to literary magazines and published his first book of poems, *Personal Sun*, in 1940. *Personal Sun* includes "To the Very Late Mourners of the Old South," which foreshadows the philosophy found in Creekmore's later novels. Creekmore used his poetic talent to describe social ills and the desperation of humanity and civilization.

In 1942 Creekmore joined the US Navy, becoming a lieutenant and serving until 1945. His experiences in World War II provided the material for his most famous book of poetry, *The Long Reprieve and Other Poems from New Caledonia* (1946). After the war, Creekmore moved back and forth between homes in Jackson and New York City. He worked as an editor for New Directions Press and as a critic for the *New York Times*, reviewing such luminaries as Carson McCullers and Langston Hughes. Creekmore was also a part of Eudora Welty's social circle (his sister married her brother), and he served as one of her early mentors.

Creekmore's novels, unlike many of his poems, specifically addressed the South. His work received praise from many for its documentary aspects, but Creekmore also received heavy criticism in the South. The *Jackson Daily News* described his first novel, *The Fingers of the Night* (1946), which depicts the life of poor whites in Mississippi, as belonging in the garbage can with *Sanctuary*, *Light in August*, *Tobacco Road*, and "any other nasty drivel purporting to picture life in Mississippi."

Hostile reviews and limited job opportunities as well as the pressure of being an openly gay man in Mississippi may have pushed Creekmore to make New York his permanent home. His other two novels, *The Welcome* (1948) and *The Chain in the Heart* (1953), also criticized southern society. *The Chain in the Heart* attacked both the contemporary treatment of African Americans and the historical legacy of slavery. *The Welcome*, Creekmore's only explicitly gay work, derided the region's stifling system of forced heterosexuality and left open the question of queer desire in the South.

Creekmore spent the last years of his life living in New York and working as a translator and editor. His final publication was a work of nonfiction, *Daffodils Are Dangerous: Poisonous Plants in Your Garden*, a serious guide that reflected his love of gardening. Creekmore died after suffering a massive heart attack on 10 February 1967 while in a taxi on his way to the airport to fly to Spain.

Courtney Chartier
Robert W. Woodruff Library,
Atlanta, Georgia

John Howard, *Men Like That: A Southern Queer History* (1999); James B. Lloyd, ed., *Lives of Mississippi Writers, 1817–1967* (1981); Ann Waldron, *Eudora: A Writer's Life* (1998); *Jackson Daily News* (23 May 1946, 11 November 1954); *Memphis Commercial Appeal* (25 May 1966); *Saturday Review* (8 August 1953); Hubert Creekmore Collection, 1928–2002, Department of Archives and Special Collections, J. D. Williams Library, University of Mississippi.

Crop Dusting

Mississippians have been dusting their crops with various substances intended to protect plants from insect pests, weeds, and other natural threats since the very earliest days of agriculture in the state. Whereas Indian farmers and later white settlers and slaves had employed a combination of techniques to increase their crop yields, after the late nineteenth century farmers began relying almost exclusively on topical, poisonous solutions, specifically arsenical compounds such as calcium arsenate and lead arsenate. Landowners usually gave the task of applying the poisons to hired hands or tenant farmers, who did so by either walking through the fields with handheld pump sprayers or by riding through the fields on horseback. Both of these methods of application were slow and costly and were never completely effective.

At the beginning of the twentieth century two factors changed forever the way Mississippians fought farm pests: the arrival of the cotton boll weevil and advances in technology. The weevil, the South's greatest agricultural enemy, began destroying the state's cotton in 1907, and extension agents as well as enterprising hucksters soon began recommending various poisonous mixtures as solutions to stem the invasion. Experts initially continued to recommend hand dusting the crop with arsenical mixtures, but businesses sprang up around the state offering alternative pesticides of dubious value to desperate farmers. As the boll weevil continued to destroy thousands of tons of Missis-

Crop duster flying over a cotton field (Bern and Franke Keating Collection, Department of Archives and Special Collections, J. D. Williams Library, University of Mississippi)

sippi cotton each year, money from the federal government, plantation owners, and banks flowed into the state to fund research into new pesticides and innovative methods of delivering the poisons.

Though the first experiments in aerial crop dusting were conducted in Ohio, engineers and farmers made the greatest developments toward commercial viability in Louisiana's Mississippi Delta. In Monroe, Louisiana, US Department of Agriculture entomologists paired with the Huff-Daland Airplane Company, which manufactured military airplanes, and began retrofitting aircraft with hoppers to drop dust onto farm fields. Though commercial crop dusters were born in Louisiana, they proved their mettle in the Mississippi Delta, where the vast, flat cotton fields with relatively few power lines and stands of trees provided an optimal training ground not only for the technology but for the pilots, who flew eight to ten feet above the tops of cotton rows and then quickly jerked their aircraft skyward to avoid the obstacles at row's end. Few planters had this expertise or could afford aircraft, so many began paying dusting companies to spray fields. This, too, was costly. By the beginning of the Great Depression, for example, the Delta and Pine Land Company in Scott was paying Delta Air Service (later Delta Airlines) eleven thousand dollars per month to dust the company's fields with calcium arsenate.

Following World War II Mississippi farmers realized that crop dusting was prohibitively expensive, but its use was also limited by the lack of pesticide options. As early as the 1910s chemists had devised synthetic organic pesticides to kill insects, but in the late 1940s and 1950s chemical companies and extension agents began pushing these chemical compounds on Mississippi growers. The most famous of these compounds was DDT, which at first appeared to be a panacea for pest problems. Used during World War II to kill mosquitoes in Asia, DDT proved equally effective against boll weevils. In addition, it was relatively inexpensive because a small quantity could be diluted to cover thousands of acres. Mississippians used DDT in huge quantities, and while it cut pest and mosquito populations, it also decimated birds and fish and damaged human health. Critics had long pointed out crop dusting did not limit poison solely to its intended targets but instead spread harmful chemicals across other fields, water sources, and populated areas. The dangers associated with DDT only bolstered this argument. Tenants usually lived on the edges of fields, and duster pilots could not avoid spraying these dwellings. Historians, sociologists, and scientists have recently uncovered damning evidence of the deleterious effects this spraying had on the health of tenant farmers as well as of crop duster pilots.

By the end of the twentieth century Mississippians used airplanes to apply fertilizers and fungicides as well as pesticides to cotton, corn, soybeans, and other crops. Although DDT is now banned, the Environmental Protection Agency has connected use of other insecticides to high rates of cancers, chronic health problems, and developmental anomalies in people living in rural areas. On average, early twenty-first-century landowners in the Mississippi Delta apply more pesticides to their fields than do farmers in other areas of the South.

James C. Giesen
Mississippi State University

Pete Daniel, *Toxic Drift: Pesticides and Health in the Post–World War II South* (2005); W. David Lewis and Wesley Phillips Newton, *Delta: The History of an Airline* (1979); Edmund Russell, *War and Nature: Fighting Humans and Insects with Chemicals from World War I to Silent Spring* (2001).

Crop Liens

Emerging in the chaos and economic devastation that followed the Civil War, crop liens were advances of credit to farmers with their future crops as collateral. When small farmers, tenants, and sharecroppers possessed little or no significant real or personal property, the only way they could get loans to purchase seed, mules, and other necessities was to mortgage their crops (and often whatever little property they did possess). When harvested, crops would be used to pay off the loan.

The crop-lien system allowed the decentralized postwar economy to function but imposed significant costs on individuals and on society as a whole. It focused on cotton production even as prices declined toward the turn of the twentieth century. Merchants and landowners advantaged themselves by exploiting dirt-poor farmers, further crippling those at the very bottom of the economic ladder.

Crop liens averaged roughly eighty dollars per year but varied depending on the amount of land to be farmed, the size of the farm family, the number of mules available to the farmer, and the farmer's reputation. However, the loans did not take the form of cash. Instead, farmers would receive credit at the merchant's store with which to purchase food, clothing, shoes, household items, feed, fertilizer, and farm implements. To cover interest accrued on the debt, farmers buying on this credit paid significantly more for these items than those paying cash. Interest rates ranged between 25 and 60 percent or more. Defenders of the system argued that these rates were justified based on such factors as the high risks involved in agriculture and high interest rates the merchants paid to their northern suppliers; critics, conversely, charged that merchants extending credit took advantage of their monopolies and of debtors' poverty. Whatever the reasons for and validity of the high interest rates, they resulted in a situation where both white tenant farmers and black sharecroppers became trapped in a cycle of perpetual debt.

Black sharecroppers in particular found themselves forced to grow cotton in a declining market, increasingly dependent on and regulated by merchants and landlords, and unable to escape the grinding poverty of this economy. In the words of Edward Royce, sharecropping and crop liens ultimately led to a devastating "constriction of possibilities."

In Mississippi, conflicts between white elite landlords and merchants and poorer whites led to political struggles over crop-lien laws. In 1875 the state gave landlords precedence over crops, preventing sharecroppers from using the crop as collateral. In 1886, with many poor whites losing their farms to banks and merchants, Mississippi rescinded the crop-lien law, ostensibly to protect small farmers, although the laws and the courts generally continued to uphold the rights of creditors.

Christopher Johnson
Palomar College

Thavolia Glymph, Harold Woodman, Barbara Jeanne Fields, and Armstead L. Robinson, *Essays on the Postbellum Southern Economy* (1985); Robert Higgs, *Competition and Coercion: Blacks in the American Economy, 1865–1914* (1977); Roger Ransom and Richard Sutch, *One Kind of Freedom: The Economic Consequences of Emancipation* (1977); Edward Royce, *The Origins of Southern Sharecropping* (1993); Gavin Wright, *Old South, New South: Revolutions in the Southern Economy since the Civil War* (1986).

Crosby Lumber Companies

Lucius Olen Crosby Sr. (1869–1948) began the first of the Crosby-related land and timber companies in the early 1900s with holdings in Southwest Mississippi and Canton. In 1916 he sold his Canton mill to Stewart Gammill Sr.; moved to Picayune after acquiring a large tract of timberland from John Blodgett of Grand Rapids, Michigan; and bought the Rosa sawmill.

Crosby and Lamont Rowlands then organized the Goodyear Yellow Pine Company, which managed the Rosa and Goodyear mills in Picayune plus several smaller mills in South Mississippi. The Pearl River Valley Railroad was organized to transport timber products to the Southern Railway in Nicholson. As midwestern industry and agriculture expanded rapidly after the conclusion of World War I, demand for timber products increased. Goodyear Yellow Pine acquired contracts related to Chicago's International Harvester Company and expanded operations in Picayune,

Cybur, Piave, Lumberton, and other Mississippi locations. It shipped millions of board feet to the Midwest for use in farm implements, homes, factories, and other industrial products.

Crosby helped organize the Mississippi Chamber of Commerce in 1923 and served as its president until 1930. In 1927 he helped Herbert Hoover manage relief operations when the Mississippi River overflowed from Memphis to the Gulf of Mexico.

L. O. Crosby's three sons, Robert Howell (1897–1973), Hollis Hobson (1899–1971), and Lucius Osmond Jr. (1907–78), worked in their father's business operations and in 1935 bought the Foster Creek Lumber Company in Stephenson. They established a large lumber operation there, renamed the town Crosby, and formed the Crosby Lumber and Manufacturing Company with Hollis Crosby as president. In 1937 Howell Crosby became president of Crosby Naval Stores, later renamed Crosby Chemical Company. It produced turpentine, rosins, and resins, largely from pine stumps salvaged from cutover timberlands. In 1941 L. O. Crosby Jr. moved from Crosby to Picayune to help his father in the Goodyear Yellow Pine Company (later renamed Crosby Forest Products). In the 1940s and 1950s the company acquired considerable land in Wilkinson, Amite, Jefferson, and Copiah Counties. During World War II Crosby Forest Products produced timber products for ammunition crates and wire-bound boxes from a veneer mill. The company twice received the Army-Navy "E" Award for excellence in manufacturing. Toward the end of the conflict German prisoners of war were used to construct creosote plants in Crosby and Picayune that produced treated telephone poles and piling used for construction in New Orleans and other expanding cities. The company became one of the state's leaders in fire protection and reforestation.

After L. O. Crosby Sr.'s death his three sons continued operating plants in Mississippi and Louisiana. In 1960 L. O. Crosby Jr. and family leased timberlands to St. Regis Paper Company, and in 1965 Crosby Lumber and Manufacturing Company was sold to St. Regis, which then established a large paper mill in Monticello. Crosby descendants continue to operate family businesses in Mississippi and Louisiana.

John Hawkins Napier III
Ramer, Alabama

John M. Barry, *Rising Tide: The Great Mississippi Flood of 1927 and How It Changed America* (1977); L. O. Crosby Jr., *Crosby: A Story of Men and Trees* (1960); Crosby Land and Resources website, www.crosbylandresources.com; James E. Fickle, *Mississippi Forests and Forestry* (2001); John Hawkins Napier III, *Lower Pearl River's Piney Woods: Its Land and People* (1985).

Crossroads Myth

One of the most recognized tales in American folklore has Mississippi roots. The story has many names, including "The Delta Legend," "The Deal with the Devil," and "The Deal at the Crossroads," among others. Yet each tells a similar story that centers on a midnight meeting between a frustrated guitarist and Satan himself at the intersection of two highways—the Crossroads. In exchange for mastery of his instrument, the musician was willing to sell his soul to the Devil. The guitarist stood at the Crossroads and played his instrument until Satan arrived in the form of a black male. The musician presented his instrument to the mysterious stranger, who tuned it, played some chords, and handed it back to its owner. A musical covenant had been reached, and the guitarist now possessed the ability to play any tune he desired. However, his soul belonged to Satan.

Scholars disagree over the origins of the Crossroads myth. Some maintain that the story originated in Africa, with Satan representing an African trickster deity such as the Dahomean Legba or Yoruba Eshu. This interpretation places the tale in a broader cultural context and elevates the musician to spiritual status. Other folklorists argue that the tale possesses many Western elements and reflects slavery's impact on African American life. Regardless of its precise origins, the myth has become most associated with early twentieth-century bluesman Robert Johnson.

Johnson was born in Hazlehurst, Mississippi, in 1911 and played harmonica with local bluesmen Willie Brown and Charlie Parker as a teen. Johnson yearned to play guitar like his idol, Son House, but possessed little feel for the instrument. In fact, Brown and Parker ridiculed his picking skills, and other bluesmen refused to play with him. Johnson left the blues circuit for months but reemerged with an unmatched proficiency on the guitar. His drastic improvement in such a brief period created suspicion that Johnson had gained his talent as a result of a deal with the Devil, and his songs encouraged such speculation. Although Johnson recorded only twenty-nine songs, many dealt with the dark themes of isolation, frustration, and personal loss. In particular, he sang of the "hellhounds" that constantly pursed him, and his most famous song, "Crossroads Blues," told the story of his experience with Satan at the lonely junction of two highways.

The legend of Johnson's Faustian pact increased after his 1938 death and continues to inspire countless musicians. The fact that Johnson is known as the King of the Delta Blues Singers and has sold millions of albums worldwide strengthens beliefs that Johnson bartered his soul for fame, because his renown came only after he joined Satan in death. Other musicians, most notably Tommy Johnson, are also associated with the Crossroads myth, which constitutes an integral part of American folklore that demonstrates the often inseparable line between the secular and the sacred in southern culture. Clarksdale, Mississippi, claims the junction of Highways 61 and 49 as the intersection of the Crossroads myth.

J. Michael Butler
Flagler College

Peter Guralnick, *Searching for Robert Johnson* (1998); Barry Lee Pearson and Bill McCulloch, *Robert Johnson: Lost and Found* (2003); Jon Michael Spencer, *Blues and Evil* (1993); Elijah Wald, *Escaping the Delta: Robert Johnson and the Invention of the Blues* (2004).

Crowe, Milburn James

(1933–2005) Community Activist and Civil Servant

Milburn James Crowe is considered a Mississippi treasure because of his devotion to preserving the history, arts, and culture of the state and particularly of the town of Mound Bayou. He was born on 15 March 1933 in Mound Bayou, one of America's oldest and largest African American towns. His father, Henry Crowe, was among the first settlers in the Delta wilderness, having followed former slave Isaiah T. Montgomery on his quest to find a land where "God dwelt and liberty." Milburn Crowe's mother, Altie, the descendant of former slaves from Louisiana, was a community activist and entrepreneur.

Isaiah T. Montgomery; his father, Benjamin; and the rest of his siblings and family were the former slaves of Joseph Davis, brother of Confederate president Jefferson Davis. Joseph Davis's plantation located at Davis Bend in Warren County was unique because of its long history of social experimentation, which began with Joseph Davis's stagecoach ride with Scottish social reformer Robert Owen. Owen, traveling to America to establish a utopian settlement in New Harmony, Indiana, espoused the idea that workers should be treated as "reasonable human beings," though a certain degree of paternalistic control was also necessary. When Joseph Davis established his five-thousand-acre plantation, Hurricane, in 1824, he instituted unheard-of reforms for his slaves, including providing well-kept cottages and allowing his workers to be judged in court by a jury of their peers. The Union Army later attempted to establish a model colony on the same land. This history and Montgomery's legacy inspired Crowe to collect and save images and memorabilia concerning Mound Bayou and the surrounding areas.

Crowe attended the Bolivar County Training School and the Southern Christian Institute in Edwards. He then relocated to Chicago, where he attended Wilson College. He became a member of the First Christian Church, which was founded by his maternal grandfather, Rev. James Turner. Crowe joined the US Air Force in 1953 and was trained in communications. He served one stint in Alaska, where he tried to organize a grassroots business cooperative among members of the local Native American community. He was honorably discharged from the Air Force in 1957 and returned to Chicago, where he worked for the Chicago Park District. He moved back to Mound Bayou in 1962 to care for his mother and began collecting information on the town.

Crowe was a community activist, businessman, and civil servant. He founded the Mound Bayou Historical Society and served as its president. He helped to incorporate the Historic Mound Bayou Foundation and establish its nonprofit status. He was a member of the Old Capital Museum's Community Advisory Committee and helped to develop the museum's *Mississippi 1500–1800* exhibits. Crowe was a member of the Mississippi Historical Society board of directors as well as of the State Historical Records Advisory Board. He served as a commissioner for the Mid-Delta Empowerment Zone Alliance and as Mound Bayou's city clerk and elections commissioner and manager. He received numerous awards for his public service, including a Public Humanities Achievement Award in 2000 and a 2005 Founders' Day Award from the Mound Bayou Civic Club, which noted, "The rich history of Mound Bayou is shared from generation to generation, because of your knowledge and kind spirit of sharing."

In the 1960s Crowe's store and restaurant, the Crowe's Nest, served as a meeting place for civil rights activists. Constance Curry, a field representative and lawyer for the American Friends Service Committee in Mississippi, remembered, "In Mound Bayou, Leon [Hall] and I stopped at a storefront—the Crowe's Nest. It was a store and restaurant as well as a meeting and gathering place for local and visiting movement people. We went inside where I met Crowe, one of Mound Bayou's longtime activists, who fed us some unforgettable barbecue ribs and then took us through a curtain-covered door to the back of the store where a poker game was in progress. Leon Hall and I played in some Atlanta games, so we poured ourselves a little scotch and joined in. I look back on that night when I sat with five black men and gambled and drank in the middle of Mississippi, and all I can say is, 'It seemed perfectly fine at the time.'"

Crowe worked tirelessly to preserve Mound Bayou's history, producing several extensive chronicles of events. He produced a newspaper, *The Voice*, as well as several other publications. He died on 10 September 2005 in Mound Bayou. Crowe's extensive archive is housed at Emory University in Atlanta.

Lynn Marshall-Linnemeier
Atlanta, Georgia

Constance Curry, *Silver Rights* (1995); Janet Sharpe Hermann, *The Pursuit of a Dream* (1981); *Mississippi History Newsletter* (October 2005).

Crowley, Mart

(b. 1935) Writer, Producer, Actor

Playwright Mart Crowley was born on 21 August 1935 in Vicksburg, where he attended St. Aloysius High School, served as equipment manager for the football team, and donated his time and talent to the Vicksburg Little Theatre. As Ellis Nassour wrote about Crowley's Vicksburg childhood, "His father operated Crowley's Smoke House. The motto was 'Where All Good Fellows Meet'—for pool, dominoes, cigars, punch-board gambling, a bit of illegal drinking, and the best hamburgers anywhere . . . but movie theatres were [Crowley's] world, where he developed his writer's imagination." Attracted by the quality of the school's drama department, Crowley went to Catholic University of America in Washington, D.C., graduating in 1957.

During the winter of 1955–56, Crowley watched the filming of Tennessee Williams's *Baby Doll* in the Mississippi Delta and hung out with Elia Kazan, Carroll Baker, Karl Malden, and Eli Wallach at Doe's Eat Place in Greenville. These experiences influenced his decision to go into show business. After working on the set of William Inge's *Splendor in the Grass* (1958) with Natalie Wood and Warren Beatty, he went on to become Wood's assistant and executive story editor for her ABC television series, *Hart to Hart*, and was named godfather to her children.

Sometimes called "the granddaddy of gay theater," Crowley is best known for his long-running 1968 play *Boys in the Band*, which opened Off-Broadway and made theater history by creating sensitive portrayals of a group of gay men attending a birthday party in New York City. *USA Today*'s David Patrick Stearns celebrated Crowley's play, which premiered before the Stonewall Riots and before ACT UP, Queer Nation, and the Gay Liberation Front, as "the *Uncle Tom's Cabin* of homosexual literature." Clive Barnes of the *New York Times* wrote, "*The Boys in the Band* is one of the best-acted plays of the season. It is quite an achievement. I have a feeling that most of us will find it a gripping, if painful, experience—so uncompromising in its honesty that it becomes an affirmation of life." A successful revival of *The Boys in the Band* appeared at the WPA Theatre in New York in 1996. In 2002 Crowley's sequel, *The Men from the Boys*, debuted in San Francisco at the New Conservatory Theatre Center.

In between, *Remote Asylum* (1970) pitted the effete masculinity of the rich against the instinctive virility of the natives of Mexico. Opening in Los Angeles and starring William Shatner, it proved a failure. Crowley's most southern play, the autobiographical *A Breeze from the Gulf*, opened at the Eastside Playhouse in New York in 1973 and received critically favorable reviews. The three-character play, which Crowley prefaced with the warning that it should not "drip with magnolias," portrays familial dysfunction as psychological violence, drug addiction, and alcohol abuse bring out the worst in parents who strive to love one another and to do their best by their son. The horrors of regular trips to Whitfield (Mississippi's psychiatric hospital), free-for-all brawls at Antoine's in "Noo Awlens," and heavy drinking on Bourbon Street are juxtaposed with moments of happiness at places such as Edgewater and Paradise Point on the Gulf Coast, with the sound of the surf and a touch of the ocean breeze.

In *For Reasons That Remain Unclear*, which premiered at the Olney Theatre in Maryland in 1993, Crowley mines his experiences as a boy who was molested by a teacher. Crowley re-creates his character from *Breeze* as an American priest who is lured to a hotel in Rome by an American writer and placed stage center.

Crowley's work has received praise for its individualized prototypes, tight structure, razor-sharp dialogue, and witty wisecracks. Lines from *Boys in the Band* have become legendary in gay culture: "Give me lithium or give me meth"; "Oh, Mary, it takes a fairy to make something pretty"; and "Show me a happy homosexual, and I'll show you a gay corpse." The 2011 documentary *Making the Boys* explored the impact, influence, and controversy surrounding the play. Themes of self-loathing and self-destruction, deep-seated homophobia, and social maladjustment appear as his characters search for love in all the wrong places and come to grips with themselves, love one another, and achieve meaningful relationships.

Colby H. Kullman
University of Mississippi

Clive Barnes, "*The Boys in the Band* Still Plays Well," *New York Times* (21 June 1996); John M. Clum, *Acting Gay* (1992); John M. Clum, *Still Acting Gay* (2000); Ellis Nassour, "The Leader of the 'Band,'" *Jackson Clarion-Ledger* (30 June 1996); Vito Russo, *The Celluloid Closet* (1987); Alan Sinfield, *Out on Stage* (1999); Claude J. Summers, *The Gay and Lesbian Literary Heritage* (1997).

Crudup, Arthur "Big Boy"

(1905–1974) Blues Musician

Arthur "Big Boy" Crudup was a blues singer and guitarist who influenced not only blues musicians but also the development of rock and roll. Arthur Crudup was born in Forest, Mississippi, on 25 August 1905. His mother, Minnie Crudup, was a musician. As a boy, Arthur, nicknamed "Big Boy" because of his large stature, sang in the church choir. Crudup did not pick up a guitar until he was thirty-two years old, and he soon began playing in juke joints and on street corners, earning small amounts of money. He sang with the Harmonizing Four gospel quartet, which moved to Chicago in 1941. He again tried to earn a living playing the blues but soon found himself broke and homeless. His big break came when talent scout Lester Melrose heard Crudup performing on a street corner and invited him to a party at bluesman Tampa Red's house. Audience members, including Lonnie Johnson and Big Bill Broonzy, were impressed enough that Melrose arranged a contract for Crudup with RCA Victor. Over the next fifteen years Crudup recorded more than eighty songs for RCA, but his lack of business acumen meant that he found himself locked into contracts that gave most of the royalties for his songs to the record company. Moreover, public musical tastes began shifting away from country blues sounds and toward more polished urban, Chicago-style blues and rock and roll. Crudup returned to Mississippi in the late 1940s, disenchanted with the music business, and continued to perform until 1956. He earned his living mostly through farm work, though he recorded a few sides for smaller labels such as Trumpet (1952), Champion (ca. 1952), Ace (1953), and Groove (1953–54), generally under pseudonyms such as Art Crudux, Arthur Crump, and Elmer James.

Elvis Presley was enamored with Crudup's music and recorded versions of his songs "That's All Right" (1954), "My Baby Left Me" (1956), and "So Glad You're Mine" (1956), earning Crudup credit as the Father of Rock and Roll. Though Presley's recordings of these songs helped launch him as an international superstar and garnered him substantial wealth, Crudup received little attention or money.

In the late 1960s Bob Koester of Delmark Records recorded Crudup and arranged for promoter-manager-photographer Dick Waterman to help get Crudup onto the festival circuit. He began touring the United States and Europe, performing until his death from a stroke on 28 March 1974 in Nassawadox, Virginia. Waterman also managed to get some past royalties paid to Crudup's estate.

Greg Johnson
University of Mississippi

Sheldon Harris, *Blues Who's Who: A Biographical Dictionary of Blues Singers* (1981); Gérard Herzhaft, Paul Harris, Jerry Haussler, and Anton J. Mikofsky, *Encyclopedia of the Blues* (1997); Dick Waterman, *Between Midnight and Day: The Last Unpublished Blues Archive* (2003).

CSS *Arkansas* (Ship)

The *Arkansas* was the only Confederate ironclad to see service in Mississippi waters during the Civil War. The vessel was one of two identical ironclads laid down in Memphis, Tennessee, by contractor John T. Shirley in October 1861. Though Shirley was to deliver both ships by 24 December, they remained incomplete when Union forces threatened the area in April 1862. Confederate authorities towed the *Arkansas* up the Yazoo River to Greenwood, where they hoped to finish the vessel. The second Shirley boat, the *Tennessee*, was destroyed on the stocks at Memphis to prevent its capture.

The saga of the *Arkansas's* completion reflected the myriad difficulties inherent in ship construction in the Confederacy and particularly in the Mississippi Delta, where industrial resources were scarce. The lack of facilities at Greenwood necessitated the vessel's removal to Yazoo City, where conditions were slightly better. Because experienced shipbuilders were unavailable, local blacksmiths, detailed soldiers, and hired slaves were pressed into service. The lack of rolled armor plate forced builders to substitute raw railroad rails. Ordnance and ordnance stores arrived piecemeal from Memphis, Vicksburg, Jackson, and Atlanta. Largely through the determined efforts of commanding officer Isaac N. Brown, work concluded in roughly five weeks, and by July the vessel was ready for a crew.

The completed *Arkansas* retained a makeshift appearance, and conditions aboard were at best primitive. Measuring 165 feet in length and 35 feet abeam, the ship featured a boxlike armored casemate housing a ten-gun battery. The gunboat's woodwork was crude, and the machinery was notoriously unreliable. Quarters were cramped and ventilation was inadequate. Heat from the engines and boilers was nearly unbearable: temperatures belowdecks held steady at 100 degrees even when the fires were banked and soared to 130 when the ship was under steam. Firemen and engineers worked in short shifts, and some even volunteered for duty on the gun deck to escape the heat.

Despite its humble origins the *Arkansas* proved formidable in its brief but eventful career. Union observers doubted that the ironclad would ever become operational, and the vessel's appearance on the Mississippi River on 15 July 1862 caught the US Navy by surprise. In a running battle the *Arkansas* fought the entire Union fleet as it ran the gauntlet between the mouth of the Yazoo and Vicksburg. The ironclad both sustained and inflicted heavy damage in the lopsided contest. Nearly crippled, the *Arkansas* reached Vicksburg, where its presence threatened Union naval superiority on the Mississippi. Moored under the city's high bluff, the ship survived two Union attempts to destroy it. It was subsequently placed under the command of the Confederate Army and ordered downriver on 2 August to support an attack against Baton Rouge. Repairs remained incomplete and mechanical problems plagued the *Arkansas* during the journey. The ship's engines broke down on 6 August, just as it encountered Union gunboats defending Baton Rouge. With the battle already joined, the vessel drifted powerless to the riverbank, where crew members set it on fire to prevent its capture. Adrift and in flames, the *Arkansas* finally exploded and sank.

The *Arkansas* illustrated the potential and the limitations of the Confederacy's home-built ironclads. Its existence altered the strategic balance on the Mississippi and forced the Union Navy to retreat downriver to New Orleans. Yet the South's limited capacity for manufacturing doomed the ironclad to destruction. Unsupported and equipped with inferior machinery, the *Arkansas* faced long odds. By the time of its destruction, the Confederacy possessed no suitable facilities in the region to replace the ironclad.

Edwin L. Combs III

Mississippi University for Women

A. Robert Holcombe Jr., "The Evolution of Confederate Ironclad Design" (master's thesis, East Carolina University, 1993); William N. Still Jr., *Confederate Shipbuilding* (1969); William N. Still Jr., *Iron Afloat: The Story of Confederate Armorclads* (1971).

Cultural Crossroads Quilters

Cultural Crossroads Quilters is a group of women who live in Port Gibson in Claiborne County, Mississippi. They work individually and in collaboration, producing a variety of quilting projects with Mississippi Cultural Crossroads, a community-based local arts agency that promotes community involvement, tolerance, and equality through the shared aesthetics of quilt making, community theater, and arts education.

Works created by Crossroads Quilters are sold at the Cultural Crossroads center and in galleries throughout the country. These quilts reflect a wide range of African American and European American traditions found in southwestern Mississippi, among them works with traditional block patterns and works made with strip and string construction techniques. The striking composition and high quality of these works has garnered attention from serious collectors across the United States.

When working alone, each quilter expresses her personal aesthetic inclinations, choosing materials, designs, and techniques that fit her unique vision. Collaborative quilts, however, are made in a variety of ways. While several quilters may produce different multiblock designs, others may strip the pieces together. The actual quilting together, binding, and finishing may be undertaken by many artists. This technique allows quilters to mix African American and European American traditions and produce expressive improvisational quilts that follow no strict pattern.

Quilting in Mississippi originally developed out of necessity as homemakers pieced together fabric scraps into bed coverings to keep warm. This utilitarian use of cast-off objects is one of the earliest examples of recycled art. Quilting becomes a decorative craft when the different elements of the piece are arranged in such a way as to increase the covering's aesthetic effect.

Mississippi Cultural Crossroads is a unique organization that has garnered awards and funding from numerous government agencies, foundations, and arts and humanities councils. Members of Port Gibson's black majority and white minority are largely racially segregated, and Cultural Crossroads is one of the few places where all area residents come together.

Since 1988 Mississippi Cultural Crossroads has organized a yearly spring quilt contest, Pieces and Strings, that highlights the work of the best contemporary quilters working within the Mississippi folk tradition. Since African American culture has long been ignored or underrepresented in this part of the country, Mississippi Cultural Crossroads has sought to promote the significance and potential inherent within the African American aesthetic. The exhibition displays African American and European American quilts side by side as a means of highlighting the accomplishments, aesthetic similarities, and differences of the two traditions.

Cale Nicholson

Little Rock, Arkansas

David Crosby, *Quilts and Quilting in Claiborne County: Tradition and Change in a Rural Southern County* (1999); David Crosby, *Teacher's Guide to Crossroads Quilters: Stitching the Community Together* (1999); Roland L. Freeman, *A Communion of the Spirits: African-American Quilters, Preservers, and Their Stories* (1996); Kyre E. Hicks, *Black Threads: An African American Quilting Sourcebook* (2003); Mary Elizabeth Johnson, *Mississippi Quilts* (2001).

Curry, Constance

(b. 1933) Activist and Author

Connie Curry has played important roles in Mississippi twice, first as a civil rights activist in the mid-1960s and since the 1990s as an author, editor, and filmmaker producing works about individuals in the civil rights movement. Born in New Jersey and raised in North Carolina, Curry attended Atlanta's Agnes Scott College, where she became a leader of the National Student Association. That involvement led her into the civil rights movement, first with the Southern Student Human Relations Project and then as a staff member and organizer in Atlanta for the Student Nonviolent Coordinating Committee.

In 1964 Curry started working for the American Friends Service Committee (AFSC), a capacity in which she became the first staff member of Mississippians for Public Education, a group dedicated to opposing the threat that massive resistance leaders might close down the public schools and use violence against supporters of school desegregation. In her work for the AFSC, she helped parents and students deal with the various difficulties involved in going to newly integrated schools.

Curry still lives in Atlanta but continues to affect Mississippi with her work as an author, editor, and documentary filmmaker. Her first book, *Silver Rights* (1995), was a popular and affectionate story of Mae Bertha Carter and her children, who were the first African American students to attend the previously all-white schools in Drew. Curry knew the Carters from her work with the AFSC and wanted to tell the story of the family's courage and perseverance. She then helped edit interviews and other material into narrative form for the 2000 book *Aaron Henry: The Fire Ever Burning*, a memoir of the Clarksdale leader of the Mississippi branch of the National Association for the Advancement of Colored People based on material Henry left at his death in 1997. In 2002 Curry and Winson Hudson published *Mississippi Harmony: Memoirs of a Freedom Fighter*, Hudson's story of his activism in Leake County. With clear prose and great respect for her subject, Curry has allowed many readers to see civil rights activists in their own words and in human terms. In 2004 Curry produced *The Intolerable Burden*, a documentary film based on *Silver Rights* with new material about public education in recent years.

Ted Ownby
University of Mississippi

Constance Curry et al., *Deep in Our Hearts: Nine White Women in the Freedom Movement* (2000).

D

Dahmer, Vernon
(1908–1966) Activist

Vernon Ferdinand Dahmer was born on 10 March 1908 in Forrest County and became a leading figure in the local civil rights movement. Dahmer owned a two-hundred-acre farm, a grocery store, and two mills in the Kelly Settlement area of northern Forrest County. He also farmed cotton commercially on three hundred additional acres. Dahmer directed music and taught Sunday school at Shady Grove Baptist Church and became a respected figure in the black community. Dahmer's economic independence enabled him to organize local blacks and support indigenous civil rights programs without fear of white financial reprisals. He served several terms as president of the Forrest County chapter of the National Association for the Advancement of Colored People and led a campaign to obtain the release from prison of Clyde Kennard, a friend who had been jailed on fraudulent charges after applying to the all-white University of Southern Mississippi. In addition, Dahmer fed, lodged, and supported Student Nonviolent Coordinating Committee volunteers who worked in the Hattiesburg area during 1964's Freedom Summer.

Dahmer realized that the vote represented the best opportunity for blacks to obtain full equality in Mississippi, so he initiated a registration campaign in Forrest County after the Voting Rights Act became law in 1965. He placed a county voter registration book in his store so that blacks could register without fear or intimidation and offered to pay the poll taxes of anyone who could not afford to do so. His activities infuriated white supremacists, who targeted the activist for assassination.

During the early hours of 10 January 1966, two cars filled with Ku Klux Klan members attacked the Dahmer home while Vernon; his wife, Ellie; and three of their eight children slept. The Klansmen riddled the house and Dahmer's nearby store with shotgun blasts and threw Molotov cocktails into the buildings. Vernon grabbed a rifle and shot back at the assailants from within the inferno as his family escaped, suffering severe burns to his head, arms, and upper body. From his hospital bed, he justified his civil rights activities by stating, "If you don't vote, you don't count" because "a man has to do his own thinking." Dahmer died of smoke inhalation on 11 January.

Pres. Lyndon B. Johnson launched a federal investigation into the crime, leading to the arrests of fourteen Klansmen on arson and murder charges. One man entered a guilty plea and juries convicted four others. KKK Imperial Wizard Sam Bowers, who was accused of ordering Dahmer's murder, finally received a life sentence in 1998 after four earlier proceedings ended in mistrials.

Vernon Dahmer remains a hero of the Mississippi black freedom struggle. A Hattiesburg park and street bear his name, testifying to one cost of the battle for racial equality in Forrest County.

J. Michael Butler
Flagler College

Taylor Branch, *Pillar of Fire: America in the King Years, 1963–1965* (1998); "Dahmer (Vernon F.)" Collection, McCain Library and Archives, University of Southern Mississippi; John Dittmer, *Local People: The Struggle for Civil Rights in Mississippi* (1994).

Ruins of Vernon Dahmer's house, Hattiesburg, after it was firebombed, 10 January 1966 (Moncrief Collection, Archives and Records Services Division, Mississippi Department of Archives and History [510])

Dairy Industry

The production and processing of milk and dairy products in Mississippi and across the country have undergone tremendous change since the antebellum era. The manner in which milk is produced on the farm and how milk is processed into dairy products has undergone especially dramatic structural evolution over the past fifty years. Technological innovations and institutional developments have resulted in many modifications in the procedures employed to market milk and dairy products from dairy farmers to processors to consumers.

Through the 1800s, milk and dairy products were usually produced and processed at home by family members who cared for and milked the cows and made butter, cheese, and other items. With no refrigeration, milk was produced and consumed on a daily basis at virtually every home. Very few commercial dairies produced and bottled milk for sale to Mississippi's urban populations prior to the 1920s.

Over the next three decades many small commercial dairies sprang up near Mississippi population centers. These operations sold raw milk to local processors that usually bottled milk and made a limited variety of dairy products and delivered them to customers' homes. This period saw the creation of numerous municipal or county "milk sheds" (like watersheds), tightly restricting the processing and marketing of milk and dairy products. Dairy farms milked between ten and fifteen cows and were located short distances from the population centers to reduce the time needed to transport highly perishable milk supplies. Farmers typically placed raw milk in five- or ten-gallon metal milk cans and set them on the side of the road for pickup by flatbed trucks, which hauled the milk to plants within the local milk shed. Estimates show that Mississippi had more than ten thousand dairy farms and perhaps as many as one hundred milk plants during the 1920s. During this era, Oktibbeha County was known as the Milk Pitcher of the South, claiming more than eight hundred dairies within its milk shed.

Post–World War II technological changes led to the elimination of local milk sheds and eventually the termination of home delivery of milk and dairy products. Innovations included the sanitary and efficient movement of raw milk over long distances, refrigeration techniques that extended shelf life, and larger, more efficient processing plants. An obvious but often overlooked feature of the structural revolution has been the development of the interstate highway system, which provided the impetus for the creation of a highly organized and sophisticated trucking industry. In the 1950s and 1960s the number of dairy farms drastically declined across the nation, especially in Mississippi, where the number of farms fell from more than 5,000 in 1950 to 1,636 in 1970. Between 1950 and 1970 advancements in dairy animal genetics, nutrition, and management more than doubled the average annual milk production from a single Mississippi dairy cow from 2,790 pounds (332 gallons) to 5,860 pounds (698 gallons). As in many other agricultural industries, the surviving farms were much larger operations.

Contributing to these fundamental changes in the dairy sector were the organization of regional milk cooperatives and the integration of corporate food chains into milk pro-

cessing. Groups of farmers established these cooperatives to ensure the sale of milk to processors and to facilitate transportation and marketing. More important, the cooperatives improved farmers' market power, enabling them to bargain with processors to raise milk prices. During the 1960s and 1970s Dairyman, Southern Milk Sales, and Gulf Coast Dairy Cooperative became prominent Mississippi institutions. Increased competition from much larger dairy processing firms during the 1990s resulted in combinations of marketing cooperatives so that by the end of the decade, a single dairy cooperative, Dairy Farmers of America, dominated the state. Dairy Farmers of America has members all across the country and claims to market about 35 percent of all the milk produced in the United States.

Since the late 1970s Mississippi and the rest of the Southeast have experienced drastic reductions in the size of the dairy industry. Dairy farms and cows have moved from the region's hot and humid weather conditions, which increase the difficulty and cost of producing milk, to the arid West and Southwest. The number of Mississippi dairy farms plummeted from 987 in 1980 to 315 in 2000. In 2005 Hurricane Katrina devastated many of Mississippi's remaining dairy farms, more than 75 percent of which were located directly along the storm's path. By July 2007 only 162 farms remained, and that number has continued to fall, reaching 120 in 2011 and 85 in 2014. That year, these farms produced 21.9 million gallons (188 million pounds) of milk valued at $48.6 million. Mississippi ranked forty-first among the states in milk production and now imports milk from Texas, New Mexico, and other states to meet consumer needs. As of 2014, Mississippi had two commercial milk processing plants, located in Kosciusko and Hattiesburg, as well as three on-farm milk bottling plants.

Cary W. "Bill" Herndon Jr.
Mississippi State University

F. J. Adcock, M. D. Hudson, P. Rosson, H. M. Harris, and C. W. Herndon Jr., *Choices* 21 (2006); C. W. Herndon Jr., *Hoard's Dairyman* (2006); *Mississippi 2015 Dairy Fact Sheet*, www.southeastdairy.org.

Dale, Ron
(b. 1949) Potter and Sculptor

Ronald Guy Dale was born on 26 January 1949 in Spruce Pine, North Carolina, and lived there for two and a half years before moving to Asheville with his parents and older brother. After graduation from high school and a turn in the US Navy he studied at the University of North Carolina at Asheville for two years (1973–75) before receiving a bachelor of fine arts degree from Goddard College (1977) and a master of fine arts degree in ceramics from Louisiana State University (1979). He taught at the University of Mississippi from 1980 until 2005, when he became a professor emeritus.

Dale was a favorite professor of numerous students and was named Teacher of the Year in 2002. He also taught ceramics at the Penland School of Crafts in North Carolina in the summers of 1985 and 1995; at Cortona, Italy, in the summer of 1987; and at Blackhills Pottery in Elgin, Scotland, in the fall of 2000. He has lectured and conducted ceramics workshops throughout the South and received numerous awards, including a Southern Arts Federation Emerging Artist Award in 1985 and the Mississippi Institute of Arts and Letters Visual Arts Award in 1992. His work is in numerous private and public collections and has been shown in twenty-five solo exhibitions and nearly one hundred group-invitational exhibitions throughout the nation.

Dale works in two modes, one making dinnerware, cups, pitchers, bowls, trays, and vases. Inspired by his teachers, Byron Temple and Cynthia Bringle, and by the work and words of potter Bernard Leach, Dale tries "to combine strong tradition with an awareness of contemporary meaning in developing, simple, straightforward forms. . . . The process is complete only when the pots are used."

For his other mode Dale uses clay and wood to create multidimensional sculptures. "My sculptural work has evolved out of the traditional vocabulary of the vessel," he explains. "Combined with architectural and furniture imagery, I am able to explore concepts of altered space and perspective, light and shadow, and the flattening of form while allowing for a more direct expression of ideas—ideas dealing with both social and personal issues."

Is This My Graceland? (1991–92, 88″ × 81″ × 12″) pays tongue-in-cheek homage to Mississippi artist George Ohr, known as the Mad Potter of Biloxi, who died in 1918. Dale duplicated twenty-one of Ohr's kinky and distorted vessels and arranged them on shelves that lean perilously outward, typical of Dale's work. Among the vessels are some elegant pissoirs and "vagina pots." Ohr also experimented with photography, and copies of his zany self-portraits hang in a gallery setting reflected in a mirror above the shelves. "It's a piece that's closer to me than any other I've done," Dale says, "since it's really autobiographical."

Inspired by Italian painter and printmaker Giorgio Morandi, Dale has created sculptures that are still-life compositions of bottles and vessels in wooden frames of various sizes and shapes. The works appear two-dimensional and flat when viewed from the front but are clearly three-dimensional when approached from other angles.

After reading *The Good Life*, Helen and Scott Nearings's 1954 book on back-to-the-land self-sufficiency, Dale became determined to combine his living and working conditions. He designed and built the home in rural Lafayette County near Oxford where he and his wife reared their daughter and son. With the opening of Irondale Studio in 1996 on land next to his home, Dale realized his dream.

Ann J. Abadie
University of Mississippi

Patti Carr Black, *Art in Mississippi, 1720–1980* (1998); Lisa N. Howorth, in *Ceramics Monthly* (June–July–August 1994); Lisa N. Howorth, *The South: A Treasury of Art and Literature* (1993); *Southern Register* (Spring 1993).

Darden, Charles R.

(1911–1994) Activist

Charles R. Darden served as the president of Mississippi's state conference of branches of the National Association for the Advancement of Colored People (NAACP) from 1955 to 1960. Darden was born in Lauderdale County in 1911, attended Meridian public schools, and became a photographer as well as a prominent voice in the local civil rights movement. Darden was instrumental in establishing a chapter of the NAACP Youth Council in Meridian and served as president of the organization's Meridian branch.

Darden's civil rights activities earned him surveillance by the Mississippi State Sovereignty Commission, which tracked his movements across the state and kept records of the attention he garnered in national and local press. Darden was employed part time by a company that sold class rings in black schools throughout the state, allowing him to become involved in NAACP branches all over Mississippi. Darden

Charles R. Darden, 1960 (Mississippi State Sovereignty Commission Records, Mississippi Department of Archives and History [1-4-0-40-1-1-1])

gained the most attention in 1959 when he was charged with disturbing the peace at Harris Junior College, a black school in Meridian. The college suspended a group of students that included Darden's sons as well as James Chaney, who was later murdered by the Ku Klux Klan during 1964's Freedom Summer, after they wore badges commemorating the fifth anniversary of the Supreme Court's *Brown v. Board of Education* decision. Darden spoke with the principal and photographed the students leaving the school following the suspensions. When he arrived home, local police confiscated the film. Darden was fined fifty dollars for disturbing the peace by encouraging the students' protest.

Darden began to disagree with the direction of the movement in Mississippi early in 1960. Students and other young African Americans began to favor the direct action taking place in other parts of the country, most notably through sit-ins. Darden argued that white business leaders had begun to arm themselves in preparation for such protests and discouraged direct action in favor of continued registration and voting. The NAACP's Mississippi field secretary, Medgar Evers, and others preferred direct action. Darden and Evers developed a professional and personal feud over the organization's direction, and in the fall of 1960 Clarksdale druggist Aaron Henry succeeded Darden as the Mississippi NAACP's president, in large part as a result of the support of Evers and his influential Jackson branch of the organization.

Darden continued his civil rights work and in 1964 was elected as an alternate Mississippi Freedom Democratic Party delegate to the Democratic National Convention. Until his death in 1994, he continued to live in Meridian with his wife, Inez.

Adam C. Evans
Washington, D.C.

Seth Cagin and Philip Dray, *We Are Not Afraid: The Story of Goodman, Schwerner, and Chaney and the Civil Rights Campaign for Mississippi* (1988); John Dittmer, *Local People: The Struggle for Civil Rights in Mississippi* (1994); Myrlie Evers-Williams and Manning Marable, *The Autobiography of Medgar Evers: A Hero's Life and Legacy Revealed through His Writings, Letters, and Speeches* (2005).

Darden, Israel Putnam

(1836–1888) Grange Leader

Worthy Master of the State and National Grange, Israel Putnam "Put" Darden was born in Jefferson County, the son of John Pendleton Darden and Martha Fleming Darden. His grandfather, David Darden, and other family members had emigrated from Georgia to the Mississippi Territory in April 1798, and John Darden was a well-to-do planter who had settled near the Red Lick community in northeastern Jefferson County. Put Darden earned a bachelor's degree from the University of Mississippi in 1856, winning acclaim for his skills in public speaking. He acquired a share of his father's land and purchased an adjoining farm several years later. By 1860 he owned a cotton plantation of more than seven hundred acres and twenty-eight slaves. At the beginning of the Civil War, he enlisted as a lieutenant in the Jefferson Flying Artillery and assumed command of the battery during the Battle of Shiloh. Promoted to captain, he led his battery in fighting in Tennessee, Georgia, Alabama, and Mississippi.

Returning to Jefferson County in May 1865, Darden sought to regain his financial stability. He was elected to the legislature in 1866, but his term ended with the beginning of military rule in 1867. To encourage agriculture, horticulture, and manufacturers of all kinds in the local area, he played an important role in the founding of the Jefferson County Planters', Mechanics', and Manufacturers' Association in 1868 and served on its board of directors for twenty years. After the Grange movement swept the state in the early 1870s, Darden spent most of his time promoting its goal of protecting the rights and interests of farmers. A national fraternal organization that encouraged sectional reconciliation, stressed the importance of education, and welcomed white men and women of all ages with agricultural interests, the Grange (formally the Patrons of Husbandry) had widespread appeal at a time when farmers were struggling to survive in a depressed agricultural economy. Darden spearheaded the move to establish the Phoenix Grange in his neighborhood and subsequently served as its head. In 1873 and 1874, as many farmers lost their land in delinquent tax sales, he and other Grangers played a decisive role in organizing Taxpayer Leagues, which urged white voters of all parties to unite and overthrow the "carpetbagger regime."

Put Darden took over the reins of the state Grange in 1876 and served as its leader until his death twelve years later. Over that time, membership declined, but the organization's political influence increased. Darden visited almost every county annually to reactivate, encourage, and establish Granges. Although many of the earlier Grange cooperatives had failed, Darden achieved limited success in the early 1880s by promoting cooperative stores on the Rochdale plan, which allocated stock and dividends to consumers based on their patronage. Largely because of Darden's leadership, the state Grange recorded its greatest achievement—the 1878 creation of the Mississippi Agricultural and Mechanical College. Grangers also initiated the 1884 move to establish the Industrial Institute and College for white females at Columbus.

Darden fought for state and national legislation to regulate railroads and advocated changes in Mississippi's lien law to ensure that property in foreclosure sales would bring at least three-fourths of its market value. Although Grange bylaws prohibited the discussion of politics, Darden told Grangers to vote only for men who promised to support their interests. In contrast to Wool Hat spokesman Frank Burkitt, who criticized the president of the agricultural college, Gen. Stephen D. Lee, and opposed his requests for legislative appropriations, Darden cooperated with Lee, praised his work at the school, and called for funding to expand its services.

Grangers backed Darden for governor at the 1885 state Democratic convention, but he received only 42 votes to Gov. Robert Lowry's 193. Despite having rejected an independent candidacy, the Grange leader received more than 800 votes in the general election. Later that year, at the meeting of the National Grange in Boston, Darden was elected its Worthy Master, the second southerner to hold that post. In his first annual address, Darden noted the group's declining membership and maintained that farmers wanted an organization that would use its influence to secure favorable legislation. He thus urged Grange leaders to play an active role in state and national politics.

A longtime member of the Christian Church, Darden endured many personal tragedies and hardships during his years of public service. His first wife died in 1860, when their son was only nine months old. Darden married again in the fall of 1865, but his second wife died about a year later. He remarried again and had four children with his third wife before she, too, died. His fourth and final marriage took place in November 1885 and resulted in three more children, one of whom was born after his death. A fire destroyed Darden's country home in 1882, and he lost all of his papers, books, and war relics.

Put Darden died at his home after a brief illness. Grangers across the state and nation held memorial services for their deceased leader. In 1891 the National Grange placed a monument honoring Darden on the grounds of the Mississippi Agricultural and Mechanical College at Starkville (now Mississippi State University). Without Darden's leadership, Grange membership in the state declined, and the organization ceased to exist in Mississippi after its 1898 meeting.

Thomas Neville Boschert
Delta State University

Darden Family Papers, Special Collections, Mitchell Memorial Library, Mississippi State University; Jefferson County Mississippi, Chancery Clerk Records; General Stephen D. Lee, "The Agricultural and Mechanical College of Mississippi: Its Origin, Object, Management and Results," Special Collections, Mitchell Memorial Library, Mississippi State University; D. Sven Nordin, *Rich Harvest: A History of the Grange, 1867–1900* (1974); "The State Grange and A&M College," Special Collections, Mitchell Memorial Library, Mississippi State University.

Davis, Alexander K.
(?–?) Lieutenant Governor

Alexander K. Davis was a central figure in Mississippi Reconstruction. A lawyer and Tennessee native about whom little is known prior to his arrival in Mississippi in 1869, he became the state's first African American lieutenant governor before being impeached in 1875 as part of the Mississippi Plan to return government to white Democrats.

Davis entered politics in 1869, when he was one of forty African Americans, most of them ex-slaves, who won seats in Mississippi's first Reconstruction legislature, which convened on 11 January 1870 in Jackson. Davis was elected to the State House of Representatives from Noxubee County, in eastern Mississippi. He served on the House Ways and Means Committee and chaired the Committee on Salaries and Fees of Public Officers. During his three years as a legislator, he authored and sponsored more than twenty-five bills, among them House Bill No. 6, which sought to extend the debt-collection period in Noxubee County, and House Bill No. 11 to "regulate, reduce and cause uniformity of tolls and charges on the Mobile and Ohio Railroad."

Davis was an active participant in Republican Party machine politics. At the state's 1873 Radical Republican convention, Davis and other elected black Republicans lobbied to have at least three African American candidates included on the statewide slate. The Republicans did so, nominating Davis for lieutenant governor, T. W. Cardozo for state superintendent of education, and James Hill for secretary of state. All three men won, as did white Republican Adelbert Ames, the party's gubernatorial nominee. In addition, black Republican candidates took 55 of the 115 seats in the House of Representatives, and Warren County's I. D. Shadd was elected Speaker.

The election inspired riots across the state in Water Valley, Louisville, Macon, Yazoo City, Friars Point, Columbus, Rolling Fork, Clinton, and Vicksburg, and the Democratic Party struck back two years later. Using both legal and illegal tactics, Democratic candidates took 97 seats in the State House and 26 of 35 seats in the State Senate.

The Democrats then turned to unseating the Republicans who occupied Mississippi's highest offices. Since Davis was the highest ranking of the three African American officeholders, Democrats regarded his ouster as essential, especially because they also intended to impeach Governor Ames. The legislature alleged that Davis had committed a series of unlawful actions while serving as acting governor—"excessive" and "illegal" granting of pardons and the "questionable" commutation and remission of sentences. Between 22 January 1874 and 2 January 1875, legislators charged, Davis had "pardoned thirty-two out of the [state] penitentiary, four out of county jails, seventeen before trial"; in addition, he had issued "six commutations and six remissions."

Davis denied all charges, but on 14 February 1876, the House committee investigating him recommended filing articles of impeachment. Five days later, the House voted to approve five articles of impeachment against Davis for "high crimes and misdemeanors" related to the pardon of Thomas Barrentine, who had been charged with murder.

The State Senate held Davis's trial, with Mississippi Supreme Court associate justice James Tarbell presiding. After nearly a month of proceedings, on 26 February 1876 the Senate voted thirty-one to four in favor of impeachment, with two abstentions. The sentencing phase of the impeachment proceedings, however, was suspended and delayed because Democrats feared that Ames would appoint a new Republican lieutenant governor. The legislature then scheduled Ames's impeachment proceedings to begin on 28 March and voted to repeal the governor's power to appoint state officials.

Davis assumed that his conviction would mean his removal from office and resigned. Also anticipating an impeachment conviction, Ames resigned and left the state even before the end of the trial proceedings. Cardozo, too, resigned after being impeached. The Democrats' Mississippi Plan had succeeded.

Dernoral Davis
Jackson State University

Eric Foner, *Freedom's Lawmakers: A Directory of Black Officeholders during Reconstruction* (1996); Eric Foner, *Reconstruction: America's Unfinished Revolution, 1863–1977* (2002); James Garner, *Reconstruction in Mississippi* (1968); James Loewen and Charles Sallis, *Mississippi: Conflict and Change* (1974); Vernon Wharton, *The Negro in Mississippi, 1865–1890* (1965).

Davis, Jefferson

(1808–1889) Confederate President

Jefferson Davis was a Mississippi war hero, congressman, and senator; US Army officer and secretary of war; and Confederate president. He was born in Kentucky to Jane Cook Davis and Samuel Emory Davis, a Revolutionary War veteran. The youngest of ten children, Jefferson was a toddler when his parents settled at Rosemont, a modest plantation near Woodville, Mississippi, and he always considered the Magnolia State home.

He began attending boarding school in Kentucky at age eight, returned to Mississippi to continue his education at

Jefferson Davis at Beauvoir, ca. 1885 (Photograph by Edward L. Wilson, Library of Congress, Washington, D.C. [LC-DIG-ppmsca-23865])

several academies, and then enrolled in 1823 at Transylvania University in Lexington, Kentucky. A year later, following the death of Samuel Davis, Jefferson's oldest brother, Joseph, a wealthy attorney and planter, arranged the boy's appointment to the US Military Academy. Not a serious student, Jefferson earned numerous demerits, narrowly escaped dismissal, and finished in the bottom third of his class. Still, he formed enduring friendships with men who became his fellow officers in the Mexican War and generals on both sides in the Civil War. After graduation in 1828, he was posted to the frontier, serving as a lieutenant of infantry and dragoons.

In June 1835 he left the army and married Sarah Knox Taylor, the youngest daughter of future US president Zachary Taylor, one of Davis's commanding officers. Sarah died just three months later, and the grieving widower lived for a decade on his plantation on land from his father's estate, working alongside his slaves to improve and cultivate it. Named for the tangled wilderness it was when Davis acquired it, the eight hundred acres of Brierfield fronted the Mississippi River on Davis Bend south of Vicksburg.

Joseph Davis prompted his younger brother, a Democrat in a predominantly Whig county, to run for the Mississippi House of Representatives in 1843. Though unsuccessful, Jefferson Davis gained more experience the following year canvassing for the national Democratic slate, and in 1845 he was elected to the US Congress. Joseph had also introduced his brother to Varina Banks Howell (1826–1906), the well-educated, vivacious daughter of a Natchez businessman, and Jefferson and Varina married in an Episcopal ceremony in February 1845 at the Briars in Natchez. They lived together for more than forty years and had six children: Samuel (1852–54), Margaret Howell (1855–1909), Jefferson Jr. (1857–78), Joseph Evan (1859–64), William Howell (1861–72), and Varina Anne (1864–98).

Jefferson Davis immediately made a name for himself as an unusually conscientious congressman and an avid participant in House debates, although he was only in Washington for seven months before he was elected colonel of the 1st Mississippi Regiment. Slated for a year of duty in the Mexican War, the Mississippians were in combat at Monterrey and Buena Vista, both key victories against numerically superior foes. Wounded at Buena Vista, Davis became a nationally known war hero and an obvious choice to fill a Senate vacancy in the summer of 1847. He served enthusiastically until 1851, when the Democrats asked him to become their candidate in the crucial Mississippi governor's race. Again he traveled the state on grueling speaking tours, but he came in a close second.

In 1853 president-elect Franklin Pierce asked Davis to head the War Department, so the Davises returned to Washington, which remained their principal residence until January 1861. As secretary of war, Davis took a personal interest in numerous issues of domestic and international importance: improving the army, West Point, and national defense; surveying routes for a railroad to the Pacific; moving westward the "chain of forts" to protect settlers; enlarging the US Capitol; constructing the Washington aqueduct; encouraging scientific advances in weaponry; sending the first-ever military commission abroad to observe the Crimean War. He also served as one of the president's closest advisers on domestic policies. Just before the end of Pierce's term, Davis was chosen to resume his favorite post, representing Mississippi in the US Senate. As a prominent and moderate spokesman for the South, he styled himself a "national Democrat," never urged separation from the North, and labored to keep the Union together. However, with Abraham Lincoln's election as president, Davis did not believe that the new Republican administration would allow the seceding states to depart peacefully and foresaw "thorns innumerable."

Davis had already accepted command of state troops in case of war when he received the news that he had been elected president of the Confederate States of America. Duty-bound, he accepted and struggled mightily for four years to simultaneously run a war and mold a nation. Like his northern counterpart, Davis was tenacious and single-minded and had epic struggles with his army commanders, the state governors, and Congress. Unlike Lincoln, Davis lacked the essential material resources to ensure success. A month after Appomattox he was captured while trying to make his way across the Mississippi River to lead Confederate forces who had not yet surrendered.

Imprisoned at Fort Monroe in Virginia, Davis endured solitary confinement and limited contact with the outside world, his health and morale declining until he was released in May 1867. Without citizenship, salary, savings, or even a home—Brierfield had been seized by Union troops in 1862 and sold in 1866—he had gambled all and lost all on the Confederacy. The Davises rambled through Canada and England until he accepted the presidency of a Memphis

life insurance company in 1869. Four years later, it, too, failed.

Finally, a longtime admirer, Sarah Ellis Dorsey, offered to rent Davis a cottage at her seaside retreat near Biloxi, a refuge where he could write his memoirs. Davis loved Beauvoir, and the property became his after Dorsey's death in 1879. There he penned his two-volume remembrance of the war, along with another book and several magazine articles. He and Varina, who had always helped him with writing, entertained friends and family members, and the former president began to travel more often, mainly to Confederate veterans' events. In 1881 he regained ownership of Brierfield after a protracted legal battle. He fell ill there in November 1889 and died three weeks later in New Orleans. In 1893 his remains were moved from Metairie Cemetery to Hollywood Cemetery in Richmond, Virginia.

Lynda Lasswell Crist
Rice University

William J. Cooper Jr., *Jefferson Davis, American* (2000); Jefferson Davis, *The Rise and Fall of the Confederate Government* (2 vols., 1881); Varina Howell Davis, *Jefferson Davis, Ex-President of the Confederate States of America: A Memoir by His Wife* (2 vols., 1890); Haskell M. Monroe et al., eds., *The Papers of Jefferson Davis* (12 vols. to date, 1971–); Papers of Jefferson Davis, Rice University, www.jeffersondavis.rice.edu; Dunbar Rowland, ed., *Jefferson Davis, Constitutionalist: His Letters, Papers, and Speeches* (10 vols., 1923).

Davis, Joseph Robert

(1825–1896) Confederate General

Joseph Robert Davis, a nephew of Confederate president Jefferson Davis, was born in Woodville, Mississippi, on 12 January 1825 to Susannah and Isaac W. Davis. After receiving his education in Nashville, Tennessee, and at Miami University in Ohio, Joseph Davis opened a law practice in Madison County, Mississippi. Following in the footsteps of his famous uncle, he entered politics, and in 1860 the people of Madison County sent him to the State Senate. His political career did not last long, however, as war broke out in 1861.

Answering the Confederacy's call, Davis entered military service as captain of an infantry company that became part of the 10th Mississippi Infantry Regiment, and on 12 April 1861 Davis was elected the regiment's lieutenant colonel. The 10th Mississippi served under Gen. Braxton Bragg and first saw duty in Pensacola, Florida. But Davis did not see much combat, as he was promoted to full colonel on 21 August and soon thereafter began a one-year stint as a military aide to Jefferson Davis. Joseph lived with his uncle and his family at the Confederate White House and visited troops throughout the South, often accompanying the president, and wrote reports on the military situation. President Davis described his nephew as "discreet, gentlemanly and of sound judgment."

On 15 September 1862 Jefferson Davis promoted Joseph to the rank of brigadier general, an assignment that carried with it command of an infantry brigade. The appointment, however, had to be confirmed by the Confederate Senate, and many in that body did not favor the promotion. The nomination was defeated on 3 October by an eleven-to-six vote. However, just five days later, the Senate reconsidered Davis's nomination and approved it by a vote of thirteen to six. Though the matter was never investigated, it was widely believed that the sudden change of events resulted from a political payoff by President Davis to Georgia senator Ben Hill, who arranged to have the vote reconsidered.

Joseph Davis received command of a brigade in Robert E. Lee's Army of Northern Virginia and fought the remainder of the war in the Eastern Theater, participating in some of the war's most horrific battles. His brigade, made up mostly of Mississippi troops, served in Henry Heth's division and took part in the Battle of Gettysburg as one of the first units to see action on 1 July. The brigade joined Gen. James J. Pettigrew on 3 July and took part in Pickett's Charge with the 2nd Mississippi Regiment, losing half its men. Davis continued to lead his men in battle, serving in all the battles of the 1864 Wilderness Campaign against Gen. Ulysses S. Grant and through the miserable stalemate at Petersburg. In April 1865 he was present at Appomattox for Lee's surrender.

Paroled by Grant at Appomattox, Davis returned to Mississippi to resume his law practice. He divorced his wife of thirty years, Frances H. Peyton Davis, in 1878 and a year later married Margaret Cary Green, who bore him three children. He later moved to Biloxi, where he died on 15 September 1896.

Ryan S. Walters

Hattiesburg, Mississippi

Charles E. Hooker, *Confederate Military History*, vol. 7, pt. 2, *Mississippi* (1899); Ezra J. Warner, *Generals in Gray: Lives of the Confederate Commanders* (1959).

Davis, Reuben

(1813–1890) Politician and Lawyer

Reuben Davis, a prolific lawyer and politician, was born on 18 January 1813 in Winchester, Tennessee. Following the

Reuben Davis, wood engraving, ca.1861–65 (Library of Congress, Washington, D.C. [LC-USZ62-105735])

wishes of his father, a Baptist preacher, Davis moved to Hamilton, Mississippi, to study medicine with his brother-in-law. He could not resist the lure of the law, however, and earned a law license and settled in Aberdeen with his bride, Mary. Known for his courtroom theatrics, Davis built a thriving law practice that later prompted historian Dunbar Rowland to rank him among the three greatest criminal defense lawyers in Mississippi history.

Davis was elected colonel of the 2nd Mississippi Infantry in the Mexican War and embarked for Mexico in 1847. Plagued by illness, Davis's regiment never saw action, and his time in Mexico was one of the unhappiest of his life.

Davis subsequently concentrated on his political aspirations and after several unsuccessful attempts won the Democratic nomination for Congress and defeated Whig Charles Clark in 1856. Davis joined the southern fire-eaters in Congress and made speeches defending slavery and advocating secession, making him a hero to many of his constituents. He won reelection in 1858 after no one stepped up to challenge him. Joining other Mississippi statesmen, Davis spoke around the state to unite Mississippians against Abraham Lincoln in the 1860 campaign and to urge secession after Lincoln's election. As the Mississippi secession convention met, Davis resigned his seat in Congress and returned home to Aberdeen.

After the Civil War started, Gov. John J. Pettus appointed Davis major general of the state military board, where he helped to raise, drill, and arm the militia. When the Confederacy asked for troops, Pettus appointed Davis commander of an ill-equipped expedition of sixty-day Mississippi volunteers into Kentucky to defend Bowling Green. The failure of this expedition earned Davis great criticism as a military leader.

Moving from the military realm back into the political one, Davis easily won the election to the Confederate Congress and began serving in 1862. He became a very vocal opponent of Pres. Jefferson Davis's administration. The two Davis men, who were not related, knew each other as members of Mississippi's prewar congressional delegation. Reuben Davis's views on conscription and other military matters often brought him into conflict with not only Jefferson Davis but also other members of Congress. Reuben Davis resigned his seat in 1863 and ran for governor, losing in a landslide to war hero Charles Clark.

After the death of his first wife in 1865, Davis married Sallie Garber, who gave birth to three children. His law practice in Aberdeen again flourished, and he soon found himself drawn back into politics. Davis joined with other whites in the state to overthrow the Reconstruction government in the 1875 election, delivering fiery speeches and employing other scare tactics to intimidate black voters and ensure a Democratic win.

Davis switched parties and ran as the Greenback candidate for Congress in the bitterly contested 1878 election, losing to H. L. Mudrow and then retiring from politics. One of the greatest achievement of Davis's life was the publication of his memoirs, *Recollections of Mississippi and Mississippians*. Popular with both his contemporaries and historians, *Recollections* provides an invaluable and unique glimpse into antebellum Mississippi life. Davis died suddenly on 24 October 1890.

Nancy Prince
Mississippi Department of
Archives and History

Reuben Davis, *Recollections of Mississippi and Mississippians* (1972); Nancy Prince, "Reuben Davis: The Biography of a Politician in Civil War Era Mississippi" (master's thesis, University of Mississippi, 1998); Dunbar Rowland, *Courts, Judges, and Lawyers of Mississippi, 1798–1935* (1935).

Davis, Tyrone

(1938–2005) Soul Singer

Soul singer Tyrone Davis was born in Greenville on 4 May 1938 to the Rev. Willie Branch and Ora Davis-Branch. (One source suggests that his family lived in a small rural community south of Leland.) After his parents divorced, Davis attended school in Arcola until age fourteen, when he left to join his father in Saginaw, Michigan. He moved to Chicago in the late 1950s and soon began hanging out in the city's blues clubs at night. Davis eventually was hired as a chauffeur and valet by bluesman Freddie King, touring with King for a year. Davis then found work in a Chicago steel mill alongside Otis Clay, another Mississippi native who also

aspired to a musical career. The two became lifelong friends. Davis was married twice. After an early union ended in divorce, he and his wife, Ann, married in 1963 and remained together until his death. He was the father of five daughters.

Fortune smiled on Davis one evening when he stationed himself near the stage during a Bobby "Blue" Bland concert. Bland offered the nattily attired Davis an opportunity to sing and then tendered some sage advice: "Be you, don't be me." Davis later credited Bland's remark with helping him forge a distinctive style. Yet Davis's early efforts singing at clubs on Chicago's South and West Sides were imitative of other singers, particularly Bland. Pianist Harold Burrage befriended Davis and arranged for him to record several songs released under the name Tyrone the Wonder Boy, but none found commercial success. After Burrage died in 1966, two years passed before Davis attracted attention with a song on the Dakar label. "Can I Change My Mind" soared to the top spot on the R&B charts and No. 5 on the pop charts. "Is It Something You've Got" continued the momentum, achieving Top 5 status on the R&B charts, but the song was eclipsed by the infectious "Turn Back the Hands of Time," which reached No. 1 among R&B songs and No. 3 on the pop charts.

Davis's success continued into the 1970s, with a string of hits that included his third R&B chart-topper, "Turning Point." Unlike fellow Mississippi expatriates in Chicago such as Otis Clay and Otis Rush, Davis relied on his smooth baritone more than on a shouted blues sound. While Davis was a versatile vocalist, on his biggest hits he sang in a penitential tone, apologizing for some misdeed or pleading for a second chance with his woman. These songs particularly resonated with the females in his audience, many of whom viewed Davis as a sex symbol and rushed the stage when he performed. Davis benefited as well from a top-notch band that he drove relentlessly in rehearsals.

Davis left Dakar in 1976 and signed with industry giant Columbia the next year. Although he continued to churn out albums and hits that ascended the R&B charts, by 1981 his sales had slipped, and he parted with Columbia. He recorded on a series of smaller labels until landing in 1996 at Jackson-based Malaco Records, which took in a number of black musical elder statesmen, among them Davis and fellow Mississippi native Little Milton. Although Davis sold twenty-five million records and recorded thirty-eight albums, he never achieved the crossover appeal of some of his R&B contemporaries. Music critics lament the relative lack of attention paid to Davis, but his main constituency of urban working-class blacks supported him throughout his career. A tireless performer, Davis was a fixture on the Chitlin' Circuit and was enormously popular when he appeared in Mississippi and elsewhere in the South. His peers recognized Davis's genius and honored him with a Pioneer Award from the Rhythm and Blues Foundation in 1998.

Davis suffered a stroke in September 2004, slipped into a coma, and died of pneumonia on 9 February 2005. Fellow musicians staged major benefit concerts for him in both

Chicago and Tunica, and Davis was lauded for having ascended from "the cotton fields of Mississippi" to become one of the iconic figures of Chicago soul music.

Christopher Losson
St. Joseph, Missouri

Chicago Public Radio, interview with Otis Clay (10 February 2005); *Delta Democrat-Times* (10 February 2005); Dave Hoekstra, *Chicago Sun-Times* (10 February 2005); Greg Kot, *Chicago Tribune* (9 February 2005); Robert Pruter, *Chicago Soul* (1992).

Davis, Varina Howell
(1826–1906) Confederate First Lady

Varina Howell was born to William Burr Howell and Margaret Kempe Howell on their plantation, the Briers, near Natchez on 7 May 1826. Varina enjoyed a loving, happy youth complete with the advantages of the wealthy planter class. Varina was exceptionally well educated for a woman in the antebellum South, attending an exclusive private girls' academy in Philadelphia, Pennsylvania, for two terms beginning when she was ten. A family friend subsequently tutored her in Latin, French, English literature, and history. In late 1843 Varina spent the Christmas season visiting Hurricane, a plantation owned by family friend Joseph Emory Davis. Here, the sixteen-year-old Howell met Joseph's brother, Jefferson, a widower more than twice her age.

They married in an Episcopal ceremony at the Briers Plantation two years later. The early years of their marriage were turbulent and fraught with conflict and separations. In 1845 Jefferson Davis was elected to the House of Representatives and moved to Washington, D.C., leaving his young bride to live with her in-laws in Mississippi. Varina had a strong personality and clashed with Joseph Davis over property, and she chafed at his attempt to have her live with a widowed sister-in-law and her eight children. Jefferson Davis left Congress to fight in the Mexican War and came home a hero with a serious injury that required Varina to nurse him back to health. Soon thereafter, he was appointed to the Senate, and he eventually allowed Varina to join him in Washington, where they resided for the next twelve years. The couple had six children, Samuel (1852–54), Margaret Howell (1855–1909), Jefferson Jr. (1857–1878), Joseph Evan (1859–64), William Howell (1861–72), and Varina Anne "Winnie" (1864–1898). Varina Davis was a devoted mother and worked as her husband's secretary to advance his political career. She also developed deep friendships with other well-connected women such as Mary Boykin Chestnut.

Wedding photograph, Jefferson Davis and Varina Howell Davis, 1845 (New York Public Library [Image ID: 97462])

When the South seceded, Jefferson Davis preferred to serve as a soldier but agreed to be president of the Confederate States of America. Varina acted as First Lady in both Montgomery, Alabama, and Richmond, Virginia, attracting criticism from political enemies. Some thought it was improper for Varina Davis to entertain while pregnant, and some Virginia blue bloods did not think her enough of a southern lady. Regardless, she strove to support her husband and the Confederacy.

As the war ended, the Davises attempted to escape to Texas and continue the fight. Union troops captured them in southern Georgia. Jefferson was considered a traitor and imprisoned in Fort Monroe, Virginia, though he was never tried and was released in 1867. Varina took her older children to Canada with their grandmother and then moved with her infant daughter to Virginia to be near the prison, writing to her husband and occasionally visiting with him during his incarceration. Varina took financial responsibility for her family and borrowed money to keep the family afloat.

The next several years were bleak for the Davises as they faced homelessness and suffered serious illnesses. The family traveled, accepting social invitations from European elites. Jefferson did not adjust well to postwar America. In 1869 he accepted a job with an insurance company in Memphis, but the company failed. The couple continued to fight with his brother, Joseph, over the family plantation, Brierfield. Jefferson eventually won the court battle, but the plantation brought in little revenue. Varina developed heart trouble during a visit to England, and she remained there for medical care, while Jefferson returned to the United States in

November 1876 and within three months had taken up residence at Beauvoir, a plantation on the Gulf Coast owned by a widow, Sarah Ellis Dorsey. Varina returned to the United States in October 1877 but did not want to join her husband at Beauvoir and remained in Memphis. She later changed her mind and moved to Beauvoir in May 1878.

Jefferson Davis began writing his account of the Confederacy, with Dorsey acting as his secretary. Davis hoped his book would restore financial security to his family, but the book sold poorly. When Dorsey died in 1879, she bequeathed Beauvoir to Jefferson and Winnie Davis, leaving Varina out of the will. Winnie joined her parents at Beauvoir, where the family received many visitors. Mother and daughter cared for Jefferson and helped him with articles and speeches until his death in December 1889.

Varina Davis devoted much of the remainder of her life to writing a voluminous account of the Confederacy in which she defended her husband and tried to ensure that he would be remembered as a hero, even taking the name Varina Jefferson Davis as she pursued her literary career. In 1892 she stunned southerners when she and Winnie moved to New York City, where she spent the last years of her life writing articles and worrying about money. Winnie died in 1898, and Varina died in October 1906 and was interred beside her husband in Richmond's Hollywood Cemetery.

Minoa D. Uffelman
Austin Peay State University

Carol K. Blesser, *Journal of Southern History* (February 1999); Joan E. Cashin, *First Lady of the Confederacy: Varina Davis's Civil War* (2006); William J. Cooper Jr., *Jefferson Davis, American* (2000); Suzanne T. Dolensy, *Journal of Mississippi History* (May 1985); Papers of Jefferson Davis, Rice University, http://jeffersondavis.rice.edu.

Davis Bend Plantation

An oddly aligned property located in Warren County, approximately twenty miles south of Vicksburg, Davis Bend occupies a unique place in Mississippi politics and social history. Its founders, Joseph Emory Davis, a well-respected Mississippi lawyer born on 10 December 1784 in Wilkes County, Georgia, and Littleton Henderson, of whom little is known, purchased what had been eleven thousand acres of uncharted swampland along a bend in the Mississippi River in May 1818 as an investment. Davis maintained control of sixty-nine hundred acres along the highly desirable western and southern portions of the plot and by the 1830s left behind his legal practice to live the life of a gentleman farmer.

In 1824 Davis had assembled a slave force of 112 under the direction of his younger brother, Isaac, to prepare the land for plantation life. In early 1827, while continuing the clearing process, Isaac was critically injured during a particularly violent storm that also killed his infant son. Later that year, Joseph Davis; his new wife, Eliza Van Benthuysen Davis; and his three daughters from previously undocumented unions settled into a lavishly decorated plantation home, Hurricane.

With Joseph Davis's parents deceased, he had assumed the role of family patriarch, and in 1835 the youngest of his nine brothers, Jefferson, purchased and began clearing a portion of the land. In 1848 Jefferson Davis and his wife, Varina Howell Davis, moved into their own newly built plantation home, Brierfield.

By midcentury a string of successful cotton harvests helped make Davis Bend plantation extremely successful. In spite of the financial successes, however, neighbors and competitors grew increasingly concerned about Joseph Davis's unique ideas regarding the plantation workforce. The theoretical blueprint for the Davis Bend labor force, which at its peak topped 450 and was extremely versatile and self-sufficient, was fostered in part by Davis's interpretation of British industrialist/philanthropist Robert Owen's theories of working-class partnership and self-governance. Determined to build the same sort of versatile and self-motivated workforce that Owen had pioneered at his textile mill in New Lanark, Scotland, and later at New Harmony, Indiana, Joseph Davis offered his slaves opportunities for advancement. They ultimately had access to a school that offered a rudimentary education and a court system to adjudicate infractions and settle disputes.

The most indispensable of Davis's slaves was Benjamin T. Montgomery, who arrived at Davis Bend in 1836. Cultured and quite ambitious, Montgomery virtually ran the Davis operation during the antebellum years and helped cement Davis's reputation as a well-rounded businessman by running a dry goods store at the back of the plantation.

In the aftermath of the war, Jefferson Davis's service as Confederate president left the family fortune exposed to northern reprisals. Joseph Davis, sickly and seeking a means to maintain some semblance of financial independence, transferred ownership of Davis Bend to Montgomery on 19 November 1866. This decision, while locally lamented, offered an expedient way to avoid a Union backlash while keeping the property under Davis family control.

However, Montgomery seized the opportunity, built a third plantation home, Ursino, on the property, and took charge of his own extremely successful cotton enterprise run solely by former slaves at Davis Bend. Until his death in 1878 Montgomery and Sons ranked among the state's top cotton producers.

In 1881 Jefferson Davis won back control of the family property, arguing that his brother had leased rather than sold Davis Bend to Montgomery. The Montgomerys retained Ursino, and no Davises returned to live on the property.

Following a crippling late nineteenth-century cotton slump and years of neglect, the once profitable plantation fell into a state of disrepair and was abandoned.

By the end of the twentieth century the Mississippi River had cut its way through the bend, rendering it an inaccessible island. Now known as Davis Island, it is a private nature preserve.

Joel Nathan Rosen
Moravian College

Frank Everett Jr., *Brierfield: Plantation Home of Jefferson Davis* (1971); Kenneth Marvin Hamilton, *Black Towns and Profit: Promotion and Development in the Trans-Appalachian West, 1877–1915* (1991); Janet Sharp Hermann, *Joseph E. Davis: Pioneer Patriarch* (1990).

Deal, Borden (Loyse Youth Deal)

(1922–1985) Author

Novelist Borden Deal was born Loyse Youth Deal on 12 October 1922 in Pontotoc, Mississippi, the youngest of three children of farmers Borden Lee Deal and Jimmie Anne Smith Deal. He spent his childhood in the farming communities of Pontotoc, New Albany, and Ingomar, where he began to cultivate his lifelong hobbies of fishing, golf, and guitar playing. When the Great Depression hit, Deal's father lost his land because of the drop in cotton prices. With assistance from federal programs, the family relocated to a communal farming project in Enterprise, and Deal graduated from Macedonia Consolidated High School near Myrtle. After his father was killed in a 1938 truck accident, young Deal decided to leave home.

Deal joined the Civilian Conservation Corps and fought fires in the Pacific Northwest, moving between camps by hitchhiking and riding freight trains. During this period he also worked on a showboat, at a lumber mill, and in wheat harvesting as a migrant laborer. Deal then moved to Washington, D.C., and became as an auditor for the US Department of Labor from 1941 to 1942. He also worked as a correspondent for Association Films in New York City. Deal served as an aviator cadet in the US Navy from 1942 to 1945 and subsequently attended college at the University of Alabama, where he studied under creative writing teacher Hudson Strode and became a student of Jungian psychology, two experiences that profoundly affected his writing. He graduated in 1949, majoring in English and minoring in creative writing. He pursued graduate studies at Mexico City College during 1950 and then worked as a skip tracer, telephone operator, copywriter, and freelance writer between 1950 and 1955.

He began publishing his writings in 1948 and went on to enjoy a long career as an author, publishing twenty-one books and more than one hundred short stories. He occasionally wrote under the pseudonyms Lee Borden and Leigh Borden and published erotica under the pseudonyms Him, Her, and Us. His final novels were published posthumously in 1985 and 1989. He was best known for works set in the American South, including *Dunbar's Cove* (1957), a novel about the Tennessee Valley Authority; and *The Insolent Breed* (1959), a story about hillbilly music and humanity's fight against encroaching civilization. The childhood farming settings of his youth featured strongly in Deal's work, particularly in the Olden Times series novels *The Least One* (1967) and *The Other Room* (1974) as well as in the somewhat autobiographical *There Were Also Strangers* (1985). Novels such as *Walk through the Valley* (1956) and *Interstate* (1970) also showcased Deal's continued commitment to the ideas of the quest for land, personal ambition, and identity. He explored Jungian psychology and human fallibility in *Dragon's Wine* (1960) and *Adventure* (1978). Deal garnered various honors and awards during his four-decade career, including a 1957 Guggenheim Fellowship.

Borden Deal died of a heart attack on 22 January 1985 in Sarasota, Florida. He once told an interviewer that he wanted his books to be a "panorama of the New South," noting that his characters "live and work in real time in real places: raising horses, building highways and TVA dams, running for public office, farming the Southern earth. The drama of their individual lives embodies the important story of the years since about 1890, when the South began gradually to emerge from the shadow of a losing war in the wrong cause, to regain at last, with the election of the first Southern president in over a hundred years, its original position as a prime mover in the destiny of the nation."

Frances Abbott
Digital Public Library of America,
Boston

Gale Group, *Dictionary of Literary Biography*, vol. 6, *American Novelists since World War II*, 2nd ser. (1980); Robert H. McKenzie, ed., *The Rising South*, vol. 2 (1976).

Dean, Dizzy

(1911–1974) Athlete and Broadcaster

The son of an itinerant Arkansas farmer, Jay Hanna "Dizzy" Dean lived much of his life in Mississippi and became one of the most prominent southerners of the twentieth century as a Major League Baseball player and colorful radio and television announcer.

Dean grew up in a hardscrabble world of cotton farming, received no formal schooling beyond the second grade, served briefly in the US Army, and then began his baseball career with the St. Louis Cardinals. He won his first game at the end of the 1930 season, posted a 26–10 record the next year, and gained baseball immortality with the 1934 season, when he was 30–7, led the league in strikeouts for the third straight year, and then was the winning pitcher in two games as the Cardinals defeated the Detroit Tigers in the World Series. Dean, along with his brother, Paul "Daffy" Dean, who also won two games in the 1934 Series, belonged to the Cardinals' Gashouse Gang, pranksters whose antics made them a prime baseball attraction everywhere. Dizzy Dean's fastball was overpowering and his boldness legendary. Dean suffered a toe injury in the 1937 All-Star Game that diminished his effectiveness, and the Cardinals traded him to the Chicago Cubs, for whom he played from 1938 to 1941. He then became a broadcaster for the Cardinals (1941–46) and the St. Louis Browns (1941–48). After he complained about the Browns' pitching staff during the 1947 season and said that he could do better, the team management brought him back to pitch the final game of the year. He backed up his words, throwing four shutout innings and singling in his only at bat before leaving with a pulled hamstring. He went on to become a broadcaster for the New York Yankees (1950–51), several national networks (1952–65), and Atlanta Braves (1966–68). He compiled a 150–83 pitching record in his twelve Major League seasons and was elected to the National Baseball Hall of Fame in Cooperstown, New York, in 1953.

With no Major League team in the Deep South during Dean's playing career, the border-state Cardinals were a special favorite of southerners, and Dean's brash southern persona intensified the bond. He played his down-home manner to the hilt, and his sayings became legendary. Newspaper reporters quoted in dialect one of his favorite lines, "'Tain't braggin' if you kin really do it." He was fond of *ain't*, and when English teachers protested he said, "A lot of people ain't saying ain't, ain't eating." Told that his toe had been fractured, Dean replied, "Fractured, hell! The damn thing's broken!" In his Hall of Fame induction speech he told the crowd that the "good Lord" had given him "a strong body, a good right arm, and a weak mind."

Dean's broadcasting career brought his wit and personality to a national audience. His southern vernacular language, identifiable regional accent, folksy sayings, and impromptu singing of "Wabash Cannonball" and other Americana songs made him for many Americans what one scholar has called "the quintessential southerner."

Dean was a longtime resident of Wiggins, Mississippi, and was buried there after his death on 17 July 1974. The Dizzy Dean Museum was established in Jackson, and its exhibitions are now a part of the Mississippi Sports Hall of Fame. Since 1977 Dizzy Dean Baseball/Softball has provided organized play for children in Mississippi and other southern states, honoring his legacy.

Charles Reagan Wilson
University of Mississippi

S. Spencer Davis, in *The Human Tradition in the New South*, ed. James C. Klotter (2005); Robert Gregory, *Diz: Dizzy Dean and Baseball during the Great Depression* (1992).

Decoration Day

In the aftermath of the Civil War, white southerners felt the need to grieve for the casualties of the conflict as well as for the defeated cause. One of the first ritualistic mediums created for communal mourning was Decoration Day, also known throughout the South as Confederate Memorial Day. This springtime regional holiday never acquired a single calendar date, as did the federal version. Even when the 1917 Mississippi legislature added Confederate Memorial Day on 26 April to the list of official state holidays, many communities continued to celebrate on dates of their own choosing. Raymond, for example, observed Decoration Day on the anniversary of a local battle, while other towns opted for the birthday of a favorite Confederate hero.

In keeping with Victorian bereavement customs, women assumed a leading and organizing role in Decoration Day commemorations, which typically included a procession of townspeople to a nearby cemetery with Confederate remains, the adornment or "decoration" of gravestones with wreaths and flowers, and prayers and speeches. The season, the blossoms, and the orations all evoked the idea of regeneration: in addition to offering an outlet for grief, a primary purpose of the ritual was to renew the community's memory of the Confederacy and its casualties. Speakers gave meaning to this sacrifice by praising the virtues of the deceased, defending the righteousness of their cause, and even proclaiming the ultimate vindication of these principles.

Several cities across the region claim to have originated the holiday. One such contender in Mississippi is Jackson, which held a ceremony on 26 April 1865. Reacting to the news of Gen. Robert E. Lee's surrender, Sue Langdon Vaughan sent a notice to a local paper requesting that "Daughters of the Southland" meet at Greenwood Cemetery to garland the graves of Confederate heroes. Large numbers of townspeople and soldiers turned out to witness the observance, and in 1891 an inscription on the Mississippi Monument to the Confederate Dead memorialized this event by asserting, "Decoration Day Originated in Jackson, Mississippi."

In 1866 three Columbus women organized a 25 April procession to Friendship Cemetery, where approximately fourteen hundred Union and Confederate graves received floral tributes. The impartiality of this homage caused accounts to spread as far as New York City, where the story inspired Francis Miles Finch to write his popular poem, "The Blue and the Gray." In 1932 the Children of the American Revolution erected a modest monument in Friendship Cemetery proclaiming it the site of the first Decoration Day.

Although audience size and participating locales have diminished dramatically since World War I, local chapters of the United Daughters of the Confederacy and the Sons of Confederate Veterans, among other organizations, continue to observe Decoration Day across Mississippi.

Leigh McWhite
University of Mississippi

Gaines M. Foster, *Ghosts of the Confederacy: Defeat, the Lost Cause, and the Emergence of the New South, 1865–1913* (1987); Sally Leigh McWhite, "Echoes of the Lost Cause: Civil War Reverberations in Mississippi, 1865 to 2001" (PhD dissertation, University of Mississippi, 2003); Charles Reagan Wilson, *Baptized in Blood: The Religion of the Lost Cause, 1865–1920* (1980).

Deer, White-Tailed

White-tailed deer (*Odocoileus virginianus*) are an important recreational and economic resource in Mississippi. They are the most hunted game species in the state, with an annual economic impact of more than $150 million.

Today, Mississippi has an estimated 1.75 million white-tailed deer, with populations in every county. Not too long ago, however, they were virtually nonexistent in the state. When the French arrived in 1699, white-tailed deer probably ranged all over the area, but the lack of undergrowth in virgin pine and hardwood stands could support only very small deer populations.

Mississippi held its first deer hunting season in 1905, with only the hunting of bucks allowed until 1915. Despite such restrictions, market hunting practically exterminated deer from the Mississippi landscape. In 1929 Aldo Leopold estimated that only a few small herds remained in inaccessible areas of the Mississippi River floodplain and in the Pearl and Pascagoula River swamps. The Mississippi Game and Fish Commission was created in 1932 and conducted the first game survey the following year, estimating that the state had only a few hundred deer scattered over thirty-four of the eighty-two counties.

White-tailed deer (Photograph by Scott Bauer, courtesy US Department of Agriculture, K-5437-3)

Between 1900 and 1925 most of Mississippi's virgin pine and hardwood stands were removed, creating abundant undergrowth and thus ideal deer habitat statewide. By 1940 the Game and Fish Commission maintained forty refuges encompassing 241,138 acres. Approximately four hundred deer were purchased, mostly from Mexico and North Carolina, and released into these refuges between 1933 and 1940. Private organizations also purchased deer from Alabama and Louisiana in the early 1930s. By 1953 almost two-thirds of the deer used for restocking came from the Leaf River Refuge in Southeast Mississippi.

At least 3,142 deer were released into Mississippi between 1931 and 1965. Deer were released in almost every county, with most receiving fewer than 75 deer. More than 75 percent of the deer came from within the state, but deer also came directly from Louisiana, Alabama, Mexico, Wisconsin, North Carolina, and Kentucky. By 1966 deer were present in every county in Mississippi; three years later, the state's deer population was estimated at 260,000, and deer seasons were open in parts of all counties. Today, deer seasons are open throughout the state, and the estimated annual harvest exceeds 300,000 deer.

While all of Mississippi's white-tailed deer are the same species, weight, antler size, and timing of breeding vary significantly across the state, apparently as a consequence of soil fertility. The deer with the largest weights, largest antlers, and earliest breeding live on the most fertile soils. Weights of mature bucks vary from an average of 147 pounds in the poorer soils of the Coastal Flatwoods to an average of 199 pounds in the rich soils of the Mississippi Delta. The antler main beams of mature bucks range from an average of 15.8 inches in the Coastal Flatwoods to an average of 20.9 inches in the Mississippi River batture lands.

Chad M. Dacus

Mississippi Department of
Wildlife, Fisheries, and Parks

Mississippi Department of Wildlife, Fisheries, and Parks, Deer Program website, www.mdwfp.com/deer; Mississippi State University Extension Service, *White-Tailed Deer*, www.msucares.com, Wiley Charles Prewitt Jr., "The Best of All Breathing: Hunting and Environmental Change in Mississippi 1900–1980" (master's thesis, University of Mississippi, 1991).

Deerskin Trade

Mississippi was part of a large southeastern regional trade in deerskins that operated from the 1680s through the early 1800s. Deer hides were an important commodity in the prehistoric Southeast and quickly became the main commodity in the trade between the numerous Native American tribes and the French, British, Spanish, and later the American powers that vied for control of the areas east of the Mississippi River. For the Native Americans, the trade quickly became part of the social and political distribution of goods that validated and maintained chiefly rank and held the allegiance of hunters and warriors. European trade goods (which included guns; powder; metalwares such as kettles, axes, and knives; and large quantities of yard goods and blankets) came to the Native Americans as gifts from Europeans to cement political and military ties and as part of a commercial trade in which prices of European goods were set in numbers of deerskins. The Europeans also used the trade to provide lucrative monopolistic rights to court favorites: for example, the French Company of the Indies (1717–31) and Spain's grants of privileged trading status to Panton, Leslie, and Company in the 1780s. These practices created two levels of trade: an official, well-documented, heavily regulated trade run from trading posts established at major ports, and a furtive, often illegal, trade carried on by numerous *coureurs du bois*, as the French called them, who traveled into the hinterlands to trade in the Indian villages and live with the different Indian nations. Much of the legislation related to the trade sought to control the disruptive behavior of these freelance traders.

For the Indians of the Southeast, the major deer hunt occurred in the late fall, when villages broke up into small bands and dispersed to different hunting grounds. In the early years of the trade, only enough deer were killed to supply the band's needs for meat, fat, and skins to purchase a few European goods. The trade, then, had natural limits, at least until rum was introduced. In his analysis of the Choctaw trade, Richard White claims that rum sales drove overhunting of deer at the end of the eighteenth century. Another evil introduced by the trade was the credit system: goods were advanced to individual hunters or a band leader against an expected return of deer hides after the fall hunt. The repayment of debts depended on the success of the season, the skill of individual hunters, and the willingness of the hunters to repay their debts. Competing traders often used rum to lure hunting bands and purchase the season's take before the skins reached the trading post. The need to pay trade debts increased the pressure on Native Americans to sell their lands.

The English, particularly traders operating from South Carolina, had extended overland trading routes into the Mississippi area by the 1680s. Transporting their trade goods and deer hides on packhorses was expensive, and the English trade consequently included a large component of Indian slaves. Traders encouraged the Chickasaw to raid their neighbors, particularly the Choctaw, for slaves who could be transported to Charles Town markets. France turned its interests to the Southeast when d'Iberville settled Biloxi in 1699, and by 1701, sixty traders were doing business there. The French and English competed aggressively for the hide trade east of the Mississippi. The French had the advantage of water transportation; the English had a greater variety of higher-quality trade goods. The French established two major posts to control the southeastern trade, New Orleans and Mobile. Smaller posts were also constructed, among them Fort Toulouse on the Alabama River to secure the trade of the Choctaw and Alabama, Fort Rosalie near Natchez, and various posts on the Tombigbee River. The rivalry between the French and the English spawned a protracted series of wars between the Chickasaw, who were generally trading partners and allies of the English, and the Choctaw, who generally favored the French. A civil war broke out among the Choctaw in 1748–50 as that nation became divided over loyalties to French and English traders.

In 1763, when the British officially gained control of the areas east of the Mississippi River, Mobile and Pensacola became centers for the English trade in deerskins, but deerskins also crossed the Mississippi to the New Orleans markets in large numbers. The American Revolution interrupted the deer hide trade. When it resumed after the war, Panton, Leslie, and Company, a British firm established in 1783 and operating out of Florida, dominated the trade. The company set up trading posts in Pensacola in 1785 and in Mobile in 1788 before establishing posts up the Mississippi River, including at Nogales (near the mouth of the Yazoo) in 1793 for the Chickasaw-Choctaw trade and at Chickasaw Bluffs near Memphis in 1796 for the Chickasaw trade. The Nogales post was important in serving hunters who had crossed the Mississippi because of declining deer populations on the eastern bank.

While Panton, Leslie, and Company dominated the trade in the Southeast, it was never without competition. The US government entered the hide trade to win the friendship of Native Americans and woo them away from hostile powers. The US Indian Factory System, which ran from 1795 to 1822, set up trading factories at Chickasaw Bluffs (1802–18) for trade with the Chickasaw and at Fort St. Stephens near Mobile in 1802 for the Choctaw and Chickasaw trade. This post later moved to Fort Confederation in 1815 and closed with the whole system in 1822. With declining deer populations east of the Mississippi River, Panton, Leslie, and Company ceased being a major player in the hide trade. After the Choctaw and Chickasaw signed 1805 treaties with the United States, the company devoted much of its energies to collecting its old trade debts from these nations through treaty payments from the US government.

Royce Kurtz
University of Mississippi

William S. Coker and Thomas D. Watson, *Indian Traders of the Southeastern Spanish Borderlands: Panton, Leslie, and Company and John Forbes and Company, 1783–1847* (1986); Verner W. Crane, *The Southern Frontier, 1670–1732* (1956); Ora Brooks Peake, *A History of the United States Indian Factory System, 1795–1822* (1954); Paul Chrisler Phillips, *The Fur Trade* (1961); Daniel H. Usner, *Indians, Settlers, and Slaves in a Frontier Exchange Economy: The Lower Mississippi Valley before 1783* (1992); Richard White, *The Roots of Dependency: Subsistence, Environment, and Social Change among the Choctaws, Pawnees, and Navajos* (1983).

Delta

The Mississippi Delta encompasses the northwestern part of the state of Mississippi, bounded on the west by the Mississippi River and to the east by the Loess Bluffs that separate the area from the hills and prairies that characterize much of Mississippi. The Delta is not the delta of the Mississippi River, which is farther to the south in Louisiana, but rather one of the largest of the numerous alluvial floodplains in the Lower Mississippi River Valley and a basin for the Mississippi and Yazoo Rivers. It measures seventy miles across at its widest point and encloses an area about two hundred miles long that writer William Alexander Percy called "a badly drawn half oval." The Delta is unusually flat, with elevation going from 205 feet above sea level below Memphis to 80 feet above at Vicksburg and averaging an elevation of 125 feet from Greenville to Greenwood. The core counties of the Delta are Bolivar, Coahoma, Humphreys, Issaquena, Leflore, Quitman, Sharkey, Sunflower, Tunica, and Washington. The counties of Carroll, DeSoto, Grenada, Holmes,

The Delta (Photograph by James G. Thomas, Jr.)

Panola, Tallahatchie, Tate, Warren, and Yazoo contain alluvial deposits as well and have been part of the Delta's human history.

For thousands of years the Mississippi River deposited silt from upstream into the Delta, slowly building up rich alluvial deposits that would make the area some of the most fertile agricultural land in the world. Its environment is part of the Southeastern Bottomland Forest Region, an area that was one of the nation's largest forests, dominated by cypress, tupelo, and sweet gum but also featuring sycamore, poplar, pecan, maple, hickory, hackberry, black gum, slash pine, honey locust, and walnut. A traveler in the 1820s noted the picturesque ecology, with migratory birds, kingfishers, herons, ducks, eagles, and soon-to-disappear Florida panthers. The Delta was swampland, with rivers and streams flowing through it and the Mississippi River flooding each spring. Wetlands in the Delta offer extensive water resources and a natural river pathway to support an "avian superhighway" for countless migrating birds. This Mississippi Flyway attracts the most diverse migratory flock in North America.

The Delta is a cultural concept as well as a physical region. Writer David L. Cohn is credited with saying that the "Mississippi Delta begins in the lobby of the Peabody Hotel in Memphis and ends on Catfish Row in Vicksburg." The Peabody is a classic grand southern hotel and was the gathering spot for the Delta elite: according to Cohn, anyone who stood in its lobby long enough would "see everybody who is anybody in the Delta and many who are on the make." Catfish Row suggested a very different Delta, with race and social class meanings: in shacks along the Mississippi River, African Americans, Cohn wrote, celebrated a culture with "the music of guitars, the aroma of love, and the soul-satisfying scent of catfish frying to luscious golden-brown in sizzling skillets." The extremes of wealth and poverty structured the cultural Delta and produced distinctive ways in differing communities.

Beginning in AD 1000, long before the Peabody and Cat-fish Row, Native Americans lived on the land that became known as the Delta. They were part of the Mississippian culture that dominated the Mississippi River Valley for seven centuries. The natives were organized into chiefdoms and had an economy based on trade and agriculture. They built flat-topped earthen mounds that were ceremonial and political centers of life. Winterville, six miles north of present-day Greenville, had a series of twenty-three mounds arranged around a plaza, at the center of which towered a fifty-five-foot mound. Today it is a National Historic Land-mark and a state park, reflecting its value as a point of origin for Delta life. Hernando de Soto and his sixteenth-century explorers of the Gulf Coast were the first Europeans to tra-verse the Delta, as he crossed the Mississippi River in June 1541, likely in what is now Tunica County. He encountered a tribe known as the Quizquiz, who later reorganized as the Tunica.

Whites had settled on farms near the Mississippi River and on higher land on the eastern fringes of the Delta in the early nineteenth century, and they and their slaves transformed the land, eventually building vast cotton plan-tations that replaced the forests, canebrakes, and swamp-lands. Successful agricultural work required large numbers of slaves and money, making the Delta a region dominated by a planter elite. Wade Hampton III, a South Carolin-ian from one of the South's most distinguished families, became one of the Delta's largest landowners, with nine hundred slaves scattered over two counties by the time of the Civil War. Greenwood Leflore, a Choctaw leader who had signed the 1930 Treaty of Dancing Rabbit Creek that ceded Indian lands to the state, was another successful planter, with four hundred slaves on his plantation near Greenwood and a taste for fine European decorations for his home, Malmaison. Davis Bend Plantation, run by Jef-ferson Davis's brother, Joseph, was an unusual antebellum experiment based on the communal teachings of socialist Robert Owen. Productivity was extraordinary in the Delta, enabling planters to accumulate wealth and become a pow-erful social group that dominated the region's economic and political life for generations.

Union and Confederate forces contended in the Delta for control of the Mississippi River during the Civil War, nota-bly fighting over the Yazoo Pass, including the Battle of Fort Pemberton near Greenwood in 1863. At the end of the war, the Delta attracted freed slaves from the eastern South who saw the region as a more open and almost frontier society compared to those southern areas with a long legacy of slav-ery and its behavioral expectations for blacks. They sought landownership in the Delta after the war and asserted their political rights during Reconstruction at a time when new Delta lands were being cleared for settlement. Even with the restriction of political rights at the end of Reconstruction, African Americans still came to the Delta in search of eco-nomic opportunity.

Outside forces helped remake the Delta in the late nine-teenth century. Timber companies clear-cut the swampy forest of its hardwoods, making land available for sale, and railroads laid tracks that connected Delta planters to out-side cotton markets. The federal government passed con-structed levees to contain the tumultuous floods that had prevented the utilization of much Delta land for farming before the Civil War. In the early twentieth century, foreign investors began buying and operating Delta plantations. The British-owned Delta and Pine Land Company became the world's largest cotton plantation, with a sixty-thousand-acre operation in 1927. All of these forces promoted the region's economic modernization, creating plantations as factories with management methods that resembled those found at industrial sites. Essential to this management was close control of costs, including the exploitation of a large pool of cheap labor. By 1910 tenants operated 92 percent of Delta farms, and 95 percent of those tenants were African Americans.

The plantation dominated the Delta's economic, social, and cultural life. As Luther Brown has noted, the plantation was a virtual company town. Plantations often had their own currencies and supported commissaries, churches, and health care facilities. Delta and Pine Land published a weekly newspaper for its black tenants. Another well-known and successful plantation, Dockery Farms, was established by Will Dockery in 1895 between Ruleville and Cleveland on the Sunflower River. Dockery Farms came to support several thousand workers who raised crops on six thou-sand acres. It relied on wage farmworkers rather than the more typical sharecroppers. Family, managers, and work-ers mailed their letters from Dockery's own US Post Office and bought train tickets at the Dockery railroad terminal. A physician tended to the sick on the plantation, ministers of two Dockery churches pastored their flocks, and a sizable Dockery cemetery provided a final resting place for those who worked on the plantation. Early bluesmen such as Charley Patton and Son House worked on Dockery, making it the plantation birthplace of the blues.

Although Delta planters embraced economic modern-ization and sold their cotton on world markets, they saw themselves as Old South gentry. Their style emphasized personalism and paternalism, and they pursued the good life, with their financial resources enabling frequent travel, elaborate parties and dances, tasteful decoration of homes, good food and drink, and education of their children at fine schools and colleges across the South and the nation. The Percy family in particular embodied this ideal, producing generations of political leaders and writers as well as savvy economic managers. Planter fortunes depended on the suc-cess of cotton growing, and cotton culture pervaded the Delta as what Cohn called "a secular religion."

As the white landowning class prospered via cotton, Afri-can American fortunes grew more desperate. Delta society was rigidly segregated along racial lines, and by the early twentieth century the post–Civil War dream of the Delta as a place for African American economic success had been frustrated. Blacks found themselves facing declining economic opportunities, political disfranchisement, increasing violence, virtual powerlessness in the criminal justice system, sparse health care facilities, and inferior schools. These social problems, along with cotton's declining fortunes because of the boll weevil and the availability of jobs for African Americans in the urban North, pushed African Americans out of the Delta by the second decade of the twentieth century, as they increasingly migrated to Chicago and other northern cities. The Illinois Central Railroad became a powerful symbol in black culture of a connection to a new world. With the paving of roads, Highway 61, which runs from New Orleans to Chicago via the Delta, became another escape route. Black migrants from the Delta transplanted southern culture to the North, including foodways, speech patterns, church life, and folklife.

African Americans produced a vibrant Delta culture that sustained them through hard times. The blues emerged there out of traditional work songs, not only expressing the black suffering but also transcending that suffering. The black church also insulated its believers from the traumas of living in an oppressive society. Baptists, especially Missionary Baptists, constituted the major denomination, but Delta blacks also became Methodists, Presbyterians, and Pentecostals, particularly joining the Church of God in Christ, which had emerged on the edge of the Delta in the early twentieth century. The rural culture featured black folk customs involving ways to ensure healthy babies, contain the spirits of the dead, bless marriages, and nurture good health. Folk magic included dreaded conjure balls, which represented physical curses; mojo hands, which were small pouches that protected against curses; and bottle trees, which captured unwanted spirits on the landscape.

Mound Bayou was a distinctive Delta place, an all-black town founded in the 1880s. Booker T. Washington noted that the town was "the heart of a Negro population more dense than can be found anywhere outside of Africa." He called it a "Negro colony, occupying 30,000 acres, all of it owned by blacks who farmed small tracts of land." Mound Bayou's Taborian Hospital opened in 1942 and represented one of the few medical centers serving blacks throughout the Delta.

Immigrant groups made the Delta ethnically diverse, although these groups lived within a world that thought overwhelmingly in terms of black and white. Chinese immigrants originally came to the Delta after the Civil War as potential tenant farmers, but they quickly left the fields and launched grocery stores, usually serving black workers. Passed down through families for generations, these stores were gathering spots for blacks; whites often came there looking for potential day laborers. The Chinese fell outside the Delta's black-white ideological framework, and some communities there maintained separate schools for Chinese children in addition to segregated schools for blacks and whites. Some of the lumberjacks who cleared the Delta of its trees came from Germany, and the Irish helped build levees. Labor recruiters in Italy brought farmworkers to the Delta for several decades around 1900. Later in the century Sicilian immigrants owned and operated restaurants in Greenwood. Lebanese came around the same time, becoming merchants in such Delta towns as Greenwood, Greenville, Leland, and Vicksburg.

Delta people experienced eleven major floods between 1858 and 1922, but the 1927 Mississippi River flood was a defining experience for the modern Delta. The Delta became covered with water from south of Cleveland all the way to Vicksburg, inundating more than 16.6 million acres and 162,000 homes and leading to the deaths of between 250 and 500 people. The flood worsened race relations, as authorities forced black tenant farmers to stay in improvised crowded camps through the ordeal and required some blacks to work without pay in recovery efforts. The flood consequently spurred increased migration to Chicago.

The federal government helped to define the Delta in the mid-twentieth century. Soon after the 1927 flood, Congress appropriated $325 million for an extensive flood control project. The New Deal introduced the most extensive federal government presence in the region since Reconstruction. Planters used New Deal appropriations to their advantage, accepting payments to take land out of production and leaving their tenants with few resources. World War II created jobs that drew tenants away to military and defense projects, creating a labor shortage that promoted the consolidation of agricultural lands, the diversification of crops beyond cotton, and the mechanization of plantations.

The Delta was a stronghold in the South's final defense of racial segregation in the 1950s and 1960s. Delta politician Fielding Wright was the vice presidential candidate of the Dixiecrat Party in 1948, and Delta whites voted overwhelmingly for that party's rhetoric of resistance to social change. In the 1950s the region birthed the Citizens' Councils, which organized intimidation of civil rights advocates and cooperated with state government agencies to defend the South's racial caste system. The brutal 1955 murder of Chicago teenager Emmett Till in Money, Mississippi, sparked racial protest across the nation.

Civil rights activists targeted the Delta with boycotts, voter registration drives, marches, and other activities designed to show the injustices rooted in race in a region where blacks comprised a majority of the population yet lacked basic democratic rights. James Meredith was shot during a 1966 march through the Delta, and protesters occupied the courthouse grounds and the Confederate monument in Greenwood, where Stokely Carmichael first used the phrase "Black Power." The Civil Rights Act of 1964 and the Voting Rights Act of 1965 empowered Delta blacks politically and economically. The region elected its first black congressman, Mike Espy, in 1986, and he served until 1993. Since that time, the seat has been held by another African American, Bennie Thompson. The Delta's historical memory has drastically changed, with civil rights leaders Fannie Lou Hamer, Aaron Henry, and Amzie Moore now central figures in a new regional iconography.

The civil rights movement coincided with changes in agricultural production, as the neoplantation emerged as a highly mechanized and capitalized cotton production system that relied on a few wage hands and had no need for the large numbers of tenants who had long made their homes on plantations. This promoted the further exodus of blacks from the Delta and began a period of agricultural reorganization that led to a new farm economy based not only on cotton but also on soybeans, rice, catfish farming, poultry production, and more recently commercial corn production. The decline in federal government price supports for agricultural production in the 1980s hit the Delta hard and promoted consolidation of farms into larger plantation systems. Casino gambling came to the Delta in the 1990s, with Tunica and Vicksburg especially profiting from increased jobs and tax-generated public funds in a region that still has high rates of rural poverty.

Despite racial divisions and the poverty of many of its citizens, the Delta has been a creative place for musicians, writers, and artists. Such classic blues performers as Robert Johnson, Muddy Waters, and B. B. King, among many others, first played their music there. Country singers Charley Pride and Conway Twitty also grew up in the Delta, as did classical music composer Kenneth Haxton. Sam Cooke sang gospel music in Delta churches before becoming a classic rock and soul performer, while the Delta's Ike Turner recorded what has been described as the first rock and roll record, "Rocket 88," in 1951. Sculptor Leon Koury and artist Valerie Jaudon called the region home, and the inimitable Jim Henson, creator of the Muppets, was raised in Leland. Tennessee Williams lived in Clarksdale as a child, and his plays feature recurring themes of Delta society. Greenville was a major literary community in the mid-twentieth century, home to William Alexander Percy, Walker Percy, Shelby Foote, Ellen Douglas, Hodding Carter, David Cohn, Beverly Lowry, Lewis Nordan, and Steve Yarbrough. Cultural tourism has become an important part of the Delta's economy, with travelers visiting literary sites as well as the Delta Blues Museum and actor Morgan Freeman's Clarksdale blues club, Ground Zero; the B. B. King Museum in Indianola; and numerous historic blues sites that now have official markers as part of the Mississippi Blues Commission's Blues Trail.

Charles Reagan Wilson
University of Mississippi

Nancy Bercaw, *Gendered Freedoms: Race, Rights, and the Politics of Household in the Delta, 1861–1875* (2003); Blues Highway website, www .blueshighway.org; Robert L. Brandfon, *Cotton Kingdom of the New South:* *A History of the Yazoo Mississippi Delta from Reconstruction to the Twentieth Century* (1967); James C. Cobb, *The Most Southern Place on Earth: The Mississippi Delta and the Roots of Regional Identity* (1992); David L. Cohn, *Where I Was Born and Raised* (1948); Tom Rankin, *Southern Space: Photographs from the Mississippi Delta* (1993); Mikko Saikku, *This Delta, This Land: An Environmental History of the Yazoo-Mississippi Floodplain* (2005); John C. Willis, *Forgotten Time: The Yazoo-Mississippi Delta after the Civil War* (2000); Nan Elizabeth Woodruff, *American Congo: The African American Freedom Struggle in the Delta* (2003); Sharon D. Wright Austin, *The Transformation of Plantation Politics: Black Politics, Concentrated Poverty, and Social Capital* (2006).

Delta and Pine Land Company

Funded with northern capital in 1886, the Delta and Pine Land Company of Mississippi (DPL) remained in existence through a variety of incarnations for more than 125 years. Formed to sell farm and timber land in post-Reconstruction Mississippi, the company helped stimulate and shape the state's land development, most notably in the Mississippi Delta. By the 1910s DPL had sold more than a half million Mississippi acres. The company might have gone out of business had it not been for its valuable perpetual charter—permitted briefly under Mississippi law—that carried no limits on capitalization or size and value of landholdings. Neither subsequent restrictions nor Mississippi's Constitution of 1890 changed that charter, leaving DPL and three others unique among Mississippi corporations. Populist efforts after the turn of the century prompted limits on corporate agricultural landholdings, but the Mississippi Supreme Court upheld DPL's exemptions in a 1917 decision, *Southern Realty Co. v. Tchula Cooperative Stores.*

DPL's special charter attracted a group of British investors who early in the century had sought prime Mississippi

Offices, stores, and clinics of the Delta Pine and Land Company, October 1939 (Photograph by Marion Post Wolcott, Library of Congress, Washington, D.C. [LC-USF34-052216-D])

farmland to supply English mills with long-staple cotton. The investors represented the Fine Cotton Spinners' and Doublers' Association of Manchester, England, a fiber conglomerate that had grown to fifty affiliates after it was organized in 1898 by some of England's ablest commercial giants. Disappointment with Egyptian long-staple cotton apparently prompted the British to investigate the highly successful cotton work of Prof. Jesse W. Fox of the agricultural experiment station in Greenville, Mississippi. Aggressive salesmanship by land promoter Lant K. Salsbury and others led the Fine Spinners to acquire tens of thousands of Delta acres in 1911, slipping through a loophole in Mississippi law limiting tillable acreage by creating two holding companies that in turn leased their land to an operating corporation, the Mississippi Delta Planting Company. Salsbury, a Michigan native who became a timber and land promoter in his adopted South, assumed the company's presidency. With boll weevil threats on the horizon, the British investment likely helped stabilize the state's volatile land market.

Fearing renewed Populism, the British conglomerate joined with minority investors to purchase DPL's name and charter in 1919, thereby acquiring immunity from future limitations of the Mississippi legislature. Nevertheless, the company's long-staple cotton proved unsuitable for British spindles, and despite scientific research and development, including prolific seed varieties bred by company geneticist Early Ewing Sr., insect infestation and floods left the company awash in red ink. With millions of dollars invested, attempts to unload the company's unprofitable American holdings fell through, and the Mississippi River Flood of 1927 destroyed the crop and scattered black sharecroppers. Salsbury left for new adventures, replaced as president by the company's general counsel, Oscar Goodbar Johnston, a Mississippi-born lawyer and former legislator and planter who had originally been retained to assist in the sale of the mammoth plantation.

Johnston led the company in fiscal retrenchment, moved DPL headquarters from Memphis to the tiny Mississippi Delta village of Scott, and changed the several thousand black tenants to half shares, meaning that they supplied only their labor while the company provided seed, mules, work implements, housing, and woodland for fuel. Half the value of the cotton crop, minus deductions for items purchased on credit, belonged to the tenants, half to the company, while they shared fertilizer and pest control costs equally. The plantation, consisting of approximately thirty-eight thousand acres, decentralized into twelve units, offered incentives for local managers, hired its own policeman, and was home to seven county schools for tenant children.

Johnson increased the paternalistic social welfare programs Salsbury had begun, using public and private resources to treat or prevent common diseases, including malaria, typhoid, and pellagra, and to provide primary care and hospitalization on the plantation. In the 1920s and 1930s, the company improved tenant housing; added recreational facilities, including a movie theater; helped fund several black churches on the plantation; encouraged live-at-home garden cultivation and improved diets; and acquired a federally funded instructor in home economics to teach food preservation.

Between the wars, the high-profile, labor-intensive plantation was the subject of frequent surveys by critics, journalists, and academics, including a Harvard-led study that credited quality diet and medical care for improved health and low mortality rates among its black labor force. DPL also became a port of call for students of agriculture from the United States and abroad. Johnston's leadership in the New Deal, where he held policy appointments in the Department of Agriculture, attracted unwanted attention. In 1936 and 1937 critics raised conflict-of-interest issues when the plantation legally received New Deal subsidies that Johnston had helped formulate. But Johnston ran what the *New York Times* called an "enlightened company" motivated by what he believed were "just sound economics."

While World War II swept agricultural labor off the farm and increased the demand for mechanization, the development of the long-awaited, long-feared cotton picker changed cotton's kingdom, including DPL, forever. Johnston was forced into retirement in 1950, and within a decade the sharecropper was also gone. The British eventually sold out, but Delta and Pine Land survived, a model of stability amid the vicissitudes of twentieth-century agriculture. In June 2007, with US Justice Department approval, DPL, the world's oldest privately held seed producer, was acquired by the Monsanto Company for $1.5 billion cash. The otherwise sleepy Delta village of Scott remained DPL's headquarters as the company began the newest phase of an expanding twenty-first-century empire that not even the most optimistic investor could have foreseen.

Lawrence J. Nelson
University of North Alabama

Robert Brandfon, *Cotton Kingdom of the New South: A History of the Yazoo Mississippi Delta from Reconstruction to the Twentieth Century* (1967); Delta and Pine Land Company Records, Special Collections, Mitchell Memorial Library, Mississippi State University; J. William Harris, *Deep Souths: Delta, Piedmont, and Sea Island Society in the Age of Segregation* (2001); Lawrence J. Nelson, *King Cotton's Advocate: Oscar G. Johnston and the New Deal* (1999).

Delta and Providence Cooperative Farms

In March 1936 a coterie of liberal Christians, ostensibly led by Reinhold Niebuhr, and the Southern Tenant Farmers' Union (STFU), under the direction of the Socialist Party of

America (SPA), established Delta Cooperative Farm near Hillhouse, Mississippi. The biracial farm was initially established to provide refuge for sharecropping families who had been evicted from their homes in the Arkansas Delta because of the crop reduction provisions of the Agricultural Adjustment Act. For a brief time, poor black and white farmers cooperated under the leadership of a fragile coalition of political socialists and evangelical utopians.

The Christian activists expected that the cooperative farm would demonstrate the redemptive nature of social and economic justice. The SPA and STFU planned to use the farm to modify the entire economic structure of staple-crop production. The SPA saw the Delta Cooperative Farm as the first in a growing phalanx of plantations liberated from their corporate owners and placed in service to the producers.

Using a twenty-thousand-dollar contribution from William H. Timken of Canton, Ohio, Sherwood Eddy purchased 2,138 acres of mostly "buckshot" Delta bottomland and established Cooperative Farms of Mississippi, with Niebuhr, America's premier theologian, as president. The board of directors of Cooperative Farms was composed of luminaries and near-luminaries: Eddy, an international missionary and troubleshooter for the YMCA; sociologist Arthur Raper; John Rust, inventor of a mechanical cotton picker; William Scarlett, bishop of the Episcopal Diocese of Missouri; and William R. Amberson, a physiologist at the University of Tennessee Medical School in Memphis. The board appointed Sam Franklin Jr., recently returned from a stint as a YMCA missionary in Japan, as resident director, and Blaine Treadway, a part-time press operator for the *Memphis Press Scimitar* and full-time socialist, as assistant resident director.

Scores of national publications covered the activities and success of the Delta Cooperative Farm. Articles in national magazines and influential newspapers spoke of economic justice, human dignity, and the surprising financial success of the farm. According to articles penned by Niebuhr, Eddy, Amberson, H. L. Mitchell, and others, the cooperators were making money and finding dignity in the very heart of cotton plantation country. At a time and place when the average cash income of sharecropper families totaled less than $200 per year, the members of Delta Cooperative Farm enjoyed the benefits of a medical clinic, a varied diet, and an annual income of almost $450 in cash and deferred certificates. In the first year, despite a slow start and bad weather, the farm produced 152 bales of cotton. Members established a sawmill; poultry, hog, and dairy operations; and a consumers' cooperative, named after England's Rochdale Cooperative. In 1937 the US Postal Service established the Rochdale post office.

Student volunteers organized by the Quaker American Friends Service Committee came to Hillhouse and labored with the Delta Cooperative Farm members. Other volunteers staffed a summer labor school under the auspices of the STFU. The farm's appeal enabled the directors to launch successful fund-raising campaigns in the midst of the Great Depression. The state of Mississippi provided funding for eight months of school for white children and only four months for African Americans, but white farm members insisted on hiring a teacher to provide a full eight months of instruction for the black children.

Indeed, Delta Cooperative Farm was successful, its supporters claimed, because of the remarkable cooperation of black and white members. The farm retained some of the traditional mores of the South regarding social equality: for example, blacks used the community house for social activities on different nights of the week from whites. However, a biracial committee selected by the members managed the farm, and the families lived in close proximity, separated only by the road that traversed the farm.

In 1938 favorable publicity; compliments from Eleanor Roosevelt, Louis Brandeis, and Jacob Coxey; and financial support from liberal Americans encouraged the directors to acquire 2,880 acres in Holmes County, on which they established a second enterprise, Providence Cooperative Farm. But all was not as the press reported. Serious dissension emerged among the board of directors. Amberson accused the board in general and Franklin in particular of misrepresenting the farm's economic success. Amberson charged the board with blatant dishonesty in its fund-raising appeals, alleging that the farms had lost money in every year of operation. Journalist Jonathan Daniels agreed, suggesting that the primary income for Delta Cooperative Farm came not from cotton but from Yankee benevolence. Amberson and Treadway castigated the board for financial chicanery and for deemphasizing membership in the STFU. In addition, the SPA faction criticized the board for its paternalistic and elite management of the farm. According to Amberson and Treadway, the farm was not managed by the members but instead was a dictatorship headed by Franklin and the board of directors, no different from any other Delta cotton plantation worked by sharecroppers.

The racial harmony and cooperation lauded by Eddy and Niebuhr deteriorated or perhaps never really existed. Arguments, charges of racial injustice, and dishonesty plagued membership meetings. Despite the farm's deteriorating financial condition, the members did have access to on-site medical care and some outstanding educational programs.

The economic morass of the Great Depression and Delta Cooperative Farm's inability to make money from its operations influenced the board to sell the property in 1942. The lure of employment in wartime industries and the inefficiency of the operations had made continued operation untenable. The board subsequently focused on Providence Cooperative Farm, but operations there gradually dwindled to providing community education and a medical clinic. The enterprise struggled along until September 1955, when a teenaged white girl reported that some black boys from the farm had whistled at her while she was waiting for the bus. In view of the recent Emmett Till case, the citizens of Holmes County met at the Tchula school, heard the taped "confessions," and voted (with only one objection) to expel the staff of Providence Cooperative Farm from Holmes County. On 12 October 1956 the stockholders and director voted to sell Providence Cooperative Farm to the Delta Foundation for one dollar.

The cooperative farms did not achieve their goals. The Christian Socialists did not usher in an age of social justice and economic success, the Socialist Party of America did not transform Mississippi sharecroppers into a rural socialist vanguard, and their vision of biracial cooperative farming died.

Fred C. Smith
Tupelo, Mississippi

William R. Amberson, *Nation* (13 February 1935); Will Campbell, *Providence* (2002); Mississippi History Now website, http://mshistorynow.mdah.state.ms.us; Jonathan Daniels, *A Southerner Discovers the South* (1938); Sherwood Eddy, *Christian Century* (3 February 1937); Jonathan Mitchell, *New Republic* (22 September 1937); Reinhold Niebuhr, *Christian Century* (10 February 1937); Fred C. Smith, *Trouble in Goshen: Plain Folk, Roosevelt, Jesus, and Marx in the Great Depression South* (Jackson: University Press of Mississippi, 2014).

Delta Blues Museum

The Delta Blues Museum resides in a restored five-thousand-square-foot freight depot in downtown Clarksdale between the blues club Ground Zero and the Delta Blues Museum Stage. Mississippi's oldest music museum, it began in 1979 as part of the Carnegie Public Library. In 1999 it moved to the restored 1918 depot and became an independent entity governed by a five-member board appointed by the mayor and board of commissioners. The museum is "dedicated to creating a welcoming place where visitors find meaning, value, and perspective by exploring the history and heritage of the unique American musical art form of the blues." The museum employs four full-time workers (a director, an exhibits and programs coordinator, a group tour manager, and a gift shop manager) as well as several part-time workers. Funded by the City of Clarksdale, admissions, gift shop revenue, memberships, grants, and donations, the museum welcomes more than twenty-five thousand visitors a year. The Delta Blues Museum was one of ten recipients of the 2013 National Medal for Museum and Library Service presented by the Institute of Museum and Library Services in Washington, D.C.

The largest artifact in the Delta Blues Museum is blues legend Muddy Waters's cabin. The structure has been reconstructed with the original cypress boards of the cabin, which was located on the Stovall family plantation outside Clarksdale. Between 1996 and 2000 the House of Blues circulated the cabin to Chicago, Orlando, New Orleans, and other major US and Canadian cities; the cabin even made a special appearance at the 1996 Olympics in Atlanta. The cabin then sat in a warehouse until 2001, when it moved to the Delta Blues Museum. Visitors can sit in the cabin and watch a video presentation about Waters's life.

Another popular traveling Muddy Waters item exhibited at the museum is the "Muddywood Guitar." In 1989 rock band ZZ Top asked Pyramid Guitars in Memphis to build a guitar from a solid cypress board that had originally been part of Muddy Waters's cabin. The result was the Muddywood Guitar, which symbolizes rock and roll's indebtedness to the blues. The guitar was exhibited throughout the United States to raise money for the Delta Blues Museum.

The museum also houses instruments played by many famous blues artists—Charlie Musselwhite's harmonica, Sam Carr's drumsticks, and the guitars of Super Chikan, John Lee Hooker, B. B. King, and Big Joe Williams. Various copies of *Living Blues* magazine hang throughout the museum. The Jelly Roll Kings' autographed wooden shoes from Holland sit in a glass case, as does a signed postcard from Musselwhite addressed "to the staff at my favorite place in the whole wide world—the Delta Blues Museum of Clarksdale." Other notable displays include a sculpture of a woman in a coffin made of Yazoo River clay by James "Son" Thomas; suits worn by Eddie Cusic, E. B. Davis, and Pinetop Perkins; and W. C. Handy's autograph on an off-white 5.5″ × 3.5″ card. Temporary exhibits of ephemera have included art, T-shirts, posters, and photographs. The museum has hosted *Delta Dogs*, a popular exhibition by Delta photographer Maude Schuyler Clay, and has displayed posters celebrating twenty-five years of the Sunflower River Blues Festival.

The Delta Blues Museum sponsors an arts and education program that works to continue the musical tradition of the Delta Blues. Classes meet four days a week to teach students musical technique and the history of the blues. Students can choose to play guitar, harmonica, keyboard, bass guitar, and drums, or any other blues instrument of their choice. Public performance opportunities enable participants to share their achievements with the community. The adjacent Delta Blues Museum Stage serves as the main venue for local blues festivals.

The Delta Blues Museum has launched the Deeper Roots Campaign, seeking $1.2 million to expand the museum, add exhibits, and further its mission of preserving and sharing the blues heritage.

Miranda Cully Griffin
Memphis, Tennessee

Delta Blues Museum website, www.deltabluesmuseum.org.

Delta Council

A group of Delta planters started meeting in the years after the 1927 Mississippi River Flood to coordinate their efforts and lobby governments to improve conditions in the Delta. Scattered efforts by this Delta Chamber of Commerce gave way to a larger organization, reorganized in 1935 as the Delta Council. The council established its headquarters in Stoneville, Mississippi, home of the Delta Branch Experiment Station.

The Delta Council initially sought to provide better health conditions, transportation, flood control, education, and economic development to residents of the Delta; to serve "as a general information and publicity bureau" for the region; and to represent the Delta before the state and federal governments. The council's early efforts included working with the federal government to increase subsidies for cotton farmers and to expand cotton sales. The Delta Council helped start the National Cotton Council and consistently supported efforts to use science and technology to limit costs and improve agricultural productivity. Delta Council leaders created a brand logo for Delta cotton and encouraged Delta women to develop a "Wear What You Sow" campaign.

The Delta Council's first leaders included Mississippi cotton planters and state and federal government officials: Oscar Johnston, head of the Delta Pine and Land and the National Cotton Council; political power broker Walter Sillers; several members of the Percy family; Will Dockery of Dockery Farms; W. T. Wynn and Hodding Carter of Greenville; and Rhea Blake of the Delta Chamber of Commerce. The council's first president was Walter M. Kethley, president of Delta State Teachers College.

The Delta Council has always had staunch supporters and harsh critics. Detractors argue that council represents the interests of wealthy planters at the expense of poorly paid workers, especially disfranchised African Americans, and that the council's actions pushed those workers off the land and offered little in return. The Delta Council has consistently opposed farmworkers' organizations on the grounds that they "cause disunity and a breach of faith." A 1944 council document contended that "the plantation system as a partnership is successful only when there is mutual understanding and mutual effort." The council also argued against limits on child labor and opposed agricultural minimum wage laws as late as the 1960s. In short, critics have charged, the council worked hard to make sure plantation owners had access to as much cheap labor and as many government subsidy payments as possible.

Supporters, conversely, believe that the council provided enlightened leadership to support the region's economic and human development. In the face of job losses as a result of farm mechanization and crop reductions, the Delta Council encouraged industrialization and agricultural diversification via the timber, rice, soybean, and catfish industries.

The council has a mixed record on race relations. It created a subcommittee on the topic as early as 1948, and it never merged with the white supremacist groups that actively opposed the civil rights movement. However, the organization's publication, the *Delta Council News*, made no mention of the *Brown v. Board of Education* decision in 1954, the controversy and violence over the desegregation of the University of Mississippi in 1962, or the Mississippi Summer Project of 1964. It opposed the Civil Rights Act of 1964 and two years later produced a film, *Daylight in the Delta*, that portrayed the region as having particularly good race relations.

The annual meeting of the Delta Council has long been a major political and social event. Speakers have included Secretary of State Dean Acheson, rocket engineer Wernher von Braun, astronaut Alan Shepherd, and future presidents George W. Bush and Bill Clinton. In his 1952 speech to the Delta Council, William Faulkner discussed how Americans had moved away from assumptions about responsibility that had been so crucial to the Founding Fathers. His criticisms of the federal government and especially its welfare policies earned Faulkner applause from his conservative listeners; however, later readers of the speech wondered if Faulkner was also critiquing twentieth-century planters' reliance on federal agricultural subsidies.

The Delta Council remains a powerful force in Mississippi, especially in setting the agenda for agricultural policy.

Ted Ownby
University of Mississippi

William M. Cash and R. Daryl Lewis, *The Delta Council: Fifty Years of Service to the Mississippi Delta* (1986); James Cobb, *The Most Southern Place on Earth: The Mississippi Delta and the Roots of Regional Identity* (1994); *Delta Council News*; Nan Elizabeth Woodruff, *American Congo: The African American Freedom Struggle in the Delta* (2003); Clyde Woods, *Development Arrested: Race, Power, and the Blues in the Mississippi Delta* (1998).

Delta Ministry

The National Council of Churches launched the Delta Ministry in September 1964 as a ten-year program of relief, community building, literacy, economic development, and racial reconciliation. The Delta Ministry concentrated its efforts in the Yazoo-Mississippi Delta and operated projects in Hattiesburg and McComb. Influenced by the biblical idea of a servant ministry and by the Student Nonviolent Coordinating Committee and the Congress of Racial Equality, the ministry sought to enable the poor to achieve self-chosen goals by acting as a facilitator rather than as a leadership organization. Directed by Art Thomas, a white Methodist minister from Pennsylvania, the ministry's staff was at first predominantly comprised of white northern Protestant clergymen. The ministry also brought hundreds of mostly short-term lay and clerical volunteers, including some Jews, to Mississippi.

The ministry never received adequate funding, in large part because opposition to the project, particularly from white southerners, limited and delayed contributions from some of the largest denominations in the National Council of Churches. Nevertheless, by 1967, with the Student Nonviolent Coordinating Committee and Congress of Racial Equality in decline and the Southern Christian Leadership Conference largely focused on the North, the ministry had the largest civil rights field staff in Mississippi. By design, most ministry staffers were now blacks from Mississippi, although two African American northerners, Owen Brooks and Harry Bowie, led the organization.

The ministry failed to achieve racial reconciliation. Its militancy, support of direct action, and working alliance with the Mississippi Freedom Democratic Party alienated the National Association for the Advancement of Colored People and moderate whites such as Greenville newspaper editor Hodding Carter III. Nevertheless, the ministry achieved some notable successes. By threatening to distribute food, it induced counties that had not joined the free federal surplus commodities program to participate. In January 1966 some Ministry staff joined unemployed agricultural workers in occupying the disused Greenville Air Force Base, which led Mississippi to implement Operation Help, a federally funded food program for the poor. The action also encouraged the federal government to restore funding to the Child Development Group of Mississippi, a Head Start program that the ministry had helped launch and that benefited thousands of deprived black children. Working with health care professionals, the ministry secured federal funding that helped expand impoverished Mississippians' access to medical care. In 1969 the ministry created the Delta Foundation, which used federal and philanthropic monies to create six thousand jobs over the next twenty-five years. The ministry also registered thousands of African American voters, trained black electoral candidates, and assisted black elected officials.

The ministry's financial difficulties precluded a literacy program and prematurely curtailed the McComb project. The group also made strategic mistakes. It supported a 1966 strike by Delta farmworkers that only hastened rural unemployment caused by mechanization and herbicides. Cooperatives founded by the ministry did not find sustainable markets, and Freedom City, a village built by displaced agricultural workers, failed to develop a viable economic base.

Budget cuts imposed by the faltering finances of the National Council of Churches reduced the ministry's staff to four in 1971, eventually led the National Council to withdraw from the project, and revealed long-simmering tensions between the group's northern leaders, who favored independent African American development, and black staff members from Mississippi, who supported integration and favored working with moderate blacks and whites in the state's Democratic Party. By the late 1970s the ministry often comprised little more than Brooks, who continued his civil rights work until his death in July 2014.

Mark Newman
Edinburgh University

James F. Findlay Jr., *Church People in the Struggle: The National Council of Churches and the Black Freedom Movement, 1950–1970* (1993); Bruce Hilton, *The Delta Ministry* (1969); Leon Howell, *Freedom City: The Substance of Things Hoped For* (1969); Mark Newman, *Divine Agitators: The Delta Ministry and Civil Rights in Mississippi* (2004).

Delta Pride Catfish Workers' Strike

With unemployment hovering around 10 percent, Sunflower County was an unlikely setting for a show of labor militancy. But for thirteen weeks in 1990, nearly one thousand African American workers struck for higher wages, safer working conditions, and an end to discriminatory managerial practices at the Indianola-based Delta Pride catfish processing company. Although it barely registered on the national radar, the strike rekindled the spirit of the state's civil rights movement and continued the long-running struggle over the value of black labor in the Mississippi Delta.

Shortly after Delta Pride's founding by a group of white farmer-owners in 1981, the African American women who made up the majority of the workforce began complaining of repetitive motion ailments, insufficient bathroom breaks, and overbearing supervisors who used stopwatches to time workers as they cut and packaged fish. "They hire you, cripple you, fire you," explained one longtime employee to a reporter. "They treat people like dogs out there. It's like being back on the plantation." The United Food and Commercial Workers Union, which had limited success in unionizing catfish and poultry plants in the region, soon set its sights on Delta Pride, believing that a victory at the nation's largest catfish producer would facilitate the organization of smaller processors and bring stability to the industry. In October

1986, despite the company's efforts to intimidate and fire union supporters, a majority of Delta Pride workers voted to be represented by Local 1529.

In the three years after unionization, however, wages remained only slightly above the federal minimum, and working conditions did not substantially improve. In 1989 the Occupational Safety and Health Administration found that Delta Pride had failed to implement controls to reduce repetitive motion disorders, ignored employees' injuries, and knowingly exposed them to safety hazards. With their first union contract set to expire in the summer of 1990, the workers hoped to raise wages and push for health and safety improvements. The company, still smarting from the union victory, aimed to stall negotiations and break Local 1529.

On 10 September, following several weeks of negotiations, workers voted 410–5 to reject the company's final contract offer of a wage increase of 6.5 cents an hour. Three days later, more than nine hundred employees walked off the job at the plants in Indianola and Inverness. The strikers' efforts initially focused on stopping strikebreakers from crossing the picket lines and taking jobs, but by the end of the first month, the union shifted strategy and began framing the strike more broadly as a civil rights issue. Union leaders pulled together sympathetic churches, labor unions, and the National Association for the Advancement of Colored People and carried out an effective campaign to pressure Delta Pride to negotiate. Donations of groceries and cash sustained the strikers, and Local 1529 leaders, among them Sarah White and Rose Turner, traveled across the country, promoting a boycott of Delta Pride and addressing a hearing of the Congressional Black Caucus in Washington, D.C.

Delta Pride officials tried to downplay the strike's racial dimensions and continued catfish production at reduced levels using replacement workers. But a series of miscues in late October forced Delta Pride back to the bargaining table. First, the National Labor Relations Board cited company officials for threatening picketers and encouraging employees to quit the union. The next day a federal grand jury indicted two shareholders for attempting to bribe a union negotiator to end the strike. A nationally televised interview with Delta Pride board chairman Turner Arant on NBC's *Today* show may have been the final blow to the company. During a segment on the strike, camera crews followed Arant as he walked proudly around his catfish ponds and through his large family home, where he pronounced that catfish had been very good to him. These scenes were contrasted with an interview with a striker, who spoke of the challenges she faced trying to feed her family of eight and pay her bills on Delta Pride wages. Arant resigned under pressure from the board of directors, and both sides returned to the bargaining table. On 12 December the company and Local 1529 reached an agreement that gave a sixty-cent hourly raise to every worker who had been employed for one year, provided for

the rehiring of the strikers, and established a health and safety committee that included workers. The contract was ratified the next day by a 479–1 vote.

Employer-employee relations improved in the years after the strike, though overproduction and foreign competition have forced periodic layoffs at Delta Pride. Several key union leaders have been involved in other efforts to organize workers in the South's growing food processing industries.

Kieran W. Taylor
The Citadel

Eric Bates, *Southern Exposure* (Fall 1991); J. Todd Moye, *Let the People Decide: Black Freedom and White Resistance Movements in Sunflower County, Mississippi, 1945–1986* (2004); Richard Schweid, *Catfish and the Delta: Confederate Fish Farming in the Mississippi Delta* (1992).

Delta Regional Commission

In October 1988 the US Congress established the Lower Mississippi Delta Development Commission (commonly known as the Delta Regional Commission) to study methods of alleviating poverty in the portions of Mississippi and six other states that comprise the Mississippi Delta, an area where the alluvial soil is rich but most inhabitants are poor. In its two years of work, the commission alerted Congress and the nation to the needs of the region and presented a plan for later aid efforts.

The creation of the Delta Regional Commission represented the culmination of years of work by the congressional delegations from Illinois, Missouri, Kentucky, Tennessee, Arkansas, Mississippi, and Louisiana. Members included the governors of these seven states (or their representatives) plus two presidential appointees. Arkansas governor and future US president Bill Clinton chaired the commission, with Mississippi governor Ray Mabus as vice chair.

With a mandate to evaluate the region's needs and recommend actions to improve the quality of life there, the commission spent more than a year meeting with residents and compiling data. In May 1990 it published *The Delta Initiatives: Realizing the Dream . . . Fulfilling the Potential*, a comprehensive report that designated 219 counties (45 in Mississippi) as either in the Delta or contiguous to it. The document listed specific steps that local, state, and federal governments could take to address endemic economic and social problems. It also detailed the support needed from private businesses and nonprofit organizations. Having completed its mission, the commission ceased its duties on 30 September 1990.

Aid for the Delta was a high priority after Clinton became president in 1993. Budget restrictions prevented large investments early in his presidency, but by the late 1990s dozens of government agencies and private philanthropies were funding programs totaling hundreds of millions of dollars.

One example is the Rural Empowerment Zones–Enterprise Communities Initiative (EZ-EC) operated by the US Department of Agriculture. Under this program, cities and counties use block grants to pay for social services or economic development. Frequently, these grants are used to match a required percentage of larger grants. Delta counties in Mississippi are home to two of the thirty-three original EZ-EC communities nationwide, and by 2006 those two had received more than $257 million in funds from public and private sources. The US Department of Health and Human Services and the Kellogg Foundation have also collaborated on Humphreys County's Delta Rural Health Network, which works to improve residents' access to doctors and other services and to encourage students to choose medical careers.

Acting on Clinton administration requests in 2000, Congress established a new entity, the Delta Regional Authority (DRA), to monitor and coordinate the various aid efforts through state and local alliances. The DRA legislation added 21 counties in Alabama, bringing the total number of districts served to 240. In its first five years, the DRA approved $48.5 million of its own grants, which have brought almost $1 billion in matching money. One notable endeavor is a visa waiver system that has allowed fifty-nine physicians from other nations to practice in Mississippi's Delta towns.

The DRA has drawn criticism for lacking an overall strategy and duplicating the work of other federal agencies. Whether these allegations are true or false, the Mississippi River Delta remains the poorest major region in the country, the same position it occupied in 1930. Of the 240 DRA counties, 227 are labeled economically distressed, including 41 in Mississippi. In addition, poverty rates are 55 percent above the national average, and deaths from circulatory diseases and cancer are far more common than in most of the United States.

The Delta Regional Commission brought attention and financial aid to a neglected backwater, and thousands of families have benefited from the many economic development efforts or the social services implemented by government and private organizations since publication of *The Delta Initiatives*. More than twenty years after the DRC closed its books, however, measurements of the health, education, and economic well-being of the Delta's citizens indicate that many tasks remain undone.

Sammy Landrum Morgan
Jonesboro, Arkansas

Delta Regional Authority website, www.dra.gov; Paul Fronstein, Issue Brief 276, Employee Benefit Research Institute (December 2004); Health Resources and Services Administration, Rural Assistance Center Network Sourcebook; US Department of Health and Human Services, Agency for Toxic Substances and Diseases Registry, *Mississippi Delta Project* (May 1995); US Department of Health and Human Services, Lower Mississippi Delta Development Commission, *Final Report: The Delta Initiatives* (14 May 1990).

Delta State University

Located in Cleveland, in the heart of the Mississippi Delta, Delta State University is a public institution offering a comprehensive curriculum to more than four thousand students from all over the United States as well as from more than twenty other countries. The university offers bachelor's degrees in more than fifty majors as well as master's degrees and doctoral programs.

Delta State Teachers College was created by Mississippi Senate Bill 236, sponsored by Senators W. B. Roberts and Arthur Marshall, and signed into law by Gov. Henry L. Whitfield on 9 April 1924. Housed in the former Bolivar County Agricultural High School buildings in Cleveland, the college opened its doors on 15 September 1925 with 123 students and 11 faculty members. James Wesley Broom was appointed as Delta State's first president.

In 1926, following Broom's death, William Marion Kethley, a native of Jackson, was appointed president. He remained in the position for thirty years, during which time the faculty and student body weathered the Great Depression, World War II, the Korean War, and the social backlash against the *Brown v. Board of Education* decision. The Kethley era also witnessed the expansion of Delta State's academic and professional course offerings and consequently the school's 1955 name change to Delta State College.

Whereas Kethley had focused on developing Delta State's curriculum and academic standards, his successor, James M. Ewing, prioritized the construction of new facilities. Between 1956 and 1971, when Ewing left office, the institution added the president's home, six groups of dormitories, two groups of apartments for married students, a coliseum, four classrooms and office buildings, a cafeteria, and a library building.

Ewing's tenure also included major changes brought about by the civil rights movement. The college's first African American student, Shirley Antoinette Washington, enrolled in the fall of 1967. The black student population subsequently grew, and on 27 February 1969 a group of fifty-two African American students declared themselves the Black Student Organization and presented Ewing with a list of grievances and demands. Items on the list included black counselors and instructors, black history courses, fair grading policies toward black students, an end to discrimination against black students by white professors, scholarship opportunities for black students, and representation for black students in the Student Government Association. When the students' demands were not met, they staged a sit-in in front of the president's office on 10 March. After refusing to leave, the students were arrested and taken by bus to Parchman State Penitentiary, where they were kept overnight before being released. The following year Delta State hired two part-time black instructors, one of whom offered a black history course and both of whom served as counselors to black students.

In 1974 the college again changed its name, this time becoming Delta State University. The school has subsequently grown dramatically, diversifying its student body and enhancing its academic, athletic, and extracurricular offerings. Its undergraduate student body is now roughly 40 percent African American and includes Hispanic and Asian/Pacific Islander students as well. It is the only school in Mississippi to offer a degree in commercial aviation.

The school's athletic teams are officially known as the Statesmen and Lady Statesmen, recognizing the role state representative Walter Sillers Jr. played in locating the school in Cleveland. However, in the mid-1990s, the student body officially adopted the Fighting Okra as an unofficial sports mascot. It has subsequently become a humorous and recognizable symbol of the university and was featured on the "Okraphobia" episode of the Food Network show *Good Eats*.

Delta State's women's basketball team was a national powerhouse in the 1970s and 1980s, winning three national titles in each decade. The National Collegiate Athletic Association (NCAA) Division I women's basketball Player of the Year receives a trophy named for Margaret Wade, Delta State's coach and a member of the Naismith Memorial Basketball Hall of Fame. The university's football team won the NCAA Division II national championship in 2000 as well as Gulf South Conference championships in 2007, 2008, 2010, and 2011. The baseball team brought home the NCAA Division II national championship trophy in 2004. Among the notables associated with the school's baseball team are former Major League pitcher Dave "Boo" Ferris, who coached the Statesmen from 1960 to 1988; Eli Whiteside, who played in the Majors between 2005 and 2014 and was a member of the 2010 World Series champion San Francisco Giants; and John Grisham, who pursued a career as an attorney and author after being cut from the Delta State squad.

Eva Walton Kendrick
Birmingham, Alabama

Delta State University website, www.deltastate.edu; Jack Winton Gunn and Gladys C. Castle, *Pictorial History of Delta State University* (1980).

Demagogues

For a century after the Civil War, Mississippi was affected by all of the elements necessary for the production of demagogues: deep racial suspicions left over from the days of slavery, lingering resentment of Reconstruction, an impoverished agrarian society, sharp class distinctions between the few haves and the many have-nots, and a poorly educated electorate.

In their 1939 book, *Dixie Demagogues*, Allan A. Michie and Frank Ryhlick wrote, "A fantastic parade of charlatans has marched across the hustings of the South since the Civil War." Nowhere was the tramping of the demagogic guard more resounding than in Mississippi, where politicians exploited the frustrations of poor people. Rabble-rousing rhetoric filled the chambers of the state legislature and echoed from the steps of county courthouses. The practitioners of demagoguery won many elective positions over the years; some rose to the highest offices in the state.

James K. Vardaman, editor of the *Greenwood Commonwealth*, emerged in the latter part of the nineteenth century as a leader of populist forces in the state, with a strong strain of racism permeating his speeches and writings. Known as the Great White Chief, Vardaman targeted Mississippi's black population in his diatribes. He characterized the Negro as "a lazy, lustful animal which no conceivable amount of training can transform into a tolerable citizen." He also singled out corporate interests as enemies of the people and waged class warfare against wealthy business owners and planters.

Vardaman was twice defeated as a candidate for governor before winning the office in 1903 and plunging the state into such quixotic initiatives as a futile attempt to repeal

James K. Vardaman at the Democratic National Convention, 1912 (Photograph by Harris and Ewing, Library of Congress [LC-H261-1506])

the Fifteenth Amendment, which extended voting rights to all races, and legislation to limit corporations to property worth no more than two million dollars. Vardaman later became involved in bitter contests for a US Senate seat against LeRoy Percy, a member of an aristocratic Delta family. Though Percy first defeated Vardaman in a special election decided by the legislature, Vardaman gained the seat and revenge in a tumultuous 1911 campaign in which the victor's followers were encouraged to call themselves *low-brows* and *rednecks*.

Though Vardaman lost his political credibility in Washington, his place was quickly taken by his protégé, Theodore G. Bilbo. As a state legislator, governor, and US senator, Bilbo dominated Mississippi's political landscape for forty years. Spewing ethnic slurs and racial epithets, Bilbo became known as the nation's most vociferous demagogue. He was involved in scandals throughout his career but was shameless about the controversies. After serving ten days in jail in Oxford for contempt of court, Bilbo compared himself to Martin Luther and St. Paul, who had also been imprisoned. Bilbo had his own newspaper, the *Mississippi Free Lance*, to counterattack his critics. In one famous tirade against Fred Sullens, editor of the *Jackson News*, Bilbo delivered a curse against his rival: "Cast him out upon the lonely seashore of despair, where the howling winds of divine retribution will bite and cut him to the ignoble death that he so justly deserves, and where like a dead mackerel in the moonlight he will, forever, of his own corruption, lie stinking and shining, shining and stinking." Bilbo died in 1947 while suspended from the Senate and under investigation for kickbacks in connection with the construction of his "dream house" in Poplarville.

Though no other politician could measure up to Bilbo's thunder, many tried. Ross Barnett, a country lawyer with roots in Leake County, rode the support of the Citizens' Council to the governor's office in 1959 and eventually led the state into its greatest crisis since the Civil War in an effort to block James Meredith from enrolling at the University of Mississippi in 1962. Barnett publicly portrayed himself as a champion of white southerners but privately engaged in a series of secret deals with the Kennedy administration during the integration struggle that triggered a riot on the University of Mississippi campus.

Barnett attempted a comeback in 1967 but was badly beaten in the last episode of raw demagoguery in Mississippi. Barnett lost to a congressman from Raymond, John Bell Williams, who ran an openly racist campaign. Another candidate, Jimmy Swan, ran a powerful insurgent campaign, declaring that Mississippi's white children would never be sacrificed "on the filthy, atheistic altar of integration."

Curtis Wilkie
University of Mississippi

John M. Barry, *Rising Tide: The Great Mississippi Flood of 1927 and How It Changed America* (1997); A. Wigfall Green, *The Man Bilbo* (1963); Erle Johnston, *I Rolled with Ross* (1980); V. O. Key Jr., *Southern Politics in State and Nation* (1949); Albert D. Kirwan, *Revolt of the Rednecks: Mississippi Politics, 1876–1925* (1965); Allan A. Michie and Frank Ryhlick, *Dixie Demagogues* (1939); Chester Morgan, *Redneck Liberal: Theodore G. Bilbo and the New Deal* (1985).

Democratic Party

Mississippi's Democratic Party traces its origins to the early nineteenth century. Before the Civil War the Democratic Party consisted mostly of rural white residents who opposed most government activity. Their hero was Andrew Jackson, who opposed large federal structures like national banks while supporting policies to move American Indians off lands desired by US citizens. Wealthy Mississippians, mostly white and from plantation areas along the Mississippi River, tended to support the Whig Party. After the Civil War almost all of the state's whites joined forces in support of the Democratic Party. During the Reconstruction period, the Republican Party, primarily a combination of African Americans and northerners, dominated the state's elected offices. With the withdrawal of federal troops in 1876, the Democrats regained their prominence, and by the 1890s Mississippi had become a one-party state. Most political battles were fought between Democratic Party candidates who represented the state's two ideological groups. These contests were often oversimplified as the Delta versus the Hills, with wealthier planters pitted against poorer farmers from the Hill and Piney Woods regions.

After the Second World War, cracks in the Democratic Party facade began to show in presidential elections. In 1948 the States' Rights Democrats (the Dixiecrats) won Mississippi's electoral votes. In 1964 Arizona Republican Barry Goldwater adopted a states' rights stand on civil rights and did not support the Civil Rights Act of 1964; he, too, carried Mississippi. In the ensuing five decades, only one Democrat, Georgia native Jimmy Carter in 1976, has won the state's electoral votes.

Until the 1970s whites held almost exclusive control over the Mississippi Democratic Party. Black Mississippians were largely disenfranchised immediately following the end of the federal occupation, and as recently as 1960 only about 7 percent of black Mississippians were registered to vote. After the passage of the Voting Rights Act of 1965, however, black Mississippians began to register in numbers not seen since Reconstruction. Many wanted to align themselves with the Democratic Party because of their fondness of Franklin D. Roosevelt's New Deal policies and John F. Kennedy's and Lyndon Johnson's support of the civil rights movement.

The Democratic Party leadership was not eager to admit the newly enfranchised African Americans into the party. In 1964 black Mississippians frustrated at their exclusion from the delegate selection process for the national convention formed the Mississippi Freedom Democratic Party and sought to have an alternate slate of delegates seated. National party leaders devised a compromise that would have seated members of both the regular and Mississippi Freedom Democratic groups, but both sides rejected the deal.

The tension between the two groups persisted for several years, and the Democratic Party became divided between the Loyalists (almost exclusively African Americans) and the Regulars (almost exclusively white). At the 1968 and 1972 Democratic National Conventions, delegates selected by the Regulars were not recognized, while Loyalist delegates were seated. At the state and county levels, however, Loyalists were generally excluded from the party's business and nominating process. By 1976 the two factions united under the Mississippi Democratic Party label when a black man and a white man were chosen as party cochairs. The party returned to a single chair in the late 1980s after an agreement was reached under which the membership and chairs of party committees would reflect the state's racial makeup. In the twenty-first century the Mississippi Democratic Party consists of a biracial coalition that varies from moderate to liberal in its ideology. This pragmatic flexibility allows white Democrats to have moderate beliefs while black Democrats in the Delta tend to be more liberal.

Over the past few decades the party's ability to send members to Congress has weakened. By the 1990s both of the state's senators and many of its representatives hailed from the Republican Party. However, state-level offices such as governor, lieutenant governor, and state auditor have until recently been competitive between the state's two dominant parties.

Democrats do best in the Delta. With its heavily black population, the Delta sends the state's only African American representative to Congress. Support for the Democratic Party's presidential candidates is also strong in this region. The Hills and Piney Woods regions typically support Democrats for local offices while backing Republicans for Congress and president. The coastal region has a history of supporting Republicans at all levels of elected office. Party identification in the Jackson metropolitan area is similar to that found in many metropolitan areas throughout the United States. The inner city of Jackson, mostly black, supports Democratic Party candidates, while the mostly white suburbs support Republicans.

Two primary factors explain why the Democratic Party does well in local politics but has less success sending its members to Washington, D.C. First, 36 percent of Mississippi's population is African American, and African Americans are especially supportive of the Democratic Party's candidates both in the state and in the country as a whole.

Because Mississippi has the nation's largest proportion of African Americans, Democrats will continue to occupy a large number of municipal, county, and state legislative offices. Second, local-level Democrats have often been able to avoid the liberal label that Mississippians often give to national Democrats. In Mississippi, which is one of the country's most conservative states, being viewed as a liberal, especially by members of the white community, is often the political kiss of death. Local Democrats who succeed must quickly master the ability to distance themselves from the party's national liberals.

James Newman
Southeast Missouri State
University

Bradley G. Bond, *Political Culture in the Nineteenth-Century South: Mississippi, 1830–1900* (1990); Dale Krane and Stephen D. Shaffer, eds., *Mississippi Government and Politics: Modernizers versus Traditionalists* (1992); Jere Nash and Andy Taggart, *Mississippi Politics: The Struggle for Power, 1976–2006* (2006); James A. Newman, Stephen D. Shaffer, and David A. Breaux, *American Review of Politics* (Summer 2003).

Dennis, David J., Sr.

(b. 1941) Activist

Born in Shreveport, Louisiana, in 1941 to a black sharecropping family, Dave Dennis knew the constraints of poverty and disfranchisement in the South, and at an early age he began to break down those barriers. As a college student at Dillard University in New Orleans, Dennis became involved in the civil rights movement, participating in lunch counter sit-ins. By November 1960 he had joined the New Orleans chapter of the Congress of Racial Equality (CORE) and had become a Freedom Rider, hoping to desegregate interstate bus travel. A year later, he was hired as a full-time CORE field secretary.

For that first year, Dennis worked in Shreveport and Baton Rouge, organizing other students to participate in boycotts and sit-ins and teaching them about Gandhian nonviolence. Having established himself as a civil rights veteran who had faced white brutality, Dennis moved to Mississippi in June 1962 to work as the only CORE activist in the state.

As field secretary of CORE and assistant program director of the newly revived Council of Federated Organizations, which coordinated activists' efforts, Dennis struggled to empower local blacks and to develop indigenous black leadership. Along with Robert Moses, who worked with the Student Nonviolent Coordinating Committee and as program director of the Council of Federated Organizations, Dennis established farm and store cooperatives, community centers, and voter registration programs.

The high point of Dennis's efforts in the state came during the Freedom Summer campaign of 1964, when the state was flooded with young civil rights workers. Stationed in the 4th Congressional District, Dennis and his small staff of CORE workers found their greatest success in Canton, just north of Jackson. Nonetheless, the harassment by white supremacists and the lack of support and protection from the federal government greatly discouraged many activists.

When CORE volunteers James Chaney, Michael Schwerner, and Andrew Goodman disappeared during the summer and were later found murdered and buried beneath a dam in Philadelphia, Mississippi, Dennis and many others felt a crushing blow. Delivering the eulogy at Chaney's funeral in Meridian, Dennis angrily called for retribution, rethinking his nonviolent stance. From then on, he openly supported groups like the Deacons for Defense, which retaliated against white violence.

After the failure of the Mississippi Freedom Democratic Party's efforts to unseat the all-white Mississippi delegation at the 1964 Democratic National Convention in Atlantic City, Dennis and many others dejectedly withdrew from Mississippi. In September 1964 Dennis returned to New Orleans to work as regional program director for CORE but resigned the next year when the organization became entrenched in budget cuts and debates over Black Power.

Dennis went to law school and opened a practice in Lafayette, Louisiana. In 1989 he was reunited with Moses at a conference in Jackson. Moses had left the state not long after Dennis and had gone on to found the Algebra Project in Cambridge, Massachusetts, to teach mathematics to African American students.

In 1992 Dennis closed his law practice and moved with his wife, Mattie Bivins, a civil rights activist whom he had met in Hattiesburg, and their family to Jackson to begin the Delta Algebra Project. As director and CEO of Positive Innovations, Dennis continues to serve as a partner in and manager of the Southern Initiative of the Algebra Project. By 2003 the Algebra Project boasted ten thousand students and three hundred teachers at twenty-eight sites across the country, and in 2006 the organization implemented the Quality Education as a Civil Right program. The Algebra Project continues to affect thousands of students and hundreds of teachers across the country.

Robert E. Luckett Jr.
Jackson State University

Algebra Project website, www.algebra.org; John Dittmer, *Local People: The Struggle for Civil Rights in Mississippi* (1994); August Meier and Elliot Rudwick, *CORE: A Study in the Civil Rights Movement, 1942–1968* (1973).

Dennis, Herman D.

(ca. 1916–2012) Visionary Artist and Minister

Born in Rolling Fork around 1916, Rev. Herman D. "Preacher" Dennis—artist, self-styled preacher, World War II veteran, and devoted husband—led a difficult life but always believed that he had been spared for a purpose. His mother died during childbirth, leaving her infant son alone with her for six days until someone discovered him, and he also survived a deadly tornado and a wound sustained during his tour of duty in the South Pacific during World War II.

In 1984 Dennis and Margaret Rogers married after he promised to transform her humble Vicksburg grocery store into something truly extraordinary. The result was a remarkable art environment, *Margaret's Grocery and Market, the Home of the Double-Headed Eagle*, located on Highway 61, five miles from the center of Vicksburg.

The brightly colored, geometric hodgepodge of structures and bold signage that comprised *Margaret's Grocery* added up to much more than the sum of individual parts. Rev. Dennis's message was a highly personal hybrid that mixes quotes from the New Testament with Masonic symbols, which did not seem to contradict each other but instead were unified by the overall aesthetic. To create the exterior, including a number of impressive towers, he added cinder blocks, sheet metal, and found objects to what was the original grocery store, painting everything predominantly bright red, white, pink, and yellow, with some blues and greens, mainly in a dynamic checkerboard motif. The interior, densely filled with Mardi Gras beads, Christmas lights, newspaper clippings, and additional mystical signs and images, provided a mysterious contrast to the vibrantly colored exterior.

As is the case with many self-taught visionary artists in the South who are also ministers, Rev. Dennis did not shun the nonbeliever. He constructed a chapel in a brightly painted bus located at the side of the central structure, complete with pews, pulpit, and King James Bible and rendered the bus impressively shiny with silver paint, duct tape, and aluminum foil. Multiple signs proclaimed, "All is Welcome / Jews and Gentiles."

At once an art installation and a devotional environment, *Margaret's Grocery* bore witness to the nature of its creator, who never distinguished between his callings as artist and preacher. Margaret Dennis died in October 2009 at the age of ninety-four. Two years later Gov. Haley Barbour and the Mississippi Arts Council commended Herman and Margaret Dennis and *Margaret's Grocery* with a Senate resolution proclaiming a week of awareness and preservation in honor of the couple and their "Bible Castle to God." Herman Dennis died in 2012. *Margaret's Grocery* has since fallen into ruins.

Jenifer Borum

New York, New York

Carol Crown, ed., *Coming Home! Self-Taught Artists, the Bible, and the American South* (2004); Chris Thompson, Chad Chisolm, and Dorothy-Dean Thomas, *Mississippi Folklife* (1999); Bruce West, *Arkansas Review* (2001); Stephen Young, *Southern Quarterly* (2000–2001).

Derian, Patricia

(1929–2016) Activist

Patricia Murphy Derian, a Mississippi social and political activist and assistant secretary of state for human rights and humanitarian affairs under Pres. Jimmy Carter, was born Patricia Sue Murphy on 29 August 1929 in New York City, where her mother was visiting. Growing up in Virginia during the Great Depression and World War II, her Irish roots and Catholic upbringing may have influenced her attitude about the Jim Crow system she saw around her. Decades later, that attitude, which reflected a desire for reform, prodded her into a career in civil rights and political activism.

In 1953, shortly after graduating from the University of Virginia's Nursing School, Patricia Murphy married Paul S. Derian, a recent medical school graduate. Derian settled into the life of a 1950s upper-middle-class housewife, focused mostly on rearing the family's three children. Prodded by extensive reading of works on philosophy and social commentary, especially the writings of French anticlerical writer André Gide, she formally broke with the Catholic Church in a resignation letter to her bishop and became an avowed agnostic.

In 1959 Paul Derian accepted a position at the University of Mississippi Medical Center in Jackson, where Patt Derian soon became involved in civil rights activism. The violence at the University of Mississippi surrounding the 1962 admission of James Meredith inspired her to help organize Mississippians for Public Education, an organization of white women who publicly supported the desegregation of Mississippi's public schools and challenged the Citizens' Council's idea of abandoning these schools. In 1965 Derian involved herself in antipoverty activism as director of the Jackson Head Start Office. A year later she took a position as adviser to Mississippi Action for Progress, a new statewide agency authorized to administer Head Start programs.

In 1968 Derian helped found the Loyalist Democratic Party of Mississippi, a biracial alternative to the segregationist Regular Democrats and the increasingly black-separatist Mississippi Freedom Democratic Party. The national Democratic Party recognized the Loyalists as the state's genuine Democratic organization, and Derian served as member of the party's national committee from 1968 to 1977. In this role she served on the commission that created a new party constitution, establishing landmark reforms in the presidential nominating process. During this period she briefly led the Southern Regional Council, one of the oldest and most important civil rights organizations in the United States.

After playing an important role in Jimmy Carter's 1976 election campaign, Derian found herself appointed coordinator for human rights (a post later upgraded to assistant secretary for human rights and humanitarian affairs) in the State Department. She emerged as the department's primary advocate for Carter's new human rights approach to US foreign policy, pushing for the elimination of military aid to authoritarian US allies such as Argentina and the Philippines. She became internationally famous for lecturing such allies on their poor human rights records. After the Soviet invasion of Afghanistan in late 1979, Derian's bureau lost influence in the Carter administration.

After Carter lost the 1980 election to Ronald Reagan, Derian and Hodding Carter III (whom she had married in 1978) remained in Washington, D.C., where Derian continued her involvement in international human rights activities. She later moved to Chapel Hill, North Carolina, where she died on 20 May 2016.

John Damico

Georgia Perimeter College

Adam Bernstein, *Washington Post* (20 May 2016); John Kelly Damico, "From Civil Rights to Human Rights: The Career of Patricia M. Derian" (PhD dissertation, Mississippi State University, 1999); Patt Derian Papers, Special Collections, Mitchell Memorial Library, Mississippi State University; Victor Scott Kaufman, *Historian* (Fall 1998).

Desegregation of Private Colleges

The desegregation of Mississippi's public universities and colleges is well documented; however, desegregation among the major white private colleges is less well known. All of these colleges were sponsored by one of the major evangelical Christian denominations. The principles of traditional Christianity, the proximity of some white colleges to historically black Rust College and Tougaloo College, and the lack of state sponsorship added unique dynamics to the desegregation stories of these colleges. The historically whites-only private colleges that faced issues of desegregation in the 1960s included Blue Mountain College (Southern Baptist), Belhaven College (Presbyterian), Millsaps College (Methodist), Mississippi College (Southern Baptist), Clarke College (Southern Baptist), and William Carey College (Southern Baptist).

In 1965 Millsaps became the first private college to desegregate, and significant evidence shows that many Millsaps supporters wanted to do so sooner. Many Millsaps students and faculty had a special relationship with their counterparts at Tougaloo. In 1965 Millsaps administrators called a meeting of representatives of all five of the state's white evangelical four-year colleges, seeking a concerted effort to eliminate racial barriers at the same time. The Millsaps delegation was supported only by the delegation from William Carey College, which began admitting black students in the fall of 1966. Just down the street from Millsaps, Belhaven did not desegregate until 1967, becoming perhaps the last Presbyterian college in the United States to desegregate. Blue Mountain College in Tippah County was a women's college, so the classic segregationist fear of black males interacting with white females did not apply. However, only Mississippi College desegregated later than Blue Mountain, which did so in 1968. Clarke College, a Southern Baptist junior college in Scott County, closed in the 1970s for several reasons, one of which was desegregation.

If the Methodists, especially Millsaps College, had the best record on integration, Southern Baptists clearly had the worst. Mississippi College was one of the last private colleges in the country to drop its segregation policy and did not do so until the 1969–70 school year. Moreover, William Carey College would have seemed to be in a good position to maintain segregation because black students in the Hattiesburg area had already gained access to the University of Southern Mississippi. Nonetheless, William Carey was the first Baptist college in the state to desegregate, and by Mississippi standards, it also integrated more fully in the late 1960s than other private colleges, even Millsaps. Soon after black students began attending William Carey, many of them became active in the college's extracurricular events and organizations.

The integration of Blue Mountain College involves several factors that were not present at any of the other schools. In addition to having an exclusively female student body, the college was considerably smaller and more rural than any of the state's other private institutions. This created a unique family-like atmosphere that included students, faculty, administrators, and staff, including African American janitorial and food service employees. Some of the first black students at Blue Mountain College were the daughters of employees. Nonetheless, no black students moved into the dorms until 1978.

J. Toby Graves
Copiah-Lincoln Community
College

Joel A. Alvis Jr., *Religion and Race: Southern Presbyterians, 1946–1983* (1994); James F. Gordon, *A History of Belhaven College, 1894–1981* (1983); Paul Harvey, *Freedom's Coming: Religious Culture and the Shaping of the South from the Civil War through the Civil Rights Era* (2005); Dwayne Keith Jones, "An Oasis of Liberalism and Academic Freedom in Jim Crow Mississippi: Millsaps College and Its Desegregation" (master's thesis, Mississippi State University, 2000); Charles Marsh, *God's Long Summer: Stories of Faith and Civil Rights* (1997); Richard Aubrey McLemore and Nannie Pitts McLemore, *The History of Mississippi College* (1979); Mark Newman, *Getting Right with God: Southern Baptists and Desegregation, 1945–1995* (2001).

Desegregation of Public Colleges and Universities

Before 1962, when James H. Meredith desegregated the University of Mississippi, white and black Mississippians attended racially segregated public colleges and universities. In the decade following Meredith's enrollment, desegregation spread gradually through the state's higher education system. By the mid-1970s, rigid segregation in Mississippi's public colleges and universities had died, and no public institution maintained a strictly all-white or all-black faculty or student body.

State leaders doggedly resisted Meredith's registration at the University of Mississippi. Even after a lengthy court battle resulted in an injunction forcing the state board of trustees to enroll Meredith, Gov. Ross Barnett promised to keep Meredith out of the university. A tense showdown between Barnett and the US Justice Department turned violent on

30 September 1962, when a mob of students and demonstrators rioted against US marshals and members of the US military outside the University of Mississippi administration building. Two people died during the incident, and the university campus suffered significant damage. Journalists from across the country covered the event, and by the time Meredith registered for classes on the morning of 1 October, media accounts of the riot had made Ole Miss synonymous with violence, lawlessness, and racism.

Desegregation at Mississippi State University went more smoothly. In 1965 Richard Holmes became the school's first African American student. Gov. Paul B. Johnson, who had served as Barnett's lieutenant governor during the desegregation crisis in Oxford, did not attempt to block the university from registering Holmes. Plainclothes law enforcement officials from Starkville, Oktibbeha County, and around the state stayed close to the Mississippi State campus on the day Holmes began summer classes, but to the relief of university president Dean Wallace Colvard, no mobs or demonstrators taunted Holmes or protested his registration.

After the peaceful desegregation of Mississippi State, the University of Southern Mississippi admitted its first two black students, Raylawni Young Branch and Gwendolyn Elaine Armstrong, in September 1965, ten years after the first of two attempts to enroll there by Clyde Kennard, a decorated Korean War veteran who was denied admission because of his race. The university now recognizes Kennard with a scholarship and a building named in his honor, though he was never admitted and was incarcerated as a reprisal for his efforts. Mississippi University for Women desegregated in 1966, and Shirley Antoinette Washington became the first African American student at Delta State College (now Delta State University) in 1967. Historically black Alcorn Agricultural and Mining College (now Alcorn State University) admitted white students beginning in 1966, while Jackson State College (now Jackson State University) and Mississippi Valley State College (now Mississippi Valley State University) followed suit in 1969 and 1970.

The faculty composition of Mississippi's higher education system also changed during the 1960s and 1970s. White faculty members began teaching at Alcorn State in the 1966–67 school year, at Jackson State in 1967–68, and at Mississippi Valley in 1968–69. Black teachers joined the all-white faculties at the University of Mississippi, Mississippi University for Women, and Southern Mississippi in 1970–71. Delta State desegregated its faculty in 1973–74, and Mississippi State hired African American teachers beginning in 1974–75.

African Americans now comprise more than one-third of Mississippi's population and make up approximately 20 percent of the student body at Mississippi State, 30 percent at Mississippi University for Women, and roughly a quarter of the student body at Southern Mississippi. At Delta State, located in majority-black Bolivar County, African Americans make up 40 percent of the student body. At the University of Mississippi, African Americans comprise less than 15 percent of the student body. While Meredith's registration began the desegregation of Mississippi's higher education system, the project of fully integrating the state's public colleges and universities remains unfinished.

Thomas John Carey
University of Mississippi

Russell H. Barrett, *Integration at Ole Miss* (1965); John K. Bettersworth, *People's History: The Centennial History of Mississippi State* (1980); Charles W. Eagles, *The Price of Defiance: James Meredith and the Integration of Ole Miss* (2009); David G. Sansing, *Making Haste Slowly: The Troubled History of Higher Education in Mississippi* (1990); David G. Sansing, *The University of Mississippi: A Sesquicentennial History* (1999); James W. Silver, *Mississippi: The Closed Society* (1964).

de Soto, Hernando
(1500?–1542) Spanish Explorer

Hernando de Soto was the leader of the first European expedition into the area that became Mississippi. His parents were Francisco Mendez de Soto and Leonor Arias Tinoco. They were minor nobility and, more important to the Spanish ethos of the time, were old Christians and not Jews, conversos, Moors, or peasants.

Hernando de Soto's birth date is unknown. In 1535, when he resigned the governorship of Cuzco, Peru, he stated in a signed affidavit that he was approximately thirty-five years old. His birth date has been estimated to be anywhere from 1496 to 1500, with 1500 the generally accepted date. His birthplace is also unknown. His father was from Jerez de los Caballeros, and his mother was from Badajoz. Both cities claim to be Hernando de Soto's birthplace. De Soto in his will asked to be buried in Jerez and throughout his life asserted that he was from there.

Hernando de Soto had two sisters, Catalina and Maria, and an older brother, Juan. As the second son, Hernando would not inherit, and he, like other second sons, saw the recently discovered New World as an avenue to wealth.

De Soto journeyed to the New World in 1514 as part of the expedition of Pedro Arias de Avila. The destination was Castilla del Oro, in modern-day Panama. Since the Spanish Crown did not fund exploration, many conquistadors formed partnerships for economic reasons. De Soto formed a partnership with Hernan Ponce de Leon and Francisco Companon. With Panama as the base, these Spanish conquistadors explored Central America, notably what is now Nicaragua, amassing wealth through the

Indian slave trade, mines, and encomiendas. They eventually added shipping to their enterprise, leading to their greatest wealth.

When Francisco Pizzaro needed men and supplies to explore Peru, de Soto and his partners contracted to provide a ship, men, and horses for Pizzaro's expedition. The partners were to be paid for the ship's cargo and would earn shares in the enterprise. In addition, de Soto was to receive a governorship of Cuzco, the chief Spanish (Inca) city. In 1532 the conquest of the Inca Empire began, and de Soto benefited monetarily from its plunder.

Not satisfied with his secondary position in the Incan conquest, de Soto wanted to be governor of a rich province. In 1535, he resigned the governorship of Cuzco and sailed for Spain, where he petitioned King Charles V for governorship of a province. While waiting for his request to be granted, Hernando de Soto married Isabel Bobadilla, the daughter of Pedro Arias de Avila, in what was probably a political marriage to maintain and increase property. The union also allied de Soto with one of Spain's more powerful families.

On 20 April 1537 Charles V granted the Capitulación de La Florida to Hernando de Soto, giving him the right to conquer and settle Florida along with several titles and honors. In 1539 de Soto arrived in La Florida, which included modern-day Mississippi. De Soto's background in Peru and Central America was essential to his interest in La Florida, where he focused on gold and precious metals. He reconnoitered the region looking for large-scale native urban civilizations like the Incas.

Since de Soto lacked a supply line, he forcibly acquired food and labor from the local populations. This approach required de Soto to be constantly moving. In 1541 he crossed into present-day Mississippi and wintered at Chicaca. The Spaniards were attacked by the Native Americans and lost most of their remaining belongings and equipment. After recuperating from the attack, the conquistadors left Chicaca and were the first Europeans to see the Mississippi River.

After crossing the river, they searched for gold and food. The Native Americans informed the Spaniards that to the west they would not find large populations. De Soto turned back to the southeast and returned to the Mississippi River.

In 1542 de Soto fell ill. He became despondent and told his men that he felt grief and sorrow for leaving them in a land where they did not know where they were. De Soto died, probably from typhoid fever, and was buried in the Mississippi River to conceal his death from the natives.

Hernando de Soto did not find the gold that he sought, and his legacy is still debated in the Southeast and Mississippi. The de Soto chronicles offer invaluable primary sources for historians, both for their information about geography and the environment and as the first written history of the southeastern Native Americans. The chronicles are especially useful for the insight they provide into Native American culture before wide-scale European influence.

De Soto was not interested in settling the land. He and his troops stole maize and food from the Native Americans, causing hardship, starvation, and conflict. De Soto treated the Native Americans brutally, using dogs to track and hunt them. He continued the policy practiced in Central America of abducting chiefs to ensure compliance with Spanish objectives. He enslaved Native Americans to use as porters and guides. Perhaps most important, his men and animals introduced the diseases that so dramatically decimated the Native American populations.

Jan Taylor
Mississippi Department of
Archives and History, Winterville
Mounds

Miguel Albornoz, *Hernando de Soto: Knight of the Americas* (1986); Lawrence A. Clayton, Vernon James Knight Jr., and Edward C. Moore, eds., *The De Soto Chronicles: The Expedition of Hernando de Soto to North America in 1539–1543*, 2 vols. (1993); David Ewing Duncan, *Hernando de Soto: A Savage Quest in the Americas* (1996); Charles Hudson, *Knights of Spain, Warriors of the Sun: Hernando de Soto and the South's Ancient Chiefdoms* (1997); Charles Hudson, *The Southeastern Indians* (1976); John R. Swanton, *Final Report of the United States De Soto Expedition Commission* (1985).

DeSoto County

Located in the northwestern corner of the state, DeSoto County is bounded by the Mississippi River to the west, Tennessee to the north, and the Coldwater River and Arkabutla Lake to the south. DeSoto was established on 9 February 1836 from land ceded to the United States by the Chickasaw Nation under the 1832 Treaty of Pontotoc. Both the county and its seat, Hernando, are named for sixteenth-century explorer Hernando de Soto. In 1872 Tate County annexed a portion of DeSoto County.

Already well populated at its first census in 1840, DeSoto County was home to 3,981 free people, who outnumbered the county's slave population by almost a thousand. Perhaps because of its proximity to Memphis, the area had a significant nonagricultural workforce early on, with nearly 100 people working in commerce and manufacturing.

DeSoto's population grew rapidly over the next twenty years, and by 1860 the county's slave population numbered 13,987, 60 percent of the total. Agricultural production in DeSoto was high on the eve of the Civil War, when the county ranked seventh in the state in its value of livestock, eleventh in the production of cotton, and thirteenth in the production of corn. County farms were also among the most productive in the state in growing potatoes and orchard products.

The Mississippi Delta was a destination for many of the South's African Americans in the post–Civil War years. During the late 1800s DeSoto's black population increased while its white population declined. Like many Delta counties, DeSoto emerged as a sharecropping county during Reconstruction, with almost half its farms (far above the state average) tended by sharecroppers in 1880. As a result, the county's farms dramatically decreased in size, averaging just 86 acres, the lowest figure in Mississippi, and well below the state average of 156 acres.

By 1900 only 9 percent of DeSoto's black farmers owned their own farms, with the rest working either as tenants or sharecroppers. In contrast, 53 percent of the county's white farmers claimed ownership. Industry remained small, but it was clearly growing, with sixty-one companies employing 124 men and 1 woman. DeSoto was now a large county, with more than 24,000 people, 77 percent of them African American.

In 1860 the county had thirty-two churches, most of them Baptist, Methodist, and Presbyterian. After the turn of the century, in contrast, religious life in DeSoto reflected its growing African American population, with Missionary Baptists the largest group and the Colored Methodist Episcopal Church stronger in DeSoto than in any other Mississippi county except Marshall. The Methodist Episcopal Church and Southern Baptist Convention also had significant congregations.

DeSoto's population stabilized in the early twentieth century, increasing only slightly from 1900 to 1930. As the Great Depression loomed, the majority of DeSoto's farming population was African American, and nearly 90 percent worked as tenants or sharecroppers.

Between 1960 and 1980, DeSoto's population more than doubled from 23,891 to 53,930. African Americans comprised 61 percent of that number. DeSoto experienced a dramatic transition in its labor market, as its farming workforce fell from nearly half the county's population in 1960 to just under 2 percent by 1980. Just under one-fifth of DeSoto's laborers worked in manufacturing, primarily in food production, timber, or textiles. Many women worked in private homes, and more than 30 percent of the population had less than five years of schooling.

In June 1966 James Meredith, who had been the University of Mississippi's first African American student, announced he would begin his March against Fear to raise awareness about black voter registration in Mississippi. He planned to walk from the Peabody Hotel in Memphis, Tennessee, to Jackson, passing through DeSoto County. Meredith's journey was aborted when he was shot several times in Hernando, but other activists completed the walk on his behalf.

DeSoto County has had its share of notable citizens. Nathan Bedford Forrest, Confederate general and first Grand Wizard of the Ku Klux Klan, moved to Hernando at age twenty-one. W. C. Faulkner, grandfather of celebrated author William Faulkner, described DeSoto County's Horn Lake as "Hell's Hole" in his novel *The White Rose of Memphis*. Author John Grisham spent several years in the 1980s working as an attorney in DeSoto County, and some readers find traces of the area in his work. In the mid-1990s the blues rock band North Mississippi Allstars formed in Hernando. DeSoto has also long had a close connection to Memphis, and the county courthouse in Hernando displays a mural originally painted for the Gayoso Hotel in the Tennessee city.

Like many counties in northern Mississippi, DeSoto County had a white majority in 2010, hosted a small but significant Hispanic/Latino minority, and had grown significantly during the last half of the twentieth century. Though DeSoto's black population had declined to 22 percent, its total population had undergone the state's largest proportional increase during this period, growing by 575 percent since 1960 to more than 130,000, making it the third-largest county in the state. Like several neighboring counties, DeSoto's white population increased over this period. Southaven has been Mississippi's fastest-growing Mississippi city in recent years, attracting Memphis residents to its suburban neighborhoods. DeSoto's convention center, proximity to gaming establishments, growing shopping facilities, and diverse recreational amenities have helped the county maintain some of Mississippi's lowest poverty rates.

Mississippi Encyclopedia Staff
University of Mississippi

Genealogical Society of DeSoto County, *Our Heritage, DeSoto County, Mississippi* (1992); Mississippi State Planning Commission, *Progress Report on State Planning in Mississippi* (1938); *Mississippi Statistical Abstract*, Mississippi State University (1952–2010); Charles Sydnor and Claude Bennett, *Mississippi History* (1939); University of Virginia Library, Historical Census Browser website, http://mapserver.lib.virginia.edu; E. Nolan Waller and Dani A. Smith, *Growth Profiles of Mississippi's Counties, 1960–1980* (1985).

Detective Fiction

Unlike most styles of fiction, detective fiction has a definite genesis. Scholars credit Edgar Allan Poe, a Virginian, with creating the first detective story, *The Murders in the Rue Morgue*, in 1841. Poe's C. Auguste Dupin was the literary model for Arthur Conan Doyle's more famous Sherlock Holmes. Subsequently, detective fiction has remained a mainstay of popular writing. Although the particulars of the detective have changed a great deal, detective fiction still bears the stamp of its nineteenth-century southern creator.

Because detective fiction has its roots in southern literary tradition, it is no surprise that Mississippi has produced its fair share of detective novelists. Mississippi's most famous writer, William Faulkner, dabbled in detective fiction. Contemporary authors John Armistead, Ace Atkins, Nevada Barr, Jim Fraiser, John Grisham, Carolyn Haines, Charlaine Harris, Thomas Harris, Greg Iles, Neil McGaughey, and Charles Wilson have also embraced tales of detection.

Faulkner, a Nobel Prize winner and Raymond Chandler contemporary, wrote several hard-boiled detective stories that are collected in *Knight's Gambit*, and critic André Malraux observed that one of Faulkner's most commercially successful works, *Sanctuary*, incorporated hard-boiled themes. Although Faulkner was not the first author to have a lawyer as detective, he embraced the character early and is a progenitor of the legal thriller fiction Grisham has excelled at writing.

Grisham is undoubtedly the most popular contemporary Mississippi author. Born in Arkansas, Grisham moved to Southaven as a child. He graduated from Mississippi State University in 1977 and the University of Mississippi School of Law in 1981. In terms of books sold, Grisham is one of the biggest names in all of contemporary fiction. The majority of his work is of the legal thriller variety—fiction with a lawyer-detective as the protagonist. The popularity of this genre represents a turn away from the hard-drinking, womanizing, gun-toting heroes of hard-boiled detective fiction and a turn back toward heroes like Dupin and Holmes. In the words of critic Larry Landrum, "Capturing with perfect pitch the obsession with money and power that began in the early 1980s and the paranoia of the 1990s, Grisham's legal thrillers tap into several different audiences." Grisham's work also features themes of racial strife and the conflict between industry and environment.

Iles has not attained Grisham's stratospheric popularity but is nevertheless an important Mississippi detective writer. Iles moved to Mississippi as a child, was educated at the University of Mississippi, and has written several best-selling legal thrillers with Natchez lawyer Penn Cage as the protagonist. Critics have consistently praised Iles's rendering of Natchez life, but like Grisham, Iles's work has proven popular with the reading public but has failed to gain serious scholarly attention.

Atkins is not a native Mississippian but has set several novels in the Delta and currently resides in the state. He was born in Alabama and played football for Auburn University before becoming a writer for the *St. Petersburg Times* and then the *Tampa Tribune*. Atkins's protagonist, Nick Travers, a former National Football League player and current college professor, seems to meld all of the hard-boiled detective's manliness with all of the Victorian detective's intellectual prowess. Enigmatic Texas musician and politician Kinky Friedman has said, "If Raymond Chandler came from the South, his name would be Ace Atkins."

Among several native Mississippi female detective writers, Haines stands out because of the size of her body of work. Haines has written fifteen Sarah Booth Delaney mysteries and a dozen other novels, with more on the way. She has also written numerous romance mysteries under the pseudonym Caroline Burnes. Born in Lucedale, Haines was educated at the University of Southern Mississippi and the University of South Alabama. Like Atkins, Haines cut her teeth as a journalist before moving on to novels.

Charlaine Harris was born in the Mississippi Delta but now resides in southern Arkansas. She was educated at Rhodes College in Memphis, Tennessee. Perhaps best known for the Sookie Stackhouse vampire novels, she has also written eight Aurora Teagarden novels about a Georgia librarian-detective; five Lily Bard novels about a Shakespeare, Arkansas, detective; and numerous other novels. Her most recent work has retained elements of the detective novel but has made a pronounced shift toward Southern Gothic fiction.

Barr has written more than a dozen novels in the Anna Pigeon series. The Nevada-born Barr came to Mississippi after receiving her education at Cal Poly, San Luis Obispo and the University of California at Irvine. Her experience as a park ranger on the Natchez Trace Parkway is reflected in her protagonist, who is both a park ranger and a detective. Critics have consistently praised Barr's use of language and descriptions of nature.

In very broad terms, Mississippi detective fiction has tended toward more educated, cultured, and erudite detectives than Mike Hammer or those in Ed McBain's 87th Precinct. Mississippi detective authors also seem to address violence as an organic fact of life rather than something outstanding or unnatural. Violence in Mississippi detective fiction tends to cross racial lines, and race typically plays an integral part in plots. In addition, the crimes featured tend to be small-town crimes committed by or against the power structure. Finally, Mississippi detective writers tend to pay more attention to the natural world than do writers from more urbanized areas.

Ben Gilstrap
University of Mississippi

Larry Landrum, *American Mystery and Detective Novels: A Reference Guide* (1999); Larry N. Landrum, Pat Browne, and Ray B. Browne, eds., *Dimensions of Detective Fiction* (1976); Martin Priestman, ed., *The Cambridge Companion to Crime Fiction* (2003).

Devine, Annie

(1912–2000) Activist

Annie Devine played a significant role in the Mississippi Freedom Democratic Party (MFDP) and the civil rights movement as a whole. Born in Mobile, Alabama, in 1912, Annie Bell Robinson moved with her family as a young girl to Canton, Mississippi, and was raised there. After attending Tougaloo Southern Christian College (later Tougaloo College), she returned to Canton, working as an insurance agent.

Devine was a leader in her church, and activists who came to Canton with the Congress of Racial Equality noted her unique and influential position in her community as a sounding board and voice of advice. According to movement historian Tom Dent, Devine served as a foil for the more outspoken C. O. Chinn, another community leader. This complementary leadership worked to unite the town's black community. Devine capitalized on this community to encourage voter registration.

Together with Fannie Lou Hamer and Victoria Gray Adams, Annie Devine helped start the MFDP, and the three women were selected as the party's delegates to the 1964 Democratic National Convention in Atlantic City, where they unsuccessfully sought to prevent the delegates from Mississippi's all-white Democratic Party from being seated. In the film *Standing on My Sisters' Shoulders* (2002), Adams notes that Devine brought the wisdom to their three-woman group. Despite their lack of political success, they kept the national media spotlight on Mississippi during a general lull in attention to the civil rights movement. According to the Mississippi State Sovereignty Commission's files, Devine also played a significant role in organizing James Meredith's 1966 March against Fear. Devine continued her public service work as a member of the MFDP by chairing a 1966 meeting of the Medical Committee on Human Rights at which the committee devised a plan to test equal rights in Mississippi hospitals and clinics. The committee planned to send African Americans to hospitals and clinics and then document the quality of their care and treatment with questionnaires.

Devine continued her work as a public servant, eventually working with National Negro Women of America and other projects. She died in Ridgeland on 22 August 2000.

Kathryn McGaw York
University of Mississippi

John Dittmer, *Local People: The Struggle for Civil Rights in Mississippi* (1994); Fannie Lou Hamer Statue Committee website, www.fannielou hamer.info; Chana Kai Lee, *For Freedom's Sake: The Life of Fannie Lou Hamer* (1999); Mississippi Department of Archives and History, Sovereignty Commission Online website, http://mdah.state.ms.us/arrec /digital_archives/sovcom/; Wolfgang Saxon, *New York Times* (1 September 2000).

Dickins, Dorothy

(1898–1975) Home Economist and Author

Dorothy Dickins was a scientist, an author, and a leader of home demonstration efforts in Mississippi. First employed by the state in 1924, Dickins became Mississippi's head of home economics research. She wrote her first publication in 1927 and continued to write about rural women until her 1964 retirement.

Born in Money in 1898, Dickins grew up in Greenwood and received a bachelor's degree in chemistry from the Industrial Institute and College in Columbus. She then earned a master's degree in nutrition at Columbia University and worked briefly in Jackson before taking a position in 1925 in Starkville, where she spent the rest of her professional life. She was the first woman to work as a scientist for the Mississippi Agricultural Experiment Station. Dickins earned a doctorate in 1933 at the University of Chicago, and she began to use the critical tools of professional social science in studying and trying to improve life for rural women.

Dickins was especially important as the author of dozens of reports on home economics. Her reports for the Mississippi Agricultural Experiment Station reflected her interests and approach as a professional social scientist. Early in her career, she joined her interest in social science to assumptions that rural life was superior to city life. To her, rigorous scientific study proved that farming people lived longer and with better health than people not living on farms. She began her numerous reports with questions she could test through empirical research and detailed her sources and methods. Her discussions of food habits, for example, analyzed calories, quantities, energy per person, and amounts of vitamins, iron, calcium, minerals, and protein. She categorized the subjects of her research by income; race; family size; status as owner, tenant, farmer, or nonfarmer; and type of soil in the area. Her first publication examined the food habits of farming families and urged more sophisticated planning and greater understanding of diet to retain the benefits of farm life. The diet and health of the typical child growing up amid the potential abundance of the southern farm, she wrote, should be "much better than the average urban child."

During the Depression, Dickins, like many southern leaders, came to challenge some earlier assumptions about the special virtues of farm life. She showed considerable subtlety and sensitivity in discussing the problems of tenant farmers. In an important 1937 report, "Occupations of Sons and Daughters of Mississippi Cotton Farmers," Dickins showed her willingness to change. After studying farm people for a decade and living in a period of depression, rural out-migration, and governmental experimentation, Dickins began to question whether farm life was always best and whether her job was to teach the skills farm people needed to stay on the farm. She studied a large group of white young adults who had grown up on farms and found that few of them owned land, that cotton planting was producing wealth for a few people but poverty for the rest, and that those who had left the farm were doing better than those who stayed.

Dickins's critique of 1930s farm life had a feminist side, and she gave voice to the grievances of rural women. Young farming women worked harder and benefited less than most farming men, and Dickins criticized situations that kept young women isolated and working too hard to notice better opportunities. "In these days of 'equal rights,' it is surprising how many out-of-school farm girls are found with a status similar to that of children of the family," she wrote. Mississippi, Dickins urged with optimism, should develop more industries, especially for working women, to help them avoid the poor health and low wages so common in southern factories.

From the 1940s through the end of her career, Dickins tended to concentrate on issues of health. She wrote an important report, "Wanted: A Healthy South," for the Southern Regional Council and worked to encourage local communities to store and market locally grown produce as a means of both helping farmers and improving consumers' health. Dickins died in 1975, leaving a legacy of concern and inspired study of the lives of rural people, especially rural women.

Ted Ownby
University of Mississippi

Dorothy Dickins, *Mississippi Agricultural Experiment Station Bulletin* (November 1927, August 1928, May 1937); Helen Sue Jolly, "Selected Leaders in Mississippi Home Economics: An Historical Inquiry" (PhD dissertation, Mississippi State University, 1995); Ted Ownby, *American Dreams in Mississippi: Consumers, Poverty, and Culture, 1830–1998* (1999); Bob Ratliff, *Mississippi Landmarks* (Spring 2005).

Diddley, Bo (Otha Ellas Bates)
(1928–2008) Blues Musician

Combining R&B and blues with eccentric onstage performances, Bo Diddley is often considered one of the pioneers of rock and roll music. Otha Ellas Bates was born on 30 December 1928, in McComb. He never knew his father, Eugene Bates; his mother, Ethel Wilson, was only fifteen or sixteen years old when Ellas was born. Ethel's first cousin, Gussie McDaniel, raised him while the family tried to make a living as sharecroppers. In 1934, in the midst of the Great Depression, they moved to Chicago, where Bates started to develop an interest in music. His first instrument was a violin, and he took lessons from classical teacher O. W. Frederick. He also taught himself to play the drums and the trombone.

At age twelve Bates received his first guitar, a Christmas present from his stepsister, Lucille McDaniel. John Lee Hooker had already become one of his heroes, and Bates wanted to play just like him. But he had trouble strumming the guitar: "I couldn't play the guitar like everyone else," Diddley later recalled. "Guitarists have skinny fingers. I didn't. I play drum licks on the guitar." This music style evolved into the distinctive "shave and a haircut, two bits" rhythm that characterized most of his repertoire.

Bates probably started to use the name *Bo Diddley* around 1940, though its origins are uncertain: it might have been a nickname acquired during his brief boxing career, or it might refer to a harmonica player he saw in Mississippi or to a southern folk instrument known as the diddley bow. Not even Diddley knew the origins of his stage name, recalling only that "the kids gave me that name when I was in grammar school in Chicago."

While he was still in high school, Diddley formed his first band, the Hipsters. The group, which later changed its name to the Langley Avenue Jive Cats, performed on Chicago's street corners and clubs. In 1955 Diddley cut a demo of two of songs, "Uncle John" and "I'm a Man," and took it to Chess Records, one of Chicago's preeminent blues labels. Leonard and Phil Chess liked the music but did not appreciate the lyrics of "Uncle John," which they viewed as derogatory to blacks. They suggested that Diddley change the words, which he did. The song "Bo Diddley" was born, and it reached the top of the R&B charts when it was released as a single in 1955. The rhumba-like beat was trademark Bo Diddley. "When I used to walk from spot to spot looking for work, everybody played like T-Bone Walker and those cats, so I tried something different," Diddley explained.

Other hits followed, among them "Diddley Daddy" and "You Can't Judge a Book by Its Cover." Diddley rocked the stage with his peculiar moves, flamboyant suits, and his square guitars, which he made himself. The Beatles, the Rolling Stones, and other British bands were influenced by his music, and the Animals celebrated him in their song "The Story of Bo Diddley," calling him "the rock 'n' roll senior general." Later artists such as Bruce Springsteen and U2 also found inspiration in Diddley's songs, but by the time these artists became popular, his fame had waned considerably. He reached the zenith of his career during the 1950s and early 1960s.

Diddley believed that his impact on the development of rock and roll had been underestimated. "What gets me is when white brothers started playing guitars and sounding like us, and folks said that Elvis started rock 'n' roll," he said. "Well, let me tell you Elvis ain't started a damn thing. I love what he did. But he came three years after me. I was already breaking records at the Apollo Theater."

During the 1970s, when his career was on a downhill slope, Diddley went to New Mexico, where he served for a time as a deputy sheriff. In 1987, the same year he was inducted into the Rock and Roll Hall of Fame, he moved to the Gainesville, Florida, area. Around that time, his popularity again started to rise. Diddley performed at the inaugurations of Presidents George H. W. Bush and Bill Clinton, and Diddley's 1996 album *A Man amongst Men*, which featured renowned musicians including Jimmie Vaughan and Keith Richards, received a Grammy Award nomination. Still, the bitterness remained. "When kids hear me play now they say, 'Hey, you sound like so-and-so.' Wow, that's an insult; it's degrading. They don't know I started the sound and the so-and-so's copied me," Diddley explained. "When I hear that, it's a bad feeling, a hurting feeling. I ask myself why I'm still out here performing when all that has happened is that I've been forgotten."

Bo Diddley died in Florida in 2008.

Maarten Zwiers
University of Groningen, the Netherlands

Bernard Weinraub, *New York Times* (16 February 2003); George R. White, *Bo Diddley: Living Legend* (1995).

Disfranchisement

Mississippi became the first southern state to disfranchise its African American voters when it called a constitutional convention in August 1890. Over the next dozen or so years, every other former Confederate state called a convention or ratified an amendment intended to eliminate as many black voters as possible. In the process, a large number of white voters also lost the right to vote. Disfranchisement was a decisive episode in southern history because it ended black voting, which had been introduced during Reconstruction, and forged the Solid South, with the one-party system and massively reduced electorate that characterized the region's politics until the implementation of the Voting Rights Act of 1965.

As was the case in all the disfranchising states, the initiators were the leaders of the Democratic Party, who had never accepted the legitimacy of African American voting after passage of the Reconstruction Act of 1867. The idea that former slaves, free blacks, and their descendants could vote threatened white privilege and supremacy, particularly because African Americans persisted in voting for Republican candidates. In the 1870s and 1880s the Democrats manipulated the black vote, principally through intimidation and violence but also by committing fraud at the ballot box. Especially in Mississippi, these illegal and vicious methods, along with white Democrats' schemes to fuse with independent black factions, had proven so effective that the Republican Party was quite weak by 1890.

The late 1880s had seen a flurry of interest in calling a convention to revise the state's constitution. Surprisingly, that interest came from farmers from predominantly white counties who were joining the Farmers' Alliance to get their economic and political grievances redressed. These rural voters wanted the constitution changed to reduce government expenditures and taxes, end tax preferences for corporations, reduce the Black Belt's representation in the legislature, and provide for an elected judiciary. As the movement grew, Black Belt legislators realized that they could defuse this challenge by agreeing to hold a convention and focusing on the agrarians' desire to eliminate the black vote. Most Democrats were also concerned with outflanking the efforts of the northern Republicans in Congress to strengthen the enforcement of voting rights through the recently introduced Federal Elections Bill (the Lodge Bill). In January 1890, therefore, the Mississippi legislature voted 84–53 to call a convention. A mere 39,000 of the state's 240,710 eligible voters participated in the convention election, choosing 130 Democrats and 4 others as delegates.

The suffrage issue dominated the convention, but finding the means of eliminating black voters proved thoroughly perplexing. The franchise committee considered a vast array of possibilities, including even such surprising suggestions as plural voting (giving more votes to wealthier whites) and woman suffrage (increasing the white vote to offset the black vote). Ultimately, the convention decided to reduce the black vote by instituting such qualifications for voting as lengthy residence requirements, payment of an annual two-dollar poll tax, and literacy tests that required voters to read a section of the state constitution. In addition, the constitution mandated the use of the secret ballot, another provision that required voters to be able to read. Moreover, voters were disqualified if they had been convicted of any of a long list of criminal offenses that blacks were believed to be more prone to commit.

Because the literacy provision would disfranchise many white voters as well, the drafters of the constitution stipulated that merely "understanding" the clause to the registrar's satisfaction might suffice. The state's leading Democratic newspaper, the *Jackson Clarion-Ledger*, described this loophole as "a transparent fraud," and observers throughout the state denounced it as corrupt and out of place in a constitution that was intended to remove blacks and thereby "purify the vote," as the disfranchisers described their aims, and to end electoral fraud. Further criticism arose from delegates in the Black Belt, who feared that the restrictions on black voting were inadequate. But their demands for an added property qualification were countered by representatives from white-dominated counties, who worried that these tests would remove white voters even though Sen. James Z. George, the chair of the Franchise Committee and an ally of the agrarian wing of the party, had already obtained a reapportionment scheme that favored the white counties. With George assuming a lead role, the entire constitution, including the suffrage provisions and the reapportionment plan, was approved. George was considered the architect of the disfranchisement scheme, which he defended at great length and with stunning self-righteousness in the Senate.

Other states studied and often emulated Mississippi's approach to disfranchisement, which proved devastatingly effective. A mere 69,905 whites and 9,036 African Americans voted in the 1892 congressional elections, the first held under the new constitution. The main objective of banishing African Americans from the state's political life had been achieved. The political dominance of the Democratic Party and the white race was secure.

Michael Perman
University of Illinois at Chicago

J. Morgan Kousser, *The Shaping of Southern Politics: Suffrage Restriction and the Establishment of the One-Party South, 1880–1910* (1975); Michael Perman, *Struggle for Mastery: Disfranchisement in the South, 1888–1908* (2001).

Dittmer, John
(b. 1939) Historian

John Dittmer is a prominent historian of the Mississippi civil rights movement. A native of Seymour, Indiana, Dittmer earned bachelor's (1961), master's (1964), and doctoral (1971) degrees from Indiana University. In the fall of 1967 he accepted an appointment as assistant professor of history at Tougaloo College, a small, historically black liberal arts college just outside Jackson. Within a year, Tougaloo appointed Dittmer academic dean. He returned to teaching in the fall of 1970 and was promoted to associate professor in 1971. He continued teaching there until 1979, when he accepted a position as visiting associate professor of history at Brown University. After three years at Brown, one year as a Rockefeller Foundation fellow, and two years at the

Massachusetts Institute of Technology, Dittmer returned to Indiana to become an associate history professor at DePauw University in Greencastle. He retired and was granted emeritus status in 2003.

While at Tougaloo, Dittmer had known many civil rights activists and had heard their stories. He knew that the struggle for civil rights was different in Mississippi than in much of the rest of the South. Mississippi lacked cities large enough to support the independent black ministers who often assumed leadership roles in the movement in other southern states—men such as Martin Luther King Jr. of Atlanta, Fred Shuttlesworth of Birmingham, and Kelly Miller Smith of Nashville. In Mississippi, King's Southern Christian Leadership Conference led no campaigns against segregation. Also, unlike other southern states, Mississippi's African American population approached 40 percent of the total in the 1960s, and blacks outnumbered whites in many counties. This demographic meant that the state's activists took voting rights, not desegregation, as their primary goal. In much of Mississippi, if blacks could vote, they could rule.

The story of civil rights in Mississippi was the story of local people refusing to continue to quietly accept segregation and disfranchisement. In *Local People: The Struggle for Civil Rights in Mississippi* (1993), Dittmer gracefully recounts how local people, encouraged by student activists, most often with the Student Nonviolent Coordinating Committee and the Congress of Racial Equality, gradually but tirelessly fought for civil rights in the face of unrelenting white violence. Dittmer argues that without local people to support, house, and even protect the student activists, the struggle for civil rights in Mississippi would likely not have occurred in the 1960s and certainly would not have succeeded. Dittmer also argues that it is impossible to overstate the importance of the leadership provided by local people. In virtually every town where student activists worked, the civil rights cause was advanced by local leaders—perhaps most notably Fannie Lou Hamer of Sunflower County. Without Dittmer's work in *Local People*, the determination, bravery, and leadership provided by Annie Devine, Unita Blackwell, Victoria Gray Adams, and others would be far less renowned. *Local People* received three major book awards: the 1994 Lillian Smith Book Award, the 1995 Bancroft Prize, and the 1995 McLemore Prize.

In addition to *Local People*, Dittmer has authored *Black Georgia in the Progressive Era* (1977) and *The Good Doctors: The Medical Committee for Human Rights, Race, and the Politics of Health Care in America* (2009). He and Danielle L. McGuire served as coeditors of *Freedom Rights: New Perspectives on the Civil Rights Movement* (2011). Dittmer has received several research fellowships as well as teaching awards. In 2010 DePauw created the John Dittmer Award to recognize the graduating history major with the highest grade point average.

Ernest M. Limbo
Huntsville, Alabama

DePauw University website, www.depauw.edu; John Dittmer, e-mail interview with Ernest M. Limbo; John Dittmer, *Local People: The Struggle for Civil Rights in Mississippi* (1993).

Dixiecrats (States' Rights Democrats)

The Dixiecrat movement was a short-lived effort by conservative white Democrats to pressure the national Democratic Party to give up its support for Harry Truman's civil rights program. When the party's 1948 national convention adopted a strengthened civil rights position, the Mississippi delegation and half the Alabama delegates walked out of the assembly and formed a splinter group. Officially called the States' Rights Democratic Party, the Dixiecrats condemned proposals to eliminate the poll tax, to pass a law against lynching, to end segregation in interstate transportation, and to make the Fair Employment Practices Commission a permanent institution. More broadly, they objected to the federal government's increasing interest in civil rights issues and upheld what they saw as the virtues of states' rights. The states' rights movement attempted to reform the party system by creating a politically conservative Solid South that could govern itself without the centralized state.

In February 1948, even before the Democratic National Convention, Gov. Fielding Wright had called Mississippi's first meeting of Democrats opposed to Truman's civil rights initiatives, referring to the group as the True White Jeffersonian Democrats. Wright remained one of the group's leaders and later was nominated as the Dixiecrats' vice presidential candidate, joining presidential candidate Strom Thurmond of South Carolina on the national ticket. The True Democrats drew up a "declaration of principles" that denounced the national party's platform. Walter Sillers, one of the most important Mississippi politicians of the mid-twentieth century and Speaker of the Mississippi House, coordinated the later walkout at the national convention and helped plan Wright's strategy of preaching the rights of individual citizens and the sovereignty of the states. The group named Wright honorary chair of the first statewide convention: he joined businessman Wallace Wright, head of campaign direction, and Mary Louise Kendall, head of the Women's Committee, as state leaders. By March of that year every county in the state had a True Democrat auxiliary.

When the dissident group failed to win concessions from the national party, the first and only convention of the States' Rights Democratic Party met in Birmingham, Alabama, in July to nominate its presidential ticket. In addition to Fielding Wright, Mississippians involved in that convention included John Bell Williams, James Eastland, John C. Stennis, Wallace Wright, and Hugh White. The Dixiecrats knew that they would not win the presidential election but hoped either to pressure the national Democrats to amend their civil rights stance or to split the election among three parties and throw it into the House of Representatives. At the least, the Dixiecrats believed, their actions would force the national party to recognize its dependence on the South.

Thurmond and Wright received a majority of the presidential vote in Mississippi, South Carolina, Alabama, and Louisiana. The ticket won 87 percent of Mississippi's votes, the highest percentage of any state. However, the Dixiecrat candidates received few votes from the Upper South and Georgia. Many of the South's politicians maintained their affiliation with the Democratic Party, while a few hard-liners began to call for a separate southern party. Dixiecrats did not run candidates in future elections, but their opposition to the civil rights platform of the Democratic Party showed in national contests. The Dixiecrat walkout initiated the first of several instances after World War II when the Mississippi Democratic Party withheld its support from the national party.

William P. Hustwit
Birmingham Southern University

Ted Ownby
University of Mississippi

Numan V. Bartley, *The New South, 1945–1980* (1995); Richard Ethridge, "Mississippi's Role in the Dixiecrat Movement" (PhD dissertation, Mississippi State University, 1971); Kari Fredrickson, *The Dixiecrat Revolt and the End of the Solid South, 1932–1968* (2001); Robert A. Garson, *The Democratic Party and the Politics of Sectionalism, 1941–1948* (1974); James Loewen and Charles Sallis, eds., *Mississippi: Conflict and Change* (1974); Ann Mathison McLaurin, "The Role of the Dixiecrats in the 1948 Election" (PhD dissertation, University of Oklahoma, 1972).

Dixon, Willie
(1915–1992) Blues Musician

Willie Dixon was a highly influential blues bassist, composer, arranger, singer, and producer, most famously for Chess records in Chicago. His work with Muddy Waters and Howlin' Wolf in the 1950s helped shape the postwar urban blues style, while his association with Chuck Berry and Bo Diddley contributed to the early development of rock and roll.

Willie James Dixon was born in Vicksburg on 1 July 1915. He gained an appreciation for reading and poetry at an early age from his mother, Daisy Dixon. While in the fourth

Willie Dixon (Courtesy Blues Archive, Department of Archives and Special Collections, J. D. Williams Library, University of Mississippi)

grade in the Depression-era South, Dixon wrote, printed, and sold thousands of copies of poems such as "The Signifying Monkey" and other ditties to local bands on the streets of Vicksburg. As a teenager Dixon learned about harmony singing from a carpenter, Theo Phelps, who added him to the Union Jubilee Singers.

Dixon moved to Chicago at age seventeen and immersed himself in the boxing world. His pugilistic talents brought him the Illinois State Golden Gloves Heavyweight Championship in 1937. He met guitarist Leonard "Baby Doo" Caston at a gym and began playing the stand-up bass when he and Caston sang together on street corners. The two formed the quintet the Five Breezes, which recorded eight sides for the Bluebird label in 1940. In 1941 Dixon, who was a conscientious objector to World War II, spent ten months in prison for draft evasion. Upon his release he formed the Four Jumps of Jive, and the group cut four sides for Mercury Records in 1945. Later that year Dixon again found himself working with Caston in the Big Three Trio, which recorded for OKeh, Delta, and Columbia Records between 1946 and 1954.

These early recordings caught the attention of Leonard and Phil Chess, who hired Dixon to do session work for the Aristocrat label, a Chess subsidiary, in 1948, beginning with a session with Robert Nighthawk. While Dixon recorded some of his own material for Aristocrat over the next two years, he remained primarily a featured artist during other musicians' sessions.

The commercial appeal of Dixon's songwriting became apparent with Muddy Waters's 1954 recording of "Hoochie Coochie Man." After this initial success, Dixon produced a

string of hits for many of Chess's high-profile performers, including Waters's follow-up, "I Just Want to Make Love to You"; Howlin' Wolf's "Evil"; and Little Walter Jacobs's "My Babe" and "Mellow Down Easy." The Chess brothers subsequently began pushing Dixon-penned songs on their stable of artists, and he became known as the label's most reliable tunesmith. Dixon continued his session work by accompanying R&B artists Lowell Fulson, Bo Diddley, and Sonny Boy Williamson II on stand-up bass. He also worked on early rock and roll recordings, including Chuck Berry's "Maybellene," "Sweet Little Sixteen," "Rock and Roll Music," and "Johnny B. Goode."

Dixon found it hard to support his family on the hundred dollars a week the Chess brothers paid him, and he began working for Chess's crosstown rival, Cobra, in 1956 while continuing his session work for his old label. At Cobra, Dixon wrote songs for pioneers of the so-called West Side sound such as Magic Sam, Buddy Guy, and Otis Rush. Rush's version of the Dixon-penned "I Can't Quit You, Baby" was the company's first single and a Top 10 R&B hit. Cobra folded in 1958.

Upon Dixon's return to Chess full time in the late 1950s, his session work gradually diminished in favor of artists who played the electric bass. At the same time, the emergence of rock and roll had a detrimental effect on Chicago's live blues scene. As playing gigs began to dwindle, Dixon joined Memphis Slim on an East Coast tour and at the Newport Folk Festival in 1957 and 1958. In the late 1950s and early 1960s Dixon performed at several successful American Folk Blues Festivals in Europe organized by Germans Horst Lippmann and Fritz Rau. Dixon's role as an organizer for these festivals brought him into contact with young British rock bands such as the Rolling Stones and the Yardbirds that had been heavily influenced by his songwriting. By the mid-1960s Dixon's relationship with Chess ended, but not before he penned singer Koko Taylor's 1966 hit, "Wang Dang Doodle."

In the 1970s Dixon focused his energies on recouping much of the royalties that Chess had failed to pay him for his services over the preceding two decades. He created the Blues Heaven Foundation to help other aging blues musicians obtain financial security. This work led to Dixon's involvement in obtaining song copyrights for Chess artists into the 1980s. Dixon's health then began to decline, and he died in his sleep in 1992 at his home in Pasadena, California.

Cale Nicholson
Little Rock, Arkansas

Lenny Carlson and Fred Sokolow, *Willie Dixon: The Master Blues Composer, 1915–1992* (1992); Bob Corritore, Bill Ferris, and Jim O'Neal, *Living Blues* (July–August, September–October 1988); Willie Dixon with Don Snowden, *I Am the Blues: The Willie Dixon Story* (1989); Benjamin Filene, *Romancing the Folk: Public Memory and American Roots Music* (2000); Paul Zollo, *Songwriters on Songwriting* (1997).

Dixon v. Mississippi

In *Dixon v. Mississippi* (1896) the Mississippi Supreme Court upheld the provisions in the 1890 Mississippi Constitution regarding the qualification of electors, voter registration, and literacy tests. In so doing, the court laid the foundation for the US Supreme Court's decision in *Williams v. Mississippi* (1898), affirming the constitutionality of the state's poll tax, disenfranchisement clauses, literacy test, and grandfather clause.

The case originated when John Henry Dixon, an African American, was indicted, convicted, and sentenced to life in prison for the murder of Nancy Minor. Dixon filed a motion to quash the indictment, asserting that the process of selecting the grand jury discriminated against him. He argued that the state jury commissioners chose potential jurors from a list from which election officers had improperly removed the names of African Americans eligible to serve as jurors. When his motion to quash was overruled, Dixon made a motion to transfer the case from state to federal court because he feared that he could not receive a fair and impartial trial in Mississippi. The trial court denied this motion as well.

Dixon appealed the denial of these motions to the Mississippi Supreme Court. He argued that the provisions providing for voter qualification, voter registration, and the literacy test resulted in discrimination in violation of the Fourteenth Amendment. He asserted that the state election officers discriminated against African Americans when compiling lists of voters to provide to the jury commissioners. The jury commissioners would then choose juries from lists that wrongfully excluded African Americans, thereby preventing them from both serving on juries and receiving fair trials.

The court rejected this argument, explaining that the operation of elections and jury selection functioned independently of one another. The court admitted that election officers had the right to turn away voters deemed unqualified even if they were registered to vote. But while election officers made lists of actual voters, the jury commissioners selected juries from a list of registered voters. Election officers had no power to remove a person from the registered voter list even if they refused to allow that person to vote. From this, the court concluded that even if election officers discriminated against African American voters, this practice had neither harmed Dixon nor deprived him of any constitutional right.

Dixon also argued that the trial court erred in denying his motion to remove the case to federal court. If there was reason to believe that a jury had been selected improperly and that a defendant could not receive a fair and impartial

trial, the case was to be removed. The Mississippi Supreme Court held, however, that where a law was not facially discriminatory but discriminatory only in its application, removal to federal court was improper. In those cases, the victim had no judicial remedy. In an effort to explain the clearly discriminatory effects of the laws, the court stated that each of the provisions at issue applied to African American and white citizens alike. It admitted that African Americans were disproportionately affected by these provisions and were prevented from voting in a greater proportionate number than white citizens. However, the court stated that these disproportionate effects arose not because of race but because "of superior advantages and circumstances possessed by the one race over the other," resulting in "a greater number of the more fortunate race possess[ing] the qualifications which the framers of the constitution deemed essential for the exercise of the elective franchise."

The Mississippi Supreme Court found that the challenged constitutional provisions did not violate the Fourteenth Amendment. It held that the jury was not improperly selected, the provisions were not facially discriminatory, and Dixon was not denied his right to a fair and impartial trial. Therefore, it held that the trial court properly denied Dixon's motions to quash the indictment and remove the case to federal court.

Dixon v. Mississippi and its predecessor, *Gibson v. Mississippi* (1896), are part of a line of cases that provided for a narrow interpretation of the Reconstruction amendments and ushered in an era of widespread discrimination against African Americans.

Amanda Brown
University of Mississippi

Dixon v. Mississippi, 20 So. 839 (1896); *Gibson v. Mississippi*, 162 US 565 (1896); *Williams v. Mississippi*, 170 US 213 (1898).

Treaties of Doak's Stand, Dancing Rabbit Creek, and Pontotoc Creek

In three treaties concluded between 1820 and 1833, the US government purchased the land of the Choctaw and the Chickasaw in exchange for land west of the Mississippi River. Pressure for the treaties came from white settlers wanting access to Mississippi land, especially in fertile cotton-growing areas, and from a federal government increasingly intent on the policy of Indian Removal. Removal caused considerable contention among the Choctaw and Chickasaw, some of whom fought the policy for years.

The Treaty of Doak's Stand was signed by the Choctaw Indians on 18 October 1820 and ratified by the United States on 8 January 1821. Andrew Jackson and Pushmataha were the chief negotiators for the treaty. In return for surrendering about one-third of their remaining land to the US government (about five million acres), the Choctaw received thirteen million acres in the Arkansas Territory, Indian Territory (now Oklahoma), and Spanish Texas from southwestern Arkansas to the western boundary of the United States. Some of this land had already been settled by whites, and few Choctaw emigrated as a result of this treaty. However, it included many new ideas regarding how native tribes would be treated, and it introduced new concepts to tribal society. The treaty stipulated that each Choctaw male would receive a rifle, bullet mold, camp kettle, and blanket as well as a year's worth of ammunition for hunting and defense and a year's worth of corn for his family. Further, all Choctaw who subsisted by traditional hunting lifestyle instead of working in the white world would be moved west. It provided for a federal Indian agent, a factor, a blacksmith, and a Removal agent. The treaty prohibited whiskey trade and provided for the establishment of police force in the Choctaw Nation.

The treaty specified that any individual Choctaw who adopted the lifestyle of an American farmer could become a US citizen, subject to the laws and jurisdictions that applied to all American citizens, and the tribal land designated by the treaty would be then divided into a family farm. It provided federal aid for education of children and included humanitarian aid. Money generated from the sale of land in Mississippi was earmarked for the support of Choctaw schools on both sides of the Mississippi River.

The Treaty of Doak's Stand defined boundaries of land that "shall remain without alteration." Nonetheless, the 1830 Treaty of Dancing Rabbit Creek forced the Choctaw to exchange this land for acreage in the Indian Territory. The Choctaw signed this treaty, also known as the Choctaw Removal Treaty, on 27 September 1830, and the United States ratified it in February 1831. By signing the treaty the Choctaw agreed to relinquish their rights to all of their lands east of the Mississippi River—more than ten thousand acres in Mississippi and Alabama—and to relocate to what is now southeastern Oklahoma. The treaty also guaranteed that "no Territory or State shall ever have a right to pass laws for the government of the Choctaw Nation of Red People and their descendants; and that no part of the land granted them shall ever be embraced in any Territory or State." The relocation began in 1831 and took three years to complete, and an estimated twenty-five hundred Choctaw died of starvation and exposure en route. They received no compensation for farm buildings, schoolhouses, or livestock that they left behind in Mississippi and Alabama.

About six thousand Choctaw chose to remain in Mississippi and Alabama, where they received allotments of land within the ceded territory and became subjects of the state governments. However, the terms of the treaty, which allowed each head of household to select a 640-acre plot of land, each child over ten to have 320 acres, and each young child 120 acres, were widely disregarded, and many Choctaw scattered across the Mississippi swampland. A reservation was later established for the Mississippi Choctaw near Philadelphia.

The Chickasaw signed the Treaty of Pontotoc Creek (the second attempt at an agreement between the nation and the US government) on 20 October 1832, and the United States ratified it on 1 March 1833. The Chickasaw ceded their lands in Alabama and Mississippi to the US government. Each family was allowed to sell its land to white settlers and received a temporary residence until Removal to Indian Territory. The tribe was to pay for its own relocation with the proceeds of the sale of land. The Chickasaw negotiated with the Choctaw for land in Indian Territory in 1837.

In 1970 the US Supreme Court revisited the Treaty of Dancing Rabbit Creek and the Treaty of Pontotoc Creek (as well as the 1835 Treaty of New Echota with the Cherokee Nation) in *Choctaw Nation v. Oklahoma*. The Court found that the treaties gave the Native Americans both the Arkansas River riverbed and oil and mineral rights.

Beth A. Stahr
Southeastern Louisiana University

D. L. Birchfield and Melissa Walsh Dolg, in *The Gale Encyclopedia of Native American Tribes*, vol. 1, ed. Sharon Malinowski and Anna Sheets (1998); Duane Champagne, ed., *Chronology of Native North American History from Pre-Columbian Times to the Present* (1994); Arthur H. DeRosier Jr., in *Forked Tongues and Broken Treaties*, ed. Donald E. Worcester (1975); Grant Foreman, *Indian Removal: The Emigration of the Five Civilized Tribes of Indians* (1966); Arrell M. Gibson, in *History of Indian-White Relations*, vol. 4 of the *Handbook of North American Indians*, ed. Wilcombe E. Washburn (1988); Francis Paul Prucha, *American Indian Treaties: The History of a Political Anomaly* (1994).

Dockery Farms

Located in Sunflower County a few miles southeast of Cleveland, Dockery Farms was a large cotton-growing plantation that started in 1895. It is most famous as the home of Charley Patton, the creative early blues musician who influenced other performers, among them Son House, Robert Johnson, Bukka White, and Howlin' Wolf. Patton's family began

Dockery Plantation (Photograph by James G. Thomas, Jr.)

working at Dockery Farms around 1900, when the area still included considerable swampland. Before long, Dockery became an economic success story—part of what historian James Cobb calls a New South plantation kingdom. Owner Will Dockery bought land, employed workers, and planted cotton with such success that the plantation grew to about ten thousand acres and had four hundred families working the land. The plantation had its own railroad line, post office, doctor, and cotton gin and plantation store.

Patton played music at house parties, at the Dockery company store, at various juke joints, and in other local settings. In 1929 record producer H. C. Speir, a Jackson furniture dealer, heard of Patton's talents, found him at Dockery Farms, and made the first recordings of his music. The plantation's railroad was the setting for Patton's "Pea Vine Blues," while "34 Blues" describes the singer's departure from the plantation: "They run me from Will Dockery's" when an overseer "told Papa Charley, 'I don't want you hangin' round on my job no more.'"

Today Dockery Farms is a site on the Mississippi Blues Trail noted as one of the birthplaces of the blues. An often-reproduced sign on a barn announces, "Dockery Farms, est. 1895 by Will Dockery, 1865–1936, Joe Rice Dockery 1908–1982." The members of the Dockery family did not take great notice of the blues performed on their plantation until scholars and fans turned it into something of a shrine, but Joe and his wife, Keith Dockery, were longtime supporters of classical music.

Ted Ownby
University of Mississippi

Stephen Calt and Gayle Wardlow, *King of the Delta Blues: The Life and Music of Charlie Patton* (1988); Steve Cheseborough, *Blues Traveling: The Holy Sites of Delta Blues* (2001); James C. Cobb, *The Most Southern Place on Earth: The Mississippi Delta and the Roots of Regional Identity* (1992); Pat Howse and Jimmy Phillips, *Peavey Monitor* (1995); Mississippi Blues Trail website, msbluestrail.org; Robert Palmer, *Deep Blues: A Musical and Cultural History of the Mississippi Delta* (1981).

Doe's Eat Place

Doe's Eat Place began in 1903 as an immigrant-owned grocery store, like many other Delta establishments. Carmel Signa sailed from Sicily, Italy, and made his way to the growing Mississippi River town of Greenville. The Signa family lived in back of what was known as Papa's Store until the Great Mississippi Flood of 1927 destroyed their livelihood. To help the family recover, Carmel's son, Dominic, "Big Doe," bootlegged whiskey until he sold his still for three hundred dollars and a Model T Ford. Big Doe worked in the cafeteria at the air force base in Greenville, where one of the enlisted men gave him a recipe for hot tamales. According to food scholar John T. Edge, black farmworkers brought their lunches of cornbread and fatback into the fields, where they met migrant Mexican workers with their lunches, which also featured cornmeal and pork, though in the form of tamales. Mamie Signa, Big Doe's wife, improved the initial recipe and began selling them from her kitchen. The tamales were popular, and soon the Signa women and children were rolling hundreds of tamales to sell to the families who showed up at Big Doe's door seeking hot tamales for their dinner.

By the mid-1940s Signa had replaced the grocery store with a juke joint, while the family still resided in the back of the building. A local doctor frequently turned up at the Signas' back door for dinner between house calls, and Big Doe would grill him a steak to go with his tamales. Word of Doe's delicious steaks began to spread, and the establishment developed into a unique business: a restaurant in the back for white patrons and juke joint up front for black customers. The juke joint eventually closed, and the Signa family focused on the restaurant, which became known as Doe's Eat Place and drew customers from all over the world. During the 1950s the cast of the movie *Baby Doll* frequented

Doe's Eat Place, Greenville (Courtesy Amy C. Evans)

the restaurant while filming outside of town, and director Elia Kazan ate Christmas dinner with the Signas.

Two of Big Doe and Mamie's four children, Dominic "Little Doe" and Charles, took over the restaurant in 1974, but the atmosphere remains unchanged. Doe's Eat Place is the same clapboard and cinder block joint on Nelson Street with autographed pictures of celebrities and Mississippi sports heroes on smoke- and grease-stained walls and beer sold from an ancient cooler on the honor system that Big Doe began. Little Doe continues to wrestle giant steaks under his daddy's old Garland broiler while patrons fight over the last hot tamale on the platter or scrape up the last bite of salad, which is still dressed and tossed in Big Doe's wooden bowl. For a time Charles Signa operated another Doe's in Oxford, and there are locations in Louisiana, Arkansas, Kentucky, and Oklahoma.

LeAnne Gault
Madison, Mississippi

Doe's Eat Place website, www.doeseatplace.com; John T. Edge, *Southern Belly: The Ultimate Food Lover's Companion to the South* (2000).

Dogtrot House

Dogtrot is the colloquial name for a house with two sides of rooms linked by a covered open passageway. The dogtrot was the second-most-common house type on the southern frontier; only the even simpler one-room cabin was more prevalent. The geographical and cultural origins of the house are murky, but evidence suggests that it did not develop in a solely southern context, although the form has deep and long-lasting connections to southern settlements. Settlers in other parts of the United States quickly replaced dogtrot houses with more refined buildings, often transforming former domestic structures into barns or other support buildings. In contrast, southern settlers continued to build in this original, unpolished form well into the nineteenth century, especially in Alabama and Mississippi.

Dogtrot houses featured logs laid horizontally on top of one another, fitted together at the corners with notched joints. The weight of the log above held each piece in place, and gravity secured the joints. Gaps between the logs were filled with clay or clay mixtures. Sometimes cracks at the meeting point between wall and joists served as windows, which were generally unglazed. Room sizes depended on the size of the timber, which often provided about twenty feet of usable length.

Dogtrot cabin of Ed Bagget, sharecropper, near Laurel, January 1939 (Photograph by Russell Lee, Library of Congress, Washington, D.C. [LC-USF34-031960-D])

The flexibility of the log house appealed to new settlers because the structures were easy to expand. In many cases, owners built single-room cabins and later enlarged them as they became more established. Simply adding another pen and connecting it to the original by an open air passage changed the tone and meaning of the house, making a more permanent statement on the land and addressing the spatial needs of a growing family. Based on contemporary reports, enclosed rooms on either side of the central hall were used for sleeping, while the open passageway was the primary living space, used for dining, socializing, and sheltering both people and animals. The tunnel created by the open passage funneled the breeze through the space, creating what was probably the most comfortable area in the house.

The most rudimentary dogtrot houses worked well in a region with abundant timber resources and few laborers to produce finished materials from those supplies. In 1818 a settler in Northeast Mississippi reported that he built a single-room log house in five days with the help of his brothers and a neighbor. A dogtrot house would not have taken much more time or effort to assemble.

Not all dogtrot houses featured rough materials and quick construction, nor were they built only by newly arrived settlers. Many southern farmers continued to use the dogtrot form even as their farms became established and prosperous because the building form suited the hot, humid climate. Some planters built in the dogtrot form but used more refined timber framing instead of rough logs. Some planters continued to build with rough logs while filling their homes with sophisticated furniture, rich carpets, plates, and books. In a few cases, more sophisticated dogtrot houses might feature folding doors at either end of the passageway to allow the space to be fully enclosed. Many southern farmers chose to invest in land and labor rather than spending money on big houses. Nineteenth-century agriculture encouraged such practices, since farmers expected to move on after their land had been depleted by overcultivation.

Emilie Johnson
University of Virginia

Terry G. Jordan and Matti Kaups, *Geographical Review* (January 1987); Mills Lane, *Architecture of the Old South, Mississippi/Alabama* (1989).

Dollarhide, Louis

(1918–2004) Art Critic and Scholar

An influential art critic, Louis Dollarhide taught English at Mississippi College and the University of Mississippi from the 1950s through the 1980s. The Oklahoma-born Dollarhide grew up in Kosciusko, Mississippi, and attended Mississippi College before earning a master's degree at Harvard and doctorate at the University of North Carolina, where his dissertation concerned the work of William Shakespeare. Most famous as the art critic for the *Jackson Clarion-Ledger*, Dollarhide published more than a thousand reviews of literature, theater, and music between 1955 and 1976.

Dollarhide started writing reviews of literature when Frank Hains of the *Jackson Daily News* asked him to contribute to a series of responses to Eudora Welty's *The Bride of Innisfallen* in 1955. That effort led to a series of columns, and by 1958 he was writing a regular column, "Of Art and Artists," in which he praised and critiqued both well-known and little-known writers and artists and made a special point of discussing works by new writers. He took particular interest and pride in Welty's success. Dollarhide occasionally wrote to address what he saw as conventional critiques of southern writing. He criticized work that seemed to fit too easily into the stereotypes of local color writing. In a 1966 article on the work of Berry Morgan, he scoffed at people who continued to use H. L. Mencken's old critique of the South as a place without culture or creativity. A year later, he criticized those who condemned William Faulkner and other writers for dramatizing only the darkest sides of Mississippi life: "The fact is, they do the state inestimable good just by being great writers."

As an art critic Dollarhide had particular affinity for events at Allison's Wells, for the work of Marie Hull and Mildred Wolfe, and for young artists such as William Dunlap, Marshall Bouldin, and Thomas Eloby. As music writer, he took clear pride in events that belied Mississippi's reputation as a backwater. He wrote with affection about Leontyne Price's appearance at Rust College and of the Jackson Symphony's performance at the city's new auditorium in 1968.

Dollarhide collected many of his favorite columns into a 1981 book, *Of Art and Artists*. He and Ann Abadie served as coeditors of *Eudora Welty: A Form of Thanks*, a 1979 collection of essays from the symposium that inaugurated the Center for the Study of Southern Culture at the University of Mississippi. Dollarhide retired from teaching in 1987 and died in 2004.

Ted Ownby
University of Mississippi

Louis Dollarhide, *Of Art and Artists* (1981); Louis Dollarhide and Ann Abadie, *Eudora Welty: A Form of Thanks* (1979); Louis Dollarhide Collection, Department of Archives and Special Collections, J. D. Williams Library, University of Mississippi.

Domestic Workers

Domestic workers and their employment in Mississippi have been intimately connected with issues of race and gender. Before the Civil War, most servants were African American slaves. While some urban employers preferred white or free black workers, the vast majority employed slaves to carry out domestic tasks. Few households in antebellum Mississippi could afford a large force of domestic workers, but many families considered having at least one servant an indispensable measure of status and made serious efforts to purchase or hire household workers. In towns, many slaveholders brought in extra income by hiring out slaves to work as domestics, though the practice was less common in rural areas. On many farms and plantations, slaves often performed both field and house duties. Most domestic workers were females who worked as cooks, laundresses, maids, nurses, and in other capacities, although wealthier households might also have male slaves serving as body servants, footmen, or gardeners. While white employers spoke of a special, paternalistic bond with their household workers, the servants themselves often resented the close supervision of their work and used their positions to help their families and the larger slave community through activities such as stealing food or gathering information.

The outbreak of the Civil War brought radical changes for domestic workers and their employers. After federal troops reached the state, enslaved domestic workers, like other slaves, began to run away to Union camps. Although slaveholders deplored all such activity, they were especially affected by the desertion of servants, having believed that they felt loyalty toward the families with whom they had worked so closely. Domestics who reached the Union lines often found themselves employed in similar work in the army's camps.

During and immediately after the war, domestic workers and their employers transitioned from slave to free labor. Many freedwomen—both domestics and field workers—initially withdrew from the labor force and dedicated themselves to working for their own families. However, women often had to rejoin the workforce for financial reasons. Postwar household workers frequently were either single mothers or married women whose husbands could not support their families. The leaders of an 1866 laundry workers' strike in Jackson wrote a petition stating that low wages and high rents made it "impossible to live uprightly and honestly."

Reconstruction constituted a transitional period during which many patterns established themselves. Most antebellum domestics had lived with their owners or employers but now began to establish their own households, and by the end of the nineteenth century, very few Mississippi servants lived with their employers. As in the antebellum period, however, African American females continued to comprise most of the state's domestic workforce, performing a variety of tasks such as cleaning, laundry, child care, and cooking. Late in the century, whites began manufacturing the Mammy myth, which fondly recalled the devoted (and imaginary) domestic slave.

The twentieth century brought many more changes for domestic workers. As massive numbers of Mississippi's African Americans migrated north, women often supported their families with domestic skills learned in their home state. World War II continued the pattern, drawing many domestics out of Mississippi in search of better jobs in the booming war industries of the western states.

After the war, the civil rights movement, too, had a tremendous impact on domestic workers. Many women began questioning not only southern institutions such as Jim Crow segregation but also the low wages and often degrading working conditions of household service, refusing to wear uniforms and demanding better pay and more respect from their employers. These developments, combined with better educational and occupational opportunities for African American women and the increased use of professional cleaning services, led to a decline in the number of black women employed as servants. However, domestic work, including in-home child care, continues to serve as a primary occupation for many Mississippi women, particularly African Americans.

Discussions about *The Help*, Kathryn Stockett's 2009 novel and the 2011 film based on it, dramatized tensions in the lives of domestic workers in 1960s Mississippi and also raised questions about white southerners' attempts to understand or speak for those workers.

Julia Huston Nguyen
National Endowment for the
Humanities

Ronald L. F. Davis, *Good and Faithful Labor: From Slavery to Sharecropping in the Natchez District, 1860–1890* (1982); Tera W. Hunter, *To 'Joy My Freedom: Southern Black Women's Lives and Labors after the Civil War* (1997); Jacqueline Jones, *Labor of Love, Labor of Sorrow: Black Women, Work, and the Family from Slavery to the Present* (1985); David Katzman, *Seven Days a Week: Women and Domestic Service in Industrializing America* (1978); Leon Litwack, *Been in the Storm So Long: The Aftermath of Slavery* (1979); Anne Moody, *Coming of Age in Mississippi* (1968); Julia Huston Nguyen, *Journal of Mississippi History* (Spring 2001); Daniel Sutherland, *Americans and Their Servants: Domestic Service in the United States from 1800 to 1920* (1981); Susan Tucker, *Telling Memories among Southern Women: Domestic Workers and Their Employers in the Segregated South* (1988).

Donald, Cleveland Jr.
(1946–2012) Activist

Cleveland Donald Jr., the second African American to graduate from the University of Mississippi, was a civil rights activist, scholar, and university administrator. A Jackson native, Donald participated in black freedom struggles in both the Deep South and the Northeast, and his research on Brazil informed discussions of race relations in both Latin America and the United States.

Born in 1946, Donald began participating in the Jackson civil rights movement as a student at Brinkley High School. During the summer of 1963 Donald landed in jail for protesting segregation at the state fair in Jackson. He earned outstanding grades at Tougaloo College and applied as a transfer student for the 1964 summer term at the University of Mississippi. Donald's application did not incite the violence and ugliness of the James H. Meredith case, but the university also did not welcome him. Administrators tied up Donald's application in hearings and delays for four months before finally giving in to a court order. The judge who ordered Donald's enrollment took the unusual step of stipulating that Donald could not participate in any civil rights demonstrations while attending. Fears of a repeat of the events of 1962 led university officials to call in extra security when Donald arrived on campus. For the most part, however, white students treated their new classmate civilly, if coldly. After a few days, the extra security left Oxford. Donald earned excellent grades and graduated in 1966 with a degree in history.

Donald attended graduate school at Cornell University, where as a member of the Afro-American Society (AAS), he participated in the April 1969 takeover of the university's student union to protest sanctions that administrators had levied against black students for their roles in previous demonstrations and to demand better social and academic treatment of African Americans at the university. AAS members had armed themselves, making the protest extremely tense and controversial. Donald initially struggled with the idea of using the threat of violence at an institution of higher learning, but he later reconciled himself to the fact that white fraternity members' attempts to use guns to remove the protesters made weapons necessary for self-defense. Inside the union, Donald, with his calm demeanor and his experience with tense situations in Mississippi, proved invaluable in soothing his nervous compatriots. The conflict ended peacefully, with administrators agreeing not to prosecute AAS members.

Donald completed his doctorate at Cornell in 1973, returning to the University of Mississippi five years later to serve as the first director of the Black Studies Program. He remained there until 1980, when he took a position with the National Endowment for the Humanities. Donald's scholarship and leadership earned him esteem in the fields of Latin American and Africana history. In addition to the University of Mississippi, he taught and served as an administrator at the State University of New York at Binghamton, the University of Massachusetts, and the University of Connecticut, Waterbury campus. He died on 26 January 2012 in New Milford, Connecticut.

Thomas John Carey

University of Mississippi

Russell H. Barrett, *Integration at Ole Miss* (1965); Cleveland Donald Jr., *Divided We Stand: Reflections on the Crisis at Cornell*, ed. Cushing Strout and David Grossvogel (1970).

Donald, David Herbert

(1920–2009) Historian

David Herbert Donald, a biographer and a historian of the US Civil War era, was born in Goodman, Mississippi, on 1 October 1920. His father, Ira Unger Donald, was a cotton planter; his mother, Sue Ella Belford Donald, had been a schoolteacher. Donald's early interests were in music and perhaps ministry, but they were eventually overtaken by his passion for history and the life of the mind. He became one of his generation's preeminent historians, a masterful literary craftsman, and twice the winner of the Pulitzer Prize in biography.

Donald's academic distinctions were blue-blooded: highest honors as a graduate of Millsaps College in 1941; a brief graduate stint at the University of North Carolina, which was then in the vanguard of the sociological inquiry that engaged him; and finally, doctoral training at the University of Illinois under James G. Randall, the era's most outstanding Civil War scholar. After receiving his doctorate in 1945, Donald taught at Columbia University, Smith College, Princeton University, Johns Hopkins University, and Harvard University, where he became the Charles Warren Professor of American History. He retired in 1991 and received emeritus status. Even at age thirty-one, Donald displayed an "erudition and courtliness" and was "appropriately tweedy in dress, with prematurely thinning hair and thick glasses."

Donald focused on political history, taking a skeptical view that often was at odds with much of the received historical wisdom: the last of Donald's elegant biographies, *Lincoln* (1995), portrayed a passive, mistake-prone president who reacted to rather than guided events. Similarly, Donald saw Massachusetts senator Charles Sumner as vain, pompous, and acutely and constantly in need of approval and his fellow abolitionists as consumed by status anxiety. But despite his origins as a white son of the segregated South, Donald did not demean their cause or the people to whom that cause was dedicated. A self-described "Christian and conservative," Donald's approach and his intellect in general were subtly shaped by theologian Reinhold Niebuhr, whose philosophy also guided the works of some scholars with whom Donald frequently disagreed.

Donald was a writer with roots in a rural Mississippi tradition. As a young man Donald was surrounded by stories and storytellers—mainly elderly women whose epic stories of pioneers, ex-Confederates, and family-defying iconoclasts imparted an oral tradition keen in vernacular language, rich in personal experience, and alive with drama, artistry, and possibility. "Inevitably," he wrote, "this tradition affected my own approach toward history—as it has affected so many of the best historians of the South. Though I was trained in the best 'scientific' methods of historical research, taught to deal with vast impersonal forces like 'class,' 'caste,' 'capitalism,' 'feudalism,' and the like, I found that when I actually sat down to write, my mind slipped into the old patterns of narration, of making readers see and understand real-life figures in the past." Indeed, although he authored and edited dozens of books and essays, the best-known and most influential of Donald's works are personal and biographical: *Lincoln's Herndon* (1948); *Charles Sumner and the Coming of the Civil War* (1960), for which he won the 1961 Pulitzer Prize; *Charles Sumner and the Rights of Man* (1970); and *Lincoln*, which received the 1996 Lincoln Prize. Reflecting his broad interests, the influences of his boyhood, and his intellectual courage and confidence, *Look Homeward: A Life of Thomas Wolfe* (1987)—an enormous professional gamble for a historian of his rank and stature—won him his second Pulitzer Prize. Donald's work embraced and experimented with many different tools of analysis—quantitative method, psychoanalysis, literary criticism—and, partly because Donald revised his views over a long career, his writings do not fit easily into any one school of historical thought.

Donald married fellow historian Aida DiPace in 1955, and they had three children. He died on 17 May 2009.

Paul Christopher Anderson
Clemson University

David Herbert Donald, "On Being an American Historian," US Department of State, Bureau of International Information Programs website, http://usa.usembassy.de/etexts/writers/donald.htm; Ari Hoogenboom, in *A Master's Due: Essays in Honor of David Herbert Donald*, ed. William J. Cooper Jr., Michael F. Holt, and John McCardell (1985); Robert Allen Rutland, ed., *Clio's Favorites: Leading Historians of the United States, 1945–2000* (2000).

Dorsey, L. C.
(1938–2013) Activist and Author

Born on 17 December 1938, Lula C. Dorsey grew up sharecropping in Tribbett, Mississippi, and from an early age took an interest in civil rights and social justice. Inspired by her mother, who read her stories out of the *Chicago Defender*, Dorsey began to study the Southern Christian Leadership Conference's techniques for organizing volunteers.

Dorsey began working for Head Start in 1964 before moving on two years later to Operation Help, a program that sought jobs and resources for the disadvantaged. Her activities brought her into contact with Fannie Lou Hamer, who inspired Dorsey to become involved in the civil rights movement and to join the Mississippi Freedom Democratic Party, for which Dorsey began organizing boycotts and demonstrations.

In 1968 Dorsey earned her general equivalency diploma through an experimental program at Tufts University before attending the State University of New York at Stony Brook, where she earned a master's degree in social work in 1973. She went on to earn a doctorate in the subject from Howard University. Dorsey subsequently returned to Mississippi and resumed her work with Head Start, this time as the director of social services in Greenville. She also began working on prison reform, serving as associate director of the Southern Coalition on Jails and Prisons from 1974 to 1983. During this time, Dorsey published numerous articles on prison reform in the *Jackson Advocate*. She also wrote and published a book, *Cold Steel*, describing life in Mississippi's Parchman Prison.

Because of her vast knowledge on the prison system, Dorsey served on Jimmy Carter's National Council for Economic Opportunity in 1978–79. In 1983, the American Civil Liberties Union honored Dorsey for her work in prison

reform. Dorsey also helped to establish the community action programs in Bolivar and Sunflower Counties and founded the Mississippi Office of Economic Opportunity. She served as the executive director of the Delta Health Center in Mound Bayou from 1988 to 1995, when she began working as a clinical associate professor in the Family Medicine Department at the University of Mississippi Medical Center. She also served as associate director of the Delta Research and Cultural Institute at Mississippi Valley State University.

The mother of six children, Dorsey resided in Jackson until her death on 21 August 2013. She appeared in several films documenting women's roles in the struggle for civil rights, including *Standing on My Sisters' Shoulders*. The Jackson-based Dr. Mary S. Nelums Foundation honors Dorsey's work with the annual Dr. L. C. Dorsey Social Activist Award.

Amy Schmidt
Lyon College

Telisha Dionne Bailey, "'Please Don't Forget About Me': The History of Crime and Punishment in Parchman Prison, 1890–1980" (PhD dissertation, University of Mississippi, 2015); John Dittmer, *Local People: The Struggle for Civil Rights in Mississippi* (1994); Karen Rutherford, Mississippi Writers Page website, www.olemiss.edu/mwp/; *Standing on My Sisters' Shoulders* website, www.sisters-shoulders.org.

Dorsey, Sarah Anne Ellis
(1829–1879) Author

Sarah Anne Ellis was born on 16 February 1829 to wealthy Natchez plantation owners Mary Routh Ellis and Thomas George Percy Ellis, an ancestor of writer Walker Percy. Thomas Ellis died when Sarah Anne was nine, and her mother married Charles Dahlgren in 1840. They raised the precocious child with the assistance of her governess, writer Eliza Ann Dupuy, in Mary's ancestral home, Routhland.

In 1853 Sarah married wealthy Marylander Samuel Worthington Dorsey and took full advantage of her privileged existence, traveling and pursuing intellectual endeavors. She published at least six Victorian romance novels in the 1860s and 1870s (*Agnes Graham*, *Athalie*, *The Vivians*, *Lucia Dare*, *Panola*, and *Vivacious Castine*) as well as her first literary offering, an 1866 tribute to Confederate general Henry Watkins Allen, a family friend.

Her achievements subsequently continued far beyond the traditional forms of writing common to women in the nineteenth century. She was the first woman admitted into New Orleans's prestigious Academy of Sciences, where one of her last projects was a paper delivered on 13 April 1874, "On the Philosophy of the University of France." This title veiled Dorsey's promotion of a philosophy grounded in the equal albeit separate treatment of women. As she attempted to reconcile religion with science, she advocated an elevated position for women based not on social and political theory but on genealogical science and eugenics: "I do not recognize any antagonism or any inequality in value, of the intellect of the sexes; the one is simply the complement of the other, of the Two, the intellect of Woman is probably more composed of the results of reflex action of the race, thought and habit than that of man. She seems to be in some sort, the granary of humanity! She has more of the treasures of race posited in her than man has. She has more and quicker intuition, and of what is called instinct, than he has; and philosophers teach that intuition is the ultimate product of voluntary race, thought and habit." Thus, she demonstrated both her feminism and her racial prejudice.

Dorsey is now best known for her connection to the former president of the Confederacy, Jefferson Davis. She offered the destitute Davis a home at Beauvoir, the Mississippi Gulf Coast antebellum mansion she had bought and renamed in 1873. A childhood friend of Confederate First Lady Varina Howell Davis, Dorsey not only provided a haven for the disgraced leader but also served as secretary-transcriber for his memoirs. When she died of breast cancer on 4 July 1879, she left the home to Jefferson Davis. The Dahlgren family contested the bequest, claiming that Dorsey was not of sound mind when she amended her will in favor of Davis, but the suit was dismissed.

Dorsey is buried in the Routh family cemetery in Natchez, where her tombstone lists the titles of her books.

Amy Pardo
Mississippi University for Women

Bertram Wyatt-Brown, *The House of Percy: Honor, Melancholy, and Imagination in a Southern Family* (1994).

Douglas, Ellen (Josephine Ayres Haxton)
(1921–2012) Writer

When Houghton Mifflin awarded Josephine Ayres Haxton a fellowship for her first novel, *A Family's Affairs* (1962), she assumed the pseudonym Ellen Douglas to protect the identity of her maternal aunts, whose lives had inspired the plot. Her cover was soon blown when her story "On the Lake" appeared in the *New Yorker* and friends Betty and Hodding Carter recognized the boating accident as a fictionalized

Ellen Douglas (Josephine Ayres Haxton) (Bern and Franke Keating Collection, Department of Archives and Special Collections, J. D. Williams Library, University of Mississippi)

version of an incident that had occurred when Haxton was fishing with her sons.

Born in Natchez on 12 July 1921, Josephine Ayres grew up in small towns in Mississippi, Arkansas, and Louisiana as her family moved to follow her father's civil engineering career. Ayres's literary life was nurtured by her mother, who read to her every night, and her paternal grandmother, who wrote children's books. Books began broadening Douglas's world early on. She devoured William Faulkner, Ernest Hemingway, and Thomas Wolfe in high school and W. J. Cash's *The Mind of the South*, Eudora Welty's *A Curtain of Green*, and Richard Wright's *Native Son* in college, while her first serious boyfriend plied her with texts ranging from *Ten Days that Shook the World* to *The Decline of the West*. Ayres enrolled at Virginia's Randolph-Macon Woman's College in 1938 but transferred to the University of Mississippi and graduated in 1942 with a degree in sociology. Although her parents lived and breathed the southern segregationist worldview, undergirded by a strong Presbyterian faith, Ayres's horizons expanded considerably when she encountered a liberal sociology professor at the University of Mississippi who directed her honors thesis on tenant farming.

In January 1945 Ayres married composer and musician Kenneth Haxton and moved with him to Greenville, where he managed his family's department store, Nelms and Blum, and collaborated in creating Levee Press, which produced limited editions of works by Faulkner, Welty, and William Alexander Percy. The Haxtons raised three sons in Greenville and enjoyed a literary society that included poet Charles Bell, newspaper editor Hodding Carter, historian Shelby Foote, novelist Walker Percy, and literary agent Ben Wasson. During the volatile 1960s, when her husband publicly supported the peaceful integration of schools, Haxton used their home to host a historic meeting of black and white women to advise the welfare department about setting up a day care center. Shortly after the couple divorced in 1980, Douglas moved to Jackson, and she subsequently taught and was a writer in residence at Northeast Louisiana University, the University of Mississippi, the University of Virginia, and Millsaps College.

Black-white relationships became a very important subject for Douglas as early as her second book, *Black Cloud, White Cloud* (1963), which included the novella "Hold On," a longer version of "On the Lake," a story for which Douglas won the O. Henry Prize. Drawing inspiration from Faulkner, Douglas planted all of her fiction firmly in Mississippi (her Homochitto is based on Natchez and her Philippi on Greenville), but she used as her models such great nineteenth-century realists as Flaubert, Dostoevsky, James, and Tolstoy, consciously reacting against the gothic and mythic elements in Faulkner's work. Douglas admired Welty but found her "too idiosyncratic a writer" to serve as an influence; instead, Douglas turned to Katherine Anne Porter to validate her preoccupation with complex family relationships. Douglas's reading of Simone de Beauvoir's *The Second Sex* and Betty Friedan's *The Feminine Mystique* helped shape her views about gender relations, which dominate the plot of her second novel, *Where the Dreams Cross* (1968). A concern with the way America warehouses the elderly and infirm became the subject of her third novel, *Apostles of Light* (1973).

Interviewers always seemed to press Douglas about how her life relates to her art. And while she was willing to talk about personal influences in her fiction, she politely but firmly pointed out that where readers see people and places, a writer also sees an artistic "problem": conflicting stories and messy emotions that have to be shaped with the conventions of fiction and worked out within or against a literary tradition. In explaining her narrative choices, Douglas repeatedly said that "each project has its own reasons, so that the reason you do something is because it works in that project." Interest in her work has increased because of the narrative versatility evidenced in her experimental novels, *The Rock Cried Out* (1979), *A Lifetime Burning* (1982), and *Can't Quit You, Baby* (1988), and in her hybrid collection, *Truth: Four Stories I Am Finally Old Enough to Tell* (1998). Douglas attributed her growing ability to match form and content in these later works to her reading of metafiction, particularly Milan Kundera's *The Book of Laughter and Forgetting*.

The Rock Cried Out features embedded narratives and focuses on a white youth's naïveté about his family and his community during the 1960s; *A Lifetime Burning*, written in the form of a journal, concerns a wife's misunderstanding of her marriage as well as her own sexuality; and the metafictional *Can't Quit You, Baby* explores a white woman's self-deception in her relationship with her African American maid. But these novels are also about writing fiction. Con-temporary theories about positionality and America's ongoing problems with race relations made Douglas especially sensitive about her characters' and her own difficulty not only in understanding someone who is different but also in fully understanding their own experiences. Douglas said that over the years she had "gotten more and more interested in what's true and what isn't true and how impossible it is to recognize the truth or to tell the truth or to read a book and know it's true." By finding just the right form for her books, Ellen Douglas sought to share with her readers her preoccupation with truth and moral responsibility.

Ellen Douglas died at her home in Jackson in 2012.

Suzanne W. Jones
University of Richmond

Ellen Douglas, interview by Suzanne Jones (19 June 2004); Margalit Fox, *New York Times* (12 November 2012); *Southern Quarterly* (Summer 1995); Panthea Reid, ed., *Conversations with Ellen Douglas* (2000).

Dow, Lorenzo
(1777–1833) Religious Leader

Lorenzo Dow gained fame as a traveling evangelist who led revivals throughout the United States, England, and Ireland. He is credited with leading the first camp meeting revival on Mississippi soil on 12 November 1804 near Washington.

Born on 16 October 1777 in Coventry, Connecticut, to Humphrey Dean Dow and Tabitha Parker Dow, Lorenzo claimed that at the age of thirteen he "was taken up by a whirlwind above the sky," where he witnessed God and Jesus sitting on an ivory throne. During this mystical experience, the angel Gabriel challenged Dow to be faithful to return to heaven. Throughout the 1790s Dow strongly felt the call to preach, though his parents opposed his efforts. In March 1796 John Wesley came to Dow in another vision, making it clear that Lorenzo had been called to preach the gospel. Dow garnered letters attesting to his moral character and set out riding circuits throughout New England. The Methodist Conference initially refused to grant Dow credentials to preach in connection with the church. Undeterred, Dow set out on his own and recalled how people were "offended" by his "*plainness* both of *dress, expressions*, and way of *address*," leading him to be known as Crazy Dow. The nickname and his consistently unkempt appearance became staples of Dow's career. By 1798 he presented the Methodist Conference with a letter signed by thirty pastors and respectable citizens and received his license.

Dow subsequently continued evangelistic work in New England, traveled to Ireland, and ventured on multiple Georgia preaching tours with stops in Tennessee, the Carolinas, and Virginia. On 3 September 1804 he married Peggy Holcomb, whom he often referred to as "his Rib."

Dow immediately launched a Mississippi tour, visiting Natchez and Washington. The Dows also traveled and toured Great Britain, North Carolina, and Virginia before coming back to Mississippi. After his return from Great Britain in 1807, Dow encountered numerous hardships including financial problems, attacks on his reputation, and declining health. The Dows consequently "retired" to the Mississippi Territory and built a cabin in "wilderness" about thirteen miles outside of Gibson Port (now Port Gibson).

From 1807 to 1820 the Dows periodically lived in the cabin while Lorenzo made frequent evangelizing tours. Peggy died on 6 January 1820, and Lorenzo married Lucy Dolbeare on 1 April 1820.

During his time in Mississippi, Dow's independent evangelical style conflicted with established churches and organized circuits. The Baltimore Conference ruled against Dow for failing to obey "rule and order." The Dows traveled to Natchez for supplies and proceeded eastward, crossing the Pearl River on their way to Georgia and eventually New England. Dow's struggles in Mississippi with the Methodist hierarchy, along with new attacks on his reputation, led him to publish a powerful pamphlet, *On Church Government* (1816), in which he attacked Methodist Church governance.

Dow possessed a forceful political consciousness shaped by the major ideological trends of his day, republicanism and Jacksonian democracy. Historians have noted that Dow amalgamated republicanism, patriotism, and evangelicalism. Fellow evangelist Jacob Young recalled an 1807 Mississippi Territory camp meeting where a man disrupted proceedings. Dow took to the podium, told the history of the American Revolution, explained the "Divine favor" bestowed upon the United States, and quoted the Constitution along with the oaths of office for the president and justices of peace. He interpreted the Constitution as keeping "order and harmony" for the nation.

Dow's mixing of politics and religion was even more evident in his statement that "monarchy, popery, slavery, and episcopacy" all had the same roots and threatened individual freedom. He maintained that slavery represented a "national evil" and often preached on the sins of the United States. Throughout his later years, Dow espoused fierce anti-Catholic rhetoric.

Dow believed that Andrew Jackson had rightfully been elected president in 1824 but had been "defrauded out of it." Eight years later, Dow visited President Jackson in Washington. In this period of national division, Dow's religious writings returned to the trademark plainness that had started his career. He implored Christians to form a "bond of union" based on love toward all men, setting aside sectarian divisions and bigotry. Dow returned to Washington, D.C., in late 1833 to renew the patent for a "family medicine" business. He died there on 2 February 1834.

Dow's prolific writings include his journal, *The History of the Cosmopolite or Exemplified Experience*, and numerous religious pamphlets and treatises.

Ryan L. Fletcher
University of Mississippi

Benjamin Griffith Brawley, *Journal of Negro History* (July 1916); Lorenzo and Peggy Dow, *The Dealings of God, Man, and the Devil: As Exemplified in the Life, Experience, and Travels of Lorenzo Dow . . . Complete Works* (1850); Nathan O. Hatch, *The Democratization of American Christianity* (1989); Charles Coleman Sellers, *Lorenzo Dow: The Bearer of the Word* (1928); Randy J. Sparks, *On Jordan's Stormy Banks: Evangelicalism in Mississippi, 1773–1876* (1994); Randy J. Sparks, *Religion in Mississippi* (2001).

Downing, Ann

(b. 1945) Gospel Musician

Virginia Ann Sanders Downing is one of the most accomplished women in southern gospel music. Born on 12 June 1945 in Pittsboro, Mississippi, she grew up on a cotton farm, where she developed a love of music via music teachers, singing schools, church singing, and listening to such popular favorites as Rosemary Clooney and Patti Page on radio and recordings. Sanders wanted to sing gospel professionally, and by the mid-1960s she had become a fan and acquaintance of Ginger Smith Laxson of the Speer Family, a southern gospel group that had been around since 1921. The Speers were looking for a female vocalist and asked Sanders to join them when she graduated from high school. She toured with them for five years, and her versions of "I Must Tell Jesus" and "On the Sunny Banks" made her a popular performer. Sanders went on to become a member of one of the most significant gospel groups of the 1970s, the Downings, after she married Paul Shirley Downing Jr. The Downings charted eighteen Top 20 gospel songs from 1969 to 1976, including "I'm Free," "I Believe What the Bible Says," and "Jesus Is Coming Soon." The group members' lively concert style made them especially popular on tour. In 1969 Ann Downing won the first Dove Award as the gospel music industry's best female singer.

The Downings disbanded in 1978, and Paul and Ann Downing began a women's retreat and other ministries. Paul Downing died in 1992, but Ann Downing has continued as a solo performer and songwriter. In 1999 her rendition of "Climbing Jacob's Ladder" became a gospel hit. Downing has long been a regular on Bill Gaither's Homecoming video concerts, and she remains active in ministries, using music as part of her work with women's groups, older people, and youth.

Charles Reagan Wilson
University of Mississippi

James Goff Jr., *Close Harmony: A History of Southern Gospel* (2002); Absolutely Gospel Music website, www.sogospelnews.com.

Drama

It is amazing to discover the amount of talent devoted to the theater in Mississippi, a state far removed from Broadway—the center of drama in America, for better or worse—both in terms of distance and interest. When *theater* and *Mississippi* are mentioned in the same sentence, Tennessee Williams automatically comes to mind: his achievement and reputation tower over those of most other twentieth-century southern—indeed, American—playwrights.

People are often astounded to learn that the South and particularly Mississippi, which is generally perceived as a backward state with a high illiteracy rate, has produced so many major writers and dramatists. In addition to Williams, who is regarded as one of the world's most significant twentieth-century dramatists, Mississippi nurtured Mart Crowley, whose groundbreaking *Boys in the Band* was the first major play to portray the gay lifestyle in a truthful manner, and Beth Henley, whose *Crimes of the Heart* deals realistically with a dysfunctional southern small-town family in a new, almost whimsical way. All three of these playwrights followed in the footsteps of Stark Young, a Mississippian who went to New York at an early age and became a potent force as both a creative writer and a critic whose perceptive reviews helped shape American drama.

What the hills of North Mississippi meant for Faulkner in terms of setting and influence, the Delta signified for Tennessee Williams, who traveled far afield but never lost his attachment to the place he called home. For all of the state's presumed flaws, Mississippi has provided for its artists some invaluable substance, some support. In Williams's words, Mississippi constituted "a deep wide world you can breathe in." The classic struggle between puritanism and romanticism, a part of Williams's own character, also appeared in many of his dramas. Blanche DuBois of *A Streetcar Named Desire* is hopelessly idealistic at the same time that she is puritanically prudish in her condemnation of Stanley Kowalski. Her romanticism has been nurtured by growing up on a plantation in the Mississippi Delta. (Even though Laurel is the name of her hometown in the play, references to Moon Lake and other elements make it clear that Williams was writing about the Delta.) Despite the fact that the family is dying off and the land has been lost bit by bit because of the sexual peccadilloes of her ancestors, Blanche remains inescapably tied to that past, which may exist only in her imagination.

Williams drew from his southern heritage and his Mississippi childhood an intense sense of place, an attachment to family, an awareness of tradition and history (even though he is perhaps the least concerned with re-creating the southern past of any Mississippi writer of his generation), a romantic sensibility, a love of both lyrical and colloquial language, and a firm grounding in religion, especially involving a deep spirituality. For Williams as for other southern authors, that love of language is often rooted in the English of the King James Version of the Bible and the words of Protestant hymns as well as the eloquent and imaginative dialogue of southerners themselves.

Although Stark Young preceded Williams by a generation, those same devotions and ties were present in Young's work. He was associated with the Agrarians and was a contributor to their seminal book, *I'll Take My Stand*. Young made a place for himself in the tightly knit society of New York theater, becoming a much admired translator of Anton Chekhov's plays, a critic for the *New Republic* and *Theater Arts*, and a staunch supporter of young southern talent. Despite the cosmopolitan circles in which he moved and worked, Young retained his Mississippi influences and sympathies, and his work clearly reflects the fact that he was the son of a Confederate soldier and felt a deep attachment to the land of his birth. He shared with Williams a fascination with Chekhov's works, which depict a world in which aristocrats are fading away as a strange and frightening new social order evolves.

As Flannery O'Connor has noted, most southern writers are Christ-haunted, and Mississippians' work is permeated by concerns regarding the age-old battle between good and evil, God and Satan, within human beings. In Mart Crowley's *Boys in the Band*, protagonist Michael is a Roman Catholic Mississippian living in Manhattan. Although he believes himself free of his ties to the past, he suffers from guilt for many of his actions: at the end of the play, for example, after he has brutalized some of his party guests with his biting insults, he hurries off to a late Mass to seek redemption. He quotes his father—"I don't understand any of it, I never did"—acknowledging perhaps unconsciously his ties to the past and family. In Crowley's sequel, *The Men from the Boys*, Michael describes himself as "the most liberal Confederate who ever lived."

Crowley observed the filming of Williams's *Baby Doll* in the Mississippi Delta and became friends with the movie's stars and staff, a connection that eventually led him to a career in Hollywood. Although *Boys in the Band* broke new ground in the portrayal of gay life in America, appreciation of the play should not be limited to that perspective, because it is first and foremost, like all good drama, a study of the human experience in general.

Beth Henley, too, has gone from Mississippi to Hollywood. Her most famous work, *Crimes of the Heart*, began as a stage play and later became a popular movie, as did Henley's *The Miss Firecracker Contest*. In those and her other works, Henley creates female characters reminiscent of those in the world of Eudora Welty and Carson McCullers—indissolubly tied to their families despite having left them in a futile attempt to escape the past. Though Henley's eccentrics may be reminiscent of the creations of other writers, her characters are uniquely her own, shaped in large part by the confining elements of small-town life and by their family ties and sympathies.

In "Person-to-Person," Williams explained the proliferation of writers in the twentieth-century South: "I once saw a group of little girls on a Mississippi sidewalk, all dolled up in their mothers' and sisters' cast-off finery, old raggedy ball gowns and plumed hats and high-heeled slippers, enacting a meeting of ladies in a parlor with a perfect mimicry of polite Southern gush and simper. But one child was not satisfied with the attention paid her enraptured performance by the others, they were too involved in their own performances to suit her, so she stretched out her skinny arms and threw back her skinny neck and shrieked to the dead heavens and her equally oblivious playmates, 'Look at me, look at me, look at me!' . . . I wonder if she is not, now, a Southern writer."

Williams's insights might equally apply to theater performers. Mississippi has produced numerous distinguished actors, many of whom first performed in school and community theater groups in their home state. Dana Andrews was for many years a leading man in motion pictures, including such memorable films as *Tobacco Road*, *The Best Years of Our Lives*, and *Laura*. Ruth Ford, who performed in both movies and stage plays, was a friend of Faulkner, Williams, and Crowley and appeared in works by all of them. Faulkner wrote *Requiem for a Nun* at Ford's request, and she starred in it with her husband, Zachary Scott. Louise Fletcher, one of several products of the University of Mississippi drama department, achieved fame with her creation of Nurse Ratched in the movie *One Flew Over the Cuckoo Nest*. Meridian native Diane Ladd has appeared frequently on television and in movies, receiving three Academy Award nominations.

Four Mississippi-born African American actors are readily recognizable to audiences. Arkabutla-born James Earl Jones's powerful baritone is instantly familiar as the voice of Darth Vader in the *Star Wars* movies and has long made him in demand as a narrator in a variety of genres. He has also delivered unforgettable performances in movies, television dramas, and theater, where he played the role of Big Daddy in the first African American staging of *Cat on a Hot Tin Roof*. Morgan Freeman, who spent much of his childhood in Charleston and Greenwood, Mississippi, has appeared in numerous movies (among them *Driving Miss Daisy* and *The Shawshank Redemption*) and in stage drama (Clifford Odets's *The Country Girl*). Vicksburg's Beah Richards gave memorable portrayals in numerous supporting roles on both stage and screen, including that of the mother in *Guess Who's Coming to Dinner*. And Kosciusko's Oprah Winfrey has become an institution, a multifaceted actress, author, producer, and talk-show host who has achieved worldwide fame.

Somewhat lesser known television actors from Mississippi include Anthony Herrera, Gerald McRaney, former Miss America Mary Ann Mobley, Carrie Nye, and Sela Ward. More recently, Parker Posey has had recurring roles in a variety of television series, among them *The Good Wife*, and has regularly appeared in Christopher Guest's comic films. Lance Bass, who first gained fame as a member of the boy band NSYNC, has gone on to appear in numerous television productions and movies. And Hollywood heartthrob Channing Tatum has had a string of hit movies, including *Magic Mike* and the critically acclaimed *Foxcatcher*.

Kenneth Holditch
New Orleans, Louisiana

C. W. E. Bigsby, *Modern American Drama, 1945–1990* (1992); Lyle Leverich, *Tom: The Unknown Tennessee Williams* (1995); John Pilkington, ed. *Stark Young: A Life in Letters, 1900–1962* (1975).

Dulaney, Burgess
(1914–2001) Sculptor

The creations of Burgess Dulaney, fashioned of unfired Mississippi mud, leave one wondering whether his hands were guided by otherworldly forces. The act of transforming a simple earthen mass into what others would later call artwork seemed intuitive for Dulaney. Led by an inner voice or a vivid imagination—and a true love of the feel of wet clay on his hands—Dulaney spent his life choosing the mud carefully, familiarizing himself with its qualities and its limits, and using this knowledge to produce astonishingly powerful raw works of art. He added store-bought marbles for eyes, occasional bits of broken china for teeth, and horsehair to some of his unusual and whimsical creations.

Dulaney, the youngest of twelve children, was born in Itawamba County on 16 December 1914 and never traveled more than a few miles from his birthplace. He spent his childhood working on the family farm, never attended school, and never learned to read or write.

In the mid- to late 1970s Dulaney began to create solid mud sculptures made of clay dug from pits behind the family home. Made without interior support, some of the solid pieces weigh nearly fifty pounds. Most are about the size of a soccer ball or bowling pin. Dulaney also built thin-walled and hollow vessel-like works that refer to utilitarian-style pottery and classic southern face jugs. Dulaney's gift of several pieces to local merchants led to the discovery of his talent. The endless supply of locally dug clay allowed him to create fascinating creatures, unusual human forms, animal caricatures, and vessels, many of which have stunning similarities to pre-Columbian and American Indian artifacts. Some of the clay, rich in iron oxide, darkens over time, adding an almost eerie effect to these amazing works.

Dulaney experimented with fashioning some pieces from cement but found that he much preferred the feel of natural clay to the harshness of concrete mix. He spent hours working on each piece, removing impurities, shaping the clay by hand, and ensuring that it did not dry too quickly.

Dulaney died on 27 June 2001, leaving behind a body of fascinating art. His work is held in numerous private collections and in a variety of institutions, including the Mississippi Museum of Art and the Mississippi Department of Archives and History in Jackson; the Art Museum of Southeast Texas in Beaumont; and the American Visionary Art Museum in Baltimore.

Terry Nowell
Austin, Texas

Baking in the Sun: Visionary Images from the South (1987); Karekin Goekjian and Robert Peacock, *Light of the Spirit: Portraits of Southern Outsider Artists* (1998).

Dunbar, William
(1749–1810) Planter and Scientist

William Dunbar was born in 1749 in Morayshire, Scotland, and attended the University of Glasgow before migrating to Pennsylvania in 1771. Dunbar established a trading outfit, moving supplies between Philadelphia and Pittsburgh for two years, before entering into a partnership with fellow Scotsman John Ross. In 1773 he traveled down the Ohio and Mississippi Rivers and established New Richmond, one of the earliest plantations in Baton Rouge, Louisiana, which was then part of British West Florida. Dunbar kept a diary of life at New Richmond, detailing his efforts to control his Jamaican-born slaves, his excitement but uncertainty about social life on the frontier, and his various economic

activities. Surveying this period of his life, historian Bernard Bailyn writes that "seen through his letters and diary," Dunbar "appears to be more fictional than real—a creature of William Faulkner's imagination, a more cultivated Colonel Sutpen but no less mysterious."

After the 1783 Treaty of Paris handed the region to Spain, Dunbar moved north into Spanish-held Natchez, establishing a plantation called the Forest. Dunbar remained in place when the area shifted hands to the United States in 1795 and lived in his plantation home until his death.

Over the years he built up a fortune trading slaves and growing tobacco, rice, corn, indigo, and sugar. However, a large portion of his wealth came from the manufacture of barrel staves. Slaves took the local white and red oaks and transformed them from trees to staves in a single operation, moving from spot to spot and sending the finished product downriver to New Orleans for shipment to the West Indies. Typical of planters in that region, Dunbar cultivated extensive trading connections with partners in Baton Rouge, New Orleans, Philadelphia, Havana, and Scotland. Though Pinckney's Treaty had shifted his allegiance from Spain to the United States, Dunbar nonetheless maintained good relations with Spanish officials.

In fact, during his time in American-held Natchez he remained in the pay of both the Spanish and American governments, mostly as a surveyor. He eventually took on the job of establishing thirty-first parallel boundary between Spanish West Florida and the United States in 1798, helping to open that region to greater settlement from both countries. He later headed the 1804 Red River Expedition, exploring the frontiers of what would become Arkansas and Texas for the United States. This final voyage probably soured his relations with the Spaniards, who viewed any American exploration in this area as little more than spying. Nonetheless, his descriptions of both the U.S.–West Florida border and the Red River area contain some of the earliest European scientific classifications of wildlife in those places. In West Florida alone he cataloged more than thirty species of trees as well as numerous fruits and vegetables cultivated by the natives.

Dunbar's one foray into politics came during his time as a magistrate under Gov. Winthrop Sargent. However, from his time at the University of Glasgow, Dunbar had displayed an inquiring, scientific mind, and he spent a great deal of time engaged in scientific observation, making astronomical observations, and conducting experiments. This southern Benjamin Franklin corresponded with Thomas Jefferson on a number of occasions, and Jefferson recommended Dunbar for membership in the American Philosophical Society. Dunbar eventually wrote twelve entries in the society's publications. He also introduced the square-bale style of cotton packing to the Deep South, developed a method for extracting cottonseed oil, and spent a great deal of time cataloging rainfall, barometric pressure, sunrise and sunset times, observations of a comet and an eclipse, and other natural phenomena in and around Natchez. At the time of his death in 1810, Dunbar was one of the wealthiest and most influential persons in southern Mississippi.

Andrew McMichael
Western Kentucky University

Bernard Bailyn, *Voyagers to the West: A Passage in the Peopling of America on the Eve of the Revolution* (1988); William Dunbar, *The Life, Letters, and Papers of William Dunbar of Elgin, Moray Shire, Scotland, and Natchez, Mississippi, Pioneer Scientist of the Southern United States*, ed. Mrs. Dunbar Rowland (1930).

Duncan, Stephen
(1787–1867) Planter and Banker

Stephen Duncan, an entrepreneur, a financier, and one of the largest slave owners in the antebellum South, was born on 4 March 1787 in Carlisle, Pennsylvania. Duncan, the second of five children of John Duncan and Sarah Eliza Postlethwaite Duncan, grew up in Carlisle and lived a comfortable childhood but received an emotional blow at the age of six when his father was killed in a duel. Four years later, his mother remarried the well-to-do Col. Ephraim Blaine. Following the standard preparatory schooling of the day, Duncan attended Dickinson College in Carlisle, which his paternal grandfather and namesake had helped found. After graduating in 1805, Duncan studied medicine at the University of Pennsylvania under the renowned Benjamin Rush. Though a promising career appeared to await him as a physician in Philadelphia, Duncan instead migrated to the Natchez District of Mississippi in 1808.

Among the factors that contributed to Duncan's move were the economic opportunities available in the newly opened territory. His maternal uncle, Samuel Postlethwaite, had migrated to the Natchez District in 1800 and stood ready to introduce his nephew to the growing inner circle of "Natchez Nabobs," which Postlethwaite had entered through his marriage to Ann Dunbar.

Duncan cemented his place among the Natchez elite with his marriage to Margaret Ellis on 19 September 1811. Duncan used Ellis's dowry lands along the Homochitto River outside of Natchez to begin his career in planting and slave owning, which soon trumped his career in medicine. The couple had two children before Margaret Duncan died of yellow fever in 1815. On 25 May 1819, Stephen Duncan married Catharine A. Bingaman, whose family helped constitute the core of the Natchez elite. In 1820 they moved into Auburn, an architecturally significant home on the outskirts of Natchez, where

they raised their five children. (Duncan's children from his previous marriage lived with relatives.) Though Auburn was considered the family's main residence, they annually spent early summer through late fall visiting friends and family in Pennsylvania, Rhode Island, and New York. Duncan's significant social, familial, and business ties in the Northeast eventually prompted him to purchase a three-story townhouse in Washington Square in New York City.

In one generation, Duncan created an economic empire built on a variety of entrepreneurial pursuits, among which slave owning and agriculture played an important role, catapulting him to the highest echelons of the mid-nineteenth-century American elite. By the eve of the Civil War, Duncan enslaved more than twenty-two hundred men, women, and children on more than fifteen cotton and sugar plantations in Mississippi and Louisiana. The harsh labor regimen on the Duncan plantations produced an extraordinary amount of cotton and sugar, and these cash crops provided Duncan with great liquidity that allowed him to survive economic disasters. In 1860, Duncan was worth at least $3.5 million, about half of that amount in slaves.

Though much of his fortune was built on the back of slave labor, he also had railroad, lumber, and shipping interests in Mississippi as well as the Northeast. However, banking provided another cornerstone of his financial empire. When Samuel Postlethwaite died in 1825, Duncan assumed his uncle's role as president of the Bank of the State of Mississippi, remaining in that position until the bank's demise in 1844. Until 1833 the bank constituted the state's only financial institution. At that point Duncan and his associates liquidated most of the bank's funds and created the Agricultural Bank. Duncan's new "pet bank" received federal deposits in the wake of Pres. Andrew Jackson's veto of the Bank of the United States, an irony not lost on those involved in Mississippi politics: Duncan was a rabid anti-Jacksonian.

In politics, Duncan identified as a National Republican and later a Whig. Representing Adams County at the 1832 Mississippi constitutional convention, he scoffed at the idea of Jacksonian democracy. Duncan also became involved in the presidential campaigns of John Quincy Adams and Henry Clay, and upper-level Whigs considered Duncan a potential candidate for secretary of the treasury if the Whigs prevailed in the 1852 presidential contest. As a Whig, Duncan believed in a national economy bolstered by high tariffs, a policy that many southerners and slave owners rejected. However, Duncan argued that tariffs would protect the southern economy by producing revenue that could then be used to transport surplus slave labor outside of the United States. According to Duncan, a plan of gradual emancipation and colonization would simultaneously address economic and racial concerns by limiting the danger of crop overproduction and reducing white fears about an increasing slave population. In 1831 Duncan and other large planters formed the Mississippi Colonization Society, and he served as the society's president from its inception until the late 1840s, when he resigned over financial and political disagreements with both the state society and the national parent organization, the American Colonization Society. In spite of the dissension, Duncan was elected vice president of the American Colonization Society in 1836 and appointed as a life director in 1858. For all Duncan's involvement in colonization, no evidence indicates that he emancipated any of those he enslaved.

Duncan's involvement in the community stretched beyond politics and included philanthropic efforts and institution building in the Natchez area. Shortly after his arrival, he became manager of the elite Natchez Dancing Assemblies. In the 1820s he launched a campaign to build Trinity Episcopal Church, and he served as its treasurer from 1822 to 1826. He also lobbied the federal government to donate land to Oakland College and served as a trustee of Jefferson College from 1830 to 1840.

As secession approached, Duncan first sided with the southern cause and accused the North of trampling on private property rights. Following secession, Duncan blamed the South for triggering war. He eventually concluded that both sides bore responsibility. Throughout the Civil War period, Duncan remained a staunch unionist, and in 1863 he moved permanently to his New York home, where he remained until he died of natural causes on 29 January 1867. He is buried in Laurel Hill Cemetery in Philadelphia.

Martha Jane Brazy
University of South Alabama

Martha Jane Brazy, *An American Planter: Stephen Duncan of Antebellum Natchez and New York* (2006); D. Clayton James, *Antebellum Natchez* (1968); Noel L. Polk, ed., *Natchez before 1830* (1989); Morton Rothstein, in *Entrepreneurs in Cultural Context*, ed. Sydney M. Greenfield et al. (1979); Morton Rothstein, in *Essays in Honor of Arthur C. Cole*, ed. Hans L. Trefousse (1977); William Scarborough, *Masters of the Big House: Elite Slaveholders of the Mid-Nineteenth-Century South* (2003).

Dunlap, William
(b. 1944) Artist

William Dunlap was raised in Webster County and earned a bachelor's degree from Mississippi College in 1967 and a master of fine arts degree from the University of Mississippi two years later. He taught at North Carolina's Appalachian State University from 1970 to 1979 and at Memphis State University in Tennessee in 1979–80. He subsequently moved to the Washington, D.C., area, and now maintains studios in Mathiston, Mississippi; McLean, Virginia; and

Coral Gables, Florida. His subject matter covers landscape, history, and memory, and in addition to working with traditional materials, he borrows from photography and from the Old Masters, incorporates found objects, and makes reference to art history and criticism. To understand his work, he says, "Read the Bible. Genesis and the Book of Revelation might hold a clue." It also helps to know something about art history, southern history and literature, and the American landscape tradition. Dunlap evokes all of these in his oeuvre, which he sometimes terms "hypothetical realism."

Dunlap's work is varied—coral-tinged Delta sunsets; large, found-object constructions with punning, postmodern titles (often incorporating paintings); a fourteen-canvas 112-foot cyclorama created for the rotunda of the Corcoran Gallery of Art in Washington, D.C., that depicts the Shenandoah Valley in the summer and Antietam battlefield in the winter. He also has worked on a serial portrait of Gore Vidal in both clay and bronze. Though his many works might not look as if they all came from the hand of one artist, viewers with an eye for detail will be able to spot continuity. Despite varying techniques, themes emerge: the body of a modern-day St. Sebastian, Sergeant Wylliams, on the verge of returning to the earth; Dunlap's favorite hunting dog, a Walker hound; Rembrandt and his son, Titus; blooming irises; arrows and arrowheads (both death-dealing instruments and enduring reminders of people long gone); the changing of seasons and the cycles of the earth.

Dunlap also wants to demystify the art-making process and the idea of the pristine art object: grids, splatters, and drips remain on his paintings as records of the work's creation; old snakeskins in various stages of decay appear in several works; and found objects as prosaic as an old mailbox become cornerstones of assemblages. His body of work has an immediate visual impact but also bears closer scrutiny and considered meditation.

Dunlap has lived outside of Mississippi for many years but has always maintained ties to his home place. He frequently returns to Mathiston, remains involved as a University of Mississippi alumnus, and continues to exhibit in Laurel, Jackson, and Oxford. He received the Mississippi Governor's Award for Excellence in the Arts in 1991 and served as master of ceremonies of the awards gala for several years. He is a three-time winner of the Mississippi Institute of Arts and Letters awards. Dunlap's work can be found in major national museums such as the Metropolitan Museum of Art in New York City, in prominent galleries around the country, and in all of Mississippi's major museums, including the Lauren Rogers Museum of Art, the Mississippi Museum of Art, and the Museums of the University of Mississippi. In addition to his work as an artist, Dunlap occasionally works as an art critic and commentator and is a renowned raconteur.

Jill R. Chancey
Nicholls State University

Ruth Stevens Appelhof, *William Dunlap: Re-Constructed Re-Collections* Exhibition Catalog, Art Museum of Western Virginia (1992); William Dunlap, *Dunlap* (2006); William Dunlap website, www.williamdunlap .com; Mary Lynn Kotz, *Museum and Arts Washington* (March–April 1989); Barbara Rose, *In the Spirit of the Land* Exhibition Catalog, Corcoran Gallery of Art (1995).

Dupree, Marcus
(b. 1964) Athlete

Marcus Dupree with his mother at a press conference, 19 October 1983 (McCain Library and Archives, University of Southern Mississippi)

Marcus Dupree was born on 22 May 1964, in Philadelphia, Neshoba County. He achieved national attention as a running back at Philadelphia High School, where he gained 5,283 rushing yards and scored a national record eighty-seven touchdowns from 1978 to 1981. Coaches from the most storied college football programs in the country recruited Dupree, and he chose to attend the University of Oklahoma. Mississippi-born author Willie Morris captured the excitement of Dupree's final high school season and the fervor surrounding his recruitment in *The Courting of Marcus Dupree* (1983), which argued that Dupree's gridiron performance created a bond between whites and blacks in racially polarized Philadelphia. Morris described Dupree's high school ability and his potential for future greatness as the "Marcus Legend."

As a freshman at Oklahoma, Dupree did not start until his seventh game but still rushed for 1,144 yards. His breakout performance came during his sophomore year at the 1983 Fiesta Bowl, where he ran for 239 yards and won the game's Most Valuable Player Award despite leaving the contest early in the third quarter with an injury. The effort established a school record for rushing yards in a bowl game.

Because of his turbulent relationship with Oklahoma coach Barry Switzer, Dupree transferred to the University of Southern Mississippi before his sophomore season ended. However, he never played a down for Southern Miss and entered the experimental United States Football League in 1984. Dupree rushed for 684 yards and nine touchdowns as a rookie for the New Orleans Breakers but suffered a devastating knee injury in his initial season. Similar injuries plagued the remainder of Dupree's career. He was drafted in 1986 by the National Football League's Los Angeles Rams and finally made it to the league in 1990, carrying the ball sixty-eight times for 251 yards and two touchdowns over two seasons. After his retirement from football, Dupree worked as a professional wrestler, general manager of an Arena Football League team, and a scout for the Washington Redskins. In 2010 Dupree was the subject of an ESPN documentary, *The Best That Never Was*. He is still best known for the athleticism and seemingly limitless potential that he demonstrated at Philadelphia High.

J. Michael Butler
Flagler College

Jonathan Hock, *The Best that Never Was* (2010, Documentary); Willie Morris, *The Courting of Marcus Dupree* (1983).

E

Earthquakes

The area that is now Mississippi has a recorded earthquake history spanning more than three hundred years. The earliest documented earthquake occurred on Christmas Day 1699. Fr. J. F. Buisson St. Cosme, a French missionary, was camped along the Mississippi River below the site of Memphis when he and the rest of his party felt an earthquake. The Mississippi Territory also felt the effects of an 1811–12 series of earthquakes on deeply buried faults in the New Madrid Seismic Zone, which includes northeastern Arkansas, western Tennessee, and southeastern Missouri. Main shocks occurred on 16 December 1811, 23 January 1812, and 7 February 1812, with thousands of aftershocks. These earthquakes shook most of the United States, caused sand blows and bank sloughing in the epicentral area, and created Reelfoot Lake in northwestern Tennessee. Winthrop Sargent, first governor of the Mississippi Territory, felt the main shocks at his home near Natchez, where furniture was jarred, dishes rattled, and water sloshed in cisterns.

About one-fifth of the nearly fifty earthquakes known to have occurred in Mississippi could not be felt by humans and were detected only by instruments. The earliest earthquake with a Mississippi epicenter took place on 11 September 1853 and shook houses and alarmed inhabitants of Biloxi. The strongest earthquake in Mississippi occurred on 16 December 1931 in the Batesville-Charleston area (estimated magnitude 4.7 on the Richter scale). It was felt over sixty-five thousand square miles in northern Mississippi and parts of Alabama, Arkansas, and Tennessee. The maximum intensity of VI–VII (on the Modified Mercalli Intensity scale, which describes the effects of shaking on the ground and structures) was felt at Charleston, where walls cracked and chimneys collapsed; intensity VI damage to plaster and chimneys occurred at Belzoni, Tillatoba, and Water Valley. The second-strongest event was on 4 June 1967, when an intensity VI (magnitude 3.8) earthquake located northeast of Greenville was felt over twenty-five-thousand square miles in Mississippi, Arkansas, Louisiana, and Tennessee. The third-strongest earthquake, on 1 February 1955, was centered at Gulfport, had an intensity of V, and was felt along the Mississippi coast from Biloxi to Bay St. Louis.

Earthquakes have occurred throughout Mississippi from the northeast corner to the coast but have clustered in northwestern Mississippi, perhaps related to the New Madrid Seismic Zone or the White River Fault Zone. Several earthquakes occurred in Clarke County in the 1970s, along the Pickens-Gilbertown Fault Zone, possibly related to oil and gas activity.

An earthquake need not be located within the state to affect Mississippi. Earthquakes have occurred in all neighboring states and in the Gulf of Mexico. Various quakes have been felt in Mississippi, as have the 31 August 1886 earthquake near Charleston, South Carolina, which rocked the Vicksburg City Hall; the 31 October 1895 Charleston, Missouri, event, which was felt in most of Mississippi; the 27 March 1964 Alaska earthquake, which was detected by water-level instruments in wells in Mississippi; and the 24 March 1976 earthquake in northeastern Arkansas, which was felt across northern Mississippi.

The greatest risk to Mississippi from earthquakes is a recurrence of a strong earthquake in the New Madrid Seismic Zone. An earthquake of magnitude 7.6 (perhaps less strong than the main events of the 1811–12 series), if located at the southern end of the zone, would be felt throughout Mississippi and would cause damage in the northern part of the state. Unreinforced masonry buildings, bridges, chimneys, and other such structures would be most vulnerable. A strong earthquake in the New Madrid Seismic Zone could cause widespread destruction from Memphis to St. Louis, require a massive emergency response, and disrupt economic activity in the center of the country. Mississippi has plans for response to an earthquake disaster and could serve as a staging area for communities in more strongly affected states. Mississippi is one of eight states around the New Madrid Seismic Zone that have joined together to form the Central United States Earthquake Consortium, a Memphis-based organization that includes emergency management directors as well as state geologists and transportation officials.

Michael B. E. Bograd
Office of Geology, Mississippi
Department of Environmental
Quality

Michael B. E. Bograd, *Earthquakes in Mississippi*, Mississippi Office of Geology, Fact Sheet 1 (June 2008); B. C. Moneymaker, *Journal of the Tennessee Academy of Science* (July 1954); Winthrop Sargent, *Memoirs of the American Academy of Arts and Sciences* (1814).

East, Charles
(1924–2009) Author and Editor

Author and editor Charles East was born 11 December 1924 in Shelby, Mississippi. The son of Elmo Montan East and Mabel Grandolph East, he married Sarah Simmons of Cleveland. After graduation from Louisiana State University, the couple moved to New York City, where East began his career as an editorial assistant for *Collier's* magazine. He went on to publish numerous short stories and nonfiction in such literary quarterlies as the *Yale Review*, *Antioch Review*, and *Virginia Quarterly Review*. While working as an editor at the Louisiana State University Press and the University of Georgia Press, he helped establish their fiction publishing programs.

Between 1981 and 2001, East served as editor of the annual Flannery O'Connor Award for Short Fiction series, which has been called the most important collection of contemporary short fiction. East selected the stories to be included in *Listening to the Voices: Stories from the Flannery O'Connor Award* (1998), which has been hailed as an invaluable contribution to the American short story.

East's first collection of his own writings, *Where the Music Was: Stories* (1965), received the Henry Bellaman Award. East paints a picture of the South in the 1930s and 1940s, often with alienated characters or those just outside the mainstream of acceptable norms. His second short story collection, *Distant Friends and Intimate Strangers* (1996), told of a South with sensibilities more universal than regional.

East also published a meticulously edited and annotated edition of *The Civil War Diary of Sarah Morgan* (1991). According to East, Morgan's story was "a life's lesson learned in the most terrible way—compounded into the span of a war instead of a lifetime."

East counted his Mississippi Delta upbringing and education as a godsend to him as a writer. In his introduction to *The New Writers of the South: A Fiction Anthology* (1987), he defined southern writers by where they lived in their early years, when they are "listening to the sound of voices, surrounded by the quirks and myths and lies that will shape [their] view of human history and that, though [they do] not know it yet, will in some mysterious way infuse [their] characters."

East died in Baton Rouge, Louisiana, in 2009.

Augusta Scattergood
St. Petersburg, Florida

Charles East, *Sewanee Review* (Summer 1999); Charles East, ed., *The Flannery O'Connor Award: Selected Stories* (1992); Charles East, e-mail interview by Augusta Scattergood (May 2004).

East, P. D., and the *Petal Paper*

P. D. East and the *Petal Paper* followed in the tradition of the satirical personal essayist and pamphleteer. East's iconoclastic style was more akin to that of his North Carolina contemporary and supporter, Harry Golden, and his *Carolina Israelite* than to the community newspaper conventions of mid-twentieth-century American journalism. The *Petal Paper*'s prickly barbs and satirical bombasts aimed at small-town segregationists, the Citizens' Council, and the Ku Klux Klan were so successful that the paper lost all its local subscribers and only barely survived with the support of a national audience.

Percy Dale East was born on 21 November 1921 in Columbia, Mississippi, and was adopted by James and Bertie East five days later. The Easts labored in Piney Woods lumber camps south of Hattiesburg, his father as a manual laborer and his mother as a boardinghouse operator. East was a lackluster student, spending "five years on what should have been a three-year job" to earn a high school diploma. Formal higher education included one semester at Pearl River Community College and a few courses at Mississippi Southern College (now the University of Southern Mississippi).

East worked briefly for Greyhound Bus Lines in Hattiesburg before becoming a ticket clerk for the Southern Railway System. He was drafted into the US Army in December 1942 but discharged a year later as "temperamentally unsuited for the rigid discipline demanded by the military." He returned to the Southern Railway System until July 1951, when he became editor of the *Union Review* and *Local Advocate*, labor union newspapers in Hattiesburg. East sought a livelihood as a full-time weekly newspaper publisher in Petal, across the Leaf River from Hattiesburg, by following the editorial formula "Love American Motherhood and Hate Sin." The *Petal Paper*'s inaugural edition appeared on 19 November 1953, with six pages and thirty-nine advertisements "designed to keep everyone happy." His first year was profitable, but a November 1954 editorial opposing a constitutional amendment to allow the state legislature to abolish the public school system in the event of integration brought the happy days to an end.

In the following months, East unleashed a barrage of screwball satire to ridicule segregation, white supremacy, and massive resistance to integration. He advocated replacing the magnolia as the state symbol with the crawfish because the crawfish's idea of progress was to move "backward toward the mud from which he came." East lampooned Mississippi's US senator James O. Eastland as "Our Jungle Gem." One satirical editorial described St. Peter interrogating blacks at the entrance to heaven. Another editorial addressed to Bible Belt Brethren translated the King James Version of the Bible into the Dixiecrat tongue: "'And he took the DIXIE CUPS, and gave thanks that they were SEPARATE BUT EQUAL, and said, Take this MINT JULEP and divide it among yourselves.' Dixiecrat Luke 22:17." East castigated the Citizens' Councils and Ku Klux Klan as the "Bigger and Better Bigots Bureau." A "news story" reprinted the text of a speech by the Honorable Jefferson D. Dixiecrat to the Mississippi Chapter of the Professional Southerners Club, extolling its progress in keeping blacks from voting.

The *Petal Paper*'s most legendary broadside took the form of a March 1956 full-page advertisement with a caricature of a mule proclaiming, "Yes, You too, can be SUPERIOR, Join the Glorious Citizens Clan Next Thursday Night!" For only five dollars, "Citizens Clan" members received ten freedoms, including "Freedom to yell 'N——' as much as you please without your conscience bothering you!" and "Freedom to be superior without brain, character, or principle!" A note at the bottom of the page declared, "This Page in Behalf of Liberalism, Fairness and Progress Donated by *The Petal Paper*." Known as the "jackass" advertisement, it was reprinted in the *Reporter* (March 1957) and *Harper's* (January 1959) and by East's account had appeared in all fifty states, Canada, Japan, Ireland, Australia, France, Italy, and Germany.

By November 1956 wholesale cancellations of local advertising and subscriptions left the *Petal Paper* struggling along on out-of-state subscriptions and donations. "Friends of P. D. East" mustered financial and moral support from Steve Allen, Harry Belafonte, Harry Golden, John Howard Griffin, and Eleanor Roosevelt, generating five thousand dollars in 1959. A year later, *Louisville Courier-Journal* editor Mark Ethridge, a native Mississippian who had encouraged East to write about race, remarked that "his paper is a hobby now rather than a business." Royalties from East's memoir provided a brief financial respite, but the *Petal Paper*, already appearing irregularly, continued only sporadically after East relocated to Fairhope, Alabama, in 1963 to escape threats and harassment. By 1968, he had accrued debts totaling twenty-five thousand dollars.

"The loner of the civil rights movement," East died of liver failure in Fairhope on 31 December 1971. His memoir, *The Magnolia Jungle: The Life, Times, and Education of a Southern Editor* (1960), ended with a fitting epitaph: "His beloved Magnolia Jungle needed a path. It needed clearing. Let it be said of P. D. East: With his heart and his hatchet he hacked like hell!"

Arthur J. Kaul
University of Southern Mississippi

P. D. East Collection, McCain Library and Archives, University of Southern Mississippi; John Howard Griffin, *Black Like Me* (1961); Gary Huey, *Rebel with a Cause: P. D. East, Southern Liberalism, and the Civil Rights Movement, 1953–1971* (1985).

Eastland, James O.

(1904–1986) Politician

Known as the Godfather of Mississippi Politics, James Oliver Eastland was one of the leaders of the massive resistance movement during the 1950s and 1960s. Eastland was born on 28 November 1904 in Doddsville, a small town in the Mississippi Delta. A year later the family moved to Forest, in the hilly eastern part of the state, where James's father, Woods Eastland, ran a personal injury law practice. Woods also owned a large plantation in the Delta. In 1911 he was elected district attorney, and both his influence and his political network grew. One of his friends was Paul B. Johnson Sr., who served as governor of Mississippi from 1940 to 1943. This friendship proved instrumental in James Eastland's rise to political prominence.

After attending public schools in Forest, James Eastland studied at the University of Mississippi (1922–24), Vanderbilt University (1925–26), and the University of Alabama (1926–27). He was admitted to the bar in 1927 and briefly practiced law before winning election to the Mississippi House of Representatives in 1928. During his four years there, he supported the populist agenda of Gov. Theodore G. Bilbo. Retiring from state politics, Eastland married Elizabeth Coleman in 1932 and returned to Doddsville two years later to help his father manage the family farm. James Eastland also opened a law firm in nearby Ruleville.

When US senator Pat Harrison died in office on 22 June 1941, Johnson had to appoint a successor until a special election could be held to fill the seat for the last eighteen months of Harrison's term. Johnson initially offered the post to Woods Eastland, but he declined and suggested his

James O. Eastland, 1946 (Library of Congress, Washington, D.C. [LC-USZ62-109670])

son. James Eastland served for three months, aggressively defending cotton planters' interests. He did not participate in the special election but defeated Wall Doxey to win the seat during the regular 1942 Democratic primary, which in practice served as the general election in one-party Mississippi. Eastland's victory resulted largely from his accomplishments in the Senate, his roots in the Delta and in the Mississippi hill country, and his father's network of political friends.

James Eastland entered national politics at the dawn of the civil rights struggle. In the decades following World War II, the planter-politician from Mississippi became a vocal opponent of racial equality. In 1948 Eastland bolted from the Democratic Party after it adopted a strong civil rights plank at its national convention. Together with Mississippi's other senator, John Stennis, Eastland was one of the few national politicians who openly supported the States' Rights Party (the Dixiecrats). Eastland ran unopposed in 1948 but faced racial moderate Carroll Gartin in the 1954 Democratic primary. Eastland secured his victory by portraying himself as a champion of white supremacy, a popular position in Mississippi in the wake of the Supreme Court's May 1954 *Brown v. Board of Education* decision. Eastland took seventy of the state's eighty-two counties.

Eastland's reputation as the guardian of the Old South grew over the next two decades as he used his position as chair to make the Senate Judiciary Committee the "graveyard of civil rights legislation." He blocked more than one hundred civil rights measures before the Senate finally maneuvered around "the Chairman" and passed the Civil Rights Act of 1964 and the Voting Rights Act of 1965. Outside the South, Eastland was often not highly regarded, with New York senator Herbert Lehman describing his colleague from Mississippi as "a symbol of racism in America" and the Protestant Episcopal Diocese of New York accusing him of "subversion just as real and, because it comes from a U.S. Senator, far more dangerous than any perpetrated by the Communist Party." However, Massachusetts senator Ted Kennedy commended Eastland for the "scrupulously fair and even-handed manner in which he presided over a committee of so many diverse viewpoints with so many issues before it."

Eastland won reelection to the Senate five times but chose not to run again in 1978 when he realized that old age and a changed political culture would prevent him from winning a seventh term. Unlike Stennis, Eastland was not able to distance himself from his segregationist past, and civil rights activist Aaron Henry bluntly told the senator, "Your chances of getting support in the black community are poor at best. You have a master-servant philosophy with regard to blacks." After retiring, Eastland moved back to Mississippi and spent his last years at the family plantation in Doddsville. When asked shortly before his death whether he would be a different politician if he had to do it over again, Eastland paused before responding, "I voted my convictions on everything."

Eastland died on 19 February 1986. A US courthouse/post office building in Jackson was named in his honor, and the James O. Eastland Collection is available to researchers in the Department of Archives and Special Collections, J. D. Williams Library, University of Mississippi.

Maarten Zwiers
University of Groningen, the Netherlands

J. Lee Annis, *Big Jim Eastland: The Godfather of Mississippi* (2016) Chris Myers Asch, *The Senator and the Sharecropper: The Freedom Struggles of James O. Eastland and Fannie Lou Hamer* (2008); Joe Atkins, *Jackson Clarion-Ledger* (27 October 1985); Don Colburn, *James O. Eastland: Democratic Senator from Mississippi* (1972); J. Todd Moye, *Let the People Decide: Black Freedom and White Resistance Movements in Sunflower County, Mississippi, 1945–1986* (2004); Wolfgang Schlauch, *Journal of Mississippi History* (August 1972), Maarten Zwiers, *Senator James Eastland: Mississippi's Jim Crow Democrat* (2015).

Economic Development Strategies

Throughout the twentieth and into the twenty-first centuries Mississippi ranked at or near the bottom of most development criteria in the United States. As recently as 2010 Census Bureau data, for example, Mississippi ranked lowest in the country in median family income and highest in percentage of families in poverty. These dismal rankings have persisted despite the state's ongoing initiatives and remarkable creativity in the field of economic development. Indeed, Mississippi has stood at the forefront of many of the most significant innovations in US economic development over the past century.

Congress created the Tennessee Valley Authority (TVA), which included several Northeast Mississippi counties, in 1933. The TVA offered a pioneering model for comprehensive regional development, inspiring similar projects elsewhere in the United States and around the world. Two of the most prominent subsequent US federal regional development initiatives also included large areas of Mississippi: the Appalachian Regional Commission (1963) in the Northeast and the Delta Regional Authority (2000) in the northwest Delta and southwestern regions of the state.

As Congress was creating the TVA, the State of Mississippi was also pioneering a very different approach to economic development. The 1936 Balance Agriculture with Industry (BAWI) program initiated the use of publicly funded state incentives—such as industrial buildings and training programs—to attract private industrial investment. These techniques continue in Mississippi and in every other state despite criticism for the rapidly escalating costs of such programs and occasional disappointment with resulting jobs and other social benefits.

National enthusiasm for free enterprise in the 1980s resulted in a second wave of economic development initiatives that sought other means of stimulating private sector investment and job creation. The hallmark of this second wave was the enterprise zone, which offered special tax and other concessions to companies investing in targeted economically lagging regions. After considerable delay, the North Delta Mississippi Rural Enterprise Community (1994) became one of the country's first such federally designated zones.

The third wave of economic development in the 1990s emphasized network building among public and private entities and the creation of industrial clusters. An ideal industrial cluster is a dynamic mixture of regional industries, suppliers, consumers, technology, and trained workers. The dream of building thriving industrial clusters in Mississippi provided further justification for massive publicly funded incentives to attract automotive industries such as Nissan and Toyota. It remains to be seen whether such investments will result in the self-perpetuating industrial growth predicted by the cluster model as well as whether recent emphasis on technology- and cluster-based development in Mississippi will have a significant economic or social impact on the state's large population in poverty.

Mark M. Miller
University of Southern Mississippi

Appalachian Regional Commission website, www.arc.gov; T. K. Bradshaw and E. J. Blakely, *Economic Development Quarterly* (February 1999); James C. Cobb, *Selling the South: The Southern Crusade for Industrial Development, 1936–1990* (1993); Delta Regional Authority website, www.dra.gov; M. E. Porter, *Economic Development Quarterly* (February 2000); Tennessee Valley Authority website, www.tva.gov.

Edelman, Marian Wright

(b. 1939) Attorney and Activist

Children's rights activist and lawyer Marian Wright Edelman spent about five eventful years in Mississippi working on a variety of civil rights activities, especially involving the law, education, and poverty. She was the first African American woman to practice law in the state.

Marian Wright Edelman (Courtesy Centers for Disease Control and Prevention)

Born in 1939, Wright was named after opera singer Marian Anderson and grew up in Bennettsville, South Carolina, where her father was a Baptist preacher. An extraordinary student, she attended Spelman College in Atlanta and won fellowships to study in Europe and in Africa as part of a Peace Corps project. She earned a degree from Yale Law School in 1963 and then started "getting ready for Mississippi" with the aid of an Earl Warren Fellowship from the Legal Defense and Education Fund of the National Association for the Advancement of Colored People (NAACP).

Wright went to Greenwood as an NAACP activist in 1963 and immediately witnessed marches over the vote—complete with police officers using dogs against marchers—and controversies about food for the poor. What she saw solidified her decision to work in Mississippi as a lawyer. She moved to Jackson and opened an office on Farish Street, working for the Legal Defense and Education Fund. To gain access to Mississippi's courts, she registered as a law clerk with Jackson's only African American attorneys, R. Jess Brown, Carsie Hall, and Jack Young. When she first went into court in 1964, white lawyers and judges refused to shake her hand, and one Meridian judge angered her by making her sit next to the sheriff and deputy sheriff from Neshoba County, where civil rights workers James Chaney, Michael Schwerner, and Andrew Goodman had been murdered in the summer of that year. Her legal work involved both lawsuits over segregation and discrimination and defense work for activists sent to jail for taking part in protests. She became a member of the Mississippi bar in November 1965.

While in Mississippi, Wright also served on the executive committee of the Student Nonviolent Coordinating Committee and the legal advisory committee for the Council of Federated Organizations. She served on the boards of both the Delta Ministry and the Child Development Group of Mississippi, and she and Henry Aronson coauthored a pamphlet, *Your Welfare Rights*, that they distributed to poor people in the state. Her career blurs any lines scholars tend to draw between the NAACP and the Student Nonviolent Coordinating Committee, between legalistic and direct action protesters, and between insiders and outsiders.

She was particularly important in supporting the Child Development Group's Head Start work. She worried that the administrative style of the group's founder, Tom Levin, opened him up for criticism both from African Americans and whites in Mississippi and from federal authorities who wanted to ensure that the group was spending federal money in responsible and accountable ways. Wright tried to find a way to further the group's goals without alienating the federal government, in part by nominating John Mudd, a Harvard graduate who had worked briefly in Mississippi, as Levin's replacement.

Wright was awed by the men and women both inside and outside Mississippi whose efforts to change life in the state showed "the ability of determined people to resist and overcome evil through personal and collective will." However, she grew frustrated with the situation in the state, and the "continuing attack on Mississippi Head Start programs was one impetus for my moving to Washington in 1968."

In 1967 she testified before a US Senate committee about poverty in Mississippi. Committee member Robert Kennedy then contacted Wright to arrange a tour of impoverished areas in the Delta, and she used her knowledge and connections to show him areas around Greenville, Marks, and Cleveland. On that trip she met Kennedy's assistant, attorney Peter Edelman, whom she married in Virginia in 1968. The Edelmans, Kennedy, and Martin Luther King Jr. were leading figures in the Poor People's Campaign that began in 1968.

In 1973 Marian Wright Edelman organized the Washington-based Children's Defense Fund (CDF), and she has remained its president for more than forty years. The CDF uses lobbying, policy study, and training to highlight and address the problems of poor children, among them poverty, inadequate health care, educational deficiencies, child abuse and other violence, and juvenile justice. The organization also runs the Black Community Crusade for Children as well as a special initiative for children affected by Hurricane Katrina. The CDF's mission statement proclaims the goal of ensuring "every child a Healthy Start, a Head Start, a Fair Start, a Safe Start, and a Moral Start in life and successful passage to adulthood with the help of caring families and communities." Edelman coined the term "Leave No Child Behind," although despite the similarity of the phrase, she rarely agreed with the George W. Bush administration's "No Child Left Behind" efforts.

Edelman has received numerous awards, among them the Presidential Medal of Freedom and a MacArthur Foundation Fellowship. Institutes and buildings have been named in her honor. She has written numerous books that mix policy statements about protecting children with words of inspiration and advice.

Ted Ownby
University of Mississippi

Children's Defense Fund website, www.childrensdefense.org; John Dittmer, *Local People: The Struggle for Civil Rights in Mississippi* (1994); Marian Wright Edelman, *Families in Peril: An Agenda for Social Change* (The W. E. B. Du Bois Lectures) (1989); Marian Wright Edelman, *Lanterns: A Memoir of Mentors* (2000); Marian Wright Edelman, *The Measure of Our Success: A Letter to My Children and Yours* (1993); Polly Greenberg, *The Devil Has Slippery Shoes* (1969); Mississippi Department of Archives and History, Sovereignty Commission Online website, http://mdah.state.ms.us/arrec/digital_archives/sovcom/; Mark Newman, *Divine Agitators: Delta Ministry and Civil Rights in Mississippi* (2004); Marian Wright, Henry Aronson, and John Mudd, *New South* (Winter 1966).

Edmondson, Belle

(1840–1873) Diarist and Confederate Smuggler

Belle Edmondson is famous for smuggling goods and information through Union lines around Memphis during the Civil War. Born into a large family in Pontotoc, Mississippi, in 1840, she moved with her family to Holly Springs in 1856, attending Franklin Female College, and then to Shelby County, Tennessee, in 1860. In 1862 she worked as a nurse, tending Confederate soldiers injured at Shiloh.

The diary Edmondson kept in 1863–64 reveals the tension between the everyday life of a young woman of some means and the new demands of wartime. On one hand, Edmondson recorded the typical activities in a fairly wealthy southern household—sewing and visiting, courting, praying and attending church, and dancing and playing cards. On the other hand, Edmondson recorded her support for the Confederacy, criticizing Union military men, discussing escaped slaves, and above all worrying about the safety of her family and friends. Religious and military discussions often intermingled: "I worship Jeff Davis and every Rebel in Dixie." The diary also offers intriguing information about wartime travel, as she was concerned about military forces, strangers, and the rising and falling of creeks and rivers. She mixed wartime hardships with the unhappiness of her personal life in a short tribute to the persistence of women: "We have had a miserable day. I am inclined to think woman can drink to the dregs any cup of trouble which is given her."

A few 1864 diary entries mention Edmondson's work smuggling contraband goods—clothing, items for Confederate uniforms, money, and letters—through Union lines in Memphis. In one, she noted that she had "brought a great deal through the lines this eve." On another occasion she pinned several articles of clothing inside her hoop skirt and "all my buttons, brass buttons, Money & c in my bosom." Union forces arrested some of her friends for smuggling in March 1864 and decided to arrest her later in the spring. Edmondson thus fled the Memphis area in favor of Waverley Plantation near Columbus.

Edmondson died in 1873.

Ted Ownby
University of Mississippi

Catherine Clinton, *Tara Revisited: Women, War, and the Plantation Legend* (1995); Belle Edmondson Diary, Southern Historical Collection, Wilson Library, University of North Carolina at Chapel Hill; Belle Edmondson, *A Lost Heroine of the Confederacy: The Diaries and Letters of Belle Edmondson*, ed. Loretta and William Galbraith (1990); Drew Gilpin Faust, *Mothers of Invention: Women of the Slaveholding South in the American Civil War* (1996); Elizabeth D. Leonard, *All the Daring of the Soldier: Women of the Civil War Armies* (1999).

Education

In an 1802 address to the Mississippi Territory's legislature, Gov. W. C. C. Claiborne spoke eloquently of the need for free schools: "The very preservation of Republican government depends upon the diffusion of knowledge among the body politic." He recommended the establishment of a system of public schools and a state university. The legislature responded by establishing Jefferson College in the territorial capital, Washington, six miles east of Natchez, but took no action on a system of free schools.

During the early years of statehood the only institutions that could be considered public schools were the township schools supported in part by the funds from Sixteenth Section Lands—the lands US policy set aside for the support of education. Franklin Academy, established at Columbus in 1821, was Mississippi's first public school supported by the revenue from Sixteenth Section Lands. Since that money was not sufficient to fully support the schools, most township schools charged some tuition.

The antebellum Mississippi government devoted little money to education. In 1846 Gov. Albert Gallatin Brown presented the legislature with a comprehensive educational package that called for the creation of a state superintendent of education and county school boards, the establishment of a uniform statewide public school system, and the enactment of a school tax. However, the measure that eventually passed did not establish a state superintendent and county school boards, and it allowed any county to exempt itself

Public school, Clarksdale, ca. 1915 (Ann Rayburn Paper Americana Collection, Department of Archives and Special Collections, J. D. Williams Library, University of Mississippi [rayburn_ann_36_04_001])

from the provisions of the law by a popular vote. Rather than establishing a direct school tax, which was very unpopular, the legislature paid for public schools with fees imposed on hawkers and street peddlers, pool halls, tenpin alleys, tippling houses and saloons, liquor stores, and "private houses of entertainment" as well as other unspecified fines. The permissive nature of the law, which vested school management in the local community, created a "bewildering maze" of separate school districts.

Mississippi's small farmers saw no compelling reason to spend any of their meager income on book learning, and antebellum artisans learned their craft through the apprenticeship system. Most farmers and craftsmen thus considered attending school a luxury for which they had neither time nor inclination. Wealthy Mississippians, in contrast, tended to send their children to private schools or to hire tutors. Historian Alma Pauline Foerster has argued that the southern gentry fostered the notion that free schools offered "a bounty to the indigent."

The most important circumstance that stymied the development of a state system of public schools was the attachment to place, the doctrine of local control, and the determination of the county oligarchies to run their own affairs without interference from the folks in the next county or from the state capital in Jackson. This sense of localism was prompted in part by travel conditions in antebellum Mississippi, where distances were measured not in miles but in days. In 1860 65 percent of the state's land mass was virgin forest, and Jackson was four days' journey from the state university in Oxford. Such conditions deepened the sense of place, and the attachment to local schools has remained very strong over the ensuing century and a half.

No public institution in antebellum Mississippi provided formal education to its slave population or free blacks. Mississippi was the only slave state that reported no free black children in school in 1850. Thomas Jones briefly conducted a school for "children of color" in Natchez, but it apparently closed after Jones was arrested for furnishing a forged pass to a slave. Although a state law prohibited the education of slaves, some slaves and free blacks managed to acquire rudimentary reading, writing, and mathematical skills.

The tension between church and state was a central theme in the early history of higher education in Mississippi. In 1811 the General Assembly of the Presbyterian Church declared that education was "the legitimate business of the church, rather than the state," and in 1818 a convention of evangelical ministers denounced authorities at Jefferson College for neglecting the religious instruction of their students. This attack severely damaged the college's public standing, and its enrollment steeply declined.

The board of trustees subsequently reorganized Jefferson College into a military academy. The cadets, some as young as five years old, displayed a "sartorial splendor" in their dashing uniforms at daily parades. Offering insight into the psychology of antebellum white Mississippians, the school's historian has written, "What southern boy would not thrill to the crack of musket shots, the smell of burning powder, and the clash of steel?"

In 1829 Gov. Gerard Brandon recommended that the Jefferson College Board of Trustees return its charter to the state so the legislature could establish a public university at a central location "more likely to meet with public patronage." Brandon also recommended that Mississippi Academy, a collegiate institution in Clinton, be designated the state university. The academy, like Jefferson College, was technically a state-supported institution, and in 1827 the legislature allocated part of the proceeds from an 1819 federal land grant to the academy. The enormous potential of that revenue encouraged the school's patrons to seek its designation as the state university. But Brandon could not persuade the legislature to create one state institution of higher learning at a central location.

Mississippi also had several other small private colleges, most prominently the University of Holly Springs, Sharon College in Madison County, Centenary College in Brandon, Semple Broaddus College in Centre Hill in DeSoto County, Jackson College in Jackson, and Oakland College in Claiborne County. All were small residential colleges with a closed classical curriculum. The Natchez College of Commerce and the Southern Scientific Institute, also located in Natchez, and the Chulahoma College and Commercial Institute in Marshall County were small and short-lived institutions that provided the rudiments of commercial and agricultural education.

Several women's colleges and academies also existed in antebellum Mississippi, most notably Elizabeth Female Academy in Natchez, the Female Collegiate Institute in Holly Springs, and Whitworth College in Brookhaven. The curriculum at the women's colleges combined the classics with other courses that collegiate officials considered appropriate for women students. According to a statement by the founders of Elizabeth Female Academy, "Female virtues relate to domestic more than public things. The education of females, therefore, should teach them to aspire to those virtues peculiar to their sex." Other educators, however, rejected such a limited view of women's intellectual capacity or interests. The president of Whitworth College believed "that the female is able to comprehend as the male" and conducted his school on that presumption.

Most of Mississippi's collegiate institutions were small denominational schools, and many members of the state's aristocracy sent their sons to college in the North or to Europe. But as the sectional crisis over slavery intensified, some Mississippians saw a danger in that tradition. Gov. Albert Gallatin Brown had long favored the founding of a state university for reasons that went beyond academics. "Those opposed to us in principle," he said, "can not safely be entrusted with the education of our sons." In response to this growing concern, the legislature founded the University of Mississippi, which opened on 6 November 1848 with eighty-three students. After Mississippi seceded, all but four of its students joined the Confederate Army, and the university, like most other Mississippi collegiate institutions, closed during the war.

The American Civil War is the central, crucial event in this nation's history. Nothing was ever the same again, certainly not in the South and in Mississippi, and one of that war's most significant legacies is Mississippi's public school system. After the emancipation of Mississippi's 436,631 slaves, the legislature established a public school system and provided scholarships to students at the University of Mississippi who agreed to teach in the new system. The legislature also established Alcorn Agricultural and Mechanical College, the first black land-grant college in the United States, and the State Normal School, a black teachers college at Holly Springs that remained in existence until 1904, when Governor James K. Vardaman, who opposed educating Mississippi's African American population, vetoed its state appropriation.

Mississippi's 1870 school law established a statewide system of free schools to be financed by a school tax and authorized school boards in counties and municipalities to build schools to meet local demands. The statute did not require public schools to be racially segregated, but racial demographics and public sentiment nevertheless resulted in separate schools for whites and African Americans. After the adoption of the 1890 constitution racial segregation in the public schools became a matter of both law and tradition. The dual system and the sparsely settled nature of the state's population resulted in the establishment of thousands of small schools in the closing decades of the nineteenth century.

In 1904 the state superintendent of education reported that the state had 4,188 rural white schools with an enrollment of 169,507 and 2,892 rural black schools with an enrollment of 205,601. The rural school year averaged 129 days. Like the antebellum common schools, most of the rural schools had just one room and did not group students by grade level. In addition to the rural school system, which was supervised by county officials, Mississippi had thirty-four town school districts supervised by municipal authorities, with a total enrollment of 29,796 white students and 18,837 black students. These schools divided students into grades and had a school year that averaged 165 days.

During the early twentieth century, with the advent of motorized transportation and the construction of hard-surface roads, Mississippi initiated a massive school consolidation program that eventually transformed the common school system. In 1910 the legislature authorized the consolidation of county schools and provided free transportation for enrolled students. After overcoming initial resistance generated by Mississippi's strong sense of localism, consolidation was enormously successful. By 1936 Mississippi had nearly a thousand rural schools with an enrollment of more than 200,000 students, 150,000 of whom were transported by school wagons and buses. More than four hundred teachers' homes had been constructed near the schools.

Most of the municipal separate school districts provided secondary education, and the 1910 legislation authorized county school boards to establish residential agricultural high schools to provide secondary education for rural students. Over the next decade, officials established fifty-one agricultural high schools across the state. A 1922 law then authorized the agricultural high schools to add the first two years of college to their curriculum. The Pearl River and Hinds County agricultural high schools immediately did so, becoming the state's first junior colleges. After World War II most of the junior colleges discontinued their high school classes and expanded their technical and vocational programs. In the 1970s the junior colleges tailored their course offerings to local needs and interests, and all but one are now known as community colleges. Mississippi's community college system is considered one of the best in the nation.

Even after three decades of massive consolidation, Mississippi still had 197 county and separate school districts and 4,921 attendance centers at the end of World War II, as well as eighteen white and three black agricultural high schools. The rising costs of public education, the demand for better schools, and the impending desegregation of Mississippi's dual system prompted wide support for the reorganization of public schools. The US Supreme Court's 1896 *Plessy v. Ferguson* ruling had permitted segregated educational facilities as long as they were "separate but equal." Beginning in the 1940s, the National Association for the Advancement of Colored People had spearheaded a legal campaign against segregation by pointing out the inequalities in southern black and white school systems. That campaign reached its climax with the Supreme Court's May 1954 decision in *Brown v. Board of Education*, which found that separate schools were inherently unequal. However, officials in Mississippi and other southern states hoped that they would be permitted to retain their segregated educational systems if

they undertook a major campaign to bring the schools for African American children into parity with the schools for white children.

As the ultimate safeguard against the integration of the public school system, however, on 21 December 1954 Mississippi voters voted by a margin of two to one in favor of a constitutional amendment authorizing the abolition of public schools if necessary to prevent their integration. In addition, the legislature rescinded the state's compulsory attendance law in 1956.

The first breach in Mississippi's wall of official school segregation occurred at the University of Mississippi in the fall of 1962. Following a night of rioting in which two people were killed, James Meredith was admitted to the university under a federal court order. Although the school's board had resisted the order for almost two years and Gov. Ross Barnett had threatened to close the institution, the Kennedy administration ultimately forced Mississippi's white power structure to abide by the court order. Following Meredith's admission to the University of Mississippi, the state's other institutions of higher learning integrated peacefully over the next several years.

Mississippi's K–12 schools had avoided integration for a decade after the *Brown* ruling, but passage of the Civil Rights Act of 1964 signaled that segregated schooling's days were numbered. Many state and local officials began to prepare for that inevitability, and integration gradually began to occur. In the spring of 1970 the state's dual, segregated school system was superseded by a unified, integrated system, and Mississippi's black and white children finally attended school together. Integration occurred more peacefully than most people had believed possible because classroom teachers and school officials focused on accepting rather than resisting the change and on the safety of the state's half a million schoolchildren.

Mississippi received significant infusions of federal funds from the National Defense Act of 1958 and the Elementary and Secondary Education Act of 1965. These funds provided a boon to the state's underfunded system just as the school curriculum was proliferating and extracurricular activities were burgeoning.

During the 1970s, under the leadership of Gov. William L. Waller, Mississippi public schools also benefited from a renewed emphasis on a more equitable use of Sixteenth Section funds, early childhood and adult education, better teacher pay, a more comprehensive system of accountability, and the reinstatement of compulsory education. The culmination of this growing popular support for public education was the ratification of a constitutional amendment creating an appointed state board of education with the authority to appoint the state superintendent. In addition, with the strong public support of the *Jackson Clarion-Ledger*, Gov. William F. Winter shepherded passage of the Education Reform Act of 1982 at a special December 1982 legislative session. The measure constituted what many consider the most comprehensive and most significant school law since the establishment of the public school system in 1870.

In 1992 the legislature passed another major education reform, the Education Enhancement Act, over the veto of Gov. Kirk Fordice. This law provided special funding to the state's public school system, community colleges, and institutions of higher learning to renovate and add facilities, to repair and add to Mississippi's aging fleet of school buses, and to upgrade school libraries.

By the early twenty-first century Mississippi's public school system included sixty-eight county school districts, eighty-one municipal separate school districts, and three agricultural high schools. The state also operates schools for the blind and the deaf as well as a math and science school and a high school for the arts. Public school enrollment was approximately five hundred thousand, with nearly thirty-six thousand classroom teachers earning an average annual salary of about forty thousand dollars.

The state's collegiate system included fifteen community colleges with thirty-three branch campuses and more than two hundred thousand students. Enrollment in the state's eight universities totaled approximately seventy thousand, with almost 80 percent receiving some form of student aid.

When Hurricane Katrina devastated the Mississippi Gulf Coast on 29 August 2005, it totally destroyed 16 schools schools along the coast and damaged another 24 as well as 263 schools further inland in South Mississippi. Recovering from the storm has been only one of the challenges facing Mississippi's educational system in the early twenty-first century. The state has made some major gains in improving education: for example, the annual dropout rate fell from 6.2 percent to 3.2 percent between 1995 and 2012, and the graduation rate for entering high school freshmen rose from 62.7 percent in 2002–3 to 68 percent in 2011–12. Moreover, between 2000 and 2013 Mississippi's students improved their fourth- and eighth-grade reading, writing, and mathematics scores on the standardized tests that are part of the National Assessment of Educational Progress (the Nation's Report Card). But Mississippians still trail the national averages on all of those tests, and graduation rates for Hispanic and African American children are lower than the rates for their white peers.

David G. Sansing
University of Mississippi

Charles C. Bolton, *The Hardest Deal of All: The Battle over School Integration in Mississippi, 1870–1980* (2005); Andrew P. Mullins, *Building Consensus: A History of the Passage of the Mississippi Education Reform Act of 1982* (1992); National Center for Education Statistics website, nces.ed.gov; David Sansing, *Making Haste Slowly: The Troubled History of Higher Education in Mississippi* (1990).

Education Enhancement Act of 1992

The Education Enhancement Act, passed by the Mississippi legislature during the 1992 regular session, augmented funding for public education through a 1 percent sales tax increase and an earmark on collected sales tax revenue. It was the first act in the state's history to earmark a tax increase specifically for public education.

The Education Enhancement Act sought to provide funding for facilities, equipment, utilities, land, textbooks, technology, instructional materials, and supplies. Whereas previous landmark Mississippi education legislation, such as the 1982 Education Reform Act, focused on directing funding toward traditional academic and curricular pursuits, the 1992 measure was intended to aid schools and institutions of higher learning in addressing facilities, overhead, and instructional needs. According to Andrew P. Mullins, assistant to the state superintendent of education at the time, while previous Mississippi education legislation was geared toward the traditional "Three Rs," the Education Enhancement Act addressed needs relating to the "Three Bs": buildings, buses, and books.

The act created the Education Enhancement Fund to collect and distribute money to Mississippi's various educational systems. The Mississippi Department of Education established guidelines for distributing this funding to the K–12 system, and the Board of Trustees of State Institutions of Higher Learning and the State Board of Community and Junior Colleges allocated funding for higher education.

The Education Enhancement Act reduced local ad valorem tax rates from 7 percent to 4 percent. Each month, 2.266 percent of the state's aggregate sales tax revenue collected is deposited into the School Ad Valorem Tax Reduction Fund until the amount totals forty-two million dollars. Any amount collected in excess of that figure is then deposited into the Education Enhancement Fund. The money deposited into the Education Enhancement Fund is generated by the 9.073 percent of total monthly sales tax revenue collected that is earmarked for that purpose.

Each fiscal year, sixteen million dollars from the Education Enhancement Fund is allocated to the Mississippi Department of Education to be distributed to the various school districts. Of the remaining funds, 16.61 percent is allocated to funding the Mississippi adequate education program, 7.97 percent is allocated for transportation operations and maintenance, and 9.61 percent is allocated for classroom supplies, instructional materials, and equipment. For higher education, 22.09 percent of the money is allocated to the Board of Trustees of State Institutions of Higher Learning to support Mississippi universities, and 14.41 percent is allocated to the State Board of Community and Junior Colleges.

Between fiscal year 1993 and fiscal year 2007, more than $4.1 billion was allocated to Mississippi schools, community colleges, and universities, with approximately 70 percent of that amount going to the K–12 schools, 17 percent to the state universities, and 13 percent to the community colleges. The state budget for fiscal year 2016 projects spending of more than $382 million from the fund, including $273 million for General Education Programs, $43.3 million for community colleges, and $65.5 million for the state universities.

Republican governor Kirk Fordice vetoed the Education Enhancement Act of 1992, characterizing it as a tax increase. In a rare move, however, the legislature overrode the veto. The legislature subsequently passed resolutions recognizing the leadership of House Speaker Pro Tempore Robert George Clark and House Speaker Tim Ford in obtaining legislative approval of the act.

Kerry Brian Melear
University of Mississippi

Karen S. Louis, Karen Febey, Molly Gordon, Judy Meath, and Emanda Thomas, *Educational Leadership in the States: A Cultural Analysis* (2006); Andrew P. Mullins Jr., *Building Consensus: A History of the Passage of the Mississippi Education Reform Act of 1982* (1992); Mississippi Institutions of Higher Learning, Office of Policy Research and Planning, *All Educational Appropriations, General and Education Enhancement Fund Appropriations, FY 1990–2007*; Mississippi Joint Legislative Budget Committee, *State of Mississippi Budget Bulletin, Fiscal Year 2016* (1 May 2015); Mississippi State Board of Education, *Rules and Regulations Regarding the Administration of Funds Appropriated for Education Enhancement Funds for Classroom Supplies and Materials* (2007).

Education Reform Act of 1982

For much of Mississippi's history, public elementary and secondary education in has often been substandard or practically nonexistent. In 1982, however, the state departed significantly from its usual approach to public education when the legislature passed landmark education reform, an effort that involved intense political maneuvering and an unprecedented campaign by the *Jackson Clarion-Ledger*.

The Mississippi Education Reform Act of 1982 established compulsory school attendance, created state-funded kindergartens, increased teacher pay, authorized the hiring of teaching assistants and truant officers, and implemented a statewide testing program for performance-based accreditation of public schools. The reforms were funded by increases in the state's sales tax and corporate and individual income taxes.

Prior to passage of the act, Mississippi's educational system received inadequate funding and was still reeling from conflict over integration. Many public officials expressed only tepid support at best for a system that had lost many white students to private segregated academies after the full desegregation of the public schools in 1971. Before 1982, for example,

- Mississippi was the only state without a public kindergarten program;
- only 45 percent of children who began first grade finished the twelfth grade;
- the state had the nation's second-highest illiteracy rate;
- about 10 percent of children did not attend school at all because of weak attendance laws;
- only one in twenty children attended preschool, compared to three out of four nationally;
- the armed forces rejected 35 percent of Mississippi applicants, nearly four times the national rejection rate of 9 percent.

Attorney and former state legislator William Winter had been elected governor in 1979 and made education reform the centerpiece of his legislative agenda. He created the Special Committee on Public School Finance and Administration "to develop programs 'that will produce the best possible educational system for the state.'"

After his education agenda stalled in the 1981 and 1982 regular legislative sessions, Winter mobilized public support for reform before calling a special legislative session in December. In addition to a public awareness campaign undertaken by his staff via a nonprofit group, Winter made 82 speeches between June and December to promote his proposals, while First Lady Elise Winter, his staff, and other officials made 362 additional speeches. Supporters of education reform also held nine regional town meetings to discuss the issue.

Winter's efforts picked up support from many of the state's newspapers, most prominently the *Jackson Clarion-Ledger*. In the weeks leading up to the special session, the paper published a series of investigative articles providing an overview of public education in Mississippi, gave extensive coverage to Winter's efforts to garner public support, and printed editorials calling for education reform. The paper also highlighted each step of the legislative process, including debates, committee meetings, negotiations, and discussions of funding.

Moving beyond usual legislative coverage, the *Clarion-Ledger* created a Hall of Shame, in which it spotlighted legislators who had voted against portions of the education reform bill. The reporting had an impact: according to Andrew P. Mullins Jr., "It was obvious from legislators' public and private comments that this kind of journalism, which had not been seen before, was devastatingly effective. Publicly criticizing individual members for their votes rather than the legislature collectively as had been the custom created a tremendous amount of pressure on lawmakers. The resulting constituent pressure influenced many of their votes." The *Clarion-Ledger*'s coverage of the issue received a 1983 Pulitzer Prize for Public Service.

On 20 December 1982 the bill passed both houses of the legislature after much debate and political wrangling. Winter, who said the bill represented "a break with the old do-nothing spirit of the past," signed it into law three days later.

The act has resulted in many improvements to Mississippi's educational system, although it continues to trail many other states. A 2002 study by the Mississippi Department of Education found that since 1982 the state had implemented uniform curricula in state schools and strengthened teacher certification and licensure programs. Statewide testing has demonstrated that students have made "slow but consistent progress, with test results inching up for the past several years." Mississippi's rate of high school completion increased by 8.6 percentage points between 1990 and 2000, and Mississippi's annual dropout rate fell from 6.2 percent to 3.2 percent between 1995 and 2012.

The Mississippi Education Reform Act of 1982 fundamentally changed the way state leaders approached education and provided a model for other states, many of which passed similar legislation in the years following Mississippi's action.

Ellen B. Meacham
University of Mississippi

Mississippi Department of Education, *Progress Report of the Mississippi Education Reform Act of 1982* (2002); Andrew P. Mullins Jr., *Building Consensus: A History of the Passage of the Mississippi Education Reform Act of 1982* (1992); National Center for Education Statistics website, nces.ed.gov; US Census website, census.gov; Kathleen Woodruff Wickham, *The Role of the "Clarion-Ledger" in the Adoption of the Mississippi Education Reform Act of 1982: Winning the Pulitzer Prize* (2007).

Edwards, David "Honeyboy"

(1915–2011) Blues Musician

Delta bluesman David "Honeyboy" Edwards has recently gained as much attention for his rich storytelling and the longevity of his life as for the blues he played for eight decades. In 1997 Chicago Review Press published his memoir, *The World Don't Owe Me Nothing*. Five years later Edwards appeared as the subject of a documentary film, *Honeyboy*, another critically acclaimed work that boosted

David "Honeyboy" Edwards, Clarksdale (Photograph by David Wharton)

the guitarist's reputation. Edwards's career extended into his nineties and carried him from the Delta towns of Mississippi to New Orleans, Memphis, Chicago, and abroad. During his early years in the South he ran in the same circles as and got to know the American blues elite—Charley Patton, Robert Johnson, Howlin' Wolf, Muddy Waters, and B. B. King. In the later years of his career he fattened his discography with studio and live recordings.

Edwards was born on 28 June 1915 in Shaw, Mississippi. He fled the rising waters of the Great Mississippi Flood of 1927, and in the fall of 1929, as the stock market collapsed and depression seized the country, his father bought him his first guitar (used, for eight dollars). At age seventeen, hurting for money but eager to avoid the hand-to-mouth existence of a sharecropper, Edwards took to the road as an apprentice to Big Joe Williams, hitching rides on trains, playing music on street corners and at house parties, hustling in dice games, and sometimes turning to admiring female fans for food and shelter. Edwards soon split from Williams and began to formulate a unique musical style, featuring acoustic guitar and a throaty, soulful voice. In the 1950s, having canvassed the South from Texas to Tennessee, Edwards joined the Great Migration north to Chicago. There he found regular work on the streets and in club venues, and he kept a home in the Windy City for the remainder of this life.

Edwards did not find the same success and renown as some of his contemporaries. In 1942 folklorist Alan Lomax tracked down Edwards in Clarksdale and recorded him for the Library of Congress. However, almost a decade passed before Edwards recorded again: under the name Mr. Honey, he cut a couple of records, "Who May Your Regular Be" and "Build a Cave," in Houston in 1951. Two years later he recorded several songs for Chicago's Chess Records, but they went unissued until "Drop Down Mama" surfaced in a 1970 anthology. It became his first hit single and was followed by "Sweet Home Chicago," "Long Tall Woman Blues," and "Just

Like Jesse James." In the 1970s he formed the Honeyboy Edwards Blues Band, and in the ensuing decades, he took to the studio more often: more than half of his recordings appeared after 1990. Edwards was inducted into the Blues Hall of Fame in 1996, and in 2002 the National Endowment for the Arts named him a National Heritage Fellow, in conjunction with which the Smithsonian Institution released an album, *Mississippi Delta Bluesman*. In 2010 Edwards won a Grammy Lifetime Achievement Award and a Mississippi Governor's Award for Excellence in the Arts.

"The last of the original Delta bluesmen" died of congestive heart failure on 29 August 2011 at his home in Chicago, having made his final public appearance at a Clarksdale blues festival the preceding April.

Hicks Wogan

New Orleans, Louisiana

David "Honeyboy" Edwards, *The World Don't Owe Me Nothing* (1997); Bill Friskics-Warren, *New York Times* (29 August 2011); Robert Palmer, *Deep Blues: A Musical and Cultural History of the Mississippi Delta* (1981); Scott L. Taradesh, *Honeyboy* (film, 2002).

Edwards, Teddy

(1924–2003) Jazz Musician

Teddy Edwards was one of the few successful jazz musicians from Mississippi. Living and playing mostly in Los Angeles, he made more than twenty jazz albums under his own name beginning in 1947 and performed on many others as a side musician.

The son and grandson of musicians, Theodore Edwards was born in Jackson in 1924 and started playing alto saxophone in jazz bands as a child. As part of the Great Migration, he moved to Detroit in 1940, playing as a professional with the Royal Mississippians. After touring in jazz bands he settled in Los Angeles in 1944, switched from alto to tenor saxophone, and joined Howard McGhee's band and became part of California's developing bebop scene. Edwards recalled the mid-1940s as "the most creative period in history because everything was at its highest tempo."

In the tradition of jazz cutting or soloing contests, Edwards made a reputation for trading extended improvisations with fellow musicians. Most famous was "The Duel," a 1947 bebop song that featured Edwards and fellow tenor saxophonist Dexter Gordon. For much of his career Edwards played in quintets and sextets with piano, bass, drums, and multiple horns. Edwards's best-known song was "Sunset Eyes," which he first recorded in 1954 as a member of a Clif-

ford Brown–Max Roach group. Five years later, Edwards released an album under that title. Edwards also played with Charlie Parker, Benny Carter, and Hampton Hawes, and his longest partnership paired him with Gerald Wilson, a trombonist and composer born in Shelby, Mississippi. A versatile jazz musician, Edwards performed as both a leader and session musician, and he was responsible for the music in at least two films.

Edwards's fans have often considered him underappreciated. Toward the end of his career, Edwards again began attracting attention both for the body of his work and for songs recorded with singer Tom Waits on a 1991 album, *Mississippi Lad*. Shortly before Edwards's death in 2003, *The Legend of Teddy Edwards*, a film biography, presented historical footage of Edwards and interviews with and about him.

Ted Ownby

University of Mississippi

Leonard Feather and Ira Gitler, *The Encyclopedia of Jazz in the Seventies* (1976); "A Fireside Chat with Teddy Edwards," *All About Jazz* website, www.allaboutjazz.com; Jean-Louis Ginibre, *Mississippi Lad* (1991), liner notes; *The Legend of Teddy Edwards* (2002).

Eggleston, William

(b. 1939) Photographer

Photographer William Eggleston, popularly known as the Father of Color Photography, was born on 27 July 1939 in Memphis, Tennessee. Raised on his family's plantation in Tallahatchie County, Mississippi, Eggleston attended classes at Vanderbilt, Delta State, and the University of Mississippi, though he never received a degree. While in school, Eggleston learned a great deal about modern art, particularly the abstract expressionists. He began photographing by 1957 and was soon inspired by the vision of photographers Robert Frank and Henri Cartier-Bresson.

Although his early work consisted of traditional black-and-white photography, by the late 1960s Eggleston shot almost exclusively with color transparency film. In contrast to Gary Winograd's confrontational street photography or Diane Arbus's studied portraits, Eggleston chose *literally* to photograph the world around him. It was as if he freed himself from photographic convention, eschewed the formulas of composition, and simply observed his environment. Images of worn shoes under a bed, a freezer brimming with packaged foods, and the interior of an oven epitomize Eggleston's curious and probing eye. Similarly arresting are his photos of the rural South. *Black Bayou Plantation, near Glendora, Mississippi* depicts white plastic containers that appear to have just spilled from a cardboard box across a dirt road. A portion of a wood structure appears at the right frame, beside which the road recedes into the sun-drenched landscape. As in many of Eggleston's images, there is a sense of something ominous afoot, as if calamity lurks just out of the frame.

In 1967 Eggleston traveled to New York and met Jon Szarkowski, director of the Department of Photography at the Museum of Modern Art, and the meeting led to a 1976 exhibition of Eggleston's work, the first one-person exhibition of color photographs in the museum's history and a watershed moment in photography. The vibrant images of seemingly banal subject matter both shocked and bewildered viewers. Eggleston's most arresting images are deceptively casual yet recklessly engaging in their ineffable sense of peril. *Untitled (Greenwood, Mississippi),* more popularly known as *The Red Ceiling,* is one of Eggleston's more celebrated images. From a garish red ceiling dangles a bare lightbulb from which the tendrils of white extension cords slither towards the walls of the room. "It is so powerful," Eggleston said of this photo, "that I have never seen it reproduced on the page to my satisfaction. When you look at the dye transfer print, it's like red blood that's wet on the wall. . . . It shocks you every time."

Perhaps it is no coincidence that Eggleston burst into the national consciousness as the South became increasingly urbanized. His images depict a region sliding ever closer to homogenization. "One of the first things that woke me up," Eggleston commented, "was walking into some alien place, a shopping center—one of the first ones in the country—and thinking, 'It's right here.'" Eggleston's juxtapositions of old money Delta interiors, newly constructed suburbs, and desolate rural landscapes suggest a land on the cusp of an uneasy transition. Furthermore, many of his environmental portraits are of individuals who appear to uneasily negotiate their personal spaces. A man leers sideways over his coffee cup; an elderly woman stares glumly from a household doorway, the room behind her both doleful and threatening. A restless anxiety pervades much of Eggleston's portraiture, as if the subjects themselves are wrestling with psychological turmoil.

In addition to exhibitions at major museums, Eggleston has published more than ten portfolios and numerous monographs, including *William Eggleston's Guide, Los Alamos, Ancient and Modern,* and *The Democratic Forest.* He is also the recipient of a National Endowment for the Arts Photographer's Fellowship and a Getty Images Lifetime Achievement Award.

Maury Gortemiller
Decatur, Georgia

Geoff Dyer, *The Ongoing Moment* (2005); William Eggleston, *Ancient and Modern* (1992); Richard Grant, *Telegraph* (29 June 2002); Charles Hagen and Nan Richardson, *Aperture* (Summer 1989); John Howell, *Aperture* (Winter 2001); Mary Werner Marien, *Photography: A Cultural History* (2006); Sean O'Hagan, *London Observer* (25 July 2004); Ingrid Sischy, *Art Forum* (February 1983); Constance Sullivan, ed., *Horses and Dogs: Photographs by William Eggleston* (1994).

Elder, William Henry

(1819–1904) Religious Leader

William Henry Elder was born on 22 March 1819 in Baltimore. His parents were commission merchant Basil Spalding Elder and Elizabeth Snowden Elder. He graduated from Mount St. Mary's College in Emmitsburg, Maryland, in 1837, and after a long period of further education, he was ordained a priest of the Roman Catholic Church on 29 March 1846. For the next ten years he served as a professor of theology at Mount St. Mary's.

In 1857 Elder was appointed bishop of the Diocese of Natchez, a small, isolated frontier diocese that covered the entire state of Mississippi and included eleven churches and five schools with twelve priests. He proved to be a talented organizer and administrator. Over the next twenty-three years, in spite of the tremendous disruption of the Civil War, he built a network of forty-eight churches and twenty-three schools supplemented by a handful of religious houses and supported by numerous associations and sodalities.

Elder began his work in the diocese with the 1859 completion of St. Mary's Cathedral in Natchez. From the beginning, he planned an ambitious program of building and growth. His efforts to carry out his plans were temporarily halted by the outbreak of the Civil War. He accepted secession as a duty to public order and the war as a fait accompli, but he did not believe his fellow Catholics should claim that the church officially sanctioned either. For example, he wrote to Catholic newspaper editor Napoléon-Joseph Perché, "It is not well for them to have the appearance of acting in a body as Catholics in sustaining any particular measure . . . urging on to steps that are most likely to lead to war." Nevertheless, he sent priests to serve as chaplains in the Confederate Army and Sisters of Mercy to nurse the sick and wounded, and he gave his blessing to a Natchez volunteer company.

In 1863 US forces seized Vicksburg and then occupied Natchez. Elder did not actively oppose the occupation, although he spoke with Confederate soldiers and bought a Confederate bond while making a circuit of his diocese, most of which remained outside Union lines. The following year, Col. Benjamin G. Farrar, a former student with Elder at Mount St. Mary's and now acting commander at Natchez, reissued an order that all local ministers should read a prayer for the elected officials of the US government, including the president, in Sunday services. When Elder refused, asserting that the order violated both church prerogative and the US Constitution, he was exiled across the Mississippi River to Vidalia, Louisiana. He was allowed to return seventeen days later without being required to read the prayer on the grounds that military authority had been sufficiently vindicated.

During Reconstruction, Elder helped guide the rebuilding and expansion of the Natchez Diocese. In 1878 a lethal yellow fever epidemic swept through Mississippi, straining the diocese's resources. Elder contracted the disease and almost died of the illness after his subordinates forced him to take charge of Catholic relief efforts in Vicksburg. He left the diocese in 1880 to become coadjutor and later sole archbishop of Cincinnati, a post he held until his death on 31 October 1904.

William Vaughan

Jackson, Mississippi

William Henry Elder, *Civil War Diary (1862–1865) of Bishop William Henry Elder, Bishop of Natchez* (1960); Richard Oliver Gerow, *Cradle Days of St. Mary's at Natchez* (1941); James L. Pillar, *The Catholic Church in Mississippi, 1837–1865* (1964); William Henry Elder Letterbooks, Archives of the Catholic Diocese of Jackson; *Sadlier's Catholic Almanac* (1881).

Elizabeth Female Academy

In the first decade of the nineteenth century, Washington, six miles from Natchez, was a thriving hamlet. The site of Mississippi's first territorial capital, Washington seemed to have a bright future, and its citizens saw the need for cultural and educational institutions that would reinforce its prominence and aid its growth. Having established Jefferson College in 1802, they turned to the instruction of girls, and Mississippi's first school for girls, Elizabeth Female Academy, opened its doors in 1818. Named for Elizabeth Greenfield Roach of Philadelphia, who donated land and a building, the school was granted a charter by the Mississippi legislature and run under the auspices of the Methodist Episcopal Church. While male presidents oversaw the school, daily operations lay in the sphere of the female principal.

Elizabeth Female Academy experienced its greatest success under the direction of Caroline Thayer, who arrived in 1825 and had published extensively on education topics. She took great interest in the educational theories and practices of the day and introduced to the school ideas such as Johann Pestalozzi's inductive learning and the use of monitors, advanced students who helped guide younger girls in their studies. Thayer attracted new students and oversaw the expansion of the school building during the 1820s.

At a time when many Mississippians continued to doubt the need for female education, Thayer and other educators at Elizabeth Female Academy held their students to rigorous academic standards in the belief that a strong academic education would benefit future wives and mothers. The curriculum included English grammar and composition, arithmetic, geography, American and ancient history, US government, natural and moral philosophy, botany, chemistry, astronomy, and Latin. Those who wished could also take lessons in French, drawing, and music. The school's directors took advantage of its close proximity to Jefferson College: girls could occasionally attend lectures given by professors at the college, and naturalist John James Audubon taught at both institutions. Elizabeth Female Academy's leaders also believed in regular exercise, which the school's rural location facilitated.

Although the charter granted by the Mississippi legislature stated that "no religious test or opinion shall be required of the pupils" and students of many different denominations attended, religion had a central place at Elizabeth Female Academy. Most presidents were also Methodist clergymen who saw training pious Methodist women as one of their central goals. Boarding students attended prayer services twice each day, and all students were expected to adhere to rules such as those that required plain dress and banned dancing.

Elizabeth Female Academy closed in 1848. Natchez's growth and development during the period after statehood had been mirrored by a sharp decline in Washington's size and importance. As Natchez grew, more and more girls' academies opened there, attracting not only city dwellers but also the rural residents of Adams County who had been Elizabeth Female Academy's primary student base. The property passed back to Elizabeth Greenfield Roach's heirs.

Julia Huston Nguyen

Washington, D.C.

Claribel Drake, *Daughters of the American Revolution Magazine* (May 1962); Charles B. Galloway, in *Publications of the Mississippi Historical Society*, vol. 2, ed. Franklin L. Riley (1899); John G. Jones, *A Complete History of Methodism as Connected with the Mississippi Conference of the Methodist Episcopal Church, South*, vol. 2 (1908); Edward Mayes, *A History of Education in Mississippi* (1970); Julia Huston Nguyen, "Molding the Minds of the South: Education in Natchez, 1817–1861" (master's thesis, Louisiana State University, 1997).

Ellicott, Andrew

(1754–1820) Surveyor

Andrew Ellicott was a skilled mathematician, inventor, and engineer who achieved his greatest fame as a surveyor. Born on 27 January 1754 in Pennsylvania to a Quaker family, Ellicott grew up studying science and its practical uses. He eventually brought his skills to the Deep South and helped the Natchez area become a part of the United States.

Ellicott spent most of his forty-plus years of service to the country determining important boundaries. He finished Charles Mason and Jeremiah Dixon's work of defining the boundary between Virginia and Pennsylvania—the famous Mason-Dixon Line. He also established the line between New York and Pennsylvania and helped settle a border dispute between Georgia and North Carolina. His exact measurements and attention to detail were all the more remarkable considering that most of his instruments were handmade. Ellicott was the first to record the height of Niagara Falls, superintended the construction of Pennsylvania's Fort Erie, and helped establish the town there. Perhaps most important, he surveyed Washington, D.C., and helped plan for the nation's new capital. In 1792 he was appointed surveyor general of the United States.

Diplomatic events brought Ellicott to the Mississippi Valley. On 27 October 1795 the United States and Spain signed the Treaty of San Lorenzo, also known as Pinckney's Treaty, which granted the United States the free usage of the Mississippi River and set the thirty-first parallel as the northern boundary of Spanish Florida, transferring the Natchez District to the young nation. Soon thereafter, Pres. George Washington appointed Ellicott as commissioner to meet with a Spanish counterpart to set the boundary.

Ellicott arrived in Natchez in February 1797. A strong proponent of American expansion, he immediately pressed Spanish governor Manuel Gayoso de Lemos on when operations would begin. Ellicott further heightened tensions when he defiantly raised an American flag at his encampment.

For more than a year, the Spanish delayed their evacuation from the territory, hoping the treaty would become invalid. Ellicott was caught in a delicate situation, wanting to press the Spanish to follow through on the terms of the treaty yet not wanting to ally himself with the region's residents who wanted to physically oust the Spanish. After much distress, intrigue, and near revolt, the Spanish finally evacuated the area in March 1798, allowing Ellicott to proceed with the boundary survey.

Ellicott remained in public service as secretary of the land office for Pennsylvania before becoming chair of mathematics at the US Military Academy at West Point. He left briefly to serve his country again when he was called to make astronomical observations associated with the Treaty of Ghent, which ended the War of 1812, but otherwise remained at West Point until his death in 1820.

Clay Williams
Mississippi Department of
Archives and History

Samuel Flagg Bemis, *Pinckney's Treaty: A Study of America's Advantage from Europe's Distress, 1783–1800* (1926); Jack D. L. Holmes, *Gayoso: The Life of a Spanish Governor in the Mississippi Valley, 1789–1799* (1965); Catherine VanCortlandt Mathews, *Andrew Ellicott, His Life and Letters* (1908); Clayton Rand, *Men of Spine in Mississippi* (1940); John C. Van Horne, *Journal of Mississippi History* (August 1983).

Ellis, Powhatan

(1790–1863) Judge

Powhatan Ellis was born on 17 January 1790 to Josiah and Jane Ellis on their family homestead, Red Hill Farm, in Amherst County, Virginia. The youngest of eleven children, Powhatan received his name in recognition of the family's descent from Pocahontas, the daughter of Chief Powhatan.

Ellis attended Washington Academy (now Washington and Lee University) in Lexington, Virginia, in 1808 before moving on to Dickinson College in Carlisle, Pennsylvania, in 1809–10. During the War of 1812 he enlisted as a private in a Lynchburg, Virginia, rifle company and rose to the rank of captain. Military service brought Ellis into contact with Gen. Andrew Jackson, and the two men became lifelong friends. Ellis completed his education by studying law in 1813–14 at the College of William and Mary, was subsequently admitted to the bar, and began practicing in Lynchburg.

With letters of introduction from General Jackson to Mississippi governor David Holmes, Ellis and several other young men set out for the Mississippi Territory in 1816. Holmes commissioned Ellis as an attorney in Natchez on 20 August 1816. Ellis then decided to make his home in Wayne County. On 21 January 1818 the legislature selected Ellis to represent his district on the first Mississippi Supreme Court. During his lifetime, one of the towns in the growing district was named Ellisville in his honor.

Ellis served on the court for seven years and was described as popular, attentive, and patient even "with the most prosy speakers." Ellis maintained a conservative judicial philosophy: in his view, even if some judicial opinions were "incorrect, it is better they should remain fixed and immutable than we should declare to the community, what may be the law of the land today, may be changed tomorrow."

In 1825 Mississippi governor Walter Leake appointed Ellis to fill a vacancy in the US Senate, and he resigned from the Mississippi Supreme Court. He served until January 1826, when his successor was elected. In March 1827 he returned to the Senate after winning the election.

Ellis met and married Eliza Rebecca Winn of Washington, D.C. in 1831. Ellis left the Senate and on 14 July 1832 was appointed as a federal judge for Mississippi. The Ellises had a son, Powhatan Jr., and a daughter, Rebecca. Powhatan Jr. lived just two years, dying shortly after Rebecca's birth in 1834. One year later Eliza Ellis also died.

On 5 January 1836 President Jackson appointed Ellis to serve as US chargé d'affaires in Mexico, a position he held until 1837, when the new president, Martin Van Buren, appointed Ellis to the post of minister plenipotentiary to Mexico, a highly sensitive job in light of the poor United States–Mexico relations as a consequence of the 1836 Texas Revolution. Ellis served in this post until 21 April 1842, when he returned to Mississippi and a private legal practice in the Wayne County area. He ultimately moved back to Virginia, where he died in Richmond on 18 March 1863.

LeAnn W. Nealey

Jackson, Mississippi

Frank E. Everett Jr., *Federal Judges in Mississippi, 1818–1968* (1968); Federal Judicial Center, Biographical Directory of Federal Judges website, www.fjc.gov; John Ray Skates Jr., *A History of the Mississippi Supreme Court, 1817–1948* (1973).

Eloby, Thomas Edward, Jr.

(1945–2001) Artist

Thomas Edward Eloby Jr. was born in Coahoma, Mississippi, on 2 April 1945. He was the first of ten children and as a young man assumed a great deal of responsibility for his siblings after his father died.

From a very early age, Eloby made art. For the most part he was self-taught, taking advantage of his good hand-eye rendering skill. He earned a bachelor's degree at Mississippi Valley State University and briefly attended the School of the Art Institute of Chicago. He was a natural artist of exceptional talent who never received accolades equal to his achievements. While well known in the Mississippi Delta, he was never recognized on a wider scale. Whenever he needed to pay a bill, he carried art to patrons in the Clarksdale area and asked them to buy it, which many did.

Eloby followed the adage "Paint what you know." He lived his life in the Delta, surrounded by floodplains and "just plain folks." When a landscape appears in the background of one of his works, it is flat and treeless and may have a barn or a small shack or house. The blues surrounded him all the time in the Delta, and many portraits show men holding guitars.

Eloby's preferred subject matter was African Americans, and he is mostly known for his Mississippi Delta people. In Eloby's portraits, the people rarely smile, instead featuring expressions best described as stoic. Many of his subjects appear in different works painted at different times, enabling viewers to see them age.

Animals, fruit, and geometric arrangements rarely appear in Eloby's work. Skulls, skeletons, pipes, and shoes, conversely, are often included and may be central to the work, in the background, or buried in a drawing so cleverly that they are hard to find. Eloby loved to layer images. According to art scholar Betty Crouther, Eloby worked from memory, primarily using pencil, pen, or oil paint, and often spent hours drawing layer upon layer, virtually obliterating the underdrawings. Even careful viewers cannot be sure they have seen everything the artist laid down.

Eloby's work can be extremely simple or aggravatingly complex. The complex pieces are layered with increasing densities of pigment, are always figurative, and sometimes have a geometrically oriented design. Eloby coined the term *translusionist* to describe this method of working in complex layers. He also said of art, "Anything that is quickly seen loses its fascination."

In a 1979 interview, Eloby summarized the relationship between his life and art: "I feel that every black artist should say something about himself. A white artist cannot capture the dignity to the fullest extent because he does not know the inner emotions of blacks, but those emotions are part of me. I am able, through my heritage and environment, to create a painting which depicts real life situations."

Eloby died on 3 December 2001.

Albert Sperath

University of Mississippi

Patti Carr Black, *Art in Mississippi, 1770–1980* (1998); Jeff Piselli, *Clarksdale Press Register* (6 December 2001).

Elzy, Ruby Pearl

(1908–1943) Musician

Ruby Pearl Elzy was a pioneering black opera singer. A soprano, she was best known for her performances in *Porgy and Bess*. Elzy was born in Pontotoc on 20 February 1908, the eldest child of Charlie Elzy and Emma Kimp Elzy. When she was five, her father abandoned the family, leaving Elzy's mother to support herself and her four children by teaching school, working in the cotton fields, and doing laundry for well-to-do white families. Elzy learned spirituals from her grandmother, who had been born a slave. Elzy sang her first solo in church at the age of four and even as a child dreamed of a singing career.

Elzy was a freshman at Rust College in Holly Springs in May 1927 when she was overheard singing by a visiting college administrator, Dr. C. C. McCracken of Ohio State University. Impressed, McCracken arranged for Elzy to transfer to Ohio State, where she graduated with honors in 1930 and received a Julius Rosenwald Fellowship to the Julliard School in New York City. Elzy received two degrees from Juilliard, graduating in 1934. While there, she joined the professional chorus directed by composer and conductor J. Rosamond Johnson, the younger brother of poet James Weldon Johnson. As a member of the Johnson Choir, Elzy made her Broadway debut in the 1930 musical *Brown Buddies*. The following year, she appeared in the revue *Fast and Furious*.

In 1933 Elzy had her first film role, playing Dolly in *The Emperor Jones*, starring Paul Robeson and written by DuBose Heyward. When Heyward and composer George Gershwin began working on *Porgy and Bess*, adapted from Heyward's novel, he recommended that Gershwin hear Elzy. Gershwin then cast her as Serena, the opera's second-most-important female role. *Porgy and Bess* had its world premiere in Boston on 30 September 1935 and ten days later opened at the Alvin Theatre in New York. Critics praised Elzy's performance, particularly her singing of the difficult aria "My Man's Gone Now," which Gershwin had written especially for her.

In 1937, following Gershwin's death, Elzy sang in memorial concerts with the New York Philharmonic and the Los Angeles Philharmonic, the latter presented at the Hollywood Bowl and broadcast worldwide by CBS radio. Elzy made her solo New York recital debut at Town Hall in October 1937. Two months later, the highlight of Elzy's career came when she was invited to sing at the White House by First Lady Eleanor Roosevelt. In 1938 Elzy appeared as Serena in the first West Coast tour of *Porgy and Bess*. When the show closed, Elzy settled in Hollywood. She sang on radio and appeared in three more films, *The Toy Wife* (1938), *Tell No Tales* (1939), and *Way Down South* (1939). Elzy starred as Ella Jones in the Federal Theatre Project's production of Hall Johnson's musical, *Run Little Chillun*, which opened in Los Angeles in July 1938 and ran for more than three hundred performances.

In 1940 Elzy returned to Broadway to star opposite Robeson in a short-lived musical adaptation of *John Henry*. That year she also made her first and only commercial recording, a solo in composer Harold Arlen's *Americanegro Suite*. In 1941 Elzy made her final screen appearance, singing "St. Louis Blues" in the Paramount film *Birth of the Blues*, starring Bing Crosby. In 1941 Elzy starred again as Serena in

producer Cheryl Crawford's revival of *Porgy and Bess*. The production was a sensation, playing for 286 performances on Broadway before embarking on a 1942–43 national tour. When Elzy gave her last performance as Serena in 1943, she had appeared in the role more than 800 times.

Elzy was scheduled to begin a solo concert tour in August 1943 and to make her grand opera debut in the title role of Verdi's *Aida* in 1944. However, she died in Detroit on 26 June 1943 following an operation to remove a benign tumor. She was buried in Pontotoc.

David E. Weaver
Ohioana Library Association,
Columbus, Ohio

David E. Weaver, *Black Diva of the Thirties: The Life of Ruby Elzy* (2004).

Emancipation

Emancipation in Mississippi constituted a multistep process involving decisions and actions by the slaves themselves, the changing policies of the federal government, and Union military victories. In 1860 the US Census counted 436,631 slaves in Mississippi. Though in many cases Union troops arrived at plantations and told enslaved men and women that they were now free, those men and women more often already had taken steps to secure their own emancipation.

Especially in counties near the Mississippi River, self-emancipation occurred when young men left in small groups to find freedom behind Union lines. During this first phase, many other slaves claimed freedom on farms and plantations, by working more for themselves, taking advantage of interruptions and new overseers, finding ways to negotiate with owners, and ultimately claiming the land and their labor for themselves. As historian Nancy Bercaw writes, "They located the meaning of emancipation in the land, the crop, and the community." For a short time in 1862, women, older men, and children worked for themselves on land left behind by former landowners, making decisions about growing and marketing crops. Even in areas where traditional owners remained in place, the nature of labor changed, and owners reported that slaves refused to work as they had prior to the war.

Throughout the war but especially in the early period, the spread of information was part of emancipation. Slaves listened to conversations about the Civil War and its possible consequences, literate slaves read what they could, and slaves who traveled took on new importance in spreading news and rumors. Even before the fighting reached Mississippi, some slaves interpreted the war as bringing slavery to an end. Moseley, an Adams County slave who participated in an 1861 plan to overturn slavery in his area, told other slaves that "Lincoln would set us free." Some slaves involved in that conspiracy imagined that Gen. Winfield Scott would be taking New Orleans for the Union in September, with Natchez falling soon after that.

The US government, however, entered the war without plans to bring an end to the institution of slavery, and when US forces first ventured into Mississippi, they did not welcome enslaved people into their ranks. Declared William Tecumseh Sherman in June 1862, "The well-settled policy of the whole army now is to have nothing to do with the Negro." By later that year, however, Union forces had begun to see the advantages both of using newly freed former slaves as workers and more generally of undermining the slave system. Federal officials began establishing camps where former slaves could work. According to historian Timothy B. Smith, "In Natchez, Federal soldiers arrived in 1863 and turned the famous slave market at the 'Forks of the Road' into a locale for freemen." In addition, "Federal authorities gathered thousands of escaped and liberated slaves" at Confederate president Jefferson Davis's plantation, Brierfield, and his brother's nearby plantation. Camps in Vicksburg and Corinth attracted thousands of newly freed people. When these "contraband camps" began to organize former slaves into work groups that resembled plantation slavery, the freedpeople bristled, with some complaining and others moving on to places where they found emancipation more meaningful.

Abraham Lincoln's Emancipation Proclamation solidified the idea that Union forces were fighting to end the institution of slavery. The proclamation stated that at the beginning of 1863 all slaves in the Confederate states would be free. Lincoln and his military leaders saw the proclamation not only as giving the Union cause the high moral purpose of opposing slavery but also as providing military benefits by destabilizing the southern economy and society. The president believed that "the bare sight of fifty thousand armed and drilled black soldiers on the banks of the Mississippi would end the rebellion at once."

The proclamation ushered in the second phase of emancipation, in which enslaved men and women aligned themselves with the US government to support emancipation. Probably the most dramatic way freedpeople claimed their own freedom was by joining the federal military forces. Historians differ about how many African Americans fought in the war. Timothy Smith concludes that "Mississippi probably sent at least 25,000 to 30,000 African American soldiers to the Union army." Many of the African American units, eventually called US Colored Troops, were organized at camps in Natchez, Vicksburg, and Corinth as well as in Arkansas, Tennessee, and Louisiana. African American military service often consisted of support work, first as servants and in construction, but the US Colored Troops eventually engaged in battle. African American troops in the 51st U.S.

Colored Infantry fought off a Confederate attack in 1863 at Milliken's Bend, and those in the 3rd Cavalry Regiment fought in Yazoo City, in Natchez, in Woodville, and around Jackson.

Mississippi political and military authorities condemned these forces as the most troubling signs of a larger crisis in the slave system. Slave owners began to fear all sorts of forms of rebellion, preventing individual slaves from traveling, trying to keep slaves ignorant of news, and sometimes taking large groups of slaves away from the sites of likely military action. Winthrop D. Jordan details how Natchez area slave owners dealt with an 1861 conspiracy not only by executing those involved but then by keeping it remarkably quiet. Local groups formed new paramilitary organizations to deter possible slave escapes and rebellion. The Mississippi state government sought not only to crack down on slave movement but also to impress slaves for use in Confederate forces. Mississippi's Civil War governors, John J. Pettus and Charles Clark, consistently looked for ways to prevent slaves from gaining freedom and joining the Union military.

Former slaves made several important changes as they became free people. Along with moving and joining the military, changing their names became another way of asserting independence and became especially important as they started signing legal documents and formalizing marriages. Many newly free people immediately began to negotiate their labor in a new setting, to attempt to become landowners, and to make demands on and assume responsibilities within government.

Emancipation very quickly became a point of conflict in public culture, as many former slaves celebrated Abraham Lincoln and dates associated with the coming of freedom, while supporters of the Confederacy began celebrating the memory of the war as having little to do with slavery and emancipation. Contests over the political, legal, economic, and social meanings of emancipation, of course, continued through Reconstruction and beyond.

Ted Ownby
University of Mississippi

Nancy Bercaw, *Gendered Freedoms: Race, Rights, and the Politics of Household in the Delta, 1861–1875* (2003); Winthrop D. Jordan, *Tumult and Silence: An Inquiry into a Civil War Slave Conspiracy* (1993); Anthony E. Kaye, *Joining Places: Slave Neighborhoods in the Old South* (2007); Leon Litwack, *Been in the Storm So Long: The Aftermath of Slavery* (1978); Armstead L. Robinson, *Bitter Fruits of Bondage: The Demise of Slavery and the Collapse of the Confederacy, 1861–1865* (2005); Timothy B. Smith, *Mississippi in the Civil War: The Home Front* (2010); Ben Wynne, *Mississippi's Civil War: A Narrative History* (2006).

Emmerich, J. Oliver, Sr.
(1896–1978) Journalist

J. Oliver Emmerich is best known as one of a handful of white Mississippi editors who publicized and criticized the worst of his community's actions in opposition to the civil rights movement. He was born in New Orleans on 2 December 1896 and raised in McComb, a growing timber and railroad town. After attending Mississippi A&M (now Mississippi State University), Emmerich worked as a county agricultural agent before buying the *McComb Enterprise* in 1923. He later bought the town's other paper and merged the two to form the *McComb Enterprise-Journal.*

For nearly three decades, Emmerich's paper showed few signs of being anything other than a supporter of boosterism and white privilege. Emmerich attended the 1948 Democratic National Convention and joined other white Democrats who walked out to protest the party's civil rights platform. The *Enterprise-Journal* seemed in most ways a typical small-town newspaper, dominated by local news and featuring only a single small column about African American life.

In the early 1950s Emmerich began to make editorial changes that attracted criticism from some white readers. In 1950 he printed a story about police brutality against a black teenager. Then, in what he called the newspaper's "first major reform in news policy," he began using courtesy titles such as Mr. and Mrs. to refer to African Americans. Emmerich and the newspaper staff incurred more condemnation when editorials condemned violence against Freedom Riders in 1961 and criticized Gov. Ross Barnett's role in inciting the riot that accompanied desegregation at the University of Mississippi in 1962.

In 1964 Emmerich cautioned opponents of Freedom Summer against violence and lawbreaking. In a front-page May editorial, he urged readers to "relax" and hoped that at the end of the summer they could look back and say, "We met a crisis with maturity. We did not panic. We exercised restraint." McComb, however, was the home of an active chapter of the National Association for the Advancement of Colored People, saw considerable activism by the Student Nonviolent Coordinating Committee, and was the site of substantial voter registration activity during the summer. Despite Emmerich's urgings, the Ku Klux Klan, Americans for the Preservation of the White Race, and others responded with arson and bombings. The homes and offices of African American leaders suffered the bulk of the violence, but a bomb also damaged the home of *Enterprise-Journal* managing editor Charles Dunagin. After the newspaper condemned the bombings and helped raise funds for a reward to assist in catching the perpetrators, opponents burned a cross on Emmerich's lawn.

In the fall of 1964, with a combination of weariness and optimism, Emmerich wrote editorials demanding that all people receive equal justice under law and criticizing "extremists" on both sides who had brought McComb "close to chaos." In one editorial he called on bankers, merchants, lawyers, industrial workers, schoolteachers, railroad men, housewives, and ministers to develop and actively promote a new sense of community responsibility.

In 1973 Emmerich published *Two Faces of Janus: The Saga of Deep South Change*, a memoir of his life in journalism as well as an analysis of the positive and troubling sides of southern life. He concluded by emphasizing the good: "No Utopia exists. But the road traveled today is in the direction of government by law as contrasted by government by men."

Emmerich died on 17 August 1978. Since 1977 the Mississippi Press Association has awarded the J. Oliver Emmerich Award for editorial writing. Recipients have included Emmerich's son, John Oliver Emmerich Jr., who won the award in 1981 for his work at the *Greenwood Commonwealth.*

Ted Ownby
University of Mississippi

David R. Davies, ed., *The Press and Race: Mississippi Journalists Confront the Movement* (2001); J. Oliver Emmerich Sr., *Two Faces of Janus: The Saga of Deep South Change* (1973); John Oliver Emmerich Sr. Papers, Special Collections, Mitchell Memorial Library, Mississippi State University; Mississippi Press Association website, http://mspress.org; Susan J. Weill, *In a Madhouse's Din: Civil Rights Coverage by Mississippi's Daily Press, 1948–1968* (2002).

Engel, Lehman
(1910–1982) Composer and Conductor

In 1958 *Time* magazine called composer, conductor, author, and teacher Lehman Engel "one of the nation's busiest and most versatile men-about-music." *A Streetcar Named Desire, The Consul, Murder in the Cathedral*, and *Li'l Abner* are a few of the many Broadway shows with which he was associated as a composer or conductor. His efforts earned him widespread recognition, including Tony Awards in 1950 (for conducting the Menotti opera *The Consul*) and 1953 (for conducting Gilbert and Sullivan operettas and *Wonderful Town*).

Born to Jewish parents in Jackson, Engel played the piano by ear until age ten, when his parents were able to afford lessons for him. He wrote that his first piano teacher was an "aristocratic southern lady" whose lessons, like those of his subsequent teachers, he quickly outgrew. He completed his first composition, *The Scotch Highlander*, shortly after he began taking piano lessons, and musical composition for the theater became one of his primary interests. A Jackson movie house, the Majestic Theater, with its small orchestra accompanying silent movies, impressed the young boy greatly and provided some of his most memorable early experiences.

Although not an extremely talented pianist, Engel entered the Cincinnati Conservatory of Music after graduating from high school. When he discovered that he had been eligible for a partial scholarship for piano lessons but was the only student not receiving funds, he became angry and immediately transferred to the Cincinnati College of Music. Two years later he turned down a faculty position there and moved to New York. With a graduate scholarship to the Julliard School, Engel took courses in composition from Rubin Goldmark and studied privately with Roger Sessions. Engel also made contacts and established his career, spending several months attempting to meet Martha Graham: when he finally did, she encouraged him to write compositions for her dance company and for other concert dancers.

Engel received his first Broadway credit for *Within the Gates* (1934). Music had already been written for the play, but Engel heard it, expressed his dislike to director Melvyn Douglas, and offered to write a new version by the next morning. The play closed after just 141 performances, but Engel's music received praise.

The Federal Music Project, a subsidiary of the Works Progress Administration, organized a group of madrigal singers and hired Engel to serve as the group's conductor from 1935 to 1939. He also composed music for the Federal Theatre Project and its subsidiary children's theater before he began working with Orson Welles and John Houseman at their Mercury Theater. During World War II he joined the US Navy, conducted a military orchestra at the Great Lakes Naval Training Station, and later served as chief composer for the navy's film division in Washington, D.C. His other pursuits included joining with Aaron Copland, Marc Blitzstein, and Virgil Thompson to found Arrow Music Press, which published the work of American composers; conducting more than sixty recordings for major record companies such as Columbia, Decca, and RCA Victor; composing four operas and music for radio, film, and television; writing books about musical theater; and teaching workshops in musical lyrics.

Known as the Poor Man's Lenny Bernstein, Engel became one of the most respected and sought-after musicians on Broadway. He never returned to the South to live but visited Jackson to conduct premieres of two of his operas. Engel died of cancer in 1982.

Jessica Foy
Cooperstown, New York

Josh Barbanel, *New York Times* (30 August 1982); Lehman Engel, *This Bright Day: An Autobiography* (1974); Lehman Engel, *Words with Music: Creating the Broadway Musical Libretto* (1972, 2006); Walter Rigdon, ed., *The Biographical Encyclopedia and Who's Who of the American Theatre* (1966); Nicolas Slonimsky, *Baker's Biographical Dictionary of Musicians* (1984); *Time* (8 December 1958).

Entergy Mississippi

Entergy Mississippi is a public utility company that provides electric power to homes and businesses in forty-five counties in the western half of Mississippi. It is regulated within the state by the Mississippi Public Service Commission, created by the Mississippi legislature in 1956. Now an operating company within the Entergy Corporation system of companies in Arkansas, Louisiana, and Texas, the company was known as the Mississippi Power and Light Company (MP&L) before 1996.

MP&L was chartered in April 1923 by Harvey Couch, an entrepreneur from Little Rock, Arkansas. He selected Jackson, the state capital, as headquarters for the new company. The company's first initiative was to purchase the municipal utility operations in Jackson, Vicksburg, Columbus, and Greenville. The company later purchased utilities with distribution lines in other large towns and connected them with transmission lines to form an integrated, interconnected electrical system. The transmission system brought service to small towns between the larger ones.

In 1924 MP&L entered into an agreement with the Arkansas Power and Light Company and the Louisiana Power and Light Company—both owned by the Couch interests—to construct a twenty-five-thousand-kilowatt plant near Sterlington in North Louisiana to supply electric power to the three utilities. A transmission line from the plant ran east across the Mississippi River at Vicksburg to supply MP&L.

In July 1925 Couch entered into a consolidation agreement with Electric Bond and Share Company (EBASCO), a subsidiary of General Electric. The agreement combined the two groups of properties into one large, coordinated system owned by Electric Power and Light Corporation, a new subsidiary of EBASCO. With EBASCO's reservoir of experience and financial expertise, MP&L continued its acquisition program. In 1926 the company was incorporated under Florida law; MP&L did not incorporate under Mississippi law until 1963. The ownership arrangement with Electric Power and Light continued until 1949, when a holding company, Middle South Utilities (MSU), was formed to own the common stock of MP&L, Louisiana Power and Light, Arkansas Power and Light, and New Orleans Public Service. MSU was based in New York City until 1963, when it moved its corporate headquarters to New Orleans. MSU's formation had been motivated by Congress's passage of the Holding Company Act of 1935, which stipulated that utilities could only be part of a regional holding company whose subsidiary companies operated in geographically contiguous areas.

In 1926 MP&L sold its operations in Northeast Mississippi to the Mississippi Central Power Company. The following year, MP&L experienced its first major natural disaster, the Great Mississippi River Flood, which put a large portion of the Delta under water. Over the years, MP&L's infrastructure has suffered costly damage from other natural disasters, among them ice storms, tornadoes, and hurricanes.

In 1930 MP&L moved to the third floor in the Lampton Building at 308 East Pearl Street in Jackson, an address that became its permanent headquarters. Beginning in the 1940s, MP&L began constructing power plants: Rex Brown Steam Electric Station in Jackson (1946), Natchez Steam Electric Plant in Natchez (1950), Delta Steam Electric Station in Cleveland (1951), Baxter Wilson Steam Electric Station in Vicksburg (1964), and Gerald Andrus Steam Electric Station in Greenville (1971). In 1972, MP&L and its sister MSU companies announced plans to build a 1.29-million-kilowatt nuclear power plant, Grand Gulf Nuclear Station, in Claiborne County near Port Gibson. Grand Gulf Nuclear Unit 1 went online in 1985, and its operation was transferred to MSU's new nuclear subsidiary, System Energy Resources, the following year.

In 1996 MSU changed its name to Entergy Corporation, and the subsidiary companies were renamed accordingly. At the end of 2014, Entergy Mississippi served 442,000 customers, and Entergy Corporation employed 2,000 people in the state.

Peggy W. Jeanes
Jackson, Mississippi

Carroll Brinson, *Always a Challenge: Mississippi Power and Light Company's First Sixty Years* (1984); Entergy Corporation website, www.entergy.com; Entergy Mississippi website, www.entergy-mississippi.com.

Environment

Mississippi is rural, with a large proportion of its human population occupied in primary production. Thus, it is no surprise that the state's history, culture, and economy are intrinsically tied to the natural environment. The state's diverse soils, forested lands, and bodies of water have always provided the basis for human subsistence. Human impact on Mississippi's natural environment has varied greatly over time, ranging from the effects of Native American subsistence systems through the heyday of cotton production and "cut out and get out" lumbering to contemporary industrial and residential development.

In the past, scholars were often reluctant to see nature as anything other than a haphazard "unimproved" setting where human activity took place. Today, however, many observers strongly reject this view. The natural environment is an active and often decisive factor in human history, influencing the economic options available and shaping the developmental paths taken. Environmental conditions set the ultimate boundaries for human societies and their activities but do not prescribe which direction people take in given situations.

Mississippi covers an area of close to forty-eight thousand square miles, with ample resources for both humans and wildlife. Mississippi's climate is noted for its long growing seasons, hot summers, and high humidity. Late summer to early fall is usually the driest part of the year. Moderate droughts occur every few years, with severe ones every two or three decades. The climate is further characterized by a long frost-free period, while prolonged periods of below-freezing temperatures are atypical. During the warmest months, violent thunderstorms frequently occur. Ice storms, tornadoes, and also hurricanes in coastal areas are occasional but characteristic and can dramatically affect local conditions.

Virtually all of Mississippi was covered by the sea during the Cretaceous period, and the resulting topography is relatively flat, with the state's highest elevation of just 806 feet found at Woodall Mountain in Tishomingo County. All of the state's major river systems—the Tombigbee, Pascagoula, Pearl, Big Black, and Yazoo—empty into the Gulf of Mexico, either directly or through the Mississippi River. The state's soils consist of sedimentary deposits that slope gently toward the Gulf. The land can be arranged into three major soil regions: the alluvial river floodplain, the loess belt of wind-blown alluvium, and the coastal plain. However, great variation in soil productivity occurs between and within these major regions. Human settlement patterns have closely mirrored these differences. The most productive soils for agriculture are found in the Black Belt region of northeastern Mississippi and in the Yazoo-Mississippi basin (the Delta) in the northwestern part of the state. The soils of the southern coastline and the so-called flatwoods belt in the northwest are the poorest for agricultural purposes. Many of Mississippi's soils are prone to erosion. The Loess Hills on the eastern edge of the Delta, also known as the brown loam region, exemplify an area where strict conservation practices are required to ensure continued productivity of the land.

The major types of natural forest vegetation found have been arranged into various subdivisions that largely correspond to the prevalent soil types. Floodplains of major rivers, including the whole of the Delta, originally supported dense hardwood forests characterized by bald cypresses, gums, and various oaks. The Black Belt and Loess Hill regions originally supported an oak-hickory forest, while the rest of northern Mississippi's uplands consisted of a mixed forest of pines and oaks. Pine forests have historically dominated central and southern Mississippi, with loblolly and shortleaf pine giving way to the longleaf and slash pine in the more southern parts of this area, known as the Piney Woods.

Considerable human impact on Mississippi's landscapes goes back much further than the twentieth century. By the antebellum era, Euro-American settlement had caused locally significant ecological changes. Further, the area settled by people of European and African origin beginning in the eighteenth century was hardly a true wilderness, as it had been inhabited and influenced by aboriginal people for millennia. Native Americans' way of life has often been romanticized and the environmental impacts of their land-use practices downplayed, even though those early inhabitants were clearly capable of manipulating animal and plant assemblages and creating habitats that suited human settlements.

Immediately prior to contact with Europeans, Native Americans in what was to become Mississippi typically combined their regular horticultural cycle with annual cycles of hunting and gathering: deer, waterfowl, and fish supplemented a diet dominated by corn. Most of the fishing likely occurred during the summer months, while an intensive period of deer and bird hunting probably took place during the late fall and winter.

European expansion to the region began during the sixteenth century with incursions by Spanish conquistadors. Unlike Hernando de Soto and his troops, subsequent European colonists recognized the region's natural resources as the basis for their material advancement. Vast trade in deerskins, initiated by Europeans, played a decisive role in the decline of white-tailed deer populations in the South. It seems probable that the Native Americans' widespread belief in the reincarnation of killed game animals made "conservationist" attitudes toward deer foreign at a time when Native Americans craved European trade goods. By the 1790s commercial hunting had severely depleted deer populations over most of the present-day state of Mississippi.

European settlers in Mississippi immediately based their economic lives on agriculture, obtaining new cropland by clearing forested areas. By the mid-1830s, Native Americans had ceded their lands in Mississippi to the United States, and the US government moved quickly to open the cessions for sale to incoming settlers. Before it could be sold, however, the former Indian land had to be surveyed according to the laws of the new nation. Throughout much of the South, the old survey systems, such as "metes and bounds" that applied in the original thirteen colonies, were replaced by a new approach to land division based on a rectangular grid. It presented a radical departure from the preceding irregular patterns of land apportionment, with no acknowledgment of "natural" boundaries.

Large-scale agriculture began in Mississippi in the early nineteenth century and came to be based on the plantation system and cultivation of staple crops, especially cotton, for the international marketplace. The scarcity of labor—resolved first by using slaves and then by using tenant workers—demanded great efficiency. Primitive agricultural techniques, cash crops, and insatiable markets ensured that Mississippians would produce major changes in the landscape. In addition to forest clearing for agriculture, trees were harvested for housing, fencing, lumber, and fuel. The intense exploitation of Mississippi's forests accelerated during the nineteenth century and has continued to this day. Much of the recent increase in forested area has come from the abandonment of marginal farmland and its conversion into evenly aged pine plantations. The effects of habitat alteration are evident in the decline of many of the state's wildlife populations.

Over the past two hundred years the area occupied by original landscapes has been tremendously reduced in Mississippi, and the remaining pristine areas are greatly influenced by human activities. In addition to physical habitat transformation, overhunting and overfishing have taken their toll on the state's wildlife populations. Abundant wildlife originally provided a convenient supply of food and made hunting and fishing an important part of the local culture and economy, often with little attention to the concept of sustainable yield. For example, many species of cranes, ducks, and shorebirds experienced severe population declines before the passage of the Migratory Bird Treaty Act of 1916, which established federally regulated hunting seasons for migratory game birds. Market hunting continued locally until at least the mid-1930s for species such as bobwhite quail, rabbits, and waterfowl. In addition to the pursuit of edible fish and game, conspicuous and "harmful" species such as hawks, eagles, and mammalian predators were customarily shot for sport and practice. Mississippi's hunters pursued white-tailed deer, black bears, and panthers to near extinction by the early twentieth century, and some animals, including the panther, never recovered.

The rapid decline of many wildlife populations aroused little attention among biologists until well into the twentieth century. Conservation ideas were still unusual, and the few laws passed for protection of threatened species prior to that time often proved impossible to enforce. Incomplete knowledge about the primeval numbers of Mississippi's wildlife species, combined with insufficient statistics on land use and fragmented data on hunting and fishing or the effects of introduced disease and predators, means that in many cases it is not possible to determine which factors contributed most to the decline of the different populations.

Hunting as an activity survived the decline of large game. Some small creatures—among them quail, rabbits, and foxes—adapted well to agricultural areas and prospered in spite of their proximity to humans. Intense hunting of these animals occurred for most of the twentieth century, with quail hunting in particular developing a large following not only in Mississippi but across the South.

As a consequence of Mississippians' love for recreational hunting and fishing, the state created the Game and Fish Commission in the 1930s. The commission established and enforced regulations based on scientific ideas of wildlife management. The commission also attempted restocking programs for deer, turkeys, and other large game. Aided by changing human ways of life, some of these efforts met with great success. Mississippi now has one of the largest deer populations in the nation for its land area, and deer hunting today generates something of the frenzy that once accompanied quail hunting.

Because Mississippi is a conservative state, enthusiasm for hunting and fishing can serve as the starting place for ecological concern. While the percentage of people who hunt and fish is in decline, many still view the activities as important traditions. The basic interaction with nature that hunting and fishing provides and the impulse to conserve game and fish often lead to the beginning of environmental consciousness.

One natural force, flooding, has always posed a physical threat to human subsistence in certain parts of Mississippi. From their arrival in the state's alluvial lowlands, Euro-American settlers realized that economic development would occur in flood-prone regions in direct proportion to the amount of control gained over the Mississippi and its tributaries. Relief from flooding—a natural phenomenon of the floodplain—made the development of agriculture, infrastructure, and industry possible in the lowlands.

The massive task of walling the river off from the floodplain, however, demanded investments on a scale unavailable to any individual landowner, county, or even state. Governmental involvement in flood control and water resource development evolved during the nineteenth and twentieth centuries, with far-reaching effects on the floodplain's natural hydrological regime. Since the disastrous 1927 Great Mississippi Flood federal funding has enabled massive human-induced change in the hydrology of the Mississippi and its tributaries. The present system of flood control in Mississippi is a compromise resulting from a long and complicated interplay among interest groups, striving to balance widely conflicting views on economy, politics, engineering, and the environment but satisfying few and facing an uncertain future.

After centuries of hard work and massive investments by individual interests and local, state, and federal governments, it has customarily been assumed that almost any amount of high water can be safely transported through the Lower Mississippi Valley. Still, as the high waters of 1973, 1993, 2008, and 2011 have demonstrated, the potential for serious flooding still exists in the region despite the remaking of hydrological systems at an enormous economic and environmental cost. Authorized by legislation passed in 1928, the Mississippi River and Tributaries Project is approaching completion, but the collapse of New Orleans levees in 2005 after a storm surge caused by Hurricane Katrina has cast doubt on the reliability of the South's entire flood-control system.

Mississippi's nineteenth- and early twentieth-century levee builders, planters, and lumber entrepreneurs can hardly be blamed for failing to understand the full environmental consequences of their actions since the science of conservation biology did not emerge until a few decades ago. Ignorance, however, no longer constitutes a valid excuse. Consequently, many measures, including important federal and state legislation, have sought to reverse some of the most negative environmental trends. Critical wildlife habitat has also been set aside, mainly by federal and state authorities, and reintroduction programs for endangered species are in progress. While some Mississippi plants and animals have been permanently lost, the ongoing attempts to enforce and expand existing conservation legislation and create preserves for imperiled species provide hope for the future of Mississippi's natural environment.

Still, unprecedented pollution of land, water, and air has taken place in Mississippi as a byproduct of industrialization and mechanized agriculture over the past century. This pollution adversely affects the natural environment and the people and wildlife occupying it. Ecologists assert that the proper test for assessing the harmfulness of environmental change is whether ecological systems retain their resilience. Do human-induced changes in our natural environment remain within bounds that enable the recovery of the systems after disturbance? William Faulkner's Ike McCaslin reflected in 1942 that Mississippi's natural environment ultimately "belonged to no man. It belonged to all; they had only to use it well, humbly and with pride." This idea is even more important today than when it was written.

Wiley C. Prewitt Jr.
Yocona, Mississippi

Mikko Saikku
University of Helsinki

Donald E. Davis, *Southern United States: An Environmental History* (2006); James E. Fickle, *Mississippi Forests and Forestry* (2001); Mikko Saikku, *This Delta, This Land: An Environmental History of the Yazoo-Mississippi Floodplain* (2005).

Environmental Organizations

A variety of natural resource conservation organizations can be found in Mississippi. In 2014 nearly one hundred were registered with the Secretary of State's Office as charitable organizations. Some of these organizations, such as the Izaak Walton League, are national in scope; others, such as the World Wildlife Fund, are international in scope and have members in Mississippi but no state or local chapters. The Audubon Society, the National Wildlife Federation, the Nature Conservancy, and other groups have both a national and a state structure, with state organizations known as Audubon Mississippi, the Mississippi Wildlife Federation, the Mississippi Chapter of the Nature Conservancy, and so forth. Individuals may be members of either the national or state organization or of both. Other statewide organizations such as the Bear Education and Restoration Group of Mississippi and the Mississippi Ornithological Society are independent state entities. In addition, many local organizations have had very specific missions, such as the Wolf River Conservation Society and Friends of the DeSoto.

These types of environmental organizations began to develop in the late 1800s and early 1900s, when people across the country became aware of the loss or decline of many wildlife species. At the federal level, Pres. Theodore Roosevelt created 150 national forests, 4 national game preserves, 5 national parks, and 18 national monuments between 1901 and 1903 and convened the first North American Conservation Conference in 1909 in recognition of the need for conservation throughout the United States. But private citizens discovered that federal and state agencies could not and sometimes would not address all conservation concerns and realized that individuals needed to take an active role in conservation efforts. In response, groups began to form to take on that role.

In 1936 Franklin Delano Roosevelt convened a North American Wildlife Conference, "the purpose being to bring together all interested organizations, agencies, and individuals on behalf of restoration and conservation of land, water, forest, and wildlife resources." Scientists and technicians discussed restoration of the continent's vanishing wildlife as well as soil erosion, restoration of impounded water, and pollution control. The conference resulted in the adoption of a program and recommendations for closer cooperation among interested groups, individuals, and government agencies and in the creation of the National Wildlife Federation.

New organizations continue to emerge in Mississippi. The Land Trust for the Mississippi Coastal Plain, for example, was incorporated in 2000 and purchases land for protection as permanent green space. The Natural Resources Initiative of North Mississippi, founded in 2001, seeks to facilitate an environmentally sustainable, healthy, and dynamic economy through proactive partnerships between government and business. The Deer Creek Watershed Association (founded in 2005) and other groups have addressed water quality issues in the Delta.

All of these organizations seek to protect some aspect of the natural world. This mission may encompass the whole of wildlife or focus on one particular species, group of species, or natural feature. These groups' efforts usually lead to protecting habitats required for plants and animals and generally include an education component.

Cathy Shropshire
Mississippi Wildlife Federation

Thomas B. Allan, *Guardian of the Wild: The Story of the National Wildlife Federation* (1987); Mississippi Secretary of State, *2007 Report on Charitable Organizations in Mississippi*; Mississippi Secretary of State, *2014 Report on Charitable Organizations in Mississippi*; National Wildlife Federation, *Conservation Directory 2005–2006* (2005); Franklin D. Roosevelt, "Letter on the North American Wildlife Conference," American Presidency Project website, www.presidency.ucsb.edu; Theodore Roosevelt Association website, http://www.theodoreroosevelt.org.

Episcopalians

The Episcopal Church in Mississippi traces its roots back to British West Florida in the late eighteenth century, about the time that the American Episcopal Church formed out of the remnants of the Church of England. The region around Natchez was the most settled area in what became Mississippi, and the Rev. Adam Cloud arrived there in 1789 or 1790 as the first Episcopal minister. The Rev. Adam Boyd came to Natchez in 1800 and conducted regular services with the Book of Common Prayer at the courthouse. Worshippers built Christ Church at Church Hill in 1815, making it the oldest Episcopal church in the state. Other early Episcopal churches were Trinity Church, Natchez; St. Paul's, Woodville; and St. John's (now St. James's) in Port Gibson. The first convention of the diocese met in Natchez on 17–18 May 1826. Five clergymen, with no bishop, served fewer than one hundred congregants as the church worked to gain a foothold in what was already becoming a culture dominated by evangelical Protestants.

Native American removal in the northern and central parts of Mississippi opened those areas to settlement by white Americans and their slaves, and Bishop James Hervey Otey of the Diocese of Tennessee began visiting the state in the 1830s, playing a supervisory role as provisional bishop beginning in 1835. The church consecrated William Mercer Green as the first permanent bishop of Mississippi in 1850. In that year, 506 congregants participated in Episcopal services in the state. Under Bishop Green, the church's most significant work included the establishment of schools, among them St. Andrew's College, which opened in 1852. Green also encouraged the church's ministry to African Americans, with clergy baptizing more than four hundred slaves in 1860.

At the beginning of the Civil War, the church was established throughout the state, but its strength remained in the southwest.

Mississippi Episcopalians helped found the University of the South before the war and joined the Protestant Episcopal Church in the Confederate States of America before reuniting with other American Episcopalians after the war. The conflict caused great upheaval in the diocese, as it did in the rest of the state, including the destruction of property and disruption of services. Green continued to encourage the church's ministry to African Americans, ordaining the state's first African American deacon, George H. Jackson, in 1874. Green served until 1883, when he was succeeded as bishop by Hugh Miller Thompson. Thompson designated St. Peter's church in Oxford to serve as a cathedral church from 1883 to 1887, with St. Columb's Cathedral in Jackson consecrated in 1894. Thompson established several congregations of black Episcopalians, expanded the church's educational work, including the 1890 establishment of St. Mary's School for African Americans in Vicksburg, and helped establish a diocesan branch of the national church's Woman's Auxiliary to the Board of Missions. In 1900, near the end of Thompson's service, twenty-seven clergy served thirty-four parishes. Thompson divided the diocese into convocations of Columbus, Jackson, Pass Christian, Natchez, and Oxford.

Theodore DuBose Brattan became bishop in 1903, serving until 1938, when he was succeeded by William Mercer Green II, grandson of Mississippi's first bishop, whose tenure extended until 1942. Between 1900 and 1940 the number of Episcopalians in Mississippi rose from 3,792 to 8,422. The Episcopal Laymen of Mississippi was established in 1927, and Green became nationally prominent for his work with rural churches. Duncan Montgomery Gray held the bishopric from 1943 until 1966, tumultuous years for economic development and social change. Within the church, Gray promoted the creation of an annual clergy conference, the Rose Hill conference center and campsite (established in 1946 and renamed the Gray Center in 1966), and new primary and secondary schools. As the civil rights movement reached Mississippi, Gray and other priests, among them Edward H. Harrison and Wofford Smith, witnessed in favor of racial reconciliation. Some laypersons responded by attempting to intimidate the clergymen, but other parishioners backed an end to Jim Crow. Over Gray's tenure, Mississippi's Episcopalians increased from eighty-three hundred members and thirty-three parish priests to thirteen thousand communicants and fifty-five priests. John Maury Allin served as diocesan bishop from 1966 to 1974, followed by Duncan Montgomery Gray Jr. (1974–94), Alfred Clark Marble (1994–2003), Duncan Montgomery Gray III (2003–15), and Brian R. Seage (2015–present).

In 1973 the national church selected Allin to serve as presiding bishop of the American Episcopal Church, while his successor in Mississippi oversaw such major changes as adoption of a new Book of Common Prayer in 1979 and the ordination of the first women in the diocese in the 1980s. Under its four most recent bishops, Mississippi's Episcopal Church has championed ministries for social justice and aid for those suffering, both in the church and in the broader society. Commissions and committees at local parishes and at the diocesan level have supported feeding ministries, halfway houses, new affordable homes, prison work, racial reconciliation, and environmental stewardship. The most divisive issue has perhaps been the ordination of the national Episcopal Church's first gay bishop.

Charles Reagan Wilson
University of Mississippi

The Episcopal Church in Mississippi, 1763–1992 (1992); The Episcopal Diocese of Mississippi website, www.dioms.org.

Espy, Mike
(b. 1953) Politician

Having served as both a US congressman and US secretary of agriculture by the time he was forty, Mike Espy seemed on his way to a long and successful political career before he was brought down by an influence-peddling scandal. Born on 30 November 1953 in Yazoo City, Mississippi, Alphonso Michael "Mike" Espy earned a bachelor's degree from Howard University and a law degree from Santa Clara Law School

Mike Espy (Courtesy Mike Espy Collection, Congressional and Political Research Center, Mitchell Memorial Library, Mississippi State University)

in 1978. He worked with Central Mississippi Legal Services from 1978 to 1980, quickly climbing the career ladder to become chief of the Mississippi Legal Services and assistant secretary of state.

Espy subsequently served as assistant secretary of Mississippi's Public Lands Division (1980–84) and as assistant attorney general and director of the state's Consumer Protection Division (1984–85). In 1986 he was elected to represent the state's 2nd Congressional District, a position he retained until 1993.

During his first congressional term, Espy played a critical role in creating the Lower Mississippi Delta Commission, which spent two years on antipoverty efforts in Mississippi and the surrounding region. Espy then formed and chaired the seven-state Lower Mississippi Delta Congressional Caucus and served on a variety of committees and subcommittees, including Agriculture, Conservation, and Community and Natural Resources, as well as the Domestic Task Force. Mississippi's catfish industry constituted one of Espy's pet projects while in Congress. He persuaded the army to purchase catfish and wielded his influence to secure block grants for two processing plants for his district.

Espy's progressive and innovative ideas caught the attention of Pres. Bill Clinton, who in 1993 appointed the Magnolia State congressman to serve as secretary of agriculture, a position he held until 1994.

But scandal in the Department of Agriculture destroyed Espy's political career. In August 1997 a federal grand jury indicted him on thirty counts of illegally accepting gifts from large food producers in exchange for political influence. Espy pled not guilty to all charges and told reporters on 10 September 1997, "I know I will prevail." He was right. On 3 December 1998 the US District Court acquitted Espy on all charges after jurors found that, although Espy had received gifts, he had not provided favors in return.

In 1999 Espy returned to Washington to serve as a senior adviser to the Department of Energy on a no-pay, part-time basis. He remains involved in Washington politics and is still one of Mississippi's most influential and dynamic politicians, having established consulting and legal firms. He also frequently appears as guest commentator on national news programs and in magazines.

Craig S. Piper
Mississippi State University

Michael Baron and Grant Ujifusa, *The Almanac of American Politics, 1988* (1988); *Biographical Directory of the United States Congress, 1774–1989 Bicentennial Edition* (1989); Phil Duncan, ed. *Congressional Quarterly's Politics in America 1992: The 102nd Congress* (1992); Mike Espy Collection, Congressional and Political Research Center, University Libraries, Mississippi State University; Mike Espy PLLC website, www.mikespy.com.

Ethnicity

Although the United States is commonly described as a nation of immigrants, the South has historically proven the least enticing region for foreign settlers. Mississippi is no exception.

A small number of immigrants had settled in Mississippi as early as the eighteenth century. Jews and Italians who first arrived on American shores through the port of New Orleans eventually made their way to Mississippi, where many of them worked as peddlers. These immigrants were loyal to their new homeland and fought with the Confederate Army during the Civil War.

After the war, however, many white employers complained that African Americans freed of the coercive influence of slavery had become indolent and insubordinate and lobbied for the recruitment of foreign laborers as an alternative workforce. The Mississippi state legislature responded by establishing the Department of Agriculture and Immigration in 1873. Nine years later, state politicians approved further laws designed to attract immigrant workers.

Plantation owners recruited a small number of Chinese to the Delta beginning in 1869–70. With the demise of Reconstruction and restoration of white supremacist rule, however, planters reverted to hiring African Americans. Those Chinese who abandoned the fields but remained in the area carved a niche in the local economy as grocery store owners who catered principally to black customers. Beginning in the 1880s Sicilians settled on the Gulf Coast, where they worked in truck-farming colonies or in the fishing and canning industries. Syrian and Lebanese immigrants pursued a similar economic route to Jews, starting out as peddlers before establishing themselves as store owners, and Jewish merchants became increasingly prominent on the main streets of many Mississippi communities.

But political and business leaders' efforts to lure foreign laborers to Mississippi largely proved unsuccessful. Economist James A. Dunlevy argues that many immigrants shared an "avoidance of the South syndrome" as a consequence of five factors: (1) the region's predominantly rural economy offered fewer and less lucrative employment prospects than the industrial North; (2) immigrants from farming backgrounds had fewer opportunities to settle their own land than were available in the West; (3) immigrants did not want to compete with African Americans in a hostile labor market; (4) the relative absence of urban centers restricted the growth of ethnic support networks; and (5) immigrants feared violent antipathy and preferred to settle in more welcoming regions.

In 1890 immigrants constituted 14.7 percent of the overall US population but only 0.98 percent of all southerners and just 0.62 percent of Mississippi residents (7,952 foreign-born persons out of a total population of 1,289,600). Only North Carolina and South Carolina had smaller shares of immigrants.

Immigrants had reason to fear that they would become the target of nativist violence. Mississippians scapegoated immigrants in times of social and economic turmoil. The economic depression of the 1890s, for example, resulted in the foreclosure of many white farms. When Jewish merchants who purchased this property rented it to black sharecroppers, resentful whites retaliated by forming themselves into vigilante groups known as White Caps. Launching a series of arson attacks, they reclaimed the land from terrorized black sharecroppers and their Jewish landlords.

Sicilians were also victims of mob violence. Late-nineteenth- and early twentieth-century stereotypes portrayed Sicilians as dangerous criminals who threatened the social order. Although nativist violence against Sicilians was more common in Louisiana, lynch mobs were also active in Mississippi. In March 1886 a mob seized Federico Villarosa from a jail in Natchez, where he was awaiting trial on a rape charge, and hanged him. A further act of lynch law occurred in July 1901 when whites in Erwin murdered Vincenzo and Giovanni Serio and wounded Salvatori Liberto. A local newspaper defended the mob's actions on the grounds that Vincenzo Serio had been "a source of trouble to the neighborhood ever since he took up his residence."

By the early twentieth century state leaders had abandoned their hope of recruiting an alternative labor force to African Americans. The influx of supposedly unassimilable Southern and Eastern Europeans stimulated an intense nativist reaction across the United States, and Mississippi politicians added their voices to the mounting chorus calling for immigration restrictions. Sens. Leroy Percy and John S. Williams supported literacy tests intended to limit the number of immigrants admitted. Williams believed that migrants from Southern and Eastern Europe threatened the social and political order because they had neither experience of nor the capacity for democratic government: "The ignorant man, whatever his race, coming to a country where he is not governed but becomes a part of the governing force, is dangerous." The Mississippi Farmers' Educational and Cooperative Union also lobbied to curtail mill owners' recruitment of immigrant field hands because it threatened to reduce raw cotton prices.

One of the most complicated issues that confronted immigrants was their position in the southern racial hierarchy, which often placed them in a liminal status between black and white. White Mississippi society considered Chinese and Sicilians to be nonwhite, resulting in their social exclusion. New immigrants often fraternized with African Americans, and immigrant merchants gained a reputation for treating black customers with courtesy and respect. In addition, some Chinese men married African American women. In other cases, however, Chinese rejected assimilation with the black minority and cultivated the white com-

munity, sending their children to white churches and giving money to causes and programs favored by white leaders. Some anglicized their Chinese family names. In some instances, such efforts gradually persuaded the white community to grant the Chinese some degree of privilege, allowing them to frequent public places from which blacks were barred. Chinese grocers improved their stores, acknowledged Jim Crow laws, and began to have white customers.

The 1890 constitution created separate school systems for African Americans and whites but did not specify which category encompassed Chinese and Sicilian children, who consequently attended white schools in many Delta communities. In 1924, however, Rosedale officials barred Chinese children from the town's white schools, prompting a lawsuit. The case, *Lum v. Rice*, ultimately reached the US Supreme Court, which upheld the Mississippi Supreme Court's ruling denying Chinese students access to white public schools.

Nevertheless, through the middle of the twentieth century, ethnic minorities generally succeeded in claiming the rights and privileges of whiteness. During the desegregation crises of the 1950s and 1960s, Citizens' Councils actively recruited participation from members of these ethnic groups. Yet the civil rights struggle also led to a resurgence of ethnic violence. Some white supremacists believed that the black freedom struggle was a conspiracy masterminded by Jewish communists. In 1967 the Ku Klux Klan bombed Temple Beth Israel in Jackson and the home of its rabbi, Perry Nussbaum, who had supported imprisoned Freedom Riders. Less than a year later, Meridian's Temple Beth Israel suffered a similar terrorist attack.

The decline of rural and small-town economies during the last decades of the twentieth century led to the outmigration of many ethnic minorities. Mississippi is nonetheless now experiencing one of the most significant ethnic transformations in its history. Changes to federal immigration and free trade policies have stimulated increased labor migration from Latin America. Between the 2000 and 2010 US censuses, the percentage of Mississippi's population that was Hispanic or Latino doubled from 1.4 percent to 3.0 percent, and demographers predict that those figures will continue to grow rapidly. Moreover, those figures may underreport the true number of Latinos in Mississippi, since those who lack the proper documentation to reside in the United States may not have participated in the census. Mississippi's Latinos have settled mostly in small towns and rural areas, where they work on farms and in poultry plants. Urban centers, especially Jackson, also have significant Latino populations. Mississippi's Latino population is predominantly Mexican but also includes people from Puerto Rico, Cuba, and other Latin American countries.

The Mississippi Immigrants' Rights Alliance formed in 2000 to protect and promote the interests of the state's emerging Latino community. The alliance has scored a number of successes, most notably recovering more than one million dollars in unpaid wages for immigrant workers who helped rebuild coastal Mississippi after Hurricanes Katrina and Rita. Latino migration will play an increasingly profound role in redefining the economic, political, and racial dynamics of a state historically shaped by a basic division between black and white.

Clive Webb
University of Sussex

Roland T. Berthoff, *Journal of Southern History* (August 1951); James C. Cobb, *The Most Southern Place on Earth: The Mississippi Delta and the Roots of Regional Identity* (1992); James A. Dunlevy, in *Research in Economic History: A Research Annual*, vol. 8, ed. Paul Uselding (1982); James W. Loewen, *The Mississippi Chinese* (1971); Mississippi Immigrants' Rights Alliance website, www.yourmira.org; Raymond A. Mohl, in *Other Souths: Diversity and Difference in the U.S. South, Reconstruction to Present*, ed. Pippa Holloway (2008); Leo E. Turitz and Evelyn Turitz, *Jews in Early Mississippi* (1983); US Census Bureau, American FactFinder website, factfinder.census.gov; Shana Walton and Barbara Carpenter, ed., *Ethnic Heritage in Mississippi: The Twentieth Century* (2012); Clive Webb, *American Nineteenth-Century History* (Spring 2002).

Ethnographies of Mississippi

Between World War I and World War II, social scientists and intellectuals perceived Mississippi as the most southern of the southern states. These scholars conducted three pioneering studies—two in Indianola and one in Natchez—that represented Mississippi as "the South." All were supported by the Rockefeller-funded Social Science Research Council, a newly formed organization that underwrote problem-oriented social science research. In Mississippi, the issue studied was the "Negro problem."

Between 1932 and 1934, Hortense Powdermaker spent twelve months in Indianola, in Sunflower County, ultimately producing *After Freedom: A Cultural Study in the Deep South* (1939), an ethnography that described the town's African American community (though she referred to it by the pseudonym Cottonville). She also surveyed middle-class whites regarding their attitudes on the "interracial situation."

John Dollard, Powdermaker's colleague at the Yale Institute of Human Relations, spent five months conducting research in Indianola (which he called Southerntown) and made broad generalizations about the nature of race relations in the South in *Caste and Class in a Southern Town* (1937). Rather than studying community norms and attitudes, as Powdermaker did, Dollard laid out a series of social, economic, and psy-

chological "gains" that whites obtained by dominating black people and explored the effects of white supremacy on African Americans. The first edition of Dollard's book contained a report by Leonard W. Doob on "Poor Whites: A Frustrated Class," the only ethnographic attention paid to this group.

Dollard adopted the concept of "caste and class" from W. Lloyd Warner, a Harvard anthropologist. While Powdermaker and Dollard were studying Indianola, Warner directed an in-depth multiyear study of Natchez, which he dubbed Old City. His research team included an African American couple, W. B. Allison Davis and Elizabeth Stubbs Davis, and a white couple, Burleigh B. Gardner and Mary R. Gardner. They produced *Deep South: A Social Anthropological Study of Caste and Class* (1941), which examined the "system of color-castes," looking at the stratification within each caste and examining the system's economic underpinnings.

These three works are now considered classics. Dollard's broad-brush analysis of white racism was poorly reviewed but remained a staple in classrooms and was read by virtually all civil rights workers in Mississippi in the 1960s. *Deep South* was used to support the US Supreme Court's *Brown v. Board of Education* decision outlawing segregated public schools. Powdermaker's well-reviewed study garnered little attention until the late 1960s and has subsequently remained continuously in print.

Three decades passed before publication of the next significant ethnographic study of Mississippi, James W. Loewen's *The Mississippi Chinese: Between Black and White* (1971). Unlike the depression-era studies, Loewen did not claim to study a general phenomenon; rather, he brought to light a group that had been largely invisible outside the Delta. *The Mississippi Chinese* can be viewed as emblematic of the revolutionary shift in the structure of race in America, marking a renewed interest in ethnicity and a recognition that "race" constituted more than simply black and white.

In 1997 political scientist Frederick M. Wirt documented the impact that federal civil rights laws had on institutions and individuals in Panola County in *"We Ain't What We Was": Civil Rights in the New South*. White attitudes, Wirt argues, changed largely because of enforcement of federal civil rights laws. The study is ethnographic because Wirt conducted large numbers of in-depth interviews and used local newspapers and other qualitative sources to explore changing attitudes and behaviors.

All of these studies occurred near the Mississippi River, primarily in the Delta, where plantation agriculture predominated. The river also allowed a vigorous commercial culture to develop, something little noted in these studies. Economic anthropologist E. Paul Durrenberger looks at these dimensions of Mississippi Gulf fisheries in his 1996 ethnography, *Gulf Coast Soundings: People and Policy in the Mississippi Shrimp Industry*. This work analyzes the history of shrimping around Biloxi, documenting the arrival of Vietnamese immigrants, relations among fishers and processors, and the international markets and ecological conditions that shift the circumstances under which fishers make their livelihoods.

Jane Adams
Southern Illinois University
Carbondale

Allison Davis, Burleigh B. Gardner, and Mary R. Gardner, *Deep South: A Social Anthropological Study of Caste and Class* (1941); John Dollard, *Caste and Class in a Southern Town* (1937); Leonard W. Doob, in *Caste and Class in a Southern Town*, ed. John Dollard (1937); Paul E. Durrenberger, *Gulf Coast Soundings: People and Policy in the Mississippi Shrimp Industry* (1996); James W. Loewen, *The Mississippi Chinese: Between Black and White* (1988); Hortense Powdermaker, *After Freedom: A Cultural Study in the Deep South* (1939); Frederick M. Wirt, *"We Ain't What We Was": Civil Rights in the New South* (1997).

Ethridge, Tom
(1911–1974) Journalist

From 1951 until his death Tom Ethridge wrote a popular column, "Mississippi Notebook," for the *Jackson Clarion-Ledger*, Mississippi's largest statewide daily newspaper. His Confederate-flag-waving column earned him a reputation as an archconservative, sarcastic, race-baiting defender of Mississippi and southern values.

Thomas Tann Ethridge was born into an influential family. His father, George Hamilton Ethridge, had been in the state legislature, served as assistant attorney general, and sat as a justice of the Mississippi Supreme Court for twenty-five years, making him one of the few men to serve in all three branches of the state government. The youngest of four children, Tom attended Jackson public schools and took classes at Tulane University, though he never graduated.

Ethridge worked as an advertising manager for the Mississippi Power and Light Company for many years and initially wrote "Mississippi Notebook" as a hobby, distributing it free of charge to the state's newspapers. As it grew in popularity, the *Clarion-Ledger* brought him onto the full-time staff as a columnist and editorial assistant in 1951.

Ethridge's column featured down-home humor and backwoods racism and appeared in the *Clarion-Ledger* and *Jackson Daily News*, both of which were owned by the powerful Hederman family, as well as in segregationist publications such as the *Citizens' Council*, the *Citizen*, and the *Southern Review*. As the civil rights movement enveloped the state, the Hederman papers and Ethridge hammered readers with the rhetoric of states' rights, white superiority and black inferiority, "communist infiltration," and "outside agitators."

Ethridge's column regularly attacked anything that he perceived as threatening the state and its customs, especially the federal government, civil rights activists, and liberals. Ethridge explained that the NAACP stood for "Niggers, Apes, Alligators, Coons, and Possums" and likened the organization's executive secretary, Roy Wilkins, to an African witch doctor who "reverted to ancient tribal instincts." In response to the University of Mississippi desegregation crisis, Ethridge applauded Gov. Ross Barnett's "courageous" stand against the federal government, labeled the Fifth Circuit judges who had ordered James Meredith's admission "nine judicial baboons," and ran a string of racist jokes about watermelons and chicken thefts. Ethridge reveled in the 1965 violence in Los Angeles's Watts neighborhood, happy to have the nation's attention turned away from the South. The Los Angeles Police Department should take a page from the Birmingham police, he claimed, but should replace fire hoses and police dogs with flamethrowers because "nothing could stop bloodthirsty savages quicker than reducing them to cinders."

The Hedermans and Ethridge served as mouthpieces for the state hierarchy, unquestioningly supporting Barnett, Sen. James O. Eastland, the Citizens' Council, and the Mississippi State Sovereignty Commission. The Citizens' Council gave Ethridge an award for his "fair stories" about the Council, and the Mississippi House of Representatives approved a resolution praising his service to the state. The Sovereignty Commission passed along information on civil rights "troublemakers" that he could use to whip up anti-integrationist sentiment in his column.

Ethridge leveled considerable criticism at fellow journalists Bill Minor, Hodding Carter Jr., and Ira Harkey, calling them "traitors" to their heritage and a "cancer to the cause." When Harkey won the Pulitzer Prize for his coverage of the University of Mississippi crisis, Ethridge editorialized that "any journalistic quisling" who "indulges in local bedwetting" apparently appealed to the "mix-minded" Pulitzer board. Harkey responded by calling Ethridge a "weird fellow, of typical cold unsmiling bigot visage," a sentiment echoed by Minor, who remembered Ethridge as an "annoying, nasty little parasite."

Many civil rights groups and newspapers outside the South quoted Ethridge's columns as an attempt to show the "problem" with Mississippi, but "Mississippi Notebook" remained the *Clarion-Ledger*'s most popular column. He received the Liberty Award from the Congress of Freedom, the Man of the Year Award from Women of Constitutional Government, and accolades from many other groups, including the American Legion, Daughters of the American Revolution, and American Coalition of Patriotic Societies.

Ethridge's death in 1974 coincided with a new day in Mississippi journalism. The preceding year, Rea Hederman had taken the helm of the *Clarion-Ledger* and vowed to turn the paper around. In 1974 the *Clarion-Ledger* hired its first black reporter. Less than a decade later it won a Pulitzer Prize of its own.

Rebecca Miller Davis
University of Missouri at
Kansas City

David G. Davies, ed., *The Press and Race* (2001); Tom Ethridge Subject File, Mississippi Department of Archives and History; Ira Harkey, *The Smell of Burning Crosses* (1967); Bill Minor, interview by Rebecca L. Miller (12 December 2008); James Silver, *Mississippi: The Closed Society* (1963); Curtis Wilkie, *Dixie* (2001); Curtis Wilkie, interview by Rebecca L. Miller (20 May 2008).

Eubanks, W. Ralph

(b. 1957) Author and Editor

W. Ralph Eubanks, an editor, publisher, and writer based in Washington, D.C., was born on 25 June 1957 in Collins, Mississippi. His father, Warren Ralph Eubanks, was employed by the Farmers Home Administration, and his mother, Lucille Richardson Eubanks, worked as a schoolteacher. Eubanks attended segregated schools in Mount Olive and Collins from 1963 until 1970, when he became one of the first African American students to integrate the Mount Olive school district. Upon graduating from high school in 1974 he enrolled at the University of Mississippi, where he received degrees in psychology and English literature in 1978. He went on to earn a master's degree from the University of Michigan the following year.

In his first book, *Ever Is a Long Time* (2003), Eubanks described his upbringing on a farm near Mount Olive. His parents, graduates of Tuskegee College and members of the National Association for the Advancement of Colored People, shielded him and his three sisters from much of the racism and violence of the period. However, sit-ins, church burnings, and the assassinations of Medgar Evers, John F. Kennedy, and Martin Luther King Jr. served as reminders of the ongoing tensions. Days before Eubanks was born, Mississippi's governor, James P. Coleman, had been asked whether Mississippi's public schools would ever be integrated. He responded, "Well, ever is a long time. . . . I would say that a baby born in Mississippi today will never live long enough to see an integrated school." Twelve years later, Eubanks's mother reminded him and his sisters of Coleman's words on their first day of classes at the newly integrated Mount Olive High School. While at the school, Eubanks began to read books by southern authors, including Mississippians William Faulkner and Eudora Welty, that helped him obtain a more nuanced understanding of the South and inspired him to pursue writing as a career.

Although primarily a memoir, *Ever Is a Long Time* also provides a history of the Mississippi State Sovereignty Commission (1956–73), a publicly funded agency that attempted to maintain white supremacy in the state by spying on citizens who favored integration. When the commission's files on eighty-seven thousand Mississippians were declassified in 1998, Eubanks learned that his parents had been under surveillance by the largest state-run spy network in American history. Eubanks spent three years conducting research in an attempt to understand why his parents had generated commission files, scouring through previously classified documents and interviewing former commission member Horace Harned, former Klansman and superintendent of education Denson Lott, and civil rights activist Ed King.

Eubanks's second book, *The House at the End of the Road* (2009), tells the story of the interracial marriage of his maternal grandparents, James Morgan Richardson and Edna Howell Richardson. After marrying in 1914, Jim, a white man, and Edna, a light-skinned black woman, made their home in the largely independent black community of Prestwick, Alabama. They raised their children, designated white on their birth certificates, to acknowledge their mixed-race background, leading several white members of the Richardson family to disown the black members of the family and ultimately to his grandparents' burials in separate cemeteries. Eubanks intertwines this narrative with a history of interracial marriages and the laws that affected these relationships. He also explores racial identity in American history, noting how the socially and culturally constructed category of race means very little to his interracial children and their generation. Eubanks credits the change to the American population's increasingly multiracial makeup as well as to Jim and Edna Richardson and other couples who chose to transcend the racial possibilities of their time.

Eubanks has also written articles for numerous publications and is a contributor to National Public Radio. He has worked as an editor for most of his career, holding positions at the American Geophysical Union, the American Psychological Association, and Taylor and Francis USA. From 1995 to 2013 he served as the director of publishing at the Library of Congress. From 2013 to 2014 he served as editor of the *Virginia Quarterly Review*. He received a 2007 Guggenheim Fellowship and has been a fellow at the New America Foundation. He is married to Colleen Delaney, and they have three children.

Xaris A. Martínez
University of North Carolina

W. Ralph Eubanks, *Ever Is A Long Time: A Journey into Mississippi's Dark Past, a Memoir* (2003); W. Ralph Eubanks, in *Beyond the Archives: Research as a Lived Process*, ed. Gesa E. Kirsch and Liz Rohan (2008);

W. Ralph Eubanks, The House at the End of the Road: The Story of Three Generations of an Interracial Family in the American South (2009).

Eugenics

Derived from Greek to mean "well born," *eugenics* was coined as a term to "express the science of improving stock ... especially in the case of man" and was first promoted in 1883 by Francis Galton, a cousin of Charles Darwin. Eugenic thought had both positive and negative components. Positive eugenics encouraged the proliferation of the "well born," while negative eugenics strove to control the population of those believed to be unfit. Negative eugenics had varied manifestations in the American South and in Mississippi specifically, including restrictions on interracial marriages or those considered mentally incompetent, sex-based segregation of mental health facilities, sterilization, and, as seen in Virginia, a drive to document the ethnic composition of citizens. Eugenic practice in Mississippi initially sought to safeguard the supposed purity of the white race through control of mentally degenerate whites but in the mid-twentieth century became a justification for the sterilization of economically disadvantaged black women.

As historian Edward J. Larson notes in *Sex, Race, and Science: Eugenics in the Deep South,* eugenic practice was introduced formally in Mississippi in 1913 by J. N. Fox, a physician at the state mental hospital in Jackson. Fox promoted the control of mental illness and disability through restrictions on marriage. At the 1913 annual meeting of the Mississippi Medical Association, Fox stated, "It is a well-known fact that when two feebleminded persons mate, their offspring is sure to be feebleminded also." He went on to state that these offspring were likely to become "murderers, sexual perverts, and pyro-maniacs."

Though Fox was the first to formally present a eugenic program to Mississippi physicians, the idea was not new. In 1912 J. M. Buchanan, superintendent of the East Mississippi Insane Asylum, wrote an article urging compulsory sterilization not only of severe cases but also of those suffering from "any form of nervous instability."

With the support of the state's physicians, Gov. Theodore G. Bilbo began to promote eugenics in 1919, pushing for a separate facility for the "mentally retarded" after Thomas H. Haines, an official of the National Committee for Mental Hygiene, observed Mississippi's prisons and noted that "imbeciles" lacked "common sense" but were "highly sexed." Haines deliberately sought to promote eugenic practice, and his biased and unscientific survey found "200 or 300 feebleminded delinquents passing through the courts of Mississippi each year." Based on his findings, he suggested the creation of a separate "colony" as a more efficient and cost-effective way to care for and sexually segregate those with mental illness or disability. Such a colony would be located in a rural area, with the "higher grade morons" able to function on self-supporting agricultural settlements near the main institution. The colony would also begin sterilizing its residents.

On 2 April 1920, after hearing testimony in support from the State Federation of Women's Clubs, the Mississippi House of Representatives approved legislation to create an institution, making it the last state in the Deep South to pass such a measure. The *Jackson Daily News* heralded the law, noting that it would "put a final stop to the increase of much useless humanity." However, poor and rural Mississippi never prioritized funding for eugenic programs, and interest in the idea declined after Bilbo left office later that year. Eugenics returned to prominence with Bilbo's reelection as governor in 1928, and the state soon had the Deep South's first comprehensive eugenic sterilization law, lauded as the "result of a social awakening." Bilbo's inaugural address implicitly argued for sterilization and the expansion of the Mississippi Colony: "The state has spent its millions in the effort to advance our civilization, to educate and uplift our people yet our feebleminded, epileptic, insane, paupers and criminals can reproduce without restriction, thus continuing to corrupt our society and increase tax burdens on our people." The appropriations bill to fund the new institution was introduced by Jacksonian Wiley Harris, who noted that "surely society owes to posterity no higher duty than by humane methods to breed out of the race such defectives as those who at once become a burden to the state and a scourge to their descendents." H. H. Ramsey, the superintendent of the Mississippi School and Colony for the Feebleminded, was a major proponent of eugenics and began working on a joint effort to identify developmentally disabled and ill children in the state's schools while expanding the sexually segregated facilities to include vocational training with plans for future sterilization of patients.

The cost of implementation and the rising demand for social services with the onset of the Great Depression meant that this comprehensive law did not have a major effect until the mid-1930s. The Mississippi Colony performed few sterilizations because the state lacked the funds to fight court appeals from patients' families, who were required to consent to the operations. Sterilizations continued at state institutions at a declining rate until World War II, when the East Mississippi Insane Asylum in Meridian lost its only surgeon to the war effort. By 1941 the Mississippi Colony's leadership no longer promoted eugenics. However, the comprehensive sterilization law remains on the books, with its only alteration the 1984 deletion of epilepsy from the conditions requiring sterilization.

In the mid-twentieth century, eugenics turned from the protection of the "purity" of the white race to population control for the poor. Mississippi's politicians and doctors began to impose eugenic practice on the black population of the Delta. With the mechanization of crops and increased civil rights activity, politicians and the Citizens' Council began to attempt to disperse the state's black population—to curb the "black tide which threatens to engulf us." According to Dorothy Roberts, surgeons commonly sterilized black women without their consent while they were hospitalized for other surgeries, with as many as 60 percent of women at one Delta hospital given postpartum sterilizations. The practice was so prevalent that it became known as the "Mississippi appendectomy," and among those affected was Mississippi Freedom Democratic Party leader Fannie Lou Hamer, who was sterilized at Sunflower City Hospital after a minor operation in 1961.

In 1972 the Mississippi House considered a bill that made it a felony for a welfare recipient to give birth to a second illegitimate child, providing penalties of between one and five years' incarceration or sterilization. The Student Nonviolent Coordinating Committee was outraged at the bill's implications for the communities in which the group worked and condemned the measure as a "genocide bill," citing Rep. Stone Barefield, who stated during the floor debate, "When the cutting starts, they'll head to Chicago." The campaign against the bill gained national attention, and the Mississippi Senate passed a less restrictive bill that nevertheless declared unmarried parenthood to be a crime. Sterilization was deleted as a penalty, the charge was changed from a felony to a misdemeanor, and the punishment was reduced to between thirty and ninety days in jail. This law remains on the books.

The practice of eugenics in Mississippi has had a variety of manifestations. From pseudoscientific actions designed to protect whites from degenerative mental illness to the involuntary sterilization of black Delta women in the 1960s and 1970s, the practice has signaled a historic drive among state officials to maintain strict class- and race-based hierarchies, with troubling implications for human rights.

Becca Walton
University of Mississippi

Susan K. Cahn, *Sexual Reckonings: Southern Girls in a Troubling Age* (2007); James C. Cobb, *The Most Southern Place on Earth: The Mississippi Delta and the Roots of Regional Identity* (1992); Edward J. Larson, *Sex, Race, and Science: Eugenics in the Deep South* (1995); Dorothy Roberts, *Killing the Black Body: Race, Reproduction, and the Meaning of Liberty* (1997); Alexandra Minna Stern, *Eugenic Nation: Faults and Frontiers of Better Breeding in Modern America* (2005); Clyde Woods, *Development Arrested: The Blues and Plantation Power in the Mississippi Delta* (2000).

Evers, Charles
(b. 1922) Activist and Politician

Charles Evers has been working as a civil rights activist, businessman, and politician since the 1950s. The older brother of Medgar Evers, Charles Evers earned recognition in his own right as a disc jockey, the first African American member of the Democratic National Committee, and the first African American mayor of a biracial town in Mississippi in more than a century.

James Charles Evers was born in Decatur, Mississippi, on 11 September 1922, the eldest of Jim and Jessie Evers's four children. Jim Evers held a variety of jobs, including stacking lumber in sawmills, working for the railroad, renting property, operating a small farm, and working as a lumber contractor. Jessie Evers supplemented the family's income by working as a maid. Beginning as a teenager, Charles earned money as a bootlegger.

In 1939 Evers left school, lied about his age, and enlisted in the US Army. He was soon discovered and dismissed from the service. Evers then moved to Forest, where he worked in a funeral home operated by his great-uncle. He reenlisted in the army when he turned eighteen and went to Camp Shelby in Hattiesburg. After training at several army bases, he was dispatched to the 334th Engineer Battalion with the Army Corps of Engineers. Evers was transferred to Fort Leonard Wood, Missouri, in 1942 and then was shipped overseas to Sydney, Australia, the following year. He served with a combat engineering unit in Australia, New Guinea, and the Philippines, rising to the rank of battalion sergeant major before being transferred back to Mississippi and mustered out of the army in 1945.

Charles and his younger brother, Medgar, subsequently attended Alcorn Agricultural and Mechanical College, where Charles earned a high school diploma as well as a college degree in social studies, though his education was interrupted when he was briefly recalled to the army. He served as class president, played center on the football team, and operated a

Charles Evers speaks at a demonstration to protest Vernon Dahmer's murder, January 1966 (Moncrief Collection, Archives and Records Services Division, Mississippi Department of Archives and History, [466])

taxi service for students. He also participated in civil rights work with Dr. Theodore Roosevelt Mason Howard and joined the National Association for the Advancement of Colored People (NAACP) in 1948.

Evers then moved to Philadelphia, Mississippi, where he managed a funeral parlor, taught history and coached football in nearby Noxapater, and continued his bootlegging operation. His involvement with the NAACP grew, and in 1953 he was elected the group's Mississippi voter registration chair. In February 1956 he organized the Philadelphia chapter of the NAACP, but financial problems and threats of retaliation by the Ku Klux Klan forced him to move to Chicago, where he held a series of jobs. He periodically visited the South to assist in voter registration drives and provide financial support to his family.

When Medgar Evers was assassinated on 12 June 1963, Charles Evers returned to Mississippi and took over for his brother as the NAACP's Mississippi field secretary. Evers remained active in the civil rights movement throughout Mississippi and the South, often serving as the NAACP's representative to other civil rights organizations and helping to run civil rights boycotts in Natchez and Fayette. In 1968 he ran for the congressional seat vacated when John Bell Williams became governor of Mississippi. Although Evers performed well in the primary, he lost in the runoff election. In 1968 he was one of three African American delegates from Mississippi to the Democratic National Convention, but he declined the position when the Mississippi delegation refused to swear loyalty to the national Democratic ticket, including its civil rights plank. Instead, he accepted a position on the Democratic National Executive Committee, the party's highest policymaking group.

Evers returned to politics in 1969, defeating an incumbent to become mayor of Fayette. In addition to his mayoral duties, Evers served as judge and prosecutor, and he further expanded his business ventures with the acquisition of a shopping center, motel, and restaurant. He repeatedly won reelection, remaining in the post until 1989. In 1974 he hosted the first Southern Conference of Black Mayors.

In 1971 Evers ran for governor, garnering 22 percent of the vote but losing to Democrat Bill Waller. Evers ran as an independent in the 1978 race to replace retiring US senator James O. Eastland, finishing third behind the Democratic candidate and the Republican victor, Thad Cochran.

Evers has written two memoirs, *Evers* (1971) and *Have No Fear: The Charles Evers Story* (1997). The federal government indicted Evers for income tax evasion in 1974, but the case ended in a mistrial in June 1975.

At the end of his political career, Evers joined the Republican Party. Since 1973 he has hosted the Medgar Wiley Evers Homecoming Celebration, which honors his brother's life and legacy. He remains active in the Fayette community and has traveled around the globe.

Carolyn Cooper Howard
University of Mississippi

Jason Berry, *Amazing Grace with Charles Evers in Mississippi* (1973); Charles Evers, *Evers*, ed. Grace Halsell (1971); Charles Evers and Andrew Szanton, *Have No Fear: The Charles Evers Story* (1997); Medgar Wiley Evers Homecoming website, medgarevershomecoming.com.

Evers, Medgar Wiley
(1925–1963) Civil Rights Activist

Medgar Evers became the first Mississippi field secretary for the National Association for the Advancement of Colored People (NAACP) in December 1954 and held this position until his death on 12 June 1963. As field secretary, Evers led and organized voter registration drives and economic boycotts and provided assistance to individuals struggling against white oppression and racism.

Medgar Wiley Evers was born in Decatur, Mississippi, on 2 July 1925 to James and Jessie Evers. The Everses were strong proponents of education and made sure their children attended school for the full term. Segregation, however, forced Medgar and his siblings to attend Newton Vocational School instead of the all-white high school in Decatur. This type of inequality, combined with a family heritage of resistance to injustice, heightened his sense of fair play. The many examples of manhood exhibited by his father and the religious convictions of his mother bolstered his belief in equality for all. Evers grew up in the Church of God in Christ but in 1956 became a member of Jackson's New Hope Baptist Church.

In 1943 Evers joined the US Army and served with the Red Ball Express, a truck convoy that brought supplies to Allied troops in the wake of the D-Day invasion. He went on to see combat in Liège and Antwerp, Belgium; and Normandy, Le Havre, and Cherbourg, France, receiving two combat stars and the Good Conduct Medal before returning to Mississippi in 1946. He and his older brother, Charles, registered to vote without incident but were denied the franchise on Election Day by an assembled white mob.

Both Everses enrolled at Alcorn Agricultural and Mechanical College in 1946. Medgar earned high school and college diplomas from the school, serving as editor of the campus newspaper and yearbook and as president of both the junior class and the student forum. He was also an active member of the debate team, college choir, football team, and track team. He married fellow Alcornite Myrlie Beasley on Christmas Eve 1951, and they went on to have three children, Darryl Kenyatta, Reena Denise, and James Van Dyke.

After graduating in 1952 Medgar and Myrlie Evers moved to all-black Mound Bayou, where he worked for the Magnolia Mutual Insurance Company. His January 1954 application to the University of Mississippi Law School was rejected because of his race, but the application brought Evers to the attention of the NAACP, which was looking to establish a stronghold in the state in the wake of the *Brown v. Board of Education* decision. He recruited for the NAACP and helped organize a successful boycott against area gas station owners who denied African Americans use of restroom facilities.

In January 1955 the Evers family relocated to Jackson. As field secretary Evers investigated instances of police brutality, murder, voter discrimination, economic intimidation, rape, and lynching, including the 1955 abduction and murder of fourteen-year-old Emmett Till in Money. Evers was also responsible for recruiting and retaining members for the NAACP and for providing African Americans with various forms of assistance.

By the early 1960s Evers had shifted toward direct action as the primary method for achieving social, political, and economic equality—for example, by organizing boycotts of discriminatory local stores and national chains in downtown Jackson. He also served as an adviser to James Meredith during his 1962 effort to integrate the University of Mississippi and supported student sit-in and read-in demonstrations in the state capital. In August 1962 the Everses petitioned the Jackson Separate School District to reorganize the schools under its jurisdiction on a nonsegregated basis. Medgar Evers also played an active role in a variety of civil rights organizations, among them the Citizens' Committee for Human Rights of Jackson and Operation Mississippi, which sought to "wipe out segregation in all phases of Mississippi life."

By June 1963 Evers had spent almost nine years working to bring national attention to the lack of respect for human life and violence—both random and deliberate—perpetrated against black Mississippians. He consistently apprised political officials in Washington of events in Mississippi as a means of linking the civil rights struggle in the state to the national struggle for equality. He sent reports of injustices and abuses to the FBI and the Justice Department for documentation and to the NAACP's national office in New York for publication. He understood that his activism made him a target but was more concerned about how his death might affect his family than about his personal safety.

Just after midnight on 12 June 1963, Evers arrived home from a strategy meeting at New Jerusalem Baptist Church. He got out of his car in the driveway and was shot in the back with a high-powered rifle. He died less than an hour later at University Medical Center. On 15 June a funeral was held in Jackson, and four days later he was buried with full military honors at Virginia's Arlington National Cemetery. Police arrested white extremist Byron De La Beckwith, and he was charged with the murder, but two 1964 trials ended in hung juries. A Mississippi jury finally convicted him of killing Evers on 5 February 1994 and sentenced him to life imprisonment. He died in prison in 2001.

Evers's contributions to the movement for civil equality in Mississippi have received extensive recognition, both within the state (his name appears on numerous streets and buildings as well as on Jackson's international airport) and elsewhere (for example, schools in Illinois and Medgar Evers College of the City University of New York). In 2003 the Mississippi legislature honored his service with House Concurrent Resolution No. 94.

Michael Vinson Williams
Tougaloo College

Charles Evers and Andrew Szanton, *Have No Fear: The Charles Evers Story* (1997); Medgar Wiley Evers and Myrlie Beasley Evers Papers, Mississippi Department of Archives and History; Myrlie Evers-Williams with William Peters, *For Us, the Living* (1967); Myrlie Evers-Williams and Manning Marable, *The Autobiography of Medgar Evers: A Hero's Life and Legacy Revealed through His Writings, Letters, and Speeches* (2005); Michael Vinson Williams, *Medgar Evers: Mississippi Martyr* (2011).

Evers, Medgar, Homecoming Celebration

Medgar Wiley Evers served as the first Mississippi field secretary for the National Association for the Advancement of Colored People from December 1954 until white extremist Byron De La Beckwith shot and killed Evers outside his Jackson home on 12 June 1963.

Charles Evers, Medgar's older brother, subsequently worked to organize services to honor his memory. Shortly after playing to a crowd of ten thousand at the 1973 memorial service in Jackson, blues icon B. B. King told Charles Evers that there "ought to be some kind of yearly event to keep Medgar's dream alive." What had been, in Charles's words, a "small Memorial Service on the second Sunday in June" became "three full days of celebrations."

The Medgar Evers Homecoming Celebration connects individuals of all backgrounds and social status in remembrance of Evers, the civil rights struggle, and all those who gave their lives in the quest for social and political parity. The objective of this celebration, according to Charles Evers, "is to try to show how far we've come since Medgar Evers's death. . . . Medgar didn't die for black folks. He died for the freedom of all folks." Until 1982 the annual event was held in Fayette, where Charles served two four-year terms as mayor. Event organizers then moved it to Jackson because of greater venues, overall convenience, and Medgar's love of the city. Over the years the event has included forums discussing the civil rights movement, gospel expos, skydiving events, rodeos, carnivals, gospel and blues concerts, and an annual parade. Attendees have included such notables as James Earl Jones, Robert F. Kennedy Jr., Danny Glover, Redd Foxx, Louis Gossett Jr., Muhammad Ali, Joe Namath, and Kris Kristofferson; Foxx and Ali have participated in the annual parade. Political figures such as the Rev. Jesse Jackson and Nelson Rockefeller have also supported the annual celebration.

The annual Medgar Evers Parade remains an integral part of the memorial celebration. Many individuals look forward to this portion of the commemoration, during which celebrity grand marshals, local political figures, organizations, schools, and community folk both stand and travel along well-marked routes to the sounds of music and neighborhood enthusiasm.

Organizers intend the event not only to celebrate the life of Medgar Evers but to inspire those in attendance to remember the struggle waged and the victories gained.

Michael Vinson Williams
Tougaloo College

Kenn D. Cockrell, in *Medgar Evers Homecoming Booklet, June 4–6, 1982*, Mississippi Department of Archives and History; Medgar Wiley Evers Homecoming website, medgarevershomecoming.com; Evers, Medgar Memorial Festival, Mississippi Department of Archives and History; *Forty-Fourth Annual Medgar Wiley Evers/B. B. King Mississippi Homecoming Booklet, May 31–June 2, 2007*; Michael Vinson Williams, *Medgar Evers: Mississippi Martyr* (2011).

Evers-Williams, Myrlie
(b. 1933) Activist and Author

Known primarily as the widow of the civil rights leader Medgar Evers, Myrlie Evers-Williams has proven to be an influential African American civil rights activist in her own right.

Myrlie Louise Beasley was born in Vicksburg on 17 March 1933. Her parents were Mildred Washington Beasley and James Van Dyke Beasley, but she was raised by her grandmother, Annie "Mama" McCain Beasley, and her aunt and namesake, Myrlie Beasley Polk. Myrlie Beasley began learning to play the piano at age four and started giving piano lessons to other children at age twelve. She enrolled at Alcorn Agricultural and Mechanical College in Lorman intending to pursue a career as a pianist but changed her major to education and minored in music.

In 1950, on the first day of her freshman year at Alcorn, Beasley met Medgar Evers, who was two years ahead of her

Myrlie Evers-Williams at University of Mississippi, 2012 (Photograph by Nathan Latil, courtesy University of Mississippi University Communications)

at the school. They married on 24 December 1951 and spent another year at Alcorn while Medgar finished his degree. Myrlie Evers hoped that they would move to Chicago, but her husband did not want to leave Mississippi, so they moved to Mound Bayou, where he accepted a job at the Magnolia Mutual Insurance Company and she had a summer job as a secretary. She planned to return to college in the fall, but a severe illness both terminated her first pregnancy and hospitalized her, depleting the money set aside for her college. They remained in Mound Bayou and had two children, Darrell Kenyatta and Reena Denise.

In December 1954 Medgar Evers became the Mississippi field secretary for the National Association for the Advancement of Colored People (NAACP), and the family moved to Jackson early the following year. Myrlie Evers enjoyed the city's African American community despite threats to her husband's life, and in 1957 the Everses reached the landmark of owning their own home—and a piano. Myrlie Evers worked part time as Medgar's secretary, chauffeur, and hostess, a partnership seeking voting rights, equal justice, and economic equality for blacks in Mississippi.

As Medgar Evers's civil rights activities attracted more attention, Myrlie Evers came increasingly to fear attacks by white extremists. She became afraid to let her children play outside or answer the telephone, and her marriage suffered. In 1959, she took the children and left for a few days. The Everses reconciled and worked to separate their private life a little more from the civil rights movement and to let Myrlie step out of Medgar's shadow, and she took charge of the family finances so that she would be prepared if something happened to her husband. Their third child, James Van Dyke, was born in 1960.

In the early 1960s the fear worsened. Myrlie and Medgar Evers slept with guns by their beds and taught their children what to do if the house were attacked. Policemen trailed Myrlie Evers whenever she drove anywhere, and a Molotov cocktail exploded in their carport. On the evening of 11 June 1963 Myrlie Evers and her two older children watched Pres. John F. Kennedy's civil rights speech on television. Shortly after midnight, they heard the sound of Medgar Evers's car in the driveway, followed by the gunshots that killed him.

After a 15 June funeral at Jackson's Masonic Temple, Medgar Evers was buried at Virginia's Arlington National Cemetery on 19 June. Myrlie Evers subsequently slipped into a deep depression, though she remained outwardly strong, giving speeches and raising funds for the NAACP. In July 1964 she moved her family to Claremont, California, and enrolled at Pomona College. She continued to work for the NAACP and published a book, *For Us, the Living* (1967), while earning a 1968 bachelor's degree in sociology. Evers held a variety of jobs, including assistant director of planning and development for Claremont College and director of community affairs for the Atlantic Richfield Company. In 1976 she married labor and civil rights activist Walter Edward Williams. Throughout this period she remained heavily involved in politics and the NAACP.

In 1989, with the help of Jerry Mitchell of the *Jackson Clarion-Ledger* and Morris Dees of the Southern Poverty Law Center and with the support of her husband, Evers-Williams persuaded prosecutor Ed Peters to reopen the case against Byron De La Beckwith, who had been charged with Medgar Evers's murder in 1964 but had not been convicted. Prosecutors led by Bobby DeLaughter spent four years preparing for the new trial, and when it began Evers-Williams was the first witness. She and her two oldest children were present when De La Beckwith was found guilty on 5 February 1994.

On 19 February 1995 Evers-Williams was elected chair of the NAACP, becoming the first woman to head the organization. She stepped down in 1998 to focus on establishing the Medgar Evers Institute, which works to preserve and advance Medgar Evers's legacy. In 2012, in anticipation of the fiftieth anniversary of his death and in recognition of Myrlie Evers-Williams's work, the organization's name was changed to the Medgar and Myrlie Evers Institute. In 2013 she delivered the invocation at Pres. Barack Obama's second inauguration.

Anna F. Kaplan
Columbia University

Charles Evers and Andrew Szanton, *Have No Fear: The Charles Evers Story* (1997); Medgar and Myrlie Evers Institute website, www.evers institute.org; Myrlie Evers-Williams with Melinda Blau, *Watch Me Fly: What I Learned on the Way to Becoming the Woman I Was Meant to Be* (1999); Myrlie Evers-Williams with William Peters, *For Us, the Living* (1967).

Ex parte McCardle

Ex parte McCardle (1869) was a landmark case in which the US Supreme Court recognized Congress's power to make exceptions to the court's appellate jurisdiction. Today, both opponents and supporters of contemporary proposals to restrict Supreme Court jurisdiction cite *McCardle* as precedent.

William McCardle, editor of the *Vicksburg Times*, published a series of articles highly critical of Reconstruction. US Army officials arrested him under the Military Reconstruction Act of 1867, which gave the military jurisdiction over much of the South following the Civil War. McCardle was charged with disturbing the peace, inciting insurrection, libel, and impeding Reconstruction. He sought release by bringing an action for habeas corpus in the US Circuit Court for the Southern District of Mississippi. The court dismissed the writ and remanded McCardle to military custody. He was released on bail subject to the disposition of an appeal of that decision to the US Supreme Court. On appeal, McCardle argued that the Military Reconstruction Act was unconstitutional.

Under the Judiciary Act of 1789, federal courts could hear habeas petitions only of those who were held in federal custody. However, the Habeas Corpus Act of 1867 had empowered the US Supreme Court to hear appeals from lower courts in habeas corpus cases, a Radical Republican–backed measure intended to protect former slaves from southern state courts. The US government argued that the new act did not give the federal courts jurisdiction to grant habeas corpus to McCardle since he was not being held by the State of Mississippi. The Supreme Court rejected that argument and set the case for argument on the merits. Radicals faced the possibility that a statute drafted with the goal of preventing southern states from impeding Reconstruction would be used to attack the Military Reconstruction Act itself.

On 9 March 1868 the Supreme Court held oral arguments on McCardle's constitutional claims. Later in the month Congress repealed part of the Habeas Corpus Act, specifically to prevent the court from hearing McCardle's case. The Supreme Court then considered whether it had jurisdiction to hear McCardle's constitutional claims. On 12 April 1869 the court held that it could not decide McCardle's case because Congress had constitutional authority to regulate the court's appellate jurisdiction. Writing for the unanimous court, Chief Justice Salmon P. Chase observed that although the court's authority stems from the Constitution, it "is conferred 'with such exceptions and under such regulations as Congress shall make.'" And the court concluded that the 1868 act was an unmistakable exception to the court's appellate jurisdiction. However, the court also expressly indicated that it still had jurisdiction in habeas corpus cases, notwithstanding the partial repeal of the Habeas Corpus Act.

Natalya Seay
Washington, D.C.

Erwin Chemerinsky, *Federal Jurisdiction* (2007); *Ex parte McCardle*, 74 US 506 (1869); Peter W. Low and John C. Jeffries Jr., *Federal Courts and the Law of Federal State Relations* (2004); William Van Alstyne, "A Critical Guide to Ex parte McCardle," *Arizona Law Review* (1973).

Ex parte Yerger

Edward M. Yerger, a newspaper editor, southern nationalist, and member of one of Mississippi's most prominent families, murdered Col. Joseph H. Crane in Jackson on 8 June 1869. The slaying of Crane, a US Army officer acting as mayor of the occupied city, set off a national firestorm and became a flashpoint in debates about Congressional Reconstruction. To some observers, Yerger's act of rage and vengeance epitomized the violent recalcitrance of the unbowed South; for others, the murder proved the dangerous infeasibility of military occupation of the former Confederate states. A lengthy and sensational trial and several appeals produced no definitive verdict, and Yerger remained a figure of both curiosity and infamy until his death.

The dispute between Yerger and Crane arose from unpaid city taxes. To satisfy the newspaperman's considerable debt, Crane had ordered a piano seized from Yerger's home. Taking the seizure as an affront to his honor, Yerger responded swiftly and publicly by berating the mayor in a drunken rage and stabbing him repeatedly on a public street. Under the authority of Reconstruction Act of 1867, a military commission brought Yerger to trial. Yerger's team of lawyers, which included his uncle, Judge William Yerger, did not contest any of the facts of the case. Instead, they used the testimony of Yerger's friends, relatives, and ex-slaves to attempt to establish his alcoholism, propensity for violence, and "moral insanity." They also filed a motion contesting the jurisdiction of the military commission to rule on a case involving the commission of a crime against Mississippi law by a private citizen.

The 5th Circuit Court denied Yerger's application for habeas corpus, but his lawyers renewed the plea before US Supreme Court chief justice Salmon P. Chase. Chase declined to grant the writ to Yerger, instead instructing Yerger's lawyers to apply for jurisdiction in the Mississippi Circuit Court. After the Circuit Court at Jackson affirmed the jurisdiction of the military commission to try Yerger, his lawyers refiled their petition with the Supreme Court, and Chase invoked the court's appellate jurisdiction.

Yerger's challenge to the jurisdiction of the military commission exacerbated tensions within the federal government about the role of the judiciary and the constitutionality of the military governments of the Reconstruction Act of 1867. But while the granting of habeas corpus in *Ex parte Yerger* implicitly undermined the authority of the military commissions, both the government and Yerger's lawyers eschewed a showdown that would have resulted in a public hearing on the merits of Congressional Reconstruction. Thus, in October 1869, the government and Yerger's lawyers reached an agreement stipulating that Yerger would stand trial before a state court after Mississippi's readmission to the Union in early 1870. Once in custody of Mississippi authorities, Yerger promptly escaped from prison and spent a week hunting and fishing before voluntarily returning to jail. In 1871, while free on bail, Yerger moved to Baltimore, where he failed spectacularly in the newspaper business and died on 22 April 1875.

Thomas John Carey
University of Mississippi

Ex parte Yerger, 75 US 85 (1869); Charles Fairman, *History of the Supreme Court of the United States: Reconstruction and Reunion, 1864–88* (1971); W. S. M. Wilkinson, *Trial of E. M. Yerger, before a Military Commission for the Killing of Bv't-Col. Joseph G. Crane, at Jackson, Miss., June 8th, 1869, Reported for the Jackson Weekly Clarion* (1869).

Exodusters

In the winter and spring of 1879, after the end of Reconstruction, approximately five thousand former slaves fled economic inequality and increasing violence in the Lower Mississippi River Valley to settle in Kansas. Newspaper writers and other observers likened the grassroots migration to the ancient movement of Hebrews from Egypt, calling the migrants Exodusters. In Mississippi, freedpeople living in the rural Delta counties bordering the Mississippi River migrated in particularly large numbers.

After Reconstruction, Redeemer governments of white Democrats who had ruled the South before and during the Civil War passed laws to immobilize former slaves and preclude blacks from owning land. African Americans living in the rural counties and parishes of the Deep South faced the worst conditions. Organized violence made political participation prohibitively dangerous, and economic and agricultural policies trapped tenant farmers in cycles of debt.

As violence escalated and chances at landownership became more limited, pockets of southern blacks began to consider leaving the region. In the mid-1870s, groups in Mississippi sent letters of inquiry to Kansas officials and formed clubs to pool resources and funds for the migration. Several black families in the Delta counties of Issaquena, Warren, and Washington traveled to Kansas in late 1877 and encouraged other families to follow. In the next year, Kansas Fever caught on quickly, and more groups of blacks began to leave Mississippi spontaneously. By the winter of 1878–79, enough African Americans had left the state's Cotton Belt that plantation owners began to worry about a labor shortage.

In the counties and parishes bordering the Mississippi River, where Mississippi and Louisiana blacks flocked to catch steamships up to St. Louis, authorities harassed prospective migrants and confiscated their belongings. The Exodusters nevertheless remained determined to leave, continuing to pour north from the Delta throughout the spring. Kansas Fever raged unabated until May, when steamboats stopped picking up Exodusters.

Most of the 1879 Exodusters who made it to St. Louis arrived without money, food, shelter, or a means of transportation to Kansas. The city's Colored Relief Board, an ad hoc group of hardworking blacks, helped the Exodusters survive before national media coverage of the movement generated large donations from across the country. St. Louis's white community and leaders reacted to the refugees indifferently and sometimes with downright hostility.

In Kansas, a historically free territory and the home of abolitionist John Brown, high-ranking officials greeted the Exodusters more warmly. A Quaker-run relief organization collected donations from old abolitionist networks that stretched all the way to England, helping Exodusters find housing and employment in several counties. The Exodusters themselves, though, did the heavy lifting of establishing communities and carving out new lives in Kansas.

Though African Americans migrated to Kansas and the Midwest from the South both before and after 1879, no other movement approached the intensity and spontaneity of the Kansas Fever migration. Most of the African Americans who left Mississippi in 1879 did not immediately succeed in purchasing land: the majority labored on farms, on railroads, in mines, or as domestics. But almost none of the blacks who made the journey returned to Mississippi. If the 1879 Exodusters did not find economic success or free land in the North, their participation in a spontaneous, grassroots movement defied the oppressive policies of post–Reconstruction Mississippi and spoke powerfully for freedom and against economic enslavement.

Thomas John Carey
University of Mississippi

Robert G. Athearn, *In Search of Canaan: Black Migration to Kansas, 1879–1880* (1978); Roy Garvin, *Journal of Negro History* (January 1948); Nell Irvin Painter, *Exodusters: Black Migration to Kansas after Reconstruction* (1976).

Extinctions and Endangered Species

Certain Mississippi plants and animals have been designated as endangered either by the state or by both the state and US governments. Under Mississippi law, such species are protected from hunting and illegal possession, while listing by federal authorities results into additional restrictions aimed at protecting the species and its habitat. As defined by the federal Endangered Species Act of 1973, endangered species are those currently in danger of becoming extinct, while threatened species consist of those likely to become endangered in the near future. Under state law, the Mississippi Department of Wildlife, Fisheries, and Parks is responsible for managing endangered species populations.

Extinction occurs when the last surviving individual of a species dies. A species will become extinct when its rate of death continually exceeds its rate of birth. Extinctions are a natural part of the evolutionary process, and innumerable species of plants and animals have evolved and eventually become extinct since the earth came into existence. The rate of extinctions, however, has increased alarmingly during recent centuries because of human activities. The extinction of a species is typically a two-stage process. First, something (for example, habitat alteration or hunting) leads to a situation in which only a small population remains. As the number of organisms subsequently decreases below the "minimum viable population," the species quickly becomes extinct. Species with narrow habitat requirements are characteristically subject to higher threats of extinction.

Species that have vanished from Mississippi in the past few hundred years include the red wolf, Florida panther (cougar), American bison (buffalo), Carolina parakeet, and passenger pigeon. Current endangered Mississippi animals and plants are at risk for a variety of reasons. In many cases, the habitats crucial for the species' survival have been modified or completely destroyed. The amount of Mississippi covered by original landscapes has been greatly reduced, and the remaining pristine areas are increasingly influenced by various human activities. Some species have disappeared or become endangered because of overexploitation: the state's Gulf sturgeon populations were wiped out by early twentieth-century fishing, while some birds and mammals, including the passenger pigeon, Carolina parakeet, black bear, and cougar, were hunted relentlessly.

E

As a by-product of industrialization and mechanized agriculture, Mississippi's land, water, and air have reached unprecedented levels of pollution during the last century. The use of pesticides and herbicides expanded enormously, and Mississippi's wildlife often became unintended victims of human chemical ingenuity. For example, the siltation and chemical pollution caused by modern agricultural and forestry practices have severely affected many of Mississippi's streams and led to population declines among many native fish and mussels. The decline of many bird species coincided with the introduction of chlorinated pesticides, especially the notorious DDT in 1947. Animals at the top of the food chain, such as the bald eagle and brown pelican, ingested high levels of the pesticide, which had contaminated their food sources. Adult mortalities increased, but the principal effect was damage to the species' ability to reproduce, as birds affected by DDT failed to lay eggs or produced thin eggshells that broke during incubation.

The environmental effects of European colonization have been magnified by deliberate and accidental introduction of various Eurasian and African life forms. Euro-American settlers brought numerous new species to Mississippi, and many of them became competitors of, predators of, or parasites on the original flora and fauna, often with devastating effects on the indigenous wildlife. The long list of such alien species includes organisms as dissimilar as hogs, cats, dogs, rats, fire ants, and kudzu. The early explorers and settlers also brought with them Old World diseases that often proved lethal for Native Americans as well as for the indigenous flora and fauna. Increasing suburbanization and recreational pressures on Mississippi's remaining prime wildlife habitats have recently created yet another unnatural proliferation of predators. For example, suburban development has resulted in an increased number of rats, skunks, raccoons, opossums, blue jays, and cowbirds, all of which adversely affect the original woodland species remaining in the altered habitat.

As famous conservationist Aldo Leopold noted in 1929, Mississippi was among the last states to realize the need to protect wildlife: the first state agency with such responsibilities, the Game and Fish Commission, was not established until 1932. Since the 1930s some species that were almost eliminated from Mississippi have rebounded because of conservation efforts by state and federal authorities and volunteer organizations. Wild turkeys and white-tailed deer, for example, today sustain healthy and harvestable populations as a consequence of successful reintroduction and conservation programs. The American alligator and brown pelican, too, have experienced significant population increases since conservation efforts began in the 1960s. In recent years, black bear sightings in the state have also been on the rise, but the return of the panther to Mississippi has yet to be validated.

The need to protect Mississippi's endangered species can be justified by various arguments. Many of the species are beautiful or immensely interesting in their own right. It has also been argued that all species have the same right to exist as humans do and that all species are intrinsically worth preserving. In addition, endangered species form an integral part of the state's biological diversity, and their disappearance could have unanticipated negative effects on Mississippi's human inhabitants.

Mikko Saikku
University of Helsinki

Mississippi Museum of Natural Science, *Endangered Species of Mississippi* (1995); Mississippi Department of Wildlife, Fisheries, and Parks website, www.mdwfp.com.

F

Falkner, William Clark

(1825/26–1889) Author

The great-grandfather of Nobel Prize–winning novelist William Faulkner, Col. William Clark Falkner was a significant figure in nineteenth-century North Mississippi, distinguishing himself as a soldier, railroad builder, and author.

There is some discrepancy regarding Falkner's birth—various accounts set his birthdate at 6 July 1825 or 1826. Another question concerns whether his last name was actually spelled *Faulkner* and he removed the *u*, which his great-grandson later either added or replaced. He was born in Knox County, Tennessee; moved to St. Genevieve, Missouri, early in his youth; and at age seventeen went to Pontotoc, Mississippi, to live with his uncle, T. I. Word. Sometime between 1842 and 1845, he moved to Ripley, where another uncle, John Wesley Thompson, lived.

Falkner spent the rest of his life in Ripley. He first emerged as a public figure in town when he interviewed A. J. MacCannon, who had killed an entire family with an ax, and published his life story. In 1846–47 Falkner fought in the Mexican War, receiving wounds in his left foot and hand. After returning to Ripley he became embroiled in a feud with the Hindman family. Difficulties started when rumors spread that Falkner had blackballed Robert Hindman's membership in the Knights of Temperance. (There is no evidence of Falkner having done so.) In 1849 Hindman attempted to shoot Falkner, but the gun misfired, and Falkner stabbed his assailant to death. Hindman's family inscribed his tombstone with the words *Murdered by W. C. Falkner* and only grudgingly changed it to *Killed by W. C. Falkner* after Falkner's acquittal. The enmity between the Falkners and Hindmans continued to grow over the next few years, resulting in Falkner's killing Erasmus W. Morris, a friend of the family's, in 1851 and culminating in a proposed duel between Falkner and Thomas Hindman Jr. The duel was averted by the intervention of M. C. Galloway, who managed finally to make peace among the enemies, but Falkner had become a much-disliked figure in town.

When the Civil War began, Falkner helped raise Company F, the Magnolia Rifles, and was elected its colonel. This company joined with others to become the 2nd Mississippi Infantry Regiment. Shortly before the first Battle of Manassas, Falkner was promoted to brigadier general of a brigade made up of the 2nd and 11th Mississippi, the 4th Alabama, and the 1st Tennessee Regiments, but he resigned the position immediately after learning that it might eventually bring about a separation from his original regiment. In the battle itself, Gen. P. G. T. Beauregard dubbed Falkner the Knight of the Black Plume, and some have argued that Falkner, not Thomas "Stonewall" Jackson, was described as "standing like a stone wall." Although Falkner later campaigned for election to command the 2nd Mississippi, he was defeated by a candidate whom the soldiers saw as more lenient. Nevertheless, Falkner maintained the title of colonel not only for the rest of the war but for the remainder of his life. In fact, his descendants referred to him after his death as the Old Colonel, partly to distinguish him from one of his sons, who moved to Oxford and was often called the Young Colonel.

Falkner married Holland Pearce in Ripley in 1847, and they had one son, John Wesley Thompson Falkner (grandfather of the Nobel laureate), before her death in 1849. Two years later, Falkner married his childhood sweetheart, Elizabeth Vance, and they went on to have eight children. Falkner also fathered at least one child by one of his slaves. Active in Reconstruction, he built the Ship Island, Ripley, and Kentucky Railroad Company, the first narrow-gauge railroad in North Mississippi. Although still a controversial figure in Ripley, he had established himself as a public figure of significant popularity. He then turned his attention to politics, campaigning for election to the state legislature. This new career path and his life ended on 5 November 1889, the eve of his successful election, when his former railroad partner and now political rival, Richard Thurmond, shot and killed him on the Ripley town square.

Although Falkner led a multifaceted and intriguing life, he is best known today as a figure connected with literature. He wrote numerous books in multiple genres. In addition to *The Life and Confession of A. J. MacCannon, Murderer of the Adcock Family*, his works included *The Siege of Monterey* (an epic poem), *The Spanish Heroine* and *The Little Brick Church* (romantic novels), *The Lost Diamond* (a play), and *Rapid Ramblings in Europe* (a travel book). His most famous book, *The White Rose of Memphis*, was reprinted several times until the mid-twentieth century.

Falkner is also remembered through the writings of his great-grandson—not only because William Faulkner sought to emulate his namesake's writing but also because the Old Colonel served as the model for numerous characters in Faulkner's novels, most obviously Col. John Sartoris, who closely resembles Falkner and whose gravesite statue as described in *Flags in the Dust* is identical to Falkner's, which still stands in Ripley. Also modeled partly on Falkner is Col. Thomas Sutpen of *Absalom, Absalom!*, who is known as the Knight of the Black Plume. Scholars have also argued that Faulkner may have been thinking of his great-grandfather when creating Flem Snopes, since the poor white character comes from someplace unknown to become a major figure in the hamlet of Frenchman's Bend and the town of Jefferson.

Taylor Hagood
Florida Atlantic University

Joseph Blotner, *Faulkner: A Biography* (1974); Robert Cantwell, introduction to *The White Rose of Memphis* (1953); Donald P. Duclos, *Son of Sorrow: The Life, Works, and Influence of Colonel William C. Falkner, 1825–1889* (1998); Arthur F. Kinney, *Critical Essays on William Faulkner: The Sartoris Family* (1985); James B. Murphy, in *Lives of Mississippi Authors, 1817–1967*, ed. James B. Lloyd (1981); Joel Williamson, *William Faulkner and Southern History* (1993).

The Atwater family reunion (Photograph by David Wharton)

Family Reunions

"Next week be the fourth of July and us plan a big family reunion outdoors here at my house," says Celie, the main character in Alice Walker's *The Color Purple*. On the day of the reunion family members analyze the custom this way: " 'Why us always have family reunion on July 4th,' say Henrietta, mouth poke out, full of complaint. 'It so hot.' " " 'White people busy celebrating they independence from England July 4th,' say Harpo, 'so most black folks don't have to work. Us can spend the day celebrating each other.' " Among the other attendees are two women who sip lemonade and make potato salad, noting that barbecue was a favorite food even while they were in Africa. The reunion day is especially joyful for the two women, who had been thought lost until their appearance at the reunion, where they are joyfully reunited with Celie and other family members.

Extended and elaborated southern families plan reunions around celebration, abundant good food, shared responsibilities, simple recreational activities, and above all talk. Although summer is the most popular season and the Fourth of July a popular date for family reunions for both black and white southern families, reunions can happen at any time. Some families have them annually, others have them on a schedule best described as "every so often," and still others have them only once or twice in a generation's lifetime, depending on some organizer's initiative.

Like the indefinite date for family reunions, there is an inexactness as to who constitutes "family" for each gathering. Some families invite only the descendants of a given couple and those descendants' spouses and children. Others invite the eldest couple's brothers and sisters and their children plus in-laws and some of the in-laws' relatives. Some gather households that have only a vague bond of kinship—people who are "like family" because of strong friendships. There is inevitably a logic of kinship and affection to each family reunion, and such a party is hard indeed to crash.

The impetus for a family reunion, if it is not an annually scheduled event, may be the birthday of an elderly family member, a holiday, a wedding anniversary, or an achievement such as paying off a home mortgage. Sometimes a family holds a reunion for a homecoming of one of its members, as in the case of Eudora Welty's novel *Losing Battles*, which is a family reunion story focused around the day a son and husband return from a stay at Parchman, the Mississippi state prison.

Families often gather in someone's home, though summer picnic versions are commonly held in state or city parks. Motels, hotels, or restaurants host them, as do clubhouses and community centers, but by far the most popular settings are homes and then churches. "Dinner on the grounds" in the churchyard, with food burdening tablecloth-covered makeshift tables, is a happy memory of family reunions in the minds of many southerners.

The occasion offers time to catch up on relatives' news and gossip, perhaps to transact a little family business, to settle—or stir up—family disputes, and generally to reestablish connections. Southern family reunions usually have no programs. Other than an occasional game or swim or boat ride, the main activities are conversation and eating. Reunions may last overnight or even several days but most frequently occur over only one meal.

The food might include barbecue with baked beans and coleslaw or fried fish with hush puppies, fried potatoes, and a salad. A restaurant meal might be ordered, but in a great many cases family reunion food is a large and generous potluck dinner where each participating household brings versions of its best offerings of food and drink—fried chicken, ham, meat casseroles, rice dishes, cooked garden vegetables, fresh raw vegetables, potato salad, gelatin salad, seafood salad, homemade rolls and breads, cakes, pies, cookies, jams, preserves, pickles, watermelon, iced tea, and lemonade. A time for eating, conversing, and sharing each other's company, a southern family reunion is a special occasion for reaffirming family ties.

Gayle Graham Yates
University of Minnesota

Alice Walker, *The Color Purple* (1982); Eudora Welty, *Losing Battles* (1970).

Farish Street

Farish Street in Jackson is the heart of one of the country's oldest African American communities, founded before the end of the Civil War. The neighborhood was home to the city's small black middle class, which developed after Reconstruction and survived until desegregation. Farish Street's identity as a hub of black life emerged from the migration of freed slaves searching for a more favorable social environment and the reality of enforced segregation.

The Farish Street neighborhood embodied the dreams, ideas, and values of these freed blacks, serving as their social, political, business, and cultural center. The district was home to a black-run hospital, funeral homes, churches, theaters, and schools. By 1908 one-third of the district was owned by blacks, and half of its black families owned their homes. From 1890 to the 1960s residents of the district could proudly claim self-sufficiency and basic freedom from white domination.

The area features numerous African American vernacular building types from ca. 1860 through the 1940s. Many of these structures were built by black carpenters, plasterers, and brick masons who were first- and second-generation freed slaves. Famous buildings in the Farish neighborhood include the Alamo Theatre and the Crystal Palace, venues for the most popular African American performers who came through Jackson.

Many early African American political leaders found a safe haven for their work in the Farish Street neighborhood. In the early twentieth century the Black and Tan Party, which consisted of the few blacks who "qualified" to vote, conducted business on Farish Street. From 1930 until his death in 1970, Dr. A. H. McCoy practiced general dentistry and dental surgery at the corner of Capitol and Farish Streets. McCoy was also passionate about equal rights and social justice. He was state president of the National Association for the Advancement of Colored People (NAACP) for many years, enduring threats, thrown bricks, and firebombs. During McCoy's tenure as NAACP president, the organization held its meetings on Farish Street, always changing the location for security reasons. Medgar Evers became the organization's state field secretary in 1954 and worked from an office at 507 North Farish Street. After his 1963 murder, most of the attendees at his funeral marched to Collins Funeral Home on North Farish Street in a mass civil rights demonstration.

For music fans, Farish Street is probably most remembered for the work of H. C. Speir and Lillian McMurry, two white furniture store owners who discovered and promoted local blues musicians. During the 1920s Speir's Furniture store at 225 North Farish Street sold phonographs and records. Noting the heavy demand for so-called race records as well as the wealth of talent literally just outside his door, Speir basically became a freelance talent scout. He would locate, audition, rehearse, and sometimes record local blues musicians. Some of the musicians he recorded or discovered include Ishman Bracey, Tommy Johnson, Charley Patton, and the Mississippi Sheiks. McMurry's furniture store opened in 1949 at 309 North Farish Street, and a year later she went into the record business. Between 1951 and 1955 McMurry's Trumpet Records label recorded some of the most important local blues musicians, among them Elmore James, Sonny Boy Williamson II, and Jerry McCain.

Farish Street has been compared to Rampart Street in New Orleans, South Parkway in Chicago, 18th and Vine in Kansas City, and Beale Street in Memphis. These streets were all hubs of black cultural life that lost their sense of neighborhood significance because of urban renewal or, ironically, because of desegregation. In 1980 the area was designated the Farish Street District and added to the National Register of Historic Places, and in 1995 it was added to the National Trust for Historic Preservation's list of Most Endangered Places as a consequence of neglect and of the demolition of two hundred of the area's nine hundred buildings. In 2002 the city of Jackson signed a forty-five-year lease with Performa Entertainment Real Estate for development and management of the Farish Street Entertainment District, located on the two blocks of Farish between Amite and Hamilton Streets. However, the project has been dormant since 2014 after the US Department of Housing and Urban Development found that federal funds for the project had been misspent, and the City of Jackson no longer considers it a priority.

Eric Feldman
New York University

Scott Barretta, *Living Blues* (July–August 2005); Adam Ganucheau, *Jackson Clarion-Ledger* (28 January 2015); Alferteen Harrison, ed., *The Farish Street Historic District: Memories, Perceptions, and Developmental Alternatives* (1984); National Trust for Historic Preservation website, www.preservationnation.org; Jim O'Neal, *Living Blues* 67 (1986); Marc W. Ryan, *Trumpet Records: Diamonds on Farish Street* (2004).

F

Farm Security Administration Photography

The work of Farm Security Administration photographers in 1930s Mississippi provided a window onto the state's complex race relations and economic situation during the Great Depression. The agency's depiction of the state created a lasting impression in the national imagination, and the photographs remain valuable to historians studying the state's distinctive cultural landscape.

Led by Roy Stryker, chief of the Information Division's historical section, the Farm Security Administration (previously known as the Resettlement Administration) sought to document poverty in rural America. Beginning in 1935, Stryker's division employed photographs to illustrate the social issues that the New Deal programs sought to address. The project included professional photographers such as Walker Evans, Dorothea Lange, Russell Lee, Carl Mydans, Arthur Rothstein, Ben Shahn, and Marion Post Wolcott, all of whom produced images of the lives of rural Mississippians. The project began as an effort to document the effects of the agricultural depression following the farm crisis of the 1920s but later expanded to cover many facets of Mississippi life, both rural and urban.

Many Farm Security Administration images of Mississippi depicted the sharecropping system, and photographers worked primarily in the Delta, documenting thirty-one counties from Coahoma in the northern part of the state to Warren in the south. Photographers also visited counties in the coastal plain as well as Lafayette and Lee Counties in the northern hill country. Some portraits and landscape views detailed cotton picking, payday at plantation commissaries, churches, and street scenes from Vicksburg to Tupelo. The 270,000 images in the Farm Security Administration's photographic collection are now housed at the Library of Congress in Washington, D.C.

Becca Walton
University of Mississippi

Pete Daniel, Merry Forrester, Maren Stange, and Sally Stein, *Official Images: New Deal Photography* (1987); Karen Glynn and Tom Rankin, eds., *A Mississippi Portrait: Farm Security Administration Photographs, 1935–1940*, Southern Media Archive at the Center for the Study of Southern Culture, University of Mississippi (2000); F. Jack Hurley, *Portrait of a Decade: Roy Stryker and the Development of Documentary Photography in the 1930s* (1972); Nathan Natanson, *The Black Image in the New Deal* (1992).

Farm Subsidies

Farm subsidies is the term for a vast array of taxpayer-supported payments from the federal government to farmers and landowners to support agriculture. US Department of Agriculture subsidies can be classified into three categories: commodity, disaster, and conservation, each of which includes subprograms targeted at different needs within the agricultural economy. Since the 1990s, commodity subsidies have comprised the largest category of Mississippi farm payments, with cotton, soybeans, corn, livestock, and peanuts receiving the biggest shares. Oats, wheat, sorghum, and honey farms also received commodity support through loan deficiency and marketing payments. Sunflower and barley farmers obtained additional payments through direct and counter-cyclical programs. Conservation ranked as the third-largest category of subsidies in the state from 1995 to 2014. The Conservation Reserve Program represented the largest conservation program for the state during the period. Disaster ranked as the fifth-most-important category for Mississippi. The federal government paid the largest share of disaster subsidies to Mississippians through the Livestock Disaster Emergency Program.

From 1995 to 2014 Mississippi ranked thirteenth in the United States for farm subsidy payments, which totaled $8.63 billion. A majority of payments went to Mississippi landlords, while about a third went to farm operators. Critics of farm subsidies point out that statistical estimates suggest that the top 10 percent of Mississippi subsidy recipients controlled 85 percent of the actual dollars paid by the Department of Agriculture to the state's farmers.

Farm subsidies in Mississippi have often been defined by struggles over racial and class hierarchies. Mississippi lawmakers' adherence to principles of state control and limited government precluded any serious support for federal intervention in state agriculture prior to the late 1920s. Overseers of sharecropping in particular opposed any federal interference in Mississippi's postslavery agricultural labor system. By 1932 mass "sheriff's sales" of farmlands across the state underscored the economic woes facing farmers. In the throes of the Great Depression, Mississippians warmed to New Deal federal involvement in farm policy. In 1933 the Agricultural Adjustment Administration (AAA) paid farmers across the Cotton Belt to destroy approximately 25 percent of their cotton crop to reduce supply and raise prices. The AAA subsequently established an allotment system, whereby farmers contracted to plant only a set number of acres and in return received payments for land left idle. The AAA, like many subsequent farm subsidy agencies, allowed local control through AAA county committees. During the New Deal, elite Mississippi Delta planters garnered an unrepresentatively high percentage of the largest AAA subsidies across the South. Landlords often controlled county AAA committees, thus exercising power over payment distributions, and AAA payments often did not filter down from landlords to tenants or croppers.

In 1936 Congress passed the Soil Conservation and Domestic Allotment Act, which basically paid farmers to place their lands in conservation agriculture. For example, under this bill, farmers received around ten dollars an acre to shift from surplus crops such as cotton and corn to conservation crops. Congress extended the Soil Conservation and Domestic Allotment Act through the 1940s.

During the 1950s the mechanized cotton harvester and expanded conservation subsidy programs exacerbated the economic hardships faced by Mississippi's poor farmers by decreasing the need for laborers, tenants, and sharecroppers. The Agriculture Act of 1956 increased conservation subsidies with the introduction of the Soil Bank program. Many wealthy Mississippi farmers welcomed new conservation subsidies, but in the process tenants and croppers lost even more acreage to subsidies. As the civil rights movement spread across Mississippi, the issue of control over farm subsidies emerged as an important dimension of the freedom struggle. In the spring of 1965 black tenants and tractor drivers went on strike across the Delta for better wages, and in 1966 African Americans engaged in a sit-in at Greenville Air Force Base to demand food and land.

In 1961 the Agricultural Stabilization and Conservation Service (ASCS) replaced the AAA and began to administer farm subsidy programs through elected local committees. In 1976, only 3 of 984 elected county committee members nationwide were African Americans: 1 of those 3 called Mississippi home. The absence of African Americans from the local ASCS power structure has been linked to the economic hardships faced by black farmers across the nation during the agency's tenure. The ASCS's role in the administration and distribution of farm subsidies meant that black farmers found themselves at the mercy of local whites for economic livelihood and physical survival. For many black farmers and tenants, civil rights in Mississippi meant more than voting rights or desegregation. Freedom for these farmers also meant freedom from a neoplanter class of whites supported by federal farm subsidies.

Throughout the 1970s and 1980s, calls increased to use farm subsidies for environmental purposes through enlarged conservation efforts. Congress offered federal payments in the Agriculture Act of 1970 to farmers who allowed hunters and fishers to use lands already in conservation. In addition, the 1985 Farm Bill significantly expanded conservation programs, including the Conservation Reserve Program, with expanded access to payments for lands beyond those identified as erosive.

During the 1990s both Democrats and Republicans attempted to reform farm subsidies. First, in 1994 Democratic secretary of agriculture Mike Espy, a Mississippi native, oversaw the reorganization of Department of Agriculture. In the process, the ASCS and other agencies were streamlined into the Farm Service Agency (FSA). Since 1994 the FSA has served as the local administrative unit for farm subsidies across Mississippi. In 1996 the Republican-controlled Congress passed the Freedom to Farm Act, which among other things sought to ease farmers off federal subsidy programs. However, faced with declining commodity prices in the late 1990s, Congress passed numerous farm relief measures that subsequently undercut the ideals of the Freedom to Farm Act.

Farm subsidies reemerged as a persuasive political issue after the turn of the century because of a declining agricultural economy. Bipartisan reformers lost key votes in Washington as farm-state senators and representatives rejuvenated farm subsidies. The 2002 Farm Security and Rural Investment Act reauthorized numerous subsidies on agricultural products such as milk that had been abolished in the 1990s. Significantly for Mississippi farmers, the 2002 measure raised cotton and grain subsidies to even higher levels than those that had existed in the 1990s. Proponents estimated that the act would cost taxpayers $190 billion over the law's five-year life span, and critics derided it as a step backward toward New Deal–era subsidies, unbalanced national budgets, and corporate welfare masquerading as farm relief. Supporters, however, noted that the rural economy had fallen on hard times and that small farmers needed help to survive.

Critics of contemporary farm subsidies in Mississippi have pointed to a number of inequalities within the system. Just like its ASCS predecessor, the FSA local control over the farm subsidies apparatus has engendered questions of racial and class equality. The administration of local and county FSA offices rests in the hands of local elected committees. In 2007 only 8 of Mississippi's 236 FSA committee members were African American. Contemporary critics of farm subsidies have maintained that the continued white domination of the FSA power structure has prevented equal access to relief for Mississippi's black farmers. Moreover, modern farm subsidies are based on farm size and production yields, not economic need, meaning that large, wealthier farmers receive a far greater share of appropriated funds than do small, poorer farmers.

Supporters of current farm subsidies maintain that Mississippi farmers must have government support to compete in a global economy. They point out that US farm subsidies level the playing field with foreign farmers who receive heavy subsidies from their home governments. Moreover, farmers contend that subsidies provide a safety net for producers and stability to the agricultural economy, enabling producers to present Mississippi consumers with a secure and modestly priced food supply. In addition, supporters argue that large, stable farm operations supported by subsidies lift other sectors of the local economy. Prosubsidy organizations such as the Mississippi Farm Bureau also contend that agriculture's prominent role in the state's economy necessitates farm stability. Farmers challenge that critics exploit nonrepresentative examples of subsidy abuse and have forgotten about the tough realities faced by the small family farms that benefit the most from subsidies. Finally, farmers are quick to point out that recent high commodity prices do not translate into high incomes for farmers. Dramatic increases in the costs of fuel, fertilizer, seed, land, and machinery have negated any increased revenue provided by high commodity prices.

Federal farm subsidies have undeniably enabled struggling farm families to weather hard times throughout Mississippi history. Nevertheless, New Deal origins and civil rights legacies remain and infuse Mississippi farm subsidies with deeper meanings related to economic and racial inequalities. Mississippians continue to debate the necessities, inequities, and realities of current federal farm subsidy programs.

Ryan L. Fletcher
University of Mississippi

Andrew Backover, *USA Today* (12 November 2002); Murray R. Benedict, *Farm Policies of the United States, 1790–1950* (1953); Zachary Cain and Stephen Lovejoy, *Choices* (4th Quarter 2004); James C. Cobb, *Journal of American History* (December 1990); Environmental Working Group, Farm Subsidy Database website, www.farm.ewg.org; Gilbert M. Gaul and Dan Morgan, *Washington Post* (20 June 2007); Becky Gillette, *Mississippi Business Journal* (3 December 2007); Valerie Grim, *Agricultural History* (Spring 1996); Donald Holley, *Uncle Sam's Farmers: The New Deal Communities in the Lower Mississippi Valley* (1975); US Department of Agriculture, 2002 Census of Agriculture website, www.agcensus.usda.gov; Jasper Womach, *Average Farm Subsidy Payments, by State, 2002,* www.nationalaglawcenter.org.

Farm Technology and Mechanization, Twentieth Century

With the most fertile Delta and prairie lands in relatively few hands and with labor cheap and abundant, Mississippi's large landowners had few incentives before the late 1940s and 1950s to make major capital investments and purchase expensive equipment. As long as owners of large farming tracts could exploit the relatively cheap labor of both tenants and sharecroppers, they had no need to invest in anything but primitive tools for turning over soil, planting seeds, hoeing weeds, and harvesting cash crops of cotton and corn.

Until the end of World War II, therefore, basic farm tools and sources of power had largely remained as they had been before the Civil War. Soil was tilled by iron-and-wood plows pulled by mules. In readiness for sowing seeds, simple spike-toothed harrows smoothed over plowed land. As staple crops of cotton and corn grew, so did weeds, meaning that adult workers and their older children returned to fields several times during the growing season with simple wooden and metal hoes, hacking away what had not been planted. When corn and cotton ripened in early and late autumn, the crops were harvested by hand: ears of corn were torn from stalks, and cotton was picked from plants and placed in bags draped over pickers' shoulders. As a rule, entire families engaged in these arduous tasks. In the dairy belts in and around Oktibbeha County and to the southwest in New Orleans's milk shed, milking was performed by hands grasping and pulling teats, and the daily job of carrying filled milk cans to the nearest road for pickup was a muscle-building routine shared by men and boys.

Mississippi's degree of technological backwardness is evident from statistics taken from the 1925 Census of Agriculture. While Mississippi had 257,228 farms, Kansas had 165,879. But Mississippians owned 1,871 tractors and 928 radios, whereas farmers in Kansas had 31,171 tractors and 13,189 radios. Mississippi had 540,782 blacks who lived on someone else's land and toiled under extremely primitive conditions—for example, using 327,646 mules.

The 1945 Census of Agriculture showed that few mechanical improvements had come to Mississippi farms over the preceding two decades. Although tractor ownership had increased to 12,417, Mississippi's 97,028 sharecroppers seldom had access to the new equipment: they operated only 476 rubber-wheeled tractors. In contrast, Kansas's farmers had 115,729 tractors, 67,636 of which had rubber wheels.

Over the next half century, however, Mississippi experienced an agricultural revolution as new technologies created a need to diversify. A 1992 agricultural census showed that the state now had a total of 31,998 farms, that sharecropping had been completely eliminated, and that tenancy existed on just 9.3 percent of the state's 10.2 million harvested acres. Mississippi's farmers had 58,625 tractors, 5,308 combines with specially designed heads for grain and soybean harvests, 3,674 mechanical cotton pickers, and 10,509 hay balers.

Mississippi's crops changed as well. Introduced to the state in 1948, rice became an important crop in the Delta, and many farmers began planting soybeans. Large-scale, sophisticated, computer-controlled poultry operations became commonplace in the area around the city of Laurel. Farmers in the Delta region and to a lesser extent in eastern Mississippi made the state the nation's top catfish producer. The commercial production of farm-raised catfish began in the 1960s and then underwent technological and scientific innovations such as aerating water; feeding for fast, uniform growth; and controlling disease. Pearl River County emerged as a key source for early season blueberries, with growers coming to rely on automated picking equipment.

Many factors contributed to Mississippi's agricultural revolution. Perhaps most important, farmworkers left the land as other opportunities became available. The state's drive to encourage industrial development brought factories and nonfarming jobs, while many African Americans in particular headed to Chicago and other northern cities in search of better jobs and living conditions. The resulting depopulation of the plantations necessitated increased investment in labor-saving equipment.

Research at agricultural universities also led to many of the changes in Mississippi's farming practices. The laboratories and extension stations of Mississippi State University, for example, developed new cotton varieties, and its county agents brought news of latest techniques and innovations directly to farmers. Similarly, Mississippi State's College of Veterinary Medicine made key discoveries that changed the practices of livestock, poultry, and catfish producers. Innovations at Alcorn State University also aided in improving the state's farm economy.

Agricultural activity in rural Mississippi today bears almost no resemblance to farming prior to the 1960s. Crop-dusting planes deposit herbicides on fields below; mammoth air-conditioned tractors pull wide plows or thirty-two-row planters; self-propelled combines harvest rice, corn, and soybeans; sophisticated mechanical cotton pickers remove more snow-white bolls each day than an entire field of workers could have picked in a week; wide-winged irrigation apparatuses creep along, sprinkling water onto fields; tank attachments to tractors measure and spread anhydrous ammonia and other fertilizers on fields, increasing yields and sustaining the soil; millions of chickens grow under technologically sophisticated conditions; and scientifically managed ponds yield megatons of uniform-sized catfish for processing in Mississippi and distribution throughout the nation.

Dennis S. Nordin
Mississippi State University

James C. Cobb, *The Most Southern Place on Earth: The Mississippi Delta and the Roots of Regional Identity* (1986); Pete Daniel, *Breaking the Land: Transformation of Cotton, Tobacco, and Rice Cultures since 1880* (1986); James C. Giesen, *Boll Weevil Blues: Cotton, Myth, and Power in the American South* (2011); Jack Temple Kirby, *Rural Worlds Lost: The American South, 1920–1960* (1987).

Farmers' Alliance and Colored Farmers' Alliance

During the late nineteenth century a number of agrarian groups formed in response to depressed agricultural prices, high freight rates, and rural isolation. The National Farmers' Alliance was the largest of these groups. Based in the South, the Midwest, and the Plains states, the organization reached a peak membership of 1.2 million in 1890. The alliance promoted economic cooperatives that favored farmers in buying, selling, and storing agricultural produce.

In 1887 lecturers from the Texas-based Southern Farmers' Alliance traveled throughout the South and rapidly established suballiances. The first Mississippi chapter was founded at Oak Hill, in Carroll County. Over the next three years the Mississippi organization grew from one thousand members to eighty thousand—more than half of the state's rural men. In 1888 the National Farmers' Alliance held its meeting in Meridian. A year later, the Southern Farmers' Alliance joined the National Farmers' Alliance.

Membership in the Southern Alliance grew throughout the state but remained concentrated in nonplantation white-majority counties. While women participated in alliance meetings, they did not receive full membership privileges. The Southern Farmers' Alliance banned African Americans from membership but recognized the Colored Farmers' Alliance and Cooperative Union as a parallel association. Founded in Texas in 1886, the Colored Farmers' Alliance later spread to Mississippi. Like the Southern Alliance, the Colored Alliance grew rapidly. In December 1890, the Mississippi Colored Farmers' Alliance included ninety thousand members. Although the two groups met separately, they engaged in similar activities. Both the Southern Alliance and Colored Alliance organized cooperative purchasing and selling efforts, held regular meetings, engaged in rituals, and founded newspapers.

From 1888 to 1891 alliance members participated in a successful regional boycott of jute-bag manufacturers and planned to open a cotton-bagging factory. In 1888 the Mississippi Alliance established a state exchange in Winona to purchase goods in bulk. Despite the short-term success of these efforts, the association failed to achieve long-term improvements, and the exchange moved to Memphis in 1890.

Events in Leflore County also demonstrated the limits of alliance success. In 1889 organizer Oliver Cromwell established several Colored Alliance branches in the county. Cromwell convinced his fellow African Americans to take their business to a Southern Alliance store in Durant. Angered by the loss of business and control over the black laborers, a group of Leflore County whites threatened Cromwell. In response, seventy-five African Americans marched military-style to deliver a note to Shell Mound whites announcing that three thousand men would defend Cromwell should whites choose to attack. Hoping to avoid racial warfare, the county sheriff called on Governor Robert Lowry for support, and three companies of national guardsmen quickly arrived in Leflore. According to state newspapers, over the next five days, the troops arrested forty African Americans, killed five ringleaders, and ended the potential for greater violence. Outside Mississippi, newspapers reported that greater atrocities occurred, resulting in at least twenty-five deaths. White planters subsequently ordered the Southern Alliance store in Durant to cease its relations with the Colored Alliance and pressured the *Vaiden Colored Farmers' Alliance Advocate* to stop distribution in Leflore and Tallahatchie Counties. While little is known about the role of Southern Alliance members in the Leflore County events, white planters succeeded on both accounts. Most historians argue that the Leflore County Massacre marked the decline of the Mississippi Colored Alliance.

Faced with the failure of the state exchange and the cotton-bagging factory and the violent suppression of the Colored Alliance, some alliance members turned to politics as a more effective means of reform. Led by *Chickasaw Messenger* editor Frank Burkitt, alliance members gained sway in the state legislature. By 1890 two congressional representatives supported the alliance, and fifty-five delegates to the state's constitutional convention received support from the organization. The farm organization encountered its greatest test in the 1891 state legislative elections. With both US Senate seats open, control of the state legislature was especially important, since the legislature would elect Mississippi's senators. Alliance candidates Ethelbert Barksdale and Burkitt supported the subtreasury plan, under which farmers could store their crops in government-owned warehouses to await higher prices while the government extended low-interest loans to farmers in the interim. Proposed at the 1890 National Alliance meeting, the subtreasury plan became the rallying cry of the agrarian organization and the central issue of the Mississippi campaign.

After an emotional campaign and a fraudulent election, alliance candidates failed to win a majority in the state legislature. The defeat ensured that Mississippi's senators would not support national legislation to implement the subtreasury plan. Suballiances fell into rapid decline as many farmers joined the Mississippi Populist Party in 1892. Other farmers quit the alliance because of its increasingly political tone, the failure of its economic cooperatives, or its turn from local initiatives to state and national reform. Internal divisions over politics and interracial and intergender cooperation ended the brief but strong surge of the Mississippi Farmers' Alliance.

Benjamin Purvis
University of Mississippi

Martin Dann, *Journal of Ethnic Studies* (Fall 1974); Gerald Gaither, *Blacks and the Populist Movement: Ballots and Bigotry in the New South* (rev. ed. 2005); Steven Hahn, *A Nation under Our Feet: Black Political Struggles in the Rural South from Slavery to the Great Migration* (2003); William F. Holmes, *Phylon* (3rd Quarter 1973); Albert Kirwan, *Revolt of the Rednecks: Mississippi Politics, 1876–1925* (1964); Michael Schwartz, *Radical Protest and Social Structure: The Southern Farmers' Alliance and Cotton Tenancy, 1880–1890* (1976); C. Vann Woodward, *Origins of the New South, 1877–1913* (1951).

Farmers Union

Founded in 1902 in Point, Texas, the Farmers Educational and Co-Operative Union of America was originally established as a secret organization that sought to raise farmer's incomes by forming cooperatives that would negotiate fair prices for its membership. If necessary, members agreed to withhold crops from the market to ensure acceptable prices. Members also negotiated collectively for better prices on commodities such as seed and fertilizer. Membership in the Farmers Union, which was open to both farmers and farm laborers as well as to teachers, ministers, and almost anyone who supported farmers' cause, expanded dramatically after it removed the veil of secrecy. The first chapters outside of Texas were established in Arkansas, Georgia, Louisiana, and Alabama. Mississippi joined the second tier of states to establish chapters, along with South Carolina, Tennessee, Florida, Illinois, Kansas, Missouri, Oklahoma, Colorado, Kentucky, North Carolina, and Washington.

In Mississippi, as in most of the South, the plight of both whites and African Americans who worked farms improved very little after the Civil War. Slavery had ended and the plantation system had collapsed, but the lien system that replaced it merely offered a new form of bondage, leaving most farmers without land and in perpetual debt. The idea of collectively negotiating for better crop prices had much appeal to individuals with little opportunity to better their plight and no political clout.

The year 1906 represented a turning point for both the National Farmers Union (NFU) and the Mississippi Farmers Union (MFU). Charles S. Barrett of Georgia was elected NFU president, and J. M. Bass took the reins for a two-year term as president of the MFU. One of the primary objectives of both groups was the establishment of courses in public schools that would teach farmers' sons economics and government. The Farmers Union agenda also included enforcement of antitrust laws, improving rural roads, and more stringent immigration laws. The MFU achieved considerable success in its efforts to reform the state's educational system. Under Gov. Edmund F. Noel (1908–12), the state established agricultural high schools, many of which later became part of the state's junior/community college system. With help from Sen. George Robert Hightower, the MFU pushed through legislation that laid the groundwork for agricultural extension programs.

Hightower resigned his position in the legislature to serve as the MFU president from 1908–12. During his presidency the NFU began to call for the direct election of all US senators, holding up Mississippi as a model for the rest of the country, since in 1902 the state had become the first to implement direct primary elections. The MFU's momentum was short-lived, however, and membership began to wane both in Mississippi and in most other southern states. The MFU declined for a variety of reasons. Hightower resigned to accept the presidency at Mississippi Agricultural and Mechanical College (now Mississippi State University). By 1916 the NFU advocated voting rights for women, an unpopular position in the state. In its early years the NFU had welcomed both white and black farmers, a policy that went against the state's segregation practices. Increasing racial tensions encouraged by race-baiting politicians, such as Theodore G. Bilbo, also played a role in the demise of the MFU and similar organizations elsewhere in the South. The NFU continues to exist and boasts considerable membership in other parts of country but has almost no presence in the states of the former Confederacy.

Donald C. Simmons Jr.

Katrina M. Jarding
Dakota Wesleyan University

Stephen E. Ambrose, *Georgia Historical Quarterly* (March 1964); Charles C. Bolton, *Poor Whites of the Antebellum South: Tenants and Laborers in Central North Carolina and Northeast Mississippi* (1994); William Tucker, *Agricultural History* (October 1947); Harold D. Woodman, *New South—New Law: The Legal Foundations of Credit and Labor Relations in the Postbellum Agricultural South* (1995).

Fat Possum Records

Perhaps most famous for its recordings of Mississippi hill country blues, Fat Possum is an independent Oxford record label. Though Fat Possum is now home to many independent rock artists, Matthew Johnson and Peter Lee founded the label in 1991 to record the music of older local bluesmen whose work would not have been available to the public. Operating at first with the remainder of his student loan money from his time at the University of Mississippi, Johnson spent time at Junior Kimbrough's juke joint in Holly Springs in the early 1990s and met three people who would shape the record label: musicians R. L. Burnside and Kimbrough and writer and musicologist Robert Palmer. Palmer initially helped Johnson and Lee decide whom to record and often produced recording sessions and wrote liner notes for albums.

Johnson's first recordings, produced with financial help from John Hermann of the band Widespread Panic, included Burnside, Kimbrough, Cedell Davis, Paul "Wine" Jones, and other Mississippi bluesmen. Fat Possum released a handful of blues albums and a series of compilation discs, *Not the*

Same Old Blues Crap. The label often had trouble meeting expenses and getting its music to the public. In 1994 Fat Possum struck a deal to have Capricorn Records distribute Fat Possum recordings, but the agreement turned sour, and the two labels spent about eighteen months embroiled in a legal battle. Fat Possum declared bankruptcy, incurred nearly a million dollars in debt, and was unable to support its artists. Fat Possum also came under attack from critics for its antipurist stance and its portrayal and marketing of the artists on the label, which occasionally strayed into stereotype, highlighting such aspects of performers' lives as violence, murder, jail time, and substance abuse.

Fat Possum bounced back in the late 1990s, making a deal with Epitaph Records and releasing Burnside's critically successful *A Ass Pocket of Whiskey*, which featured alternative rock musician Jon Spencer from the Jon Spencer Blues Explosion. Other critically acclaimed albums by Kimbrough, T-Model Ford, and Robert Belfour followed. Fat Possum also generated good sales with several albums of Burnside and others' material remixed with hip-hop beats. However, Johnson and new partner Bruce Watson continued to struggle into the twenty-first century, in part as a consequence of the deaths of many of their artists, including Kimbrough in 1998 and Burnside in 2005. Asie Payton, Charlie Caldwell, and King Ernest died before the label could release their records.

The label's offices moved to Water Valley for several years before returning to Oxford in 2010. Fat Possum has recently focused on working with indie rock artists, among them the Black Keys, the Heartless Bastards, Paul Westerberg, the Walkmen, Dinosaur Jr., Modest Mouse, and Andrew Bird. They have also pursued one-album recording deals with well-known artists such as Solomon Burke and acquired or licensed back catalogs by Townes Van Zandt, Al Green, and Hi Records as well as George Mitchell's archival recordings of Furry Lewis and other Mississippi bluesmen. The diverse composition of Fat Possum's roster has made the formerly blues-based label a favorite among rock fans, critics, and musicians. In 2016 Fat Possum celebrated its twenty-fifth anniversary with a series of new and new-to-vinyl blues recordings.

Ellie Campbell
University of Mississippi

Michael Dixon, *Blues Access* (Winter 1997); Richard Grant, *London Observer* (16 November 2003); Andrea Lisle, *Memphis Flyer* (18 December 2001); Jay McInerney, *New Yorker* (4 February 2002).

Fatherland Site (Grand Village of the Natchez Indians)

The Fatherland Site, also known as the Grand Village of the Natchez Indians, is a National Historic Landmark archaeological site owned by the State of Mississippi and administered by the Mississippi Department of Archives and History. A close correlation has been established between archaeological findings there and the ethnohistory of the Natchez Indians. Eighteenth-century European visitors who described the site include Iberville, Pénicaut, Gravier, Charlevoix, and du Pratz. At that time, the mound center was the home of the Great Sun, the hereditary chief of the Natchez tribe.

The first archaeological work at the Fatherland Site (named for a nineteenth-century plantation) was Warren K. Moorehead's limited testing in 1924. In 1930 archaeologist Moreau B. C. Chambers led the first extensive excavations at the site for the Mississippi Department of Archives and History, and over the following decade, he and James A. Ford identified it as the place mentioned frequently in French colonial records as the Grand Village of the Natchez. In 1962 and 1972 Robert S. Neitzel carried out further archaeological investigations for the department, eventually leading to state acquisition of approximately 126 acres for preservation and public interpretation.

The site's three mounds have been designated A, B, and C. French colonial descriptions focus on the Great Sun's mound (Mound B) and the temple mound (Mound C). Mound A was evidently not in use by the Natchez during the French colonial period. Excavations at Mounds B and C revealed that these two earthworks were built up incrementally, and radiocarbon dates from all three mounds indicate construction between AD 1200 and historic contact. Very little remained of the archaeological footprint of the last structure atop Mound B, which would have been the chief's house seen by European visitors to the site.

Mound C was identified as the temple mound based on its location and on the presence of twenty-six human burials, recalling French colonial accounts of burial activity in and around the temple building. A significant portion of the historic Natchez temple's archaeological footprint was documented atop Mound C. The temple's floor plan reveals a two-room structure—a smaller northern room, or portico, adjoining a larger southern (or rear) enclosure, with the whole building measuring about sixty feet in length and forty-two feet in width.

In addition to the structures on the mounds, colonial visitors to the Grand Village mentioned a few dwellings near the mounds and ceremonial plaza. Neitzel's 1972 excavations uncovered evidence of four off-mound building locations.

In 1983 a fifth building location came to light during excavations connected with an erosion-control project. No further archaeological excavations are planned.

The Grand Village of the Natchez Indians is located within the Natchez city limits. A museum features exhibits about the Natchez Indians and the French colonial period as well as a reconstructed Natchez Indian house and outdoor interpretive signs.

James F. Barnett Jr.
Mississippi Department of
Archives and History

James F. Barnett Jr., *The Natchez Indians: A History to 1735* (2007); Robert S. Neitzel, *Archaeology of the Fatherland Site: The Grand Village of the Natchez* (1965); Robert S. Neitzel, *The Grand Village of the Natchez Revisited: Excavations at the Fatherland Site, Adams County, Mississippi, 1972*; John R. Swanton, *Indian Tribes of the Lower Mississippi Valley and Adjacent Coast of the Gulf of Mexico* (1911).

Faulkner (Falkner), John Wesley Thompson, III

(1901–1963) Author, Pilot, Artist

The great-grandson of famous Mississippian William Clark Falkner and younger brother of Nobel Prize laureate William Faulkner, John Faulkner was born in Ripley on 24 September 1901. Faulkner married Lucille "Dolly" Ramey of Oxford in 1922. The couple had two sons, James Faulkner, born in 1923, and Murry "Chooky" Falkner, born in 1928. After earning a bachelor's degree in civil engineering from the University of Mississippi in 1929, John Faulkner lived in the Mississippi Delta for several years, working as an engineer for the Mississippi Highway Department. In 1936–37 he served as part owner and chief pilot for Mid-South Airways in Memphis. In 1938 he moved his family to Greenfield Farm, a 320-acre property sixteen miles northeast of Oxford owned by his brother, William. In 1940 the family moved into town, taking up residence in Memory House, a large antebellum home that belonged to Dolly's parents. John worked for the City of Oxford and occasionally taught writing classes at the university. During World War II he served as a US Navy pilot, achieving the rank of lieutenant commander, although he was too old for combat duty. In 1962 he achieved a degree of national notoriety by siding with the segregationists who opposed federal intervention in the integration of the University of Mississippi.

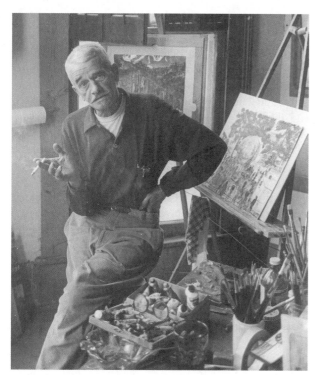

John Faulkner, 1961 (Martin J. Dain Collection, Department of Archives and Special Collections, J. D. Williams Library, University of Mississippi)

Faulkner was also a writer and painter whose works depict characters, scenes, and events typifying his native region. His first published novel, *Men Working* (1941), which has been favorably compared to John Steinbeck's *The Grapes of Wrath* (1939), dramatizes the trials of a sharecropper family victimized by the Great Depression and an inept government bureaucracy. His second novel, *Dollar Cotton* (1942), the plot of which may owe something to William Faulkner's *Absalom, Absalom!* (1936), describes the rise and fall of a Mississippi Delta plantation owner during the early twentieth century. In addition to these works of social realism, Faulkner also produced a popular series of humorous paperback novels treating rural southerners in a style that combines the tall-tale humor of the southwestern yarn spinners and the pathos of Erskine Caldwell: *Cabin Road* (1951), *Uncle Good's Girls* (1952), *The Sin Shouter of Cabin Road* (1955), *Ain't Gonna Rain No More* (1959), and *Uncle Good's Weekend Party* (1960). Faulkner also wrote two books of personal reminiscences, *Chooky* (1950), a semifictional composite based on the experiences he, his three brothers, and his two sons had during childhood, and *My Brother Bill: An Affectionate Reminiscence* (1963).

Lesser known but just as significant as his writings are John Faulkner's oil and watercolor paintings. A self-taught but talented artist, he sought to capture scenes of Oxford and Lafayette County that were fast disappearing under the onslaught of modernization that historian C. Vann Wood-

ward has called the "Bulldozer Revolution." One group of paintings, which Faulkner nostalgically titled *The Vanishing South*, includes such representative subjects as *Carnival Time*, *Sorghum Mill at Night*, *Brush Arbor*, *Ginnin' Time*, and *Possum Hunt*. He also created two oil paintings based on stories by William Faulkner, *The Bear* and *Red Leaves*. John Faulkner explained the main theme of his creative work: "Before I forget all the places in Mississippi that I love I want to put them down in color and stories. I hope my paintings and writings are an accurate picture of the land that bred me and in which I have lived." Faulkner died on 28 March 1963 in Oxford.

Robert Hamblin
Southeast Missouri State
University

Mississippi Quarterly (Fall 2001); John B. Padgett, Mississippi Writers Page website, www.olemiss.edu/mwp; S. Redding Jr., *South Atlantic Quarterly* 68 (1969).

Faulkner, William

(1897–1962) Author

When Allen Tate described the generation of writers that produced the Southern Renaissance as having a "double focus, a looking two ways," he doubtless was including William Faulkner. That dual perspective—backward to the antebellum South and the Civil War, forward to the modernist revolution in Western thought and the arts—invested Faulkner's fiction with a perpetual tension, the depth of

William Faulkner (J. R. Cofield Collection, Department of Archives and Special Collections, J. D. Williams Library, University of Mississippi)

which was great enough to convert an oeuvre largely confined to a tiny portion of the US South into an expression of national, hemispheric, and world relevance. Born in 1897 in New Albany and moving to Oxford in 1902, Faulkner was the eldest child in a family that had been prominent in the area for three generations, highlighted by his paternal great-grandfather, William C. Falkner, whose extravagant life and career—lawyer, planter, decorated Civil War officer, politician, railroad builder, and novelist—seemed to impose on all his descendants, even the most successful, a sense of inevitable decline.

This family history, combined with a Lost Cause mentality prevalent among southern white males born at the turn of the century, gave Faulkner what Nietzsche called the inclination to "monumentalism." Fortunately for Faulkner's writing, he also acquired the capacity to distance himself from or at least radically complicate his inheritance, largely through his growing familiarity with modernist thought. One source of that familiarity was an Oxford townsman, Phil Stone, who took Faulkner under his superbly educated wing in 1914. For more than a decade Stone conducted a literary tutorial with the young high school dropout, exposing him to everything from the classics to the contemporary, with particular emphasis on nineteenth-century British poetry, the French Symbolists, and the recent poetry and fiction of Wilde, Yeats, Joyce, Pound, and Eliot. Another source was Faulkner's 1925 sojourn in New Orleans's Vieux Carré while waiting to arrange passage to Europe: during those six months, he associated with a number of writers, artists, and journalists, including Sherwood Anderson, William Spratling, Lyle Saxon, Roark Bradford, and Hamilton Basso. Faulkner was an avid listener in a group of notable raconteurs, becoming privy to discussions of current art and literature as well as to the thought and writings of Marx, Nietzsche, Frazer, Bergson, and Freud. He would never again experience an extended participation in a community of intellectual peers.

Following his 1926 return to the United States after a six-month stay in Europe, much of it in Paris, Faulkner spent a good deal of time shuttling among Oxford, New Orleans, and New York. After his 1929 marriage to his former high school sweetheart (the recently divorced Estelle Oldham Franklin), Faulkner settled permanently in Oxford, ready to combine a profound historical sense rooted in the South with the modernist tendency to hold in suspicion virtually all that had been thought and said: the urge, in Pound's terms, to "make it new." Except for several trips to Hollywood as a screenwriter to improve his often precarious financial situation, Faulkner lived and wrote in Oxford. It became part of the model for his fictitious Yoknapatawpha County, which apparently required and justified his decision to remain—in contrast to most modernist American writers—within the narrow arena of his beginnings.

Faulkner's fourth novel, *The Sound and the Fury* (1929), was his great breakthrough, as he brought his double focus to major fictional expression. On the one hand, the novel portrays a 1920s southern family whose central voices are obsessed with a past—located in the diverse images of an absent sister—they can neither restore nor convincingly clarify. On the other hand, the novel represents this imprisonment in an irrecoverable past as a narrative revolution: a combination of abrupt scene shifts, looping chronology, and the perversely allusive prose of interior monologue. The backward look may paralyze the Compsons and by extension the impotent upper-class South they represent, but Faulkner asserted his creative vitality with stunning self-assurance.

For his works through *Go Down, Moses* (1942), Faulkner expanded what might seem a narrow and insufficiently representative southern drama into an examination of broader social and cultural conditions. From the sexual rebellion of Caddy Compson in *The Sound and the Fury*, which both dismays and fascinates her brother, Quentin, emerged a series of hetero- and homosexual encounters that constitute a kind of initiatory challenge that stimulates in women a passion for experience and in men a fear of contamination. It is as if the double focus of inherited codes and the quest for autonomy assumed a sexual correspondence. Characters such as Addie Bundren in *As I Lay Dying* (1930), Temple Drake in *Sanctuary* (1931), Lena Grove in *Light in August* (1932), and Charlotte Rittenmeyer in *If I Forget Thee, Jerusalem* (1939) boldly pursue sexual intimacy, while Quentin Compson, in *The Sound and the Fury* and *Absalom, Absalom!* (1936), the "tall convict" of "Old Man" (1939), and Ike McCaslin of *Go Down, Moses* withdraw from heterosexual engagement, finding comfort in latent homoerotic relations and a protective celibacy restricting any fulfilled sexual intimacy. Complicating this withdrawal is the fact that the power of original imaginative insight, especially in Quentin and Ike, seems to require that restriction.

With *As I Lay Dying* and *The Hamlet* (1940), Faulkner turned to the country people (never "poor whites") of Frenchman's Bend, discovering a community capable of realizing its own version of Jefferson's tensions of past and present, memory and desire, as a productive dynamic. Frenchman's Bend is "hill-cradled and remote, definite yet without boundaries, straddling into two counties and owning allegiance to neither." The dilemma of Frenchman's Bend is that it gives rise to Flem Snopes, who aggrandizes a laissez-faire trading ethic inseparable from the community's own individualistic value system. The result is Faulkner's representation in a small rural town of the power of the twentieth-century US market system and its sometimes crushing effects on people who can no longer reconcile their demands for autonomy and a cohesive and humane social fabric.

Race, however, remained the great social and moral issue of Faulkner's time and place and the driving force of his greatest fiction. In *Light in August*, *Absalom, Absalom!*, and *Go Down, Moses* the clash of tradition and originality is embodied in Faulkner's effort to deny the validity of racism by empowering the human imagination as the vehicle of truth, the only means of grasping the inhumanity, the destructiveness—for all involved—and the criminal illogic of racist thinking. Both *Light in August* and *Absalom!* make central the "invention" and murder of a black man—Joe Christmas and Charles Bon, respectively—as the key to understanding the history of southern violence and decline. In *Light in August* Faulkner identifies the cultural rather than biological origins of racial difference, portraying Christmas's ultimate autonomy as his refusal to live according to that culture's binary basis. As one unnamed character puts it, "He never acted like either a nigger or a white man. That was it. That was what made the folks so mad."

In *Absalom* and *Go Down, Moses* it is not so much the social creation of race as the violation of kinship that constitutes the primal sin of southern history. Henry Sutpen's murder of his "black brother," Charles Bon, Carothers McCaslin's incestuous intimacy with his own slave daughter—these unforgivable transgressions are revealed only through the unique imaginative breakthroughs of Quentin Compson, his narrative partner Shreve McCannon, and Ike McCaslin.

With *Go Down, Moses* Faulkner concluded his treatment of southern history and the need to reinterpret it. His later post–World War II fiction focused primarily on contemporary southern life, somewhat diminished in narrative intensity but nevertheless proposing an inhabitable, possible South, with its Snopes energy of acquisition reduced to a need for "respectability" in *The Town* (1957) and *The Mansion* (1957) and its racism reconceived as the possibility of justice for a black man accused of murdering a white man in *Intruder in the Dust* (1948). The greatest exception to a fiction more accommodating to existing conditions is *A Fable* (1954), a World War I novel that is largely remote from Mississippi, in which humanity is destined to perpetual warfare and perpetual hierarchical control, with its only glory lying in the fact that "man and his folly" will endure and prevail. If the imagination retains its power, it does so only in its desperate claim, "I'm not going to die. Never."

Respected yet popularly unacknowledged during the years of his greatest output, Faulkner became widely recognized as the most important twentieth-century American novelist near the end of his career. In 1950 he received the Nobel Prize for Literature, and he received the Pulitzer Prize for two novels, *A Fable* (1954) and *The Reivers* (1962). William Faulkner died in Byhalia, Mississippi, 1962.

Donald Kartiganer
University of Mississippi

André Bleikasten, *The Ink of Melancholy: Faulkner's Novels from "The Sound and the Fury" to "Light in August"* (1990); Joseph Blotner, *Faulkner: A Biography* (1984); Joseph Blotner, ed., *Selected Letters of William Faulkner* (1977); Cleanth Brooks, *William Faulkner: The Yoknapatawpha Country* (1963); Malcolm Cowley, ed., *Faulkner-Cowley File* (1961); Thadious Davis, *Games of Property: Law, Race, Gender, and Faulkner's Go Down, Moses* (2003); Richard Godden, *Fictions of Labor* (1997); Frederick L. Gwynn and Joseph Blotner, eds., *Faulkner in the University* (1959); Robert W. Hamblin and Charles A. Peek, eds., *A William Faulkner Encyclopedia* (1999); John T. Irwin, *Doubling and Incest/Repetition and Revenge: A Speculative Reading of Faulkner* (1975); Donald Kartiganer and Ann J. Abadie, eds., *Faulkner at 100: Retrospect and Prospect* (2000); John T. Matthews, *The Sound and the Fury: Faulkner and the Lost Cause* (1991); James B. Meriwether and Michael Millgate, eds., *Lion in the Garden* (1968); David Minter, *William Faulkner, His Life and Work* (1980); Michael Millgate, *The Achievement of William Faulkner* (1966); Richard C. Moreland, ed., *A Companion to William Faulkner* (2007); Noel Polk, *Children of the Dark House: Text and Context in Faulkner* (1996); Eric Sundquist, *Faulkner: The House Divided* (1983); Linda Wagner, ed., *William Faulkner: Six Decades of Criticism* (2002); Philip Weinstein, *Faulkner's Subject: A Cosmos No One Owns* (1992), Dean Faulkner Wells, *Every Day by the Sun: A Memoir of the Faulkners of Mississippi* (2012).

Faulkner's Geography

Most of William Faulkner's works are set in Yoknapatawpha County, a fictional place inhabited by fictional persons. However, Faulkner integrated it into a geographical setting that included prominent actual places, combining the real, the modified, and the imaginary. Yoknapatawpha County is in north-central Mississippi, seventy miles south of Memphis, Tennessee, the same geographical position as the real Lafayette County, and the geography of the fictional place is based heavily on Lafayette's geography. Like Lafayette, Yoknapatawpha County is drained in the north by the Tallahatchie River and in the south by the Yoknapatawpha, Faulkner's fictional name and the older Indian name for the Yocona River. Jefferson, the political seat of Yoknapatawpha County, has many geographical similarities to Oxford, the political seat of Lafayette County.

Despite these similarities, many differences also exist between Yoknapatawpha County and Lafayette County. The geography of Lafayette County and Oxford were changed in four principal ways—locations were shifted, place-names were changed, components were omitted, and reality was blended with fabrication. Objects, places, and events were sometimes shifted among counties and eras. In addition to Lafayette, Faulkner also drew from Marshall, Tippah, and Panola Counties.

Faulkner intended Yoknapatawpha County to be neither Lafayette County thinly disguised nor the entire South in microcosm. Rather, he viewed Yoknapatawpha as a place located in the South that he could use to describe the universal experience of humankind.

Charles S. Aiken
University of Tennessee

Charles S. Aiken, *Geographical Review* (January 1977, July 1979); Calvin S. Brown, *A Glossary of Faulkner's South* (1976); Don Doyle, *Faulkner's County: The Historical Roots of Yoknapatawpha* (2001).

Favre, Brett

(b. 1969) Athlete

Brett Favre, 1990 (McCain Library and Archives, University of Southern Mississippi)

Brett Lorenzo Favre was born on 10 October 1969 in Gulfport, the second of Irvin and Bonita Favre's four children, who were raised in the nearby town of Kiln. Brett played multiple positions on the Hancock North Central High School football team, coached by his father. In 1987 Favre enrolled at the University of Southern Mississippi (USM), his father's alma mater and the only school to offer him a scholarship. Coaches wanted him to play defensive back, but Favre opted to compete for the starting quarterback position. In his second game as a freshman, Favre entered the contest against Tulane in the third quarter and led USM to a 31–24 comeback victory. He started all but one of his remaining games at Southern Miss and led the Golden Eagles to a 30–26 upset victory over sixth-ranked Florida State in the first game of his junior year. The only game he missed was the season opener during his senior year: six weeks earlier, he had been involved in a near-fatal automobile accident that resulted in the loss of thirty inches of his intestines. On 8 September 1990 he returned to lead USM to a 27–24 win over thirteenth-ranked Alabama. By the end of his time at Southern Miss, Favre had set school records in numerous passing categories, including career yards (7,695), completions (613), attempts (1,169), touchdowns (52), and 200-yard games (15). During 1989, he set the school's single-season records for passing attempts (381), completions (206), yards (2,588), and touchdowns (16). That year, he also established school records for completions in a game (26 against East Carolina) and yards in a game (345 versus Memphis State). The Atlanta Falcons drafted Favre with the thirty-third pick in the 1991 National Football League (NFL) draft.

Favre spent one unremarkable season with the Falcons: Washington linebacker Andre Collins intercepted Favre's first regular-season pass and returned it for a touchdown, and Favre attempted only three other passes. Atlanta subsequently traded Favre to the Green Bay Packers in exchange for a first-round pick in the 1992 draft. With Green Bay, the man who wore jersey number 4 reached legendary status.

Favre played sixteen seasons in Green Bay, starting every game as the Packers' quarterback from 20 October 1992 through 20 January 2008. He led Green Bay to seven National Football Conference (NFC) Central/North Division Championships, four NFC Conference Championships,

two Super Bowl berths, and the 1997 Super Bowl Championship, a 35–21 victory over the New England Patriots in Super Bowl XXXI in New Orleans, just sixty miles from his childhood home. Favre holds every major Packers' passing record.

In 2005 Favre had one of his statistically worst seasons. He threw a career-high 29 interceptions, had a career-worst 70.9 passer rating, and threw only 20 touchdowns. When the season ended, Favre said that 2006 would be his last. However, he subsequently changed his mind, and declaring that a year would be his last but then playing longer became a common theme in his final seasons. In fact, 2007 proved a renaissance year in Favre's career. He led the Packers to 13 regular-season wins, tying a franchise mark, and an appearance in the NFC Championship game. Favre also reached numerous personal milestones, setting NFL career records career for wins as a starting quarterback (149), touchdown passes thrown (421), pass attempts (8,393), touchdown passes of 75 yards or more (13), three-touchdown games (63), passing yards (61,362), and interceptions thrown (278). *Sports Illustrated* named Favre its Sportsman of the Year, and he started for the NFC in the 2008 Pro Bowl. He then formally announced his retirement on 4 March 2008.

Favre later stated that he had felt pressured to make a decision regarding his playing future and regretted his choice. He applied for and was granted reinstatement, and in August 2008 the Packers traded him to the New York Jets. Favre led the team to a 9–7 record before retiring again, and the Jets released him from all contractual obligations. Favre again changed his mind about retiring and signed with the Minnesota Vikings on 18 August 2009. The Vikings went 12–4 in the regular season and lost to eventual Super Bowl champion New Orleans in the NFC Championship game. He played a second season with the Vikings, starting 13 games for the team and compiling a 5–8 record, before injuries finally ended his career in December 2010.

Favre is one of the most decorated quarterbacks in NFL history. He started a league record 297 consecutive regular-season games and holds career regular-season records for passes attempted (10,169), passes completed (6,300), and victories as a starting quarterback (186, tied with Peyton Manning). He was elected to eleven Pro Bowls and selected to six first- or second-team all-pro rosters.

Favre has always made his permanent home in Sumrall, Mississippi, near Hattiesburg. USM retired his jersey number in 1993, inducted him into the university's Sports Hall of Fame in 1997, and named him to its Football Team of the Century in 2001. On 18 July 2015 the Green Bay Packers inducted Favre into the team's Hall of Fame and retired his number. He appeared on the 2016 ballot for the NFL Hall of Fame and easily won election.

Since his retirement, Favre has remained one of Mississippi's most recognizable public figures. He has served as a football coach at Lamar County's Oak Grove High School, has done extensive charitable work, and has appeared in numerous commercials.

J. Michael Butler

Flagler College

Stan Caldwell, *Jackson Clarion-Ledger* (6 May 2014); Brett Favre website, www.officialbrettfavre.com; Brett and Bonita Favre with Chris Havel, *Favre* (2004); Brett Favre with Chris Havel, *Favre: For the Record* (1997); National Football League website, www.nfl.com; Pro Football Reference website, www.pro-football-reference.com; Steve Serby, *No Substitute for Sundays: Brett Favre and His Year in the Huddle with the New York Jets* (2009); *Brett Favre: The Tribute* (2008).

Featherston, Winfield Scott

(1820–1891) Confederate General and Politician

The son of transplanted Virginians, Winfield Scott Featherston was born on 8 August 1820 near Murfreesboro in Rutherford County, Tennessee. He volunteered for military service against the Creek Indians before studying law, moving to Mississippi, and gaining admission to the bar. Featherston built a successful law practice and entered the political arena, winning election to the US Congress as a Democrat in 1846 and 1848 but losing his bid for reelection in 1850. He remained a leading political voice in Mississippi, and in 1860 the state sent him to Kentucky to discuss secession with officials there.

With the outbreak of the Civil War, Featherston served as colonel of the 17th Mississippi Infantry. In 1862 he received a promotion to the rank of brigadier general. He participated in a number of battles in Virginia, including First and Second Bull Run, Ball's Bluff, Yorktown, Williamsburg, and Fredericksburg, and he was wounded at Glendale. He was later transferred to the Western Theater, where he served during the Vicksburg and Atlanta Campaigns before accompanying John Bell Hood on his ill-fated invasion of Tennessee. Featherston was among the Confederate forces who surrendered with Joseph E. Johnston at Durham Station, North Carolina, in 1865.

Featherston returned to Mississippi after the war, reestablishing both his law practice and his political career. Once Reconstruction ended, he served two terms in the Mississippi legislature, and in 1882 he became judge of the state's second judicial circuit. In 1890 he served as a delegate to the Mississippi Constitutional Convention, where he contributed as a member of the judiciary committee. Featherston lived to see the new state constitution ratified but died in 1891 at his home in Holly Springs.

Ben Wynne

Gainesville State College

Winfield Scott Featherston, Subject Files, Mississippi Department of Archives and History; Stewart Sifakis, *Who Was Who in the Civil War* (1988).

Fennelly, Beth Ann

(b. 1971) Writer

Born in New Jersey and raised in Lake Forest, Illinois, poet Beth Ann Fennelly settled in Oxford, Mississippi, in 2001 with her husband, author Tom Franklin. She received her BA from the University of Notre Dame and an MFA from the University of Arkansas, and had a postdoctoral fellowship at the University of Wisconsin. She is professor of English at the University of Mississippi, where she teaches poetry and nonfiction writing. She served for six years as the director of the MFA program at the University of Mississippi, before stepping down in 2016 when she was named the state's fifth poet laureate, succeeding Natasha Trethewey. On being named poet laureate, Fennelly said, "Southerners in general and Mississippians in particular are known to have produced many of our nation's greatest writers. It will give me joy to help promote literary arts throughout the state and encourage future generations of Mississippi storytellers and writers."

Fennelly has published three books of poetry, *Open House*, *Tender Hooks*, and *Unmentionables*, and a book of nonfiction, *Great with Child: Letters to a Young Mother*, all with W. W. Norton. She has been included three times in the *Best American Poetry* series. Her work is challenging in both its themes and its structure, and Fennelly experiments widely with poetic form. She sometimes writes autobiographically, and the poems in *Tender Hooks* were inspired by the first year in the life of her first child. Her book-length poem "The Kudzu Chronicles," published in *Unmentionables*, is grounded in her experience of living in Mississippi and reflects on how a Midwestern transplant can take root as a southern writer, just as the kudzu vine flourishes. One reviewer wrote, "Acknowledging the intractable problems of uprootedness, indebtedness, and inheritance—writing about them rather than ignoring them—may be the best solution available for a contemporary poet. In the end, an imaginary grave next to the plots of one's literary forebears, a place in a personally constructed canon, may be the most secure station the contemporary American poet can hope for."

Fennelly has also written in multiple voices and in conversation with poets and artists of the past, and the settings of her poems range across the world. When an interviewer asked about her subject matter, she replied, "If I could think of anything I wouldn't put in a poem, I'd put it immediately, rather perversely, in a poem."

She also writes essays on travel, culture, and design for *Country Living, AFAR, Southern Living, Garden & Gun,* the *Oxford American,* and other periodicals. In 2013 Fennelly and her husband Tom published the coauthored *The Tilted World,* a novel set during the backdrop of the historic Mississippi flood of 1927. Her grants and fellowships have included a 2003 National Endowment for the Arts Award, a 2006 United States Artist Grant, a 2009 Fulbright Fellowship in Brazil, and three awards from the Mississippi Arts Commission. Prizes include the Pushcart Prize, the *Kenyon Review* prize in 2001, and the 2016 Lamar York Prize in Creative Nonfiction. Her sixth book, *Heating & Cooling: 52 Micro-Memoirs,* published in 2017, combines the extreme brevity of poetry with the truth-telling of creative nonfiction.

An inspiring teacher and an ambassador for poetry, Fennelly was named Outstanding Teacher of the Year and Humanities Teacher of the Year in 2011, and a Top 20 Arts and Humanities Professor in Mississippi in 2013. After Barry Hannah's tenure as director of the MFA program ended when he passed away in 2010, Fennelly filled the role. In 2016 CollegeMagazine.com recognized the quality of the program when it ranked the University of Mississippi a "Top 10 University for Aspiring Writers." She is an active member of the Poetry Out Loud initiative, sponsored by the National Endowment for the Arts, which encourages high school students to recite poetry. She once said, "I find myself being a proselytizer . . . when I travel for readings in other states, and even countries, and come across an ignorant person who asks, 'Why do you live in Mississippi?' Literature has a cultural currency here that feels very healthy to me. I notice (it) in stark relief when I travel to other parts of the country where people think they're more cosmopolitan but don't really have a sense of the power of the written word."

Rebecca Lauck Cleary
University of Mississippi

Jackson Clarion-Ledger (11 August 2016); "Unmentionables," *Smartish Pace* website, www.smartishpace.com.

Ferns

Ferns are a class of plants that includes more than twelve thousand species. From the florist's shop they move to special events and occasions such as weddings, funerals, homecoming ceremonies, parties, and numerous other locales where flower arrangements add beauty and warmth to the setting. They provide background greenery for sprays, wreaths, and flower carpets using a host of other plants that produce colorful flowers. They are not difficult to grow and can be cultivated by the novice plant grower with a little practice. Home sites often have fern beds in conjunction with flower beds and flower gardens. Some people find ferns unappealing because of their lack of brilliant, diversely colored flowers, but they provide reliable, attractive greenery.

Ferns are among the oldest groups of living land plants. Fern fossils are found in the rocks of the Upper Devonian period (about 365 million years ago) and Upper Paleozoic period (about 345 million years ago). Early records of fern distribution in Mississippi and the other sixteen or so states of the Southeast indicate that their presence can be ascribed to two hurricanes that brought spores to the area. These "invasions" occurred during two different geologic periods as far back as 15 million years, with other individual species arriving in subsequent years.

Ferns are widely distributed and vary greatly in appearance. Most are less than six feet tall. In temperate zones, ferns produce an underground stem called a rhizome; roots grow out from rhizomes below ground while the leaves, called fronds, grow out above ground. All ferns are vascular plants, meaning that they have a tubular system that brings water and minerals from the roots to the leaf tips. These features as well as roots, stems, and leaves are considered advancements over more primitive plants and allow ferns to attain greater size. Most temperate zone ferns are terrestrial, growing on rocks and soil, and they thrive in different habitats. Though ferns are often associated with low, wet, shady, rich substrate environments, there are some exceptions, such as bracken ferns, which thrive on dry, sunny hillsides with poor soils. Some of the smallest ferns grow in water—on the surfaces of streams, ponds, lakes, and rivers.

Ferns are cosmopolitan, and only a few ecosystems worldwide are uninhabited. Mississippi lies below what is called the Fall Line, the position of the seashore about 125 million years ago. Many Mississippi ferns are found near the Fall Line.

The best tallies of fern species in Mississippi (those officially reported in scientific publications) indicate roughly thirty to thirty-five different species. Many of these studies were conducted in the 1930s, and some of the ferns identified have apparently never been found again.

Some more common Mississippi ferns include the Christmas fern (*Polystichum acrosticoides*), a widely spread form that may be considered an evergreen; lowland lady (*Athyrium asplenoides*); resurrection fern (*Polydium polypodioides*), which grows on the bark of hardwood trees; and cinnamon fern (*Osmunda cinnamomea*) and royal fern (*Osmunda regalis*), which are larger and somewhat more majestic forms. Many gardeners are particularly partial to the Venus maidenhair (*Adiantum capillus-veneris*), which is abundant in North Mississippi and does quite well in cultivation in containers or moist places.

Some areas of Mississippi provide numerous habitats suitable for luxuriant growth of these remarkable spore-producing plants whose rich green fronds attract both the casual and the serious, the amateur and the professional.

George H. Dukes Jr.
Brandon, Mississippi

A. M. Armitage, *Armitage's Native Plants for American Gardens* (2005); George H. Dukes Jr., *A Mississippi Woodland Fern Portfolio* (2000); Sue Olsen, *Encyclopedia of Garden Ferns* (2005).

Ferris, William
(b. 1942) Folklorist and Educator

From taking photographs while a teenager to serving as head of the National Endowment of the Humanities (NEH), Bill Ferris has sought to document the American South through film, books, photographs, oral histories, audio recordings, and lectures.

Born on 5 February 1942, William Reynolds Ferris grew up on his family farm south of Vicksburg, Mississippi. His upbringing and the cultural specificity of the region—in particular, his exposure to rural African American music and artistic traditions—shaped his professional and personal life. Much of Ferris's work has documented historically overlooked African American communities in Mississippi.

By age twelve Ferris was taking photographs of his family, his neighbors, and natural scenes. He subsequently attended Brooks School in Andover, Massachusetts; Davidson College in North Carolina; Northwestern University in Evanston, Illinois; Trinity College–Dublin; and the University of Pennsylvania, where he received a doctorate in folklore in 1969. Throughout these years, he continued to take photographs of the area where his family lived whenever he was home from school. As a young professor Ferris merged his oral history and documentary projects with classroom lectures, teaching at Jackson State College (1970) and Yale University (1972–79).

In 1979 he became the founding director of the Center for the Study of Southern Culture at the University of Mississippi, the first program devoted to the academic study of the region. Ferris remained at the center until 1997, when Pres. Bill Clinton appointed him to chair the NEH. He returned to academia in 2002 and currently serves as professor of history and associate director of the Center for the Study of the American South at the University of North Carolina at Chapel Hill.

Ferris's doctoral dissertation became his first publication, *Blues from the Delta* (1970), a collection of oral histories from Delta bluesmen framed by cultural studies and folkloric approaches. He has written and edited nine additional books on topics as varied as literary Mississippi, folk art practice, and livestock trader Ray Lum. Ferris has also created audio and visual records of his subjects and produced films, photographs, and recordings to accompany his written work. He and Charles Reagan Wilson served as coeditors of the *Encyclopedia of Southern Culture*, which features the work over more than eight hundred scholars and garnered national media acclaim and a variety of awards, including one from the American Library Association. Ferris has also been honored by the Mississippi Institute of Arts and Letters and has received France's Order of Arts and Letters and the Charles Frankel Prize in the Humanities.

As a bookend of sorts with *Blues from the Delta*, Ferris created a book, DVD, and audio recording collection, *Give My Poor Heart Ease: Voices of the Mississippi Blues* (2009), based on interviews with Delta blues musicians. Rather than offering academic or narrative commentary, Ferris allows his subjects—some well known, others obscure—to tell their stories. Another multimedia collection, *The Storied South: Voices of Writers and Artists* (2013), collects twenty-six interviews Ferris conducted with such notables as Eudora Welty, Pete Seeger, Alice Walker, William Eggleston, Bobby Rush, and C. Vann Woodward. A third work, *The South in Color*, appeared in 2016.

Odie Lindsey
Nashville, Tennesseew

William Ferris, documentary films at *Folkstreams* website, www.folk streams.net; William Ferris, *Images of the South: Visits with Eudora Welty and Walker Evans* (1978); William Ferris, *"You Live and Learn. Then You Die and Forget it All": Ray Lum's Tales of Horses, Mules, and Men* (1992); Marc Smirnoff, *Oxford American* website, www.oxfordamerican.org.

Ferriss, Dave "Boo"
(b. 1921) Athlete and Coach

Born in Shaw on 5 December 1921, David Meadow "Boo" Ferriss has devoted his life to baseball on both the national and local levels. Ferriss first gained recognition for a brief but exceptional career with the Boston Red Sox of Major League Baseball's American League. After a shoulder injury ended his career, Ferriss returned to Mississippi and embarked on a twenty-six-year career as the head coach of Delta State University's baseball team.

After graduating from Shaw High School, Ferriss played baseball at Mississippi State University, where he was an All–Southeastern Conference pitcher. In 1942, after his junior season, the Boston Red Sox signed Ferriss to a professional contract. His rise to the Major Leagues was interrupted by his service in the US Army from 1942 to 1945, but he made his debut with the Red Sox on 29 April of that year and went on to post a 21–10 record in his rookie season. In 1946 he went 25–6 for the Red Sox, helping them to an American League pennant. He beat the St. Louis Cardinals 4–0 in Game 3 of the World Series and started Game 7, though he did not get the decision as the Red Sox lost the game and the Series.

In 1947 Ferriss was expected to play a major role in Boston's pitching rotation, but he sustained a shoulder injury and never again showed the brilliance that he had exhibited during his first two years in the league. His final Major League appearance came in 1950, and he finished with a career 65–30 record. Ferriss returned to the Red Sox as pitching coach in 1955, remaining in that role for five seasons.

Ferriss returned to Mississippi in the fall of 1959 to become the head baseball coach and athletic director at Delta State College (now Delta State University). He served in that role until 1967, when he left to become the athletic director at Mississippi State. Ferriss returned to Delta State a year later and resumed his head coaching duties in 1970. Ferriss compiled an overall record of 639–387–8 at Delta State, leading the Statesmen to four Gulf South Conference championships and three trips to the National Collegiate Athletic Association Division II College World Series (1977, 1978, and 1982). His 1978 team finished second in the nation. He retired after the 1988 season and was selected as a member of the American Baseball Coaches Hall of Fame. He has also been inducted into the Mississippi Sports Hall of Fame and the Boston Red Sox Hall of Fame.

Ferriss's impact on baseball in Mississippi continues to be felt even after his retirement from coaching. Beginning in 2004, the Mississippi Sports Hall of Fame and Museum began presenting the Boo Ferriss Award to the state's top college baseball player. The baseball facility at Delta State bears his name, and a museum dedicated to his life is located on campus. In 2012 he received the Mississippi Sports Hall of Fame's Rube Award for his contribution to sports in the state. Ferriss lives in Cleveland with his wife, Miriam.

Christopher J. Hedglin
Jackson, Mississippi

Baseball-reference.com website, www.baseball-reference.com; Rick Cleveland, *Boo: A Life in Baseball, Well Lived* (2009); Sam Gwynne, *Boston Globe* (19 February 2006); David Halberstam, *Summer of '49*; David Halberstam, *The Teammates*; Mississippi Sports Hall of Fame and Museum website, www.msfame.com.

Fiction

> The sorry, shabby world that don't quite please you, so you create one of your own.
> **—William Faulkner**

> Because we've got a lot of explaining to do.
> **—Richard Ford**

The old question still applies: Why Mississippi? Why should or how could a state at the bottom of practically every imaginable quality-of-life list have produced and continue to produce so much world-class fiction? William Faulkner, Eudora Welty, Richard Wright, Elizabeth Spencer, and Ellen Douglas would of course be enough to establish Mississippi's credentials as a cornerstone of American fiction, but Mississippi in fact has many, many more writers, so that the question elaborates itself, ravels out into multiple strands that ultimately provide no real answers. Every possible line of argument (so far, at any rate) generates its own objections or tut-tuts. The question itself may be mostly an academic parlor game, though it is, to be sure, an interesting one.

The question assumes that a reasonable explanation for the phenomenon must exist. Over the years people have proposed answers ranging from the ridiculous—*It's the water, stupid!*—to more thoughtful and provocative considerations of cultural, political, historical, and economic forces: fiction as a response to oppression and hard times, fiction as a reaction against current circumstance rather than as an intellectual attempt to master it, to see through the current circumstance into something larger. It might be nice to explain Mississippi's outpouring of fiction as some sort of response to the shabby, chaotic, poverty-stricken, and backward world Mississippians inhabit, but that explanation simply won't wash, if only because it would imply an equal outpouring of fiction from the other states of the Old South that for all practical purposes have had pretty much the same history as Mississippi.

Why? and *How?* invariably seem to originate in a patent condescension toward Mississippi: reciting the faults of Faulkner's *Intruder in the Dust* in the *New Yorker*, Edmund Wilson suggested that it would have been a better novel and Faulkner would have been a better writer if he had spent more time in such places as New York discussing literature with such writers as Edmund Wilson. The review prompted Welty's acid response, which the magazine published the following week, that she shuddered at the idea of novel writing as a kind of assembly line at which Faulkner worked only to show up for payday and have bossman Wilson dock him for having a bad address. Welty wanted slightly more purity of judgment than Wilson showed and even had the temerity to suggest that Faulkner's intelligence rather than his address might be the source of all that was good in his fiction.

Faulkner's early reviewers indeed worried about his address, perhaps understandably—how could he write such transcendent prose in a benighted state like Mississippi? Significantly, the question never seemed to bother intelligent readers and reviewers in Europe—or, truth to tell, in this country—though it continued to burble along in American criticism for years, its pernicious effects on understanding culminating in the all but unanimous assumption among reviewers and critics (even southerners, who, one might have hoped, should have known better) that southern writers' strength was directly tied, Antaeus-like, to their contact with the southern soil. In 1954, when Faulkner published *A Fable*, and in 1955, when Welty published *The Bride of the Innisfallen*, the critical world was aghast, patronizing, tsk-tsking and clucking that these writers could have so deliberately committed literary suicide by presuming to try to operate outside of Mississippi, *in Europe, of all places*, so far from those sturdy roots of place, home, and tradition that were their perceived strengths—as though a writer abandons those strengths when crossing a border, as though Faulkner and Welty wrote their best fiction with their bare feet encased securely in Mississippi mud. The effects of that immediate reaction have been long-lasting: such silly and critically indefensible impositions on Faulkner and Welty have meant that only now, more than half a century later, are we just beginning to take proper account of these two splendid and important works of fiction, though criticism of Faulkner, Welty, and other Mississippi writers is now much less concerned with such parochialism. When the old chestnut of place emerges in the criticism, it does so energized by new theoretical and conceptual contexts.

Welty was right that the fiction itself simply demonstrates the high range of intelligence in Mississippi. To account for the wealth of Mississippi fiction, we should begin with the fiction itself, stripped of the overlay of location, and suggest, as Welty does, that the *fact* of "Mississippi fiction" is more important than the *why* of it. At least as far as fiction is concerned, Mississippi may quite simply be smarter than the rest of the country. Even if, as Richard Ford quips, we somehow have more explaining to do than other states have had, that would not in itself account for the quality of the fiction.

Ford's witticism points toward at least a partial answer, though it does not explain why other states have not produced such an extensive range of writers. Ford suggests that Mississippi fiction at some level springs from inherited guilt over the state's racial history—from some necessary or perhaps inevitable engagement with and/or resistance to that history, which so completely overwhelms our national and state self-images. Welty's work has often been criticized for lacking that political dimension, a consciousness of the racial networks that created the pervading social tensions that seem to define Mississippi in the minds of so many, friend and foe alike. Faulkner has been bashed on numerous occasions because of his perceived lack of distance (that home address again) and resulting blundering naïveté in political and racial matters. But the insistence on overt political content is itself a shrill political attack, an un-Jamesian imposition of a donnée on writers of any address, an assumption that racial history is the single and unequivocal given in Mississippi. There would thus seem to have been a contradiction: the same criticism that insists on fidelity to place has often assumed that that fidelity worked against a Mississippian's capacity to understand Mississippi. Thus, when we go to Europe or Boston, we are too far from place; when we stay at home, we are too close. How *did* we ever learn to write?

But Faulkner's work, writ large, is not the race-dominated oeuvre that we generally take it to be, although there is some consensus that *Light in August, Absalom, Absalom!*, and *Go Down, Moses* would be on any list of his greatest works. Though black characters are as much a part of his fictional landscape as of the actual landscape of North Mississippi, they are by and large part of the given and are often centrally involved in a work's fictional situation without the work's being "about" race—except as their circumstances as poor and historically disadvantaged help to create the fictional situation from essential elements of the social and cultural landscape. In *Requiem for a Nun*, Nancy Mannigoe, who murders Temple Drake's baby, would almost certainly not have done so had she not been so positioned by poverty and circumstance; race is crucial in *Requiem* but is not its source or the reservoir of its meaning, and the novel is not "about" race in the same sense as *Absalom, Light in August*, and *Go Down, Moses*. Faulkner nearly always deals with poverty and injustice and family dysfunction as they appear in white families; when black characters are central to his narratives, they are heroic, intelligent, complicated people who cope heroically even if sometimes tragically not so much with poverty as with a white world to which they are connected by the intimacies of blood and tradition. Minor black characters in his fiction are marginalized—faces on the street, snapshots as we pass them. Faulkner never dealt directly—either in his fiction or, I suspect, in his life—with the particularly anguished, tumultuous world of Mississippi that Richard Wright describes so powerfully in *Black Boy*. *Black Boy* faces things that Faulkner for some reason simply avoided. That is perhaps why Faulkner, still in his high-modernist, nonpolitical phase, liked *Native Son* much more than he liked *Black Boy*: he wrote to Wright that what *Black Boy* said certainly needed to be said but that it would be much better said in fiction—as if fictional artists could not write autobiography.

Ford's fiction does not at first seem to engage the state's racial history at all. However, that history is a major presence, and he treats it more as a current political fact than as a historical problem and as a wider and more profoundly American problem than the narrowly focused, though of course, powerfully dramatic problems of lynching and other forms of racial violence: his New Jersey has problems of immigration, and he sets *Independence Day* around 4 July and *The Lay of the Land* during the week of Thanksgiving, dates that allow a wide range of meditations on the meaning of America. Blacks in the work of Walker Percy and Barry Hannah seem as confused and befuddled as whites are. Ellen Douglas marks out her own racial territory in *Can't Quit You, Baby*, depoliticizes it as much as possible to concentrate on the relations between a white woman and the black woman who cooks and cleans for her. No one slices more intimately than Douglas into the intricacies of race relations as they are lived day to day, exploring how friendship, love, and hate happen simultaneously even through years of misunderstanding and assumption, at some distance from Faulkner's and Wright's more public dramas. For Richard Wright, of course, race is the defining and all-consuming landscape of fiction and of his important polemical nonfiction writings about Africa's emergence as a primary factor of world politics in the post–World War II world, though even he needed to escape the topic in a voluminous series of haiku.

We can best define "Mississippi fiction" as fiction written by Mississippians, without attaching any preconditions as to its subject matter. In fact, Mississippi's fiction writers cast a very wide net indeed for subject and setting: Augustus Baldwin Longstreet's and Joseph Beckham Cobb's treatments of backwoods Mississippi and Alabama rednecks; Joseph Holt Ingraham's fabulously best-selling historical and religious epics; Evans Harrington's exploration of the penal system at Parchman; Thomas Hal Phillips's depiction of the problems of young male friendships; Thomas Harris's serial-killer epics; Elizabeth Spencer's lights in various piazzas; James Street's extremely popular dramas of antebellum Mississippi and of Columbus's voyage to the New World; Stark Young's antebellum Mississippi planters and aristocrats; Willie Morris's exploration of the social and political scene in New York and Washington, D.C.; Larry Brown's Vietnam returnees; John Grisham's and Greg Iles's best-selling thrillers; and Barry Hannah's depiction of a postmodern Mississippi and Alabama, where all traditional assumptions about Mississippi and everything else simply dissolve in a chaos of the current, where black and white are fellow travelers no matter what our history, where we are all equally befuddled and confused and doing our best, whatever that is. Mississippi fiction is a sumptuous examination not just of Mississippi but of the rest of the world and of Mississippi's inextricable relationship to it.

Noel Polk
Mississippi State University

Dorothy Abbott, *Mississippi Writers: Reflections on Childhood and Youth*, vol. 1, *Fiction* (1985); Patti Carr Black and Marion Barnwell, *Touring Literary Mississippi* (2003); Noel E. Polk and James R. Scafidel, *An Anthology of Mississippi Writers* (1979).

Fiddling Tradition

Fiddling is playing traditional folk music on the violin, generally without the aid of written music (although many fiddlers are musically literate to at least some degree). No clear line existed between violin performance and fiddling in eighteenth-century America, since plenty of what were already traditional dance tunes—as well as tunes that would become traditional—were fashionable in both Britain and the United States. But during the first half of the nineteenth century, American fiddling took on an identity of its own, partly as a consequence of rural fiddlers who still drew on repertoires that had fallen out of favor and partly as a result of the widespread popularization of blackface minstrelsy, which incorporated white performers' interpretations and caricatures of slave fiddling.

Fiddlers usually play in styles specific to the regions where they live, though those regions are now more broadly defined than was the case in the past: "old-timey" fiddlers in the Southeast perform rustic "breakdowns" in heterophony with banjos, a style that evokes blackface minstrelsy, while Texas fiddlers using "contest" style systematically vary their breakdowns, waltzes, polkas, and rags. Today, most fiddlers' repertoires still focus on genres of bipartite dance tunes and songs that date back to the eighteenth through early twentieth centuries, although the contest stage and bluegrass venues have become the focus for most fiddle traditions over the past half century.

Widespread immigration to Mississippi from the southeastern United States included fiddlers playing in a variety of old-timey styles. When fiddling again briefly became part of popular music as part of so-called hillbilly music during the 1920s and 1930s, Mississippi string bands such as the Leake County Revelers, Narmour and Smith, Freeny's Barn Dance Band, the Mississippi Possum Hunters, and Hoyt Ming's Pep Steppers (mistakenly recorded as Floyd Ming's Pep Steppers) became widely known through radio broadcasts and 78 rpm records. These string bands, which included a fiddler, a guitarist, and often a mandolinist and/or banjoist, often included family members. Many of their recordings have been reissued, and revivalist ensembles such as the Old Hat String Band from near Vicksburg still play such music. However, many contemporary fiddlers play in contests at the Mississippi State Fair, in rural locations in the northern part of the state and surrounding areas, or most frequently in bluegrass bands. The vigorous Magnolia State Bluegrass Association, whose approximately fifteen hundred members include several hundred fiddlers, sponsors dozens of bluegrass festivals, gospel sings, and jam sessions each year.

Chris Goertzen
University of Southern Mississippi

David Freeman, *Mississippi String Bands*, vols. 1–2 (1998), liner notes; Chris Goertzen, *American Music* (Fall 2004); Tony Russell, *Country Music Originals: The Legends and the Lost* (2007).

Filipinos

Filipinos constitute a small but increasingly significant minority group on the Mississippi Gulf Coast. Filipino immigrants have a relatively short history in the state. In 1960, according to the US census, Mississippi was home to only 59 people of Philippine ancestry, about half of them in Harrison County. That number grew steadily over the rest of the century, reaching 1,043 in 1980, 1,565 in 1990, and 3,845 in 2000. The 2010 census counted 3,562 Filipinos, making them the state's fourth-largest Asian immigrant group, behind Vietnamese, Indians, and Chinese. By far the largest number of Filipinos in the state live in Harrison County, and very few live in rural areas.

Changes in American immigration laws account for a good deal of that dramatic increase in population. The 1965 Immigration and Nationality Act replaced national origin quotas with preferences for people with particular skills and for unifying families. Since 1965 about half a million Filipinos have come to the United States every decade.

In Mississippi, as in many parts of the United States, many Filipinos are doctors and nurses. According to historian Barbara Posadas, "Filipino American health care professionals veritably define the ethnic group in the minds of many Americans." Those health care professionals who came to the United States because of their especially desirable skills are also notable in that they came with family members. Unlike many American immigrant groups, Filipinos tend to have relatively even gender ratios and to live in large family groups.

Ted Ownby
University of Mississippi

Hazel McFerson, ed., *Blacks and Asians: Crossings, Conflict, and Commonality* (2006); *Philippine News* website, www.philippinenews.com; Barbara M. Posadas, *The Filipino Americans* (1999); Maria P. P. Root, ed., *Filipino Americans: Transformation and Identity* (1997); US Census Population Reports, www.census.gov.

Finch, Charles Clifton

(1927–1986) Fifty-Seventh Governor, 1976–1980

Cliff Finch campaigned for governor in 1975 on the promise of more and better-paying jobs for Mississippians. To dramatize his concern for the hardships of the state's working people, Finch spent one day a week during the late stages of his campaign bagging groceries at supermarkets, driving bulldozers, and working at other ordinary jobs, bringing a sack lunch. His campaign tactics were very popular and helped him reach the governor's office in his first try.

The oldest of five children, Finch was born in Pope, in Panola County, on 4 April 1927. He enlisted in the US Army at age eighteen and served in Italy during World War II. Finch subsequently signed on with a construction company and spent a year doing heavy construction work in Guam before working his way through the University of Mississippi. After graduating from the law school in 1958, he opened a law office in Batesville.

In 1960 Finch entered politics, winning election to the Mississippi House of Representatives. He won the post of district attorney for the 17th Judicial District in 1964 and was reelected four years later. His first statewide campaign was an unsuccessful race for lieutenant governor in 1971.

In 1975 Finch conducted a populist gubernatorial campaign that united working-class black and white voters. In the general election, Finch, a Democrat, narrowly defeated Republican Gil Carmichael and Henry Kirksey, a black independent. In 1977 Finch signed a bill abolishing the Mississippi State Sovereignty Commission.

In 1978 Sen. James Eastland retired from the US Senate, surrendering the seat he had held since 1941. Although he still had two years remaining on his four-year gubernatorial term, Finch ran for the Senate seat but lost in the Democratic primary. Republican Thad Cochran went on to win the post.

Finch also sought the 1980 Democratic nomination for the US presidency, entering the New Hampshire primary. He garnered little support and withdrew from the campaign soon thereafter to return to his Batesville law practice. He remained a practicing attorney until his death on 22 April 1986.

David G. Sansing
University of Mississippi

Cliff Finch Subject File, Mississippi Department of Archives and History; *Mississippi Official and Statistical Register* (1976–80); Jere Nash and Andy Taggart, *Mississippi Politics: The Struggle for Power, 1976–2006* (2006).

First Monday Trade Days (Ripley)

Every month since 1893 Ripley has held its First Monday Sale and Trade Day. The town's merchants originally designated the first Monday of every month a "Grand Bargain Day" in hopes of attracting rural trade to town by allowing cash-poor farmers to gather on the courthouse square to trade produce, livestock, tools, and labor among themselves. The Tippah County government helped promote the event by holding sheriff's office auctions of stray livestock and other unclaimed property from the courthouse steps on the same day. First Monday quickly became very popular, with rural people from throughout the area traveling to Ripley every month. Early twentieth-century photographs show the town's courthouse square packed full of people, mules, and horse-drawn wagons.

Because of congestion on the courthouse square, First Monday moved to another part of Ripley's business district in the 1910s. In the early 1940s it moved again, this time because of sanitation and noise issues, to the intersection of Highways 15 and 4, about a quarter mile from downtown. A decade or so later, First Monday relocated to the Tippah County Fairgrounds, a mile to the south on Highway 15. It

Larry Sinclair selling corn, First Monday, Ripley (Photograph by David Wharton)

settled in its present location, on the east side of Highway 15 about two miles south of downtown Ripley at what was once a drive-in movie theater, in 1978.

The event now takes place on the weekend before the first Monday of every month. Hundreds of vendors rent booths on the fifty-acre grounds, offering a wide variety of merchandise, both new and used. Some of the vendors are professionals who come to First Monday as a regular part of their travels on the southern flea market circuit. Others are locals who come more for fun than profit and who generally sell only at First Monday. The town normally has a population of about five thousand, but thousands more flock to Ripley on First Monday weekends, eager to trade, buy, talk, and gawk. They come from throughout the South and often from much farther away. In July 1999 cars from Texas, Missouri, Ohio, Arizona, Indiana, and New York were noted in the parking lot along with vehicles from Mississippi and other southern states.

Items available for sale or trade include sunglasses, guinea fowl, videos, baby strollers, sweet potatoes, bumper stickers, shotguns, porch swings, farm implements, dolls, microwave ovens, dogs, T-shirts, artificial floral arrangements, homemade music CDs, and just about anything else. There are also many refreshment booths offering such American standards as hamburgers, corn dogs, sausage on a stick, French fries, popcorn, ice cream, and soft drinks—but no alcoholic beverages. Foods with a more southern flavor include pork rinds, boiled peanuts, fried pies, sweet tea, and fresh-squeezed lemonade.

As with any long-standing tradition, First Monday has changed over the years. At first, virtually all transactions were trades—"an old hound dog for an old single barrel shotgun or plow tools for a mule," as one lifelong resident of Ripley put it—with little or no cash changing hands. Such trading now seems a thing of the past, though as recently as the 1960s and 1970s, some old-timers disdained cash sales for the more subtle art of barter. One Ripley native recalls trying to buy a shotgun at First Monday from a man who was willing to trade but would not consider taking cash. Another remembers an elderly farmer wandering the grounds, holding a large pipe wrench over his head, and shouting, "Who will trade me a billy goat for this pipe wrench? I need a good billy goat, who needs a good pipe wrench?" Today, even though price is sometimes open to negotiation, nearly all First Monday business is transacted in cash. Some people mourn this change, believing it has turned First Monday into just another flea market that has lost its connections to its rural past.

David Wharton
University of Mississippi

David Wharton, *Mississippi Folklife* (Fall 1999).

Fish, Native

Mississippi possesses one of the richest freshwater fish faunas in the United States, with a total of at least 292 species, of which 212 are native freshwater or diadromous (moving between freshwater and saltwater for purposes of spawning). In addition to native freshwater species, 66 species are primarily estuarine or marine but are capable of entering freshwater, 9 species have been introduced into Mississippi from regions outside North America, and 4 are native to North America but transplanted into Mississippi. Only four states support more native freshwater fish—Tennessee (297), Alabama (295), Kentucky (220), and Georgia (219).

The minnows (family *Cyprinidae*) contain the greatest number of species (59), followed by darters (family *Percidae*, 45), suckers (family *Catostomidae*, 20), catfish (family *Ictaluridae*, 18), and sunfish (family *Centrarchidae*, 18). Anglers and commercial fishers will be familiar with fish in some of these families, especially *Centrarchidae* (shadow bass, warmouth, bluegill, long-ear and red-ear sunfish, largemouth and spotted bass, white and black crappie), *Ictaluridae* (channel and blue catfish; black, yellow, and brown bullheads; flathead catfish), *Catostomidae* (smallmouth, bigmouth, and black buffalo; blacktail redhorse), and *Percidae* (walleye, sauger). Other sport or commercial fish include paddlefish (family *Polyodontidae*), grass and chain pickerel (family *Esocidae*), white, yellow, and striped bass (family *Moronidae*), freshwater drum (family *Sciaenidae*). The 28 or so native species that are sometimes harvested for sport or commercial purposes thus make up only a small portion of the total native freshwater fish fauna. Nongame fish comprise most of the diversity and

are beautiful and fascinating in their own right. Along with sport fish, the nongame fish are vital to the health of Mississippi's aquatic systems.

Three species (table 1A) are endemic to Mississippi, meaning that they are found nowhere else. The bayou darter (*Etheostoma rubrum*) occurs only in the Bayou Pierre system south of Vicksburg. The Yazoo shiner (*Notropis rafinesquei*) and the Yazoo darter (*Etheostoma raneyi*) are restricted to streams of the Yazoo drainage in northwestern Mississippi. Ten species are endemic to drainages that occur in Mississippi and one adjoining state (table 1B), further highlighting the unique elements of the Mississippi fauna. Seven of these species are endemic to the Mobile Basin (shared between Mississippi and Alabama). One species is endemic to the Mobile and Pascagoula drainages (shared with Alabama), one species is endemic to the Lake Pontchartrain drainage (shared with Louisiana), and one species is endemic to the Pearl River drainage (shared with Louisiana) and the Pascagoula River drainage. Unfortunately, this species, the pearl darter, has been extirpated from the Pearl River drainage and is now restricted solely to the Pascagoula River drainage. This river is unique in that it is the last large (mean annual discharge of more than 350 cubic meters per second) river system in the lower forty-eight states that is not seriously altered by mainstream dams or diversions. The natural flow regime of the Pascagoula River makes it an important refuge for fish that have been eliminated from other stream systems as a consequence of habitat modification or loss.

Mississippi owes its rich fish fauna to its location adjoining upland areas to the north and east and to the Mississippi River along its western border. The Mississippi River Basin, which supports at least 31 families and 375 species of native fish, has had a major influence on the state's fish fauna. The basin has variously functioned as a refuge for more northern clear-water fish during the Pleistocene glaciations (which ended approximately ten thousand years ago), as an area of speciation, as a conduit for dispersal for some species between stream systems, and as its character has changed since the last ice age, a barrier to clear-water, upland fish. The size, longevity, and positioning of the Mississippi River Basin have all contributed to the richness of the fish fauna. In particular, the north-south alignment allowed for a southward displacement of many species during the Pleistocene glacial advances, when what is now the northern United States was covered with ice sheets, with subsequent northward recolonization when the ice retreated. Most of Mississippi (with the exception of the extreme northeastern corner, including Tishomingo County) was inundated by shallow seas during various Cenozoic marine transgressions, whereas areas immediately to the east (northern Alabama) and north (Tennessee) were not. These areas are above the Fall Line, the boundary between the more upland Tertiary areas and the soft marine deposits of the Coastal Plain. Also, the Tennessee-Mississippi Basin of Alabama and Tennessee was south of

Table 1. Fish Endemic Solely to Mississippi (A) or Endemic to a Body of Water Shared with an Adjoining State (B)		
A.		
Body of Water	**Common name**	**Scientific name**
Bayou Pierre	Bayou darter	*Etheostoma rubrum*
Yazoo River Drainage	Yazoo shiner	*Notropis rafinesquei*
Yazoo River Drainage	Yazoo darter	*Etheostoma raneyi*
B.		
Body of Water	**Common name**	**Scientific name**
Mobile Basin (Mississippi & Alabama)	Alabama sturgeon	*Scaphirhynchus suttkusi*
	rough shiner	*Notropis baileyi*
	silverside shiner	*Notropis candidus*
	fluvial shiner	*Notropis edwardraneyi*
	southern sand darter	*Ammocrypta meridiana*
	Tombigbee darter	*Etheostoma lachneri*
	backwater darter	*Etheostoma zonifer*
Mobile Basin and Pascagoula drainage (Mississippi & Alabama)	southeastern blue sucker	*Cycleptus meridionalis*
Lake Pontchartrain Drainage (Mississippi & Louisiana)	broadstripe topminnow	*Fundulus euryzonus*
Pearl and Pascagoula Drainages (Mississippi & Louisiana)	pearl darter	*Percina aurora*

the maximum penetration of the Pleistocene ice sheets. Thus, this area represents an ancient faunal region that, with its high topographic diversity, has provided ample opportunity for isolation and diversification of fish species. Tennessee's Central Highlands region is considered a center of abundance and evolution for both darters and minnows, and Mississippi's location near this area further explains the high diversity of its fish population.

Mississippi's diverse fish fauna currently face some threats. Although the US Fish and Wildlife Service lists only two fish species from Mississippi as endangered (Alabama sturgeon and pallid sturgeon) and two as threatened (bayou darter, Gulf sturgeon), data compiled by the Mississippi Department of Wildlife, Fisheries, and Parks; the Mississippi Museum of Natural Science; and the Mississippi Wildlife Heritage program indicate that 70 species (35 percent of Mississippi's native fish fauna) are to some degree imperiled. The primary reasons for imperilment include physical habitat loss or damage, chemical pollution, overexploitation, and introduction of nonnative (exotic) species. Thus, we must meet the challenge of maintaining this rich biological legacy for future generations.

Stephen T. Ross
University of New Mexico,
Museum of Southwestern Biology

Herbert T. Boschung Jr. and Richard L. Mayden, *Fishes of Alabama* (2004); Brooks M. Burr and Richard L. Mayden, in *Systematics, Historical Ecology, and North American Freshwater Fishes*, ed. Richard L. Mayden (1992); Mats Dynesius and Christer Nilsson, *Science* (4 November 1994); David A. Etnier and Wayne C. Starnes, *The Fishes of Tennessee* (1993); Maurice F. Mettee, Patrick E. O'Neil, and J. Malcolm Pierson, *Fishes of Alabama and the Mobile Basin* (1996); Lawrence M. Page, *Handbook of Darters* (1983); Henry W. Robison, in *Zoogeography of North American Freshwater Fishes*, ed. C. H. Hocutt and E. O. Wiley (1986); Stephen T. Ross, *Inland Fishes of Mississippi* (2001); W. Todd Slack, Mississippi Museum of Natural Science, personal communication (November 2006); Melvin L. Warren Jr. and Brooks M. Burr, *Fisheries* (January 1994).

Fishing

Fishing has always provided sustenance and recreation to the native peoples of what would become Mississippi and to the Europeans and Africans who largely supplanted them. Before World War II most Mississippians lived on farms, and they fished within the context of the agricultural cycle and according to the rise and fall of the streams and rivers. In addition to small farm ponds, mill ponds, and beaver impoundments, fishing took place in naturally occurring streams and rivers and their associated oxbows. When farmwork permitted, Mississippians took fish by every conceivable method, including seines, traps, poisons such as crushed buckeye (*Aesculus* species), and even bare hands. Hand fishing, or grabbling, as it is often called in Mississippi, probably evolved in part from a Native American fishing technique. It is still practiced: folks reach into the

Spanish mackerel caught in Biloxi (Ann Rayburn Paper Americana Collection Department of Archives and Special Collections, J. D. Williams Library, University of Mississippi [rayburn_ann_36_30_001])

spawning cavities of blue and especially flathead catfish during the early summer. Catfish bite the offending hands, allowing the grabbler to grip inside their mouths and gills and haul them out onto the bank or into the boat.

Farming folks particularly looked forward to the lay-by time during late summer, after crops had been planted and cultivated, when a lull in labor demands occurred until the fall harvest. Water levels were usually low at this time. Families might set baited lines for catfish or use poles and lines to fish for bluegill, bass, or crappie. The low water made seining easier, and those without nets might simply wade through the isolated pools to muddy the water until the fish rose to the surface.

People often purchased fish from commercial fishermen who worked the rivers and oxbows with specialized tackle, such as gill nets, hoop nets, and trammel nets. In earlier times commercial fishermen might sell any species of fish, but conservation legislation of the 1930s restricted catches to nongame fish, such as catfish, gar, and, most important, buffalo. Members of the sucker family, the three species of buffalo found in Mississippi waters are bony but delectable and could survive considerable handling and captivity in live nets, an important trait in the days before refrigeration. Weighing up to sixty pounds and available year-round, the buffalo was the foundation of the inland commercial fishery. The buffalo and other nongame fish appealed to the rural poor and quickly lost favor once folks moved to town and had access to other foods. Catfish endured as an important commercial species but are now mostly a product of aquaculture rather than wild caught. A few commercial fishers still catch buffalo and wild catfish, and persistent consumers can still find the occasional fish market, mostly in the Mississippi Delta.

Recreational fishing grew in importance after World War II as people earned more and enjoyed more leisure time. Delta oxbow lakes became important destinations for folks seeking bluegill, crappie, or bass. At the same time, farmers began using powerful new pesticides that had long-term ill effects on fish populations. As the primary agricultural region, the Delta received the brunt of such pesticide use, and all types of fishing suffered. While Delta fisheries languished, the Corps of Engineers was completing a series of large flood-control reservoirs in the hill country. Intended to keep floodwater off the Delta farmland, these huge impoundments, including Sardis, Enid, and Grenada, also created a new fishery that was somewhat less affected by agricultural runoff. Reservoir fishing became immensely popular, and the lakes and their surrounding lands remain important as vast government-owned and thus publicly accessible recreational areas.

In recent years, good fishing has returned to many Delta rivers and oxbows. Pesticide residues of the 1950s and 1960s are buried under more recent layers of sediment, and while consumption advisories are widespread, many Delta fish are safe to eat.

The estuarine and coastal waters of Mississippi have always yielded a rich harvest of shrimp, crabs, oysters, and various finfish enjoyed by local inhabitants, but by the late nineteenth century, railroads, ice houses, and canneries made the coast an important supplier of seafood to the rest of the country. The area around Biloxi emerged as a center of the industry. The fisheries and the businesses they supported attracted a diverse community, including Cajuns from Louisiana, Slavonians from the countries that would become Yugoslavia, Polish immigrants from Baltimore, and much later the Vietnamese. The familiar problems of overfishing and foreign competition have diminished the coastal fisheries in recent years. Shrimpers in particular have suffered from an influx of a cheaper farm-raised product from overseas. Recreational anglers enjoy a vibrant fishery for such popular species as speckled seatrout, flounder, and redfish. One may even still see folks throwing cast nets for mullet, a fish once known as Biloxi bacon for its importance as a subsistence food.

At its best, fishing encourages a sense of stewardship of the natural world. Fishing opportunities still abound in Mississippi, and considering the state's history of intense use, the freshwater and marine fisheries remain in remarkable health. Overdevelopment and apathy may be more serious threats than overexploitation to today's fishing. Water for urban growth and agriculture is becoming precious even in the traditionally water-rich South. Accessing and fishing the state's wilder river systems can be intimidating for many. And in a time when casinos are a growth industry and virtual reality is more seductive than an afternoon on a creek, fishing is losing some of its appeal.

Wiley C. Prewitt Jr.
Yocona, Mississippi

Fannye A. Cook, *Freshwater Fishes in Mississippi* (1959); Pete Daniel, *Toxic Drift: Pesticides and Health in the Post–World War II South* (2005); Donald C. Jackson and John R. Jackson, *Fisheries* (May–June 1989); Aimee Schmidt, *Mississippi Folklife* (1995); Donald G. Schueler, *Preserving the Pascagoula* (1980).

Five Blind Boys of Mississippi
Gospel Singers

In the 1930s four blind students at the Piney Woods School south of Jackson—Lawrence Abrams, Archie Brownlee, Joseph Ford, and Lloyd Woodard—began singing together as the Cotton Blossom Singers, performing sacred and popular songs at fund-raising events for the school. Alan Lomax recorded them on 9 March 1937 for the Library of Congress. By the early 1940s the group performed religious music as the Jackson Harmoneers, singing in the ensemble jubilee style first popularized in the late nineteenth century by the Fisk Jubilee Singers. By 1942 the original quartet was joined by Melvin Henderson.

After moving to Chicago in the mid-1940s, the group became known as the Five Blind Boys of Mississippi. Some sources claim that a promoter billed them alongside the Five Blind Boys of Alabama to market their performances as a competition. Robert H. Harris, lead singer of the popular Soul Stirrers, was a major influence on the Five Blind Boys of Mississippi in this period. His "hard gospel" style featured emotive sounds that made full use of his vocal range, and Brownlee, the Blind Boys' lead singer, had one of the most powerful voices in gospel music, able to growl, shout, and moan to provide a counterpoint to gospel rhythm. According to Anthony Heilbut, Brownlee's singing and stage presence made him "king of the road with his bloodcurdling shrieks and his sixteen-bar-blues tributes to Mother"—for example, "Mother, Don't Worry If Your Child Should Go to War" and "Keep Your Lamp Trimmed and Burning till Your Child Comes Home." Brownlee could also sing with "an unresolved falsetto shriek that conjured up images of witchcraft or bedlam." Brownlee's style was an early influence on Ray Charles and later soul singers.

The Five Blind Boys of Mississippi achieved national popularity in the late 1940s, and their 1950 bluesy recording of "Our Father" for Peacock Records became one of the first gospel records to hit Billboard's R&B charts. Rev. Percell Perkins, a hard gospel shouter like Brownlee and the group's business manager, began performing with the Blind Boys during this period.

Brownlee died of pneumonia in New Orleans on 8 February 1960, when he was only thirty-five years old. Roscoe Robinson replaced Brownlee as lead singer, and the group also included Willmer "Little Ax" Broadnax, Rev. Sammy Lewis, Rev. George Warren, and Tiny Powell. The group toured through the 1990s.

Charles Reagan Wilson
University of Mississippi

The Best of the Five Blind Boys (CD 2006); Anthony Heilbut, The Gospel Sound: Good News and Bad Times (2002).

Flag, State

Mississippi has had two state flags, and both have been closely associated with the state's Confederate history. Mississippi and most other states did not adopt official flags until the Civil War. When Mississippi seceded on 9 January 1861 and thus became a de facto independent entity, the need for a state flag became obvious. Accordingly, on 26 January the state secession convention approved a committee report recommending a state flag "of white ground, a Magnolia tree in the centre, a blue field in the upper left hand corner with a white star in the centre, the Flag to be finished with a red border and a red fringe at the extremity of the Flag." The blue field with the white star was the Bonnie Blue Flag made famous by Harry McCarthy's 1861 song by that title. Mississippi was one of five southern states to incorporate the single-star motif into its new flag.

Apparently not widely used, the Magnolia Flag served as the official state flag for the remainder of the Confederacy. In August 1865 a constitutional convention renounced secession and repealed many of the laws passed by the convention, including the law adopting the Magnolia Flag. For the next three decades, Mississippi had no flag.

In January 1894 Gov. John Marshall Stone asked the legislature to correct this oversight, and on 6 February legislators passed a measure declaring that the state's new banner would have "width two-thirds of its length, with the union, square in width, two-thirds of the width of the flag; the ground of the union to be red and a broad blue saltier thereon bordered with white and emblazoned with thirteen (13) mullets or five-pointed stars, corresponding to the number of the original States of the Union; the field to be divided into three bars of equal width, the upper one blue, the center white, the lower one red." This turgid language masked the

Presentation of Mississippi state flag, 7 July 1925 (Library of Congress, Washington, D.C. [LC-F81-36522 [P&P]])

fact that the new flag's field resembled the Confederate Stars and Bars and that its union or canton was the blue cross on a red field of the Confederate battle flag. This resemblance was of course no accident. The flag was likely designed by Sen. E. N. Scudder, a member of the Joint Legislative Committee for a State Flag. In 1924 his daughter told the Mississippi Division of the United Daughters of the Confederacy, "My father loved the memory of the valor and courage of those brave men who wore the grey [and] he wanted to perpetuate in a legal and lasting way that dear battle flag under which so many of our people had so gloriously fought." On 7 February 1894, Gov. Stone, a Confederate veteran, signed the flag bill.

Mississippi was the first state to incorporate the Confederate battle flag into its official symbolism, and no serious challenge to this iconography arose for nearly a century. In 1988, 1990, 1992, and 1993, Aaron Henry, an African American state legislator, introduced bills to change the state flag, but they never reached the floor. In April 1993 the Mississippi Conference of the National Association for the Advancement of Colored People filed suit in state chancery court contending that the state flag violated equal protection clauses in the state constitution, particularly a prohibition against "symbols or vestiges of slavery" on the state flag. The state allowed the Mississippi Division of the Sons of Confederate Veterans to intervene as a defendant in the case, and in May 2000 the Mississippi Supreme Court ruled that the state flag did not demonstrably violate the plaintiffs' constitutional rights to free speech and expression, due process, and equal protection as guaranteed by the state's constitution.

The court decision also dropped a political bombshell: Mississippi had not had an official state flag since 1906, when the flag law had inadvertently been omitted from the revised state code. Gov. Ronnie Musgrove, a Democrat, appointed a seventeen-member advisory commission chaired by former governor William Winter, a progressive Democrat and flag opponent. The commission held a series of five public hearings that brought out large and vocal audiences divided primarily along racial lines.

The commission unveiled a proposed new flag and announced that the state's voters would have the opportunity to decide between it and the 1894 flag. The new flag retained the 1894 flag's field but substituted for the blue diagonal cross a circle of twenty stars: thirteen on the outside, representing the original thirteen states, six representing the sovereign entities (including the Confederacy) that have ruled over Mississippi, and one on the inside of the circle, representing Mississippi itself. A vote for the new flag would also approve two pieces of legislation that were intended to assuage fears of a wholesale assault on Confederate heritage. One act would prohibit the removal of any monument or memorial on public property or the renaming of streets, bridges, parks, or structures named for historical figures. A second act would designate the 1894 flag a "historical flag"

that "shall be honored, protected and flown wherever historical flags are flown" and that could be displayed by historical or heritage groups, citizens, and businesses. The proposals asked supporters of the 1894 flag to surrender only the blue cross in the canton.

The flag vote became in effect a referendum on the larger issue of Mississippi's image. As in the other southern states facing flag issues, Mississippi's business leaders and major media urged adoption of the new flag not only as a gesture of respect toward the state's black minority but also as a way of "improving the negative image the state has outside our boundaries." Predictably, national and international media dredged up Mississippi's past racial troubles and the statistics on education that demonstrated the state's stereotypical backwardness. Just as predictably, many white citizens resented implications that the state was backward and resisted demands that they perceived as renunciations of the state's Confederate heritage.

On 17 April 2001 Mississippians voted by a two-to-one margin for the old flag over the proposed new one. Voters split primarily but not exclusively along racial lines. African American leaders were mortified to find that some majority-black counties supported the old flag and complained that black voters simply did not appreciate the importance of the flag change. In the aftermath of the referendum, flag opponents threatened boycotts and vowed to simply stop displaying the state flag. Flag supporters vowed to consolidate their victory by using the state's "indirect initiative" law to force a vote to have the 1894 flag incorporated into the state constitution.

The issue of the Confederate emblem on the Mississippi flag returned to prominence in June 2015 in the wake of shootings in Charleston, South Carolina, perpetrated by a gunman who used the Confederate battle flag as a symbol of white supremacy. Yazoo City, Alcorn State University, Jackson State University, Mississippi Valley State University, and the University of Mississippi announced that they would no longer fly the state flag as long as it contains the Confederate emblem. In addition, prominent Mississippians in literature, music, sports, and government publicly called for the emblem's removal from the state flag.

On 18 February 2016 more than two hundred people gathered at the Capitol in Jackson to support changing the flag. On 23 February twelve different bills to change, remove, or redesign the state flag died in committee.

John M. Coski
Museum of the Confederacy

David G. Sansing
University of Mississippi

Donesha Aldridge, wjtv.com (2 September 2015); John M. Coski, *The Confederate Battle Flag: America's Most Embattled Emblem* (2005); Sally Leigh McWhite, "Echoes of the Lost Cause: Confederate Reverberations in Mississippi from 1865 to 2001," University of Mississippi, PhD Dissertation, 2002; Jerry Mitchell, *Jackson Clarion-Ledger* (17 August 2015); John Shelton Reed, *Southern Cultures* (Spring 2002); David G. Sansing, Mississippi History Now website, http://mshistory.k12.ms.us.

Yazoo and Mississippi Valley Railroad Station, Egremont, 2 April 1927 (Archives and Records Services Division, Mississippi Department of Archives and History [000078054])

Flood, 1927 Mississippi River

The great Mississippi River Flood of 1927, known as the nation's most destructive, actually began in the summer of 1926, when heavy rains pummeled the Mississippi River's central basin. By September, the river's swollen tributaries were flowing at an alarming rate through Kansas and Iowa. On the morning of 1 January 1927 the residents of Nashville, Tennessee, awoke to find that the raging waters of the Cumberland River had risen above the city's fifty-six-foot levees. In the spring of that year melting snows up north joined with heavy rains to spell disaster. On the morning of Good Friday, 15 April 1927, the *Memphis Commercial Appeal* warned readers, "The roaring Mississippi River, bank and levee full from St. Louis to New Orleans, is believed to be on its mightiest rampage. . . . All along the Mississippi considerable fear is felt over the prospects for the greatest flood in history."

The US Army Corps of Engineers assured the concerned public that the levee system built to confine the Mississippi River would hold, but the river was so powerful that it broke through. At greatest risk were the agricultural lands of the Mississippi Delta below Memphis. On 22 April 1927, when the levees broke just upriver from Greenville, a huge crevasse one hundred feet deep and half a mile wide opened up. By May, the rampage of the Big Muddy created a watery basin sixty miles wide below Memphis before rejoining the Mississippi, cascading over the Louisiana lowlands, and then rushing on to the Gulf of Mexico. Although the flooding directly affected seven states, Mississippi, Louisiana, and Arkansas suffered the greatest destruction.

When the waters began to recede by the 1 July, the river was still seventy miles wide in some areas, and at least 1.5 million acres still remained under water. By August 1927 more than a thousand people had died as a direct consequence of the flood, nearly seven hundred thousand others had been displaced, and at least twenty-seven thousand square miles of land lay submerged under water up to thirty feet deep. The torrential rains had fallen at a rate more than ten times the yearly average, and property damage was estimated at one billion dollars.

Throughout the Mississippi Delta the flooding had an especially devastating impact on African Americans, tens

Birdsong Camp, Cleveland, 29 April 1927 (Archives and Records Services Division, Mississippi Department of Archives and History [000097135])

of thousands of whom lived as impoverished cotton tenants, sharecroppers, and plantation wage hands in the lowlands. Most of the flood's black victims, perhaps as many as 330,000, became refugees, crammed into "relief" camps set up by the Red Cross; the men and women in these 154 camps were impressed into service, stacking sandbags atop the remaining levees. The bluff city of Vicksburg was engulfed as thousands of flood victims sought shelter from the raging waters.

Flood control in Mississippi prior to the 1927 disaster was largely the responsibility of town, county, and district levee boards. Congress subsequently passed the Flood Control Act of 1928, transforming the entire Mississippi River Valley within a generation. The Army Corps of Engineers constructed the world's longest system of levees, this time incorporating floodways, locks, dams, and runoff channels. Vicksburg became the new home of the Mississippi River Commission in 1930, and the US Waterways Experiment Station was established there to study problems associated with controlling the flow of the Mississippi River.

The 1927 flood had national political effects. Secretary of Commerce Herbert Hoover, who directed the Red Cross's efforts to provide massive flood relief, won national attention for his humanitarianism. The subsequent publicity he received was a large factor in his successful 1929 bid for the presidency. The end of the flood also signaled a political upheaval in Louisiana and may have opened the door for populist leaders such as Huey Long. Finally, the flood became a major factor prompting the migration of African Americans from the South to cities in the North and West.

Joyce L. Broussard
California State University at
Northridge

John M. Barry, *Rising Tide: The Great Mississippi Flood of 1927 and How It Changed America* (1997); Pete Daniel, *Deep'n as It Come: The 1927 Mississippi River Flood* (1996); Federal Writers' Project of the Works Progress Administration, *Mississippi: The WPA Guide to the Magnolia State* (1938).

Flush Times Myth

The Flush Times myth is only partly mythological. The term refers to a period of rapid development and speculation on the antebellum southwestern frontier, which was composed primarily of the newly recognized states of Alabama and Mississippi as well as parts of western Tennessee, Arkansas, and Louisiana. A number of factors contributed to the area's economic boom, which spanned the 1820s and stretched beyond the economic depression of the late 1830s. Most notable among them was the incipient sense of Manifest Destiny, which entitled the United States to the continent and authorized the forcible removal of native peoples from the path of progress. The South's seemingly endless supply of land and natural resources attracted not only settlers but also speculators, and the liminal nature of the borderland itself suspended the more codified regulations that governed land acquisition and the practice of law in the East. Immigrants to the South reported two main goals—profit and adventure—and exemplified a kind of restless spirit that foreign observers to the young nation would increasingly link with the character of its people.

The phrase *Flush Times* was likely coined by Joseph Glover Baldwin, a lawyer who moved from Virginia to Mississippi in 1836 and later wrote about his experiences in *The Flush Times of Alabama and Mississippi* (1853), a curious collection of humorous sketches and serious autobiographies of legal figures. By the time Baldwin published his volume, the world he was re-creating had become more staid, but he

invokes a time of intensely competitive masculinity acted out not only in physical violence but in a sort of lawlessness that made every man a lawyer who dared to call himself one. In "The Bench and the Bar," Baldwin describes the southwestern frontier as "a legal Utopia" populated mainly by young men who "had come out on the vague errand of seeking their own fortune, or the more definite one of seeking somebody else's." The title character of another sketch, Ovid Bolus, exemplifies the sort of lawyer who survives in Baldwin's world: he "had long torn down the partition wall between his imagination and his memory."

Baldwin's frontier exemplifies the genre of southwestern humor, a writing style that flourished between the mid-1830s and the mid-1860s. Its lawlessness spills beyond Baldwin's makeshift courtrooms to summon a world of trickster figures and crude but darkly comic violence. One of the genre's most famous figures, Johnson Jones Hooper's Captain Simon Suggs, sums up his world with an aphorism: "It is good to be shifty in a new country." If the times were less flush for some settlers than others, stories about the antebellum southwestern frontier have nourished a steady mythology about a region that threatened to make its inhabitants both wealthy and wily.

Kathryn McKee
University of Mississippi

Hennig Cohen and William B. Dillingham, eds., *Humor of the Old Southwest* (1994); M. Thomas Inge and Edward J. Piacentino, eds., *The Humor of the Old South* (2001); James H. Justus, *Fetching the Old Southwest: Humorous Writing from Longstreet to Twain* (2004).

Folklife and Folklore Research

Mississippi's folk culture has attracted interest from scholars since the early twentieth century. The state has provided ample opportunities for those studying traditional music, material culture traditions, folk belief, and many other areas of folk culture. A long line of folklorists and other cultural researchers have come to the state to conduct research, while homegrown scholars have helped to expand knowledge of the state's folk culture.

Folklore research in Mississippi began in 1907 with Georgia native Howard Odum (who went on to become a prominent sociologist), a graduate student in classics at the University of Mississippi. Interested in studying the psychology of African Americans through an examination of their music, Odum utilized a relatively new piece of technology, the cylinder recorder. The young researcher traveled by horseback throughout Lafayette County, recording itinerant African American musicians in what is believed to have been one of the earliest field recording projects documenting African American traditional music. Odum's recordings did not survive, but he referenced the work in later writings, most notably *The Negro and His Songs* (1925). The song titles and lyrics that he included in this work demonstrate strong connections to the earliest commercially recorded blues songs.

Folklore research within Mississippi began in earnest during the early 1920s. Two native researchers, Arthur Palmer Hudson and Newbell Niles Puckett, were among the first to publish information on Mississippi folk culture. Hudson was born in Attala County in 1892 and grew up on a farm there. He attended the University of Mississippi and by 1920 was a member of the school's English faculty. While working on a master's degree at the University of Chicago, he took a course on folk song and became captivated by the music. He returned to Mississippi and began teaching a course on English and Scottish ballads. When a student told him about relatives who were still singing these songs, Hudson visited with the singers and soon realized the potential for collecting folk songs in Mississippi. Hudson's students helped him gather folk songs and ballad texts from singers living throughout the state, many of which he published in *Folksongs of Mississippi and Their Background* (1936). Hudson also gathered together a group of folklore enthusiasts in 1927 and established the Mississippi Folklore Society, which focused on supporting the collection and publication of the state's folklore. The society published Hudson's *Specimens of Mississippi Folklore* (1928) but became inactive when he left Oxford in 1930 to pursue doctoral work at the University of North Carolina.

Columbus native Newbell Niles Puckett was a contemporary of Hudson but focused on a different area of Mississippi culture. Born in 1897, Puckett earned a bachelor's degree at Mississippi College and a doctorate from Yale University. Puckett had been exposed to African American culture through his interactions with the workers at his father's brick factory, and at Yale he began researching African American folk beliefs. He conducted fieldwork during the early 1920s in and around Columbus as well as in other parts of the South, and his doctoral dissertation, *Folk Beliefs of the Southern Negro* (1926), received widespread acclaim in academic circles. Puckett's book presents examples of African American belief in the Black Belt region of Mississippi, Alabama, and Georgia, with detailed information on burial customs, voodoo, folk medicine cures, and omens. Puckett's fieldwork was also notable for his use of photography, a documentation tool not used by many folklore scholars of the time. His images of river baptisms, brush arbor revivals, and grave decorations thus provide a unique record of the era's practices.

The most prominent Mississippi-born folklorist of the early 1900s made his name as a folk song collector during the 1910s but did not conduct field research in the state until the early 1930s. John A. Lomax was born in Goodman in 1867 but grew up and spent most of his life in Texas. He first came to prominence in folk song circles with *Cowboy Songs and Other Frontier Ballads* (1910). Although he was well known for his song-collecting efforts, Lomax worked a variety of jobs to support his family. He conducted his first field research in Mississippi in 1933, recording traditional songs sung by prisoners at Parchman Penitentiary and Oakley Prison near Jackson. During his later recording expeditions through the South, Lomax regularly stopped at Parchman, conducting additional recording sessions there in 1936, 1939, and 1940 as part of his work for the Library of Congress. Lomax's recordings from Mississippi and the other southern states became an important part of the library's collection of folk music. Lomax also utilized these recordings as sources for his popular songbook collections, such as *Folk Song U.S.A.*

Other state and federal projects were also active in Mississippi during the 1930s. The Federal Writers' Project and the Federal Music Project (both part of the Depression-era Works Progress Administration) helped to launch various state-level folklore and folk music collection projects. The directors of the Mississippi office took this project seriously, and within months of beginning their work in 1936, the researchers had collected eighteen hundred folk songs from singers around the state. This office continued its work until 1941.

To more thoroughly document the singers whose songs were being collected by the state-level projects, the Works Progress Administration dispatched Herbert Halpert, a young folk song collector from New York, to the Southeast during the spring of 1939. Traveling in a converted ambulance outfitted with recording equipment, Halpert spent more than a month in Mississippi, filling 169 recording discs with ballads, children's songs, work songs, sacred music, and traditional fiddling. Halpert's discs were deposited in the Library of Congress but were not released to the public through commercial recordings until many years later.

By the early 1940s John Lomax's son, Alan, began visiting Mississippi to record musicians. The younger Lomax had begun working with his father as a teenager, accompanying him on his 1933 recording trip. Alan Lomax returned to Mississippi in the summer of 1941 as part of his work for the Library of Congress's Archive of American Folk Song. Working in partnership with the traditional music scholar John Work and sociologist Lewis Jones, faculty members from Fisk University in Nashville, Lomax made two trips to Coahoma County between 1941 and 1942, recording many different examples of African American sacred and secular music, among them the first recordings of legendary Mississippi blues musicians Muddy Waters (McKinley Morganfield) and David "Honeyboy" Edwards.

Alan Lomax went on to become one of the most prolific American researchers documenting traditional music.

During his sixty-year career, he traveled all over the world to record the music of traditional cultures. Mississippi remained important in Lomax's work. He returned several times, documenting important traditional musicians and releasing recordings that brought them wider attention. Lomax made his final trip to Mississippi in 1978, documenting a group of blues musicians (including Jack Owens and Sam Chatmon) for his film, *The Land Where the Blues Began*. In 1993 Lomax published a book by the same title, a memoir of his work with blues musicians.

The early 1960s brought a new generation of researchers interested in Mississippi's blues performers from the 1920s and 1930s. Several young enthusiasts, among them photographer Dick Waterman, came to Mississippi to track down these musicians. Those found included Mississippi John Hurt, Skip James, and Son House, and the attention helped them to relaunch their performing careers.

This era also saw the beginning of Mississippian William Ferris's efforts to document the folk culture of his community. Born in 1942, Ferris grew up on a farm near Vicksburg and began recording church services and blues performers near his home while an undergraduate at Davidson College. He built on this work as a graduate student, traveling throughout the Mississippi Delta to interview and record blues musicians for his doctoral dissertation (later published as *Blues from the Delta* [1988]). Ferris went on to teach at Jackson State University and at Yale University and remained active as a field researcher. He documented a wide range of Mississippi traditional artists, including blues musicians, storytellers, and embroidery artists, and featured their work in books, in films, and on record albums. These projects highlighted Mississippi artists' ties to tradition as well as their individual visions.

With the growth of interest in documenting and studying the state's folk culture, a group of academics and enthusiasts reactivated the Mississippi Folklore Society in December 1966. The group began holding an annual meeting at which members presented research on Mississippi folk culture and began publishing the *Mississippi Folklore Register* (later *Mississippi Folklife*), offering researchers a venue for articles on such topics as the origins of place-names and local dialect, the songs of railroad track workers, Sacred Harp singings, and many others. The group remained active until the early 1990s, while the journal was published until 2000.

By the 1970s, folklore research began to receive support from state and local institutions in Mississippi. The Craftsmen's Guild of Mississippi was formed in 1973, while Mississippi was featured at the 1974 Smithsonian Festival of American Folklife in Washington, D.C. The Smithsonian project brought a number of researchers from outside Mississippi into the state, including folklorist Worth Long and documentary photographer Roland Freeman, who traveled throughout the state in 1974, documenting musicians and craftspeople. The duo returned to Mississippi the following year to conduct an in-depth survey of African American folk culture in the southwestern corner of the state. Their findings were featured in a 1977 exhibition at the State Historical Museum.

The 1977 creation of the University of Mississippi's Center for the Study of Southern Culture helped to bring the study of folk culture into new prominence within the state's university system. Ferris's appointment as the center's first director and his nearly twenty years leading the organization helped to ensure folklore's place as a core subject of the center's ongoing classes and projects.

Folklore penetrated another area of state government with the 1982 creation of the position of folk arts director at the Mississippi Arts Commission. The director was tasked with documenting traditional artists and recruiting them for the agency's grants and other services. The folklorists who worked for the agency during the 1980s included Tom Rankin, who went on to do extensive documentation of African American religious life in the Delta (published in his book *Sacred Space* [1993]) while teaching at Delta State University and the University of Mississippi.

The growing support for folk culture research also inspired more local documentation projects. Mississippi Cultural Crossroads, a community arts organization in Port Gibson, began working with local high school students in the early 1980s, teaching them photography and interviewing skills. The students then used those skills to document local history and community folk traditions, with their material presented in a journal (*I Ain't Lyin'*), a series of original plays, and other programming.

As folk culture research begins its second century in Mississippi, some previously gathered materials are finding new use as part of a statewide tourism effort. The Mississippi Blues Commission began work on a statewide Mississippi Blues Trail in 2006, placing historical markers to commemorate notable blues musicians and venues. Within a decade, the number of markers had topped 150, and the popularity of this project and growing interest in promoting the state's unique culture demonstrate that those documenting Mississippi's folk culture will continue to find outlets for their work.

Larry Morrisey
Mississippi Arts Commission

William R. Ferris, *Local Color: A Sense of Place in Folk Art* (1982); Roland L. Freeman, *A Communion of Spirits: African-American Quilters, Preservers, and Their Stories* (1996); Bonnie J. Krause, *Mississippi Folklife* (Fall 1999); Mississippi Blues Trail website, msbluestrail.org; Mississippi Department of Archives and History, *Made by Hand: Mississippi Folk Art* (1980); *Mississippi Folklife* website, www.mississippifolklife.org; John W. Work, Lewis Wade Jones, and Samuel Adams, *Lost Delta Found: Rediscovering the Fisk University–Library of Congress Coahoma County Folklore Study*, ed. Robert Gordon and Bruce Nemerov (2005).

Folsom, David

(1791–1847) Choctaw Leader

David Folsom was born in the village of Bok Tuklo in Mississippi Territory on 25 January 1791. His father was Nathaniel Folsom, a descendant of Scot-Irish traders who traveled to Choctaw territory during the 1770s and took two wives, both nieces of Choctaw chief Miko Pushkush. David's mother was Aiahnichih Ohoyoh. One of twenty-four children, David became a principal instrument of change within the Choctaw Nation during the first half of the nineteenth century.

At age seven, Folsom left his parents' home to live with his sister, Molly, and her husband, Samuel Mitchell, a US Indian Agent, who taught David to speak English. Molly died three years later, and David returned home to work at his father's tavern and trading post at Pigeon Roost on the Natchez Trace. At age sixteen, after earning enough money to buy a horse and new clothes, he traveled 250 miles to attend school on the Elk River in Tennessee, staying there for six months. Upon his return, he received another month of education from James Allen, a friend of the Folsoms.

Between 1812 and 1814 the United States fought Shawnee Chief Tecumseh's pan-Indian alliance, the Creek, and the British. For three years, Folsom served under Andrew Jackson and renowned Choctaw chief Pushmataha. Folsom also aided Jackson in the capture of Pensacola and rose to the rank of colonel before leaving military service. After the war, Folsom married Rhoda Nail, the daughter of American Revolutionary War figure Henry Nail and his Choctaw wife. Folsom's marriage was the first Choctaw union performed by law rather than tribal custom.

In 1819 Folsom wrote to the American Board of Commissioners for Foreign Missions and requested that it start schools to convert and educate Choctaw children. Supported by Folsom's private funds, missionaries built two schools, Elliot and Mayhew. Folsom argued that the Choctaw could survive settler encroachment and federal corruption only by embracing Christianity, reading, and writing. His home at Pigeon Roost, located between the two schools, allowed him to monitor and manage the institutions, missionary curricula, and goods shipped to them. During the mid-1820s he established a 150-acre estate, including a house, a barn, and stables, at Yoknokchaya on Robinson Road. Folsom also owned a tavern and trading post, cattle and horses, and ten slaves.

In 1824 Folsom traveled to Washington, D.C., as part of the Choctaw delegation that would negotiate with the Pres. James Monroe. Folsom and his close friend, James McDonald, a Choctaw lawyer, argued for Choctaw rights and fair treatment while refusing to sell land at low prices. The delegation signed the 1825 Treaty of Washington, which stipulated that the United States would protect schools, relinquish debts, and permit the Choctaw to stay in Mississippi Territory.

Folsom vehemently opposed Removal, a view that earned him the position of chief of the Northeast District of the Choctaw Nation in 1826. He thus deposed full-blood chief Mushulatubbee, who had opposed missionary schools and condoned Removal. With fellow chiefs Greenwood Leflore and John Garland, both of whom had white fathers and Choctaw mothers, Folsom established the first police force, the light horsemen, and the first constitutional government in the Choctaw Nation.

In 1830 Garland and Folsom gave their power as chiefs to Leflore. Although Leflore had claimed to oppose Removal, in September of that year he orchestrated the Treaty of Dancing Rabbit Creek, which provided that the Choctaw would move to the west of the Mississippi River. Fearing Leflore's new power, deteriorating relations with the federal government, and threats from Pres. Andrew Jackson and his treaty commissioners, Folsom signed the treaty. He was scorned for his signing but aided in the Removal efforts to Oklahoma Territory.

Rhoda Folsom died in 1837, and four years later Folsom married Jane Ball. He fathered a total of thirteen children and died on 24 September 1847 in Doaksville, Oklahoma.

Cole Cheek
Spartanburg Methodist College

Taylor Carson, *Searching for the Bright Path: The Mississippi Choctaws from Prehistory to Removal* (1999); Czarina C. Conlan, *Chronicles of Oklahoma* (December 1926); James H. B. Cushman, *History of the Choctaw, Chickasaw, and Natchez Indians* (1899); Angie Debo, *The Rise and Fall of the Choctaw Republic* (1934); Clara Sue Kidwell, *Choctaws and Missionaries in Mississippi, 1818–1918* (1995); Theda Perdue, *"Mixed Blood" Indians: Racial Construction in the Early South* (2003).

Foodways

Long before the arrival of Europeans, the Chickasaw and Choctaw and other native tribes living in present-day Mississippi cultivated corn, pounding and soaking the grain for use in porridge-like dishes and breads. Primary among the Choctaw was *tanfula*, made by boiling corn kernels with wood ash lye.

Historian Daniel Usner has cataloged the centrality of corn in eighteenth-century Choctaw foodways. For an elemental bread, Choctaw stirred boiling water into dried and ground corn, added chestnut or hickory oil, fashioned a firm dough, tucked rolls made from that dough into corn shucks, and baked the rolls in hot ashes. For *buhana*, a mix of ground corn, beans, and hickory meats, cooks again employed shucks, but they boiled the bundles in the manner of tamales.

Beans and squash were staples as well. Native Americans foraged for hickory nuts and pecan nuts and for wild persimmons and other native fruits, which they ate out of hand. In the ashes of a dwindling fire, they roasted sweet potatoes, an indigenous crop like corn, beans, and squash. Choctaw ground the leaves of sassafras trees into a powder, now commonly known as filé, later selling it at city markets in Biloxi and other trading centers. Along the coast Native Americans fished the salt waters for pompano and shrimp; from the mudflats they harvested oysters. Deer, bear, and smaller game such as squirrels and rabbits were the primary meats. A typical meal was a hunter's stew cooked over an open flame or a roast cooked in the embers from a fire.

Native to Europe, pigs were introduced early to present-day Mississippi. During his exploratory expedition of 1541, Spaniard Hernando de Soto traversed the state and crossed the Mississippi River with pigs, intended as on-the-hoof provisions for troops. Feral pigs were soon rooting the Mississippi soil. Early settlers adopted the animals as livestock, preferring swine to cows because of their efficiency in converting feed to flesh.

European settlers arrived with a taste for rye and wheat but soon adopted corn, which was far easier to cultivate, harvest, and transform into meal for bread. From native peoples, settlers learned to eat green corn as a vegetable; to dry it in the manner of a grain and boil it until tender; and to grind it into flour for dumplings and breads. Though numerous other foodstuffs, among them peppers, peanuts, and black-eyed peas, were introduced in ensuing years, corn and pork, the bedrock components of what would become the modern Mississippi diet, were in place at an early date.

Many of the dishes and drinks considered distinct to Mississippi—everything from souse meat to desserts such as pecan pie—owe their origins to European recipes and techniques. But the introduction of enslaved Africans thoroughly transformed the diet. African Americans reinterpreted European cookery and Native American ingredients. Some of the foodstuffs we now recognize as elemental to the southern diet owe their presence to the slave trade. Watermelons arrived by way of Africa. Okra, too, is an African plant. But African techniques practiced by cooks of African ancestry had the most cultural and culinary impact.

African American cooks have dominated Mississippi's kitchens. Outdoor cooking, especially for barbecues and fish fries, was often the work of black men. Black women often cooked in white households and white-owned restaurants. Such relationships, historian Karen Hess has observed, had their roots "in the antebellum South when any house of pretension had skilled slaves in the kitchen. . . . The white mistress may have taken an interest in the kitchen . . . but she never actually toiled in the kitchen. The excruciating labor and the 'stirring of the pots' were done by black women cooks."

Following the Civil War, modern Mississippi foodways emerged as blacks and whites and the rich and the poor adopted similar diets and similar habits of consumption. Reliance on a cotton monoculture discouraged row crop farming of vegetables. Poverty and malnutrition took their toll in the guise of pellagra, a nutritional deficiency linked to workers' diet of meat, meal, and molasses.

In the first half of the twentieth century, as roads and rails reached more of the population, Mississippi distinguished itself as a locus for truck farming. Both black and white sharecroppers tended truck patch gardens on land that was not dedicated to cotton and other high-yield cash crops. Vardaman, in Calhoun County, emerged as a center of sweet potato production. Crystal Springs, in Copiah County, earned such a reputation for growing and shipping vegetables that the town became known as the Tomatopolis of the World.

Along the Gulf Coast and especially in the Mississippi Delta, newly arrived immigrants complicated Mississippi foodways. Although the influence of West Africans and Scots-Irish remained predominant, Croatian and Serbian immigrants made the Gulf Coast their home and soon came to dominate the seafood industry. In the Delta, Chinese immigrants initially arrived to build railroads but remained and opened groceries and restaurants in the late nineteenth century. Greeks settled across the state, most notably in Jackson, where restaurants such as the Rotisserie, the Black Cat, and the Mayflower honed a creolized Greek style that relied on fresh seafood trucked up from the Gulf and local vegetables flavored with preserved pork.

Those multiethnic influences remain, especially in the Delta. Chinese grocery stores still dot Greenville and other towns. Sicilian Creole restaurants such as Lusco's and Giardina's, both established in the 1930s, remain Greenwood stalwarts. Across the Delta, hot tamale vendors, a likely legacy of the early twentieth-century arrival of Mexican cotton pickers, sell what many now recognize as a traditional snack food. And the Chamoun and Abraham families of Clarksdale and other Lebanese restaurateurs serve kibbe and fried chicken, baklava and barbecue.

For much of its modern history Mississippi has struggled with poverty and with feeding its people, bestowing great symbolic importance on food and thus leading it to figure large in Mississippi music and letters. If blues music reflects African cultural mores, it also reflects African American foodways. In 1968 bluesman Little Milton, a native of Inverness, tapped the zeitgeist when he sang, "If grits ain't groceries / Eggs ain't poultry / And Mona Lisa was a man." Catfish, another definitively southern foodstuff and more recently associated with Mississippi, where the great majority of pond catfish is now raised, serves as the focal point in what music scholar Scott Barretta believes may be "the most widely shared Delta blues standard of the folk repertoire." Recorded by Mississippi artists ranging from Robert Petway to Elmore James, "Catfish Blues," like many a blues song, mixes food imagery and sexual imagery: "Well, I wish I was a catfish, swimming in the deep, blue sea / I would have all you good looking women, fishing after me." Muddy Waters employed the lyrics and tempo of "Catfish Blues" in "Rollin' Stone."

The state's writers often made food central to their works. Richard Wright first titled his biography *American Hunger*, and Eudora Welty employed food imagery to great effect in her novels. As a chronicler of domestic life, she gave voice to everyday folks such as bakers and cooks. In addition to her fiction, Welty wrote at least three cookbook introductions for local nonprofit organizations, including *The Country Gourmet: Recipes Compiled by the Mississippi Animal Rescue League*. In an introduction to *The Jackson Cookbook*, Welty wrote about her hometown, but the sentiments could apply to any place at any time. She employed food to examine the importance of oral traditions handed down from one generation of women to the next: "I daresay any fine recipe used in Jackson could be attributed to a local lady, or her mother—Mrs. Cabell's Pecans, Mrs. Wright's Cocoons, Mrs. Lyell's Lemon Dessert. Recipes, in the first place, had to be imparted—there was something oracular in the transaction—and however often they were made after that by others, they kept their right names. I make Mrs. Mosal's White Fruitcake every Christmas, having got it from my mother, who got it from Mrs. Mosal, and I often think to make a friend's recipe is to celebrate her once more, and in that cheeriest, most aromatic of places to celebrate in, the home kitchen."

The movement of Mississippians from farms to cities and suburbs spurred an increased reliance on prepackaged foods and a spike in the number and quality of restaurants. During the middle years of the twentieth century, as roads improved and discretionary income increased, humble cafés and restaurants proliferated. Some, like the slugburger and doughburger cafés of Booneville and Corinth—serving economical hamburgers made with meat extended by soy and wheat products—were local phenomena. (Weidmann's, in Meridian, was a grand exception on the other end of the socioeconomic spectrum.) But others came to define statewide genres.

Revolving-table restaurants emerged as definitive category. In 1915 the proprietors of the Mendenhall Hotel in Mendenhall installed a trio of Lazy Susan–style tables in their dining room, a solution to the effrontery of the "boardinghouse reach." Other restaurants soon followed suit, including Walnut Hills in Vicksburg and the Dinner Bell in McComb. The bottom tier of the Lazy Susan remained stationary, while the buffet of meats and vegetables spun by on the top tier like a carousel of calories.

Country stores also emerged as a specific sort of Mississippi restaurant. Taylor Grocery, in the village of Taylor, eight miles south of Oxford, is typical of a style popular in northern Mississippi, where grocery cafés like Stareka's in Greenville are popular and every other convenience store seems to stock a steam table with fried meats and long-simmered vegetables. The Taylor store began life in the early 1900s as a true grocery, selling cornmeal and cured meats and such. A shopper could pick up a little something to eat, such as a fried apple pie or in later years a plate of fried catfish. By the 1970s, as residents of Taylor grew accustomed to shopping in Oxford and elsewhere, the sale of dry goods declined and the sale of catfish improved. Oxford college students and others began making the trek to eat fried catfish in a onetime country store where the shelves were still stocked with jars of mayonnaise and cans of tomatoes. As Oxford gentrified, Taylor Grocery emerged as a rough-and-tumble redoubt, with a wide front porch, a screen door, and rustic interior.

African American restaurateurs long had only restricted opportunities. Capital was hard to come by, and Jim Crow laws limited the appeal of black restaurants. But they nevertheless proliferated in Mississippi. The Big Apple Inn on Farish Street in Jackson dates to the 1930s, when Juan Mora began selling hot tamales from a cart. By 1939 he had moved into a permanent location, and he soon added pig ear sandwiches to the mix. Today, his great-grandson, Gene Lee, works the griddle, selling sandwiches and tamales.

Downstate, in Foxworth, near Hattiesburg, Leatha Jackson opened Leatha's Bar-B-Que Inn in 1976. Born in 1923, Jackson was one of fourteen children. She picked cotton for twenty years beginning at the age of five and did not learn how to read until she reached seventy. She worked in restaurants for nearly three decades before opening her own establishment, and despite the odds, it became a postintegration success. White and black customers alike clamored for her pork and beef cooked on monstrous cylindrical smokers set alongside the railroad tracks near the family compound. In 2000 Jackson relocated the restaurant to Hattiesburg, where she remained at the helm until she suffered a stroke in 2009. Her daughter, Bonnie Jackson, then took over until her death in September 2015.

One of the central struggles of the civil rights movement was the integration of lunch counters, diners, cafés, and restaurants. The reasons were practical. It was absurd that a black man or woman, shopping in a department store equipped with a lunch counter, could not take a break from that shopping, take a seat on a stool, and eat. Yet that was the norm until Pres. Lyndon Johnson signed the Civil Rights Act of 1964, outlawing segregation in places of public accommodation.

White Mississippians reacted swiftly and angrily. Gov. Paul B. Johnson, for example, called the measure "vicious" and vowed to resist integration. However, the law of the land gradually won acceptance in most—but not all—of the state's establishments. Jackson's Belmont restaurant; Dinty Moore's Shaw café, the Shady Nook; and others converted to "private clubs," where admittance was available to those who paid a nominal fee—and had white skin. The Subway in the basement of Jackson's Robert E. Lee Hotel and other restaurants closed rather than admit African Americans. As late as the early 1980s Mississippi still had between ten and twenty restaurants that refused to serve African Americans: Moore died in 1984 having never served a black man or woman.

In 1908, ten years before the rest of the United States, Mississippi banned the sale of alcoholic beverages. Prohibition also persisted in the Magnolia State long after the rest of the country abandoned the idea: beer with an alcohol content of 3.2 percent of less was allowed in 1945, but other alcoholic beverages effectively remained illegal until 1966. Nevertheless, the *Jackson Clarion-Ledger* estimated in 1950 that Mississippi had more retail liquor dealers than any of the legally wet states in the region. Founded in 1966, Greenville's Jigger and Jug was the first legal liquor store to open in the state in more than fifty years.

Soft drinks have long mattered in Mississippi, too. Coca-Cola was first bottled in Vicksburg in 1894 by Joseph A. Biedenharn. Four years later chemist Edward C. Barq Sr. began bottling and selling soft drinks in Biloxi. Barq's Biloxi Pop came in a variety of flavors including strawberry and peach, but root beer emerged as the most popular. As soft drinks evolved from local and regional products to national brands, Barq's remained competitive, especially on the Gulf Coast, until 1995, when the Coca-Cola Company bought Barq's and transformed the brand into the most popular root beer product in the nation.

In the last third of the twentieth century regional foods, including southern cuisine, gained national attention. Some Mississippi cookbooks touted "new southern cooking," while others highlighted traditional ways and localized food traditions. Community cookbooks such as *Bayou Cuisine*, first published in 1970 by St. Stephen's Episcopal Church of Indianola, celebrated the Delta's middle-class culinary traditions. Kathy Starr's 1992 volume, *The Soul of Southern Cooking*, featured stories and recipes that pay homage to the African American cooks of Hollandale and other small Delta towns, including instructions for "How to Kill a Hog at Home" and recipes for gar stew and fried buffalo fish ribs.

Delta native Craig Claiborne became the food editor of the *New York Times* in 1957 and used the post to introduce America to a multitude of new foods and new perspectives on the dinner table. In addition to editing the food section of the *Times* and writing features, Claiborne reviewed restaurants and published more than twenty cookbooks, including *Southern Cooking* (1987), and an autobiography, *A Feast Made for Laughter* (1982), both of which pay tribute to the cuisine of his youth.

In the 1960s and 1970s, Mississippi became the leader in commercial catfish farming, and in the late 1980s the Catfish Institute, a Belzoni-based aquaculture industry group, started selling Americans on the mild fish that had long been a staple of Mississippi cuisine. By 1998 catfish had become the fourth-most-popular fish in the United States, though by 2014 it had dropped to eighth.

In the early 1980s Greenwood's Fred Carl conceived the idea of manufacturing commercial-style appliances for the home market. He incorporated Viking Range in 1984 and five years later opened a facility in his hometown to build stainless-steel home ranges with the power of commercial stoves. By the early 1990s Viking ranges were recognized as an industry standard, thanks to the quality of the product and a keen public relations campaign. Carl expanded the company's reach, developing a Viking Life division that focused on cooking schools, travel programs, and a complex of culinary-related businesses centered on the Alluvian, a boutique hotel in Greenwood.

By the 1990s the state's major cities—most notably Oxford, Hattiesburg, and Jackson—featured restaurants that offered updated takes on traditional recipes, such as fried green tomatoes topped with crab or shrimp and grits capped with bacon and mushrooms. John Currence opened Oxford's City Grocery in 1992. A restaurant veteran, Currence interpreted traditional southern ingredients in nontraditional ways: for example, a fried oyster appetizer was inspired by a chicken-on-a-stick dish served to late-night revelers by a local gas station.

In 1999, in part as a consequence of these developments, the Southern Foodways Alliance, an institute of the Center for the Study of Southern Culture at the University of Mississippi, launched an ongoing campaign to document and celebrate southern foodways by staging symposia, collecting oral histories, and making documentary films. The projects include an oral-history-driven culinary tourism effort focusing on the Mississippi Delta's hot tamale makers.

John T. Edge
University of Mississippi

Craig Claiborne, *A Feast Made for Laughter* (1982); Yolanda Cruz, *Hattiesburg American* (23 September 2015); John T. Edge, Southern Foodways Alliance website (1 July 2014), www.southernfoodways.org; John Egerton, *Southern Food: At Home, on the Road, and in History* (1987); *Hattiesburg American* (17 September 2013); *Mississippi Folklife* (Winter 1997); National Fisheries Institute website, www.aboutseafood.com; *New York Times* (1 June 1981); Ted Ownby, *American Dreams in Mississippi* (1999); Susan Puckett, *A Cook's Tour of Mississippi* (1980); Katherine Rawson, *"Eating Pie": Digesting Food Production and Consumption in Faulkner* (2007); Richard Schweid, *Catfish and the Delta* (1992); Kathy Starr, *The Soul of Southern Cooking* (1989); Joe Gray Taylor, *Eating, Drinking, and Visiting in the South: An Informal History* (1982); Daniel Usner, *Southern Exposure* (November–December 1983).

Football

Football is a civil religion in Mississippi. Evidence of the Magnolia State's fascination with the sport is abundant, from the popularity of Friday night high school games through the number of professional players born and reared in Mississippi. *Jackson Clarion-Ledger* columnist Rick Cleveland argues that "Mississippi's signature sports event is small-town high school football" because "nothing, nowhere, matches it for passion and competition." Indeed, the high school accomplishments of Philadelphia native Marcus Dupree, for one, made him a statewide celebrity before he attended his senior prom. Mississippi high schools have also produced numerous players who achieved fame in the professional ranks, including Walter Payton, Jerry Rice, Archie Manning, Brett Favre, Lance Alworth, Deuce McAllister, Steve McNair, Jake Gibbs, Eric Moulds, and Charlie Conerly. A 1986 study published in *American Demographics* concluded that Mississippi produced more professional football players per capita than any other state in the nation despite the fact that the state possesses few urban areas and has no professional teams to enhance the sport's popularity. Not surprisingly, a June 2004 *Sports Illustrated* poll revealed that eight of Mississippi's ten greatest sports figures played high school football in their home state. Although the high school game unites communities and produces heroes, it pales in comparison to the devotion and fanatical followings that Mississippi colleges claim.

The college game is the largest denomination in Mississippi's secular gridiron worship. The two largest schools in the state, Mississippi State and the University of Mississippi, possess one of the most intense rivalries in college sports. The contempt of the institutions' fans for each other peaks during the Egg Bowl, the annual football contest between the teams. The victor receives yearlong possession of the Golden Egg trophy as a symbol of victory over its most hated foe. In 1926 a brawl broke out between the players and fans of each school after the University of Mississippi won a 7–6 contest that ended a string of thirteen straight losses to their adversaries. The next year, in hopes of deterring violence, student representatives from the two schools agreed to award the Golden Egg, a gold-plated football mounted on a wooden base, to the winner in a dignified postgame presentation. Ironically, however, the physical evidence of superiority over their archrivals only increased the yearly clash's importance to players, students, and supporters of both colleges.

The intensity of the rivalry has its origins in class differences. Mississippi State, previously known as Mississippi A&M, "the people's college," was established as an agricultural school in 1878. The college is located in Starkville, in the middle of Mississippi's eastern hill country, and initially attracted primarily economically and politically powerless citizens from throughout the state. In contrast, the University of Mississippi fashioned itself the school of the aristocrats and political leaders. Its curriculum centered on the liberal arts and teaching professional trades to its elite student body. The class-based antagonism students developed for each other carried over into and found a natural outlet in the violent game of football. The two schools played their first contest in the sport in 1901, making it the second-longest rivalry in the Southeastern Conference (SEC). After the 2015 season, the University of Mississippi held a commanding 63–43–6 edge.

Although the Egg Bowl is the Magnolia State's most intense contest, other aspects of college football make its prominent role in Mississippi culture undisputable. The state's historically black colleges also possess a proud pigskin heritage. Columbia native Walter Payton played at Jackson State from 1971 to 1974, was named to two all-American teams, and set a National Collegiate Athletic Association (NCAA) scoring record with 464 points before going on to play thirteen seasons with the Chicago Bears of the National Football League (NFL), retiring as the league's all-time leading rusher. Crawford wide receiver Jerry Rice set eighteen NCAA Division I receiving records while attending Mississippi Valley State University from 1981 to 1984 and holds nearly every major NFL receiving record. Mount Olive native Steve McNair, who played quarterback at Alcorn State University from 1990 to 1994, became the only player in college football history to record 16,000 yards of total offense. Mississippi Valley State and Alcorn State possess a heated rivalry of their own. On 4 November 1984 63,808 fans—the largest crowd to attend a game in the state at the time—watched the two undefeated teams face off in Jackson. Even Division III schools with ties to religious groups are not immune to the state's obsession. Student violence at a 1960 basketball game led to the termination of football contests between Baptist-supported Mississippi College and Methodist-affiliated Millsaps College for forty years. The football rivalry meant so much to players and fans at each school that they referred to it as the "Holy War."

Gridiron success has only fueled the state's passion for college football. The University of Mississippi has won six SEC championships and three national championships and was named the Team of the 1960s by several sports publications. The University of Southern Mississippi owns eight conference titles and claims two national championships. Jackson State (fourteen conference titles) and Alcorn State (nine) have dominated the Southwestern Athletic Conference. Mississippi Valley State University made headlines in the 1980s with Coach Archie Colley, quarterback Reggie Totten, and receiver Jerry Rice. Southern Miss alum Brett Favre had a long and impressive career as an NFL quarterback. Cleveland's Delta State University won a Division II national championship in 2000, and Mississippi College won national titles at the same level in 1989 and 1990. Although

Mississippi State has not won an SEC championship since its lone 1941 title, the program made news in 2004 by hiring the conference's first black head football coach, Sylvester Croom.

The variety of levels, intensity of intrastate contests, number of stars who represent the state professionally, and support that state football squads receive make the sport an indispensable part of Mississippi's culture.

J. Michael Butler

Flagler College

William G. Barner, *The Egg Bowl* (2007); William G. Barner, *Mississippi Mayhem* (1982); Mike Butler, *Journal of Mississippi History* (Summer 1997); John W. Cox and Gregg Bennett, *Rock Solid: Southern Miss Football* (2004); Jim Fraiser, *For Love of the Game: The Holy Wars of Millsaps College and Mississippi College Football* (2000).

Henry S. Foote, ca. 1844–60 (Photograph by Mathew B. Brady, Library of Congress, Washington, D.C. [LC-USZ62-110163])

Foote, Henry Stuart

(1804–1880) Nineteenth Governor, 1852–1854

Henry Stuart Foote was born in Fauquier County, Virginia, on 28 February 1804. He graduated from Washington College (now Washington and Lee University) in Lexington, Virginia, in 1819, studied law, and migrated to Mississippi in the 1826, settling in Vicksburg and becoming active in state politics. He was noted for regularly changing political affiliations, earning the moniker Colonel Weathercock. Like many political figures in his day, Foote affected a number of characteristics of the planter elite, including taking on the title *Colonel* and engaging in "affairs of honor," most notably in two shootouts with Sargent S. Prentiss.

Beginning in 1847, he represented Mississippi in the US Senate, serving until 1852, when he resigned to become governor. Foote was a staunch advocate of slavery, employing his oratorical skill to deliver several memorable addresses on the subject, including one in Congress in which he warned that abolitionists might meet the noose in Mississippi. His fire-eating oratory earned him yet another moniker, Hangman Foote, which he proudly kept.

Nevertheless, Foote did not truly fit the mold of the extreme secessionists. During the Crisis of 1850 Foote actively worked to find a solution and was instrumental in hammering out the details of what became the Compromise of 1850. As partisan lines in Mississippi collapsed and reformed into states' rights and Unionist camps, Foote fell firmly into the Unionist group. When Foote returned home, the states' rights Mississippi legislature censured his actions. Foote defended his position by running for governor against Jefferson Davis

in 1851, winning handily and considering his efforts vindicated. Within two years, support for Unionists had weakened considerably, and in January 1854 Foote resigned the governorship, departing for California.

Foote subsequently became involved in Know-Nothing circles, but his proslavery past prevented him from winning office in California. By the late 1850s he had settled in Nashville, Tennessee. He campaigned against secession, but after Tennessee left the Union, he was elected to the Confederate Congress. He used his position as a soapbox to criticize the Davis administration. In 1863 Foote fled to the North, attempting to negotiate a peace settlement, but he was unwelcome there and went into exile in England and later Canada.

After the Civil War Foote continued his attempts to match his earlier political successes. He worked with Horace Greeley and Carl Schurz to garner southern support for the Liberal Democrats in the 1872 presidential election, but the movement developed little momentum. In 1876 he endorsed the Republican ticket and was rewarded with the directorship of the New Orleans mint. He authored four books, *The Bench and the Bar of the South and South-West, Texas and the Texans, The Civil War*, and *Casket of Reminiscences*. Henry Foote died in Nashville on 20 May 1880.

David Libby

University of Texas at San Antonio

Biographical Directory of the United States Congress, 1774–1989 Bicentennial Edition (1989); Henry S. Foote, *Casket of Reminiscences* (1874); John E. Gonzales, "The Public Career of Henry Stuart Foote" (PhD dissertation, University of North Carolina, 1957).

Foote, Shelby

(1916–2005) Historian and Novelist

Novelist and author of the acclaimed three-volume *The Civil War: A Narrative*, Shelby Foote was born in Greenville, Mississippi, on 17 November 1916. Foote's paternal great-grandfather was a Confederate cavalry colonel who saw action at Shiloh and assembled a family fortune by acquiring plantations in Noxubee County and the Mississippi Delta. His grandfather, Hugh, built on this legacy, at one time owning five Delta plantations, but he gambled away his fortune after moving to Greenville in 1910. In July 1915 Hugh's son, Shelby Dade Foote, married Lillian Rosenstock, the daughter of a prominent Jewish planter who had arrived in the Delta in the late 1870s. Although her father had hoped that she would marry a Jewish suitor and was angered by her choice, he arranged for his son-in-law to obtain a job with Chicago-based Armour Meats. Shelby Foote Sr. worked assiduously, with promotions taking him to Jackson, Vicksburg, Pensacola, and Mobile. When the couple's only child, named Shelby after his father, was five, Shelby Sr. died of a bacterial infection. Suddenly widowed, Lillian accepted an offer from her sister and brother-in-law to live with them in Greenville. Her father was unable to help her financially, having lost his own fortune in cotton speculation, so Lillian was forced to work outside the home.

Greenville was unusual by Mississippi standards, with a diverse ethnic and religious population. Young Shelby attended local public schools, reputedly the best in the state, and was doted on by his mother. He struggled to fit in, refusing to accept prevailing standards in either behavior or dress. Some Greenville residents disapproved of his antics and found him enigmatic and headstrong. William Alexander Percy, scion of the Delta's most influential family, was not among them. Lillian was a secretary in a law office that adjoined Percy's, and he requested that the young Foote show some teenage Percy cousins around town when they came for a summertime visit in 1930.

Percy's request transformed Foote's life, bringing him into contact with Walker, LeRoy, and Phinizy Percy, whose father had recently committed suicide. When their mother died in an automobile accident in 1932, William Alexander Percy adopted his young cousins. Foote reveled in their friendship, finding in them the siblings he lacked, and he soon spent enormous time at the Percy home. As time elapsed he gravitated increasingly to Walker, and the two future novelists developed a lifelong friendship. An added boon was Foote's access to Will Percy, whose home was the artistic and cultural center of the Delta. The young Foote eagerly took advantage of the large family library, devouring the works of Shakespeare and other authors, including James Joyce, Thomas Mann, William Faulkner, and Marcel Proust. He later remarked on the

Shelby Foote (Bern and Franke Keating Collection, Department of Archives and Special Collections, J. D. Williams Library, University of Mississippi)

importance of Proust's *Remembrance of Things Past* in his formation as a writer.

Foote first tried writing in high school, where he served as editor of the school newspaper. The *Pica* was no ordinary school publication. It was a sophisticated endeavor that included poems, essays, stories, book reviews, and wide-ranging editorials. Following his 1935 graduation, Foote followed Walker and LeRoy Percy to the University of North Carolina but remained in Chapel Hill for just two years. Although he was awed by the immense campus library and wrote for the school's literary publication, he became increasingly apathetic and reclusive. He attended class sporadically and spent most of his time writing. When he departed in 1937, he undoubtedly intended to become a full-time writer.

For his first novel, Foote drew on the figure of his grandfather, Hugh, who became the protagonist of *Tournament*. Foote labored on the manuscript for months and sent it to Alfred A. Knopf's New York publishing house. The editors there liked it but cautioned that they did not think it would sell well. Disappointed, Foote stored the manuscript away. In 1940 Foote joined the Mississippi National Guard in an artillery unit, eventually serving on active duty with the US Army and receiving an officer's commission. Foote craved combat, as did many other southern males. Stationed in Northern Ireland in late 1943 and seemingly destined to participate in the invasion of Europe, a run-in with a superior officer resulted in his abrupt discharge. Stunned, Foote joined the Marine Corps but did not see combat before the Japanese surrendered in 1945.

Foote returned to work on *Tournament* and on some short stories, several of which were accepted for publication. Buoyed by this success, Foote began writing an account of the Battle of Shiloh as the first of what he projected would be three Civil War novels. The others would center on Brice's

Crossroads and Vicksburg. Random House rejected the Shiloh novel, though editors at the smaller Dial Press were interested but worried about its appeal. When they asked if he had any other works, Foote recounted the plot of *Tournament*, which he hurriedly polished and sent off. Dial accepted the book, and its 1949 publication marked a turning point in Foote's literary career. Four more novels followed over the next five years: *Follow Me Down* (1950), *Love in a Dry Season* (1951), *Shiloh* (1952), and *Jordan County* (1954). Four of the five centered on the Delta, with fictional Jordan County and its county seat, Bristol, closely resembling Washington County and Greenville. Reviewers noted his growing maturity as a writer, and Foote believed that his literary apprenticeship was over. He set his sights on writing an ambitious novel that he tentatively called *Two Gates to the City* and believed might vault him into the first ranks of American writers.

However, in 1954 Random House president Bennett Cerf suggested that Foote pen a one-volume history of the Civil War. The publishing firm envisioned a two-hundred-thousand-word book, and Foote eagerly assented, calculating that he could finish it in eighteen months. After completing an outline, Foote recognized that doing justice to his subject would require far more than the allotted word limit, and he suggested a three-volume work instead. Random House agreed, and Foote spent the next twenty years on the project. From the outset he took various strands and wove them into a narrative based on a particular campaign or battle. He deplored the analytical method employed by academic historians and scorned their inability to make the events and personalities of the war come alive. He unashamedly employed a novelist's techniques, maintaining that historians and novelists seek the same truth but that novelists can make the information breathe in a way that historians cannot. He eschewed footnotes and extensive bibliographies, considering them the province of pedantic historians.

The three parts of *The Civil War: A Narrative* appeared in 1958, 1963, and 1974, respectively. Many reviewers noted his dramatic flair, lively writing, and adroit balancing of the war's operational theaters. Yet academic historians took issue with Foote's approach and methodology. Several criticized his reliance on secondary sources. Frank Vandiver questioned Foote's omission of economic factors, while others noted his emphasis on military events and wondered why slavery and political events were shortchanged. And the absence of footnotes came in for particular—and predictable—criticism. C. Vann Woodward's review of the third volume noted that professional historians had essentially abdicated their role as storytellers, a void filled by writers such as Foote.

Foote conceded that if he had known that the work would consume the most productive two decades of his life, he would never have embarked on it. And although he feigned indifference, his failure to win the National Book Award or Pulitzer Prize left him angry and embittered. Foote threw himself into a new novel, *September September*, about three white Mississippians who kidnap and attempt to ransom the child of a wealthy black Memphis resident. Foote set the novel in 1957, at the same time as the Little Rock crisis, and characteristically sought to accurately capture the milieu. Published in 1978, the novel garnered mixed reviews. He returned to *Two Gates to the City* but never managed to commit the work to paper. His inability to write the novel may have stemmed from his unwillingness to challenge his own conception of the South, which was ultimately based in the Civil War and the aristocratic environment of the Percy household. By the early 1980s he had given up on the novel.

With Ken Burns's 1990 documentary, *The Civil War*, Foote became a popular icon. Burns's eleven-hour series became the most-watched Public Broadcasting System program of all time, and Foote made nearly ninety on-camera appearances, far more than any other figure. He used his encyclopedic knowledge to tell anecdotes that humanized the conflict and its participants, both great and small, speaking in a mellow southern drawl and avuncular style that captivated the nation. Foote immediately found himself overwhelmed by letters, phone calls, and requests for interviews and appearances. He eventually wearied of the attention, but his participation in the documentary reaped him a financial whirlwind. His books, especially the Civil War trilogy, flew off the shelves.

After a long illness, Foote died in Memphis 27 June 2005. He was survived by his third wife, Gwyn, and two children.

Christopher Losson
St. Joseph, Missouri

William C. Carter, ed., *Conversations with Shelby Foote* (1989); C. Stuart Chapman, *Shelby Foote: A Writer's Life* (2003); Tony Horwitz, *Confederates in the Attic: Dispatches from the Unfinished Civil War* (1998); Robert L. Phillips Jr., *Shelby Foote: Novelist and Historian* (1992), in *The History of Southern Literature*, ed. Louis D. Rubin, Jr. (1985); Jay Tolson, ed., *The Correspondence of Shelby Foote and Walker Percy* (1996); C. Vann Woodward, *New York Review of Books* (6 March 1975).

Ford, Charles Henri

(1913–2002) Author and Artist

Born in Brookhaven, Mississippi, in 1913, Charles Henri Ford cannot be considered a southern writer in the traditional sense. The themes in his artwork, photography, poetry, and prose do not focus on the South or the southern experience. Instead, much of Ford's work reflects a more broad homosexual American and expatriate American experience. Although his literary career began in Mississippi, Ford soon left the South and evolved into a prolific member of the American avant-garde. Ford is best known as America's first surreal poet.

In 1929 Ford and two friends started *Blues: A Magazine of New Rhythms* in Columbus, Mississippi. Although *Blues* lasted only nine issues, it published authors including William Carlos Williams, Gertrude Stein, and Ezra Pound. After the failure of *Blues*, Ford moved to Paris and joined Gertrude Stein's salon, through which he met other expatriate luminaries, among them Peggy Guggenheim, Man Ray, and Djuna Barnes. Ford later lived with Barnes and worked as her typist while she wrote the novel *Nightwood*.

In 1933 Ford published his first novel, *The Young and Evil*, which he wrote with Parker Tyler, another of the founders of *Blues*. *The Young and Evil* describes the lifestyle and adventures of a group of gay artists living in Greenwich Village in the 1930s. It has been called the first gay novel and presents evidence of an openly gay community existing in New York in the first half of the twentieth century. It was banned in the United States and England until 1975.

Ford returned to the United States in 1934 with the Russian painter Pavel Tchelitchew, who was Ford's lover and companion until Tchelitchew's death in 1957. The years that they spent together in New York proved to be the most productive of Ford's career. They enjoyed the company of such luminaries as Stein, Williams, Guggenheim, Edith Sitwell, Glenway Wescott, George Platt Lynes, Jean Cocteau, Orson Welles, e. e. cummings, and Salvador Dalí, and Ford wrote about that period in *Water from a Bucket: A Diary, 1948–1957* (2001).

In 1938 Ford published his first full-length book of poems, *The Garden of Disorder*, with an introduction by William Carlos Williams. Two years later Ford started *View* magazine, which attracted talent from all over the world, including Albert Camus, Georgia O'Keefe, Marc Chagall, Paul Klee, Pablo Picasso, Henry Miller, and Jorge Louis Borges. In the 1940s View Editions published the first monograph on Marcel Duchamp and the first English translations of André Breton's poems.

In the 1950s Ford turned away from literature and to the visual arts. A close association with Andy Warhol and his circle introduced Ford to pop art, and he started to produce collage poetry and films, including one full-length feature, *Johnny Minotaur* (1971). Ford continued to work as a multimedia artist until his death on 27 September 2002. He was a longtime resident of the Dakota apartment building in New York City, living in a studio provided by his sister, actress Ruth Ford. Although Ford, like many American surrealist painters, photographers, and authors, is not well known by the standards of his most productive time, he was a member of a group of American innovators who pushed the era's boundaries. His legacy is vast and impressive, and because of the focus on the still-controversial subject of homosexuality in most of his work, it remains avant-garde.

Courtney Chartier
Robert W. Woodruff Library,
Atlanta

Charles Henri Ford, interview by Allen Frame, *Journal of Contemporary Art* website, www.jca-online.com; Charles Henri Ford, *Modern American Poetry* website, www.english.illinois.edu/maps; Charles Henri Ford Papers, 1928–1981, Harry Ransom Humanities Research Center, University of Texas at Austin; *New York Times* (30 September 2002).

Ford, Richard
(b. 1944) Author

Pulitzer Prize–winning author Richard Ford grew up living in a Jackson home across the street from writer Eudora Welty as well as in the home of his maternal grandparents, the Marion Hotel in Little Rock, Arkansas. His father, Parker Ford, was a traveling starch salesman whose wife, Edna, often accompanied him on the road. The fluidity of this living situation and the consequent idea that home is conceptual rather than geographically fixed permeates much of Ford's fiction.

Parker Ford died of a heart attack when his son was sixteen, prompting Richard and his mother to permanently relocate to the Marion Hotel, a move that further exposed him to the idea of itinerant life. He was also thrust into a role of responsibility within the family, another theme that pervades many of his characters' circumstances. Ford earned a bachelor's degree in literature at Michigan State University in 1966. His time in the Midwest represented yet another challenge, leaving him feeling both unsettled in his native South and out of place in the Midwest. Following graduation and a brief stint in law school, Ford enrolled in the master of fine arts program at the University of California at Irvine. At this time he married Kristina Hensley, a researcher of urban and regional planning whom he had met in Michigan. All of Ford's books are dedicated to his wife.

Ford has taught at the University of Michigan, Williams College, and Princeton University. His debut novel, *A Piece of My Heart* (1976), is the only one of his works set in Mississippi. Themes in the novel discuss and/or debunk some of the uniqueness often attributed to the South, but Ford has subsequently addressed the idea of the South or of southern literature only outside his work, if at all. He explained in 1997, "I'm a southerner, obviously; I like the South . . . but the South is just not a subject on which I have any interesting

Richard Ford at Square Books, Oxford (Photograph by Robert Jordan, courtesy University of Mississippi University Communications)

an American fictional icon but establishing Ford as one of the literary giants of his generation.

Ford released two additional volumes of short fiction, *Women with Men* (1997) and *A Multitude of Sins* (2002), and edited *The Granta Book of the American Long Story* (1998) before returning to Bascombe's evolving life and viewpoints in *The Lay of the Land* (2006). Ford returned to his home state in 2010 as a writing professor at the University of Mississippi before joining the writing faculty at Columbia University in 2012, the same year he released another novel, *Canada*. His most recent book is *Let Me Be Frank with You* (2014), a collection of four novellas featuring Bascombe.

Odie Lindsey
Nashville, Tennessee

Dictionary of Literary Biography: American Novelists since WWII, 6th ser. (2000); Huey Guagliardo, ed., *Conversations with Richard Ford* (2001); Deborah Treisman, *New Yorker* (21 August 2006).

things to say or any curiosity about. . . . It would seem to me that if the South could find a vocabulary adequate for all of its equal component parts, it would quit being the South and just become part of America. But by insisting on itself the way some wanton southerners enjoy doing, what it's basically doing is resisting useful change."

Ford's next novel, *The Ultimate Good Luck* (1981), received mixed reviews, which combined with the death of his mother to prompt him to stop writing fiction and instead to become a reporter for New York–based *Inside Sports* magazine. When the magazine folded, Kristina Ford challenged her husband to resume his fiction, resulting in *The Sportswriter* (1986), the pivotal text of Ford's career. The novel introduced Ford's most recognized character, sportswriter Frank Bascombe, whose hypercontemplative narrative explores the parameters of consumerist Middle America. Echoing themes learned from Ford's upbringing, Bascombe also mulls the ideas of personal agency, accountability, and home and community. Critics and readers championed the novel, which earned a PEN/Faulkner citation.

Next came a short story collection, *Rock Springs* (1987), and another novel, *Wildlife* (1990). Ford subsequently moved to Montana, published short fiction and essays, and wrote his most famous novel to date, *Independence Day* (1995). The second installment in the life of Frank Bascombe, *Independence Day* picks up five years after *The Sportswriter* and again chronicles the themes of home and community and determination or the lack thereof. Meditating on his place in the world, Bascombe, now a real estate agent in a New Jersey shore town, must interact with family, romantic interests, tenants, and others over the course of the holiday weekend. The novel became the first ever to win both the Pulitzer Prize and PEN/Faulkner Award, not only solidifying Bascombe as

Ford, Ruth

(1915–2009) Actress

Ruth Elizabeth Ford, stage, film, and television actress, was born in Hazlehurst, Mississippi, the second child of Charles Lloyd Ford and Minnie Gertrude Cato Ford, who owned a hotel there. Ruth attended Mississippi State College for Women in Columbus during the 1920s before transferring to the University of Mississippi, where she received a bachelor's degree in French in 1932 and a master's degree in philosophy the following year. Ford subsequently worked as a fashion model in New York, Paris, and London, posing for well-known photographers Man Ray, Cecil Beaton, and Carl Van Vechten and appearing on the covers of *Vogue*, *Harper's Bazaar*, and *Mademoiselle*.

In 1938 Ford joined Orson Welles's Mercury Theater and made her Broadway debut in the Welles-directed revival of *The Shoemaker's Holiday*. She appeared in two other Broadway productions before moving to Hollywood in 1941 and acting in *Truck Buster*, *The Gorilla Man*, *Lady Gangster*, and other films that led Tennessee Williams to describe her as the "Bernhardt of Grade B pictures." After returning to New York in 1946 Ford appeared in thirteen Broadway plays, including Jean-Paul Sartre's *No Exit*, Federico García Lorca's *The House of Bernarda Alba*, Tennessee Williams's *The Milk Train Doesn't Stop Here Anymore*, and fellow Mississippian Mart Crowley's *A Breeze from the Gulf*. Ford appeared in fifty films and television productions between 1941 and 1985, among them Moss Hart's autobiographical *Act One*;

Frederick King Keller's homage to Ingmar Bergman, *The Eyes of the Amaryllis*; and the live television series Armstrong Circle Theater and Studio One.

Ford is best known for her role as Temple Drake (Mrs. Gavin Stevens) in William Faulkner's *Requiem for a Nun*, a stage adaptation of his 1931 novel, *Sanctuary*. Ford first met Faulkner when she was a student at the University of Mississippi in the 1930s. During a dinner at Oxford's Tea Hound restaurant, Faulkner approached Ford and remarked that she had a "very fine face." In the 1940s Faulkner and Ford renewed their acquaintance in Hollywood, where he was a screenwriter and she an actress at Warner Brothers. Ford allegedly requested that Faulkner write a screenplay for her, and he obliged with *Requiem*. Ford assisted with the adaptation and starred in the play with her husband, Zachary Scott, at the Royal Court in London in 1957 and later in New York. Although Faulkner presented Ford with the English rights to the stage version of *Requiem* in 1950, the production did not open in the United States until January 1959. Touted as the first play ever written for an American actress by a Nobel Prize winner, *Requiem* opened on Broadway at the John Golden Theater and ran for forty-three performances. In 1987 Ford revived *Requiem* at the Faulkner and Yoknapatawpha Conference at the University of Mississippi, starring in and directing the play.

Ford married German American actor Peter van Eyck in 1940 and divorced him after the birth of their daughter, Shelley, the next year. In 1952 Ford married actor Zachary Scott, who adopted her daughter. After Scott died of a brain tumor in 1965, Ford bought an apartment in Manhattan's historic Dakota apartment building, where her brother, poet and artist Charles Henri Ford, also lived. Ruth Ford's art-filled apartment became a salon, and for the next forty years she was a muse to writers, artists, and musicians and hosted parties for Faulkner, Williams, Edward Albee, Truman Capote, George Balanchine, Robert Mapplethorpe, Andy Warhol, Isak Dinesen (Karen Blixen), and other visitors from abroad, including those Charles Henri Ford knew when he was part of Gertrude Stein's Paris salon during his youth. "If Ruth Ford had lived in another century," lyricist-composer Stephen Sondheim said, "she would have been one of the great solonnières of all time."

Following her brother's death in 2002, Ruth Ford became reclusive, spending her last years in her apartment. She died in 2009.

Ann J. Abadie
University of Mississippi

Lisa K. Speer
Arkansas History Commission

Joseph Leo Blotner, *Faulkner: A Biography* (2005); Dennis Hevesi, *New York Times* (14 August 2009); Internet Broadway Database website, www.ibdb.com; Barbara Izard and Clara Hieronymus, *"Requiem for a Nun"*: *On Stage and Off* (1970); Dennis McLellan, *Los Angeles Times* (16 August 2009); Robert Simonton, *Playbill* (17 August 2009); Marion Nancy Dew Taylor, *Mississippi Quarterly* (Summer 1967).

Fordice, Kirk
(1934–2004) Sixty-First Governor, 1992–2000

In 1991, having never before held public office, Kirk Fordice was elected Mississippi's first Republican governor in 118 years. In his successful reelection bid in 1995, he became the first Mississippi governor to succeed himself in more than a century.

Daniel Kirkwood Fordice was born in Memphis, Tennessee, on 10 February 1934. He attended Purdue University, earned a bachelor's degree in 1956 and a master's degree one year later. Fordice then served two years' active duty with the US Army, followed by eighteen years in the Army Reserve, retiring with the rank of colonel in 1977.

At the time of his election to the governorship, Fordice was the CEO of Fordice Construction, a heavy-construction general contracting firm in Vicksburg. He had previously served as president of the Associated General Contractors of America, a position in which he often dealt with state and federal governments.

Fordice joined the Republican Party in 1964 and developed strong and long-lasting connections to party leaders and financial contributors. He campaigned as a business leader and benefited from voters' frustration about incumbent Democratic governor Ray Mabus's reform efforts. Fordice narrowly defeated Mabus in 1991 and won reelection four years later over Dick Molpus by a much wider margin, campaigning on platforms to lower taxes, encourage more local control over schools, and create a climate for business growth. Fordice also supported the goals of religious conservatives, such as limiting access to abortion and supporting prayer in schools.

As governor, Fordice became famous for his bluntness, which he attributed to the fact that he was not a conventionally polished politician. He attracted considerable criticism for remarks about the possibility of calling out the National Guard to oppose raising taxes to improve historically African American universities, and his second race for the governor's office included bitter disagreements about whether his marital difficulties should be part of political discussions.

While governor, Fordice chaired the Southern Governors' Association and the Southern Growth Policies Board and was instrumental in bringing the annual meetings of both organizations to Biloxi. An avid sportsman, outdoorsman, and horseman, Fordice held lifelong memberships in the National Rifle Association, the Nature Conservancy, and the American Quarter Horse Association. He was also a member of the Game Conservation International Club and Safari International.

After leaving the governor's office, Fordice remained in Jackson and played an active role in business and civic affairs. Twice divorced, he died in Jackson in 2004.

David G. Sansing
University of Mississippi

Mississippi Official and Statistical Register (1992–2000); Jere Nash and Andy Taggart, *Mississippi Politics: The Struggle for Power, 1976–2008* (2nd ed. 2009).

Portable logging camp, Jones County (New York Public Library [Image ID: 110169])

Forests and Forest Products before 1930

Mississippi is blessed with an abundance of luxuriant forests. The 1900 US Census of Manufactures reported, "The state was originally nearly all covered with timber, consisting of pine in the southern third, of which a long tongue extended nearly to the north line of the state, following roughly the divide between the Mississippi and the Tuscaloosa rivers. There was also a small area near the Tennessee River in the northeastern corner. Elsewhere the timber consisted almost entirely of hard wood with much cypress in the Yazoo Bottom." From the towering longleaf pines in the south to the hardwoods of the northern hills and the cypress of the bottomlands, Mississippi's trees have played major roles in its culture and economy.

At the time of the first European contact, members of the de Soto expedition described a land of cathedral-like longleaf pine forests and stands of other pine species in the southern and central parts of the region, giving way to hardwoods and areas of mixed pines and hardwoods farther north. The explorers described forests that had been somewhat altered by Native Americans as they burned areas for ceremonial reasons and for hunting and cleared lands for agriculture. More than a century passed between the Spaniards' departure from the New World and the establishment of permanent European settlements in Mississippi. During that period the Native American population was drastically reduced by disease, and the forests grew more crowded. However, the newly arrived settlers believed they were seeing virgin forests, largely untouched and unaffected by human activity.

During the early periods of Spanish, French, and British control, Mississippi settlers actively used the forest resources. Along the Gulf Coast and inland in the Tombigbee region,

the area south of Natchez, and north of Lake Pontchartrain, pine trees were felled to construct ships, tapped to produce naval stores, and cut to produce barrel staves. Early farmers produced hand-hewn lumber and posts to construct buildings and fences, and some produced materials for sale in the surrounding area. Small water-powered mills produced wood products commercially, and steam-powered sawmills appeared in the early nineteenth century, with the earliest engines salvaged from steamboats.

Some say Eleazer Carver built the first sawmill in Mississippi at Washington in 1807. The first steam sawmill along the Gulf Coast may have been erected at Pascagoula in 1835, but it operated only briefly. Later in the 1830s several more steam sawmills were constructed at the junctions of waterways and the Mississippi Sound. The early operations were mostly located along rivers and streams, which then carried the mills' products to New Orleans and other markets. By 1840 Hancock County (including the area that became Harrison County in 1843) had ten sawmills, Jackson County had two mills, and Lawrence had ten.

Most of the raw material to feed these mills was rafted down rivers and streams from the logging sites, some of which were far in the backcountry. The Crescent City became a destination point for lumber from the interior, which was either used locally or shipped to the Caribbean and other overseas markets. Along the Mississippi River and other navigable waterways, "woodhawks" stripped the timber from neighboring forests to supply fuel for passing steamboats. Early farmers and planters regarded the forests as impediments, girdling, cutting, and burning trees to clear land for cultivation.

Increasing numbers of early Mississippians harvested and processed the state's abundant trees during the early nineteenth century, selling most of their production in local and regional markets. At Natchez in 1828 Andrew Brown, a Scottish immigrant, established a mill that employed loggers and purchased felled timber from outside suppliers and from swampers who ventured into the lowlands in boats to harvest cypress. Brown used both free white and African American slave laborers in his mill. From 1850 to 1870 Mississippi had about 250 lumber mills, and in 1860 they turned out products worth roughly two million dollars annually. The patterns of Mississippi lumbering remained largely unchanged through the Civil War and Reconstruction eras until developments in other parts of the country, the growth of national markets, and the construction of railroads changed the industry's dynamics.

During this time Mississippi's most important manufactured products came from its forests. At the 1876 Philadelphia Centennial Exposition, sixty-eight varieties of Mississippi-grown lumber were exhibited. Mississippi lumber products again impressed visitors to the New Orleans exposition of 1885, attracting the attention of northern lumbermen and investors whose operations in the New England and Great Lakes states were running out of raw materials. By 1890 Mississippi had 338 sawmills, a number that grew to 500 two decades later. The longleaf pine lumber boom began along the Gulf Coast during the last quarter of the century, with the firm of Poitevant and Favre constructing one of the world's largest mills at Pearlington.

Spurring the industry's rise was the tremendous growth of US cities and population, which created an enormous demand for lumber and other forest products. With forests in the northeastern and Upper Great Lakes states leveled, lumbermen found new sources of timber not only in the intermountain West and the Pacific Northwest but also in the South's huge old-growth forests, which had scarcely been touched and could be purchased at bargain basement prices. And the era's extensive railroad construction meant that lumber could be shipped from Mississippi to markets in Chicago, St. Louis, Kansas City, and other northern cities.

In 1880 Mississippi had an estimated 24,975 million feet of standing yellow pine, and at the turn of the century, the state had roughly 32,300 square miles of timberlands—seven-tenths of its land area. Mississippi moved to the forefront among lumber-producing states, with more than three-fourths of the 1900 cut consisting of yellow pine and the remainder largely oak. The state's sawmills produced more than six million dollars worth of lumber in 1890, and a decade later the state had more than 800 mills whose products had a value of more than twelve million dollars. Over the next decade the number of mills again doubled and the value of their production nearly tripled.

In 1909 the state produced more than 2.5 billion board feet of lumber, nearly 6 percent of the national harvest. More than 2.1 billion feet was southern pine, the nation's most important species. Cypress was also in great demand, with prices increasing as much as twenty-fold in a few years. The value of various hardwood species was much lower, leading landowners to girdle and burn thousands of board feet to make way for agricultural production. In 1919 Mississippi had just over fifteen hundred mills that produced nearly one hundred million dollars in forest products, and the industry employed more than thirty-seven thousand workers, about twelve thousand of whom labored in the woods.

In 1925 Mississippi's lumber industry ranked second in the South and fourth in the nation, and four years later Mississippi had become the nation's leading lumber-producing state. Many of the state's lumbermen had migrated from other regions, some were native Mississippians, and all were shaped by the dynamics of the industry. While land was cheap, the steam-powered mills and logging railroads were expensive, and capital was scarce. Most operations were financed with money borrowed through the sale of timber bonds, meaning that trees had to be harvested and processed as rapidly as possible to meet debt obligations. The state of knowledge concerning the cultivation and growth cycle of trees was rudimentary, so most lumbermen did not even consider the possibility of sustainable harvesting and reforestation. In any case, new forests always seemed to be available for exploitation, so the prevailing practice was to cut out and get out, leveling the forests and then moving the entire operation to a new location. Cutover lands were considered of low value, and tax laws worked against those who might have considered reforestation.

The industry's boom period was relatively short-lived. The lumbermen quickly cut through the longleaf, shortleaf, and loblolly pines of the southern and middle parts of the state, and the Delta saw rapid harvesting of cypress and other bottomland hardwoods, which were processed at mills in Vicksburg and other Mississippi locations and in Memphis, which for a time billed itself as the "hardwood capital of the world" because of the sale and marketing of timber and lumber that came in torrents from Mississippi and other neighboring areas. During the 1920s the last of the old-growth forests were being cut, and many of the forty thousand Mississippians who worked in the woods and mills were forced into other occupations or unemployment. By the late 1920s the state had vast tracts of cutover land and areas of scrub trees that were considered too marginal for harvesting. Adding to the difficulties was the prevalence of woods arson, committed by people who hated the large companies, thought burning helped to control insects and snakes, and/or simply enjoyed seeing the woods burn.

James E. Fickle
University of Memphis

James E. Fickle, *Mississippi Forests and Forestry* (2001); James E. Fickle, *Timber: A Photographic History of Mississippi Forestry* (2004); Nollie W. Hickman, *A History of Mississippi*, vol. 2, ed. Richard Aubrey McLemore (1973); Nollie W. Hickman, *Mississippi Harvest: Lumbering in the Longleaf Pine Belt, 1840–1915* (1962); John Hebron Moore, *Andrew Brown and Cypress Lumbering in the Old Southwest* (1967); Mikko Saikku, *This Delta, This Land: An Environmental History of the Yazoo-Mississippi Floodplain* (2005).

Forests and Forest Products since 1930

After the boom in the Mississippi timber industry and its decline in the 1920s, new developments on the land and in forest knowledge produced a rebirth of the forest products industry in a relatively short period. Americans began to grow concerned about cutting forests without providing for their regeneration. Fears of a looming timber famine—as well as Progressives' penchant for the idea of managing society efficiently and rationally—created an interest in European forestry. Europeans had long managed forests to ensure their health and continued productivity, and a few Americans were inspired by their example. Gifford Pinchot briefly studied at a French forestry school before returning to the United States and becoming the first chief of the US Forestry Service. Prussian forester Carl Alwyn Schenck came to North Carolina to manage George Vanderbilt's forestlands and establish the Biltmore Forest School. Pinchot's family funded the new Yale Forest School, and a third early forestry school was created in New York.

The prevailing philosophy among the early professional foresters was "wise use," and forestry education typically included a good deal of fieldwork, usually conducted in spring or summer "camps." Yale had an especially strong impact on the South, conducting an annual summer camp on the lands of Louisiana's Urania Lumber Company and later those of Arkansas's Crossett Lumber Company. Urania's Henry Hardtner, to the derision of most of his contemporaries, began to practice selective cutting and reforestation, managing his forests on a permanent or "sustained yield" basis.

Inspired by the Urania example, the Great Southern Lumber Company of Bogalusa, Louisiana, which depended on both its home state and Mississippi for timber, undertook the largest reforestation effort in the South up to that point. At Yale, Prof. Herman H. Chapman became an expert on the growth and management of southern pine, training generations of foresters who went to Mississippi and other southern states with a sense of mission to manage and rebuild the forests. In addition, Mississippi's Posey Howell and other self-trained local foresters learned about the life cycles of the forests on the ground while working in the lumber industry.

Another important factor in the regeneration of the forests was the discovery of new uses for timber in the early twentieth century. In Georgia, Charles Holmes Herty developed a process for making paper from southern pine, while in Laurel, Mississippi, William H. Mason's experiments produced the process for manufacturing Masonite, which became a popular fiberboard product. Both of these industries created markets for young and marginal trees, thus reducing the time cycle for managing a forest from planting or natural regeneration to producing revenue.

Piney Woods lumberjacks lead oxen to logging truck, 1958 (Moncrief Collection, Archives and Records Services Division, Mississippi Department of Archives and History [814])

Landowners and managers discovered that far more timber remained on cutover and marginal lands than they had realized. Leaving only a few seed trees meant that the pine forests would regenerate naturally, and trees grew in Mississippi's warm and moist climate far more rapidly than most observers had expected. By the late 1930s Mississippi's second-growth forest was nearing maturity. The activities of the Yale Forest School and a few pioneering lumber companies inspired foresters and other lumbermen to believe there might be a profitable future in regeneration and selective cutting of their timberlands.

The State of Mississippi began to put its weight behind the reforestation effort. In 1926 Gov. Henry L. Whitfield, concerned about the disappearance and condition of the state's forests, pushed for the creation of the State Forestry Commission. Soon, lookout towers were constructed and educational programs were conducted to fight Demon Fire. The state offered a ten-year tax exemption on lands devoted to reforestation. The Mississippi Forestry Association, an organization of forest landowners and companies, was born in 1938 and joined the State Forestry Commission to promote wise use through a variety of programs and publicity. In 1954 Mississippi State University established a School of Forestry. The "tree farms" program encouraged landowners to put trees back on the land and manage forests responsibly.

As a result of these efforts and the speed with which Mississippi's trees grew, by the 1950s more than half of the state's land area—some 16,508,900 acres—was covered by what came be known as the third forest. More than three-quarters of some counties was covered by trees—longleaf and slash pines in the south, shortleaf and loblolly pines in the northern hills, and hardwoods in the Delta and northern valleys and prairies. By 1959 Mississippi had only 117 pine sawmills, but more than half were at least medium-sized (with annual production of more than two million board feet annually). The small "peckerwood" or "muley" mills that had sold to concentration yards were disappearing. The state also had six large pulp mills. The number of facilities subsequently declined, so that only ninety-two sawmills remained in 2002, although six pulp mills still functioned. Big companies came to be the order of the day. For example, Weyerhaeuser bought out the long-established Molpus and DeWeese lumber companies of Philadelphia, Mississippi, a phenomenon repeated elsewhere around the state. Ironically, some of the companies that had abandoned Mississippi for the West, such as those of prominent lumberman Edward Hines, now returned and established major presences.

By 1958 only three southern states exceeded Mississippi in total lumber production. Attracted by low land and labor costs and abundant water, International Paper, St. Regis, Weyerhaeuser, Great Northern Nekoosa, Georgia Pacific, Louisiana Pacific, Crown Zellerbach, Champion, and other pulp and paper companies moved into the state, making it a major paper producer. While the forest products industry experienced ups and downs as a consequence of the dynamics of the market, large companies harvested substantial quantities of timber and maintained significant staffs of foresters and other professionals to keep the lands productive. In the forests, genetics and improved management techniques improved timber productivity, while new machinery and processes enabled faster and greater harvesting and processing. Chipping mills and other developments increased the variety and manufacturing techniques of the forest products industry. By the turn of the twenty-first century, Mississippi's roughly 18.5 million acres of forestland covered approximately 62 percent of the state. One in four of the state's manufacturing jobs was in the forest products industry, and nonindustrial private landowners controlled the majority of the forestlands.

During the latter part of the twentieth century the burgeoning environmental movement began to affect Mississippi. The forest products companies and community became more conscious of public relations. Companies adopted responsible harvesting techniques and began to manage the forests under guidelines called the Sustainable Forestry Initiative. "Green-certified" products were marketed as having been produced in accordance with good environmental practices. Companies started to manage their lands to provide benefits in addition to timber, such as recreation, wildlife management, and aesthetic enjoyment. The Nature Conservancy and other groups worked with private companies to acquire some timberlands for public use and preservation.

After decades of fearing a future timber famine and of maintaining large forest land bases and armies of professional foresters to manage these lands, major companies began to dispose of the lands, with plans to secure their timber requirements from other landowners, including some in other countries.

International Paper closed its Moss Point paper mill in 2001 and in 2003 had a reported 200,000 acres of forested land on the market in Mississippi, part of an anticipated sale of 1,500,000 acres across the South between 2002 and 2007. In 2006 the company announced plans to sell thirteen lumber mills in the South to a company headquartered in British Columbia. Other industry companies also rapidly disposed of their lands during this period, with more than half of the sales to institutional investors, such as timber investment management organizations and real estate investment trusts.

The reasons for divestiture included poor stock performance, pressure to increase shareholder returns, debt reduction, tax considerations, and minimization of capital gains. Also contributing were decreasing international demand for US timber products, industry consolidation, fear of hostile takeovers, and depreciation and closure of older processing facilities. Ironically, Richard Molpus, a member of one of Mississippi's prominent early lumbering families, became head of a firm brokering land sales from forest products companies to investment organizations.

Differing investors' objectives meant that the future of these lands was uncertain, but aging of landowners and worries that lands were being mismanaged, fragmented, and sold for nontimber development caused some concern. In addition, Hurricanes Katrina and Rita killed or damaged an estimated 320 million trees in Mississippi and Louisiana. Thus, the first two decades of the twenty-first century have represented an unsettled and transitional time for the Mississippi forest products industry.

James E. Fickle
University of Memphis

James E. Fickle, *Mississippi Forests and Forestry* (2001); James E. Fickle, *Timber: A Photographic History of Mississippi Forestry* (2004); Mikko Saikku, *This Delta, This Land: An Environmental History of the Yazoo-Mississippi Floodplain* (2005).

Forrest, Nathan Bedford
(1821–1877) Confederate General and Ku Klux Klan Leader

Nathan Bedford Forrest was born on 13 July 1821 in Bedford County, Tennessee, to an impoverished backwoods family. Although he received no formal education, Forrest amassed a considerable personal fortune as a planter and slave dealer before the war, and by its end Ulysses S. Grant had come to regard Forrest as "an officer of great courage and capacity" and "about the ablest cavalry general in the South." Many military historians rank him as the most effective cavalry officer ever produced on the North American continent, and he is certainly among the most controversial.

The outbreak of the Civil War coincided with the advent of long-range rifles, and every commander should have realized that the massed, knee-to-knee saber charge of Waterloo had passed and that mounted infantry, utilizing horses for rapid transportation but armed and trained to fight on foot, was the future of the cavalry. Nevertheless, many officers on both sides of the conflict failed to grasp rifles' significance and continued to employ horse soldiers in the traditional Napoleonic mode. But, wrote Maj. Gen. Dabney H. Maury, "the rigorous intellect of Forrest, unclouded by precedents or the dogmas of military critics," made him a prophet of modern mobile warfare. His philosophy was best summed up in his perhaps apocryphal dictum, "Get there first with the most men."

As lieutenant colonel of the 7th Tennessee Cavalry, Forrest first gained public acclaim by cutting his way out of the encircling Union ranks at Fort Donelson to join Albert Sidney Johnston's army at Corinth. He fought with distinction as colonel of the 3rd Tennessee Cavalry at Shiloh, earning promotion to the command of a cavalry brigade with the rank of brigadier general on 21 July 1862. In that capacity he operated against Grant's communications in western Tennessee. Among the most daring of his exploits during this period was his capture of Col. Abel D. Streight's raiders. From 11 April through 3 May 1863, Forrest's six hundred troopers chased Streight's two thousand mule-mounted Union infantrymen across northern Alabama, finally forcing their surrender near Lawrence.

In May 1863 he rejoined the Army of Tennessee, then under Gen. Braxton Bragg, with command of a cavalry division. Following Bragg's failure to pursue and crush William S. Rosecrans's defeated army after the Confederate victory at Chickamauga, however, Forrest quarreled bitterly with his commander, calling him "a damned scoundrel" and "a coward" and offering to "slap [Bragg's] jaws." Forrest demanded and received a transfer to an independent command in northern Mississippi, where he conducted a series of brilliant raids into western Tennessee and Kentucky. These actions disrupted William Tecumseh Sherman's communication network and captured prisoners far in excess of Forrest's numbers, earning him a promotion to major general on 4 December 1863 and causing Sherman to declare that "Forrest is the very devil" and to vow to hound him "to death, if it cost 10,000 lives and break the Treasury."

As the defender of northern Mississippi, Forrest conducted a number of small but classic set-piece battles, among them his rout of Brig. Gen. William Sooy Smith's seven-thousand-man cavalry command at Okolona on 21–22 February 1864 and his flawless performance at Brice's Cross Roads on 10 June

1864, which virtually annihilated Maj. Gen. Samuel D. Sturgis's twelve-thousand-man column at Tishomingo Creek near Tupelo.

More problematic was Forrest's 12 April 1864 capture of Fort Pillow, Tennessee, which involved the deliberate massacre of the largely African American garrison. Reassigned to the Army of Tennessee to accompany Gen. John Bell Hood's ill-starred invasion of Tennessee, Forrest's cavalry corps undertook rearguard actions that were almost solely responsible for saving the remnant of Hood's shattered army after its defeats at Franklin and Nashville. Although he was promoted to lieutenant general on 28 February 1865, Forrest's command was finally overwhelmed at Selma, Alabama, in April 1865.

Following the war, he returned to his Memphis plantation and for a time served as president of the Selma, Marion, and Memphis Railroad. During the Reconstruction period, Forrest was active in and served as the imperial wizard of the Ku Klux Klan.

Forrest was an ardent believer in the restoration of home rule to the occupied southern states and was certainly an advocate of the destruction of the Republican Party in the former Confederacy—by violence, if necessary. Forrest died in Memphis on 29 October 1877, probably of diabetes, and is buried beneath a colossal equestrian statue of himself in Forrest Park in Memphis, Tennessee.

Thomas W. Cutrer
Arizona State University–West

Dabney H. Maury, in *Battles and Leaders of the Civil War*, vol. 5, ed. Peter Cozzens (2002); Brian Steele Wills, *A Battle from the Start: The Life of Nathan Bedford Forrest* (1992).

Forrest County

Located in the Piney Woods of southern Mississippi, the northern half of Forrest County is traversed by the Pascagoula River. Formally established on 6 January 1908 from land ceded to the United States by the Choctaw Nation, Forrest includes the area formerly comprising the Second District of Perry County. The county is named for Nathan Bedford Forrest, Confederate general and first grand wizard of the Ku Klux Klan. Hattiesburg, the county seat, takes its name from Hattie Hardy, the wife of the city's founder, Capt. W. H. Hardy.

At its first census in 1910, Forrest County had a population of 20,722 and was 65 percent white. Forrest grew quickly as the railroad hub of the Piney Woods region and

Pine Street, Hattiesburg, seat of Forrest County, ca. 1908 (Ann Rayburn Paper Americana Collection, Department of Archives and Special Collections, J. D. Williams Library, University of Mississippi [rayburn_ann_24_106_001])

educational center of southern Mississippi. The founding of Mississippi Normal College (now the University of Southern Mississippi) in 1910 was a momentous occasion for both the county and the city of Hattiesburg. Mississippi Woman's College, which later became William Carey University, opened in Hattiesburg the following year.

Forrest County's population grew to 30,115 by 1930, with the county's racial profile remaining largely unchanged as whites made up two-thirds of the population. Forrest was one of the few counties in Mississippi at the time with more nonagricultural laborers than farmers: as the Great Depression set in, the county had 2,244 industrial workers and just 1,026 farm owners and tenants. With the growing city of Hattiesburg and its population of 13,270, Forrest was also one of the five Mississippi counties with more urban dwellers than rural residents. Forrest had a small but substantial immigrant population of about 200, with Russians making up the largest group.

Writers have been a crucial part of the creative life of Hattiesburg and Forrest County. Novelists James Street and Elliott Chaze as well as several other authors developed their skills while working for the *Hattiesburg American*. Cliff Sessions went to the University of Southern Mississippi and worked in radio before becoming one of the most notable journalists of the civil rights era. P. D. East's publication, the *Petal Paper*, developed a reputation in the 1950s for unconventional and challenging work. Other local writers, such as poet Angela Ball, fiction writer Frederick Barthelme, and scholars including Noel Polk and Neil McMillen have taught at the University of Southern Mississippi.

Hattiesburg has long been a media leader. WDBT was one of the first radio stations in Mississippi, while WDAM was one of the state's first television stations. Forrest County was also an important stop on the High Hat Chitlin' Circuit.

Hattiesburg has played a significant role in Mississippi's labor history. The city was the site of substantial Knights of Labor activity, and Hattiesburg fireman Ray Bryant became the first president of the state AFL-CIO. In 1911 nursing organizer Jennie Mae Quinn started the Hattiesburg Association of Graduate Nurses, the first group of its kind in Mississippi. Mississippi's first Federation of Business and Professional Women's Clubs also started in Hattiesburg.

Forrest County was home to a number of civil rights activists as well as the site of some of the movement's tragedies. Victoria Gray Adams, a founder of the Mississippi Freedom Democratic Party, was born in Palmer's Crossing in 1926, and Dorie and Joyce Ladner were born in the same community in the 1940s. In 1955 Forrest County native Clyde Kennard applied to become the first African American to attend what is now the University of Southern Mississippi. His application was denied, and he spent considerable time in jail on dubious charges. Vernon Dahmer, a business owner and leader of the National Association for the Advancement of Colored People (NAACP), spearheaded voter registration movements in his home county until 1966, when he was murdered by members of the Ku Klux Klan. The Congress of Racial Equality, the Student Nonviolent Coordinating Committee, the Delta Ministry, and other major civil rights organizations also had activists working in Hattiesburg, among them Lawrence Guyot, Mattie Bivins, Hollis Watkins, and Curtis Hayes.

Forrest's population had grown to 52,722 by 1960, with whites still comprising 72 percent of the county's residents. Forrest was one of only three Mississippi counties whose population boasted a median level of schooling of eleven or more years, and the county registered in the top five for nonagricultural employment, retail sales, bank deposits, and per capita income. The county also had the state's largest retail workforce, though chemical manufacturing was Forrest's largest industry. The county boasted a small international contingent, most of them Mexican. Forrest's population continued to increase over the next two decades, and by 1980 the county was home to more than 66,000 people.

As in many counties in southeastern Mississippi, Forrest County's 2010 population remained predominantly white (60 percent), and the 74,943 residents included a small but significant Latino community. Like neighboring Lamar and Jones Counties, Forrest's proportion of African Americans also grew over the previous half century.

Mississippi Encyclopedia Staff
University of Mississippi

Forrest County, Mississippi Genealogy and History website, http://msgw.org/forrest; Mississippi State Planning Commission, *Progress Report on State Planning in Mississippi* (1938); *Mississippi Statistical Abstract*, Mississippi State University (1952–2010); Charles Sydnor and Claude Bennett, *Mississippi History* (1939); University of Virginia Library, Historical Census Browser website, http://mapserver.lib.virginia.edu; E. Nolan Waller and Dani A. Smith, *Growth Profiles of Mississippi's Counties, 1960–1980* (1985); William Carey University website, www.wmcarey.edu.

Fort Adams, Treaty of

Delegates from the Choctaw Nation and commissioners for the United States signed the Treaty of Fort Adams on 17 December 1801. Located some thirty-eight miles below Natchez on the Mississippi River, the fort, named for Pres. John Adams, was constructed in 1799 on Loftus Heights overlooking the Mississippi. While under the command of Brig. Gen. James Wilkinson, it served as the port of entry from Spanish Louisiana into the United States and collected export-import duties until 1803.

On 12 December 1801 Wilkinson, Benjamin Hawkins, and Andrew Pickens welcomed the Choctaw to Fort Adams on behalf of their "new father," Pres. Thomas Jefferson. While Jefferson's administration continued to emphasize pacification, it cloaked expansion and pressure for more roads and land in a policy of "civilizing" Native Americans. After a successful conference with the Chickasaw in October, the commissioners anticipated no problems in extending a road across Choctaw country from Nashville to Natchez. In his opening remarks, Wilkinson told the Choctaw delegates of Jefferson's concern for "his red children" and his desire "to lead & protect you in the paths of peace & prosperity."

Asking the "Mingos, chiefs, and warriors" to open their minds and state their wishes, Wilkinson outlined the conference agenda. He explained the need to improve the path from Nashville to Natchez and provide accommodations for travelers and reported that the Chickasaw had agreed to open the road through their lands. Without making a specific request to build a road between the Lower Tombigbee River and Natchez, Wilkinson suggested that opening a road could "prevent disagreement and mischief" because of the constant travel back and forth. In the same vein, he told his Choctaw audience, "We come not to ask lands from you, nor shall we ever ask for any unless you are disposed to sell." To prevent any future misunderstandings, he asked that the old boundary line separating the Natchez settlers and the Choctaw "be retraced and marked anew." He ended his remarks by reminding them that the president had generously sent presents for several years but had not received anything in return.

Except for the pipe ceremony on the first day, only four of the twelve Choctaw speakers used the traditional symbolism and speech followed at Hopewell and Nashville. Tuskonahopoie, Tootehoomuh, and Oak-chume offered to take the commissioners "by the hand and hold fast." Oak-chume covered his hands if not his entire body with white clay as a gesture of peace and friendship. Elautaulau Hoomah invoked the power of the sun to bring honest talks by acknowledging that the clouds had cleared when he began to speak. Tuskonahopoie, a chief of the lower towns, opened the second day and told the commissioners that seven chiefs would speak for their towns and then the young warriors should be heard. Like those who followed him, he granted permission to cut the road and agreed to redraw the boundary line, but he denied receiving annual gifts or pay for the lands occupied by "white peoples."

Subsequent speakers agreed to the creation of the road and the redrawing of the boundary but reflected the changing dynamics of the frontier exchange economy. Apukshunnubbee, chief of the Western District, asked for an interpreter, a blacksmith, and spinning wheels for his towns. Homastubbee, chief of the Northeastern District, asked for a wheelwright and for women to teach his women to spin and weave, and he asked that farm implements and blacksmith tools be sent to his people. The mixed-blood Robert McClure asked for a cotton gin and a blacksmith for the lower towns. Wishing to conduct their business "sober," Homastubbee asked the commissioners not to distribute the whiskey they had brought to the conference. Buc-shun-abbe asked that traders be prevented from introducing liquor to his people.

On the morning of 17 December, the commissioners greeted the Choctaw delegation, promised to faithfully report the conference to their new father, and apologized that the presents sent by the president had "not reached your hands." General Wilkinson read the treaty and interpreted the six articles that provided for cutting the Natchez Trace and redrawing the demarcation lines for the land bounded on the south by the thirty-first parallel, on the north by the Yazoo River, and on the east by a line paralleling the Mississippi River on the west. The sixteen Choctaw chiefs, "principal men and warriors," made their marks on the treaty below the signatures of Wilkinson, Hawkins, and Pickens.

Before departing for their towns, Tuskonahopoie received a copy of the treaty, and the commissioners distributed $2,038 in goods—primarily guns and ammunition—and twelve days of rations and tobacco for each delegate. In exchange for the three sets of blacksmith tools discussed in Article 5, the Choctaw had effectively confirmed the transfer of 2.5 million acres of land to the US government. While there would be no less deception at the next six treaty conferences, American demands for Choctaw land cessions continued through their Removal to the West under the 1830 Treaty of Dancing Rabbit Creek.

James P. Pate
University of Mississippi, Tupelo

Benjamin Hawkins, *A Combination of a Sketch of the Creek Country, in the Years 1798 and 1799, and Letters of Benjamin Hawkins 1796–1806* (1982); Florette Henri, *The Southern Indians and Benjamin Hawkins, 1796–1816* (1986); Greg O'Brien, *Choctaws in a Revolutionary Age, 1750–1830* (2002).

Fort Maurepas

Fort Maurepas was the first European settlement in Mississippi and the first capital of the French colony of Louisiana. Pierre LeMoyne, Sieur d'Iberville, a Canadian military hero, authorized construction of the fort during his expedition to fortify the mouth of the Mississippi River and establish a colony to secure the region for France. Anchoring his ships off Ship Island in February 1699, he set out to explore portions of the Gulf Coast and the Mississippi River. Failing to find a suitable site for settlement along the Mississippi, Iberville returned to Biloxi Bay. After locating a channel of sufficient depth to accommodate seagoing ships, he ordered the construction of a fort on the eastern side of the bay.

Construction began 8 April 1699 and was completed by 25 April. The fort, named in honor of the French minister of marine and colonies, is believed to have been designed by Remy Reno, a draftsman with knowledge of military construction techniques who participated in Iberville's expedition. Featuring four bastions made of squared logs, the fort mounted twelve guns. Its interior contained several structures, among them barracks, a storehouse, and a chapel.

Upon completion of Fort Maurepas, Iberville returned to France, leaving a garrison of approximately eighty men. He named Jean de Sauvole as commandant and Iberville's brother, Jean-Baptiste LeMoyne, Sieur d'Bienville, as lieutenant. Over the next few months the fort served as a base of operations for further exploration of the area. On one such trip up the Mississippi, Bienville encountered an English ship at a spot now known as English Turn and managed to bluff the English forces into believing that the French had firm military control of the river, temporarily halting their rival's colonization in the region. Also during this period, Bienville's forces attempted to obtain the friendship of local tribes, and two members of the garrison were sent to live among the natives to learn their languages.

The first summer of the fort's existence proved especially harsh, as heat killed the garrison's crops and freshwater became scarce. Illness spread, and as boredom set in, discipline among the troops declined. Iberville increased the garrison to approximately 120 when he returned in January 1700. He also ordered more expeditions into the interior and authorized construction of a fort on the Mississippi. During this time, the Spanish commandant at Pensacola arrived off Biloxi Bay and demanded that the French leave the area, claiming that the garrison was in violation of a treaty. After being refused by Sauvole, the Spanish left, only to be wrecked in a storm so destructive that they had to go back to ask for help from Fort Maurepas.

Illness struck the garrison again after Iberville's second return to France. Sauvole died of a fever, and Bienville assumed command of the fort in August 1701. Iberville returned to the Gulf Coast for the last time late in the year with orders to move the settlement to Mobile to be closer to France's ally, Spain, because of a looming war with England. By the spring of 1702, Fort Maurepas was totally abandoned.

Mike Bunn
Historic Chattahoochee
Commission

Edward N. Akin and Charles C. Bolton, *Mississippi: An Illustrated History* (2002); John K. Bettersworth, *Mississippi: A History* (1959); Jay Higginbotham, *Fort Maurepas* (1968); Charles Sullivan and Murella H. Powell, *The Mississippi Gulf Coast: Portrait of a People* (1999).

Fort Rosalie

Organized by the French in 1716, the Natchez District grew rapidly, soon boasting the third-largest population in the Lower Mississippi Valley. To attract settlers, the French built Fort Rosalie on a bluff overlooking the Mississippi River. Three failed attempts to find qualified leaders yielded uneasy diplomacy with the Natchez Indians. Relations mended, albeit briefly, after Captain de Merveilleux came to Fort Rosalie. In 1728, however, Gov. Étienne Boucher de Périer severed ties by appointing Sieur de Chepart to the post. Rarely sober and purportedly bitter, Chepart abused his native neighbors and demanded their tribute.

Among many concerns, sexual exchanges especially disturbed local tribesmen. Complained one elder, the French intended "to seduce our women, to corrupt our nation, to lead our daughters astray, [and] to make them proud and lazy." Those words surely resonated with Chief Sun. Born to a Natchez princess and a French soldier, Chief Sun embodied his people's complaints. Obeying not only tribal consensus but perhaps psychological forces, Chief Sun plotted against the French. Not even his mother could deter him from waging war against his father's nation.

On 28 November 1729 the Natchez sprang a surprise attack on Fort Rosalie. Disguised as a hunting expedition, the war party borrowed guns from the armory and then turned them on the unsuspecting soldiers and settlers. During the ensuing Massacre at Fort Rosalie, Chief Sun smoked near the tobacco shed, where a warrior delivered Chepart's severed head. More than two hundred French were killed, with another three hundred women, children, and slaves taken prisoner.

Officials soon learned that the natives had black allies, a factor the French found just as disturbing as the carnage.

Colonial lawmakers codified prohibitions that regulated contact between settlers and slaves but incorrectly relied more on cultural rifts to separate Native Americans from Africans and African Americans. The interracial rebels, however, could only briefly appreciate their union and enjoy their victory.

The governor immediately launched a reprisal after news of the massacre reached New Orleans, driving the rebels across the Mississippi River. The French never abandoned Fort Rosalie, but they never revived it as a settlement after 1729. Fort Rosalie fell into disuse until the Treaty of Paris in 1763. It was occupied by the British from 1763 to 1779, by the Spanish from 1779 to 1798, and by the Americans from 1798 until 1804, when it was abandoned.

Christopher Waldrep
San Francisco State University

Seymour Feiler, ed., *Jean-Bernard Bossu's Travels in the Interior of North America, 1751–1763* (1962); Gwendolyn Midlo Hall, *Africans in Colonial Louisiana: The Development of Afro-Creole Culture in the Eighteenth Century* (1992); D. Clayton James, *Antebellum Natchez* (1968); Julie Sass, in *Natchez before 1830*, ed. Noel Polk (1989); Garland Taylor, *Mississippi Valley Historical Review* (September 1935); Daniel H. Usner Jr., *Indians, Settlers, and Slaves in a Frontier Exchange Economy: The Lower Mississippi Valley before 1783* (1992).

Fossils

Mississippi is rich and diverse in fossils—the preserved remains of ancient life. Paleontology (the study of fossils) has a long history in the state, dating back nearly two hundred years. Among the first fossils to be described from Mississippi are petrified wood, giant oysters and other mollusks, the elephantine mastodon, an ancient serpentine whale, giant marine lizards, and giant ground sloths. Perhaps most unusual to early Mississippi fossil collectors was the discovery of ancient marine life throughout the state as far north as the northeastern corner of the state, well inland from the modern coastline. This was an indication that Mississippi had spent a large part of its geologic history under water. In fact, only sixty-six million years ago, a small, shallow inland sea called the Mississippi Embayment finally began its slow retreat from the Lower Mississippi River Valley to expose the area on its eastern shores we now call Mississippi.

Six particularly fossil-rich time periods are recorded in Mississippi's geologic history. From oldest to youngest, these are (in millions of years) the Devonian period (409–363),

Mississippian epoch (350–320), Cretaceous period (95–66), Eocene epoch (55–34), Oligocene epoch (34–24), and Pleistocene epoch (0.10–0.01). Although fossiliferous deposits representing other periods occur in the geologic record of the state, these are the most fossiliferous in Mississippi. Most fossils are recovered from rocks and sediments exposed at the surface, although fossils are also recovered from drilling projects that go deeper. In Mississippi, fossils are found only in sedimentary deposits, which get younger moving from the far northeastern corner of the state (Tishomingo County) to extreme southwestern and southern Mississippi. These sedimentary layers, laid down across the Southeast over the past four hundred million years, include deposits of limestone, chalk, gravel, quartz sand, clay, silt, mud, organic debris, and various combinations thereof. Most ancient rocks and sediments lying beneath Mississippi's blanket of soils were deposited by the Mississippi Embayment, an extension of the Gulf of Mexico. However, thinner layers of nonmarine deposits also exist, largely formed by streams. All fossil-bearing Pleistocene deposits found north of the modern coastline are of stream origin.

The oldest rock formations exposed at the surface in Mississippi are found in in Tishomingo County. Millions of years of erosion have weathered and eroded fragments of these rocks of Devonian and Mississippian age, carrying them all over the state and depositing them as thick gravel lenses. These gravel deposits are mined today for use in paving rural roads and driveways. Many people with gravel driveways know about the bounty of fossils contained within the pebbles, which are primarily composed of chert (petrified siliceous ooze). Marine invertebrates such as corals, crinoids (sea lilies), gastropods (snails), bryozoans (moss animals), brachiopods (lampshell), and trilobites populate this nearly ubiquitous chert gravel.

Moving to the west (Boonville, Ripley, and New Albany) and south (Tupelo, Aberdeen, and Columbus), deposits of Late Cretaceous age are encountered. The Cretaceous is the last period in the Age of Dinosaurs, or Mesozoic era. During this period, the sea floor supported a variety of bottom-dwelling invertebrates, including a variety of clams, gastropods, urchins, and bryozoans. The most abundant and easily recognized bottom-dwellers common to the Cretaceous chalks of northeastern Mississippi are the large, thick-shelled oysters Exogyra and Pycnodonte. Fragments of thick-shelled aberrant clams called rudists are not uncommon, identified by their unusual macrocellular (honeycombed) texture. Fish teeth and bones are common in these deposits, especially teeth belonging to several species of sharks, like the crow shark Squalicorax and the goblin shark Scapanorhynchus. Shell fragments of sea turtles and individual backbones of giant marine lizard-snakes called mosasaurs are common in Mississippi's Cretaceous deposits. As dinosaurs were strictly terrestrial animals, very few bones of this extinct group are found in marine Cretaceous deposits.

However, dinosaurs were occasionally washed to sea by hurricanes and rivers.

Moving further west (Holly Springs, Oxford, and Grenada) and south (Jackson, Meridian, and Quitman), overlying deposits of Cretaceous age are deposits dating to the Eocene epoch. In Mississippi, Eocene deposits frequently contain archaeocetes, or premodern whales. Several different types have been discovered to date, the oldest (forty-one million years) with well-developed hind limbs. Zygorhiza is the smallest of the Late Eocene archaeocetes, which also include Basilosaurus, the largest known archaeocete, and Cynthiacetus, a medium-sized form named for Cynthia, Mississippi, a small community on the edge of Jackson. Because of the abundance of fossil whales in central Mississippi, the Mississippi state legislature designated archaeocetes the State Fossil in 1981. Exposed along several watercourses in the central part of the state from Yazoo County in the west to Clarke County in the east are layers of sand rich in the Eocene sand dollars Protoscutella and Periarchus.

Fossil-rich lime pits scattered throughout central Mississippi expose limestone dating to the Oligocene epoch. Like the underlying and thus preceding sedimentary layers, this relatively soft limestone contains a variety of bottom-dwelling creatures, including many of the same basic groups that lived as far back as the Cretaceous period. The species, however, are quite different—much closer to modern forms. Ubiquitous in the Oligocene age limestone are the wafer-like, coin-sized tests of the giant foraminiferan Lepidocyclina. Foraminiferans are a very diverse group of single-celled animals that inhabited the oceans in great abundance for hundreds of millions of years. The same soft limestone contains the sand dollar Clypeaster and heart urchin Schizaster.

The last important time period in the state's fossil record is the Pleistocene (100,000 to 10,000 years ago), the most recent Ice Age, which some scientists believe is still ongoing today. The major compositional difference between the animal life of the present and that of the Pleistocene is the extinction of many large terrestrial vertebrates from the Northern Hemisphere 10,000 years ago. Otherwise, the animals (and plants) are basically the same. Most of the extinct megafauna were mammals. In Mississippi, this group includes the mammoth, mastodon, horse, tapir, stag moose, llama, sabertooth cat, and American lion as well as giant forms of bison, ground sloth, armadillo, beaver, short-faced bear, and wolf. The disappearance of most of North America's large mammals at the end of the Pleistocene is thought to have been caused by warming climate coupled with the arrival of the first migrants from Asia.

George Phillips
Mississippi Museum of Natural Science

Alvin R. Bicker Jr., *Geologic Map of Mississippi* (1969); Eleanor Daly, *A List, Bibliography, and Index of the Fossil Vertebrates of Mississippi* (1992); David T. Dockery III, *Windows into Mississippi's Geologic Past* (1997); David T. Dockery III, James E. Starnes, David E. Thompson, and Laura Beiser, *Rocks and Fossils Found in Mississippi's Gravel Deposits* (2008); Earl M. Manning and Michael B. E. Bograd, *Mississippi Geology* (December 1999).

4-H Clubs

Mississippi's 4-H program started before the passage of federal legislation to support education for rural youth. In the spring of 1907, William Hall Smith, Holmes County's superintendent of schools, began Corn Clubs for boys as a way to supplement the educational opportunities and to fill a void in public schools. "Corn Club" Smith, as he became known, believed that by working through youth he could improve the diet and agricultural methods of the county's farm families. At the same time, Smith began a Home Culture Study Club for girls, focusing on domestic topics. That fall 82 of the original 120 corn club members exhibited their goods at the local fair. Winners earned prizes from local merchants in categories such as most ears on a stalk, largest ears, and highest yield.

Having learned about the success of Smith's clubs from representatives of the General Education Board and from the US Department of Agriculture's Office of Farmer's Cooperative Demonstration Work, educator and government agricultural expert Seaman A. Knapp hired Smith, paying him one dollar a year to collaborate with the department, and Mississippi became the first state with federal funds for boys' and girls' demonstration clubs. The Smith-Lever Act, passed in 1914, expanded Smith's concept into a program to teach rural youth through the Cooperative Extension service at land-grant institutions.

In 1911 Knapp hired Susie V. Powell to start Tomato Clubs for girls, and two years later, M. M. Hubert, working in Jefferson County, became the state's first Negro Extension agent. In 1916 Alice Carter Oliver became Mississippi's first Negro Home Demonstration agent. Agents subsequently formed clubs to study such projects as poultry, beef, swine, and dairy; in 1926 Lee County even formed a baseball club.

4-H gradually changed its missions and programs. During the Great Depression, it supported "Live-at-Home" programs designed to make rural populations subsistent. During World War II only limited projects and programs specializing in food, feed, fiber, and conservation took place. The 4-H's war motto, "One unit for home use, one for our soldiers, and one for our allies," encouraged club members to grow victory gardens and preserve their bounty. In 1942 Mississippi's 4-H members had 23,036 gardens, producing nearly 1.2 million cans of fruits and vegetables. Starting in the 1950s, projects expanded beyond agriculture-related topics to include electronics, computers, wildlife and fisheries, health, public speaking, graphic arts, child care, citizenship, and service learning, and many others.

In 2002 4-H celebrated its centennial. Among the events in Mississippi was the groundbreaking of the Peter Frierson Mississippi 4-H Museum at the Mississippi Agricultural and Forestry Museum in Jackson. Though Mississippi is not the sole birthplace of the 4-H movement, it is home to one of the most important events in the organization's history.

Sara Morris

University of Kansas

4-H Vertical Files, Special Collections, Mitchell Memorial Library, Mississippi State University; Lee Howard Moseley, *History of Mississippi Cooperative Extension* (1976); Franklin M. Reck, *The 4-H Story: A History of 4-H* (1951); Roy V. Scott, *The Reluctant Farmer: The Rise of Agricultural Extension to 1914* (1970); Thomas Wessel and Marilyn Wessel, *4-H: An American Idea, 1900–1980* (1982).

Franchimastabé
(?–1801) Choctaw Chief

Franchimastabé was the title of a major eighteenth-century chief of the western division of the Choctaw. The record of his life during both war and peace provides insight into the political and economic changes in the Gulf and Lower Mississippi Valley brought about by sustained contact between Native Americans and Euro-Americans in the last half of the century. He developed considerable political skill in exploiting rival French, British, Spanish, and American imperial interests to advance his own. Other chiefs did the same, however, and as events of the 1780s and 1790s reveal, Franchimastabé often found himself in competition with and isolated from other important chiefs, all of whom sought goods from Europeans and Americans as a means of sustaining authority.

The first evidence in the historical record of a Franchimastabé emerges in the 1760s, toward the end of the French and Indian War. The title suggests that he had established himself in a traditional way for young male warriors—that is, by killing an enemy, in this case a Frenchman. In 1763 John Stuart, the British superintendent for Indian affairs in the southern district in North America, sent a letter to his "friend and brother" Franchimastabé to express continued

dependence on his friendship. Two years later, the chief led a party of Choctaw up the Mississippi River to assist the British in establishing a post at the mouth of the Missouri River. Continuing a practice begun by the French to create some sort of useful hierarchy among native groups, British officials made him a small-medal chief.

The American Revolution afforded Franchimastabé more opportunities to sustain British confidence and through it to secure goods that would enable him to fulfill the basic expectation that chiefs be generous. By the end of that conflict, he had defined himself in the minds of some as the "English chief." In 1777 he attended a meeting in Mobile called by Stuart to secure Choctaw approval of boundaries for a Natchez District. He affixed his sign to the treaty document. The next year he led Choctaw to help the British secure Natchez after a raid by American rebel James Willing. In 1781 Franchimastabé led a force to help the British resist the Spanish expedition against Pensacola. In the context of that failed enterprise, Franchimastabé strongly complained about a lack of help from the British and their failure to provide promised presents.

Franchimastabé subsequently employed trade and diplomacy to secure goods. He developed an especially close association with trader Turner Brashears, who had come into the region during the American Revolution. Like so many other traders, Brashears acquired a Native American wife—the daughter of another Choctaw chief, Taboca, and the niece of Franchimastabé. Franchimastabé and Brashears thus established kinship ties that proved useful for both men.

In the closing days of the American Revolution, Franchimastabé and Taboca traveled to Savannah and St. Augustine to secure a continued supply of goods. That journey proved futile, and Franchimastabé and others had to look to both the Spanish and Americans for the goods they wanted. Along with more than two thousand other Choctaw and Chickasaw, Franchimastabé attended a summer 1784 congress held by the Spanish in Mobile and signed a treaty of friendship and commerce. As problems developed with regard to this trade, Franchimastabé hosted a late 1787 meeting in his village of West Yazoo at which he and other chiefs complained of the Spaniards' failure to abide by the terms of the Mobile treaty. The Spanish governor's representative assured Franchimastabé that these problems would be remedied, and with the encouragement of Chickasaw chief Taskietoka, Franchimastabé agreed to exchange his English medals for Spanish ones. Taboca and other Choctaw had already agreed to a treaty with the United States to secure American goods.

Three important congresses of the 1790s provided opportunities for Franchimastabé to enhance his chiefly role, but records of those meetings indicate that he did much to alienate other chiefs. In 1791 he and Taboca agreed to a letter in which Brashears protested the Spaniards' establishment of a military and trading post at the mouth of the Yazoo River. The Spanish governor of Louisiana, Manuel Gayoso, and other Spanish officials had concluded that such a post was needed to deter a projected American settlement, but Brashears saw the initiative more as a way to expand the interests of the other traders on whom the Spanish had come to rely for goods for the Indian trade. That letter began a year of intense diplomatic activity that culminated in a Natchez congress attended by almost one thousand Choctaw and Chickasaw. Other Choctaw and Chickasaw chiefs, including Taskietoka, had decided to support the Spanish initiative, but Franchimastabé resisted until he was assured of ample gifts, receiving a scolding from Taskietoka. Later that year Franchimastabé and others traveled to New Orleans to meet with the Spanish governor-general and agree to an initiative to create a confederation of the major Native American groups of the Gulf region (Choctaw, Chickasaw, Creek, and Cherokee) that would reduce violence among them and deter what all agreed was increasing US pressure for land. The agreement was formalized in late 1793 at the new Spanish post of Nogales, at the mouth of the Yazoo. In what was no more than a symbolic gesture given the nature of Choctaw polity, Gayoso announced that he would regard Franchimastabé as the principal chief of the entire Choctaw nation.

Franchimastabé met a serious challenge to his position and indeed his life after the 1795 Treaty of San Lorenzo provided for the Spanish to withdraw south of what the United States had insisted since 1783 to be its southern boundary. Many Native American leaders felt betrayed and threatened. That feeling, combined with Franchimastabé's age, envy of his ability to extract goods from outsiders, and younger male warriors' need to assert themselves resulted in a plot to assassinate him. It failed, and Franchimastabé lived on until early 1801. Expressing regret at his death, the governor of the recently created Mississippi Territory, Winthrop Sargeant, called Franchimastabé "a universal Friend of the White People."

Charles A. Weeks
Jackson, Mississippi

James Taylor Carson, *Searching for the Bright Path: The Mississippi Choctaws from Prehistory to Removal* (1999); Greg O'Brien, *Choctaws in a Revolutionary Age, 1750–1830* (2002); Charles A. Weeks, *Paths to a Middle Ground: The Diplomacy of Natchez, Boukfouka, Nogales, and San Fernando de las Barrancas, 1791–1795* (2005).

Franklin, C. L.
(1915–1984) Religious Leader and Activist

Born in Sunflower County on 22 January 1915, Clarence LaVaughn Franklin became one of the most influential ministers on the twentieth-century national black religious scene and an activist on behalf of racial justice and equality. Franklin barely knew his biological father, Willie Walker, and in 1920 his mother, Rachel Pittman, married Henry Franklin, who adopted the boy. A member of a sharecropping family, C. L. Franklin and his two sisters found peace of mind through their faith in God. He confessed his faith in Christ at St. Peter's Rock Baptist Church in Cleveland, Mississippi, in 1929. A year later, at the height of the Great Depression, he declared his calling to the ministry. Excelling as a speaker, Franklin was ordained and promoted to associate pastor at St. Peter's Rock. In 1936 Franklin married Barbara Vernice Siggers of nearby Shelby, and they had four children, Erma, Cecil, Aretha, and Carolyn. Franklin preached at several different Delta churches as a circuit rider.

Franklin and his family moved to Memphis in 1939, when he became pastor of New Salem Baptist Church. During World War II he hosted a weekly radio broadcast in which he sang, preached, and analyzed events concerning black Americans. In part as a response to Franklin's encouragement, Memphis's black community bought more than a million dollars in war bonds. In 1944, seeking more financial security, Franklin accepted a position to lead Friendship Baptist Church in Buffalo, New York, where he worked with his congregants who were members of the local black trade union to obtain higher wages. His 1945 sermon at the National Baptist Convention brought him national acclaim, enlarging his audience from the hundreds to the thousands. The following year he accepted a position at Detroit's New Bethel Baptist Church.

There, Franklin broadened his position as spiritual leader and became more politically active, traveling across the country to preach racial equality. In addition, Franklin's 23 June 1963 Walk to Freedom, in which he and Dr. Martin Luther King Jr. led 125,000 people down Detroit's Woodward Avenue to demand racial equality and raise funds for King's Southern Christian Leadership Conference, transformed city politics. King later described the event as "one of the most wonderful things that has happened in America," and he gave an early version of the "I Have a Dream Speech" that he delivered at the March on Washington a few months later.

Franklin's civil rights activities and his preaching took a toll on his marriage, and he and Barbara divorced in 1951. She died the following year, and shortly thereafter, their daughter, Aretha, began singing during services at New Bethel. She subsequently switched to performing secular songs and became the queen of American soul singers.

In one of his most famous sermons, "Give Me This Mountain," C. L. Franklin lamented, "Blackness is not a curse it is just the same as whiteness. . . . All colors are beautiful in the sight of God." Franklin's zeal for racial unity and justice galvanized religion in America. He was shot during an attempted robbery at his Detroit home in 1979 and remained in a coma until his death on 27 July 1984.

Marco Robinson
Rust College

"Detroit's Walk to Freedom," http://reuther.wayne.edu/node/7858; Nick Salvatore, *Singing in a Strange Land: C. L. Franklin, the Black Church, and the Transformation of America* (2005); Jeff Titon, ed., *Give Me This Mountain: Life History and Selected Sermons of C. L. Franklin* (1989).

Franklin, Tom
(b. 1963) Author

Tom Franklin was born on 7 July 1963 in the small town of Dickinson in southwestern Alabama and lived there until his family moved to Mobile in 1981. Franklin earned a bachelor's degree in English from the University of South Alabama in 1989. While in college Franklin worked at a variety of jobs, including a four-year stretch as a heavy-equipment operator in a sandblasting-grit factory, a stint as a clerk at the Mobile Infirmary morgue, and a time as a construction inspector on a hazardous-waste cleanup crew at a chemical plant. Franklin published short stories in both the *Chattahoochee Review* and the *Nebraska Review* before receiving a master of fine arts degree from the University of Arkansas in 1998. He subsequently held residencies or taught at the University of South Alabama, Bucknell University, Knox College, and the University of the South before accepting the position of John and Renée Grisham Writer in Residence at the University of Mississippi in 2001. Both he and his wife, poet Beth Ann Fennelly, now teach in the university's creative writing program.

The stories in Franklin's first collection, *Poachers* (1999), were revised while he was in graduate school. The title piece, first published in the *Texas Review*, won the 1998 Edgar Allan Poe Award. The story is set in the swamps of Alabama, along the banks of the Alabama River, and involves three brothers who are caught illegally poaching game. They murder a young and ambitious game warden to conceal their crime, and the local sheriff sends for an infamous game warden, Frank David, to search out the brothers. He does, tracking them to their home in the swamp and meting out a brutal justice. Other stories in the volume draw inspiration from Franklin's various jobs, mining his native Alabama for settings and characters and portraying a world that is distinctly southern and uniquely South Alabaman.

Franklin's next book, *Hell at the Breech* (2002), is a historical novel based on real events that occurred a few miles from his childhood home. The novel is set in 1897 and follows the vigilante justice that occurs after the accidental killing of an aspiring politician in rural Mitchum Beat, Alabama. Friends and relatives of the slain man form a night-riding society, Hell-at-the-Breech, to terrorize the townsfolk they believe are responsible for his death, driving a wedge between people who are perhaps not very different.

Franklin's third book and second novel, *Smonk* (2006), is set in 1911 and follows the one-eyed, dwarflike, goitrous, sickly, and excessively violent E. O. Smonk just days before his trial for general mayhem in Old Texas, Alabama. He has resolved to kill every male citizen of the town before they can try him, and he nearly does, but not before he encounters the boyish waif Evangeline, a fifteen-year-old prostitute who is every bit Smonk's violent equal. *Smonk* counts among its themes incest, fratricide, insanity, violence, and the emotional detritus left scattered across the rural South even decades after the Civil War. Violent though *Smonk* is, it is not without the dark comedy that can be compared to that of humorists of the Old Southwest such as Henry Clay Lewis and Johnson Jones Hooper. The settings and characters in Franklin's work remind his readers that some areas of the South remain part of the nation's frontier.

Franklin's highly regarded work has been compared to such gothic southern authors as Flannery O'Connor, William Faulkner, Larry Brown, Cormac McCarthy, and Harry Crews. Franklin's writings have appeared in the *Black Warrior Review*, the *Southern Review*, the *Oxford American*, *Best American Mystery Stories of the Century*, and *New Stories from the South, 1999*. Franklin's third novel, *Crooked Letter, Crooked Letter* (2010) moved from his native Alabama to rural Mississippi, and in 2013 Franklin and Fennelly published a coauthored novel, *The Tilted World*, set in Mississippi during the Great Flood of 1927.

James G. Thomas, Jr.
University of Mississippi

Greg Johnson, *Atlanta Journal-Constitution* (27 August 2006); Veronica Pike Kennedy, *Birmingham News* (3 September 2006); Fredric Koeppel, *Memphis Commercial Appeal* (8 October 2006); Mary A. McCay, *New Orleans Times-Picayune* (24 September 2006).

Franklin County

Located in the southwestern part of the Yazoo-Mississippi Delta, Franklin County was founded in 1809 and named for Benjamin Franklin. One of Mississippi's earliest counties, Franklin's notable geographical features include the

Bude Hotel, Bude, Franklin County, ca. 1911 (Ann Rayburn Paper Americana Collection, Department of Archives and Special Collections, J. D. Williams Library, University of Mississippi [rayburn_ann_23_90_001])

Homochitto River and part of the Homochitto National Forest. Towns include Meadville (the county seat, named for political, military, and financial leader Cowles Mead) and Bude and Roxie.

In the state's first full census of 1820, Franklin County had a population of 3,821, 60 percent of them free and 40 percent enslaved. The great majority worked in agriculture, with just 38 people employed in manufacturing or commerce.

By 1840 Franklin County's 2,699 slaves comprised 57 percent of the population, a proportion that grew slightly to 60 percent over the next two decades. By 1860 its primary agricultural product was cotton, and the county's five manufacturing establishments employed just 23 men in lumber work and making shoes.

In 1880 Franklin County had 9,729 residents and was roughly half African American and half white. Manufacturing remained minimal, with eight firms employing 12 people. Fifty-eight percent of the county's 1,236 farmers owned their land. Franklin was one of several Mississippi counties with high numbers of Populist voters in the 1880s and early 1890s.

In 1900 the county had a population of 13,678, divided almost evenly between African American and white residents. As in much of Mississippi, dramatic differences existed between white and black landowning. While 72 percent of white farmers owned their land, only 19 percent of black farmers did so. Most African Americans working in agriculture were tenants and sharecroppers. Novelist Richard Wright was born into a family of agricultural workers in the Roxie area, about twenty miles east of Natchez. Industry and immigration remained relatively limited. The county had only 19 foreign-born residents, and its thirty-three industrial establishments employed just 114 workers, all of them male. Most of Franklin County's churchgoers were Baptist, with the Southern Baptist Convention dominant. The National Baptist Convention and the Methodist Episcopal Church, South, also had significant numbers of adherents.

In 1930 the population had decreased slightly, and whites made up 60 percent of Franklin County residents. About half of the white farmers and 87 percent of the African American farmers worked as tenants.

By 1960 Franklin County's population had decreased to 9,286, making it one of five counties in Mississippi with a population density of less than 20 people per square mile. Whites continued to hold the majority, but the number of people employed in furniture manufacturing now outstripped those in agriculture. Franklin also had thirty-one proven oil wells, providing the county with the third-highest mineral production value in the state.

In May 1964 members of the Ku Klux Klan in Franklin County kidnapped and murdered African Americans Charles Moore and Henry Dee. Not until 2007 was Klansman James Ford Seale convicted of one count of conspiracy and two counts of kidnapping and sentenced to three life terms. The families of Moore and Dee filed a civil lawsuit against Franklin County, stating that the county sheriff and one of his deputies had collaborated with the Klan to cover up the murders. Franklin County settled with the families in 2010.

Like many counties in or near the Mississippi Delta, Franklin's population decreased between 1960 and 2010, when it reached 8,118, with 65 percent of its residents white.

Mississippi Encyclopedia Staff
University of Mississippi

Mississippi State Planning Commission, *Progress Report on State Planning in Mississippi* (1938); *Mississippi Statistical Abstract*, Mississippi State University (1952–2010); National Public Radio, "Miss. Officials Agree to Settlement in '64 Slaying" website, www.npr.org/templates/story/story.php?storyId=127991862; Charles Sydnor and Claude Bennett, *Mississippi History* (1939); University of Virginia Library, Historical Census Browser website, http://mapserver.lib.virginia.edu; E. Nolan Waller and Dani A. Smith, *Growth Profiles of Mississippi's Counties, 1960–1980* (1985).

Free Blacks in Antebellum Mississippi

In 1840 Mississippi had 1,366 free blacks, most of whom lived in Natchez and other towns in southwestern counties along the Mississippi River. By 1860 that number had declined to 773, principally because local and state governments had made it increasingly difficult to emancipate slaves. As agitation over the morality of slavery grew in northern states and southerners increasingly feared that free blacks might assist in slave rebellions, the plight of the state's free people of color worsened, even when those African Americans themselves owned slaves and accommodated to the larger social order of slavery.

In a world where all blacks were presumed to be enslaved, African Americans could achieve free status in a few relatively simple ways. A child born to a free black woman was free. A slave owner could manumit a slave when a legal authority such as the state legislature or a judicial officer endorsed the manumission. And a slave who had been legally manumitted in another state could move to Mississippi. In many cases, manumitted blacks were the sons and daughters of the same white owners who freed them: in 1860, 601 of Mississippi's free blacks were mulattoes.

Antebellum Mississippi's free blacks were constrained by a social order rooted firmly in the institution of slavery. Free blacks were forbidden by law to serve on juries or testify against whites, carry weapons unless licensed, move about without documented evidence of their freedom and proof of employment, vote or run for any public office, set type or work for a newspaper, sell or trade goods in other than designated towns, operate grocery stores or taverns, work on boats or river craft, serve as ministers, and assault or use abusive language toward whites. Violation of these laws could result in fines, imprisonment, whippings, and even enslavement.

However, blacks who had been emancipated in Mississippi could own property in the state. They also could marry, learn to read and write (although no schools for free blacks existed), have recourse to the law for the enforcement of contracts, and enjoy the security of family life not subject to sale or enslavement unless specific laws were violated. Natchez barber William Johnson and a few other enterprising free blacks accumulated small amounts of wealth and even owned slaves. Such free men and women worked as farmers, barbers, hack drivers, woodcutters, carpenters, brick masons, laundresses, and cooks, and some inherited property from white fathers and relatives.

Many of the state's slave-owning free blacks enjoyed a relatively protected status in their communities principally because they accommodated themselves to and at least publicly supported dominant white racial mores. Deference to all whites and knowing one's place might help to safeguard free African Americans' well-being but also circumscribed their freedom, keeping them from being truly free. And no matter how well they followed the rules, they remained vulnerable to outbreaks of white hysteria.

Joyce L. Broussard
California State University at
Northridge

Ira Berlin, *Slaves without Masters: The Free Negro in the Antebellum South* (1974); Ronald L. F. Davis, *The Black Experience in Natchez, 1720–1880* (1994); Virginia Meacham Gould, ed., *Chained to the Rock of Adversity: To Be Free, Black, and a Female in the Old South* (1998); William Ransom Hogan and Edwin Adams Davis, eds., *William Johnson's Natchez: The Antebellum Diary of a Free Negro* (1951); D. Clayton James, *Antebellum Natchez* (1968); Charles Sydnor, *American Historical Review* (July 1927); Charles Sydnor, *Slavery in Mississippi* (1933); Wilbur Zelinsky, *Population Studies* (March 1950).

Free Southern Theater

Inspired by and part of the civil rights movement, the Free Southern Theater started at Tougaloo College in Jackson in 1963. The small group of activist actors and directors began with the twin objectives of using drama as a form of social protest and inspiration and taking serious theater to isolated, impoverished people, especially African Americans in the South.

The founders were artist Doris Derby, journalist Gilbert Moses, and actor-playwright John O'Neal, northern-born African Americans who had moved to Mississippi as part of the civil rights movement. Moses and O'Neal worked for the Student Nonviolent Coordinating Committee. The theater group soon added Richard Schechner, a drama professor at Tulane University. For its first performance, the leaders chose *In White America*, a historical play about African American oppression and resistance written by Martin Duberman. The cast included three African American and three white actors who performed the play on small stages, at freedom schools, and in other public areas beginning on 31 July 1964 at Tougaloo and continuing on to at least fifteen other Mississippi towns and cities over the next five months. Because the group's first season coincided with the Mississippi Summer Project, it added the murders of James Chaney, Andrew Goodman, and Michael Schwerner, along with some freedom songs, to the script.

The Free Southern Theater emphasized its commitment to poor people facing discrimination by presenting all plays for free and by holding discussions during intermission and after the plays. At a 1965 performance in Ruleville, Fannie Lou Hamer rose at the intermission of *Waiting for Godot* to announce that food was on its way from Chicago and made a point of comparing African American men who merely sat around waiting for change to the characters in the play.

The Free Southern Theater faced numerous challenges in the mid- and late 1960s. In the midst of the civil rights movement, some whites opposed the tours. In Indianola, police watched as two hundred people attended *In White America*. For a while in 1965, the Deacons for Defense rode with the group for protection. Other problems included a persistent lack of funds and disputes over the content and direction of the performances. In 1966 the Free Southern Theater took up headquarters in the Desire neighborhood of New Orleans, in part to be closer to a larger community of African American professional actors. Under the direction of New Orleans native Tom Dent, the Free Southern Theater focused on material that came from and was exclusively about African Americans, not just the broader themes of power and liberation common in the theater's first two years.

In 1985 John O'Neal staged a jazz funeral in New Orleans to mark the death of the Free Southern Theater. But the theater inspired several other groups to take drama and poetry into southern African American communities, in part to encourage a wider range of expression and in part to continue the political work of the Free Southern Theater. In 1968 BLKARTSOUTH formed a network of creative artists who, according to poet-playwright Nayo Barbara Watkins, considered their work "part of the movement, part of the struggle." In the 1970s Watkins worked with O'Neal to create a character for solo performance, Junebug Jabbo Jones, who used African American vernacular language, the blues, and migration stories. In 1976 Watkins, O'Neal, and others started Alternate Roots (Regional Organization of Theaters South) to use African American settings and speech for alternative drama in the South.

Ted Ownby
University of Mississippi

Jan Cohen-Cruz, *Local Acts: Community-Based Performance in the United States* (2005); Thomas C. Dent, Richard Schechner, and Gilbert Moses, *The Free Southern Theater* (1969); James Harding and Cindy Rosenthal, eds., *Restaging the Sixties: Radical Theaters and Their Legacies* (2006); James Edward Smethurst, *The Black Arts Movement: Literary Nationalism in the 1960s and 1970s* (2005); Ellen L. Tripp, "Free Southern Theater: There Is Always a Message" (PhD dissertation, University of North Carolina at Greensboro, 1986).

Free State of Jones

The Free State of Jones is perhaps Mississippi's most enduring Civil War legend. Long a staple of folklore, fiction, and history, this anti-Confederate uprising has inspired five full-length books and countless articles and essays. Fascination with the legend endures not only because white men and women of a Deep South state fought against the Confederacy but also because of interracial collaboration between Newt Knight, captain of the Knight Company, a band of deserters, and Rachel, a slave. Their alliance led to the growth of a mixed-race community that survives today.

More than simply a local Civil War tale, the Free State of Jones is important for what it reveals about class, race, and gender relations in the Old South. Few large slaveholders lived in Mississippi's Piney Woods, and most families that opposed the Confederacy came from the nonslaveholding yeomanry. Women and children from closely related families protected their male relatives from Confederate authorities, while resourceful slaves provided deserters with food and supplies pilfered from their masters.

The true facts and significance of the Jones County uprising have long been disputed. There is no hard evidence, for example, to support the *Natchez Courier*'s 1864 claim that the county had formally seceded from the Confederacy and formed its own republic, although the Jones County region certainly was a hotbed of internal dissent. The majority of Jones County voters initially opposed the state's secession from the Union, and by 1863 widespread desertions from the Confederate Army contributed to an already explosive social and political climate, producing violent clashes between community factions and between deserters and Confederate militia.

The Knight Company maintained its camp on the Leaf River at the intersection of Jones, Covington, and Jasper Counties. At the height of the company's power, it included between one hundred and three hundred men. In early 1864 reports that Jones County deserters had killed or threatened Confederate officials convinced Confederate leaders to send two expeditions into the region to quell unrest. Col. Henry Maury led the first expedition on 2 March 1864, and Col. Robert Lowry (future governor of Mississippi) headed the second on 14 April. During a weeklong raid, Lowry's men executed eleven suspected deserters but failed to capture Knight and some twenty members of his band. During Reconstruction, Republicans rewarded several members or supporters of the band with local political appointments, but their influence was eroded by the return to power of pro-Confederate Democrats.

By 1900 the image of the Free State of Jones had been reshaped by the myth of the Lost Cause, which insisted that the Confederacy had been formed to protect liberty and independence by defending states against a too-powerful federal government and that the issue of slavery was peripheral to antebellum sectional tensions. Conceptions of a Solid South, accompanied by campaigns of white supremacy and implementation of racial segregation, left little room for white southerners who armed themselves against the Confederacy and allied with slaves. Knight's forces increasingly became dismissed as a gang of poor white outlaws and bandits.

Lost Cause versions of the Free State of Jones have been revised in the wake of historians' current emphasis on studying the Civil War's home front as well as its battlefields. Like various other unionist strongholds throughout the South, Jones County's inner war indicated deep political fissures within the white South that blurred gender and racial boundaries and threatened the slaveholding patriarchy from within.

A 2016 Hollywood film, *The Free State of Jones*, revived and expanded interest in the story.

Victoria E. Bynum
Texas State University, San Marcos

Victoria E. Bynum, *The Free State of Jones: Mississippi's Longest Civil War* (2001); G. Norton Galloway, *Magazine of American History* 8 (1886); Richard Grant, "The True Story of the 'The Free State of Jones,'" *Smithsonian* (March 2016); Ethel Knight, *The Echo of the Black Horn: An Authentic Tale of "the Governor" of "the Free State of Jones"* (1951); Thomas J. Knight, *The Life and Activities of Captain Newton Knight and His Company and the "Free State of Jones"* (1935); Rudy Leverett, *Legend of the Free State of Jones* (1984); Goode Montgomery, "Alleged Secession of Jones County," *Publications of the Mississippi Historical Society* (1904); James Street, *Tap Roots* (1943).

Freedmen Schools

On the eve of the Civil War, Mississippi was home to an estimated 436,000 enslaved African Americans. By 1865 the war, the Emancipation Proclamation, and the Thirteenth Amendment to the US Constitution meant that all of these people were now free. But very few of them had received any education at all, leaving them ill equipped for their new lives.

As early as 1862 aid organizations from the North sent emissaries southward to assist the former slaves in making the transition to citizens. In Mississippi, this process began by the spring of 1863 and continued until 1870. These organizations established a network of grassroots "freedmen schools" to educate and uplift the freed slaves. These schools directly challenged the prewar ideology and laws that explicitly forbade African Americans—free or enslaved—from attending school.

The most active organization throughout the South was the US Bureau of Refugees, Freedmen, and Abandoned Lands (the Freedmen's Bureau), which assisted freedmen and poor whites in negotiating labor contracts, purchasing land, settling disputes and judicial affairs, voting, and attending school. The bureau consolidated three types of schools: private schools founded and maintained by free blacks; missionary schools staffed by northern-born teachers; and private schools started by Mississippi whites.

Between 1865 and 1870 approximately 10 percent of Mississippi's former slaves attended schools consolidated by the bureau. The schools peaked in 1868, when 128 institutions enrolled a total of 6,250 pupils. The schools served as the foundation for the state's first tax-supported public school system, which was established in 1870. Many more former slaves would likely have attended school if greater resources had been available and white opposition had been less intense: newly freed African Americans had an intense interest in education, which symbolized equality and societal uplift as well as provided vital skills for everyday living.

But the movement to provide education for Mississippi's former slaves ended quickly. In 1875 Mississippi voters replaced Reconstruction-era Republican officeholders with white supremacist Democrats, who quickly moved to roll back many of the advances the state's African Americans had gained over the preceding decade.

Christopher M. Span
University of Illinois at
Urbana–Champaign

Lerone Bennett, *Before the Mayflower: A History of Black America* (1968); Christopher M. Span, in *Chartered Schools: Two Hundred Years of Independent Academies in the United States, 1727–1925*, ed. Nancy Beadie and Kim Tolley (2002); Christopher M. Span, *Journal of African-American History* (Spring 2002); Randy Sparks, *Journal of Mississippi History* 54 (Summer 1992).

Freedmen's Bureau

The US Bureau of Refugees, Freedmen, and Abandoned Lands was established in March 1865 to facilitate a free labor economy, found an educational system, provide health care for newly freed slaves, and mediate conflicts between blacks and whites and between Unionists and former Confederates. The bureau's commissioner, Gen. Oliver Otis Howard, and agents faced the monumental task of mending social rifts following centuries of slavery and a bloody war.

In June 1865 the Mississippi Freedmen's Bureau issued regulations regarding fair labor contracts between employers and newly freed African Americans. The bureau sought to encourage negotiations between the two parties, with bureau agents advising the former slaves. Policies promoted by Col. Samuel Thomas, the assistant commissioner of the Mississippi Bureau, included share tenancy, in which lands would be leased to former bondspersons in return for the crop and these workers assured a "share" of the property if employers failed to pay wages. Thomas believed that such an economy would enable former slaves to obtain the capital necessary to become independent, and they likely expected that their situations would gradually improve. Thomas's successors, Thomas J. Wood and Alvan Gillem, promoted sharecropping as a means to make freedpeople ineligible for government aid. Agents of the Mississippi Bureau felt that

F

promoting free labor would ensure economic equality, but the sharecropping system was in some ways akin to slavery.

The bureau was understaffed, with only twelve agents serving the entire state in 1866. In Mississippi, as in all of the former Confederate states, violence was often employed to intimidate freedpeople. In Amite County, men with blacked faces often flogged freedpeople. At least thirty black men and women were killed in an 1871 riot in Meridian following the arrest of three black leaders. Because the Union Army rapidly demobilized following the war, the bureau told black victims of violence that they must find protection through local and federal institutions, often an impossible task.

Education was central to the bureau's aims, and several southern black colleges were founded to educate teachers for newly opened black schools. Among those institutions was Jackson's Tougaloo College, which was opened by the American Missionary Association in 1869.

The Mississippi Freedmen's Bureau also focused on health care, as smallpox, yellow fever, and cholera were rampant in the postwar years. Hospitals were built in Vicksburg and Natchez in 1870. However, treatment for mentally ill freedpeople was grossly inadequate, and many were jailed because of the lack of facilities.

Pres. Andrew Johnson's June 1865 restoration of former plantation owners' property displaced many freedpeople. A ten-thousand-acre plantation in Davis Bend held by the bureau was restored to the prior owner, Jefferson Davis, and those living there were evicted. In Natchez, Thomas, a proponent of ownership of lands by former slaves, saw his hopes for redistribution end with Johnson's program of amnesty.

Some scholars have argued that the Mississippi Bureau did not adequately challenge the implementation of the Black Codes in 1865. For example, one regulation permitted orphaned African American children to be apprenticed to white planters under conditions that resembled those under slavery, but according to some reports, planters kidnapped children. Nancy Bercaw notes that apprenticeship "ignored black household and community structures" in which grandparents, siblings, aunts and uncles, or close friends would informally adopt children whose parents had died.

The Mississippi Bureau undoubtedly improved the lives of many freedpeople; however, extreme challenges and limited resources meant that officials continually had no choice but to compromise in their efforts to provide aid. Congress dissolved the Freedmen's Bureau in 1872.

Becca Walton
University of Mississippi

Nancy Bercaw, *Gendered Freedoms: Race, Rights, and the Politics of Household in the Delta, 1861–1875* (2003); Ronald L. F. Davis, *Good and Faithful Labor: From Slavery to Sharecropping in the Natchez District, 1860–1890* (1982); Eric Foner, *Nothing but Freedom: Emancipation and Its Legacy* (1983); Eric Foner, *Reconstruction: America's Unfinished Revolution, 1863–1877* (1988); Donald G. Nieman, *Journal of Mississippi History* (May 1978); Dale Edwyna Smith, *The Slaves of Liberty: Freedom in Amite County, Mississippi, 1820–1868* (1999); Vernon Lane Wharton, *The Negro in Mississippi,1865–1890* (1947).

Freedom City

Advised and supported by the Delta Ministry, ninety-four African Americans moved to four hundred acres of land in Wayside, Mississippi, to begin Freedom City in July 1966. Influenced by Israeli kibbutzim, the ministry's plan called for residents to build their own houses and establish an industrial and agricultural cooperative. The ministry hoped that the community would become a model to be emulated by other blacks who had lost their plantation jobs to mechanization and chemicals as well as provide African American Mississippians with an alternative to migrating to urban northern ghettoes that were bedeviled by increasing unemployment and other social problems.

Difficulties beset Freedom City from the beginning. Unskilled, ill educated, and unaccustomed to acting without the direction of plantation owners, many residents could not adopt disciplined work patterns, and their growing sense of freedom made them balk at direction from others and undermined the cooperative ideal. The residents were largely uninterested in farming, which they associated with deprivation, and the money earned from the harvests did not cover the mortgage on the land. The federal government at first rejected and then stalled grant applications from the Delta Opportunities Corporation (DOC), which the Delta Ministry had created with sympathetic Mississippians to provide adult basic education and vocational training for Freedom City residents and other unemployed agricultural workers. A storm destroyed most of the temporary plastic huts in which the families at Freedom City had been living. Concerned by the Delta Ministry's financial problems, the National Council of Churches, the ministry's sponsor, refused to allow Freedom City to be included in the ministry's budget, forcing money for the project to be raised separately and consequently depriving Freedom City of adequate funding. The site's poor conditions, the extensive training required by its workforce, and the fear of a hostile business environment deterred potential industrial employers despite the ministry's extensive efforts to attract them.

Freedom City children integrated the local school, and with assistance from the ministry's tutoring project, half of them completed the school year with passing grades. Some of the children made rapid progress despite their previous poor schooling. After considerable discussion, the residents agreed to allow two white families to join them in the summer of 1967.

The following November, the DOC began its federally funded training program. The Ford Foundation agreed to pay for building materials for fifty homes at Freedom City, and ground was broken for houses in May 1968. Families moved into ten new homes in August 1969, but eight of their ceilings collapsed; another eight houses remained under construction. In 1970 Freedom City's residents decided to lease 320 acres of the site to a white farmer; the remaining 80 acres became Freedom Village, and the focus turned to building houses and amenities. Internal disagreements and staff turnover plagued the DOC, and in 1971 the Nixon administration ended funding for the self-help housing training program. The ministry was unable to find alternative backers for the program. Only twenty of the planned fifty houses ultimately were built. With support from the United Methodist Church and the United Presbyterian Church in the United States, the ministry sponsored a small ceramics cooperative at Freedom Village, but the project was not economically viable and closed in February 1973. Plagued by budget and staff cuts, the ministry scaled down and then ended its involvement in Freedom Village. The site remains in existence and began hosting the annual Delta Blues Festival in 1977.

Mark Newman
University of Edinburgh

Bruce Hilton, *The Delta Ministry* (1969); Leon Howell, *Freedom City: The Substance of Things Hoped For* (1969); Mark Newman, *Divine Agitators: The Delta Ministry and Civil Rights in Mississippi* (2004).

Freedom Riders

Freedom Rides, undertaken by the Congress of Racial Equality (CORE) in 1961, were designed to test the US Supreme Court's 1960 ruling in *Boynton v. Virginia* that segregation of facilities in interstate bus terminals violated the Interstate Commerce Act. The first two groups of Freedom Riders left Washington, D.C., on 6 May 1961, bound for New Orleans, where they planned to attend a 17 May rally celebrating the seventh anniversary of the landmark *Brown v. Board of Education* decision. The Trailways and Greyhound buses made their way relatively peacefully until they reached Alabama. They encountered violence at Anniston, where mobs burned one bus, and at Birmingham and Montgomery, where angry mobs attacked and severely beat many of the riders. After the violence in Birmingham, many of the riders chose to continue on to New Orleans by airplane, and Student Nonviolent

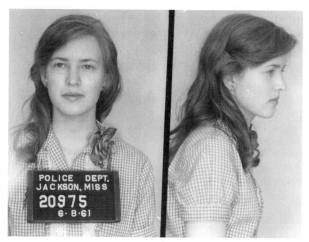

Freedom Rider Joan Trumpauer, 1961 (Archives and Records Services Division, Mississippi Department of Archives and History [2-55-3-85-1-1-1])

Coordinating Committee (SNCC) activists stepped in to continue the journey by bus.

US attorney general Robert F. Kennedy arranged for federal marshals to protect the riders as they traveled between Birmingham and Montgomery. For the journey to Jackson, Mississippi, state law enforcement officials agreed to protect the riders; in exchange, Kennedy agreed not to intervene when Jackson police arrested the riders. This behind-the-scenes deal displeased the Freedom Riders, who believed that Kennedy should have supported their right to use integrated facilities. On the journey from Montgomery to Jackson, the bus bearing the Freedom Riders was escorted by a caravan of highway patrol cars, FBI spotter cars, helicopters, and US Border Patrol airplanes flying high-altitude reconnaissance in response to threats to bomb the bus. Jackson police then arrested the riders when they attempted to integrate the bus station waiting room. The riders refused bail and pled guilty to charges of breaching the peace, choosing to serve their thirty-nine-day sentences in the hopes that the preservation of segregation would become too expensive for white Mississippi to maintain. Over the course of the summer, police arrested 328 Freedom Riders in Mississippi, two-thirds of them college students, three-quarters male, and more than half black. When the Jackson city jail could no longer hold all the arrestees, authorities transferred many of the riders first to the Hinds County Prison Farm and later to the maximum-security wing at Parchman Penitentiary. There the prisoners endured sweltering heat and excruciating boredom. When they sang freedom songs, prison officials took away mattresses as punishment. On 7 July 1961 the last riders were released from Parchman.

As a result of the Freedom Rides, CORE and SNCC eclipsed the National Association for the Advancement of Colored People, which did not support the rides, as the leading civil rights group in Mississippi. The US Justice Department subsequently worked quietly with movement leaders to steer activities toward voter registration, which officials believed would have less incendiary effects.

Lisa K. Speer
Arkansas History Commission

Raymond Arsenault, *Freedom Riders: 1961 and the Struggle for Racial Justice* (2006); Taylor Branch, *Parting the Waters: America in the King Years, 1954–63* (1988); John Dittmer, *Local People: The Struggle for Civil Rights in Mississippi* (1994); Charles M. Payne, *I've Got the Light of Freedom: The Organizing Tradition and the Mississippi Freedom Struggle* (1995).

Freedom Schools

The idea of the freedom schools originated as part of the 1964 Mississippi Freedom Project when Charles Cobb, a Student Nonviolent Coordinating Committee worker in Mississippi, suggested a two-month school session for tenth- and eleventh-grade students. The freedom schools initially sought to fill gaps in what African American youth were learning in Mississippi schools, to give African American youth a broad summer intellectual and academic experience that they could share with their fellow students, and to form the basis for statewide student action such as school boycotts. The freedom schools subsequently changed to conform to conventional academic standards, offering leadership development, remedial academics, information on contemporary issues, and a nonacademic curriculum.

In the summer of 1964, Mississippi had forty-one freedom schools in twenty communities across the state, with a total of seventy-five teachers and 2,138 students—twice as many as Cobb and other leaders had expected. Most schools had five or six teachers and between seventy-five and one hundred students, who ranged in age from preschoolers to seventy-year-olds, requiring modifications to the original teaching program, which had been designed for high school students.

Most freedom schools offered core curriculum courses in black history and civics in the morning and "special interest" courses in the afternoons. Classes for adults were held during the evenings and usually included informal civics discussions and reading instruction. The students were fond of the special interest courses in creative writing and foreign languages as well as the new knowledge that they obtained about African American history in the core curriculum courses. The freedom school teachers reported that they learned a great deal from working with the adults in the evening classes.

The freedom schools cooperated with the Mississippi Caravan of Music (a project of the Council of Federated Organizations), while the Free Southern Theater provided cultural entertainment for freedom school students. The Mississippi Caravan of Music was organized by Robert and Susan Cohen, who presented folksingers such as Pete Seeger, Judy Collins, Phil Ochs, and Cordell Reagan in concerts and informal workshops around the state.

Perhaps the freedom schools' greatest contributions were their publications and the Mississippi Student Union. The freedom schools published an excellent volume of poetry written by students. In addition, local freedom schools published newspapers with engaging titles such as the *Freedom Flame*, the *Freedom Journal*, and the *Freedom Press*. The publications contained essays, poems, and other material written by the students.

Freedom schools held a statewide convention in a Baptist seminary in Meridian in August 1964. All of the state's freedom schools sent delegates, and they accepted as their main ideological statement the Palmer's Crossing Declaration of Independence, a reworking of the original Declaration of Independence. In addition, the students called for school boycotts and drafted position statements on public accommodations, housing, education, health, foreign affairs, federal aid, job discrimination, the plantation system, civil liberties, law enforcement, city maintenance, voting, and direct action. The students passed a resolution in support of the Mississippi Student Union and founded the Young Democratic Clubs of the Mississippi Freedom Democratic Party.

Donald Cunnigen
University of Rhode Island

Clayborne Carson, *In Struggle: SNCC and the Black Awakening of the 1960s* (1981); John Dittmer, *Local People: The Struggle for Civil Rights in Mississippi* (1994); John F. McClymer, *Mississippi Freedom Summer* (2004); Charles M. Payne, *I've Got the Light of Freedom: The Organizing Tradition and the Mississippi Freedom Struggle* (1995); Daniel Perlstein, *History of Education Quarterly* (Autumn 1990); Mary Aickin Rothschild, *A Case of Black and White: Northern Volunteers and the Southern Freedom Summers, 1964–65* (1982); William Sturkey and Jon N. Hale, ed., *To Write in the Light of Freedom: The Newspapers of the 1964 Mississippi Freedom Schools* (2015).

Freedom Songs

Based in traditional and popular forms of African American music such as spirituals, folk music, blues, and even popular rock and roll and rhythm and blues formats, freedom songs have long been an important type of civil rights song. Freedom songs convey positive messages of unity and perseverance rather than antagonistic responses to oppression. Most of the songs that came to be known as freedom songs had roots in African American religious music, in protest songs associated with American labor movements, or both. By the early 1960s protesters had changed the wording of some religious songs—for example, shifting discussion of salvation in "Keep Your Eyes on the Prize" to an emphasis on freedom. Other songs emphasized overcoming fear, claimed the ultimate righteousness of the activists' cause, and helped people stay together as a group.

In the summer of 1961, more than three hundred Freedom Riders were arrested and incarcerated in Mississippi's Hinds County Jail and Parchman Penitentiary. Many civil rights activists cite this period as pivotal in establishing freedom songs as an important tool for demonstrators. Their extended confinement resulted in the expansion of the freedom song repertoire, as they modified existing civil rights songs and created versions of folk or popular songs that applied to the movement. Songs developed during this era included "Mississippi Goddam," "Which Side Are You On?," "Hallelujah I'm A-Travelin'," and "Freedom Train a' Comin'" (an adaptation of a union song). In addition, imprisoned Freedom Riders transformed "Yankee Doodle," "The Midnight Special," "On Top of Old Smokey," "The Battle Hymn of the Republic," and even "Dixie" into parodies discussing prison conditions, reflecting on the Freedom Rides, and commenting on personalities such as Mississippi governor Ross Barnett.

The Mississippi Caravan of Music also helped boost the importance of freedom songs. Headed by Bob Cohen, the caravan traveled throughout the state, teaching freedom school students freedom songs and their origins. Caravan members also often kept up the morale of civil rights workers, who had little opportunity for after-hours recreation.

Rebecca Camarigg
Fayetteville, Arkansas

Guy Carawan and Candie Carawan, *Sing for Freedom: The Story of the Civil Rights Movement through Its Songs* (1990); Guy Carawan and Candie Carawan, eds., *We Shall Overcome!: Songs of the Southern Freedom Movement* (1963); Benjamin Filene, *Romancing the Folk: Public Memory and American Roots Music* (2000); Shana L. Redmond, *Anthem: Social Movements and the Sound of Solidarity in the African Diaspora* (2014); Kerran L. Sanger, *"When the Spirit Says Sing!": The Role of Freedom Songs in the Civil Rights Movement* (1995); Pete Seeger and Robert S. Reiger, *Everybody Says Freedom: Including Many Songs Collected by Guy and Candie Carawan* (1989).

Freedom Summer, Narratives of

Discrimination, segregation, and violence in Mississippi became subjects of national fascination during the 1964 Mississippi Summer Project. One of the project's goals was to focus national attention on the injustices African Americans faced in the state and on the experiences of activists fighting those injustices. At least five very different books were published shortly after Freedom Summer to document their authors' responses to Freedom Summer and more broadly to describe Mississippi at a dramatic moment in its history: *Three Lives for Mississippi* (1965) by William Bradford Huie, *The Summer That Didn't End* (1965) by Len Holt, *Stranger at the Gates* by Tracy Sugarman (1966), *Mississippi Notebook* (1964) by Nicholas Von Hoffman, and *Letters from Mississippi* (1965), edited by Elizabeth Sutherland. Written by journalists and activists sympathetic to the project, these books used a documentary style to convey the drama of the fight, the enormity of the oppression black Mississippians faced, and the zeal of the activists. All of the authors were not from Mississippi.

Despite their different points of focus and styles of documentation, all of the books suggested that conditions in Mississippi were part of a larger national issue. Huie argued, "We must see the link between a rotting shack in Mississippi and a rotting America," and Holt agreed, writing that the racial discrimination so obvious in Mississippi was present in different forms in Chicago, Detroit, Los Angeles, New York, and other cities: "For the worse, not for the better, Mississippi is America." A northern student quoted in *Letters from Mississippi* wrote home, "Has everybody in the U.S. asked himself—asked himself! am I prejudiced? Asked himself persistently until he arrives at that prejudice that is inevitably there by the nature of our society?"

Sugarman was a New England illustrator who traveled with the young northern activists from Oxford, Ohio, to Mississippi to contribute his artistic talent to the movement. *Stranger at the Gates* contains sketches of scenes he encountered deep in the Delta, showing meetings, homes, and faces. He sought to convey physical sensations: the dirt floors of the homes of Delta farmworkers, the dripping of leaky faucets, the hostile stares of white Mississippians driving by in pickup trucks, and the heat of the Delta summer.

Mississippi Notebook consisted of a collection of snapshots and fragmented images from Freedom Summer. Von Hoffman used short, three- to four-sentence paragraphs to create subtle portraits of Mississippians. The book opened with black and white photographs of African Americans taken by Henry Herr Gill, while the text began with a vivid image: "Devil's Dust, the little wind-stirred geysers of dry earth that blow up between rows of cotton plants, puff here and there across the fields." He moved from the land to the people on it, their expressions, and their words, and he recorded overheard conversations, interviews, and numerous physical images. Perhaps above all, he portrayed activists' and African Americans' feelings of fear.

The missives published in *Letters from Mississippi* were written by northern activists working in the state and collected by the Mississippi Project Parents Committee, and the book sought to inspire support for the activists and their cause. The correspondence begins with preparations in Oxford, Ohio, and moves chronologically through the summer, offering accounts of travel to Mississippi; volunteers' first experiences living in African American communities; efforts to register voters and teach schools; difficulties with law enforcement officials and other white supremacists; concerns about the disappearances of James Chaney, Andrew Goodman, and Michael Schwerner in Neshoba County and later reflections on their murders; the details of office work; the political efforts of the Mississippi Freedom Democratic Party; and reflections on their Mississippi activism, its challenges, and its shortcomings. Most of the writers were white college students, and their first names were included, though their surnames were not. Many letters showed a youthful earnestness and great respect for fellow activists who had spent more time in Mississippi. Many volunteers found conditions worse than they had imagined: one activist wrote, "I really cannot describe how sick I think this state is." Some letters were humorous; others revealed fears about safety, about the work's effectiveness, and about romanticizing the experience.

Huie, a novelist, screenwriter, and author of several nonfiction works, faced the difficult challenge of writing about a murder investigation as it took place. *Three Lives for Mississippi* included considerable information about the lives and work of Chaney, Goodman, and especially Schwerner as well as about their murders and the subsequent investigation and trial. He summed up the enormity of the issue early in the book: "For most normal human beings, including those in Mississippi, much of what follows will be incomprehensible." To address such an issue, he used an abundance of quotes, included diagrams showing the details of the murders, and thoroughly described the trial of the accused perpetrators.

Holt, who described himself as a "Negro lawyer," offered a more straightforward account of the Mississippi Summer Project, beginning with the Neshoba County murders and continuing through the Student Nonviolent Coordinating Committee, the Congress of Federated Organizations, the Mississippi Freedom Democratic Party, and other groups; the Freedom Schools; the so-called White Folks' Project; and the Democratic National Convention. Holt included a great deal of primary source material—newspaper and trial reports, demands of activists, school curricula, and policy papers.

Caroline Myers Millar
Arkansas Historic Preservation Program

Ted Ownby
University of Mississippi

Len Holt, *The Summer That Didn't End* (1965); William Bradford Huie, *Three Lives for Mississippi* (1965); Elizabeth Sutherland Martinez, ed., *Letters from Mississippi* (2002); Tracy Sugarman, *Stranger at the Gates* (1966); Elizabeth Sutherland, ed., *Letters from Mississippi* (1965); Nicholas Von Hoffman, *Mississippi Notebook* (1964).

Freedom Summer Project

The Mississippi Summer Project of 1964, known as the Freedom Summer Project, sought to use multiple methods to change race relations in the state. An effort primarily of the Student Nonviolent Coordinating Committee, the National Association for the Advancement of Colored People, the Congress of Racial Equality, the Southern Christian Leadership Conference, the National Council of Churches Commission on Race Relations and its Delta Ministry, and the Medical Committee for Human Rights, the Freedom Summer Project brought to Mississippi more than 700 college students from thirty-seven states, 150 experienced civil rights workers, and 100 clergy. In addition, 150 lawyers, doctors, photographers, and others worked with specific groups to provide legal services for civil rights workers, provide health care for indigent African Americans, and document the civil rights movement via photographs.

The Freedom Summer Project began with a two-week training session at the Western College for Women in Oxford, Ohio. One week focused on voter registration, while the other provided guidance on working with the freedom schools. Volunteers also participated in workshops and heard speeches by veteran civil rights workers.

Mississippi's whites greeted the arrival of the summer volunteers with violence and a military-style buildup. On 21 June 1964 volunteers Michael Schwerner, James Chaney, and Andrew Goodman left their local Congress of Federated Organizations office in Meridian to investigate the burning of Mount Zion Methodist Church, an African American church in Philadelphia, where some members had agreed to sponsor a freedom school. The three civil rights workers were arrested and subsequently disappeared. On 3 August their bodies were discovered in an earthen dam. Many other civil rights activists suffered less lethal violence and degradation: over that summer, the Mississippi State Advisory Committee to the US Commission on Civil Rights cataloged 164 civil rights complaints, 52 beatings or injuries, 250 arrests, 4 gunshot wounds, and 13 African American churches destroyed by fire. The violence made the Freedom Summer Project a memorable media story.

The 1964 Freedom Summer Project featured (1) voter registration and the organization of the Mississippi Freedom

PROGRESS IN MISSISSIPPI
DEPENDS ON YOU

The Mississippi Summer Project needs money now to establish and support the activities described in this pamphlet. We are asking the people of America—individuals as well as institutions—to contribute now to assist SNCC in its commitment to the struggle for justice in the state of Mississippi.

A contribution in any amount will be of help. For example:

$5 will supply school materials for one day-student for the entire summer.

$25 will pay the utility bills for one Freedom School for the summer.

$50 will buy office materials for one voter registration field office.

$100 will buy materials for a home nursing and baby care class for one Community Center.

$125 will buy one tape recorder for a Freedom School.

$400 will provide scholarship money for one Southern Negro college student, enabling him to return to school after working in Mississippi for the summer.

$2000 will rent and remodel a building for one Community Center.

$3000 will buy one used bus for transporting vote workers and registrants.

Send your contribution to:
MISSISSIPPI SUMMER PROJECT
Student Nonviolent Coordinating Committee
8½ Raymond Street, N. W.
Atlanta 14, Georgia

MISSISSIPPI **SUMMER PROJECT**

Freedom Summer Project pamphlet, 1964 (McCain Library and Archives, University of Southern Mississippi)

Democratic Party, (2) the operation of freedom schools, (3) the establishment of community centers for African Americans, (4) the white community project, and (5) federal programs research to bring aid to the African American community. Most of the civil rights workers came to assist African Americans in voter registration, inform them of their rights as American citizens, and integrate public facilities. By summer's end, twelve hundred African Americans had registered, and forty-one freedom schools and community centers had been established. Because of the media attention received by the civil rights workers, the Freedom Summer Project became in many ways the most significant aspect of the Mississippi civil rights movement.

Donald Cunnigen
University of Rhode Island

Clayborne Carson, *In Struggle: SNCC and the Black Awakening of the 1960s* (1982); John Dittmer, *Local People: The Struggle for Civil Rights in Mississippi* (1994); Doug McAdam, *Freedom Summer* (1988); Charles M. Payne, *I've Got the Light of Freedom: The Organizing Tradition and the Mississippi Freedom Struggle* (1995); Mary Aickin Rothschild, *A Case of Black and White: Northern Volunteers and the Southern Freedom Summers, 1964–1965* (1982).

Freedom Vote

The Council of Federated Organizations (COFO) sponsored two mock statewide "freedom elections" in 1963. These elections sought to provide African Americans with exposure to the voting process, to inform them about the inadequacies of the Democratic and Republican Parties with regard to race relations and voting, and to support the development of African American political institutions. The mock elections were spearheaded by Allard K. Lowenstein, a Yale-trained lawyer and activist with the Student Nonviolent Coordinating Committee (SNCC). In August 1963, 733 African Americans presented affidavits at the official polls regarding voter registration illegalities. Then 27,000 unregistered African Americans cast protest ballots at special polling stations within their communities.

COFO activists then began working in earnest on a statewide mock election. A COFO convention in support of the freedom vote took place in Jackson on 6 October, with delegates from all over the state backing a platform that called for racial justice, school desegregation, and voting rights. In addition, the convention advocated the elimination of the literacy section of the state's voting laws and selected activist Aaron Henry to run for governor and Rev. Edwin King as Henry's running mate.

Lowenstein enlisted approximately seventy students from Yale University and Stanford University to assist workers throughout the state when the freedom vote was held in November 1963. Members of Mississippi's police force jailed and harassed campaign workers, and several SNCC staffers had their lives threatened. Henry and King ultimately received 83,000 votes, mostly but not entirely from African Americans.

Donald Cunnigen
University of Rhode Island

Clayborne Carson, *In Struggle: SNCC and the Black Awakening of the 1960s* (1982); John Dittmer, *Local People: The Struggle for Civil Rights in Mississippi* (1994); Frank R. Parker, *Black Votes Count: Political Empowerment in Mississippi after 1965* (1990); Charles M. Payne, *I've Got the Light of Freedom: The Organizing Tradition and the Mississippi Freedom Struggle* (1995).

Freeman, John
(b. 1942) Poet

Poet John Freeman was born on 20 December 1942 in Jackson, Mississippi. After graduating from Madison-Ridgeland High School north of Jackson, he earned a bachelor's degree in English from Millsaps College and a master's degree from Mississippi College and did further graduate work at the Universities of Iowa and Arkansas. Freeman recalled having "the very good fortune to study under James Whitehead at Millsaps and Arkansas and J. Edgar Simmons at Mississippi. These wonderful Mississippi poets and human beings largely shaped me as a writer and a person." Freeman's childhood in Jackson and at his grandparents' farm in Lake shaped his writing, so that, in Freeman's words, "Mississippi *is* the subject of my poetry."

Freeman taught English and creative writing at Tarleton State University and Mississippi State University before spending several years working as an assistant manager of a marina, an industrial manager, and a preacher. In 1976 he began teaching high school English and implemented a remedial English program at Oakley Training School, Mississippi's reform school for incarcerated boys. He also served as the school's interim principal, assistant principal, staff development coordinator, state testing coordinator, and computer literacy director. Freeman is also a former professional musician and songwriter. Since retiring, Freeman has lived in Hattiesburg, Biloxi, Gulfport, Fort Walton Beach, and New Orleans. He is the current poetry editor of *Magnolia Quarterly*, a literary journal associated with the Gulf Coast Writers Association.

Freeman has published three volumes of poetry. His poetry is distinguishably southern yet often transcends the regional label, incorporating universal themes of love and pain. His sparse yet elegant language and thematic poignancy rank highly among contemporary poets. Some of his best works are the Choctaw poems in his third collection, *In the Place of Singing*. In the South the past is often not past, and reconnecting to it is nothing new. However, by exploring a southern heritage that is largely lost and using the Choctaw language, Freeman puts a new spin on a tested formula.

Ben Gilstrap
University of Mississippi

John P. Freeman, *Illusion on the Louisiana Side* (1994); John P. Freeman, *In the Place of Singing* (2005); John P. Freeman, *Standing on My Father's Grave* (2001); Gulf Coast Writers Association website, www.gcwriters.org.

Freeman, Morgan
(b. 1937) Actor

Academy Award–winning actor Morgan Freeman was born on 1 June 1937 in Memphis, Tennessee. After living in Charleston, Mississippi; Chicago; and Gary, Indiana, he graduated from high school in Greenwood, Mississippi.

Freeman attended Los Angeles Community College and spent several years in the US Air Force before seeking acting jobs in Hollywood. He traveled between the West Coast and New York, accumulating roles in small productions until his November 1967 Broadway debut as Rudolph in *Hello, Dolly!* From 1971 to 1976 Freeman played the role of Easy Reader on the PBS children's program *The Electric Company*. His 1978 portrayal of Zeke in Richard Wesley's *The Mighty Gents* earned excellent critical reviews and the Clarence Derwent Award as the season's most promising male newcomer, the Drama Desk Award for outstanding featured actor in a play, and a Tony Award nomination for best actor in a featured role. He continued working in live theater through the early 1980s, earning the *Village Voice*'s Obie Award for performances in *Coriolanus* (1979) under the auspices of the New York Shakespeare Festival and Bertolt Brecht's *Mother Courage and Her Children* (1980).

Freeman's first film appearance was an uncredited role in *A Man Called Adam* (1966). He made intermittent film and television appearances through the 1970s and early 1980s before his film work began gathering widespread critical acclaim. His portrayal of the pimp Fast Black in 1987's *Street Smart* earned an Oscar nomination as Best Supporting Actor. His portrayal of principal Joe Clark in *Lean on Me* (1989) was widely praised, although the film itself was not a commercial or critical success. That same year Freeman played Sgt. Maj. John Rawlins in the Civil War epic *Glory*, which he describes as the most satisfying role he has ever done. His other noteworthy parts include an aging gunfighter in *Unforgiven* (1992) and four more performances for which he received Academy Award nominations: the chauffeur in *Driving Miss Daisy* (1989), a prisoner in *The Shawshank Redemption* (1994), a boxing trainer in *Million Dollar Baby* (2004, for which he won the Oscar as Best Supporting Actor), and South African president *Nelson Mandela* in *Invictus* (2009). He has also played God—twice.

Freeman's work has been lauded by critics as well as others in the movie industry. In a rave review of *Street Smart*, *New Yorker* writer Pauline Kael asked, "Is Morgan Freeman the greatest American actor?" Directors mention his name in the same breath with such industry heavyweights as Robert De Niro and Meryl Streep. Freeman remains highly regarded and in high demand as both an actor and a narrator. He was also featured in the documentary film *Prom Night in Mississippi* (2009), which detailed his funding of Charleston's first integrated prom. In 2007 Freeman received the Lifetime Achievement Award from the Mississippi Institute of Arts and Letters. He received the American Film Institute's Lifetime Achievement Award in 2011 and the Cecil B. DeMille Award at the 2012 Golden Globes ceremony.

Freeman has also worked behind the camera, making his directorial debut with *Bopha!* (1993) and forming a production company, Revelations Entertainment, with producer Lori McCreary in 1997. In addition, he is part owner of Clarksdale's Ground Zero Blues Club.

Kevin Herrera
University of Mississippi

Sandra Brennan, All Movie Guide website, www.allmovie.com; Jill Daniel, in *Biography*, vol. 6 (2002); Ground Zero Blues Club website, www .groudzerobluesclub.com; Internet Movie Database website, www.imdb .com; Charles Moritz, ed., *Current Biography Yearbook* (1991); Miranda Spencer, in *Biography*, vol. 7 (2003).

French, Samuel Gibbs
(1818–1910) Confederate General

Samuel Gibbs French was born in Gloucester County, New Jersey, on 22 November 1818. He graduated from West Point in 1843 and served in garrison duty as an artillery lieutenant until the Mexican War, where he fought in several battles and won two brevet promotions. French was severely wounded in the thigh at Buena Vista in February 1847. He was appointed to the Quartermaster's Department in January 1848 and remained in that post until 1856, when he resigned from the army to manage a plantation along Deer Creek near Greenville, Mississippi. In 1853 he married Eliza Matilda Roberts, the daughter of a prominent Natchez banker, helping to facilitate his entry into the planter elite. They had one child before her death in 1857. When Mississippi seceded, Gov. John J. Pettus appointed French chief of ordnance for state forces. In the spring of 1861 he accepted a commission as major of artillery in Confederate service, and in October Jefferson Davis offered him a brigadier general's commission and summoned him to Richmond.

French saw duty in Virginia and North Carolina between late 1861 and May 1863, winning promotion to major general and working to strengthen defenses at Richmond and Petersburg. Secretary of war James A. Seddon solicited information from French in 1863 about defending the Mississippi River, and French wrote a detailed report that undoubtedly came too late to be of value during the Vicksburg Campaign.

Nevertheless, the report may have convinced Davis that French would prove useful in defending Mississippi, and he was dispatched there in May 1863. Gen. Joseph E. Johnston suggested that French's northern background might arouse prejudice and hinder his acceptance, but Davis tartly replied that French had been a wealthy Mississippi planter and cited his service to the state after secession.

Illness compelled French to take a leave of absence from early August to October 1863. He remained in Mississippi until the spring of 1864, when he and his division joined Johnston's army in North Georgia. French's command fought in various engagements during the Atlanta Campaign and maneuvered north of the city after it fell to Federal forces in September 1864. French attacked a Union supply depot at Allatoona on 5 October 1864 but disengaged after learning of the impending arrival of reinforcements from William Tecumseh Sherman's army. During John Bell Hood's disastrous Tennessee invasion, two of French's brigades suffered dreadful casualties at Franklin on 30 November 1864. French reported that more than one-third of his men engaged were killed, wounded, or missing. French subsequently suffered an infection that severely damaged his eyesight and relinquished command to Claudius Wistar Sears, remaining on sick leave until February 1865. He fought in the defense of Mobile that spring and surrendered and was paroled near the city in April.

In January 1865 he married Mary F. Abercrombie, the daughter of a US general in the War of 1812. They went on to have three children. French labored to rebuild his ruined Mississippi plantation before moving to Georgia in 1876 and Florida in 1881. French published a memoir, *Two Wars: An Autobiography of General Samuel G. French* (1901), in which he criticized Governor Pettus and Confederate generals William J. Hardee, Hood, and Leonidas Polk. According to a modern assessment of the memoir, the apparently unreconstructed French "blasts the Yankees for nearly everything wrong in civilization," and "the bitter partisanship of many passages mars the work's credibility." French died on 20 April 1910.

Christopher Losson
St. Joseph, Missouri

Confederate Veteran (May 1910); David J. Eicher, *The Civil War in Books: An Analytical Bibliography* (1997); Howard Barclay French, *Genealogy of the Descendants of Thomas French*, vol. 2 (1913); Charles Hooker, *Confederate Military History: Mississippi*, ed. Clement A. Evans (1899); Dunbar Rowland, *Mississippi: Comprising Sketches of Counties, Towns, Events, Institutions, and Persons, Arranged in Cyclopedic Form* (1907); Jack D. Welsh, *Medical Histories of Confederate Generals* (1995).

French

Mississippi's state flower, the magnolia, was named for Pierre Magnol, a seventeenth-century French botanist at the University of Montpellier. And Bay St. Louis, French Camp, LeFleur's Bluff, Rosalie in Natchez, Cat Island, Ship Island, the coastal town of D'Iberville, and Bienville National Forest are just a handful of the many places named by the French people who colonized the land that later became the state of Mississippi.

The first European settlements in what is now Mississippi were established by French explorers in the late 1600s. René-Robert Cavelier, Sieur de La Salle, was the first European to navigate the great river later named the Mississippi all the way to the Gulf of Mexico, establishing peaceful alliances with the Indian inhabitants along the way. On 9 April 1682 he claimed the entire watershed for France, naming it the Colbert River after Louis XIV's finance minister. The name later became the St. Louis River, after Louis IX of France, and finally the Mississippi, from an Indian word meaning Father of Waters or Great River.

In 1685 the king, believing that the New World might become an important element in the Europeans' continuous struggle for power, decided to ensure France's control of the continent by building defenses at the mouth of the Mississippi. That year he financed La Salle's voyage into the Gulf of Mexico. Serious miscalculations caused La Salle to land nearly four hundred miles to the west of the river's mouth, in Matagorda Bay.

The Spanish threat to French control of the Mississippi became more serious, finally prompting Louis XIV to send another emissary to the region. Pierre Le Moyne, Sieur d'Iberville, arrived on the Gulf Coast in 1699 and explored the coastline from Dauphin Island to Ship Island and Biloxi Bay and back toward the Chandeleur Islands before accidentally discovering the mouth of the Mississippi while attempting to outrun a vicious storm. Because of the treacherous waters and unprotected anchorages in that area, Iberville chose the eastern shore of Biloxi Bay as the site of Fort Maurepas, the first capital of La Louisiane, the new colony that encompassed all of present-day Mississippi and the land on both sides of the river as far north as the Great Lakes. Iberville became governor of this new colony, which gave France a north-south waterway through the center of the continent as well as Gulf Coast fortifications.

Jean-Baptiste Le Moyne, Sieur de Bienville, was named governor after the 1706 death of his brother, Iberville. La Louisiane suffered greatly from lack of material and financial support, but its greatest difficulty was the lack of permanent colonists. Most of those who came were soldiers, sailors, or trappers hoping to further their careers or make a fortune. The colony had very few women and virtually no families. After several requests from Bienville, the king began to send young women hoping to marry and begin new lives. These were called *filles à la cassette* because they carried small trunks containing their dowries. Many men and women who had been lured by promises of quick wealth were disappointed, but those in search of a fresh beginning remained and became permanent inhabitants.

Hard winters and a lack of supplies caused the deaths of hundreds of colonists, but nearby Indian villages generously offered food and lodging to starving colonists and soldiers. Arrival of supply ships continued to be sporadic, and French farmers had difficulty adjusting to the humid southern climate.

Disappointed in the lack of progress, the king decided in 1712 to grant the colony to Antoine Crozat, a financier who agreed to send colonists and to establish profitable trade. However, Crozat's chosen governor, Antoine de la Mothe Cadillac, was a dismal failure, alienating colonists, Indians, and his own administrators. In 1717 Crozat gave up his grant and returned it to the new king, Louis XV, who then granted it to John Law, a Scottish financier. Law moved quickly to populate the colony through joint-stock concessions or land grants whose value inflated until the "Mississippi Bubble" burst. Law narrowly escaped the angry stockholders by fleeing France, but he had brought to Louisiana thousands of colonists as well as black slaves from West Africa. The Company of the Indies ran the colony after Law's fall in 1720, but it again returned to the Crown in 1732. During this period La Nouvelle Orléans became the colony's new capital.

The British constantly threatened the new French colony. The Choctaw generally supported the French during this struggle, while the Chickasaw were more loyal to the British. For a while the French became more dependent on the Natchez Indians, especially because of their fertile, easily defended land on the Natchez Bluffs. Friction between the French and the Natchez erupted in a 1729 rebellion after the French demanded a Natchez sacred site. The French commandant rejected several offers of compromise made by the Great Sun, the Natchez chief, leading the natives to kill all French males in the settlements around Fort Rosalie and possibly further north at Fort St. Pierre on the Yazoo River. In 1730 the French asked the Choctaw to join in punitive attacks against the Natchez. The Chickasaw sympathized with the Natchez, increasing the enmity that led to the Chickasaw Wars of 1736 and 1740 under the leadership of Bienville, whose efforts resulted in a stalemate.

After Bienville's recall to France, Pierre de Rigaud, Marquis de Vaudreuil, arrived in New Orleans in 1743 to become the colony's new governor. During his years in office, the European war was strongly reflected in the colonies, pitting French against English along with their Choctaw and Chickasaw allies. The Choctaw Civil War further weakened France's control.

Louis Billouart de Kerlérec succeeded Vaudreuil as governor in 1753. Territorial disputes between the French and English in Acadia and the Great Lakes region finally resulted in the Seven Years' War (1756–63). The Acadians were expelled from their homes in 1755, and although most of them settled in present-day Louisiana, some came to Mississippi.

The 1763 Treaty of Paris ended the long struggle between England and France for control in North America, with Great Britain assuming authority over all French possessions east of the Mississippi River and a secret treaty giving Spain all possessions west of the river. The majority of existing French settlers remained behind, mostly on land grants along the great river or on the Gulf Coast.

One notable exception to that majority was Louis LeFleur, the son of a French soldier, who developed lucrative trade with the Indians and established several posts on small rivers and on the Natchez Trace during the late 1700s. LeFleur's Bluff, on the Pearl River in Jackson, is believed to have been the site of one of those posts. LeFleur married Rebecca Cravat, a niece of a respected Choctaw chief, Pushmataha, and built a home on the Natchez Trace, which developed into a trading community, Frenchman's Camp (now French Camp). One of his sons, Greenwood, changed his last name to Le Flore and was elected chief of the Choctaw people in 1822.

Although the colony lost its French status after the Seven Years' War, Mississippi retains an indelible French heritage, especially along the Gulf Coast. Those early families are ancestors of many Mississippians. Some names have been Americanized, such as Horn Island instead of *Isle à la Corne* or Pearl River instead of *Rivière aux Perles*, but others, including Bellefontaine and Gautier, have remained French.

Gail Buzhardt
Millsaps College

Jean Bernard Bossu, *Nouveaux Voyages aux Indes Occidentales* (1768); Gail A. Buzhardt and Margaret Hawthorne, *Rencontres sur le Mississippi, 1682–1763* (1993); Pierre Margry, ed., *Découvertes et Établissements des Français dans l'Ouest et dans le Sud de l'Amérique Septentrionale (1614–1754)* (1974); Mississippi Department of Archives and History, *Correspondance Générale: Louisiane*, Archives des Colonies, ser. C13A, 13B, Archives Nationales de Paris (microfilm); Antoine-Simon Le Page du Pratz, *Histoire de la Louisiane Française* (1758); Daniel H. Usner Jr., *American Indians in the Lower Mississippi Valley: Social and Economic Histories* (1998); Daniel H. Usner Jr., *Indians, Settlers, and Slaves in a Frontier Exchange Economy: The Lower Mississippi Valley before 1783* (1992).

French-Natchez War

In 1701 Sieur de Sauvole sent an expedition of four men to explore the high bluffs 150 miles upriver from New Orleans. They found the area "perfectly good and agreeable," but the French experience there later proved otherwise. The land was named the Natchez District after the powerful tribe whose members preferred that the French stay far from the bluffs.

Violence marred the first attempt to colonize the Natchez District in 1715. Irritated by the construction of a trading house, a band of natives murdered several frontier traders and looted the outpost, commandeering goods, horses, and slaves. Hearing news of the atrocities, Gov. Antoine de la Mothe Cadillac ordered Jean-Baptiste Le Moyne, Sieur de Bienville, to lead thirty-five soldiers to punish the tribe. Bienville somehow cowed tribal leaders into executing the guilty, returning the stolen merchandise, and constructing a fort for the future protection of the French.

After the erection of Fort Rosalie in 1716, the Natchez District experienced incredible growth. Its population topped 300 settlers and slaves by 1723 and 750 by 1729. Many of the new arrivals began clearing land for the cultivation of tobacco, wheat, and indigo. The steady encroachment on tribal lands angered native inhabitants, and their hostility prompted Bienville, now governor of Louisiana, to send 500 troops on a 1722 "peace offensive" that destroyed two tribal villages.

Relations worsened after Sieur de Chepart received the commission to govern the Natchez District in 1728. A notorious drunk, Chepart mistreated natives and settlers alike. His bad behavior led to his dismissal from office after the Superior Council found him guilty of abusing power. Gov. Étienne Boucher de Périer, however, pardoned Chepart and restored his commission. The commandant returned to Fort Rosalie and banished the Natchez Indians from the village of White Apple. The enraged tribal sovereign, Chief Sun, immediately began plotting an attack on the garrison and the surrounding settlements.

On 28 November 1729 Chief Sun led what the French called the Massacre at Fort Rosalie. Disguised as peaceful visitors on a hunting expedition, the war party borrowed guns from the armory and then fired on surprised soldiers and settlers. Once the massacre commenced, Chief Sun watched the carnage from a perch near the tobacco storehouse, where he received Chepart's severed head. The Natchez inflicted more than two hundred casualties and captured more than three hundred women, children, and slaves.

The Natchez won the first battle but decisively lost the war. The French-Natchez War (1729–30) ultimately led to the annihilation of the Natchez as a nation, which some tribal elders had considered a French objective all along. Most died as warriors in battle; some died as slaves in Saint-Domingue, and others continued their struggle as adopted members of the Chickasaw or Yazoo.

The Natchez inspired other native uprisings. The Yazoo killed eighteen soldiers in March 1730, and the Chickasaw launched a guerrilla war in 1731. Despite two decades of military campaigns, the French never managed to suppress the rebellious tribes.

Christopher Waldrep
San Francisco State University

Jean-Bernard Bossu, *Travels in the Interior of North America, 1751–1762*, ed. Seymour Feiler (1962); Gwendolyn Midlo Hall, *Africans in Colonial Louisiana: The Development of Afro-Creole Culture in the Eighteenth Century* (1992); D. Clayton James, *Antebellum Natchez* (1968); Richard Aubrey McLemore, ed., *A History of Mississippi*, vol. 1 (1973); Julie Sass, in *Natchez before 1830*, ed. Noel Polk (1989); Garland Taylor, *Mississippi Valley Historical Review* (September 1935); Daniel H. Usner Jr., *Indians, Settlers, and Slaves in a Frontier Exchange Economy: The Lower Mississippi Valley before 1783* (1992).

French Period, Government in

Robert Cavelier de La Salle (1643–87) was the first European to follow the Mississippi River to its mouth. On 9 April 1682 he claimed it and its tributaries for France, calling the territory Louisiana after his king, Louis XIV. To forestall claims by England and Spain, Pierre Le Moyne, Sieur d'Iberville (1661–1706) founded a colony, landing on 25 January 1699, and constructing Fort Maurepas at Old Biloxi (now Ocean Springs). Louisiana encompassed the entire Mississippi River basin from the river's source in what is now Minnesota to the Gulf of Mexico. It included outposts in southern Indiana and Illinois, but as a practical matter the government, based in New Orleans after its transfer from Biloxi in 1722, exercised minimal authority north of present-day Natchez.

As a result of the Seven Years' War (also known as the French and Indian War), France ceded the land west of the Mississippi (including New Orleans) to Spain on 3 November 1762. On 10 February 1763 the Treaty of Paris gave England the land east of the river (including what is now Mississippi) and free navigation of the river, plus Spanish Florida. The Indians living in the immense territories were of course not consulted.

To the French government, a colony—any colony—was worth only what it contributed to the power and wealth of France. The Louisiana Territory was valued for three reasons: (1) it would keep England out of the Mississippi Valley and thus protect New France; (2) it would control the mouth of the river and provide a naval base to protect the immensely profitable West Indies sugar islands; and (3) it might be a base from which France could gain a share of Spain's colonial trade. Even if Louisiana had become a profitable exporter to France or its colonies, only strategic purposes justified its retention. Hence, in the government's eyes, after England conquered Canada in the French and Indian War, Louisiana became expendable. It could no longer be defended from the English, but everything west of the river might be given to Spain, France's ally, to cement the friendship and block further English expansion. Spain and England finally agreed to the deal. French Louisiana was gone—until 1800, when Spain, under duress, gave its share back to Napoleon, who sold it to the United States three years later although he had assured Spain that he would not do so.

Louisiana's government was part of New France (except for the 1720–31 period) and thus subject to the governor-general in Quebec. In practice, however, Louisiana's governors (or their interim substitutes) answered only to the Ministry of Marine in Paris. Louisiana remained a royal colony until 1763, and French authority over the Spanish cession continued on an interim basis until 1769.

As in all French colonies, Louisiana's government was hampered by entangled responsibilities. The governor exercised general oversight and full military authority. After the 1706 death of Iberville, who had mostly been absent, Louisiana's governors included Antoine de la Mothe Cadillac (1713–17); Jean Michele de Lépinay (1717); Étienne Boucher de Périer (1729–33); Jean-Baptiste Le Moyne, Sieur de Bienville (1733–43), Iberville's younger brother, who as king's lieutenant, commandant, and finally commandant-general was the colony's most consequential figure; Pierre Rigaud de Vaudreuil (1743–53); and Louis Billouart de Kerlérec (1753–63).

As historian W. J. Eccles has observed, "In one respect Louisiana surpassed all the French colonies: the constant bickering, intrigue, and open quarrelling among the officials." Aside from turf battles, reasons abounded: the great distances from Paris and Quebec, which hindered supervision and provisioning; perpetual shortages of food and trading goods; miserable salaries, when paid; the inferior talents of many civil and military appointees; intense rivalries between the military and administrative nobilities; plentiful opportunities for graft, corruption, and illicit trading; feuding religious orders and a lack of discipline in the clergy; fear of revolt by the black slaves; and the stress of relations with the Indians—many times more numerous than the colonists—regarding trade, customs, and warfare.

David S. Newhall
Centre College

Arthur S. Aiton, *American Historical Review* (July 1931); W. J. Eccles, *France in America* (1972); Marcel Giraud, *Mississippi Valley Historical Review* 36 (1949–50); Giraud, *Histoire de la Louisiana Française*, 5 vols. (1953–87); Donald J. Lemieux, *Southern Studies* (Spring 1978); John Francis McDermott, ed., *The French in the Mississippi Valley* (1965); K. Saadami, in *French Colonial History* (2003); Jennifer M. Spear, *William and Mary Quarterly* (January 2003); Daniel H. Usner Jr., *Indians, Settlers, and Slaves in a Frontier Exchange Economy: The Lower Mississippi Valley before 1783* (1992).

Fried Dill Pickles

Fried dill pickles are one of Mississippi's most memorable appetizers, served in taverns featuring hamburger steak and pinball, at roadside catfish houses, and on white tablecloths in temples of New Southern cuisine. Cooks across the Magnolia State favor hamburger dills cut into slices rather than spears, but the unanimity ends there. The origin of the dish is debatable, the dipping sauce varies widely, and the batter may have no spices at all or liberal sprinklings of cayenne pepper and garlic powder.

Robinsonville's Hollywood Café has long declared itself the originator of fried dill pickles. One version of the story dates the creation to 1969, when the catfish supply was exhausted one evening and the cook substituted pickles. However, other establishments in Mississippi and Arkansas also claim to have devised the dish. Considering southern cooks' propensity for frying almost anything, "fried dill pickles were just bound to happen eventually," writes Sweet Potato Queen Jill Conner Browne. Hal White, co-owner and chef at Hal and Mal's Restaurant and Brewery in downtown Jackson, theorizes that the first fried dill pickle resulted when an errant hamburger chip was inadvertently tossed into onion ring batter and fried.

White's pickles undergo a three-step dunk: into a wash of eggs and milk, then into seasoned flour, and then back into the wash before deep-frying. Some cooks use a single-step process in which the pickles are dipped into a batter made from some combination of milk, buttermilk, beer, pickle juice, flour, hot sauce, red pepper, garlic, and paprika. Because of the saltiness of the pickles, some recipes do not include salt. Some call for no seasoning whatsoever.

Cock of the Walk restaurants in Jackson and Natchez bring fried dill pickles to the table without dipping sauce. Beer joints often serve ketchup as a condiment, and some diners stir in shots of hot sauce. At the Blue and White Restaurant in Tunica, the preferred accompaniment is ranch dressing. Some Mississippi establishments serve Comeback Sauce with fried dill pickles. An unusual creation of Jackson's Greek-owned restaurants, Comeback has been described as a spicier, pureed version of Thousand Island dressing minus the chopped pickles. New Orleans–style remoulade sauce is another dipping option. White labels fried dill pickles a "Mississippi thing," while *Gourmet* magazine's "Road Food" columnist, Michael Stern, has portrayed them as both a "weird Delta specialty" and a "favorite Delta munchie."

Whether invented or accidental, fried dill pickles have been more passionately embraced in Mississippi than in any other state. Thin, round, briny, crunchy, spiced, sauced, and steaming hot, they epitomize the creative and resourceful use of common southern kitchen pantry staples.

Fred Sauceman
East Tennessee State University

Jill Conner Browne, *The Sweet Potato Queens' Big-Ass Cookbook (and Financial Planner)* (2003); John T. Edge, *Southern Belly: The Ultimate Food Lover's Guide to the South* (2007); Michael Stern, Road Food website, www.roadfood.com; Hal White, Interview by Fred Sauceman (27 August 2003).

Fulkerson, Horace S.
(1818–1891) Editor and Author

Horace S. Fulkerson was born in 1818 in Kentucky and moved to Rodney, Mississippi, in 1836. He became deputy US marshal in Port Gibson in 1840 and in 1845 married Charlotte McBride, with whom he went on to have five children. In the 1850s he worked in New Orleans as an agent for the Southern Pacific Railroad. When the Civil War broke out, Fulkerson traveled to Europe as a Confederate agent, buying war materials. He then worked with the Confederate Cotton Bureau and proposed a plan to build Confederate gunboats in Texas.

After the Civil War, he moved to Vicksburg and became a merchant. In 1885 he founded the *Vicksburg Sun*, serving as the paper's manager and editor. The first three issues featured Fulkerson's reminiscences, which he then published as *A Civilian's Recollections of the War*. Fulkerson also published a memoir, *Random Recollections of Early Days in Mississippi* (1885), that contained anecdotes about frontier life, with considerable details about fighting, dueling, steamboat races, land speculation and other forms of gambling, and yellow fever epidemics. Two years later, he published *The Negro; as He Was; as He Is; as He Will Be*, which he dedicated to "The Old South" "Out of an Affection respectful and a just remembrance of her." The volume discussed the supposed retrogression of African Americans into criminality after emancipation. According to Fulkerson, African life was uncivilized, and the racial characteristics of Africans were "as immutable as any of the laws of nature." Through slavery, Africans could be civilized, taught work habits, and converted to Christianity, but emancipation and especially gaining the right to vote were tragic mistakes, leading to unrealizable expectations and inevitable conflict. Fulkerson concluded that physical separation was the only solution to southern race relations and urged the US government to take the money being spent on African American education and instead use it to "give [the African] a country all to himself," perhaps in the Caribbean or Central America.

Ted Ownby
University of Mississippi

Stephen Cresswell, *Rednecks, Redeemers, and Race: Mississippi after Reconstruction, 1877–1917* (2006); Percy L. Rainwater, *Mississippi Valley Historical Review* (1937).

Fusion Politics

In the late 1870s and early 1880s, Mississippi's Republicans, Greenbackers, and independents joined forces to attempt to overthrow the entrenched Democrats. After some brief successes in the early 1880s, the experiment in fusion and cooperation declined, and Democrats moved the state toward the disfranchisement of African Americans in the 1890s. A solid, one-party state emerged.

Fusion politics arose for several reasons. First, an economic downturn and decline in cotton prices led many agrarians to support the new Greenback Party, which promised an inflated currency and government intervention in the economy. Beginning in the late 1870s, the Mississippi Greenback Party found support among former Whigs, some African Americans, and some white small farmers. Greenback strength was concentrated in the north-central section of the state. Second, the Democratic Party, controlled by merchants, lawyers, and railroad interests, refused to accede to the small farmers' demands. Third, straight tickets of Republicans, Greenbackers, and independents at the county and congressional levels could not win in four-way fights, so leaders and activists advocated fusion tickets. Fusion was a marriage of convenience, not an ideological or programmatically coherent enterprise: the parties never formally fused but merely saw cooperating as the only way to defeat the Democrats. To coalesce, fusionists focused on securing federal supervisors of elections (and thus, honest elections) and local control of government (home rule).

To siphon off Democrats and appeal to more than just activists, the fusionists persuaded several important Democrats to bolt their party. Former Democrat Benjamin King, a state senator from Copiah County, ran for the governorship in 1881, winning 40 percent of the vote but losing to Robert Lowry. Other converts included lawyer Elza Jeffords and Confederate hero James R. Chalmers. Despite massive fraud and violence across the state, the fusionists captured two congressional districts in 1882—one after a contested election case—and won scores of local offices. However, not all opponents of Democrats favored fusion. Some Republicans and Greenbackers ran independently. Some African Americans, including Republican leader John R. Lynch, preferred sharing offices with Democrats to guarantee that at least some Republicans would hold office, particularly in the Black Belt, where political fraud and violence were common.

Fusionists' victories proved sporadic and short-lived. The Democrats, seeing their power erode and fearing that fusion politics might expand, co-opted much of the Greenbackers' platform; used fraud and violence to steal scores of elections, leading to a US Senate investigation in 1883; and used the color line to lambaste their opponents. In addition, the fusionists began to divide over strategy and office sharing. Many fusionists became disillusioned and demoralized as their newspapers closed down and the Democrats controlled the national government. By 1886 fusion forces were in disarray, and by the end of the decade, in the face of terrible violence and massive fraud, the experiment was dead. Not until the rise of the Populist Party in the 1890s would Democratic hegemony again come under threat.

Despite the fusion forces' failure to sustain their opposition to the Democrats, capture the governorship, or control the state legislature, the fusion experiment affected Mississippi politics. It showed that alliances could oust the Democrats and that grassroots oppositional movements could work, a legacy on which the Populists built. Fusion forced the Democrats, at least for a time, to acknowledge farming interests, though the party's leadership quickly returned to ignoring agrarian issues in the 1890s.

James M. Beeby
University of Southern Indiana

Stephen Cresswell, *Multiparty Politics in Mississippi, 1877–1902* (1995); Michael R. Hyman, *The Anti-Redeemers: Hill Country Political Dissenters in the Lower South from Redemption to Populism* (1990); Albert D. Kirwan, *Revolt of the Rednecks: Mississippi Politics, 1876–1925* (1951).

G

Gaines, George Strother
(1794–1873) Negotiator and Businessperson

George Strother Gaines is most famous for his role in negotiating and then leading the Choctaw Removal from Mississippi. Born 1 May 1794 in Stokes County, North Carolina, Gaines moved with his family (including his older brother, Edmund Pendleton Gaines, a noted US Army officer) to the area around Gallatin, Tennessee; ten years later Gaines moved to Fort St. Stephens in the Mississippi Territory (now Alabama) to apprentice as an Indian factor, assuming full duties at the Choctaw Trading House in 1807. After moving the Trading House to the west bank of the Tombigbee River, he resigned his position in 1818 to pursue new business opportunities, especially banking, relocating to Demopolis, Alabama, in 1822. While there, Gaines served two terms in the Alabama State Senate.

Gaines's trading relationships with a number of Choctaw leaders, including Pushmataha, led to his involvement in the negotiations in Macon, Mississippi, that led to the 1830 Treaty of Dancing Rabbit Creek. A year later he served as the federal liaison overseeing the groups of Choctaw who traveled through Arkansas to survey Oklahoma lands for Choctaw settlement, and he subsequently supervised Choctaw movement into that territory. In 1831, as Gaines watched hundreds of Choctaw boarding boats in Vicksburg, he wrote, "The feeling, which many of them evince in separating, never to return again, from their long cherished hills, as poor as they are in this section of the country, is truly painful to witness; and would be more so to me, but for the conviction that removal is absolutely necessary for their preservation and future happiness."

Gaines moved to Mobile in 1832 and became president of the Bank of Mobile and established a dry goods business. In 1844–45 he served on a three-member committee that met in Philadelphia, Mississippi, to investigate land claims by Choctaw who felt that the US government had not kept its promises to them. He also became deeply involved in the establishment of the Mobile & Ohio Railroad through the Tombigbee Valley.

Sometime after 1850, Gaines moved to a ranch in Perry County and then to other landholdings in Wayne County. In 1856 he began a final business venture, Peachwood Nurseries, near State Line. By the standards of southwestern Mississippi, he and his family were large slave owners, with more than twenty slaves. Gaines was elected to the Mississippi House of Representatives, making him one of the few men to serve in the legislatures of two states. A Confederate supporter, he resigned in 1863 because of poor health.

Gaines married Ann Lawrence in 1812, and they had nine children, most notably businessmen George Washington Gaines and Abner Strother Gaines. Ann Gaines died in 1868, and George Strother Gaines died five years later.

Gene C. Fant Jr.
Palm Beach Atlantic University

George Strother Gaines, *The Reminiscences of George Strother Gaines: Pioneer and Statesman of Early Alabama and Mississippi, 1805–1843*, ed. James P. Pate (1998).

Gaines, Marion Viola Stark
(1850–1942) Photographer

Marion Viola Stark Gaines, Mississippi's earliest known published woman photographer, was born in Columbus on 10 August 1850 to Peter Stark and Sarah Bradford Short Stark. Shortly thereafter, the Starks moved to Mobile, Alabama, where her father worked as a cotton merchant. On 13 February 1879 Marion married Capt. Abner Strother Gaines and moved to Peachwood, his family's plantation and nursery at State Line in Wayne County, Mississippi, where their four children were born.

While at Peachwood in the 1890s and early 1900s Gaines experimented with photography and was influenced by pictorialism, a cultural and artistic movement that regarded photographs as true art and not simply records of reality. Gaines's photographs depict floral themes and life in her home and community. Her still lifes of native flowers and plants include magnolias and camellias, pinecones and peaches, as well as some exotic horticultural varieties. Her images of family, neighbors, and places—her daughter, Viola, reading a book in a vine-covered doorway; her son, Edmund, holding a dead rabbit and a gun after a hunting trip; African Americans packing bales of cotton on the porch of a log cabin; a young woman shelling peas; and Choctaw women and girls holding flower chains—provide insight into life in South Mississippi more than a century ago.

Marion Stark Gaines, ca. 1890s (Marion Stark Gaines Photograph Collection, Billups-Garth Archives, Columbus-Lowndes Public Library)

Gaines's photographs were published in various ladies' and photography magazines. In 1900 she won an award in portraiture from the Association Camera Club in Mobile for a picture of her daughter. In June 1901 *Photo-Eye* published "By the West Window," in which Gaines discussed the difficulties and challenges of photographing flowers. The same month *Ladies' Home Journal* showcased one of her pictures of Peachwood Plantation in a competition featuring images of log cabins. Gaines's interest in photography diminished after the death of her husband in 1905. Shortly thereafter, she moved back to Mobile, where she lived until her death on 11 August 1942.

More than half a century after her death, the work of this pioneering photographer began attracting academic and public interest. In 1999 both the Old Capitol Museum and the Mississippi Museum of Art in Jackson mounted exhibitions featuring Gaines's photographs, and in 2003 the Columbus-Lowndes Public Library showed her artwork and photography. The Mississippi Digital Library provides a portal for researching and exploring images from the Marion Stark Gaines Photography Collection at the Columbus-Lowndes Public Library.

Mona Vance-Ali
Columbus-Lowndes Public Library

Gene Fant Jr., *Mississippi Magazine* (May–June 1997); Marion Stark Gaines, *Photo-Era* (June 1901); Marion Stark Gaines Photography Collection, Billups-Garth Archives, Columbus-Lowndes Public Library, Columbus, Miss.; Mississippi Digital Library website, http://collections.msdiglib.org; N. C. Wyeth, *Ladies' Home Journal* (June 1901).

Galloway, Charles Betts
(1849–1909) Religious Leader

Born in Kosciusko, Mississippi, in 1849, Charles Galloway became a bishop in the Methodist Episcopal Church, South and one of the state's leading postbellum religious figures.

Galloway attended the University of Mississippi as a teenager after the Civil War. Following his graduation, he married Harriet Willis of Vicksburg, and the two moved to Black Hawk for his first ministerial position. The young couple were strong supporters of education, including Sunday schools, and Harriet Galloway became the first president of the Women's Missionary Union in Mississippi. Charles Galloway quickly became a Methodist leader, beginning his work as editor of the *New Orleans Christian Advocate* in 1882 and serving as minister at churches in Vicksburg and Jackson. At his urging, First Methodist Church of Jackson completed a new building in 1883. In 1886, at age thirty-seven, he was named a bishop, earning the nickname the Boy Bishop.

Galloway provided leadership and commentary on the most important issues in religious life. An ardent supporter of missionary work, he traveled to Latin America, Asia, Europe, and the Middle East to spread the Gospel, detailing his travels in *A Circuit of the Globe* (1895).

As the head of one of Mississippi's most popular denominations, Galloway became a popular speaker at graduations, dedications, and other ceremonial events, among them the founding of Millsaps College and the dedication of the New Capitol. His language tended to be lofty and optimistic, with

Charles Betts Galloway (Archives and Records Services Division, Mississippi Department of Archives and History [PI 2001.0018 Box 257 R67 B554 Folder 13 #223])

great hopes that education, good government, and Christianity were leading to a better nation and world.

At a time when many ministers preferred not to take a stand on the issue, Galloway was a public proponent of Prohibition laws, and in 1887 he debated Jefferson Davis in the press on the issue of alcohol sales. The two public figures argued, often in debater's language that alternated between great esteem and irritated rebuke. Galloway lamented that such an eminent figure as Davis could let his words be used by supporters of saloons, and Davis criticized Galloway for moving toward the "forbidden union of church and state." Galloway emphasized that opposing the sale of alcohol was simply part of the "duties of citizenship."

Galloway was a leading supporter of higher education and uplift. He was crucial to Millsaps's founding and served as president of the Methodist Episcopal Church, South Board of Education as well as on the boards of trustees at Vanderbilt University and the University of Mississippi. His interest in education informed his ideas about race relations. He always advocated the education of African Americans, particularly industrial training, and openly opposed James K. Vardaman and others who sought to cut funding to African American schools.

Historian Ray Holder argues that Galloway was torn between a desire for kindness and brotherhood with African Americans on one hand and participation in the life of white southerners of his generation on the other. He grew up among Confederate supporters and heard sermons as a child that "proved to my perfect satisfaction that the South was bound to win." He was an insistent supporter of the Lost Cause, celebrated the Confederacy, and denounced the policies of Reconstruction. In a 1903 address, "The South and the Negro," the bishop made clear that he supported segregation and political discrimination. According to historian Charles Reagan Wilson, Galloway advanced "four principles for race relations: no social mixing, separate schools and churches, white control of politics, and opposition to the colonization of blacks." However, Galloway was frustrated by the violence and hatred found in turn-of-the-century Mississippi, declaring that "any policy which tends to inflame prejudice and widen the racial chasm postpones indefinitely the final triumphs of the Son of Man among the sons of men." He condemned lynching, overt displays of hatred, and the politicians who benefited from heated language about preserving white supremacy. Without ever holding up possibilities of equality, Galloway urged that white Mississippians had two main duties with regard to African Americans—making sure all people were protected under the law, and improving education.

After Galloway's death in 1909, First Methodist Church in downtown Jackson was renamed Galloway Memorial United Methodist Church.

Ted Ownby
University of Mississippi

Charles Betts Galloway, *Christianity and the American Commonwealth* (1898); Charles Betts Galloway, *Great Men and Great Movements: A Volume of Addresses* (1914); Ray Holder, *Mississippi Methodists, 1799–1983: A Moral People "Born of Conviction"* (1984); Charles Reagan Wilson, *Baptized in Blood: The Religion of the Lost Cause, 1865–1920* (1980).

Gambling

In 1992 dockside gambling became legal on navigable waterways in Mississippi, leading to unprecedented growth and challenges. However, gambling has existed in the state for centuries; only the means and scope differ today. Native Chickasaw, Choctaw, and Natchez, the three most historically significant indigenous peoples in pre-European Mississippi, regularly engaged in gambling practices, often centered on the outcome of games such as stickball and chunky, which resembles handball. Hundreds of players spent days competing, while both spectators and players wagered their valuables on its conclusion.

As Spain, France, and England sought control of North America during the seventeenth century, their cultural pastimes diffused across what is now Mississippi. In the 1790s, when the region was a Spanish possession, the Fleetfield Race Track in the early urban center of Natchez provided citizens with opportunities for betting and socializing. By the early 1800s "gambling houses" crowded the narrow strip of land at Natchez-under-the-Hill along the Mississippi River, and as steamboats became common over the next two decades, the area offered ample opportunities to travelers.

The Tivoli Hotel in Biloxi, built in 1926–27, provided legal gambling with slot machines in its lobby. The hotel was demolished after being damaged by Hurricane Katrina. Photo ca. 1929 (Ann Rayburn Paper Americana Collection, Department of Archives and Special Collections, J. D. Williams Library, University of Mississippi [rayburn_ann_29_159_001])

Organized religious groups in Natchez, Vicksburg, and other river towns attempted to curb gambling activities, especially after the revivalism of the Second Great Awakening in the 1830s, but Mississippians continued to enjoy betting on activities such as yacht racing, billiards, and bowling. In 1849, Pass Christian, a small town along the Gulf Coast, became home to the first yacht club in the South, regularly hosting races for tourists.

As early as 1847, however, Biloxi had become the most popular tourist destination along the coast. Steamboats brought visitors from New Orleans to such establishments as Madame Pradat's, the Nixon Hotel, the Shady Grove Hotel, and the Magnolia Hotel, where they enjoyed dancing, hunting, boating—and gambling. After the devastation of the Civil War, passenger rail service was inaugurated between Mobile and New Orleans in 1870, returning Biloxi to its antebellum prominence in the tourist industry.

New Orleanians legalized the lottery in 1868 and prizefights in 1890. Because of the Mississippi Gulf Coast's proximity and popularity among vacationers and investors from Louisiana, the Magnolia State offered many of the same gambling opportunities. Reciprocity appeared to exist between the two locations. For example, John L. Sullivan fought Paddy Ryan in Mississippi City on 7 February 1882, claiming the title of heavyweight champion of the world in bareknuckle fighting. Sullivan also battled Jack Kilrain in 1889 at Richburg, near present-day Hattiesburg, the last bareknuckle event in Mississippi, which had outlawed such fights. Louisiana subsequently legalized prizefighting, likely in response to the Mississippi ban.

By the early twentieth century shell roads and trolley lines crisscrossed the twenty-two-mile coast, transporting visitors as well as residents. After the United States enacted Prohibition on 1 July 1919, ships from Biloxi and other coastal localities continued to bring illegal liquor from the Caribbean Islands to various Mississippi Sound ports and barrier islands. One attractive location for these clandestine activities was Dog Key (also known as the Isle of Caprice). Three Biloxi entrepreneurs, Col. Jack W. Apperson, developer of the Buena Vista Hotel; Walter H. "Skeet" Hunt; and Arbeau Caillavet pooled resources and opened the Isle of Caprice casino, dance hall, bathhouse, and refreshment pavilion on 30 May 1926. The resort remained in operation until 1932, when the key disappeared into the sound's waters, taking the casino with it. However, the lure of gambling did not disappear.

Grand Gulf Coast hotels such as the Pine Hills, the Edgewater Gulf, the White House, and the Tivoli enticed tourists even after Prohibition ended in 1933 and into the Great Depression. On 8 July 1937 the *Biloxi Daily Herald* reported that 254 slot machines had been checked in Gulfport. The Edgewater Hotel was famous for high-stakes poker games and other gambling activities known as the "lounge business." In addition, some individuals owned gambling machines and paid federal gambling taxes to operate these devices.

Gulf Coast gambling operations expanded during the 1940s and 1950s, driven in part by the thousands of World War II–era troops training at Biloxi's Keesler Air Force Base. The string of nightclubs along Highway 90 became known as the Strip.

In the 1950s the Biloxi Protestant Ministerial Association called for an investigation into the open nightlife and gambling machine operations. Tennessee senator Estes Kefauver's Organized Crime Committee investigated gambling in the region, leading to a backlash against some types of gambling machines, including slots, but pinball machines quickly filled that niche. The Fiesta, the Beach Club, Mr. Lucky's, and Gus Stevens's Club all offered opportunities for betting in the 1960s along the Gulf Coast. The *Biloxi Daily Herald* reported 362 residents of Harrison, Hancock, and Jackson Counties had paid 408 gaming device stamps in 1964. After 1969's Hurricane Camille destroyed many of the clubs along the Strip, the coast rebuilt by courting a new image as a family resort area, not a gaming destination.

In 1988 the federal Indian Gaming Regulatory Act allowed Indian tribes to open casinos, and the Mississippi Band of Choctaw Indians opened the Silver Star Casino in Neshoba County. Coastal interests began lobbying to reinstate gambling, and on 29 June 1990 the state legislature passed the Mississippi Gaming Control Act, which permitted gambling on vessels docked along the Mississippi River or on the Mississippi Sound if a majority of county residents voted to allow it. Hancock County voters approved dockside gambling in December 1990, with Harrison County following three months later.

On 1 August 1992 the Isle of Capri opened its doors to legalized riverboat gambling in Biloxi, with other establishments soon following that lead. In 2002, according to the American Gaming Association, Mississippi's thirty casinos employed more than thirty-two thousand workers, had $2.7 billion in revenue, and contributed more than $322 million in taxes to the state.

Hurricane Katrina caused massive damage to the coast's casinos and hotels, destroying the lower floors of land-based establishments and pushing some floating casinos inland, where they crashed into hotels and other structures. Mississippi subsequently changed its laws to permit casinos to operate on land rather than solely on barges, and the gambling industry helped fuel recovery from the hurricane, especially in Biloxi. As of 2013 Mississippi's gaming establishments had rebounded to employ twenty-three thousand people, generate gross revenues of $2.25 billion, and provide nearly $273 million in tax revenue. In addition, the Mississippi Band of Choctaw Indians now operates casinos in Philadelphia, Choctaw, and Heidelberg.

Deanne Stephens Nuwer
University of Southern Mississippi
Gulf Coast

American Gaming Association website, www.americangaming.org; Deanne Stephens Nuwer, Mississippi History Now website, http://ms history.k12.ms.us; Greg O'Brien, *Choctaws in a Revolutionary Age, 1750–1830* (2002); Denise Von Herrman, ed., *Resorting to Casinos: The Mississippi Gambling Industry* (2006).

Gandy, Evelyn
(1920–2007) Politician

The first woman to hold several important positions in state government, Evelyn Gandy was born in Hattiesburg, graduated from Hattiesburg High School, and attended the University of Southern Mississippi. In 1943 she graduated from the University of Mississippi Law School, where she was the first woman president of the student body. Her politically active parents, Kearney C. and Abbie Whigham Gandy, always encouraged her interest in the law, politics, and public service and instilled in her the idea that gender need not impede her success in whatever she chose to do.

In 1947 Forrest County voters elected Gandy to represent them in the State House of Representatives, thus launching a political career that spanned almost four decades. In addition to serving in the House until 1952, she held the posts of assistant attorney general (1959), state commissioner (1972–76), and lieutenant governor (1976–80). Gandy was the first woman to serve in each of these state offices and became

Evelyn Gandy (Archives and Records Services Division, Mississippi Department of Archives and History [PI 2001.0018 Box 257 R67 Box 554 Folder 13 #224])

a role model for women—and men—in interested in seeking public office in Mississippi. Betsy Rowell, a Hattiesburg councilwoman, said, "Growing up, I actually believed I could do this because Ms. Gandy told me I could. She's dedicated her life to public service, and she made it look easy. I can tell you from where I sit that it's not. There were many times she was the only woman in a room making decisions."

As state treasurer Gandy implemented a program to ensure the fair and equitable distribution of state funds to all banks in Mississippi. Her actions also led to the placement of state funds in interest-bearing accounts. As commissioner of insurance, she worked to strengthen the regulation of insurance companies and standards for the licensing of agents. She also helped in the establishment of a state academy to train firefighters. As commissioner of public welfare, she worked to expand and strengthen programs and brought the department into compliance with the federal Civil Rights Act.

A progressive lieutenant governor, Gandy labored effectively for improvements in education, economic development, and health care, issues that she championed throughout her career. She was always especially sensitive to the needs of the mentally ill and the mentally disabled. She guided through the Senate a bill that established the State Ethics Commission. Her most important legacy was the passage of the Sixteenth Section Reform Act of 1978, which reformed the leasing of these lands and increased school revenues from between two and three million dollars per year to approximately seventy million dollars in 2014.

Evelyn Gandy twice sought the Democratic Party nomination for the Mississippi governorship, leading the field in the first primary but losing in runoffs to William Winter in 1979 and Bill Allain in 1983. Although friends and supporters urged her to run again in 1987, she declined.

After 1984 she practiced law with Ingram and Associates in Hattiesburg. Gandy remained politically active, lent her support to candidates, and encouraged women to become involved in politics. Her numerous honors and awards included the Margaret Brent award from the American Bar Association for paving the way to success for other female attorneys. In accepting the award Gandy stated, "Our civilization will truly never be refined until men and women work together in every phase of our society . . . in full equality, equal partnership, and mutual respect." In 2002 the State of Mississippi honored her by naming a segment of State Highway 42 encircling Hattiesburg the Evelyn Gandy Parkway. She died in 2007.

Martha Swain
Mississippi State University

Evelyn Gandy, interview by author; *Jackson Clarion-Ledger* (4 August 1997); *Hattiesburg American* (12 June 2002); Mississippi Department of Education website, www.mde.k12.ms.us.

Gay Life

Mississippi, the nation's poorest state, upsets dominant notions of lesbian, gay, bisexual, and transgender (LGBT) community and history. Though in many places queer life is conceived as an urban phenomenon, in Mississippi it more commonly has been characterized by the careful negotiation of local institutions—home, church, school, and workplace. Such sites are often assumed to be hostile to sexual and gender nonconformity, but such nonconformity has flourished in precisely these settings in Mississippi. Older LGBT Mississippians recall meeting sexual partners at church socials and family reunions, in classrooms and on shop floors, on athletic fields and at roadside rest areas. If households and employers, educational and religious organizations sometimes condemned "deviant" sexualities and genders, those institutions' buildings and grounds often became the most common sites for queer sexual activity.

Finding friends and partners across a largely rural landscape, queer Mississippians have relied on circulation as much as congregation. The state has long harbored queer networks but has only recently developed lesbian and gay cultures. Before the 1960s same-sex play between adolescents was tacitly condoned, and queer sex between adults was clandestine but common. Though an 1839 sodomy law criminalized oral and anal sex and seven men were imprisoned under the statute over the next four decades, homosexual activity was quietly accommodated with a prevailing pretense of ignorance. By the 1970s, however, LGBT identity politics and organized Christian resistance had grown hand in hand.

For women in particular, education and separatist organizations have proved critical in the forging of same-sex worlds and relationships. In the early 1890s suffragist Pauline Orr and Miriam Paslay created a life together as professors at the first state-funded women's college in the United States, the Industrial Institute and College (now Mississippi University for Women) in Columbus, where they promoted a broad curriculum rather than a focus on "domestic science." They also advocated equal pay for equal work at other state universities. A century later, Brenda and Wanda Henson founded Camp Sister Spirit near Ovett, a feminist retreat that hosted events for women only, lesbians, and gay men. Despite facing death threats, the Hensons also cultivated a nonprofit organization that worked to alleviate hunger, poverty, and bigotry in the region. Though anchored in state and local struggles for social change, Orr and Paslay and the Hensons became key figures in national and international women's reform movements.

When male public figures have been implicated in homosexual acts, mainstream media scandals historically have erupted. In the 1890s newspapers exposed Prof. William Sims, who was kicked off the faculty at the University of Mississippi, as well as planter-politician Dabney Marshall, who murdered his accuser. Jon Hinson represented Mississippi's 4th District in the US House of Representatives from 1979 until 1981, when he was forced to resign after being charged with sodomy. Two years later, gubernatorial candidate Bill Allain faced rumors that he had engaged in homosexual acts with two male transvestites but nevertheless won election. While oppressive discourses continually cast homosexuality as new or as elsewhere, a number of Mississippians have produced queer narratives with local settings—playwrights Mart Crowley and Tennessee Williams, novelists Hubert Creekmore and Thomas Hal Phillips, poets and memoirists William Alexander Percy and Kevin Sessums, physique artist and pulp novelist Carl Corley.

Scandals involving black civil rights activist Aaron Henry and white advocate Bill Higgs marked a crucial turning point in regional queer history. When accused in the early 1960s of intercourse with younger men, the two movement leaders denied the allegations, a required response given the cultural climate of the times. But these charges linked queer sexuality and racial equality, both in alarmist rhetoric and in practice, and the strident legal-political crackdown against members of the LGBT community that emerged elsewhere in the 1950s did not reach Mississippi until the following decade and formed part of the massive resistance to African American freedom struggles.

Establishments that accommodated or were friendly to the LGBT community date back nearly a century, with "gay bars" existing from the 1940s onward in Mississippi. Most of these establishments catered to mixed clienteles—young and old, women and men, gender normative and nonnormative. Mirroring larger divides, however, these businesses often have remained racially segregated. When towns and cities achieved the critical mass to support more than one queer bar, separate black and white establishments usually resulted. In Jackson in the 1970s and 1980s, for example, the two were located directly across the street from one another.

Although fundamentalist preachers from Mississippi have founded some of today's most prolific vehicles of homophobia (Donald Wildmon's American Family Association and Fred Phelps's Westboro Baptist Church), many queer Mississippians, black and white, have retained strong commitments to Christian spirituality. While the Mississippi Gay Alliance, founded in 1973, and its longtime leader, Eddie Sandifer, often advocated a radical political agenda linking various left causes, the most successful organizing, Sandifer concedes, has occurred through LGBT congregations such as the Metropolitan Community Church, which opened in Jackson in 1983. The twenty-first-century political struggle has largely been led by Equality Mississippi and its executive director, Jody Renaldo.

Transgender persons have occasionally found amenable physicians, including gay doctor Ben Folk, and hospitals for treatments, as at the University Medical Center in Jackson. More frequently they have traveled abroad for lower-cost sex reassignment surgery. While only a minority of queer Mississippians have moved to major out-of-state cities, many have returned regularly throughout their lives and permanently in retirement. Ironically, as mainstream media fixate on rural prejudice and brutality, American antiviolence projects report a far greater incidence of homophobic assault and murder in urban centers, with their high LGBT visibility. Thus, some LGBT people find greater safety in Mississippi, whereas many queer urbanites consider the form of selective visibility practiced there an ideological impossibility. Often belittled as backward or exceptionally repressive, Mississippi continues to hold a deep emotional grip on many of its queer natives.

In recent years, issues of law and politics have been central to gay and lesbian life. Beginning in 1993 state and federal courts, the US Congress, state legislatures, and state referenda tackled the issue of same-sex marriage, with some states permitting it and others as well as the federal government defining marriage as solely involving a man and a woman. In response to this patchwork of laws, numerous gay and lesbian residents of Mississippi and other states where same-sex marriage remained illegal began traveling outside their home states to be married elsewhere. In 2015, however, the US Supreme Court ruled in *Obergefell v. Hodges* that all laws against same-sex marriage were unconstitutional, and Mississippi's first same-sex marriages took place.

In the spring of 2016 the Mississippi legislature passed House Bill 1523, dubbed by its sponsors the "Religious Liberty Accommodations Act," and Gov. Phil Bryant signed it into law on 5 April. The act declared that public employees, businesses, and social workers could not be punished for denying services based on the beliefs that marriage is strictly between a man and a woman, that sexual intercourse should only take place within such a marriage, and that gender is determined at birth. In addition, the measure said that the government could not prevent businesses from firing transgender employees, clerks from refusing to license same-sex marriages, or adoption agencies from refusing to place children with unmarried couples believed to be having sex. Finally, the law declared that businesses and other institutions could not be prevented from establishing "sex-specific standards or policies concerning employee or student dress or grooming, or concerning access to restrooms, spas, baths, showers, dressing rooms, locker rooms, or other intimate facilities or settings." Authors claimed that the law protected business owners and public officials from being forced to violate their religious beliefs. Opponents, however, argued that the measure in fact sanctioned religious discrimination, permitting people to impose their religious views on others, and compared it to earlier religion-based arguments for racial segregation. As with North Carolina's better-known "Bathroom Bill," other states and localities responded by banning employees from nonessential travel to Mississippi, and several governments warned LGBT travelers about visiting the state. In late June, just before the law was to go into effect on 1 July, a US district court judge issued a series of injunctions against the law, declaring that it violated the Equal Protection Clause and the Establishment Clause of the US Constitution.

John Howard
King's College London

Michael Bibler, *Cotton's Queer Relations: Same-Sex Intimacy and the Literature of the Southern Plantation, 1936–1968* (2009); Kate Greene, *Women and Politics* 17 (1997); John Howard, in *Queer Studies: An Interdisciplinary Reader*, ed. Robert J. Corber and Stephen Valocchi (2003); John Howard, ed., *Carryin' On in the Lesbian and Gay South* (1997); Sarah Kaplan, *Washington Post* (31 March 2016); Sarah Wilkerson-Freeman, "Love and Liberation: Southern Women-Loving-Women and the Power of the Heart," Paper Presented to the Organization of American Historians (April 2003); Benjamin E. Wise, *William Alexander Percy: The Curious Life of a Mississippi Planter and Sexual Freethinker* (2012).

Gayoso de Lemos, Manuel
(1747–1799) Spanish Governor

Manuel Gayoso de Lemos was the most famous Spanish ruler of Natchez. He was born in 1747 in Portugal to a Spanish diplomat and Portuguese woman. His education included languages, diplomatic skills, and military training, all of which proved beneficial to his career as an administrator of Spanish colonies in North America.

Spain gained control of the Natchez District after its victories over the British in the Lower Mississippi Valley during the Revolutionary War and decided to upgrade the settlement from an isolated military post to what they hoped would be a more prosperous colony. Gayoso was appointed as governor of the district in 1787 with orders from the Spanish Crown to bolster the region so that it would provide better protection for Spain's more lucrative possessions in Mexico.

He faced a monumental task. When Gayoso arrived in 1789, Natchez was a small frontier settlement built around a dilapidated fort on the river. He oversaw the creation and development of the town and initiated policies to entice settlers to the region. He encouraged agricultural innovation to find a cash crop that would strengthen the local economy. Unlike many Spanish colonial rulers, he did not force Catholicism on the city's residents. Persons of other denominations could not preach in public but could worship in their own homes. He improved the district's defenses by building forts at present-day Vicksburg and Memphis and helped conclude important treaties with Native Americans to prevent the United States from encroaching on Spanish territory.

Gayoso had a congenial personality and charmed Natchez. He frequently held lavish social and political gatherings at his mansion, Concorde. Under his regime, the Natchez District grew and gained new settlers; however, Spain's hold on the territory remained tenuous.

In 1795, with the United States expanding, its leaders negotiated the Treaty of San Lorenzo (also known as Pinckney's Treaty) with Spain. The agreement granted the United States free usage of the Mississippi River and set the thirty-first parallel as the northern boundary of Spanish Florida, transferring the Natchez District to the young nation. Gayoso and other Spanish leaders subsequently attempted to nullify the treaty, offering excuses to American officials and delaying the Spanish evacuation of the area. Spain finally relinquished control in March 1798.

By that time Gayoso had already departed. He had received a promotion to governor-general of Louisiana and West Florida and reported to New Orleans in 1797. He died there of yellow fever on 18 July 1799.

Clay Williams
Mississippi Department of
Archives and History

Jack D. Elliott Jr., *Journal of Mississippi History* (Winter 1997); Jack D. L. Holmes, *Gayoso: Life of a Spanish Governor in the Mississippi Valley, 1789–1799* (1965); Jack D. L. Holmes, in *A History of Mississippi* (1973).

Genealogy and Genealogists

In Mississippi, where introductions are commonly followed by questions such as "Where are you from?" and "Who is your mother?," it is easy to understand why genealogy is a common hobby. Genealogy is defined as the history of the descent of a person or family from a particular ancestor. It is an interdisciplinary pursuit, involving geography; local, state, and national history; sociology; political science; economics; and archaeology, among other areas. Compiling the history of a family usually requires the use of original contemporary records such as censuses (both state and federal), tax rolls, land grants and deeds, wills or estate records, church records, county histories, and vital records (birth, marriage, and death certificates). Newspaper articles and obituaries as well as personal journals and manuscripts often provide details about daily life. Maps of the area and cemetery transcriptions can help to pinpoint the family's original home site. And photographs of the family or individual are a bonus if they have been preserved. Tracing a family's history may require the skills of a detective, who must uncover clues to connect one generation to another, and of a puzzle solver, who can take one piece of information and fit it into the picture of a family.

When doing genealogy, some people concentrate on one family and compile family stories and documentation going back to an immigrant ancestor or even further. Others research only a few generations. And still others become so captivated by the search that they work on one family and then move on to another until they have documented grandparents and great-grandparents for ten generations or more.

While genealogy is the history of a family, a genealogist researches and prepares genealogies or family histories. Most genealogy in Mississippi is done by individuals researching their own families, and they may refer to themselves not as genealogists but as family historians or researchers. A few individuals become professionals and provide genealogical research services for others. One of Mississippi's first professional genealogists was Richard Lackey of Forest, who developed a national reputation and has been inducted into the National Genealogical Society Hall of Fame. Other Mississippians have earned varying levels of accreditation from the Board for Certification of Genealogists. Most of the state's libraries and archives provide lists of persons who have some expertise in local and/or statewide research and who will do research for individuals for a fee. Major genealogical research collections are held by the Mississippi Department of Archives and History, Cook Library at the University of Southern Mississippi, the Laurel-Jones County Library, the Pascagoula Library, and the Aberdeen Public Library. Most county and regional libraries collect local and family information on their area, and nearly all libraries offer online catalogs, enabling researchers to look for specific holdings without leaving their homes.

Genealogists benefit from sharing questions and research findings with others, often through genealogical organizations in the relevant geographic area. Mississippi has two statewide genealogical organizations. The Mississippi Genealogical Society bases membership on the recommendation of two current members, while the Family Research Association of Mississippi is open to anyone who wants to join. Most counties also have genealogical and/or historical societies that preserve and publish local history and help researchers looking for local contacts and information.

Sandra Boyd
Mount Olive, Mississippi

Val D. Greenwood, *The Researcher's Guide to American Genealogy* (1990); Anne S. Lipscomb and Kathleen S. Hutchison, *Tracing Your Mississippi Ancestor* (1994).

General Stores

General stores were vital to economic and social life in rural Mississippi from the early 1800s through the early 1900s. Today, the long and narrow wooden buildings stir nostalgia in many people by evoking rural community. In their day, with their walls lined with various goods and their owners trying to keep up with the latest trends, these stores connected farming people to an intriguing range of tastes and experiences. In frontier areas, proud settlers often believed that general stores were signs of civilization and good taste.

Shopping corresponded to the social divisions in rural Mississippi. Men drank alcohol and lounged on the buildings' front porches, making general stores primarily male institutions. Women sometimes felt uncomfortable and stayed away, especially on weekends. Postbellum general stores usually accepted African American customers' money but often forced them to enter via the back door and refused to allow them to try on clothing before purchasing.

The white men who did the majority of shopping concentrated on what they saw as necessities—tools, shoes, hats, flour, tobacco. About half of their purchases were cloth or sewing notions. Few bought luxury goods, although general store merchants consistently advertised that they had the latest items from urban centers. Mississippians who bought luxuries generally traveled to cities or had agents buy goods for them.

Most shoppers at general stores did business on credit. Store owners recorded purchases in a ledger, and customers planned to pay in the fall when the crops came in. A minority paid with produce. Farmers who worried about staying out of debt tended to keep their purchases to a minimum. Many traveled to general stores only once a month, enjoyed a day at or around the general store, and then loaded their wagons and returned home. Most general stores were independent businesses, some owned by Russian Jews or other immigrants who started out as traveling peddlers. Some general stores served the interests of powerful economic institutions by dealing only in scrip issued by plantations or timber companies.

Novelists and memoirists frequently mention general stores as important sites for crossroads social life. In *Light in August* William Faulkner's Lena Grove has to summon all of her courage to brave the "man-eyes" that watch as she enters a general store to buy sardines. Faulkner's Ab Snopes makes his first stop in Yoknapatawpha County at a general store in search of land to farm. In memoirs by Clifton Taulbert and Charles Evers and stories by Mildred Campbell, black children encounter ridicule and terror at white-owned general stores. Eudora Welty's "The Little Store" emphasizes the magic she felt as a child when she first had the freedom to choose among small luxuries.

In the early twentieth century, department stores, chain stores, cash stores, and mail-order catalogs all offered a wider variety of goods and different types of shopping than did general stores. Department stores and the new grocery stores encouraged shoppers to walk around and choose goods for themselves rather than asking the storekeeper for one item at a time. Many general store buildings today have closed or sell secondhand items or antiques.

Ted Ownby
University of Mississippi

Thomas D. Clark, *Pills, Petticoats, and Plows: The Southern Country Store* (1944); Ted Ownby, *American Dreams in Mississippi: Consumers, Poverty, and Culture, 1830–1998* (1999).

Gentry, Bobbie (Roberta Lee Streeter)
(b. 1944) Musician

Bobbie Gentry is a singer-songwriter whose persona and work have come to be identified with Mississippi. Born on 27 July 1944 in Chickasaw County, Roberta Lee Streeter lived with her parents on a farm near Greenwood until she was thirteen, when the family moved to Palm Springs, California. Her interest in and aptitude for music appeared early—she wrote her first song, "My Dog Sergeant Is a Good Dog," at age seven.

While still in her teens, Streeter taught herself to play piano, banjo, guitar, bass, and vibes. She began performing at a country club during high school and continued to play in nightclubs while majoring in philosophy at the University of California at Los Angeles. She transferred to and graduated from the Los Angeles Conservatory of Music before moving to Las Vegas and becoming a dancer and actress and taking her stage name from a 1952 film, *Ruby Gentry*.

Gentry signed with Capitol Records in 1967, recording first a blues song, "Mississippi Delta," and then the song that made her world-famous, "Ode to Billie Joe." Originally a seven-minute song recorded with only her guitar accompaniment, "Ode to Billie Joe" was cut to five minutes and strings were added before it was released as her first single. Telling the story of how the narrator's friend, Billie Joe, dropped "something" (perhaps an illegitimate child) off the Tallahatchie Bridge before committing suicide, the song enjoyed tremendous success, moving past the Beatles' "All You Need Is Love" to No. 1 on the United States popular music charts. "Ode to Billie Joe" also rose to No. 13 in Britain and into the top 20 on the country music charts. The song won three Grammies, was recorded by multiple artists, and inspired a 1976 movie, *Ode to Billy Joe.*

G

In the wake of her success, Gentry became a headliner in Las Vegas while continuing to record both alone and with Glen Campbell. During this time, she married and divorced Bill Harrah, manager of the Desert Inn hotel and casino. After a series of moderate successes, including a handful of hits with Campbell, Gentry's recording of "I'll Never Fall in Love Again" became a No. 1 hit in the United Kingdom, prompting her to move to England. In 1974 she had a short-lived British television series, *The Bobbie Gentry Show*, before retiring from performing. After a second brief marriage to songwriter Jim Stafford, she returned to Los Angeles. Her retreat from the spotlight and continuing musical influence were the subject of a 2012 BBC documentary, *Whatever Happened to Bobbie Gentry?*

Although much of Gentry's life and career have been spent away from Mississippi, "Ode to Billie Joe" has become a classic, representing the rich blend of romance, exoticism, and horror that characterize popular conceptions of the singer's native state.

Taylor Hagood
Florida Atlantic University

Donald Clarke, ed., *The Penguin Encyclopedia of Popular Music* (1998); Colin Larkin, ed., *The Guinness Encyclopedia of Popular Music* (1995).

Geography

People around the world know of a place called *Mississippi*. Given the same Ojibwa name as the "great river" that runs along the area's western side (recorded far upstream in 1666 as *Messipi* by French explorers), the place is legendary. As a bounded area or an ordered unit of space—a state—Mississippi is one thing. As a place, it is quite another—or at least it is more. In the geographical imaginations and the mental maps of many people, Mississippi holds a place. While those imaginings may not please us all, this, too, is part of who we are, who we have been, and what this place is. Mostly, though, this place we call *Mississippi* is many things. It is many different places with different landscapes and different cultures.

From its highest land surfaces (Woodall Mountain, 806 feet) in the northeastern Tishomingo Hills near Tennessee and Alabama, Mississippi gently undulates downhill toward both the Mississippi River and the Gulf of Mexico. There, a narrow coastline faces the shallow Mississippi Sound and its barrier islands, beyond which lies the Gulf. Within the belted coastal plain of which Mississippi is a part, different landform (physiographic) regions, defined by surface formations, soils, and vegetation, provide subtle diversity both physically and culturally.

This geography makes Mississippi quite fascinating. Just like forests, hills, prairies, and coasts, expressions of culture change from place. Physical and cultural geographical characteristics interact and contribute to making places. The food we eat, the way we pray, the houses we build, the plants we grow, the cities we make, and the things we do for a living are as much a part of Mississippi's geography as our forests, hills, and rivers. Seeing how these things change across the state helps us understand a little more about who and what Mississippi is.

On a variety of Mississippi landscapes—pine-forested hill lands, narrow strips of plains, river valleys, and a coastal plain—humans have long found different ways to make livings and function as complex societies. In so doing, we produce distinct cultures and cultural landscapes. The landscapes that we make, then, serve both as rich contexts for life and as archival repositories, stores of information on who we are and were. Reading these landscapes throughout Mississippi can be as captivating, intriguing, and enlightening as any great book.

Mississippi is part of the Gulf Coastal Plain, mostly lowlands and low rolling hills. A humid subtropical climate provides general warmth and moisture throughout the year. Average temperatures vary from 82° F in July to 48° F in January, with the north becoming much cooler than the south in the winter months. Northern portions of the state receive approximately fifty inches of rainfall annually, with that number increasing toward the south to approximately sixty-one inches per year on the Gulf Coast. As a result of these climatic conditions, the environment sees rapid and significant plant growth, leading to an abundance of forestlands and long growing seasons, both of which have been integral to Mississippi's historical development.

Mississippi generally can be divided into four geographic regions: Pine Belt (Piney Woods or Southern Pine Hills), Northern Hills, Gulf Coast, and Yazoo Basin (Delta). Finer distinctions within these regions, especially the Pine Belt and Northern Hills, help distinguish more specific landform regions, which often have distinct cultural expressions. For example, the Northern Hills region contains the Northern or Red Clay Hills, Flatwoods, Pontotoc Ridge, Black Prairie, and Tishomingo (or Northeastern) Hills. The Black Prairie, a flat narrow strip of limestone-derived soil extending from Alabama (again, a former coastal plain), differs from the rest of the Northern Hills in its soil and related older plantation history and high African American population. However, most of the Northern Hills has a relatively high degree of cultural similarity. Mississippi's geographical diversity is probably best seen within this landform region classification system.

Understanding the origins of these landform regions even helps explain where Mississippi came from. Beginning about two hundred million years ago, the Appalachian and

Ouachita Mountain systems were basically connected in a single range that faced a southern coastline. Around ninety-five million years ago this chain was broken. Many think that this gap formed when it passed over a geologic hot spot, which pushed the land up two or three kilometers before it began to erode back down. When the land surface was no longer over the hot spot (about eighty-five million years ago), the land slowly sank back to where it had been, but the top two or three kilometers was missing. This gap—a depression called the Mississippi Embayment—created an opening for the new Mississippi River. At that time, the region now known as the Northeastern Hills or Tishomingo Hills—geologically distinct in Mississippi and the foot of the Appalachian Mountains—was the only land surface of modern Mississippi that existed.

Glaciers, droughts, and floods subsequently came and went across North America, and temperatures and the sea level rose and fell. Sediment steadily washed down from the Appalachians and into the embayment, slowly settling along the coast and building land.

Successive waves of deposition during different climatic regimes built more land, leaving exposures along or near former coastlines. Fossil sand dollars on the Chickasawhay River north of Waynesboro and other evidence testifies to the existence of these earlier coastlines. The belted coastal plain that is the Gulf Coast South, including most of Mississippi, slowly developed.

As rivers brought different types of sediment to the growing coast, different types of land surfaces came into existence. Some were built and then modified through erosion. The northwest-southeast trend of the natural regions testifies to their history as former gulf and/or river coastlines. The infamous and remarkably flat Delta is simply an alluvial flood basin lying next to these higher former coastlines and filled with the sediment of Mississippi and Yazoo River floods.

One distinct and more recent landform, the Loess Plateau or Loess Bluff region, is characterized by a fine silt deposited (presumably by wind) along the terraces overlooking the Mississippi River during and following the last North American glacial period. This layer, thickest at the western edge of the terrace overlooking the river valley (up to twenty-seven meters at Vicksburg), overlays other landform surfaces and thins toward the east. Easily eroded, high bluffs drop sharply to the river valley, providing protective sites for early important river towns such as Natchez and Vicksburg. These bluffs also housed ancient hardwood forests—for example, the big trees and numerous waterfalls of Clark Creek Natural Area near Fort Adams. The fertility of loess soil provided a context for Mississippi's early settlement in the Natchez District and its early plantations. However, the soil's tendency to erode hindered expansion. In fact, some scholars still define the Natchez District as a distinct culture region within Mississippi based on this early settlement and the related cultural diversity that characterizes the area.

An important part of who we are is where we are. In making our way in the world, we humans always influence environmental landscapes, at times with dramatic results. This, too, is part of our cultural imprint. Mississippi is certainly not immune to the human imprint, and practically everywhere in the state has been affected—our forests, pastures, lakes, and rivers. The postbellum removal of the giant hardwood forests of the Yazoo Basin and the destruction of more than 98 percent of the Pine Belt's great longleaf pine forests are good examples of our potential to effect change. That Mississippi has no place unaltered by humans is more or less certain.

Within Mississippi's different landform regions, settlement has taken many forms over time. The landscapes of Mississippi have experienced different cultures and histories as different groups of people have deployed a variety of adaptive strategies for different things and at different times, leaving a mosaic of cultural patterns.

The cultural and historical geography of Mississippi reflects the human drama that has unfolded in this warm, humid place. Historically, Native Americans hunted and farmed river valleys large and small. These groups eventually built cities, particularly along the edge of the Mississippi River Valley. Emerald Mound, near Vicksburg, is the second-largest mound in North America and provides a good example of the achievements of what is widely known as Mississippian culture. These complex societies experienced dramatic disruption as soon as the first Europeans passed through.

Europeans colonized the region beginning on the coast in 1699 and along the Mississippi River, particularly near Natchez in 1716. The slow processes of land appropriation and indigenous genocide that characterized European colonization may have started here with Hernando de Soto. By 1817 the territory was defined by its admission as a US state, and the process of colonization sped up, particularly after the 1831 Treaty of Dancing Rabbit Creek removed most indigenous inhabitants from the territory, opening it up for others.

The state generally was settled throughout the 1800s, largely by farmers and loggers and the towns that provided services to those settlers. Migrants from the East trickled in as land was opened for settlement, slowly cleared of its native inhabitants, and repopulated by Anglo and Celtic Protestants and African Americans. Some of the earlier Europeans were Anglo-Celtic cattle herders who practiced open-range herding in the grassy savanna landscape of the longleaf pine forests. Early plantations developed in the Natchez District and eastern Black Belt. Peasant farmers, mostly Anglo-Celtic, cleared farmland throughout the state. The Delta was cleared and settled primarily in the decades after the Civil War. The Pine Belt was settled more substantially around the turn of the twentieth century as the giant longleaf pine forests were cut for export.

Race constitutes an important component of this settlement history. The history of race in Mississippi is inherently a matter of geography. From the processes of migration and cultural diffusion to settlement patterns, voting patterns, and economic patterns, race manifests itself spatially. Segregation is among the most obvious examples. An understanding of race and race relationships is imperative to any attempt to understand Mississippi. In addition to indigenous genocide and the Trail of Tears, the long drama of "blacks" and "whites" in Mississippi has left a marked cultural geography, affecting where and how we live, how we worship, where we go to school, where we work, where we eat, where we socialize, and with whom. From the well-known Map of Mississippi Blues Musicians to Nina Simone's song "Mississippi Goddam," this geographical legacy has left imprints at many levels.

Until the 1930s African Americans were Mississippi's largest ethnic group, meaning that African American culture has had a tremendous impact. However, many other groups have moved, lived, cooked, worshipped, and spoken here—Choctaw, Lebanese, Vietnamese, Italians, Jews, French, Chinese, and others—creating a more complicated story that is also inherently a story of geography.

Like the river from which the state takes its name, Mississippi's geography continues to change. People move in and move out, changing cultural values and behavior. Rivers meander and change their courses, confusing political borders. Economic developments change lifestyles, environments, and towns. The evolution of technology and social values changes lands and lives throughout the state. How it all looks in the future is up to us.

J. O. Joby Bass
University of Southern Mississippi

S. S. Chapman, G. E. Griffith, J. M. Omernik, J. A. Comstock, M. C. Beiser, and D. Johnson, *Ecoregions of Mississippi* (2004); Ralph Cross and Robert Wales, *Atlas of Mississippi* (1974); Igor I. Ignatov, "Natural History and Phytogeography of the Loess Hills and Ravines, Lower Mississippi Embayment" (PhD dissertation, Louisiana State University, 2001); Terry G. Jordan, *North American Cattle Ranching Frontiers: Origins, Diffusion, and Differentiation* (1993); Arthell Kelley, *Mississippi Geographer* (1975, 1976, 1978, 1981); Arthell Kelley, *Southern Quarterly* (July 1963); James W. Loewen, *Mississippi Geographer* (1974); Stewart G. McHenry, *Mississippi Geographer* (1979); Mikko Saikku, *This Delta, This Land: An Environmental History of the Yazoo-Mississippi Floodplain* (2005); Roy B. Van Arsdale and Randel T. Cox, *Scientific American* (January 2007).

Geophagia (Eating Dirt)

Known throughout the world as the act of eating dirt, geophagia was noted as early as 460–370 BC by Hippocrates,

who wrote about the desire of pregnant women to engage in the practice. Geophagia, first described as a medical issue in 1563 as a form of pica (intentionally eating things that have no nutrient value), is practiced on almost every continent.

African slaves are thought to have brought the practice to the New World. Soil or clay eating later became a cultural tradition among southern, rural African American women and children. Geophagia is most often seen in pregnant and postpartum women. Dirt eating is reported among whites as well as African Americans, generally in the poorest areas of the South, though scholars debate the practice's connection to socioeconomic or educational status. Elders teach younger generations geophagia.

Psychological, economic, social, cultural, and biological or medical factors are recorded reasons for the practice of dirt eating, although the debate continues. Some people simply find that dirt tastes good, describing it as sour and smooth. Biological factors include eating dirt as a filler to suppress hunger; as a general health practice; as a medicine to satisfy iron, calcium, and/or zinc deficiencies (although some researchers dispute this); as a pregnancy craving; as a treatment for disease; as a method to absorb toxins; as a way to settle the stomach, especially during pregnancy; and as a means of softening or lightening skin. From an evolutionary standpoint, eating dirt may have been a way to adapt to the environment. Eating soil is also thought to strengthen the immune system.

The South has known dirt hills where diggings are visible. Dirt is dug from below the surface: deeper soil is considered to have fewer parasites. The dirt ideally should be smooth and without grit and usually is gray with red streaks when dug from the hillside. The soil is spread on a cookie sheet, seasoned with vinegar or other flavorings, and then baked in a wood-burning oven for an hour or smoked in the chimney.

After preparation, dirt is sour with an acidic taste, crunchy, and smooth; it melts in the mouth like chocolate. Some southerners mail dirt to family members in the North, and prepared dirt can be purchased on the Internet. White clay contains kaolin and tastes like aspirin. Kaolin is similar to medicines routinely used as antacids and antidiarrheal treatments.

Some scientists consider dirt eating harmful as well as a psychological disorder, and the amount eaten and the consequences of such consumption determine the degree of pathology. Problems associated with the practice include the ingestion of microorganisms, worm infestation, ingestion of lead or other toxins, altered electrolytes, intestinal obstruction, and constipation. The kaolin in dirt can be harmful during pregnancy, possibly causing low birth weight and mental disabilities, although research has not confirmed these effects. Dirt eaters may not get the nutrients needed if dirt is replacing food. Geophagia may decrease iron and zinc in the body but supplement calcium. Soil in populated areas may contain toxins, but in rural areas, the risk of harm from pollution is considered less threatening.

In 1942 it was reported that as many as 25 percent of African American children in one Mississippi county engaged in dirt eating; as recently as 1971, eating dirt was common in the state. The practice is now disappearing, although some people persist in private to avoid social stigma. In some cases, people suffering from pica eat starch or soda rather than dirt.

Jennie Gunn
University of Mississippi

Tom Corwin, *August Chronicle* (March 1999); Dorothy Dickens and Robert N. Ford, *American Sociological Review* (February 1942); Cynthia R. Ellis, EMedicine from WebMD website, http://emedicine.medscape.com; Dennis Frate, *Mississippi Folklife* (Fall 1999); Hilda Hertz, *Social Forces* (March 1947); Marc Lallanilla, *ABC News* (3 October 2005); Matt Rosenberg, About.com website, www.about.com; Alexander Woywodt and Akos Kiss, *Journal of the Royal Society of Medicine* (March 2002); Patrick Yao, "A Case of Geophagia," UCLA Department of Medicine (May 2007).

James Z. George (Archives and Records Services Division, Mississippi Department of Archives and History [PI PER G46 Box 16 Folder 42 #3])

George, James Z.
(1826–1897) Judge and Senator

Known as both the Great Commoner and as the author of disfranchisement provisions in Mississippi's Constitution, James Zechariah George was born in Monroe County, Georgia, on 26 October 1826. His family moved to Carroll County in 1836.

George served in the Mexican War in the First Mississippi Regiment, commanded by Jefferson Davis. On 27 May 1847, George married Elizabeth Brooks Young. He gained admission to the bar and became clerk of the High Court of Error and Appeals, prospering enough to increase the number of slaves he owned from twelve in 1850 to thirty a decade later. George won election to the state secession convention of 1861 and signed the Ordinance of Secession. During the Civil War he served as an officer in the 20th Mississippi Volunteers and the 5th Mississippi Cavalry, was captured twice by the Union Army, and spent two years as a prisoner of war.

After the conflict ended, George resumed the practice of law, establishing a profitable and high-profile partnership with Wiley P. Harris. In 1879 George was appointed to the Mississippi Supreme Court and elected chief justice. He also served on the board of trustees of both the University of Mississippi and the Agricultural and Mechanical College of the State of Mississippi (now Mississippi State University). He was elected to the US Senate in 1880 and won reelection in 1886 and 1892, though his final campaign was tainted by fraud and violence. He served for many years on the Senate Judiciary Committee and chaired the Agriculture and Forestry Committee.

George authored three books, *Decisions of the High Court of Errors and Appeals*, *Digest of the Decisions of the High Court of Errors and Appeals*, and *The Political History of Slavery in the United States*, which was not published until nearly two decades after his death.

George was generally popular and greatly respected among white Mississippians, in large part as a result of his effective defense of white supremacy. During the 1875 election, George persuaded Republican governor Adelbert Ames not to arm the African American militias by promising to try to ensure that the election was fair and peaceful. The Democrats won the election and assumed complete control of state government, ending Reconstruction in Mississippi.

George also devised the provisions of Mississippi's 1890 constitution that denied the franchise to African Americans without violating the letter of the Fifteenth Amendment and provided the "understanding clause" as a loophole for illiterate whites. He supported increasing the representation in the state legislature for the predominantly white counties. When Republican senators in Washington criticized the new Mississippi Constitution, George defended its voting provisions on the Senate floor. His approach was scholarly and legalistic. He pointed out northern states had for decades used the same sorts of franchise provisions and had maintained them even after the Civil War. George declared that African Americans should be treated fairly but also that they were incapable of responsible citizenship.

George died in Mississippi City, Mississippi, on 14 August 1897. More than three decades later, the state honored him and Davis with bronzes in the National Statuary Hall in the US Capitol. George's home, Cotesworth, near North Carrollton, is listed on the National Register of Historic Places.

Daniel C. Vogt
Jackson State University

Biographical Directory of the United States Congress; Dictionary of American Biography, vol. 4 (1931); James W. Garner, Publications of the Mississippi Historical Society (1903); Lucy Henderson Horton, Family History (1922); Lucy Bryan Peck, "The Life and Times of James Z. George" (master's thesis, Mississippi State University, 1964).

George County

Located in the Piney Woods region of southeastern Mississippi, George County is bounded to the east by the Alabama state line. The Chickasawhay and Leaf Rivers flow into the Pascagoula River near George's northern boundary, while the Escatawpa River traverses the county's southeastern corner. George was established on 16 March 1910 from lands formerly included in Jackson and Greene Counties. The county is named for James Z. George, a US senator from Mississippi. Lucedale, the county seat, takes its name from Gregory Luce, a lumber entrepreneur who moved to the area in the late nineteenth century, and is the hometown of mystery author Carolyn Haines and football star Eric Moulds, who played receiver for Mississippi State University and the NFL's Buffalo Bills.

In the 1910 census, George County had a total of 6,599 residents, of whom 72 percent were white and 28 percent were African American. Among the county's agricultural workforce, 96 percent owned their land, the highest percentage in the state.

George County experienced little overall population growth over the next two decades, with only 7,523 people in 1930. However, whites accounted for 87 percent of that total. George County had no cities and one of the state's lowest population densities. Landownership rates remained high.

George County's population topped eleven thousand in 1960 and fifteen thousand two decades later, when 88 percent of residents were white. George developed a small but significant manufacturing industry that produced transportation equipment. Although public administration was

George's largest employer, a significant portion of the county's laborers also worked in retail. Agriculture, which employed 14 percent of George's workforce, was concentrated on soybeans and hogs.

In 2010, George, like many southeastern Mississippi counties, remained predominantly white, included a small but significant Hispanic/Latino minority, and had experienced continued population increases, surpassing twenty-two thousand.

Mississippi Encyclopedia Staff
University of Mississippi

George County, Mississippi Genealogy and History Network website, http://George.msghn.org; Mississippi State Planning Commission, Progress Report on State Planning in Mississippi (1938); Mississippi Statistical Abstract, Mississippi State University (1952–2010); Charles Sydnor and Claude Bennett, Mississippi History (1939); University of Virginia Library, Historical Census Browser website, http://mapserver.lib.virginia.edu; E. Nolan Waller and Dani A. Smith, Growth Profiles of Mississippi's Counties, 1960–1980 (1985).

Germans

Some of the first Europeans to settle lands that subsequently became Mississippi and Louisiana were Germans. An influential force in early settlement, Germans created communities in many Gulf Coast territories, including the Côte des Allemands (German Coast), in present-day St. John the Baptist and St. Charles Parishes in Louisiana. The Mississippi Gulf Coast often served as entry into these other settlements in what are now Louisiana and Florida.

Early German settlers, seeking refuge from continual upheavals in their homeland, found refuge with French and English settlement companies that promised riches to all who would immigrate to North America. Among these early immigrants was Hugo Ernestus Krebs, a German from the disputed Alsace-Lorraine region. Settling in Pascagoula in 1730, Krebs married the daughter of influential Frenchman Joseph Simon de La Pointe. The Krebs family wielded great influence over the development of the Singing River area. Participating in local politics and commerce, the Krebses established a thriving nineteenth-century lumber shipping and shipbuilding community along the Gulf Coast. The Krebs name graces buildings such as the Old Spanish Fort, also known as the Krebs–La Pointe House, and Lake Chatahoula, now known as Krebs Lake.

Prior to the Civil War, many immigrants who settled in Mississippi congregated along the Gulf and in the Delta region. Many of these new arrivals did not engage in agriculture but instead pursued trades or railroad work. In Claiborne County, a region that experienced marked antebellum growth, foreign immigrants comprised roughly 18 percent of the total population. Germans, including members of the Bernheimer, Dischinger, Englesing, Frankenbush, Rinehart, Rohnbacker, and Seidlitz families, settled in Port Gibson and Grand Gulf, working primarily as laborers, merchants, and tradesmen.

German immigrants such as Ludwig Hafner (anglicized as Lewis Harper) and Eugene W. Hilgard participated in the growth of Mississippi's educational system. Employed as a professor of agricultural and geological studies at the University of Mississippi in 1854, Hafner soon became state geologist in Jackson. His replacement at the university, Hilgard, not only produced a geological survey for the state but also helped the Confederate cause with his knowledge of chemistry.

Land settlement agencies, often associated with railroad companies, enticed immigrants to settle along railroad lines in the late nineteenth century. Advertisements induced a group of immigrants from the Treia region of Germany who were living in the Chicago area to move south. Buying land from the Highland Colony Company, later known as the Gluckstadt Land and Improvement Company, members of the Schmidt, Klaas, Fitsch, Kehle, Hasse, and Weilandt families rode the Illinois Central Railroad's "immigration car" to Calhoun, Mississippi, which soon became known as Gluckstadt. Other families journeyed south on the railroad and settled in Ridgeland.

Many of these settlers established small farms, where they endured not only harsh agricultural conditions but smallpox and other diseases. Although some families decided to return to the North, most worked together to help Gluckstadt thrive. Predominantly Catholic, they initially focused on building churches, cemeteries, and religious schools, and the church, in turn, helped the community.

During the two world wars, those of German descent often encountered resentment and fear of their heritage. In Gluckstadt, Germans drew strength from one another and the Catholic Church. Many community members served in the United States armed forces, yet Madison County had the post office renamed *Calhoun* during World War I. By 1940, however, the German community was accepted as ethnically German but not "foreign," according to a Works Progress Administration survey that recorded the county as having no foreign population. Commemorating their German heritage and struggle to build a thriving town in Mississippi, Gluckstadt annually hosted Harvest Festivals until the 1950s.

In the latter part of the twentieth century, German families increasingly made the Gulf Coast their home after retirement from active military duty. In 1970 Germans accounted for nearly a third of all foreign-born persons in Mississippi and Alabama. While more recent years have seen a decline, Mississippi continues to attract German immigrants.

German culture remains a formidable influence as historical societies and heritage groups maintain links to their immigrant past. Since the mid-1980s Gluckstadt's St. Joseph Catholic Church has hosted an annual fall GermanFest, attracting fifteen thousand or more visitors. Other Oktoberfest celebrations can be found in smaller historically German communities such as Heidelberg, northeast of Laurel, and on the Gulf Coast, where the German American Society hosts a festival in the Biloxi-Gulfport area.

Elizabeth Ladner
University of Virginia

J. Hanno Deiler, *The Settlement of the German Coast of Louisiana and the Creoles of German Descent* (1909); Katharine Donato and Shirin Hakimzadeh, *Migration Information Source* website, www.migrationinformation.org; George A. Everett Jr., *Journal of Mississippi History* (November 1976); Jay Higginbotham, *Pascagoula: Singing River City* (1967); Harris Gaylord Warren, *Journal of Mississippi History* (April 1947); Herbert Weaver, *Journal of Mississippi History* (July 1954); D. C. Young and Stephen Young, in *Ethnic Heritage in Mississippi*, ed. Barbara Carpenter (1992).

G

Gerow, Richard
(1885–1976) Religious Leader

Born in Mobile, Alabama, longtime Catholic bishop and activist Richard Oliver Gerow spent most of his life in Mississippi. He was the only son of Warren Gerow, who was a maker of Mardi Gras floats and a volunteer fireman, and Ann Vickers Skelan Gerow, an Irish immigrant.

Gerow received his education at Mobile's cathedral school and McGill Institute before attending St Mary's College in Emmitsburg, Maryland. While there, he decided to become a priest. Under the tutelage of Bishop E. P. Allen, Gerow spent five years at the North American College in Rome and was ordained on 5 June 1909 in the Cathedral of St. John Lateran by Cardinal Pietro Respighi, the vicar of Rome.

Gerow's first priestly assignment was in a black parish in Pensacola, Florida. From there, he went to the cathedral in Mobile, remaining there and moving up the clerical hierarchy until 23 June 1924, when the thirty-nine-year-old Gerow was named bishop of Natchez. He was a scholar and a man of peace who hated violence in any form. He chose for his coat of arms and motto "In Thee, O Lord, Have I Hoped," an apt choice given the challenging situation he was about to face.

Gerow began to make changes as soon as he became bishop. He moved his residence from Pass Christian (where his predecessor, Bishop John Gunn, had been) to Natchez and decided to keep a diary of his daily activities and to organize the diocesan archives. Gerow was so faithful in carrying out these decisions that his diary grew to more than seven volumes, and his archives were among the best organized in the Catholic Church.

Gerow oversaw the renovation of St. Mary's Cathedral (at a cost of nearly eighty thousand dollars) during the desperate years of the Great Depression. Often paternalistic, he stayed close to his clergy through semiannual retreats and conferences. He consistently sought to recruit new members for the priesthood, especially from Ireland, where he traveled almost yearly. He brought more than two dozen religious orders to his diocese to help in every area of Catholic life from education to hospital ministry. He always made sure that the clergy and religious received decent salaries and lived in decent conditions. Gerow was especially concerned with property rights, making it clear that only the bishop would hold rights to any land or buildings. He was also very interested in the diocese's two orphanages, D'Evereux Hall and St. Mary's.

In addition to his activities with the Boy Scouts, the Catholic Laymen's Association, and the Catholic Committee of the South, Gerow paid special attention to the Diocesan Conference of Catholic Women. He felt that the Catholic faith was often treasured by and passed on through the women in Catholic families. Gerow also showed special interest in African Americans and Native Americans, consistently seeking funds for them and working to make sure that their spiritual needs were met. On 22 July 1948, after much thought and consideration and with the help of Monsignor Joseph Brunini, Gerow moved the chancery from Natchez to Jackson.

Between 1948 and 1966 the diocese faced challenges resulting from its growth. Gerow emphasized Catholic education and had Father Joseph Koury take over as superintendent of Catholic schools. Churches were built around the vast diocese so that every Catholic would have the opportunity to go to Mass and receive the sacraments. The diocese started its first newspaper, the *Mississippi Register*. Gerow's most significant accomplishments included his establishment of Catholic Charities in 1962. He also asked Rome to change the diocese to the Diocese of Natchez-Jackson, which occurred in 1957. He continued to recruit and work on behalf of his clergy. In 1956 he approved the creation of Pax Christi and endorsed the church's Greenwood movement. He was perhaps most proud when he saw two native Mississippians, Joseph Brunini and Leo Fahey, elevated to the bishopric.

Gerow did not challenge segregation but set up separate black parishes and schools so that African Americans could practice their faith. If any form of discrimination occurred, Gerow usually acted very quickly to stop it and punish those involved. St. Augustine's Seminary (the only seminary for black candidates for the priesthood) was located in his diocese and received his wholehearted support. He ordained more black priests than any other bishop in America.

Gerow was shaken by the turbulence of the 1960s and particularly by Medgar Evers's murder, which he publicly condemned. With the support and encouragement of his auxiliary bishop, Brunini, Gerow ordered the integration of all first grades in diocesan schools and followed up by fully integrating all levels. By then, Gerow was aging and his strength diminishing. He left these matters and other diocesan issues to Brunini, who became his successor. Gerow went into retirement and stayed active with fishing and photography. He died on 20 December 1976 at the age of ninety-one, living long enough to see his diocese have one of the first black bishops in the United States, Joseph Howze.

Michael V. Namorato
University of Mississippi

Richard O. Gerow, *Catholicity in Mississippi* (1939); Richard O. Gerow, ed., *Civil War Diary of Bishop William Henry Elder* (1961); Richard O. Gerow, *Cradle Days of Mississippi* (1941); Richard O. Gerow, *St. Mary's Parish, Natchez, Bishop Janssens' Administration* (1961); Michael V. Namorato, *The Catholic Church in Mississippi, 1911–1984* (1998).

Gholson, Samuel Jameson

(1808–1883) Confederate General and Politician

A politician and Confederate general, Samuel Jameson Gholson was born on 19 May 1808 in Madison County, Kentucky. He relocated as a youth to Alabama, where he studied law and was admitted to the bar in 1829. The next year he moved to Monroe County, Mississippi, and practiced law in Athens. Gholson served several terms in the state legislature during the 1830s before becoming a member of the US House of Representatives from 1836 to 1838. His congressional service was enlivened by a quarrel with Henry A. Wise of Virginia that would have resulted in a duel between the two men if not for the intervention of John C. Calhoun and other friends. In 1839 Pres. Martin Van Buren appointed Gholson to serve as a federal district judge for Mississippi, a post he held until 1861, when he resigned as a consequence of his support for secession. An ardent Democrat, he served as a member of the state secession convention.

Although he had been a major general in the state militia, Gholson enlisted as a private in the 14th Mississippi Infantry. After being mustered into state service in Aberdeen in April 1861, he was elected captain of a company; he subsequently received promotions to major and colonel. Gholson first saw action at Fort Donelson, where he was wounded on 13 February 1862. Taken prisoner when the garrison surrendered, Gholson was exchanged seven months later. He fought at both Iuka and Corinth, suffering a wound in the left thigh at Corinth that resulted in a long, painful recovery.

Gov. John J. Pettus appointed Gholson a major general in the Mississippi state militia in April 1863 and sent him to Northeast Mississippi to organize state troops. Gholson faced criticism from other Confederate officers who resented what they perceived as his interference with their recruitment and supply efforts, but both Nathan Bedford Forrest and Gov. Charles Clark recommended Gholson for a cavalry brigade command in the Confederate Army. In contrast to Forrest's and Clark's enthusiasm, Gen. Wirt Adams regarded the command as unreliable and suggested, to no avail, that the troops be dismounted and dispersed among other commands.

Gholson's brigade fought in central Mississippi, where Gholson was wounded at Jackson on 7 July 1863. When his brigade was transferred to Georgia to reinforce the Army of Tennessee, Gholson remained behind because his health prevented him from returning to field duty. He resumed activity in the fall of 1864 and suffered a wound on 28 December at Egypt that necessitated the amputation of his left arm. He was captured and saw no further field service. He was paroled at Meridian in May 1865.

Gholson was again elected to the Mississippi legislature in 1865 but was removed from office after passage of the Reconstruction Act of 1867. He returned to his law practice in Aberdeen, sought to overthrow the Republican government, and won election to the state legislature in 1878. He died on 16 October 1883 in Aberdeen.

Christopher Losson

St. Joseph, Missouri

John H. Eicher and David J. Eicher, *Civil War High Commands* (2001); Charles E. Hooker, *Confederate Military History: Mississippi*, ed. Clement A. Evans (1899); Dunbar Rowland, *Military History of Mississippi, 1803–1898*, taken from *Mississippi Official and Statistical Register* (1908).

Gibson, Tobias

(1771–1804) Missionary

In 1799 Tobias Gibson made an epic journey from the Carolinas to establish Mississippi's first Methodist church, near Natchez. Gibson was born on 10 November 1771 to Jordan Gibson and Mary Middleton Gibson, who lived along the Great Pee Dee River in South Carolina. In 1789 Tobias Gibson met Francis Asbury, who was organizing a Methodist meetinghouse near the Gibson family home. In 1771 John Wesley, the founder of Methodism, had appointed Asbury to go to America and minister to the emerging Methodist societies in the colonies. Friendship with Asbury influenced

Gibson's entire life, and he entered the itinerant ministry in February 1792 and served appointments to the Bush River and Santee Circuits in South Carolina.

Gibson briefly served the Union Circuit after being ordained an elder in 1794 and then became Bishop Asbury's traveling associate. On 20 March 1794 Gibson rescued Asbury from the swirling Catawba River during a trip to the Kentucky Conference. Asbury appointed Gibson to Kentucky's Lexington Circuit in 1794, Tennessee's Holston Circuit in 1795, and South Carolina's Edisto Circuit in 1796 and Charleston Circuit two years later.

In 1799 Asbury appealed for a volunteer to go to the "Natchez Mission" in the newly formed Mississippi Territory. Gibson responded, and after serving with the Little Pee Dee Circuit in South Carolina and Anson Circuit in North Carolina, he made his pioneering trip to Natchez.

Gibson's journey took him through the Cumberland Gap and Nashville, Tennessee. There, he sold his horse and descended the Cumberland, Ohio, and Mississippi Rivers to Natchez by canoe and flatboat, arriving during the summer of 1799. Gibson traveled an estimated one hundred thousand miles in his tenure as a Methodist circuit rider, visiting small settlements, holding camp meetings, and spreading Wesleyan theology.

Gibson became engaged to Sarah Griffing, daughter of Judge John Griffing, but they never married because of Gibson's declining health. Gibson preached his last sermon on New Year's Day 1804 and died of tuberculosis on 5 April of that year.

William L. Jenkins

San Diego, California

William L. Jenkins, *Mississippi United Methodist Church, Two Hundred Years of Heritage and Hope* (1986); William L. Jenkins, *Tobias Gibson: Mississippi Methodist Missionary by Rivers and Long Roads* (1999); Randy J. Sparks, *On Jordan's Stormy Banks: Evangelicalism in Mississippi, 1773–1876* (1994).

Gibson v. Mississippi

In *Gibson v. Mississippi* (1896) the US Supreme Court upheld Mississippi's 1890 constitution and statutes providing for the qualification of electors and jury selection. In doing so, the court added *Gibson* to a line of cases narrowly interpreting the Reconstruction amendments, resulting in widespread discrimination against African Americans.

The case originated when John Gibson, an African American, was indicted by an all-white jury for the January 1892 murder of Robert Stinson, a white man. Gibson filed a motion to remove the case to federal court on the grounds that the jury was improperly selected, violating his constitutional right to equal protection and preventing him from receiving a fair and impartial trial. He asserted that the jury commissioners discriminated when selecting potential jurors and that jury selection should have occurred under the provisions of the Mississippi Code of 1880 rather than the Code of 1892, which was not adopted until after the date of the alleged murder. The later code added the requirement that jurors be qualified electors and pass the literacy test.

The trial court refused to accept Gibson's argument and denied his motion to remove. Gibson then requested that a special venire be summoned to try his case. The trial court summoned special jurors, but Gibson was unhappy with the notice used to summon them and filed a motion to quash the special venire. The trial court denied this motion as well, and the jury found Gibson guilty of murder. The Mississippi Supreme Court accepted the case on appeal and affirmed the trial court's decision.

Gibson appealed to the US Supreme Court, arguing that the jury commissioners discriminated when selecting the jury and therefore violated his right to equal protection, making it impossible for him to receive a fair and impartial trial in state court. He asserted that under those circumstances, removal to federal court was proper. The Court, in an opinion by Justice John Marshall Harlan, held that Gibson's motions to remove and to quash the special venire were properly denied because neither the constitution nor the laws of the state were facially discriminatory and that under those circumstances, the possibility that a state court might not enforce a defendant's Fourteenth Amendment rights during a trial did not constitute grounds for removal, despite the fact that black citizens would not receive a fair and impartial trial.

The court also found that the trial court's application of the Code of 1892 did not constitute improper ex post facto application of the laws. It noted that the Constitution of 1890 was in effect at the time of the alleged murder, and it required that jurors be qualified electors and pass the literacy test. It also provided for the selection of jurors from a list of registered voters. The court found that because the Constitution of 1890 contained the substantive provisions at issue, Gibson was unaffected by court's application of the Code of 1892, which included largely procedural provisions that did not materially affect Gibson's rights.

With regard to Gibson's motion to quash the special venire, the court held that unless a state court criminal trial was conducted under a law that invaded or denied a defendant's constitutional rights, it could not review errors in the method of selecting jurors.

In sum, according to the court, although the US Constitution forbade laws that were racially discriminatory, if discrimination resulted from the application of a law rather than the facial construction of a law, the victim had no judicial remedy. *Gibson v. Mississippi* is one in a line of cases, including *Plessy v. Ferguson* (1896) and *Williams v. Mississippi* (1898), that narrowly interpreted the Reconstruction Amendments, ultimately allowing states to strip African Americans of their civil rights.

Amanda Brown
Nashville, Tennessee

Gibson v. Mississippi 162 US 565 (1896).

Gilchrist, Ellen
(b. 1935) Writer

Despite interruptions caused by family circumstances, Ellen Gilchrist has been a writer since the age of fifteen, publishing both fiction and nonfiction in a wide array of genres over more than a half century. Gilchrist was born in Vicksburg on 20 February 1935 and grew up primarily in Indiana, Illinois, and Kentucky, though her family regularly visited Mississippi. She began publishing a newspaper column but had to give it up at the age of fifteen when her family moved again. She enrolled at Vanderbilt University in 1953, transferred to the University of Alabama in 1954, and then dropped out to marry Marshall Walker in 1955. She and Walker had two sons before they divorced. She subsequently married and divorced James Nelson Bloodworth before remarrying Walker, having another son, and divorcing again in 1963. She then finished a bachelor's degree at Millsaps College, where she took classes with Eudora Welty.

In 1968 Gilchrist married Frederick Sidney Kullman of New Orleans and resumed newspaper work in 1975 as a

Ellen Gilchrist (Bern and Franke Keating Collection, Department of Archives and Special Collections, J. D. Williams Library, University of Mississippi)

contributing editor of the *Vieux Carré Courier*. The next year she entered the creative writing master of fine arts program at the University of Arkansas, dividing her time between Fayetteville and New Orleans. While she was enrolled, she published her first collection of poems, *The Land Surveyor's Daughter* (1979), and her first book of fiction, *In the Land of Dreamy Dreams* (1981). Her first novel, *The Annunciation* (1983), soon followed, as did *Victory over Japan* (1984), a collection that won the American Book Award. Gilchrist has subsequently remained prolific, publishing poetry, fiction (including short stories, the genre for which she is best known, as well as novellas, novels, and historical fantasy), and nonfiction in both books and magazines.

In the Land of Dreamy Dreams introduces Rhoda Manning, an autobiographical character who is paradoxically both spoiled and oppressed by her father. Like her creator, Rhoda is a talented writer with the promise of a career ahead of her, but she drops out of college after eloping, and soon has several children. She divorces her husband but continues to focus most of her energy toward finding a mate rather than on writing. She is never able to overcome her conflict with her dominating father and brother or the resulting belief that her value as a woman depends on the opinions of the men in her life.

Rhoda became Gilchrist's most popular recurrent character and the prototype for the protagonists of most of the author's fiction. That prototype evolved in her second novel, *The Anna Papers* (1988), which features Anna Hand, who fulfills the promise that Rhoda cannot. Though Anna is also unsuccessful with marriage, she does not have children and is a published author who has set her own priorities and disregards familial obligations when necessary, chooses lovers according to her own desires without regard for whether society or her family would approve, and takes her own life rather than succumbing to cancer.

Other recurring characters include Nora Jane Whittington, also introduced in the first collection, and Crystal Manning Mallison Weiss, who is introduced by her African American housekeeper and confidante, Traceleen, the narrator of several stories in *Victory over Japan*. Gilchrist's protagonists are divided between manifestations of the original prototype and characters that reflect its evolution. By continuing to create characters with Rhoda's weaknesses, including women of the next two generations, Gilchrist shows that overcoming gender strictures remains difficult, even into the twenty-first century. Careers may be more accessible and socially acceptable, but southern families continue to emphasize the need for daughters to find appropriate husbands and provide heirs. Even Rhoda, in her sixties in recent collections, such as *I, Rhoda Manning, Go Hunting with My Daddy* (2002), has begun to echo her father's concerns about the consequences of her granddaughters' rebellious natures.

Gilchrist never completed her master of fine arts degree but settled in Fayetteville after she and Kullman divorced and in 2001 became a member of the University of Arkan-

sas's creative writing faculty. She divides her time between Fayetteville and Ocean Springs, Mississippi.

Margaret Donovan Bauer
East Carolina University

Margaret Donovan Bauer, *The Fiction of Ellen Gilchrist* (1999); Encyclopedia of Arkansas History and Culture website, www.encyclopediaofarkansas.net; Ellen Gilchrist, *A Dangerous Age* (2008); Ellen Gilchrist, *Falling through Space* (2000); Ellen Gilchrist, "Keeping Houses," in *O: The Oprah Magazine* (Summer 2008); Mary McCay, *Ellen Gilchrist* (1990); Carolyn Perry and Mary Louise Weaks, eds., *The History of Southern Women's Literature* (2002).

Gilley, Mickey
(b. 1936) Country Musician

Mickey Leroy Gilley was born on 9 March 1936 in Natchez to Irene and Arthur Gilley. He grew up across the Mississippi River in Ferriday, Louisiana, where his father operated a grocery, a taxi service, and restaurants and his mother worked in a café. As a boy Gilley learned to sing and to play guitar and piano, and he was reared in the Pentecostal faith of the Assembly of God church. With his cousins Jerry Lee Lewis and Jimmy Swaggart, he absorbed hillbilly, blues, and boogie-woogie music on the radio and in the clubs of Ferriday and Natchez. In 1953 he married Geraldine Garrett and moved to the booming city of Houston, Texas, working in construction and in the parts department of an engineering company. Three years later, watching Lewis's musical career take off at Sun Records, Gilley tried to record his own music on a variety of labels but met with little success. He struggled, traveling and playing clubs in Louisiana, Mississippi, and Alabama, and he and Geraldine divorced.

In 1959 Gilley scored a regional hit with "Is It Wrong?," a rockabilly number on Dot Records. This success launched him into work as a full-time musician in the clubs along Spencer Highway in Pasadena, a working-class suburb of Houston. He spent ten years performing at the Nesadel Club, where he met Vivian McDonald, who in 1962 became his second wife. In 1971 Gilley and local bar owner Sherwood Cryer transformed a decrepit dance hall into Gilley's Club. Advertised as the "biggest honky-tonk in the world," the club quickly became a major success and expanded to a floor area of almost four acres and a holding capacity of five thousand.

In 1974 Gilley recorded a song for the club jukebox, and its B-side, "Room Full of Roses," became an unexpected radio hit. Picked up for national distribution by Playboy Records, it reached No. 1 on the country charts. The style on "Room Full of Roses" was not rockabilly, like his earlier work, but rather honky-tonk, a country music form that had originated in the mid-1930s in the oil towns of Texas. With electrified instruments and a steady dance beat, honky-tonk songs dwelt on lyrical themes of romantic trouble, mistreatment, and the brief release provided by alcohol and festivity in the club. Gilley continued to record songs in this vein and scored a string of No. 1 hits, among them "Don't the Girls All Get Prettier at Closing Time" and "A Headache Tomorrow (Or a Heartache Tonight)." These commercial successes led to opportunities for Gilley to tour the country, and singer and guitarist Johnny Lee became house bandleader at Gilley's Club.

The club received wide publicity through a 1978 *Esquire* cover story and the 1980 film *Urban Cowboy*, boosting the sales of Gilley's and Lee's new records and inspiring a brief national craze for cowboy boots, country dancing, and mechanical bull riding. After the fad waned in the mid-1980s, Gilley scored fewer hits. He eventually severed business relations with Cryer, and in 1989 the club burned to the ground. By the next year, Gilley had slowed touring and recording and had moved to Branson, Missouri, where his Mickey Gilley Theatre and Gilley's Texas Café became popular draws for a predominantly older crowd of vacationers. Thus, though Gilley grew up in the rich cotton-producing region of Natchez-Ferriday, his sound and public image have been tied not to agricultural Mississippi but rather to the honky-tonk culture of Sunbelt Texas.

John Hayes

Georgia Regents University

Ken Burke, *Country Music Changed My Life: Tales of Tough Times and Triumphs from Country's Legends* (2004); Elaine Dundy, *Ferriday, Louisiana* (1991); Peter Guralnick, *Lost Highway: Journeys and Arrivals of American Musicians* (1999); Joel Whitburn, *The Billboard Book of Top 40 Country Hits* (1996).

Gillom-Granderson, Peggie

(b. 1958)

Gillom, Jennifer

(b. 1964)
Athletes

Natives of Abbeville, the Gillom sisters have earned accolades for their many accomplishments in women's basketball. Their mother was Ella Gillom, and both attended Lafayette County High School.

Peggie Gillom was born on 14 April 1958 and played basketball for the University of Mississippi from 1976 to 1980, setting school records with 2,486 points and 1,271 rebounds. She played for one year with the Dallas Diamonds of the Women's Professional Basketball League before returning to the University of Mississippi to serve as an assistant women's basketball coach under Van Chancellor. Gillom remained at the university for sixteen years, during which the team captured the 1992 Southeastern Conference (SEC) regular-season championship and appeared in fourteen National Collegiate Athletic Association (NCAA) Tournaments, reaching the Elite Eight four times. In 1997 and 1998 she coached for the Houston Comets of the Women's National Basketball Association (WNBA), again as Chancellor's assistant. The Comets won the league title in both of those years. Between 1998 and 2003, Gillom served as head women's basketball coach at Texas A&M, compiling an overall record of 53–86. In addition, she served as assistant coach of the 2000 US Olympic women's basketball team that captured the gold medal in Sydney, Australia. From 2003 until her retirement in 2011, Gillom served as women's basketball associate head coach at the University of Mississippi. She married Anthony Granderson in 2005 and resides in Abbeville.

Jennifer Gillom was born on 13 June 1964 and attended Lafayette County High School. Gillom played basketball for the University of Mississippi from 1982 to 1986: her sister served as one of her coaches. She garnered four all-SEC first team selections and was named the conference's Female Athlete of the Year in 1986. Jennifer Gillom's career total of 2,186 points trails only Peggie among Rebel players . During Gillom's career the team appeared in four NCAA Tournaments, reaching the Sweet 16 in 1983 and 1984, and she was named the Most Valuable Player of the 1986 NCAA Midwest Regional. Gillom played on the gold-medal winning US women's basketball teams at the 1986 World Championship and the 1988 Olympics. Gillom played professionally in Italy from 1986 to 1996 and for the WNBA's Phoenix Mercury from 1996 to 2002, averaging 15.3 points per game. Gillom's WNBA teams reached the playoffs three times, including 1998, when they lost in the finals. After one year with the league's Los Angeles Sparks, she retired at the end of the 2003 season. Gillom went on to coach at Xavier College Preparatory School in Phoenix before becoming an assistant coach for the WNBA's Minnesota Lynx in 2008 and the team's head coach the following year. She returned to the Sparks as head coach in 2010–11, spent the 2012 season as an assistant with the Washington Mystics, and since 2013 has been an assistant coach with the Connecticut Sun.

Both Gillom sisters have been inducted into the Mississippi Sports Hall of Fame and the Women's Basketball Hall of Fame. The University of Mississippi's Gillom Sports Center is named in their honor.

Ryan L. Fletcher

University of Mississippi

Mississippi Legislature, *House Concurrent Resolution 159*; Mississippi Sports Hall of Fame website, msfame.com; University of Mississippi, Official Athletic website, www.olemisssports.com; WNBA website, www.wnba.com; Women's Basketball Hall of Fame website, www.wbhof.com.

Goff, Bruce, Houses

Architect Bruce Goff (1904–82), long associated with Oklahoma and the Midwest, built two houses along the Gulf Coast of Mississippi, the Emil Gutman House (1958–60) in Gulfport and the W. C. Gryder House (1960) in Ocean Springs. These houses, with their formal oddities, unorthodox colors, and simpler-than-it-appears planning and structure, are not atypical for Goff, although there is no typical Goff house. The designs embodied the peculiar spirit that marked Goff's modern architecture throughout his career—an individualism and creative freedom that have been compared to the democratic spirit of Frank Lloyd Wright but that elitists of the eastern establishment, as Asa Louise Huxtable observed, dismissed as outré fantasies. Goff remained a maverick, unconstrained by any traditional formalities and creating some of the most unusual building forms of the twentieth century. Rather than conforming to architectural or social theories of the day, Goff focused on client needs, producing a consumer-driven and highly personal architecture. His houses display an idiosyncratic play of ornament and color, the latter contrasting with high modernism's colorless abstraction and predisposition to avoid ornament. His is an organic architecture in which the natural forms and space of houses are continuous and unified, expressing a quality of space that he called the "continuous present" in an open architecture informed by geometric discipline.

Goff's use of geometry to generate orderly plans is evidenced in his best-known house, built in 1956–66 for Joe Price in Bartlesville, Oklahoma, as well as in the Gutman House. The Gutman House, built for a site with a high water table on a bayou property that was open to storm and flooding, was raised fifteen feet on three points of support, balancing the house on exposed angular pipe columns. The house appeared to float above its carport and play area. Built on a triangular module, its simple structure of wood frame and light steel shaped geometric interior spaces: enclosed bedrooms, kitchen, and baths surrounded a central conversation pit and modular family living room open to the hexagonal dining area. After surviving several hurricanes, it was destroyed by fire in the mid-1980s.

In contrast to the geometric order of the Gutman House, the Gryder House features unusual organic shapes. Deceptively symmetrical, the ordering axis is marked by an entry bridge crossing a water garden to a foyer that leads past curved stairs and a central fireplace to a double-height reception room and porch beyond. Balconies off upper bedrooms overlook the principal living area, and the central space expands laterally to a lounge on one side and to the dining room and kitchen on the other. Inasmuch as one arrives via a tubular bridge crossing a large pond, one appears now to inhabit a spatial expression of the organic forms in nature that envelop the house. The residence's muted purple stucco exterior and turquoise interior tiles, together with its organic teardrop windows and soaring rooflines, prompted Jeffrey Cook to describe the Gryder House as "an exotic living orchid."

However, the organic unorthodox form of the Gryder House is particularly unusual; the house resembles a weird architectonic praying mantis. In his personal play with ornament and color, Goff displayed a unique and at times eccentric expression. The Gryder House's teardrop windows, conical balconies, and gesturing roof lines are mirrored in water and feature textured tiling accents inside and out. Even Hurricane Katrina caused only minimal damage, and the Gryder House remains one of Goff's most exotic and fanciful houses.

When nonclassical angularities or sweeping curves join Goff's unconventional use of materials and his romantic decorative richness of surface and light, the result can move the modern aesthetic from the new to the novel and can transform a rational art to what appears to be irrational fantasy. Critics have called Goff's houses bizarre, but clients have embraced these unique responses to individual needs.

Robert M. Craig
Georgia Institute of Technology

Jeffrey Cook, *The Architecture of Bruce Goff* (1978); David Gilson DeLong, "The Architecture of Bruce Goff: Buildings and Projects, 1916–1974," (PhD dissertation, Columbia University, 1976); David Gilson DeLong, *Bruce Goff: Toward Absolute Architecture* (1988); J. François Gabriel, *Beyond the Cube: The Architecture of Space Frames and Polyhedra* (1997); Takenobu Mohri, *Bruce Goff, Architect* (1970); Pauline Saliga and Mary Woolever, eds., *The Architecture of Bruce Goff, 1904–1982: Design for the Continuous Present* (1995); John Sergeant and Stephen Mooring, *AD Profiles: Bruce Goff* (1978).

Goldberger, Joseph

(1874–1929) Doctor

Joseph Goldberger, a physician and scientist, holds a prominent position in the annals of Mississippi's medical history for his critical work battling pellagra, a dreaded disease. In

G

1915 Goldberger conducted a controversial medical trial with prisoners at the Rankin State Prison Farm, near present-day Whitfield, that determined that pellagra was a nutritional disorder.

The son of a sheepherder who later became a grocer, Goldberger was born near Giralt in the Austro-Hungarian Empire (now Giraltovce, Slovakia) on 16 July 1874 and immigrated with his large German-speaking family to New York City by 1883. His parents, Samuel and Sarah Goldberger, were Orthodox Jews who valued education, and in 1895 Goldberger received a medical degree from the city's Bellevue Hospital Medical College. He soon began a career in public health, working as a physician with the US Marine Hospital Service (now the US Public Health Service). He came south by the late 1890s to battle epidemics such as yellow fever and malaria.

Goldberger's work in Mississippi began in the summer of 1905 when he was assigned to Vicksburg for quarantine duty during the last substantial US yellow fever epidemic. Goldberger married Mary Humphreys Farrar on 19 April 1906 in New Orleans. The daughter of a prominent New Orleans attorney, Mary was the great-grandniece of Confederate president Jefferson Davis as well as the great-granddaughter of Mississippi governor B. G. Humphreys. Mary was intelligent, idealistic, and extremely committed to her husband's scientific work, and her Mississippi ties facilitated her husband's work in the state.

Goldberger subsequently turned his attention to pellagra, a major cause of death and illness. Mississippi had the highest pellagra fatality rate in the South, with almost eleven thousand cases (more than a thousand of which resulted in death) reported in 1914. In the spring of that year, Goldberger studied the prevalence of pellagra at the Methodist and Baptist orphanages in Jackson and concluded that the disease was not infectious but rather resulted from the common diet of the southern poor—cornbread, pork, and cane syrup. The following August, he initiated feeding experiments at the Methodist orphanage, largely eliminating the disease there.

His success encouraged him to propose to Gov. Earl Brewer and the Mississippi State Board of Health a demonstration to test his hypothesis that pellagra was a dietary deficiency. With the authorities' full cooperation, Goldberger, assisted by Dr. George A. Wheeler, induced the disease in healthy volunteer convicts at the Rankin Farm by changing their diet. Twelve of the institution's seventy white male convicts accepted Gov. Brewer's offer of a pardon in exchange for participation in the experiment. The men were observed from 4 February to 19 April 1915 as they performed their usual work routine and ate their usual diet, which included a variety of vegetables grown at the farm and dairy products. No evidence of pellagra appeared during this period. Beginning on 19 April, however, the prisoners received a diet typical of many southerners: biscuits, mush, grits, brown gravy, cornbread, sweet potatoes, cane syrup, and coffee.

Although one of the twelve subjects was discharged from the experiment in July because of prostatitis, the remaining eleven, whose ages ranged from twenty-four to fifty, remained on the restricted diet until the study ended on 31 October 1915. Six of the eleven men developed pellagra symptoms, including the typical dermatitis as well as gastrointestinal complaints. All twelve men subsequently received full pardons, and the six men who had developed pellagra symptoms fully recovered.

The experiment proved that the disease was caused by dietary deficiencies and was not infectious or communicable. After further research, Goldberger concluded that the important pellagra preventative was "a heretofore unrecognized or unappreciated dietary factor," which he designated "factor P-P," for "Pellagra Prevention." Subsequent scientists determined that pellagra is caused by a lack of niacin.

Most Mississippians embraced Goldberger's work. In April 1916 the state legislature authorized any county or group of counties to establish pellagra hospitals, and the number of pellagra deaths in the state fell from 1,535 in 1915 to 561 in 1925. Goldberger returned to the state during the Great Flood of 1927 to battle the disease again. He died of renal cell cancer on 17 January 1929.

Lucius M. Lampton
Magnolia, Mississippi

Alan M. Kraut, *Goldberger's War: The Life and Work of a Public Health Crusader* (2003); Lucius M. Lampton, *Journal of the Mississippi State Medical Association* (February 2005); Robert P. Parsons, *Trail to Light: A Biography of Joseph Goldberger* (1943); Milton Terris, ed., *Goldberger on Pellagra* (1964).

Goldring/Woldenberg Institute of Southern Jewish Life

Founded in 1986 as the Museum of the Southern Jewish Experience (MSJE), the Jackson-based Goldring/Woldenberg Institute of Southern Jewish Life (ISJL) works to preserve and document the practice, culture, and legacy of Judaism in the southern United States. The original idea for the museum came from Macy B. Hart, a longtime director of the Union of American Hebrew Congregations's Henry S. Jacobs Camp in Utica, Mississippi. Hart recognized that many of the region's smaller Jewish communities were experiencing population decline, forcing synagogues to close their doors. The MSJE began as an effort to preserve the artifacts and history of these communities. The MSJE completed its first building in 1989 on the grounds of Jacobs Camp. Three years later the museum entered into a preservation agreement with Temple B'nai Israel in Natchez, with the congregation deeding its historic 1906 building to the museum. The museum has created several award-winning exhibits, including *From Alsace to America: Discovering a Southern Jewish Heritage*, and *Bagels and Grits: Images of Southern Jewish Life*. The MSJE's History Department worked to gather information about every southern Jewish community. The museum also worked to restore and preserve historic Jewish cemeteries in communities that no longer had a Jewish presence.

In 2000, under Hart's leadership, the museum expanded its mission to become the ISJL and to provide Judaic services and cultural programs in Alabama, Arkansas, Florida, Georgia, Kentucky, Louisiana, Mississippi, North Carolina, Oklahoma, South Carolina, Tennessee, Texas, and Virginia. Incorporating the research and historic preservation work of the museum, the ISJL created new departments of rabbinic services, education, and cultural programs. Many small congregations around the country do not have full-time rabbinic leadership, so in 2003 the ISJL revived the practice of circuit-riding rabbis. The ISJL's first itinerant rabbi served more than two dozen small congregations in a four-state region. In 2015 ISJL rabbis visited twenty-nine congregations in eleven states (all of the targeted states except Oklahoma and Virginia). The ISJL also sought to raise the level of Jewish education in small cities and towns. The ISJL Education Department developed a complete and detailed nondenominational religious school curriculum administered by a team of Jewish educators who travel across the region making site visits. In 2015–16, fifty-nine congregations used the ISJL curriculum. The ISJL also brings cultural programs to small communities through its Jewish Cinema South film series and its Southern States Jewish Literary Series.

Funded by both large foundations and individual members, the ISJL represents an innovative attempt to fulfill the spiritual, educational, and cultural needs of isolated and underserved Jewish communities. Working outside the national institutions of American Judaism, the ISJL envisions the Jews of the thirteen southern states as one community and synagogue.

The problems of isolated and underserved Jewish communities are not limited to the South. In every region, small congregations lack the resources to support full-time rabbis or Jewish educators. The ISJL is shaping a model of living Judaism and Jewish preservation that can be replicated in other parts of the country.

Stuart Rockoff

Mississippi Humanities Council

Andrea Oppenheimer Dean, *Preservation* (July–August 2000); Goldring/Woldenberg Institute of Southern Jewish Life website, www.isjl.org; Brenda Goodman, *New York Times* (26 November 2005); Lewis Lord, *US News & World Report* (25 May 1998); Michael Schuman, *Philadelphia Inquirer* (14 April 2002).

Golf

Until recently most of Mississippi's golf courses were small concerns. Many were country club courses, racially segregated and open only to club members and their friends. Only in recent decades has golf become part of a broader effort to present the state as an attractive destination for tourists, and as of 2015 golfers can choose from among more than 140 courses in all areas of Mississippi.

Golf first came to Mississippi along the Gulf Coast, which later was nicknamed the Golf Coast. The state's first course, the Great Southern Golf Club, built by respected architect Donald Ross, opened in 1908, and by 1930, additional courses had been constructed along the coast as well as in Natchez and Vicksburg.

The increasing popularity of golf seems to owe much to the declining number of people who make their livings in agriculture and to the dramatic increase in tourism. American golf has grown popular as a game for urbanites and suburbanites searching for sports in the outdoors. Until recently, Mississippians in general spent plenty of time farming, hunting, and fishing, and relatively few felt a need to embrace a time-consuming and potentially expensive sport as a way to get close to nature. Perhaps more important, Mississippi's business and government leaders have promoted golf as part of a broader effort to attract tourists that has also involved highlighting the state's casinos, beaches, and public parks. Many of the state's most impressive new courses are located in casino areas, in state parks, or along the Gulf Coast.

The state has hosted professional tournaments since men competed in the Gulfport Open in 1944 and 1945. From 1968

Great Southern Hotel, Gulfport, ca. 1906 (Library of Congress, Washington, D.C. [LC-D4-19408])

to 1993 the Professional Golfers' Association (PGA) held the Magnolia Classic at the Hattiesburg Country Club. The tournament subsequently moved to the Annandale Golf Club in Madison, outside of Jackson, and became known as the Deposit Guaranty Classic until 1999, the Southern Farm Bureau Classic from 1999 to 2006, the Viking Classic from 2007 to 2011 (though the tournament was canceled in 2009), the TrueSouth Classic in 2012, and since then as the Sanderson Farms Championship. From 2014 onward it has been held at the Country Club of Jackson. Never among the top tier of PGA tournaments, it has frequently been scheduled at the same time as more elite tournaments such as the Masters, the British Open, or the Tour Championship. In 2015 winner Peter Malnati took home $738,000 of the $4,100,000 purse. Since 2010, Biloxi's Fallen Oak course has hosted an event on the PGA's Champions Tour (for golfers age fifty and older). Winner David Frost's share of the $1,600,000 in 2015 prize money totaled $240,000. Mississippi hosted its first major national golf event in 1999, when the Old Waverly Golf Club in West Point was the site of the US Women's Open, won by Juli Inkster.

The state has produced a handful of successful professional golfers. Mary Mills won the 1963 US Women's Open and eight other Ladies Professional Golf Association tournaments in the 1960s and 1970s. Mills was a prodigy, winning eight consecutive Mississippi women's amateur tournaments beginning when she was just fourteen and continuing through her years at Millsaps College. Male pro golfers from Mississippi include Pete Brown, Jim Gallagher Jr., and Vance Veazey. Brown, born in Port Gibson and raised in Jackson, made headlines as the first African American golfer to win a PGA tournament when he posted the low score at the 1964 Waco Turner Open.

Only on rare occasions has golf had a hand in the issues that most scholars see as central to Mississippi history. Once when University of Mississippi history professor James Silver and the school's first African American student, James Meredith, played golf in 1963, Silver noted that the crowds observing and protecting Meredith did not help his game: "The walkie-talkies used by the marshals and the military weren't exactly conducive to good golf."

Ted Ownby
University of Mississippi

Mississippi Golf: 2006 Official Golf Guide; David R. Holland, GulfCoast Golf.com website, www.gulfcoastgolf.com; Visit Mississippi website, www.visitmississippi.org; James W. Silver, *Mississippi: The Closed Society* (1964).

Good Roads Movement

The Good Roads Movement began in the early 1900s as an effort to enhance the quality of rural life, allowing farm people to keep the benefits of rural life while having connections to markets and cultural possibilities of towns and cities and increasing economic investment and tourism. The movement sought to have hard-surfaced roads standardized under the direction of state authorities, thereby modernizing transportation to allow travel by car and truck.

In the early twentieth century most Mississippi counties continued the antebellum practice of requiring all men to work a few days a year to build or improve roads. When county leaders announced Good Roads Days, they usually called on younger men to fill potholes with sand and dirt. Good Roads movement supporters, in contrast, wanted state authority over roads designated as state highways and wanted some new taxes to support building and improving those roads.

The main difficulties for the movement were a lack of coordination among counties and the South's long history of low taxes, as the construction of the Bankhead Highway through northeastern Mississippi in 1920 illustrates. According to historian Corey Lesseig, the goal was to build an 18-foot-wide road from Memphis to Birmingham, but each county bore responsibility for constructing its stretch of the highway. While wealthier Lee County could afford to build its section of the highway, nearby Itawamba County could not and consequently constructed a 9-foot-wide paved road with 4.5 feet of gravel on either side: people "just drove on the middle of the road."

The Illinois Central Railroad organized the state's first Good Roads conference in 1901, but the movement progressed unevenly. Mississippi started its Highway Commission in 1916, in part because the Federal Aid to Roads Law of that year gave federal money only to states that had high-

Parade supporting better roads, McComb, 1913 (Cooper Postcard Collection, Archives and Records Services Division, Mississippi Department of Archives and History [PI_1992/Box 102/Folder 1])

way departments. The commission received limited funding until 1922, when the legislature inaugurated a one-cent tax on gasoline. In 1924 Mississippi designated its first state highways. In 1930 the state's Stansel Highway Bill called for uniformity in state highways and a network of paved roads connecting all towns of at least five hundred people.

Ted Ownby
University of Mississippi

Stephen Cresswell, *Rednecks, Redeemers, and Race: Mississippi after Reconstruction, 1877–1917* (2006); Corey T. Lesseig, *Automobility: Social Change in the American South, 1909–1939* (2001); Howard Lawrence Preston, *Dirt Roads to Dixie: Accessibility and Modernization in the South, 1885–1935* (1991).

Gordon, Eva L.
(1888–1982) Educator

Eva Lois Williams Gordon was an educational and civic leader in southern and central Mississippi for more than five decades. The daughter of Celia Ann Berkley Williams, Eva was born on 29 October 1888 in Magnolia. After her mother's death, Williams was raised by her grandparents, Aaron and Hannah Berkley, both of whom were ex-slaves. Her early life revolved around education and religion, and she attended Magnolia's St. James United Methodist Church for her entire life. Williams was educated in the local black public schools, and by age fifteen she graduated from Mississippi and Louisiana Normal and Industrial College, a short-lived black institution located in Magnolia. She began her career in 1903 as a supply teacher in the nearby Lundy Lane Community, and in 1904 Prof. J. E. Johnson, who later established Prentiss Institute in Jefferson Davis County, hired her as a primary teacher in the Magnolia school system. Williams continued her education during several summers at Hampton Institute and Tuskegee Institute.

In 1906 she married Emory Urias Gordon, a native of Gillsburg who worked as a mill and compress worker. The couple had four children, one of whom died at eighteen months.

In 1919 Eva Gordon became principal of the Magnolia black schools, which occupied a substandard building and offered education only through the eighth grade. Learning of the recently established Julius Rosenwald Fund, she raised one thousand dollars in matching funds to erect a Rosenwald School in Magnolia, with most of the money coming in pennies, nickels, dimes, and quarters contributed by blacks and whites in the community. The Pike County Training School opened in the early 1920s.

Gordon continued to focus on the underprivileged in her community. In 1937 she went into home demonstration work and accepted a teaching position in Gloster, and she later became a Jeanes teacher in Hinds County. At that time, black schools were in session only when children's labor was not needed in the cotton fields, resulting in abbreviated terms, but Gordon persuaded Hinds officials to lengthen the school term for blacks to equal that of whites. She later returned to Pike County as a Jeanes supervisor and became the Pike County Extension Service's first black home demonstration agent for women and girls. Her 4-H Club activities were highly regarded, winning state and national awards. The exhibit hall at the Pike County Fairgrounds bears her name. In 1958 a new Magnolia school, located directly across Highway 51 from the site of the Pike County Training School, was named in her honor.

She retired as a demonstration agent in 1955 after fifty-two years of public service and remained active in church, educational, agricultural, and civic organizations until her death in Jackson on 26 March 1982.

Lucius M. Lampton
Magnolia, Mississippi

"Celebration of the Home Going of Mrs. Eva L. Gordon," Funeral Program (30 March 1982); Dorothy Gordon Gray, interview by author (15 January 1999); *Jackson Advocate* (23 May 2002); *Magnolia Gazette* (2 November 2006, 18, 22, 26 February 2007, 27 March 2008); George A. Sewell and Margaret L. Dwight, *Mississippi Black History Makers* (1984); Louretta Smith, *Magnolia through the Years* (1975).

Gothic Revival Architecture

Gothic Revival architecture originated in England during the second half of the eighteenth century. This style came to prominence in the United States in 1832 with Alexander Jackson Davis's design of Glen Ellen, a palatial home in Towson, Maryland. One of Davis's contemporaries, Andrew Jackson Downing, promoted Gothic Revival with the publication of *Victorian Cottage Residences* and *Architecture of Country Houses*, which popularized the style in rural areas.

The first American Gothic Revival buildings were made of stone and suggestive of medieval European castles, with battlements, pinnacles, parapets, and quatrefoil windows. Eventually, structures were built of brick or wood, and many of the highly decorative architectural elements fell by the wayside. The steam-powered scroll saw allowed for the mass production of lacy ornamentation that became known as gingerbread trim and gave rise to the substyle known as

Episcopal Chapel of the Cross, Mannsdale (1852), considered a perfect example of Gothic Revival architecture (Charles Reagan Wilson Collection, Center for the Study of Southern Culture, University of Mississippi)

Carpenter Gothic, characterized by steeply pitched roofs, pointed arched doorways and windows, and single-story porches.

The majority of Gothic Revival architecture in Mississippi can be found in houses of worship. One of the earliest examples is St. Mary's Basilica in Natchez. Construction began on the building in 1841, making it Mississippi's oldest Catholic structure still in use. The exterior is notable for its spindle-like spires and tall arched windows. Its elaborate interior, completed in the 1850s, includes magnificent stained glass and an ornate altar.

Designed by British architect Frank Willis and modeled after thirteenth-century rural English churches, the Episcopal Chapel of the Cross in Madison County was consecrated in July 1852. Its bell tower and steeply pitched roof are classic Gothic Revival elements. Two Gothic Revival buildings, the Sisters of Mercy convent at St. Francis Xavier Academy in Vicksburg and the Sacred Heart Catholic Church in Rodney, were built in 1868. The convent, which is listed on the National Register of Historic Places, is a four-story brick structure with multiple chimneys. Today it is one of five buildings that make up the Southern Cultural Heritage Complex. Sacred Heart Catholic Church is a simple wooden Carpenter Gothic structure with an arched doorway and windows. Sacred Heart was moved to Grand Gulf Military State Park in 1983 and now serves as a nondenominational Confederate Memorial Chapel.

One example of residential Gothic Revival architecture is Manship House in Jackson. Built in 1857 by Charles Henry Manship, Jackson's mayor during the Civil War, this one-story frame house with a steeply pitched roof was patterned after a design from Downing's *Architecture of Country Houses*. Manship added floor-to-ceiling windows and a gallery that bisects the house, thereby improving ventilation. The Manship House has been restored and is now operated by the Mississippi Department of Archives and History as a museum.

Another 1857 home, Cedarhurst in Holly Springs, was the residence of writer Sherwood Bonner. The house has a balcony with an iron lacework balustrade that was made at a local foundry. Its multiple chimneys, finials, and gingerbread ornamentation on the gables and the archways over the front porch are characteristic of the Gothic Revival style.

The intricate decorative details of residential Gothic Revival fell out of public favor at the end of the nineteenth century, and residential architecture moved toward the Queen Anne style.

Linda Arrington Lusk
Nashville, Tennessee

Chapel of the Cross Episcopal Church website, www.chapelofthecrossms.org; Mary Wallace Crocker, *Historic Architecture in Mississippi* (1973); Elmo Howell, *Mississippi Home-Places: Notes on Literature and History* (1988); Mary Carol Miller, *Great Houses of Mississippi* (2004); Mississippi Department of Archives and History, Manship House Museum website, http://mdah.state.ms.us/museum/manship/index.html; Visit Holly Springs website, www.visithollysprings.org; Visit Natchez website, www.visitnatchez.com.

Govan, Daniel Chevilette
(1829–1911) Confederate General

Confederate general Daniel Chevilette Govan was born in Northampton County, North Carolina, on 4 July 1829. He was the son of Andrew Robison Govan, a former South Carolina congressman, and Mary Pugh Jones Govan. After a short time in Tennessee, the family settled near Holly Springs, Mississippi. After attending the University of South Carolina, Govan went to California with a party led by his cousin, future Confederate general Ben McCullough. McCullough became sheriff of Sacramento County, while Govan served as his deputy until his return to Mississippi in 1852. The following year he married Mary Otey, daughter of the Episcopal bishop of Tennessee, James Hervey Otey. The newlyweds moved to Arkansas, where they lived until Govan enlisted in the Confederate Army in 1861. He recruited a company and became its captain.

After his company was attached to the 2nd Arkansas Regiment early in 1862, Govan became a colonel and led the regiment at Shiloh, the invasion of Kentucky, Murfreesboro, and Chickamauga. By that time, the 2nd Arkansas was so reduced by battle and disease that it and the 15th Arkansas were consolidated into a single regiment.

Govan was promoted to brigadier general in December 1863. His brigade, mostly of Arkansas troops, was part of Patrick Cleburne's division. On 22 July 1864, during the Battle of Atlanta, Govan's brigade captured the entire 16th Iowa Regiment. The following September, at the Battle of Jonesboro, Govan's brigade was posted at the apex of a sharp angle of the Confederate lines. The brigade was overwhelmed and Govan and many of his men were captured. He was exchanged shortly thereafter for Brig. Gen. George Stoneman and returned to the army.

On 30 November 1864 at the Battle of Franklin, in Tennessee, Govan was wounded while his brigade was in the thick of the fighting that wrecked the Confederate Army of Tennessee. Govan and what was left of his unit later served with Lt. Gen. Joseph E. Johnston during the Carolinas Campaign and surrendered with him at Durham, North Carolina, on 26 April 1865. By that time, Govan's brigade consisted of two consolidated regiments that comprised the remnants of twenty former regiments.

After the war, Govan returned to Arkansas. In 1883 he attended a reunion of the 16th Iowa and returned its flag. In 1894 Pres. Grover Cleveland appointed Govan to serve as Indian agent of the Tulalip Agency in Washington State, a post he held until 1898, when he returned east. Govan spent the rest of his life in Tennessee and Mississippi and died on 12 March 1911.

David A. Norris

Wilmington, North Carolina

David S. Heidler and Jeanne T. Heidler, *The Encyclopedia of the American Civil War* (2000); William S. Powell, ed., *Dictionary of North Carolina Biography* (1996); Daniel E. Sutherland, *Arkansas Historical Quarterly* (Autumn 1995); Craig L. Symonds, *Stonewall of the West* (1997); Ezra J. Warner, *Generals in Gray: The Lives of the Confederate Commanders* (1959); US War Department, *The War of the Rebellion: A Compilation of the Official Records of the Union and Confederate Armies* (1901).

Governor and Lieutenant Governor, Offices of

Since achieving statehood in 1817, Mississippi has demonstrated a determined, independent streak and willingness to depart from national norms. This uniqueness is clear when considering the offices of governor and lieutenant governor. While the federal model and the model in many other states provide for a strong chief executive and a weak second in command, Mississippi embarked on a different path. Political scientists and interested observers routinely rank Mississippi's governor as one of the nation's weakest while describing the office of lieutenant governor as one of the most powerful. This contrast results from both deliberate choices and unintentional consequences, from political considerations and traditions that have evolved over almost two centuries.

Mississippi's first constitutional convention reflected the wariness of strong executives that permeated the newly independent country. Determined to avoid the autocratic executives they opposed in the past, such as the British Crown and even the territorial governors appointed by the newborn United States, the delegates adopted a constitution limiting the governor to a single two-year term and providing the office with little control over appointments. Subsequent constitutions adopted by Mississippi in 1832, 1869, and 1890 continued the tradition of a weak governor.

The Constitution of 1890, which remains in effect, provides for a governor who performs the common duties of a chief executive, serves as commander in chief of the state militia or National Guard, grants pardons, and temporarily appoints people to fill vacancies until the next election. The governor is charged with enforcing the state's laws but has little real authority to carry out this role. The constitution intentionally diffused executive power by creating independently elected executive officers such as lieutenant governor and attorney general who faced little or no term limits. Much of the Mississippi bureaucracy has more recently come under the control of seven other independently elected statewide officials, six elected commissioners for public utilities and transportation, and more than 130 largely independent boards and commissions. However, legal action and the personal political skills of recent governors have begun to increase the powers of the office.

In 1983 the Mississippi Supreme Court declared that the large number of legislators serving on the boards and commissions of executive agencies was an unconstitutional violation of separation of powers. The legislature passed a major 1984 reorganization of the executive branch that among other things gave the governor exclusive power to propose the annual executive budget. In 1986 citizens adopted a constitutional amendment allowing governors to serve two consecutive terms, giving governors much more leverage since they have more time to make appointments to agency governing boards.

Governors historically assumed a passive stance toward legislating and day-to-day government operations but more recently have pursued a more aggressive approach. Their tools include the item veto, the two-thirds vote required to override a veto, and the power to call special sessions of the legislature and to set the agenda. Television and social media networking have greatly increased the governor's power to appeal directly to the people for policy changes.

The advent of the competitive two-party system in Mississippi has enabled the governor to use party discipline when dealing with the legislature. When the Democrats were the only party of note in Mississippi, geographical, racial, and other factions existed and political party discipline did not.

The rebirth of the state's Republican Party introduced a new dynamic into the relationship between the governor and legislature.

Mississippi's lieutenant governorship was not intentionally designed to be one of the nation's most powerful but evolved as such. Much of this power can be credited to the fact that the lieutenant governor is elected independently of the governor, to the original lack of term limits, and to the traditional rules of the State Senate, which are not enshrined in the constitution itself. The lieutenant governor is president of the Senate, can vote in case of a tie, assigns bills to committees and largely sets the agenda, and appoints committees and their chairs. The lieutenant governor also becomes governor when the governor travels out of the state. Some controversy has resulted from this provision when lieutenant governors acting as governors have called special sessions of the legislature or pardoned criminals without the sitting governors' consent. The Mississippi Senate does not use a seniority system for committee assignments similar to Congress, so the lieutenant governor is free to leverage assignments for assistance with public policy goals. One of the few checks on the office's power was the 1992 adoption of a constitutional amendment limiting the office to two terms.

Brian Wilson
University of Mississippi

Dana B. Brammer and John W. Winkle, eds., *A Contemporary Analysis of Mississippi's Constitutional Government: Proceedings of a Forum, May 2–3, 1986* (1986); Dale Krane and Stephen D. Shaffer, *Mississippi Government and Politics: Modernizers versus Traditionalists* (1992); Thomas E. Kynerd, *Administrative Reorganization of Mississippi Government: A Study in Politics* (1978); Jere Nash and Andy Taggart, *Mississippi Politics: The Struggle for Power, 1976–2006* (2006); John W. Winkle, *The Mississippi State Constitution: A Reference Guide* (1993).

Governors

David Holmes, 1817–20
George Poindexter, 1820–22
Walter Leake, 1822–25
Gerard Chittocque Brandon, 1825–26
David Holmes, 1826
Gerard Chittocque Brandon, 1826–32
Abram M. Scott, 1832–33
Charles Lynch, 1833
Hiram G. Runnels, 1833–35
John Anthony Quitman, 1835–36
Charles Lynch, 1836–38
Alexander Gallatin McNutt, 1838–42
Tilghman Mayfield Tucker, 1842–44
Albert Gallatin Brown, 1844–48
Joseph W. Matthews, 1848–50
John Anthony Quitman, 1850–51
John Isaac Guion, 1851

James Whitfield, 1851–52
Henry Stuart Foote, 1852–54
John Jones Pettus, 1854
John J. McRae, 1854–57
William McWillie, 1857–59
John Jones Pettus, 1859–63
Charles Clark, 1863–65
William Lewis Sharkey, 1865
Benjamin G. Humphreys, 1865–68
Adelbert Ames, 1868–70
James Lusk Alcorn, 1870–71
Ridgley Ceylon Powers, 1871–74
Adelbert Ames, 1874–76
John Marshall Stone, 1876–82
Robert Lowery, 1882–90
John Marshall Stone, 1890–96
Anselm Joseph McLaurin, 1896–1900
Andrew Houston Longino, 1900–1904
James Kimble Vardaman, 1904–8
Edmond Favor Noel, 1908–12
Earl Leroy Brewer, 1912–16
Theodore Gilmore Bilbo, 1916–20
Lee Maurice Russell, 1920–24
Henry Lewis Whitfield, 1924–27
Dennis Murphree, 1927–28
Theodore Gilmore Bilbo, 1928–32
Martin S. Conner, 1932–36
Hugh Lawson White, 1936–40
Paul Burney Johnson Sr., 1940–43
Dennis Murphree, 1943–44
Thomas Lowry Bailey, 1944–46
Fielding L. Wright, 1946–52
Hugh Lawson White, 1952–56
James Plemon Coleman, 1956–60
Ross Robert Barnett, 1960–64
Paul Burney Johnson Jr., 1964–68
John Bell Williams, 1968–72
William Lowe Waller Sr., 1972–76
Charles Clifton Finch, 1976–80
William Forrest Winter, 1980–84
William A. Allain, 1984–88
Raymond Edwin Mabus Jr., 1988–92
Daniel Kirkwood Fordice, 1992–2000
David Ronald Musgrove, 2000–2004
Haley Reeves Barbour, 2004–12
Dewey Phillip Bryant, 2012–

Lieutenant Governors

Duncan Steward, 1817–20
James Patton, 1820–22
David Dickson, 1822–24
Gerard Chittocque Brandon, 1824–26
Abram M. Scott, 1828–32

Fountain Winston, 1832

Charles Lynch, 1833–34

P. Briscoe, 1834–36

W. Van Norman, 1836–37

Alexander G. McNutt, 1837–38

A. L. Bingaman, 1838–40

G. B. Augustus, 1840–42

Jesse Speight, 1842–43

A. Fox, 1843–44

Jesse Speight, 1844–46

G. T. Swan, 1846–48

Dabney Lipscomb, 1848–51

James Whitfield, 1851–54

John J. Pettus, 1854–58

James Drane, 1858–65

John M. Simonton, 1865–69

Ridgley Ceylon Powers, 1870–71

Alexander K. Davis, 1871–76

John M. Stone, 1876–78

William H. Sims, 1878–82

G. D. Shands, 1882–90

M. M. Evans, 1890–96

J. H. Jones, 1896–1900

James T. Harrison, 1900–1904

John Prentiss Carter, 1904–8

Luther Manship, 1908–12

Theodore Gilmore Bilbo, 1912–16

Lee Maurice Russell, 1916–20

Homer H. Casteel, 1920–24

Dennis Murphree, 1924–27

Clayton B. Adams, 1928–32

Dennis Murphree, 1932–36

Jacob Buehler Snider, 1936–40

Dennis Murphree, 1940–43

Fielding L. Wright, 1944–46

Samuel Edgerton Lumpkin, 1948–52

Carroll Gartin, 1952–60

Paul B. Johnson Jr., 1960–64

Carroll Gartin, 1964–66

Charles L. Sullivan, 1968–72

William F. Winter, 1972–76

Evelyn Gandy, 1976–80

Brad J. Dye Jr., 1980–92

Eddie Jerome Briggs, 1992–96

David Ronald Musgrove, 1996–2000

Amy Tuck, 2000–2008

Dewey Phillip Bryant, 2008–12

Jonathon Tate Reeves, 2012–

Governor's Mansion

The 1841 Mississippi Governor's Mansion is the second-oldest continuously occupied governor's residence in the United States. Designed by English-born architect William Nichols, who also designed the 1839 Mississippi Capitol, the mansion is an outstanding example of domestic Greek Revival architecture. The 334 BC choragic monument of Lysicrates in Athens was the basis for Nichols's design of the mansion's semicircular front portico supported by Corinthian columns. Nichols designed ornately carved architraves with the anthemion (Greek honeysuckle) for the large entrances, with pocket doors between the dining room and the east parlor and between the double west parlors as well as for the front door and doors of first-floor rooms. These architraves were patterned after engravings published in Minard Lafever's *The Beauties of Modern Architecture* (1839). Lafever's publication was also the source for Nichols's rosette design for the carved wooden mantel in the southwest bedroom, one of the four original second-floor bedrooms.

With the coming of the Civil War, Gov. John Jones Pettus ordered the removal of most of the mansion's furniture, which was shipped to Macon, the temporary state capital, for safekeeping. At the war's end, however, this furniture—undoubtedly some of the mansion's finest—could not be located. Wounded Confederate soldiers were housed in the mansion for part of the first half of 1863. Then, on 18 July, Gen. William Tecumseh Sherman celebrated the fall of Vicksburg with a victory dinner at the mansion.

The mansion survived the war but subsequently suffered neglect and fell into disrepair. By 1904 many citizens were calling for its demolition, and the legislature considered disposing of the mansion to make room for commercial development. After

Governor's Mansion, 316 East Capitol Street, Jackson, ca. 1936 (Photograph by Jack E. Boucher, Library of Congress, Washington, D.C. [HABS MISS, 25-JACK, 6-58])

his January 1908 inauguration, Gov. Edmond Noel announced that because of the structure's poor condition, he and his family would reside at the Edwards House. Patriotic women's organizations and other groups urged that the mansion be saved, and in March 1908 the legislature allocated thirty thousand dollars for a renovation, which was to be directed by local architect William S. Hull.

The 1908–9 renovation included the construction of a two-story family annex to the rear of mansion. The three-part window on the rear facade was bricked in, and the original twelve-pane windows were replaced with the more modern double-pane style. The original staircase was removed and replaced with a center staircase to give access to the family annex. New entrances from the back hall to the dining room and from the back hall to the northwest parlor were constructed to match the 1841 entrances in both size and form. The original front door was replaced with a beveled glass door. Thin hardwood floors were placed over the original wide heart pine plank floors. A layer of yellow pressed brick was applied to the original mansion exterior to match the yellow pressed brick of the family annex. The mansion remained yellow until it was painted white during the 1940–43 term of Gov. Paul B. Johnson Sr.

Despite occasional appropriations for repair and furnishings, the mansion deteriorated structurally until a 1971 inspection indicated that the building was no longer safe for occupancy. Gov. John Bell Williams and his family moved out, and the mansion's future again looked bleak.

During the 1971 gubernatorial campaign, candidate William Waller and his wife, Carroll, recommended a complete restoration of the mansion, as did the Mississippi Department of Archives and History. Public support for preservation grew, and shortly after Waller's January 1972 inauguration as governor, the legislature allocated $2.7 million for a major restoration and renovation between 1972 and 1975. The State Building Commission appointed Charlotte Capers, who had served as director of the Department of Archives and History during the restoration of the Old Capitol and who now held the post of director of publications and special projects for the department, to serve as principal executive for the mansion project. Consultants on the project included architectural historian Charles E. Patterson, noted for his work on Independence Hall and the Historic American Buildings Survey, and architect and interior designer Edward Vason Jones, who had worked on the White House and the US State Department Diplomatic Reception Rooms.

Investigation of the house and historical records led to discoveries such as the location of the original staircase. Sliding doors that had been encased in walls were uncovered. The hardwood flooring was removed to expose the original wide heart pine plank floor. A geometric painted border was found on the original floor in the double west parlors. Jones oversaw the acquisition of museum-quality furnishings that would be compatible with the mansion's Greek Revival style.

Carroll Waller spearheaded fund-raising to match a twenty-thousand-dollar grant from the Mississippi American Revolution Bicentennial Commission. In 1975 landscape architect William Garbo designed formal gardens with walkways, benches, two gazebos, and a columned fountain. Around a rose garden was placed a miniature replica of the cast iron fence that had surrounded the perimeter of the mansion grounds from 1855 to 1908.

On 24 April 1975 the National Park Service designated the Governor's Mansion a National Historic Landmark. On 8 June a formal dedication ceremony was held and the mansion again opened its doors to the public.

In 1980 the legislature gave the Mississippi Department of Archives and History authority over the use of the historic section and grounds of the Governor's Mansion. The building still serves as the residence for the state's chief executive, while the 1841 section is open for free guided tours, meaning that the mansion welcomes visitors from schoolchildren to tourists to dignitaries from the United States and abroad.

Mary Lohrenz
Mississippi Governor's Mansion

Helen Cain and Anne D. Czarniecki, *An Illustrated Guide to the Mississippi Governor's Mansion* (1984); Mary Lohrenz, *Mississippi Governor's Mansion Docent Manual* (March 2006); Mississippi Department of Archives and History website, www.mdah.state.ms.us; C. Ford Peatross and Robert O. Mellown, *William Nichols, Architect* (1979); David G. Sansing and Carroll Waller, *A History of the Mississippi Governor's Mansion* (1977).

Graham, Alice Walworth
(1905–1994) Author

Born in Natchez on 24 February 1905, novelist Alice Walworth Graham was the daughter of John Periander Walworth and Alice Leslie Gordon Walworth. She attended Mississippi State College for Women (now Mississippi University for Women) in 1922–23. She married Richard Norwood Graham, a civil engineer, in 1936 and gave birth to one son, Richard Jr. After living in her paternal family home in Natchez from 1936 to 1939, the Grahams moved to New Orleans, where she developed her writing career.

Graham was a popular mid-twentieth-century novelist who wrote in the damsel-in-distress genre. While elements of realism appear in her work, romantic entanglements and family heritage are the overwhelming factors. *Lost River* (1938) depicts the aftermath of the Civil War from the traditional white landowners' perspective of devastation and loss. *Romantic Lady* (1952) continued this tradition, as did *Indigo*

Bend (1953) and *Cibola* (1962), both of which focused on the Natchez area. *The Vows of the Peacock* (1955), *Shield of Honor* (1957), and *The Summer Queen* (1973) were all historical romances set among the royalty of England.

Graham's second novel, *The Natchez Woman* (1950), rose above this genre with its first-person point of view and setting between the world wars. Far from the conventional moonlight and magnolias heroine of the Old South, Jane Elliston can be characterized as a modern woman whose sexual feelings outweigh her commitment to her aging maiden aunts and their values, such as preserving her virginity by discouraging marriage. In fact, this tale of passion includes a celebration of breaking with the sexual mores of the post–World War I era, as Jane rejoices after her first sexual encounter, which she initiates: "According to everything I'd been taught, after having flung my bonnet over the windmill, I should have wept bitter tears into my pillow. I didn't." Later in the same passage, Jane admits to understanding her newly claimed status in the world by intentionally subverting societal expectations: "I've never set myself up as a rebel against society. A façade of invulnerable respectability often allows more leeway. If I want something beyond the limits of the established code, I just make a little sortie and retire again, unsuspected." Jane has not only agency but the courage to use it, waging a private war on double standards. The novel concludes with the advent of World War II, and Jane, though now a cynic, divorced from her first lover and remarried without passion, dismisses the supposed "fruits of old age" at the coming of her first grandchild: "How tedious they sounded. My God! Who wanted that!" Thus she regrets not her unconventional life choices but the fact that her life is ending conventionally. This novel breaks with the romanticized past of her other works to portray a heroine whose actions empower her rather than function as a tribute to a lost civilization.

Graham returned to Natchez in 1962 and lived there until her death in 1994.

Amy Pardo
Mississippi University for Women

Alice Walworth Graham Papers, Louisiana and Lower Mississippi Valley Collections, Special Collections, Louisiana State University Library.

Granberry, Edwin

(1897–1988) Author

Edwin Granberry was a celebrated writer and teacher whose works engaged the interaction between the southern land-holding class and laborers in the early twentieth century. Born in Meridian, Mississippi, Granberry moved with his family to Jacksonville, Florida, as a child and attended the University of Florida. After serving in the US Marine Corps during World War I, he attended Columbia University, graduating in 1920. He became a professor of romance languages at Miami University of Ohio before attending the renowned 47 Workshop at Harvard from 1922 to 1924, during which time he wrote the play *Hitch Your Wagon to a Star.*

In March 1924 Granberry married Mabel Leflar, and they went on to have three sons. From 1925 to 1933 Granberry served as Latin and French master at Stevens School in New Jersey. During this era he published *The Ancient Hunger* (1927), *Strangers and Lovers* (1928), and *The Erl King* (1930). His 1932 "A Trip to Czardis" won the O. Henry Memorial Award as the year's best short story; Granberry later expanded the story into a novel, which was released in 1966. In addition to writing fiction, Granberry worked with artist Roy Crane and later Henry Schlensker on the cartoon *Buz Sawyer.*

In 1933 Granberry became writer in residence at Rollins College in Winter Park, Florida, and in 1940 he was named the school's Irving Bacheller Professor of Creative Writing. He was an inspiring and innovative professor, often holding class outdoors or at his home. He developed friendships with writers Sinclair Lewis, Thornton Wilder, Irving Bacheller, and Marjorie Kinnan Rawlings, who sometimes appeared in his classes as guest lecturers.

In 1936 Granberry reviewed Margaret Mitchell's *Gone with the Wind* in the *New York Sun*, proclaiming the work a *War and Peace* for twentieth-century America and comparing it to the writings of Hardy and Dickens. Granberry viewed the work as an antidote to southern writing of the time, which was concerned primarily with barren, cruel landscapes rife with incest and abject poverty and provided no redeeming view of the contemporary South. Mitchell wrote to Granberry a few weeks after the review was published, beginning a close friendship between the authors and their families.

Critics described Granberry's work as examining the romantic "feudal" South, a space where noble plantation or ranch owners interact with poor whites, who are often (though not always) portrayed as noble. Granberry's novels evoke the wild landscapes of Florida (*A Trip to Czardis*, *Strangers and Lovers*, and *The Erl King*) and of the western prairies (*The Ancient Hunger*), with settings particularly attuned to the environment. Granberry wrote evocatively of seasonal change and of human interaction with the natural world and was known as a "backyard agriculturalist, zoologist, and ornithologist." Sexuality is an important theme in Granberry's work, with issues of infertility and gender roles driving his narratives.

Granberry died on 5 December 1988.

Becca Walton
University of Mississippi

G

Edwin Granberry, *New York Sun* (July 1936); Edwin Phillips Granberry Collection, Department of Archives and Special Collections, J. D. Williams Library, University of Mississippi.

Grange

Founded in 1867 in Washington, D.C., by Minnesota farmer Oliver H. Kelley and six friends, the Grange, also known as the Order of Patrons of Husbandry, was the first US national organization of farmers. A fraternal organization similar to the Masons, with secret rituals and seven degrees of rank, the Grange served chiefly as a social club for isolated rural families in the West and the South in the 1870s and 1880s. Although technically apolitical in the sense that its members did not run for office or endorse parties or candidates, it engaged heavily in lobbying Congress and state legislatures for reforms that would benefit rural America, such as regulation of railroad shipping rates, rural free delivery of the US mail, and more and better schools and colleges in the hinterlands.

By 1871 the National Grange had established two of its first three southern chapters in Mississippi. The Mississippi state Grange grew rapidly in the early 1870s, owing partly to the convenience that Ku Klux Klansmen found in using the Grange, with its secretive nature, as a front for violent activities during Reconstruction. Nationally, Grange membership began to dissipate after 1875, and Mississippi's state Grange followed suit, but not before accomplishing one of its main goals—stripping the University of Mississippi of its Morrill Land Grant and establishing a separate state agricultural and mechanical college, which was founded in Oktibbeha County in 1878. This college is now Mississippi State University and was the second of its kind in the South.

In the 1880s many state Granges struggled for survival, but the Mississippi Grange remained the most consistently vibrant and active in the South, rivaled only by the Texas Grange. One reason for this organizational strength lay in the fact that the Mississippi agricultural and mechanical college administration and faculty used Grangers as students in out-of-class laboratories of experimental farming techniques. Another reason was the leadership of Mississippi's US senator, James Z. George, who cosponsored the 1887 measure that established agricultural experiment stations around the nation. A third and more important reason was that in 1886 state grange master Putnam Darden was elected national grange master, an exalted position that filled Mississippi Grangers with pride. However, Darden died in 1887 and thus held the position only briefly.

Darden's death, coupled with the rise of the National Farmers' Alliance at about the same time, led to another decline in Grange membership in Mississippi. The Farmers' Alliance destroyed the Grange in several southern states, but the Mississippi organization hung on despite its diminished membership. In the mid-1890s the Grange made a strong and semieffective effort to woo back Alliance members, but the Mississippi Grange finally folded in 1898, by which time much of the National Grange's political agenda had been accomplished and the changing needs of rural farmers no longer justified the continuation of the organization.

Thomas Adams Upchurch
East Georgia College

Stephen Cresswell, *Rednecks, Redeemers, and Race: Mississippi after Reconstruction, 1877–1917* (2006); David H. Howard, *People, Pride, and Progress: 125 Years of the Grange in America* (1992); Albert Kirwan, *Revolt of the Rednecks: Mississippi Politics, 1876–1925* (1965); Sven D. Nordin, *Rich Harvest: A History of the Grange, 1867–1900* (1974); Thomas Adams Upchurch, *Journal of Mississippi History* (Fall 2003).

Grant, Ulysses S., in Mississippi

By the time Ulysses S. Grant contemplated a campaign in Mississippi in 1862, he was no longer an obscure officer from Illinois. Victory at Fort Donelson in February 1862 made him a national hero, and a ferocious battle at Shiloh followed 6–7 April. Grant was initially surprised at Shiloh, but his troops recovered and on the second day of the fighting compelled the Confederates to retreat to Corinth. Grant was temporarily superseded by Henry W. Halleck but was restored to departmental command after Halleck went to Washington as general in chief. That autumn Grant contemplated a two-pronged assault against Vicksburg. He would move overland through the state while William Tecumseh Sherman sailed from Memphis; together the two might capture Vicksburg. Grant's plan went awry after Confederate cavalry under Earl Van Dorn captured and burned the Union supply depot at Holly Springs while Nathan Bedford Forrest wreaked havoc on Grant's communications line. Grant abandoned his plan and withdrew to Memphis while Sherman debarked above Vicksburg and was repulsed at Chickasaw Bayou in late December.

Despite this inauspicious beginning, an undaunted Grant took charge of an assortment of Federal units on both sides of the Mississippi River. He did so in part because an army rival, Maj. Gen. John A. McClernand, was contemplating the idea of leading a force down the river against Vicksburg. Both Grant and Sherman distrusted McClernand's abilities and eventually loathed him. Throughout the winter and spring of 1862–63 Grant attempted to gain ground and thus position himself to attack Vicksburg: his unsuccessful efforts included several canal projects designed in part to bypass Vicksburg batteries, an ambitious plan to utilize the waterways of the Yazoo-Mississippi Delta (the Yazoo Pass expedition), and another involving naval vessels moving through a labyrinth of bayous, rivers, and streams (the Steele's Bayou expedition). Grant later downplayed these efforts, but he may have harbored greater hopes than he later implied. He defended the canal projects as a means of keeping the men busy, but disease stalked the regiments and stirred criticism.

In mid-April, Grant and Adm. David Dixon Porter agreed to a bold venture. Porter ran several gunboats and transports past the Vicksburg batteries while army units marched down the Louisiana side of the river. On 30 April 1863 the navy began ferrying Grant's forces across the Mississippi. Grant felt enormous relief when his men had safely reached "dry ground on the same side of the river with the enemy." He rapidly spread out his army, keeping the Confederates unsure of his movements and intentions. His soldiers carried just a few days' rations. Battles were fought and won at Grand Gulf, Port Gibson, Raymond, Jackson, Champion Hill, and the Big Black River. Two assaults on Vicksburg were repelled in May, and Grant reluctantly settled down to a siege that ended with Confederate capitulation on 4 July. It was a masterful campaign of maneuver and combat, boldly conceived and expertly executed. Sherman had remonstrated against Grant's plan, arguing that it might end disastrously, and Lincoln confessed in a congratulatory message that he had viewed Grant's movements after his initial successes at Grand Gulf and Port Gibson as mistaken. Grant allayed those fears.

Grant also paid attention to political realities. The 1862 elections had not gone well for the administration, and he recognized that victories were needed to buoy spirits in the North. Unlike Sherman, who disliked African Americans and resented the idea of enlisting black men, Grant accepted the Emancipation Proclamation and supported humanitarian efforts on behalf of escaped slaves. When Adj. Gen. Lorenzo Thomas came to the Mississippi Valley in 1863 to enlist black men into military service, Grant allowed Thomas to work unfettered and posed no obstacles. All of these things help to explain why Lincoln sustained Grant despite some considerable false starts in late 1862 and early 1863. One can only speculate how Lincoln would have reacted if Grant had suffered a dreadful reverse after crossing the Mississippi.

Vicksburg was Grant's greatest campaign. Lost Cause apologists later assailed Grant as a butcher, citing his high casualties during the 1864–65 campaign in Virginia. But Grant was no butcher in Mississippi in the spring and summer of 1863. He abandoned his supply base, moved quickly, landed one blow after another, and kept one eye on Gen. Joseph E. Johnston's forces while attacking Vicksburg. Grant suffered relatively low casualties while keeping the enemy confused and off balance, and military officers still study his campaign.

Grant subsequently went from Vicksburg to Chattanooga, where he won fresh laurels that resulted in his being summoned to Washington and placed in charge of the entire Union war effort. His efforts in Mississippi transformed Grant and dealt the Confederacy an incalculable blow.

Christopher Losson
St. Joseph, Missouri

Michael B. Ballard, *Vicksburg: The Campaign that Opened the Mississippi* (2004); Ulysses S. Grant, *Personal Memoirs of U. S. Grant* (1885–1886); Brooks D. Simpson, *Ulysses S. Grant: Triumph over Adversity, 1822–1865* (2000); Ulysses S. Grant Collection, Mississippi State University.

G

Gray, Duncan Montgomery, Jr.

(1926–2016) Religious Leader

Episcopal bishop and activist Duncan Montgomery Gray Jr. was born on 21 September 1926 in Canton, Mississippi. His father, Duncan Montgomery Gray Sr., served as the fifth coadjutor bishop of the Diocese of Mississippi from 1943 to 1966. The younger Gray spent his early childhood and adolescence in Columbus, Meridian, and Greenwood. After graduating from Jackson's Central High School, he participated in the US Navy's V-12 program. He earned a bachelor's degree in electrical engineering at Tulane University and in 1948 took an engineering position with Westinghouse in Pittsburgh. On 9 February of that year, he married Ruth Miller Spivey, and they went on to have four children.

From 1950 to 1953 Gray studied theology at the University of the South in Sewanee, Tennessee, receiving a master of divinity degree. He was ordained a priest in October 1953 and served in small congregations in Cleveland, Rosedale, and Oxford, Mississippi, over the remainder of the decade.

Gray became a noted southern spokesperson for integration in the 1950s and 1960s. During his tenure as president of the Sewanee seminary student body, he and others met with the board of trustees regarding the integration of the seminary. In 1956 he was asked to leave the Mississippi State College campus after presenting a pro-integration speech during a Religious Emphasis Week program. Most notably, however, during the days of rioting that followed James

Duncan Montgomery Gray Jr., St. Peter's Episcopal Church, Oxford, 1962 (Martin J. Dain Collection, Department of Archives and Special Collections, J. D. Williams Library, University of Mississippi)

Meredith's 1962 enrollment at the University of Mississippi, Gray was a voice of calm and moderation, attempting to persuade students to discontinue their irrational behavior. He preached a similar sermon as part of the Day of Repentance that followed the riots.

Gray continued his activism through the 1980s. As rector of St. Peter's Church in Meridian, he and other clergy formed the Committee of Conscience that helped to rebuild African American churches bombed and burned by Ku Klux Klan members. He worked with the Lauderdale Economic Assistance Program, the first community action agency sponsored by white liberals and one of the groups that competed for control of the state's Head Start Centers in the mid-1960s.

In addition, he served as president of the Mississippi Council on Human Relations from 1963 to 1967, was a board member of the Southern Regional Council, and chaired Meridian's Title I Advisory Committee. He served as a member of the Mississippi State Advisory Committee to the US Commission on Civil Rights, the Mississippi Hunger Coalition, Jacksonians for Public Education, the Committee of Southern Churchmen, the Mississippi Religious Leadership Conference, the Mississippi Chapter of the American Civil Liberties Union, and Community Relations Service.

He was consecrated bishop coadjutor of the Diocese of Mississippi in 1974 and remained in that post until his retirement in 1993. His son, Duncan Montgomery Gray III, became bishop coadjutor of the Diocese of Mississippi in 2000.

Donald Cunnigen
University of Rhode Island

Will D. Campbell, *And Also with You: Duncan Gray and the American Dilemma* (1997); Donald Cunnigen, *Anglican and Episcopal History* (December 1998); Araminta Stone Johnson, *And One Was a Priest: The Life and Times of Duncan M. Gray Jr.* (2011); Gardiner H. Shattuck Jr., *Episcopalians and Race: Civil War to Civil Rights* (2000); Donald Williams, *An Oral History with the Right Reverend Duncan Gray Jr., D.D.* (1999).

Great Depression

While some accounts state that no people suffered more during the Great Depression than Mississippians, a majority of residents of the Magnolia State were impoverished long before 1929 and knew little but hard times. According to the 1920 census the state was 86.6 percent rural, two-thirds of the population farmed, and 70 percent were tenants or sharecroppers dependent on the price of cotton. After fetching nearly a dollar a pound during World War I, the staple's price fell sharply during the 1919–23 recession. Recovering to twenty cents per pound over the rest of the decade, the price eroded to less than a nickel per pound in 1932. Planters, tenants, and sharecroppers watched helplessly as farm income dwindled from $191 million in 1929 to a mere $41 million in 1932. No other state experienced such a precipitate drop in farm income. Moreover, any discussion of the farmer's dilemma after 1930 must include crimes of nature: boll weevils; the floods of 1927, 1932, and 1936; and the great southern drought of 1930–31. Paradoxically the drought reduced the amount of cotton grown without raising the price, leading to widespread support for various crop-reduction schemes in Mississippi and other cotton states.

Farmers were not alone as victims of diminishing income. The state's tiny manufacturing sector also suffered. Between 1929 and 1932, 1,165 small plants, more than 800 of them sawmills, ceased operations. The number of jobs in lumbering, fishing, manufacturing, and railroading dropped from 52,000 in 1929 to 28,000 in 1932, and payrolls dropped from $42 million to $14 million. In turn, the lack of consumer purchasing power devastated the state's retail business. In the supposedly prosperous 1920s, wholesale and retail prices were 44 percent lower than they had been during World War I, even before the crest of the Depression. After 1930, prices hit rock bottom.

Advertisements for grocery and dry goods stores indicate the depths to which the economy had plunged. Prices appearing in the *New Albany Gazette* in 1931 were typical: ten bars of soap for twenty-nine cents, potatoes at two cents a pound, boys' tennis shoes at seventy-five cents, and cotton-yard goods at ten cents a yard. But consumers had little or no income to spend. The entire stock of many stores was sold at public auction, and nearly one thousand stores closed, leaving an additional nine thousand people out of work. News notices told a vivid picture of deflation. In April 1932 the *Jackson Clarion-Ledger* reported that the Delta State Teachers College dining hall offered a full breakfast for ten cents and a dinner for twenty cents.

As individuals and businesses went broke, tax collections fell to a trickle, leaving state and county officials strapped for funds. Property assessments fell by $80 million between 1928 and 1932. In January 1932 state coffers contained a paltry $1,347, while the state debt reached $50 million. Lack of adequate revenue resulted in drastic cuts in services. Public schools, hospitals, and health units closed or operated with seriously curtailed funds. Many school districts were unable to pay teachers for a year, and others paid teachers only in scrip, often discounted up to 20 percent. Even members of the state legislature were unable to cash their salary warrants. Gov. Martin S. Conner used his own money to buy food for patients at the state's mental hospital. Only the adoption of the nation's first sales tax led to a balanced budget, but even that was a mixed blessing because of its regressive effect on low-income taxpayers. In the words of historian John Ray Skates, "The Great Depression harshly underlined the defects in Mississippi's economic order."

Because of the deflation in property values, the state treasury's 1932 receipts totaled only 64 percent of the preceding year's ad valorem taxes. Many private citizens now found themselves burdened with mortgages larger than the values of their homes or businesses. Even ex-governor Theodore G. Bilbo lost his pecan farm to the hard times. A staple of most survey histories of the Great Depression is a May 1932 headline from the *Literary Digest* declaring that on a single day in April, "One-Fourth of a State Sold for Taxes." How many Mississippians lost their homes in the Depression is hard to measure, but a good indication is that within eighteen months of Congress's passage of the 1933 Home Owners Loan Act, the Home Owners Loan Corporation received more than eighteen thousand applications from Mississippi totaling an estimated $30 million in property. The corporation eventually acted favorably on eight thousand of the applications.

With agriculture, manufacturing, and retail sales languishing, the banking system—never one of the nation's strongest—began to buckle. Property values shrank to their lowest level since 1850, payrolls dropped, and savings deposits fell by 50 percent from 1930 to 1933. Bank failures began in 1930, when fifty-nine banks went under, followed by fifty-six in 1931 and twelve in 1932. After the March 1933 national bank holiday, only four closed.

The Depression also had enormously high social costs. Whites replaced blacks in menial jobs. Lack of public funds for schools and health services punished blacks and poor whites alike. Most factory owners, either by willful neglect or by economic necessity, paid low wages to workers who had virtually no access to union protection. By 1939 the Congress of Industrial Organizations had only one hundred members in the state.

Unemployment figures fluctuated throughout the decade. Some indication of the serious nature of unemployment emerges from the fact that by June 1943, when the New Deal's Works Progress Administration was liquidated, $117 million had been allocated for the state, mostly for wages.

Significant recovery did not begin until 1936, when Gov. Hugh L. White's Balance Agriculture with Industry initiatives joined the massive injection of federal money into Mississippi by Pres. Franklin D. Roosevelt's New Deal ($450 million from 1933 to 1939). The onset of World War II brought robust economic growth and a modicum of social reform that neither Mississippi's political leaders nor New Deal largesse could achieve.

Martha H. Swain
Mississippi State University

Roger D. Tate Jr.
<NONE>

James C. Cobb, *The Most Southern Place on Earth: The Mississippi Delta and the Roots of Regional Identity* (1992); Oliver Emmerich, in *A History of Mississippi*, vol. 2, ed. Richard A. McLemore (1981); Martha H. Swain, *Pat Harrison: The New Deal Years* (1978); Roger D. Tate Jr., "Easing the Burden: The Era of the Great Depression in Mississippi" (PhD dissertation, University of Tennessee, 1978); William Winter, in *Mississippi Heroes*, ed. Dean Faulkner Wells and Hunter Cole (1980).

Great Migration

Scholars and other observers have long used the Great Migration to refer to a significant movement of African Americans from the South to other parts of the United States from 1914 until the early 1920s. People chose to leave the South in response to a combination of broad difficulties since the late 1800s—disfranchisement, segregation laws and Jim Crow practices, the rise of lynching and other forms of violence, and the gradual but clear decline in chances for owning land. People were also responding to the lure of jobs that opened up during World War I, when many northern industrial workers went to Europe and immigration of potential workers came to a halt. The availability of jobs was the specific reason for the timing of the Great Migration, but African Americans left Mississippi with a mixture of relief about putting many of the difficulties and fears of southern life behind them and excitement about the possibilities of city life.

Many migrants left Mississippi and the South after a series of internal moves—from the farm to the city or from sharecropping to seasonal work on levees or other construction projects. Members of sharecropping households had moved from place to place looking for labor arrangements with less debt and more possibility for owning land, but such opportunities diminished as the boll weevil destroyed crops and as large-scale agribusiness developed. Individuals often left Mississippi for Chicago or other northern cities where acquaintances lived and then became contacts for other migrants. South Chicago's Bronzeville neighborhood became home to a large community of African Americans from the South, especially Mississippi.

One of the greatest advertisers of life in the urban North was the nation's leading African American newspaper, the *Chicago Defender*, which had high circulation in Mississippi and especially in the Delta. The *Defender* touted the economic, cultural, and political potential of urban life and kept migrants in touch with news from Mississippi.

As historian Neil McMillen has detailed, Mississippi's population changed relatively little as a consequence of migration from 1880 to 1910. In fact, from 1880 to 1900, white migration from Mississippi was slightly greater than African American migration, and the numbers of white and African American migrants were roughly equal in 1910. The net population loss of African Americans dramatically increased over the next decade, far outstripping the number of white Mississippians who left. Precise statistics about migration are always problematic, but it seems clear that from 1914 to 1920, about one hundred thousand African Americans left Mississippi—about one-fifth of all the migrants who left the South.

The Great Migration resulted in significant population declines in most but not all parts of Mississippi. The number of African Americans fell in most Mississippi counties between 1910 and 1930, but the African American population of Hinds County increased as a consequence of migration to the city of Jackson. More dramatically, several Delta counties saw substantial population increases.

Black and white commentators on Mississippi life used the Great Migration as a way to discuss the place of African Americans in the United States. In *Black Boy*, Richard Wright divided his life into two sections, before and after he moved from the South, and near the end of the southern section, he wrote, "I was leaving the South to fling myself into the unknown, to meet other situations that would perhaps elicit from me other responses. And if I could meet enough of a different life, then, perhaps, gradually and slowly I might learn who I was, what I might be." African Ameri-

can religious leaders compared train travel from the South to biblical stories of movement to the Promised Land, and numerous blues musicians sang about the pains and potential of ramblin', sometimes with "Sweet Home Chicago" as a destination. African American leaders in Chicago, including antilynching activist and club organizer Ida B. Wells-Barnett, counseled migrants on how to find jobs, where to live, and how to reject appearances and mannerisms the leaders associated with rural poverty and Jim Crow. White Mississippians had varying responses to African American migration. Some condemned labor agents, and many agreed with the man who told Wright, "The North's no good for your people, boy." Greenville native William Alexander Percy, who identified himself as a "planter's son," wrote of African Americans who left Mississippi on a whim, suffered as individuals when they were accustomed to the community of plantation life, and were likely to need help returning to the South.

In recent years, some scholars have questioned whether the Great Migration was quite as distinctive as it long seemed. First, African Americans had left the South in substantial numbers in the decades before and after the Great Migration period and then in even greater numbers in the 1940s and 1950s. Second, larger numbers of white southerners moved to the North and West, but social commentators at the time generally neglected that migration, as have scholars until recently. Despite those important points, the Great Migration of the 1910s and 1920s stands as a turning point in black migration from the 1910s through the 1960s and as a dramatic response to the injustices of the Jim Crow South.

Ted Ownby
University of Mississippi

Davarian L. Baldwin, *Chicago's New Negroes: Modernity, the Great Migration, and Black Urban Life* (2007); John M. Giggie, *After Redemption: Jim Crow and the Transformation of African American Religion in the Delta, 1875–1915* (2008); James N. Gregory, *The Southern Diaspora: How the Great Migrations of Black and White Southerners Transformed America* (2005); James R. Grossman, *Land of Hope: Chicago, Black Southerners, and the Great Migration* (1989); Steven Hahn, *A Nation under Our Feet: Black Political Struggles from Slavery to the Great Migration* (2005); Neil McMillen, *Dark Journey: Black Mississippians in the Age of Jim Crow* (1990).

Greek Revival Architecture

The Greek war for independence in 1821 spawned a fascination in the United States with architectural finds from antiquity and heralded the Greek Revival period in architecture. Like the Federal style that immediately preceded it, Greek Revival elements first appeared in the design of public buildings such as schools, churches, and banks. Temple-like facades, symmetrical structural design, bas-relief friezes, and grand columns recalled classical times and are the hallmarks of Greek Revival design.

One of the first significant Greek Revival buildings in Mississippi was the Agricultural Bank of Natchez. Built around 1833, this structure incorporated Doric columns and a facade resembling an Ionic temple. Three of the state's best examples of public architecture in this style are Jackson's Old Capitol building, the Governor's Mansion, and the Lyceum on the campus of the University of Mississippi, all of them designed by British architect William Nichols. The Old Capitol, completed in 1839, includes a domed rotunda and stately Ionic columns. Construction on the Governor's Mansion was completed in 1842. With its massive portico and grand Corinthian columns, this building is the second-oldest continuously occupied governor's mansion in the nation. The Lyceum, completed in 1848, is the oldest building on the campus of the University of Mississippi and features the fluted Ionic columns typical of this period.

While Greek Revival architecture in Mississippi originated in the state's public buildings, it reached its apex in residential design. It is synonymous with the archetypal image of the columned antebellum plantation mansions of the South. Many design features of Greek Revival architecture served a practical purpose, helping to alleviate the heat of the Mississippi summers. Deep porches, high ceilings, and tall windows aided in ventilation. The simple design at the core of Greek Revival style permitted its replication in remote areas.

Holly Springs, the site of substantial prosperity in the late antebellum period, showcases one of the largest collective representations of decorative and elaborate Greek Revival residential architecture in the state. Montrose, built in 1858 by Alfred Brooks, contains an extravagant curved staircase and ornate ceiling medallions. Oakleigh, built the same year, has faux marble painted baseboards in its dining room, a fashionable design treatment at the time.

Natchez is synonymous with elegant elaborate mansions. Its two greatest examples of Greek Revival architecture are in Stanton Hall and Dunleith. The palatial Stanton Hall, built in 1857, covers an entire city block. Its facade contains a bas-relief frieze and Corinthian columns. Dunleith, with twenty-six Doric columns, is the last surviving example of a fully colonnaded home in Mississippi and features a two-tiered gallery that encircles the entire structure.

Perhaps the most recognizable and grandest colonnaded structure in the state is no longer standing. The remains of Windsor lie approximately ten miles southwest of Port Gibson. Built by Smith Coffee Daniell II, it was completed in 1861, only a few weeks prior to Daniell's death. The forty-foot-tall Corinthian columns that surrounded the mansion were its defining architectural element. In February 1890 an accidental fire destroyed the home, and only twenty-three of the original twenty-nine columns still stand.

Greek Revival architecture held sway in Mississippi long after the national obsession waned. Its popularity paralleled the state's strongest period of sustained economic growth, from 1830 to 1860. When the rule of King Cotton came to an end, so did the prevalence of Greek Revival architecture. Many of the great Greek Revival mansions of Mississippi were abandoned after the Civil War, some were destroyed by fires, and others were divided and used for tenant farmer and sharecropper housing.

Linda Arrington Lusk
Nashville, Tennessee

Mary Wallace Crocker, *Historic Architecture in Mississippi* (1973); Marc R. Matrana, *Lost Plantations of the South* (2009); Mary Carol Miller, *Great Houses of Mississippi* (2004); Mississippi Department of Archives and History, Old Capitol Museum website, www.mdah.state.ms.us/museum/oldcap/; National History Landmarks Program website, www.nps.gov/history/nhl; Oxford Convention and Visitors Bureau website, www.oxfordcvb.com; Ruins of Windsor website, http://home.olemiss.edu/~kcozart/ruins.html; Visit Holly Springs website, www.visithollysprings.org; Visit Natchez website, www.visitnatchez.com.

Greeks

For most of its history, Mississippi had few Greek immigrants. In 1910 the US census recorded only 117 people of Greek birth in the state, but that number slowly increased, reaching 207 in 1920, 342 in 1930, and 378 in 1960. Mississippi ranked near the bottom among all US states (along with the Dakotas, Arkansas, Vermont, Alaska, and Hawaii) in the number and percentage of Greek Americans.

Greeks started moving to America in significant numbers in the first two decades of the twentieth century. Most immigrants consisted of relatively poor young men, many of whom hoped to make some money and return to Greece. Immigration to the South was slow, and the region had few significant Greek communities but a number of successful individuals. Through most of the century, Mississippi's Greeks were spread out along the Gulf Coast, in Hinds County and Warren County, and in even smaller numbers in the Delta. In the 1940s no county had more than thirty-four Greek residents. Some of the more prominent Greek immigrants built on traditional skills to open restaurants. Arthur Fokakis moved to Hattiesburg in 1920 and soon started a café, the Coney Island, near the train station. James Zouboukos moved from Greece to Texas in 1935 and then to Jackson after World War II. He and his brother, Peter, opened the Elite Restaurant, which remains a fixture on East Capitol Street. Jackson, Madison, Biloxi, and Oxford have long been proud of their Greek restaurants.

Beginning in 1960, some individual counties had substantial numbers of Greeks—156 in Hinds County and 96 in Harrison County. The Greek population subsequently has increased steadily, reaching 3,703 in the 2010 census, most of them in Hinds County and on the Gulf Coast. In addition to older immigrants and their descendants, a second wave of Greeks has taken advantage of the Immigration Act of 1965, which encouraged immigration by people with skills, education, and American relatives.

Each May Jackson's Greek Orthodox Holy Trinity Church hosts the two-day Greekfest. According to popular chef Cat Cora, a Jackson native, church members walked into "a completely different world: long dark wooden pews, deep red altar curtains, golden icons catching the light from dozens of candles along the walls." On Celebration Sundays, the Zouboukos brothers prepared *kotopoulo psito*, a roast chicken dish with lemon and herbs, for "at least two hundred hungry Greek southerners." Cora, whose father, Spiro, was born in the Mississippi Delta after his parents left Skopelos and whose mother, Virginia, grew up making Greek dishes, recalls, "In Jackson, my mother and father were part of an extended family of Greeks for whom cooking and eating were the center of life." Cora, now living in Northern California, takes pride in mixing Greek and Mississippi food traditions.

Although Mississippi has not been home to a large Greek population, many of its residents have long shown interest to the point of reverence for some parts of ancient Greek tradition. Most obviously, Greek Revival architecture, emphasizing columned buildings that reflect balance, order, and a nearly timeless tradition, was extremely important in antebellum Mississippi and in the architecture, including many university and government buildings, that recalls that period. In addition, Greek-style statues are a common part of Mississippi gravestone design.

Ted Ownby
University of Mississippi

Charles C. Moskos, *Greek Americans: Struggle and Success* (1989); D. C. Young and Stephen Young, in *Ethnic Heritage in Mississippi*, ed. Barbara Carpenter (1992); Cat Cora, *Cat Cora's Kitchen* (2004); US Census, Population Reports.

Green, Martin Edwin
(1815–1863) Confederate General

Confederate general Martin Edwin Green was born in Fauquier County, Virginia, on 3 June 1815. In 1836 he moved with his wife to Lewis County, Missouri, where he and his brothers operated a steam sawmill. One brother, James, served as a US senator from Missouri between 1857 and 1861. In the summer of 1861 Martin Green recruited Confederate troops in Northeast Missouri and formed a cavalry command. After participating in minor engagements in the region, Green and his forces joined Gen. Sterling Price's army south of the Missouri River.

Green was elected colonel of a cavalry regiment formed in part by his original command and participated in the campaign that led to the capture of a Federal garrison at Lexington, Missouri, in September 1861. He also fought at Pea Ridge (or Elkhorn Tavern) the following March. Commissioned a brigadier general from 21 July 1862, Green led a brigade in Price's army and saw combat at Iuka, Corinth, and Hatchie Bridge. Green's brigade was attached to John S. Bowen's division in October 1862 and remained there through the Vicksburg Campaign, earning a reputation for combat prowess.

Green's Arkansas and Missouri troops were thrust into battle on 1 May 1863 as part of a Confederate force sent to check the advance of Federals under Gen. John A. McClernand toward Port Gibson. Although they fought valiantly over rough terrain, Green's men and the remainder of Bowen's troops were forced to withdraw through the town that evening. Two weeks later, Green's brigade was heavily engaged at Champion Hill, where they joined with Bowen's other units to temporarily stop the Union advance. Shortly thereafter, the brigade retreated across the Big Black River in the face of Yankee pressure. Bowen's division withdrew into the Vicksburg defenses, where commanding general John C. Pemberton used the Bowen's men as a ready reserve force.

In early June, Green's brigade was placed in line at a site where Federals employed mining operations to draw closer to the Confederate position. Green was slightly wounded on 25 June 1863 but returned to the front lines two days later. Although warned to fire a few shots before reconnoitering the enemy position, Green reportedly remarked that the bullet that would kill him had not yet been molded. A Union sharpshooter proved Green wrong, sending a slug into his head as he peered over the edge of a parapet. He died instantly.

Christopher Losson
St. Joseph, Missouri

Michael B. Ballard, *Vicksburg: The Campaign That Opened the Mississippi* (2004); Ezra Warner, *Generals in Gray: Lives of the Confederate Commanders* (1959); Jack D. Welsh, *Medical Histories of Confederate Generals* (1995).

Green, William Mercer

(1798–1887) Religious Leader

William Mercer Green was the first Episcopal bishop of Mississippi, a position he held from 1850 until his death in 1887. He also participated in the founding of the University of the South in Sewanee, Tennessee, and served as its chancellor from 1866 until 1887.

The Green family arrived in America in 1771 when Dr. Samuel Green of Liverpool, England, settled on the Cape Fear River near Wilmington, North Carolina. His son, William Green, became a wealthy rice planter and the father of William Mercer Green, who was born in Wilmington on 2 May 1798. William Mercer Green graduated from the University of North Carolina at Chapel Hill in 1818 and married Sally W. Snead of Williamsborough, North Carolina. After studying for the ministry, he became a rector at two North Carolina churches and then a chaplain and professor at the University of North Carolina from the 1820s through the 1840s. He received a doctor of divinity degree from the University of Pennsylvania in 1845.

In 1850 Green was unanimously elected bishop of Mississippi. Although the Episcopal Church had been active in the area that became the state since the 1790s, Green became its first bishop. He began his tenure by traveling extensively and estimated that during his first year he logged more than 4,500 miles, preached 124 times, baptized 44 people, confirmed 106 people, and celebrated Holy Communion 25 times. Much of his work was as a missionary, bringing his message to communities that lacked Episcopal congregations. The first decade years of his episcopate saw the church grow steadily, as he completed the diocese's organization, increased its resources, and undertook extensive pastoral efforts with his fellow clergymen. Green was well liked and highly respected by his contemporaries, and he and many other Episcopal clergymen welcomed instances in which African Americans joined whites in worship.

In 1857 Green and members of ten other dioceses across the Deep South sponsored the formation of a new university at Sewanee, Tennessee. Green suggested the name the University of the South and served for many years as a trustee of the institution. When Mississippi seceded in 1860, he participated in the organization of the Episcopal Church in the Confederacy and continued his ministry throughout the Civil War. After the conflict ended, he helped reorganize the Episcopal Church in the South to reincorporate it into the American Episcopal Church.

Green was named chancellor of the University of the South in December 1866 and moved to Sewanee, where he worked to raise funds to ensure the university's survival. Green also continued to serve as bishop of Mississippi. In 1880 the Mississippi Diocese was granted an assistant bishop, and Hugh Miller Thompson assumed the post. In 1884 Green turned full charge of diocesan affairs over to Thompson but continued to supervise the diocese and travel in Mississippi. Green died in Sewanee on 13 February 1887 and was buried in Jackson, Mississippi.

Carolyn Cooper Howard
University of Mississippi

Arthur Benjamin Chitty Jr., *Reconstruction at Sewanee: The Founding of the University of the South and Its First Administration, 1857–1872* (1954); Mississippi Historical Records Survey Project, *Inventory of the Church Archives of Mississippi, Protestant Episcopal Church Diocese of Mississippi* (1940).

Greene, Percy

(1897–1977) Editor

Percy Greene, a conservative African American newspaper editor, was born in Jackson to George Washington Green and Sarah Stone Green. Percy later added an *e* to the family surname. Greene grew up in a family of twelve children and was educated at various Jackson schools, including Jackson College High School. In 1915 he joined the segregated US Army and served in the 25th Infantry during World War I. He was honorably discharged in 1922 and five years later organized the National Association of Negro War Veterans, which served black veterans denied admission into veterans' organizations. He also founded the group's newspaper, the *Colored Veteran*.

After leaving the army, Greene returned to Mississippi and reenrolled at Jackson College. He married Frances Lee Reed in 1921, and they went on to have two daughters, Frances Lorraine and Gwendolyn Louise. Greene studied law under a Jackson attorney but failed the bar exam in 1926 following an altercation with a white man. After 1928 he worked as a journalist for two Jackson newspapers, the *Negro Citizen* and the *Mississippi Enterprise*.

He founded the *Jackson Advocate* in 1939 and spent the next four decades as its owner, editor, and publisher. In the early years of his career Greene received several recognitions for his journalism, including an award for courage in journalism from the *Chicago Defender* (1946), a citation from the Washington, D.C., Institute on Race Relations (1947), and awards from the Mississippi Association of Colored Teachers and the *Pittsburgh Courier*. He was invited to the inauguration of Pres. Harry S. Truman.

By the 1950s Greene's position on segregation and civil rights led to a split with much of the African American community. He and others in Mississippi's small black middle class wanted to see the status quo maintained. He supported voting rights and equal education for blacks as necessary to social progress but believed that segregation should continue. Greene subscribed to Booker T. Washington's accommodationist philosophy and believed that blacks and whites could live peacefully in separate but equal environments and that African American advancement depended on maintaining southern whites' goodwill. Furthermore, he opposed the National Association for the Advancement of Colored People and other civil rights organizations.

His position on civil rights caused many members of the African American community to cancel their subscriptions to the *Advocate*, and by the late 1950s his newspaper was in financial jeopardy. He accepted funding from the Citizens' Council and the Mississippi State Sovereignty Commission, which used the *Advocate* as a mouthpiece in favor of segregation. He opposed African Americans' civil rights for the remainder of his life, a position that damaged his paper's credibility. Greene suffered a heart attack in 1976 and subsequently sold the newspaper to Charles W. Tisdale, and it continues to publish today. In 1977 Pres. Jimmy Carter posthumously honored Greene's service in the armed forces.

Lisa K. Speer
Arkansas History Commission

Caryl A. Cooper, in *The Press and Race: Mississippi Journalists Confront the Movement*, ed. David R. Davies (2001); "Oral History with Percy Greene" (1972), Center for Oral History and Cultural Heritage, University of Southern Mississippi, digilib.usm.edu/cdm/compoundobject/collection/coh/id/15364/rec/5; Julius E. Thompson, *Percy Greene and the Jackson Advocate: The Life and Times of a Radical Conservative Black Newspaperman, 1897–1977* (1994); Julian Williams, *Journalism History* (Summer 2002).

Greene County

Greene County is located in the Piney Woods region of southeastern Mississippi along the Alabama border. The Leaf and Chickasawhay Rivers traverse the county; both are tributaries of the Pascagoula River, which empties into the Gulf of Mexico. Greene County was established on 9 December 1811 and is named for the Revolutionary War general Nathanael Greene. Founded in 1906, Leakesville, the county seat, is named for Walter Leake, governor of Mississippi from 1822 to 1825.

In the 1820 census, Greene County had a small population—1,065 free people and 380 slaves. Virtually everyone in the county worked in agriculture, with only seven people employed in commerce and manufacturing. Twenty years later, Greene's population had hardly changed, reaching only 1,207 free people and 429 slaves.

While much of Mississippi had experienced dramatic population growth by 1860, Greene County was still home to only 1,527 free people and 705 slaves. On the eve of the Civil War, Greene's agricultural yields ranked near the bottom of the state in most categories: with just 146 bales, the county's cotton production was second-lowest; corn output had the same rank, and the value of livestock was third-lowest in the state. However, antebellum Greene County ranked near the top in rice production, coming in fourth among Mississippi counties. Like other Piney Woods counties, Greene maintained both considerable support for and opposition to the Confederacy.

Greene County's population grew following the Civil War, reaching 3,194 (75 percent of them white) by 1880. Virtually all of Greene's farmers owned their land (96 percent), so the county had almost no renting or sharecropping. Greene County farms averaged 268 acres, far above the state average. The county had two manufacturing firms that employed eleven men and one child. Like other Piney Woods counties, Greene did not attract immigrants: only seven people born outside the United States lived in the county.

By the opening decades of the twentieth century, Greene County's distinction as a haven for yeoman farmers was beginning to change. In 1900, twenty-five manufacturing firms, including some lumber companies, employed 282 male industrial workers. However, the county continued to maintain high rates of landownership: 94 percent of Greene County's white farmers and 122 of the total of 141 African American farmers (87 percent) owned the land they farmed. Moreover, the county's farms remained fairly large.

Prior to the Civil War, Greene County had been home to fourteen churches—seven Methodist, five Baptist, and two Presbyterian. These denominations continued to dominate the county's religious landscape into the twentieth century. In 1916 Baptists, both Southern and Missionary, Methodists, and Presbyterians reported the largest church memberships in the county.

In 1930 the county's 10,644 residents (75 percent of whom were white) lived in a rural area with the fourth-lowest population density in Mississippi. Most white and African American farmers still owned their farms, but the industrial workforce had grown dramatically, topping 1,000.

Thirty years later, Greene's population had decreased to 8,366, giving it the second-lowest population density in the state. Likewise, Greene's labor force was the second-smallest in Mississippi, with more than 40 percent of workers engaged in the production of corn and winter wheat and the care of livestock. Although Greene contained more than 408,000 acres of commercial forest, the second-highest acreage in the state, by 1980 only 470 workers were employed in manufacturing, few of them in timber-related industries.

As with many of the state's southeastern counties, in 2010 Greene County's population had a white majority (72.5 percent). A total of 14,400 people lived there.

Mississippi Encyclopedia Staff
University of Mississippi

Mississippi State Planning Commission, *Progress Report on State Planning in Mississippi* (1938); *Mississippi Statistical Abstract*, Mississippi State University (1952–2010); Charles Sydnor and Claude Bennett, *Mississippi History* (1939); University of Virginia Library, Historical Census Browser website, http://mapserver.lib.virginia.edu; E. Nolan Waller and Dani A. Smith, *Growth Profiles of Mississippi's Counties, 1960–1980* (1985).

Greenfield, Elizabeth Taylor

(1813–1876) Musician

Elizabeth Taylor Greenfield was one of the first African American singers to cross nineteenth-century America's formidable racial barrier and garner serious attention from white audiences. Taylor's father was an African-born slave and her mother a Seminole Indian. Taylor was unschooled in social graces and received no formal voice or music lessons. Moreover, she was often considered an eyesore: a critic later admitted that fairly assessing her talent required him to listen to her without looking. However, she possessed an astonishing twenty-seven-note range, traversing it with ease and great emotion and leaving nearly every music critic of her generation in raptures.

The story of her unlikely journey to the public eye began in Natchez, where she was born into a family owned by Elizabeth Holiday Greenfield, a wealthy Quaker. Early in her childhood young Elizabeth Taylor and her family moved with Greenfield to Philadelphia, Pennsylvania, and, as a consequence of both the political climate of the North and Greenfield's religious beliefs, Taylor's family was freed and given money to start a new life in Liberia. While the rest of the Taylors left for Africa, Elizabeth elected to stay behind in America in Greenfield's household and added her mistress's last name. While in Greenfield's home, the girl began teaching herself to play the guitar and harp, instruments that served as accompaniments to her voice. Several of her friends and neighbors encouraged her to develop her musical gifts.

Elizabeth Holiday Greenfield died in 1844, and Elizabeth Taylor Greenfield, now in her thirties, made her way to Buffalo, New York, to live with friends. On the train ride north, a wealthy general's wife overheard Greenfield singing and, impressed by her voice, invited her to sing for a party the following week at her home in Buffalo. The general, his wife, and their guests were awed by her untrained yet brilliant voice, and she was soon invited to sing at other events around town. Over the next few years, Greenfield sang before large audiences in New York and the Midwest. Reviewers raved about her effortless skill, comparing her to Jenny Lind and Teresa Parodi, the vocal superstars of the 1850s, and dubbing her the Black Swan.

To receive formal training, Greenfield traveled to London in 1853 with the financial support of her fans in Buffalo. In England, she met Harriet Beecher Stowe and several aristocratic English women. Greenfield was an instant success, and in the summer of 1854 she found herself before a most impressive audience—Queen Victoria and her court.

Despite her popularity, Greenfield lacked the funds to remain in London longer than a year, and in late summer of 1854 she returned to the United States, where she resettled in Philadelphia. Over the next twenty years, she gave voice lessons and occasional concerts. She died on 31 March 1876. Half a century later, Harry Pace borrowed her nickname for the first African American record company, Black Swan.

Katherine Treppendahl
University of Virginia

Tonya Bolden, *The Book of African-American Women* (1996); Benjamin Brawley, *The Negro Genius* (1937); Monroe Alphus Majors, *Noted Negro Women: Their Triumphs and Activities* (1893).

Greenville Delta Leader

The *Greenville Leader* began publication in 1930. In 1938 Rev. H. H. Humes, an African American, was serving as the paper's editor, while Levye Chappel was its publisher; by the following year, Humes had changed the paper's name and assumed publishing responsibilities along with the H. H. Humes Publishing Company. The newspaper's primary audience consisted of black Mississippians living in and around Greenville. In 1939 the *Delta Leader* was published every Saturday, and subscriptions cost two dollars per year. Like the *Greenville Leader*, the *Delta Leader* proudly displayed the phrase "Advocate of the Mid-South" at the top of each front page. The paper's platform was "to promote the interest of the people of the Mid-South in economics, civics, education, religion, and a better relationship." After one year of publication the *Delta Leader* claimed five thousand paid subscribers.

Reverend Humes utilized the paper not only to educate the public but also to further his own interests. Humes had a great desire to improve the relationship between blacks and whites but had a strong distaste for those who "irritate and agitate." In his opinion, the friction between the races was unproductive, and he believed that blacks would fare better by setting and working toward higher goals. *Delta Leader* editorials frequently condemned the juvenile delinquency and lack of morals that Humes encountered among black citizens in Greenville. However, Humes also did not hesitate to publicize accomplishments of local and nationally known blacks. Humes's effort drew some glowing local praise. In a 1939 letter to the editor, Hodding Carter, editor of Greenville's *Delta Democrat-Times*, declared that the *Delta Leader* constituted "a fine and dignified expression of the Negro's determination to better himself in every sphere."

Proof of Humes's desire to combat racial agitation by blacks is found in the records of the Mississippi State Sovereignty Commission. Shortly before Humes's death in 1958 it was disclosed that he had accepted payments for services and travel expenses from the Sovereignty Commission and was indeed considered one of its most important nonwhite friends. Some black organizations in Mississippi criticized his actions, perceiving them as harming the cause of civil rights.

The *Delta Leader* did not attempt to lead the black population toward more political success and also did not make demands on whites in this realm. It stressed that black Mississippians should not migrate to the North but remain in Mississippi, where they had a better chance for success in life.

The full run of the *Delta Leader* is no longer extant. The Mississippi Department of Archives and History holds the most complete collection, which includes microfilm copies of scattered issues from 1939–41, 1943, and 1947. Microfilm copies of the issues from 1951 and 1955 are held by the Greenwood-Leflore Public Library System.

Barton Spencer
University of Southern Mississippi

Greenville Delta Leader newspaper; *Greenville Leader* newspaper; Mississippi Department of Archives and History, Sovereignty Commission Online website, http://mdah.state.ms.us/arrec/digital_archives/sovcom/; Henry Lewis Suggs, ed., *The Black Press in the South, 1865–1979*; World-Cat website, www.worldcat.org.

Greenwood Civil Rights Movement

Greenwood sits on the banks of the Yazoo River in Leflore County in the eastern Mississippi Delta. In the 1960s the city, sometimes called the Cotton Capital of the World, exported eight hundred thousand bales a year. When the civil rights movement erupted in Greenwood, blacks comprised nearly two-thirds of the county residents, but only a small percentage had registered to vote. Further, segregation in housing divided the genteel homes of the upper-class white population from the African American neighborhood across the river and railroad tracks. Greenwood's African American community drew strength from Wesley United Methodist and other old churches; its historic neighborhoods, such as the Browning community; and its academic institutions, which included Mississippi Valley State University in nearby Itta Bena. Greenwood also harbored the state headquarters of the white Citizens' Council.

Although a chapter of the National Association for the Advancement of Colored People was founded in the city in 1952, voting among blacks remained limited, and in June 1962 organizer Bob Moses of the Student Nonviolent Coordinating Committee (SNCC) arrived in Greenwood to begin a renewed effort to register blacks. He established connections with local leaders, but initial resistance to civil rights efforts proved strong, and activists struggled to find places to meet, holding mass gatherings in the city junkyard, Rev. Aaron Johnson's First Christian Church, and the home of local civil rights veteran Dewey Greene, among other locations. Throughout 1963 activists and members of SNCC endured arrests and violence, fighting back with meetings and marches. During the Freedom Summer of 1964, Greenwood became the nerve center of SNCC's efforts in the Delta. In 1965 federal registrars arrived to ensure the vote for Greenwood blacks, the Greenwood Voters League encouraged citizens to register, and African American students integrated Greenwood's middle school.

After these important victories, Greenwood activists decided to tackle economic problems, and the area's civil rights protests reached their climax. Greenwood native James Moore and others built on their previous gains and found new allies. In the fall of 1967 Father Nathaniel Machesky, the head of Greenwood's St. Francis Center, a poor-relief organization, and African American ministers William Wallace of the Christian Methodist Episcopal Church and M. J. Black of the African Methodist Episcopal Church orchestrated what became an eighteen-month boycott of local merchants to protest racial discrimination. Members of Greenwood's African American community were rallied by clerics and other activists, including Mary Boothe, who became director of what became known as the Greenwood Movement, and many National Association for the Advancement of Colored People and Mississippi Freedom Democratic Party members. Whites responded to the nonviolent boycott with a firebombing and repeated drive-by shootings at the St. Francis Center and with court orders to prevent picketing. By early 1969, however, the campaign had forced white store-keepers to hire blacks and brought paved streets and street lighting to Greenwood's African American neighborhoods.

The Greenwood Movement remains important for at least three reasons. First, it derived potency from community energy and challenged discrimination on both the political and economic levels. Second, its sustained mass demonstrations, rare in Mississippi, resembled the earlier protest campaigns of Albany, Georgia, and Selma, Alabama. Third, the involvement of nuns, monks, and priests in the boycott made Greenwood a notable example of the Catholic Church's participation in the civil rights struggle.

William P. Hustwit
Birmingham Southern University

Townsend Davis, *Weary Feet, Rested Souls: A Guided History of the Civil Rights Movement* (1998); John Dittmer, *Local People: The Struggle for Civil Rights in Mississippi* (1994); Michael V. Namorato, *The Catholic Church in Mississippi, 1911–1984* (1998); Mark Newman, *Journal of Mississippi History* (Winter 2005); Charles M. Payne, *I've Got the Light of Freedom: The Organizing Tradition and the Mississippi Freedom Struggle* (1995).

Grenada County

Located in north-central Mississippi, Grenada County is traversed from east to west by the Yalobusha River. A significant portion of Grenada Lake lies in the county's northeastern corner. Grenada was established on 9 May 1870 from areas formerly included in Yalobusha, Tallahatchie, and Carroll Counties. These lands were originally acquired from the Choctaw and Chickasaw Indians under the 1830 Treaty of Dancing Rabbit Creek. Both the county and its seat, Grenada, are named for the Spanish province of Granada.

The 1870 census counted 10,571 Grenada residents, a number that grew to 12,071 (73 percent of them African American) ten years later. The county's people worked primarily in agriculture, raising a mix of grains, cotton, and livestock. Only 44 percent of Grenada's farms were cultivated by their owners, with tenants and sharecroppers tending the remaining farmland. Grenada also had a small manufacturing base, with twenty-three companies employing forty-five

industrial workers. Germans comprised the largest share of the county's sixty-five immigrants.

Influential Mississippians who called Grenada home in the late nineteenth century included activist Sallie Reneau, who campaigned to acquire funding for a state college for women. Former Confederate general Edward Cary Walthall moved to Grenada in 1871 and became a leading lawyer for the railroad companies that eventually dominated Mississippi's transportation system. He also was a leading voice in the Democratic Party's efforts to bring an end to Reconstruction.

At the turn of the century, Grenada remained largely a farming county, but most of the county's white farmers owned their land, whereas most African American farmers did not. Grenada's manufacturing sector supported a workforce of 133, including 6 women. The county was home to 14,122 people in 1900.

In 1916 Missionary Baptists were the largest religious denomination in Grenada County, followed by the African Methodist Episcopal Church and the Methodist Episcopal Church, South; the Southern Baptist Convention; and the Presbyterians. In 1922 the West Harmony Convention of shape-note singers began in Grenada County.

By 1930 Grenada had a population of 16,802, 9,987 of them African American. The county's urban population had grown to 4,349, and its industrial sector employed almost 600 workers. The majority of Grenada's farmers were tenants. Camp McCain, south of Grenada, became a major military training site for soldiers during World War II.

Several of Mississippi's most important political figures have hailed from Grenada County. William Winter, who as governor made great efforts to address generations of inequitable education in the state, was born in Grenada in 1923. Delta-based civil rights activist Amzie Moore was born on a Grenada County plantation in 1911. Erle Johnston, head of the Mississippi State Sovereignty Commission, was born in Grenada, as was Trent Lott, congressman, senator, and longtime Gulf Coast resident. In 1966 the town of Grenada was the site of a substantial civil rights boycott.

Donna Tartt, author of the novels *The Secret History* (1992), *The Little Friend* (2003), and *The Goldfinch* (2013) was born in 1963 in Grenada and grew up in the county.

By 1960 the county's population, almost evenly divided between African Americans and whites, had grown to 18,409. Grenada's industrial workforce comprised almost 2,000 people, a number that nearly doubled to 3,850 a decade later. Textile production, retail, and domestic work became the county's largest employment sectors. By 1980, less than 2 percent of the county's more than twenty thousand residents worked in agriculture, focusing on cotton, soybeans, winter wheat, and cattle.

Like many counties in northern Mississippi, Grenada's population continued to grow in the early twenty-first century, reaching almost 22,000 in 2010. The county's racial profile had shifted, with whites comprising a 57 percent majority. Hugh White State Park, home to a Corps of Engineers lake, park, and golf course, is in Grenada County. Grenada also hosts at least three annual festivals.

Mississippi Encyclopedia Staff
University of Mississippi

Grenada County, Mississippi, Mississippi Genealogy and History Network website, http://grenada.sandysfamilytree.com/countyhistory.html; Mississippi State Planning Commission, *Progress Report on State Planning in Mississippi* (1938); *Mississippi Statistical Abstract*, Mississippi State University (1952–2010); Charles Sydnor and Claude Bennett, *Mississippi History* (1939); University of Virginia Library, Historical Census Browser website, http://mapserver.lib.virginia.edu; E. Nolan Waller and Dani A. Smith, *Growth Profiles of Mississippi's Counties, 1960–1980* (1985).

Grierson's Raid

By the spring of 1863 the Confederate West was in disarray, and one of the most strategically important points in the South was under threat from the advancing Union Army. Ulysses S. Grant was bringing a large force down the western side of the Mississippi River, intent on capturing Vicksburg. Grant planned to cross the river just above Natchez and move steadily north toward Jackson. After capturing the state capital, he would then turn his full attention toward Vicksburg, advancing on the port city from the east. Though Grant had assembled a formidable force, he knew he would face stiff resistance from Confederate troops and consequently planned several diversions in hopes of dividing or distracting the rebel forces while he moved the bulk of his army through the state. Among these diversions was a major cavalry raid led by Col. Benjamin H. Grierson.

At the Civil War's outset, Grierson was an unlikely candidate to lead such a raid. He was not a professional soldier. Born in Pittsburgh in 1826 and educated in Ohio, he was a music teacher and bandleader. He enlisted in the US Army as a private in 1861 and rose steadily through the ranks. After serving on the staff of his friend, Brig. Gen. Benjamin Prentiss, Grierson received his own cavalry command and a promotion to colonel. He then made a name for himself leading minor raids through Tennessee and North Mississippi. On 17 April 1863 Grierson began the raid for which he would become famous, moving out from La Grange, Tennessee, just north of the Mississippi border, with three regiments of cavalry totaling around seventeen hundred men. The raid was designed to disrupt Confederate supply and communication lines that serviced Vicksburg and siphon off Confederate troops from Vicksburg's defense. Among other things, Grant charged Grierson with "destroying all telegraph wires, burning provisions, and doing all mischief possible." As they carried out their orders, Grierson's men left a "smoldering path of destruction" through many Mississippi communities, including Pontotoc, Louisville, Philadelphia, Decatur, Newton, Raleigh, Hazlehurst, and Brookhaven, before moving south into Louisiana. The raid ended on 2 May when Grierson and his men arrived at Baton Rouge. In just over two weeks they had traveled more than six hundred miles, taken five hundred Confederate prisoners, and captured thousands of arms and other property, including more than one thousand mules. They had also kept a significant number of Confederate cavalry and infantry occupied and, as Grant later wrote, "taken the heart out of Mississippi." In the process Grierson lost fewer than fifty men.

The raid was a great success, as was Grant's overall strategy. Vicksburg fell on 4 July 1863 after a forty-seven-day siege, marking the beginning of the end for the Confederacy. After the war Grierson remained in the service as a cavalry commander until his retirement in 1890. He died on 1 September 1911 in Omena, Michigan. Grierson's Civil War exploits were the basis for a 1959 John Wayne film, *The Horse Soldiers*.

Ben Wynne
Gainesville State College

D. Alexander Brown, *Grierson's Raid* (1954).

Griffith, Richard
(1815–1862) Confederate General

Richard Griffith, an officer in the Mexican War and a Confederate general, was born on 11 January 1814 near Philadelphia, Pennsylvania. He graduated from Ohio University in 1837 and moved to Vicksburg, where he was employed as a teacher in a private school. Griffith remained there until the Mexican War, when he enlisted in the 1st Mississippi Rifles. Elected first lieutenant, Griffith became the regimental adjutant and forged a close bond with his commanding officer, Jefferson Davis.

After returning from Mexico, Griffith worked as a banker in Jackson, became a US marshal, and subsequently served two terms as state treasurer. He was present when Mississippi passed the ordnance of secession and soon thereafter recruited the Raymond Fencibles, a company that eventually became part of the 12th Mississippi Infantry. Griffith was elected colonel of the regiment, which was assigned to duty in Virginia. He was promoted to brigadier general on 2 November 1861 and placed in charge of a brigade of four

Mississippi regiments. The promotion was directly related to machinations by Davis, who created a vacancy for Griffith by transferring Charles Clark, the previous brigade commander, to the western theater. By the spring of 1862 Griffith's brigade consisted of the 1st Louisiana Battalion; the 13th, 18th, and 21st Mississippi Regiments; and one battery, with a combined effective strength of 2,534 men.

In the opening stages of the Peninsula Campaign Griffith's command engaged in minor skirmishing and remained in reserve at Seven Pines. During the Seven Days' Battles, which resulted in Union forces under George McClellan being driven from the Virginia Peninsula, Griffith's brigade served in John B. Magruder's division. On 29 June 1862 Magruder advanced as part of a general Confederate movement. As he extended his lines to the left, Union artillery opened fire from long range as the Battle of Savage's Station began. A portion of a Federal artillery shell tore through Griffith's inner thigh, causing profuse bleeding. He fell from his horse into the arms of a colonel and was borne to the rear. William Barksdale took command of Griffith's brigade and led it into its first significant combat.

Davis found the mortally wounded Griffith, attempted to console him, and arranged for his transportation to Richmond, where he died later that night. His funeral the next day was attended by Davis, members of the Confederate cabinet, and hundreds of other mourners.

Christopher Losson
St. Joseph, Missouri

Harold A. Cross, *They Sleep beneath the Mockingbird: Mississippi Burial Sites and Biographies of Confederate Generals* (1994); Charles E. Hooker, *Confederate Military History: Mississippi*, ed. Clement A. Evans (1899); Ezra Warner, *Generals in Gray: Lives of the Confederate Commanders* (1959).

Grisham, John
(b. 1955) Author

Since his first book was published in 1989, John Grisham has been one of America's most popular novelists. Grisham has a unique talent for writing compelling legal stories people enjoy reading. Many of his novels portray likable but flawed characters facing challenges that involve contemporary social issues such as racism, environmental destruction, homelessness, revenge violence, the death penalty, health insurance, the rights of children, the power of tobacco companies, organized crime, and government corruption. Many of his lawyers are young, hardworking, and unsure whether the law really does much to help ordinary people.

Born in Jonesboro, Arkansas, in 1955, John Grisham grew up in Arkansas and northern Mississippi. He graduated from Mississippi State University in 1977 and the University of Mississippi Law School four years later. He married Renée Jones and began practice in Southaven. From 1983 to 1990 he was a member of the Mississippi House of Representatives. Intrigued by cases he saw and heard about, he started writing fiction about legal issues.

Grisham's novels set in and near Mississippi show an intriguing dichotomy between an older small-town South in the fictional Ford County and a showy, wealthy, sometimes scary New South. Grisham's books about the edges of Mississippi—Memphis, New Orleans, and the Mississippi Gulf Coast—present a Sun Belt South marked by new wealth, powerful and often corrupt corporations, organized crime, a potent federal government, and the facelessness of modern society. Part of the uniqueness of Grisham's rise to popularity was the juxtaposition of the southern setting of Memphis and organized crime in his extraordinarily popular *The Firm* (1991).

In the interior of Mississippi, the fictional Ford County, Grisham deals with traditionally southern settings and issues—racial segregation and white supremacy, face-to-face community life held together through families, and long traditions. Grisham's first book, *A Time to Kill* (1989), addresses traditional southern themes of race, rape, revenge violence, and community standards, but he twists those themes by portraying an African American man who avenges the rape of his child by killing a white man and then relies on community traditions about protecting one's family to overturn community traditions of white supremacy. After three books set in Memphis and New Orleans, Grisham returned to Ford County with *The Chamber* (1994), a book about confronting Mississippi's worst traditions in which young lawyer Adam Hall attempts to keep his grandfather, Sam Cayhall, from execution for the murders of civil rights workers in the 1960s. An exile's Ford County homecoming is also the theme of *The Summons* (2002), in which a lawyer son returns after the death of his father, a judge. Finding a fortune in hidden cash, the son ponders how to legally and ethically deal with both the money and his father's legacy. Grisham returned to the Ford County setting in *The Last Juror* (2004), the story of a free-spirited young editor who comes to know an older African American woman serving as a juror in the 1970s trial of an accused rapist and murderer.

Grisham's novels frequently deal with uncertainties about the law and the temptations of wealth. Many of Grisham's lawyers are young and somewhat rebellious figures who know the law and use it for the benefit of their clients but do so outside the courtroom and sometimes outside conventional structures of the legal system; some tire of the system and leave it. In novels such as *The Partner* (1997), *The King of Torts* (2003), and *The Appeal* (2008) and the nonfiction work *The Innocent Man* (2006), Grisham takes a dark view of the law as a haven for self-interest. Some of his more recent books address an issue surely important in Grisham's own life—what to do with extraordinary wealth. In *The Testament* (1999), *The Summons* (2002), and especially *The King of Torts*, large and unexpected amounts of money raise complicated moral and legal issues.

Since moving from Mississippi to Virginia in the late 1990s, Grisham has expanded the range of settings and topics of his work. *A Painted House* (2001), a slowly paced semiautobiographical novel set in 1950s rural Arkansas, discusses childhood, baseball, cotton, Mexican labor, and relative poverty but no legal issues. The first Grisham novel in which the setting is largely irrelevant to the story, *Skipping Christmas* (2001), involves a couple who decide to avoid the typical expectations of Christmas. Other recent novels deal with high school football and Central Intelligence Agency intrigue. *The Innocent Man*, Grisham's first nonfiction work, details the life an Oklahoma man whose conviction for murder was overturned after years of effort and some new evidence. *Theodore Boone, Kid Lawyer* (2010) introduced a different approach to legal fiction. Two of his recent works, the short story collection *Ford County* (2009) and the novel *Sycamore Row* (2013) return to the Mississippi county Grisham created in *A Time to Kill*.

Grisham's books have become so popular that his book signings are events with virtually unprecedented popularity, and many of his works have been made into movies.

Ted Ownby
University of Mississippi

John Grisham website, www.jgrisham.com; John Grisham, interview by Tom Mathews, *Newsweek* (15 March 1993); Beth Pringle, *John Grisham: A Critical Companion*.

Grits

Grits, the quintessential southern food, are so versatile that they can be served for breakfast, lunch, or dinner and are so popular that there are almost as many grits recipes as great gumbos. Grits became essential to southern cooking at least in part because almost all farming people—Indian, white, and black—grew corn; they have remained popular in part because they are so easily adaptable to different tastes. Success in preparing grits is all in the flavor-enhancing seasonings and delicate hand of the chef. Too much seasoning, as in red pepper, can bring tears to the eyes of grits lovers, while too little produces a bland blend that begs to be dressed up.

And dressed up grits dishes are—as shrimp and grits, garlic cheese grits, grits soufflé, grits and greens, seafood with roux over grits. The list is as extensive as the creative cook wants to make it. Craig Claiborne, a Mississippi native and a longtime food writer for the *New York Times*, offered numerous recipes using grits in his best-selling cookbooks. Grits are not the in-home breakfast staple they once were, perhaps because they have also been claimed by dark-wood-and-candlelit uptown restaurants, as exemplified by dishes such as the popular shrimp and grits.

Grits are a corn product, coarsely ground and served in many different ways. Grits are tasty, healthy, and easy to prepare—even easier if the cook knows the secret of cooking them. The true grits aficionado will not use instant grits (as memorably depicted in the 1992 movie *My Cousin Vinny*) or overcook them to the "mushy" stage. Knowing how to cook and enjoy grits involves taking a tradition born of necessity and turning it into both a treat and a point of regional pride.

Sylvia Higginbotham
Columbus, Mississippi

S. R. Dull, *Southern Cooking* (2006); John Egerton, ed., *The New Encyclopedia of Southern Culture*, vol. 7, *Foodways* (2007); Sylvia Higginbotham, *Grits 'n Greens and Deep South Things* (2005); Sylvia Higginbotham, *Grits 'n Greens and Mississippi Things* (2002); Susan Puckett, *A Cook's Tour of Mississippi* (2005).

Guerrilla Warfare in the Civil War

Guerrilla (irregular) warfare erupted in a number of areas in Mississippi during the Civil War. It was particularly prevalent in portions of the state where loyalty to the Confederacy was tenuous or waned as the war progressed. Historian John K. Bettersworth has described this "disloyal country" as stretching from northeastern Mississippi, near the Tennessee border, down through the central prairie into the Piney Woods and along the Gulf Coast. Within these areas Confederate authority during the war was challenged by deserters who formed bands to resist conscription and payment of taxes, especially the onerous taxes in-kind; committed acts of sabotage; and battled Confederate forces sent against them. Regular civil government often disintegrated in counties where guerrillas operated. Bettersworth listed two dozen counties where evidence of opposition to the Confederacy occurred: it was particularly powerful in Attala, Choctaw, Covington, Greene, Jones, Leake, Perry, Scott, Smith, and Tishomingo. The Gulf Coast counties, virtually abandoned by Confederate forces early in the war, also were havens for guerrillas.

Although some of these guerrillas sought to make contact with or enlist the aid of Union forces, disloyalty to the Confederacy was not always synonymous with Unionism.

Opposition was generated by a number of factors. Class differences played a major role. The vast majority of guerrillas did not own slaves and had no vested interest in a Confederate victory. In areas of fiercest resistance, residents possessing a strong antiauthoritarian streak deeply resented conscription, taxation, and the loss of property to roving Confederate cavalry. A band of guerrillas led by Newt Knight in Jones County achieved mythic status after the war, when they were widely reported to have seceded from the Confederacy and established the Free State of Jones. According to Victoria E. Bynum, these men were frequently aided and sustained by both women and slaves, were bound together by intricate familial connections, and were both perpetrators and victims of violence. In Jones and other counties where wartime disloyalty vexed Confederate authorities, evidence suggests that guerrilla warfare was at times driven by feuds and personal antagonisms that predated the war.

Pro-Confederate politicians and residents complained persistently to Gov. Charles Clark and Confederate military authorities about the depredations committed by guerrillas. As a result, a number of efforts were made to bring guerrillas to heel. Forays into Jones County in 1864 by Confederate cavalry and infantry resulted in the capture and execution of a number of Knight's followers, but the invaders also suffered casualties and did not decisively quell resistance.

Elsewhere in the state, guerrillas operated for both sides in the Yazoo-Mississippi Delta. Pro-Confederate groups sparred with Union expeditions into the Delta, fired on vessels traveling down the Mississippi and Delta waterways, and provoked retaliatory measures. Plantations and towns were raided and buildings were often burned by Federal forces to punish guerrilla activity. Guerrillas who supported the Union raided Mississippi from Arkansas and from islands in the river, stealing crops and livestock, skirmishing with Confederate scouts and state troops, and providing intelligence to Federal troops. As in other regions, whites involved in these ventures often enlisted the help of escaped slaves.

The pervasive nature of guerrilla warfare reveals that disillusionment deepened as the war wore on; it is telling that a majority of guerrillas were Confederate deserters. The deep animosity and resentment generated by guerrilla activity persisted long into the postwar era, evidence that a sizable minority of Mississippians never embraced the Lost Cause mythology that extolled Confederate solidarity and the sacred nature of the Confederate experience.

Christopher Losson
St. Joseph, Missouri

John K. Bettersworth, *Confederate Mississippi: The People and Policies of a Cotton State in Wartime* (1943); Victoria E. Bynum, *The Free State of Jones: Mississippi's Longest Civil War* (2001); William D. McCain and Charlotte Capers, eds., *Memoirs of Henry Tillinghast Ireys: Papers of the Washington County Historical Society, 1910–1915* (1954); Daniel E. Sutherland, *A Savage Conflict: The Decisive Role of Guerillas in the American Civil War* (2013).

Guion, John Isaac
(1802–1855) Seventeenth Governor, 1851

On 3 February 1851 authorities arrested Gov. John A. Quitman in Jackson and took him to New Orleans to be arraigned for violating American neutrality laws in relation to his dealings with Cuban insurgents. When the *Jackson Mississippian and State Gazette* announced that Quitman had resigned and that John Isaac Guion had assumed the governor's office, the editor hailed the new governor as "a true Southron in heart and head."

Guion, who was born in Adams County on 18 November 1802, was one of antebellum Mississippi's most notable lawyers. After studying law in Lebanon, Tennessee, Guion opened a practice in Vicksburg with William Sharkey, a classmate at Lebanon. After Sharkey was elected to the state supreme court, Guion formed a partnership with Seargent S. Prentiss.

From 1842 to 1846 Guion represented Warren County in the state legislature. In 1846 he moved to Jackson, and two years later he was elected to represent the city in the State Senate. (In antebellum Mississippi several large cities elected representatives to the legislature.) Guion, a strong supporter of states' rights, played a prominent role in the Jackson Convention of 1849, which was called to discuss the South's response to the possibility of California's admission to the Union as a free state.

When Quitman resigned in February 1851, Senate president Dabney Lipscomb of Columbus was seriously ill and unable to perform his duties; Guion was president pro tempore of the Senate. Consequently, when the office of governor became vacant, Guion became governor, serving until his Senate term expired on 4 November.

In the general election Guion had not run for reelection to the Senate and instead had been elected a circuit judge. Since the term of the Speaker of the House had also expired with the 4 November general election, there was no one in the line of succession as established by the constitution of 1832. The office of governor, therefore, remained vacant until 24 November.

Guion assumed his judgeship and remained on the Mississippi bench until his death in Jackson on 6 June 1855.

David G. Sansing
University of Mississippi

Mississippi Official and Statistical Register (1912); Dunbar Rowland, *Encyclopedia of Mississippi History*, vol. 1 (1907).

Gulf Coast Architecture and Hurricane Katrina

Prior to Hurricane Katrina, the Mississippi Gulf Coast had one of the largest and densest concentrations of historic beachfront architecture in the United States. Because the Mississippi coast is comparatively low (about twenty-eight feet above sea level at Bay St. Louis, the highest point) and prone to storm surges, most of the older homes were elevated, some as much as eight feet above the ground, and thus had endured countless storms. Until Katrina, the greatest single loss of historic architecture had come as a result of Hurricane Camille (1969), the most powerful hurricane to strike the US mainland until that time. The storm destroyed scores of beachfront homes in a comparatively narrow band between Biloxi and Pass Christian.

Following Camille, the Gulf Coast began to become more of an architectural hodgepodge, a trend that escalated after the advent of dockside casino gambling in the 1990s, when theme architecture (including such additions as a glaringly fake pirate ship) and high-rises began to proliferate. Nevertheless, dozens of historic districts remained intact in 2005, and many new homes followed the prevailing architectural styles. The most impressive concentration was along Pass Christian's tony East Scenic Drive.

Katrina first made landfall on the eastern edge of the Louisiana coast, then delivered its full impact on the Mississippi coast, raking the beachfront with winds up to 150 miles per hour and a storm surge as high as 30 feet across a swath perhaps 150 miles wide. Thousands died across the coast and in New Orleans. In the aftermath, it became clear that the storm had caused what was arguably the greatest loss of historic architecture from a single cataclysmic event in US history.

The worst damage took place along the Mississippi coast, where in some areas no buildings were left standing for miles. Across the state's three coastal counties an estimated 65,000 buildings were completely destroyed, among them more than 800 historic structures, 250 of them listed in the National Register of Historic Places. Several entire historic districts were lost. The frenzied cleanup that followed saw the razing of another 200 National Register–listed buildings that had been damaged by the storm.

Among the buildings that were destroyed were the Spanish Customs House (ca. 1790), the Breath House (ca. 1820), and Elmwood Plantation (ca. 1805) in Bay St. Louis; the imposing Grass Lawn Mansion (1836) and the Robinson-Maloney-Dantzler House (1849) in Gulfport; the Tullis-Toledano Manor (1856) in Biloxi; structures dating to the 1820s in Ocean Springs's Shearwater Pottery compound; and numerous historic churches and commercial buildings. Also severely damaged was Gulfport's Turkey Creek neighborhood, characterized by modest homes built by freed slaves.

The few survivors included Beauvoir, the last home of Confederate president Jefferson Davis (1852), which was severely damaged and lost its library and other outbuildings; the iconic Biloxi Lighthouse (1848); and the La Pointe–Krebs House in Pascagoula (ca. 1720).

Amid the miles and miles of empty lots, where lonely porch steps are all that remain of countless historic homes, the survivors have since sparked a determined preservation effort. Soon after the storm the Gulf Coast Field Office of the Mississippi Department of Archives and History, collaborating with the National Trust for Historic Preservation, the Mississippi Heritage Trust, and the Mississippi Mainstreet Program, began advising property owners about saving damaged historic buildings and processing grants through a forty-million-dollar congressional appropriation earmarked for historic structures. The State of Mississippi also published a handbook on Gulf Coast architecture, encouraging builders of new homes to make use of traditional styles.

The only surviving section of the US 90 route that still evokes the old Mississippi coast is a truncated, one-mile stretch of Pass Christian's East Scenic Drive, where Greek Revival–and French Provincial–style mansions, Creole Cottages, and coastal vernacular homes represent the region's architectural archetype. An estimated 80 percent of Pass Christian's beachfront homes were lost to the storm and subsequent demolitions, but because East Scenic Drive occupies comparatively high ground (about twenty-five feet above sea level), more buildings survived there than elsewhere.

A coastwide architectural vision articulated during a series of poststorm public meetings was largely discarded in the rush to recover, and high-rise condos, casino complexes, and fast-food restaurants have set the tenor for much of the new construction. Likewise, the concepts embodied in new residential construction vary widely, encompassing historically sympathetic replications, steel-reinforced concrete fortresses, and structures that are clearly designed to be disposable.

Many buildings, including some higher-profile properties, remain in limbo, caught between competing visions of the Gulf Coast's architectural redevelopment. On one side are those who believe in a mixed-use development showcasing historic architecture; on the other are proponents of a clean-slate approach who believe that damaged properties should be cleared for whatever new development might come along.

Alan Huffman
Bolton, Mississippi

Atlanta Journal-Constitution (25 September 2005); Alan Huffman, *Lost* (September 2006); Alan Huffman, *Preservation* (January–February 2006, September–October 2007).

Gulf Coast Architecture before Hurricane Katrina

Architecture along the Mississippi Gulf Coast can be divided into four categories, folk, vernacular, popular, and polite. The distinctions between these classifications sometimes are blurry, but they adequately differentiate Gulf Coast architecture. The history of building along the Mississippi Gulf Coast reflects the influences of climate, outside practice, and historical events. The influence of New Orleans can be seen throughout the coast, as can the imprint of cities such as Chicago.

Folk buildings usually were owner-built and reflected the builder's cultural heritage, not outside sources. As colonial powers assumed control during various eras, engineers designed forts, not habitations. An important drawing from 10 December 1720 shows some of the earliest constructed folk types. Temporary gable-roofed huts were of colombage (half-timber and thatch). Mississippi's coastal architecture often shared elements with Louisiana architecture because of the cultural and colonial history. Folk houses also had bousillage (mud-and-moss walls and hewn frames). The fronts of these structures often were plastered and whitewashed under galleries. Needing to adapt to the tropical climate along the coast, Creole folk types' construction contained architectural elements that helped keep the structure cool. Galleries, high roofs, and provisions for cross-ventilation, such as outside entrances to each room, allowed air circulation. This style had a number of distinguishing characteristics, including a gable roof parallel to the front, an undercut gallery, a central chimney, either a two- or a five-room floor plan, and often either two or four openings across the main facade. Natural disasters such as hurricanes, fire and other human-induced calamities, and the march of progress mean that folk types from the eighteenth century are now rare.

Vernacular buildings were indigenous to the Gulf Coast area but constructed by professional builders. These builders often worked from standard plans but adjusted the overall form and decorative detail according to the owners' wishes or financial situation. Biloxi census records from the mid-nineteenth century list builders.

The vernacular Creole Cottage, similar to the folk variety, featured a particular roof form, undercut gallery, and four-bay front. The basic plan nearly always had four rooms, square or almost so, and usually contained a four-bay front with doors in the central two bays. Chimneys and fireplaces had no standard position. Creole Cottages occasionally contained stock ornaments on galleries.

Another vernacular type, the Biloxi Cottage, had a hip roof and appeared in Natchez, Port Gibson, and other towns along the coast in the 1880s and 1890s but were especially concentrated in Biloxi. The Biloxi Cottage could have either a hip roof or a gabled roof but always had a four-bay front, with the main roof extending to cover a gallery. The plan was basically four rooms, as in the Creole Cottage.

Another vernacular house type is the shotgun, which had three basic variations—the straight shotgun, the lateral-wing shotgun, and the three-bay shotgun—all of which were found on the Gulf Coast. The shotgun house may have originated in Haiti and Africa, but the shotguns in Mississippi dated from the late nineteenth century and resulted from New Orleans influences. The main characteristic of the shotgun was narrowness—many were only one room wide. The roof extended to cover a small gallery or porch across the main facade. The roof could be hip, gable-on-hip, or gable, but the hip form predominated. Shotgun homes were single-family dwellings along the coast, but construction stopped around the middle of the twentieth century.

Popular building types reflected national trends rather than local tradition, gaining widespread acceptance and popularity. Sources for popular types included outside builders, nearby examples, pattern books, periodicals, and newspaper articles.

An early popular type, the American Cottage, was a house with a symmetrical facade with an uneven number of bays—usually three or five—and a central door. Symmetry was the outstanding characteristic. American Cottages often were bayed, with a projecting semioctagonal bay constituting the most prominent element of some main facades.

The bungalow type appeared in the late nineteenth century and with Craftsman styling became a dominant form of new construction along the coast by 1920. The orientation of the roof determined its variation. Along the coast, the roof was always gabled and ran perpendicular to the main facade. The gable-fronted type always had a gabled porch, sometimes centered and sometimes off to one side. The treatment of the porch gable was the same as the main gable. One side of the porch often featured a pergola. The gable-sided version often had a shed-roofed porch across the main facade and a larger dormer on the front slope of the roof. Features adapted for Craftsman style included shallow roof pitch; gabled porches with wide overhangs fronted with rafters supported on extended purlins; visible rafter ends in a stylized pattern; multiple windows; massive porch posts, often tapering upward; and brick bases.

Polite architecture was the domain of the architect and professional designer who built with attention to both function and aesthetics while heeding national trends of style and technique. Several polite types of houses appeared along the coast.

The oldest polite examples were in the Greek Revival style. Decorative Greek detail often was applied to older building types with elements such as Ionic columns. Inside moldings, mantles, and doorways also reflected Greek detail. New Orleans businessmen constructed many antebellum Greek Revival homes along the coast.

G

As downtown areas developed, particularly 1890s Biloxi, architects constructed buildings in Commercial Romanesque style. The massive solidity of the style gave the buildings a secure, almost invincible appearance, particularly popular for banks.

However, the Queen Anne style was most popular for 1890s houses, with multiple galleries and stock detail. The style appeared irregular in composition. The gallery detail used on these houses included turned posts, sawn brackets, spindle bands, and sometimes balustrade railings.

Reacting to the irregular composition, the Colonial Revival created a more formal facade with columned and porticoed houses appearing along the Gulf Coast in the late 1890s. Chicago businessmen lured by the Gulf breezes constructed two-story houses with Corinthian porticos, elliptical fanlights, and Federal-style decorations.

The Colonial Revival style was not suited to smaller houses, so the Mission style became popular for those homes at the turn of the twentieth century. Based on Spanish influence, universal Mission style featured stucco walls; tile roofs (if the roof was visible); often flat roofs; flat projecting bands; and extensive use of arches. Spanish Colonial style differed from Mission by including more decorative Spanish details such as twisted columns and iron grills.

From 1910 to 1930, the Tudor Revival style was popular. Its most common characteristics were the jettied upper floor, high-pitched gabled roofs, and half-timber construction with stucco infill. Windows had small multilights, usually in diamond patterns in the upper sash of double-hung windows. Bay windows were also very common.

After the late 1930s, Minimal Traditional emerged as a popular national style. Simplicity and lack of traditional detail characterized this style used for one-story, low-roofed homes. These homes also featured at least one large front-facing gable. This style lasted until approximately the 1950s, when the rapid urbanization of the Mississippi coast resulted in large subdivisions of ranch-style homes.

Coastal architecture reflected historical movements and aesthetics while maintaining optimal climate adaptation prior to widespread air-conditioning.

Deanne Stephens Nuwer
University of Southern Mississippi

A. J. Bicknell and William T. Comstock, *Victorian Architecture: Two Pattern Books* (1975); Clay Lancaster, *Art Bulletin* (September 1958); Virginia and Lee McAlester, *A Field Guide to American Houses* (1996); Milton B. Newton Jr., *Melanges* (27 September 1971); John Michael Vlach, "Sources of the Shotgun House: African and Caribbean Antecedents for Afro-American Architecture" (PhD dissertation, Indiana University, 1975); Eugene M. Wilson, *Alabama Folk Houses* (1975).

Gulf Coast Cuisine

The cuisine of the Mississippi Gulf Coast is primarily determined by the bountiful supply of seafood in the waters of the Gulf of Mexico. Children grow up gigging for flounder at low tide and using nets to snare crab in the shallow surf on warm afternoons. The search for the freshest and best treasures from the deep is a way of life for many coastal residents. Crowds gather at the docks to buy fish and shellfish straight from the boats, pack the fish in coolers, and take them home to make gumbo, jambalaya, and crab West Indies. Chefs from local restaurants purchase the makings of soft-shell crab, stuffed flounder, oyster bisque, and seafood platters.

The curve of coastline between Alabama and Louisiana has for centuries attracted those who love the sea. The Biloxi Indians first came to fish in the Sound, leaving behind shell mounds to be discovered by future generations. In 1699 the king of France sent Pierre Le Moyne, Sieur d'Iberville, and his brother, Jean-Baptiste Le Moyne, Sieur de Bienville, to claim the region for France. Although the flags of Spain and England have also flown over the Gulf Coast, the French left the greatest influence on food. French sauces and cooking methods have mellowed the spiciness of Cajun and Creole dishes to develop the cuisine the coast enjoys today. Classic French dishes on restaurant menus include escargot en bordelaise, tournedos, duchesse aux champignon, and velouté of oysters en croute.

After years of rule by European powers, Mississippi became the twentieth state in the Union in 1817. As the antebellum South prospered, the coast began to become a mecca for New Orleanians seeking to escape the city's heat and the plague of yellow fever. Before and well after the Civil War, wealthy merchants and planters built mansions near the water and spent the summers enjoying the Gulf breezes. These vacationers brought their Creole and Cajun recipes and their refined taste for gourmet dining with them. New Orleans cuisine took root and became the coast's strongest gastronomic influence. Popular New Orleans dishes today include trout meunière, oysters Rockefeller, oysters Bienville, and crawfish étouffée. During the Civil War, when Federal forces captured Fort Massachusetts on Ship Island and imposed a blockade that prevented coast residents from reaching vital supply ships, many vowed to survive on the Gulf's plentiful mullet, which they dubbed Biloxi Bacon.

In the late 1800s and early 1900s the Gulf Coast turned to manufacturing. The construction of canneries, lumber mills, railroads, and ice plants attracted workers from Europe and elsewhere. Today, descendants of this wave of immigrants weave the cultural fabric of the towns of Bay St. Louis, Pass Christian, Long Beach, Gulfport, Biloxi, Ocean Springs, and Pascagoula. Nationalities include Italian, Irish, Greek, Swiss, Austrian, Slavonian, Croatian, German, and English.

The cuisines of all of these countries have affected the coast in subtle ways, but their cookery is most evident at festivals. Examples include St. Patrick's Day, the Greek Orthodox Church Festival, and St. Joseph's Altar, a celebration featuring Sicilian food.

The coast is very much a part of the Deep South, as is especially obvious in recipes for vegetables and desserts. Vegetable dishes popular with both white and African American home cooks and chefs include squash casserole, fried green tomatoes, and eggplant fritters. Favorite desserts are bread pudding, Mississippi mud cake, banana pudding, pecan pie, and peach cobbler.

Bread choices run the gamut from farm favorites such as cornbread and hush puppies to the French bread used to make po'boy sandwiches, another New Orleans specialty that the coast has embraced. The venerable Ole Biloxi Schooner, a popular restaurant, uses French bread to make po'boys filled with oysters, shrimp, crawfish, and soft-shell crabs.

The arrival of casinos in 1992 brought gambling palaces with sleek restaurants and introduced international dishes such as Kobe beef from Japan, beluga caviar, and Dover sole. The success of these casinos has brought a measure of prosperity to restaurants on the coast. Emeril Lagasse, celebrity chef and television star, has become a frequent visitor since his marriage to Gulf Coast native Alden Lovelace.

Mary Leigh Furrh
Jackson, Mississippi

Gulf Coast Symphony Orchestra Guild, *Encore! Encore!* (1999); Edith Ballard Watts with John Watts, *Jesse's Book of Creole and Deep South Recipes* (1954); Mary Ann Wells, *A History Lovers Guide to Mississippi* (1988); Westminster Academy Mother's Club, *The Gulf Coast Gourmet* (1979).

Gulf Coast Geography

In 1951, just four years after a major but unnamed hurricane struck what he called the "Gulf Coast Country," Mississippi writer Hodding Carter Sr. described the area as "a soft, near-tropic abode of chameleon sea and white sand." The natural elements he described—"the rustling beauty of tall pines and moss-drenched water oaks and redolent magnolias"—contribute to the breeziness of quotidian life on the Mississippi Gulf Coast. But the gentle sea lapping the coast periodically changes more than just its color, rising up like an angry dragon—twice so far since his observation, by Hurricanes Camille (1969) and Katrina (2005)—and slapping at the foundations of coastal life. Since the Mississippi Gulf Coast runs east-west for forty-four miles slightly north of 30 degrees north latitude, and because of its south-facing situation on the east side of a landmass near semitropical waters, it is subject to tropical storms, including hurricanes, churning northward from the Atlantic tropics, sometimes blasting over the West Indies and roiling through the Caribbean Sea and Gulf of Mexico.

Regions lie nested within larger regions. Such is the case with the coast, which is part of the large physiographic province known as the Gulf-Atlantic Coastal Plain (sometimes Atlantic Coastal Plain) that stretches from the middle Rio Grande Valley, in Texas, to southern New Jersey and even Long Island, New York. This large physiographic province is divided into Upper and Lower Coastal plains. The Mississippi section constitutes a portion of the seaward edge of the Lower Coastal Plain, which is made up of two physiographic subregions, the Coastal Terrace and the Barrier Islands. Beyond the barrier islands to the south lie the Continental Shelf and the Gulf of Mexico. Between the barrier islands and the coast is the narrow and shallow body of saltwater (a lagoon) called the Mississippi Sound. Thus, the coast as a natural region is the seaward edge of the Lower Coastal Plain, itself the seaward section of the wide Gulf-Atlantic Coastal Plain.

The mainland part of the Mississippi Gulf Coast, the Coastal Terrace, is between five and ten miles wide and made up of lowlands (e.g., the highest elevation in Bay St. Louis is approximately twenty-five feet), bayous, salt marshes, beaches, and rivers and their narrow floodplains running northward. Much of the coastal plain was once covered by shallow seas.

Mississippi's territory includes five sandy barrier islands, formed between thirty-five hundred and six thousand years ago. From east to west, they are Petit Bois, south of Pascagoula; Horn Island, about twelve miles out and once the haunt of artist Walter Anderson; Ship Island (actually two islands, East Ship and West Ship), which once provided the only deep-water harbor between New Orleans and Mobile; and Cat Island. In addition, there are two near-shore islands: Round, a small island near Pascagoula, and Deer Island, now entirely owned by the State of Mississippi and angling obliquely from within a few hundred meters of the Biloxi beach to about two miles offshore directly seaward of Biloxi Bay. Petit Bois, Horn, and Ship Islands are part of the Gulf Islands National Seashore. The islands, like all barrier islands, are in flux. Littoral drift tends to cause erosion on their eastern ends and build up sand spits on their western ends. In addition, Hurricane Katrina severely damaged the barrier islands' pine trees, as can be seen on Deer Island viewed from the mainland. Another barrier island, the Isle of Caprice, formerly lay two miles beyond Horn but disappeared into the sound's waters in 1931–32.

The coast is interrupted by bays and bayous. Toward the east is the Back Bay of Biloxi on the north side of the Biloxi peninsula, and Fort Bayou, forming the northern border of Ocean Springs. They meet and form a *T* where they merge in Biloxi Bay, an opening to the sound. Toward the west is St. Louis Bay, surrounded by the towns of Pass Christian on the east side and Bay St. Louis and Waveland on the west.

Rivers also intersect the coast. The main rivers, from east to west, are the Pascagoula, said to be the largest non-dammed river in the eastern United States; the meandering Tchoutacabouffa and Biloxi, which together flow into Big Lake at the western end of the Back Bay of Biloxi; the Wolf; the Jourdan; and the Pearl, a large river flowing south from Mississippi's capital city, Jackson, and forming part of the state's western border. The barrier islands and the discharge of the rivers keep the waters of the Mississippi Sound in conditions of relatively low salinity (about half as much as the Gulf in normal years) and high turbidity.

The Mississippi Gulf Coast is classified as having a moist subtropical climate, with mild winters and hot summers. In a normal year, the area receives between sixty-three inches of precipitation (in the western corner) and sixty-six inches (in the east), some of the highest totals in the continental United States. Nearly all of this precipitation is rain (snow is rare), and it is fairly evenly distributed throughout the year.

Despite the area's low relief, a surprisingly large number of vegetative habitats may be found within a few miles of the coast. The bayous and rivers add complexity. Habitats include maritime communities typically found on the barrier islands and within a few hundred meters of open ocean on the mainland edge. Tidal marshes are wet grasslands that occur along shorelines and tidally influenced portions of coastal rivers. Wet pine savannas were historically a fire-maintained plant assemblage occurring on the wettest (hydric) soils that overlay perched water tables and consisted of a widely spaced canopy of longleaf pine and diverse understory. The Mississippi Sandhill Crane Wildlife Refuge, in Jackson County, maintains this habitat with controlled burns. Pine flatwoods share flat terraces with wet pine savanna but occupy areas with fewer days of standing water.

The coast comprises a cultural landscape exhibiting traits of the wider Gulf of Mexico culture region overlaid on a natural region on the seaward edge of the Gulf-Atlantic Coastal Plain. Post-Katrina recovery along the entire coast has not been a time of large-scale relocation and risk reduction. Instead, beachfront properties have been rebuilt in Pascagoula, Ocean Springs, and other cities. Casinos have been repaired, and high-rise condominiums are being built in Biloxi, Gulfport, and cities to the west. The continued force of global climate change, with the resulting rise in sea levels and more intense tropical storms, has disturbing implications for the future of the Mississippi Gulf Coast. It is, after all, a low-lying coastal region facing a warm, capricious, chameleon-like sea.

Lee Durham Stone
Ocean Springs, Mississippi

Ralph D. Cross and Robert W. Wales, eds., Charles T. Traylor, chief cartographer, *Atlas of Mississippi* (1974); Alan Strahler and Arthur Strahler, *Introducing Physical Geography* (2006).

Gulf Coast Tourism

The Mississippi Gulf Coast tourism industry, concentrated primarily between Ocean Springs in the east and Bay St. Louis in the west, dates to the arrival of the railroad after the Civil War. During the antebellum period, a few New Orleanians escaped the city's frequent yellow fever epidemics and heat by vacationing along the coast, but most travelers ferried past the area on the steamboat route between New Orleans to Mobile. The completion of the New Orleans, Mobile, and Chattanooga Railroad in 1870 facilitated access to the once-isolated shoreline and placed the Mississippi Gulf Coast on a popular rail route that eventually linked Florida and California. The retirement of former Confederate president Jefferson Davis to Beauvoir likewise bolstered national interest in the Mississippi Gulf Coast. After purchasing the smaller lines operating along the coast during the 1880s, the Louisville and Nashville Railroad became the major promoter of travel to the Mississippi beachfront. The company also introduced commuter service between Ocean Springs and New Orleans in 1880, thereby bringing many more weekend vacationers as well as an influx of summer homeowners.

Belief in the healthful properties of coastal air attracted tourists even though the area suffered from occasional, well-publicized yellow fever outbreaks into the early twentieth century. The Mexican Gulf Hotel, which opened in 1883

Mexican Gulf Hotel, Pass Christian, ca. 1908 (Ann Rayburn Paper Americana Collection, Department of Archives and Special Collections, J. D. Williams Library, University of Mississippi [rayburn_ann_32_90_001])

in Pass Christian, was the first winter hotel on the coast. The completion of the Gulf and Ship Island Railroad by Capt. Joseph Jones in 1899 established a direct rail link to the North. By the early twentieth century, large hotels dotted the beach, catering primarily to northerners during the winter months. The most famous vacationer was Pres. Woodrow Wilson, who spent the winter of 1913–14 in Pass Christian.

After a destructive 1915 hurricane, officials constructed a twenty-six-mile-long seawall, completed in 1926, similar to that built by Galveston. A waterfront highway that eventually became US 90 paralleled the wall. Improved storm protection, a better mosquito eradication program, and a real estate boom inspired in part by land speculation in Florida during the 1920s increased interest in the Mississippi Gulf Coast as a vacation destination. The decade became known as the golden age of tourism in the area, as the Edgewater Gulf Hotel, the Buena Vista Hotel, and other large resorts opened. Surf bathing and the fad of beauty contests made Mississippi beaches ever more popular. The construction of roads and bridges, especially under New Deal programs, bolstered the tourism industry, with automobiles slowly replacing trains as Americans' preferred mode of travel. A region of Mississippi tied more closely to the urbane culture of New Orleans than to the conservative values of the hinterland, coastal communities protected visitors' access to gambling, alcohol, and until the 1980s prostitution as well as more acceptable attractions such as golf courses, boating, and fishing. The opening of Keesler Air Force Base in 1941 solidified the year-round tourism industry as entertainment venues catered to the large permanent presence of military personnel.

The Mississippi Gulf Coast's tourism industry became a key site in the civil rights struggle. In 1951 engineers began dredging sand from the Gulf to add a lengthy beach in front of the seawall for tourists' enjoyment and for better hurricane protection. The investment of tax revenues into public beach maintenance projects encouraged African Americans to challenge segregation laws that restricted their access to shore. In 1959 Dr. Gilbert Mason led an ultimately successful "wade-in" in Biloxi, the civil rights movement's first nonviolent protest in Mississippi. The resulting negative publicity spawned by violent resistance to integration caused a decline in travel to the coast. Combined with the devastating effects of Hurricane Camille in 1969 and the development of beach tourism in the Florida Panhandle, the Mississippi Gulf Coast tourism industry struggled through the 1970s and 1980s. During this period, the so-called Dixie Mafia, a cabal of local officials, businessmen, and criminals, made the coast a center for prostitution and drug trafficking until a series of convictions dismantled the network by the mid-1980s.

In 1992 dockside casino gambling rejuvenated tourism on the Mississippi Gulf Coast, with large gaming barges, resort hotels, and entertainment venues converting the beachfront into the third-largest casino market in the United States, trailing only Las Vegas and Atlantic City. Hurricane Katrina in 2005 demolished virtually all of the structures along the coast. To quickly rebound from the devastation, the state authorized the introduction of land-based casinos within eight hundred feet of the shoreline. As of 2016, the Mississippi Gulf Coast had no fewer than sixteen casinos featuring everything from golf courses and Minor League Baseball to fine dining and top-name entertainment.

Anthony J. Stanonis
Queen's University Belfast

Mary Allen Alexander, *Rosalie and Radishes: A History of Long Beach, Mississippi* (1980); Gerald Blessey, interview by Angela Sartin, 2 January 2000, Community Bridges Oral History Project, Center for Oral History and Cultural Heritage, University of Southern Mississippi; J. Michael Butler, *Journal of Southern History* (February 2002); Philip Hearn, *Hurricane Camille: Monster Storm of the Gulf Coast* (2004); Edward Humes, *Mississippi Mud: Southern Justice and the Dixie Mafia* (1995); Gilbert R. Mason, *Beaches, Blood, and Ballots: A Doctor's Civil Rights Struggle* (2000).

Gulfside Assembly

The Gulfside Assembly is located in Waveland, on Mississippi's Gulf Coast. Founded in 1923 by Bishop Robert E. Jones of the Southwestern District of the Methodist Episcopal Church, it was the first permanent African American Chautauqua-style coastal resort in the nation. Elected to the episcopacy in 1920, Jones was the church's first African American bishop. A tireless advocate of racial uplift and interracial cooperation, Jones had previously served as the editor of the *Southwestern Christian Advocate*, the organ of black Methodism in New Orleans. As bishop, Jones devoted his energies to making the church more responsive to the social and educational needs of its congregants, especially those residing in the rural South.

Gulfside grew out of Jones's desire to provide religious recreational facilities that would inculcate middle-class values among a populace inundated by what he consented unhealthy commercial amusements. In the summer of 1923 Jones purchased more than three hundred acres of mostly undeveloped coastal property from several landowners. These purchases included Jackson House, a seaside mansion that had been owned by Andrew Jackson's son, and rumors held that Jones had passed as a white man to buy the property. Gulfside's survival in the Jim Crow South resulted in large part from the slightly more racially tolerant attitudes of Gulf Coast whites and from the seemingly nonthreatening nature of a religious resort. Soon after securing title to the land, Jones and his cofounders began clearing the land and refitting Jackson House as a dormitory.

Jones envisioned the resort as the first phase in a larger program of progressive racial reform. Assembly members formed Gulfside Clubs in black communities across the South. As part of the "Gulfside movement," these clubs solicited donations for a school for underprivileged boys, encouraged social and fraternal organizations to hold annual meetings at Gulfside, and served as "enthusiastic and intelligent field agent[s] for" what one pamphlet called the "biggest venture ever started for and by colored people." Gulfside's charter stated that "the purpose of the Assembly is to establish, own, operate and maintain a school under the auspices of the Methodist Church for assemblies, conventions, conferences, orphan homes, camp meetings and religious resorts with both temporary and permanent dwellings on the Gulf of Mexico, for health, rest and recreation, for children, the aged, disabled and others." More than thirty additional buildings were constructed on the grounds, including cabins, classrooms, and a one-thousand-seat auditorium.

Gulfside hosted a variety of groups, including training institutes for ministers and teachers, camps for Boy Scouts and Camp Fire Girls, recuperative summer retreats for "tired mothers," and an industrial training school for impoverished young black men. Many of those educated at Gulfside's boys' school went on to become leaders in the church. Gulfside's mission and programs were comparable to an earlier generation of Progressive-era reform organizations such as Jane Addams's Hull House. Gulfside camps offered strictly regimented daily activities and preached the productive and uplifting use of leisure time. Alongside camps and institutes, middle- and upper-class black families from New Orleans and the surrounding area vacationed at the resort throughout the summer.

In his interactions with white neighbors and benefactors, Jones stressed the resort's racially conservative mission, a strategy that enabled him to secure financial support from the Julius Rosenwald Fund for Gulfside's construction and operation and from the states of Mississippi and Louisiana for Gulfside's educational training institutes. Beginning in 1931 Gulfside hosted an annual performance of spirituals sung by black college choirs before a segregated audience. The resort also hosted interracial and interdenominational conferences aimed at improving race relations in the region.

In the mid-1930s Gulfside struggled to remain financially solvent. After a fire of suspicious origins burned Jackson House to the ground in 1935, Gulfside nearly folded; it rebuilt, only to suffer further damage from a tidal wave in 1947 and Hurricane Camille in 1969. After each disaster, the members' resolve strengthened, and Gulfside remained the sole African American resort on the Gulf Coast. In the autumn of 1964 the members of the Student Nonviolent Coordinating Committee met at Gulfside, which, attendee Mary King recalled, was the only place where a "racially integrated group [could] stay together and not trigger violence in Mississippi." At this meeting, King and Casey Hayden introduced a petition for gender equality in the organization.

Desegregation proved as much of a challenge to Gulfside's continued existence as did fires and natural disasters. By the late 1960s, as African Americans gained access to other coastal beaches and resorts, the institution struggled to attract guests and refashion its identity in the desegregated South. Leaders stressed its nondenominational character, and into the twenty-first century it remained a popular site for African American and interracial groups from the Gulf Coast and for black Methodists from across the country.

Hurricane Katrina struck the Gulf Coast in September 2005 and destroyed every structure on the Gulfside grounds, including the Norris Center, a three-million-dollar lodging and meeting building that had been dedicated just sixteen days earlier. By 2015 a new open-air chapel had been built and an outdoor prayer pavilion was under construction, while the United Methodist Church continued to consider other plans for rebuilding the site.

Andrew W. Kahrl
University of Virginia

Kathy L. Gilbert, "Gulfside Assembly Re-Imagining Future of Historic Site" (28 August 2015), www.umc.org/news-and-media/gulfside-assembly-reimagining-future-of-historic-site; Gulfside Assembly Vertical Files, Mississippi Department of Archives and History; Robert E. Jones Papers, Amistad Research Center, Tulane University; Henry N. Oakes, "The Struggle for Racial Equality in the Methodist Episcopal Church: The Career of Robert E. Jones, 1904–1944" (PhD dissertation, University of Iowa, 1973).

Gunter, Sue

(1939–2005) Basketball Coach

Born in 1939 in Walnut Grove in Leake County, Sue Gunter witnessed and contributed to major transformations in American women's basketball. She became a coach while still in her twenties and spent most of her life coaching women's basketball at Stephen F. Austin State University and Louisiana State University (LSU).

Gunter started playing basketball as a small child, shooting at a hoop on her family's farm. Like many young women, she went to a teachers' college, graduating from Peabody College in Nashville in 1962. While in Nashville Gunter played guard on the Amateur Athletic Union national championship team supported by Nashville Business College.

The fact that Gunter was playing for Nashville Business College while attending Peabody reveals an important reality about women's basketball in the mid-twentieth century.

In the early 1900s, women had played basketball, but college and university administrators discouraged female participation on the grounds that the game was too strenuous, competitive, and unladylike for polite young women. From the 1930s through the 1950s, women's basketball became a game for working-class people, supported by factories, churches, and vocational schools like Nashville Business College, whose squad played at the city's YMCA.

Gunter played on an American team chosen to play a team from the Soviet Union in the early 1960s and then became the coach of women's basketball at Middle Tennessee State University. From there she went to Stephen F. Austin State University in Nacogdoches, Texas, where she coached basketball along with three other women's sports from 1965 to 1980. Five of her teams reached the playoffs of the Association of Intercollegiate Athletics for Women, an organization Gunter helped organize in 1971.

Her success at Stephen F. Austin attracted national attention. Gunter served as an assistant coach for the US Olympic team in 1976, the first year women's basketball was a medal sport. She became head coach in 1980, when the team did not get to compete because the United States boycotted the games.

In 1983 she moved on to the position of head coach of women's basketball at LSU, where the women's teams were known as the Ben-Gals. Renamed the Lady Tigers, Gunter's teams became a force in the Southeastern Conference. Between 1983 and 2004 LSU posted a 442–221 record. The National Collegiate Athletic Association began holding women's basketball championships in 1984, and the Lady Tigers participated in fourteen tournaments before Gunter retired. Over this period, women's college basketball grew dramatically, with increased administrative support, budgets for recruiting and training, attendance, and television coverage.

Gunter received numerous honors, including induction into the Women's Basketball Hall of Fame and the Mississippi and Louisiana Sports Halls of Fame. She retired in 2004 with a lifetime record of 708–308 and was elected to the Naismith Memorial Basketball Hall of Fame on 4 April 2005. She died on 4 August of that year.

Ted Ownby
University of Mississippi

Susan K. Cahn, *Coming on Strong: Gender and Sexuality in Twentieth-Century Women's Sport* (1994); Pamela Grundy, *Learning to Win: Sports, Education, and Social Change in Twentieth-Century North Carolina* (2001); Rosemary Skaine, *Women's College Basketball Coaches* (2001); TigerBait.com website.

Guyot, Lawrence

(1939–2012) Activist

On 17 July 1939 Lawrence Thomas Guyot Jr. was born in Pass Christian, the oldest of five sons of a domestic worker and a carpenter. He attended Catholic parochial schools before earning his diploma from Randolph High School in 1957. He then attended Tougaloo College in Jackson, graduating in 1964 with a bachelor's degree in biology and philosophy. While attending Tougaloo, Guyot joined the struggle for civil rights and became a member of the Student Nonviolent Coordinating Committee (SNCC).

Working as a SNCC field secretary, Guyot helped register African American voters in communities across the state, including McComb, Greenwood, and Hattiesburg. Guyot and other SNCC members participated in a student-led march to the McComb City Hall to protest Brenda Travis's expulsion from school and Herbert Lee's murder. Guyot and other marchers were beaten and arrested. Out on bond, the SNCC workers organized and opened Pike County's Nonviolent High, a freedom school for the students who refused to attend the public school to protest Travis's expulsion.

After a fellow SNCC worker was attacked in Greenwood, Guyot was sent there to organize and register voters. While participating in a protest march, Guyot and seven other SNCC leaders were arrested and charged with disturbing the peace. He served a prison sentence, partly in Parchman. After his release, Guyot was notified that June Jordan, Fannie Lou Hamer, and several other civil rights workers were in jail in Winona. Arriving there to try to arrange the women's bail, Guyot was again arrested and beaten. Other SNCC workers feared that Guyot's life was in danger and persistently called the jail and demanded to speak with him. He and the others were released the next morning.

Guyot also worked for SNCC in Hattiesburg, where he directed the Freedom Summer Project in 1964. He organized a 1964 Freedom Day there that included registration of African American voters and a protest march, which resulted in another jailing. Though he was elected chair of the Mississippi Freedom Democratic Party (MFDP), he did not attend the Democratic National Convention in Atlantic City with Hamer and other MFDP delegates because he was still in jail in Hattiesburg.

After his release, Guyot remained active in the party and led a group of students in a silent march to the Capitol in Jackson. Halfway there, the marchers were stopped by police, arrested, and taken to the state fairgrounds, where conditions were deplorable. Protesters continued to march and for several days, and by the end of the week, the number of arrests surpassed one thousand.

As SNCC members proposed an expansion of their work into other southern states, Guyot continued to champion efforts in Mississippi. He also supported white involvement in the movement at a time when other members of the Council of Federated Organizations were questioning it. After disillusionment with what many perceived to be the MFDP's failure at the 1968 Democratic Convention in Chicago, Guyot left Mississippi to pursue other civil rights causes.

Guyot earned a law degree from Rutgers University in 1971 and went to work as a fund-raiser for Mississippi's Mary Holmes Junior College. He then moved to Washington, D.C., where he worked first for Pride, Inc., and then for the US Department of Health and Human Services. Guyot remained politically active both locally and nationally until his death in 2012. He coauthored *Putting the Movement Back into Civil Rights Teaching* (2004) and appeared in numerous film documentaries about the civil rights movement in Mississippi, including *Eyes on the Prize*. His forty-seven-year marriage to Monica Klein Guyot produced two children.

Amy Schmidt
Lyon College

Clayborne Carson, *In Struggle: SNCC and the Black Awakening of the 1960s* (1981); John Dittmer, *Local People: The Struggle for Civil Rights in Mississippi* (1994); History Makers website, www.thehistorymakers.com; Charles M. Payne, *I've Got the Light of Freedom: The Organizing Tradition and the Mississippi Freedom Struggle* (1995); Howard Zinn, *SNCC: The New Abolitionists* (2002).

Guyton, Arthur C.

(1919–2003) Physician, Educator, and Scholar

Dr. Arthur C. Guyton spent his career as chair of the Department of Physiology and Biophysics at the University of Mississippi Medical Center in Jackson. During his five decades there, he became one of the most highly regarded physiologists in the world and authored the widely used *Textbook of Medical Physiology*, in publication since 1956. He wrote forty other books and more than six hundred articles for scientific publications. His work led to a new understanding of the cardiovascular system and changed the entire field of physiology.

Guyton was born in Oxford in 1919, the son of Dr. Billy S. Guyton and Mary Katherine Smallwood Guyton. Billy Guyton, an ophthalmologist in Oxford, also taught part time at the School of Medicine, at that time located in Oxford, and served as its dean from 1935 to 1944, guiding it through an accreditation crisis that threatened its closure. Kate Guyton was a mathematics teacher who had been a missionary in China before her marriage.

Arthur Guyton graduated from the University of Mississippi with the highest academic average in his class, the Taylor Medal in physics, and the short story award. He went on to Harvard Medical School, where he earned his degree in 1943. He subsequently married Ruth Weigle, the daughter of the dean of the Yale Divinity School and chair of the committee responsible for the Revised Standard Version of the Bible. They ultimately had ten children, all of whom became physicians.

After a year's internship at Massachusetts General Hospital in Boston, Guyton served in the US Navy for two years at the National Naval Medical Center in Bethesda, Maryland, and at the state's Camp Detrick. Back in Boston to complete a residency in surgery at Massachusetts General, Guyton contracted polio in 1946. He and Ruth spent months in Warm Springs, Georgia, where he regained the use of some of his paralyzed muscles, though he had residual paralysis in his right lower leg, left upper arm, and both shoulders.

"It was clear," Guyton wrote, "that I couldn't be a surgeon as I had planned. But that meant that I could devote myself to the two things that meant the most to me: medical research and raising a family." The Guytons moved back to Oxford in 1947, and he began teaching physiology and doing research. He was named chair of physiology in 1948 and moved to Jackson in 1955 when the University of Mississippi Medical Center opened and the school expanded to a full four-year curriculum.

In 1956 the first edition of his textbook was published, and he received a presidential citation for devices he designed for those disabled by polio—an electronic wheelchair (though he never used one), a special hoist for moving patients from bed to chair, and an automatic locking and unlocking leg brace. At the same time, he worked to discover the cause of hypertension (high blood pressure). His research found that most of what had been written about the heart, blood flow, blood vessels, and blood pressure control was wrong.

His first major breakthrough was the discovery that cardiac output—the amount of blood pumped by the heart—depended not on the heart but on the demand of tissues for oxygen. This theory significantly advanced the understanding of circulation. He filled in another missing link in the understanding of cardiovascular physiology when he proposed and then proved that the pressure in the fluid between cells is negative, an understanding that was vital to comprehending fluid retention in tissue and congestive heart failure.

Having worked out some of the basic mechanisms of circulation, Guyton turned again to blood pressure. Working with an analog computer and the first computer model of the circulatory system, he found that the only factor that could control blood pressure long term was fluid control by the kidney. This idea flew in the face of prevailing notions but was eventually accepted by the scientific community and has provided the basis for much drug development in the treatment of hypertension.

Guyton received nearly every conceivable prize offered in the field of physiology. Most notably, however, the Royal College of Physicians in London invited him to give the William Harvey Lecture at the 1978 symposium commemorating the four hundredth birthday of Harvey, the scientist who first described the circulation of blood.

Guyton's research and teaching changed physiology from a science of verbal descriptions to one of quantitative analysis. He brought mathematics and physics into the discipline. He was a pioneer in the use of computers to study body function and taught scientists all over the world computer simulation. Scientists at the National Aeronautics and Space Administration now use a descendant of his original computer model of the cardiovascular system to determine ways to counter the effects of weightlessness on astronauts.

More than two dozen of Guyton's students went on to become heads of physiology departments around the world, and at least six have served as president of the American Physiological Society. His *Textbook of Medical Physiology* has been and remains enormously influential. It is now in its thirteenth edition (coauthored by Dr. John Hall, who took over after Guyton's death) and has been translated into at least a dozen languages. The textbook earned Guyton the 1996 Abraham Flexner Award for Distinguished Service to Medical Education, awarded by the Association of American Medical Colleges. It is used in more medical schools around the world than any other physiology text.

Guyton and his wife died in 2003, the result of injuries sustained in an automobile accident.

Janis Quinn
University of Mississippi Medical
Center

Carol Brinson and Janis Quinn, *Arthur C. Guyton: His Life, His Family, His Achievements* (1989); Arthur C. Guyton, "A Brief History of Cardiovascular Physiology at Mississippi," unpublished manuscript, Department of Physiology and Biophysics, University of Mississippi Medical Center; Arthur C. Guyton, interview for the Rowland Medical Library Oral History Project, University of Mississippi Medical Center (16 November 2001); Janis Quinn, *This Week at UMC* (30 November 1996, 22 September 2000).

G

H

Hains, Frank
(1926–1975) Art Critic

A native of Parkersburg, West Virginia, Frank Hains became important to Mississippi arts in the 1950s as the arts editor for the *Jackson Daily News*, for which he wrote the "On Stage" column. After attending Marietta College in Ohio and serving in the military, Hains arrived in Vicksburg in 1951 to work in radio. He moved on to Jackson in 1955 and from 1956 to 1975 wrote lively critiques of stage performances, music, and movies. Hains also directed plays, especially at Jackson's Little Theatre. In his columns, he admired good theater and music and wrote disparagingly of works he considered simple or unambitious. He was especially interested in performances in Mississippi and considered himself something of an ambassador for improving the arts in the state.

An openly gay man, Hains negotiated the realities of gay life at a time and place that discouraged discussion of anything but heterosexual relationships. Hains praised Tennessee Williams's *Cat on a Hot Tin Roof* and pushed audiences to recognize the lead character's homosexual relationship even when the Hollywood version left the issue unclear. Hains also defended other works by Williams and wrote highly of works by Lillian Hellman and Kenneth Anger that addressed issues of homosexuality. He allowed readers of his column to consider the nature of his life—joking about living alone and never marrying, enjoying musical theater, and celebrating literature that addressed complex sexual issues—without ever explicitly discussing his own sexuality.

To the horror of his readers and friends, including numerous writers, artists, and theater lovers, a drifter beat Hains to death in his Jackson home in 1975.

Ted Ownby
University of Mississippi

Louis Dollarhide, *On Art and Artists* (1981); Leonard Gill, *Memphis Magazine* (April 2007); John Howard, *Men Like That: A Southern Queer History* (2001).

Haise, Fred
(b. 1933) Astronaut

Astronaut Fred Wallace Haise Jr. was born in Biloxi, Mississippi, on 14 November 1933. He attended Biloxi public schools and graduated from Biloxi High School before earning an associate's degree from Perkinston Junior College. He then joined the naval aviation cadet program and became a fighter pilot with the US Marines between 1954 and 1956. He subsequently returned to school, receiving a bachelor of science degree in aeronautical engineering from the University of Oklahoma in 1959.

During his military career, Haise had served as a research pilot for the National Aeronautics and Space Agency (NASA), and in April 1966 he was among nineteen pilots selected as part of NASA's Astronaut Group 5. He served as a backup pilot for the Apollo 8, 11, and 16 missions before going into space in 1970 as the lunar module pilot for the Apollo 13 mission to the moon. About fifty-five hours into the flight, a ruptured oxygen tank forced the crew to scuttle the mission. With assistance from Houston ground controllers, Haise and his fellow crew members, James A. Lovell and John L. Swigert, managed to return safely to earth. The mission was dramatized in a 1995 film, *Apollo 13*, in which Bill Paxton

Fred Haise (Courtesy Biloxi Historical Society)

played Haise. The film was nominated for the Academy Award for Best Picture.

From April 1973 to January 1976 Haise served as technical assistant to the manager of the Space Shuttle Orbiter Project. In 1977 he commanded a two-man crew that piloted space shuttle approach and landing test flights. Haise resigned from NASA in 1979 to take a position with Grumman Aerospace Corporation. He retired in 1996.

Haise's awards include the Presidential Medal of Freedom, the NASA Distinguished Service Medal, the AIAA Haley Astronautics Award, the American Astronautical Society Flight Achievement Award, and the City of New York Gold Medal.

Ben Gilstrap
University of Mississippi

Lyndon B. Johnson Space Center website, www.jsc.nasa.gov; Jim Lovell and Jeffrey Kluger, *Lost Moon: The Perilous Voyage of Apollo 13* (1994); Space.com website, www.space.com.

Hall, Martha Lacy
(1923–2009) Author

Born in Magnolia, Mississippi, to William and Elizabeth Lacy, Martha Lacy attended Whitworth College for Women in Brookhaven from September 1941 to June 1943, earning an associate's degree. She then married Robert Sherrill Hall Jr. and went on to have three children. Her conventional start in life and profession, including her first publication, *An Historical Sketch of Magnolia, Mississippi* (1956), belied the dedication to southern writing that she demonstrated through her influence as an editor for Louisiana State University Press from 1968 to 1978 and subsequently as managing editor. Among her projects at the press was the Pulitzer Prize–winning novel *A Confederacy of Dunces* (1980) by John Kennedy Toole. She retired from the press in 1984.

Hall's power of storytelling came to light with the publication of *Call It Living: Three Stories* (1981) and the subsequent collection *Music Lesson* (1984). Her finest literary achievement can be found in the short story collection *The Apple-Green Triumph, and Other Stories* (1990), published by Louisiana State University Press. The title story earned an O. Henry Award in 1991, bringing her national recognition. Originally published in the *Virginia Quarterly Review* (1990), "The Apple-Green Triumph" describes the main character's journey in her late husband's ancient British sports car, a Triumph, to retrieve her errant younger brother,

who is returning to Mississippi for his twin sister's funeral. Hall skillfully uses Welty-like humor in both character development and dialogue and creates strong southern female characters.

She died on 1 November 2009.

Amy Pardo
Mississippi University for Women

Martha Lacy Hall obituary, www.charlestonfunerals.com; Whitworth College for Women Archive, Lincoln-Lawrence-Franklin Regional Library, Brookhaven, Miss.

Hamblett, Theora
(1895–1977) Artist

A shy, unassuming farm girl from northern Mississippi, Theora Hamblett became one of the South's most distinguished self-taught artists. Noted for her colorful depictions of the Mississippi countryside, often showing children at play, and her idyllic memory paintings of the rural South, Hamblett is perhaps best known today for her eerie, sometimes wistful renditions of her daydreams and visions.

The daughter of Samuel Fielder Hamblett and his second wife, Tamzy Sophia Cobb Hamblett, Theora grew up with one brother, Samuel Hubert Hamblett, on the family's farm near Paris, Mississippi. The Hambletts lived in a dogtrot house her father had built before the Civil War and maintained a farm of several hundred acres with tenant families: they plowed, planted, and harvested cotton and tended cattle,

Theora Hamblett, *Cotton Picker*, ca. 1965, oil on canvas, 24'⅝" × 36'¾" (Courtesy Brooks Museum of Art, Memphis, Tennessee, Brooks Fine Art Foundation Purchase 65:51)

sheep, hogs, and chickens. Theora walked a mile and a half to school, and her family regularly attended church, alternating between the Methodists and the Baptists. Hamblett's memories of her early life—feeding chickens, picking cotton, sorghum making, spring cleaning, walking to school on frosty mornings—created an idyllic vision of her early life.

A gift of crayons that Hamblett received when she was about eight years old seems to have sparked her interest in painting. The gift, coupled with the girl's first trip to see a traveling circus, left an indelible impression: "When I went home [from the circus], oh, how I drew and colored." Hamblett's descriptions of her childhood certainly reveal a girl with an extraordinary aesthetic sensitivity. She was struck by the vibrancy, brilliance, and manifold colors of nature: "During the early days of my youth I became aware of how much I adored beautiful colors. Many times I have . . . made mental pictures of the . . . many trees all colored with the profuse colors of late autumn. There were sweet gums with their reddish purple, sometimes deep, almost black purple; persimmons with their yellow and orange; beechnuts and sycamores with their golden yellows; hickory trees and scaly barks with various shades of yellows; many kinds of oaks; and several types of evergreens. How I longed to paint that landscape!"

After graduating from Lafayette County Agricultural High School in 1915, Hamblett began teaching in one- and two-teacher schools, a career she followed intermittently for nearly two decades. On occasion, she attended summer school at the University of Southern Mississippi. After her mother's death in 1935 and several dismal years of trying to support herself by raising poultry, she moved from the family home to Oxford. In 1939 she bought a large house and divided it into four apartments, renting out three to students and reserving the fourth for herself.

Not until Hamblett was fifty-five years old did she finally succumb to the allure of making art, signing up for an adult education course offered by the University of Mississippi. She soon enrolled in a correspondence course sponsored by Connecticut's Famous Artists School. Although she learned basic painting techniques from such efforts, Hamblett determined to become her own teacher, saying she had to find her own way. In the mid-1950s Betty Parsons, a New York art dealer, purchased *The Golden Gate*, a painting inspired by a vision Hamblett had experienced some thirty years earlier. Parsons then sold the painting to Albert Dorne, the president of the Famous Artists School, who gave it to the Museum of Modern Art, which exhibited it under the title *The Vision* in 1955.

Over the next twenty-two years, Hamblett developed an extraordinary oeuvre, exact in workmanship and meticulous in style. Using oil paint on canvas or Masonite, she developed a unique pointillist technique that invested her paintings with a distinctive look. Although she embraced figurative representation, Hamblett employed few of the techniques used in Western art, such as one-point perspective or modeling, to simulate nature. Instead, she developed an approach that was both conceptual and decorative, conveying her thoughts in a language that is wonderfully ornate yet extremely refined.

Hamblett's subject matter can be divided among four basic themes—(1) pure landscape paintings; (2) landscape paintings with children playing games; (3) memory paintings, often with scenes set within a landscape; and (4) dreams and visions. Almost all demonstrate her love of nature and her beloved trees. The last category is the most personal, detailing the visions that she first experienced at age seventeen and that occurred more regularly in later life. She took these visions as a sign that God wanted her to paint her dreams, and, indeed, the images inspired by her visions often have religious connotations. They also suggest an understanding of symbolism. Hamblett's paintings, however, share little similarity with traditional religious iconography and are instead highly idiosyncratic.

In addition to the Museum of Modern Art, Hamblett's paintings hang in the permanent collections of the Morris Museum of Art and the Ogden Museum of Southern Art. Her work has been exhibited at the Corcoran Gallery of Art, the American Visionary Art Museum, the Walter Anderson Museum of Art, and the Memphis Brooks Museum of Art. In Mississippi, Hamblett's paintings can be found in the collections of the Mississippi Museum of Art, the Lauren Rogers Museum, and the University of Mississippi Museum, which today maintains Hamblett's archive, including some six hundred of her paintings.

Carol Crown
University of Memphis

Patti Carr Black, *Art in Mississippi, 1720–1980* (1998); William Ferris, in *Local Color: A Sense of Place in Folk Art*, ed. Brenda McCallum (1982); Paul Grootkerk, *Woman's Art Journal* (Autumn 1990–Winter 1991); Theora Hamblett, as told to Betty Tackett, *I Remember* (1971); Theora Hamblett in collaboration with Edwin E. Meek, *Dreams and Visions* (1975); Theora Hamblett in collaboration with Edwin E. Meek and William S. Haynie, *Theora Hamblett Paintings* (1975).

Hamer, Fannie Lou

(1917–1977) Activist.

A civil rights activist and role model for other activists, Fannie Lou Townsend Hamer was born in 1917 in Montgomery County, Mississippi, the youngest of the twenty children of sharecroppers James Lee and Lou Ella Bramlett Townsend. Townsend grew up on the E. W. Brandon Plantation in Sunflower County, where her parents moved in 1919. She began

Fannie Lou Hamer on her front porch (McCain Library and Archives, University of Southern Mississippi)

picking cotton on the plantation at age six and after sixth grade left school entirely to help support her family by working in the fields. In 1944 she married Perry "Pap" Hamer, also a sharecropper, and the two moved to the W. D. Marlow Plantation outside Ruleville.

On the Marlow Plantation, Fannie Lou Hamer worked with her husband in the fields, performed domestic work for the white family, and served as timekeeper for the plantation. Her life during this period was no less difficult than the years of her youth. For example, in 1961, during surgery to remove a small cyst in her stomach, a white doctor performed a hysterectomy without her knowledge or permission. In 1962, after Hamer attempted to register to vote, W. D. Marlow evicted the Hamers. That year the Student Nonviolent Coordinating Committee (SNCC) came to the Mississippi Delta, and Hamer worked with the group on voter registration drives. Whites responded by threatening her with violence, and in 1963 she and several other SNCC workers returning from a voter registration conference in South Carolina were arrested and taken to the Winona jail and severely beaten. Hamer never completely recovered from injuries sustained in the attack.

Despite such physical and emotional intimidation, Hamer persisted in her work with SNCC, becoming one of the most visible and influential of Mississippi's grassroots activists. In 1963 she passed the voter registration test, and the following year she cast her first vote in a Mississippi election. Later in 1964 Hamer became one of the founding members of the Mississippi Freedom Democratic Party, which challenged the seating of the state's all-white delegation to the Democratic National Convention in Atlantic City. Hamer's "I Question America" speech at the convention catapulted her to national prominence despite President Lyndon Johnson's attempts to prevent the nation from seeing and hearing her. When the Democratic Party offered to give two convention seats to the Mississippi Freedom Democrats, she replied, "We didn't come all this way for no two seats." While she failed to win a seat at the 1964 convention, she served as a delegate to the 1968 and 1972 Democratic National Conventions.

With a powerful voice rooted in African American religious traditions, and determined to face obstacles and opponents directly, Hamer could inspire awe in fellow activists and great irritation in her opponents. Many of her words—phrases such as "I question America," "Sick and tired of being sick and tired," "Nobody's free until everybody's free"—became memorable rallying points and expressions of both discontent and resilience.

She twice ran unsuccessfully for the US Congress from Mississippi's 2nd District. Legal action that she initiated against Sunflower County voter registration officials (*Hamer v. Campbell*, 1965) eventually led to the eradication of discriminatory procedures such as the poll tax.

After 1964 Hamer devoted much of her energy to alleviating the plight of other economically impoverished Delta residents. She organized clothing and food drives, worked with the Head Start program in Sunflower County, and supported the Mississippi Freedom Labor Union, which represented day laborers, domestics, and truck drivers. Most significant were two efforts Hamer undertook with assistance from charitable organizations outside the South: the Pig Bank, established in 1968 with help from the National Council of Negro Women, and the Freedom Farm Cooperative, founded in 1969, with funding from several outside sources. Both programs provided food for local residents; in addition, Freedom Farm Cooperative provided agricultural jobs, food stamps, housing, and scholarships for young people; support for African American entrepreneurial efforts; and assistance with acquiring home loans, including down payments. Hamer served as assistant director until Freedom Farm dissolved in 1974.

Hamer was also a driving force in the desegregation of Sunflower County schools, initiating legal action that resulted in the creation of one merged public school system and protected the jobs of African American teachers and administrators (*Hamer et al. v. Sunflower County*, 1970).

Hamer's health declined, and she died on 14 March 1977 of heart failure brought on by cancer, hypertension, and diabetes. Her legacies of courage, straight talk to powerful people, and activism on behalf of poor people continue to offer inspiration.

Lisa K. Speer
Arkansas History Commission

Chris Myers Asch, *The Senator and the Sharecropper: The Freedom Struggles of James O. Eastland and Fannie Lou Hamer* (2008); Fannie Lou Hamer, *To Praise Our Bridges* (1967); June Jordan, *Fannie Lou Hamer* (1972); Susan Kling, *Fannie Lou Hamer: A Biography* (1979); Chana Kai Lee, *For Freedom's Sake: The Life of Fannie Lou Hamer* (1999); Charles Marsh, *God's Long Summer: Stories of Faith and Civil Rights* (1999); Kay Mills, *This Little Light of Mine: The Life of Fannie Lou Hamer* (1993); J. Todd Moye, *Let the People Decide: Black Freedom and White Resistance Movements in Sunflower County, Mississippi, 1945–1986* (2004); Charles Payne, *I've Got the Light of Freedom: The Organizing Tradition and the Mississippi Freedom Struggle* (1995).

H

Hamer, Fannie Lou, "I Question America" Testimony

On Saturday, 22 August 1964, the Mississippi Freedom Democratic Party appeared before the Credentials Committee at the Democratic National Convention in Atlantic City, New Jersey, to challenge the seating of the all-white delegation elected by the state's Democratic Party. Fannie Lou Hamer delivered dramatic testimony before the committee, provoking President Lyndon Johnson to take to the airwaves in an attempt to prevent the nation's citizens from seeing and hearing her. Hamer utilized the power of personal narrative, offering an emotional recollection of her struggle to vote that galvanized listeners in the convention hall.

Hamer detailed her attempts to register to vote and the harassment and violent intimidation she and other activists received at the hands of law enforcement officials. She also told the committee of her family's eviction from their long-time home because of her refusal to withdraw her registration. Her narrative reached its climax when she described her arrest and beating after attending a voter registration conference:

> After I was placed in the cell I began to hear sounds of licks and screams. I could hear the sounds of licks and horrible screams [as they beat another woman].
>
> They beat her, I don't know how long. And after a while she began to pray, and asked God to have mercy on those people.
>
> And it wasn't too long before three white men came to my cell. . . .
>
> I was carried . . . into another cell where they had two Negro prisoners. The State Highway Patrolmen ordered the first Negro to take the blackjack. . . . And I laid on my face, the first Negro began to beat me. . . .
>
> After the first Negro had beat until he was exhausted, the State Highway Patrolman ordered the second Negro to take the blackjack.
>
> The second Negro began to beat. . . . I began to scream and one white man got up and began to beat me in my head and tell me to hush.

Hamer closed with a powerful appeal: "All of this is on account of we want to register, to become first-class citizens. And if the Freedom Democratic Party is not seated now, I question America. Is this America, the land of the free and the home of the brave, where we have to sleep with our telephones off of the hooks because our lives be threatened daily, because we want to live as decent human beings, in America?"

Evening news programs aired Hamer's testimony, prompting a deluge of telegrams and phone calls in which citizens urged White House officials to seat the Freedom Democrats. The Democratic Party establishment resisted those calls, but Hamer's testimony left a powerful mark on the American consciousness, and four years later, party officials seated an integrated Mississippi delegation.

Adria Battaglia
Angelo State University

American Rhetoric Online Speech Bank website, www.americanrhetoric.com; Nick Kotz, *Judgment Days: Lyndon Baines Johnson, Martin Luther King Jr., and the Laws that Changed America* (2005); Kay Mills, *This Little Light of Mine: The Life of Fannie Lou Hamer* (1993); PBS, *Eyes on the Prize: America's Civil Rights Years* (DVD 1986).

Hamilton, Mary Ann Mann

(1866–1937) Writer

Mary Ann Mann Hamilton was a white frontier settler whose touching and historically revealing autobiography, *Trials of the Earth*, provides insight into life in the Mississippi Delta at the turn of the twentieth century. Mary Ann Mann was born on 19 May 1866 in Illinois to William Calvin Mann and Elizabeth Ritchie Mann. The family subsequently moved to Arkansas, where Mary left school by the second grade. When she was seventeen, both of her parents died, leaving her to care for her brothers and sisters as well as several boarders.

She subsequently met an Englishman, Frank Hamilton, and married him on 28 July 1885. He proposed to her by declaring, "I am tired of boarding around from pillar to post, with nowhere I can call home. You can make a home for me." Though the two struggled together, with five of their ten children dying before the age of six, Mary retained her self-confidence and optimism. She recalled, "I had nothing to live for but to make every house we lived in a home."

In *Trials of the Earth*, Mary Hamilton relied on her vivid memory and storyteller's voice to recapture life in the Delta from 1896 to 1932. The stories reveal her courage and wit, physical strength, and efforts on behalf of her family. After arriving in the Delta with her husband and two small children, Hamilton encountered what seemed to her a "new world." It was January 1896, and she thought she might be the first white woman to cross the frontier: "We drove down the Mississippi River levee about a mile, then turned off the levee down into the thickest timber I had ever seen. Oak, gum, ash, hackberry, and poplar stood so thick, with no underbrush, only big blue cane growing rank and tall, almost to the limbs of the trees. It looked so odd, but what looked odder still to me was the black mud, 'gumbo.' . . . [W]hen we came out on the Mississippi River, the ground was sandy, but it was black sand, and cottonwoods and sycamores that seemed to me when I looked up like their tops were lost in the sky. It was a pretty sight, except the road. The soft black sand was almost hub deep." From there, her stories went on to detail life in Delta boardinghouses; the threats of timber work, malaria, floods, typhoons, wild boars, and poverty; and the treachery and lunacy of certain neighbors. The book also included violent moments that revealed the racism of the white settlers.

Hamilton's volume gives a sense of the roles of the pioneer men, women, and children. There was little time for play or affection between parents and their children, who began laboring as soon as they could walk. Men worked long days clearing the land and bought all the family goods; some abused alcohol. Women cooked, kept house, and managed the family. Yet Hamilton treasured her life on the frontier, recalling the efforts to live "day by day, young and full of life and fun, trying to make our home pleasant and home for dozens, yes hundreds, of men. To me they will all live as long as I do, laughing and joking, sympathizing with each other and us, in sickness and trouble, working, toiling to blaze a way and build a home in this dear old Delta where the happiest part of my life has been spent."

In 1931, when she was living near Greenwood, Hamilton began to set down her recollections with the encouragement of Delta writer Helen Dick Davis, who had family connections to the elderly Hamilton. Two years later she turned over a draft of the book to Davis, who edited it and offered it to a publisher. It was rejected, and Hamilton subsequently changed her mind about publishing it. She died on 19 May 1937 and is buried in Yazoo City's Glenwood Cemetery. The manuscripts were rediscovered in a box in 1991 and published the following year.

Caroline Myers Millar
Little Rock, Arkansas

Mary Hamilton, *Trials of the Earth*, ed. Helen Dick Davis (1992); Larry Primeaux, Better Chancery Practice Blog, chancery12.wordpress.com/2014/02/ (28 February 2014).

Hancock County

Hancock County is located on the Gulf Coast, with the Pearl River and Louisiana border forming much of its western boundary. The county was established on 14 December 1812 and is named for John Hancock, signer of the Declaration of Independence. Bay St. Louis is the county seat.

City Hall, Bay St. Louis, seat of Hancock County, ca. 1907 (Ann Rayburn Paper Americana Collection, Department of Archives and Special Collections, J. D. Williams Library, University of Mississippi [rayburn_ann_33_36_001])

Like Mississippi's other coastal counties, Hancock is distinctive for its early emphasis on tourism and connection to New Orleans, its cultural and religious diversity, its nonagricultural economy, and its beaches. The presence of fresh seafood, ethnic diversity, and a tourist trade have contributed to the development of a unique cuisine and economy.

In its first census in 1820, Hancock had a small population of 1,142 free whites, 321 slaves, and 131 free blacks, the second-largest such group in Mississippi. Hancock was also the only county in the new state in which the majority of laborers (161) worked in manufacturing and commerce, as compared to 153 who worked in agriculture.

By 1840 Hancock had ten sawmills, the most in Mississippi. The free population had grown to 2,311, of whom only 74 were African Americans, while the slave population numbered 1,056. Although nonagricultural laborers no longer dominated the county's workforce, more than a quarter of its people—still the highest percentage in the state—were employed in commerce and manufacturing. By the 1840s the town of Shieldsboro had a quality hotel and a number of boardinghouses and was developing a reputation as a tourist destination.

Hancock County's population did not change a great deal during the late antebellum period. As in most of Mississippi, the number of free blacks was declining. A decade before the Civil War began, the county was home to only twelve free blacks, a number that dropped to zero ten years later. By 1850 a relatively small proportion of the county's farmland had been improved. Hancock ranked last in the state in cotton production, second-to-last in corn, and third-to-last in the value of its livestock. However, Hancock ranked fifth in Mississippi in rice production. In 1860, Hancock's 27 percent constituted one of the smallest slave populations in the state.

In the postbellum period, whites comprised 4,635 of the county's 6,439 people (72 percent). With only 364 farms, most of them owned by the people who ran them, the county's agricultural sector remained fairly underdeveloped. By 1880 Hancock and Harrison, a neighboring county to the east, had the highest proportions of immigrants in Mississippi, with 4.27 percent and 6.88 percent, respectively. These counties were home to small but substantial German, French, and English contingents, and a number of Italian and Austrian immigrants arrived in the late 1800s. To advance and profit from the Mississippi timber industry, the firm of Poitevant and Favre built one of the largest sawmills in the country in Hancock County in the final decades of the nineteenth century.

In 1875 leaders in Shieldsboro changed the town's name to Bay St. Louis. Several years later, the Louisville and Nashville Railroad purchased the coastal track, permanently linking New Orleans and the Mississippi Gulf Coast. With the expansion of its gambling infrastructure, Bay St. Louis quickly became a popular resort area and weekend destination for New Orleans residents.

Over the next few decades the county's population increased dramatically, reaching 11,886 people in 1900. With only 530 farms, Hancock was now a trading and industrial county. The great majority of the county's small agricultural community (90 percent of white farmers, and 34 percent of the forty-four African American farmers) owned the land they farmed. The county had fewer than fifty tenants and sharecroppers.

During the opening decades of the twentieth century, the county boasted a unique industrial sector and immigrant population. In the early 1900s, Hancock had 349 foreign-born residents, with Italians slightly outnumbering Germans and French. It was one of only ten Mississippi counties with more than 1,000 industrial workers: 1,077 people, most of them men, worked in the county's forty industrial establishments, many of them involved in either timber or seafood.

In 1850 Hancock County had three Methodist churches, one Baptist church, and one Catholic church. By 1916 Hancock and Harrison were among the few counties in the state in which Catholics comprised the largest religious contingent. In addition to the county's 4,374 Catholics, Hancock also had just over 2,000 Baptists (1,237 Missionary Baptists and 827 Southern Baptists), while its Methodist congregants numbered fewer than 1,000. A Methodist campground, Gulfside, was established in Waveland in 1923.

A host of artists and writers grew up in or chose to move to Hancock County. John F. H. Claiborne moved to Bay St. Louis in the mid-1800s and stayed there for the remainder of his life, writing numerous works on the history of Mississippi. Eliza Jane Poitevant, better known by her pen name Pearl Rivers, grew up in Pearlington before becoming an important journalist in New Orleans in the late nineteenth century. Sculptor Richmond Barthé, born in Bay St. Louis in 1901, was an important artist in the Harlem Renaissance, and self-taught artist William Beecher was also born in the city in 1902. In recent years, the county has worked to support creative people, celebrating and supporting art through the production of public murals in churches, libraries, and other downtown buildings.

With a substantial immigrant population and unique economy, Hancock remained unusual by Mississippi standards in 1930. The county's population had remained stable over the previous three decades, and as the Great Depression set in, Hancock was home to 11,415 residents, 8,596 of whom identified as white, 2,815 as black, and 4 as "other." More than a quarter of the county's population lived in urban settings, and Hancock had the lowest percentage of farmland and very few tenant farmers.

Hancock has maintained an important connection to the U.S. military since Bay St. Louis native Henry Jetton Tudbury became the state's best-known soldier during World War I. During World War II, the county was home to a Merchant Marine academy. In 1961 the John C. Stennis Space Center started operations in Hancock. This facility for testing National Aeronautics and Space Administration rocket engines has been a major employer and influence on the Gulf Coast, encouraging the development of new technologies, related research, and industry.

By 1960 Hancock's population had grown to 14,039, 84 percent of them white. Hancock's agricultural sector continued to shrink, employing fewer than 100 people by 1970. Manufacturing employment, conversely, grew from 90 workers in 1960 to more than 1,000 in 1970. The county's per capita income doubled over the same decade. By 1980 the county was home to almost 25,000 residents.

Hurricanes Camille and Katrina did extraordinary damage to Hancock County. Camille made landfall near Bay St. Louis in August 1969, with winds gusting to two hundred miles per hour. The severe destruction ultimately led to opportunities to build larger, newer structures, but many of them did not survive Katrina thirty-six years later. Katrina was even more devastating, killing fifty-one people in Hancock County; destroying all buildings near the beach in Bay St. Louis, Pearlington, and Waveland; and reshaping the environment and economy of the entire area.

Like many counties in Southeast Mississippi, in 2010 Hancock County was predominantly white, had a small but significant Hispanic/Latino minority, and had experienced significant population growth during the last half of the twentieth century. With an increase of more than 200 percent since 1960, Hancock County's population has undergone one of the largest proportional expansions in the state during this period, reaching 43,929 residents.

Mississippi Encyclopedia Staff
University of Mississippi

Hancock County, Mississippi, GenWeb website, www.rootsweb.ancestry.com; Mississippi State Planning Commission, *Progress Report on State Planning in Mississippi* (1938); *Mississippi Statistical Abstract*, Mississippi

State University (1952–2010); Charles Sydnor and Claude Bennett, *Mississippi History* (1939); University of Virginia Library, Historical Census Browser website, http://mapserver.lib.virginia.edu; E. Nolan Waller and Dani A. Smith, *Growth Profiles of Mississippi's Counties, 1960–1980* (1985).

Hannah, Barry
(1942–2010) Author

Barry Hannah (Photograph © Tom Rankin)

Acknowledged as a master of the short story and highly regarded as a novelist, Barry Hannah emerged in the last quarter of the twentieth century as one of the most critically acclaimed American fiction writers. He was born on 23 April 1942 in Meridian, Mississippi, to William Hannah, an insurance agent, and Elizabeth King Hannah, a homemaker. He grew up in Clinton, where his experience in his school's all-state band later influenced both his subject matter and his style.

While an undergraduate at Mississippi College, Hannah worked as a research assistant in pharmacology at the University of Mississippi Medical School in Jackson. After receiving a bachelor's degree in 1964, he elected to follow his interest in literature and writing and attended the University of Arkansas, where he completed master's and master of fine arts degrees.

Hannah taught writing and literature at Clemson University from 1967 to 1973. His first novel, *Geronimo Rex*, was published in 1972 and was nominated for the National Book Award. The book won the William Faulkner award and received extensive critical praise.

After the publication of his second novel, *Nightwatchman* (1973), an unsuccessful murder mystery, Hannah began to focus more on short stories, working primarily with Gordon Lish at *Esquire*. These stories were collected in *Airships* (1978), which brought him acclaim and the Arnold Gingrich Award for short fiction. Hannah wrote most of the stories while teaching creative writing at the University of Alabama from 1975 to 1980.

Hannah then moved to Hollywood but was generally unsuccessful in his attempts to write film scripts. After seeking and receiving treatment for alcoholism, Hannah returned to the academic environment, holding writer in residence positions at the University of Iowa, the University of Mississippi, and the University of Montana at Missoula. In 1983 he was awarded a Guggenheim Fellowship and settled into a long-term position at the University of Mississippi.

Although Hannah continued to battle problems with alcohol through the 1980s, he maintained his productivity as a writer, publishing a collection of short stories, *Captain Maximus* (1985), and four novels, *The Tennis Handsome* (1983), *Hey Jack!* (1987), *Boomerang* (1989), and *Never Die* (1991). Early in the 1990s he began talking openly about his problems with alcohol and noted that his early fascination with drinking came from an awareness that his literary idols—William Faulkner, James Joyce, and Ernest Hemingway—were all, in his words, "drunks." When Hannah realized that he needed to give up alcohol, he feared that he would be unable to write without it. Those concerns proved unwarranted: a 1993 collection of stories, *Bats Out of Hell*, won the Faulkner Award for literature, while a 1996 collection, *High Lonesome*, was nominated for the Pulitzer Prize in fiction.

The Fellowship of Southern Writers gave Hannah the 1999 Robert Penn Warren Award for fiction and invited him to become a member four years later. His 2001 novel, *Yonder Stands Your Orphan*, further solidified his reputation.

Hannah married three times and had three children. By the end of the twenty-first century, he began experiencing major health problems, and he suffered a heart attack and died on 1 March 2010. His posthumous publications include a collection of short stories, *Long, Lost, Happy: New and Selected Stories* (2010).

Although Hannah's fiction focuses primarily on the South, his works have a universal appeal. His unique voice, his deftness with language, and his effective analysis of the human psyche through a fusion of the humorous and the tragic established him as a significant contemporary writer.

Verbie Lovorn Prevost
University of Tennessee at Chattanooga

Martyn Bone, ed., *Perspectives on Barry Hannah* (2006); Mark J. Charney, *Barry Hannah* (1992); Sharon R. Gunton and Jean Cistine, eds., *Contemporary Literary Criticism* 23 (1983); Daniel Jones and John D.

Jorgenson, eds., *Contemporary Authors: New Revision Series* 68 (1998); Richard E. Lee, *Dictionary of Literary Biography*, vol. 234, *American Short-Story Writers since World War II*, ed. Patrick Meanor and Richard E. Lee (2001); James G. Thomas, Jr., ed., *Conversations with Barry Hannah* (2016); Ruth D. Weston, *Barry Hannah, Postmodern Romantic* (1998).

Hardy, James D.

(1918–2003) Surgeon

Dr. James D. Hardy served as chair of the Department of Surgery at the University of Mississippi Medical Center in Jackson from its opening in 1955 until his retirement in 1987. Hardy and a team of surgeons from the medical center performed the world's first lung transplant in 1963. The patient lived for eighteen days before dying of kidney failure. The following year Hardy performed the world's first heart transplant when he and his team took the heart from a chimpanzee and transplanted it to a man dying of heart disease, who lived for eighteen days.

Hardy grew up in Newala, Alabama, about thirty-five miles south of Birmingham, where his father owned a lime manufacturing plant. He graduated from the University of Alabama and from medical school at the University of Pennsylvania before serving in the military during World War II. He subsequently did a surgical residency at Penn, finishing in 1951, and became the director of surgical research at the University of Tennessee. In 1953 Dr. David Pankratz, dean of the School of Medicine at the University of Mississippi, tapped Hardy to chair the Department of Surgery at the nascent University of Mississippi Medical Center. Hardy, by then married to Louise Scott Sams Hardy and the father of four daughters, moved his family to Jackson in 1955.

Recognizing that organ transplantation was the next advancement in surgery, Hardy began equipping labs for transplant research. From 1956 to 1963 Hardy, along with Drs. Watts Webb, Martin Dalton, and Fikri Alican, performed nearly one thousand lung transplants in animals. He sought permission from the medical center's vice chancellor, Dr. Robert Marston, to proceed to human lung transplantation, assuring Marston that the team would follow prescribed guidelines, which included finding a recipient who had a fatal disease and who would benefit from the transplant. John Russell met all the criteria and agreed to the surgery, which was performed on 12 June 1963. Though Russell died less than three weeks later, Hardy considered the operation a success because the lung was still functioning with no signs of rejection at his death. The transplant attracted little local notice, however, because of Medgar Evers's murder, which occurred the same night.

With the success of the lung transplant, Hardy wanted to do a human heart transplant. He again got permission and readied surgical teams to take care of both the donor and the recipient. On 23 January 1964 Boyd Rush, the patient Hardy had identified as a heart recipient, was dying of heart failure. Because of difficulties in obtaining a donor human heart, however, Hardy decided to proceed with a chimpanzee's heart, which beat for ninety minutes before failing.

Hardy had prepared himself for a certain amount of criticism, but he thought most of it would come from the general public. He did not count on the outcry from his colleagues. He was maligned at national surgical meetings and his clinical integrity was questioned. The criticism abated after *Journal of the American Medical Association* published a June 1964 paper wherein Hardy detailed the strict guidelines he used in selecting both donor and recipient, his work in the labs leading up to transplant, and the strong scientific basis for the act.

A national moratorium on organ transplantation followed Hardy's heart transplant because doctors still had to overcome the problem of organ rejection, but his pioneering work played a vital role in making organ transplants the viable clinical option that they have become.

Hardy amassed a scholarly record that is rarely equaled. He wrote or edited twenty-three books, including two autobiographies, and published nearly six hundred papers in medical journals. He served as president of every major surgical society in the world prior to his death on 19 February 2003.

Janis Quinn
University of Mississippi
Medical Center

Martin Dalton, *Annals of Thoracic Surgery* (November 1995); James D. Hardy, *The World of Surgery, 1945–1985: Memoirs of One Participant* (1986); Mary Jo Festle, *Journal of Mississippi History* (Summer 2002); Jurgen Thorwald, *The Patients* (1971).

Hardy, William Harris

(1837–1917) Businessman and City Founder

A businessman, lawyer, and the founder of both Hattiesburg and Gulfport, William Harris Hardy was born in Collirene, Lowndes County, Alabama, on 12 February 1837, the son of Robert William Hardy and Temperance L. Toney Hardy. After establishing Sylvarena School near Raleigh, in Smith County, Mississippi, William Harris Hardy began practicing law in Raleigh in 1858; two years later, he married Sallie Ann

Johnson of Brandon, Mississippi, with whom he went on to have six children.

When Mississippi seceded in January 1861, Hardy raised a militia company, the Smith County Defenders, which became Company H of the 16th Mississippi Infantry, Army of Northern Virginia. He later served as an aide-de-camp to Gen. James Argyle Smith.

Hardy practiced law after the Civil War, built railroads in South Mississippi, and served the state as a legislator and circuit court judge. In 1872 Hardy served as grand master of the Grand Lodge of Mississippi, Ancient Free and Accepted Masons.

Following Sallie's death in 1872, Hardy married Hattie Lott of Mobile, Alabama, in 1874. She bore him three children before she died in 1895. Hattie was the namesake for the city that Hardy founded in 1882 along the railroad he built from Meridian to New Orleans. Hattiesburg was to be the seat of a new county to be created out of Perry County: the Mississippi legislature voted to name the new county in Hardy's honor, but Gov. Anselm McLaurin vetoed the measure, and the new county became Forrest County instead. In *No Compromise with Principle*, Hardy is also credited with naming Laurel, Mississippi.

In 1900 Hardy married Ida V. May, and they had three sons. Hardy died in 1917 in Gulfport, which he also founded. In May 1945 the USS *William Harris Hardy*, an eighteen-thousand-ton cargo vessel, was christened in Pascagoula.

Hon. Robert G. Evans
Raleigh, Mississippi

Robert G. Evans, *The Sixteenth Mississippi Infantry: Civil War Letters and Reminiscences* (2002); Toney A. Hardy and William Harris Hardy, *No Compromise with Principle: The Epic Story of William Harris Hardy and the Mississippi He Loved* (1946); William H. and Sallie J. Hardy Papers, McCain Library and Archives, University of Southern Mississippi; Dunbar Rowland, ed., *Biographical Sketches of Mississippians*, vol. 3 of *A History of Mississippi* (1976).

Harkey, Ira

(1918–2006) Journalist

Pulitzer Prize–winning newspaperman and civil rights advocate Ira B. Harkey Jr. was born on 15 January 1918 in New Orleans. Raised in an affluent household, Harkey starred in football and track during high school, briefly headed out west, and then earned a degree in journalism from Tulane University in 1941. He served in the US Navy in the Pacific theater during World War II. In 1946 Harkey began his journalism career at the *New Orleans Times-Picayune*. Three years later, he purchased the *Pascagoula Chronicle-Star*, a small-circulation weekly serving Mississippi's eastern Gulf Coast, for $102,000.

Harkey radically reconfigured the paper's policy on how it would report race-related stories. Specifically, he barred the use of the word *colored*; dropped the segregated Jim Crow section and incorporated news about African Americans into the rest of the paper; and declared that the word *Negro* would be used only when it was relevant to a story. Most controversially, the *Chronicle-Star* would begin using the courtesy designation *Mrs.* to identify what Harkey described as "carefully selected Negro women." These radical changes prompted an outcry from editors and journalists around the state, but Harkey's journalistic and business acumen quickly turned the newspaper into a thriving enterprise.

On 1 September 1954, a few months after the *Brown v. Board of Education* ruling declared school segregation illegal, the local Ku Klux Klan burned a six-foot cross in Harkey's front yard and left him a note: "We do not appreciate niggerlovers. We are watching you." The incident gave Harkey the title of his autobiography: *The Smell of Burning Crosses*.

Never one to back down from a public fight, Harkey counterattacked with the logic of Christianity, law, history, and economics, going after the hatemongers with his own fiery zeal. Harkey's biting humor, a key rhetorical tactic in generating a large and dedicated readership, was often on display in his editorials. Harkey's fictitious foil, Colonel Myopia Heartburn, stood in for hardcore Mississippi segregationists and always took a beating.

Harkey offered strong editorial support for James Meredith's integration of the University of Mississippi in September 1962 and savaged the "Fascist" tactics employed by Gov. Ross Barnett in attempting to prevent Meredith from enrolling. Harkey's outspokenness and level-headed reasoning earned him the Pulitzer Prize for Editorial Writing in May 1963.

In Pascagoula, however, Harkey's commentary provoked first a boycott of the *Chronicle-Star* and then violence. A rifle slug ripped through the front door of the newspaper's office, and less than a month later shotgun blasts took out several windows. Harkey countered with a .38 revolver and dedicated practice at a local range, refusing to be intimidated by the "goons" of Jackson County.

But Harkey was ostracized and alone in Pascagoula, and in July 1963 he sold the *Chronicle-Star* and left Mississippi. (Financial issues caused by a divorce apparently also played a role in his decision to sell the paper.) He had turned a stagnant weekly into a thriving five-day-a-week progressive voice, winning awards for his courage and journalism, including the Sidney Hillman Foundation Award, the Sigma Delta Chi medallion for distinguished public service in newspaper journalism, and the Silver Em Award from the University of Mississippi. The paper's new owner, Ralph Nicholson, despite promises to Harkey, quickly reversed editorial course and returned the paper to its race-baiting roots.

Harkey subsequently enrolled at Ohio State University, earning a master's degree in journalism and a doctorate in political science. After the 1967 publication of his memoir, he became a frequent visiting professor and guest lecturer on college campuses around the country. He published three more books. The state's journalists even made their peace with Harkey, inducting him into the Mississippi Press Association's Hall of Fame in 1993. He died on 8 October 2006 near his home in Kerrville, Texas.

Davis W. Houck

Florida State University

David L. Bennett, in *The Press and Race*, ed. David R. Davies (2001); G. McLeod Bryan, *These Few Also Paid a Price: Southern Whites Who Fought for Civil Rights* (2001); Ira Harkey Papers, Wisconsin Historical Society Archives, Madison; Nick Marinello, *The Tulanian* (2004); Susan Weill, *In a Madhouse's Din: Civil Rights Coverage by Mississippi's Daily Press, 1948–1968* (2002).

Harkins, Greg

(b. 1952) Furniture Maker

Greg Harkins is a furniture maker working in the central Mississippi community of Vaughan. Since 1976 he has been crafting benches, tables, beds, and straight-back chairs. His rocking chairs are his specialty and have earned him the most attention. Among those who have owned his chairs are Pope John Paul II, astronaut John Glenn, comedians George Burns and Bob Hope, and every US president beginning with Jimmy Carter. Harkins has received four invitations to the White House, attending twice. The subject of more than forty newspaper and magazine articles, he appeared on the cover of *American Woodworker* magazine in October 1995.

Harkins was born on 21 March 1952 in Jackson and graduated from Mississippi State University. After college he became an apprentice to chair maker Tom Bell, who was based in Carthage. Bell started making chairs at age eleven and kept at it for seventy-three years, working for the first forty-five without electricity. Harkins learned time-tested, nineteenth-century techniques from Bell. "I've been blessed," Harkins says of the experience. "I had the opportunity to look through a window that no longer exists." In 1979, after three years under Bell, Harkins established his own shop, which he maintains today.

To create a rocking chair, he combs his tract of land for appropriate hardwoods such as hickory, persimmon, red oak, and walnut. After he selects the timber, a nearby friend mills it. Then, in an old and beautiful barn alongside Interstate 55, Harkins turns, shapes, and assembles the pieces into a chair. His process, called shrink-fitting, requires no nails or glue; in 1987 he explained it to *Nation's Business* magazine: "The vertical pieces (posts) are green, and the horizontal pieces (rounds) are dry. And when that green post dries down around those dry rounds, it is not going anywhere." He finishes each piece of furniture with a beeswax mixture, then signs it and dates it. The entire process takes about twenty hours.

Like Bell, Harkins shares his expertise with others, hosting chair-making classes in his workshop. He considers each new project his most important to date, and he aspires always to improve on his last effort, maintaining, "I make the best chair that Greg Harkins physically is able to make."

Hicks Wogan

New Orleans, Louisiana

Harkins Rocking Chairs and Furniture website, www.harkinschairs.com; Del Marth, *Nation's Business* (June 1987); Mississippi Folklife and Folk Artist Directory website, www.arts.state.ms.us/folklife.

Harney, Richard "Hacksaw"

(1902–1973) Blues Musician

Richard Harney was born on 16 July 1902 to Mary Howard and Dick Harney of Money. Although Dick Harney had forgone secular music to become a church deacon, he did not hesitate to teach his children to play together as long as they did not practice in the house. This early musical training served Harney well, as he took to playing on the street corners of Greenville with his oldest brother, Joe, at the age of twelve.

Richard Harney later found a number of ways to earn a living. After farming and then playing guitar on the street, he worked as a bassist for a Cincinnati jazz band in the early 1920s and subsequently supported himself as a piano tuner and repairman. Although his nickname has sometimes been erroneously attributed to a short stint as a boxer, musician Pinetop Perkins insisted that the moniker resulted from Harney's ability to fashion replacement piano parts on the spot, using virtually any materials and the tool that became his namesake. The nickname may also have reflected the frequent statement that Hacksaw's ability on the guitar could cut other musicians in two.

Though Harney was a master of piano, he was best known among his fellow musicians for his guitar work. Returning to the Delta, Harney formed a guitar duo with his brother, Maylon. Known by their family nicknames, Pet and Can, they recorded two sides backing vocalist and accordion player Walter "Pat" Rhodes as well as another two sides with Pearl Dickson. Pet and Can's musical career came to a sudden end when Maylon was stabbed to death in a juke joint.

Hacksaw Harney apparently met and admired both Blind Lemon Jefferson and Charley Patton; however, his guitar work is more consistent with the ragtime-influenced Piedmont style prevalent in Georgia and the Carolinas. Using an intricate and percussive finger-picking technique in combination with chord progressions heavily colored by his background in jazz, Harney developed a unique sound. Hacksaw's signature style influenced Delta legend Robert Johnson, with whom he often traded licks, as well as sometime member of the Mississippi Sheiks Eugene "Sonny Boy Nelson" Powell.

In addition to the death of his brother, a speech impediment and naturally shy disposition prevented Harney from achieving fame in his youth. When he attempted to play with other musicians he was often ridiculed for his disability, at least until his superior ability made them look like amateurs. Though he possessed remarkable skill on a number of instruments, work as a piano tuner in Clarksdale and Jackson became his primary source of income until he was rediscovered in 1969. Although he no longer owned a guitar and claimed not to have played in twenty years, Harney was soon filmed and recorded by Adelphi Records and began playing festivals and workshops in 1971. Despite suffering a minor stroke, he toured with recording partner Houston Stackhouse in 1972–73. He died of stomach cancer on Christmas morning 1973.

Robert Hawkins
Bradley University

Denise Tapp, Richard "Hacksaw" Harney, *Sweet Man* (1996), liner notes.

Harrington, Evans B.
(1925–1997) Author and Educator

Evans Burnham Harrington, educator, author, editor, and civil rights activist, was born in Birmingham, Alabama, on 5 October 1925. The son of a Baptist minister, he grew up in a succession of small towns and churches in southern and central Mississippi, graduating from Ellisville Agricultural High School in 1943. After serving in the US Naval Reserve from 1943 to 1945, he earned a bachelor's degree from Mis-

sissippi College in 1948. For the next two years he taught high school English and social studies in Decatur. In 1951, following the completion of a master's degree at the University of Mississippi, the university hired him to supervise the English practice teachers at University High School. Four years later he was appointed to the university's English faculty. He received a doctorate in English from the university in 1968.

During a teaching career that spanned more than three decades, he taught courses in creative writing and American literature and served as chair of the English department at the University of Mississippi from 1979 to 1987. A cofounder of the annual Faulkner and Yoknapatawpha Conference, which he directed from 1974 until 1993, Harrington was also a longtime participant in the Southern Literary Festival, serving as president of that organization in 1965, 1976, and 1987.

Harrington's published writings include *The Prisoners* (1954), a realistic novel about the struggle to maintain personal dignity and integrity under the dehumanizing effects of penal conditions; several short stories, including "The Knife in the Dark," published in the *Saturday Evening Post* (1954) and subsequently dramatized on television by Rod Serling; the script for the documentary film *Faulkner's Mississippi: Land into Legend* (1965); and a 1976 musical adaptation of William Faulkner's comic story "My Grandmother Millard and General Bedford Forrest and the Battle of Harrykin Creek." He published three novels under the pseudonym Gilbert Terrell: *Willa* (1961), *Missy* (1962), and *Lily* (1964). These three books, published by Dell as paperbacks with rather provocative covers, all had southern settings, mixed themes of love and frustration, sexual relationships, small-town life, and the occasional literary reference. One character in *Missy*, for example, says of a visiting writer, "Well, I just hope [he] doesn't write like Williams or Faulkner or Caldwell, or so many of our Southern writers." *The Prisoners*, the only novel Harrington published under his own name, occasionally reads more like the works of Faulkner, with unusually long sentences and complex but inevitable relationships among characters. Harrington also published a number of personal and critical essays, and he and Ann J. Abadie coedited four volumes of papers presented at the Faulkner and Yoknapatawpha Conference.

A passionate advocate for individual liberties and civil rights, Harrington was an active member of the American Civil Liberties Union, Mississippi Council on Human Relations, American Association of University Professors, and Common Cause. His identification with such liberal organizations made him a frequent target for the ire and occasionally the threats of Mississippi's political reactionaries. In 1962, along with historian James Silver and other University of Mississippi liberals, Harrington openly supported the enrollment of James Meredith, the first black student to attend the university. In 1965 state politicians and even some of his colleagues at the University of Mississippi castigated him for inviting African American students from Tougaloo

College to attend the Southern Literary Festival hosted by the university—the first meeting of that organization to be integrated. In 1972, as faculty sponsor of *Images*, the University of Mississippi literary journal, he joined with his student writers in a successful suit against the university's attempt to suppress an issue of the magazine that contained controversial language.

Harrington's ambivalent feelings about being a liberal in a conservative state and region that he dearly loved find poignant expression in "Living in Mississippi," an essay that appeared in the *Yale Review* in 1968. Harrington died in 1997.

Robert W. Hamblin
Southeast Missouri State
University

Robert W. Hamblin, *Journal of Mississippi History* (May 1991); Evans Harrington, *Yale Review* (Spring 1968); Evans B. Harrington Collection, Department of Archives and Special Collections, J. D. Williams Library, University of Mississippi.

Harris, Nathaniel Harrison

(1834–1900) Confederate General

Nathaniel Harrison Harris, a lawyer, Confederate general, and businessman, was born on 22 August 1834 in Natchez. After receiving a law degree from the University of Louisiana, he practiced with his brother in Vicksburg. At the outbreak of the Civil War he organized the Warren Rifles and was elected captain. The unit was mustered into state service in April 1861 and entered the Confederate Army in Richmond as Company C of the 19th Mississippi Infantry Regiment.

In July 1861 Harris and his troops joined Gen. Joseph E. Johnston's army confronting Union forces in Virginia's Shenandoah Valley. On 21 July they were ordered to Manassas, but they arrived too late to take part in the battle there. Harris spent the rest of 1861 in Northern Virginia and in the spring of 1862 was ordered to Yorktown to meet George B. McClellan's advance on Richmond. Col. L. Q. C. Lamar praised Harris for gallantry after the Battle of Williamsburg on 5 March 1862, and he received a promotion to major. Harris subsequently took part in the Battle of Seven Pines, the Seven Days' Campaign, and the Second Battle of Manassas. Following the Battle of Antietam he received a promotion to lieutenant colonel. Later in 1862 he commanded troops at the Battle of Fredericksburg.

In April 1863 Harris became a full colonel. His command was heavily engaged at the Battle of Chancellorsville, where it participated in Stonewall Jackson's flank attack, and at

Gettysburg, where it assaulted the Union position on Cemetery Ridge. Following the Battle of Bristoe Station, Harris was promoted to brigadier general. He took part in the Battles of the Wilderness and of Spotsylvania Courthouse, where he was involved in fighting at Bloody Angle. He also commanded troops at the Battle of Cold Harbor.

Harris's command was placed along the lines around Petersburg when the city came under siege in June 1864, and his troops took part in several efforts to prevent Union forces from cutting the Weldon Railroad. In March 1865 he was sent to the inner defense lines of Richmond to meet Philip Sheridan's raid. Harris's forces were hurriedly sent back to Petersburg when the lines there appeared on the verge of breaking, and his troops were called on to man Fort Gregg and Fort Whitworth. There, despite high casualties, they delayed the Union Army long enough for Robert E. Lee to evacuate his army. Harris ultimately surrendered at Appomattox on 9 April 1865.

After the war Harris returned to Vicksburg to resume his law practice and later became president of the Mississippi Valley and Ship Island Railroad. In 1885 he was appointed registrar of the US Land Office in Aberdeen, South Dakota. In 1890 he moved to San Francisco to pursue business opportunities there. He died while on a trip to Malvern, England, on 23 August 1900.

Mike Bunn
Historic Chattahoochee
Commission

Dictionary of American Biography (1931); Dunbar Rowland, *Military History of Mississippi, 1803–1898* (1908); Jack Welsh, *Medical Histories of Confederate Generals* (1995).

Harris, Thomas

(b. 1940) Author

The author of *The Silence of the Lambs* and other novels of suspense, William Thomas Harris was born in Jackson, Tennessee, in 1940. When he was a young boy, he and his parents, William and Polly, moved to a farm in his father's hometown, Rich, Mississippi. Harris attended Clarksville High School, where his mother taught biology. Harris exhibited a love of books at an early age and spent much of his time reading. Ernest Hemingway was one of his favorite authors.

Harris earned a bachelor's degree in English from Baylor University in Waco, Texas, in 1964, while working at night as a police reporter for the *Waco Tribune-Herald*. Though he found the job uninspiring, the experience and insight he gained into police work served him well in his later writings. While at Baylor, Harris wrote and submitted dark, meticulously crafted short stories to publications such as *True* and *Argosy*.

In 1968 Harris took a job with the Associated Press in New York, working as a crime reporter and editor and learning about police procedure in homicide investigations. Harris was intrigued by criminal psychology and forensic pathology, interests that added great depth to his fiction, enriching his characterizations and enabling him to take dark suspense in a new direction.

Harris and co-workers Sam Maull and Dick Riley created the idea for a novel about a group of Arab terrorists who conspired with a disturbed Vietnam veteran to commandeer the Goodyear Blimp and use it to bomb the Super Bowl. *Black Sunday* was published in 1975, becoming a best seller and a successful movie and enabling Harris to begin writing full time.

Harris spent eighteen months in 1979–80 living in his hometown, where he wrote *Red Dragon* (1981), the novel that introduced to readers his most famous character, Dr. Hannibal Lecter. Two film adaptations were made from this novel, *Man Hunter* (1986) and *Red Dragon* (2002).

Excitement surrounding the character of Lecter set the stage for a second novel with the psychotic doctor as one of the principal characters. *The Silence of the Lambs* (1988) is considered a masterpiece of dark suspense. The novel redefined the serial killer story, profoundly influencing the horror and thriller genres and winning several awards. The 1991 film adaptation, directed by Jonathan Demme, swept the Academy Awards, taking the top five honors: Best Actor, Best Actress, Best Screenplay, Best Director, and Best Motion Picture.

The third novel in the Lecter series, *Hannibal* (1999), allows readers a glimpse into Lecter's childhood and the trauma that profoundly shaped his life and psyche. Despite mixed reviews, the novel was a success. The 2001 movie version, however, disappointed many readers. Director Ridley Scott not only changed the ending but also sacrificed suspense by focusing only on the grisly aspects of the story.

In 2006 Harris published *Hannibal Rising*, which chronicles Lecter's early life. The 2007 film version, with a screenplay written by Harris, garnered generally negative reviews.

In 2006 Harris received the Lifetime Achievement Award from the Horror Writers Association. Between 2012 and 2015, NBC aired *Hannibal*, a television series featuring one of Harris's most famous characters.

Harris eschews publicity and lives in Florida and New York.

Shannon Riley
Ripley, Mississippi

Jason Cowley, *The Observer* (19 November 2006); Thomas Harris, "Foreword to a Fatal Interview," *Red Dragon* (2000); Shannon Riley, *Surreal Magazine* (2005).

Harris-Stewart, Lusia
(b. 1955) Athlete

One of the first two women inducted into the Naismith National Basketball Hall of Fame, Lusia Harris-Stewart has made her mark on the basketball world as well as on culture at large since embarking on her groundbreaking athletic career in the 1970s. Born in 1955, the tenth of eleven children of Willie and Ethel Harris, Harris spent her childhood on a vegetable farm in Minter City, frequently playing basketball with her siblings. She continued to play through middle school and high school and was recruited by Delta State University.

Harris's Delta State teams won the championship of the Association of Intercollegiate Athletics for Women (AIAW) in 1975, 1976, and 1977. Harris was the top scorer at the 1975 World Games and the Pan American Games. She notched the first two points ever scored by a women's basketball player at the Olympics, leading the US team to a silver medal in 1976 in Montreal. She was selected three times to the Kodak All-American Team and the AIAW All-Tournament Team. In 1976 she was named Most Valuable Player at the AIAW National Championship as well as Mississippi's first Amateur Athlete of the Year. The following year, Harris won the Broderick Award as the AIAW's top basketball player and the Broderick Cup as female collegiate athlete of the year. In 1977 the New Orleans Jazz made her the first and only woman ever officially selected in a National Basketball Association draft, though she never tried out for the team. While at Delta State she also became the first black woman named Homecoming Queen. Also in 1977, she married George Stewart; they have four children.

Harris-Stewart holds bachelor's and master's degrees from Delta State and has worked as a teacher and basketball coach at the college and high school levels, primarily in Mississippi. She also played professionally in 1979–80 in the Women's Professional Basketball League.

Harris-Stewart has been inducted into the Delta State Hall of Fame, the Women's Basketball Hall of Fame, the International Women's Sports Hall of Fame, and the Mississippi Sports Hall of Fame. In 1992 she became one of the first two women inducted into the Naismith Memorial Basketball Hall of Fame. In 2007 she was honored by NBA superstar LeBron James's James Family Foundation for her work as an educator and coach and because of her groundbreaking achievements.

Emily Bowles-Smith
Lawrence University

Seale Ballenger, *Hell's Belles: A Tribute to the Spitfires, Bad Seeds, and Steel Magnolias of the New and Old South* (1997); Lusia Harris-Stewart, Oral

History Files, Delta State University; Darlene Clark Hine, Elsa Barkley Brown, and Rosalyn Terborg-Penn, eds., *Black Women in America: An Historical Encyclopedia* (1994); Ernestine Gichner Miller and Carole A. Oglesby, *Making Her Mark: Firsts and Milestones in Women's Sports* (2002); "Oral History with Ms. Lucia Harris-Stewart" (1999), Center for Oral History and Cultural Heritage, University of Southern Mississippi, http://digilib.usm.edu/cdm/compoundobject/collection/coh/id/3087.

Harrison, Juanita

(28 December 1891–?) Writer

Juanita Harrison's only book, *My Great, Wide, Beautiful World* (1936), is one of the earliest examples of autobiographical travel writing by an African American woman. The book presents the accounts of her journeys around the world in an unedited, vernacular text that illustrates Harrison's vigorous autonomy and transcendence above the race and class drawbacks she experienced as a young girl growing up in rural Mississippi.

Little is known about Harrison's life beyond *My Great, Wide, Beautiful World*, and the book's preface relates the few details known regarding her youth. Juanita Harrison was born in 1891 somewhere in Mississippi. Her formal schooling ended by the time she was ten, at which point she began doing household labor—cooking, washing, and ironing—to help support her family.

The travel pictures Harrison saw in magazines instilled a wanderlust that became the defining aspect of her life. She began her travels at age sixteen, finding employment in Canada and Cuba. During this time she took classes in conversational Spanish and French at the Young Women's Christian Association, gaining skills that would prove a great asset in her future travels.

For the next twenty years Harrison saved her earnings, and at age thirty-six she set out from California, traveling through twenty-two different countries from June 1927 to April 1935. In France, her employer, Felix Morris, suggested that she write a book about her experiences. Morris's daughter, Mildred, helped Harrison approach the Macmillan publishing firm, and *My Great, Wide, Beautiful World* was born. The book was dedicated to Harrison's employer in Los Angeles, Myra K. Dickinson, and her husband, who helped Harrison invest and save her money to finance her travels.

It was rare for an African American writer to accomplish such lofty goals at the height of the Great Depression, and a recurring theme in *My Great, Wide, Beautiful World* is Harrison's staunch autonomy. Harrison refused to be bound by conventions of gender and race, and she often wrote of her pride in being an unmarried woman able to choose which of her numerous male suitors she allowed to accompany her on her travels.

Harrison praises different cultures' pageantry and delights in the exotic sights, sounds, and foods that she experiences. She attends bullfights, the theater, and Greek, Catholic, and Protestant churches, all with equal fervor. These passages point toward Harrison's understanding and appreciation of the variety of customs she encountered.

My Great, Wide, Beautiful World was initially serialized in the March and November 1935 issues of *Atlantic Monthly*. Its publication in book form in 1936 garnered warm reviews from the *New Republic*, the *Saturday Review of Literature*, and the *New York Times*. The book fell out of print until 1996, when it was reissued with a critical introduction by Adele Logan Alexander as part of Henry Louis Gates Jr.'s series, African American Women Writers, 1910–1940.

My Great, Wide, Beautiful World concludes with Harrison on Waikiki Beach in Hawaii in 1936. Having traveled through Israel, Burma, Thailand, Russia, and Europe, she pitches a tent and decides to end her journey amid the tropic beauty and harmony of Honolulu rather than returning to the harsher American homeland. Harrison appears not to have written any more in her lifetime, and details of her death are unknown.

Cale Nicholson
Fayetteville, Arkansas

Rebecca Chalmers Barton, *Witnesses for Freedom: Negro Americans in Autobiography* (1948); Lean'tin L. Bracks, in *Black Women of the Harlem Renaissance Era*, ed. Lean'tin L. Bracks and Jessie Carney Smith (2014); Cathryn Halverson, *Maverick Autobiographies: Women Writers and the American West, 1900–1936* (2004); Emmanuel S. Nelson, *African American Autobiographers: A Sourcebook* (2002); Lorraine E. Roses and Ruth E. Randolph, *Harlem Renaissance and Beyond: Literary Biographies of 200 Black Women Writers, 1900–1945* (1990).

Harrison, Pat

(1881–1944) Politician

A US congressman and senator who was especially important during the New Deal years, Byron Patton Harrison was born in Crystal Springs to Robert A. Harrison, a disabled Civil War veteran, and Anna Patton Harrison, a housewife and later boardinghouse proprietor. Harrison received his education in the Crystal Springs public schools and entered Louisiana State University on a baseball scholarship but left after two years to begin work. He taught school and was a high school principal in Leakesville while studying law in the evenings. He was admitted to the bar in 1902 and soon

Pat Harrison, 1 October 1938 (Photograph by Harris and Ewing, Library of Congress, Washington, D.C. [LC-H22-D-4618])

New Deal legislation: the National Industrial Recovery Act; the Reciprocal Trade Agreement Acts of 1934 and 1940; fourteen revenue bills, including the Wealth Tax Act (1935) and the undistributed profits tax (1936); and the 1935 Social Security Act and its 1939 amendments. Circumstances of the Great Depression and his loyalty to the Democratic Party motivated Harrison to support the New Deal, but the social engineering tendencies of Pres. Franklin D. Roosevelt and tax measures that redistributed wealth led Harrison to become disenchanted. He grew estranged from the president, a gulf exacerbated when Roosevelt supported Alben W. Barkley as Senate majority leader in 1937. Harrison lost that contest by one vote without the support of Mississippi's other senator, Theodore G. Bilbo, a fierce opponent of Harrison. The breach between Harrison and Roosevelt healed in 1940 when the president turned to the senator, always a supporter of national defense efforts, to manage passage of what became the Lend-Lease Act.

In 1939 Washington correspondents named Harrison the most influential senator. His popularity with the press and his colleagues never waned. His seniority earned him the post of president pro tempore in January 1941, six months before he succumbed to colon cancer.

Martha H. Swain
Mississippi State University

Chester Morgan, *Redneck Liberal: Theodore G. Bilbo and the New Deal* (1985); James T. Patterson, *Congressional Conservatism and the New Deal Coalition* (1967); Martha H. Swain, *Pat Harrison: The New Deal Years* (1978); Martha H. Swain, *Journal of Mississippi History* (November 1976); Pat Harrison Collection, Department of Archives and Special Collections, J. D. Williams Library, University of Mississippi.

entered politics, winning two terms as a district attorney. In 1905 Harrison married Mary Edwinna McInnis of Leakesville, and they went on to have three children.

At age twenty-nine, Harrison was elected to the US Congress from Mississippi's 6th District after a campaign during which he became known simply as Pat. While in the House of Representatives (1911–19), Harrison strongly supported Pres. Woodrow Wilson but was too constrained by a states' rights stance to support all New Freedom social legislation. In 1918, with the support of Wilson and Mississippi's senior senator, John Sharp Williams, Harrison defeated Sen. James K. Vardaman, one of the "little group of willful men" who had opposed the president's call for war in 1917. Harrison won reelection to the Senate in 1924, 1936, and 1940.

As a member of the Democratic minority from 1921 to 1933, Harrison garnered popular favor by harassing Republican presidential administrations. His witty yet effective style of debate aptly suited the role of a minority senator. When his party took the White House in 1933, Harrison assumed enormous power as chair of the Senate Committee on Finance. In that role, Harrison oversaw passage of major

Harrison County

Located on the Gulf Coast, Harrison County was established on 5 February 1841 from portions of Hancock, Jackson, and Perry Counties. The county is named for William Henry Harrison, ninth president of the United States. Gulfport and Biloxi are the county seats.

Mississippi's Gulf Coast was crucial to the history of the colonial period as a meeting point for European and Native American people. In 1699 the French, led by Pierre Le Moyne, Sieur d'Iberville, established Fort Maurepas as the first European capital in Mississippi. For three years the settlement was organized under the leadership of Jean de Sauvole and Iberville's brother, Jean-Baptiste Le Moyne, Sieur de Bienville. As a military and political leader, Bienville remained on the

St. Mark's Episcopal Church, Mississippi City (Ann Rayburn Paper Americana Collection, Department of Archives and Special Collections, J. D. Williams Library, University of Mississippi [rayburn_ann_32_22_001])

Gulf Coast for many years, residing in the area that eventually became Harrison County until 1722.

At its first census in 1850, Harrison County was home to 3,378 whites, 56 free blacks, and 1,441 slaves. Like other Gulf Coast counties during the antebellum period, Harrison did not have a well-developed agricultural economy. The county ranked among the bottom in the state in the value of its cotton, corn, and livestock. However, by 1860 Harrison produced more rice than any other county in Mississippi. That year, 138 of Harrison's laborers worked in manufacturing and commerce, the majority of them employed by the county's eight sawmills and two steam engines. Antebellum Harrison County was notable for its large foreign-born population. On the eve of the Civil War, 584 people born outside the United States lived in the county, the third-highest number in the state. In 1860 slaves made up 21 percent of the county's population.

Though few Civil War battles took place on the Gulf Coast, Harrison County became a significant site for former Confederates after the war. Jefferson Davis moved to the Beauvoir Plantation in Biloxi in 1877 and spent much time writing his memoirs. After his death in 1889, Beauvoir became a home for Confederate veterans.

In the years after the Civil War both Harrison's population and its agricultural sector remained relatively small. However, the county had the state's largest proportion of foreign-born people, with immigrants, the majority of them either Germans or Irish, comprising nearly 7 percent of the population. In 1880 Harrison had only 190 farms, the fourth-fewest in Mississippi, and almost all of the county's farmers owned their land. That year, Harrison's 2,146 African Americans comprised 27 percent of the county's population of 7,895.

Rapid expansion occurred in Harrison County during the late 1800s, with the total population more than doubling to 21,002 by 1900. Though the county's farming workforce continued to dwindle, the number of industrial laborers increased rapidly as the residents of coastal counties found jobs in industry and fishing rather than agriculture. Between the 1890s and 1930s the Biloxi schooner emerged as a distinctive type of Mississippi fishing boat, primarily for oystering. By 1900 the county's nearly one hundred industrial firms employed 1,577 people (1,172 men, 270 women, and 135 children), the second-highest number of nonagricultural workers in the state.

Harrison's immigrant population also grew dramatically during this period. Germans and Irish still comprised the largest foreign-born groups, but the turn of the century also found the county home to French, Austrian, English, Italian, Swedish, Danish, Russian, and Canadian residents. Harrison likewise had the highest number of second-generation immigrants. Several foreign-born groups, including those from Italy and Greece, came from countries with well-developed fishing cultures. Immigrant laborers from such backgrounds moved quickly into fishing and canning industries. Beginning in 1887 the Knights of Labor found success organizing unions in several of Biloxi's canning factories.

Religious life in antebellum Harrison County did not center on the Baptist and Methodist groups that dominated most of Mississippi. Of the eight churches in the county in 1860, three were Methodist, two were Baptist, two were Catholic, and one was Episcopalian. By 1916, with its diverse population of newly arrived European immigrants, Harrison County was home to 8,434 Catholics, by far the most in the state. With more than 800 congregants, the county's Episcopalian contingent was also Mississippi's largest. Since the 1920s and 1930s, Biloxi and Pass Christian have hosted Blessing of the Fleet ceremonies, where Catholic priests confer benedictions for the safety and progress of fishing people. In the 1930s the Church of Our Lady of the Gulf had more than 3,000 members, Mississippi's largest Catholic community.

Like other coastal counties, Harrison developed an arts community, which, along with the county's beaches, sports, and hospitality, attracted tourists. Since the antebellum period, the county has also maintained a reputation as a desirable destination for gamblers. The first hotels designed to accommodate northerners looking to spend winters on the Gulf Coast opened in 1883 in Pass Christian. The expansion of railroads in Harrison and the county's proximity to New Orleans brought increasing numbers of tourists and winter residents, especially during the 1920s.

George Ohr, known as the Mad Potter of Biloxi, opened Biloxi Art and Novelty Pottery in 1879. From about 1880 to 1910 Ohr made some of the most ingenious pottery of the era. Painter Dusti Bongé was born in Biloxi in 1903, and Mary Kimbrough Sinclair, author of the memoir *Southern Belle*, spent much of her childhood in the city. The county's connection to New Orleans is also evident from the founding of Barq's Root Beer, which was invented in Biloxi in 1898 by New Orleans native Edward Barq.

Harrison County experienced several developments related to the military during the first half of the twentieth century. In 1941 Beauvoir Plantation became a museum honoring Jefferson Davis, and Confederate veterans continued to live there until the 1950s. In 1941 the Air Force opened Keesler Field in Biloxi, bringing thousands of people to the area during World War II. The town of Saucier also operated a prisoner-of-war camp throughout the war.

By 1930 the population had reached 44,143, the sixth-highest in the state, with whites comprising 82 percent of the total. Biloxi was the third-largest city in Mississippi, and Harrison was one of only nine counties in the state with more than 1,500 industrial workers. As the Great Depression set in, officials generally did not consider farming men and women unemployed. However, in coastal Harrison, with its large urban workforce, 1,300 men and more than 300 women—the highest numbers reported in Mississippi—were classified as unemployed.

From 1930 to 1960 Harrison County experienced dramatic population growth, reaching nearly 120,000 residents. In 1960 the county had the second-largest population in Mississippi and boasted the second-highest population density in the state. Whites continued to comprise a large majority. Harrison also continued to draw new immigrants, many of them Mexican, and was now home to smaller but substantial Vietnamese, Indian, Japanese, and Filipino communities. Indeed, the county had Mississippi's highest concentration of Vietnamese natives, the majority of whom worked in fishing and related industries.

In 1960 Harrison's large nonagricultural labor force was distributed among fishing, shrimping, manufacturing, retail, construction, and service jobs. Those working in agriculture were few. The county had the second-highest percentage of high school graduates in Mississippi and the lowest percentage of residents with less than five years of schooling.

Harrison County has a unique civil rights history. In 1960 Dr. Gilbert Mason headed one of the state's first direct-action demonstrations, organizing a "wade-in" to protest beach segregation. Mason also helped establish the county's chapter of the National Association for the Advancement of Colored People. Activist Lawrence Guyot, an important figure in the movement and member of both the Student Nonviolent Coordinating Committee and Mississippi Freedom Democratic Party, was born in Pass Christian.

A diverse range of celebrated individuals hail from Harrison County. Natasha Trethewey, who served as US poet laureate in 2012–13, is a native of Gulfport. Her work, perhaps most notably the poems in her collection, *Native Guard*, has dealt with coastal life and issues of race. Fred Haise, one of the astronauts on the 1970 Apollo 13 flight that suffered a crippling mechanical failure but nevertheless returned to earth, was born in Biloxi in 1933. Journalist Robin Roberts, who has worked for both ESPN and national morning news programs, grew up in Biloxi and Pass Christian. Gulfport native Mahmoud Abdul-Rauf (born Chris Jackson) led a notable career as a basketball player at Louisiana State University and in the National Basketball Association. Writer

Jesmyn Ward was born in DeLisle outside Pass Christian. Her novel, *Salvage the Bones*, deals with characters on the Gulf Coast after Hurricane Katrina and won the 2011 National Book Award. The Ohr-O'Keefe Museum of Art opened in Biloxi in 1992.

Hurricanes Camille and Katrina wreaked havoc on Harrison County's population and economy. In 1969 Camille leveled Pass Christian, killing more than 100 people in Harrison County and leaving more than 40,000 homeless. Thirty-six years later Katrina led to the deaths of 126 people and destroyed countless buildings, from historic sites to newer commercial and gambling establishments.

Like other counties in coastal Mississippi, in 2010 Harrison County's population remained composed of a white majority. Harrison's 187,105 people represented an increase of 56 percent since 1960 and made it the second-largest county in Mississippi. The county also possessed a small but significant Hispanic/Latino minority as well as a significant Asian minority.

Mississippi Encyclopedia Staff
University of Mississippi

Harrison County, Mississippi History and Genealogy Network website, http://Harrison/msghn.org; Mississippi State Planning Commission, *Progress Report on State Planning in Mississippi* (1938); *Mississippi Statistical Abstract*, Mississippi State University (1952–2010); Charles Sydnor and Claude Bennett, *Mississippi History* (1939); University of Virginia Library, Historical Census Browser website, http://mapserver.lib.virginia.edu; E. Nolan Waller and Dani A. Smith, *Growth Profiles of Mississippi's Counties, 1960–1980* (1985).

Harvey, Clarie Collins

(1916–1995) Activist and Businesswoman

Clarie Collins Harvey was a prominent businesswoman and social activist. Born in Meridian, Mississippi, on 27 November 1916, Collins was the daughter of Rev. Malachi C. Collins and Mary Augusta Rayford Collins, a schoolteacher. An only child, young Clarie lived a relatively privileged life for an African American in the predominantly white town of Meridian. In 1916 her father opened a funeral and insurance business, which his daughter later owned and operated. Collins had opportunities for education uncommon to most African Americans in the South, attending Smith Robertson Elementary School in Jackson and Tougaloo College, where she completed high school and one year of college. She then earned a bachelor's degree in economics from Atlanta's Spelman College in 1937 as well as a certificate in mortuary technique (1942) from the Indiana College of Mortuary

Science and a master's degree (1950) in personnel administration from Columbia University in New York. In 1943 Collins married Martin L. Harvey, dean of Southern University.

Both of her parents were committed to political and social activism in their church and various other organizations, and Harvey developed her own ideas on women's activism. Harvey initially worked through the Methodist church and the Young Women's Christian Association. Through her activism in the male-dominated National Association for the Advancement of Colored People and Methodist Church organizations, Harvey learned the formal procedures for running meetings and organizations. However, she also witnessed the exclusion of women from leadership positions and sought to create a forum where women's energies could be fully utilized. She devoted a great deal of her time to working with women's organizations such as the National Council of Negro Women, Women Strike for Peace, and Church Women United, becoming the group's first African American president in 1971. In 1961 she organized Womanpower Unlimited to mobilize African American women to support the efforts of the Freedom Riders. The organization engaged in voter registration, assisted with school desegregation efforts, and collaborated on the Mississippi Box Project before disbanding in 1968. Harvey also provided support to the Wednesdays in Mississippi project and for ten years served on the Mississippi Advisory Committee to the US Commission on Civil Rights.

Harvey's humanist perspective included a commitment to activism on the international level as well. She began her international travel in 1939 as a student representative at the World Conference of Christian Youth in Amsterdam. This event marked the beginning of her commitment to international affairs, which went on to include participation in Kwame Nkrumah's 1962 World without the Bomb Peace Conference in Accra, Ghana; the Eighteen Nation Committee on Disarmament in Geneva (1962); and a 1963 Women's Peace Pilgrimage to the Vatican as well as membership in the World Council of Churches.

Harvey's civic and professional leadership earned her local, national, and international recognition. In 1974 Gov. William Waller declared Clarie Collins Harvey Day, and she was named Woman of the Year by the National Funeral Directors Association in 1955 and Churchwoman of the Year by the Religious Heritage of America Foundation in 1974. Harvey remained an active contributor to her church, community, profession, and state until her death on 27 May 1995.

Tiyi M. Morris
Ohio State University

Raymond Arsenault, *Freedom Riders: 1961 and the Struggle for Racial Justice* (2006); Tiyi M. Morris, in *Groundwork: The Local Black Freedom Movement in America,* ed. Jeanne Theoharis and Komozi Woodard (2005); Tiyi M. Morris, *Womanpower Unlimited and the Black Freedom Struggle in the Twentieth-Century South* (2015); George Alexander Sewell, *Mississippi Black History Makers* (1977).

Hattiesburg American

The first issue of the *Hattiesburg American* appeared on 1 October 1917, but the paper originated in 1897 as the *Hattiesburg Progress*. William Henry Seitzler published the paper twice a week until 1899, when it began appearing every day and changed its name to the *Daily Progress*. In 1907 the paper became the *Hattiesburg Daily News*, and by 1923 it was headquartered in a three-story wood frame building on Front Street. It continued as the *Daily News* until Howard S. Williams acquired the paper in 1917. The new name, *Hattiesburg American*, was inspired by the US entry into World War I. The first issue of the *Hattiesburg American* had eight pages and sold for five cents. The circulation was 2,206, and twenty-two "carrier boys" serviced Hattiesburg and the army's Camp Shelby, located just south of Hattiesburg.

In early 1923 Williams announced the sale of the paper to Rev. Gus Shaw Harmon for seventy-five thousand dollars. Williams wanted Harmon, a Methodist minister for the past two and a half decades, to use the *American* as a conduit for the ministry. The Harmon family owned the paper for the next thirty-seven years, with business manager Thomas St. John acquiring a partial stake. Circulation grew from 6,402 in 1926 to 14,795 in 1957.

In 1960 the Harmons and St. John sold the paper to Robert, Zach, and Henry Hederman, owners of the *Jackson Clarion-Ledger* and *Jackson Daily News*. St. John stayed aboard as general editor until two months before his death in 1963. His role was taken over by his son, Larry, who had previously been the assistant general manager and had worked for the *American* in various capacities since he was eleven years old.

According to an interview with *American* editorial page editor Ben Lee, under the Harmons and Hederman, the paper's basic editorial tenet involved "not opposing anything except forest fires and drownings, being in favor of everything else, making no one mad, rocking no boats, and endorsing no political candidates." However, in the early 1960s, the paper became an outspoken opponent of the Republican Party, arguing that its development in Mississippi would benefit "the 920,000 Negroes who dwell here" and denouncing national party figures for their opposition to continued segregation. In 1972, the *American* moved to a building on Main Street that would serve as its home for the next four decades. Leonard Lowery served as a reporter and editor at the paper from 1938 until he succumbed to a heart attack in the *American*'s newsroom on Christmas Eve 1982.

In 1982 the Hederman brothers sold their daily newspapers in Hattiesburg and Jackson along with several weeklies to the Gannett Company. The sale led to major changes in the newspaper's facilities as well as in its appearance and content. The newspaper's Main Street headquarters underwent a $5.6 million expansion, almost doubling its square footage and increasing the press capacity by 75 percent. Gannett began printing *USA Today* in Hattiesburg.

In early 2006 the *Hattiesburg American* switched from afternoon delivery to morning delivery; the following year, its layout was redesigned and the paper began to emphasize local news. By 2013 the paper had a weekday circulation of sixty-five hundred and a weekend circulation of thirty-four thousand, though additional readers accessed the online edition via the *American*'s website.

In 2009 printing operations were moved to the *Clarion-Ledger*'s facility in Jackson, and the following year Gannett announced that the *American*'s Main Street building was for sale. In 2014 the paper's staff moved to new offices on Mamie Street in Hattiesburg.

Barton Spencer

University of Southern Mississippi

Tim Doherty, *Hattiesburg American* (28 June 2014); Billy Hathorn, *Journal of Mississippi History* (November 1985); *Hattiesburg American* website, www.hattiesburgamerican.com; Patt Foster Roberson, "A History of the Hattiesburg American" (PhD dissertation, University of Southern Mississippi, 1985); WDAM-TV website, www.wdam.com (6 October 2010).

Hattiesburg Civil Rights Movement

The 1962 arrival in Hattiesburg of Hollis Watkins and Curtis Hayes marked the beginning of the Hattiesburg civil rights movement. The two volunteers from Pike County were sent by the Student Nonviolent Coordinating Committee (SNCC) to organize African Americans attempting to register to vote in Forrest County. At the time one-third of Forrest County's population was African American, but only about fifty African Americans were registered to vote.

The main obstacle to African American voter registration was the county's circuit clerk and registrar of voters, Theron Lynd, elected in 1959. Although the Hattiesburg community was more sympathetic to civil rights struggles than were other Mississippi communities, the town remained segregated. Lynd denied African Americans the vote by refusing to answer their questions about the registration form and by selecting the most difficult sections of the Mississippi state constitution for them to interpret, a requirement of the literacy test for registration. In 1960 Lynd refused to open his records to federal government officials, who then filed a lawsuit against him. In 1961 Lynd was found guilty of violating the Civil Rights Act of 1957, but federal district judge

Rev. J. C. Killingsworth (tall, black male in hat and suit) and Rev. Milton Barnes (black male in shirtsleeves and sunglasses) lead a march up Hattiesburg's Batson Street to the Forrest County Courthouse to protest the shooting of Lonnie Charles McGee, 29 July 1967 (Moncrief Collection, Archives and Records Services Division, Mississippi Department of Archives and History [477])

Harold E. Cox, an avowed racist, refused to force Lynd to comply with the government's requests.

In 1962 the Fifth Circuit Court of Appeals overruled Cox and placed an injunction on Lynd to cease his discrimination. Lynd ignored the injunction, but these court decisions encouraged SNCC and the National Association for the Advancement of Colored People (NAACP) to send Watkins and Hayes to establish Hattiesburg's voter registration drive.

The Hattiesburg headquarters for SNCC, the Council of Federated Organizations (COFO), and later the NAACP was located in the African American hotel run by Mrs. Lenon E. Woods: activists called it Freedom House. The Hattiesburg movement consisted primarily of older and younger African Americans, including many activists too young to even apply to vote. Middle-aged African Americans supported these efforts with donations of money, food, and lodging. However, the best-known participants in the movement were African American and white clergymen.

Those activists included Rev. L. P. Ponder of St. John's Methodist Church in Palmer's Crossing, a tiny hamlet just outside Hattiesburg. In 1962 Ponder and a group of his parishioners attempted to register to vote at the county courthouse in Hattiesburg. Although none passed the registration test, that group included three important figures in the Hattiesburg movement: Virgie Robinson, the Rev. J. W. Brown, and Victoria Gray Adams. They remained involved in the movement in any way they could, and Robinson even went to jail. Adams, one of the few middle-aged activists and a mother of three, became the manager of the Hattiesburg movement in September 1962, when Watkins and Hayes left to work in the Mississippi Delta. A few of those in the Palmer's Crossing group, including Brown, were employed as school bus drivers, and all were fired by the next day. However, the involvement of St. John's Methodist Church inspired many other religious leaders and citizens to join the civil rights movement. An exception was the Rev. R. W. Woullard of Hattiesburg's largest Baptist church, who opposed the movement. In 1959 Clyde Kennard, a black man, had applied for admission to Mississippi Southern College (now the University of Southern Mississippi), and Woullard had used his influence to help block Kennard's entrance.

In the summer of 1962 Watkins and Hayes established the Forrest County Voters League. By the end of the summer more than one hundred African Americans had attempted to register to vote, and under pressure from the federal government, Lynd had acknowledged four of those applicants as qualified to vote. When Watkins and Hayes left, Adams addressed organizational disagreements between SNCC and the local NAACP, led by Vernon Dahmer, and the two organizations united their efforts in 1963.

After assuming leadership of the movement, Adams attended a workshop that inspired her to begin citizenship classes around the Hattiesburg area, teaching African Americans to read and write. These classes allowed Adams access to groups of people who hesitated to join the movement but who desired the basic skills she taught. By using the state constitution and Mississippi's voter registration forms as the texts for her classes, Adams not only taught her students to read but prepared them for the literacy requirement of the voter registration test.

Despite Adams's attempts, the Hattiesburg movement moved too slowly for the civil rights organizations. Another Fifth Circuit Court of Appeals ruling found Lynd in contempt and ordered him to register forty-three African Americans. Lynd appealed the ruling to the US Supreme Court, which upheld the lower court decisions against Lynd. Bob Moses, codirector of the COFO, called for his fellow activists to converge on Hattiesburg before the 1964 elections. In the fall of 1963 the *Voice of the Movement* newsletter was created and distributed among African Americans. In addition, civil rights leaders in Mississippi staged a mock election, the Freedom Ballot, and Hattiesburg had the largest African American turnout in the state.

On 22 January 1964 the Hattiesburg movement staged the first Freedom Day, during which picketers would march in front of the courthouse while large numbers of African Americans applied to vote. In anticipation of mass arrests, experienced activists Fannie Lou Hamer, Amzie Moore, James Forman, John Lewis, and Ella Baker traveled to Hattiesburg with the intention of going to jail to keep up the morale of the locals arrested. Everyone agreed to refuse bail to draw more attention to the cause.

Inspired by speeches given the night before, around two hundred people from all over the South braved the rain to demonstrate at the courthouse, with newspaper reporters and television cameras documenting the protest. The police ordered the picketers to disband, but they refused. By the time the courthouse closed that day, seventy-five African Americans had stood in line all day to register to vote, but

only twelve had been allowed inside. They were not notified of the results of their tests.

Only two people were arrested on Freedom Day: Moses, for refusing to leave the sidewalk across the street from the courthouse, and Oscar Chase, an African American who had recently graduated from Yale Law School and who was arrested for failing to report that he had hit a parked truck with his car (though the incident caused no damage to the truck). In jail Chase was beaten by a white cellmate while guards watched, and his bail was paid the next day. Moses refused bail and had no problems in jail awaiting his court date with Judge Mildred W. Norris. Norris requested that those in attendance who were sitting on the "wrong" sides of the courtroom segregate themselves. However, Howard Zinn, an adviser for SNCC, brought to her attention to the fact that the US Supreme Court had ruled segregated courtrooms unconstitutional, and Norris continued with the case. She found Moses guilty of obstructing sidewalk traffic and refusing to move when police asked.

By the end of that week, 150 African Americans had completed the voter registration test in Hattiesburg, and more continued to picket outside, earning the name the "Perpetual Picket." More activists were arrested as the movement ushered in Freedom Summer 1964. Freedom House hosted the largest organization in the state, and Hattiesburg was a center of activity, including founding freedom schools and libraries.

Hattiesburg movement members were active in founding the Mississippi Freedom Democratic Party, which challenged the white delegates at the 1964 Democratic National Convention. In the mid-1960s Hamer, Adams, and the Rev. John Cameron ran for Congress from Mississippi, a landmark event for the state's African Americans.

Anna F. Kaplan
Columbia University

Townsend Davis, *Weary Feet, Rested Souls: A Guided History of the Civil Rights Movement* (1998); John Dittmer, *Local People: The Struggle for Civil Rights in Mississippi* (1994); *United States v. Lynd*, 301 F.2d. 818 (1962), 371 US 893 (1963) cert. denied, 375 US 968 (1963) cert. denied; William Sturkey, "The Heritage of Hub City: The Struggle of Opportunity in the New South" (PhD dissertation, Ohio State University, 2012); Howard Zinn, *SNCC: The New Abolitionists* (2002).

Haxton, Brooks

(b. 1950) Poet and Translator

Brooks Haxton can attribute at least some of his love of language and his ear for its rhythms to his lineage: his mother was novelist Josephine Haxton, who published her fiction under the pen name Ellen Douglas, and his father was composer and writer Kenneth Haxton. The youngest of their three sons, Brooks is one of the most acclaimed American poets at work today. He has published eight collections of poetry, four translations, and *Fading Hearts on the River* (2014), about his son's experiences as a professional poker player.

Haxton was born on 1 December 1950 in Greenville, Mississippi. He began writing poetry during junior high school, when the town was in the midst of school integration, and he and his friends became interested in the protest songs of Bob Dylan. He received a bachelor's degree from Wisconsin's Beloit College in 1972 and a master's degree in creative writing from Syracuse University nine years later.

Haxton's first published volume, *The Lay of Eleanor and Irene* (1985), is a narrative poem set in New York City that, like many of Haxton's other works, focuses on human relationships and specific moments of everyday life. His poetry often touches on his childhood and adolescence while moving easily between the worlds of personal memory and world history, often blurring the line. Haxton's translations include ancient Greek poems, Victor Hugo, Heraclitus, and German Jewish poet Else Lasker-Schüler.

Organizations that have honored Haxton include the Academy of American Poets, the Ingram Merrill Foundation, and the National Endowment for the Arts and National Endowment for the Humanities. He has also received a Guggenheim Fellowship and the Hanes Award for Poetry. He teaches poetry and world literature at Syracuse University.

J. E. Pitts
University of Mississippi

Dorothy Abbott, ed., *Mississippi Writers; Reflections on Childhood and Youth*, vol. 3, *Poetry* (1988); David Kirby, *New York Times Book Review* (30 May 2014); Syracuse University, College of Arts and Sciences, Faculty Directory website, asfaculty.syr.edu/pages/eng/haxton-brooks.html.

Hayes, Randy

(b. 1944) Artist

Painter Randy Hayes is known for realist paintings that display expressionist and other distortions and that draw on theatrical lighting. Randolph Alan Hayes was born in Jackson in 1944 and grew up near Clinton. At age sixteen Hayes moved to Tupelo, where he met artist Ke Francis and spent time with him drawing and painting. Hayes studied at Rhodes College in Memphis from 1962 to 1965 and received a bachelor of fine arts degree from the Memphis Academy

of Art in 1968. He next studied sculpture and worked toward his master of arts at the University of Oregon before moving to Seattle in 1968 as a VISTA volunteer. Hayes had his first solo exhibition there in 1971 and spent most of the next forty-five years in the city.

In 1973 Hayes moved to Boston to work as a set designer for Boston's PBS affiliate, WGBH. This experience significantly influenced his art. He became fascinated with the possibilities of dramatic lighting, and he experimented with constructions, combining drawings, light, and three-dimensional space. With these influences, Hayes returned to Seattle in 1979 and began working with shadowboxes. According to Hayes, "There are several prevailing themes in my work: the loss of innocence, the allure of glamour, the taboos of sex and race. Perhaps I am most drawn to the struggle of the individual with the unknown. My interest in these themes can be traced, at least in part, to my having spent my early years in the South. While my subjects may be hustlers in Times Square, prostitutes in Rome, or rollerskaters on Venice Beach, this southern inheritance is at the heart of much of my work."

Hayes's figurative work, while realistic in aspect, borrows brilliantly from the repertoire of modernism, and the inherent drama of his painting bespeaks the narrative tradition. Critics have pointed out that his painting has expressionist distortion, fauve color, the motion of futurists, and the light and brushwork of impressionism. Though Hayes says, "I think of myself as a traditionalist," his techniques belie that assessment. In an early mode, he made life-size pastel drawings using high-contrast photographs of the models for gestures and patterns of light and dark. He then cut out the figures, sandwiched them between sheets of fiberboard and acrylic cut into the shapes of the figures, and mounted them directly onto a black-painted gallery wall. Under heavy theatrical lighting, the paintings glowed with the energy of his subjects: boxers, strippers, pool players, prostitutes, and other urban dwellers.

Hayes later began oil painting. A 1984 installation commissioned for the Seattle Center, *The Pool*, was a transitional work in both form and content. Life-size cutout figures were executed with a severely limited palette of oil paint on canvas mounted on board. The subject matter, couples by a swimming pool, focused on interactions between people. Hayes continued the use of theatrical lighting to give a heightened dramatic cast to the paintings. In more recent work, he has embraced the conventionally framed oil painting truncated by the picture edge, but his aggressive realism, concerned with social alienation and personal isolation, is thoroughly modern. Hayes's work has been called erotic, but the eroticism is more a function of the physical monumentality and motion of his figures than the sexual content.

Since the beginning of his career Hayes has used photographs as source material for his paintings, but in 1991 photographs became a part of his medium. Using a grid of snapshots to present a scene from all perspectives, Hayes covered the photographic images with new images rendered in semitranslucent washes of paint. This technique produced complex and layered surfaces with narrative content and provocative commentary. Hayes frequently uses Mississippi iconography in his work, and in 2013 he returned to the state, setting up his studio in Holly Springs.

Hayes's 1996 exhibition in Seattle, *The South So Far*, included *Moon over Vicksburg*. The series *Baby Doll Suite* (2006) was inspired by the film adaptation of the Tennessee Williams play and the steamy work's effect on the people of Clinton. Hayes's 2008 series, *Ruins of Mississippi and Other Places in the World*, thematically juxtaposed the loss of the Mississippi Gulf Coast after Hurricane Katrina with iconic ruins in Rome, Athens, Mombasa, Oaxaca, and elsewhere. His art has been the subject of numerous shows as well as articles in *Artweek*, *ARTnews*, *Art in America*, and other prominent art magazines. He has received a National Endowment for the Arts Regional Visual Arts Fellowship (1988) and the Mississippi Institute of Arts and Letters Visual Arts Award (1990). His work is in the collections of the US Department of State, Microsoft Corporation, McDonald's Collection, the Seattle Art Museum, the Mississippi Museum of Art, and the Tacoma Art Museum, among others.

Patti Carr Black
Jackson, Mississippi

Odie Lindsey
Nashville, Tennessee

Patti Carr Black, *Art in Mississippi, 1720–1980* (1998); Patti Carr Black, *The Mississippi Story* (2007); Randy Hayes website, www.randyhayes.net.

Haymond, Saul
(b. 1947) Artist

Saul Haymond Sr. of Pickens is a self-taught painter who has been documenting life in Holmes County's African American community for more than forty years. Born in 1947 on a plantation near Ebenezer, Haymond was first exposed to painting and the art world through a mail-order book that featured the paintings of Michelangelo and Leonardo da Vinci. Haymond began copying these artists' works, tracing them on the ground in the dirt. Haymond subsequently drew on grocery sacks using charcoal from the fireplace. His stepfather felt that the drawings were a waste of paper and often used them as kindling in the family's fireplace, so Haymond began drawing under the house. He eventually

accumulated enough money to buy a watercolor set, beginning his experiments with color.

When he was seventeen, Haymond left home for a Job Corps position in Maryland. There he took some painting classes and had the first public exhibition of his work, at which several political figures from the Washington, D.C., area purchased his paintings. Haymond returned to Mississippi and went to work as a farm laborer while continuing to paint in the evenings, sometimes depicting African Americans in the cotton fields. Haymond's friends initially objected that his paintings portrayed depressing local scenes, but he argued that his art depicted the history of African Americans in the Delta.

Much of Haymond's work focuses on scenes from his life and those of his neighbors and friends. Some of his favorite topics include former homes, local stores, workers picking cotton, and landscapes of the places where he previously lived and worked. Because of his emphasis on local subjects, other Holmes County residents frequently commission pieces from Haymond. Using photographs and stories from his clients, he creates paintings that depict scenes from the community's or local families' history.

Haymond's work began to garner greater recognition in the 1990s, when he received fellowships from the Guggenheim Foundation and the Mississippi Arts Commission. His work also began to be exhibited outside of the state, including an exhibition at the Atelier A/E Gallery in New York. He was also one of the artists featured in the Mississippi Museum of Art's 1999 Mississippi Invitational show. He retired from work as a farm laborer in November 2004 and now devotes himself full time to his art.

Larry Morrisey
Mississippi Arts Commission

Saul Haymond, interview by Larry Morrisey, Mississippi Arts Commission Folklife Archive (6 August 2005); Mississippi Invitational 1999 Exhibit Catalog, Mississippi Museum of Art.

Haywood, Spencer
(b. 1949) Athlete

Despite winning a gold medal at the 1968 Olympics, his excellence in the American Basketball Association (ABA) and National Basketball Association (NBA), and a publicized battle with drugs, Spencer Haywood's most lasting legacy may prove the 1971 Supreme Court victory that enabled him to enter the NBA.

Haywood was born in Silver City, near Belzoni, on 22 April 1949. His father, John Haywood, died three weeks earlier, leaving his mother to raise Spencer and his nine siblings. Eunice Haywood worked both in the cotton fields and as a domestic, often laboring eighteen- to twenty-hour days. Because the infant Spencer was sickly, Eunice Haywood took him into the fields when he was a week old to monitor and nurse him. The family lived in abject poverty, often gleaning clothes from a nearby dump and receiving government rations. According to Haywood, he was shot at several times while walking roads at night during his early years and ordered to act as target on a driving range while working at the county's all-white country club. At the same time, however, Haywood recalls his boyhood in Mississippi as being marked by the strongest family bond he has ever experienced.

After Haywood's mother sewed together a basketball made of croaker sack and rags, he began shooting hoops whenever possible. By age thirteen, Haywood had grown to 6'6", and on his first day at McNair High School Coach Charles Wilson, an eleven-time Mississippi Black Coach of the Year, recruited him to play basketball. Though success on the court at times earned him a modicum of respect from white citizens in Belzoni, Haywood moved to Detroit to live with relatives after his sophomore year. There, he helped lead Pershing High School to the 1967 Michigan Class A championship.

Haywood attended Trinidad State Junior College, where his dominant play led to a position on the 1968 US Olympic basketball team. At the time, the nineteen-year-old Haywood was the youngest player ever offered a spot on the roster. He set a US team record in Mexico City, shooting 71.9 percent, and led the team with 145 points scored. The following year, playing for the University of Detroit, he averaged 32.1 points per game and led the nation with an average of 21.5 rebounds per game. Haywood then decided to turn professional, joining the ABA's Denver Rockets in 1969. He was named Rookie of the Year and Most Valuable Player for the 1969–70 season, leading the league in scoring and rebounds.

The next year Haywood and Seattle SuperSonics owner Sam Schulman defied NBA rules by completing a contract. At the time players were not permitted to sign with or be drafted by any NBA team until four years after their high school graduation (their designated college class graduation year). When the league threatened to punish the SuperSonics and Haywood, Haywood and Schulman filed an antitrust suit, claiming that the NBA's draft policy was in effect a restriction of trade, violating the Sherman Act of 1890. Haywood played for the Sonics while the case worked its way through the courts, with fans frequently booing him and players physically threatening him both off and on the court. In 1971, the US Supreme Court ruled in favor of Haywood and Schulman, paving the way for future players to join the league before finishing—or even beginning—college careers.

Haywood proved one of the NBA's most dominating forces, averaging a career 9.3 rebounds and 19.2 points per game while playing for Seattle and several other teams. He was named to two all-NBA first teams, played in four NBA All-Star Games, and was a member of the 1979–80 NBA champion Los Angeles Lakers. Like many players of the era, however, he also began using cocaine, eventually developing a serious habit that ultimately led to his dismissal from the Lakers. Haywood sobered up and played one year in the Italian league before spending two more seasons with the NBA's Washington Bullets.

In 2010, nearly four decades after *Haywood v. National Basketball Association*, the league honored Haywood during its annual All-Star Game. Of the twenty-four players selected as all-stars that year, twenty-one had come into the league as beneficiaries of Haywood's efforts. In 2015 he was inducted into the Naismith Memorial Basketball Hall of Fame.

Odie Lindsey
Nashville, Tennessee

Spencer Haywood with Scott Ostler, *Spencer Haywood: The Rise, the Fall, the Recovery* (1992); *In re. Spencer Haywood v. National Basketball Association*, 401 US 1204 (1971); Tim Povtak, NBA Fanhouse website, http://nba.fanhouse.com; Dan Raley, *Seattle Post-Intelligencer* (22 November 2006).

Hazen, Elizabeth Lee

(1885–1975) Scientist

Candida albicans, more commonly known as a yeast infection, can be uncomfortable and painful and if left untreated can have serious long-term health effects. Prior to important discoveries in microbiology by Mississippi native Elizabeth Lee Hazen during the 1950s, no treatment was available to counteract the effects of an imbalance in the bacteria integral to the functions of the human body. But Hazen and her research partner, Rachel Brown, made the widespread treatment of the common yeast infection both safe and effective.

Born on 24 August 1885 in Rich, in Coahoma County, Elizabeth Lee Hazen (known as Lee) was orphaned early in life. Laura and Robert Hazen, an aunt and uncle who lived in Lula, adopted the girl and her two sisters. Though Robert and Laura had little formal schooling, they were staunch advocates of education, and Lee graduated as Lula's valedictorian in 1904. After one year of private tutoring in Memphis, she matriculated at Mississippi Industrial Institute and College (later Mississippi University for Women), graduating in May 1910 with a bachelor's degree in science. Hazen then taught high school in Jackson while continuing her education during summers at the University of Tennessee and the University of Virginia. Hazen eventually moved to study full time at Columbia University in New York, earning a master's degree in 1917.

After a brief break to work in army laboratories during World War I, Hazen returned to study at Columbia in 1923. In 1927 she became one of the first women to receive a doctorate in biomedicine from the school. Hazen stayed on to continue her research and to teach, and in 1931 the head of the New York State Department of Health's Division of Laboratories hired Hazen to head its Bacterial Diagnosis Laboratory in New York City. During the 1930s and 1940s she researched the origins of a variety of infectious bacteria, including anthrax and tularemia.

World War II saw the exciting discovery and subsequent widespread use of both penicillin and streptomycin, but these medicines had costs as well as benefits. While both antibiotics killed infectious bacteria, they also upset the delicate balance of the body's bacteria. In 1944 Hazen's director had her return to Columbia to do research on fungal infections caused by this bacterial imbalance and work to find a fungicide that would combat such illnesses. Using soil samples, Hazen identified bacteria that grew actinomycetes, described by David D. Carson as "a particular class of moldlike microbes containing many antibiotic-producing species," but she needed a chemist's expertise to isolate and grow these actinomycetes. Reconnecting with the New York State Health Department, Hazen began working with Brown, and they developed nystatin, a medication that was effective in fighting *Candida*, *Crytococcus*, and fourteen other species of fungi. In 1951, after patenting the fungicide, Hazen and Brown sold the manufacturing rights to E. R. Squibb and Sons, which eventually produced a wide range of antifungal medications.

Nystatin still remains the safest and most effective antifungal medication on the market. Yet Hazen and Brown declined personal profit from the sale of the drug. Instead, they split the proceeds between the nonprofit Research Corporation and the Brown-Hazen Fund, which focused specifically on microbiology research. Both women remained active administrators of this fund, especially encouraging young women in the field of science and scientific research. Among other awards, in 1994 Hazen and Brown were inducted into the National Inventors Hall of Fame, the second and third women to receive that honor. Hazen died in Seattle in 1975.

Kathryn McGaw York
University of Mississippi

David D. Carson, in *Mississippi Women: Their Histories, Their Lives*, ed. Martha H. Swain, Elizabeth Anne Payne, Marjorie J. Spruill, and Susan Ditto (2003).

Head Start

Head Start, the innovative preschool education program created as part of Pres. Lyndon Johnson's War on Poverty, had substantial success and also generated controversy in Mississippi between 1965 and the early 1970s. Serving six thousand impoverished children in the summer of 1965, Head Start centers became an immediate target of the state's white segregationist politicians. Many Mississippi whites objected to the civil-rights-movement-based identity of local Head Start centers, fearing that the program's largely African American students were receiving a "radical" education in the preschool classes. White elites also opposed Head Start because the program employed large numbers of African American movement activists as teachers' aides, outreach workers, bus drivers, cooks, and janitors. In Mississippi the War on Poverty's goal of "maximum feasible participation" of the poor came close to reality in Head Start projects because of the extensive involvement of parents and community members.

The grassroots movement that had fueled the direct-action civil rights demonstrations and the voter registration campaigns provided an initial model for Head Start educational programs through the freedom schools organized by the Student Nonviolent Coordinating Committee and Congress of Federated Organizations in the summer of 1964. Committed white activists were among the creators of the federal program, and movement-related organizations such as the Delta Ministry were heavily involved in training community members to organize and staff the first Head Start programs. These networks of movement activists became the direct beneficiaries of federal funds granted to the Child Development Group of Mississippi (CDGM) in 1965. Because federal salaries of between sixty and one hundred dollars a week far exceeded the prevailing wage rates of three dollars a day, especially in Delta counties, demand was high for jobs in Head Start programs and other programs funded by the War on Poverty.

By late 1966 a sustained power struggle developed among white segregationist elites, CDGM activists and their allies, and a new coalition of "Loyal Democrats" that consisted of middle-class African American activists and white liberals who supported Johnson. In 1966 Mississippi Action for Progress, a hastily organized coalition of agencies, competed directly with CDGM for federal funding and control of local programs. Between 1966 and 1968 CDGM organizations were forced to join programs administered by the Mississippi Action for Progress, and federal pressures tightened educational requirements and regulations for Head Start employees. The resulting programs became more bureaucratic and less innovative.

Mississippi's Head Start history illustrates the conflicts that arose when state and federal authorities took control of programs and agencies begun by activists. War on Poverty programs disrupted established power relationships in communities across the United States. In a poor state such as Mississippi, federal funds constituted a highly contested source of local and state political power. Head Start teachers' aides and outreach workers increased their skill levels and education and consequently better educated their own children. Roles as students and leaders conferred increased status within their communities and became a prized source of empowerment.

Head Start has remained a subject of debate and occasional controversy. Nevertheless, in 2013–14, Mississippi's more than three hundred Head Start Centers received just over $185 million to serve twenty-seven thousand children.

Kim Lacy Rogers
Dickinson College

James F. Findlay Jr., *Church History* (June 1995); James F. Findlay Jr., *Church People in the Struggle: The National Council of Churches and the Black Freedom Movement, 1950–1970* (1993); Mark Newman, *Divine Agitators: The Delta Ministry and Civil Rights in Mississippi* (2004); Kim Lacy Rogers, *Life and Death in the Delta: African American Narratives of Violence, Resilience, and Social Change* (2006); US Department of Health and Human Services, Head Start Program Facts, Fiscal Year 2014 (April 2015).

Hederman Family
Publishers and Printers

The Hederman family interests have included newspapers, a printing business, a television station, banking, and real estate. As longtime publishers of the *Jackson Clarion-Ledger* and *Jackson Daily News*, they used the newspapers to promote their conservative views.

The family empire began in 1894 when Robert "Bert" Hederman and Tom Hederman moved with their widowed mother, Susan Virginia Hederman, to Jackson from Hillsboro. Although only in their teens, the boys began working for Col. Robert H. Henry, a cousin, at the *Clarion-Ledger*. The brothers purchased the newspaper's small job printing division in 1898. In 1902 the printing business was moved to Capitol Street, adjacent to the *Clarion-Ledger*, and the business was named Hederman Brothers. The business moved to South State Street in 1907 and to East Pearl Street in 1909. The Hedermans acquired the *Clarion-Ledger* in 1922 from Henry and co-owner Col. J. L. Power. Bert Hederman, who

married Jennie Belle Taylor, took over the printing business, and Thomas Hederman, who married Pearl Smith, became the paper's business manager and editor. Bob, Zach, and Henry, sons of Jennie and Bert Hederman, and Tom Jr. and Arnold, sons of Pearl and Thomas Hederman, worked in the businesses.

In 1954 cousins Robert M. Hederman Jr. and Thomas M. Hederman Jr. acquired the *Jackson Daily News* and merged its printing plant with that of the *Jackson Clarion-Ledger*. Tom Jr., who graduated from Mississippi College and Columbia University, served as editor of the two dailies and six weekly papers beginning in 1948. Bob Hederman, a graduate of Mississippi College and New York University, served as publisher. Their brothers also earned undergraduate degrees at Mississippi College, left Mississippi for graduate degrees, and then returned to Jackson. Arnold Hederman became sports editor of the *Clarion-Ledger*; Zach and Henry Hederman received graduate degrees in printing engineering from Carnegie Mellon University and then went to work at the printing company. The pattern continued into the next generation. Cousins Robert Hederman III, Rea Hederman, Hap Hederman, and Zach Hederman Jr. began their publishing careers at the family-owned *Madison County Herald*. Zach Jr. and Hap subsequently focused on the printing business; Robert III and Rea worked at the newspaper. In 1960, Bob, Zach, and Henry purchased the *Hattiesburg American*.

The family's power and influence extended to state politics. Family members worked with Gov. Ross Barnett in his unsuccessful effort to keep James Meredith from enrolling at the University of Mississippi in Oxford in 1962 and supported the Mississippi State Sovereignty Commission. The *Jackson Clarion-Ledger* headline about the June 1963 arrest of Byron De La Beckwith in the murder of Medgar Evers, "Californian Is Charged with Murder of Evers," covered up De La Beckwith's long residence in Greenwood and his membership in right-wing groups in Mississippi. The papers also editorialized against the sale of alcohol, and the Hedermans' influence helped maintain Prohibition in Mississippi until 1966, when it became the last state in the South to permit alcohol sales. Family members also served on governmental boards and bodies and were active members of Jackson's First Baptist Church. The family-owned Capitol Broadcasting Company also owned WJTV, which went on the air on 20 January 1953. The station was known for upholding the goals of white supremacy and faced licensing challenges during the civil rights era. The station is now owned by Media General.

Rea Hederman, Robert Hederman Jr.'s son, joined the staff of the *Clarion-Ledger* in 1973 and served as city editor and managing editor before becoming executive editor in 1980. He worked to change the tone of the newspaper, and during his tenure the paper won several national awards, including a Robert F. Kennedy Memorial Award in 1978, a Heywood Broun Award in 1979, a George Polk Award in

1981, and a National Education Reporting Award in 1982. The paper won a Pulitzer Prize in 1983 for its stories on Mississippi's educational system. Rea Hederman did not control the editorial page, however, and the family was sharply divided over his coverage of issues such as police brutality toward blacks in Jackson and the plight of poverty-stricken black farmers in the Delta. In 1984 Rea Hederman; his brother, Robert; and his two sisters, Jan Hederman Lipscomb and Sara Hederman; purchased the *New York Review of Books* for about five million dollars. Rea Hederman left Mississippi.

In 1982 the Hederman family sold the morning *Jackson Clarion-Ledger* (circulation 66,620), the afternoon *Jackson Daily News* (40,147), the *Hattiesburg American*, and newspapers in Canton, Clinton, Petal, Senatobia, Ocean Springs, and Lumberton to the Gannett Company. At that time, Hap Hederman became president and CEO of the printing company. The Hederman Brothers printing building, adjacent to the newspaper building, was sold to Gannett in 1993, and the printing company was moved to Ridgeland. Doug Hederman joined his father and grandfather in the company in 1997, and the following year the firm became a division of Master Graphics. Family members continue to be important in Mississippi philanthropy and economic development.

Kathleen Woodruff Wickham
University of Mississippi

Marcel Dufresne, *American Journalism Review* (October 1991); Peggy Elam and Loretta Pendergrast, *Jackson Clarion-Ledger* (2 April 1982); Kathy Lally, *Baltimore Sun Journal* (5 January 1997); *New York Times* (8 January 1985); Bill Prochnau, *Washington Post* (25 April 1983); David Remnick, *Washington Post* (12 December 1984); James Silver, *Mississippi: The Closed Society* (1964); Kathleen Wickham, *Winning the Pulitzer Prize: The Role of the "Clarion-Ledger" in the Adoption of the 1982 Education Reform Act* (2007).

Hemphill, Jessie Mae

(1923–2006) Blues Musician

Singer, guitarist, percussionist, and songwriter Jessie Mae Hemphill was born between Como and Senatobia, near the Tate-Panola County line, in 1923. (It was believed for many years that she was born much later, in 1933 or 1934.) Her family had a long musical tradition, contributing to her multi-instrumental abilities and the richness of her North Mississippi hill country sound. Hemphill's great-grandfather, Dock Hemphill, was a fairly well-known fiddle player from the area around Ackerman. In 1942 Library of Congress folklorist Alan Lomax recorded her grandfather, Sid Hemphill,

Jessie Mae Hemphill (Courtesy Blues Archive, Department of Archives and Special Collections, J. D. Williams Library, University of Mississippi)

performing ballads, country dance tunes, and spirituals on various instruments, such as a cane fife, quills (pan pipes), banjo, drums, and fiddle. Jessie Mae Hemphill's mother, Virgie Lee, and two aunts, Rosa Lee Hill and Sidney Lee, sang, played various string instruments, and played drums at family picnics. Jessie Mae's father played piano. Like many in her family, Jessie Mae began performing on bass and snare drum with African American fife and drum ensembles for community picnics. Sid Hemphill and Rosa Lee Hill taught Jessie Mae to play the guitar, which she used to accompany her singing at church gatherings and other functions. Like her grandfather and other musicians from this region, Hemphill played the one-string guitar, better known as the diddley bow.

Although she played some Chicago- and Delta-style blues, Hemphill's overall musical style was rooted in the North Mississippi hill country tradition: strong, repetitive dance rhythms (which she called the "hypnotic boogie") and little harmonic variation outside a single tonal center. She sang gospel, spiritual, blues, and original songs to distinct hill country guitar accompaniments, often backed by a tambourine or bells attached to her foot.

Although Hemphill played semiprofessionally in Memphis and the Mississippi Delta in the 1950s and 1960s, she failed to garner extraregional attention for another thirty years. To supplement her performing, Hemphill supported herself by cleaning houses and working in cafeterias and grocery stores. In the 1970s, at the suggestion and with the help of University of Memphis ethnomusicologist David Evans, Hemphill ventured toward a more professional musical career, performing across the United States, Canada, and throughout Europe. Her first recordings were released in

1979 as a set of singles Evans produced for the University of Memphis's High Water Records label. Hemphill's first album, *She-Wolf*, was released by the French label Vogue in 1980.

A 1993 stroke resulted in partial paralysis of her left side, slowing Hemphill's performing and recording schedules. Nevertheless, she appeared on several more recordings, including Richard Johnston's *Foot Hill Stomp* (2002) and the collaborative tribute album *Dare You to Do It Again* (2004).

Hemphill received four 1991 W. C. Handy Awards for Traditional Blues Female Artist and Best Country Blues Album for *Feelin' Good*. She died on 22 July 2006.

Greg Johnson

University of Mississippi

David Evans, *Feelin' Good* (1980), liner notes; David Evans, *She-Wolf* (1980), liner notes; George Mitchell, *Blow My Blues Away* (1971); Luigi Monge, in *Encyclopedia of the Blues*, ed. Edward Komara (2006); Robert Mugge, *Deep Blues: A Musical Pilgrimage to the Crossroads* (film, 2003).

Henley, Beth

(b. 1952) Playwright

Playwright and screenwriter Elizabeth Becker Henley was born on 8 May 1952 in Jackson to Charles Boyce Henley, a lawyer and Mississippi political figure, and Elizabeth Josephine Becker Henley, an amateur actress. Beth Henley showed an interest in the theater even as a child; she often accompanied her mother to rehearsals at Jackson's New Stage Theatre and enrolled in an actor's workshop there. Henley attended Jackson's public schools and then went to Southern Methodist University, where she received a bachelor of fine arts degree in theater in 1974. Though Henley's primary interest was acting, a one-act play she wrote for a class assignment, *Am I Blue*, was produced at Southern Methodist in 1973. Hoping to pursue a career as an actress rather than a writer, she spent a year as a graduate student in the theater department at the University of Illinois, Urbana-Champaign before moving to Los Angeles in 1976.

Unable to land the types of acting jobs she wanted, Henley turned to writing. Her first full-length play, *Crimes of the Heart*, was a dark comedy focusing on the relationship of three adult sisters in Hazlehurst, Mississippi. The play was first staged in at the Actor's Theatre in Louisville, Kentucky, in 1979. It was produced on Broadway in November 1981 and garnered a Tony nomination, the 1981 New York Drama Critics Circle Award for Best New American Play, and the 1981 Pulitzer Prize for Drama, making Henley the first woman to win the Pulitzer for drama in twenty-three

years. Henley's play, which contains several well-drawn, colorful, and somewhat eccentric characters, also elicited a number of favorable comparisons to the works of Flannery O'Connor and Eudora Welty. Henley's plays generally tend to explore the comedy inherent in human relationships.

Although Henley's next few plays—*The Miss Firecracker Contest* (first produced in 1980), *The Wake of Jamey Foster* (1982), and *The Debutante Ball* (1985)—were set in small Mississippi towns, several of her other plays explore life far away from her native state. Most notable among those are perhaps *The Lucky Spot* (1986), which takes place in the Old West, and *Signature* (1995), set in Hollywood in the year 2052. Henley's other plays are *Abundance* (1989), *Control Freaks* (1992), *L-Play* (1995), *Revelers* (1996), *Impossible Marriage* (1998), *Family Week* (2000), *Sisters of the Winter Madrigal* (2003), and *Ridiculous Fraud* (2006). *The Jacksonian*, which premiered in Los Angeles in 2012, is set in the playwright's Mississippi hometown. Her most recent play, *Laugh*, had its premiere at Studio Theatre in Washington, D.C., in March 2015.

Henley has also written for the screen, including the adaptations for her plays *The Miss Firecracker Contest* (1989), *Abundance* (1998, released as *Come West with Me*), and *Crimes of the Heart* (1986), for which she received an Academy Award nomination for Best Adapted Screenplay. Her other screenwriting credits include *Nobody's Fool* (1986), *True Stories* (1986), which she wrote with actor Stephen Tobolowsky (with whom she was also romantically involved for more than two decades) and rock musician David Byrne, and the PBS teleplay *Survival Guides* (1985), which she wrote with Budge Threlkeld.

Jennifer Southall

Jackson, Mississippi

Robert Bain and Joseph M. Flora, eds., *Contemporary Poets, Playwrights, Essayists, and Novelists of the South: A Biographical-Bibliographic Sourcebook* (1994); Mary Dellasega, in *Speaking on Stage: Interviews with Contemporary American Playwrights*, ed. Philip C. Kolin and Colby H. Kullman (1996); Julia A. Fesmire, ed., *Beth Henley: A Casebook* (2002); Alexis Greene, ed., *Women Who Write Plays: Interviews with American Dramatists* (2001); Janet L. Gupton, in *Southern Women Playwrights: New Essays in Literary History and Criticism*, ed. Robert L. McDonald and Linda Rohrer Paige (2002).

Henry, Aaron

(1922–1997) Activist and Political Leader

Aaron Edd Henry, a pharmacist, civil rights activist, entrepreneur, and Mississippi political leader, was born on a

Aaron Henry speaks before the Credentials Committee at the Democratic National Convention, Atlantic City, N.J., August 1964 (Photograph by Warren K. Leffler, Library of Congress, Washington, D.C. [LC-U9-12470E-28])

plantation outside Clarksdale. His parents died before he was six years old, and a maternal uncle, Ed Henry, reared him. His uncle was a cobbler with relative independence, inspiring Aaron to become an independent businessman. He and his family moved to Clarksdale, where he completed elementary school. In the absence of a high school for African Americans, he attended the nearby boarding school at Coahoma.

Henry enlisted in the army in 1942 and after serving as a truck driver returned to Clarksdale in 1946. He immediately registered to vote and proudly noted that the 1946 mayoral election was his first exercise of the franchise. Even then, he exhorted others to join him. He went on to study pharmacy at Xavier University, graduating in 1950 and opening the Fourth Street Drug Store in Clarksdale. His business prospered, and his store became the hub of a broad range of social and political activity, particularly after he established a local chapter of the National Association for the Advancement of Colored People (NAACP) in 1953.

Over the next thirty-five years Henry became one of the state's most powerful political leaders. He assumed the presidency of the state NAACP in 1960 and held the office for more than thirty years. In the early 1960s his hometown chapter anchored a widespread social movement challenging racial exclusion in Clarksdale. He led NAACP members in demonstrations and boycotts against virtually every segregated public facility and merchant in the small town.

Henry subsequently led a statewide movement organized around the Council of Federated Organizations, an umbrella group of other civil rights groups that worked to overturn social and political segregation. Henry stood at the center of most major state mobilization campaigns through the 1960s, including leadership of two challenges to the segregated Democratic Party (the Regulars), which was unseated at the 1968 national convention. He led the new Loyalist faction in gaining control of the party, thus demolishing a century-old racially exclusive hierarchy. He served first as chair of the

Mississippi Party and then as cochair when the Loyalists and Regulars merged. In the interim he also achieved great influence within the national Democratic Party, had entrée to every president beginning in 1960 and many members of Congress, and affiliated with every major civil rights organization in the period. Following an earlier challenge to the WLBT-TV station, he and others acquired the business. Henry later chaired its board and earned considerable wealth from his partial ownership. He won a seat in the Mississippi legislature in 1979. Aging and ailing, he gave up the presidency of the NAACP in 1993 and lost his legislative post in 1995. He died in Clarksdale two years later.

Minion K. C. Morrison
Mississippi State University

Raymond Arsenault, *Freedom Riders: 1961 and the Struggle for Racial Justice* (2006); Françoise Hamlin, *Crossroads at Clarksdale: The Black Freedom Struggle in the Mississippi Delta after World War II* (2012); Aaron Henry with Constance Curry, *Aaron Henry: The Fire Ever Burning* (2000); Minion K. C. Morrison, *Aaron Henry of Mississippi: Inside Agitator* (2015).

Henson, Jim
(1936–1990) Puppeteer

America's greatest and most popular puppeteer, James Maury Henson was born on 24 September 1936 in Greenville, Mississippi. Henson was in fifth grade when his father accepted a new job and the family moved to Hyattsville, Maryland, a suburb of Washington, D.C. Fascinated with television, Jim began looking for ways to work in the expanding medium, and after graduating from Northwestern High School, he and a friend landed jobs as puppeteers for the *Junior Morning Show* on a local station.

Henson enrolled at the University of Maryland in 1954, and met Jane Nebel, who became his first important performing partner and later his wife. In 1955 Henson debuted *Sam and Friends* on Washington's NBC station, WRC-TV: one of the characters was an early version of Kermit the Frog. The show ran until 1961 and won a local Emmy in 1958. With this award, Henson began to seriously consider puppetry as a career and art form.

After graduating from the University of Maryland, Henson began making television commercials, and his characters Rowlf the Dog and other Muppets began appearing on the *Ed Sullivan Show*, the *Tonight Show*, and the *Jimmy Dean Show*. During the next few years Henson brought in colleagues Jerry Juhl, Don Stahlin, and Frank Oz, who would play significant roles in the development of the Muppets.

Oz became Henson's key performing partner on characters as diverse as Grover, Cookie Monster, Fozzie Bear, and Miss Piggy.

In 1965 Henson wrote, produced, directed, and starred in an experimental film, *Timepiece*, that was nominated for an Academy Award. In 1966 the Carnegie Institute conducted a study of children's television programming that resulted in the establishment of the Children's Television Workshop (now Sesame Workshop), which began developing a new show for preschoolers. The basic proposal included puppets, and Henson's Muppets were suggested.

Debuting in 1969, *Sesame Street* was an instant success. Featuring a greatly expanded cast of Muppets, the show introduced preschoolers to letters, numbers, and shapes as well as more complicated themes such as friendship, pregnancy, and death. Many of its characters—Bert, Ernie, Oscar the Grouch, Grover, Elmo, Big Bird, the Count, Cookie Monster, and Kermit the Frog, among others—have become American icons. By the early 1970s *Sesame Street* was being watched by approximately half of the twelve million children aged three to five in the United States. The program is currently shown in more than 140 countries with 20 international versions using indigenous characters, puppets, sets, and stories.

In September 1976 Henson introduced *The Muppet Show*. Despite the Muppets' obvious appeal to adults, Henson had a hard time convincing American network television to air a prime time show using his characters. Lord Lew Grade of the British-based Associated Communications Corporation ultimately took a chance and syndicated the program to TV stations in more than one hundred countries. Adults made up three-fourths of the show's audience. Muppet regulars Sam the Eagle, the Swedish Chef, Statler and Waldorf, Kermit the Frog, and Miss Piggy played host to an impressive array of guest stars such as Vincent Price, Zero Mostel, Danny Kaye, George Burns, and Julie Andrews. One of the show's proudest moments came when one of Henson's greatest inspirations, ventriloquist Edgar Bergen, visited the show with his characters, Charlie McCarthy and Mortimer Snerd.

The popularity of *The Muppet Show* led to a variety of feature films, including *The Muppet Movie* (1979), *The Great Muppet Caper* (1981), *The Muppets Take Manhattan* (1984), *Muppet Treasure Island* (1996), *Muppets from Space* (1999), *The Muppets* (2011), and *Muppets Most Wanted* (2014). The talents of Henson and his team led to other film work, including *The Dark Crystal* (1982) and *Labyrinth* (1986). Other television shows also followed. *Fraggle Rock* premiered on HBO in 1983 and ran for four years. *Muppet Babies*, an animated Saturday morning program, was launched in 1984 and ran for eight years. In the fall of 2015, ABC launched a new series, *The Muppets*.

Henson died of a bacterial infection in 1990 at the age of fifty-three. Memorial services were held at the Cathedral of St. John the Divine in New York City and at St. Paul's Cathedral in London. In true Jim Henson style, both services started with "Sunny Day," the theme song from *Sesame Street*. Henson wanted the memorials to be happy and had requested that mourners not wear black. Instead, they waved colorful butterflies on stems made by the Muppet Workshop. Big Bird sang "It's Not Easy Being Green," a song usually voiced by Henson in the character of Kermit the Frog. A Dixieland band played, and Muppeteers sang a medley of Muppet-related songs.

Kevin Herrera
University of Mississippi

Kiley Armstrong, "Thousands Attend Memorial for Muppet Creator," Associated Press (21 May 1990); Matt Bacon, *No Strings Attached: The Inside Story of Jim Henson's Creature Shop* (1997); Rhea R. Borja, *Education Week* (2 October 2002); Christopher Finch, *Jim Henson: The Works, the Art, the Magic, the Imagination* (1993); Susan Andre George, *Follow Your Enthusiasm: The Jim Henson Performance Aesthetic* (1993); Ann Donegan Johnson, *The Value of Imagination: The Story of Jim Henson* (1991); Brian Jay Jones, *Jim Henson: The Biography* (2013); John J. O'Connor, *New York Times* (1 June 1990); Jean Seligmann and Elizabeth Ann Leonard, *Newsweek* (28 May 1990).

Herdahl v. Pontotoc County School District

Lisa Herdahl and her family moved from Wisconsin to the northern Mississippi town of Ecru in 1993. There, her family began attending a Lutheran church. Though Herdahl was a Christian and was raising her children to follow her faith, she was appalled to learn that the Pontotoc County public schools offered Bible classes and read prayers over the school intercom systems every morning. Herdahl told school officials that she would not allow her children to be involved, a stance that brought retaliation from teachers and students. In one instance, a teacher put headphones over the ears of Herdahl's son during the morning prayers, prompting other students to tease him. In December 1994 Lisa Herdahl and her family took the school district to federal court with the help of attorneys from the American Civil Liberties Union and People for the American Way, a nonpartisan organization that acts to protect constitutional rights. The lawsuit provoked further harassment of the Herdahls, including angry letters to the local newspaper and signs opposing the case posted on virtually every house and business in Ecru. In addition, Lisa Herdahl received at least one death threat, and her convenience store received a bomb threat.

On 6 March 1996 Judge Neal Biggers Jr. of the US District Court for the Northern District of Mississippi found in the Herdahls' favor, declaring that prayers in Pontotoc's public school classrooms and over the intercom systems were unconstitutional. Bible history classes, however, were permissible as long as they did not endorse a specific religion or doctrine. Wrote Biggers, "The Bill of Rights was created to protect the minority from tyranny by the majority. . . . To say that the majority should prevail simply because of its numbers is to forget the purpose of the Bill of Rights."

Andrew Tillman
University of Mississippi

CNN website, www.cnn.com (3 June 1996); Charles Levendosky, *Casper Star-Tribune* (27 August 1995); *Herdahl v. Pontotoc County School District*, 933 F.Supp. 528 (N.D. Miss. 1996); *School Prayer: A Community at War*, ITVS POV Documentary website, http://archive.itvs.org/schoolprayer /index.html; D. W. Steel, *Oxford Eagle* (7 March 1996); Nadine Strossen, *William and Mary Bill of Rights Journal* 4, no. 2 (1995); Charles Raymond Westmoreland, "Southern Pharisees: Prayer, Public Life, and Politics in the South, 1955–1996" (PhD dissertation, University of Mississippi, 2008).

Herrera, Anthony

(1944–2011) Actor

Anthony Herrera, best known for his role as James Stenbeck on the CBS soap opera *As the World Turns*, was born in Wiggins, Mississippi, on 19 January 1944 and was raised there by his maternal grandparents. After graduating from Wiggins High School and receiving a bachelor's degree in zoology and English literature from the University of Mississippi, Herrera moved to New York to study acting. He performed with the Will Geer Shakespeare Theater for five years before crossing over to television series and soap operas. After small roles on *Search for Tomorrow* and *The Young and the Restless*, Herrera began appearing in the mid-1970s as Mark Galloway on *As the World Turns*. In 1980 he took on the role of villain James Stenbeck on the show, and over the next twenty years he murdered, blackmailed, robbed, lied to, and cheated countless characters in the fictional town of Oakdale. The character was believed to have died at least five times, and Herrera appeared on other programs during those interludes, including a recurring role on *Loving* between 1985 and 1991.

In 1997 Herrera was diagnosed with mantle cell lymphoma. After various treatments failed, he received a pioneering stem cell transplant that induced a long-term remission. Herrera wrote about his recovery in his book, *The Cancer Wars*, and testified on Capitol Hill in 2005 about the benefits of stem cell research.

In addition to acting, Herrera tried his hand at screenwriting, directing, and producing. In 1984 he produced and directed *Mississippi Delta Blues*, a documentary on blues musician James "Son" Thomas. In 1987 he wrote and directed *The Wide Net*, an adaptation of a short story by Eudora Welty. He also coauthored *Smoke and Mirrors* (1991), a comedy-mystery play originally presented in twelve Mississippi cities. Herrera founded www.poetrytheatre.org, a website that "gives poetry to everyone to inspire, to enjoy and to learn" by offering video clips of actors and musicians reciting their favorite poems.

Herrera's cancer subsequently returned, and he died on 21 June 2011 in Buenos Aires, Argentina. His survivors included his daughter, actress Gaby Hoffmann.

Katherine Treppendahl
University of Virginia

Internet Movie Database website, www.imdb.com; *Soap Central* website, www.soapcentral.com; Poetry Theatre website, www.poetrytheatre.org.

Hester Site

Holding great significance for archaeologists, the Hester Site is located in Monroe County, just west of the town of Amory, on the Tombigbee River. Excavations conducted in the 1970s revealed this site as the earliest occupation yet found in Mississippi.

Spear-point types from the site indicate a date in excess of ten thousand years ago. Hester is a stratified site, occupied for a long period and later sealed by flood events. The site thus resembles a layer cake, with the oldest remains on the bottom and the most recent on top. Hester was occupied almost continuously from about ten thousand years ago to six thousand years ago. It was then abandoned until around AD 500, reoccupied until AD 900, and then abandoned again until the 1920s. Hester is listed as a National Historic Landmark.

The earliest occupation was by Paleo-Indians. All tools found from this early habitation are hunting and butchering tools, indicating that only males occupied the Hester site, since most early people had a strict sexual division of labor and hunting was a male activity. Further, tools were not being manufactured at the site. Hester was probably a deer hunting camp, where animals were brought and processed before being taken back to the base camp.

Hester subsequently served as a base camp. The presence of adzes indicates heavy woodworking activities such as house construction and dugout canoe manufacture. Also present are stones used to process nuts, a class of tools that indicates that females lived at Hester. Nut harvest was an important activity for early people, who competed with many animals for this important resource. In addition, end scrapers have been found, suggesting the preparation of hide, another activity assumed to have been carried out by females. These people had no knowledge of pottery, agriculture, or the bow and arrow. (In fact, the bow and arrow do not appear in Mississippi until around AD 800.)

At about 4000 BC the site was abandoned for unknown reasons. It remained unoccupied until around AD 500, when hunter-gatherers who practiced an early form of agriculture arrived. These inhabitants used pottery, leaving many potsherds. Hester remained occupied for approximately five hundred years before again being abandoned until the 1920s, when a small wood frame house was constructed on the site.

Samuel O. Brookes
National Forests in Mississippi

Samuel O. Brookes, *The Hester Site, an Early Archaic Occupation in Monroe County, Mississippi: A Preliminary Report* (1979).

Highway 61/Blues Highway

Like an asphalt shadow snaking the land by the river, Highway 61 works its way through Mississippi from Memphis in the north down to the Louisiana line in the south. Though its full length stretches from Wyoming, Minnesota, to New Orleans, Mississippi's 61 is arguably the most famous and infamous link in a highway whose history touches the core of the American narrative. Known for its modern association with blues history, Highway 61 also witnessed the movement of countless African American migrants escaping the harsh realities of Jim Crow and shifting agricultural patterns in the Mississippi Delta and Deep South. This iconic stretch of road passes through Tunica, Clarksdale, Cleveland, Vicksburg, and Natchez, following the river as it carries the weight of myriad histories down to the Gulf of Mexico.

Though Highway 61 runs the length of the state, its passage through Mississippi's Delta contributes to its widely known moniker, the Blues Highway. In the twentieth century many African Americans in the Delta labored as sharecroppers on vast plantations. After a brief post–Civil War period of limited landownership and increased political representation, southern governments realigned to maintain white supremacy under the Jim Crow system. The mechanization of agricultural labor and sustained political, economic, and social inequities combined to push African Americans out of Mississippi in great numbers in the early to middle part of the century. Known as the Great Migration, this exodus was also aided by the *Chicago Defender*, an African American newspaper that disseminated to southern blacks information about industrial employment opportunities and favorable living conditions in the North. As World War II mobilization efforts created labor shortages in northern industrial centers, African Americans increasingly left the harshly segregated South in hopes of finding better fortune, treatment, and opportunity in Chicago, Detroit, St. Louis, Philadelphia, and other cities. Highway 61 served as a primary conduit for thousands of these migrants. More recently, their descendants have begun to return to their southern roots in search of family, familiar landscapes, and employment opportunities in the gaming and tourism industries. Highway 61 remains an important channel for this reverse migration.

In the late twentieth century, Mississippi sought to develop and transform its economy through the engines of casino gambling and tourism. As a primary link in this developing chain, Highway 61 slips through cotton fields, dropping visitors into the neon glitz of Tunica. Farther south, the association with Mississippi blues history and culture is clearly evident. The town of Clarksdale and the state tourism office promote the connection between Highway 61 and an enticing blues narrative. Publicity for the town claims, for example, that Robert Johnson sold his soul to the devil at the intersection of Highways 61 and 49 in Clarksdale. In 1941 a sharecropper named McKinley Morganfield sat down for an interview and field recording session with John Work and Alan Lomax at the Stovall farm near Clarksdale. After hearing his recorded voice and guitar for the first time, Morganfield decided to leave the heat and labor of the Delta and travel the Illinois Central Gulf rail line that paralleled Highway 61 to Chicago. Within a few years, Morganfield changed his name to Muddy Waters, forever shaping American music and cultural history. These images are routinely employed in Clarksdale's tourism literature and within Mississippi's continuing effort to brand itself as a blues cultural mecca. As Mississippi's Blues Highway, Highway 61 serves a critical modern function by providing a touristic experience in which distinctive mythic landscapes and histories are promoted, encountered, and interpreted.

As its tourism economy gathers steam, Mississippi needs to involve local communities along the Highway 61 corridor in the creation and packaging of heritage-based narratives. Like many unique southern locales, the Mississippi Delta obtains significant economic benefits from heritage tourism efforts. As blues culture continues to form the core of these efforts, local input is critical to maintaining historical integrity within highly complex and at times controversial themes.

Brian Dempsey
Middle Tennessee State University

Alan W. Barton, *Attitudes about Heritage Tourism in the Mississippi Delta: A Policy Report from the 2005 Delta Rural Poll*, Policy Paper no. 05–02,

Center for Community and Economic Development, Delta State University (December 2005); James Cobb, *The Most Southern Place on Earth: The Mississippi Delta and the Roots of Regional Identity* (1992); Alferdteen Harrison, ed., *Black Exodus: The Great Migration from the American South* (1991); Benita J. Howell, ed., *Cultural Heritage Conservation in the American South* (1990); Stephen A. King, *Arkansas Review* (April 2005); Randall Norris, ed., *Highway 61: Heart of the Delta* (2008); Elijah Wald, *Escaping the Delta: Robert Johnson and the Invention of the Blues* (2004).

Hiking

Hiking as a form of outdoor recreation in Mississippi is an enjoyable and increasingly popular pastime, largely because of the state's varying terrain, numerous public lands, relatively mild climate, and long-standing tradition of engagement in outdoor recreation by its citizens.

While outdoor recreational activities such as hunting, fishing, boating, and picnicking have long been popular with Mississippians, they have been somewhat slower than residents of other states to develop interests in more adventurous and physically challenging outdoor activities (often called outdoor pursuits). Evidence indicates that variables such as age, income, and regional residency may affect Mississippians' interest in hiking. In a 2004 study, residents of rural areas of the state rarely cited hiking among their favorite activities. Yet according to the National Sporting Goods Association, an estimated 638,000 Mississippians aged seven years or older hiked at least twice in 2006. Within the same demographic group, 169,000 persons reported having backpacked two or more times during that same year. Both of these statistics place Mississippi above the national average for participation in these outdoor pursuits.

Mississippi has extensive public and private lands suitable for hiking. One of the state's most widely used resources is the Natchez Trace, which not only provides a contemporary resource for hikers but represents a historical artifact of one of the state's very first trails. Native Americans used the Natchez Trace as a corridor for foot travel throughout present-day Mississippi, northern Alabama, and Tennessee. By the early nineteenth century this trail was also an important overland return route for travelers who had journeyed downriver on boats through the Tennessee, Cumberland, and Ohio River Valleys. Today the National Park Service manages the 444-mile Natchez Trace corridor, and it serves as a central artery that connects many excellent public hiking trails. From Donivan Slough in northern Mississippi to Bullen Creek near the southern terminus, the Natchez Trace offers a number of short nature trails and day hikes that can be completed in less than an hour as well as longer and more challenging routes. Hiking trails at another National Park Service site, Vicksburg National Military Park, include Trek Hike and Al Scheller Scout Trail. The Scheller Trail was originally designed as a compass course, and its 12.5 miles of footpaths feature rugged terrain, steep elevation changes, and stream crossings.

Other federal resources within the state include extensive US Army Corps of Engineers holdings and the 1.2 million acres of land located in Mississippi's six national forests. Trails at Holly Springs National Forest's Upper Sardis Wildlife Management Area, for example, were built with volunteer assistance and are open for hiking and other nonmotorized activities. In De Soto National Forest hikers can enjoy the Tuxachanie Trail and Black Creek Wilderness Trail.

Most of Mississippi's twenty-two state parks and other state lands offer hiking and walking trails. Parks notable for their trails include Tishomingo State Park and Wall Doxey State Park in northern Mississippi, Great River Road State Park in the Delta, and Paul B. Johnson State Park in the south.

Many local and community trails exist throughout the state, and special events and festivals often feature planned hikes. The trail through Bailey's Woods to William Faulkner's Rowan Oak estate has been used for guided nature hikes during Oxford's Double Decker Festival, and Rolling Fork's Great Delta Bear Affair regularly features both general nature hikes and birding tours.

Mississippians also enjoy hiking on private lands, as many large farms and woodlots offer opportunities for families and friends to walk familiar terrain. In addition, nonprofit organizations such as Audubon Mississippi and the Nature Conservancy both offer guided hikes and allow hikers to explore on their own. The Strawberry Plains Audubon Center near Holly Springs has fifteen miles of hiking trails within its twenty-five hundred acres.

As long as humans have lived in Mississippi, they have hiked, first as a principal means of travel and now primarily for recreation. This activity remains an important part of Mississippi's culture.

David M. Zuefle
University of Mississippi

Mississippi Development Authority—Tourism Division, "Mississippi Adventure Guide" (2005); National Park Service website, www.nps.gov; David M. Zuefle, "Environmental Knowledge and Attitudes of North Mississippi Residents" presentation to the University of Mississippi Faculty Research Program (November 2004).

Hill, Faith (Audrey Faith Perry)
(b. 1967) Country Musician

Country music and pop superstar Faith Hill was born Audrey Faith Perry on 21 September 1967 in Ridgeland, Mississippi, and was raised by her adoptive parents, Edna and Ted Perry, in Star, twenty-five miles southeast of Jackson, along with two brothers in a devout Christian family. As she sang in church, family and neighbors took note of her vocal talent, and before long she was performing wherever the town afforded her the opportunity. By the time she was in high school, she knew she wanted a career singing country music.

After briefly attending Hinds Junior College, Perry moved to Nashville in 1987, holding a series of jobs that included a stint as a receptionist at singer Gary Morris's company. She was overheard singing along with the radio and became a demo singer for the company as well as a backing vocalist for Gary Burr, performing with him at Nashville's Bluebird Café. During this time, she married and divorced music publisher Daniel Hill. An executive with Warner Bros. Records heard Hill's work and signed her to a contract.

In 1993 Warner Bros. released her first album, *Take Me as I Am*, which produced two No. 1 hits, "Wild One" and "Piece of My Heart." Hill's subsequent recordings have yielded numerous hits, including chart-toppers "It Matters to Me," "This Kiss," "Let Me Let Go," "Breathe," "The Way You Love Me," and "Mississippi Girl." She has released six studio albums and two compilations and has had forty-one singles appear on the Billboard Country Chart. Her albums have sold more than forty million copies worldwide, and she has achieved pop crossover success as well.

In 1996 Hill teamed with Tim McGraw for a concert tour: they married on 6 October of that year. In 1997, their first vocal collaboration, "It's Your Love," topped the country charts. The pair have recorded other songs together and toured jointly again in 2006 and 2007, with tremendous success. They also have three daughters.

Hill has won five Grammy awards and numerous Academy of Country Music and Country Music Association awards. In December 2015 she was honored with a marker on the Mississippi Country Music Trail at the corner of Mangum and Main Street in Star.

Hill has also become an actress, performing on television in *Promised Land* and *Touched by an Angel*, and in a 2004 movie, *The Stepford Wives*, and in 2015's critically acclaimed *Dixieland*. From 2007 to 2012, Hill performed the opening theme song for NBC's *Sunday Night Football*, and she sang the national anthem before Super Bowl XXXIV in 2000 and "America the Beautiful" before Super Bowl XLIII in 2009. In 2015 it was announced that Hill would become executive producer of a new Nashville-based daytime talk show. Hill and McGraw's philanthropic efforts have included support for literacy programs, Hurricane Katrina relief, and a benefit concert for victims of a devastating 2010 Nashville flood.

Edward Morris
Nashville, Tennessee

James L. Dickenson, *Faith Hill: Piece of My Heart* (2001); Faith Hill website, www.faithhill.com; Internet Movie Database website, www.imdb.com; Sterling Whitaker, Taste of Country website, tasteofcountry.com (23 December 2015), Joel Whitburn, *Top Country Songs: 1944 to 2005* (2006).

Hill, Robert Andrews
(1811–1900) Judge

Judge Robert A. Hill served in the federal judiciary during one of the most challenging times in Mississippi history—Reconstruction after the Civil War. Hill was born in Iredell County, North Carolina, on 25 March 1811, the grandson of Scots-Irish immigrants. His father, David Hill, and mother, Rhoda Andrews Hill, were well-read for their time. When Hill was young, the family moved to Williamson County, Tennessee, to farm.

Hill was the only son among four daughters, and at age ten he began to support the family after his father's declining health precluded the heavy labors of farming. He attended school when not tending crops, but the balance of his education was gained at home with his father. In 1831 he taught at a county school in addition to farming. In 1833 he married Mary Andrews.

Hill was elected a constable in 1834 and later became a justice of the peace, thereby acquiring legal training. He resigned in 1844 to take up the practice of law. He practiced law in Waynesboro, Tennessee, until 1847, when the legislature selected him as a state district attorney general. He held that position until his defeat in an 1855 popular election. That year he moved to Tishomingo County, Mississippi, to form a law partnership with John F. Arnold. In 1858 he returned to public office when he was elected probate judge of Tishomingo County, a post he held until 1865.

Hill opposed secession but did not take a side during the Civil War. A Whig before the war and a Republican after it, he favored the Lincoln-Johnson plans for constitutional measures for the restoration of the South. He served as a delegate to the 1865 Mississippi constitutional convention, which was charged with undoing the work of the 1861 constitution.

In 1866, Pres. Andrew Johnson recognized Hill's dedication to a reconciled government by appointing him to the federal judiciary for the two districts (northern and southern) that comprised Mississippi. The court moved from Pontotoc to Oxford, where Judge Hill took up residence. With Hill's support, the state rescinded its legislation that conflicted with federal laws, and as a federal judge he was the only one with jurisdiction to intercede with the military command of the state. In Ku Klux Klan prosecutions during 1871 he ruled regarding the constitutionality of certain congressional acts while preserving the peace. In the fall of 1875 he publicly called on the voters of Mississippi "of both races and all parties" to peaceably register and vote in congressional elections and thereby show "to the world that, though composed of different races and entertaining different opinions, we are capable of self-government and can live in peace."

Mississippi's 1868 constitutional convention invited Hill to prepare the part of the Mississippi constitution concerning the judiciary. Calling on his earlier experience in the chancery courts of Tennessee, he drafted the article blending probate and equity into the chancery court system as a separate court for each county. His work was so well received that the judiciary article was not changed in the new constitution of 1890.

Hill was elected president of the Mississippi State Bar Association in January 1889 while a sitting federal judge. He retired from the federal bench in 1891 and continued to live in Oxford, where he served as a trustee of the University of Mississippi, until his death on 2 July 1900.

Camille H. Evans
Jackson, Mississippi

Biographical and Historical Memoirs of Mississippi (1891); Judge Billy G. Bridges and James W. Shelton, eds., *Griffith's Mississippi Chancery Practice* (2000); Frank E. Everett Jr., *Federal Judges in Mississippi, 1818–1968* (1968); Robert A. Hill Subject File, Mississippi Department of Archives and History.

Hinds County

As the home of Mississippi's capital city, Hinds County has long been the center of the state's government as well as a hub of educational, economic, and cultural life. Jackson is Mississippi's largest city, and Hinds County, a largely urban county in a primarily rural and agricultural state, has been the most populous county in the state since 1860. Chosen in part for its central location, Jackson has great importance to Mississippians as the site of state government, as the headquarters of numerous businesses and other organizations, and as a location for meetings, conferences, entertainment, and even the state fair. The Pearl River runs through Hinds County and Jackson. The county seat is Jackson, and other notable towns include Raymond, Bolton, Cayuga, Clinton, Edwards, Learned, Oakley, Pocahontas, Terry, Tougaloo, and Utica.

Founded in 1821 on land ceded by the Choctaw in the Treaty of Doak's Stand, Hinds County was named for Gen. Thomas Hinds. Jackson, named for Gen. Andrew Jackson years before he became president, became the capital in 1821, four years after Mississippi statehood. The plan for the city had roots in Thomas Jefferson's goal for state capitals to be small cities with numerous green spaces. The state government began meeting in Jackson in 1822 in a small brick building that served as the state's first capitol. The larger, more impressive Greek Revival structure that eventually became known as the Old Capitol was designed by architect William Nichols and constructed in the 1830s, opening in 1839. In 1842 Gov. Tilghman Tucker became the first governor to move into the Governor's Mansion, also designed by Nichols.

Despite a growing urban core, antebellum Hinds County was an agricultural powerhouse. In its first census in 1830, the county had a population of 5,433 free people and 3,212 slaves. Just ten years later, Hinds County had the state's second-largest overall population, including the second-largest slave population. In 1840 Hinds had almost twice as many slaves (12,275) as free people (6,823). Jackson had about three hundred people working in manufacturing.

By 1860 Hinds County was the largest in the state, with 8,776 free people and 22,363 slaves, the largest such population and a ratio that ranked thirteenth among Mississippi counties. With its 3,199 people, Jackson was the state's fourth-largest city, with the second-most people born outside the United States. In 1860 Jackson had the fifth-highest number of manufacturing workers in the state, most of them making woolen goods, but Hinds remained devoted to agriculture. It ranked second in the state in cotton production and was among Mississippi's top seven counties in corn, livestock, oats, peas and beans, and sweet potatoes.

Hinds County had twenty-three churches in 1860—eight Baptist, seven Methodist, three Presbyterian, two Christian, two Episcopal, and one Catholic. In 1861, fifteen Jewish families founded Beth Israel Congregation.

Jackson was the site of Mississippi's secession convention and home of the state's leading secessionist newspaper, the *Mississippian*, edited by Ethelbert Barksdale. The state government operated in the city until Union forces took it in May 1863. As part of a broad effort to take Vicksburg and weaken the forces that might defend it, Union troops led by Ulysses S. Grant fought back Confederates first at Raymond and then at Jackson. William Sherman's men quickly burned a considerable number of Jackson buildings and railroads, leading some to begin referring to the city as Chimneyville. The state government had to flee the city.

Postbellum Hinds County grew dramatically, reaching 43,958 people (73 percent of them African Americans) in 1880. About half of the county's farmers owned their land, while the rest were renters or sharecroppers. The county employed 206 men and 14 women in industry, a number higher than most in the state but not as large as might be expected for a growing urban area. In 1880 Hinds had the state's second-highest number of foreign-born people, with 501 men and women, mostly from Ireland, Germany, and England.

By 1900 Hinds County's 186 industrial establishments were the most in the state, while its 6,607 farms were second. Its population of 52,577 included almost 40,000 African Americans. For such a large county, Hinds had a relatively small number of foreign-born residents, with Irish, German, and English immigrants making up the majority of the county's 275 nonnatives. As a consequence of the county's large African American majority, Missionary Baptists were the most popular religious group in the 1916 religious census, followed by the Methodist Episcopal Church, South; the Southern Baptist Convention; the Methodist Episcopal Church; the Colored Methodist Episcopal Church; the Catholic Church; and the Presbyterian and Episcopalian churches. Charles P. Jones, a leader of the Church of God in Christ and later of the Church of Christ (Holiness), pastored a church in Jackson in the 1890s and early 1900s.

By the turn of the twentieth century, Jackson was growing in numerous ways. The expansion of government, with new departments and responsibilities, led to the building of the New Capitol, a large and impressive Beaux Arts building designed by Theodore Link that opened in 1903. Farish Street and the surrounding neighborhood became a site for African American business and leadership, with churches, funeral homes, restaurants, and entertainment catering to and mostly run by African Americans.

Hinds County also became a center of the state's educational activity, with numerous offices dealing with public education as well as a large and diverse array of colleges and universities. Tougaloo College, Millsaps College, and Mississippi College have roots in the 1800s and connections to religious institutions. Hinds was also home to many other institutions that are now defunct, among them Mount Herman Seminary near Clinton; Hillman College (a women's college that became part of Mississippi College); the Southern Christian Institute in Edwards; St. Andrew's College in Jackson; Campbell College (a predecessor of Jackson State University); and Utica Normal and Industrial School. The growth of Jackson State University and Hinds Community College expanded educational opportunities, and Jackson State changed from a teachers' college for African American students to a broad-ranging university with numerous

strengths. The University of Mississippi Medical Center opened in Jackson in 1955 and attracted international attention in 1963 and 1964 when surgeon James D. Hardy and his team performed the world's first lung and heart transplants.

Sometimes in partnership with the city's educational institutions, Jackson writers have produced an extraordinary body of work. The importance of books and reading showed in one of the key events of the city's civil rights history, when students from Tougaloo College staged a sit-in at an whites-only library. Eudora Welty was born in Jackson in 1909 and resided there for most of her life. Living near the Belhaven campus and with friends throughout the city, Welty used Jackson and many other Mississippi locations as settings for her work. Richard Wright spent part of his childhood in Jackson and in *Black Boy* memorably detailed frustrations with his education in the city. Margaret Walker Alexander, author of "For My People," *Jubilee*, and many other works, spent much of her professional life teaching at Jackson State University. Playwright Beth Henley was born in Jackson, as were novelist Richard Ford and poets James T. Whitehead, Turner Cassity, John Stone, and John Freeman. John Alfred Williams, a leader of the Black Arts movement, was born in Jackson in 1925, and poet and literary scholar Jerry Ward helped lead a movement of artists connected to Tougaloo College in the 1980s. Barry Hannah grew up in Clinton, attended Mississippi College, and set some of his work there. Poet Sterling Plumpp grew up outside Clinton and moved to Jackson before leaving the state. Novelist Kathryn Stockett grew up in Hinds County and set her best-selling novel, *The Help*, in 1960s Jackson.

Hinds is far less famous for its music scene than are New Orleans, Memphis, and the Mississippi Delta, but the county has been important both as a place to play and record and as the home of numerous notable musicians. Early blues artists such as Charley Patton, Tommy Johnson, and the Chatmon family grew up in rural Hinds, and Patton made his first recordings in Jackson. Farish Street has been the home of extraordinary music of various genres, and record labels Trumpet Records, Ace Records, and Malaco Records started in Jackson. Blues and jazz singer Cassandra Wilson was born in Jackson in 1955, and rap musician David Banner (Levell Crump) is a Jackson native whose lyrics frequently comment on Mississippi issues. Country musician Faith Hill and R&B singer Dorothy Moore also have roots in Hinds. Musicians not affiliated with distinctively southern forms of music also hail from Jackson. Conductor and composer Lehman Engel, born in 1910, grew up in the city, as did innovative contemporary musician Milton Babbitt. Jackson's festivals, concert halls, colleges, and churches have offered settings for a great deal of music, and the Mississippi Mass Choir got its start in the city in 1988.

The state's capital city and largest urban area is also home to one of Mississippi's most active and eclectic settings for the visual arts. The Mississippi Art Association began in 1911

H

to solicit work for the state fair, and its efforts eventually led to the creation of the Mississippi Museum of Art. Painter William Hollingsworth, born in 1910, has been called the Faulkner of Visual Arts because of his range of work about the people of Mississippi. Marie Hull did extraordinary work while teaching from her home in Jackson. Many artists had affiliations with Jackson colleges. While Karl and Mildred Wolfe were establishing the Wolfe Studio, for example, they also taught at Millsaps College. The Mississippi Art Colony has met in Utica since the 1970s, and the Tougaloo Art Colony began operation in 1997. Recent artists with strong Hinds County connections include painters Randy Hayes, Mary Lovelace O'Neal, Lynn Green Root, Laurence Arthur Jones, and Wyatt Waters; sculptor James Seawright; and stained glass artist Andrew Young. Architect N. W. Overstreet and his firm, working in Jackson from the 1910s through the 1960s, helped define the look of the city, creating many modernist buildings of reinforced concrete. The firm's work included the monumental Bailey School (designed by Overstreet and A. H. Town), an Art Deco building with sculptural concrete reliefs of Andrew Jackson and Chief Pushmataha; the Walthall Hotel; and the First National Bank building (now Trustmark).

In 1930, with more than eighty-five thousand people, Hinds County was Mississippi's leading urban center. With about one thousand people per square mile, Hinds had the densest population in the state as well as the most whites and second-most African Americans. Hinds had the second-highest number of industrial workers (more than twenty-five hundred), and it still had more than sixty-six hundred farms. As in most of the state, by 1930 the majority of the county's farmers, black and white, were tenants.

Hinds County's population more than doubled to 187,045 between 1930 and 1960 and grew to 250,998 by 1980, maintaining its standing as most populated county with the highest density. Sixty percent of the population was white, and almost 50 percent had a high school education or more, the highest percentage in the state. Fewer than 4,000 members of the labor force of more than 80,000 were involved in agriculture. Many important Mississippi businesses—among them McRae's Department Stores, the Jitney Jungle groceries, Mississippi Power and Light, and WorldCom—maintained headquarters in Hinds County.

As the state capital, Jackson has been the primary location for Mississippi's media, beginning with the *Eastern Clarion*, predecessor of the *Jackson Clarion-Ledger*. Other newspapers have included or still include the *Jackson Daily News*; the city's leading African American–run newspaper, the *Jackson Advocate*; the Prohibition newspaper *Mississippi White Ribbon*; the civil rights newspaper *Eagle Eye*; the 1960s counterculture publication the *Kudzu*; and the current *Mississippi Magazine* and *Jackson Free Press*. The *Clarion-Ledger* has long had the state's highest newspaper circulation, and its notable journalists and columnists have included Tom Ethridge, Bill Minor, and Jerry Mitchell. Jackson was also home to Mississippi's first and largest television stations and now hosts the state's public television and radio network.

In the 1950s and 1960s, with its combination of a large African American population, key institutions, and inspired and creative leadership, Jackson became one of the centers of the state's civil rights movement. The National Association for the Advancement of Colored People (NAACP) and other groups had operated in Jackson for years, with voting rights work and the development of educational institutions among the most notable efforts. Many more recent protesters attended Tougaloo College, while others came from other colleges, especially Jackson State, and the city's churches, labor and civic groups. In the early 1960s protesters began a series of efforts to integrate all-white libraries, lunch counters, bus stations, other business locations, churches, and public facilities. In 1961 Freedom Riders dramatized transportation segregation and many spent part of the summer in jail. An extended boycott in 1962–63, led primarily by NAACP secretary Medgar Evers, called for an end to racial segregation, and Evers's June 1963 murder demonstrated the lengths to which opponents of civil rights would go. Hinds County is also important because numerous activists who grew up there, including Carpenter's A. M. E. Logan, Terry's Robert C. Smith, Edwards's George Lee, and Jackson's Gladys Noel Bates, Charles McLaurin, Constance Slaughter-Harvey, Colia L. L. Clark, Gilbert Mason, and Henry T. Wingate, among many others.

Jackson was also notable for opposition to civil rights work. While civil rights activists started Womanpower Unlimited to help jailed activists, Jackson was also the home of Women for Constitutional Government, a southern organization that condemned federal efforts to desegregate schools. Jackson was the headquarters of the Citizens' Council and its first school, Citizens' Council School Number 1. While the Jackson Chamber of Commerce called for obeying federal laws requiring desegregation, the Mississippi State Sovereignty Commission, also headquartered in the city, worked to maintain segregation. In 1967 the bombing of the Temple Beth Israel, where Rabbi Perry Nussbaum had criticized racial segregation, demonstrated further divisions in the community.

In recent years, Hinds County has become the center for an expanding institutional base for a multiethnic Mississippi. The Goldring/Woldenberg Institute of Southern Jewish Life began work in Jackson in 1986, continuing the work of the Henry S. Jacobs Camp in Utica. In 1992 some Jackson ministers founded Mission Mississippi to encourage better relations between white and African American Christians, and in 2000 the International Museum of Muslim Cultures opened to encourage study and understanding of that faith. Jackson is home to Mississippi's largest community of Indian immigrants, many of them drawn to the city's computer industry. Festivals celebrating Irish culture, Italian life, and Greek life (building on the city's history of Greek restaurants) are important annual events.

By 1980 the number of Hinds County residents involved in agriculture had declined to less than 1,000. Conversely, the manufacturing workforce continued to grow, reaching 9,450 in 1960 and 15,500 in 1980. Industry in Hinds revolved around the production of furniture, durable goods, and food products. More than 6,500 persons were employed in retail trade, with finance, insurance, and real estate employing another 4,421. Hospitals, public administration, and education were other large employers. In 1980 Hinds boasted the highest personal income, bank deposits, and retail sales in the state and had the second-highest per capita income.

During the second half of the twentieth century Hinds's population increased by about 58,000 people, and between 1980 and 2010, it grew by nearly 70,000, reaching 245,285. The county's racial profile shifted dramatically, as a two-thirds white majority became a two-thirds black majority, a consequence not only of new African American arrivals but also of white flight to neighboring counties. By the second decade of the twenty-first century, small Latino/Hispanic and Asian minorities had emerged in Hinds County as well as in neighboring Madison County.

Mississippi Encyclopedia Staff
University of Mississippi

Mississippi State Planning Commission, *Progress Report on State Planning in Mississippi* (1938); *Mississippi Statistical Abstract*, Mississippi State University (1952–2010); Charles Sydnor and Claude Bennett, *Mississippi History* (1939); University of Virginia Library, Historical Census Browser website, http://mapserver.lib.virginia.edu; E. Nolan Waller and Dani A. Smith, *Growth Profiles of Mississippi's Counties, 1960–1980* (1985).

Hip-Hop

The vibrating bass and jabbing wit of southern hip-hop provide a soundtrack for contemporary life in Mississippi, and young people throughout the state define themselves and their communities through their engagement with a regional hip-hop aesthetic they call the Dirty South. The global hip-hop movement, which includes dance, art, clothing, and musicianship, emerged as a genre of popular music throughout the 1970s and 1980s, but hip-hop is rooted in the practice of rap, a rhythmic form of black poetic speech that has historically been central to the Mississippi cultural landscape. Mississippians have, in turn, contributed important sounds and styles to the development of hip-hop as a global genre. Rather than representing a break with traditional forms of song and speech, the synthesizer riffs and chanting cadence of 'Sip-hop represent the latest version of Mississippi's complex black oral and musical traditions.

Mississippi's best-known commercial hip-hop artists include Jackson's David Banner and DJ Kamikaze (originally of the group Crooked Lettaz), Batesville's Soulja Boy, and Hattiesburg's Afroman. Many Mississippians are involved in national and regional groups and are pioneers in the deep southern hip-hop subgenre of crunk music—a slow, bassy, chanting dance floor production style that reached its commercial apex in the first decade of the twenty-first century. Mississippi artists such as Nate Dogg have brought the gospel-infused sounds of southern rap to the West Coast gangsta aesthetic and influenced hip-hop styles in larger southern cities including Memphis, Atlanta, and New Orleans.

Far from the big-city recording studio or sound stage, however, most Mississippi artists prefer a kind of improvisatory hip-hop poetry called freestyle, a practice of poetic improvisation and rhythmic vocal play that emerges in the living rooms and on street corners of everyday creative community life. This poetry can be accompanied by an oral technique called beatboxing, which uses the mouth and breath to mimic drum sounds, improvised over instrumental versions of popular hip-hop songs, or "spit" in a rapid-fire a capella that recalls a host of Mississippi oral-musical styles. The freestyle artist must show a deep knowledge of hip-hop slang and lyrics while improvising new commentaries on the situation at hand.

The deep-rooted Mississippi blues are perhaps the strongest strain present in current regional pop styles; the improvised, spoken-word blues boasts of artists such as Muddy Waters, Howlin' Wolf, and Koko Taylor portray the themes of physical prowess, vocal strength, and masterful wordplay that anchor 'Sip-hop today. Further, the bass-heavy sounds and rhythmic interplay of the Mississippi blues are echoed in the deep sounds of crunk music. Classic rapping blues artists such as Ike Turner and Early Wright can still be found in clubs and locally owned radio stations in the region. These Mississippi mainstays not only weave verbal riffs, shout-outs, song lyrics, and poetic fragments into their performance but also juggle multiple records or CDs on their equipment, cutting and mixing in a down-home version of hip-hop's scratching, remixing and MC-ing techniques. In Mississippi today, many local radio stations feature hip-hop DJs who talk to callers, announce community events, and encourage listeners to dance over the sounds of remixed hip-hop records. They also feature home recordings of local hip-hop artists in their musical mixes and host on-air freestyle battles.

Although conventional hip-hop histories place the genesis of hip-hop on the East Coast in the mid-1970s and the movement itself was named and organized by New York artist Afrika Bambaataa, the poetic, musical, and stylistic techniques of hip-hop have been firmly rooted in the American South for centuries. Many hip-hop researchers recognize the importance of an African American insult-trading practice called the dozens (typically an exchange of improvised "yo' mama" jokes) in the formation of early rap styles, particularly in the practice of rap battling, in which two rappers trade poetic boasts and insults with coolness and wit. Hip-hop also draws from the barroom toasts, or long epic poems involving an unlikely hero outwitting oppressive opponents; these include tales drawn from African proverbs such as the Signifying Monkey and tales of plantation rebels or badmen such as Railroad Bill. The prison work songs and levee hollers documented by folklorists John W. Work, Alan Lomax, and William Ferris also underline the chugging call-and-response, sparse rhythms, and droning sound of Mississippi crunk styles.

These hip-hop roots continue to thrive throughout Mississippi today, as kids weave popular rap lyrics into their schoolyard dozens games and young people underline their hip-hop performances with story lines drawn from the classic badmen toasts. Collaborations between blues musicians and rappers, gospel singers, and hip-hop producers are common. Many Mississippi clubs feature classic blues, southern soul, R&B, pop, and hip-hop in a single Saturday-night mix, and older club patrons are often familiar with emerging hip-hop dances. Children create homemade Internet videos in which they parody the lyrics of a popular hip-hop song to represent their community and state.

Although the most recognized commercial practitioners of 'Sip-hop are young men, women are critical to the local hip-hop movement in a number of ways, both as artists and less visibly through family and religious traditions. Many women in Mississippi cultivate a poetic talent and stage dramatic readings at family reunions and community gatherings; young rappers often learn the skills of rhyme and elocution in this setting. Gospel preaching and song, particularly with the African American Holiness and Church of God in Christ churches of the region, infuses 'Sip-hop with its signature rich vocals and biblical phrasing. Much Mississippi hip-hop is religious in nature, and performances often take place inside the church. Mississippi's rich African American rhythmic, musical, spiritual, and poetic heritage continues to nourish new global movements in music.

Ali Colleen Neff

Virginia Tech

Roger D. Abrahams, *Singing the Master: The Emergence of African American Culture in the Plantation South* (1992); William Ferris, *Blues from the Delta* (1979); Murray Forman and Mark Anthony Neal, eds., *That's the Joint! A Hip-Hop Studies Reader* (2004); Ali Colleen Neff, *Let the World Listen Right: The Mississippi Delta Hip-Hop Story* (2009); John Wesley Work, Lewis Wade Jones, and Samuel C. Adams Jr., *Lost Delta Found: Rediscovering the Fisk University–Library of Congress Coahoma County Study, 1941–1942*, ed. Robert Gordon and Bruce Nemerov (2005).

Historic Preservation

Historic preservation in Mississippi began in the prehistoric era with the continual care of ceremonial mounds by native Mississippians. Contemporary preservation is still best seen though stewardship of the historic environment by individuals and the public sector.

In 1899 the Vicksburg Military Park was established when the federal government set aside almost eighteen hundred acres to commemorate the Civil War Battle and Siege of Vicksburg. Civil War battlefield preservation remains an important component of historic preservation, with continued involvement by governmental entities with important partners from the private sector.

Natchez is one of the state's oldest and historically wealthiest regions and possesses some of its finest early architecture. Economic hardships in the area, beginning after the Civil War and continuing through the Depression, affected many homeowners' ability to maintain these large architectural treasures. Several iconic homes were in danger of being lost in 1932, when the women of the Natchez Garden Club established the nation's second-oldest home tour. The profits of the Natchez Pilgrimage have been continuously used to restore some of Natchez's most endangered buildings.

With the 1936 publication of *Gone with the Wind* and the upcoming centennial of the Civil War, interest in antebellum architecture increased. New industries were coming to Natchez, and the city began to suffer from some of the schizophrenic traits affecting most of the New South—reverence for the past and a mania to modernize. In 1951 a master plan designated a small, one-block-wide, U-shaped residential historic district that wrapped around three sides of the downtown. In 1952 a weak city ordinance was passed requiring the City Planning Commission to review plans for exterior alteration in the small district. This measure was the nation's third ordinance that granted the local government the right to protect the historic architecture for the common good of the public.

Recognition of the destructive effects of massive federal projects conceived and executed with little or no regard for historic properties led Congress to enact the National Historic Preservation Act of 1966. This legislation established a coordinated governmental historic preservation program to be administered by the federal and state governments through state historic preservation offices—in this case, the National Park Service and the Mississippi Department of Archives and History (MDAH). Created in 1902, MDAH is the second-oldest state archives in the nation. The Historic Preservation Division was established to help lessen the destructiveness of federal programs by having historians and archaeologists review these programs at the state level.

The National Register of Historic Places was created to serve as a master list of those properties that had been recognized by the federal government as being historically significant and especially worthy of preservation.

During the early history of the National Register program in Mississippi, architectural historians and archaeologists looked only at buildings and sites that had national significance, such as the site of the Treaty of Dancing Rabbit Creek, Beauvoir, Rowan Oak, and the I. T. Montgomery House. In 1972, however, the Natchez Bluffs and Under-the-Hill Historic District became the first historic district to be listed, signaling a move toward recognizing the importance of neighborhoods and commercial districts in addition to individual buildings and sites.

In the 1970s interest in historic preservation experienced a resurgence as the nation began to prepare for the Bicentennial, and historical societies and civic organizations targeted buildings in their community for preservation. Citizens formed several local nonprofit organizations—among them the Woodville Civic Club, the Historic Natchez Foundation, and the Vicksburg Foundation for Historic Preservation—and they continue to lead the preservation movement at the local level.

The Mississippi Landmark program was established in 1970 to protect historic properties against changes that might alter their historic character. The program primarily protects public buildings, although some individuals have requested Mississippi Landmark status to ensure the perpetual preservation of their historic private property. Through this program and subsequent grant programs administered by MDAH, a number of courthouses, city halls, university buildings, and local history museums have been restored.

Amendments to the National Preservation Act have strengthened the federal-state-local government partnership to foster individual investment in preservation. Since 1976 the Federal Investment Tax Credit program has encouraged reinvestment in historic neighborhoods and districts and emphasized the importance of the National Register. A 1986 amendment to the National Historic Preservation Act established the Certified Local Government program to provide grants and technical assistance to enable communities to add a preservation component to their planning process. Only a handful of communities previously had the local expertise to implement a local preservation program; however, the technical assistance provided through the Certified Local Government program has allowed the number of preservation programs in the state to grow as more cities and towns pass preservation ordinances to protect the historic buildings that define their community.

The Mississippi Main Street Association is an economic development program based in historic preservation. The association has facilitated the economic revitalization of historic downtown districts through an incremental and comprehensive community-driven process that looks at organization, promotion, design, and economic restructuring.

The Mississippi Heritage Trust was established in 1992 as the nonprofit, statewide voice for historic preservation. The trust has raised public awareness of the importance of Mississippi's historic resources and worked to preserve the irreplaceable throughout a variety of preservation programs.

In the early twenty-first century, the historic buildings, landscapes, and sites that define Mississippians are being recognized as important touchstones. Public and private investment in the protection of these places remains important to the local and state economy. Historic preservation in Mississippi has become a major planning tool, a large component of the tourism industry, an important part of the construction industry, and a defining element in communities throughout the state.

Michelle Jones
Mississippi Department of
Archives and History

Diane L. Barthel, *Historic Preservation: Collective Memory and Historical Identity* (1996); James M. Fitch, *Historic Preservation: Curatorial Management of the Built World* (1990); Mississippi Department of Archives and History, Historic Preservation Division, website, http://mdah.state.ms.us/hpres/; Norman Tyler, *Historic Preservation: An Introduction to Its History, Principles, and Practice* (1999).

History Textbooks and Race

Historically, Mississippi schoolchildren have read from state history textbooks featuring tone, content, and perspective that reflected contemporary racial conditions in larger society. For much of the twentieth century, a white-supremacist narrative defined these textbooks, but an alternative narrative arose during the era of civil rights in the 1960s and 1970s to challenge that version of events.

The first state history texts were written by white Mississippians at a time when Civil War veterans still walked the streets and when memories of Reconstruction remained fresh. The United Daughters of the Confederacy, the Daughters of the American Revolution, the American Legion, and later the Citizens' Council screened textbooks to ensure that they upheld the principles of the Lost Cause, southern pride, states' rights, and white cultural superiority while avoiding suggestions of black autonomy and discontent. Working in cooperation with the state textbook ratings committee (created in the 1940s) and the state superintendent of schools, these organizations set forth an ideologically pure agenda not only to teach "correct, fair, and unbiased" facts, as the United Daughters of the Confederacy put it, but also to instill the values of white culture, principles of good citizenship and patriotism, and a faith in the racial hierarchy.

One early textbook that met these standards and that was used by teachers in both black and white classrooms was *History of Mississippi: A School Reader*, written by Mabel B. Fant and John C. Fant and published by the Mississippi Publishing Company in 1927. It advanced a mythic southernized version of history constructed around a narrative that was selective rather than comprehensive. Whites were regarded with the nomenclature *Mississippian* and inclusive pronouns (*we, us*), while blacks (and Indians) were characterized with exclusionary pronouns (*they, them*). From this perspective, whites were the true history makers, while blacks were shunted to the margins. Readers were led to believe that except during the unfortunate period of Reconstruction, harmony and goodwill prevailed between the races.

Published in 1935, Pearl Guyton's *The History of Mississippi: From Indian Times to the Present Day* followed the Fant formula. Guyton portrayed slavery as a benign institution of uplift for African savages and Reconstruction as a benighted era of black supremacy, ineptness, and corruption. Her heroes were a noble Ku Klux Klan that rescued the South from the scourge of Yankee carpetbaggers, southern white scalawags, and deluded blacks. When all was over, "the hard feelings that existed between the blacks and whites during reconstruction times gave way to understanding and cooperation."

Guyton's book remained an approved text until it went out of print in the 1960s. By then, *Mississippi: Yesterday and Today*, by John K. Bettersworth, became the standard in classrooms, and it was the only option available in the late 1960s and 1970s. Bettersworth refrained from the romanticism and pathos that characterized his predecessors' books, but he, too, ignored the historical contributions of blacks, offered a traditional interpretation of Reconstruction, and portrayed Gov. Ross Barnett—a rabid white supremacist—as a defender of constitutional government.

The first challenge to the segregationist narrative came in 1974 with the publication of *Mississippi: Conflict and Change*, by James Loewen, Charles Sallis, and other authors, black and white. Unabashed in its criticism of Mississippi's racial past, the book recognized the historical agency of blacks and debunked the myth of harmonious race relations. It also dealt with other issues previously considered too controversial for a textbook: poverty, lynching, labor unrest, and white political corruption. Although the book captured the prestigious Lillian Smith Award, given by the Southern Regional Council to recognize authors whose books represent "outstanding creative achievements which demonstrate through literary merit and moral vision an honest representation of the South, its people, its problems, and its promises," Mississippi's textbook commission refused to approve the volume for classroom use. With the aid of the National Association for the Advancement of Colored People, the authors sued, and in 1980 a US district court ordered the state to approve the textbook. Other books with more balanced interpretations of Mississippi's racial past were then introduced, giving school districts a broad selection of state history textbooks with more comprehensive and inclusive narratives.

Jack E. Davis
University of Florida

Jack E. Davis, *Race against Time: Culture and Separation in Natchez since 1930* (2001); Georgia Center for the Book website, www.georgiacenterforthebook.org.

Hog Production

Mississippi is not famous for hogs, but hogs and pork have long had considerable importance in the state's history. An early breed of hog descended from the era of Spanish explorers is called the Choctaw hog. Once fairly common in Mississippi, the only remaining Choctaw hogs live among Native American nations in Oklahoma.

The hog was justly famous as one of the two food sources of the southern yeomanry in the nineteenth century. (Corn was the other.) The idea of living high on the hog from branded hogs that more or less fed themselves running free on open range was part of a yeoman ideal. Hogs were common in most areas of antebellum Mississippi: in 1840 the state had almost three hogs per person, and by 1860 there were slightly less than two hogs per person. The number of hogs per person was highest in the Piney Woods, where Greene County residents had six hogs per person, and in central Mississippi, where Leake County residents averaged seven hogs per individual. The rest of the state averaged about two hogs per person, except in the Mississippi River counties, where hogs were far more unusual. Adams County, home of the state's greatest cotton and slave wealth as well as its largest urban population, had by far the fewest hogs per person.

In the postbellum period, hog production slowly and steadily declined until the 1920s, when the drop became precipitous. Scholars generally attribute the decline of hog farming to a rise in production for national and international markets, often generated by debt and the demands of landlords who wanted farming people to produce cotton for a market and not pork for themselves. The 1880 census was the last in which Mississippi had more hogs (1,151,000) than people (1,131,000), and through the 1920s the total number of hogs in the state decreased from 1,300,000 to 730,000. Hogs increasingly were penned and fed rather than allowed to run free to feed themselves.

Richard Wright described his "speechless astonishment" at "seeing a hog stabbed through the heart" in the Mississippi of his youth, and Anne Moody memorably wrote that too many African Americans were "just shot and butchered like hogs." William Faulkner put hogs and especially hog trading in several of his stories, perhaps most notably "Barn Burning." Eudora Welty photographed "Pigs and Laundry on Farish Street" in Jackson in the 1930s. Mississippi has never had a distinctive or famous style of pork barbecue, but barbecue has a long history in the state.

The 2012 agricultural census counted 401,898 hogs. In recent years, raising hogs ceased to be the province of small family farms and has instead become an industrial process. In 1980 Mississippi had more than twenty thousand operations, a number that declined to one thousand by 2006. Many of the state's hogs are now raised at industrial hog facilities known as confined animal feeding operations (CAFOs), where large numbers of hogs are raised in small spaces.

Economic losses in pork production in 1998 drove many of Mississippi's independent producers out of business or increased their risk of losing their family-run operations. This economic loss was an incentive for out-of-state hog corporations to bring industrial swine production to Mississippi. The new trend of large-scale production involves a high density of hogs grown in confinement houses and producing vast amounts of waste. The hog waste is collected and stored in "lagoons"—open pits in the ground where the waste is broken down by microbes. The liquid from the hog waste is later sprayed onto fields as fertilizer. This system introduces several problems for human health and environmental quality. Toxic gases, chemicals, and pollutants can cause health problems for individuals who work in the confinement houses. In addition, residents who live close to the operations may have adverse health effects such as irritation to their eyes, noses, and throats; headaches; vomiting; decrease in proper lung functioning; negative impacts on their immune systems; respiratory ailments; and a decrease in the overall quality of life in communities that neighbor CAFOs.

The number of large-scale packers across the South has declined rapidly. Bryan Foods was the last in Mississippi, but the plant closed its doors in 2007, putting around 1,200 employees out of work.

Sacoby M. Wilson
University of South Carolina

Iowa State University and the University of Iowa Study Group, *Iowa Concentrated Animal Feeding Operations Air Quality Study, Final Report* (2003), www.public-health.uiowa.edu/ehsrc/CAFOstudy.htm; National Research Council, *The Scientific Basis for Estimating Air Emissions from Animal Feeding Operations* (2002); Sacoby M. Wilson, F. Howell, S. Wing, and M. Sobsey, *Environmental Health Perspectives Supplement* (2002); S. Wing, G. Grant, and D. Cole, *Environmental Health Perspectives* (2000); S. Wing and S. Wolf, *Environmental Health Perspectives* (2000).

Holland, Endesha Ida Mae
(1944–2006) Playwright and Activist

Endesha Ida Mae Holland was an activist, educator, and playwright. Ida Mae Holland (she added Endesha as an adult) was born on 29 August 1944 in Greenwood to midwife Ida Mae Holland and grew up with three older siblings, Simon Jr., Bud, and Jean. Holland's childhood reflected the prevailing racism encountered by African Americans living in the South. She and her family worked seasonally in the cotton fields of Leflore County, the same county where fourteen-year-old Emmett Till was murdered on the day before Holland's eleventh birthday. Less than a year later a white man raped her.

At age thirteen she was compelled to quit school and find employment to help provide for her mother and siblings. Over the next several years she worked as a prostitute and served time on a prison farm for shoplifting. Holland gave birth to her only child, Cedric, in 1961, only months after being released from the prison farm. She married Cedric's father, Ike, in 1963 and divorced in 1966. Holland later married and divorced two more times.

After a chance encounter with Bob Moses in 1962, Holland gave up prostitution and devoted herself to the civil rights movement as a volunteer for the Student Nonviolent Coordinating Committee in Greenwood. From 1962 to 1965 Holland traveled extensively, promoting civil rights outside of the South. She was arrested on several occasions as a result of her activities and became the target of violence when her Greenwood home was firebombed in 1965. Her mother burned to death in the flames.

Five months later, Holland left Mississippi and traveled north. Through the help of activist friends, she enrolled at the University of Minnesota, where she studied playwriting and remained active in black issues. She also helped establish the school's African American studies program and founded Women Helping Offenders, a program designed to provide aid to women in prison. Holland ultimately earned bachelor's, master's, and doctoral degrees from the university and became a professor of American studies and women's studies at the State University of New York at Buffalo. She later worked at the University of Southern California in Los Angeles as a playwright in residence and a professor.

In 1981 Holland's *The Second Doctor Lady* won the New York Drama Critics' Circle's Lorraine Hansberry Award for Best Play. Holland revised the play into an autobiographical two-act drama, *From the Mississippi Delta*, that was produced in London and Off-Broadway in 1991. The play includes some of the more harrowing incidents from Holland's life, including her rape, and has been acknowledged as an intense and inspirational work. Commenting on the dramatization of her life and her triumph over poverty and abuse, Holland declared that today's "young people need to know that they can do wrong things and yet still change and grow." In 1997 Holland published *From the Mississippi Delta* (1997) as a memoir.

On 18 October 1991 Greenwood declared Dr. Endesha Ida Mae Holland Day to celebrate her contributions to the city's culture and history. She died in 2006 from complications of a degenerative neurological disease.

Frances Abbott
University of Alabama

Margalit Fox, *New York Times* (1 February 2006); Gale Group, *Contemporary Black Biography*, vol. 3 (1992); Gale Group, *Contemporary Theatre, Film, and Television*, vol. 11 (1993); Mississippi Writers and Musicians website, www.mswritersandmusicians.com/.

Hollingsworth, William

(1910–1944) Artist

William Robert "Hollie" Hollingsworth Jr. was one of Mississippi's most productive artists of the 1930s and 1940s. His ability to capture the regional landscape and people of Mississippi in his sketches, oil paintings, and watercolors led him to be known as the Faulkner of Visual Arts. Along with his contemporary, Eudora Welty, whom he had known since childhood, Hollingsworth played an integral part in elevating the perception of the arts in his home state.

Hollingsworth was born on 17 February 1910 in the house on Jackson's President Street where his parents and thirteen-year-old sister, Isabel, lived. His mother, Willie Belle Van Zile Hollingsworth, herself a watercolorist, died when the boy was not quite a year old, forcing his father, William Robert Hollingsworth Sr., to the forefront of young William's life. The elder Hollingsworth became a partner in Hollingsworth and Tyson Real Estate and Rental Agents, working alongside his son-in-law, Fred A. Tyson. Among the firm's most significant contributions was the development of Jackson's Belhaven neighborhood.

The young Hollingsworth was keenly aware of the activities and the people in his downtown Jackson neighborhood; later in life he expanded on these early observations. The black community along Jackson's Farish Street provided the inspiration for much of his art, as in his oil painting *High Farish* (1941) and his watercolor *Sudden Shower* (1937).

Hollingsworth graduated from Jackson High School in 1928. He studied at the University of Mississippi and the School of the Art Institute of Chicago, graduating in 1934. He married fellow student Celia Jane Oakley in 1932, and the two had a son, William Robert Hollingsworth III, in 1933. The family returned to Jackson after Hollingsworth was unable to find work in Chicago, and he began work as a clerk with the Federal Emergency Relief Agency. He held this position for four years, until the agency was disbanded, and then focused on earning a living as a working artist.

Hollingsworth began to receive recognition for his artwork in the mid-1930s, when his paintings *Vagabond's Respite* and *Tired, Oh Lord, Tired* won awards from the Mississippi Art Association. In 1937 he won the William Tuthill Prize from the Art Institute of Chicago for his work *Siesta*.

In 1941 Hollingsworth played a key role in the establishment of the Millsaps College Art Department, where he worked as an art instructor alongside his friend, fellow Mississippi artist Karl Wolfe. Throughout this time Hollingsworth suffered from varying degrees of depression as he worried about his family's finances, his father's ailing health, and the destruction brought on by World War II. Hollingsworth enlisted in the US Navy in 1942 but was released after only two weeks because of his poor eyesight. Crestfallen, he came back to Mississippi, where his depression deepened and he developed alcoholism. The following year saw the realization of one of Hollingsworth's greatest fears, the death of his father, further increasing his depression, although his work continued to garner praise and awards.

On 1 August 1944 Hollingsworth took his own life. The Mississippi Museum of Art's permanent collection now contains more than three hundred of his works.

Linda Arrington Lusk
University of Mississippi

René Paul Barilleux, ed., *Passionate Observer: Eudora Welty among Artists of the Thirties* (2002); Jane Oakley Hollingsworth and O. C. McDavid, eds., *Hollingsworth: The Man, the Artist, and His Work* (1981); Mississippi History Now website, http://mshistory.k12.ms.us; St. Joseph Abbey website, www.saintjosephabbey.com.

Holmes, David

(1769–1820) First and Fifth Governor, 1817–1820, 1826

When the constitutional convention met in July 1817 to draft Mississippi's first constitution, David Holmes was named president of the convention and was subsequently elected without opposition as the state's first governor. Holmes had served as territorial governor for several years, and his election facilitated Mississippi's transition from territorial status to statehood.

Holmes was born in York County, Pennsylvania, on 10 March 1769, and moved with his family to Virginia when he was very young. In 1797 he was elected to represent the state in the US Congress, and he remained in office until 1809, when he was appointed governor of the Mississippi Territory. Holmes was a popular choice for governor, and his appointment marked the end of a long period of bitter factionalism in the territory. During his administration the territorial capital was located at Washington, a small town six miles east of Natchez.

Holmes directed the territory during very difficult times. Border incidents with Spanish adventurers below the thirty-first parallel sparked frequent violence along Mississippi's southern frontier, and the War of 1812 incited numerous Indian raids in the eastern half of the territory.

The Mississippi Territory grew rapidly after the war and by 1817 had reached the population required for statehood. Holmes was inaugurated as governor on 7 October 1817 at Natchez, the new state capital, and Mississippi was formally granted statehood on 10 December. Under Mississippi's first constitution the governor served a two-year term and was allowed to succeed himself. During Holmes's first administration the judicial system was established and the state's judges were appointed, the legislature was organized, the militia was created, and the Choctaw Indian land cession east of the Pearl River was organized.

Holmes did not seek reelection in 1819, and the following year the state legislature appointed him to the US Senate, where he served until he was again elected governor in 1825, receiving nearly 90 percent of the vote. Holmes's health soon began to fail, however, and he resigned on 25 July 1826. His eleven years and one month as territorial and state governor ranks him second among Mississippi's chief executives.

Holmes subsequently returned to Virginia, where his health continued to decline until his death on 28 August 1832. Holmes County was named in his honor.

David G. Sansing
University of Mississippi

Biographical Directory of the United States Congress (1950); *Mississippi Official and Statistical Register* (1912); Dunbar Rowland, *Encyclopedia of Mississippi History*, vol. 1 (1907).

Holmes, Verner Smith

(1909–2000) Physician and Educator

A physician from McComb, Verner Smith Holmes was appointed to the Board of Trustees of the Mississippi Institutions of Higher Learning in 1956. During his twenty-four years on the board, Holmes consistently opposed efforts to use higher education for purposes that were purely political or white supremacist. Holmes faced criticism for those efforts but was the only person ever appointed to serve two terms.

Holmes was born on 10 July 1909 in Walthall County. He attended Mississippi College and the University of Mississippi before earning a medical degree from Tulane University. He served in the US Army's Medical Corps from 1942 to 1945 and then returned to his home state and began practicing as an otolaryngologist in McComb.

After his appointment to the Board of Trustees of the Mississippi Institutions of Higher Learning, Holmes opposed white supremacists' efforts to defy the federal government and prevent the integration of the University of Mississippi and other universities. He was one of the few board members to urge compliance with federal court rulings requiring desegregation and was the only member to vote against the board's September 1962 decision to transfer authority for dealing with the issue of integrating the University of Mississippi to Gov. Ross Barnett. When the board finally realized that the full force of the federal government stood behind the desegregation effort and voted unanimously to enroll James Meredith, Holmes was excoriated for the position he had held throughout the controversy.

Other issues of race and reputation were important to Holmes. He voted to allow sports teams at Mississippi universities to play in athletic events that involved African American athletes. In response, opponents burned a cross at a hunting lodge Holmes used on the Bogue Chitto River. Rejecting the speaker bans some universities instituted during controversies of the 1950s and 1960s, he also spoke up for the right of colleges and universities to invite whatever speakers they wanted to their campuses.

Holmes was an important influence in the development of the University of Mississippi Medical Center in Jackson, which opened the Verner Smith Holmes Learning Resource Center in 1982. Holmes died in 2000.

Ted Ownby
University of Mississippi

Find a Grave website, www.findagrave.com; Verner Smith Holmes Papers, Department of Archives and Special Collections, J. D. Williams Library, University of Mississippi; *Journal of the Mississippi State Medical Association* (July 2000); David Sansing, *Making Haste Slowly: The Troubled History of Higher Education in Mississippi* (1990).

Holmes County

Holmes County, created in 1833 from part of Yazoo County and located in central Mississippi, was named for former governor David Holmes. Notable features in Holmes County include Tchula Lake and the Hillside National Wildlife Refuge, Mathews Brake National Wildlife Refuge, Morgan Brake National Wildlife Refuge, and Theodore Roosevelt National Wildlife Refuge. The county is also home to Holmes County State Park. The county seat is Lexington, and other towns include Durant, Goodman, and Pickens.

In 1840 the county had a population of 5,566 slaves and 3,886 free people. By 1860 the slave population had grown to 11,975, more than twice the free population of 5,816. The county was a leading producer of cotton (ninth among counties in the state), was sixth in the value of its livestock, and ranked twelfth in growing corn. In 1860 only 41 residents worked in manufacturing. Of the fourteen churches in Holmes in 1840, eight were Methodist, three were Presbyterian, two were Baptist, and one was Episcopalian.

Holmes County grew rapidly in the postbellum period, as numerous migrants came to farm the rich Delta land. The African American population almost doubled to 20,233 in 1880, while the white population grew by only 1,000. But population expansion did not mean the growth of farm-owning prosperity—almost half of Holmes County's farmers worked as sharecroppers, and the county had only 45 industrial workers.

By 1900 Holmes had a population of 36,838, including more than 28,000 African Americans. The area remained agricultural, with more than 5,000 farms. Whereas 57 percent of the 1,000 white farmers owned their own land, only 12 percent of African American farmers did so, meaning that the county had more than 3,400 black tenant farmers and sharecroppers. Holmes County employed 214 industrial workers, all but 4 of them men. Durant was home to an active Colored Farmers' Alliance, and the county's superintendent of schools, William Hall Smith, started Mississippi's first Corn Clubs, the precursors to 4-H Clubs. The Order of the Eastern Star, a women's Masonic organization, claimed Holmes County's Eureka Masonic College (known as the Little Red Schoolhouse) as its birthplace. Edmond F. Noel, the thirty-seventh governor of Mississippi, was from Holmes County.

As in many counties with African American majorities, Missionary Baptists dominated the religious landscape, with more than three times as many as the Methodists, Baptists, and Presbyterians who called the county home. Holmes County was also important in the history of the Church of God in Christ, a holiness group. In 1897 minister and denominational founder Charles Harrison Mason led a Lexington revival that formed the basis for the group's first church. In the 1920s Illinois native Arenia Mallory moved to Holmes

County, where she founded Saints Industrial and Literary School as a Church of God institution; she served as its principal for more than fifty years. In the 1930s the Mississippi Health Project, a program originated by the Alpha Kappa Alpha sorority, began at the Saints school.

From 1900 to 1930 the population changed very little, although the rate of farm ownership decreased, so that 89 percent of African American farmers and 64 percent of white farmers were now tenants or sharecroppers. The industrial population grew to 639, although the county remained primarily agricultural. Two experimental agricultural communities, Providence Farm and Mileston, began in the late 1930s and 1940s to address farmworkers' problems. Providence Farm included a substantial Southern Tenant Farmers' Union.

Holmes County was the birthplace to several scholars interested in the history and culture of Mississippi and the South. John A. Lomax was born near Goodman in 1867 before moving to Texas. Lomax was a folklorist and musicologist famous for collecting American music, including the music of rural African Americans. Historian David Herbert Donald, known for his scholarship on Abraham Lincoln, was also born in Goodman. Tchula native Chalmers Archer Jr., an author and educator born in 1938, described his upbringing in *Growing Up Black in Rural Mississippi*. Other notable natives of Holmes County include blues musicians Lester Davenport, Jimmy Dawkins, and Lonnie Pitchford as well as Monroe Saffold Jr., who won the Amateur Athletic Union's US masters'-level bodybuilding championship in 1990.

By 1960 Holmes County's population had decreased to 27,096, with African Americans holding a 71 percent majority. Almost half of the 1960 workforce was still involved in the agricultural production of cotton, soybeans, oats, and livestock, but agricultural employment dropped to less than 8 percent by 1980. In that year Holmes had a small but growing manufacturing sector that concentrated on furniture and apparel.

The Holmes County civil rights movement grew in part from organized community efforts at Mileston. Beginning in 1963 a group of local activists including Hartman Turnbow joined with Student Nonviolent Coordinating Committee organizers to make sustained efforts to register African Americans to vote. Just four years later, Holmes County schoolteacher Robert Clark became the first African American elected to the Mississippi House of Representatives since Reconstruction. Hazel Brannon Smith, the white editor of the *Durant News* and *Lexington Advertiser*, never officially joined the movement but consistently wrote articles condemning racial violence. In 1964 Smith became the first woman to win the Pulitzer Prize for editorial writing.

As in many Delta counties in Mississippi, Holmes County's population was predominantly African American and decreased overall during the last half of the twentieth century. The 2010 population of 19,198 represented a drop of

29 percent (7,898) since 1960 and was 83.4 percent African American and 15.6 percent white. In recent years Holmes County has consistently had one of Mississippi's highest poverty rates, topping 40 percent.

Mississippi Encyclopedia Staff
University of Mississippi

Mississippi State Planning Commission, *Progress Report on State Planning in Mississippi* (1938); *Mississippi Statistical Abstract*, Mississippi State University (1952–2010); Charles Sydnor and Claude Bennett, *Mississippi History* (1939); University of Virginia Library, Historical Census Browser website, http://mapserver.lib.virginia.edu; E. Nolan Waller and Dani A. Smith, *Growth Profiles of Mississippi's Counties, 1960–1980* (1985).

Holmes County Civil Rights Movement

The seeds for the emergence of the civil rights movement in Holmes County were planted during the Great Depression. The federal government, through the Farm Security Administration, bought five foreclosed plantations in the county as part of the effort to turn poor tenants and sharecroppers into landowners. The agency divided these ninety-five hundred acres into more than one hundred farms, all of which contained at least sixty acres. The original tenants received the land, a home, and all the tools, equipment, and mules needed to be independent farmers. After five years, those who continued on the farms received low-interest, long-term mortgages. The landowning blacks in this community, Mileston, had their own cooperative cotton gin and mercantile store. They shared tools with each other and swapped labor. Mileston farmers developed a sense of pride and independence through owning land and being relatively free from the interference and control of whites.

In late 1962 student workers from the Student Nonviolent Coordinating Committee (SNCC) sought to establish contacts in the county of Leflore and the city of Greenwood, thirty miles north of Mileston. Some Mileston residents, among them Annie Mitchell Carnegie and her brother, Ozell Mitchell, had secretly been involved with the National Association for the Advancement of Colored People (NAACP) and other groups. They and other Mileston blacks asked SNCC workers to come to Mileston, and by the spring of 1963, SNCC workers were conducting a citizenship school at the church of Rev. J. J. Russell, concentrating on lessons about interpreting sections of the state constitution, a part of the literacy test required for registration.

On 9 April 1963, fourteen African Americans from Mileston made their way to the county seat of Lexington to register.

Word had leaked out about their coming, and a group consisting of the deputy sheriff, his deputies, thirty auxiliary policemen, and other white officials stood in front of the courthouse, attempting to intimidate the farmers and deter them from registering. Led by Hartman Turnbow, all fourteen took the literacy test over the next two days, but all failed.

A month later white night riders firebombed Turnbow's home and fired shots at him. A key component of the Holmes County movement was that its participants believed in self-defense: Turnbow returned fire, and his assailants fled. The Mileston community stood firm and began holding mass meetings to drum up support. Turnbow and others traveled across the county and rallied other blacks.

Landownership played a key role in the early part of the movement. The Mileston farmers and other landowning blacks had the economic independence to weather white oppression. With the exceptions of teacher Bernice Montgomery and Rev. Russell, most educators and ministers did not join the early movement because they depended on whites for their livelihoods.

Holmes County activists took part in some of the central moments of the Mississippi civil rights movement. They played a major role in the Mississippi Freedom Democratic Party, which challenged the seating of the all-white Mississippi delegation at the 1964 Democratic National Convention. The Holmes County movement benefited from the influx of northern students during the Freedom Summer of 1964 as well as from the passage of the federal Civil Rights Act of 1964 and Voting Rights Act of 1965. By the mid-1960s Holmes County activists pushed not only for the vote but also for the integration of all public facilities, launching a selective-buying campaign that eventually forced white merchants and politicians in Lexington to acquiesce to many of the demands. The dedication and intensity of the Holmes County activists efforts paid off in 1968. Robert Clark, a teacher from the small hamlet of Ebenezer, became the first African American elected to the Mississippi state legislature since the 1890s.

Jeffery B. Howell
Mississippi State University

Kenneth A. Andrews, *Freedom Is a Constant Struggle: The Mississippi Civil Rights Movement and Its Legacy* (2004); John Dittmer, *Local People: The Struggle for Civil Rights in Mississippi* (1995); Jay MacLeod, in *Minds Stayed on Freedom: The Civil Rights Struggle in the Rural South* (1991); Charles M. Payne, *I've Got the Light of Freedom: The Organizing Tradition and the Mississippi Freedom Struggle* (2007); Susan Lorenzi Sojourner, Civil Rights Movement Veterans website, www.crmvet.org.

H

Holtzclaw, William Henry

(1870–1943) Educator and Author

William Henry Holtzclaw, a student and follower of Booker T. Washington, was the founder and leader of Utica Normal and Industrial School for the Training of Colored Young Men and Women. In 1915 Holtzclaw published his autobiography, *The Black Man's Burden*.

Born into a poor family of former slaves in Alabama in 1870, Holtzclaw went to Tuskegee Institute in 1890. Impressed and influenced by Booker T. Washington's doctrines of hard work, agricultural science, and high moral character, Holtzclaw left school ready to take the Tuskegee model to other parts of the South. After marrying fellow Tuskegee student Mary Ella Patterson and teaching briefly in Snow Hill, Alabama, he moved to Mississippi.

In 1902 he worked to organize a small public school, but he soon began raising money and organizing construction workers to build the private school that became Utica Normal and Industrial School. Following the Tuskegee model, Holtzclaw wanted students to work as part of their tuition, and he also relied on the Tuskegee model to attract fund-raisers, with support from both benefactors within Mississippi and distant philanthropists such as Andrew Carnegie and publisher F. A. Ginn. The school's offerings included teaching, agriculture, printing, carpentry, construction, steam and electrical engineering, and dressmaking. In debates about whether African American education should emphasize practical job training or more academic subjects, Holtzclaw emphasized the former.

As part of his work at Utica Normal and Industrial, Holtzclaw helped organize an annual Negro Farmers Conference in 1905 and the Black Belt Improvement Company, and he published two newspapers, the monthly *Utica News* and the school newspaper, *Southern Notes*. The school attracted some notoriety with the Utica Jubilee singers, a group of musicians modeled on singers from Fisk and Tuskegee.

Holtzclaw clearly modeled *The Black Man's Burden* on Washington's popular *Up from Slavery* (1901). Both autobiographies told stories of people overcoming impoverished upbringings through education, hard work, and example. Both stressed uplift and self-reliance. Holtzclaw wrote that one of his greatest goals was to teach African Americans, especially in rural areas, "to depend upon themselves, to find in their own communities and about their own doors a means of progress and betterment, and not to look to any outside source whatever." Holtzclaw seemed a bit more willing than Washington directly to criticize white southern abuses. He spoke out against James Vardaman for cutting funds to African American schools, stood up to local opposition to his school, and condemned white violence against black men and women.

William Henry Holtzclaw and his family, 1915 (New York Public Library [Image ID: 1230989])

Eleven years after Holtzclaw's death in 1943, Utica Normal and Industrial School became Utica Institute Junior College; it later became the Utica campus of Hinds Community College, and the school's William H. Holtzclaw Library is named in his honor. In December 2015 the college announced that it had received a grant from the National Endowment for the Humanities to highlight Holtzclaw's work. In 1991 Holtzclaw's home on the college campus, the Holtzclaw Mansion, which had been vacant since the mid-1960s, was designated a Mississippi Landmark. Despite attempts to restore the building, it continued to deteriorate, and in 2011 it was named one of the 10 Most Endangered Historic Places in Mississippi. In April 2014 the Board of Trustees of the Mississippi Department of Archives and History approved its demolition.

Ted Ownby
University of Mississippi

James D. Anderson, *The Education of Blacks in the South* (1988); Robert Fulton Holtzclaw, *William Henry Holtzclaw, Scholar in Ebony, Founder of Utica Junior College* (1977); Preservation in Mississippi website, misspreservation.com; *Southern Notes*, Department of Archives and Special Collections, J. D. Williams Library, University of Mississippi.

Home Demonstration

Work to improve the daily lives of Mississippi's rural women began before passage of the Smith-Lever Act in 1914. Mississippi A&M College faculty organized Farmers' Institutes shortly after the school's opening in 1880. Although the college was originally designed for male farmers, women received encouragement to attend, and organizers eventually added special sessions on domestic-oriented topics.

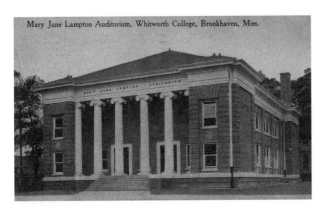

Mary Jane Lampton Auditorium, Whitworth College, Brookhaven, Miss.

Susie V. Powell, with assistance of the Mississippi Federation of Women's Clubs, established tomato clubs, or "canning clubs," in the early 1900s. The first canning demonstration took place at Whitworth College in Brookhaven, and by that fall 152 girls had tomatoes canned and displayed at local fairs. (Ann Rayburn Paper Americana Collection, Department of Archives and Special Collections, J. D. Williams Library, University of Mississippi [rayburn_ann_23_08_001])

After the success of William Smith's Corn Club in Holmes County, Seaman Knapp hired Susie V. Powell, school improvement supervisor at the Mississippi State Department of Education, to organize Tomato Clubs for girls. Promoters of club work for girls believed that they would gain responsibility and learn skills that would make them better homemakers and mothers. In addition, agents expected that girls would bring their new home economics knowledge to their mothers back on the farm. With assistance from the Mississippi Federation of Women's Clubs, Powell established clubs in Lincoln and Copiah Counties in 1911. The first canning demonstration took place at Whitworth College in Brookhaven, and by the fall of that year 152 girls had tomatoes canned and displayed at local fairs. As clubs formed across the state, markets and other avenues developed where the girls could sell their products.

After passage of the Smith-Lever Act Powell became the state home demonstration agent for Mississippi A&M College's Extension Service. Alcorn A&M also had an extension program that worked mostly in the southwestern area of the state. Counties hired white and African American women to serve as agents and to develop programs for both women and girls. After the United States entered World War I extension programs refocused on educating farm women and their families about producing and conserving food and fiber. Agents formed mother-daughter Canning Clubs to further the war effort. Club members sold their canned goods to the US Army and Navy, filling entire railroad cars with products. Agents also taught conservation through the adoption of wheatless and meatless days.

With the end of the war, home demonstration again shifted gears, this time emphasizing ways to improve Mississippians' home lives. Local clubs run by county councils became commonplace throughout the state's rural communities. Programs reflected the growth of home economics and the adoption of scientific homemaking. Women learned food preparation, dairy and poultry techniques, clothing construction, and home and kitchen improvement. The Extension Service also began hosting on-campus short courses that provided women and girls with intensive training on particular subjects.

With the start of the Great Depression, the concept of living at home became the major theme of extension work, as agents encouraged impoverished farm families to become self-sufficient and thus eliminate the need to purchase goods. Home demonstration programs now featured instruction on refinishing furniture or making usable home decorations out of packing crates. By the mid-1930s, agents had begun teaching about the benefits that electrification would bring to rural homesteads.

World War II again altered home demonstration programming, returning it to a focus on food preparation and preservation. Clubs throughout the state adopted horticulture and canning programs to make the nationwide program for victory gardens a reality in Mississippi. In the decades after the war agents continued to teach improved homemaking skills and added projects regarding civil defense, voting, health and safety, Head Start, family finances, and numerous other topics. By the 1960s, home demonstration had shifted from emphasizing the improvement of the rural home to working with women to improve their rural communities. This focus led to the end of home demonstration programs, as extension agents concentrated on social problems and working with food industries.

Sara Morris
University of Kansas

Lu Ann Jones, *Mama Learned Us to Work: Farm Women in the New South* (2002); Danny Blair Moore, "'Window to the World': Educating Rural Women in Mississippi, 1911–1965" (PhD dissertation, Mississippi State University, 1991); Lee Howard Moseley, *History of Mississippi Cooperative Extension* (1976); Minoa Dawn Uffelman, "'Rite Thorny Places to Go Thro': Narratives of Identities, Southern Farm Women of the Late Nineteenth and Early Twentieth Century" (PhD dissertation, University of Mississippi, 2003).

Home Front, Civil War

Mississippi's January 1861 secession inaugurated a four-year struggle that profoundly affected the state's citizens. Although support for leaving the Union was not universal, when war came, tens of thousands of men attempted to enlist in various military units. Most did so unaware of the potentially deadly consequences that awaited them, either in camp or on the battlefield. They left behind wives and children, many of whom would become widows or fatherless. Yet aside from excitement engendered by the creation of the Confederacy and war preparations, life followed familiar patterns for many Mississippians, especially those living in rural areas and during the first year of the war. Change subsequently came rapidly, as the government sought to limit cotton production and encouraged the transition to food crops such as corn and wheat. Enterprising agriculturists recognized cotton's enduring value, and production declined but never entirely ceased. As the war progressed, a thriving cotton trade with the enemy ensued, sometimes with the blessing of state and Confederate authorities. Movement toward a sustenance economy faltered in 1862, when drought severely curtailed corn yields, and again in 1864, when the northern part of the state endured another prolonged dry spell. The government encouraged livestock production, but the scarcity of salt posed a major problem for beef and pork growers.

Although antebellum amusements such as horseback riding, fishing, and hunting continued for some residents, at least early in the war, social life increasingly came to revolve around soldiers and their needs. The elite held balls and parties, and hasty courtships and marriages were conducted before regiments departed. News of disease striking within the ranks soon began filtering back, and in April 1862 casualties from the fighting at Shiloh were transported to communities throughout North Mississippi, offering a glimpse of the human toll that such battles exacted.

Mississippi's lack of industry meant that residents had to make adjustments early in the war. Home manufacture of clothes began soon after the outbreak of hostilities, with old looms and spinning wheels pressed into service. As the war continued, medicine and other necessities became increasingly scarce. Inflation sent prices of basic commodities soaring. Federal troops began to reach parts of Mississippi in 1862 and gained control over large portions of the state by the next autumn. Some areas saw repeated visits from Confederate and US forces, with both sides eager to appropriate crops and livestock and to raid chicken coops and smokehouses, although Union troops were more likely to loot and torch dwellings. Urban areas did not escape unscathed, with Jackson, Meridian, Oxford, and Prentiss, among others, suffering extensive damage. By early 1864 the state's railroads were wrecked and its textile mills destroyed.

Conscription and heavy taxation eroded support for the Confederacy. Some regions of the state had never supported secession, and opposition grew as the war continued. Both state and Confederate authorities attempted to round up deserters, stanch opposition, and enforce conscription, but these efforts often led to open violence. War weariness set in, and the fall of Vicksburg generated doubts about the Confederacy's prospects. Hardships increased. In December 1863 the legislature ordered county boards of police to compile lists of enlisted soldiers and their dependents and assessed a special tax to aid with relief efforts. The next August it empowered county commissioners to impress provisions for distribution to the indigent. Assessing the success of these efforts is difficult, since much of the state was under US control and many local governments had ceased to function.

Women bore many of the burdens as the war dragged on. White women not only fulfilled their traditional child-rearing and housekeeping duties but sewed, nursed sick and wounded soldiers, and managed farms and plantations. Some affluent women were forced to shoulder tasks they had never anticipated, especially late in the war. With husbands absent, many women attempted to manage and care for slaves. Petitions sent to Govs. John J. Pettus and Charles Clark worried that not enough able-bodied men remained in some locales to keep the slaves subdued. Thousands of women learned that their fathers, husbands, sons, or other male relatives had died in faraway locales. Despair must have gripped many such women. Women banded together, often with other kinfolk, for mutual support. Some fled to live with relatives in safer areas, including other states.

Numerous southern postwar accounts stress the faithfulness and loyalty of beloved family slaves, and some undoubtedly existed. But enormous numbers of slaves fled when Union boats or columns appeared. So many African Americans left their masters that they became a headache for Federal commanders, who resorted to placing them in contraband camps in Corinth, Natchez, Vicksburg, and elsewhere. Some Union officers discouraged females, children, and old slaves from leaving their plantations but encouraged younger males to flee, recognizing the economic impact of their absence. Some slaveholders responded by sending their bondsmen away from threatened regions.

In 1863 the US War Department authorized Adj. Gen. Lorenzo Thomas to recruit African Americans throughout the Mississippi Valley into the ranks. Former Mississippi slaves enrolled in various locales, including Helena, Arkansas; Louisiana; Memphis; and Vicksburg. Eager to play a part in their own liberation, thousands served under white officers in US Colored Troops regiments. Although they were subject to racial discrimination and often employed in menial pursuits, black men in Union uniforms epitomized the shocking transformation of Mississippi society that the war unleashed. Emancipation destroyed the cornerstone on which Mississippi's antebellum prosperity had rested, and losses in slaves and other property devastated the state's economy.

The war disrupted the normal contours of life. Most but not all clergy supported the Confederacy; the most famous exception was James A. Lyon, a Presbyterian minister in Columbus. Higher education came to a standstill. By 1864 only one daily newspaper, the *Meridian Clarion*, still published in the state. Agricultural production plummeted. Levees broke and water flooded much of the Delta in 1865, causing further misery. Although defeat embittered some Mississippians, by mid-1865 most wanted peace under any circumstances. Estimates suggest that more than a quarter of all Mississippi's Confederate soldiers perished. Others returned with physical or psychological wounds to a landscape that was drastically altered, matching their devastation both physically and psychologically. One of the most prosperous states in the Union in 1860, five years later Mississippi was shattered.

Christopher Losson
St. Joseph, Missouri

John K. Bettersworth, *Confederate Mississippi: The People and Policies of a Cotton State in Wartime* (1943); Mississippi, Governor, Correspondence and Papers, John Jones Pettus and Charles Clark, Mississippi Department of Archives and History; James W. Silver, ed., *Mississippi in the Confederacy: As Seen in Retrospect* (1961); Timothy B. Smith, *Mississippi in the Civil War: The Home Front* (2010).

Hooker, John Lee

(1917–2001) Blues Musician

John Lee Hooker was born on 22 August 1917 in Vance, Mississippi, near Clarksdale, to William Hooker, a Baptist preacher and sharecropper, and Minnie Ramsey Hooker. His mother later left her husband for Will Moore, a minor blues player who had a major influence on John Lee Hooker's early blues training by teaching him the boogie. Exposed to the early blues tradition of Son House, Robert Johnson, and Charley Patton, Hooker left Mississippi for Memphis while still in his teens, with no formal education and unable to read or write. Though he learned much in Memphis, he could not break into the Memphis scene. He spent seven years in Cincinnati before heading to Detroit in 1943.

Hooker worked odd jobs and became a minor part of the Detroit blues scene. In 1948–49 his recording, "Boogie Chillun" (or "Boogie Chillen"), became a hit and brought him to the attention of recording studios. Hooker followed up with an even bigger hit, "I'm in the Mood" (1951), as well as with other releases under his own name and under pseudonyms. During the 1960s Hooker was part of the British blues movement, traveling to Europe to play alongside such artists as B. B. King, Albert King, Howlin' Wolf, and Muddy Waters. Hooker's shuffling blues style influenced the Rolling Stones' Keith Richards, the eclectic folk-ballad sound of Van Morrison, the disciplined blues articulation of Eric Clapton, and the tribal island rhythms of Carlos Santana, all of whom later collaborated with Hooker on such albums as *The Healer* (1989), *Mr. Lucky* (1991), and *Chill Out* (1995). Hooker's 1962 hit "Boom-Boom," which returned to

the rhythm of "Boogie Chillun," became the cornerstone for a later album, while his "One Bourbon, One Scotch, One Beer" became a centerpiece for hard blues artist George Thorogood. Hooker's career reignited following a collaboration with the band Canned Heat, *Hooker 'n Heat* (1971), and he appeared in John Belushi and Dan Ackroyd's 1980 film, *The Blues Brothers*.

The Healer included a Grammy-winning remake of "I'm in the Mood" with blues diva Bonnie Raitt. Hooker was inducted into the Rock and Roll Hall of Fame in 1991. His final studio album, *Don't Look Back* (1997), won the Grammy for Best Traditional Blues Album, while the title duet with Van Morrison earned the Grammy for Best Pop Collaboration with Vocals.

Unlike most blues artists, Hooker did not return to his native South but brought his South to the world. As Hooker said in "Boogie Chillun," the blues is "in 'im and it's gotta come out." After receiving the Grammy Lifetime Achievement Award in 2000, Hooker died at his California home on 21 June 2001.

Thomas Eaton
Southeast Missouri State
University

Bill Dahl, AllMusic.com website, www.allmusic.com; Phillip Gallo, *Variety* (July 2001); John Lee Hooker website, www.johnleehooker.com; Greg Kot, *Chicago Tribune* (6 July 1997); Charles S. Murray, *Boogie Man: The Adventures of John Lee Hooker in the American Twentieth Century* (2000); Tony Russell, *The Guardian* (June 2001).

Hopewell, Treaty of

The Treaty of Hopewell refers to three treaties negotiated with the Cherokee, Choctaw, and Chickasaw Nations in 1785 and 1786 by commissioners appointed by the US government under the Confederation Congress. The original commission appointed by Congress on 21 March 1785 included Benjamin Hawkins, Joseph Martin, and Andrew Pickens. Lachlan McIntosh was added when two others refused to serve. The commissioners sought to impose a federal Indian policy on the postrevolutionary South and to nullify the Spanish influence among the southern Indians.

All three treaty documents extended the peace, friendship, and "protection of the United States of America, and of no other sovereign whosoever." The documents were virtually identical except for the articles that described their national boundaries, and the Cherokee treaty contained thirteen articles, while the Choctaw and Chickasaw treaties had only eleven. Several articles provided for the restoration of prisoners and property captured during the Revolutionary War, prohibited American citizens from settling on Indian lands, forbade retaliation, and required that criminals be delivered up and punished. Two articles provided for trade and the exclusive right of trade by the United States, and a third article required notice "of any designs . . . against the peace, trade or interests of the United States of America." In addition, an article in the Cherokee treaty guaranteed justice "respecting their rights" and the right to send a representative to Congress. Otherwise the treaties used the same language, contrived assurances of peace and friendship, and concluded that the "hatchet shall be buried forever."

Despite internal and external opposition to dealing with the American government, Cherokee, Choctaw, and Chickasaw delegations traveled to Pickens's plantation home, Hopewell, on the Keowee River in northwestern South Carolina. Each nation contained anti-American factions, especially the militant Chickamauga Cherokee, or pro-Spanish factions that sought trade and alliances with Spain. In addition to internal opposition, Alexander McGillivray, the pro-Spanish leader of the Creek Confederacy, prevented his nation from reaching an agreement with the commissioners and attempted to dissuade and intimidate the Chickasaw and Choctaw.

The Cherokee delegation, which included 918 men and women, arrived over a period of several days and delayed the opening session until midmorning on 22 November 1785. Along with speeches and the presentation of symbolic tokens of friendship, discussions centered on disputes about boundaries between Cherokee and US territory. Despite the protestations of some Cherokee leaders, the US commissioners and 37 Cherokee chiefs and warriors signed the treaty on 28 November.

While the commissioners doled out presents to the departing Cherokee, the Choctaw delegation continued its trek eastward, losing most of its horses to the Creek and arriving at Hopewell on 26 December. Worn down by their exhausting two-and-a-half-month journey, the 127 Choctaw men and women presented quite a contrast with the recently departed Cherokee party, whose members had arrived dressed in their finest clothing, leather leggings, gorgets, medals, and feathers. The Choctaw demanded food and new clothing before proceeding with their talks, and like the Cherokee before them, their men and women followed a regimen of rituals and ceremonies in their discussions with the commissioners. They marched in carrying white poles with white deerskins attached as peace tokens, performed the Eagle Tail Dance while painted in white clay, and exchanged gifts with the commissioners, including the calumet pipe and eagle feathers. Each Choctaw speaker from Yockonahoma on the first day through Mingohoopie four days later emphasized the sunny weather and the importance of the sun in helping to create friends and allies out of the Euro-Americans.

The Choctaw delegation, handpicked by Franchimastabé, headman or "first chief," included men known for their pro-British connections as well as Taboca, "second chief of the Choctaw," noted for his diplomatic finesse as leader and chief spokesperson. While the commissioners talked about peaceful relations and boundaries, the Choctaw journeyed to South Carolina to establish trade relations with the Euro-Americans on the Atlantic Coast and to supplement the flow of manufactured goods from the Spanish. Unlike the Cherokee, the Choctaw felt no need to discuss boundaries because their land had not been invaded by the Euro-Americans, and the Choctaw failed to understand Article 3, which described the boundaries and reserved three tracts of land six miles square for trading posts controlled by the United States. After several days, thirty-one Choctaw medal chiefs and "captains" concluded their negotiations on 3 January 1786 and placed their marks on the treaty document signed by Hawkins, Martin, and Pickens.

A much smaller Chickasaw delegation, including men and women, arrived four days after the Choctaw signed the second Hopewell treaty. Hawkins, Martin, and Pickens opened their third treaty session at 10:00 on 9 January 1786 and addressed the Chickasaw using the same speeches promising peace and "the blessings of the new changes of sovereignty over this land which you & us inhabit." Following an explanation of a draft of the treaty by the commissioners, Piomingo, Mingotushka, and Latopoia, who represented the pro-American faction of their nation, addressed the conference and presented several strands of white beads and a broad wampum belt as tokens of friendship and peace. Piomingo boldly presented himself as the "head leading warrior" of the Chickasaw Nation, and Mingotushka presented a medal "worn by our great man, he is dead" but sent by his daughter as a token of peace. Although Piomingo questioned Article 1, stating that he had taken no American prisoners to surrender, he agreed to Article 3, which described the boundaries of the Chickasaw Nation and provided for the establishment of a trading post on a circular tract of land five miles in diameter near the mouth of Bear Creek.

When the commissioners and Chickasaw chiefs convened the next day, 10 January, they presented two copies of the treaty and a map of the Chickasaw lands. After reading the treaty and explaining each article, the commissioners asked the Chickasaw to sign the document, and Piomingo, Mingotushka, and Latopoia made their marks below the signatures of the commissioners.

The treaties signed at Hopewell left US relations with the southern Indians in a precarious situation. Despite their marks on the treaties, none of the delegations recognized the sovereignty of the United States over their lands.

James P. Pate
University of Mississippi, Tupelo

American State Papers: Documents, Legislative and Executive, of the Congress of the United States, 38 vols. (1832–61); James R. Atkinson, *Splendid Land, Splendid People: The Chickasaw Indians to Removal* (2004); Arrell M. Gibson, *The Chickasaws* (1971); Charles J. Kappler, ed., *Indian Affairs: Laws and Treaties*, 5 vols. (1904–41); Greg O'Brien, *Choctaws in a Revolutionary Age, 1750–1830* (2002); Greg O'Brien, *Journal of Southern History* (February 2001); Alice Noble Waring, *The Fighting Elder: Andrew Pickens, 1739–1817* (1962); Grace Steele Woodward, *The Cherokees* (1963).

Hopson Plantation

In the first decades of the twentieth century, the Hopson Plantation, near Clarksdale, Mississippi, spearheaded the adoption of mechanization for large-scale commercial agriculture in the Delta, becoming the first plantation to use a mechanical cotton picker.

The Hopson family purchased the tract of land that would become the plantation from the State of Mississippi in 1852. As in much of the Mississippi Delta, the level, well-drained alluvial soil on the Hopsons' land was ideally suited for cotton production. During the late nineteenth century the plantation grew to four thousand acres, with approximately thirty-one hundred under cultivation.

The Hopson family subsequently became interested in utilizing new technology to improve crop yield and reduce labor costs. In 1914 the plantation became one of the first in the region to use a tractor and soon followed that innovation with the use of pickup trucks. During the 1930s the plantation halved its cotton acreage as a result of the Agricultural Adjustment Administration's cotton program. To help increase the yield on the reduced acreage and to decrease costs, the family permitted the International Harvester Company to use the plantation as a developmental station for a mechanical cotton picker beginning in 1935.

The first public demonstration of the device took place at the Hopson Plantation on 2 October 1944 in front of three hundred onlookers. This picker was capable of harvesting six acres per day—far more than even a skilled worker could harvest by hand. The family estimated that the machine reduced the cost of production from $39.41 per bale to $5.26. Shortly thereafter, the plantation became the testing ground for a flame cultivator, which mechanized the process of clearing weeds.

These advances coincided with and helped further the decline of the sharecropping system in southern commercial agriculture. The Great Migration to northern cities had dramatically reduced the supply of agricultural laborers throughout the South. By the 1920s the Hopson Plantation was one of many that had come to rely largely on day workers and seasonal migrant laborers. For this reason, most cotton plantation owners eagerly anticipated the perfection of a mechanical picker and other devices that would minimize the need for human labor.

By 1950 the Hopson Plantation had become fully automated, and all elements of premechanized production had been eliminated. As a state-of-the-art operation, the plantation became a model for other plantations, and it remained a testing ground for agricultural machinery. It operated as an independent commercial cotton farm until 1972.

In the 1970s Clarksdale's role in the development of blues music became more widely appreciated, and the Hopson Plantation began a second life as a tourist destination. During the 1990s local businessmen purchased the core of the plantation and converted the buildings into a hotel, a concert hall, and a meeting venue. The plantation now serves as a hot spot for those seeking to better understand the history and culture of the Mississippi Delta.

Trevor A. Smith
Mississippi Gulf Coast
Community College

Donald Holley, *The Second Great Emancipation: The Mechanical Cotton Picker, Black Migration, and How They Shaped the Modern South* (2000); Howell Hopson, *Mechanization of a Delta Cotton Plantation as Applied to Hopson Planting Company* (1944); Hopson Plantation Commissary website, www.hopsonplantation.com; Nicholas Lemann, *The Promised Land: The Great Black Migration and How It Changed America* (1992); Bill Tipton, "Mechanical Cultivation and Picking of Cotton, Dream of Industry, Comes True," *ACCO Press* 22 (November 1944); Bill Talbot and James Butler, interviews by Trevor A. Smith (September 2007).

House, Son (Eddie James House Jr.)
(1902–1988) Blues Musician

Born Eddie James House Jr. on 21 March 1902 in the Riverton community near Clarksdale, Mississippi, Son House was one of the most influential Delta bluesmen of the twentieth century. His protégés included Robert Johnson and Muddy Waters (McKinley Morganfield) as well as a number of post-1960s blues revivalists.

House's father was an amateur musician who played guitar as well as tuba in a local brass band. House's parents separated when he was eight years old, and House moved with his mother and two brothers to Louisiana. Leaving school after the eighth grade, House worked temporary jobs, and by the age of fifteen he was preaching in Baptist churches. He eventually returned to the Clarksdale area to visit his father, and for several years thereafter House wandered around the Delta working as a sharecropper. Initially disliking his father's blues music, Son House preferred church music as a teenager, singing in a choir and learning shape-note singing from an uncle. But after he realized that singing and playing the blues at various venues was an easier way to earn money than sharecropping, he began to perform. In 1928 he studied the guitar—particularly slide techniques—from widely respected Delta musician Willie Brown.

House spent about two years in the second half of the 1920s imprisoned at Parchman Farm, apparently after killing a man in self-defense, though the details of the incident remain unclear. By 1930 he had returned to performing music throughout the Delta, and he met bluesman Charley Patton, who told House about the Paramount label's interest in recording blues musicians. In May of that year House traveled to Paramount's studio in Grafton, Wisconsin, where he made his first recordings. While few copies sold on the commercial "race records" market, House's three double-sided Paramount 78s featured his dynamic vocal interpretations and his innovative slide guitar arrangements of blues learned from other Delta musicians, particularly Lyon bluesman James McCoy.

House's Paramount recordings attracted the attention of folklorist Alan Lomax, who in 1941 journeyed to the Delta to record House performing blues solo and with Willie Brown and a small band. Returning to Mississippi the following year, Lomax made additional field recordings of House's blues music. Recorded onto acetate on portable equipment and intended primarily as documentation for the Library of Congress, these recordings were not widely heard for years.

In 1943 House moved to Rochester, New York, where he lived in obscurity and stopped making music for two decades. He was rediscovered in June 1964 by three white blues aficionados, Dick Waterman, Nick Perls, and Phil Spiro, who encouraged House to resume performing. Since House had forgotten much of what he knew about guitar playing, Alan Wilson, a white guitarist and student of House's records, demonstrated his former performing style. House soon began performing at coffeehouses and festivals, and he made new recordings of his blues repertoire for the Columbia label. In 1965 he appeared at Carnegie Hall, and he toured Europe in both 1967 and 1970. Although poor health slowed him, House continued to tour through the mid-1970s. Thereafter, he lived in Detroit, where, after years of suffering from both Parkinson's and Alzheimer's diseases, he died of cancer on 19 October 1988.

Ted Olson
East Tennessee State University

Daniel Beaumont, *Living Blues* (September–October 2003); Daniel Beaumont, *Preachin' the Blues: The Life and Times of Son House* (2011); Paul Oliver, *Popular Music* 8 (1989); Jeff Titon, *Living Blues* (March–April 1977); Dick Waterman, *Living Blues* (January–February 1989).

House Parties

The house party is important in southern musical forms as diverse as blues, country, jazz, and hip-hop. Country music fiddlers play at rural house parties, which Bill Malone calls "one of the great seedbeds of country music." Jazz is associated with rent parties, where people gather and raise money to pay the next month's rent. In William Miller's children's book, *Rent Party Jazz* (2001), New Orleans musicians perform to raise rent money for a friend who has lost her job. Jazz rent parties in Chicago and New York are associated with pianists such as Speckled Red, James P. Johnson, and Fats Waller. And today in Clarksdale, young hip-hop artists such as Jerome Williams (TopNotch the Villain) perform at house parties.

For more than a century house parties have been home to blues in the Mississippi Delta, with audiences gathering each Friday and Saturday night to hear a guitarist or pianist play and sing, sometimes accompanied by a harmonica player and a drummer. At times, a musician rubs a broom handle across the floor to provide rhythm. Once the music begins, audience members join in with their own verses and verbal encouragement. Stories, jokes, and music are all part of the blues performance at a house party. As small rooms fill with smoke and the smell of alcohol, couples talk, dance the Slow Drag, and sing along with the performer. Blues house parties are found in Delta neighborhoods such as Kent's Alley, Black Dog, and the Brickyard in Leland.

At the house party, dancers speak to the singer, who responds through the music. Blues singers learn to "talk the blues" with the audience as they integrate conversation among the blues verses. After singing each verse, musicians continue their instrumental accompaniment and develop a talk session. Then they sing another verse while the audience recalls rhymes and jokes to tell at the next verse break. The audience influences the length and structure of each blues song, forcing singers to integrate the songs with the responses. Experienced blues singers know that audience response is a measure of their musical skill, and a successful blues session is filled with comments and jokes that are told as the music is played. This call-and-response exchange between blues performers and their audiences is also familiar in the black church service, where a similar pattern develops between the preacher and the congregation.

Constant verbal interplay occurs between the singer and the audience during a blues performance at a house party. The role of performer shifts back and forth between the singer and the audience. After an audience member tells a joke, the performer recaptures the audience by changing the musical beat or striking louder chords. The singer allows the center of attention to shift to members of the audience but maintains overall control through his music.

During house party performances, the distinction between music and talk blurs as performer and audience respond to each other. Blues talk mixes with verses and at times becomes the focus of the performance. The form of blues talk at a house party can be either short phrases or lengthy conversations. Short phrases such as "Play the blues, Pine" appear during musical breaks after each line. These phrases are reminiscent of how the blues disc jockey speaks as he plays a record. Rather than interrupt the blues verse, both the disc jockey and the blues audience insert phrases during instrumental breaks. More lengthy blues talk pulls the center of attention away from the verses. For example, a long conversation between the singer and the audience can be inserted like a verse within the song. Lengthy blues talk can also feature obscene tales, toasts, and dozens that are performed with instrumental accompaniment.

Blues house parties remain common in the Mississippi Delta. When a musician finds an audience and a comfortable room, the party begins early in the evening and will last "into the wee, wee hours."

William Ferris

University of North Carolina at Chapel Hill

William Ferris, *Blues from the Delta* (1988); William Ferris, *Mississippi Delta Blues* (film 1983); Bill C. Malone, *Country Music, U.S.A.* (2002); William Miller, *Rent Party Jazz* (2001); Ali Colleen Neff, *Let the World Listen Right: The Mississippi Delta Hip-Hop Story* (2009); Eudora Welty, in *The Collected Stories of Eudora Welty* (1980).

Hovis, Guy

(b. 1941) Musician

Guy Hovis is best known for his appearances on *The Lawrence Welk Show* as half of the singing duo Guy and Ralna. He was born in Tupelo on 24 September 1941 to Guy Hovis Sr., an original member of the Mississippi Highway Patrol, and Frances Hovis. As a child, Guy developed a strong interest in music through singing at the Harrisburg Baptist Church, participating in a gospel quartet and singing regularly at weddings and civic clubs. Hovis's musical interests followed him to the University of Mississippi, where he met Allen Pepper, Trent Lott, and Gaylen Roberts, with whom he formed a musical group, the Chancellors. After graduating in 1963 with a degree in accounting, Hovis spent two years in the US Army at Oklahoma's Fort Sill. After returning to the University of Mississippi for a semester of graduate work, Hovis headed to Los Angeles in hopes of breaking into the entertainment industry.

Hovis made his first appearance on national television in 1967 on *Art Linkletter's House Party*. He subsequently spent several years performing with singer David Blaylock as Guy and David. They toured the country, recorded an album, and appeared on popular television variety shows. Hovis began dating Ralna English, a performer from Texas who was part of the cast of *The Lawrence Welk Show*, and they married in 1969. English asked Welk to let Hovis perform, and Guy and Ralna sang a duet on the December 1969 Welk Christmas show. By the following February Hovis was a regular performer, and Guy and Ralna became the show's most popular duet act.

Hovis appeared on *The Lawrence Welk Show* for twelve years, during which time he cultivated his music production skills. Hovis produced eight of the ten records that he made with Ralna. In 1974 their popular album, *How Great Thou Art*, was nominated for Dove Awards for Producer and Artist of the Year. Guy and Ralna's popularity peaked in the late 1970s, and the last episode of *The Lawrence Welk Show* aired in 1982. The couple divorced two years later, temporarily ending the Guy and Ralna act.

From 1990 to 2007 Hovis served as director of Mississippi senator Trent Lott's state office, and in 2005 Hovis performed at the second inauguration of Pres. George W. Bush. Hovis has also written and starred in two successful musical revues and performed around the country with the Welk Musical Family. Audiences continued to see Guy and Ralna performing on reruns of *The Lawrence Welk Show*, and they have reunited professionally, occasionally appearing together in concert. Hovis also continues to perform solo at revivals, private concerts, and other events and to do charitable work with such organizations as the American Cancer Society and Childhelp USA and with veterans' organizations. He performed for *Mississippi Rising*, a televised benefit for Hurricane Katrina relief. Hovis and his wife, Sarah "Sis" Lundy, live in Jackson.

Sarah Taylor Condon

Houston, Texas

Guy Hovis, e-mail interview by Sarah Taylor Condon (27 August 2007); Guy Hovis website, www.guyhovismusic.com; *The Lawrence Welk Show* website, www.welkshow.com; Oeta, the Oklahoma Network website, www.oeta.onenet.net.

Howard, T. R. M.

(1908–1976) Physician and Civil Rights Leader

Civil rights leader Theodore Roosevelt Mason Howard was born on 4 March 1908 in Murray, Kentucky. His father was

Dr. T. R. M. Howard, 1950s (Mississippi State Sovereignty
Commission Records, Mississippi Department of Archives and
History [2-79-1-4-1-1-1])

a tobacco twister, while his mother worked as a cook for Will Mason, a prominent white doctor. Mason hired the boy to perform menial hospital jobs and was so impressed that he helped pay for Howard's medical education. In gratitude, Howard added *Mason* to his name. Howard attended three Adventist colleges: the all-black Oakwood College in Huntsville, Alabama; Union College in Lincoln, Nebraska; and the College of Medical Evangelists in Loma Linda, California. At Union College, he won the American Anti-Saloon's League's 1930 national oratorical contest.

While in California, Howard was active in civil rights and politics and wrote a regular column for the *California Eagle*, the main black newspaper in Los Angeles. He was also the president of a self-help political organization, the California Economic, Commercial, and Political League. In 1935 he married prominent black socialite Helen Boyd.

In 1942 Howard became chief surgeon at the hospital of the Knights and Daughters of Tabor in the all-black town of Mound Bayou, Mississippi. Within five years, he had founded an insurance company, a hospital, a home construction firm, and a large farm, where he raised cattle, quail, hunting dogs, and cotton. He also built a small zoo and a park as well as Mississippi's first swimming pool for blacks. In 1947 he broke with the Knights and Daughters, organized the rival United Order of Friendship, and opened the Friendship Clinic.

Howard entered the civil rights limelight in 1951 when he founded the Regional Council of Negro Leadership. One of its officials was Medgar Evers, whom Howard had hired as an agent for his Magnolia Mutual Life Insurance Company. The council mounted a successful boycott against service stations, distributing twenty thousand bumper stickers bearing the slogan, "Don't Buy Gas Where You Can't Use the Restroom."

The council organized yearly rallies for civil rights and voter registration, sometimes drawing audiences of ten thousand or more. The rallies featured nationally known speakers such as Rep. William Dawson of Chicago, alderman Archibald Carey of Chicago, Rep. Charles Diggs of Michigan, and attorney Thurgood Marshall of the National Association for the Advancement of Colored People.

In 1954 Howard ran afoul of a credit squeeze that the white Citizens' Councils launched against civil rights activists. He was instrumental in organizing a counteroffensive to encourage black businesses, churches, and voluntary associations to transfer their accounts to the black-owned Tri-State Bank of Memphis. The $280,000 that poured into the bank were made available for loans to victims of the squeeze.

The fallout from Emmett Till's August 1955 murder represented the beginning of the end of Howard's career in Mississippi. When Till's mother came to testify at the trial of his attackers, she stayed at Howard's house, and he played a highly visible role in tracking down witnesses and evidence. Faced with death threats, Howard sold most of his property in Mound Bayou and permanently relocated to Chicago in 1956.

In early 1956 the *Chicago Defender* gave Howard the top spot on its annual national honor roll of black leaders. He founded a successful clinic on the city's South Side and served as president of the National Medical Association and as chair of the board of the National Negro Business League.

In 1958 Howard ran for Congress as a Republican against Dawson, the powerful Democratic incumbent. Howard's campaign struggled in the face of Dawson's well-oiled political machine and voter discontent with the Republicans because of the 1958 recession. Nevertheless, his bid helped pave the way for the black independent movement, which eventually propelled two of Howard's friends to higher office: Ralph Metcalfe took Dawson's seat in Congress in 1970, while Harold Washington not only held the same seat from 1981 to 1983 but subsequently became Chicago's mayor.

By the early 1960s Howard was largely forgotten as a national leader but remained important in Chicago, where he helped to found Operation PUSH (People United to Save Humanity). He increasingly indulged in his favorite pastime, big-game hunting, and made several trips to Africa for this purpose. He died in Chicago on 1 May 1976.

David T. Beito
University of Alabama

Linda Royster Beito
Stillman College

David T. Beito, *From Mutual Aid to the Welfare State: Fraternal Societies and Social Services, 1890–1967* (2000); David T. Beito and Linda Royster Beito, *A.M.E. Church Review* (2001), in *Before Brown: Civil Rights and White Backlash in the Modern South*, ed. Glenn E. Feldman (2004).

Howard, Volney E.
(1809–1889) Editor and Judge

Volney Erskine Howard, a prominent newspaper editor and jurist, practiced law in four states and held governmental positions in three. He played a role in the admission of Texas to the Union, the negotiation of the Compromise of 1850, and the settlement of California.

Born in Norridgewock, Maine, on 22 October 1809, Howard spent his early years on a farm before attending nearby Bloomfield Academy and Waterfield College. In 1832 Howard left Maine to practice law with an uncle living in Brandon, Mississippi. Howard quickly rose to local prominence, gaining a seat in the Mississippi House of Representatives in 1836 and carrying the state's electoral vote for Martin Van Buren to Washington, D.C. While in the capital, he met and married Catherine Elizabeth Gooch of Massachusetts.

Upon his return to Mississippi, Howard became the reporter for the state's high court. Howard's most notable and controversial activities in Mississippi revolved around his ownership and publishing of the *Mississippian* newspaper. His aggressive editorials and dogged partisanship made the *Mississippian* one of the Southwest's leading Democratic papers, and his fierce opposition to a bill in the state legislature to guarantee the issues of the Union Bank led him to fight duels with Sergeant S. Prentiss, Alexander G. McNutt, and Hiram G. Runnels. The duel with Runnels left Howard with severe wounds in his chest and ribs. His position was vindicated when the bank later became insolvent.

Howard made an unsuccessful run for the US Congress before leaving Mississippi in 1840 for New Orleans, where he established a law practice. Four years later, he moved on to San Antonio, Texas, and won election to the state constitutional convention of 1845. Howard subsequently represented Bexar County in the House of the First Texas Legislature. He represented Texas in the US Congress from 1849 to 1853, served briefly as US attorney to the Land Commission of California in the 1850s, and spent the remainder of his life as a lawyer and judge in California. He sat on the superior court of Los Angeles and helped frame the 1879 California Constitution. Howard declined a seat on the US Supreme Court owing to poor health and retired from public life in 1884. He died in Santa Monica on 14 May 1889.

Thomas John Carey
University of Mississippi

Biographical Directory of the United States Congress (1950); Zachary T. Fulmore, *Quarterly of the Texas State Historical Association* (October 1910).

Howell, Bailey
(b. 1937) Athlete

Born in Middleton, Tennessee, on 20 January 1937 to Walter and Martha Howell, Bailey Howell developed into one of the finest and most consistent basketballers ever to play the game. Playing for Middleton High School between 1953 and 1955, Howell scored 1,187 points, a Tennessee high school record at the time. He was selected all-conference each season, all-state his junior and senior seasons, and all-American his senior year.

From a list that included Memphis State, the University of Mississippi, the University of Tennessee, Vanderbilt, the University of Kentucky, and others, Howell chose to continue his education and playing career at Mississippi State. During his three varsity seasons, Howell led the Bulldogs to a 64–14 record. Averaging 27.1 points and 17.0 rebounds per game (both of which are still school records), Howell concluded his career as Mississippi State's leading scorer (2,030 points) and leading rebounder (1,277 rebounds). Howell's 47 points against Union in 1958 and his 34 rebounds against Louisiana State University in 1957 remain single-game records for a Bulldog basketball player. He also continues to rank at or near the top in several other statistical categories.

One of the greatest players in Southeastern Conference (SEC) history, Howell was named first team all-conference each of his three seasons. He was the conference's Sophomore of the Year in 1957 and won the SEC's scoring title the following two seasons (averaging 27.8 and 27.5 points per game, respectively). In both 1958 and 1959 Howell earned the SEC's Most Valuable Player award, and in his senior season Howell led the Bulldogs to the conference championship.

Howell finished in the Top 10 nationally in scoring and rebounding every year, led the nation in field-goal percentage (56.8 percent) as a sophomore, finished fourth in scoring as a junior and senior, and finished second in rebounding as a senior. In 1958–59, Howell's senior season, the Bulldogs posted a 24–1 record and were ranked third in the nation. However, because the State of Mississippi prohibited its collegiate sports teams from competing against teams with African American players, Howell's Bulldogs never appeared in the National Collegiate Athletic Association Tournament. Despite this lack of national exposure, Howell was named an all-American following both his junior and senior seasons.

In 1959 the Detroit Pistons selected Howell with the second overall pick in the National Basketball Association (NBA) draft. Between 1959 and 1971 Howell played for Detroit, Baltimore, Boston (with whom he won the 1968 and 1969 NBA championships, averaging nearly 20 points per game), and Philadelphia. He posted a career scoring average of 18.7 points per game and made the NBA All-Star Team six times. Howell finished his career ranked in the league's Top 10 in nine statistical categories. In September 1997 he was inducted into the Naismith Memorial Basketball Hall of Fame.

Since the end of his basketball career, Howell and his wife, Mary Lou, have lived in Starkville, where he has remained active in business, the community, and the Starkville Church of Christ. He is also a member of the Tennessee, Mississippi, and Mississippi State University Halls of Fame, and the Bailey Howell Award is given annually to the best collegiate basketball player in the Magnolia State. Mississippi State retired his No. 52 jersey in 2009 and in 2015 named the street running past the school's basketball arena *Bailey Howell Drive*.

John Richard Duke
Harding University

Bailey Howell, interview by John Richard Duke (20 January 2004); *Mississippi State University Men's Basketball Media Guide* (2015–16); Mississippi State University website, www.msstate.edu.

Howell, Elmo
(1918–2013) Author

Elmo Howell was a teacher, writer, scholar, and poet whose work contributed significantly to the discussion of and preservation of Mississippi places, people, and art. Born on 5 August 1918 in Itawamba County, Howell attended Tremont High School and the University of Mississippi, where he received a bachelor's degree in English in 1940. He then earned master's and doctoral degrees in English at the University of Florida before taking a teaching position at Alabama's Jacksonville State College from 1955 to 1957. He then moved to Memphis State University (now the University of Memphis), where he taught southern literature and the English novel along with other English courses until his retirement in 1983.

Most of Howell's early publications were scholarly articles and notes on such writers as William Faulkner, Flannery O'Connor, William Gilmore Simms, and Mark Twain. Many of these essays, especially those on Faulkner, explored the interconnections between literature and southern culture, perhaps leading to Howell's later focus on Mississippi culture and history. He began traveling and collecting information about various locations in his native state and in 1988 published *Mississippi Home-Places: Notes on Literature and History*, a travel book that offered directions to significant homes in the state and their histories. His subsequently published two additional books, *Mississippi Back-Roads* and *Mississippi Scenes*, both of which bore the same subtitle as their predecessor.

Howell then turned his hand to poetry, and he produced eight volumes of poems—*Winter Verses, The Apricot Tree, I Know a Planted Field, Have You Been to Shubuta?, Tuesday's Letter and Other Poems, Mount Pleasant, A Roosting Place*, and *The Old Settlement*. These texts primarily examine and discuss life in Northeast Mississippi, drawing on Howell's travels and knowledge of history to offer a rich blend of nostalgia and pithy observations and insights. In 2005 he returned to literary criticism with *Notes on Southern Lit*.

He died on 3 October 2013 in Memphis.

Taylor Hagood
Florida Atlantic University

Lucius Lampton, *Journal of Mississippi History* (August 1994); *New Albany Gazette* (11 October 2013).

Howlin' Wolf (Chester Arthur Burnett)
(1910–1976) Blues Musician

Chester Arthur Burnett, better known as Howlin' Wolf, was among the greatest architects of early electric blues, a seminal presence not only in blues history but in the development of popular music in the last half of the twentieth century. A recording star through much of the 1950s and 1960s at Chicago's Chess Records, Burnett, who tailored the field hollers and folk blues of his upbringing to the amplified, small ensemble settings of a nascent postwar blues scene, also wielded direct influence on a generation of blues-indebted rock performers, especially those of the British Invasion.

Though Burnett was skilled on harmonica and guitar, his main instrument was his voice, one of the most distinctive in all of blues. Informed by such models as Charley Patton, Tommy Johnson, and Jimmie Rodgers (as well as the ravages of childhood tonsillitis), Burnett treated his singing as if it were the amp-distorted equal of the guitar and harmonica in urban blues combos. His range ventured from guttural growls to a falsetto moan that played up his stage name (hinting as well at the rich tonal masking of voice modifiers in some African cultures). Sun Records founder-producer Sam Phillips, a lover of unique voices, proclaimed Howlin' Wolf his greatest find. Standing 6′3″ and weighing close to "three hundred pounds of heavenly joy," as he famously described himself, Burnett was both literally and figuratively larger than life, performing with an oft-noted visceral energy and abandon—crawling on all fours one minute,

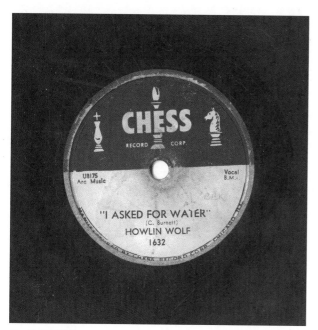

Howlin' Wolf (Chester A. Burnett) (Courtesy Blues Archive, Department of Archives and Special Collections, J. D. Williams Library, University of Mississippi)

climbing stage curtains the next—in an embodiment of the blues that made for both legendary theater and cathartic ritual.

Named after the twenty-first president of the United States, Burnett, the son of a sharecropper, was born on 10 June 1910, in White Station, near West Point, Mississippi. His parents separated when he was one, and he lived for a time with his mother, Gertrude Jones, and then a great-uncle. His maternal grandfather, who would frighten the boy with tall tales of wolves in the area, gave him his nickname, which stuck after Funny Papa Smith had a 1930 hit with "Howling Wolf Blues." At thirteen Burnett went to live with his father, Leon "Dock" Burnett, on the Young and Morrow Plantation, near Dockery Farms. As a result, Burnett came into contact with Delta blues giant Charley Patton, who mentored the teenager musically—the first song he learned on guitar was Patton's "Pony Blues"—and Burnett built on several elements of Patton's playing, from a gruff vocal style and the preference of riff-based blues structures to a strong sense of showmanship. Burnett also picked up ideas and techniques from other regional players as well as recordings, notably those by Tommy Johnson. One of Burnett's more fruitful relationships was with Sonny Boy Williamson II, who had married Burnett's stepsister, Mary, and who taught him how to play the harmonica. Williamson and Burnett would later play on Chess Records.

Throughout the 1930s and into much of the 1940s Burnett farmed in Mississippi and Arkansas, working also as a musician both in solo contexts and with other players including Williamson, Son House, Willie Brown, and briefly Robert Johnson. In 1941 Burnett enlisted in the US Army, and he was honorably discharged in 1943, having been stationed stateside the entire time. He returned to farming but by 1948 had moved to West Memphis, Tennessee, where in 1950 he began performing and pitching products on radio station KWEM in a fifteen-minute slot on Monday through Saturday afternoons. There, he assembled his first band, the House Rockers, in which such Memphis/Mid-South electric blues pioneers as James Cotton, Junior Parker, Auburn "Pat" Hare, Matt "Guitar" Murphy, and Willie Johnson all came through the ranks.

Phillips, who had recently set up his Memphis Recording Service, learned of the Wolf and brought him into the studio in 1951. At age forty Burnett was far older than most musicians launching their careers, but Phillips was so impressed he used nothing less than gospel song hyperbole to describe Burnett's music: "This is where the soul of man never dies." Burnett recorded for Phillips for little more than a year, with his efforts, including his first single, "Moanin' at Midnight," licensed to Chess. Unbeknownst to Phillips, Ike Turner, who played with Wolf on some of his recordings, had also negotiated a deal for Burnett with Los Angeles label RPM. That debut, a not-so-sly remake called "Morning at Midnight," fueled litigious ire, and after some negotiation Burnett ended up at Chess, while another Phillips client, Rosco Gordon, went to RPM.

To ensure their investment, Chess relocated Burnett to Chicago in 1953, and he became a bona fide titan of the electric blues scene alongside peer and rival Muddy Waters. Burnett's repertoire at Chess was a combination of songs culled from the Delta blues tradition and his own rural past ("Sitting on Top of the World," "I Asked for Water") and those provided him by Chess songwriter and session bassist Willie Dixon ("Hidden Charms," "Built for Comfort," "Three Hundred Pounds of Joy"), who sometimes tricked Burnett into recording songs by saying that they were going to Muddy Waters instead. Among other milestone recordings were 1961's "The Red Rooster" (which became a United Kingdom No. 1 covered by the Rolling Stones) and his signature tune at Chess, the 1956 classic "Smokestack Lightnin'." Burnett's stylistic shift from country to city is particularly notable in the latter song, which he performed as early as the 1930s and first recorded in 1951 for RPM as "Crying at Daybreak." What began as a rural field holler set to loose, open-ended ensemble riffing in the RPM version became dramatically more standardized and arranged if no less compelling, the metamorphosis of a still largely rural blues into a fully realized expression of the city. Lyrically, the central image of a train's smokestack reflects the changeover, the perfect industrial, migratory metaphor for this new urbanized form of music.

A "compulsive performer," in the words of Peter Guralnick, Burnett remained active to the end, playing blues clubs and festivals and opening for rock acts. He joined a number of his devotees, including Eric Clapton and members of the Rolling Stones, for a 1970 album, *The London Howlin' Wolf*

Sessions. After years of declining health, including several heart attacks and dialysis for kidney problems, Burnett died on 10 January 1976 after complications from brain tumor surgery. He has been inducted into both the Blues and Rock and Roll Halls of Fame.

William Lee Ellis

Memphis, Tennessee

Nadine Cohodas, *Spinning Blues into Gold: The Chess Brothers and the Legendary Chess Records* (2000); John Collis, *The Story of Chess Records* (1998); Colin Escott with Martin Hawkins, *Good Rockin' Tonight: Sun Records and the Birth of Rock 'n' Roll* (1991); Robert Gordon, *Can't Be Satisfied: The Life and Times of Muddy Waters* (2002); Peter Guralnick, *Feel Like Going Home: Portraits in Blues and Rock 'n' Roll* (1971); Peter Guralnick, *Lost Highway: Journeys and Arrivals of American Musicians* (1979); Sheldon Harris, *Blues Who's Who: A Biographical Dictionary of Blues Singers* (1981); Mark Humphrey, *Howlin' Wolf: His Best* (1997), liner notes; Chris Morris and Dick Shurman, *Howlin' Wolf: The Chess Box* (1991), liner notes; Robert Santelli, *The Big Book of Blues: A Biographical Encyclopedia* (1993); James Segrest and Mark Hoffman, *Moanin' at Midnight: The Life and Times of Howlin' Wolf* (2004).

Howorth, Lucy Somerville

(1895–1997) Lawyer, Feminist, Politician

Lucy Somerville Howorth was born on 1 July 1895 in Greenville, Mississippi, the youngest of four children of Robert Somerville and Nellie Nugent Somerville, the first woman elected to the Mississippi legislature. "Judge Lucy," as she came to be known, participated in some of the most important historical movements of the twentieth century.

Appropriately for a life devoted to social justice and the rights of women, Lucy Somerville's first political cause was the suffrage movement. Nellie Somerville was an officer in both the state and the national suffrage movements and took her infant daughter to meetings. Lucy sorted pamphlets by color at her mother's knee and later served as a page at suffrage meetings. As a freshman at Randolph-Macon Woman's College (now Randolph College) in Virginia, she organized an Equal Rights Club. On 26 August 1920 she sat in the gallery and watched as the Tennessee legislature ratified the Nineteenth Amendment, giving women the vote.

After graduating from Randolph-Macon in 1916, Somerville went to New York City to study at Columbia University. She also worked at an aircraft factory during World War I and later conducted industrial research for the Young Women's Christian Association.

Convinced that her calling was the law, Somerville went home to Mississippi and enrolled in the University of Mississippi School of Law in Oxford. She was active in campus

Lucy Somerville Howorth (Bern and Franke Keating Collection, Department of Archives and Special Collections, J. D. Williams Library, University of Mississippi)

life, including helping found the Marionettes, a drama club that included William Faulkner. She graduated at the top of the Class of 1922, delivering the commencement address, "Intellectual Integrity and College Education." The speech was covered by the newspapers and incurred the lasting wrath of the college president, whom she took to task for banning the teaching of Darwin's theory of evolution.

For the next four years she practiced law with a Cleveland, Mississippi, firm operated by her brother-in-law, Audley Shands, and worked with other community leaders to establish Delta State Teachers' College. She continued her work in women's organizations, serving on the national board of the Young Women's Christian Association and speaking throughout the state at high school and vocational conferences to urge young women to consider the legal profession.

In 1926 she moved to Greenville and established her own law practice. During the Great Mississippi River Flood of 1927, she volunteered with the Red Cross and navigated the streets of Greenville in a boat for five months. The same year she was appointed US commissioner of the Southern District of Mississippi, earning herself the title *Judge*.

Her 1928 marriage to another young lawyer, Joseph Howorth, precipitated her move to Jackson, where the pair established the firm of Howorth and Howorth. Three years later she was elected to the state legislature from Hinds County. With her as chair, the Public Lands Committee wrote legislation creating the state parks system and establishing a board to regulate drilling for gas and oil on state-owned land. In an amendment to a bill establishing the Game and Fish Commission, Howorth proposed that people be allowed to raise and sell game and fish on their property. Though some observers ridiculed the amendment, she lived to see the Delta become the nation's catfish capital.

Howorth's outstanding record and her support of Franklin Roosevelt at the 1932 Democratic National Convention led to a 1934 presidential appointment to the Board of Appeals of the Veterans Administration. She and her husband moved to Washington and spent the next twenty-five years in public service. During World War II she coordinated the volunteer work of the Veterans Administration. Howorth ultimately became general counsel of the War Claims Commission, the first woman to hold the top legal post in a federal agency.

A firm believer in the power of organizations to bring about change, Howorth worked steadily for women's rights through a network of New Deal women and through groups such as the American Association of University Women and the Business and Professional Women's Club. Widely known as a public speaker, she gave the keynote address at Eleanor Roosevelt's 1944 White House Conference on Women in Post-War Policy Making.

Lucy and Joe Howorth retired to Cleveland, Mississippi, where Joe painted and taught art classes and Lucy edited a collection of her grandfather's Civil War letters, served as chair of the Cleveland Library Commission, and traveled. Her honors included a Lifetime Achievement Award from Radcliffe College and outstanding alumni awards from Randolph-Macon and the University of Mississippi.

Joe Howorth died in 1980. Prior to her death in 1997, Lucy advised a young historian, "There's nothing like living a long time. Try to see that you do."

Dorothy Shawhan
Delta State University

William M. Cash and Lucy Somerville Howorth, eds., *My Dear Nellie: The Civil War Letters of William L. Nugent to Eleanor Smith Nugent* (1977); Lucy Somerville Howorth, interview by Constance Myers (20–23 June 1975), Southern Oral History Program Collection, Southern Historical Collection, Wilson Library, University of North Carolina at Chapel Hill; Leila J. Rupp and Verta Taylor, *Survival in the Doldrums: The American Women's Rights Movement, 1945 to the 1960s* (1987); Anne Firor Scott, Dorothy Shawhan, and Martha H. Swain, *Lucy Somerville Howorth: New Deal Lawyer, Politician, and Feminist from the South* (2006); Somerville and Howorth Family Papers, Schlesinger Library, Radcliffe Institute, Harvard University, Cambridge, Mass.; Susan Ware, *Beyond Suffrage: Women in the New Deal* (1981); Lucy Somerville Howorth Collection, Charles W. Capps Jr. Archives and Museum, Delta State University.

Civil, and Spanish-American Wars and during Reconstruction. Collecting and preserving folk songs and folklore became his lifelong passion.

His mother, Lou Garnett Palmer Hudson, and his father, William Arthur Hudson, enjoyed reading from a library of several hundred volumes housed in a log cabin school. They passed their enthusiasm to their son, who qualified for the University of Mississippi despite his farm-boy background. He received a bachelor's degree in 1913 and served as principal of Gulfport High School from 1913 to 1918. On 12 September 1916 he married Grace McNulty Noah of Kosciusko, and they went on to have three children.

Hudson taught English at Gulf Coast Military Academy for a year before becoming superintendent of schools in Oxford in 1919–20. He reenrolled at the University of Mississippi, teaching English and earning a master's degree in 1920. Under the influence of E. C. Perrow, Hudson became an enthusiastic collector of folk songs. He earned another master's degree from the University of Chicago in 1925 and a doctorate from the University of North Carolina five years later, writing his dissertation on Mississippi folk songs. He then returned to teach at the University of Mississippi, serving as an assistant professor in 1920–24 and a professor in 1927–30. On 24 May 1927 he organized the Mississippi Folklore Society. Its first publication was Hudson's *Specimens of Mississippi Folklore* (1928). Hudson went on to write numerous books on folklore in Mississippi and the rest of the South, including *Folksongs of Mississippi and Their Background* (1936). In 1930 he returned to the University of North Carolina, where he taught until his retirement in 1963. He subsequently was named Kenan Distinguished Professor Emeritus. Hudson died in 1978.

Abbott L. Ferriss
Emory University

Arthur Palmer Hudson, *Journal of Mississippi History* (April 1942); Arthur Palmer Hudson Papers, Southern Historical Collection, Wilson Library, University of North Carolina at Chapel Hill; Bonnie J. Krause, "Arthur Palmer Hudson, Mississippi Folklorist," *Mississippi Folklife* (1999); Hal May, ed., "Hudson, Arthur Palmer 1894(?)–1978," *Contemporary Authors* (1984); North Carolina Folklore Society Records, Southern Historical Collection, Wilson Library, University of North Carolina at Chapel Hill.

Hudson, Arthur Palmer
(1892–1978) Folklorist

Arthur Palmer Hudson grew up in Hesterville (formerly known as Palmer's Hall) in Attala County, Mississippi, listening to stories of his ancestors' exploits in the Mexican,

Hudson, Winson
(1916–2002) Activist

In 1963 Winson Hudson finally registered to vote in Leake County, interpreting part of the state constitution by saying, "It meant what it said and it said what it meant." Hudson, born in the county's hill country in 1916, had made her first attempt in 1937. Hudson lived her entire life in Harmony, a five-thousand-acre rural all-black community where families owned their land and homes and were highly protective of both.

Winson Hudson and her sister, Dovie, also filed the first lawsuit to desegregate the public schools in a rural Mississippi county, and in 1964 Debra Lewis entered first grade at the previously all-white grammar school. She was escorted to the school by Jean Fairfax of the American Friends Service Committee and Derrick Bell, the attorney from the National Association for the Advancement of Colored People (NAACP) Legal Defense Fund who had filed the lawsuit. Both groups continued to support Winson Hudson and her work in the county.

Hudson had helped to establish the county NAACP chapter in 1962 and served as its president for thirty-eight years. Her work included voting rights, school desegregation, health care, government loans, telephone service, good roads, housing, and child care—all intertwined with the black freedom struggle. She helped to welcome and house the young volunteers who came to work in Leake County during the 1964 Freedom Summer. She perceived current challenges and faced them individually or through the NAACP chapter, and in the closing years of her life she tried to convince young people about the importance of education and avoiding the fast track to prison, particularly for young black men. She had been heartbroken in 1978, when one of her early Head Start students, Earl Johnson, was executed at Parchman Penitentiary at age eighteen. She also stressed the importance of "saving our people's land and houses. There will be people, buildings, and cars and things going to the moon and people living on another planet, but there won't be no more land."

The role that Hudson and other African American women played in the civil rights movement at the local level in black communities is sometimes overlooked. She was friends with another Mississippi freedom fighter, Mae Bertha Carter, of Drew, and recalled with pleasure a visit to the University of Virginia where the two of them met Max Kennedy, Robert Kennedy's son, and sang to him, "Has anyone here seen my old friend Bobby?" Hudson received many honors and awards, including the NAACP Freedom Award for Outstanding Community Service. She died in April 2002.

Constance Curry
Emory University

Winson Hudson and Constance Curry, *Mississippi Harmony, Memoirs of a Freedom Fighter* (2002); Brian Lanker, *I Dream a World: Portraits of Black Women Who Changed America* (1999).

Hughes, Henry
(1829–1862) Proslavery Author

Henry Hughes wrote one book, *Treatise on Sociology, Theoretical and Practical*. Published in 1854, that book was significant as one of the first American works of sociology and especially as an idiosyncratic contribution to the proslavery argument.

Hughes was born on 17 April 1829 in Port Gibson and grew up there before attending Oakland College. He apprenticed with lawyers in New Orleans and became licensed to practice in 1850. He soon became disenchanted with the profession and grew more interested in scholarship and politics.

Treatise on Sociology, Theoretical and Practical is notable in part because it attempts to fit slavery into a broad definition of human relations. Hughes began with the theoretical points that human societies most need subsistence and then order to guarantee that subsistence: "In every society there must therefore be both orderers and orderees. Some must order; some, be ordered."

Hughes addressed issues of slavery in a long section on practical sociology. *Treatise* repeated many points common to the proslavery argument. It argued that southern slaves enjoyed better physical conditions than northern or European industrial workers; that slavery created a system without poverty, labor strife, frustrated ambitions, or the potential for revolution; and that slavery worked best when everyone involved acted out of a sense of mutual responsibility. However, the book was also unique in at least two ways. First, Hughes discarded the terms *slave owner* and *slave* in favor of *warrantor* and *warrantee* and replaced the term *slavery* with a new word, *warranteeism*. His goal was not merely semantic: Hughes believed that, in an ideal society, people with power owned the labor but not the bodies of people without power. Thus, he wrote that warrantors bore responsibility for providing necessities and an orderly society for their warrantees; in return, warrantees bore responsibility for working hard. Second, Hughes's work stressed the power of the government. While many southern slave owners and their political representatives condemned the growth of any government—state or federal—Hughes argued that government should set and enforce standards for working hours, housing and health conditions, and family relationships. In warranteeism, he wrote, "The supreme orderer is the State." The final two pages of the book left behind its scholarly approach and language and rhapsodized about the possibilities of a time "when the budding poetry of an all-hoping sociologist, shall ripen to a fruitful history" and the world would "praise the power, wisdom, and goodness of a system, which may well be deemed divine."

Treatise has had an uneven career, sometimes going unpublished and perhaps unread for decades, sometimes attracting attention either for its importance in the early history of sociology or more commonly as a contribution to proslavery literature. Sections of *Treatise on Sociology* appear in at least two collections of proslavery writing.

Hughes also wrote a few magazine pieces on the desirability of reopening the slave trade and the need to keep political balance between the North and South. He served as a colonel with the 12th Mississippi Regiment during the war and died of illness on 3 October 1862 at his home in Port Gibson.

Ted Ownby
University of Mississippi

Douglas Ambrose, *Henry Hughes and Proslavery Thought in the Old South* (1996); Drew Gilpin Faust, ed., *The Ideology of Slavery* (1981); Henry Hughes, *Treatise on Sociology, Theoretical and Practical* (1854); Henry Hughes, *Selected Writings of Henry Hughes*, ed. Stanford M. Lyman (1985); Eric McKitrick, ed., *Slavery Defended* (1963).

Hull, Marie
(1890–1980) Artist

Painter Marie Atkinson Hull was born on 28 May 1890 in Summit, Mississippi, to Ernest and Mary Katherine Atkinson. She graduated from Belhaven College in Jackson in 1909 with a degree in music. After two years of private lessons in art she continued her education at the Pennsylvania Academy of Fine Arts (1911–12) and studied for two summers at the Colorado Springs Art Center and in 1922 at the Art Students League in New York. She taught art in 1913–14 at Hillman College (which later merged with Mississippi College) and gave private lessons at her home in Jackson for more than fifty years.

One of the founding members of the Mississippi Art Association in 1911, Atkinson was elected president in 1916. Her 1917 marriage to architect Emmett J. Hull, who designed their home on Belhaven Street, led to some collaborative work. She began making drawings for his architectural designs but soon turned away from commercial art as being too "mechanical and rigid." Many of her paintings represent people and scenes she observed in Mississippi, but she also traveled extensively. She recorded her impressions of trips to France, Spain, and Morocco as well as the western United States, Canada, and Mexico in more than sixty sketchbooks now owned by the Mississippi Museum of Art.

Hull exhibited widely, most notably at the Art Institute of Chicago in 1929, the Spring Salon in Paris in 1931, the New York American Annual Exhibition in 1937, the New York World's Fair in 1939, and the Golden Gate Exhibition in San Francisco in 1939, as well as in museums and galleries in Cincinnati, Philadelphia, Washington, and throughout the southern states. She received many prizes for her work, starting with a gold medal from the Mississippi Art Association in 1920 and a first place from the Southern States Art League in 1926. A painting of yucca won her second prize in the 1929 Texas Wild Flower Painting Competition. Hull used the twenty-five-hundred-dollar award to study landscape and figure painting in Europe for several months with a group of professional artists.

Hull worked in a variety of media, primarily oil and watercolor, and her stylistic approach varied considerably throughout her career. She noted, "One must keep experimenting, seeking and finding new ways of working in art.... When art ceases to become vital and moving forward, expanding, then the artist begins to copy himself." Hull was influenced by numerous movements throughout her career, including the sober naturalism of American regionalism; the vibrant colors and looser brushwork of impressionism, postimpressionism, and fauvism; and finally, in some of her later work, the intensity of abstract expressionism. Refusing to settle on a single defining personal style, Hull searched for the approach that best suited the subject. She preferred a more direct realism of constructed form in her commissioned portraits, such as the seven paintings made for the Mississippi Hall of Fame from 1938 to 1968. The noncommissioned portraits in the *Sharecropper* series from the late 1930s are close in style to such regionalists as Grant Wood. Hull focused on the effect of the Great Depression on these men, whom she hired as models, but gave them a quiet dignity. Her portraits of black servants, such as *Annie Smith* (1928), show freer, more lively brushwork and bold colors that create a vibrant foil for the serious expressions and upright poses.

Hull's landscapes are often more experimental, revealing her interest in the underlying geometry of trees, rocks, and buildings enlivened by rich colors and rapid touches of the brush. The watercolor sketches made during her travels, such as *Granada* (ca. 1929), evoke a sense of light and atmosphere reminiscent of Monet and Cezanne, and she applied what she learned from the work of the impressionists and postimpressionists to her paintings of local scenes in Jackson in the mid-1930s for the Federal Arts Project of the Works Progress Administration. Even *Sedge Field* (ca. 1965), *Mississippi Red Clay* (1972), and other later nonobjective paintings, which she described as "lyrical abstraction," were often inspired by the landscape of her native state. The energy created by the broken brushwork and vivid colors is controlled by her overriding sense of order and discipline: as she observed, "Art is a balance between the emotional, imaginative and original, plus the discipline of art."

Hull's importance to the cultural history of Mississippi results not only from her lively experimentation with portraits, landscapes, still lifes, and abstract paintings but also from her impact on the many young artists to whom she gave private lessons. She painted until shortly before her death on 21 November 1980.

Elise Smith
Millsaps College

Patti Carr Black, *Art in Mississippi, 1720–1980* (1998); Mississippi History Now website, http://mshistorynow.mdah.state.ms.us; Bruce Levingston, *Bright Fields: The Mastery of Marie Hull* (2015); Malcolm M. Norwood, Virginia McGehee Elias, and William S. Haynie, *The Art of Marie Hull* (1975); Estill Curtis Pennington and J. Richard Gruber, *Celebrating Southern Art* (1997); Elise Brevard Smith and Liliclaire C. McKinnon, *Marie Hull and Her Contemporaries Theora Hamblett and Kate Freeman Clark* (1988).

Humes, H. H.
(1903–1958) Editor and Religious Leader

Rev. H. H. Humes is an oddity of racial uplift ideology. The tall, eloquent editor of the *Greenville Delta Leader* and president of the Negro State Baptist Convention, Humes viewed the state's black population as separate but equal and therefore requiring little assistance from whites. In 1954 he proudly called Mississippi's blacks a "distinct" race, noting that the separate schools for black and white children planned in Greenville were "the same, penny for penny"— clear evidence, he reasoned, of equal opportunities for both races. His editorials decried the US Supreme Court's efforts to lift the ban on segregation in public schools, and he railed against "northern agitators" seeking to disrupt what he saw as a happy system of tenant farming.

The Mississippi State Sovereignty Commission apparently paid Humes four hundred dollars to enforce segregation, listing the payments as travel and investigative expenditures. After those payments were revealed in 1957, the Negro State Baptist Convention attempted to oust him, though he held onto his post. The extent to which the Sovereignty Commission determined the content of the six-page weekly *Leader* may never be known. Percy Greene, editor of another of the state's successful black newspapers, the *Jackson Advocate*, printed entire articles generated by the Sovereignty Commission. Ideological allies, Humes and Greene had attended Jackson College in Jackson during the 1920s. Like Greene, Humes was a strong proponent of accommodation, describing Greenville as a thriving cotton town where the black man "gets justice in the courts and has his own swimming pool, the same as white, his own Negro policeman and his own Negro welfare worker."

Such views reflected a conservative, successful black middle-class perspective in Greenville and the other Delta towns where the *Leader* circulated. This outlook was reflected not only in the paper's editorials but also in news items featuring successful black businessmen and college graduates as well as in the *Leader's* advertising. On the paper's second anniversary, for example, Leland Oil Works recognized the *Leader* "for its conservative policy," and a funeral business located in the town of Marks hailed the newspaper as the greatest medium of advertising the business had tried in eleven years. A similar advertisement from Greenville's Watson Funeral Home congratulated Humes for "bringing to the public and its readers one of the most ably edited Negro newspapers in circulation anywhere."

In the late 1930s and early 1940s Humes advocated on behalf of the race's talents and abilities, stressing traditional themes of uplift in the black press such as hard work, frugality, and patience. Unlike other editors who employed this strain of racial uplift ideology, however, Humes did not view skin color as a barrier: "The color of the skin and the locality in which you live holds no hindrance to an individual who wants to make progress." Such progress was also reflected in the paper's advertising for events at local entertainment venues, such as the Harlem Theatre, which during World War II hosted a "Who's Who in Greenville" competition to select the best singer, best dancer, best orchestra, most popular lady, and best-dressed person from among the three hundred attendees.

Cotton farming fueled such prosperity, Humes wrote in the *Leader*, which was located on Washington Avenue, in the city's black business district. Numerous articles profiled black farmers, their success defined by their resourcefulness and willingness to eke out a living in Mississippi rather than join the throngs of blacks who had migrated north, an endeavor that Humes saw as a cruel mirage. Humes vowed to devote the *Leader* to showing that blacks outnumbered white farmers, an indication of their success, though he did not indicate in what capacity these black farmers worked.

He dwelled on manners and propriety, identifying such disturbing social trends as black children cursing on Greenville's streets and the jitterbug craze sweeping the Delta. He advised business leaders to form larger associations of merchants on Nelson Street and called for the closing of black-owned roadside restaurants as health hazards, suggesting instead that black entrepreneurs merge to open a grand cafeteria that would draw patrons from miles around for Sunday dinner. In the spirit of such a separatist vision he wrote, "It isn't the policy of *The Delta Leader* to either irritate or agitate. But, our policy is to persistently advocate for those things that are helpful to Negroes."

In sum, Humes was a conflicted figure. Although he advocated voting rights for blacks, his complicity in the caste system that disenfranchised them on so many other levels sullies his efforts. On 2 January 1958 Humes was taken ill while en route home from visiting friends in Leland, and he died of heart attack in a doctor's office.

Mark K. Dolan
University of Mississippi

Greenville Delta Leader (1938–41); Julius E. Thompson, The Black Press in Mississippi, 1865–1985 (1993); Us (February 1954); Patrick S. Washburn, The African American Newspaper: Voice of Freedom (2006).

Hummer, T. R.
(b. 1950) Poet

Terry Randolph Hummer was born in Macon, Mississippi, on 7 August 1950 and raised on a farm in Noxubee County. His father, C. V. Hummer of Prairie Point, traced his Mississippi ancestry to the late nineteenth century, when his family emigrated from Bavaria. Hummer's mother, Marion Kate Slocum Hummer, was a "Mississippian displaced from Louisiana." His parents met in the 1930s, and Hummer was born at what he calls the "statistical crossroad" of the Hummer family's rise into the middle class and the Slocum family's "gradual, but considerable, decline." After C. V. Hummer's death, the family moved to Macon, where the boy attended school. During the summer of 1965 Hummer worked on his uncle's farm, saving "a third of a tenth" of his earnings toward the purchase of an electric guitar.

Despite his farming background, Hummer remembers his Mississippi childhood not idyllically but as part of an increasingly homogenous, facade-focused America divided by land, class, and especially race. Hummer's poem, "Mississippi 1955 Confessional," in The 18,000-Ton Olympic Dream: Poems (1990) confronts the racist ideology of his own upbringing: "A white boy brought up believing the wind isn't even human, the wind is happy / To live in its one wooden room with only newspaper on the walls."

Hummer acknowledges the artistic influences of James Dickey and jazz music as well as a continued deep emotional attachment to Prairie Point and its environs, but he prefers to see himself as a poet "who happens to be from the South" rather than as a southern poet.

Hummer attended the University of Southern Mississippi, earning a bachelor's degree in 1972 and a master's degree two years later. In 1980 Hummer completed a doctorate at the University of Utah, where he studied with poet Dave Smith. Hummer taught at various colleges and universities outside the South until 1997, when he became senior poet in the creative writing program at Virginia

Commonwealth University. In what can be seen as a symbolic return to the South, Hummer joined the blues band Little Ronnie and the Grand Dukes, reinventing the lyric sounds that he remembered from the 1960s.

Hummer published his first chapbook, Translation of Light, in 1976, and has now published ten collections of poems. Hummer received a National Endowment for the Arts Fellowship in 1987, a Guggenheim Fellowship in 1993, and two Pushcart Prizes (1990 and 1992). Walt Whitman in Hell (1996) won the 1999 Hanes Prize for Poetry from Fellowship of Southern Writers. Five of his books have been included in Louisiana State University's Southern Messenger Poets series, including Ephemeron (2011), which won the 2012 Mississippi Arts and Letters Award for Poetry.

In 2006, after spending several years as a professor at the University of Georgia and editor of the Georgia Review, Hummer joined the creative writing program at Arizona State University, where he continues to teach and write poems.

Sean Harrington Wells
Auburn University

Phil Paradis, Cimarron Review (April 1985); T. R. Hummer, e-mail interview with Sean Harrington Wells; T. R. Hummer, James Dickey Newsletter (Fall 1986); T. R. Hummer, Southern Review (Winter 1995); Louisiana State University Press website, www.lsupress.org; Ernest Suarez, in Southbound: Interviews with Southern Poets, ed. Amy Vermer (1999).

Humphreys, Benjamin Grubb
(1808–1882) Twenty-Sixth Governor, 1865–1868

For five years after the Civil War, martial law and civil authority existed concurrently in Mississippi. That phenomenon created a constitutional entanglement that scholars have yet to unravel. Gov. Benjamin Grubb Humphreys had the misfortune of being caught in that knot of conflicting and often competing authority. When Humphreys was inaugurated on 16 October 1865, he shared power with a provisional governor, and he was eventually removed by a military governor whose authority Humphreys challenged and whose orders he countermanded.

Humphreys was born on 26 August 1808 at Hermitage, his father's plantation in Claiborne County along the Bayou Pierre. He was appointed to the US Military Academy at West Point but was expelled with about forty other cadets after they were involved in a Christmas frolic. He then returned to Mississippi to help his father manage the plantation. For almost a decade, Humphreys, a Whig, represented

Benjamin Grubb Humphreys (Archives and Records Services Division, Mississippi Department of Archives and History [PI STA H86.6 Box 19 Folder 18 #2])

Biographical Directory of the United States Congress (1950); William C. Harris, *Day of the Carpetbagger: Republican Reconstruction in Mississippi* (1978); William C. Harris, *Presidential Reconstruction in Mississippi* (1967); *Mississippi Official and Statistical Register* (1912); Dunbar Rowland, *Encyclopedia of Mississippi History: Comprising Sketches of Counties, Towns, Events, Institutions and Persons*, vol. 1 (1907).

Humphreys County

Claiborne County in the state legislature, serving in both the House and the Senate.

In 1846 Humphreys purchased some land in Sunflower County and established a plantation at Roebuck Lake. Humphreys opposed secession, but when the war began, he organized the Sunflower Guards and was soon elected colonel of the 21st Mississippi Regiment. Union troops destroyed his plantation during the Vicksburg Campaign. In July 1863 Humphreys received a promotion to brigadier general and command of Gen. William Barksdale's brigade after Barksdale fell at Gettysburg. Humphreys was seriously wounded at Berryville in September 1864 and was reassigned to duty in South Mississippi.

On 2 October 1865 Humphreys was elected as Mississippi's governor. Among the uncertainties during this difficult and confusing time was the possibility that a Confederate brigadier general might not be eligible for high office in postwar Mississippi. More broadly, Mississippi and other southern states were expected to reconstruct themselves and extend the rights of citizenship to their former slaves. White Mississippians, however, would not voluntarily do so.

Humphreys criticized state legislators' efforts to return African Americans to peonage and to deny them access to the courts and other Black Codes. But when Mississippi and other ex-Confederate states failed to reconstruct themselves under Pres. Andrew Johnson's lenient plan, Congress placed the southern states under military law and installed military governors. While that action did not automatically remove the civil governor, it did create a rivalry between the military and civil authorities that led to Gov. Humphreys's removal from office in 1868.

Humphreys subsequently retired from public life and engaged in business and planting until his death on 22 December 1882. Humphreys County is named in his honor.

David G. Sansing
University of Mississippi

Located in the central Delta and named for Confederate general and Mississippi governor Benjamin Humphreys, Humphreys County was founded in 1918. The Yazoo River flows through the county, and part of the Theodore Roosevelt National Wildlife Refuge lies within its boundaries. The county seat is Belzoni. Other towns include Isola, Louise, and Silver City.

In 1930 Humphreys had a population of 24,729, of whom 17,032 (69 percent) were African American. A rural and agricultural county with fewer than 200 industrial workers, Humphreys had more than fifty-six hundred farms, the majority of them worked by tenants and sharecroppers. During World War II, a site near Belzoni hosted a branch of Hinds County's Camp McCain for prisoners of war.

By 1960 Humphreys's population had declined to 19,093. Its racial demographics remained largely unchanged, though a small Chinese community had developed. Agricultural employment accounted for more than half of the workforce, and the crops grown included cotton, soybeans, winter wheat, rice, and oats. About 300 people worked in furniture and textile manufacturing. In 1976 Gov. Cliff Finch named Humphreys County the Farm-Raised Catfish Capital of the World because of its new efforts at catfish production. The county remained the top catfish-producing county in the United States until changes in the industry in the early twenty-first century.

Belzoni was the site of civil rights activity in the 1950s and some violent opposition. Minister George Lee and businessman Gus Courts helped organize a chapter of the National Association for the Advancement of Colored People in 1953. Lee was murdered in 1955—no charges were ever filed in the case—and Courts was driven from the area.

Humphreys County has been home to an impressive number of artists, musicians, and athletes. Blues musicians Elmore James and Pinetop Perkins spent part of their childhoods there, as did rhythm and blues performer Denise LaSalle. Jazz musician George Cartwright of the band Curlew was born in 1950 in the Humphreys town of Midnight. Artist Ethel Wright Mohamed lived in Belzoni for decades beginning in the 1920s, embroidering pictures of rural life, often specific to the Mississippi Delta. Basketball star Spencer Haywood's long journey through the University of Detroit, the Olympics, the American Basketball Association, and the National Basketball Association began in Silver City. Lawrence Gordon, former president of Twentieth Century Fox and producer of numerous movies, including *Die Hard*, *Predator*, *Field of Dreams*, *Hellboy*, *Watchmen*, and *Boogie Nights*, is a native of Belzoni.

From 1960 to 1980 the county's population again declined, reaching 13,931. Humphreys added a number of new industrial jobs, but private household work followed agriculture as the largest employer. More than 30 percent of the population, a figure considerably higher than the Mississippi average, had fewer than five years of education.

As in many core Delta counties, Humphreys County's 2010 population was predominantly African American and had declined over the last half of the twentieth century. In fact, Humphrey County's population had undergone one of the largest proportional decreases in the state, shrinking by 50.9 percent since 1960. By 2010 population of 9,375 was 74.5 percent African American and 23.5 percent white.

Mississippi Encyclopedia Staff
University of Mississippi

Mississippi State Planning Commission, *Progress Report on State Planning in Mississippi* (1938); *Mississippi Statistical Abstract*, Mississippi State University (1952–2010); Mississippi History Now website, http://mshistorynow.mdah.state.ms.us; Charles Sydnor and Claude Bennett, *Mississippi History* (1939); University of Virginia Library, Historical Census Browser website, http://mapserver.lib.virginia.edu; E. Nolan Waller and Dani A. Smith, *Growth Profiles of Mississippi's Counties, 1960–1980* (1985).

Hunting

People have hunted in what is now Mississippi for at least the past twelve thousand years. Some of the earliest hunters, known as Clovis people to archaeologists, created beautiful stone projectile points and might have been so efficient that they hastened the extinctions of mastodons, giant ground sloths, and other creatures. Later native peoples pursued white-tailed deer, black bears, and a multitude of smaller animals and birds in seasonal rounds of hunting and gathering. As tribes came to depend more on agriculture, they probably hunted less and did so at times that did not interfere with planting and harvest.

By the time Hernando de Soto and his men reached the Mississippi area around 1540, most natives lived in well-established towns near substantial cornfields. Intensive farming and hunting around the towns kept large game well away from the population centers. The Spaniards who traveled from town to town depended for subsistence mainly on pilfered Indian corn, rarely mentioning access to deer and usually short of meat. This dichotomy between settled, farmed land with a complement of small game and the more remote areas with large game such as deer persisted for hundreds of years.

Natives and ever-increasing numbers of Europeans and Africans hunted for subsistence and for hides. Deerskins in particular became a major commodity for the entire Southeast and the primary means by which Native Americans obtained European goods throughout most of the eighteenth century. Overhunting reduced the white-tailed population to a point where the skin trade was no longer commercially viable by the nineteenth century. Hunting generally returned to a means of supplemental subsistence and recreation.

By 1840 most natives had been removed to the West and agriculture was spreading over more of the state. The dichotomy between settled and wild land still held true, as vast river bottoms too flood-prone for farming provided big-game hunting grounds. The settled lands proved an ideal habitat for small game such as rabbit and quail that could withstand persistent hunting by the farm population. During the nineteenth century game of most kinds was available if not abundant, depending on the area and local hunting pressure.

The situation began to change with the turn of the twentieth century as lumber interests began cutting virgin forests and agriculture continued to expand. As the population grew, widespread hunting pressure began to take a toll on larger species such as deer, bears, and turkeys. Theodore Roosevelt's famous 1902 Delta hunt led to the creation of one of the world's most famous toys but came at a time when most of the state's bears were already gone. When Aldo Leopold completed his 1929 survey of Mississippi's game, he estimated that only a remnant population of deer and turkeys remained—too few, in his opinion, to justify hunting. Black bears were too scarce to mention.

Great enthusiasm for small-game hunting remained, however. In particular, quail hunting developed a vast following. Both rich and poor hunted bobwhite quail, usually known simply as *birds*, although the rich appropriated the literature of the quail hunt across the Southeast. People shot squirrels in second- and third-growth forests, ran foxes and coons with hounds, and hunted possums. Waterfowling was also popular, but early on the best spots belonged to wealthy individuals or clubs. It is difficult to overestimate the widespread love of hunting in the state. Both white and black, rich and poor participated. Even though waterfowling and some types of quail hunting remained the province of the wealthy, some facet of the chase was available to almost everyone.

Like most southerners, Mississippians used dogs to hunt just about everything. Feists and curs treed late-season squirrels, pointers and setters located quail, redbones found coons, beagles chased rabbits, and Walker hounds ran deer. However, individual dogs or any mix of dog might turn out to be perfect for certain game, and pedigree was never as important as performance. As reflections of their owners, dogs also added to the element of competition among hunters who might meet for a night of coon hunting or a week at deer camp.

The general affection for hunting helped gain acceptance for the Game and Fish Commission, established in 1933. Fannye Cook and other conservationists had begun working toward an organized game law enforcement agency in the 1920s. Like most government agencies of the time, the new Game Commission had few resources, but it laid the foundation for the conservation programs and restocking efforts in the wake of World War II.

The 1940s marked the beginning of significant changes in game populations and hunting. Work in war-related industries lured the rural poor away from the land, and the postwar mechanization of agriculture drove away even more people. Agriculture continued to characterize the Delta and blackland prairie regions of the state, but much of the upland reverted to or was planted in forest. Population in the countryside dropped dramatically, while an invigorated Game and Fish Commission continued and refined the restocking of large game such as deer and turkeys. Fewer hungry people and modern wildlife-management techniques combined to encourage a remarkable expansion of large game populations. By 1975 breeding populations of deer existed in virtually all parts of Mississippi, and the total herd numbered around half a million. The human reaction to game had fundamentally changed, and a deer in the yard could be simply a spectacle or garden pest, not necessarily a vital food item.

Some of the same changes that led to an increase in large game also led to declines in small game, particularly quail. The weedy field margins and unimproved pastures of small-patch premechanized farming had produced fabulous numbers of quail. As technology allowed, farmers enlarged their fields, eliminating much of the edge effect of numerous hedgerows. Herbicides and pesticides controlled many of the weeds and insects that had made the margins of old-fashioned cotton fields into bird nurseries. New varieties of pasture grass stood up to intense bovine grazing but formed a continuous turf that young quail could not traverse. By the 1980s quail numbers were in steep decline. The conditions that had encouraged quail were by-products of a rural way of life that most people were glad to leave behind. Quail are not endangered, though the few coveys that remain offer only limited hunting. The state manages certain public areas for quail, and some individual landowners attempt to replicate decent habitat conditions. Nevertheless, quail hunting, even poor quail hunting, is probably as rare today in Mississippi as deer hunting was in 1929.

Small-game hunting has by no means disappeared. Squirrel hunting remains popular with or without dogs. Rabbit hunting and coon hunting still have a following, and waterfowling draws as many hunters as ever. Even so, most hunting activity in the state today is connected with deer.

Mississippi enjoys a long deer season that begins with archery around October and allows hunting for whitetails with one weapon or another until the end of January and longer in some areas. A huge industry has evolved to support modern deer hunting. Hunters buy such items as deer calls, camouflage clothing, and deer-urine-based lures in addition to archery equipment and firearms. And while some people still use dogs, hunters are more likely to use deer stands than hounds. Nearly every year, Mississippians debate whether to legalize the practice of hunting over bait such as corn. And some new gadget or practice always seems to challenge the notion of "fair chase."

While individual hunters are spending more money on their pursuit, the number of hunters is falling. This issue is of great concern with regard to deer, which have no serious predators other than humans in Mississippi and no winter kill. Unchecked numbers of white-tails degrade habitat for themselves and other wildlife. Deer do significant damage to certain crops, including soybeans, and are factors in a growing number of traffic accidents. Overpopulation can ultimately lead to malnutrition, disease, and violent fluctuations in deer numbers, problems that are looming in some areas. Biologists have long looked to hunting as a means to control deer, and with no viable alternative, the decline in hunting may be the major wildlife management problem of the future.

Wiley C. Prewitt Jr.
Yocona, Mississippi

Charles Hudson, *Knights of Spain, Warriors of the Sun: Hernando de Soto and the South's Ancient Chiefdoms* (1997); Stuart A. Marks, *Southern Hunting in Black and White: Nature, History, and Ritual in a Carolina Community* (1991); Jim Posewitz, *Beyond Fair Chase: The Ethics and Traditions of Hunting* (1994); Wiley C. Prewitt Jr., "The Best of All Breathing: Hunting and Environmental Change in Mississippi, 1900–1980" (master's thesis, University of Mississippi, 1991); Richard White, *The Roots of Dependency: Subsistence, Environment, and Social Change among the Choctaws, Pawnees, and Navajos* (1983).

Hunting Camps (Hunt Clubs)

Hunt clubs were formally introduced in Mississippi in the early twentieth century. As William Faulkner depicted in

Go Down, Moses, the hunting camp allowed an escape from civilization or at least an opportunity to behave outside normal social conventions. Camp life often blurred the strict racial lines that existed in early twentieth-century Mississippi. Black men served as hunting guides and cooks and often hunted alongside white doctors, lawyers, and prominent businessmen.

Many of Mississippi's hunt clubs were organized by settlers who were clearing the Delta wilderness for farmland and sought to rid the state of its indigenous black bears. US president Theodore Roosevelt went to Issaquena and Sharkey Counties in 1902 to assist in the eradication efforts with a kill of his own. When he refused to shoot a bear supplied by hunting guide Holt Collier at Smedes Plantation in Sharkey County, the incident became the subject of national folklore and the inspiration for the teddy bear.

The Ten Point Deer Club in the Steele Bayou wilderness of Issaquena County became a legendary hunting camp starting in the mid-1920s, playing host to Mississippi's elite white lawyers, doctors, and businessmen. Despite its name, the club initially focused primarily on hunting bears, turkeys, and occasionally squirrels or foxes. Mississippi had only a small deer population for most of the first four decades of the twentieth century, and not until 1942 did the club report its first official deer hunt.

Today, most of the state's hunting clubs concentrate on deer or waterfowl. After massive repopulation efforts over the preceding thirty years, hunters killed an average of 25,000 deer per year statewide by 1970; in 2013, by contrast, Mississippi's 149,046 hunters harvested 263,705 deer. In 2006 white-tailed deer hunting was a $860 million industry, while waterfowl hunting generated $192 million.

Hunting as an economic boost is only a recent phenomenon. In 1937 Mississippi commissioner of agriculture J. C. Holton expressed hope that land control and hunting restrictions could preserve the wildlife population, but he was also concerned about the state being overrun by "game preserves owned by rich men on which others may not hunt and fish." In 1948 Hendrix Dawson, editor of *Mississippi Game and Fish*, compared restricted hunting practices to European aristocratic hunting laws, under which peasants could not kill wild game without permission. In 2001, 92 percent of Mississippi's hunters reportedly hunted on private land, and an estimated 90 percent of the state's available hunting land was privately owned.

For hunters unwilling or unable to purchase or lease hunting land, hunt club memberships are one of few remaining alternatives. Hunt clubs are not required to register with the state, and there is no way to know how many such clubs exist. Nearly 42 percent of resident and nonresident hunters polled in 2001 belonged to a hunt club. Club organizers' responsibilities vary, but officers generally are elected to collect dues, map out hunters' assigned areas, decide where to put the tree stands, pay employees for maintenance, listen to grievances, and ensure that members follow the rules.

Modern camp clubhouses include house trailers, primitive cabins, million-dollar lodges, and everything in between. Upscale cabins can feature deer antler chandeliers hanging over linen-adorned tables bedecked with McCarty pottery and high-definition flat-screen televisions to accompany the traditional storytelling and card-playing entertainment. Each camp has its own characteristics. For example, hunters at Beaver Dam Lake vie for the position of caller—the person responsible for making duck calls—a tradition handed down in some families with as much significance as the first rifle or inheriting the land itself. *Wild Abundance* (2010) is a cookbook anthology that celebrates food and recreational traditions at various Mississippi camps. Traditional camp cooks were apt to grill fish or roast rattlesnake or frog legs over a campfire or bring chicken, steak, or even chili from home.

Traditionally, women were not allowed to join hunt clubs. They could participate in club activities but could not vote on club rules. However, many women still joined in hunting rituals such as having faces smeared with the blood of the first kill or having shirttails cut off if they missed a shot. In the twenty-first century, entire families—daughters and wives as well as sons—are beginning to hunt together. Thirty thousand of the 240,000 Mississippians who reported hunting in 2006 were female. In addition, women participate in female-only hunts. Mississippi's Ward Lake Hunting Club, for example, hosts a club of six women who call themselves the Swamp Witches. This nontraditional group follows more conventional duck hunting methods than many male-only clubs, paddling their own canoes and often waiting in naturally formed duck blinds rather than driving or motorboating to the prefabricated camouflaged blinds that many hunters now use.

Whether a club follows traditional or modern hunting and entertaining practices, camaraderie remains a constant. During the season, members of some clubs have a big Sunday dinner together or eat breakfast before leaving the cabin for the day. Many hunters visit their clubs in the off-season to go fishing or horseback riding or to participate in other outdoor recreational activities.

Michelle Bright
University of Mississippi

Karen Brasher, "Hunting and Fishing Boost Economy, Improve Habitat," *Mississippi State University Forestry, Wildlife, and Fisheries News* (21 October 2010); Brian Broom and Jacob Threadgill, *Jackson Clarion-Ledger* (21 November 2014); Chad M. Dacus, Mississippi Department of Wildlife, Fisheries, and Parks, interview (January 2011); "Economic Impacts of White-Tailed Deer Hunting in Mississippi," paper presented at the Southeastern Association of Fish and Wildlife Agencies (2007); Alan Huffman, *Ten Point: Deer Camp in the Mississippi Delta* (1997); Wiley C. Prewitt Jr., "The Best of All Breathing: Hunting and Environmental

Change in Mississippi, 1900–1980" (master's thesis, University of Mississippi, 1991); Susan Schadt, ed., *First Shooting Light: A Photographic Journal Reveals the Legacy and Lure of Hunting Clubs in the Mississippi Flyway* (2008); Susan Schadt, ed., *Wild Abundance: Ritual, Revelry, and Recipes of the South's Finest Hunting Clubs* (2010).

Hurt, Mississippi John
(1892–1966) Blues Musician

Mississippi John Hurt was born on 8 March 1892 in Teoc, just north of Greenwood in the Mississippi Delta. Hurt grew up one of three children in a farming family in nearby Avalon. He began his musical career by singing in church choirs as a young child. He picked up three-finger style guitar around age nine and soon began playing at local house parties when he was not working as a farmhand around Avalon. Hurt's initial repertoire favored country, pop, and ragtime rather than the gentle blues that came to define most of the rest of his career.

In the early 1920s Hurt met Willie Narmour, a popular local fiddle player, and the two began performing at square dances, to much acclaim. Several years later, Narmour brought Tommy Rockwell of OKeh Records to Hurt's home, where the producer was so impressed by "Monday Morning Blues" that he offered to pay Hurt to come to Memphis for a February 1928 recording session. Only two of the eight sides that Hurt recorded there were ever released, but the label asked him to record again in New York later in the year. Other sessions sporadically followed, but these recordings resulted in only a few, small-selling singles, and Hurt failed to gain any real success.

Hurt likely would have died in obscurity were it not for the folk music revival of the early 1960s. Thirty-five years after Hurt made his first recordings, musicologist Tom Hoskins discovered that Hurt was still living in Avalon. Following the path detailed in Hurt's "Avalon Blues," Hoskins found Hurt, now in his seventies, working as a farmhand. Hurt's musical ability remained intact, and after he played at the 1963 Newport Folk Festival, he toured university campuses, coffeehouses, and concert halls and made a series of recordings for small labels. Hurt eventually made his most memorable live and studio recordings at Vanguard Records under the supervision of folksinger Patrick Sky. Hurt appeared on Johnny Carson's *Tonight Show* in 1963.

Hurt died on 2 November 1966 in Grenada after suffering a heart attack. In 1999 Hurt's granddaughter, Mary Frances Hurt, founded the Mississippi John Hurt Foundation to preserve his musical legacy and provide musical and educational opportunities to disadvantaged young people.

The foundation operates Avalon's Mississippi John Hurt Museum and hosts the annual Mississippi John Hurt Music Festival.

Mark Coltrain
Charlotte, North Carolina

Hugh Barker and Yuval Taylor, *Faking It: The Quest for Authenticity in Popular Music* (2007); Bruce Eder, AllMusic.com website, www.allmusic.com; Sheldon Harris, ed., *Blues Who's Who: A Biographical Dictionary of Blues Singers* (1981); Mississippi John Hurt Foundation website, http://www.mississippijohnhurtfoundation.org/.

I

I-House

The I-house was first recognized as a recurring vernacular house form by Fred Kniffen of Louisiana State University. He coined the name in 1936, deriving it from the fact that the house form was often found in the midwestern states of Indiana, Illinois, and Iowa. Kniffen also recognized that the term was appropriate since the profile of the core house form, which consists of two main rooms set side-by-side on the first story and a matching pair on the upper story, has a distinct vertical orientation that suggests a capital *I*. Most commonly in the South, a central passageway separates the main rooms on both stories. The I-house is a vernacular house type characterized by a recurring physical form rather than by features associated with any particular architectural style. Stylistic features were applied to the recurring form and changed over time in keeping with popular tastes.

The origins of the I-house are unclear. Some scholars believe that it is derived from sixteenth-century English antecedents, while others think that it is an American form related to log-building traditions. The I-house emerged as a recognizable form in Pennsylvania, Delaware, Maryland, and Virginia by the 1750s and in the Carolinas by the 1780s. By the end of the eighteenth century regional variations of the basic I-house form had emerged. I-houses with porticoes and small porches tended to dominate in Virginia, while single-story, full-width porches or galleries were widespread on the I-houses of the Piedmont area of the Carolinas and Georgia. In the coastal areas of the Carolinas many I-houses featured full-width porches on both stories.

The I-house form appeared in Mississippi around 1800, brought to the Natchez area by settlers from the Eastern Seaboard. The I-house was widely built throughout Mississippi in the antebellum period, reaching the peak of its popularity and consistency of form in the 1840s and 1850s. Most Mississippi I-houses are wood-frame buildings with weatherboard siding. Brick I-houses are much less common and are located mostly in towns, with the highest concentration in Holly Springs.

I-houses in Mississippi are generally categorized into several subtypes on the basis of porch configuration and the arrangement of rooms beyond the core form. These subtypes include

- basic I-house with no porch
- I-house with one-story portico
- I-house with monumental portico
- I-house with double-tiered portico
- I-house with composite porch (combining a one-story, full-width porch and a two-story or monumental portico)
- single-galleried or Carolina I-house (one-story, full-width porch)
- double-galleried I-house (two-story, full-width front porch)
- full-colonnaded I-house
- I-house with dual overlapping colonnades

Of these subtypes, the most popular were the monumentally porticoed, single-galleried, and double-galleried variants. The porticoed I-house was preferred in the northern third of the state; the single-galleried I-house was preferred in the central and southern uplands; and the double-galleried I-house was most prevalent in the southwest corner of the state, in and around Natchez.

I-houses continued to be built after the Civil War but declined in popularity after about 1875 because of changing architectural tastes and technologies. Few were built after the turn of the twentieth century.

Todd Sanders
Mississippi Department of
Archives and History

Richard J. Cawthon, *The I-House and Expanded I-House in Mississippi, 1800–1875: Variations of a Traditional Form* (1992).

Iberville, Pierre Le Moyne, Sieur d'

(1661–1706) French Military Leader

Pierre Le Moyne, Sieur d'Iberville, founded the French colony of Louisiana and the first European settlement in what is now Mississippi at Biloxi in 1699. The third son of noted New France emigrant Charles Le Moyne de Longueuil et de Châteauguay, Iberville was born in Montreal, in the French colony of Canada, in 1661. From 1686 to 1697 he took part in several expeditions to drive the English from the Hudson Bay region and claim Canada for France. His successes earned him a reputation as a bold and ruthless warrior, while plunder and trade licenses granted by the French government made him very wealthy.

In 1697 the French government selected him to lead an expedition to fortify the mouth of the Mississippi River and establish a colony in the Gulf Coast region. The French hoped to secure the area for themselves and prevent English colonial expansion in the region. René-Robert, Cavalier de La Salle, had claimed the area in 1682 and named it Louisiana in honor of the French king but had failed to solidify the claim by establishing a settlement.

Iberville departed France in October 1698 with two ships, the *Badine* and the *Marin*, and arrived on the Gulf Coast in January 1699. Finding the Spanish already in possession of the excellent harbor at Pensacola, he continued westward, exploring Mobile Bay and portions of the Mississippi Sound. Anchoring off of Ship Island on 10 February, he took a canoe over to the mainland three days later. He moved quickly to obtain the friendship of local tribes by providing them with food and gifts. From them he learned of a river to the west that he believed was the Mississippi and set out to explore it. Only after returning from his expedition up the river did he obtain conclusive proof that he had indeed found the Mississippi: a local tribe presented members of his expedition with a letter written more than a decade earlier to La Salle.

Iberville did not find a suitable site for a fort along the Mississippi and authorized the construction of a fort on Biloxi Bay. The settlement, Fort Maurepas, served as the first capital of French Louisiana. When the post was completed, Iberville returned to France, returning in January 1700 to further explore the Mississippi. He authorized construction of Fort Boulaye, located in present-day Plaquemines Parish, Louisiana, to deter English intrusion before leaving for France once again. He returned in December 1701 with instructions to move the colony to Mobile Bay to be closer to France's ally, Spain, at Pensacola, in case of war with England. Iberville left the area for the final time after the construction of Fort Louis at Mobile in 1702.

In 1706 Iberville took part in an expedition charged with attacking British colonies in the West Indies. He captured the island of Nevis from the English but caught yellow fever in Havana soon thereafter and died on 9 July 1706.

Mike Bunn
Historic Chattahoochee
Commission

Nellis M. Crouse, *Le Moyne d'Iberville, Soldier of New France* (2001); Richard A. McLemore, *A History of Mississippi* (1973); Richebourg G. McWilliams, ed., *Iberville's Gulf Journals* (1991); Charles L. Sullivan and Murella H. Powell, *The Mississippi Gulf Coast: Portrait of a People* (1999).

Ibrahima, Abdul-Rahman
(1762–1829) Slave and Public Figure

Born into royalty in the Futa Jallon region of West Africa (present-day Guinea) in 1762, Abdul-Rahman Ibrahima was educated in the Muslim cites of Jenne and Timbuktu. Following the completion of his education, Ibrahima served as an officer in the military and was given the rank of colonel at the age of twenty-six. In 1788 Ibrahima led a troop of two thousand men against the Hebohs, a group of non-Muslim Africans who were disrupting his father's slave trade with Europeans. Ibrahima was captured and sold to British slavers for two bottles of rum, eight hands of tobacco, two flasks of powder, and a few muskets.

Ibrahima was transported nearly three thousand miles to the Caribbean island of Dominica; after a brief stay, he was shipped another sixteen hundred miles to New Orleans, at the time under Spanish control. From New Orleans, Ibrahima and other slaves were loaded onto a barge and sent upriver to Natchez, Mississippi, where a young planter, Thomas Foster, purchased Ibrahima and his friend, Samba, for around $950.

Foster greatly valued Ibrahima because of the respect other slaves accorded him, his loyalty and trustworthiness, his skill in tending cattle, and his managerial abilities in supervising slaves in the cultivation of cotton. Foster renamed his new slave *Prince* and occasionally allowed him to walk to a rural market a few miles north of Natchez to sell vegetables. In 1807, at a market crossroads, Prince asked a white man if he wanted to buy some vegetables and was surprised when the man responded by addressing the slave as *Ibrahima*. The man was Dr. John Coates Cox, and he had met Ibrahima in Africa. For the next twenty years, Cox, and his son, William, worked to obtain Ibrahima's freedom.

In the 1820s William Cox and Natchez newspaper editor Andrew Marschalk joined forces to call national attention to Ibrahima's plight. Marschalk's articles drew the attention of leaders of the American Colonization Society, a group founded in 1816 that sought to send free American blacks to settle in West Africa. After the intervention of Henry Clay, secretary of state under Pres. John Quincy Adams, a leading opponent of slavery, Foster agreed to sell Ibrahima for two hundred dollars on the condition that he immediately leave for Liberia. After receiving his emancipation in 1827 or 1828, however, Ibrahima toured northern cities as part of a campaign to raise funds to buy his family's freedom. Often dressed as a Muslim prince, Ibrahima thrilled audiences with his remarkable story, and he met many influential Americans, including Pres. Adams. His supporters included noted abolitionists, including some northern merchants who hoped to partner with him in trading ventures, as well as

African Americans, among them John Russwurm, the editor of the nation's first African American newspaper, *Freedom's Journal.*

However, Ibrahima's willingness to seek the support of abolitionists alienated his Natchez-based supporters, particularly Marschalk. In his opinion, Ibrahima had betrayed his promise to leave immediately for West Africa, and the editor published numerous articles both locally and in the national press attacking Ibrahima. This agitation became caught up in national politics when supporters of proslavery presidential candidate Andrew Jackson attacked the Adams administration for using Ibrahima to undermine the institution of slavery.

In the summer of 1829 Rahman and his wife, Isabella, whose freedom he had managed to secure, departed for Africa, leaving behind their children and grandchildren. He became seriously ill shortly after they arrived in Liberia and died on 6 July 1829. Ibrahima's New York supporters purchased two of his sons and their families, who were reunited with Isabella in Liberia, but eight of their other children and their families remained enslaved in Mississippi.

Dawn Dennis

Northridge, California

Terry Alford, *Prince among Slaves: The True Story of an African Prince Sold into Slavery in the American South* (1997); Allen D. Austin, *African Muslim Slaves in Antebellum America: A Sourcebook* (1984); Allen D. Austin, *African Muslims in Antebellum America: Transatlantic Stories and Spiritual Struggles* (1997); Sylviane A. Diouf, *Servants of Allah: African Muslims Enslaved in the Americas* (1998); "From African Prince to Mississippi Slave: Abdul Rahman Ibrahima," Documenting the American South website, http://docsouth.unc.edu/highlights/ibrahima.html; P. J. Staudenraus, *The African Colonization Movement, 1816–1865* (1961); Bertram Wyatt-Brown, *Southern Honor: Ethics and Behavior in the Old South* (1982).

Ice Plants

Manufactured block ice had a profound impact on the Deep South, leaving a legacy still apparent today. Agriculture, poultry, dairy farming, and seafood became well-established industries with the introduction of plants that produced three-hundred-pound blocks of ice, the region's first inexpensive means of refrigeration.

In Mississippi, manufactured ice plants appeared first in Natchez and later in Jackson in 1880. The Natchez plant was built on the banks of the Mississippi River, while Jackson's Morris Ice Company was located along the Pearl River. By the early 1900s plants had been constructed on the coast and in North Mississippi. Run by steam engines, the plants produced their own electricity and often supplied excess energy to neighboring businesses or to the town itself.

Ice was at first a luxury used for cooling in the summertime, but both home and commercial usage grew steadily throughout the 1900s and 1910s. By World War I ice was so vital that men who worked at ice plants could be excused from war duty. During the Great Depression people were so dependent on ice that most plants suffered little setback. According to a 1934–35 Mississippi Bureau of Census study, sixty-seven of Mississippi's eighty-two counties had ice plants, and their value totaled $3,630,000.

Well into the 1940s, ice plants relied on home delivery routes throughout the summer months. The homeowner would place a card, supplied by the ice plant, in the front window with the desired amount of ice needed—generally twenty-five, fifty, or seventy-five pounds. Two or three times a week, the deliveryman would chop off the appropriate amount from a three-hundred-pound block, carry it into the home, and place it in the icebox.

Along the Mississippi Gulf Coast, the seafood industry developed hand in hand with ice plants. Ships used ice in the hull to preserve the daily catch. Local markets used ice to store and display the seafood. Customers kept the seafood in their home iceboxes until they were ready to prepare it. The Pascagoula Ice and Freezer Company, purchased by Hermes Gautier in 1936 from the Electric Light and Power plant, is Mississippi's only remaining block ice plant using an ammonia compressor system.

In the produce region in the middle of the state, ice was critical for refrigeration during transportation, enabling the shipment of produce to regional and national markets. One of the most notable ice plants, McComb Ice House and Creamery, was opened in McComb in 1904 by brothers Hugh and William McColgan. Located at the crossroads of the produce markets of Mississippi and Louisiana, the plant became the largest in the South in 1924, producing two hundred tons of ice a day. In 1926 Xavier Kramer purchased the plant, and it became the largest railroad-icing complex in the world. Using electronic conveyors, the icing galleries could load sixty rail cars simultaneously and ice an entire trainload of cars in less than an hour—less than half the usual time.

In the Delta, ice plants sold much of their product to cotton farmers for drinking water. When cotton choppers were replaced by herbicides, some ice plants relied on the catfish farming industry for their customer base. Ice supplied oxygen and refrigeration when transporting live catfish to processing plants.

Numerous technological advances chipped away at the usefulness of the block ice business. From the invention of refrigerated trucks and railcars to the use of modern ice machines in restaurants and chicken-processing plants, the ammonia block ice plants became obsolete by the 1960s and 1970s.

Elli Morris

Richmond, Virginia

Mississippi, Bureau of Census, *Ice Plants 1934–35: Study of Ad Valorem Assessments in Various Mississippi Industries* (1935); Elli Morris, *Cooling the South: The Block Ice Era, 1875–1975* (2008); Bernard Nagengast, *Mechanical Engineering* magazine website, www.memagazine.org.

Imes, Birney
(b. 1951) Photographer

Vinton Birney Imes III is a photographer whose endeavors have included commercial and studio photography and photojournalism. He is a self-taught artist who depicts the people, places, and landscapes of rural Mississippi.

Museum collections in the United States and France contain his photographs. From coast to coast, galleries and museums have exhibited his pictures. His work has appeared alongside that of other fine American photographers, including Walker Evans, Margaret Bourke-White, Clarence John Laughlin, and Robert Frank.

According to Mississippi-born writer Richard Ford, the photographs in Imes's *Juke Joint* evoke a "thrilling otherness." That could mean the color picture of a juke joint with a blue front and a blue truck by it. Or it could mean a black-and-white image of rabbits hanging lifeless from the waist of a young hunter, a close-up of his torso and torn and bloodied pants' legs. In the background another hunter with torn pants rests a gun barrel on his shoulder.

The oldest of the five sons and one daughter of Vinton Birney Imes Jr. and Nancy McClanahan Imes, Birney was born on 21 August 1951 in Columbus, Mississippi. Educated in Columbus public schools and at the University of Tennessee, where he majored in history, he points out, "When my high school was integrated in the late 60s, the veil began to part, and I started to see the richness and diversity of culture that till then had been hidden from me. When I began photographing six or seven years later, it was in part my wish and my need to overcome this ignorance that helped make my choice of subject an obvious one." As a young white man he increasingly photographed African Americans in Northeast Mississippi and to the west in the Delta.

For a time, he worked as a photojournalist for his family's newspaper, the *Columbus Commercial Dispatch*. He moved into commercial and studio photography and was drawn to black-and-white images. By 1983 he was photographing juke joints with a large-format camera, making long exposures with small apertures and color film. In her introduction to Imes's *Whispering Pines*, curator Trudy Wilner Stack wrote, "The camera allows him to cross the unseen lines of familial, racial, and class territory." Imes says, "When I show these pictures or try to talk about them, someone invariably wants me to explain myself in terms of race—my being white and the subjects being black. . . . Maybe the answer they are looking for is in the pictures."

Singer Lucinda Williams has acknowledged the debt her songwriting owes to *Juke Joint*. An Imes picture, *Turk's Place, Leflore County, 1989*, graces the cover of her Grammy-winning *Car Wheels on a Gravel Road*.

Imes is married to Beth Hickel Imes, to whom he dedicated *Juke Joint*, and they are the parents of two sons and one daughter. In 1996 Imes followed in the footsteps of his father and grandfather, becoming editor and publisher of the *Commercial Dispatch*, where he also writes a column and sometimes takes pictures.

Berkley Hudson

University of Missouri

Birney Imes, *Juke Joint* (1990); Birney Imes, *Partial to Home: Photographs by Birney Imes* (1994); Birney Imes, *Whispering Pines* (1994).

In the Heat of the Night

Set in Sparta, Mississippi, but filmed mostly in Sparta, Illinois, and Dyersburg, Tennessee, the 1967 film *In the Heat of the Night* won five Academy Awards and presented an important view of both racial tensions and the potential for human respect in a 1960s Mississippi torn by conflict over civil rights. The film's source is John Ball's novel *In the Heat of the Night* (1965), winner of an Edgar Award for Best First Mystery Novel. At the core of both the film and the novel is the dramatic relationship between Virgil Tibbs, a sophisticated black homicide detective from outside the South, and Bill Gillespie, a shrewd, small-town white sheriff, who eventually come to work together to solve the murder of a prominent citizen.

The police take Tibbs into custody because he is black and a stranger. Gillespie learns that Tibbs is a police officer and then is pressured by a relative of the murder victim to ask Tibbs to help find the killer. Outraged that a black man is involved in the investigation, members of the town council and a group of young punks harass Gillespie and Tibbs, seeking to get Tibbs off the case and out of town. Both men are proud, willful, and despite their prejudices intelligent enough to know that they need each other to solve the case. Much of the story revolves around the two men's struggle to work through their difficulties and achieve their goals. In the process, they not only solve the crime but earn each other's respect.

In the film, directed by Norman Jewison, Sidney Poitier and Rod Steiger play the roles of Tibbs and Gillespie. Both actors give outstanding performances: Steiger received the Academy Award for Best Actor, and Poitier won much praise across the country. The *New York Times*, for example, declared, "It is most appropriate and gratifying to see Mr. Poitier coming out at this moment of crisis in racial affairs in a film which impressively presents him as a splendid exponent of his race." The film also won the Oscar for Best Film (beating out *Bonnie and Clyde*; *The Graduate*; *Guess Who's Coming to Dinner*, another Poitier film concerned with racial issues; *Cool Hand Luke*; and *In Cold Blood*) as well as Academy Awards for its screenplay, sound, and editing.

Three significant changes in the screenplay sharpen the film's focus on civil rights issues. First, in the book, Tibbs is from Pasadena, California, while in the movie he is from Philadelphia, Pennsylvania, a shift that highlights the North-South tensions over race. Second, the film's murder victim is from the North and plans a factory that will economically enhance the town but also will employ both blacks and whites equally. In the novel the victim is a music impresario whose music festival will save the town's economy. Third, and most significant, the book is set in South Carolina, whereas the movie is set in Mississippi, which had become the center of the racial conflicts that beset the country in the 1960s.

The *Time* magazine review of the film states that *In the Heat of the Night* shows "that men can join hands out of fear and hatred and shape from base emotions something identifiable as a kind of love." On the film's thirtieth anniversary, *Salon* said that its "message was profound: that education, intellect, decency and elegant self-comportment are the surest and best ways to eradicate racism."

Larry Vonalt
Missouri University of Science and
Technology

Bosley Crowther, *New York Times* (6 August 1967); Mark Gauvreau Judge, *Salon.com* website, www.salon.com (1998); *Time* (11 August 1967).

Indian Removal Act of 1830

In the early years of the republic, the US government adopted an Indian policy that emphasized education for native peo-

ple and the cultivation of family-sized farms. In this period the United States did not mandate that tribes move west across the Mississippi River. In 1817 secretary of war John C. Calhoun of South Carolina added to current policy the statement that the national goal was to preserve Indians and that they should never be forced to abandon ancestral lands. In 1828, however, the nation elected Andrew Jackson to the presidency. The westerners who assumed control of the government wanted Indians removed across the Mississippi River, allowing rich eastern lands finally to become farms and plantations for white encroachers without fear of raids or legal objections.

Jackson tended to be a pragmatist, shifting from nationalistic to states' rights stances without missing a beat. On removing Indians to the West, Jackson was clearly a states' rights advocate. On 30 July 1829 his secretary of war issued a directive declaring that individual states had dominion over their resident Native Americans, and on 19 January 1830 both houses of the Mississippi legislature extended the state's laws "over the persons and property of the Indians resident within its limits." With the governor's signature, Indians could no longer claim special privileges. Violations of the measure would result in fines of up to one thousand dollars and as many as twelve months in prison. The only way that Indians could retain their heritage and uniqueness, according to supporters of Removal, was to move west of the Mississippi River.

The controversy in Mississippi spread across the country and led to one of the most bitter congressional battles during the Jacksonian era. Northern liberals opposed Removal, while frontiersmen backed the policy. On 6 April 1830 the Senate began to discuss a bill to move Indians to the West. Sen. Hugh L. White of Tennessee headed the supporters, while opponents were led by Sen. Theodore Frelinghuysen of New Jersey, who requested the passage of a resolution perpetually guaranteeing Indians sovereignty over all their current lands and a resolution declaring that Indian land could be acquired only through a negotiated treaty acceptable to both sides. On 10 April both resolutions were defeated in close votes.

Those votes sealed the fate of native people on ancestral lands in Mississippi and other southern states. Later that day Jacksonian senators offered a bill "to provide for an exchange of . . . lands with the Indians residing in any of the states or territories and for their removal west of the river Mississippi." Opponents could only revisit the policies in place since George Washington's presidential days, which required coexistence with Indians. The Removal bill passed the Senate by a 28–19 vote and was sent to the House of Representatives for concurrence.

In the House, Rep. William R. Storrs of Connecticut introduced the two Frelinghuysen resolutions on 7 April. The debate was every bit as fierce as that in the Senate, and western expansionists won the day only through the personal involvement of Pres. Jackson. He met individually with northern Democrats, using the bully pulpit and congressional pork to secure their votes. On 29 May the House voted 103–97 in favor of a measure that had only minor differences from the Senate bill. The two houses ironed out the inconsistencies during the following month, and on 30 June Jackson signed the Indian Removal Act of 1830 into law.

The act led to Mississippi's Treaty of Dancing Rabbit Creek on 27 September 1830 and the removal of all but a few of Mississippi's Choctaw Indians between 1831 and 1833. Other tribes followed. The Indian Removal Act of 1830 was the most important piece of legislation affecting US-Indian relations.

Arthur H. DeRosier Jr.
Rocky Mountain College

Thomas Hart Benton, *Thirty Years View; or, A History of the Workings of the American Government for Thirty Years from 1820 to 1850* (1856); Arthur H. DeRosier Jr., *The Removal of the Choctaw Indians* (1970); A. Hutchinson, ed., *Code of Mississippi, Being an Analytical Compilation of the Public and General Statutes of the Territory and State with Tabular References to the Local and Private Acts, from 1789 to 1848* (1848); *Journal of the House of Representatives of the State of Mississippi, at Their 1830 Session Held in the Town of Jackson* (1830).

Indians, East

Indians began immigrating to Mississippi from the Indian subcontinent in perceptible numbers in the early to mid-1960s. These immigrants had generally come to the United States to further their education and then moved to the state to take jobs. The population gradually grew, and Indians began coming to Mississippi directly from their home country, with some of the largest concentrations in Jackson, Starkville, Oxford, and Hattiesburg. As of 2014, the US Census Bureau's American Community Survey estimated that Mississippi was home to approximately 5,400 Indians.

The earliest immigrants worked primarily in the areas of medicine and higher education. While these professions continue to be well represented among Indians in Mississippi, the employment picture is now much more diverse. In the early 1980s, with the growth of Jackson's wireless communication industry, Indians began seeking jobs in this area of information technology. Indian entrepreneurs began establishing motels, even in smaller towns, across the state. Mississippi now has a considerable number of Indian-owned small businesses, among them convenience stores, gas stations, fast-food restaurants, and other franchises. Though these businesses are most visible in Jackson, they can be seen throughout the state. Indian physicians, too, have ventured into even the smallest of communities, sometimes serving as the sole health care providers in rural areas.

As the number of Indians has grown, so has the range of services that they require. Jackson now has places of worship for Hindus and Sikhs that employ full-time priests, stores that stock a full range of Indian groceries and the inevitable Bollywood DVDs, Indian restaurants, and a beauty salon that also sells ethnic clothing and jewelry. Periodically, one of the grocery stores hosts a show by a jeweler from a large city. A movie theater in nearby Madison occasionally screens Hindi movies. All of these enterprises appeal to non-Indians as well as Indians.

The population of Indians in Mississippi represents the mosaic that is India, and although most of the state's Indian community is Hindu, other faiths are represented. All of the country's major festivals are celebrated with verve across the state, with the size of the Indian community deciding the scale. In particular, Indian students at the University of Mississippi, Mississippi State University, and the University of Southern Mississippi mark major holidays. As the number of Indians has grown, some splintering into narrower segments has naturally occurred. These groups, usually united by language, commemorate occasions that may be particular to them. In addition, Indian and other South Asian students at both the University of Mississippi and Mississippi State University have formed cricket clubs, while students at Southern Miss have staged demonstrations of the sport.

In all instances, Indians take pleasure in inviting non-Indians to participate in their celebrations and to share their country's foods and cultural practices. College and school groups visit Indians' places of worship in Jackson, and other institutions and civic groups across the state make attempts to educate their members about the culture and religions of India.

As is true of most immigrant groups, Indian families emphasize education and academic success, and members of the younger generation have distinguished themselves scholastically and in extracurricular activities. Taken together, Indian immigrant parents and their first-generation American-born children in Mississippi can be considered an example of a "model minority." Though this designation carries some negative connotations, it also signifies a level of achievement that is generally typical of this demographic in Mississippi. Parents and grandparents work to ensure that youngsters learn about their heritage and culture, and young Indian Americans seem to move with ease between their homes that have a largely Indian flavor (in all senses) and the world beyond. While some initiatives have sought to teach the Hindi language, Indian religious beliefs, and Indian cultural practices in formal settings, most of the instruction in these areas takes place as it does in India—at home, both by example and by osmosis. Many of the children speak the language of their parents.

Seetha Srinivasan
Jackson, Mississippi

US Census Bureau, American FactFinder website, factfinder.census.gov; Seetha Srinivasan, in *Ethnic Heritage in Mississippi*, ed., Barbara Carpenter (1992).

Industry and Industrial Labor

Mississippi's historic failure to develop significant industry was in part a product of attitude and preference, as reflected in John Sharp Williams's 1916 statement that Mississippi was a "'wonderful state,' untroubled by industries, cities, and ambition!" However, from its earliest days the area that is now Mississippi enjoyed a small amount of nonagricultural economic activity, often connected to the region's abundant forests and waters. West Florida produced barrel staves for sale to the sugar planters of the West Indies, ships as large as twenty tons were built in Pascagoula, and naval stores were produced for export. While manufacturing was limited in the Mississippi Territory, by 1810 the area had twenty spinning mills as well as 1,330 looms producing 350,000 yards of cotton cloth annually. In addition, there were producers of linen and woolen fabric, tanneries, and distilleries.

The first major new industrial enterprise of the 1830s was at Bankston, the location of a tannery, shoe manufactory, brickyard, and wheat, grist, saw, and textile mills. These operations, founded by J. M. Wesson, employed slaves and northern workers. By 1840, in an age dominated by cotton production, Mississippi had fifty textile factories, but they were extremely small and employed only eighty-four people. A spinning mill was constructed at Natchez to provide cotton and woolen thread for home looms. The state's major industries were lumber mills, grist and flour mills, and tanneries.

Edward McGehee built a large steam cotton mill in Woodville in 1850, and Joshua and Thomas Green opened a textile

J. Bound's Mill, Moss Point, ca. 1913 (Ann Rayburn Paper Americana Collection, Department of Archives and Special Collections, J. D. Williams Library, University of Mississippi [rayburn_ann_32_30_001])

mill in Jackson five years later. Mississippi's largest industry in 1860 was lumbering, with 228 firms employing more than 1,400 workers. Other important industries included grain milling, blacksmithing, carriage and wagon making, metalworking, machinery and implement manufacturing, leather finishing, and cotton ginning. Between 1850 and 1860 the number of employees grew from 3,154 to 4,775. The industrial labor force was mostly white, including many immigrants in the textile industry.

Industry's rise from the ashes of the war began with Wesson's establishment of the Mississippi Mills in 1866. Later acquired by a New Orleans firm and then by cotton planter Edward Richardson, the factory burned in 1873 and was replaced by a new facility considered the largest textile mill south of the Ohio River. The operation employed eight workers and won national notice for the high quality of its products. By the end of Reconstruction, several other textile operations had entered the industry, including Stonewall Cotton Mill at Enterprise and Corinth's Whitfield Manufacturing Company.

Some historians argue that during the late nineteenth century Mississippi failed to attract industry as rapidly as neighboring states because its resources were primarily extractive and lacked coal, hydroelectric, and other power facilities. Observers in the early twentieth century cited the absence of major population centers as an impediment, noting that cities on Mississippi's borders acted as barriers to its urban development. Other perceived problems included a predominantly agricultural labor force and the low level of education among Mississippi's workers, especially African Americans.

In 1882 the state legislature passed a law exempting new industries from taxation during their first decade of operation. This action stimulated investment, and by 1890 the state had nine cotton mills. Most of the workers were white, although African Americans were sometimes employed as firemen or janitors. Most of the white workers were natives of the area, although there were some immigrants from abroad or from other parts of the country. Still, these mills employed an average of only about twelve hundred workers and constituted only 1 percent of the country's mills.

A longleaf pine lumber boom began along the Gulf Coast during the last quarter of the century, with the firm of Poitevant and Favre constructing one of the world's largest mills at Pearlington. However, despite an abundance of timber, only seven ships with a total value of six thousand dollars were constructed in Mississippi yards during 1890. In that year the state ranked thirty-eighth (out of forty-four states) in the gross value of products and thirty-ninth in the average number of employees. In addition to the textile mills, in 1890 Mississippi had 338 sawmills, 408 flour and grist mills, and 8 planing mills and door manufacturers. To stimulate industrialization the tax exemptions for factories were extended in 1900 to include five-year exemptions for state taxes and ten-year exemptions for city taxes.

From 1890 to 1920 dramatic increases occurred in the number of manufacturing establishments in the state, the value of products, and capital investment. But while the increases were well above the national averages, Mississippi's relative position among the states did not improve. Much of the increase occurred in lumbering, which accounted for nearly half of the value of manufacturing in the state and employed 21,223 out of 33,994 industrial workers in 1905.

Lumbering was a short-term proposition governed by a prevailing "Cut out and get out" philosophy. With the advent of railroad logging and steam-powered mills, lumbermen cut Mississippi's forests rapidly, without providing for regeneration; once the trees were leveled, the industry moved on to other venues, especially in the West. Mississippians resented the exploitation of their forests to enrich investors and lumbermen from other areas. Such anger was channeled through Gov. James K. Vardaman's attacks on the "lumber trust" and corporate interests generally. The rate of corporate expansion in the state slowed.

Gov. Henry L. Whitfield attempted to create a more favorable industrial climate by pushing for the repeal of laws limiting landholding by large corporations (a change that particularly affected lumber companies) and by encouraging railroad construction and the establishment of cotton mills. Signs of progress were evident: for example, although the lumber industry had eliminated some forty thousand jobs by 1930, all but five thousand were replaced by other employment. Also, lumber manufacturing began its evolution into the forest products industry as the Dantzler family began to make paper at Moss Point and William H. Mason developed a fiberboard process, turning out Masonite at Laurel. Because these industries used young pine trees and because officials wanted to revive the lumber industry on a more stable basis, Mississippi implemented a tax-exemption program for reforestation to encourage the growth of forests and their resulting jobs.

During the 1920s canning of fish produced rapid industrial growth along the Gulf Coast. However, during the early twentieth century, overall industry declined in importance, with manufacturing employment growing by only about seven thousand workers between 1910 and 1920 and then declining by nearly five thousand over the ensuing decade. By 1930 the state had only ten textile mills. Mississippi was hit hard by the Great Depression and lost population as people moved to other states to look for jobs.

State leaders struggled to attract investment and industry. A train with exhibits promoting Mississippi's industrial potential traveled across other sections of the country. Gov. Martin Conner promoted industrialization, and Gov. Hugh White was elected in 1935 on a platform of industrial development. White's program, Balance Agriculture with Industry (BAWI), led to the creation of the Mississippi Industrial Commission, which was empowered to issue certificates to local governments that sought to build plants for lease to prospective manufacturers. Citizens were asked to vote for local bond issues to finance plant construction. From 1936 to 1940, twelve plants were constructed under BAWI-approved bond issues. Most were in the garment industry, but there were also the Armstrong plant at Natchez and the Ingalls Shipyard at Pascagoula. By the end of World War II, BAWI-financed plants supplied nearly a quarter of the state's industrial payroll, and the plants attracted during the 1930s accounted for 14 percent of the state's industrial workers.

World War II brought industrial progress, including tremendous growth at Pascagoula, where Ingalls built commercial and US Navy ships, and at Flora and Prairie, where large ordnance plants operated. During the wartime boom from 1939 to 1947, the number of manufacturing establishments in Mississippi grew by 61 percent, factory employment rose by 47 percent, and workers' income increased by 286 percent. Still, Mississippi ranked last among the states in federally financed war production facilities and total war contracts and tied for last in privately financed facilities.

In 1944, to facilitate the transition to peacetime industry and promote industrialization, Gov. Thomas L. Bailey set up the Agricultural and Industrial Board. The effort included tax exemptions for industry and public bond issues to build plants. By the late 1950s the program had sponsored some 188 industrial projects, including 141 new industries and 47 plant expansions. Other industries were attracted by the state's welcoming attitude. In 1957 Gov. J. P. Coleman increased funding for activities associated with industrial development, and his successor, Ross Barnett, created a "research park" in Jackson and pushed for a reduction in corporate taxes. In addition, railroads and power companies maintained industrial promotion programs, as did many other private groups, including the Mississippi Manufacturers Association and the Delta Council.

Mississippi industries grew rapidly during the 1950s. Industrial output reached $175 million in 1937, $759 million in 1947, and $1.605 billion a decade later. Wages rose by more than 100 percent. The leading industries were lumber, food processing, and pulp and paper, with textile manufacturing lagging far behind. Among the most spectacular stories was that of the Ingalls Shipbuilding, which had thrived during and after the war and by the late 1950s was the state's largest single employer. Other large enterprises with significant industrial workforces included producers of shoes, garments, and chemicals.

In 1956 state industrial and financial leaders established the First Mississippi Corporation, which issued and sold bonds for new industries and industrial expansion. One of the first beneficiaries was the Coastal Chemical Corporation at Pascagoula, the world's largest producer of sulfuric acid. By 1957 Mississippi chemical manufacturers employed six thousand workers and produced $181 million in goods annually. Natural gas was discovered near Amory in 1928 and near Jackson in 1930. At the end of the decade, major oil discoveries took place, and oil refining became a significant enterprise. In 1958 the state's largest refinery began producing gasoline for Gulf Oil, and by 1970 Mississippi ranked ninth nationally in production and value of petroleum and tenth in natural gas production, employing more than fourteen thousand workers.

By 1957 Mississippi had a total workforce of 750,000, more than half in nonagricultural work. Almost 100,000 were in business operations, with most of the remainder in construction, professional work, and public employment. Lumbering was the leading industry, followed closely by apparel, with 24,000 employees and annual output of $208 million; food processing, with 14,000 workers and $334 million in output; and pulp and paper, with 8,000 workers and $236 million in product.

The state's industrial growth continued over the 1960s, but the displacement of agricultural labor by mechanization resulted in a net loss of jobs. However, major gains accrued as a consequence of the expansion of employment in such industries as textiles and manufacturers of wood products. Among the wood products companies that established facilities in the state was Hillenbrand Industries, whose Batesville Casket Company had plants in Batesville and Vicksburg. The Vicksburg operation was named a Top 10 facility in *Industry Week*'s 2007 Best Plants competition.

Shipbuilding remained one of the glamour industries. Through various changes in corporate ownership, the Ingalls Shipyard at Pascagoula has continued to produce vessels for the US Navy (including nuclear-powered submarines), US Coast Guard, US Marine Corps, and foreign and commercial customers. An expansion of the Pascagoula facility completed in 1970 brought the total number of workers at Ingalls to more than ninety-six hundred. Employment at the facility peaked at twenty-five thousand in 1977 before dropping to about twelve thousand in the early twenty-first century. Ingalls remains the state's largest industrial employer.

Despite the state's commitment to recruiting and encouraging industry, Mississippi has continued to rank at the bottom nationally in per capita income and toward the bottom in industrialization. However, some bright spots have appeared on the horizon. In the 1970s northern Rust Belt states began to lose factories and jobs for a variety of reasons, including outdated facilities, the presence of unions and labor-management conflict, high tax rates, and burdensome environmental regulations. Some of these industries and jobs gravitated toward Third World counties, where tax rates and wages and other labor costs were lower. Others looked toward the South.

As some American companies joined the movement toward globalization, manufacturers in foreign lands began to challenge US companies in the American market. Led by Germany's Volkswagen and then by a coterie of Japanese manufacturers, foreign automakers began to compete with the Detroit's Big Three. As the quality of the imports rose and many Americans became disenchanted with domestic vehicles, the face of this important industry changed. Rather than simply shipping vehicles to America, foreign manufacturers began to build plants in the United States. These facilities were typically ringed by ancillary plants that manufactured components for the automobiles. Sun Belt states attracted a number of these operations, including Nissan in Tennessee and Mercedes in Alabama, but Mississippi was originally frozen out despite the state's ongoing efforts to attract industry.

Mississippi recorded a significant breakthrough on 6 April 2001, when Nissan broke ground on a $1.4 billion vehicle assembly plant near Canton, just north of Jackson. At full capacity, the plant could produce four hundred and fifty thousand pickup trucks, sport-utility vehicles, and minivans annually. Eight additional new plants (valued at some $140 million) would supply the Nissan facility, while various Mississippi-owned suppliers would also benefit. The Nissan plant and the auxiliary facilities were expected to employ about thirty thousand people. Between 2003, when Nissan opened its Mississippi doors, and 2015, more than three million vehicles were produced in Canton. The most recent news of new industry was the 2016 announcement that Continental AG was moving a large new plant to the Jackson area.

The enormous Nissan facility elevated Mississippi's profile as an emergent manufacturing location, and in February 2007 Toyota chose Mississippi over Arkansas and Tennessee for a new plant. Opened in November 2011 at Blue Springs, near Tupelo, Toyota's facility cost $800 million to construct. In less than four years, the factory's two thousand employees produced five hundred thousand Toyota Corollas.

Toyota's decision to locate in Northeast Mississippi capped efforts to attract industry to what had once been one of the most impoverished areas in the nation. The industrial recruitment effort was led by the Pontotoc Union Lee Alliance, Mississippi's first regional economic development alliance. The alliance was a product of 2003 state legislation that allowed collaboration among various governmental jurisdictions for economic development. The alliance located industrial sites, obtained land options, and secured environmental, geological, wetland, and archaeological clearances to market the sites at industry meetings and trade shows and among industry experts. Toyota's decision to build in Mississippi illustrated the state's enhanced industrial image as it entered the twenty-first century.

Long before the Toyota factory, the rise of industry had brought occasional conflicts between capital and labor. As the Knights of Labor sought to establish a presence in the state they were involved in numerous strikes over wage and hour issues. The Knights encountered strong opposition from employers and community leaders. One strike occurred in the textile industry at Wesson in the late 1880s. Another took place among forest products industry workers in the Moss Point–Pascagoula area. Additional conflicts in that industry occurred at Handsboro in 1888, 1889, and 1900. By 1888 the Knights of Labor had thirty-three locals in Mississippi, some of them racially mixed, but as a result of their liberal philosophy and their national decline, the Knights were gone by the early twentieth century.

The first permanent unions in the state were in the railroad industry, with a local of the Brotherhood of Locomotive Engineers established at Water Valley in 1869. The Brotherhood of Railroad Trainmen chartered their first Mississippi local in 1888, establishing four additional units by 1904. By 1910 the firemen and engine men had five lodges, with the first four chartered before 1894. Legendary engineer Casey Jones was a member of two of the early Water Valley lodges and in 1893 was elected president of the local firemen's lodge. Railroad shops were established in Water Valley, Meridian, Jackson, Vicksburg, and McComb. The railroads brought jobs and encouraged immigration—at Water Valley, for example, the railroad company brought in four hundred Swedes in 1877.

The decline of the Knights of Labor coincided with the rise of the American Federation of Labor (AFL), a national organization built on the craft union concept. Craft unions, organized around trades, became the dominant form of labor organization in Mississippi during the early twentieth century. Early craft unions were established at Natchez, Vicksburg, Gulfport, Biloxi, Jackson, Meridian, Hattiesburg, and McComb. Unions were apparently well accepted in these communities, including even McComb, where the local merchants, newspaper, and citizens supported the workers during a large and violent two-month strike in 1911 by shop craftsmen against the railroad. In 1918 the State Federation of Labor was organized to act as a coordinating body for all Mississippi AFL unions.

During the 1920s and the early 1930s the State Federation worked with the legislature to pass measures favorable to workers and cooperated with the Mississippi State Board of Development to attract industry to the state. By 1927 the State Federation of Labor's membership numbered around fifteen thousand. Craft and railroad union membership topped eighteen thousand. Blacks and whites often attended unsegregated union meetings during this period. Blacks dominated some of the organizations numerically but were not allowed to hold important offices. In other cases, however, conflict arose between the races, particularly when they were competing for scarce jobs.

From the mid-1930s onward Mississippi political leaders assumed an antiunion attitude. Gov. Hugh White's Balance Agriculture with Industry program was built on the assumption that Mississippi's ability to attract industry would improve if labor unions were weak. The Congress of Industrial Organizations (CIO) began to challenge the AFL on the national scene, although Mississippi had only one hundred CIO members by 1939. Mississippi was virtually untouched by the southern unionization drives of the AFL and CIO, probably because of the absence of major industries.

Union membership boomed after World War II. Nationally, membership reached seventeen million, and in the South a fierce organizational war erupted between the AFL and the CIO. The CIO's Operation Dixie was especially successful in Mississippi between 1946 and 1949, winning more union recognition elections than it lost, but the union's efforts in the state were terminated after 1948 because of a change in leadership. Prior to that date, the CIO had more success organizing Mississippi workers than did the AFL. The two unions merged in 1955, when the state's two largest industrial unions were the Amalgamated Clothing Workers of America and the International Woodworkers of America, each of which had more than five thousand members.

During the 1950s and early 1960s union growth in Mississippi stagnated, although industrial employment increased significantly. Antiunion sentiment was strong, particularly in the northern part of the state, where industrial growth was most significant, and from 1950 to 1962 overall union membership increased only from fifty thousand to fifty-two thousand. Some of the industries attracted to the state came at least in part to avoid labor unions, including low-wage apparel, textile, and furniture manufacturers. Adding to the problems of unions and union organizers was the legislature's 1954 passage of a right-to-work law followed by a special 1960 election that added the bill as an amendment to the state constitution. In addition, the state courts were almost unfailingly willing to issue injunctions against picketing and other union activities in labor disputes. Still, with strong industrial job growth during the 1960s, union membership increased by twenty-eight thousand during the decade, reaching about eighty thousand by 1970.

Union growth was in part a product of moderating attitudes among state and community leaders and of the 1964 federal Civil Rights Act, which had a section on equal employment opportunity that led employers to hire greater numbers of African Americans. Blacks constituted at least half of the workforce in many plants and were more receptive to union organizing efforts than their white co-workers.

As low-wage textile and garment firms and other industries migrated to Third World countries during the 1980s and 1990s, Mississippi and other traditionally low-wage southern states launched campaigns to attract newer high-tech industries, including automobile manufacturers and their many suppliers. Again, the lures included an abundant labor force and a considerable amount of antiunion sentiment. As in the earlier industrial recruitment drives, the new jobs created were largely nonunion jobs, but now they were no longer low-wage, low-benefit jobs. Mississippi manufacturing and workers entered a new and better industrial age.

James E. Fickle
University of Memphis

James C. Cobb, *Industrialization and Southern Society, 1877–1984* (1984); James C. Cobb, *The Selling of the South; The Southern Crusade for Industrial Development, 1936–1990* (1993); James E. Fickle, *Mississippi Forests and Forestry* (2001); Nollie W. Hickman, Donald C. Mosley, and Ralph J. Rogers, in *A History of Mississippi*, vol. 2, ed. Richard Aubrey McLemore (1973); John Hebron Moore, *The Emergence of the Cotton Kingdom in the Old Southwest: Mississippi, 1770–1860* (1988); Donald C. Mosely, "A History of Labor Unions in Mississippi" (PhD dissertation, University of Alabama, 1965); Nissan Canton Vehicle Assembly plant website, www.nissan-canton.com; Toyota USA Newsroom website, pressroom .toyota.com.

Influenza Epidemic of 1918

Mississippi was not immune to the worldwide influenza pandemic that struck in 1918–19, killing as many as forty million people around the globe. The Spanish flu reached the state in September 1918 and was acute for only a little over a month, but by the end of the year, 6,219 Mississippians had died, most of them infants and adults aged twenty-five to thirty-five. Adams and Sunflower Counties had the highest death rates, while George and Stone Counties had the lowest rates. The epidemic peaked in Mississippi on 22 October, when 9,842 new cases were reported. The incidence of disease subsequently declined gradually, with a brief recurrence in January 1919.

As in the rest of the United States, the epidemic began on Mississippi's military bases. Officials at the Extra-Cantonment Zone at Payne Field in West Point telegraphed the State Board of Health regarding the appearance and rapid spread of the disease. By the end of the first week in October, Dr. W. S. Leathers, the board's executive officer, ordered all county health officers to close public meetings, public schools, and "places of amusement" in towns where cases of influenza appeared. However, educational institutions that housed their students were asked to remain open and restrict the students to campus. In spite of community protest, county fairs were suspended. The State Board of Health subsequently imposed further restrictions on public gatherings, ordering funerals to be held privately and banning the practice of taking bodies into churches.

In the second week of October, the situation became more serious. Meridian alone reported at least one hundred new flu cases each day. People were not sure how to recognize or prevent the illness and panicked at its rapid onset and tendency to progress to pneumonia and at the increasing number of deaths. Whole families became ill, and neighbors rendering aid were likely to succumb. Parents began to demand the return of children boarding at school, either out of fear for their health or out of a need for help in nursing family members at home. The US Public Health Service sent seventeen doctors and twenty-four nurses to Mississippi, but the state still faced a shortage of medical assistance.

Dr. Leathers asked Red Cross chapters in the state to organize and train women to assist in the emergency.

The disease had begun to abate in many communities by the end of October. Clergy, school boards, and business owners pushed the State Board of Health to rescind the regulations restricting public gatherings. Many schools reopened, and church services resumed during the first week of November. However, because the disease was especially prevalent in black communities, black schools remained closed.

Newspapers in Jackson reported the discovery and testing of an influenza vaccine in New York on 4 October, but the vaccine did not reach Mississippi until mid-November. The US Public Health Service tested it at Brookhaven's Whitworth College, which had remained free of influenza throughout the epidemic.

Diane DeCesare Ross
University of Southern Mississippi

John M. Barry, *The Great Influenza: The Epic Story of the Deadliest Plague in History* (2004); Mississippi State Board of Health, *Report of the Board of Health of Mississippi from July 1, 1917 to June 30, 1919* (1919); Mississippi State Medical Association, *Transactions of the Mississippi State Medical Association* (1919).

Ingalls Shipbuilding

Ingalls Shipbuilding, located in Pascagoula, is a division of Huntington Ingalls Industries that develops and produces technologically advanced, highly capable warships for the surface US Navy fleet, US Coast Guard, US Marine Corps, and foreign and commercial customers. Since its founding in 1938 Ingalls has had a varied building program and has been one of Mississippi's leading industrial employers.

The company began as the Ingalls Shipbuilding Corporation, an operation of the Ingalls Iron Works Company of Birmingham, Alabama. Under a five-year exemption from ad valorem taxes granted under Mississippi's Balance Agriculture with Industry industrial revenue bond program, the shipbuilding facility was constructed on a 160-acre tract on the east bank of the Pascagoula River.

Ingalls has been the state's largest employer since 1939, when it built its first ship, the cargo ship SS *Exchequer*, using a technique that revolutionized shipbuilding: the steel plates of the hull were welded end to end rather than overlapped and riveted. The company grew, winning cargo and passenger ship contracts from the US Maritime Commission.

With the onset of World War II Ingalls switched from building commercial ships to building ships for defense.

Jennie Mae Turner, welder, Ingalls Shipyard, Pascagoula, 1943 (Photograph by Underwood and Underwood, Library of Congress, Washington, D.C. [LC-USZ62-99892])

Ingalls operated around the clock during the war, building all types of military vessels. The first ship Ingalls completed for the war effort was the USS *Arthur Middleton,* a combat-loaded transport launched in December 1941. Ingalls's aircraft carriers, troopships, and combat, cargo, and passenger vessels sailed around the world. After the war, many of these warships returned to Ingalls to be converted to cargo carriers, and the company resumed building ships for maritime commerce.

In the 1950s Ingalls began production of highly sophisticated ships for the US Navy. In 1952 the shipyard launched the USS *Vernon County,* the first of five landing ships, tanks under construction for the navy. Three years later the company began to build submarines and established a nuclear power division. In 1957 it received its first submarine contract, producing three navy submarines and twelve nuclear-powered attack submarines. Ingalls's next naval contract resulted in the production of the destroyers USS *Morton* and USS *Parsons* in the late 1950s, and that ship type became the basis of the shipyard's business for the next three decades.

In 1961 Ingalls was acquired by California-based Litton Systems. By that time Ingalls had produced more than 250 vessels, including more than 200 for the US Navy. Later in the decade the United States sought to build new ships to replace the aging naval fleet and other vessels, and in 1967 Litton announced plans to build a new manufacturing facility on a 611-acre tract of land on the west bank of the Pascagoula River. The Mississippi legislature approved an agreement to enter into a partnership with Litton Industries to sell industrial revenue bonds for the construction of the new shipyard.

Production at the new facility began 12 March 1970 as the shipyard worked to fill two large US Navy contracts to design and build a series of assault ships and multimission destroyers. In addition, the Maritime Administration issued contracts for eight commercial container ships. Between 1975 and 1980 Ingalls delivered 60 percent of all US Navy ships constructed, employing an all-time high of twenty-five thousand people in 1977. In 1978 the US Navy selected Ingalls as lead shipbuilder for the Aegis guided missile cruiser program, and the company built nineteen of the program's twenty-seven cruisers over the next decade. By 2015 Ingalls was the builder of record for thirty-five Aegis DDG 51 guided missile destroyers.

A US economic downturn in the late 1980s and early 1990s combined with huge cuts in military spending to produce a slump in the shipbuilding industry. Though the navy contracted for fewer ships during the early 1990s, Ingalls continued to produce large, high-tech ships for the service. To augment its defense-related work, Ingalls renewed its efforts to enter the commercial shipbuilding industry and to focus on international expansion. Ingalls had been constructing drilling rigs since the 1950s and in 1998 signed a contract with Zentech to design and construct deepwater jack-up drilling rigs.

In April 2001 Northrop Grumman Corporation, based in Los Angeles, acquired Litton Industries. Under Northrop Grumman's Ship Systems Division, Ingalls Shipbuilding was renamed Ingalls Operations. In March 2011 Northrop Grumman announced that it would spin off Huntington Ingalls Industries as an independent and publicly traded company. It is the largest supplier of US Navy surface vessels, responsible for building nearly 70 percent of the naval fleet. It is also Mississippi's largest industrial employer, with about twelve thousand workers.

Peggy W. Jeanes
Jackson, Mississippi

GlobalSecurity.org website, www.globalsecurity.org; R. I. Ingalls Sr., *An Address before the Mississippi Press Association, May 21, 1943* (1943); Ingalls Shipbuilding website, ingalls.huntingtoningalls.com; Mississippi, Department of Economic and Community Development, Port of Pascagoula Files, Series 2101, Mississippi Department of Archives and History; Northrop Grumman website, www.northropgrumman.com; Jeffrey L. Rodengen, *The Legend of Litton Industries* (2000).

Ingraham, Joseph Holt

(1809–1860) Author

Despite being one of the most prolific writers of his time, Joseph Holt Ingraham has almost been forgotten in ours.

Born in Portland, Maine, on 26 January 1809, Ingraham spent most of his life moving from one state to another, but he considered Mississippi his home and died in Holly Springs in 1860. Ingraham published more than one hundred novels and another hundred contributions to magazines and journals.

In 1830 Ingraham traveled to Natchez and New Orleans and settled in Washington, Mississippi, as a faculty member at Jefferson College. His tenure there was probably the basis for the title *Professor*, which appears on many of his novels. In 1832 he married a native Mississippian, Mary Elizabeth Oldin Brookes, a planter's daughter. In 1835 Ingraham published his first book, *The Southwest*, based on a series of letters that had been published by the *Natchez Courier*. *The Southwest*, a travel book, sought to bolster the image of Ingraham's adopted region.

In 1836 Ingraham's first novel was published with great success. *Lafitte: The Pirate of the Gulf* was a melodramatic adventure novel. Contributing to the rise of Ingraham's literary star was the dramatization of *Lafitte*, which played in both New York and Philadelphia.

Ingraham continued writing historical adventures, often set in the Old Southwest, and became the best-paid American novelist of the 1840s. Between 1842 and 1847 he published just over eighty novels, most of them moralistic tales of pirates or country life and all of them cheap, paperbound editions that could be quickly printed and distributed. Despite his success, Ingraham was constantly beset by money troubles, and his novels, though best sellers, were not as well received critically. Edgar Allan Poe, for example, wrote of *Lafitte*, "Upon the whole, we could wish that men possessing the weight and talents and character belonging to Professor Ingraham, would either think it necessary to bestow a somewhat greater degree of labor and attention upon the composition of their novels, or otherwise, would *not* think it necessary to compose them at all."

In 1847 Ingraham began to look in a new direction. He enrolled as a theological student in Nashville, Tennessee, working toward his ordination as an Episcopal minister. Ingraham continued to write fiction, but his morality tales took on a very different nature. Instead of pirate adventure, Ingraham turned to biblical history. In 1855 he published his most famous novel, *The Prince of the House of David*, which follows the life of Adina, a Jewish girl living in the time of Christ. Although *The Prince of the House of David* constituted a marked departure from Ingraham's early work (which now seemed to embarrass the new minister), it was his most popular book, selling more than four million copies by 1931.

As a minister, Ingraham moved between states and congregations, sometimes serving in Mississippi. In 1858 he returned to the state as a minister of Christ Church in Holly Springs. Over the next two years Ingraham published two more biblical novels and *The Sunny South*, a defense of the region and a direct response to *Uncle Tom's Cabin*. On 9 December 1860, while in the vestibule of his church, Ingraham dropped a loaded pistol and was fatally wounded. He was survived by his wife and son, Col. Prentiss Ingraham, who reached even greater fame than his father as a dime novelist.

Courtney Chartier
Robert W. Woodruff Library,
Atlanta

Joseph Holt Ingraham Collection, Clifton Waller Barrett Library of American Literature, Albert and Shirley Small Special Collections Library, University of Virginia; James B. Lloyd, ed., *Lives of Mississippi Authors, 1817–1967* (1981); Edgar Allen Poe, *Southern Literary Messenger* (August 1836).

Ingraham, Prentiss
(1843–1904) Author

Prentiss Ingraham was one of the most prolific writers in the history of American literature and was easily the most fertile Mississippi writer. He is credited with writing six hundred novels and four hundred novelettes but may have written even more. Primarily dime novels, Ingraham's writings may not be considered great works of literature, but they were extremely popular in the late 1800s. They made him famous and remained in demand after his death.

Prentiss Ingraham was born near Natchez on 28 December 1843. His mother was Mary Brooks Ingraham, the daughter of a wealthy planter. His father, Joseph Holt Ingraham, was born in Portland, Maine, but moved to Natchez in the 1830s, taught foreign languages at Jefferson College in Washington, Mississippi, and wrote romance novels.

Prentiss Ingraham received his early education at Jefferson College and later attended St. Timothy's Military Academy in Maryland. When the Civil War began, Ingraham was attending Mobile Medical College but left to enter the Confederate Army in Withers's Mississippi Regiment of Light Artillery. He later transferred to Ross's Texas Cavalry Brigade, rising to the rank of commander of scouts. He was wounded in the foot while fighting at the siege of Port Hudson, Louisiana, and the injury troubled him for the rest of his life. He was taken prisoner but escaped. He received a second wound while fighting at the Battle of Franklin, Tennessee.

Following the Civil War Ingraham went to Mexico and fought with Benito Juárez against the French under Emperor Maximilian. By 1866 Ingraham was fighting with the Austrians against the Prussians in the Austro-Prussian War. He later fought the Turks on the island of Crete and then served for a time with the khedive's army in Egypt. Ingraham eventually joined rebels fighting against Spain in Cuba, becoming a colonel in the Cuban rebel army as well as a captain in the navy. Captured by the Spanish while trying to smuggle arms into Cuba, Ingraham later escaped and thereafter always used the title *colonel*.

His literary career began in 1869, while he resided in London; by the following year he had moved to New York City and begun writing novels and plays. His first dime novel, *The Masked Spy*, was published in 1872. So many works in this genre followed that he is sometimes referred to as the King of the Dime Novels. His novels covered a wide range of subjects, from pirates to private detectives, but after the early 1870s most of his novels were Westerns. His Westerns were so popular that some historians credit him with popularizing the cowboy hero and shaping a popular perception of the western frontier that exists today. He published under at least thirteen different pen names, complicating any effort to count the total number of books he wrote.

Even though many of Ingraham's Westerns were based on fictional characters, he also wrote more than one hundred novels about Buffalo Bill Cody, including some that were written two years before Ingraham actually met the Wild West showman in 1879. They became good friends, and Ingraham briefly served as the press agent for Buffalo Bill's Wild West Show.

In 1903 Ingraham was diagnosed with Bright's disease, a fatal kidney disorder that was attributed to his foot wound. He retired to the Confederate home at Beauvoir in Biloxi for treatment and died on 16 August 1904.

H. Clark Burkett
Historic Jefferson College

Albert Johannsen, *The House of Beadle and Adams* (1950); James B. Lloyd, ed., *Lives of Mississippi Authors, 1817–1967* (1981); Linda Zimmerman, Dime Novels and Penny Dreadfuls website, www-sul.stanford.edu /depts/dp/pennies/cover.html.

Insurance

Insurance is a way to provide protection against loss. Since the risk of loss is only a probability—usually a very low probability—insurance is often called risk management. Since individuals have risk of loss in many parts of their lives, a number of types of insurance exist. The most common lines of insurance are life, automobile, flood, marine, health, property, accidental death and dismemberment, worker's compensation, and unemployment compensation. As protection for risk, insurance dates back to the Babylonians, more than four millennia ago.

The Mississippi Insurance Department is led by the commissioner of insurance, one of the six statewide elected state officials. In 2014, Mississippi's insurance industry comprised 2,253 firms with over $12.5 billion in premiums written.

In 2014, 379 companies wrote life insurance policies in Mississippi. Premiums totaling over $1.7 billion were written, with almost $750 million benefits paid. The three firms that wrote the highest percentages of life insurance were Southern Farm Bureau Life Insurance Company (5.5 percent), State Farm Life Insurance Company (5.2 percent), and Metropolitan Life Insurance Company (4.1 percent). Each of the remaining companies wrote 4 percent or less of the state's policies. Fifty-five companies wrote zero.

Also in 2014, 230 companies wrote annuity policies in Mississippi. Premiums totaled almost $1.5 billion, and more than $328 million in benefits were paid. The four firms that wrote the highest percentages were Jackson National Life Insurance Company (9.2 percent), Lincoln National Life Insurance Company (7.1 percent), Pruco Life Insurance Company (6.2 percent), and Variable Annuity Life Insurance Company (5.9 percent). None of the remaining companies wrote more than 5 percent of policies.

Six health insurance companies wrote policies in Mississippi in 2012. More than $615 million in premiums were written, and almost $505 million in losses were paid. The four companies with more than a 4 percent market share were Magnolia Health Plan (32.5 percent), Windsor Health Plan (30.2 percent), United Health Care of Mississippi (21.1 percent), and HealthSpring of Tennessee (10.1 percent).

Property/casualty insurance was written by 824 companies in Mississippi in 2012, with almost $4.4 billion in premiums written and more than $2.3 billion in losses paid. The three largest companies for this insurance line were Mississippi Farm Bureau Casualty Insurance Company (8.7 percent), State Farm Mutual Automobile Insurance Company (8.4 percent), and State Farm Fire and Casualty Company (6.8 percent). None of the remaining companies had more than a 3 percent market share.

In addition to traditional corporate, profit-seeking companies, insurance protection can be provided by private associations, usually based in member-owned trade or occupational groups. Nine of these fraternal companies operated in Mississippi during 2012: the Order of United Commercial Travelers of America (67.3 percent) and Assured Life Association (23.0 percent) had the bulk of the business. Other fraternal companies included Woodmen of the World Life Insurance Society, Royal Neighbors of America, Thrivent Financial for Lutherans, Knights of Columbus, United States Letter Carriers Mutual Benefit Association, Independent Order of Foresters, and Modern Woodmen of America. None had more than a 3.5 percent market share, and they collected only $31 million in premiums and paid only $10 million in losses.

Mississippi's insurance industry was severely affected by Hurricane Katrina, which hit the Gulf Coast on 29 August 2005 and caused substantial damage in the southern portion of the state and totally devastated the coastal margin. Less than a month later, Hurricane Rita wreaked further havoc. Business-as-usual losses were completely overwhelmed by hurricane-related losses. The Mississippi Insurance Department has calculated Katrina-related damage at $125 billion and insured losses at $45–60 billion. By 1 August 2006, 483,693 insurance claims related to the two storms had been filed in Mississippi, and insurers had paid out more than $10.5 billion. Of those totals, 236,372 claims and $7.6 billion involved coastal Hancock, Harrison, and Jackson Counties.

One issue that arose in the storm-related claims was whether wind or water caused the damage. Homeowner policies cover only wind-caused damage; to obtain coverage for water damage, homeowners must purchase separate policies from the Federal Emergency Management Administration's National Flood Insurance Program, and many Mississippians had not done so. Many insurance companies argued that damage had resulted from the storm surge (water) rather than from the wind and denied claims on that basis. In addition, many of those with flood policies discovered that they were capped well below the amount of the damage.

In the wake of 2012's Superstorm Sandy, rate hikes proposed by the National Flood Insurance Program threatened to exacerbate the still unresolved post-Katrina insurance concerns of Mississippi Gulf Coast residents. In response, the Mississippi Insurance Department filed suit against the program in 2013, with five other states filing supporting briefs. In April 2014, reacting to Congress's passage of the Homeowner Flood Insurance Affordability Act, the department withdrew its lawsuit, though it retained the right to refile if the Federal Emergency Management Administration's implementation of the new legislation fails to meet Mississippians' needs. Because of legal controversy and the losses connected to Katrina, some insurance companies are refusing to issue new homeowner policies in Mississippi. More than a decade after the storm, the greatest difficulty for coastal Mississippi reconstruction and redevelopment remains adequate and affordable insurance.

Edward Nissan

George Carter
University of Southern Mississippi

Mississippi Insurance Department website, www.mid.ms.gov; Liam Plevin, *Wall Street Journal* (4 May 2007).

International Museum of Muslim Cultures

Located in Jackson, the International Museum of Muslim Cultures (IMMC) is dedicated to educating the American public about Islamic history and culture and the contributions of diverse Muslim communities to the world. IMMC is a venue for presenting examples and reflections of Islamic thinking, inspiration, and enlightenment, and it serves as an educational resource and partner for advancing and teaching about Islam as well as for strengthening global consciousness, historical literacy, and multicultural appreciation.

American Muslims throughout the United States have long created strong community institutions, including mosques, schools, and local and national Muslim associations. But those communities placed little emphasis on communicating to the general public the influences of Islamic culture and history. IMMC got its start in late 2000, when a group of Jackson Muslims set out to develop a six-month companion exhibition to the Mississippi Arts Pavilion exhibition *The Majesty of Spain*, which excluded the more than eight hundred years of Islamic influence on the Iberian Peninsula. The IMMC mounted its inaugural exhibition, *Islamic Moorish Spain: Its Legacy to Europe and the West*, in April 2001, and it remains a part of the museum's permanent collection.

In October 2006 the IMMC relocated to the Arts Center of Mississippi in downtown Jackson and opened its second exhibition, *The Legacy of Timbuktu: Wonders of the Written Word*, which featured forty-five ancient African manuscripts from among an estimated one million recently rediscovered in the Republic of Mali. By revealing that a sophisticated, highly literate culture flourished in the city of Timbuktu beginning in the fourteenth century, these ancient documents have worked to refute stereotypical depictions of Africa as a primitive society with a strictly oral history tradition. Other exhibitions at the museum have included two photography exhibits, *Capture the Spirit of Ramadan* and *Mosques of America*.

After the tragic events of 11 September 2001, the Iraq War, and the tension between America and some Islamic countries, the IMMC has taken a more prominent role in educating the public about Islamic civilization and its influence. The IMMC serves as a national and international cultural tourism destination, as a research and educational center, and as a repository for Islamic objects with cultural, artistic, aesthetic, and historical significance. The museum researches, collects, preserves, exhibits, and interprets objects, stories, and history. Further, the IMMC develops educational workshops, seminars, and other programs for teachers and the general public and offers a curriculum for grades 6–12 and institutions of higher learning. In recent years, the museum has featured texts from Timbuktu, an exhibit on Moorish Spain, and a collection of images illustrating Ramadan celebrations from throughout the world.

The museum facilitates multicultural and interfaith dialogue to promote understanding and illustrates to the American public the diversity of the Muslim community—past, present, and future. The museum has hosted more than thirty thousand visitors from all over the United States and more than thirty foreign countries. Approximately half of its visitors are students and teachers.

Okolo Rashid
Jackson, Mississippi

Joshua Hammer, *Smithsonian* (December 2006); *Jackson Clarion-Ledger* (9 August 2005, 28 November 2006); International Museum of Muslim Cultures website, www.muslimmuseum.org; Ann Walton Sieber, *Saudi Aramco World* (January–February 2006).

International Sweethearts of Rhythm

The International Sweethearts of Rhythm was an all-female jazz band of the 1940s. Though it was not the first all-female jazz band, it was the first racially integrated jazz band. Founded in 1937 at the Piney Woods Country Life School (now Piney Woods School) in Rankin County, the group raised money for the predominantly African American school, although some band members also possessed Mexican and Chinese heritage.

Laurence Clifton Jones, the creator of the Piney Woods Country Life School, began organizing singing groups in 1921 to help raise money for the institution. In 1937 he helped form an all-girl dance band, which became known as the International Sweethearts of Rhythm. With piano, bass, drums, full brass and reed sections, and one or two featured singers, the group began touring the southern United States. After receiving positive press in the *Chicago Defender*, the band began to play higher-profile tours in New York, Chicago, and other metropolitan centers. The Sweethearts played several European venues as part of a 1945 USO tour and made several recordings and movie shorts in the mid-1940s. The pressures of touring and expectations to perform well academically led band members to leave the school and continue the band while based in Arlington, Virginia. The band existed until 1949.

Greg Johnson
University of Mississippi

D. Antoinette Handy, *The International Sweethearts of Rhythm* (1983); Rosetta Reitz, *The International Sweethearts of Rhythm* (1984), liner notes.

International Women's Year, Mississippians and

The United Nations declared 1975 International Women's Year. In response, the US Congress mandated that each state and territory would hold a women's convention and send delegates to the National Women's Conference in Houston in November 1977. In addition, Pres. Gerald Ford convened the National Commission on the Observance of International Women's Year. When Jimmy Carter became president, he changed the commission's membership and charged it with gathering ideas for a national plan of action to further women's issues, particularly with regard to the Equal Rights Amendment, which had been passed by Congress on 22 March 1972. For the amendment to go into effect, thirty-eight states needed to ratify it by 22 March 1979. Thirty did so within the first year, but the effort then stalled, and at the beginning of 1977 the amendment still needed ratification by three more states. Despite some support from political leaders such as Lt. Gov. Evelyn Gandy and William Winter, Mississippi was not among the ratifying states.

The commission received a five-million-dollar budget and announced plans to revive the ERA ratification effort and push for support for other feminist initiatives. Conservatives across the country saw the plan as a government-funded initiative to force unwanted and unnecessary changes on society. The commission received heavy criticism and suffered a backlash in several states, including Mississippi.

As the Mississippi Organizing Committee (MOC) planned the state conference, to be held on 8–9 July 1977 in Jackson, it publicized its efforts via most major media outlets. The MOC expected a mostly progressive audience that would support the ERA and other feminist initiatives. However, some Mississippi conservative women alleged that the MOC had failed to publicize the gathering in an attempt to keep them from coming. Though only 350 women signed up for the state conference, more than 1,100 attended, with overcrowding and friction arising between groups with competing political views. The conservative women staged a "takeover" of the conference, voted to block every initiative suggested by the commission, and elected only conservative delegates to represent the state at the national convention.

When the National Women's Conference opened, delegates from other states attempted to have the Mississippi women unseated, claiming that they did not fairly represent the state's women and their ideas. That effort failed, and the Mississippi delegates participated, opposing some measures but supporting parts of the plan of action. The conservative women were outvoted, however, and the plan of action that the conference presented to the president and Congress reflected a liberal feminist viewpoint.

The Mississippi conservatives had lost the battle but ultimately won the war. Though Congress subsequently extended the deadline for passing the ERA by three years, it failed to win ratification, and the plan brought no further results. In addition, the events connected with International Women's Year brought together Mississippi's previously apolitical conservative women and motivated them to become politically active. They formed strong bonds that reached across race and class lines and that subsequently helped to facilitate the growth of a conservative women's activist network.

Kathryn McGaw York
University of Mississippi

Marjorie Julian Spruill, in *Mississippi Women: Their Histories, Their Lives*, vol. 2, ed. Elizabeth Anne Payne, Martha H. Swain, and Marjorie Julian Spruill (2010).

Irish

While some Irish settlers moved to what is today Mississippi when the British ruled West Florida, the first major Irish presence in the state came when the Spanish took the colony back after the American War of Independence. With Roman Catholicism the established religion, Irish priests came to serve in the Natchez District. These priests were exiles from British rule in Ireland who came from the Irish seminary in Salamanca, Spain. Some of these priests were well liked by the predominantly American and Protestant population, but a few could be overzealous in their Catholicism, resulting in trouble for the Spanish governors.

These priests left with their Spanish sponsors in 1798. For the next few decades, the predominant Irish presence in the state was Protestant. Political refugee Alexander Campbell became the Natchez city clerk in 1811. Gerard Brandon, who served as Mississippi's governor in the mid-1820s, was the son and grandson of Irish immigrants. Frederick Stanton arrived in Natchez from Ireland via New Orleans in 1818 to practice medicine, but by the time of his death in 1859, he had become a very substantial planter. His house, Stanton Hall, originally called Belfast, takes up a Natchez city block, providing a testament to his wealth and status. Other descendants of Scots-Irish settlers in Virginia and the Carolinas made their way to Mississippi after Indian Removal in the 1820s and 1830s, seeking land and cotton wealth.

Some Irish Catholics also began to take advantage of the "Flush Times" in Mississippi. Unlike their Protestant Scots-Irish compatriots, however, they lacked large amounts of capital and family connections. Nonetheless, members of this wave found niches in the rapidly growing state. For example, a sizable community grew near Paulding, in Jasper County, a stagecoach stop on the line between New Orleans and Nashville. In 1837 residents there founded the state's second Catholic parish. Irish Catholic farmers from East Georgia came to Camden and Madison Counties in search of new cotton land in the 1840s and founded the settlement of Sulphur Springs. It attracted Irish immigrants from New Orleans and soon boasted a Catholic church and school.

The advent of the Great Famine pushed more than two million people out of Ireland between that 1845 and 1855, and some came to Mississippi. For the most part, these immigrants were very poor and found opportunity in urban areas. In 1860 the state boasted almost four thousand Irish-born residents, most in either Natchez or Vicksburg but with other groups concentrated in Jackson, Port Gibson, Biloxi, and Holly Springs. The most rural parts of the state had the fewest Irish: for example, Issaquena County had one Irish-born resident, while Jones and Greene Counties had none.

Most of these famine Irish were laborers who found a niche at the lower end of the cotton economy. They dug ditches for planters, loaded and unloaded steamboats, and waited tables in hotels along the coast. The burgeoning public works projects of the 1850s also provided opportunity. For example, the construction of the Mobile and Ohio Railroad brought gangs of Irish laborers to eastern Mississippi in the 1850s. Those higher on the socioeconomic scale usually worked as artisans or in merchandising. Irish women worked primarily as washerwomen and in other menial jobs but occasionally could improve their condition. In general, however, the Irish lived in the worst housing and were prone to serious problems, including alcoholism, violence, and crime.

Despite the harsh conditions, the Irish stayed in antebellum Mississippi thanks to community institutions, particularly Catholic churches and schools, usually operated by Irish and Irish-American nuns. While the early church leadership in Mississippi was not Irish, Irish priests, nuns, and laity formed the backbone of the Diocese of Natchez, which had been founded in 1837.

More prosperous Irish immigrants founded their own societies. The most active was the Hibernian Society in Natchez. Middle-class Irish also took an active interest in Irish and American politics, showing a particular penchant for political journalism. James Hagan edited the *Vicksburg Sentinel*, for example, and Logan Power edited the *Jackson Mississippian*. The most important antebellum Irish editor, Richard Elward, made Natchez's *Mississippi Free Trader* the most important proponent of states' rights outside of South Carolina. Less prominent Irish also took part in politics, strongly supporting the proimmigrant Democratic Party, especially in the mid-1850s.

The Irish followed the Democratic Party in support of secession after Abraham Lincoln's election to the presidency in 1860. The vast majority of Irish did not own slaves, and a few challenged the racial status quo. Most notably, Patrick Lynch married a Louisiana slave, and their son, John Roy Lynch, became Mississippi's first black congressman. However, most Irish did not object to slavery. Irishmen fought in numerous Confederate units, including the Natchez Fencibles, the Adams Light Guards of Natchez, and the Jasper Grays of Paulding. The Vicksburg Irish staffed two units, the Shamrock Guards and the Sarsfield Southrons (named for a late seventeenth-century Irish hero).

The Irish sealed their place as white southerners through their Confederate service, and the Civil War marked the high point of Irish immigration to Mississippi. The state subsequently plunged into grinding poverty, losing its allure for Irish immigrants. The Catholic Church continued to feature a notable Irish influence, however. Irish-born bishops Thomas Heslin and John Gunn led the church in Mississippi between 1889 and 1924, and Irish priests and nuns continued to come to the state until the 1980s. Indeed, the greatest institutional legacy of the Irish in Mississippi is the numerous Catholic churches and schools.

In the 2010 census, more than 109,000 Mississippians (5.3% of the population) claimed Irish ancestry.

David T. Gleeson
Northumbria University

William Henry Elder, *Civil War Diary (1862–1865) of Bishop William Henry Elder, Bishop of Natchez*, ed. R. D. Gerow (1961); David T. Gleeson, *The Irish in the South, 1815–1865* (2001); Jack D. L. Holmes, *Journal of Mississippi History* (March 1987); Michael Namorato, *The Catholic Church in Mississippi, 1911–1984: A History* (1998); Charles E. Nolan, *St. Mary's of Natchez: The History of a Southern Catholic Congregation, 1716–1988* (1992); James J. Pillar, *The Catholic Church in Mississippi, 1837–1865* (1964).

Isom, Sarah McGehee

(1850–1905) Educator

Hired to teach elocution at the University of Mississippi in 1885, Sarah "Sallie" Isom was the first woman in the state to hold a teaching position at a coeducational college or university. The daughter of physician Thomas Dudley Isom and Sarah McGehee Isom, Isom was born in 1850. She attended August Seminary in Virginia and studied drama and public speaking in Boston and Philadelphia.

The University of Mississippi had for years taught public speaking as part of the work of other departments, especially English, but in 1884 the board of trustees decided to hire an instructor of elocution. Isom, an Oxford native with a strong educational background, was hired, but only after

some considerable argument among members of the board. The early 1880s were an important time for the development of public education for women in the state. The University of Mississippi first admitted women as full students in 1882 and hired its first full-time female employee, librarian Julia Wilcox, in 1884, the same year that the Mississippi legislature established Mississippi Industrial Institute and College (now Mississippi University for Women) in Columbus.

From the 1880s until her death in 1905, Isom was the only instructor of elocution at the university. She taught two courses whose primary goal was "to substitute *natural* methods of express for the faulty delivery which commonly prevails in the reading circle, the college, the pulpit, on the platform and the stage." From the beginning of her teaching career, she encouraged her students to compete in public speaking in front of the entire university.

The University of Mississippi's Sarah Isom Center for Women and Gender Studies is named in her honor.

Ted Ownby
University of Mississippi

Historical Catalogue of the University of Mississippi, 1849–1909 (1910); David G. Sansing, *The University of Mississippi: A Sesquicentennial History* (1999); Sarah Isom Center for Women and Gender Studies website, http://sarahisomcenter.org/.

Isom, Thomas Dudley

(1816–1902) Pioneer and Physician

In 1835 Chisolm, Martin, and Craig, a trading firm located in Pontotoc, Mississippi, was looking to establish new trading venues with the Chickasaw. To do so, the firm sent partner John J. Craig's nephew, Thomas Dudley Isom, born in Maury County, Tennessee, on 5 April 1816, to a part of Mississippi known as the Ridge. Isom built a three-room log cabin at what is now the site of the Oxford square and set up a successful trading business, winning the confidence of his Chickasaw neighbors and becoming the first white settler in what was to become Lafayette County.

The trade business waned after the 1832 Treaty of Pontotoc Creek, which removed most of the Indians from Mississippi. But Isom's friendship with Chief Toby Tubby and Princess Hoka led the Chickasaw to deed a large tract of land to Chisolm, Martin, and Craig. The firm immediately donated fifty choice acres to Lafayette County to serve as the county seat. Isom suggested that the new town be named *Oxford*, hoping to entice a state university to rival the famous namesake in England.

With no further business to transact, Isom chose to pursue a career in medicine. He first trained at Transylvania College and then earned his degree in medicine at Jefferson Medical College in Philadelphia. He returned to Oxford, where he set up practice in the small log cabin that had served as his trading post. In 1840 Isom met Sarah McGehee of Abbeville, South Carolina, who was visiting her sister in Lafayette County. He followed her back to South Carolina and married her in 1841. The new couple returned to Oxford. Their children included Sarah Isom, who became the first woman to hold a teaching position at a coeducational college or university in Mississippi.

Over the next twelve years Isom's medical practice and reputation prospered. In 1860, he and L. Q. C. Lamar represented Lafayette County at the state secession convention in Jackson. Isom made a strong plea to maintain the Union, but he voted for secession after recognizing that his voice was in the minority.

At the start of the Civil War, Isom enlisted in the 17th Mississippi Infantry as the company surgeon and accompanied the unit to Virginia. He was soon recalled to Oxford and placed in charge of the University Hospital, where he treated Confederate wounded from the Battle of Shiloh. When it appeared that Gen. Ulysses S. Grant's army would invade Oxford, Isom, operating under the cover of darkness, led an evacuation of the hospital and all eighteen hundred patients to Granada, thus preventing their capture by Union forces. In 1863 he was called to Jackson and appointed to the Army Medical Board, serving until the end of the war.

With the collapse of the Confederacy, Isom returned to Oxford to resume the practice of medicine. He received renown for his innovative medical treatments. In 1869 he was elected vice chair of the Mississippi State Medical Association. In 1883 he served as a delegate to the American Medical Association convention in New Orleans. He died at his Oxford home on 5 May 1902.

Walter H. Eversmeyer
Metairie, Louisiana

"Isom Place," Skipworth Historical and Genealogical Society, Oxford, Mississippi; *Oxford Eagle* (8 May 1902); Harris D. Riley, *Journal of the Mississippi State Medical Association* (May 1999).

Issaquena County

Founded from land ceded to the United States by the Choctaw Indians in 1820, Issaquena County was established on 23 January 1844. The county's name is taken from a Native American phrase that roughly translates as "deer river." Issaquena is located along the Mississippi-Arkansas border in the Delta, and the Mississippi River forms the county's snaking western edge. Mayersville, Issaquena's county seat, is named for landowner David Mayers.

Antebellum Issaquena County had a large slave majority. At the county's first census, in 1850, Issaquena had a free population of 373 and a slave population of 4,105. A decade later, the free population had grown to 587, while the slave population had increased to 7,244. With slaves making up 93 percent of the population, Issaquena had the highest percentage of slaves in Mississippi on the eve of the Civil War.

Despite its small population, in the late antebellum period Issaquena County had the state's ninth-most-valuable farmland. The county's farms, with their large slave workforce, were among the top cotton producers in Mississippi. Conversely, Issaquena farmers concentrated far less on corn and livestock, ranking among the middle in output in these agricultural categories. According to the 1860 census, only one person in the county, a laborer earning three hundred dollars a year at a lumber mill, worked in manufacturing.

Postbellum Issaquena County continued to represent a distinctive socioeconomic profile within the Mississippi Delta. In 1880 African Americans accounted for 92 percent of the county's 10,004 people. Issaquena also maintained the state's smallest industrial workforce, with a single manufacturing firm employing just three people.

In 1880 Issaquena's farms were far larger than the state average, but the county experienced extraordinary changes in its agricultural sector over the remainder of the century. While the county's population size and racial profile remained stable, by 1900 the average farm size had decreased to fifty-five acres, far smaller than Mississippi's average of eighty-three acres.

Issaquena County was home to W. E. Mollison, a powerful figure in education and the law in the late 1800s and early 1900s. Born in Issaquena County, Mollison left Mississippi to attend Fisk University and Oberlin College. He later served in a variety of positions, including as the county's school superintendent. Mollison was one of the few practicing African American attorneys in Mississippi during this period.

On the eve of the Civil War, Issaquena County had three churches, all of them Methodist. More than half a century later, Missionary Baptists were the largest denomination, followed by the African Methodist Episcopal Church.

In 1930 Issaquena had a population of 5,734 people and the third-lowest population density in the state. As the Great Depression set in, African Americans comprised 81 percent of the county's population. Tenants operated 86 percent of all farms.

Issaquena County natives of note include two important Mississippi political figures, at least one notable artist, and one of history's most revered blues musicians. C. B.

"Buddie" Newman, the powerful Speaker of the Mississippi House during the 1970s and 1980s, was born in Valley Park, the son of a railroad foreman. Unita Blackwell, an activist, organizer, and Mayersville political figure, grew up in Coahoma but moved to Issaquena County with her husband in the 1950s. Blackwell was an ardent supporter of African American enfranchisement in the 1960s and 1970s and played a key role in the incorporation of Mayersville. In 1977 she became the town's first mayor and the first African American woman to hold that office in Mississippi. Rev. H. D. Dennis, famous for Margaret's Grocery, a folk art destination and general store (named after his wife), was born in Issaquena County in 1916. Electric blues musician Muddy Waters (McKinley Morganfield) was born in Issaquena County on 4 April 1913, though he soon relocated with his grandmother to the Stovall Plantation, near Clarksdale.

By 1960 Issaquena's population had shrunk to 3,576, and the county possessed the lowest population density in Mississippi. The depopulation continued in the 1960s and 1970s, and by 1980 only 2,513 residents called Issaquena County home. African Americans still comprised a majority but made up only 67 percent of the total population. Two-thirds of the labor force worked in agriculture, and much of the county's acreage was used for cultivating cotton, soybeans, winter wheat, oats, and cattle. One of the poorest counties in the state, Issaquena had Mississippi's lowest per capita income in 1980 and struggled to provide education for its residents. Almost 40 percent of the population had fewer than five years of education, and less than 12 percent had graduated from high school.

Like many Delta counties in Mississippi, Issaquena County's 2010 population remained predominantly African American and had shown an overall decline in size during the last half of the twentieth century. Indeed, the county's population had undergone one of the greatest proportional decreases in the state, shrinking by about 60 percent since 1960 and making it the smallest county in Mississippi, with only 1,406 residents. Issaquena continued to suffer from some of the highest poverty rates in the state.

Mississippi Encyclopedia Staff
University of Mississippi

Unita Blackwell, *Barefootin'*: *Life Lessons from the Road to Freedom* (2006); Issaquena Genealogy and History Project website, www.roots web.ancestry.com/~msissaq2; Mississippi State Planning Commission, *Progress Report on State Planning in Mississippi* (1938); *Mississippi Statistical Abstract*, Mississippi State University (1952–2010); Charles Sydnor and Claude Bennett, *Mississippi History* (1939); University of Virginia Library, Historical Census Browser website, http://mapserver.lib.vir ginia.edu; E. Nolan Waller and Dani A. Smith, *Growth Profiles of Mississippi's Counties, 1960–1980* (1985).

Italians

The rural Deep South, including Mississippi, never attracted large numbers of immigrants. There were few large cities, and would-be laborers were plagued by competition from slavery and by prejudice toward Catholic foreigners. As a result, Italian immigration was slow, concentrated in specific areas, and radiated from New Orleans.

The first Italians entered Mississippi as members of the de Soto expedition in the 1540s. Among them was Berardo Peloso, who in 1558 piloted a ship and became the first European to see Pascagoula Bay. In 1699, when the French settled the Gulf Coast in the vicinity of Biloxi and later at Fort Maurepas (Ocean Springs) and Fort Rosalie (Natchez), immigrants from the Italian Piedmont came as convicts, settlers, and soldiers. One of the more famous was Enrico Tonti, who had been born in Naples and received military training in France. Prior to his death in 1704 of yellow fever, he served as a skilled Indian agent and successful soldier when diplomacy failed.

During the nineteenth century many Italians entered Mississippi through the port of New Orleans. Carrying produce into the Mississippi Basin, they were attracted to Natchez and Vicksburg, where their small numbers and the cosmopolitan atmosphere of the communities allowed them social access. Among the Italian names appearing in city directories was L. A. Cusmani, who sold "family groceries, tobacco, cigars, liquor and plantation supplies."

When the Civil War began in April 1861, Mississippi was home to more than one hundred Italian immigrants, and men named Grillo, Leoni, and Rietti joined the state's Confederate cavalry and infantry regiments. They served with distinction on the battlefield, with some paying the ultimate price. During the 1863 Siege of Vicksburg, Italians and other residents lived in caves and tightened their belts as Gen. Ulysses S. Grant's army threatened the city.

In the late nineteenth century, massive emigration began from Italy because of lack of economic and social opportunities and compulsory military service. Italians from Calabria, Sicily, and the Marches entered Mississippi through New Orleans, where many maintained family ties. Italians worked as farmers, merchants, or employees in the fishing and canning industries along the Gulf Coast at Biloxi, Ocean Springs, and Gulfport. The Caruso family operated one of the largest canning plants on the Gulf Coast, while the Deangelo family operated the Italian Shipyard at Moss Point (1881–1934). In Mississippi, where foreigners and Catholics were few in number, Italian shopkeepers took steps to maintain a low profile and sold primarily "American" goods. Italians who settled in Hattiesburg, Laurel, Granada, and other towns maintained strong ties with relatives and friends in New Orleans.

In the 1880s the first Italians were attracted to the Mississippi Delta to work on levee repair and remained to farm or work as laborers on cotton plantations. Many lived in plantation housing, and some developed small stores or "rolling stores" (wagons laden with merchandise) to serve the rural communities.

Throughout the state, Italians brought their culture with them. Families carried the tradition of baked bread, and beehive-shaped ovens appeared next to shacks and homes. To supplement their diets they developed large gardens and raised poultry and hogs. Frugal in their ways, few Italians ran up large debts at the plantation commissaries.

In 1904 Natchez had two hundred Italian residents working as merchants, small proprietors, and truck farmers, while Canton had one hundred Italians and Gulfport had thirty. In 1910 more than a thousand Italians lived in Bolivar and Washington Counties in the Delta, while another thousand were scattered around the rest of the state.

Italians established mutual benefit societies to serve as social and assimilative centers in Bay St. Louis, Clarksdale, Shaw, Greenville, Jackson, and Natchez. Although some Italians joined Protestant denominations, the majority remained Catholic, and their presence helped to expand the Catholic Church in Mississippi. Bishop Joseph Brunini, who came from a Vicksburg Italian American family, served as bishop of the Diocese of Jackson-Natchez from 1968 to 1984 and worked to promote his faith and ecumenical ties with non-Catholics. Delta cuisine often incorporates Italian tastes and recipes, as is demonstrated by the menus at restaurants such as Giardina's and Lusco's in Greenwood or the iconic Doe's Eat Place in Greenville.

Beginning in the late nineteenth century, Italian Americans became involved in local and state politics. Mississippi-born Frank J. Arrighi served as Vicksburg's city assessor around the turn of the twentieth century. The Botto family played a prominent role in the community as well. Andrew Houston Longino, born in Lawrence County to a family whose roots stretched back through eighteenth-century North Carolina to Italy, served as governor from 1900 to 1904.

In the early twenty-first century the last of the original immigrants could still be found working the land and enjoying the fruits of their labors. Younger Italian Americans continue to enter politics and the professions. In Jackson, in the Delta, and along the Gulf Coast, Italian Americans maintain their cultural and social ties and their traditions.

Russell M. Magnaghi
Northern Michigan University

Russell M. Magnaghi, *Louisiana History* (Winter 1986); Emily Fogg Meade, *South Atlantic Quarterly* (1905); Girolamo Moroni, *Bollettino dell'Emigrazione* (1913).

Itawamba County

Named for Chickasaw leader Itawambe Miko (Levi Colbert), Itawamba County was founded in 1836 on land ceded by the Chickasaw in the Treaty of Pontotoc. Itawamba County is located in northeastern Mississippi, on the Alabama border. The Tombigbee River flows through Itawamba, as does the Tennessee-Tombigbee Waterway. The Natchez Trace Parkway travels through the county. The seat is Fulton, and other towns include Mantachie and Tremont.

In the 1840 census, Itawamba had 4,655 free residents and 720 slaves. Ninety-four people worked in commerce and manufacturing. By 1860 the population had grown to 14,167 free people and 3,528 slaves, one of the lowest percentages among the state's counties. Itawamba ranked thirty-fifth in the state in cotton production and also grew corn, sweet potatoes, peas, and beans. Itawamba's manufacturing sector employed one hundred people at a variety of companies. The county's seventeen houses of worship included eight Baptist churches, six Methodist churches, and three Presbyterian churches.

After the Civil War, Itawamba continued to have a large white majority, with whites making up 90 percent of the county's 10,663 people in 1880. Most of those residents worked in agriculture, and 80 percent of farmers owned their land. Only twelve people worked in manufacturing. In 1900 African Americans still comprised less than 10 percent of the county's 13,544 residents. Most farmers owned their land, and as in many such counties, the average farm size was fairly large, at 121 acres. Itawamba had only fifty-three industrial workers in 1900. The 1916 religious census found the Methodist Episcopal Church, South, to be the largest religious group, followed by the Southern Baptist Convention and the Churches of Christ.

In 1930 Itawamba was one of Mississippi's least populated counties, with the second-lowest population density in the state. Only 6 percent of the county's 18,225 residents were African Americans, giving Itawamba the lowest percentage of African Americans per square mile in the state. In a dramatic change since 1900, tenant farmers ran about two-thirds of the county's farms, and the number of industrial workers had grown to 317.

Itawamba's population declined to just over fifteen thousand by 1960 but topped twenty thousand two decades later. The county's labor force followed state trends, with agriculture losing workers and manufacturing gaining them. Although Itawamba's industry was slow to grow, it employed more than twenty-five hundred people in 1980, largely in textile and clothing production. Those who worked in agriculture relied on corn, soybeans, and livestock.

Singer Tammy Wynette, born Virginia Wynette Pugh in 1942, grew up in Itawamba County. Poet and author Elmo

Howell, born in Itawamba County in 1918, wrote widely on Mississippi's small towns and country roads. Sculptor Burgess Delaney, born in 1914, grew up in rural Itawamba County and spent his entire life there, using local clay in his work. Congressman John Rankin was born 1882 in rural Itawamba County. From the 1920s through the 1940s he was an outspoken conservative on issues of race and the power of government. Sharion Aycock, the first female federal district court judge in Mississippi and first woman elected head of the Mississippi Bar Association, grew up in Tremont. In 2010 the county's Constance McMillen joined with the American Civil Liberties Union in a successful suit that forced the Itawamba County School District to allow her to attend the Itawamba Agricultural High School prom with her girlfriend.

In 2010 Itawamba's population of 23,401 was 92.4 percent white and roughly 6.5 percent African American.

Mississippi Encyclopedia Staff
University of Mississippi

Mississippi State Planning Commission, *Progress Report on State Planning in Mississippi* (1938); *Mississippi Statistical Abstract*, Mississippi State University (1952–2010); Charles Sydnor and Claude Bennett, *Mississippi History* (1939); University of Virginia Library, Historical Census Browser website, http://mapserver.lib.virginia.edu; E. Nolan Waller and Dani A. Smith, *Growth Profiles of Mississippi's Counties, 1960–1980* (1985).

Iuka, Battle of

In the summer and fall of 1862, Confederate leaders planned key offensives in both major theaters of operation. As Gen. Robert E. Lee strategized for his invasion of Maryland, Gen. Braxton Bragg, commander of the Army of Tennessee, hoped to move north from Mississippi and Tennessee to seize Kentucky. But to do so, he would need help. Gen. Ulysses S. Grant's forces, fresh off a major victory at Shiloh in the spring, sat in western Tennessee, and Union troops under his command had advanced on Corinth, Mississippi, forcing the Confederates to retreat to Tupelo. Additional Confederate forces would have to hold Grant in the northern part of the state and perhaps even push him further north to allow Bragg to invade Kentucky. One result of this holding action was the Battle of Iuka.

Bragg began shifting his forces to Chattanooga, Tennessee, in late July, and by early September he was on his way to Kentucky. Bragg placed Sterling Price, the commander of the Army of the West, in charge of the District of Tennessee. Earl Van Dorn and his force guarded Vicksburg against a threat from Adm. David Farragut. Bragg wanted both small armies to occupy Grant while Bragg's forces operated in Kentucky, thereby preventing Grant from reinforcing Don Carlos Buell's Union troops in Middle Tennessee. Van Dorn eventually left Vicksburg to combine forces with Price, who had moved on the small town of Iuka. Grant, troubled with Bragg in Kentucky, did not want Price to maneuver around Grant's flank and toward the Ohio River in a possible move to join Bragg, so the Union general began to plan the destruction of Price's force at Iuka.

Van Dorn, moving his small army toward Iuka, had been given overall command of the Army of the West because of his seniority. He urged Price to redeploy his troops to Rienzi, where the two armies could be combined and a campaign could be launched into West Tennessee. But on the afternoon of 19 September, with Price finishing preparations to evacuate Iuka, Confederate and Union forces clashed as Grant's forces drove Rebel pickets from their positions south of the town. Grant had launched a two-pronged assault on Price, with Gen. William S. Rosecrans and Gen. Edward Ord attacking Iuka from different directions.

Grant's strategy, had it succeeded, might have destroyed Price's army at Iuka. But problems occurred, as they do with most military plans. Rosecrans and Ord's assaults did not occur simultaneously, and Price and his army escaped destruction. Price rushed brigades from Henry Little's division to face Rosecrans. Little was killed during the battle, and Price then deployed his whole division against Rosecrans in a counterattack. Rosecrans had not been able to get his entire division into the battle, and Price's forces pushed him back six hundred yards, capturing nine cannons before night fell and the battle had to be suspended. Confused, Ord never moved his forces one inch to aid Rosecrans.

Price wanted to renew the battle the next morning, but reluctant subordinates urged against it. With a road to the south open, Price withdrew during the night and marched west to link up with Van Dorn. By dawn on 20 September, the Confederates had abandoned Iuka. A total of fourteen hundred men had been killed or wounded. Both sides claimed victory, but Grant treated the engagement as a loss because Price's army had not been destroyed. With Price and Van Dorn now combined, Grant would soon face them again.

Ryan S. Walters
Hattiesburg, Mississippi

Albert Castel, *General Sterling Price and the Civil War in the West* (1996); Bruce Catton, *Grant Moves South, 1861–1863* (1960); Thomas Lawrence Connelly, *Army of the Heartland: The Army of the Tennessee, 1861–1862* (1967).

J

Jackson, Andrew
(1767–1845) US president

No national leader is associated with the early history of Mississippi as closely as the seventh president, Andrew Jackson. Indeed, he rose to prominence as a consequence of events that took place in the Mississippi Territory and just a few miles to the south in New Orleans. One of the earliest notable Americans to travel the Natchez Trace, Jackson first arrived in Natchez in 1789, probably in response to the proclamation welcoming Americans to Spanish Louisiana, which included the Natchez District. Like all Americans who wished to conduct business there, Jackson signed an oath of allegiance to the Spanish Crown, clearly an act of expediency and pragmatism by the xenophobic frontiersman.

In addition to his extensive business interests in Natchez, Jackson owned property along Bayou Pierre north of the town. And the Natchez Trace seems to be intertwined in his life. For example, in 1790 Jackson accompanied Rachel Donelson Robards on a boat journey to seek refuge from her estranged husband, Lewis Robards, returning to Nashville on the Trace. Probably in the spring or summer of 1791, Jackson rode back down the Trace to marry her, mistakenly believing that she had obtained an official divorce. Though no written record of the marriage has been found, according to tradition Col. Thomas Green, a former magistrate, performed the ceremony at the estate of his son, Thomas Marston Green, near Natchez. Later that year, accompanied by a large retinue of friends and relatives to assure safety, Jackson and his bride returned to Nashville via the Natchez Trace. When Jackson realized that the marriage had occurred before Rachel was legally divorced, they exchanged vows again in 1794 before a justice of the peace in Tennessee. No issue caused Andrew and Rachel Jackson as much grief throughout their lives as charges by political opponents that they had committed adultery.

Two decades after his marriage, Jackson became involved in a feud with the Choctaw Indian agent, Silas Dinsmoor. Some travelers on the Trace thought Dinsmoor was overzealous in his enforcement of an 1802 federal law that required persons escorting slaves through Indian territory to have a passport signed by an appropriate territorial official. The Choctaw Agency was located on the Trace just north of present-day Jackson. In 1811 Dinsmoor posted a notice that he intended to arrest and detain slaves traveling in the Choctaw nation whose masters lacked a passport and proof of ownership. Jackson, a partner in a firm that dealt in slaves, planned to challenge Dinsmoor with armed force while escorting some slaves from Natchez back to Nashville. However, Dinsmoor was away when Jackson arrived to confront him. Jackson's traffic in slaves later became an issue in his presidential campaigns.

The events most closely associated with Jackson's rise to fame relate to the War of 1812 and the concurrent Creek War, which was fought in Mississippi Territory. In January 1813 Jackson commanded some two thousand Tennessee troops. With two regiments of infantry he floated down the Cumberland, Ohio, and Mississippi Rivers to Natchez, where cavalry forces that had ridden down the Trace awaited him. In Natchez, Jackson also found a letter from the secretary of war ordering him to dismiss all of the men under arms. Jackson ignored those orders and used his own credit to organize a march back up the Trace to Nashville, during which he displayed such personal toughness that his men affectionately described him as "tough as hickory." He carried the nickname Old Hickory for the rest of his life.

After the Fort Mims Massacre north of Mobile, Alabama, on 30 August 1813, Jackson was chosen to lead a punitive expedition against the hostile Red Stick faction of the Creek Indians. During this campaign, known as the Creek War, Jackson and his men suffered tremendous privation. However, Jackson displayed remarkable courage and leadership, and his Tennessee troops concluded the campaign with a historic victory at the Battle of Horseshoe Bend.

Jackson was now a full-fledged military hero. After a brief respite the secretary of war appointed him the chief commissioner responsible for negotiating a treaty with the Creek at Fort Jackson on the Alabama River. In this highly punitive document signed on 9 August 1814, the Creek ceded half of their domain, foretelling Jackson's Removal policy and endearing him further to land-hungry southern frontiersmen. From Fort Jackson, the general hurried to Mobile to prepare for the anticipated invasion by the British. When he learned that the British armada was headed for New Orleans, Jackson marched his army from Mobile at a furious pace across Mississippi Territory, roughly following the thirty-first parallel to the Pearl River. From there he veered south to the northern shore of Lake Pontchartrain and then sailed across to New Orleans to prepare for his historic confrontation with the British on 8 January 1815. Mississippians were among the diverse group that composed his victorious forces at New Orleans. After the battle, Jackson triumphantly returned to Tennessee via the Natchez Trace.

While Jackson was already a hero to white citizens of Mississippi when it became a state in 1817, they particularly appreciated him as the chief negotiator of the 1820 Treaty of Doak's Stand, just north of present-day Jackson on the Natchez Trace. That treaty opened for settlement some five million acres of prime farmland now known as the Mississippi Delta. So appreciative were the members of the legislature that in 1821 they named the newly designated capital city on the Pearl River for the general.

Jackson remained highly popular in Mississippi. In his futile 1824 campaign for the White House, he carried every county in the state. Winning the presidency four years later, he again won every county but recorded much larger margins. En route to New Orleans for the 1840 celebration of the silver jubilee of the Battle of New Orleans, the former president stopped briefly in Vicksburg; on his return to Nashville, he stayed in Jackson for several days. His health had already begun to fail, and that proved to be his last visit to Mississippi.

John D. W. Guice

University of Southern Mississippi

H. W. Brands, *Andrew Jackson: His Life and Times* (2005); Thomas D. Clark and John D. W. Guice, *The Old Southwest, 1795–1830: Frontiers in Conflict* (1996); John D. W. Guice, *Journal of Mississippi History* (Summer 2007); Jon Meacham, *American Lion: Andrew Jackson in the White House* (2008); Robert V. Remini, *Andrew Jackson and the Course of American Democracy 1833–1845* (1984); Robert V. Remini, *Andrew Jackson and the Course of American Empire, 1767–1821* (1977); Robert V. Remini, *Andrew Jackson and the Course of American Freedom, 1822–1832* (1981); Sean Wilentz, *The Rise of American Democracy: Jefferson to Lincoln* (2005).

Jackson, Angela

(b. 1951) Writer

A native of Greenville, Angela Jackson is a writer of poetry, fiction, and drama. She is the fifth of nine children born to George Jackson Sr. and Angeline Robinson Jackson. Raised on Chicago's South Side, Jackson later earned a bachelor's degree from Northwestern University. Although she entered Northwestern on a premedical scholarship, two visiting professors, Margaret Walker and Hoyt William Fuller, influenced her in the direction of literature. She also holds a master's degree in Latin American and Caribbean studies from the University of Chicago.

Jackson is best known for poetry that draws on modernist techniques, folklore, and myth to explore issues of identity and gender. Her poetry collections include *VooDoo/Love Magic*, *The Greenville Club*, *Solo in the Boxcar Third Floor E*, *The Man with the White Liver*, *Dark Legs and Silk Kisses*, *And All These Roads Be Luminous*, and *Warm Earth*. Jackson uses symbols such as spiders, roots, and rituals and relies on the empirical to construct biting images of race and memory. Her poetry grapples with themes of personal and cultural identities of the African diaspora, a trademark of Jackson's style. Jackson cites Gwendolyn Brooks as a great influence on her work.

She has also written four plays: *Witness!*, *Shango Diaspora: An African-American Myth of Womanhood and Love*; *Comfort Stew* (also known as *When the Wind Blows*); and *Lightfoot: The Crystal Stair*. Her poetry and short fiction have also appeared in various journals and anthologies, including the *Chicago Review*, *Triquarterly*, and *Callaloo*. In 2009 she published her first novel, *Where I Must Go*. Jackson has participated in Illinois's Poets-in-the-Schools Program and has worked with the Organization of Black American Culture.

Jackson has received numerous honors for both fiction and poetry, including the Pushcart Prize and the Poetry Society of America's Shelley Memorial Award, and has received fellowships from the National Endowment for the Arts and the Illinois Arts Council. *All These Roads Be Luminous* was nominated for the National Book Award, while *Where I Must Go* won the American Book Award.

Jayetta Slawson

Southeastern Louisiana University

Marianna White Davis, Maryemma Graham, and Sharon Pineault-Burke, eds., *Teaching African American Literature: Theory and Practice* (1998); Laurie Levy, ed., *Chicago Works: A Collection of Chicago Authors' Best Stories* (1990); D. Soyini Madison, *The Woman That I Am: The Literature and Culture of Contemporary Women of Color* (1994); Carole A. Parks, ed., *Nommo: A Literary Legacy of Black Chicago (1967–1987)* (1987); Poetry Foundation website, www.poetryfoundation.org.

Jackson Advocate

Flourishing amid fear, segregation, and mob violence, the *Jackson Advocate* emerged in 1938 as perhaps Mississippi's most successful though ideologically conflicted black newspaper. One of three black weeklies operating in the state at the end of the Great Depression, the *Advocate* campaigned vigorously for voting rights and education yet secretly supported the caste system that kept blacks disenfranchised. The paper is difficult to consider apart from its founding editor, the controversial and flamboyant Percy Greene, who for years accepted payments from the Mississippi State Sovereignty Commission in exchange for supporting segregation as the best means for blacks and whites to get along. Many members of the black community never forgave Greene for his association with the Sovereignty Commission, which even took the form of publishing stories from the commission word for word. Nonetheless, the *Advocate* also expressed outrage over violence by the Ku Klux Klan, though fear of reprisals led the paper to restrict its criticism mostly to incidents in other parts of the South. Six decades passed before the paper directly challenged such violence, and during the 1990s the *Advocate* was often called the most firebombed newspaper in America.

With offices on Hamilton Street, the *Advocate*, a standard-sized newspaper of six to eight pages, existed within an atmosphere of oppression. Like many black newspapers in the South, the *Advocate* chronicled lynching and other atrocities on its front page yet focused heavily on black achievement on its inside pages. As evidence of race progress, the *Advocate* printed stories about successful businessmen, prominent black educators, and gifted college graduates. In addition, black athletes in the sports section, fair-skinned debutantes in society news, and jazz musicians on the entertainment page provided surefire proof, the paper reasoned, of race potential. This strain of racial uplift ideology reached back to the appearance of the nation's first black newspaper, *Freedom's Journal*, in 1827. The black press sought from its inception to undo the racist logic that condemned an entire race for the misdeeds of the individual by identifying successful individuals as reflecting the potential of the entire race.

The *Advocate* functioned in this vein for many years, though Greene was secretly filling his coffers with money from those who sought to deny black readers their humanity. Greene's editorials reflected his strong ties to the views of Booker T. Washington yet supported the mechanism that prevented blacks from elevating themselves, rendering the editor paradoxical at best. During World War II, front-page stories about patriotic black servicemen and their contribution to defeating Hitler became frequent items, though the *Advocate*'s editorial page often blamed blacks for their own problems, arguing that racial progress required frugality, industry, and clean living as personified by the individuals touted as race achievers. Editorials routinely exhorted blacks to lead moral lives, reporting, for example, on the high rates of venereal disease among black soldiers, a malady that prevented them from completing their duties.

The necessity for the black press to print news that both informed and had relevance to the black community helped shape the *Advocate*'s content, which in many regards was aimed at the city's black middle class. For example, Greene's column, "Up and Down Farish Street," contained observations about prominent black residents whom the publisher encountered on his evening strolls—a sort of who's who of the neighborhood where the *Advocate* circulated.

The *Advocate* failed to address many of issues affecting blacks in the state, especially with regard to civil rights during the 1950s. What had begun as a strategy of indirectly addressing racial violence became a tepid reliance on wire service copy gleaned from the Associated Negro Press. Only in small ways did readers interact with the newspaper. For example, the entertainment section featured articles chronicling black entertainers such as Ella Fitzgerald and Louis Armstrong and a "Rate the Records" column that encouraged readers to vote on their favorite songs, sold at local music shops. In most respects, however, the newspaper had lost touch with readers by the mid-1970s.

In 1978, after Greene's death the preceding year, Alabama publisher Charles Tisdale purchased the paper and began deepening its racial consciousness. He appointed as editor Colia Liddell LaFayette, an activist, poet, actress, and teacher who turned the paper into a record of insight and inquiry. Tisdale risked his life by leading local marches against racial injustice. According to the black news website Mississippi Link, Tisdale viewed Greene as a brilliant man who "just didn't have any character."

Tisdale's writings led to many threats. In 1982 two former Klansmen were convicted of firing eighty-four bullets into his office, and in 1998 Molotov cocktails were thrown into the *Advocate*'s offices—one of more than twenty times that the paper was vandalized or bombed. Most news items reflected protest on the local level and included court reporting on Mississippi's judicial system as well as the hiring and firing of black employees by area businesses. Under Tisdale, "Up and Down Farish Street" became a column on local black history.

The *Advocate*'s circulation gradually declined from seventeen thousand in 2000 to about eight thousand in 2010. According to Tisdale, "The thing that has become more complicated is African Americans themselves. They no longer see the need to identify with their own race"—a further irony in the history of one of the state's most successful black newspapers.

Tisdale remained the paper's publisher until his death on 7 July 2007. His widow, Alice Tisdale, took over as publisher afterward.

Mark K. Dolan
University of Mississippi

Jacqueline Bacon, *Freedom's Journal: The First African American Newspaper* (2007); Mississippi Link website, themississippilink.com; Julius E. Thompson, *The Black Press in Mississippi, 1865–1985* (1993); Julius E. Thompson, *Percy Greene and the Jackson Advocate: The Life and Times of Radical Conservative Black Newspaperman, 1897–1977* (1994); Patrick S. Washburn, *The African American Newspaper, Voice of Freedom* (2006).

Jackson, Battle and Siege of

Songwriter Harry McCarthy first played his song "The Bonnie Blue Flag" in Jackson in the spring of 1861. Its lilting tune and defiant words expressed the jubilation unleashed by secession. By 1862 Jackson had become an important Confederate manufacturing and railroad center, thanks in part to the Southern Railroad of Mississippi and the New Orleans, Jackson, and Great Northern Railroad, both of which passed through the town. The Southern offered a direct connection with Vicksburg, forty-four miles to the west by way of Clinton and Edward's Station.

During the Vicksburg Campaign (1863), Maj. Gen. Ulysses S. Grant crossed the Mississippi below Vicksburg and then turned north, instantly demonstrating the frailty of Vicksburg's only rail link with points east. Jackson, even more vulnerable, was doomed to both a battle (14 May) and, following the fall of Vicksburg, a siege (10–16 July). In the looting and destruction that followed the siege, a Union colonel from Missouri saw amid the wreckage "pianos smashed so that the 'Bonnie Blue Flag' may never be played on them again."

On 30 April–1 May Grant crossed two corps of his army (about twenty-five thousand men) to the east bank of the Mississippi at Bruinsburg, downstream from Vicksburg. When Gen. William T. Sherman's 15th Corps crossed, the force totaled about forty thousand men in all. Grant was to fight five battles south and east of Vicksburg, capturing Jackson in the third of these, on 14 May, and sealing Vicksburg's fate.

In addition to its instructions to Gen. John C. Pemberton in command at Vicksburg, the Confederate government offered a threefold response to Grant's coup. All of the elements involved the defense of Jackson. On 1 May, Richmond ordered reinforcements to Mississippi from Gen. P. G. T. Beauregard's command in the Carolinas and Gen. Braxton Bragg's Army of Tennessee at Tullahoma. These forces, which on 9 May came to include Lt. Gen. Joseph E. Johnston, were all directed to Jackson by rail. Had this force been allowed to concentrate there with Gen. John Gregg's brigade, already in the town, Johnston's force would have numbered about thirteen thousand.

On 3 May Gov. John J. Pettus ordered the construction of earthworks to ring the city on the west from points on the Pearl River up- and downstream. After the Battle of Port Gibson on 1 May, Grant planned to move northeast to reach the line of the Southern Railroad and turn west toward a crossing of the Big Black River east of Vicksburg. At Dillon's Plantation, where he had established headquarters with Sherman's corps, Grant learned of the Battle of Raymond, fourteen miles southwest of Jackson, on 12 May. Gregg had brought his brigade out of the Jackson entrenchment and

fought for fourteen hours against a division of Gen. James B. McPherson's 18th Corps. Gregg left McPherson with the distinct impression that his force was far larger than it was, betokening a Confederate buildup at Jackson. Grant then decided to move east against Jackson rather than west against Vicksburg. McPherson was ordered farther north, to approach Jackson on the Clinton Road, while Sherman advanced through Raymond toward Jackson.

Grant had surmised correctly. By 11 May Confederate reinforcements began arriving in Jackson. Part of Gen. W. H. T. Walker's brigade moved through town to join Gregg at Mississippi Springs. On the morning of 13 May, Col. Peyton Colquitt, commanding the first elements of Gen. States Rights Gist's brigade arrived. Gen. Johnston came in on one of the trains bearing Colquitt's men and took up headquarters at the Bowman House, where he met with Gregg.

Confederate forces then at hand, including Mississippi state troops and civilian volunteers, numbered only about six thousand, but more were approaching fast. Gregg believed (incorrectly) that the Union advance would be from one direction only, on the Clinton Road, yet Johnston concluded almost immediately that the situation was lost. Johnston gave orders to evacuate Jackson, wiring secretary of war James Seddon, "I am too late." His reference was certainly to Jackson but may also have included Vicksburg. Johnston ordered his infantry to march out to the north, on the Canton Road. While Gregg fought a delaying action west of town, Gen. John S. Adams gathered stores and movable property and followed the infantry north.

The Battle of Jackson comprised two separate actions. Battles northwest of town, on the Clinton Road at the O. R. Wright Farm, featured the heaviest fighting. Gregg had moved aggressively on the morning of 14 May, placing three regiments and the Brookhaven Artillery to resist the advance of Gen. M. M. Crocker's division of McPherson's 17th Corps. Gregg's force included the 24th South Carolina under Lt. Col. Ellison Capers, which suffered the heaviest losses of any Confederate command (eleven killed, thirty-eight wounded, fifty-six captured). Gregg envisioned a hard-fought rearguard action, and it lasted until the advance of Gen. J. M. Tuttle's division of Sherman's 15th Corps from the southwest on the Mississippi Springs Road and over Lynch Creek. To try to hold that line, Gregg created a scratch force under Col. A. P. Thompson of the 3rd Kentucky Mounted Infantry and Martin's Georgia Battery. After Thompson fell back into the Jackson earthworks, Sherman chose not to continue the assault but rather probed the Confederate line closer to the Pearl River. A column of engineers leading the 95th Ohio discovered a gap in the line where the railroad from New Orleans passed through the works. The Ohio regiment was soon well behind Confederate lines. By then, however, the Confederates were mostly gone, having completed their mission. They had left behind seventeen artillery pieces with the state troops and volunteers, which fell into Federal hands. Confederate losses have been estimated at five hundred, Union losses at about four hundred. By late afternoon the flag of the 59th Indiana flew over the State Capitol. Grant headed west almost immediately, fighting again at Champion Hill on 16 May. Sherman stayed behind to destroy the railroads and other public property.

The significance of the battle lay in its impact on the two Confederate forces nearest Grant. Pemberton, at Vicksburg, was now isolated. Johnston, pushed out of Jackson, saw half of his new command, in the words of Edwin C. Bearss, "scattered to the winds." Once his force had been reconstituted, it was by necessity nearer to Yazoo City than to Jackson. The Federals left behind a scene of desolation and ruin, not only of railroad facilities but also of foundries, factories, gins, and mills.

The Siege of Vicksburg began on 18 May. Johnston's forces, now near Yazoo City, grew to about thirty-one thousand men, but Johnston did little either to relieve Vicksburg or to enable Pemberton's besieged garrison to break out. On 1–2 July, Johnston probed for any possible weakness in Grant's ring around Vicksburg, but the end was near. On 3 July Grant ordered Sherman to prepare to move against Johnston as soon as the surrender came; when it came the next day, Johnston drew off toward Jackson. His force comprised infantry divisions commanded by Gens. John Breckinridge, Samuel French, William W. Loring, and W. H. T. Walker. Gen. William Jackson's cavalry acted as rear guard for the march, which ended at Jackson late on 7 July. Johnston spent 8 July improving the Jackson earthworks before his infantry units took up their positions the next day: Loring between the Pearl River and the Canton Road, Walker as far as the Southern Railroad tracks, French from there to the Raymond Road, and Breckinridge from that road back to the Pearl. Johnston's artillery included two thirty-two-pound rifled guns and the four guns of the Cotton Bale Battery, which were stationed at the northernmost point of the line, covering the Canton Road.

The line was stronger than that of 14 May but was compromised in two ways. This time, an attack could be expected down the Canton Road, Johnston's line of retreat in May. And the New Orleans Railroad bridge over the Pearl remained in ruins. Supplies from the east could not come by rail any closer than a mile from the river, where wagons waited. Johnston did not believe he could withstand a siege, and he hoped merely to repel any frontal assaults the enemy might launch.

The force Sherman moved from Vicksburg east to Jackson was far larger than that of 14 May. It included three full infantry corps: the 9th under Gen. James Parke, the 13th under Gen. E. O. C. Ord, and the 15th under Gen. Frederick Steele. In all, Sherman had just under fifty thousand men at his disposal. By 8 July, after a sharp skirmish at Clinton, Sherman's force was within striking distance of Jackson.

There was to be no great strike, however. Sherman's corps—the 9th aiming at the Canton Road, the 15th on the Clinton Road, and the 13th on the Raymond Road—were not linked by any good north-south roads. The Confederate line was strong in itself, and the Confederates might counterattack into any gaps in the advance. Furthermore, Sherman's artillery ammunition supply was low. The wagon train carrying his reserve supply would not reach him until 16 July. Sherman made little progress on 9–10 July and then ordered his forces to begin siege operations. Only north of Jackson, where Parke's corps was aiming to reach and then turn south on the Canton Road, did substantial movement occur. Sherman's lines were generally about fifteen hundred yards from the Confederate works, but in some places, such as the high ground of the Deaf and Dumb Asylum, artillery was as close to the enemy as four hundred yards.

On 11 July a sharp fight took place in front of the Cotton Bale Battery's position, on the crest of a ridge north of today's Fortification Street and just east of State Street. The hard-pressed battery, supported by Company A of the 14th Mississippi Regiment, turned back a Federal thrust down the Canton Road

On the night of 11 July, Sherman gave orders for a bombardment of Jackson to commence at 7:00 the following morning and last an hour. In all, artillerists fired some three thousand rounds into the city. Even an hour's firing seriously depleted the ammunition on hand.

The bloodiest fighting of the siege came on 12 July, between Bailey's Hill on the Union right and the Confederate lines about one thousand yards away. The previous afternoon, Hovey's division of the 13th Corps had crossed Lynch Creek between the Raymond Road and the New Orleans Railroad, dislodging the 1st Arkansas Mounted Rifles. On 12 July, Isaac Pugh's brigade of Jacob Lawman's division was sent forward from Bailey's Hill with orders to cross the railroad to its left and rectify the Union front beyond the creek. They faced a huge cornfield beyond which were concealed two well-placed Confederate infantry regiments, the 32nd Alabama and the 14th Louisiana, who knew the Union forces were coming. Two batteries, with twelve guns in all, lay just behind the Confederate infantry. The Federals hesitated before entering the corn and then advanced—to their destruction. In the tornado of artillery and rifle fire that engulfed the brigade, 68 men were killed, 302 more were wounded, and 149 were later captured. Confederates lost only 7 men.

The next day was uneventful, and a truce occurred on 14 July. A general cease-fire held from noon until 5:00 in the evening as soldiers from two Louisiana regiments, the 13th and the 20th, buried the dead from Pugh's attack two days earlier.

Both Sherman and Johnston watched closely for the arrival of Sherman's artillery reserve wagons. On 15 June Gen. William Jackson's cavalry tried but failed to intercept the all-important wagons. Johnston, however, decided to evacuate the town before Sherman's wagons arrived. He withdrew his infantry across the Pearl River bridges that evening. By the night of 17 July his force, largely intact, went into camps at Brandon. The Confederates left a flag flying over the Capitol, but by midday on 17 July it had been replaced with a flag from the 35th Massachusetts. Johnston also left behind his two thirty-two-pound rifled guns, twenty-four thousand artillery rounds, and fourteen hundred rifles. His casualties totaled 71 men killed, 504 wounded, and 25 taken prisoner. Sherman's losses were greater but light considering the enormity of what had been done: 129 killed, 752 wounded, and 231 captured.

Severe destruction attended and followed the evacuation, the second in two months' time. City Hall, the Governor's Mansion, the Capitol, and the mayor's house survived, in stark contrast to the rest of "Chimneyville." On 23 July, according to Col. James Peckham of Missouri, "As I write the sky is illuminated by the light of burning buildings. Jackson is in ruins."

Brandon H. Beck
Shenandoah University

Edwin C. Bearss, *The Campaign for Vicksburg* (1991); Edwin C. Bearss and Warren Grabau, *The Battle of Jackson, May 14, 1863; The Siege of Jackson, July 10–17, 1863; Three Other Post-Vicksburg Actions* (1981); Luther S. Bechtel, Diary, Mississippi Department of Archives and History; Samuel Carter III, *The Final Fortress: The Campaign for Vicksburg, 1862–1863* (1980); Civil War Scrapbook, Battles of Raymond and Jackson, Mississippi Department of Archives and History; Richard N. Current, ed., *Encyclopedia of the Confederacy* (1993); Warren E. Grabau, *Ninety-Eight Days: A Geographer's View of the Vicksburg Campaign* (2000); Wiley Sword, *Blue and Gray* (Spring 2004).

Jackson, City Plan of

Jackson's founding was part of an early southern tradition of planned state capitals on the frontier that also included Columbia, South Carolina; Louisville and Milledgeville, Georgia; Raleigh, North Carolina; Cahaba, Alabama; and Tallahassee, Florida. Convenient to the shifting center of population growth, encouraging further development, and exerting new political power over older tidewater or colonial centers, these new capitals reflected planning possibilities before strong central governments disappeared in the face of Jacksonian democracy.

In 1821, four years after Mississippi achieved statehood and one year after the Treaty of Doak's Stand ceded a portion of Choctaw homelands in the center of the state, the Mississippi legislature moved the state capital from the Natchez area to a high bluff overlooking the Pearl River, in the midst of the formerly Choctaw lands. With legislative approval the commissioners of the new city created an enlightened and ambitious city plan with north-south rows of ten square blocks. Along the east margin of this grid were three large public greens, the center one for the future capitol, and the other two for a courthouse and a college. The three greens were positioned on the edge of the bluff, ensuring the prominence of the anticipated public buildings. The greens were connected by a curved street.

The streets themselves had an order dictated by their widths. Capitol Green was fronted by State Street and was the terminus for Capitol Street, each of which was one hundred feet wide. College Street and Court Street were also one hundred feet wide but were landscaped boulevard-style and terminated on the east at their respective greens. All other streets were sixty feet wide.

Such a clear vision for a seat of government was impressive on the American frontier. However, what really made Jackson's plan special was the fact that public parks or groves were sprinkled throughout the city in a checkerboard pattern, with alternating squares left open. Public commons for recreation or daytime pastures were not unusual in American cities, but leaving every other square as green space was extraordinary. Pres. Thomas Jefferson had suggested this plan to Gov. William Henry Harrison of Indiana, resulting in a short-lived checkerboard at Jeffersonville in 1802, and to Gov. W. C. C. Claiborne as a healthy extension of New Orleans in 1804. That the checkerboard came with a stamp of approval from Jefferson and the popular Claiborne may have convinced the legislature of the plan's value.

But the idea may have been too ambitious. As funds were needed for constructing state buildings over the next three decades, green squares were platted in lots and sold. Today City Hall and its park and Smith Park are America's only remnants of Jefferson's ambitious plan for half-green cities.

Four of the original squares were taken in the 1840s for the State Penitentiary and are now a park setting for the New Capitol, built in 1903. Of the three public greens along the bluff, only the Capitol Green survives, with its original Capitol (1839) at the nexus of the major downtown streets. The squares of the original plan remain the city's only blocks with that shape.

Cavett Taff
Mississippi Department of
Archives and History

Michael W. Fazio, *The Chequer Board Plan of Jackson, Mississippi: A Chapter in the Origin and Disposal of the American Public Domain* (1980); Michael W. Fazio, *Arris: Journal of the Southeast Chapter of the Society of Architectural Historians* (1989); John Reps, *The Making of Urban America* (1965).

Jackson Civil Rights Movement

The civil rights movement in Jackson encompassed the direct action protests in Mississippi's capital city in the early 1960s. The grassroots campaign to end racial discrimination in Jackson emerged out of the Tougaloo College and North Jackson Youth Councils of the National Association for the Advancement of Colored People (NAACP). The wave of sit-ins that began in Greensboro, North Carolina, in February 1960 inspired similar protests in Mississippi, but the state NAACP's conservative leadership, fearful of violent reprisals against African Americans, remained focused on voter registration drives. Nevertheless, Medgar Evers, the NAACP's field secretary for Mississippi since 1954 and only paid worker in the state, recognized Youth Council members' desire to engage in coordinated protests in the capital city and helped organize a boycott of downtown businesses around Easter 1960. In March 1961, nine Tougaloo students and members of the NAACP Youth Council carried out a meticulously planned sit-in at the whites-only Jackson Public Library on North State Street. After explaining to the librarians that they needed books that they could not obtain at the "colored branch," the nine Tougaloo students were confronted by police and arrested for breach of the peace. The prolonged incarceration and trial of the Tougaloo Nine prompted prayer assemblies at Jackson State and outside the courthouse. The police saw these gatherings as unlawful demonstrations and responded with dogs, clubs, and tear gas.

According to Myrlie Evers, the Tougaloo Nine sit-in represented "the change of tide in Mississippi." Jackson-area students and Youth Council members throughout the state now attempted sit-ins at various public spaces, among them the zoo and Jackson's buses, parks, and swimming pools. Outsiders also spurred local movement activity: two months after the library sit-in, waves of Freedom Riders began arriving at the Trailways station in downtown Jackson, provoking more than three hundred arrests by the end of the summer. With most riders choosing to remain in Parchman Prison and the Hinds County jail rather than posting bond, African American churchwomen in Jackson organized Womanpower Unlimited to help the riders while they were in jail and after their release. For the next several years, Womanpower Unlimited, led by Clarie Collins Harvey, raised funds and coordinated support for local and out-of-state activists whom police detained during peaceful protests. The arrests and trials of the Freedom Riders also brought in a new group of civil rights workers, as David Dennis and Tom Gaither of the Congress of Racial Equality (CORE) and James Bevel, Diane Nash, and Bernard Lafayette of the Student Nonviolent Coordinating Committee (SNCC) continued to organize in Mississippi after their release from jail. In early 1962 the Council of Federated Organizations brought the NAACP, CORE, SNCC, and local groups into a state-wide civil rights coalition.

From late 1961 through 1962 much of the Jackson NAACP's efforts centered on voter registration drives and legal challenges, including an ultimately successful lawsuit to enroll Jackson State student James Meredith at the University of Mississippi. A suit to remove segregated seating aboard Jackson's privately owned buses won in court, but many white drivers ignored the court order. The newly organized Jackson Nonviolent Movement, led by Gaither and Tougaloo student Joan Trumpauer, then spearheaded further boycotts of buses. Yet, like an attempted boycott campaign of white-owned downtown businesses in December 1961, the bus boycott failed to garner massive support from local blacks.

With the desegregation of the University of Mississippi and the renewed hope that change was possible, civil rights activity picked up once again. In October 1962 the NAACP's North Jackson Youth Council, advised by Tougaloo sociology professor John Salter, coordinated a boycott of the Mississippi State Fair for Negroes. This time, most people stayed away from the fairgrounds, and the Youth Council planned a more comprehensive campaign. Recognizing that the holiday shopping season typically drew thousands of African Americans to the white-owned businesses along Capitol Street, Salter and the Youth Council members coordinated an economic boycott of downtown businesses. Activists demanded equal hiring practices, the use of courtesy titles, and an end to segregated seating and restrooms. With the campaign receiving endorsements from Evers and the local SNCC and CORE representatives, the boycott leaflets now officially bore the name *Jackson movement*.

Black students distributed leaflets and spoke in churches throughout the community, and by Christmas 1962 Evers deemed the boycott "60–65 percent effective." When neither Mayor Allen Thompson nor white business owners gave in to any of the demands, movement leaders extended the economic boycott into 1963. Emboldened by the campaign in Birmingham, where city officials finally agreed to form a biracial commission and begin dismantling racial discrimination in businesses, movement leaders hoped to utilize direct action tactics in Jackson. In May, with the boycott in its sixth month, the state NAACP announced the possibility of future mass marches, picketing, and demonstrations. In addition to the earlier demands, the movement called for the mayor to create a biracial committee, hire black policemen and school crossing guards, and desegregate all public facilities. In a final effort to avert a Birmingham-like confrontation, Rev. Edwin King Jr., Tougaloo's new chaplain, organized a series of interracial ministers' meetings to encourage dialogue among city and state religious leaders. After white ministers refused to join their black counterparts in demanding an end to racial discrimination in Jackson, and with Mayor Thompson refusing to budge, the direct action phase of the movement commenced on 28 May.

J

For a week and a half in late May and early June 1963, coordinated protests took place throughout the city. On the first day, five students and teachers were arrested on Capitol Street for carrying signs that declared, "Jackson Needs a Bi-Racial Committee," while at nearby Woolworth's lunch counter, one of the most violent sit-ins of the civil rights movement began to unfold. For more than two hours, Tougaloo students and adults sat on stools while a growing white mob hurled racist insults and sprayed ketchup and mustard on them. As police watched from outside the store, some in the mob threw the students on the floor: at one point an ex-police officer pulled student Memphis Norman to the ground and stomped repeatedly on his head. When members of the mob began to pick up merchandise to use as projectiles, the manager finally intervened and ordered everyone out. The nationwide media coverage of the violence at Woolworth's provoked a temporary change of heart for Mayor Thompson, who privately told some black ministers that he would agree to some of the movement's demands. The ministers reported the concessions to a jubilant crowd at a mass meeting that night, but the mayor announced that he had not agreed to any deal, and demonstrations resumed. During the next week, Jackson police arrested more than six hundred people, most of them high school and college students, for picketing and attempted sit-ins. Police arrested several Lanier High School students who gathered at lunch to sing freedom songs, while movement leaders and ministers staged a kneel-in on the steps of the Federal Building on Capitol Street. The largest demonstration occurred on 30 May, when police clubbed several marchers and arrested four hundred students as they walked down Farish Street. The city incarcerated those arrested in makeshift jail cells at the livestock area of the State Fairgrounds.

The direct action protests diminished as the national NAACP grew weary of supplying bail funds and the Hinds County Chancery Court granted the mayor an injunction that prohibited the movement from coordinating future demonstrations or acts of civil disobedience. Convinced that any civil rights activity would result in arrests and recognizing that mass demonstrations were no longer financially feasible, Evers and King argued for smaller, targeted protests. Evers and King sought to confront white Christians more directly regarding the immorality of segregation and planned a series of church visits throughout Jackson. On 9 June, black students attended worship at St. Peter's Catholic Church, while ushers at several Baptist and Methodist churches turned other students away. However, police refrained from making any arrests. The easing of tensions did not last long, for two days later, a sniper killed Evers in the driveway of his home.

Anger over Evers's murder awakened people's activism. Mass meetings filled to capacity, and people took to the streets of Jackson in spontaneous marches. Thousands packed into the Masonic Temple for Evers's 15 June funeral, where friends and civil rights leaders from across the country eulogized the NAACP leader. In keeping with an arrangement with city officials, the mourners marched silently from the temple down Farish Street to the funeral home. When the end of the procession reached the funeral home, after most of the out-of-town leaders had departed, the hundreds still present began singing freedom songs. They then marched back toward the intersection at Capitol Street, the central target of the movement's boycotts, sit-ins, and protests for the past six months. A verbal back-and-forth with the assembled police soon turned violent, as stones flew through the air and police ran forward with dogs and clubs. Police arrested more than two dozen people, including Salter and King.

The funeral procession and the unplanned protest on Capitol Street marked the final demonstrations of the Jackson movement. On 18 June Mayor Thompson, pressured by the Kennedy administration, agreed to meet some of the movement's demands, including hiring black policemen and crossing guards. This agreement fell well short of the original demands, failing to provide for desegregated public facilities and businesses or for a biracial committee. Yet encouraged by NAACP leaders and more conservative local ministers, a majority at a mass meeting at a Pearl Street African Methodist Episcopal Church voted to accept the compromise. While this decision represented the end of Jackson's mass movement, smaller protests and activities continued. King led students, faculty, and out-of-state ministers back to local white-only churches for the next ten months, resulting in more than forty arrests. Tougaloo activists also waged an increasingly successful campaign to desegregate the city's entertainment venues by encouraging performers to cancel scheduled appearances. In the end, the desegregation of Jackson's public accommodations and businesses occurred through federal law and reluctant local compliance. In July 1964 Jackson Chamber of Commerce leaders called on the city's businesses to comply with the new Civil Rights Act, a request reluctantly seconded by Mayor Thompson.

Carter Dalton Lyon
St. Mary's Episcopal School,
Memphis, Tennessee

Daphne Chamberlain, "And a Child Shall Lead the Way: Children's Participation in the Jackson, Mississippi, Black Freedom Struggle, 1946–1970" (PhD dissertation, University of Mississippi, 2009); John Dittmer, *Local People: The Struggle for Civil Rights in Mississippi* (1994); Susan Erenrich, ed., *Freedom Is a Constant Struggle: An Anthology of the Mississippi Civil Rights Movement* (1999); Myrlie Evers-Williams with William Peters, *For Us, the Living* (1967); Debbie Z. Harwell, *Wednesdays in Mississippi: Proper Ladies Working for Radical Change, Freedom Summer 1964* (2014); Carter Dalton Lyon, "Lifting the Color Bar from the House of God: The 1963–1964 Church Visit Campaign to Challenge Segregation" (PhD dissertation, University of Mississippi, 2010); M. J. O'Brien, *We Shall Not Be Moved: The Jackson Woolworth's Sit-In and the Movement It Inspired* (2013); John R. Salter Jr., *Jackson, Mississippi: An American Chronicle of Struggle and Schism* (1979); Michael Vinson Williams, *Medgar Evers: Mississippi Martyr* (2011).

Jackson Clarion-Ledger

The *Clarion-Ledger* was founded in 1837 in Paulding, Jasper County. Known initially as the *Eastern Clarion*, the paper was sold later that year and moved to Meridian. After the Civil War, the paper moved to Jackson, merged with the *Standard*, and became known as the *Clarion*. Owners Col. J. L. Power and Col. Robert H. Henry renamed the paper the *Daily Clarion-Ledger* after combining it with the *State Ledger* (printed in Brookhaven and Newton) in 1888. The company is listed as the second-oldest corporation in Mississippi.

Henry was a member of the Hederman family, and when he retired in 1912, other family members began managing the paper. Scott County printers Robert M. "Bert" Hederman (1877–1944) and Thomas M. Hederman (1878–1948) acquired control of the *Clarion-Ledger* in 1922. Bert Hederman took over the printing business that Henry had started, while Tom Hederman became the paper's business manager and editor. In 1954 Robert M. Hederman Jr. (1910–96) and Thomas M. Hederman Jr. (1911–85) acquired the *Jackson Daily News* (an afternoon paper founded in 1892) and merged its printing plant with that of the *Clarion-Ledger*.

On 1 April 1982 the Hederman family sold the morning *Jackson Clarion-Ledger*, the afternoon *Jackson Daily News*, the *Hattiesburg American*, and six weeklies to Gannett for $110 million. The *Clarion-Ledger* had a circulation of 66,620,

Jackson Clarion-Ledger Building, ca. 1912 (Al Fred Daniel Photograph Collection, Archives and Records Services Division, Mississippi Department of Archives and History, [17])

mostly in the communities surrounding the state capital. The *Daily News* had a circulation of 40,147.

Gannett consolidated the two Jackson newspapers in 1989. Over the next decade Gannett launched a multistep expansion that included moving the newspaper from 311 East Pearl Street to 201 South Congress Street in 1996. Other changes included acquiring the Hederman Brothers printing building in 1993, adding a second press line in 1995 (expanding from eight units to fifteen units and providing the capability to print up to sixty thousand papers per hour), and the renovation on the west side of the building, which houses circulation and production facilities.

Prior to 1970 the *Clarion-Ledger* and the other Hederman papers were known for their racist politics, promoting segregation and supporting the efforts of the Mississippi State Sovereignty Commission, a quasi-secret government agency. Rea Hederman became the *Clarion-Ledger*'s editor in 1970 and made dramatic changes in the newspaper's tone. It subsequently won numerous national prizes, including a 1979 Heywood Broun Award and the Robert F. Kennedy Memorial Award, a National Education Reporting Award, and a George Polk Award, all in 1981. The newspaper also won the Pulitzer Prize for Public Service in 1983 for its robust coverage of the dire state of public education in Mississippi and the marathon legislative initiative that led to the adoption of the 1982 Education Improvement Act.

Reporter Jerry Mitchell, credited with reopening many old civil rights cases, has added to the newspaper's list of awards. He was named a Pulitzer Prize finalist in 2006. His other awards include a 2005 George Polk Award for Justice Reporting, a 1999 Heywood Broun Award, the 1999 Sidney Hillman Award, and the 2005 Columbia Journalism School Citation for Coverage of Race and Ethnicity. In 2009 he was named a Macarthur Foundation Fellow, receiving five hundred thousand dollars because his "life and work serve as an example of how a journalist willing to take risks and unsettle waters can make a difference in the pursuit of justice."

Distributed throughout the state, the *Clarion-Ledger* has the largest circulation in Mississippi. However, like most other newspapers, its circulation has dropped in recent years, falling to about sixty thousand by the 2010s.

Kathleen Woodruff Wickham
University of Mississippi

Peggy Elam and Loretta Pendergrast, *Jackson Clarion-Ledger* (2 April 1982); Kathy Lally, *Baltimore Sun Journal* (5 January 1997); Andrew P. Mullins Jr., *Building Consensus: A History of the Passage of the Mississippi Education Reform Act of 1982* (1992); R. L. Nave, *Jackson Free Press* (2 September 2014); Bill Prochnau, *Washington Post* (25 April 1983); James Silver, *Mississippi: The Closed Society* (1964); Kathleen Wickham, *Winning the Pulitzer Prize: The Role of the Clarion-Ledger in the Adoption of the 1982 Education Reform Act* (2007).

Jackson Country Club Liquor Raid

On the night of 4 February 1966 Hinds County chief deputy sheriff Tom Shelton and three of his deputies conducted a liquor raid at a reception at the Jackson Country Club. For years the Junior League of Jackson's annual Carnival Ball had been an important social event, and that night the country club was playing host to the king's reception, which followed the ball itself. Much to the displeasure of the partygoers, Shelton and his men seized roughly ten thousand dollars' worth of liquor from the club, arrested the assistant bar manager, and produced one of the more subdued receptions in the history of the Carnival Ball. More important than this immediate result was the way in which public reactions to this raid and its legal consequences led to the repeal of Prohibition in Mississippi.

While the Twenty-First Amendment had ended national Prohibition in 1933, the State of Mississippi had chosen to continue the "noble experiment" by outlawing the sale, possession, or consumption of hard liquor and wine within the state's borders. In 1959 Oklahoma repealed its Prohibition laws, leaving Mississippi the only remaining dry state. However, much as had been the case during national Prohibition, drinkers found a way to get their liquor. In fact, the State of Mississippi even facilitated the process of obtaining liquor, and it did so quite efficiently.

Although the sale of liquor had been illegal in Mississippi since 1908, the state had long imposed some form of tax on alcoholic beverages. As long as the "penalty" tax had been paid, state officials did not obstruct liquor sales. The most famous of these taxes was undoubtedly sec. 10108–01 of the 1942 Mississippi Code, better known as the Black Market Tax. The code imposed a tax of roughly 10 percent on the sale of all illegal goods but was collected exclusively on the sale of liquor. The tax came into use in 1944, but not until more than a decade later was its full potential unleashed.

In 1956 William Winter took office as Mississippi's state tax collector and immediately saw the deficiencies in the application of the black market tax. Winter knew that all the liquor in Mississippi came from Louisiana, so he worked with the Louisiana Department of Revenue to give the process more transparency, thus greatly improving his office's efficiency in collecting the taxes. Over time, the revenue generated from this system became vital to the state's annual budget. Winter himself benefited from the tax as well, because he received a percentage of the taxes his office collected. A 1962 *Life* magazine article noted that Winter's annual income of sixty thousand dollars more than doubled the governor's salary of twenty-five thousand dollars and that Winter was the second-highest-paid public official in the United States, trailing only the president. Despite the fact he benefited substantially from this hypocritical system of taxing an illegal item,

Winter, like many others, had for some time advocated the abolition of both his office and the state's Prohibition laws.

The Jackson Country Club raid exposed many of these hypocrisies to the general public, and support grew for addressing the Prohibition issue. Pressure on the legislature to act increased further as a result of the court case resulting from the arrest of the assistant club manager, Charles Wood. Wood and his attorneys claimed that the state had implicitly repealed Prohibition laws by taxing liquor and by randomly enforcing those laws—for example, Vicksburg, Natchez, and the Gulf Coast had open liquor sales, while other parts of the state were totally dry.

The case went to the Mississippi Supreme Court, raising the specter that the court would overturn the Prohibition laws and leave the state with no controls on the sale of liquor. With the Supreme Court ruling imminent, legislators began considering a variety of bills to repeal Prohibition, leading wets and drys to reach a compromise under which the state government became the sole wholesaler for all liquor stores in Mississippi. Gov. Paul B. Johnson signed the bill into law in May 1966, and the Mississippi State Tax Commission created the Office of Alcoholic Beverage Control.

Joseph Green
University of Mississippi

Clayton Sledge Allen, "The Repeal of Prohibition in Mississippi" (master's thesis, University of Mississippi, 1992); Joseph Stone Green, "The Last Drinking Drys: The Repeal of Prohibition in Mississippi" (honors thesis, University of Mississippi, 2008); Norman Ritter, *Life* (11 May 1962).

Jackson County

Jackson County on the Gulf Coast played an important role in Mississippi's early development. Founded in 1812, it was named after Andrew Jackson. For much of its history, artists have flocked to Jackson County, establishing a unique art community. Compared to other parts of Mississippi, Jackson County is ethnically diverse and has few farms. Instead of depending on agriculture, the county developed mammoth timber and transportation industries. The county's recent history boasts population growth, industrial development, and increased government spending. Major cities include Escatawpa, Gautier, Moss Point, and Ocean Springs. The county seat, Pascagoula, became one of Mississippi's largest cities in the mid-twentieth century. Because of its geography, Jackson County is vulnerable to the natural disasters common in coastal areas.

Washington Avenue, Ocean Springs, Jackson County, ca. 1913 (Ann Rayburn Paper Americana Collection, Department of Archives and Special Collections, J. D. Williams Library, University of Mississippi [rayburn_ann_36_29_001])

The founding of Jackson County dates to the 1600s, when French and then Spanish colonists encountered Native Americans on the Gulf Coast. These Europeans as well as some English and German settlers in the area interacted with the Biloxi, Pascagoula, and Moctobi tribes.

In the 1690s French colonizer Pierre Le Moyne, Sieur d'Iberville, established several Gulf Coast forts and settlements, some of which eventually became Gautier and Ocean Springs. Iberville's commandant, Jean de Sauvole, built Fort Maurepas (the foundation of what became Ocean Springs) and developed relations with the Biloxi and other tribes. These relationships assisted the French in obtaining land for municipal development. Spanish settlers later took control of the area until 1810, when Spain relinquished this land to the US government and the area became part of Mississippi Territory. In 1812 the Mississippi government divided the area into three counties: Mobile County to the east, Hancock County on the west, and Jackson County in the middle.

Jackson County had few residents in the early 1800s. According to the 1820 census, the population consisted of 1,300 free whites, 321 slaves, and 61 free blacks. The county subsequently experienced significant growth, doubling by 1840 to 2,955 whites, 1,087 slaves, and 80 free African Americans, the second-highest number in the state.

Jackson contained the fewest improved acres of farmland in the state in 1860. Unlike most of Mississippi, its farms produced very little corn or livestock, and it exported the smallest amount of cotton in the state. Jackson County did, however, rank thirteenth in rice production and eleventh in the value of its orchards. It relied on a growing timber industry, with two sawmills in operation by 1840. In 1875 the state's first wood treatment establishment opened in Pascagoula. These industries continued to grow. In 1880 Jackson County had only twenty-three farms, almost all of them run by their owners.

A cotton depot opened in Jackson County in 1819, the Round Island Lighthouse began its work in 1832, and Pascagoula was a popular steamboat stop. All of these factors made Jackson one of the earliest areas in the state to attract tourists, initially drawing travelers intrigued by salt water and seafood. Because of its proximity to waterways, the county built a reliable transportation industry.

Mirroring other counties in the state, Jackson contained a high number of Methodist and Baptist congregations. In 1860 Jackson County had fifteen Methodist churches and six Baptist churches. The county's two Catholic churches expanded as Jackson attracted more immigrants than did other parts of Mississippi, including substantial numbers of German and Irish workers.

In 1900 Jackson had 478 foreign-born residents and 1,200 white residents born in the United States to immigrant parents. The majority of those immigrants were Germans, while others were English, Irish, Italian, Canadian, Danish, and Swedish. There were twice as many men than women, and many worked in fishing or canning factories. The importance of immigration and past immigrant settlement meant that cultural life on the Gulf Coast stood out within Mississippi. According to the 1916 religious census, Catholics were the largest religious group in Jackson County, making up more than a quarter of all church members. Various Methodists, Baptists, Presbyterians, and Episcopalians also lived in the county.

Jackson County's population grew dramatically around the turn of the century. Between 1880 and 1900 the population mushroomed from 7,607 to 16,513, about a third of them African American. The increase in population paralleled the rise of the Jackson County industrial economy. The county ranked near the top in the state in industrial employment, with 1,329 county residents, all but 21 of them men, holding industrial jobs. Michigan lumberman Delos Blodgett bought considerable timberland and employed numerous South Mississippi workers in the late 1800s and early 1900s. By the early twentieth century the L. N. Dantzler Lumber Company, with headquarters in Moss Point, was one of the largest in the state. Jackson remained a largely nonagricultural county, but its total number of farms rose to 544 in 1900. Almost all farmers owned their farmland.

Jackson County began welcoming artists and developed a unique arts community. Shearwater Pottery began as an Anderson family business in the 1920s, and numerous visual artists flourished there. Walter Anderson, born in 1903, served as a phenomenal force for creativity in Ocean Springs. Opened in 1991, the Walter Anderson Museum features many of his works, including wall murals he created in the 1950s. Many other artists, some with connections to New Orleans, have lived and worked in Jackson County. The county is also home to buildings designed by Frank Lloyd Wright and Bruce Goff. An ornamental cottage tradition with roots in the 1800s contributes to the unique architecture in Ocean Springs. Jackson and other coastal counties host numerous art groups and festivals year round.

In 1930 white residents made up about three-quarters of the county's 16,000 residents. Jackson was one of the few

Mississippi counties with more urban than rural residents. In the late 1930s and 1940s Ingalls Shipbuilding, spawned by the Balance Agriculture with Industry program, brought significant changes to the area. The company quickly became the state's largest industrial employer.

Through World War II, industrial and military employers used high wages to lure large numbers of people to the Gulf Coast, and the small town of Pascagoula suddenly became a small city. One of many migrants to the area was Chester Paul Lott, who moved to the coast to work at Ingalls. His son, Trent, grew up in Pascagoula and went on to become a long-time Mississippi senator.

A number of creative individuals have called the coastal county home. Singer-songwriter Jimmy Buffett, though more associated with the Caribbean and Florida beach life, was born in Pascagoula in 1946. Writer Al Young was born in Ocean Springs in 1939 before moving with his family to Detroit. Born in 1897, Jacob Reddix grew up in Vancleave and became a scholar and served as president of Jackson State College for twenty-five years. Journalist Ira Harkey bought the *Pascagoula Chronicle-Star* in 1949 and started a long career as editor and columnist, winning a Pulitzer Prize.

Jackson County's population more than tripled between 1930 and 1960, with the white majority growing to 80 percent. At midcentury, Jackson had the state's highest per capita income. The number of residents reached almost 120,000 by 1980, making Jackson the third-most-populous county in the state. The county's industrial base continued to grow, employing more than 20,000 people—more than half the county's workforce and the highest number of industrial workers in Mississippi. The majority of those employed worked producing transportation equipment, specifically ships. More than one-fifth of the county's female laborers also worked in manufacturing. Retail accounted for another large segment of the workforce. Jackson County also claimed one of the better educational systems in the state, no doubt as a consequence of its industrial success. The county also had Mississippi's fourth-largest Mexican immigrant community.

Jackson County suffered extraordinary architectural and human damage from Hurricane Katrina in 2005, but by 2010 Jackson County's population of nearly 140,000 placed it among the largest in the state. That number represented an increase of more than 150 percent since 1960. Seventy-two percent of the population was white, while 21 percent was African American, 4.5 percent was Hispanic, and 2 percent was Asian.

Mississippi Encyclopedia Staff
University of Mississippi

Mississippi State Planning Commission, *Progress Report on State Planning in Mississippi* (1938); *Mississippi Statistical Abstract*, Mississippi State University (1952–2010); Charles Sydnor and Claude Bennett, *Mississippi History* (1939); University of Virginia Library, Historical Census Browser website, http://mapserver.lib.virginia.edu; E. Nolan Waller and Dani A. Smith, *Growth Profiles of Mississippi's Counties, 1960–1980* (1985).

Jackson Daily News

The *Jackson Daily News* traces its origins to a post–Civil War merger of the *Clarion*, based in Meridian, and the *Standard*, based in Jackson. Four men displaced by the merger founded the *Jackson Evening Post* in 1882. Frederick Sullens acquired the paper in 1907 and renamed it the *Jackson Daily News*. Sullens, who was born in 1877, was a colorful but antagonistic editor. In 1940 he challenged gubernatorial candidate Paul B. Johnson to a duel and ended up in a fight with the judge in the lobby of the Walthall Hotel. He was also a staunch segregationist whose front-page editorial the day after the 1954 US Supreme Court's *Brown v. Board of Education* ruling forcefully denounced the decision.

In 1937 the *Jackson Clarion-Ledger* and *Jackson Daily News* incorporated under a charter issued to Mississippi Publishers Corporation for the purpose of selling joint advertising. The arrangement required advertisers to purchase ads in both publications.

In 1954 the Hederman family bought the *Jackson Daily News* from Sullens for about five hundred thousand dollars after a court battle between the two newspaper owners over the Hedermans' purchase of *Daily News* stock. The Hederman family consolidated the two newspaper plants, and Sullens remained editor of the *Daily News* until his death in 1957. At the time of the sale the *Daily News* had a circulation of 41,361, while the *Clarion-Ledger*'s circulation was 47,396.

The Gannett chain purchased the *Jackson Daily News*, *Jackson Clarion-Ledger*, *Hattiesburg American*, and six weeklies on 1 April 1982 for $110 million. The *Daily News* had a circulation of 40,147 at the time of the sale. In 1989 Gannett consolidated the two papers, eliminating the *Daily News*.

Kathleen Woodruff Wickham
University of Mississippi

Kathy Lally, *Baltimore Sun Journal* (5 January 1997); Gene Roberts and Hank Klibanoff, *The Race Beat* (2006); *Time* (13 May 1940, 18 January 1943, 8 November 1954).

Jackson Eagle Eye

The *Eagle Eye*, a Jackson newspaper published by Arrington W. High (1910–88), was the most strident of Mississippi's five black newspapers in the 1950s. At a time when the state's other black newspapers took a conservative approach to race relations, High's newspaper was known for its explicit demands for social equality and bold criticism of white authorities. His criticism extended to black teachers and clergy who did not join his call for immediate integration and voting rights.

High wrote and published the newspaper from his home on Jackson's Maple Street, and it usually took the form of a one- or two-page mimeographed sheet measuring eight by fourteen inches. The banner proclaimed itself "America's greatest newspaper, bombarding segregation and discrimination." Though the price fluctuated, individual copies of the newspaper sold for ten cents, and a yearly subscription ranged between five and eight dollars. The frequency of publication varied but at times was as often as three times a week. The paper could be purchased directly from High or at the Farish Street Newsstand in Jackson. Available archival documents (incomplete because of the informal mode of production and dissemination) show that High published the newspaper from 1954 to 1967, though its run may have been longer.

Steven D. Classen characterizes the *Eagle Eye* as offering "blunt provocative commentary" that defied typical journalistic convention and functioned as "aggressive advocacy journalism." High employed colorful language in his attacks on the state and white supremacist organizations, calling Mississippi "Murder, Inc." and the Citizens' Council "the baby of Murder, Inc." After researching the educational backgrounds of Mississippi's state legislators, High asserted, "The average member of our State Legislature cannot tell the Constitution of both the State and the U.S. from that of a Sears-Roebuck catalog." He regarded Mississippi and Alabama as "the restrooms for white hoodlumism" and asked, "What is the difference between Southern white supremacy and communism? They both stand for enslavement." According to Julius Eric Thompson, issues that recurred in the newspaper included the gross inequality of segregated education. High predicted in September 1954 that black students would soon attend the University of Mississippi, Mississippi State, Delta State, and the University of Southern Mississippi. Another theme was the willingness of white men to achieve "bedroom integration" with black women while maintaining segregation in public life. High also often urged black domestics to take care of their own children rather than those of their white employers. In March 1956 High wrote that Martin Luther King Jr. was a "dynamic young leader" and lauded the National Association for the Advancement of Colored People for "wrecking the hell out of white supremacy in the South." High also praised Dr. T. R. M. Howard, a Mound Bayou doctor and leader who founded the Regional Council of Negro Leadership in 1951.

As a native Mississippian with a white father and a black mother, High characterized his experience in the state as a "life of Hell." High's militant stance on civil rights led agents of the Mississippi State Sovereignty Commission to collect the *Eagle Eye* and track his movements. Also under surveillance was the Farish Street Newsstand, which sold not only High's paper but also other liberal black newspapers, such as the *Chicago Defender*, while refusing to sell the conservative *Jackson Advocate*. Commission agents described High as a "troublemaker among the Negroes." In August 1954 High was arrested for "distributing literature without a permit," but a judge declared that the *Eagle Eye* was a newspaper and was covered by freedom of the press laws. The following year, according to High, he was declared a "lunatic" and was held behind bars for five months at the Mississippi State Asylum in Whitfield, finally escaping to Chicago in a coffin. According to High, his confinement resulted from the fact that any African American in Mississippi who "will not be cowed by cross burning, frequent jailings, floggings and threats must be insane." High continued to publish the *Eagle Eye* from Chicago. However, he was later diagnosed with paranoia, and at least some issues of the paper contain bizarre writings: for example, in November 1967, under the heading "White Lesbians Secrets," High alleged that "every [Mississippi] county but one have a White Lesbians Association" and reported that "A Yazoo City White woman was elected state chairman of the 'Lesbians Murder Committee,'" which would execute any "'White Lesbians' who fail to live up to the oath of loyalty to the 'Lesbians Association.'"

Becca Walton
University of Mississippi

Steven D. Classen, *Watching Jim Crow: The Struggles over Mississippi TV, 1955–1969* (2004); *Jackson Eagle Eye* (September 1954–May 1967); *Jet* (16 May 1988); Mississippi Department of Archives and History, Sovereignty Commission Online website, http://mdah.state.ms.us/arrec/digital_archives/sovcom/; Charles M. Payne, *I've Got the Light of Freedom: The Organizing Tradition and the Mississippi Freedom Struggle* (1995); Julius Eric Thompson, *The Black Press in Mississippi, 1865–1985* (1993); *Time* (17 January 1955).

Jackson State College Killings, 14 May 1970

The shootings on the campus of Jackson State College on 14 May 1970 began with the throwing of rocks at passing cars on Lynch Street, a sporadic occurrence in preceding years. Lynch Street, a four-lane thoroughfare that bisected the campus and that was named for John Roy Lynch, the state's first African American member of Congress, connected West Jackson's white suburbs to the city's business district. Businesses serving the black neighborhoods just east of the campus on Lynch Street included a few bars and pool halls that attracted students and a group of nonstudents known as cornerboys. Fear and resentment between the two groups sometimes boiled over into physical confrontations, including a May 1969 rock-throwing fight.

Yet racial tension provoked most of the conflict on Lynch Street. In February 1964 a white motorist hit a black student in front of her dormitory, breaking her leg. After police let the driver continue, students blocked traffic and later that night threw bottles and rocks at a barricade of city policemen. Claiming to see a sniper, the police fired their shotguns into the air and then into the crowd, wounding three. The incident provoked further distrust of white policemen and white motorists, many of whom taunted students as they passed through campus. On 10 May 1967 students again blocked traffic on Lynch Street, this time to thwart the capture of a black student whom the police had accused of speeding. Groups of students and cornerboys threw projectiles at the police, set small fires, and looted a few businesses. The next night, officers and a large contingent of black youth confronted each other once again: this time a bottle thrown from the crowd seriously cut a police officer's neck. The injured officer discharged his shotgun in the air, and as the crowd moved toward the barricade, policemen opened fire. Ben Brown, a twenty-two-year-old nonstudent, was hit with buckshot on Lynch Street and later died. In addition, two students were wounded by birdshot. Another confrontation arose eleven months later when a crowd of demonstrators and rock throwers gathered to express outrage over the assassination of Martin Luther King Jr., but police seemed more restrained, using tear gas instead of bullets to disperse the protest.

On the night of 13 May 1970 a crowd in front of Alexander Hall, the women's dorm, again began throwing rocks and bottles at white motorists on Lynch Street, eventually hitting a passing patrol car. No one is certain what provoked this latest volley of projectiles, but many students had come to regard throwing rocks as an annual springtime ritual to express dissatisfaction with the white establishment. Just nine days earlier, National Guardsmen had opened fire on antiwar demonstrators at Ohio's Kent State University, killing four students and injuring nine. Yet neither antiwar nor civil rights activism was prevalent among the student body at Jackson State.

Hundreds of students began to gather on Lynch Street between Alexander Hall and Stewart Hall, the men's dorm. Many ignored a 10:30 p.m. curfew set by college president John Peoples, and students and nonstudents struck campus security cars and set fire to two trash trailers. Some attempted to burn down the ROTC building, but members of the Jackson police and the highway patrol arrived to secure the area, and the students began to disperse. The next day, Peoples chastised his students for "the annual riot," while Jackson mayor Russell Davis downplayed the incident, assuring residents that officers "did a good job" and that the situation could have been much worse. Neither expected a repeat of the violence.

But at about 9:30 the following night, a small group in front of Stewart Hall began tossing stones at white drivers as police and highway patrolmen arrived to close off the street. False rumors began spreading that civil rights leader Charles Evers and his wife had been murdered. Evers was the mayor of Fayette, the brother of the slain Medgar Evers, and the father of a Jackson State student. Some nonstudents commandeered a nearby dump truck, intending to dump its load of dirt in the middle of Lynch Street. When it stalled near Stewart Hall, a young man pulled out his revolver and shot at the engine and the gas tank, setting the truck ablaze. Crowds continued to build in front of Stewart and Alexander Halls, throwing rocks and other objects and shouting insults. Patrolmen fired shotguns, and National Guardsmen began leaving their posts to come to the aid of the police officers. Accompanied by a tank, Guardsmen moved into positions along the fence in front of Alexander Hall, flanked by city police and highway patrolmen.

As bottles began crashing on either side of the officers, members of the highway patrol and city police opened fire, mostly in the direction of Alexander Hall. Officers claimed to see a sniper in an upper window of the dormitory and fired shotguns, rifles, and submachine guns at the building for approximately twenty-eight seconds, unleashing more than four hundred rounds. Students sought cover, but a buckshot slug killed James Earl Green, a senior at Jim Hill High School who had stopped across the street from Alexander Hall on his way home after work at a nearby grocery store. Three buckshot pellets killed Phillip Gibbs, a junior at Jackson State. Twelve others were wounded, most of them students and all of them either inside or in the vicinity of Alexander Hall.

For weeks thereafter, black and white students gathered at the Governor's Mansion to protest the tragedy. After reading a report from the highway patrol, Gov. John Bell Williams announced on television that "the responsibility must rest with the protesters." Mayor Davis tried to quell the tension by appointing a biracial committee to investigate the incident. US attorney general John Mitchell arrived in Jackson and requested a federal grand jury because the highway patrolmen refused to cooperate with an FBI investigation. The federal grand jury, presided over by Judge Harold Cox, declined to indict any of the officers.

In September 1970 the President's Commission on Campus Unrest released its report on the Kent State and Jackson State shootings. While the commission did not intend to assign guilt, its findings disputed many of the central claims of the highway patrol and the grand jury. The commission ultimately found fault with the officers' actions that night, concluding that the indiscriminate twenty-eight-second fusillade "was an unreasonable, unjustified overreaction."

Following the violence in 1970, the city closed Lynch Street between Barrett Drive and Dalton, a move the college had long urged. The university later converted the space into the Gibbs-Green Plaza, a popular outdoor area where students congregate. The city later modified the street's name to J. R. Lynch Street. The Jackson State Class of 1971, to which Gibbs had belonged, erected a memorial to the "Martyrs of May 14, 1970," in front of Stewart Hall. Every May, the Jackson State community gathers for Gibbs-Green Memorial activities.

Carter Dalton Lyon
St. Mary's Episcopal School,
Memphis, Tennessee

John A. Peoples Jr., *To Survive and Thrive: The Quest for a True University* (1995); *The Report of the President's Commission on Campus Unrest* (1970); Lelia Gaston Rhodes, *Jackson State University: The First Hundred Years, 1877–1977* (1979); Tim Spofford, *Lynch Street: The May 1970 Slayings at Jackson State College* (1988).

Jackson State University

Jackson State University, located in downtown Jackson, is Mississippi's only urban historically black public university. Founded in 1877 as Natchez Seminary, the school was funded and operated by the American Baptist Home Mission Society of New York "for the moral, religious, and intellectual improvement of Christian leaders of the colored people of Mississippi and the neighboring states." The private school offered religious training for Mississippi's newly freed and underprivileged black citizens for sixty-three years.

The society purchased J. A. P. Campbell's fifty-two-acre estate in Jackson in 1882 and moved the school there from Natchez the following year. At that time the school's name was changed to Jackson College. The campus moved again to new facilities southwest of the city in the early twentieth century, and the former Camp estate now houses Millsaps College, a private Methodist institution.

Jackson College awarded its first bachelor's degree at the close of the 1924 school year. A decade later, the American Baptist Home Mission Society withdrew its financial support, and the school came under public control as part of the state educational system in 1940. Now named the Mississippi Negro Training School, it featured academic programs geared toward training rural and elementary schoolteachers. In 1944 the school became Jackson College for Negro Teachers. In 1956 after a division of graduate studies and a four-year liberal arts program were added, the school was reclassified as Jackson State College. On 15 March 1974 it became Jackson State University in recognition of the expanded quality and breadth of the school's academic offerings and faculty.

On 14 May 1970 law enforcement officials, stationed on campus in the wake of recent protests, opened fire on students assembled on a nearby campus lawn. A Jackson State student and a local high school student were killed, and twelve others were injured. No one was ever charged in the shootings.

The past four decades have been a period of tremendous growth for Jackson State University. The school now has more than eight thousand traditional and nontraditional undergraduate and graduate students who can choose from among more than thirty major programs of study in six schools—Business; Education and Human Development; Liberal Arts; Lifelong Learning; Science, Engineering, and Technology; Public Service. It offers Mississippi's only academic programs studying urban life. In 2010 the university elected its first female president, Dr. Carolyn Meyers.

In 1968 the university founded the Institute for the Study of the History, Life, and Culture of Black People. Now known as the Margaret Walker Center, its archival collections, exhibitions, and public programs honor Walker's legacy. The university shows its dedication of both studying and honoring African American history by being home to the Hamer Institute, the W. E. B. Du Bois Honors College, the Richard Wright Center for the Written Word, and the Walter Payton Health and Wellness Center.

Jackson State's athletic teams compete in the Southwestern Athletic Conference. The university's athletic teams are commonly known as the Blue Bengals. Jackson State is well known for its marching band, the Sonic Boom of the South, which was inducted into the National Collegiate Athletic Association's Hall of Champions in 2003.

Famous alumni of Jackson State include Rep. Robert G. Clark Jr., the first African American elected to the Mississippi legislature since Reconstruction; Walter Payton, who played running back for the National Football League's Chicago Bears and is a member of the league's Hall of Fame; US congressman Bennie G. Thompson; professional golfer Shasta Averyhardt; and Weather Channel meteorologist Vivian Brown.

Jackson State University has five colleges—Liberal Arts, Business, Education and Human Development, Public Service, and Science, Engineering, and Technology—along with schools of Journalism and Public Health. With almost 10,000 students in 2015, JSU had the fourth-largest number of students of all historically black colleges and universities in the nation.

Eva Walton Kendrick
Birmingham, Alabama

Jackson State University website, www.jsums.edu; John A. Peoples Jr., *To Survive and Thrive: The Quest for a True University* (1995); Lelia Gaston Rhodes, *Jackson State University: The First Hundred Years, 1877–1977* (1979).

Jails and Prisons

Like other jurisdictions, Mississippi utilizes a broad array of correctional measures, among them local county jails, state prisons, regional jail facilities, and juvenile facilities. The sheriff of each county is charged with operating the local facility, hiring personnel to supervise inmates, and providing transportation and services such as meals, recreation, and medical treatment. Local jails are extremely diverse in terms of inmate capacity, physical size and structure, and number and type of personnel, ranging from one- or two-cell facilities in rural areas to the Harrison County Jail and other facilities with inmate capacities exceeding five hundred.

The inmate population in local jails is extremely diverse. Local jails were originally developed to provide housing for suspects awaiting trial on either state or local charges and for local inmates serving sentences for misdemeanor criminal offenses or violations of city ordinances. However, for a variety of reasons, most local jails now also house state inmates on a long-term basis. State inmates customarily remain in local jails for thirty days following their convictions while awaiting transfer to the Central Mississippi Correctional Facility for processing and classification. Depending on the availability of beds in state facilities, state inmates may remain in local jails for longer periods of time. In addition to state inmates awaiting transfer, local jails are typically approved to retain state inmates who qualify for trusty status or who will participate in approved work programs. While in the local facility, these inmates provide services to the county or municipality, including building and property maintenance, construction, and beautification projects for public facilities, roads, and parks. Funding for local jails is a county responsibility. As with other county expenditures, the Board of Supervisors is responsible for funding the operation of the jail and the provision of inmate services.

The Mississippi Department of Corrections is the agency responsible for the operation and maintenance of the state prison system. Mississippi currently operates three public prison facilities: the Mississippi State Penitentiary at Parchman, the Central Mississippi Correctional Facility at Pearl, and the South Mississippi Correctional Institution at Leakesville. All are accredited by the American Correctional Association.

Officially opened in 1901, the Mississippi State Penitentiary at Parchman is the oldest state prison in Mississippi and is located on approximately eighteen thousand acres in Sunflower County. The only maximum security prison in the state, Parchman, as it is known, is also the largest facility, with approximately 3,350 beds. Mississippi's death row inmates are held at Parchman.

The Central Mississippi Correctional Facility opened its doors in 1986 and is situated on 171 acres in Rankin County, near Jackson. The facility currently serves as the receiving and classification center for all inmates sentenced to the custody of the Mississippi Department of Corrections. During this process, inmates receive medical and psychological examinations, screening for sexually transmitted diseases, and educational and intelligence testing. In addition to serving as the classification center, the institution houses approximately thirty-four hundred inmates and is the only state facility authorized to house female offenders, including those on death row. The institution is also authorized to house male offenders. The Central Mississippi Correctional Facility has minimum-, medium-, and maximum-security units and provides housing for male inmates with medical or physical conditions that require ongoing or specialized treatment.

The South Mississippi Correctional Center was established in 1989 and is located in Greene County. It is the smallest state facility, with an inmate capacity of approximately thirty-two hundred. This institution has minimum-, medium-, and maximum-security areas and offers the regimented inmate discipline program, a paramilitary-style boot camp to which offenders can be sentenced.

To augment the number of beds available at the three major state prisons, the Mississippi legislature approved the creation of fifteen regional facilities that are jointly operated by the county and state. Each facility is authorized to house 280 state inmates. Private companies operate six facilities throughout the state. While the majority of state inmates remain housed in public facilities, Mississippi utilizes private prisons more than any other state per capita.

Mississippi also has two training schools for juvenile offenders who are adjudicated delinquent by the youth court. Juveniles may be held in the training school until their twentieth birthday. Columbia Training School in Marion County is authorized to house female offenders and younger males. The Mississippi Youth Correctional Complex, more commonly known as Oakley, is located in Raymond, in Hinds County, and houses older males. In addition, a private juvenile facility was established in 2001 in Walnut Grove. Operated by Cornell Companies, this facility is authorized to house approximately one thousand juvenile offenders.

Lisa S. Nored
University of Southern Mississippi

Mississippi Code Annotated, secs. 43-27-2, et seq. (2008); Mississippi Code Annotated, sec. 43-27-29 (2008); Mississippi Code Annotated, sec. 47-5-3 (2008); Mississippi Code Annotated, sec. 47-5-110 (2008); Mississippi Department of Corrections website, www.mdoc.state.ms.us; Mississippi Department of Human Services website, www.mdhs.state.ms.us; David Oshinsky, *"Worse Than Slavery": Parchman Farm and the Ordeal of Jim Crow Justice* (1996); William Banks Taylor, *Down on Parchman Farm: The Great Prison in the Mississippi Delta* (1999).

James, Elmore
(1918–1963) Blues Musician

One of the founders of the Chicago style of blues, Elmore James was born on 27 January 1918 on a farm near Richland, Mississippi. His mother was Leora Brooks, and his father has been assumed to be Joe Willie James, who took on that role to the child. James and his family were sharecroppers, and they traveled widely throughout the Delta region of Mississippi, looking for better working conditions. By 1937 they had moved to the town of Belzoni, where Elmore James met legendary Mississippi bluesman Robert Johnson. The still-unknown James was trying to create his own style of playing. He had long exhibited a passion for making music, first with a diddley bow and later with a guitar, but he had not distinguished himself from other itinerant bluesmen performing in the Delta's juke joints. Johnson heavily influenced James's playing, and James went on to record Johnson's "Dust My Broom" in 1951 for the Trumpet label. It became James's biggest hit.

James's musical development was sidetracked when he was drafted into the US Navy during World War II, serving in the Pacific and participating in the invasion of Guam. After his discharge, James returned to Mississippi and formed occasional partnerships with his friends Aleck Miller (Sonny Boy Williamson II) and Homesick James Williamson. In the late 1940s James toured the South, playing in small clubs and beginning to establish a reputation as a frenetic electric guitar player and soulful singer. By 1951 he came to the attention of Lillian McMurry, who recorded his first sessions for her fledgling Trumpet label. The exceptional sales of these early recordings prompted James to move to Chicago, where he played for large urban audiences hungry for aggressive electric blues.

With his band, the Broomdusters, James excited Chicago audiences with a snarling, fiery electric guitar sound that foreshadowed the work of Jimi Hendrix, who later acknowledged this debt when he recorded James's "Bleeding Heart." Never quite comfortable in Chicago or any other big city, James repeatedly returned to Canton, Mississippi, home of his half-brother, Robert Holsten. Various labels enticed James to travel to such diverse locations as Los Angeles, Chicago, New Orleans, and New York City to record. Although better known for covering the work of others, such as Tampa Red's "It Hurts Me Too," James wrote songs, including "The Sky Is Crying" and "Hand in Hand."

Throughout the 1950s and early 1960s, James split his time between Chicago and Mississippi. On 24 May 1963 he died of a heart attack in Chicago, never realizing much fame in his lifetime but becoming an important stylistic influence on a later generation of bluesmen, both black and white, including Hound Dog Taylor, B. B. King, George Thorogood, and Stevie Ray Vaughan.

Mark Allan Jackson
Middle Tennessee State University

Alan Balfour, *Soul Bag* (May 1983); Mike Leadbitter, *Nothing but the Blues* (1971); Robert Palmer, *Deep Blues: A Musical and Cultural History of the Mississippi Delta* (1981).

James, Skip
(1902–1969) Blues Musician

Blues musician Nehemiah "Skip" James was born on 9 June 1902 on the Whitehead Plantation near Bentonia, Mississippi, on the edge of the Delta. His mother was the plantation's main cook; his father, a blues guitarist and bootlegger, soon left the family, eventually becoming a respected Baptist minister. An only child, James received his childhood nickname, Skippy, because of his penchant for dancing at social gatherings. He was musically inclined from an early age, and when he was twelve, his mother arranged for him to study piano at a local school, the only formal music lessons of his career. Accompanying church services on piano and listening to secular music at juke joints, James began learning guitar in 1917 by observing local musician Henry Stuckey.

James initially played guitar in a traditional African American style. Modified from banjo playing and known as rapping or frailing, this technique involved sounding individual guitar strings or groups of strings with fingernails. He later developed a more complex three-finger picking style, with the strings often keyed down in an open D-minor tuning. This style combined with his high-pitched, often falsetto voice to give James's music its distinctive sound, which many blues music fans have described as "haunting" and "eerie."

After graduating from high school, James left Bentonia and worked as a laborer in, among other places, Marked Tree, Arkansas, where he also played piano in dance halls for both black and white audiences. He moved to Memphis and performed regularly in a barrelhouse. By playing piano in such diverse settings, secular as well as sacred, James developed a sophisticated if at times seemingly anarchic piano style that was as unique as his guitar style. His early blues music repertoire included many of the traditional blues songs then circulating around the Delta. By the mid-1920s James was listening to commercial blues records, and he endeavored to learn and personalize a number of the popular songs of that era. He also began to compose his own blues, including such renowned compositions as "I'm So Glad," "Cypress Grove Blues," and "Hard Times Killin' Floor Blues."

In 1931 James traveled to Grafton, Wisconsin, to record for the Paramount label. While many blues scholars have lauded these recordings for their individuality and emotional power, James viewed the experience as a failure because the records sold poorly. Disillusioned with his prospects of making a living as a bluesman during the Great Depression, James remained primarily in Mississippi and Alabama and spent the next three decades serving as a Baptist preacher and working various manual labor jobs. During this period, his only musical activity consisted of occasionally singing in a black gospel group.

"Rediscovered" in June 1964 by John Fahey, Bill Barth, and Henry Vestine, white blues aficionados who were familiar with his Paramount recordings, James enjoyed a successful career as a bluesman for the rest of his life. James moved from Mississippi to Philadelphia, Pennsylvania, and performed at the Newport Folk Festival and other major festivals, toured in Europe, and recorded two critically acclaimed albums for the Vanguard label (*Today!* and *Devil Got My Woman*). His commercially released Paramount records influenced several significant blues performers during the 1930s (most famously Robert Johnson), while the Vanguard recordings inspired cover versions of his songs by more recent musical luminaries, including the British rock group Cream, blues performer Rory Block, and the acoustic blues duo Cephas and Wiggins. James died of cancer on 3 October 1969.

Ted Olson
East Tennessee State University

Stephen Calt, *I'd Rather Be the Devil: Skip James and the Blues* (1994); Ted Olson, *Living Blues* (May–June 1992).

Jasper County

Located in southeastern Mississippi, Jasper County's lands have a long Native American history. Red Shoe, an eighteenth-century Choctaw chief and important leader in negotiations with the Chickasaw, English, and French, was from the area that became Jasper. The county was officially established from Jones and Wayne Counties in 1833 and is named for Sgt. William Jasper, a Revolutionary War hero. Jasper's two county seats are Bay Springs and Paulding, which is named for another Revolutionary War figure, John Paulding. Just four years after founding the county, Jasper's leaders established the publication that eventually became the state's preeminent newspaper, the *Jackson Clarion-Ledger*.

In its early years Jasper had a substantial majority of free people relative to its slave population. By 1860 both the free and slave populations had nearly tripled, reaching 6,458 and 4,549, respectively. Like most Mississippi counties, antebellum Jasper was largely agricultural: the county's first census in 1840 shows only 40 people working in commerce and manufacturing. Jasper's farms practiced mixed agriculture, concentrating on corn, livestock, and sweet potatoes more than cotton.

In 1880, 251 of the county's citizens identified as Native Americans, one of the largest such populations in Mississippi. The county's population had increased to 15,394 by the turn of the century, with whites comprising a slight majority. Farming experiences differed markedly along racial lines; while 80 percent of white farming families owned their land, only a third of the African American farmers did so, with the rest working as either sharecroppers or tenants. Several books by Mississippi historian and memoirist S. G. Thigpen, born in Jasper County in 1890, detail rural life in South Mississippi during this era.

Jasper County has been home to a variety of churchgoing populations. In the 1830s a group of Irish settlers there founded the state's second Catholic parish. Thirty years later, only five counties had more churches than did Jasper, and most of its congregations were Methodist or Baptist. *The Southern Minstrel*, a popular nineteenth-century shape-note compendium compiled and edited by Lazarus Jones, had roots in Jasper County. The religious census of 1916 shows Missionary Baptists as the county's largest denomination, followed by the Methodist Episcopal Church; the Methodist Episcopal Church, South; the Southern Baptist Convention; and the Presbyterian Church.

By 1930 Jasper's population had reached 18,634. Nonagricultural work opportunities were clearly on the rise, as the county's industrial workforce, primarily laboring in timber, had grown to 400. While Jasper remained a largely agricultural county with more than three thousand farms, the majority of its farmers were now tenants.

The population declined slightly over the next three decades, falling to just under 17,000 in 1960. Jasper's population was roughly split between white and black residents but also included a significant number of South Asian immigrants. The county's agricultural sector, focused on corn and cattle, now employed only about half of Jasper's workforce. The county's more than three hundred thousand acres of commercial forest contributed to employment opportunities as well, and many of the county's other laborers worked in either machinery or furniture production.

Since the 1960s, the Jasper County economy has benefited from significant natural gas and petroleum reserves. In 2010 Jasper produced more gasoline and oil than any other county in Mississippi. The 2010 census showed that the majority of Jasper's 17,062 citizens were African American and that the county's population had shown no significant change in size since 1960.

Mississippi Encyclopedia Staff
University of Mississippi

Mississippi State Planning Commission, *Progress Report on State Planning in Mississippi* (1938); *Mississippi Statistical Abstract*, Mississippi State University (1952–2010); Charles Sydnor and Claude Bennett, *Mississippi History* (1939); University of Virginia Library, Historical Census Browser website, http://mapserver.lib.virginia.edu; E. Nolan Waller and Dani A. Smith, *Growth Profiles of Mississippi's Counties, 1960–1980* (1985).

Jaudon, Valerie

(b. 1945) Artist

Abstract artist Valerie Jaudon was born on 6 August 1945 in Greenville, Mississippi. As early as elementary school she became fascinated with art and art history. She developed an appreciation for the works of Paul Cézanne, Georges Seurat, Piet Mondrian, Paul Klee, Pablo Picasso, Jackson Pollock, and Andy Warhol. These and other artists, plus the highly structured elements of music and architecture, influenced Jaudon's artistic choices and career path.

She attended Mississippi University for Women in Columbus in 1963 and then Memphis Academy of Art in 1965. She studied art at the University of the Americas in Mexico City in 1966 and two years later went to St. Martin's School of Art in London. Not until 1975 did she make her debut in a two-person show with artist-designer Sonia Delaunay in New York. Two years later, New York's Holly Solomon Gallery presented Jaudon's first solo exhibition.

In the 1970s Jaudon linked herself with the female-dominated pattern and decoration movement, which emphasized art's aesthetic values and usefulness. Both her work and her philosophy have subsequently evolved, yet she continues to follow that movement's basic tenets. Her imagery at first comprised gridlike, geometric abstractions. Indeed, her oil paintings from the 1980s reflect Gothic and Romanesque architectural influences, with their rounded and pointed arch and gable formations. More recently her focus has shifted to painting ornamental figures that, though still symmetrical and abstract in form, do not overwhelm the canvas. The strict, interlaced lines of her earlier creations gave way to floating figures that rest in larger planes of color and space.

Her work has appeared solo at the Corcoran Gallery in Los Angeles, Sidney Janis Gallery in New York, Amerika Haus in Berlin, and the Mississippi Museum of Art in Jackson. She has also participated in group exhibitions in London; New York; Washington, D.C.; Belgium; Germany; and Norway. Jaudon has also completed fourteen public art commissions, including several in New York City: *Long Division* (1988) for the MTA Lexington Avenue Subway, *Reunion* (1989) at the Police Plaza/Municipal Building, and *Free Style* (1989) at the Equitable Building.

Jaudon's work appears in numerous museum collections, among them the Museum of Modern Art, New York; the National Museum of Women in the Arts, Washington, D.C.; the Hirshhorn Museum and Sculpture Garden, Smithsonian Institution, Washington, D.C.; and the Mississippi Museum of Art.

Jaudon lives and works in New York, where she also serves as a professor of art at Hunter College. Among her numerous honors are the 1981 and 1997 Art Awards from the Mississippi Institute of Arts and Letters.

Kathy Greenberg
Tampa, Florida

René Paul Barilleaux, *Valerie Jaudon* (1996).

Jefferson College

Chartered in 1802, Jefferson College constituted one of the first attempts at higher education in Mississippi. Incorporated by the first session of the Mississippi Territory's General Assembly, the college's antebellum benefactors included territorial governor J. C. C. Claiborne, geologist B. L. C. Wailes, and John A. Quitman. The founders located the institution in Washington, a small but flourishing village six miles from Natchez, the territorial capital. One of the few settled areas of the frontier territory, Adams County already had many wealthy planters, who, organizers hoped, would send both their sons and their financial contributions to the college.

From the beginning, Jefferson College struggled. The school did not begin operating until 1811, when there were no students ready for a collegiate curriculum. The institution consequently operated as a preparatory school rather than as a college, and it never awarded a bachelor's degree. Jefferson College was hurt by conflict between rural Adams County planters and the Natchez nabobs. While many planters from Washington and Adams County sent their sons to Jefferson, the Natchez elite preferred other institutions, including

Gateway to Jefferson College (Archives and Records Services Division, Mississippi Department of Archives and History [PI ED 534 Box 11 R72 B4 S2 Folder 35 #53])

William B. Fowler, "The History of Jefferson College of Washington Mississippi, prior to the War for Southern Independence" (master's thesis, Louisiana State University, 1937); William B. Hamilton, *Journal of Mississippi History* (Fall 1941); Aubrey Keith Lucas, in *A History of Mississippi*, ed. Richard Aubrey McLemore (1973); Edward Mayes, *A History of Education in Mississippi* (1970); Julia Huston Nguyen, "Molding the Minds of the South: Education in Natchez, 1817–1861" (master's thesis, Louisiana State University, 1997); David Sansing, *Making Haste Slowly: The Troubled History of Higher Education in Mississippi* (1990).

Oakland College in neighboring Claiborne County and schools in New Orleans and the North. The conflict between Washington and Natchez also led to financial troubles. Although Congress had granted several lots in Natchez for the support of Jefferson College, attempts to lease those lots met with opposition from the city and led to a lengthy court battle.

The death of the college's president forced its closure from 1826 to 1829, and financial difficulties led to another closure in 1838. Fire struck the campus in 1841, destroying the main building, including the library and part of the territorial archives, which had been stored there. In the midst of such misfortunes, the college also had difficulty attracting and retaining students. The curriculum repeatedly changed as administrators sought to attract students with features such as military drill and a technical course in engineering, surveying, and agricultural science. Notable students included Jefferson Davis and Mississippi governor Albert Gallatin Brown. Naturalist John James Audubon taught at Jefferson College, as did novelist Joseph Holt Ingraham. The school functioned as the center of Washington's social and cultural life, but as the town declined in population and importance, so too did the college.

The Civil War brought additional problems to Jefferson College. The bulk of the student body enrolled in the Confederate military, and much of the faculty left as well. The college closed in 1863 and did not reopen until 1866. During the late nineteenth and early twentieth centuries, the school, now known as Jefferson Military College, continued to educate young men as a preparatory school, but it never achieved the level of stability or renown that its founders had intended, and it permanently shut its doors in 1964.

The Mississippi Department of Archives and History has preserved the college as an official state historic site. Today, visitors can tour the college grounds, which also host educational programs and camps.

Julia Huston Nguyen
Washington, D.C.

Jefferson County

Originally named Pickering County, Jefferson County was one of Mississippi's first counties and was established on 2 April 1799 by the proclamation of Mississippi's first territorial governor, Winthrop Sargent. On 11 January 1802 Gov. C. C. Claiborne divided Pickering into Claiborne and Jefferson Counties. Jefferson County was named for Pres. Thomas Jefferson. The county seat is Fayette.

Though never as large as Adams County immediately to its south, Jefferson County was home to numerous influential Mississippi residents. Families from the Carolinas, Virginia, and Maryland settled in the area as early as 1768. One of their descendants, Thomas Maston Green, served as the second delegate to Congress from the territory. The family's home, the Green Mansion, near Cole Creek, allegedly hosted Gen. Andrew Jackson's 1791 wedding. Early political figures such as Cowles Mead, a delegate to the Mississippi assembly in 1807, and Cato West, a delegate to the 1817 constitutional convention, lived in Jefferson County. Rush Nutt developed the Petit Gulf cottonseed on his plantation outside Rodney.

Many first settlers to the area traveled by the Natchez Trace, a public road that ran north from Natchez through Jefferson County to Cumberland, Tennessee. Samuel Mason, a member of the Mason and Harp Gang, which was accused of attacking and robbing travelers along the Trace, was killed in 1802 and his head was delivered to Jefferson County for a reward of two thousand dollars. His killers were identified as members of another violent gang, and both were hanged in Greenville.

In 1820 Jefferson had a population of 6,822, making it the fourth-largest county in the young state. Throughout the county's antebellum history, most people living in Jefferson County were slaves. By 1830 the number of slaves increased to 69 percent of the population, and ten years later, 9,146 of Jefferson's 11,650 people were slaves. On the eve of the Civil War, only 19 percent of the county's 15,000 residents were free people. In its early years Jefferson County landowners concentrated on plantation agriculture, raising substantial quantities of cotton, vegetables, and livestock. A small manufacturing industry emerged around 1860, when three Fayette establishments employed 27 men making carriages, saddles, and harnesses.

In 1880 only 36 percent of the county's farmers owned their land. As in many counties with high percentages of tenants and sharecroppers, the farms in Jefferson County were divided up into small units, averaging sixty-one acres, well below the state average. In addition, sixteen manufacturing companies in Jefferson employed forty-five men and one woman.

Jefferson County stands out as one of the few counties without a Baptist congregation during the antebellum period. In 1860 the county had ten Methodist churches, six Presbyterian churches, and one Episcopal church. Over time the Baptist church developed an influential presence in Jefferson County, and by 1916 the Missionary Baptists stood among the largest religious groups. The Methodist Episcopal Church, South, and the African Methodist Episcopal Church were also significant in the county. The first racially integrated Methodist church in Mississippi, Union Church, is located in Jefferson County. Other notable firsts in Jefferson County included the state's first agent for the Negro Extension Service, M. M. Hubert, and the first publication of the *Mississippi White Ribbon*, a newspaper run by Prohibition leader Harriet Kells.

Unique not only for its religious profile but also for its immigrant population, Jefferson County witnessed an influx of German, Irish, and English families around 1880. African Americans now made up the majority of the 17,314 people living in the area; by 1900, 81 percent of the residents were black. At the turn of twentieth century only 7 percent of Jefferson's African American farmers owned land, compared to 54 percent of the county's white famers. These percentages altered only slightly after a sharp decline in population in the 1930s. Tenancy dominated Jefferson County in the Depression era: among the county's 14,291 residents, 6 percent of black farmers owned land, as did 37 percent of white farmers.

Like many parts of Mississippi, Jefferson County experienced population decreases beginning in the mid-twentieth century. By 1960 just over ten thousand people, three-quarters of them African Americans, lived in Jefferson County. Despite a declining agricultural economy, the county relied on corn, winter wheat, soy, and livestock production. A small furniture industry also provided employment, as did a few wells that produced petroleum and natural gas. Through the 1970s Jefferson County ranked among the lowest in the state in per capita income. At the beginning of the decade, fewer than 20 percent of county's residents had graduated from high school.

In 1969 Fayette elected civil rights activist and businessman Charles Evers as mayor, making him Mississippi's first African American mayor after the passage of the Voting Rights Act of 1965. Prior to his election, Evers led civil rights boycotts in Natchez from 1965 to 1966 and in Fayette in 1966. With Evers in office, Fayette hosted the first Southern Black Mayors Conference. Evers ran unsuccessfully for governor in 1971 but returned to Fayette and won a second term as mayor.

As of 2010, Jefferson County had 7,726 residents, 85.6 percent of them African Americans.

Mississippi Encyclopedia Staff
University of Mississippi

Mississippi State Planning Commission, *Progress Report on State Planning in Mississippi* (1938); *Mississippi Statistical Abstract*, Mississippi State University (1952–2010); Charles Sydnor and Claude Bennett, *Mississippi History* (1939); University of Virginia Library, Historical Census Browser website, http://mapserver.lib.virginia.edu; E. Nolan Waller and Dani A. Smith, *Growth Profiles of Mississippi's Counties, 1960–1980* (1985).

Jefferson Davis County

Named for the president of the Confederacy, Jefferson Davis County was created in 1906 from parts of Covington and Lawrence Counties. The county is located in the south-central part of the state, and the seat is Prentiss.

In the 1910 census, the county's population totaled 12,860 and was 53 percent African American and 47 percent white. About 60 percent of all farming families owned their land, while the rest worked as tenants. White farmers were slightly more likely to own their land than were African American farmers.

In 1907 Bertha and Jonas Johnson established Prentiss Normal and Industrial Institute in Jefferson Davis County. Founded on principles Bertha Johnson had learned at the Tuskegee Institute, the school initially emphasized agricultural and vocational training, later added a high school and junior college, and supported at least one Rosenwald building. Among the leading individuals who attended Prentiss Normal and Industrial prior to its closure in 1989 was religious leader and activist Dolphus Weary.

In 1930 Jefferson Davis County had a population of 14,281, including 7,901 African Americans and 6,380 whites. A rural and agricultural county, Jefferson Davis County had no urban centers and just seven people born outside the United States. Of the county's 2,958 farms, 40 percent were run by owners—tenants worked the rest. Farmers grew more corn than other crops, and the county's nine manufacturing establishments employed 77 workers. Both of those numbers were among the lowest in the state. In 1934 Jefferson Davis County became one of the first areas to gain power via the Tennessee Valley Authority.

The religious census of 1916 found that most of Jefferson Davis County's church members were either Baptists or Methodists. About two-thirds of all church members belonged to the Missionary Baptist or Southern Baptist Churches, and the other largest groups were the Methodist Episcopal Church, South; the Colored Methodist Episcopal Church; and the Roman Catholic Church.

From 1930 to 1960 the population declined slightly to 13,540, and Jefferson Davis County continued to have a small African American majority. Agricultural employment dropped from 2,030 in 1960 to 200 in 1980. Major crops included soybeans, cotton, and corn. Even in 1960 the county had relatively little industry, employing 457 people in some small furniture and clothing factories. In 1960 about 34 percent of the county's workers were employed in agriculture, and just 13 percent worked in industry. Seven gas wells promised profits.

Notable people from Jefferson Davis County include professional basketballer Al Jefferson. Steve McNair, a National Football League player who attended Alcorn State University and was selected to the Pro Bowl three times, is buried in Prentiss.

Unlike most counties in southern Mississippi, Jefferson Davis County's 2010 population was predominantly African American and had remained relatively stable in size since 1960. In 2010 the county's population of 12,487 was 60 percent African American and 38.7 percent white.

Mississippi Encyclopedia Staff
University of Mississippi

Mississippi State Planning Commission, *Progress Report on State Planning in Mississippi* (1938); *Mississippi Statistical Abstract*, Mississippi State University (1952–2010); Charles Sydnor and Claude Bennett, *Mississippi History* (1939); University of Virginia Library, Historical Census Browser website, http://mapserver.lib.virginia.edu; E. Nolan Waller and Dani A. Smith, *Growth Profiles of Mississippi's Counties, 1960–1980* (1985).

Jews

Jews have never made up as much as 1 percent of Mississippi's population. Yet despite their small numbers, Jews have had a significant impact on life in the state.

Jews have lived in Mississippi since the eighteenth century, though the first significant Jewish community was not established until the 1800s in Natchez. The first Jewish religious service was reportedly held in Natchez in 1800. The state's oldest congregations are B'nai Israel, formed in Natchez in 1840, and Anshe Chesed, formed in Vicksburg in 1841.

Joe Martin Erber and his uncle, Meyer Gelman, Congregation Ahavath Rayhim, Greenwood, ca. 1993 (Photograph by Bill Aron, courtesy Golding/Woldenberg Institute of Southern Jewish Life)

During the nineteenth century, Jewish immigrants from the German states and Alsace settled in Mississippi. Late in that century and early in the next they were joined by Jewish immigrants from Eastern Europe, many of whom initially worked as traveling peddlers. Since most Jews had been legally prevented from owning land in Europe, they had no experience with farming, and most had supported themselves through business ownership. When they came to the United States, they drew on this entrepreneurial experience and became involved in commerce, traveling from town to town to sell supplies to farmers and their families.

After these peddlers, most of them young single men, saved enough money, they opened stores in the towns through which they had traveled. As Mississippi and the rest of the South began to move toward a capitalist, commercial economy in the wake of the Civil War, merchants played an essential role in linking southern farmers to the national market. In towns throughout Mississippi main streets were dominated by Jewish merchants. The most notable success was Stein Mart, now a national department store chain, which had its roots in a dry goods store founded by Russian Jewish immigrant Sam Stein in 1908 in Greenville.

This economic role brought great opportunity as well as real challenges. Since laws prevented Jewish merchants from opening their stores on Sunday, most had no choice but to work on Saturday, the Jewish Sabbath. It was also very difficult to follow Jewish dietary restrictions in the absence of a ready supply of kosher meat. Mississippi Jews adapted their traditional religious practices to fit their new environment.

For the most part, Jews have enjoyed acceptance in Mississippi, in part because they quickly assimilated to southern culture. While remaining faithful to their unique religion and culture, southern Jews have worked to lessen the barriers and differences between themselves and their Gentile neighbors. Many Jews have held positions of civic leadership, including serving as mayors of Natchez, Meridian, Vicksburg, and Rolling Fork. They have embraced the cultural values of the South, for better or worse. More than two hundred Mississippi Jews fought for the Confederacy during the Civil War, and even Jews who had not even been in the United States at the time of the war later celebrated Confederate Memorial Day. Many embraced the symbolism and mythology of the Old South. Jane Wexler, a Jewish woman whose mother was one of the founders of the Natchez Pilgrimage organization, was the queen of the Pilgrimage in 1932. During the civil rights movement many Jews shared the prejudices of their white non-Jewish neighbors, although others, inspired by Jewish values, spoke out in favor of racial equality and integration.

Indeed, anti-Semitism was most pronounced during the struggle over civil rights. In 1967 the Ku Klux Klan bombed Jackson's Temple Beth Israel and the home of its rabbi, Perry Nussbaum, who supported integration. Several months later the Klan bombed Temple Beth Israel in Meridian. The incidents galvanized much of the local non-Jewish community to denounce these violent acts.

Although Mississippi Jews worked hard to fit in, they also sought to maintain their distinct identity. Jewish parents encouraged their children to marry other Jews, a difficult task in towns with only a few Jewish families. As a result, Mississippi Jews built statewide and regional social networks to ensure that their children had access to Jewish peers. Utica's Henry S. Jacobs Camp, founded in 1970, has become one of the most significant Jewish experiences for young Jews in Mississippi and the surrounding areas.

Mississippi's Jewish population has declined from more than four thousand in 1968 to perhaps fifteen hundred after the turn of the twenty-first century. The children of the Jewish merchants who settled in Mississippi attended college, became professionals, and had little interest in taking over the family business. The decline of Mississippi's rural economy and the rise of national retail chains have also pushed Mississippi Jews to such booming Sunbelt cities as Atlanta, Dallas, and Houston. The Museum of the Southern Jewish Experience, with branches in Utica and Natchez, was created in 1986 to ensure that the legacy of Mississippi Jews lives on even if their numbers continue to decline.

Stuart Rockoff
Mississippi Humanities Council

Edward Cohen, *The Peddler's Grandson: Growing Up Jewish in Mississippi* (2001); Marcie Cohen Ferris and Mark Greenberg, *Jewish Roots in Southern Soil: A New History* (2006); Goldring/Woldenberg Institute of Southern Jewish Life, *Cultural Corridors: Discovering Jewish Heritage across the South* (2002); Mississippi Historical Records Survey Project, *Inventory of the Church and Synagogue Archives of Mississippi: Jewish Congregations and Organizations* (1940); Jack Nelson, *Terror in the Night: The Klan's Campaign against the Jews* (1993); Leo E. Turitz and Evelyn Turitz, *Jews in Early Mississippi* (1983).

Jitney Jungle

Founded in 1919, Jitney Jungle remained a private, family-owned grocery chain until 1996. The history of this Mississippi-based firm documents important changes in food retailing in the twentieth century, from the earliest stages of self-service store design in the 1920s to the rise of the supermarket in the 1930s and the discount megamarket of the 1970s.

In 1919 Judson McCarty Holman; his brother, William Henry Holman Sr.; and their cousin, William Bonner McCarty, founded the Jitney Jungle in Jackson. The Holman-McCarty partnership had begun in 1912 as the McCarty-Holman Company, and within a few years the partners had created a small chain of Jackson grocery stores. Like most of their competitors, these stores offered credit and delivery services to customers, whose food orders were assembled by clerks in each store. During the World War I era, rising food costs and the difficulty of collecting from credit customers inspired McCarty-Holman to join a growing number of grocers converting their stores to cash-and-carry, experimenting with trends in self-service store design popularized by the Memphis-based chain Piggly Wiggly, founded in 1916. Shifting to cash-and-carry reduced the costs associated with credit and delivery, and self-service reduced the need for clerks and thus the cost of wages.

Local legend held that the name *Jitney Jungle* resulted from a printer's error in the first newspaper advertisement that transformed *Jingle* to *Jungle*. According to W. H. Holman Sr., however, the name was a play on slang terms of the early twentieth century. *Jitney* was a popular name for the cheap taxis many customers used to travel to the store as well as a slang term for a nickel, thus echoing the firm's slogan and advertising emphasis on saving money: "Every Jitney would be a jungle of bargains that could save the customer a 'jitney' on a quarter." The Jitney partners estimated that customers could save 20 percent based on the cash-and-carry policy and self-service design, a viewpoint that inspired the longtime Jitney Jungle slogan, "Save a Nickel on a Quarter."

The first self-service Jitney Jungle store opened on 19 April 1919 on East Capitol Street in downtown Jackson, just down the street from a rival Piggly Wiggly store. McCarty applied for a patent on the new store's self-service design on 7 June 1919. The patent, issued 27 July 1920, asserted distinctive improvements in self-service store design by eliminating the problem of shoplifting, minimizing the number of clerks, and providing multiple entry and exit points that enabled customers to find the goods they sought without traversing the entire store. Soon thereafter, Piggly Wiggly filed a patent infringement suit against the McCarty-Holman Company. In the 1920s the Jitney Jungle expanded from Jackson to other towns in Mississippi, including Greenwood, Yazoo City, and Canton. The US District Court ruled in 1930 that Piggly Wiggly was not the inventor of self-service retail practices and could not claim patent infringement protection. Settlement of the lawsuit opened the door to McCarty-Holman's expansion, largely through Jitney Jungle franchises in small towns across Mississippi.

Jitney Jungle weathered the Great Depression and continued to update its stores. In 1934 the company opened its first real supermarket in Jackson, with a parking lot to serve the increasing number of customers arriving by automobile. The store was also innovative as the second Jitney to be air-conditioned and the first to contain a women's bathroom, amenities that signaled the increasing importance of women as grocery customers. By 1946 the partners estimated that 90 percent of their customers were women, and the company's gross sales had reached $7.5 million. Jitney incorporated in 1946 as a strategic response to new tax policies.

The company embraced post–World War II trends that linked supermarkets and suburban expansion. Jitney Jungle was Jackson's first supermarket to open an anchor store in a new suburban shopping center in the 1950s, with its supermarket at Morgan Center. While Jitney advertisements of the 1920s had stressed the bargains made possible by self-service, the new supermarkets were designed to promote the comfort and convenience of female customers. Holman described the store as a "super social institution," where clerks were required to wear ties and women not only came to buy groceries but also made appointments to socialize and shop together.

Jud Holman died in 1950, and a second generation of Holmans and McCartys began to assume the leadership of the company. During the 1950s W. H. Holman Sr. managed the wholesale operations of the firm and the McCarty-Holman Company became the distribution and service warehouse for Jitney Jungle stores. In 1954 Jitney bought a bakery in Columbia, Tennessee, and began making its own bread and baked goods. Such wholesaling functions enabled the firm to keep retail prices low and compete with larger supermarket chains. In the 1960s Jitney launched Topco, a national cooperative purchasing association that enabled the company to obtain high-quality food products at the discount prices offered to much larger supermarket chains.

W. H. Holman Jr. became presiding officer of the board of the McCarty-Holman Company after his father's death in 1962. Five years later the younger Holman was elected president of Jitney Jungle Stores of America, and he served as the company's chief executive officer until 1998. Under Holman's leadership, Jitney expanded from a chain of thirty-two stores, all located in Mississippi, to a southeastern regional chain of almost two hundred stores in six other states. Much of this expansion resulted from the strategic acquisition of other small chains in Gulf Coast states. In the 1970s Jitney opened a megastore in Jackson, just off I-55 North—a giant food discount store with a pharmacy and gas station.

In 1996 management of the company passed from the Holman and McCarty families to a New York–based investment firm, Bruckmann, Rosser, Sherril, and Company. With these new resources, Jitney began an aggressive expansion, including the acquisition of stores in new market areas—most significantly, the 1997 purchase of Mobile-based Delchamps. The expansion increased annual sales but also required corporate reorganization to manage stores beyond the Mississippi base and larger expenses for building and remodeling stores. Jitney Jungle filed for bankruptcy protection on 12 October 1999. In early 2001 Jitney Jungle Stores of America sold 125 stores to Winn-Dixie Stores and Bruno's Supermarkets. The company's bankruptcy marked an end of an era for Mississippi food shoppers.

Lisa Tolbert
University of North Carolina at Greensboro

Tracey A. Deutsch, *Untangling Alliances: Social Tensions at Neighborhood Grocery Stores and the Rise of Chains* (2002); John W. Fiero, *International Directory of Company Histories* (1999); Mike Freeman, "Clarence Saunders, the Piggly Wiggly Man" (master's thesis, Memphis State University 1988); William Henry Holman Jr. *"Save a Nickel on a Quarter": The Story of Jitney Jungle Stores of America* (1974).

John Ford Home (Ford's Fort)

Located near Sandy Hook in southern Marion County, the John Ford Home, also known as Ford's Fort, is the oldest frontier-style structure in the Pearl River Valley. Located on a plateau about a mile and a half west of the Pearl River, it is less than a mile north of the Louisiana border. Although oral tradition in the Ford family speculates that the house was built by a Spanish squatter before 1792, most evidence suggests that it was built by Rev. John Ford soon after his arrival in the state during the first decade of the nineteenth

John Ford Home (also known as Ford's Fort), Columbia (Library of Congress, Washington, D.C. [LC-USZ62-83684])

century. The house served as an important territorial military post, inn, and post office as well as the site of historic events in the state's history, including the Pearl River Convention and early Methodist assemblies.

John Ford was born in 1767 in South Carolina, one of several sons of Capt. James Ford, a North Carolina patriot in the Revolutionary War, and his second wife, Ann Townsend Ford. John Ford married Catherine Ard, also a South Carolina native, in 1790. The two converted to Methodism in their thirties and resided in South Carolina's Marion District. Becoming a Methodist minister, Ford was elected to and served in the South Carolina legislature for two terms beginning in 1798. By 1807 Ford joined and soon became a leader of a small colony of South Carolina relatives and neighbors who moved west into the Tennessee River Valley, originally settling near present day Huntsville, Alabama, and then moving to Mississippi, where they settled in Jefferson County near the mouth of the Bayou Pierre. Between 1809 and 1811 Ford and several of his brothers moved to the west bank of the Pearl River in what was then Amite County in the Mississippi Territory. That area, which became Marion County on 9 December 1811, was populated by many South Carolinians, who named the county after Ford's home district in South Carolina.

The geographic importance of the house was magnified by its proximity to Ford's Ferry, two and a half miles away on the Pearl River. Operated by John Ford's older brother, Joseph (1763–1825), this ferry was a significant crossing on the Pearl and gave access to roads east and west in the Mississippi Territory. The major post road from Fort Stoddard to New Orleans came to Ford's Fort, intersecting with other post roads going west to Pinckneyville and Natchez, southwest to Baton Rouge, and south to Lake Pontchartrain and New Orleans. One of the first post offices in the territory was established at the house on 26 December 1812, and Ford served as postmaster until his death. The post office was originally known as Ford's and before 1826 came to be called Fordsville.

During the War of 1812 and the Creek War of 1813 settlers on the Mississippi frontier became the targets of Native

American attacks, often encouraged by the British. In August 1813 Ford wrote to territorial governor David Holmes of the erection of a stockade and other defenses at the house. The fortified enclosure behind which the Fords and their neighbors gathered when the region was threatened came to be known as John Ford's Fort. The high wooden palisade, located fifty feet from the house, surrounded it as a garrison. Parts of this stockade survived into the twentieth century.

Ford became one of the territory's most prominent leaders. A man of wealth, he owned 2,597 acres of land in 1819 and possessed forty-four slaves in 1815. Respected by his peers, Ford played a critical political role during Mississippi's territorial period, especially in the creation of the state. As factions within the Mississippi Territory battled for statehood, the division of the vast territory became a contentious issue. On 29 October 1816 county delegates chosen by vote during local meetings of settlers gathered at the Ford Home to discuss the issue of statehood at what became known as the Pearl River Convention. Its primary purpose was to express to Congress support for admission of the Mississippi Territory as a state with its territorial boundaries intact. The memorial drafted to Congress argued strongly against the division of the territory and criticized earlier petitions supporting division as representing "a *small section* of our Territory, and from a *small minority* of our fellow citizens." Seventeen delegates from fifteen counties attended, including Cowles Mead, who presided over the convention; noted Indian fighter and scout Sam Dale; and Joseph E. Davis. Ford served as the convention's secretary. The convention dispatched Judge Harry Toulmin as its special delegate to Washington, D.C. Although he could not convince Congress to admit the whole territory as one state, the convention's memorial was referred to a select committee and dominated discussions in Washington on this matter, much to the chagrin of Mississippi's pragmatic territorial representative, Dr. William Lattimore.

On 1 March 1817 Pres. James Madison signed the congressional act that enabled the inhabitants of the western part of the Mississippi Territory to form a constitution and state government. In June 1817 Ford was elected to represent Marion County as one of forty-eight delegates to the state's first constitutional convention. Held at the territorial capital, Washington, this event lasted for six weeks in July and August. Ford served on the committee on rules and later on the committee that drafted the constitution. The constitution was approved and signed by its delegates, including Ford, on 15 August 1817. On 10 December Pres. James Monroe signed a congressional resolution that proclaimed the constitution a republican document and declared Mississippi a state.

Ford's house has also been called the Cradle of Mississippi Methodism. On 14 November 1814 the second conference of the Mississippi Methodist Church assembled there. Three years later Methodist bishop William McKendree visited Ford's house and ordained him a minister before becoming ill with pneumonia, and he remained there for several months while Ford's family nursed him back to health. On 29 October 1818 "Ford's Meeting-house," as Methodist records term it, was again the site of the Methodist annual conference. The feeble McKendree, still recovering from his illness, presided at the session, conducting many of the conference meetings in his bedroom. Four of Ford's sons became Methodist ministers and circuit riders, and two of his daughters married Methodist ministers. One son, Thomas Ford, established Jackson's first Methodist congregation in 1837. It is now Galloway United Methodist Church.

Ford died on 14 February 1826 at his home and is buried in an unmarked grave in the nearby Ard Family Cemetery. Ford's descendants retained ownership of the house and property, preserving it largely without change, until November 1962, when the Marion County Historical Society purchased about six acres of land, including the house and barn (built in 1909), to preserve the site for future generations. The restored house has been open to the public since June 1963. In 1971 the site was placed on the National Register of Historic Places.

Lucius M. Lampton
Magnolia, Mississippi

Cyril Edward Cain, *Four Centuries on the Pascagoula*, 2 vols. (1953, 1962); Clarence Edwin Carter, *The Territorial Papers of the United States*, vol. 6, *The Territory of Mississippi. 1809–1817* (1937); J. F. H. Claiborne, *Mississippi as a Province, Territory, and State* (1880); John G. Jones, *A Complete History of Methodism, 1799–1845*, 2 vols. (1887); William K. McDonald and Alex H. Townsend, *John Ford House, Sandy Hook, Miss.: A Report of Archaeological Excavations Undertaken by National Heritage Corporation for the Mississippi Department of Archives and History, November 1974–January 1975*.

Johnson, Aaron
(b. 1924–2009) Minister and Activist

The pastor at the First Christian Church in Greenwood in the 1950s and 1960s, Aaron Johnson was one of the earliest Mississippi ministers to support the National Association for the Advancement of Colored People (NAACP) and then the Student Nonviolent Coordinating Committee (SNCC). Johnson grew up in a sharecropping family, served in the military, and became both a barber and a minister in Greenwood. Johnson belonged to the NAACP in the 1950s as well as to the Citizens' League, a voting rights group for African Americans in the town. He was one of many African Americans refused the right to vote: in his case, the court clerk declared that he was "mentally incapacitated."

When SNCC student activists came to Greenwood, Johnson allowed them to use his church as a temporary headquarters. In 1963, after arsonists set fire to buildings next to SNCC headquarters and the local police arrested activist Sam Block, Johnson helped organize a meeting that led to what historian John Dittmer calls "the largest single registration effort in Mississippi since Reconstruction," involving more than 150 African Americans. For these efforts and for participating in boycotts and efforts to integrate Greenwood schools, Johnson faced both economic pressure and threats of violence. Johnson opened his church to activists earlier than many southern churches, perhaps in part because some of his salary came from the national Disciples of Christ office in Indianapolis.

Johnson was unanimously elected as the first chair of Leflore County's Mississippi Freedom Democratic Party, and he was very active in the group in 1964–66. After Martin Luther King Jr.'s April 1968 assassination, Johnson served as a member of the executive committee of the Greenwood movement boycott, which, according to the *Jackson Clarion-Ledger*, sought "jobs for Negroes on the police and fire departments and in city and county government, better streets in the Negro sections, equal garbage collection, courtesy titles and other changes."

Johnson sent his children to newly integrated schools and continued his work as a minister and barber in Greenwood for many years.

Ted Ownby
University of Mississippi

John Dittmer, *Local People: The Struggle for Civil Rights in Mississippi* (1994); Paul Harvey, *Freedom's Coming: Religious Culture and the Shaping of the South from the Civil War through the Civil Rights Era* (2005); Aaron Johnson Files, Mississippi Department of Archives and History, Sovereignty Commission Online website, http://mdah.state.ms.us/arrec/digital_archives/sovcom/; Charles M. Payne, *I've Got the Light of Freedom: The Organizing Tradition and the Mississippi Freedom Struggle* (1995).

Johnson, Bertha LaBranche
(1882–1971) Educator

Bertha LaBranche Johnson was a leading advocate for black education, founding two schools and serving as a leader and member of many civic and political organizations. Born in Wesson, Mississippi, to Jule LaBranche and Orrie Smith LaBranche, Bertha attended Tuskegee Institute, graduating with a bachelor's degree in 1902. In 1904 she married Jonas Edward Johnson (1873–1953), and they went on to have three children, Alcee, Onette, and Eva.

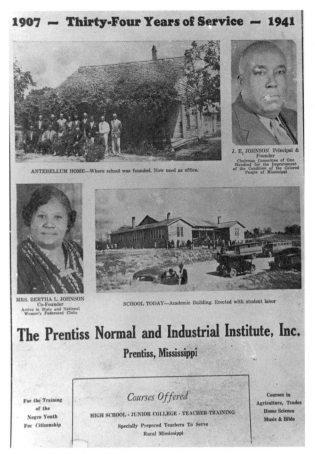

Advertisement for the Prentiss Normal and Industrial Institute showing cofounder Bertha Johnson (Archives and Records Services Division, Mississippi Department of Archives and History [PI ED 1982.0044 Box 12 R72 B4 52 Folder 2 #1])

Bertha and Jonas Johnson cofounded the Prentiss Normal and Industrial Institute in Jefferson Davis County to continue the Tuskegee Institute's emphasis on the training of the "head, heart, and hand." With financial backing from local black farmers, the Johnsons secured a six-hundred-dollar loan from a white banker. The original school, an elementary, was situated on forty acres, and the founders recruited the first students by traveling to rural areas. When the school opened its doors in 1906, many of its forty students paid for their education with produce and chickens from their farms. By 1953 the school had expanded to include a high school and junior college, with forty-four faculty members serving seven hundred students on a five-hundred-acre campus.

In 1927 Bertha Johnson also founded Laurel's Oak Park Vocational School, the state's first municipally maintained agricultural and vocational school for African Americans. Situated on 259 acres, the school had buildings for manual arts and home economics and a large area for agricultural production. Both Oak Park and the Prentiss Institute received acclaim from Johnson's former teacher, Booker T. Washington, and from George Washington Carver. In

1941 Johnson received an honorary master's degree from Tuskegee.

Despite Prentiss's success, enrollment dwindled with integration and the opening of other educational opportunities to black students, and the school closed its doors in 1989. After the school closed, the building served various community groups and the local Head Start. The campus included a classroom building built in 1926 and paid for by the Rosenwald Foundation, a philanthropic organization that funded one in five rural black schools in the South in the first decades of the twentieth century. In 2006 the National Trust for Historic Preservation identified the building as an endangered historic place, and in 2006 and 2009, the Prentiss Institute Board of Trustees obtained grants from the Mississippi Department of Archives and History and the Lowe's Charitable and Educational Foundation Preservation Fund to restore the structure. With additional funding from alumni and supporters, the Rosenwald School was restored, and it reopened in 2013 as a venue for weddings and other special events. The Mississippi Department of Archives and History has recognized it as a historic landmark, and it is listed on the National Register of Historic Places.

Alcee Johnson (1905–95) was a member of the National Association for the Advancement of Colored People (NAACP), and because he served as Prentiss's manager, the school came under the surveillance of the Mississippi State Sovereignty Commission, which called the institution a "hotbed of NAACP activity" and noted Johnson's support for integration. The commission files also noted Bertha Johnson's backing of a student strike at Alcorn State and followed the activity of several other family members.

Bertha Johnson held numerous posts with civic organizations. She served as president of the Mississippi State Federation of Colored Women's Clubs for six years and vice president for ten years and as the statistician for the national federation for five years. Johnson championed issues such as the care and housing of elderly black Mississippians, the creation of libraries in black schools, and the addition of African American history to the state's curriculum. The federation also worked to address the needs of black tuberculosis patients and to build educational facilities for special needs children. In addition, Johnson was a member of the executive council of the Committee of Interracial Cooperation and a member of the Mississippi Association of Teachers in Colored Schools.

In 1940 Johnson wrote *Lifting as We Climb*, a book about the history of the Mississippi Federation of Colored Women's Clubs. She died on 24 February 1971 and is buried with her husband at a church near the Prentiss Institute. A marker in front of the school's original building honors the Johnsons and bears the inscription, "Lives dedicated to unselfish service to their fellow man."

Becca Walton
University of Mississippi

Jaman Matthews, Heifer International website, www.heifer.org; Jefferson Davis County Economic Development District website, http://jeffda visms.com/ESW/Files/Prentiss_Institute_History_(Museum).pdf; Neil R. McMillen, *Dark Journey: Black Mississippians in the Age of Jim Crow* (1990); Mississippi Department of Archives and History, Sovereignty Commission Online website, http://mdah.state.ms.us/arrec/digital _archives/sovcom/; *Who's Who in Colored America* (1950).

Johnson, Paul B., Jr.

(1916–1985) Fifty-Fourth Governor, 1964–1968

Paul B. Johnson Jr. beside a portrait of his father, Paul B. Johnson Sr., 1964 (Moncrief Collection, Archives and Records Services Division, Mississippi Department of Archives and History [846])

When Paul Burney Johnson Jr. was inaugurated as Mississippi's fifty-fourth governor on 21 January 1964, he became the only son of a Mississippi governor to ascend to the state's highest office. "Little Paul," as he was fondly known among his supporters, was born in Hattiesburg on 23 January 1916. He earned bachelor's and law degrees from the University of Mississippi and married Dorothy Power in 1941 at the Governor's Mansion.

In August 1947, shortly after his discharge from the Marine Corps, Johnson ran in the special election to fill the unexpired term of Sen. Theodore Bilbo but was defeated by John C. Stennis. Later that year Johnson ran for the governorship, losing in the Democratic primary. He again ran unsuccessfully for governor in 1951 and in 1955. In 1959 Johnson was elected lieutenant governor in the first primary.

He was serving in that office in 1962, when James Meredith attempted to integrate the University of Mississippi. Johnson supported Gov. Ross Barnett's defiance of the US Supreme Court. On one occasion Johnson stood in the middle of University Avenue and personally blocked Meredith's entrance onto the campus. From that incident came the slogan Johnson used in his 1963 campaign for the governorship, "Stand Tall with Paul." He defeated J. P. Coleman in a runoff election.

In his inaugural address Governor Johnson encouraged the people of Mississippi to accept the changes that were occurring throughout the South and the nation and pledged that law and order would prevail in Mississippi. He urged people not to "fight a rear guard defense of yesterday" but to conduct "an all out assault on our share of tomorrow."

During Johnson's administration Mississippi reached a milestone in its economic development. In May 1965 the number of Mississippians employed in industry exceeded the number of agricultural workers for the first time in the state's history.

In 1967, while he held the office of governor, Johnson ran unsuccessfully for lieutenant governor. He then returned to his law practice in Hattiesburg and eventually assumed the role of an elder statesman in Mississippi politics. Johnson died at his home in Hattiesburg on 14 October 1985.

David G. Sansing
University of Mississippi

Joseph Crespino, *In Search of Another Country: Mississippi and the Conservative Counterrevolution* (2009); Paul B. Johnson Jr. Subject File, Mississippi Department of Archives and History; *Mississippi Official and Statistical Register* (1964–68).

Johnson, Paul B., Sr.

(1880–1943) Forty-Sixth Governor, 1940–1943

During his unsuccessful 1931 and 1935 races for the Mississippi governorship, Paul Burney Johnson Sr. called himself the Champion of the Runt Pig People, and in his winning 1939 campaign he promised to bring New Deal measures to the state. In supporting government programs for the poor and unemployed, Johnson explained that he was trying to give the common people their fair share of the nation's wealth, pledging, "I will never balance the budget at the expense of suffering humanity."

Johnson was born into a poor farm family, and he readily identified with Mississippi's "redneck" dirt farmers, sharecroppers, and day laborers. When he became a lawyer he vowed to "save a little from everything I made." He saved some of bills he received as payment for his first law case for the rest of his life.

Born in Hillsboro in Scott County on 23 March 1880, Johnson studied law at Millsaps College and opened a successful law practice in Hattiesburg in 1903. After a four-year term as city judge, he was appointed a judge of the 12th Circuit, and he was subsequently elected to the court in 1911 and 1915.

In 1918 Johnson defeated Theodore Bilbo in the contest to represent Mississippi's 6th District in the US House of Representatives. After serving three terms in Congress, Johnson did not seek reelection and began to pursue his lifelong dream of becoming governor of Mississippi. After two unsuccessful campaigns, Johnson achieved his dream in 1939 and was inaugurated on 16 January 1940.

Johnson was skeptical of the Balance Agriculture with Industry (BAWI) program and took steps to curtail industrial expansion in Mississippi. His legislative program emphasized more direct measures to increase the purchasing power of the state's poor and unemployed workers. Among his two most important achievements were an increase in pensions for senior citizens and a law providing free textbooks for schoolchildren. Both measures provoked controversy: in particular, opponents of free textbooks accused Johnson of socializing Mississippi and claimed that the state's involvement in the textbook business would undermine the free enterprise system.

Johnson was ill during much of his administration, and the long and bitter struggle over the textbook bill put an enormous strain on him and his family. His health declined rapidly in late 1943, and Gov. Johnson died on 26 December. Paul B. Johnson State Park in Hattiesburg is named in his honor.

David G. Sansing
University of Mississippi

Biographical Directory of the United States Congress (1950); *Jackson Daily News* (27 December 1943); *Jackson State Times* (6 December 1959); Thomas E. Kelly, *Who's Who in Mississippi* (1914).

Johnson, Robert
(1911–1938) Blues Musician

Easily the most controversial and speculated upon figure in pre–World War II Mississippi blues, guitarist and singer Robert Johnson was born on 8 May 1911 in Hazlehurst, south

Robert Johnson's "Me and the Devil Blues" (1938) (Courtesy Blues Archive, Department of Archives and Special Collections, J. D. Williams Library, University of Mississippi)

of Jackson in Copiah County. His recorded body of songs includes examples of instrumental virtuosity, emotionally evocative lyrical poetry, and spine-tingling vocal range. Nonetheless, his most successful record during his lifetime sold only about ten thousand copies, a modest figure even for the late 1930s. The bare facts of his short life offer little insight into his emergence as a transcendent musical figure, and the scant number of verifiable facts and the conjectural nature of most of the assembled biographical data contribute to the myths that complicate our understanding of his life.

At least some of the mystery emanates from Johnson's birth to Julia Dodds outside of her marriage to Charles Dodds Jr. Reliable recollections of Johnson's childhood have been difficult to come by as he carried the last names *Dodds*, *Spencer*, and *Willis* before learning that his biological father was Noah Johnson and adopting that surname in his early teens. Johnson's boyhood proved no more stable than his name. While his conception had occurred after Charles Dodds fled Hazlehurst following a feud with a prominent white family between 1907 and 1909, Julia and Charles Dodds reunited around 1914 in Memphis, where Charles had settled and adopted the last name *Spencer*. The reconciliation proved short-lived, and Julia was back in Mississippi, around Robinsonville in Tunica County, by 1918.

By the early 1920s Robert was living with Julia and her new husband, Dusty Willis, on the Abbay and Leatherman Plantation. Johnson's aptitude for music and reluctance to labor in either the cotton field or the classroom were apparent by the mid-1920s, and he drew inspiration and tutelage from elder musicians Son House and Willie Brown, both

Robinsonville locals and barrelhouse performers born near the turn of the century.

By 1929 Johnson's personal life temporarily stabilized as he married and prepared for fatherhood, but his wife and baby died in childbirth in the spring of 1930. Immediately thereafter, Johnson left the Delta in search of his father in Hazlehurst. There, Johnson apprenticed with guitarist Ike Zinnerman and remarried, settling in South Mississippi. Whether he reunited with his father is unknown.

In the 1960s House recalled that Johnson returned to the Delta after about six months, during which time Johnson became an expert guitarist. It seems more likely, however, that Johnson stayed around Hazlehurst for about two years—long enough to practice and hone his musical skills in an apprenticeship with Zinnerman. House's mistaken reckoning of the amount of time Johnson spent away from the Delta provided anecdotal evidence for the Faustian explanation of Johnson's talent that later arose—that is, that he sold his soul to the devil.

The bulk of Johnson tales come from the period between his return to the Delta around 1932 and his death six years later. The number of 1930s bluesmen with stories about Johnson attests to the breadth of his travels and tells us something about his latter-day marketability. If accounts of Johnson's activities are beyond verification, the experiences of his colleagues who lived to tell about their own careers at least offer details of the professional context in which Johnson operated.

During the 1930s Mississippi's African American musicians earned most of their income from live performances, meaning that substantial travel was required. Most, including Johnson, did not own cars and consequently traveled on foot, by rail, and by hitching rides. Musicians' sporadic earnings compared favorably with those of day laborers, and musicians were often fed and housed during engagements. Though Johnson performed in St. Louis, Chicago, Detroit (on a minister's radio program), and possibly New York, he made most of his living in Mississippi.

Recording provided musicians with another source of income, and in 1936 Johnson made contact with H. C. Speir, a Jackson-based furniture and record store owner and self-styled talent broker. Speir had earned a reputation for arranging recording sessions for Mississippi blues musicians, and he referred Johnson to Ernie Oertle of the American Recording Company. Oertle invited Johnson to San Antonio, Texas, in November 1936 for a session at which he recorded sixteen songs, including the enduring "I Believe I'll Dust My Broom," "Sweet Home Chicago," and "Terraplane Blues," the biggest seller of his lifetime. Another number from this session, "Cross Road Blues," has been cited as evidence of Johnson's supernatural dealings, though the lyrics lack any otherworldly reference. Johnson recorded again in Dallas the following June, cutting the provocatively titled "Hellhound on My Trail," "Me and the Devil Blues," and eleven other songs.

Enamored with Johnson's recordings, producer John Hammond summoned him to New York City for the Spirituals to Swing concert, a December 1938 presentation of black music to New York's elite at Carnegie Hall. But Johnson had died in Greenwood on 16 August 1938. According to legend, a juke joint operator poisoned Johnson's whiskey after learning of the musician's involvement with his wife. Johnson's death certificate lists syphilis as the cause of death.

The Johnson legend grew with the blues revival of the 1960s, when significant numbers of white listeners became aware of pre–World War II blues recordings. The posthumous coronation of Johnson as King of the Delta Blues (a subgenre that never existed as such before the revival) followed. Ever-opportunistic bluesmen—storytellers and performers by trade and usually by nature—recognized the chance to elevate their status through association with Johnson, who fascinated many latter-day interviewers. Musicians unknowingly contradicted one another's recollections and deliberately challenged the validity of others' associations with Johnson. At the same time, an exotic interpretation of the blues began to emerge in revivalist circles, with Johnson among its most romanced figures. His untimely demise and lyrics concerning the devil (a common theme among his contemporaries) and the crossroads became conflated with African American myths about musicians trading their souls to Satan in return for accelerated abilities. The bluesman's three gravesites are monuments to the unreliability of recollections about Johnson. Johnson's death certificate lists "Zion Church" as his burial site, though none of the current markers sits at such a place.

Preston Lauterbach
Nellysford, Virginia

Steven C. LaVere, *The Complete Recordings: Robert Johnson* (1991), liner notes; Mississippi Blues Trail website, www.msbluestrail.org; Robert Palmer, *Deep Blues: A Musical and Cultural History of the Mississippi Delta* (1982); Elijah Wald, *Escaping the Delta: Robert Johnson and the Invention of the Blues* (2004).

Johnson, Tommy

(1896–1956) Blues Musician

Tommy Johnson helped create the Delta blues sound and its accompanying mythology. Ever the entertainer, Johnson claimed to have sold his soul to the devil, showboated on stage by playing his guitar behind his head and between his legs, and used a falsetto voice that is unmistakable to contemporary blues fans.

Tommy Johnson (Courtesy Blues Archive, Department of Archives and Special Collections, J. D. Williams Library, University of Mississippi)

Born on George Miller's plantation in Terry, Mississippi, in 1896, Johnson was one of thirteen children. His uncles and two of his brothers, Mager and LeDell, played guitar, while other family members played various instruments in a brass band. After his family relocated to Crystal Springs around 1910, Johnson's brother LeDell taught Tommy the basics of the guitar, and by the time he turned eighteen, he and his brothers were playing gigs across Copiah County and beyond. In 1916 Johnson moved to Webb Jennings's plantation near Drew with his first wife, Maggie Bidwell Johnson. There he fell under the artistic influence of the Mississippi Delta's first blues superstar, Charley Patton, who lived at nearby Dockery Farms. Johnson nevertheless developed his own unique sound, complete with syncopated bass notes. After a year of playing in the Delta with Patton, Dick Bankston, and Willie Brown, Johnson began playing jukes across Mississippi, Arkansas, and Louisiana. Johnson moved back to Crystal Springs in 1920 and resumed sharecropping, traveling to the Delta to play with Patton after the season's crops were in.

By this time Johnson had developed an alcohol addiction along with a reputation as a notorious gambler and womanizer. His drinking was the subject of one of his most well-known songs, "Canned Heat Blues," which Johnson recorded along with eight other tracks for the Victor label in Memphis in February 1928. In the song he lamented his habit of drinking Sterno, a denatured and jellied alcohol used as fuel that he mixed with water and drank when alcoholic beverages were unavailable or too expensive: "Crying, canned heat, canned heat, mama, crying, sure, Lord, killing me. / Crying, canned heat, mama, sure, Lord, killing me. / Takes alcorub to take these canned heat blues." Other tracks recorded at this session include "Big Road Blues," "Maggie Campbell Blues," and "Cool Drink of Water Blues."

In 1930 Johnson traveled to Grafton, Wisconsin, for a Paramount session at which he recorded eleven more tracks, among them "Slidin' Delta" and another song that refers to his alcoholism, "Alcohol and Jake Blues": "I woke up, up this morning, crying, alcohol on my mind. / Woke up this morning, alcohol was on my mind. / I got them alcohol blues and I can't rest easy here." Once the economic hardships of the Great Depression set in, limiting the record-buying public's expendable income, Johnson's short recording career abruptly ended.

Until his alcoholism-related death on 1 November 1956 in Crystal Springs, Johnson continued playing the blues in his signature style, mainly at local dances, juke joints, and fish fries around South Mississippi. Although demand for his records had waned, interest in seeing and hearing his dynamic performances had not.

Johnson started and publicized the rumor that he had sold his soul to the devil, mystifying himself and enhancing his reputation much in the way that the similar legend regarding Robert Johnson (no relation) did. Filmmakers Joel and Ethan Coen revived the legend of deal-making Tommy Johnson, played by contemporary musician Chris Thomas King, in their 2000 film *O Brother, Where Art Thou?* His music was a powerful influence on other bluesmen of his day, including Robert Nighthawk, Houston Stackhouse, Howlin' Wolf, Floyd Jones, and Otis Spann, and it continues to shape the sound of the blues today.

James G. Thomas, Jr.
University of Mississippi

David Evans, *Big Road Blues: Tradition and Creativity in Folk Blues* (1982); David Evans, "The Blues of Tommy Johnson: A Study of a Tradition" (PhD dissertation, University of California at Los Angeles, 1967); David Evans, *The Legacy of Tommy Johnson* (1972); Stefan Grossman, *Delta Blues Guitar* (1969); Gérard Herzhaft, *Encyclopedia of the Blues* (1997); Robert Palmer, *Deep Blues: A Musical and Cultural History of the Mississippi Delta* (1982); Jeff Todd Titon, *Early Downhome Blues: A Musical and Cultural Analysis* (1977); Gayle Dean Wardlow and Edward M. Komara, *Chasin' That Devil Music: Searching for the Blues* (1998).

Johnson, William

(1809–1851) Businessman

William Johnson was a freedman who lived in Natchez and kept a diary from 1835 to 1851. The diary, discovered in the attic of the Johnson home in 1938 and first published in 1951, portrays the economic, social, and political life of Natchez in the 1830s and 1840s. It is one of the few surviving narratives by an African American in the antebellum South.

Johnson was born a slave in Natchez in 1809. His master, William Johnson, freed the diarist's mother, Amy, in 1814 and the boy six years later, and William adopted his former master's name. Despite speculation that the elder Johnson had fathered both of Amy's mulatto children, the diarist never identified his father. In the early 1820s young William went to work for his brother-in-law, James Miller, a freedman from Philadelphia, Pennsylvania, who had operated a successful Natchez barbershop. By 1828 William was running his own barbershop in Port Gibson, but he returned to Natchez two years later and bought Miller's business when Miller moved his family to New Orleans. In 1835 Johnson married Ann Battles, and they had eleven children over the course of their sixteen-year marriage.

Johnson prospered throughout the 1830s and 1840s. As a barber, Johnson catered almost exclusively to whites. As his business grew, he opened a bathhouse and two smaller barbershops where he employed several barbers, both free and slave, and trained a number of apprentices. He also owned sixteen slaves. Johnson also developed a side business as a moneylender and broker. Again, most of his clients were white, and some received loans of up to one thousand dollars. Johnson engaged in a number of other economic activities, selling everything from toys to wallpaper, operating a horse and dray, speculating in land, renting buildings, and hiring out his slaves to work for others. Johnson also purchased land in the swampy areas of Adams County and started a farm he named Hard Scrabble. Although the farm produced corn, vegetables, fruits, wool, and cattle, most of its revenue came from timber sales. All of Johnson's business ventures succeeded, and at the time of his death his personal assets were valued at almost twenty-five thousand dollars.

In the late 1840s, however, a bitter boundary dispute erupted between Johnson and a neighbor. On 16 June 1851 Johnson was shot in an ambush as he returned to his farm. Before he died the next morning, Johnson regained consciousness and identified the shooter as his neighbor, Baylor Winn, who claimed to be of Native American descent and thus white rather than a free person of color. Winn was arrested and brought to trial three times over the next two years. The first two trials centered on Winn's racial heritage, since the only witnesses to the murder were African Americans, who were legally barred from testifying against whites. The prosecutor ultimately concluded that he could not obtain a conviction and dropped the charges against Winn.

Johnson used his diary primarily to keep business records, but he also recorded the weather, court cases, fights, social functions, births, deaths, marriages, political campaigns, holiday celebrations, epidemics, and recreational activities such as horse races, parades, cockfights, circuses, and balls. The diary thus paints a vivid picture of Natchez as the center of a thriving community of free and enslaved African Americans who displayed a variety of personalities in their dealings with one another and with whites, who lived in a variety of economic circumstances, and who had distinct social levels.

Carolyn Cooper Howard
University of Mississippi

Edwin Adams Davis and William Ransom Hogan, *The Barber of Natchez* (1973); Virginia Meacham Gould, *Chained to the Rock of Adversity: To Be Free, Black, and Female in the Old South* (1998); William Johnson, *William Johnson's Natchez: The Ante-Bellum Diary of a Free Negro*, ed. William Ransom Hogan and Edwin Adams Davis (1993); Winthrop D. Jordan, *Tumult and Silence at Second Creek: An Inquiry into a Civil War Slave Conspiracy* (1995); Natchez National Historical Park website, www.nps.gov/natc/index.htm.

Johnston, Erle

(1917–1995) Journalist and Director of the Mississippi State Sovereignty Commission

Journalist Erle E. Johnston Jr. gained his greatest fame as director of the Mississippi State Sovereignty Commission. Born on 10 October 1917 in Garyville, Louisiana, Johnston moved with his family to Grenada in 1928, graduated from high school there, and then was employed by newspapers in Grenada and Jackson before going on to work for and then buying the *Scott County Times* in Forest in 1941. Always interested in politics, Johnston ran James Eastland's 1942 campaign for the US Senate and later worked on campaigns for other prominent Mississippi Democrats, including Fielding Wright, John Stennis, and Ross Barnett.

In 1960 Gov. Barnett, hoping to strengthen the Mississippi State Sovereignty Commission, hired Johnston as the commission's public relations director, replacing Hal DeCell. Johnston had the job of publicizing Mississippi to the rest of the country, especially by arguing that racial segregation was a positive aspect of society appreciated by both whites and African Americans within the state but misunderstood by many outsiders. Johnston set up a speakers' bureau to send Mississippians to give talks before numerous groups outside the state and oversaw the production of a 1962 film, *The Message from Mississippi*, that showed residents speaking positively about race relations.

In May 1962 Johnston surprised many defenders of segregation when he gave a commencement address at Grenada High School, "The Practical Way to Maintain a Separate School System in Mississippi." Calling his approach that of a "practical segregationist," Johnston criticized what he termed the extremism of both the National Association for the Advancement of Colored People and the Citizens'

Erle Johnston (McCain Library and Archives, University of Southern Mississippi)

Council and suggested obeying the law and cooperating with African Americans rather than threatening or intimidating those who tried to challenge the system. William Simmons of the Citizens' Council condemned the speech as a type of surrender, and many supporters of massive resistance called for Johnson to resign or be fired.

Instead, Barnett named Johnston director of the Sovereignty Commission, a position he held from 1963 through the turbulent mid-1960s. The commission opposed the Civil Rights Act and the desegregation of schools; investigated numerous activists, describing many of them as agitators, communists, and lawbreakers; sent informers to infiltrate civil rights groups; investigated activities at Tougaloo College; and sought to counter negative images of the state during Freedom Summer activities in 1964.

Johnston continued to look for a way to oppose the civil rights movement without working with lawbreaking extremist groups. He criticized the Ku Klux Klan and the Americans for the Preservation of the White Race, suggested that the commission he ran might be doing public relations harm, and in 1965 gave a speech that encouraged young Mississippians to "profit by some of the mistakes made by my generation." Amid debates about the future of the commission and his part in it, Johnston resigned in 1968.

Johnston wrote three books showing his transformation from a firm supporter of massive resistance to someone who tried to understand a wider range of opinions. *I Rolled with Ross: A Political Portrait* (1980) told affectionate stories about Barnett as a campaigner, governor, and supporter of industrial development. Some stories were humorous, but the book clearly sought to praise Barnett's character. It began with a statement from someone who heard a Barnett speech in 1979: "No man can make you feel prouder to be a Mississippian than Ross Barnett." Johnston's next book,

Mississippi's Defiant Years, 1953–1973 (1990), consisted of a narrative of civil rights activism and massive resistance taken both from Johnston's experiences and from evidence from Mississippi newspapers. That book, with testimonials from a wide variety of perspectives, including those of Simmons, William Winter, John Salter, Neil McMillen, and with tributes to Aaron Henry and Charles Evers, made no attempt to defend massive resistance. In *Politics: Mississippi Style* (1993), Johnston told stories of state politicians' conflicts, friendships, and campaigns.

Johnston served as mayor of Forest from 1981 to 1985. He and his wife, Fay, had three children. Fay served as editor of the *Scott County Times* when Erle worked at other jobs, and their son held that position from 1979 until the Johnstons sold the newspaper in 1983. Erle Johnston died on 27 September 1995, soon after organizing a forty-year reunion of players from Mississippi's Jones County Junior College and California's Compton Community College who had participated in a 1955 football game in defiance of Mississippi's rules about racial segregation.

Ted Ownby
University of Mississippi

Joseph Crespino, *In Search of Another Country: Mississippi and the Conservative Counterrevolution* (2007); Yasuhiro Katagiri, *The Mississippi State Sovereignty Commission: Civil Rights and States' Rights* (2001); Erle E. Johnston Jr. Papers, McCain Library and Archives, University of Southern Mississippi.

Johnston, Oscar Goodbar

(1880–1955) Agricultural Leader

By consensus of his peers, including critics, Oscar Goodbar Johnston, a lawyer, planter, politician, civic leader, and federal government official in the field of agricultural policy, possessed one of Mississippi's and the South's most agile and gifted minds. Born in Jackson on 27 January 1880, Johnston, the son of businessman and public servant John Calvin Johnston and Emma Goodbar Johnston, spent part of his adolescence in the Delta before graduating from Kentucky Military Institute in 1899 and Tennessee's Cumberland School of Law in 1901. Johnston served in the Mississippi legislature and joined the Tank Corps as a private during World War I before returning to Mississippi and running for governor in 1919 against Lee M. Russell, a protégé of Piney Woods demagogue Theodore G. Bilbo. Though Johnston won better than 47 percent of the statewide vote in the primary runoff, his identification with wealthy plantation river counties against the hill and Piney Woods area in the era of the redneck revolt ensured his defeat. Johnston fondly quoted Bilbo's perhaps apocryphal statement, "I told you I could take the worst man in the state and beat the best one with him."

Johnston's eclectic career in the early 1920s included civic leadership in Clarksdale as well as banking and planting. He joined other prominent Delta planters in founding the Staple Cotton Cooperative Association, a Greenwood-based agency that sought to promote orderly and profitable marketing of long-staple cotton. In 1926 Johnston became the Memphis general counsel for the British-owned Delta and Pine Land Company of Scott, Mississippi. Delta and Pine Land owned thirty-eight thousand acres of land, making it one of the South's largest long-staple cotton producers. During the Great Flood of 1927, Johnston helped direct the plantation's recovery, including providing for the company's sharecroppers who had scattered in the chaos. That same year, the British bondholders named him president of the sprawling Mississippi plantation. During the Great Depression, however, the well-managed and generally well-funded and retrenched corporate plantation wobbled on the edge of financial collapse.

With agriculture languishing, Johnston was appointed director of finance for the newly created Agricultural Adjustment Administration (AAA) in 1933 while continuing to serve as Delta and Pine Land's president. Heading to Washington as a pragmatic conservative who sought to fortify American agriculture, particularly cotton, within the welfare-capitalist consensus, Johnston found himself among northeastern liberal social engineers, some of whom wanted to employ the AAA to change landlord-tenant relationships in the South. Interpreting his mandate broadly, Johnston persuaded Pres. Franklin Roosevelt to lend ten cents per pound on the 1933 cotton crop—a loan desperately needed by southern growers—and then helped set up and became one of the original directors of the Commodity Credit Corporation, the agency designed to distribute the loans. Further, to liquidate nearly 2.5 million bales of US-government-held cotton accrued through defaults on loans issued by the old Federal Farm Board, Johnston organized and became manager of the Federal Cotton Pool, developing a complicated scheme to allow participating farmers to purchase an interest in the government cotton while reducing acreage in return for subsidy or parity payments. The plan essentially offered farmers a no-lose proposition, since the loans were "non-recourse"—that is, if farmers defaulted, the government got the cotton, nothing more—while if prices improved (which they did), farmers pocketed the profits. Millions of farmers joined the program. Along the way, Johnston fended off interference from both the Senate Agriculture Committee and the AAA's Legal Division, which argued that he had too much power and too little accountability. But cotton farmers benefited, and the program was a success. Johnston's Delta and Pine Land Company also participated legally in New Deal subsidies, but in 1936–37 the unwanted notoriety of federal payments to an essentially British-owned corporation raised political questions about the New Deal.

Johnston's management of thousands of black sharecroppers on the company's highly visible cotton plantation defied the stereotype of the oppressive landlord by promoting a paternalistic welfare-capitalist system that delivered more cash, health care, and a superior lifestyle than most black agricultural workers had during the Great Depression. One Christian socialist admitted in 1942 that Johnston's operations were "purely capitalistic money-making schemes although I think his workers are well paid."

Within the New Deal and throughout the South, Johnston emerged as King Cotton's chief advocate. Never a New Dealer, he became convinced that solutions to his industry's perennial problems of overproduction, underconsumption, and intramural jealousies had to be solved by the industry itself. Initially planning to organize only producers, he soon broadened his vision to include the larger cotton industry, eventually coaxing producers, ginners, merchants, mills, cooperatives, warehousers, and cottonseed crushers into the National Cotton Council of America. The Cotton Council became a model of agricultural organization and a chief industry advocate before Congress. Though Johnston's leadership was not unchallenged, cotton leaders in the late 1930s and early 1940s generally agreed that only he had the skills and political capital within the industry to make it work.

After World War II, Johnston brought order to an otherwise chaotic industry and enjoyed a brief period of elder statesmanship before declining physical and mental health forced his retirement by 1950. Shielded by Martha Anderson Johnston, his wife of half a century, he disappeared from public view and died in Greenville on 3 October 1955, just weeks before the new facilities of the National Cotton Council were dedicated in Memphis, Tennessee.

Lawrence J. Nelson
University of North Alabama

Lawrence J. Nelson, *King Cotton's Advocate: Oscar G. Johnston and the New Deal* (1999); Oscar Johnston Papers, Delta and Pine Land Company Records, Mitchell Memorial Library, Mississippi State University.

Jones, Casey
(1864–1900) Engineer and Folk Hero

John Luther "Casey" Jones was born on 14 March 1864 in southwestern Missouri. He was the son of Frank F. Jones, a schoolteacher, and Anna Nolen Jones. When he was thirteen he and his family moved to Cayce, Kentucky, the town that gave him his nickname. In 1886 he married Janie Brady of Jackson, Tennessee, and they went on to have three children. From 1890 to 1899, he worked as an engineer for the Illinois Central on a fast freight run from Jackson, Tennessee, to Water Valley, Mississippi.

As was the custom among engineers of his day, Jones made his own train whistle. His had a distinctive sound, resembling the call of the whippoorwill, an unmistakable signature to every hearing person along his route. Some black Mississippians who listened as Jones and his fellow engineers raced their engines past their homes incorporated the sound of the train whistle into blues harmonica playing, often as a counterpoint, just as the rhythm of the pistons driving the wheels of the locomotive was one of the underpinnings of blues guitar.

Jones built a reputation as the Illinois Central's fastest engineer, a specialist in bringing overdue freights in on time. In 1900 he became engineer on the passenger train popularly known as the Cannonball, which ran between Canton and Memphis on the New Orleans–Chicago route. An Illinois Central engineer could receive no more prestigious assignment.

On 29 April 1900, just north of Vaughan, Mississippi, Jones allegedly failed to heed a flagman's lantern signal. The Cannonball rounded the next curve at seventy miles an hour. In front of him, too close to avoid a collision, were the rear four cars of a freight train that had been unable to pull completely onto a side track. Jones applied the emergency brake. He stayed with the Cannonball up to the moment of collision, although he might have had time to jump. His body was found in the wreckage of his cab, but all of his passengers and crew survived. He went to his grave with a perfect record, never having lost a single passenger or railroad employee in his charge. His widow, represented by Earl Brewer, future governor of Mississippi, received a $2,650 settlement from the Illinois Central.

Jones's heroic death and the often inaccurate songs it inspired have made him one of the major figures in Mississippian and American folklore. Wallace Saunders, a black engine wiper at the Canton roundhouse who cleaned up the Cannonball's locomotive after the wreck, wrote the first song about Jones, which was later recorded under the supervision of noted folk music collector Alan Lomax. Two vaudevillians, T. Lawrence Siebert and Eddie Newton, composed the best-known song about Casey Jones, containing the refrain "Casey Jones was a brave engineer." This version portrayed Jones, who avoided saloons and was a faithful husband, as a "rounder"—a hard-drinking womanizer. In 1938 his widow composed and published "Casey Jones, My Husband" as a rejoinder.

In 1912 fellow folk legend Joe Hill published "Casey Jones, the Union Scab," in which the engineer operated his train while his fellow railroad workers were on strike. The song ended with Casey thrown into hell for scabbing on the angels. In 1970 rock band the Grateful Dead released "Casey Jones" by Robert Hunter and Jerry Garcia, a version that described Jones as "driving that train, high on cocaine."

William Ashley Vaughan
Jackson, Mississippi

Carleton Jonathan Corliss, *Main Line of Mid-America: The Story of The Illinois Central* (1950); Fred J. Lee, *Casey Jones: Epic of the American Railroad* (1940); Alan Lomax, *The Folk Songs of North America* (1960); James Alan McPherson and Miller Williams, *Railroad, Trains, and Train People in American Culture* (1976); B. W. Overall, *The Story of Casey Jones, the Brave Engineer* (1956); Graham Seal, *Encyclopedia of Folk Heroes* (2001).

Jones, Charles Price
(1865–1949) Religious Leader

A bishop, theologian, hymnist, poet, and newspaper editor, Charles Price Jones was born in Texas Valley, near Rome, Georgia, on 9 December 1865. He grew up in the Methodist home of his mother and stepfather, Berry Latimer, in Kingston, Georgia. After his mother's death in 1882, Jones bounced around before settling in Arkansas in 1884 and converting at Locust Grove Baptist Church in Cat Island, Crittenden County. Jones became a lay Baptist preacher in 1885, was licensed to preach in 1887, enrolled in Arkansas Baptist College that same year, and in 1888 became a schoolteacher as well as the pastor of Pope Creek Baptist Church in Grant County. Jones held various pastorates in Arkansas before moving to Mount Helm Baptist Church in Jackson, Mississippi, in 1895.

A major turning point in Jones's life occurred when he received the sanctified experience in 1894. In 1895, while pastoring in Mississippi, he met Walter S. Pleasant, Charles Harrison Mason, and other Baptist holiness advocates, and together they initiated a Baptist holiness movement. In 1896 Jones began publishing a Baptist holiness newspaper, *Truth*. In 1897 he held a regional holiness convention in Jackson. Later in the year the Baptist holiness movement in the Mid-South embraced a nondenominational stance, advocating the substitution of biblically based names for congregations instead of the term *Baptist*. The nondenominational stance galvanized an antiholiness opposition led by Patrick Henry Thompson and others.

During the battles over nondenominationalism, various congregations associated with the Baptist holiness movement split, other congregations withdrew from Baptist conventions, and new holiness fellowships were formed. From 1897 through the early twentieth century, Jones was a leading pastor in the nondenominational holiness movement. From 1895 to 1917 he pastored in Jackson and in other congregations in Hinds County. His Christ Temple developed a major congregation and campus by 1906, with an eight-hundred-member congregation, a sanctuary that seated one thousand, a printing shop, a school building, and girls' dormitory.

In 1906 Jones was elected general overseer of the Church of God in Christ, a nondenominational holiness fellowship of more than 110 congregations in the Mid-South, most of them in Mississippi. In 1907 ten congregations, including one in Lexington, Mississippi, led by Mason, were dismissed from Jones's fellowship because of their embrace of Pentecostalism. Jones continued to lead his faction of the Church of God in Christ until it changed its name to the Church of Christ (Holiness) in 1915. In 1917 he moved to Los Angeles.

Jones remained president of the Church of Christ (Holiness) until 1926 and then served as bishop from 1927 to 1944. During part of 1926 and 1927 Jones resigned from the presidency and denomination to work with a predominantly white holiness organization. Under Jones's leadership, the Church of Christ (Holiness) entered discussions with the predominantly white Church of the Narazene about a merger in 1923–24 and with the Pilgrim Holiness Church about joint mission projects in 1944. While these discussions failed, various predominantly black holiness fellowships such as the Virginia and North Carolina Convocation merged with the Church of Christ (Holiness).

Jones's church supported a mission in Liberia beginning in 1902 and Christ's Missionary and Industrial School in Jackson, organized in 1897. It also ran Virginia's Boydton Institute during the 1920s.

Jones was the author of various poems, most famously "An Appeal to the Sons of Africa," and numerous hymns, including the popular holiness hymn "Deeper, Deeper." His published theological works included treatises, memoirs, and a collection of sermons.

He married Fannie Brown of Little Rock, Arkansas, in 1891. In 1918, two years after her death, he married Pearl E. Reed. He died on 19 January 1949.

David H. Daniels III
McCormick Theological Seminary

David Douglas Daniels, "The Cultural Renewal of Slave Religion: Charles Price Jones and the Emergence of the Holiness Movement in Mississippi" (PhD dissertation, Union Theological Seminary, 1992); Dale Irwin, in *Portraits of a Generation: Early Pentecostal Leaders*, ed. James R. Goff and Grant Wacker (2002); Randall J. Stephens, *The Fire Spreads: Holiness and Pentecostalism in the American South* (2010).

Jones, E. Fay
(1921–2004) Architect

Euine Fay Jones was a renowned architect, most famous for designing Thorncrown Chapel in Eureka Springs, Arkansas, voted by the American Institute of Architects as one of the top five buildings designed by an American architect in the twentieth century. He designed two structures in Mississippi that recalled the features of Thorncrown Chapel.

Jones was born in Pine Bluff, Arkansas, on 31 January 1921. While still in high school, he saw a film on architect Frank Lloyd Wright and decided to follow in his profession. Jones enrolled in the University of Arkansas's School of Engineering, since the institution had no architecture program. In 1941, after two and a half years of college, Jones became a US Navy pilot, and he fought in the Pacific theater during World War II. He married Mary Elizabeth "Gus" Knox in 1943. At the war's conclusion, he reenrolled in the University of Arkansas, joining the first class of the newly created School of Architecture. While still a student, Jones met his hero, Wright, at the 1949 American Institute of Architects Convention. Jones attended graduate school at Rice University before teaching for two years at the University of Oklahoma, where he met Bruce Goff, who would become both a mentor and a friend. Jones reconnected with Wright and apprenticed with him both at Taliesin West in Arizona and at Taliesin East in Spring Green, Wisconsin. Jones then accepted a faculty position in the University of Arkansas's architecture program, teaching there for thirty-five years and becoming professor emeritus in 1988.

Jones also set up a Fayetteville architectural practice. His earliest commissions were houses for university faculty. In the late 1950s Jones expanded his firm but chose to keep it small, concentrating primarily on domestic buildings in Arkansas and surrounding states. In the late 1970s Jones met a prospective client, Jim Reed, to discuss the possibility of a wayfarers' chapel in the Ozarks outside of Eureka Springs, a resort town. The building that resulted, Thorncrown, brought Jones's designs to national prominence and added a new typology to his body of work. He subsequently designed several more chapels in Arkansas and in Texas.

He also received two significant Mississippi commissions that emulate his chapel architecture. According to scholar Robert A. Ivy, Pinecote Pavilion at the Crosby Arboretum in Picayune "rivals Thorncrown Chapel." The pavilion is a light and transparent structure whose columns and roof beams evoke the canopy of trees adjacent to the pond. The roof structure reveals itself toward the gable ends of the building so that its latticework seems to dissolve into the surrounding forest. The pavilion houses exhibition and educational space for the arboretum. The Pine Eagle Chapel at Camp

Tiak in Wiggins is a small, pagoda-like chapel on the shore of a lake. Both Mississippi commissions were gifts in memory of L. O. Crosby Jr., with Pinecote Pavilion given by Lynn and Stewart Gammill and Pine Eagle Chapel by the Dorothy and Osmond Crosby Family. Jones also designed two private homes in the state, one in Clarksdale and one in Iuka.

Jones died in Fayetteville in August 2004.

Justin Faircloth
University of Virginia

Sheila Farr, *Fay Jones* (2000); Robert Adams Ivy Jr., *Fay Jones: The Architecture of E. Fay Jones* (1992); E. Fay Jones: *Outside the Pale: The Architecture of Fay Jones* (1999); Fay Jones Collection, Special Collections University of Arkansas Libraries.

Jones, Grace Allen
(1876–1928) Teacher and Club Organizer

A native of Iowa, Grace M. Allen first met Laurence Clifton Jones at a church in Iowa City when both were students. When Jones became the organizer and principal of the Piney Woods Country Life School in Rankin County, he corresponded with Allen, and they married in Iowa City in 1912. They later had two sons, Turner and Laurence Jr.

Grace Allen Jones quickly became crucial to the Piney Woods School not only as a teacher and speaker but also as an organizer of clubs for women. She founded and led Mothers' Clubs that set standards for and discussed child rearing, cooking, quilting, and sewing. From that start, Jones used women's clubs to address important issues in Mississippi. She helped start an American Red Cross organization for African Americans. She made connections between the Mothers' Clubs and the Mississippi State Federation of Colored Women's Clubs, and as that group's president in 1920, she urged more communities to start women's clubs. Those groups worked to improve child care, to teach African American history, to start libraries for African American children, and to provide resources so that physically handicapped African American children could learn.

Laurence Jones liked to use the story of his family's housing situation as a lesson in modesty and progress. He and Grace began their marriage living in a one-room log cabin at the Piney Woods School before moving into the corner room of a school building, another room in an academic building, an old mill house, and finally a comfortable cottage in 1922. They named the cottage the Community House

because it was the setting for so many meetings. Grace Allen Jones died of pneumonia in 1928.

Ted Ownby
University of Mississippi

Alferdteen B. Harrison, *Piney Woods School: An Oral History* (1982); Grace Morris Allen Jones Papers, Iowa Women's Archives, University of Iowa Libraries; Laurence C. Jones, *Piney Woods and Its Story* (1922); Laurence C. Jones, *The Spirit of the Piney Woods* (1931).

Jones, James Earl
(b. 1931) Actor

Actor James Earl Jones was born on 17 January 1931 in Arkabutla, Mississippi. When he was very young, his mother, Ruth Connolly Jones, moved away, leaving him to be raised by her parents. When he was five, the family moved to Michigan, traumatizing the boy and causing him to develop a stutter. The problem was so severe that Jones resolved not to speak and lived as a mute until his high school years, when teacher Donald Crouch began challenging him with poems, debating, and speech contests. Jones is now widely known for his powerful, dignified voice.

Jones graduated from high school and attended the University of Michigan on a scholarship to study medicine. After appearing in several student theatrical productions, he abandoned medicine in favor of acting in his junior year. Jones never completed his degree because he expected to be called to active duty in the Korean War: "I'd be off to war and probably dead the same fall."

Jones did serve in the US Army, though not in Korea, and after his discharge in 1955 he went to New York. He moved in with his father, Robert Earl Jones, a former prizefighter who had turned to acting. The younger Jones studied with drama coaches Lee Strasberg and Tad Danielewski and earned a diploma from the American Theatre Wing. In 1957 he had a role in an Off-Broadway production of *Wedding in Japan*. He continued to land roles in various productions and joined the New York Shakespeare Festival in 1960. In 1961 he played Oberon in the company's production of *A Midsummer Night's Dream* and the Lord Marshall in *Richard II*.

Jones made his film debut in *Dr. Strangelove; or, How I Learned to Stop Worrying and Love the Bomb* (1963) and made guest appearances on television series such as *East Side/West Side*, *Channing*, and *The Defenders*. In 1965 he received an Emmy Award for a performance in *Beyond the Blues*, a television documentary. His 1968 performance as Jack Jefferson in the Broadway hit *The Great White Hope* proved to be a major milestone in Jones's career, earning him rave reviews as well as a Tony Award and a Drama Desk Award. He won a Grammy award in 1969 for his recording of the play and received an Academy Award nomination for the 1970 film version.

Jones continued to turn in well-received stage, television, and film performances. Even his most controversial work, the title role in Phillip Hayes Dean's monodrama *Paul Robeson* (1978), won critical accolades. Jones uses his powerful acting skills and voice to portray characters who expect and demand respect. He has played an enormous array of roles—political, legal, and military characters as well as fathers and grandfathers.

Jones's film credits include radical activist/baseball fan Terence Mann in *Field of Dreams* (1989); the 1990 thriller *The Hunt for Red October* and its two sequels, *Patriot Games* (1992) and *Clear and Present Danger* (1994); and Montgomery minister-activist Vernon Johns in *The Vernon Johns Story* (1994). More recently, he has appeared on such television shows as *Everwood* (2004), *The L Word* (2004), *House M.D.* (2009), and *The Big Bang Theory* (2014). But Jones is perhaps best known as the voice of Darth Vader in *Star Wars* (1977), *The Empire Strikes Back* (1980), *Return of the Jedi* (1983), and other film and television productions. He has also loaned his rich bass to Mufasa in Disney's *The Lion King* (1994), to various characters on *The Simpsons*, and to the CNN television network.

In 1985 Jones was elected to the Theatre Hall of Fame. In 1992 he received the National Medal of the Arts from Pres. George H. W. Bush. In 2011 he received an honorary Academy Award for lifetime achievement.

Kevin Herrera
University of Mississippi

Academy of Achievement Website, www.achievement.org; David Bianculli, "James Earl Jones Discusses His Life and Career," transcript of interview from *Fresh Air*, National Public Radio (1 October 2004); Rebecca Flint, in *All Movie Guide* (2005); Internet Movie Database website, www.imdb.com; John F. Kennedy Center for the Performing Arts website, www.kennedycenter.org.

Jones, Laurence Clifton

(1888–1975) Educator and Author

Laurence Clifton Jones was the founder of and a major figure in the Piney Woods Country Life School, an ambitious institution for African Americans on the edge of Rankin County, near Braxton in Simpson County. Born in St. Joseph, Missouri, in 1888, Jones received his education in Iowa before moving south to answer, as he wrote in his 1922 book, *Piney Woods and Its Story*, "the cries of my people for the opportunities of education which were being denied them." An admirer and correspondent of Booker T. Washington, Jones believed that African Americans needed to work for their education and gain practical skills that would help them in their work. Students labored to build and keep up the school, and the curriculum concentrated on manual training, farming, carpentry, cooking, and sewing.

While teaching in Hinds County, Jones visited the Piney Woods area, where he heard Sunday school leaders discussing how they had long wanted to begin a high school for African American students. The Piney Woods Country Life School opened in 1909, and Jones received a charter for the school in 1913. Along with five teachers, including his wife, Grace Allen Jones, whom he married in 1912, the school was soon teaching African American students from throughout southern Mississippi, Florida, and Louisiana.

Like Washington, Robert Holtzclaw, and other African American educational leaders, Jones spent much of his time and effort raising funds, both in Mississippi and in the North, especially Iowa. He cultivated friendships with numerous donors and employed the first Jeanes Foundation teacher in the state.

Jones described most of his dealings with whites in Mississippi as cordial and positive. He consistently referred to white men and women who donated money or time to the school as "southern white friends." But on at least one occasion, angry whites interpreted his heated language at a revival meeting as a challenge to white supremacy and threatened to lynch him. By the 1930s Jones was praising interracial groups and speaking optimistically of white Mississippians who had given up their opposition to African American education.

Jones lived long enough to see his success lead to a bit of celebrity. In the 1950s his life was the subject of two biographies, and he appeared frequently on radio, along with the Piney Woods Singers, and on television. A 1954 appearance on Ralph Edwards's *This Is Your Life* turned into a successful fund-raising campaign when the show included an appeal for donations. He remained at the school's helm until 1974, just a year before he died.

Ted Ownby
University of Mississippi

Beth Day, *The Little Professor of Piney Woods* (1955); Alferdteen B. Harrison, *Piney Woods School: An Oral History* (1982); Laurence C. Jones, *The Bottom Rail* (1935); Laurence C. Jones, *Piney Woods and Its Story* (1922); Laurence C. Jones, *The Spirit of the Piney Woods* (1931); Neil McMillen, *Dark Journey: Black Mississippians in the Age of Jim Crow* (1990); Leslie Harper Purcell, *Miracle in Mississippi* (1956).

Jones, Lawrence Arthur

(1910–1996) Artist

Artist Lawrence Arthur Jones was born in 1910 in Lynchburg, Virginia, to Napoleon Jones and Nanni Hemings Jones, a descendant of Thomas Jefferson's slave, Sally Hemings. He believed his ancestry earned him special privileges, including access to the Lynchburg public library; art studies with Sally Mahood, a local white artist; and mentoring from poet Anne Spencer. Jones studied at the School of the Art Institute of Chicago from 1934 to 1936, enrolling with letters of reference from poet James Weldon Johnson and Virginia senator and secretary of the US Treasury Carter Glass. Jones served as artist in residence at Jane Addams's Hull House in Chicago before leaving for New Orleans to establish and head the art department at Dillard University. His Art Institute degree incomplete, Jones was required to enroll at Dillard from 1937 to 1940 while teaching art. He also produced prints for the Works Progress Administration's Federal Arts Project.

Jones painted his first mural, *Negro Homemaking in Georgia* (ca. 1940–41), for Georgia's Fort Valley State College. He won a Rosenwald Fellowship in 1941 and used it to study in Mexico, associating with the Taller de Gráfica Popular. Jones was drafted into the US Army, designed training aids, and painted *Courage, Fraternity, Strength*, a mural for the Fort McClellan Enlisted Men's Service Club. Returning to the School of the Art Institute in 1946, Jones met architect Frank Lloyd Wright and toured his Wisconsin home, Taliesen. Jones then returned to Fort Valley State College, where he founded the art department; met and married María Luisa Ramírez of Cienfuegos, Cuba; and befriended artist Benny Andrews. In 1947 Jones painted *The Rape of Ethiopia*, which protested Italian expansionism and dominion in Africa. As in many of Jones's major works, this painting is layered with symbolism emphasizing humankind's inhumanity.

In 1949 Jones moved to Mississippi to establish and head the art department at Jackson College for Negro Teachers (now Jackson State University). In 1957 his painting *Many Years of Growth* won honorable mention at Atlanta University's annual exhibition. In 1964 his triptych *Past, Present, and Future* (1962–63) took second in the painting category at the Chicago Centennial Show of Black Progress. The triptych is an allegory of the black experience in America and Jones's guarded hopes for the future of the race. He painted murals for Jackson churches, Jackson State University (1976–78), and Morris Brown College in Atlanta (1982) as well as collaborated with high school students on a portable mural for Jackson's Smith Robertson Museum (1983).

Jones earned a master's degree in art education from the University of Mississippi (1970–71) and visited Ghana, Nigeria, Togo, and the Republic of Benin with the Educators to Africa Association in 1974. He produced prints throughout his career, including *Disasters of War* (1971) and *Mammy Wagon* (1981). Jones retired from Jackson State University in 1978 and died in Jackson in 1996.

Betty J. Crouther
University of Mississippi

Patti Carr Black, *Art In Mississippi, 1720–1980* (1998); Elton C. Fax, *Seventeen Black Artists* (1971); G. James Fleming and Christian E. Burckel, *Who's Who in Colored America* (7th ed. 1950); Lawrence A. Jones lecture, Tennessee State University (30 March 1992); Lawrence A. and Maria L. Jones, interviews by Betty J. Crouther.

Jones County

Founded in 1826 from portions of Covington and Wayne Counties, Jones County is located in southern Mississippi's Piney Woods region. The Leaf River traverses Jones's western region from north to south, while Tallahoma Creek wends its way through the county's eastern section. In the 1820s and 1830s the lands now incorporated into Jones County were ceded to the United States by the Choctaw Indians through the Treaty of Mount Dexter, the Treaty of Doak's Stand, and the Treaty of Dancing Rabbit Creek. The county is named for Revolutionary War hero John Paul Jones. Its two seats are Laurel and Ellisville.

An economic depression contributed to emigration from Jones County during its early years. Antebellum Jones remained sparsely populated, reporting only 1,309 free people and 161 slaves in its first census in 1830. By 1860 the population was growing again, and the population had climbed to

Central Avenue, Laurel, seat of Jones County, ca. 1927 (Ann Rayburn Paper Americana Collection, Department of Archives and Special Collections, J. D. Williams Library, University of Mississippi [rayburn _ann_25_13_001])

2,916 whites and 407 slaves (12 percent), the smallest number and percentage in the state.

As in other Piney Woods counties, economic activity in Jones did not revolve around agriculture, and the county was among the lowest in Mississippi in raising cotton, corn, and cattle during the antebellum period. Its residents owned considerably more hogs than average, and Jones ranked eleventh in the state in rice production. In 1860 the county's industrial workforce included only nineteen people working in flour or lumber mills.

Jones County is most famous for the story of the Free State of Jones. The county was the site of considerable dissent before and during the Civil War. While it is unclear whether Jones ever officially declared that it had seceded from Mississippi or the Confederate States of America, the Knight Company of deserters stubbornly resisted the Confederacy's efforts to disperse, arrest, and even execute some of the participants. Generations of debates have occurred over the legacy of Newt Knight and his group, who are variously considered heroic defenders of local control who seceded from the secessionists, thuggish outlaws, or mavericks who defied all rules, including the racial conventions of marriage. The tale has been dramatized in a 2016 movie, *The Free State of Jones*.

Fifteen years after the end of the Civil War, Jones County's population had increased only slightly to 3,828. Still rural and agricultural, with only four manufacturing firms, Jones was a rare Mississippi county that produced little corn or cotton. By contrast, Jones was among the top counties in the state in growing rice and rearing sheep. In 1880 Jones had the state's smallest African American community, comprising only 9.4 percent of the population.

Jones's population grew dramatically at the end of the nineteenth century, reaching 17,846 in 1900, with African Americans accounting for more than a quarter of residents. The county's rate of landownership was relatively high, as 79 percent of white farmers and 65 percent of black farmers owned the land they worked. Jones had a growing industrial economy, with fifty-four establishments employing 1,148 workers. The Eastman-Gardiner timber company and mill, headquartered in Laurel, grew quickly in the late 1800s and by the early 1900s became one of Mississippi's largest firms. In 1907 the Gilchrist-Fordry Company began similar work in the Laurel area, with a huge mill and substantial timber acreage.

On the eve of the Civil War, Jones had eighteen churches—eleven Methodist, six Baptist, and one Presbyterian. A half century later, most of Jones County churchgoers were either Southern Baptists or Missionary Baptists.

The county's population continued its impressive expansion during the early twentieth century. By 1930 Jones was home to 41,492 people, with whites outnumbering African Americans almost three to one. Landownership in the county had declined during the previous three decades, and as the Great Depression set in, 54 percent of white farmers and 26 percent of African American farmers owned their land. However, the county's industrial sector had grown substantially, employing 4,037 workers, the most in Mississippi. The majority of these laborers worked in large sawmills and pulp mills. Laurel was also home to Masonite, a product developed by William H. Mason that turned young trees into fiberboard. Increased job opportunities in manufacturing attracted the Congress of Industrial Organizations, which had some success organizing the county's workforce.

In the 1940s surveys in Jones County resulted in the discovery of oil. In 1944 the Helen Morrison Well in neighboring Jasper County became the area's first productive well, and by the end of that year Jones County led the state in oil production.

Beginning in the 1920s Jones County became an important location for the arts. In 1923 the Lauren Rogers Museum of Art was established in Laurel. It features an exciting combination of American, European, and Japanese art and is currently the state's oldest art museum. In 1922 Laurel teacher Ernestine Clayton Deavours edited and published *Mississippi Poets*, the first substantial literary anthology of Mississippi writers. Born in Laurel in 1927, opera singer Leontyne Price began her musical career in her hometown schools and churches before becoming one of the world's leading opera singers in the 1950s and breaking numerous racial barriers. Author Carolyn Bennett Patterson, *National Geographic*'s first female editor, was born in Laurel in 1921.

By 1960 Jones's population had increased to almost sixty thousand people, with whites holding a three-quarters majority. Industry maintained its strong presence in the county, and many workers were employed in construction and retail. Livestock, soybeans, corn, and oats dominated the agricultural sector. The county also had numerous oil wells and almost three hundred thousand acres of commercial timberland.

Jones County is associated with several important events and figures in Mississippi's turbulent twentieth-century racial history. In 1945 Willie McGee, an African American, was convicted of raping a white woman in Laurel. McGee claimed the relationship was consensual, and his multiple trials attracted international intention, with critics seeing his conviction and 1951 execution as a form of legal lynching. In 1955 Jones County Junior College played a football game against a Compton Community College team that included African American players, defying the state law barring all-white teams from competing against racially integrated squads. In 1966 Sam Bowers, a Laurel businessman and leader of the White Knights of the Ku Klux Klan, murdered civil rights activist Vernon Dahmer. After four mistrials in the 1960s, Bowers was finally convicted of the crime in 1998.

Like most counties in the southern part of the state, Jones County's 2010 population of 67,761 was predominantly white. However, the county was also home to a Latino minority (primarily Mexicans from Veracruz, Chiapas, and Oaxaca) as well as a small but growing South Asian community. As in neighboring Jasper, Jefferson Davis, Lamar, and Forrest

Counties, Jones's African American minority had also shown a significant proportional increase.

Mississippi Encyclopedia Staff
University of Mississippi

Victoria E. Bynum, *The Free State of Jones: Mississippi's Longest Civil War* (2004); Jones County Mississippi, Genealogy and History website, www .jones.msgenweb.org; Mississippi State Planning Commission, *Progress Report on State Planning in Mississippi* (1938); *Mississippi Statistical Abstract*, Mississippi State University (1952–2010); Charles Sydnor and Claude Bennett, *Mississippi History* (1939); University of Virginia Library, Historical Census Browser website, http://mapserver.lib.virginia.edu; E. Nolan Waller and Dani A. Smith, *Growth Profiles of Mississippi's Counties, 1960–1980* (1985).

Jordan, Winthrop D.
(1931–2007) Historian

Winthrop D. Jordan was a renowned historian, admired professor, and award-winning author on the topics of race and slavery in American history. Best known for the book *White over Black: American Attitudes toward the Negro, 1550–1812* (1968), which earned him the National Book Award, the Bancroft Prize, and other honors, Jordan spent the last twenty-two years of his career as the William F. Winter Professor of History and F. A. P. Barnard Distinguished Professor of Afro-American Studies at the University of Mississippi. In *White over Black* Jordan asserted that English perceptions about color, Christianity, manners, sexuality, and social hierarchy contributed to the "unthinking decision" to commence the trans-Atlantic slave trade and crystallized by the late eighteenth century into a race-based justification for chattel slavery. This argument profoundly affected historians' understanding of both slavery and racism. The book's erudite discussion of interracial sex is credited with inspiring serious scholarly inquiry into that topic—particularly the relationship between former president Thomas Jefferson and his slave, Sally Hemings. In 1993 Jordan won a second Bancroft Prize for *Tumult and Silence at Second Creek: An Inquiry into a Civil War Slave Conspiracy*. In this work, Jordan not only brought to light details of a previously unstudied slave revolt near Natchez but also provided a model of the investigative skill, devotion to source materials, and keen insight that goes into the making of a consummate work of historical scholarship.

A native of Worcester, Massachusetts, Jordan was born on 11 November 1931 into a family of scholars and liberal thinkers. His father, Henry Donaldson Jordan, was a professor of history at Clark University specializing in nineteenth- and early twentieth-century British and American politics. Winthrop Jordan's mother, Lucretia Mott Churchill Jordan, was descended from pioneering feminist and Quaker abolitionist Lucretia Coffin Mott. His great-great uncle, Edward N. Hallowell, was a commanding officer of the 54th Massachusetts Infantry Regiment, a celebrated African American Civil War unit. True to these roots, Jordan's midcareer decision to live and teach in Mississippi was fueled in part by a missionary impulse to improve the quality of higher education in the state. In addition, he was a founding member of Mississippi's first official Quaker meeting, which met weekly at the Jordan home in Oxford.

Jordan attended high school at Massachusetts's prestigious Andover Academy and graduated from Harvard University in 1953 without having taken a single course in history (because, he later explained, he was a history professor's son). Although his degree was in social relations, his real major was performing with the Krokodiloes, an a cappella singing group. After a brief stint with the Prudential Life Insurance Company, Jordan began his teaching career as an instructor at Phillips Exeter Academy in New Hampshire while earning a master's degree in history from Clark in 1957. In 1960 he received a doctorate in history from Brown University. His doctoral dissertation formed the foundation of what became his masterwork, *White over Black*.

In 1963, after a two-year fellowship at the College of William and Mary's Institute of Early American History and Culture, Jordan joined the department of history at the University of California at Berkeley, where he remained until he joined the faculty of the University of Mississippi in 1982. Jordan taught courses in African American history and early American social and intellectual history and a graduate seminar in research methods. In 2005, a year after Jordan's retirement, ten of his former doctoral students from both Berkeley and Mississippi published *Affect and Power: Essays on Sex, Slavery, Race, and Religion*, a collection of essays he inspired.

In 2006 Jordan discovered he was suffering from amyotrophic lateral sclerosis (Lou Gehrig's disease). Until days before his death on 23 February 2007, Jordan continued to pursue his scholarly interests, particularly his search for the origins of the one-drop rule—the uniquely American concept that only a small amount of African ancestry is sufficient to categorize a person as black, which he had originally explored in the *William and Mary Quarterly* in 1962.

Ironically, the Oxford funeral home in charge of filing Jordan's death certificate incorrectly recorded his race as black. This was not the first time the son of New England seafaring stock had been presumed to have African roots. In 1993 the *Journal of Blacks in Higher Education* listed him among the year's "most highly cited black scholars." Although Jordan's family and friends viewed his posthumous racial recategorization as an appropriate homage to the man whose life's work contributed more to our understanding of what he called the "American chiaroscuro" than any other historian, the incident also revealed the enduring significance of racial labels. Mississippi law required the certificate to be amended and refiled, a process that proved an arduous and prolonged obstacle to the administration of his estate. To paraphrase Jordan's 1999 assessment of public debate concerning the paternity of Hemings's children, the wonder is not that a man with no known African ancestry was mistaken for black but that it mattered to some people.

Susan Ditto
Washington, D.C.

Winthrop D. Jordan, in *Sally Hemings and Thomas Jefferson: History, Memory, and Civic Culture*, ed. Jan Ellen Lewis and Peter S. Onuf (1999); David Libby, Paul Spickard, and Susan Ditto, eds., *Affect and Power: Essays on Sex, Slavery, Race, and Religion in Appreciation of Winthrop D. Jordan* (2006); History News Network, History Doyens, "Winthrop D. Jordan" (2 July 2006).

Judiciary

The Mississippi judiciary is a four-tiered system composed of trial and appellate courts. The Mississippi Constitution created four courts, including the Supreme Court of Mississippi, the circuit courts, chancery courts, and justice courts. The constitution provides that the legislature may create and establish inferior courts as necessary. The four tiers of the judicial structure include the courts of limited jurisdiction, courts of general jurisdiction, the intermediate appellate court, and the court of last resort.

Courts of limited jurisdiction include municipal courts, justice courts, and county courts. These courts have concurrent jurisdiction over civil and criminal matters, and appeals from these courts may be made to the circuit or chancery court.

Municipal courts are widely referred to as city or police courts. Municipal courts exist in all cities, towns, and villages with populations greater than ten thousand. In 2016 there were 226 municipal courts in Mississippi. Municipal courts hear cases involving violations of municipal ordinances, misdemeanor criminal offenses, and traffic violations that occur within the city limits. In limited cases, the municipal court may serve as the juvenile court for the jurisdiction. Municipal court judges are attorneys appointed by municipal authorities—typically, the mayor or the city council. Municipal court judgeships are considered part-time posi-

tions, and most municipal judges also maintain active law practices.

The justice court is the only court of limited jurisdiction created by the Mississippi Constitution of 1890. While the constitution originally granted justice courts jurisdiction over civil matters in excess of five hundred dollars, the legislature has modified the jurisdictional amount of justice courts to include civil actions under thirty-five hundred dollars. Justice courts also have limited jurisdiction over certain criminal matters. Typically, justice courts adjudicate misdemeanor criminal offenses, including traffic offenses that occur in the county; conduct initial and preliminary hearings in felony cases; make bail decisions; and entertain requests for search and arrest warrants. Justice court judges are elected to four-year terms via partisan elections. Qualifications include state and county residency, a high school diploma or general equivalency diploma, and, once elected, completion of annual legal training provided by the Mississippi Judicial College. As of 2016 there were 197 judges presiding over 83 Justice Courts.

County courts are authorized by the legislature and are required in counties with populations greater than fifty thousand and optional in all other counties. Mississippi currently has twenty-one county courts, with thirty county court judges. They have jurisdiction over a variety of civil and criminal matters, including misdemeanor criminal offenses as well as noncapital felony cases transferred by the circuit court. County courts also have jurisdiction over civil matters that involve amounts less than two hundred thousand dollars and have exclusive jurisdiction over matters involving eminent domain, the partition of personal property, and unlawful entry and detainer.

In addition, county courts function as youth courts. In counties that lack county courts, the chancery or family court serves as the youth court. In Mississippi, youth courts hear matters involving juveniles including but not limited to delinquency cases, cases of abuse and neglect, dependency cases, and cases involving children in need of supervision. The youth court is a civil court whose primary focus is the protection of the best interest of the child.

Mississippi currently has twenty-one county court judges. To qualify as a county court judge, individuals must be at least twenty-six years of age, residents of the state, and practicing attorneys for five years. Candidates must meet all voter eligibility requirements and cannot have been convicted of certain felonies. County court judges serve four-year terms in office.

The Mississippi Constitution of 1890 created two courts of general jurisdiction, circuit and chancery courts. The state currently has twenty-two circuit court districts. Circuit courts are authorized to hear civil matters with two hundred dollars or more in controversy. As such, they have considerable concurrent jurisdiction with the justice and county courts. Circuit courts also hear all criminal cases involving adults charged with felony offenses. Moreover, circuit courts possess appellate jurisdiction over appeals from justice or municipal courts and certain administrative proceedings. Mississippi currently has fifty-three circuit court judges. Candidates for circuit court judge must be at least twenty-six years of age, residents of the state, and practicing attorneys for five years.

Chancery courts are courts of equity created by the Mississippi Constitution of 1890. Chancery courts have jurisdiction over cases involving matters in equity, divorce and alimony, testamentary and of administration, minors' business, idiocy and lunacy, certain real estate actions, and a variety of other actions. Mississippi has twenty chancery court districts and forty-nine chancery court judges. Like county and circuit court judges, chancellors must be at least twenty-six years of age, residents of the state, and practicing attorneys for five years. In addition, candidates seeking the office of chancery court judge must meet all voter eligibility requirements and cannot have been convicted of certain felonies. Chancery judges serve four-year terms in office.

In 1993 the legislature created the Court of Appeals to serve as the intermediate appellate court for the state. While all appeals proceed directly to the Supreme Court of Mississippi, the Court of Appeals is authorized to hear cases assigned by the Supreme Court. Decisions handed down by the Court of Appeals may be reviewed by the Supreme Court if a party files a petition for writ of certiorari. However, the decision to grant or deny the petition is discretionary, and the Supreme Court does not choose to hear all cases. The Court of Appeals is composed of ten judges who serve eight-year terms following nonpartisan and staggered elections in five districts. Candidates for the Court of Appeals must possess the same qualifications as individuals seeking election to the Supreme Court.

The Supreme Court of Mississippi (the court of last resort) is the only appellate court created by the Mississippi Constitution. While it is authorized to assign cases to the Court of Appeals, state law requires the Supreme Court to retain cases involving the death penalty, election contests, utility rate regulation, and public bond issues as well as cases in which a lower court has held a statute unconstitutional. In addition, the Supreme Court will retain cases involving fundamental and urgent issues of broad public importance; cases involving the constitutionality of a statute, ordinance, court rule, or administrative rule or regulation; and cases involving inconsistency or conflict between the decisions rendered by the Court of Appeals and Supreme Court. In addition to appellate jurisdiction, the Supreme Court of Mississippi is responsible for rules involving trials and appeals. The rule-making power of the Supreme Court has resulted in the Mississippi Rules of Civil Procedure, Mississippi Rules of Evidence, Mississippi Rules of Appellate Procedure, Mississippi Uniform Rules of Circuit and County Court Practice, Mississippi Uniform Chancery Court Rules, and Uniform Rules of Procedure for Justice Court. The Supreme Court is also the final arbiter of complaints regarding the conduct and performance of judges throughout the state.

The Supreme Court has nine sitting justices who serve eight-year terms following nonpartisan elections. Three justices are chosen from each of three Supreme Court districts—the Northern District, the Central District, and the Southern District. Justices must be at least thirty years of age, be state residents for at least five years, be practicing attorneys for five years prior to service, meet all voter eligibility requirements, and must not have been convicted of certain felonies.

Lisa S. Nored
University of Southern
Mississippi

Michael H. Hoffheimer, *Mississippi Law Journal* (1995); James Robertson, in *Encyclopedia of Mississippi Law*, ed. Jeffrey Jackson and Mary Miller (2003); Leslie Southwick, *Mississippi Law Journal* (1996).

Juke Joints

The origins of the term *juke* or *jook* remain uncertain. Some scholars have speculated that the word derives from an African word, *juga*, meaning "bad" or "wicked," while others believe *juke* comes from *juice*, often used to describe early electric guitars and music players (juice boxes). Whatever the term's origins, juke joints remain important spaces for blues musicians and audiences.

In 1934 Zora Neale Hurston wrote that "musically speaking, the Jook is the most important place in America." Spatially speaking, juke joints are difficult to define, because they are a conceptual space rather than a template. The earliest juke joints were defined by the live blues music played there, whether the site was an abandoned sharecropper shack, an open field, or someone's home.

Juke joints are never built; rather, they appropriate previous spaces. The buildings adapted for juke joints have different layouts and definitions, but juke joints carry certain elements that redefine the previous space. Almost all contemporary juke joints contain a bar of some sort (even if it consists only of a few cases of beer and a garbage can full of ice), a pool table, a stage area, seats for patrons, and colorful decorations. The interior walls often are roughly painted with scenes of celebration (people drinking, dancing, and singing) or with idyllic pictures of paradise (palm trees and islands). Celebratory decorations of various kinds adorn the walls—*Happy Birthday* signs, Christmas lights, confetti and

Jitterbugging in a juke joint on Saturday evening outside Clarksdale, November 1939 (Photograph by Marion Post Wolcott, Library of Congress, Washington, D.C. [LC-USF34-052594-D])

tinsel. Juke joints need only the lowest common denominators of celebration, relying on basic decorations and design elements like the bar to establish itself.

The malleability of juke joints developed out of the subversive nature of early blues music itself. During slavery, African Americans were not permitted to gather; in some cases, dancing and singing also were not allowed. Despite these constraints, music played an important role in the development of the African American community. As blues music gained popularity in the Jim Crow South, juke joints became safe places for African Americans to gather without white supervision. The basic principles that kept juke joints covert during segregation have become the defining elements of juke joints since that time.

Juke joints are not simply a rural phenomenon, although even in towns and cities they tend to serve an established community. Unlike a club or bar, patrons at a particular juke joint tend to know each other. This lack of anonymity was certainly necessary to ensure safety under Jim Crow and remains a fundamental principle of modern juke joints. Certain elements that are a given for other businesses are often lacking at juke joints, such as set hours of operation or public phone numbers. Instead, juke joints tend to run when musicians are available to play, with notice of a performance spreading through community networks rather than via official advertising. News of a performance depends on the path of information already established within a given community, reaffirming the familiarity of the crowd that attends a particular juke joint. As a result, some prior knowledge of the juke's existence and possible operating hours is required. This does not mean newcomers are not allowed: those who are willing to talk to local citizens about attending juke joints will most often be welcome. While juke joints tend to serve a specific core group of people, they are not private functions. Patrons must often pay to enter, and liquor and food are frequently sold. Still, juke joints tend not to be moneymaking endeavors for the proprietors, and almost all proprietors hold full-time

jobs. Unlike a party, juke patrons pay for food and drinks, and musicians are paid—albeit minimally—from the money raised. In Mississippi and much of the rest of the South, proprietors are supposed to purchase juke joint licenses from the state.

Defining a juke joint has less to do with the decoration or style of the space and more to do with the interaction between the crowd and the music. Live music is no longer an absolute, as many juke joints employ deejays or house jukeboxes, but the lack of anonymity among the crowd at a juke joint remains one of the elements that distinguishes it from a club. Juke joints are a function of blues, and the physical spaces mimic the metaphorical in many ways. The call-and-response nature of blues, for example, can be seen in the interaction required of juke joints. Unlike clubs or bars, juke joints rely on an atmosphere of familiarity among the patrons, proprietors, and musicians. The communal nature of blues music also imprints the space. Just as any given blues tune can have an infinite number of lyrics or chords, particular design or decorative principles do not bind the spaces.

The Mississippi Blues Trail has identified numerous past and present juke joints, and the establishments remain important both to local blues fans and to traveling enthusiasts. Photographers and filmmakers have long found—and continue to find—juke joints to be subjects of great beauty and intrigue.

Jennifer Nardone
Columbus State Community
College

Steve Cheseborough, *Blues Traveling: The Holy Sites of the Delta Blues* (2009); Katrina Hazzard-Gordon, *Jookin': The Rise of Social Dance Formations in African-American Culture* (1990); Zora Neale Hurston, *The Sanctified Church* (1981); Birney Imes, *Juke Joint: Photographs* (1990); Jennifer Nardone, in *Perspectives in Vernacular Architecture 9* (2002); Lorenzo Turner, *Africanisms in the Gullah Dialect* (1959).

Juneteenth Celebrations

Independence Day in the United States is officially celebrated on 4 July, but for many Americans the 1776 Declaration of Independence did not signal freedom. Instead, Pres. Abraham Lincoln's 1863 Emancipation Proclamation recognized and proclaimed freedom for the slaves, even though the news did not reach all of the slaves for several years. Juneteenth celebrations commemorate Maj. Gen. Gordon Granger's 1865 ride through the South carrying the news of emancipation and his announcement on 19 June in Galveston, Texas, that slavery had been abolished. That date was eventually shortened to *Juneteenth*.

As populations subsequently shifted and migrated, Juneteenth celebrations spread to other states, including Mississippi. Typical festivities for the day include rodeos, parades, reenactments of Granger's ride, concerts, sports tournaments, car shows, and elaborate picnics. Many of the celebratory activities seek to fulfill possibilities not available to slaves during their captivity, such as being free from hunger, and the dress is traditionally Sunday best. Because different groups of slaves were freed at different times, not everyone celebrates Juneteenth on the same day or even in the same month, but the most common day remains 19 June.

In 1979 Texas became the first state to officially recognize Juneteenth as a holiday. From 2004 until 2010, several Mississippi legislators, including Rufus Straughter, Bryant Clark, Omeria Scott, Erik R. Fleming, John Hines, and John Mayo, proposed legislation making Juneteenth a state holiday. In 2010, Mississippi became the thirty-sixth state to do so, and by 2016, forty-three states had recognized Juneteenth as a state holiday or special day of observance. In 2012 the US Postal Service issued a Juneteenth "Flags of Freedom" stamp. In 2014 the US Senate unanimously recognized 19 June of that year as "Juneteenth Independence Day." Supporters continue to work to persuade Congress to declare the occasion a National Day of Observance, like Flag Day.

Many Mississippi communities and groups hold Juneteenth celebrations. In 2015 festivities took place in Hattiesburg, Itta Bena, Biloxi, and Jackson, among other towns and cities.

Anna F. Kaplan
Columbia University

National Juneteenth Holiday Campaign website, www.juneteenth.us; William H. Wiggins Jr., in *Juneteenth Texas: Essays in African-American Folklore*, ed. Francis Edward Abernethy (1996).

J

K

Katrina, Hurricane

The storm that became known as Hurricane Katrina formed over the Bahamas on 23 August 2005. It became a Category 1 hurricane (winds of 74–95 miles per hour) two days later and crossed southern Florida. Over the warm waters in the Gulf of Mexico, the storm strengthened, packing 175 mile-per-hour winds that made it a Category 5 hurricane—the strongest possible. Moving north through the Gulf of Mexico, the 450-foot-wide storm made landfall 40 miles east of New Orleans, coming ashore early on 29 August over Southeast Louisiana and into Mississippi as a Category 3 storm (111–130 miles per hour). Its powerful right-front quadrant passed over coastal and central Mississippi, causing a twenty- to thirty-foot tidal surge and fifty-five-foot sea waves. Moving north, the storm drenched most of the state, with rainfall totaling between eight and ten inches. Hurricane-force winds battered Mississippi for seventeen hours, spawning at least eleven tornadoes along the Gulf Coast. Winds measuring 80–85 miles per hour were recorded as far north as Jackson, approximately 150 miles from the coast. The hurricane did not downgrade to a tropical storm until it crossed out of Mississippi and into Tennessee, where it finally dissipated on 30 August.

Katrina was one of the five most deadly hurricanes in US history, with 1,836 people killed in the storm itself and the subsequent floods. It was also the most costly hurricane ever to hit the United States, causing an estimated $125 billion in damage. Katrina leveled 65,380 homes on the coast and washed away city after city—antebellum houses, businesses, schools, hotels, marinas—from Pascagoula to Bay St. Louis. Flooding reached as far as twelve miles inland. One third of the state's population—approximately 800,000 people—remained without power for days following the storm. Across Mississippi, 238 residents lost their lives.

In the few days before Katrina made landfall, the National Hurricane Center warned residents of the impending storm. On 26 August Mississippi activated its National Guard, and by 29 August, forty-one counties and sixty-one cities had issued evacuation orders, with fifty-seven emergency shelters opening along the coast and thirty-one in reserve if needed later. More than one million people left the storm's path.

All of Mississippi's eighty-two counties were affected by the storm, and forty-seven were declared full disaster areas. However, the state's three coastal counties—Harrison, Jackson, and Hancock—suffered the most damage.

Hancock's cities of Waveland, Bay St. Louis, Pearlington, and Clermont Harbor were almost completely destroyed as water took out every structure within half a mile of the beach. Fifty-one deaths were recorded in the county.

The death toll was highest to the east, in Harrison County, where 126 people were killed. The cities of Long Beach and Pass Christian were flattened, while Gulfport and Biloxi suffered extensive damage. The Biloxi–Ocean Springs Bridge was obliterated. Biloxi's nine casino-hotels were destroyed, with several of the barges on which they sat washed onto land. In 2003 the casinos generated $879 million in revenue and were the second-largest employer along the Coast. After Katrina, their loss meant that unemployment skyrocketed. In addition, the seafood industry, primarily shrimp processing, had employed about three thousand people and accounted for $450 million per year but was decimated by the hurricane. The county also suffered from the flooding of Biloxi's Keesler Air Force Base and from shipping disruptions at the Mississippi State Port Authority in Gulfport, the third-busiest US container port on the Gulf. The casino and shipping industries and the military presence helped Harrison County recover in the years following Katrina.

Jackson County also experienced the tremendous storm surge, with 90 percent of the city of Pascagoula flooded and twelve people killed. Other communities in the county suffered extensive damage, as did Ingalls Shipbuilding.

In the wake of Hurricane Katrina, volunteers from around the world came to help Mississippi recover. Nongovernmental organizations such as the American Red Cross, Americorps, North Carolina Baptist Men, the Salvation Army, Catholic Charities, and hundreds of individuals arrived within days of the storm. Just two weeks after the hurricane made landfall, corporate relief donations reached approximately $409 million. Officials from national organizations and the Mississippi Commission for Volunteer Service estimate that more than

Wrecked car at Long Beach condo complex after Hurricane Katrina (Photograph by David Wharton)

two hundred organizations with more than eight hundred thousand volunteers provided relief to Mississippi through more than eighteen million hours of work.

Deanne Stephens Nuwer
University of Southern Mississippi,
Katrina Research Center

Betty Plombon, *Katrina and the Forgotten Gulf Coast* (2006); Michael Tracey, *She Was No Lady: A Personal Journey of Recovery through Hurricane Katrina* (2006); Timothy H. Warneka, *Healing Katrina: Volunteering in Post-Hurricane Mississippi* (2007).

Hurricane Katrina, Environmental Impact

After making landfall in Florida and Louisiana, Hurricane Katrina struck the northern Gulf Coast near the mouth of the Pearl River at the Mississippi-Louisiana border on 29 August 2005. The 125-mile-per-hour winds, exceptional storm surge, and heavy precipitation and flooding associated with the hurricane caused tragic loss of life and extensive damage to human infrastructure as well as to ecosystems throughout Mississippi.

The most widespread ecological impact of Hurricane Katrina was damage to millions of trees caused by high winds. The US Department of Agriculture's Forest Service estimated timber losses of up to 3 billion cubic feet with a commercial value of about $1.3 billion across nearly 3.5 million acres of forestland in Mississippi alone. Damage was particularly severe within sixty miles of the coast, although forests throughout the state were affected. Even where trees were not blown down, the combination of high winds and intense precipitation defoliated trees and damaged tree crowns, depositing large amounts of leaf litter and woody debris on the ground and in streams.

The wind caused a variety of immediate damage. Most directly, Hurricane Katrina resulted in a reduction in standing forest biomass and shifts in forest composition because of differences in species susceptibility to high wind speeds. Nearly 20 percent of the standing volume of timber was destroyed, with up to a 40 percent loss near the coast; by comparison, 1969's Hurricane Camille made an almost identical landfall but resulted in an average loss of only 11 percent of standing volume. Such changes influenced suitability and usage of habitat for animal species. For example, roughly half of all cavity trees for the endangered red-cockaded woodpecker in the De Soto National Forest were lost, and migratory birds had to shift their habitat usage in the Pearl River bottoms and likely on several barrier islands off the Mississippi coast. Exposure to higher levels of sunlight caused by fallen trees increased the susceptibility of forestlands to invasive nonnative species such as Chinese tallow tree (*Triadica sebifera*) and cogon grass (*Imperata brasiliensis*), which are prevalent in the damaged areas.

In addition to altering plant and wildlife habitat, the dead and damaged trees greatly increased fuel for wildfires a problem exacerbated by a moderate to severe drought in the months after the hurricane. The downed trees also served as a haven for forest insects and diseases, including southern pine beetle and black turpentine beetle, which thrive on fallen trees and can harm living trees. Decomposition and combustion of dead and downed trees has also led to the release of large quantities of carbon dioxide into the atmosphere.

The second major cause of ecological damage associated with Katrina was the storm surge, which was exceptionally high as a consequence of the massive size of the hurricane, the strength of the system just prior to landfall, the intense low central pressure at landfall, and the shallow offshore waters. Estimates from a range of sources indicate that the surge was between twenty-four and thirty feet along the portion of the Mississippi coast centered on St. Louis Bay (including the communities of Waveland, Bay St. Louis, Pass Christian, and Long Beach) and was between seventeen and twenty-two feet along the eastern half of the Mississippi coast from Gulfport to Pascagoula. It penetrated at least six miles inland and up to twelve miles inland along bays and rivers, crossing Interstate 10 in many locations.

The storm surge affected coastal ecosystems through two mechanisms. Mechanical damage resulted from the dynamic force of the water itself—for example, when the surge moved sediment from wetlands, beaches, and coastal barrier islands to other land areas. The storm surge and waves from Hurricane Katrina completely inundated several barrier islands off the Mississippi coast, including Petit Bois, Horn, East Ship, West Ship, Cat, and the Chandeleur Islands, resulting in significant land loss, submersion of wildlife habitat, and damage to seagrass beds. These islands serve as buffers against hurricanes and storm surges and provide important wildlife habitat, and the loss of associated seagrass beds can affect the aquatic life that spawns, nests, and feeds there. Damage to oyster beds from siltation and contamination was also high along the northern Gulf Coast. Mechanical damage to vegetation, such as bark stripping and uprooting, as well as burial by deposited sediments was particularly notable on barrier islands and in the narrow belt along the coastline near US Highway 90.

In addition, inundation by seawater in the surge zone led to extensive changes in soil characteristics, including salinity, pH, conductivity, and soil chemistry, and salt spray contributed to defoliation of trees, particularly pines. Such changes can lead to extended tree mortality and slow forest recovery.

While Hurricane Katrina had a number of short-term ecological effects, the longer-term impacts will be under investigation for years to come. Many of the initial effects will likely

K

be short-lived, but in some coastal systems storm effects may have pushed ecosystems past a threshold, resulting in extensive and potentially irreversible damage.

John A. Kupfer
University of South Carolina

Douglas Brinkley, *The Great Deluge: Hurricane Katrina, New Orleans, and the Mississippi Gulf Coast* (2007); by William H. Cooke, Katarzyna Grala, David Evans, and Curtis Collins, *Journal of Forestry* (December 2007); Gaye S. Farris, Gregory J. Smith, Michael P. Crane, Charles R. Demas, Lisa L. Robbins, and Dawn L. Lavoie, eds., *Science and the Storms: The USGS Response to the Hurricanes of 2005* (2007); Hermann M. Fritz, Chris Blount, Robert Sokoloski, Justin Singleton, Andrew Fuggle, Brian G. McAdoo, Andrew Moore, Chad Grass, and Banks Tate, *Journal of Geotechnical and Geoenvironmental Engineering* (May 2008); John A. Kupfer, Aaron T. Myers, Sarah E. McLane, and Ginni Melton, *Ecosystems* (February 2008); Pervaze A. Sheikh, *Congressional Research Service Report for Congress* (February 2006); James Patterson Smith, *Hurricane Katrina: The Mississippi Story* (2012).

Kearney, Belle
(1863–1939) Temperance Lecturer and Political Activist

A leader in Mississippi's movement for suffrage for women, Belle Kearney was born in Madison County on 6 March 1863, the daughter of Walter Gunston Kearney, a planter and politician, and Susannah Owens Kearney. Belle was educated at nearby Canton Ladies Academy and tutored students at home before accepting a teaching position in the Mississippi public school system. During the summer Kearney furthered her own education, attending the Normal College at Iuka and an adult lecture program at the Southern Chautauqua at Monteagle, Tennessee.

Inspired by the oratory of Frances E. Willard, president of the Woman's Christian Temperance Union (WCTU), Kearney abandoned teaching for a career as a lecturer and exponent of prohibition. At the 1889 Mississippi WCTU convention in Crystal Springs, she was appointed state superintendent and organizer of the Young Woman's Christian Temperance Union and the Loyal Temperance Legion. Describing the WCTU as "the discoverer, the developer of Southern women," Kearney traveled throughout Mississippi, lecturing, organizing local chapters, and conducting business meetings. In 1891 she became a national lecturer and organizer for the WCTU, and four years later she was elected the organization's state president, though she soon resigned to attend the WCTU's international convention in London.

After lecturing and traveling through Europe, Kearney returned to the United States and wrote an autobiography, *A Slaveholder's Daughter* (1900), which included her thoughts on race, class, and the role of women in the postwar South. She also took up the cause of woman suffrage, a movement that was closely allied with the WCTU. She was appointed vice president of the Mississippi Woman Suffrage Association in 1897 and became an outspoken advocate for the need to enfranchise literate white women to "insure immediate and durable white supremacy, honestly attained." Her whites-only position was not endorsed by the National American Woman Suffrage Association, and in 1906 Kearney established the Southern Woman Suffrage Conference, which tried but failed to persuade the Mississippi legislature to enfranchise literate white women.

Undeterred, Kearney remained a strong advocate of suffrage while becoming active in the Social Purity Movement, which promoted higher moral standards and sex education. In 1907 Kearney served as field secretary for the World Purity Federation, and in 1921 she published *Conqueror or Conquered*, a novel that warned of the dangers of venereal disease.

The passage of the Nineteenth Amendment in 1919 opened up the possibility of a political career. Kearney ran unsuccessfully for the US Senate in 1922 but became the first woman elected to the Mississippi State Senate the following year. She devoted her time in office to improving opportunities for women and campaigning for tougher Prohibition legislation, with limited success. While she helped to win the introduction of prayer at the commencement of each Senate session, she failed to garner support for antilynching laws. After completing her term, Kearny embarked on another series of lecture tours, finally returning to Vernon Heights, where she died in 1939.

Giselle Roberts
La Trobe University, Melbourne,
Australia

Belle Kearney Papers, Mississippi Department of Archives and History; Nancy Carol Tipton, "'It Is My Duty': The Public Career of Belle Kearney" (master's thesis, University of Mississippi, 1975); Marjorie Spruill Wheeler, *New Women of the New South: The Leaders of the Woman Suffrage Movement in the Southern States* (1993).

Keaton, Russell
(1909–1945) Cartoonist

Russell Keaton was a noted cartoonist and one of the first to use a woman as the main character in an aviation cartoon. Born in Corinth, Mississippi, on 15 May 1909 to Ernest and Velma Rinehart Keaton, he began drawing after his father's death in 1913. Keaton attended school in Corinth until his senior year, when he went to live with an aunt in Huntsville, Alabama. After graduating in 1927, Keaton briefly attended the University of Tennessee. Dismayed to find that he could not take art courses until his junior year, Keaton left in 1928 to attend the Chicago Academy of Fine Arts.

The same year, the National Newspaper Service began the comic strip *Buck Rogers* and contacted the Chicago Academy in search of an artist to draw the strip's Sunday version. Keaton was recommended, and he began his work on *Buck Rogers* in January 1929. In 1932, Keaton married Virginia LaGarde, also of Corinth.

Keaton's work on *Buck Rogers* was uncredited, and in 1933 he left the strip to become an artist for the aviation comic strip *Skyroads*, where he was allowed to sign his own name. In addition, *Skyroads* did not require Keaton to live in Chicago, so he returned to Corinth, where he became a member of the local Rotary Club and the Corinth First Presbyterian Church, serving as deacon and president of Men of the Church and teaching the boys' Sunday school class.

Keaton dreamed of creating his own strip, however, and on 2 October 1939 *Flyin' Jenny* made its debut. Keaton's choice of subject matter came from the interwar popularity of aviation comic strips, his own interest in flying, and the then-novel idea of a female protagonist in an action cartoon. The Keaton family, which now included a daughter, Julie Virginia, moved to Memphis in 1939 so Keaton could take flying lessons. He often sketched *Flyin' Jenny* at the Memphis airport and put the names of Memphis residents in his strip because he "got a kick out of seeing how many find themselves." The Keatons moved back to Corinth in 1941. In an effort to remove some of the strip's work from his own shoulders, Keaton partnered with a number of writers, including famed naval aviator and scriptwriter Frank Wead. In 1943 Keaton joined the Army Air Corps Reserve and served as a flight instructor at the Jackson, Tennessee, Army Contract School while continuing his work on the weekday version of the strip. His family joined him in Jackson, and a second daughter, Mary Janalee, was born in 1943.

The Keatons returned to Corinth in 1944, but Russell Keaton was soon diagnosed with acute leukemia, and he died on 13 February 1945. The artist for the Sunday version of *Flyin' Jenny*, Marcus Swayze, took over the strip, which folded in 1946.

Brian S. Miller
Charleston Southern University

Virginia Keaton Anderson, *The Aviation Art of Russell Keaton* (1995); *Memphis Press-Scimitar* (14 February 1945).

Kells, Harriet B.
(1841–1913) Prohibition Leader and Editor

Harriet Kells helped establish the first chapter of the Woman's Christian Temperance Union (WCTU) in Mississippi and served as editor of the organization's *Mississippi White Ribbon*. Kells played a primary role in inviting the nation's leading Prohibition speaker, Frances E. Willard, to speak in Jackson, a visit that inspired the first serious attempts to form Prohibition organizations in the state.

Born in Natchez, Harriet Barfield Coulson spent parts of her childhood in Jefferson County and later in Jackson. After marrying William H. Kells in 1864, Harriet taught school in East Tennessee, served as a principal in Pass Christian, and worked as a health officer at the Industrial Institute and College (now Mississippi University for Women) in Columbus and taught school in Jackson. Kells became the *White Ribbon*'s first editor in 1889 and remained the major figure in its publication until her death.

Like many Prohibitionists, Kells condemned alcohol for destroying home lives. She spoke idealistically of the ways women could uplift male society, condemned "drunken, ignorant black men," and believed that Prohibition would solve problems of crime and racial conflict. Like many WCTU leaders, Kells also supported the goal of suffrage for women. Fellow temperance and women's rights advocate Belle Kearney called Kells "one of the brainiest, most cultured and advanced women in the South."

In the 1890s, Kells's editorial talent allowed her to work with Willard as the editor of Chicago's *Union Signal*, the nation's leading WCTU journal. The *Mississippi White Ribbon* suspended publication during her absence. She returned to Mississippi and to her job as editor in 1904, living first in Fayette and then Jackson.

Kells used her editorial position to dramatize differences between her opinions and those of her opponents and critics. The *Jackson Daily News* once criticized Kells for her "sharp tongue." As a leader of the wing of the Mississippi Prohibition movement that demanded a state law, she criticized supporters of local-option laws, primarily Methodist minister Charles B. Galloway, for compromising with evil. In 1904 she criticized ministers more broadly for their lack of interest in the politics of Prohibition: "The supine negligence and criminal silence of the church is responsible mainly for present liquor-soaked, law-defying conditions in Mississippi."

Kells participated in the successful campaign that resulted in Mississippi's passage of a 1907 law banning the sale of alcohol and then used the power of the WCTU to demand enforcement of statewide Prohibition. She believed that women should have the vote and that until they did, they should work to convince men to support their causes: "Every woman can *talk* [Prohibition] into every man's consciousness."

K

Kells served as president of the state WCTU from 1909 to 1913, spending part of 1910 in Scotland as a representative to the organization's international conference. She died in 1913.

Ted Ownby
University of Mississippi

Ruth Bordin, *Woman and Temperance: The Quest for Power and Liberty, 1873–1900* (1990); William Graham Davis, "Attacking 'The Matchless Evil': Temperance and Prohibition in Mississippi, 1817–1908" (PhD dissertation, Mississippi State University, 1975); Belle Kearney, *A Slaveholder's Daughter* (1900); *Mississippi White Ribbon* (January 1914); Mary Jane Smith, "Constructing White Womanhood in Public: Progressive White Women in a New South" (PhD dissertation, Louisiana State University, 2002).

Kelly, Patrick
(1954–1990) Fashion Designer

Celebrated fashion designer Patrick Kelly was born in Vicksburg, Mississippi, on 24 September 1954. Raised primarily by his mother, Letha Kelly, a home economics teacher, and his grandmother, Ethel Rainey, a cook and maid, Kelly developed an interest in fashion at a young age. By his junior year in high school, the self-taught Kelly was creating dresses for neighborhood girls while designing department store windows and sketching newspaper ads. After his 1972 graduation from high school, Kelly enrolled at Jackson State University, where he studied art history and African American history before moving to Atlanta two years later.

There, a job sorting clothes for AMVETS gave him access to clothing, including designer wares, which he refashioned and sold along with some original creations. He also began decorating windows for Rive Gauche, an Yves Saint Laurent boutique. His friendship with model Pat Cleveland subsequently transformed his life. Cleveland encouraged Kelly to move to New York, where he briefly attended the Parsons School of Design.

With Kelly financially unstable, Cleveland then suggested a move to Paris and anonymously sent Kelly a one-way ticket in 1979. Kelly became a costume designer for Le Palace, a nightclub, and freelanced for designer Paco Rabanne. When Kelly began adorning his signature body-hugging jersey dresses with colorful buttons, a practice inspired by his grandmother, his star began to shine.

Kelly's personal clothing—oversized overalls and a cap—the southern dinners he sold when money was tight, and the "honey chiles" and other southern expressions that peppered his speech charmed the French. He closed his fashion shows with gospel music. However, his practice of pinning a miniature doll resembling a pickaninny on his designs as well as on people he encountered proved controversial, especially as his fame grew in the United States.

Victoire, an exclusive Paris boutique, began selling his designs in 1985, and the next year he created Patrick Kelly Paris with his business and personal partner, Bjorn Amelan. A 1987 interview with Gloria Steinem on NBC's *Today Show* led to an introduction to Linda Wachner, CEO of apparel manufacturer Warnaco. Negotiations tipped in Kelly's favor when actress Bette Davis appeared on *The David Letterman Show* wearing a body-hugging Patrick Kelly original and raved about him. Significant licensing deals with Vogue Patterns for his designs and Streamline Industries for his buttons also followed. In 1988 Kelly became the first American and the first black admitted to the Chambre Syndicale du Prêt-à-Porter des Couturiers et des Créateurs de Mode, the governing body of the French fashion industry, and showed his collection at the Louvre. Kelly sought to design clothes that would "make you smile," and his dresses featured bright colors, bold patterns, and eye-catching trim. On the brink of becoming a household name, Kelly died in Paris on 1 January 1990. Bone marrow disease and a brain tumor were announced as the cause of death; in reality, however, Kelly had contracted AIDS and died of complications of the disease.

Kelly's work has garnered critical attention since his death. A 2004 exhibition, *Patrick Kelly: A Retrospective*, at the Brooklyn Museum of Art was guest curated by Thelma Golden and revealed that Kelly was far from racially naive. The exhibition included not only his designs but also more than eight thousand examples of advertising, dolls, and other items employing racial stereotypes from Kelly's personal collection of black memorabilia, including items celebrating Diana Ross, Michael Jackson, and Josephine Baker. In 2014 the Philadelphia Museum of Art presented another exhibition, *Patrick Kelly: Runway of Love*, again featuring not only his ensembles but also videos of his fashion shows, photographs, and items from his memorabilia collection.

Ronda Racha Penrice
Atlanta, Georgia

Robin Givhan, *Washington Post* (30 May 2004); *Patrick Kelly: Runway of Love* exhibition website, www.philamuseum.org/exhibitions/799.html; Horacio Silva, *New York Times* (22 February 2004).

Kemper County

Located east of Jackson, along the Alabama-Mississippi border, Kemper County was founded on 23 December 1833. The Tombigbee River crosses Kemper in the east, and the Chickasawhay River wends its way through the county's southern region. The lands now incorporated into Kemper were ceded to the United States by the Choctaw Tribe under the 1830 Treaty of Dancing Rabbit Creek. The county is named for Reuben, Nathan, and Samuel Kemper, a trio of brothers who fought under Gen. Andrew Jackson in the War of 1812. De Kalb, the county's seat, is named for Revolutionary War general Baron Johann de Kalb.

Kemper County emerged in the 1830s as a rapidly growing part of eastern Mississippi. In the 1840 census, the county reported 4,623 free people and 3,040 slaves; twenty years later the county's population neared twelve thousand and was about half free and half slave. Kemper's farms and plantations practiced mixed agriculture, concentrating on cotton, corn, sweet potatoes, and livestock. John J. Pettus, Mississippi's governor during the Civil War, hailed from Kemper. Though no battles took place in the county, it was subject to a number of raids by US troops, and exceptionally high numbers of Kemper citizens fought as Confederate soldiers.

By 1880 Kemper had grown to 15,719 people, with African Americans slightly outnumbering whites. The county also had a small Native American population as well as forty-one foreign-born residents. Agriculture was typical of Mississippi in both the size of Kemper's farms and the percentage of farm ownership. Industry was slow to develop in the county, and its twenty manufacturing establishments employed only twenty-nine men.

By the late nineteenth century the county was known as Bloody Kemper because of its high homicide rate during the Reconstruction era. The most notorious example of county's postbellum hostilities was the Chisholm Massacre. Political conflicts between Democrats and Republicans led to the 1875 murder of Republican sheriff W. W. Chisholm, his family, and a number of African Americans. A mysterious series of murders in the 1890s by a Kemper County doctor helped to seal the county's violent reputation.

In 1900 Kemper was home to 20,492 people, about half of them African American. Although Kemper remained primarily agricultural, it had forty-seven manufacturing establishments employing almost a hundred workers. Only a quarter of Kemper's African American farmers owned their land, while more than two-thirds of white farmers did so.

On the eve of the Civil War, Kemper County had forty-two churches, the fifth-highest number in the state. Most were either Baptist or Methodist. By 1916 most of Kemper's church members were Baptist, with those belonging to Missionary Baptist and Southern Baptist congregations comprising well over half of the county's churchgoing population. Most of Kemper's remaining congregants were either Methodist or Presbyterian.

By 1930 Kemper's population had increased slightly to about twenty-two thousand, more than half of them African Americans. The county's industrial sector had undergone significant expansion, employing almost a thousand workers. The largest industrial employer was the Sumter Lumber Company in Electric Mills, which was unique both for its tremendous size and for its use of electric rather than steam power. Only 37 percent of the county's farmers owned their land as the Great Depression set in.

Over the next thirty years Kemper's population decreased dramatically, falling to 12,277 in 1960. Kemper was home to a large Choctaw community. A majority of the labor force was employed in agriculture, with fewer than five hundred manufacturing workers, almost all of them in furniture production. Most of the county's farmland was devoted to corn, cotton, cattle, and soybeans. Kemper was one of the poorest Mississippi counties throughout the 1980s and ranked last in the state in per capita income in both 1960 and 1970.

John C. Stennis was born in De Kalb in 1901 and went on to represent Mississippi in the US Senate from 1947 to 1989.

By 2010 Kemper's population had declined to 10,456, and the county was one of very few in east-central Mississippi with an African American majority.

Mississippi Encyclopedia Staff
University of Mississippi

Charles Ray Fulton, "A History of Kemper County, Mississippi, 1860–1910" (master's thesis, Mississippi State University, 1968); Kemper County Historical Association, *Kemper County: Sesquicentennial Celebration, 1833–1983* (1983); Mississippi State Planning Commission, *Progress Report on State Planning in Mississippi* (1938); *Mississippi Statistical Abstract*, Mississippi State University (1952–2010); Charles Sydnor and Claude Bennett, *Mississippi History* (1939); University of Virginia Library, Historical Census Browser website, http://mapserver.lib.virginia.edu; E. Nolan Waller and Dani A. Smith, *Growth Profiles of Mississippi's Counties, 1960–1980* (1985).

Kemper Rebellion

Reuben, Samuel, and Nathan Kemper, sons of a Virginia Baptist preacher, migrated to the Feliciana Parish area of West Florida in 1799. There they helped found and manage a "settlement store" for John Smith, a US senator from Ohio. The business dovetailed with Spanish efforts to encourage American settlement in the area, but the store's failure devolved into a dispute over nearly forty-eight hundred pesos Reuben Kemper owed to Smith.

The Kempers remained in and around West Florida. They owned land and slaves in Feliciana and worked Smith's land for him but seemed to have no real ties to the community. At the same time, the brothers had purchased an inn in Pinckneyville, Mississippi, just over the border. By early June 1804 Smith was attempting to expel the Kempers from his property, and Nathan, Samuel, and four companions resisted the eviction with force, fighting off authorities for several days. Nathan and Samuel Kemper eventually fled across "the line," as residents called the West Florida–Louisiana border, to Pinckneyville, beyond the range of Spanish officials. Assembling a gang of about twenty men, they returned to Spanish territory in mid-June, accosted some locals, and spent a few weeks stealing cattle, slaves, and anything else they could carry away. Spanish officials captured some of the men, though a raiding party led by the Kempers subsequently freed them.

Reuben Kemper had escaped to New Orleans, where he wrote to American officials in Mississippi, New Orleans, and Washington, D.C., urging them to intervene in the West Florida affair on the Kempers' behalf. When the US government pardoned the gang members, Spanish officials began to suspect that the Kempers had American backing. In large part because the Kempers' actions in June 1804 were not directed at any institution or group of officials, Spanish officials never viewed the violence as a true rebellion in the sense that it had any larger organization and never filed complaints with the US government. Instead, the Spaniards treated the incidents as simple banditry of the type that had plagued the area for decades and issued an order to take the gang members "dead or alive," confiscated their West Florida property, pardoned members of the gang willing to lay down their arms and leave Florida peacefully, and forbade the Kempers from returning to Spanish territory.

Nathan and Samuel crossed into Spanish territory in early August, bearing a declaration of independence as well as a flag featuring blue and white stripes and two stars on a blue field. This act, combined with confessions from some gang members, made the Kempers' actions a true attempt at political rebellion, and the Spaniards began to label them traitors. Chased back across the line within a few days, the Kempers reverted to cattle and horse thievery until a Spanish militia crossed the Mississippi border, snatched Nathan and Samuel from their beds, and put them on a boat to Baton Rouge. A raiding party freed the brothers, who made their escape to New Providence in the British Caribbean, where they spent several years attempting without success to raise support for a British invasion of West Florida. Some historians have glorified this event as evidence of nascent anti-Spanish sentiment in West Florida. Nevertheless, the Kemper "rebellion" was nothing more than a series of border raids led by a few disgruntled settlers.

Andrew McMichael
Western Kentucky University

Archives of the Spanish Government of West Florida: A Series of 18 Bound Volumes of Written Documents Mostly in the Spanish Language, vols. 2, 4, 7; Isaac Joslin Cox, *The West Florida Controversy, 1798–1813: A Study in American Diplomacy* (1918); Andrew McMichael, *Louisiana History* (Spring 2002); Vicente Sebastián Pintado Papers, Library of Congress; Robert W. Wilhelmy, *Cincinnati Historical Society Bulletin* (1970).

Kennard, Clyde

(1927–1963) Activist

The landscape of the modern civil rights era is replete with untold episodes of human tragedy. In civil-rights-era Mississippi, among the less known human tragedies is that of Clyde Kennard.

Born on 12 June 1927, one of five children of Will and Laura Kennard, Clyde Kennard grew up near Hattiesburg. At age eighteen he joined the US Army, serving from 1945 to 1952 and earning both a high school diploma and numerous awards, including the Korean Service Medal, the United Nations Service Medal, the Good Conduct Medal, and the Bronze Service Star. While in the military, Kennard began studying at Fayetteville Teachers College, near Fort Bragg, North Carolina, where he was stationed. Kennard transferred to the University of Chicago soon after leaving the military but returned to Forrest County after a couple of semesters to assist his mother with her chicken farm.

In 1955 Kennard telephoned Mississippi Southern College (MSC, now the University of Southern Mississippi), an all-white school in Hattiesburg, and requested a catalog. Several weeks later he called again, this time requesting an application for admission and indicating that he was African American. After failing to receive an application, Kennard visited the campus, where he met with MSC president W. D. McCain and college registrar M. W. Kenna, who told Kennard that he would have to satisfy all entrance requirements, including recommendation letters from five alumni from his county. McCain told the Mississippi State Sovereignty Commission that Kennard's grades were "above average" and that he had "met all of the requirements with the exception of furnishing the five recommendations from alumni in the county from which he was applying." Officials refused to provide Kennard with the names of alumni from Forrest County, and he was denied admission.

In September 1958 Kennard resumed his efforts. The Sovereignty Commission worked to find "derogatory information" on him and enlisted conservative black leaders to "persuade him that it was in the best interest of all concerned that he withdraw and desist from filing an application for admission to Mississippi Southern College." In early 1959, Gov. J. P. Coleman met with Kennard and told him that "it was not the appropriate time" for him to attend MSC. Kennard temporarily withdrew his application but decided to try again that fall.

On 15 September, Kennard attempted to register but was told that he would not be admitted because he had failed to supply a transcript from the University of Chicago, a point he disputed. As Kennard was leaving campus, local law enforcement officials stopped him and arrested him on charges of "driving at an excessive speed" and of illegal possession of "five pints of whiskey and other liquor under his front seat." Justice Court judge T. C. Hobby found him guilty of both charges and imposed a six-hundred-dollar fine.

Kennard remained undeterred, but in September 1960 he was arrested and charged with possession of stolen chicken feed worth twenty-five dollars, a felony offense under Mississippi law. An all-white jury convicted Kennard, and circuit judge Stanton Hall sentenced Kennard to the maximum term allowed under law, seven years at Parchman Penitentiary.

Kennard endured brutal treatment and was forced to work six days a week in Parchman's cotton fields. He began experiencing severe abdominal pains and suffered significant weight loss, and doctors at the University of Mississippi Hospital in Jackson found a large lesion on his colon. Nevertheless, Kennard was denied medical care and forced to continue working at Parchman, where other prisoners carried him between his cell and the fields. As information about Kennard's condition became known in late 1962, civil rights leaders and Kennard's mother launched a public campaign to persuade Gov. Ross Barnett to grant Kennard clemency, but Barnett resisted until February 1963. Kennard then traveled to Chicago for treatment, but his cancer had reached an advanced stage, and he died on 4 July 1963.

Despite attempts by John Howard Griffin, author of *Black Like Me*, and others to tell Kennard's story, he remained largely forgotten, overshadowed by such events as James Meredith's desegregation of the University of Mississippi in September 1962 and Medgar Evers's murder less than a month before Kennard's death. In 1991, however, the *Jackson Clarion-Ledger* published secret documents that showed that the Sovereignty Commission had framed Kennard. Over the next fifteen years, supporters waged a campaign to win him a posthumous pardon, and these efforts finally bore fruit on 12 May 2006, when circuit judge Robert Helfrich declared Kennard innocent of all charges.

The student services building at the University of Southern Mississippi is named in honor of Kennard and Walter Washington, the first African American to receive a doctorate from the institution. In addition, the school offers the Kennard Scholars Program, an honors program for "students committed to academic excellence, leadership development, and citizenship" that "gives particular attention to students from underrepresented and diverse communities."

Dernoral Davis
Jackson State University

Erle Johnston, *Mississippi Defiant Years, 1953–1973: An Interpretive Documentary with Personal Experiences* (1990); Timothy J. Minchin and John A. Salmond, *Journal of Mississippi History* 81 (Fall 2009); Mississippi History Now website, http://mshistorynow.mdah.state.ms.us; David Sansing, *Making Haste Slowly: The Troubled History of Higher Education in Mississippi* (1990); Southern Miss Now website, news.usm.edu.

Key, Al
(1905–1976)

Key, Fred
(1909–1971)
Aviation Pioneers

In the mid-1930s Meridian, Mississippi, like many midsized southern cities, began seeking funds to build a modern airport. The bumpy grass runway had little appeal to the new commercial airlines of the day, and Meridian's boosters wanted their city to appear on the world's air map. The airport's operators, Algene Earl Key and Frederick Maurice Key, thought that a publicity stunt would generate interest in the project, and they decided to establish a new world record for sustained flight. To do so, they had to overcome numerous obstacles, including finding safe ways to refuel and service their plane while in flight.

Securing the help of A. D. Hunter and James Keeton, the Key Brothers located a Curtis-Robbins high-wing monoplane powered by a 165-horsepower Wright Whirlwind engine. They named the little plane the *Ole Miss*. The aircraft was modified with a one hundred fifty-gallon fuel tank and a catwalk from the enclosed cockpit out toward the propeller. The Key Brothers would take turns making the hazardous journey along the catwalk to service the engine and refuel the plane. They also designed a spill-free air-to-air refueling nozzle to keep fuel from splattering over the aircraft and starting a fire. During the record-setting flight, Hunter and Keeton would fly a similar plane above *Ole Miss*, lowering engine oil and food as well as refueling via the nozzle-hose contraption. The brothers' wives, Louise and Evelyn, would provide meals for Hunter and Keeton to deliver.

The Key Brothers promoted their proposed adventure in the local media, and after two unsuccessful attempts in 1934, on 4 June 1935 a modest crowd watched as they lifted off the grass strip at 12:32 p.m. Their flight plan took them on looping patterns above the greater Meridian area. As the Keys remained aloft for first one week and then two and three, intrigued local citizens watched from the ground, joking that Louise and Evelyn would divorce their husbands for desertion.

For nearly four weeks, the brothers took turns flying and servicing the plane, enduring a lack of restful sleep, thunderstorms, and filthy conditions that inflamed their eyes. In addition, an electrical fire broke out on board, and the Curtis nearly collided with the refueling plane on several occasions.

At 6:06 p.m. on 1 July 1935 the Key brothers landed the *Ole Miss* in the middle of the grassy strip in front of more than thirty thousand onlookers. A few months later, the City of Meridian began building a new airport, Key Field.

During their twenty-seven-days aloft, the Key Brothers flew for 653 hours, 34 minutes, and covered 52,320 miles—enough to circle the earth twice. The Wright engine made more than sixty-one million revolutions, consumed six thousand gallons of fuel, and used three hundred gallons of oil while maintaining an average airspeed of eighty miles per hour. It received fuel and supplies from the other aircraft 432 times. The Keys' record for sustained flight would not be broken until the Apollo moon missions of the 1960s.

In 1955 Fred Key had the *Ole Miss* restored and flew the plane to Washington, D.C., where it remains on display at the Smithsonian National Air and Space Museum. The Army Air Corps adopted the Keys' style of in-flight refueling during World War II, and a modified version of the valve that Hunter invented for their flight remains in use by US military aircraft.

Both Al and Fred Key served as bomber pilots during World War II, winning the Distinguished Flying Cross and other honors. Al Key remained in the US Air Force until 1960, when he retired with the rank of colonel. He served as mayor of Meridian from 1965 until 1973. Fred Key ran Key Brothers Aviation Service at Key Field until his death.

David L. Weatherford
Northwest Florida State College

Stephen Owen, *The Flying Key Brothers and Their Flight to Remember* (1985); Edward Park, *Smithsonian Magazine* (1997); Smithsonian National Air and Space Museum website, www.airandspace.si.edu.

Kimbrough, Junior
(1930–1998) Blues Musician

Rockabilly pioneer Charlie Feathers referred to his friend, fellow musician, and teacher Junior Kimbrough as "the beginning and end of music." While Feathers was famous for his idiosyncratic theories about music, his assessment of Kimbrough highlighted the fact that the bluesman's music was almost a genre unto itself. David Kimbrough Jr. was born in Hudsonville, Mississippi, just north of Holly Springs, on 28 July 1930. His father, three older brothers, and a sister were blues musicians. At age eight he learned guitar from his father, whom he cited as his most important influence, and he was soon playing and singing for friends and family. He recalled that musicians who visited the family home included Fred McDowell, Eli Green, Johnny Woods, and early blues pioneer Gus Cannon.

As a teenager Kimbrough sang in a gospel group, and by the late 1950s he had formed the first incarnation of the Soul Blues Boys, who played at weekend functions in the area. Kimbrough's early electric band was relatively rare among traditional North Mississippi blues artists, and performing in this format differentiated his music from that of other locals such as R. L. Burnside and Mississippi Fred McDowell, who played largely solo or in duos. Feathers, who farmed on the same Hudsonville plantation as Kimbrough, called Kimbrough's music "cottonpatch blues."

In 1968 Kimbrough recorded a session for the Memphis-based Philwood label: a single issued under the name "Junior Kimbell" included a cover of Lowell Fulson's "Tramp." The following year Feathers, who had recorded at Philwood around the same time, recorded with Kimbrough at Kimbrough's juke joint. The song "Feel Good Again" appeared in 1986 on a limited-issue 78 single on the Perfect imprint; it later appeared on the Revenant Charlie Feathers CD *Get with It*.

Kimbrough was otherwise not recorded during the great wave of field recordings in the 1960s and early 1970s. In 1982 he was recorded by Sylvester Oliver of Rust College, resulting in a single on the Highwater label. Kimbrough subsequently gained recognition in blues circles and began appearing at festivals. Several of his songs from a 1984 festival appearance in Georgia appeared on the LP *National Downhome Blues Festival*, vol. 2 (1986).

In 1984 Kimbrough began hosting Sunday afternoon house parties, which soon became a popular local institution, and in 1991 he opened a juke joint in Holly Springs. Kimbrough gained more exposure in 1992 when Oxford's Fat Possum label recorded a CD, *All Night Long*, at Kimbrough's new juke joint in Chulahoma, located on Route 4 about ten miles southwest of Holly Springs. Kimbrough and R. L. Burnside, who also recorded a CD for Fat Possum at the juke joint, played at Junior's Place every Sunday evening, often accompanied by their children. Kimbrough usually played in a trio, accompanied by his son, Kenny Malone (aka Kent Kimbrough), on drums and Burnside's son, Garry, on bass. Rock stars made pilgrimages to the club, which was oddly shaped and adorned with folk art, and it eventually became a popular destination for University of Mississippi undergraduates.

Kimbrough typically performed original songs that were longer than ten minutes each, and writer and critic Robert

Palmer, who produced *All Night Long* and Kimbrough's second Fat Possum CD, *Sad Days, Lonely Nights*, emphasized his music's droning and hypnotic qualities. Kimbrough's music did not sell very well, but it was embraced by critics and many fans of alternative music who appreciated his music's unorthodox qualities and bought into Fat Possum's marketing strategy of offering "Not the Same Old Blues Crap."

Kimbrough performed on a few national tours, including serving as an opening act for proto-punk icon Iggy Pop, but he was otherwise not very interested in traveling outside the area. He continued to host his Sunday evening gatherings and made two more CDs for Fat Possum. He slowed down for health reasons in the mid-1990s and died of a heart attack on 17 January 1998.

After his death, Fat Possum issued a greatest hits package and organized a tribute record consisting of alternative rock bands covering Kimbrough's songs. One of Kimbrough's sons, David Malone (aka David Kimbrough Jr.), has recorded several CDs and consciously pays tribute to his father's music, and Kenny Malone usually sings his father's signature "All Night Long" when performing.

Scott Barretta
Greenwood, Mississippi

Anthony DeCurtis, *You Better Run: The Essential Junior Kimbrough* (2002), liner notes; Sylvester Oliver with David Evans, *Do The Rump!* (1997), liner notes.

Kinard, Frank "Bruiser"
(1914–1985) Athlete

Frank M. "Bruiser" Kinard played offensive and defensive tackle for the University of Mississippi football team from 1935 to 1937. Kinard became the school's first all-American athlete, and his play with Brooklyn Dodgers of the National Football League (NFL) and the New York Yankees of the All-America Football Conference (AAFC) made him a charter member of the Pro Football Hall of Fame.

Born outside Jackson in Pelahatchie, Mississippi, on 23 October 1914, Kinard earned the nickname Bruiser as a punishing tackler and blocker at Jackson Central High School. After graduating in 1933, Kinard briefly attended the University of Alabama but left because Coach Frank Thomas did not like coaching married players. Kinard and his wife, Midge, then moved to Oxford, where he enrolled at the University of Mississippi.

Kinard helped establish the school's football team as a national powerhouse. In the final regular-season game of the 1935 season, Kinard led the Rebel defense in a dominating effort against rival Mississippi State, penetrating the Bulldog backfield and ending plays before they could begin. The 14–6 victory helped earn the University of Mississippi its first postseason bowl invitation.

Though the University of Mississippi recorded a disappointing 5–5–2 finish in 1936, Kinard impressed sportswriters and coaches and earned all–Southeastern Conference and all-America honors at the end of the season. In 1937 Kinard served as team captain, closing out his college career with repeat selections to the all–Southeastern Conference and all-America teams.

In 1938 Kinard began his professional career with the NFL's Brooklyn Dodgers. Kinard's size (around two hundred pounds) made him small for an NFL tackle, but he more than compensated with his speed, durability, and aggressiveness. As in college, Kinard played both offense and defense, and he missed time because of injuries only once. Kinard earned all-NFL honors for Brooklyn five times between 1938 and 1944. After a brief stint in the US Navy during 1945, Kinard played two more years for the New York Yankees of the new and short-lived AAFC. In 1946 Kinard became the first player to have earned both all-NFL and all-AAFC honors.

Kinard retired from professional football in 1948 and returned to the University of Mississippi as an assistant to Coach John Vaught. Kinard remained in the position until 1970 and helped to oversee some of its most successful teams in the school's football history. He then served as the university's athletic director until 1973.

Kinard won election as a charter member of the Mississippi Sports Hall of Fame, the Orange Bowl Hall of Fame, and the Pro Football Hall of Fame.

Thomas John Carey
University of Mississippi

W. G. Barner, *Mississippi Mayhem: A Game-by-Game History of the Ole Miss–Mississippi State Football Rivalry, 1901–1980* (1982); *Jackson Clarion-Ledger* (8 September 1985); *New York Times* (9 September 1985); William M. Sorrels and Charles Cavagnaro, *Ole Miss Rebels: Mississippi Football* (1976).

King, Albert (Albert Nelson)
(1923–1992) Blues Musician

Born Albert Nelson on 25 April 1923 in Indianola, Mississippi, Albert King was an influential blues singer and guitarist. In 1931 he moved with his mother, Mary Blevins; stepfather, Will Nelson; and twelve siblings to Osceola, Arkansas, where

Albert King (Courtesy Blues Archive, Department of Archives and Special Collections, J. D. Williams Library, University of Mississippi)

an album recorded with a group of white southern rock singers; an Elvis Presley tribute album, *Blues for Elvis: Albert King Does the King's Things*; and a comedy album with Albert Brooks. King retired from recording in the 1980s but continued to perform, influencing and encouraging younger blues players such as Stevie Ray Vaughan and Robert Cray. He was inducted into the Blues Foundation Hall of Fame in 1983.

King died of a heart attack on 21 December 1992, two days after a concert in Los Angeles. His funeral procession was held on Memphis's Beale Street, and he was buried in Edmondson, Arkansas.

Taylor Hagood
Florida Atlantic University

Sheldon Harris, *Blues Who's Who: A Biographical Dictionary of Blues Singers* (1994); Gérard Herzhaft, *Encyclopedia of the Blues* (1997); Greg Johnson, *Blues Notes: A Monthly Publication of the Cascade Blues Association* (September 1999); Robert Santelli, *The Big Book of Blues: A Biographical Encyclopedia* (2001).

they worked as sharecroppers. His early musical influences included Blind Lemon Jefferson, Robert Nighthawk, Elmore James, and Lonnie Johnson as well as his stepfather, who played guitar. King taught himself to play first a homemade cigar box guitar and then a real guitar, which he purchased for $1.25 when he was nineteen years old. He developed a unique style in which he played the guitar left-handed but held the instrument upside-down and strung for a right-hander.

Supporting himself primarily by driving a bulldozer, King first performed with the In the Groove Boys. By the late 1940s he traveled to St. Louis and Chicago to become a professional musician. His first recordings were cut on the Parrot label, with "Bad Luck Blues" and "Be on Your Merry Way" enjoying reasonable popularity. After recording on the Bobbin, King, and Coun-Tree labels, King moved to Memphis in 1966 and began recording on Stax, a new soul label. Various singles were compiled into a 1967 album, *Born under a Bad Sign*, which included a number of hits, including the title track, "As the Years Go By," and "The Hunter." The album catapulted King into international fame among both black and white audiences. A top-selling live album, *Live Wire/Blues Power*, followed, further securing his importance in the music world.

King continued to perform and record throughout the 1970s. A large man (6' 4" and 250 pounds) who played a Flying V–model Gibson guitar he called Lucy, King resembled another famous blues artist, B. B. King. Both men were from Indianola, and Albert occasionally claimed to be B. B.'s half-brother. Albert King's varied and innovative musical efforts included a performance with the St. Louis Symphony; a show at the all-white Jackson First Baptist Church; *Lovejoy*,

King, B. B. (Riley B. King)
(1925–2015) Blues Musician

Riley B. King was born to Albert Lee King and Nora Ella King on 16 September 1925 just outside the towns of Itta Bena and Berclair, Mississippi. When Riley was four, his mother went to live with another man, and the boy moved from household to household for several years, living mostly with his maternal grandmother, Elnora Farr, in Kilmichael. Though he was raised in a Baptist tradition, the sanctified preaching of the Holiness Church had the greatest impact on King. His uncle's brother-in-law, Archie Fair, often played the guitar during church services and taught the boy a few chords. He had a powerful voice and often sang solos in church. During the winter months when he was not working the fields, King attended the Elkhorn Baptist School in Kilmichael, where teacher Luther Henson instilled a zest for learning and self-improvement that drove King throughout his life.

King toiled in the fields around Kilmichael until he was almost eighteen years old, when he moved to the Johnson Barrett Plantation outside Indianola. Here, he helped form a five-member group, the Famous St. John Gospel Singers, that performed in churches and on a few live radio broadcasts. King also began playing blues on street corners and listening to other bluesmen, such as Robert Jr. Lockwood and Sonny Boy Williamson II. In 1946, just over two years after moving to Indianola, King moved to Memphis to make his living as a musician.

B. B. King (Courtesy Blues Archive, Department of Archives and Special Collections, J. D. Williams Library, University of Mississippi)

In Memphis, King lived with his second cousin, Bukka White, for about ten months, learning from White and other musicians. King found it difficult to compete with the numerous Beale Street bluesmen, however, and returned to Indianola and the Barrett farm in 1947. Back in Memphis the following year, King benefited from some good luck. Williamson had mistakenly booked himself for two shows at the same time and allowed King to perform for a live blues show on KWEM. Listeners loved King's sound, and his career took off. King sang an advertising jingle for another Memphis radio station, WDIA, and soon became host of the station's *Sepia Swing Club*, which showcased African American musicians. As a disc jockey, he cultivated the nickname Beale Street Blues Boy, which was later shortened to Blues Boy and ultimately B. B.

King recorded his first songs for the Bullet label in 1949 and went on to record primarily for Modern Records subsidiaries RPM, Kent, and Crown until 1962, when he began recording for ABC-Paramount. King's first big hit came in 1951, with a cover of Lowell Fulson's "Three o'Clock Blues." King's first national tour followed, and other songs, among them "Every Day I Have the Blues" and "Sweet Little Angel," rose up the R&B chart. His biggest crossover hit, "The Thrill Is Gone" (1970), made it to No. 3 on the R&B chart and No. 15 on the pop music chart. The King of the Blues went on to perform with many noted R&B, soul, and rock musicians, including Bobby "Blue" Bland, John Lee Hooker, Etta James, Eric Clapton, the Rolling Stones, and U2, and maintained a rigorous touring schedule well into his eighties. King's music is often defined by his powerful voice, rooted in a gospel tradition, and his distinctive guitar sound, which uses linear melodic lines and sustaining key notes to fuse clean jazz soloing and gospel cries.

A staunch supporter of civil rights, King helped Charles Evers, brother of Medgar Evers, organize the Medgar Evers Homecoming Festival and performed there for many years. King also performed at an annual homecoming festival in Indianola. In 1972 he helped start the Foundation for the Advancement of Inmate Rehabilitation and Recreation, and he frequently performed at prisons.

King was inducted into the Blues Hall of Fame in 1980 and into the Rock and Roll Hall of Fame in 1987. He won fifteen Grammy Awards, including Best Male R&B Vocal (for "The Thrill Is Gone") and eight Best Traditional Blues Albums. His many and varied contributions to music and the arts as well as his spirit of giving back to local communities earned him honorary degrees from Tougaloo College, Yale University, Berklee College of Music, Rhodes College of Memphis, and Mississippi Valley State University. The University of Mississippi named him honorary professor of southern studies.

A widely acclaimed 2012 documentary, *The Life of Riley*, told the story of King's life and music. In addition, on 21 February of that year, he performed at the White House, and Pres. Barack Obama sang along with King on a few lines of "Sweet Home Chicago." He gave his final performance at Chicago's House of Blues on 3 October 2014 and died in his sleep at his Las Vegas home on 14 May 2015. He was buried at Indianola's B. B. King Museum and Delta Interpretation Center, which opened in 2008 "to honor the life and music of one of the most accomplished musicians of our time" and "to share the rich cultural heritage of the Mississippi Delta."

Greg Johnson
University of Mississippi

B. B. King website, www.bbking.com; B. B. King Museum and Delta Interpretive Center website, www.bbkingmuseum.org; Sebastian Danchin, *"Blues Boy": The Life and Music of B. B. King* (1998); B. B. King, *Blues All Around Me: The Autobiography of B. B. King* (1996); Richard Kostelanetz, *The B. B. King Companion* (1997); Chris Richards, *Washington Post* (21 February 2012); Tony Russell, *Guardian* (15 May 2015); Charles Sawyer, *The Arrival of B. B. King* (1980).

King, Clennon
(1920–2000) Activist

Clennon Washington King Jr., the first African American to attempt to attend the University of Mississippi and the first black man to run for president of the United States, spent five decades fighting for civil rights as a controversial and eccentric professor, minister, and political candidate.

Clennon Washington King Jr., 1960s (Mississippi State Sovereignty Commission Records, Mississippi Department of Archives and History [1-28-0-94-1-1-1ph])

King's behavior ranged from the audacious to the downright bizarre. His independence, his frequent support of segregation, his cooperation with the Mississippi State Sovereignty Commission, and his criticism of groups such as the National Association for the Advancement of Colored People (NAACP) earned King as many enemies in the African American community as in the white power structure.

Born 18 July 1920 in Albany, Georgia, King grew up the oldest of seven children in a middle-class family. He earned a bachelor's degree at Tuskegee Institute and a master's degree from Case Western Reserve University before teaching at various black colleges during the 1940s and 1950s. In 1957, as a history professor at Alcorn Agricultural and Mechanical College (now Alcorn State University), King assailed NAACP members as the "real Uncle Toms" for allegedly attempting to soothe their inferiority complexes through integration and disrupting race relations between whites and "ordinary" blacks. In response, a group of Alcorn students hanged King in effigy, and more than six hundred students boycotted his classes. At the end of the 1958 school year, the college let King's contract lapse.

In the summer of 1958 King attempted to enter the graduate program in history at the University of Mississippi. No African American had ever applied to the university, and the white power structure struck back quickly and devastatingly. When King arrived in Oxford to register, Gov. J. P. Coleman, members of the state highway patrol, and several plainclothes officers greeted him. After forcibly removing King from the registration area, state authorities carried him to jail. Two physicians then declared King insane, and he spent nearly two weeks in a state asylum before his younger brother, civil rights lawyer C. B. King, secured his release.

In 1960 King became the first black man to run for president. Running on the Independent Afro-American Party ticket, King won 1,485 votes in Alabama and finished eleventh nationally in a twelve-candidate field. During the 1970s he waged unsuccessful gubernatorial, state legislative, and local commission campaigns in Georgia. King made national news during the 1976 presidential campaign by attempting to desegregate Democratic nominee Jimmy Carter's whites-only Plains Baptist Church. King moved to Miami in 1979 and established All Faiths Church of Divine Mission, the Arenia Mallory School of Religion, the Miami Council for Church and Social Action, and the Party of God. King ran in local elections on the Party of God ticket into the 1990s, behaving increasingly bizarrely: his 1993 campaign used intentionally outlandish profanity, while in 1996 he wore lipstick and sweatpants to campaign events. King died of prostate cancer on 12 February 2000.

Thomas John Carey
University of Mississippi

James H. Barrett, *Integration at Ole Miss* (1965); Charles W. Eagles, *The Price of Defiance: James Meredith and the Integration of Ole Miss* (2009); *Miami New Times* (25 July 1996); *New York Press* (8 March 2000); *Time* (18 March 1957).

King, Ed
(b. 1936) Religious Leader and Activist

A native of Vicksburg, Rev. Edwin King Jr. became one of the key white leaders in the civil rights movement of the 1960s. Born on 20 September 1936, King began questioning the morality of segregation at an early age and was involved in Methodist Church youth activities that promoted integration. After a 1953 tornado ravaged Vicksburg, King realized the extent of the unequal infrastructure of black and white neighborhoods and the extreme poverty of many black residents.

In 1954 he enrolled at Millsaps College in Jackson and became active in interracial student gatherings. Graduating in 1958 with a bachelor's degree in sociology, King felt called to the ministry and entered Boston University. In addition to absorbing the teachings of theologians who championed racial equality, King continued to volunteer for civil rights causes. On a trip to Montgomery, Alabama, during which he facilitated communication between activists and churches, police twice arrested King for eating with black colleagues. With newspapers in Mississippi trumpeting his arrests, King's parents faced accusations that their son was a communist and felt compelled to move out of the state.

The turmoil surrounding James Meredith's 1962 enrollment at the University of Mississippi convinced King and his wife, Jeannette, that Mississippi needed homegrown activists to help steer the state toward peaceful change. After completing two master's degrees at Boston University, King accepted a position as chaplain of Tougaloo College, a predominantly black college in North Jackson. The Kings arrived at Tougaloo in January 1963, and Ed King became involved in the growing Jackson freedom movement, joining with Medgar Evers and John Salter, a professor at Tougaloo, to organize a boycott of downtown businesses. As talks with Mayor Allen Thompson reached an impasse, King organized a series of interracial meetings that included the heads of all of Mississippi's major religious groups. He was convinced that dialogue among church leaders was key to avoiding massive demonstrations and potential violence. When the white ministers declined to join with black colleagues in a joint statement of solidarity, picketing and sit-in demonstrations commenced. Over ten days in late May and early June 1963 Jackson police arrested six hundred people, mostly black high school and college students. King personally led and participated in many of the acts of civil disobedience. During the first day, he directed students during a two-hour sit-in at a Woolworth's lunch counter. On 29 May police arrested King and others for trespassing when they attempted a kneel-in on the steps of the Federal Building on Capitol Street. The next day, King's actions convinced his fellow Methodist ministers to discontinue his status with the conference, effectively expelling him from his home church.

When the National Association for the Advancement of Colored People ended demonstrations in the face of an injunction that allowed police to arrest anyone engaging in civil disobedience, King and Evers decided to try to visit white churches. Believing that the sight of blacks being turned away from churches would stir the consciences of white Christians, they initiated a campaign in which students and later out-of-state ministers attempted to attend various white churches in Jackson. While most churches refused to allow the students to enter, the visits sparked debates about the morality of segregation within churches, and after police began arresting visitors in October 1963, some denominations, particularly Methodists, began to reevaluate their racial policies.

In addition to helping set up freedom schools and organize voter registration drives, King served a crucial role in encouraging other activists in their daily struggle to maintain hope and strength. King also stood at the forefront of several challenges to the state's political structure. Protesting the lack of enforcement of voting rights and the exclusion of blacks from the Mississippi Democratic Party, King served as Aaron Henry's running mate in 1963's Freedom Vote: the ticket received eighty-three thousand votes. The next year, King was one of the delegates from the newly formed Mississippi Freedom Democratic Party that challenged the all-white Mississippi Democratic Party at the Democratic National Convention in Atlantic City, New Jersey. In 1964 and 1965 King spoke to church audiences throughout the Midwest, helping to convince them of the need to push their congressional leaders to adopt new civil and voting rights legislation. In 1966 King ran as the Freedom Democratic nominee for US Congress against incumbent John Bell Williams in Mississippi's 3rd District, receiving 22 percent of the overall vote.

King left Tougaloo in 1967 to work for the Delta Ministry, an ecumenical development program that targeted the state's poorest communities. He remained active in various political causes in the 1960s and 1970s. Since 1974 King has taught sociology at the Medical Center of the University of Mississippi in Jackson and served as an adjunct professor at Millsaps College and the University of Mississippi in Oxford. In 2014 he and Trent Brown published *Ed King's Mississippi: Behind the Scenes of Freedom Summer*. He remains an ordained minister in the United Methodist Church and continues to speak throughout the world about the civil rights movement.

Carter Dalton Lyon
St. Mary's Episcopal School,
Memphis, Tennessee

John Dittmer, *Local People: The Struggle for Civil Rights in Mississippi* (1994); Ed King, in *Freedom Is a Constant Struggle: An Anthology of the Mississippi Civil Rights Movement*, ed. Susan Erenrich (1999); Ed King, in *Mississippi Writers: Reflections on Childhood and Youth*, vol. 2, ed. Dorothy Abbott (1986); Charles Marsh, *God's Long Summer: Stories of Faith and Civil Rights* (1997); John R. Salter Jr., *Jackson, Mississippi: An American Chronicle of Struggle and Schism* (1979).

Kirksey, Henry

(1915–2005) Activist and Political Figure

When Henry J. Kirksey died on 9 December 2005, Mississippi's largest newspaper, the *Jackson Clarion-Ledger*, wrote, "He wasn't a very good politician . . . but Kirksey . . . probably did more to change the political landscape of Mississippi than any individual in the last 30 years by his persistent legal battles for equal representation for black voters."

Born on 9 May 1915 in Tupelo, the crusty, salty-tongued Kirksey studied at North Carolina Central University in Durham and served in the US Army during World War II. He went on to have a great impact on Mississippi politics despite losing campaigns for governor, lieutenant governor, and Jackson mayor. Using demographic and mapmaking skills honed during his military service, he filed a lawsuit against countywide legislative elections in 1965, resulting in the establishment of single-member districts fourteen years later. This and other Kirksey actions eventually helped open the door to the election of hundreds of African Americans to public office in the state.

K

Kirksey waged a seven-year legal battle that finally brought down Jackson's commission form of government in the mid-1980s, leading to a mayor-council form and the election of the city's first modern-era black mayor and black council members. In the early 1960s, he was a sharp critic of county government, claiming deep-seated political corruption, and he felt vindicated decades later when the Federal Bureau of Investigation conducted a sting operation, Operation Pretense, that led to corruption charges against dozens of county supervisors, forty-six of whom pled guilty, and the dumping of the beat system.

For years, Kirksey waged a lonely battle to open the legislatively sealed records of the Mississippi State Sovereignty Commission, a civil rights–era agency that spied on citizens in an effort to preserve racial segregation. In the mid-1980s he could be seen on the streets of downtown Jackson carrying signs in one-man protests. The records were finally opened in 1998 and helped set the stage for convictions in several unresolved civil-rights-era murders. "One of the problems of Mississippi is you want to paint over the reality of the past," Kirksey said. "If you don't tell the truth about history, how the hell are you going to do anything?"

Kirksey served in the Mississippi State Senate from 1980 to 1988 but readily admitted that he was not an effective legislator. Backroom deals and compromises were not his style. However, the fiery and passionate Kirksey spoke loudly on important issues with a stinging eloquence. He once charged that the state legislature "still operate[s] in the Confederacy." He called the state Ethics Commission "a brick wrapped in paper to look like a loaf of bread . . . the pus from the political cancer that pervades government in Mississippi." He referred to Jackson's mayor as "His Imperial Highness, Emperor Dale Danks," and said that Danks's "attempts to clothe himself with an image of democratic concern and action leave him buck naked in public."

Kirksey lost as many battles as he won. He never succeeded in persuading the state to remove the Confederate battle flag from the upper left corner of the Mississippi flag, which he called a "Confederate slave flag." He was fined after he protested the embargoed Sovereignty Commission records by refusing to turn over the financial disclosure statement required of elected officials. His campaigns for office never resulted in more than a temporary platform for his ideas. However, his many achievements won him national recognition, including the William Dawson Award from the Congressional Black Caucus Foundation in Washington, D.C., and the James White Award from the National Association for the Advancement of Colored People.

Kirksey spent his later years teaching at Tougaloo College near Jackson. After he lost his home to foreclosure, friends and an anonymous donor came up with forty thousand dollars and land to establish a lifetime estate for the retired warrior.

"For Kirksey it was never about the politics or self-aggrandizement," wrote his friend and colleague Don Manning-Miller, vice president for finance at Rust College in Holly Springs, after Kirksey's death. "Much like the Hebrew prophets of old, Kirksey was a truth teller—telling the hard truth to the powerful and calling them to account."

Joe Atkins
University of Mississippi

Joe Atkins, *Jackson Clarion-Ledger* (3 March 1985, 15 September 1991); Kelli Esters, *Jackson Clarion-Ledger* (12 December 2005); Don Manning-Miller, *Rustorian* (9 January 2006).

Knight, Etheridge, Jr.
(1931–1991) Poet

Etheridge Knight Jr. was born to Etheridge "Bushie" Knight Sr. and Belzora Cozart Knight on 19 April 1931 in Corinth, the third of seven children. Knight attended the Scales Street School until the financially struggling family moved to Paducah, Kentucky, where his father worked on the Kentucky Dam. After the move, Knight spent several summers in Corinth. He quit school in the ninth grade and frequented bars and pool halls, where he was introduced to "toasting," an African American tradition of telling long narratives. Knight's brand of toasting focused on drugs, sex, violence, and crime. In 1947 he enlisted in the US Army, serving as a medical technician during the Korean War and developing addictions to drugs and alcohol. After his discharge, Knight turned to crime to support his habit, and a 1960 armed robbery netted him a sentence of between ten and twenty-five years in the Indiana State Prison.

There, Knight's toasting entertained fellow prisoners and led him to begin "poeting" (his term for writing poetry). He corresponded with prominent African American literary figures, including Gwendolyn Brooks, Sonia Sanchez, and Dudley Randall. His first book, *Poems from Prison*, was published in 1968, the same year he received his release. Knight went on to serve as poetry editor for *Motive* magazine; receive grants from the National Endowment of the Arts (1972 and 1981); win appointments as writer in residence at the University of Pittsburgh, University of Hartford, Lincoln University, and Butler University's Writers Studio; and publish two more books, *Black Voices from Prison* (1970) and *Belly Song and Other Poems* (1973). *Belly Song* earned Knight nominations for the National Book Award and the Pulitzer Prize as well as a Guggenheim Fellowship, which enabled him to study African American oral history as the basis of black poetry. *Born of a Woman* (1980) reflected this knowledge. His final work, *The Essential Etheridge Knight* (1986), won the 1987

American Book Award. Knight also founded the Free People's Workshop, which educated residents of Indianapolis, Philadelphia, New York, Toledo, and Memphis about publishing. Knight also won a Shelley Memorial Award from the Poetry Society of America (1985); was the subject of a play, *Knight Song* (1985); and received the Before Columbus Foundation American Book Award in Poetry (1986). Knight earned a bachelor's degree from Martin University in Indianapolis in 1990 and became the school's first poet laureate.

Knight married three times, adopting two children with his second wife, Mary Ann McNally, and fathering a son with his third wife, Charlene Blackburn. After losing a long battle with lung cancer on 10 March 1991, Knight received the 1993 Indiana Governor's Award for Literature and was inducted into the Gwendolyn Brooks Hall of Fame. In 1992, his sister, Eunice Knight-Bowens, and her family founded the Etheridge Knight Festival of Arts, which was held annually in Indianapolis until his sister's death in 2013.

Kristi White
Corinth, Mississippi

Dorothy Abbott, ed., *Mississippi Writers: Reflections of Childhood and Youth* (1985); Etheridge Knight Festival of the Arts Collection Description, www.indianahistory.org; Patricia L. Hill, *Mississippi Quarterly* (Winter 1982–83); Miles Raymond Hurd, *Notes on Mississippi Writers* (January 1993); Charles Rowell, *Callaloo* (Fall 1996).

Knights of Labor

During the tumultuous "great upheaval" of American labor in the mid-1880s, the Knights of Labor became the largest and most powerful labor organization in the nation's history to that point. Organizing skilled and unskilled workers (including farmers and farm laborers), male and female, white and black, the Knights claimed a national membership of more than seven hundred thousand in 1886. In Mississippi, membership peaked two years later at about three thousand in forty-four chapters, or "local assemblies." Although the Knights of Labor all but disappeared in the 1890s, the organization nevertheless led some significant labor conflicts and local political challenges in Mississippi and across the nation.

Formed in Philadelphia, Pennsylvania, in December 1869, the Knights of Labor first appointed southern organizers nine years later. In 1880 the Knights chartered Mississippi's first local assembly in the rural community of Back Creek. The group lapsed by the end of the year, however, and the Knights did not make another foray into Mississippi until 1882, when the first of Jackson's five locals received its charter.

Not until 1886 did the Knights begin to organize a significant number of Mississippi workers. Local assemblies already existed in Jackson and Meridian, and the Knights added chapters in Hattiesburg, Natchez, and Vicksburg as well as in lumbering communities along the Gulf Coast. The Knights entered Biloxi in 1887, organizing one hundred employees of canning and fish pickling plants in one local assembly and African American male and female packers and shippers in another.

Although the national leader of the Knights of Labor, General Master Workman Terence V. Powderly, opposed strikes, Knights across the country participated fully in the wave of walkouts that swept the nation during the mid-1880s. In 1887 the Knights struck against a foundry and machine shop in Vicksburg because of late payment of wages, with strikes soon following in Gulf Coast lumber mills to protest fourteen-hour workdays. The Knights won at least some of these strikes and, in keeping with another national trend, ran a labor ticket in Vicksburg's municipal elections in the spring of 1888, electing the mayor and justice of the peace as well as an alderman.

As in the rest of the nation, however, the Knights of Labor could not maintain momentum in Mississippi. Lumber mill owners banded together and crushed strikes in 1889, and the Knights' political success in Vicksburg proved an isolated victory. Furthermore, many white farmers left the Knights and joined the fledgling (and ultimately much larger) Farmers' Alliance. By the early 1890s the Knights' dwindling membership in Mississippi became increasingly rural and African American. The organization soon faded into oblivion, although local assemblies still existed as late as 1894 in Jackson and Vicksburg and as late as 1900 in rural Harrison and Jackson Counties. Nevertheless, the Knights of Labor played a pioneering role in organizing Mississippi workers in a large variety of occupations, and the Knights' recruitment of African Americans (albeit into segregated local assemblies) made the organization more racially egalitarian than many labor unions that would follow.

Matthew Hild
University of West Georgia

Leon Fink, *Workingmen's Democracy: The Knights of Labor and American Politics* (1983); Matthew Hild, *Greenbackers, Knights of Labor, and Populists: Farmer-Labor Insurgency in the Late Nineteenth-Century South* (2007); Melton A. McLaurin, *The Knights of Labor in the South* (1978); Donald C. Mosley, "A History of Labor Unions in Mississippi" (PhD dissertation, University of Alabama, 1965).

K

Knox, Bishop

(b. 1955) Educator

Bishop Knox was born in 1955 in Washington County. The tall, thin black man climbed the ranks of the Mississippi public school system during the 1970s and 1980s, earning a doctorate from the University of Southern Mississippi along the way. A biology teacher, coach, and principal, Knox became the center of controversy over religion in public schools in the early 1990s.

During the fall of 1993, in just his second year as head principal at Jackson's Wingfield High School, students at the majority-white school approached Knox about having morning prayers over the intercom system. A devout Christian and believer in religious exercises in public schools, he found nothing wrong with their wishes. Before making his decision, however, Knox sought the counsel of Jackson school officials. The deputy superintendent and school board attorney advised against the prayers, calling them "inappropriate" and "constitutionally impermissible." The principal had conducted his own research, however, and reached a different conclusion. Knox found that the Fifth Circuit Court of Appeals in New Orleans had ruled that prayers and other religious exercises were permitted as long as school officials did not coerce students to participate. He spoke with the Wingfield student council and expressed his support for their request. On 5 November 1993 Wingfield High students voted overwhelmingly in favor of the student-led prayers, and four days later, the student council president began the practice of reading a short prayer over the intercom: "Almighty God, we ask that you bless our parents, teachers, and country throughout the day. In your name we pray. Amen."

The prayers continued for the next two days, but Jackson school officials stepped in and disciplined Knox. After Knox refused to stop the prayers, Superintendent Ben Canada placed Knox on administrative leave, ultimately firing him on 24 November. Readers of the *Jackson Clarion-Ledger* flooded the editorial pages with passionate letters applauding Knox and the students who voted for morning prayers. On 29 November nearly three hundred of Wingfield High's eight hundred students staged a walkout opposing Knox's dismissal, with the demonstration dominated by signs reading "We Want Knox" and "We Want Prayer" along with the sounds of "Jesus Loves Me."

This protest galvanized others around the state to defend school prayer and Knox. From Tupelo in the northeast to Hattiesburg in the south, white and black Mississippians took a stand for religion in public schools by holding rallies and walkouts. Predominantly white, conservative Christian groups such as the Tupelo-based American Family Association and the Mississippi Baptist Convention endorsed Knox's decision and called for his reinstatement. Sixteen black ministers from Jackson gave a press conference announcing their support for Knox and prayer in public schools.

Diverse print media such as *Time*, *Jet*, and *National Review* covered the Knox controversy and the subsequent protests. The biracial nature of these rallies and the pro-Knox sentiment captured the attention of many. In Mississippi, Gov. Kirk Fordice, a conservative Republican with very little support among African Americans, praised Knox and the prayer rallies, frequently comparing the demonstrators to the civil rights marchers of the 1960s. Conservative Christian activists at the national level also saw Knox as a rallying point. "In a statement that could have been made by Pat Robertson or Jerry Falwell," Christian Coalition leader Ralph Reed wrote, "Knox argued that anything that restored moral values in our young people, including prayer, could hardly be viewed as harmful."

The controversy lost steam by April 1994, when Knox returned to Wingfield High. The Mississippi Supreme Court upheld a lower court judge's reinstatement of Knox. Unlike the lower court, however, the Supreme Court did not require the school district to provide Knox with back pay. The Knox controversy also inspired the Mississippi legislature to pass legislation allowing voluntary student-led prayer in public schools, just as Knox and his students sought. The American Civil Liberties Union challenged the legislature, and in 1996 the state's high court struck down the school prayer law.

After years of working in pupil assessment, Knox became principal at a Jackson middle school and later an associate superintendent and executive director of student support services for Jackson Public Schools.

Charles Westmoreland
Delta State University

W. O. "Chet" Dillard, *Caveats from the Bench: Warnings about the Erosion of Our Constitutional Rights from a Mississippi Trial Court* (1994); *Jackson Clarion-Ledger* (November 1993–April 1994); Roxanne Christine Radzykewycz, "Voluntary, Student-Initiated Prayer: The Case of Mississippi" (EdD dissertation, Vanderbilt University, 1996).

Ku Klux Klan

The white hoods and burning crosses of the Ku Klux Klan are arguably the most powerful and recognizable symbols of white power and violence in the South. Although the Klan has always been a secretive terrorist organization espousing white supremacy, its character and goals have varied

Mississippi Ku Klux Klan members, 1872 (Library of Congress, Washington, D.C. [LC-USZ62-49988])

throughout its history. This history, in Mississippi and elsewhere, consists of three distinct phases: the Reconstruction era, the "second Klan" of the 1920s, and the period of the civil rights movement. From the outset Mississippi Klansmen used violence and intimidation to impede struggles for black freedom. However, until the civil rights era, the Klan in Mississippi was less violent and had less extensive power than Klans in other states.

Following the Civil War, a number of vigilante groups formed, protesting black enfranchisement and Republican rule in the South. These various organizations eventually became subsumed into the Ku Klux Klan, which had initially organized in Pulaski, Tennessee, in 1866 as a recreational fraternity of Confederate veterans. As it developed into a political organization, spreading its "Invisible Empire" across the South to restore white supremacy, the Klan in effect acted as the terrorist arm of the Democratic Party. It used threatening night rides, whippings, shootings, and lynchings to tyrannize African American voters, landowners, and leaders as well as white Republicans and other backers of black equality.

The Klan did not become active in Mississippi until 1870. Night riding and violence increased at this time but were largely confined to a dozen counties in the northern and eastern parts of the state, particularly Panola, Alcorn, and Tishomingo. Because the Klan was much more prominent in Alabama and Tennessee, counties bordering these states experienced higher rates of Klan activity. In these areas, Klan membership crossed social and economic lines, although planters and professionals were more likely to hold leadership positions.

Although Mississippi's Klansmen had less political power than Klansmen in other states, the Mississippi Klan was notable for its stand against public schools and black education. Klansmen tore or burned down many schools and threatened, whipped, and killed numerous teachers. On 8 March 1871 Mississippi Klansmen also instigated a riot in Meridian, attracting national attention and helping to prompt federal intervention to control Klan activity. The riot began during the trial of three men accused of inflammatory speech after publicly promoting the organization of black militias as a means to resist Klan vigilantism. The courtroom, filled with armed Klansmen, erupted into violence, with shots fired and three people, including the presiding judge, killed. The chaos spilled into the streets, where white mobs beat and killed perceived black leaders, thwarting any nascent black resistance.

Soon after taking office in 1870, Mississippi governor James Alcorn, a Republican, commissioned a "Secret Service" of police to seek out and combat mounting Klan activity. Klan terror began to wane after 1871 congressional hearings and the passage of federal laws banning mask wearing and night riding. Although the Klan had officially disbanded by 1873, unofficial bands of vigilantes, or whitecappers, continued to terrorize black leaders, landowners, and laborers long after Reconstruction ended.

The Klan officially reorganized in 1915 in Atlanta and reached a peak strength of five million members in the early 1920s. Unlike the Reconstruction-era Klan, the second Klan was a national, Protestant organization, championing "100 percent Americanism" and targeting not only African Americans but Jews, Catholics, and others whom they believed flouted Protestant morality. These Klansmen adopted their most notorious symbol, the burning cross. The Klan was prominent throughout the country, particularly in the Midwest, but was notably more violent in the South. While the Mississippi Klan was similarly terroristic, it was weaker than in neighboring states, never achieving power above local precincts and undertaking relatively restrained activities. William Percy's *Lanterns on the Levee* (1941) detailed how the author's father, US senator LeRoy Percy, challenged the rise of Klan power in Greenville in 1922. As Percy suggested, white elites in the 1920s, unlike those in the Reconstruction era, tended to distance themselves from the Klan, which was dominated by middle- and working-class men. The Klan saw its strength wane by the mid-1920s, when a series of scandals and internal conflicts crippled the organization. Theodore Bilbo, who was elected governor in 1928 and served as a US senator from 1935 to 1947, was a former Klansman, a fact that had little impact on his popularity.

The Klan re-formed again in 1946 and became active across the South in the 1950s and 1960s largely in response to the civil rights movement. Revived Klan activity in Mississippi

K

was first reported in 1954 (following the *Brown v. Board of Education* decision), and the Klan attained prominence in the state after 1963. Indeed, Klan terror in Mississippi during the 1960s was arguably its most notorious. At this time, "the Klan" consisted of a series of separate factions, including the United Klan and the White Knights of the Ku Klux Klan, all of which promoted white supremacy and sought to preserve racial segregation and black disenfranchisement. The White Knights was by far the largest and most infamous of these groups. Led by Sam Bowers, it boasted some six thousand members and became one of the most violent Klans in the South. Bowers, a Laurel businessman, was a dynamic and fanatical leader who, like his 1920s predecessors, infused militant Christianity into Klan rhetoric. During the 1960s the White Knights were responsible for more than thirty bombings of black homes, churches, and synagogues and at least ten murders, including those of civil rights workers Andrew Goodman, Michael Schwerner, and James Chaney outside Philadelphia, Mississippi, in 1964 and the 1966 firebombing death of Vernon Dahmer, a leader of the National Association for the Advancement of Colored People in Forrest County. After four mistrials, Bowers was eventually convicted of Dahmer's murder in 1998 and sentenced to life in prison.

Klan strength waned by the 1970s because of federal infiltrations and indictments as well as internal conflicts, although it experienced a brief resurgence in the late 1970s and early 1980s, holding marches and burning crosses. As of 2014 Mississippi still had three active Klan organizations, including the White Knights, though their power and strength had weakened considerably.

Amy Louise Wood
Illinois State University

David Chalmers, *Hooded Americanism: The First Century of the Ku Klux Klan, 1865–1965* (1965); Michael Newton, *The Ku Klux Klan in Mississippi: A History* (2010); Patsy Sims, *The Klan* (1996); Southern Poverty Law Center website, www.splcenter.org; Allen W. Trelease, *White Terror: The Ku Klux Klan Conspiracy and Southern Reconstruction* (1971); Wyn Craig Wade, *The Fiery Cross: The Ku Klux Klan in America* (1987).

Ku Klux Klan during the Civil Rights Period

Across the South, one product of the 1954 *Brown* school desegregation decision was the revitalization of militant segregationist groups, including more than a dozen competing Ku Klux Klan (KKK) organizations. In Mississippi, however, staunch support for the segregationist status quo by elected officeholders and a thriving network of Citizens'

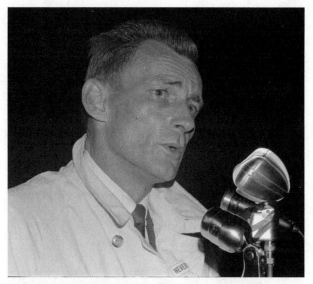

Robert M. Shelton, imperial wizard of the United Klans of America, speaks at a Ku Klux Klan rally, Hattiesburg, 28 October 1965 (Moncrief Collection, Archives and Records Services Division, Mississippi Department of Archives and History [306])

Councils meant that the Klan's brand of vigilante politics had little appeal among Jim Crow supporters. Not until 1964, in the face of escalating civil rights activity, did any Klan group mobilize a significant following in the state. But before declining sharply in the late 1960s, Mississippi's Klan membership displayed shocking brutality, perpetrating hundreds of burnings, bombings, and other violent acts, including at least ten murders.

The civil-rights-era Klan's first move into Mississippi occurred in the fall of 1963, when an organizer for the Louisiana-based Original Knights of the Ku Klux Klan arrived in Natchez, where he recruited approximately three hundred Mississippians to his organization. Infighting soon resulted in the expulsion of Original Knights state officer Douglas Byrd, who promptly recruited two-thirds of the group's Mississippi membership into a new organization, the White Knights of the Ku Klux Klan. In April 1964 Sam Holloway Bowers, a forty-year-old World War II veteran, assumed leadership of the White Knights, transforming it into a militant and highly secretive organization dedicated to a brand of Christian patriotism that viewed the encroaching civil rights threat as a Jewish-communist conspiracy against sovereign white Mississippians.

The influx of civil rights workers associated with the 1964 Freedom Summer voter registration project undertaken by the Council of Federated Organizations increased the urgency of the White Knights' mission. Membership in the Klan grew rapidly, peaking at an estimated six thousand members spread over fifty-two "klaverns" (chapters) statewide. Bowers was clear that the group would use "force and violence when considered necessary," and throughout that summer the White Knights engaged in hundreds of acts of intimidation, including the burning of forty-four black churches and the killing of civil rights workers Andrew Goodman, James Chaney, and Michael Schwerner in Neshoba County. Those crimes became one of that summer's biggest media stories, and subsequent pressure exerted by the council and its allies resulted in a large-scale investigation of the Klan by the FBI.

The controversy also provided an opening for a rival Klan organization, the United Klans of America (UKA), to begin a Mississippi recruiting campaign. The UKA was headed by Robert Shelton, a talented organizer who had built his operation into the largest KKK outfit in the nation, with hundreds of klaverns spread across the South. Unlike the secretive White Knights, the UKA hosted large open rallies and cross burnings to recruit members and publicly at least eschewed the sort of violence associated with Bowers.

The UKA had first entered Mississippi in the spring of 1964 with the establishment of klaverns in McComb and Natchez, taking members primarily from the White Knights. During the summer of 1965, Shelton embarked on an ambitious string of public rallies, several of which drew audiences in the thousands, leading to the formation of seventy-four additional UKA klaverns across the state. By 1966 membership in the White Knights had been reduced to a few hundred, while several times that number had joined the UKA.

But the fortunes of both Klan organizations soon declined. Continued violence perpetrated by the White Knights—including the 1966 killing of Vernon Dahmer, a Forrest County leader of the National Association for the Advancement of Colored People, and a later bombing campaign targeting Jews in Jackson and Meridian—sharply eroded the Klan's public appeal. Gov. Paul Johnson referred to Dahmer's killers as "vicious and morally bankrupt criminals," and district attorneys and juries became less reluctant to indict and convict Klan adherents. In addition, federal action—including a congressional investigation and a highly successful FBI campaign to infiltrate and neutralize the Klan—sapped the KKK's resources. Organizational strife cut into membership as well: amid accusations of financial improprieties, Shelton expelled the state's UKA officers in 1966.

By the close of 1968, both the White Knights and the UKA were shells of their former selves. Despite sporadic attempts by Shelton to revive his organization with early 1970s recruiting drives in McComb and elsewhere, the Klan made headlines primarily in the courtroom. Bowers and seven other Klansmen served prison time after a 1967 trial for the Freedom Summer murders. Bowers also weathered four mistrials in the Dahmer killing before finally being convicted of murder and arson in 1998. He died in prison in 2006.

Edgar Ray Killen, a central player in the Freedom Summer murder conspiracy, was found guilty of manslaughter in 2005. Two years later, another former White Knights member, James Ford Seale, was convicted of kidnapping and conspiracy in the 1964 murders of Charles Moore and Henry Dee, two young black men who were abducted, beaten, and dropped into the Mississippi River amid unfounded fears

that "Black Muslims" had been stockpiling weapons around Natchez. Still more trials could result from a renewed emphasis on FBI investigation of civil rights cold cases, further cementing the brutal legacy of the state's civil-rights-era KKK.

David Cunningham
Brandeis University

David Cunningham, in *The Civil Rights Movement* in Mississippi, ed. Ted Ownby (2013); David Cunningham, *There's Something Happening Here: The New Left, the Klan, and FBI Counterintelligence* (2004); Charles Marsh, *God's Long Summer: Stories of Faith and Civil Rights* (1997); Jack Nelson, *Terror in the Night: The Klan's Campaign against the Jews* (1993); US House of Representatives, Committee on Un-American Activities, *The Present Day Ku Klux Klan Movement* (1967); Don Whitehead, *Attack on Terror: The FBI against the Ku Klux Klan in Mississippi* (1970).

Kudzu (Newspaper)

A group of current and former college and university students started the *Kudzu* newspaper in Jackson in 1968, at the height of the American countercultural movement. Founders David Doggett and Everett Long, both of whom had attended Millsaps College, and a small staff that included Cassell Carpenter and Mike Kennedy published the paper, which featured news and opinion about youth and rebellion both locally and worldwide, until 1972. The paper began as a biweekly but was eventually published on a six-week schedule.

Doggett, a leader of the Southern Student Organizing Committee in Mississippi, had helped publish a few issues of *Free Southern Student* in 1965, and similar publications—*Mockingbird* (1966) and *Unicorn* (1968)—followed. By those standards, the *Kudzu*'s four-year run was quite a success. The first issue featured a drawing of the state of Mississippi covered in kudzu and a few other images—black and white hands clasping, a peace sign, a lynching tree, a burning cross, a mushroom, and a bong or hookah. The second issue clarified that its organizers hoped "A New Spirit Rising in the South" would, like kudzu, spread everywhere.

The *Kudzu* mixed protest news and philosophy with music and lifestyle issues. A columnist using the pen name Colonel Sartoris Snopes discussed issues specific to the South. Several other authors wrote lengthy pieces about philosophical and ethical issues, especially the meaning of revolution. Staff sought to make the newspaper a collective effort, with no clear authority figure determining content. Like many underground newspapers, the *Kudzu* struggled with funding, finding outlets for sale, and printing deadlines.

Kudzu staff covered student protests and condemned violence against protesters at Mississippi Valley State College,

Jackson State College, and Tougaloo; consistently called for an end to the Vietnam War; and showed support for civil rights and revolution in the South and beyond. According to an early piece by Doggett, *Kudzu* staff members "strive to ally ourselves with unemployed and working class whites and with the black movement for liberation." More broadly, the *Kudzu* staff hoped that the newspaper would help put them "in contact with our generational brothers in San Francisco, New York, Paris, and Prague." Most articles were written by staff members, but the paper also reprinted stories from the Underground Press Syndicate.

Part of the significance of the *Kudzu* lay in the severity of the responses to the newspaper and its staff. In the fall of 1968 the principal of Jackson's Callaway High School alerted the police that *Kudzu* staff members were selling copies on campus, and the police arrested the staff on obscenity charges related to the newspaper's content as well as on charges of pandering to minors and littering. When *Kudzu* staff helped organize the Mississippi Youth Jubilee in Edwards in 1969, "featuring music & poetry & guerilla theatre & politics & music & art & people & love & freedom," the entire event took place under close police supervision. In 1970 Jackson police had staff members under surveillance for some time before ransacking the house where most *Kudzu* staff members lived and arresting them for the possession of one bag of marijuana. Staff members claimed the police must have planted the drugs in the house. Jackson's two major white newspapers, the *Clarion-Ledger* and the *Daily News*, opposed the *Kudzu* and its causes. The *Clarion-Ledger* referred to the newspaper's staff as "the Kudzu House hippies," while the *Daily News* published names of all *Kudzu* staff members and in 1970 ran an editorial condemning the magazine's open support for marijuana, overall opposition to respectability and authority, and its poor spelling and editing: "It's all based so strongly on trash and tripe and error and an overweening obscenity of thought and word that trying to read and discuss it boggles the mind."

Volunteers bucking a system that had the power to make their lives difficult had difficulty sustaining the publication. By the fall of 1969 a *Kudzu* column reported that only three of the original eight staff members still lived in Jackson and worked for the publication: "Pigs make life in Jackson hazardous but it's mostly the little things that drive people away—dope's scarce and expensive, nobody hires long-hairs, even bands can't find work, nobody has any bread, there's no place to hang out, people curse you on the street, and it's almost impossible to find a place to live without being evicted." Nevertheless, publication continued for two more years. The newspaper demonstrates the presence and challenges faced by Mississippi's youth counterculture.

Ted Ownby
University of Mississippi

Donald Cunnigen, *Journal of Mississippi History* 2 (2000); *Kudzu* Subject File, Mississippi Department of Archives and History; Gregg L. Michel, *Struggle for a Better South: The Southern Student Organizing Committee* (2004).

Kudzu (Plant)

Its name has appeared as an adjective, describing such words as *economics*, *politics*, and *terminology*. It has been compared to horror films in which the monster is killed, only to reappear in the sequel. It is, in fact, all of these things and more. As a noun it has worked its way into the modern southern language in a way that no other plant has. As an invasive it has deeply affected the economy of the American South. It arrived here politically, and it has left the region littered with the silver bullets of failed attempts to control its menace. It is kudzu, and it has left a permanent imprint on Mississippi's environment.

In 1876 countries from around the world were invited to take part in the Centennial Celebration of the United States held in Philadelphia, Pennsylvania. The Japanese government designed an exhibition of lush gardens to showcase the country's plants. The large leaves and sweet fragrance of the kudzu blossoms garnered much notice from gardeners, who soon began planting the vine as an ornamental. By 1900 the plant was being sold through mail-order companies as an inexpensive livestock forage, and by 1934 approximately ten thousand acres of kudzu had been planted across the South. In 1933 the US government's Soil Erosion Service (later renamed the Soil Conservation Service) began to encourage the use of kudzu to help control agricultural erosion. The Civilian Conser-

Kudzu (Photograph by James G. Thomas, Jr.)

vation Corps hired hundreds of men to plant kudzu along drainage ditches, highways, and waterways, distributing as many as eighty-five million seedlings as part of the effort. In the Piedmont regions of Mississippi, Georgia, and Alabama, the planting of kudzu was encouraged as a way to hold soil in place in gullies and newly deforested regions. Farmers were paid as much as eight dollars an acre to plant the vine and received assistance from state agricultural extension services. As many as 1.2 million acres were planted under this program, but its proponents had little understanding of the potential outcome.

As early as 1902 botanist David Fairchild, who was ultimately responsible for the introduction to the United States of more than two hundred thousand exotic species, began his own experiments with kudzu and warned that it could become an invasive. That concept, however, was new, and his concerns went largely unheeded. Kudzu plantings continued until 1953, when the US Department of Agriculture noted an inability to adequately control the plant and began discouraging its use as a cover crop. Campaigns began in the 1960s to eradicate kudzu throughout the Southeast, but by the 1970s the vine was spreading faster than it was being controlled, and the Agriculture Department listed it as a "common weed of the South." In 1998 Congress listed kudzu as a "federal noxious weed." Today, estimates vary but most agree that millions of acres of land are kudzu-infested across the South, with between a quarter and half a million acres reported in Mississippi alone.

Environmentally, kudzu is considered an opportunistic species. The same qualities that made it attractive as a drought-resistant high-nitrogen forage crop have enabled it to thrive even where it is unwanted. The plants develop extensive root systems that can penetrate six feet or more into the ground and reach weights of four hundred pounds, permitting the vines to resist both dry periods and freezing conditions. Kudzu thrives under a wide range of conditions but grows especially well in a warm humid climate. Its large leaves promote high rates of photosynthesis, and under ideal conditions, a kudzu vine can grow up to a foot in a single day and sixty feet in a season. As the vines make their way into the forest canopy, they overtake their host, preventing light from getting through. The vine girdles woody stems and tree trunks, preventing nutrients from traveling between the root system and the canopy. Some trees are literally uprooted by the weight of the infestation. As competing native vegetation is choked out, food sources and habitats of native animals are lost, resulting in a large-scale alteration of local ecology. Kudzu is also highly flammable. The vine acts as a fuel ladder from the forest floor to the forest canopy, creating intense crown fires that can be difficult to control and can have devastating consequences for wildlife, forest regeneration, and property owners. Much farmland has been lost to kudzu infestations, but agricultural concerns are generally based on the ability of kudzu to act as a host for various pests or fungi that can affect crop productivity.

Property damage and the funding of kudzu eradication programs throughout the Southeast are costly. Hard numbers have not been published regarding the impact of kudzu on the timber industry, but the problem is well understood in Mississippi, which depends greatly on the economics of timber and agriculture. The US Forest Service has recognized kudzu as "a threat to the economy and diversity" of the state's forested lands, and managing timber in areas of kudzu infestation is financially unfeasible. Farmers continue to spend a great deal to curb potential infestations.

People affected by the plant have made numerous efforts to solve the kudzu problem, but there are no easy answers. Extensive use of herbicides creates its own set of problems, including killing native plants and animal populations that kudzu eradication should bolster. The Mississippi Kudzu Coalition has worked to utilize state and federal grants to provide education to the public about kudzu and control methods and have set a goal of eradicating 90 percent of the kudzu in North Mississippi. Other proposals would utilize kudzu as a source for ethanol and for folk medicines. Cookbooks have suggested using kudzu for salad greens and in kudzu flower wine. Basket makers and other folk artists have found their own uses for the vine. There is certainly more than enough to go around, and until other solutions to the kudzu problem are found, it will remain "the plant that ate the South."

Newt Lynn
Prescott, Arizona

Kerry Britton, David Orr, and Jianghua Sun, *Invasive Plants of the Eastern United States* (2002); Amanda Harris, *Fruits of Eden: David Fairchild and America's Plant Hunters* (2015); Mississippi State University Extension Service website, http://msucares.com; Max Shores, *The Amazing Story of Kudzu* (DVD 1996); US Department of Agriculture, National Forest Service website, www.fs.usda.gov/mississippi; Beryl Williams and Samuel Epstein, *Plant Explorer, David Fairchild* (1963).

K

L

Ladd, Diane (Rose Diane Ladner)

(b. 1935) Actress

Diane Ladd, a talented actress, writer, director, and singer who has received three Academy Award nominations, was born Rose Diane Ladner on 29 November 1935 in Meridian. She remained in her hometown until she graduated from high school at age sixteen and moved to New Orleans to attend finishing school. There, she studied singing, dancing, and fencing while acting at a community theater, modeling professionally, and singing with a French Quarter band. After a touring cast member of John Carradine's *Tobacco Road* spotted Ladd during a performance, she was hired as a replacement actress for a San Francisco production. She made her way to New York City, where she enrolled at the Actors Studio and found a job dancing at the Copacabana.

Her first major stage role came in the 1959 Off-Broadway production of *Orpheus Descending* by Tennessee Williams, who was Ladd's first cousin. The following year, she married Bruce Dern, one of her *Orpheus Descending* costars. Before divorcing in 1969, the couple had two children, Laura Dern, who went on to become a noted actress, and Diane Elizabeth Dern, who died in an accident at age eighteen months. Ladd performed in many theater productions, including the Broadway play *Carry Me Back to Morningside Heights* (1968), the Off-Broadway production of *Noisy Passengers* (1970), and Preston Jones's renowned Texas Trilogy, *Lu Ann Hampton Laverty Oberlander* (1976).

After appearing in Roman Polanski's *Chinatown* (1974), which received numerous Oscar nominations, Ladd had her breakthrough film role as the wisecracking waitress Flo in Martin Scorsese's *Alice Doesn't Live Here Anymore* (1974), for which she earned the first of her Best Supporting Actress Academy Award nominations. In 1980–81 she played waitress Belle Dupree in CBS's television adaptation of the film, *Alice*. Her second Academy Award nomination acknowledged her portrayal of Marietta in David Lynch's *Wild at Heart*, in which she played the obsessive and malicious mother of her real-life daughter, Laura Dern. In 1991 she and Dern again acted together in Martha Coolidge's *Rambling Rose*, for which both mother and daughter received Academy Award nominations.

From 1969 to 1977 Ladd was married to William A. Shea Jr., and in 1999 she married businessman Robert Charles Hunter. Ladd continues to act on stage, on television, and in films, frequently playing the role of a southern woman, replete with a heavy accent. In addition to guest appearances on *E.R.*, *Cold Case*, *Touched by an Angel*, *Grace under Fire*, and numerous other shows, she appeared as Helen Jellicoe on television's *Enlightened* from 2011 to 2013. Other notable films have included *Ghosts of Mississippi* (1996), *Primary Colors* (1998), *28 Days* (2000), *The World's Fastest Indian* (2005), and *Joy* (2015).

Katherine Treppendahl
University of Virginia

Diane Ladd website, www.dianeladd.com; Hollywood.com website, www.hollywood.com; Internet Movie Database website, www.imdb.com; US Census (1940).

Ladner, Dorie Ann

(b. 1942) Activist

Dorie Ann Ladner is an activist for civil and human rights who was born on 28 June 1942 in Palmer's Court, Mississippi, a small community near Hattiesburg. Named after African American World War II hero Dorie Miller, who shot down Japanese planes at Pearl Harbor despite having received no weapons training, Ladner grew up in a nurturing environment that ultimately gave her the courage and determination of her namesake. During her youth, Ladner was mentored by local civil rights activist Clyde Kennard and exposed to the vision and leadership of Vernon Dahmer, both of whom later became martyrs in the struggle for equal rights.

Like many others, Dorie Ladner and her sister, Joyce, were deeply affected by the death of Emmett Till, a fourteen-year-old African American boy who was abducted and murdered in Money during the summer of 1955. Dorie Ladner subsequently enrolled at Jackson State University, and after nine students from Tougaloo College attempted to integrate the Jackson public library in March 1961, the sisters developed a close relationship with Medgar Evers, a leader of the National Association for the Advancement of Colored People whose office was a short distance from the Jackson State campus. In the fall of 1961, after Jackson State students were prohibited from openly supporting the Tougaloo students, the two women enrolled at Tougaloo College. In 1962 Dorie and another Tougaloo student, Charles Bracey, were arrested for attempting to desegregate a Woolworth's lunch counter.

Ladner moved deeper into activist circles and closer to the violence that defined the lives of countless black Mississippians. She worked with the Student Nonviolent Coordinating Committee (SNCC) and the Congress of Racial Equality and was a founding member of the Council of Federated Organizations. In a movement laced with sexism and egotism she developed a reputation as a gutsy individual who stood up for her principles.

Ladner and other Mississippi activists were distraught over Evers's June 1963 assassination, and two months later she took part in the March on Washington, which she thought offered hollow promises and selfish agendas and was remote from the struggles of black folks in Mississippi. She went on to participate in the 1965 Selma-to-Montgomery March and the 1968 Poor People's March.

Ladner served as an organizer during the 1964 Freedom Summer Project and as SNCC's Natchez project director from 1964 to 1966. She remained politically active, working to oppose the Vietnam War and to support the presidential campaigns of Eugene McCarthy and George McGovern. After marrying and giving birth to a child, she returned to school, graduating from Tougaloo in 1973 and earning a master's degree in social work from Howard University two years later. Ladner spent the next three decades as a social worker in Washington, D.C., and continued her antiwar and political activism through the Iraq War and Barack Obama's presidential campaign. She is featured in *Standing on My Sisters' Shoulders* (2002), an award-winning documentary about the civil rights movement. In 2011 Ladner received the Humanitarian Award from the Fannie Lou Hamer National Institute on Citizenship and Democracy. In 2014 Tougaloo College awarded Ladner an honorary doctorate, and on 23 October 2015 Natchez celebrated Dorie Ladner Day.

Jelani M. Favors
Duke University

Jelani M. Favors, "Shelter in a Time of Storm: Black Colleges and the Rise of Student Activism in Jackson, Mississippi" (PhD dissertation, Ohio State University, 2006); History Makers website, www.thehistorymakers .com; Dorie Ladner, interview by Jelani M. Favors (23 June 2004); Zinn Education Project website, zinnedproject.org.

Ladner, Joyce Ann
(b. 1943) Activist and Educator

Joyce Ann Ladner was born on 12 October 1943 in Battles, Mississippi, and grew up in Palmer's Crossing, a small community on the outskirts of Hattiesburg. After graduating in 1960 as the salutatorian of her high school class, she enrolled at Jackson State College but transferred with her sister, Dorie, to Tougaloo College a year later after Jackson State students were barred from publicly supporting efforts to desegregate public facilities in the Mississippi capital. Joyce Ladner was arrested after attempting to worship at Jackson's all-white Galloway Methodist Church. She earned a bachelor's degree in sociology from Tougaloo in 1964 and went on to earn master's and doctoral degrees in sociology from Washington University in St. Louis. She subsequently taught at Southern Illinois University, Hunter College, and Howard University.

In 1959, while still in high school, Ladner helped organize Hattiesburg's first National Association for the Advancement of Colored People Youth Council. She worked closely with Vernon Dahmer, Clyde Kennard, and Medgar Evers, all of whom gave their lives to the civil rights struggle. Ladner became a field representative for the Student Nonviolent Coordinating Committee, and worked to register voters in Albany, Georgia, during the summer of 1963. She worked closely with organizers of the March on Washington in 1963 and the following year was a member of the Mississippi Freedom Democratic Party delegation that challenged the state's all-white delegation at the Democratic National Convention in Atlantic City, New Jersey.

Ladner received critical acclaim for her book *Tomorrow's Tomorrow: The Black Woman* (1971), which explores the influences shaping the construction of identity for African American adolescent girls living in St. Louis's Pruitt-Igoe Housing Project. She is also the author of *The Ties That Bind: Timeless Values for African American Families* (1999) as well as numerous other books, scholarly articles, reports and conference proceedings, and popular magazine and newspaper articles. Her scholarly contributions have focused on African American female socialization, teenage pregnancy, cross-racial adoption, the history of sociology, race and ethnic relations, and poverty.

She served as the vice president for academic affairs and interim president of Howard University and was appointed by Pres. Bill Clinton to the Financial Responsibility and Management Assistance Authority for Washington, D.C. Previously married to US diplomat Walter Carrington, Ladner has one son. In 1997 her work in education earned her *Washingtonian* magazine's Washingtonian of the Year Award. After retiring to Florida in 2003, she became a strong supporter of Barack Obama's presidential campaign and was seated on the steps of the US Capitol during his 2009 inauguration. She continues to speak publicly on topics related to civil rights and is working on a memoir.

Donald Cunnigen
University of Rhode Island

American Program Bureau website, www.apbspeakers.com; Bettye Collier-Thomas and V. P. Franklin, *Sisters in the Struggle: African American Women in the Civil Rights–Black Power Movement* (2001); Vicki L. Crawford, Jacqueline Anne Rouse, and Barbara Woods, *Women in the Civil Rights Movement: Trailblazers and Torchbearers, 1941–1965* (1993); History Makers website, www.thehistorymakers.com; Belinda Robnett, *How Long? How Long?: African American Women in the Struggle for Civil Rights* (1997).

Lafayette County

Site of the University of Mississippi and the home of William Faulkner and the subject of much of his work, Lafayette County has since the antebellum period been the educational and literary center of northern Mississippi.

Named for the Marquis de Lafayette, the county was founded in 1836, shortly after treaties forced most of the native Chickasaw population to leave Mississippi. In 1840 the new county had a population of 3,689 free people and 2,842 slaves. According to the census, 162 people worked in commerce and manufacturing. Thomas Dudley Isom, member of a firm that traded with the Chickasaw and later a medical doctor, suggested naming the local town *Oxford* as a way to attract the state university, which state officials began discussing in the 1840s. The strategy worked, and the university was founded in 1844 and opened its doors for classes in 1848; the country's fourth public law school opened there just nine years later. Southwestern humor author Augustus Baldwin Longstreet and noted scientist Frederick Augustus Barnard were among the school's early chancellors.

By 1860 Lafayette County's population had increased to 8,906 free people and 7,129 slaves. As in most of north-central Mississippi (east of the Delta but west of hillier country), the county's farms and plantations concentrated on corn (ranking sixteenth among the state's counties) rather than on cotton (twenty-fifth). The county was home to thirty-two churches: twelve Methodist, eight Baptist, six Presbyterian, five Cumberland Presbyterian, and one Episcopalian.

Part of Oxford was burned during the Civil War, and the University of Mississippi closed when most of its students left to join the Confederacy. In the 1880s the university recovered slowly. Sarah McGehee Isom became Mississippi's first female university professor when she was hired to teach elocution in 1885. The state's first medical school opened in Oxford as part of the University of Mississippi in 1903.

Lafayette County's population continued to grow in the postbellum period, reaching 21,671 in 1880 and remaining evenly divided between African Americans and whites. Lafayette had 108 foreign-born residents (primarily from England, Ireland, and Germany), a higher number than most Mississippi counties. The county's agriculture continued to mix cotton, corn, and livestock, and owners cultivated about 62 percent of the farms. Lafayette ranked eleventh among the state's counties in number of mules: quipped Oxford's most famous native, William Faulkner, whose stories relied on the county scenes and characters as background, "A mule will labor willingly and patiently for ten years for the privilege of kicking you once."

Lafayette County grew little in the late 1800s. When Faulkner was born in 1897, the county's population had grown by just five hundred since 1880. Industry employed 110 people, among them 8 women. Outside Oxford, in life as in Faulkner's fiction, agriculture dominated. About half of all white farmers owned their land, compared to only about one-fifth of black farmers. Most African Americans made their living as sharecroppers and tenants. Southern and Missionary Baptists, Methodists (both Methodist Episcopal Church, South, and Colored Methodist Episcopal), and Presbyterians were the largest religious groups in the early twentieth century.

When Faulkner wrote his major works in the late 1920s and 1930s, Oxford had relatively few other artists, though his mother was a painter and his great-grandfather had been a novelist. Faulkner created a set of images, stories, and characters that continues to dominate thinking about Mississippi and the South. During his lifetime, the number of artists, writers, and other creative thinkers who lived in Oxford increased dramatically. Howard Odum, who went on to a career as a prominent sociologist, studied classics at the University of Mississippi and spent a great deal of time recording African American musicians. Arthur Palmer Hudson served as Lafayette County's school superintendent before becoming a leading University of Mississippi folklorist. John Faulkner was a significant writer whose works for some time outsold those of his brother. In the visual arts, Theora Hamblett made paintings based on her dreams and observations, and Sulton Rogers, born in 1922, whittled wooden images of scenes from the Bible as well as from his nightmares. John McCrady made Lafayette County the subject of many of his greatest paintings. Political figure Ellen Woodward was born in Oxford, as was Arthur Guyton, professor of physiology and author of the major textbook in his field.

The county's population remained steady at about twenty thousand in the early twentieth century. In 1930, 59 percent of the population was white, 41 percent was African American, and one person was identified as "other." Still rural with a small population of factory workers, Lafayette County at the time of the Great Depression had an economy dominated by agricultural tenancy, with only one-third of farmers owning their land.

In 1960 Lafayette County was home to 21,355 people, of whom two-thirds were whites and one-third were African Americans. Agriculture remained the county's primary employer, with corn, soybeans, livestock, and cotton the major crops. Education was the second-highest employer, and about 10 percent of laborers worked in manufacturing.

The University of Mississippi was still a small institution in 1962 when James Meredith applied to become the first African American to enroll. His attempt resulted in a riot in which two people died as well as in shame and negative publicity for the university. University figures who tried to open up the university to both African American students and to a broader spirit of criticism included history professor James Silver, whose 1964 book, *Mississippi: The Closed Society*, criticized policies of the university and more broadly the state. While some students and alumni embraced Confederate imagery, the university, starting in the 1970s, began making significant efforts to study the South as part of a broader set of improvements.

Beginning in the 1970s authors Willie Morris and Barry Hannah, who wrote while teaching at the University of Mississippi, and Larry Brown, an Oxford-born writer who lived in rural Tula, added to the town's reputation as a place that valued creativity, especially on topics central to Mississippi life. Novelist Cynthia Shearer lived in Oxford for nineteen years, and Dean Faulkner Wells and her husband, Larry Wells, started Yoknapatawpha Press to publish southern writers. Less famous Lafayette County natives have included Naomi Sims, born in Oxford in 1948 and sometimes called the first African American supermodel, and Philip Cohran, an Oxford-born jazz musician who helped establish the Association for the Advancement of Creative Musicians in Chicago. Notable athletes at the university have included football stars Archie Manning, Deuce McAllister, Eli Manning, and Michael Oher (subject of the 2007 book and Academy Award–winning 2009 movie, *The Blind Side*) and basketball stars Jennifer Gillom and Peggie Gillom-Granderson from the Lafayette County community of Abbeville. Major scholars in recent decades have included folklorist William Ferris, a Mississippi native who served as director of the university's Center for the Study of Southern Culture from 1978 to 1998, and slavery historian Winthrop Jordan. In the 1990s Lafayette County's Fat Possum record label began recording North Mississippi blues, often in innovative ways.

In 1980 Lafayette County's population was 31,030; over the next thirty years, that number grew to more than 47,000. Like many counties in North Mississippi, Lafayette was predominantly white in 2010 (72 percent), with a sizable African American population (24 percent). In the twenty-first century the county was also home to small but growing Hispanic/Latino and Asian populations, each making up about 2 percent of county residents.

Mississippi Encyclopedia Staff
University of Mississippi

Don H. Doyle, *Faulkner's County: The Historical Roots of Yoknapatawpha* (2001); Mississippi State Planning Commission, *Progress Report on State Planning in Mississippi* (1938); *Mississippi Statistical Abstract*, Mississippi State University (1952–2010); Charles Sydnor and Claude Bennett, *Mississippi History* (1939); University of Virginia Library, Historical Census Browser website, http://mapserver.lib.virginia.edu; E. Nolan Waller and Dani A. Smith, *Growth Profiles of Mississippi's Counties, 1960–1980* (1985).

Lake George Site

The Lake George site is a late prehistoric multimound center located at the western edge of Yazoo County in the Yazoo Basin region of west-central Mississippi. An alluvial floodplain of the Mississippi River, the Yazoo Basin is one of the richest agricultural areas in North America as well as one of the richest archaeological zones, with an unusually abundant concentration of prehistoric sites. The largest of these sites is Lake George, which was built during the peak of aboriginal development in the basin.

The vicinity of the Lake George site reveals a long sequence of prehistoric occupations. Beginning at least by the second millennium BC, peoples of the Poverty Point culture had taken up residence. This widespread culture is distinguished by its fine lithic technology that often utilized exotic stones from distant sources and by a system of food preparation that utilized clay balls for cooking. Pottery was introduced just before the Common Era by the Tchefuncte culture, which also briefly occupied the site. Shortly thereafter, the Marksville variation of the famous Hopewell culture made an appearance and was followed by components of a local culture known as Baytown.

Although there may have been some movement of earth at the site before, real mound building began at Lake George around AD 800, when peoples of a strong new local development identified as the Coles Creek culture began their occupation. The earliest mound was a platform, on the summit of which a structure was placed. This was the beginning of the late prehistoric temple mound tradition. Over the last centuries of the first millennium, several additional mounds were constructed around a central plaza. The site covered only a few hectares, and the mounds were relatively small— less than six meters high. Not all of the buildings placed on top of these mounds were temples. Some may have served as charnel houses or fulfilled other public functions, while others were residences for the elite elements of society. Otherwise, few people lived at Lake George.

The Coles Creek peoples relied on the rich resources of the Mississippi Valley, supplemented by corn-based horticulture. They achieved a comfortable existence that was finely tuned to their environment. Their material culture was characterized by a plain clay pottery and few stone artifacts.

This modest development, however, changed around AD 1200. New influences suddenly appeared at the site, and a program of large-scale public works was implemented. Within a generation or two, dozens of additional mounds were built around a double plaza dominated by a huge central mound that was twenty meters high and covered a couple of hectares. The entire site grew to more than twenty hectares and was surrounded by a palisaded embankment on three sides, while the fourth fronted on a natural lake. The staggering amount of earthwork construction and emphasis on a great focal mound represented a major departure from the native Coles Creek ceremonial center but was characteristic of the Mississippian culture, a dynamic new development that influenced most of the midwestern and southeastern United States at this time.

The Mississippian culture was not unified but rather represented a series of innovations in lifestyle, including subsistence, social and political structure, economic and trade relations, and probably ceremonial activities. These innovations resulted in an intensive corn-bean-squash agriculture, the command and control to effect large public works programs, the exchange of exotic materials and finished artifacts over great distances, and new religious iconographies. Many local peoples adopted these innovations and participated in the "Mississippian coprosperity sphere" during the concluding centuries of prehistory. In the case of the Coles Creek people at Lake George, the agent of Mississippianization can be identified.

During the twelfth century the greatest Mississippian site—in fact, the largest prehistoric site in all of the United States—was Cahokia in west-central Illinois, near the confluence of the Mississippi and Missouri Rivers. This metropolis had contact with vast stretches of the continent, and its influence reached as far as the southern part of the Mississippi Valley and the Yazoo Basin. Stone and pottery artifacts distinctive of Cahokia and its environs have been found at Lake George and nearby sites, dating to about AD 1200, just at the beginning of the great program of mound construction.

Lake George flourished for another two centuries as the center of a large population descended from the local Coles Creek peoples. In keeping with the earlier tradition, however, and quite different from other contemporary Mississippian sites such as Cahokia, the Lake George site remained a "vacant ceremonial center" with only a small resident population.

By the middle of the fifteenth century, Lake George had been abandoned; in its place several smaller mound sites scattered around the Yazoo Basin assumed the functions it had fulfilled. Reasons for this change are unclear, but it did not result from population collapse, since the Yazoo remained one of North America's most densely inhabited regions well into the sixteenth century.

Jeffrey P. Brain
Peabody Essex Museum, Salem, Massachusetts

Jeffrey P. Brain, in *Mississippian Settlement Patterns*, ed. Bruce D. Smith (1978); Stephen Williams and Jeffrey P. Brain, *Excavations at the Lake George Site, Yazoo County, Mississippi, 1958–1960* (1983).

Lakes

Most major lakes in Mississippi did not form naturally but have been constructed for particular purposes. Lakes fall into one of six classifications according to their origin or primary purpose: oxbow, flood control, water supply, recreation, navigation, and hydroelectric.

The naturally occurring oxbow lake is created by changes in a river's course. As rivers flow, particularly through flat areas, they take the path of least resistance. Such a path is typically not a straight line but a series of bends known as *meanders*. Over time or through channelization, the river erodes away part of its bank, and the meander shifts and/or expands. These shifts allow meanders farther upstream to connect to those downstream, bypassing the old channel and forming a new one. Sediment begins to build and eventually cuts off part or all of the old channel, which becomes

Lake Lee, near Tupelo (Courtesy Tupelo Convention and Visitors Bureau)

isolated as an oxbow lake (named for the typical *U* shape). Oxbow lakes are usually found along larger rivers, and most of Mississippi's oxbow lakes occur along the Mississippi River or on the southern reaches of the Pearl and Pascagoula. Examples of oxbow lakes in Mississippi include Eagle Lake in Warren County, Moon Lake in Coahoma County, and Old River Lake in Wilkinson County.

Most of Mississippi's large lakes, including Arkabutla, Sardis, Enid, and Grenada Lakes, are classified as flood control lakes. After the Great Flood of 1927 the US Army Corps of Engineers devised a plan to prevent the Yazoo Basin (also known as the Delta) from again being deluged by floodwaters. In the western part of the Delta, the levee system was modified and improved to hold back the Mississippi River. In addition, the Corps of Engineers constructed several lakes east of the Delta to prevent flooding from the hills. The corps dammed the Coldwater River (forming Arkabutla Lake), the Tallahatchie (Sardis Lake), the Yocona (Enid Lake), and the Yalobusha (Grenada Lake), building the dams in the loess and red clay hills because doing so was easier than damming the rivers in the Delta. While Arkabutla Lake was being constructed in 1942, the entire town of Coldwater moved 1.5 miles to the south to avoid encroaching waters. Sardis, the state's third-largest lake, was the first completed. Enid is known for its world-record crappie and gar. Grenada, the largest lake in the state at normal pool, was the last of the four to be built. A few smaller lakes also serve as flood control lakes, but the only other one maintained by the Army Corps of Engineers is Okatibbee Lake, near Collinsville, which prevents flooding on the tributaries of the Pascagoula. During dry seasons Okatibbee also serves as a source of water for the delicate ecosystem further south, near the mouth of the Pascagoula.

Mississippi's water supply lakes are typically smaller in number and scale with the exception of Ross Barnett Reservoir, the state's second-largest lake. It was built in the 1960s primarily to serve as a source of drinking water for the Jackson area.

Although many Mississippi lakes provide forms of recreation, certain lakes have been created primarily to serve that purpose, and many are maintained by the Mississippi Department of Wildlife, Fisheries, and Parks. Some provide only fishing, while others also offer swimming, skiing, and boating. The twenty-two state-maintained lakes include Oktibbeha County Lake near Starkville, Kemper County Lake near De Kalb, Lee Lake near Tupelo, and Lake Lincoln near Wesson. Many private lakes provide similar conveniences.

Lakes for navigation provide water along waterways that use a lock-and-dam system for boats traveling to port. These lakes also render wider and deeper channels through which boats can travel. Navigation lakes in Mississippi are located along the Tennessee-Tombigbee Waterway and include Columbus Lake, Aberdeen Lake, and Lake Bay Springs.

Finally, Mississippi has one hydroelectric lake, built to provide cheap electricity through hydroelectric power. Pickwick Lake, in the far northeastern corner of the state and stretching into parts of Tennessee and Alabama, is part of the Tennessee Valley Authority.

Caleb Smith
William Carey University

History of the Town of Coldwater, Jessie J. Edwards Public Library, Coldwater, Miss.; Tom L. McKnight, *Physical Geography: A Landscape Appreciation* (1999); Mississippi Department of Wildlife, Fisheries, and Parks website, www.mdwfp.com; Pearl River Valley Water Supply District website, www.rossbarnettreservoir.org; US Army Corps of Engineers, Vicksburg District website, www.mvk.usace.army.mil.

Lamar, L. Q. C.

(1825–1893) Political Leader

Lucius Quintus Cincinnatus Lamar is one of only two men in history to serve in the US president's cabinet, in both the US Senate and the US House of Representatives, and on the US Supreme Court. He is also the only Mississippian ever to serve on the Court. In his Pulitzer Prize–winning book, *Profiles in Courage*, John F. Kennedy featured Lamar and seven other prominent American leaders, among them John Quincy Adams, Daniel Webster, and Sam Houston. Lamar was a national figure with celebrity appeal, considered by many to be one of the greatest speakers of the nineteenth century. His efforts to promote national reconciliation after the Civil War included an eloquent eulogy for Massachusetts senator Charles Sumner, a Radical Republican, and Lamar's transformation from a slave owner and reluctant secessionist to a defender of black civil rights and education is one of the great American stories of personal redemption.

L. Q. C. Lamar, the fourth of eight children of Lucius Quintus Cincinnatus Lamar and Sarah Williamson Bird Lamar, was born in Putnam County, Georgia, on 17 September 1825. His uncle, Mirabeau B. Lamar, served as president of the Republic of Texas. Lamar graduated from Emory College, where he met his future father-in-law and mentor, Augustus Baldwin Longstreet, then serving as the school's president. Lamar married Virginia Longstreet in 1847, and they moved to Oxford soon after her father became president of the University of Mississippi.

A lawyer and professor at the university, Lamar first won election as to the US Congress in 1857. Sometimes mistakenly referred to as a fire-eater because of his impassioned speeches defending the South's point of view, Lamar knew the destructive consequences of secession and advised Mississippi's governor and the rest of the state's congressional delegation against it. Nevertheless, he resigned from Congress in 1860 after secession became inevitable. Expressing concern that the more radical elements supporting secession might experiment with new models of government, Lamar assumed responsibility for drafting Mississippi's ordinance of secession.

During the Civil War Lamar served as a colonel of the 19th Mississippi Infantry and earned praise for heroism under fire at the Battle of Williamsburg before resigning because of poor health. Lamar subsequently served as Confederate minister to Russia and special envoy to France and England and as a judge advocate for the Confederacy and witnessed Gen. Robert E. Lee's surrender at Appomattox.

In 1872 Lamar became the first former Confederate and Democrat from Mississippi elected to Congress; five years later he was elected to the Senate. Lamar promoted reconciliation through important symbolic actions such as his famous eulogy of Sumner, negotiated the Compromise of 1877, and was the only southerner to support a pension for an ailing and broke Ulysses Grant, positions that at times invoked the wrath of constituents still bitter over losing loved ones and homes in the war. But Lamar also encouraged the South to accept the new social realities by taking the extraordinary step of publicly encouraging the appointment of a black cabinet member (though almost a century passed before an African American would gain that distinction). In addition, Lamar defended black voting rights in general and specifically opposed James Z. George's 1890 push for a new state constitution with the express purpose of disenfranchising blacks. Lamar also joined a few other southerners in supporting direct federal aid to local public schools, emphasizing the benefits for the former slaves. These positions were quite radical for a leading white southern politician of the time. Responding to frequent yellow fever epidemics, Lamar broke with convention again by introducing bills giving the federal government responsibility for public health instead of relying on the various state health boards, efforts that eventually led to the creation of what is now the US Public Health Service.

In 1884, when Grover Cleveland became the first Democratic president since the Civil War, he appointed Lamar secretary of the interior. While in office, Lamar introduced a distinctly more progressive policy of relations with American Indians and fought to protect their lands from homesteading. His environmental policies, such as protecting Yellowstone National Park, were enlightened for the time and helped prepare the way for the first national conservation policy under Theodore Roosevelt a few years later. In 1888 Cleveland named the Mississippian to serve on the US Supreme Court.

Lamar died on 23 January 1893 and is buried in St. Peter's Cemetery in Oxford. His home in Oxford has been restored and is open to the public as a museum.

In the 1970s a group of southern writers, politicians, business leaders, and journalists, including Willie Morris and William Winter, created the L. Q. C. Lamar Society, which sought to improve race relations and encourage economic development. The group's founders declared that Lamar's "struggle for reconciliation between the races and the regions of the country in the divisive 1870s is worthy of emulation by his fellow Southerners in the 1970s."

Brian Wilson
Jackson, Mississippi

Wirt Armistead Cate, *Lucius Q. C. Lamar: Secession and Reunion* (1935); Charles Betts Galloway, *Great Men and Great Movements: A Volume of Addresses* (1914); John F. Kennedy, *Profiles in Courage*, memorial ed. (1964); L. Q. C. Lamar, *You Can't Eat Magnolias*, ed. H. Brandt Ayers and Thomas H. Naylor (1972); Edward Mayes, *Lucius Q. C. Lamar: His Life, Times, and Speeches, 1825–1893* (1896); Thomas Naylor, *New South* 25, no. 3 (1970); David G. Sansing, *The University of Mississippi: A Sesquicentennial History* (1999); James W. Silver, *Mississippi: The Closed Society* (1966).

Lamar County

Located in southeastern Mississippi and named for congressman, secretary of the interior, and US Supreme Court justice Lucius Quintus Cincinnatus Lamar, Lamar County was founded in 1904. While for much of its history the county has been rural, the northeastern part of the county has become part of the Hattiesburg metropolitan area. The Wolf River flows through Lamar County. The county seat is Purvis; other towns include Lumberton and Sumrall.

Southeastern Mississippi was a prominent area for the timber industry, which, along with the expanded railroad system, brought people to the area in the late 1800s. In the 1910 census, Lamar County had a population of 11,741. Seventy-eight percent of the county's farmers owned their own farms, while the remainder were tenants or sharecroppers. In 1930 Lamar County's population was 12,848 and was 78 percent white. As in many parts of the state, Baptists and Methodists dominated church life in Lamar County.

Lamar County's population changed very little through 1960, though the concentration on agriculture and timber had given way to a more diverse economy. In a county of 13,675 residents, only 14 percent of working people made their living in agriculture. Twice that number were employed in manufacturing, primarily in the timber, furniture, and clothing industries, and Lamar County was one of the Mississippi's leading producers of petroleum, ranking fifth in the state's mineral wells and with three functioning oil wells. The Baxterville Field, where oil was discovered on the border between Lamar and Marion Counties, was one of the state's earliest successful wells.

Notable events in Lamar County's history include a major tornado that struck Purvis on 24 April 1908, killing eighty-three people and destroying the railroad depot and other structures. In 1964 and 1966 the US Department of Energy and the Advanced Projects Research Agency conducted underground nuclear detonations at the Tatum Salt Dome, an endeavor known as Project Dribble. Journalist and novelist James H. Street was born in Lumberton. Lillian McMurry was born in Purvis and went on to become an important figure in the blues, owning Trumpet Records and recording musicians in Jackson.

Significant population growth began in the 1970s, and by 1980 Lamar County had a population of almost 24,000, 50 percent more than in 1960. By 2010, like many Southeast Mississippi counties, Lamar County had a majority white population and a small but significant Hispanic/Latino minority: Lamar's population of 55,658 was 77 percent white, 20 percent African American, and 2 percent Latino/Hispanic. With a 300 percent increase in size since 1960, the county's population had undergone the third-largest proportional expansion in the state during this period.

Mississippi Encyclopedia Staff
University of Mississippi

Mississippi State Planning Commission, *Progress Report on State Planning in Mississippi* (1938); *Mississippi Statistical Abstract*, Mississippi State University (1952–2010); Charles Sydnor and Claude Bennett, *Mississippi History* (1939); University of Virginia Library, Historical Census Browser website, http://mapserver.lib.virginia.edu; E. Nolan Waller and Dani A. Smith, *Growth Profiles of Mississippi's Counties, 1960–1980* (1985).

Land Sales, Public, 1800–1840s

As a federally regulated practice, the sale of public land in the early 1800s was deeply permeated with issues of class, politics, and sectionalism. Mississippi politicians emerged as leading voices on congressional public land policy. The Harrison Land Act of 1800 created the framework for US public land policy for twenty years. Under the act, half sections of 320 acres were to be sold at two dollars per acre, and purchases were allowed on credit. In 1803 Congress passed the Mississippi land bill, which established two land offices in the Mississippi Territory, with one responsible for lands west of the Pearl River and the other administering land sales to the east. Under the bill, the president appointed a registrar and receiver for each office to conduct the land transactions. The act also authorized the appointment of a government surveyor for the Mississippi Territory and the establishment of a commission to mediate land disputes. Land sales would take place for three weeks at the offices,

after which time registrars and receivers could arrange and approve private sales for any unsold lands. Although the Mississippi land act set the price at two dollars per acre, the local auction and bidding process meant that quality public lands commonly sold at higher prices.

In 1804 Congress reformed public land sales by reducing the minimum purchase size to 160 acres. Faced with a disadvantageous federal land policy and economic hardships, squatters inundated the Mississippi Territory along with other western states and territories. Squatters were typically poor settlers who developed and improved land they did not own. In 1807 Congress passed the Intrusion Act, which made illegal settlement punishable by jail time and authorized the president to use "military force" against squatters. New England congressmen criticized the bill as tyranny and bayonet justice that denied constitutional and equal rights to squatters simply because of their class.

In Mississippi, however, the hard-line approach seemed to work. By the start of the War of 1812 approximately five hundred thousand acres of public land had been sold in the Mississippi Territory, mainly to planters and speculators. The freedoms epitomized by squatters and open cattle ranges slowly vanished behind the property boundaries and consequent changes brought by public land sales.

In the wake of the war, demand for cotton increased. In response to this boom, small farmers, planters, and speculators aggressively used both cash and credit to purchase quality Mississippi farmland, and the area's population nearly doubled from 1810 to 1820. The Panic of 1819 brought the cotton boom to a halt, and land prices dropped as well. The subsequent financial crisis produced a political backlash against the credit system, and Congress moved to reform land policy yet again. At the center of this effort, Mississippi senator Thomas Hill Williams shepherded passage of the Land Act of 1820, which banned the use of credit in the purchase of public land, reduced the minimum size of land purchase to eighty acres, and cut the price to $1.25 per acre. The ban on credit further impeded poor whites' access to the public land market.

Perhaps the most decisive moments in Mississippi public land sales occurred during the 1830s, when the US government adopted the policy of Indian Removal. The Choctaw Treaty of Dancing Rabbit Creek (1830) and the Chickasaw Treaty of Pontotoc (1832) removed those tribes from Mississippi and opened new swaths of lands for public sale. The federal government sold 236,894 acres of Mississippi public land in 1832. Land sales climbed to 1,126,232 acres in 1833, after preliminary Indian removal, and peaked at 3,267,299 acres in 1836. Congress responded to the boom in 1833 by creating new land offices in the Choctaw Purchase and Chickasaw cession.

Speculation reached a fever pitch in the 1830s. Individual speculators purchased anywhere from 320 to 75,000 acres of land, while joint-stock companies backed by eastern capital purchased land in 100,000-acre increments. This practice not only devoured the best lands but also substantially increased prices, preventing poorer settlers from entering into the market. Companies active in Mississippi included the American Land Company, Boston and Mississippi Cotton Land Company, and New York and Mississippi Land Company, which purchased 35 percent of the Chickasaw allotments. With help from land agents, the companies resold lands to wealthy planters, turning profits as high as 200 percent.

Two political issues dominated 1830s discourse on public land policy: preemption rights and distribution. Preemption allowed squatters first purchase rights for land they settled and improved prior to any public land sale, while distribution involved the question of what to do with the surplus proceeds of the land sales. Democrats used their support for preemption to appeal to the "common man" of the frontier. Congress approved limited preemption laws from 1830 to 1840 that applied to settlers who were already squatting on land, but westerners wanted those rights extended universally and permanently into the future. At the same time, National Republicans and later the Whigs fought hard for a distribution bill that would allocate the surplus proceeds from public land sales to the states for internal improvements and education.

In 1833 Kentucky senator Henry Clay introduced a distribution bill to which his ally, Mississippi senator George Poindexter, offered an amendment granting Mississippi, Louisiana, and Missouri five hundred thousand acres each for internal improvements. Poindexter's lengthy speeches in favor of distribution envisioned a cultural and economic renaissance for Mississippi that would feature the building of seminaries, colleges, common schools, and internal improvements, including good roads that would connect planters with market towns. However, Mississippi's other senator, John Black, maintained that distribution represented corruption by empowering the federal government at the expense of the state and that it would raise prices on inferior lands. Black also argued that poor whites needed to settle those inferior public lands to prevent Mississippi from developing a "dense colored population" of slaves. From this perspective, public land sales were intertwined with Mississippi's efforts to regulate class, race, and slavery. In spite of Black's efforts, the Senate narrowly passed Clay's bill.

The Whig Party swept to power in 1841, taking control of Congress and the White House. To win support for the party's distribution policy, the Whigs proposed a land bill that coupled distribution with liberal preemption rights. Democrats fumed that that distribution component of the bill translated into higher tariffs. Pres. John Tyler signed the bill after it passed both the House and the Senate by narrow margins. Mississippi's senators exemplified the partisan split, with Whig John Henderson voting in favor and Democrat Robert Walker voting against. This landmark law finally secured sweeping rights for poor whites against speculators and planters, but they had long since gobbled up

Mississippi's best public lands, forcing many poor whites to travel farther west.

Ryan L. Fletcher
University of Mississippi

Charles C. Bolton, *Poor Whites of the Antebellum South: Tenants and Laborers in Central North Carolina and Northeast Mississippi* (1996); Bradley Bond, *Political Culture in the Nineteenth-Century South: Mississippi, 1830–1900* (1995); Thomas D. Clark and John D. W. Guice, *Frontiers in Conflict: The Old Southwest, 1795–1830* (1989); R. S. Cotterill, *Mississippi Valley Historical Review* (March 1930); Benjamin H. Hibbard, *A History of the Public Land Policies* (1924); Edwin Arthur Miles, *Jacksonian Democracy in Mississippi* (1960); Roy M. Robbins, *Mississippi Valley Historical Review* (December 1931); Elizabeth Young, *Redskins, Ruffleshirts, and Rednecks: Indian Allotments in Alabama and Mississippi, 1830–1860* (1961).

Land Speculators

Land speculators played a prominent role in Mississippi history, most notably in the antebellum period. Even during the territorial period, however, competing groups of speculators laid claim to parts of the Mississippi Territory, leading to disputes that ultimately limited settlement. A number of individuals or land companies acquired rights to certain tracts of Mississippi real property from the British or Spanish governments. Other speculators received grants of land from the State of Georgia, which in 1795 created Bourbon County, encompassing parts of what would become the Mississippi Territory. One of the central issues of the factional politics of the territorial period involved sorting out rival land claims and balancing the rights of speculators against the interests of settlers.

The Choctaw and Chickasaw owned much of the land acquired by the early speculators, who assumed that they could resell the land after the Indians were removed. When removal finally came in the 1830s, cotton prices were high, and credit terms were easy. As a result, land speculators, including wealthy planters and their agents from the Atlantic seaboard and land companies formed in the Northeast, acquired much of the Choctaw and Chickasaw land cessions before the federal government had the chance to organize public land auctions. The New York and Mississippi Land Company, for example, at one point held four hundred thousand acres of the Chickasaw cession in North Mississippi—10 percent of the entire area ceded by the tribe in 1836.

By 1837 the land speculation craze had begun to abate, and those who had bought land in hopes of realizing big profits ultimately did not make as much money as they had hoped. The Panic of 1837 ended the easy credit of the early

1830s, and the opening of Texas lands further west offered new opportunities for land speculators. Many of the speculators that acquired Chickasaw or Choctaw land in the 1830s held on to the property for a number of years, still hoping to receive a sizable return on their investment. In 1841, five years after the Chickasaw lands were ceded to the US government, a group of twenty land speculators still owned almost one-third of the land in Pontotoc County in Northeast Mississippi. It soon became apparent, however, that much of the eastern part of the Indian cessions would never be converted to large cotton plantations, so speculators began to sell off their holdings in small plots to yeoman farmers at prices lower than the speculators had initially anticipated but substantially higher than the federal government's proposed minimum price of $1.25 an acre.

Charles C. Bolton
University of North Carolina at Greensboro

Charles C. Bolton, *Poor Whites of the Antebellum South: Tenants and Laborers in Central North Carolina and Northeast Mississippi* (1994); Robert V. Haynes, *Journal of Mississippi History* (October 1962).

Landforms

The total relief of Mississippi, from the coastline to the highest elevation at Woodall Mountain, near Iuka in Tishomingo County, is 806 feet. Mississippi's eleven physiographic regions can be described as alternating bands of ridges and prairies. As a generalization, the hills are underlain by sand or gravel deposits, and the prairies or plains are underlain by clay formations. The physiographic regions map of Mississippi resembles the state geologic map because the terrain formed on the underlying geologic formations. For related reasons, similar patterns can be seen in state maps of soil types and forest types.

The Paleozoic Bottoms are confined to eastern Tishomingo County and are stream valleys underlain by Paleozoic rocks—the oldest exposed in Mississippi. The Tombigbee Hills lie west of the Paleozoic Bottoms and are bounded to the west by a line running through Alcorn, Prentiss, Lee, Monroe, and Lowndes Counties. These hills are underlain by unconsolidated sands and gravels deposited during the Cretaceous period. The Black Prairie or Black Belt is a crescent-shaped strip of level or gently sloping terrain underlain by chalk and marl of the Cretaceous Selma Group. It has rich soils; the northern part of the region is more wooded and has more relief, while the southern part, extending into Alabama,

exhibits more continuous plains. To the west of the Black Prairie is a narrow range of hills, the Pontotoc Ridge, that extends as far south as Chickasaw County. This rugged terrain is underlain by Cretaceous sands and sandstones and includes the high points of Lebanon Mountain at 790 feet in elevation and Geeville Mountain at 710 feet.

The Flatwoods is a narrow region (just two to eight miles wide) of low, wooded terrain. It is underlain by the Paleocene Porters Creek Clay and forms an arc from the Tennessee line in Tippah County to the Alabama line in Kemper County. The North Central Hills region is a broad area of uplands underlain by sand and clay formations from the Paleocene and Eocene ages that are noted for containing deposits of lignite, a low-grade form of coal. Stream erosion has created areas of rugged terrain. To the south, the North Central Hills grade into the gently undulating plains of the Jackson Prairie. This region extends from northern Hinds and southern Madison Counties southeast into Clarke County. The Jackson Prairie is underlain by marine clay of the Eocene Yazoo Formation, infamous in central Mississippi for its shrink-swell properties that can damage roads and buildings. South of the Jackson Prairie, the southern third of the state is in the Piney Woods, also known as the Pine Hills region. The Piney Woods is an eroded highland noted for its pine trees and is underlain in the valleys by sands and clays of Miocene age and in the uplands by gravels and sands of the Pliocene Citronelle Formation. Citronelle gravels are mined extensively, particularly in Copiah County.

The Loess Hills or Bluff Hills in western Mississippi extends from the Tennessee line in DeSoto County to Louisiana in Wilkinson County. It is about fifteen to twenty-five miles wide and is underlain by loess, an eolian silt deposited during the Ice Age, and preloess gravel deposits. The loess is thickest—one hundred feet or more—in the Vicksburg-Natchez region. The eastern boundary of the Loess Hills is indistinct, but the western boundary is formed by the very distinctive Bluff Line that separates the hills to the east and the Delta to the west. The Mississippi Alluvial Plain, better known as the Mississippi Delta, lies to the west of the Loess Hills. Also called the Yazoo River Basin, this agriculturally rich area slopes gently from 210 feet above sea level at the Tennessee line to 94 feet at Vicksburg. The Coastal Meadows form a low, flat strip of land between the Piney Woods and the coastline. The region contains sandy ridges that were once barrier islands or beach ridges.

Other landforms include the Mississippi River, which forms much of the state's western border; alluvial plains of rivers, with their oxbow lakes, meander scars, and terraces; drowned river valleys such as Back Bay of Biloxi; and the chain of barrier islands that define the Mississippi Sound.

Michael B. E. Bograd
Office of Geology, Mississippi Department of Environmental Quality

Mississippi Department of Environmental Quality website, http://www
.deq.state.ms.us; Mississippi Office of Geology, *Physiographic Regions of
Mississippi* (2009).

Landowners, African American

In Mississippi as elsewhere in the South, a few African Americans acquired significant antebellum holdings, but the bulk of black landholdings were acquired after 1865. During the postbellum period, the number of African American landholders in Mississippi grew rapidly, with the state soon ranking near the top in both numbers and acreage. For a variety of reasons, however, black landownership declined over the second half of the twentieth century before rebounding in the twenty-first.

African Americans in different regions of the South acquired land differently. In Mississippi and the Lower South, African Americans who obtained land during the antebellum period typically benefited from piecemeal and complicated manumission and were often related to white plantation owners. Across the region by 1860 nearly one-third of freed black heads of families owned land totaling $3,166,000 of real estate.

In 1860 Mississippi had only seventeen rural black landowners, the second-fewest among states in the Lower South. Their holdings had a total value of approximately $45,100. By comparison, Louisiana's 567 rural black landowners had holdings valued at $2,669,800. Mississippi and many other states passed laws that obstructed black ownership of real estate. In an 1859 case, *Heirn v. Bridault and Wife*, Mississippi's courts held that free nonresident African Americans were considered alien enemies and therefore were incapable of receiving property within the state. Mississippi permitted African Americans who acquired their freedom in the state to own property, but freed African Americans from other states lacked that right, a provision that closed one avenue to property ownership; additional laws that limited the ways that African Americans could be freed within the state closed the other. In 1870 Mississippi had 1,600 black farm owners; two decades later, that number had grown to 11,526. At the turn of the twentieth century, Mississippi's 20,973 black farm owners were outstripped only by Virginia's 26,527. By 1950 Mississippi African Americans were full owners of 23,293 farms and part-owners of another 5,647 farms, with a total of 2,120,539 acres. After 1950, however, black owner-operator farms and acreage consistently decreased as a result of a variety of factors, among them racism, discrimination in lending and operating the enterprises, difficulties in adequate estate planning, transformations in the economic viability of small-scale agriculture, and demographic changes.

Small to medium-sized farms declined precipitously during the second half of the twentieth century. Since most black farms are small, most of the owners have been unable to capitalize on efficiencies of scale common in contemporary agricultural practices. Further, discriminatory lending and general difficulty in securing access to operating capital made expansion extremely difficult. Consequently, most of Mississippi's black landowners found themselves unable to secure an adequate living on the land. It is likely that much of the black-owned farmland across the South and in Mississippi specifically is being rented out to white farmers. Such arrangements can provide owners with a modicum of income.

There is widespread agreement that African Americans have disproportionately lost land because of intestate transfer of property across generations. The typical legal mechanism used to distribute property among legal heirs treats them as tenants in common, allowing any individual to transfer his or her interest in the property. These individual interests are often extremely small, especially after multiple generations of intestate transfers. Each of these fractions of the total property can be sold or transferred as the owner sees fit, including to nonfamily members. Problems arise when an individual interest holder asks for his or her proportion of the physical property. Subdividing the property into multiple small yet equal parcels tends to be impossible. To settle such fractionated heir claims, forced sales of property often occur, with the proceeds divided according to percentage interest among the heirs. Many observers believe that at least some black-owned land has been lost when individuals familiar with the legal process have intentionally manipulated this form of ownership. According to this argument, whites who desire black-owned farmland identify heirs who no longer live in the area and purchase their interest in the property, force a sale, and then purchase the entirety of the property. Though this process is widely acknowledged to have occurred, there is disagreement about how often it has happened.

Complicating these problems, African American farmers in Mississippi and across the South have been victims of systematic discrimination and racism both in terms of their farming operations and as a matter of course in their daily lives. Perhaps most damaging, the US Department of Agriculture long discriminated against African American farmers, and black farmers sued the department in 1997. *Pigford v. Glickman* (1999) became the largest class-action civil rights settlement in the country's history. The department admitted a history of discriminatory practices, particularly with regard to operating loans, and provided fifty-thousand-dollar payments to farmers who had their claims approved. In many cases, these payments amounted to too little, too late. Nevertheless, the number of African American farmers nationwide grew by 9 percent between 2002 and 2007 and another 9 percent over the next five years. In 2002, 5,145 of Mississippi's 42,186 farm operators were African American; ten years later, 6,627 of 54,778 farm operators were African American. However, black Mississippians' farms on average remain far smaller than those of their white counterparts.

Spencer D. Wood

Kansas State University

Pete Daniel, *Dispossession: Discrimination against African American Farmers in the Age of Civil Rights* (2013); W. E. B. Du Bois, in *Special Reports: Supplementary Analysis and Derivative Tables, Twelfth Census of the United States, 1900*, Department of Commerce and Labor, Bureau of the Census (1906); Loren Schweninger, *Agricultural History* (Summer 1989); Charles S. Sydnor, *American Historical Review* (July 1927); US Commission on Civil Rights, *The Decline of Black Farming in America: A Report of the United States Commission on Civil Rights* (1982); US Department of Agriculture, Census of Agriculture (2002, 2007, 2012); Spencer D. Wood and Jess Gilbert, *Review of Black Political Economy* (Spring 2000).

Langfitt, Howard

(1919–1997) Journalist

From 1945 to 1961 Howard Langfitt was in charge of agricultural programming at WJDX radio and then WLBT television in Jackson. He used the media to connect farmers to agricultural experts, portrayed many Mississippi farmers as modern and innovative, and encouraged other farmers to follow their example. He also supported agricultural extension work and 4-H Clubs.

Langfitt grew up on farms in Iowa and studied speech and radio at the University of Iowa. He first lived in Mississippi during World War II when his Army Air Force Squadron was stationed in Jackson. He and his Mississippi-born wife, Gloria, moved to Iowa briefly but returned in 1945 when Langfitt was offered a job as Farm Services director at WJDX. In 1954 Langfitt's job expanded to cover farm services for both WJDX and WLBT, which reached most of the state's televisions.

Langfitt started a daily television show, *RFD Televisit*, which combined farm news with Agricultural Extension Service advice. In 1955 he began a more unusual program, *Farm Family of the Week*, which offered personal and detailed portrayals of farmers, especially smaller farmers, who used innovative agricultural techniques to thrive at a time when agriculture was becoming dominated by larger plantations. Through personal accounts, the program offered stories about diversifying crops and mixing crops with livestock; relying on government experts; economizing in farm production and at home; and taking part in contour farming,

flood control, and numerous other innovations. Langfitt's show usually focused on white small farmers, and he took care to show them in the fields, at home, and dealing with government and university experts.

Michael Thompson

Pfeiffer University

Ted Ownby

University of Mississippi

CHARM (newsletter of the Consortium for the History of Agricultural and Rural Mississippi), Mitchell Memorial Library, Mississippi State University; Michael Dodson Thompson, "Educating Mississippi's Farmers, 1944–1961" (master's thesis, University of Mississippi, 1995).

LaSalle, Denise (Ora Denise Allen)

(b. 1939) Soul Blues Singer

Known as the Queen of Soul Blues, Denise LaSalle has sung the blues, soul, gospel, funk, disco, and all genres in between for more than thirty years, appealing to her fans with her lively and often inspirational personality.

Ora Denise Allen was born in LeFlore County on 16 July 1939 to Nathaniel and Nancy Allen. Her family moved to Belzoni when she was seven years old and to Chicago when she was thirteen. There, she took Denise LaSalle as her stage

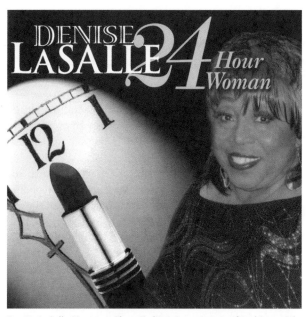

Denise LaSalle (Courtesy Blues Archive, Department of Archives and Special Collections, J. D. Williams Library, University of Mississippi)

name and met Billy "the Kid" Emerson, who recorded her song "A Love Reputation" (1967) on his Tarpon label. In 1969 she married Bill Jones, who helped her found Crajon Productions, which released the Goldstar, Parka, and Crajon labels. She and Jones divorced in 1974. LaSalle subsequently signed with Westbound Records, and from 1970 to 1976 she recorded hits such as "Trapped by a Thing Called Love" (1971), "Man Sized Job" (1972), and "Married, but Not to Each Other" (1976). She also made recordings for MCA and ABC, including "Love Me Right" (1977). LaSalle moved to Jackson, Tennessee, in 1977, and married disc jockey James Wolfe.

Most of LaSalle's early hits fit more into the R&B category than blues or soul. In the late 1970s LaSalle began connecting more with blues sounds while retaining elements of soul, helping to shape the sound of soul blues. Most of her well-known soul blues songs have appeared on the Malaco label, though she has also recorded for Ecko. LaSalle has released several gospel and R&B albums, including *God's Got My Back* (1999), but somewhat paradoxically is also known for her risqué and often humorous lyrics. She was inducted into the Blues Hall of Fame in 2011 and into the Rhythm and Blues Music Hall of Fame four years later. In 2013 and 2014, LaSalle was nominated for the Blues Music Award in the Soul Blues Female Artist of the Year category.

Greg Johnson
University of Mississippi

Blues Foundation website, www.blues.org; David Nelson, *Living Blues* (January–February 1992); Robert Pruter, in *Encyclopedia of the Blues* (2006).

Latinos, Poultry Industry and

In economics, culture, and politics, the poultry industry has had dramatic effects on central Mississippi. Since the mid-1990s its recruitment of Latino immigrant workers has reshaped the region's demographics.

The state's poultry industry began in Scott County, and it remains home to the greatest concentration of poultry plants. Since the 1950s chicken processing has been the primary source of employment for many local working families. The budding industry originally employed a largely white workforce but shifted to a mostly black labor pool in the 1960s as technological advances deskilled and increased poultry production; mechanization eliminated jobs in cotton; government incentives spurred industrial growth in the area, producing new job opportunities for white workers; and struggles for civil rights increasingly turned to economic concerns. When black workers began to organize in the 1970s for better pay and working conditions, the industry responded by turning to Latino immigrant labor.

B. C. Rogers Poultry, headquartered in Morton, was the first Mississippi poultry operation to recruit Latino migrants. Asserting that "there was no labor available to us here," the company brought in Mexican and Mexican American workers from El Paso, Texas, in 1977. This experiment lasted only a few years, and almost no Latino families stayed in the area. The 1980 defeat of a union organizing drive at B. C. Rogers, coupled with Reagan-era reforms to federal welfare policy, enabled management to maintain power over its workforce and continue to reap profits without imported labor.

The industry grew considerably in the 1980s, as health concerns and corporate advertising campaigns dramatically increased US chicken consumption. Furthermore, Mississippi's poultry processors cultivated an international export market. By the early 1990s, according to a Scott County newspaper, "it has become difficult for local poultry producers to staff late shifts because of labor shortages." B. C. Rogers executives claimed 90 percent turnover rates, 50 percent absentee rates on the night shift, and 300 employment vacancies.

In 1993 B. C. Rogers agents headed to South Texas in search of workers. The company brought in between seven hundred and eight hundred workers over a six-month period, but few stayed. Seeking new ways to lower turnover rates, the company began advertising jobs in a Miami newspaper. B. C. Rogers soon instituted a formal Hispanic Project, transporting a bus full of Latino migrants to Mississippi each week and providing them with corporate housing, though it was often cramped and uncomfortable. Housing and transportation costs were deducted from workers' paychecks, frequently leaving them with extremely low earnings. Between 1994 and 2001 the Hispanic Project brought thousands of workers from Miami, and other poultry processors in central Mississippi quickly inaugurated similar programs.

During the 1990s most of these Latino immigrants to Scott County came from Cuba, Nicaragua, Honduras, and the Dominican Republic. In Leake County, Guatemalans came from South Florida to work slaughtering chickens at Choctaw Maid Farms. By the turn of the century migrants from Miami increasingly came from Argentina, Peru, and Uruguay, and communities in Veracruz, Chiapas, and Oaxaca, Mexico, subsequently began sending migrants to Scott, Leake, Madison, and Jones Counties. Mississippi's Latin American community is exceptionally diverse, with significant differences in nationality, class, race, ethnicity, gender, language, and legal status creating obstacles to collective organizing. Scott County alone has Latino immigrants from more than a dozen countries. Nevertheless, much of this heterogeneity is elided, with most native Mississippians calling the migrants simply "Hispanic" or even "Mexican."

Recent immigration from Latin America has changed the landscape of central Mississippi. Local economies have grown, especially the niches of Hispanic groceries, international wire transfer services, rental housing, and used car sales. Schools have had to adapt to students whose first language is not English. Health care providers struggle to communicate with Spanish-speaking patients. For their part, undocumented immigrants struggle with increasingly punitive federal, state, and local policies that make it difficult for them to drive cars, open bank accounts, or get decent jobs.

Poultry companies often ignore these problems, finding ways around federal immigration and employment laws and using third-party labor contractors to staff portions of their production lines.

Angela C. Stuesse
University of North Carolina

Anita Grabowski, "La Pollera: Latin American Poultry Workers in Morton, Mississippi," Institute of Latin American Studies, University of Texas at Austin (2003); D. C. Griffith, *Jones's Minimal: Low-Wage Labor in the United States* (1993); L. E. Helton and Angela C. Stuesse, "Race, Low-Wage Legacies, and the Politics of Poultry Processing: Intersections of Contemporary Immigration and African American Labor Histories in Central Mississippi," paper presented at Southern Labor Studies Conference, Birmingham, Alabama (2004); Human Rights Watch, *Blood, Sweat, and Fear: Workers' Rights in US Meat and Poultry Plants* (2004); Steve Striffler, *Chicken: The Dangerous Transformation of America's Favorite Food* (2005); Angela C. Stuesse, "Globalization 'Southern Style': Transnational Migration, the Poultry Industry, and Implications for Organizing Workers across Difference" (PhD dissertation, University of Texas at Austin, 2008); Angela C. Stuesse, in *Heading North to the South: Mexican Immigrants in Today's South*, ed. M. Odem and E. Lacy (2009); Angela C. Stuesse, in *Public Anthropology in a Borderless World*, ed. Sam Beck and Carl A. Maida (2015); Angela C. Stuesse, *Scratching Out a Living: Latinos, Race, and Work in the Deep South* (2016); Donald D. Stull, Eric Schlosser, and Michael J. Broadway, eds., *Slaughterhouse Blues: The Meat and Poultry Industry in North America* (2003).

Lauderdale County

Founded in 1833 and named for Col. James Lauderdale, a US military officer killed during the War of 1812, Lauderdale County is located in eastern Mississippi, on the Alabama border. The Choctaw traditionally inhabited the area that now makes up the county; the United States took possession of the land under the terms of the 1830 Treaty of Dancing Rabbit Creek. Home of Meridian, a large and active railroad city that serves as the county seat, Lauderdale County may be best known as the home of country musician Jimmie Rodgers. Other towns in the county include Marion and Russell. Okatibbee Lake is located within the county, as is Meridian Naval Air Station.

In its first census in 1840, Lauderdale's population consisted of 4,005 free people and 1,353 slaves (25 percent). By 1860 the free population had grown to 8,225, while the county had 5,088 slaves (38 percent). The county's farms and plantations practiced mixed agriculture, growing cotton and corn and raising livestock. Lauderdale ranked in the top ten of the state's counties in growing rice and sweet potatoes. The county's businesses employed 1,000 industrial workers, most of them at lumber mills. In 1860 Lauderdale County had thirty-one churches—seventeen Baptist, twelve Methodist, and two Presbyterian. In February 1864 Union forces led by Gen. William Tecumseh Sherman entered Meridian, destroying property and railroad infrastructure.

By 1880 the population had increased, primarily because the number of African Americans had more than doubled to account for 54 percent of the county's 21,501 people. Lauderdale County farmers continued to practice mixed agriculture, growing cotton, grains, rice, and sweet potatoes as well as raising livestock.

In 1888 the National Farmers' Alliance held its first meeting in Mississippi in Meridian. The Daughters of the Confederacy first gathered in Meridian in 1893, the year before the national United Daughters of the Confederacy formed. In 1897 the Mississippi Woman Suffrage Association formed in Meridian, with Nellie Nugent Somerville and Belle Kearney serving as its first officers.

With the growing city of Meridian, Lauderdale County stood out as unique in its number of industrial establishments and workers. In 1880 it ranked fourth in the state in industrial production, with forty-three manufacturing firms and 373 industrial workers, including 18 women and 11 children. With the exception of the Gulf Coast counties, Lauderdale also had a higher number of immigrants than most of Mississippi, with 203 foreign-born residents, mostly from Ireland and Germany. In 1870 one of those immigrants, Felix Weidmann, opened a restaurant that continues to serve customers today.

By 1900 Lauderdale County had grown dramatically. Its population of 38,150 ranked fifth in the state. African Americans and whites each made up about half of the population, and Lauderdale had more immigrants and residents born to immigrant parents than most Mississippi counties. In 1900 Lauderdale led the state in the number of manufacturing establishments (194) and the number of industrial workers (1,639, more than 1,400 of them men), and it ranked second only to Jackson County in the amount of capital invested in industry. About two-thirds of white farming families owned their land, twice the rate for black farming families. Missionary Baptists and Southern Baptists made up about half of all churchgoers, with various groups of Methodists and Presbyterians constituting most of the rest.

Transportation was key to Meridian's growth and character. Jimmie Rodgers's first nickname was the Singing Brakeman because of his experience on trains. The son of a railroad worker, Rodgers, born in Meridian in 1897, worked on and then sang about trains and eventually took on the persona of the rambler who always dreamed of home. Meridian became the home of Mississippi air transportation in 1935, when an impressive stunt by pilots Al and Fred Key inspired the building of Mississippi's first airport, Key Field. Four years later, the Mississippi National Guard organized an air squadron at the site, and during World War II the army had a pilot training program at Key Field.

By 1930 Lauderdale's population had grown to 52,748 and was about 60 percent white. Lauderdale was more densely populated than most other counties, and Meridian was the state's largest city. The county's 65 manufacturing establishments employed 1,674 workers. The county had substantial ethnic diversity, with numerous residents from Palestine and Syria, Russia, Iceland, England, and Greece.

Lauderdale's population continued to grow in the mid-twentieth century, and by 1960 the county was home to 67,119 people, about two-thirds of them whites. Lauderdale County was also home to 15 Native Americans. The county ranked in the top five in the state in population, population density, per capita income, and the percentage of the population with a high school education. About 18 percent of Lauderdale's workforce had jobs in industry, primarily furniture, food, apparel, and textiles, and a large number of people worked in hospitals. The county no longer had an agricultural economy: only 4 percent of its workers were employed in agriculture, primarily growing corn and raising livestock. More than 2,800 people, most of them women, were employed in personal service.

Organized civil rights efforts in Lauderdale County began with Charles R. Darden of the National Association for the Advancement of Colored People, who became the organization's state president in 1955 and led school desegregation efforts in Meridian. In 1961 Meridian native Clarie Collins Harvey organized Womanpower Unlimited in Jackson and led and participated in numerous other organized campaigns. In 1963 Congress of Racial Equality activist James Chaney worked with Michael and Rita Schwerner to set up community centers in Meridian; in 1964 Chaney, Michael Schwerner, and fellow activist Andrew Goodman were murdered in Neshoba County. In the summer of 1964 a Freedom Schools convention met in Meridian.

Other notable people from Lauderdale County include many in creative professions. Novelist Edwin Granberry and Barry Hannah were born in Meridian, though Granberry grew up in Florida and Hannah was raised in Clinton. Actresses Diane Ladd, born in 1932, and Sela Ward, born in 1956, grew up in Meridian. Architect Samuel Mockbee grew up in Meridian and became a leading force in new architectural design to address the needs of low-income people. Musician Pat Sansone, best known for his work as a member of the band Wilco, is from Meridian.

Lauderdale's population spiked between 1960 to 2010, growing by nearly ten thousand in the 1970s alone. In 2010 the county's population was 80,261, of which 54 percent were white, 43 percent were African American, and the remaining 3 percent were primarily Asian or American Indian.

Mississippi Encyclopedia Staff
University of Mississippi

Mississippi State Planning Commission, *Progress Report on State Planning in Mississippi* (1938); *Mississippi Statistical Abstract*, Mississippi State University (1952–2010); Charles Sydnor and Claude Bennett, *Mississippi History* (1939); University of Virginia Library, Historical Census Browser website, http://mapserver.lib.virginia.edu; E. Nolan Waller and Dani A. Smith, *Growth Profiles of Mississippi's Counties, 1960–1980* (1985).

Lauren Rogers Museum of Art

The oldest art museum in Mississippi, Laurel's Lauren Rogers Museum of Art (LRMA), was founded in 1923 as a memorial to Lauren Eastman Rogers, who had died suddenly two years earlier. Rogers was the only heir of his parents and his maternal grandparents, who had a substantial timber fortune. In the wake of Rogers's death, the family created the Eastman Memorial Foundation "to promote the public welfare by founding, endowing and having maintained a public library, museum, art gallery and educational institution, within the state of Mississippi." The LRMA's Georgian Revival building was designed by Rathbone DeBuys of New Orleans and completed in 1923, with major additions in 1924 and 1983. Ironwork inside was created by noted craftsman Samuel Yellin. The LRMA was originally both a museum and a public library, but most library holdings not related to art were transferred to the Jones County Library in 1978–79, leaving the museum to focus solely on promoting, teaching about, and exhibiting the fine arts.

LRMA maintains five collecting areas: American Art, European Painting, Native American Basketry, Japanese Ukiyo-e Woodblock Prints, and British Georgian Silver. All except the silver collection originated with major early gifts from Rogers's extended family; the silver collection originated with a gift in the 1970s from Thomas and Harriet Gibbons, owners and editors of the local newspaper, the *Laurel Leader-Call*. The museum continues to collect works in these five areas, with a permanent gallery devoted to each. Highlights include works by Mary Cassatt, Winslow Homer, John Singer Sargent, Camille Corot, Jules Adolphe Breton, Hiroshige, Hokusai, Paul Storr, and Hester Bateman. The Native American basket collection is one of the finest and most representative in the Southeast. In addition to historic basketry, the museum continues to collect contemporary Choctaw basketry, in keeping with the LRMA's location in lands historically inhabited by the Choctaw.

The LRMA also hosts numerous exhibitions. In addition to featuring internationally known artists such as Ansel Adams, Sam Gilliam, and Dale Chihuly, exhibitions have been devoted to textiles, ceramics, glass, basketry, watercolors, pastels, paintings, and sculpture. The LRMA has always participated in Mississippi arts community, holding early exhibitions of works by Walter Anderson, Andrew Bucci, Kate Freeman Clark, Marie Hull, John McCrady, and Karl and Mildred Wolfe, among others. Involvement in arts education has led to exhibitions of the Mississippi Art Colony and of work by college students and professors. The LRMA Library is today devoted to art reference books and clipping files, local history archives, and a small collection of rare Mississippiana. Highlights of the library collection include a rare 1840 edition of *Audubon's Birds of America* and first editions of several William Faulkner novels.

Efforts to reach out to the surrounding community are ongoing, with free admission, a docent program, and a busy art education schedule for both children and adults. Notable publications include the *Handbook of the Collections*, *By Native Hands: Woven Treasures from the Lauren Rogers Museum of Art*, and *Mississippi Portraiture*.

Jill R. Chancey
Nicholls State University

Lauren Rogers Museum of Art website, www.lrma.org.

Law

Law in Mississippi has reflected the confusions, disagreements, and contradictions characteristic of all Americans' ambivalence about the role of law in society. Mississippi's lawyers have sometimes distinguished themselves as among the best in the nation and at other times have disgraced themselves with racist appeals. At the same time that Mississippi's judges and lawyers built the state's judicial edifice, the state saw more lynchings than anywhere else in the Union. Lynching measures ordinary citizens' lack of faith in law, and that brutal record is just as much a part of Mississippi's legal history as the learned opinions published by the state supreme court.

From its beginnings, Mississippi law had an uncertain connection to the nation's organic laws. Mississippi's court sys-

Reuben V. Anderson, the first African American to serve on the Mississippi Supreme Court, 1960s (McCain Library and Archives, University of Southern Mississippi)

tem has its roots in the Mississippi Organic Act of 1798, which established a territorial government. This law authorized Pres. John Adams to appoint three territorial judges and a governor. By all accounts, Adams chose badly. Historians have described Gov. Winthrop Sargent from Massachusetts as overly authoritarian and judges Peter Bryan Bruin, Daniel Tilton, and William McGuire as representing varying degrees of incompetence. Bruin may have been an alcoholic and was certainly untrained in the law, while McGuire, who was educated as a lawyer, stayed in Mississippi for only a few months in 1799, returning to Virginia to complain that he could not live on the salary provided. Working largely without law books, Sargent, Bruin, and Tilton authored Sargent's Code, the harsh series of statutes, often criticized as unconstitutional, that comprised Mississippi's first set of laws.

Mississippi's supreme court has its roots in an 1814 law that created the Mississippi High Court of Errors and Appeals. Judges serving on Mississippi's High Court militantly and aggressively defended the basic ideas of Mississippi's white society, making the court a bastion of the states' rights ideology associated with John C. Calhoun. At the same time, Mississippi's highest court adopted and accepted many of the most cherished ideals enshrined in the US Constitution, defending due process and judicial review. Mississippi's High Court defended due process in an 1855 case sparked by a Vicksburg city ordinance directing a marshal to seize stray hogs. The judges struck down the ordinance as unconstitutional, pointing out that it failed to provide proper notice or a trial before authorizing the sheriff to take private property.

Judicial review fared as well in Mississippi as it did before the US Supreme Court. The High Court first held an act of the legislature unconstitutional in *Runnels v. State* (1823), articulating the necessity for judicial scrutiny of legislative acts, a position staked out by the US Supreme Court and many other state courts decades earlier. Judge Powhatan Ellis approached the task with "caution and circumspection" and with concern for the "delicacy of the situation." Although he had repeatedly expressed "diffidence and reluctance" toward legislative acts, the legislature could not exercise unlimited discretionary power without converting "our boasted freedom and independence" into "a mere delusion."

While upholding due process and judicial review according to national standards, Mississippi's highest court articulated its own version of popular sovereignty. The court equated the state with its white population. The states are the people, the court said, and the people cannot speak other than through their states.

In criminal law, the Mississippi High Court of Errors and Appeals did very well, turning in well-written and carefully researched opinions that relied on precedent drawn from many states and showed impressive research. The judges ruled that those accused in capital cases were entitled to counsel and based their denunciation of double jeopardy on the US Constitution, which was "the paramount law of the land." The court also protected suspects' rights against self-incrimination.

In *George (a Slave) v. State* (1859), however, Mississippi's High Court ruled that slaves never had the rights articulated in English common law except in "one or two very early cases" where overly "humane" North Carolina indulged itself in "unmeaning twaddle." But Mississippi's judges acted under common law influences when they required magistrates to warn slaves that their statements might be used against them in court. The judges, in fact, thought that the mere presence of armed and hostile white men around a slave prisoner made any confession questionable. The High Court told Mississippi magistrates that they must establish "very clear and strong evidence" that they had cautioned slaves against confession before admitting those confessions into evidence. From its beginnings the court recognized a problem with private individuals working in concert with state officers to extract confessions from accused persons.

Mississippi, like all other states, also maintained a system of inferior courts, operated by magistrates or justices of the peace (JPs). JPs were supposed to be accessible, close to the people, and efficient. JPs held court in the backs of stores, under trees, or in their homes. Magistrates could try suits for breach of contract, for the recovery of personal property or for damage done by wandering livestock, or for injury to personal property where the damage did not exceed fifty dollars. Much of these courts' business involved small debts. The JPs also heard minor criminal complaints. For example, they could jail vagrants for ten days or fine anyone caught selling liquor within two miles of a church.

JPs also functioned as a kind of slave court. Any white person could complain to a magistrate when assaulted verbally by a slave or by a free person of color. Upon receipt of such a complaint, a justice would summon two slave owners to sit as judge and jury; they could administer thirty-nine lashes or order the defendant pilloried. These JP courts subjected slaves to informal procedures and lax processes that would not have been tolerated for white defendants.

Magistrates also heard cases headed for circuit court. White victims of felonies began their journey through their state's criminal justice system by taking their complaints to their local JP, who would decide whether the complaint sounded reasonable enough to order an arrest. He also would decide whether the accused person awaited trial in jail or out on bond. Waiting in jail could mean months of incarceration, since circuit courts met only twice a year.

Antebellum Mississippi had no police force. JPs encouraged ordinary citizens to investigate crimes and bring evidence to justify issuance of a warrant to be served by a constable. Mississippi did, however, maintain slave patrols, with leaders selected by county governing bodies known as boards of police. Patrol leaders made lists of all persons in their districts eligible for duty and once a month assembled patrols to search slaves' quarters. Patrol leaders simply rounded up a body of citizens, with no supervision from political leaders. Slave patrols kept no records and swiftly administered whatever punishments they saw fit. They could order whippings on the spot. As with JP courts, slave patrollers administered a kind of informal justice that the state would not have tolerated for white suspects.

In fact, race relations in Mississippi before emancipation rarely passed before any kind of judicial review. Slave owners disciplined their slaves largely outside the criminal justice system. Slave patrols and the JPs' slave courts largely kept slaves who somehow escaped their owners' discipline from entering circuit court. Even circuit courts meeting in counties with black-majority populations had few black defendants because Mississippi allowed slaves access to circuit court only when charged with the most serious crimes: murder, arson, and rape. Though sanctioned by law, slavery was essentially a lawless institution in Mississippi in the sense that slave owners faced few regulations on their relations with their slave property.

Emancipation put an end not only to slavery but to white Mississippians' primary system for controlling their state's black population. White Mississippians tried to use law to do what had once been done outside the law—that is, to discipline their labor force. Between 22 November and 1 December 1865, Mississippi passed what northerners described as Black Codes—six laws that attempted to substitute law for the lash. For the first time, African Americans were permitted to marry, but marriage across racial lines was forbidden. Black plaintiffs could testify when they sued white people but under no other circumstances. The new laws defined vagrancy to include insufficient vigor by employees, so that a person with a job might be deemed a vagrant if his employer thought he was not working hard enough.

Mississippi's Black Codes included a statute creating a system of county courts that would always be in session and therefore always accessible to the white victims of black criminals. These courts would make it easy for complainants to file charges—a simple, half-page "information" sheet substituted for the cumbersome grand jury system required in circuit court. Whites intended their new county courts to control blacks' supposed propensity for thievery and other small crimes, tendencies previously shackled by slavery's chains.

The Black Codes tried but failed to institutionalize race relations within the law. Mississippi withdrew its Black Codes in the face of the US Civil Rights Act of 1866, which defined citizenship in a way that made obviously discriminatory state laws illegal. Most white Mississippians likely had grown disenchanted with their legal approach to labor control even before Congress acted. Whites called the county courts "nigger courts" and complained about their cost. White defendants found themselves hauled before county courts about as often as blacks did. Creditors used the new courts as a handy way to pursue debtors, much to the disgust of white debtors. Black parents used the courts to pry their children out of the hands of former slave owners through the habeas corpus process. And lawyers readily defended blacks accused of crimes in county courts, regularly winning acquittals. Many whites began looking to vigilantism and lynching as a more effective way to control blacks. The Ku Klux Klan, organized in 1866 in Tennessee, became active in Mississippi in 1868.

The federal civil rights law marked the beginnings of a change in national policy. Congress took control of Reconstruction policies in 1867, leading to Republican government in Mississippi. Former slaves served on juries and as justices of the peace. In 1870 Mississippi organized a Supreme Court after the adoption of a new constitution in 1869. Mississippi's Republican-dominated legislature passed a state civil rights law in 1873. Black Mississippians wasted little time in testing its provisions, seating themselves in previously all-white public accommodations and at times sparking violent reactions from angry whites.

By 1877 white "Redeemers" had come to power in Mississippi, largely through illegal means, and had ousted Republicans from office. For years Democrats joked about stealing votes and cheating at the polls to end Reconstruction. Some argued that Mississippi needed a new state constitution to eliminate black voting by legal rather than illegal means. The 1890 constitution accomplished this goal, but electoral irregularities continued.

For years before Mississippi convened its 1890 constitutional convention whites debated how to eliminate black voting without violating the US Constitution's Fifteenth Amendment barring racial discrimination in voting. The solution—poll taxes and literacy tests—was supposed to obviate the need for vote stealing and other corrupt practices common in Mississippi elections. The lone black delegate at the convention, Isaiah T. Montgomery, endorsed voting restrictions in hopes that whites would curb their vigilante violence. Instead, lynching became more open and prominent in Mississippi.

Article III of the 1890 constitution articulated an extensive bill of rights. Section 26 guaranteed that no Mississippi citizen could be compelled to give evidence against himself—in other words, it forbade police torture of suspects. Nonetheless, Mississippi law enforcement officers routinely flouted the constitution, torturing suspects to elicit confessions. In *Brown v. Mississippi* (1936), which went to the US Supreme Court, a sheriff's deputy testified in court that he had beaten three black suspects, a procedure so routine that he did not hesitate to speak on the record as a court reporter transcribed his words. The Supreme Court threw out the convictions.

In 1888 Mississippi's legislature amended its laws to require that train companies segregate passengers by race and authorized railroad conductors to enforce segregation. Railroads resisted, but the Mississippi Supreme Court ruled that segregation was constitutional in *Louisville, New Orleans and Texas Ry. Co. v. State of Mississippi* (1889). The railroad contended that only Congress could legislate on questions involving interstate commerce, but the Mississippi court rejected this argument, authorizing segregation in Mississippi for three-quarters of a century.

Through much of the twentieth century courts across the state failed to try the killers of African Americans and civil rights workers. Not until 2005 did state authorities make an arrest in the 1964 murders of James Chaney, Michael Schwerner, and Andrew Goodman. In 1964 prosecutor William Waller unsuccessfully prosecuted Byron De La Beckwith for the murder of Medgar Evers the preceding year. When Waller asked prospective jurors if they thought it was a crime to "kill a nigger" in Mississippi, some thought so, some did not, and some were not sure. When African American Reuben V. Anderson began practicing law in 1967, some Mississippi courthouses still maintained segregation and refused to allow Anderson use the same bathroom as his white colleagues. Anderson ultimately watched the fall of legal segregation, and in 1985 he became the first African American to serve on the Mississippi Supreme Court.

At the end of the twentieth century another Mississippi lawyer, John Grisham, wrote a series of legal thrillers depicting the continuing corruption in courthouses and law firms. But even Grisham recognized that Mississippi law was changing profoundly. Mississippi allowed blacks and women to serve on juries. In 1992 the Mississippi Supreme Court ruled 4–3 that prosecutors could retry De La Beckwith for Evers's murder, and De La Beckwith was subsequently convicted. Mississippi also became the first state to sue tobacco companies to recover smokers' health care costs. Mississippi attorney general Michael Moore engineered this strategy, endorsed by the Mississippi Supreme Court in 1997 and copied by scores of other states and the federal government.

At the end of the twentieth century Mississippi became notorious for its tort litigation. Large law firms set up offices in counties known for generous awards, seeking to pursue lucrative cases. Business groups routinely ranked Mississippi last when judging states' fairness in tort lawsuits.

Critics identified judicial campaigning as contributing to the problem. Since 1832 Mississippians have elected their state judges, and these campaign costs have risen astronomically—from an average of twenty-five thousand dollars in 1990 to one million dollars in 2002. Business groups and lawyers have made large contributions to the judges before whom they litigate. One tort reform association labeled several Mississippi counties "judicial hellholes." In 2004 Mississippi enacted a law restricting malpractice awards to five hundred thousand dollars and awards in other cases to one million dollars, a provision that Gov. Haley Barbour said he hoped would make Mississippi more attractive to business.

Like courts, lawyers, judges, and litigants in every other corner of the nation, Mississippi has only occasionally lived up to the ideals enshrined in the state and federal constitutions.

Christopher Waldrep
San Francisco State University

Howard Ball, *Murder in Mississippi: United States v. Price and the Struggle for Civil Rights* (2004); Richard Cortner, *A Scottsboro Case in Mississippi: The Supreme Court and Brown v. Mississippi* (1986); Meredith Lang, *Defending the Faith: The High Court of Mississippi, 1817–1975* (1977); Dunbar Rowland, *Courts, Judges, and Lawyers of Mississippi, 1798–1935* (1935); Maryanne Vollers, *Ghosts of Mississippi: The Murder of Medgar Evers, the Trials of Byron De La Beckwith, and the Haunting of the New South* (1995); Christopher Waldrep, *Roots of Disorder: Race and Criminal Justice in the American South, 1817–80* (1998).

Lawrence County

Located in south-central Mississippi and founded in 1814, Lawrence County is named after naval officer James Lawrence, known for his famous last words, "Don't give up the ship!" during a battle during the War of 1812. The two primary towns in Lawrence County are the county seat, Monticello, and New Hebron. In the 1820 census, Lawrence had 3,925 free people and 991 slaves. Seventy people worked in commerce and manufacturing, ranking Lawrence fourth among Mississippi's seventeen counties.

In 1840 the county still had a majority of free people, but the ratio had narrowed, with 3,648 free people and 2,272 slaves. Monticello, which had once briefly served as the capital of the Mississippi Territory, was a steamboat stop on the Pearl River, and Lawrence County had ten sawmills, as many as any county in Mississippi. Farmer Charles Lynch became a judge and then a state senator; in 1835 he became the state's governor.

By 1860 Lawrence County was home to 5,517 free people and 3,696 slaves. The county's farms and plantations grew a mixture of products, including cotton, corn, and other food crops. Yet Lawrence farmers concentrated more heavily on livestock than did their counterparts in other counties. The county's businesses employed 45 industrial workers, most of them in lumber mills. Lawrence had twenty churches: fourteen Baptist and six Methodist. Among the county's most noted natives, historian Franklin Riley was born in Lawrence County in 1868.

In 1880 Lawrence continued to have a fairly small population of 9,420, with a small increase in both the African American and white populations. Lawrence had 1,256 farms, 906 of them cultivated by their owners. The county's farmers grew less cotton than most of the state, concentrating instead on livestock as well as corn and other grains, including rice. Lawrence County ranked third in Mississippi in the production of rice. Industry remained small, with only fourteen firms.

Between 1880 and 1900 the county's population increased by a third, to 15,103. For the first time, African Americans made up half of Lawrence's population. Industry was growing, but it remained small, with forty-three companies employing 77 workers. Slightly more than half of all farmers owned their own land, with more whites and fewer blacks owning their farms.

In 1916 five-sixths of all the county's churchgoers were Baptists, either in the Southern Baptist Convention or the National Baptist Convention. Most of the remaining church members were Methodists.

Lawrence's population began to decrease in the early twentieth century. In 1930 the county was home to 12,471 people, 62 percent of them whites. Even by Mississippi standards, Lawrence was sparsely populated, and agriculture remained the county's primary economic activity.

Religious leader and activist John Perkins was born in New Hebron in 1930. Perkins said the killing of his brother, Clyde, by a New Hebron official led him to leave the state, though he later returned to take up a ministry of action and reconciliation as founder of Voice of Calvary Ministry. Thomas Jefferson Young, author of the successful novel *A Good Man*, grew up in Oma and returned there in retirement. Earl W. Bascom, the Father of Modern Rodeo, worked on the Hickman Ranch in Arm. Educator Rod Paige, secretary of education in the George H. W. Bush administration, was born in Monticello in 1933.

By 1960 Lawrence County's population had declined to just over 10,000 people. About a quarter of the county's workers were employed in agriculture, emphasizing corn, soybeans, and livestock, while 29 percent of its workers had jobs in industry, especially furniture, timber, and apparel. From 1960 to 1980 the population increased slightly to 12,518.

Lawrence County's population grew to 13,258 in 2000 but dropped to 12,292 over he next decade. Like many counties in southern Mississippi, Lawrence County's 2010 population was predominantly white, with a substantial number of African Americans and a small but significant Hispanic/Latino minority.

Mississippi Encyclopedia Staff
University of Mississippi

Mississippi State Planning Commission, *Progress Report on State Planning in Mississippi* (1938); *Mississippi Statistical Abstract*, Mississippi State University (1952–2010); Charles Sydnor and Claude Bennett, *Mississippi History* (1939); University of Virginia Library, Historical Census Browser website, http://mapserver.lib.virginia.edu; E. Nolan Waller and Dani A. Smith, *Growth Profiles of Mississippi's Counties, 1960–1980* (1985).

League of Women Voters

The League of Women Voters (LWV) began in 1920 at the recommendation of Carrie Chapman Catt of the National American Woman Suffrage Association as a means of educating white women to vote. When the Nineteenth Amendment went into effect despite Mississippi's rejection of it, the same women who had lobbied the Mississippi legislature on behalf of woman suffrage organized the state LWV and then began working to form local chapters. By the first state convention in 1921, the group had more than one thousand members, with chapters in Greenwood, Hattiesburg, Laurel, Columbus, Brookhaven, Jackson, and other towns; by the following year 2,080 members had joined twenty-eight official state chapters.

Early efforts of the Mississippi LWV included support for legislation benefiting children and women, such as the 1921 Sheppard-Towner Maternal and Infancy Act, which made federal funds available for pre- and postnatal care. The LWV's national president, Maud Wood Park, addressed a 1921 joint session of the Mississippi legislature, advocating on behalf of the Sheppard-Towner Act as well as denouncing national efforts to introduce an equal rights bill on the grounds that it would threaten existing laws protecting women's interests, such as the right to alimony. The league also supported an equal guardianship law that passed during this legislative session.

League organizers in Mississippi faced resistance from women suspicious of the national organization's aims. National LWV representative Liba Peshakova first found that Mississippians believed that the organization was "militant, aggressive and a political party," but recruitment efforts improved when civic leaders such as Helen G. Yerger, women's

editor of the *Jackson Clarion-Ledger*, threw their support behind the group. The Mississippi LWV nevertheless continued to struggle to gain members and faced a dearth of leadership.

According to a 1931 report, the Mississippi LWV's priorities included prevention of war, child-labor reform, maternal and infant hygiene, women's representation on the state textbook committee, and public employment opportunities for women. By the following year, however, the records of the national LWV show no evidence of any activity in Mississippi, and the state organization remained defunct until 1950, though activity in local chapters might have continued. In one-party Mississippi, the group struggled to gain a following as a nonpartisan voter education organization.

In 1946 a group of Jackson women invited representatives from the national office to help restart a unit, and by 1956 the LWV again had active chapters in Bay St. Louis, Greenville, Jackson, Meridian, and Natchez, with a total of 568 members. However, many Mississippians remained suspicious of the national organization's engagement with international relations and civil rights, areas perceived as having ties to communism. League leaders in the state tried desperately to provide reassurance, emphasizing noncontroversial programs and the LWV's nonpartisan stance and remaining silent on controversial topics. In addition to focusing on basic voter education, water resource management, fire prevention, and city planning, the league worked on behalf of children's issues, such as poor conditions in juvenile detention centers.

The LWV's avoidance of civil rights issues created a curious situation for an organization ostensibly devoted to voters' rights and political engagement. Feminist Lucy Somerville Howorth left the LWV because she found it a "studious, lady-like group that wouldn't really tangle." And indeed, league minutes show repeated calls for extensive "study" of contentious issues rather than action. Perhaps because of such silence or because of the national LWV's reputation, the statewide membership dropped to 347 in 1959. The group's failure to publicly support segregation resulted in a "loss of prestige" as many white southerners perceived the organization as integrationist. Following the 1962 integration of the University of Mississippi, the founding of conservative groups such as Women for Constitutional Government siphoned off women uncomfortable with the LWV's public perception.

Through the early 1960s, Mississippi LWV meetings continued to avoid the topics of voting rights, segregation, and violence. The 1963 annual meeting, for example, made no mention of the bloody September 1962 integration of the University of Mississippi or its political implications for the Oxford chapter or Mississippi more broadly. Despite violent reprisals against boycotts in Jackson and the assassination of Medgar Evers, the minutes of another meeting later in 1963 merely noted that "members . . . expressed opinions

L

that certain subjects were not as they should be." Such studied disengagement made it difficult for the organization to demonstrate its relevance at a time when voting rights was a central national concern and Mississippi the key battleground. For much of its history, the LWV supported the poll tax and literacy tests, the most prominent methods of disfranchising African Americans, if those practices were "uniformly administered." As activists risked and gave their lives to register black voters, the league instructed members to go about their voter registration work by "talk[ing] quietly with your acquaintances" lest their efforts be confused with those of the civil rights groups.

By 1964, however, the Mississippi LWV could no longer avoid civil rights, and many did not expect the league to survive the civil rights movement. The state league president during the 1960s, Betty Rall, corresponded frequently with June Morgan of the national office, describing the loss of twenty-five Jackson members amid fears about the planned Freedom Schools and voter registration efforts by the Student Nonviolent Coordinating Committee and the Congress of Racial Equality. When she received letters from league women in other states whose children were planning to be Freedom Summer volunteers, Rall responded with ambivalence. She applauded the voters' basic educational mission but warned of Mississippians' violent mistrust of activists from outside the state. The League of Women Voters in Mississippi remained all-white until the 1960s.

In the mid-1960s a shift occurred as more conservative members left the league. The Oxford chapter, founded in 1962 and including a number of women professors and others affiliated with the University of Mississippi, remained quite active. The state league advocated on behalf of public education as legislators began exploring the diversion of funds to private schools to avoid integration. League women worked with public schools and Head Start programs and began interacting with black and interracial civic groups, an activity that chased off additional conservative women. In 1969 the Mississippi LWV had 238 members divided among chapters in Jackson, Meridian, Vicksburg, Long Beach, and Oxford.

In the late 1960s the league began to collaborate with the American Association of University Women to sponsor Legislative Days on which women attended sessions of the state legislature. In 1968 the league finally saw the success of its four-decade-long effort to gain Mississippi's women the right to serve on juries. The LWV began to support the Equal Rights Amendment in the early 1970s and adopted a pro-choice stance in 1990, positions that alienated some members. By the second decade of the twenty-first century, the state had only two local LWV groups, the Mississippi Gulf Coast League of Women Voters and the League of Women Voters of the Jackson Area.

Becca Walton
University of Mississippi

League of Women Voters of Mississippi Collection, Archives and Special Collections, J. D. Williams Library, University of Mississippi; League of Women Voters of Mississippi website, www.lwv-ms.org; Debra Lynne Northart, *The League of Women Voters in Mississippi: The Civil Rights Years, 1954–1964* (1997); Martha H. Swain, in *Mississippi Women: Their Histories, Their Lives*, vol. 2, ed. Elizabeth Anne Payne, Martha H. Swain, and Marjorie Julian Spruill (2010); Martha H. Swain, in *Southern Studies: Interdisciplinary Journal of the South*, 23, no. 1 (1984).

Leake, Walter

(1762–1825) Third Governor, 1822–1825

Although his term began on 7 January 1822, Gov. Walter Leake did not deliver his inaugural address until 24 June because the capital city was being relocated. When he finally spoke, the capital was temporarily situated at Columbia, in Marion County. Five days later, the legislature located the state capital at the new town of Jackson, which was being built near LeFleur's Bluff, a trading post on the Pearl River. In December 1822 members of the legislature and other state officials moved to Jackson. During Leake's first year in office, the state's first capitol, a small two-story brick building on Capitol Street, was constructed at a cost of three thousand dollars.

Walter Leake was born in Albemarle County, Virginia, on 25 May 1762 and came to the Mississippi governorship with a great deal of experience in political and governmental affairs. He was a Revolutionary War veteran and had served in the Virginia legislature. Pres. Thomas Jefferson appointed Leake judge of the Mississippi Territory in 1807, and he moved to Claiborne County, which he represented in the constitutional convention of 1817. Following Mississippi statehood, Leake was appointed one of the state's first two US senators. In 1820 he was appointed to the state supreme court to fill the vacancy caused by the death of Judge John Taylor. He served on the high court until his inauguration as governor.

During his first administration Leake signed a law abolishing imprisonment for debt, making Mississippi one of the first states to do so. Leake also tried unsuccessfully to persuade the legislature to pass a law prohibiting dueling.

Leake arranged for the formal transfer of the 1819 federal land grant that had been given to Mississippi to support a state university, and the state's first major road system was begun during his term, with roads leading out from Jackson to Natchez, Vicksburg, Winchester (Yazoo City), Holmesville, Liberty, and other points. The towns of Jackson (1823) and Vicksburg (1825) were incorporated during his administration.

In 1823 Leake became Mississippi's first governor reelected to a second term, but he died on 17 November 1825 at his home in Mount Salus (now known as Clinton). He was succeeded by Lt. Gov. Gerard C. Brandon.

Leake County and Leakesville, the county seat of Greene County, were named in Leake's honor.

David G. Sansing
University of Mississippi

Biographical Directory of the United States Congress (1950); *Mississippi Official and Statistical Register* (1912); Dunbar Rowland, *Encyclopedia of Mississippi History*, vol. 2 (1907).

Leake County

Located in the center of Mississippi, Leake County was founded in 1833 with a small population of free people and slaves. Named for antebellum governor Walter Leake, the county is located between Attala and Scott Counties to the north and south and Madison and Neshoba Counties to the west and east. A portion of the Natchez Trace Parkway runs through Leake County. The county seat is Carthage, and other towns include Edinburg, Thomastown, and Walnut Grove.

In 1840 Leake's population consisted of 1,620 free people and 542 slaves. Twenty years later slaves made up a third of the county's population, which had grown to 6,268 free people and 3,056 slaves. Leake's farms and plantations practiced mixed agriculture, concentrating on both cash crops and food crops for home use. Leake had very few industrial laborers, with just nineteen people working in lumber mills and other small industries. Of Leake's twenty-five churches in 1860, twelve were Baptist, ten were Methodist, and single Lutheran, Union, and Cumberland Presbyterian congregations existed.

In 1880 Leake remained an agricultural county. Its farmers practiced mixed agriculture, concentrating especially on dairy farming. The county ranked second in the state in the production of milk. The population was 13,146, including 8,104 whites, 4,660 African Americans, and 382 Choctaw—the second-highest number of Native Americans in the state.

By 1900 Leake County had a population of 17,360, of whom 6,231 were African American. Leake had little industrial growth, with just 69 men and no women or children working in manufacturing.

Leake County played a role in the rise of string band music in the early 1900s with the success of the Leake County Revelers and other groups. Carthage was the home of author Katherine Bellamann, born in 1877.

By 1930 Leake had 21,803 residents, with whites outnumbering African Americans by an almost two-to-one ratio and with 297 Choctaw. Still a completely rural county, Leake had almost four thousand farms, half of them operated by tenants.

Over the next three decades, Leake's population declined to 18,660, with whites accounting for 56 percent of residents, African Americans for 41 percent, and Native Americans for 3 percent in 1960. Leake County had a large number of agricultural workers, employed primarily in raising corn and livestock; the 15 percent of its workers employed in manufacturing worked mostly in the apparel industry. Population figures remained steady until the twenty-first century.

Important figures in Mississippi's civil rights history had roots in Leake County. Winson and Dovie Hudson grew up in Harmony and spent much of their lives working with the National Association for the Advancement of Colored People to address issues of equal opportunity in voting and education. Ross Barnett, governor from 1961 to 1964 and one of the state's most influential opponents of the civil rights movement, was born and raised in the Leake County community of Standing Pine.

Leake County has produced some very successful sports figures. Sue Gunter, born in 1939 in Walnut Grove, contributed to changes in women's basketball, including its development as an Olympic sport and as a major part of college athletics. Deuce McAllister grew up in Lena and went on to excel at football for the University of Mississippi and the New Orleans Saints.

Leake County has been in the news in recent years, both as the center of Operation Pretense, an investigation of corruption among local governments that began in Carthage in the 1980s, and for the opening of a private juvenile prison in Walnut Grove in 2001.

From 2000 to 2010 Leake County's population increased from 20,940 to 23,805. Like many central Mississippi counties, Leake County had a white majority, while African Americans made up 40 percent of the population and Choctaw accounted for 6 percent, making it one of the state's most significant Native American minorities (along with neighboring Neshoba and Newton Counties). A small but significant Guatemalan and Mexican minority had also emerged in Leake.

Mississippi Encyclopedia Staff
University of Mississippi

Mississippi State Planning Commission, *Progress Report on State Planning in Mississippi* (1938); *Mississippi Statistical Abstract*, Mississippi State University (1952–2010); Charles Sydnor and Claude Bennett, *Mississippi History* (1939); University of Virginia Library, Historical Census Browser website, http://mapserver.lib.virginia.edu; E. Nolan Waller and Dani A. Smith, *Growth Profiles of Mississippi's Counties, 1960–1980* (1985).

Leake County Revelers
Musicians

The Leake County Revelers were an old-time string band from the 1920s and 1930s. Its members were Will Gilmer (1897–1960), fiddle; R. O. Moseley (1884–1931), mandolo (a banjo-mandolin hybrid); Jim Wolverton (1895–1969), five-string banjo; and Dallas Jones (1889–1985), guitar. Only Wolverton was actually from Leake County. All the other members lived in or near Sebastapol in Scott County.

The band formed in 1926 and went on to record forty-four 78s for OKeh and Columbia Records between 1927 and 1930. The band does not seem to have toured or recorded as widely as contemporaries such as Narmour and Smith, who recorded as far afield as New York and San Antonio; most of the Revelers' recordings were made in Atlanta and New Orleans.

Despite remaining close to home, the Revelers were probably the most sophisticated and distinct of all the era's old-time string bands. Discovered by H. C. Speir, a Jackson record store owner and talent scout better known for finding blues artists, the Revelers played tunes with relaxed, easy tempos and complex vocal arrangements. This style set their recordings apart from other string band 78s of the era, which tend toward raucous breakdowns and field-holler-style singing. In addition to such standards as "Leather Britches" and "Listen to the Mockingbird," they recorded an extensive array of ragtime blues, vaudeville tunes, and waltzes.

Gilmer, the most restless and best-traveled of the Revelers, spent time in Texas, where he learned "Wednesday Night Waltz," a compelling but oddball tune that includes sections in both waltz and breakdown timing. It became the Revelers' best-selling record, topping 195,000 copies sold by 1931, and one of the best-selling string band recordings of all time. Their works have been rereleased by Document and County Sales (and included in many compilation packages), and they have a large audience even today. Contemporary bands play "Monkey in a Dog Cart" and other Revelers' tunes as part of a general revival of Mississippi fiddle tunes.

In the 1930s the Revelers were recruited to play at whistle stops and schoolhouses as part of one of Huey Long's Louisiana gubernatorial campaigns. Frank Buckley Walker, a talent scout for Columbia Records, remembered, "They would attract the crowd, and when they had the crowd there, Huey used to speak to them about how wonderful a governor he'd make and he was elected hands down. But it was really the Leake County Revelers that won the election."

Under the name Leake County String Band, descendants of the band members provided music for the 1976 movie *Ode to Billie Joe.*

Ed McAllister
Belhaven University

Eugene Chadbourne, AllMusic.com website, www.allmusic.com; Mississippi Country Music Trail website, www.mscountrymusictrail.org; *Mississippi String Bands*, vols. 1 and 2 (1998), liner notes; Frank Buckley Walker, interview, Johnson's Depot website, www.johnsonsdepot.com.

Lebanese and Syrians

Arab immigrants from the Ottoman Empire province of Syria, which included modern-day Lebanon, first began to arrive in America in the late 1870s, fleeing religious persecution, economic distress, and military duty in the Ottoman army. Like most immigrants, they also were attracted by the lure of America. About 25 percent of them settled, either initially or eventually, in southern states, and by the late 1880s Mississippi had small but established Syrian and Lebanese communities. Some migrants were attracted to the state because of its relatively warm climate, while others came from New Orleans, their port of entry. After the first immigrants became established, family members and relatives from Syria and Lebanon often followed, swelling their numbers.

Nearly all of these early Arab immigrants to Mississippi were Christian, representing sects affiliated with both the Roman Catholic Church (Maronites, Melkites, and Chaldean Catholics) and the Eastern Orthodox Church.

The overwhelming majority were poorly educated and had survived in their native land by cultivating small family farms. Farming in Mississippi, however, was based on a modified plantation system characterized by tenancy and sharecropping that was completely alien to Syrians and Lebanese. Moreover, many of the immigrants came intending to make as much money as possible and then return to their

Lebanese merchant James Ellis in front of his dry goods store in Port Gibson (Courtesy James G. Thomas, Jr.)

homeland; they were not interested in settling on farmland. As a result, the early immigrants' preferred occupation was peddling household goods, which required little capital and minimal command of English. Because Mississippi's population lived largely in rural areas without easy access to stores, the state was fertile ground for peddlers. Syrians and Lebanese settled predominantly along the Mississippi River and near railroad towns as well as in Jackson and Meridian.

By 1900 many of the early peddlers had become suppliers and eventually shopkeepers, mostly selling dry goods and groceries. Syrian and Lebanese communities thrived in Vicksburg, Greenville, Clarksdale, Port Gibson, Yazoo City, and Natchez. A yellow fever epidemic in Jackson at the turn of the century drove many of that city's Syrian and Lebanese inhabitants to outlying towns. The *Syrian Business Directory*, published in New York in 1908, listed approximately sixty-five Arab-owned businesses in Mississippi, with concentrations in Natchez and Vicksburg. More than 70 percent of these businesses were groceries or dry good stores, but there were also a few clothing stores, restaurants, and bakeries.

According to 1930 US census data, the state had nearly eighteen hundred Syrians and Lebanese (including immigrants and their Mississippi-born children). Around 20 percent lived in Vicksburg, virtually all of them Eastern Orthodox from the al-Kurah district in northern Lebanon. They established the state's first Orthodox Church in 1906.

In part as a reaction to prejudice and in part to preserve their heritage from the forces of assimilation, Syrians and Lebanese began to form local clubs—usually called Cedars Clubs, after the cedar tree, Lebanon's national symbol. In 1931 more than four hundred representatives from dozens of such clubs throughout the South created an umbrella organization, the Southern Federation of Syrian Lebanese American Clubs. The federation held its annual convention in Jackson in 1935 and has met frequently in the state since then. Along with local clubs, churches served as centers of social and cultural life for Syrians and Lebanese. Most of these early immigrants were members of uniquely Middle Eastern Christian sects and thus tended to build their own churches instead of joining established ones. This practice allowed them to preserve religious services in the Arabic language.

The flow of new immigrants began to dwindle by 1930 as a result of tightened US immigration laws. By this time, an entire generation of Syrians and Lebanese had grown up in Mississippi, considered themselves Americans, and were rapidly assimilating. Many sought spouses from within their ethnic community, but many others—often to the dismay of their parents—married non-Arabs. Like many immigrant communities the Syrians and Lebanese emphasized education and strong family bonds. This combination produced a community that by World War II was thriving economically and beginning to make inroads into the professions.

The pressures to more thoroughly assimilate were strong, especially in the South, where these Arabs feared that they would not be regarded as sufficiently white. Many Syrians and Lebanese changed or modified their names—Tannous became Thomas; Elias became Ellis; Haddad became Smith. Some left their ethnic churches for traditional Roman Catholic or Protestant ones. Perhaps trying to prove their whiteness, Syrians and Lebanese typically adhered to the dominant hostile position toward civil rights in the 1950s and 1960s.

The second and third generations of Syrians and Lebanese were less likely to marry within their ethnic community. Their links to their Middle Eastern heritage remained strong but were primarily cultural: church affiliation, food, and the use of a few Arabic words of endearment. Many Mississippians who are of only partial Syrian or Lebanese descent nevertheless identify culturally with the community. In this regard, the pattern of Syrian and Lebanese assimilation is typical of most immigrant communities in the United States.

A new wave of immigration from the Middle East began in the 1970s as a consequence of civil war in Lebanon, general regional conflict, and changes to US immigration laws. Many of these newer arrivals have been Muslims and hail from Palestine, Egypt, Iraq, Yemen, and Morocco in addition to Lebanon and Syria. They have also tended to be better educated than the early immigrants: many are professionals or academics. As a result, they more commonly seek jobs and settle in cities, especially Jackson.

The 2000 US census counted 4,215 people of Arab descent in Mississippi. If those who have only one parent or grandparent of Arab descent are included, the figure probably would have been closer to 10,000.

William Mark Habeeb
Georgetown University

Eric J. Hooglund, ed., *Crossing the Waters: Arabic-Speaking Immigrants to the United States before 1940* (1987); Gregory Orfalea, *Before the Flames: A Quest for the History of Arab Americans* (1988); Afif Tannous, *American Sociological Review* (June 1943); James G. Thomas, Jr., in *Ethnic Heritage in Mississippi*, ed. Barbara Carpenter (1992); James G. Thomas, Jr., "Mississippi *Mahjar*: The History of Lebanese Immigration to the Mississippi Delta and the Role of the Group within a Traditionally Black-and-White Social System" (master's thesis, University of Mississippi, 2007); *The Naff Arab-American Collection*, Archives Center, National Museum of American History, Smithsonian Institution, Washington, D.C.; US Census Bureau.

Lee, George Washington

(1904–1955) Minister and Activist

Rev. George Washington Lee was a pioneering civil rights activist in the Delta whose unsolved 1955 murder illustrates the tremendous risks associated with advocating racial and political equality in Mississippi in the 1950s. Born in 1904, the son of a white father and a black sharecropper, Lee grew up in Edwards, a rural town about thirty miles west of Jackson. Lee's mother died when he was young, and he was raised by an aunt until he graduated from high school. He moved to New Orleans and worked on the banana docks while he took a correspondence course in typesetting.

In the 1930s Lee returned to Mississippi, moving to the Delta town of Belzoni to become a preacher. Like most Delta preachers, Lee ministered to multiple rural congregations, at times juggling as many as four, and supplemented his income with a variety of entrepreneurial ventures. He and his wife, Rosebud, established a print shop in their home and ran a grocery store that catered to black customers. These enterprises gave Lee the personal contacts and the independent financial means to become a community leader and an early civil rights activist. Other early grassroots leaders such as T. R. M. Howard, Aaron Henry, and Amzie Moore were also businessmen.

Lee's involvement with civil rights blossomed in the early 1950s as black Mississippians began pushing for equality. In 1953 he joined with his friend and fellow grocer, Gus Courts, to organize the Belzoni branch of the National Association for the Advancement of Colored People (NAACP). He also became a vice president of the Regional Council for Negro Leadership, a Delta-based group founded by Howard that focused on voting rights and economic self-sufficiency.

By 1955 Lee had become perhaps the most visible civil rights leader in Humphreys County. Described by *Jet* reporter Simeon Booker as a "tan-skinned, stumpy spell-binder," Lee regularly spoke about the importance of voting, predicting that if all the blacks in the Delta were to register, they could send an African American representative to the US Congress. He was among the first blacks to register to vote in the county since Reconstruction, and he helped to register nearly one hundred new black voters. At an April 1955 Regional Council rally, Lee told a crowd of nearly ten thousand, "Pray not for your Mom and Pop. They've gone to heaven. Pray you can make it through this hell." His "down-home dialogue and his sense of political timing," Booker noted, "electrified" listeners.

Lee may have thrilled his supporters, but he also frightened and angered local whites, who vigorously defended voting as a whites-only privilege. Citizens' Council members confronted Lee, demanding that he destroy his poll-tax receipts and refrain from voting. He not only refused but even sued the local sheriff after the latter stopped accepting poll-tax payments from prospective black voters.

On the evening of 7 May 1955 Lee was driving along a Belzoni road when a convertible pulled alongside his vehicle and a white gunman shot him in the face. He died on the way to the hospital. An autopsy reported that lead fragments filled Lee's mouth and that his face resembled something that had "gone through a meat grinder," but Humphreys County sheriff Ike Shelton insisted that Lee had been killed in a car accident and that the lead in his mouth must have been tooth fillings. "Negro Leader Dies in Odd Accident" read the headline in a Jackson newspaper the next day.

Lee's murder outraged local blacks and activists throughout the state. The NAACP, led by its new field secretary, Medgar Evers, immediately launched an investigation and demanded that federal authorities get involved. Lee's funeral attracted national attention as more than one thousand mourners (and readers of the *Chicago Defender*) viewed his mutilated body—Rosebud Lee had insisted on having an open casket. NAACP pressure prompted the federal Justice Department to investigate.

No one was ever charged with Lee's murder. The FBI built a circumstantial case against two members of the Citizens' Council, Peck Ray and Joe David Watson Jr., but the local prosecutor refused to take the case to a grand jury. Later that year, in another act of violence for which no one was convicted, Gus Courts was shot and driven from town.

Chris Myers Asch
Colby College

John Dittmer, *Local People: The Struggle for Civil Rights in Mississippi* (1994); Jack Mendelsohn, *The Martyrs: Sixteen Who Gave Their Lives for Racial Justice* (1966); Mississippi Civil Rights Project website, mscivil rightsproject.org; J. Todd Moye, *Let the People Decide: Black Freedom and White Resistance Movements in Sunflower County, Mississippi* (2004).

Lee, George Washington
(1894–1976) Writer and Business Leader

George Washington Lee was a successful African American businessman and politician who wrote his first book to promote racial pride during the Great Depression by praising black-owned businesses on Beale Street in Memphis. As a novelist, short story writer, and essayist, Lee also used his writings to provide a realistic portrayal of the corruption of the tenant farming system. In his final works he wrote short political essays.

Lee was born on 4 January 1894 in Indianola, the son of Rev. George Lee and Hattie Lee. George's parents separated soon after his birth, and the family moved into a sharecropper's shack following his father's death. Lee's mother insisted on her sons' education, but young George also worked as a cotton planter and picker, grocery clerk, house worker, and dray driver. He enrolled at Alcorn Agricultural and Mechanical College in Lorman and from 1912 to 1917 worked each summer as a bellhop at the Gayoso Hotel in Memphis to earn money to help his family and pay his tuition. At Alcorn, Lee was inspired by reading abolitionist Wendell Phillips's message of racial understanding and black pride.

In 1917 the War Department acquiesced to demands put forth by the National Association for the Advancement of Colored People (NAACP), establishing a black officer's training camp in Des Moines, Iowa. Lee was admitted to the program, rose to the rank of lieutenant, and fought for two years in France during World War I before his honorable discharge in 1919.

Lee then moved to Memphis, where he undertook a variety of activities, including working a number of jobs, leading fraternal and political organizations, and writing. Lee served as vice president of the Mississippi Life Insurance Company from 1922 to 1924 and later held various executive positions with the Atlanta Life Insurance Company and the Universal Life Insurance Company. His active career as a civic and political organizer endowed him with a keen knowledge of contemporary social issues and later served as subject matter for Lee's writings. He served on the Tennessee executive committee of the American Legion and delivered a seconding speech for Robert Taft at the 1952 Republican National Convention. Lee frequently spoke out against poverty and discrimination, praised racial pride, and stressed the need for blacks to organize and support their own businesses.

When the Great Depression halted Beale Street's economic prosperity, Lee wrote a history of the area's leading black-owned businesses to help renew his political theme of black pride. *Beale Street: Where the Blues Began* (1934) was historical fiction, featuring a foreword by blues composer and musician W. C. Handy. The book highlights blacks who achieved great financial success despite segregation and economic deprivation. Lee credited Robert R. Church Sr., who gained his freedom following the Civil War and went on to become worth millions of dollars, with helping to establish Beale Street as a black economic center. Through the frame of Church's narrative, Lee praised the success of local bankers, lawyers, real estate agents, ministers, doctors, business professionals, and insurance executives, all of whom Lee knew.

Lee balanced Beale Street's financial success with other civic accomplishments by including citizens who achieved artistic success and exemplified a high moral standing. He highlighted Julia A. Brooks, founder of a local integrated music school, and praised blacks who stayed to help save the city after the majority of whites fled during an 1878 yellow fever epidemic. At the risk of damaging his message of black pride, Lee tempered *Beale Street* with stories of corrupt and uneducated blacks. Through the inclusion of scenes with pimps, prostitutes, and poor men and women scavenging garbage cans for food, Lee provided an honest portrayal of Depression-era life.

The book garnered wide public and critical praise, prompting his rise within the Republican Party but a reduced role with the NAACP and the Urban League. He wrote his second book only after Walter White, the NAACP executive secretary, claimed that *Beale Street*'s success resulted from the area's prominence rather than Lee's writing skills.

Lee's literary response came in the form of a 1937 novel, *River George*. Introduced in the third chapter of *Beale Street*, Aaron George, the novel's hero, mirrors Lee's life in several ways. George attends Alcorn A&M before returning to sharecropping to support his mother. While in college he gains a sense of social responsibility, and he later discovers that he has been cheated by the local plantation bookkeeper. At this point, George begins to organize his fellow tenant farmers to question the sharecropping system. After the local white postmaster is killed in a struggle with George, he joins the army, becomes a lieutenant, and serves in France before returning home to die at the hands of a lynch mob. Critics praised the book's autobiographical elements as well as its depiction of a black hero exposing the corruption of the tenant farmer system.

By the early 1940s Lee's involvement with the Republican Party increased and his writing emphasized folklore rather than racial pride as his political stance shifted from protest to forms of accommodation. *Beale Street Sundown*, his final book, reflected these changes. The short stories collected there, which originally appeared in the *Negro Digest*, the *World's Digest*, and the *Southern Literary Messenger*, are more aesthetic vignettes than social tracts.

Lee's political essays appeared in black periodicals and newspapers throughout the 1950s and 1960s. He maintained his role within the Republican Party by actively supporting the Eisenhower administration and working in the Goldwater presidential campaign. He became grand commissioner of the Elks in the 1960s and helped raise money for the United Negro College Fund. Lee died on 1 August 1976.

Cale Nicholson
Fayetteville, Arkansas

Trudier Harris, *Dictionary of Literary Biography*, vol. 51, *Afro-American Writers from the Harlem Renaissance to 1940* (1987); David M. Tucker, *Lieutenant Lee of Beale Street* (1971).

Lee, Herbert
(1912–1961) Civil Rights Activist

Herbert Lee was an early martyr in the Mississippi civil rights movement. A land-owning dairy farmer with a nine children, Lee, an Amite County native, was a charter member of the Amite County chapter of the National Association for the Advancement of Colored People, founded in 1953.

Lee was a supporter of the students who started voter registration efforts in the McComb area in 1961, and he offered to drive organizer Robert Moses of the Student Nonviolent Coordinating Committee (SNCC) around and help him contact potential voters.

On the morning of 25 September 1961, Lee got into an argument with a white neighbor, E. H. Hurst, who was a representative in the state legislature, a member of the Citizens' Council, and the father-in-law of Billy Ray Caston, who had assaulted Moses a few days earlier. Hurst then shot Lee, claiming to have acted in self-defense after he brandished a tire iron. Although there were numerous witnesses to the shooting, the local sheriff intimidated them into supporting Hurst's story, and the local coroner's jury refused to indict him. One witness, Louis Allen, later told the Federal Bureau of Investigation that he had been forced to lie to the jury. Although Hurst was never charged, local whites retaliated against Allen by harassing and beating him. Then, on 31 January 1964 Allen, too, was gunned down. No one was ever charged in his murder.

Martin Luther King Jr. and leaders of SNCC, the Congress of Federated Organizations, and the Mississippi Freedom Democratic Party all cited Lee's name in discussing the need to build on the sacrifices of older activists. A Delta Ministry building in Greenville was named in his honor. A 1963 SNCC film, *We'll Never Turn Back* showed Lee's large family, without their murdered father, as a living sign of the people whom the movement was fighting to serve.

Ted Ownby
University of Mississippi

Kerry Bradford, "Terror in Liberty: Death and Civil Rights in a Mississippi Community" (master's thesis, University of Mississippi, 1993); Civil Rights Teaching website, www.civilrightsteaching.org; John Dittmer, *Local People: The Struggle for Civil Rights in Mississippi* (1994); Bruce Hilton, *The Delta Ministry*; Mississippi Civil Rights Project website, www.mscivilrightsproject.org; Mississippi Department of Archives and History, Sovereignty Commission Online website, http://mdah.state.ms.us/arrec/digital_archives/sovcom/; Northeastern University Civil Rights and Restorative Justice Project website, nuweb9.neu.edu/civilrights; Charles M. Payne, *I've Got the Light of Freedom: The Organizing Tradition and the Mississippi Freedom Struggle* (1995).

Lee, Muna
(1895–1965) Writer and Activist

Writer, translator, and activist Muna Lee was born in Raymond, Mississippi, on 29 January 1895 to Mary Maud Lee and Benjamin Lee, a druggist. The family moved to Hugo, Oklahoma, in 1902. Lee was a reader from an early age, and her father's stores provided her with a ready source of reading material. She started reading poetry and then writing while a teenager at Blue Mountain College, where her favorite teacher was David Guyton. After completing her education at the University of Mississippi in 1913, she taught school in Oklahoma and began publishing poems before she turned twenty, winning an award from *Poetry* magazine in 1916.

Two years later, she moved to New York to take a position as a translator for the Postal Censorship Division of the US Secret Service. She almost immediately published two of her poems, in both English and Spanish, in a new magazine, *Pan-American Poetry*. In 1919 Lee married Luis Muñoz Marin, a poet and the son of a Puerto Rican political leader who later became the island nation's first democratically elected governor. The couple moved to Puerto Rico in 1920 and went on to have two children. Through the 1920s and early 1930s she published widely in New York and Chicago magazines, including H. L. Mencken's *Smart Set* and *Others: A Magazine of the New Verse*. Most of Lee's early poems are first-person quatrains and sonnets. Macmillan published her only book of poetry, *Sea-Change*, in 1923.

Lee became an expert translator and a spirited proponent of Spanish-language literature written in the Americas. In 1925 she selected and translated the poems for the first issue of *Poetry* to feature Latin American works, and she began to translate other works, including histories and memoirs. In addition, she worked in the publicity office of the University of Puerto Rico.

In the late 1920s and 1930s, Lee became active in the modern women's movement, helping to found the Inter-American Commission of Women and working with the National Woman's Party. She combined her interests in feminism and Pan-American history and culture by working on behalf of the right of Puerto Rican women to vote. At the 1928 convention of the twenty-one-nation Pan-American Union. Lee compared the situation of women to the situation of Puerto Rico: "Our position as women, amongst you free citizens of Pan America, is like the position of my Porto Rico in the community of American States. We have everything done for us and given us by sovereignty. We are treated with every consideration save the one great consideration of being regarded as responsible beings. We, like Porto Rico, are dependents. We are anomalies before the law." Writing in the 1930s under the pen name Newton Gayle, Lee coauthored five well-received detective novels that featured dialogue in both English and Spanish.

Lee and Muñoz Marin legally separated by 1938 and divorced in 1946. Beginning in 1941 Lee worked for the US State Department in Washington, D.C., encouraging and organizing cultural exchanges with Latin American countries. She continued her work as translator and sought novel ways to connect US and Pan-American history. In 1944 the Library of Congress organized a radio series, *The American*

Story, with Lee providing content that showed connections among the various settlements in the Americas. In 1947 Lee and a fellow State Department employee, Ruth Emily McMurry, published *The Cultural Approach: Another Way in International Relations*, which described cultural exchanges as part of twentieth-century diplomacy, criticized exchanges that served only as propaganda, and encouraged programs that were truthful and "directed by the best minds of the several countries." Lee worked for the State Department until 1965, retiring shortly before her death from lung cancer on 3 April 1965.

Lee apparently visited Mississippi only twice after graduating from college, giving talks during the 1940s at Hinds Junior College and at Blue Mountain College, where David Guyton introduced her to the audience. In a 1940 interview in Puerto Rico she said that her writing drew on her range of experiences, beginning with the place of her birth: "Whatever poetic gift I have has also been fostered by every favoring environment: the beautiful simplicity, dignity, and pride of Mississippi; the thrilling sweep and color of the Indian Territory prairie; the heartening friendliness of great cities, New York, Washington, Paris, Madrid; the remoteness and completeness and intensity on this tropic island that has been a rich port to me."

Ted Ownby
University of Mississippi

Jonathan Cohen, *Muna Lee: A Pan-American Life* (2004); Elaine Hughes, *Lives of Mississippi Authors*, ed. James B. Lloyd (1981); Ruth Emily McMurry and Muna Lee, *The Cultural Approach: Another Way in International Relations* (1947); Southern Literary Festival Association, *Four Talks on Writing, Delivered at the Southern Literary Festival* (1947).

Lee, Stephen D.

(1833–1908) Confederate General, Politician, and Educator

Born on 22 September 1833, in Charleston, South Carolina, Stephen Dill Lee was the first child of Dr. Thomas Lee Jr. and Caroline Allison Lee. His mother died in 1835, shortly after giving birth to Caroline Kezia Rachel Lee, and Stephen and his sister were raised by their financially unsuccessful father and his second wife, Elizabeth Cummings Humphreys Lee, whom he married in 1839.

In part as a consequence of the family's financial situation, Lee received his early formal education at a military boarding school run by the uncle for whom he was named. He later secured an appointment to the US Military Academy, graduating in 1854. Lee served in the US Army for

Statue of Stephen Dill Lee, Vicksburg (Library of Congress, Washington, D.C. [LC-D4-73328])

nearly seven years and saw action in Florida in the Third Seminole War and along the Kansas-Missouri border.

On 20 February 1861, following the secession of several southern states, he resigned from the army and was commissioned a captain in South Carolina forces and later in the Confederate Army. Lee first served as an aide-de-camp to Gen. P. G. T. Beauregard in Charleston, and on 11 April 1861 he delivered an ultimatum to Union major Robert Anderson demanding the evacuation of Fort Sumter. When the demand was refused, South Carolina troops fired on the fort and civil war began.

Lee served as an artillery officer in the early campaigns of the war in Virginia and Maryland. In action at Seven Pines, on the Peninsula, at Second Manassas, and at Antietam, he exhibited personal bravery and exceptional skill. Lee rose steadily in rank and on 6 November 1862 was promoted to brigadier general and sent to the fortress city of Vicksburg, known as the Gibraltar of the Confederacy.

In December 1862 Lee commanded the Confederate forces that defeated William Tecumseh Sherman's US troops along the banks of Chickasaw Bayou, north of Vicksburg. He led a brigade of Alabama troops throughout the Vicksburg Campaign and during the siege of the city, which surrendered to Ulysses S. Grant on 4 July 1863. Following his exchange, Lee was elevated to major general on 3 August 1863; on 23 June 1864 he received another promotion, becoming the youngest Confederate lieutenant general. Given command of John Bell Hood's old corps in the Army of Tennessee, Lee fought valiantly in the battles around Atlanta and in the disastrous Tennessee Campaign. During the retreat from Nashville, Lee's corps served as the army's rear guard and clashed frequently with the enemy.

On 17 December 1864, while in action along the Harpeth River near Spring Hill, Tennessee, he was wounded in the foot. After being taken to a hospital in Florence, Alabama, Lee was moved to the home of his fiancée, Regina Harrison, in Columbus, Mississippi, and they married on 9 February 1865, during his convalescence. He rejoined the army under Joseph E. Johnston in North Carolina and served with distinction for the remainder of the war. He and his wife subsequently moved to Devereaux, a 770-acre plantation in Noxubee County that the couple received as a wedding gift from Regina Lee's grandfather.

Despite his energy and determination, Stephen Lee was unable to make his plantation a financial success. His failure gave rise to his belief that education and the application of science to agriculture provided the best hope for farming in Mississippi. His interest in promoting agriculture led him to the political arena, and he was elected to the State Senate in 1878. Lee supported a bill to create Mississippi Agricultural and Mechanical College (now Mississippi State University) and was appointed the school's first president in 1880, serving until 1899.

Although his duties at the college were demanding, Lee remained active in politics and was a delegate to the convention that drafted the state's 1890 Constitution. He also pursued interests in other fields and served as president of the Mississippi Historical Society. He slowly became interested in honoring his fellow veterans, and his efforts to serve them soon became a passion that dominated the last twenty years of his life. In 1895 he became president of the Vicksburg National Military Park Association, which sought to secure congressional establishment of a national military park at Vicksburg. In February 1899, when Pres. William McKinley signed the bill creating the park, Lee was appointed to the park commission. Elected by his fellow commissioners as chair, Lee served in that capacity until 1901.

After Regina Lee's death on 3 October 1903, Stephen Lee devoted his remaining energies entirely to honor veterans who had fought in the Civil War. In 1904 he was named commander in chief of the United Confederate Veterans. On 22 May 1908, shortly after speaking at a reunion of Union veterans in Vicksburg, Lee suffered a stroke, and he died six days later. On 11 June 1909 a standing statue of Lee, sculpted by Henry Kitson, was dedicated on the grounds of the park at Vicksburg.

Terrence J. Winschel
Vicksburg National Park

Herman M. Hattaway, *General Stephen D. Lee* (1976); *New York Times* (29 May 1908); Terrence J. Winschel, *Journal of Mississippi History* (Spring 2001).

Lee County

Known to many as the county where Elvis Presley grew up and made his first music, Lee County in northeastern Mississippi has a long history of events central to story of the state. In one legend explaining the story of the Chickasaw, members of the tribe wandered from far in the West and chose to settle in "old fields" west of what became Tupelo. The area became a main location for the Chickasaw, and the crucial 1736 Battle of Ackia took place there. The county seat is Tupelo, while other communities include Plantersville, Saltillo, Shannon, Baldwyn, and Verona.

As part of Itawamba and Pontotoc Counties, the area became a growing farming area in the 1830s after the removal of most Chickasaw. Civil War military forces moved through the area in 1862, prior to the Battle of Iuka, and returned in 1864 as part of movements that led to the Battle of Brice's Cross Roads near Baldwyn.

Lee County was formed during Reconstruction and was named after Robert E. Lee. It was from the start a sizable county, with a population of 15,955 in its first census in 1870 and 20,470 in 1880. About a third of its population was African American, and in 1880 Lee had about 100 people born outside the country, most of them from Ireland. Owners cultivated 61 percent of the county's farms, practicing mixed agriculture with grains, cotton, and livestock. The county particularly concentrated on the production of butter (ranking third in the state) and orchard products (eighth). Northeastern Mississippi has a reputation as an area for yeoman farmers, but by 1880 Tupelo already had thirty-seven manufacturing establishments, employing sixty-two workers.

In 1900 Lee's population remained steady at 21,956, with whites accounting for about 60 percent of residents and African Americans for the remainder. It remained an agricultural county, with thirty-five hundred farms. Forty-four percent of all white farmers owned the land they farmed, while only 9 percent of the African American farmers did so. Industry continued to increase in importance, and by 1900, 175 industrial workers, all but 9 of them men, were employed at seventy-five firms. Lee County was home to fifty-seven immigrants, most of them from Ireland and Germany.

In the 1916 religious census the churches of Lee County, as in much of Mississippi, were mostly Methodist and Baptist. The leading denominations were the Missionary Baptists; the Methodist Episcopal Church, South; the Colored

Methodist Episcopal Church; and the Southern Baptists; with smaller but substantial numbers in the Methodist Episcopal Church and the Presbyterian Church.

By 1930 Lee County's population had grown to 35,313 and was just over two-thirds white. Tenants worked more than 70 percent of the county's 5,289 farms. Lee County was home to thirty-two manufacturing establishments with more than nine hundred workers, many of them women employed in garment factories, and Tupelo had grown to more than six thousand people, making Lee one of Mississippi's more densely populated counties.

Lee County's most famous resident was Elvis Aron Presley, born in 1935. Before he moved with his parents to Memphis in 1948, the young Presley sang in an Assemblies of God church, performed at the local fair, and had some experience with the county's African American population. The small shotgun house where he was born is now a major tourist attraction. Other creative individuals from Lee County include fiddler Hoyt Ming, Lawrence Welk show singer Guy Hovis, and *Sweet Potato Queen* author Jill Connor Browne. Internationally acclaimed painter Sam Gilliam was born in Tupelo in 1933.

The New Deal brought a new and important series of relationships between the federal government and Lee County. Tupelo became famous in 1934 as the first city to receive power through the Tennessee Valley Authority. That year, Pres. Franklin Roosevelt and First Lady Eleanor Roosevelt visited the city for the opening of the Tupelo Homesteads, a twenty-five-building planned community for people displaced from their homes by the economic changes of the Great Depression. The buildings are now connected to Tupelo's welcome center for the Natchez Trace Parkway.

In the 1930s George McLean bought the *Tupelo Journal* and started a campaign for economic and community development that involved improved education, new industry that would pay wages that were high by Mississippi standards, and greater cooperation between rural and urban areas. Those points later became central to the concept of the Tupelo Miracle, a period of economic and educational improvement.

By 1960 Lee's population had topped forty thousand and the county ranked in the state's top ten in population and population density. Lee had the fourth-highest number of industrial workers in Mississippi, with more than twelve hundred women and four hundred men working in the apparel industry and many others working in food and furniture industries. About 15 percent of the county's workers were employed in agriculture, primarily producing soybeans and corn and raising cattle. Population growth continued, and by 1980 Lee County had 57,061 residents; two decades later, the population had boomed to 75,755.

Recent developments in Lee County include the growth of a tourist industry related to Elvis Presley and the increasing influence of the Tupelo-based American Family Association, a group that supports conservative religious causes.

Like many counties in northeastern Mississippi, in 2010 Lee County had a significant white majority, an African American minority, and a small but growing Hispanic/Latino community. Lee County nearly doubled between 1960 and 2010, and its population of 82,910 made it one of the state's largest counties. In addition, it had Mississippi's fourth-highest per capita income.

Mississippi Encyclopedia Staff
University of Mississippi

Mississippi State Planning Commission, *Progress Report on State Planning in Mississippi* (1938); *Mississippi Statistical Abstract*, Mississippi State University (1952–2010); Charles Sydnor and Claude Bennett, *Mississippi History* (1939); University of Virginia Library, Historical Census Browser website, http://mapserver.lib.virginia.edu; E. Nolan Waller and Dani A. Smith, *Growth Profiles of Mississippi's Counties, 1960–1980* (1985).

LeFlore, Greenwood

(1800–1865) Choctaw Chief

L

A leader of the Choctaw in the crucial period of the 1820s and 1830s, Greenwood LeFlore was born in 1800 to Nancy Cravat, a Choctaw woman, and Louis LeFleur, a Canadian fur trader. The kinship connections of his mother's clan and his father's dealings with the fur trade made LeFlore well positioned to straddle the native and European worlds that were merging as settlers moved ever westward. Indeed, the parents took steps to ensure that he obtained the skills and connections necessary to prepare him to lead his people during a challenging time.

When LeFlore was twelve, his family sent him to live with Maj. John Donly and his family in Nashville, Tennessee. Little is known of LeFlore's stay there, but he probably acquired a basic education and witnessed firsthand the inner workings of slavery and the cotton economy. Much to the Donlys' dismay, his efforts to cultivate connections led him to elope with their daughter, Rosa, back to his home in the Choctaw nation in 1817.

LeFlore returned to a nation in turmoil and entered politics with a handful of allies who shared his reformist leanings. In 1825 he and another young man, David Folsom, challenged the three national chiefs whose tendency to cede land to settle personal debts had caused increasing alarm among the people. In 1826 Folsom unseated Chief Mushulatubbee in the eastern towns, and in the western towns where LeFlore lived, people agitated for the removal of his uncle, Robert Cole. Acclaimed by the public, LeFlore pledged never to "turn his coat" on his people.

LeFlore won widespread backing by supporting mission schools where children learned to read, write, and speak English as well as a host of trades that would give them opportunities in the changing economy. At the same time, he made his fortune with thirty-two slaves who worked a 250-acre cotton plantation in the Yazoo River Valley. LeFlore appeared to be the consummate southern planter, but he also adhered closely to Choctaw traditions of generosity and obligation. His wealth, for example, underwrote his support for a network of leaders who governed the western towns and enabled him to host anyone who might come to visit or ask his advice. As one observer wrote, his home "must be free to all who visit them, and as they wish to elevate their people, their tables must be well supplyed."

In addition to ministering to the needs of his people, LeFlore had to rebuff the federal government's constant clamor for more land. He wrote to the Office of Indian Affairs that the government's endless demands pressured his people so that they could find neither the time nor the energy to accommodate the cultural and political expansion of Anglo-America. His plea for a few years of "rest," however, ended with Andrew Jackson's election to the presidency in 1828. Jackson's victory signaled that the Native Americans' tenure in Mississippi would be tolerated no longer, and in 1830 the federal government enacted the Indian Removal Act to hasten that departure.

The act dashed LeFlore's hopes for a strong and independent Choctaw nation, and he predicted in a speech to the national council that "bad white men will soon come among us, and settle on our vacant land, and cheat us out of our property." Accordingly, in September 1829, LeFlore called a public meeting where he announced his despair and counseled his audience to accept Removal because armed resistance offered no hope. The national council responded by electing LeFlore as the nation's sole chief and authorizing him to negotiate the nation's Removal to the West.

In September 1830 nearly six thousand Choctaw convened on a small patch of land between the two forks of Dancing Rabbit Creek to hear the federal government's proposal for Removal. In the early going a number of men and women spoke out against Removal; feeling that their will had been made clear, the people then packed up and returned to their homes. Two days later the federal commissioners called together a handful of leaders including LeFlore and concluded the Treaty of Dancing Rabbit Creek, in which the Choctaw agreed to leave Mississippi.

Nearly fifteen thousand of the approximately eighteen thousand Choctaw moved to Indian Territory over the next three years, but LeFlore was not among them. He remained behind after receiving death threats for his role in the Removal treaty. He expanded his plantation holdings, served briefly in the Mississippi legislature, and became a leading cotton planter. His plantation home, Malmaison, was one of the finest in the state, and he modeled it after in the French style favored by his hero, Napoleon Bonaparte. When Mississippi seceded from the United States, LeFlore cast his lot with the Union despite his ownership of slaves, and when he died in August 1865 his body was wrapped in an American flag and interred on his plantation grounds. Malmaison burned to the ground in 1942.

James Taylor Carson
Queen's University

James Taylor Carson, *Journal of Mississippi History* (2003); James Taylor Carson, *Searching for the Bright Path: The Mississippi Choctaws from Prehistory to Removal* (1999); Arthur H. DeRosier Jr., *The Removal of the Choctaw Indians* (1970); Clara Sue Kidwell, *Choctaws and Missionaries in Mississippi, 1818–1918* (1995).

Leflore County

Located in the Mississippi Delta, Leflore County was formed during Reconstruction from portions of Carroll and Sunflower Counties. The Tallahatchie and Yalobusha Rivers meet in Greenwood, the seat of Leflore County, to form the Yazoo River. The county was named for Choctaw leader Greenwood LeFlore.

Leflore began as a cotton-growing area with high numbers of African Americans working as tenant farmers. In its first census in 1880, 78 percent of the county's 10,246 residents were African Americans, far higher than the state average of 57 percent. Leflore was also home to 16 Native Americans and 84 foreign-born immigrants. Two-thirds of the county's farmers were renters or sharecroppers. As in most plantation areas operated by tenants, those farms concentrated on cotton, by far the most abundant crop.

Howard Street, Greenwood, seat of Leflore County, ca. 1909 (Ann Rayburn Paper Americana Collection, Department of Archives and Special Collections, J. D. Williams Library, University of Mississippi [rayburn_ann_36_15_001])

Leflore's population more than doubled from 1880 to 1900 as African Americans moved to the area in search of economic opportunity. In 1900 the proportion of African Americans had risen to 88 percent, with whites accounting for fewer than 3,000 of the county's 23,834 people. The county was also home to a small group of German and Russian immigrants. Leflore was a cotton-growing powerhouse using sharecroppers and tenant farmers. Only 5 percent of the county's four thousand African American farmers owned their land, while 42 percent of the 271 white farmers did so. A growing manufacturing base employed 363 men and no women. Leflore County was home to substantial Colored Farmers' Alliance activity, led by organizer Oliver Cromwell in the late 1880s.

In 1916, Leflore's largest religious group was the Missionary Baptists. In fact, Leflore's more than eight thousand Missionary Baptists gave it the fourth-highest concentration in the state. The county also had a substantial number of Methodists (divided among four denominations) and smaller numbers of Southern Baptists, Presbyterians, Catholics, and Episcopalians.

In 1930 Leflore County was remarkable because of the number of African Americans growing cotton as tenant farmers. Leflore was home to more than eight thousand farms, 95 percent of them operated by tenant farmers—the highest percentage in the state. Leflore had a total population of 53,506, fourth-highest in the state, including 40,884 African Americans (76 percent). Leflore had a substantial population born outside the United States, with 57 natives of Italy, 41 from Russia, 38 from Palestine and Syria, and 23 from Greece. An unknown number of migrant workers from Mexico worked in Leflore and other Delta counties in the 1920s and 1930s. The county had the third-highest population density in Mississippi. The city of Greenwood, with about 8,000 residents, was the business center for the county, and Leflore had 589 industrial workers.

A variety of creative individuals grew up Leflore County. Blues musician B. B. King was born Riley B. King outside Itta Bena and Berclair in 1925. Soul blues singer Denise LaSalle (Ora Denise Allen) was born in Leflore in 1939, and blues performer Furry Lewis was born in Greenwood in 1899. As a child, singer Bobbie Gentry, famous for the song "Ode to Billie Joe," lived with her family on a farm outside Greenwood. Blues legend Robert Johnson died in Greenwood in 1938.

Numerous writers spent their childhoods in the area and went on to use Leflore County as setting and subject for their work. Lewis "Buddy" Nordan grew up in Itta Bena and wrote about the town in numerous works of fiction. Mary Craig Kimbrough Sinclair's family had homes in Greenwood and on the Gulf Coast, and she detailed her youth and her life with Upton Sinclair in a 1957 memoir, *Southern Belle*. Donna Tartt, author of several novels, including the Pulitzer Prize–winning *The Goldfinch* (2013), was born in Greenwood in 1963. Agricultural scholar Dorothy Dickins, who spent most of her career in Starkville, grew up in Money. Actress Carrie Nye was born in Greenwood. Basketball star Lusia Harris Stewart grew up in Minter City and gained acclaim playing at Delta State in the 1970s before representing the United States in the Pan American and Olympic Games.

Mississippi Vocational College opened in Itta Bena in 1950 as a segregated institution for African Americans. It changed its name in 1962 to Mississippi Valley State College and in 1974 became a university. A small public school, it is best known to sports fans as the alma mater of National Football League star Jerry Rice, who played there in the 1980s.

By 1960 Leflore's population had begun to shrink. Of the county's 47,142 residents, 64 percent were African American, 35 percent were white, and nearly 1 percent were Chinese. About a third of the employed in Leflore County worked in agriculture. The county ranked third in Mississippi in the production of soybeans, fourth in rice, and fifth in cotton. The prominence of cotton led to the creation of Greenwood's Cottonlandia Museum, which in 2012 became the Museum of the Mississippi Delta. Though manufacturing remained a small part of the economy, a substantial number of women worked in the clothing industry.

The county was significant in several ways during the civil rights years. Teenager Emmett Till was murdered in 1955 after white supremacists overheard remarks he made at a grocery store in the Leflore County community of Money. Robert "Tut" Patterson was working in Leflore in 1954 when he helped form the first Citizens' Council in the Sunflower County town of Indianola. In 1963 Student Nonviolent Coordinating Committee workers began organizing in Leflore, and Greenwood civil rights workers declared 25 March 1964 Freedom Day, with numerous demonstrators attempting to register to vote. Civil rights activists Amzie Moore, Hollis Watkins, Lawrence Guyot, Bob Zellner, and Willie Peacock worked in Leflore County. Both James Bevel and Marion Barry were born in Itta Bena in 1936, Laura McGhee and her children lived in the community of Browning, and Greenwood native Endesha Ida Mae Holland detailed her youth and her turn toward activism in a 1997 memoir, *From the Mississippi Delta*.

The population decline that began in the mid-twentieth century has persisted into the twenty-first. Greenwood experienced an economic resurgence when Viking Range started building kitchen appliances there in the 1980s. Nevertheless, Leflore lost 31.4 percent of its residents between 1960 and 2010. In 2000, the county had 37,947 residents, but ten years later, that number had fallen to 32,317: 72 percent of those inhabitants were African American, 25 percent were white, and 2.3 percent were Hispanic/Latino. Catfish farming began in the county in the 1970s and by 2007 provided 786 jobs.

Mississippi Encyclopedia Staff
University of Mississippi

Mississippi State Planning Commission, *Progress Report on State Planning in Mississippi* (1938); *Mississippi Statistical Abstract*, Mississippi State University (1952–2010); Charles Sydnor and Claude Bennett, *Mississippi History* (1939); University of Virginia Library, Historical Census Browser website, http://mapserver.lib.virginia.edu; E. Nolan Waller and Dani A. Smith, *Growth Profiles of Mississippi's Counties, 1960–1980* (1985).

Levee Camps

Oh, you got to roll,
Just like a hunter's hound,
Lord, if you can't roll, get your britches down.
—David "Honeyboy" Edwards, "You Got to Roll" (recorded in Clarksdale, 1942)

Levee camps were temporary settlements erected along the Mississippi River from roughly 1880 to 1940 to support the construction, repair, and enlargement of the great earthen levees that run along both sides of the river's banks. The typical levee camp that flourished during this period housed an almost exclusively black male workforce of seasonally employed mule drivers, overseen by white foremen and levee contractors, though black women also came to the camps to live with and cook for individual workers or to serve as paid cooks in camp commissaries. This style of levee camp was especially numerous in the low-lying Arkansas-Mississippi Delta (located along both sides of the river between Memphis and Vicksburg), which saw some of the most extensive levee construction projects during this period.

The vast majority of black levee workers were either cotton sharecroppers attempting to earn cash during down periods in the plantation cycle or other workers who came from a sharecropping background and thus had the expert

Unscreened and unfloored tents at a typical community levee camp on the Mississippi River, (National Archives and Records Administration, RG 77, Entry 109, file 2525-1110/1)

mule-handling skills required for levee construction. Typically located in remote areas along the river's edges, levee camps gained a notorious reputation for long work hours, exploitative commissary and pay practices, harsh forms of white disciplinary violence, and a wild and violent after-hours work culture characterized by drinking, gambling, fighting, and sex. Indeed, these aspects gave levee camp life a prominent place in early blues hollers, songs, and folklore from the region.

The traditional style of levee camp was a product of the mule-based construction practices that increasingly characterized levee building after 1880. The first mule-powered equipment used for levee building was the slip scraper, or slip, which had a cutting blade on the front of an open receptacle that filled up with earth as it dragged along the ground behind the mule. Wheeled scrapers, or wheelers, were developed shortly thereafter, using a larger blade and bucket that could be lowered and lifted; each one was pulled by multiple mules. (The blues song "You Got to Roll" referred to the work of rolling a wheeler.) Shortly after 1900 wagons attached to elevating graders were used alongside slips and wheelers. Elevating graders, which were pulled by mules or sometimes by steam or diesel tractors, lifted excavated earth to the wagon by means of a conveyor belt powered by the turning of the equipment's wheels. Increased federal funding for flood control following the Great Mississippi River Flood of 1927 dramatically speeded mechanization in levee building, though traditional mule teams continued to work alone or alongside more mechanized equipment for at least another decade. The full mechanization of levee construction culminated with huge drag-line levee-building machines, which were in general use throughout the Delta and Lower Mississippi by 1940 and made the traditional mule-team levee camp mostly a thing of the past.

As a labor site, levee camps provided the promise of mobility and cash wages to sharecroppers otherwise bound to the land by debt. Levee work therefore posed a potential threat to the Delta's racial-economic order, especially during the Great Migration, when white planters were already concerned about sharecroppers' increased mobility. White contractors and foremen organized the levee camp work site so that it reproduced patterns of racialized subordination common to the region as a whole, using an exploitative commissary system and administering ritually humiliating beatings in which workers were stripped naked and beaten on their bare hindquarters (reflected in the blues line, "If you can't roll, get your britches down"). Although these conditions had long been the subject of blues songs and hollers from the region, they were further confirmed in a series of 1930s investigations initially spearheaded by the National Association for the Advancement of Colored People and later continued by the American Federation of Labor and the US Army Corps of Engineers. Levee contractors also organized gambling, prostitution, and the sale of alcohol in the camps, taking a share of the profits and lending workers money under usurious terms to participate in these activities. Evidence suggests that contractors also supported a certain level of black-on-black violence in the camps as a means of labor control, as reflected in contractors' reported instruction to workers, "Keep yourself out of the grave, and I'll keep you out of jail."

Perhaps not surprisingly, the after-hours activities in the levee camps attained an almost mythic status in black oral culture from the Delta region and attracted the early attention of Alan Lomax and other folklorists. However, Lomax and others generally accepted oral accounts of these activities as testimonies of fact. In what was likely a more accurate assessment, Fisk University sociologist Lewis Wade Jones (who collaborated with Lomax in 1941 and 1942) acknowledged that the levee camp was indeed "wild and lawless" yet also observed that "it is difficult to get at facts behind the legend and lore of the levee camp." Ultimately, he concluded, "For the folk of the Delta the legend and lore are the facts." Indeed, more recent scholarship has suggested that the tales of after-hours activities represented an effort by black men in the Delta to reinscribe a sense of masculine autonomy and authority in a social order that offered them few freedoms.

Michael McCoyer

Northwestern University

James Cobb, *The Most Southern Place on Earth: The Mississippi Delta and the Roots of Regional Identity* (1992); John Cowley, *Journal of Folklore Research* (May–December 1991); Allison Davis, Burleigh B. Gardner, and Mary R. Gardner, *Deep South: A Social Anthropological Study of Caste and Class* (1941); Adam Gussow, *Seems Like Murder Here: Southern Violence and the Blues Tradition* (2002); Alan Lomax, *The Land Where the Blues Began* (1993); Michael McCoyer, *International Labor and Working-Class History* (Spring 2006); US Congress, House Committee on Labor, *Regulation of Wages Paid to Employees by Contractors Awarded Government Building Contracts* (Hearings), 72nd Cong., 2nd sess. (13, 22 January 1932); Roy Wilkins, *The Crisis* (April 1933); John Wesley Work, Lewis Wade Jones, and Samuel C. Adams Jr., *Lost Delta Found: Rediscovering the Fisk University–Library of Congress Coahoma County Study, 1941–1942*, ed. Robert Gordon and Bruce Nemerov (2005).

Leventhal, Mel

(b. 1945) Human Rights Lawyer

A native of Brooklyn, New York, Melvyn Roseman Leventhal began his work in the Mississippi civil rights movement in 1965. While attending New York University Law School, he spent summers in Jackson through the Boston-based Law Students Civil Rights Research Council. Upon graduating in 1967 he set up practice in Jackson and married Alice Walker, an author and fellow activist whom he had met during his summers in Mississippi. Walker referred to Leventhal as "a human rights lawyer who sues a large number of racist institutions a year (and wins)." Their daughter, Rebecca Leventhal (now Rebecca Walker), born in 1969, was known as a "movement child" because of her parents' involvement in the civil rights movement and because of the promise suggested by such an interracial relationship.

The harshness of the struggle for civil rights and its accompanying violence were very real to Leventhal both inside and outside the courtroom. According to Walker, she and Leventhal were "the only interracial, married, home-owning couple in Mississippi," and their presence in public life often caused "an angry silence." Leventhal's work for the National Association for the Advancement of Colored People was complicated by the anti-Semitism of many Mississippi judges. In his book chronicling the work of the organization's lawyers, Jack Greenberg recalled that Judge Harold Cox refused to accept legal documents from Leventhal unless he attached *A.D.* to all dates. However, Cox later confided in Leventhal after sentencing those involved in the 1964 murders of Jewish civil rights activists Michael Schwerner and Andrew Goodman as well as African American James Chaney, "It's one thing to beat them up, but another to kill them."

Leventhal worked for the Legal Defense and Education Fund, which focused on issues of school desegregation to encourage equal educational opportunities for children across Mississippi. Despite the Supreme Court's 1954 *Brown v. Board of Education* decision, public schools in Mississippi remained segregated throughout the 1960s. Predominantly white school boards used tactics such as districting to maintain segregation. In addition, private schools became havens for the children of white Mississippi segregationists. Leventhal fought to assure that such segregated academies did not detract from the quality and funding of public schools. An example was his fight for the integration of the faculties of Coahoma County High School and Coahoma Agricultural High School, where he argued that integration required equal opportunities for teachers as well as students.

Leventhal returned to New York in 1975, and his marriage to Walker ended the following year. He maintained a successful career as a lawyer, serving in the state attorney general's office as head of the Consumer Frauds and Protection Bureau and later as assistant attorney general.

Adam C. Evans

Washington, D.C.

Jack Greenberg, *Crusaders in the Courts: How a Dedicated Band of Lawyers Fought for the Civil Rights Revolution* (1994); Alice Walker, *In Search of Our Mother's Gardens: Womanist Prose* (2004); Rebecca Walker, *Black, White, and Jewish: Autobiography of a Shifting Self* (2001).

Lewis, Furry
(1899–1981) Blues Musician

Walter "Furry" Lewis was born in 1899 in Greenwood, the son of Walter Lewis and Victoria Coleman. His father left the family before Walter was born, and when the boy was six, his mother moved him and his two sisters to Memphis. At an early age Lewis learned both a country and ragtime style of blues from an obscure bluesman named Blind Joe. Lewis attended school through the fifth grade before taking up work as a delivery boy to help his family financially. He acquired the nickname Furry from a childhood friend, and following a train-hopping accident as a teenager, Lewis lost a leg, pushing him into music full time.

While still a teenager, Lewis left Memphis to work in a traveling medicine show, crisscrossing the South first as vaudeville comedian and later playing his particular strain of blues to gather crowds for the show's medicine barker. He also played for house parties and family picnics in and around Memphis and as far away as southern Arkansas.

Lewis became an expert in the "bottleneck blues" style particular to Mississippi bluesmen, which involves slide slapping and string muffling along the guitar neck with a pocketknife or other blade or a bottleneck slide. In the 1920s blues musician W. C. Handy discovered young Lewis in Memphis and bought him his first manufactured guitar. From this start, Lewis sang his own versions of folk songs, including "Kassie Jones" ("Casey Jones"), "Stack-o-Lee" ("Stagger Lee"), and "John Henry." Lewis's renditions of these folktales first brought him to the attention of Vocalion Studios. The better-known Victor label signed Lewis in 1928, and he recorded eight songs. Lewis returned to Vocalion to record

Furry Lewis (Courtesy Blues Archive, Department of Archives and Special Collections, J. D. Williams Library, University of Mississippi)

four more songs before the Great Depression pushed him back into obscurity, where he remained until 1959.

Lewis lived in Memphis and worked odd jobs as a laborer until he was rediscovered during the same blues resurgence that brought many other older musicians to world attention. Lewis gained notoriety as part of the Blues Revival, making some new recordings and performing as part of the Memphis Blues Caravan. He was not pleased with folksinger Joni Mitchell's portrayal of him in her 1976 song, "Furry Sings the Blues," in which she describes "Old Furry" as "Fallen to hard luck / And time and other thieves." Lewis never attained the fame of some more celebrated blues artists, but he opened twice for the Rolling Stones, appeared on *The Tonight Show*, and had a part in a 1975 movie, *W. W. and the Dixie Dancekings*, starring Burt Reynolds. His recordings document the unique jackknife slide, his low string–high vocal harmony, and his use of the oral tradition of black American heroes. He died in Memphis on 14 September 1981.

Thomas Eaton
Southeast Missouri State University

Arne Brogger, Blue Highway website, www.thebluehighway.com; Ian Eagleson, *Smithsonian Folkways* (2002); Greg Johnson, Blue Notes website, www.cascadeblues.org.

Libraries

When nine students from Tougaloo College considered a location for a civil rights protest in 1961, they concluded that sitting in at the Jackson Public Library would serve their goals. First, the public library was a government institution, and the state had for years said access to reading was a citizen's right. Further, the idea that access to books should be open to all people celebrated reading's potential for encouraging new ideas.

Mississippi has had libraries almost as long as it has had Euro-American settlers. Organizations such as Natchez's Mississippi Republican Society and Mississippi Society for the Acquirement and Dissemination of Useful Knowledge, the Library Company of Gibson-Port, and the Adams Athenaeum in Washington began lending books in the early 1800s. In the 1820s Liberty, Franklin, Yazoo, Tchula, and other places had debating and lecturing societies that also had small libraries. The rise of religious colleges, the organization of the state law library in Jackson, the beginning of the University of Mississippi in Oxford, and the rise of Sunday schools were landmarks in the start of organized libraries for specific groups. According to the US census, by 1870

Mississippi churches were home to more than five hundred Sunday schools with libraries.

Efforts to begin free public libraries began in the late 1800s and accelerated in the early 1900s with the assistance of women's organizations. The State Federation of Women's Clubs supported libraries, and individual groups frequently crusaded on the county level. For example, as soon as Bolivar County's Daughters of the American Revolution chapter formed in 1916, it began to work to create a county library. In 1924 Starkville Woman's Club leader Mena Blumfield told her organization, "This town should have a library. I want every one of you to give me a dollar and a book."

The Mississippi Library Organization formed in 1911 and held its first meeting at Houston High School. In 1926 the legislature created the Mississippi Library Commission to offer professional leadership to local groups, set standards, and clarify laws about books and library access. Ten years later, the group started its newsletter, *Library News.* Funding for new libraries often came from the Andrew Carnegie fortune, and the Works Progress Administration helped build and improve libraries in the 1930s. A 1926 survey found that Jackson, Clarksdale, Meridian, and Greenville had the public libraries with the largest collections of books, while some counties with poorly funded libraries had fewer than one thousand books.

By the 1940s Mississippi State College for Women (later Mississippi University for Women) and Mississippi Southern College (later the University of Southern Mississippi) had library science programs, and Tougaloo College and the University of Mississippi offered library science classes. By 1949 the state had thirty-one county libraries. In 1950 DeSoto, Tate, Panola, and Lafayette Counties in northern Mississippi created the state's first regional library system. By the following decade, every county had some kind of public library, though many librarians had little training.

Moreover, African Americans were not permitted to use most of these facilities. In the 1920s Coahoma County started Mississippi's first "book wagon," a service that sometimes made books available to African Americans. A 1916 study found that of the state's twenty public libraries, only Meridian Library No. 2 served African Americans. A 1950 report concluded that Mississippi's African Americans had access to only eight public libraries. Though African American churches and colleges often had books, public schools for black children almost always were deficient in this arena. In fact, discussions of Mississippi schools before and after the 1954 *Brown v. Board of Education* decision often mentioned libraries as especially vivid signs of inequality. State law required libraries only in public schools that offered multiple English classes, and the great majority of such schools were for whites only. Civil rights activists teaching in Freedom Schools beginning in 1964 were consistently troubled by the lack of books in African American schools and worked to bring new reading materials to their students.

Library building surged in the late 1960s, partly as a result of the Public Library Construction Act of 1964, which offered federal funds for the enterprise. Forty-two new public library buildings opened in Mississippi between 1964 and 1971. Subsequent initiatives to improve the state's education and quality of life have consistently included libraries.

In recent years, the state's libraries have focused on improving access to Mississippi's civil rights history. Tougaloo College is home to the Mississippi Civil Rights Collection, and the University of Southern Mississippi's library hosts the Civil Rights in Mississippi Digital Archive; the Mississippi Department of Archives and History has a wide range of materials on the civil rights movement and massive resistance and has made many of them available online; and other colleges and universities have become central locations for civil rights research.

Mississippi's twenty-first-century libraries reach far into the life of the state. A 2010 survey found 285 public libraries, including branch establishments, 58 academic libraries, 61 special libraries, and dozens of school libraries. Public libraries play many roles, lending books and other materials, offering computer access, hosting programs for children, housing adult education services, and serving in many ways as community centers.

Ted Ownby
University of Mississippi

Whitman Davis, *The Library Situation in Mississippi* (1916); Mississippi Library Commission, *Directory of Mississippi Libraries* (2010); Mississippi Library Commission, *Long Range Program for Library Development in Mississippi* (1972); Mississippi Library Survey, *People without Books: An Analysis of Library Services in Mississippi* (1950); Margarete Peebles and J. B. Howell, eds., *A History of Mississippi Libraries* (1975); *Public Library Buildings in Mississippi, 1964–1971* (1971); Augusta B. Richards et al., eds., *Libraries in Mississippi: A Report of a Survey of Library of Facilities* (1949).

Lighthouses

Lighthouses were once ubiquitous fixtures on the Mississippi coast, with as many as nine in operation in the late nineteenth century. Their numbers diminished because of recurrent storm damage and the increasing reliance on more modern navigational aids. After Hurricane Katrina in 2005, Mississippi's only remaining operational lighthouse was in Biloxi.

Pass Christian Lighthouse was the state's first. Spurred by the increasing traffic of steamers carrying cotton, Congress authorized its construction in 1829. The brick lighthouse stood twenty-eight feet high (small in comparison to others) but forty-two feet above sea level. Although briefly extinguished

Biloxi Lighthouse, ca. 1901 (Photograph by Detroit Photographic Company, Library of Congress, Washington, D.C. [LOT 13923, no. 351])

during the Civil War, the lighthouse continued in operation until 1882. When a nearby property owner refused to trim or cut some trees that obscured the beam from the lighthouse, the government discontinued operation.

Workers constructed a duplicate of the lighthouse in Pass Christian on Cat Island in 1831. Built directly on sand without a foundation, the thirty-four-foot brick lighthouse suffered from frequent storm damage. After Confederate troops burned the tower, the government commissioned a new structure, completed in 1871. By this time, however, most New Orleans–bound ships took a different route, and the Cat Island Lighthouse's usefulness had diminished. The prefabricated lighthouse continued in operation until 1937, and the structure burned in 1961.

The Round Island Lighthouse, located at the entrance to the Pascagoula Estuary, three miles from the mainland, began operation in 1832. National attention temporarily focused on Round Island in 1849, when a group of men seeking Cuban independence attempted to organize an expedition from there. The men damaged the lighthouse and briefly kidnapped the keeper and his two sons before being overrun by federal forces. The government completed the rebuilding of the forty-eight-foot brick lighthouse in 1859. The Round Island Lighthouse suffered storm damage over the years and became inactive in 1944. After Hurricanes Georges (1998) and Katrina, only about a third of the structure remained intact on the island. In 2010 the City of Pascagoula relocated that portion to the foot of the Pascagoula River Bridge on US Highway 90 at the entrance to the city. Another third of the lighthouse, including most of the lantern gallery, was salvaged from the island, and by 2015 interior and exterior renovations of the structure had been completed.

In 1847 the federal government commissioned the Biloxi Lighthouse to be made of cast iron, a more durable and portable alternative to its brick predecessors on the coast. Jefferson Davis specifically asked for the appropriation, expressing resentment of the disproportionate number of lighthouses constructed along the East Coast of the United States. Built

in Baltimore, the sixty-two-foot lighthouse began operating in 1848 and served as an important guide to passenger steamers visiting the area's resorts. The lighthouse suffered hurricane damage in 1860 and began to lean during the Civil War. When officials restored it to use in 1867, they covered the exterior with black tar to prevent rust. Many coastal residents interpreted this as a gesture of mourning for Pres. Abraham Lincoln, a view many local businesses echoed in advertisements aimed at attracting northern visitors. Painted white again in 1869, the lighthouse became electrified in 1929. Women served as keepers of the Biloxi Lighthouse for most of the period before the US Coast Guard assumed responsibility in 1939. The Coast Guard deeded the lighthouse to the City of Biloxi in 1968. The lighthouse survived Hurricane Katrina, although the structures around it did not, and a flag draped over its top railing served as a symbol of hope for coastal residents. In 2007 the Mississippi Department of Transportation put the image of the Biloxi Lighthouse on license plates. It remains in operation.

The Ship Island Lighthouse received its appropriation at the same time as the Biloxi Lighthouse, but conflicts over land claims with Spain meant that construction of the fifty-one-foot structure did not conclude until 1853. The US Army Corps of Engineers began work on a fort on Ship Island in the late 1850s, but it remained unfinished at the start of the Civil War. Confederates seized the island and maintained control for a few months. When Union forces retook the island in 1861, Confederate troops set fire to the interior of the lighthouse. Union troops finished the fort and repaired the lighthouse, though they took care that it did not shine to the north, where Confederates still operated. The Union troops on the island included some of the first African American regiments of the war. After storms battered the lighthouse, officials condemned it in 1886. A new, taller lighthouse constructed on the site operated until 1964, when it was deactivated, and it burned down in 1972. In the 1990s the Friends of Gulf Islands National Seashore led a campaign to rebuild the Ship Island Lighthouse. Using the second tower's foundation, the Navy Seabees completed a replica in 2000, but Hurricane Katrina destroyed it.

Other defunct Mississippi lighthouses were located at the Broadwater Beach Marina (1965–2005), East Pascagoula River (1854–1906), Lake Borgne (1889–1937), Horn Island (1874–1906, 1908–61), Merrill's Shell Bank (known as the Pass Marianne Lighthouse, 1860–1943), Natchez (1828–49), Proctorsville (1858–60), and St. Joseph Island (1861–93).

Carter Dalton Lyon
St. Mary's Episcopal School,
Memphis, Tennessee

"Biloxi Lighthouse Stands as Beacon of Hope," *USA Today* (20 October 2005); Dan Ellis, *Lighthouses and Islands of the Gulf* (2000); Donna Harris, *Biloxi Sun Herald* (31 December 2007); Round Island Lighthouse Preservation Society website, www.roundislandlighthouse.org.

Lincoln County

Lincoln County in southern Mississippi was formed in 1870, during the brief period of Republican Reconstruction, and was named after Abraham Lincoln. Brookhaven serves as the county seat, and smaller communities include Ruth, East Lincoln, Auburn, and Bogue Chitto. In the 1870 census, Lincoln had a population of 10,184, a number that grew to 13,547 (including 7,701 whites) ten years later. Lincoln's farmers grew relatively small amounts of cotton and ranked in the bottom quarter in most areas of farm production but had Mississippi's eighth-largest rice harvest. Landowners cultivated about 63 percent of Lincoln County's farms. In 1880 Lincoln had a small but growing manufacturing industry, with twenty-five establishments employing 132 workers. The county ranked ninth in the value of manufactured goods produced.

In 1900 Lincoln had a population of 21,552. The county's eighty-nine manufacturing establishments employed 997 workers, nearly all of them men working in the timber industry. As in most of Mississippi, far more white farmers (72 percent) owned their land than did African American farmers (44 percent).

About half of the thirteen thousand Lincoln County churchgoers recorded in the 1916 religious census were Southern Baptists. The rest belonged to churches of the National Baptist Convention and the Methodist Episcopal Church, South, with the African Methodist Episcopal Church, Methodist Episcopal Church, and Church of Christ each having about six hundred members. Lincoln County had the state's second-highest Church of Christ membership. Constructed in 1896, Brookhaven's Temple B'nai Sholom served the area's Jewish residents until 2009.

Commercial Bank, Brookhaven, seat of Lincoln County, ca. 1907 (Ann Rayburn Paper Americana Collection, Department of Archives and Special Collections, J. D. Williams Library, University of Mississippi [rayburn_ann_23_88_001])

Brookhaven has a long history as an educational center. Methodists established Whitworth College in 1859, and it continued to teach Mississippi women until 1964. Annie Coleman Peyton graduated from Whitworth in 1872 and taught there briefly before working for the establishment of Mississippi Industrial Institute and College (now Mississippi University for Women) in Columbus, the state's first public college for women. Susie Powell spent her childhood in Brookhaven and attended Whitworth College before going on to a career in home demonstration work. Through Powell's efforts at Whitworth, Lincoln County became home to Mississippi's first canning clubs. Copiah-Lincoln Community College was founded in 1928. Today, Lincoln is home to the Mississippi School for the Arts, which moved into the buildings on the old Whitworth campus.

Brookhaven has also produced several important writers. Author and artist Charles Henri Ford was born there in 1913, and author Martha Lacy Hall, a native of nearby Pike County, attended Whitworth College. Brookhaven's Cid Ricketts Sumner, born in 1890, was a popular mid-twentieth-century author whose novels became the basis for the movies *Pinky* (1949) and *Tammy and the Bachelor* (1957).

By 1930 Lincoln had a population of 26,357 (including 36 natives of Italy) and was 64 percent white. About five thousand Lincoln County residents lived in the growing city of Brookhaven, and almost a thousand people worked in industry. Still, farming dominated, with thirty-six hundred farms divided evenly between owners and tenants. The county's farmers grew considerably more corn than cotton or other crops.

In 1960 Lincoln's population remained virtually unchanged, though the percentage of African Americans had dropped from 36 to 31. At least two important figures in Mississippi's civil rights struggle and its opposition were Lincoln County natives. Hollis Watkins grew up on a farm on the edge of Lincoln and Pike Counties before becoming an activist in McComb as a teenager and then going on to work for numerous civil rights causes. Judge Tom Brady gained fame as the author of a short publication, *Black Monday*, a condemnation of the 1954 *Brown v. Board of Education* decision primarily on constitutional grounds.

As in many southern Mississippi counties, Lincoln County's 2010 population remained predominantly white and had grown over the last half of the twentieth century, gaining more than eight thousand people since 1960. Among Lincoln's 34,869 residents, 68.4 percent were whites and 30 percent were African Americans.

Mississippi Encyclopedia Staff
University of Mississippi

Mississippi State Planning Commission, *Progress Report on State Planning in Mississippi* (1938); *Mississippi Statistical Abstract*, Mississippi State University (1952–2010); Charles Sydnor and Claude Bennett, *Mississippi History* (1939); University of Virginia Library, Historical Census Browser website, http://mapserver.lib.virginia.edu; E. Nolan Waller and Dani A. Smith, *Growth Profiles of Mississippi's Counties, 1960–1980* (1985).

Literacy and Illiteracy

Low levels of adult literacy have plagued Mississippi since the state's founding. Though Mississippi's illiteracy rate decreased considerably during the twentieth century, pockets of illiteracy have endured in the state's rural, African American, and impoverished communities, and the state currently ranks dead last in national literacy statistics.

Between 1870 and 1920 Mississippi's illiteracy rate declined from 53.9 percent to 17.2 percent; nevertheless, only Louisiana's rate was worse. Moreover, improving literacy figures for the state as a whole obscured the endurance of illiteracy in the state's poorest, blackest, and most rural counties. In 1940, for example, a full sixty years after the state's illiteracy rate had dropped below 50 percent, a survey of 220 heads of farm-labor households in the Delta showed a 53 percent illiteracy rate.

In 1990 the Mississippi Employment Security Commission and the Social Science Research Center at Mississippi State University sponsored the Mississippi Literacy Assessment Project (MLAP), a study designed to produce the first set of comprehensive data on literacy levels throughout the state. The project's 1991 report concluded that significant numbers of Mississippians lacked the reading skills necessary to complete everyday tasks such as reading a bus schedule, understanding a newspaper article, or filling out paperwork. The report also highlighted the pervasive discrepancies in literacy levels between black and white Mississippians, between residents in rural areas and those in suburban or college-town communities, and between poor and middle-class Mississippians. Literacy levels remained lowest in the Delta counties. In short, the MLAP confirmed that Mississippi had made little progress in ameliorating illiteracy in the places that suffered the most from it.

Mississippi carried the nation's worst literacy rates into the twenty-first century: a 1998 study estimated that 30 percent of the state's inhabitants did not possess functional literacy skills and that another 34 percent possessed extremely low reading skills. In 2000 James L. Barksdale, a native of Jackson, a graduate of the University of Mississippi, and the founder of Netscape, a computer services company, donated one hundred million dollars to fight illiteracy in the state. While Barksdale's gift allowed the University of Mississippi and schools throughout the state to establish an ambitious set of programs to teach reading skills, it also continued a Mississippi tradition of private donations taking the place

of public welfare programs and highlighted the state government's failure to provide the necessary funds to address Mississippi's endemic poverty.

The MLAP and other literacy studies suggest a direct correlation between poverty and illiteracy. An inability to file paperwork or complete an application makes achieving in school, acquiring a better job, or voting knowledgably in an election very difficult, and cycles of poverty and illiteracy appear to perpetuate themselves. A legitimate effort to combat illiteracy thus would have to grow from a comprehensive government program to eliminate poverty. As long as Mississippi remains the poorest state in the country, it will likely remain the most illiterate state in the country.

Thomas John Carey
University of Mississippi

James C. Cobb, *The Most Southern Place on Earth: The Mississippi Delta and the Roots of Regional Identity* (1992); Arthur G. Cosby et al., *The Mississippi Literacy Assessment: A Report to the Mississippi Employment Security Commission and the Governor's Office for Literacy, State of Mississippi* (1991); Kevin Sack, *New York Times* (20 January 2000); Sanford Winston, *Illiteracy in the United States* (1930).

Literary Anthologies

According to an old joke, Mississippi has more people who can write than can read. Unfair though the joke may be, the state has unquestionably produced a disproportionate number of authors, including some of the nation's best—William Faulkner, William Alexander Percy, Margaret Walker Alexander, Tennessee Williams, Eudora Welty, and Richard Wright, among others. With such a rich literary tradition, it should come as no surprise that Mississippians have put together some fine literary anthologies.

Though notable anthologies were produced in the nineteenth century, they are no longer readily available. The earliest easily obtained anthology, *The Mississippi Poets* (1922), was edited by Ernestine Clayton Deavours, a teacher in the city schools of Laurel, and published by E. H. Clarke and Brother of Memphis. It contains works by William Alexander Percy and Stark Young, who are still well known, but as is often the case with older literary anthologies, the names of authors who have dropped out of the canon are at least as interesting. Among those Deavours judged worthy of inclusion were Henry M. Arney, T. A. S. Adams, Julia K. Wetherhill Baker, Newton S. Berryhill, Isabel Folsom, Layfayette R. Hammerlin, S. A. Jonas, and Lulah Ragsdale.

Another early anthology, *Mississippi Verse* (1934), was edited by Alice James and published by the University of

North Carolina Press. Unlike *The Mississippi Poets*, which was published with some notion of turning a profit, *Mississippi Verse* was a scholarly endeavor. James included one of Faulkner's few poems as well as works by Young and Percy. Again, however, the volume featured works by other largely forgotten pre–World War II authors—Lemuella Almond, Elizabeth Austin, Rodney M. Baine, Horace Polk Cooper, Jamie Sexton Holme, and Kummer Wrinn, among others.

In 1975 Noel E. Polk and James R. Scafidel coedited *An Anthology of Mississippi Writers*, which was published by the University Press of Mississippi. Arranged chronologically, the anthology begins with southwestern humor and ends with William Mills; in between are works by Faulkner, Williams, Wright, Welty, Richard Bell, Barry Hannah, and others. Probably its most remarkable feature is its balance of canonized highbrow authors and great popular writers.

Of all available Mississippi literary anthologies, Dorothy Abbott's four-volume *Mississippi Writers: Reflections of Childhood and Youth* (1985–91) is the most comprehensive, featuring works by canonized fiction writers and poets, nonfiction pieces pertaining to relatively obscure civil rights workers, Medgar Evers's essays, and selections from Shelby Foote's epic Civil War history. The set was published by the Center for the Study of Southern Culture at the University Press of Mississippi, which also released a one-volume edition for use in schools and accompanied by a teachers' manual. Two additional anthologies of note are Marion Barnwell's *A Place Called Mississippi: Collected Narratives* and *Mississippi Writers Talking*, a collection of interviews conducted and compiled by John Griffin Jones.

Edited by Thomas McNeely Jr. and Peter Buttross Jr. and published by Red Dawn Press, *Beyond the Bars* (2004) is a collection of poetry and prose written by inmates at the Wilkinson County Correctional Facility at Woodville. The raw emotionalism of the poems is hardly surprising, but many of the poems also exhibit a high degree of technical proficiency.

In 2016 University of Mississippi writer in residence Tom Franklin edited *Mississippi Noir*, a collection of stories set in rural and urban areas across the state.

Whereas older collections tended to neglect the work of African American authors, their writings are better represented in recent anthologies, in keeping with the trend toward inclusiveness that has appeared in American and especially southern letters. Also, where verse dominated early twentieth-century compilations, later anthologies generally feature a greater variety of poetry, prose, and drama.

Ben Gilstrap
University of Mississippi

Dorothy Abbott, ed., *Mississippi Writers: An Anthology* (1991); Dorothy Abbott, ed., *Mississippi Writers: Reflections of Childhood and Youth*, 4 vols. (1985–91); Ernestine Clayton Deavours, *The Mississippi Poets* (1922); Alice James, ed., *Mississippi Verse* (1934); Thomas McNeely Jr. and Peter Buttross Jr., eds., *Beyond the Bars: An Anthology of Poetry and Prose from a Mississippi Prison* (2004); Noel E. Polk and James R. Scafidel, eds., *An Anthology of Mississippi Writers* (1979).

Living Blues

Founded in 1970 in Chicago, *Living Blues* magazine is America's oldest and most respected blues magazine. It focuses largely on the living tradition of contemporary African American performers, leaving coverage of white blues artists to other forums. In addition to articles on well-known stars such as Howlin' Wolf and Muddy Waters, *Living Blues* devotes attention to lesser-known blues artists from across the United States. The magazine is also known for publishing the *Living Blues Directory* (an annual industry guide to blues clubs, radio stations, societies, festivals, artists, and agents) and for its annual Living Blues Awards. In 1983 the University of Mississippi bought *Living Blues*, and the magazine's home moved to Oxford, where it is published by the Center for the Study of Southern Culture.

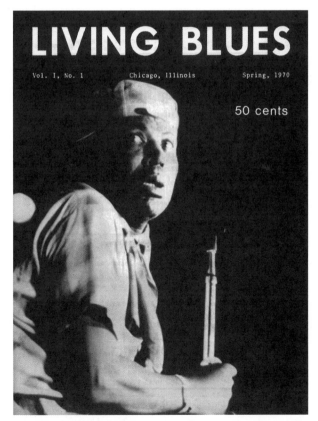

First issue of *Living Blues* magazine, 1970 (Courtesy *Living Blues* magazine)

Jim O'Neal, Amy van Singel, and Bruce Iglauer founded the magazine and ran it while it was based in Chicago. The first issue featured Howlin' Wolf on the cover and began the magazine's practice of printing long articles, extensive reviews, and shorter news segments. The editors resisted the urge to define the blues on the grounds that "blues speaks for itself. We do not intend to explain, define, or confine the blues. We believe the blues to be a living tradition, and we hope to present some insights into this tradition." In the introduction to *The Voice of the Blues*, a 2002 collection of the magazine's "classic interviews," O'Neal wrote, "The *Living Blues* approach was simply to get the artists to tell the stories of their lives and their careers, to trace the development of the music, and to tell us what they knew about other musicians." That approach revealed history, social commentary, humor, and sometimes distrust among the blues community. *Living Blues* became known for the length and depth of those interviews as well as for its photo essays, which document performers, clubs, festivals, and other blues events.

When the magazine was founded, people interested in the music and its history had few resources, and *Living Blues* provided a way to preserve the history, document the present, and find a future for the music by opening it up to both new and old audiences. By featuring more established artists as well as newcomers and performers ignored by other blues sources, *Living Blues* has encouraged, extended, and made possible many blues careers and has showcased some of the best music journalism in the business. Its writers have included David Evans, Samuel Charters, Paul Garon, William Ferris, Barry Lee Pearson, John Brisbin, David Whiteis, Jim DeKoster, and Roger Wood, while its editors have included Peter Lee, David Nelson, Scott Baretta, and Brett Bonner.

Ellie Campbell
University of Mississippi

Evan Hatch, *Southern Register* (Fall 2000); *Living Blues* website, www.livingblues.com; Jim O'Neal and Amy van Singel, *The Voice of the Blues: Classic Interviews from Living Blues Magazine* (2002); Melanie Young, "A Historical Analysis of *Living Blues* Magazine" (master's thesis, University of Mississippi, 2012).

Log Cabins

Log cabins represent a significant part of vernacular architectural history and settlement heritage in Mississippi. Some rural portions of Mississippi retained traditional log construction as the principal building method into the early twentieth century. The modern term *log cabin* is synonymous with the historic term *log house*. Historically, however, *log cabins* were small, crude, more temporary buildings or in some cases slave quarters, while *log houses* were usually the first permanent shelter built by settlers and were more neatly constructed and finished.

The log house has its origins in the Middle Atlantic region, particularly southeastern Pennsylvania and Delaware. The region's first settlers, Swedes and Finns, began log construction in America. The Germans, Scots-Irish, and English who came to that area a little later added their own building traditions, and American log construction was born. As people migrated south and west, they took their log building tradition with them. In the Upland South, including northern Mississippi, it became a defining characteristic of the nineteenth-century architectural landscape.

While exact construction methods varied from community to community, some basics of assembly were common for most nineteenth-century log cabins. Starting with the foundation, the simplest example began simply with log sills left flat on the ground or a single course of flat stones. This type of foundation meant that the cabin had a dirt floor. Better log cabins were raised on sills, either with wooden blocks or stone piers, and had wood flooring laid on joists. The best foundations were of continuous masonry. Cabins with wood flooring usually had puncheon floors—long, thick slabs of wood hewn roughly to an even surface. Later in the nineteenth century, as sawmills became more prevalent, floors were sawn or planed.

The walls of log cabins were constructed by horizontally stacking hewn logs and joining them at the corners using one of several notching techniques. In general, preferred notching methods were half-dovetail, V-notch, or saddle notch, but in some cases full dovetailing, diamond notching, or square notching was employed. Any spaces between the logs were chinked with short boards, rocks, straw, or rags. The fill was then covered with river clay or lime mortar plaster and smoothed. Later, siding could be added to cover the exposed logs and give the house a more finished look.

Interior walls of the log cabin could be finished in several ways. Some interior walls left the hewn logs exposed; others were whitewashed or painted. More prosperous owners had interior walls plastered over or covered with vertical boards, paneling, or wallpaper. These improved surfaces would have been reserved for the more formal rooms.

Log houses had several different forms. Settlers frequently started by building a single-pen or one-room house and then added on to it over time as their means improved. The single-pen is a square or rectangular building with a side gable roof and an exterior gable-end chimney; historically, they were one story or one and a half story. The latter had an enclosed interior staircase leading to a sleeping loft. Rectangular single-pens that followed the hall-parlor plan had a partition wall that divided the structure into two rooms of unequal size. The hall was the larger of the two rooms and the center of familial activities. The head of the household often slept in the hall, and the parlor was reserved as a more private area.

As families expanded, they added on to single-pen houses, typically, though not always, one room at a time. Multiroom houses could take several forms, including the double-pen, saddlebag, dogtrot, central passage, and I-house. The saddlebag form had a room added to the chimney side of the original pen, resulting in a central chimney flanked by two rooms. If the second room was added to a wall without a chimney, the result was a double-pen. Both forms frequently had dual entries because of the difficulty of cutting into existing log walls. The pens could be of different sizes and could be one or two stories high.

Log cabins lost their dominance in rural Mississippi by the turn of the twentieth century. Many extant examples are hidden on the modern landscape by siding, plaster, new roofs, and other exterior features. They can be recognized by their thick window and door openings, large stone chimneys, and small upstairs windows.

Summer J. Chandler
Austin, Texas

Terry G. Jordan, *Texas Log Buildings: A Folk Architecture* (1982); Fred B. Kniffen, in *Common Places: Readings in American Vernacular Architecture*, ed. Dell Upton and John Michael Vlach (1986); William J. Macintire, *The Pioneer Log House in Kentucky* (1998); John Morgan, *The Log House in East Tennessee* (1990).

Logan, A. M. E.

(1915–2011) Activist

A. M. E. Logan, the Mother of the Jackson Civil Rights Movement, was born A. M. E. Marshall in 1915 in Myles, in Copiah County. She was the eighth of twelve children of Nellie Carrie Jane Rembert Marshall and John Collins Marshall. Her father was an African Methodist Episcopal minister with great love for the church, leading her parents to name her A. M. E. Most of Marshall's formative years were spent in the Carpenter community in Hinds County. Frequent childhood illnesses prevented her from completing high school, but she later earned a diploma from the American School of Correspondence in Chicago. She inherited her work ethic, passion for helping others, and economic independence from her father. After marrying Style Logan in 1932 and starting a family, she instilled those same values in her four children, Style Jr., Vivian, Shirley, and Willis.

A. M. E. Logan moved to Jackson with her family in October 1943, working as a cashier at Campbell College and later for the Illinois Central Railroad Station. In 1954 Logan's presence in the community grew when she began selling A. W. Curtis Rubbing Oil, developed by scientist George Washington Carver. With an acute understanding of the importance of social, political, and economic freedom, Logan encouraged her customers to join the National Association for the Advancement of Colored People (NAACP) and register to vote as she went door-to-door selling her product.

During a tumultuous time for black Mississippians, Logan made a profound impression on civil rights activists who arrived in the capital city in May and June 1961. On 29 May 1961 Logan assisted Clarie Collins Harvey in forming Womanpower Unlimited, a Jackson-based organization that provided a safety net, motherly nurturing, and support to the Freedom Riders who were testing the integration of interstate transportation in the wake of the US Supreme Court's 1960 *Boynton v. Virginia* decision. As the executive secretary for Womanpower Unlimited, Logan opened her home to hundreds of young men and women, provided clothing and other essentials to activists detained at Parchman Penitentiary, and called parents to inform them that their children were safe. Logan often solicited support for these efforts through her door-to-door sales.

Logan served as the first secretary of the Jackson branch of the Southern Christian Leadership Conference and was a member of the Jackson branch of the NAACP. In an effort to make quality education available for all of the city's black children, Logan joined Medgar and Myrlie Evers and other parents in filing a 1963 petition to desegregate the Jackson Municipal Schools.

Logan was also active in the Order of the Eastern Star, the Elks, and the African Methodist Episcopal Church, and well into her nineties she checked on her neighbors and others in her community and sold products door-to-door for Avon. In August 2010 the company recognized her as the oldest salesperson in its history. She died on 5 February 2011 after falling at home. She was believed to have been ninety-six years old, but whenever she was asked about her age or date of birth, she responded, "I am as old as my tongue, and a little older than my teeth!"

Daphne R. Chamberlain
Tougaloo College

A. M. E. Logan, interview by Daphne R. Chamberlain and Freddi W. Evans (2009–10); A. M. E. Logan, interview by Tiyi Morris (n.d.); Clarie Collins Harvey, interview by John Dittmer and John Jones, Mississippi Department of Archives and History (21 April 1981); Daphne R. Chamberlain, "'And a Child Shall Lead the Way': Children's Participation in the Jackson, Mississippi, Black Freedom Struggle, 1946–1970" (PhD dissertation, University of Mississippi, 2009); Tiyi M. Morris, *Womanpower Unlimited and the Black Freedom Struggle in Mississippi* (2015); Tiyi M. Morris, in *Groundwork: Local Black Freedom Movements in America*, ed. Komozi Woodard and Jeanne Theoharis (2005).

Lomax, Alan
(1915–2002) Folklorist

Alan Lomax began his career by assisting his folklorist and academic father, Mississippi-born John Lomax, during extended trips made to record folk tunes. Alan became a prodigy as a collector, enthusiast, and promoter. Despite the scholarly emphasis of his later years, this array of activities remained his true focus.

Alan Lomax's early fieldwork and attempts at advocacy inspired colorful reminiscences of the black South, Haiti, and Spanish-language Texas. He wrote book reviews and gave public lectures and radio shows, anticipating what public sector folklorists do today. Beginning in 1937 he served as head of the Library of Congress's Archive of American Folk Song. In 1941–42 he joined with John C. Work, Lewis Wade Jones, and Samuel C. Adams Jr., all of whom were African American academics connected with Fisk University, in designing and executing a pair of fruitful collecting trips to Coahoma County, providing money and supplies from his position at the Library of Congress. The team recorded blues performances by Muddy Waters, David "Honey Boy" Edwards, and Son House, among many others.

In the 1950s Lomax lived in England, out of reach of McCarthyist hysteria, and completed fruitful collecting trips to Spain and Italy. In the 1960s he returned to the United States, where he arguably became more famous—and certainly had more success as a fundraiser—than any other American music academic before or since. He played numerous roles in the decade's folk revival, functioning as a partial cause, an observer, an influential—and often controversial—participant, and a careful critic. While continuing to stimulate interest in what the public had come to call folk music, he cautioned enthusiasts against reproducing the sounds of folk performers without sufficiently understanding cultural contexts.

Later in his life, Lomax emphasized broad academic theorizing in his "cantometrics," an all-encompassing scheme correlating culture with musical sound. He advocated moving beyond the pitches and words of songs to look more closely at performance, embodiment, timbre, gender, style, and the use of ethnographic film, topics, and techniques that the field of ethnomusicology did not fully embrace for decades. The system was far too general, but his narration of the nuts and bolts of cantometric coding, while never serving as a scholarly model, constitutes a rich thesaurus of terms to describe aspects of music and social organization.

Energetic collecting, vivid description, eloquent advocacy, and grandly intended theoretical syntheses all twined together in Lomax's life and work. Above all, Lomax will be remembered for his calls to arms both in words and by example. He was personally and professionally eclectic, often arrogant, but always aggressively and endearingly populist.

Chris Goertzen
University of Southern Mississippi

Ronald Cohen, ed., *Alan Lomax: Selected Writings, 1934–1997* (2005); Benjamin Filene, *Romancing the Folk: Public Memory and American Roots Music* (2000); John Wesley Work, Lewis Wade Jones, and Samuel C. Adams Jr., *Lost Delta Found: Rediscovering the Fisk University–Library of Congress Coahoma County Study, 1941–1942*, ed. Robert Gordon and Bruce Nemerov (2005).

Lomax, John
(1867–1948) Folklorist

John Avery Lomax collected more than ten thousand folk songs throughout his life, providing a valuable archive for future use by scholars seeking to understand various forms of American music. Lomax asserted that his life's work sought the "intimate poetic and musical experience of unlettered people," and his efforts spanned decades and drew attention to the musical traditions of the American South and West.

Lomax was born near Goodman, in Holmes County, Mississippi, in 1867. Two years later, his family moved to a farm in Bosque County, Texas, because Lomax's father, James, was having conflicts with his wealthier brother and was unwilling to raise his family near recently freed African Americans. John Lomax's childhood experiences with music included church camp meetings and hearing the songs of cowboys on the Texas frontier, a fascination that shaped much of his work. Lomax studied for a year at Granbury College and then taught in rural schools for seven years. In 1895 he enrolled at the University of Texas at Austin and after graduation stayed on the campus, working several jobs. In 1903 he taught English at Texas Agricultural and Mechanical College.

Lomax next enrolled in graduate studies at Harvard University with professors who encouraged his interest in cowboy songs. He received a Sheldon Grant from Harvard to record these songs, and he researched and wrote his 1910 *Cowboy Songs and Other Frontier Ballads* with the money from the award. At the same time, Lomax cofounded the Texas Folklore Society to preserve folk material against the perceived encroachment of mainstream commercial music.

In 1910 Lomax accepted an administrative job at the University of Texas, but he continued to record and began lecture tours, an endeavor he continued throughout much of the rest of his life. Lomax and other administrators were fired in 1917 as a consequence of a political conflict between the university president and the Texas governor, though the dismissal was later rescinded following the governor's impeachment. In the interim, however, Lomax began work as a banker in Chicago, doing little collecting for the next fifteen years. In 1931 his wife, Bess Brown Lomax, died, and his four children—Shirley, John Jr., Alan, and Bess, all of whom later assisted their father with collecting—encouraged him to return to folk music to raise his spirits. He began a lecture tour, traveled to New York, and reached an agreement with a publishing company to produce an extensive anthology of folk material. After traveling to Washington, D.C., to review the Archive of American Folk Song, Lomax arranged to use the archive's equipment to make recordings across the country.

He set out in June 1933 on his first recording trip, taking with him his eighteen-year-old son, Alan. In July they acquired a 315-pound acetate disc recorder, which they placed in the trunk of their Ford sedan. They began by visiting prison farms in Texas, Louisiana, and Mississippi. Lomax believed prisons provided the isolation necessary to gather what he perceived as "authentic" field hollers, blues songs, ballads, and songs left from slavery. While at Parchman Prison Farm in Mississippi in 1939, Lomax wrote in his field notes, "In the solitude and confinement the Negro recalls the songs that he learned as a child, and readily learns others from his prison associates as they work together." Because the inmates at Parchman worked from four o'clock in the morning until dark, the Lomaxes had only the noon lunch hour and a short period of time before lights-out to record the men working in the fields, though they were able to record the spirituals sung by the female inmates as they worked at sewing machines in the mornings.

As a collector of folk songs, John Lomax was noteworthy for several reasons. First, he turned from the manuscript-based collection method advanced by Francis Child to the use of recording. Second, Lomax worked to popularize individual musicians (such as Louisiana bluesman Huddie "Leadbelly" Ledbetter), crafting an image in the public eye of what a "real" folksinger looked like. While promoting Leadbelly, Lomax frequently encouraged him to make his singing more accessible, altering his accent and speaking during songs to better explain the lyrics. Lomax published several books, including *Cowboy Songs and Other Ballads* (1910), *American Folksongs and Ballads* (1934), *Our Singing Country: Folk Songs and Ballads* (1941), and *Adventures of a Ballad Hunter* (1947).

In 1934, the same year he married classics professor Ruby Terrill, Lomax was named honorary consultant and curator of the Archive of American Folk Song and worked to expand the archive. He was active in two New Deal programs, serving as adviser on collecting for both the Historical Records Survey and the Federal Writers' Project.

In 1947 a friend from Greenville sought to arrange a celebration in Lomax's birth state to coincide with his eightieth birthday. After an initial postponement, the event, which included John Lomax Day and a visit from Gov. Fielding L. Wright, was scheduled for January 1948. However, at an informal press conference on the day he arrived in Greenville, Lomax suffered a heart attack. He remained in a coma for several days and died at a Greenville hospital on 26 January 1948.

Becca Walton
University of Mississippi

Hugh Barker and Yuval Taylor, *Faking It: The Quest for Authenticity in Popular Music* (2007); Benjamin Filene, *Romancing the Folk: Public Memory and American Roots Music* (2000); John A. Lomax, *Adventures of a Ballad Hunter* (1947); Nolan Porterfield, *Last Cavalier: The Life and Times of John A. Lomax, 1867–1948* (1996); "Southern Mosaic: The John and Ruby Lomax Southern States Recording Trip," American Memory Archive of the Library of Congress website, www.memory.loc.gov.

Longfellow House (Bellevue)

Pirates and buried treasure, a "renegade" priest, a baby falling from a third-story window, and bloodstains on floors—these are the legends that surround Pascagoula's most treasured antebellum home, the Longfellow House. Constructed in the 1850s for the Daniel Graham family, it has long been the subject of local lore. The three-story structure originally stood on an extensive piece of property, boasting four hundred feet of waterfront land on Pascagoula Bay. Craftsmen constructed the home of native pine and cypress and topped it with a slate roof, punctuated by three dormers and two chimneys at each end. The grandest architectural feature of the house was and still is a self-supporting winding staircase that leads to the third floor.

Over the years this magnificent estate has been home to many different people, generating fascinating stories about the property. The first owners, the Grahams, were slave traders with a reputation for extreme cruelty to their slaves that supposedly resulted in bloodstains on the third-story floors. The Grahams occupied the home for a time, and the house subsequently sat empty for a number of years, prompting locals to believe that it was haunted.

Between 1873 and 1902 the home, known as Bellevue, changed hands at least nine times. Some owners resided on the estate, though others did not, and at one time it served as a girls' school. The Longfellow House's history has become

Longfellow House (Bellevue), Pascagoula, built 1852 (Charles Reagan Wilson Collection, Center for the Study of Southern Culture, University of Mississippi)

quite muddled, perhaps opening the door to many of the legends surrounding it.

In 1902 W. A. Pollock purchased the house. His family lived there until 1938, a longer tenure than any other family. Members of the Pollock family then sold the house to Mayor Frank Canty, who resold it just three years later to Ingalls Shipbuilding Corporation. Ingalls owned the estate for several decades and transformed it from a private residence to an exclusive club and resort. It featured all the amenities of a luxurious beachfront resort: cottages, hotel rooms, dining rooms, a lounge, a swimming pool, and a golf course.

After some success, patronage of the resort declined, and the Longfellow House fell into disrepair. A real estate developer eventually purchased the estate, divided the land to sell as individual lots, and sold the house to Dianne and Richard Scruggs, who spent countless hours researching the history of the home and restoring it to grandeur before donating it to the University of Mississippi Foundation. The home was damaged by Hurricane Katrina in 2005 and was purchased the following year by Drs. Tracy and Randy Roth, who lost their own historic home in the storm. The Roths undertook repairs, and the house once again serves as a private residence.

Numerous legends regarding the house have arisen, perhaps the best known of which is the one that gave the home its current name. Poet Henry Wadsworth Longfellow supposedly was visiting the estate when he was inspired by Pascagoula Bay and penned "The Building of a Ship." Despite the authority with which locals often tell this story, it is simply a legend. The poem in question describes the process of a ship's construction, and it does mention Pascagoula. Locals likely drew a connection to this reference and the town's shipbuilding tradition and concluded that the poet must have witnessed shipbuilding in Pascagoula. However, a closer reading of the poem reveals that Pascagoula, one of the country's largest exporters of timber at the time, was simply a source for the lumber used to build the ship: "Brought from regions far away, / From Pascagoula's sunny bay." Longfellow apparently never traveled south of Virginia, so the idea that he visited the home is simply a myth.

Having taken on lives of their own, the myths have romanticized the historic home for generations and have enshrined the Longfellow House in the hearts of locals. The house is now one of the few antebellum homes left on the Mississippi Gulf Coast, a beloved community landmark and a symbol not only of local history but also of the area's resilience.

Alice Hull Lauchaussee
Spring Hill College

Longfellow House Vertical File, Local History and Genealogy Department, Jackson-George County Library, Pascagoula; Mary Carol Miller, *Must See Mississippi: Fifty Favorite Places* (2007); *Pascagoula Chronicle-Star* (7 February 1941, 16 January 1966); Cynthia Rush, *Beach Boulevard, South Mississippi's Magazine* (June–July 2007).

Longino, Andrew Houston
(1854–1942) Thirty-Fifth Governor, 1900–1904

Andrew Longino was the first governor elected after the Civil War who was not a Confederate veteran, and he was the last governor nominated by a state party convention. In 1903 the state adopted the popular primary system of nominating all candidates for public office.

Longino was born in Lawrence County on 16 May 1854 and went on to graduate from Mississippi College in Clinton, making him the first governor to hold a degree from one of the state's institutions of higher learning. After studying law at the University of Virginia, he was admitted to the Mississippi state bar in 1881. Longino served in the state legislature, as a district attorney, and as chancellor of the 7th Judicial District before winning election to the governorship in 1899.

As the first governor of the twentieth century, Longino warned the people of the state to brace themselves for enormous changes. He especially urged Mississippians to embrace the new age of technology that could revolutionize the state's economy and provide thousands of new jobs. In his inaugural address, Longino condemned lynching, proposed that counties compensate the families of lynching victims, and suggested that law enforcement officials who allowed lynching be held accountable. Political opponents later used these words against him.

Longino's administration was noted for several major achievements. A bill authorizing a new capitol was passed, and the cornerstone was laid on 3 June 1903. In addition, a new state penitentiary was built at Parchman, the Mississippi Department of Archives and History was established, a constitutional amendment providing for the election of state judges was passed, and a textile school was started at Mississippi A&M College (now Mississippi State University) in Starkville.

Longino ran for the US Senate in 1903 but was defeated by Hernando DeSoto Money. After leaving the governor's office in January 1904, Longino maintained a law practice in Jackson. In 1919 he again sought the state's highest office but lost in the runoff election to Lee Russell. Longino subsequently retired from public life and died in Jackson on 24 February 1942.

David G. Sansing
University of Mississippi

Stephen Cresswell, *Rednecks, Redeemers, and Race: Mississippi After Reconstruction, 1877–1917* (2006); Thomas E. Kelly, *Who's Who in Mississippi* (1914); *Mississippi Official and Statistical Register* (1912); Dunbar Rowland, *Encyclopedia of Mississippi History*, vol. 2 (1907).

Longstreet, Augustus Baldwin
(1790–1870) Educator and Author

Augustus Baldwin Longstreet served as president of four southern colleges, including the University of Mississippi, and was the author of *Georgia Scenes* (1835), the first major work of southwestern humor. Born on 22 September 1790 in Augusta, Georgia, to Hannah Randolph Longstreet and William Longstreet, he studied at Rev. Moses Waddel's academy in Willington, South Carolina, and at Yale, where he graduated with honors. After reading law in Litchfield, Connecticut, he was admitted to the Georgia bar in 1815 and became a circuit-riding attorney for a seven-county district. Longstreet and Frances Eliza Parke, whom he married on 3 March 1817, had eight children, only two of whom survived to adulthood.

A states' rights activist, Longstreet was well known as an assemblyman, criminal trial lawyer, circuit court judge, political satirist, and newspaper owner-editor. Although his popular comic collection *Georgia Scenes, Characters, Incidents, &c. in the First Half Century of the Republic* (1835) was published anonymously, Longstreet was quickly identified as the author. His articulate narrators, Lyman Hall and Abraham Baldwin (both named after Georgia politicians), tell tall tales of men's horse-trading and women's gossip, incorporating the sometimes vulgar voices of rural Georgians. Edgar Allan Poe reviewed *Georgia Scenes* enthusiastically in the *Southern Literary Messenger*, and a fashion developed for the vernacular dialogue and robust physicality of the southwestern humor genre, which took its name

from the Old Southwest, a region extending from Georgia to Mississippi and Arkansas. Antebellum practitioners included Thomas Bangs Thorpe, Johnson Jones Hooper, and even a Mississippi governor, Alexander G. McNutt. Mark Twain and contemporary humorists such as Clyde Edgerton and Mississippi's Barry Hannah have continued the literary tradition.

Longstreet never completed his plans to publish a second volume of comic sketches. He became a Methodist preacher in 1838 and was subsequently elected president of the Methodist-sponsored Emory College in Atlanta, where he also taught and wrote proslavery pamphlets. In the years before the Civil War, Longstreet also served as a professor and chief administrator at Centenary College in Louisiana, the University of Mississippi, and South Carolina College.

Between 1849 and 1856, while serving as chancellor at the University of Mississippi, he wrote on political and theological subjects and worked on *Master William Mitten; or, A Youth of Brilliant Talents, Who Was Ruined by Bad Luck* (1864), a moralistic novel that never achieved the fame of his early humorous fiction. Longstreet's son-in-law, L. Q. C. Lamar, chaired the committee that drafted Mississippi's Ordinance of Secession; Confederate general James Longstreet was Longstreet's nephew. Through much of the Civil War, Judge Longstreet and his wife lived as refugees in Elon, Alabama, but they subsequently returned to Oxford, home of both of their daughters. Longstreet published essays in the *Nineteenth Century* in 1869 and 1870 and was working on a treatise about biblical interpretation when he died on 9 July 1870. The Longstreet-Lamar House on Oxford's North 14th Street has been restored as a national historic landmark.

Joan Wylie Hall
University of Mississippi

Joan Wylie Hall, *Writers of the American Renaissance: An A–Z Guide* (2003); M. Thomas Inge and Edward J. Piacentino, eds., *The Humor of the Old South* (2001); Kimball King, *Augustus Baldwin Longstreet* (1984); Augustus Baldwin Longstreet, *Georgia Scenes, Characters, Incidents, &c. in the First Half of the Republic: By a Native Georgian* (1992); David Rachels, ed., *Augustus Baldwin Longstreet's "Georgia Scenes" Completed: A Scholarly Text* (1998); Scott Romine, *The Narrative Forms of Southern Community* (1999); Jessica Wegmann, *Southern Literary Journal* (Fall 1997).

Lott, Trent
(b. 1941) Political Leader

Chester Trent Lott served more than thirty-four years as a US representative and US senator from Mississippi. Son of

Chester Paul Lott, a sharecropper, laborer, and pipefitter at Ingalls Shipbuilders in Pascagoula, and Iona Watson Lott, a schoolteacher, Lott was born in Grenada on 9 October 1941. An only child educated in the public schools of Pascagoula, Lott was active in music and drama and enjoyed wide popularity, winning election as homecoming king and student body president. Lott enrolled at the University of Mississippi in 1959 and went on to earn degrees in public administration (1963) and law (1967). While in school Lott joined the Sigma Nu social fraternity, was a cheerleader, and served as president of his fraternity and of the Interfraternity Council. Lott worked industriously to make friends, build alliances, and hone the political skills that would serve him well during his years in Washington.

After briefly practicing law in Pascagoula, Lott went to Washington as a legislative assistant for US Rep. William M. Colmer of the state's 5th District. Colmer, a Democrat who represented the Gulf Coast in the House from 1933 to 1973, was the powerful chair of the House Rules Committee. Like many southern Democrats, Colmer had become uncomfortable with the party's attention to civil rights measures. He joined the rest of Mississippi's congressional delegation in signing the 1956 Southern Manifesto denouncing the *Brown* decision and increasingly threw his support to Republican candidates for the presidency. Colmer announced his intention to retire in 1972, and local Republicans recruited Lott to run under their banner. Colmer offered his endorsement. Lott was elected as Republican Richard Nixon won 78 percent of the state's votes. Lott was joined in Congress in 1973 by fellow freshman representative Thad Cochran, a strong indication of the state's growing attachment to the Republican Party.

Lott served in the House from 1973 to 1989, easily winning reelection every two years and running unopposed in 1978. Lott became the first southern Republican elected minority whip and held that position from 1981 to 1989. Lott also followed in Colmer's footsteps in serving on the House Rules Committee from 1975 to 1989. Lott was known for his interest in tax and budget measures, for his skill in compromise and making deals, and for his support of defense spending and farm subsidy programs. He ran for the Senate in 1988 when veteran Democrat John C. Stennis retired after more than forty years of service. Lott defeated a fellow member of Congress, Wayne Dowdy, a Democrat who represented Mississippi's 4th District and was the former mayor of McComb. Lott handily won reelection to the Senate in 1994, 2000, and 2006. From 1995 to 1996 Lott served as his party's whip in the Senate, making him the first person to hold that position in both houses of Congress. In 1996 Lott was elected Senate majority leader, a post he held until the Republicans lost control of the Senate in the 2000 elections. He then became Senate minority leader.

During his time in the House and Senate, Lott followed two consistent principles: to support the fortunes of the Republican Party in Mississippi and the nation, and to bring economic development to the state, either through federal spending on military bases and highway programs or through recruiting aerospace and automobile companies. Lott's conservative voice on social issues, combined with his ability to deliver services to his constituents, gained him a wide political following in the state.

Lott generated national controversy at a December 2002 party celebrating the one hundredth birthday of South Carolina senator Strom Thurmond, who in 1948 had run for the presidency on the segregationist Dixiecrat ticket with Mississippi governor Fielding Wright as his running mate. Mississippi supported the Dixiecrats, and Lott remarked that the nation would have been better off if it had followed Mississippi's lead. Criticism of Lott's remarks forced him to resign as minority leader. The Bush White House's conspicuous lack of support became a sore point for Lott, but his popularity at home remained undiminished, and he won reelection in 2006 with 64 percent of the vote. In 2007 he gained a measure of redemption when he defeated Tennessee's Lamar Alexander in the race for minority whip.

In November of that year, however, Lott surprised most constituents and political observers by announcing his intention to resign from the Senate effective 18 December 2007. Gov. Haley Barbour appointed US representative Roger Wicker to fill the remainder of Lott's term. In January 2008 Lott and former senator John Breaux, a Louisiana Democrat, announced the formation of the Breaux-Lott Leadership Group, a Washington-based consulting and lobbying firm.

Lott, a Mason and a Southern Baptist, married Patricia Thompson in 1964, and they went on to have two children, Chester Trent Lott Jr. and Tyler Lott Armstrong. Lott and his wife live in their Gulfport home, which they rebuilt after Hurricane Katrina. In 2005 Lott published a memoir, *Herding Cats: A Life in Politics*.

Trent Brown
Missouri University of Science and Technology

Joseph Crespino, *In Search of Another Country: Mississippi and the Conservative Counterrevolution* (2007); Jere Nash and Andy Taggart, *Mississippi Politics: The Struggle for Power, 1976–2006* (2006).

Lovering, Amos
(1805–1879) Judge

Born in Medway, Massachusetts, in 1805, Amos Lovering was best known for his role as a Republican commissioner on the committee tasked with revising the Mississippi Code of Laws in 1871. Lovering received his early education at Day's Academy in Massachusetts, an institution that prepared him for study at Brown University in Rhode Island, from which he graduated in 1828. Lovering then studied law and apprenticed with other lawyers before moving to Louisville, Kentucky, to begin his practice. His search for better positions and more stimulating environs prompted moves to St. Joseph, Missouri, and then to Scott County, Indiana. Lovering soon established himself as an able lawyer, becoming a justice of common pleas for Scott and Clark Counties. In 1862, after ten years of service as a judge, Lovering moved to Nashville.

In 1869 Lovering moved to Jackson to become a judge in Mississippi's 9th Judicial District. In the highly charged environment of Presidential and Congressional Reconstruction, many white Democrats perceived the presence and governing role of Lovering and other Republicans in Mississippi as evidence that the oppressive North was seeking to punish a defeated South. Gov. James Alcorn, a Republican and a scalawag, attempted to introduce progressive reforms to Mississippi, and Lovering participated in these endeavors, directly confronting issues of race, education, and law. In the December 1871 edition of the *Mississippi Educational Journal*, Lovering expressed his opinion that the way to defeat the Ku Klux Klan could be found in "universal education in morals and mind" for both races. Such views only incited passions against him.

Lovering became a commissioner on the committee to revise Mississippi's Code of Laws to conform with the newly passed amendments to the US Constitution regarding the abolition of slavery, a prerequisite for readmission to the Union. Appointed by Gov. Alcorn, Lovering joined two Democratic judges, J. A. P. Campbell and Amos R. Johnson. Lovering's Republican affiliation and presence on the committee, combined with his outspoken beliefs, sparked hatred against the new code. The Code of 1871 greatly resembled the Code of 1857, yet white southerners detested the laws and blamed problems within the legal system on Lovering and the Republican Party. Gov. John M. Stone, a Democrat who took over for Ames in 1876, blamed his inability to stop racial violence on the Code of 1871.

Lovering contracted malaria while in Mississippi and was enfeebled by the disease. He ended work in the legal profession and returned in 1876 to Louisville, where he died on 28 January 1879.

Elizabeth Ladner
University of Virginia

William C. Harris, *Journal of Southern History* (May 1974); E. O. Jameson, *The Biographical Sketches of Prominent Persons, and the Genealogical Records of Many Early and Other Families in Medway, Mass., 1713–1886* (1886).

Lower Mississippi River

"The people of the Delta fear God and the Mississippi River." So begins "The Mississippi River," a chapter in David Cohn's memoir, *Where I Was Born and Raised* (1948). After describing how the people increasingly turned to God as the river approached flood, he writes, "For God and the river are immortal and immemorial. Like life, the river gave birth to this land; like death it comes to reclaim what it has given. Then the hand of man is impotent and refuge is in God alone." William Alexander Percy echoed this theme: "With us, when you speak of 'the river,' though there be many, you mean always the same one, the great river, the shifting, unappeasable god of the country, feared and loved, the Mississippi."

Both authors refer to the Lower Mississippi River, which historically forms the western border of Mississippi. (Because of changes in the channel by nature and the Army Corps of Engineers since creation of the state, some parts of Mississippi are now on the western side of the river, while some parts of Arkansas and Louisiana are on the eastern side.) By the time the river leaves Mississippi and enters Louisiana, it has collected water from thirty-one states and two Canadian provinces, a drainage basin stretching from New York to Montana and encompassing more than 1.2 million square miles. Major tributaries include the Missouri, Ohio (largest by volume), Tennessee, Arkansas, and Yazoo River systems. The Atchafalaya is the only distributary stream, draining water out of the Mississippi through the Sidney A. Murray Jr. Hydroelectric Station and Old River Control Structure south of Natchez. Consequently, the greatest volume in the entire Mississippi River drainage basin flows along Mississippi's western border. At flood stage, almost twice as much water flows past Rosedale, Greenville, Vicksburg, and Natchez as passes New Orleans or exits the mouth of the river.

The Lower Mississippi begins at an elevation of 270.5 feet above sea level at the confluence of the Mississippi and the Ohio Rivers at Cairo, Illinois. It proceeds to the sea over a natural course of 954 river miles (although the straight-line distance is only 600 miles), giving it an average slope of only six inches per mile. From just north of Vicksburg to its mouth, the bed of the river lies below sea level. Ranking fifth among the world's rivers in average discharge, the Lower Mississippi is very turbulent and powerful. Historically it meandered through the Mississippi Alluvial Valley in a sinuous pattern, with each meander cutting into the bank on the convex edge and depositing sediments on the concave edge. As meanders become more extreme, the point of land inside the meander becomes connected to its neighboring bank by a narrow neck, which can be cut off during floods. This natural process allows the river to shorten its route to the sea and leaves behind oxbow lakes, which eventually fill in with sediment. Prior to human intervention, this process occurred more or less continuously over several thousand years, with the river channel or the channels of tributary streams moving across the floodplain and leaving behind oxbows and new land as older land was eroded.

The floodplain of the river is filled with alluvium that is several hundred feet deep in some places. This waterborne sediment is fine-grained and composed primarily of sand, silt, and clay. In the northwestern part of the state, all or parts of nineteen counties lie within the alluvial plain called the Mississippi Delta, but the floodplain itself continues along the river south of the Delta until it exits into Louisiana. This plain was created by the river, which historically enriched it by regular flooding that deposited new alluvium incrementally and sometimes destroyed the land as the river reclaimed its sedimentary burden. In such alluvial systems, the highest ground is adjacent to the channel because floodwaters lose momentum, drop their sediment load, and build natural levees when they overflow the channel proper. This high ground is both convenient to river travel and safer in time of flood; hence it was settled before the rest of the floodplain. It is also sandier because sand settles more quickly from the water than does silt, and sandier soils are preferred for cotton culture. Finer-grained particles such as clay precipitate farther from the river channel, creating back swamps with heavier "gumbo" soils.

In the absence of human intervention, the river naturally flooded on a regular basis, and the floodplain, including all of the Delta, was a swampy bottomland hardwood forest interspersed with canebrakes, cypress stands, and oxbow lakes. Early European and African settlers encountered huge trees and forests filled with panthers, red wolves, black bears, deer, alligators, and diverse smaller creatures, including the ivory-billed woodpecker. Clearing the forests, either by logging or creating deadenings (girdling of trees), was usually the first order of business. Permanent use of the cleared land for agriculture required construction of levees walling off the river, but once done, the only obstacle to large-scale agriculture was the tree stumps. The arrival of railroads beginning in the 1870s allowed immigrants easier access to the land and carried lumber and commodities to shipping points.

Flooding on the Lower Mississippi River became more problematic after human settlement increased in the Delta region, with major flood events in 1782, 1828, 1858, and as recently as 1993 and 2011; lesser floods in 1844, 1850, 1851; and troublesome floods in 1862, 1865, 1867, 1882, 1883, 1884, 1890, 1897, 1903, 1912, 1913, and 1922. During the Great Flood of 1927 the river carried a volume of 2.5 million cubic feet per second and reached a width of sixty miles below Memphis. The levees crevassed (broke) near Scott, Mississippi, and forty-one other locations in Arkansas, Louisiana, and Mississippi, eventually flooding twenty-seven thousand square miles (nearly 16.6 million acres) and displacing more than seven hundred thousand

people in the Lower Mississippi Valley. This flood caused direct economic losses estimated between $3.3 and $12.6 billion (in 2016 dollars) and was so catastrophic that prior to Hurricanes Katrina and Rita it was considered the greatest natural disaster in US history. Levee construction had previously been the responsibility either of individual landowners or of local levee boards, but after the US Congress passed the Flood Control Act of 1928, the US Army Corps of Engineers bore responsibility for levee construction to prevent flooding and promote economic development.

In late April and early May 2011, as a result of a fourteen-day rainfall and northern snowmelt, the Delta experienced flooding from the Mississippi River and her major tributaries of a magnitude unseen since 1927. The Mississippi reached flood stage in Greenville (48 feet) on 28 April, eventually cresting at 62.22 feet on 16 May. The Delta south to Natchez remained at flood stage until the first and second weeks of June. Major highways, including portions of US Highway 61, were cut off by floodwaters, and more than 350 residences from Greenville to Natchez were destroyed. More than 1,400 homes suffered damage, and more than 2,600 residences, businesses, and other structures ultimately were affected by the flood. Damage in Mississippi was estimated to exceed one billion dollars.

The river created the land of the Delta, provided it with fertile, rock-free soil, and predisposed it to large-scale agriculture, especially the growing of cotton. Until the second half of the twentieth century, cotton culture required large numbers of field hands and mules. Today, walled off by massive levees from view and mind, the Lower Mississippi River is primarily a conduit for shipping and conveying floodwaters. Much of the batture land (the land on the river side of the levee) is owned by timber companies and leased to hunting clubs. Army Corps of Engineers wetland regulations protect some forested wetlands, and the land's potential to support new natural-resource-based economic development ventures is being explored.

Luther Brown
US Fish and Wildlife Service

Ron Nassar
US Fish and Wildlife Service

Stephen Ambrose and Douglas Brinkley, *The Mississippi and the Making of a Nation* (2002); John M. Barry, *Rising Tide: The Great Mississippi Flood of 1927 and How It Changed America* (1998); David L. Cohn, *Where I Was Born and Raised* (1948); Pete Daniel, *Deep'n as It Come: The 1927 Mississippi River Flood* (1997); Anuradha Mathurand and Dilip da Cunha, *Mississippi Floods* (2001); Mikko Saikku, *This Delta, This Land: An Environmental History of the Yazoo-Mississippi Floodplain* (2005).

Lower Mississippi Survey

The Lower Mississippi Survey (LMS) was established in 1939 as a collaborative long-term research program to systematically survey and study the archaeological record of a large section of the Lower Mississippi River Alluvial Valley. The program was conceived and jointly founded by three individuals: James A. Ford (1911–68) of Louisiana State University, James B. Griffin (1905–97) of the University of Michigan Museum of Anthropology, and Philip Phillips (1900–1994) of the Peabody Museum at Harvard University. Their combined efforts and involvement in LMS investigations laid the foundation for archaeological research in the Lower Mississippi Valley, and the program they created engaged in regional research since its conception. For more than half a century, the LMS played a major role in illuminating the cultural history of one of the most archaeologically significant regions in the United States and stood as one of the most pivotal research endeavors in the history of Eastern North American archaeology.

Although the geographic range of LMS projects later expanded, the initial research focused on an area of the Mississippi River Alluvial Valley from northeastern Arkansas to the southern part of Mississippi's Yazoo Basin. At the time, the prehistory of this portion of the Mississippi River landscape was poorly understood. Archaeologists were beginning to reconstruct prehistoric chronologies and define cultural sequences for adjacent regions of the floodplain to the north and south. However, little was known about the pre-Mississippian cultural history within the vast floodplain bottomlands extending from the mouth of the Ohio River near Cairo, Illinois, south to Vicksburg.

To address the void in archaeological knowledge of this region, a large-scale systematic survey project was devised. Fieldwork commenced in 1940 and was implemented over five field seasons (each lasting no longer than two months) between 1940 and 1947. During the fieldwork, more than twelve thousand square miles were surveyed and 382 archaeological sites were documented (only 60 of which had previously been known to archaeologists). In addition, twenty stratigraphic test pits were excavated at eleven different sites, and more than 346,000 potsherds were examined during subsequent laboratory analysis.

The research findings and the vast quantity of data amassed from this initial ambitious project were compiled in a 457-page monograph, *Archaeological Survey of the Lower Mississippi Valley, 1940–1947* (1951). The landmark publication defined the standard for archaeological research and reporting in the region and remains a paramount reference for scholars working in the Southeast. The researchers established the basic chronology and ceramic typology for the entire Yazoo Basin of Mississippi as well as for much of eastern Arkansas. In the process, they refined existing analytical methods of ceramic seriation and pottery classification techniques. Previously undocumented earlier pre-Mississippian cultural manifestations were identified in the study area, and a cultural sequence that spanned a greater period of antiquity was constructed to accommodate this new information. In addition to greatly enhancing our understanding of the breadth and time depth of the region's prehistoric record, the project addressed the geological context of the study area. Phillips, Ford, and Griffin realized the importance of geomorphology to understanding the archaeology of the region, forming the foundation for a long tradition of collaboration between geologists and archaeologists working in the Lower Mississippi Valley.

The initial LMS publication provided the base for and source of much of the subsequent work in the Lower Valley. Data and insight provided by the text gave birth to a series of new, more specific regional research issues that engendered the next phase of LMS-affiliated investigations. In 1949 Phillips, who served as the first LMS director, began a six-year focused survey project of the Lower Yazoo Basin. The resulting two-volume monograph, *Archaeological Survey in the Lower Yazoo Basin, Mississippi, 1949–1955* (1970), included notable sections on method and theory and advanced the discourse on regional cultural chronologies. The work also made significant contributions to southeastern ceramic typologies, and the publication's detailed descriptions and illustrations are still used to aid pottery classification. Two additional large-scale LMS research projects were undertaken in the Yazoo Basin of Mississippi during the 1950s. The 1951 excavations at the Jaketown site in Humphreys County helped define the position of Poverty Point culture in relation to the existing southeastern prehistoric sequence and generated an acute research interest in the Late Archaic culture. Stephen Williams of Harvard University was appointed LMS director in 1958 and began intensive investigation of the Lake George Site in Yazoo County that year. The Lake George research helped to outline the developmental history of the large multicomponent settlement, tracing the cultural changes among its inhabitants as well as the evolution of the site's natural and constructed landscape through time.

Williams remained the LMS director until 1993, and during his tenure the number of participants and areal scope of LMS projects expanded considerably. Field research was conducted from southeastern Missouri and southwestern Kentucky to the mouth of the Mississippi River. The Boeuf Basin in northeastern Louisiana and coastal areas were also investigated. In additional to advancing our understanding of the regional prehistoric record, the numerous LMS projects trained a diverse group of archaeologists. Until 2003 the LMS program remained involved in regional archaeological research under director Tristram R. Kidder of Washington

University in St. Louis. An archive of past LMS work is housed at the University of North Carolina Research Laboratories of Archaeology.

Lee J. Arco

Washington University in St. Louis

Jay K. Johnson, in *Histories of Southeastern Archaeology*, ed. Shannon Tushingham, Jane Hill, and Charles H. McNutt (2002); LMS Archives Online, Research Laboratories of Archaeology, University of North Carolina at Chapel Hill, http://rla.unc.edu/Archives/LMS1/index.html; Philip Phillips, *Archaeological Survey in the Lower Yazoo Basin, Mississippi, 1949–1955* (1970); Philip Phillips, James A. Ford, and James B. Griffin, *Archaeological Survey in the Lower Mississippi Alluvial Valley, 1940–1947* (1951); Vincus P. Steponaitis, Stephen Williams, Steve Davis Jr., Ian W. Brown, Tristram R. Kidder, and Melissa Salvanish, University of North Carolina, LMS Archives Online website, www.rla.unc.edu/Archives/LMS1/index.html; Stephen Williams, in *Archaeological Survey in the Lower Mississippi Valley, 1940–1947*, ed. Stephen Williams (2003).

Lowndes County

Located in eastern Mississippi on the Alabama border, Lowndes County was formed in 1830 out of a portion of Monroe County and was named after congressman William Lowndes. Columbus serves as the county seat. Artesia, Caledonia, and Mayhew are other towns in the county.

In its first census in 1830, Lowndes County had a small population of 2,109 free people and 1,065 slaves. It grew dramatically in the next decade and by 1840 had the state's sixth-largest population. In 1840 Lowndes had 5,742 free people and a substantial slave majority of 8,771.

By 1860 Lowndes had Mississippi's fourth-largest population, with 6,895 free persons and 16,730 slaves (71 percent). Lowndes was a prosperous agricultural area. Its farms and plantations grew the third-most corn and fourth-most cotton in Mississippi, and the county ranked twelfth in the value of its livestock. In addition, Lowndes County's 335 industrial workers ranked fourth in the state. More than a hundred of those men were employed in blacksmithing, brickwork, lumber mill work, and carpentry—all jobs indicative of a growing area. Author Joseph Beckham Cobb, best known for *Mississippi Scenes*, lived in Columbus from 1844 until his death in 1858.

In 1860 Lowndes County had thirty-two churches, among them six Presbyterian churches and four Cumberland Presbyterian churches, giving the county more of a Presbyterian concentration than most of the rest of the state. It was also home to twelve Baptist, eight Methodist, and two Christian churches.

Main Street, Columbus, seat of Lowndes County, ca. 1906 (Ann Rayburn Paper Americana Collection, Department of Archives and Special Collections, J. D. Williams Library, University of Mississippi [rayburn_ann_23_118_001])

Columbus was an important site for Civil War leadership, transportation, production, and memory. Confederate generals William Barksdale, William Edwin Baldwin, and Jacob Hunter Sharp all spent considerable time in Lowndes County. As a railroad center, Columbus was the location of the Briarfield Arsenal, one of the major facilities supplying weapons to the Confederacy. Lowndes County was briefly home to the Mississippi legislature, which met in Columbus after Union forces took Jackson. In 1866 three women put flowers on the graves of numerous Confederate and Union soldiers at Columbus's Friendship Cemetery, and it subsequently became known as the site of the first Decoration Day.

In 1870 Lowndes County had the second-highest population in the state. A decade later the population had grown to 28,244 despite the fact that a portion of the county became part of Clay County in 1872. African Americans made up a substantial majority of Lowndes's population. Lowndes remained a very productive agricultural county: its farmers grew the third-most corn in the state, ranked fifteenth in cotton, and had the eighth-most mules. Lowndes, like many black-majority counties, had high rates of tenancy and low rates of farm owning. Landowners cultivated only 37 percent of the county's farms, a figure well below the state average. While 505 of the 713 white farmers were owners (71 percent), only 195 of the 2,754 African American farmers owned their land (7 percent). The county's manufacturing firms employed the fifth-most industrial workers in the state, and Lowndes had a particularly high number of foreign-born residents, many of them from Germany.

The Industrial Institute and College for the Education of White Girls of the State of Mississippi, the nation's first public university for women, opened in Columbus in 1884 after years of lobbying efforts led by educators Sallie Eola Reneau, Olivia Valentine Hastings, and Annie Coleman Peyton. Over the following century, changes in the name and mission of the school marked changes in Mississippi education. In 1920 it became the Mississippi State College for Women, reflecting the broad educational and curricular goals of the institution. In 1966 the college accepted its first black students, and in 1974 it became Mississippi University for Women. Eight years later, as a result of *Hogan v. Mississippi University for Women*, the school admitted its first men. Among the notable and dedicated faculty members have been Emma Ody Pohl, physical education professor from 1907 to 1955; literature professor Pauline Orr, who taught from the 1880s to 1913; and Bridget Smith Pieschel, an English professor who has served as director of the school's Center for Women's Research and Public Policy since 2005 and who helped to establish an oral history program to study Mississippi women. Alumnae of the institution include artists Valerie Jaudon and Eugenia Summer; home demonstration leader Dorothy Dickins; actress Ruth Ford; educator Blanche Colton Williams; scientist Elizabeth Lee Hazen; novelist Alice Walworth Graham; author, scholar, and editor Patti Carr Black; and legal figures Helen Carloss and Lenore Prather.

As in most of Mississippi, various groups of Baptists and Methodists made up the majority of Lowndes County's church members in the early twentieth century. The largest groups were the Missionary Baptists; members of the Methodist Episcopal Church, South; and members of the Southern Baptist Convention. The Methodist Episcopal Church, Colored Methodist Episcopal Church, and Presbyterian Church of the United States also had substantial memberships.

Numerous creative individuals were born or grew up in Lowndes County. Thomas Williams III was born in 1911 in Columbus, where his grandfather, Walter Dakin, was a minister at the Episcopal Church. After changing his name to Tennessee Williams, he went on to become one of America's greatest playwrights. Blues musician Big Joe Williams, born in 1903, grew up in the western Lowndes community of Crawford. Folklorist Newbell Niles Puckett, author of *Folk Beliefs of the Southern Negro* (1926), photographer Marion Gaines, and baseball broadcaster Red Barber grew up in Lowndes County.

In the early 1900s the Lowndes County population remained substantial, increasing slightly to 29,987 by 1930, when African Americans accounted for almost 60 percent of residents. Columbus had a population of 10,501, but the county's economy still concentrated on agriculture, with more than thirty-five hundred farms. Seventy-three percent of Lowndes County's farmers were tenants, and their interests were divided among cattle, hogs, corn, cotton, and forage crops.

Lowndes County's population jumped to 46,639 by 1960. It ranked fifth in the state in per capita income and near the top in population density and the percentage of its residents who had finished high school. As the home of the Mississippi University for Women, it employed more than one thousand people in education. Twenty-two percent of workers were employed in industry, including in electrical equipment, metalwork, and apparel. Farmers comprised 12 percent of the labor force, concentrating on soybeans, corn, livestock, and some cotton.

In recent years, Columbus has been notable as the home of documentary photographer Birney Imes and for Genesis Press, one of the nation's leading publishers of books by and about African Americans. In 1988 Columbus became the site of the new Mississippi School of Mathematics and Science, which attracts students from throughout the state.

Like most counties in eastern Mississippi, Lowndes County grew between 1960 and 2000, when its population reached 61,586, before declining slightly to 59,779 a decade later. As in neighboring Oktibbeha and Noxubee Counties, the white proportion of the county had increased over the previous half century, and by 2010 just over half of Lowndes's population was white, African Americans made up more than 40 percent of residents, and Hispanics represented a small but growing minority.

Mississippi Encyclopedia Staff
University of Mississippi

Hogan v. Mississippi University for Women, 653 F.2d 222 [1981]); Mississippi State Planning Commission, *Progress Report on State Planning in Mississippi* (1938); *Mississippi Statistical Abstract*, Mississippi State University (1952–2010); Charles Sydnor and Claude Bennett, *Mississippi History* (1939); University of Virginia Library, Historical Census Browser website, http://mapserver.lib.virginia.edu; E. Nolan Waller and Dani A. Smith, *Growth Profiles of Mississippi's Counties, 1960–1980* (1985).

Lowrey, Mark Perrin

(1828–1885) Confederate General, Minister, and Educator

Mark Perrin Lowrey was born in McNairy County, Tennessee, on 20 December 1828. At the age of fifteen he moved with his family to Farmington in what was then part of Tishomingo County (now Alcorn County). After volunteering for service in the Mexican War, he was mustered out in Vicksburg in July 1848. Although he did not see action, he learned to respect the discipline of military life.

After the war Lowrey married Sarah Holmes and began what he thought would be a lifetime as a brick mason. He was good at his job and began to accumulate money, but in 1853 he became a Baptist minister. As Mississippi moved toward secession, he attempted to remain politically neutral, but he was nevertheless asked to lead men into war because of his prior military service, slim as it was. Lowrey soon found himself serving as colonel of the 32nd Mississippi Regiment. Opposed to human bondage and owning no slaves, he saw himself solely as defending his home and family from invasion by Union forces.

He saw action between the Battle of Shiloh and his resignation on 14 March 1865, attaining the rank of brigadier general. Confederate soldiers remembered him as the Fighting

Mark Perrin Lowrey (Courtesy Blue Mountain College)

Baptist Message (31 October 1940); Larry Wells Kennedy, "The Fighting Preacher of the Army of Tennessee" (PhD dissertation, Mississippi State University, 1976); Mark Perrin Lowrey, Unpublished Autobiography, 30 September 1867, Archives of the National Alumnae Association of Blue Mountain College, Blue Mountain, Mississippi; *Memphis Commercial Appeal* (12 February 1906); *Ripley Enterprise* (6 March 1912); *Ripley Southern Sentinel* (15 March 1923); Robbie Neal Sumrall, *A Light on a Hill: A History of Blue Mountain College* (1947).

Lowry, Beverly
(b. 1938) Author

Parson of the Army of Tennessee, declaring that he would "preach like hell on Sunday and fight like the devil all the week."

Lowrey returned to Mississippi, resumed his pastoral duties, and worked to reorganize Baptist churches that had suffered from the war. He was a well-respected man, and in 1872, while he was preaching in Jackson, the state legislature asked him to become a US senator. He declined, saying, "I can not sacrifice the commission I hold as a minister of the gospel even for a commission as U.S. Senator." That year he also declined an offer from the Southern Baptist Convention to become executive secretary of the Foreign Mission Board because he believed that Mississippi offered a safer environment for his children than did Richmond, Virginia.

Lowrey served as president of the Mississippi Baptist Convention from 1868 to 1877 as well as on the board of trustees for the University of Mississippi and Mississippi College. He edited the Mississippi Department of *The Baptist* from 1870 to 1877. In 1869 he and a friend, Dr. J. B. Gambrell, decided to start a school for girls. Later that year he traded property with Randolph Gipson, taking possession of a farm on a hillside in Tippah County known as the Brougher Place. There, on 12 September 1873, he established Blue Mountain Female Institute (later renamed Blue Mountain College). He devoted the remainder of his life to the cause of female education, serving as the school's president and as a history professor. While accompanying several students and two faculty members to catch the train to New Orleans, the general collapsed and died at the railway station in Middleton, Tennessee, on 27 February 1885. Gambrell remembered his friend as "a Christian and minister, a writer and editor, a soldier and citizen, an educator, a man."

Thomas D. Cockrell
Northeast Mississippi Community College

Born in Memphis, Tennessee, on 10 August 1938, novelist Beverly Fey Lowry moved to Greenville with her family when she was six years old. An excellent student, Fey was also a competitive swimmer and majorette in high school. She spent two years at the University of Mississippi before transferring to Memphis State University (now the University of Memphis), where she earned a bachelor's degree in 1960.

Fey soon married stockbroker Glenn Lowry and moved with him to New York City, where she took acting classes, spent a great deal of time writing a journal, and gave birth to the first of two sons. In 1965 the Lowrys moved to Houston, where their second son was born the following year.

In 1973 Lowry enrolled in a writing workshop at the University of Houston, where she met Mississippi fiction writer Donald Barthelme, who read and edited her work. She joined the creative writing faculty at Houston in 1976 and published her first novel, *Come Back, Lolly Ray* (1977), about a female high school football hero in the fictional town of Eunola, Mississippi, modeled after Greenville. Her next novel, *Emma Blue* (1978), is also set in Eunola, while her third novel, *Daddy's Girl* (1981), is set in Houston.

In 1980 Lowry moved to San Marcos, Texas, where she taught creative writing at Southwestern Texas State University. Lowry ultimately followed her somewhat whimsical and overtly humorous first novels with more darkly ironic works of fiction—*The Perfect Sonya* (1987) and *Breaking Gentle* (1988). This turn in tone is most likely attributable to the death of both of Lowry's parents and of her younger son, who was killed in a 1984 hit-and-run accident. In addition, she and her husband divorced after thirty years of marriage.

Lowry turned to nonfiction with *Crossed Over: A Murder, a Memoir* (1992), in which she recounts her struggle to cope with her son's death through her relationship with Karla Faye Tucker, convicted and ultimately executed for her role in a Houston double homicide. The book drew wide critical praise and comparisons to Truman Capote's *In Cold*

Blood. Lowry followed *Crossed Over* with a return to Eunola in *The Track of Real Desires* (1994). After a nine-year hiatus, she published *Her Dream of Dreams: The Rise and Triumph of Madam C. J. Walker* (2003), a nonfiction account of the first female African American millionaire, and a speculative biography, *Harriet Tubman: Imagining a Life* (2007).

Lowry's short stories, reviews, and articles have appeared in countless publications. She has served as president of the Texas Institute of Letters (1982–84) and has taught in creative writing programs at schools across the country, including the Universities of Alabama and Montana and George Mason University.

Jennifer Southall

Jackson, Mississippi

Joe David Bellamy, *Literary Luxuries: American Writing at the End of the Century* (1995); Joseph M. Flora and Robert Bain, eds., *Contemporary Fiction Writers of the South: A Biographical-Bibliographic Sourcebook* (1993); *Houston Chronicle* (9 November 2008); Merril Maguire Skaggs, in *Women Writers of the Contemporary South*, ed. Peggy Whitman Prenshaw (1984).

Lowry, Robert

(1829–1910) Confederate General and Thirty-Second Governor, 1882–1890

Robert Lowry occupied the office of governor for eight years and was Mississippi's first governor to remain in office for two consecutive four-year terms.

Lowry was born in the Chesterfield District of South Carolina on 10 March 1829. In the 1840s his family moved to Raleigh, Mississippi, in Smith County. After reading law and being admitted to the state bar in 1859, he established a practice in Brandon. When the Civil War began, he enlisted as a private and rose to the rank of brigadier general. After the war he resumed his practice of law in Brandon and won election as a Democrat to the state legislature in 1865.

In 1881 Lowry won the governorship, defeating Republican Benjamin King by a vote of 77,727 to 52,009. During Lowry's first administration a bill was introduced to move the state capital from Jackson to Meridian, a rapidly growing railroad town located at the junction of the Southern and Mobile and Ohio Railroads. That effort failed, and the 1890 constitution established Jackson as the permanent state capital.

During Lowry's first term, Jefferson and Varina Howell Davis visited Jackson at the request of the Mississippi legislature, and Lowry honored them with a formal state dinner at the Governor's Mansion. Twenty years earlier the State of Mississippi had commissioned Lowry to seek Davis's release from prison at Fort Monroe, where he had been sent awaiting his trial for treason against the United States. The federal government eventually dropped the charges against the Confederate president. That state dinner was one of Davis's last public appearances. Also during Governor Lowry's first administration, Mississippi established the Industrial Institute and College at Columbus, the first state-supported college for women in the United States.

Lowry was a proponent of industrial development and strongly supported the expansion of Mississippi's railroad system, which grew spectacularly during his eight years in office. During the 1880s the amount of track in Mississippi more than doubled from 1,118 miles to 2,366 miles, and in 1883 more track was laid in Mississippi than in any other state.

After Lowry left office, he moved his permanent residence to Jackson and spent much of his time collaborating with William H. McCardle, the former editor of the *Vicksburg Times*, on *A History of Mississippi* and on a textbook for use in the state's public school system. Lowry briefly reentered politics in 1901, running unsuccessfully for the US Senate. He died in Jackson on 19 January 1910.

David G. Sansing

University of Mississippi

Mississippi Official and Statistical Register (1912); Dunbar Rowland, *Encyclopedia of Mississippi History*, vol. 2 (1907); David G. Sansing and Carroll Waller, *A History of the Mississippi Governor's Mansion* (1977).

Lum, Ray

(1891–1976) Mule Trader

Ray Lum was born on 25 June 1891 in Rocky Springs, Mississippi, a rural community of about seventy-five people located on the Natchez Trace. His grandmother reared him, and during childhood he milked cows, herded cattle and goats, and trained horses. At the age of twelve he moved to Vicksburg and spent two years as a delivery boy for local stores. His trading career began at fourteen, when he bought a horse for $12.50 and sold it for $25.00. However, in another of his earliest transactions, he sold his wagon and team of goats in Port Gibson for $20 after being promised $25. He later recalled, "That was one of the best lessons I ever got. That was the best five dollars ever I earned." He was beaten in this trade but afterwards was "awake." He learned from his mistakes and quickly became a shrewd judge of animals and people, embarking on a career during which he bought and sold livestock in every area of the United States. His base of operations was Vicksburg, where at one time he owned five stables and hundreds of horses and mules.

As a young man, Lum traded with gypsies who were said to "hoodoo" horses, making plugs look like fine animals. From Vicksburg he traveled up the Sunflower River into the Mississippi Delta to sell horses and mules to farmers. Shortly thereafter he began making regular trips to Texas to acquire the trainloads of stock that he auctioned at his three barns in Vicksburg.

Lum moved to Texas in 1922 and established a central sale barn in Fort Worth that was managed by his partner and ring man, Harry Barnett. Lum then set up local sales throughout West Texas. He shipped stock to every barn in the region and personally auctioned the animals on a partnership basis with his local managers. During this time he introduced night sales, where both buyers and stock could escape the Texas heat. In 1937 Lum returned to live in Vicksburg and introduced registered Hereford cattle into the Deep South to upgrade the quality of beef.

As late as 1967 he auctioned uninterrupted for hours at large sales in Atlanta and Birmingham. Failing eyesight eventually forced him to withdraw from the extended auctions of his earlier years because he could no longer see bids. Until just prior to his death, Lum drove each week to sales in Lorman, Vicksburg, Port Gibson, Natchez, and Hazlehurst, filling his large car with "everything pertaining to a horse." Bridles, bits, and currycombs were piled on the dashboard; boxes of hats and boots covered the backseat; saddles filled the trunk; and cans of ribbon cane syrup lined the back floor.

As a trader, Lum was adept at both humor and deception. At times he offered customers veiled truths that only seasoned traders would understand. He defined a trader as "a man that trades in everything. A real trader don't never find nothing that he can't use. If he is a trader—and you're looking at one right now—he will trade you for anything you have got. If he can't use it, he'll find someone else that can. There is lots of people that can take a pocketknife and run it into a barrel of money, and there are a lot of people that you can give a barrel of money and won't be long until they won't even have the pocketknife. It's all in who it is trading. Yes sir, I think traders are born." Lum preserved his world through tales of men and animals he knew: "When you get eighty-five years old, you outlive all your friends. That's the bad part of being old; you can't find nobody to talk to about things that happened back there. They're all gone. You live and learn. And then you die and forget it all."

William Ferris
University of North Carolina at
Chapel Hill

William Ferris, *You Live and Learn. Then You Die and Forget It All: Ray Lum's Tales of Horses, Mules, and Men* (1992); Ben Green, *Some More Horse Tradin'* (1972); Edward Mayhew, *Illustrated Horse Management,*

Containing Descriptive Remarks upon Anatomy, Medicine, Shoeing, Teeth, Food, Vices, Stables (1864).

Lum v. Rice

During the second half of the nineteenth century, Chinese immigrants began settling in the Mississippi Delta. The 1890 Mississippi Constitution created a dual school system for whites and blacks but said nothing about the Chinese, who attended white schools in communities throughout the Delta. In 1924, however, Rosedale officials declared that Chinese children could no longer attend white schools, prompting Gong Lum, a Chinese grocer, to petition the state circuit court of Mississippi so that his American-born daughter, Martha, could attend the town's all-white high school. Lum argued that because Martha "is not a member of the colored race nor is she of mixed blood," she should not have to attend a black school. Moreover, because neither Rosedale nor Bolivar County operated a school for children of Chinese descent and because Lum was a taxpayer who helped to support and maintain the Rosedale high school, he contended that Martha was entitled to attend that school.

The court denied Lum's petition on the grounds that Martha "is a member of the Mongolian or yellow race, and therefore not entitled to attend the schools provided by law in the state of Mississippi for children of the white or Caucasian race." The trial court overturned this ruling and ordered the board of trustees and state superintendent to desist from discriminating against Martha because of her race. The defendants then appealed to the Mississippi Supreme Court, which held that the state constitution "divided the educable children into those of the pure white or Caucasian race, on the one hand, and the brown, yellow, and black races, on the other, and therefore that Martha Lum, of the Mongolian or yellow race, could not insist on being classed with the whites."

The case then moved to the US Supreme Court, which was primarily interested in "whether a state can be said to afford a child of Chinese ancestry, born in this country and a citizen of the United States, the equal protection of the laws, by giving her the opportunity for a common school education in a school which receives only colored children of the brown, yellow or black races." The court answered yes: excluding Martha Lum from white schools fell "within the discretion of the state in regulating its public schools, and does not conflict with the Fourteenth Amendment."

Lum v. Rice had both immediate and long-lasting effects. A year later the Supreme Court of Mississippi cited the case *Lum v. Rice* in denying a mandamus plea by Joe Tin

Lun, who also was of Chinese ancestry, to "compel the state superintendent of education and the teachers of the Dublin consolidated school to permit him to enroll" in an all-white school. More significantly, until *Brown v. Board of Education* (1954), the US Supreme Court continually cited *Lum v. Rice* to uphold segregation in public education.

Vivian Wu Wong

Milton Academy, Milton,
Massachusetts

"Exclusion of Chinese from Mississippi Schools," *School and Society* (29 September 1928); *Gong Lum v. Rice* (275 US 78 [1927]); James W. Loewen, *The Mississippi Chinese: Between Black and White* (1988); Ruthanne Lum McCunn, *Chinese American Portraits: Personal Histories, 1828–1988* (1996); *Rice v. Gong Lum* (139 Miss. 760).

Lumumba, Chokwe (Edwin Finley Taliaferro)
(1947–2014) Activist, Attorney, and Political Leader

An activist, lawyer, and briefly the mayor of Jackson, Chokwe Lumumba was born Edwin Finley Taliaferro on 2 August 1947 in Detroit. Taliaferro learned a sense of social responsibility from his parents' civil rights efforts in Michigan. As he recalled, "I developed a political consciousness because I had a mother who knew. She knew about justice and injustice, about self-determination."

Following the assassination of Martin Luther King Jr. in 1968, Taliaferro joined the Black Action Movement at Western Michigan University, where student protesters seized a campus building and demanded that administrators examine racism on campus. Inspired, Lumumba helped establish the Black United Front at Kalamazoo, and in 1969 he joined the provisional government of the Republic of New Afrika (RNA), a liberation movement that sought financial reparations for slavery and land in the southeastern United States to establish an independent black nation. During this period he changed his name, taking *Chokwe* (warrior) from an Angolan tribe that never succumbed to slavery and *Lumumba* to honor fallen Congolese nationalist Patrice Lumumba.

After graduating from Kalamazoo College with a degree in political science, Lumumba enrolled at Detroit's Wayne State University Law School but left in 1971 when his RNA responsibilities called him to Mississippi. The group's headquarters had relocated to a house near Jackson State University, and in August 1971 agents from the Federal Bureau of Investigation and the Jackson Police Department raided the property. During the resulting exchange of gunfire, police lieutenant William Louis Skinner was killed, and eleven RNA members were charged with murder and treason. Lumumba temporarily moved to Jackson to provide assistance to the RNA legal defense.

Lumumba subsequently returned to Detroit, finished his law degree, and worked briefly in the Detroit public defender's office. He then entered private practice, retaining his commitment to the goal of liberation and self-determination for African Americans and frequently accepting cases that placed him at odds with mainstream politics. In 1978 Lumumba defended the Pontiac Brothers, sixteen inmates charged with murder during a riot at Illinois's Pontiac Correctional Facility. In 1981 Lumumba served as counsel for Black Liberation Army members Fulani Sunni-Ali, Bilal Sunni-Ali, and Mutula Shakur, accused of involvement in an armored car robbery that resulted in the death of two police officers. Lumumba also worked to uncover evidence to support the release of Geronimo Pratt and briefly provided counsel for exiled Assata Shakur, both of whom were high-profile members of the Black Panthers.

Lumumba and his family moved to Mississippi in 1988, but his activist past and affiliation with controversial legal clients made his admittance into the Mississippi Bar Association difficult. Lumumba established a Jackson firm in 1991 and continued "working for people caught up in racial or political situations." Among several politically charged cases, Lumumba helped orchestrate the release of sisters Gladys and Jamie Scott, who were serving consecutive life sentences for a 1994 armed robbery in Forest. Based on the perceived severity of the Scott sisters' sentences, the case gained attention from the National Association for the Advancement of Colored People, the American Civil Liberties Union, and other human rights organizations. In December 2010, with Jamie Scott suffering from kidney failure, Gov. Haley Barbour ordered the sisters' release from prison on the condition that Gladys donate a kidney to Jamie.

Away from the courtroom, Lumumba cofounded the Malcolm X Grassroots Movement and the Malcolm X Center for Self Determination and continued his involvement with the New Afrikan People's Organization. In the wake of Hurricane Katrina in 2005, Lumumba organized "people's assemblies," assisting in community-driven recovery efforts.

Lumumba shifted into more conventional public service, winning election to Jackson's City Council in 2009. After one term representing Jackson's Ward 2, he ran for mayor. Lumumba neither distanced himself from his radical past nor viewed a run for public office as a departure from the goals of the RNA and New Afrikan People's Organization. While still committed to increasing political agency for African Americans, Lumumba made his mayoral campaign more inclusive, promoting "an agenda of compassion, justice, and human rights." Lumumba envisioned that Jackson could build a "solidarity economy" based on localized cooperatives and municipal partnerships with citizen-run businesses.

L

After a decisive win, Lumumba took office in July 2013 and immediately focused on Jackson's neglected infrastructure, fighting to raise water and sewer rates to finance internal improvement projects.

Lumumba died unexpectedly on 25 February 2014. Formerly skeptical political foes found his seven months in office promising, surprisingly amenable, and effective. At his funeral, former governor William Winter stated, "I was afraid that he would divide our city. I could not have been more wrong."

Chris Colbeck
University of Mississippi

Herbert Buchsbaum, *New York Times* (10 March 2014); Robert Caldwell, *Against the Current* (May–June 2013); Chokwe Lumumba File, Mississippi Department of Archives and History; National Conference of Black Lawyers website, www.ncbl.org; Bhaskar Sunkara, *The Nation* (26 February 2014); Western Michigan University Archives website, https://wmich.edu/library/collections/archives.

Lusco's

Once a place where cotton farmers went to drink Papa Lusco's Prohibited libations, this iconic Greenwood restaurant has changed little in appearance and atmosphere since it opened on 4 March 1933, though it has done away with its long-standing tradition of allowing patrons to fling butter pats onto the ceiling. The second-oldest restaurant in Mississippi and the oldest maintaining the same location as a family-owned and -operated enterprise, Lusco's has a history that remains a strong presence.

Italian immigrants Charles and Marie Lusco established Lusco's Grocery on the corner of Johnson and Main in Greenwood in 1921. The Luscos set up a table in the shop's back room, near the kitchen, and local cotton men would sit, play cards or dominoes, eat whatever Marie and her three daughters prepared, and drink Charles Lusco's homemade wine. Prohibition laws made the privacy of Lusco's back room essential. After this building burned, the business moved to its present location at 722 Carrollton Avenue. Only patrons who provided the secret password would be admitted into the store's nether regions, where the restaurant booths are now located.

Though the food and waitstaff attract interest and draw crowds, the booths are Lusco's truly extraordinary feature. Each booth is enclosed by curtains to protect patrons' privacy, and each was originally equipped with a bell that diners would ring to signal a need for service. The bells have been replaced by buzzers, but the curtains remain, preserving the clandestine quality of the Prohibition-era dining experience.

When the restaurant first opened, all of the waiters were African American men, who would recite the menu to patrons from memory and then take diners' orders, again committing everything to memory. In 2012 a documentary film, *Booker's Place*, told the story of Booker Wright, who caused controversy and lost his job when he demonstrated how he had to use different forms of language to please customers who expected deferential treatment from an African American waiter.

Fourth-generation owners Andy and Karen Pinkston continue to use the recipes Mama Lusco and her daughters perfected, though dishes have evolved to allow for shifting tastes and new ingredients. The Luscos came from Italy to Mississippi by way of Louisiana, and their cuisine fused Creole, Italian, and southern cookery. In addition to Mama's famous spaghetti, Lusco's is known for its broiled shrimp in butter sauce, tender steaks, exceptional salads, and seasonal broiled pompano. Some of Lusco's sauces can now be purchased from gift and gourmet retailers and online. Travel and food writers from across the globe have noted Lusco's distinctive character, and the restaurant is a genuinely unique establishment worthy of a trip to the Mississippi Delta and of a return visit.

Brooke Butler
New Orleans, Louisiana

Joe Atkins, *Daily Mississippian* (30 June 1998); John T. Edge, *Southern Belly: The Ultimate Food Lover's Companion to the South* (2000); Amy Evans, Southern Foodways website, www.southernfoodways.com; Lusco's website, www.luscos.net.

Lyells, Ruby Elizabeth Stutts
(1904–1994) Activist and Educator

An educator and a leader of numerous civic and women's organizations, Ruby Elizabeth Stutts Lyells spent four decades advocating for improvements in African American education and helping to create an infrastructure for Mississippi's civil rights movement. Impressive writing skills and a powerful speaking voice made Lyells a force in both scholarly journals and public venues, and she participated not only in educational and policy debates but also in direct action protests.

Born in 1908 in Yazoo County, Lyells attended Alcorn Agricultural and Mining College (now Alcorn State University), where she compiled an impressive academic record and became valedictorian in 1929. Lyells subsequently stepped into a leadership role at Alcorn, working as a librarian and student counselor and helping to form and develop the Library Division of the Mississippi Teachers Association.

In 1942 Lyells completed her master's thesis at the University of Chicago and became the first black Mississippian to earn a degree in library science. Throughout the 1940s and 1950s Lyells contributed regularly to publications such as the *Journal of Negro Education* and continued the research she had begun for her thesis. Lyells often wrote about reforms in African American library systems, but her articles and speeches always emphasized broader educational issues. Above all, Lyells consistently advocated creating a curriculum for black colleges that went beyond satisfying accreditation requirements or providing vocational training to foster a legitimate environment for scholarship and inquiry.

Lyells left Alcorn in 1945 and became the head librarian at Jackson State College (now Jackson State University). After a successful two-year stint during which she helped modernize and expand the school's library system, Lyells moved to the Jackson Public Library and headed the College Park and Carver branches. Lyells not only improved the library system but also used her leadership skills to agitate in favor of school desegregation and build networks of black women committed to social change. The boldness of her speeches and the doggedness of her campaigns made Lyells an inspiring and attractive leader. As a Republican and the president of the Negro State Federation of Women's Clubs, Lyells helped bring African American women into public life at a time when white men and Democrats ruled Mississippi politics.

Lyells did much of her work during the 1940s and early 1950s, before the civil rights movement erupted full-blown in Mississippi. As national organizations such as the National Association for the Advancement of Colored People expanded their presence in the state, men took on most of the leadership positions. Though the Student Nonviolent Coordinating Committee and other organizations included women in their leadership, these more radical and innovative groups tended to attract young people and college students. Thus, while Lyells participated in many of the direct action protests of the 1950s and 1960s, she did not align herself directly with those groups but instead remained an independent voice for change as the movement gained momentum. Her independence, her gender, and her age precluded Lyells from starring in the most publicized dramas of the civil rights era, but her tireless efforts to improve African American education and her commitment to bringing black women into public life helped pave the way for the movement's watershed accomplishments.

Thomas John Carey
University of Mississippi

John Dittmer, *Local People: The Struggle for Civil Rights in Mississippi* (1994); Ruby E. Stutts Lyells, *Journal of Negro Education* (Spring 1945); Josephine McCann Posey, *Against Great Odds: The History of Alcorn State University* (1994); Leila Gaston Rhodes, *Jackson State University: The First Hundred Years, 1877–1977* (1979).

Lynch, Charles
(1783–1853) Eighth and Eleventh Governor, 1833 and 1836–1838

Charles Lynch is one of the few men to have held office in all three branches of state government. He is also one of the very few Mississippians to have served as a judge even though he was not a lawyer.

Lynch was born in South Carolina in 1783 and migrated to Mississippi, where he became a farmer. In 1821 the Mississippi legislature appointed him probate judge of Lawrence County, and from 1827 to 1833 he represented the county in the State Senate. He was a leader of the Jacksonian Democrats in Mississippi, and he strongly opposed South Carolina's attempt to nullify the tariff. The 1832 Mississippi Constitution abolished the office of lieutenant governor, so when Gov. Abram Scott died in June 1833, Lynch, who was serving as president of the State Senate, was next in line for the governor's office. He served until the following November and urged the legislature to establish a state system of public schools; however, the legislature considered his plan too expensive and did not enact it.

In 1835 Lynch ran for the governorship as a Whig and won election by 426 votes, the second-smallest margin in state history. Lynch's 7 January 1836 inauguration represented the first time the state's chief executive held an elaborate inaugural ceremony. He was formally escorted into the chamber of the House of Representatives and introduced to a joint session of the state legislature, whose members watched as the chief justice of the Mississippi Supreme Court administered the oath of office and officially installed Lynch as the governor and commander in chief of the state's army, navy, and militia. Prominent Mississippi statesman Adam L. Bingaman read Lynch's inaugural address to the assembly.

During his administration, Lynch brought about extensive changes in Mississippi's criminal code, which he called the "Bloody Code" because it imposed the death penalty for a large number of offenses. He also recommended the establishment of a state penitentiary, which was authorized by the legislature and opened in 1840.

The first year of Lynch's tenure coincided with a period of great economic prosperity, but the Panic of 1837 caused Mississippi's economy to collapse. Several years of severe depression followed, during which time thousands of Mississippians fled to Texas to escape foreclosure on their farms and slaves.

In an effort to shore up the state's banking system and alleviate the shortage of money and credit, Mississippi issued five million dollars in bonds and invested them in the Union Bank, a newly established state bank. But land prices continued to decline, and the Union Bank failed within a year. The state was left with the worthless bank stock and a huge debt. Lynch, whose popularity declined along with the state's economy, did not seek reelection in 1837.

L

Lynch then served briefly as president of the Alabama and Mississippi Railroad Company and as commissioner of public buildings before retiring to his plantation home near Jackson. He died there on 9 February 1853.

David G. Sansing
University of Mississippi

Mississippi Official and Statistical Register (1912); Dunbar Rowland, *Encyclopedia of Mississippi History*, vol. 2 (1907).

Lynch, James D.
(1838–1872) Religious Leader and Politician

From 1864 to 1872 James Lynch was an important figure in Mississippi politics and religion. The son of free African Americans, Lynch was born in 1838 in Baltimore. He started his education there before moving on to Kimball Union Academy in New Hampshire. He became a minister of the Methodist Episcopal Church, North and served congregations in Indiana and Illinois. In 1860 Lynch moved to Pennsylvania, where he became editor of the *Philadelphia Advocate*. In late 1864 he traveled to Savannah, Georgia, where he met with African American clergy, Gen. William Tecumseh Sherman, and Secretary of War Edwin M. Stanton. At times during the meeting, Stanton polled the African Americans present to see if they agreed on various points: on two occasions, Lynch was the sole dissenter, arguing that African Americans would not need to live in separate colonies and declining to support General Sherman on the grounds of lack of familiarity. Lynch soon returned north.

In 1867 Lynch settled in Mississippi as a representative of his denomination, reporting that the group had six thousand members and had established twenty meetinghouses and many schools. He helped to establish Shaw University (now Rust College) in Holly Springs. Lynch resided on Jackson's Capitol Street with his wife and two sons and bought several other town lots.

While he continued his interest in religion, education, and Masonry, Lynch soon became actively engaged in politics, serving as vice president of several state Republican conventions. His fame and influence rested primarily on his oratorical skills, which received praise from both whites and blacks. African Americans traveled for miles to hear him speak. Lynch could orchestrate the emotions of his audience and was an effective political debater and campaigner.

In the factional struggles between conservative and Radical Republicans in Mississippi, Lynch allied himself with the conservatives led by James L. Alcorn. For example, Lynch campaigned for the ratification of the constitution of 1868 even though he had not supported its most controversial provisions, which prohibited supporters of secession from holding public office and required voters to subscribe to a declaration of civil and political racial equality. He was elected secretary of state in 1869 on a ticket headed by Alcorn. In fact, he received more votes than Alcorn. He did a creditable job in that post and served on the State Board of Education. Hiram Rhoades Revels, who completed Lynch's term as secretary of state, stated that he found the office and records in good condition. Lynch did not object to the establishment of a segregated school system, but he was concerned that school funds be distributed fairly. Lynch believed that former slaves should rely on landowning rather than sharecropping and argued that government policies should make it possible for freed blacks to purchase between 40 and 160 acres of land and pay for it over five years at 6 percent interest.

In 1870 he contended briefly for nomination for the US Senate, but the position went instead to Revels. Radical Republican criticism of Lynch increased, but he also faced allegations that he was a heavy drinker. These allegations helped George McKee defeat Lynch for nomination to Congress in 1872, although bribery may also have played a role. Lynch was also accused of rape but was acquitted. Disappointed by these events, Lynch did not participate in the 1872 presidential election in Mississippi, though he did serve as a delegate to the Republican National Convention that year. He addressed the convention so effectively that he was invited to campaign for the reelection of Pres. Ulysses S. Grant in Indiana and Illinois.

Soon after his return to Jackson, he was diagnosed with Bright's disease of the kidneys (glomerulonephritus), and he died on 18 December 1872. He was buried in Greenwood cemetery in Jackson, and the Republican-controlled legislature appropriated money for a statue there in his honor.

Daniel C. Vogt
Jackson State University

Eric Foner, *Freedom's Lawmakers: A Directory of Black Officeholders during Reconstruction* (1996); William C. Harris, *Historian* 34 (1971); "Minutes of Interview between Colored Ministers and Secretary of War and General Sherman" (12 January 1865), in *Official Records of the War of the Rebellion*, Series i, vol. 47, pt. 2; George Alexander Sewell and Margaret Dwight, *Mississippi's Black History Makers* (1984); Vernon Lane Wharton, *The Negro in Mississippi, 1865–1890* (1965).

Lynch, John Roy
(1847–1939) Politician and Author

A planter, Reconstruction-era politician, Republican civil servant, and important historian, John Roy Lynch was born on 10 September 1847 on Tacony plantation, near the town of Vidalia, Louisiana, in Concordia Parish. The biracial progeny of plantation manager Patrick Lynch, an Irish immigrant, and slave Catherine White, Lynch followed his mother's status into slavery. While saving to buy the family, his father died and left them enslaved. Later sold across the Mississippi River to Natchez, Lynch finally gained freedom after Union troops occupied the city in 1863. Lynch remained in Natchez and worked as a photographer during the day and attended school at night.

In 1869 Gov. Adelbert Ames appointed Lynch to serve as a justice of the peace. Later that year he was elected to the Mississippi House of Representatives, where his intellect and oratorical skill apparently impressed both black and white colleagues. His legislative record led not only to his reelection but also to his 1872 selection as Speaker of the House.

In 1872 Lynch won a seat in the US House of Representatives, and he was reelected two years later. He lost the seat in 1876 but he returned to Congress for almost a year after contesting Gen. James R. Chalmers's election in 1882. Lynch again failed to win reelection in 1884 and retired to his plantation in Adams County. On 18 December 1884 he married Mobile native Ella Wickham Somerville.

Although he considered himself a planter, Lynch continued to study law and engage in politics. From 1883 to 1889 he served the Republicans in several key state and national positions, ultimately receiving a federal appointment from Pres. Benjamin Harrison to serve as an auditor in the Navy Department, a post Lynch held from 1889 to 1893. He briefly returned to Mississippi and gained admittance to the state bar in 1896. He practiced law in Washington, D.C., from 1897 to 1898, when Pres. William McKinley appointed him to serve as a US Army paymaster during the Spanish-American War. Lynch divorced his wife in 1900 and remained in the army, attaining the rank of major and spending three years in Cuba before moving on to postings in San Francisco, Hawaii, and the Philippines.

He retired from the army in 1911, married Cora Williamson, and moved to Chicago, where he reestablished his legal practice and launched his writing career. Having experienced Reconstruction firsthand, Lynch was offended by the scholarship written under the direction of William Archibald Dunning, which was sympathetic to white southerners and portrayed Reconstruction as an era of Republican corruption, former slaves' barbarity, and federal vindictiveness. In 1913 he

John Roy Lynch, 1911 (New York Public Library [Image ID: 1239435])

published *Facts of Reconstruction*, an alternative to the Dunning School and an inspiration to later revisionist historians. Lynch further challenged scholarly consensus in *Reminiscences of an Active Life: The Autobiography of John Roy Lynch* and *Some Historical Errors of James Ford Rhodes*. Lynch died in Chicago on 2 November 1939 and was interred at Arlington National Cemetery.

Christopher Waldrep
San Francisco State University

Biographical Directory of the United States Congress (1950); W. E. B. Du Bois, *Black Reconstruction in America, 1860–1880* (1935); John Roy Lynch, *The Facts of Reconstruction* (1913); John Roy Lynch, *Reminiscences of an Active Life: The Autobiography of John Roy Lynch*, ed. John Hope Franklin (1969); John Roy Lynch, *Some Historical Errors of James Ford Rhodes* (1922); US House of Representatives, History, Art, and Archives website, history.house.gov; Vernon Lane Wharton, *The Negro in Mississippi, 1865–1890* (1947).

Lynching and Mob Violence

In Mississippi, lynching—an extralegal, often ritualized execution for alleged crimes—and other forms of mob violence were inextricably linked with racial domination. From the dawn of the Civil War to the civil rights movement in the 1960s, white Mississippians attempted to preserve white supremacy through racial murder and terror.

Although mob violence occurred in antebellum Mississippi, it was not an interracial phenomenon. White cotton planters frequently used limited forms of coercive violence to enforce the labor discipline of their African American slaves, but most victims of vigilantism were white. Only during the Civil War did lynching and mob violence begin to be directed toward the black population, and African Americans became the prime targets for mob attacks after 1865, reflecting white southerners' determination to maintain social, economic, and political control. During Reconstruction, vigilante groups such as the Ku Klux Klan intimidated, tortured, and murdered hundreds of African Americans in Mississippi as well as in other states of the former Confederacy.

Despite federal legislation that outlawed the Klan, mob violence against blacks continued unabated after the end of Reconstruction in 1877. In the 1880s lynching emerged as the dominant method to enforce the region's racial hierarchies. White southerners of all classes participated in these public rituals of murder, which turned increasingly barbaric in the ensuing decades. In many cases, hundreds of spectators watched as white men tortured, mutilated, and finally killed the black victims. Most were hanged, though others were burned alive or died in a hail of bullets. Many whites justified these heinous crimes as necessary to protect their wives and daughters against "black beast rapists." Yet few of the victims, most of whom were young men, were actually accused of interracial rape. More often, this charge served as a pretext for punishing violations of the region's racial etiquette.

Lynchings took place in rural areas of Mississippi as well as in cities such as Hattiesburg, Meridian, and Natchez. Because lynchings were not recorded until the 1890s, the real number of victims will never be known. Conservative estimates put the number at 476 victims (including 24 whites) in Mississippi between 1889 and 1945—almost 13 percent of the 3,786 lynchings in the United States during that period and the highest total of any state. White southerners' support for this brutal vigilantism was almost unanimous, reflecting their belief that lynching was a legitimate form of informal law enforcement. Police officers, too, condoned the violence, and white newspapers frequently commended the murderers. And local, state, and federal officials made no effort to stop the violence, forcing African Americans to protect themselves. Blacks occasionally repelled white mobs with gunfire, but resistance was difficult. Supported by local police and state militia, heavily armed white mobs crushed most black protection efforts and brutally retaliated against the defenders.

In the mid-1930s the number of lynchings in the South began to decline, and Mississippi saw almost no incidents of mob violence against blacks between 1940 and 1945. The National Association for the Advancement of Colored People and other antilynching groups launched publicity campaigns that brought the prospect of federal intervention and changed public opinion. In addition, the increasing mechanization of the region's cotton plantations reduced the need for a submissive African American labor force and thus undermined the socioeconomic roots of lynching.

But these changes did not bring an end to white violence. Rather, racial murder became an increasingly secret and covert affair that could generate national indignation if the incident became publicly known. In 1955, for example, white men beat and shot black teenager Emmett Till after he allegedly whistled at a white woman in Money, a small town in the Mississippi Delta, dumping his body in the Tallahatchie River. In stark contrast to earlier lynchings, the Till case made front-page news across the nation, leading to the indictment (though not the prosecution) of the killers.

Mob violence and extralegal killings persisted into the 1960s in Mississippi. In 1962 several thousand whites rioted on the campus of the University of Mississippi in Oxford when James Meredith attempted to integrate the all-white school. Voter registration drives in rural areas of the state also ran into violent resistance, especially from the revived Ku Klux Klan. Although concerned about the region's rampant lawlessness, the federal government refused to protect civil rights activists until 1965, when officials began taking legal action against white extremists and attempting to disrupt the Ku Klux Klan. In addition, African Americans organized informal defense groups across the state, guarding their own communities. By the late 1960s, Mississippi's traditional forms of lynching and mob violence had ceased to exist.

Simon Wendt
University of Heidelberg

John Dittmer, *Local People: The Struggle for Civil Rights in Mississippi* (1994); Neil McMillen, *Dark Journey: Black Mississippians in the Age of Jim Crow* (1990); Stephen J. Whitfield, *A Death in the Delta: The Story of Emmett Till* (1988); Akinyele O. Umoja, *Radical History Review* (Winter 2003).

Lyon's Bluff Site

Lyon's Bluff is a large prehistoric to early historic period Indian mound and village complex in northeastern Oktibbeha County. It is located in the Black Prairie region, where the chalk bedrock weathers into a rich soil with relatively low acidity, leading to extraordinarily good preservation of bone and shell remains. The site was occupied over several centuries, providing a long-term record of a remarkably stable native farming community.

Excavations at Lyon's Bluff began in the mid-1930s, when Moreau Chambers of the Mississippi Department of Archives and History spent two seasons digging in the single mound and in the deep village deposits. Chambers uncovered numerous human burials and encountered many house floors, marked by layers of clean, white sand obtained by the Indians from the bed of Line Creek, a Tibbee Creek tributary that flanks the site on the north. Chambers also discovered something unique in the archaeology of Mississippi—an alligator skull resting on a bed of turtle shells. Local folklore that the site was the scene of a massacre of the Chakchiuma Indians by a combined force of Choctaw and Chickasaw warriors was not substantiated by Chambers's or later work.

Further excavations at Lyon's Bluff took place from the mid-1960s through the early 1970s, including one "amateur" dig and a joint Mississippi State University–University of Mississippi field school. Most of the work from this period took place under the direction of Richard Marshall from Mississippi State University. In 2001 and 2003 summer digs directed by the university's Evan Peacock were again held at the site. This work focused on establishing basic site chronology and community layout, especially during the final phase of occupation. Radiocarbon dating indicates that the site was occupied continuously from about AD 1200 to 1650. It certainly was inhabited when Hernando de Soto passed through the area in AD 1540 and continued to be inhabited for a century or more thereafter. Although a very few artifacts of European origin have been found at the site, no certain de Soto–period diagnostics have been recovered. The effects, if any, of de Soto's expedition on the occupants of the site have yet to be determined.

A mixture of English-made and Indian ceramics recovered from the western part of the site shows that it was reoccupied for a time during the early 1800s. No ethnic identification of these inhabitants has yet been made.

One striking feature found during the most recent work at Lyon's Bluff is a series of palisade lines. The main palisade was discovered fortuitously in the summer of 2001, when an excavation unit encountered a deep, narrow ditch that had been dug through the clay subsoil down into the chalk bedrock. This suspected palisade trench was confirmed through the use of a magnetic gradiometer, a device that detects changes in the earth's residual magnetic signature. The gradiometer image clearly revealed the palisade trench, which encircles the main part of the site containing the mound. The palisade had at least one four-sided defensive tower or bastion protruding outward. This would have allowed archers to defend the wall, which would have been made of upright wooden posts. The palisade enclosed an area of more than three acres that included the mound and the densest concentrations of village debris. Extensive archaeological remains are found outside the palisaded areas as well and cover an area of more than twenty acres.

The gradiometer image also shows the locations of at least six houses, some well inside the palisades and some abutting the inner palisade walls. These structures are visible because, like the palisades, they were built by setting upright wooden posts in narrow ditches known as wall trenches. Excavation has confirmed that magnetic anomalies in the centers of these rectangular structures represent central fire hearths. The houses were coated in a thick layer of mud packed on interwoven cane mats lashed to the posts, a construction method known as wattle and daub.

Excavations have shown the existence of hundreds of smaller sites in the Black Prairie not far from Lyon's Bluff—one- or two-household sites whose occupants practiced a mixed economy of maize-based agriculture supplemented by hunting and fishing. Lyon's Bluff was central to these smaller farmsteads and likely served as a political and religious center and as a place of refuge in times of war. Chemical and stylistic analysis of pottery from Lyon's Bluff indicates trade with other settlements in the region. Large amounts of artifacts, animal bones, freshwater mussel shells, and charred plant remains reveal that the inhabitants enjoyed a long period of stability.

Evan Peacock
Mississippi State University

Samuel O. Brookes, *Mississippi Archaeology*, no. 1 (2000); Patricia K. Galloway, *Mississippi Archaeology*, no. 1 (2000); Terry Lolley, *Mississippi Archaeology*, no. 1 (2000); Richard A. Marshall, *Journal of Alabama Archaeology* (1977, 1986); Evan Peacock and S. Homes Hogue, *Southeastern Archaeology*, no. 1 (2005).

Lytle, Emma Knowlton
(1911–2000) Artist and Filmmaker

Emma Knowlton Lytle's work as a filmmaker and artist was rooted on Perthshire plantation in Bolivar County. Born in 1911, Knowlton was the daughter of Sam and Susie Knowlton. Sam's father, Pole Knowlton, had moved to the Delta from Arkansas in the 1880s and bought Perthshire plantation in 1905. Emma attended Sweet Briar College in Virginia and graduated from Radcliffe College in Massachusetts. When her first husband, Jack Rose Humphreys, died in 1940, Emma and her daughter, Eleanor, moved back to Perthshire. In 1945 she married Chicago native Stuart Lytle; they went on to have two children, Robert and Susan.

From 1939 to 1941 Emma Lytle filmed scenes at Perthshire plantation, turning them into an intriguing color documentary, *Raisin' Cotton*. The film moved through the year, showing workers at various stages of the cotton-growing process—breaking ground with mule-driven plows, planting, chopping cotton, dealing with pests, picking, and ginning. With scenes of airplanes and tractors, the film also dramatized the mechanization of cotton plantation labor. Later scenes filmed in black and white showed cotton being milled into cloth at a North Carolina textile mill. Lytle subsequently said that she was disappointed in the scenes in North Carolina cotton mills because she did not understand what was going on in the factories the way she understood plantation agriculture.

Raisin' Cotton also showed African Americans spending Saturdays at general stores and baptisms held in the fall after revival services. Lytle was impressed by what she later termed the "profound reverence" of the baptisms, and she repeatedly returned to such images in her painting. She concentrated much of her painting and sculpture on scenes of African American life at Perthshire.

In 1997 the Center for the Study of Southern Culture at the University of Mississippi completed *Voices of Perthshire*, a project featuring two versions of *Raisin' Cotton*, one with commentary from Lytle, the other with commentary from some of the workers she filmed.

Lytle died in 2000.

Ted Ownby
University of Mississippi

Guide to the Gilbert-Knowlton-Lytle Papers, Charles W. Capps Jr. Archives and Museum, Delta State University; *Voices of Perthshire* (film, 1997).

M

Mabus, Ray

(b. 1948) Sixtieth Governor, 1988–1992

Although Ray Mabus was the youngest governor in America at the time of his inauguration on 12 January 1988, he had already accumulated an impressive record of public service and academic achievements. Mabus had earned three degrees: a bachelor of arts from the University of Mississippi, a master's from Johns Hopkins in political science, and a law degree from Harvard. He had received two distinguished academic awards—a Fulbright Scholarship and a Woodrow Wilson Fellowship—and had traveled widely throughout Europe, the Middle East, Russia, and Latin America.

In addition to a two-year tour of duty in the US Navy aboard a guided-missile cruiser, Mabus had also served as a law clerk for the US 5th Circuit Court of Appeals, as a congressional aid, and as legal counsel to a subcommittee of the House Agriculture Committee. As legal counsel to Gov. William Winter, Mabus was instrumental in the drafting and passage of the Education Reform Act of 1982, a stricter law against driving under the influence of alcohol, and an open-records law.

Raymond Edwin Mabus was born in Starkville, Mississippi, on 11 October 1948 and grew up in Ackerman. His father, Raymond Mabus, was a hardware store owner turned timber businessman, while his mother, Lucille Curtis Mabus, was a former basketball coach. Mabus attended public school in Ackerman before enrolling at the University of Mississippi.

In 1983, undertook his first campaign for public office, winning election as state auditor and becoming a highly visible and at times controversial public figure. A Democrat, he vigorously enforced the state's financial documentation laws and held public officials to a strict accounting for the expenditure of state funds. Mabus's investigations of the finances of county officials led to Operation Pretense, an FBI investigation that resulted in the indictment of fifty-seven county officials. In 1988, just before he turned forty, Mabus ran for governor, using the campaign slogan "Mississippi Will Never Be Last Again" and defeating Republican Jack Reed in the general election.

Soon after his inauguration, Mabus presented a comprehensive and ambitious legislative package to the state legislature. Among his most significant achievements were a teacher pay raise that temporarily brought Mississippi teachers up to the southeastern average, a reorganization of the executive branch (although it was less comprehensive than he had proposed), and a law providing for the unit system of county government. His proposals for educational reform, which he pushed in regular legislative sessions and in a special session, were not enacted, in part because he did not want to raise taxes to fund new programs.

The 1987 gubernatorial succession amendment made Mabus eligible for a second term, and he sought to become the first Mississippi governor to serve two successive terms in more than one hundred years. However, he lost to Republican Kirk Fordice in the 1991 general election, clearly illustrating the decline of Mississippi Democrats' traditional political dominance.

Pres. Bill Clinton appointed Mabus as US ambassador to Saudi Arabia, a position he held from 1994 to 1996. He also served the executive branch as secretary of the navy under Pres. Barack Obama (2009–17).

David G. Sansing
University of Mississippi

Carroll Brinson, *Our Time Has Come: Mississippi Embraces Its Future* (1988); *Mississippi Official and Statistical Register* (1988–92); Andrew P. Mullins Jr., *Building Consensus: A History of the Passage of the Mississippi Education Reform Act* (1982); Jere Nash and Andy Taggart, *Mississippi Politics: The Struggle for Power, 1976–2006* (2006).

Madison County

Formed in 1828 from a part of Yazoo County, Madison County takes its name from Pres. James Madison. Located in central Mississippi, Madison County began as a growing frontier area with a substantial slave population. Now part of the Jackson metropolitan area, it borders the Ross C. Barnett Reservoir and contains a portion of the Natchez Trace Parkway. Madison County towns include Camden, Farmhaven, Madison, Ridgeland, and Flora, and Canton serves as the county seat.

In the 1830 census, Madison County's population consisted of 2,806 free people and 2,167 slaves. Ten years later, as a cotton-producing area, Madison's free population had increased to 3,997, while its slave population had mushroomed to 11,533—third-most among the state's counties.

Liberty Street, Canton, seat of Madison County, ca. 1916 (Ann Rayburn Paper Americana Collection, Department of Archives and Special Collections, J. D. Williams Library, University of Mississippi [rayburn_ann_23_92_001])

The growing county also had a small but substantial nonagricultural population, with 253 people working in commerce and manufacturing.

By 1860 the free population had reached 5,260, while the slave population had nearly doubled again to 18,118, a number that trailed only Hinds County. With 77 percent of its residents enslaved, Madison ranked tenth among Mississippi's sixty counties. Madison's soil and labor force were extraordinarily productive, ranking third in the state in growing corn, fourth in cotton, fifth in Irish potatoes, and first in sweet potatoes. The county had only 169 industrial workers, most of them employed in small mills and blacksmith shops.

In 1860 Madison County's thirty-nine churches ranked it fourth in Mississippi, and the variety of denominations was greater than in most of the state. Madison was home to fourteen Methodist churches, eleven Baptist churches, six Presbyterian congregations, three Episcopalian houses of worship, two Cumberland Presbyterian churches, two Catholic churches, and one Christian church.

Madison County's population remained roughly the same in the decades after the war, with 19,907 African Americans and 5,946 whites in 1880. The county continued to practice mixed agriculture, with substantial concentrations of cotton, corn, and sweet potatoes. Madison ranked sixth in the state in the number of hogs. Like many black-majority counties, Madison County had a high number of tenant farmers and relatively few landowning farmers (28 percent).

By 1900 Madison's population numbered 32,493, of whom 25,918 (79 percent) were African American. Madison County had almost 200 immigrants, mostly from England, Germany, and Ireland. While still rural, Madison had 260 industrial workers. About half of Madison County's 11,000 church members were Baptists, most of them either Missionary Baptists or Southern Baptists. The county was also home to about 3,500 Methodists, most of them in the African Methodist Episcopal Zion Church or the Methodist Episcopal Church, South.

With more than 800 Catholics, the seventh-highest number in Mississippi, and close to 500 Presbyterians, Madison maintained a greater variety of churches than much of the state. The German community in Gluckstadt was largely Catholic.

Madison County native Belle Kearney was born in 1863 and attended Canton Ladies Academy before emerging as a leader in Mississippi movements for temperance and woman suffrage. In the twentieth century, members of the powerful Hederman family owned and ran the *Madison County Herald*.

By 1930 Canton was a growing town of 3,252, but the large county continued to have an agricultural economy, with well over six thousand farms, more than 80 percent of them operated by tenant farmers. Major crops included cotton, corn, and cattle.

The Canton civil rights movement began with efforts at voter registration in the 1950s and picked up strength when the Congress of Racial Equality, the Student Nonviolent Coordinating Committee, and eventually the Council of Federated Organizations addressed issues of voting, segregation, education, and violence. These groups organized a boycott, a Freedom House, and a Freedom School. Activists faced violence during the Freedom Summer of 1964 and again in 1966 during the March against Fear. Madison County landowner and businessman C. O. Chinn was a relentless organizer whose courage Anne Moody documented in *Coming of Age in Mississippi*, and Canton native Annie Devine was one of the organizers of the Mississippi Freedom Democratic Party.

By 1960 Madison County's population had declined slightly to 32,904 but remained overwhelmingly African American (72 percent). Despite growing economic diversity, the county remained an agricultural center, with more than 36 percent of workers employed in agriculture. Madison County farms grew the third-most corn in Mississippi and produced substantial amounts of livestock, cotton, oats, and soybeans. Manufacturing workers, especially in furniture and wood products, accounted for 17 percent of the labor force. Madison County was also home to two oil wells. By 1980 the county's population had increased to 41,613.

In 2010 Madison County, like many of its neighbors, had a white majority and a small but significant Hispanic minority, primarily from Mexico. With 95,203 people, the county had grown 190 percent since 1960, one of the state's greatest proportional increases during this period, and had become among the largest in Mississippi. As in neighboring Hinds County, Madison had developed a small Asian population.

In the twenty-first century, Madison County has one of Mississippi's lowest poverty rates and highest rates of per capita income, in large part as a consequence of the 2002 opening of a major Nissan plant.

Mississippi Encyclopedia Staff
University of Mississippi

Mississippi State Planning Commission, *Progress Report on State Planning in Mississippi* (1938); *Mississippi Statistical Abstract*, Mississippi State University (1952–2010); Charles Sydnor and Claude Bennett, *Mississippi History* (1939); University of Virginia Library, Historical Census Browser website, http://mapserver.lib.virginia.edu; E. Nolan Waller and Dani A. Smith, *Growth Profiles of Mississippi's Counties, 1960–1980* (1985).

Magnolia, Southern

Southern magnolia (Photograph by James G. Thomas, Jr.)

The southern magnolia (*Magnolia grandiflora*), with its shiny, heavy, evergreen leaves and its fragrant, creamy-white blossoms, is one of the best-loved trees of the South. Its large, waxy flowers (which can be as big as dinner plates) gave rise to the species name *grandiflora*, given to this tree in 1759 by famed Swedish botanist Carl Von Linne (Linnaeus). The common and generic name *Magnolia* honors French botanist Pierre Magnol, who helped develop the method of classifying plants in the 1700s. Colonial naturalist Mark Catesby called it the Carolina laurel, and the tree is also known as bull bay, a name used by early botanists.

Although native to the Gulf Coastal Plain from East Texas to central Florida and to the Atlantic Coastal Plain from central Florida to coastal Virginia, the southern magnolia has been widely planted as an ornamental and is now found throughout the Southeast and in warm temperate and tropical areas around the world.

The 80–120 living magnolia species are descendants of some of the earliest of flowering plants, and early magnolias may have coexisted with dinosaurs. Some botanists believe that magnolias originated before bees, leading the tree to depend on beetles for pollination. Magnolias lack the uniquely different petals and sepals that characterize most flowering plants, and botanists coined the word *tepals* to describe magnolias' showy white flower parts. Southern magnolia leaves can measure between five and eight inches long, have smooth edges, and are often nearly elliptical, with a distinct rusty felt-like pubescence on the underside.

Southern magnolias are well adapted for the southern Coastal Plain, with deep roots that hold the trees firm in hurricane winds and tough bark that makes them somewhat resistant to the region's frequent fires. They are somewhat tolerant of shade but intolerant of a lengthy cold season or drought.

Under optimum conditions of rich, well-drained soils and good sunlight within forest habitat, a southern magnolia can grow to more than ninety feet tall and develop a trunk with a diameter of more than three feet. When grown as an ornamental in the open, magnolias are not so tall but can develop massive limbs, resulting in a stocky tree with a broad reach. Magnolias have long been planted as ornamentals in front of southern homes. Few plants can grow beneath a magnolia because of the shade created and the slow-to-decay magnolia leaves that accumulate on the ground.

Magnolia flowers appear most frequently during May and June but also occasionally in the fall. Seeds mature in late fall or early winter in fleshy, cone-like structures. At maturity the seeds have a red, fleshy covering and are pushed from the cone-like structure, with each one suspended by a short fiber and thus "hanging ready" for consumption by birds. These fruits, which measure between a quarter of an inch and half an inch, attract numerous birds and other wildlife. The seed ensconced inside the coating passes intact through a bird's digestive tract, dispersing southern magnolias and helping them establish in the wild in many areas where the tree was introduced.

The southern magnolia has come to symbolize the South and southern culture. Associated with this symbolism, ideas and actions that are uniquely southern are sometimes referred to as coming from "behind the magnolia curtain."

In 1861, the year that his state of Arkansas seceded from the Union, Albert Pike, who served as a Confederate general, wrote a tribute to the tree that became something of a national song for the Confederacy:

What, what is the true southern symbol,
The symbol of honor and right,
The emblem that suits a brave people
In arms against number and might!—
'Tis the ever green stately Magnolia,
Its pearl-flowers pure as the truth,
Defiant of tempest and lightning,
Its life a perpetual youth.

French blood stained with glory the lilies,
While centuries marched to their graves;

And over bold Scott and gay Irish
The thistle and shamrock yet wave:
Ours, ours be the noble Magnolia,
That only on Southern soil grows
The symbol of life everlasting;—
Dear to us as to England the rose.

On 26 January 1861 the Mississippi secession convention adopted what has been called the Magnolia Flag as the official flag of the "Sovereign Republic of Mississippi." The Magnolia Flag bore a single white star on a field of blue at the upper left, and most of the remainder of the flag was a white field with a southern magnolia tree somewhat centered to the right of the blue. A strip of red sometimes bordered the right edge of the flag. The Magnolia Flag served as the official Mississippi flag for thirty-three years. In the twenty-first century, some people have suggested restoring the Magnolia Flag as the official state flag.

In November 1900 schoolchildren across Mississippi voted overwhelmingly in favor of the southern magnolia as the state flower. In 1935 schoolchildren selected the southern magnolia as the state tree, a choice that the legislature ratified on 1 April 1938. The state legislature did not make the southern magnolia the official state flower until 1952. Neighboring Louisiana has also adopted the southern magnolia as the state flower.

The wood of the southern magnolia has been used in making veneer, furniture, packing crates, interior trim, cabinets, and doors. Native Americans of the South used decoctions made from magnolia bark to treat skin and kidney ailments. Modern pharmaceutical companies are investigating chemicals derived from magnolias for potential medicinal use. The major human use of southern magnolias today is as an ornamental, and more than one hundred varieties have been developed for the horticultural trade.

Jerome A. Jackson
Florida Gulf Coast University

Mark Catesby, *The Natural History of Carolina, Florida, and the Bahama Islands, Containing the Figures of Birds, Beasts, Fishes, Serpents, Insects, and Plants* (1730); E. F. Gilman and D. G. Watson, *Magnolia Grandiflora Southern Magnolia*, US Department of Agriculture Forest Service, Fact Sheet ST-371 (1994); F. Griffin, *Magnolia, Newsletter of the Southern Garden Historical Society* (Fall 1984); L. A. Taylor, *Plants Used as Curatives by Certain Southeastern Tribes*, Botanical Museum of Harvard University (1940); N. G. Treseder, *Magnolias* (1978).

Malaco Records

The roots of Jackson-based Malaco Records stretch back to 1961, when cofounder Tommy Couch Sr. began booking R&B bands at the University of Mississippi while serving as social chair of his fraternity, Pi Kappa Alpha. After graduation Couch moved to Jackson to work as a pharmacist and partnered with his brother-in-law, Mitchell Malouf, to form a booking agency, Malaco Productions. Couch's fraternity brother, Gerald "Wolf" Stephenson, subsequently joined the agency, and it moved into recording in 1966. Around this time Malaco moved to its present location at 3023 Northside Drive.

In their first years Malaco released few recordings, concentrating instead on leasing master recordings to other labels. One of the most notable—if untypical—sessions resulted in a 1970 Capitol LP, *I Do Not Play No Rock 'n' Roll*, by downhome bluesman Mississippi Fred McDowell. The label gained momentum the same year via productions by New Orleans arranger Wardell Quezergue that yielded two major hits, Jean Knight's "Mr. Big Stuff" on Stax Records, and King Floyd's "Groove Me" on Malaco's own Chimneyville label. "Groove Me" marked the beginning of a distribution and production arrangement with Atlantic Records, but the relationship ultimately did little for Malaco's shaky finances. Salvation came in the form of Dorothy Moore, whose ballad "Misty Blue,"

Dorothy Moore's hit single, "Misty Blue" (1975), on the Malaco Records label (Living Blues Collection, Archives and Special Collections, University of Mississippi)

released on Malaco, reached the Top 5 on both the R&B and pop charts in early 1976. She subsequently scored many other hits for the label.

The company finally found its niche in the early 1980s following the signing of Texan Z. Z. Hill, whose 1982 smash hit "Down Home Blues," penned by Memphis–Muscle Shoals songwriter George Jackson, alerted the record industry to a seemingly untapped, mostly southern market for "soul blues." Malaco's eventual conquest of this market resulted from a number of factors: the hiring of veteran record promotion man Dave Clark; the development of a distinctive studio sound, aided by Malaco's purchase of Muscle Shoals Sound in the mid-1980s; and a pool of talented songwriters, including Jackson, Larry Addison, Rich Cason, and Frederick Knight.

In tandem with the rise of disco and the "urban contemporary" radio format, veteran soul stars including Denise LaSalle, Little Milton, Johnnie Taylor, Latimore, and Bobby "Blue" Bland lost major label contracts, and Clark helped bring them to Malaco. With these artists Malaco became the major force on the largely southern Chitlin' Circuit, garnering impressive record sales but relatively little national attention. During the 1990s Malaco added veterans including Shirley Brown and Tyrone Davis, and Tommy Couch Jr., a University of Mississippi graduate and booking agent like his father, started the Waldoxy subsidiary, bringing aboard artists including Artie "Blues Boy" White, Carl Sims, Mel Waiters, Bobby Rush, and blues comedian Poonanny. The label has more recently signed many younger southern soul stars.

Less well known but of great importance to Malaco's prosperity is its gospel catalog. The label ventured into this market in the mid-1970s with the Jackson Southernaires and subsequently signed the Soul Stirrers, the Sensational Nightingales, the Williams Brothers, the Angelic Gospel Singers, and others. After purchasing the catalog of pioneer gospel label Savoy Records in 1986, Malaco became the leading gospel label, scoring hits with artists including the Mississippi Mass Choir, Rev. Clay Evans, Dorothy Norwood, and Rev. James Cleveland.

Malaco's offices suffered some damage when Hurricane Katrina hit in 2005 and were destroyed by a tornado on April 15, 2011. The company decided to rebuild and took the opportunity to refocus and strengthen its business, and Malaco continues to thrive long after better-known soul labels Motown and Stax have closed their doors.

Scott Barretta
Greenwood, Mississippi

Peter Guralnick, *Living Blues* (January–February 1989); Jeff Hannusch, *Rolling Stone* (2 June 1988); MS News Now website, www.msnewsnow .com; Jacob Threadgill, *Jackson Clarion-Ledger* (February 6, 2016).

Mallory, Arenia
(1904–1977) Educator

Dr. Arenia Conelia Mallory was a leader in education, religion, social welfare, and civil rights. Born in Jacksonville, Illinois, on 28 December 1904, Mallory moved to Mississippi in 1926. She earned a bachelor's degree from Simmons College in Louisville, Kentucky, master's degrees from Jackson State University and the University of Illinois, and a law degree from Bethune-Cookman College in Daytona Beach, Florida, in 1951.

Mallory's most important achievement was as founder and long-standing head of the Saints Industrial and Literary School in Lexington, Mississippi. She served as president of the school from 1926 to 1976. In 1954 the school was renamed Saints Junior College, and in the 1970s it became Saints Academy, a private religious secondary school for students in grades one through twelve operated by the Church of God in Christ, the largest African American Pentecostal denomination. Mallory was a leader in the national church, particularly its Women's Department.

Mallory encouraged not only education but also the provision of health and welfare services for sharecroppers in Holmes County, where African Americans predominated. She frequently traveled across the country with a girls' choir, the Jubilee Harmonizers, raising money and gathering books and clothing for her students and county residents. On a stop in Oakland, California, she convinced former Mississippi resident Ida Louise Jackson, president of Alpha Kappa Alpha, a black sorority, to work in the Mississippi Delta, and Mallory's school served as headquarters for the organization's Summer School for Rural Teachers in 1934 and for its Mississippi Health Project the following year.

Mallory advocated on behalf of black rights and women's rights at the national as well as local levels. As a member of the National Council of Negro Women, an umbrella organization of black women's groups, Mallory was one of sixty-five attendees at a 1938 conference in Washington, D.C., on "The Participation of Negro Women and Children in Federal Programs." She subsequently served as the council's vice president from 1953 to 1957 and as a consultant for the US Department of Labor in 1963. In 1968 Mallory became the first woman and the first African American elected to the Holmes County Board of Education.

She left Saints Junior College in 1976 and died on 8 May 1977. Today, the Arenia C. Mallory Community Health Center in Lexington and the Arenia Mallory School of Religion in Miami, Florida, honor her legacy.

Susan L. Smith
University of Alberta

M

Anthea D. Butler, *Women in the Church of Christ: Making a Sanctified World* (2007); Linda Gordon, *Pitied but Not Entitled: Single Mothers and the History of Welfare* (1994); Arenia C. Mallory Subject File, Mississippi Department of Archives and History; George Alexander Sewell and Margaret L. Dwight, *Mississippi Black History Makers* (1984); Susan L. Smith, *Sick and Tired of Being Sick and Tired: Black Women's Health Activism in America, 1890–1950* (1995).

Malone, Dumas
(1892–1986) Historian and Editor

Dumas Malone, best known for his six-volume biography of Thomas Jefferson, was born in Coldwater, Mississippi, on 10 January 1892 to Methodist minister John Malone and Lillian Kemp Malone, a teacher. The family soon moved to Georgia, where Dumas received a bachelor's degree from Emory University in 1910 before moving on to earn a divinity degree from Yale University in 1916. When the United States entered the First World War, Malone joined the Marine Corps and served stateside as a second lieutenant until 1919. Malone subsequently returned to Yale, where he earned master's and doctoral degrees in history.

In 1923 Malone began teaching European and American history at the University of Virginia, where he remained until 1929. He then joined the *Dictionary of American Biography*, where he served as an editor, editor in chief, and eventually director, and became director of Harvard University Press. In 1944 Malone received a fellowship from the Rockefeller Foundation to begin work on a biography of Jefferson. Malone became a history professor at Columbia University from 1945 to 1958 before returning to the University of Virginia in 1959 as the first Thomas Jefferson Professor of History. He retired from teaching in 1962 but retained the title of emeritus professor and continued his scholarly writing career.

Malone's major publications include *The Public Life of Thomas Cooper* (1926), which was based on his doctoral dissertation and which won the John Addison Porter Prize at Yale; *Edwin A. Alderman* (1940), a book about a former president of the University of Virginia; and *Empire for Liberty*, a two-volume textbook cowritten with Basil Rauch (1960). However, Malone is most noted for his six-volume biography of Thomas Jefferson, *Jefferson and His Time* (1948–81): *Jefferson the Virginian* (1948), *Jefferson and the Rights of Man* (1951), *Jefferson and the Ordeal of Liberty* (1962), *Jefferson the President: The First Term, 1801–1805* (1970), *Jefferson the President: The Second Term, 1805–1809* (1974), and *Jefferson and His Time: The Sage of Monticello* (1981). The first five volumes won Malone the 1975 Pulitzer Prize for history. Malone's scholarship was thorough, with an eye for detail, and his writing style was fluid, which made the reading enjoyable. He received the Presidential Medal of Freedom in 1983 and resided in Charlottesville until his death on 27 December 1986.

James C. Foley
St. Andrew's Episcopal School

Eric Pace, *New York Times* (28 December 1986); Merrill D. Peterson, *William and Mary Quarterly* (April 1988).

Mammy's Cupboard

Mammy's Cupboard is a roadside business located ten miles south of Natchez on Highway 61. It is a popular culture icon much like other oversized figures across the nation—Paul Bunyan in the Upper Midwest, Indian teepees in the West—that draw from regional or state imagery to attract travelers. Mammy's Cupboard is linked to evolving southern ideology, and it is especially connected to Natchez's celebration of the Old South.

Natchez businessman Henry Gaude built Mammy's Cupboard in 1939 to attract visitors headed to the Natchez Pilgrimage, an elaborate tour of plantation homes that began in 1932. The twenty-eight-foot high building was constructed in the shape of a slave woman with hoop skirt—a mammy figure. She originally had earrings made from horseshoes

Mammy's Cupboard, south of Natchez, October 2008 (Photograph by Carol M. Highsmith, Library of Congress, Washington, D.C. [LC-DIG-highsm-04148])

and a serving tray in her hands, with white hair and a red head scarf that suggested maturity and modesty. The figure's exaggerated black color, white circles under the eyes, and bright red rouge drew from minstrel makeup conventions and from standard racist imagery of blacks at the time.

Designers of Mammy's Cupboard drew from the long-established mammy icon, a deeply rooted symbol of the plantation household. The black domestic servant was a key to the functioning of the antebellum plantation, and families sometimes invested her with moral authority and status not given to other slaves. But her position created special tensions and anxieties with white plantation women who owned such servants but at times relied inordinately on them. Southern writers, artists, and promoters created the myth of mammy—a loyal, maternal slave woman who devoted herself to the nurture of her master's family. She was strong, innocent, and fundamentally asexual, supposedly making her a natural to live happily as a human chattel. The mammy figure assured white southerners that their households, with slave and free people living intimately together, were organic and harmonious, without jealousies, sexual attractions, or conflicts. The mammy became a sentimental image, reflecting the sometimes real feelings of affection and dependence across racial lines but also revealing white cultural expectations about black subservience.

After the Civil War the myth of mammy became an emblem of North-South reconciliation, as songs, stories, plays, paintings, and advertisements from Broadway to Hollywood as well as below the Mason-Dixon Line promoted the long-suffering figure of the contented black domestic worker. The Natchez Pilgrimage created an idealized world of Old South beauty, represented by the city's mansions. Promoters soon added a Confederate Pageant to celebrate the Lost Cause. This historical memory had only a limited role for black Natchez residents, who wore bandanas or livery for the pilgrimage and sang spirituals for the pageant. As Lori Robbins notes, Mammy's Cupboard was a "low culture" attraction that survived symbiotically with the "high culture" Natchez Pilgrimage, surprisingly presenting a giant black woman as the featured figure.

Originally a café, Mammy's Cupboard went on to house a gas station, convenience store, gift shop, and an arts and craft center before again becoming a restaurant. During the era of the civil rights movement, racial tensions led the Gaude family to paint the figure as an Indian woman instead of a black slave, but this change was short-lived. Subsequent owners have softened the figure's decorations, downplaying harsher racial stereotypes. They removed the horseshoe earrings and most of the figure's makeup while lightening the skin to suggest ethnicity but not necessarily race. These changes have been in keeping with the spirit of the times. The nearby Natchez Pilgrimage has added a Freedom's Road black history presentation, and black historical buildings are now part of touristic Natchez. Still, this figure's physical build, age, and dress (especially the hoop skirt and head scarf) portray a stereotypical slave in line with the old mammy imagery. Today, Mammy's Cupboard serves up pies and other delicacies for Natchez residents and travelers attracted by the giant figure.

Charles Reagan Wilson
University of Mississippi

Lori Robbins, *Mississippi Folklife* (1999); Kenneth W. Goings, *Mammy and Uncle Mose: Black Collectibles and American Stereotyping* (1994).

Manning, Archie
(b. 1949) Athlete

No Mississippi athlete has been more revered than University of Mississippi quarterback Archie Manning. During the late 1960s and early 1970s, the state caught what one sportswriter labeled "Archie Fever." "The Ballad of Archie Who" immortalized Manning in song, while water towers screamed Manning's name across the state's landscape. James O. Eastland, a US senator from Mississippi from 1943 to 1978,

Archie Manning, ca. 1968–70 (John Leslie Collection, Department of Archives and Special Collections, J. D. Williams Library, University of Mississippi [MPAP_b9_f55_228])

claimed that Manning "has done more good for the state on the national scene than any man of the generation." At a time when the Magnolia State conjured up images of racism, poverty, and backwardness in the minds of many Americans, Manning's football career provided a symbol of success. One Mississippian even said, "When outsiders pointed to James Meredith, the Philadelphia murders, the Ku Klux Klan—everything that was wrong with the Deep South in the 1960s—there was always an answer: Yeah, but we've got Archie Manning." State politicians and journalists referred to Manning as the ideal all-American youth, a patriotic, humble young man who was the antithesis of the young radicals found across college campuses in the 1960s.

Born on 19 May 1949, Elisha Archibald Manning III grew up in Drew, a small town in the Delta. He led a busy childhood, participating in church-related activities and numerous sports. Manning starred for Drew High School in football, basketball, and baseball and was valedictorian of his graduating class. He attended the University of Mississippi, and after spending his freshman year on the school's junior varsity squad, Manning led the Rebels to a 7-3-1 record during the 1968 season, capping the year with a Liberty Bowl win over Virginia Tech. Over his junior season, Manning posted some remarkable statistics—1,762 passing yards, 502 rushing yards, and 23 total touchdowns—as the team notched an 8-3 record. On 1 January 1970 the Rebels defeated Arkansas in the Sugar Bowl, 27-22. In addition to earning the game's Most Valuable Player award, Manning took home the Southeastern Conference's Offensive Player of the Year award, the Walter Camp Memorial Award for the outstanding back in college football, and a spot on the all-American team. He also finished fourth in the Heisman Trophy balloting.

Manning and the Rebels had a strong start to the 1970 season, defeating their first four opponents by an average of nearly 20 points. After a surprise defeat by in-state rival Southern Mississippi, however, the team suffered two more losses and Manning broke his left arm. Hampered by the injury, Manning kept the Rebels close in the Gator Bowl, but the Rebels lost 35-28 to Auburn. Manning finished third in the 1970 Heisman Trophy vote and ended his college career with a litany of school records.

In the spring of 1971, the New Orleans Saints selected Manning with the second overall pick in the National Football League draft. Manning remained in the league for fourteen seasons, playing for the Saints (1971-81) as well as the Houston Oilers (1982-83), and Minnesota Vikings (1983-84). Playing for some of the league's worst teams, Manning never appeared in the playoffs and sustained numerous injuries. Nevertheless, he was selected to the Pro Bowl in 1978 and 1979 and was named the National Football Conference's Player of the Year in 1978. In 1989 he was inducted into the College Football Hall of Fame. He has worked as a football broadcaster and in 2013 became one of the inaugural members of the College Football Playoff Selection Committee, though he resigned for health reasons the following year. Participants in a 1999 *Jackson Clarion-Ledger* poll overwhelmingly chose Manning as Mississippi's Athlete of the Century, giving him nearly three times as many votes as the second-place finisher, Hall of Fame running back Walter Payton.

Manning remains a popular figure in New Orleans, where he still makes his home, and across the Gulf South, though many younger football fans may know him best as the father of Super Bowl–winning quarterbacks Peyton and Eli Manning.

Charles Westmoreland
Delta State University

Thomas BeVier, *Memphis Commercial-Appeal* (9 January 1970); Jerry Gilbreath, *Mississippi Magazine* (Spring 1970); Archie Manning and Peyton Manning, *Manning: A Father, His Sons, and a Football Legacy* (2000); William W. Sorrels and Charles Cavagnaro, *Ole Miss Rebels: Mississippi Football* (1976); John Vaught, *Rebel Coach: My Football Family* (1971).

Map Resources

Map resources for Mississippi are plentiful and include both hard copy and digital map data as well as aerial photographs and satellite images, which are also commonly available in digital format and on the Internet.

Among the numerous widely available road atlases, DeLorme offers highly detailed, large-format topographic and street map atlases of all fifty US states, with substantial recreational information and detail. Other recreational maps exist for Mississippi's six national forests.

Perhaps the most well-known maps produced by the federal government covering all of Mississippi are the 7.5 minute topographic quadrangles produced by the US Geological Survey. These are useful for general reference, urban and regional planning, and development and recreation, with detailed information at a scale of 1:24,000 (one inch = 2,000 feet). Each map measures 22 inches by 27 inches and covers an area of about 64 square miles. The University of Mississippi has the state's most complete holdings, with all current maps as well as older federal maps, which are useful for tracking land use changes through time. In addition to the 1:24,000 map series, the University of Mississippi also has the 1:100,000 and 1:250,000 topographic maps. Other state public universities hold some federal maps. Mississippi State University, for example, has complete holdings of the 1:24,000 scale quadrangles for the whole state but generally keeps only the most current maps.

Finally, the Special Collections Department at Mississippi State holds a collection of Sanborn Fire Insurance Maps from the late 1800s to early 1900s for more than one hundred Mississippi cities, showing detail down to outlines of specific buildings. As the library website states, "They are an excellent resource for anyone researching specific buildings, communities, or industries. The maps generally show commercial or industrial districts, nearby residential neighborhoods, or rapidly growing parts of town."

Aerial photography and satellite images provide insightful perspectives on Mississippi's present and historic landscape. Aerial photographs were taken between 1980 and 1989 through the National High Altitude Program, which produced 1:80,000-scale maps, and subsequently through the National Aerial Photography Program, which provides standardized sets of cloud-free photographs at 1:40,000 scale covering the United States over five- to seven-year cycles. This program's products offer the most recent and consistent source of high-quality aerial photography.

Since 1955 the Aerial Photography Field Office of the US Department of Agriculture's Farm Service Agency has acquired aerial photography during the growing season in the continental United States as part of the National Agriculture Imagery Program. In addition, the department's Natural Resources Conservation Service creates black and white aerial photographs with annotation regarding soil-type boundaries, as an important component of its information-rich county soil surveys.

Satellite images of Mississippi are available at the US Geological Survey website. Typically, these data are intended for professional and scientific use and are distributed in digital formats that require specialized training and software. However, Google Maps, Google Earth, the US Geological Survey's National Map website, and other sources now make satellite images, aerial photography, and interactive maps accessible to the general public.

Finally, the Mississippi Automated Resource Information Service provides digital map data for the state that can be downloaded or viewed interactively. Users can choose which "themes" they want to see, such as utilities, political, transportation, geographic, and many others.

Jerry Griffith
University of Southern Mississippi

Google Earth website, www.google.com/earth; Google Maps website, www.google.com/maps; J. D. Williams Library, University of Mississippi; Mississippi Automated Resource Information Service website, www.maris.state.ms.us; Special Collections Library, Mitchell Memorial Library, Mississippi State University; US Department of Agriculture, Farm Service Agency, Photography Field Office website, www.apfo.usda.gov; US Department of Agriculture, Natural Resources Conservation Service, Web Soil Survey website, http://websoilsurvey.sc.egov.usda.gov/App/HomePage.htm; US Geological Survey website, www.usgs.gov; US Geological Survey National Map website, nationalmap.gov.

Mara, Thalia

(1911–2003) Dancer, Teacher, Arts Supporter

Thalia Mara, a celebrated ballet teacher, dancer, and author of several textbooks on ballet, founded and directed the USA International Ballet Competition in Jackson. In 1994 the City of Jackson changed the name of the Jackson Municipal Auditorium to Thalia Mara Hall in recognition of her profound influence on the city's cultural community.

Born on 28 June 1911 to Russian émigrés in Chicago, Mara began studying ballet as a young child and by age fourteen was a company member of the Chicago Opera Ballet and Ravina Park Opera Ballet. At sixteen, she was a soloist in Paris with the Ballet Suedois de Carina Ari, performing throughout Europe and South America. She returned to the United States several years later and appeared as a soloist with several prominent ballet companies.

She soon developed a passion for teaching ballet to others, and in 1962 Mara and her husband, fellow dancer Arthur Mahoney, founded the National Academy of Ballet and Theater Arts. Mara felt that contemporary ballet had declined into "sharp, cold movement," and she insisted on a return to "lyricism, romanticism, classicism, and musicality [in which]

Thalia Mara (Bern and Franke Keating Collection, Department of Archives and Special Collections, J. D. Williams Library, University of Mississippi)

M

the expressiveness of the individual must be encouraged." Mara instructed and encouraged many young ballerinas who went on to become principals and soloists with renowned ballet companies. The school closed a decade later because of increasing educational costs, but Mara continued to contribute to ballet instruction by writing respected textbooks for young dancers and teachers.

In the mid-1970s, the Jackson Ballet Guild invited Mara to create a professional ballet troupe in the Mississippi capital. She believed strongly that the future of American ballet lay in broadening the focus from major cities and building organizations in smaller areas. After six years with the guild, she resigned to develop the USA International Ballet Competition in Jackson. The first competition, organized by Mara and Robert Joffrey, artistic director of Joffrey Ballet, was held in 1979 and brought the world's best young dancers to Jackson. The two-week competition took place again in 1982 and has subsequently been held every four years. It remains one of the most important ballet competitions in America.

Mara also contributed to Jackson's artistic community through the nonprofit Thalia Mara Arts International Foundation, which sponsors teacher training scholarships, a piano competition, and various dance performances. She died in Jackson on 8 October 2003.

Katherine Treppendahl
University of Virginia

Jennifer Dunning, *New York Times* (11 October 2003); Internet Movie Database website, www.imdb.com; Thalia Mara, *First Steps in Ballet* (1955); Richard Philip, *Dance Magazine* (1 October 2004); USA International Ballet Competition website, www.usaibc.com.

Marion County

Located in southern Mississippi, Marion County was formed in 1811. Named after Gen. Francis Marion, the county borders Louisiana to the south. Columbia serves as the county seat. In 1816 the Pearl River Convention assembled in Marion County to debate the conditions under which Mississippi would enter the Union as a new state. The convention met at the home of Rev. John Ford, twenty miles south of Columbia, in a house that had served as an inn and military post. Six years later, Columbia was the state's temporary capital for the inauguration of Gov. Walter Leake.

Marion County's population remained relatively small throughout the antebellum period. In its first census, in 1820, it had 1,884 free people and 1,232 slaves. By 1840 Marion County had grown slightly, with 2,121 free people and 1,709 slaves.

In 1860, though much of Mississippi grew dramatically, the population of Marion County remained small—just 2,501 free people and 2,183 slaves. Like many southern Mississippi counties, Marion ranked low in various categories related to agricultural production, including total value of farmland, production of cotton, and production of corn. The county had just eight churches—four Methodist and four Baptist.

By 1880 Marion County was home to 6,901 people, with virtually all of its population growth occurring among white residents. Marion County retained its low rankings in the value of farmland and in cotton production but produced the second-highest amounts of rice and sheep in the state. A total of 84.5 percent of Marion County's farmers owned their own farms, a figure far higher than most parts of Mississippi. With its emphasis on smaller farming, Marion County became one of the centers of the state's Populist movement.

In 1900 Marion County's population was 13,501 and was approximately two-thirds white. Marion County remained notable for its high number of landowners—more than 80 percent of white farm families and almost 60 percent of African American farm families owned their land. The county's forty-three manufacturing establishments employed 258 men and 2 women. The timber industry accounted for most of the industrial growth.

In the 1916 religious census, more than two-thirds of Marion County's churchgoers were Baptists, with Southern Baptists making up about half of the county's church members and Missionary Baptists making up another quarter. A substantial number of county residents also belonged to the Methodist Episcopal Church and Methodist Episcopal Church, South.

Two of the state's most prominent twentieth-century architects designed buildings in Marion County. A. Hays Town designed the Lampton House in Columbia, and his partner, N. W. Overstreet, designed Columbia High School.

By 1930 Marion County's population increased to almost 20,000 even though the county had lost some of its land to other counties. Whites made up almost two-thirds of Marion's population. Outside the growing town of Columbia (population 4,833), Marion continued to have an agricultural economy, with farm owners slightly outnumbering tenants. The county's manufacturing establishments employed 755 industrial workers. In 1945 oil was discovered on the Marion-Lamar County line.

The most famous native of Marion County is likely football star Walter Payton (1954–99). Payton was a running back at Jefferson High School and Jackson State University before playing for the National Football League's Chicago Bears and ultimately ending up in the league's Hall of Fame. Another Marion County native, Dolphus Weary, born in Sandy Hook in 1946, played important roles in the Voice of Calvary ministry and Mission Mississippi.

Population growth continued in the mid-twentieth century, and by 1960 Marion County was home to 23,293 people. A quarter of Marion's workers were employed in manufacturing, where there was a mixture of furniture and wood products, textiles, and apparel. Sixteen percent of the county's employees worked in mixed agriculture, concentrating on livestock, corn, and soybeans. Natural gas and petroleum also remained part of Marion County's economy.

By 2010, as in most southern Mississippi counties, Marion's population was predominantly white and had grown slightly over the preceding half century, increasing from 23,293 in 1960 to 27,088 in 2010.

Mississippi Encyclopedia Staff
University of Mississippi

Mississippi State Planning Commission, *Progress Report on State Planning in Mississippi* (1938); *Mississippi Statistical Abstract*, Mississippi State University (1952–2010); Charles Sydnor and Claude Bennett, *Mississippi History* (1939); University of Virginia Library, Historical Census Browser website, http://mapserver.lib.virginia.edu; E. Nolan Waller and Dani A. Smith, *Growth Profiles of Mississippi's Counties, 1960–1980* (1985).

Married Women's Property Act

Introduced in the Mississippi Senate in 1839 by Sen. T. B. J. Hadley at the urging of his wife, Piety Smith Hadley, the Married Women's Property Act was repeatedly voted down before finally passing on 15 February. Gov. Alexander G. McNutt signed it the following day, making it the first law of its kind enacted by any state in the United States. It granted married women the right to own property in their own names rather than requiring them to list all property in the names of their husbands.

While some historians credit the act's passage to the Hadleys, others assert that the bill originated from the experience of Elizabeth Love, a Mississippi Chickasaw Indian. In the late 1780s Betsy Love was born into a slave-owning Chickasaw family in what was then Mississippi Territory, and in the late 1790s she married a white man, James Allen, in a Chickasaw ceremony. Allen subsequently defaulted on a debt and was sued, and the sheriff confiscated one of Love's slaves along with other property to pay the debts. American law recognized coverture, which transferred all of a woman's property to her husband when they married. Under Chickasaw law, however, the wife kept the property she owned before her marriage as separate from that of her husband. Therefore, the husband had no rightful claim to Love's slave,

and the sheriff had no right to confiscate the slave to cover the husband's debts.

In *Fisher v. Allen* (1837) the Mississippi courts ruled in favor of Love and Allen, setting a precedent for the Mississippi's Married Women's Property Act of 1839. In the case of debt-threatened husbands such as Sen. Hadley, the law served a much more practical purpose: it provided a safeguard against property seizure. Men could place property such as slaves or private businesses such as Piety Hadley's boardinghouse under their wives' ownership and thereby prevent that property from being confiscated to settle debts.

Anna F. Kaplan
Columbia University

Mississippi History Now website, http://mshistorynow.mdah.state.ms.us; Phyllis J. Read and Bernard L. Witlieb, *The Book of Women's Firsts* (1992); Bertram Wyatt-Brown, *Southern Honor: Ethics and Behavior in the Old South* (25th anniv. ed. 2007).

Mars, Florence
(1923–2006) Author

Writer Florence L. Mars is most famous for opposing and writing about racist violence in her hometown. Born in Philadelphia, Mississippi, in Neshoba County, on 1 January 1923, she was the only child of Adam Longino Mars and Emily Geneva Johnson Mars. Mars's father was a prominent lawyer, and her grandfather was one of the county's largest landowners. Her family also owned Philadelphia's leading department store. Florence attended the Philadelphia public schools and later Millsaps College in Jackson before transferring to the University of Mississippi, from which she graduated in 1944.

An early supporter of African American civil rights, Mars first came under fire in her community when she expressed support for the US Supreme Court's 1954 *Brown v. Board of Education* decision, which barred segregated schools. She spent the next several years outside of Mississippi, working as a photographer in New Orleans and traveling in Europe. In 1962 she returned to Philadelphia to raise cattle on a farm inherited from her paternal grandfather and to manage the Neshoba County stockyards, which she had purchased in 1957.

Mars is best known for her involvement in the FBI investigation into the 1964 killings of civil rights workers Andrew Goodman, Michael Schwerner, and James Chaney. Her book, *Witness in Philadelphia* (1977), relates Neshoba County's troubled racial history during the 1960s, particularly focusing on the murders, which were perpetrated by local law enforcement and Klansmen. Mars and her aunt, Ellen Spendrup, cooperated with the FBI to provide background information on the community and Klan activity in the area. The two women also testified before a federal grand jury in Biloxi about Sheriff Lawrence Rainey's history of brutality toward African Americans. Mars's actions resulted in threats to her physical safety and a Klan-orchestrated boycott of her stockyard that forced its closing and the sale of her cattle farm. Rainey retaliated against Mars by arresting her in 1965 on charges of drunk driving, an incident that shocked the white community and led to a decline in his influence.

Mars also wrote *The Bell Returns to Mount Zion* (1996), a sequel to *Witness*, and *The Fair: A Personal History* (2001), concerning the annual Neshoba County Fair. Mars's photographs appeared in the *New York Times* and *Time* magazine. In June 2005, less than a year before her death on 23 April 2006, she was in the courtroom when Edgar Ray Killen was finally convicted in the deaths of the three civil rights workers.

Lisa K. Speer
Arkansas History Commission

Seth Cagin and Philip Dray, *We Are Not Afraid: The Story of Goodman, Schwerner, and Chaney and the Civil Rights Campaign for Mississippi* (1988); Lynne Olson, *Freedom's Daughters: The Unsung Heroines of the Civil Rights Movement from 1830 to 1970* (2001); "Oral History with Miss Florence Mars, Native Mississippi Author" (1978), Center for Oral History and Cultural Heritage, University of Southern Mississippi, http://digilib.usm.edu/cdm/compoundobject/collection/coh/id/5022/rec/3.

Marschalk, Andrew

(1767–1838) Publisher

Andrew Marschalk, called the Father of Mississippi Journalism for his pioneering newspaper work in early nineteenth-century Natchez, was born on 4 February 1767 in New York City to Andrew Marschalk, a baker, and his wife, Anna Hardenbroeck Marschalk. The first Marschalks had come to New York about 1700. Andrew Marschalk grew up among New York's Dutch community and witnessed a naval bombardment of New York City and the furious activity associated with the preparation of the city's defenses prior to its abandonment to the British. He fought in the American Revolution at age fourteen.

Marschalk began his education in the printing trade as an apprentice in New York but ran away in 1787. He lived in England for part of the 1780s and seems to have continued work in the printing trade: he brought a press with him when he returned to the United States in 1790. For most of the 1790s Marschalk served in the US military on the frontier under the commands of Anthony Wayne and Arthur St. Clair. Marschalk also acted as quartermaster at Fort Jefferson near present-day Greenville, Ohio.

In 1798, while stationed at Walnut Hills (later Vicksburg), Marschalk printed "The Galley Slave," a poem that became the first work printed in Mississippi. The following year, Winthrop Sargent, the governor of the newly formed Mississippi Territory, encouraged Marschalk to print the territorial laws. Marschalk printed some of this work in Natchez, and after finishing his military service, he returned to the city and started the *Mississippi Herald* in 1802. Three other newspapers had begun publishing during the interim, and Marschalk's paper merged with the *Mississippi Gazette* to become the *Mississippi Herald and Natchez Gazette*, which lasted until 1808. Marschalk published newspapers in Natchez and nearby Washington almost continuously until 1833, and he aided in establishing newspapers in Woodville and Port Gibson.

Marschalk supported the Jeffersonian Democrats in the early decades of the century and the Jacksonian Democrats in the 1820s. The nature of partisan journalism in the Mississippi Territory led to conflict and violence, and Marschalk seldom shrank from controversy. In one famous incident, territorial judge George Poindexter chased Marschalk into his printing shop and beat him for an article that appeared in the *Washington Republican*, which Marschalk edited from 1813 to 1815. Marschalk subsequently operated the *Mississippi State Gazette* (1818–25), the *Natchez Gazette* (1825–27, 1830–32), and the *Mississippi Statesman and Natchez Gazette* (1827–29).

In 1797 Marschalk married Susannah McDonald, who died in 1814. His second marriage, to Sydney Johnson, lasted from 1817 to his death in Natchez on 8 August 1838. Several of his sons followed in his footsteps, starting newspapers in Port Gibson, Natchez, and Macon.

Tony Seybert
Palmdale, California

Journal of Mississippi History 2 (April 1940); Dunbar Rowland, *History of Mississippi: Heart of the South*, vol. 2, L–Z (1925); Charles S. Sydnor, *Journal of Southern History* (February 1935).

Marshall County

Founded in 1836, Marshall County borders Tennessee and was named for Supreme Court justice John Marshall. The county seat is Holly Springs, and other communities include

Byhalia, Potts Camp, Red Banks, and Chulahoma. Marshall County is home to the Holly Springs National Forest.

This northern Mississippi county was an economic powerhouse in the antebellum years, with large populations of slaves and free people, considerable agricultural productivity, and a growing number of commercial and industrial workers. In its first census in 1840, Marshall County had a population of 9,266 free people and 8,260 slaves. Its total population of 17,526 ranked third among Mississippi's counties, and it ranked first in the number of free people. In 1840 Marshall County ranked fourth in the state, with 349 commercial and manufacturing workers.

Marshall County continued to grow through the antebellum period and by 1860 trailed only Hinds County in population, with the increase coming primarily in the number of slaves. Marshall was home to 11,384 free people and 17,439 slaves. Like most areas with substantial numbers of slaves, Marshall County grew a large amount of cotton, ranking sixth in the state. Yet unlike most northern Mississippi areas, it also concentrated on food production. In 1860 the county ranked second in the state in the value of its livestock, sixth in corn, second in peas and beans, eighth in sweet potatoes, and first in Irish potatoes. In 1860 the county's businesses employed the state's third-most industrial workers (338), many of them in railroads and construction.

The county had fifty-six churches in 1860, tying it for second in the state. Thirty-two of the churches were Methodist, eleven were Baptist, five were Presbyterian, three were Cumberland Presbyterian, and three were Episcopalian. The county also had a Union church and a Catholic church. Marshall was an antebellum educational leader, hosting several small colleges, including Chalmers Institute (later the University of Holly Springs), the Holly Springs Female Collegiate Institute, Franklin Female College, and North Mississippi Presbyterian College.

Marshall County was home, at least for short periods, to a substantial number of Confederate military leaders or their families, and it became the site of considerable Civil War military action. Before he was a Confederate general, Claudius Wistar Sears taught math and then served as president at St. Thomas's Hall, a military academy in Holly Springs. Samuel Benton was a teacher, lawyer, and political figure in Holly Springs before joining the Confederacy and rising to the rank of general. The families of Confederate generals Daniel Govan, Edward Cary Walthall, and James Chalmers all spent time in Marshall County.

As a railroad center, Holly Springs played an important role in the Civil War. In 1862 Union forces built a large new supply depot there. A December 1862 strike led by Confederate general Earl Van Dorn destroyed the depot, captured more than a thousand Union soldiers, and temporarily delayed Gen. Ulysses S. Grant's plans to take Vicksburg. Nonetheless, Holly Springs remained under Union control for the majority of the war.

In the 1870s parts of Marshall County were incorporated in Benton and Tate Counties. Nevertheless, Marshall remained one of Mississippi's largest counties, with 29,330 people in the 1880 census. About two-thirds of the county's residents were African American. Marshall remained a productive agricultural center, ranking second in Mississippi in corn, eighth in cotton, fourth in wheat and potatoes, eleventh in cattle, and twelfth in swine. The majority of the farms were run by tenants, and only 46 percent of the farms were cultivated by their owners. Marshall also ranked tenth in the value of manufacturing products and was home to 195 foreign-born residents, most of them from Ireland and Germany.

Postbellum Marshall County became an exciting center of African American educational and religious activity. In 1866 a combination of former slaves and the Freedman's Aid Society of the Methodist Episcopal Church formed Shaw School, which later became Shaw University and then Rust University. A public institution, Mississippi State Normal School, opened in 1870 to teach African American teachers, though it closed because of pressure from white politicians in 1904. The following year, Elias Cottrell, a bishop in the Colored Methodist Episcopal Church who had been born into slavery in the Marshall County community of Old Hudsonville, helped found Mississippi Industrial College in Holly Springs.

Two women born and raised in Holly Springs in the nineteenth century became important cultural figures. Ida B. Wells (1862–1931) attended Shaw College before becoming a journalist, popular author, and speaker. A civil rights activist and a leading opponent of lynching, Wells published a pamphlet, *Southern Horrors*, and a memoir, *Crusade for Justice*. Katharine Sherwood Bonner McDowell (1849–83) also became a writer, publishing works including the novel *Like unto Like* under the name Sherwood Bonner.

In 1900 Marshall County had a population of 26,764. As in much of Mississippi, white and black farmers had dramatically different experiences. Only 11 percent of African American farmers owned their land, while 56 percent of white farmers did so. With Holly Springs as a railroad center, Marshall County had 161 industrial workers.

In the early twentieth century, Methodists and Baptists accounted for all but about 700 of the county's 12,800 church members, with various Methodist groups slightly outnumbering the Baptists. As the home of Rust College and several denominational leaders, Marshall County also had 3,300 members of the Colored Methodist Episcopal Church, the highest number in Mississippi.

Marshall County's population declined slowly in the early 1900s, and the county lost its place near the top of state rankings in agricultural production. By 1930 Marshall was home to 17,770 African Americans, 7,093 whites, and 6 persons whom the census listed as "other." The number of industrial workers declined to 78, and agricultural tenancy came to dominate farm life, as only 24 percent of farms were run by their owners.

One of many creative Marshall County natives, Rufus Thomas (1917–2001), was born in the small community of Cayce and made his fame as a showman and musician in Memphis. Rural Marshall County has been crucial to the hill country blues and was the home of R. L. Burnside (1926–2005), Junior Kimbrough (1930–98), and several important places to play and hear the music. Other writers and artists with roots in the area include Margaree King Mitchell, who was born in Holly Springs in 1953 and is perhaps best known for children's books that involve issues of race in twentieth-century Mississippi, and Kate Freeman Clark (1875–1957), whose paintings now reside in the Kate Freeman Clark Gallery in her native Holly Springs. William Faulkner died in a Byhalia institution in 1962.

Among the many important figures to attend Rust College in the twentieth century were Jackson State University leader Leslie Burl McLemore, who helped start Rust's chapter of the National Association for the Advancement of Colored People; Wiley College president Matthew Dogan; legal figure Perry Howard; opera singer Ruby Elzy; country musician O. B. McClinton; and civil rights activist Willie Peacock.

Marshall County's population remained near 25,000 between 1930 and 1970 before increasing to 29,296 by 1980. In the 1960s agriculture remained central to Marshall's economy, with 43 percent of the county's workers employed growing corn, cotton, and soybeans or raising cattle and hogs. Twelve percent of the county's workers were employed in industry, and a great percentage of employed women worked in household service.

Tourism is important to Marshall County, which showcases its unique historic homes and relies on music events and other festivals; a pilgrimage; and the Ida B. Wells-Barnett Museum. Prior to its closure in 2014, Paul MacLeod's shrine to Elvis Presley, Graceland Too, and the colorful MacLeod himself attracted visitors to Holly Springs.

As in many northern Mississippi counties, Marshall County's 2010 population included a small but significant Hispanic/Latino minority and had increased over the previous half century. Its 37,144 residents were nearly equally divided between African Americans and whites.

Mississippi Encyclopedia Staff
University of Mississippi

Mississippi State Planning Commission, *Progress Report on State Planning in Mississippi* (1938); *Mississippi Statistical Abstract*, Mississippi State University (1952–2010); Charles Sydnor and Claude Bennett, *Mississippi History* (1939); University of Virginia Library, Historical Census Browser website, http://mapserver.lib.virginia.edu; E. Nolan Waller and Dani A. Smith, *Growth Profiles of Mississippi's Counties, 1960–1980* (1985).

Martin, Phillip
(1926–2010) Choctaw Chief

Chief Phillip Martin was the elected leader of the Mississippi Band of Choctaw Indians from 1979 to 2007, when he was defeated in a reelection bid. During his tenure in office, Martin's efforts to recruit manufacturers from throughout the United States to build plants in the Mississippi Choctaw Industrial Park brought steady jobs and decades of economic prosperity for the Choctaw people.

Born on the Mississippi Choctaw Indian reservation on 13 March 1926, during difficult years of poverty in Neshoba County, Martin channeled many of his childhood experiences into efforts to bring about economic change within his community. Martin escaped the economic and social struggles of his boyhood when he left Mississippi to attend a Bureau of Indian Affairs boarding school in Cherokee, North Carolina. After his graduation, Martin enlisted in the US Air Force and served in World War II in France and Germany. The postwar rebuilding efforts he witnessed profoundly affected him, and nearly five decades later he recalled, "If rebuilding could happen in France and Germany, then why not in Neshoba County, Mississippi? If seed money could jump-start an economy in Frankfurt, then why not on an Indian reservation? If the survivors of World War II could draw strength from adversity and form their own cultural traditions, then why not the Choctaws?"

Martin retired from the military in 1955 with the rank of sergeant and returned to Mississippi. After failing to find a job in Neshoba County, Martin moved to Meridian, where he worked as a clerk at the Meridian Air Naval Station and

Phillip Martin (Courtesy NASA Public Affairs Office)

attended community college classes. He graduated in 1957 with an associate's degree and a fresh interest in tribal politics, returned to Neshoba County, and won election as chair of the tribal council at a salary of $2.50 an hour.

Martin's leadership brought revolutionary changes to the reservation. After familiarizing himself with voluminous records on relations between Indian tribes and the US government, Martin led a delegation of his fellow Choctaw to Washington, D.C., to plead with agency heads and representatives for funding to replace poor schools and condemned homes and to pave the reservation's dirt roads. Under Martin's leadership, the Choctaw received one of the state's first federal Community Action Program grants as well as further federal and state grants.

The key to Martin's vision for the Choctaw nation's economic prosperity was attracting corporate money to the reservation, which was exempt from state and local taxes and regulations, by offering the Mississippi Choctaw Industrial Park as a plant site for corporations throughout the world. Martin established a tribal company, Chahta Enterprise, which grew from just fifty-seven employees in 1979 to more than nine hundred by the mid-1990s. Martin's efforts and the tribe's track record of productive and efficient workers fostered further expansion as the Choctaw nation and the renamed Choctaw Manufacturing Enterprise added three plants that provide products for such dominant corporate names as Ford Motors, McDonald's, and American Greetings. During Martin's three decades at the helm of the Mississippi Band of Choctaw Indians, the tribe also began operating a construction company and other public service enterprises, including the Choctaw Transit Authority and Choctaw Utility Commission, as well as the tribe's biggest moneymaker, the Pearl River Resort, which includes two casinos, a water park, and a golf course. Martin's efforts created more than four thousand new jobs in his community, and by 2010, the Choctaw businesses employed seven thousand people and generated $180 million per year in wages alone, while the reservation's 4 percent unemployment rate was less than half the national rate.

Martin served not only as tribal chief but also as business manager, director of the Choctaw Community Action Agency, and chair of the Tribal Housing Authority. He oversaw the modification of the Choctaw nation's system of tribal government to resemble state political systems and established the Mississippi Band of Choctaw as a national leader in transferring the administration of government programs from the Bureau of Indian Affairs to the tribes themselves. In addition, Martin created a scholarship fund that pays full tuition for all tribe members who are accepted to college. Between 1985 and 2000, life expectancy for members of the Mississippi Band of Choctaw rose by two decades.

Shortly before his death on 4 February 2010, Martin published a memoir, *Chief: The Autobiography of Phillip Martin* (2009), in which he "recount[ed] the major events of my life because I believe I owe it to the Choctaw people, especially the young and those yet to be born."

Eva Walton Kendrick
Birmingham, Alabama

Dennis Hevesi, *New York Times* (15 February 2010); *Neshoba Democrat* (4 February 2010); Katherine M. B. Osburn, *Choctaw Resurgence in Mississippi: Race, Class, and Nation Building in the Jim Crow South, 1830–1977* (2014); Benton R. White and Christine Schultz, in *The New Warriors: Native American Leaders since 1900*, ed. R. David Edmunds (2001).

Martin, William Thompson

(1823–1910) Confederate General

A lawyer, state legislator, and Civil War general, William Thompson Martin was born on 25 March 1823 in Glasgow, Kentucky. He was the eldest son of Emily Monroe Kerr Martin and John Henderson Martin, a lawyer; a native of Albemarle County, Virginia; and a veteran of the Battle of New Orleans. Martin graduated from Centre College in Danville, Kentucky, in 1840 and moved to Vicksburg, Mississippi, where his parents then lived, and studied law in his father's office. Martin relocated to Natchez in 1842 and was admitted to the Mississippi bar in 1844. He won election as district attorney the same year, serving until 1860.

A Whig and staunch unionist, Martin opposed secession in both 1851 and 1860, but after Mississippi seceded, he organized a cavalry unit, the Adams County Troop, and was elected its captain in the spring of 1861. After Fort Sumter he led his men to Richmond, where they became part of the 2nd Mississippi Cavalry in the Jeff Davis Legion.

Martin received a series of rapid promotions, becoming a major in October 1861, lieutenant colonel in February 1862, and colonel in July 1862. During the Peninsula Campaign he commanded the rear third of J. E. B. Stuart's column when he rode around Gen. George B. McClellan and commanded the legion in the Seven Days' Battles. Martin served as Gen. Robert E. Lee's personal aide at the Battle of Antietam. Martin's performance won him a brigadier general's commission in December 1862, and he was ordered to the West, where he served under Gen. Joseph Wheeler. Martin again distinguished himself in Tennessee, commanding a division in the Tullahoma Campaign and the Battle of Chickamauga. He received a promotion to major general in November 1863 and subsequently led a portion of Gen. James Longstreet's cavalry in the capture of Knoxville. Martin then returned to Wheeler's cavalry in the Army of Tennessee and led a division through the Atlanta Campaign. In December 1864 Martin was transferred to the Subdistrict of Northwest Mississippi, where he rounded up deserters and protected the region from guerrillas. There is no record of his surrender, but he was paroled at Meridian on 11 May 1865 and pardoned on 5 October 1866.

After the war Martin returned to practice law in Natchez. He served as a delegate to the state constitutional conventions of 1865 and 1890 and to every Democratic National Convention between 1868 and 1880. He represented Adams County in the State Senate from 1882 to 1894 and served as president of the Natchez, Jackson, and Columbus Railroad, overseeing the completion of a rail line from Natchez to Jackson in 1884. Martin also spent a dozen years as a trustee of the University of Mississippi and presided over the board of trustees of Jefferson College in Washington, Mississippi. In 1905 Pres. Theodore Roosevelt appointed Martin postmaster of Natchez.

In 1854 Martin married Margaret Dunlop Conner. They went on to have ten children and resided near Natchez at Monteigne, which Martin had built in 1854. He died in Natchez on 16 March 1910.

Tara Laver
Louisiana State University

John H. Eicher and David J. Eicher, *Civil War High Commands* (2001); Dumas Malone, ed., *Dictionary of American Biography*, vol. 6 (1933); Jon L. Wakelyn, *Biographical Dictionary of the Confederacy* (1977).

Mary Holmes College

A historically black two-year institution of higher education operated by the Presbyterian Church, Mary Holmes School was founded in 1892 in Jackson by the church's Board of Missions for Freedmen. Originally known as Mary Holmes Seminary, the institution was named by the school's principal founders, Rev. Mead Holmes and his daughter, Mary, in honor of his wife and her mother, also named Mary, who dedicated her life to helping former slaves.

The school originally sought to educate young women in the domestic arts and Christianity, offering classes in home economics, cooking, sewing, and biblical studies. It opened in Jackson on 28 September 1892 and continued its work there until 30 January 1895, when the buildings burned to the ground. The Board of Missions for Freedmen chose to rebuild the school in West Point, which had a population of thirty-five hundred and was the center of a large black community. In addition, the town had three railroads—the Mobile and Ohio, the Southern, and the Illinois Central—and was the site of the Southern Female College, an institution that ranked among the best in the South for the education of white women. Mary Holmes was constructed on approximately 192 acres in what became Clay County and opened in West Point on 1 January 1897, becoming Mississippi's only single-sex educational institution for African American women.

In 1932 Mary Holmes School became coeducational, created its first college department, and changed its mission to training teachers. It and other private schools became the primary producers of black teachers in the South. In 1959 Mary Holmes dropped its high school program and became Mary Holmes Junior College. It sought to guide students in the pursuit of knowledge, academic achievement, cultivation of religious conviction, and dedication to community service.

Mary Holmes College served many first-generation students as well as its surrounding community. In the 1960s the school was the site of a pilot project to develop catfish farming and legal services for the poor. In 1965 the college trained Head Start volunteers. However, integration brought difficulties for many historically black colleges and universities, and in December 2002 the Southern Association of Schools and Colleges removed Mary Holmes College from its list of accredited institutions. The school suspended classes in the fall of 2003, and on 3 March 2005 the Presbyterian Church (USA), through its Office of Racial Ethnic Schools and Colleges, announced the official closing of the institution. For more than a century, Mary Holmes College had provided hope and possibility to young men and women who otherwise might not have had a path to higher education.

Evelyn Kelsaw Bonner
Wiley College

Evelyn Kelsaw Bonner, Speech Delivered to Rotary Club, West Point, Mississippi (13 February 2003); Evan Silversteen, *Presbyterian News Service* (7 March 2005); Eva Stinson, *Presbyterians Today* (January–February 2006); *The Voice, Synod of Living Water* (April 2005).

Mary Mahoney's Old French House Restaurant

Mary Mahoney's Old French House Restaurant opened its doors at 110 Rue Magnolia in the Biloxi Historic District on 7 May 1964 and has subsequently achieved national acclaim as a fine-dining establishment, serving political leaders, celebrities, and guests from all over the world. Mahoney herself became a local celebrity and was invited to share her dishes at the White House.

Located in a home built by French colonist Louis Frasier in 1737, the main restaurant features a Cajun- and European-inspired seafood menu enhanced by memorable local flavor. An Irish pub that offered an intimate, laid-back atmosphere and a twenty-four-hour café that served beignets, po'boys, and other comfort foods were destroyed by Hurricane Katrina.

The original proprietor, born Mary Antonia Cvitanovich on 1 July 1924 to Yugoslavian parents in the seafood business, graduated from high school and attended community college in Perkinston for a year before returning to the Gulf Coast. She married Robert F. Mahoney on 25 November 1945. Six years later, the couple took advantage of an opportunity provided by Arkansas businessman A. B. Minor, who needed someone to manage his newly purchased Tivoli Hotel. There, Mary Mahoney gained experience in the hospitality industry. After several unsuccessful business ventures, she, her husband, and her brother, Andrew Cvitanovich, purchased the Old French House, which still served as a residence, and planned to turn it into a restaurant.

The old home, which had previously served as headquarters for colonial governor Jean-Baptiste Le Moyne, Sieur de Bienville, needed renovation. The Mahoneys consulted with friends, family, and business associates to determine how to preserve the structure while creating an inviting atmosphere for dining. Mary Mahoney started the restaurant with furniture and table settings gleaned from secondhand stores, a necessity after the expensive renovation of the old home. Menus were typed by Mahoney and stapled into legal-sized folders. Mahoney surrounded herself with family, trusted friends, and talented employees recruited from other local establishments, and the restaurant soon became a hit, garnering local and ultimately national renown. The Old French House is mentioned in two of John Grisham's novels, and Mahoney catered a party for Pres. Ronald Reagan on the White House Lawn.

The house and restaurant have survived not only Hurricane Camille in 1969 and Hurricane Katrina thirty-six years later but Mary Mahoney's death in 1985. The Mahoney family continues to operate the establishment, which shares its lot with another longtime survivor—Patriarch, a live oak believed to be more than two thousand years old.

Jill Clark
University of Mississippi

Lee Eschler and Linda Eschler, *Mississippi Gulf Coast Restaurants Post Hurricane Katrina* (2009); Edward J. Lepoma, *A Passion for People: The Story of Mary Mahoney and Her Old French House Restaurant* (1998); Mary Mahoney's Old French House Restaurant website, marymahoneys.com.

Mason, Charles Harrison

(1864 or 1866–1961) Religious Leader

Charles Harrison Mason organized and for many decades led the largest black Pentecostal denomination in the United States, the Church of God in Christ, now based in Memphis. Born on 8 September 1864 or 1866 in Bartlett, Tennessee, to parents who had been slaves, Mason grew up intending to be a minister. "It seemed that God endowed him with supernatural characteristics," his daughter wrote, "which were manifested in dreams and visions that followed him through life." In 1878 Mason's parents moved to Plumersville, Arkansas, where Mason was saved and called to preach. However, Mason forsook his mission until he was stricken with tuberculosis. He saw his healing as a miraculous reprieve and divine message to pursue his spiritual duty.

Mason attended Arkansas Baptist College briefly in the early 1890s but left school after a few months, declaring that God had showed him that "there was no salvation in schools and colleges." Mason received his preaching license in 1893 from a Baptist congregation. Four years later Mississippi Baptists ordered him to vacate his pulpit for the offense of preaching holiness doctrines, especially sanctification. Seeking to find a place for his own church, he received permission to use an abandoned gin house for a revival in 1897, and what became the Church of God in Christ was born.

In the early 1900s Mason walked from town to town in the Mississippi Delta, spreading the holiness teachings. Yet he was not satisfied with the second blessing of sanctification. Like other early Pentecostals, he sought an even more profound spiritual experience. He found it at the Azusa street revival in Los Angeles, where he received the final Holy Spirit baptism and spoke in tongues. During a night of prayer, Mason saw a vision. "When I opened my mouth to say glory," he later remembered, "a flame touched my tongue which ran down in me. My language changed and no word could I speak in my own tongue."

Mason returned from Los Angeles and split with his holiness compatriots. Legal tussles ensued, resulting in Mason's establishing the Church of God in Christ in Memphis. Early Pentecostals recognized Mason's special powers of discernment and saw him as supernaturally gifted. Criticized for importing conjure into the churches, Mason pointed to the scriptures indicating that Jesus taught the same kinds of healings and spirit possessions. Mason's preaching skill garnered considerable attention. As he proudly recounted his early career, the Holy Spirit through him "saved, sanctified and baptized thousands of souls of all colors and races."

For two decades, Mason traveled and preached throughout the entire Mississippi Delta region. With the migration of African Americans to the North, the Church of God in Christ increasingly established a presence in Chicago,

Detroit, and other cities. The church became well known for its spirited singing, accompanied by tambourines, trumpets, and other instruments and by the kinds of "shouts" and emotional ecstatic release that had been driven out of many of the more respectable black Baptist and Methodist churches. Mason remained the church's senior bishop until his death on 17 November 1961.

Paul Harvey
University of Colorado at
Colorado Springs

Ithiel C. Clemons, *Bishop C. H. Mason and the Roots of the Church of God in Christ* (1996); Ithiel C. Clemons, *History and Formative Years of the Church of God in Christ with Excerpts from the Life and Works of Its Founder—Bishop C. H. Mason* (1969); Karen Lynell Kossie, "The Move Is On: African American Pentecostal-Charismatics in the Southwest" (PhD dissertation, Rice University, 1998); E. W. Mason, *The Man ... Charles Harrison Mason* (1979); Elsie Mason, *From the Beginning of Bishop C. H. Mason and the Early Pioneers of the Church of God in Christ* (1991); Mary Mason, *The History and Life Work of Bishop C. H. Mason* (1924); Cheryl Sanders, *Saints in Exile: The Holiness Pentecostal Experience in African American Religion and Culture* (1996); Calvin White Jr., *The Rise to Respectability: Race, Religion, and the Church of God in Christ* (2012).

Mason, Gilbert R.

(1928–2006) Physician and Activist

Gilbert Rutledge Mason, the Mississippi Gulf Coast's "civil rights doctor," was born in Jackson on 7 October 1928. He graduated from Tennessee State University in 1949 and completed medical school at Howard University in 1954. After he interned in St. Louis, Mason and his wife, Natalie, moved to Biloxi in July 1955, attracted in part by the majestic twenty-six-mile beach that borders the Gulf of Mexico. Soon after settling on the coast, however, Mason discovered only whites were permitted to use the facility.

On 14 May 1959 Mason and seven other local residents walked on the Biloxi beach and into the Gulf. A city policeman soon ordered the group to leave the area, explaining that it was reserved for whites. In response, Mason formed the Harrison County Civic Action Committee with the primary intention of integrating area beaches. The group planned a massive nonviolent protest, Operation Surf, for 17 April 1960 to challenge the segregated beach statutes. Despite months of planning, Mason alone appeared at the beach. Officers arrested him and charged him with disorderly conduct. Undaunted, Mason planned another demonstration for the following weekend. His courage inspired the

Gilbert Mason (McCain Library and Archives, University of Southern Mississippi)

local black community, whose members responded to the new campaign with unprecedented enthusiasm.

On 24 April more than one hundred black men, women, and children held a nonviolent wade-in on Biloxi beach. It was the first indigenous nonviolent direct action protest in Mississippi during the civil rights era. A mob of agitated whites awaited the protesters and attacked them with pool cues, clubs, chains, blackjacks, lead pipes, and baseball bats, leading to what the *New York Times* called "the worst race riot in Mississippi history." White mobs grew larger and more agitated as the day progressed, and violence spread throughout the city. Dozens of blacks required hospitalization for their injuries, and police arrested Mason for disturbing the peace and obstructing traffic. The incident attracted the attention of the National Association for the Advancement of Colored People, which sent state organizer Medgar Evers from Jackson to the coast to investigate the event. Evers assisted Mason in establishing a Biloxi chapter of the group, and Mason became its first president.

The beachfront attacks also inspired the federal government to file a lawsuit against Harrison County officials because federal funds built and maintained the segregated beaches. The case eventually opened Mississippi's beaches to all races.

Mason built on the wade-in's successes to achieve racial equality in Biloxi during the 1960s. He started the Biloxi Youth Chapter of the National Association for the Advancement of Colored People, initiated local voter registration drives, and ensured that area restaurants served black customers. Mason and twenty-one other parents also filed suit to integrate Biloxi's public school system in 1963. Black children attended city classrooms with whites for the first time in August 1964 with no violence. On 23 June 1963 Mason led another beachfront demonstration to protest the slow pace of local integration. Unlike the initial wade-in, white mobs did not attack protesters, but police arrested all seventy-one demonstrators.

Mason was part of other efforts to improve race relations in his home state. He served as a delegate for the Mississippi Freedom Democratic Party in 1968 and 1972. Mason also criticized the state government for withholding relief assistance from the local poor and blacks in the aftermath of 1969's Hurricane Camille. The evidence Mason presented persuaded the federal government to investigate relief aid distribution practices in Mississippi, and Pres. Richard Nixon ordered Gov. John Bell Williams to appoint blacks to his all-white Hurricane Emergency Relief Council. Williams named Mason to the group, marking the first time a Mississippi governor appointed a black representative to a state policymaking body.

Mason continued to work for civil rights on the Mississippi Coast through the 1980s and 1990s. He investigated claims of racial discrimination at Kessler Air Force base, led the struggle to restructure Biloxi voting districts in the 1980s, initiated a campaign against police brutality in area jails, worked to remove the Confederate flag from public display, and mobilized African American voters to elect Biloxi's first black city council member and police chief. Four Mississippi governors and Presidents Nixon, Jimmy Carter, and Bill Clinton recognized Mason's achievements with appointments to civil rights advisory boards.

In 2000 Mason published a memoir recounting his four decades of work to promote racial equality on the Mississippi Coast. He died in Biloxi on 8 July 2006.

J. Michael Butler
Flagler College

J. Michael Butler, *Journal of Southern History* (February 2002); Gilbert R. Mason and James Patterson Smith, *Beaches, Blood, and Ballots: A Black Doctor's Civil Rights Struggle* (2000).

Massive Resistance

In February 1956 Virginia's senior senator, Harry Flood Byrd, called on southern states to undertake "massive resistance" to the growing pressure for racial desegregation from both the federal government and increasingly astute African American activists. Byrd's phrase became an umbrella term for the intricate network of barriers that individual southern states designed and deployed to halt—or at least retard—the drive toward desegregation. In Mississippi as in the rest of the South, massive resistance was a tangled and often uneven affair that gained its coherence from a common goal of maintaining racial segregation rather than from any single overarching strategy. It reached its apogee in the Magnolia State between the spring of 1954 and the autumn of 1962, but even within those dates its breadth and pace changed subtly, encompassing both the shrewd "practical segregation" of Gov. J. P. Coleman (1956–60) and the aggressive populist racism of Gov. Ross Barnett (1960–64). Throughout its history, massive resistance involved the passage of specific legislative acts, appeals to states' rights, propaganda campaigns, grassroots organization, and carefully choreographed campaigns of violence and intimidation, all of which were designed to maintain long-established traditions of white supremacy. Daily oppression of African Americans was intense and ongoing, but the resistance years were also characterized by grand set pieces of public political theater as Mississippi's segregationists clashed openly with federal forces, testing the doctrine of states' rights to its limits.

The rallying cry of massive resistance was intended for all southern states, but Mississippi set the tenor of segregationists' legislative intransigence, provided a template for grassroots organization, and refined the ideological canon. Although historians often point to the US Supreme Court's 1954 *Brown v. Board of Education* decision as a catalyst for truly massive southern resistance, Mississippi's segregationists took decisive steps well before that date. As early as 1948, for example, Gov. Fielding Wright introduced many of the themes and much of the rhetoric of later resistance when he ran as the Dixiecrat vice presidential candidate, and Mississippi's state legislature sought to outmaneuver the Supreme Court by appropriating millions of dollars for a 1950 school equalization program that was specifically designed to forestall future calls for desegregation.

In the years following *Brown*, massive resistance reached its peak. After an abortive start in late 1953, the first real signs of organization at Mississippi's grassroots came in July 1954 when plantation manager Robert B. "Tut" Patterson met with fourteen other men in Indianola to form the nation's first Citizens' Council. Patterson's original purpose was to provide an updated and less embarrassing version of the Ku Klux Klan that would eschew open violence in favor of support for firmly prosegregation politicians and for economic intimidation to mute local dissent against the segregationist line. In October 1954 the state's groups were so vibrant, especially in the Delta, that Patterson established the Mississippi Association of Citizens' Councils to coordinate activity. Within two years some ninety Council groups with an estimated quarter of a million members existed across the South. Mississippi's Citizens' Councils remained at the forefront of organizational activity throughout the massive resistance years, especially in terms of producing propaganda. In October 1955 William J. Simmons founded the influential *Citizens' Council* newspaper, and its circulation reportedly grew to between forty thousand and sixty thousand. Eighteen months later he oversaw the production of the *Citizens' Council Forum* television show from his native Jackson.

A symbiotic relationship connected the grassroots forces that gathered in the Citizens' Councils to Mississippi's most prominent politicians, many of whom played important roles in stimulating and coordinating resistance activity. Circuit Judge Tom P. Brady's "Black Monday" speech, named after Rep. John Bell Williams's label for the date of the *Brown* decision, became one of the most important and widely reproduced pamphlets produced by the Citizens' Councils. Sen. James O. Eastland publicly stated that Mississippians had a duty to disobey the Supreme Court's school desegregation decisions. Mississippi's other senator, John C. Stennis, was one of the drafters of the Southern Manifesto, in which 101 of the 128 southern members of Congress pledged to resist desegregation by "all lawful means." And although Governor Coleman distanced himself from the Citizens' Councils, his successor, Barnett, was widely known to be a long-standing supporter. Under the guidance of proresistance politicians, the state legislature passed a swath of laws designed to stave off desegregation and retard black political progress. A special September 1954 legislative session, for example, agreed to the closure of white schools faced with imminent desegregation, a move ratified two months later in a referendum in which sixty thousand voters indicated their approval. Other laws were designed to hamstring black protest and curtail the effectiveness of the National Association for the Advancement of Colored People: perhaps most notably, all school employees were required to list their organizational memberships over the previous five years. The legislature also sanctioned the 1956 creation of the Mississippi State Sovereignty Commission, which used state funds to underwrite propaganda campaigns designed to convince northerners that segregation should be allowed to continue below the Mason-Dixon Line.

Throughout Mississippi's massive resistance, those legislative measures were underpinned by brutal acts of intimidation and violence at the local level. Some of those episodes received national and even international attention: for example, the August 1955 murder of Emmett Till, which caused such a furor that the murderers, Roy Bryant and J. W. Milam, were ostracized even by their fellow Mississippians, and the 1964 abduction and murder of voter registration volunteers James Chaney, Andrew Goodman, and Michael Schwerner. Elsewhere, violence and intimidation against blacks were less well reported but no less systemic. In a typical act of segregationist retribution, thirty-eight of the fifty-three Yazoo City blacks who signed a petition calling for the desegregation of local schools were forced to flee the city, while many of those who remained were summarily fired from their jobs, denied bank loans, or refused service in local stores.

In 1962 Mississippi provided one of the most high-profile incidents of the resistance era when Barnett spearheaded an attempt to prevent African American James Meredith from enrolling at the University of Mississippi. In an indication of the increasing tensions between state and federal government, the Kennedy administration deployed twenty-three thousand troops to force Meredith's enrollment even after officials had secretly agreed with Barnett on a way to defuse the situation. Widespread rioting followed as a mob of three thousand, many of them reputedly members of the Citizens' Council, roamed the campus. Ultimately, however, the showdown at the university signaled that the federal government would prevail in such open confrontations, and the Citizens' Councils' close association with the forces of failed resistance in Oxford precipitated their decline.

Early histories suggested that as soon as it became clear that presidential administrations would not tolerate continued racial segregation and as soon as the Civil Rights Act of 1964 and Voting Rights Act of 1965 had been signed, massive resistance dissipated. Recent scholarship, however, has forcefully argued that resistance metamorphosed rather than collapsed. Segregationists learned more subtle, coded ways of denying nonwhites' equality: in 1966, for example, the Mississippi legislature considered thirty bills designed to dilute nonwhite voting strength in the state without contravening the US Constitution. Three years after passage of the Voting Rights Act, the number of Mississippians of voting age who were registered to vote was 23.3 percent higher for whites than for blacks. Mississippi's segregationists had not given up their battle, but stripping their actions and rhetoric of the most egregious and open racism enabled them to find legally acceptable means of achieving their objectives.

George Lewis
University of Leicester

Chris Myers Asch, *The Senator and the Sharecropper: The Freedom Struggles of James O. Eastland and Fannie Lou Hamer* (2008); Numan V. Bartley, *The Rise of Massive Resistance: Race and Politics in the South during the 1950s* (1969); Charles W. Eagles, *The Price of Defiance: James Meredith and the Integration of Ole Miss* (2009); Neil McMillen, *The Citizens' Councils: Organized Resistance to the Second Reconstruction, 1954–64* (1971); Joseph Crespino, *In Search of Another Country: Mississippi and the Conservative Counterrevolution* (2007); George Lewis, *Massive Resistance: The White Response to the Civil Rights Movement* (2006); J. Todd Moye, *Let the People Decide: Black Freedom and White Resistance Movements in Sunflower County, Mississippi, 1945–1986* (2004); Maarten Zwiers, *Senator James Eastland: Mississippi's Jim Crow Democrat* (2015).

Matthews, Burnita Shelton
(1894–1988) Judge

Burnita Shelton Matthews was a lawyer committed to women's rights in the law and the political system who became an activist and then a federal district court judge in Wash-

Burnita Shelton Matthews (Archives and Records Services Division, Mississippi Department of Archives and History [PI 2003.0008 Box 476 R66 B1.53 Folder 5 #1])

ington, D.C. According to scholar Kate Greene, "Like many talented and creative Mississippians before and since, Matthews left her home state and eventually the Deep South in pursuit of a calling. For Matthews, that calling was to advance the rights of women through the law."

Burnita Shelton was born on 28 December 1894 in Copiah County, Mississippi, to Lora and Burnell Shelton, a plantation owner and sometime elected official. Young Burnita developed an interest in the law by watching her father deal with political issues, and after winning a speech contest, the eleven-year-old overheard someone tell her father, "You ought to make a lawyer out of that little girl." Shelton's father assumed that his daughter would become a schoolteacher, so he sent her to the Cincinnati Conservatory of Music to learn piano. She taught music for a short time in Texas, Georgia, and Fayette, Mississippi, but always felt drawn to the law.

In 1917 Shelton married Percy Matthews, a New Orleans lawyer, a soldier, and later an army court judge. While Percy Matthews was involved in the World War I effort, Burnita Matthews grew interested in government jobs. She moved to Washington, D.C., worked for the Veterans Administration, and took law classes at night at the National University Law School. She received her law degree in 1919; passed the Washington, D.C., bar in 1920; and practiced law there for twenty-five years.

While preparing for her career as a lawyer, Matthews joined the National Woman's Party as a legal researcher and soon became the head of the Legal Research Department, preparing arguments against state laws that discriminated against women. Matthews helped research the proposed Equal Rights Amendment and frequently spoke in support of the amendment during the 1930s.

After an energetic lobbying campaign from Matthews's associates, Pres. Harry Truman appointed her to serve on the US court for the District of Columbia in 1949, making her the first woman to serve as a federal district court judge.

During the confirmation process and early in her career, she faced frequent suggestions that women were unfit to serve as judges.

Matthews retired from active district court duty in 1968 but remained a senior judge for the next two decades. She also served as a judge for the US Court of Appeals for the District of Columbia from 1970 until 1977. Matthews suffered a stroke and died on 25 April 1988 and was buried in Copiah County.

Ted Ownby
University of Mississippi

Kate Greene, in *Mississippi Women, Their Histories, Their Lives*, ed. Martha H. Swain, Elizabeth Anne Payne, Marjorie Julian Spruill, and Susan Ditto (2003); Burnita Shelton Matthews Papers, Mississippi Department of Archives and History; Martha Swain, *Southern Studies* (1984).

Matthews, Joseph W.
(1812–1862) Fifteenth Governor, 1848–1850

Joseph Warren Matthews was a plain and unlettered frontiersman who lacked the flair for oratory that many Mississippians expected from their statesmen. During the 1847 governor's race, Matthews, a Democrat and surveyor by trade, was jeered by the more aristocratic Whigs, who called him "Jo Salem," "Jo the well digger," and "Old copperas breeches," all of which were references to his common background. But Mississippi apparently had more plain folks than aristocrats, because Matthews defeated his Whig opponent by thirteen thousand votes.

Matthews had come to Mississippi from Alabama, where he was born near Huntsville in 1812. He settled near the town of Salem, in Tippah County (now Marshall County). Matthews was elected to the State House of Representatives in 1840 and to the State Senate four years later. In 1847 the Democratic Party nominated him as its candidate for governor on the third ballot.

By the time Matthews was inaugurated on 10 January 1848, Mississippi's economy had recovered from the Panic of 1837, and the Mexican War had created another period of prosperity for the Cotton Kingdom. Matthews proclaimed in his inaugural address, "Our citizens are most free from debt, our storehouses abound with plenty [and] our march is onward and upwards toward prosperity and happiness."

Matthews's administration was almost entirely free from the political turmoil that had so often characterized Mississippi politics. That relative tranquillity resulted largely from

M

popular excitement and preoccupation with the war with Mexico and the general prosperity of the late 1840s.

Although Matthews's two years in office were free from controversy, they were not uneventful. During his administration, the state adopted a new legal code and established an institution for the blind, and the University of Mississippi opened for its first session in the fall of 1848. The Jackson-Brandon railroad also began operation, and telegraph service became available in Jackson and other parts of the state.

The Mexican War and the admission of California to statehood agitated the slavery issue, and the Mississippi Democrats passed over Matthews in 1851 and nominated Gen. John Anthony Quitman, the hero of Mexico.

After his term expired, Matthews retired from politics, although he served briefly in the Confederate diplomatic corps during the Civil War. Matthews died on 27 August 1862 in Palmetto, Georgia.

David G. Sansing
University of Mississippi

Mississippi Official and Statistical Register (1912); Dunbar Rowland, *Encyclopedia of Mississippi History*, vol. 2 (1907); David G. Sansing and Carroll Waller, *A History of the Mississippi Governor's Mansion* (1977).

Maxwell, John Caldwell
(b. 1944) Actor and Playwright

John Caldwell Maxwell is best known for his one-man play *Oh, Mr. Faulkner, Do You Write?* Born to Mignonne Caldwell Maxwell and Hoover Maxwell on 12 July 1944 in Jackson, Mississippi, Maxwell spent his early years in Pickens. He attended the University of Mississippi, earning a bachelor's degree in 1966 and a master's degree two years later.

In his twenties Maxwell began reading works by William Faulkner and became interested the Mississippi author. Maxwell then conducted extensive research on Faulkner's professional and personal life, and the result was *Oh, Mr. Faulkner, Do You Write?*, which features some of Faulkner's own words and made its debut at Jackson's New Stage Theatre in 1981. Maxwell has subsequently presented his play to audiences at colleges, universities, arts organizations, and theaters in the United States as well as around the world.

Other works by Maxwell include a 1989 religious play, *The Salvation of Sunshine Billy*. First produced at the Heritage Repertory Theatre of the University of Virginia, the play was restructured as *Buck-Nekkid* and has been produced

in Atlanta, Birmingham, Jackson, and Fort Worth. Known widely as a Christian actor, Maxwell is dedicated to revitalizing interest in the Bible through drama. In 2002 he founded a nonprofit theatrical organization, the Fish Tale Group. With three original monologues profiling John the Baptist, Paul, and Peter, Maxwell has also written and produced several short mock documentary videos depicting modern-day versions of well-known Bible stories.

Maxwell has been a principal player in many productions of Jackson's New Stage Theatre, where he spent six years as artistic director. He is a member of both Actor's Equity and the Screen Actors Guild and has appeared on television programs including *Northern Exposure, Medicine Ball, Issaquena, The Rising Place*, and *Infidelity*. Maxwell lives in Jackson and pursues acting and expanding his Fish Tale Group. A filmed performance of *Oh, Mr. Faulkner, Do You Write?* was released in 2006.

Marilyn H. Smith
Jackson, Mississippi

Mississippi Writers Page website, www.olemiss.edu/mwp; John C. Maxwell, interview by Marilyn H. Smith (28 September 2004).

Mayfield, M. B.
(1923–2005) Artist

M. B. Mayfield, a Northeast Mississippi folk artist, was probably the first black student to attend the University of Mississippi, although he never registered there. He is significant for his art, for unofficially integrating the school, and for a life in which he overcame segregation and stereotype without openly fighting them. He used his art and gentle personality as tools for achieving his goals in a hostile world.

Mayfield (*M. B.* was his full name) was born on 26 April 1923 in Ecru, Mississippi, a small town near Pontotoc. His father died before the boy turned three, and his mother, Ella Tabitha Judon, raised him and his eleven brothers and sisters, many of whom did not live to adulthood. He had a twin brother, L. D. The Mayfield family owned a farm of about one hundred acres on which they raised cotton. Mayfield began drawing as a child. He attended a one-room schoolhouse in Ecru through eighth grade but had no further formal education.

As a teenager, Mayfield was diagnosed with tuberculosis, the same disease that had killed his father and five siblings, so he took the diagnosis as a death sentence. He was bedridden for eight years and became depressed and introverted, but he began to paint, using a watercolor set his mother purchased. As he recovered toward the end of that period, Mayfield began to sculpt, using native clay he dug and mixed. He made large heads of famous people, including Gen. Dwight Eisenhower and boxer Joe Louis.

Mayfield's mother displayed the Louis head on the family's front porch, which faced a major highway. One passer-by who took a keen interest was Stuart Purser, the chair of the new art department at the University of Mississippi. Purser spoke with Mayfield's mother, looked at more of the young man's work, and in June 1949 offered him a job as janitor. Mayfield accepted. Purser gave Mayfield some oil paints and supplies and the bus fare to Oxford, and he began work in October 1949.

After Mayfield finished his chores each day, he would retire to a broom closet off Purser's classroom. With the door ajar and an easel set up, Mayfield would listen to the lectures and complete the assignments just as the official students did. The other students gave him encouragement, supplies, and sometimes friendship. The shy Mayfield enjoyed working in the closet, which he called "my little private one-student classroom." Years later, he painted a picture of himself painting in the classroom closet. That and other images from youth and childhood, including his father's funeral, became the principal subject of his art. He called these depictions "memory scenes." He also painted fine landscapes, portraits, and still lifes.

Mayfield worked and painted at the university for two and a half years. During that time, students and townspeople (including William Faulkner) raised money to send him to the Art Institute of Chicago to see a Van Gogh show. After Purser left the department, Mayfield briefly moved back to Ecru before returning to the university in 1954 under the art department's new chair. However, Mayfield's mother became ill, and he left Oxford to care for her.

After a short period in Wisconsin, he moved to Memphis in 1958 to take another art-related janitorial job, this time at the Brooks Memorial Art Gallery (later Memphis Brooks Museum of Art). Mayfield worked there for twelve years and threw himself back into painting. He had a one-man exhibition at the gallery and won first prize in the amateur division of an art competition. Mayfield left that job to buy a house in Ecru and paint full time with the help of an agent who sold his work. The Pontotoc Historical Society featured an exhibition of his work. The University of Mississippi also hosted a Mayfield exhibition and has several of his paintings in its museum collection. In 1987 he wrote a short autobiography, *The Baby Who Crawled Backwards*, which he self-published in 2004. Other autobiographical pieces remain unpublished.

Mayfield died of a heart attack on 3 June 2005 in Ecru. Although proud of his artistic abilities, Mayfield shunned the spotlight and did not enjoy parties or large gatherings, even in his honor. He dismissed the idea that he had integrated the University of Mississippi. Speaking of James Meredith, who in 1962 became the first African American to register as a student at the university, Mayfield said, "I didn't accomplish the things he did. He was the one who took the punishment." The two men never met.

Steve Cheseborough
Portland, Oregon

Bryan Doyle, *Daily Mississippian* (8 June 2005); M. B. Mayfield, interview by Steve Cheseborough (February and April 1998); David Magee, *The Education of Mr. Mayfield: An Unusual Story of Social Change at Ole Miss* (2009); Jennifer Southall, *Southern Register* (Winter 2004); Neta Gooch Stringer, interview by Steve Cheseborough (April 1998).

McAllister, Deuce
(b. 1978) Athlete

Professional football player Dulymus Jerod "Deuce" McAllister was born on 27 December 1978 in Lena, Mississippi. The son of a truck driver, McAllister, an honor student and president of the student body at Morton High School, said he was inspired by fellow Mississippian Walter Payton. He was an all-state selection by the *Jackson Clarion-Ledger* after his senior season and was recruited by a number of southern colleges.

McAllister chose to attend the University of Mississippi, where between 1997 and 2000 he set numerous career, season, and single-game records. He still holds the school marks for rushing yards (3,060), rushing touchdowns (37), and total touchdowns (41). At the end of the 2000 season, the Associated Press named him to its all–Southeastern Conference team, and he was selected to play in the Senior Bowl. The New Orleans Saints chose McAllister in the first round of the 2001 National Football League draft, making him the twenty-third overall selection.

McAllister played with the Saints from 2001 to 2008 and became the team's all-time leading rusher. He was selected to the Pro Bowl in 2002 and 2003. The Saints released McAllister in February 2009 but re-signed him in January 2010 to serve as an honorary captain during the playoffs. The Saints went on to win Super Bowl XLIV, and McAllister received a championship ring. He then officially retired from the league.

Since 2002 McAllister has worked through his Catch 22 Foundation to enhance the lives of children in the Gulf South region. He was inducted into the Mississippi Sports Hall of Fame in 2014 and remains involved in business and

M

civic activities in his home state. During the 2015 and 2016 seasons, he served as an analyst on radio broadcasts of Saints games.

Richie Caldwell
Dallas, Texas

New Orleans Saints website, www.neworleanssaints.com; Ole Miss Football website, http://www.olemisssports.com/sports/m-footbl/ole-m-footbl-body .html; Pro Football Reference website, www.pro-football-reference.com.

McAllister, Jane Ellen
(1899–1996) Educator

Jane Ellen McAllister was a leader in African American teacher education at Jackson State College and other institutions. She was born in Vicksburg on 24 October 1899 to Richard McAllister, a postman, and Flora McAllister, a teacher. Both of her parents had been educated at Natchez Seminary and were members of Mississippi's small African American middle class. Ellie McAllister later recalled, "The place where I was born and raised was essentially a family neighborhood," and from her parents and neighbors she learned the value of education and service. In addition, her relatives who had been enslaved taught her "a tradition of overcoming."

After graduating from high school at age fifteen, McAllister attended Alabama's Talladega College, graduating in 1919. McAllister then earned a master's degree from the University of Michigan. Through the 1920s she taught education, Latin, and piano at Louisiana's Southern University and helped to establish extension classes for African American teachers. In 1929 she became the first African American woman to receive a doctorate from the Columbia University Teachers College, where her doctoral thesis, "The Training of Negro Teachers in Louisiana," was based on her work at Southern.

McAllister taught briefly at Virginia State University and at Nashville's Fisk University, where she became head of the department of education in 1929. Her attempts to establish an extension program that would allow Fisk student teachers to work in Nashville's African American schools generated criticism that she was moving too quickly. Fisk's president failed to support her, and she moved on to Miner Teachers College (now the University of District of Columbia), where she taught from 1930 to 1951.

McAllister encountered state governments that saw education, especially for African Americans, as a low funding priority, and she challenged African American parents to press for more education for their children. She worked initially with the Rosenwald and Jeanes Funds and subsequently with federal and other funding agencies to remedy the historic lack of teacher training for African Americans.

McAllister helped develop programs at Grambling in Louisiana and served as a consultant in 1940 when the private Jackson College transitioned to become a state institution, the Mississippi Negro Training School. (The school later became Jackson College for Negro Teachers, Jackson State College, and ultimately Jackson State University.) In 1951 she moved back to Mississippi as a professor of education at Jackson State. Until her retirement in 1970, she campaigned for federal funding and pursued educational innovations such as televised lecture courses.

Jackson State University remembers McAllister's work with lectures and a dormitory named in her honor. She died in Vicksburg on 10 January 1996.

Ted Ownby
University of Mississippi

Antrece Lynette Baggett, "A History of the Political, Social, and Financial Struggle to Establish and Sustain the Teacher Training Program at Jackson State University, 1877–1977" (master's thesis, University of Mississippi, 1995); Betty J. Gardner, in *Encyclopedia of African-American Education*, ed. Faustine C. Jones-Wilson, Charles A. Asbury, Margo Okazawa-Rey, D. Kamili Anderson, Sylvia M. Jacobs, and Michael Fultz (1996); Jane Ellen McAllister, *Integration and Education* (1973); Jane Ellen McAllister Papers Inventory, Mississippi Digital Library website, collections.msdiglib.org; Lelia Gaston Rhodes, *Jackson State University: The First Hundred Years, 1877–1977* (1978); Winona Williams-Burns, *Journal of Negro Education* (Summer 1982).

McBryde, Addie
(1883–1958) Teacher and Activist

Adeline Wiseman was born on 31 October 1883 in Cotton Plant, Mississippi. After graduating from college in Mississippi, she became a schoolteacher until her 1905 marriage to David W. McBryde. She returned to teaching in 1927 after her husband's death. Two years later, she resigned to work for the Commission for the Blind, serving as its assistant executive secretary until 1938, when the commission was abolished and its work transferred to the State Department of Public Welfare. During these nine years she traveled across the state, teaching skills to blind Mississippians and encouraging them to feel that they had a right and opportunity to go forth and earn their livelihood. In 1932, when the appropriation for her work was cut from thirty thousand dollars to fifteen thousand dollars, she voluntarily cut her salary in half to seventy-five dollars per month. She also helped set up and maintain a school at Piney Woods.

In 1938 McBryde was appointed director of the Department of Public Welfare's Division of Services for the Blind, a position she held until her retirement on 31 December 1953. Under her stewardship, the division grew, and in 1942 it established the Mississippi Industries for the Blind (1942). Near the end of her life, she created the Addie Wiseman McBryde Fund for the Needy Blind. She died on 23 October 1958.

A decade after her death, the Mississippi legislature created an adjustment center for blind persons at the University of Mississippi Medical Center in Jackson. In 1970 the facility was named the Addie McBryde Memorial Rehabilitation Center for the Blind, and it began operating in May 1972. Over the ensuing half century, the center's numerous clients have included Martha Wiseman, Addie McBryde's youngest sister.

Mary Jane Morgan

Addie W. McBryde File, Mississippi Department of Archives and History; Mississippi Department of Rehabilitation Services Facebook Page, www.facebook.com (23 March 2016).

McCarty, Oseola
(1908–1999) Philanthropist

In 1995 Oseola McCarty surprised the University of Southern Mississippi and gained national renown when she donated $150,000 of her life savings to the university. The attention and honor that resulted from the gift took her by complete surprise, but to those who were amazed by her decision to give more than half of her $280,000 estate to a scholarship fund for African American students, she said, "I don't regret one penny I gave. I just wish I had more to give."

McCarty was born in Shubuta, Mississippi, on 7 March 1908, the only child of Lucy McCarty. Oseola was raised by her grandmother, Julia Smith McCarty, and in 1916 the family moved to Hattiesburg, where Julia McCarty purchased a seven-acre truck farm and took in laundry to support the household. Oseola McCarty left school in the sixth grade to help take care of her family and for the next three-quarters of a century earned her living by taking in washing and ironing, retiring at age eighty-six because of arthritis. She never married and beginning in 1967 lived alone in a house inherited from her aunt. McCarty never owned a car, walking everywhere she went and pushing a shopping cart nearly a mile to get groceries. She seldom read the newspaper and

Oseola McCarty, (McCain Library and Archives, University of Southern Mississippi)

had a television with only one local channel. She bought an air conditioner after her retirement but turned it on only when she had company. Her social life centered on her church and her Bible.

Living so frugally, McCarty saved much of the money she earned, and at age eighty-seven, she decided to donate most of her savings to help Southern Miss students achieve the educational goals that she had long ago abandoned. Although McCarty lived just blocks away from the university, she did not set foot on the campus until August 1995, when she came as an honored guest at the fall convocation and received a one-minute standing ovation from an estimated one thousand faculty, staff, and community members in attendance. Local business leaders quickly matched her grant, creating the Oseola McCarty Endowed Scholarship. Over the next four years, donations from more than six hundred individuals, companies, and other organizations from more than thirty states raised the endowment's value to almost a quarter of a million dollars.

McCarty's story touched an amazing range of people, whether because of her gift, her work, her savings, her donation to a university that for much of her life had denied entry to African Americans, or her humble philosophy of life. When asked why she lived such a simple life without luxuries while giving away her wealth, she replied with a smile, "I *am* spending the money on myself."

McCarty received at least 150 awards, including an honorary doctorate of humane letters from Harvard University and the first honorary doctorate ever awarded by the University of Southern Mississippi. After learning that she would have liked the opportunity to study nursing, Southern Miss's School of Nursing made her an honorary alumna. New York City mayor Rudy Giuliani asked McCarty to flip the switch that lowered the ball in Times Square on New Year's Eve. The woman who had rarely traveled beyond the Hattiesburg city limits ventured all over the United States and appeared on the *Oprah Winfrey Show, Late Show with*

David Letterman, and *Today*. In recognition of her generosity, Pres. Bill Clinton awarded her the nation's second-highest civilian honor, the Presidential Citizens Medal, and has often cited McCarty as a role model for others.

The first recipient of the Oseola McCarty Endowed Scholarship, Stephanie Bullock, became close to her benefactor while in school. After McCarty became ill with cancer, she told Bullock that her only wish was to see her first scholarship recipient graduate. Bullock graduated in May 1999; McCarty died at her home on 26 September.

Although McCarty resisted the university's requests to name a building in her honor, in 2002 a new campus residence was named Oseola McCarty Hall. In the two decades since her death, the scholarship endowment has continued to receive donations: by 2014 the fund's value had topped seven hundred thousand dollars, and forty-four students had received McCarty Scholarships.

Karen Saucier Lundy
University of Southern Mississippi

Van Arnold, Southern Miss Now website (30 January 2014); Rick Bragg, *All Over but the Shoutin'* (1999); Rick Bragg, *New York Times* (13 August 1995); Rick Bragg, *Somebody Told Me* (2000); Evelyn Coleman, *The Riches of Oseola McCarty* (1999); Joyce Ladner, *The Ties That Bind: Timeless Values for African American Families* (1998); "Oral History with Miss Oseola McCarty" (1996), Center for Oral History and Cultural Heritage, University of Southern Mississippi, http://lib.usm.edu/legacy/spcol/coh /cohmccartyo.html.

McCarty Pottery

For nearly fifty years, potters Pup and Lee McCarty transformed the earth of Mississippi and its plants into clays and glazes through their work near Merigold. Perhaps it is the element of natural beauty mixed with the couple's creative spirit that attracts so many to the pottery. Their products are neither dull and uncultivated nor overly refined; rather, they combine rusticity and grace, making them suitable for everyday use, special gifts, or art exhibitions.

Born in 1923, Lee McCarty grew up in Merigold, while his wife, Erma "Pup" Rone McCarty, was born in 1923 and raised in Ethel. The two met at Delta State College and married in the 1940s. They later moved to Oxford and enrolled in pottery classes at the University of Mississippi, and Lee McCarty taught art at a high school run by the university. The McCartys soon decided to devote their lives to art. In 1954 they moved to Merigold, where they bought a mule farm and converted a barn into their living space and studio. The space formerly overlooked by the hayloft is now a lush Mondrian-inspired garden filled with vegetable and ornamental plants. McCarty vases, handcrafted seashells, and wind chimes are visible among the greenery, bamboo, flowers, and birdbaths.

McCarty clay comes from the couple's land near Macon. The pottery is thrown on a Soldner pottery wheel the couple bought in 1949 and is fired in an electric local reduction kiln without pollutants, lead, or gas. The glazes have unique names such as matte nutmeg, tea, and waterbottom. The pieces include vases, plates, bowls, wind chimes, angels, and an assortment of animals, including birds, rabbits, cats, pigs, hippopotamuses, and fish. Lee McCarty has said that he and Pup tried to employ the colors of the Mississippi Delta in their work.

The pottery is known worldwide. The McCartys showed their work at the Smithsonian Museum, the Hamlin Museum in Germany, and the Paris offices of the United Nations Educational, Scientific, and Cultural Organization as well as in Japan, at the Samuel P. Horn Museum at the University of Florida, and at the Lauren Rogers Museum in Laurel, Mississippi.

Describing their work, art historian Lisa Howorth observes, "A McCarty piece . . . seems to suggest all the rawness and earthliness and endurance of Mississippi." Since Pup McCarty's death on 8 February 2009 and Lee McCarty's passing on 7 September 2015, their godchildren, Stephen and Jamie Smith, have carried on the McCarty Pottery tradition.

Caroline Millar
Arkansas Historic Preservation
Program

Lana Lawrence Draper, *Delta Magazine* (July 2003); McCarty's Pottery website, www.mccartyspottery.com; Rex Jones, dir., *So Wonderfully Connected*, vimeo.com/39734799 (2012).

McClinton, O. B.
(1940–1987) Country Musician

A black country music singer who placed several hit records on the country singles chart in the 1970s, Obie Burnett McClinton was born on 25 April 1940 in Senatobia. Growing up on the farm of his Baptist minister father, McClinton picked cotton by day and by night listened to radio programs from such regional stations as WHBQ (Memphis) and WLAC (Nashville). While his musical tastes included blues, R&B, soul music, and rockabilly, McClinton was particularly fond of country music, and he regularly listened to *Grand Ole Opry* broadcasts on Nashville's WSM. To escape the agricultural work, the teenaged McClinton ran away to nearby Memphis, where he spent all his savings to buy a guitar, forcing him to return home. After completing high school, McClinton attended Holly Springs's Rust College, which had given him a scholarship to sing in the college choir. McClinton graduated in 1966 and found a job as a disc jockey on a Memphis radio station, WDIA. In December 1966 he enlisted in the US Air Force and began performing at military talent shows. He also began writing songs for a number of soul music artists, including Otis Redding, Clarence Carter, James Carr, and Arthur Conley.

In 1971, while working as a staff songwriter for Memphis-based Stax Records, McClinton signed a recording contract with a Stax subsidiary, Enterprise, which wanted to market him as a country singer. A fan of Hank Williams Sr. and Merle Haggard, McClinton also emulated the breakthrough success of another black Mississippian, Charley Pride, to whom McClinton self-deprecatingly compares himself in "The Other One." McClinton and Oklahoman Stoney Edwards became virtually the only other African American musicians to achieve sustained commercial success in country music in the 1970s. For Enterprise, McClinton notched two Top 40 country hits—the singles "Don't Let the Green Grass Fool You" and "My Whole World Is Falling Down"—as well as such minor hits as "Six Pack of Trouble" and "Something Better." Not entirely pleased with the studio production on his first two Enterprise albums, *O. B. McClinton Country* (1972) and *Obie from Senatobia* (1972), McClinton requested and received permission to serve as producer on his next album, *Live at Randy's Rodeo* (1973). When Enterprise went out of business in the mid-1970s, McClinton recorded albums and had minor country hits for several other recording companies, including Mercury, Epic, Sunbird, and Moonshine. He died of abdominal cancer in Nashville on 23 September 1987.

Ted Olson
East Tennessee State University

Pamela Foster, *My Country: The African Diaspora's Country Music Heritage* (1998); *From Where I Stand: The Black Experience in Country Music* (1998), liner notes.

McComb Civil Rights Movement

Located in Pike County, in southwestern Mississippi, McComb was founded in 1872 as a repair station for the Illinois Central Railroad. From its inception, McComb was segregated by railroad tracks and was the site of labor unrest, particularly conflicts over unionized African American labor. When workers from the Student Nonviolent Coordinating Committee (SNCC) arrived in 1961, McComb had approximately 13,000 residents (9,000 whites and 4,000 blacks) but no more than 250 black registered voters. Voter registration efforts, however, began long before SNCC workers arrived. As early as 1928, residents sought to register voters via the McComb Independent Lodge of the Benevolent Elks. Nathaniel and Napoleon Lewis, sons of one of the lodge's founders, continued their father's efforts by testifying at the 1946 Bilbo hearings in Jackson and creating the Pike County Voters' League.

Founded in 1944, McComb's chapter of the National Association for the Advancement of Colored People (NAACP) became quite active in the 1950s. After the Supreme Court's 1954 *Brown v. Board of Education* decision, chapter president C. C. Bryant and Webb Owens recruited new members, several of whom proved instrumental in McComb's civil rights struggle. In 1957 representatives from the chapter went to Washington, D.C., to testify in favor of the Civil Rights Act. With the help of Medgar Evers, Bryant founded a youth group to protest police brutality and to study black literature. Bryant also owned a barbershop that functioned as a center of information for the black community. Increased white violence and intimidation caused the McComb NAACP chapter and its activities to become covert.

With NAACP efforts somewhat thwarted, Bryant read in *Jet* magazine that SNCC's Bob Moses was coming to Mississippi to organize voter registration efforts and asked him to come to McComb, which thus became the site of one of Mississippi's first organized large-scale civil rights efforts. Indeed, SNCC workers used their experiences in McComb to organize communities across the entire southeastern United States.

Bryant's invitation caused Moses to scrap his original plan to begin work in Cleveland and go to McComb. After the 1961 Freedom Rides, Moses moved in with the Bryants and set up a SNCC office. Owens and another local NAACP officer, Jerry Gibson, helped Moses canvas neighborhoods, and Owens persuaded the local community to donate money for SNCC's operation. Such local involvement proved integral to SNCC's success, and Moses capitalized on the leadership in the community, relying on residents to support and protect him as he set up SNCC's voter registration school.

With backing from local NAACP leaders, SNCC workers encouraged residents to go to Magnolia, the county seat, to take the voting test. On 7 August 1961 the first voter registration class was held in the Masonic Temple, above the Burglund Supermarket, owned by Pete Lewis. About twenty-five people attended the first classes, but only four took the test, and the white registrar accepted only two.

As part of another SNCC initiative, Charles Sherrod and Marion Barry conducted nonviolence workshops for high school students. Two of the first attendees, Hollis Watkins and Curtis Hayes, staged a sit-in at Woolworth's in August

1961. After their arrest on charges of disturbing the peace, Hayes and Watkins, along with Emma Bell, Bobby Talbert, and Ike Lewis, became full-time SNCC workers.

Several days after the Woolworth's sit-in, more than two hundred black McComb residents attended a SNCC a mass meeting where Rev. James Bevel spoke on nonviolent direct action. The following day, several students, including fifteen-year-old Brenda Travis, sat in at the Greyhound bus station and were expelled from Burglund High, McComb's public African American high school. A few weeks later, on 25 September, Herbert Lee of Amite County was shot and killed by a white state legislator, E. H. Hurst, near Liberty for helping register voters. Hurst was absolved on grounds of self-defense. Just a week after the murder, the Burglund students were released from jail, but principal Commodore Dewey Higgins refused to readmit them.

On 4 October 1961 more than a hundred Burglund students marched to protest Lee's murder and the expulsion of their classmates. SNCC workers joined the students, who congregated on the steps of McComb's City Hall to pray. When the protesters refused to leave, they were arrested and charged with disturbing the peace; all those who were over age eighteen also faced charges of contributing to the delinquency of minors. The SNCC workers were beaten by police while FBI agents took notes, and Travis, who was on probation, received an indeterminate sentence in a juvenile detention center in Oakley.

After the march to City Hall, Burglund High's principal asked students to pledge not to participate in demonstrations and demanded that they return to school or be expelled. On 16 October 1961 more than one hundred students arrived at the school to turn in their books. SNCC workers then opened the Nonviolent High of Pike County, where the students took classes until the SNCC workers were tried, convicted, and jailed for several months. St. Paul United Methodist Church and the Masonic Temple housed the freedom school until the students began attending Campbell Junior College in Jackson.

Despite pleas from the US Justice Department not to send any more workers to McComb because of dangerous levels of violence, SNCC returned to McComb in the fall of 1963 for a Freedom Vote campaign, and in 1964 the Council of Federated Organizations (COFO) selected McComb as one of its Freedom Summer sites. Movement workers often met in the Summit Street District, an area of African American businesses, at Holmes Pool Hall and Holmes Chicken Shack, and SNCC established a freedom house complex. McComb residents formed housing and food committees to support COFO workers and to buy a plot of land for the Martin Luther King Memorial Center, a community center that still operates today.

White resistance intensified over the Freedom Summer. McComb's mayor, Gordon Burt Jr., served as county chair for the Citizens' Council, and police chief George Guy led a local branch of the Americans for the Preservation of the White Race. Numerous black homes and businesses were bombed, with targets chosen without regard for whether their owners supported the movement.

The first Freedom Day occurred in mid-August 1964, just a week after the Klan burned crosses in front of the homes of two white movement supporters. Libby Price, a white woman who opened her home to movement activists and helped set up the freedom house, was threatened so often that she moved to Jackson, and Red and Malva Heffner, whose daughter was the reigning Miss Mississippi, were harassed to the point that they also left McComb.

With the escalation in violence, black residents often took turns guarding each other's houses at night, and churches temporarily closed their doors to the movement. Aylene Quin opened her restaurant in the Summit Street District so that business leaders could meet secretly with COFO workers. On 30 August 1964 her café was raided by police, and when a bomb exploded at her home on 20 September, local police claimed that she had done it herself. The bombing occurred while Quin's two young children slept, and black residents armed themselves and waited at Quin's home until she returned from a Mississippi Freedom Democratic Party meeting in Jackson. COFO and SNCC workers, including Joe Martin, frantically worked to defuse the situation, but over the next several days, police jailed numerous black residents and movement workers. Twenty-four people ultimately were charged with "criminal syndicalism."

Quin, Matti Dillon, and Ora Bryant went to the White House to report to Pres. Lyndon Johnson about conditions in McComb and to request that he send federal troops. Putting McComb into the national media, they held a press conference and met with several members of Congress. In October the *New York Times* published an editorial describing the violence and stigmatizing the town. With his town in the national spotlight, Oliver Emmerich, the editor of the *McComb Enterprise-Journal*, finally broke white McComb's silence, publishing an editorial on the negative effects of white terrorism, and he and several other white residents met with the Justice Department officials. The committee recommended that prominent white citizens sign a statement calling for law and order.

When news of the statement circulated, the head of Mississippi's highway patrol, T. B. Birdsong, met with Gov. Paul Johnson, Pike County district attorney Joseph Pigott, and all of the McComb and Pike County elected officials. After Johnson threatened to bring in the National Guard before federal troops could arrive, local officials promised to defuse the situation. In less than twenty-four hours the first Klansmen suspected of bombings were arrested, and within a week eleven men were in custody on charges of attempted arson and bombing. In late October, however, the charges were dropped, and the same day that the bombers were released, thirteen COFO workers were arrested on charges of operating a food-handling establishment without a permit. In addition, opponents of the movement vandalized the *McComb Enterprise-Journal*'s office and burned a cross in Emmerich's front yard.

On 18 November 1964 the *Enterprise-Journal* published the statement by McComb's white residents and the state NAACP tested the new Civil Rights Act. With local and state police as well as FBI agents watching, Charles Evers led a group of twenty activists that included Bryant, Ernest Nobles, and several other black McComb residents that desegregated McComb's Holiday Inn, Continental Motel, Palace Theater, Trailways Bus Station, and Woolworth's lunch counter.

While white residents and FBI agents thought the McComb movement would be over by the end of 1964, numerous SNCC workers stayed, and local people remained active. In 2006 McComb High School hosted "McComb Legacies: Reclaiming Our Past for a Brighter Future: A Civil Rights Summit Honoring C. C. Bryant." Involving the William Winter Institute for Racial Reconciliation and members of the McComb community, the McComb Legacies program has gone on to provide "middle and high school youth with the opportunity to learn about, document, and share their local civil rights movement and labor history." The project's activities have included compiling oral histories of the movement, developing a civil rights driving tour, and creating a website.

Amy Schmidt
Lyon College

Clayborne Carson, *In Struggle: SNCC and the Black Awakening of the 1960s* (1981); John Dittmer, *Local People: The Struggle for Civil Rights in Mississippi* (1994); McComb Legacies website, www.mccomblegacies.org; Charles M. Payne, *I've Got the Light of Freedom: The Organizing Tradition and the Mississippi Freedom Struggle* (1995); Howard Zinn, *SNCC: The New Abolitionists* (2002).

McCrady, John
(1911–1968) Artist

Artist John McCrady was born in the rectory of Grace Episcopal Church in Canton, Mississippi, on 11 September 1911, the seventh child of Rev. Edward McCrady and Mary Tucker McCrady. The family moved to Greenwood and then to Hammond and Lake Charles, Louisiana, before settling in Oxford, where Rev. McCrady assumed the rectorship at St. Peter's Episcopal Church and served as head of the philosophy department at the University of Mississippi. John graduated from University High in 1930 after starring on the football team and occasionally contributing illustrations to the school newspaper. His nascent artistic talent was further evident at the University of Mississippi, where he illustrated sections of the school's 1931 and 1932 yearbooks.

McCrady left the University of Mississippi after his sophomore year to attend the New Orleans Art School but soon moved to New York after winning a one-year scholarship to the prestigious Art Students League. He studied with Kenneth Hays Miller and Thomas Hart Benton, two luminaries of the American Scene, a popular arts movement emphasizing native scenes and regional subject matter. However, McCrady felt uninspired by his urban surroundings and ultimately realized that his artistic muse would be the South—specifically, Oxford and the surrounding Lafayette County countryside. He returned to New Orleans in 1934.

Working in his French Quarter studio, McCrady began painting evocative representations of rural life, colorful scenes of the Oxford square, and detailed renderings of the town's vernacular architecture. Although he spent only four years in North Mississippi, he made the region the subject of nearly fifty works over his thirty-five-year career. McCrady was particularly drawn to Lafayette County's African American residents, whom he depicted in an affectionate yet often caricatured manner.

Early in his career, McCrady supplemented his meager income via the Works Progress Administration's Federal Art Project. He had his first one-man show in Philadelphia in 1936; a solo exhibition in New York came the following year. The shows brought him national recognition in *Newsweek*, *Time*, *Life*, and the *New Republic*. In 1938 he married Mary Basso, a former classmate of McCrady's at the New Orleans Art School and sister of author and Faulkner cohort Hamilton Basso. Within three years the couple had their only child, Mary Tucker McCrady.

In 1939 McCrady received a Guggenheim fellowship to document black cultural and religious life in the South. Guided by his ecclesiastical upbringing, the artist was drawn to black spirituals and religious narratives, making them the subject of several paintings from this period. One such work, *Judgment Day*, was included in a 1941 Carnegie Institute exhibit in Philadelphia and a show at the Corcoran Gallery of Art in Washington, D.C.

When the United States entered World War II, McCrady illustrated government propaganda posters and designed tools for a New Orleans manufacturer of military seaplanes. In August 1942 the success of the evening art classes he held for his coworkers at the seaplane plant led him to establish the John McCrady Art School, where many recognized Louisiana artists began their careers. It remained in operation until 1983.

As abstract, European-influenced idioms gained artistic popularity and racial inequalities were less openly tolerated, McCrady's unassuming regional aesthetic and often caricatured depictions of African Americans appeared increasingly provincial and outmoded. Thus, when McCrady exhibited his work in New York in 1946, the American Communist Party's *Daily Worker* called the show a "flagrant example of racial chauvinism." McCrady reeled from the criticism and nearly ceased painting until the National Institute of Arts and Letters awarded him a 1949 grant in recognition of his "warm poetic vision of life in the South."

For the next two decades, McCrady focused on teaching, though he continued to depict his beloved Oxford and Lafayette County in numerous easel paintings as well as in a large triptych, *The Square*, *The Courthouse*, and *The Campus*. McCrady's works are held by the Mississippi Museum of Art in Jackson, the New Orleans Museum of Art, the St. Louis Art Museum, the San Francisco Museum of Modern Art, and many private collections in Mississippi and Louisiana. He died on 24 December 1968 in New Orleans.

Teresa Parker Farris
Tulane University

Patti Carr Black, *Art in Mississippi, 1720–1980* (1998); Robert L. Gambone, *Art and Popular Religion in Evangelical America, 1915–1940* (1989); *Life* (October 1937); Keith Marshall, *John McCrady, 1911–1968* (1975); Matthew Martinez, *Louisiana Cultural Vistas* (Winter 1992); Tom Payne, *Oxford American* (February 1995); Patricia Phagan, *The American Scene and the South: Paintings and Works on Paper, 1930–1946* (1996); Stark Young, *New Republic* (November 1937).

McDew, Chuck
(b. 1938) Activist

Born on 23 June 1938 in Massillon, Ohio, Charles Frederick McDew moved to the South when he enrolled at South Carolina State College in Orangeburg. During his first semester, he was arrested several times for failing to comply with Jim Crow laws, and he converted to Judaism after being denied admittance to a white Christian church. Inspired by the sit-ins in Greensboro, North Carolina, he began leading a local sit-in movement.

In April 1960 McDew helped found the Student Nonviolent Coordinating Committee (SNCC). The following year SNCC activists met in Atlanta for the organization's second conference and decided to take a more active role in the struggle for civil rights. McDew was elected SNCC's chair, a position he held until 1964, during which time he inaugurated the practice of hiring field secretaries to go into communities to establish local leadership and register African American voters.

To register voters and desegregate public facilities throughout the South, SNCC members turned their attention to Mississippi. McDew traveled across the state to register voters, working in Greenwood, Natchez, and McComb, among other communities. In 1961 McDew participated in a student-led march to McComb's city hall, protesting Brenda Travis's expulsion from high school and the murder of Herbert Lee. Along with other protesters, McDew was beaten and arrested for breach of the peace and for contributing to the delinquency of minors. While out on bond, McDew and other SNCC organizers set up the Nonviolent High of Pike County, where he taught history to students who were boycotting the public high school. The new school closed when the SNCC organizers went on trial, and McDew and others were convicted and sentenced to between four and six months in jail.

In 1962 McDew and Bob Zellner, another SNCC worker, left McComb to visit Dion Diamond, a Freedom Rider who was in jail in East Baton Rouge, Louisiana. McDew and Zellner were arrested and kept in isolation for four weeks. Though initially they were not told the charges against them, they were later accused of criminal anarchy. The charges ultimately were dropped.

Acutely aware of the violence and injustice civil rights workers and local residents were facing, McDew repeatedly requested federal intervention in Mississippi to protect workers and citizens trying to register to vote as well as US Justice Department investigations of murders and attacks on civil rights workers.

McDew subsequently returned to school, receiving a bachelor's degree from Chicago's Roosevelt University in 1964. Between 1965 and 1980 he served as the director of community service organizations in Washington, D.C.; Cambridge, Massachusetts; Jacksonville, Florida; and Minneapolis. He has also taught civil rights and African American history at Metropolitan State University in Minneapolis and served as a guest lecturer at Harvard University, Stanford University, the University of Virginia, and numerous historically black colleges and universities.

Amy Schmidt
Lyon College

Raymond Arsenault, *Freedom Riders: 1961 and the Struggle for Racial Justice* (2006); Charles McDew website, charlesmcdew.com; Clayborne Carson, *In Struggle: SNCC and the Black Awakening of the 1960s* (1981); John Dittmer, *Local People: The Struggle for Civil Rights in Mississippi* (1994); Charles M. Payne, *I've Got the Light of Freedom: The Organizing Tradition and the Mississippi Freedom Struggle* (1995); Howard Zinn, *SNCC: The New Abolitionists* (2002).

McDonald, James L.
(1801–1830) Choctaw Negotiator

The short life of James L. McDonald, a Choctaw negotiator in the 1820s and early 1830s and the "first Indian lawyer," illustrates the options Choctaws faced in the period leading to Removal.

McDonald was born in the Choctaw tribal homeland in Mississippi in 1801. Very little is known about his father, a European, and mother, a Choctaw trader and landowner. McDonald's mother sought to educate her son to be a tribal leader, first enrolling him in a local Quaker-run mission school and later sending him to Baltimore, where he studied under Philip E. Thomas of the Baltimore Yearly Meeting. Thomas wrote to the Department of War about McDonald's potential as a tool for Indian Removal, and Thomas McKenney, a Quaker and US government official, provided McDonald with lodging and employment at a dry goods store under the supervision of the Indian Office after his 1818 graduation. McKenney became so impressed with McDonald that he convinced secretary of war John C. Calhoun to obtain federal funds to further the youth's education. While McDonald worked for the US government, he attended school during holidays and studied Greek, Latin, philosophy, business, surveying, and science.

When pressured by McKenney and Calhoun to earn a degree in law, science, or theology, McDonald expressed his desire to return to Choctaw territory, where he might farm and live near his mother. However, he also noted his fear that he would relapse into "savagism." Beginning in 1821 McDonald studied law under Ohio Supreme Court justice John McLean, a close friend of Calhoun. McDonald gained admittance to the Ohio bar in 1823. Calhoun and McKenney subsequently attempted to convince McDonald to help the federal government persuade Choctaws to remove or assimilate. Instead, McDonald returned to Choctaw territory, where he became the first Choctaw lawyer and a strong opponent of Removal.

In 1824 the three principal chiefs of the Choctaw Nation, Pushmataha, Mushulatubbee, and Apukshunnubbee, organized the Choctaw Delegation to negotiate a treaty with the president. McDonald and his friend, David Folsom, served as the principal negotiators. When the treaty was completed in 1825, McDonald had used his education, knowledge of surveying, and relationships with Calhoun and McKenney to protect mission schools, obtain high annuity payments, and relinquish Choctaw debts while retaining land in Mississippi.

McDonald supported schools and acculturation, but he opposed assimilation into white society. His experiences during the negotiations and the harsh treatment he received from Calhoun convinced him that Removal was the only option for Choctaw survival, and he signed the 1830 Treaty of Dancing Rabbit Creek. He remained in Mississippi and fell in love with a white woman, who refused to marry him because he was an Indian. Apparently depressed and suffering from alcoholism, McDonald committed suicide in September 1831.

Cole Cheek
Spartanburg Methodist College

John C. Calhoun, *The Papers of John C. Calhoun*, ed. W. Edwin Hemphill, vols. 4, 9 (1969, 1976); James Taylor Carson, *Searching for the Bright Path: The Mississippi Choctaws from Prehistory to Removal* (1999); Gary Coleman Cheek Jr., "Cultural Flexibility: Assimilation, Education, and the Evolution of Choctaw Identity in the Age of Transformation, 1800–1830" (master's thesis, Mississippi State University, 2005); Frederick E. Hoxie, *This Indian Country: American Indian Activists and the Place They Made* (2013); Clara Sue Kidwell, *Choctaws and Missionaries in Mississippi, 1818–1918* (1995).

McDowell, Mississippi Fred
(1904–1972) Blues Musician

Mississippi Fred McDowell is widely viewed by blues aficionados as the most talented artist of his generation to be "discovered" during the blues revival of the late 1950s and 1960s. Despite his nickname, McDowell was a native of Tennessee, born in Rossville on 12 January 1904. He began playing guitar as a teenager and recalled that his main influences in Rossville were Raymond Payne, a native of Mount Pleasant, Mississippi, who taught McDowell to play in the open G or "Spanish" tuning, and an uncle who played guitar with a slide made from a dried steak bone. McDowell subsequently developed his own distinctive and influential slide technique using a pocketknife.

In Rossville, McDowell worked on his father's small farm and performed at Saturday night fish fries and country dances. At around age twenty-one he moved to Memphis, where his jobs included building rail cars, stacking logs, and working at an oil mill and a dairy. McDowell traveled around Mississippi in the late 1920s, learning "Pea Vine Special" and other songs directly from blues pioneer Charley Patton while visiting the Cleveland area. McDowell moved to Como around 1940 and performed widely around the region until his music reached a broader audience after he was recorded by folklorist Alan Lomax in 1959. McDowell features prominently on a four-volume set of Lomax's field recordings, *Sounds of the South* (1960).

M

McDowell began performing on the festival and coffee-house circuits, often receiving equal billing with other rediscovered blues artists who had been documented during the heyday of country blues recording in the late 1920s and early 1930s. Managed by Dick Waterman, McDowell appeared at many prominent venues, including the Newport Folk Festival in 1964. The following year he toured Europe with the American Folk Blues Festival tour.

Throughout the 1960s McDowell recorded widely in a variety of contexts. Albums on the Arhoolie and Testament labels feature McDowell performing with his wife, Annie Mae. Another Testament LP, *Amazing Grace*, features religious songs with McDowell accompanied by a group from his church, the Hunter's Chapel Singers. Field recordings by George Mitchell feature McDowell with harmonica player Johnny Woods, and on the 1968 LP *Levee Camp Blues*, producer Pete Welding captured songs McDowell performed in his youth. One of the most popular of McDowell's many recordings was *I Do Not Play No Rock and Roll* (1969). The album, recorded at the Malaco Records studio in Jackson and issued by Capitol Records, featured McDowell on electric guitar with a rhythm section and extended monologues on various topics.

McDowell's slide guitar playing had already influenced young white artists, most notably Bonnie Raitt, and in 1971 the Rolling Stones covered McDowell's version of the gospel standard "You've Got to Move" on *Sticky Fingers*. In the 1990s and 2000s his North Mississippi Hill Country blues style was popularized by his student R. L. Burnside and younger interpreters including the North Mississippi Allstars.

McDowell died of cancer in Memphis on 3 July 1972.

Scott Barretta
Greenwood, Mississippi

Mississippi Fred McDowell, interview by Pete Welding, *Blues Unlimited* (July–August 1965); Tom Pomposello, *Mississippi Fred McDowell* (1995), liner notes; Pete Welding, *Levee Camp Blues* (1998), liner notes; Joe York and Scott Barretta, *Shake 'em on Down* (2016).

McGee, Willie
(1915–1951)

Just minutes after midnight on 8 May 1951, Willie McGee, an African American laborer, was executed in the Jones County courtroom where he had been convicted of raping a white woman more than five years earlier. Fifty witnesses watched as McGee was strapped down and killed in an electric chair placed in front of the jury box, while five hundred white men, women, and children celebrated on the courthouse lawn. The execution brought to an end an international campaign to free McGee on the grounds that his conviction was racist and grossly irregular. The case proved an embarrassment to the United States, which was growing increasingly concerned about its image abroad.

McGee was arrested in November 1945 after Laurel housewife Willette Hawkins accused him of crawling through an open window and raping her as she lay next to her sick child while her husband and two other children slept in nearby rooms. After more than a month in confinement, McGee confessed and was quickly tried, convicted, and sentenced to death. The members of all-white jury took less than three minutes to reach their decision. The Mississippi Supreme Court reversed the trial court's decision on the grounds that McGee was not provided a change of venue despite the constant presence of mobs and numerous attempts to intimidate defense lawyers.

A second trial the following year was moved to Hattiesburg, but McGee was again found guilty after the jury deliberated for a mere eleven minutes. He was convicted largely on the strength of a confession that he had allegedly written shortly after his arrest, though prosecutors had failed to introduce that confession during the first trial. The Mississippi Supreme Court again overturned the decision and returned the case to the lower court because African Americans had been excluded from the jury pool.

During a third trial in 1948, lawyers affiliated with the Civil Rights Congress (CRC), a legal defense organization with ties to the Communist Party, put McGee on the witness stand, where he testified that he had been tortured into confessing. Feeling threatened by the increasingly restless mobs that milled about the courthouse during the trial, the CRC attorneys fled Mississippi without offering a closing argument, and the jury again found McGee guilty. The state Supreme Court upheld this decision, and the US Supreme Court rejected several appeals over the next three years.

Following the third trial, the CRC increased its efforts to build an international defense campaign on McGee's behalf. The organization argued against the racist application of the rape law, under which no Mississippi white man had been executed, and alleged that Hawkins and McGee had been involved in a romantic relationship until McGee's threats to end the affair drove Hawkins to charge rape. The CRC also arranged for delegations of supporters to travel to Mississippi to lobby the governor and flooded the offices of other state officials with petitions demanding justice. A CRC-sponsored rally at the State Capitol ended in the arrests of more than forty protesters. Outside Mississippi, one thousand Chevrolet workers in Flint, Michigan, held a prayer meeting for McGee; in addition, thousands of black workers from the docks of New Orleans, the meatpacking plants of Chicago, and the clothing factories of New York organized mass protests, engaged in work stoppages, and donated money to the campaign to "Save Willie McGee." In France, Jean Cocteau, Jean-Paul Sartre, Albert Camus, and Richard Wright organized a demonstration on McGee's behalf, and various foreign governments sent letters of protest to Pres. Harry S. Truman. None of these efforts, including several last-minute appeals to the US Supreme Court and an ongoing vigil in front of the White House, saved Willie McGee.

While some Mississippi segregationists boosted their political careers by pandering to the fear and outrage among the state's white voters, McGee's highly publicized trials and execution complicated American efforts to appeal to nonaligned nations in Asia and Africa. The US Department of State closely monitored world reaction to the case, and the 1952 Republican nominee for vice president, Richard Nixon, recounted that while traveling in Switzerland his car had been pasted with bumper stickers protesting "the legalized lynching of Willie McGee." Nixon complained that the incident provided evidence that southern racism undermined the American case for democracy.

Kieran W. Taylor
The Citadel

Charles Grutzner, *New York Times* (20 October 1952); Alex Heard, *The Eyes of Willie McGee: A Tragedy of Race, Sex, and Secrets in the Jim Crow South* (2010): Gerald Horne, *Communist Front?: The Civil Rights Congress, 1946–1956* (1987); Charles H. Martin, *Georgia Historical Quarterly* (Spring 1987); Craig Zaim, *Journal of Mississippi History* (Fall 2003).

McGhee, Laura
(1907–1984) Activist

Laura McGhee, born on 5 March 1907, and her three sons represented the kind of activists who proved crucial to the civil rights movement in Mississippi. In the 1950s and 1960s, the widowed McGhee owned a fifty-eight-acre farm outside Greenwood in the Browning Community, and she welcomed workers from the Student Nonviolent Coordinating Committee (SNCC) to stay and to hold rallies. Throughout the 1960s McGhee was the matriarch of a determined family that fought discrimination in Leflore County, especially during the 1964 Freedom Summer Project. McGhee instilled a fierce sense of responsibility and self-worth in her children, and the family tested the applicability of the 1964 Civil Rights Act and won notoriety for its boldness.

McGhee's sons—Silas, who later became a member of SNCC's national executive committee; Jake, a future officer in

the National Association for the Advancement of Colored People and member of the Mississippi Freedom Democratic Party; and Clarence, a paratrooper—took on segregation as individuals and as a group. In 1964 Silas, a high school senior, attempted to integrate Greenwood's all-white movie theater, but a crowd assaulted him. In July 1964 three Klansmen kidnapped and beat Silas, an incident that led to the first arrests under the 1964 Civil Rights Act. Silas and Jake returned to the Leflore Theater seven more times to desegregate it. During one effort a mob attacked and injured the brothers, and when FBI agents failed to rescue them in the hospital, Clarence, who was home on leave, arrived with armed protection. By August 1964 white authorities arrested all the McGhees on a variety of minor criminal charges, and on 16 August gunmen shot and wounded Silas for leading sit-ins at local restaurants. The shooting stimulated the first daytime demonstrations and youth marches in Greenwood.

Laura McGhee became famous among activists for her refusal to be cowed by intimidation and violence. McGhee came into the movement after the 1955 shooting of her brother, Gus Courts, a Belzoni activist. During the 1960s the McGhee farm became a center where African Americans and activists received lessons in self-defense and voter registration techniques. McGhee demanded respect from whites and rejected what she considered illegitimate authority. In a life of struggle against night riders, firebombings, discrimination, and people who wanted her land, McGhee resisted aggressors by any means available. She kept a rifle inside the front door to defend the family and warned the local sheriff that if he failed to stop drive-by shootings on her home, he would pick up dead bodies the next time she called. She also beat up a policeman during a demonstration in Greenwood and struck an officer who arrested one of her sons. McGhee also served as one of Leflore County's eight delegates at the 1964 Mississippi Freedom Democratic Party state convention in Jackson. The family earned the respect of many movement activists for fighting discrimination with or without outside help. The McGhees, in the words of historian Charles M. Payne, "out-SNCCed SNCC."

She died on 30 April 1984.

William P. Hustwit
Birmingham Southern University

Clayborne Carson, *In Struggle: SNCC and the Black Awakening of the 1960s* (1981); John Dittmer, *Local People: the Struggle for Civil Rights in Mississippi* (1994); Charles M. Payne, *I've Got the Light of Freedom: The Organizing Tradition and the Mississippi Freedom Struggle* (1995); Townsend Davis, *Weary Feet, Rested Souls: A Guided History of the Civil Rights Movement* (1997); Taylor Branch, *Pillar of Fire: America in the King Years, 1963–1968* (1998).

M

McLaurin, Anselm Joseph

(1848–1909) Thirty-Fourth Governor, 1896–1900

Anselm McLaurin, the oldest of eight brothers and the father of ten children, was the last Confederate veteran elected governor of Mississippi.

McLaurin was born in Rankin County on 26 March 1848 and enlisted in the 3rd Mississippi Artillery at the age of sixteen, becoming a captain. After the war ended, he resumed his education at the Summerville Institute and studied law. After being admitted to the bar in 1868, he opened a practice in Raleigh, Mississippi, in Smith County. In 1871 he was elected district attorney. After serving one term, McLaurin moved back to Brandon and was elected to the state legislature from Rankin County. He and two of his brothers served as delegates to the constitutional convention of 1890, where McLaurin unsuccessfully introduced a measure that would have disfranchised any man convicted of wife abuse.

Following the death of US senator Edward C. Walthall in 1894, McLaurin was appointed to fill the remainder of the term, serving until 3 March 1895. McLaurin then ran for governor, defeating Frank Burkitt, the Populist Party candidate.

When McLaurin took office in 1896, the state treasury was virtually depleted, and he called a special session of the legislature to increase ad valorem taxes and to authorize him to secure a loan to meet the state's financial obligations. He called a second special session of the legislature to consider the construction of a new State Capitol, since the original structure, built in 1839, was in extremely poor condition. The legislature authorized a new building, but McLaurin vetoed the measure because he considered the size and the design of the proposed building unsuitable for the state's needs.

During McLaurin's second year in office, Mississippi suffered a yellow fever epidemic that virtually closed Jackson. Almost 90 percent of the population evacuated the city in the summer of 1898, and McLaurin was forced to move to his home in Brandon and to conduct state business by telephone.

After completing his term as governor, McLaurin was elected to the US Senate in 1900, defeating Congressman John Allen of Tupelo, one of Mississippi's most popular politicians. McLaurin won reelection in 1906 and served until his death at his home in Brandon on 22 December 1909.

David G. Sansing
University of Mississippi

Biographical Directory of the United States Congress (1950); *Mississippi Official and Statistical Register* (1912); Dunbar Rowland, *Encyclopedia of Mississippi History*, vol. 2 (1907).

McLaurin, Charles

(b. 1941) Activist

For five decades, Charles McLaurin has served Sunflower County as a community organizer and a civil rights activist. McLaurin played a prominent role in every major campaign of the civil rights movement in the Mississippi Delta, and he remains active in educational and social projects. McLaurin's history as a foot soldier in the early freedom movements injects the values and the spirit of older civil rights struggles into the continued daily struggle for social and economic justice in impoverished black communities.

Born in 1941 in Jackson, McLaurin heard stories and learned lessons about demanding freedom early in his life. His grandmother had graduated from Tuskegee Institute and owned a restaurant, and McLaurin's grandfather had defied the Ku Klux Klan until night riders ran him out of Mississippi. As a student at Jackson State, McLaurin landed in jail for protesting segregation at the 1961 state fair, and he earned the respect of Medgar Evers and other activists by agreeing to remain in jail until the National Association for the Advancement of Colored People (NAACP) could publicize the case. McLaurin subsequently began attending Student Nonviolent Coordinating Committee (SNCC) meetings.

In the summer of 1962 McLaurin volunteered to lead SNCC's voter registration drive in Ruleville. To ingratiate himself with the small Delta community, McLaurin attended the Williams Missionary Baptist Church and ate Sunday dinners with families. He also sipped whiskey with farm laborers and spent hours on porches and street corners, learning the dynamics of the town. McLaurin earned the trust of Ruleville's blacks, but election officials doggedly resisted the registration of black voters. During the first half of 1963, more than six hundred African Americans traveled from Ruleville to the county seat in Indianola to take the voter registration test; eleven passed.

Two years of painstaking work in Ruleville paid off across Sunflower County during the Freedom Summer Project of 1964. McLaurin had learned in Ruleville that students made the most eager and effective canvassers. Teenagers formed enthusiastic and enduring cores around which older blacks with mortgages and jobs to lose could rally as the community's confidence increased. When McLaurin took this tactic directly to Indianola during Freedom Summer, residents broke the planters' hegemony and developed an alternative worldview of defiance and self-determination. This new spirit infused the Mississippi Freedom Democratic Party (MFDP), which directly assailed the source of white power by challenging one-party rule. McLaurin served as the manager of Fannie Lou Hamer's 1964 congressional campaign and later ran for a State Senate seat. The MFDP candidates did not win elections, but their campaigns nourished the political consciousness of local people and dispelled segregationist claims that blacks lacked the interest or the knowledge to vote and hold office.

In the Delta, McLaurin experienced police brutality, spent untold hours and nights in jail, and endured taunts, degradation, and threats on a daily basis. But no Jim Crow policemen ever beat the thirst for freedom or the love of Sunflower County's people out of McLaurin. To the amazement of white leaders such as Ruleville mayor Charles Dorrough, who in 1965 predicted that McLaurin would "make some money . . . and move out of the Negro neighborhood," the activist graduated from Mississippi Valley State and settled in Indianola.

With the exception of a brief period in the 1980s, McLaurin has remained in Indianola. Today, he speaks about Hamer and other old friends, guides tours of civil rights movement sites, and works with the Sunflower County Freedom Project.

Thomas John Carey
University of Mississippi

J. Todd Moye, *Let the People Decide: Black Freedom and White Resistance Movements in Sunflower County, Mississippi, 1945–1986* (2004); Tracy Sugarman, *Stranger at the Gates: A Summer in Mississippi* (1966).

McLean, George A.
(1904–1983) Journalist

George A. McLean was an educator, sociologist, and journalist who took a bankrupt Tupelo newspaper and turned it into the largest-circulation newspaper in the nation for a city its size. He then used the newspaper's profits to fund projects that became a national model for economic development.

Born in Winona on 30 July 1904, McLean graduated from the University of Mississippi and went on to receive his master's degree in religion from Boston University in 1928. He also did graduate work in psychology and sociology at Stanford University and the University of Chicago.

In 1934 McLean found himself out of work after being fired as a sociology and education instructor at Memphis's Southwestern College (now Rhodes College) for helping to organize the interracial Southern Tenant Farmers' Union in neighboring Arkansas. That same year he used some of his family's money to buy "a bankrupt biweekly from a bankrupt bank in the middle of a Depression." At the time, the *Tupelo Journal* had fewer than five hundred paying subscribers. With no background in journalism or newspaper management,

McLean quickly turned the newspaper around so that it began to show a profit. On 1 June 1936 it became the *Tupelo Daily Journal*. McLean funneled the paper's profits back into the community through a series of economic development projects.

One of the first was the promotion of dairy farming, calling on local businesses to fund the purchase of cattle and start an insemination program that allowed those merchants to recoup their investments many times over while providing farmers with a steady income. McLean saw Tupelo and the surrounding Lee County area as a grand experiment in social reconstruction and economic diversification. On 6 April 1936, just a day after a tornado leveled most of the town and killed 230, McLean declared in an editorial, "Tupelo will build on this wreckage a better and greater city."

Another of his early efforts was the formation of rural community development councils in Lee and surrounding counties. The councils initiated local community development projects and sought to erase the divide between rural areas and towns and cities. With the local economy based almost exclusively on agriculture, McLean saw the need to find new avenues for both income and employment. The US Department of Agriculture adopted the community development council idea as a nationwide model for rural development in the 1950s.

Community leaders did not always appreciate McLean's efforts. In 1937 he and his newspaper sided with striking workers at the Tupelo Cotton Mill who were seeking an increase in their ten-dollar weekly salaries and a reduction in working hours from forty-six to forty. According to sociologist Vaughn Grisham, the first director of the George McLean Institute for Community Development at the University of Mississippi, this stance "rankled industrialists across the state by accusing them of betraying Mississippi's workers." The feud caused a marked divide within the community but earned McLean recognition as *Nation* magazine's Man of the Year. With the outbreak of World War II, the rift healed, and McLean put his personal involvement in his experiment on hold while serving in the US Navy.

After returning home, McLean resumed his efforts to diversify the local economy and create a regional identity. In 1948 he was one of the organizers of the Community Development Foundation, which promoted industrialization over agriculture and became a nationwide model for economic development. During the civil rights era, McLean's promotion of the community as a whole—rural and urban, black and white—helped the region survive integration with no major conflicts.

In the 1970s McLean put up one million dollars of his and the *Journal*'s money to fund teachers' aides in all first- and second-grade classes in Lee County's public schools. The program sought to raise students' reading levels, and the Mississippi legislature later adopted the idea statewide. In 1973 McLean gave his newspaper to his nonprofit foundation, Christian, Research, Education, Action, Technical,

Enterprises (CREATE), which became the sole stockholder in what is now the *Northeast Mississippi Daily Journal*. As McLean stipulated, a portion of the foundation's dividends is used for early childhood development and education, job training, and "the conscious, planned development of competent, unselfish leaders."

McLean received many national honors for his work. *Progressive Farmer* named him its Man of the Year in 1948, and he was the first recipient of the Tennessee Valley Authority's Distinguished Citizen Award and of the University of Mississippi Journalism Department's Silver Em award for outstanding journalistic achievement. McLean also served as a lay pastor at Tupelo's First Presbyterian Church for many years.

McLean died on 1 March 1983 in Tupelo of complications from a stroke. His widow, former schoolteacher Anna Keirsey Rosamond McLean, a native of Paragould, Arkansas, continued as owner and publisher of the *Daily Journal* until her death in 2000.

Marty Russell
University of Mississippi

Danny Duncan Collum, *Sojourners Magazine* (October 2004); Sandy Grisham, George McLean Institute for Community Development website, www.mcleancommunitydev.org; Vaughn L. Grisham Jr., *Tupelo: The Evolution of a Community* (1999); Phyllis Harper, *Northeast Mississippi Daily Journal* (21 May 1995); *New York Times* (2 March 1983); Joe Rutherford, *Northeast Mississippi Daily Journal* (21 May 1995).

McLemore, Leslie Burl

(b. 1940) Activist and Scholar

Leslie Burl McLemore, political scientist, civil rights activist, director of the Fannie Lou Hamer National Institute on Citizenship and Democracy at Jackson State University, and Jackson City Council president, has deliberately integrated the theory and practice of political change into his personal and professional lives. Born in Walls, Mississippi, on 17 August 1940 to Christine Williams McLemore and Burl McLemore, he attributes his earliest political consciousness to the influence of his maternal grandfather, Leslie Williams, a store owner. While growing up in the Jim Crow South, McLemore observed the influence Williams's political acumen gave him within the white community. During McLemore's years at Rust College in Holly Springs, where he earned a bachelor's degree in social science and economics, he was the founding president of the college chapter of the

National Association for the Advancement of Colored People. In 1962, after leading local demonstrations for integration and access to the ballot, McLemore became involved with the Student Nonviolent Coordinating Committee, working on voter registration campaigns in Benton, Marshall, Tate, and DeSoto Counties. As the northern regional coordinator for the 1963 Freedom Vote campaign, he was named to the executive committee of the Mississippi Freedom Democratic Party. McLemore also served as a delegate to the Democratic National Convention in Atlantic City, where the Freedom Democratic Party challenged the seating of the all-white delegation from the Mississippi Democratic Party.

McLemore earned a master's degree in political science from Atlanta University and a doctorate in government from the University of Massachusetts at Amherst, where his dissertation, "The Mississippi Freedom Democratic Party: A Case Study of Grass-Roots Politics," was the first formal study of the impact and influence of this local political movement. After postdoctoral work at Johns Hopkins University and Harvard University, McLemore moved into an academic career, teaching first at Southern University and then in 1971 moving to Jackson State University, where he founded the political science department. McLemore served as president of the Council of Historically Black Graduate Schools and as the dean of Jackson State's Graduate School and founding director of the school's Office of Research Administration.

As an academic, he focused his research on southern black electoral politics and held leadership roles in the National Conference of Black Political Scientists and the Southern Political Science Association. Throughout his life McLemore has maintained his interest in the potential impact of political engagement in making substantive change. As he has noted, "We've done these great things as a people and as a country, but we are so inconsistent. Obviously, democracy is always evolving. One would hope that, a year from now, two years from now, five years from now, this democratic system we know now will be even better." In support of this philosophy, McLemore has mentored young people through the Jackson Chapter of 100 Black Men. In 1997 McLemore and some academic colleagues founded the Fannie Lou Hamer National Institute on Citizenship and Democracy, which hosts workshops, programs, seminars, and tours focusing on the civil rights movement and the creation of engaged, active citizens. The Hamer Institute works to engage schoolchildren, community members, teachers, and college faculty more directly in the work of democracy.

McLemore ran unsuccessfully for the US Congress from Mississippi's 4th Congressional District in 1980. In 1999 he won a special election to fill a vacant seat on the Jackson City Council. He remained on the council for the next decade, holding the post of council president for five years and serving as the city's acting mayor for two months in 2009 following the death of Frank Melton. McLemore has served on the board of the Mississippi Municipal League, as chair of the Leadership Training Council of the National League of Cities, and as interim president of Jackson State University. He retired from politics and teaching in 2009 to focus on his work with the Hamer Institute and on mentoring.

Michelle D. Deardorff
Jackson State University

Michelle D. Deardorff, Jeff Kolnick, T. R. M. Mvusi, and Leslie Burl McLemore, *History Teacher* (November 2004); John Hicks, *Planet Weekly* (3–9 March 2004); Leslie Burl McLemore, in *Black Politics and Political Behavior: A Linkage Analysis*, ed. Hanes Walton Jr. (1994); Leslie Burl McLemore, *Negro Educational Review* 40 (1988); Rachel Reinhard, "Politics of Change: The Emergence of a Black Political Voice in Mississippi" (PhD dissertation, University of California at Berkeley, 2005).

McLemore, Richard Aubrey

(1903–1976)

McLemore, Nannie Pitts

(1900–1980)
Historians

Richard Aubrey McLemore was a historian who taught and served as president at two Mississippi institutions, directed the Mississippi Department of Archives and History, and wrote and edited several important books about Mississippi history. His wife, Nannie Pitts McLemore, coauthored some of those books.

Born in Perry County, Mississippi, on 6 June 1903, Richard McLemore was raised in Petal and graduated from Hattiesburg High School before receiving a bachelor's degree from Mississippi College in 1923 and a master's degree from George Peabody College for Teachers in 1926. Nannie Pitts was born on 21 September 1900 in Harvest, Alabama, and earned a bachelor's degree from Athens College in 1921 and a master's degree from Peabody College in 1927, the same year she married McLemore. Both of the McLemores did graduate work in history at Vanderbilt University, where Richard received his doctorate prior to teaching history at Mississippi Southern College from 1938 to 1955. After serving as the school's acting president for most of 1955, he was president of Mississippi College from 1957 to 1968 and head of the Mississippi Department of Archives and History from 1969 to 1973.

Richard McLemore began his scholarly career with two books on antebellum Franco-American diplomacy. The couple's work in Mississippi led to their interest in the state's history, and in 1945 they coauthored *Mississippi through Four Centuries*, which took a traditional line on topics in southern society and politics.

As director of the Mississippi Department of Archives and History, Richard McLemore made his most important mark on scholarship by editing *A History of Mississippi* (1973), a sprawling, two-volume work of scholarship by more than forty professional and amateur historians. Along with thorough coverage of politics and law, the history covered a wide and impressive range of topics, including religion, industry and labor unions, education, the arts, and medicine. The collection showed a clear effort to adhere to professional standards and to fit Mississippi's history into the celebration of the American bicentennial in 1976. The book, published by the University and College Press of Mississippi in Hattiesburg, had the support of the Mississippi legislature and the state's three major traditionally white universities. Written in the late 1960s and early 1970s in the wake of the civil rights movement, *A History of Mississippi* lacked the celebratory quality of much of the scholarship by white Mississippi authors (including the McLemores three decades earlier). The work included an essay on the civil rights movement by Neil McMillen of the University of Southern Mississippi and a revisionist essay on Reconstruction by David G. Sansing of the University of Mississippi. Still, the book also contained statements such as former governor James P. Coleman's assertion that "for nearly a century the Mississippi Constitution of 1890 has represented a high watermark for government."

Late in their career, the McLemores turned to the history of religion and education. Richard McLemore wrote a thorough history of Baptists in the state and two short histories of individual Baptist churches. After his death on 31 August 1976, Nannie McLemore completed a book he had started, *The History of Mississippi College*. She died on 24 January 1980.

Ted Ownby
University of Mississippi

James B. Lloyd, ed., *Lives of Mississippi Authors, 1817–1967* (1981); Richard Aubrey McLemore, *A History of Mississippi*, 2 vols. (1973); Richard Aubrey McLemore, *A History of Mississippi Baptists, 1780–1970* (1971); Richard Aubrey McLemore and Nannie Pitts McLemore, *The History of Mississippi College* (1979); Richard Aubrey McLemore and Nannie Pitts McLemore, *Mississippi through Four Centuries* (1945); Chester M. Morgan, *Dearly Bought, Deeply Treasured: The University of Southern Mississippi, 1912–1987* (1987).

M

McMillen, Neil R.
(b. 1939) Historian

Neil McMillen taught history at the University of Southern Mississippi from 1969 until his retirement in 2001. A native of Michigan, McMillen earned bachelor's and master's degrees from Southern Miss and returned to teach there after receiving his doctorate from Vanderbilt University. As a teacher, scholar, and editor, he has been a leading figure in the study of Mississippi race relations.

McMillen's first book, based on his 1969 dissertation, was *The Citizens' Council: Organized Resistance to the Second Reconstruction, 1954–1964* (1971), the first scholarly study of its subject. Written while the Council remained a force in Mississippi life, the book was remarkable for its thorough and thoughtful treatment of the white supremacist group.

Among academics, McMillen is best known for his 1989 book, *Dark Journey: Black Mississippians in the Age of Jim Crow*, the winner of the Bancroft Prize for the year's best book in American history and a finalist for the Pulitzer Prize. McMillen introduced the work as "a history of Mississippi's black people, its majority people, and their struggles to achieve autonomy and full citizenship during the critical period of disfranchisement, segregation, and exclusion following 1890." The book, he wrote, attempted to see the Jim Crow system "as black Mississippians saw it," complete with violence, fear, and limited opportunities. Based on a wide and impressive variety of sources, *Dark Journey* begins with racial segregation inside and outside the law, moves to disfranchisement and segregated and poorly funded education, and then details limited economic opportunities and injustice inside the courts and in illegal lynchings. The final two chapters describe two related options: northern migration and the "gathering challenge" of

Neil R. McMillen, 1990 (McCain Library and Archives, University of Southern Mississippi)

nascent forms of protest. Often quoted and cited by academics and frequently assigned in college classes, *Dark Journey* has had extraordinary influence on subsequent scholarship on Mississippi history.

McMillen has continued his work on African Americans in the state into the New Deal and World War II years, in part through his own scholarship and in part by editing works on Mississippi history during World War II. McMillen also has written broadly about American history by updating an older and much respected textbook, *A Synopsis of American History*. In 2005 McMillen won the B. L. C. Wailes Award, the highest honor given by the Mississippi Historical Society.

Ted Ownby
University of Mississippi

Neil McMillen, *Dark Journey: Black Mississippians in the Age of Jim Crow* (1989); University of Southern Mississippi Department of History website, www.usm.edu/history.

McMullan, Margaret
(b. 1960) Author

Margaret McMullan, author and teacher, was born in 1960 in Newton, Mississippi, to Mississippi native James M. McMullan and Austrian-born Madeleine Engel de Janosi. The family, which also included Margaret's older sister, Carlette, lived in Jackson until 1969, when they moved to Lake Forest, Illinois. Her native state is important in McMullan's writing and provides the setting for three of her novels and a collection of stories about the aftermath of Hurricane Katrina, which wrecked her family's historic home in Pass Christian.

McMullan recalls, "When we moved to the Chicago area I was in the fourth grade. My classmates heard my accent and made fun of me. A lot. So I grew very quiet. That's when I started making notes," recording "the weather, my overly dramatic feelings, what people said, everything. Writing became a habit." In high school, her story, "Bees," won a prize from Scholastic Magazines: "I got $50 and a gold pen with my name on it and I was officially hooked."

McMullan earned a bachelor's degree in religious studies from Grinnell College and then spent three years as associate entertainment editor for *Glamour* magazine in New York City. She went on to receive a master of fine arts degree in fiction from the University of Arkansas–Fayetteville. For twenty-five years, she held the Melvin M. Peterson Endowed Chair in Literature and Writing at the University of Evansville in Indiana. McMullan is the author of six novels—*When Warhol Was Still Alive* (1994), *In My Mother's House* (2003), *How I Found the Strong* (2004), *When I Crossed No-Bob* (2007), *Cashay*, (2009), and *Sources of Light* (2010). Her stories and essays have appeared in *Glamour*, the *Chicago Tribune*, *National Geographic for Kids*, *Southern Accents*, *Ploughshares*, and *TriQuarterly* and in anthologies such as *Christmas Stories from the South's Best Writers* and *Tanzania on Tuesday: Writing by American Women Abroad*. Her first story collection, *Aftermath Lounge*, and *Every Father's Daughter*, an anthology she compiled and edited with an introduction by Phillip Lopate, appeared in 2015.

The recipient of the Mississippi Institute of Arts and Letters Fiction Award in 2004 and 2008, a 2010 National Endowment for the Arts Fellowship in literature, a 2010 Fulbright at the University of Pécs in Hungary, and the 2011 Eugene and Marilyn Glick Indiana Authors Award, McMullan has also been recognized with two Pen/Faulkner nominations and awards from the Chicago Public Library, the New York Public Library, the *School Library Journal*, the Mississippi Library Association, and the American Library Association. She now lives in Pass Christian and writes full-time.

Ann J. Abadie
University of Mississippi

Lewis La Plante, *Evansville Living* (September–October 2010); Margaret McMullan, *Montréal Review* (March 2011); Margaret McMullan, website, www.margaretmcmullan.com; National Endowment for the Arts website, www.arts.gov.

McMurry, Lillian Shedd, and Trumpet Records

Lillian McMurry owned the Diamond Record Company and served as producer for its Trumpet label, which strongly influenced the development of modern blues. Lillian Shedd was born into a musical family in Purvis, Mississippi, on 30 December 1921. Her mother, Grace Smith Shedd, was an organist and pianist, while her father, Julius Milton Shedd, was a singer. In addition to performing music at home, Lillian took piano lessons. In the 1940s Lillian moved to Jackson to work at a pharmacy and later as a secretary to the governor. She married Willard F. McMurry, who owned the State Furniture Company and later Record Mart–Furniture Bargains.

Lillian Shedd McMurray (Courtesy Vitrice McMurry)

McMurry moved from selling 78 rpm records out of her husband's store to producing the sound recordings she would sell, founding the Diamond Record Company with her husband in 1951. Diamond's main label was Trumpet, named in reference to the archangel Gabriel, an indicator of Lillian's fondness for gospel music. She also formed Globe Music, which served as the publishing company for Trumpet. With McMurry's musical interests, business skills, and vision, Trumpet became the first label to record blues legends Elmore James and Sonny Boy Williamson II (Aleck Miller), though Williamson had for years been performing live on the *King Biscuit Time* radio show from Helena, Arkansas. Lillian McMurry also recorded blues artists such as Arthur "Big Boy" Crudup, Big Joe Williams, Willie Love, and Jerry "Boogie" McCain. Gospel groups appearing on the label included the St. Andrews Gospelaires, the Southern Sons Gospel Quartette, the Argo Gospel Singers, and the Famous Blue Jay Singers. McMurry also recorded country-rockabilly artists such as Lucky Joe Almond, Werly Fairburn, Jimmy Swan, and Tex and Wally Dean.

Trumpet's biggest commercial success was 1951's "Dust My Broom," by James (credited as Elmo James)—his sole recording for the label. Williamson recorded a number of successful sides for Trumpet, including "Eyesight to the Blind," "Mr. Downchild," "She Brought Life Back to the Dead," "Mighty Long Time," and "Nine below Zero." A young B. B. King played lead guitar behind Williamson on "From the Bottom." Although he had already recorded for Columbia and Bluebird, Williams recorded eight sides for Trumpet in the fall of 1951, including "Mama Don't Allow Me" and "She Left Me a Mule."

Just as Trumpet was achieving success, the label began losing artists to larger companies that could offer more money. Because of this competition, the disbanding of the Southern Sons, trouble with the local musicians' union for recording black and white musicians in the same studio, and financial difficulties, Lillian and Willard McMurry closed down Trumpet in 1956, though Lillian spent many more years fighting companies that had infringed on the label's copyrights. Many Trumpet songs have been reissued by Arhoolie, Acoustic Archives, Alligator, and other record labels. In 1995 Lillian McMurry donated the business files for the Diamond Record Company to the Blues Archive at the University of Mississippi.

Although the Diamond Record Company was short-lived, the Trumpet label was very important to the worlds of southern blues and gospel and to a lesser extent rockabilly. By forming the record label, recognizing and recruiting talented musicians, recording a variety of musical styles, and at times standing up to larger, wealthier companies, Lillian McMurry firmly established herself as a role model for women wishing to get into the business of music. For her work with Trumpet, McMurry was inducted into the Blues Hall of Fame in 1998. She died of a heart attack in Jackson on 18 March 1999.

Greg Johnson
University of Mississippi

Diamond Record Company/Trumpet Records Papers, Blues Archive, Department of Archives and Special Collections, J. D. Williams Library, University of Mississippi; Jeff Hannusch, *Living Blues* (May–June 1999); Marc Ryan, *Trumpet Records: Diamonds on Farish Street* (2004).

McNair, Evander

(1820–1902) Confederate General

Confederate general Evander McNair was born on 15 April 1820 near Laurel Hill, in Richmond County, North Carolina, the son of John E. McNair and Nancy Fletcher McNair. The family moved to Wayne County, Mississippi, when the boy was about a year old and moved again to Simpson County a few years later. After working on the family farm and teaching school, McNair opened the firm of McNair and Company in Jackson in 1843. He enlisted in the 1st Mississippi Rifles, a regiment commanded by Col. Jefferson Davis, when war broke out with Mexico in 1846, rising to the rank of orderly sergeant.

After the war, McNair returned to his store in Jackson until 1856, when he moved to Washington, Arkansas, and opened another store. On 11 August 1859 he married Hannah Merrill, a native of New York who taught at a school for girls.

In 1861 McNair raised a seven-company battalion for the Confederate service. Three more companies were added, the battalion was reorganized as the 4th Arkansas Infantry,

and McNair was elected colonel on 17 August 1861. McNair temporarily commanded his brigade at the Battle of Pea Ridge, Arkansas, on 7–8 March 1862 after the senior officers were killed or wounded.

McNair's regiment was transferred east of the Mississippi to Maj. Gen. Kirby Smith's army to take part in an invasion of Kentucky in late 1862. At the Battle of Richmond, Kentucky, on 30 August, McNair commanded a brigade that contributed greatly to the Confederate victory. After this action, he was promoted to brigadier general. His brigade consisted of Arkansas units and one North Carolina regiment.

McNair's brigade fought at Murfreesboro (31 December 1862–2 January 1863). In May 1863 the unit was transferred to Lt. Gen. Joseph E. Johnston's army in an unsuccessful effort to relieve the Siege of Vicksburg. While with Johnston, McNair's brigade was involved in fighting around Jackson. The brigade was transferred to the command of Gen. Braxton Bragg in time for the Battle of Chickamauga. At that battle, McNair was wounded while his brigade played an important role in Longstreet's breakthrough of the Union lines on 20 September 1863.

After recovering from his wound, McNair was transferred back to the Trans-Mississippi Department in 1864 to command another unit, the 2nd Arkansas Brigade of Brig. Gen. Thomas J. Churchill's Division. The last months of McNair's Confederate service were uneventful. The units of the Trans-Mississippi Department surrendered in May 1865.

After the war, McNair returned to Arkansas, relocated to New Orleans, and then moved to Magnolia. After the death of his wife, McNair moved to Hattiesburg, where he lived until his death on 13 November 1902. He is buried in Magnolia.

David A. Norris
Wilmington, North Carolina

Confederate Veteran (June 1912); William S. Powell, ed., *Dictionary of North Carolina Biography* (6 vols., 1979–96); US War Department, *The War of the Rebellion: A Compilation of the Official Records of the Union and Confederate Armies* (128 vols., 1880–1901); Ezra J. Warner, *Generals in Gray: The Lives of the Confederate Commanders* (1959).

McNair, Steve

(1973–2009) Athlete

One of Mississippi's most heralded quarterbacks, Stephen LaTreal McNair was born in Mount Olive on 14 February 1973, the fourth of Lucille McNair's five children. His father left when he was a young child, and the onus of raising the family was left to Lucille. Following the example of his older brother, Fred, Steve became Mount Olive High School's starting quarterback, leading the team to a state title in 1989.

In 1991 McNair enrolled at Alcorn State University, where Fred had started at quarterback for three years. While Steve had offers to play defensive back at other schools, only Alcorn State offered him the opportunity to play quarterback. Following an injury to the starting quarterback in the season's first game, McNair threw for three touchdowns to lead the squad to a 27–22 upset of Grambling. Over the next four years, McNair put on a show, earning the nickname Air McNair and throwing and running for a combined 16,823 yards to become college football's career yardage leader.

McNair finished third in the balloting for the 1994 Heisman Trophy, and the Houston Oilers selected him with the third pick in the first round of the National Football League draft—at the time the highest selection ever for a black quarterback.

McNair played sporadically during his first two seasons with the Oilers, starting a total of six games. Before the 1997 season the team moved to Nashville, and McNair became the starter at quarterback. After two mediocre years and an injury-shortened 1999 season, McNair and the newly renamed Titans hit their stride in 2000, compiling a 12–3 record and reaching the Super Bowl, where they lost to the St. Louis Rams, 23–16.

McNair played eleven seasons with the Oilers/Titans before being traded to the Baltimore Ravens, for whom he played two more years before retiring in April 2008. Over his career, he threw for 174 touchdowns and ran for 37 more, and he accounted for nearly 35,000 offensive yards. He shared the 2003 Most Valuable Player honors with Peyton Manning and was selected to the Pro Bowl three times.

On 4 July 2009 McNair was killed by his girlfriend as part of a murder-suicide.

P. Huston Ladner
University of Hawai'i at Manoa

Thomas George, *New York Times* (28 September 1994, 22 January 1995); Peter King, *Sports Illustrated* (28 November 1994, 20 February 1995); S. L. Price, *Sports Illustrated* (26 September 1994); Pro Football Reference website, www.pro-football-reference.com.

McNeal, P. Sanders

(b. 1949) Painter

P. Sanders McNeal paints figurative studies, portraits, and still lifes as well as landscapes and murals. Born in Greenwood, Mississippi, in 1949, Sandy McNeal grew up in Green-

Sanders McNeal, 2010 (Courtesy Randall Teasley)

ville and Indianola. She earned a bachelor of fine arts degree from Mississippi University for Women and moved to Jackson in 1962, becoming an important member of the city's art community.

McNeal has studied in New York, France, Italy, and Ireland, honing her skills in classical realism. She is versatile in oil, watercolor, pastel, and pencil, and her paintings portray scenes from Mississippi and beyond. Whether depicting the blue-sky expanse of the Mississippi Delta, a fog- and snow-drenched mountain range in Utah, or the green bog waters of County Kerry, Ireland, McNeal's paintings interact with the natural light of their surroundings. McNeal also paints nonrural subjects: for example, *The Rehearsal* (1997) depicts a musician playing his saxophone in an alleyway, with his long shadow on a wall. The positioning of the saxophonist indicates his enjoyment of performing. His only audience is a small cluster of wildflowers growing in the cracks of the alleyway. Described as a salute to Mississippi's musicians, *The Rehearsal* was commissioned for Jackson's 2002 Jubilee!-JAM and was later featured in the Mississippi Museum of Art's *The Mississippi Story* exhibition.

Sanders's work has been included in numerous exhibitions throughout the United States as well as in France and Ireland. She was commissioned to paint a mural for Union Station in Jackson in 2002, and in 2004 she accepted a commission for a painting, *Au Seuil de la Renaissance* ("At the Threshold of the Renaissance"), commemorating the sixtieth anniversary of the Mississippi Symphony Orchestra. McNeal was also selected as the official artist for the 2006 US International Ballet Competition in Jackson. McNeal's Mississippi-related works also include pastel courtroom drawings she did of the 1994 retrial of Byron De La Beckwith for the murder of civil rights icon Medgar Evers. McNeal received the Governor's Award for Excellence in Visual Arts in 1999 and the Mississippi University for Women's Alumnae Achievement Award in 2005.

Patti Carr Black
Jackson, Mississippi

Patti Carr Black, *Art in Mississippi, 1720–1980* (1998), *The Mississippi Story* (2007); P. Sanders McNeal website, www.sandersmcneal.com.

McNutt, Alexander G.

(1802–1848) Twelfth Governor, 1838–1842, and Author

When Gov. Alexander Gallatin McNutt was inaugurated in January 1838, Mississippi was entering a period of severe economic depression that lasted through both of his two terms. Although as a member of the State Senate McNutt had opposed the bill creating the Union Bank, as governor he signed the bill into law in the hope that the new financial institution could ease Mississippi's depressed economy. Those hopes were dashed, however, when the bank failed in 1839. McNutt was then forced to take a stand on the question of honoring or repudiating the state bonds that had been invested in the earlier Planters Bank as well as those invested in the Union Bank. That question became one of the most volatile political issues in antebellum Mississippi.

Because the state treasury was depleted, McNutt believed that Mississippi had no alternative but to repudiate the bonds. His position prevailed, and the legislature declared that they would not be honored. The repudiation of those bonds remained a political issue until the 1890 constitution prohibited the state from redeeming the bonds.

McNutt had migrated to Mississippi from Rockbridge County, Virginia, where he was born on 3 January 1802. After graduating from Washington College (now Washington and Lee University), McNutt moved to Jackson, where he practiced law briefly before moving to Vicksburg. In 1833 he married Elizabeth Cameron, the wealthy widow of his business partner, and acquired a large plantation along Deer Creek in Warren County. Opponents at times derided him as "Alexander the Great McNutt" and ridiculed his lack of personal courage because he had never fought a duel.

McNutt, a large man, was a gifted speaker and an accomplished though little known humorist who published a number of very popular hunting tales in the New York *Spirit of the Times*, which had forty thousand subscribers and was popular in the Old Southwest. His writings included tales of frontier life, and his characterizations of frontiersmen resembled the better-known *Georgia Scenes* by Augustus Longstreet. Two of McNutt's most famous characters were Chunky and Jem. On one occasion, after whipping a black panther, Chunky boasted, "I walks on water, I out-betters the deer, and when I get hot the Msppi hides itself."

McNutt ran unsuccessfully for the US Senate in 1842. While trying to make a political comeback, he died on the campaign trail at Cockrum's Crossroads in DeSoto County on 22 October 1848. At one time, the Sunflower County seat was McNutt, but when Leflore County was established, the county seat was moved to Greenwood, and the town of McNutt gradually became extinct.

David G. Sansing
University of Mississippi

Bradley G. Bond, *Political Culture in the Nineteenth-Century South: Mississippi, 1830–1900* (1995); *Mississippi Official and Statistical Register* (1912); Dunbar Rowland, *Encyclopedia of Mississippi History*, vol. 2 (1907).

McRae, John J.

(1815–1857) Twenty-First Governor, 1854–1857

Known to his friends and followers as Johnny McRae of Chickasawhay, John J. McRae sailed his steamer *Triumph* up and down the Chickasawhay River "as if it were the Mississippi itself." A contemporary described McRae, a folk hero who was extremely popular with the people of Mississippi, as "bright . . . humorous and fascinating."

McRae was born in Sneedsboro, North Carolina, on 10 January 1815 and was only two years old when his family moved to Winchester, Mississippi, in Wayne County. After graduating from Ohio's Miami University, McRae returned to Paulding, the seat of Jasper County, to practice law. McRae also published the *Eastern Clarion*, the forerunner of the *Jackson Clarion-Ledger*.

McRae was elected to represent Clarke County in the legislature in 1847 and was named Speaker of the House three years later. On 1 December 1851 he was appointed to replace Jefferson Davis in the US Senate after he resigned to run for the Mississippi governorship. McRae served until 17 March 1852, when the legislature appointed Stephen D. Adams to complete the term. In 1853 McRae was the States' Rights Democrats' nominee for the governorship, and he defeated the Whig candidate by several thousand votes. He easily won reelection in 1855.

During McRae's first administration Mississippi opened its first mental hospital and established an asylum for the deaf and speechless. The state also started a levee program in the Delta and adopted the Mississippi Code of 1857. In McRae's second term, the state adopted a constitutional amendment designed to prevent the recurrence of the situation caused by Gov. John A. Quitman's 1851 resignation. The amendment set the state's general elections for the first Monday in October and moved the inauguration of the governor from the first Monday in January following the general election to the first

Monday in November. That amendment shortened McRae's second term by about two months.

In 1858, McRae was elected to Quitman's seat in the US House of Representatives following his death. McRae remained in Congress until 12 January 1861. McRae subsequently won election to the Confederate Congress, where he served from 1862 to 1864.

McRae left public affairs after the Civil War. He died suddenly on 31 May 1868 while visiting Belize.

David G. Sansing
University of Mississippi

Biographical Directory of the United States Congress (1950); *Mississippi Official and Statistical Register* (1912); Dunbar Rowland, *Encyclopedia of Mississippi History*, vol. 2 (1907); David G. Sansing and Carroll Waller, *A History of the Mississippi Governor's Mansion* (1977).

McRae's Department Stores

In 1902 Samuel Proctor McRae founded a fifteen-hundred-square-foot store that sold clothes and home goods on Capital Street in downtown Jackson. The establishment of McRae's coincided with the development of America's modern consumer culture, which was best expressed at the time by the tremendous popularity of mail order catalogs such as those from Sears and J. C. Penney.

Primarily rural Mississippi had few department stores in the early twentieth century, and McRae's quickly became a popular destination for residents with the financial means to travel and purchase manufactured consumer goods. Building on this success in 1916, McRae moved his store to a much larger building near the original location.

After World War II a new generation of McRae family members significantly enlarged the downtown store and opened a second location northeast of the city to serve residents of Jackson's growing suburbs. McRae's ultimately became the state's largest department store chain and an icon of Mississippi business development.

McRae's merged with rival Kennington's department stores in 1970 and opened a Vicksburg location—the chain's first outside of Jackson—the following year. Over the next several years McRae's became common midpriced anchor stores in shopping malls throughout the Southeast. In 1986, the chain purchased the Alabama-based Pizitz department store chain, and by 1990 McRae's operated twenty-seven stores throughout the Southeast. In 1994 the company merged with the Proffitt's group, which assumed control of the stores but retained the independence of the McRae's

brand. Five years later this corporation merged with Saks Holdings, operator of Saks Fifth Avenue. In 2005 Saks sold the chain to Belk, which retired the McRae's brand name the following year and converted most of the McRae's stores into Belk stores.

Trevor Smith
Mississippi Gulf Coast Community College

Jackson Clarion-Ledger (14 April 2002, 4 May 2005).

McRaney, Gerald
(b. 1947) Actor

Gerald Lee McRaney, the star of television series *Simon & Simon* (1981–85) and *Major Dad* (1989–93), was born on 19 August 1947 in Collins, Mississippi. He grew up in Picayune and Natchez, and after injuring his knee during junior high school, McRaney turned to acting in school plays. He studied theater for a year at the University of Mississippi before moving to New Orleans to pursue his acting career. During this time, he supported himself by working in the Louisiana oil fields and on offshore rigs in the Gulf of Mexico.

After four years in New Orleans and acting in several plays, McRaney moved to Hollywood. While taking acting lessons and auditioning for television series, he made his living by driving a cab. In 1969 he received his first TV role, a small part in an episode of *Night Gallery*, and in 1975 he appeared on four episodes of *Gunsmoke*, playing the last challenger to meet US marshal Matt Dillon in a gunfight. In 1981 McRaney was cast in the CBS series *Simon & Simon* as private investigator Rick Simon, a role he played for eight years. McRaney then moved on to star in *Major Dad*, another successful CBS television series. McRaney's numerous subsequent television appearances have included *Touched by an Angel* (1996–98), *Promised Land* (1996–99), *Deadwood* (2005–6), *Jericho* (2006–7), *Undercover* (2010–12), *Fairly Legal* (2011–12), *Mike & Molly* (2012–13), *Longmire* (2012–15), *Agent X* (2015), and *House of Cards* (2013–16). An avid hunter, he has also hosted an outdoor adventure show on the OLN Network.

McRaney has remained loyal to his native state. He narrated Mississippi Public Broadcasting's production of *The Singing River: Rhythms of Nature*, an educational video about the Pascagoula River Basin, wrote a 2001 article about Natchez for *National Geographic Traveler Magazine*, and played a part in *Mississippi Rising* (2005), a telethon benefiting Louisiana and Mississippi hurricane recovery efforts. Since 1989 he has been married to actress Delta Burke, best known for her work on the TV series *Designing Women*.

Katherine Treppendahl
University of Virginia

Lynn Elber, *Entertainment News* (June 2006); Ken Hall, *Southeastern Antiquing and Collecting Magazine* (2005); Internet Movie Database website, www.imdb.com.

McWillie, William

(1795–1859) Twenty-Second Governor, 1857–1859

William McWillie migrated to Mississippi from South Carolina, but unlike many antebellum migrants, he did not come during his early childhood. McWillie moved to Mississippi during his middle years, after a very successful banking career in Camden, South Carolina. Born in the state's Kershaw District on 17 November 1795, McWillie had also served four years in the South Carolina legislature.

In 1845 McWillie and his large family moved to Madison County, where he had purchased a plantation. He built a colonial-style mansion, Kirkwood, where he lavishly entertained most of Mississippi's prominent citizens of that era.

Although most other wealthy planters were Whigs and generally opposed secession, McWillie was an ardent advocate of states' rights and aligned himself with that wing of the Mississippi Democratic Party. He began his political career in Mississippi in 1849 by winning election to the US Congress as a Democrat in a Whig district. However, Whigs and Democrats formed the Union Party under Henry Foote to quash McWillie's 1851 reelection bid.

At the 1857 Democratic Party convention McWillie received the party's nomination for governor on the fourteenth ballot, winning by only three votes. He easily defeated the Whig candidate in the general election and was inaugurated on 16 November 1857.

In his inaugural address, McWillie alluded to the great sectional issues of slavery and states' rights and predicted that secession of the slave states would become inevitable if those divisive issues were not resolved. Contending that northern reformers sought the "overthrow of the social institutions of the South," he promised that Mississippians were "full ready, and willing and able to take care of ourselves in the Union if we can; out of it if we must." He called on the nation's leaders in both the North and the South to seek a solution to those issues.

During McWillie's administration the levee system was greatly improved and railroad construction increased substantially, with the state purchasing stock in the newly organized railroads to encourage their growth. McWillie recommended the creation of a public school system with a state superintendent of education to supervise Mississippi's free schools. He commended the legislature for supporting higher education for young men and urged legislators to do the same for Mississippi's college-age women. However, the legislature did not enact any of this educational legislation. Just before McWillie's term expired, John Brown's raid at Harpers Ferry caused great alarm in Mississippi, and McWillie, fearing a large-scale slave revolt, persuaded the legislature to enlarge the state militia.

After leaving office in 1859, McWillie retired from public life and spent his remaining years at Kirkwood. He was an active supporter of the Confederacy, and his eldest son, Adam, was killed at the First Battle of Bull Run. McWillie died at Kirkwood on 3 March 1869.

David G. Sansing
University of Mississippi

Biographical Directory of the United States Congress (1950); Robert W. Dubay, *John Jones Pettus, Mississippi Fire-Eater: His Life and Times, 1813–1867* (1975); *Mississippi Official and Statistical Register* (1912); Dunbar Rowland, *Encyclopedia of Mississippi History*, vol. 2 (1907).

Mead, Cowles

(1776–1844) Legislator

Cowles (pronounced *Coals*) Mead was a legislator, administrator, statesman, and orator who served in the Mississippi Territory and in Mississippi's early statehood. Mead was born in Bedford County, Virginia, on 18 October 1776. Details are elusive, but Mead was privately educated, read law, and had political connections to Pres. Thomas Jefferson, an association that later helped Mead gain his administrative post in the territories.

After moving to Georgia, Mead launched a fierce 1804 campaign for a seat in the US Congress. The election was close, and ballots from three counties were delayed by a hurricane. Georgia's governor certified the election without the missing counties, declaring Mead the winner by 169 votes. Mead took his congressional seat in 1805, but his opponent, Thomas Spalding, refused to concede. A November 1805 recount that included the delayed ballots gave Spalding the seat by a thirty-nine-vote margin. This political reversal was temporary, however, and on 20 January 1806 Jefferson appointed Mead secretary of the Mississippi Territory, which then included the present states of Mississippi and Alabama. The secretary's powers were nearly absolute, and nearby foreign disputes with the Spanish on the Louisiana border and near Mobile helped to expand Mead's emergency powers.

Mead's powers as secretary were further increased because territorial governor Robert Williams was away in his native North Carolina on 10 January 1807 when Aaron Burr, a former US vice president, landed in the territory at Bruinsburg. Mead received reports that Burr had a force of two thousand men and feared that he planned to cause unrest. Mead used his powers as acting territorial governor to arrest Burr and imprison those suspected of aiding him.

Mead remained active in early Mississippi politics, though he was often unsuccessful. Mead found it difficult to return to his secretarial duties when Williams resumed his governorship. In May 1807 Mead drew a reprimand from Williams for trying to designate an acting territorial secretary. A series of clashes with Williams over records and appointments led to Mead's ouster from his secretarial post, but Mead was soon elected as a Jefferson County representative to the territorial assembly, where he continued his political struggle against Williams.

In 1809 Mead was chosen as one of thirteen superintendents of the newly formed Bank of Mississippi, created by the assembly for the "agricultural and commercial interests" of the territory. In 1813 Mead was commissioned a colonel in the 1st Regiment of the Mississippi Territory but resigned his commission to run for the post of territorial delegate to the US Congress. Mead strongly opposed dividing the Mississippi Territory into two states and based his campaign largely on this issue. Mead's defeat by William Lattimore of Adams County, a supporter of division, indicates public opinion within the Mississippi Territory. Mead was elected to the Territorial Assembly in 1817, and one of his proposals was to name the soon-to-be state Washington rather than Mississippi. The vote was close, but Mead lost 23–17, and the new state kept its territorial name. In 1823 Mead was elected Speaker of the Mississippi House, a post he had previously occupied in the territorial assembly. In 1825 Mead ran for governor but lost decisively, polling 1,499 votes to David Holmes's 7,846.

Mead was a popular speaker and statesman, but he consistently failed to win statewide office or to fully persuade the legislature to accept his proposals. After his gubernatorial defeat, Mead continued to serve in the state legislature but remained primarily retired. Sometime during the late 1820s Mead moved his family to Clinton, where Mount Salus Presbyterian Church was founded as a mission in 1826. That same year, Hampstead Academy (now Mississippi College) was founded as a Presbyterian-supported institution, and in 1833 Mead was appointed to the college's board of trustees. In 1842 Mead was named president of the board, but he later resigned over doctrinal controversies within the Clinton congregation.

In 1807 Mead married Mary Lilly Green of Jefferson County. The couple had two surviving children, Cowles G. Mead (1818–40) and Mary Mead (1821–75). After Mary Green Mead's death in Cincinnati, Ohio, in 1828, the senior Cowles Mead remarried twice—in 1883 to Mary Mills, who died seventeen months later, and in 1835 to Mary Magruder, who survived him after his 12 September 1844 death. Meadville, the seat of Franklin County, is named in his honor.

Chad Chisholm
Rust College

Chad Chisholm, *Images of America: Clinton* (2007); J. F. H. Claiborne, *Mississippi, as a Province, Territory, and State* (1880); Gordon A. Cotton, *Vicksburg Post* (7 March 1999); Richard A. McLemore, *Journal of Mississippi History* (April 1943); Howard Mitcham, *Journal of Mississippi History* (October 1953); George C. Osborn, *Journal of Mississippi History* (October 1941); Dunbar Rowland, *Encyclopedia of Mississippi History*, vol. 2 (1916); Dunbar Rowland, *History of Mississippi: The Heart of the South* (1925); Robert C. Weems Jr., *Journal of Mississippi History* (July 1953).

Medicine

Ancient Greek physician Hippocrates described the importance of place (climate, water supply, and environment) in medicine. The earliest records of the area known as Mississippi indicate that the region indeed possessed a distinctive medical sense of place, with the state's sultry clime and native diseases influencing its history. Before the arrival of European explorers and settlers, Mississippi's Native Americans confronted disease and illness through healers, conjurers, and shamans. These medical practitioners held prominent positions in early Native American culture, often as part of the priestly class, and treated sickness with medicine made from native herbs and roots as well as with religious ceremony and ritual. In the eighteenth century, their skill as herbalists and the success of their treatments impressed some Europeans. Le Page du Pratz praised the cures of the Natchez "surgeons" as superior to those of the French physicians. Although they called the Choctaw and Yazoo medicine men "charlatans," both Jean-Bernard Bossu and Dumont de Montigny acknowledged Native Americans' talent in using botanical and nonbotanical medicines to treat wounds, snakebites, and other ailments.

Clear archeological evidence suggests a significant decline in the Indian populations after the earliest arrival of European immigrants. Historians argue that pandemic diseases erupted in the sixteenth century, with new European maladies such as measles, smallpox, and influenza ravaging the native populations, who had little immunity. These epidemics decimated entire nations and cultures, reshaping which Indian groups dominated the Mississippi landscape. In the

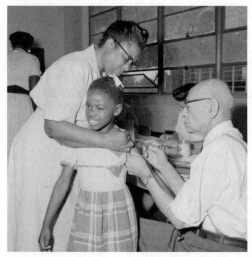

A second-grade girl receives the experimental polio vaccination during a 1954 field trial in Laurel (Moncrief Collection, Archives and Records Services Division, Mississippi Department of Archives and History)

aftermath of Hernando de Soto's expedition, disease effected a massive cultural change in the Southeast. Choctaw stories suggest that the tribe migrated to central Mississippi to find a land free of disease during a period of widespread death and sickness. Europeans also brought many diseases that became endemic to the area, such as malaria, typhoid, dysentery, and smallpox.

Europeans, too, were ravaged by illness and suffered high death rates after arriving in Mississippi. In June 1542 the once-vigorous warrior de Soto, then forty-two years of age, died of a slow, wasting fever. The French suffered similar afflictions in subsequent years. In 1701 colonial French governor Sauvolle reported that at Fort Maurepas, near Biloxi, he had thirty sick men who could not "recover from a tertian fever that saps their strength." Sauvolle himself died at the Mississippi fort that same month, the state's first recorded death of yellow fever.

The area's first physicians and surgeons were French and arrived as part of the earliest European settlements. Biloxi and Natchez had numerous physicians and even hospitals in the French colonial period, largely as a consequence of the French military presence, which usually provided surgeons with medical supplies. Spanish and English physicians were also present during those countries' colonial periods. The American period, which began in 1798, brought the dominance of English and American medical traditions, with Americans in the isolated Natchez District quickly realizing the dangers of disease and the importance of public health.

The Legislative Assembly of the Mississippi Territory passed the first law focused on disease prevention on 18 March 1799. The "Law Concerning Aliens and Contagious Diseases" sought to prevent the spread of epidemic disease—specifically, the plague, yellow fever, and smallpox—and authorized the governor, with the advice of a physician, to take measures to prevent the spread of disease

and to aid the sick. The first public health emergency of the American period was a smallpox epidemic in New Orleans in the spring of 1802. Territorial governor William C. C. Claiborne utilized the law to establish a smallpox "hospital camp" to separate those with the illness from the rest of the population. Virginia-born physician brothers William and David Lattimore oversaw the camp and led a mass vaccination of more than two-thirds of the population of the Natchez District. At Claiborne's urging, the Territorial Legislature passed a 13 May 1802 act that provided fines and imprisonment for anyone found guilty of the "importation and spread" of smallpox. These efforts prevented a serious outbreak of the disease and were the most significant early uses of public health measures in Mississippi.

Natchez's early physicians registered a number of impressive medical accomplishments, creating the area's earliest public hospital and its first board of health. Natchez Hospital, the territory's first charity hospital and one of the first in the United States, was incorporated in January 1805 to care for poor city residents as well as indigent boatmen who became sick while there. Soon after statehood, in February 1818, an extensive public health act created a board of health for Natchez with five appointed commissioners as well as a physician to serve as health officer. These commissioners of health and police oversaw cleanliness and hygiene from the city's sewers to its burial ground and worked to protect of the city from communicable diseases.

The Lattimore brothers, who had arrived in Natchez in 1801 and advised Claiborne during the smallpox epidemic, became prominent medical and political leaders in Mississippi's territorial and early statehood era. William, who moved to Amite County, served as Mississippi's first territorial congressman from 1803 to 1817. In that capacity he selected the line of division of the Mississippi Territory and led the admission of the territory as a state. He also was one of the three men who in 1822 selected the site for the state capital, which became Jackson.

While Lattimore's political accomplishments are significant, his medical accomplishments, especially in advancing the state on the path of medical licensure, were also critical. He helped create and served alongside his brother on the state's first board of medical licensure, the Board of Medical Censors. On 12 February 1819 the General Assembly passed the state's first law to regulate physicians and surgeons. Gov. David Holmes made the first appointments to the seven-member Board of Censors, which was "to license those who practice Physic and Surgery." The legislature created additional boards in 1821 and 1827, and the license laws further strengthened the board until 1836, when the state Supreme Court required that the boards have limitations on tenure to comply with the Mississippi Constitution of 1832. The Jacksonian-era decision resulted when a Wilkinson County man appealed his conviction for practicing medicine without a license. He not only won his case but invalidated the state's entire licensing process. The ruling effectively removed any state control over the practice of medicine for the next forty-six years, although in 1844 the well-organized physicians of Natchez persuaded the legislature to pass a state law creating a board of medical censors for Adams County.

The process of creating a statewide organization of physicians began in January 1829, when the legislature incorporated the Medical Society of the State of Mississippi. A decade later Jackson physicians led an effort to organize the Grand K. A. Society of Hippocrates of the State of Mississippi. An attempt to organize the various local medical societies into a statewide organization resulted in the creation of the Mississippi State Medical Society in Jackson on 14 January 1846, with physician Samuel A. Cartwright of Natchez elected as its first president. This group was officially recognized by the American Medical Association, but it, too, dissolved several years later, after Cartwright moved to New Orleans. In December 1856 the Mississippi State Medical Association (MSMA) was established in Jackson. William Young Gadberry of Benton led the effort and became the association's first president, with M. S. Craft as secretary. The association planned to meet in November 1857 but did not reconvene until 20 April 1869, when many of the same physicians gathered in Vicksburg to reestablish the association, which became a potent medical and political force.

Other health professionals also established state associations. Led by Matthew F. Ash, John F. Buck, and William P. Creecy, pharmacists established the Mississippi State Pharmaceutical Association in 1871. In April 1875 at Vicksburg, state dentists established the Mississippi Dental Association, with J. D. Miles serving as the group's first president. The Mississippi Nurses Association was founded in 1911 by a small group of nurses at the Natchez Hospital in Natchez, with Jennie Quinn serving as its first president.

Many of the state's earliest and most talented writers and scholars were physicians, including George Elliott Pendergrast, George Pfeiffer, Henry Tooley, C. H. Stone, John Wesley Monette, Samuel A. Cartwright, William H. Holcombe, and Henry Clay Lewis of Yazoo County. Holcombe was a national leader in the homeopathic medical movement and wrote prolifically in areas of medicine and poetry. Lewis achieved national fame by writing frontier humor under the pseudonym of the Louisiana Swamp Doctor, Madison Tensas. Many other Mississippi physicians published extensively in the nation's antebellum medical journals, and after the Civil War the reestablished state medical association began publishing the annual *Transactions of the Mississippi State Medical Association*. John Monette published an extensive treatise on yellow fever in the Washington Lyceum's *South-Western Journal* in 1837–38, but the state lacked a medical journal until 1891, when the *Mississippi Medical Monthly*, edited by Drs. N. L. Clarke and Hugh H. Haralson of Meridian, appeared. It morphed into the *Medical Record of Mississippi* (printed in Biloxi by Haralson) and subsequently into the *Journal of the Mississippi State Medical Association*

after the MSMA assumed its management and moved it to Vicksburg. It then ceased publication, and by 1929 the *Mississippi Doctor*, published by W. H. Anderson in Booneville, had become the MSMA's official organ. In January 1960 the MSMA began publishing the *Journal of the Mississippi State Medical Association*, which remains an influential scientific publication and one of the last remaining monthly medical journals in the South.

Prior to the early 1800s, Mississippi's physicians generally studied not in medical school but rather under other physicians. Subsequently, however, most Mississippi physicians received their training from medical schools in New York; Philadelphia; New Orleans; Augusta, Georgia; and Louisville and Lexington, Kentucky. Mississippi's first medical school was the short-lived Kirk's Clinical Institute of Medicine and Surgery, chartered in 1882 in Meridian. The University of Mississippi considered establishing a medical school as early as 1871, but because of poor resources the school did not open in Oxford until June 1903, when it was a two-year institution that did not offer clinical training. From 1908 to 1910 the university offered a four-year medical course in Vicksburg, but the University Board chose to discontinue that program and return to the two-year curriculum. In 1906 the Mississippi Medical College, a full four-year school, was organized in Meridian. This ambitious institution, which admitted two women in its first class, graduated hundreds of physicians who received their clinical training at the Matty Hersee Hospital. The school closed by 1913, leaving Mississippi with no four-year school of medicine for almost a half century.

In 1871 Dr. J. P. Moore of Yazoo City listed the diseases that embraced the "great aggregate of the death-rate of the state, the most fatal in the order as mentioned": pneumonia; malarial fever; inflammation of the brain and membranes, mostly affecting children; typhoid fever; dysentery; diarrhea; consumption; cholera infantum; influenza; scarlet fever; diphtheria; and irritative fever. Mortality schedules recorded for the state from 1850 to 1880 substantiate Moore's assertions, with a wide range of diseases noted as causes of death alongside childbirth, hives, suicide, and teething. Medical practitioners soon progressed beyond the long-established therapeutics of bloodletting, purgatives, mercury, digitalis, opiates, and "counter-irritation."

The most dreaded of all diseases in the state in the nineteenth century was yellow fever. Epidemics occurred almost annually from the 1820s to 1905. The Union blockade of southern ports during the American Civil War significantly restricted the Caribbean shipping trade, instituting an unintentional yellow fever quarantine that freed Mississippi of yellow fever for the war's duration. After trade was reestablished, yellow fever returned in 1867 and became the primary public health threat for Mississippians until eradication measures were discovered in 1905.

Race and poverty have played roles in both the complexity of illness and the delivery of health care in the state.

Antebellum physicians recognized the role of genetics in illness, such as improved yellow fever and hookworm resistance in those of West African descent. In 1854 Drs. Luke Pryor Blackburn and A. H. Brenham opened Natchez's Infirmary for the Cure of All Diseases of Colored Persons, a for-profit hospital to care for slaves and Natchez's large population of free persons of color. Cartwright became the state's most prominent antebellum specialist on slave physiology and health, although his research and writings were poisoned by his political and racial views.

Vicksburg gained its first black physician in 1865, and a handful of others followed. In 1890 only thirty-four black physicians and surgeons practiced in the state. A decade later, thirteen of the state's black physicians formed the Mississippi Medical and Surgical Association, which remains a vital professional association focused on the needs of the black physician. The MSMA began to allow black physicians to participate in scientific and society meetings in 1955 and by end of the decade granted full member status to its first black doctor. Early hospitals operated by black physicians included Alcorn A&M College Hospital (Lorman), Afro-Americans Sons and Daughters Hospital (Yazoo City), and the Taborian Hospital (Mound Bayou). Prior to 1962, when the University of Mississippi School of Medicine began admitting African Americans, most of the state's black physicians were trained elsewhere—usually at Meharry Medical College or Howard University Medical School—often assisted by the Mississippi Medical Education Program, which was created in 1946 to provide black Mississippians with scholarships to out-of-state medical schools in an attempt to prevent admitting them to in-state schools. In 1947 Meharry established one of the earliest rural training programs in the United States, sending residents and interns to Mound Bayou's Taborian Hospital until 1974. The Tufts-Delta Health Center, also in Mound Bayou, opened its doors in November 1967 as one of the nation's first comprehensive community health centers.

Well before these twentieth-century developments, the Civil War advanced the surgical skills of the average Mississippi physician, as the conflict retarded most public health and organized medicine initiatives in the state. The return of yellow fever in the postwar period resulted in the creation of boards of health in coastal counties by 1876 to quarantine ports and prevent the spread of disease. By 1877 a multiyear effort of the revived MSMA produced legislation to create the Mississippi State Board of Health. Originally unfunded and granted few powers, the board's creation was the most important medical event in Mississippi's history. Over the next decade physicians further refined its purpose and activities, including the registration of marriages, births, and deaths; sanitary regulations; quarantine powers; county health officer nominations; physician licensure; and legislative funding. The board played a major role in Mississippi's three epidemic outbreaks: yellow fever in 1878, smallpox in 1900–1901, and influenza in 1918–19. Smaller epidemics included smallpox in 1878 and yellow fever in 1897, 1898, and 1905.

Waller Leathers, a Virginia-born academic physician educated at Johns Hopkins and Harvard, organized the University of Mississippi Medical School in 1903 and served as its dean until 1924. In addition, Leathers served as the executive director of the State Board of Health from 1910 to 1924. His leadership helped create a full-time Department of Health, and he was a nationally recognized authority on public health and medical education. Leathers embraced research and encouraged aggressive attacks on hookworm infestation, influenza, pellagra, and malaria, working closely with Joseph Goldberger and the Rockefeller Foundation. His successor as state health officer, Felix Underwood, served until 1958 and created a nationally respected health agency. Assisting Underwood was registered nurse Mary D. Osborne, who served as the department's supervisor of public health nursing from 1922 to 1946. Also prominent during this period was Henry Boswell, Mississippi's "Conqueror of the White Death," who served for decades as superintendent of the Mississippi State Tuberculosis Sanatorium at Magee.

In the early 1940s Underwood and other physician-leaders began the drive to create a four-year school of medicine as a means of addressing the state's physician shortages. The idea's legislative champion was Hinds County senator Hayden Campbell, who authored the 1950 measure that established a four-year school and teaching hospital in Jackson on the site of Mississippi's first insane asylum on North State Street. The institution was dedicated on 24 October 1955 and awarded its first medical degrees in 1957. Among its most prominent physician-professors were David Pankratz, Robert Q. Marston, J. Robert Snavely, James D. Hardy, Herbert Langford, Thomas Brooks, Blair Batson, and Arthur C. Guyton. By the mid-1970s schools of dentistry, nursing, and health-related professions joined the School of Medicine and University Hospital to create the University of Mississippi Medical Center.

The Mississippi Regional Medical Program, created in 1965 and led by Guy Campbell and T. D. Lampton, had a monumental impact on the state's health delivery system. Some of the program's major accomplishments included the first stroke intensive care unit, the state's blood bank system, a statewide cardiopulmonary resuscitation program, the first renal transplant program, the first regional newborn care system, the first regional renal program, the first radiation therapy program, the first coronary care units, and the first ongoing effort to provide continuing health education for all types of health care providers. But the program did not transition into a functional health planning agency and was phased out in 1977.

The State Department of Health, under the leadership of Alton Cobb, reasserted itself as a national leader in public health from 1973 to 1993. Cobb had previously served as the first director of Mississippi's Medicaid program. As state health officer, Cobb introduced the district system and the certificate of need program, resulting in declines in infant mortality. He also oversaw the development of home health programs and the Special Supplemental Nutrition Program for Women, Infants, and Children.

Cobb was succeeded by longtime state epidemiologist Ed Thompson, who served as state health officer from 1993 to 2002. During this period the department achieved the highest immunization rates in the country and lowered tuberculosis and syphilis case rates below the national average. Thompson returned as state health officer in 2007 after a crisis in leadership at the State Department of Health that also resulted in the reconstitution of the Board of Health with a higher percentage of physician members and the requirement that the board chair be a physician. After Thompson's December 2009 death, state epidemiologist Mary Currier became state health officer. Under her leadership Mississippi's Department of Health has garnered national praise for its public health work and has opened a new state-of-the-art public health laboratory, which bears Thompson's name.

At the beginning of the twenty-first century the medical community faced a tort liability crisis, physician shortages, and a poorly coordinated trauma system. After "white coat" rallies by physicians at the State Capitol and significant grassroots public pressure, comprehensive tort reform legislation was passed in special sessions in 2002 and 2004. The 2007 creation of the Mississippi Rural Physician Scholarship Program also represented a major step toward improving the number of physicians in the state's rural and underserved areas. And the 2008 opening of the William Carey University College of Osteopathic Medicine in Hattiesburg gave the state its second medical school. Legislation passed the same year created a funded mandatory "pay or play" trauma system network that became a model for rural states across the country.

Lucius M. Lampton
Magnolia, Mississippi

Lucie Robertson Bridgforth, *Medical Education in Mississippi* (1984); John Duffy, *The Rudolph Matas History of Medicine in Louisiana*, 2 vols. (1958); T. D. Lampton, *Twelve Years of Challenge and Change . . . 1965–1977, Mississippi Regional Medical Program* (1977); Felix Underwood and R. N. Whitfield, *Public Health and Medical Licensure in the State of Mississippi, 1798–1937* (1938); Tom Ward, *Black Physicians in the Jim Crow South* (2003).

Americans, Africans, and Europeans. Members of each group acquired botanical knowledge from intergenerational contact with their elders. Beginning with an initial study of nature and proceeding to the transference of knowledge through oral traditions and into modern-day usage of folk medicine via written recipes, Mississippians have relied on each other for health care.

The migration of folk medicine among Mississippians occurred slowly and through necessity. White explorers valued Native Americans' medicinal knowledge as well as enslaved Africans' skills in faunal knowledge that kept both the planter class and the enslaved community healthy.

Folk medicine was administered as decoctions (an extraction of plant essence through boiling), elixirs or tinctures (infusions of plant matter in grain alcohol ointments of liniment containing animal fat), or infusions of plant matter or teas (simple plant matter with water). In addition, each cultural group believed that the quality of the medicinal product rested on a host of planetary configurations. Harvesting plant matter during a full moon or making an elixir under a waning moon either enhanced or depleted the remedy.

By the end of the nineteenth century, a shift occurred in public opinions regarding religion and medicine, and many Mississippians started to view folk medicine with suspicion and disdain. For example, the folk medicine ways of enslaved Africans once utilized by whites were now perceived as evidence of "African savagery." Folk medicine became synonymous with superstitions and "backward thinking," while medical physicians were becoming more respected. Nonetheless, many whites, enslaved Africans, and Native Americans lacked access to physicians and continued to rely on folk medicine, especially in the area of midwifery, well into the twentieth century and on into the twenty-first. Modernity brought with it the desire for consistent efficaciousness that skeptics of folk medicine claimed was impossible to obtain.

Phoenix Savage
Campti, Louisiana

Kay K. Moss, *Southern Folk Medicine, 1750–1820* (1999); Phoenix Savage, "The Evolution of Hoodoo in Mississippi and Contemporary Black Health" (master's thesis, University of Mississippi, 2001).

Medicine, Folk

Folk medicine is a cultural practice that derives from a basic human need to heal and regenerate. In Mississippi the three main cultural pathways of folk medicine come from Native

Melrose and the Natchez Mansion House

By the time John T. McMurran constructed Melrose around 1845, successful Natchez residents had already established the tradition of building large, stately, well-appointed homes

M

on large parcels of land in or around the town. By the late eighteenth century, when Natchez was the outpost seat of the Spanish regional governor, local houses were renowned for their luxury.

After the region became a US territory in 1797, planters and builders from New England, the southern seaboard, and Great Britain flocked to Natchez. The émigrés brought knowledge of architectural styles and techniques for executing forms inspired by the numerous English and American pattern books that enjoyed great popularity and authority during the early nineteenth century. Natchez elites chose to display their wealth by building extravagant houses in the region's economic and cultural center. The first significant houses, including Gloucester (1803–7) and Auburn (1812), foreshadowed some characteristics of later Natchez mansions, with skillful brickwork, gracious scale, and polished interior trim work. The iconic Natchez mansion house was a product of the city's culture between 1812 and 1861, with most houses built during the 1830s and the 1850s—not coincidentally the zenith of the cotton industry.

Arlington and Rosalie, brick mansions with grand Tuscan and Roman Doric porticos, brought Federal-style architecture to Natchez by 1825. These houses established the basic form associated with Natchez mansions of the period: monumental porticoes on two-story houses. In the 1830s, older houses such as Linden were significantly modernized and enlarged in the latest styles, Gloucester and others received their signature porticoes, and Ravenna, Choctaw, and many other new houses were constructed in the newly popular Greek Revival style. The 1850s saw the emergence of houses that blended elements of Italianate architecture such as the cast iron porch with the preexisting formula of a two-story building with a double-height portico and gracious classical columns. A good example is Stanton Hall (ca. 1857).

Melrose differs slightly from most of Natchez's large antebellum houses. It was constructed in the middle of the 1840s, when the cotton market suffered a depression and little building activity occurred in the town. Melrose is also notable as a pure Greek Revival structure, devoid of elements from the earlier Federal style and without Italianate forms. The house's most striking element is the pedimented two-story portico, which stretches across three of the house's five bays. Two pairs of unfluted Doric columns, perfect expressions of monumental and austere Greek Revival architecture, support the pediment. Six large, square Doric pillars march across the back of the house, supporting a double-tiered piazza and creating a colonnaded courtyard in the back of the main house with a flanking support building. Melrose was an urban showplace rather than a working plantation house, a point made clear by the finished back courtyard: on a working plantation, the service area would have been less prominently displayed and less highly articulated.

One of the striking characteristics about Natchez domestic structures is the absence of the typical townhouse—tall, thin domestic structures packed densely on narrow lots in an urban center. The number of mansions built in and directly outside the city center on massive tracts influenced builders of smaller houses, who also tended to situate their houses on sizable parcels. Examples include Green Leaves and the Burn, both constructed in the 1830s. The Natchez mansion houses, particularly Melrose, created and promoted the ideal of the stereotypical antebellum southern plantation house, complete with commodious porches, massive columns, and extensive grounds.

Emilie Johnson
University of Virginia

Randolph Delehanty, *Classic Natchez* (1996); Mills Lane, *Architecture of the Old South, Mississippi and Alabama* (1989); Irene S. Tyree, *Natchez Ante-Bellum Homes* (1964).

Meredith, James
(b. 1933) Activist

Known primarily for integrating the University of Mississippi, J. H. Meredith, the son of Moses Arthur "Cap" Meredith and Roxie Patterson Meredith, was born on 25 June 1933 in Kosciusko, Mississippi, in Attala County. He later adopted the names James Howard. Raised a Methodist, he was the sixth of Cap Meredith's ten children and the first of Roxie's five.

From Meredith's birth his parents believed that he might bring equality between the races in the United States, which he called his "Divine Responsibility." Nevertheless Cap Meredith secluded his children in the black community. In a

James Meredith walks to class at the University of Mississippi, accompanied by US marshals, 1 October 1962 (Photograph by Marion S. Trikosko, Library of Congress, Washington, D.C. [LC-DIG-ppmsca-04292])

unique position among blacks as the owner of the eighty-four-acre farm on which his family lived, Cap Meredith did not allow his children to visit friends living on white-owned farms or to work for white employers.

As a child, J. H. Meredith and all of his siblings worked in the fields when not at school. Cap Meredith shared all of his knowledge with the significant exception of the inferiority complex blacks were supposed to adopt in the presence of whites. In 1936, at the age of three, J. H. began attending Marble Rock School, which his father helped build, and in 1941 the boy continued his education at the Attala County Training School, a four-mile walk each way every day. In 1950 he left Mississippi to live with his uncle in St. Petersburg, Florida, and attend Gibbs High School for his senior year. There he had his first encounters with whites.

In 1951 Meredith graduated from high school and followed in the footsteps of his older brother, Leroy, by enlisting in the US Air Force. Meredith trained at Sampson Air Force Base in New York as part of the Air Force's new integration experiment. For nine years he moved around the United States and Japan on assignment, rising to the rank of staff sergeant and earning five good conduct medals. He attended nearby universities when he could, including the University of Maryland, Washburn University, and the University of Kansas. In December 1956 he married Mary June Wiggins, and their son John Howard was born four years later.

Meredith returned to Kosciusko in August 1960, fully intending to wage the war on white supremacy he had planned throughout his Air Force career. He later declared, "My objective was to force the federal government—the Kennedy administration at that time—into a position where they would have to use the United States military force to enforce my rights as a citizen." James and Mary June Meredith enrolled at Jackson State College, and he attended classes for two years. The day after John F. Kennedy was inaugurated as president, Meredith requested an application from the University of Mississippi, and on 31 January 1961 he applied to enroll. His application was denied based on what he felt was racial discrimination. With the help of Medgar Evers, the head of the Mississippi Branch of the National Association for the Advancement of Colored People, Meredith contacted the organization's Legal Defense and Educational Fund, which appointed attorney Constance Baker Motley to his case. She and Mississippi lawyer R. Jess Brown filed a lawsuit against the university and eventually won their case in the US 5th Circuit Court of Appeals.

Accompanied by federal marshals, Meredith made multiple attempts to enroll at the university but was blocked by Gov. Ross Barnett. Meredith finally entered the campus on the night of 30 September 1962 in the midst of a violent riot that left two people dead. He registered for classes on 1 October. On 18 August 1963 Meredith graduated from the University of Mississippi with a major in political science and minors in French and history. That same day he and his family left Mississippi at the request of the federal government. They spent the next year in Washington, D.C., and traveling around Europe, where Meredith gave public speeches. In 1964 he accepted an invitation to study at the University of Ibadan in Nigeria. He returned to New York City to study law at Columbia University in 1965, the same year his father died.

In June 1966 Meredith launched the March against Fear, a planned walk from Memphis, Tennessee, to Jackson, Mississippi, to protest racism in the Mississippi Delta. Two days after leaving Memphis on 5 June, Meredith was shot in Hernando. Other civil rights activists took over for Meredith, who recovered and rejoined the march. On 26 June more than fifteen thousand marchers, among them not only Meredith but Dr. Martin Luther King Jr., reached Jackson in what had become the largest civil rights demonstration in the state's history.

Despite Barnett's attempts to thwart Meredith's enrollment at the University of Mississippi, he endorsed the former governor in 1967 when he unsuccessfully sought to regain the governorship. Meredith earned a law degree from Columbia University Law School in 1968, at around the same time his wife gave birth to twin sons. Meredith remained in New York City until June 1971, when he returned to Mississippi. He dabbled in various professions, including stockbroker, and ran as a Republican for the Senate in 1972 and for the House of Representatives in 1974.

Mary June Meredith died in 1979, and James subsequently married Judy Alsobrooks, who bore him a daughter in 1983. A year later, Meredith accepted a one-year position at the University of Cincinnati. After unsuccessfully running for the board of education in Ohio, Meredith began working for Republican senator Jesse Helms of North Carolina in Washington, D.C., in 1989.

Meredith returned to Mississippi in 1991 and subsequently made two unsuccessful bids for Congress. He also published numerous books and continued to run for political office, give public speeches, and establish programs to further black education. He has maintained that he worked for equality for all Americans rather than for the civil rights movement, saying "Nothing could be more insulting to me than the concept of civil rights. It means perpetual second-class citizenship for me and my kind." Despite declaring that he did not want to be remembered for his role in integrating the university, he participated in commemorations of the fortieth anniversary of his admission. And exactly four years later, the university unveiled a commemorative statue depicting Meredith walking through the door of higher education.

He and his wife continue to live in Jackson.

Anna F. Kaplan
Columbia University

Sheila Hardwell Byrd, *Athens Banner-Herald* (21 September 2002); William Doyle, *An American Insurrection: James Meredith and the Battle of*

Oxford, Mississippi, 1962 (2003); Charles W. Eagles, *The Price of Defiance: James Meredith and the Integration of Ole Miss* (2009); Aram Goudsouzian, *Down to the Crossroads: Civil Rights, Black Power, and the Meredith March against Fear* (2014); James H. Meredith, *J. H. Is Born* (1995); James H. Meredith, *Letters to My Unborn Grandchildren* (1995); James H. Meredith, *"Me and My Kind": An Oral History with James Howard Meredith* (1995); James H. Meredith, *Mississippi: A Volume of 11 Books* (1995), James H. Meredith, *Three Years in Mississippi* (1966); James H. Meredith and William Doyle, *A Mission from God: A Memoir and Challenge for America* (2012); "Mississippi and Meredith Remember," CNN.com, http://edition.cnn.com/2002/US/South/09/30/meredith/index.html (1 October 2002).

Meridian Campaign

After the successful conclusion of the Vicksburg Campaign, Maj. Gen. William Tecumseh Sherman did not want to sit idle waiting for weather sufficient to support the upcoming spring campaign. Instead, he developed a plan to raid Meridian, about 150 miles from Vicksburg, and return in time to be ready for future operations. The Meridian Campaign not only succeeded in and of itself but also constituted an excellent proving ground for Sherman's later March to the Sea.

Meridian was a key strategic point, lying roughly halfway between the Mississippi capital of Jackson and the cannon foundry and manufacturing center of Selma, Alabama. Meridian served as a storage and distribution center not just for the industrial products of Selma but also for grain and cattle from the fertile Black Prairie region just to the north. It also had a hospital on the edge of town, a prison, and the headquarters for several military ordnance, quartermaster, and paymaster activities. But what made Meridian most important was its location at the junction of the Mobile and Ohio Railroad and the Southern Railroad. On 3 February 1864 Sherman began his campaign against this tempting target "to break up the enemy's railroads at and about Meridian, and to do the enemy as much damage as possible in the month of February, and to be prepared by the 1st of March to assist General [Nathaniel] Banks in a similar dash at the Red River country."

Sherman knew that his success depended on speed. He would travel light, ordering, "Not a tent will be carried, from the commander-in-chief down." He explained, "The expedition is one of celerity and all things must tend to that." In spite of his overriding concern for speed, Sherman would not compromise in the size of his force. His army consisted of four divisions—two from Maj. Gen. James B. McPherson's corps at Vicksburg and two from Maj. Gen. Stephen Hurlbut's at Memphis—for a total of twenty thousand infantry plus some five thousand attached cavalry and artillery. Sherman's Confederate adversary, Lt. Gen. Leonidas Polk, mustered a force just half that size, and his men were widely scattered, with a division each at Canton and Brandon and cavalry spread between Yazoo City and Jackson.

Polk was also handicapped by Sherman's effective deceptions, which led Polk to believe that the Union general's true objective was Mobile, Alabama. Sherman further played on Polk's fears for the safety of Mobile by having Gen. Nathaniel Banks, commander of the Department of the Gulf at New Orleans, conduct naval maneuvers and foraging operations designed to "keep up the delusion of an attack on Mobile and the Alabama River." By threatening Polk with feints, Sherman forced the Confederates to retain forces at Mobile that could have protected Meridian.

Sherman began his march from camps outside Vicksburg, with McPherson and Hurlbut advancing in separate columns to facilitate both speed and foraging. Confederate resistance was light, and Sherman refused to be distracted by minor skirmishes. By 9 February he was in Morton, having covered more than half the distance from Vicksburg to Meridian in less than a week. There he spent several hours tearing up the railroad track, using the usual method of burning crossties to heat the rails and then bending the metal into useless configurations dubbed "Sherman's neckties."

At Lake Station on 11 February Sherman destroyed "the railroad buildings, machine-shops, turning-table, several cars, and one locomotive." By midafternoon on 14 February, his lead elements were in Meridian. By then, Confederate resistance had evaporated. Sherman had also ordered Brig. Gen. William Sooy Smith to move his large cavalry force from Memphis southeast to arrive at Meridian by 10 February. A combination of a slow start and the efforts of Confederate cavalryman Nathan Bedford Forrest prevented Smith from accomplishing his mission, and he was forced to return to Memphis. Although this frustrated Sherman, it did not deter him from his objective of destroying Meridian.

For five days Sherman dispersed detachments in four directions with instructions to "do the enemy as much damage as possible." McPherson went to the south and west and destroyed 55 miles of railroad, 53 bridges, 6,075 feet of trestlework, 19 locomotives, 28 steam cars, and 3 steam sawmills. Hurlbut went north and east and wrecked 60 miles of railroad, 1 locomotive, and 8 bridges. Sherman reported, "10,000 men worked hard and with a will in that work of destruction, with axes, crowbars, and with fire, and I have no hesitation in pronouncing the work as well done. Meridian, with its depots, store-houses, arsenal, hospitals, offices, hotels, and cantonments no longer exists." His work done, Sherman returned to Vicksburg on 28 February.

Considered in a vacuum, the Meridian Campaign was a huge success, but its effects stretched far beyond the Confederate war materiel Sherman laid to waste in Mississippi. Meridian served as small-scale rehearsal for Sherman's later

March to the Sea. Meridian showed Sherman that he could march through Confederate territory, destroy Confederate war-making infrastructure and will, and all the while live off the land. This larger impact marks the Meridian Campaign as an important milestone in the evolution of strategy and the Civil War's relentless advance toward total war.

Kevin Dougherty
University of Southern Mississippi

Michael Ballard, *Civil War Mississippi: A Guide* (2000); S. M. Bowman and R. B. Irwin, *Sherman and His Campaigns: A Military Biography* (1865); Buck Foster, *Sherman's Mississippi Campaign* (2006); John Marszalek, *Sherman: A Soldier's Quest for Order* (1993); Mississippi History Now website, http://mshistorynow.mdah.state.ms.us; William Tecumseh Sherman, *Memoirs of General William T. Sherman* (1990).

Meridian Museum of Art

The Meridian Museum of Art began life in February 1933, when city residents formed the Meridian Art League and held an exhibition at the Lamar Hotel featuring works by Charles Le Clair, director of the Arts Department at the University of Alabama. Other exhibitions followed, and in 1949 the league changed its name to the Meridian Art Association. The first exhibition under the new name took place on the second floor of Marks Rothenberg Company (now Mississippi State University's Riley Center) on 8 March 1949 and featured works by a series of New Orleans–based artists. Over the next two decades, the association held exhibitions, gallery talks, and workshops around the city, most often in the 1870 Room in the original Weidmann's Restaurant. In October 1956 a painting group was formed to give local artists a chance to share and learn together and to select paintings to be hung in the 1870 Room.

In 1967, the Meridian Public Library moved out of its longtime downtown home, the historic Carnegie Library building. The structure had opened in 1884 as the First Presbyterian Church, and in 1911 the City of Meridian bought it and turned it into the Carnegie Library. In January 1968 the Meridian Art Association began planning to renovate the facility into the Meridian Museum of Art. With seed money from the association's membership and bond money from the City of Meridian, the museum opened in 1970.

The museum has four galleries (Burdette, Davidson, Weidmann, and South) and hosts about a dozen exhibitions each year featuring work by the finest artists in Mississippi and Alabama. The museum's permanent collection includes eighteenth- and nineteenth-century European portraits, twentieth-century American photography, sculpture and works on paper, contemporary decorative arts, and a growing collection of twentieth-century southern art emphasizing Mississippi and Alabama aritsts. Artists with work in the collection include Walter Anderson, Homer Casteel, Thomas Eloby, William Hollingsworth, Marie Hull, and Alex Loeb.

In addition, the museum offers art classes for children and adults, supports artists' groups, and is active in the Meridian community, helping to promote art programs in the schools, economic development, and other community events. Since 1974 it has sponsored the Bi-State Art Competition, the region's oldest juried art competition, and two decades later it added the People's Choice Art Competition. It also hosts special programs for Black History Month, art auctions, and social events and can be rented out for private gatherings such as weddings.

Terry Heder
Meridian Museum of Art

First Presbyterian Church of Meridian website, fpcmeridian.com; Ann McKee, *Meridian Star* (26 April 2007); Meridian Museum of Art website, www.meridianmuseum.org.

Methodists

Methodists have been present in Mississippi from the earliest days of European settlement. When Tobias Gibson moved from South Carolina to Natchez in 1799, he formed the first Mississippi Methodist church at Washington with eight members, including two African Americans. Methodism entered North Mississippi in 1819 and prospered over the remainder of the century because of the labors of circuit riders—itinerate Methodist ministers who traveled by horseback to spread the Gospel of Jesus, often at personal peril.

In 1813 ten ministers held the denomination's first Mississippi Annual Conference at Newit Vick's home near Fayette. Three years later, Robert Roberts became the first bishop to attend a Mississippi Annual Conference: the ministers present reported that the conference, which included present-day Mississippi, Alabama, and Louisiana, had thirteen hundred members. From 1837 to 1839 the Mississippi Conference also included Texas.

In the 1840s, many US Protestant denominations began to split over the issue of slavery, and the Methodists were no exception, splintering along geographic and racial lines for the next half century. In 1845, after the Methodist Episcopal

Methodist Church, Grenada, ca. 1910 (Ann Rayburn Paper Americana Collection, Department of Archives and Special Collections, J. D. Williams Library, University of Mississippi [rayburn_ann_24_37_001])

Church censured Bishop J. O. Andrew of Georgia over his ownership of slaves, the church's southern conferences, including the Mississippi Conference, broke away to form the Methodist Episcopal Church, South. In 1865 African American Methodists formed the Mississippi Mission Conference, which was affiliated with the Methodist Episcopal Church, and a few years later, the Mississippi Conference of the Methodist Episcopal Church, South gave birth to the North Mississippi Conference. The African American Mississippi Conference created its own Upper Mississippi Conference in 1891.

After the turn of the century, the various Methodist conferences began to reunite. In 1939 the Mississippi Conferences of the Methodist Protestant Church and Methodist Episcopal Church, South merged, as did the corresponding North Mississippi Conferences. Following the 1968 merger of the Evangelical United Brethren and the Methodist Church, the African American Mississippi Conference merged with the predominantly white Mississippi Conference in 1973, as did

their corresponding Upper and North Mississippi Conferences. In 1989 the Mississippi and North Mississippi Conferences merged, forming today's single Mississippi Conference, uniting Methodists, African American and white, throughout the state.

Mississippi's Methodists sponsored the Elizabeth Female Academy (1818–47), which was located in Washington and may have been the first American institution chartered exclusively for the higher education of women. In 1859 Whitworth College at Brookhaven succeeded Elizabeth Academy. Whitworth closed in 1976, and its former building now houses the Mississippi School of the Arts. Centenary College, now located in Shreveport, Louisiana, began its life in 1841 in Brandon Springs, Mississippi. The state's Methodists now support Holly Springs's Rust College, established in 1866 by the Freedman's Aid Society of the Methodist Episcopal Church; Mathiston's Wood College, a two-year institution established in 1886; and Jackson's Millsaps College, founded in 1890 and home of the Mississippi Conference Archives.

Notable Mississippi Methodists have included missionary Tobias Gibson (1771–1804); William Winans (1788–1857), who served as the first conference secretary; and Benjamin Drake (1800–1860), who served as president of Elizabeth Female College before founding Centenary College. Charles Galloway (1849–1909) was elected bishop at age thirty-six and was among America's premier pulpiteers. J. Lloyd Decell (1887–1946) served as bishop beginning in 1938. Both Galloway and Decell also served as editors of the *New Orleans Christian Advocate*. Bishop Nolan Harmon (1892–1993) was born in Meridian and graduated from Millsaps College. The North Mississippi Conference produced Bishops W. B. Murrah (1852–1925), who served as Millsaps College's first president (1890–1910), and Homer Ellis Finger (1916–2008), who held the same office from 1952 to 1964. Bishop Robert E. Jones (1872–1960), founder of Gulfside Assembly, was elected one of the first African American bishops in the Methodist Church in 1920. More recently, Mary Ann Swenson, who was raised in Jackson and graduated from Millsaps College, was elected a bishop in 1992, while another Millsaps graduate, Larry Goodpaster, was elected a bishop eight years later. Methodist laity have also played prominent roles in the state as governors, public servants, and educators.

Campgrounds conduct annual revivals at Shiloh near Pelahatchie, Felder's in Pike County, South Union in Choctaw County, and Salem and New Prospect in Jackson County. Mississippi Methodist assemblies include Seashore, in Biloxi, which houses the United Methodist Women's Arlean Hall; Gulfside, in Waveland, founded in 1923; Camp Wesley Pines, in Gallman; and Camp Lake Stephens, near Oxford.

In 1963 a group of twenty-eight white Methodist ministers published the "Born of Conviction" statement, which opposed racial discrimination and supported the freedom of ministers to speak out on issues of race. The ministers received mixed responses, including a significant amount of angry criticism.

In addition to a dozen social ministry centers, Mississippi Methodists sponsor the Methodist Choctaw Mission, Children's Home, Rehabilitation Center, Mississippi United Methodist Foundation, United Methodist Hour of Mississippi, and United Methodist Senior Services of Mississippi. The conference publishes a newspaper, the *Advocate*.

At the beginning of 2016 the Mississippi Methodist Conference had 1,003 churches with 1,368 clergy and 176,555 members. Since 2012 the conference has been led by Bishop James E. Swanson Sr., headquartered at the United Methodist Building on Briarwood Drive in Jackson.

William L. Jenkins

San Diego, California

Ray Holder, *The Mississippi Methodists, 1789–1983: A Moral People "Born of Conviction"* (1984); William L. Jenkins, *Mississippi United Methodist Churches: Two Hundred Years of Heritage and Hope* (1998); Mississippi Conference of the United Methodist Church website, www.mississippi-umc.org; Joseph T. Reiff, *Born of Conviction: White Methodists and Mississippi's Closed Society* (2015); Randy J. Sparks, *On Jordan's Stormy Banks: Evangelicalism in Mississippi, 1773–1876* (1994); *Encyclopedia of World Methodism* (1974).

Mexican-American War, Mississippians in

Hostilities between the United States and Mexico commenced with the ambush of a small American reconnaissance patrol north of the Rio Grande River near Matamoros, Mexico, on 25 April 1846. By the time Pres. James K. Polk, a Democrat, received news of the ambush on the evening of 9 May, Maj. Gen. Zachary Taylor's army had fought and won major battles at Palo Alto and Resaca de la Palma. On 11 May Polk asked Congress to recognize that a state of war existed between the United States and Mexico and to pass legislation enabling the nation to protect its honor, rights, and interests. (Polk failed to mention his desire for Mexican territory.) On 13 May, after almost no debate, Congress obliged the president with a war bill that authorized a call-up of fifty thousand men and appropriated ten million dollars for military expenses. Mississippi's congressional delegation, Democrats all (Sens. Joseph W. Chalmers of Holly Springs and Jesse Speight of Plymouth, and Reps. Steven Adams of Aberdeen, Jefferson Davis of Warrenton, Robert W. Roberts of Hillsboro, and Jacob Thompson of Oxford), supported Polk's call to war. With the president's signature, the United States—and with it, Mississippi—went to war.

With few exceptions, Mississippians welcomed the war, for reasons that reflected a range of emotions, interests, and ideas. Manifest Destiny, a romantic nationalism that justified territorial expansion on idealistic and racist grounds,

played a role for many. Some embraced the prospect of opening new land in the Southwest to slavery, which they deemed an economic and political necessity. Others were caught up in the *rage militaire* that swept across the nation with news of the opening of hostilities: young men dreamed of winning a reputation for selfless courage on Mexican battlefields, while their older counterparts knew full well that laurels won on the battlefield could bring tangible political and social rewards. Both men and women, publicly at least, jumped at the opportunity to demonstrate themselves worthy of their revolutionary forbears. Democrats marshaled behind their president and castigated any Whig who dared to critique war policy. Mississippi's Whigs, however, joined the forces heading off to Mexico and supported war-funding measures: no Mississippi Whig publicly called for an immediate end to the war, although Whig dissent became more vocal as the war progressed.

The most substantial manifestation of support for the war was enlistment in the volunteers. Gov. Albert Gallatin Brown expected that at least twenty-five hundred men would be requested from the state. Accordingly, on 9 May 1846 he ordered the organization of twenty-eight companies. By 1 June, according to estimates, as many as seventeen thousand men had gathered at Vicksburg. The news that Secretary of War William L. Marcy required only one regiment of approximately one thousand men for twelve months' service placed the governor in a precarious political situation. As Brown anxiously beseeched Marcy for a bigger allotment, angry would-be volunteers and their friends burned him in effigy in front of the Governor's Mansion and berated him in the press. Many of those spurned joined units from other states or sullenly bided their time until more men were needed. Still, the one-regiment quota stood.

The unit raised under the first call for troops was the 1st Mississippi Rifles, which mustered into service with 941 men at Vicksburg in June 1846. The elected field officers of the regiment were Col. Jefferson Davis (Democrat), Lt. Col. Alexander K. McClung (Whig), and Maj. Alexander B. Bradford (Whig). Davis used his Washington connections to arm his men with Model 1841 percussion rifled muskets (often referred to as Mississippi Rifles), as distinguished from the more common, less accurate, and shorter-ranged smoothbore. Under Davis's leadership, the regiment compiled a distinguished combat record, playing a prominent role in the major American victories at Monterrey in September 1846 and Buena Vista in September 1847. It suffered more battle deaths, fifty-nine, than any other volunteer unit, and its roughly equal number of nonbattle deaths (sixty-three) made it exceptional among volunteer units, where disease generally killed many more soldiers. The 1st Mississippi's 427 men mustered out of service at New Orleans in June 1847 as arguably the most celebrated volunteer regiment of the war.

The other units raised for federal service in Mississippi could not duplicate the success of the 1st Mississippi. The

2nd Mississippi Rifles and Anderson's Battalion of Mississippi Rifles were raised as the result of later federal calls for troops. Neither unit participated in major combat operations. The 2nd Mississippi mustered into service with 1,037 men at Vicksburg in January 1847. This unit spent the majority of its tour of duty in Mexico in and around Saltillo. It mustered out of service at Vicksburg in July 1848 with 606 men, having suffered no battle deaths and 187 other deaths, mainly as a result of disease. Anderson's Battalion of Mississippi Rifles mustered into service at Vicksburg in September 1847 with 445 men, spent most of its war service in garrison at Tampico, and mustered out of service at Vicksburg in July 1848 with 342 men. It suffered no battle deaths and lost thirty-eight men to other causes.

It is impossible to say exactly how many Mississippians served in the Mexican War, but the number likely falls between twenty-five hundred and three thousand. Many individuals and even complete companies joined units from other states. Others joined regular US Army formations, especially the Regiment of United States Voltigeurs and Foot Riflemen.

On 30 May 1848 the Mexican-American War officially ended with the exchange of ratifications of the Treaty of Guadalupe Hidalgo, in which the United States agreed to pay fifteen million dollars to Mexico and up to three million dollars in claims by American citizens against the Mexican government in exchange for more than five hundred thousand square miles of territory. By the end of July, all Mississippi soldiers had returned home.

The war experience had immediate and lasting effects on Mississippi. The conflict propelled some established leaders to new heights. For example, President Polk appointed John Quitman to serve as major general of volunteers, and he went on to become governor and a member of the US Congress, and Davis later served as a US senator and secretary of war and as Confederate president. The conflict also helped to develop new leaders, such as future Confederate generals Carnot Posey, who served with the 1st Mississippi Rifles, and William Barksdale, who served with the 2nd Mississippi Rifles. The issue of the expansion of slavery into the newly acquired lands subsequently came to dominate both national and state politics. War veterans, especially Quitman and Barksdale, led the fight to see that the land gained from Mexico would remain open to the South's peculiar institution. The fire that such men had breathed against their Mexican foes now turned increasingly against their own countrymen. Perhaps most significantly, the Mexican-American War prepared a generation of Mississippians to march off to the battlefield in 1861.

Gregory S. Hospodor
US Army Command and General Staff College, Fort Leavenworth, Kansas

Robert A. Brent, *Journal of Mississippi History* (August 1969); Joseph E. Chance, *Jefferson Davis's Mexican War Regiment* (1991); Donald S. Frazier, ed., *The United States and Mexico at War: Nineteenth-Century Expansion and Conflict* (1998); Gregory S. Hospodor, *Journal of Mississippi History* (Spring 1999); Dunbar Rowland, *Military History of Mississippi, 1803–1898* (1908); Richard Bruce Winders, "Mr. Polk's Army: Politics, Patronage, and the American Military in the Mexican War" (PhD dissertation, Texas Christian University, 1994); Richard Bruce Winders, *Mr. Polk's Army: The American Military Experience in the Mexican War* (1997).

Mexicans and Mexican Americans in the Mississippi Delta

Though the lumber industry in south-central Mississippi recruited Mexican laborers as early as 1908, World War I and the Great Migration of blacks to northern and western cities most acutely forced the Delta's white planters to confront the dilemma of their dependence on blacks and to think seriously about recruiting Mexican workers as an alternative. By the mid-1920s, Mexicans could earn more picking cotton in Arkansas, Louisiana, Alabama, or Mississippi than anywhere else in the country. Farmers in those states paid Mexicans an average of $4.00 per day to pick cotton, compared to $1.75 in Texas and $3.25 in California.

The Mexican migration to Mississippi peaked in 1925. As the cotton picking season arrived that fall, a Catholic priest in Clarksdale claimed that five thousand "Mexicans" (a term he applied to Mexican citizens as well as to Texas-born Mexican Americans, known as Tejanos) were picking cotton on plantations in Clarksdale, Greenwood,

Mexican cotton pickers inside the Knowlton Plantation store, Perthshire, October 1939 (Photograph by Marion Post Wolcott, Library of Congress, Washington, D.C. [LC-USF34-052247-D])

Greenville, Cleveland, Tunica, and Hollandale. And "more are coming every day," he wrote. Indeed, by the end of 1925 the priest had visited every plantation in his Clarksdale parish and found "Mexicans" on all of them. Food historians believe these migrants introduced tamales to the Mississippi Delta.

Most of these workers were Mexican immigrants who had left during the Mexican Revolution, spent some time in Texas, and then moved on. Though they had first lived in South Texas, five-sixths of ethnic Mexican household heads, wives, and boarders enumerated by census takers in the Delta's Bolivar County during the 1930 planting season were Mexican-born, while one-sixth were Tejanos. While most Mexicans and Mexican Americans left the Delta after the last of the cotton crop had been picked in December, some tried to stay in Mississippi, buying a few chickens, hogs, and cows to provide food to get them through the winter.

Many Mexican families in the Delta sent their children to school there, but a 1926 ruling of the Bolivar County Schools Board of Trustees prohibited Mexicans and Mexican Americans from attending the Gunnison Consolidated School along with white children. Instead, the county paid a Mexican community leader to offer instruction at a separate school on the plantation of J. G. McGehee. By 1928 the Mexican teacher had left the area, the number of Mexican children had dwindled, and the county was unable to convince a young Tejana woman to assume the role of teacher at the Mexican school. Hortensia Landrove, daughter of local community leader Rafael Landrove, and her young uncle, George Pérez, thus attended the white school for a few weeks during the winter of 1928–29. The following year, another family, the Robledos, enrolled children in the second grade after the cotton was picked. While Telesforo and María Robledo pulled their son, Freddo, out in February to help seed the next crop, their daughter, Jubertina, finished out the school year, struggling with English but otherwise earning As and Bs. She was promoted to the third grade at the end of the year, even as many of her peers were left behind. She became the first Mexican to complete the academic year at Gunnison's white elementary school.

In early 1930, however, school officials decided to enforce the 1926 school board ruling and told the Mexican families that their children could not attend the white school. Landrove appealed to the Mexican consulate in New Orleans for help, and the consulate in turn asked Gov. Theodore Bilbo to intervene. By April the governor's intervention had resolved the matter in Landrove's favor, and the following school year Hortensia Landrove, George Pérez, and Telesforo Robledo's son, Trinidad, again enrolled in the white school after the cotton was picked. All three finished out the academic year and were promoted to the next grade. The victory was crucial for Landrove. His children would be educated at a white school in the Delta, leaving open the possibility of gaining economic stability and becoming culturally middle class.

However, Mexicans had entered sharecropping in the Delta at the beginning of its end. As cotton prices crashed from 16.78 cents per pound in 1929 to 5.66 cents per pound in 1931, white, black, and Mexican sharecroppers alike found themselves unable to pay the debts they had incurred to purchase seed and equipment, let alone turn any profit. For most of the Delta's Mexicans, the experiment with Mississippi was over. Neither deported by local officials nor able to secure consular help in repatriating, the destitute Mexican sharecroppers of the Mississippi Delta were effectively abandoned, left to finance their own returns to Mexico or Texas.

Smaller numbers of Mexican workers continued to come to Mississippi's cotton fields seasonally throughout the 1930s and early 1940s. As World War II accelerated rural-urban migration and increased wages off the farm, the Delta's planters once again looked to Texas and Mexico for labor. In 1947 Mississippi farmers began to take advantage of the bracero guest worker program. The leadership of Mississippi's Delta Council lobbied Congress to continue the program and to minimize its financial requirements, and the US House Agriculture Committee held farm labor hearings in Greenville in 1950.

Yet bracero contracting required organized farmers' associations, minimum standards for housing and wages, and the threat of supervision and intervention from the Mexican consulate. Thus, for most of the era, Mississippi's cotton farmers preferred to bring Tejanos up to the Delta, taking advantage of Texas farmers' bracero recruitment and of Mississippi's slightly later picking season to recruit Texas's surplus labor. Tejanos picked cotton alongside African Americans, German POWs, and braceros during the war years. During the 1950s hundreds of Tejano families settled in the Delta, where they performed agricultural labor.

While braceros and Tejanos labored in the same fields, their lives differed markedly. Braceros came as single men; Tejanos were more likely to come as families. Braceros remained only seasonally, while many Tejanos stayed in the area for longer periods or even settled there. Braceros were almost entirely isolated on plantations, while many Tejanos had cars and trucks and could gather with their families on weekends, traveling up to twenty miles each Saturday night to dance to the sounds of visiting Tejano bands. By contrast, bracero Luís Gutiérrez Velásquez, who worked in Mississippi during 1947–48, was so isolated during his sojourn that he saw not a single black person. While other braceros sometimes went to town on Saturdays, Gutiérrez saw only rows of cotton during his weeks of picking.

While Tejanos led a largely private cultural and communal life, many—especially those with some education—found a limited acceptance by Delta whites. The Soto family, for example, arrived in Rosedale in 1962 having heard that Mississippi would offer a welcome escape from the abysmally low wages and Anglo-Mexican tensions of Texas. They were not disappointed: father Daniel, a trained electrician, found well-paid work in his profession—something the anti-Mexican racism of Texas had never allowed. In Texas, Soto had "worked out in the field sometimes. He didn't make any money there," recalled his wife, Alice, "maybe $5.00 a day. Here [in Mississippi] it was $1.25 an hour. We felt rich!" Their daughter, a high school student, felt shunned by whites in Texas; in Mississippi, she became friends with them.

Mexican Americans' limited possibilities for assimilation were not without condition, and most avoided association with blacks. The feeling may have been mutual: when the Sotos mistakenly went to a black lunch counter, they were told, "This is the black side, you go to the white side." Intermarriage between Mexican Americans and whites had become acceptable in the Delta by this era, while other Tejanos married each other or the children of Mexican immigrants who had come to the area in the interwar years. As the civil rights movement began to build in the Mississippi Delta during the 1950s, the region's Mexican Americans remained silent, on the sidelines. By the time the movement reached its zenith in the early 1960s, most Tejanos had been replaced by mechanical cotton pickers and had moved on to pick fruit in Florida's orchards.

Julie M. Weise
University of Oregon

Manuel Gamio, *Mexican Immigration to the United States: A Study of Human Migration and Adjustment* (1971); Alice Soto, interview by Richard Enriquez (1991), Charles W. Capps Jr. Archives and Museum, Delta State University; Southern Foodways Alliance, Mississippi Delta Hot Tamale Trail, website, www.tamaletrail.com; Julie M. Weise, *Corazón de Dixie: Mexicanos in the US South since 1919* (2015); Nan Elizabeth Woodruff, *Agricultural History* (Spring 1990).

are as large as 15 feet across and 6.6 feet thick. Common features of these mounds are pits and fire hearths, and some point to burials that date from 6,000–8,000 BP (before the present).

The midden study sought to provide a better understanding of the environmental changes and human adaptations of the region in various stages of prehistoric times. Since the holes in the archaeological records occurred mainly in the late Paleo-Indian (13,000–10,000 BP) and the Archaic (10,000–2,500 BP) periods, the project focused on those eras. However, the project also considered archaeological evidence from other prehistoric stages, such as the Middle Gulf Formational and Late Woodland, to establish a more complete timeline of life adaptations from the prehistoric evidence. The mineral analysis suggests that the composition of the soil accounts for the well-preserved condition of artifacts in the middens.

The principal investigator for the Midden Mound Project was Judith Bense, who worked with varying staff members and consultants during the project's three phases. The first two phases operated from Fulton, Mississippi. By Phase III (1984–87), fieldwork was over, and a more detailed and refined analysis took place on the University of Western Florida campus in Pensacola as the final report was prepared. At the end of each phase a progress report was published, and the results of the project constitute one of the largest collections of data of its type in the southeastern United States.

Anna F. Kaplan
Columbia University

Judith A. Bense, *Archaeology of the Southeastern United States: Paleoindian to World War I* (1994); Judith A. Bense, ed., *The Midden Mound Project* (1987).

Midden Mound Project

The Midden Mound Project, run by the Office of Cultural and Archaeological Research of the University of West Florida in cooperation with the US Army Corps of Engineers, Mobile District, developed as a byproduct of the Tennessee-Tombigbee Waterway Project. The waterway is a canal built by the Corps of Engineers to connect the Tennessee and Tombigbee Rivers to facilitate shipping across the South. The Midden Mound Project, which lasted from late 1979 or early 1980 until 1987, examined eleven prehistoric sites, including four midden mounds, in or near the Tennessee and Tombigbee floodplains in northeastern Mississippi between Aberdeen and Ryan's Well. Some of these mounds of midden (deposits of human artifacts or plant and animal remains)

Midwives

According to the Mississippi State Board of Health, from 1920 until the mid-1960s midwives were at the heart of Mississippi's public health work. In a 1994 *Nursing History Review* article, Susan Smith wrote, "Nurses, most of whom were white, and midwives, most of whom were black, worked together to implement the modern public health care system in Mississippi." Paradoxically, the state regulation of midwifery that brought public health nurses into close contact with lay midwives led to the formation of an unforeseen cadre of public health workers. Beginning in the 1920s Mississippi endorsed limitations on the practice of midwifery as health officials alleged that midwives failed to maintain sanitary surroundings and used unscientific and therefore hazardous folk medicine. Nevertheless, health officers and public health nurses quickly realized that midwives afforded indispensable assistance in applying health policy in African American communities.

In the 1920s, in an attempt to regulate the practice of midwifery, the state developed an outline that dealt with the fundamentals of midwifery. Because most midwives lacked a great deal of formal education, public health nurses gave simple directions. Small groups of midwives met monthly with instructors, who provided information and demonstrated proper techniques. The public health nurses focused primarily on two areas: sanitation (cleanliness of utensils and of the midwife and future mother and her home) and the need to call a doctor for any irregularity before, during, or after delivery. Record cards documented a full history of each midwife and included confirmation of her attendance at conferences and readiness to follow directions, a log of her equipment, and notations regarding her advances in her work. By 1947, 58 percent of Mississippi's births were still taking place in the home, and midwives attended 36 percent of those women. That year Mississippi had 2,192 midwives, all but 35 of them African Americans, and they played a pivotal role in upgrading maternal well-being in the state. The guidelines, instruction agenda, and certification of midwives by the State Board of Health helped bring about a 47 percent decline in the maternal death rate from 1920 to 1947.

In Mississippi, black midwives were the most prominent and honored members of their communities—the female equivalent of preachers. They were at the core of the time-honored healing networks in rural African American communities and served as counselors and spiritual leaders. Although already held in high esteem by their own communities, midwives rose in status among whites as a consequence of state certification.

Black mothers-to-be and some of their white counterparts favored midwives over physicians for monetary and cultural reasons. Midwives were less expensive than doctors and were willing to journey to isolated areas. They offered reassurance and assistance for expectant women before, during, and after delivery. Many midwives cooked and cleaned as well as cared for the mother and newborn.

Many African American midwives believed that they were doing the work of the Lord and thus did not insist on compensation, although a few dollars or payment in kind was standard. One woman whose husband had no money gave a cow to the midwife. In the 1920s Mississippi midwife Bessie Sutton received around $1.50 for a delivery, and when she retired "in 1962 the fee had increased to $20." She worked because she loved people, not for the money: "If I'd a stopped 'cause they didn't pay me, I'd a stopped a long time ago."

Even though many nurses remarked in their reports on the indispensable public health work achieved by lay midwives, the Board of Health eventually eradicated the practice of midwifery. In an attempt to hasten the removal of midwives, Nurse Supervisor Lucy E. Massey in 1948 introduced a retirement program initially recommended by her district nurses. The arrangement promoted the retirement of elderly midwives by notifying them and their relatives that they were too old to renew their licenses and then honoring them with ceremonies. Massey suggested that these "occasions be marked by as much ceremony as possible so that the retirement would be taken more seriously." A retirement badge was presented to midwives who were perceived as too old to practice. Any midwife who obtained this badge was known as a Mary D. Osborne Retired Midwife. When she obtained this badge, the midwife was required to return her permit and pledge that she would no longer practice, and she would wear the emblem to community gatherings and to church for the rest of her life.

Today, midwifery is still practiced in the state by two types of midwives. The first, direct-entry midwives, are often self-educated or trained through apprenticeship, attend births in out-of-hospital settings, do not have to be state-licensed, and are exempt from state medical practice laws. The second, nurse midwives, are both registered nurses and certified as midwives. Nurse midwives can deliver babies in hospitals (often in collaboration with a physician), in medical clinics, in birthing clinics, or in out-of-hospital settings such as the home. In 2009, .26 percent of all babies born in Mississippi were home births, delivered primarily by either direct-entry midwives or nurse midwives.

Lane Noel
University of Mississippi

Mississippi State Board of Health Papers, Mississippi Department of Archives and History; Laurel Lane Noel, "Midwives of Mississippi" (master's thesis, University of Mississippi, 2012); Susan L. Smith, *Nursing History Review* (January 1994).

Mileston

Located south of Tchula in the western third of Holmes County on flat, prime Delta agricultural land, Mileston was one of the resettlement communities created through an experimental poverty eradication program of the Farm Security Administration (FSA) of the US Department of Agriculture and the earlier Resettlement Administration. The projects coupled landownership with training, cooperative management, and economic assistance to facilitate upward mobility for a chronically poor stratum of sharecroppers and tenants. Of nearly one hundred such communities nationwide, Mileston was one of approximately thirteen that were entirely African American.

Mileston was part of the W. E. Jones estate until around 1940, when the FSA purchased roughly ten thousand acres of land pieced together from several plantations and converted the land into seventy individual farm units by building houses, barns, chicken coops, outhouses, wells, and smoke shacks. Mileston also contained one larger cooperative farm operated collectively by about thirty households. The parcels, each of which contained between forty and sixty acres, were originally rented to the settlers but were ultimately sold outright for around five thousand dollars each. Eighty-three of the roughly one hundred farm families involved in the project had previously sharecropped on the Jones estate. To coordinate the settlers' efforts, the FSA used cooperatives to manage the farming operations, purchase home-related materials, and deliver health care. By 1943 the community boasted a farming cooperative, a new and fully appointed public high school, and a health clinic staffed by a community nurse. The farm families received training from the FSA on matters of nutrition, planning, and home management. Today, roughly six thousand acres of the original land is still owned by families of the early project participants.

At the core of the Mileston community lay the FSA-established Mileston Cooperative Association, one of the oldest black farmers' cooperatives in the state. While individual families operated seventy of the Mileston Farms, thirty-six worked the cooperative or collective farm, Marcella Farms. The collective owned the mules, tractors, and other equipment, while each family owned its own subsistence livestock—a milk cow, hogs, and chickens. From the outset the cooperative farm idea was a difficult sell both nationwide and in Mileston, as the similarities between working the cooperative farm owned by the government and working as a sharecropper on a plantation were all too apparent. Further, given that nearly seventy of the project families were operating individual farms, cooperative participants must have felt at least somewhat envious. Beginning in 1944 the FSA sold the land to the individual families.

By 1945 the cooperative had most of the ingredients for success, with 120 members, a cotton gin, a store, a blacksmith shop, and land. The Mileston Cooperative was the center of activity, especially on Friday nights, when people gathered to play music and visit. Mileston farmers ginned their own cotton and loaded their produce directly onto train cars for sale at regional markets. The cooperative served the community for two decades.

A key community institution coordinated by the cooperative was the Mileston Medical Association. Beginning on 1 April 1940 Mileston families received home and office visits, weekly clinics, and ordinary drugs for fifteen dollars per year. By January 1942 community members finished constructing a four-room Community Health Center and dedicated it in a celebratory program that included FSA state and national leaders. Under the guidance of nurse Earless Hope, the Health Center delivered an impressive array of services. She held numerous special conferences for midwives in the area, acquired cribs for newborns, enrolled expectant mothers in education programs, and conducted home visits.

By 1946 the FSA had been dismantled and replaced by the more conservative Farmers Home Administration. Full-scale support for the resettlement communities became a thing of the past. Applying what they had learned, community members continued administering their cooperative, participated in the National Association for the Advancement of Colored People, served in the military, and worked to raise and educate their children.

The landownership base and cooperative management experience became a powerful combination for action during the civil rights movement. Mileston farmers were crucial to the success of both the Holmes County and Mississippi movements. The connection between land, the democratic process, and citizenship was so powerful in Milestone that Hartman Turnbow, Ozell Mitchell, Ralthus Hayes, Rev. Jesse James Russell, and Alma Carnegie—individuals who had little more than land—aggressively demanded their rights. Organizers and activists recognized the power as well. Inspired by Mileston, Fannie Lou Hamer, Stokely Carmichael, H. Rap Brown, and other leaders dreamed of larger visions of land reform. Mileston farmers built one of the first community centers used for citizenship classes in Mississippi, formed one of the strongest chapters of the Mississippi Freedom Democratic Party, and ultimately led the way in the election of Robert Clark to the Mississippi legislature in 1967.

Spencer D. Wood
Kansas State University

Kenneth T. Andrews, *Freedom Is a Constant Struggle: The Mississippi Civil Rights Movement and Its Legacy* (2004); Paul K. Conkin, *Tomorrow a New World: The New Deal Community Program* (1959); Ray Marshall and Lamond Godwin, *Cooperatives and Rural Poverty in the South* (1971); Spencer D. Wood, "The Roots of Black Power: Land, Civil Society, and the State in the Mississippi Delta, 1935–1968" (PhD dissertation, University of Wisconsin, 2006); Youth of the Rural Organizing and Cultural Center, *Minds Stayed on Freedom: The Civil Rights Struggle in the Rural South, an Oral History* (1991).

Military Bases

Mississippi's state motto, "Virtute et Armis" (By Valor and Arms), reflects two centuries of the state's military history. From the War of 1812 to the wars in Afghanistan and Iraq,

Cadets at the Army Air Forces training field, Greenville (Bern and Franke Keating Collection, Department of Archives and Special Collections, J. D. Williams Library, University of Mississippi)

Mississippi's soldiers have fought for their state and nation, and Mississippi has been home to important American military posts, camps, and stations.

Mississippi's premier military installation, now known as Camp Shelby, opened in 1917, ten miles south of Hattiesburg. It was first called Camp Crawford, but Kentucky and Indiana National Guardsmen of the 38th Infantry Division soon had it renamed Camp Shelby for Revolutionary War hero Col. Isaac Shelby, the first governor of Kentucky. After the 11 November 1918 armistice, Camp Shelby was closed. In 1934 the State of Mississippi acquired the facility for National Guard summer training. In 1940 Camp Shelby reopened as a federal installation, and within three years it had sprawled over three hundred thousand acres of Piney Woods and trained seventy-five thousand soldiers at a time. Seven infantry divisions trained there before fighting overseas in World War II: the 31st, 37th, 38th, and 43rd, which fought in the Pacific, and the 65th, 69th, and 85th, which fought in Europe. In addition, the Japanese American 442nd Regimental Combat Team, the most decorated US Army unit in history, trained at Camp Shelby. After V-J Day, the camp returned to state control, but in 1956 it became a permanent US Army training site, preparing troops for the Vietnam and Gulf Wars. In the first decade of the twenty-first century it trained one hundred thousand troops annually from all services for combat in Afghanistan and Iraq.

Mississippi's second major military base, Keesler Field (now Keesler Air Force Base), began in 1941 as America rearmed for World War II. Its core was the Biloxi Country Club, whose clubhouse became the Officer's Open Mess (O Club). Named for World War I aviator Lt. Samuel Reeves Keesler Jr. of Greenwood, who was shot down near Verdun in October 1918, it became an important basic and technical training base, peaking at 69,000 troops, when it was the world's largest air base. In all, 336,000 basic trainees and 142,000 mechanics served at Keesler Field during World War II, and that era is depicted in *No Time for Sergeants*, a novel by Georgia author Mac Hyman that subsequently became a play and a movie starring Andy Griffith, Roddy McDowell, and Don Knotts.

After World War II, Keesler became the US Air Force's electronic training center, and today it serves as the headquarters of the 2nd Air Force, responsible for basic and technical training for most nonflying Air Force personnel. Keesler currently hosts about fifty-one hundred active-duty members of the military, more than sixteen hundred civil service employees, thirteen thousand retirees, nearly forty-eight hundred family members, and twenty-seven hundred contractors.

During World War II two military posts were built in Mississippi to train US Army infantry divisions. Camp Van Dorn near Centerville, named for Confederate Maj. Gen. Earl Van Dorn, trained the 63rd and 99th Infantry Divisions, which fought in Europe. Camp McCain, south of Grenada, was named for World War I Maj. Gen. H. P. McCain, a Mississippian. At its peak the camp housed fifty thousand troops, including the 87th Infantry Division, which fought in Europe. Both camps were sites of serious racial disturbances, hushed up at the time, and both closed at war's end. Ten of the army's eighty-nine World War II combat divisions trained in Mississippi.

Other World War II army installations included Jackson's Foster General Hospital and ordnance plants near Flora and Prairie. Smaller service installations included a small naval station at Gulfport (still active), a Merchant Marine academy at Bay St. Louis, and a Coast Guard auxiliary air station at Biloxi.

Also during World War II, the Army Air Forces established flying training fields at Greenville and Columbus as well as smaller fields at Meridian, Greenwood, Laurel, and Hawkins Field at Jackson, which trained Dutch pilots. Auxiliary airfields were located at Clarksdale, Grenada, Gulfport, Hattiesburg, Madison, and Starkville. All closed at war's end, but the field at Gulfport became a training field for the Air National Guard. After the Korean War began in 1950, both Greenville and Columbus reopened for pilot training. Greenville subsequently closed, but Columbus continues to train pilots. In 1961 Naval Air Station Meridian opened among east-central Mississippi's hills and piney woods. This base turns out US Navy and Marine fighter pilots and has a technical training center for enlisted personnel. The Naval Construction Battalion Center, established at Gulfport in 1952, is home to the Atlantic Fleet Seabees and accommodates about forty-five hundred active-duty personnel and their families.

In 2010 there were about 10,000 Mississippi Army and 4,000 Air Guardsmen, most of whom have served in Afghanistan or Iraq.

John Hawkins Napier III
Ramer, Alabama

M

R. A. McLemore, ed., *History of Mississippi* (1961); Public Affairs Offices: Camp Shelby, Columbus Air Force Base, Keesler Air Force Base, Naval Air Station Meridian, Naval Construction Battalion Center Gulfport, Stennis Space Center, and Mississippi National Guard, in *The Army Almanac* (1959); US Department of Defense Military Installations website, www.militaryinstallations.dod.mil;.

Mills, William
(b. 1935) Writer

William Mills was born on 17 June 1935 in Hattiesburg. His literary career started with several poetry collections, moved into fiction and then nonfiction, and culminated with complex books about travel, place, and human and cultural interaction with the world. Mills grew up in Baton Rouge, Louisiana; attended Centenary College for a year; and spent two years in the army before earning bachelor's (1959), master's (1961), and doctoral (1972) degrees at Louisiana State University. His dissertation was published as *Stillness in Moving Things: The World of Howard Nemerov* (1975). He has taught at the University of Arkansas and at Oklahoma State University, and he now lives in Columbia, Missouri.

Mills has published poetry (*Watch for the Fox* [1974], *Stained Glass* [1979], and *The Meaning of Coyotes* [1984]), edited a volume on John William Corrington, written books on the Arkansas River and bears, and authored a novel and two collections of short stories. His overall literary impetus is probably best summarized in the closing lines from a poem in his first collection, *Watch for the Fox*: "Listening is better / Than not listening." His understanding of and empathy for Mississippi are displayed in "Unemployment," from the same collection:

A young hound howls.

I am almost slumbering
In a rocking chair.
The soft rain pats
A Mississippi road.

I feel like the road.

Jeffrey Klingfuss
Jackson, Mississippi

Robert M. Bain and Joseph M. Flora, eds., *Contemporary Poets, Dramatists, Essayists, and Novelists of the South: A Bio-Bibliographical Sourcebook* (1994); Joseph M. Flora and Amber Vogel, eds., *Southern Writers: A New Biographical Dictionary* (2006).

Millsaps College

Located on a one-hundred-acre urban campus in the heart of Jackson, Millsaps College is a private liberal arts college affiliated with the United Methodist Church.

Millsaps College was founded in 1890 by Reuben Webster Millsaps, a Confederate major and Harvard-trained business, finance, and church leader from Pleasant Valley, Mississippi. Inspired by his appreciation for education and concern for educational opportunities, Millsaps presented the Mississippi Methodist community with a personal gift of fifty thousand dollars for the establishment of a Christian college. Mississippi's Methodist community matched the gift, and with the help of Bishop Charles Betts Galloway, Millsaps College was soon established.

Throughout its early years Millsaps offered the state of Mississippi new opportunities for recreation and education. In 1901 the college built the state's first golf course, and in 1902 Mary Letitia Holloman became the school's first female graduate. In 1965 Millsaps became Mississippi's first all-white college to voluntarily desegregate.

Ten men and one woman have occupied the president's office: Dr. William Belton Murrah (1890–1910), Dr. David Carlisle Hull (1910–12), Dr. Alexander Farrar Watkins (1912–23), Dr. David Martin Key (1923–38), Dr. Marion Lofton Smith (1938–52), Dr. Homer Ellis Finger Jr. (1952–64), Dr. Benjamin Barnes Graves (1965–70), Dr. Edward McDaniel Collins Jr. (1970–78), Dr. George Marion Harmon (1978–2000), Dr. Frances Lucas (2000–2010), and Dr. Robert Wesley Pearigen (2010–).

Millsaps provides its more than eleven hundred domestic and international undergraduate and graduate students with thirty-three major and thirty-four minor programs of study and a faculty of more than ninety full-time professors. Along with its traditional programs in Jackson, Millsaps also affords students opportunities to participate in internship and study abroad programs within their individual fields. The college also offers academic opportunities to the greater Jackson community through the Continuing Education program and Community Enrichment Series for adult students and its summer programs for children. Millsaps College boasts a proud legacy of academic and social enrichment within the state as well as an alumni network that includes more than thirteen thousand people around the world.

Millsaps students and alumni take pride in the college's challenging academic offerings and in the Millsaps Majors, the school's sports teams. The Majors, whose colors are purple and white, compete in the National Collegiate Athletic Association's Division III and the Southern Collegiate Athletic Conference. Many students also participate in intramural athletics and in some of the more than eighty student-led clubs and organizations, including a thriving fraternity and sorority community. The college publishes a student newspaper, the *Purple and White*; a yearbook, the *Bobashela*; and a literary magazine, the *Stylus*.

In keeping with the beliefs of the Methodist Church, the college welcomes students from all religious backgrounds—or no religious background. The college maintains its relationship with the Methodist Church through partnerships such as the Center for Ministry and the Faith and Work Initiative, which are open to all students. Students at Millsaps also have the opportunity to join a number of ecumenical religious organizations. The library houses the J. B. McCain Archives of Mississippi Methodism.

Millsaps's urban campus plays host to numerous special events, among them the Millsaps Arts and Lecture Series, and the Elise and William Winter Speaker Series. In addition, the school operates the Lewis Art Gallery.

Eva Walton Kendrick
Birmingham, Alabama

George Lott Harrell, *History of Millsaps College* (1943); Millsaps College website, www.millsaps.edu.

Milton, Little (James Milton Campbell Jr.)
(1934–2005) Blues Musician

James Milton Campbell Jr. was born on 7 September 1934 on Duncan's Plantation on the outskirts of Inverness, Mississippi, the son of blues singer Big Milton Campbell. Little Milton fell in love with the guitar while listening to the *Grand Ole Opry* and bought his first six-string instrument for $14.40 from a Marshall Field catalog with money he saved from picking cotton. He cited influences such as Eddie Arnold, Ernest Tubb, Frank Sinatra, Roy Brown, and Sammy Davis Jr. His first professional job was with Leland bluesman Eddie Cusic. Little Milton later moved north and along with Ike Turner helped establish East St. Louis as a hub for blues music, playing at juke joints such as the Dynaflow, the Birdcage, and Chappie's Lounge.

Little Milton made his debut in the mid-1950s on Memphis's Sun Records. Soon after Milton cut his raucous sides, however, renegade producer Sam Phillips turned his attention to a young white singer with matinee idol looks, Elvis Presley. Undaunted, Milton traveled to St. Louis and recorded for the Bobbin label. Not until the 1960s did Little Milton truly develop his style and make his name on the Chess record label, home to such stars as Chuck Berry, Bo Diddley, and Muddy Waters. Little Milton had a No. 1 R&B hit single in 1965 with "We're Gonna' Make It," a song that resonated with the civil rights movement.

Little Milton (Courtesy Blues Archive, Department of Archives and Special Collections, J. D. Williams Library, University of Mississippi)

Milton's Chess sides reveal a soulful baritone, stinging guitar licks from his hollow-bodied Gibson, and lyrics reflecting his independence as both a musician and a man. This combination provided all the elements of a form of blues recognized as soul blues, a musical genre distinguished by passionate, gospel-tinged singing, punchy horns, "chicken-scratch" plucked guitars, and tight rhythm sections. Artists who wanted to move stylistically beyond the three-chord confines of conventional blues forms found the rhythm and blues strain of the 1950s and the southern soul style of the mid-1960s more to their creative liking. Soul blues was a fusion of Memphis blues and popular soul music that since its inception has been played by black artists for black audiences. The audience for Little Milton's music was on the Chitlin' Circuit, the string of black-owned clubs and theaters serving the entertainment needs of the often-segregated black community. Milton's music, particularly "We're Gonna Make It," spoke to the revolutionary possibilities of the 1960s.

Little Milton signed with the Memphis-based soul label Stax in 1971. At Stax, Milton expanded his studio sound, adding bigger horn and string sections and spotlighting his soulful vocals more than traditional blues. His Stax-era hits included "Annie Mae's Café," "Little Bluebird," and "That's What Love Will Make You Do." After Stax went bankrupt in 1975, Little Milton moved to Jackson-based Malaco, which found a niche with a core group of session musicians and songwriters, many of them former Stax employees. Little Milton's first Malaco single, "The Blues Is Alright," became the signature blues anthem and reestablished his presence as a major blues artist. Milton's later work for Malaco incorporated strings, horns, and background vocals to full effect. In 1988 Little Milton won the W. C. Handy Award for Blues Entertainer of the Year and was inducted into the Blues Hall of Fame. He on died 4 August 2005 in Memphis.

Mark Camarigg
University of Arkansas

Steve Huey, in *All Music Guide to the Blues*, ed. Michael Erlewine, Chris Woodstra, Cub Koda, and Stephen Thomas Erlewine (2003); Jim O'Neal, *Living Blues* (March–April 1994).

Ming, Hoyt, and His Pep Steppers
Musicians

Hoyt Ming and His Pep Steppers were an old-time string band from Lee County. The band consisted of Ming on fiddle; his wife, Rozelle, on guitar; his brother, Troy, on mandolin; and caller A. D. Coggins. Ming (at times mistakenly listed as Floyd Ming) was born on 6 October 1902 in Choctaw County into a family that included eight brothers, at least four of whom played instruments. Ming began fiddling at fifteen after his father invited a string band to perform at a house party. Hoyt and Rozelle Ming, who was born on 25 April 1907, farmed and played small dances until they were discovered at a Tupelo fiddle contest and the Troy Drug Company sponsored them to go to Memphis to record for Victor. They recorded four songs at the Peabody Hotel on 13 February 1928, including the "Indian War Whoop," a tune that included Ming's imitation of a Native American war cry. Ming impressed audiences by whooping along with the drawn-out final note of the phrase so closely that he could stop playing the fiddle without changing the sound at all. The illusion so impressed at least one man that he insisted that Ming put the fiddle into its case to prove it was not somehow still making the sound.

Ralph Peer, the talent scout who recruited and named the Pep Steppers, was particularly enamored with the sound of Rozelle Ming's feet tapping as she kept time on the gui-

tar. While most recording engineers of the day insisted that musicians mute the sound of their feet, Peer encouraged Rozelle to stomp as loudly as she could while the band recorded. Although Rozelle felt that this spoiled the recordings, most listeners find it unique and compelling aspects of the Pep Steppers' sound.

After their brief recording career, Hoyt and Rozelle Ming settled down and farmed potatoes and continued to play locally until the late 1950s. Ming was rediscovered in the early 1970s by County Records producer David Freeman, who had heard "Tupelo Blues." Freeman tracked down the Mings, who were delighted to return to their musical career. The Mings played at the National Folk Festival in Washington, D.C., in 1973 and recorded an excellent album of fiddle tunes, *Hoyt Ming and His Pep Steppers: New Hot Times* (Homestead Records, 1973). The Mings also played at the 1974 Smithsonian Festival of American Folklife. Forty years later, Hoyt and Rozelle had lost none of the unique charm and fluidity that marked their early recordings, and Rozelle's feet are clearly audible. Hoyt and Rozelle Ming made a brief cameo in the 1976 film *Ode to Billy Joe*, and John Hartford's recording of "Indian War Whoop" was featured in the Coen Brothers' 2001 film *O Brother, Where Art Thou?* Rozelle Ming died on 29 September 1983, while Hoyt Ming died on 28 April 1985. Their recording of "Ain't Gonna Rain No More" appears on a 2007 Smithsonian Folkways collection, *Classic Old-Time Fiddle*.

Edward McAllister
Belhaven University

Eugene Chadbourne, AllMusic.com website, www.allmusic.com; *Classic Old-Time Fiddle* (2007), liner notes; David Freeman, *Mississippi String Bands*, vols. 1 and 2 (1998), liner notes; Tony Russell, *Country Music Originals: The Legends and the Lost* (2007).

Minor, Bill
(b. 1922) Journalist

New Orleans Times-Picayune journalist Wilson F. "Bill" Minor was born in Hammond, Louisiana, and received a scholarship to attend Tulane University, graduating in 1943 with a degree in journalism and a minor in political science. While in school, he worked with the New Deal's National Youth Administration, and after graduation he joined the US Navy, serving on a destroyer in the Pacific.

Minor began his newspaper career in Mississippi in 1947 when the *Times-Picayune* assigned him to its Jackson bureau.

He remained in that position until 1976, leaving only when the paper closed the office. He declined an offer to run the *Los Angeles Times*'s new bureau in Houston and the *Times-Picayune*'s offer to move him to Washington, D.C. Instead, Minor remained in Jackson, launched a career as a syndicated columnist, and developed a legislative reporting service. He bought the *Northside Reporter*, a small suburban weekly, in 1973 and a few years later transformed it into the *Capitol Reporter*, which focused on covering politics. The paper was forced to close in 1981 because of an advertising boycott, threats from the Ku Klux Klan, and insufficient capital.

During his three decades in Jackson, Minor covered the state's battles over desegregation, the Emmett Till trial, James Meredith's efforts to enroll at the University of Mississippi, and the loosening of Mississippi's liquor laws. His reporting was noted for its accuracy, a feature not common among the state's newspapers, most of which opposed desegregation.

Minor attributes his liberalism to growing up in poverty under the New Deal and its programs. His father, Jacob Wilson, was an alcoholic from Mississippi who worked only sporadically as a printer. The family often survived on commodity programs. Minor continues to write hard-hitting syndicated columns on state politics. He is considered the dean of Mississippi political reporters, and his sometimes fiery writing often serves as readers' conscience.

He received the 1966 Louis Lyons Award from the Nieman Foundation at Harvard University, the 1997 John Chancellor Award for Excellence in Journalism presented by the Annenberg School for Communications of Pennsylvania, the 2001 Richard Wright Literary Excellence Award presented by Natchez Newspapers, and a 1972 Silver Em from the University of Mississippi. The Mississippi Press Association has also named its Best Reporting Prize and its General News Reporting Prize awards after Minor.

Minor is the author of *Eyes on Mississippi: A Fifty-Year Chronicle of Change*, which is based on more than 160 of his columns. He also contributed to Alexander Lamis's book, *Southern Politics in the 1990s*. Minor is the subject of a 2015 documentary film, *Bill Minor: Eyes on Mississippi*, by Ellen Ann Fentress and Lida Gibson.

Kathleen Woodruff Wickham
University of Mississippi

Michael L. Cooper, *Southern Changes* (August–September 1992); David R. Davies, ed., *The Press and Race: Mississippi Journalists Confront the Movement* (2001); Wilson F. Minor Papers, Special Collections, Mitchell Memorial Library, Mississippi State University; Jerry Mitchell, *Jackson Clarion-Ledger* (27 May 2003); Gene Roberts and Hank Klibanoff, *The Race Beat: The Press, the Civil Rights Struggle, and the Awakening of a Nation* (2006); *Time* (21 August 1978).

Mission Mississippi

Mission Mississippi is a statewide ecumenical organization working to build relationships between individual Christians and congregations across racial and denominational lines. Activities sponsored by the organization include regular prayer breakfasts, church partnerships, and the Annual Governor's Prayer Luncheon. In 2016, Mission Mississippi reported twenty-one gatherings that met monthly in cities across the state.

Founded in Jackson in 1992, Mission Mississippi owes its origins to a citywide crusade proposed by white evangelist Patrick Morley and supported by white businessmen Victor Smith and Lee Paris. Morley suggested that the campaign required a demonstration of unity between African American and white Christians and invited nationally known African American evangelist Tom Skinner to join. The effort received support from an informal interracial coalition of Jackson's ministers led by James Washington of St. Peter Missionary Baptist Church and James Baird of First Presbyterian Church.

In October 1993 Mission Mississippi held a series of three rallies in Mississippi Veterans Memorial Stadium with an attendance of approximately twenty-four thousand. Mission Mississippi's board, chaired by Paris, considered the rallies a success and made these "Celebration of Reconciliation" rallies an annual event. The board also chose Jarvis Ward, a young African American, to serve as Mission Mississippi's executive director.

While ecumenical in membership (participants include African American and white Protestants, Catholics, and Pentecostals), Mission Mississippi was and remains broadly evangelical in character. With its slogan, "Changing Mississippi one relationship at a time," Mission Mississippi is part of a national movement of evangelicals calling for racial reconciliation that includes the men's movement Promise Keepers. Though white evangelicals had been largely indifferent or even opposed to the civil rights movement in the 1960s, in the 1990s they proposed to address racial divisions in the church and nation by calling on Christians to form intentional interracial relationships.

The energy surrounding the first rallies in Jackson gradually dissipated, and attendance at the annual celebrations dwindled. In 1998 Dolphus Weary replaced Ward as the organization's director, bringing expertise in community organizing from his years with the Voice of Calvary and Mendenhall Ministries. Weary accepted the position with a mandate to develop Mission Mississippi as a statewide organization.

Under Weary and his team, Mission Mississippi's emphasis on intentional interracial relationships has survived, while the large-scale rallies have gone by the wayside. Preaching in

M

black and white pulpits the length and breadth of the state, Weary challenges congregation members to seek out interracial friendships. Mission Mississippi hosts a range of events to facilitate such relationships, including twice-weekly prayer breakfasts in different locations in Jackson, monthly businessmen's prayer breakfasts and women's prayer luncheons, restaurant discounts for two couples who eat together, and churches partnering for everything from picnics to preaching. Mission Mississippi also offers diversity training programs for schools, churches, businesses, and other organizations.

In 2005, in the wake of Hurricane Katrina, Mission Mississippi, with its unique links to African American and white congregations in the affected area, its support network of churches and Christian organizations across the country, and its connections with local community development organizations, played a significant role in coordinating faith-based aid to the Mississippi Gulf Coast. Within a month of the disaster, the Federal Emergency Management Agency listed Mission Mississippi as a key organization in the coordination of relief.

Mission Mississippi is perhaps the largest sustained ecumenical racial-reconciliation initiative in the United States.

Peter Slade
Ashland University

Mission Mississippi website, missionmississippi.net; Peter Slade, *Open Friendship in a Closed Society: Mission Mississippi and a Theology of Friendship* (2009).

Missionaries to Mississippi Indians

Frontier Mississippi provided staging grounds for religious experimentation involving southeastern Amerindian tribes and Christian missionaries. During the seventeenth and eighteenth centuries, Catholic missionaries such as Father Anthony Davion and Father Francis de Montigny planted crosses, sought to convert the tribes, and experienced culture shock amid the geopolitics of the frontier. When they sought to prevent the Natchez from ritually murdering relatives of the Great Sun, these missionaries braved the wrath of aggrieved tribesmen. Conflict among tribes and European powers, with the Choctaw of Central Mississippi favoring the French and the Chickasaw of Northeast Mississippi favoring the English, also affected missionaries. Some, including Father Nicholas Foucault, suffered martyrdom, while Davion and others merely suffered expulsion.

Protestant missionary efforts coincided with treaties that between 1801 and 1837 removed the tribes from Mississippi to Oklahoma, but the inspiration for these efforts came from John Eliot in Massachusetts and David Brainerd in New Jersey and the 1806 Haystack Prayer Meeting at Williams College. Baptists, Methodists, and Presbyterians sent missionaries to Mississippi and developed organizations for their support. In 1817 agents of the American Baptist Foreign Mission Society, headquartered in New England, established the Mississippi Society for Baptist Missions Foreign and Domestic to tell the "aborigines of the west" about the "Great Father." The missionary organizations hoped that each station would produce more converts, who in turn would generate support for other missions around the world. As early as 1815 the Mississippi Association subscribed $67.93 for such purposes.

Early Protestant missionaries, among them Yale graduate Joseph Bullen, wandered in and out of tribal lands much as other frontiersmen did. Subsequent missionaries had to draw wagons across "deep creeks and gutters on poles," accumulated debts, and accepted two-month delays for letters. But the term *mission* carried religious and diplomatic overtones. In March 1819 the US Congress passed An Act Making Provisions for the Civilization of the Indian Tribes Adjoining the Frontier Settlements. The Choctaw were entitled to six thousand dollars annually for seventeen years for sale of their land, with much of the money supporting mission schools.

The American Board of Commissioners for Foreign Missions, a venture of Congregationalists and Presbyterians, opened eight mission stations among the Choctaw and Chickasaw. Directed by Cyrus Kingsbury, these stations bore revealing names. Elliot and Mayhew in Oktibbeha County commemorated earlier missionary efforts. Goshen and Hebron bespoke a timeless affiliation with the Bible. Tribal names such as Yoknokchaya and Hikashubbaha preserved the sounds if not the culture of Amerindians. In 1820 Elliot had "seven log-dwelling houses" and a mill. By the 1830s associated mission stations claimed 250 scholars and about 400 members. A former missionary to Palestine hailed one of the stations as the "loveliest spot my eyes ever saw."

Kingsbury associate Cyrus Byington learned the Choctaw language, reducing reliance on interpreters, but misunderstandings remained. Missionaries claimed that the Choctaw were "hardened stupefied sinners" who acknowledged a "Great Spirit" who was "very seldom the subject of contemplation" and exerted "no effect on their conduct." The Choctaw at first distrusted the prosperity of the mission stations but were swayed by tribal leader Pushmataha to accept certain forms of mission benevolence. Some Choctaw resented missionary requirements for student labor at their schools, preferring their own emulative approach to child rearing. Apukshunnubbee wanted to spend tribal annuity money on blacksmith shops rather than schools. As younger mixed-blood leaders replaced full-blooded chiefs, school enrollments increased. Full-blooded chiefs favored traditional hunting and festive culture; mixed-bloods favored schools, farming, and Christianity. When missionaries allied with the mixed-bloods, they forfeited full access to the Choctaw.

Land claims, better prospects, and personal exhaustion affected missionary tenure. Maintained by the Synod of the Cumberland Presbyterian Church in Tennessee, the Cotton Gin and Monroe Station missions continued until the Chickasaw moved West in 1837. Several stations, like the nine-year mission in Jasper County, were abandoned during the 1830s to make way for white settlement. Ventures such as French Camp in North Mississippi endured.

Unlike colleagues in the Caribbean and India, Mississippi missionaries were not self-consciously radical. Baptist Isaac McCoy thought that the Choctaw should not live with whites, while Kingsbury opposed Pres. Andrew Jackson's Removal policy. Slave laborers were at times retained despite the qualms of some missionaries. The American Board and the US government alike were uncomfortable with missionaries' promotion of native languages. Missionaries also recognized oppression, theft of Indian land, and the vexatious ways of civil courts in Mississippi. Kingsbury negotiated with Pres. James Madison for a subsidy in 1816, journeyed to the Brainerd mission near Chattanooga, requited Choctaw aspirations for more schools, and opposed Methodist activities that produced immediate conversions. After the Removal of the Choctaw tribe, Kingsbury traveled to Pine Ridge, Oklahoma, in 1836 and became involved in controversy regarding slave ownership by the Choctaw.

In the later nineteenth century a second wave of missionary efforts led by Baptists, Catholics, and Methodists ministered to those who had not taken the Trail of Tears. In the twentieth century William Ketcham, a Catholic priest, helped to safeguard Choctaw rights.

Mission efforts increased literacy, produced dictionaries and Bibles in tribal languages, and encouraged the Choctaw association of church and ball ground as the focus of tribal activity and identity. Missionaries indirectly abetted white settlement and Amerindian Removal and ensured that Christianity would become part of that mixture of blood, motive, and metaphors characterizing the Amerindian experience in Mississippi.

Myron C. Noonkester
William Carey University

G. H. Anderson, ed., *Biographical Dictionary of Christian Missions* (1999); *Annual Reports of the Baptist Board of Foreign Missions for the United States* (1815, 1816); David W. Baird, in *Churchmen and the Western Indians, 1820–1920*, ed. Clyde A. Milner II and Floyd A. O'Neil (1985); Center for Study of the Life and Work of William Carey, DD (1761–1834), "An Abridgement of Mr. David Brainerd's Journal among the Indians" www.wmcarey.edu/carey/brainerd/journal.htm; B. B. Edwards, *The Missionary Gazetteer* (1832); William L. Hiemstra, *Journal of Mississippi History* (January 1948); Clara Sue Kidwell, *Choctaws and Missionaries in Mississippi, 1818–1918* (1995); Robert T. Lewit, *Mississippi Valley Historical Review* (1963–64); Isaac McCoy, *History of Baptist Indian Missions* (1840); Percy L. Rainwater, *Journal of Mississippi History* 1 (1966); Harry Warren, *Publications of the Mississippi Historical Society*, ed. Franklin L. Riley, vol. 8 (1904).

Missionary Baptists

The largest concentration of African American Baptist congregations in Mississippi identify as Missionary Baptist. A recent estimate has the total number of Mississippians who attend Missionary Baptist churches at more than 350,000. Most of these churches were formed in the immediate postemancipation years when African American congregations separated from their primarily white mother churches, which were often affiliated with the Southern Baptist Convention.

In keeping with the evangelical spirit of the white Baptist faith tradition in the South, newly formed and independent African American congregations across the state adopted the title of Missionary Baptists. Missionary Baptists believe in the classic tenets of the historic Baptist polity: the autonomy of local congregations and the view that baptism and church membership are reserved for mature congregants. Missionary Baptist services are characterized by the dynamic and expressive style of black Baptist worship.

The defining characteristic of Missionary Baptist churches remains the enduring insistence on church autonomy. Each church is led by a pastor and in most cases his wife, the first lady. Laypeople account for the remainder of the church leadership. Men can become deacons and ushers. Women hold the titles of church mothers and sisters. Few Missionary Baptist churches allow women to serve as pastors. Unlike other denominations, Missionary Baptists do not have required allegiances to national or state organizing bodies, and most choose to remain independent.

Nevertheless, statewide organizations have had an important historical presence. The most notable statewide organization is the General Missionary Baptist State Convention of Mississippi. Founded in 1890 by Rev. Randle Pollard, "the Father of Negro Baptists in Mississippi," the Baptist State Convention arose from the merger of two earlier organizations, the General Missionary Baptist Association of Mississippi and the General Convention, and originally included four hundred churches with more than seventy thousand members. The convention soon established Natchez College to provide African American youth in Mississippi with the opportunity for a private, religious-based education. Pres. Samuel Henry Clay Owen and his wife, Sarah Mazique, led Natchez College for many years before it moved to Jackson and subsequently evolved into Jackson State University. Headquartered in Jackson, the Baptist State Convention continues to promote Christian education, wellness, and community enrichment across the state.

Mississippi boasts an impressive roster of historically influential Missionary Baptists. Born in Noxubee County, Richard Henry Boyd (1843–1922) received theological training in Texas before establishing himself as a major figure in the first national African American Baptist convention, the

National Baptist Convention, USA. His "Boyd Faction" later divided the National Baptist Convention over the issue of the development of a publishing board, and Boyd's successors ultimately founded the National Missionary Baptist Convention of America, which boasts more than 2.5 million congregants. Other prominent Mississippi Missionary Baptists have included Joseph Harrison Jackson (1900–1990), who was born in Rudyard and served as president of the National Baptist Convention USA from 1953 to 1982, and Clarence La Vaughn Franklin (1915–84), a Sunflower County native who became a pioneering radio broadcast preacher and was the father of legendary songstress Aretha Franklin.

Whereas the majority of Mississippi's churches and individuals identifying as Missionary Baptist are African American, the state also has some primarily white Interstate and Foreign Landmark Missionary Baptist Churches, whose memberships exceeded 100,000 in 2000.

Eva Walton Kendrick
Birmingham, Alabama

Association of Religion Data Archives website, www.thearda.com; C. Eric Lincoln and Lawrence H. Mimaya, *The Black Church in African American Experience*; Marvin A. McMickle, *An Encyclopedia of African American Christian Heritage*.

Mississippi Action for Progress

Mississippi Action for Progress (MAP) was founded in 1966 to receive federal funds to run Head Start programs. It challenged and ultimately superseded the Child Development Group of Mississippi (CDGM) as the primary group to run Head Start in the state.

As an important part of the War on Poverty in the mid-1960s, the US government's Office of Economic Opportunity (OEO) made a commitment to Head Start programs to improve the education and health of young children in poor areas of the country. The CDGM was a private group that hoped to carry on the goals of the freedom schools of the Student Nonviolent Coordinating Committee, as evidenced by its headquarters at Mount Beulah, which shared space with the Delta Ministry and the Mississippi Freedom Democratic Party; its conscious interracialism; its rhetoric of local control over local affairs; and many of its leaders, such as founder Tom Levin, Student Nonviolent Coordinating Committee member Fred Smith, and Marian Wright. In 1965 the CDGM received a large federal grant to run Head Start programs in Mississippi.

Conservatives in the state condemned the CDGM as a leftist organization that was challenging the racial hierarchy, in part by creating jobs for young troublemakers. Gov. Paul B. Johnson, Sen. John Stennis, and other government leaders criticized the CDGM for putting up bail money for jailed demonstrators and more broadly for not knowing how to handle money, especially large federal grants. Stennis and Sen. James Eastland were among the Mississippi leaders who urged OEO director Sargent Shriver not to give more money to CDGM.

At the end of 1966, the US Congress hesitated to give another large grant to CDGM to run Head Start programs. In response, some Mississippi leaders, including Hodding Carter III and Aaron Henry of the National Association for the Advancement of Colored People, founded MAP. Other leaders included Owen Cooper, Leroy Percy, and Oscar Carr of the traditionally conservative Delta Council and Robert L. T. Smith and Charles Young, two younger African Americans who wanted to work with the existing Democratic Party. MAP received considerable criticism because it competed with the CDGM for funds and respectability. Critics saw MAP as one sign of the difficulties faced by innovative, countercultural forces in turning the energy and activism of the civil rights movement into platforms for local control and a new type of education. The OEO, happy to get away from controversies surrounding the CDGM, granted most Head Start funding and authority to MAP. Fannie Lou Hamer condemned the decision: "We aren't ready to be sold out by a few middle-class bourgeoisie and some of the Uncle Toms who couldn't care less." Wright saw the decision as another example of powerful Mississippians trying to prevent African Americans from obtaining funds to run programs for themselves.

Members of MAP and CDGM argued over the proper direction and leadership for Head Start until 1967, when the OEO stopped giving funds to CDGM. In an attempt to quell the controversy, MAP hired Helen Bass Williams of Tougaloo College, a former CDGM worker, as its director and offered a compromise between federal and local control over Head Start.

MAP remains an idealistic organization dedicated to improving the health and education of the state's poor children. By 2016 it ran sixty-one Head Start centers offering education, health care, meals, and other programs for more than six thousand children in its twenty-five-county service area, and it has expanded its range of services to include family literacy and environmental health concerns.

Ted Ownby
University of Mississippi

John Dittmer, *Local People: The Struggle for Civil Rights in Mississippi* (1995); Polly Greenberg, *The Devil Has Slippery Shoes: A Biased Biography of the Child Development Group of Mississippi (CDGM), a Story of Maximum Feasible Poor Parent Participation* (1990); Kay Mills, *Something Better for My Children: The History and People of Head Start* (1998);

Mississippi Action for Progress website, www.mapheadstart.org; Kim Lacy Rogers, *Life and Death in the Delta: African American Narratives of Violence, Resilience, and Social Change* (2006); Crystal R. Sanders, *A Chance for Change: Head Start and Mississippi's Freedom Struggle* (2016); Clyde Woods, *Development Arrested: Race, Power, and the Blues in the Mississippi Delta* (1998).

Mississippi Art Association/Mississippi Museum of Art

In 1911 a small group of art-conscious Mississippians founded the Mississippi Art Association (MAA). From the start, the Jackson-based organization strove "to seek out and foster the creatively artistic talents of the people of the state." The group's efforts resulted in the present-day Mississippi Museum of Art (MMA), currently located in downtown Jackson.

The MAA originated from the Art Study Club, which Bessie Cary Lemly (1871–1947) organized in 1903. Club members and their supporters participated in an oil exhibition held at the 1911 state fair. After an enthusiastic response to this first exhibition, the group became the Mississippi Art Association. The first meeting took place at the Mississippi State Fairgrounds, and members elected Lemly president.

The MAA's sole purpose initially was to exhibit at the state fair. Within five years, however, the association began collecting funds to hold juried exhibitions at the fair. Purchase awards went to first-prize winners, thereby allowing the association to begin acquiring works in 1912. The first piece acquired was an oil on canvas, *The Shower* (ca. 1911), by William P. Silva (1859–1948). The MAA's collection, in turn, provided the foundation for the MMA.

Over the next ten years members focused on spreading art within the community. The organization was instrumental, for example, in bringing formal art education into the public schools. Members of the MAA and the Art Study Club lobbied successfully for legislative funding. In the 1950s the organization introduced a program under which Jackson artists instructed local children every Saturday at such places as Wolfe Studios, the Junior Red Cross, and the YWCA. This program eventually expanded to include the cities of Hazlehurst, Vicksburg, and Clinton.

The MAA also began pushing for a permanent home for its collection, which by 1916 had grown to include works by Ellsworth Woodward (1861–1938), Betty McArthur (ca. 1865–1944), and the organization's own Lemly. The association continued to hold its annual show at the state fair and to acquire paintings via purchase awards. Members stored these works in their private homes. In 1926 Thomas Gale presented his family home on North State Street to the City of Jackson for educational, civic, and cultural purposes. The MAA held its annual meeting there, and the association was incorporated the same year. In 1927 the collection moved there, and the building subsequently became the Municipal Art Gallery.

In 1931 the Municipal Art Gallery premiered the Annual Watercolor Exhibition to complement the popular oil exhibition. The collection grew slowly over the next forty-five years, reaching fifty-eight pieces by the end of World War II. Though small, the collection still required more functional gallery space. On 3 March 1955 a building fund was established.

Two decades later, the collection, which had grown to include more than four hundred pieces, moved to the First Federal Savings and Loan of Jackson. In 1978 the MMA opened its doors at 201 East Pascagoula Street. Today it is the largest art museum in the state, housing more than four thousand objects in its permanent collection. The collection includes nineteenth- and twentieth-century American landscape paintings, American and European works on paper, and southern and Mississippi art; photographs; eighteenth-century British paintings; Japanese prints; pre-Columbian ceramics; folk art; and contemporary art.

Currently under the directorship of Betsy Bradley, the MMA fulfills its founders' mission to promote the work of Mississippi artists and bring art education to the public. The museum offers nearly twenty exhibitions each year, including the annual watercolor exhibition; provides summer art classes for children as well as with other youth-oriented activities; and offers film screenings, lecture series, group tours, volunteer programs, and online teaching materials.

Kathy Greenberg
Tampa, Florida

Patti Carr Black, *Art in Mississippi, 1790–1980* (1998); Patricia Odom Drake, "A Historical Study of the Mississippi Art Association from 1911 to 1975" (master's thesis, University of Southern Mississippi, 1976); Mississippi Museum of Art website, www.msmuseumart.org; Cantey Venable Sutton, *History of Art in Mississippi* (1929).

Mississippi Baptist Convention

Baptist settlers from South Carolina moved into the Natchez area in the late eighteenth century. Their first church was probably Salem Baptist Church (1791), located on Cole's Creek in what became Jefferson County. By 1806 five churches in the region formed the Mississippi Baptist Association. The

Baptist polity is fiercely independent, and associations or conventions exert no control over member churches apart from the power to expel them. This impulse toward independence prevented the association from gaining strength. Likewise, an early shortage of trained clergy not only impaired growth but also instilled a desire to develop educational opportunities. These restraints, however, did not keep the Baptists from developing an early influence on politics through leaders such as George Poindexter.

By 1824 enough churches and associations existed to generate the first statewide convention. That convention dissolved in 1829, only to re-form permanently in 1836. At that time there were 9 associations, 122 churches, and 4,287 church members. The events leading up to the Civil War generated controversy over the control of missions agencies and slave ownership among American Baptists, leading to a denominational schism in 1845. Most Baptists in the South affiliated themselves with the Southern Baptist Convention.

In 2001 the state convention reported 2,080 churches, with 1,723,149 total members. Current denominational structure involves a full-time staff headed by the executive director–treasurer. Annual conventions meet in Jackson to elect a president and various committees and boards, all of which work with the professional staff to oversee convention activities. The missions enterprises encompass work within the state, across the nation, and internationally. The early interest in providing educational training in a Baptist context led to the 1850 acquisition of Mississippi College along with several other institutions of higher learning. Current colleges include Blue Mountain College in Blue Mountain, Mississippi College in Clinton, and William Carey University in Hattiesburg, Gulfport, and New Orleans. The Mississippi Baptist Convention maintains close ties with Baptist Memorial Hospital in Memphis and the Mississippi Baptist Medical Center in Jackson. The Baptist Children's Villages are important providers of child welfare. The Christian Action Commission leads in campaigns concerning issues that influence the moral climate of the state, including recent campaigns against gambling and in favor of improved race relations. The Baptist men's association, the Brotherhood, and the ladies' auxiliary, the Women's Missionary Union, provide social action through literacy, job skill, and disaster relief activities. Since 1887 the means of communication among Baptist churches and members has been the *Baptist Record*, the state's largest-circulation weekly newspaper.

More than a third of Mississippi's population is Baptist, and the denomination wields considerable political influence. Most of the state's recent US senators, representatives, and governors have been Baptists. The historical archives of the Mississippi Baptist Convention are located at the Speed Library at Mississippi College.

Gene C. Fant Jr.
Palm Beach Atlantic University

R. A. McLemore, *A History of Mississippi Baptists, 1780–1970* (1971); Mississippi Baptist Convention, Book of Reports (2001).

Mississippi Blues Trail

The Mississippi Blues Trail celebrates the people and places that have influenced the development of the blues, the soulful musical genre that combines lyrical tales of tragedy, hardship, and lost love with creative and evocative harmonics. Perhaps the greatest creation to come out of Mississippi, the blues have inspired musicians around the world and shaped popular culture in America. The Blues Trail consists of markers placed at sites around the state, each recounting the story of an artist, venue, or event that played an important role in the development of the blues. The markers serve as a source of civic pride, keep alive local stories and sentiments, stimulate economic growth, attract tourists, and provide opportunities for education about the cultural heritage of Mississippi communities.

Each marker documents an important legacy that has local, national, and global significance. Some capture stories at risk of being lost forever, as they have persisted only through oral history or have been suppressed by those who have devalued the blues as the "devil's music." Once in place, the markers create greater interest in the roots of American music, attracting blues fans and heritage tourists from around the world. Visitors are eager to experience the places that have been immortalized in song and that gave the blues life and want to learn more about the people who made the music. The sites along the Blues Trail convey these stories from a hometown perspective.

Tourism benefits the communities where markers are placed, as it stimulates economic growth, creates opportunities for local jobs, and brings visitors from all over the world to Mississippi towns. Residents who are unaware of their local heritage can learn about people and events that crafted the fabric of their community and can take pride in sharing these stories with others. The Blues Trail also provides schools with a tangible means to educate young people about Mississippi's cultural history.

Heritage preservation efforts such as the Mississippi Blues Trail frequently enjoy broad public and institutional support because they bring together diverse interests. By linking cultural stewardship and economic development, the Blues Trail appeals to artists and musicians, historians, fans of popular culture, travelers, business and economic growth advocates, educators, and conservationists, among others.

Several trends inspired the creation of the Mississippi Blues Trail. Tourism grew as an engine of economic growth and gained institutional support in Mississippi after casino gaming was legalized in 1990. As the state built a tourism infrastructure, interest in heritage tourism increased, especially after the US National Park Service sponsored a 1996 conference to explore the cultural heritage of the Lower Mississippi Delta region. The blues emerged as an important theme, and early in the twenty-first century parallel efforts spearheaded by the Delta Center for Culture and Learning at Delta State University, the Delta Research and Cultural Institute at Mississippi Valley State University, and the B. B. King Museum in Indianola coalesced to increase interest in blues tourism and opened the possibility for political action. When the Memphis-based Blues Foundation declared 2003 the Year of the Blues, Mississippi governor Ronnie Musgrove created a commission to find ways of recognizing and promoting the role the blues has played in Mississippi's culture. The following year the state legislature passed and new governor Haley Barbour signed a measure drafted by the commission that created the eighteen-member Mississippi Blues Commission to oversee blues preservation and development.

The Mississippi Blues Commission took on administering the Mississippi Blues Trail as the centerpiece of its activities. A blue-ribbon panel identified more than one hundred sites worthy of commemoration. Blues historians and scholars carefully research and write each story, which is then placed on a marker with raised lettering on the front and a variety of text, photos, maps, and other artifacts on the back. The first marker, honoring Charley Patton, was unveiled on 11 December 2006 in Holly Ridge, and over the next decade nearly two hundred other markers were added. The dedication ceremonies have taken on tremendous meaning for the communities where the markers are located and have attracted families of those honored, blues artists involved in the story, and dignitaries, some of whom have traveled great distances to attend.

The thirteen-member nonprofit Mississippi Blues Foundation was created to raise money for the Blues Trail and other efforts to preserve and honor blues legends, and the Mississippi Development Authority's Division of Tourism Development provides statewide institutional support for the Blues Trail. The Blues Trail's success led to similar efforts, including the Mississippi Freedom Trail, which honors civil rights activities, and trails honoring country and gospel music.

Alan W. Barton

Blues Foundation website, www.blues.org; Luther Brown, director of the Delta Center for Culture and Learning at Delta State University and member of the Mississippi Blues Commission, interview by Alan W. Barton (1 August 2007); Marvin Haire, director of the Delta Research and Cultural Institute at Mississippi Valley State University and chair of the Mississippi Blues Foundation, interview by Alan W. Barton (7 September 2007); Mississippi Blues Commission website, www.msbluestrail.org; Mississippi Development Authority website, www.visitmississippi.org; Alex Thomas, director of heritage trails, Mississippi Development Authority, and member of the Mississippi Blues Commission, interview by Alan W. Barton (14 September 2007).

Mississippi Burning

The plot of Alan Parker's 1988 film, *Mississippi Burning*, is drawn from the 1964 disappearance of civil rights workers Andrew Goodman and Michael Schwerner, who were white northerners, and James Chaney, a black native of Meridian, Mississippi. The three activists were working to register African American voters in Meridian as part of the Freedom Summer project. On the night of 16–17 June, members of the Ku Klux Klan burned a church in Longdale, where activists planned to open a freedom school. On 21 June Goodman, Schwerner, and Chaney drove to see the burned-out church but disappeared outside Philadelphia on their way back to Meridian. FBI agents began investigating the disappearances the next day. On 4 August the bodies of the three men were found buried in an earthen dam.

In *Mississippi Burning*, Gene Hackman and Willem Dafoe portray fictional FBI agents who set out to find the murderers of the three activists. After realizing that the local people will not cooperate with the investigation—the whites apathetic and the blacks scared—the agents use blackmail and intimidation to persuade some KKK members to confess their involvement and implicate others. Although suspenseful and powerful in the film, these extralegal measures, including a scene in which a fictional black FBI agent holds a knife to a white man, were fabrications. Intimidation was minimally used in the actual investigation.

Hackman's and Dafoe's characters have opposite personalities and ideologies but eventually develop a friendship and mutual respect for each other. Various other characters make brief appearances that add a bit of romance, intrigue, and turmoil to the story—the villainous deputy (Brad Dourif), his decent yet misguided wife (Frances McDormand), and a brave black boy who endures much racism and emotional harm (Darius McCrary). These characters are loosely based on real people but are included primarily to give depth to the film.

Mississippi Burning hit theaters in December 1988 and grossed more than $34.6 million during its run. It received six Academy Award nominations, including Best Picture and Best Director. The film won an Oscar for Best Cinematography. However, historians and civil rights groups criticized the movie, primarily on the grounds that it portrayed African Americans as passive bystanders while the white FBI agents swooped in and saved the day. Writing in the *Chicago*

M

Sun-Times, Vernon Jarrett commented, "The film treats some of the most heroic people in black history as mere props in a morality play." Parker countered that white FBI agents had to be the heroes in the film to secure box-office popularity in 1988.

Caroline Jalfin
Somerville, Massachusetts

Harvey Fireside, *The "Mississippi Burning" Civil Rights Murder Conspiracy Trial: A Headline Court Case* (2002); Internet Movie Database website, www.imdb.com; Jerry Mitchell, *Jackson Clarion-Ledger* (24 November 2014); Robert Brent Toplin, *History by Hollywood: The Use and Abuse of the American Past* (1996).

Mississippi Choctaw Indian Federation

On 12 May 1934 in Union, the leadership of the Mississippi Choctaw communities met with allies Earl Richardson, a state senator, and E. T. Winston, a newspaper editor and friend of Gov. Theodore Bilbo, to draft a government under the auspices of the 1934 Indian Reorganization Act (IRA), which permitted Indians to create tribal councils. Naming the organization the Mississippi Choctaw Indian Federation (MCIF), these leaders proclaimed the political rebirth of the Choctaw nation in Mississippi. Choctaw superintendent Archie C. Hector, however, had already created a Tribal Business Committee (TBC) to consider acceptance of the IRA. Despite the fact that two-thirds of his committee supported the MCIF, Hector denounced it as the work of a handful of malcontents. Over the next year, Hector and the MCIF engaged the federal government's Office of Indian Affairs (OIA) in a passionate debate over which organization had the right to construct the new tribal government, and the MCIF ultimately failed to win recognition. At first glance, this story appears to be a simple tale of a political initiative that failed. Yet the MCIF's campaign reveals a Choctaw political strategy deeply rooted in historical patterns of activism. The Mississippi Choctaw used the conflict over the government to strengthen their relationships with their political allies at the state level and thus assert greater control over their lives.

The struggle to establish a tribal government in the 1930s represented the continuation of a century of Choctaw assertions of political sovereignty. Article 14 of the 1830 Treaty of Dancing Rabbit Creek had promised that the Choctaw who remained in Mississippi would receive land and that anyone who resided on the land for five years would hold the political status of a free white citizen. The allotment process was hopelessly corrupt, however, and the Choctaw became poor sharecroppers without political standing. In response, they retreated into ethnic enclaves, organized around churches and schools, where they could preserve their cultural distinctiveness. They also pressed their treaty claims at every opportunity, building up a network of political allies. In 1918 the Choctaw and their elected officials won the establishment of an OIA agency in Mississippi, which offered schools, reimbursable farm allotments, and vocational training; it did not, however, provide the tribal government that the Choctaw had desired since 1830.

Hector's TBC was a start, but the Choctaw had reservations about how it functioned and consequently created another organization to address these concerns. The committee had been appointed, not elected, and Indians living outside of the seven official communities had no representation. In contrast, the MCIF granted membership to any half-blood Choctaw over age twenty-one who headed a family as husband, wife, or guardian. Choctaw leaders also feared that they lacked education in governmental affairs, so the MCIF aligned with Richardson and Winston, who was an expert in Indian history, to provide political expertise. Finally, the TBC had noted the Choctaw people's dire need for financial assistance. The MCIF and its allies addressed that anxiety, planning to seek compensation for lost land and funding to develop tourism on Choctaw lands. The MCIF thus met needs that the TBC did not.

Moreover, the federation's actions were crucial when all the Choctaw voted on the IRA on 19 March 1935. Heeding the MCIF's complaints, Hector allowed Indians outside the seven communities to participate in the vote. Moreover, rather than appointing people to form the new government, as he had with the TBC, Hector called for elections during the vote on the IRA. The majority of the Choctaw approved the IRA and elected a new TBC to construct the government. Hector assumed that this new committee would disband the MCIF. It did not.

Instead, the Choctaw used the federation to lobby for greater control over their lives. Several members of the state's congressional delegation contacted the OIA on behalf of the MCIF, and their interventions appear to have affected decisions regarding agency matters. For example, the OIA transferred several employees whom the MCIF had criticized. The OIA also instructed Hector to include delegates from the federation in all meetings to construct the new government. The committee's refusal to disband the "rival" MCIF government, then, suggested that the Choctaw viewed the federation as another method of protecting Choctaw interests.

A few months later, however, the OIA decided that the Choctaw were not eligible for the IRA because they were not a tribe and did not live on trust lands. The savvy Choctaw political strategies had failed. Then, in 1944, Shell Oil became interested in oil leases on Choctaw lands in the Pearl River district. After much legal wrangling, Choctaw lands were reclassified as a reservation and the OIA declared that the Choctaw were indeed a tribe, meaning that a tribal council could negotiate oil leases.

The Choctaw elected another council to draft a constitution. Following the example of the all-inclusive MCIF, these representatives then called meetings in their communities to gather input for the new constitution. On 20 April 1945 the Choctaw approved this council and constitution by a 346–71 vote, and the Mississippi Choctaw officially became a tribe under the IRA.

While the MCIF eventually disbanded, its campaign for recognition had demonstrated the continuing political acumen of the Choctaw. Choctaw interactions with elected officials through the federation reinforced the Indians' position as constituents within Mississippi political networks. The Choctaw subsequently worked with their elected officials to access federal funds to help them fight the poverty of rural Mississippi. In upholding the MCIF as one means of asserting their interests, the Mississippi Choctaw maneuvered around the OIA and used the implementation of the IRA to strengthen their relationship with Mississippi's elected officials and thus to buttress their self-determination.

Katherine M. B. Osburn
Arizona State University

Bureau of Indian Affairs Records (Record Group 75), Central Classified Files: Choctaw, National Archives and Records Administration; "Condition of the Mississippi Choctaws," Hearings at Union, Mississippi, 16 March 1917; Vine Deloria Jr. and Clifford Lytle, *The Nations Within: The Past and Future of American Indian Sovereignty* (1984); Lawrence Hauptman, *The Iroquois and the New Deal* (1981); Lawrence C. Kelly, *The Navajo Indians and Federal Indian Policy, 1900–1935* (1968); Katherine M. B. Osburn, *Choctaw Resurgence in Mississippi: Race, Class, and Nation Building in the Jim Crow South, 1830–1977* (2014); Donald Parman, *The Navajos and the New Deal* (1976); Kenneth R. Philp, *John Collier's Crusade for Indian Reform, 1920–1954* (1977); Kenneth R. Philp, *Termination Revisited: American Indians on the Trail to Self-Determination, 1933–1953* (1999); Graham D. Taylor, *The New Deal and American Indian Tribalism: The Administration of the Indian Reorganization Act, 1934–1945* (1980); US House of Representatives, *Hearings before the Committee on Investigation of the Indian Service*, 12–14 March, 1917, vol. 1.

Mississippi College

The state's oldest college, Mississippi College, is also its largest private university. Chartered as Hampstead Academy on 24 January 1826 by the citizens of Mount Salus (now Clinton), the school was renamed Mississippi Academy in 1827 and Mississippi College in 1830. The college's first graduating class in 1831 included two female students.

Mississippi College Chapel, 6 April 1936 (Photograph by James Butters, Library of Congress, Washington, D.C. [HABS MISS,25-CLINT,1A-])

The school was originally unaffiliated with any religious denomination, but an 1840–41 alliance with the Methodist Conference convinced the college's board that denominational support would stabilize enrollment and finances. The college remained under Presbyterian control from 1842 to 1850, when financial difficulties returned it to the ownership of local citizens. Led by Rev. Benjamin Whitfield, the Mississippi Baptist Convention the assumed ownership, beginning a relationship that continues to the present. The Female Department disbanded in the 1850s in conjunction with the 1853 establishment of the Central Female Institute (later Hillman College), also in Clinton. In 1860 the chapel building, which doubled as the home of the First Baptist Church of Clinton, was completed. It is the only antebellum building remaining on campus.

After difficult Civil War and Reconstruction eras, the college prospered through the early twentieth century, securing full accreditation from the Southern Association of Colleges and Schools in 1922. Mississippi College regained its coeducational status in 1942 when it merged with Hillman. Graduate education began in 1950, and the School of Law opened in 1981. The same year, Clarke (Memorial) College in Newton, another Baptist institution, consolidated with Mississippi College, operating as a branch campus before closing in the early 1990s. In 1994 the school's board of trustees changed the charter to make the board more independent, with the Baptist convention approving trustees from a list selected by the college. However, the school's relationship with the Mississippi Baptist Convention continues.

Notable alumni include several governors (including A. H. Longino, H. L. Whitfield, and Ross Barnett), six presidents of the Southern Baptist Convention, more than one hundred college and university presidents, several judges, several members of the Hederman family, educator R. A. McLemore, Episcopal leader John Allin, and author Barry Hannah, who used Mississippi College settings and people in some of his work.

Gene C. Fant Jr.
Palm Beach Atlantic University

R. A. McLemore and N. P. McLemore, *The History of Mississippi College* (1979); Mississippi College website, www.mc.edu.

Mississippi College School of Law

Mississippi College School of Law (MCSOL) is located in downtown Jackson near the State Capitol, federal and state courts, and major law firms. The school has built a reputation for excellence in both practical and theoretical legal education.

MCSOL began as the Jackson School of Law, a part-time institution founded in 1930. Mississippi College acquired the school in 1975, moved it to the college's campus in Clinton, and instituted a full-time program. In 1980 the law school moved back to Jackson to its current location on Griffith Street, and in 2007 MCSOL completed an ambitious construction and renovation project to expand the campus. The law school is accredited by the American Bar Association, and its graduates may take the bar examination in all fifty states.

MCSOL's downtown location offers students access to the capital city's resources. Students may supplement classroom learning by interacting with local attorneys and judges. Students also have opportunities for externships and clerkships with private law firms, government agencies, and nonprofit organizations.

MCSOL offers options outside of the traditional law school experience, including a program that allows students simultaneously to earn law degrees and master's degrees in business administration by enrolling for one extra semester. The school also offers an executive law school program, various certificate programs, and master of laws programs.

MCSOL offers students the opportunity to participate in numerous clinical experiences: the Adoption Legal Clinic, Child Advocacy in Youth Court Clinic, Child Advocacy in Chancery Court Clinic, Mission First Legal Aid Clinic, and HIV and the Law. These clinics offer students the opportunity to gain real-world legal experience by interacting with judges, practicing attorneys, and members of the public who may not otherwise have access to legal services.

Jim Rosenblatt
Mississippi College School of Law

Mississippi College School of Law website, http://law.mc.edu.

Mississippi Council on Human Relations

The Mississippi Council on Human Relations was the state's arm of the Southern Regional Council (SRC). The council began in 1919 in Atlanta as the Commission on Interracial Cooperation, which sought to promote racial harmony and created branch groups in each of the twelve southern states. The organization's existence indicates that some white southerners realized the extent of racial problems early in the twentieth century. In the late 1920s Episcopal bishop Theodore D. Bratton founded the Mississippi Council on Interracial Cooperation in Jackson "to improve race relations" by holding interracial meetings to mediate differences and solve grievances that arose in the segregated society. Most of the MCIC's early leaders were affiliated with Christian churches, but Jewish and nonreligious members later became active.

The Commission on Interracial Cooperation was superseded by the SRC in 1944, and in the 1950s the MCIC became the Mississippi Council on Human Relations (MCHR), but the name change did not bring life to the struggling group. By the late 1950s conflict had arisen between the MCHR's white chair and Ruby Stutts Lyells, an African American woman who served as associate director. The SRC sent several staff members from Atlanta to mediate the crisis, but they failed to resolve the situation. In addition, on 12 March 1957 New York Communist Manning Johnson testified before a Louisiana legislative committee that the SRC was part of a broader Communist Party effort to infiltrate the South. Though false, the accusation caused many MCHR members to distance themselves from the group. Further, the scarcity of white members strained the group's existence, as did intimidation by members of the White Citizens' Council. In 1957 the SRC's board of directors terminated funding for the MCHR, and it entered a period of dormancy.

In the autumn of 1961, individuals interested in reviving the MCHR met in Waveland, where they formed a steering committee to select officers for the council. However, three members of the steering committee backed out as a result of pressure from groups such as the White Citizens' Council. A. D. Beittel, the white president of Tougaloo College, became president of newly reorganized MCHR, and on 3 May 1962 the revived group held its first meeting on the college campus. Members of the earlier version of the council were joined by several new black and white members. The MCHR adopted a new statement of purpose affirming its belief "in the fundamental equality of men before God" and proclaimed that it was "desirous of promoting respect for all men regardless of race, color, or creed." The council expressed its support for the Supreme Court's 1954 *Brown v. Board of Education* decision and its opposition to the Citizens' Council and the state-funded Mississippi State Sovereignty Commission.

During the 1960s and 1970s, as the civil rights movement progressed and segregation began to slowly crumble, the MCHR expanded its focus to include issues other than conciliation across the color line. The MCHR began to work to educate the public about issues of poverty in the state, relying on surveys, sociological studies, and statistical data. The group also made James Silver's *Mississippi: The Closed Society* and other publications available to doctors, lawyers, and politicians across the state.

The MCHR registered its greatest success under the leadership of Rev. Kenneth Dean, who served as executive director from 1965 to 1970. Dean helped organize US Senate committee hearings on poverty in Mississippi and on the relief effort following Hurricane Camille, and the MCHR opened local councils on the Gulf Coast, in the Oxford area, and in the Starkville-Columbus area. However, the council lost support in the 1970s and disbanded in 1979 because of lack of finances.

Aaron Watkins
City University of
New York–Baruch College

Donald Cunnigen, *Southern Studies* (Winter 1992); Kenneth Dean, interview by Betsy Nash (9 June 1992), John C. Stennis Digital Collection, Mississippi State University Libraries website, http://digital.library.msstate.edu/cdm/singleitem/collection/jcs1/id/881/rec/1; Anthony P. Dunbar, Southern Regional Council, Mississippi Council on Human Relations (1969); Aaron Watkins, "White Moderates in Mississippi: The Mississippi Council on Human Relations" (master's thesis, University of Southern Mississippi, 2007).

Mississippi Delta Blues and Heritage Festival

Held on the third Saturday in September, Greenville's Mississippi Delta Blues and Heritage Festival is one of the South's longest-running blues music festivals. Mississippi Action for Community Education (MACE), a nonprofit Greenville-based community development organization, began staging the festival in 1977. Mississippi's first celebration of the music so closely tied to the Delta, it regularly attracts fans from throughout the United States and Europe and has inspired many other blues festivals around the state.

The festival initially took place at Freedom Village, outside Leland, one of several sites where Mississippi's African Americans who had been displaced from their work and homes because of their involvement in civil rights activities had lived temporarily during the 1960s. Beginning in the mid-1980s, MACE held the festival on eighty acres of land south of Greenville, and it now takes place at the Washington County Convention Center in Greenville.

Over four decades, the festival has featured many legendary Mississippi blues musicians, including Muddy Waters, Big Joe Williams, John Lee Hooker, Sam Chatmon, and countless others. MACE has also used the festival to showcase blues musicians from the mid-Delta, among them such regular performers as guitarists Eddie Cusic and John Horton, vocalist Mamie Davis, and pianist Jerry Kattawar.

MACE operates various other programs as part of its mission to create physical, social, and economic development in the rural Delta. Since 1990, as part of its Delta Arts Project, MACE has sponsored the Blues in Schools program, which brings musicians to perform in Washington County schools.

Among Mississippi's dozens of blues festivals, the Mississippi Delta Blues and Heritage Festival stands out for its size, its longevity, and its roots in a community-organizing group.

Larry Morrisey
Mississippi Arts Commission

Stephen King, *I'm Feeling the Blues Right Now: Blues Tourism and the Mississippi Delta* (2011); Mississippi Action for Community Education, Mississippi Delta Blues and Heritage Festival Program Booklet (1980, 1998).

Mississippi Department of Archives and History

The Mississippi Department of Archives and History (MDAH) is the state repository charged with collecting, maintaining, preserving, and managing the state's official records, a vast collection of materials that pertain to the history of the territory and state. Located in Jackson, the state capital, and officially established by an act of the Mississippi legislature on 26 February 1902, MDAH is the second-oldest department of archives in the nation. While offering public access to its archives and library, MDAH also oversees the Old Capitol Museum, Historic Jefferson College, the Eudora Welty House, and other historical sites. In addition, MDAH administers historic preservation programs, public records management, and a publication program. The department's holdings document Mississippi from prehistory to the present, including more

M

than sixty thousand cubic feet of records. Among its notable holdings are the papers of civil rights activists Medgar and Myrlie Evers.

In addition to its manuscript records collections, the department holds a variety of electronic records as well as books, illustrations, maps, oral histories, photographs, microfilm, and video and audiotapes. Some collections have been digitized and are available in their entirety at the MDAH website, including the records of the Mississippi State Sovereignty Commission and of Jefferson Davis's estate, Confederate Pension applications, and numerous photographs, including those of the 1927 Great Mississippi Flood and Hurricanes Camille and Katrina. Finding aids, indexes, and archivists and librarians facilitate access to these materials by researchers, scholars, genealogists, and anyone else who is interested. MDAH is affiliated with the Mississippi Historical Society and holds institutional membership in the American Association for State and Local History, the American Association of Museums, and the Mississippi Museums Association.

The 1902 legislative act authorized the appointment of a five-member Mississippi Historical Commission, which recommended the department's creation. A board of trustees was then appointed, and shortly thereafter Dunbar Rowland was named the agency's first director. His successors have included William D. McCain (1938–55), Charlotte Capers (1955–69), Richard A. McLemore (1969–73), Elbert R. Hilliard (1973–2004), Hank T. Holmes (2005–15), and Katherine Drayne Blount (2015–).

Prior to MDAH's creation, Mississippi's official records were housed in several different locations, including Old Concord (the residence of the Spanish governors); Natchez and the Natchez District (1798); Jefferson College in Washington, Mississippi (1819); Columbia (1821); and Jackson (1822). During the Civil War the records bounced from Meridian to Enterprise to Columbus to Macon. In 1865, in accordance with orders issued by Gov. Charles Clark, the records were returned to the Capitol in Jackson, along with additional records that had been hidden in the Jackson City Hall. They remained there until 1896 when they were relocated to the State Penitentiary. By 1903 the new capitol building on Mississippi Street was completed, and the department moved into the first floor. In 1941 the archives were transferred to the War Memorial Building. In 1971 the department moved into the new Capers Building (which was designed and constructed specifically to serve as an archival repository) on South State Street. MDAH remained at that location until September 2003, when the administrative offices, collections, library, and research facilities moved to their new and present location in the William F. Winter Archives and History Building on North Street in Jackson. The Historic Preservation Division remains in the Capers Building.

In October 2013 the Mississippi Department of Archives and History broke ground on the 2 Museums Project. The Museum of Mississippi History and the Mississippi Civil Rights Museum will open in downtown Jackson in December 2017. The Civil Rights Museum will be the first state-constructed and state-operated civil rights museum in the nation.

Joyce L. Broussard
California State University at Northridge

Charlotte Capers, in *A Mississippi Reader: Selected Articles from the Journal of Mississippi History*, ed. John Edmond Gonzales (1980); Anne S. Lipscomb and Kathleen S. Hutchison, *Tracing Your Mississippi Ancestors* (1994); Mississippi Department of Archives and History website, www.mdah.state.ms.us; Dunbar Rowland, *History of Mississippi: The Heart of the South*, 2 vols. (1925; reprint, 1978); John Ray Skates, *Mississippi's Old Capitol: Biography of a Building* (1990).

Mississippi Federation of Business and Professional Women's Clubs

Established in 1924, the Mississippi Federation of Business and Professional Women's Clubs (BPW/MS) is a voluntary federation with an average membership of thirty clubs and is affiliated with the National Federation of Business and Professional Women's Clubs, the first and largest US organization of career women. Many local clubs that eventually joined to form the BPW/MS grew out of the efforts of the Young Women's Christian Association (YWCA). One of the first organizations catering to the needs of working women was established in Laurel in 1912 by women associated with the YWCA, with similar business clubs established in Jackson, Hattiesburg, Gulfport, Vicksburg, Clarksdale, and Meridian soon thereafter. Eighteen members from Mississippi clubs participated in the national federation's 1919 charter meeting, and Mississippian Earlene White was elected vice president of the national organization.

The BPW/MS was formed to advance the cause of women working in white-collar jobs and to use their gains to help other women, their communities, and their country. Women had just won the right to vote, and the national and state BPW groups believed that organizing would enable women to take advantage of the opportunities available through the political process.

The organization sought to elevate the standards for women in business and in the professions, promote the interests and cooperation of business and professional women, and extend opportunities to business and professional women through industrial, scientific, and vocational education.

The BPW engaged in political activism, civic activities, health and wellness pursuits, and educational efforts. In the

1930s the BPW/MS worked to achieve gender equality in civil service and merit exams, gain equal pay for women, and restrict child labor. In later decades the organization took on issues such as increasing the number of women in public office and serving on juries, promoting laws against obscenity, and providing civic education via legislative forums on public safety and the environment. However, the BPW/MS remained silent or did very little in the civil rights movement, and although the national organization strongly backed passage of the Equal Rights Amendment, the Mississippi branch offered only tepid support because many of the women did not want to be dubbed feminists or "women's libbers."

The BPW/MS worked to improve health care facilities and create new ones and conducted educational sessions regarding health issues. In addition, members lobbied for the creation of a state medical school, efforts that reached fruition with the 1948 creation of the University of Mississippi School of Nursing and School of Medicine. The group also has a long tradition of encouraging women's involvement in local school systems.

Salli Vargis
Georgia Perimeter College

Geline MacDonald Bowman and Earlene White, *A History of the National Federation of Business and Professional Women's Clubs, Inc., 1919–1944* (1944); Mariwyn D. Heath, *A History of the National Federation of Business and Professional Women's Clubs, Inc. (BPW/USA)*, vol. 3 (1994); *History of the Mississippi Federation of Business and Professional Women's Clubs, 1919–1950* (1951), *1950–1960* (1961).

Mississippi Folklore Society

Arthur Palmer Hudson, a professor at the University of Mississippi, founded the nonprofit Mississippi Folklore Society on 24 May 1927 to study the folklore and folklife of the South. The society remained small, comprised primarily of university students, and became dormant when Hudson left Mississippi in 1930.

George Boswell revived the society in 1966 "to study folklore in general and to collect and preserve specimens of Mississippi folklore, ranging from proverbs and riddles to art objects and the process of their manufacture." At its first meeting, on 10 December, Hudson served as honorary president and Boswell held the post of acting president. Membership was open to anyone who paid the three-dollar annual fee, and by 1972 more than 315 people had joined.

Bylaws put in place in 1968 declared that the society could not lobby or hold shares of stock and existed for the "research, compilation, and publication of pamphlets and books." A journal would be published "to promote folklore collection." Elected officers included a president, a vice president/president-elect, another vice president, a secretary-treasurer, and a council of five or six members. In addition, the society had an appointed executive secretary and editor. Each year, the society hosted an annual meeting that featured lectures and presentations of folklore, sometimes including film and music. The president's primary duty was to organize and host this gathering, which alternated between northern-central and southern-central Mississippi. The last meeting of the Mississippi Folklore Society took place in April 1992 at the Old Capitol building in Jackson.

The society first published the quarterly *Mississippi Folklore Register* in 1967. Each issue featured an introductory note from the editor, a list of the year's officers, and reviews, essays, studies, and photographs of southern culture. In 1989 the *Register* moved from the University of Southern Mississippi in Hattiesburg to Delta State University, which copublished the journal. By 1994 the journal had changed its name to *Mississippi Folklife* and was published biannually by the Folklore Society and the Center for the Study of Southern Culture at the University of Mississippi. The Mississippi Arts Commission and the National Endowment for the Arts helped fund the journal. The journal ceased print publication in 1999 but was revived online in 2015 by the Mississippi Arts Commission under the editorship of Jennifer Joy Jameson.

Betsy Martin
Jackson, Mississippi

Andrew Badger, *Mississippi Folklore Society Newsletter* (4 December 1972); Jacob Threadgill, *Jackson Clarion-Ledger* (2 November 2015); Mississippi Folklore Society Bylaws (1968); *Mississippi Folklife*, vols. 27, 28, 29 (1994); *Mississippi Folklife* website, mississippifolklife.org.

Mississippi Freedom Democratic Party

On 26 April 1964 the Mississippi Freedom Democratic Party (MFDP) was officially named at a statewide meeting held in Jackson, which was attended by two hundred of Mississippi's most active civil rights organizers. Its formation was a direct response to the Mississippi Democratic Party's singular control of the state's political process and its exclusion of black participation.

In the four years following its founding, the MFDP served as the primary advocate for the inclusion of black Mississippians in the political process. The MFDP's actions challenged the legitimacy of the all-white Mississippi Democratic Party

M

while offering a way for black Mississippians to practice political participation via voter registration, mock elections, and the selection of black candidates.

Lawrence Guyot, a political science student at Tougaloo College and a field secretary with the Student Nonviolent Coordinating Committee, became the MFDP's first chair, signaling the continued influence of the youth movement in Mississippi. Guyot directed the MFDP until the fall of 1968, when Rev. Clifton Whitley, the chaplain at Rust College, assumed leadership.

The MFDP served as the institutional home for the 1964 Summer Project, in which volunteers and full-time organizers erected a parallel political process. Canvassers began by registering voters into the dissident political party, eliminating literacy tests and other discriminatory aspects of the state-mandated registration process. Organizers then mobilized local communities to participate in and help direct parallel precinct, county, and district meetings in which they selected alternative delegations to those selected by the Mississippi Democratic Party. In early August, Freedom Democrats representing the state's five congressional districts assembled at the Masonic Temple in Jackson and chose sixty-six delegates to challenge the seating of the regular delegation at the Democratic National Convention to be held in Atlantic City, New Jersey.

At the convention, the MFDP and its supporters faced an intransigent national Democratic Party. Freedom Democrats had amassed testimony and evidence detailing the abuses committed and sanctioned by Mississippi's elected officials to prevent black political participation. Numerous state delegations pledged their support for the MFDP delegates, but Pres. Lyndon Johnson and other national leaders feared that recognizing the Freedom Democrats' claims would further alienate the southern wing of the Democratic coalition. The MFDP was offered a compromise under which the regular Democratic delegates would be seated but two of the Freedom Democrats—Aaron Henry, the president of the Mississippi branch of the National Association for the Advancement of Colored People, and Edwin King, the chaplain of Tougaloo College—would be named at-large delegates. The MFDP delegates rejected the compromise and left the convention.

The MFDP nevertheless continued to support the national Democratic Party while challenging the party's legitimacy at the state level. In the fall of 1964 Freedom Democrats campaigned for Johnson's reelection, and he garnered more votes in an MFDP-sponsored Freedom Vote than in the state-sanctioned general election. The MFDP also ran a Freedom Vote involving candidates for the US House of Representatives and Senate.

In 1965 the MFDP challenged the seating of the state's five congressmen, contending that the political preferences of black Mississippians remained unrecognized in Mississippi's elections. The MFDP collected affidavits from black Mississippians who had been denied access to the ballot and subpoenaed elected officials to testify. When the challenge came before the House of Representatives in September 1965, the MFDP's claims were denied on the grounds that the Voting Rights Act, which had passed one month earlier, would rectify these abuses in the future.

The MFDP continued to prepare black Mississippians for inclusion in a broadly defined civic life by helping them navigate and access national resources. It kept Mississippians informed through the *Mississippi Freedom Democratic Party Newsletter* as well as county newsletters. In 1965 and 1966 the MFDP encouraged black farmers to run in the Agricultural Stabilization and Conservation Service elections. Historically, white landowners controlled these local boards, which determined which farmers would receive federal agricultural subsidies. Freedom Democrats also supported black Mississippians' applications for federal poverty funds, encouraging the creation of the Child Development Group of Mississippi, the state's first Head Start program, and other programs. *Whitley v. Johnson* (1967), one of many MFDP-initiated lawsuits, sought federal redress for state-sponsored efforts that continued to limit black Mississippians' political opportunities. Consolidated for the US Supreme Court under *Allen v. State Board of Elections* (1969), *Whitley* ensured the broadest interpretation of Section 5 of the Voting Rights Act, requiring federal preclearance of a number of state-initiated alterations to voting laws and elections. This interpretation remained in force until 2013, when the Court declared that this approach was no longer constitutional in light of current conditions.

The MFDP regularly ran candidates for election either in the Democratic primary or as independents in the general election. In 1967, when black voter registration significantly increased in Mississippi, the MFDP had its greatest electoral success. More than one hundred black candidates, many affiliated with the MFDP, ran for political office, and twenty-two won election. Robert Clark, an educator supported by the Holmes County Freedom Democratic Party, became the first black state legislator since the end of Reconstruction.

As early as 1965 alternatives to the MFDP emerged to represent and direct the increasing black electorate. Charles Evers, state field secretary for the National Association for the Advancement of Colored People, aligned with white moderates to develop an institutional alternative to the MFDP, which remained overwhelmingly black and working class. In 1968 this coalition, referred to as the Loyalists, sought to replace the regulars at the Democratic National Convention. Although the MFDP was one part of this biracial coalition, responsible for half of its black delegates, the Loyalists, not the Freedom Democrats, inherited the state Democratic Party structure. The Loyalist delegation was recognized at the 1968 and 1972 Democratic Conventions. In 1976 the Loyalists gained control of the Mississippi Democratic Party.

Rachel B. Reinhard
University of California at Berkeley
History–Social Sciences Project

Unita Blackwell with JoAnne Prichard Morris, *Barefootin': Life Lessons from the Road to Freedom* (2006); Emilye Crosby, *A Little Taste of Freedom: The Black Freedom Struggle in Claiborne County, Mississippi* (2005); John Dittmer, *Local People: The Struggle for Civil Rights in Mississippi* (1995); Frank Parker, *Black Votes Count: Political Empowerment in Mississippi after 1965* (1990); Charles M. Payne, *I've Got the Light of Freedom: The Organizing Tradition and the Mississippi Freedom Struggle* (1995); Youth of the Rural Organizing and Cultural Center, *Minds Stayed on Freedom: The Civil Rights Struggle in the Rural South* (1991).

People Decide: Black Freedom and White Resistance Movements in Sunflower County, Mississippi, 1945–1986 (2004); Mark Newman, *Divine Agitators: The Delta Ministry and Civil Rights in Mississippi* (2004).

Mississippi Freedom Labor Union

The Mississippi Freedom Labor Union (MFLU) was a short-lived agricultural union that formed in the Bolivar County town of Shaw in 1965 as a collaboration between about forty-five cotton workers troubled by low wages and poor conditions and activists in the Congress of Federated Organizations. The union's main goal was to increase agricultural wages to $1.25 an hour and more broadly to help agricultural workers bargain with their employers at a time when they had little political power or economic leverage. At its height the MFLU numbered close to one thousand workers in ten Delta counties.

Members of the MFLU faced significant pressure from plantation owners, who were well along in the process of mechanizing their establishments, a process that decreased the number of workers needed and meant that workers who were hired were needed for only two or three months per year. Several plantation owners evicted tenants who joined the MFLU and engaged in labor strikes. The union had a few promising moments when workers struck against Sen. James Eastland's plantation in Sunflower County. Another group of workers, supported by the Delta Ministry, struck the Andrews Plantation in Washington County. When those strikers, led by plantation timekeeper Wallace Greene, were evicted, they took up residence in a new community they called Strike City, consisting primarily of tents. The Delta Ministry and a Jackson group, Neighborhood Developers, helped some of those workers build small homes in 1966.

The MFLU had an abbreviated life, in part as a consequence of changes in southern agriculture. According to John Dittmer, "MFLU was a bold and romantic venture, but it was anachronistic, and activists began to explore other initiatives to deal with the changing agricultural economy."

Ted Ownby
University of Mississippi

John Dittmer, *Local People: The Struggle for Civil Rights in Mississippi* (1995); Bruce Hilton, *The Delta Ministry* (1969); J. Todd Moye, *Let the*

Mississippi Health Project

The Mississippi Health Project was a Great Depression–era program of Alpha Kappa Alpha (AKA), an African American sorority, that brought free medical care to poor women. The program was a brainchild of AKA president Ida L. Jackson, a Mississippi native. Jackson, a schoolteacher in Oakland, California, had initially hoped to establish a summer education program in the rural South to help illiterates and make amends for the poor education provided by segregated schools. However, the AKA volunteers who arrived to teach in Mississippi in 1934 discovered that many poor blacks were too sick to attend class regularly and too malnourished to concentrate on lessons. In response, AKA designated funds for a health program to be headed by an AKA member, Dr. Dorothy Boulding Ferebee. A staff physician at Howard and Tufts Medical Schools, Ferebee specialized in obstetrics.

The program initially sought to immunize three thousand Delta children against diphtheria and smallpox and only incidentally to provide medical help to anyone who came to a clinic. Ferebee planned to hold the clinic six days a week for six weeks at the Saints Industrial School in Holmes County as well as to offer temporary clinics in small towns for those who could not travel to Lexington. The original staff included Ferebee and sixteen AKA volunteers as well as two public health nurses from Tuskegee University in Alabama. Holmes County health officer Dr. C. J. Vaughn provided two more nurses and, more importantly, official permission to proceed.

Unable to obtain seats on a Jim Crow train from Washington, D.C., the women drove to Mississippi, providing them with a fleet of eight automobiles that proved useful when thirteen of the fourteen plantation owners in Holmes County refused to allow their tenants to visit clinics on the grounds that they were run by communist agitators. Refusing to be dissuaded, AKA organized the nation's first mobile health clinic. Nevertheless, many sharecroppers were too intimidated to visit the clinic.

In 1936 the project moved to friendlier Bolivar County. As in Holmes, many residents had never received proper medical care, knew little about the prevention of disease, and relied on folk medicine. The sharecroppers not only received immunizations but also learned about modern health care practices, personal hygiene, and sanitation. In

1937 dental care was added to the program. AKA also offered prenatal and well-baby care along with screenings for syphilis and malaria, but malnutrition remained a concern. In 1940 AKA began a traveling kitchen to teach the preparation of nutritious meals. The project ultimately benefited fifteen thousand black Mississippians before it ended in 1941 as a casualty of gasoline rationing during World War II.

Caryn E. Neumann
Miami University at Middletown

Alpha Kappa Alpha Sorority Papers, Mississippi Health Project, Moorland-Spingarn Research Center, Washington, D.C.; Dorothy Boulding Ferebee Papers, Moorland-Spingarn Research Center, Washington, D.C.; Marjorie H. Parker, *Alpha Kappa Alpha: 60 Years of Service* (1996); Dorothy Boulding Ferebee, interview by Merze Tate (28, 31 December 1979), Black Women Oral History Project, Schlesinger Library on the History of Women in America, Harvard University, website, http://guides.library .harvard.edu/schlesinger_bwohp; Tom Ward, *Journal of Mississippi History* (Fall 2001).

Mississippi Historical Society

Although some scholars identify the original Historical Society of Mississippi as a different organization from the later Mississippi Historical Society (MHS), the MHS claims they are the same. The Historical Society of Mississippi was created on 9 November 1858 in Jackson by B. L. C. Wailes, who served as its first president. At the time the society had twenty-six members and held closed meetings, but by the 1859 meeting membership had dropped to three. Wailes donated the organization's small historical collection to the state library, ending the Historical Society of Mississippi's short run.

In 1890 faculty at the University of Mississippi revived the idea of a historical society. The new Mississippi Historical Society held annual open meetings and selected university chancellor Edward Mayes and former governor Robert Lowry as presidents and professor William Rice Sims as secretary-treasurer. The state legislature incorporated the MHS the same year, but the society suspended activities in 1894 after Sims's interest in history withered. Franklin Lafayette Riley became secretary-treasurer in 1898, and the society flourished under his leadership, laying the groundwork for what became a nationally recognized organization during the twenty-first century. The MHS began to collect historical documents and to produce the *Publications of the Mississippi Historical Society*, which increased Mississippians' awareness of and interest in their history.

In 1902 the state legislature created the Mississippi Department of Archives and History (MDAH) with Dunbar Rowland as its first director. With the department in charge of collecting and housing Mississippi's historical documents, the MHS concentrated on publications and recognition awards, releasing Riley's *Opinions of Men of Letters on the Work of the Mississippi Historical Society* in 1908. In 1939 the MHS and the MDAH began jointly publishing the quarterly *Journal of Mississippi History*, first edited by MDAH director William D. McCain. However, the MHS held no meetings between 1912 and 1953, when the interim chair of the MHS Executive Committee, James W. Silver, planned a meeting at which Frank Everett was elected the organization's president. The MHS subsequently experienced another renaissance and has produced a steady stream of major publications that includes J. F. H. Claiborne's *Mississippi as a Province, Territory, and State* (reprint, 1964), R. A. McLemore, ed., *A History of Mississippi* (2 vols., 1973), Edward Akin, *Mississippi: An Illustrated History* (1987), and the Heritage of Mississippi Series. The MHS also publishes the monthly *Mississippi History Newsletter*.

The MHS also recognizes exemplary work in Mississippi history, offering a variety of awards, including the McLemore Prize for the best Mississippi history book, the Bettersworth Award for an outstanding history teacher, the Franklin L. Riley Prize for an exemplary dissertation, the Glover Moore Prize for a notable master's thesis, the Willie D. Halsell Prize for the best *Journal of Mississippi History* article, the Mississippi History Now award for other noteworthy articles, the Frank E. Everett Jr. Award for efforts to preserve and understand local history, and the Elbert R. Hilliard Oral History Award.

The MHS also gives grants in support of school programs sponsored by the Junior Historical Society, provides educational materials for the public, and sponsors speakers and tours. The society holds annual meetings and maintains a website and an online publication, *Mississippi History Now*, designed to stimulate public interest in Mississippi history.

Anna F. Kaplan
Columbia University

Leslie W. Dunlap, *American Historical Societies, 1790–1860* (1944); Elbert R. Hilliard, *Journal of Mississippi History* (Summer 2008); Mississippi Historical Society website, www.mississippihistory.org; "Mississippi Historical Society: Historical Sketch," Mississippi Department of Archives and History website, www.mdah.state.ms.us/; Mississippi History Now website, http://mshistorynow.mdah.state.ms.us; Hans Rasmussen, *Journal of Mississippi History* (Summer 2008); Franklin L. Riley, *Publications of the Mississippi Historical Society* (1908).

Mississippi Industrial College

Holly Springs was home to several colleges for African Americans—Shaw University, which became Rust College, associated with the Methodist Episcopal Church, the public Mississippi State Normal College, which closed because of state government opposition in 1904, and Mississippi Industrial College (MIC). MIC was an enterprise of the Colored Methodist Episcopal Church (CME), and the particular project of Elias Cottrell, a CME Bishop. Cottrell began working to start a school, from first grade through college, in northern Mississippi in the early 1890s, and he set up a board of trustees and started raising money in 1900. Cottrell briefly named the future institution Mississippi Theological and Normal Seminary, but when it opened in 1906, it was called Mississippi Industrial College. By 1908 the school had 450 students, the majority of whom were in grades 1 to 8.

One of the intriguing features of Mississippi Industrial College, as historian Alicia K. Jackson has noted, is that it did very little industrial training. In the atmosphere of opposition to African American education of the early 1900s, Cottrell and other school leaders apparently made the decision to promote the respectability and uncontroversial nature of industrial education even though the school emphasized teacher training and liberal arts education. Students who aspired to the BA degree took multiple years of Latin and Greek, and literary study emphasized the classics of England and New England. The "industrial" feature of Mississippi Industrial College lay primarily in requiring students to sew, cook, and farm as part of their contribution to campus life.

Starting a private school for African Americans in the early 20th-century South was a challenge. Public money was unavailable; the CME Church, with its headquarters in Jackson, Tenn., did not have a wealthy group of supporters from throughout the country; and not many African Americans in Mississippi were making much money. Cottrell and future leaders relied on a combination of requests to the CME boards in Mississippi, occasional requests to a philanthropist like Andrew Carnegie, and the financial decisions of African American parents. Cottrell repeatedly mentioned the sacrifices of "struggling farmers . . . uneducated themselves, [who] have sacrificed much to promote facilities for their children."

Mississippi Industrial College sat—and indeed, some of its former buildings still sit—across the street from Rust College, and the proximity of the two Methodist-affiliated institutions encouraged students and faculty to make comparisons in the size of the two schools and in the nature of their leadership. It was important to the identity of MIC that black educators and trustees were in charge, while they noted that Rust College had some white supporters and trustees. In the 1910s almost all MIC faculty members, led by Pres. D. C. Potts, educated at Howard University, came from historically black institutions—Fisk, Walden, Philander Smith, Lane, Mary Holmes, Payne, and Tuskegee, along with one faculty member from Berea College in Kentucky.

The nature of MIC as a church-related school dedicated to moral propriety and uplift was clear. All students wore uniforms, went to daily devotionals and a Wednesday prayer service, and many campus organizations, like the YWCA, YMCA, and the Epworth League, had religious elements. Later in the history of the institution, CME Bishop Oree Broomfield, a graduate of MIC, supported the efforts of young people to enroll in the college by allowing some of them to live free in his home and by offering scholarships to some students studying to become ministers.

In 1923 Mississippi Industrial College opened Carnegie Auditorium, a large and impressive auditorium whose size—seating for 2,000 people—reflected the ambitious goals of the college. For much of its history, MIC emphasized the training of teachers and candidates for the ministry.

In the 1960s MIC was, compared to many African American college campuses, relatively uninvolved in the civil rights movement. College president Edgar Everett Rankin discouraged student activism, but a number of students joined students at Rust College to protest segregation in Holly Springs businesses and to attend protest meetings.

After years of financial difficulties, Mississippi Industrial College closed in 1982. Some of its buildings, now owned by Rust College, house social service and educational organizations while some are in need of repair. MIC alumni organizations continue to meet.

Ted Ownby
University of Mississippi

Oree Broomfield obituary, Christian Methodist Episcopal Church website, www.c-m-e.org; Alicia K. Jackson, "The Colored Methodist Episcopal Church and Their Struggle for Autonomy and Reform in the New South" (PhD dissertation, University of Mississippi, 2004); Mississippi Industrial College, *Catalogue* 1913–1914; Joy Ann Williamson, *Radicalizing the Ebony Tower: Black Colleges and the Black Freedom Struggle in Mississippi* (2008).

Mississippi Industrial Institute and College

What is now the Mississippi University for Women was known as the Mississippi Industrial Institute and College from its founding in 1884 until 1920. The struggle to establish the school began in 1856 when Sally Eola Reneau prepared a presentation for the legislature urging the creation of an institution to provide a specifically southern higher education for the women of Mississippi. The legislature passed the bill but allocated no funds. After the Civil War, Reneau renewed her efforts, and in 1872 she again received legislative approval to establish a women's college but no funding.

In the early 1880s Annie Coleman Peyton and Olivia Valentine Hastings took up the cause. Peyton published numerous newspaper editorials under the pseudonym "A Mississippi Woman" and made presentations throughout the state. Hastings earned the support of Sen. J. McCaleb Martin of Claiborne County, who brought the Establishment Bill to the Mississippi legislature on 12 March 1884. The bill passed by just two votes in the House and one vote in the Senate. The legislature also appropriated forty thousand dollars to support the new school. Students were required to take courses in liberal arts and to learn a practical skill to prepare them to support themselves. Each county received an enrollment quota, and education was to be free for any student appointed by her county's superintendent of education.

Although many Mississippi towns and cities actively vied to become the site of the new school, the board of trustees chose Columbus because the facilities of the Columbus Female Institute were available for free and the city offered an additional fifty thousand dollars in bonds. Richard W. Jones, a professor of chemistry at the University of Mississippi and the new school's first president, hired seventeen female faculty members, including Pauline Van de Graaf Orr, who served as "mistress of English" until 1914.

The Mississippi Industrial Institute and College opened with great fanfare on 22 October 1885, with 341 students from all parts of Mississippi and from all economic circumstances. These students were largely unprepared for higher education. As young as fifteen, many had completed no schooling past the primary grades. Student life was strictly regulated and regimented, down to such matters as types of buttons and underwear. Almost immediately, considerable controversy developed both on and off campus as to whether the school should focus on providing a liberal arts education or job skills for poor girls.

Jones resigned after three years, and the school endured four changes of administration during its first six years of operation. Charles Hartwell Cocke, the second president, was mediocre and unqualified, and the board removed him from office in March 1890, naming Mary S. J. Calloway to serve as temporary president. Arthur H. Beals, the third president, proved another poor choice, and the board did not ask him to return for a second year. For those who opposed women's education, the lack of administrative stability reflected the futility of the enterprise. However, the board's next choice, Robert Frazer, was more successful, and he remained president for eight years, although his administration was hampered by a significant financial downturn in the 1890s. Following Frazer's resignation in 1898, the Mississippi legislature sent a ten-man investigative committee to evaluate the presidential turnover. Although the committee members found the school in administrative disarray, they recognized that it had done much good for Mississippi's young women.

The board appointed native Mississippian Andrew Armstrong Kincannon to be the school's fifth president. Kincannon had previously served as the state superintendent of education, which made him both politically savvy and well connected. Before accepting the position, he demanded that the board seek additional funding and pledge not to interfere with his administration. Kincannon became a tireless promoter of the school, visiting many parts of the state and seeking to reassure citizens about the school's aims and policies. He took a particular interest in teacher training, establishing a model school and offering summer sessions for both male and female teachers. Kincannon resigned after nine years to accept the chancellorship of the University of Mississippi.

In 1907 Henry Lewis Whitfield became the school's final president. Whitfield felt that the school should offer both liberal arts and industrial courses, and his decisions about curriculum led to much controversy and dissension. In 1914 a statewide scandal erupted when someone distributed pamphlets highly critical of Whitfield and signed them only "S. T. Payer." During Whitfield's presidency, student preparation for higher education had improved to the point that the school abolished its remedial program in 1914. In 1918 the last two-year diplomas were issued to prospective teachers, who thereafter took a four-year program.

In early 1920 the legislature considered changing the Industrial Institute and College into a junior college for women. After Whitfield invited the legislators to visit the school, they voted to keep the school autonomous and changed its name to the Mississippi State College for Women in recognition of its primary academic purpose.

Sheldon S. Kohn
Zayed University, Abu Dhabi,
United Arab Emirates

Deborah A. Hall, "'Coming of Age' in the Progressive Era: The Role of Southern Women's Higher Education between 1900 and 1917" (PhD dissertation, University of Kentucky, 1991); Loyce Braswell Miles, "Forgotten Scholars: Female Education in Three Antebellum Deep Southern States" (PhD dissertation, Mississippi State University, 2003); Sarah D. Neilson, "The History of the Mississippi State College for Women" (1954); Bridget Smith Pieschel and Stephen Robert Pieschel, Loyal Daughters: One Hundred Years at Mississippi University for Women, 1884–1984 (1984); David G. Sansing, Making Haste Slowly: The Troubled History of Higher Education in Mississippi (1990).

"Mississippi—Is This America? (1962–1964)"

"Mississippi—Is This America? (1962–1964)" is the title of the fifth episode of the first part of the documentary series *Eyes on the Prize: America's Civil Rights Movement, 1954–1985* (1987). The series, created and produced by Henry Hampton and narrated by Julian Bond, explores the history of the US civil rights movement between 1954 and 1965. Topics highlighted in the episode include the formation of the South's first White Citizens' Council; the 1963 assassination of Medgar Evers; the 1964 Freedom Summer; Bob Moses's role in organizing a massive voter registration drive and establishing freedom schools; the 1964 murders of activists Andrew Goodman, James Chaney, and Michael Schwerner; and Fannie Lou Hamer and the Mississippi Freedom Democratic Party.

The title of the episode is a rhetorical question that can be understood on multiple levels. It stresses the idea that Mississippi was a racist violent place and the absolute antithesis of America. The question also suggests that while the state was the most regionally distinctive in the South, its problems constituted a matter of national concern. Footage shows Pres. John F. Kennedy admonishing the nation that "it is not enough to pin the blame on others, to say it is the problem of one section of the country or another"; rather, everyone must take responsibility. Finally, the episode demonstrates that black Mississippians and their allies very much believed that Mississippi was a part of the United States and were willing to fight for their rights as American citizens in the face of persistent violence. The documentary shows Hamer speaking at the Democratic National Convention, asking the same question of the American public: "I question America. Is this America, the land of the free and the home of the brave, where we have to sleep with our telephones off of their hooks because our lives be threatened daily because we want to live as decent human beings in America?"

The episode begins with Roy Wilkins, executive director of the National Association for the Advancement of Colored People, announcing, "There is no state with a record that approaches that of Mississippi in inhumanity, murder, and brutality and racial hatred. It is absolutely at the bottom of the list." Viewers later learn that Wilkins's assessment represented a response to the disappearance and murder of Goodman, Chaney, and Schwerner. Wilkins also asserts, "We view this as a cold, brutal, deliberate killing in a savage, uncivilized state; the most savage uncivilized state in the entire fifty states." The bulk of the episode underscores the ferocious commitment to violence evidenced by most of Mississippi's white population. The stories of Evers's assassination and the discovery of Goodman, Chaney, and Schwerner's bodies buried in an earthen dam incorporate emotional footage from the victims' families. More than twenty years

later, Myrlie Evers, Medgar's widow, recalled how danger "was simply in the air": "you knew something was going to happen." When Medgar Evers arrived at home, the family heard gunfire outside, and the children immediately "fell to the floor as he had taught them to do." Then she opened the door, discovered her husband bleeding in the driveway, and began to scream at the neighbors. The narrator then explains how "civil rights leaders and sympathetic whites traveled to the South to see firsthand the state called the 'closed society,'" invoking the title of a book by James Silver that coincidentally was published on the day Goodman, Chaney, and Schwerner disappeared. The film uses the metaphor of the closed society, in which white Mississippians defend white supremacy against any social change at all costs, to underscore the conviction that Mississippi's violence was the most virulent in the South.

The idea of Mississippi exceptionalism juxtaposed with the democratic ideals of American equality not only permits the filmmakers to highlight the state as a vulgar, sadistic society but also allows them to hold the nation responsible. Broadly speaking, Mississippi can be seen as a reflection of America's bigotry and tolerance of inequality. The documentary shows footage of Dave Dennis, a member of Congress of Racial Equality who lent his vehicle to the three murdered civil rights activists, offering a passionate yet defiant eulogy at Chaney's funeral: "I not only blame the people who pulled the trigger or did the beating or dug the hole with the shovel . . . but I blame the people in Washington D.C. This is our country, too."

Natalie J. Ring
University of Texas at Dallas

American Experience, "Eyes on the Prize, America's Civil Rights Movement, 1954–1985," PBS website, www.pbs.org; Clayborne Carson, David J. Garrow, Gerald Gill, Vincent Harding, and Darlene Clark Hine, *The Eyes on the Prize Reader: Documents, Speeches, and Firsthand Accounts from the Black Freedom Struggle* (1991); Joseph Crespino, in *The Myth of Southern Exceptionalism*, ed. Matthew D. Lassiter and Joseph Crespino (2010); Juan Williams, *Eyes on the Prize: America's Civil Rights Years, 1954–1965* (1987).

Mississippi Magazine

Founded by four Jackson businessmen—Neal Clement, Howard Stover, former copublisher Robert Temple, and current publisher Richard Roper—*Mississippi Magazine* is a descendant of *Jackson Magazine*, which changed its name to *Mississippi Magazine* during 1979, its fourth and final year of operation. Clement, Stover, Temple, and Roper bought the

M

rights to the name and launched the current *Mississippi Magazine* with the September–October 1982 issue.

According to its editors, *Mississippi Magazine* is the state's premier lifestyle publication and is dedicated to "celebrating the positive aspects of the Magnolia State." The bimonthly magazine publishes features on famous Mississippians (including John Grisham, Eudora Welty, and Morgan Freeman) and historical sites as well as gardening and decorating tips. Circulation has quadrupled from 11,500 in 1982 to 46,000 in 2016. Since 1993 the January–February issue has featured a popular wedding register that now includes more than three hundred listings. The twentieth anniversary issue, published in September–October 2002, surveyed readers on their choices in such categories as Best Mississippi Museum and Best Musician, which it continues to do annually. The magazine has run under the helm of several editors since its beginning. *Mississippi Magazine*'s editorial offices are located in Jackson.

Jennifer Southall
Jackson, Mississippi

Kelly Ingebretsen, *Mississippi Business Journal* (16 September 2002); *Mississippi Magazine* website, www.mismag.com.

Mississippi Manufacturing Company

Industrial operations in the antebellum South tended to be small affairs that primarily served local markets. In the 1850s, however, the state's largest and most profitable textile manufacturer, Mississippi Manufacturing Company, had become a significant exception. Five businessmen from Columbus, Georgia, led by James M. Wesson, asked for and received a charter from the Mississippi legislature to build a textile mill on a tributary of the Big Black River in Choctaw County in 1848. They built the first buildings at Drane's Mill, the site of what had been a water mill. The Mississippi Manufacturing Company began with a sawmill and machine shop, then quickly added a textile mill, a gristmill, a flour mill, and a wool-carding machine. It used Mississippi cotton to produce cotton cloth and clothing, encouraged Mississippi planters to grow wheat for processing into flour, and used Mississippi timber in its sawmill. By the 1850s the company had begun importing wool from New Orleans to make clothing and marketing some of its products to distributors rather than relying solely on local planters and farmers.

Wesson ran Mississippi Manufacturing as a company town, and that town soon developed into Bankston. Wesson brought in preachers, helped build churches, and outlawed alcohol. Most of the workers in the cotton and woolen mills were white men and women, while a few slaves worked the steam engine. Wesson wrote late in the 1850s, "178 Souls are fed by labour for us in and about the Mills. All of whom have the benefit of weekly preaching, as well as sabboth [sic] school instruction, so that while the children are brought up to industrious sobriety, and taught the doctrine of economy of time, as well as money, they are instructed in letters and elevated in morals."

During the Civil War, the Mississippi Manufacturing Company made uniforms for Confederate troops from the state and took on the job of making shoes. Union troops burned down the company's building in January 1865.

Ted Ownby
University of Mississippi

John Hebron Moore, *The Emergence of the Cotton Kingdom in the Old Southwest: Mississippi, 1770–1860* (1988).

Mississippi Masala

Mississippi Masala (1992) is a film that tells the story of an Asian Indian family's expulsion from Uganda and relocation to the middle of the Mississippi Delta and the interracial love affair that results. In 1972 Ugandan dictator Idi Amin confiscated the property of thousands of his nation's Indian-descended residents and expelled them as punishment for "sabotaging the economy of Uganda." In the film, an attorney, Jay (Roshan Seth), and his wife, Kinnu (Sharmila Tagore), leave behind a well-appointed residence for the small cotton-dominated community of Greenwood, where Jay manages a run-down motel and Kinnu operates a liquor store. *Mississippi Masala* was directed by Mira Nair and filmed on location in Kampala, Uganda, and Greenwood.

A minor automobile accident in downtown Greenwood brings together the Indian family's daughter, Mina (Sarita Choudhury), and Demetrius (Denzel Washington), an African American who makes his living by cleaning carpets. They soon begin dating, much to the disapproval of Mina's parents, who expect her to marry within the Indian community although they have also told her that her skin is too dark for her to be a desirable wife. Mina ignores her parents' directive to have no further contact with Demetrius.

Demetrius's African American relatives initially are most hospitable to Mina at a backyard picnic. However, after Mina's relatives discover the couple in a Biloxi motel room, the lovers are shunned by the entire Greenwood community—Indians, African Americans, and whites. The bonds among the city's black, white, and Asian communities go no deeper than economics, and each group is generally unconcerned about the other until the two young people fall in love, when racism returns to the surface. Despite the fact that his boycotted carpet-cleaning business suffers deeply and the bank considers repossessing his van, Demetrius remains loyal to Mina.

Mina's father remains obsessed with regaining his Ugandan property, and he eventually returns to his homeland, but his visit is hollow, since his Ugandan friend, Okelo (Konga Mbandu), a schoolteacher whom Jay shunned as he was fleeing the country, has died. "I never said goodbye to him," Jay laments. *Mississippi Masala* ends with Demetrius dancing through a Delta cotton field with Mina in his arms.

"The movie is about people who, having survived . . . upheavals, nevertheless have no curiosity about those outside their own social and racial circles—and about a few who do," wrote critic Roger Ebert in the *Chicago Sun-Times*. Rita Kempley of the *Washington Post* described *Mississippi Masala* as "a 'West Side Story' for the '90s."

The movie features much local color, including a trip down the aisles of the Piggly Wiggly supermarket in Greenwood and a look inside the curtained private booths at Lusco's, a downtown restaurant opened by Italian immigrants.

The Indian word *masala* describes a blend of spices that is often added to savory dishes such as curries.

Fred Sauceman
East Tennessee State University

Roger Ebert, *Chicago Sun-Times* (14 February 1992); Internet Movie Database website, www.imdb.com; Rita Kempley, *Washington Post* (14 February 1992).

Mississippi Mass Choir

Since its formation in 1988 the Mississippi Mass Choir has topped recording charts and toured internationally, in keeping with its motto, "Serving God through Song."

The Mississippi Mass Choir was the brainchild of gospel singer Frank D. Williams, who sought to put together a massive choir to showcase all that Mississippi gospel had to offer. Nearly a decade after first broaching the idea with colleagues at Jackson-based Malaco Records, Williams encouraged singers from across Mississippi to submit taped vocal performances. After poring through hundreds of entries, Williams—a longtime member of the Jackson Southernaires gospel group and an executive at Malaco—selected more than one hundred hopefuls and began putting together the choir.

Pastor and composer David R. Curry of the Liberal Trinity Church of God in Christ in Jackson became musical director, and composer and Malaco Gospel chair Jerry Mannery signed on as executive director. The group performs contemporary versions of established songs as well as new material written by Williams, Curry, and other noted composers. After beginning rehearsals in May 1988, the choir's first release was a performance recorded at Jackson's Municipal Auditorium in October of that year. Malaco put out *The Mississippi Mass Choir Live* in the spring of 1991, and it rose to the No. 1 position on the *Billboard* Gospel Chart, remaining there for forty-five weeks. As a result, the choir won several James Cleveland, *Billboard*, and Stellar awards in 1989. The choir's follow-up, *God Gets the Glory* (1990), also topped the charts, as did 1993's *It Remains to Be Seen*, which outstripped its predecessors by occupying the No. 1 position on the *Billboard* Gospel Chart for a record fifty-two weeks.

Williams's March 1993 death dealt a tremendous blow to the choir, though members, alongside Curry, Mannery, cominister of music Jerry Smith, and spiritual adviser Rev. Benjamin Cone, continued recording and performing. The choir has released seven additional albums, among them 2002's *Amazing Love*, which features a track Williams recorded prior to his death. The Mississippi Mass Choir's most recent release is *Declaration of Dependence* (2014), a recording of the choir's 2013 twenty-fifth anniversary concert in Jackson that debuted at No. 8 on the Billboard Gospel Chart. The choir has received numerous Dove, Stellar, Grammy, and other music awards and has been inducted into the Mississippi Musicians Hall of Fame. With a roster of more than 150 members, the group has performed around the globe, including in Spain and Italy, in Japan, in the Bahamas, and in South Africa. In 1990 the choir received the Governor's Award for Excellence in the Arts. That year Mississippi Mass Choir leaders joined choir director Dorcas Thigpen in forming the associated Mississippi Children's Choir, which released three acclaimed albums.

Executive director Jerry Mannery noted of the choir, "There's been so much negative that comes with Mississippi. Not only are we ambassadors for Christ, but we realize that we are also ambassadors for the state of Mississippi."

Odie Lindsey
Nashville, Tennessee

Malaco Music Group website, http://malaco.com; Mississippi Musicians Hall of Fame website, www.msmusic.org; PBS River of Song website, http://www.pbs.org/riverofsong/.

Mississippi Mud Pie

The name *Mississippi mud pie* derives from the pie's appearance, which could remind casual observers of Mississippi River mud. Out of the oven, this dense chocolate dessert looks like Mississippi River clay that the sun has parched, crusted, and cracked. On the palate, the top surface is a crunchy counterpoint to the soft, chewy center.

The cooks of Mississippi, like other American cooks, bake apple, sweet potato, and cream pies. They are proud of their peach, mincemeat, and million dollar pies. But unlike the cooks of some other regions, Mississippians also make fig, peanut butter, key lime, bourbon, and black walnut pies, and they are famous for Mississippi mud pie.

To prepare mud pies, cooks whisk together sugar, melted butter, chocolate, and eggs. Then they pour the filling into a pie shell and bake it at moderate heat. The steps are easy and the results sweet. Some call the pie a confection, while others call it a sensation or decadence. Mississippians often serve the mud pie with whipped cream, boiled custard, vanilla yogurt, or vanilla ice cream and may add sliced bananas and strawberries.

Mark F. Sohn
Pikeville College

Craig Claiborne, *Southern Cooking* (1987); Mark F. Sohn, *Mountain Country Cooking: A Gathering of the Best Recipes from the Smokies to the Blue Ridge* (1996); Mark F. Sohn, *Southern Country Cooking* (1992).

Mississippi Nurses Association

The Mississippi Nurses Association (MNA) was established on 7 June 1911 in Natchez by nurses Leola Steele and Jennie Quinn Cameron with the primary goal of ensuring the "advancement and regulation of nursing." At that time the only training nurses received was in hospitals from physicians in an unregulated and inconsistent manner. The MNA's bylaws and code of ethics formed the basis of the licensing Nurse Practice Act (NPA) signed by Gov. Earl Brewer in 1914, the same year that the State Board of Nursing was established. The MNA began efforts to make licensure compulsory in 1958 but did not succeed until 1970. The act has been revised several times at the initiative of the MNA to reflect changes in health care delivery.

The MNA held its first convention in October 1911 with forty attendees and has subsequently held a convention every year except 1918. Held at various locations around the state, MNA conventions convey information about changes in the profession and in the delivery of health care and create an esprit de corps. The MNA's newsletter, *Miss RN*, began publication in 1939 as another way of informing and uniting the constituency.

Keeping in touch with its members is crucial to the MNA, which needs their voices to help fulfill its dual mission of representing the interests of its members and caring for patients. Even from its earliest years the MNA reached out to make political and community leaders aware of its concerns. The association held its first legislative conference in 1976, and by 1991 no gubernatorial aspirant would miss the gathering. In 1984 the MNA codified its activities by establishing a Political Action Committee to endorse candidates for public office who support its interests.

The success of MNA's strategic political savvy is clear in the role of nurse practitioners (NPs). Mississippi was one of the first states to allow NPs to be reimbursed directly by Medicaid providers (1990), to sign third-party reimbursement claim forms without physician countersignature (1994), and to write prescriptions for controlled substances (2002). In 1998 the MNA required that all NPs have master's degrees; four years later, the association mandated that NPs be educated in the use of controlled substances.

In keeping with its understanding of the value of outreach, the MNA joined the American Nurses Association in 1914 and has been a visible presence in the national body. It also collaborates with agencies across Mississippi that are concerned with providing health care. The MNA has lobbied on behalf of such larger public health concerns as children's health insurance programs, antismoking efforts, insurance coverage for mammograms, school nurses, seat belt laws, and legislation allowing law enforcement officers to follow up as soon as older persons are reported missing, without a waiting period.

On the subject of race relations, the MNA often offered leadership to place health care above issues of Jim Crow. During the 1912 legislative session, a representative from Warren County proposed a bill that would "prohibit white nurses from caring for Negro patients in Mississippi hospitals." Although the bill passed the House, MNA members joined forces with doctors to prevent it from coming to a vote in the Senate. In 1947 the MNA voted to accept black members.

Seetha Srinivasan
Jackson, Mississippi

Mississippi Nurses Association website, www.msnurses.org; *Passing on the Flame: The History of the Mississippi Nurses' Association, 1911–1986* (1986).

Mississippi Picnic in Central Park

Every summer since 1980, Mississippians and others have gathered in New York City's Central Park to eat catfish and peach cobbler, listen to blues music, and celebrate and preserve Mississippi's culture. The event began when several homesick Mississippians organized the New York Society for the Preservation of Mississippi Heritage to combat the negative misconceptions about each other possessed by southerners and New Yorkers. The picnic also provides Mississippians living in New York City the opportunity to meet one another and to celebrate their common heritage. From about five hundred attendees the first year, the picnic has grown to attract several thousand each summer and has become a reunion and recruiting event of sorts for alumni from various Mississippi colleges and universities.

Featuring many of the characteristics of a University of Mississippi tailgate party, the picnic begins around noon and lasts throughout the afternoon. Attendees can enjoy fried catfish, hushpuppies, and other Mississippi delicacies as they listen to musicians performing on stage and visit various booths promoting Mississippi cultural activities and tourism, some with the help of the Mississippi Development Authority. Various contests are held, with prizes awarded in such categories as best dessert and best hat and to the winner of the watermelon seed-spitting contest. The 2015 picnic celebrated the eightieth anniversary of Elvis Presley's birth with an Elvis look-alike contest.

The 2016 picnic was canceled after the legislature passed HB 1523, the Religious Liberty Accommodations Act, which some observers perceived as discriminatory. According to organizers, "For almost four decades, the Mississippi Picnic in Central Park has consistently celebrated the best of Mississippi, without regard to race, religion, or gender orientation. We took pride in sharing our rich heritage and diversity with the rest of the world through these annual gatherings. Any law such as HB 1523 that discriminates against even a single member of our community cannot be tolerated, and therefore we have decided to stand up for all Mississippians by canceling the 2016 picnic in the park."

Katherine Treppendahl
University of Virginia

Denise Gee, *Southern Living* (June 1998); New York Mississippi Society website, www.thenyms.com.

Mississippi Sandhill Crane

The sandhill crane (*Grus canadensis*) is believed to be among the oldest of living species, having existed in much its current form for perhaps the past ten million years. Found through wet prairie regions across North America, these long-legged, long-necked birds of wet grassy prairies are distinguished by their overall gray plumage with rust accents and prominent fleshy red foreheads. Birds from northern populations migrate and can stand nearly four feet tall; those from southern populations are resident and about three and a half feet tall.

Known as a breeding bird in Mississippi since at least 1929, the Mississippi sandhill crane (*Grus canadensis pulla*) was designated as a subspecies (in this case, a unique geographic variant) in 1972. At that time it was noted that although its plumage was slightly darker, differences between the Mississippi sandhill cranes and Florida populations were minimal, and the naming of the Mississippi population as a unique form would likely serve primarily as an avenue for including it on endangered species lists. The Mississippi crane population had been listed as "rare" in the 1968 list of *Rare and Endangered Wildlife of the United* States, and in 1973 it was included on the official US list of endangered species. On 25 November 1975 more than sixteen thousand acres were set aside as the Mississippi Sandhill Crane National Wildlife Refuge to protect the birds. It was the first national wildlife refuge established under the Endangered Species Act of 1973.

Mississippi sandhill cranes are primarily found in Jackson County. Other resident populations of sandhill cranes occur in Florida and previously occurred in Alabama. Ancestors of these southern birds were almost certainly found in wet grassy prairies across the Lower Gulf Coastal Plain from Florida to East Texas. Overhunting and human alteration of habitats diminished and fragmented the ancestral population, and the Mississippi sandhill crane is today the smallest of the relict descendant populations. During the 1970s what became known as the "cranes and lanes" controversy defined both the primary cause of the endangerment of Mississippi sandhill cranes (habitat loss) and perhaps their salvation. It was feared that construction of Interstate 10 through Jackson County would result in the extinction of the population. The Mississippi Sandhill Crane National Wildlife Refuge and a reduced number of interstate exits in the crane habitat provided concessions and hope for the birds.

In 1965 cranes from the Mississippi sandhill crane population had been taken into captivity to begin a captive breeding program at the Patuxent Wildlife Research Center near Laurel, Maryland. By the early 1980s fewer than thirty Mississippi sandhill cranes remained in the wild, and annual

M

mortality was higher than annual productivity. Since 1981, captive-bred cranes have been annually introduced to the population, and by 1992 it was estimated that 75 to 80 percent of the Mississippi sandhill cranes in the wild in Mississippi had been hatched in captivity. As of January 2016, 129 Mississippi sandhill cranes remained in the wild.

The Mississippi Sandhill Crane National Wildlife Refuge provides only part of the habitat needed and used by the birds. From mid-fall to early midwinter each year, Mississippi sandhill cranes gather to feed and roost in the Pascagoula River marsh and nearby fallow agricultural fields or pastures. Sandhill cranes from migrant populations also winter on the Gulf Coast but are easily distinguished from their small, slightly darker resident relatives.

Jerome A. Jackson
Florida Gulf Coast University

J. W. Aldrich, "A New Subspecies of Sandhill Crane from Mississippi," in Proceedings of the Biological Society of Washington (1972); D. H. Ellis, G. F. Gee, S. G. Hereford, G. H. Olsen, T. D. Chisolm, J. M. Nicolich, K. A. Sullivan, N. J. Thomas, M. Nagendran, and J. S. Hatfield, *The Condor* (February 2000); Aldo Leopold, "Report on a Game Survey of Mississippi Submitted to the Game Restoration Committee, Sporting Arms, and Ammunition Manufacturers' Institute," unpublished manuscript, Mississippi Museum of Natural Science Library (1929); T. C. Tacha, S. A. Nesbitt, and P. A. Vohs, in *Birds of North America*, ed. A. Poole, P, Stettenheim and F. Gill (1992); William H. Turcotte and David L. Watts, *Birds of Mississippi* (1999); US Fish and Wildlife Service, Mississippi Sandhill Crane National Wildlife Refuge website, http://www.fws.gov/refuge/mississippi_sandhill_crane/; J. M. Valentine Jr. and R. E. Noble, *Journal of Wildlife Management* (July 1970).

Mississippi School for Mathematics and Science

In 1983, acting on the initiative of Mississippi state representative Charlie Capps from Cleveland, the legislature began the process that would result in the creation of the Mississippi School for Mathematics and Science (MSMS). Capps and other legislators believed that gifted students were not appropriately challenged by Mississippi's public schools, citing the small number of teachers certified to teach higher-level mathematics and science courses and correspondingly low numbers of school districts that offered such courses and of Advanced Placement math and science exams taken by high school students.

Appointed by the Board of Trustees of the State Institutions of Higher Learning, a nine-member committee devised a plan for a residential high school for academically able juniors and seniors. Committee members visited residential schools for gifted students in other states and were particularly influenced by the North Carolina School for Mathematics and Science and the Louisiana School for Math, Science, and the Arts. The committee found available classroom and dormitory space on the campus of Mississippi University for Women in Columbus, just twenty-six miles from Mississippi State University, a major research institution.

In 1984 the legislature received the committee's 157-page plan for a state-funded magnet school that would recognize the unique value, needs, and talents of academically advanced students and challenge each student through a multidimensional teaching program. Its students would come from across Mississippi without regard for racial, social, or economic background and would receive a qualitatively different, tuition-free educational program. The committee argued that the school would be an economic engine for the state by attracting more educated families and helping to produce better-educated and more highly skilled workers.

After some disagreement between the legislature and Gov. Bill Allain, legislation to establish MSMS was enacted in 1987, and in January 1988 the State Board of Education hired Johnny Franklin, principal of Warren Central High School, to serve as the new school's first director. MSMS opened on 6 September 1988.

Since 2008, the legislature has required MSMS students to pay five hundred dollars per semester in tuition. The school graduates between 100 and 125 students each year, with about two-thirds going on to attend college in the state of Mississippi. Other alumni have enrolled at Harvard, Yale, Stanford, the US military academies, and numerous other highly selective colleges around the world. Members of the Class of 2015 accepted nearly eight million dollars in college scholarships, and MSMS is currently ranked fifty-seventh among the nation's high schools by both *Newsweek* and the *Daily Beast*. Eleven members of the Class of 2016 were named National Merit Semifinalists.

Fred Wayne McCaleb
Mississippi School for
Mathematics and Science

Columbus Commercial Dispatch (5 September 1988, 11 February 1989, 25 May 1990); Debbie Francher, Alumni Survey Data Analysis, Classes of 1990–99, Mississippi School for Mathematics and Science; *Jackson Clarion-Ledger* (3 July 1988, 25 September 1988); Mississippi School for Mathematics and Science website, www.themsms.org.

Mississippi School for the Blind

Established in 1848 as the Institution for the Instruction of the Blind, the Mississippi School for the Blind (MSB) currently serves more than 150 blind and visually impaired students. The school educates students from kindergarten through twelfth grade, offering both day and residential services. MSB also operates several outreach programs for members of Mississippi's visually impaired population either too young or unable to attend the school.

MSB opened in 1848 on North Jefferson Street in Jackson and remained there until the Civil War. The facility served as a military hospital during the war, forcing MSB to move to Monticello. The school returned to North Jefferson Street after the war and did not move again until 1882, when the state built a new facility on North State Street. In 1948 MSB moved to a larger and more modern facility on Eastover Drive. As part of a comprehensive building project to consolidate the services and physical plants of MSB and the Mississippi School for the Deaf, MSB moved in December 1999 into a new facility on Eastover Drive.

The state did not offer educational services for African American blind children until 1929, when a program for those children was added at the Piney Woods Country Life School in Rankin County. In 1951 the state built a new school for the African American blind on Capers Avenue in Jackson. Black students remained at the Capers Avenue location until they joined the white students at Eastover Drive in 1980.

The expansion of MSB's facilities during the second half of the twentieth century coincided with a program to improve and refine the school's curriculum. Kindergarten through sixth-grade students study in the elementary school, which uses a specialized process to place students and set individual goals according to need. The elementary school core curriculum focuses on mathematics, social studies, language arts, and science. Students also receive training in Braille, orientation and mobility, daily life skills, and the use of computers and adaptive technology. Junior high and secondary school students build on their elementary training and take classes in history, algebra, geometry, biology, physical science, music, and drama. The secondary school also offers classes in health and wellness, physical education, and personal finance. Both the elementary and secondary schools allow qualified students to take some courses at local public schools.

In addition to its academic program, MSB offers a wide range of extracurricular activities. Students can receive either individual or group training in musical and vocal performance, and the MSB band and concert choir perform regularly at the school and at community functions. At regional and local meets, MSB athletes compete in swimming, cheerleading, wrestling, and track.

Thomas John Carey
University of Mississippi

Alferdteen B. Harrison, *Piney Woods School: An Oral History* (1982); Mississippi School for the Blind Annual Reports (1973, 1976); Mississippi School for the Blind website, www.msb.k12.ms.us.

Mississippi School for the Deaf

Founded in 1854 in Jackson, the Mississippi School for the Deaf (MSD) educates hearing-impaired children from prekindergarten through twelfth grade. As early as 1829, the state provided grants-in-aid for deaf children to attend special schools outside the state and occasionally paid tutors to educate individual deaf children. In 1854 the state founded the Mississippi Institution for the Deaf and Dumb (renamed the Mississippi School for the Deaf in 1924), but low salaries made faculty recruitment and retention difficult, and the school closed after operating for less than a year. The school reopened in 1857 with a larger budget and moved from its original location across the street from the governor's mansion to a tract of land just west of the Jackson city limits.

When Mississippi joined the Confederacy, the school closed and became a military hospital. In 1863 the facility burned to the ground, and the fire consumed the school's records. In the chaotic aftermath of the war, deaf children in Mississippi again received grants-in-aid to attend schools outside the state, and the school in Mississippi did not reopen until late 1871, when it was located in a new facility on North State Street in Jackson.

For a century after the Civil War, MSD suffered from the state's endemic poverty and deplorable public health. Outbreaks of yellow fever, measles, and other illnesses frequently shortened school terms, and the Great Depression exacerbated MSD's funding crisis. As late as 1944, Mississippi's per-capita funding for deaf education amounted to less than half the national average, and even the allocations of Alabama, Arkansas, Louisiana, and other Deep South states dwarfed that of Mississippi. Poor funding made hiring qualified teachers difficult, and MSD's curriculum remained primarily vocational well into the twentieth century.

A small number of deaf African Americans began attending MSD in the 1870s. Before the state built a separate facility, black students apparently attended classes in the same rooms with the same instructors as white students but

M

studied at different hours of the day. In 1882 the state converted the facility on North State Street into a separate facility for African American students. Administrators referred to the tract of land as "the farm," and the male students living there raised crops and livestock; black female students learned domestic skills such as sewing, cooking, washing, and ironing.

In the 1950s MSD began to expand and modernize. The state opened a new multibuilding facility in Jackson's Eastover neighborhood in 1951. The complex, which included nine buildings when it opened, allowed MSD to serve more students. After desegregating, MSD not only greatly improved the opportunities for the state's African American deaf population but also secured full accreditation from the Southern Association of Colleges and Schools.

MSD now offers an elementary school, which serves children through sixth grade, and secondary school, which offers grades seven through twelve. Specialized curricula track students' progress according to individual goals. Elementary school students learn American Sign Language and written English and meet individualized goals in language arts, math, science, social studies, and physical education. Secondary school students can choose to pursue a high school diploma, an occupational diploma, or a certificate of life skills. Both elementary and secondary school students participate in extracurricular activities and school clubs, and MSD competes in four sports sanctioned by the Mississippi High School Athletic Association: football, basketball, track, and volleyball.

Thomas John Carey
University of Mississippi

Robert S. Brown, *History of the Mississippi School for the Deaf* (1954); Mississippi School for the Deaf Handbook (2007); Mississippi School for the Deaf website, www.msd.k12.ms.us.

Mississippi State Colonization Society

During the Revolutionary era Thomas Jefferson and other prominent whites supported the establishment of a colony of free blacks in West Africa. The American Colonization Society (ACS) was formed in 1816 in Washington, D.C. Many northern whites and some white southerners supported colonization as a means to rid society of a large free black population.

The Mississippi State Colonization Society (MSCS) began in 1831 as the state auxiliary of the ACS. The following year the MSCS sent two free blacks from Natchez to the

Pepper Coast of West Africa (what is now known as Liberia) to report on conditions in the colony. Their account was favorable, so colonization agent James G. Birney collected funds, and within three years the society outfitted an expedition of seventy-one freed blacks aboard the *Rover* under the direction of colonization agent Robert S. Finley. In 1836, however, the MSCS and the national organization split.

In the wake of the split, Natchez citizens funded the creation of a separate colony, Mississippi in Africa, 130 miles south of the Monrovia at the base of the Sinoe River. The settlement's capital was named Greenville, after James Green, a major Natchez-area planter who supported the cause both by freeing a significant portion of his slaves and by contributing money. Josiah C. Finley, the brother of Robert, was appointed the first governor of the colony. In 1838 the first thirty-seven blacks arrived on the ship *Mail* from New Orleans.

Most the MSCS members were planters; a smaller number of clergymen also joined. Planters such as Stephen Duncan, Dr. John Ker, James R. Railey, and Judge Edward McGehee were among the wealthiest members and took an active part in colonization plans. In addition, most were either vice presidents or life members of the national organization. Members of the Presbyterian, Methodist, and Episcopalian clergy served as MSCS elected officials.

The MSCS collapsed in the early 1840s as a consequence of lack of funding, national events, and natural disasters. Further, the MSCS and the ACS remained at loggerheads over twenty-five thousand dollars Edward B. Randolph of Lowndes County had left to the state society in the mid-1830s.

In addition, the MSCS was hampered by a twelve-year court battle involving the heirs of Capt. Isaac Ross of Jefferson County, who died in 1836. In his will, Ross gave his adult slaves the option of obtaining their freedom and immediately emigrating to Liberia or being sold as slaves, with the profits from slave sales and the proceeds of the estate to go to the ACS to establish a university in Liberia. One of Ross's grandsons contested the will, and nine years passed before the Mississippi Supreme Court upheld the document's terms. Another three years passed before the former Ross slaves went to Liberia.

In 1838 the ACS expressed its desire for rapprochement with the MSCS as well as an interest in assuming control of Mississippi in Africa. The MSCS, active only from 1831 to 1840, entered into a Plan of Union with the ACS in 1841. Both organizations agreed that funds collected from the state would be used for the expenses of the Mississippi emigrants, though little was done to remove free blacks from Mississippi.

Mississippi in Africa collapsed in the late 1840s, at least in part because migrants did not want to return to the agricultural jobs they associated with the oppressive nature of slavery.

Dawn Dennis
Northridge, California

Alan Huffman, *Mississippi in Africa: The Saga of the Slaves of Prospect Hill Plantation and Their Legacy in Liberia Today* (2004); Clayton D. James, *Antebellum Natchez* (1968); Norwood Allen Ker, *Journal of Mississippi History* (February 1981); Franklin L. Riley, *Publications of the Mississippi Historical Society* (1909); Charles Sydnor, *Slavery in Mississippi* (1965).

Mississippi State Normal School for Colored Youth

The Mississippi State Normal School for Colored Youth, generally called State Normal and located in Holly Springs, educated African American teachers from its inception during Congressional Reconstruction in 1870 to its closing during Gov. James K. Vardaman's administration in 1904. One of the more idealistic efforts of Radical Reconstruction leaders was their interest in improving education for former slaves and their children. In 1870 the Mississippi legislature passed a law creating a teacher-training school in each of the state's five congressional districts. Shaw University in Holly Springs offered to give the state its teaching department, and the legislature happily accepted.

State Normal opened in 1871 with 50 students and a small faculty. Attendance at State Normal ranged between 120 and 200 beginning in the late 1870s. Its attendance was slightly lower than that of other state institutions. For example, in 1888–89, when the State Normal School had 171 students, Mississippi A&M in Starkville had 313, the Industrial Institute and College in Columbus had over 300, the University of Mississippi had 232, and Alcorn A&M had 216.

Leaders of schools for African Americans in the Deep South walked a narrow line between inspiring young people with ideals of uplift and respectability while teaching numerous skills and trying not to cause controversies that might lead white leaders to cut off funding. For much of its history, leaders of the Mississippi State Normal School faced that tension. First, the state government tended to be suspicious of any spending on African Americans and allotted only three thousand dollars per year for State Normal from 1876 to 1889. Funding then dropped to twenty-five hundred dollars in 1890 and to two thousand dollars beginning in 1891. Second, legislators required State Normal's curriculum to emphasize teacher training at the expense of other forms of education. The school had initially offered an impressive four-year program building from reading, spelling, arithmetic, and geography in the first term to metaphysics, rhetoric, algebra, history, chemistry, theories of education, physics, astronomy, literary criticism, calculus, Latin, and Greek. In response to complaints from white political figures who objected to such a complete liberal education for African Americans, the school cut its offerings down to a two-year program that concentrated on basic skills and pedagogy. Principal W. D. Highgate reported in 1891, "We have long since displaced the dead languages and in their stead put studies that will be in actual use in the school room." But while emphasizing education designed to be of "actual use," Highgate and other leaders also upheld egalitarian ideals that led to controversies with local whites, who accused Highgate of being "insolent and overbearing" and of encouraging his students "to be disrespectful and discourteous toward the white citizens of the town."

Mississippi State Normal School withstood poor funding, criticisms from local whites, and a yellow fever crisis in 1879. It could not survive Vardaman, who worked to close the school as part of a broad effort to severely limit funding for African American education. He vetoed the appropriation for the school, arguing that "after forty years of earnest effort and the expenditures of fabulous sums of money to educate [the black man's] head, we have only succeeded in making a criminal out of him and impairing his usefulness and efficiency as a laborer."

African American leaders in northern Mississippi were outraged by the decision. According to Colored Methodist Episcopal church leader Elias Cottrell, State Normal "had given more colored men and women a Normal Education, at a normal cost, than any Institution of its kind in the South, and this Bigoted Governor is still doing all in his power, as the intelligent world knows, to take every dollar of public school money from us."

Ted Ownby
University of Mississippi

James D. Anderson, *The Education of Blacks in the South, 1860–1935* (1988); Alicia K. Jackson, "The Colored Methodist Episcopal Church and Its Struggle for Autonomy and Reform in the New South" (PhD dissertation, University of Mississippi, 2004); Chiquita Gail Willis, "The History of the Mississippi State Normal School for Colored Youth, 1870–1904" (master's thesis, University of Mississippi, 1990); Stuart Grayson Noble, *Forty Years of the Public Schools in Mississippi* (1918).

Mississippi State Sovereignty Commission

On 17 May 1954—soon known to many white southerners as Black Monday—the US Supreme Court issued its *Brown v. Board of Education* decision, which did away with the idea of "separate but equal" racially segregated schools. Some white southerners, including many in Mississippi, resented

M

the end of their cherished and supposedly divinely ordained "southern way of life" and resorted to violence to defend the region's racial status quo. Others resurrected interposition, a nineteenth-century doctrine under which the state had a right to "interpose" its sovereignty to protect citizens from federal actions that the state deemed unconstitutional, even though the US Supreme Court had rejected that theory a century earlier.

An overwhelming mood of defiance of the federal government dominated the 1956 state legislative session, which featured a parade of bills and resolutions designed to protect Mississippi's racial customs. On 29 February the legislature unanimously passed an "interposition resolution" that declared the *Brown* decision "invalid." The same day, lawmakers created the Mississippi State Sovereignty Commission "to do and perform any and all acts and things deemed necessary and proper to protect the sovereignty of the state of Mississippi" from "encroachment . . . by the Federal Government or any branch, department or agency thereof." A tax-supported state agency that was part of the executive branch, the Sovereignty Commission included the governor (who also served as chair), the lieutenant governor, the Speaker of the House, the attorney general, two state senators, three state representatives, and three citizens.

Neither the word *segregation* nor the word *integration* appeared in the carefully crafted legislation, but federal "encroachment" meant "forced racial integration," and the Sovereignty Commission soon became identified as Mississippi's segregation watchdog agency. With the aura of sophistication and respectability emanating from the word *sovereignty*, the commission was expected to maintain segregation and to wreck the National Association for the Advancement of Colored People (NAACP) and other civil rights organizations in Mississippi.

Under the administration of Gov. James P. Coleman (1956–60), the commission took a muted approach, comparing itself to the FBI, "during times of war seeking out intelligence information about the enemy and what the enemy proposes to do." By the fall of 1957, the public relations department had sent more than two hundred thousand pamphlets and other forms of direct mail to newspaper editors, television stations, and state lawmakers above the Mason-Dixon Line, trying to convince northerners that resistance to the *Brown* decision resulted not from racism but from principled objections to constitutional violations. At the same time, the Sovereignty Commission used paid and unpaid informants throughout the state to keep the NAACP and the Mississippi Progressive Voters' League under surveillance. By the summer of 1959, these informants and agency investigators had enabled the Sovereignty Commission to accumulate more than four thousand index cards and several hundred investigative files containing baseless rumors, random information, and bizarre details. The commission also paid members of the state's African American community, including H. H. Humes, editor of the *Greenville Delta Leader*, to oppose integration.

In 1959 Ross R. Barnett won election to the Mississippi governorship after a campaign in which he promised to preserve rigid racial segregation. Reflecting his more confrontational approach, the Sovereignty Commission became more aggressive in the early summer of 1960. Erle E. Johnston, director of the agency's public relations branch, organized a speakers bureau program. More than 100 Sovereignty Commission members, state officials, legislators, judges, attorneys, newspaper editors, and businesspeople delivered approximately 120 addresses in northern and western states, painting a rosy picture of the state's race relations and attempting to raise alarm about federal actions. In addition, the Sovereignty Commission sponsored a film, *Message from Mississippi*, that similarly extolled the benefits of segregation. Also on Barnett's watch, the Sovereignty Commission's investigators embarked on a broadly defined "subversive hunt" as Mississippi's white power structure defined civil rights movement leaders, activists, and sympathizers as subversives for their opposition to racial conformity. During the final two years of Barnett's administration, after the 1962 University of Mississippi desegregation crisis, the Sovereignty Commission became involved in a number of bizarre incidents, including inspections of allegedly "integrated" outdoor toilets on construction sites and investigations of suspected cases of miscegenation.

Under Barnett's successor, Gov. Paul B. Johnson (1964–68), the Sovereignty Commission's role changed again, in part as a consequence of increasing violence and incidents such as the murders of NAACP leader Medgar Evers in 1963 and of civil rights activists Andrew Goodman, James Chaney, and Michael Schwerner in 1964. The Sovereignty Commission began investigating the activities of such unreconstructed white supremacist groups as the Ku Klux Klan and the Americans for the Preservation of the White Race as a way of distancing the agency from openly violent organizations. However, the commission continued its work against the civil rights movement—for example, via the Mississippi Negro Citizenship Association, a Sovereignty Commission creation that sought to co-opt the "thinking Negroes of Mississippi" and blunt the work of the Council of Federated Organizations and other more radical groups. Johnson's successor, Gov. John Bell Williams (1968–72), dismantled the agency's public relations functions and concentrated its resources on investigating anti–Vietnam War demonstrators, black nationalists, and campus radicals.

On 17 April 1973, true to a vow he made during his gubernatorial campaign, Gov. William L. Waller vetoed the Sovereignty Commission's annual appropriation bill, bringing the agency's activities to a close. The 1956 act that had created the Sovereignty Commission remained on the state's law books until 1977, when the legislature abolished the agency and voted to seal its official records until 2027. Shortly thereafter, the American Civil Liberties Union initiated a legal effort to open the records to the public. Twenty-one years later, those efforts began to reach fruition with the release of the first commission records, and in 2002 all of the agency's documents were made available via the Mississippi Department of Archives and History's Sovereignty Commission Online website.

Yasuhiro Katagiri
Arlington, Texas

Joseph Crespino, *In Search of Another Country: Mississippi and the Conservative Counterrevolution* (2007); Erle Johnston, *Mississippi's Defiant Years, 1953–1973: An Interpretive Documentary with Personal Experiences* (1990); Yasuhiro Katagiri, *Humanities in the South: Journal of the Southern Humanities Council* (2002); Yasuhiro Katagiri, *The Mississippi State Sovereignty Commission: Civil Rights and States' Rights* (2001); Neil R. McMillen, *The Citizens' Council: Organized Resistance to the Second Reconstruction, 1954–64* (1994); Mississippi Department of Archives and History, Sovereignty Commission Online website, http://mdah.state.ms.us/arrec/digital_archives/sovcom/; Sarah Rowe-Sims, *Journal of Mississippi History* (Spring 1999).

Mississippi State University

A public comprehensive university, Mississippi State University (MSU) provides opportunities for academic study at the baccalaureate, master's, and doctoral levels plus research and service functions appropriate to its role as a land-grant school accredited by the Commission on Colleges of the Southern Association of Colleges and Schools. The university's main campus is located east of and adjacent to the city of Starkville. The primary academic area covers eight hundred acres, and together with the agricultural research farms, MSU comprises a total of forty-two hundred contiguous acres. A branch campus in the city of Meridian is located on a twenty-six-acre campus.

On 18 February 1878 the Mississippi legislature created the Agricultural and Mechanical College of the State of Mississippi under the US Congress's 1862 Morrill Land-Grant College Act. In keeping with the philosophy of the original land-grant legislation, Mississippi State cherishes its role as a "people's college."

For its first fifty years, the college functioned as an all-white and all-male military school, though a few local female students were allowed to register prior to 1912. Students were required to wear military uniforms at all times, from registration in the fall until the end of the academic year in May. The school initially offered only two programs of study, the Agricultural Course and the Mechanical Course, with supporting classes in mathematics, biological and physical sciences, English, and the humanities required of all students.

In 1902 a more formalized academic program emerged with the creation of the School of Engineering, School of Agriculture, and Science School. The School of Business and Industry was organized in 1915, and the School of Education followed in 1934. In 1932 the college's name changed to Mississippi State College, and in 1957 it became Mississippi State University. The College of Arts and Sciences emerged in 1957, the College of Architecture in 1973, and the College of Veterinary Medicine in 1974. The School of Forestry became the College of Forest Resources in 1990. In the twenty-first century the university consists of the College of Agriculture and Life Sciences, including the School of Human Sciences; the College of Architecture, Art, and Design; the College of Arts and Sciences; the College of Business, including the Adkerson School of Accountancy; the College of Education; the Bagley College of Engineering, including the Swalm School of Chemical Engineering; the College of Forest Resources; the Office of the Graduate School; and the College of Veterinary Medicine. The university offers more than 175 programs leading to a baccalaureate, master's, or doctoral degree. MSU's Meridian Campus is a regional upper-division campus offering bachelor's and graduate degrees, while graduate centers in Vicksburg and at the Center of Higher Learning at the Stennis Space Center offer master's degrees in engineering.

Mississippi State began admitting African Americans in 1965, when Starkville's Richard Holmes transferred in after spending two years at a Texas college. Although Holmes lived alone in a two-bed dorm room and endured some harassment by white students, his enrollment did not provoke the violent reaction that greeted James Meredith's matriculation at the University of Mississippi or the police abuse that resulted when Clyde Kennard attempted to enroll at the University of Southern Mississippi.

By the fall of 2015 MSU's enrollment had reached 20,873, including 17,421 undergraduates. That number is nearly evenly divided between women (49 percent) and men (51 percent). A total of 71 percent of undergraduates are white, 21 percent are African American, and 2 percent are Hispanic. Mississippi is home to 71 percent of undergraduates, with 28 percent coming from other parts of the United States and 1 percent coming from other countries.

Mississippi State University campus, Starkville (Courtesy Russ Houston [R3H5875])

Among the many alumni of note are authors John Grisham and Lewis Nordan, business leaders Fred Carl and Hartley Peavey, political figures John Stennis and Sonny Montgomery, basketball stars Bailey Howell and LaToya Thomas, and baseball stars Rafael Palmeiro and Will Clark.

MSU faculty members conduct organized research in thirty-five research centers, institutes, or laboratories on campus plus a small research unit at the Stennis Space Center. The Mississippi Agriculture and Forestry Experiment Station conducts extensive research in all areas of agriculture on campus as well as at seventeen branch stations located across the state.

MSU broadened its focus beyond organized agricultural research in 1949 with the Raspet Flight Research Laboratory and the Social Science Research Center. As at many research institutions, MSU's grant- and contract-sponsored research mushroomed during the 1970s and 1980s, primarily in engineering but also in biology, education, and business.

In 1989 the National Science Foundation established an Engineering Center of Excellence at Mississippi State, building on the university's expertise in computational fluid dynamics and numerical grid generation. In 2015 the Federal Aviation Administration selected a team headed by MSU to create a new Center of Excellence for Unmanned Aircraft Systems, making the school a leader in drone-related research.

The Mississippi State University Extension Service (formerly the Mississippi Cooperative Extension Service) is headquartered on campus and maintains county offices staffed by county agents and home agents, bringing campus research to the local level throughout the state.

J. Chester McKee
Mississippi State University

Michael Ballard, *Maroon and White: Mississippi State University, 1872–2003* (2008); John Knox Bettersworth, *People's College: A History of Mississippi State* (1979); Mississippi State University website, www.msstate.edu; Mississippi State University College Portraits website, http://www.collegeportraits.org/MS/msu/print; Sid Salter, *Jackson Clarion-Ledger* (15 July 2015); *Undergraduate Bulletin of Mississippi State University* (2007–8).

Mississippi Statehood

If one were to describe the circumstances under which the Mississippi Territory was created in April 1798 and evolved toward statehood nineteen years later, *constant chaos* might be the most appropriate term. Perhaps no territory has had

such a confused past. Over the preceding century Mississippi was claimed at various times by France, Spain, England, and the United States as well as by the State of Georgia. Each entity passed laws, awarded land grants, and negotiated with Indian residents. Spain and the United States quarreled over boundary lines. Georgia claimed what is today Mississippi and Alabama and scandalized the nation with fraudulent land sales. And the livelihood of many territorial residents depended on the Mississippi River and the right to deposit goods in New Orleans, which at times was not available because of political crises. Events that affected the statehood process included illegal Georgia land sales in Mississippi Territory (1789–95); tension among Spain, France, and the United States surrounding the purchase of Louisiana (1803); Aaron Burr's expedition (1806–7); the West Florida Revolt (1810); and the War of 1812.

The territorial political climate could hardly have been worse. The bulk of the territory's population of US citizens lived in and around Natchez, a bastion of conservatism ruled by the gentry. The rest of the territory was Republican in sentiment, and that faction grew after 1798 and particularly after Thomas Jefferson's 1800 election as president. The first territorial governor was Massachusetts Federalist Winthrop Sargent, who was serving as secretary of the Northwest Territory and shared the political philosophy of Pres. John Adams and the Natchez ruling class. Sargent aspired to do a good job but lacked political sense, was ill-tempered, and knew little about the Mississippi region. His biggest problem was the fact that the territory was created at the "first-stage" level, allowing rule by a governor, secretary, and three judges without a legislative body until the territory had five thousand free male residents. Sargent's enemies, especially Cato West and former Virginians Thomas Green and Peter Brian Bruin, maintained that the territory already had five thousand free males at the time of its creation and should have been established at the "second-stage" level, with a legislature sharing power with the governor.

For two years, Sargent and his supporters withstood efforts to allow a legislature in the territory, as the governor appointed officials, including local judges and militia officers, and created Adams and Pickering Counties while organizing the Pearl River country to the east into Washington County. These were not unwise moves, but by refusing to seek second-stage status he infuriated the growing number of Republicans, who sent Narsworthy Hunter to Congress to seek second-stage status that all but Sargent and his circle wanted. By the summer of 1800 Congress authorized a territorial assembly, including a nine-member House of Representatives and a legislative council of five members selected by Congress from a list submitted by the territorial House of Representatives. Republicans won control of the first House, which, along with Jefferson's election, spelled the end of Sargent's tenure as governor.

His successor, W. C. C. Claiborne, was bright, young, energetic, and politically perceptive, seeking support from Federalists as well as Republicans. He used the skills and enhanced the power of William Dunbar, a successful, well-informed, and respected conservative. In addition, much of what Claiborne did was symbolic as well as practical, pleasing his Republican followers. For example, Pickering County became Jefferson County, Federalist-dominated Adams County became two counties as the governor lopped off its southern half and created Wilkinson County, and the new Claiborne County was created north of Jefferson County. The result was a smaller Adams County surrounded by Republican-dominated counties. To further emphasize Natchez's loss of power, Claiborne moved the territorial capital six miles east to the small town of Washington. Natchez retained economic power and still constituted the territory's social center, but, Claiborne reasoned, Natchez would no longer dominate politically.

The Claiborne years were comparatively stable for Mississippi Territory. Relative political peace prevailed, cotton became king, settlers arrived in record numbers, and Louisiana became part of the United States, making the movement of goods through New Orleans more predictable. However, in December 1803 Claiborne was transferred to New Orleans as governor. Territorial secretary Cato West served as interim governor until March 1805, when North Carolinian Robert Williams took over. Williams chose to remain in his home state most of the time and did little to address such pressing territorial problems as brigands on the Natchez Trace, growing discontent among neglected settlers between the western Georgia border and the Mississippi River counties, and lingering border and access problems.

Thanks to others, especially congressional delegate George Poindexter, political reforms occurred during the Williams years. A petition was forwarded to Congress in 1807 to remove property qualifications for voting; the following year Poindexter was appointed chair of a congressional committee to study the petition. Out of those deliberations came new, more democratic voting qualifications for free males—ownership of fifty acres of land or a town lot worth one hundred dollars. The number of members in the territorial House of Representatives was increased from nine to twelve, and the territorial delegate to Congress was to be chosen by popular vote.

In March 1809 Williams was replaced by Virginian David Holmes, who served for the remainder of the territorial period and then became Mississippi's first governor. He was a mild-mannered man who brought to Mississippi a political philosophy that stressed a bipartisan approach to problem solving.

Backcountry disaffection remained an issue during Mississippi's territorial period. Mississippi had been settled by the French on the Gulf Coast and by English, Spanish, and Americans in its southwestern section along the eastern shore of the Mississippi River. But the territory stretched east to Georgia and north to Tennessee—a vast, thinly settled, and disregarded area. As early as 1803 the region from the Pearl River east threatened to separate from Natchez domination, and a more serious 1809 secession threat was defused only by the outbreak of the War of 1812.

With Natchez's support, congressional delegate William Lattimore recommended that the entire region be incorporated as one state, but the US Senate rejected the recommendation. Division of the territory was now inevitable, but where? The backwoods folks wanting nothing to do with Natchez met at the home of John Ford at what became known as the Pearl River Convention of 1816 to fight against continued inclusion in Mississippi Territory. Though those along the Pearl River would, in the final analysis, be sacrificed, the division that evolved proved to be a fair one. The line that divides Mississippi and Alabama begins in the north where Bear Creek empties into the Tennessee River and moves straight south to the northeastern corner of Wayne County, turning slightly to the southeast to avoid cutting a corner of that county, before continuing south and reaching the Gulf ten miles east of the Pascagoula River. In 1817 the western part became the state of Mississippi, while the eastern section became Alabama two years later.

Pres. James Madison signed the enabling legislation for Mississippi statehood on 1 March 1817, with a convention to be held at the territorial capital in July. Forty-seven delegates representing fourteen counties met in the Methodist church in Washington with Gov. Holmes presiding. Despite Holmes's ability to foster bipartisanship, the convention began in bad humor and got worse. In disgust, backwoods folks moved that the convention not seek statehood because Natchez was dominating the convention, but the motion to disband failed. The delegates then crafted a conservative constitution with Natchez calling the shots, even becoming the state's capital once again. Voting was restricted to white males who had lived in Mississippi for a minimum of one year and had lived in the precinct for at least six months. Senators were required to own 300 acres of land or other real estate valued at one thousand dollars, while representatives must have 150 acres or real estate valued at five hundred dollars. Gubernatorial candidates must be at least thirty years of age, must have lived in the United States for twenty years and in Mississippi for five years, and must own 600 acres or real estate valued at two thousand dollars and have owned that property for at least six months before the election.

The constitution was signed on 15 August 1817 and was declared in effect without being presented to the voters. In September Holmes was elected the state's first governor, and the first General Assembly was held in Washington because of a yellow fever outbreak in Natchez. Walter Leake and Thomas Williams were selected as the first Mississippi senators, while George Poindexter became the first representative. The Mississippi Territory ceased to exist on 10 December 1817 when the state was formally admitted to the Union.

Arthur H. DeRosier Jr.
Rocky Mountain College

Clarence C. Carter, ed., *The Territorial Papers of the United States* (1937, 1938); J. F. H. Claiborne, *Mississippi as a Province, Territory, and State* (1889); William Dunbar, *Life, Letters, and Papers of William Dunbar of Elgin, Scotland, and Natchez, Mississippi* (1930); Andrew Ellicott, *The Journal of Andrew Ellicott* (1962); Dunbar Rowland, ed., *The Mississippi Territorial Archives, 1798–1803*, vol. 1, *Executive Journals of Governor Winthrop Sargent and Governor William Charles Cole Claiborne* (1905); Robert C. Weems Jr., *Early Economic History of Mississippi, 1699–1840* (1953).

Mississippi University for Women

When the Industrial Institute and College for the Education of White Girls of the State of Mississippi (II&C) was chartered on 12 March 1884, it made educational history as the first state-supported college for women in America. Its curriculum was a unique hybrid: a high-quality collegiate education coupled with practical vocational training. One legislator described the school as a "Godsend" for the "poor girls of Mississippi." At a time when many people considered intellectual training for women to have disastrous consequences, legislators in economically ravaged Mississippi recognized that women needed to learn not only to think for themselves but also to support themselves. The II&C's curriculum served as a model for other state-supported women's colleges, among them Georgia State College for Women (1889), North Carolina College for Women (1891), Alabama College (1893), Texas State College for Women (1901), Florida State College for Women (1905), and Oklahoma College for Women (1908).

Two decades of effort preceded the II&C's establishment. Sallie Eola Reneau of Grenada had campaigned energetically for the creation of a public college for white women during the 1860s and 1870s, winning legislative approval but no appropriations. A decade later, Olivia Valentine Hastings of Copiah County and Annie Coleman Peyton of Claiborne County joined forces to lobby legislators and journalists, including as part of their argument the fact that black women were receiving education at Mississippi colleges created during Reconstruction for people of color. Hastings's friend, legislator John McCaleb Martin of Claiborne Country, drafted a bill to create the II&C. Strong political support from a few key representatives, combined with the backing of Gov. Robert Lowry, helped Martin's bill win passage by a single vote in the Senate and by just two votes in the House.

II&C opened on 22 October 1885 in Columbus, a longtime supporter of women's education that donated to the state the buildings and grounds of the Columbus Female Institute, a private school founded in 1847, and fifty thousand dollars raised via city bonds for improvements to the property. The first session opened with 341 blue-uniformed girls entering the school's new chapel to hear Gov. Lowry exclaim, "Men and women of Mississippi, you have a jewel! Preserve it!" He also reminded the crowd that it was fitting that Mississippi should give the opportunity of a free college education to its "white girls" since "white boys" and "black boys and girls" already had similar opportunities. Tuition was free, with students selected through a quota system based on the counties' population of "educable white girls." According to the charter, the students had to be "at least fifteen years of age, in good health, and . . . of good moral character." In 1889 the first ten graduates received their diplomas.

The II&C's first president, Richard Watson Jones, also taught physics and chemistry and presided over an otherwise all-female faculty whose members influenced the state's political and educational life for decades. Pauline Orr, mistress of English, Mary Callaway, mistress of mathematics, and Sallie McLaurin, mistress of industrial and decorative arts, became powerful mentors for the young women who began leaving the II&C to attend graduate schools, to teach, or to work as bookkeepers or telegraphers. Orr was active in the woman suffrage movement, and after retiring from teaching in 1913, she served as president of the state suffrage association and spoke up and down the eastern seaboard, using her connections with former students and faculty to further the cause. Other early faculty members became well known in Mississippi for their innovative teaching and their passion for their disciplines. Emma Ody Pohl, who taught at the school from 1907 to 1955, brought mandatory physical education courses to all students and created some of the most distinctive campus traditions: the Junior-Freshman Wedding and the Zouave marching drill. Weenona Poindexter, a member of the music faculty from 1894 to 1945, initiated the diploma in music and began decades of highly successful concert series by personally guaranteeing the funding for an Ignace Paderewski concert on campus in 1905. Mabel Ward, the first home economics professor in Mississippi, created innovative programs such as the Home Management Practice House, which set the standard for home economics departments all over the country,

In 1920, when the II&C became Mississippi State College for Women, the new name more clearly reflected the institution's merging of professional training with four-year collegiate degrees. In 1966 the college admitted its first African American women, and in 1974, the school became Mississippi University for Women (MUW). In 1982 the US Supreme Court voted five to four that MUW had to admit male applicants to the School of Nursing. To avoid further litigation, the state's Board of Institutions of Higher Learning then directed MUW to open all academic programs to men. Shortly thereafter, however, the board reaffirmed the original mission focused on women's education, and in 1989 Dr. Clyda Stokes Rent became MUW's first female president. Since 2012 James Borsig has headed the school.

MUW still provides a liberal arts education with a distinct emphasis on professional development and leadership opportunities for women. The institution remains an educational model and pioneer not only in Mississippi but in the nation. Among the many notable MUW alumni are scientist Elizabeth Lee Hogan, author Eudora Welty, educators Blanche Colton Williams and Bettye Rogers Coward, actress Ruth Ford, and legal figures Kay Cobb, Lenore Prather, Helen Carloss, and Mary Libby Payne.

Bridget Smith Pieschel
Mississippi University for Women

Janet R. Langley, *Mississippi Industrial Institute and College: Forerunner of Women's Higher Education in the New South* (master's thesis, Mississippi University for Women, 1999); John McCaleb Martin, *Publications of the Mississippi Historical Society, Centenary Series* (1921); Edward Mayes, *History of Education in Mississippi* (1889); Richard Aubrey McLemore, ed., *A History of Education in Mississippi* (1973); Mississippi University for Women website, www.muw.edu; Sarah Neilson, "The History of Mississippi State College for Women" (unpublished, 1954); Bridget Smith Pieschel and Stephen Robert Pieschel, *Loyal Daughters: One Hundred Years at Mississippi University for Women* (1984).

Mississippi University for Women Founders

Mississippi University for Women, originally Mississippi Industrial Institute and College, was founded in 1884 as the first publicly supported college for women in the United States. This school's creation resulted largely from the combined political efforts of a trio of Mississippi educational activists, Sallie Eola Reneau, Olivia Valentine Hastings, and Annie Coleman Peyton.

The Tennessee-born Reneau (1836–78) was the first woman to lobby the Mississippi legislature to appropriate funds for higher education for women. A resident of Grenada County and later of Batesville in Panola County, Reneau was an 1854 graduate of the Holly Springs Female Institute, one of the best private schools for women in the state. Entering the teaching profession immediately after graduation, she soon realized that the only option for higher education, private female seminaries and institutes, lay beyond the reach of most Mississippi women, although the state had offered men a public university education at the University of Mississippi since 1848. By the late 1850s, strongly supported by her father, Nathaniel Smith Reneau, a veteran of the Mexican War and later US ambassador to Mexico, she began a writing campaign focused on persuading the Mississippi legislature to support free higher education for women so that "the indigent as well as the opulent may receive . . . the imperishable riches of a well-cultivated mind." She was only twenty when her essay, "Memorial to the Mississippi Legislature," persuaded the legislature to approve the creation of a women's college in Yalobusha County. However, the legislative support was more enthusiastic than practical, since no funds were appropriated to build or operate the college. Reneau continued to press for a public college for women into the 1870s: in 1872 the legislature approved the creation of a branch of the University of Mississippi to be called Reneau Female University of Mississippi and designated Reneau as the first president. But this bill and a similar one approved in 1873 again had no financial backing, so Reneau Female University never came into existence.

Reneau continued to teach and to lobby for women's education but in 1878 took on a new cause. Yellow fever was raging in parts of Mississippi, Louisiana, and Tennessee. The Memphis area was ravaged by the infection, and the poor who were unable to flee to a cooler climate died by the thousands. Reneau volunteered for nursing duty in Memphis, intending not only to take care of the sick but to write letters describing the epidemic to her father in Washington, D.C., for publication in northern newspapers. For a time their plan succeeded, prompting several northern philanthropists to send food and medicine south to affected towns and cities. But Reneau herself caught the fever and died.

Born in Claiborne County, Olivia Valentine (1842–96) was just a few years younger than Reneau, but there is no evidence that the two women ever corresponded about their similar interests. Valentine's family had considerable wealth and property before the Civil War but suffered substantial financial losses afterward. Her parents died while she was still a young girl, and she and her siblings were raised by their grandparents near Port Gibson. She received a private education at a female seminary in Kentucky, including instruction in music, and probably also studied at a girls' school in Pennsylvania or Maryland. After the war she came to understand the financial difficulties women faced when they had lacked the skills to earn a living. In 1877 Valentine married John G. Hastings, a widower with several children. Together they had one daughter, Adeline.

Almost immediately after her marriage, Olivia Hastings began advocating for public women's education in Mississippi. She was interested primarily in the promotion of industrial or vocational education, believing that a skill or a trade would help the poor women of her impoverished state support themselves. By the early 1880s she was writing regular letters to the *Jackson Clarion-Ledger* under the pen name "Olive," advocating free public industrial education for the white girls of Mississippi. About that same time, in 1881, the state Grange, an agricultural organization, declared itself in favor of public industrial education for women. In 1884 State Senator John McCaleb Martin, a neighbor and family friend of the Hastingses in Claiborne County, decided that he would work with Olivia Hastings to write a bill for a public industrial college for women.

M

Since 1883 Hastings had been corresponding with another Mississippian, Annie Coleman Peyton (1852–98), who under the pen name "A Mississippi Woman" had since 1879 been submitting legislative petitions, writing letters to newspapers, and publishing pamphlets promoting the creation of a public liberal arts college for women. Hastings and Peyton agreed to work together to promote a state institution that would offer an educational hybrid to Mississippi girls—a curriculum that was part industrial instruction and part collegiate liberal arts education, an "industrial institute and college." In 1884 Peyton had waited for the Grangers to sponsor a bill, as they had in 1882, but when it did not materialize, she accepted Hinds County senator J. K. McNeilly's offer to sponsor a "Bill for the Establishment of a State Normal and Industrial School for the White Girls of Mississippi." She commented in a later memoir that she knew that *normal* would "attract the schoolmen" and that *industrial* "might win the farmers to its support." Not long after McNeilly's bill was filed, Peyton learned of Senator Martin's bill and asked McNeilly to compare the bills and withdraw their version if Martin's was superior. Martin's bill called for the immediate establishment of the institution, while McNeilly and Peyton's merely requested a small appropriation and the formation of a board of trustees. McNeilly withdrew his bill, and both women and their senator allies threw all their support behind the Martin bill, which narrowly passed both houses of the legislature in March 1884.

Annie Coleman was a baby when her father died, but her mother sent her to Whitworth College, a Methodist school for women in Brookhaven, and she graduated as valedictorian in 1872. After teaching for two years at her alma mater, she married Ephraim Peyton, a Hazlehurst attorney and a judge, and they eventually had eight children. Her years as a student and as a faculty member at Whitworth made her aware of the nearly constant financial problems suffered by the church-supported school, and she was convinced that only state support would ensure the survival of a liberal arts college for women. Peyton campaigned to have the state take over the operation of Whitworth College but discovered that restrictions in the will that had created the school would return its property to members of the Whitworth family if the college left the control of the Methodist church. Like Hastings, Peyton concluded that women needed to be able to support themselves, since "especially for women, ignorance is death." Rather than industrial training, however, Peyton advocated a broad liberal arts curriculum as the best route for women's survival.

Both women served on the committee that planned and designed the curriculum for the new college for women, and Peyton chaired the group. By October 1885 their plans resulted in the opening of the Mississippi Industrial Institute and College for White Girls (II&C) on the former location of the private Columbus Female Institute in Columbus. Hastings and Ellen Martin soon helped to establish a loan fund for girls who could not afford to pay even the small boarding expenses at the II&C. In 1889, the same year that the II&C produced its first graduating class, the widowed Peyton moved with several of her children to Columbus, and for the remainder of her life she taught history at the II&C. Her daughters Annie, Artie, and Mary Lou eventually graduated from the college.

All three of the founding mothers are honored at the institution they helped to create. Mississippi University for Women's Reneau Hall, originally built as a residence hall, now houses the College of Business and the Offices of Academic Advising and Institutional Research, and both Hastings-Simmons Hall and Peyton Hall are dormitories.

Bridget Smith Pieschel
Mississippi University for Women

Bridget Smith Pieschel and Stephen Robert Pieschel, *Loyal Daughters: One Hundred Years at Mississippi University for Women, 1884–1984* (1984).

Mississippi University for Women v. Hogan

In *Mississippi University for Women v. Hogan* (1982), the US Supreme Court ruled by a five-to-four vote that the single-sex admissions policy of the Mississippi University for Women (MUW) violated the Equal Protection Clause of the Fourteenth Amendment. The Court made clear that individuals may not be excluded from educational institutions based on gender alone.

MUW, a state-supported institution, was established in Columbus in 1884 as the Mississippi Industrial Institute and College for the Education of White Girls of the State of Mississippi. MUW's School of Nursing was established in 1971. Joe Hogan, a registered nurse, applied for admission to MUW's nursing program in 1979. He was otherwise qualified but was denied enrollment because he was a male. He was permitted to audit nursing courses but could not enroll for credit.

Hogan filed suit in the US District Court for the Northern District of Mississippi, claiming that the female-only admissions policy violated the Equal Protection Clause. The court granted summary judgment in favor of MUW because it found that "the maintenance of MUW as a single-sex school bears a rational relationship to the State's legitimate interest 'in providing the greatest practical range of educational opportunities for its female student population.'"

Hogan appealed to the 5th Circuit Court of Appeals, which reversed the district court's decision and held that the admissions policy was unconstitutional because it discriminated on the basis of gender. It imposed a higher standard than the district court and found that the state had to show that the gender-based classification was substantially related to an important governmental objective. The 5th Circuit ruled that the state failed to meet this burden.

MUW then appealed to the US Supreme Court. Writing for the Court, Justice Sandra Day O'Connor began by noting that because the admissions policy expressly discriminated against applicants to the School of Nursing on the basis of gender, it was subject to scrutiny under the Fourteenth Amendment. The party seeking to uphold the gender classification had to show an exceedingly persuasive justification for it, a burden that could be met "only by showing at least that the classification serves important governmental objectives and that the discriminatory means employed are substantially related to the achievement of those objectives." The objective could not be excluding or protecting members of one gender because they were "presumed to suffer from an inherent handicap or to be innately inferior."

The Court pointed out that under limited circumstances, gender-based classifications may be justified if the classification assists members of the sex facing disproportionate discrimination. The state argued that this was the goal of its single-sex admissions policy. The Court disagreed with this argument, pointing out that women earned more than 98 percent of US nursing degrees and thus did not face discrimination in pursuing that type of education. In the Court's view, rather than compensating for discrimination against women, MUW's admissions policy tended to "perpetuate the stereotyped view of nursing as an exclusively woman's job."

The Court therefore found that the state had failed to prove that the alleged objective of educational opportunity for women was the actual purpose of the discriminatory classification. The state had also failed to show that the females-only policy was substantially and directly related to its proposed compensatory objective because the practice of allowing men to audit the nursing courses completely undermined the state's claim that men adversely affected women in the nursing program.

The Court affirmed the judgment of the 5th Circuit and held that MUW's School of Nursing admissions policy limiting enrollment to women violated the Equal Protection Clause of the Fourteenth Amendment. Justices Warren Burger, Harry Blackmun, Lewis Powell, and William Rehnquist dissented, primarily on the grounds that the majority required too rigid requirements of the state and that Hogan's only injury was one of inconvenience.

Mississippi University for Women v. Hogan has become important precedent for cases involving single-sex educational institutions, establishing that individuals cannot be refused admission to public educational institutions based solely on their gender. This decision proved instrumental in *United States v. Virginia* (1996), in which the Supreme Court required the Virginia Military Institute, the last state-supported all-male university in the United States, to admit women.

Amanda Brown
University of Mississippi

Frances Elizabeth Burgin, *Journal of Women and the Law* (2001); Debra Franzese, *American University Law Review* (February 2007); *Mississippi University for Women v. Hogan*, 458 US 718 (1982); Mississippi University for Women website, www.muw.edu.

Mississippi v. Johnson

Mississippi v. Johnson (1867) was a landmark Reconstruction-era case. In 1867 the State of Mississippi sued Pres. Andrew Johnson, seeking an injunction to prevent him from enforcing the Reconstruction Act of 1867, which had established military rule in the southern states. Lawyers for Mississippi argued that the act was unconstitutional because its enforcement would convert the US government "into a military despotism, in which every man may be deprived of his goods, lands, liberty, and life by the breath of a military commander" appointed by the president.

The US Supreme Court unanimously held that it had no jurisdiction to issue an injunction to prevent the president of the United States from performing his official duties. Writing for the court, Chief Justice Salmon P. Chase distinguished between mere ministerial acts, which could be enjoined under the precedent of *Marbury v. Madison*, and large discretionary executive acts such as enforcing an act of Congress. Relying on the principles of separation of powers, the court held that an injunction could not be issued against an executive acting in his official capacity.

The argument that such an injunction could be obtained against President Johnson as a citizen of Tennessee was also rejected. According to the Court, "A bill praying an injunction against the execution of an act of Congress by the incumbent of the presidential office cannot be received, whether it describes him as President or a citizen of a State."

Natalya Seay
Washington, D.C.

David P. Currie, *University of Chicago Law Review* (Winter 1984); Alfred H. Kelly and Winfred A. Harbison, *The American Constitution: Its Origins and Development* (1976); *Mississippi v. Johnson*, 71 US 475 (1867).

M

Mississippi Valley State University

A historically black institution of higher education, Mississippi Valley State University opened in 1950 as Mississippi Vocational College. The school's origins go back to 1943, when the Delta Council recommended an expanded "program in the study of race . . . relations and the maintenance of harmonious understanding between the two races of the Delta." The Mississippi legislature responded in 1946 by authorizing the creation of an institution in the Delta that would "train teachers for the rural and elementary schools and to provide vocational education." Legislators and other members of the state's white power structure hoped that increasing the educational opportunities available for African Americans would forestall the movement toward desegregation of educational institutions.

The new Mississippi Vocational College held its formal groundbreaking in the small Leflore County town of Itta Bena on 19 February 1950. Dr. J. H. White was selected to serve as the school's first president. While the campus was envisioned as consisting of forty buildings, two barns, and a stadium, the school at first had just fourteen regular students and seven faculty members, and classes were conducted at the old Leflore County High School building.

Nine of the first twelve graduating students in 1953 received degrees in elementary education. Most students who pursued courses of instruction in vocational terminal programs received certificates of completion in the field of agriculture. In 1954 Mississippi Vocational College had finally constructed enough student dormitories to accommodate its growing student population and began to phase out its early bus transportation and extension services and to concentrate on its majority residential student population. Much of the construction was financed by private donations from such wealthy individuals as Jacob Aron of New York, and by 1960 White was referring to the school as the "College with a Million Friends." The school began offering academic courses in the liberal arts, nursing, and business administration, and in 1964 it changed its name to Mississippi Valley State College.

By the late 1960s many college campuses faced major problems related to social unrest and racial issues. A black college located in the middle of the Mississippi Delta, Mississippi Valley State could not help but get caught up in this turbulent era. This growing student unrest culminated in at least two riots in 1968 and 1970, and in February 1969 eight hundred students staged a nonviolent boycott, demanding black history courses, an increase in the number of works by black writers in the library, remedial courses in English and math, lectures and presentations by prominent black speakers, and fewer curfew restrictions. Student enrollment dropped dramatically. White attempted to bolster admissions by abandoning entrance requirements and returning to the school's former open-enrollment policy before resigning effective 1 July 1971.

Under his successor, Dr. Earnest A. Boykins, the school became Mississippi Valley State University on 15 March 1974 and entered an era of what future university administrator Dr. Roy Hudson subsequently characterized as "a growth period for the institution in terms of enrollment, program expansion, and physical plant." However, Hudson noted, "it was also a period which portended future problems with the university," with a "decline in college student population, stricter admission standards, inflationary costs in education, and internal and external political problems."

During Boykins's tenure, the school implemented thirty-two new academic programs, including the Academic Skills Program, which was designed to help disadvantaged students. In 1976 the school added its first master's degree program. In the spring of 1977 campus enrollment reached thirty-one hundred, a new peak. By the following fall semester, however, enrollment had dropped to twenty-five hundred as a consequence of the board's insistence that the school raise both admission standards and tuition. Boykins resigned in August 1981 and was replaced by Dr. Joseph Boyer the following January.

Boyer's administration initially saw increased enrollment, and the school gained national attention through its football program. During the 1983–86 "Satellite Express" era, football coach Archie Cooley directed a squad that included quarterback Willie Totten and future Pro Football Hall of Fame receiver Jerry Rice. (Another Hall of Fame member, Deacon Jones, attended the school during the 1950s.) The school faced closure in both 1984 and 1985, and Boyer resigned in January 1988.

Dr. William H. Sutton took over six months later "with an operating deficit and declining enrollment." In addition, the school faced closure yet again as part of the fallout from the 1975 *Ayers v. Mississippi* case, in which the father of a student at one of the state's three predominantly black colleges challenged the state's funding of the institutions. Mississippi Valley State again survived, and by the mid-1990s it had begun "the quest to move from the mode of surviving to that of thriving."

Sutton retired on 1 July 1998 and was replaced by Dr. Lester C. Newman, who launched an expansion program, "From Excellence to Preeminence." Newman oversaw a reorganization of the curriculum and instituted other innovations in time for Mississippi Valley State's fiftieth anniversary celebration in 2000. The following year, the school opened the off-campus Greenville Higher Learning Center. Newman retired in 2007, and Donna H. Oliver became the school's first female president in January 2009. William B. Bynum Jr. succeeded Oliver in 2013 to become the university's seventh president.

Mississippi Valley State currently serves an undergraduate population of about nineteen hundred students, more than 90 percent of them African American and about 57 percent of them female. The university is divided into the College of Arts and Sciences, the College of Education, the College of Professional Studies, the Honors Program, and the Graduate School, which offers master's degrees in environmental health, elementary education, criminal justice, business administration, special education, rural public policy, and teaching.

Harvey Hudspeth

Mississippi Valley State University

Greenwood Commonwealth (13 April 1983, 18 May 2003); Roy C. Hudson, "Mississippi Valley State University: Historical Reflections," *The Presidential Inaugural of Dr. Lester C. Newman* (program) (24 April 1999); *Jackson Clarion-Ledger* (3 April 1973); Mississippi Valley State University website, www.mvsu.edu; William L. Ware, *Greenwood Commonwealth* (27 December 2007); J. H. White, *Up from a Cotton Patch: J. H. White and the Development of Mississippi Valley State College* (1979).

Mississippian Decline

Archaeologists have documented the abandonment of major Mississippian ceremonial centers and other secondary mound centers in the Black Warrior Valley in Alabama by the mid-sixteenth century, a period often referred to as the decline of the Mississippian tradition. Populations moved from the mound sites and resettled in nucleated villages in the river valley. Researchers have developed several explanations for these changes, including the introduction of European diseases, social and economic collapse, and soil depletion.

Several scholars have documented nutritional stress associated with the collapse of Mississippian societies in Alabama. This physiological stress coupled with Native American immune systems provided little protection against European diseases such as smallpox, measles, and influenza that were introduced in the early 1500s. Spanish slavers Francisco Gordillo and Pedro de Quejo are known to have made first contact along the South Carolina coast in 1521, with other European explorers closely following. Consequently, depopulation created by poor nutrition or disease could account for a decline in traditional social and political structures. However, the exodus from Moundville began before Europeans reached the North American coast, meaning that other factors must have been involved.

Climatic and ecological instability in the southeastern United States between AD 1300 and 1400 have been cited as the possible cause for soil depletion, particularly in Tennessee's Little River Valley. Maize agriculture provided an important food source for large Mississippian settlements and populations. If crop production declined because of poor soils or climatic factors, populations would have been forced to relocate to new agricultural areas or to separate into smaller groups to forage on naturally occurring food resources. Population movement and a decrease in group size may have necessitated the adoption of different social and economic organizations, especially if agricultural production declined. Soil depletion and a decreased labor force have been cited as possible causes for the drop in dietary maize associated with the Mississippian decline at the Moundville Ceremonial center in Alabama.

In addition to relocating to the river valley, several other cultural changes begin to appear during the later Mississippian time. At several archaeological sites the tradition of primary articulated burials, some very elaborate, was replaced by a new and more popular custom of disarticulated secondary burials. These defleshed burials were sometimes placed in urns or in mass graves. In addition to the adoption of a new burial mode, warfare iconography associated with the height of the Mississippian period disappeared during this time, along with many large palisaded villages and ceremonial centers.

Although population movement and resettlement from many ceremonial centers and other villages occurred during this time, not all secondary mound centers were abandoned. One example is the Lyon's Bluff site, a single-mound village located approximately nineteen kilometers northeast of Starkville. Researchers have documented continuous occupation of the Lyon's Bluff site from AD 1200 to 1650. Another example is the Lubbub Creek single-mound village site in western Alabama, which was also occupied well into the seventeenth century. Populations at the Lyon's Bluff and Lubbub Creek sites may have relied more on natural resources than did Moundville and other larger ceremonial sites where maize may have been the most important food source. Both the Lyon's Bluff and Lubbub Creek sites are situated in the Black Belt physiographic province, which extends from north-central Mississippi to west-central Alabama. This geological formation is known for its fertile soils. The location of the Lyon's Bluff and Lubbub Creek mound sites in this agriculturally productive area, combined with different social and economic conditions, may have led to the continued use of these sites long after the decline of Mississippian mound and ceremonial centers located elsewhere.

S. Homes Hogue

Ball State University

William W. Baden, *A Dynamic Model of Stability and Change in Mississippian Agricultural Systems* (1987); S. Homes Hogue, *Southeastern Archaeology* (Winter 2007); Vernon James Knight Jr., James A. Brown, George E. Lankford, *Southeastern Archaeology* (Winter 2001); Vernon James Knight Jr. and Vincas P. Steponaitis, in *Archaeology of the Moundville Chiefdom*, ed. Vernon James Knight Jr. and Vincas P. Steponaitis (1998); Evan Peacock and S. Homes Hogue, *Southeastern Archaeology*

(Summer 2005); Christopher S. Peebles, *Mississippi Archaeology* (June 1987); Margaret J. Schoeninger and Mark R. Schurr, in *Archaeology of the Moundville Chiefdom*, ed. James Vernon Knight Jr. and Vincas P. Steponaitis (1998).

Mississippian Period

The Mississippian (or Mississippi) period, named for the Mississippi River, is an archaeological unit that at its simplest is defined by the presence of pottery tempered with crushed mussel shell. Other artifact types, including flat-topped rectangular earthen mounds, small triangular stone projectile points, and buildings constructed with wall trenches into which posts were set, also may identify sites used in this period. The definition has been extended to encompass a dependence on maize agriculture and the existence of chiefdom-type political organization. Because all of these traits appeared and disappeared at different times and places, they cannot necessarily be used to define a coherent unit. Of them, political organization is the most difficult to identify, as it is based on many inferences from the archaeological record. The practice of adding shell to pottery was adopted rapidly over much of eastern North America around AD 1000–1100 and lasted until sustained European contact, around AD 1700, so it provides a useful temporal marker.

The pottery made in the Mississippian period prominently included cooking and storage jars. Bowls often were highly decorated, with polished surfaces that might display engraved or incised designs. Red-slipped and red-and-white painted bottles and bowls also were made. Vessels might have animal head and tail effigies on the rims, with frogs, birds, bears, and other mammals and human heads commonly used. Large assemblages of whole pottery vessels were recovered through unsystematic and destructive digging from graves at the Walls site in DeSoto County and the Humber-McWilliams site in Coahoma County. Many examples from the latter collection are displayed at Greenwood's Museum of the Mississippi Delta.

Some of the largest earthen mound groups in North America date to the Mississippian period. Several of these sites are located in Mississippi's Yazoo Basin. The most well studied of these are Winterville Mounds near Greenville in Washington County and the Lake George Site in Yazoo County. By the time mound construction ended at these sites, each had more than two dozen mounds, including in each case one mound taller than sixty-five feet. The mounds surrounded a main and one or more subsidiary plazas, open areas that presumably did not contain houses. Atop and under some of the mounds were wall trenches, postholes, and other evidence of buildings. Lake George is surrounded by a nearly 1.5-mile-long earthen embankment with an exterior ditch. Mound construction and use at both sites began in the Coles Creek period (AD 700–1150) and continued through Plaquemine (AD 1150–1325) before a major increase in earthwork construction occurred during the Mississippian period, as marked by shell-tempered pottery. Winterville was partly excavated by Jeffrey P. Brain of Harvard University in 1967–68 and by H. Edwin Jackson of the University of Southern Mississippi beginning in 2003. Part of the Lake George Site was dug by Brain and Stephen Williams of Harvard University in 1958–60.

Mississippian mound sites in other parts of the state are smaller. Owl Creek Mounds, the largest such group in Chickasaw County, has five mounds, the tallest of which is sixteen feet high, arranged around a plaza. Evidence of structures was found on four of the mounds during Mississippi State University excavations in 1991–92. The Mississippian occupation there apparently did not include a significant resident population, as relatively few artifacts were recovered anywhere within it. In contrast, slightly later mound sites in the region, such as Lyon's Bluff, were the location of small villages.

The other component of the Mississippian settlement pattern was farmsteads, many of which have been found by archaeologists. Most of the population lived at these one- or two-house sites, and primary agricultural production of maize, beans, and other crops occurred there.

Archaeologists often state that Mississippian societies were made up of people placed into ranks that varied in access to power. In support of this theory, archaeologists have argued that buildings on top of mounds were chiefly residences, but evidence sometimes indicates other uses—as temples, structures for feasting, or storage buildings. Differences in burial location (under houses or in mounds) and in amount and kinds of grave goods included with burials (none or only utilitarian items versus quantities of fancy artifacts or objects made of exotic materials such as copper) also have been used as evidence of ranking. At the Lake George Site, for example, seventy-seven Coles Creek burials were excavated from what archaeologists identify as Mound C. The only artifacts found, each in a different grave, were an awl made of bone, bark lining in one of the grave pits, a pottery vessel, and some green pigment. An interesting contrast is offered by Burial 11 at Lyon's Bluff, excavated by Moreau B. C. Chambers in 1935. Near the burial was a carefully arranged deposit of two dozen or more turtle shells on which was placed an alligator skull. This unusual burial mode might be interpreted as indicating a high-status person, unlike the many burials found at Lyon's Bluff that had no associated artifacts.

Archaeologists seek to document variability in prehistoric artifacts through both time and space. The Mississippian period previously was considered culturally homogeneous, but additional archaeological work has revealed that it encompassed much variation.

Janet Rafferty
Mississippi State University

David H. Dye and Cheryl Ann Cox, eds., *Towns and Temples along the Mississippi* (1990); Patricia K. Galloway, *Mississippi Archaeology* 1 (2000); Evan Peacock and S. Homes Hogue, *Southeastern Archaeology* 1 (2005); Janet Rafferty, *Owl Creek Mounds: Test Excavations at a Vacant Mississippian Mound Center* (1995); Bruce D. Smith, ed., *Mississippian Settlement Patterns* (1978); Stephen Williams and Jeffrey P. Brain, *Excavations at the Lake George Site, Yazoo County, Mississippi, 1958–1960* (1983).

Mississippians for Public Education

In 1963 a small group of white Mississippi women concerned about violence and the possible closing of public schools began meeting in Jackson to discuss their support for public education and their worries about the consequences of massive resistance. In 1964 five members of that group—Patricia Derian, Winifred Falls, Elaine Crystal, Mary Ann Henderson, and Joan Geiger—organized Mississippians for Public Education. Henderson, from Jackson, served as the group's first president. The organization avoided overtly supporting integration but instead urged Mississippi's state and local governments to obey federal court decisions and criticized plans to provide vouchers for parents who wished to send their children to private schools.

In July 1964 Mississippians for Public Education held public meetings, hired American Friends Service Committee worker Constance Curry to organize the group's efforts, formed new chapters in at least ten Mississippi towns, and took out newspaper advertisements to clarify the organization's position. The advertisements explained that the tuition grants program was a bad idea because the grants would cost too much, would leave other students in poorly funded public schools, would put money into unaccredited new private schools, and would perpetuate divisiveness that might encourage violence. Winifred Falls Green later recalled that the group hoped "to attract large numbers of white women across the state of Mississippi to, if in no other way, stand up in the bedroom and say to their husbands, 'We won't have this. We are not going to be Prince Edward County, Virginia, and we're not going to be Little Rock, Arkansas.'"

Mississippians for Public Education walked a line between the goal of keeping public schools open and the fear of being branded an organization of radicals. The newspaper adver-

tisement stated that they were not "debating the pros and cons of desegregation or state's rights," and Curry pretended to be Falls's old college roommate rather than a veteran of the Student Nonviolent Coordinating Committee.

Historian Charles S. Bolton concludes that Mississippians for Public Education "encouraged white parents to stick with the public schools and ultimately had more success than the Jackson's [sic] Citizens' Council chapter's effort to create a system of white-only private schools."

Ted Ownby
University of Mississippi

Charles C. Bolton, *The Hardest Deal of All: The Battle over School Integration in Mississippi, 1870–1980* (2005); Constance Curry, *Deep in Our Hearts: Nine White Women in the Freedom Movement* (2000); *Jackson Clarion-Ledger* (19 July 1964).

Mitchell, Jerry Jr.
(b. 1959) Journalist

Jerry Mitchell Jr., an investigative reporter with the *Jackson Clarion-Ledger*, has won more than twenty national journalism awards and is credited with writing the stories that led to new arrests in multiple civil rights cases dating back to the 1960s.

Mitchell was born in 1959 in Springfield, Missouri, and earned a bachelor's degree in journalism in 1982 from Harding University in Searcy, Arkansas, and a master's in 1997 from Ohio State University, where he attended the Kiplinger Reporting Program. He married Karen O'Donaghy in 1983, and they have two children, Katherine and Sam. Mitchell began working as a journalist as an editor of his high school newspaper and continued as a columnist and news editor on his college paper, but he did not become interested in investigative journalism until he became a reporter at the *Hot Springs (Arkansas) Sentinel-Record*, where he exposed a theme park scandal. He joined the *Clarion-Ledger* in 1986.

The fictional 1988 film *Mississippi Burning* inspired him to begin investigating murders from the civil rights era for which the perpetrators had never been convicted. His reporting for the *Clarion-Ledger* has led to the convictions of Byron De La Beckwith for the 1963 assassination of Medgar Evers, the leader of the Mississippi branch of the National Association for the Advancement of Colored People (NAACP); Ku Klux Klan imperial wizard Sam Bowers for ordering the 1966 murder of NAACP leader Vernon Dahmer; Bobby Cherry for the 1963 bombing of a Birmingham, Alabama, church that killed four girls; Edgar Ray Killen for helping orchestrate the 21 June 1964 killings of Michael Schwerner, James Chaney, and Andrew Goodman; and James Ford Seale for the 1964 abduction and killing of two African American teenagers, Henry Hezekiah Dee and Charles Eddie Moore. In addition, Mitchell's efforts have motivated investigations into other civil rights–era cold cases, resulting in dozens of additional convictions. Mitchell's work in 2012 and 2013 led to the arrest of Felix Vail, who is suspected of killing two of his wives and his longtime girlfriend between 1962 and 1984. In 2014 Mitchell began investigating Mississippi's corrections system, detailing corruption and abuse that have resulted in charges against at least one official. In addition, Mitchell's investigation of the murder conviction of Michelle Byrom not only led the Mississippi Supreme Court to order her off of death row but ultimately resulted in her release from prison.

The Pulitzer Prize board named Mitchell a finalist in 2006 for his work leading to Killen's imprisonment. He has twice won the Gannett Company's Outstanding Achievement by an Individual Award and has received numerous other honors, including the William Ringle Outstanding Achievement Career Award from Gannett, which owns the *Clarion-Ledger*. He has been named Journalist of the Year by the American Board of Trial Advocates and received the George Polk Award for Justice Reporting. In 2002 Judith and William Serrin featured Mitchell's reporting in an anthology of three centuries of the nation's best journalism, *Muckraking! The Journalism That Changed America*. He has also been honored with the Heywood Broun Award, the Abraham Lincoln Marovitz Award, the Sidney Hillman Award, the Inland Press Association Award, the University of Mississippi's Silver Em Award, and the Columbia University Journalism School's John Chancellor Award, which goes "to a reporter with courage and integrity for cumulative professional accomplishments." And in 2009 he received a five-hundred-thousand-dollar "Genius Grant" from the MacArthur Foundation because his "life and work serve as an example of how a journalist willing to take risks and unsettle waters can make a difference in the pursuit of justice."

Mitchell has been featured in the movies and on television. In *Ghosts of Mississippi*, the 1996 Rob Reiner film about the reopening of the Evers case, Mitchell is portrayed by Jerry Levine. Mitchell appears in a 2000 Learning Channel documentary, *Civil Rights Martyrs*, and served as a consultant on a 1999 Discovery Channel documentary, *Killed by the Klan*.

Kathleen Woodruff Wickham
University of Mississippi

R. Hayes Johnson Jr., *Human Rights* (Fall 2000); MacArthur Foundation website, www.macfound.org; Jerry Mitchell Biography, *Jackson Clarion-Ledger* website, www.clarionledger.com; Joe Treen, *Mother Jones* (24 January 2007).

Mitchell, Margaree King

(b. 1953) Author

A multitalented author known especially for her children's books, Margaree King Mitchell was born on 23 July 1953 in Holly Springs, Mississippi, to Joe King Jr. and Susie Mae Bowen King. She earned a bachelor's degree from Brandeis University in 1975 and married Kevin Lee Mitchell seven years later. They went on to have one son, Nelson.

After volunteering in her son's first-grade class and noticing that many children lacked parental support and self-esteem, she decided to create characters who could serve as role models for young children. To that end, she has written four works of historical fiction: *Uncle Jed's Barbershop* (1993), in which a barber in the rural South in the 1920s pursues his dream until he finally realizes it at age seventy-nine; *Granddaddy's Gift* (1997), in which a Mississippi man braves white intimidation to register to vote during the civil rights era; *Susie Mae* (2000), about an African American third-grader who integrates a previously all-white school; and *When Grandmama Sings* (2012), which tells the story of a girl traveling with her grandmother across the Jim Crow South in the 1940s.

More recently, Mitchell has turned to young adult literature with *The People in the Park* (2013), the story of a privileged African American teenager who must learn to cope after her father is charged with investment fraud, and to religious fiction for adults with *Woman in the Pulpit* (2015), which explores the challenges faced by women in the ministry.

Uncle Jed's Barbershop was named a Coretta Scott King Honor Book, won the International Reading Association Children's Book Award, and has been adapted as a dramatic musical. Mitchell has also composed several dramatic works, including *Once upon a Dream* (Arkansas Screen Writers Association, 1992), *Corporate Lies* (finalist, East Foundation Fellowship Program, Writers Guild of America), *The Hi-Rise* (finalist, Theatre Memphis New Play Competition, 1991), and *School's Out*, a television script (1994).

Preselfannie E.
Whitfield-McDaniels
Jackson State University

Robert Cummings, *The Mississippi Writers Page* (2007); Gale Reference Team, *Contemporary Authors Online* (2006); Ben Peterson, *Children's Advocate* (July–August 2001); Margaree King Mitchell, telephone interview with Preselfannie E. Whitfield-McDaniels (15 August 2007).

Mize, Sidney Carr

(1888–1965) Judge

Sidney Carr Mize was the US district judge who presided in the case of *Meredith v. Fair*, which resulted in the integration of the University of Mississippi in Oxford. Mize was born in Scott County on 7 March 1888 and went on to earn a bachelor's degree from Mississippi College in 1908. He earned a law degree from the University of Mississippi School of Law in 1911 and entered private practice in Gulfport. He served as a district attorney in 1914 and as a Harrison County judge and chancery judge in the 1930s. In 1937 Pres. Franklin Delano Roosevelt appointed Mize to succeed Edwin R. Holmes as US district judge for the Southern District of Mississippi. Mize held the post of chief district judge from 1961 to 1962.

In 1961 James Meredith filed suit against the University of Mississippi, which had denied his application for admission. Mize heard the case, during which the university registrar testified that he "gave no consideration whatsoever to the race or color of the plaintiff." On 3 February 1962 Mize ruled that the University of Mississippi did not have a policy of denying admission to qualified African Americans and that Meredith's rejection had not resulted from his race.

On appeal, the US Court of Appeals for the Fifth Circuit overturned Mize's decision and remanded the case with instructions to order Meredith's admission to the University of Mississippi. Mize did so, and Meredith registered on 1 October 1962.

Mize collapsed on the bench and died on 26 April 1965.

Natalya Seay
Washington, D.C.

Meredith v. Fair, 202 F. Supp. 224 (1962), 298 F.2d 696 (1962), 305 F.2d 343 (1962); James Meredith, *Three Years in Mississippi* (1966).

Mobley, Mary Ann

(1937–2014) Miss America and Actress

Crowned Mississippi's first Miss America in 1959, Mary Ann Mobley became one of the most successful women to hold the title. Born on 17 February 1937, in Brandon, Mississippi, and raised there, Mobley went on to graduate from the University of Mississippi in 1958. In September of that year, she was named Miss America 1959, and she used the crown to

Miss America Mary Ann Mobley, Idlewild Airport, New York, 1959 (Library of Congress, Washington, D.C. [LC-USZ62-130049])

launch an acting career. She appeared on television and in a few movies in the early 1960s before starring with fellow Mississippian Elvis Presley in two 1965 films, *Girl Happy* and *Harum Scarum*. She made a handful of other feature films later in the decade but was a television regular until the mid-1990s, with recurring roles on *Diff'rent Strokes*, *Falcon Crest*, and *Hearts Afire* as well as more than one hundred guest appearances on other shows. She starred on stage in numerous musical productions and was a daredevil performer on the popular television program *Circus of the Stars*. Mobley also filmed documentaries showing the impact of war on the children of Cambodia, Ethiopia, Mozambique, Somalia, Kenya, Zimbabwe, and the Sudan.

Mobley married Emmy Award–winning actor and talk show host Gary Collins in 1967, and they had a daughter, Clancy. Though Mobley lived primarily in California for the rest of her life, she and her husband always maintained a home and farm in Mississippi, and she remained devoted to her home state. She served on the boards of the Eudora Welty Foundation, the Gertrude Ford Center for the Performing Arts at the University of Mississippi, and the Mississippi Arts and Entertainment Center. She was inducted into the Mississippi Musicians Hall of Fame. In 1985 the pediatric wing of Rankin General Hospital in Brandon was named in her honor.

Mobley died of breast cancer on 9 December 2014. Her funeral was held in Jackson, and both she and her husband are buried at Parkway Memorial Cemetery in Ridgeland.

Brenda West

Oxford, Mississippi

Billy Watkins, *Jackson Clarion-Ledger* (11 December 2014); Mary Ann Mobley, interview by Brenda West; Emma G. Fitzsimmons, *New York Times* (10 December 2014).

Mockbee, Samuel
(1944–2001) Architect

Samuel Mockbee (Courtesy Timothy Hursley)

"Shelter for the soul" was the phrase architect and teacher Samuel Mockbee used to describe the functional and strikingly beautiful houses built by his students for impoverished residents of Hale County, Alabama. In 1993 Mockbee and colleague D. K. Ruth founded the Rural Studio, an innovative teaching and community service program for undergraduate architecture students at Auburn University. Using salvaged, often curious materials such as hay, rammed earth, telephone polls, and even tires and windshields, the Rural Studio builds houses and community buildings for residents of one of the poorest communities in America. More than 30 percent of Hale County residents live in poverty, many in substandard housing. The Rural Studio combines social responsibility, experimental design, and cues from the regional vernacular to create what author Andrea Oppenheimer Dean has called the "architecture of decency."

A fifth-generation Mississippian, Mockbee was born on 23 December 1944 in Meridian. As a youth he enjoyed drawing and developed an interest in architecture. Growing up in Mississippi on the eve of the civil rights revolution made him keenly aware of the social injustices that permeated southern society. He earned a bachelor's degree in architecture from Auburn University in 1974 and in 1977 formed a partnership with Thomas Goodman, an Auburn classmate. Mockbee established Mockbee-Coker-Howorth Architects with Coleman Coker and Tom Howorth in 1986. Howorth left to form Howorth & Associates Architects in 1990, while the Mockbee-Coker partnership continued until 1999.

Mockbee began teaching architecture at Auburn University in 1991 and launched the Rural Studio after obtaining a $250,000 grant from the Alabama Power Foundation. The program is predicated on the belief that architecture as a discipline is rooted in community. Students live in Hale County and participate in the local community as they learn the critical skills of planning, designing, and building. Whereas architectural training at most universities is largely theoretical, the Rural Studio gives students hands-on experience in every step of the building process. Working alongside the local residents who will be living in the houses, students learn firsthand about the influence of social and cultural values on architecture. Today, the Rural Studio continues to craft houses and other buildings from unlikely materials, each serving as a powerful statement about the social relevancy of architecture.

Mockbee routinely cited the "hay bale house" as one of the Rural Studio's most satisfying projects. Built for the Bryants, an elderly couple who had lived for decades in what Mockbee described as an "old shack," the house is made of stacked and stuccoed hay bales. The forty-two-inch-thick walls are strong, and their natural insulating characteristics allow the Bryants to heat the entire three-room house with only a wood-burning stove. Acrylic panels cover the long front porch, which provides outdoor living space. Warm, light, and dry, the house is but one example of the Rural Studio's innovative, human-centered approach to design.

Known to almost everyone as "Sambo," Mockbee possessed a humble, soft-spoken demeanor that made him an unlikely candidate for international acclaim, but widespread interest in the Rural Studio led to visiting professorships at Harvard University, Yale University, and the University of California at Berkeley. Mockbee also won several major awards, including a five-hundred-thousand dollar John D. and Catherine T. MacArthur Foundation "Genius Grant" in 2000. He received the Mississippi Governor's Lifetime Achievement Award for Artistic Excellence the same year.

Since Mockbee's death from complications of leukemia on 30 December 2001, the Rural Studio has continued its work under Andrew Freear and to date has built more than 150 projects and educated more than six hundred "citizen-architects." In 2004, the American Institute of Architects posthumously awarded Mockbee its Gold Medal. By refocusing attention on the human dimension of the built environment, Mockbee's approach to design and work with the Rural Studio provided a powerful counterpoint to the increasingly impersonal architecture of late twentieth-century America.

Dan Vivian
University of Louisville

Andrea Oppenheimer Dean, *Rural Studio: Samuel Mockbee and an Architecture of Decency* (2002); Christopher Hawthorne, *New York Times* (19 September 2002); Julie V. Iovine, *New York Times* (6 January 2002); Rural Studio website, www.ruralstudio.org; Curtis Sittenfeld, *Fast Company* (November 2000).

Mockingbird, Northern

Mississippi's official state bird, the northern mockingbird, is known to science as *Mimus polyglottos*—"mimic of many voices." Initially selected through a campaign of the Mississippi Federation of Women's Clubs, the clubs later lobbied for the mockingbird's official acceptance by the state. Both the House and the Senate unanimously passed bills favoring the choice, and Gov. Thomas Lowry Bailey signed the bill into law on 23 February 1944.

The northern mockingbird is nowhere more common than in the southeastern states, and its vocal prowess, conspicuousness, and close association with humans have led to its selection as the state bird not only of Mississippi, which was the last to do so, but also of Florida and Texas (1927), Arkansas (1929), and Tennessee (1933).

While the northern mockingbird can be found as a breeding bird from southern New England to California, it is a strong part of regional culture in the Southeast. A singing mockingbird often adds local color to stories focused on the South, as in Eudora Welty's *The Optimist's Daughter*.

In the early nineteenth century the genus name of the mockingbird was given as *Orpheus*, a name derived from a figure in Greek mythology sometimes called the Father of Songs. The bird is familiar through much of North America because of its loud and frequent singing and its ability to mimic not only other birds but other animals and mechanical sounds such as a tractor engine, the squeak of a gate, or even the ring of a cell phone. The mockingbird has readily adopted suburban and backyard habitats and sings from open perches where it is easily seen.

Naturalist John James Audubon, who lived for a time in Woodville, Mississippi, noted in 1840, "It is where the great magnolia shoots up its majestic trunk, crowned with evergreen leaves, and decorated with a thousand beautiful flowers that perfume the air; where the forests and fields are adorned with blossoms of every hue . . . that the mockingbird should have fixed its abode, there only that its wondrous song should be heard." A little over a decade later, Benjamin Wailes, Mississippi's state geologist, wrote, "In form, attitude, and motion, nothing exceeds the grace of our matchless 'Orpheus.' . . . In music and mimicry unrivalled, proud of his gift of song, he is not content with its daily exhibition, but for hours in the 'stilly night' pours forth a flood of melody."

While the mockingbird is its own best advertisement and has been heralded by Mississippians since the colonial period, the crescendo of support it received from residents during the campaign organized by the Mississippi Federation of Women's Clubs may well have been influenced by a recording of a singing mockingbird made on a golf course in Greenville in 1940. John A. Fox, manager of the Greenville Chamber of Commerce, was playing golf when he heard and saw a mockingbird singing from a low perch nearby. It occurred to him that thousands of people in northern states had never heard the mockingbird's song, so he recruited Paul Thompson of Greenville radio station WJPR to help him record the bird. They strung nearly four hundred feet of wire from the nearest electrical outlet to the No. 3 tee where the bird sang and ultimately recorded the mockingbird singing within three feet of the microphone. The Greenville Chamber of Commerce then produced a phonograph record.

Mockingbirds are very territorial, defending their entire home range against not only other mockingbirds but almost all birds as well as cats, dogs, and sometimes people. Unlike some species, mockingbirds show their defensive behavior year-round. Mockingbirds are generalists when it comes to food, eating insects, snails, worms, berries, and other fruits. Because of their catholic diet, almost any other bird might be considered a competitor for food, which might explain mockingbirds' defensiveness. Since songbirds typically defend their territory with song, it has been suggested that the mockingbird's mimicry might trick competitors into thinking that the area is already occupied by birds of an intruder's species, with the result that the intruder moves on. Of course, the mockingbird's efforts do not always succeed. When a flock of cedar waxwings or European starlings arrives, a mockingbird resorts to a frenzy of aggressive chases but often loses the berries that remain on a shrub or tree and that might have supported the mockingbird through the winter.

Another mockingbird behavior that has attracted attention is wing flashing. A northern mockingbird often moves slowly across a lawn, stopping intermittently to quickly spread both wings, revealing large white areas. This behavior seems to be associated with the search for food: the quick flash might startle insects, causing them to move and thus making them easier for the mockingbird to discover. The white spots may also reflect light ahead of the bird, casting a little light into recesses in the grass and, again, making it easier for the mockingbird to find food.

Mockingbirds typically build nests composed of twigs and lined with finer materials and locate their nests in dense shrubs or small trees. The rim of a mockingbird nest is often composed of twigs with thorns or short stubs of branches that the birds carefully place so that the thorns or stubs slip into crevices and help hold the structure together. The end result is that mockingbird nests are very sturdy, often lasting more than a season, though normally they are used only once to hold blue-green eggs and raise a brood of three to five young.

Jerome A. Jackson

Florida Gulf Coast University

James J. Audubon and J. B. Chevalier, *The Birds of America* (1840–44); K. C. Derrickson and R. Breitwisch, in *The Birds of North America*, ed. A. Poole, P. Stettenheim, and F. Gill (1992); Robin W. Doughty, *The Mockingbird* (1988); B. L. C. Wailes, *Report on the Agriculture and Geology of Mississippi, Embracing a Sketch of the Social and Natural History of the State* (1854).

Mohamed, Ethel Wright

(1906–1992) Artist

At the age of sixty Ethel Wright Mohamed of Belzoni began to create embroidered pictures that illustrated her life. By age eighty she had created more than 125 of these extraordinary "memory pictures," and they had been featured at the Mississippi State Historical Museum, the Festival of American Folklife, the Smithsonian Institution's Renwick Gallery, and two world's fairs (1982 and 1984).

Wright was born on 13 October 1906 and grew up near Eupora. Working in a bakery at age sixteen, she met thirty-two-year-old Hassan Mohamed, owner of the local dry goods store. The two married in 1924 and soon moved to Belzoni, where they opened the H. Mohamed general merchandise store and raised eight children.

When her husband died in 1965, Ethel Mohamed continued to run the family store, but she was lonely. "I was a successful businesswoman. I had brought up eight wonderful children. I had been married to a marvelous man for forty-one years. Now here I was coming home at night to this big empty house. I needed a hobby." First she tried painting, but one of her grandchildren was embarrassed by her art. "People will think you're weird," he said. When Mohamed was a child, her mother had encouraged her to draw and to embroider, to take scraps of cloth and make her own "coloring books." She decided to take up embroidery: "That way I could fold up the work and put it away quickly when people came by." She kept her stitchery hidden in a closet.

Her secret art brought her great happiness. "I began to stitch pictures, a family album of sorts, of my family's history. Of graduations, of family stories, of pets and trees and flowers in our yard. I felt a great joy when I was stitching, as if this was what I was meant to do. The needle sang to me." When Mohamed was persuaded to show her pictures to a local artist, she found a waiting audience for her work.

Mohamed created whole miniature worlds in her pictures of family and community events: births, holidays, scenes at home and at the store. One picture shows an ancestor leaving to fight for the Confederacy; a Sacred Harp singing group is the subject of another. Twelve pictures tell sequentially the story of the Mohamed family farm. *The Beautiful Horse* is about a favorite story that Hassan Mohamed brought from his native Lebanon.

The joy and the intimacy of Ethel Mohamed's memories are evident in the animation, the brilliant colors, and the fanciful detail of each child, animal, plant, tree. In many of them the trees and plants are truly animated—each leaf with a smiling face. As she stitched, all parts of the needlework came to life to her, each tiny part of the picture with its own story. Mohamed never took out a stitch. If a face turned out ugly, she would tell it, "That's too bad; you were just born that way." She never sold her pictures.

In 1991 Ethel Mohamed received the Governor's Lifetime Achievement Award for Excellence in the Arts from the Mississippi Arts Commission. Her work is included in permanent exhibits of the Smithsonian Institution and has been featured on UNESCO greeting cards. She died on 15 February 1992.

Christine Wilson

Mississippi Department of
Archives and History

William Ferris, *Local Color: A Sense of Place in Folk Art* (1982); Ethel Wright Mohamed Stitchery Museum website, www.mamasdreamworld.com; Ethel Wright Mohamed, interview by Christine Wilson (1984); Emily Wagster, *Jackson Clarion-Ledger* (7 February 1992); Christine Wilson, ed., *Ethel Wright Mohamed* (1984).

Mollison, W. E.

(1859–1924) Lawyer and Political Leader

Born in Issaquena County in 1859, Willis Elbert Mollison became a teacher, newspaperman, county official, banker, lawyer, and leading African American Republican in post-Reconstruction Mississippi. During the Civil War he learned to read from a white teacher from the North, and after the war he worked on a farm with his parents. By 1880 he had attended Fisk University in Tennessee and Oberlin College in Ohio, married his wife, Martha, in Ohio, and returned to Mississippi to teach.

Soon after his return, Mollison was appointed school superintendent and then elected clerk of the circuit and chancery courts of Issaquena County, serving from 1883 to 1891. Before becoming clerk of court, he studied law with Congressman Elza Jeffords, a native of Ohio who had been a member of the Mississippi High Court of Errors and Appeals. After examination in open court by three lawyers, Mollison was admitted to the bar in 1881 by Judge B. F. Trimble. Mollison practiced law in Issaquena County and sought statewide office. After he failed to secure the Republican nomination for secretary of state, Mollison was recruited to run on John Roy Lynch's reform ticket. Although not elected to the statewide office, Mollison moved to Vicksburg, where he served for a time as acting district attorney. This appointment by a white Democratic judge created a stir in the community but likely resulted simply from the recognition of Mollison's skill in the courtroom. One biographical sketch claimed that Mollison "had the largest criminal practice in the state." While that statement is probably an exaggeration, Mollison represented both black and white clients. He served as co-counsel with some prominent white lawyers and won nine appeals in the Mississippi Supreme Court. His most celebrated victory was overturning a murder conviction because of racist language used by the white prosecutor. Although Mississippi had adopted a Jim Crow Constitution in 1890, Mollison continued to have success in the Mississippi courts, winning three appeals as late as 1916.

Mollison, who was closely associated with Booker T. Washington, became a successful entrepreneur. He was president of Lincoln Park Land Company, a major stockholder in the Lincoln Savings Bank of Vicksburg, a director of the Mound Bayou Oil Mill and Manufacturing Company, and owner of the *National Star* newspaper. In addition, he had an active civil law practice representing fraternal benefit organizations and the Union Guaranty Insurance Company. He was a successful trial lawyer in suits against the Illinois Central and other railroads. Mollison remained active in Republican Party politics and was a strong supporter of Theodore Roosevelt.

As his son Irvin C. Mollison wrote in the *Journal of Negro History* in 1930, the life of the black lawyer in Mississippi after 1900 grew increasingly tenuous. W. E. Mollison told his son that after one trial, the judge informed Mollison that he had almost been killed during the trial. In another case, Mollison's objections to some questions asked by a white lawyer nearly caused him to assault Mollison. In yet another case, Mollison's white cocounsel went through the transcript and struck out the word *Mister* every time it appeared before Mollison's name.

The combination of the ascendancy of Jim Crow politicians, the faltering economy, and the start of World War I led to the loss of both power and business for Mollison, and like many other black Mississippians, he moved to Chicago around 1917. He practiced law in Chicago with his son, Irvin, served as president of the Cook County Bar Association, and remained active in Republican politics and the National Businessmen's Association. Mollison died on 11 May 1924.

W. Lewis Burke
University of South Carolina

Green Polnius Hamilton, *Beacon Lights of the Race* (1911); Irvin C. Mollison, *Journal of Negro History* 15, no. 1 (1930); J. Clay Smith Jr., *Emancipation: The Making of the Black Lawyer, 1844–1944* (1993).

M

Moman, Zipporah Elizabeth

(1883–1965) Educator

Zipporah Elizabeth Moman, born 10 August 1883, was a teacher who championed the rights of domestic workers. Moman graduated from Tougaloo College and became an elementary teacher in Ridgeland, worked as a home demonstration agent in Madison County, and as an adult education teacher at Lanier High School in Jackson.

In 1933 Moman helped form and became president of the National Association of Domestic Workers. The group presented a petition to the federal government calling for them to create equitable standards for domestic workers, especially in the South. The "Code of Fair Competition for Personal and Domestic Workers" requested fair compensation and adequate facilities, including a work week not exceeding 56 hours with at least two half days off, one week paid vacation, and a minimum wage of $14.40 a week. Moman also spoke out publicly about the need for domestic workers to maintain their independence and autonomy from employers by not "living in."

In 1950 Moman was appointed by Gov. Fielding Wright to the Mississippi Committee on Children and Youth. That same year, Pres. Harry S. Truman invited her to Washington, D.C., to attend the Mid-Century White House Conference on Women, Children, and Youth.

Moman went on to become matron at the Oakley Training School, an all-black juvenile reformatory opened in 1948 that remained segregated until 1969. She was the first municipal recreation supervisor of Jackson. Moman also served as the first director at College Park Recreation Center. She died in Jackson in 1965.

Kathryn McGaw York

University of Mississippi

Mississippi Department of Archives and History, Collected Papers of Zipporah Elizabeth Moman website, www.mdah.state.ms.us; Rebecca Sharpless: *Cooking in Other Women's Kitchens: Domestic Workers in the South, 1860–1960* (2010).

Monette, John Wesley

(1803–1851) Physician and Historian

John Wesley Monette, MD, of Washington, Mississippi, was the state's most prolific antebellum writer on historical, scientific, and medical topics. Born near Staunton, Virginia, on 5 April 1803, he was the son of ordained Methodist minister and physician Dr. Samuel Monett and his wife, Mary Wayland Monett. (John added the *e* to *Monett* as an adult.) In 1809 the Monetts settled in Chillicothe, Ohio, where John was reared and received his early education. In 1821 Samuel moved his family to Washington, the former Mississippi territorial and state capital six miles northeast of Natchez. There, Samuel established his medical practice, with John beginning medical training under his father. John soon left Washington to attend medical school at Transylvania University in Kentucky, from which he graduated in 1825. His inaugural thesis, submitted in January of that year, was "The Endemial Bilious Fever as It Generally Occurs in the Vicinity of Natchez."

Monette returned to Washington to practice medicine and on 10 December 1828 married Cornelia Jane Newman. Of the couple's ten children, only four survived to adulthood. He purchased a house, Propinquity, and lived there while building the three-story Sweet Auburn at Washington, where he lived for the rest of his life. Adjacent to and in front of the main house at Sweet Auburn, Monette constructed two one-story brick buildings: one served as his office, while the other served as a general library, where he wrote many of his lengthy histories, medical treatises, magazine and journal articles, and occasional poetry. He was a prominent civic leader, serving as Washington's mayor and as a councilman and as a trustee at Jefferson College for more than two decades.

The emergence of yellow fever in an epidemic form was a major concern to the antebellum medical community of the Old Southwest, especially Natchez and Washington. A viral disease transmitted to humans by various mosquitoes, yellow fever presents with such symptoms as fever, jaundice, headache, and gastrointestinal hemorrhage; its malignant form usually results in death. The disease was common in American ports such as New York, Philadelphia, and Charleston in the colonial period, but by the turn of the nineteenth century, ports in the southern United States, such as New Orleans, Mobile, Savannah, and Charleston, bore the brunt of the American attacks. In the late summer of 1817, soon after the introduction of steamboats on the Mississippi River, Natchez suffered its first epidemic, with more than one hundred lives lost. This feared disease became a regular visitor, with epidemics sweeping through Natchez in 1819, 1823, and 1825 and causing many deaths. The yellow fever epidemics that plagued the Old Southwest usually began in the Caribbean, then struck New Orleans in the mid- to late summer before slowly ascending the Mississippi River to ports in the Lower Mississippi Valley such as Natchez and spreading inland. The epidemics usually ended after the fall's first frost.

In the 1825 epidemic, yellow fever had for the first time extended into Washington, which had previously been considered safe from the disease. Witnessed by Monette in his first year of medical practice, the epidemic took the lives of more than 150 Natchez residents as well as 60 Washingtonians. These horrific local outbreaks in the 1820s birthed in Monette a lifelong interest in the disease, and he devoted significant effort and research to improving ways to prevent and treat the dreaded illness. In 1827 he published "An Account of the Epidemic of Yellow Fever That Occurred in Washington, Mississippi in the Autumn of 1825" in the first volume of the *Western Medical and Physical Journal*, edited by his highly regarded former medical professor, Dr. Daniel Drake.

In the late summer of 1837 Natchez suffered its first major yellow fever epidemic since 1825. Monette presented a paper, "The Epidemic Yellow Fevers of Natchez," later published in the *South-Western Journal*, in which he was among the first to suggest quarantine to prevent yellow fever's spread. In the summer of 1841, at his suggestion, Natchez for the first time instituted a strict prohibition on steamboat intercourse with New Orleans. When the fever erupted in New Orleans and spread up the river, it decimated river ports south and north of Natchez but left Natchez untouched.

Monette's yellow fever work culminated in a significant 1842 treatise, *Observations on the Epidemic Yellow Fever of Natchez and of the South-West*. In this ambitious book, Monette, "a man of science and deep medical learning," questioned the prevailing medical doctrine that yellow fever was "produced locally by local causes" from "certain putrescent matters" that could be found in ordinary city filth. Refuting long-held medical teachings by such influential physicians as Benjamin Rush, Monette argued that yellow fever was an imported epidemic disease of tropical origin rather than an endemic but malignant form of an indigenous fever. He concluded that the disease reached Natchez via trade with New Orleans and came to New Orleans from Cuba and the West Indies and argued that strict quarantine in southern commercial cities, towns, and ports would prevent the disease from taking hold there. Although his research was hampered by antebellum medicine's dearth of scientific knowledge (the mosquito as vector was not proven for another half century), his brilliant epidemiological work constituted a major step forward in public health and in understanding the terrible disease. His central argument, which encouraged strict quarantine during July, August, and September, was and remained for sixty years the best way to prevent yellow fever epidemics.

His financial success as a practicing physician, a cotton planter with two Louisiana plantations, and a land speculator provided him the leisure necessary to pursue more aggressively his scholarly research and writing. As early as 1833 Monette initiated work on his greatest literary achievement, *History of the Discovery and Settlement of the Valley of the Mississippi*, which was published to much acclaim in two volumes by Harper and Brothers in 1846 and reprinted two years later. The book was an expansive history of the discovery and settlement of the Mississippi Valley by Spain, France, and England as well as of the region's subsequent occupation, settlement, and establishment of civil government. This monumental work was among the first to emphasize the Mississippi Valley's importance in American history, and it remains one of the most important American histories written in the antebellum period. By 1850 he had largely completed a second edition, but he did not submit it to a publisher before his death. Much of it survives in manuscript, however, and one chapter, "The Progress of Navigation and Commerce on the Waters of the Mississippi River and the Great Lakes, AD 1700 to 1846," appeared in the *Publications of the Mississippi Historical Society* in 1903.

Beginning in the early 1830s, Monette also worked on another elaborate scholarly book, "Physical Geography of the Mississippi Valley," that also remained unpublished at the time of his death. This work included four books: "Mississippi River," "Regions of the Upper Valley," "Antiquities and Aboriginal Inhabitants," and "Zoology." Chapter 3 of the first book, "The Mississippi Floods," later appeared in the *Publications of the Mississippi Historical Society* (1903). Much of this manuscript, as well as portions of the manuscript of his *History of the Discovery and Settlement of the Valley of the Mississippi*, were acquired in 1935 by the William L. Clements Library at the University of Michigan.

Despite his early economic success, Monette experienced financial reverses toward the end of his life and was forced to spend long periods away from his home, managing his Islington Plantation in Madison Parish, Louisiana. He struggled financially and lacked time for his literary work. Leaving a mass of manuscripts unpublished, Monette died suddenly from "erysipelas of the brain" at Islington on 1 March 1851. Historian Franklin L. Riley described Monette as "the pioneer historian of the Mississippi Valley." His medical contributions, which challenged long-held shibboleths of his profession, reveal him to be a scientific pioneer as well.

Lucius M. Lampton
Magnolia, Mississippi

Lucie Robertson Bridgforth, *Journal of Mississippi History* 46 (May 1984); John L. Cotter, *Journal of Mississippi History* 13 (January 1951); Kim Monette Garrett, "John Wesley Monette," speech given to William Dunbar Chapter, Daughters of the American Revolution (13 October 2003); Lucius Lampton, *Journal of the Mississippi State Medical Association* (January 2006, December 2007, January 2008); John W. Monette, *History of the Discovery and Settlement of the Valley of the Mississippi* (1846); John W. Monette, *Observations on the Epidemic Yellow Fever of Natchez and of the South-West* (1842); John W. Monette, *South-Western Journal* (15, 28 February 1838, 15 March 1838, 30 April 1838); John W. Monette Papers, Mississippi Department of Archives and History; John W. Monette Papers, William L. Clements Library, University of Michigan.

Monroe County

The area that became Monroe County has evidence of the earliest human activity in the Mississippi area. The Hester Site, an archaeological site just west of Amory, is the location of apparent Paleo-Indian activity dating to about ten thousand years ago. The area was important in much of Native American history, including some Choctaw movements during the Chickasaw War in the 1730s. In the 1800s it became an important plantation area. The county seat is Aberdeen, located on the banks of the Tombigbee River.

Located in northeastern Mississippi, just south of the hilliest areas of the state, Monroe County was founded in 1821. In its first census in 1830, Monroe's population consisted of 2,918 free people and 943 slaves. By 1840 both populations had increased dramatically, to 5,167 free people and 4,083 slaves.

By 1860 Monroe had 12,279 slaves and 8,554 free people. In the late antebellum period, it was an agricultural powerhouse, ranking high among the state's counties in corn (fourth), cotton (seventh), sweet potatoes (second), and livestock (eleventh). The county's 120 industrial employees worked in small lumber mills, cotton gins, and businesses making carriages and saddles. In the late antebellum period, Monroe County had one of the largest populations in Mississippi. In 1860 Monroe was home to twenty-five churches—fifteen

M

Aberdeen, the seat of Monroe County (Ann Rayburn Paper Americana Collection, Department of Archives and Special Collections, J. D. Williams Library, University of Mississippi [rayburn_ann_23_67_001])

Methodist churches, seven Baptist churches, and single Presbyterian, Christian, and Episcopalian churches.

In 1872 part of Monroe County became part of Clay County. Despite this loss of territory and population, Monroe continued to grow and by 1880 was home to 28,553 people—18,001 African Americans and 10,551 whites. The county's farmers ranked first in the state in the production of corn and wheat, second in hay and tobacco, and third in livestock. Owners cultivated 46.5 percent of the farms, while tenants and sharecroppers ran the rest.

Some of Mississippi's most important political figures and political action had roots in Monroe County. Reuben Davis, an Aberdeen lawyer, was an impassioned supporter of secession and an opponent of Republicans during and after Reconstruction. Samuel Gholson, a supporter of secession and later a Confederate general, served in the state legislature and supported the overturning of Republican authority. Monroe County's postwar Ku Klux Klan committed a notorious political murder, killing Jack Dupree, an African American leader of the Republican Party.

In 1880 Monroe County had fifty-three manufacturing establishments, but most were small, and they employed only one hundred men, four women, and nine children. The county was home to 134 immigrants, most of them from Germany, Ireland, and Sweden.

By 1900 the Monroe County population had grown to 31,216, and manufacturing employed more than 500 workers. While 59 percent of the county's white farmers owned their land, only 8 percent of African American farmers did so.

About half of the Monroe County church members counted in the 1916 religious census were Baptists, with Missionary Baptists standing out as the largest group. Methodists, especially the Methodist Episcopal Church, South, and Methodist Episcopal Church, had substantial numbers as well, and the county was home to Mississippi's largest groups in the Stone-Campbell traditions—the Disciples of Christ and Churches of Christ.

Monroe County's notable figures include F. S. McKnight, Felix Underwood, and Lucille Bogan. McKnight ran a photography studio in Aberdeen for more than thirty years, and his work documented the life of the community. Underwood, born in Nettleton in 1882, became a doctor and leader in reforming Mississippi's public health system. Bogan, a blues singer, was born in Amory in 1897.

By 1930 Monroe County's population had reached 36,141, with about 20,000 whites. Aberdeen was a growing town with more than 6,000 people, and the county had more than 400 industrial workers. Still, agriculture remained the central feature of the county's economy. Tenants worked 68 percent of county farms, emphasizing corn followed by cotton and livestock.

After more than twenty years of effort, Mississippi's oil and gas industry began when the Carter No. 1 well east of Amory started yielding gas in 1926. Monroe County also became the home of one of the state's first cooperative electric power associations.

In 1960 Monroe County's population had dropped below thirty-four thousand residents, about two-thirds of them white and one-third African American. Monroe was one of eastern Mississippi's leading manufacturing centers, with 32 percent of the county's workforce employed in manufacturing, including almost two thousand women in the apparel industry. Monroe County had by far the state's largest number of apparel workers. Agriculture remained crucial to Monroe's economy, with nearly 18 percent of the county's workers growing soybeans, corn, cotton, and wheat and raising livestock. By 1980 the population had increased to 36,404, slightly higher than its 1930 numbers.

As in many of its neighboring counties, Monroe County's 2010 population was predominantly white and had shown no significant change in size since 1960. The county's 36,989 residents represented only a slight increase over 1900.

Mississippi Encyclopedia Staff
University of Mississippi

Mississippi State Planning Commission, *Progress Report on State Planning in Mississippi* (1938); *Mississippi Statistical Abstract*, Mississippi State University (1952–2010); Charles Sydnor and Claude Bennett, *Mississippi History* (1939); University of Virginia Library, Historical Census Browser website, http://mapserver.lib.virginia.edu; E. Nolan Waller and Dani A. Smith, *Growth Profiles of Mississippi's Counties, 1960–1980* (1985).

Montgomery, Benjamin Thornton
(1819–1877)

Benjamin Thornton Montgomery was born a slave in Loudoun County, Virginia, in 1819. His early childhood was as privileged as was possible for a slave: he served as a companion to his owner's son, who taught him to read and write. However, in 1836 Montgomery was taken to Natchez and sold to Joseph E. Davis, who was the older brother of future Confederate president Jefferson Davis and whose large plantation holdings lay south of Vicksburg in a large bend in the Mississippi River. Montgomery soon became the beneficiary of the elder Davis's unconventional ideas regarding slave ownership.

Montgomery quickly displayed his intellectual potential, and Davis allowed the young man free access to the Hurricane Plantation library. Montgomery improved his literacy and developed skills as both a mechanic and a surveyor. In 1840 he married Mary Lewis, with whom he had four children who lived to adulthood. Their two surviving sons, William Thornton Montgomery and Isaiah Thornton Montgomery, became noted figures in Mississippi business and politics.

In 1842 Benjamin Montgomery opened a retail store on Hurricane Plantation, selling general merchandise to both slaves and their owners. Montgomery developed a personal line of credit with wholesalers in both Natchez and New Orleans and bought and sold goods in his own name. Montgomery demonstrated his mechanical ability by inventing a boat propeller that Joseph Davis attempted to have patented in Montgomery's name. US law, however, did not allow a slave to hold a patent, so Davis's effort failed, and Montgomery's invention went unrecognized.

In the years leading to the Civil War, the Montgomery retail enterprise flourished, and the family's stature increased. Davis and his family fled Davis Bend in 1862, but Montgomery remained behind, organizing and directing the Hurricane and Brierfield Plantation slaves as they planted and harvested crops. Benjamin and Mary Montgomery fled to Ohio with their daughters, Rebecca and Virginia, in 1863 and were soon joined by Isaiah and Thornton. Benjamin Montgomery worked at a canal boat yard in Cincinnati and was allowed to show his boat propeller at the Western Sanitary Fair there in December 1864.

The Montgomerys returned to Davis Bend in 1865, and Ben Montgomery reassumed his leadership role among the former slaves. Davis Bend had been the location of a grand experiment in freedman-operated farming conceived by Union general Ulysses S. Grant and administered by local US Army authorities.

In 1865 Montgomery began regular correspondence with Joseph Davis, opening his letters "Dear Master." Beginning in 1866, however, Montgomery started his letters with "Kind Sir," a form of address that clearly indicates a more equal relationship between the two men. In October 1866 Montgomery asked Davis to lease the Hurricane and Brierfield Plantations to him. Davis countered with an offer to sell his plantation holdings to his former slave. They agreed on a price of three hundred thousand dollars, with yearly interest-only payments of eighteen thousand dollars and

the principal due in nine years. As a result of this sale, it is quite probable that Benjamin Montgomery owed more money than any other ex-slave in the country. Montgomery wasted no time in publicizing his purchase and in setting up what he hoped would be a great opportunity for himself and other former slaves. Less than a week after the sale papers were signed, Montgomery placed an advertisement in the 21 November 1866 issue of the *Vicksburg Daily Times*: "The undersigned having secured for a term of years the 'Hurricane' and 'Brierfield' plantations in Warren County . . . proposes on the 1st day of January, 1867, to organize a community composed exclusively of colored people, to occupy and cultivate said plantations, and invites the cooperation of such as are recommended by honesty, industry, sobriety, and intelligence, in the enterprise." The ad went on to outline the rules of the "Association," as Montgomery called the undertaking. Montgomery signed the ad simply, "B. T. Montgomery, Colored, formerly a slave and one of the business managers of Joseph E. Davis, Esq." It was an audacious beginning of an effort that endured for twenty years.

Raising a cotton crop on lands that were only a weakened levee away from the Mississippi River floods was a perilous business. The farmers succeeded admirably in some years, with Montgomery raising and shipping some two thousand bales of cotton in 1870, the year that Davis died. But far too many years found prime cotton lands covered with floodwaters well into late spring, and Montgomery found it impossible to plant and harvest a sizable crop. As a result, he was frequently unable to pay his former master or his heirs the yearly interest, though he did make partial payments. The Montgomery and Sons grocery and dry goods business flourished, however, and the R. G. Dun Mercantile Agency assessed Benjamin Montgomery's net worth in 1873 as $230,000, placing him among the top 7 percent of all southern merchants and planters.

In September 1867 Maj. Gen. E. O. C. Ord, commander of the Fourth Military District of Mississippi and Arkansas, appointed Montgomery to serve as justice of the peace for Davis Bend, making him perhaps the first former slave to assume political office in Mississippi. In 1872 Montgomery sent his daughters, Virginia and Rebecca, to Oberlin College, where they studied for two years.

Montgomery was severely injured in late December 1874 when part of a wall fell on him as he was helping to demolish a house. His spinal cord was damaged, and he never quite recovered from the accident. He died on 12 May 1877.

James Tyson Currie
National Defense University

James T. Currie, *Enclave: Vicksburg and Her Plantations, 1863–1870* (1980); Janet Sharp Hermann, *The Pursuit of a Dream* (1981).

Montgomery, Isaiah Thornton
(1847–1924) Political and Business Leader

Isaiah Thornton Montgomery was born into slavery on 21 May 1847 on the Davis Bend Plantation in Warren County to Benjamin Thornton Montgomery and Mary Lewis Montgomery. The younger Montgomery played a leading role in the history of Mound Bayou and in Mississippi's business and political history.

Groomed for success at an early age by his father, who even in slavery essentially ran the Davis Bend plantation, Isaiah Montgomery experienced the watershed moment in his life at age ten, when he was sent to the master's quarters to serve as personal servant to Joseph E. Davis, the plantation's founder and older brother of Jefferson Davis. Joseph Davis, who modeled his considerably liberalized methods of plantation governance on theories first espoused by British industrialist-philanthropist Robert Owen, initially used Montgomery for basic services. By the time the young man turned twelve, he had become Davis's personal secretary, certainly one of the most important and influential positions available to a plantation slave.

In addition to his clerical duties, which included filing and supervising Davis's business appointments, Montgomery was in charge of the vast array of Davis's business and personal correspondence. In this capacity, Montgomery is thought to have honed his reading and writing skills while receiving a most extensive education in business. He also received free and unfettered access to Davis's well-stocked library.

During the Civil War, while his family sought refuge in Cincinnati, Ohio, Isaiah Montgomery served for a brief time

Isaiah Thornton Montgomery, 1910 (New York Public Library [Image ID: 1157792])

as a cabin boy under Union admiral David O. Porter before rejoining his family near the end of the conflict. When the Montgomerys returned to Davis Bend after the war, they found it under Union control and in danger of being confiscated, a condition that helped convince the exiled Davis to sell the property to Benjamin Montgomery. For the better part of the next decade, the Montgomery-owned Davis Bend operation was the third-largest cotton concern in the state.

Following the collapse of the cotton market in the aftermath of Reconstruction and his father's death in 1877, Isaiah Montgomery ascended to the role of head of the Montgomery family, but with the plantation business in ruins, the Montgomerys found their financial situation bleak. A good portion of their money had fled to Kansas in the form of sharecroppers who had left Davis Bend long before settling their debts. Montgomery, desperate to explore any avenue of future profits, tried to reorganize many of these Kansas-bound Exodusters in a Davis Bend–type colony, but the venture was short-lived and financially unsuccessful.

With growing concern over his family's financial future, Montgomery settled in Vicksburg and opened a small mercantile business while biding his time looking for the next big venture. When he was contacted by a land agent of the Louisville, New Orleans, and Texas Railroad during the summer of 1887, he and his cousins, Benjamin T. Green and Joshua P. T. Montgomery, collaborated on an extensive entrepreneurial project that culminated in the founding of Mound Bayou, the Mississippi Delta's first African American town. Mound Bayou became a booming center of African American economic and social life.

While Davis Bend and Mound Bayou tend to dominate his legacy, Isaiah Montgomery's more controversial political legacy involves his role in the 1890 state constitutional convention, where he was the lone black delegate. On 12 August he stood before the other delegates and supported the measures that effectively disfranchised nearly every African American voter in Mississippi as well as more than 111,000 landless white voters. Scholars still struggle to understand his decision, but as a businessman, Montgomery faced enormous pressure to maintain a relationship within the state's predominantly white political and economic leaders. Thus, by offering to speak on behalf of a measure that was sure to pass with or without his support, Montgomery placated fellow planters while steering clear of the sort of controversy certain to place him at odds with the state's power brokers. Against the backdrop of his relationship to Booker T. Washington, who espoused independence based on self-reliance and economic autonomy rather than political tactics, Montgomery's controversial role in the convention seems easier to comprehend.

He died on 6 March 1924.

Joel Nathan Rosen
Moravian College

Kenneth Marvin Hamilton, *Black Towns and Profit: Promotion and Development in the Trans-Appalachian West, 1877–1915* (1991); Janet Sharp Hermann, *The Pursuit of a Dream* (1981); Neil R. McMillen, *Dark Journey: Black Mississippians in the Age of Jim Crow* (1989).

Montgomery, Gillespie V. "Sonny"

(1920–2006) Politician

A longtime Mississippi politician and champion of the interests of veterans, Gillespie V. "Sonny" Montgomery was born on 5 August 1920 in Meridian. His father, Gillespie Montgomery Sr., worked in the gasoline and oil wholesale business but suffered from tuberculosis and died when his son was ten. Although Sonny's mother, Emily Jones Montgomery, remarried about two years later, the family went through a hard time during the early years of the Great Depression. They moved around Mississippi in search of jobs, and Sonny frequently changed schools. With the financial aid of his wealthy great-aunt, Alice Pope, he eventually enrolled in McCallie School, a military boarding school in Chattanooga, Tennessee. Montgomery had long been fascinated by the military, and he was inspired by the drilling and battalion parades at McCallie. His family had a strong military tradition. His great-grandfather, Col. W. B. Montgomery, ran a Confederate ammunition factory in Montgomery, Alabama, before serving in the Mississippi state legislature in the late 1890s.

After completing high school, Montgomery enrolled at Mississippi State College, majoring in business and joining the school's Reserve Officer Training Corps program. He graduated in 1943 and served as a lieutenant in the 12th Armored Division in Europe, earning medals including the Bronze Star for Valor for his World War II service.

Montgomery returned from the war and worked as an insurance agent and a car salesman. He also joined the Mississippi National Guard and was sent to Korea in late 1951. In 1956, he won election to the Mississippi State Senate, building on the network of friends he had made by traveling to sell insurance and beating his opponent by fewer than one hundred votes. In May 1961 his National Guard unit escorted a group of Freedom Riders from the Alabama border to Jackson.

In 1966 Montgomery was elected as a Democrat to the US House of Representatives, filling the seat of Republican Prentiss Walker, who was challenging James Eastland for the US Senate. During his first years in Congress, Montgomery served on the Veterans Affairs Committee and the Agricultural Committee. He served as chair of the House Select Committee on US Involvement in Southeast Asia, which toured South Vietnam, Laos, and Cambodia to evaluate the military situation. In 1975 Montgomery chaired the Select Committee on Americans Missing in Action in Southeast Asia. By then, he had also been appointed to the Armed Services Committee.

In 1980 Montgomery retired from the National Guard with the rank of major general. A year later, he became chair of the Veterans Affairs Committee. In his new capacity, Montgomery started working on a revamped GI Bill, which passed after much debate in 1984. The new law sought primarily to improve the recruitment and retention of quality army personnel by providing educational assistance to active-duty soldiers as well as to members of the National Guard and the reserves. Officially labeled the Educational Assistance Act of 1984, the law is more commonly known as the Montgomery GI Bill, which Montgomery considered a great honor. Another of Montgomery's landmark achievements was the Department of Veterans Affairs Act, which he cosponsored with Rep. Gerald Solomon of New York. The bill, which went into effect on 15 March 1989, turned the old Veterans Administration into an official cabinet department. Pres. George H. W. Bush offered Montgomery the position of secretary of the new department, but he decided to remain in the House.

As a conservative southern Democrat, Montgomery was often at odds with the political agenda of his own party. During the Reagan years, he was an active member of the House's boll weevil faction, a group of conservative Democrats who supported the Republican administration's economic plans, particularly the reduction of the federal income tax. In 1995 Montgomery ardently backed a constitutional amendment to ban the desecration of the American flag.

Montgomery retired from Congress in 1997. During his last session, Congress voted to name the Department of Veterans Affairs Medical Center in Jackson in his honor. Montgomery subsequently ran a Washington-based lobbying firm, the Montgomery Group, before returning to Mississippi in 2004. A year later, Pres. George W. Bush awarded Montgomery the Presidential Medal of Freedom.

Montgomery died on 12 May 2006. On the day of his funeral, President Bush ordered US flags to be flown at half-staff to honor "Mr. Veteran."

Maarten Zwiers
University of Groningen, the
Netherlands

Sonny Montgomery, *Sonny Montgomery: The Veteran's Champion* (2003); Crystal O'Connell, *G. V. (Sonny) Montgomery: Democratic Representative from Mississippi* (1972); *Washington Post* (13 May 2006).

M

Montgomery County

Located in central Mississippi, Montgomery County was founded in 1871 from parts of Carroll and Choctaw Counties. In its first census in 1880, Montgomery was evenly divided between white (6,671) and African American (6,677) residents. Focused on agricultural production, the county's farmers grew cotton and grains and raised livestock. Montgomery County had the third-most cattle in the state. Unlike many Mississippi counties in the postwar years, Montgomery's farms were run overwhelmingly by owners (about 73 percent) rather than by tenants or sharecroppers.

Montgomery County was one of the centers of Mississippi Populist activity in the late 1880s. In 1888 the Mississippi Farmers' Alliance started a cooperative store in Winona, the county seat, to make it easier for its members to market their crops and buy affordable goods.

In 1900 the county's population of 16,536 had a slight African American majority. It also had a growing industrial workforce of more than 200 individuals. Two-thirds of all white farm families owned their land, while only one-fifth of black farmers did so.

By 1930 Montgomery County's population had declined to 15,009. Whites made up 56 percent of this total, while African Americans comprised 44 percent. Montgomery remained an agricultural county, and tenancy rather than sharecropping had become common for both black and white farmers. Alongside agricultural labor, thirty-four industrial firms employed 343 people. The 1930 census was the first in which Winona was classified as a city, with slightly over 2,500 people.

More than 90 percent of Montgomery County's church members in the 1916 religious census belonged to either Baptist or Methodist churches. The largest groups were the Missionary Baptists and the Methodist Episcopal Church, South.

Notable individuals associated with Montgomery County include bluesman B. B. King (born Riley King), who spent a great deal of his childhood in Kilmichael. Roebuck "Pops" Staples, another famous blues musician, was born near Kilmichael but grew up in the Delta before leading his family band, the Staples Singers, to success in the 1960s and 1970s. Other notable residents of Montgomery County have included A. Boyd Campbell, a state and national leader in the Chamber of Commerce, and George McLean, a journalist and community development leader in Tupelo, both of whom were born in Winona. Civil rights leader Fannie Lou Hamer was born in Montgomery County, though she spent most of her life in the Mississippi Delta. In 1963 she and other Student Nonviolent Coordinating Committee workers were returning from a conference when she was put in a Winona jail and severely beaten.

In 1960 Montgomery County's population had declined to 13,320, with whites continuing to make up a small majority of the residents. About 24 percent of Montgomery's working people were employed in agriculture, primarily raising corn, cotton, soybeans, and livestock, while 23 percent worked in manufacturing, specifically in the apparel and furniture industries.

By 2010 whites comprised 53 percent of Montgomery County's population. The total population, which had dropped by about 18 percent since 1960, was 10,925 in 2010.

Mississippi Encyclopedia Staff
University of Mississippi

Mississippi State Planning Commission, *Progress Report on State Planning in Mississippi* (1938); *Mississippi Statistical Abstract*, Mississippi State University (1952–2010); Charles Sydnor and Claude Bennett, *Mississippi History* (1939); University of Virginia Library, Historical Census Browser website, http://mapserver.lib.virginia.edu; E. Nolan Waller and Dani A. Smith, *Growth Profiles of Mississippi's Counties, 1960–1980* (1985).

Moody, Anne
(1940–2015) Author and Activist

Essie Mae Moody, who became an activist and author of one of the most powerful autobiographies written during the civil rights movement, was born on 15 September 1940 in Wilkerson County, Mississippi. Moody survived poverty, racism, and patriarchy—problems that only accelerated her eagerness for the freedom and civil rights of African Americans. Her parents were sharecroppers on a white-owned plantation, and at age nine she went to work for white women to help support her siblings. She began calling herself Anne as a teenager, attended Natchez Junior College for a time, and then earned a bachelor's degree from Tougaloo College in 1964. At Tougaloo she became a member of the National Association for the Advancement of Colored People and an organizer and fundraiser for the Congress of Racial Equality. She participated in a sit-in at Woolworth's cafeteria in Jackson, where she and her coworkers were abused by white students for almost three hours until the Tougaloo president and others arrived. Other activities led her to jail.

After graduation, she spent a year coordinating a civil rights project at Cornell University. In 1967 she married Austin Straus. The couple had a son, Sascha, before divorcing.

By 1967 Moody set aside activism in favor of writing, publishing her autobiography, *Coming of Age in Mississippi* the following year. She described how she and her white playmates were forced to sit separately at a movie theater, and later how one of her white employers told her to come into the house through the back door. The 1955 murder of fourteen-year old Emmett Till shocked her: "I hated the white men who murdered Emmett Till and I hated all the other whites who were responsible for the countless murders" she had learned about or "vaguely remembered from childhood. But I also hated Negroes. I hated them for not standing up and doing something about the murders." She wrote about her admiration of the resilience and resolve of C. O. Chinn and other activists in Canton but also described the exhaustion and frustrations of day-to-day activism. Moody increasingly wondered about the direction the civil rights movement was taking. She grew tired after the deaths of Medgar Evers, the Birmingham church bombing victims, and Pres. John F. Kennedy. She felt isolated on a bus heading toward Washington, D.C., listening to her coworkers sing "We Shall Overcome." The autobiography ends with her skepticism about the movement. Moody retired from activism because she felt that nothing seemed to change.

She won a German Academic Exchange Service grant in 1972 and spent a year in Berlin as an artist. She received the silver medal from *Mademoiselle* magazine for her story "New Hopes for the Seventies" and published an anthology, *Mr. Death: Four Stories*, in 1975. Over the next two decades, she granted no interviews and held a series of nonwriting jobs, including a position as an antipoverty counselor in New York City. She returned to Mississippi in the early 1990s and died there on 5 February 2015 after developing dementia. Her autobiography remains one of the most frequently taught books on the civil rights movement, in part because it dramatizes the events from the perspective of a particularly sensitive young person engaged in the act of interpreting those events.

Mayumi Morishita

Hiroshima, Japan

William L. Andrews, *Southern Review* (Winter 1988); Lynn Z. Bloom, in *Home Ground: Southern Autobiography*, ed. J. Bill Berry (1991); Margalit Fox, *New York Times* (17 February 2015); Minrose Gwin, *Southern Spaces* (11 March 2008); Emmanuel S. Nelson, *African American Biographers* (2002).

Moore, Amzie

(1911–1982) Activist

Amzie Moore worked throughout his life to address racial injustice in the Mississippi Delta, helping as early as the 1930s to create the groundwork for later civil rights activism in the state.

Moore was born on Wilkin Plantation in Grenada County on 23 September 1911. Moore's parents separated when he was a child, and his mother died when he was fourteen. He attended Stone Street High School in Greenwood, finishing tenth grade, the most advanced grade offered. After moving to Bolivar County in 1935, Moore got a job as a post office custodian and became active in a variety of civic organizations. One group was the Black and Tan Party, an organization of African American Republicans that was banned in most areas of the state. As a young man, he started what may have been the first black Boy Scout troop in the Mississippi Delta. These activities formed the basis for Moore's later civic and political activism.

While attending a 1940 conference of Delta blacks regarding economic and educational improvement, Moore became aware of the black movement for racial equality. When Moore was drafted in 1942, he was shocked by the segregation and racism of army bases in the United States and abroad, experiencing the ironic life of a black soldier—"Why were we fighting? Why were we there? If we were fighting for the four freedoms that Roosevelt and Churchill had talked about, then certainly we felt that the American soldier should be free first." Moore was asked to speak to black troops to raise their morale and obscure the injustices they daily experienced, a task that angered him and strengthened his resolve for activism when he returned home. He joined the National Association for the Advancement of Colored People (NAACP) while serving abroad.

Returning to Cleveland, Mississippi, in 1946, Moore witnessed an increase in white-on-black violence that he believed served to intimidate returning black servicemen. With Dr. T. R. M. Howard, Moore helped start the Regional Council of Negro Leadership, a group designed to represent black economic interests. The group launched boycotts of businesses that denied blacks full access to their facilities while accepting their patronage. He also led voter registration drives and made appeals to stop the brutalization of blacks by highway patrolmen. As an owner of a gas station on Highway 61, Moore refused to put up "colored" and "white" signs over the restrooms. An effective recruiter in area churches, Moore often performed with the choir and then pitched the NAACP to the congregation. As a devout Christian, Moore drew biblical parallels to contemporary social issues as he spoke to congregations throughout the Delta.

Following the Supreme Court's 1954 *Brown v. Board of Education* decision, intimidation of blacks increased in the Delta with the rise of the White Citizens' Council. In 1955 the Cleveland chapter of the NAACP elected Moore president, and despite an increasingly oppressive atmosphere, he oversaw a membership drive that resulted in 439 new members and made it one of the largest chapters in the state. When Mississippi legislators passed a 1957 law requiring voters to interpret a portion of the state constitution to the approval of the registrar, Moore, working with Medgar Evers, the first Mississippi field secretary for the NAACP, unsuccessfully sought to involve the Eisenhower administration. Undeterred, they set up citizenship schools where local activists taught reading skills and the constitution to black Mississippians.

In August 1955 Moore and Evers began a search for Emmett Till when the teenager was reported missing. Their investigation among Delta sharecroppers revealed that countless black Mississippians had been murdered over the years. Till's murder and the resulting international media attention signaled the beginning of the civil rights movement to Moore—"From that point on, Mississippi began to move."

In addition to owning the service station, Moore continued to work for the US Postal Service, and he and his wife, Ruth, also had rental property. However, because of his reputation as an activist, he found it difficult to obtain credit to run his business. Moore also received numerous death threats, and his marriage dissolved. Despite such personal difficulties, Moore often provided his home in Cleveland as a base for activists in the movement.

Moore expressed frustration at the hands-off approach taken by the NAACP's national office. During the 1960s, he became very involved with the Student Nonviolent Coordinating Committee, attracted by the organization's work to empower local people. Moore worked with Bob Moses to plan voter registration drives throughout the state as well as with Head Start programs and the National Council of Negro Women. Moore also served as the first chair of the Mississippi Action Committee on Education between 1967 and 1970.

Moore served as a foundational figure in the civil rights movement, empowering local people to demand change and inspiring countless younger activists. He died on 1 February 1982.

Becca Walton
University of Mississippi

Raymond Arsenault, *Freedom Riders: 1961 and the Struggle for Racial Justice* (2006); John Dittmer, *Local People: The Struggle for Civil Rights in Mississippi* (1994); Charles M. Payne, *I've Got the Light of Freedom: The Organizing Tradition and the Mississippi Freedom Struggle* (1995); Howell Raines, *My Soul Is Rested: Movement Days in the Deep South Remembered* (1977).

Moore, Dorothy

(b. 1946) Soul Blues Singer

Internationally recognized for her 1976 hit "Misty Blue," soul blues, R&B, and gospel singer Dorothy Moore is one of

Dorothy Moore, 2014 (Courtesy Thor M. Renslemo)

the many musicians associated with Jackson's Farish Street area. Born in Jackson on 13 October 1946 to parents who were singers, Moore counts the maternal grandmother who raised her as her greatest musical influence. Moore began her singing career in high school, performing in church and local clubs and singing backup on releases from a small Clinton label. Foreshadowing her lifelong connection to Farish Street, she repeatedly won the weekly contests at Jackson's fabled Alamo Theater while still a teenager. Moore's first recording deal, however, was with Epic Records in Nashville, which signed her as a member of the Poppies. The girl group's debut album was recorded in 1966 with producer Billy Sherrill, most noted for his work with country stars such as George Jones, Tammy Wynette, and Charlie Rich.

Following limited regional success Moore decided to pursue a solo career, in large part because of the control it provided her both in production and while performing. A handful of recordings followed, and in 1968 she teamed up with Jackson-based Malaco Records. The release of her 1976 album, *Misty Blue*, and the title track's ascendance to the top spot on the R&B chart propelled her to international acclaim. The song earned a Grammy nomination (one of four in Moore's career) and continues to serve as her signature. "Misty Blue" was followed by two more hits—Moore's version of the Willie Nelson–penned "Funny How Time Slips Away" (1976) and "I Believe in You" (1977). In the 1980s Moore recorded both gospel and R&B albums for the Rejoice and Volt labels, and in the 1990s she rekindled her partnership with Malaco, recording four albums with the label before a falling out over past royalties ensued.

Moore has subsequently recorded for her own independent label, appropriately named Farish Street. Her most recent release is *Blues Heart* (2012). In 1996 she received the Mississippi Governor's Award for Excellence in the Arts, and she and the Alamo Theater have been honored with a marker on the Mississippi Blues Trail. She has been inducted into both the Mississippi Musicians Hall of Fame and the Official Rhythm and Blues Music Hall of Fame.

Odie Lindsey
Nashville, Tennessee

Vladimir Bogdanov, Chris Woodstra, and Stephen Thomas Erlewine, ed., *All Music Guide to the Blues: The Definitive Guide to the Blues* (2003); Farish Street Records website, www.farishstreetrecords.com; Mississippi Blues Trail website, msbluestrail.org; Official Rhythm and Blues Music Hall of Fame website, rhythmandblueshof.com.

Morgan, Albert Talmon
(1842–1922) Politician

Albert Talmon Morgan was a controversial Republican politician in Reconstruction-era Mississippi who gained some fame by writing an account of his time in the state. Born in Wisconsin to George and Eleanor Morgan, devout Baptists and abolitionists who migrated from New York, Morgan attended Oberlin College in Ohio, served in the Union Army, and then settled with his older brother, Charles, in Yazoo County in 1866. After failing as a planter and a merchant, he turned to politics. The 1867 federal mandates to register and protect black voters provided Morgan the opportunity to represent his county as a delegate at the constitutional convention.

Although previously apprehensive about black suffrage, he eventually supported both political and social equality, identifying with the Radical faction at the convention and crusading to end concubinage in the state he called a "hot-bed of miscegenation." Morgan's crusade to recognize common-law unions and punish concubinage portended his mission to legalize intermarriage—a mission realized when his bill repealing discriminatory marriage laws survived both houses of the Mississippi legislature and received the governor's tacit approval in 1870.

Having removed all obstacles to intermarriage, Morgan married Carolyn Victoria Highgate, a biracial schoolteacher from New York. The newlyweds quickly became fodder for the state's Democratic newspapers, and the headlines severely damaged his local reputation. Commonly called "Miscegenationist Mawgin," he endured attacks not only from Democrats, who thought his marriage confirmed native white suspicions about carpetbaggers, but also from Republicans, who thought it alienated native white recruits from the party.

The 1874 Republican convention for Yazoo County nominated Morgan for sheriff, but F. P. Hilliard (a former political associate and a former sheriff) ran against him. Fraught with intraparty squabbles and desertions, the election left Morgan claiming victory and Hilliard crying fraud. Foregoing an official inquiry, the two factions settled the contested election via violence that ended with Hilliard's body riddled with bullets.

Public outrage over the shootout centered on Morgan. After a local newspaper blamed the sheriff for local woes, a book, *Sister Sallie*, urged native white men to reclaim local government, by force if necessary, to prevent the intermarriage of their sisters. An extralegal society, the White Liners, attempted to reestablish "home rule" by purging northerners from Mississippi's communities through intimidation and violence. Overwhelmed by the insurrection, Morgan implored Gov. Adelbert Ames to rescue the party in Yazoo County. The governor, however, lacked both the commitment and the influence to stop the purge, and a year after the vigilantes launched their violent campaign, federal investigators were told that only one northern man still resided in Yazoo County.

Morgan fled to Washington, D.C., where he published his memoirs, *Yazoo; or, On the Picket Line of Freedom in the South: A Personal Narrative*. He then moved his family to Lawrence, Kansas, before leaving them there to prospect for gold and silver in Colorado. Morgan died on 15 April 1922 in Denver. His children included well-known poet Angela Morgan.

Christopher Waldrep
San Francisco State University

Martha Hodes, *White Women, Black Men: Illicit Sex in the Nineteenth-Century South* (1997); Albert T. Morgan, *Yazoo; or, On the Picket Line of Freedom in the South: A Personal Narrative* (1884); David Overy, *Wisconsin Carpetbaggers in Dixie* (1961); C. B. Waldrep, *Journal of Mississippi History* (Summer 2002).

Morgan, Berry
(1919–2002) Author

Betty Berry Taylor Brumfield was born on 20 May 1919 in Port Gibson, Mississippi, the daughter of John Marshall Brumfield and Bess Betty Berry Taylor Brumfield. In 1940 she married Aylmer Lee Morgan III of Arlington, Virginia., and they went on to have four children. She attended Loyola University in 1947 and Tulane University in 1948–49.

After her divorce in 1972 Morgan became a creative writing instructor at Northeast Louisiana University (now University of Louisiana at Monroe) and several schools in Washington, D.C. She also worked as a farmer, secretary,

M

and real estate specialist, and she was active in the Mississippi civil rights movement.

Her first novel, *Pursuit*, was published in 1966 and earned her the Houghton Mifflin Literary Fellowship, given to new authors who show potential. She also began publishing short stories in the *New Yorker*, a practice she continued until 1988. *The Mystic Adventures of Roxie Stoner* (1974), a collection of sixteen short stories, earned Morgan another Houghton Mifflin Literary Fellowship. Her third novel, *The Mississippian*, was never completed.

Most of Morgan's stories take place in or near the mythical King's Town, Mississippi, which resembles Port Gibson. They focus on the Ingles family—like her own family, Catholics who lived on a plantation. The main character in *Pursuit*, Ned Ingles, returns to King's Town after trying to teach at a New Orleans university. He expects to find things unchanged: "The land, with its familiar rises and falls, the remembered contours of the trees, gave him the impression that he never left off looking at it, but was coming back, as from an illness or coma, to an original and authentic viewpoint." In fact, his return forces him to confront numerous uncertainties about sex and race, paternity, responsibility, religion, and alcohol. *Mystic Adventures* is more episodic, telling numerous stories from the perspective of the African American title character.

Morgan died on 19 June 2002 in Summit Point, West Virginia.

Tina Harry
University of Mississippi

Martha Adams, in *Dictionary of Literary Biography*, vol. 6, ed. James E. Kibler Jr. (1980); W. Kenneth Holditch, in *Lives of Mississippi Authors 1817–1967*, ed. James B. Lloyd (1981); Susan Furlong-Bolliger Literary Reference Center, EBSCOhost; *Winchester Star* (22 June 2002).

Morrill Act and Land-Grant Schools

Mississippi State University and Alcorn State University, along with the nation's other seventy-four land-grant institutions, owe their existences in large part to the work of one man, Justin Smith Morrill. Concerned by farmers' lack of scientific training, Morrill, who represented Vermont in the US House of Representatives from 1855 to 1867 and in the US Senate from 1867 to 1898, proposed a series of bills to use public lands to help fund education. The idea of government-sponsored schools had been around since the early 1600s, but Jonathan Baldwin Turner, an Illinois College professor, promoted this new approach to funding schools during the 1850s. Morrill drew on Turner's ideas and on the success of Europe's agricultural colleges to build an argument for federal support to create "people's colleges."

In 1857 Morrill introduced the "Bill Granting Lands for Agricultural Colleges" and suggested that each state receive twenty thousand acres of public land for each representative and senator. The bill met resistance among many southern politicians, including Mississippi senator Jefferson Davis, and among many westerners, but it ultimately passed both the House and the Senate. However, Pres. James Buchanan vetoed the bill in 1859 because he thought it was unconstitutional. The following year, with a new president and with representatives and senators from the thirteen seceded southern states absent from Washington, Morrill reintroduced his bill. After increasing the amount of land to be allotted to thirty thousand acres per representative or senator, Congress passed the measure, and on 2 July 1862 Pres. Abraham Lincoln signed it into law.

The Morrill Act of 1862 provided that states could sell public lands or land scrip provided by the secretary of the interior, with the proceeds of these transactions going "to the endowment, support, and maintenance of at least one college where the leading object shall be, without excluding other scientific and classical studies and including military tactics, to teach such branches of learning as are related to agriculture and the mechanical arts."

In 1871, in the middle of Reconstruction, Mississippi formally rejoined the Union. Gov. James Lusk Alcorn wasted no time in petitioning the secretary of the interior for the state's land scrip. Alcorn and many others supported separate but equal education for blacks, and on 13 May 1871 the state legislature accepted the terms of the Morrill Act by decreeing that two-fifths of the money from the land sales would go to the University of Mississippi and three-fifths would go to establish a university for African American students. The state purchased the Lorman site where Oakland College, a former Presbyterian school, had stood. The college, renamed Alcorn University, opened the same year, becoming the country's first black land-grant college. Hiram Rhoades Revels, a state senator from Adams County and later the school's first president, worked with Alcorn to prepare the bill that established the university.

The University of Mississippi used its portion of the scrip to hire a soil chemist as head of the new agriculture department. The program failed to interest students, however, and closed after four years. Angered by this failure, local chapters of the Patrons of Husbandry, a national farm organization, were determined to establish a land-grant school for whites in Mississippi. To that end, Grangers lobbied the legislature, and on 28 February 1878 the bill to create the Agricultural and Mechanical College of the State of Mississippi (now Mississippi State University) became law. In that same year, Alcorn University became Alcorn Agricultural and Mechanical College. It is now known as Alcorn State University.

Marybeth Grimes
Mississippi State University

An Act Donating Public Lands to the Several States and Territories Which May Provide Colleges for the Benefit for Agriculture and Mechanical Arts, Stat. 12:503, 2 July 1862; John K. Bettersworth, *People's University: The Centennial History of Mississippi State* (1980); Craig L. LaMay, in *A Digital Gift to the Nation: Fulfilling the Promise of the Digital and Internet Age*, ed. Lawrence R. Grossman and Newton N. Minow (2001); Edward Mayes, *History of Education in Mississippi* (1899); Mary Fisher Robinson, *Journal of Mississippi History* 12 (January 1950); William B. Parker, *The Life and Public Services of Justin Smith Morrill* (1971); Josephine McCann Posey, *Against Great Odds: The History of Alcorn State* (1994); Roy V. Scott, *Agricultural History* (October 1969).

Morris, Willie

(1934–1999) Author and Editor

Willie Morris (Bern and Franke Keating Collection, Department of Archives and Special Collections, J. D. Williams Library, University of Mississippi)

Although Willie Morris's reputation rests largely on his nonfiction works, particularly his first autobiography, *North toward Home* (1967), he also achieved widespread recognition as an editor, newspaper journalist, children's author, essayist, and editorial writer. Commentators and critics have often singled out his perceptive understanding of and deep affection for the South as well as his passionate convictions about the importance of race relations in America.

Sixth-generation Mississippian William Weaks Morris was born on 29 November 1934 in Jackson, the only son of Henry Rae Morris, a bookkeeper, and Marion Harper Weaks Morris. Before his first birthday, the family moved to Yazoo City, a small town located on the edge of the Mississippi Delta, where he acquired a strong sense of history, place, and family, themes that he often explored in his books.

After graduating from high school in 1952 as class valedictorian, Morris left his familiar Mississippi Delta for the University of Texas at Austin, where he joined the staff of one of the best student newspapers in the country, the *Daily Texan*. Immersing himself in journalism and books, he became editor his senior year. He soon achieved campus—and even national—notoriety for his no-holds-barred editorials on segregation, censorship, and other controversial issues.

Morris received a bachelor's degree in English in 1956 and went on to study history at Oxford University as a Rhodes Scholar, earning bachelor's and master's degrees. From 1960 to 1962, as the crusading editor of the liberal *Texas Observer*, Morris honed his reportorial skills while covering topics that the mainstream press generally ignored, such as illiteracy, racial discrimination, and the inequities of the death penalty.

Morris became associate editor of *Harper's* magazine in 1963 and editor in chief four years later, shortly before the publication of *North toward Home*. Throughout this "autobiography in mid-passage" he struggles to understand his regional identity as he challenges the complex and emotionally charged issues that confronted Americans during the mid-twentieth century.

As the youngest editor in chief in the history of the nation's oldest magazine, Morris aggressively sought contributions from such well-known writers as William Styron, Larry L. King, David Halberstam, Robert Penn Warren, and Norman Mailer. Despite creating a widely read and often quoted periodical, Morris eventually became embroiled in editorial disputes with the publication's owner and resigned in 1971.

Morris's departure from *Harper's* followed a painful divorce from his wife, Celia Buchan Morris, and he moved to Bridgehampton, New York, to concentrate on writing. In early 1980 he returned to Mississippi to accept a position as writer in residence and instructor in the University of Mississippi's English department.

In 1990 Morris married his longtime friend and editor, JoAnne Prichard, and the following year he resigned his position at the University of Mississippi. At their home in Jackson, he chronicled his exhilarating years at *Harper's* in a second memoir, *New York Days* (1993), which he followed with the widely popular *My Dog Skip* (1995). This bittersweet tribute to the canine companion of his boyhood and poignant memoir of a bygone era became a successful 2000 motion picture.

Morris, who served as an on-site consultant for the film, did not live to see its final version. In late July 1999 he and his wife flew to New York to view a preliminary screening. On 2 August, several days after they returned home, he suffered a heart attack and died. He is buried in Yazoo City's Glenwood Cemetery, just thirteen paces from the grave of the Witch of Yazoo, a character he immortalized in his children's book *Good Old Boy* (1974).

Several of Morris's books have appeared posthumously, including *My Cat Spit McGee* (1999), *My Mississippi* (2000, a joint project with his son, photojournalist David Rae Morris), and the novel *Taps* (2001). The author often said that *Taps*, written over much of his thirty-year literary career, was "my baby" and "my life work." In an interview shortly after the book's publication, JoAnne Prichard Morris remarked that he had wanted to say "all he felt and had learned over a lifetime." Morris's coming-of-age story captures the ideas and beliefs that not only consumed him but also played significant roles in much of his writing: the importance of the past, the allegiance to a place and the power of land, loyalty to family and friends, the intricacies of personal relationships, the unquestioning love of a dog, the glory and disappointment of sports, the meanness and tragedy of racial injustices, and the fragility of human life as well as the intense, complex emotions of love, joy, sacrifice, and grief.

Halberstam affirmed in his eulogy for Morris that his friend "loved good writing and good books, but what he loved best was this region and this country." The hallmarks of Morris's best works are his gracefully lyrical writing and his enduring love for Mississippi.

Jack Bales
University of Mary Washington

Peter Applebome, *New York Times* (3 August 1999); Jack Bales, ed., *Conversations with Willie Morris* (2000); Fred Brown and Jeanne McDonald, *Growing Up Southern: How the South Shapes Its Writers* (1997); Larry L. King, *In Search of Willie Morris: The Mercurial Life of a Legendary Writer and Editor* (2006); Teresa Nicholas, *Willie: The Life of Willie Morris* (2016).

Moses, Bob

(b. 1935) Activist and Educator

Civil rights activist Bob Moses has played two important roles in Mississippi—first as a movement organizer with the Student Nonviolent Coordinating Committee (SNCC) in the 1960s and later as a founder of the Algebra Project. Born on 23 January 1935 in New York City's Harlem, Robert Parris Moses grew up living in a housing project. In 1952 he graduated from the highly competitive Stuyvesant High School and received a scholarship to attend Hamilton College in Upstate New York, where he was one of three African American students. During his college years he spent summers in France and Japan, exploring his interests in pacifism and Eastern philosophy. He earned a bachelor's degree from Hamilton in 1956 and then moved on to Harvard University, where he received a master's degree in philosophy. Because of his mother's sudden death and father's illness,

he left Harvard in 1958 for a job at New York's Horace Mann School, where he taught mathematics for two years.

While in Virginia visiting an uncle, William Moses, an architect and Hampton Institute faculty member, Bob Moses joined a Newport News picket line, where he met Wyatt T. Walker of the Southern Christian Leadership Conference (SCLC). Late in 1960 Moses went to the SCLC's Atlanta headquarters to work with the organization's Ella Baker and Jane Stembridge. Stembridge invited Moses to go to Mississippi to recruit student participants for a special conference of civil rights activists. The conference resulted in the development of SNCC. In Mississippi, he met Aaron Henry and Amzie Moore, National Association for the Advancement for Colored People (NAACP) leaders in the state. In 1961 C. C. Bryant, the president of McComb's NAACP chapter, invited Moses to organize voter registration efforts in the Pike County area. He served as a SNCC field secretary and the director of the Council of Federated Organizations (COFO) during the 1964 Freedom Summer project. COFO resulted from Moses's efforts to encourage cooperation among the numerous civil rights groups working in the state.

By example and through his soft-spoken leadership style, Moses encouraged activists to listen to other people and to become part of communities they wanted to help. He said that black Mississippians had spent much of their lives having wealthier, more educated people tell them what to do, and he did not want civil rights activists, no matter how well-meaning, to do the same. Moses advocated nonviolent protest, spoke highly of the potential of freedom schools to set examples for new ideas about education, and above all promoted a creative, participatory approach to community life.

In 1965 Moses left Mississippi. Between 1968 and 1976, he and his family lived in Tanzania. In 1982 he received a prestigious MacArthur Fellowship of five hundred thousand dollars. He used the money to found the Algebra Project, an educational enrichment program developed with Charles E. Cobb that provides underprivileged youngsters with mathematical skills. Moses has also received the Heinz Award and the Margaret Chase Smith Award, and in 2006 Harvard University awarded him an honorary doctorate. He currently teaches math in Jackson.

Donald Cunnigen
University of Rhode Island

Raymond Arsenault, *Freedom Riders: 1961 and the Struggle for Racial Justice* (2006); Taylor Branch, *Parting the Waters: America in the King Years, 1954–63* (1988); Eric Burner, *And Gently Shall He Lead Them: Robert Parris Moses and Civil Rights in Mississippi* (1994); Clayborne Carson, *In Struggle: SNCC and the Black Awakening of the 1960s* (1981); John Dittmer, *Local People: The Struggle for Civil Rights in Mississippi* (1994); William Heath, *The Children Bob Moses Led: A Novel of Freedom Summer* (1995); Wesley C. Hogan, *Many Needs, One Heart: SNCC's Dream for a New America* (2007); Robert P. Moses and Charles E. Cobb Jr., *Radical*

Equations: Math Literacy and Civil Rights (2001); Charles M. Payne, *I've Got the Light of Freedom: The Organizing Tradition and the Mississippi Freedom Struggle* (1995).

Mosley, Jessie Bryant

(1903–2003) Activist, Educator, Writer

Jessie Bryant was born in Houston, Texas, on 30 November 1903 to Grant Hamilton Bryant and Emma Bryant. She earned bachelor's and doctoral degrees from Jarvis Christian College in Hawkins, Texas, and became certified in teaching and library science. She married Dr. Charles Clint Mosley, who served as dean of Southern Christian Institute before becoming a long-serving professor at Jackson State, and they went on to have three children. Though community activism and cultural preservation remained central to her mission, Mosley also worked as a teenage program director for the YWCA in Jackson in the 1950s, a teller at State Mutual Federal Savings and Loan in the early 1960s, and a social science teacher in the Jackson public schools from 1965 to 1970.

Jessie Mosley wrote several historical works on African Americans in Mississippi, including *The Negro in Mississippi* (1950). Recognizing that contemporary textbooks overlooked the accomplishments of African Americans, she wrote her own, highlighting black Mississippians' successes in government, education, business, industry, the arts, and religion. She intended to "remind some and acquaint others of the contributions and achievements of the Negro within the State of Mississippi and to create better understanding between the races." She updated that book in 1969 and wrote two shorter works, *The Story of Negro Disciples in Mississippi* and *The History of the Women's Movement in Mississippi.*

In the early 1960s Mosley was part of a core group of black women who were at the forefront of the civil rights movement in Jackson. She served as treasurer of Womanpower Unlimited, a group formed in 1961 to coordinate community support for the jailed Freedom Riders. A shoe store that she and her husband owned served as a safe houses for riders. In 1967 Mosley helped found the Jackson chapter of the National Council of Negro Women (NCNW), the group started by Mary McLeod Bethune to encourage leadership roles for black women in community activities and social causes. Mosley supervised the Jackson Unit's day care, nursery, and kindergarten centers and served as the NCNW's state convener from 1977 to 2001.

Building on her commitment to uncover and share the achievements of black Mississippians, she founded the Negro in Mississippi Historical Society in 1963. Mosley and

the organization helped lead the effort to preserve the Smith Robertson School, which had opened in 1894 as Jackson's first public school for African Americans. After the school closed in 1971, the city abandoned the building, and it faced demolition. Mosley, Alferdteen Harrison, and others organized a petition drive to save the structure, and in 1984 the Smith Robertson Museum and Cultural Center opened in the old school with Mosley as its founding director. The museum, the state's first dedicated to preserving African American history, is located in the heart of the Farish Street neighborhood, which at one time was the central business district for black Jacksonians.

Mosley worked with other state and local organizations, including the Mississippi State Federation of Colored Women's Clubs, the Mary Church Terrell Club, and the Mississippi Humanities Council. She organized the first Women, Infants, and Children program in Jackson and founded Wednesdays in Mississippi to encourage more interracial communication. She received numerous honors, including the Carter G. Woodson Award for her efforts in promoting Black History Month and the NCNW's 1998 Mary McLeod Bethune Living Legend Award. The City of Jackson named Dr. Jessie B. Mosley Drive in her honor.

Mosley died at her Jackson home on 6 June 2003. In 2015, her daughter, filmmaker Wilma Mosley Clopton, released a book and accompanying documentary film, *Jessie: One Woman, One Vision: A Look at the Life of Dr. Jessie Bryant Mosley.*

Carter Dalton Lyon
St. Mary's Episcopal School,
Memphis, Tennessee

Eva Hunter Bishop and Geneva Brown Blalock White, eds., *Mississippi's Black Women: A Pictorial Story of Their Contributions to the State and Nation* (1976); Thyrie Bland, *Jackson Clarion-Ledger* (12 June 2003); Jana Hoops, *Jackson Clarion-Ledger* (11 April 2015); Tiyi Morris, *Womanpower Unlimited and the Black Freedom Struggle in Mississippi* (2015).

Mound Bayou

Located along US Highway 61 in the central Mississippi Delta, Mound Bayou was at one time the nation's largest and most self-sufficient African American town. Founded in 1887 by cousins Isaiah T. Montgomery, Joshua P. T. Montgomery, and Benjamin T. Green, all of whom had been slaves at the Davis Bend Plantation in Warren County, the initial settlers of this once-storied community carved out a productive and prosperous standard of living in the midst of

Mound Bayou Foundation, Mound Bayou, January 1939
(Photograph by Russell Lee, Library of Congress, Washington, D.C.
[LC-USF33-011948-M1])

what had been for most African Americans of the period a uniquely treacherous and unforgiving part of the American South.

The prototype for Mound Bayou was the former Davis Bend Plantation, which under the administration of Joseph E. Davis, older brother of Jefferson Davis and a devotee of Robert Owen's theories regarding the cultivation of a labor pool, allowed for the creation of a versatile, self-sufficient, cooperative, and pragmatically educated workforce. The Montgomerys and Green gained expertise from their slave-era experiences that served the budding town they helped establish: Isaiah Montgomery and Benjamin Green in business matters and Joshua Montgomery in the practice of law.

In July 1887 Isaiah Montgomery was commissioned to serve as land agent for the Louisville, New Orleans, and Texas Railroad, which sought to build passenger rail links through the heart of the Delta region but desperately needed towns to create a customer base. Although primarily focused on white settlers, railroad officials also sought to exploit the heretofore untapped possibilities provided by black laborers looking to establish their own communities. This search ultimately led the railroad to recruit Montgomery and a handful of other African American agents.

Once all involved agreed on an exact location for the Mound Bayou settlement, in the hinterlands of Bolivar County near the Chickasaw burial mounds some seven miles west of the Sunflower River and fifteen miles east of the Mississippi River, Montgomery set out in search of potential settlers. The first wave brought members of his extended family and included both Joshua Montgomery and Benjamin Green. Isaiah Montgomery eventually targeted other former Davis Bend residents, many of whom had worked both with and for the Montgomerys. He later traveled to other parts of the Deep South to entice former slaves to come to Mound Bayou, where they would engage in the all-too-familiar clearing out of swamplands but would now do so for their own benefit. As a result of his inspired planning and recruiting, Montgomery developed

an enviable revenue stream from a combination of commissions and land sales, and as settlers poured in from throughout the region, Montgomery and Green founded the town's only sawmill, another boon for the family coffers.

Under any other circumstances, Mound Bayou, nicknamed by its residents the Jewel of the Delta, would have been deemed an unmitigated success, but as an African American venture in the center of Mississippi's most productive plantations during the peak years of Jim Crow, its accomplishments were nothing short of miraculous. At a time when few Delta communities could organize themselves effectively, Mound Bayou, through the work of another astute businessman, Charles Banks, developed a thriving business infrastructure complete with a governing body, banks, merchants, cotton gins and warehouses, and a public school system, all outside the reach of the surrounding white-dominated towns. These successes began to draw notice from around the country, as Booker T. Washington, Theodore Roosevelt, Andrew Carnegie, Julius Rosenwald, and other noted figures became de facto supporters of the town's vast enterprises. In 1942 Mound Bayou became home to the central Delta's first hospital when the Knights of Tabor, a progressive African American fraternal order, built a forty-two-bed facility staffed by physicians from the Meharry Medical School in Nashville, Tennessee. With the hospital, schools, parks, and a small but impressive array of African American professionals, Mound Bayou offered hope, examples, and a central location for many African Americans in the Delta.

The second half of the twentieth century was not nearly as kind to Mound Bayou. As an oasis from white-run politics and white-owned business, it was a safe place for some civil rights leaders, especially early in the movement. But a series of business setbacks, fluctuating markets, mounting antagonism from surrounding areas, and severe political infighting began to wear away at its legacy, and by the late 1960s the once proud and self-sufficient town had been reduced to the level of many other small, struggling Delta communities. Though it remains a part of the Delta landscape, it has yet to regain its status as one of the region's most successful ventures in town building.

Joel Nathan Rosen
Moravian College

Kenneth Marvin Hamilton, *Black Towns and Profit: Promotion and Development in the Trans-Appalachian West, 1877–1915* (1991); Janet Sharp Hermann, *The Pursuit of a Dream* (1981); A. P. Hood, *The Negro at Mound Bayou* (1910); David Jackson, *A Chief Lieutenant of the Tuskegee Machine: Charles Banks of Mississippi* (2002); Neil R. McMillen, *Dark Journey: Black Mississippians in the Age of Jim Crow* (1990).

Mound Builders

The vast terrain stretching from the Great Lakes to the Gulf of Mexico and from the Mississippi Valley to the Atlantic seaboard is dotted with thousands of ancient man-made earthen and shell mounds and embankments. More than five thousand mounds have been recorded outside of the Mississippi Valley, among them a few in coastal Labrador and the Desert Southwest. Some mounds are taller than oaks, while others are barely waist high. There are domes, cones, flat-topped platforms, other geometric forms, and animal effigies as well as raised rings, spans, and facades. Many were built in a single stage, but larger mounds were often capped or mantled several times. Some mounds are devoid of artifacts and interior features, others cover dismantled wooden buildings, and still others contain burials or form foundations for walled buildings. Embankments encircle plazas or connect buildings in cosmic or magical arrangements. Sometimes there is only one mound; sometimes there are a score or more. Invested labor ranges from modest (the equivalent of a mere handful of people working for a day or two) to monumental (the equivalent of hundreds of people toiling for years).

So who built these mounds? Ignoring more than a century of eyewitness accounts, some nineteenth-century antiquarians refused to admit that the mounds were the work of the American Indians, claiming instead that the architects were refugees from sunken continents, lost races, conquering foreign legions, or the mighty Aztec or Toltec. These perceptions lasted until 1894, when the Smithsonian Institution's thirteen-year mound study definitively showed that Native Americans were the builders.

With the identity of the Mound Builders resolved, twentieth-century archaeologists turned to the history of mound building. Boosted by radiocarbon dating in midcentury, archaeologists have traced Mound Builder roots back at least seven millennia. The oldest known mound group in mainland North America is Monte Sano on the banks of the Mississippi River in what is now Louisiana. The larger of its two conical mounds covers a crematorium and dates to sometime around 7,300–7,400 years ago (calibrated). Early mound building flourished between 5,000 and 6,000 years ago, when Lower Mississippi Valley natives erected solitary mounds as well as mound complexes with between two and eleven structures. Early mounds were empty but were occasionally built over demolished wooden structures. Denton is the oldest known mound complex in Mississippi, dating to around 6,200–6,300 years ago. South Atlantic coastal groups continued to build shell mounds and rings through the ensuing millennium, but the falling population in the Lower Mississippi Valley quieted mound building. It resumed in grand fashion around 3,700 years ago, when a giant earthwork incorporating nearly a million cubic yards of dirt was erected at Poverty Point in northeastern Louisiana. Another population decline followed Poverty Point's abandonment, and when mound building returned some six centuries later, small domed mounds had begun to assume burial duty. A few hundred years later, around the turn of the Christian era, they often became lavishly appointed conical tombs that incorporated homespun mortuaries with grave goods fashioned in international Hopewell style.

Later, the Lower Mississippi population plummeted again, and when mound building recommenced a few centuries later, mound form and function changed—flat-topped platforms, often true truncated pyramids, supported temples and elite residences—but a few mounds continued to be used for burial. Large earthwork towns came and went as the winds of war and local politics dictated: Cahokia in Illinois; Moundville in Alabama; Troyville, Pritchard Landing, and Mott in Louisiana; and Toltec and Lakeport in Arkansas.

Two of the most important mound sites in Mississippi are Lake George and Winterville. The first is located on the south side of Lake George, a half mile east of the Sunflower River and southeast of what is now Holly Bluff. Archaeologists recognized twenty-five mounds there, ranging from gentle rises that were likely house foundations to a fifty-five-foot high mound that covered almost two acres. The other large mounds at the site served as ceremonial centers. An earthen wall and a trench surround the site. The location was a fortunate one for the Mound Builders, with fertile Delta soils and wetlands supporting food supplies, primal hardwood forests providing resources for the shelter, streams and rivers containing fish and shellfish, and natural levees from Mississippi River sandy and silty loams protecting the site from flooding.

The Winterville site, near the present city of Greenville, has at least twenty-three mounds and several plazas. Like other Mississippian societies, the people at Winterville had a well-defined social hierarchy based on heredity through the female line and expressed at the top through affiliation with a powerful chief. A fire in the late fourteenth century

Pharr Mounds, one of six mound groups along the Natchez Trace Parkway, is a ninety-acre complex of eight burial mounds built between about 1,800 and 2,000 years ago. (Courtesy US National Park Service)

destroyed the original structure at Winterville, and the population declined thereafter, moving to other locations in the Yazoo River Basin. The powerful Natchez tribe was among the last of the Mound Builders, but its unity was destroyed in a prolonged war with the French in 1731.

The Mound Builders were not a single tribe but comprised many independent groups that built mounds as a traditional way of celebrating the creation and the cosmos. Natives called mounds *navels*, the mini mountains where first humans rose from their watery birth cave deep in the earth, and many of the multiple-mound complexes, especially the older ones, employ standard measures and mound placement to portray the cyclical march of the sun, moon, and Venus across the sky. Mound arrangements thus not only diagram the tiered cosmos but accurately measure the day counts of the heavenly cycles: they are native North America's first calendar, predating similar Mesoamerican almanacs by centuries. Mound form and use changed over the seven-millennium history of mound building, but Mound Builders remained true to the ancient core beliefs until the last basketload of earth was tamped into place.

Jon L. Gibson
Homer, Louisiana

George R. Milner, *The Mound Builders* (2004); Robert Silverberg, *The Mound Builders* (1968); Cyrus Thomas, *Report on the Mound Explorations of the Bureau of Ethnology* (1894).

Movies

Many of the movies filmed in or featuring Mississippi are based on the works of the state's famous literary figures. Among others, the works of William Faulkner (*As I Lay Dying, Intruder in the Dust, The Sound and the Fury, Sanctuary, The Story of Temple Drake, Tomorrow, Barn Burning, The Reivers, A Rose for Emily*), Willie Morris (*My Dog Skip, Good Ole Boy: A Delta Boyhood*), Eudora Welty (*The Wide Net, Why I Live at the P.O., The Ponder Heart*), Tennessee Williams (*Cat on a Hot Tin Roof, Orpheus Descending, Baby Doll, This Property Is Condemned, The Loss of a Teardrop Diamond*), Stark Young (*So Red the Rose*), Beth Henley (*Miss Firecracker, Crimes of the Heart*), John Grisham (*A Time to Kill, The Client, The Chamber, The Pelican Brief*), Larry Brown (*Big Bad Love*), and Clifton Taulbert (*Once upon a Time . . . When We Were Colored*) have all reached the silver screen, with scenes either shot in the state of Mississippi or staged there.

Mississippi has also been the site and/or subject of many documentaries, especially those dealing with the Missis-

sippi Freedom Summer (*Murder in Mississippi*) and other aspects of the civil rights movement (such as *Eyes on the Prize*). African American life, particularly dealing with music (*Mississippi Blues, Mississippi Delta Blues, You See Me Laughin'*) and poverty (*LaLee's Kin: The Legacy of Cotton, Baby Business*) is also a popular subject.

The Mississippi Film Office, under the umbrella of the Mississippi Development Authority and the Mississippi Division of Tourism, works to promote the movie industry in the state. Established in January 1973 by executive order of Gov. Bill Waller, the organization was one of the first three film commissions in the world. The Mississippi Film Office encourages and supports on-location shooting and the hiring of local businesses, talent, and crew. The Film Office has liaisons in Corinth, Holly Springs, Oxford, Tupelo, Greenville, Yazoo City, Columbus, Meridian, Canton, Metro Jackson, Natchez, Vicksburg, Harrison County, and Hattiesburg. Attributes of Mississippi touted by the Film Office include the state's beautiful landscapes, historic homes, and town squares.

Promoting Mississippi history casts the state in both a good and bad light. Despite the lushness of the landscape and the beauty of Mississippi towns, many Mississippi-made or Mississippi-based films focus on the state's negative heritage of race relations. The film *Mississippi Burning* (1988) was not well received in the state because of both its loose interpretations of the truth and harsh indictment of Mississippi. Even comedies like *The Jerk* (1979) and *Life* (1999), neither of which was filmed in Mississippi, drew attention to the race-based poverty and discrimination that are often the most visible part of Mississippi's heritage.

Only since the 1990s has a kind of independent film scene emerged in and about Mississippi. Films such as Ira Sachs's *The Delta* (1996), which looks at gay life in Mississippi, and John Michael McCarthy's *Tupelo Trilogy* (*Damselvis: Daughter of Helvis; Teenage Tupelo;* and *The Sore Losers*), three exploitation films about poor white life in Tupelo, explore modern problems normally untouched by documentarians and adaptations of the works of Mississippi's literary masters. In addition, the state currently hosts film festivals in Jackson, Oxford, Tupelo, Biloxi, Clarksdale, and other cities.

Select Mississippi Filmography

500 Nations (1993); *A Century of Women* (1994); *The Adventures of Huck Finn* (1993); *America's War on Poverty* (1994); *Angels of Death: Executioners in America* (1999); *As I Lay Dying* (Canton, 2013); *The Autobiography of Miss Jane Pittman* (1973); *Baby Business* (Benoit, 1995); *Baby Doll* (1956); *Ballast* (2008); *Barn Burning* (1978); *Beah: A Black Woman Speaks* (2003); *The Beast Within* (Raymond and Jackson, 1982); *Believe It or Not* (Holly Springs, 1931); *Beyond the Forest* (2008); *Big Bad Love* (Holly Springs and Oxford, 2001); *Biker Zombies* (Livonia, 2001); *Black Snake Moan*

(2006); *Blind Vengeance* (DeSoto County, 1990); *Blossom Time* (Columbus, 1996); *The Blue and the Gray* (Vicksburg National Military Park, 1935); *The Blues* (documentary series, 2001–2); *Brain Machine* (1977); *Cajun Heat* (1988); *The Chamber* (Greenwood, Indianola, Jackson, Parchman, and Parchman Prison, 1996); *The Client* (Clinton, 1994); *Cookie's Fortune* (Holly Springs, 1999); *Courtship* (1986); *Cremains* (Biloxi, 2000); *Cries of Silence* (1993); *The Crisis* (Vicksburg National Military Park, 1916); *Crossroads* (Delta, 1986); *Damselvis: Daughter of Helvis* (Tupelo, 1994); *The Dark Secret of Black Bayou* (1981); *The Dawn of Truth* (Mound Bayou, 1918); *Deep Blues* (1990); *Dixieland* (2015); *The Dynamiter* (Glen Allan, 2011); *Don't Look Back: The Satchel Paige Story* (1980); *Double Jeopardy* (Stennis Space Center, 1999); *Down by Law* (1986); *Eyes on the Prize* (1985); *The Fifties* (1997); *Finding Graceland* (Hollywood and Tunica, 1998); *First Nations Removed* (2000); *Forgetting Youth* (1998); *Freedom on My Mind* (1993); *Freedom Road* (1978); *From Mound Bayou to Lady Selbourne* (1999); *The Further Adventures of Tom Sawyer and Huckleberry Finn* (1981); *Get on Up* (2014); *Ghosts of Mississippi* (Jackson, 1996); *Good Ole Boy: A Delta Boyhood* (Natchez Trace Parkway, 1988); *Goofy Golf* (Biloxi, 1983); *The Gun in Betty Lou's Handbag* (Oxford, 1992); *Heart of Dixie* (Holly Springs and Oxford, 1989); *Heart of Maryland* (1920); *The Help* (Greenwood and Jackson, 2011); *Highway 61 Revisited* (1995); *The Historian* (2014); *Home from the Hill* (Oxford, 1960); *The Horse Soldiers* (1959); *Huckleberry Finn* (Natchez, 1974); *I Know Why the Caged Bird Sings* (1979); *The Insider* (Pascagoula, 1999); *Intruder in the Dust* (Oxford, 1949); *Issaquena* (2001); *Jesse James' Women* (1954); *John John in the Sky* (1999); *The Lady Killers* (2004); *LaLee's Kin: The Legacy of Cotton* (Tallahatchie County, 2001); *Leningrad Cowboys Go America* (Natchez, 1989); *Leopold Bloom* (2002); *Life at These Speeds* (2016); *Life on the Mississippi* (1978); *Lomax: The Hound of Music* (2008); *The Loss of a Teardrop Diamond* (2009); *Lost Junction* (2001); *Lost in Mississippi* (1996); *Love's Savage Fury* (1979); *Lured Innocence* (1997); *Lurking Terror* (Livonia and Unadilla, 2002); *M Is for Mississippi* (2008); *Midnight Special* (2016); *The Minstrel Man* (1975); *Miss Firecracker* (Yazoo City, 1989); *Mississippi* (1994); *Mississippi Burning* (Bovina, Jackson, Varden, and Vicksburg); *Mississippi Grind* (2015); *Mississippi Masala* (Biloxi, Greenwood, Grenada, and Ocean Springs, 1991); *Mississippi Queen* (2010); *Mistress of Paradise* (1981); *The Musical Adventures of Huckleberry Finn* (1973); *My Dog Skip* (Canton, 2000); *Natchez Trace* (1960); *New Nation* (Vicksburg 1996); *Nightmare in Badham County* (1976); *North and South: Books 1 and 2* (1985); *O Brother, Where Art Thou?* (Canton, Jackson, Valley Park, Vicksburg, and Yazoo City, 2000); *Ode to Billy Joe* (Greenwood and Itta Bena, 1976); *Oh, Mr. Faulkner, Do You Write?* (2006); *Old Natchez on the Mississippi* (1940); *Orbis Romanus* (2008); *Pale in Your Shadow* (1996); *Part of the Family* (1974); *The People vs. Larry Flynt* (Oxford, 1996); *The Ponder Heart* (Canton, 2001); *Popular Science* (1943); *Portrait of America* (1985); *The Premonition*

(Grenada, 1976); *Pretty Baby* (Hattiesburg, 1978); *The Princess of Patches* (1917); *The Promised Land* (1993); *A Public Voice* (1994); *Raintree County* (Windsor Ruins and Port Gibson, 1957); *Red Dirt* (Meridian, 2000); *The Reivers* (Carrollton and Carroll County, 1969); *Return to the River* (1989); *The Rising Place* (Jackson, 2002); *Rites of Spring* (2011); *The Road to Graceland* (1997); *Roads and Bridges* (1998); *Roll of Thunder, Hear My Cry* (1977); *Rumors of Wars* (Jackson and Madison County, 2013); *The Search for Robert Johnson* (1991); *Shark* (Tupelo, 1997); *Shake 'Em on Down: The Blues According to Fred McDowell* (2016); *Slippy McGee* (1921); *So Red the Rose* (1935); *Southern Justice: America Undercover* (1991); *Standing on My Sisters' Shoulders* (1997); *Standing in the Shadows of Motown* (Grenada, 2002); *Stone Cold* (Bay St. Louis, 1991); *Stop Breakin' Down* (1998); *Southern Writers* (1993); *Swept off My Feet* (1996); *Taking Back My Life: The Story of Nancy Ziegenmeyer* (1991); *Teenage Tupelo* (Tupelo, 1995); *Texas Heart* (2016); *Thieves Like Us* (Pickens and Canton, 1973); *This Is Elvis* (Tupelo, 1981); *This Property Is Condemned* (Bay St. Louis, 1966); *A Time to Kill* (Canton and Jackson, 1996); *Tomorrow* (Alcorn and Itawamba Counties and Tupelo, 1972); *Transplants* (1995); *Two Rivers* (Clarksdale, 1996); *Uncle Tom's Cabin* (Natchez, 1987); *Under Cover* (Pearlington, 1987); *Waking in Mississippi* (Canton, 1998); *Walk the Line* (2005); *Warheads* (1993); *WCW Uncensored '96* (Tupelo, 1996); *White Light* (2001); *Why I Live at the P.O.* (1997); *The Wide Net* (1986); *Wild at Heart* (1989); *A Worn Path* (1993); *You See Me Laughin'* (2002).

Courtney Chartier
Robert W. Woodruff Library,
Atlanta

Internet Movie Database website, www.imdb.com; Mississippi Film Office website, www.visitmississippi.org/film/.

Muhammad, Curtis Hayes
(b. 1943) Activist

Curtis Hayes, a native of Summit, Mississippi, was a field secretary for the Student Nonviolent Coordinating Committee (SNCC) in Mississippi during the 1960s. Hayes also worked with the Forrest County Voters League in Hattiesburg to promote voter registration among the county's African American population. Hayes and Hollis Watkins were the first students recruited by Bob Moses to join burgeoning SNCC efforts in the McComb area. In late August 1961 Hayes and Watkins staged a sit-in at the Woolworth's drugstore on Main Street in McComb. After taking a seat at the lunch counter and refusing to move, both men were arrested on charges of breach of the peace.

Hayes and Watkins's sit-in and arrest served as the catalyst for the McComb movement: only three days later a capacity crowd attended a community meeting to hear James Bevel speak on nonviolent protest. The next day, three black youths, one of them only fifteen, were arrested after attempting to integrate the local Greyhound bus station. Hayes was a key player in the Pike County Nonviolent Movement. Both he and Watkins had spent the beginning of the 1960s working for voting rights in Hattiesburg, with little success. The sit-in movement presented Hayes with an opportunity to become enthusiastic about action after months of frustrating voter registration drives.

After the initial McComb movement Hayes took on a prominent role in SNCC and Council of Federated Organizations (COFO) efforts across the state. As planning began for the Freedom Summer initiative, Hayes originally opposed an expanded role for white activists in the Mississippi movement. According to John Dittmer, Hayes and others "were concerned that the proposed summer project, with its heavy emphasis on untrained volunteers, would divert resources away from SNCC's primary mission: organizing local communities and developing indigenous leadership." Freedom Summer planning sessions eventually refocused SNCC efforts on Hayes's native McComb region.

As SNCC redirected its focus back toward McComb, where the organization had initiated the state's first voter registration project three years earlier, Hayes became the area's SNCC project director. He guided divided factions of black leadership to compromise, uniting them under the COFO umbrella. In July 1964 Hayes survived a Klan bombing of the McComb freedom house, although he was knocked unconscious and received glass cuts over his entire upper body. As the movement progressed, Hayes helped to organize the Mississippi Freedom Democratic Party's election and trip to Atlantic City, New Jersey. After that experience, however, his "hopes and dreams of being part of the National Democratic party were dead."

Hayes's postmovement life follows the pattern of many of his civil rights movement contemporaries. After the disbanding of SNCC and COFO, he traveled north to Chicago, where he organized a citywide school boycott protesting racism and segregated schools. In the early 1970s, he lived underground, hiding from the FBI and changing his name to Curtis Hayes Muhammad. Like scores of other movement veterans, Muhammad then traveled to the revolutionary nations of East and North Africa. He joined the Liberian revolutionary struggle and was arrested, nearly executed by a firing squad, then held prisoner and tortured for five months before he was released in response to efforts of his former civil rights network and Liberian student activists. Muhammad later returned to Liberia to establish an orphanage for abandoned children.

Muhammad's personal life has been as volatile as his postmovement activism. He has been married several times and has fathered ten children, often raising them as a single parent. He continues to advocate for human rights and social justice both in the United States and around the world.

Eva Walton Kendrick
Birmingham, Alabama

John Dittmer, *Local People: The Struggle for Civil Rights in Mississippi* (1994); Charles Marsh, *God's Long Summer: Stories of Faith and Civil Rights* (1997); Veterans of the Civil Rights Movement website, www.crmvet.org.

Mule Farming

For much of its history, farming in Mississippi was inextricably linked to mules, which were hitched to plows, planters, cultivators, and wagons. While mules were used to a limited extent in other regions, between 1850 and 1950 southerners adopted and employed the animals to a degree unprecedented anywhere else in the nation. Mules are a crucial part of Mississippi's agricultural, economic, and social history and heritage, a part of the state's history that disappeared as capital-intensive, mechanized agriculture replaced tenancy and sharecropping. Before the advent of tractors, mules provided the draft power for practically every aspect of Mississippi agriculture, from plowing to planting to hauling crops to market. Acknowledging the importance of the animals, the Mississippi Department of Archives and History mounted a 1981 exhibition, *Mules and Mississippi*.

Mules on Knowlton Plantation, Perthshire, July 1940 (Photograph by Marion Post Wolcott, Library of Congress, Washington, D.C. [LC-USF34-055153-D])

During the years that mules prevailed as the chief draft animals on Mississippi farms, nearly all Mississippians, regardless of race, gender, or economic status, had some contact with the animals. Mule farming was a labor-intensive process that required long hours behind a mule, often with old and inefficient equipment. Because labor was required to pick cotton at the end of the season, landowners had little incentive to modernize other aspects of cotton production even when doing so was possible. Thus, one-row cultivators and walking plows remained standard items on many cotton farms and plantations as long as they used mules, whether the farmer owned one mule or, like the Delta and Pine Land Company plantation, a thousand mules.

Statistics from agricultural censuses highlight the relative importance of mules, horses, and tractors in Mississippi. In 1930 the state's 312,663 farms had roughly 370,000 mules, just over 102,000 horses, and 5,542 tractors. The state's mules were valued at $32 million and horses at $6.2 million. By 1960, however, machines had replaced draft animals to the extent that the government no longer deemed it necessary to count mules.

Mules are hybrid animals, the result of a cross between a donkey and a horse—usually a jack or jackass (male donkey) and a mare. (A male horse can also be bred to a female donkey, or jenny, but that union was rare.) Mules are sterile and do not produce offspring. The jack provides long ears, small hooves, surefootedness, and toughness. The mare contributes an active disposition and size. Mules were produced in many sizes for various purposes, with mining mules the smallest and draft mules the largest. Most mules used in Mississippi were bred and raised outside the state, however, since it was usually more convenient to rely on specialized suppliers than it was to raise mules on one's farm. During the 1930s and 1940s, however, Mississippi farmers raised significant numbers of home-grown mules because the outside supply had begun to diminish. Tractors catalyzed a significant decline in mule use during the same years, but the development of a viable mechanical cotton picker truly heralded the end of the mule era, removing the last bottleneck in mechanizing cotton production. Along with the cotton picker and tractor, herbicides and pesticides also removed much of the need for manual labor in cotton production.

Because they dominated as draft animals in Mississippi for nearly a century, mules took on iconic status. As such, they symbolized the best and worst of cash-crop agriculture. Mules evoked the hardiness and vibrancy of rural culture, but they also came to be equated with sharecropping, poverty, inefficiency, and resistance to change. Mules represented an integral component of rural folk life and music. The passing of the mule era constituted much more than the simple end of farming with draft animals. The decline of mule farming in Mississippi was part of a much larger reshaping of the state's social and economic landscape. Rural Mississippi was deeply altered by highly mechanized agricultural practices that required substantially fewer laborers, but the more profound changes related to race, politics, and economics are still under way more than half a century after the end of the mule era.

George B. Ellenberg
University of West Florida

Patti Carr Black, *Mules and Mississippi* (1980); James C. Cobb, *The Most Southern Place on Earth: The Mississippi Delta and the Roots of Regional Identity* (1992); George B. Ellenberg, *Mule South to Tractor South: Mules, Machines, and the Transformation of the Cotton South* (2007); William Ferris, *"You Live and Learn, Then You Die and Forget It All": Ray Lum's Tales of Horses, Mules, and Men* (1992).

Mule Racing

Men who worked mules always found time to race them as well. By 1900 nearly 2.5 million mules worked in the fields of the American South. Racing provided entertainment at a range of social gatherings from antebellum agricultural fairs to the Kentucky Derby to informal barbecues. Mules often shared the racing program with ponies, harness horses, and native running horses. At the 1835 Maury County Fair in Tennessee, planters organized mule races on the last day of the fair, using slaves as jockeys. The mule population peaked at more than 4.4 million in 1925, before the growing presence of tractors began to shift the southern agricultural economy from manual labor to mechanized labor.

Despite the diminishing numbers of mules, mule racing surged in popularity in the Mississippi Delta during the Great Depression, with farmers holding races on their plantations to provide entertainment. Washington County planter Larry Pryor held an annual "Pryor Derby" on Silver Lake Plantation in the 1930s and helped women in the towns of Rosedale and Greenwood organize their first races in 1938 and 1941, respectively. The large public events featured pari-mutuel betting and were advertised on the radio as far north as Chicago.

Planter family home-movie footage of mule races in the Mississippi Delta towns of Rosedale and Greenwood provides a rare glimpse of the popular social event attended by whites and African Americans during segregation. Footage of the 1946 Rosedale races documents the grounds and audience as well as the racetrack. The 8mm film reveals a county fair atmosphere with speakers' platforms draped in patriotic bunting, sound trucks, announcers, large scoreboards, decorated concession stands, betting booths, musical groups, crowds of white people, and grandstand seating covered by enormous pavilion-style tents with flying pennants. The African American presence on the film is limited to mounted riders gliding through the white crowds on their way to and from the racecourse and a small section of track where black men and women stand to watch the races.

Federal Emergency Relief Administration payments to displaced Delta tenants and sharecroppers in the 1930s threatened white control over the labor pool. The annual mule races reinforced the premechanical social order that linked African Americans with the lowly mule, reassuring whites of continued social and political control. The Rosedale races were operated by the female members of the local country club known as Walter Sillers Memorial Park, while the women's Junior Auxiliary sponsored the Greenwood races. Temporary, makeshift tracks were staked out with rope at the Rosedale country club golf course and at the American Legion baseball diamond in Greenwood. The women modeled the mule races on thoroughbred horse racing to provide a comic spectacle for white audiences as contrary plow mules wreaked havoc on a circular race course. The male members of the white community cooperated with the race organizers in supplying animals and riders but took the competition much more seriously than did the women.

African American men competed among each other to ride in the races. Interviews with planters and former riders reveal that many of the large farmers invested time and money in acquiring and training fast mules. Such animals developed reputations, and planters tried to disguise fast-running mules by dyeing their hair and changing their names from year to year. Some planters used the same winning riders every year, while others held competitions on their farms to select the best hostlers from among their employees. African American farmhands vied for the chance to participate in the races. The home movie footage shows that the mules were ridden bareback by African American men wearing everyday clothing with large numbers attached to the backs of their shirts. In addition to public recognition of their superior animal handling skills, riders benefited financially as the job provided a rare opportunity to make hard cash in a sharecrop economy. The men were paid to ride and received tips and bonuses if they won.

Though widely advertised as mule races, the Rosedale and Greenwood programs also included horse racing. White men rode against black men in the horse races but not in the mule races. Because of their close association with blacks, mules were considered inferior mounts, unfit for white men. The exception was the "Gentlemen's Jockey," a spoof on thoroughbred racing in which white planters rode against each other on their prize mules. A second exception occurred during World War II when white soldiers from outside the South who were stationed at the Greenwood Army Air Field and at Camp McCain attended the races and competed on the mules. World War II interrupted the Rosedale races, which resumed in 1946 and continued into

the 1950s, when the lack of mules brought them to a natural end. Greenwood held races from 1941 to 1948.

Karen Glynn
Cape Town, South Africa

Melvin Bradley, *The Missouri Mule: His Origin and Times*, vol. 2 (1993); Robert Allen Carpenter, *Delta Review* (Summer 1964); James C. Cobb, *The Most Southern Place on Earth: The Mississippi Delta and the Roots of Regional Identity* (1992); Pete Daniel, *Breaking the Land: The Transformation of Cotton, Tobacco, and Rice Cultures since 1880* (1985); William Ferris, *"You Live and Learn, Then You Die and Forget It All": Ray Lum's Tales of Horses, Mules, and Men* (1992); Karen Glynn, "Mule Racing in the Mississippi Delta: 1938–1950," (master's thesis, University of Mississippi, 1995); Robert Byron Lamb, *The Mule in Southern Agriculture* (1963); "Mule Races Off to a Fine Start," *Greenwood Commonwealth* (6 August 1941).

Murals

Because of their size, public murals tend not to be simply decorative but informative, often focusing on the historical background of an area or representative of the interests of the community. The art form was most common during the Great Depression (1930–41), but contemporary projects indicate a recurring interest in community murals. Some of these more modern works have been created by professional artists, but the popularity of murals extends to the often charming or unusual projects of local citizens or children.

An example of early mural art in Mississippi is displayed in the DeSoto County Courthouse. In 1902 artist Newton Alonzo Wells completed a series of murals depicting the journey of explorer Hernando de Soto for the Gayoso Hotel in Memphis. The murals were acquired in 1948 by Fred Goldsmith of Goldsmiths Department Store. In 1953 they were donated to DeSoto County and put on display in the courthouse. Legend has it that the courthouse marks de Soto's campsite on the evening before he discovered the Mississippi River, making the donation particularly appropriate.

Other early historical murals include three panels commissioned by the Mississippi Department of Archives and History and executed by New Orleans artist Alexander Alaux. They were originally designed for the Hall of History in the New Capitol but have ended up in the Old Capitol Museum. Titles include *The Discovery of the Mississippi by Hernando de Soto*, *The Departure of Governor W. C. C. Claiborne and General James Wilkenson from Fort Adams Mississippi on December 10, 1803 for New Orleans to Receive the Louisiana Purchase from France*, and *Jefferson Davis at the Battle of Buena Vista*.

In Mississippi as in most of the United States, murals were not widespread until the late 1930s and early 1940s.

This resurgence was partially inspired by the Mexican government's support of muralists such as Diego Rivera, David Alfaro Siqueiros, and José Orozco, although it was also influenced by the success of American Regionalists such as John Stuart Curry and Thomas Hart Benton.

In 1931 federally supported art in America became a reality through the public art programs of the New Deal. Three government-sponsored programs commissioned a number of public murals. The Public Works Art Program and Federal Arts Program were responsible for artworks in public buildings—libraries, courthouses, hospitals, schools, and community centers. These were not necessarily murals but included sculptures, bas-reliefs, and other forms of public art. The Treasury Department's Section of Fine Arts was responsible for artworks in post offices across the United States. Thirty-one murals were proposed for Mississippi post offices, though those in Poplarville, Charleston, and Meridian were never executed, and those in Okolona and Indianola have been painted over. Surviving murals include those in Amory, Batesville, Bay St. Louis, Booneville, Carthage, Columbus, Crystal Springs, Durant, Eupora, Forest, Hazlehurst, Jackson, Leland, Louisville, Macon, Magnolia, New Albany, Newton, Pascagoula, Picayune, Pontotoc, Ripley, Tylerville, and Vicksburg. Most are in good condition and feature themes of cotton, farming, industry, local historical events, and community life in general.

The old Greenwood Leflore Library is currently being renovated, but it houses two Federal Art Project murals by local artist Lalla Walker Lewis. Other, more famous Works Progress Administration murals include those of Walter Inglis Anderson at Ocean Springs High School. The theme of the murals is historical, and Anderson's stylized figures act out the early history of Mississippi. Anderson created other community-sponsored murals during the 1950s in the Ocean Springs Community Center. Themes include animals and the life of the Gulf Coast. These colorful designs were not immediately popular, but today they coexist in the Walter Anderson Museum of Art along with the wall paintings found in Anderson's cottage after his death.

Ocean Springs boasts several additional murals. Anderson's grandson, Chris Steble, created *Past, Present, and Future* near Washington Avenue, and Stig Markenson painted another mural on Government Street. The current Ocean Springs Community Center is decorated with a mosaic mural by Elizabeth Veglia, while several other large mosaics by the same artist are located in downtown Gulfport and at the Ohr-O'Keefe Museum of Art.

Nearby Bay St. Louis has one of the most interesting church murals in Mississippi. St. Rose de Lima, a traditionally African American Catholic church, features Auseklis Ozols's mural, *Christ in the Oaks*, which depicts a black Christ. The downtown boasts six contemporary murals by local artists depicting scenes of the bay and local history, while the Hancock County Library has another mural by Veglia.

Other communities with contemporary murals based on local history are Newton, Leland, Tutwiler, and Vicksburg. In Vicksburg, a series of thirty-two realistic murals by Louisiana artist Robert Dafford decorate the floodwall. Mural topics for the Vicksburg project include scenes of the river, early industry, a legendary Mississippi bear hunt by Teddy Roosevelt, and downtown at the beginning of the twentieth century. Community projects also include murals produced in schools and libraries by children and others. Joseph Barras of Van Winkle created bas-relief murals for several schools in the Jackson area. Many schools have invited local artists or paid an artist in residence to work in the school and guide production of murals.

Similarly, many libraries have created murals in their children's areas or reading rooms. Among them are the Pike-Amite-Walthall Library in McComb, Pontotoc County Library, Starkville Public Library, Ocean Springs Municipal Library, Bay St. Louis–Hancock Library, and Union County Library. At the Library of Hattiesburg, Petal, and Forrest County, William Baggett, longtime art professor at the University of Southern Mississippi, created a fifteen-hundred-square-foot mural painted on metal that depicts the evolution of the community. It includes images of Native Americans and early Mississippi history as well as the segregated school classrooms of the 1960s and the teachers and students of today.

Mary Jane Zander
Virginia Commonwealth
University

Sue B. Beckham, *Depression Post Office Murals and Southern Culture: A Gentle Reconstruction* (1989); Patti C. Black, *Art in Mississippi, 1720–1980* (1998); Randolph Delehanty, *Art in the American South: Works from the Ogden Collection* (1996); Lisa N. Howorth, *The South: A Treasury of Art and Literature* (1993).

Murphree, Dennis

(1886–1949) Forty-Second and Forty-Seventh Governor, 1927–1928, 1943–1944

Dennis Herron Murphree served as Mississippi's governor on two separate occasions but was never elected to the office. Murphree won the position of lieutenant governor in 1923, 1931, and 1939 and held the post when two of the state's chief executives died—Henry Whitfield in 1927 and Paul B. Johnson Sr. in 1943. Murphree ran for governor as the incumbent in 1927 but lost, as he did when he ran while holding the lieutenant governorship in 1935 and 1943.

Murphree was born in Calhoun County on 6 January 1886. At age twenty-five he was elected to represent his home county in the state legislature, winning reelection in 1915 and 1919. As a legislator and later as governor, Murphree was one of the state's strongest advocates of the "pay-as-you-go" system of state finances, and he was instrumental in passing the law requiring Mississippi to balance its budget.

During his first term as lieutenant governor, Murphree and several businessmen, educators, and other leaders developed the "Know Mississippi Better" train. From 1925 to 1948 the specially equipped train traveled through three hundred cities in forty-seven states, Canada, and Mexico, showcasing Mississippi products and resources and advertising the state.

Shortly before Whitfield's death, Murphree announced that he would seek reelection as lieutenant governor. However, after he ascended to the governorship, his friends and supporters convinced him not to seek the state's second-highest office while holding its highest office, so he chose to run for governor but lost to Theodore Bilbo.

Murphree won another term as lieutenant governor in 1931 and again tried for the governorship in 1935, finishing third in the Democratic primary behind Johnson and Hugh L. White, who won the runoff and the office. Four years later, Murphree retook the post of lieutenant governor, positioning himself for another bid for the state's top office. However, he came in third in the 1943 Democratic primary, trailing Martin S. Conner and Thomas L. Bailey, who took the runoff on 24 August and the general election the following November.

However, Johnson, the incumbent governor, died on 26 December, leaving Murphree to serve the remainder of the term until Bailey's inauguration on 18 January 1944. Murphree then retired from public life, and he died in Jackson on 9 February 1949.

David G. Sansing
University of Mississippi

Jackson Daily News (20 March 1927); William D. McCain, *Journal of Mississippi History* (October 1950); *Mississippi Official and Statistical Register* (1924–28).

Murray, Judith Sargent
(1751–1820) Author

Judith Sargent Murray was at the center of the discussion over women's nature that informed the debates about gender and class of her day. Born on 1 May 1751, she was the oldest child of Winthrop Sargent and Judith Saunders Sargent, both of whom were wealthy and respected members of the merchant elite in Gloucester, Massachusetts. Murray's first husband, Gloucester merchant John Stevens, died insolvent in 1787. Her second husband, John Murray, was the first Universalist minister in America. He, too, was unable to maintain his wife in the style to which she had been accustomed.

As someone whose life was characterized by downward social mobility and who embraced a religion that most Americans viewed with distrust, Judith Murray occupied the margins of polite society. At the same time, her inherited status gave her a sense of entitlement that she never lost. This sense that she somehow deserved better gave her the confidence to challenge what she saw as the unfair disadvantages under which eighteenth-century women operated. In particular, Murray resented the deficiencies in education that even the most privileged women of her day took for granted. Taking a page from philosopher John Locke, she argued that women and men were intellectual equals but that a lack of education turned women into the silly and frivolous creatures that she disdained.

To prove her point, Murray wrote and published poetry and essays. Two of her plays, *The Medium* (1795) and *The Traveller Returned* (1796), were produced at Boston's Federal Street Theater, making her the first American-born woman to see her work performed in the Massachusetts capital. *The Gleaner* (1798), a three-volume compilation of essays, plays, and poetry, brought her at least a modicum of the fame that she so fervently sought. The volumes include her novel-like story of "Margaretta" and her most well-known piece, a four-part essay, "Observations on Female Abilities." In style and in substance, her poems, plays, and especially her essays blurred the intellectual lines dividing men and women. Simply by writing about politics and war as well as philanthropy and piety, she was claiming the right as a citizen to comment directly on public affairs. Because she always wrote under a pseudonym, appearing sometimes as the female "Constantia" and other times as the male "Gleaner," "Reaper," or "Mr. Vigillius," her disguises personified the fluidity of gender identities.

While she spent most of her life in either Gloucester or Boston, Murray moved to Natchez in 1818 to live with her daughter, Julia Maria Murray Bingaman, and son-in-law, planter and lawyer Adam Bingaman. Historians know virtually nothing about Murray's short life in Mississippi. A New Englander to the core, she no doubt was puzzled and perhaps repelled by her new home. She had always expressed her doubts about the institution of slavery, although like most of her compatriots she disliked the system for the way that it corrupted white owners rather than for the harm it did to African Americans. She thought the southern climate was unhealthy and that it did special damage to New Englanders not used to the heat and humidity. And as a staunch Federalist, she felt uncomfortable in a society whose inhabitants tended to be Jeffersonian Republicans. Finally, she saw the frontier as an uncivilized place, full of "ferocious and savage people" who lacked the polish and gentility of the men and women who inhabited her native New England. A whiff of the discomfort with which she viewed her adopted home appears in a codicil to her will, devised on 5 July 1820, the day before she died. She wanted to be buried in "some sequestered spot," safe from the "invasions of the Planter, or from intrusion of any description." It was also her "express wish, that said spot be enclosed by a decent railing." And she wanted her grave marked with a "monumental marble" that would announce the place of her birth and her parents' names. Natchez was too wild and forbidding for someone whose notion of nature was redolent of fields tamed by the plow and land marked by neatly defined boundaries. As she requested, her gravestone in Natchez's Bingaman Cemetery continues to proclaim for future generations that she was a Sargent of Gloucester, Massachusetts.

Sheila L. Skemp

University of Mississippi

Find a Grave website, www.findagrave.com; Madelon Jacoba, *Studies in the Humanities* (December 1991); Amelia Howe Kritzer, *Early American Literature* (January 1996); Judith Sargent Murray, *Selected Writings of Judith Sargent Murray*, ed. Sharon M. Harris (1995); Sheila L. Skemp, *Judith Sargent Murray: A Brief Biography with Documents* (1998).

Murrell, John

(1806–1844) Bandit and Folk Hero

John Andrews Murrell was a small-time thief along the Natchez Trace whose exploits became mythologized during the 1830s and who became widely known as the Great Western Land Pirate or the Rob Roy of the Southwest.

The facts of Murrell's life are rather pedestrian. Born in 1806 in Lunenberg County, Virginia, Murrell moved with his family to Williamson County, Tennessee, as a young child. In 1823 he was charged with stealing a horse and served a year in prison for the crime. After his release, he married, fathered two children, and continued to engage in petty thievery and counterfeiting. In July 1834 Murrell was convicted of stealing a slave and sentenced to ten years of hard labor. He reformed while incarcerated, contracted tuberculosis, and was granted an early release in in April 1844. He died of the disease in Pikeville, Tennessee, on 1 November of that year.

However, the mythology that sprang up around Murrell was far more exciting and was emblematic of the frontier nature of Mississippi in its early statehood. In 1835, writing under the pseudonym Augustus Q. Walton, Virgil A. Stewart published *A History of the Detection, Conviction, Life and Designs of John A. Murel, the Great Western Land Pirate*. Stewart alleged that Murrell was not only a highwayman and slave thief but also a leader of slave rebellions. Stewart portrayed Murrell as motivated by class resentments against the wealthy planters of the South and alleged that he led slaves into rebellion, only to take advantage of the disorder and plunder plantations of their wealth, escaping with the treasure.

The Murrell legend worked its way through central Mississippi in the summer of 1835. In towns from Vicksburg and Clinton to Canton and Livingston, slaves and alleged conspirators were publicly whipped and executed. Most scholars find it unlikely that an actual slave conspiracy existed at the same time, but if so, it is unlikely that it was connected to Murrell's plan.

According to folklore, Murrell's band of thieves continued to range the Old Southwest and to meet in the Devil's Punch Bowl, a land formation along the Natchez Trace, long after his incarceration and death. His story, originally told as a cautionary tale to warn planters of the dangers of the frontier, resonated and was retold among the common folk living and working on the Mississippi River. As late as the 1870s thorough descriptions of his actions and the details of his hiding places could be found in Mark Twain's *Life on the Mississippi*. Indeed, a century after his death, Murrell remained part of the physical and cultural landscape of Eudora Welty's and William Faulkner's Mississippi and was one of the many cultural reference points in their literature. Even in the mid-twentieth century, a traveling carnival claimed to feature the "head of Murrell." Many modern residents of Mississippi have heard of Murrell and are aware of his purported exploits.

David J. Libby

University of Texas at San Antonio

Encyclopedia of Arkansas History and Culture website, www.encyclopediaofarkansas.net; David J. Libby, *Slavery and Frontier Mississippi, 1720–1835* (2004); James Lal Penick Jr., *The Great Western Land Pirate: John Murrell in History and Legend* (1981); Joshua Rothman, *Flush Times and Fever Dreams: A Story of Capitalism and Slavery in the Age of Jackson* (2014).

Musgrove, Ronnie

(b. 1956) Sixty-Second Governor, 2000–2004

After serving in the Mississippi State Senate from 1988 to 1996 and as lieutenant governor from 1996 to 2000, Democrat Ronnie Musgrove was elected governor under circumstances unique in Mississippi history. Under the 1890 state constitution, because neither Musgrove nor any other gubernatorial candidate received a majority of the votes cast in the November 1999 general election, the legislature elected the governor. And in a special vote on 4 January 2000, legislators elected Musgrove.

Born in the Tocowa Community in Panola County on 29 July 1956, David Ronald Musgrove earned degrees from Northwest Mississippi Junior College, the University of Mississippi, and the University of Mississippi Law School. In 1980 he was elected president of the law school student body.

Musgrove, a member of the Mississippi and American Trial Lawyers Associations, served as president of the Panola County and Tri-County Bar Association and on the Board of Directors of the Mississippi Young Lawyers Association. He was selected for membership in the Inns of Court in 1988 and two years later was elected to the Board of Bar Commissioners of the Mississippi State Bar Association. In 1995 Musgrove was inducted as a fellow in the Mississippi Bar Foundation.

In 1998 Musgrove served as chair of the National Conference of Lieutenant Governors. During his term as governor, he served on the Executive Committee of the Southern Regional Education Board, the National Board of Professional Teaching Standards, the National Assessment Governing Board, the National Board of Directors of Jobs for America's Graduates, and the Executive Committee of the Democratic Governors Association. In addition he chaired the Southern States Energy Board and the Executive Committee of the National Governors Association.

Musgrove won the close election over Republican Mike Parker by emphasizing his work as lieutenant governor and in part because of divisions in the Republican Party. He ran as a conservative on fiscal and social issues, and his time as governor generally revealed this conservative perspective. His term included a special legislative session to enact tort reform, and Musgrove helped persuade the Nissan Motor Company to build a large facility in Mississippi. However, during a period of increasing Republican popularity, Musgrove supported efforts to remove the image of the Confederate battle flag from the state flag. He ran for reelection in 2003, but challenger Haley Barbour used his political and business experience, along with Musgrove's support for changing the flag, to win the office.

Since 2004 Musgrove has practiced law, worked as a political consultant, and taught classes at the University of Mississippi and at the Mississippi College School of Law. In 2008 he ran for the US Senate but lost to incumbent Roger Wicker.

David G. Sansing
University of Mississippi

Mississippi Official and Statistical Register (1988–92, 1992–96, 1996–2000); Jere Nash and Andy Taggart, *Mississippi Politics: The Struggle for Power, 1976–2006* (2006).

Mushrooms

Anyone who travels through Mississippi, from coastal Ocean Springs to the extreme northern city of Olive Branch, from the Mississippi River on the west to the Alabama border to the east, can find mushrooms or similar fungi. At some point in the year, mushrooms—both poisonous and nonpoisonous—are present in each county.

Fungi occupy their own exclusive niche in the biological system of classification of living organisms. They are a separate kingdom, similar to the plant and animal kingdoms. Like plants, fungi produce spores, and at one time fungi were classified as plants. Mushrooms, however, lack chlorophyll and also have no true roots, stems, leaves, flowers, or seeds, features that eventually led to their classification as their own kingdom. Unlike most plants, which have chlorophyll and can manufacture their own food, mushrooms cannot live independently and must absorb food from the surrounding medium—usually rotting wood, soil, leaf mold, or similar substrates. The ubiquitous nature of the Fungi (the mushroom group name) is equaled somewhat by the bacteria and other microorganisms.

Many mushrooms have received monikers motivated by the finders' first impressions—Devil's Snuffbox, Hen-of-the-Woods, Wolf's Milk Slime, Death Angel, Giant Stinkhorn, all of which exist in Mississippi. Some mushrooms found in the southern part of the state may not grow in the north and vice versa, but common varieties such as *Boletes, Russulas, Amanitas, Agaricus, Lactarius,* and *Armillaria,* exist in both areas and most points in between.

Mushrooms have recently experienced a culinary renaissance, with an increasingly diverse array of forms and species available at restaurants and in grocery stores. Most of these mushrooms are commercially grown for the market and are sold both fresh and preserved.

Many Mississippi localities have edible fungi that can be found at or near the same sites year after year. One popular but not abundant mushroom, the morel, can be used in almost any culinary undertaking. Orange-yellow chanterelles often abound in patches. Some members of the genus *Boletus* are most desirable, as are some *Agaricus, Lactarius,* and *Russula.*

Roughly a dozen mushrooms found in Mississippi produce chemical toxins or poisons. One of the more deadly of these is the genus *Amanita*. Ironically, most members of this genus are very attractive. The Destroying Angel, *Amanita caesarea* (Caesar's mushroom), is a brilliant orange, yellow, and red, and its caps are speckled with scales or tissue flakes.

George H. Dukes Jr.
Brandon, Mississippi

C. J. Alexopoulos, C. W. Mims, and M. Blackwell, *Introductory Mycology* (1996); David Arora, *Mushrooms Demystified* (1986); Will H. Blackwell, *Poisonous and Medicinal Plants* (1990); George H. Dukes Jr., *Mushrooms of Mississippi and Other Fungi and Protists* (2000).

Mushulatubbee

(1770–ca.1838) Choctaw Chief

Mushulatubbee was an important early nineteenth-century Choctaw chief. He first made his mark as a warrior, leading Choctaw men in support of the United States in its 1813–14 war against the Red Stick Creeks. In addition to his exploits on the battlefield, kinship ties positioned Mushulatubbee for leadership. His uncle, Homastubby, had been chief of the eastern towns where Mushulatubbee lived, and his sister's marriage to trader John Pitchlynn gave Mushulatubbee access to trade goods, translating services, and two nephews, John and Peter, who worked tirelessly to support him.

In 1820 Mushulatubbee declared that the deerskin trade had come to an end and that the Choctaw had to produce goods for the American market economy. He set an example for his followers in the eastern towns by raising cattle that he marketed in Alabama and by purchasing slaves to work his fields of corn and cotton. The chief also identified schools as important resources for his people. Mushulatubbee hoped that the children who attended the Choctaw mission schools and an academy that he helped sponsor in Kentucky would learn how to read and write in English, enabling them to make a living and to defend their land and sovereignty against American expansion.

In spite of his popularity, Mushulatubbee's political fortunes waned in 1824 when he led an effort to cede Choctaw land to the federal government in exchange for the cancellation of his substantial debts. His advocacy for the resulting Treaty of Washington garnered universal scorn, and his efforts to win back his former supporters came to nought. The disgraced chief had to hide in the US agent's cabin for some nights for fear of assassination. In April 1826 Mushulatubbee's rival, David Folsom, convinced the eastern council to turn the chief out of office and elect Folsom as the eastern towns' new leader.

Mushulatubbee had come to believe that the Choctaw nation could survive only by leaving Mississippi for Indian Territory (present-day Oklahoma). In 1829 he called a council to discuss Removal and found some support, so he began to correspond with Pres. Andrew Jackson on the subject. Old Hickory rewarded Mushulatubbee with the gift of a blue officer's uniform that marked him as an important player in the politics of Removal. Emboldened, Mushulatubbee began denouncing his opponents, and in 1830 he attracted enough support to unseat Folsom as chief of the eastern towns. Mushulatubbee went on to participate in the negotiations for the Treaty of Dancing Rabbit Creek, which fulfilled his plans for the Choctaw Removal to Indian Territory.

After Removal, Mushulatubbee resigned as chief and was succeeded by his nephew, Peter Pitchlynn. Mushulatubbee settled in the Arkansas River Valley, where he died of smallpox on 30 August 1838.

James Taylor Carson
Queen's University, Kingston, Ontario

James Taylor Carson, *Searching for the Bright Path: The Mississippi Choctaws from Prehistory to Removal* (1999); Horatio B. Cushman, *History of the Choctaw, Chickasaw, and Natchez Indians* (1899); William A. Love, *Publications of the Mississippi Historical Society* (1903).

Music

In 2000 acclaimed filmmakers Joel and Ethan Coen released *O Brother, Where Art Thou?* Set in late 1930s Mississippi, the film was an artsy exercise in camp, a collage of characters and characterizations that recognized no state boundaries and took liberal artistic license with its subject. The result was a compelling yet not necessarily bona fide composite containing geographical and historical ambiguity. With an intriguing story (a modern-day *Odyssey*) and fine cast, including the charismatic George Clooney, the film appealed to a large and appreciative audience and surprisingly emerged as the hit of the year. The true star of the film may have been the music. An accompanying compact disc served as an entertaining souvenir of the movie; according to the liner notes, it contained songs of various styles and genres, from "blues, gospel, string-band hoedowns, [and] Appalachian balladry [to] work songs and vaudeville hokum." Yet the music's popularity outside of the movie theater arguably owed its success to how the songs were presented on-screen, performances that served as a touchstone of common images that many people associated with rural Mississippi.

Whether it was the authentic work songs emanating from a fictional chain gang, a gospel call to a baptism beyond the banks of a muddy river, or an overall-clad itinerant trio singing "into a can" within the confines of a recording studio located in the middle of nowhere, the imagery conformed to universal perceptions of Mississippi inhabitants as inherent makers and consumers of music. Mississippians apparently tolerated tedious political campaigns and pompous windbags and blowhards—that is, politicians—because musicians were hired to perform at their rallies. Excited rural dwellers headed to town on Saturdays to enjoy live musical entertainment on the square, avidly listening to and watching energetic hillbilly bands and only grudgingly meandering in and out of nearby shops and stores to fill essential supply and grocery needs. Of course, everyone sang in sync at Ku Klux Klan meetings, and shackled black grave diggers did the same as they prepared some poor soul's final earthly resting place. There even is a plotline that echoes the well-known legend of a nondescript African American rambler who became a phenomenal bluesman after having sold his soul to the devil at midnight at a crossroads. Indeed, *O Brother, Where Art Thou?* conveys the message that music, at least in Mississippi, is everywhere.

Although the movie may have overstated its case, it nonetheless made its point. Many outsiders view Mississippi as a faraway land of melody and melisma, a place where natives are as apt to break out in song as they are to talk or even breathe. After all, the Magnolia State has produced more than a few figures conventionally viewed as the stylistic pioneers of various celebrated strains of American music. Charley Patton and Robert Johnson (Delta blues), Jimmie Rodgers (country music), Muddy Waters (electric blues), B. B. King (rhythm and blues), the Blackwood Brothers (gospel), Elvis Presley (rock and roll), and Sam Cooke (soul) are but a few of the musical innovators whose lives began in Mississippi. Other prominent musicians and musical celebrities who have called Mississippi home, at least during some part of their lives, include such luminaries as David Banner, Lance Bass of NSYNC, Jimmy Buffett, Ace Cannon, Gus Cannon, John and Sam Chatmon of the Mississippi Sheiks, Hank Cochran, Bo Diddley, Bobbie Gentry, Faith Hill, Howlin' Wolf, Albert King, Chris LeDoux, Brandy Norwood, Charlie Pride, Jimmy Reed, LeAnn Rimes, David Ruffin of the Temptations, Britney Spears, Roebuck "Pop" Staples of the Staples Singers, Marty Stuart, Ike Turner, Conway Twitty, Edgar Winter, Tammy Wynette, and Lester Young.

As any list highlighting the state's accomplished performers would demonstrate, Mississippi has turned out a wide variety of musical genres and personalities. And while several styles or related derivations that are affiliated with folk or "roots music" certainly have flourished—those tethered to the blues, country music, or gospel—in no way did they corner the musical market. Nearly all categories of music have accrued adherents within the state. Classical, fine art,

and theater traditions have fared well, with many favorite sons and daughters rising to prominence in privileged fields commonly thought to be exclusive to supposedly more sophisticated areas. The Mississippi Musicians Hall of Fame, with its slogan, "Mississippi, birthplace of America's music," has inducted several individuals who may have been more comfortable performing at New York City's Carnegie Hall or Metropolitan Opera House than they would have been at the Apollo Theater in Harlem or the Ryman Auditorium in Nashville. Those who have been honored as Hall of Fame inductees for their work in non-folk-related fields include such artists as John Alexander (opera), Dee Barton (classical composer), Lehman Engel (Broadway conductor), Elizabeth Taylor Greenfield (concert vocalist), Samuel Jones (classical composer and conductor), Willard Palmer (classical pianist), Leontyne Price (opera), William Grant Still (classical composer), and Walter Turnbull (opera). They are a few of the maestros who have served as constant reminders that Mississippi's musical roster and repertoire cannot be grouped into one or two genres. The obvious influence of national and international high art standards within the state's borders reveals that Mississippi's "closed society" may not have been as culturally isolated as conventional wisdom would have observers believe.

While classical and fine art musical legacies have been very important to the state's cultural development, however, no one would deny that Mississippi's most recognized musicians have sprung from and adhered to working-class traditions. People the world over have honored and revered native performers associated with the blues, country music, gospel, rock and roll, rhythm and blues, soul, dance music, hip-hop, and pop, genres that first gained a hearing not in symphony halls and musical conservatories but in juke joints, honky-tonks, bordellos, nightclubs, and churches; at festivals; and through radio, television, and the Internet. Such artists have captured the popular imagination at least in part because they represented art forms to which nearly everyone had access. The music they produced generally did not require formal training to be appreciated or replicated. It originated with ordinary people who sang in styles or played instruments that likewise could be mastered by others of similar socioeconomic and educational backgrounds and circumstances. Most important, perhaps, the music's lyrical content addressed universal themes that corresponded to the daily experiences and needs of people everywhere. Whether they represented joy or sorrow or a response to freedom or oppression, the sounds of music seemed always to accompany work, play, and worship. Indeed, music was a constant presence in situations where people loved, laughed and cried, celebrated and mourned, lived and died.

The majority of Mississippians, therefore, like their counterparts throughout the American South, were indeed a musical people. The state's Native American, Anglo-Celtic, and West African groups all claimed age-old musical traditions. Such ancient practices, of course, were not identical, but music was central all of the groups. Native Americans, for example, believed that music (and dance) possessed magical qualities that could be summoned to benefit those who performed or otherwise participated in its creation and reception. Music thus constituted a major component of public celebrations and religious rituals and maintained an importance in more private and personal quarters. Moreover, music served as the transmitter of an indigenous people's history, keeping alive the stories and legends of bygone eras.

Music, particularly ballads, functioned in a similar fashion for Anglo-Celtic migrants, the large majority of whom were illiterate. In the absence of a written literature, ballads provided a journalistic perspective on past as well as more recent events. In addition, they offered guides for morality, often producing narratives that described in graphic (and frequently superstitious) detail the harmful consequences of waywardness. Yet ballads, like other forms of Anglo-Celtic music brought to Mississippi, also furnished entertainment, whether in the home or in public. Dancing to fiddle tunes during celebrations such as weddings and community gatherings, for example, represented a standard practice, a piece of cultural baggage readily transplanted to the Mississippi frontier.

As for West Africans forcibly relocated to the antebellum American South, their engagement with music was even more pronounced. Music seemed to be rooted within their cultural makeup to a degree that could be distinguished from their European counterparts. From both individual and communal settings, music served as an important connection to another world, a spiritual realm where one's gods and ancestors dwelled in harmony. With its deep-seated emphasis on polyphonic and polyrhythmic tendencies, African music also connected enslaved people to each other. Indeed, through the melodic sounds of voices and the rhythmic swinging and swaying of bodies, West African exiles merged present with past and one with all in a manner that helped deny slavery's power to nullify a people and a culture.

The legacies established by these original inhabitants, especially those from West Africa and Great Britain, cannot be overstated. They were central to the evolution of music in Mississippi. Yet neither can one take too lightly the rural and agricultural milieu from which the music emerged. Working behind a mule and plow, often separated by long distances from neighbors, farmers frequently sang out or hollered simply so that they could hear a human voice, even if it was only their own. Of course, those within earshot might respond, making for a distinctly convivial exchange. If nothing else, such activities helped break the monotony of rural seclusion. In addition to establishing a regimented pace, the work songs and field hollers of slave laborers relieved the boredom of isolation and repetitious toil. Characterized by improvisation and the give-and-take of call-and-response between leader and chorus, the songs could reflect either a spiritual or secular bent, referencing

concerns or topics that all understood. In a rural folk society that relied almost exclusively on an agricultural existence, the emphasis on such verbal expression reiterated the importance of oral communication. For many who worked the land, whether their own or someone else's, formal education received little attention and was routinely dismissed as unnecessary, superfluous, or out of reach. Inhabitants tended to rely on the spoken rather than the written word for information, inspiration, and entertainment. It is no coincidence, then, that music flowed from an environment where public oratory, whether in the form of political posturing, fire-and-brimstone preaching, or commodity auctioneering, played a very prominent role. Like its formidable literary tradition, which developed around the aural art of storytelling, Mississippi's musical heritage has rested heavily on a long-standing and pervasive oral culture.

Most important to the state's musical evolution, however, has been the relationship of its people to power. Simply put, the large majority of its citizens have possessed little real access to social, economic, political, or even racial authority and security. In a state legendary for sustaining a rigid hierarchical social and governmental structure that favored the few while ignoring the many, both black and white, the masses were marginalized. And the ramifications of systemic discrimination along racial, class, and gender lines have been horrendous. For generations, Mississippi has endured as one of the most economically challenged and politically oppressive states in the Union. Yet one unintended consequence of this situation relates directly to music. Enjoying little satisfaction associated with material acquisition, political prerogative, or social status, ordinary Mississippians turned to music, a cost-effective and seemingly apolitical means of enjoyment, release, creative sustenance, and self-expression. The blues, for example, which developed in the Mississippi Delta at the turn of the twentieth century, established a modern framework for such musical manifestations. Created by a generation of African Americans that came of age in the late nineteenth century expecting a just racial environment, the blues represented a response to the realities of lynching, political disenfranchisement, economic subordination, and the final implementation of Jim Crow segregation. It conveyed a strong sense of realism that allowed disillusioned performers and listeners to identify and relieve themselves of repressed emotions that harmed their psychological well-being. Recognizing that life epitomized a series of ups and downs, the blues embodied a perspective that encouraged perseverance in the face of defeat, failure, and oppression. It was a worldview that became the essence of working-class musical expression.

At no other time has the roots music phenomenon so central to the film *O Brother, Where Art Thou?* and perceptions of the state carried greater weight than in the early twenty-first century. Rarely seen as a vanguard, Mississippi, which habitually has languished at the bottom of all major social indexes, such as those concerned with income,

M

education, health care, infant mortality, and environmental safety, ironically may have anticipated what the future holds for a majority of Americans. Mississippians unfortunately can relate in personal and historical terms to a transnational world of permeable borders, less governmental concern or protection for the underrepresented, and the seemingly endless growth of corporate wealth and power at the expense of workers and citizens. Yet as residents of the Magnolia State have demonstrated, resistance to such oppressive versions of modern society can be mounted—through music.

Michael T. Bertrand
Tennessee State University

William Barlow, *Looking up at Down: The Emergence of Blues Culture* (1989); Samuel Charters, *The Country Blues* (1959); James L. Dickerson, *Mojo Triangle: Birthplace of Country, Blues, Jazz, and Rock 'n' Roll* (2005); Dena Epstein, *Sinful Tunes and Spirituals: Black Folk Music to the Civil War* (1977); David Evans, *Big Road Blues: Tradition and Creativity in the Folk Blues* (1987); William Ferris, *Blues from the Delta* (1984); Benjamin Filene, *Romancing the Folk: Public Memory and American Roots Music* (2000); Charles Hamm, *Music in the New World* (1983); Charles Joyner, *Shared Traditions: Southern History and Folk Culture* (1999); Lawrence Levine, *Black Culture and Black Consciousness: Afro-American Folk Thought from Slavery to Freedom* (1977); Alan Lomax, *The Land Where the Blues Began* (1992); Bill C. Malone, *Country Music USA* (2nd rev. ed., 2002); Bill C. Malone, *Don't Get above Your Raisin': Country Music and the Southern Working Class* (2002); Bill C. Malone and David Stricklin, *Southern Music, American Music* (rev. ed., 2003); Grady McWhiney, *Cracker Culture: Celtic Ways in the Old South* (1988); Robert Palmer, *Deep Blues: A Musical and Cultural History of the Mississippi Delta* (1982); Jeff Todd Titon, *Early Downhome Blues: A Musical and Cultural Analysis* (1977); Craig Werner, *A Change Is Gonna Come: Music, Race, and the Soul of America* (1998).

Music, Religious

Religious music in Mississippi emerged from the musical forms that early settlers brought to the state, the dynamic cultural cauldron of the nineteenth-century frontier, the influence of northern urban religious styles, the continuing importance of the rural cultural context, the commercialization of traditional music, and the state's abiding biracial context. It remains a flourishing community and commercial form today.

Church people in the early nineteenth century sang old British hymns and carols and the evangelical songs of Methodist writers such as Charles Wesley, John Newton, and William Cowper. Camp meetings saw the use of new melodies, and choruses were sometimes added to older songs to engage worshippers. Songs in early Mississippi circulated in shape-note form, whereby the shape of the note indicated

its musical pitch—*fa* was a triangle, *sol* a circle, *la* a square, and *mi* a diamond. This system had previously been popular in New England, but it died out there while becoming pervasive in the South after 1800. Singing schools served as training grounds for shape-note teachers, who spread through the countryside, and tunebooks such as the *Sacred Harp* (1844) provided a musical repertoire for religious singing, public and private. The book has gone through endless revisions and remains popular in Mississippi.

Black Mississippians attended early camp meetings and sometimes worshipped in biracial churches, with evangelical music entering deeply into black religious culture during the antebellum era, when slaves increasingly embraced Protestantism. In praise sessions held in slave quarters at night or at funerals, African Americans used music to articulate a distinctive religious worldview and nurture a sense of identity. African inheritances emphasizing the importance of body movement while singing promoted preservation of the ring shout, where religion was danced as well as sung. The spirituals provided a singular body of religious songs that influenced black as well as white religious music. After the Civil War the Fisk Jubilee Singers traveled across the nation, helping to popularize spirituals. In the South, campus choirs at Mississippi's Rust College and other newly formed African American schools followed the Fisk lead.

The late nineteenth century saw the spread into Mississippi of evangelistic music associated with urban revivalism. Gospel music had become defined by the 1870s in the publications of Ira Sankey, song leader for the era's leading evangelist, Dwight L. Moody. This predominantly northern urban music became part of southern religious traditions when its revival songs were published in shape-note form, enabling rural people to sing the songs. The Ruebush-Kieffer Company of Dayton, Virginia, and the Anthony J. Showalter publishing house in Dalton, Georgia, led the way, with paperback hymnals that were used in country churches but were especially noteworthy for their role in a defining Mississippi religious-musical ritual—the weekend singing conventions that became legendary as "all-day-singings with dinner on the grounds." The lyrics of southern gospel music were rooted in a biblically based theology that was aware of sinfulness and assured of salvation for believers in Christ and that celebrated the joys of heaven. These often nostalgic and sentimental songs told of country churches, the family hearth, and spiritually nurturing mothers but above all of a comforting Savior, helping to create intimate possibilities for singers to know the love of Jesus. "What a Friend We Have in Jesus," "Washed in the Blood of the Lamb," and "In the Garden" are good examples. Mississippians sang the new gospel songs as well as traditional church hymns in such denominational hymnals as the Methodist *Cokesbury Hymnal* (1923) and the Southern Baptist Convention's *Broadman Hymnal* (1940).

Pentecostal and Holiness churches became important religious traditions in Mississippi in the early twentieth century and embraced these tunes. These churches began as attempts to restore a Wesleyan piety to the Methodist Church, stressing a religion of the heart that was open to the emotional appeals of stirring music. Pentecostal and Holiness people moved beyond the traditional church piano and organ and embraced tambourines, horns, and electric guitars. They welcomed the shape-note paperback hymnals, and Pentecostal composers wrote such classic gospel songs as "When the Saints Go Marching In" and "Great Speckled Bird." Tupelo's Elvis Presley grew up a Pentecostal, and his love of gospel music, which deeply influenced his early rock performances, came from that background.

The performance style of much modern black gospel music originated among African American Pentecostals in Memphis in the first decade of the twentieth century. The Church of God in Christ, whose founders included Charles Harrison Mason from Lexington, Mississippi, instituted services with new rhythmic intensity, including clapping of hands, swaying, shaking of heads, and occasional shouted interpolations. Rhythmic music was encouraged in this context. Gospel quartets that subsequently became popular grew partly out of the Fisk Jubilee ensemble singing tradition, sometimes augmented by secular barbershop harmonies from the late nineteenth century, but they also drew from this Pentecostal-Holiness style of music.

Both white and black gospel traditions became commercialized beginning in the early twentieth century. James Vaughan's publishing company in Lawrenceburg, Tennessee, and the Stamps-Baxter Company in Jacksonville, Texas, blanketed the South with paperback hymnals and pioneered other ways to spread gospel music. Both companies used traveling quartet singers and radio to market songbooks, with Vaughan launching WOAN, one of the first broadcasting stations in Tennessee, and Stamps-Baxter sponsoring noon and Sunday broadcasts on Dallas's KRLD beginning in 1937. The Stamps-Baxter Quartet recorded for Victor Records in 1928 and became enormously successful, leading most white gospel quartets to affiliate with Stamps-Baxter. The Gospel Singers of America was a Mississippi Gulf Coast singing school affiliated with Stamps-Baxter. It was run out of a stately white building by Videt Polk, one of the company's main composers. Mississippi produced one of the most famous white gospel quartets, the Blackwood Brothers, who were organized in Ackerman in 1934, sang in churches in Choctaw County, and became prominent through radio broadcasts on Kosciusko's WHEF and Jackson's WJDX. Spending time during the 1940s in Iowa and California before settling in Memphis in 1950, they helped to nationalize gospel music.

Since the 1930s Mississippians have heard a variety of black gospel styles, such as solo performers in the mold of Mahalia Jackson or Rosetta Tharpe; guitar-accompanied blues-gospel singers; half-spoken, half-sung preacher sermons; local church choirs; and interdenominational church choirs. However, the gospel quartet long dominated religious performance in the state, and Mississippi produced some of the nation's most successful groups. The Five Blind Boys of Mississippi organized in the 1930s as a quartet of students from the Piney Woods School south of Jackson. Originally known as the Cotton Blossom Singers, the group changed its name in the mid-1940s and adopted a "hard gospel" sound that utilized screams, growls, and thigh-slapping rhythmic accompaniment. Frank Crisler organized the Jackson Southernaires in 1940, and they were among the first gospel groups to diversify their instrumental sound, using bass, drums, keyboard, and guitars. The Canton Spirituals made a name for themselves blending rock and soul in a new gospel sound. Elgie Graham and Willie Johnson began the Pilgrim Jubilees in Houston, Mississippi, in 1944, and they made Billboard's Top 25 list with such albums as *Back to Basics*, *Family Affair*, and *I'm Getting Better All the Time*.

As with white gospel groups, radio and recordings were crucial to the success of Mississippi's black gospel performers. The Jackson Southernaires, for example, hosted a Jackson radio show for four decades and had a local television show, *Gospel Unlimited*, in the 1970s. The Southernaires signed in 1963 with a leading gospel recording company, Duke/Peacock, and the Pilgrim Jubilees recorded on Mashboro Records before moving to Peacock/Songbird, Savoy, and Malaco. Malaco had specialized in blues and rhythm and blues music but released its first gospel record, the Golden Nuggets' *Gospel Train*, in 1973. The company's gospel division, long overseen by Franklin D. Williams, has been crucial to providing recording opportunities for the state's performers. In 1991 the Williams Brothers from Smithdale founded Blackberry Records, the state's first recording company run by African Americans.

After World War II gospel groups increasingly reflected secular styles and performed in nonchurch settings, traveling in large buses for concerts at community auditoriums. In 1948 Wally Fowler pioneered the "package show," where many individual acts performed together. Fowler also popularized the all-night gospel singings in Mississippi and other parts of the South. More recently, Bill and Gloria Gaither have promoted concert and television programs that highlight one particular gospel theme—songs of wonder and amazement at God's glory. Overlooking denominational theologies, they concentrate on an underlying spirituality that comes out of an evangelical sensibility. The Gaither programs draw from the close ties between white gospel and country music, with the gospel ballad and bluegrass gospel, which often features dobros, banjos, and electric guitars. The Gaithers' Homecoming concerts often take place in Mississippi's larger towns and are televised on Mississippi Public Broadcasting.

Mississippi remains a leader in gospel music. Organized by Franklin L. Williams in 1988, the Mississippi Mass Choir has won *Billboard's* Gospel Artist of the Year award several times. Songwriter Jimmy Owens of Clarksdale helped

M

pioneer contemporary Christian music. Religious music also survives as a daily and special occasion pastime for many people. Events such as Sacred Harp singings and fifth Sunday singing conventions take place in county courthouses and local churches. Evangelicals continue to value family gospel singing, and religious music is heard on local radio stations across the state.

Charles Reagan Wilson
University of Mississippi

James H. Brewer, ed., *Mississippi Musicians Hall of Fame: Legendary Musicians Whose Art Has Changed the World* (2001); Bob Darden, *People Get Ready! A New History of Black Gospel Music* (2005); James Downey, in *Sense of Place, Mississippi*, ed. Peggy W. Prenshaw (1979); Anthony Heilbut, *The Gospel Sound: Good News and Bad Times* (1971); James R. Goff, *Close Harmony: A History of Southern Gospel* (2002).

Many of Mississippi's state universities, including Jackson State University, the University of Mississippi, Mississippi State University, and the University of Southern Mississippi, have Muslim Student Associations that provide opportunities for Muslim students and faculty to practice their religion, promote Islamic awareness, and increase understanding of the Islamic faith among non-Muslims.

Jackson is home to the International Museum of Muslim Cultures, which is dedicated to educating the public about Islamic history and culture. It opened to the public in 2001 and five years later moved to its current location at the Mississippi Arts Center.

Houssain Kettani
Fort Hays State University

Kathy Hanrahan, *Associated Press* (7 January 2007); Brannon Ingram, Pluralism Project at Harvard University website, www.pluralism.org (2008); International Museum of Muslim Cultures website, www.muslimmueum.org; Muslim Students Association website, www.msanational.org.

Muslims

Muslims are playing a vital role in the development of the state of Mississippi. They cover all spectrums of society. The state's Muslims are university professors, medical doctors, government officials, students, and members of virtually every other profession. They live in communities all over the state.

Most of Mississippi's Muslims are either African Americans or immigrants and their descendants. In the twentieth century and particularly after the 1960s, significant numbers of African Americans began converting to Islam, mostly following the guidance of Imam W. Deen Muhammad. And though a handful of Muslims came to the United States as early as the 1840s, immigration from Muslim countries in the Middle East and South Asia grew dramatically in the twentieth century.

Regardless of race and country of origin, all Muslim communities pray, celebrate, and engage in cultural activities. Some mosques are operated by the African American Muslim community and are associated with Imam Muhammad and the Mosque Cares Ministry. Mosques operated by immigrant Muslims are affiliated with the Islamic Society of North America and the North American Islamic Trust.

By the second decade of the twentieth century, Mississippi had more than fifteen Islamic centers and mosques, located in cities and towns throughout the state: Biloxi, Clarksdale, Greenville, Hattiesburg, Hickory Flat, Jackson, Madison, Meridian, Mound Bayou, Oxford, Silver Creek, Starkville, Sumrall, Vicksburg, and Waynesboro. Most have prayer halls, and several have religious schools for children.

Myths and Representations: European Colonization through 1900

The notion of Mississippi as an especially southern place did not occur to Native Americans or early European explorers and settlers—and certainly not in the ways and for the reasons that later definitions of the South were created. The place we call Mississippi was colony and frontier well before it was a state with a widely shared sense of its history, traditions, and image. The land was the home of thousands of Choctaw, Chickasaw, Natchez, Tunica, Biloxi, and Pascagoula, all with their own cultures, foundational narratives, and sense of the land and their place in it.

Early descriptions of Mississippi resemble those found in explorers' narratives of other areas of what became known as the Gulf South. Spanish and French explorers commonly marveled at the land's bounty and beauty, viewing the South as a new Eden ripe to fall into their hands. At the same time, and often in the same accounts, Europeans painted the land as a savage and uncivilized place, teeming with dangerous Indians. Spanish explorer Hernando de Soto led an expedition through the Southeast that spent the winter of 1540–41 in Mississippi. Journals kept by members of the expedition show that the explorers were fascinated by the native peoples and by the native flora and fauna. The journals also record Spanish misunderstanding and abuse of the Indians, leading to what would become a familiar pattern of violence and retaliation. Over time, Mississippians' stories about the state's original inhabitants became consistent with larger heroic American narratives of discovery, exploration, conquest, and settlement.

More than one hundred years passed between the de Soto expedition and the establishment of the first permanent European settlement in Mississippi. Between 1699 and 1702 French explorers (and brothers) Jean-Baptiste Le Moyne, Sieur de Bienville, and Pierre Le Moyne, Sieur d'Iberville, established bases on Cat Island and near what are now Ocean Springs and Biloxi. From that point through the end of the eighteenth century, stories and representations of Mississippi fit within broader tales of the struggle between the British and the French and their Native American allies for hegemony in North America. Following the construction of Fort Rosalie on the Natchez Bluffs in 1716, the Natchez District and the Mississippi River became rich producers of Mississippi images and myths. During the eighteenth and early nineteenth centuries Natchez developed a reputation, still celebrated, as a rough and cutthroat gambling den, with coarse men from Mississippi riverboats drawn to the city's Under-the-Hill port district. Myth and legend also grew surrounding the Natchez Trace, which connected the city with Nashville, Tennessee, especially the road's robber gangs such as the Masons and Harpes.

Before Mississippi became a southern state, it was the southwestern frontier of the United States. The new country asserted a claim to Mississippi in 1783, but the land remained essentially in Spanish hands until the end of the century, when it became a US territory before achieving statehood in 1817. By the 1830s the state's population, both free and enslaved, boomed as part of the southwestern Cotton Kingdom. In *Flush Times of Alabama and Mississippi* (1853), Joseph G. Baldwin memorably described the state's raw conditions, social and economic fluidity, and boom-and-bust mentality. Mississippi in the early decades of the nineteenth century is just as accurately described as the West as it is the South. Like many other Americans in states such as South Carolina and Tennessee that later seemed quite southern, Mississippians in this period were ardent nationalists who embraced the expanding Union and saw its values as their own.

Some of the most persistent narratives and representations of Mississippi stem from the state's experience with slavery, Confederate defeat in the Civil War, and struggles during Reconstruction. As in other Deep South states, Mississippi's economy and broader culture became deeply invested in the production of cotton using slave labor. That is not to say that most Mississippians owned slaves or became wealthy cotton barons. The state's surviving antebellum mansions, particularly those in Natchez, are singularly unrepresentative. Most white Mississippians lived under much more modest, frontier-like conditions. Further, the Delta, the area of the state most typically associated with cotton production, did not come under broad cultivation until the late nineteenth century. Whatever the average white Mississippian's economic relationship to the South's peculiar institution, the white population in the decades before the Civil War largely viewed slavery as a positive good and almost universally supported white supremacy as a doctrine and political program. The state's African American population, of course, rejected these ideas and constructed beliefs and practices that told a much different story of their aspirations and sense of how the world should be. Nevertheless, the white population's defense of slavery and white supremacy demanded and created myths and narratives that continue to influence the state and its people to the present day.

Most white Mississippians became ardent defenders of slavery after the 1830s, when federal treaties opened the northern two-thirds of the state to white settlement. In this period, Mississippi's black population rose dramatically, and white Mississippians, slave owners or not, largely came to believe that control of the enslaved population constituted a vital state interest. From the 1830s through the coming of the Civil War, white Mississippians, like other southerners, grew increasingly sensitive to northern and international criticism of the region's manners and institutions.

Mississippi had a vigorously competitive two-party system into the 1850s, but the polarization caused by the politics of slavery fractured the Mississippi Whigs so completely that for many generations the memory of an antebellum two-party system disappeared beneath exhortations that all white Mississippians had always shared the same basic political faith. The state cast its lot with the Confederacy, experienced what whites perceived as a galling and inexplicable defeat, and by the end of the century joined the rest of the white South in remembering the experience as a tragic Lost Cause. Such myths were not without foundation. Battle and disease killed thousands of Mississippians; thousands more returned maimed. Memories of civilian hardship in cities burned or besieged by Union forces lingered well into the twentieth century. Particularly with Jefferson Davis's postwar residence at Beauvoir on the Gulf Coast, many Mississippians came to believe that they had a special responsibility for ensuring that the Confederate experience was piously remembered. Conversely, black Mississippians regarded Confederate defeat as the deliverance for which they had long hoped.

In the wake of the war, black Mississippians aspired to economic advancement and the enjoyment of basic civil rights. White Mississippians rejected these aspirations, and the state soon became nationally known for its commitment to racial segregation and white supremacy. White recollections of Reconstruction and its meaning became one of the state's most fundamental and orthodox tenets. For more than a century after the Civil War, one of the most enduring Mississippi narratives was that of Reconstruction as a carnival of vice and folly. This impression of Reconstruction animated generations of white Mississippians and seemed

M

to offer self-evident proof that black Mississippians had no capacity for self-government. At the same time, the vociferousness with which the state's newspapers, textbooks, and politicians denounced Reconstruction persuaded many black Mississippians that most whites would never accept African American political participation. During the late nineteenth century, white Mississippians searched for the meaning of Confederate defeat and how to make sense of that legacy as well as the recent and frightening insistence by black Mississippians that they deserved the same constitutional rights and economic opportunities as did whites.

Following Reconstruction certain stories became staples of white belief: the Civil War was a response to northern interference and invasion; during the war, the loyalty and docility of slaves offered touching evidence of the essential benignity of the institution; Reconstruction was a misguided festival of corruption that forever proved the folly of black political participation; a group of valiant white Democrats, the Redeemers, restored democracy and offered the only safe political leadership for the state; and finally, both races found segregation the best way to handle race relations. At the same time, both native whites and many outsiders wished to see in Mississippi some of the remnants of a way of life that elsewhere was gone with the wind. These accounts stressed the courtly manners and hospitality of the state's residents and commonly presented slaveholding as admirable and enviable. Mississippi suffragist Belle Kearney's memoir, *A Slaveholder's Daughter* (1900), neatly summarizes what became a widely held if exaggerated view of a "very rich and very proud" Old South: "Its wealth consisted of slaves and plantations. Its pride was masterful from a consciousness of power. The customs of society retained the color of older European civilization, although the affairs of state were conducted according to the ideals of a radical democracy. Its social structure was simple, homogeneous." By the end of the nineteenth century, dominant voices in Mississippi society proclaimed that the state's white population stood as one in honoring the sacrifices of the Confederate generation and safeguarding the Jim Crow society that now seemed central to the Mississippi Way of Life.

Trent Brown
Missouri University of Science
and Technology

Dorothy Abbott, ed., *Mississippi Writers: Reflections of Childhood and Youth*, vol. 1, *Fiction* (1985); Joseph G. Baldwin, *Flush Times of Alabama and Mississippi* (1853); Marion Barnwell, ed., *A Place Called Mississippi: Collected Narratives* (1997); Bradley G. Bond, ed., *Mississippi: A Documentary History* (2003); Paul Conkin, *Journal of Southern History* (February 1998); Fred Hobson, *Southern Cultures* (Spring 2000); Belle Kearney, *A Slaveholder's Daughter* (1900); James W. Loewen and Charles Sallis, eds., *Mississippi: Conflict and Change* (1974).

Myths and Representations since 1900

Especially since the end of the nineteenth century and for good or for ill, the state of Mississippi has been viewed as particularly and intensely southern. The state's name conjures up a variety of intense images: stately Natchez homes, Delta plantations, cotton fields, and magnolias; demagogic politics, racism, poverty, hardship, and want; anti-intellectualism alongside stunning achievements in creative writing and music; searing images of violent resistance to social change along with an intense concern with manners, hospitality, and courtesy. For much of the twentieth century many other Americans and not a few Mississippians and former Mississippians viewed the state as backward if not actually evil. "Everybody knows about Mississippi," sang Nina Simone in 1963, the same year that Bob Dylan declared that he wasn't "a-goin' down to Oxford town." More than most other states, Mississippi has generated sharp and often dissonant narratives and myths: the land where a blues musician might offer his soul to the devil at a crossroads, the most southern place on earth, the worst state in America to be black, a land the ambitious leave, a place that offers a warm Magnolia State welcome and grace and sense of place, a land of slow-paced down-home living and traditional values—and more recently a place attempting to preserve the best of its customs and culture while coming to terms with and perhaps overcoming the tragic and painful legacies of its past.

Many iconic images and impressions of Mississippi seem indistinguishable from broader southern myths and narratives: sharp and lingering memories of the Civil War as a tragic Lost Cause; front-porch hospitality, storytelling, and iconic southern foods such as fried chicken, iced tea, greens, and a variety of dishes involving pork and corn; an enthusiasm for sports, particularly football, amounting practically to a civil religion; evangelical Christianity, religious revivals, and river baptisms; mules, cotton fields, country stores, a love of the outdoors and the traditions of fishing and hunting, especially such landmarks as the opening day of deer season, and a pattern of life still influenced by rural and agricultural ways; and a lingering respect for traditionally defined roles for men and women, manifesting themselves in ways such as a veneration of military service for men and a respect for beauty pageants.

Scholars have long argued that whatever it means to be southern, Mississippi is it. Historian Dunbar Rowland's admiring *Mississippi: The Heart of the South* (1925) represented what was by the twentieth century a common view of the state. John Shelton Reed often points out that almost any definition of the South today begins with Mississippi and Alabama and moves out. Fred Hobson has written that "Mississippi is the guts of the beast, the stomach with a Bible Belt wrapped around it. . . . Mississippi . . . is visceral."

Indeed, some have argued that Mississippi images have overly influenced people's impressions of the larger South: Paul Conkin notes that in talking about the South, some people really mean "a South largely defined by Alabama and Mississippi . . . or even the area around Oxford, Mississippi."

As with any stock of myths and narratives, many of those generated by Mississippians are quite self-conscious and serve a variety of ends. Certainly since the late 1800s Mississippians have engaged in very deliberate acts of memorialization and assertions of identity. Obvious examples would include the Confederate monuments that stand in front of many of the state's courthouses, joined later in the twentieth century by memorials to those who died in later wars. Many Mississippians not only deeply prize kinship and family ties but also avidly trace their genealogy at local and state historical societies and more recently via the Internet. Because of their interest in tradition, custom, and history, Mississippians are sometimes accused of living in the past. But Mississippians' interest in the past and the way that it is remembered have always been very closely tied to arguments about the present and its values, whether the issue is the design of the state flag or the erection of memorials to heroes of the civil rights movement. As with many traditions, Mississippi's are often of relatively recent vintage, beginning with the commonly held idea that Mississippi's customs, institutions, and general way of life have always existed in what is basically their present form. Like all people's myths and narratives of identity, those generated by Mississippians explain to themselves and others their views of the world and how it works.

White Mississippians have generated most of the memorials, textual or otherwise, that laud the state's virtues. Black Mississippians have understandably been less praiseful of a place that long denied them basic civil rights, decency, and respect. For example, Richard Wright's novels and autobiographical writings and Anne Moody's memoir *Coming of Age in Mississippi* (1968) demonstrate that neither time nor distance could provoke nostalgia for the place they were born. James Meredith, on the other hand, expressed the complex mixed feelings that many other black Mississippians have held as he described coming home: "There is the feeling of joy . . . to enter the land of my fathers, the land of my birth, the only land in which I feel at home. . . . There is a feeling of sadness . . . because I am immediately aware of the special subhuman role that I must play, because I am a Negro, or die. [And] I feel love because I have always felt that Mississippi belonged to me and one must love what is his." Since the mid-twentieth century Mississippians have produced a flood of memoirs and fictional works about their home state. While residents' experiences of race vary widely, of course, one notable feature of these narratives is that they show that Mississippians of all races, especially in rural areas, praised and valued and experienced many things in common—an attraction to the land, attention to agricultural rhythms, and church, family, and kinship ties. These

factors and many others provided a texture to everyday life that was more alike than most Mississippians recognized.

Myths and representations of Mississippi have long followed a broader national pattern of viewing the South in conflicting and sometimes irreconcilable ways. Are the state and the region the last refuge of a religious sensibility or of a broader way of life uncorrupted by twentieth-century materialism and consumerism? Is Mississippi somehow a cultural and social backwater, a place that has failed to evolve and progress? Or is the state perhaps the nation's pathological abyss in which one can view cracked and warped perversions of American dreams and aspirations? As with any symbols or cultural practices, those created by and about Mississippians are open to multiple interpretations. One example might be the powerful if sometimes frustratingly amorphous confection of manners and etiquette noticed by Mississippians and other Americans alike. These manners, such as respect for one's elders and regard for kin and neighbors, have often drawn favorable comment, while other practices, such as Jim Crow racial etiquette, stultifying gender roles, and an emphasis on hierarchy and rank, have been central to a much less flattering image of southern culture. This Janus-faced presentation, or duality, one might call it, was observed by Bernard Lafayette, a cofounder of the Student Nonviolent Coordinating Committee, a 1960s civil rights organization, as he recollected his first visit to the state: "The first sign I saw was a huge billboard that said, 'Welcome to Mississippi, the Magnolia State,' and a beautiful white magnolia blossom. . . . [T]he next sign I saw said, 'Prepare to Meet Thy God.'"

While white Mississippians have long winced at one-dimensional representations of the state, other Americans and many black Mississippians have unquestionably associated the state with a fundamental racial consciousness and commitment to white supremacy that by the 1960s seemed anachronistic compared even to other states of the Deep South. Civil rights worker Robert Moses said that Mississippi in 1964 was "a little apartheid." The state's name, then, long served as shorthand for racial discrimination. Perhaps understandably, many Mississippians have resented the broad strokes in which the state has been painted, insisting that there is more to Mississippi than racial discrimination. Many of these Mississippians praise themselves for their devotion to family, church, and community. In their eyes, the state has held firm to values, manners, and practices of which the rest of the nation has lost sight. Like many Mississippi self-images, devotion to these practices can be seen as a negative as well as a positive. To outsiders, the state can feel clannish and exclusive in its definition of community and hostile to those who challenge or simply do not share the majority's adherence to conservative values and evangelical Christianity. One finds this sense of Mississippi as essentially one homogeneous community in the Works Progress Administration's *Guide to Mississippi* (1938), which described the state as "the great neighborhood called Mississippi, a neighborhood where the birthright of knowing the drive of the plow in the puissant earth binds the sections more closely than geographical boundaries, a neighborhood of earth-rooted individuals who know and understand one another."

The state and its customs, particularly Jim Crow and the politics associated with racial segregation, attracted the attention of social scientists in the 1930s and 1940s. John Dollard's *Caste and Class in a Southern Town* (1937), a study of "Southerntown" (actually Indianola) and Hortense Pow-dermaker's *After Freedom: A Cultural Study in the Deep South* (1939), another study of Indianola, helped circulate the image of Mississippi as race-obsessed and caste-ridden. Other critics were more vociferous if less scholarly. H. L. Mencken, while a fan of the values that he believed the Old South to embody, enjoyed tweaking Mississippi in the 1920s and 1930s, consistently terming it the most "barbaric" state in the Union. Most white Mississippians dismissed this criticism, while some, such as David Cohn, in *Where I Was Born and Raised* (1948), and William Alexander Percy, in *Lanterns on the Levee: Recollections of a Planter's Son* (1941), attempted to explain the state and its customs to a national audience.

Business and progressive interests in Mississippi have long been sensitive to the stereotypes that other Americans hold about the state. Campaigns in the 1930s such as Gov. Hugh White's Balance Agriculture with Industry aimed to convince investors that the state's folkways could accommodate the development of business. By the 1950s and 1960s many white Mississippians certainly knew that in the eyes of other Americans, the state conjured up images not only of violent resistance to civil rights but also of the rejection of broader American myths of equality, opportunity, and progress. As newspapers and television began covering the civil rights movement in Mississippi and the rest of the South, black and white Mississippians were well aware of the light that the media threw on their state and its customs. Many white Mississippians maintained that the civil rights movement was the product of outside agitators—a way of preserving their belief that black Mississippians were largely content with the Mississippi Way of Life. White Mississippians also commonly declared that Yankees unfairly maligned and picked on the state, failing to see their own prejudices and provincialisms. Some Mississippians' automobiles displayed license plates declaring that Mississippi was "The Most Lied about State in the Union." The state song, "Go, Mississippi," adopted by the legislature in 1962, clearly responds to official white Mississippi's impressions of outside criticism: the state is "on the right track," "cannot go wrong"; "ev'rything's fine," and the state is "leading the show." At the time the song was adopted, only the last assertion seemed indisputable—and not necessarily in a positive way.

Mississippi has always produced its own dissenters and critics. In the 1960s, however, dissent less often produced progressive change than excited popular denunciation that merely confirmed many existing conceptions regarding the state. In the wake of what he perceived as the failure of the state's political leadership during the integration of the University of Mississippi, history professor James W. Silver wrote *Mississippi: The Closed Society* (1964). For that, Silver was hounded from the state. Hodding Carter's *So the Heffners Left McComb* (1965) seemed to most readers not the story of one family's attempt to understand the social change in their community but rather a familiar tale of Mississippi intolerance. Other critical voices held out hope not only that Mississippi might accept social change but also that the state might have lessons to teach the rest of the nation.

Mississippi's musical and literary traditions have provided powerful and not always flattering representations of the state to the nation and the world. Blues lyrics, to take one example, provide a powerful testimony of the meaning of Mississippi to many of its black citizens. Similarly, for much of the twentieth century, the state's writers commonly took as their material Mississippi's struggles with race and poverty and the weight of the past on the present. To many readers, Yoknapatawpha County is Mississippi, with Thomas Sutpen, Quentin Compson, and Joe Christmas all representing something true about the state's encounter with history. Most white Mississippians scorned William Faulkner and other Mississippi writers such as Richard Wright during their most productive years for their critical representations of the state. For several decades, Willie Morris made a career of reflecting on the state's recent past and his feelings about it. From his father's admonition to leave the state for the better educational opportunities that Texas provided to his encounter with Robert Frost during which he said that Mississippi was the worst state in the Union, Morris relished examining and discussing the history of his family and state.

Artists from outside the state also helped to fashion myths and representations of Mississippi. Bob Dylan's "Oxford Town" casts a familiar image of white Mississippians as violent, prejudiced, and essentially un-American. On the other hand, Jerry Jeff Walker's "Mississippi, You're on My Mind" reminds us that not all representations of Mississippi center on race. That song presents the state's hold on the narrator via a procession of familiar images: barbed wire fences, honeysuckle, tar paper shacks, John Deere tractors, lazy dogs, and oven-like heat. Along with press and television coverage of the state, Hollywood has created and perpetuated lasting images of Mississippi. As with many other movie representations of the South, those of Mississippi tended to fall into one of two broad categories: comic, sassy, colorful, and favorable, such as *Crimes of the Heart* (1986), or coarse, crude, racist, and unregenerate, such as *In the Heat of the Night* (1967) and *Mississippi Burning* (1988), which is also notable for its condescending view of black Mississippians as powerless but prayerful.

In recent years many Mississippians have hoped that the state can escape, atone for, or simply stop thinking and talking about its history of racial prejudice and discrimination. In some accounts, the state has arrived at a sort of promised land beyond racism, and if Mississippi is not yet a beloved community of racial harmony, it is at least a workable and useful model of honest attempts at racial reconciliation and a day-to-day ability to live and work together. Attempts to carry myths and representations of Mississippi beyond stories of black-white conflict surely are not without merit. Characterizations of the state's population and history as Anglo-Saxon versus African American do not take into account the plain fact that the state has always been home to a variety of people with stories about themselves and their history that sometimes stand as counternarratives to and at other times weave easily into familiar Mississippi stories. Broader, more inclusive, and perhaps more workable narratives of Mississippi might include the long-standing communities of Chinese and Italians in the Delta, Choctaw Indians in eastern Mississippi, Southern and Eastern Europeans and Vietnamese on the Gulf Coast, and an increasing number of Spanish-speaking residents.

Recent years have seen a great deal of good-faith effort to craft narratives and representations of Mississippi that are race-neutral if not colorblind. The state's media, universities, and most public forums honor Mississippi's writers, musicians, and other public figures through the lens of race. Mississippians have begun incorporating the civil rights movement into the stories they tell about who they are. The Mississippi Department of Archives and History's State Historical Marker program has commemorated more than eight hundred significant people, places, and events, a large number of which focus on black Mississippians' experiences and history. The state's Department of Travel and Tourism, to take another example, offers resources for those interested in visiting sites related to Mississippi's African American history, including frank discussions of the civil rights movement that would have been unthinkable in a state publication a generation or two ago.

One of the clearest ongoing arguments over narratives and representations of the state is the extent to which past racial inequities deserve public attention and remediation. Perhaps the best reason not to declare a moratorium on the discussion of race in the state in that for most of Mississippi's history, the conversation was very much one-sided. Black Mississippians long formed their own judgments regarding the state and its promise. Until recently, however, those views were largely confined within the black community, as the danger of expressing discontent with the status quo outweighed the likelihood of effecting change. The Great Migration is itself a testimony to many black Mississippians' view of the state as an unpromising land, but census figures have begun to show an African American return migration to the state, itself a commentary on the state's image. African Americans' narratives of Mississippi have recently displayed an increasing desire to claim the state as their own and on their own terms. W. Ralph Eubanks's *Ever Is a Long Time* (2003) describes the author's attempts to learn about the history of the state during the 1960s, a story his parents shielded from him as he grew up during those years. Clifton L. Taulbert's *Once upon a Time When We Were Colored* (1989) tells a story of warmth, community, and identity during the Jim Crow years and is not far removed from other celebrations of growing up in rural Mississippi. Musician Afroman's "Mississippi" brags of his sexual exploits but also expresses pleasant surprise that he attracts white fans, possibly because of their shared love for marijuana. And rapper David Banner's "Mississippi" is the state "where yo grandmamma from" and invites the listener, "Now come on home get you somethin' to eat." Conversely, he also describes the state as a place "where a flag means more than me."

The state flag controversy is an indication that Mississippi still struggles to craft inclusive narratives of community and identity. On one level, of course, many white Mississippians see the argument as a referendum not so much on a particular flag as on whether they accept the version of the state's history that other people insist that the flag represents. Symbols such as the state flag are highly meaningful within and across various communities of Mississippians, even if those meanings are highly contested. Mississippians argue about the meaning of flags, statues, college mascots, and street names, and those arguments are often so heated because these symbols do not have absolute meanings.

Many Mississippians recognize that the state continues to have an image problem. While some merely resent what they consider an inaccurate and exaggerated stereotype, others make efforts to correct it. Indeed, a state advertising agency's public relations campaign, "Mississippi . . . Believe It!," promotes the state's achievements in the arts, sports, science, and technology.

Mississippians continue actively to craft representations of and stories about the state. Many have learned that money can be made in marketing the state as a provider of culture, especially literature, music, and history. Where the state once had a reputation for shunning outsiders, Mississippians now avidly seek patrons to gamble in casinos and to make movies in picturesque small towns. Every year, the calendar is filled with festivals, homecomings, and reunions, drawing on and promoting an image of the state as family and kin. Tourists and native Mississippians come to century-old events such as the Neshoba County Fair and to decades-old celebrations such as the Natchez Pilgrimage as well as to events of more recent vintage, such as the Medgar Evers Homecoming Celebration, the Mississippi Delta Blues and Heritage Festival, or the Oxford Conference for the Book. Mississippians have discovered that culture is a commodity that can be marketed to burnish the state's image to investors as well as cultural arbiters. Even authenticity can be marketed or even created. Today, tourists come to Mississippi to find the "real South," and entrepreneurs and local people have learned to supply it.

Unflattering representations of Mississippi continue to appear in the media, as the state consistently ranks near the top (or bottom, as the case may be) in national rankings of obesity, teenage pregnancy, and venereal disease. Unfairly or not, to many other Americans, the state's name still conjures up images of the 1962 riot in Oxford or the 1964 murders of civil rights workers Andrew Goodman, James Chaney, and Michael Schwerner in Neshoba County. A younger generation of Americans became familiar with that image of the state from *Eyes on the Prize*, a history of the civil rights movement televised on PBS in 1987. Many Mississippians complain that the rest of the country and the world view the state wrongly, that the Mythic Mississippi that Hollywood, the media, and many academics see is harsh and distorted and bears little resemblance to the state today. However, the state's past does not change simply because current conditions have changed. Myths and representations are often tenacious and are famously oblivious to fact and reason. So Mississippians continue to tell about themselves and their culture. Whenever the national spotlight shines on the state, many residents attempt to show the rest of the country a New Mississippi, one in which the real story is the state's "racial evolution" and not its "murderous past," as an Associated Press story on the 2008 presidential debate in Oxford put it. However they wish its story to be told, those who call Mississippi home can broadly agree with Faulkner's reflection on the state: "You don't love because; you love despite; not for the virtues, but despite the faults."

Trent Brown
Missouri University of Science
and Technology

Dorothy Abbott, ed., *Mississippi Writers: Reflections of Childhood and Youth*, vol. 1, *Fiction* (1985); Charles Angoff and H. L. Mencken, *The American Mercury* (September, October, and November 1931); Marion Barnwell, ed., *A Place Called Mississippi: Collected Narratives* (1997); Bradley G. Bond, ed., *Mississippi: A Documentary History* (2003); Hodding Carter, *So the Heffners Left McComb* (1965); David Cohn, *Where I Was Born and Raised* (1948); Paul Conkin, *Journal of Southern History* (February 1998); John Dollard, *Caste and Class in a Southern Town* (1937); W. Ralph Eubanks, *Ever Is a Long Time* (2003); Federal Writers' Project of the Works Progress Administration, *Mississippi: The WPA Guide to the Magnolia State* (1938); Fred Hobson, *Southern Cultures* (Spring 2000); Bernard Lafayette, in *Cornbread Nation 4: The Best of Southern Food Writing* (2008); James W. Loewen and Charles Sallis, eds., *Mississippi: Conflict and Change* (1974); James Meredith with William Doyle, *A Mission from God: A Memoir and Challenge for America* (2012); Anne Moody, *Coming of Age in Mississippi* (1968); William Alexander Percy, *Lanterns on the Levee: Recollections of a Planter's Son* (1941); Willie Morris, *North toward Home* (1967); Willie Morris, *Terrains of the Heart and Other Essays on Home* (1981); Hortense Powdermaker, *After Freedom: A Cultural Study in the Deep South* (1939); John Shelton Reed, *My Tears Spoiled My Aim and Other Reflections on Southern Culture*, 1993; Dunbar Rowland, *Mississippi: The Heart of the South* (1925); James W. Silver, *Mississippi: The Closed Society* (1964); Clifton L. Taulbert, *Once upon a Time When We Were Colored* (1989); Richard Wright, *Black Boy* (1946); Richard Wright, *Uncle Tom's Children* (1938).

N

Nanih Waiya

Rising a majestic 25 feet out of the Mississippi earth is an enormous mound measuring 218 feet by 140 feet that has been celebrated for centuries as a legendary birthplace of Choctaw civilization. Located near Louisville in Winston County, Nanih Waiya is among the most mysterious and enticing Native American sites in the southeastern United States. The site actually encompasses two mounds: the main (or temple) mound and the nearby Nanih Waiya Cave, which may be the setting for the Choctaw emergence myth. At one time the site was enclosed by an earthen embankment and moat, though only a short segment remains.

The emergence myth describes the birth of several southeastern tribes. When humans were first created, they were too weak to survive in the elements and remained protected inside the Mother Mound until they grew stronger. The first to emerge were the Creek, who dried themselves on the side of the mound and began to make their way toward the east.

The next to emerge were the Cherokee, who looked to find the trail left by the Creek. The Creek, however, had been careless while smoking tobacco and caused a fire that destroyed their path. The Cherokee decided to turn north and settle. They were followed by the Chickasaw, who also chose the northern path. Finally came the Choctaw, who chose not to migrate but to remain near the mound.

Archeological evidence indicates that the mound was first built in the Middle Woodland period (approximately AD 0–300) and remained occupied until about AD 700. Historical data suggest that the modern Choctaw tribe moved to the Mississippi area in the late 1500s or early 1600s. By the eighteenth century the Choctaw began to venerate the site as an earth mother. However, Choctaw tradition also included another legend that described the Choctaw as immigrants to the area. Historical evidence tends to support the immigrant theory: the Choctaw were most likely a confederacy of groups that survived the diseases brought to Mississippi by Europeans.

Although the immigration legend remained a part of Choctaw tradition, Nanih Waiya was still regarded as Choctaw sacred ground. In 1828 Choctaw leader Greenwood LeFlore called a tribal assembly at Nanih Waiya to discuss the threat posed by growing numbers of white settlers. However, LeFlore's efforts to maintain Choctaw control of the site failed. The 1830 Treaty of Dancing Rabbit Creek, which provided for the Removal of the Choctaw, and subsequent US government pressure eventually coerced the Choctaw to give up their Mother Mound.

The antebellum period ushered in an influx of white settlers as well as a dependence on agriculture. This new industry began slowly to erode the Nanih Waiya site, and an 1854 visitor noted that plows had leveled areas of the mound.

Nanih Waiya received a new lease on life when twentieth-century preservationists organized movements focused on native sites. In 1959 the Luke family sold the site to the Mississippi State Park Commission. The site opened to visitors in 1962 and was added to the National Register of Historic Places nine years later. In 2006, the Mississippi legislature returned control of the site to the Luke family, and T. W. Luke deeded it to the state on the condition that it be maintained as a park. In 2008, the Luke Family deeded control to the Mississippi Band of Choctaw Indians.

As the mound enters its third millennium, its future once again is in jeopardy. In an age of government budget cuts, the conservation of Nanih Waiya remains uncertain. Yet despite its many trials, the old mound still greets the Mississippi morning as it has for the past two thousand years.

Jodie Cummings
Ridgeland, Mississippi

Kenneth H. Carleton, *Common Ground Magazine* 1 (Spring 1996); Kenneth H. Carleton, *Mississippi Archaeology* 34 (1999); Heather Jackson, *Winston County Journal* (23 December 2004); George E. Lankford, ed., *Native American Legends* (1987); Mississippi Band of Choctaw Indians website, www.choctaw.org; National Park Service website, www.cr.nps.gov; National Register of Historic Places website, www.nationalregister ofhistoricplaces.com.

Narmour and Smith
Musicians

Narmour and Smith was a popular old-time string band in the 1920s and 1930s. Fiddler William Thomas Narmour was born in Ackerman, Mississippi, on 22 March 1889. His family moved to Carroll County when he was seven, and he lived there the remainder of his life. Narmour first learned to play on a cigar box fiddle built for him by his father, who was also a fiddler, and was "discovered" by OKeh Records at the 1927 Winona Fiddle Contest. Together with guitarist and neighbor Shellie Walton Smith, born on 26 November 1895, Narmour recorded more than fifty 78s between 1928 and 1934, first for OKeh Records and after its collapse for Victor. Narmour and Smith recorded during five sessions—one in Memphis, two in Atlanta, one in New York, and one in San Antonio. Smith played guitar on all these sides except "Rose Waltz," where he and Narmour swapped instruments.

Their records sold very well. "Carroll County Blues," their most popular tune, was one of the biggest-selling records of 1929. It remains a standard for old-time fiddlers all over the country and can still be heard frequently today at fiddler's conventions and old-time jams. Other influential tunes include "Little Star" and "Charleston #1," "Charleston #2," and "Charleston #3," named for the county seat of neighboring Tallahatchie County. OKeh promoted Narmour and Smith's 78s by including them in a series of "Medicine Show" recordings made in September 1929 with other OKeh artists such as Emmett Miller and the Georgia Crackers, Fiddlin' John Carson, slide guitarist Frank Hutchison, and pianist Bud Blue. One measure of their popularity was their longevity. After OKeh collapsed, Narmour and Smith signed with Victor Records in 1934, rerecording sixteen of their most popular tunes. Narmour and Smith's recordings seem to have been most popular in Texas, Mexico, and the West. They continued to play and record long after most string bands had been retired by the Great Depression.

Both musicians returned to Carroll County after their recording careers ended.

Narmour played locally in later years but never again with Smith, who stopped playing after the birth of his children. Willie Narmour farmed, drove a school bus, and owned a garage in Avalon until his death on 24 March 1961. Shell Smith farmed and worked as a high school custodian prior to his death on 28 August 1968. In 2014 Narmour and Smith were honored with a marker on the Mississippi Country Music Trail on Lexington Street in Carrollton.

Edward McAllister

Belhaven University

Harry Bolick website, www.harrybolick.com; David Freeman, *Mississippi String Bands*, vols. 1 and 2 (1998), liner notes; Mississippi Country Music Trail website, ww.mscountrymusictrail.org.

Nash, Diane
(b. 1938) Activist

Diane Judith Nash was a leader in the civil rights movement. Though not a Mississippian, Nash was integral to the movement in the state, from the Freedom Rides of 1961 to later work on voter registration drives and citizenship schools.

Born into a middle-class Chicago family on 15 May 1938, Nash grew up a devout Catholic and considered devoting her life to the church. She studied English at Howard University before transferring to Nashville's Fisk University in 1959. Appalled by segregation in the city, she began to study nonviolence with James Lawson, a theology student at Vanderbilt University, as well as at the Highlander Folk School with activists such as Rosa Parks and Septima Clark. Students from Nashville sought to challenge segregation in department stores with whites-only eating facilities. Two days after a sit-in by North Carolina A&T State students in Greensboro on 1 February 1960, the already-trained Nashville students began a massive effort to desegregate the city's lunch counters, with Nash devoting herself to recruiting other students for direct action while frequently participating in the sit-ins. An eloquent public speaker, Nash became the unofficial spokesperson for the Nashville group.

Nash played an important role in the April 1960 founding of the Student Nonviolent Coordinating Committee (SNCC) and advocated the group's independence from existing civil rights organizations such as the National Association for the Advancement of Colored People and the Southern Christian Leadership Conference (SCLC). At SNCC's inception, Nash served as the unofficial leader of the direct action branch.

Nash's first work in Mississippi occurred in 1961, when she received word that the Congress of Racial Equality planned to halt the Freedom Rides after violent attacks on activists in Birmingham. Nash wanted to show that the movement would not be halted by violence and recruited other veterans of the Nashville sit-in movement to continue the planned ride through Mississippi to New Orleans. Two days after Nash and other Freedom Riders were arrested and transported by the police to the state line, they returned to Birmingham and resumed the ride, this time reaching Jackson before being arrested. They spent thirty-nine days imprisoned at Parchman Prison Farm, a time that unified them and strengthened their dedication to the movement.

Following her imprisonment, Nash and James Bevel, whom she married in 1962, opened the SNCC office in Jackson. They sought to implement a plan they termed "Move on Mississippi," in which all segregated institutions would face challenges from SNCC. In the fall of 1961 Nash and other SNCC members worked to empower local high school and college students to take direct action, founding the first "freedom house" on Rose Street in Jackson. The Jackson nonviolent movement began many projects, such as picketing the segregated Mississippi State Fair, challenging segregated waiting rooms in bus stations, and in the spring and summer of 1962, organizing a boycott of the city bus system, which remained unconstitutionally segregated. For her involvement in encouraging high school students to buy bus tickets and then sit in white waiting rooms, Nash was arrested for contributing to the delinquency of minors. In April 1962, facing the prospect of two years in jail, she decided not to appeal: "This will be a black child born in Mississippi and thus wherever he is born he will be in prison. I believe that if I go to jail now it may help hasten the day when my child and all children will be free." Ultimately, she spent ten days in jail.

The SCLC hired Nash and Bevel in 1961. She remained a member of the organization's staff until 1965, working with the student wing of the movement and applying her experience in the Nashville movement and with SNCC. She helped to organize the 1963 March on Washington, and she and Bevel served as the key architects of the movement's Selma voting rights campaign. She later questioned SCLC's male-dominated leadership structure, recalling, "I never considered Dr. King my leader. I always considered myself at his side and I considered him at my side. I was going to do what the spirit told me to do. So If I had a leader, that was my leader." In addition, Nash distanced herself from SNCC with the organization's turn from nonviolent direct action to Black Power in 1965 under the leadership of Stokely Carmichael. With her lifelong dedication to nonviolence, Nash also became active in the anti–Vietnam War movement.

Nash has received numerous honors, among them the SCLC Rosa Parks Award, the Distinguished American Award from the John F. Kennedy Library, and the Lyndon B. Johnson Award for Leadership in Civil Rights.

Nash and Bevel divorced after having two children. She lives in Chicago and remains politically active. Tessa Thompson portrayed her in the movie *Selma* (2014). In March 2015, on the fiftieth anniversary of the March on Selma, she reflected, "It took many thousands of people to make the changes that we made," she says, "people whose names we'll never know. They'll never get credit for the sacrifices they've made, but I remember them."

Becca Walton
University of Mississippi

Raymond Arsenault, *Freedom Riders: 1961 and the Struggle for Racial Justice* (2006); "Diane Nash, Civil Rights Movement Leader, Reflects on Selma" (5 March 2015), ABC7 website, abc7chicago.com; John Dittmer, *Local People: The Struggle for Civil Rights in Mississippi* (1994); Howard Dukes, *South Bend Tribune* (16 January 2005); David Halberstam, *The Children* (1999); Aldon Morris, *The Origins of the Civil Rights Movement: Black Communities Organizing for Change* (1984); Charles M. Payne, *I've Got the Light of Freedom: The Organizing Tradition and the Mississippi Freedom Struggle* (1995).

Natchez Civil Rights Movement

The civil rights movement came later in Natchez than in many of Mississippi's other towns and cities but had moments of drama and violence, made demands with clarity and conviction, and ended with considerable success. After George Metcalfe, the president of the Natchez chapter of the National Association for the Advancement of Colored People (NAACP), survived a nearly fatal car bombing, Natchez's African American community began a boycott of white-owned businesses that ended late in 1965 with an agreement that stood as a rather dramatic success in mid-1960s Mississippi.

A group of leaders had started the city's chapter of the NAACP in the 1940s and sustained it through the 1950s and early 1960s. Male and female church leaders and owners of businesses such as funeral homes, groceries, and the African American newspaper, the *Bluff City Bulletin*, made up much of the early NAACP membership. Activists called for legal and political equality, job training, and improvements in education.

On 27 August 1965 Metcalfe, a union member who worked at Armstrong Tire and Rubber, was seriously injured when his car exploded at the Armstrong plant. The longtime NAACP leader had already been in the news twice that week, once for appearing at a school board meeting to ask that Natchez implement the Supreme Court's decade-old *Brown v. Board of Education* decision by desegregating its schools, once for leading a boycott against the Jitney Jungle stores owned by Mayor John Nosser.

The assault on Metcalfe inspired the local civil rights community to call in statewide leaders, especially NAACP field secretary Charles Evers, and the group quickly issued a list of demands: the Board of Aldermen should denounce the Ku Klux Klan and the Citizens' Council; the police should end acts of brutality and offer protection for African American funerals; the school board should immediately desegregate the schools; the welfare and social security offices should stop withholding or threatening to withhold checks from people involved in protests; store employees should use the courtesy titles *Mr.*, *Mrs.*, and *Miss* when dealing with all customers; and stores should hire more African American employees. In addition, the city should hire African Americans, desegregate swimming pools and parks, appoint African Americans to the school board, equalize services such as sewers and street sweeping in all neighborhoods, enact new housing standards to govern relations between landlords and renters, and guarantee that all citizens could engage in free speech and political protest without the fear of arrest.

At least two groups of activists were at work in Natchez—the NAACP, which continued to call for discussions with

N

the Natchez aldermen, and younger protesters, including Dorie Ladner, Rudy Shields, and Chuck McDew from the Council of Federated Organizations, who combined voter registration with marching, picketing, and other forms of direct action. Both groups called on African Americans in Natchez and Adams County to boycott white-owned businesses until the city complied with the activists' demands. The mayor and aldermen, who had long envisioned Natchez as an exceptionally peaceful community, called for calm and planned negotiations with protest leaders but stressed that they would not negotiate under the threat of violence. Scattered violence, especially bombings and rock-throwing incidents, and fears that it would escalate inspired Gov. Paul Johnson to send six units of the Mississippi National Guard to the city—the first time the state had used the Guard since the fall of 1962 at the University of Mississippi.

Street picketing continued in September and October 1965, with dozens of protesters arrested every day for parading without a permit. The city's jail overflowed, and city police started sending some prisoners to Parchman Prison.

In October and again in early December, protest leaders Evers, minister Shead Baldwin, and businessman Archie Curtis met with the Natchez aldermen. The first meeting failed when city officials declared that many of the protest demands fell outside their control, so the boycott continued, with African Americans staying away from the downtown shopping area. Many Natchez whites wanted to crush the boycott and its leaders, whom they labeled "outside agitators." At a November meeting of about 175 businesspeople affiliated with the Chamber of Commerce, some white leaders suggested firing all African Americans, including household workers, who participated in the boycott. Another group that started in Natchez, the Americans for the Preservation of the White Race, condemned the protests and called for Mississippi and Louisiana whites to take part in a "buy-in" campaign to shop in Natchez that would counteract the boycott. Many business leaders, however, wanted the protests to end and hoped to restore what they could of the small city's peaceful reputation.

At the beginning of December 1965, city officials met again with protest leaders. On 4 December, the *Natchez Democrat* announced, "Agreement Reached Ending Negro Boycott in Natchez." The story detailed the city's plans to meet the demands point by point. According to Evers, "Everything we asked for we have gotten concessions on, and then some."

The end of the boycott certainly did not resolve all civil rights issues in the area. The NAACP and Student Nonviolent Coordinating Committee continued to disagree over protest strategy. Americans for the Preservation of the White Race took their buy-in strategy to nearby Fayette. Violence returned to Natchez in 1967 when NAACP member Wharlest Jackson was killed in a car bombing shortly after he had been promoted to a job once open only to whites at Armstrong Tire and Rubber. Still, the Natchez movement stands as a success in the sense that activists made specific demands with the support of the African American community and local authorities eventually agreed to meet those demands.

Ted Ownby
University of Mississippi

Marjorie Baroni Papers, Department of Archives and Special Collections, J. D. Williams Library, University of Mississippi; *Bluff City Bulletin*, 1964–65; Jack E. Davis, *Race against Time: Culture and Separation in Natchez since 1930* (2001); John Dittmer, *Local People: The Struggle for Civil Rights in Mississippi* (1994); Akinyele Omowale Umoja, *We Will Shoot Back: Armed Resistance in the Mississippi Freedom Movement* (2013).

Natchez Democrat

A daily newspaper located in Natchez, the *Natchez Democrat* was founded in 1865 by Capt. James W. Lambert and Paul A. Botto. A few months after the paper's establishment, Lambert bought Botto's interest and became the sole owner. Lambert and members of his family operated the newspaper until 1970, when it was purchased by James B. Boone Jr. of Tuscaloosa, Alabama. The newspaper is currently published by Natchez Newspapers, which is part of the Boone Newspaper publishing group.

As the city's leading newspaper, the *Natchez Democrat* has historically published local news and business and social information, celebrated local developments such as the Natchez Pilgrimage, and taken conservative stances on major political issues. Its editorials tended to fit historian Jack Davis's argument that Natchez leaders envisioned their community as exceptionally peaceful, marked by affection and respect among all community members. In 1954 James Lambert criticized the *Brown v. Board of Education* decision for overstepping the proper role of the judiciary. Perhaps more unusual, during a 1965 civil rights boycott, Lambert ran short front-page editorials calling for calm, condemning lawlessness, and taking pride in Natchez's white and African American community for avoiding riots and violence.

The newspaper is published every morning and covers Adams County and the nearby Mississippi counties of Franklin, Wilkinson, Amite, Claiborne, and Jefferson as well as Concordia Parish in Louisiana. Over the years the *Natchez Democrat* has established itself as an award-winning local newspaper. In the 2006 Mississippi Press Association Better Newspaper Contest the newspaper won twenty-four awards, including second place for general excellence in

Daily Division B and a first-place award for best editorial page. In 2016 its daily circulation was about 8,500.

Melissa Smith
Mississippi University for Women

Boone Newspapers website, www.boonenewspapers.com; *Natchez Democrat* website, www.natchezdemocrat.com.

Natchez Indians

Residing on the east side of the Mississippi River in present-day Adams County, the Natchez Indians played a significant role in colonial history, interacting with the French and English as well as with the region's other Native American groups. Documentation gathered before the breakup of the Natchez group in the mid-1730s reveals a matrilineal society supported by maize horticulture, fishing, hunting, and gathering. Once considered a ranked society split between what the French called "nobles" and "commoners," the Natchez ranks have more recently been interpreted as moieties, with one moiety having an elder-brother status in relation to the other moiety. French descriptions of elaborate tribal ceremonial activities serve as ethnographic examples for the interpretation of late prehistoric southeastern societies known only through archaeology.

The Natchez have been tentatively linked to the powerful sixteenth-century chiefdom known as Quigualtam, whose warriors harassed the de Soto expedition with a fleet of enormous wooden dugout canoes, some capable of transporting up to one hundred warriors. After de Soto's death in 1542 and the departure of his companions, no Europeans entered the Lower Mississippi Valley for more than a century. During this interval the Indian populations of the region experienced a severe demographic decline that continues to puzzle archaeologists. When the La Salle expedition traveled through this same area less than 150 years later, the populous mound-building chiefdoms of de Soto's time were gone. In their place were a few relatively small tribal groups such as the Natchez, Taensa, Tunica, and Quapaw.

Archaeology in southwestern Mississippi securely links the Natchez Indians of the French colonial era with the local prehistoric population that occupied ceremonial centers such as Emerald Mound and the Fatherland site, also known as the Grand Village of the Natchez. However, colonial accounts present a picture of a native society that was probably altered in significant ways from its prehistoric counterpart. The people the colonial writers called *the Natchez* were not a single ethnic group but a confederation representing speakers of two or more different languages. Attached to the core Natchez-speaking community during the 1720s were two small tribes, the Tiou and Grigra. Both of these groups probably spoke languages in the Tunican family, named for the Tunica group living on the Lower Yazoo River in the late seventeenth century. French colonists learned to differentiate between Natchez and the Tunican languages because the latter had the *r* sound, which was missing from Natchez languages. Another probable Tunican-speaking group, the Koroa, had a village a few miles downriver from the Natchez in La Salle's time, though the settlement was later abandoned. It is not known whether this Koroa group was temporarily part of the Natchez confederation. By forming confederacies, small tribal groups increased their odds of survival during the violent period of the English-driven Indian slave trade, Indian population depletion from European diseases such as smallpox, and the fierce eighteenth-century client warfare between pro-French and pro-English tribes.

The French observed the Great Sun, a Natchez chief, in his role as ceremonial leader and assumed that he was the ruler of the Natchez nation. In fact, however, political power in the Natchez confederacy was distributed among the chiefs of five villages or settlement districts: Flour, Tiou, Grigra, White Apple, and Jenzenaque. In response to the conflicting demands on the Natchez by French and English interests, the district chiefs negotiated autonomously with both colonial powers. By 1716, when the French established Fort Rosalie on the Natchez bluff, the Natchez group was divided in its allegiance to the two European nations.

Because of its distance from French ports at New Orleans and Mobile, the colony that grew up around Fort Rosalie depended on the Natchez Indians for food and other necessities, which the Natchez exchanged for guns, blankets, iron tools, and other European goods. As the local colony expanded to include two tobacco plantations, friction between the Natchez and French helped to sway the Natchez settlement districts toward alliances with the English. Assured by English traders of a reliable supply of merchandise to replace that coming from the French, the Natchez attacked the French colony on 28 November 1729. With the help of Indian allies, the French retaliated early the following year. In the war that followed, the Natchez people abandoned their homeland for refuge with pro-English groups including the Chickasaw, Creek, and Cherokee. Today, groups of Natchez descendants are recognized in South Carolina and Oklahoma.

James F. Barnett Jr.
Mississippi Department of
Archives and History

James F. Barnett Jr., *The Natchez Indians: A History to 1735* (2007); Antoine-Simone Le Page du Pratz, *The History of Louisiana or of the*

Western Parts of Virginia and Carolina (1774); John R. Swanton, *Indian Tribes of the Lower Mississippi Valley and Adjacent Coast of the Gulf of Mexico* (1911; reprint, 1998).

Natchez Nabobs

The Natchez Nabobs constituted one of the largest single aggregations of wealthy and socially prominent slaveholders in the antebellum South, rivaled only by the affluent planters and merchants in the aristocratic citadel of Charleston, South Carolina. The stately mansions that still grace the picturesque streets of the Mississippi River town bear eloquent testimony to the wealth and power once enjoyed by these nabobs. Indeed, on the eve of the Civil War, the per capita wealth in Adams County was reputedly the highest of any county in the United States.

Of the seventy-one Mississippi planters who owned more than 250 slaves during the 1850s, fifty-five (71 percent) resided in Natchez and its environs. The most affluent of these planter nabobs were Francis Surget Sr., Levin R. Marshall, and Stephen Duncan. Surget, the son of a French sea captain, settled near Natchez in 1785 and eventually accumulated an estate that included a dozen plantations and thirteen hundred slaves and was valued at more than two million dollars at his death in 1856. Marshall, a true capitalistic entrepreneur, migrated to Mississippi from Virginia in 1817 to become cashier of the United States Bank in Woodville. He subsequently made a fortune in banking, mercantile, and planting enterprises, and by 1860 he owned more than a thousand slaves on plantations in three states. Similarly, Stephen Duncan, a native of Carlisle, Pennsylvania, settled in Natchez a decade before Marshall. Aided by two propitious marriages and uncommon entrepreneurial skills, Duncan ultimately amassed a fortune by exploiting the labor of more than a thousand slaves on his seven cotton plantations in the Mississippi Delta and two sugar plantations in Louisiana.

These men exemplify one of the salient characteristics of the Natchez nabobs. Nearly two-thirds of this cohort had migrated to Natchez from other parts of the country, especially from the Northeast. Nine of the nabobs were natives of that region, and nearly half of the native Mississippians had parents or spouses from that area. For example, the parents of Natchez-born William J. Minor were born in Pennsylvania and Connecticut, and after attending the University of Pennsylvania, Minor married a woman from that state.

Minor and Duncan were two of the central figures in a complex family network spawned initially by marriage alliances both within the Natchez District and with other families in the Northeast. This network was subsequently enhanced by a business relationship that developed between the Natchez planters and the Leverich brothers, owners of a New York factorage house. A key element in the family and business relationships that connected the nabobs to the Northeast was the Gustine family of Carlisle, Pennsylvania. Shortly before Duncan arrived in Natchez in 1808, his sister married Samuel Gustine, and the Gustines had four daughters before relocating to Natchez in the 1830s. The two youngest daughters married Natchez nabobs William C. Conner and William J. Minor, while their older sisters married brothers Charles P. and Henry S. Leverich. Numerous additional marriages bound other prominent Natchez families to this group.

Unlike their wealthy counterparts in such long-settled Atlantic seaboard states as Virginia and South Carolina, most of the Natchez elite accumulated their vast estates not through inheritance but through an assiduous application of the Protestant work ethic; the investment of capital derived initially from legal, medical, and mercantile pursuits; and the labor of slaves. These nouveau riche Natchezians were capitalists in every sense of the word, not only diversifying their economic portfolios by investing in banks, railroads, and other enterprises outside the agricultural sector but also by behaving in capitalistic ways in their exclusively agricultural pursuits. Thus, when cotton prices plummeted in the wake of the Panic of 1837, both Duncan and Minor began transferring their resources to more lucrative areas. By the 1850s both men had virtually liquidated their holdings in Adams County. Duncan shifted his huge slave force to the virgin lands of the Yazoo Delta, while Minor established a sugar empire consisting of nine thousand acres of land and six hundred slaves in the parishes of Ascension and Terrebonne, Louisiana. Indeed, by the last decade of the antebellum period, a majority of the slaves owned by the Natchez nabobs were located across the river in Concordia and adjacent Louisiana parishes.

With few exceptions, the nabobs tended to be Whiggish in their political allegiance before the Civil War and Unionists during and after the sectional crisis of 1860 erupted into bloodshed. Although many other elite slaveholders throughout the South were Whigs and Unionists before secession, most of them supported the Confederacy once the die was cast. They did so despite the fact that, like the Natchezians, many had business, educational, travel, and residential connections with the Northeast. But the nativity and familial ties with that region were stronger among the Natchez aristocrats than among their counterparts elsewhere in the slave South. Nowhere else featured such a concentration of northern-oriented planters and professional men, and nowhere else did elite slaveholders maintain such a precarious regional identity.

Because many of the nabobs had never developed a strong emotional attachment to their adopted homeland, most gave at most grudging support to the fledgling Confederacy. Indeed, five of the most prominent members of the group picked up stakes and moved to New York City during the height of the conflict. When he departed Natchez in the spring of 1863, Duncan, perhaps the wealthiest of the nabobs at that time, presented the Confederate government with a bill for $185,000 to compensate him for his wartime losses, all of which he attributed to the act of secession. Ironically, the actions of Duncan and his Unionist cohorts during the war contributed to the demise of the civilization they had struggled to build. Today only the mansions and the memories remain to mark the opulent society that once existed in Natchez.

William K. Scarborough
University of Southern Mississippi

Martha Jane Brazy, *An American Planter: Stephen Duncan of Antebellum Natchez and New York* (2006); D. Clayton James, *Antebellum Natchez* (1968); Robert E. May, *John A. Quitman: Old South Crusader* (1985); William K. Scarborough, *Journal of Mississippi History* (August 1992); William K. Scarborough, *Masters of the Big House: Elite Slaveholders of the Mid-Nineteenth Century South* (2003); William K. Scarborough, *Prologue* (Winter 2004); Michael Wayne, *The Reshaping of Plantation Society: The Natchez District, 1860–1880* (1983).

Natchez Rhythm Club Fire

On 23 April 1940 the Rhythm Club on St. Catherine Street in Natchez was the scene of a great tragedy in American history. Around 11:15 p.m. a fire broke out in the hall, where a crowd of a few hundred people, mostly young African Americans and their teachers, were dancing to the music of the Walter Barnes Band. More than two hundred people, including nine of the twelve members of the band plus the leader, died of asphyxia or were burned by the flames after being trampled while trying to reach the venue's door. The high number of fatalities resulted from many factors: the only accessible exit could only be opened inward, the windows had been boarded up, and the rear door had been bolted to prevent people from watching or entering without paying. Moreover, the interior walls had been festooned with highly flammable dried Spanish moss, which caught fire quickly because a fan was turning at top speed. The exact cause of the blaze is thought to be a lighted cigarette dropped by a careless person, though the unproven suspicion of arson committed either for racial reasons or by an angry young man who had not been allowed to enter the dance hall was aroused and promptly rejected a few days after the disaster.

Journalistic coverage of the fire was extensive in light of the fact that the event struck a highly segregated black community in the midst of the rampant discrimination that existed in the South in the 1940s. The white-owned *Natchez Democrat*, a daily, dealt with the news item the day after it took place but devoted most of the coverage to matters such as voluntary donations, the role of the American Red Cross, and updated lists of contributors and victims. In addition, the paper expressed concern about growing tensions in town. Black-owned weekly national newspapers did not publish until five days after the event, but they provided much more detailed and extensive coverage. The *Chicago Defender* gave particular prominence to Barnes's heroic and fatal decision to urge his band members to continue playing to calm the trapped revelers. J. Robert Smith, the first *New York Amsterdam News* correspondent to arrive on the scene, interviewed Natchez mayor W. J. Byrne, who said he had received words of condolence from many African American organizations but not from Pres. Franklin D. Roosevelt.

Music seems to have been the most vital way that the memory of this tragedy has remained alive in the African American community. Over the rest of the twentieth century, no fewer than ten original compositions were recorded about the tragedy, plus some covers belonging to musical genres ranging from vocal group harmony to blues, from gospel to juke joint music. The first two songs, the Lewis Bronzeville Five's "Mississippi Fire Blues" and "Natchez Mississippi Blues" (Bluebird B8445), were waxed immediately after the disaster. Most of the rest of the songs feature lyrics that display a remarkable preoccupation with the concept of memory: Gene Gilmore's "The Natchez Fire" and Leonard "Baby Doo" Caston's "The Death of Walter Barnes" (Decca 7663); Charles Haffer Jr.'s "The Natchez [Theater] Fire Disaster" (Library of Congress 6623-B-2, unreleased); Howlin' Wolf's "The Natchez Burnin'" (Chess 1744); Robert Gilmore's "Wasn't That a Awful Day in Natchez" (Louisiana Folklore Society LFS-1); and John Lee Hooker's "Natchez Fire [Burnin']" (Riverside LP 008), "Fire at Natchez" ("The Great Disaster of 1936") (Galaxy LP 8201), and "The Mighty Fire" ("Great Fire of Natchez") (Vee-Jay 1078).

Luigi Monge
Genoa, Italy

Blues Unlimited (January 1969, February–March 1970); Alan Lomax, *The Land Where the Blues Began* (1993); Albert McCarthy, *Big Band Jazz* (1974); Luigi Monge, in *Nobody Knows Where the Blues Come From: Lyrics and History*, ed. Robert Springer (2006); John Wesley Work, Lewis Wade Jones, and Samuel C. Adams Jr., *Lost Delta Found: Rediscovering the Fisk University–Library of Congress Coahoma County Study, 1941–1942*, ed. Robert Gordon and Bruce Nemerov (2005).

N

Natchez Slave Market

In the late eighteenth century, slave auctions and sales in Natchez took place at the landing along the Mississippi River known as Under-the-Hill. For the most part, slaves sent to Natchez arrived in New Orleans and were transported upriver, though slaves reached town overland as well.

By the 1790s the center of the trade in humans began shifting away from the river, and after an 1833 city ordinance barred the sale of slaves within city limits, the market moved to the Forks of the Road, the intersection of Washington Road/Natchez Trace (today's D'Evereaux Drive), Old Courthouse Road (Liberty Road), and St. Catherine Street at the northwest edge of town. Reasons for the move are varied and could be related to the town's concern with presenting a genteel appearance (the market's original name, Niggerville, may have been changed to a geographic descriptor because of such concerns) or to residents' fears that keeping slave pens in the raucous Under-the-Hill neighborhood was exceedingly dangerous. A more direct reason for the move was that Isaac Franklin of the slave-trading firm Franklin and Armfield managed his company from this location.

The growing profit potential of cotton as well as the decline in tobacco production helped to shift the center of slavery away from the Upper South states of Virginia and Maryland toward Mississippi and Louisiana. These shifts, along with the end of US importation of slaves, increased the value of those born in the United States and created an almost boundless market for enslaved men and women in the Old Southwest. As a result of these large-scale economic and demographic changes and the efforts of Franklin and Armfield, Natchez became the second-largest slave market in the United States, trailing only New Orleans.

By the antebellum period, slaves made their way overland to the Forks of the Road as part of coffles traveling from Virginia to Tennessee and then along the Natchez Trace. The journey was brutal. Usually taking place in the late summer and early fall under the presumption that cooler temperatures would have produced illness, the enslaved were manacled, chained, and forcibly marched to their destination under the watchful eyes of drivers on horseback. In the 1830s Franklin and Armfield began sending slaves via ship from Virginia to New Orleans and then upriver via steamboats equipped to hold between 75 and 150 slaves. Shipments to New Orleans could contain nearly 400 slaves, and by 1835 these ships were leaving Virginia every two weeks.

While Joseph Holt Ingraham famously described the market at the Forks of the Road as an orderly place where content, well-dressed, well-fed slaves were marketed, such outward appearances belied the conditions the enslaved endured. William Wells Brown, an enslaved man who made several trips to Natchez before escaping to freedom, indicated that slaves at the market were not as well treated as slave traders presented to their potential clients. Measles, cholera, and other diseases killed slaves confined to coffles and pens waiting to be sold, and traders concerned themselves with the health of slaves only when it might harm profits. Traders hoped to unload diseased slaves to unsuspecting purchasers. Moreover, as Rice Ballard, a partner of Franklin and Armfield, wrote, "The more Negroes lost in that country, the more will be wanting if they have the means of procuring them." In other words, slaves killed by epidemics might cause short-term losses for the company but might also increase the value of the survivors.

The most despicable aspect of the trade at the Forks of the Road was the treatment of "fancy maids"—attractive, young female slaves. These girls and women, usually of mixed race, were essentially marketed as sexual slaves, and they commanded the highest prices. Franklin and Armfield's partners frequently wrote to one another of their sexual exploits with these girls as well as their profitability, demonstrating perhaps that planters and slave traders were not so different in their desires.

Though the enslaved rarely receive much discussion in tours of Natchez, the Forks of the Road and the men, women, and children bought and sold there have recently been acknowledged by local activists with a monument presenting the history of the market.

Timothy R. Buckner
Troy University

Edward E. Baptist, *American Historical Review* (December 2001); William Wells Brown, *Narrative of William W. Brown, Fugitive Slave, Written by Himself* (1847); Joseph Holt Ingraham, *The Southwest by a Yankee, 2 vols.* (1835); Walter Johnson, *Soul by Soul: Life inside the Antebellum Slave Market* (1999); David J. Libby, *Slavery and Frontier Mississippi, 1720–1835* (2004); Preservation in Mississippi website, misspreservation.com.

Natchez Trace

The Natchez Trace was a series of ancient paths that connected the Lower Mississippi River Valley to the Cumberland River Basin. The trail predates human occupation of the areas and may have been started by bison and other large animals that followed a small ridge that led to salt licks along the Cumberland River. One of the earliest sites of human occupation along the Natchez Trace is found in the Bear Creek Village site, which dates to about 8000 BC. Other evidence of human occupation can be seen along the Old Trace in the form of mounds. During the Woodland

(2000 BC to AD 1000) and Mississippian (AD 900 to 1700) periods, Mound Builders occupied the area and constructed burial and ceremonial mounds that remain visible today.

The first Europeans to see any part of the Natchez Trace were Hernando de Soto and his band of explorers. They camped during the winter of 1540–41 among the Chickasaw, along the Natchez Trace in what is now Mississippi. More than a century passed before the next European encounter occurred. In 1682 French explorers led by La Salle sailed into the region via the Mississippi River. A decade later, British traders from the Carolinas were trading with the Chickasaw. For the next century England, France, and Spain allied and competed with the Choctaw, Chickasaw, and each other to colonize the region known as the Old Southwest. The trail was known by a number of names, including the Chickasaw Trace, the Choctaw Trace, and the Nashville Road. (*Trace* is the French word for "track.")

In 1783 a new contender sought control of the Natchez Trace—the United States. The years from the 1780s to the 1820s, known as the boatmen period, saw the heaviest use of and fastest change along the path. Owners of agricultural products, livestock, coal, and other materials from the Ohio River Valley shipped their goods down the Ohio and Mississippi Rivers on flatboats and keelboats to the port cities of Natchez and New Orleans. The sailors who accompanied the goods were known as "Kaintuck" boatmen. Once the goods were sold, the boat itself was often sold for the lumber it contained, and the boatmen traveled home overland by the Natchez Trace.

By the boatmen period the Natchez Trace did not simply connect the Lower Mississippi River to salt licks. Instead, it had become a five-hundred-mile series of trails that connected Natchez to Nashville, Tennessee, and could be traversed by horseback in three to four weeks. Established roads from Nashville connected the boatmen back to their homes to the northeast. Near the end of the boatmen period, the name *Natchez Trace* became popular.

Traveling the Natchez Trace during this period was dangerous. Outlaws quickly learned that boatmen carried large sums of money as they traveled through the wilderness, and horses and weapons were highly sought after by the Choctaw, Chickasaw, and other boatmen. Traveling in groups provided an effective defense against some of these dangers, but crossing the Tennessee River and other waterways was treacherous for all travelers. Though the threat of robbery was real, some stories of bandits on the Old Trace were embellished through oral history and literature. Stories about Sam Mason and the Harp brothers, for example, took on mythic qualities over the years.

Beginning in 1800 significant changes took place along the Natchez Trace. That year, the federal government designated it a National Post Road. Soon thereafter, Pres. Thomas Jefferson, seeing the importance of improving the defense of the Mississippi Territory and newly acquired Louisiana, began widening the Trace. Also during this time, with permission from the Choctaw and Chickasaw, small and primitive "stands" were established to provide basic food and shelter for travelers.

During the War of 1812. Gen. Andrew Jackson used the Natchez Trace to march some of his troops to and from the January 1815 Battle of New Orleans. By this time, though, the future of the Natchez Trace was in jeopardy. Steamboats began to appear on the Mississippi in the 1810s and by the following decade offered boatmen safer and quicker passage back north. In addition, other federal roads siphoned traffic off the Natchez Trace, and the Choctaw and Chickasaw Indians were removed to Indian Territory in modern-day Oklahoma during the 1830s. By this time much of the Natchez Trace was abandoned. Though some local communities adopted sections of the Trace into more modern road systems, others were left to nature. The National Park Service has preserved numerous portions of the old Natchez Trace as part of the Natchez Trace Parkway.

Ernie Price
National Park Service

Timothy Davis et al., *Paving the Way: A Bibliography of the Modern Natchez Trace Parkway* (1999); William C. Davis, *A Way through the Wilderness: The Natchez Trace and the Civilization of the Southern Frontier* (1995); Natchez Trace Parkway, National Park Service website, www.nps.gov /natr/; Dawson A. Phelps, *Tennessee Historical Quarterly* (September 1962).

N

Natchez Trace Parkway

The Natchez Trace Parkway, one of nine parkways under the jurisdiction of the US Department of the Interior's National Park Service, was authorized on 18 May 1938 to commemorate the Natchez Trace. Also known as the Old Trace, the path was a series of foot trails used by prehistoric Native Americans that became the primary route between the East and the Old Southwest during the late eighteenth and early nineteenth centuries.

At 444 miles long and an average of 800 feet wide, the meandering two-lane twentieth-century road starts just southwest of Nashville, Tennessee, and heads diagonally southwest across Tennessee, through thirty miles of northwestern Alabama, and from the northeast corner of Mississippi to Natchez. The route roughly follows the historic Old Trace. About 97 miles of Old Trace are contained and preserved in the parkway's right-of-way.

Only about 60 percent of the Old Trace was still in use by the mid-1930s when a confluence of events set the stage

Natchez Trace Parkway (Photograph by Carol M. Highsmith, Library of Congress, Washington, D.C. [LC-DIG-highsm-04324])

for the commemorative parkway: a federal Depression Era public policy aimed at providing employment, a new class of roads to serve automobile-oriented recreation, and a revered but antiquated thoroughfare ideally suited to modern historic preservation and cultural marketing.

The earliest commemoration of the Old Trace came with the Mississippi State Society of the Daughters of the American Revolution, established 1896 in Natchez. The project, to identify the Old Trace with granite markers placed in each county through which the path passed, was introduced at the Daughters' first statewide conference in 1905. The first marker was installed in 1908 in Tishomingo County, with a Natchez marker following in 1909, and a marker at the Alabama-Mississippi state line in 1913. Seventeen stone boulders were erected by 1933 in Mississippi and Tennessee.

There is some evidence that the Natchez Chamber of Commerce may also have initiated a movement to "pave the Trace" in 1915, and a convention met in Kosciusko to formalize the idea, but only limited documentation of the effort survives. The first incarnation of the Natchez Trace Military Association may have occurred at this time. The marking project undertaken by the Daughters of the American Revolution was winding down in the early 1930s, just as the Military Association was germinating, and the roles and relationship of the two organizations are unclear. Commemoration of the Old Trace in a new parkway was more than romantic nationalism: it provided economic vitalization through cultural marketing in the antebellum city of Natchez and much-needed transportation infrastructure for Mississippi.

By most accounts, the Natchez Trace Military Association officially formed on 21 January 1934 in Jackson as a self-described "civic and patriotic organization trying to induce the Federal Government to pave the ancient Trace and preserve it as a National Parkway." Within a few months the group officially dropped *Military* from its name as the project was to be headed by the US Department of the Interior rather

than the War Department. Each county through which the Old Trace ran established an association chapter.

A primary figure in this endeavor was Mary Roane Fleming Byrnes, who joined the Natchez Trace Association as corresponding secretary of the Adams County chapter. She quickly rose to become vice president of the state organization in 1934 and president in March 1935. She remained in the post for the next thirty-five years. Byrnes was born into an old Natchez family and resided at Ravennaside, where evidence of her passion was displayed in two rooms until the late 1990s. "The War Room" contained a site plan of the parkway, and the "Trace Room" was dominated by an oversized, hand-painted mural of the Old Trace.

In 1934 federal legislation authorized fifty thousand dollars for a study of the Natchez Trace "with a view to constructing a national road on this route to be known as the Natchez Trace Parkway." Mississippi congressman Jeff Busby had introduced two bills that year: the first, for the Natchez Trace survey, passed with a little help. Sen. Pat Harrison, chair of the Senate Finance Committee, and other members of the Mississippi delegation paid a convincing visit to Pres. Franklin Roosevelt, who signed the legislation. Busby's second bill, which would have provided twenty-five million dollars in construction funds, failed, but the success of the survey legislation offered reason to celebrate. Adams County hosted a grand rally in July 1934 "for the purpose of enlisting interest in and support for paving the Natchez Trace," which was envisioned, too optimistically, as "the first link of the proposed great international highway of strategic value connecting South and Central America with this country, and following the direct route of historic interest from the southwest to Washington and the east." With funding from the Emergency Relief Appropriation Act of 1935, construction began two years later. That fall, groundbreakings were held for three discontiguous sections of Mississippi parkway, even before the land was designated a unit of the National Park Service.

The Old Trace was researched and mapped by the NPS's Branch of Historic Sites and Building and its Branch of Plans and Designs with the cooperation of planner John Nolen. The US Bureau of Public Roads flagged the alignment in the field. The states would acquire land and deed it to the federal government. With historical research complete, planners had to decide whether to attempt a route "with only minor deviations, [that] may follow faithfully the line of the old road—for merely historical reasons" or whether "the parkway itself should [follow] the general direction of that historic route, but essentially satisfying the technical and esthetic standards of modern parkway construction." The NPS defined parkways in the 1930s using several criteria, including a ban on commercial traffic and unsightly roadside development and frontage rights but calling for the use of previously undeveloped land with native scenery, preserved through a wide right-of-way buffer and limited at-grade crossings. The southernmost portion of this parkway "would introduce the traveling public to an area where scenery, architecture, and historical associations combine to portray graphically the story of the Old South. . . . [T]he scenic beauty, historic associations of the Trace, and the existing need for a good highway from Jackson, the State capital, to Natchez, make the construction of this parkway justifiable."

Parkway construction continued apace between 1937 and 1941, paused during World War II, and then resumed through the late 1960s. By this time, however, people and priorities were changing. The parkway concept was threatened after funding shifted to pay for the war in Vietnam and the Bureau of Public Roads grew into the interstate-building Federal Highway Administration. Locally, longtime superintendent Malcolm Gardner, at the park since 1936, retired in 1967. And after more than three decades at the Natchez Trace Association's helm, the forceful Byrnes resigned just before her death in 1970. During the effort to complete the Trace over the following decade, the association relocated from Natchez to Tupelo and realigned as an organization. Funds gradually were appropriated for missing segments, and by the end of the twentieth century, Mississippi's congressional delegation worked to assure completion of the parkway. The final two sections officially opened on 21 May 2005.

The sinewy parkway offers a serene drive through a sequence of indigenous natural backdrops—creek bottoms and prairie, a cedar swamp and loess soil. The route is also studded with cultural sites and artifacts telling the stories of residents from the prehistoric era through the nineteenth century. Mount Locust is the lone restored "stand" of the many lodgings that lined the Old Trace; Emerald Mound is the nation's second-largest prehistoric ceremonial mound, covering nearly eight acres; and evocative sections of sunken Old Trace are southern highlights. One unadvertised historic resource is found at park headquarters: the Tupelo Homesteads was a twenty-five-dwelling New Deal demonstration project built in 1934. When the project failed, the dwellings became housing for park staff. Toward the north end of the Natchez Trace Parkway is the grave of Meriwether Lewis, who died in 1809, and its restored 1848 monument. A span supporting the parkway road over TN 96 became an unintended attraction when it was completed in 1996 as the first US segmentally constructed concrete arch bridge, measuring a lofty 155 feet high and 1,648 feet long. The US Federal Highway Administration designated the parkway an All-American Road in 1996.

Sara Amy Leach

National Cemetery Administration, Department of Veterans Affairs

Timothy Davis, Todd Croteau, and Christopher Marston, *America's National Park Roads and Parkways: Drawings from the Historic American Engineering Record* (2004); *History of the Mississippi State Society Daughters of the American Revolution, 1896–1996* (1996); Sara Amy Leach, in *Looking beyond the Highway: Dixie Roads and Culture*, ed. Claudette Stager and Martha Carver (2006); Sara Amy Leach, *Ranger: Journal of the Association of National Park Rangers* (Summer 1996); Natchez Trace Parkway Association Collection, Natchez Trace Parkway Headquarters, Tupelo, Miss.; Verbie Lovorn Prevost, "Roane Fleming Byrnes: A Critical Biography" (PhD dissertation, University of Mississippi, 1974); Fred Smith, *Journal of Mississippi History* (Summer 2006).

Natchez-under-the-Hill

Natchez-under-the-Hill is the area of Natchez below the bluffs overlooking the Mississippi River. Like other river towns in the frontier Southwest, Natchez-under-the-Hill was notorious for lawlessness, debauchery, and violence. Residents and officials alike were appalled and attempted to clean up the area but had little success until the 1830s.

Brothels, gambling houses, and saloons under the hill catered to boatmen, travelers, and poor whites. The flow of alcohol from these establishments often led to fights over women, cheating at cards, or even simple misunderstandings, and an insult or wrong look might result in fisticuffs. Many Natchez whites lamented these activities and worried that such men would encourage slaves to gamble and drink. Indians and slaves sometimes frequented establishments at Natchez-under-the-Hill, and white critics often complained about both drunkenness and interracial fraternization.

Natchez officials during both the Spanish and American periods used legal means in attempt to reform Natchez-under-the-Hill. Manuel Gayoso de Lemos, Spanish governor of the Natchez District, issued laws in 1792 that banned gambling, public rowdiness, and liquor sales to slaves and Indians under the hill. Gayoso also instituted a curfew, but the Spanish could not enforce those laws. The Mississippi territorial government restricted the sale of liquor to Indians

Natchez-under-the-Hill, ca. 1910 (Ann Rayburn Paper Americana Collection, Department of Archives and Special Collections, J. D. Williams Library, University of Mississippi [rayburn_ann_35_10_001])

beginning in 1798, and Gov. Winthrop Sargent remarked that Natchez had become an abominable place. The Mississippi Territory passed a 1799 law regulating slave activity on Sundays.

Sometimes what went on under the hill spilled over into Natchez proper. In 1807 boatmen came up from the landing and rioted in the town, and one person was killed. A more serious incident occurred in May 1817 when a mob of Kentucky boatmen seized control of the landing but soon began fighting among themselves. The three-day riot ended only when the Kaintucks, as the boatmen were called, surrendered in fear after Natchez officials aimed a cannon at the rioters from the bluffs above.

"Respectable" citizens blamed these instances of violence and rioting on the vices common in Natchez-under-the-Hill. In 1816 the city government expelled most of the prostitutes who worked in the area, placing the women on boats and taking them to other ports. Nevertheless, many returned, and new prostitutes were always arriving. The same attitude applied to gambling. In July 1835, for example, city authorities demanded that gamblers vacate the landing within twenty-four hours. Men and women, along with various kinds of gambling equipment, were seen leaving on the Citizens' Rail Line, but many returned.

Natchez citizens blamed gamblers for a series of fires that began under the hill and spread to the city. In January 1836, twenty-eight houses caught fire and burned at the landing. These fires threatened the city and incited fear among townspeople, who extinguished the fires and saved the city. Some whites believed that slaves had started the fires, and the number of slave patrols was increased markedly in hopes of preventing any further rebellion. Other observers believed that the real culprits were gamblers bent on revenge after having been forced to leave.

In the 1830s Natchez finally gained headway in cleaning up under the hill. Although gambling still existed in the area, it continued on a much reduced scale. Many gamblers had departed for New Orleans, Memphis, or Vicksburg, and a number of saloons and brothels had closed and been replaced by commercial establishments. Yet boatmen still stopped under the hill. In his diary, William Johnson mentioned that a group of Irishmen rioted over the city's tax on flatboats in December 1836.

Even today, gambling remains a big attraction under the hill, where riverboat casinos now draw visitors—legally.

Jaime Elizabeth Boler
Jones County Junior College

Jaime Elizabeth Boler, *City under Siege: Resistance and Power in Natchez, Mississippi, 1719–1857* (2005); William C. Davis, *A Way through the Wilderness: The Natchez Trace and the Civilization of the Southern Frontier* (1995); William Ransom Hogan and Edwin A. Davis, eds., *William Johnson's Natchez* (1993); D. Clayton James, *Antebellum Natchez* (1968); Joshua D. Rothman, *Flush Times and Fever Dreams: A Story of Capitalism and Slavery in the Age of Jackson* (2013).

National Association for the Advancement of Colored People (NAACP)

The National Association for the Advancement of Colored People (NAACP) first came to Mississippi less than a decade after the organization's 1909 founding, but the group was obscured in its early days by a racial caste regimen that severely punished activity in opposing that system. Since the NAACP sought to destroy the Jim Crow system, its members suffered loss of jobs, intimidation, and physical violence. Nevertheless, the organization's activists persevered, and by the twenty-first century, change had indeed come.

The presence of the NAACP in Mississippi can be divided into four periods, the last of which began in the early 1960s when the group consolidated into a powerful outlet of political expression. The first period was associated with the expansion of the national organization into organized southern state chapters from World War I into the early 1920s. The second period occurred immediately after World War II, when the organization experienced a growth spurt. The third period coincided with the emergence of the modern civil rights movement in the mid-1950s and saw the legal demolition of "separate but equal" public schools. The fourth period, after 1962, focused on political mobilization via the courts and structural integration into the political process.

During the first period, branches organized but then dissolved almost immediately in Vicksburg in 1918 and in the entirely African American town of Mound Bayou the following year. Other chapters followed in Jackson, Meridian, and Natchez, urban centers where some African Americans were independent of the white economic structure. These chapters, too, had short life spans. Leaders and chapters everywhere faced the perils of public discovery, since state law prohibited membership in organizations such as the NAACP and since those identified as "troublemakers" faced violence from white individuals and organizations intent on crushing any threat to the established social order. Membership also posed an economic burden, with the result that few chapters attained the required fifty members. These constraints severely limited even furtive activity. Membership throughout the state remained small, perhaps well below five hundred.

The second period began after World War II and saw the ascendancy of the Jackson chapter, where a member sued the school district for equal pay and was promptly fired. The incident helped inspire the creation of other chapters and the appointment of the state's first paid NAACP official, William Bender, a chaplain at Tougaloo College, an integrated private institution that afforded Bender some protection. This appointment also situated the state chapter to stimulate public debate on some of Mississippi's most important race-related issues, particularly segregated schools and disfranchisement.

During the third period, the organization came into its own, significantly aided by the Regional Council of Negro Leadership, which in the late 1940s organized the first mass meetings of the type that became commonplace a decade and a half later. These carefully planned events brought together large crowds of African Americans in black-owned venues in racially segregated enclaves. Aaron Henry emerged from within this local structure to become the state's most successful NAACP leader.

Events outside Mississippi helped propel the growth of the state organization during this era. The national NAACP was waging an intense legal battle against segregated schools, recording a resounding victory with the US Supreme Court's 1954 *Brown v. Board of Education* decision. Although the Court declared "separate but equal" education to be unconstitutional and required the desegregation of schools, the State of Mississippi moved to equalize schools for African American children in hopes of forestalling integration with support from certain African American community leaders. The plan failed, as black leaders associated with the NAACP refused to cooperate with the plan and insisted on full integration. The organization mushroomed across Mississippi, with chapters springing up in new towns. Less than a year later, Medgar Evers was appointed the group's Mississippi field secretary, and plaintiffs began to petition for school desegregation, though they achieved no immediate results. In 1960 Henry became the president of the Mississippi NAACP, joining with Evers to form an unabashedly aggressive team at the forefront of an escalating civil rights movement. The two men traversed the state, ramping up the pressure for school desegregation and with it social change. In addition, Henry headed up an NAACP-sponsored street movement in his hometown of Clarksdale. The organization soon joined the Student Nonviolent Coordinating Committee, the Congress of Racial Equality, and the Southern Christian Leadership Conference to form the Council of Federated Organizations (COFO), an umbrella civil rights group for the state. Henry became head of COFO and subsequently played a leadership role in virtually every Mississippi entity that challenged segregation.

Mississippi's white political leaders and prosegregation organizations such as the Citizens' Council continued to identify the integrated NAACP as their chief enemy. Its chief symbol and spokesman, Evers, became a marked man, and he was murdered in June 1963.

The fourth period saw the NAACP's most intensive activity, much of it in coordination with the other COFO members. Henry remained president of the NAACP until 1993, overseeing street protest campaigns, boycotts, and above all legal challenges. One of the most notable efforts involved the 1962 admission of James Meredith to the University of Mississippi, which brought the national spotlight on the state. The Mississippi NAACP's later challenges included segregated public accommodations, disfranchisement, and media discrimination. In addition, working with the national organization and other groups, the Mississippi NAACP was a major force in securing passage of the Civil Rights Act of 1964 and the Voting Rights Act of 1965.

The civil rights coalition splintered in the mid-1960s, leaving the NAACP as the state's predominant civil rights organization. As street mobilization waned, the NAACP intensified challenges to school segregation. The victories were piecemeal, keeping the NAACP and its Legal Defense Fund busy for years. Similarly, as the Voting Rights Act was implemented, the Legal Defense Fund collaborated with others in challenging reapportionment plans for the state legislature and other political bodies.

In the mid- to late 1960s politics in Mississippi entered a new phase, marked by new types of competition for political power. The NAACP became a major political player with its members most active in registration campaigns and electioneering. The greatest indicator of the new phase was the struggle for control of the state Democratic Party. After the Mississippi Freedom Democratic Party failed to unseat the segregated Mississippi delegation at the 1964 Democratic National Convention, members of the NAACP collaborated with Mississippi whites to develop the Loyalist Democrats. The new party, chaired by Henry, quickly increased the number of black Democrats elected to office, and eight years later the Loyalists merged with the "Regular" Democratic faction, with Henry serving as cochair of the unified party.

While the NAACP today is less visible, its footprints remain omnipresent. Mississippi now has enormous numbers of African American elected officials, and black Mississippians enjoy routine access to public facilities, public conveyances, and full voting rights, all as a direct consequence of the work of the NAACP.

Minion K. C. Morrison
Mississippi State University

David Beito, *Black Maverick: T. R. M. Howard's Fight for Civil Rights and Economic Power* (2009); John Dittmer, *Local People: The Struggle for Civil Rights in Mississippi* (1994); Aaron Henry with Constance Curry, *Aaron Henry: The Fire Ever Burning* (2000); Neil McMillen, *The Citizens' Council: Organized Resistance to the Second Reconstruction, 1954–1964* (1994); Neil McMillen, *Dark Journey: Mississippians in the Age of Jim Crow* (1990); Minion K. C. Morrison, *Aaron Henry of Mississippi: Inside Agitator* (2015); Minion K. C. Morrison, ed., *Black Political Mobilization, Leadership, and Power: African Americans and Political Participation* (1987); Frank Parker, *Black Votes Count: Political Empowerment in Mississippi after 1965* (1990); Patricia Sullivan, *Lift Every Voice: The NAACP and the Making of the Civil Rights Movement* (2009).

N

National Cotton Council of America

Organized in 1939, the National Cotton Council of America represented the loose consolidation of an old industry that had long defied unity. The council's creation proved difficult and was made possible only by the desperate state of the cotton industry during the Great Depression. Plunging cotton exports, bulging warehouses, and growing international competition jeopardized the industry's viability, and synthetics soon posed another challenge. Getting cotton from field to fiber also lent itself to intramural warfare among the industry's components, with conflicting interests among producers, mills, processors, warehousers, shippers, and cottonseed crushers. One segment might reap benefits at the expense of others. Greater production, for example, meant lower prices for producers while generating revenue for processors and handlers, who trafficked in volume. The various components organized individual trade associations to protect their particular interests.

Producers were the largest and most disorganized of the industry's segments. Cotton farmers were buffeted by the vagaries of weather, interest rates, and labor supply, along with market fluctuations. The need for unity became acutely apparent in 1937, when cotton farmers, with acreage restrictions off for the first time during the New Deal, produced the largest crop in US history—nearly nineteen million bales. The glut destroyed the cotton market and helped plunge the nation into the so-called Roosevelt Recession. With the addition of international trade restrictions and a large foreign crop, US cotton exports plummeted to a half-century low.

During the Great Depression, the New Deal had intervened in the cotton economy with acreage restrictions, subsidies, and crop loans. If farmers defaulted on their loans, their cotton was moved into federally approved warehouses. By the late 1930s, however, the New Deal had run its course. If the American cotton industry was to survive, it needed to save itself.

That salvation originated in the Mississippi Delta. In the mid- to late 1930s leaders of the Delta Chamber of Commerce wanted to promote new uses for cotton but realized that such ideas required a more aggressive organization. One of the agency's talented leaders, William Rhea Blake, thought the Delta Chamber (renamed the Delta Council in 1938) might spawn a national body to do just that and helped sell the idea to William T. Wynn, a highly respected and prominent Greenville lawyer, banker, and businessman. Wynn, in turn, apparently recruited the most prominent cotton man in the United States, Oscar Goodbar Johnston, president of the Delta and Pine Land Company in Scott, Mississippi.

Johnston, a planter, lawyer, and orator, had held several appointments in the New Deal, including serving on the board of the Commodity Credit Corporation, an agency he helped organize in 1933 to distribute loans to cash-starved southern farmers. As head of the Federal Cotton Pool, which he also organized, he liquidated 2.4 million bales of government-held cotton between 1934 and 1936 without breaking the market, in the process returning profits to southern cotton farmers. The highest-profile cotton planter in America, with an almost reverential following in the cotton industry, Johnston had been contemplating an organization of cotton producers only. Among the often-jealous segments of cotton's kingdom, the idea of an industry-wide body—once thought too visionary to achieve—percolated in the South as the cotton economy floundered. Most interest-group executives were prepared to yield leadership to Johnston, and in 1938 he abandoned his original goal of a producers' organization in favor of a national body dedicated to finding new uses for cotton and speaking for a united industry.

At the June 1938 annual meeting of the Delta Chamber of Commerce on the campus of Delta State Teachers College in Cleveland, King Cotton's retainers, led by Johnston, brought together leaders of allied cotton associations; got seed money pledged by Mississippi's governor, Hugh White; and reached consensus on the need for a national council. Strenuous organizational work throughout the South soon followed, including establishing state units and blunting territorial and leadership jealousies and fears west of the Mississippi River, notably in Texas. According to Mississippi editor Hodding Carter, "By airliner, by train, more frequently by automobile," organizers "had traveled separately and together, persuading dubious state groups to whom they are strangers, smoothing internal differences, bringing together clashing producers, ginners, compressors, seed crushers, merchants to whose divergent doors the name and purpose of Oscar Johnston is a ready passkey."

Organizational efforts culminated at the Peabody Hotel in Memphis in November 1938 with eighty-six delegates from fourteen cotton states responding to Johnston's plea for unity. An intricate plan developed, including requiring two-thirds majorities and veto options over policy for each branch of the industry. Two cents per bale from each state unit would provide funding. The Cotton Council sought to advance "consumption of American cotton, cottonseed, and the products thereof."

Two months later, with sufficient funding in sight, the National Cotton Council of America held its first annual convention in Dallas and named Johnston as president and twenty-five leading cotton men as members of the board. Unseen challenges lay ahead, including closed markets occasioned by war, conflict with the American Farm Bureau Federation, financial issues, and the council's intense and incessant lobbying of Congress. Had industry leaders known about the looming challenge of synthetics, Blake later said, "it might have just made us quit before we started." Mills and cooperatives joined the original five segments—producers, ginners, merchants, crushers, and warehousers—and, over the years, spin-offs included Cotton Incorporated and the Institute for Cotton International. If the National Cotton Council of America could not restore King Cotton to his throne, it could claim its share of credit for unifying and saving a vital American industry.

Lawrence J. Nelson
University of North Alabama

Hodding Carter, "Cotton Fights Back! The Story of the National Cotton Council," *Greenville Delta Democrat-Times* (1939); Lawrence J. Nelson, *King Cotton's Advocate: Oscar G. Johnston and the New Deal* (1999).

Native American Women

Mississippi's native women have played an important if largely unremarked role in the state's history. Among their earliest achievements was the cultivation of corn, a crop that remains vital to Mississippi's agriculture. Some time in the eighth or ninth century AD a vast trade network that connected the Valley of Mexico with North America delivered corn to the American South. Women and men cleared thick stands of river cane and created fields along the many rivers and creeks that cut across the region. Women turned the loose alluvial soils with digging sticks and planted both family plots and community fields that remained under the women's control. After the corn had sprouted, female farmers heaped soil around the green shoots to push them higher, forming the hills that gave native fields their most distinctive feature. Their produce fed the rise of the Mississippian societies that had their first encounters with Europeans in the early sixteenth century.

Diseases introduced to the region by Hernando de Soto and other erstwhile conquistadors decimated the region's native population, but the women who survived kept growing corn. Pierre Le Moyne, Sieur d'Iberville, who founded Fort Maurepas at Biloxi in 1699, encountered these women and the plant that was their lifeblood. His ship had reached the Mississippi coast during harvest time, and a Biloxi woman welcomed him and his men with a dish of corn porridge. To signal his acceptance of the woman's graciousness, Iberville presented her group with axes, knives, shirts, beads, and tobacco.

If corn that was raised, prepared, and served by native women opened the European settlement of what is today Mississippi, female farmers also became engaged in the struggle to hold onto their land against the rising tide of European and American settlement and expansion. For example, in 1830, when the US government called on representatives of the Choctaw to discuss their Removal from Mississippi, the women who attended the talks steadfastly refused to cede an inch, threatening the life of any man who dared to do so. Chickasaw women also spoke out against ceding their land. When the United States pledged to assign plots of land to Chickasaw heads of household as part of an agreement to remove to Indian Territory in present-day Oklahoma, government officials assumed that the group would consist only of men. After the United States refused to assign land reserves to female heads of household, Chickasaw chiefs, under pressure from the women, explained to Pres. Andrew Jackson that tribal custom allowed women to own land and homes separately from their husbands and insisted that the women be allowed to register as heads of household.

Whether the Chickasaw women succeeded in that effort is unclear, but one Chickasaw woman, Betsy Love, transformed state property law. In 1837 Love filed suit to prevent the seizure of her slave to settle her American husband's debts. In *Fisher v. Allen* Love argued before the Mississippi Supreme Court for the Chickasaw custom of separate ownership of property, and the presiding justices found in her favor. Two years later the state assembly codified the *Allen* decision by legislating that any property a woman owned before marriage could not be used to cover her husband's debts after marriage. Love's tenacity and intelligence ensured that Mississippi's property laws and gender jurisprudence reflected the influence of the countless generations of corn mothers who had come before her.

James Taylor Carson
Queen's University, Kingston,
Ontario

James Taylor Carson, in *Neither Lady nor Slave: Working Women of the Old South*, ed. Susanna Delfino and Michele Gillespie (2002); LeAnne Howe, *Mississippi History Now* (2005); Pierre Le Moyne D'Iberville, *Iberville's Gulf Journals* (1981).

Native Americans

The story of Mississippi's Native Americans is inextricable from that of the state itself, beginning with the river that gives the state its name. *Mississippi* is derived from the Objibwe for "big river," and the names of many towns and counties reflect the Choctaw and Chickasaw presence: Panola (cotton), Tchula (fox), and Neshoba (wolf). Other place-names—Natchez, Pascagoula, and Biloxi—are reminders of tribes that no longer exist in the state. The influence of Mississippi's Native Americans has been and remains multifaceted. Before Europeans came to the part of the earth now known as Mississippi, Native Americans made it their home, naming the animal and plant life that sustained them; developing the religion, economy, and infrastructure that characterizes society; and ultimately leaving a record of their presence in the form of earthen mounds, place-names, and stories. The Mississippi Band of Choctaw Indians still maintains a presence in the state, influencing its economic and cultural life as strongly as their ancestors did before Removal.

The physical evidence of the Mississippian tribes is scattered throughout the state, most notably in the form of the mounds they built. Some, like the Parr and Bynum sites near Tupelo, were burial mounds, yielding artifacts that provide a window into the customs and lives of those buried there. In addition to human remains, these archeological sites have yielded various ceremonial artifacts, including copper spools and other copper objects; decorated ceramic vessels; lumps of galena, a shiny lead ore; a sheet of mica; and a greenstone platform pipe. The fact that copper, galena, mica, and greenstone are not naturally found in Mississippi points to a trade network that predated European contact.

Across the state in Natchez is Emerald Mound, one of the largest remaining Indian mounds in North America. Built by the ancestors of the Natchez Indians between AD 1250 and 1600, the mound was a ceremonial site until the latter part of the seventeenth century, when the Natchez abandoned it for the newly built Grand Village some twelve miles to the southwest, nearer the river. This site served as both a political and religious center for the Natchez, according to French colonists who recorded their observations of events there.

Nanih Waiya, a mound located near the Choctaw community of Bogue Chitto, holds particular significance for Mississippi Choctaw. It is central to their creation legends. In one version, each of the southeastern tribes emerged from the mound, newly brought to life by the Creator. Each tribe lingered at the mound for a while and then departed, each in a different direction. Last to emerge, the Choctaw rested on the slopes of Nanih Waiya and remained near the mound. Another version has wandering brothers Chata and Chickasa leading their people from the west in search of a place with fertile soil and abundant game. Each night, the travelers would plant a pole in the ground, taking care that it was standing erect. In the morning the pole would be leaning, pointing the direction they were to take on that day's journey. When they arrived at Nanih Waiya, they camped at the base of the mound, with Chickasa and some of the party moving on across the creek. In the morning, the pole stood straight, an indication that they had found the place they were to call home. Chata and the others who had remained tried to catch up with Chickasa's group but failed to locate them. Those who had departed went on to become the Chickasaw tribe, while the Choctaw established a homeland in the shadow of Nanih Waiya.

Such stories are not limited to Nanih Waiya. Folklore connected with Mississippi's Native Americans is associated with many of the state's communities. The Pascagoula River, for example, is known as the Singing River not only for the characteristic humming sound of its current but for a tale that seeks to explain the phenomenon. According to the version on the City of Pascagoula's website, the Pascagoula were peaceful people whose idyllic existence was threatened by the more warlike Biloxi. Rather than face enslavement, the Pascagoula joined hands and walked into the river, chanting until the last voice was silenced by the waters.

The falls on the Strong River at D'Lo are said to be the site of an annual Choctaw ritual described on the website for the water park there as "an initiation to manhood for Choctaw boys of puberty age that involved unknown rituals but lasted for the four days leading up to the full moon of October." These and other examples of community lore exemplify the place that Native Americans hold in Mississippi's collective imagination.

Native Americans played a conspicuous role in Mississippi's political and economic history as well. The tribe now known as the Mississippi Band of Choctaw was particularly active in trade, first taking part in what anthropologist John Peterson called a "complex of aboriginal trade linking the shell of the coastal areas with stone and related products of the interior" and later trading deer hides and other items to the French and British in exchange for European goods. The Mississippi Band has become a major player in the state's twenty-first-century economy, resuming the role it was forced to abandon when most of the tribe left the state following the final cession of tribal lands through the Treaty of Dancing Rabbit Creek.

In 1699 the French established a settlement where the city of Biloxi is now located. The Choctaw established trade relations with the Europeans, acquiring guns and other goods and over time enlisting the French as allies against the Natchez and Chickasaw. Nearly forty years later Choctaw in the western division of the tribe began to trade with the British. The factionalism created by this trade rivalry led to a situation tantamount to civil war. Choctaw from the eastern division, along with their French allies, attacked several western division towns, burning them to the ground. Hundreds of Choctaw were killed in this conflict, and when it ended, tribal leaders worked to unite their people more closely.

After the intertribal warfare was resolved, some Choctaw continued to seek trade with Great Britain, while others maintained their trade relationships with France. This gave the tribe a certain advantage in relations with the two countries, enabling them to play one nation against another. The French and Indian War broke out in 1750, effectively ending trade with France. The Choctaw continued trading with the British until the American Revolution forced them to seek new partners. By the end of the eighteenth century the United States had become the only major source of trade for the Choctaw.

The Choctaw entered a period of prosperity as well as great wariness. They expanded their interests from the deerskin trade to the same kinds of enterprises that supported their non-Indian neighbors: agriculture, livestock, operating inns and ferries, and selling baskets and foodstuffs. They sought out education in English, mathematics, and agriculture, welcoming Protestant missionaries who established schools in the Choctaw Nation and helped the tribe develop a written constitution and representative form of government. In the midst of this prosperity, the Choctaw remained mindful of the growing pressure for westward expansion and the eagerness of state and federal governments to acquire ever-growing amounts of Choctaw territory.

Despite their efforts to support the United States in the Creek War and the War of 1812, the Choctaw ceded more than twenty-three million acres of their territory to the United States in a series of agreements signed between 1801 and 1830, when the Treaty of Dancing Rabbit Creek outlined the terms of Choctaw removal to the West. When the treaty was signed, Mississippi had more than nineteen thousand Choctaw, approximately thirteen thousand of whom were removed between 1831 and 1833.

Some Choctaw remained in Mississippi, where they had been promised allotments of land in exchange for renouncing their status as tribal members and registering with the government. Within a short time, however, most of the remaining Choctaw had sold their land to survive. Some assimilated into non-Indian society, while others subsisted as sharecroppers, living for decades as a shadow nation within the state.

At the turn of the twentieth century only 1,253 Choctaw remained in Mississippi. They had minimal access to health care, education, and employment other than sharecropping. A congressional hearing held in Union in 1916 resulted in the establishment of the Choctaw Indian Agency in Philadelphia two years later. The Bureau of Indian Affairs initially built schools and a hospital, laying the groundwork for the establishment of a tribal government. This milestone came after the passage of the Indian Reorganization Act of 1934, legislation that reversed five decades of expectation that the Choctaw would acculturate into the surrounding Anglo society.

The remainder of the century saw incredible change. Nearly forty years after the first tribal council was seated, Calvin Isaac won election as the first tribal chief. In 1979 Phillip Martin took over that post and instituted an aggressive program of economic development that began with the opening of manufacturing plants on the reservation. A decade later the tribe had developed a diversified economy that included manufacturing, retail, service, and government jobs. After the 1988 passage of the National Indian Gaming Act, the Choctaw negotiated an agreement with the state of Mississippi that enabled them to open the Silver Star Resort and Casino in 1994. A second casino, golf courses, and a water park followed, creating jobs on the Choctaw reservation and surrounding communities. In

2001 a Mississippi State University study of the tribe's economic impact indicated that the tribal government and its business enterprises had created more than fourteen thousand jobs and payroll in excess of $356.8 million. By 2010, the Choctaw businesses employed seven thousand people and generated $180 million per year in wages alone, while the reservation's 4 percent unemployment rate was less than half the national rate. In addition, a scholarship fund pays full tuition for all tribe members who are accepted to college. Between 1985 and 2000, life expectancy for members of the Mississippi Band of Choctaw rose by two decades.

Throughout this period of economic growth, Mississippi Choctaw have not lost sight of the cultural traditions that define them as a people. In particular, the Choctaw language remains an essential element of tribal identity. In the past, most tribal elders spoke Choctaw as a first language and learned English only when they began to attend school. With an increase in the number of Choctaw homes in which English is spoken, the Mississippi Band has created a program to promote the use of the Choctaw language, which is still heard in tribal schools and administrative offices. And the language remains deeply rooted in Choctaw communities and homes—most Choctaw parents not only encourage their children to hone their communications skills in English but also make sure that their sons and daughters speak Choctaw.

Other aspects of traditional life coexist with and complement the reservation's thriving economy. The ancient tradition of swamp cane basketry is thriving and adapting. The traditional forms that once held farm produce are now found in collections around the country. Traditional clothing is still worn for special occasions, the old tribal dances are taught in the schools, and stickball is played by more than a dozen community teams, using sticks and balls that differ little from the ones used before Removal. These and other traditions are showcased each summer at the Choctaw Indian Fair, an event that combines a celebration of traditional culture with the midway rides and musical performances found at county fairs. A highlight is a tournament in which stickball teams from around the reservation compete in what is billed as the World Series of Stickball. Choctaw baskets and beadwork are offered for sale, as is the work of craftspeople from other tribes, such as turquoise and silver jewelry from the Southwest, quillwork from midwestern tribes, and items such as dream catchers and beadwork that represent a growing "pan-Indian" aesthetic that is also evident in the Plains-style dancing and drumming that also take place at the fairground. This style of Native American dance is also found at various powwow gatherings around Mississippi. The Natchez Powwow held annually at the Grand Village of the Natchez Indians is probably the oldest event of this kind in the state. Others include the Native American Indian Intertribal Council Powwow held at D'Iberville; the annual Southern Miss Golden Eagle Intertribal Society Powwow, held on the campus of the University of Southern

N

Mississippi; and the Veterans Day Powwow sponsored by the Mississippi Band of Choctaw Indians.

The popularity of gatherings such as the Choctaw Fair and the Natchez Powwow are evidence of a strong appreciation for the culture and traditions of Mississippi's Native Americans. The success of the state's only remaining Native American tribe is a tribute to both the tenacity of the Choctaw people and their willingness to remain deeply involved in Mississippi's economic and cultural life.

Deborah Boykin

Alabama Center for
Traditional Culture

James Taylor Carson, *Searching for the Bright Path: The Mississippi Choctaws from Prehistory to Removal* (1999); H. B. Cushman, *History of the Choctaw, Chickasaw, and Natchez Indians*, ed. Angie Debo (1884; abridged ed., 1961); Robbie Ethridge, *From Chicaza to Chickasaw: The European Invasion and the Transformation of the Mississippian World* (2010); Patricia Galloway, *Choctaw Genesis, 1500–1700* (1996); Dennis Hevesi, *New York Times* (15 February 2010); Mississippi History Now website, http://mshistorynow.mdah.state.ms.us; National Park Service, Indian Mounds of Mississippi website, www.nps.gov/nr/travel/mounds; Greg O'Brien, *Choctaws in a Revolutionary Age, 1750–1830* (1996); Katherine M. B. Osburn, *Choctaw Resurgence in Mississippi: Race, Class, and Nation Building in the Jim Crow South, 1830–1977* (2014); John Reed Swanton, *Source Material for the Social and Ceremonial Life of the Choctaw Indians* (1931).

Native Americans, Relations with the French

From start to finish (1699–1763), French Louisiana suffered from lack of settlers, persistent shortages of goods for trade, and competition from English traders from Charleston and Georgia. In what is present-day Mississippi, fewer than five hundred farmers, traders, and soldiers huddled mainly near Forts Rosalie (Natchez) and St. Pierre (on the Lower Yazoo). Repeated wars with England (1701–14, 1744–48, 1754–63) diverted French ships and resources. Exportation of deerskins supported Louisiana's economy, gradually supplanted by growing quantities of tobacco, timber, pitch and tar, indigo, cotton, silk, and rice after black slaves began to arrive (1717–31). French relations with the Indians, ordinarily better than those enjoyed by the Spaniards and English, benefited from a relative lack of racial prejudice and especially from the fact that the French tended to have a greater desire for furs than for land. The exception that proved this rule was the massacre of the French by the Natchez Indians in 1729, after the French tried to put in place a grossly mismanaged plan to confiscate land that the Natchez considered sacred to turn it into tobacco plantations. The French and

their Choctaw, Chakchuima, and Tunica allies crushed and scattered the Natchez and their Koroa and Yazoo supporters, but the plantation scheme was aborted.

The French initially wanted friendly relations with all the tribes. In addition to deerskins, the colonists, facing starvation during the first two decades, needed Indian-produced food. Furthermore, the Indians far outnumbered the French in the Lower Mississippi Valley, though the number of Indians declined precipitously from sixty-seven thousand in 1700 to twenty-two thousand in 1750, primarily as a consequence of smallpox and other European diseases. The dominant tribes in Mississippi proper in 1725 were the Natchez (population around seventeen hundred), soon obliterated or fleeing to the Chickasaw and Upper Creek; the Chickasaw (population around thirty-five hundred), mainly in present-day Union and Pontotoc Counties in the north; and the Choctaw (around fourteen thousand), located in some fifty villages in the Pearl, Pascagoula, and Tombigbee watersheds. By 1705, however, the peace policy had broken down, and for the remainder of their time in Louisiana, the French and the Choctaw almost continuously promoted war against the Chickasaw.

The reasons became obvious. English traders, the bane of the French, persistently established themselves among the Chickasaw, although some Chickasaw approached the French whenever English trade faltered. Moreover, the Choctaw and Chickasaw were perennial foes despite their common origin. The English use of their allies, including the Chickasaw, to capture Choctaw and sell them into slavery stoked Choctaw hatred of the Chickasaw even after the English abandoned slaving expeditions following the Yamassee War (1715–17). The French, moreover, understood almost immediately that they needed Choctaw backing if Louisiana were to survive. Keeping the Choctaw meant fighting the Chickasaw to prevent English traders from enticing the Choctaw. The French at times encouraged quarrels among the Choctaw, notably during the Choctaw Civil War (1747–50) as a means of maintaining leverage and promoting Choctaw dependency. Last but certainly not least, hostile Chickasaw endangered Louisiana's communications with posts in Illinois and Canada.

The French presence profoundly affected the tribes. Western diseases, introduced by Hernando de Soto's expedition in the sixteenth century, devastated the Indians throughout the French period until survivors' immunities began to raise population levels slowly after around 1750. The deerskin trade generated changes at many levels. When the French appeared, deer were plentiful because disease and slave raiding had reduced the human population. The French also paid better than the English for the skins of smaller deer from the pine forests of the Choctaw country. In roughly four generations the Indians moved from the Stone Age to the Iron Age because of Western goods on which they grew to depend. They wanted woolen (*limbourg*) and cotton cloth (preferable to rawhide in Mississippi's climate); French-made lightweight muskets, suitable for hunting; powder and bullets; metal kettles, axes, hoes, and knives; glass beads, silver single-shell necklaces, combs, mirrors, pipes, and buttons; tiny bells for leggings; and after midcentury, *tafia*, a cheap rum.

Commerce, a relatively unimportant activity among Indian tribes devoted to hunting, gathering, and agriculture (notably the Choctaw), inexorably transformed these societies. The European market economy, featuring prices governed by supply and demand, cost accounting, and unlimited personal gain as its motive, was alien to Indian concepts. Barter based on traditional "just price" values was familiar; variable prices reflecting production levels or shipping costs were not and struck the Indians as unfair or thievery. Furthermore, agreeing to trade involved a friendship confirmed by gifts. If the French wanted to trade and use Indian lands, the Indians expected gifts. Furthermore, any Indian chief was expected to be generous in sharing his gifts with the members of his tribes. The French resented what they perceived as polite extortion but were compelled to allocate increasing sums of scarce government money for gifts for an annual ceremony with all the chiefs as a means of continuing trade, affirming the rejection of the English, or fighting the Chickasaw. The only saving grace was that Choctaw demand for European goods, while growing slowly, was fairly inelastic—that is, it was confined to a limited quantity of quality items. Thus, the French could—barely—supply Choctaw demand and thus keep them loyal.

To regularize matters, the French tried but failed to impose a European-style hierarchical order on the Choctaw by appointing a head chief. Choctaw organization, a tangle of traditional and family relationships, baffled the Europeans. The new "head chief" acquired no real authority, and gift distribution created an elite of chiefs, subchiefs, and their relatives that alienated large numbers of poor warriors. That the chiefs had always controlled the distribution of guns and used it to preserve their leverage only made matters worse. Factions formed, and some Choctaw inevitably turned to the English. The ambitious and wily Chief Red Shoes spent a decade alternately instigating pro-French or pro-English factions until he was assassinated in 1747 by a warrior who collected a French scalp bounty.

Other exploitative methods the French used included slavery, alcohol, and credit. The French concluded early that Indian enslavement was unpromising and instead turned to importing black slaves. By 1763 the Lower Mississippi Valley had only one hundred Indian slaves along with five thousand black slaves and two hundred mulattos. The English used alcohol and credit liberally to expand Indian demand, whereas the French used both reluctantly, partly because with short supplies they did not need to increase demand. French administrators and especially priests expressed regret over the ravages of alcohol, which included the point that drunken Indians made unreliable allies or fighters. Credit also was problematic, for Indians did not understand why whites could be so demanding regarding prompt repayment. A quarrel over a debt, in fact, ignited a dangerous 1722 uprising by the Natchez. The French began offering scalp bounties by the 1720s while fighting the Chickasaw. The lure of bounties tended over time to turn many Choctaw warriors into mercenaries, altering warfare from contests of pride and honor to something resembling a commercial enterprise carried on regardless of winter or planting or harvesting. Warfare also cost hunters time and safety, thus damaging the deerskin trade.

Other, less obvious, changes ensued. The deerskin trade gravely damaged Choctaw agriculture. Women had controlled the land and cultivation; consequently, their social status declined despite employment as skilled dressers of deerskins. Guns made hunting a solitary or small-group enterprise not involving a large band surrounding game for a collective kill. Sexual relations were affected when French traders, settlers, or soldiers, lacking white female companionship, acquired Indian wives, concubines, or lovers. A growing mixed-race component confused traditional family ties and weakened tribal authority and values. Missionaries—few in number and almost wholly unsuccessful in making converts—deplored the aborting of mixed-race babies and the disorder introduced in both French and Indian society by clashing sexual mores. Furthermore, contrasting conceptions of honor, justice, and vengeance muddied negotiations about why and how to wage war.

The arrival of Europeans forced the Indians to adapt to more unpredictability in their lives. Tradition and yearly cycles gave way to out-of-season activities using implements and technology that could alter the environment. The gun alone dramatically affected the size of Indian and animal populations as well as the extent and density of the woodlands and the amount of land needed for agriculture.

Nevertheless, the Choctaw avoided simple subordination to the French, though smaller Mississippi tribes had less success in doing so. There were too few French; intratribal divisions and traditions frustrated their attempts to impose a controllable organization; and above all, the presence of the English handed the Choctaw an opportunity to pit foreigners against each other. The Choctaw apparently did not fully grasp that when the French era ended in 1762–63, leaving only the English east of the Mississippi, the prospects of avoiding dependency had suffered a mortal wound.

David S. Newhall
Centre College

Patricia Galloway, *Journal of Mississippi History* 4 (1982); Jesse O. McKee and John A. Schlenker, *The Choctaw: Cultural Evolution of a Native North American Tribe* (1980); William C. Sturtevant, ed., *Handbook of North American Indians*, vol. 4, *History of Indian-White Relations*, ed. Wilcombe E. Washburn (1988); Daniel H. Usner Jr., *American Indians in the Lower Mississippi Valley: Social and Economic Histories* (1988); Daniel H. Usner Jr., *Indians, Settlers, and Slaves in a Frontier Exchange Economy: The Lower Mississippi Valley before 1783* (1992); Daniel H. Usner Jr.,

N

Proceedings of the 10th Meeting of the French Colonial Historical Society, April 12–14, 1984 (1985); Richard White, *The Roots of Dependency: Subsistance, Environment, and Social Change among the Choctaws, Pawnees, and Navajos* (1983); Patricia Dillon Woods, *French-Indian Relations on the Southern Frontier* (1980).

Native Americans, Relations with Spanish

By 1784 Spain possessed a transcontinental frontier empire in North America that stretched from New California through the Lower Mississippi Valley and Gulf Coast, including Louisiana (acquired from France in 1762) and East and West Florida (which had been returned to Spain in 1783). While one Treaty of Paris restored the Floridas, a second treaty between Great Britain and the new United States of America established American claims westward to the Mississippi River and an uncertain southern boundary. The architects of Spain's resurgence, Carlos III and José de Gálvez, secretary of the Indies, understood the strategic value of this northern fringe of the Spanish empire and the importance of renewed relations with the Native Americans in the Gulf and Lower Mississippi.

In the spring of 1784 Spanish officials launched a bold strategy to deny American claims south of the Ohio River and west of the Appalachian Mountains and to develop relations with the southern tribes designed to stem American expansion. The Cherokee, Chickasaw, Choctaw, and Creek—the Four Nations—signed treaties with the United States as well as treaties of friendship and fealty with Spanish representatives at conferences held in disparate venues from Pensacola to the Chickasaw Bluffs. These Native Americans, pro-American and pro-Spanish, used their considerable diplomatic skills to play the new American republic and the Spanish against each other to maintain the status quo and gain trade advantages.

Esteban Miró, acting governor-general of Louisiana and West Florida, and other Spanish officials signed four 1784 treaties with the Chickasaw, the Choctaw, and the Tallapoosa and Alabama of the Creek federation. Alexander McGillivray, a prominent mixed Scots-Creek, initiated the first treaty on behalf of the Tallapoosa at the Pensacola Congress on 30 May–1 June 1784. Eight Tallapoosa chiefs received "great medals" and six received "small medals" when they signed a defensive alliance with Spain and promised to maintain peace and friendship with Spain and other tribes. The Tallapoosa left Pensacola with a generous supply of powder, provisions, and rum.

Delegations from the Chickasaw, Choctaw, and Alabama traveled to Mobile, where they negotiated three treaties with Miró. The Alabama danced and performed an elaborate calumet ceremony and signed a treaty of friendship and fealty to Spain on 23 June 1784. The Chickasaw signed a similar agreement on the same day, marking the emergence of Ugulayacabé as a war chief. In July, Miró welcomed a much larger Choctaw delegation of 185 great- and small-medal chiefs, captains, warriors, and women representing fifty-nine villages led by Taboca and Franchimastabé. The Choctaw signed a treaty on 14 July 1784 similar to the treaties signed by the other delegations but insisted on receiving gifts and provisions whenever they traveled to Mobile or New Orleans.

Although American commissioners negotiated treaties with the Cherokee, Chickasaw, and Choctaw at Hopewell, South Carolina, in 1785–86, the Spanish quickly responded to this American threat. McGillivray prevented the Creek from sending delegates to Hopewell and attempted to dissuade the Chickasaw and Choctaw from attending. Miró sent Juan de la Villebeuvre on a mission to the Choctaw that ended in a successful meeting with the principal chiefs of the Chickasaw and Choctaw at "Grand Yazoo" in late October 1787. Following the Yazoo Conference several influential Choctaw and Chickasaw traveled to New Orleans in January 1788 and met with Miró, exchanged their English medals for Spanish medals and gifts, and renewed their pledge of loyalty to Spain. Miró guaranteed fair trade and the delivery of quality merchandise by Panton, Leslie, and Company traders.

In December 1791 Francisco Luis Héctor, Baron de Carondelet, replaced Miró as governor-general of Louisiana and West Florida and implemented policies to check American land grabbing and contacts among the southern Indians. Before his arrival in New Orleans, Manuel Gayoso de Lemos, the governor at Natchez, moved up to the Yazoo River in April 1791 and constructed a fort near its mouth to prevent the South Carolina Yazoo Company from starting a settlement at Los Nogales or Walnut Hills (present-day Vicksburg). Franchimastabé and Taboca challenged the Spanish land claims, causing Gayoso to negotiate for a year before concluding a treaty with Taskietoka, Franchimastabé, Ugulayacabé, and some three hundred Choctaw and Chickasaw at Natchez on 14 May 1792.

Following Gayoso's success at Natchez, Carondelet launched an aggressive plan to control the Indian trade, stifle American influence over the Four Nations, and build an Indian confederacy to defend Spain's claim to the Lower Mississippi Valley south of the Ohio and west of the Appalachians. Carondelet's confederacy received its first endorsement from Bloody Fellow, who led a Cherokee delegation to a November 1792 New Orleans conference that included Choctaw, Chickasaw, and Shawnee. He urged Carondelet to construct posts at Muscle Shoals on the Tennessee and at the site of the old French Fort Tombecbé on the Tombigbee River and to halt American intrusions on Indian lands. Carondelet proposed that Spain serve as a mediator between the Four Nations and the United

States and suggested the creation of a congress with representatives from each nation to prevent conflicts and maintain peace.

Despite the efforts of George Washington's administration to counter the Spanish influence, Carondelet's plan met with success through the diplomacy of Gayoso and Villebeuvre. At Boucfouca (present-day Jackson), Villebeuvre signed a three-article treaty with twenty-six Choctaw chiefs and captains on 10 May 1793. Article 1 provided for the transfer of approximately 25.5 acres to the Spanish for the construction of a fort at the site of the former French fort on the Tombigbee River, where the Choctaw would receive "gifts and provisions." In the other articles, the Spanish promised to protect and defend the Choctaw and their lands, and the chiefs and captains pledged to remain "steadfast friends" of the Spanish. Six months later at Fort Nogales, Gayoso welcomed two thousand Chickasaw, Choctaw, Tallapoosa, and Alabama, and they signed the Treaty of Nogales on 28 October 1793. By this treaty, Ugulayacabé, Franchimastabé, and four great-medal chiefs representing the Creek and Cherokee agreed to form "an offensive and defensive alliance" and accepted "His Catholic Majesty" as their protector, empowering the Spanish to regulate trade and mediate boundaries with the United States.

The Treaties of Boucfouca and Nogales led to the construction of Fort Confederation on the Tombigbee in 1794 and Fort San Fernando de las Barrancas on the Chickasaw Bluffs (present-day Memphis) in 1795 with the approval of the Chickasaw. While Choctaw and Chickasaw visited the new Spanish posts to trade and to receive gifts and munitions, Spanish and American representatives negotiated the Treaty of San Lorenzo in October 1795. The treaty established the thirty-first parallel as the boundary between Spanish and American territory east of the Mississippi River. It effectively ended Carondelet's Indian confederacy and in 1797 and 1798 forced the evacuation of Spanish fortifications north of the new boundary, including Nogales, Confederation, San Fernando de las Barrancas, and San Esteban de Tombecbé, north of Mobile. The treaty left the Four Nations exposed to the demands of the southern states and the policies of the federal government.

James P. Pate
University of Mississippi, Tupelo

Jack D. L. Holmes, *Florida Historical Quarterly* (October 1969, April 1980); Jack D. L. Holmes, *Gayoso: The Life of a Spanish Governor in the Mississippi Valley, 1789–1799* (1965); Jack D. L. Holmes, *Publications of the East Tennessee Historical Society* 34 (1962); Manuel Serrano y Sanz, *Spain and the Cherokee and Choctaw Indians in the Second Half of the Eighteenth Century*, trans. Samuel Dorris Dickinson (1995); Charles A. Weeks, *Paths to the Middle Ground: The Diplomacy of Natchez, Boukfouka, Nogales, and San Fernando de las Barrancas, 1791–1795* (2005).

Neshoba County

Located in east-central Mississippi, Neshoba County was founded in 1833. Its name comes from a Choctaw word meaning "wolf." The county may be best known for three things: (1) the notorious murders of three civil rights workers in 1964, (2) the presence and prominence of the Mississippi Band of Choctaw Indians, and (3) a county fair popular far beyond the county's borders.

After its founding, Neshoba County almost doubled in population during each decade in the antebellum period. In its first census in 1840, only 1,693 free people and 744 slaves lived in Neshoba County. By 1850 the population had increased to 4,729, including 3,393 free people and 1,335 slaves. Ten years later, Neshoba County's population had risen to 6,131 free people and 2,212 slaves (26 percent of the total). Antebellum Neshoba was not a large producer of agricultural goods, but it ranked considerably higher in the value of its livestock. The county had 49 industrial workers, most of whom worked at four lumber mills.

Neshoba's 1880 population of 8,741 had grown little since the antebellum period. Neshoba County's 418-person Choctaw community gave it the state's largest Native American contingent and the highest percentage (about 5 percent) of Native American residents. Owners rather than tenants ran 82 percent of the county's farms and concentrated more on corn, swine, and sheep than on cotton. Neshoba remained a farm economy, with only 23 people working in industry.

Between 1880 and 1900 the county's population grew by about 50 percent to 12,726. The rates of landowning for both black and white farmers were higher than state averages, with 77 percent of white farmers and 43 percent of black farmers owning their land. In 1900 Neshoba had only 23 industrial workers and the lowest total manufacturing wages in the state.

In 1891, with the organization of the Neshoba County Fair, the county became a central location for annual visits and campaign speeches. In the twentieth century the fair became famous for unique cabins that housed generations of families and friends visiting the area.

Methodists and Baptists made up more than three-quarters of the county's church members in the early twentieth century. The Southern Baptist Convention and Methodist Episcopal Church, South were the largest religious groups, while Catholics accounted for about 7 percent of churchgoers.

By 1930 Neshoba's population had risen to 26,691, including 20,516 whites, 5,469 African Americans, and 695 Native Americans. Despite having the eleventh-most industrial workers in Mississippi (1,080 people), Neshoba remained an agricultural county with more than 4,600 farms evenly divided between those run by owners and those operated by tenants.

The Choctaw Fair began in the Pearl River community in 1949 and has subsequently become a major gathering of both Choctaw and nonnative people. At the fair, numerous events celebrate Choctaw culture through food and sports. In addition, the Mississippi Band of Choctaw Indians has aggressively recruited industry since the late 1970s and has run successful casinos since the 1990s. The Mississippi Band has also become one of the state's major employers and runs a school system where more than 1,500 students learn the Choctaw language as part of their education.

Between 1930 and 1960 Neshoba's population declined to 20,927. Whites made up 72 percent of the population, with African Americans totaling 22 percent and the Choctaw 6 percent. Farmers made up about 26 percent of the work-force, while manufacturing provided another quarter of all jobs. The majority of industrial workers produced either clothing or furniture. Farming concentrated first on corn, then cotton and soybeans.

In 1956 Charles Evers organized the Philadelphia chapter of the National Association for the Advancement of Colored People, and by the early 1960s Neshoba County had an active civil rights movement. In June 1964 three movement workers—Meridian native James Chaney and New Yorkers Michael Schwerner and Andrew Goodman—disappeared while investigating the burning of Mount Zion Methodist Church outside Philadelphia in retaliation for the church's support for civil rights efforts. The three men were later found dead, and their murders attracted national condemnation and a long series of investigations that finally ended with the conviction of Edgar Ray Killen for manslaughter in 2005. The movie *Mississippi Burning* (1988) offered a fictionalized version of these events.

Marcus Dupree was a football star at Philadelphia High School before playing at the University of Oklahoma and in the United States Football League and National Football League. Willie Morris's 1983 book, *The Courting of Marcus Dupree*, details how Dupree's talent helped to smooth over racial divisions and brought football scouts to rural Mississippi.

Race relations in the county again received more national attention and criticism when presidential candidate Ronald Reagan made a 3 August 1980 stop at the Neshoba County Fair, where he attracted attention and controversy for using the language of states' rights.

Between 1960 and 2010 Neshoba County's population increased by nearly 42 percent, reaching 29,676. Whites made up a majority of the population, African Americans comprised a substantial minority, and the Choctaw minority showed significant growth.

Mississippi Encyclopedia Staff
University of Mississippi

Mississippi State Planning Commission, *Progress Report on State Planning in Mississippi* (1938); *Mississippi Statistical Abstract*, Mississippi State University (1952–2010); Charles Sydnor and Claude Bennett, *Mississippi History* (1939); University of Virginia Library, Historical Census Browser website, http://mapserver.lib.virginia.edu; E. Nolan Waller and Dani A. Smith, *Growth Profiles of Mississippi's Counties, 1960–1980* (1985).

Neshoba County Fair

The Neshoba County Fair is one of Mississippi's most notable social, political, and cultural institutions. A true campground fair, the event has been held annually (except for an interruption during World War II) since 1891. Located eight miles southwest of the county seat, Philadelphia, the fair features political oratory, late-night gospel singing, popular musical acts, a triathlon, livestock and produce exhibitions, a midway with games and carnival food, a beauty contest, mule racing, and the only legal horseracing in the state. The fair's patrons and admirers praise the sense of community and nostalgia that the event embodies. Indeed, the fair represents nothing so much as an annual weeklong family reunion for thousands of Neshoba County residents, their kin, and their friends.

The fairgrounds resemble a small Mississippi town, with neighborhoods such as Happy Hollow and Sunset Strip, streets, and even a post office, all fanning out from centrally located Founder's Square. The most distinctive feature of the fair is the cabins, now numbering more than six hundred, in which thousands of people live for a week in late July each year. These magnificent specimens of vernacular architecture are decorated and feature such names as The Fox Den, Green Acres, and Ye Old King's Kastle. Traditionally, these two- and three-story structures have been self-consciously spartan, in keeping with the fair's early history as a camp meeting; some early cabins were log houses. Cabin owners have more recently installed air-conditioning and even Mississippi-manufactured Viking ranges. Almost all of the cabins feature broad front porches and balconies that allow for long afternoons and evenings of visiting with family and friends. Most cabins display some signs of life twenty-four hours a day. Upstairs, one typically finds row upon row of bunk beds. Most of the cabins are decorated with family names and even family trees; state, national, and Confederate flags; and banners declaring allegiance to one of the state's universities. And while Neshoba is a dry county, alcohol is in plentiful if discreet supply in many cabins.

The Neshoba County Fair traces its origins to 1889 and to Patron's Union meetings and other fairs in surrounding counties and communities. Fairgoers and their families initially traveled the red clay roads to the fair in ox-drawn wagons, camping at night in makeshift shelters. In 1891 nine men formed the Neshoba County Stock and Agricultural Fair Association. With an initial tract of 20 acres, the Fair Association began construction of a pavilion and later a hotel. Fairgoers soon began building the cabins that make the fairgrounds so distinctive. Early fairs featured the sorts of exhibitions of livestock, agricultural products, and handcrafts common at county fairs across the South. Incorporated under state law in 1933, the Neshoba County Fair, unlike other state and county fairs, was and remains a private, nonprofit corporation owned by local stockholders. The Fair Association still owns all 150 acres on which the cabins stand and must approve any sale, transfer, or significant alteration to any cabin.

For the past one hundred years the fair has played an important role in Mississippi politics. Governors since Anselm McLaurin (1896–1900) have spoken at the fair, as has practically every serious candidate for state and local office, including constable and supervisor. In recent decades the fair has even drawn the occasional presidential candidate, including such figures as Jack Kemp, Michael Dukakis, John Glenn, and Ronald Reagan. Would-be officeholders have long enjoyed the opportunity to woo the very large (by Mississippi standards) and politically savvy crowds. Unlike many state and county fairs, Neshoba's is held in late July, not at harvest time. Mississippi's primary elections are held in August, which gave candidates the chance to brave the heat and the dust (or mud) and reach voters before the election that mattered most when Mississippi was a one-party state. For most of the twentieth century the vast majority of dozens of candidates who spoke at the fair each year were Democrats, though Republican hopefuls are now in the majority and receive the warmest welcome, a change that reflects broader currents in Mississippi and southern politics.

As with almost any Mississippi institution, the fair carries its own history of race. In the 1950s and 1960s politicians speaking at the fair strove to outdo each other in claiming the power to defend the state's "traditional way of life" from the menaces of the federal government and outside agitators. Ross Barnett became a fair favorite in the years after he served as governor. The old ways of speaking about race have disappeared from the fair, and Mississippi politicians today sometimes use the fair's Neshoba County setting to point to the recent successful prosecutions of civil rights era killers as evidence of the state's movement away from the old days.

The cabins, the food, and the political speaking all contribute to the unique sense of place and community that makes the Neshoba County Fair "Mississippi's Giant Houseparty" for its patrons.

Trent Brown
Missouri University of
Science and Technology

Robert Craycroft, *The Neshoba County Fair: Place and Paradox in Mississippi* (1989); Steven H. Stubbs, *Mississippi's Giant Houseparty: The History of the Neshoba County Fair* (2005).

Neshoba County Murders

On the night of 21 June 1964 three civil rights workers—James Chaney, Andrew Goodman, and Michael Schwerner—disappeared in Neshoba County. Federal law enforcement officials were called in to search for the missing men. That effort and the investigation that continued after their bodies were found forty-four days later focused national attention on the county and the state. The Federal Bureau of Investigation (FBI) labeled the case "Mississippi Burning."

Lawrence Rainey had been elected sheriff of Neshoba County in 1963. Rainey, previously a police officer in Canton and Philadelphia, had campaigned with the promise to "take care of things," a phrase white residents of Neshoba County understood to mean preserving white supremacy. Black residents interpreted those words to mean that law enforcement officials would escalate the level of violence against black citizens. Soon after Rainey became sheriff, Cecil Price, who had worked with Rainey in Canton, was hired as a deputy and quickly gained a reputation for being hard on blacks. Within his first year on the job, two black residents were killed while Price was arresting them.

During the "Freedom Summer" of 1964, civil rights workers traveled to Mississippi from across the country to help African Americans register to vote. An umbrella organization, the Council of Federated Organizations (COFO), was created to coordinate actions by various civil rights groups and opened a headquarters in Meridian, near Neshoba County. On 21 June three men met at the office: Goodman, a twenty-year-old history major from Queens College in New York; Michael Schwerner, a twenty-four-year-old graduate of Cornell University; and James Chaney, a twenty-one-year-old civil rights activist from Lauderdale County. The three men left Meridian for Sandstown, a community in eastern Neshoba County, where the Mount Zion Church had recently been burned because it was to be the home of a freedom school. Schwerner told others at the office that if he, Goodman, and Chaney were not back by 4:00 p.m., COFO should "start trying to locate us."

After visiting the church, the activists got into their car and decided to drive back to Meridian via Philadelphia, which they thought would be the fastest route. However, their station wagon got a flat tire near Philadelphia, and Deputy Price stopped the vehicle at around 3:00. He arrested Chaney, the driver, for speeding and held Schwerner and Goodman for questioning. Price released the men from jail at about 10:30 that night. COFO leaders had already begun to search, but when they called the Neshoba County Jail, they were falsely told that Goodman, Chaney, and Schwerner were not there.

On 22 June COFO told the media about the missing men, sparking demands for a federal effort to find them. The FBI sent special agent John Proctor into Neshoba County to see if local law enforcement was involved in the disappearance. Proctor initially found no evidence of illegal activity on the part of local law enforcement, and white Neshoba residents began claiming that COFO had filed the missing persons' case to gain sympathy and financial support. However, within forty-eight hours Goodman, Chaney, and Schwerner's station wagon was found in a swamp about twenty-seven miles from where Price told the FBI he had last seen the vehicle.

Over the next six weeks, 150 FBI agents scoured Mississippi for the men. US Navy divers brought in to assist the effort found the bodies of eight other African Americans—three civil rights activists, plus five men who were never identified. On 4 August FBI agents found the bodies of the three missing men inside an earthen dam in the southwestern corner of Neshoba County.

While Goodman, Chaney, and Schwerner were being held in the Neshoba County Jail, Klansmen had been assembling. As the three activists attempted to leave the county after their release from the jail, Price stopped them again after a high-speed chase, and Klansmen took them to an isolated area, tortured Chaney, shot all three men, and buried them in the dam. Motivated by a large reward offered by the FBI, one of the conspirators had told agents where the bodies could be found.

Several months later, after Mississippi officials showed little interest in prosecuting the perpetrators, the federal government charged eighteen men with conspiring to violate Goodman, Chaney, and Schwerner's civil rights. Seven were found guilty and sentenced to prison terms ranging from three to ten years. Deputy Price and Sam Bowers, imperial wizard of the White Knights of the East Mississippi Ku Klux Klan, received the longest sentences, though no one served more than six years. Eight defendants, including Sheriff Rainey, were acquitted, and the jury hung on the guilt or innocence of three others, including Edgar Ray Killen.

After the 1967 election, Philadelphia's board of aldermen experienced a complete turnover, Rainey and Price left law enforcement, and school integration in Neshoba County occurred smoothly and without major incident. Whites generally sought to put the case into the past and avoid revisiting it. Nevertheless, memories lingered, and a 1988 film, *Mississippi Burning*, offered a fictionalized version of the events. Inspired by the movie, *Jackson Clarion-Ledger* investigative reporter Jerry Mitchell began looking into various civil rights–era cold cases, and his work, along with that of a biracial local group known as the Philadelphia Coalition, and an Illinois high school teacher and three of his students, led the

State of Mississippi to bring charges against Killen. Although the jury declined to convict him of murder, on 21 June 2005, exactly forty-one years after the crime, it did find him guilty on three counts of manslaughter for recruiting the mob that carried out the killings. He received the maximum punishment on each count—twenty years imprisonment.

James Newman
Southeast Missouri State
University

Howard Ball, *Murder in Mississippi: United States v. Price and the Struggle for Civil Rights* (2004); Seth Cagin and Philip Dray, *We Are Not Afraid: The Story of Goodman, Chaney, and Schwerner, and the Civil Rights Campaign for Mississippi* (2006); William Bradford Huie, *Three Lives for Mississippi* (1965, repr., 2000); Florence Mars, *Witness in Philadelphia* (1977).

New Capitol

Mississippi's current capitol building, commonly referred to as the New Capitol, is actually well over a century old. Dedicated in 1903, the building is the third capitol facility constructed in the city of Jackson and has now served as the seat of Mississippi's government longer than all of the previous capitols combined.

The New Capitol was born of dire necessity. By the 1890s the Old Capitol, which had been constructed in 1839, stood in desperate need of repair. The building was also not large enough to house the growing government. Leading citizens began advocating for a new building by 1890 as conditions in the Old Capitol steadily worsened, and in 1896 the legislature appointed a committee to solicit bids.

Constructing the New Capitol proved contentious. The legislature and Gov. Anselm J. McLaurin spent four years debating where to locate the building and how to choose a design. Many politicians wanted to tear down the Old Capitol and build the new facility on the same site, but others preferred the spot a few blocks away where the State Penitentiary stood. Disillusioned by the lack of progress, McLaurin's successor, Andrew H. Longino, made construction of a new capitol a top priority when he took office in 1900. Within a matter of weeks, he had appointed a new State House Commission to oversee construction of a capitol on the State Penitentiary site. St. Louis architect Theodore Link was chosen for the job, and construction began on 1 January 1901. The structure ultimately cost just over one million dollars, money that came from back taxes owed by railroad companies.

Designed in the Beaux Arts style, the New Capitol incorporates elements from several classical architectural forms

New Capitol, ca. 1916 (Al Fred Daniel Photograph Collection, Archives and Records Services Division, Mississippi Department of Archives and History [26])

Mississippi History Now website, http://mshistorynow.mdah.state.ms.us; Dunbar Rowland, *History of Mississippi* (1925); John Ray Skates, *Mississippi's Old Capitol: Biography of a Building* (1990); Mississippi Department of Archives and History, *Proceedings of the Dedication Ceremonies, Mississippi State Capitol Restoration and Renovation 1980–1983* (1983).

typical of the late French Renaissance. The building is 402 feet long and 225 feet wide and is topped by a solid copper eagle coated in gold leaf. The pediment of the main portico is decorated with fourteen figures symbolizing Mississippi's artistic, intellectual, and economic heritage. Its elaborately decorated interior includes Bedford limestone and Georgia granite as well as Vermont, Black Belgian, Italian, and New York marble. More than four thousand electric lights (a recent invention at the time of its construction) illuminate the interior. A massive dome rises 180 feet above the floor and features four murals depicting important scenes in the state's history.

The building was dedicated at a daylong public ceremony on 3 June 1903. The event, attended by a wide variety of citizens and reporters from throughout Mississippi and neighboring states, included the laying of the cornerstone and addresses by Gov. Longino; Bishop Charles B. Galloway of the Methodist Episcopal Church, South; and Chief Justice A. H. Whitfield. The celebration culminated with an evening reception in the illuminated building.

After three-quarters of a century of service, the New Capitol, like its predecessor, required extensive repair. After renovations that took four years and cost more than nineteen million dollars, the facility was rededicated on its eightieth anniversary, 3 June 1983. The New Capitol has been designated a Mississippi landmark building and is listed on the National Register of Historic Places. It continues to serve as the headquarters for the state's legislative and executive branches of government and remains open to the public.

Mike Bunn
Historic Chattahoochee
Commission

Clay Williams
Mississippi Department of
Archives and History

New Deal Jobs Programs

In 1933 Mississippi was experiencing the depths of the Great Depression. Cotton, which accounted for nearly 80 percent of Mississippi's gross farm income, had fallen from twenty cents per pound to just under five cents between 1927 and 1932. As farmers fell deeper into debt, farms were auctioned off for unpaid property taxes, and tenant farmers were thrown off the land. As landownership reverted to the banks, more than a million acres were taken out of production, and depressed property values resulted in eighty million dollars in lost state revenues from 1931 to 1933. The production of timber, the state's other main agricultural resource, also fell drastically, and more than a thousand small plants closed and twenty-four thousand manufacturing jobs evaporated. With the decline in agriculture and industry across the state, annual per capita income fell from $239 to $117 between 1929 and 1933.

In December 1932 Gov. Martin "Mike" Conner named George B. Power the director of the Mississippi Board of Public Welfare. Using funds from Pres. Herbert Hoover's Reconstruction Finance Corporation, Power organized state welfare programs on a county level, emphasizing work relief and home garden programs. Those programs expanded after Franklin D. Roosevelt became president in January 1933 and inaugurated the New Deal, a series of programs designed to advance economic and social recovery in the nation's financial, industrial, and agricultural sectors. The New Deal also provided both direct relief and work programs to assist the poor and unemployed. Power became the state coordinator of New Deal relief programs.

In April 1933 Power became the state administrator of the Civilian Conservation Corps, a New Deal program designed to put men between ages eighteen and twenty-five to work in reforestation projects, road and park construction, flood control, and fire prevention. More than ten thousand people applied for the four thousand job positions. Because of a shortage of state social workers, county eligibility committees chose job applicants. These committees often denied jobs to African Americans as a means of controlling labor during the fall cotton harvest.

The Board of Public Welfare also oversaw the distribution of Federal Emergency Relief Administration (FERA) funds

N

in 1933–35. The FERA provided grants to states on a matching basis—for every three dollars the state provided, the federal government would provide one dollar. Because of the state's desperate financial condition, however, Mississippi was exempted from the federal matching provision of the program. By the end of June 1933 more than seventy-nine thousand Mississippi families had received FERA relief. Also that year, the Civil Works Administration (CWA) was created to provide emergency relief through the winter of 1933–34. The Mississippi CWA spent nine million dollars during the six months of its existence and employed seventy-four thousand people in jobs ranging from repairing schools and hiring teachers to building roads and reservoirs.

Disparities and discrimination were common in the administration of many New Deal programs. The Mississippi CWA employed sixty thousand men but only fourteen thousand women. Men received forty-five cents per hour, while women received thirty-two cents. Women were often relegated to sewing rooms and clerical positions, which paid considerably less than the construction jobs offered to men. In the spring of 1934, with the expiration of the CWA, relief and work programs reverted back to the control of the state-managed FERA. The Mississippi Emergency Relief Association transferred women from direct relief to work relief programs and employed women as clerks, nutritionists, health technicians, social workers, library assistants, school lunch workers, and teachers.

In 1935 President Roosevelt initiated a second wave of New Deal programs that provided federal assistance on a much broader scale. Mississippi established a permanent state welfare agency to coordinate federal relief programs begun under the Social Security Act. The State Planning Commission worked closely with the federal Works Progress Administration (WPA) to build and improve parks, libraries, schools, roads, drainage basins, and reservoirs.

From 1935 until the beginning of World War II, the WPA provided Mississippians with a wide range of employment opportunities. Music education courses were offered in public schools, summer camps were conducted for youth and recreation, and community centers were opened for senior adults. The state also benefited from various WPA projects that collected and cataloged cultural, religious, and historical records.

James S. Kinsey
Jackson State University

Sue Bridwell Beckham, *Depression Post Office Murals: A Gentle Reconstruction* (1989); Eric C. Clark, *Journal of Mississippi History* (November 1990); Mississippi Planning Commission, *The Industrial Status of Mississippi* (April 1937); Martha Swain, *Journal of Mississippi History* (February 1984); Roger D. Tate Jr., *Journal of Mississippi History* (February 1984); William Winter, *Journal of Mississippi History* (August 1979).

Newman, C. B. "Buddie"
(1921–2002) Politician

Clarence Benton "Buddie" Newman was born on 8 May 1921 in Valley Park, Mississippi, the son of a state legislator who also worked as a section foreman for the Yazoo and Mississippi Valley Railroad (later part of the Illinois Central line). As a boy, Newman accompanied his father to Jackson to serve as a legislative page. There, he met many of the state's major politicians, such as Fielding Wright, Speaker of the Mississippi House of Representatives and a future governor. After high school, Newman went to work for Southern Natural Gas Company, but with the outbreak of World War II he enlisted in the military, serving in the Pacific Theater from 1942 to 1945. When Newman returned to Issaquena County after the war, he resumed his job with the gas company and began farming. In 1947 he won election to the Mississippi Senate, and politics soon became his primary vocation. He served one term in the upper chamber of the legislature before moving to the Mississippi House, where he won reelection eight times, serving through 1988. During his forty-year legislative career, Newman became one of the state's most powerful and ultimately most controversial politicians.

Very early in his stint in the Mississippi House, Newman developed a close relationship with Walter Sillers, the forceful Speaker who ruled from 1944 to 1966. Sillers placed the young lawmaker on the influential Ways and Means Committee and in 1964 made him chair of the committee, a post he held until 1975. While in the legislature in the 1960s he strongly supported segregation, and he was closely involved with Gov. Ross Barnett during the crisis over the integration of the University of Mississippi. In a 1993 interview, Newman declared that African Americans "should have an opportunity to vote. They should have an opportunity for an education, but I would be lying to tell you today if I believe they ought to go to school together. I don't believe that. . . . I don't believe they ought to be in school together. And I don't think they ought to marry. I think that there's a place that they ought to be separated."

In 1976 Newman became Speaker, serving in that capacity until his retirement. Like Wright and Sillers before him, Newman closely guarded the power of the state's most influential body, but by the mid-1980s he faced challenges to his rule. Some observers trace the decline of Newman's power to his initial lackluster support for Gov. William Winter's Education Reform Act. During the 1982 legislative session, Newman killed Winter's public kindergarten bill by adjourning the House on a crucial deadline day without a vote. The press pummeled Newman for his action. The Speaker soon changed his position and went on to play a key role in securing passage of the education reform package during a special session later in the year. In 1983, however, a group of freshman legislators tried to change the rules to reduce Newman's power. Newman responded by punishing the rebels, a tactic Sillers had used to great effect. Times, however, had obviously changed, and resentment over Newman's actions festered. By 1987 the reformers had a majority, and it was clear that Newman would not be reelected Speaker after the 1988 elections.

Newman chose to withdraw from politics and returned to Valley Park, where he operated a farm and a railroad museum until his death on 13 October 2002.

Charles Bolton
University of North Carolina at
Greensboro

Bill Minor, *Eyes on Mississippi: A Fifty-Year Chronicle of Change* (2001); Andrew P. Mullins Jr., *Building Consensus: A History of the Passage of the Mississippi Education Reform Act of 1982* (1992); "Oral History with Mr. C. B. Newman" (1992, 1993), Center for Oral History and Cultural Heritage, University of Southern Mississippi, http://digilib.usm.edu/cdm/ref/collection/coh/id/5953.

Newspapers during the Civil War

As Mississippi anticipated war in 1861, its primary method of getting information suffered several nearly fatal blows. Among the hundreds of men who volunteered for militias and military companies were the bulk of the state's newspaper publishers, writers, and printers. The state's official newspaper, the *Jackson Mississippian*, reported that by midyear two-thirds of the state's professional newsmen had gone to war. A second severe handicap hit the state's newspaper industry even harder: Mississippi had no paper mills at the outbreak of the Civil War. Newspaper publishers depended on paper supplies from Alabama and Georgia, and as the war progressed, paper became more difficult and much more expensive to obtain, rising to ten times prewar prices by 1862 alone.

It is difficult to establish exactly how many newspapers were published in Mississippi when the state seceded on 9 January 1861. An early twentieth-century researcher, using information from the census, set the number at seventy-three, but later surveys have documented only thirty papers, a mere fifteen of which remain available for research in archives and libraries.

The state's most influential newspaper in 1861 was the *Mississippian*, published by fire-eating secessionist Ethelbert Barksdale until shortly after the war began, when he sold the paper to F. T. Cooper and A. N. Cooper. By 1863 only a few Mississippi towns had access to newspapers. Jackson and Vicksburg each had two papers, while Natchez, Meridian, and Canton had one apiece. In each paper, reliable news was scarce. The papers reported news of battles as best they could, receiving dispatches by telegraph transmissions, which were expensive and unreliable. In March of that year, Jackson's *Daily Southern Crisis* merged with the *Mississippian* for "business reasons." That summer, with the end of the three-month Siege of Vicksburg, Union forces seized both of that city's newspapers. The *Vicksburg Citizen* had been publishing on the back side of wallpaper, since no other paper was available, but the publication's final issue, dated 2 July, remained defiant: "The great Ulysses—the Yankee Generalissimo, surnamed Grant—has expressed his intention of dining in Vicksburg on Saturday next, and celebrating the 4th of July by a grand dinner and so forth. . . . Ulysses must get into the city before he dines in it. The way to cook rabbit is 'first catch the rabbit.' &c." However, the final item in that edition of the paper, printed in the lower right corner and dated 4 July, was added by Union troops after they took the city: "Two days bring about great changes. The banner of the Union floats over Vicksburg. Gen. Grant has 'caught the rabbit'; he has dined in Vicksburg, and he has brought his dinner with him. The 'Citizen' lives to see it. . . . This is the last wall-paper edition, and is, excepting this note, from the types as we found them. It will be valuable hereafter as a curiosity." In addition, Union forces took over publication of the *Natchez Courier* and destroyed the offices of the *Canton Gazette*.

The *Mississippian* alone escaped Union control, moving some of its equipment to Selma, Alabama. The paper continued to cover local news in Jackson and to distribute within the city, even though its editorial offices were in Meridian and its press in Selma. In 1864, however, even the *Mississippian* began to agitate for peace. Only once did the Confederate government complain about a Mississippi newspaper. In January 1865 the *Meridian Eastern Clarion* published a false report about the location of Union forces, resulting in a warning from the Confederacy about alarming citizens unnecessarily. No further action was taken.

Mississippians first learned of a report that Robert E. Lee had surrendered from a headline in the 12 April 1865 *Vicksburg Daily Herald* and received the official news on 18 April from the *Natchez Weekly Courier*. On 15 April the *Herald* reported the assassination of Abraham Lincoln in an official dispatch from US secretary of war E. M. Stanton. Early the next month the *Herald* told its readers, "Return to your homes and become quiet and peaceable citizens. . . . The strong arm of government has taken hold of you and checked you in the mad career of your folly and saved you from utter ruin."

Nancy McKenzie Dupont
University of Mississippi

John K. Bettersworth, *Confederate Mississippi: The People and Policies of a Cotton State in Wartime* (1943); Nancy McKenzie Dupont, "The Gathering Tempest: The Role of Mississippi Newspapers in the Secession Crisis, 1860–1861" (PhD dissertation, University of Southern Mississippi, 1997); William David Sloan and James Glen Stovall, *The Media in America: A History*, ed. James D. Startt (1993).

Newton County

The area in east-central Mississippi that became Newton County had a substantial Choctaw population that moved west in the 1830s as part of policies of Indian Removal. Reportedly named after Isaac Newton, the county was formed from the southern part of Neshoba County in 1836. Its county seat is Decatur. In the frontier period, Newton County was a small but growing community with a large majority of free people. In the 1840 census, Newton had 1,980 free people and 454 slaves, one of the smallest slave populations in the state.

By 1860 Newton's population had increased to 6,131 free people and 2,212 slaves (approximately 35 percent of the total). Despite its small size, Newton ranked thirty-sixth among the state's sixty counties in cotton production. Among Newton County's twelve churches, five were Baptist, five were Methodist, and two were Presbyterian.

By 1880 the county had grown to 13,436 people, with substantial increases in the numbers of both African Americans and whites. Newton was also home to 322 Choctaws, the third-highest Native American population in the state. Newton's postbellum farmers practiced mixed agriculture, concentrating on corn and other grains rather than on cotton. Owners cultivated about 73 percent of the county's 1,493 farms, a figure well above the state average, while tenants and sharecroppers farmed the rest.

Population growth continued in the late 1800s, and by 1900 Newton's population totaled about 20,000. Of the county's white farmers, 72 percent owned their own land, compared to just 27 percent of the African American farmers. Manufacturing was increasing, with 63 firms employing 172 industrial workers, all but 3 of them male. One of the first four agricultural experiment stations in Mississippi started in Newton County.

The religious census of 1916 showed that Baptists—almost evenly divided between Southern Baptists and Missionary Baptists—made up 70 percent of all church members in Newton County. Methodists and Presbyterians accounted for most of the remainder. Notable events in the county's religious life included the 1908 establishment of Clarke Memorial College, a Baptist institution as well as a state singing convention for gospel musicians that took place in Newton in 1934.

Civil rights leaders Charles and Medgar Evers were born in Decatur in the 1920s and attended Newton Vocational School. Eugenia Summer, born in Newton in 1923, taught at Mississippi University for Women and was a noted artist.

In 1930 Newton's population grew to almost 23,000. The county's farms were divided evenly between those run by owners and those operated by tenants. Corn and livestock were the primary agricultural products, followed by cotton and swine. Newton County's twenty industrial establishments employed 434 people.

The county's population declined to 19,517 in 1960, with whites making up two-thirds of residents, African Americans 32 percent, and Native Americans 2 percent. About a quarter of the county's workforce labored in industry. Both men and women worked in apparel factories, while furniture production primarily employed men. Another quarter of the workforce raised livestock and mixed crops. Newton's population remained steady through the 1980s.

Like many counties in central Mississippi, Newton's population has remained relatively stable in the late twentieth and early twenty-first centuries. In 2010 Newton County was home to 21,720 people, 63.2 percent of them white, 30 percent of them African American, and 5 percent of them Native American.

Mississippi Encyclopedia Staff
University of Mississippi

Mississippi State Planning Commission, *Progress Report on State Planning in Mississippi* (1938); *Mississippi Statistical Abstract*, Mississippi State University (1952–2010); Charles Sydnor and Claude Bennett, *Mississippi History* (1939); University of Virginia Library, Historical Census Browser website, http://mapserver.lib.virginia.edu; E. Nolan Waller and Dani A. Smith, *Growth Profiles of Mississippi's Counties, 1960–1980* (1985).

Nichols, William
(1777–1853) Architect

Over a prolific career that spanned more than five decades, architect William Nichols designed major public and institutional buildings in four southern states, becoming among the most accomplished architects of his generation and a leading figure of the Greek Revival. He produced his most mature work while serving as state architect of Mississippi in the late 1830s and 1840s. The State Capitol, the Governor's Mansion, the State Penitentiary, and the Lyceum at the University of Mississippi rank among his finest accomplishments. Nichols was a versatile stylist who stayed abreast of changing tastes by moving adeptly from Federal- and Palladianinspired designs in the early stages of his career to the Greek Revival by the late antebellum period.

Nichols was born in 1777 in Bath, England. He arrived in New Bern, North Carolina, in 1800 and began working as an architect and surveyor. The elegant Federal-style Hayes Plantation House near Edenton (1814–17) was the most important of his early designs. He remodeled the State House in Raleigh between 1820 and 1824 and then sought new opportunities in Alabama, where he was appointed state architect. In 1827 he began drafting plans for a new capitol at Tuscaloosa. Completed in 1831, the capitol was built on a cruciform plan and featured a projecting central pavilion with engaged Ionic columns. Nichols also designed the University of Alabama, where he created a broad quadrangle and built along its periphery a temple-like Lyceum, a three-story Rotunda, and professors' houses and dormitories. Construction began in 1828; the university opened three years later. In December 1833, when the fiscal conservatism of the Alabama legislature led to his dismissal, Nichols accepted an appointment as assistant state engineer of Louisiana and moved to Baton Rouge, where he oversaw the completion of the state penitentiary and remodeled and enlarged Benjamin H. Latrobe's Charity Hospital of 1815 for temporary use by state legislature. In New Orleans, Nichols saw the Greek Revival designs of James Gallier and James Dakin, which significantly influenced his later work.

Nichols was appointed state architect of Mississippi in December 1835. Upon arriving in Jackson, he immediately set to work on the new state capitol, which had been plagued by problems since construction began in 1834. Nichols prepared new plans and oversaw the project through to its completion in 1839. The exterior was loosely modeled on the US Capitol in Washington, D.C.; the interior, brilliant in its ornamentation and rationally ordered plan, was uniquely Nichols. During the same era Nichols also designed the Gothic-style State Penitentiary (1836–40) and the Governor's Mansion (1839–42), which is today considered a Greek Revival masterpiece. In the mid-1840s Nichols prepared a master plan for the University of Mississippi at Oxford and built the Lyceum (1846–48), a three-story structure that housed lecture halls, a library, and a laboratory. He on died 12 December 1853 in Lexington while supervising construction of a building for the Lexington Female Academy.

Dan Vivian
Johns Hopkins University

Catherine W. Bishir, *North Carolina Historical Review* (October 1991); Mills Lane, *Architecture of the Old South: Mississippi and Alabama* (1989); C. Ford Peatross and Robert O. Mellown, *William Nichols, Architect* (1979).

Noel, Edmond Favor

(1856–1927) Thirty-Seventh Governor, 1908–1912

Shortly before Gov. Edmond F. Noel's inauguration on 21 January 1908, several Jackson businessmen recommended the sale of the Governor's Mansion and the commercial development of the city block that the 1842 mansion occupied. The *Jackson Clarion-Ledger*, calling the mansion a "ramshackled old barn," also urged the legislature to dispose of the sixty-six-year-old building, which was in very poor condition. Some businessmen also wanted to demolish the Old Capitol, which had been replaced in 1903. Governor Noel and the First Lady, Alice Tye Neilson Noel, did not favor either proposal and saved the mansion from destruction, spearheading the historic structure's first major renovation.

While the mansion was being renovated, Noel and his family lived in the Edwards Hotel. The original family cottage on the north side of the mansion was replaced by a modern, two-story family annex, and the original staircase was replaced by a single flight of stairs leading to an interior balcony.

Born on his family's plantation in Holmes County on 4 March 1856, Edmond Noel was an influential state legislator before his election as Mississippi's chief executive. After serving in the Mississippi House and as a district attorney, Noel was elected to the State Senate in 1895 and reelected in 1899. As a state senator he authored a constitutional amendment providing for an elective judiciary and the Noel Primary Election Act. After an unsuccessful bid for the governorship in 1903, Noel won the office four years later. His administration was characterized by many progressive reforms, especially in education, among them the consolidation of rural school districts, the establishment of agricultural high schools (later the state's junior/community college system), the establishment

Edmond Favor Noel, 1908 (Photograph by Bain News Service, Library of Congress, Washington, D.C. [LC-DIG-ggbain-00423])

of a teachers college at Hattiesburg, and the beginning of agricultural extension work.

Other major reforms achieved during Noel's administration included a child labor law, a pure food law, the establishment of a state charity hospital, and the enactment of a statewide Prohibition law. In response to violence between railroad workers striking against the Illinois Central and strikebreakers hired by the railroad company, Noel sent in the National Guard.

After his term expired in January 1912, Noel remained active in state affairs. In 1918 he ran for the US Senate but was defeated by Pat Harrison. Two years later he again won election to the State Senate. He was reelected in 1924 and died at his home in Lexington on 30 July 1927.

David G. Sansing
University of Mississippi

Thomas E. Kelly, *Who's Who in Mississippi* (1914); *Mississippi Official and Statistical Register* (1912, 1920).

Nonfiction

In the introduction to *Humor of the Old Deep South* (1936), Arthur Palmer Hudson comments on a fundamental issue that confronts any anthologist or encyclopedist: "History and literature, philosophy and folklore: we separate them for purposes of study and try to pretend that they are different. We dedicate foundations and dissect them, endow chairs to support them in grand isolation, pay professors to subdivide and scrutinize them. Then, as good laymen, we sweep away the messy fragments and forget them, or feed them to school boys." To be useful, an encyclopedia needs to be divided into topics and categories. Anyone who attempts to treat very many of the topics "in grand isolation" is soon frustrated: always things overlap; always there are "messy fragments." When subdividing the general category *literature* into its constituents, it is relatively easy to identify prose fiction, poetry, and drama, but what about the rest? What about memoirs, biographies, general histories, or collections of essays? What happens to a novelist who writes a prizewinning history? Thus this encyclopedia has a rather amorphous category, *nonfiction*, for what remains after fiction, poetry, and drama are peeled away from the huge and fascinating body of English prose produced by writers who enjoy some connection to Mississippi. It is the glory of Mississippi's attachment to the written word that there is so much left over, so many juicy if also messy "fragments," when the purely imaginative is removed.

Nothing figures quite so pervasively in Mississippi's non-fictional prose as the issues of race and civil rights. During the civil rights movement of the 1960s Mississippi became the locus of some of the most significant events of the twentieth century. Because of the centrality of these issues to the state's history, Mississippians have written voluminously about race, and because the issues directly or indirectly affect almost every feature of life in the state, texts not ostensibly about race often take on the burdens of unintentional complexity as readers—with good reason—examine them for nuances of racial imagery and symbolism.

It is not surprising that during the first half of the nineteenth century Mississippians, having invested much of their wealth in the ownership of human beings, would feel the need to join their fellow southerners in the defense of the peculiar institution. Regarding Africans and their American descendants as inferior to those of European descent, authors Henry Hughes and Matthew Estes argued that slavery provided civilizing amelioration for a people who otherwise would lack that advantage. Hughes and Estes joined their voices to those of many editors and preachers who sought to justify the antebellum slave economy on the grounds that it was good for the enslaved and that it imposed the dignity of noblesse oblige on the owners.

After the Civil War and well into the mid-twentieth century Mississippians made significant contributions to the narrative of the Lost Cause, relying on representations of the pastoral beauty of the antebellum arrangements Hughes and Estes endeavored to defend. These narratives bolstered the reassertion of white dominance after Reconstruction and defended the sharecropping system as it emerged. Memoirs, many of them written under guidelines supplied by the United Daughters of the Confederacy and southern veterans' organizations, added to the underlying ideology of white supremacy and the consensus that condoned the activities of the Ku Klux Klan and supported racial segregation. Until the 1970s schoolchildren read history texts endorsing white supremist viewpoints. Horace Fulkerson's *The Negro: As He Was, as He Is, as He Will Be* (1887), Alfred Holt Stone's *Studies in the American Race Problem* (1908), and Laura Rose's *The Ku Klux Klan; or, Invisible Empire* (1914) made the prevailing ideology seem reasonable, even beneficial, for black Mississippians, depicting them as happy in their rural place.

The black community had few means and little opportunity to make its case against the dominant racial narrative. Following the lead of Booker T. Washington, Laurence Clifton Jones (*Piney Woods and Its Story* [1922]) and William Henry Holtzclaw (*The Black Man's Burden* [1915]) opened private schools to teach the useful trades to black students, raising funds from northern philanthropists. Several decades passed, however, before the ideas of Washington's principal opponent, W. E. B. Du Bois, gained a following in Mississippi.

Some of Mississippi's more moderate whites were inclined to agree with Jones and Holtzclaw. Leroy Percy gave a 1907 speech to the Mississippi Bar Association supporting education for African Americans, and his son, William Alexander Percy, as his cousin, novelist Walker Percy, notes, "was regarded in the Mississippi of his day as a flaming liberal" in matters of race. Nevertheless, Will Percy, who once entertained African American poet Langston Hughes in Greenville, believed that "the Negro" should "before demanding to be a white man socially and politically, learn to be a white man morally and intellectually." Will Percy used his 1941 autobiography to passionately advocate noblesse oblige, which dictated an obligation for white men of high breeding to care for their "tragic, pitiful, and lovable" culturally younger black brothers, who were "not adult, not disciplined." Because southern whites of privileged economic and social standing believed that they knew "the Negro" better than did working-class southerners or northerners, they also believed that they occupied a better position to act in the black community's interests. Will Percy's good friend and sometime houseguest, David Cohn, published three editions of his Mississippi memoirs in which he professed views similar to and appreciative of his host's. Most of these more moderate whites, among them the Percys and Cohn, vigorously opposed the Ku Klux Klan. A number of journalists throughout the state, most notably Clayton Rand, also supported the moderate viewpoint.

Will Percy's *Lanterns on the Levee* appeared in 1941, six years after Hodding Carter Jr. had moved, largely at Percy's urging, from Hammond, Louisiana, to Greenville to edit first the *Delta Star* newspaper and then the *Delta Democrat-Times*. Carter's views surpassed his benefactor's in moderation, and he was soon regarded as a truly liberal voice in racial matters. In 1946 Carter received the Pulitzer Prize for his courageous criticism of Sen. Theodore Bilbo, among others.

The previous year, Richard Wright had published the first part of his autobiography, *Black Boy*, which earned public condemnation from Bilbo. Wright's bare, surrealistic prose narrative depicts his boyhood in the Deep South amid privations and injustices that denied him not only economic and educational opportunities but sometimes life's basic necessities—food, clothing, and shelter.

The civil rights movement brought a number of books by black Mississippians. Lerone Bennett, editor of *Ebony Magazine*, and William Raspberry, a columnist for the *Washington Post*, were among the first to contribute their considerable talents to the movement. John Alfred Williams published *This Is My Country Too* (1965) two years before the novel for which he is best known, *The Man Who Cried I Am*. Anne Moody's *Coming of Age in Mississippi* (1968) chronicled growing up in and near Centreville, her college days as a waitress in New Orleans and as a student at Tougaloo College in Jackson, and her work in the civil rights movement in Canton and Jackson. It has become a classic text of the movement.

Chalmers Archer Jr.'s *Growing Up Black in Rural Mississippi: Memories of a Family, Heritage of a Place* (1992) depicts his life growing up near Tchula. Endesha Ida Mae Holland's play, *The Second Doctor Lady*, served as the basis for her

1991 drama, *From the Mississippi Delta*, which she rewrote and published as a memoir six years later. Clifton Taulbert's three memoirs, *Once upon a Time When We Were Colored* (1989), *The Last Train North* (1992), and *Watching Our Crops Come In* (1997), focus on his experiences growing up in Glen Allan. Archer, Holland, and Taulbert write about life in the Delta and the often harsh conditions there for young black children in the 1940s and 1950s—the same time and place that Percy observed from a very different perspective. For Taulbert more than for the others and certainly more than for Moody or Wright, African American folkways offered a sustaining foundation that in its better manifestations made for pleasant memories.

The number of distinguished Mississippi historians and literary critics who, while often concerned with race, turn to other topics is far too large for each of them to have a separate entry in this encyclopedia. For example, John Knox Bettersworth's high school history text, *Mississippi: A History* (1959), remained the standard until James Loewen and Charles Sallis published *Mississippi: Conflict and Change* (1974); Thomas Daniel Young was an authority on the literature of the American South; and Suzanne Marrs has written the standard biography of Eudora Welty. Among those who are included in this volume are Shelby Foote, whose three-volume history of the Civil War helped make him a television personality late in his life; David Herbert Donald, whose biographies of Charles Sumner and Thomas Wolfe won Pulitzer Prizes; Dumas Malone, whose biography of Thomas Jefferson also won a Pulitzer; and Charles Sydnor, who served as head of the history department at the University of Mississippi.

In addition to the distinguished reputations earned by some of Mississippi's literary and academic historians, the state's local history and folklore have engendered a noteworthy library of books. A wide variety of purposes drives or sometimes inspires writers to shape the memories and history of a place into prose. One of the better of those reasons is the sheer joy of producing descriptive language for its own sake and the humor a particular angle of vision can generate. Among the reasons for Jill Connor Browne's success is the obvious pleasure she takes in the Sweet Potato Queen, and the same can be said for Jerry Clower's anecdotes.

Preserving the memory of a vanishing way of life has long provided motivation for local and folk historians. Humor easily mixes with nostalgia. Augustus Baldwin Longstreet, who became president of the University of Mississippi in 1849, claimed that he was doing nothing more than preserving a memory of images and incidents in the sketches he collected in *Georgia Scenes* (1835). A great deal of the material that Hudson included in *Humor of the Old Deep South* presents itself as local history. Hudson's collection includes selections by J. F. H. Claiborne, W. H. Sparks, Reuben Davis, and John Sharp Williams, who wrote about the settlement and development of the state and in the process assessed the prevailing estimates of the general character of the populace.

Several of these writers attempted to defend Mississippians' character from the depictions of them in the more raucous backwoods, frontier humor of the half-horse, half-alligator variety. Horace Fulkerson's *Random Recollections of Early Days in Mississippi* (1885) preserves some engaging episodes he believed to be representative of the early settlement of the region. Much more recently Grady Thigpen's accounts of life in and around Picayune preserve local history that escapes more formal accounts. Thigpen found the visitors to his hardware store to be a vast source for a communal life worth saving from oblivion.

Journalists, too, have made enormously worthwhile contributions by preserving their impressions of communal, political, and social events. Some of the more distinguished such authors—William Raspberry, Bill Minor, and Curtis Wilkie, for example—have organized into books some of their widely read columns on topics of local, state, national, and international news.

Construction of the past in language enables memoirists to objectify the personal and explore its meaning, confronting memory to understand it and articulate its values. The intellectual honesty of Noel Polk's examination of his Baptist upbringing in *Outside the Southern Myth* (1997) is enriched by his engagement with William Faulkner's prose and the history of ideas as well as by Polk's considerable talent as a writer. But for Polk and for most recent writers, language is at best an inexact medium. When Alfred Holt Stone wrote in 1908 that he intended to explore the minds of black Mississippians "to learn what and how the Negro thinks and feels," Stone likely believed that such a task was possible, and he obviously believed that language offered a reliable means for conveying what he thought he learned. Recently, however, such confidence has largely disappeared. Writers of nonfiction increasingly employ practices more often associated with imaginative writing. Describing the jazz musicians he first encountered as a high school student, Polk provides a good example: "They sang to parts of me that were eons old and I memorized them instantly: they were poems that I have never forgotten."

Hudson observes that the writers represented in his anthology "did not bring to their work an active artistic imagination" and that the appeal of their work derives from "the inherent interest of the life which they record." Hudson believed that the reason his writers "originated something new in writing was that they had the wit to realize that something old in talking might look new in writing." Subsequent students of a few of these gifted amateurs have found considerable literary skill. Mississippi nonfiction in the twentieth century—the best of it—has capitalized on the earlier experiments. Some more recent writers have created prose of a very high artistic caliber indeed, and their work is likely to assume a place among the fundamental and formative texts of our culture. *North toward Home* (1967) and *New York Days* (1993), the two installments of Willie Morris's memoir,

employ imaginative, highly nuanced language to get at that part of the self that is "eons old." Morris writes about his need to "take the language to its limits." One of the more interesting constructs in Morris's memoir is the Dixie Theater in Yazoo City, where as a boy Morris saw movies that "sent [him] into the bright roil of the afternoon with the pulsing mystery and promise of the world."

Shelby Foote's three-volume history of the Civil War also seems destined to become a permanent part of the national narrative. Convinced that history and fiction are very nearly identical in light of the language in which both must be told, Foote worked on his history for twenty years, shaping not simply sentences and paragraphs but the entire work into a unity that is a metaphor for his sense of a universal order limited only by the shape of time.

When fiction, and drama, and poetry are subtracted from the body of Mississippi prose, what is left may not, after all, be very different from what has been taken away. Perhaps that is one reason the "messy fragments" have a strong appeal.

Robert Phillips
Mississippi State University

William L. Andrews, ed., *African-American Autobiography: A Collection of Critical Essays* (1992); Jack Bales, *Willie Morris: An Exhaustive Annotated Bibliography and Biography* (2010); J. Bill Berry, ed., *Home Ground: Southern Autobiography* (1991); J. Bill Berry, ed., *Located Lives: Place and Idea in Southern Autobiography* (1990); Will Brantley, *Feminine Sense in Southern Memoir: Smith, Glasgow, Welty, Hellman, Porter, and Hurston* (1995); Fred Brown and Jeannie McDonald, *Growing Up Southern: How the South Shapes Its Writers* (2005); James G. Hollandsworth Jr., *Portrait of a Scientific Racist: Alfred Holt Stone of Mississippi* (2008); James B. Lloyd, ed., *Lives of Mississippi Authors, 1817–1967* (1981); Ed Piacentino, ed., *The Enduring Legacy of Old Southwest Humor* (2006); Robert Stepto, *From behind the Veil: A Study of Afro-American Narrative* (1991); Julius E. Thompson, *The Black Press in Mississippi, 1865–1985* (1994); Benjamin E. Wise, *William Alexander Percy: The Curious Life of a Mississippi Planter and Sexual Freethinker* (2012).

Nordan, Lewis

(1939–2012) Author

Lewis Alonzo "Buddy" Nordan, a novelist and short story writer, was born on 23 August 1939 in Forest, Mississippi. Nordan grew up in Itta Bena, a Delta town whose landscape and residents provided much of the raw material for his three short story collections, four novels, and memoir. Nordan's childhood home appears in his fiction as a realm of mystery and magic where the lines between the grotesque and the beautiful, the comic and the tragic are always blurry and

Lewis Nordan (Photograph © David G. Spielman)

indistinct. His work has drawn comparison not only to southern chroniclers of the gothic and grotesque such as William Faulkner and Flannery O'Connor but also to Latin American magic realists such as Gabriel García Márquez and Jorge Luis Borges and comic writers such as James Thurber.

Nordan's father, Lemuel Bayles, died when the boy was eighteen months old. His mother, Sara, married Gilbert Nordan, and for much of his life Lewis believed that Gilbert was his biological father. Nordan's early family life in Itta Bena, especially his complicated relationship with his stepfather, plays a major role in his fiction, particularly the stories about Sugar Mecklin, who bears Nordan's childhood nickname and whose stepfather, like Nordan's, is a loving but distant alcoholic housepainter named Gilbert. As Nordan put it, "I've been writing about wanting a father all my life." His frequent visits to blues bars as a young Deltan exposed him to the music that so powerfully informs both the style and theme of his fiction and that he has called "a visceral and early literary influence."

After leaving Mississippi for a two-year stint in the navy, Nordan enrolled at Millsaps College, where he met his first wife, Mary Mitman. Their troubled marriage and the deaths of two of their three sons—one as an infant, one from suicide—contributed to Nordan's careful examination of tortured family relations in his fiction. Nordan graduated from Millsaps in 1963 and taught public school in Titusville, Florida, from 1963 to 1965 before returning to his home state to pursue a master's degree at Mississippi State University. He went on to receive a doctorate in 1973 from Auburn University, where he wrote a dissertation on Shakespeare's dramatic poetry. Dissatisfied with literary scholarship, Nordan decided in 1974 to pursue writing as a vocation.

Nordan's first notable success came with his story "Rat Song," for which he received the University of Arkansas's John Gould Fletcher Award. Continuing to write, Nordan soon took a position teaching creative writing at the University of Arkansas at Fayetteville. In 1983 Nordan's first collection of short stories, *Welcome to the Arrow Catcher Fair*, appeared, and he accepted a job as professor of creative writing at the University of Pittsburgh. In these stories and those included in his next collection, *The All-Girl Football Team* (1986), Nordan explored the fictional Delta town of Arrow Catcher, a richly imagined hamlet to which he would often return in his fiction, populating it with fantastic creatures such as freshwater swamp dolphins and talking parrots as well as human citizens both freakish and ordinary. All of them struggle with the awareness that "we are all alone in the world." In *Music of the Swamp* (1991), a novel in stories about Sugar Mecklin and his family, Sugar "senses the tragic limitations of a society defined by racial hatred and alcoholism and geographical isolation." *Wolf Whistle* (1993), perhaps Nordan's finest achievement, reimagines the 1955 murder of Emmett Till from the perspective of the white community, probing the social and personal traumas that drive some individuals to horrific acts and others to sit silently by. Nordan's 1995 novel, *The Sharpshooter Blues*, a meditation on grief and loss and an investigation into the American preoccupation with firearms and outlaws, tells the story of hydrocephalic Hydro Raney, who, traumatized by the events surrounding his shooting of two would-be thieves, eventually takes his own life. *Sugar among the Freaks* appeared in 1996 and collected all but three of the stories in his first two volumes of short stories. Nordan's next novel left Arrow Catcher behind: set on a hill country llama farm, *Lightning Song* (1997) follows twelve-year-old Leroy Dearman's sometimes comic, sometimes terrifying initiation into the mysterious world of love and sex amid the near collapse of his parents' marriage. Nordan published a memoir, *Boy with Loaded Gun*, in 2000, chronicling the misadventures and tragedies of his Delta boyhood as well as his adult life. However, he cautions readers that "the ratio of fiction to nonfiction is about the same, in inverse proportions, as in the novels."

Nordan retired from the University of Pittsburgh in 2005 and lived there with his second wife, Alicia Blessing Nordan, until his death on 13 April 2012.

Brannon Costello
Louisiana State University

Barbara A. Baker, *Southern Quarterly* (Spring 2003); Thomas Aervold Bjerre, *Mississippi Quarterly* (Summer 2001); Mary Carney, *Southern Quarterly* (Spring 2003); Edward Dupuy, *Southern Literary Journal* (Spring 1998); Edward Dupuy, *Southern Quarterly* (Spring 2003); Margalit Fox, *New York Times* (16 April 2012); Huey Guagliardo, *Southern Quarterly* (Spring 2003); Russell Ingram and Mark Ledbetter, *Missouri Review* (Summer 1997); Blake Maher, *Southern Quarterly* (Fall 1995); James F. Nicosia, *Southern Studies* (Spring 1993); Robert Rudnicki, *Southern Quarterly* (Spring 2003).

N

Norman, Cora

(b. 1926) Educator

In her 2009 book, *Mississippi in Transition: The Role of the Mississippi Humanities Council*, Cora Norman describes a phone call she received in 1972 from Thomas Flynn, a professor of philosophy at the University of Mississippi, asking her to become the staff administrator of the new Mississippi Humanities Council (MHC). Norman listened to the offer, hung up the phone, and immediately went to the dictionary to look up *humanities*. It was a funny introduction to the word for the woman who became the MHC's first executive director and embodied the pursuit of problem solving through humanities for Mississippians for more than two decades.

Cora Ellen Garner was born on 7 November 1926 to Robert Everett Garner and Jewel Beasley Garner and grew up an only child in rural Columbia County, Arkansas. At a time when most people, especially women, did not seek higher education, Garner dreamed of going to medical school. She graduated from Magnolia Agriculture and Mechanical College (now Southern Arkansas University) and upon graduation was one of a handful of women who enrolled in the University of Arkansas Medical School. Financial pressures and discrimination caused her leave the school after one semester but did not weaken her resolve for higher education. She married Bill Norman in 1946, and they moved to Texas so he could attend graduate school. Cora Norman received a bachelor's in chemistry from Texas Western College and worked to support her husband through school.

The Norman family, which now included two children, moved to Oxford in 1961 when Bill took a job in the biology department at the University of Mississippi. Cora subsequently returned to school and earned a master's degree in chemistry and a doctorate in education administration from the university. Oxford was in the midst of its protracted struggle with opponents of segregation, and Norman initially hesitated to step into the fray. She had grown up in a segregated society but had developed an understanding that friendships could cross the color line. Those friendships eventually encouraged her to question and then challenge the status quo. Shortly after her arrival in Oxford, while on a family trip, Norman's car overturned, injuring her and her African American housekeeper. Norman refused segregated treatment at the hospital, instead sharing a table in the emergency room with the housekeeper. Through such experiences and witnessing James Meredith's attempt to enroll at the university, Norman concluded that those with the advantage of education were more open to differing perspectives. She also joined many civic-minded organizations in an attempt to help the community move forward and acted on her commitment to discussion, public and private, as a way to resolve community issues.

While finishing work on her doctorate she received the phone call that began her relationship with the MHC. In 1965 Congress established the Foundation for the Arts and Humanities (subsequently the National Endowment for the Arts and the National Endowment for the Humanities). States were to receive federal money to establish humanities programs that would educate local communities about public policy issues. Through cooperation with universities and academics, the MHC sought to teach adults to address problems through learning and discussion.

Through a series of community meetings across the state, the MHC board determined that the most pressing problem facing Mississippi was education. In addition to the state's high dropout rate (around 50 percent at the time of the MHC's inception), conflicts over integrating the public school system raged. White families were pulling their children out of schools, and superintendents were resigning. The MHC spent its first three years trying to address these issues, accepting proposals on how to best address the problems and allocating money. The MHC initially encountered significant resistance both from professors, who were expected to get out of the classroom and into the community, and from school superintendents, who were struggling simply to find places where blacks and whites could sit down together. Norman's candor in talking about sensitive issues and her willingness to listen and learn made her the ideal person to shepherd the MHC through this turbulent time.

Norman headed the MHC for twenty-four years, steering the agency in accordance with the state's needs. At times the council focused on local and regional history; at other times it worked to educate people about how to find a more dynamic civic voice. Norman retired in 1996 and traveled extensively, studying the changing role and status of women around the world. The MHC's Cora Norman Lecture Fund is named in her honor, and on 25 October 2012 Norman herself delivered the Cora Norman Lecture on the University of Mississippi campus. She has received many other honors, including the Fannie Lou Hamer Humanitarian Award in 2009.

Danielle Andersen
University of Mississippi

Cora Norman, *Mississippi in Transition: The Role of the Mississippi Humanities Council* (2009); Gayle Graham Yates, *Mississippi Mind: A Personal Cultural History of an American State* (1990).

North Mississippi Allstars
Musicians

Owing in large part to heavy touring, the North Mississippi Allstars have become one of Mississippi's most recognized rock bands. Versed in the traditional music of the region, the group's sound is a contemporary mash of hill country blues, southern rock, gospel, and other popular music from Mississippi and across the South.

Since forming the group in Hernando in 1996, bassist Chris Chew, guitarist Luther Dickinson, and drummer Cody Dickinson have released both studio albums and live recordings. Cody and Luther are the sons of producer Jim Dickinson, noted for his impact on the Memphis music scene and for his work performing, recording, and producing work by the Rolling Stones, Big Star, the Replacements, Ry Cooder, and Bob Dylan, among others. Though their father was most associated with Memphis, the Dickinson brothers grew up in Hernando and spent their formative years in the company of North Mississippi blues legends including R. L. Burnside, Otha Turner, and Junior Kimbrough. The particulars of hill country blues—in particular, the upbeat focus on a single, repeated chord—served as foundation for the North Mississippi Allstars music.

After spending several years on the road as show openers, the North Mississippi Allstars released their debut album, *Shake Hands with Shorty*, in 2000. The recording earned the group a Grammy nomination in the Best Contemporary Blues Album category, and the band received a 2001 W. C. Handy award for Best New Artist Debut. The albums *Phantom 51* and *Electric Blue Watermelon* earned Grammy nominations, and the band has garnered critical praise from *Rolling Stone*, *Spin*, and other publications. In 2011, following Jim Dickinson's death, the band released *Keys to the Kingdom*, a studio album described as a "song cycle" related to his death. Complementing the group's studio work are live recordings, including a *Live in the Hills* series of releases recorded at the North Mississippi Hill Country Picnic festival in Potts Camp. Their most recent studio release is *World Boogie Is Coming* (2013).

The North Mississippi Allstars are best known for their energetic concerts. They are often grouped in the "jam band" category because of their onstage improvisation and their adherence to both a stripped-down production and instrumental approach. The Allstars are mainstays on the festival circuit and have played with such other well-known jam bands as the Tedeschi Trucks Band, Los Lobos, and Phil Lesh and Friends. Musically, the Dickinsons' take on hill country trance blues and southern rock is paired with Chew's gospel-influenced walking bass. Echoing Burnside and other forebears, the group's original material is often paired with contemporary takes on such hill country blues staples as "Goin' Down South" or "Po Black Maddie."

The Allstars frequently work on stage or in the studio with guest musicians of note, including Robert Plant, Duwayne Burnside, Lucinda Williams, Robert Randolph, the Dirty Dozen Brass Band, and Otha Turner's legacy, the Rising Star Fife and Drum Band. Side projects include recording with touring peers John Medeski and Robert Randolph as the Word (2001) and serving as backing band for roots rocker John Hiatt. Cody Dickinson and Chew are also members of contemporary blues outfit the Hill Country Revue, and Luther Dickinson has performed and recorded with Alvin Youngblood Heart and Jimbo Mathis as the South Memphis String Band. For several years Luther Dickinson has also performed with southern rock group the Black Crowes.

Two constants for the Allstars remain their acclaimed live performances and their North Mississippi base. When not on tour the band members may be found producing music at the Zebra Ranch studio in Coldwater.

Odie Lindsey
Nashville, Tennessee

Hap Fry, *Fort Collins Coloradoan* (4 February 2010); Bob Mehr, *Commercial Appeal* (23 August 2009); North Mississippi Allstars website, www.nmallstars.com; Ernest Suarez, *Washington Post* (26 February 2010); Zebra Ranch website, www.zebraranch.com.

Northeastern Hills

An old argument, often identified with political scientist V. O. Key Jr., divided Mississippi society and politics in the early twentieth century between the Delta and the Hills. The Delta was identified with cotton plantations, extremes of wealth and poverty, and a powerful white minority and a large African American majority. In contrast, the Hills region was characterized by smaller farms, mixed agriculture, a large white majority, and the potential for a more populist politics. While such dichotomies often oversimplify complex realities and ignore the variations in other regions of the state, the image of northeastern Mississippi as a part of the southern upcountry, historically characterized by small-scale agriculture and a predominantly white population, is in many ways accurate. The northeastern corner of the state is also important as a longtime center of Chickasaw life, significant Civil War activity, the first sites powered by the Tennessee Valley Authority, the location of the "Tupelo Miracle," and the birthplaces of William Faulkner and Elvis Presley.

Northeastern Mississippi was the home of ancient populations during the Woodland and Mississippian periods. For generations, the area was the home of the Chickasaw. A Chickasaw origin story says the group moved from a distant site in the West and settled at a spot on the Tombigbee River in present-day Lee County. The Chickasaw spread over northern Mississippi and beyond, generally in small communities. They combined hunting with agriculture and developed a reputation for successful military campaigns. In 1736, Chickasaw forces turned back Choctaw and French attackers in the Battle of Ackia, which took place near what is now Tupelo. The 1832 Treaty of Pontotoc Creek ceded Chickasaw land east of the river to the United States, and almost all Chickasaw left the state for reservations in Indian Country (now Oklahoma).

Between the 1830s and 1870, the Northeastern Hills region consisted of Pontotoc, Itawamba, Tippah, and Tishomingo Counties. In the 1870s, the Mississippi legislature created five new counties in the area—Alcorn, Union, Benton, Lee, and Prentiss. Tishomingo County is home to Mississippi's highest point, Woodall Mountain (elevation 806 feet).

With Chickasaw Removal, land in northeastern Mississippi opened up for settlement by US citizens, primarily from eastern parts of the South. In the antebellum period, northeastern Mississippi had some of the largest numbers of free people in the state. In 1840 the percentage of slaves in the four hill counties ranged from 10 percent in Itawamba County to 35 percent in Pontotoc County. Over the next twenty years, those numbers increased only slightly. In 1860, hill country counties had Mississippi's lowest percentages of slaves: free people accounted for 80 percent of the populations of Itawamba and Tishomingo Counties, 72 percent in Tippah County, and 67 percent in Pontotoc County.

Small farming dominated the economy of the Northeastern Hills, and the migration of free people from the eastern South made the region one of the more heavily settled parts of antebellum Mississippi. Farmers concentrated on corn and hogs, mixing the traditional practices of yeoman households with other grains, tobacco, and cotton. In the mid-1800s Tippah County was one of the state's leading producers of corn. Most antebellum industry involved timber, blacksmithing, and construction.

Northeastern Mississippi was an important site for military activity early in the Civil War, with battles in Corinth and Iuka in 1862. Confederate troops moved through the area in late 1862, followed by Union forces in the spring of 1863. Troops clashed again at Brice's Crossroads near Baldwyn in 1864. Much of the area had come under Union control by the middle of the Civil War, and Corinth was home to a Union Army camp for escaped slaves, a hospital, and a military cemetery.

In the postbellum period, many farmers increasingly turned to cotton, growing more by far than in the Piney Woods and Gulf Coast regions though less than in most of the state. In the early twentieth century, northeastern Mississippi remained an agricultural area, but the yeoman ideal was becoming difficult to sustain. In 1900, only about half of the area's farming people owned their land, with rates far higher for white farmers than for black farmers. Tishomingo County, where more than two-thirds of farming people owned their land, was an important exception.

The Northeastern Hills have been the location for some of Mississippi's more ambitious ways to use government action and industrial planning to promote economic development. First, political leaders in the region welcomed the Tennessee Valley Authority for its possible benefits in creating jobs and providing inexpensive electricity. In 1934 the Alcorn County Power Association became the nation's first organization to distribute power, and Tupelo and other areas joined later in the year. In 1938 Pickwick Lock and Dam opened in Tishomingo County. The New Deal's Civilian Conservation Corps built Tishomingo Park in the 1930s, and the Tupelo Homesteads represented a New Deal attempt to settle displaced people into communities of subsistence farmers.

Industrial leaders imagined northeastern Mississippi as a good place to develop factories that might avoid the problems southern leaders associated with a permanent factory class—low wages, poor health, and separation from what they saw as the supportive community life of farming families. The "Tupelo Miracle" consisted of a program to improve education, encourage high-wage employment, and sustain connections between people in Tupelo and surrounding rural areas.

After decades of discussion, study, lobbying, and construction, the Tennessee-Tombigbee Waterway opened in 1985, allowing river navigation through northeastern Mississippi, and in 2010 Toyota opened Mississippi's second-largest automobile factory in Union County.

One intriguing feature of hill country culture is that the region of Mississippi with the smallest percentage of African Americans has produced two of the most significant white artists to deal with issues of race with great energy and creativity. Before moving with his family to Oxford, William Faulkner was born in the Union County town of New Albany in 1897, when African Americans made up about a quarter of the county's population. Faulkner's attention to the whole range of characters meant that he imagined the perspectives of Native Americans, African Americans, whites, and people who did not fit into racial categories. Elvis Presley was born in Tupelo in 1935, when African Americans made up about a third of Lee County's population. Other creative people of note from the hill region include writers Borden Deal, William Clark Falkner, Thomas Hal Phillips, Etheridge Knight, Jill Conner Browne, and James Autry. Musical natives of the region include country star Tammy Wynette, opera singer Ruby Elzy, and singer-songwriter Delaney Bramlett. Artists include Sam Gilliam, Elijah Pierce, Burgess Dulaney, the craftspeople active in Peppertown Pottery, and cartoonist Russell Keaton.

Since the antebellum period, religious life in northeastern Mississippi has revolved primarily around the Baptists and Methodists, by far the largest two groups. In 1873 the Southern Baptists in Tippah County started Blue Mountain College, a small institution for young women. In recent decades the area's religious conservatism has been showcased by *Herdahl v. Pontotoc County School District* (1996), a lawsuit against public prayer in school, and by the rise of the American Family Association, which originated and maintains its headquarters in Tupelo.

In the twenty-first century, the Northeastern Hills counties maintain their large white majorities, with African American populations ranging from about 15 percent in Pontotoc, Tippah, and Union Counties to less than 3 percent in Tishomingo County. Latinos now comprise about 4 percent of the area's people. Across the region, the population grew by about 40 percent between 1960 and 2010, a rate considerably higher than in most parts of Mississippi.

Ted Ownby
University of Mississippi

Vaughn Grisham, *Tupelo: The Evolution of a Community* (1999); Ted Ownby, in Elizabeth Anne Payne, Martha H. Swain, and Marjorie Julian Spruill, eds. *Mississippi Women, Their Histories, Their Lives*, vol. 2 (2010); US Census Reports; Joel Williamson, *William Faulkner and Southern History* (1993).

Notaro, Tig
(b. 1971) Comedian, Writer, and Actor

From an early age, Tig Notaro knew she was funny: "In kindergarten I was a funny kid. As soon as you can be funny, I think I was funny." Born Mathilde O'Callaghan Notaro on 24 March 1971, Notaro spent her childhood in Pass Christian, reveling in the wilds of the Gulf Coast and cultivating a comic sensibility that would eventually help her become a successful comic performer and writer. Notaro credits the influence of her mother, Susie, for much of her success. In 2015 Notaro recalled, "My mother was a very, very free-spirited, wild, gregarious, funny person. She was born in New Orleans and grew up in southern Mississippi and raised in a pretty structured, conservative environment. And she was an artist, she was a painter and a dancer, and very creative, funny person. And she really encouraged me to be who I was and do what I wanted to do."

When Notaro was six, she moved with her mother and stepfather to outside of Houston, Texas. The girl earned the nickname "Huckleberry Tig" and remembers being "very into animals and nature," returning often to Mississippi to spend summers with family. With "zero interest" in school,

Notaro "failed eighth grade twice, and then they moved me up to ninth grade. Then I failed that and dropped out." She found her joy either outdoors or playing guitar and drums. Notaro eventually settled in Denver, Colorado, and worked in music promotion before heading to Los Angeles at age twenty-five and trying standup comedy.

Honing her material during open mic nights and in coffee shops, Notaro, with deadpan delivery and subtle observational humor, developed a loyal following. In 2004 Notaro starred in a Comedy Central Network television special; two years later, she appeared on NBC's *Last Comic Standing*. Notaro made multiple appearances on network talk shows hosted by Conan O'Brien, Jimmy Kimmel, and Jimmy Fallon and enjoyed guest roles in episodes of *The Office* and *Community*. From 2007 to 2010, Notaro was also a regular contributor to the *Sarah Silverman Program*.

In 2012 a series of personal tragedies transformed Notaro's life and career. Following a bout with pneumonia, Notaro was diagnosed with a life-threatening intestinal disease. She recovered, but her mother died shortly thereafter. A few months later, Notaro was diagnosed with stage 2 breast cancer. Scheduled to appear at a Los Angeles comedy club, Notaro contemplated canceling. Her decision to perform and the intimate nature of her material that night garnered high praise from fellow comedians. Notaro recalled, "I would've felt dishonest or inauthentic, I think, if I was on stage just talking about— just observing life in general from afar. That wasn't where I was. I was very ill."

Championed by fellow comedian Louis C.K., a recording of Notaro's seminal performance went public, and *Tig Notaro Live* became the No. 1 comedy album in the country. Since her successful treatment for cancer, Notaro has continued to challenge audiences with exceptionally personal shows. At New York City's Town Hall, Notaro performed part of her routine topless, revealing scars from her double mastectomy and winning widespread critical acclaim for her ability to balance vulnerability, truthfulness, and humor. In 2013 Notaro began work on Comedy Central's *Inside Amy Schumer* and had a role in her first feature length film, *In a World. . . .* In 2014–15, she had a recurring role on Amazon's critically acclaimed *Transparent* and released three projects: *Knock, Knock, Its Tig Notaro* (Showtime), *Tig* (Netflix), and *Tig Notaro: Boyish Girl Interrupted* (HBO).

Notaro married Stephanie Allynne in October 2015 in Pass Christian, and in January 2016 the couple announced that they were expecting twins. In December 2015 Amazon announced that it would be airing Notaro's semi-autobiographical television series, *One Mississippi*, about a woman who returns to her hometown, Bay St. Lucille, Mississippi, after the death of her mother. She received the Mississippi Governor's Arts Award for Artist Achievement in 2016.

Chris Colbek
University of Mississippi

Sydney Brownstone, *Mother Jones* (May–June 2013); Vanessa Grigoriadis, *Vanity Fair* (January 2013); Internet Movie Database website, www.imdb.com; Tig Notaro Facebook page, https://www.facebook.com/tignotarocomedy/; Tig Notaro website, www.tignotaro.com; Arun Rath, *All Things Considered*, National Public Radio (18 July 2015); Alyssa Rosenberg, *Washington Post* (17 July 2015); Don Steinberg, *Wall Street Journal* (13 July 2012).

Noxubee County

Long before its official founding in 1833, the area that became Noxubee County, in eastern Mississippi along the Alabama line, had been the site of significant historical events. Choctaw chief Pushmataha, a critical figure in the growth of American migration to the region, was born there in the 1760s.

In September 1830 representatives of the federal government met with a group of Choctaw leaders in Noxubee County to sign the Treaty of Dancing Rabbit Creek. The treaty, negotiated by Noxubee County natives Peter Pitchlynn and family (members of the Choctaw Nation) and George Strother Gaines (liaison for the federal government), removed most Choctaws from Mississippi.

Newly available for American settlement, Noxubee County quickly developed into a productive agricultural county with a rapidly growing population. In the 1840 census, it had a population of 3,818 free people and 6,157 slaves. There, plantation leaders such as Joseph Beckham Cobb and Stephen D. Lee made and expanded the fortunes that helped start their political careers. Between 1840 and 1860 the county's population doubled, with the number of free persons growing to 5,171 and the number of slaves growing to 15,496 (75 percent of the total). One of Mississippi's most productive agricultural areas, Noxubee County ranked first in the production of corn, fifth in cotton, fourth in livestock, and sixth in sweet potatoes. Its farmland had the third-highest value in the state. Seventy-two people labored in industry, with most making bricks or working in lumber mills. In 1860 Noxubee County was home to thirty churches: fifteen Methodist, ten Baptist, four Presbyterian, and one Catholic.

In the postbellum period Noxubee became a popular destination for African Americans looking to improve their lives. While the number of whites remained stable, the African American population increased by almost 10,000 between 1860 and 1880, making the county one of the state's largest, with 29,572 people. Noxubee had by far the largest number of Alabama natives who relocated to Mississippi. As in many black-majority counties, Noxubee had a large number of tenant farmers. Only 38 percent of the county's farms were run by their owners, a figure well below the state average. At the same time, Noxubee remained an important center for agricultural production, ranking first in the state in production of corn and oats, tenth in cotton, and sixth in the total value of farms. The county's 4,373 mules constituted the fourth-highest total in the state.

In 1880 Noxubee's manufacturing firms employed 113 men, 6 women, and 18 children. In addition, the county was home to 89 foreign-born residents, mostly from Ireland and Germany.

From 1880 to 1900 Noxubee's population increased minimally to 30,846, with African Americans comprising 85 percent of residents. The county also had an extraordinary number of African American tenant farmers (more than 3,300) but only 269 African American farm owners. By comparison, only about 200 of Noxubee's 693 white farmers were tenants. Noxubee's religious census for 1916 was unique in that Missionary Baptists made up more than half of all churchgoers. Methodist Episcopal; Methodist Episcopal Church, South; Southern Baptist; and Colored Methodist Episcopal churches accounted for most of the remainder.

Noxubee County's population declined steadily in the early twentieth century, falling to just 25,560 in 1930. African Americans outnumbered whites by a ratio of four to one. In many ways, the demography of this East Mississippi county resembled a Delta county, with a large but decreasing African American population and a small white population. Still an agricultural county with more than 4,600 farms, Noxubee employed 449 industrial workers. Eighty percent of Noxubee's farms were run by tenants rather than owners.

Notable natives of Noxubee County include poet T. R. Hummer, born in Macon, the county seat, in 1950, and home demonstration leader Sadye Hunter Wier, who was born in 1905 and attended Noxubee Industrial School, founded by her parents, Samuel and Minnie Hunter.

By 1960 Noxubee County's population had decreased to 16,826 and was 78 percent African American. Noxubee also ranked in the bottom five counties in the state in per capita income. Only 11 percent of its workers were employed in industry (primarily furniture and apparel firms), whereas 45 percent had jobs in agriculture. The county stood out for its large numbers of hogs and cattle (second and third in the state). The population decline continued, and by 1980 the county was home to only 13,212 people.

Unlike most eastern Mississippi counties, Noxubee had a predominantly African American population in 2010. The number of residents continued to decline, falling to 11,545.

The county seat is Macon, and other towns include Brooksville and Shuqualak.

Mississippi Encyclopedia Staff
University of Mississippi

Mississippi State Planning Commission, *Progress Report on State Planning in Mississippi* (1938); *Mississippi Statistical Abstract*, Mississippi State University (1952–2010); Charles Sydnor and Claude Bennett, *Mississippi*

History (1939); University of Virginia Library, Historical Census Browser website, http://mapserver.lib.virginia.edu; E. Nolan Waller and Dani A. Smith, *Growth Profiles of Mississippi's Counties, 1960–1980* (1985).

Nursing

Nursing practice and the people who provide care vary from generation to generation depending on society's needs and situations. The history of nursing in Mississippi may be divided into two large chapters, each covering a century of change.

The initial chapter may be described as the pretraining period for nurses. From the early antebellum period until the 1898 opening of the first nurses' training program in Natchez, Mississippians had extensive need for nursing care. Nurses fell into two categories, domestic and community. Domestic nurses practiced within families in times of illness, injury, or epidemic. All women were considered nurses. Their cookbooks and marriage and home medical guides were filled with sick diets, cures, and home remedies. Slaves or hired servants might assume the role of sick nurse. Families tended to provide all care when sickness struck. Domestic nurses often remain obscured in the shadows of history because their service was personal. Their practice consisted of following orders when a physician could be summoned or relying on home and folk remedies when a doctor's care was not available.

Community nurses, conversely, served people outside of the home during times of crisis. Community nurses might list themselves in local business directories or answer calls for volunteers during epidemics. The records of the great epidemics in the 1800s list many nurses who volunteered or were paid to serve during outbreaks of yellow fever and other communicable diseases. Community nursing practices were shaped by current medical practices. For example, in the early years of the century, yellow fever victims were given no fluids but were purged, bled, blistered, and cupped as the fever developed. Nurses were expected to provide all care to patients without removing any of the bedclothes piled high even in summer in an attempt to break the fever. By the end of the century, there was less purging and blistering, and patients were given mustard baths, allowed to drink iced champagne if available, and given other fluids.

Surviving public records reveal that nursing in the community, especially during fever outbreaks, was a field dominated by African Americans, both male and female. Doctors and patients strongly preferred black nurses, believing them better suited for this type of difficult work. In addition, hiring black nurses cost less than hiring white ones.

Training programs for nurses began in the state a full twenty-five years after they were established in the northern states. In the North, the years after the Civil War were marked by movements that called for hospital reform, leading to early training programs for nurses. In Mississippi, however, former hospital matrons were coping with the problems of Reconstruction and crises from annual disease outbreaks. The state had few physicians ready to build hospitals, and limited public resources slowed the growth of a health system that would require nurses. Large family networks, the rural nature of the state, and the home focus of medical care also limited the need for trained nurses.

The second chapter in Mississippi's nursing history opened with the creation of the nursing program at Natchez Charity Hospital in 1898. Trained nurses had to be brought to the state from other regions to lead the initial efforts. Hospitals and training programs grew rapidly between 1900 and 1920, when more than forty facilities were established. Students learned cooking, sanitary measures, and caring for equipment. They worked twelve-hour days and sporadically attended classes in the evenings. They had a half day a week off for religious services and another partial day off to deal with personal issues.

The early hospital-trained nurses had vision and courage that came from the difficulties of their educational process. Just ten nurses from this first generation met at the Natchez Hospital in June 1911 to establish the Mississippi State Association of Graduate Nurses. They approved a code of ethics, made organizational plans, and set out to persuade the legislature to require licensing of nurses, a goal that was reached with the creation of the Mississippi Board of Nurse Examiners in 1914. Two years later the first examination was held, and the state had its first registered nurses.

The First World War stimulated interest in the field because of public image of war nursing. During the Great Depression years hospitals reduced student numbers to cut costs and hired graduates who would work for room and board, leading to the development of the idea of the staff nurse. During the Second World War the innovative cadet nursing program again stimulated nursing school enrollments, but a severe shortage followed during the 1950s as nurses left practice to marry and start families. Most of Mississippi's registered nurses graduated from hospital diploma programs and were competent and hardworking, but the profession continued to advocate the creation of higher education programs in nursing. In 1948 the School of Nursing opened at the University of Mississippi, and the state's first associate degree nursing program opened nine years later at Northeast Mississippi Junior College in Booneville.

In the final years of the twentieth century the profession's focus shifted from educational change to the rapidly changing practice environment and expanding roles of the nurse. When the century opened, nurses were not considered skilled enough to manage even clinical thermometers, which remained a tool for doctors alone. By the end of the century nurses were certified to start IVs, administer medications, and resuscitate patients. With the development of nurse practitioners, advanced practice became part of the mainstream in nursing education and practice.

Linda Sabin
University of Louisiana at Monroe

Reita Keyes, "History of Nursing Education in Mississippi" (PhD dissertation, University of Mississippi, 1984); Mississippi Historical Committee, *Passing the Flame: The History of the Mississippi Nurses' Association, 1911–1986* (1986); Linda Sabin, "From the Home to the Community: A History of Nursing in Mississippi, 1870–1940" (PhD dissertation, University of Mississippi, 1995); Linda Sabin, *Struggles and Triumphs: The Story of Mississippi Nurses, 1800–1950* (1998).

Nussbaum, Perry E.
(1908–1987) Rabbi and Activist

Rabbi Perry E. Nussbaum became a controversial proponent of civil equality in Mississippi during the 1950s and 1960s. Raised in Toronto, Ontario, Nussbaum was the son of working-class Eastern European Jewish immigrants. Nussbaum's family attended a small orthodox synagogue, and he did not encounter Reform Judaism until shortly after his graduation from Toronto's Central High School of Commerce. Unable to gain acceptance to the Chartered Accountants of Toronto (a rejection he attributed to being a Jew), Nussbaum began working as secretary to Rabbi Barnett R. Brickner of Toronto's Holy Blossom Temple. Brickner encouraged Nussbaum to apply to the Hebrew Union College in Cincinnati. Matriculating in the fall of 1926, Nussbaum earned his undergraduate diploma from the University of Cincinnati in 1931 and received his rabbinic ordination from Hebrew Union in 1933. He seriously considered enrolling in a social service school after his ordination but instead decided to take a congregation.

During his student years, Nussbaum maintained a correspondence with Rabbi Ferdinand Isserman, who had succeeded Brickner at Holy Blossom in Toronto. Isserman's passionate concern for social justice issues impressed Nussbaum, and Isserman soon came to serve as a rabbinic role model.

Nussbaum's direct and forceful personality played an important role in shaping his rabbinate. By his own admission, Nussbaum was "never a diplomat." He had little capacity for catering to superiors, even those who might be in a position to further his career. He was the last member of his class to be offered a pulpit by Hebrew Union president

Dr. Julian Morgenstern, who sent the neophyte rabbi as far from Cincinnati as possible: Melbourne, Australia. When the congregation dismissed Nussbaum six months later, Morgenstern urged Nussbaum to pursue another career altogether. Nevertheless, Nussbaum persevered. In the fall of 1934 he went to Amarillo, Texas, to officiate for the High Holy Days and managed to translate this temporary assignment into a permanent position.

Nussbaum's difficult experience in Melbourne presaged two peripatetic decades in the American rabbinate. Between 1937 and 1954 Nussbaum served pulpits in Pueblo, Colorado; Wichita, Kansas; Trenton, New Jersey; Long Beach, New York; and Pittsfield, Massachusetts. In 1954 a rabbinic colleague urged Nussbaum to apply for the open pulpit at Beth Israel in Jackson. Nussbaum landed the position and arrived in Jackson only a few months after the US Supreme Court's *Brown v. Board of Education* decision outlawing racial segregation in public schools. The Court's decision was a watershed event for the nation and for Nussbaum. As the new rabbi in the state's capital, he promptly became the spokesman for Mississippi Jewry.

Nussbaum was embroiled in the struggle over civil rights throughout his nearly two decades in Jackson. His actions provoked criticism and even enmity from many quarters. On one hand, he distressed some members of his congregation when he publicly criticized Mississippi segregationists and urged Jackson's Jews to accept the Supreme Court's decision as the law of the land. Many of his congregants worried that their rabbi's outspokenness would provoke a violent backlash that would endanger the synagogue and the larger Jewish community. Yet Nussbaum refused to be censored, and he continued publicly to condemn racism and injustice. At the same time, Nussbaum vigorously defended southern Jews to their northern coreligionists who the rabbi believed had little appreciation for the genuine dangers that existed during this turbulent era.

Nussbaum's reputation as a man of courage grew when he volunteered to minister to civil rights activists imprisoned in Mississippi's state penitentiary in the early 1960s. Although some of his congregants begged him to remain above the fray, Nussbaum refused to keep silent. He helped to integrate the city's ministerial association, and to the chagrin of many in Jackson, the rabbi invited the integrated ministerial association to meet in the temple itself. Nussbaum repeatedly told his congregants that as Jews they were obligated to promote justice and defend liberty.

On 18 September 1967 a bomb destroyed a significant portion of Temple Beth Israel's new synagogue building. On 22 November, the rabbi's home was bombed. Nussbaum and his wife escaped without physical injury, but these experiences left the rabbi traumatized and embittered. A leading Southern Baptist minister who came to Nussbaum's home to express sympathy regarding the bombing was told to spare his regrets. "If you really want to show your sympathies," Nussbaum lectured the minister, "then tear up whatever you're preparing for your sermon next Sunday morning and speak to the people in the front pews about their culpability in everything that's happened not just to me . . . but to the blacks and their churches over the years."

A few days later, Nussbaum resigned from Jackson's Rotary Club, where he had been active for nearly fourteen years. Despite appeals from the community, the rabbi refused to reconsider his decision. Years later, Nussbaum expressed regret over these displays of pique. Justified or not, his hot-headed conduct in the aftermath of the bombings diminished his standing in the Jewish community and among Jackson's social elite. Jackson's Jewish leaders expected their rabbi to function as a goodwill ambassador to the community at large, not as a harsh social critic. Though he was nearing retirement, the thought of remaining in Jackson's charged environment seemed increasingly intolerable to Nussbaum. He applied for other positions but found no takers for a sixty-year-old rabbi. With no other viable options, Nussbaum completed his contract, remaining in Jackson until 1973, when he and his wife, Arene Talpis Nussbaum, retired to San Diego.

Nussbaum died on 30 March 1987. During his lifetime, he received little recognition for his civil rights activities. However, his intrepid refusal to keep silent and his determination to follow his moral conscience in the face of life-threatening violence mark him as a noteworthy religious leader in Mississippi during the 1950s and 1960s.

Gary Phillip Zola
Hebrew Union College–
Jewish Institute of Religion

Richard J. Birnholz, *Central Conference of American Rabbis Yearbook* (1987); Edward Cohen, *The Peddler's Grandson: Growing Up Jewish in Mississippi* (2002); Allen Krause, "The Southern Rabbi and Civil Rights" (Rabbinic thesis, Hebrew Union College–Jewish Institute of Religion, 1967); Charles Marsh, *God's Long Summer: Stories of Faith and Civil Rights* (1997); Murray Polner, *Rabbi: The American Experience* (1977); Gary Phillip Zola, in *The Quiet Voices: Southern Rabbis and Black Civil Rights, 1880s to 1990s*, ed. Mark K. Bauman and Berkley Kalin (1997).

Nutt, Haller, and the Octagon House

Haller Nutt was best known for ambitious architectural plans for a Natchez house that was never finished. Nutt was born on 17 February 1816 at Laurel Hill Plantation in Jefferson County, Mississippi. He was one of seven children born to Dr. Rushworth Nutt, developer of Petit Gulf cotton, a rot-resistant strain, and his second wife, Eliza Ker Nutt. Haller Nutt is often erroneously referred to as "Dr.," and while he

Longwood, in Natchez, the largest octagonal house in the United States (Charles Reagan Wilson Collection, Center for the Study of Southern Culture, University of Mississippi)

did attend the University of Virginia from 1832 to 1835, he earned neither a medical nor a doctoral degree but instead earned a fortune in sugar and cotton. Following in his father's footsteps, Haller Nutt developed a successful hybrid cotton strain, Egypto-Mexican, and by 1860 his plantations in Louisiana and Mississippi covered 42,947 acres and required the labor of eight hundred slaves. While his vast fortune topped three million dollars before the outbreak of the Civil War, he amassed an enormous amount of debt prior to his death in 1864. His unfinished home, Longwood, came to be known as Nutt's Folly, a symbol of his financial fall.

Haller Nutt married Julia Augusta Williams of Natchez in 1840 at Evergreen Plantation in Louisiana, and they went on to have eleven children, some of whom did not survive to adulthood. Julia Nutt had always been fond of Natchez and was the inspiration behind her husband's 18 September 1850 purchase of Longwood Plantation, located on eighty-six acres two miles south of Natchez in Adams County.

On 24 December 1859 Nutt wrote to Pennsylvania architect Samuel Sloan to express an interest in building an octagonal house (a popular midcentury design) at Longwood. Sloan completed plans in April 1860, and construction began shortly thereafter.

The arabesque design included thirty-two rooms, eight verandas, four porches, 115 doors, twenty-six fireplaces, twenty-four closets, and a rotunda that opened to a Moorish cupola. Each floor was to have at its center an eight-sided room with eight doors leading to eight outer sections. The 30,000-square-foot structure measured 104 feet across and is the largest octagonal house in America. Excluding the costs of land and furnishings, building supplies totaled twenty-eight thousand dollars. Unique to Longwood were Sloan's plans to harness indirect lighting through the use of mirrors and a progressive fireplace venting system.

The final drawings for Longwood were published in 1861 in *Homestead Architecture* as "Design I—Oriental Villa." That same year the exterior and nine rooms on the basement level were completed. However, construction halted in April when the Civil War broke out, and the first through third floors remain a "vast, empty, and unfinished shell." The Nutt family moved into the basement—the only finished living space—and Haller Nutt resided there until his death from pneumonia on 15 June 1864. Julia Nutt resided at Longwood until her death in 1897.

Ownership of Longwood remained with members of the Nutt family until 1968, when it was purchased by the Pilgrimage Garden Club of Natchez, which now operates it as a museum and offers tours. On 16 December 1969 Longwood was designated a National Historic Landmark and added to the National Register of Historic Places. Five of the original plantation outbuildings still stand: the necessary (privy), kitchen, slave quarters, stables, and carriage house.

Linda Arrington
University of Mississippi

Alma K. Carpenter, *Journal of Mississippi History* (Summer 1998); Joanne V. Hawks, *Journal of Mississippi History* (November 1994); Hugh Howard, *Natchez: The House and History of the Jewel of the Mississippi* (2003); D. Clayton James, *Antebellum Natchez* (1968); Harnett T. Kane, *Natchez on the Mississippi* (1947); National Register of Historic Places Inventory—Nomination Form, https://www.apps.mdah.ms.gov/nom/prop/2109.pdf; Pilgrimage Historical Association Collection: Nutt Family Papers, Mississippi Department of Archives and History; William T. Whitwell, *The Heritage of Longwood* (1975).

until the 1989, Nye often performed at the Williamstown Theater Festival in Massachusetts. Her Williamstown performances included starring roles in *Cat on a Hot Tin Roof* (1958), *Bus Stop* (1958), and *A Streetcar Named Desire* (1959) and culminated with the role of the eccentric Zelda Fitzgerald in *Clothes for a Summer Hotel* (1989). At age twenty-four, she made her Broadway debut in *A Second String* (1960), and she was quickly recognized as a promising and talented young actress. In 1965 she earned a Tony nomination for her role in *Half a Sixpence*.

In the mid-1960s Nye added film and television to her repertoire. She received much praise for her portrayal of Alabama-born Hollywood icon Tallulah Bankhead in a made-for-television film, *The Scarlett O'Hara War* (1980).

After 1997 Nye did little acting and instead devoted herself to rebuilding Tick Hall, the century-old Long Island cottage she and Cavett owned, after it was destroyed by fire. A documentary, *From the Ashes: The Life and Times of Tick Hall* (2003), chronicles Nye's efforts to create an exact replica of the cottage.

Nye died of lung cancer on 14 July 2006. She is remembered as a distinctive character both on and off the stage. In 2003, when asked to name her favorite career role, she answered with her typical wit: "None of them. I only became an actress so I wouldn't have to cook or make a bed."

Katherine Treppendahl
University of Virginia

Internet Movie Database website, www.imdb.com; Dennis McLellan, *Los Angeles Times* (18 July 2006); "Tony-Nominated Actress Carrie Nye Dead at Age 69," Broadway.com website, www.broadway.com.

Nye, Carrie
(1936–2006) Actress

Carrie Nye, a Tony-nominated actress and a native of Greenwood, Mississippi, is best remembered for her throaty, southern dialect and sharp wit. While she appeared in numerous films and television shows, she gained her greatest acclaim on the stage.

Carolyn Nye McGeoy was born on 14 October 1936 and began acting at an early age: by fourteen, she was starring in local plays. She attended Stephens College in Columbia, Missouri, and later the Yale School of Drama, where she met and married fellow actor Dick Cavett, who went on to become a well-known television host. From the late 1950s

O Brother, Where Art Thou?

O Brother, Where Art Thou? denotes two early twenty-first-century mass media phenomena: a film by Joel and Ethan Coen and its influential roots-music soundtrack. The title comes from Preston Sturges's classic 1941 film, *Sullivan's Travels*, in which it is the name of the social allegory that fictional filmmaker John L. Sullivan wishes to make to redeem a career he thinks he has wasted on light comedies.

In the 2000 film Ulysses Everett McGill (George Clooney) and two associates escape a 1937 Mississippi chain gang and struggle to return to excavate buried treasure on McGill's farm before a Tennessee Valley Authority dam project floods it. Like *Sullivan's Travels*, the movie follows the picaresque format of the road picture. The fugitives crisscross Mississippi at an impossible pace, make a hit recording, and alter the course of a gubernatorial campaign in which the "reform" candidate is climactically revealed to be a Klansman.

Like most Coen films, *O Brother, Where Art Thou?* brims with allusion. As most of the film's promotional materials proclaimed, the plot—though much less than that of James Joyce's *Ulysses*—is based on events of the first and greatest road saga, the *Odyssey*. John Goodman plays Cyclops, a one-eyed Bible salesman; three washerwomen singing by a stream are the Sirens; joyful southern evangelicals getting baptized in a river are the Lotus Eaters; and McGill struggles to reach his wife, Penny, in fictional Ithaca, Mississippi. Yet more complex cinematic and literary allusions abound as well. The dance of the Klansmen is lifted from the *Wizard of Oz*. The title is taken from Sturges's dark satire about the relation between the literally unwashed masses (represented in the Coens' film by any number of Mississippians) and the mass media they consume (represented here by radio, which incumbent governor Pappy O'Daniel calls "mass communicatin"). Near movie's end, McGill floats on a coffin à la Herman Melville's Ishmael.

Yet despite the film's superficially comic tone, McGill's closing prophecy that rural electrification will mean "out with the old spiritual mumbo-jumbo, the superstitions, and the backward ways" and the appearance in the South of "a veritable Age of Reason—like the one they had in France"

employs a dramatic irony so heavy that in 2000 it verged on pathos. Though the Depression setting softens the satire of the South, the film nods as much to contemporary events as to literature and film. At least since *Barton Fink* (1991), the Coen brothers have dramatized tensions and complicities between intellectuals and a mindless mob portrayed with a touch of Nazi imagery. Raised in an observant Jewish home, the Coens wrote the screenplay immediately after the Southern Baptist Convention (the Lotus Eaters) had called for the conversion of the Jews. The chief Klan character disparages Jews and lauds "heritage" and the Confederate flag, which were sources of debate in several southern states—including Mississippi—at the time of the film's composition and remain so today. McGill's representative rural southern sidekicks, Pete (John Turturro) and Delmar (Tim Blake Nelson), are two of the stupidest characters ever put on film, and the forward-looking McGill repeatedly explodes when confronted by other characters' torpor and stubborn backwardness. Clooney delivers his lines in a fast-talking Kentucky accent based on his uncle's, while Turturro, Nelson, and most of the other supporting actors strive for more Mississippian cadences and inflections.

This contrast is most evident in the film's music. The escapees' band, the Soggy Bottom Boys (a nod to Lester Flatt and Earl Scruggs's Foggy Mountain Boys), makes its name bringing Appalachian "hillbilly" music to notoriously unmountainous Mississippi. The Coens have called the film "a valentine to the music"—but none of it comes from Mississippi. Even the lone real-life bluesman who appears in the film, Chris Thomas King, hails from Baton Rouge. The bulk of the film's old-timey soundtrack is performed by bluegrass and alt-country musicians and the black Nashville gospel group the Fairfield Four. If the film satirizes the mores of the Lower South, its soundtrack unambivalently lauds the music of the Upper. Effectively launched by a concert at the Ryman Auditorium in May 2000—before the film was released in the United States—the soundtrack went on to sell nearly eight million copies by 2015. Famously, it did so without the benefit of airplay on mainstream country music radio. *Down from the Mountain*, D. A. Pennebaker's documentary film of the Ryman concert, was released in theaters and on DVD in 2001. The documentary's soundtrack became another recording, its musicians toured nationally, and dozens more spinoff records were released. Bluegrass acts saw increased music sales and concert attendance as the genre succeeded the Cuban music of 1997's *Buena Vista Social Club* as the nation's "authentic" alternative music du jour.

Jon Smith
Simon Fraser University

Hugh Ruppersburg, *Southern Cultures* (Winter 2003).

Oakland College

Founded in 1830 by the Presbytery of Mississippi, Oakland College was located in Claiborne County. The founding of the college was part of a larger trend of college building undertaken by religious denominations around the United States during the early 1800s. Oakland, like many other religious colleges, was founded to train an educated ministry. Fearing the morally and physically unhealthy impact a town or city might have on students, the founders located the college on 250 acres near Rodney.

Oakland College found the early success that eluded its nearby rival, Jefferson College. In 1831 Oakland College awarded the state's first bachelor's degree to James M. Smylie, and the school went on to attract many other young men, including several sons of the Natchez elite. Although some Mississippians, among them Natchez minister Joseph B. Stratton, complained that Oakland's secluded rural location deterred prospective students, enrollment soared from an initial three students to more than one hundred by the 1850s. Many Mississippi observers pointed to Oakland College as proof that southern institutions could attain the same level of success and prominence as the northern institutions to which many planters sent their sons. As sectional tensions grew during the antebellum period, Oakland College and other such schools grew increasingly more important.

Supporters included Rev. James Smylie, Dr. John Ker, David Hunt, and Rev. Benjamin Chase, and the college flourished despite the murder of its president, Jeremiah Chamberlain, in 1851. Local planter George Briscoe felt that Chamberlain, a staunch Unionist, did not support southern rights and stabbed him in front of his residence at the college. R. L. Stanton replaced Chamberlain. Later presidents included James Purviance and William Breckinridge.

Although most Oakland students did not pursue religious careers, ministerial training remained an important part of the school's mission. From 1837 to 1841, Ker endowed a special chair in theology at the institution. At the same time, the Presbyterian churches in nearby Bethel and Rodney gave considerable support to Oakland. In turn, students from the college contributed both money and energy to the churches.

By 1861 Oakland was the oldest college in continuous operation in Mississippi, but the Civil War brought serious challenges. Students and professors alike left to join the fight, and the college closed in 1862. During the war, Union forces occupied the campus. The institution never reopened, and in 1871 the state of Mississippi purchased the campus and reopened it as Alcorn University to educate newly freed slaves. In 1878 Alcorn became the nation's first land-grant college for black students. The Synod of Mississippi used the proceeds from the sale to start Chamberlain-Hunt Academy in Port Gibson.

Julia Huston Nguyen
Washington, D.C.

Melvin Kellogg Bruss, "History of Oakland College (Mississippi), 1830–1871" (master's thesis, Louisiana State University, 1965); Aubrey Keith Lucas, in *A History of Mississippi*, ed. Richard Aubrey McLemore (1973); Edward Mayes, *A History of Education in Mississippi* (1970); Julia Huston Nguyen, "Molding the Minds of the South: Education in Natchez, 1817–1861" (master's thesis, Louisiana State University, 1997); Tommy Wayne Rogers, *Journal of Mississippi History* (Spring 1974); David Sansing, *Making Haste Slowly: The Troubled History of Higher Education in Mississippi* (1990).

Obesity

Obesity, or excessive body fat, is a complex condition involving the interaction of genetics, environment, and behavior. This is especially evident in Mississippi, where cultural practices, lifestyle choices, policy, and environmental factors have combined to place the state at the forefront of the national epidemic in obesity. Between 1990 and 2014 Mississippi's adult obesity rate more than doubled, from 15 percent (the highest in the country) to 35.5 percent (third-highest). Another 35.2 percent of adult Mississippians were classified as overweight (having excessive body fat but less than obese levels). Rates are significantly higher among African Americans, among women, and among those aged twenty-six to sixty-four as well as in lower-income households.

Obesity is also a problem among Mississippi's younger people, although signs of improvement are evident. The obesity rate for high school students fell from 18.1 percent in 2009 to 15.4 percent in 2013, while the number of overweight high school students declined from 17.7 in 2007 to 15.4 percent in 2013. Mary Currier, the state health officer, attributed the improvement to the Healthy Schools Act of 2007, which mandated healthy lunches, eliminated sugary drinks and snacks from schools, and required 150 minutes of physical activity a week for students. In addition, the obesity rate for two- to four-year-olds from low-income families dropped from 14.6 percent in 2008 to 13.9 percent in 2011.

Mississippians continue to suffer serious health conditions as a result of being overweight/obese. The adult diabetes rate has climbed from 6.9 percent in 1990 to 13.0 percent in 2014 (the second-highest rate in the country), while the adult hypertension rate rose from 28.2 percent to 40.0 percent (third-highest) over that span. Rates of obesity-related heart disease, arthritis, and cancer have also risen and are projected to continue increasing. In children, obesity not only is a harbinger of adulthood obesity and morbidity but carries current risks for metabolic, respiratory, hepatic, orthopedic, endocrine, and psychological problems, including low self-esteem and depression. Obesity places significant stress on the health care system: in 2008, the state incurred $925 million in health care costs directly related to obesity, a number that could reach an estimated $3.9 billion by 2018. Mississippi's mortality rates from cardiovascular disease, diabetes, and stroke are among the nation's highest, owing in part to obesity.

The role of genetics in appetite, metabolism, and other facets of obesity research is under intensive investigation. In addition, ecological factors such as nutrition knowledge, coping skills, body image, comorbid conditions, level of health literacy, overall literacy level, and self-efficacy play a role. Behavioral factors include decreased physical activity, increased sedentary activity, and decreased fruit and vegetable intake, especially associated with a high calorie/high fat diet. Family influences are crucial in the development of obesity, particularly childhood obesity, and range from food budget to dietary quality, frequency of fast-food meals, and family attitudes toward nutrition and physical activity. Other environmental factors that affect obesity within Mississippi are its levels of poverty and education, the local availability of fresh produce, the availability of recreational facilities, the ubiquitousness of fast-food and buffet-style restaurants, deeply ingrained cultural patterns, and the humid climate. Mississippi's cultural legacy includes hospitality that often takes the form of delicious but calorie-laden cuisine, traditions that incorporate feasting, and strong feelings related to individual choices.

More than half of Mississippi's population lives in rural areas, with a large percentage of commuters. Fast-food restaurants abound in areas with high cardiovascular mortality, often to the exclusion of grocery stores with fresh produce, thus increasing the rates of fast-food consumption as snacks before and after school or work. More than one in five Mississippians live in poverty, which has been linked to food insecurity and obesity. A lack of physical activity is associated with an increased risk of developing obesity, and in 2014 nearly a third of Mississippi adults engaged in no leisure time activity. Moreover, a 2013 study found that barely a quarter of all high school students participated in daily physical activity.

Alongside the Healthy Schools Act, Mississippi has implemented a number of additional measures to help combat its obesity problem. Since 2010 the state has participated in the Safe Routes to School National Partnership's State Network Project, which works to encourage and increase the safety of walking and bicycling. Two years later the Move to Learn initiative began encouraging teachers across the state to lead students in short physical activity breaks, and various faith-based organizations have also implemented programs to encourage healthy eating and exercise habits. The Mississippi Grocery Access Task Force has worked since 2012 to address the lack of supermarkets and other retailers that offer healthy, affordable foods in underserved areas. And the Just Have a Ball program run by the Partnership for a Healthy Mississippi has offered thousands of elementary school students not only a playful, interactive assembly about the importance of eating healthy and remaining active but also a playground ball to take home.

In short, the national, state, and local governments are working with schools as well as community- and faith-based agencies and groups to develop innovative educational and intervention programs to help Mississippians become healthier and lower the state's obesity rates.

Gerri A. Cannon-Smith
Nationwide Children's Hospital,
Columbus, Ohio

Gerri A. Cannon-Smith, "Journey to Success Preschool Obesity Prevention Pilot Program: Implications for Practice," Poster Presentation, US Department of Health and Human Services, National Prevention Summit, Washington, D.C. (26 October 2006); Centers for Disease Control and Prevention, *Nutrition, Physical Activity and Obesity: Data, Trends, and Maps* website, https://nccd.cdc.gov/NPAO_DTM/Default.aspx; David S. Freedman, Laura Kettel Khan, William H. Dietz, Sathanur R. Srinivasan, and Gerald S. Berenson, *Pediatrics* (3 September 2001); Siobhan C. Maty, John W. Lynch, Trivellore E. Raghunathan, and George A. Kaplan, *American Journal of Public Health* website, www.ajph.org (June 2008); "Mississippi," Robert Wood Johnson Foundation website, http://www.rwjf.org/en/library/articles-and-news/2013/07/mississippi—signs-of-progress.html; Mississippi Department of Health, Behavioral Risk Factor Surveillance System Report Annual Prevalence Report (2007); Mississippi Preventing Obesity with Every Resource (POWER) Project, Mississippi Department of Health website, www.msdh.state.ms.us; Jerry Mitchell, *Jackson Clarion-Ledger* (21 September 2015); Astrid Newell, Amy Zlot, Kerrey Silvey, and Kiley Ariail, *Preventing Chronic Disease* website, www.cdc.gov/pcd/issues/2007/apr/06_0068.htm; State of Obesity website, http://stateofobesity.org/states/ms/; University of Mississippi Medical Center website, www.umc.edu.

Ocean Springs Ornamental Cottages

The ornamental cottage owes its origins to the European cottage orné, which arose as a result of the picturesque movement of the late eighteenth and early nineteenth centuries. Architect John Nash (1752–1835), who designed London's Regency Street and Trafalgar Square, designed smallish houses built in an artificial rustic manner. Architect Andrew J. Downing described such cottages as "sources of beauty and picturesque," giving "an air of rustic modesty . . . expressive of honest, lovely, unaffected country character."

These cottages evolved during the Edwardian, Italianate, Gothic Revival, and Eastlake periods, acquiring elements of each style in the various locations where they were erected. These elements include rustic-work post and bracket, rustic wood cresting, bargeboard, flat-board and turned-wood balustrades, turned colonnettes, chamfered posts, shallow pitched roofs with gable overhangs, cross-gable roofs, piercework, and openwork friezes.

It is not surprising that such a picturesque house found its way to bucolic but flamboyant Ocean Springs in the late nineteenth and early twentieth centuries. The town boasts six historical districts with houses representing numerous architectural styles. Two examples of ornamental cottages are the Honor-Attaya House (built by John B. Honor in 1917) and the Geiger-Friar House (constructed in 1898 by German immigrant Peter Geiger). A raised-basement structure, the Honor-Attaya House was smashed off its piers by Hurricane Katrina but has been restored and raised to flood level. The two-bay porch has a wood rail, turned-wood posts with jigsaw brackets, and an ornamented frieze.

The Geiger-Friar House has a cross-gable roof with overhang and ornamented panelwork. The three-bay porch features an openwork frieze, a balustrade rail, and posts similar to those of the Honor-Attaya House. Ocean Springs preservationists have kept this building in excellent shape.

Jim Fraiser
Tupelo, Mississippi

Lynn Lofton, *Mississippi Business Journal* (15 December 2008); Mississippi Department of Archives and History, Historic Resources Inventory Database website, http://www.apps.mdah.ms.gov/Public/search.aspx.

Ogden, Florence Sillers

(1891–1971) Conservative Activist

"Where the men faltered, the women have led out for constitutional government. They have been far ahead." Writing just before the 1964 presidential election, Florence Sillers Ogden confidently predicted that the white women of her native state, Mississippi, would raise their voices and cast their ballots for a "Conservative president of the United States," Barry Goldwater. She ticked off reasons why Mississippi's women should support the Republican candidate: spiraling taxes, federal infringements on free enterprise, creeping socialism in America's churches and schools, and most importantly for Ogden, civil rights. A triumphant rise of the Right did not materialize in 1964, but Ogden's prognostication for her home state proved on target. She was certainly well positioned to judge. Beginning in the late 1940s, Ogden's political organizing placed her at the hub of the Deep South's metamorphosis from Democratic to Republican stronghold. Through her weekly newspaper column, her leadership in women's clubs, and her position as a member of one of Mississippi's most elite families, Ogden promoted conservative principles and tried to prod like-minded white women to political action.

Ogden's involvement with politics grew naturally out of her family background. The granddaughter of slaveholders, Florence Sillers was born on 2 October 1891 to Walter Sillers Sr. and Florence Warfield Sillers. The wealthy Sillers family embodied the archetypical image of Delta planter-aristocrats, relying on African American tenant labor to operate immense cotton plantations in the small Bolivar County town of Rosedale. Ever leery of threats to their economic and political power, the members of the Sillers family wielded their substantial influence in state government to shore up Mississippi's repressive racial hierarchy. Walter Sillers Sr. helped engineer the legal disfranchisement of African Americans in the 1890s, and Florence Warfield Sillers was an active member of the Daughters of the American Revolution who authored a history of Bolivar County that valorized the Confederate-era South. Their only son, longtime Speaker of the Mississippi House of Representatives Walter Sillers Jr., relentlessly worked to hobble the forces of organized labor and civil rights reform. On 29 June 1911 Florence Sillers married Harry Cline Ogden.

Aside from the prominence she enjoyed from her family name, Florence Sillers Ogden built her own statewide reputation through her regular newspaper column, "Dis an' Dat." Her writings appeared in the *Delta Democrat-Times* in the late 1930s and subsequently in the *Jackson Clarion-Ledger* as well. Her weekly feature ran the gamut from lighthearted reports on local social gatherings to scathing denunciations of liberal politicians. Ogden also built networks through her work in women's organizations. Like her mother, Ogden served as a leader in the Daughters of the American Revolution and collaborated with other white women to celebrate and preserve Mississippi's Confederate past. The United Daughters of the Confederacy and the right-wing Congress of Freedom also counted Ogden among their dedicated members.

Although she and her husband had no children, Ogden frequently invoked the responsibilities of motherhood and womanhood in her political writings and speeches. In 1948 she stood before eight hundred women who had gathered to support the third-party Dixiecrat movement and told her audience, "We, the women, have a big stake in these issues." Four years later, Ogden expressed her bitter disappointment at Mississippi's male leaders, who had consented to liberal Adlai Stevenson as the Democrats' 1952 presidential nominee. Disgusted, Ogden formed a chapter of Democrats for Eisenhower in Bolivar County and declared, "Now I've got to elect Ike all by myself—with the help of the women."

Ogden insisted that her conservative principles involved more than the politics of race, yet the flashpoints of her activism coincided with key moments in the civil rights struggle, and she unabashedly and unswervingly defended white supremacy. Ogden decried the Supreme Court's 1954 *Brown v. Board of Education* decision as "the most outrageous seizure of power in all the history of our country, worthy of Stalin and Russia." Along with her vigorous support for the segregationist Citizens' Councils, Ogden was a founding member of the Women for Constitutional Government, an organization born in the wake of the fall 1962 integration crisis at the University of Mississippi. Nearly two thousand women flocked to Jackson for the group's inaugural meeting, where they heard Ogden, one of the keynote speakers, call for a return to constitutional and judicial conservatism. Anticivil-rights activism dominated the organization's agenda, although it also fiercely opposed US participation in the United Nations and later the Equal Rights Amendment.

Christianity, patriotism, and conservatism mingled together in Ogden's political philosophies. Her address to the Women for Constitutional Government opened by asking God to guide the organization "as He guided the Founders of this Nation." She despised the liberal drift of the National Council of Churches and accused many southern churches of "falling right in to the Communist plan." For Ogden, communism and liberalism seemed synonymous, as did conservatism and true Americanism. When the US Congress considered liberalizing immigration policy, for example, Ogden was among the grassroots warriors who rushed to defend the existing quota system, based on a 1924 law, that disproportionately favored Western European immigrants over those from Asia, Africa, and Latin America. She passionately maintained that the quota system protected the American way of life and American freedoms.

Ogden died on 23 June 1971, nearly a decade before the apex of the conservative counterrevolution—Ronald Reagan's 1980 ascent to the presidency—yet she and countless other white Mississippi women undeniably left a deep imprint on the movement.

Ann Ziker
Houston, Texas

James C. Cobb, *The Most Southern Place on Earth: The Mississippi Delta and the Roots of Regional Identity* (1992); Elizabeth Gillespie McRae, in *Massive Resistance: Southern Opposition to the Second Reconstruction*, ed. Clive Webb (2005); Florence Sillers Ogden Papers, Charles W. Capps Jr. Archives and Museum, Delta State University; *The Sillers: A Mississippi Delta Family* website, https://sillersfamily.wordpress.com/; *Woman Constitutionalist*.

Ohr, George
(1857–1918) Potter

George Edgar Ohr, the self-proclaimed Mad Potter of Biloxi, was a ceramic artist active from 1882 to 1907. Born in Biloxi on 12 July 1857 to Eastern European immigrants Johanna Wiedman Ohr and George Edgar Ohr Sr., he spent his early career training in his father's blacksmith shop.

Ohr went on to learn the mechanics of the pottery trade with Joseph Fortune Meyer, a Biloxi native living and working in New Orleans. In 1881 Ohr left New Orleans to begin a two-year trip across the eastern United States, where he visited a variety of well-established folk potteries such as the Kilpatrick Brothers pottery in Anna, Ohio. In 1883 Ohr settled back in Biloxi and opened his first studio, selling utilitarian and folk pottery. The studio was run solely by Ohr, who dug and processed local clay, built and stoked his wood-burning kiln, and prepared glazes from traditional recipes.

George Ohr, *Petticoat Vase*, ca. 1898 (Collection of the Ohr-O'Keefe Museum of Art, gift of David Whitney in honor of Frank and Berta Gehry)

Ohr married Josephine Gehring on 15 September 1886, and they went on to have ten children, five of whom lived to adulthood. George Ohr opened the Biloxi Art and Novelty Pottery in 1890, establishing himself not only as a craftsman of utilitarian pottery but also as a clay artist. On 12 October 1894 fire consumed much of Biloxi, including Ohr's studio and an estimated one thousand pieces of pottery. Facing the destruction of much of his hometown, life's work, and family income, he produced the most innovative work of his career, creating a variety of paper-thin vessels known for their undulating pinches, folds, and twists. Ohr borrowed shapes and lines from his early blacksmith training to create curling ribbon handles for vases, teapots, and mugs. The intensity and brilliant color of Ohr's glazes provoked much comment, and Ohr represented the state of Mississippi at many world's fairs and expositions, including the World's Columbian Exposition in Chicago (1893) and the St. Louis World's Fair (1904).

Sometime around 1905 George Ohr stopped glazing his pottery, leaving it in the bisque form to create his most abstract and sculptural ceramic objects. Soon after his explorations with bisque, Ohr stopped potting altogether, and by 1910 his studio was disassembled and his work packed away. Ohr spent the remainder of his life experimenting with motorcycles and automobiles and died in Biloxi on 7 April 1918 of throat cancer.

Ohr's work stayed packed away on his family property until the 1970s. In 1972 Ohr's surviving children sold the entire pottery collection to New Jersey antiques dealer James Carpenter, who disseminated Ohr's work to the New York City art world.

The Old Capitol Museum hosted the first exhibition of Ohr's pottery, which has also been shown at New York's Metropolitan Museum of Art and in *Ohr Rising: The Emergence of an American Master*, an exhibition that traveled widely across the United States and Canada in 2007–9. Biloxi's Ohr-O'Keefe Museum of Art, designed by famed architect Frank Gehry, opened in 2010 and is the major depository in the state for Ohr's work.

Anna Stanfield Harris
Biloxi, Mississippi

Garth Clark, Robert A. Ellison Jr., and Eugene Hecht, *The Mad Potter of Biloxi: The Art and Life of George E. Ohr* (1989); Robert A. Ellison Jr. with Martin Edelburg, *George Ohr, Art Potter: The Apostle of Individuality* (2006); Eugene Hecht, *After the Fire, George Ohr: An American Genius* (1994); Ellen J. Lippert, *George Ohr: Sophisticate and Rube* (2013); Richard D. Mohr, *Pottery, Politics, Art: George Ohr and the Brothers Kirkpatrick* (2003); Ohr-O'Keefe Museum of Art website, georgeohr.org.

Ohr-O'Keefe Museum of Art

The Ohr-O'Keefe Museum of Art is the third incarnation of a private nonprofit art museum originally established in Biloxi in 1992 by the Jackson-based Mississippi Museum of Art as a satellite facility located in a wing of the Biloxi Library and Cultural Center. The museum closed its Coast branch on 1 July 1994, and the George E. Ohr Arts and Cultural Center opened in the same location.

A decade earlier, pottery created by George Ohr (1857–1918) had graced a number of Jasper Johns paintings exhibited at New York's Leo Castelli Gallery, garnering critical acclaim for the relatively unknown and long-deceased potter. As early as the 1950s, Ohr's pottery had appeared on the secondary market and had attracted the attention of abstract expressionist collectors such as Johns and Andy Warhol. After a series of one-man shows of Ohr's work, celebrity collectors Steven Spielberg and Jack Nicholson helped fuel an increase in the prices fetched by Ohr's pottery. In the fall of 1989, ninety-one pieces of Ohr pottery were presented in the American Craft Museum's retrospective exhibition, *George Ohr: Modern Potter*, and Abbeville Press released the book *George Ohr: Mad Potter of Biloxi*.

Another hundred-piece exhibition, *After the Fire: The Later, Greater George Ohr*, opened at New York's Kurland-Zabar Gallery in 1994. At the same time the upstairs library space in Biloxi opened as the Pot-Ohr-E-Gallery, displaying 140 pieces, the largest number of Ohr works assembled to that date. In the gallery a statue of the potter at his wheel presented viewers with a life-size diorama, while a re-creation of the family's Victorian parlor displayed artifacts loaned by the potter's descendants. Pottery loans from across the Mississippi Coast comprised the inaugural display in the nation's first museum dedicated to an individual ceramicist. Holding a "Mad Potter's Ball" and premiering Mississippi ETV's documentary *Mad Potter of Biloxi*, the museum enlivened Biloxi's Fall Festival with a juried art show. Transformation from branch operation to stand-alone arts center was completed with the establishment of the Mud Dauber summer camp for children.

In 1998 Biloxi's former mayor, Jerry O'Keefe, donated a million dollars to the museum in memory of his wife, Annette Saxon O'Keefe. This donation fueled a movement to construct a freestanding museum on Delauney Street, where George Ohr's shop once stood. However, plans for the downtown location soon gave way to a four-acre beachfront site proposed by new mayor A. J. Holloway. The mayor's vision for a campus called Tricentennial Park included the antebellum Tullis-Toledano Manor, along with piers for the Seafood Museum's two Biloxi schooners, the art museum, and the relocated Pleasant Reed House. City leaders agreed that the park was ideally situated for commemorating Biloxi's history, and the nation's top museum designer, Los Angeles architect Frank Gehry, was commissioned to plan the cultural complex.

In 2000 the institution was incorporated as the Ohr-O'Keefe Museum of Art, and Gehry walked the beachfront site where Lynoaks, a turn-of-the-century mansion, had stood until Hurricane Camille struck in 1969. The live oaks that survived that storm inspired Gehry to design structures that dance with the trees. The model revealed a year later, with porches on all the buildings, evidenced Gehry's respect for regional architecture traditions. Five separate structures were designed to house the Ohr-O'Keefe Museum of Art. Three serve as gallery space—one for African American artworks, another for contemporary exhibitions, and the third as the signature pavilion space for Ohr's pottery. Additional buildings house the Mississippi Sound Welcome Center and the museum's Center for Ceramics. Respecting the museum's neighborhood, Gehry's humanistic endeavor situates the campus entrance on its north side, where the Pleasant Reed House stands as the touchstone vernacular structure in a streetscape of similar buildings.

A 2003 celebration kicked off construction, but in August 2005 Hurricane Katrina struck, decimating the site. Only the foundation remained from the George Ohr Gallery, and the Biloxi Grand Casino barge had been jammed into the partially constructed African American Gallery. The Contemporary Gallery sustained damage, but the four-story Center for Ceramics weathered the storm well. Though the Pleasant Reed House had been washed away, its archives had been saved, as had the museum's collection of Ohr pots. Museum staff returned to work in a twenty-eight-foot trailer parked in the wreckage of downtown Biloxi, and construction resumed in June 2007. The demolished historic house was reconstructed as the Pleasant Reed Interpretive Center, and the Mississippi Sound Welcome Center, the IP Casino Resort Spa Exhibitions Gallery, the Gallery of African American Art, the Pleasant Reed Interpretive Center, and the Creel House opened in 2010. The City of Biloxi Center for Ceramics opened in 2012, followed by "the Pods" (formally the John S. and James L. Knight Gallery and home to the permanent exhibition of Ohr's work) two years later. The museum is just the second Mississippi institution to earn Smithsonian affiliation.

Susan McClamroch

New Orleans, Louisiana

Garth Clark, Robert A. Ellison Jr., and Eugene Hecht, *The Mad Potter of Biloxi: The Art and Life of George E. Ohr* (1989); Robert A. Ellison Jr., *George Ohr, Art Potter: The Apostle of Individuality* (2006); Ellen J. Lippert, *George Ohr: Sophisticate and Rube* (2013); Richard Mohr, *Pottery, Politics, Art: George Ohr and the Brothers Kirkpatrick* (2003); Ohr-O'Keefe Museum of Art website, georgeohr.org; Rita Reif, *New York Times* (24 September 1989, 16 October 1994); Bruce Watson, *Smithsonian Magazine* (February 2004).

Oil and Gas Industry

In 1860 state geologist Eugene Hilgard first reported Mississippi's potential as a petroleum-producing state, predicting that the Jackson Dome would produce oil. But the state's first oil well was not drilled until 1903. That attempt, near Enterprise in Clarke County, proved unsuccessful. Additional ventures failed in Tishomingo, Jones, Hancock, and Lauderdale Counties before success arrived on 7 October 1926 at the Carter No.1 well about six miles east of Amory, which produced gas until 1938.

The discovery of gas prompted major petroleum companies to come to Mississippi and explore. The most active of the companies was Gulf Refining, which opened a Meridian office and employed geologists, aerial photographers, and magnometer operators to map the surface. The Jackson Oil and Gas Company's No.1 Mayes began producing natural gas on 16 February 1930, and by 1944 more than 100 million cubic feet of gas were produced at Jackson Field. Oil was also discovered at Jackson, but it was not of commercial quality.

A 1939 Works Progress Administration project to find suitable clay for school tableware in Yazoo County eventually led assistant state geologist Frederic Mellen to a geological structure he believed had the potential to produce oil. He was correct, and on 5 September of that year the first commercially significant oil strike took place southwest of Yazoo City at what became Tinsley Field, attracting representatives of independent and major oil companies.

Most of Mississippi's significant oil and gas fields were discovered during the World War II era. Following Tinsley, fields were discovered in Pickens, Cary, and Brookhaven in the western part of the state. In 1943 oil and gas were discovered near Natchez. Gulf Refining also began drilling in eastern Mississippi, and Eucutta Field, twelve miles northeast of Laurel in Wayne County, became the area's first commercial oil-producing field. Gulf Refining then started drilling in Heidelberg. Indications of oil were found on Christmas Eve 1943, and the Helen Morrison well was completed in 1944. By the end of that year, Heidelberg had several wells capable of producing more than fifteen hundred barrels per day. At the time it was considered the most significant discovery in the eastern United States. Later in 1944 gas was discovered at what became known as Gwinville Field in Jefferson Davis County, which ultimately produced the most gas in the state. In 1945 oil was discovered along the border of Lamar and Marion Counties. In subsequent years Baxterville Field often ranked as the highest producer of Mississippi oil.

In some areas, education benefited from oil's discovery. School districts with producing wells earned severance tax revenues and royalties. The Heidelberg Consolidated School earned enough money from the well on its property to build a cafeteria and gymnasium, erect lights for the football field, beautify the campus, and extend the school term to nine months. The school's athletic teams also gained a new nickname, the Oilers.

Oil and gas exploration continued after World War II, with Laurel becoming the center of the oil and gas industry in the southeastern part of the state. By 1956 eight hundred producing wells were located within fifty miles of the city. Natchez had a similar role in the southwest. In 1980 Adams County had fifty-six oil and gas companies employing about 1,700 people, while Jones County had forty-two companies employing about 770 people. In 1965 oil was discovered in deeper strata in Bay Springs, prompting further new exploration.

But the wave had already crested. Gas production peaked at just over 253.5 million cubic feet in 1956, while oil production topped out at slightly over 65.1 million barrels in 1970. Petroleum production subsequently has declined dramatically. As oil from outside the United States became cheaper, unprofitable American wells were shut down, and oil investors lost interest in Mississippi, which traditionally had a high "dry hole" rate and where wells tended to be deeper and thus more expensive. Less production meant that fewer people were employed, and by 1982, twelve thousand Mississippians had lost oil- and gas-related jobs. In 2010 Mississippi ranked thirteenth in the United States, producing just over 24 million barrels of oil. That year, the state produced just under 87 million cubic feet of gas, ranking twentieth in the country. Oil production has subsequently remained between 24 and 25 million barrels annually, while gas production has continued to fall, reaching 57 million cubic feet in 2015.

James Kennedy
Hinds Community College

John S. Ezell, *Journal of Southern History* (August 1952); Dudley J. Hughes, *Oil in the Deep South: A History of the Oil Business in Mississippi, Alabama, and Florida, 1859–1945* (1993); James Beauregard Kennedy, "The Oil and Gas Industry in Mississippi" (master's thesis, Mississippi State University, 1993); Mississippi Oil and Gas Board website, www.ogb .state.ms.us; US Energy Information Administration website, www.eia .gov/state/.

Oktibbeha County

Like many other Mississippi counties, Oktibbeha County was formed in 1833 from lands ceded to the United States by the Choctaw Nation in 1830. The name is said to have come from the words *okti abeha bok*, meaning "ice, there in the creek." The county is the site of multiple Choctaw burial sites. Native American artifacts more than two thousand years old have been discovered near Choctaw mounds just east of Starkville, the county seat.

Located in northeastern Mississippi, Oktibbeha began as a profitable agricultural county with success in corn crops and orchard products. Although livestock did not dominate Oktibbeha's industry, the prairie grasses and ample supply of water from the Noxubee River made the county conducive to raising cattle, mules, and horses. By the 1920s Oktibbeha became Mississippi's main dairy producer, and the region was known as the Milk Pitcher of the South.

In 1840 Oktibbeha had 2,197 enslaved residents and 2,079 free people. The county witnessed a dramatic increase in the number of slaves in the late antebellum period, and by 1860 the county's 7,631 slaves comprised 59 percent of the population of 12,977. Oktibbeha lost some of its territory and population with the establishment of Clay County to the north in 1872 and of Sumner County to the northwest two years later.

According to some evidence, the first church services held in the county occurred in 1835, led by Horatio Baldwell, a Presbyterian minister. Over time, Baptist churches came to dominate Oktibbeha's religious organizations, and by 1860 Oktibbeha had thirteen Baptist churches, eleven Methodist churches, five Presbyterian congregations, and two Cumberland Presbyterian congregations.

In response to lobbying by white farmers in the Grange, the state founded Mississippi Agricultural and Mechanical College in Starkville in 1878, bringing significant changes to the community. Mississippi A&M was the state's first land-grant college, created with Morrill Act funds, which allowed states to sell federal land to establish institutions for higher education. Classes began at the "people's college" in 1880, though women were not admitted until half a century later.

Another major contribution to the farming industry in Oktibbeha County was the opening of the state's first agricultural experiment station in 1888. The stations served as teaching centers where Mississippi farmers could learn new ways of selecting seed and plowing, planting, and rotating crops. In 1908 the boll weevil destroyed Mississippi's cotton crop, and A&M extension services received funds to work to prevent similar devastations. With the help of the US Department of Agriculture and the Hatch Act of 1914, new extension agents were hired to travel throughout the state and demonstrate productive farming techniques. For more than a century, the extension services have conducted and published research on significant subjects in Mississippi agriculture—the boll weevil, dairy farming, catfish, soybeans, forestry, kudzu. The extension agents and home demonstration researchers funded by the Hatch Act operated out of offices in Starkville and maintained close connections to the university. Some prominent scholars and faculty members from this era include Dorothy Dickins, a leader in home economics research, and David Phares, author of *The Farmers Book of Grasses and Other Forage Plants.*

In 1900 Oktibbeha's population topped twenty thousand, with African Americans accounting for almost two-thirds of the total. The county had a small but growing industrial sector, with 106 employees. Only 10 percent of Oktibbeha's 3,115 African American farmers owned their land, compared to more than two-thirds of white farmers. In 1916 the majority of Oktibbeha churchgoers attended Missionary Baptist and Southern Baptist services, while many others joined Methodist Episcopal and Methodist Episcopal Church, South congregations.

In the 1930s Oktibbeha's population declined slightly to 19,119 (11,367 African Americans and 7,752 whites). The growing college town of Starkville had a population of almost 2,600. The county's businesses employed almost 400 workers, and Starkville's dairy condensery (which opened in 1926) and other factories expanded manufacturing employment in the region. Agriculture remained the center of Oktibbeha's economy, with two-thirds of the 2,827 farms run by tenant farmers.

Mississippi A&M became Mississippi State College in 1932 and Mississippi State University in 1957. The school's notable graduates have included agricultural reformer Cully Cobb; political figures John Stennis, Sonny Montgomery, and Sharion Aycock; novelists John Grisham, Louis Nordan, and Thomas Hal Phillips; food writer Craig Claiborne; children's author Laurie Parker; chair maker Greg Harkins; and longtime coaches Ron Polk (baseball) and Babe McCarthy (basketball). Famous Mississippi State athletes include basketball stars Bailey Howell, Jeff Malone, and Erick Dampier; football stars Eric Moulds and D. D. Lewis; and Major League Baseball players Will Clark, Rafael Palmeiro, and Jonathan Papelbon. In 1965 Mississippi State University admitted its first African American student, Richard Holmes.

Among notable Starkville natives not associated with Mississippi State University are James "Cool Papa" Bell, a Negro League baseball star, and National Football League Hall of Fame receiver Jerry Rice, who was born in Starkville and grew up in Crawford.

By midcentury, Oktibbeha County's workers relied a great deal on Mississippi State University and other schools. In 1960 more than seventeen hundred county residents earned their living in education, giving Oktibbeha the state's fourth-highest percentage of people with high school and college degrees. With the growth of the university and concerns connected to it, Oktibbeha County's population soared to 36,018 by 1980.

In 2010 Oktibbeha County's population reached 47,671 and was 59 percent white, 36.6 percent African American, and 2.4 percent Asian and Asian American, making Oktib-

beha one of six counties in Mississippi with significant Asian populations.

Mississippi Encyclopedia Staff
University of Mississippi

Mississippi State Planning Commission, *Progress Report on State Planning in Mississippi* (1938); *Mississippi Statistical Abstract*, Mississippi State University (1952–2010); Dunbar Rowland, *Encyclopedia of Mississippi History: Comprising Sketches of Counties, Towns, Events, Institutions, and Persons* (1907); Charles Sydnor and Claude Bennett, *Mississippi History* (1939); University of Virginia Library, Historical Census Browser website, http://mapserver.lib.virginia.edu; E. Nolan Waller and Dani A. Smith, *Growth Profiles of Mississippi's Counties, 1960–1980* (1985); Sadye H. Wier and George R. Lewis, *Sadye H. Wier: Her Life and Work* (1993).

Old Capitol

Regarded by many observers as the most historic building in Mississippi, the Old Capitol is a centerpiece of the state's history and a National Historic Landmark. The building—the second capitol facility constructed in Jackson—was authorized after the 1832 constitution confirmed that Jackson would remain the state capital until at least 1850. Leaders envisioned a more expansive capitol that would serve the rapidly growing state for years to come.

William Nichols, designer of the North Carolina and Alabama capitols and one of the South's premier architects, was hired to build the capitol after an earlier false start by another architect. Nichols's plan called for a Greek Revival–style statehouse, a popular form at the time for public buildings because of its association with classical Greek and

Old Capitol, 100 North State Street, Jackson, 1940 (Photograph by Lester Jones, Library of Congress, Washington, D.C. [HABS MISS, 25-JACK,3-2])

O

Roman societies. The style was also practical in the southern climate because several of its features, such as galleries, large windows, and high ceilings, facilitated air circulation.

Despite many handicaps such as economic depression and a lack of skilled labor, the capitol was largely completed by January 1839, when the legislature first met in the new building. The imposing three-story structure was topped by a massive copper-plated rotunda rising nearly one hundred feet from the limestone ground floor. Throughout the interior, intricate handmade Greek Revival architectural elements adorned the building.

Several key moments in Mississippi's history transpired within the walls of the Old Capitol. In 1839 the Mississippi legislature became the first in the nation to confer property rights on married women, and the secession convention, which voted to take Mississippi out of the Union, met there in January 1861. The election of Hiram Rhodes Revels, the first African American to serve in the US Congress, took place there in 1870, and in 1884 the legislature created the first state-supported college for women in the United States, the Industrial Institute and College for the Education of White Girls of the State of Mississippi (now Mississippi University for Women). In 1890 the building hosted the state constitutional convention. In addition, national figures including Andrew Jackson, Henry Clay, and Jefferson Davis visited the Old Capitol.

Though Union forces captured the city of Jackson during the Civil War, the Old Capitol escaped destruction. By 1900, however, the building had fallen into disrepair, and a new, larger capitol was constructed nearby. Although there were plans at the time to destroy the Old Capitol and sell the land it occupied, patriotic organizations and leading citizens including Dunbar Rowland, the first director of the Mississippi Department of Archives and History, persuaded the legislature to restore the building. From 1917 to 1959 it was used as a state office building, housing such agencies as the Board of Health, Department of Education, and Department of Agriculture.

Under the leadership of Gov. James P. Coleman, the building underwent an extensive restoration from 1959 to 1961 to serve as the state historical museum, administered by the Mississippi Department of Archives and History. Damage caused by Hurricane Katrina in 2005 resulted in the closure of the museum. It reopened after extensive restoration in 2009 with a focus on the interpretation of Mississippi's political and governmental heritage, the importance of historic preservation, and the storied past of the Old Capitol itself.

Mike Bunn
Historic Chattahoochee
Commission

John Ray Skates, *Mississippi's Old Capitol: Biography of a Building* (1990).

Old Southern Tea Room

Vicksburg's Old Southern Tea Room opened in 1941 under the leadership of Mary McKay. It eventually became one of the best restaurants in the South, lauded by the *Saturday Evening Post* and featured in the 1955 edition of Duncan Hines's *Adventures in Good Eating*.

The restaurant began as a civic project, brainstormed at a meeting by the Vicksburg Ladies Spring Pilgrimage Committee. The group was determined to make the city a premier destination for the many visitors who flocked to the South every year to tour antebellum homes. Yet they worried that Vicksburg lacked quality eateries like those found in Natchez and New Orleans and resolved to sponsor a seasonal restaurant to cater to tourists during pilgrimage.

They turned to McKay, whom the *Vicksburg Post* described as "a strong-willed and feisty blue-blood, a waspish little lady who grew up in the decaying splendor of Millbrook [Plantation] in east Mississippi." Her grandfather had built the plantation before the Civil War, operated steamboats on the Chickasawhay River, and signed a treaty with the Choctaw on behalf of Andrew Jackson. The family fortune declined after the war years, but McKay—now the wife of a Vicksburg attorney and the mother of two grown children—remained a prominent socialite and community volunteer who heralded her ties to the Old South.

The city pooled resources to launch the restaurant. An old drugstore on Monroe Avenue was offered rent-free. The women of the pilgrimage committee donated pots, plates, and even a dilapidated old stove. McKay hired Elvira Coleman, who had for many years cooked at Millbrook Plantation, to prepare the food.

The project was to last no longer than six weeks, but the restaurant was so popular with tourists and locals that McKay decided to continue it after pilgrimage ended. When the ladies of the community took back their cookware, McKay got more. She borrowed money to purchase an old stove and negotiated an affordable rent. "Aunt" Elvira continued to work in the kitchen with others she mentored, creating the southern dishes that her diners relished: stuffed ham, fried chicken, catfish, corn pudding, and filled cakes, among others.

The Old Southern Tea Room, first by law and later by custom, was a whites-only dining establishment. McKay managed the kitchen and dining room with a staff of six African American women: two prepared food, two cooked, and two waited tables, with staff members switching duties each day. Except for McKay, each employee wore a calico dress, a white apron, and a bandana on her head. Especially during the civil rights era, many members of the black community criticized the mammy costume, but according to former employee Herdcine Williams, for some of the women, the steady income and good tips outweighed some of the humiliation of the costume.

With six different women contributing their skills in the kitchen, the restaurant offered a variety of daily specials. Many diners lunched there multiple times per week. In the years that Warren County was a dry community, the tea room also featured a hideaway in the back where mint juleps were served. In time, the restaurant earned a national reputation. Duncan Hines included it in his 1955 edition of *Good Eating*: when asked what he would like to do first after returning from Europe, he offered, "I would like to be at The Old South Tea Room, in Vicksburg, Mississippi; enjoying the Stuffed Garden Egg-plant and Corn Pudding." The quip proudly appeared on the back cover of the restaurant's cookbook, along with compliments from representatives of *Life* magazine, the *Chicago Sunday Tribune*, and the *Minneapolis Star*.

Mary McKay managed the restaurant on her own for many years. Though she could not even boil water, she possessed a fiery temper and demanded high quality from the kitchen. The popularity of the restaurant was testament to its success. In 1951, at age sixty-four, she sold one-third of the restaurant to Warren Asher. He bought her out nine years later with an agreement that reserved McKay's right to consult in the kitchen and obligated Asher to serve her three meals a day for the rest of her life. He arranged for her meals even after she moved to a nursing home and fed her until her death in 1974.

In 1960 McKay published the *Old Southern Tea Room Cookbook*, a paperback collection of recipes featuring a photograph of a young woman in an antebellum ball gown on the front cover. The book opens with "Recipe for Nationally Famous Restaurant," penned by Vicksburg native Charlotte Khan, which offers an embellished tale of the tea room's history. Inside, recipes for Aunt Elvira's little hot biscuits (including lard), Aunt Fanny's spoon bread, Delta luncheon rice casserole, old southern "cawn puddin," and the Old Southern Tea Room's famous mint juleps are decorated with pen-and-ink drawings, including images of slaves working in fields and kitchens.

The restaurant subsequently changed ownership and location several times before the final owners declared bankruptcy and closed the tea room's doors forever.

Mary Beth Lasseter
University of Mississippi

Gordon Cotton, *Vicksburg Post* (15 April 2007); Charles Faulk, *Vicksburg Post* (15 March 1987); Mary McKay, *Old Southern Tea Room Cookbook: A Collection of Favorite Old Recipes* (1960).

Old Spanish Trail (Highway 90)

In September 1915 representatives from Mississippi, Louisiana, and Alabama met in Mobile, Alabama, and created the Alabama–Gulf Coast Highway Association, seeking to spur the creation of a new highway along the Gulf Coast. The association sprung from the Good Roads Movement, which beginning in the 1910s sought to create better transportation routes for the increasingly popular automobile. In the days before the 1926 creation of the US federal highway system, such associations played an important role in road building. Supporters initially hoped for a road that would link Mobile to New Orleans via cities along the Mississippi Gulf Coast. Just one month later, however, the Alabama–Gulf Coast Highway Association floated a more ambitious proposal—a highway from Miami, Florida, up the Florida Gulf Coast, through Mobile, and across coastal Mississippi to New Orleans. This future road was dubbed the Old Spanish Trail.

Harrison County, Mississippi, began issuing bonds to construct a twenty-five-mile beachfront road as a result of advocacy from the Alabama–Gulf Coast Highway Association, but the effort soon lost momentum. Good Roads advocates from Florida, Alabama, Mississippi, Louisiana, and Arizona met again in Mobile on 10–11 December, and this time they created the Old Spanish Trail Highway Association, which took as its mission the creation of a highway that would connect the East to the West. Any efforts previously initiated by towns along the proposed route would be incorporated into this thoroughfare. The 419 delegates in attendance at the meeting expanded their vision even further, planning a southern national highway from St. Augustine, Florida, to San Diego, California. Travelers crossing the country would experience the wonders of the nation and bring tourist dollars into the areas through which the route passed.

In Mississippi, those areas would include the municipalities of Pascagoula, Gautier, Ocean Springs, Biloxi, Mississippi City, Gulfport, Long Beach, Pass Christian, and Bay St. Louis. Even though it would be identified as part of the Old Spanish Trail, this portion had no historical connection to the Spanish. It would be simply a coastal highway. Mississippi cities already had graded many miles of road on the front beach, but with the coming of World War I, efforts halted.

By 1919 the Old Spanish Trail Highway Association resumed work under the direction of Harral B. Ayers. The biggest challenge was waterways. Efforts varied from city to city and county to county, with each one passing road bonds. Some areas still had dirt tracks, while others had improved bridges and roads. Mississippi's three coastal counties—Jackson, Harrison, and Hancock—moved forward with construction.

On 17 November 1925 the road known as the Old Spanish Trail became US Highway 90, and by 1928 the last ferry on the

O

highway route was replaced by the East Pascagoula Bridge in Jackson County. Over the next decades, projects such as the Biloxi–Ocean Springs Bridge and the Bay St. Louis Bridge continued to improve the route from Mobile to New Orleans, and Highway 90 remained the main road for travelers. During the 1980s, the completion of Interstate 10 about six miles further inland provided a second route across the Mississippi coast, linking states to the east to those to the west.

Highway 90 in Mississippi suffered significant damage when Hurricane Katrina struck in August 2005. The bridges between Bay St. Louis and Pass Christian and between Biloxi and Ocean Springs were destroyed, as were significant sections of the roadbed, especially in Harrison County. By 2008, however, all repairs had been completed.

Deanne Stephens Nuwer
University of Southern Mississippi,
Katrina Research Center

"Minutes of the Convention of 'The Old Spanish Trail,'" Mobile, Alabama, 10–11 December 1915, Old Spanish Trail Association Archives, Louis J. Blume Library, St. Mary's University, San Antonio, Texas; *Old Spanish Trail Magazine* (August 1920); Charles Sullivan, in *The Story of a Modern American Highway* (2003).

O'Neal, Mary Lovelace

(b. 1942) Artist

Painter, art educator, and civil rights activist Mary Lovelace O'Neal has been a force in American art since the mid-1970s. Lovelace was born in Jackson on 10 February 1942 to Ariel M. Lovelace, a professor at Tougaloo College, and Edna R. Lovelace. Mary Lovelace received a bachelor of fine arts degree from Howard University in 1964 and a master of fine arts degree from Columbia University in 1969. She went on to teach at the University of California at Berkeley, where she was the first African American to earn tenure and the first to chair the Department of Art Practice. Although her dynamic compositions and vibrant colors place her work decidedly in the abstract school, her approach creates a provocative balance between narrative and pure abstraction.

O'Neal developed her interest in art, education, and social issues while growing up in Mississippi and Arkansas. As a child, she and her brother drank from "whites only" fountains and ran through Woolworth's and other off-limits establishments to spin the stools at the lunch counters. Later, at Howard University in Washington, D.C., O'Neal focused both on art and on the civil rights movement. While studying under art historian David Driskell, she helped organize rallies, voter drives, and other actions. For a time she had a serious relationship with future Black Panther Party icon Stokely Carmichael. During this era she gave speeches in Canton, Mississippi, and elsewhere; served as an educator in a Mississippi freedom school; and went to New York to console the family of slain civil rights activist Michael Schwerner.

In 1963 O'Neal received a fellowship to the Skowhegan School of Painting and Sculpture, where she spent the summer focusing on her artwork. Inspired by Willem de Kooning, Mark Rothko, and especially Franz Kline, she developed her abstract expressionist style. In graduate school at Columbia University, where she was the only African American in her class, O'Neal soon began to fuse her political awareness with her work—no easy task, given the nonnarrative context of her aesthetic. A striking characteristic of the works she ultimately produced was the lampblack pigment ground into the canvas. The process created a striking black background on which she added minimal strikes of color to make a social statement without betraying her minimalist, abstract style.

In the 1970s O'Neal completed her *Whale Series*, which is among her most noted work. While still featuring the lampblack canvasses, these paintings also feature large, vibrant shapes of color, the primary form of which resembles a whale. In general, the figures and broad swaths of color represent a departure from the minimalism of her earlier work. In the decades that followed, O'Neal's painting continued in this fashion, with contrasting colors and (at times less abstract) shapes evading literal interpretation in favor of an emotional exchange with the viewer. In many cases her paintings became more crowded by color and shape as well as layers of color and texture. The titles of the paintings offer a window into the political influences behind the work, complementing the limited subject narrative of the paintings themselves: *Running with Black Panthers and White Doves*; *Racism Is Like Rain, Either It Is Raining or It Is Gathering Somewhere*; *Running Freed More Slaves Than Lincoln Ever Did*.

O'Neal retired from the University of California at Berkeley in 2006 and became professor emerita. Married to Chilean painter Patricio Toro, O'Neal continues to make art and spends time between the Bay Area and Santiago, Chile. She is described as a raconteur with a highly flamboyant personality. Her works are in the collections of the San Francisco Museum of Modern Art, the Oakland Museum of California, and the National Museum of Fine Arts, Santiago, Chile. She has received the Artiste en France Award from the French government.

Odie Lindsey
Nashville, Tennessee

René Paul Barrilleux, ed., *Mary Lovelace O'Neal* (2002); Patti Carr Black, *Art in Mississippi, 1720–1980* (1998).

Operation Pretense

Operation Pretense was a 1980s undercover investigation of corruption in county purchasing in Mississippi. The investigation resulted in felony convictions or guilty pleas involving 56 of the 410 supervisors in twenty-six of the state's eighty-two counties.

Mississippi's "beat system" of county administration led itself to widespread corruption. Each county was divided into five districts, or beats, each of which elected a supervisor who controlled all activities related to building and maintaining roads in the district. On routine matters, each supervisor had complete control of purchasing activities from initiation to payment approval, a system that was open to abuse, since it was easy to provide fraudulent documentation for materials that were not delivered. For purchases that could not be controlled directly, bids could easily be rigged. Counties were not required to keep inventory or asset records.

Rumors had long swirled that many supervisors were on the take, but sheriffs and county prosecuting attorneys had little stomach for pursuing supervisors who approved the budgets for those county offices. District attorneys, for their part, hesitated to offend politically powerful supervisors, and the state attorney general has no subpoena power. Thus, catching corrupt supervisors required involvement by the US attorneys and the Federal Bureau of Investigation (FBI) as well as a sting that would catch supervisors in the act of taking payoffs from vendors.

Because John Burgess, a Pentecostal minister and businessman from Carthage, was a key figure in the investigation, the FBI code-named its investigation Operation Preacher's Ten Percent Supervisors' Expense, or Pretense. In 1982, after investing in a company that manufactured pipes, Burgess learned that the company's salesmen had to pay kickbacks to supervisors to do business with counties. Burgess told federal authorities what he knew and agreed to cooperate in an undercover investigation. He opened an FBI front, the Mid-State Pipe Company, and taped conversations as he took kickbacks from several county supervisors. He ultimately testified against supervisors before grand juries and in two criminal trials.

Other key players in Operation Pretense were FBI special agents Jerry King and Cliff Chatham. Using the aliases Jerry Jacobs and Cliff Winters, these agents worked undercover as salesmen for Mid-State and conducted most of the stings. US attorneys James Tucker and John Hailman prosecuted the cases. State auditor Ray Mabus and his staff provided leads, secured records, and testified in court. Auditor Sheila Patterson's testimony in the first trial, that of Perry County supervisor Trudie Westmoreland, was a very important factor leading to conviction. This trial demonstrated the strength of the government's cases and caused many supervisors to seek plea agreements.

But Operation Pretense did not eliminate the corruption. Several supervisors continued their illegal practices even after they were indicted. One supervisor threatened to kill an undercover agent. The brother of an indicted vendor offered to help an indicted supervisor by "fixing" the jury if he went to trial. Boards of supervisors subsequently appointed relatives of convicted supervisors as their replacements.

Boosted by his Pretense involvement, Mabus was elected governor on a reform platform in 1987 and spearheaded the 1988 passage of legislation to reform county government. All counties were required to institute central purchasing systems and to hold referenda to choose between the beat and unit systems, under which professional managers would be in charge of all county activities.

Although the reform legislation constituted a major step forward, it also contained major flaws. Only forty-eight counties adopted the unit system, leaving thirty-four under the old beat system. Moreover, the law allows citizens to petition to put the question on the ballot again, and Jones and Lincoln Counties subsequently voted to go back to the beat system.

The conditions that Operation Pretense revealed seem almost unbelievable: the lack of rudimentary controls over purchases made with taxpayer money, the lack of county planning and control over roads, and supervisors' almost unlimited power within their beats. Operation Pretense devastated lives, derailed political careers, and resulted in significant reforms in county government. However, those reforms were far from perfect or complete.

James R. Crockett
University of Southern Mississippi

James R. Crockett, *Operation Pretense: The FBI's Sting on County Corruption in Mississippi* (2003).

Orr, Pauline Van de Graaf

(1861–1955) Educator

Pauline Van de Graaf Orr was one of the most important educators in the South before 1920. Orr was born in 1861 in Chickasaw County to Cornelia Van de Graaf Orr and Jehu

O

Orr, a well-known attorney and judge in Columbus. Both of her parents had been educated in the North, and her father had earned a master's degree from Princeton University.

Pauline Orr demonstrated a precocious love of learning and spent her childhood days reading through the family's collection of classics. In Columbus she took the unprecedented path of appealing directly to the headmaster of a boys' school for admission to the college preparatory course of study. At sixteen she entered New York's Packer Collegiate Institute, one of the nation's best schools for girls. After graduation she traveled to Germany and studied at the University of Hanover. Orr apparently expressed little interest in the effort to create a state-supported institution of higher education for Mississippi's women, but after the legislature founded the Industrial Institute and College for the Education of White Girls of the State of Mississippi in 1884 and Columbus was chosen as the site of the new school, Pres. R. W. Jones met Orr and immediately asked her to serve as "mistress of English."

Over the next thirty years, Orr strove to make the school the equal of any women's college. She was known as an extremely demanding yet inspiring instructor. Experience had taught her that women could perform well in difficult academic environments, and she insisted on only the best from her students. Orr's dedication to high standards led to almost constant conflicts with those who felt that the school should focus more on vocational training than on liberal arts education. Attrition rates for students in Orr's classes were high because students as young as fifteen enrolled without adequate preparation, and Orr endured strained relations with a series of school officials who she felt lacked a firm commitment to high academic standards.

During the early 1890s Orr began what would become a lifelong relationship with Miriam Greene Paslay, one of the first baccalaureate graduates of the Industrial Institute and College. In addition to teaching, the two periodically traveled together in Europe between 1893 and 1905, studying at the University of Munich and the University of Zurich as well as touring Italy. Orr was influenced by the spirit of European romanticism and particularly by Thomas Carlyle, and she wrote poetry as well as insightful studies of contemporary writers such as Robert Browning.

Orr's best students often went on to distinguished careers. Both Blanche Colton Williams and Rosa Peebles earned doctorates and became chairs of departments of English. Frances Jones Gaither became a best-selling novelist, chronicling the Old South. Along with teaching, Orr was a frequent lecturer at literary and cultural clubs throughout Mississippi and gave a December 1906 talk on Browning at the University of Mississippi that the school's chancellor found exceptional.

In 1913, after years of conflict with the Industrial Institute and College's president, Henry Whitfield (later the governor of Mississippi), Orr resigned from the faculty. At the time she said, "I have desired, above everything else, the mental enfranchisement of the girls of Mississippi. I have tried to help them to realize and express themselves."

Orr subsequently devoted herself to the cause of voting rights for women, twice serving as president of the Mississippi Woman Suffrage Association. Following the death of Orr's mother in 1917, Orr and Paslay moved to New York City, where Orr resided until she died on 21 November 1955. Orr maintained lifelong correspondences with many former students, and her brownstone became a stopping place for many visitors and migrants from Mississippi. On 30 October 1954, the school where she had spent so much of her life dedicated the Orr Chapel in recognition of her contributions.

Sheldon S. Kohn
Zayed University, Abu Dhabi,
United Arab Emirates

Myra Mason Lindsey, "Life of Pauline Orr," Mississippi Department of Archives and History; Rosa Peebles, "Remembrance of Miriam Greene Paslay," Mississippi University for Women Archives (1932); Bridget Smith Pieschel and Stephen Robert Pieschel, *Loyal Daughters: One Hundred Years at Mississippi University for Women, 1884–1984* (1984); Stephen Pieschel, "The Orrs of Orr's Hill," Special Collections, Mississippi University for Women (1985); Sarah Wilkerson-Freeman, in *Mississippi Women: Their Histories, Their Lives*, ed. Martha H. Swain, Elizabeth Anne Payne, Marjorie Julian Spruill, and Susan Ditto (2003).

Osborn, Mary D.

(1875–1946) Public Health Nursing Leader

Mary D. Osborn was born in Ohio and graduated from Akron City Hospital School of Nursing in 1902. She subsequently worked at the hospital and by 1906 occupied the post of assistant director of nursing. Her intense interest in maternal nursing led her in 1912 to New York City, where she became assistant director of nursing at Women's Hospital. Soon thereafter, a charitable organization asked for help, and she became the nursing director of the Association for Improving the Condition of the Poor. Later known as the Community Service Society, the group sought to reduce maternal and infant deaths among the city's poor. Osborn also became active in the American Red Cross, particularly its outreach to the poor. During this period she worked closely with Harry Hopkins, an American Red Cross leader who went on to play a major role in the relief effort in Mississippi after the 1927 flood.

Osborn first came to Mississippi in 1921 to observe granny midwives, most of whom had little formal education but who played a major role in maternity care in the state. Most of the midwives were African American, and records indicate that they were delivering approximately 80 percent of the state's African American babies. Osborn did not plan to remain in Mississippi for long, but the American Red Cross recommended her to the State Board of Health for a planned maternal health program. She became first the supervisor of the Division of Maternal Child Health and within a year the supervisor of public health nursing. She spent the rest of her career leading Mississippi's nurses in public health efforts.

At the time of Osborn's arrival, Mississippi's death rates for mothers and infants were among the highest in the country. In 1917 almost 10 percent of all babies died, as did more than four hundred mothers. Osborn viewed the granny midwife as a significant member of the team who could help save some of those lives. She knew that the midwives varied in education and skill but also recognized their valued role in poor communities, especially those without doctors. Her goal became clear within a year of taking the health department position. The midwives needed to be educated and trained in modern methods to help lower death rates. By 1922 Osborn had written a *Manual for Midwives*, which became the handbook for all midwives practicing in Mississippi. She then prepared public health nurses to travel throughout the state, training groups of midwives.

Osborn hoped to build a network of public health nurses and midwives, creating midwives' clubs and instituting badges for trained midwives. As the groups grew and matured, Osborn added further education to increase skills in basic hygiene and health management. The midwives ran demonstrations and became models in their communities in areas such as home care for the sick and immunization education. As the programs in Mississippi grew, Osborn's staff of nurses grew from 7 in 1921 to more than 160 when she left the department in 1946, and by 1950 the infant death rate had dropped to just 3.6 percent.

Osborne resigned from the State Department of Health in June 1946 and died on 7 July after a short illness. Her picture hangs in the department's headquarters, and in 1996 she was inducted into the American Nurses Association Hall of Fame in recognition of her service to Mississippi mothers, children, and midwives.

Linda Sabin
University of Louisiana at Monroe

Mississippi Nurses Association Historical Committee, *Passing the Flame: The History of the Mississippi Nurses' Association, 1911–1986* (1986); Public Health Nursing Papers, Mary D. Osborn Biographical Materials, Mississippi Department of Archives and History.

Overseers

No figure was more indispensable to the success of plantation agriculture in Mississippi than the overseer, an individual charged with the general oversight of all operations on the plantation. Usually employed on units with twenty or more working field hands, the overseer occupied a position in the managerial hierarchy between the owner or his agent and the black drivers who directly supervised the work of their fellow slaves under the gang system that most cotton plantations utilized. Chiefly responsible for slave discipline and crop production, overseers assigned gangs to work, administered corporal punishment to those who violated plantation rules, enforced a night curfew, distributed food and clothing, treated minor medical ailments, maintained various record and account books, and executed other routine duties associated with the operation of slave plantations.

In 1860 Mississippi had nearly four thousand overseers, a number exceeded only in Virginia, Georgia, and Alabama. Each Mississippi overseer was responsible for roughly sixty to one hundred slaves, a markedly lower ratio than was found in the rice districts of South Carolina and sugar parishes of Louisiana, where in some counties one overseer had charge of as many as three hundred slaves. In contrast to their counterparts in the older Atlantic seaboard states, the overseers on Mississippi's cotton plantations tended to be young, unmarried, relatively inexperienced, and disposed to move frequently from one plantation to another in search of more attractive conditions.

Most overseers came from yeoman farmer families and had little formal education. Although they were universally enjoined to treat their black charges with justice and humanity, the intense pressure from their employers to produce bountiful cotton crops frequently resulted in merciless exploitation of chattel laborers. When one overseer neglected stock, farm utensils, and sick workers, planter Haller Nutt observed that the man seemed to think "his whole salvation depend[ed] upon this crop alone—whatever the sacrifice to me." On another occasion, Nutt attributed the deaths of six slaves in a single year to the "cruelty" of his overseer.

Few men aspired to enter the business of overseeing as a lifetime occupation. Rather, a man became an overseer in hopes of saving sufficient money to purchase a small parcel of land and perhaps a few slaves and thus to reenter the yeoman farmer class. Such a goal was realistic for plantation managers who lived frugally and soberly: in addition to an annual salary of between four hundred and five hundred dollars, overseers received lodging, basic provisions, and the use of one or more slaves to perform such chores as cutting wood and washing. Gulf-state planters often offered added incentives in the form of bonuses tied to production quotas, an arrangement that encouraged maximum production at the expense of slave welfare. Whatever his compensation, the overseer was an isolated figure, living a lonely and spartan existence. Viewed with a condescending and often critical eye by their employers, forbidden to fraternize with the slaves, discouraged from entertaining company, and obliged by the nature of their duties to maintain a physical presence on the plantation, overseers had little opportunity to enjoy the fruits of their managerial labors.

This isolation was exacerbated by overseers' alienation from both slaves and slaveholders. As the most visible representatives of the authoritarian and often brutal slave regime, overseers frequently incurred the animosity of those who labored under the duress of the whip. Overseers fared little better with their employers, who constantly criticized a variety of shortcomings, both real and imagined, and who changed overseers frequently and capriciously, failed to pay adequate salaries, and expressed class biases. Even under the best of circumstances, a certain degree of conflict was inherent in the owner-manager relationship. With no direct proprietary interest in laborers, stock, or equipment and under constant pressure to maximize production, overseers had difficulty appreciating owners' concerns regarding the property that constituted the bulk of their capital investment. Overseers also believed that they should receive greater control over plantation routines if they were to be held accountable for the results. Slaves often exploited this inherent conflict between proprietor and overseer to their advantage, in some cases undermining the overseers' authority by going over their heads to masters.

Whatever its deficiencies, the overseer system remained an integral part of plantation management until after the Civil War. Indeed, during that conflict, the role of the overseer became even more crucial as hundreds of thousands of able-bodied whites entered military service. Overseers initially comprised one of the exempted occupational groups under the Confederate Conscription Act of 1862, though the number of exempted managers was reduced as Confederate military fortunes declined, thereby undermining slave discipline and contributing to the demoralization of the home front.

William K. Scarborough
University of Southern Mississippi

Robert F. W. Allston, *The South Carolina Rice Plantation as Revealed in the Papers of Robert F. W. Allston*, ed. James H. Easterby (1945); John S. Bassett, *The Southern Plantation Overseer as Revealed in His Letters* (1925); Eugene D. Genovese, *Roll, Jordan, Roll: The World the Slaves Made* (1974); William K. Scarborough, *The Overseer: Plantation Management in the Old South* (1966; reprint, 1984); William K. Scarborough, *Agricultural History* (January 1964); Kenneth M. Stampp, *The Peculiar Institution: Slavery in the Ante-Bellum South* (1956).

Overstreet, N. W.
(1888–1973) Architect

N. W. Overstreet was arguably the most prolific and influential architect practicing in Mississippi through much of the twentieth century. His significance stemmed from the large number, wide distribution, and high quality of his built work as well as from his forceful mentorship of the many young architects who interned in his office. He has been called Mississippi's First Architect.

Noah Webster "Webb" Overstreet was born on 4 July 1888 in Eastabouchie, a small sawmill town in the Piney Woods of southern Mississippi. He received a degree in engineering from Mississippi State College in 1908 before moving on to complete his studies at the University of Illinois, where he received a degree in architectural engineering. His education gave him a thorough grounding in the technical aspects of the profession and a familiarity with and dedication to the principles of modern architecture as exemplified by Frank Lloyd Wright and his Prairie Style contemporaries in the American Midwest and by Otto Wagner and other European Secessionist architects. Overstreet returned to Mississippi in 1912 to begin his architectural practice with the desire to introduce progressive architectural styles to his home state.

Overstreet practiced for fifty-seven years, retiring from his firm, then known as Overstreet, Ware, Ware, and Lewis, in 1969. Through much of this time his office was the state's largest architectural firm. Overstreet's buildings help tell the story of Mississippi's history. His early public service buildings, including the Bolivar County Courthouse, often featured modern architectural forms emblematic of the progressive spirit of the times. His post–World War I institutional buildings, such as Jackson's Central Presbyterian Church, sometimes borrowed from more traditional styles, thereby reflecting the growing conservatism of these years. His Art Deco buildings of the 1920s, including the Standard Life Building in downtown Jackson, announced the renewed optimism of the business community. The streamlined Depression-era public works buildings, such as the boldly composed Columbia High School, resounded with the era's curious mixture of disillusionment and determination. And his many post–World War II International Style buildings, including the Bolivar County Health Services Building, revealed the restless pragmatism of the moment.

The success of the office resulted in large part from Overstreet's friendships and associations. He was a longtime member of the Jackson Rotary Club, a deacon in Jackson's First Baptist Church, and class president of the Mississippi State Alumni Association. Overstreet's outgoing personality and genuine sympathy for the needs of his clients made him a persuasive salesman on behalf of his firm and a powerful advocate for the cause of modernism. In addition to marketing, Overstreet was concerned primarily with the engineering and construction of his projects. He entrusted much of the firm's design work to his younger assistants, thus helping to build the skills and confidence of many men who would later become leaders of their own firms. In particular, A. Hays Town worked with Overstreet from 1926 to 1939 and designed many of the firm's most widely recognized projects, including Jackson's Bailey Junior High School.

Overstreet was the first Mississippian inducted into the American Institute of Architects' College of Fellows, which recognized his firm's excellence in design. His buildings reflected the latest trends of their day and the aspirations of his clients. Most of the nine hundred buildings for which he was responsible continue to serve the needs of Mississippians. Overstreet's mentorship of several generations of Mississippi architects helped to set the high aspirations and ethical standards that his profession continues to uphold.

David Sachs
Kansas State University

David Sachs, *The Work of Overstreet and Town: The Coming of Modern Architecture to Mississippi* (1986).

Oysters

While the Mississippi coastline may be small compared to that of neighboring states, oyster harvesting accounts for a significant portion of the state's seafood industry, and oysters figure prominently in the local diet. Along with shrimp and blue crab, oysters are the most widely harvested seafood in the state. While shrimp and crabs are considered shellfish, oysters are actually bivalve mollusks with two shell valves hinged at one end and a single muscle attaching the shells at the other end.

Archaeological evidence shows that humans have cultivated and farmed oysters for centuries. Naturally grown oysters are almost nonexistent today, but seeding programs using existing oyster beds have created a successful and healthy industry. Young oysters (spats) are used to seed the beds. An oyster requires about three years to mature. During that period the seed oysters may be transplanted several times to waters of varying salinity and food supply to stimulate growth. Oysters filter their food as water passes through their shells. Thus, water temperature, salinity, mineral content, and biotoxins can affect the oyster's taste and health.

Crassostrea virginica (Eastern or American oyster) is one of the four major species of oysters and is found along the

Child oyster shuckers, Pass Packing Company, Pass Christian, February 1911 (Photograph by Lewis Wickes Hines, Library of Congress, Washington, D.C. [LC-DIG-nclc-00857])

Atlantic seaboard and the Gulf of Mexico, including Mississippi. The state Department of Marine Resources (DMR) manages the state's natural oyster reefs, and the overwhelming majority of the state's commercially harvested oysters come from the reefs in the western Mississippi Sound. Mississippi oyster-processing plants accept catches from other states because in-state landings are not enough to sustain operations.

Hurricane Katrina in 2005 and the Deepwater Horizon oil spill of 2010 decimated Mississippi's oyster industry by more than 80 percent. For example, in 2004, fishermen harvested nearly a half million sacks of oysters from Mississippi's coastal waters. In 2014 that number was just over 78,000 sacks. Katrina alone damaged 80–90 percent of the near and offshore reefs, breaking them, moving them, and covering them in debris and silt. Larval oysters need a hard surface on which to attach to begin the growth process. This surface, or cultch material, is often made of recycled oyster shells. The DMR's "shell planting" project, which required depositing recycled shells on existing reefs, was the first step in restoring the damaged environment.

Those familiar with oysters know the old adage that they should be eaten only in months containing the letter *R*. This advice resulted in part from the possibility of spoilage in warmer temperatures (late spring and summer months). In addition, *Vibrio vulnificus*, an extremely virulent marine bacterium, becomes dormant in cold weather and thus poses much less of a threat. Further, oysters just taste better during the colder months: during the spring and summer, as oysters prepare to spawn, they become fatty and less flavorful.

Now, of course, oysters are available year-round thanks to refrigeration and a number of postharvest processing technologies. Individual quick-freeze, high hydrostatic pressure, and heat-cool pasteurization are the most commonly used techniques for bringing raw oysters to market. While raw oysters may be dangerous for certain at-risk groups (especially diabetics and those with depressed immune systems), oysters offer a number of health benefits. They are a good source of calcium, iron, B12, and zinc. They also have a well-established if not completely accurate reputation as an aphrodisiac.

Live oysters are available for sale by the dozen, half bushel, or bushel (approximately ten dozen). Shucked (removed from the shell) oysters are sold by weight, volume, or count and are either frozen or canned or in plastic containers. The best way to shuck is with an oyster knife, which has a strong steel blade designed for prying open the hinged end of the shell. Steaming them for a few seconds can ease the opening process because the heat softens the muscle.

Oysters are delicious prepared in many different ways—raw on the half shell, with a lemon wedge, or with a bit of hot sauce. The DMR published a cookbook, *Mississippi Oyster Recipes*, featuring cooking suggestions developed with the Gulf and South Atlantic States Fisheries Foundation to increase consumer awareness, consumption, and sales of oyster products. The cookbook includes recipes that push the gastronomical limits. Along with oyster cornbread dressing and oyster soup, more adventurous cooks can try their hands at pepper and pineapple oyster stew or tofu spinach oyster dip. Like its saltwater neighbor, shrimp, oysters are a staple item at most Coast restaurants, served in soup, on po'boys, atop salads, or as part of bountiful seafood platters.

The famed dishes oysters Rockefeller and oysters Bienville created in New Orleans are also available on the Mississippi Coast. Fried oysters, oyster dressing, oyster pie, smoked oysters, and oyster shooters are but a few other ways to serve them. Another is what many consider a classic Mississippi seven-course meal: a half dozen on the half shell and a Barq's Root Beer.

Aimée Schmidt
Decatur, Georgia

M. F. K. Fisher, *Consider the Oyster* (1988); Mississippi Department of Marine Resources website, www.dmr.state.ms.us; National Marine Fisheries Service website, www.st.nmfs.gov; Joan Reardon, *Oysters: A Culinary Celebration with 185 Recipes* (2004).

P

Paige, Rod

(b. 1933) Educator and US Secretary of Education

Roderick Raynor Paige was born in Monticello, Mississippi, on 17 June 1933. Though many people in segregated Mississippi expected little in the way of educational achievement from African American children, Paige's mother was a librarian, and his father was a school principal. Paige earned a bachelor's degree from Jackson State University and master's and doctoral degrees from Indiana University.

After serving in the US Navy from 1955 to 1957, Paige started his career as a teacher and coach at Hinds Agricultural High School and Utica Junior College from 1957 to 1963. He then moved to Jackson State, where he served as head football coach from 1964 to 1968. In 1971 he accepted the same position at Texas Southern University, a historically black institution in Houston, coaching until 1975, when he switched his focus to administration and became the school's athletic director. He taught at Texas Southern from 1980 to 1984 before becoming dean of the university's College of Education. While serving in that role, he created the Center for Excellence in Urban Education.

Paige served as a trustee and officer of the Board of Education of the Houston Independent School District from 1990 to 1994, when he left Texas Southern and became the district's superintendent. In 2001 the American Association of School Administrators named Paige National Superintendent of the Year.

In 2001 Pres. George W. Bush selected Paige to serve as secretary of education, the first school superintendent to hold that office. Paige played an instrumental role in securing passage of the No Child Left Behind Act of 2001, a controversial reform measure that sought to increase public school accountability. Paige's belief that programs such as affirmative action represented a poor way to fight racial discrimination raised a critical eye among liberals, but Paige consistently challenged the National Association for the Advancement of Colored People and other organizations that claimed to speak for all African Americans: "I have a message for the NAACP's Julian Bond and Kweisi Mfume, who have accused black conservatives of being 'puppets' of white people, unable to think for ourselves: You do not own, and you are not the arbiters of, African American authenticity." In 2004 Paige sparked a firestorm when he called the largest US teachers' union, the National Education Association, a "terrorist organization," though he immediately apologized for his "inappropriate choice of words."

Paige resigned from the Department of Education in 2005 and became chair of a consulting firm, the Chartwell Education Group. Paige continued his support for strict accountability and his criticism of some teacher unions with his 2007 book, *The War against Hope: How Teachers' Unions Hurt Children, Hinder Teachers, and Endanger Public Education*. In 2010 he and Elaine Witty coauthored *The Black-White Achievement Gap: Why Closing It Is the Greatest Civil Rights Issue of Our Time*. He has served as a public policy scholar at the Woodrow Wilson International Center for Scholars as well as on the boards of numerous education-related organizations. He continues to speak publicly on education issues, remaining a staunch advocate of school-choice programs. In November 2016, Paige became interim president of Jackson State University.

Ben Gilstrap
University of Mississippi

Dallas Morning News, 6 February 2015; Rod Paige, *The War against Hope: How Teachers' Unions Hurt Children, Hinder Teachers, and Endanger Public Education* (2007); Rod Paige website, www.rodpaige.com.

Paleo-Indians

Paleo-Indians were the first people to enter the Americas and Mississippi. Originally, it was thought that these people came across an ice-free corridor from Asia about thirteen thousand years ago. Now, however, some archaeologists believe that the first people arrived around twenty thousand years ago, and a few push the date as far back as fifty thousand years ago. At present we have no firm evidence for these early dates, and some scholars have recently suggested that these people may have come from Europe or Africa. Hard evidence is lacking.

The first people to enter Mississippi appear to have arrived about thirteen years ago from the Northeast, according to evidence from chert, the material employed to manufacture their spear points. Most of the chert is from the Tennessee Valley, and none is from western sources, as would be expected if the people had come from Asia. They traveled south along the Tennessee, Tombigbee, and Mississippi

Rivers and then moved east up the tributary streams into the interior of what is now the state. Another factor that suggests an eastern origin for these people is that thousands of their distinctive spear points have been found in the East, while only hundreds have been found in the West.

Paleo-Indians were hunter-gatherers who arrived near the end of the ice age, when many now-extinct animals were still present. The Indians' spear points and other tools have been found at a number of sites, but remarkably few skeletal remains of humans have been recovered. In the western United States some of these spear points have been recovered with animal skeletons—mostly wooly mammoth and bison. Killing such large animals with spears tipped with stone was dangerous work and is a testament to the Paleo-Indians' hunting prowess. The extinction of the Pleistocene megafauna is a mystery. Some people have attributed the extinction to the Paleo-Indians, but several smaller species went extinct at this time, as did species that were certainly not prey animals. Most researchers now believe that climate changes combined with other factors contributed to the extinctions during this period.

Samuel Brookes
National Forests in Mississippi

Samuel O. McGahey, in *The Paleoindian and Early Archaic Southeast*, ed. David G. Anderson and Kenneth E. Sassaman (1996).

Panic of 1837

In the nineteenth and early twentieth centuries Americans used the word *panic* to describe an economic depression. Because they associated depressions with banking crises, they evocatively labeled severe financial downturns *panics* and captured the popular response to currency restriction and bank closings. The Panic of 1837 signaled the start of the country's worst depression in the nineteenth century, which wreaked havoc in Mississippi for almost ten years.

During the scant two decades that separated Mississippi's entrance into the Union and the panic, the state grew at a remarkable pace. The development of the cotton gin and, more important, the hybridization of several varieties of cottonseed prompted East Coast residents to migrate to the southwestern frontier. Many veterans of the War of 1812 received land grants, which they exercised on the vast public domain of Mississippi. Statehood in 1817 encouraged more migrants to turn southwest, since the Union's familiar protections and stability were now available.

But substantial growth in the state awaited the Removal of Native Americans from the vast central portion of the state. When Choctaw Removal began in 1830, white settlers traveling with their slaves flooded into the middle third of Mississippi, and when the US government removed the Chickasaw from their ancestral home later in the decade, white migration shifted to the upper third of the state. This era has been labeled the Flush Times in antebellum Mississippi.

Between 1830 and 1835 the state grew exponentially, and thirty new counties were created from Indian cession lands. As potential farmers flowed into the public domain, they brought with them a desire for land and the need for capital. But Mississippi had few banks, and for much of the first twenty years of statehood, only the Bank of the State of Mississippi stood ready to lend money. To meet the credit crisis, Mississippi chartered twenty-seven banks between 1832 and 1837. Waterworks, railroads, and insurance companies received legislative charters to function as banks. They could accept deposits and issue currency. To meet the demand for credit, these banks freely printed currency notes, frequently without the gold and silver (specie) needed to back the paper money.

Inflationary currency policy caused notes issued by most Mississippi banks to be severely discounted when not exchanged at the issuing bank. Essentially then, banks in Mississippi produced a currency that met local demand but lacked credibility outside the immediate community. By itself, the currency policy of state-chartered banks was not conducive to long-term prosperity, but the international flow of specie and federal policy hastened the demise of the Flush Times.

In the mid-1830s the international flow of gold and silver began to shift away from the United States. Great Britain had traditionally been a primary customer for American raw materials (including cotton) and supplied the United States with specie in exchange. However, in the 1830s, the British government and entrepreneurs looked to Southeast Asia for new products to buy—tea and opium. The diminution in the US specie supply rapidly became evident.

In 1836 Pres. Andrew Jackson sought to shore up the federal government's supply of specie by issuing his Specie Circular Act of 1836, which required that all debts owed to the United States be paid in gold or silver. The regulation placed a premium on gold and silver for all manner of financial transactions. Mississippians turned to their local banks to exchange currency for specie but discovered that they had none to back the notes, and banks begin closing almost as rapidly as they opened. Currency, once readily available for conducting everyday transactions, suddenly became scarce.

Owners of businesses and farmers found themselves hopelessly in debt and unable to buy or sell goods. Official statistics about the depth of the depression are unavailable, but its effects remained evident as late as 1845. Jehu Amaziah Orr, who traveled from Jackson into northeastern Mississippi, noted countless abandoned plantations, which he described as "bits of wreckage and flotsam" that marked "the unseen graves of those who have perished there." Courts routinely seized property, and to escape bankruptcy proceedings debtors packed their households and fled to Texas in the middle of the night, a practice so common that another resident referred to Texas as "the stronghold of evil-doers."

The Panic of 1837 devastated Mississippi's economy. Perhaps more important, political debate over the causes of and cure for the panic led to the development of a competitive two-party political system dominated by discussion of economic issues.

Bradley G. Bond
Northern Illinois University

Bradley G. Bond, *Political Culture in the Nineteenth-Century South: Mississippi, 1830–1900* (1995); J. A. Orr, *Mississippi Historical Society Publications 9* (1906); Larry Schweikart, *Banking in the American South from the Age of Jackson to Reconstruction* (1987); Peter Temin, *The Jacksonian Economy* (1969).

Panola County

Panola County, located in northwest Mississippi in the Mississippi Delta, was established in 1836. According to oral tradition, its name comes from an Indian term for cotton. Its county seat is Batesville, with other notable towns including Como, Crenshaw, and Sardis. Shortly after its establishment, the 1840 census found that Panola County had slightly more slaves than free people (2,415 to 2,242). Part of an agricultural economy, antebellum Panola County had no industrial or manufacturing workers.

By 1860 the growing county had 5,237 free people and 8,557 slaves. Farmers raised cotton, corn, and livestock, and Panola County ranked seventh among the state's counties in growing potatoes. Only twelve people were employed by manufacturers. Thirteen of the county's twenty-seven churches were Methodist, seven were Baptist, four were Presbyterian, and three were Cumberland Presbyterian.

African Americans moved to Panola and other Mississippi Delta counties in great numbers after emancipation with the hope of finding and working available land. Despite losing part of its territory to Quitman County in 1877, Panola grew to 28,352 people by 1880, with two-thirds of them African Americans. Many had moved to Mississippi from other parts of the South. Only two counties produced more cotton than Panola did, and it ranked second in the number of cat-

tle and eighth in the production of corn. Forty-six percent of the county's farms were run by their owners, with the rest operated by tenants and sharecroppers. Panola's thirty-one manufacturing establishments, all located in Batesville, employed seventy men and three children.

Between 1880 and 1900 Panola's population remained stable. Small-scale manufacturing was rapidly increasing, with eighty-five establishments employing 110 workers. Only 16 percent of black farmers owned their own land, while 47 percent of white farmers did so.

Early in the twentieth century, Panola County's Methodists and Baptists comprised more than 90 percent of all church members. The largest groups were the Missionary Baptists (more than five thousand), the Methodist Episcopal Church, South (more than three thousand), the Colored Methodist Episcopal Church (more than two thousand), and the Southern Baptists (about sixteen hundred). Panola County also had many small but substantial groups of Presbyterians and Church of Christ members.

In 1930 Panola was home to 28,648 people, including almost 18,000 African Americans (63 percent of the population). Like several Delta counties, Panola had a low number of industrial workers—just 123. Almost 80 percent of its farms were operated by tenants, and cotton was the primary crop, followed by corn and forage crops.

Ties to the federal government brought changes to Panola County in the 1930s and 1940s. During World War II, Camp Como housed Italian and German prisoners of war. A more lasting change came with the construction of Sardis Lake, a US Army Corps of Engineers flood-control reservoir that was designed both to protect Delta agricultural land from flooding and to provide an important source for recreation, including fishing.

Though the county's overall population numbers remained stable, in 1960 whites accounted for 44 percent of residents while the African American population declined to 56 percent. Panola remained agricultural, ranking near the top of Mississippi's counties in growing corn and soybeans and high in the production of cotton and livestock. Textile work was the primary form of industry, and manufacturing jobs made up about 12 percent of the county's employment.

Panola County has been the home of some uniquely creative citizens. The state's first home demonstration agent, Susie Powell, was born in Batesville. Writer and critic Stark Young was born in Como in 1881. In the 1920s blues singer Jessie Mae Hemphill grew up near the Tate County line. Poet James Seay was born in rural Panola County in 1939. Mississippi Fred McDowell played most of his career around Como, where folklorist Alan Lomax recorded him in 1959. Hip-hop artist Soulja Boy was born in Batesville. Panola County is also the home of the Como Opera Guild and the Panola Playhouse.

In 2010, like many northern Mississippi counties, Panola County's population was growing: its 34,707 residents constituted an increase of about 20 percent over the previous half century. The county's racial profile shifted over this period, with whites accounting for 49.4 percent of the population and African Americans for 48.6 percent, while most of the remainder were Latinos.

Mississippi Encyclopedia Staff
University of Mississippi

Mississippi State Planning Commission, *Progress Report on State Planning in Mississippi* (1938); *Mississippi Statistical Abstract*, Mississippi State University (1952–2010); Charles Sydnor and Claude Bennett, *Mississippi History* (1939); University of Virginia Library, Historical Census Browser website, http://mapserver.lib.virginia.edu; E. Nolan Waller and Dani A. Smith, *Growth Profiles of Mississippi's Counties, 1960–1980* (1985).

Parchman Prison

Officially known as the Mississippi State Penitentiary, Parchman Prison is one of three state prisons administered by the Mississippi Department of Corrections. Located in rural Sunflower County, it is the oldest and largest of the state's adult penal institutions, consisting of some eighteen thousand acres of bottomland in the Yazoo Delta on which are situated eighteen housing units with a bed capacity of 5,768. Staffed by more than 1,700 employees, the penitentiary incarcerates felons of all security classifications, including males under sentence of death, and is the site at which the State of Mississippi carries out capital punishment.

With the exception of its vast acreage, far-flung physical plant, and token tribute to the ideal of penal farming, Parchman is nowadays unremarkable among American prisons, reflecting the homogenized "justice model" of criminal corrections the federal judiciary imposed during the 1970–80s.

Female prisoners, Parchman Penitentiary, 1930s (Archives and Records Services Division, Mississippi Department of Archives and History [PI/PEN/P37.4-67])

The Mississippi State Penitentiary, in fact, was the target of one such important ruling. In 1972 the US District Court for the Northern District of Mississippi found in *Gates v. Collier* that the institution was in violation of the First, Eighth, and Fourteenth Amendments. In the words of the presiding judge, subsequent judicial oversight transformed it from "a very backward, shabby, trusty-run plantation, to a modern operation."

The prison today consists of grim structures surrounded by razor wire rising ominously from the flatlands. There are few reminders of when the institution's land was cultivated for cotton, when convicts "under the gun" dragged their burlap sacks along the sweltering floor of the Yazoo Delta, and when "Parchman Farm" was a focus in the fiction of William Faulkner and Eudora Welty and was lamented in the music of Leadbelly, Muddy Waters, Bukka White, and a host of other blues artists.

Both the legend and actual life and labor at the penal farm were influenced profoundly by slavery, Jim Crow, and the agricultural poverty and dependence of the sharecropping system. One could argue, however, that Parchman Farm had ameliorating features that accrued to the advantage of black (if not white) convicts and that by some standards—financial productivity, rates of escape and recidivism, and absence of riots—it was also a very effective penal institution. Therein lies a paradox, and it has recently inspired lively debate among not only litigators but also historians, criminologists, journalists, and prison administrators.

The story of Parchman begins in 1900, when the state of Mississippi, following the example of the Carolinas, embraced the ideal of penal farming on public lands and concluded the first of a series of land deals delivering acreage in Sunflower County to the state's troubled penal system. Among the lands purchased was the "old Parchman place," a large tract that once had been owned by a prominent county family, whose patriarch, J. M. Parchman, came with the deal as the first warden.

In establishing the penal farm, state actors considered the existence of a large and rapidly growing African American convict population and the unrealized public revenues of a brutal policy that since the Civil War had delivered the captive labor of black convicts to private business interests. The idea was to terminate a scheme of penology that might well have been worse than slavery and to generate revenues for the public weal.

In 1904 Parchman Farm became the pet project of Gov. James K. Vardaman, Mississippi's "White Chief," who regarded the undeveloped penal farm as a possible solution to the problem of what he called "criminal negroes" who were migrating to the state's cities, seeking "a way to live without honest toil," and menacing "the safety of the white man's home." Vardaman exploited racial fears and his virtual stranglehold on Mississippi politics to carry his plan to fruition. In 1912 the chair of a visiting legislative committee expressed astonishment: "Think of 16,000 acres of land stretching out before us as level as a floor and as fertile as the Valley of the Nile, in the very finest state of cultivation," he wrote in his official report, adding that Mississippi now had "one of the best, if not the best, Penitentiary systems in the United States." By the end of 1914 Parchman Farm was the hub of a huge, self-sufficient plantation system, with five penal farms and two lime plants situated on 23,910 acres.

The penitentiary was organized on principles that were consistent with what had been the ideal of large-scale southern agriculture for well over a century. Front Camp, on the easternmost part of the plantation, was the axis on which everything turned. There, a central administration coordinated purchasing, allocated labor and other resources, received and processed raw cotton, and conducted sales. In 1917 Front Camp had a barnlike administration building; a pretentious "Big House" for the "super" (superintendent); a number of shabby cottages inhabited by subordinates and their families; a guesthouse, at which visiting politicians and other favored parties drank and caroused in splendid isolation; a hospital of sorts; and a rather sad chapel for employees. Immediately outside the front gate, to which nothing resembling walls or fences was attached, was a railroad depot, Parchman Station, and across the tracks were a cotton gin and warehouses.

West of Front Camp were Parchman's field camps—the equivalents of what were known as working plantations in free-world agriculture—and to each of them was allocated acreage for the cultivation of the cash crop, cotton, and truck crops for the sustenance of the convicts. The field camps were widely dispersed over the sprawling acreage, facilitating the proper classification of "gunmen" (convicts under the gun) and confining trouble to defensible space. Field camps were equipped with "cages"—dormitories resembling military barracks—and each was supervised by a white sergeant whom the black convicts dubbed "da Main Mos' Man." Camp sergeants were assisted by "drivers"—white men who supervised and literally drove gunmen in the cotton rows. Black gunmen assigned them the title *Cap'n*. Dressed in baggy "ring-a-rounds" (uniforms with horizontal stripes), the gunmen rose before dawn, rode mules to the fields, and worked under the guns of trusties in tight files known as "long lines" until dusk, helped along by the rhythmic chants of fellow convict "callers." Scattered about the plantation were specialized units that housed convict carpenters, convict brick masons, and others who maintained the physical plant as well as a wide assortment of plants and shops where convicts performed services. Parchman had a canning plant, a dairy, a laundry, a newspaper, and a picture show. The facility also had a women's camp, where sewing machines hummed, producing uniforms and crude suits of clothing distributed to convicts at the time of release.

Early in the twentieth century, the state's satellite penal farms were important pieces of the puzzle. The largest of them, the unit in Quitman County known as Lambert, absorbed whatever surplus convicts Parchman could not accommodate. The others—Oakley Farm in Hinds County, Belmont Farm in Holmes County, and Rankin County Farm—housed convicts who were judged too young, too old, too sick, or too white and socially prominent for the rigors of Parchman.

At midcentury Parchman was notable for a number of reasons, not the least of which was its size. Six full miles separated Front Camp from the back side of the penitentiary, and within the grounds were forty-six square miles of cultivated bottomland. The prison was also unique among American prisons because of its financial productivity, functioning as what one observer described as a "profit-making machine" and providing the State of Mississippi with its greatest source of income other than tax revenues. But Parchman's most remarkable feature was its racial orientation. It was, simply put, an African American institution: the language, the music, the food, the labor, and the recreation all were distinctly African American. American penologists dubbed it the "Mississippi System."

Whites accounted for no more than about 25 percent of Parchman's convicts before 1972, much less earlier in the century: in the words of one employee, the white boys were "incidental." That, to be sure, was not a coincidence. Vardaman, Parchman Farm's philosophical and political architect, had designed the prison to be an African American institution. The goal, expressed very explicitly by the White Chief, was to inculcate among the felonious members of the black underclass habits and expectations of work that might make them responsible citizens within the confines of the state's racial caste system.

A succession of superintendents contended that the only problematic convicts at Parchman were white men and, finding their presence at odds with the institution's mission, did everything imaginable to get rid of them. In 1916, when the Columbia Training School was established, the penitentiary's staff happily bid adieu to most of the white males under age eighteen. That left a large number of troublesome white men under the age of twenty-five, but they were foisted on Oakley Farm in the 1920s amid much high-sounding talk of salvaging youth gone wrong. Then, during the early 1940s, Superintendent Lowery Love began construction on but never completed a special unit for those he discreetly termed "hardened criminals"— unmanageable convicts in the white camps. In 1953, when Superintendent Marvin Wiggins reluctantly began construction on Parchman's maximum security unit, "Little Alcatraz," he did so because of chaos in the white cages and much bad press.

Every convict, black or white, began his sentence to "penal servitude" in Parchman's cotton rows. There, amid searing heat and choking yellow dust, many white gunmen faltered or flat-out rebelled, whereas the majority of the black gunmen worked through the tasks of hoeing or picking. Black gunmen were encouraged to make their quotas in the rows via a series of calculated incentives, the most effective of which was the prospect of a little time with "Rosie" (convict jargon for women, but in this case specifically a prostitute) after weighing up on Saturday. Prison administration considered the ready availability of recreational sex perfectly consistent with the black man's normal lifestyle and thus a necessary inducement for hard work. The flip side of this racial profiling mandated that white convicts had to go without. Other incentives offered solely to black convicts early on included a ration of moonshine, which was produced at the camp stills by smiling "hooch-boys," and visitation privileges. Visitation brought black families to Front Camp on Sundays, often aboard the fabled Midnight Special, a train chartered by the state that traveled the Yellow Dog Line through the little towns of the Delta. The train, marked by its headlight, arrived at Parchman Station before dawn and was memorialized by some of the blues artists who also served as inmates. The conjugal relations allowed during "mama's visit"—a first in American prisons—were celebrated as well.

The penitentiary was presided over by a large and almost exclusively African American force of trusties, whose elevated status was confirmed by their "up-and-downs" (uniforms with vertical stripes). These men provided security, serving quite effectively as "shooters" in the fields, where their lethal marksmanship felled more than one "rabbit in the row" (a would-be escapee). The trusties presided as bosses in the black cages as well, allied with the white sergeants and drivers in maintaining order. The trusties commanded a convict hierarchy and at times maintained the status quo by whipping recalcitrant black gunmen with their sergeant's "strop." Perhaps nothing says more about the Mississippi System than this ritual. While the white sergeants readily applied "Black Annie" in the white cages, where convict leadership was often counterproductive, they rarely did so in the black cages, where virtually everything was done to acknowledge and support the ascendancy of a functional prison social hierarchy. Indeed, black "cagebosses" and "canteen-men"—the white sergeants' "Main Mos' Snitches"—were often quite influential in the delivery of the greatest incentives of all: furloughs, suspended sentences, and even pardons.

Black men also served as middle managers in virtually all of the penitentiary's plants and shops, supervising apprentices of their race, and managed the homes of the white employees, directing domestic staffs composed of convict underlings and caring very attentively for children. But the "Main Mos' Trusties" were the graying black men at Front Camp. They had considerable influence, keeping the penitentiary's financial records, allocating precious resources, and coordinating almost everything with the blessings of the super. The slow but steady evolution of these distinctly functional internal arrangements ultimately changed the nature of the institution.

The advent of parole in 1944 and probation in 1956 resulted in the departure of the penitentiary's senior black trusties.

Accompanying the resulting erosion of management and security during the 1950s, a substantial and progressive increase in the number of white commitments posed insurmountable difficulties. The solution adopted by the legislature—the construction of a maximum-security unit and the placement of a gas chamber within it—only compounded the problem by changing the penitentiary's social chemistry. At about the same time, Mississippi's cotton economy collapsed, producing financial deficits at Parchman, inspiring free-world complaints about the ruinous effect of convict labor on the private sector, and resulting in a decline in legislative appropriations, the degeneration of the physical plant, and mounting fiscal difficulties.

The state placed Freedom Riders in the sweltering cells of Little Alcatraz in 1961, drawing attention to the facility. Frustrated white sergeants reacted with a number of atrocities, producing unprecedented political and legal pressure from new foes, including the US 5th Circuit Court of Appeals, which reminded penal administrators that they dealt with human beings, "not dumb driven cattle."

The penitentiary was also hamstrung by a woeful void in leadership in Jackson, where state politicians condemned the federal government and never seemed to understand that a faltering penal institution patterned after an antebellum slave plantation simply would not do. Old Parchman Farm was dead in the water when Nazareth Gates and his fellow inmate-plaintiffs filed suit in US District Court in 1972: far from destroying the old penal farm, the federal judge merely presided over the institution's autopsy while attempting to chart a course for a future that even now remains uncertain.

William Banks Taylor
University of Southern Mississippi

Donald Cabana, *Death at Midnight: The Confession of an Executioner* (1996); David M. Oshinsky, *"Worse Than Slavery": Parchman Farm and the Ordeal of Jim Crow Justice* (1996); William Banks Taylor, *Brokered Justice: Race, Politics, and Mississippi Prisons, 1798–1992* (1993); William Banks Taylor, *Down on Parchman Farm: The Great Prison in the Mississippi Delta* (1999).

Parker, Laurie
(b. 1963) Author

As a children's author and illustrator, collage artist, and jewelry maker, Laurie Parker has artistic talents that make her work in demand across Mississippi. Parker was born in Bruce on 24 July 1963, though her family—parents, Sam and Ruth Parker; brother, Tommy; older sister, Lynn; and fraternal twin, Nancy—moved to Starkville when she was a baby. After graduating as valedictorian from Starkville High School in 1981, Parker earned an education degree from Mississippi State University in 1985, worked as a schoolteacher, and returned to Mississippi State to study engineering before turning to full-time jewelry making.

After several years of selling collages and jewelry at solo shows and at crafts markets, Parker thought books would be another way to put her collage talents to work. In 1997 Quail Ridge Press published Parker's first book for children, *Everywhere in Mississippi*, the story of Skippy the dog. Other books followed, including *All over Alabama* (1997), *Mississippi Alphabet* (1998), *Texas Alphabet* (2000), and *Louisiana Alphabet* (2001). The books featuring rhyming text, enjoyable illustrations, and lessons in geography within the verse.

In 2002 Parker took a new direction with *The Turtle Saver*, a longer story about a turtle lost on the Natchez Trace. The work marked a significant change for Parker, moving beyond her stock-in-trade geographical stories to a more lyrical theme with a moral—small kindnesses can reap great rewards.

In 2003 Parker left Quail Ridge and launched her first holiday offering, *It Really Said Christmas*, which she chose to self-publish "to make more money from my hard work." She also found it "exciting to be able to create how I wanted to create." The following year, she released *Mad for Maroon*, a story that grew out of her love for the Mississippi State University Bulldogs. Her subsequent children's books have included *Tales of the Good Life* (2005), *A for Angels* (2007), *The Sweet Dreams Book* (2009), *Garden Alphabet* (2011), and *Everywhere in Mississippi* (2012).

Parker shifted gears again with *The Matchstick Cross* (2013), a novel for adults about a Mississippi woman living in New York who returns home after her mother's death. Two more novels, *Yonder Breaks the Morning* (2014) and *Hush, Swing, Hush* (2015), are set in Oxford and Meridian, respectively.

A resident of Starkville, Parker continues to write and to create pins and other decorative works, which she sells at art shows, festivals, and holiday markets.

Julie Whitehead
Brandon, Mississippi

Yolanda Cruz, "Parker Pens First Novel," *Hattiesburg American* (May 16, 2014); Lynne Willbanks Jeter, *Mississippi Business Journal* (2002); Laurie Parker, interview by Julie Whitehead (2003); Laurie Parker website, http://www2.netdoor.com/~lauriep/writer/about.html; Quail Ridge Press website, www.quailridge.com.

Parks, State

Mississippi state parks evolved not out of the conservation impulses of the Progressive era but out of the pragmatic need to employ Mississippians and create recreation areas during the Great Depression. Mississippi state parks, like state and national forests, were created with an eye toward multiple uses rather than specifically preservation. The first Mississippi parks, created by the Civilian Conservation Corps (CCC), offered immediate employment opportunities with the promise of wise resource stewardship and recreational facilities for the future. And though few in the state had a long-term vision for these new parks, most agreed that the jobs they provided and conservation of the lands they encompassed made them worthwhile.

Between 1935 and 1941 the CCC created ten state parks. Leroy Percy State Park was first, followed by Legion, Holmes County, Clarkco, Tombigbee, Wall Doxey (originally Spring Lake), Percy Quinn, Tishomingo, Roosevelt, and Magnolia (now part of the Gulf Islands National Seashore). Because few Mississippians had the wherewithal to travel out of state during the Great Depression, they began looking closer to home for recreation. Though none of the parks was completed, 42,000 people visited in 1937; four years later, with most of the original parks still under construction as a consequence of funding shortages, that number had skyrocketed to 450,000. Despite pressures placed on them by increasingly mobile travelers, especially after World War II, and financial issues, Mississippi continued adding state parks.

Prior to the 1956 creation of the Mississippi State Park Commission, the Mississippi Forestry Commission administered the parks. The parks subsequently became the purview of the Bureau of Recreation and Parks, which became

P

John W. Kyle State Park, Panola County (Courtesy Andy Young, Forever Young Photography)

part of the Department of Natural Resources in 1978 before moving to the newly created Department of Wildlife, Fisheries, and Parks in 1989.

Mississippi now has twenty-five state parks: Buccaneer, Clark Creek, Clarkco, Florewood, George P. Cossar, Golden Memorial, Great River Road, Holmes County, Hugh White, J. P. Coleman, John W. Kyle, Lake Lincoln, Lake Lowndes, LeFleur's Bluff, Legion, Leroy Percy, Natchez, Paul B. Johnson, Percy Quin, Roosevelt, Shepard, Tishomingo, Tombigbee, Trace, and Wall Doxey. In addition to hiking, fishing, and camping, the parks offer a variety of other recreational opportunities, including water parks, equestrian trails, mountain bike trails, disc golf, and miniature golf. The parks also include four golf courses: Mallard Pointe, the Dogwoods, LeFleur's Bluff, and Quail Hollow.

Andy Harper
University of Mississippi

Justin C. Eaddy, *Journal of Mississippi History* (Summer 2003); Mississippi Commission on Natural Resources, "A History of Mississippi's State Parks" (1985); Mississippi Department of Wildlife, Fisheries, and Parks website, www.mdwfp.com.

Pascagoula River

The Pascagoula River Basin of southeast Mississippi has been compared to the Serengeti Desert of Africa, the Amazon Basin of South America, and the Mekong River Delta of Vietnam. It is to Mississippi what the Everglades is to Florida, the Okefenokee Swamp to Georgia, the Atchafalaya Basin to Louisiana, the Big Thicket to Texas—in other words, an ecological treasure.

Scientists have deemed the Pascagoula to be the last major river system in the lower forty-eight states and southern Canada unaltered by dams, channelization, levees, or similar human impact. While there are dams on its extreme upper tributaries, the Pascagoula's flow essentially remains natural.

The ninety-six-hundred-square-mile basin is wild in other ways, too, flanked by approximately six hundred thousand acres of public lands, including state parks and wildlife management areas, national wildlife refuges and forests, and a pair of Nature Conservancy preserves. The Nature Conservancy purchased some forty-two thousand acres of riverside land from the Pascagoula Hardwood Company in the 1970s and sold it to the state, which set it aside in wildlife management areas—a pioneering effort in conservation that served as an example to other states. In addition, conservationists

Pascagoula, Mississippi, ca. 1908 (Ann Rayburn Paper Americana Collection, Department of Archives and Special Collections, J. D. Williams Library, University of Mississippi [rayburn_ann_32_41_001])

used the presence of the Gulf sturgeon, a giant fish that spawns in the Pascagoula, to help block a proposal to dam the Bowie River, a Pascagoula tributary, in the 1990s.

The Pascagoula has two major tributaries. The 159-mile Chickasawhay River begins at the town of Enterprise, just south of Meridian. To the west, the 185-mile Leaf River heads up near Raleigh, just south of Interstate 20. The pale, silty Chickasawhay meets the dark, clear Leaf just above the village of Merrill in southeastern Mississippi to form the main Pascagoula, which meanders 81 miles south to the Gulf Coast at the towns of Pascagoula and Gautier. Other sizable tributaries include the Chunky River, Buckatunna Creek, Okatoma Creek, the Bowie (also spelled Bouie) River, Tallahala Creek, Bogue Homa Creek, Black Creek, Red Creek, and the Escatawpa River.

On the upper reaches of the Leaf and Chickasawhay, rapids alternate with long, slow stretches where the water barely moves over its sandy bed. There are some rollicking rapids, including a double-decker that drops two or three feet and a foaming chute one hundred yards long on the Leaf. Mossy clay banks are topped with sycamore, river birch, water oak, hickory, cypress, and beech trees. Spicing up the greenery in the springtime are white-blooming dogwoods and fringe trees, pink-flowered native azaleas and mountain laurels. Other blooming plants include red buckeyes, dewberries, honeysuckles, wisterias, yellowtops, privets, black haws, and trumpet vines.

Visitors may observe hawks carrying snakes in their talons, ospreys toting fish, deer sipping at the riverside, swallows circling above rapids, black vultures hulking on rock bars, kingfishers diving for minnows, turtles gliding along the bottom, herons and egrets gracefully taking flight, turkeys fleeing in panic, and snakes pausing in midswim to stare. An especially distinctive Pascagoula species is the swallowtail kite. These beautiful black-and-white birds have a sharply forked tail and narrow wings that spread more than four feet, but they rarely flap, instead soaring on the air currents like kites.

The riverside environment deteriorates in places on the lower Leaf and Chickasawhay, with cutovers, rusty oil wells, eroded sand mines, traffic noise, industries, sewage lagoons, a paper mill, and camps whose owners have thrown rubbish down the bank in futile attempts to stop erosion. Things improve at the juncture of the rivers, where the Charles M. Deaton and Herman Murrah Nature Conservancy preserves lie.

The Pascagoula River itself is wide and slow. In high water the river spreads out over its banks into the woods, creating a network of lakes and bayous. When low, it exposes vast sandbars and leaves bayous nearly dry. Sandy beds and sandbars show tracks of minks, muskrats, snakes, beavers, raccoons, possums, armadillos, mice, wild hogs, squirrels, coyotes, deer, herons, nutrias, bobcats, and alligators.

Nearer the coast, the Pascagoula splits into east and west rivers, both affected by tides from the Mississippi Sound. The east river goes by industrial Moss Point and Pascagoula, while the west takes a more remote route to Gautier. Sandbars and dry banks subside into a wet jungle of mud, cypress, and palmettos. Sloughs, bayous, and oxbow lakes branch in every direction. Rustic camps line the west river at Poticaw Landing and Rogers Bend. Trees give way to marsh north of Interstate 10 and then to open bays as the river enters the Mississippi Sound through a sieve of marshy islands.

Pascagoula means "bread people," and legend has it that when the Pascagoula Indians faced extinction, they agreed to commit mass suicide by wading into the river singing. To this day people report hearing a singing noise on the lower river, leading to its nickname, Singing River.

Ernest Herndon
McComb, Mississippi

Mats Dynesius and Christer Nilsson, *Science* (4 November 1994); Ernest Herndon, *Canoeing Mississippi* (2001); Ernest Herndon and Scott B. Williams, *Paddling the Pascagoula* (2005); Donald Schueler, *Preserving the Pascagoula* (1980); Scott B. Williams, *Exploring Coastal Mississippi* (2004).

Paternalism

Paternalism is a term used to describe the relatively humane system or method of governance and management of individuals and societies through the guise of a father's benevolence toward his children. This benevolent manner, however, can mask the male's real underlying desire and intent to dominate, often characterized by intrusive and controlling behavior. The term is often used interchangeably with *patriarchy*.

The meanings of the two words are nuanced, however, and ultimately differ. Patriarchy in its purest sense denotes absolute male authority, wherein unconditional power resides with the male head of household. The patriarchal system is thought to be paternalistic when male patriarchs exercise their absolute authority constrained by a sense of affection, compassion, and noblesse oblige toward their dependents—women, children, enslaved and free workers, and members of the larger community.

For the South, the relationship between enslaved people and the men who owned them, according to historian Eugene D. Genovese (the scholar most associated with this perspective), involved a complex set of reciprocal arrangements between masters and slaves, commonly held assumptions about what to expect, and clear constraints on the treatment of enslaved people. The end result was a social order governed by an overall paternalistic ethos. Other factors that influenced the emergence of the South's paternalistic society included the importance of kinship relations, especially in an agrarian society; the racial assumption of the supremacy of all whites over blacks regardless of class; the cultural acceptance of the subordination of all females, children, and slaves by white men, who expected deference and faithful service; a feudal sense of honor and a dreaded fear of dishonor as a valid state of mind; an evangelical yet conservative and patriarchal religious belief that defends racial slavery; an economic- and class-based system dependent on racial slavery as its mooring; and the social expectations of a largely rural and rigidly hierarchical social order. The paternalistic rules that culturally governed the exercise of authority by white male slaveholders over almost all others in society were, it is argued, codified in law and institutionalized in custom over time.

Historians disagree about the extent to which the term *paternalism* describes the antebellum South. Some contend, for example, that the term's usefulness depends on what part of the South is studied. The time period can also make a difference. Perhaps, some argue, the idea holds more validity for the Upper South and less for the Lower South. As planters (patriarchs) moved westward (that is, to the Mississippi frontier) in the 1820s, they may have lost their commitment to the gentler, kinship-enforced version of paternalism and regressed to a more tyrannical form of absolute patriarchal authority over their families and slaves. Nevertheless, over time, this form of domination marked by a sense of constraint and deference (paternalism) softened the more brutal aspects of patriarchy and helped to enlarge the arena in which servile and subordinate people participated in shaping their own lives.

Joyce L. Broussard
California State University at
Northridge

Joyce L. Broussard, "Female Solitaires: Women Alone in the Lifeworld of Mid-Century Natchez, Mississippi: 1850–1880" (PhD dissertation, University of Southern California, 1998); Catherine Clinton, *The Plantation Mistress: Woman's World in the Old South* (1982); Drew Gilpin Faust, *James Henry Hammond and the Old South: A Design for Mastery* (1982); David Foster, *Review of Politics* (Fall 1994); Elizabeth Fox-Genovese, *Within the Plantation Household: Black and White Women of the Old South* (1988); Eugene D. Genovese, *Roll, Jordan, Roll: The World the Slaves Made* (1972); Eugene D. Genovese, *The World the Slaveholders Made: Two Essays in Interpretation* (1969, 1988); Gerda Lerner, *The Creation of Patriarchy* (1986); Ulrich B. Phillips, *American Negro Slavery: A Survey of the Supply, Employment, and Control of Negro Labor as Determined by the Plantation Regime* (1966); William K. Scarborough, *Masters of the Big House: Elite Slaveholders of the Mid-Nineteenth Century* (2003); Bertram Wyatt-Brown, *The Shaping of Southern Culture: Honor, Grace, and War, 1760s–1880s* (2001); Bertram Wyatt-Brown, *Southern Honor: Ethics and Behavior in the Old South* (1982).

Patriotic American Youth

Patriotic American Youth (PAY) was founded in 1961 in Jackson. The first edition of the group's monthly newsletter, *Pay Day*, announced that it sought to provide leadership development for young people opposed to communist encroachment. According to PAY's founders, one of the most glaring examples of communist activity was Mississippi's burgeoning civil rights movement. According to PAY's student president, George Monroe of the University of Mississippi, the movement signaled a "war" that was "destroying . . . the very roots of American civilization." Contrary to the thinking of what Monroe described as "liberal welfare do-gooders . . . America was built over a period of many years with the sweat and blood of many people, people young like you and I, people who were willing to lay down their lives, their fortunes, and their sacred honors so that we might have freedom." This unironic statement willfully ignored the fact that the black movement for civil rights was seeking to claim the freedom owed to those whose sweat and blood built the nation.

PAY's first high school chapter was organized in Itta Bena, and the state office was located in Jackson's War Memorial building. In 1968 the organization had five thousand high school and college members. The group ran the Freedom Book Store on State Street in Jackson, disseminating anti-civil-rights pamphlets along with leaflets detailing communist infiltration. PAY sponsored an essay contest on "What America Means to Me"; showings of films such as the House Un-American Activities Committee's *Operation Abolition*; classes in Hinds and other counties on the US Constitution; and lectures by Senators Strom Thurmond, James O. Eastland, and John Stennis.

The members of PAY's board of advisers represented a who's who of conservative Mississippi leaders. The group garnered support from administrators at the University of Southern Mississippi, Mississippi State University, and the University of Mississippi; the state judiciary; members of the legislature; and business leaders. The inaugural edition of *Pay Day* thanked the Mississippi State Board of Education for the "blessings conferred upon the organization of PAY." Judge Henry Lee Rodgers of the Mississippi Supreme Court served as chair, and the state on several occasions provided PAY with financial support.

The organization had close ties to the Citizens' Councils. Judge Tom Brady, a member of PAY's board, was a leader in efforts to found the Councils following the 1954 *Brown v. Board of Education* decision. In addition, PAY's executive director, Sara C. McCorkle, also headed the Citizens' Council youth organization for a time.

Becca Walton
University of Mississippi

Charles Hills, *Jackson Clarion-Ledger* (19 December 1968); Mississippi Department of Archives and History, Sovereignty Commission Online website, http://mdah.state.ms.us/arrec/digital_archives/sovcom/; *Pay Day* (November–December 1961).

Patterson, Carolyn Bennett
(1921–2003) Travel Author

As a child in Kosciusko, Mississippi, Carolyn Bennett read Robert Louis Stevenson's *Travels with a Donkey in the Cevennes*. She was especially captivated by his commitment: "I travel for travel's sake . . . to come down off this featherbed of civilization, and find the globe granite underfoot and strewn with cutting flints." As an adult, Carolyn Bennett Patterson lived out Stevenson's call for adventure by writing articles for *National Geographic*. Patterson was hired by that publication in 1949 and remained there for her entire professional life. In 1962 she became its first woman senior editor.

Bennett was born in Laurel, Mississippi, on 12 April 1921. While in high school, she recalled, "I was editor of the high school paper—but in name only. My every idea was rejected by the sponsor who informed me that I would never be a journalist so had better abandon the idea before I made a fool of myself. I ignored her." After attending Blue Mountain College and Mississippi State College, she earned an undergraduate degree from Louisiana State University and a graduate degree in journalism from the University of Missouri. She then went to work for the *New Orleans States* newspaper.

Bennett's interest in travel conflicted with the wishes of her mother, whose "dearest desire was that I would marry a rich Mississippi man—maybe in Jackson." Instead, Bennett married Frederick G. Patterson—not a Mississippi man—and raised two children from their home base in Washington, D.C. In 1949 she secured a job as a library assistant at *National Geographic*. She moved from librarian to writer after suggesting to the managing editor that the publication send an author to retrace the steps of Jesus.

Patterson traveled widely, writing stories from such far-flung places as Tasmania, New Zealand, and Haiti and covering Winston Churchill's 1965 funeral in London. In 1978, she retraced Stevenson's route through the mountains of France. That story, "Travels with a Donkey," was particularly important to Patterson, and she told it with a mixture of respect for Stevenson, awe at the landscape, interest in what had changed and not changed about the people she met, and alternating admiration for and frustration with her donkey. Patterson's *National Geographic* contributions also included articles on the Tennessee-Tombigbee Waterway, the Neshoba County Fair, the comparisons between Gettysburg and Vicksburg, and Mardi Gras in New Orleans.

After retiring from *National Geographic* in 1986, Patterson published a memoir, *Of Lands, Legends, and Laughter: The Search for Adventure with "National Geographic"* (1998). The chapters on Mississippi set the stage for her later life, detailing how she loved a band trip to Texas and concluded a high school newspaper article with the realization, "I am a traveler." Each chapter emphasized adventure.

Patterson donated her papers to the Mitchell Memorial Library at Mississippi State University. Patterson died on 7 July 2003.

Ted Ownby
University of Mississippi

Carolyn Bennett Patterson, *National Geographic* (October 1978); Carolyn Bennett Patterson, *Of Lands, Legends, and Laughter: The Search for Adventure with National Geographic* (1998); Carolyn Bennett Patterson File, Mississippi Department of Archives and History; Carolyn Bennett Patterson Papers, Special Collections, Mitchell Memorial Library, Mississippi State University.

Patterson, Robert "Tut"

(b. 1921)

After the US Supreme Court declared segregated schools unconstitutional in its May 1954 *Brown v. Board of Education* decision, Tut Patterson organized the Citizens' Council to resist the ruling. The group held its first meeting in Indianola on 11 July with the backing of fourteen prominent Mississippians, including the town's mayor. Indianola selected Patterson as its Citizen of the Year. A few months later, representatives from twenty-two counties created the Citizens' Councils of Mississippi, headquartered in Greenwood, and chose Patterson to serve as executive secretary, the organization's only salaried administrator in its early days. Beginning in 1956 he also served as secretary of the Association of Citizens' Councils of America.

Robert Boyd Patterson was born on 13 December 1921 in Clarksdale. He attended Mississippi State College, where he starred on the football team. During his senior year he served as team captain and was named all–Southeastern Conference. Patterson graduated in 1943 and immediately entered the army, where he served as a paratrooper with the 82nd Airborne Division and fought in Europe from the D-Day invasion to the occupation of Germany, rising to the rank of major. After the war Patterson became a plantation manager in LeFlore County and married Mary Agnes Chism of Clarksdale. Under his wife's influence he became a Methodist.

"History proves," Patterson once declared, "that the supreme power in the government of men has always been public opinion." The Council's purpose was clear—stirring opposition to integration. The group's first task was ensuring the passage of a state amendment giving the legislature power to close public schools and provide tuition grants for segregated private schools. Patterson warned that integrated schools were only the beginning. The future of the nation, he told Council members, depended on "Southern white people." "If we white Southerners submit, . . . the malignant powers of mongrelization, communism and atheism will surely destroy this Nation from within. Racial intermarriage has already begun in the North and unless stopped will spread to the South."

Patterson relied on exaggeration and even fabrication. In 1955 he released what was allegedly a recording of a speech by Roosevelt Williams, a professor at Howard University and a leader of the National Association for the Advancement of Colored People. According to the tape, the group's "real" agenda was "integration of the white bedroom," since white women longed for black men. The tape was widely distributed, with the attorney general of Georgia mailing transcripts in official envelopes. However, the recording was a fake, and Williams did not exist. Patterson downplayed the hoax, declaring, "We never claimed it to be authentic."

Membership in the Citizens' Councils peaked at around one million, and southern resistance delayed significant school desegregation for a decade, allowing whites time to organize private schools and flee the public school system. In 1966 Patterson helped to found Greenwood's Pillow Academy, from which his two sons and two daughters graduated. After the Methodist Church began to espouse what Patterson saw as "its social gospel," he also helped organize an Independent Methodist Church.

Around 1961 William Simmons, editor of the *Citizens' Council* magazine, quietly surpassed Patterson among the Council's leaders. The organization had developed from its rural grassroots origins into a sophisticated publicity machine, and Patterson lacked the social standing and boardroom polish of Simmons, who came from a prominent banking family. Simmons's corporate background advanced the organization's long-standing goal of marshaling the region's elite. Patterson continued to play a pivotal role as executive secretary and as a public speaker throughout the former Confederate states.

By 1970 the successes of the civil rights movement led Patterson to conclude that the "Federal Government is now fully committed to the amalgamation of the white and black races." Integration was in evidence everywhere, even "our national news media" and "entertainment such as television." "The Negro is thrust into every situation on television, obviously and unnaturally." Patterson hoped others shared his disgust: "I believe most people resent it." However uneasy whites felt about integration, Patterson and his allies overestimated American racism. Southern segregation and the Council's resemblance to Nazism made many uncomfortable. Patterson himself published in neo-Nazi journals.

The Citizens' Council formally disbanded in 1989 but was replaced by the Council of Conservative Citizens, which Gordon Baum had founded four years earlier based on the Citizens' Council's mailing list. The Southern Poverty Law Center classifies the Council of Conservative Citizens as a white nationalist hate group, but it retains some influence. It has approximately fifteen thousand members and continues the Citizens' Council's mission of raising money for private white academies. Patterson carries on his career in organized racism as a member of the advisory board and a columnist for the *Citizens Informer*, the Council of Conservative Citizens' primary publication. The *Informer*'s editor has described him as "our revered elder statesman."

Bryan Hardin Thrift
Johnston Community College

Heidi Beirich and Bob Moser, "Communing with the Council," *Intelligence Report* (Southern Poverty Law Center) (Fall 2004); Hodding Carter III, *The South Strikes Back* (1959); Citizen Council Publications Subject File, Mississippi Department of Archives and History; Hank Klibanoff, *Jackson Clarion-Ledger* (19 June 1983); Neil McMillen, *The Citizens' Council: Organized Resistance to the Second Reconstruction, 1954–1964* (1994); Jerry Mitchell, *Jackson Clarion-Ledger* (7 January 1993); Robert Boyd Patterson Subject File, Mississippi Department of Archives and History; Southern Poverty Law Center website, www.splcenter.org.

Patton, Charley
(ca. 1891–1934) Blues Musician

Few people have had as large an impact on American music as Charley Patton, the Father of Delta Blues. Not only was Patton the first blues superstar, but many other forms of music, among them gospel, R&B, soul, and especially rock and roll, show the direct influence of his work.

Patton was born to Bill and Annie Patton around 1891 near the central Mississippi towns of Bolton and Edwards. He showed an early predilection for making music, and he learned to play the guitar as a very young child. But Patton grew up in a hardworking farming and religious family, and his father considered playing the guitar a sin. Despite frequent punishments for playing music, Patton continued performing ragtime, folk songs, and spirituals at picnics and parties in Henderson Chatmon's string band, most likely for all-black audiences at first and then for whites who could afford to pay better.

Seeking to capitalize on the economic opportunities that the Mississippi Delta had begun to offer planters and day laborers, Bill Patton packed up his family in 1897 and relocated north to Will Dockery's farm in Sunflower County. There, Charley Patton turned his musical ability toward the blues. He began to study the raw and rhythmic blues-playing technique of guitarist Henry Sloan, eventually crafting an inventive style that incorporated heavy bass notes and playing slide guitar with a knife.

In the twenty-two years that followed his arrival at Dockery Farms, Patton never completely disavowed his religious upbringing. He oscillated between the roles of hard-drinking, womanizing rambler and God-fearing preacher. The rambling bluesman in him won out most often, but even then he stayed close to home, never traveling farther than western Tennessee, eastern Arkansas, or northeastern Louisiana to play gigs. While Patton was in Jackson in the summer of 1927, Henry C. Speir, a white music store owner, arranged for him to go to Richmond, Indiana, where on 14 June 1927 he recorded fourteen songs in a Gennett Records studio. That session produced some of his most celebrated work, including "Pea Vine Blues," "Tom Rushen Blues," and "Pony Blues," which became an immediate "race record" hit. Later that year Patton traveled to Grafton, Wisconsin, to record with fellow Delta bluesman and fiddler Henry "Son" Sims. Patton recorded several more times, with his final session taking place in New York City in January 1934.

Ever the Delta performer, Patton sang and recorded songs that included people, places, and events in his community. "Tom Rushen Blues" bemoaned the possibility that a friendly sheriff might be replaced by one less amenable to public drunkenness: "Laid down last night, hopin' I would have my peace / I laid down last night, hopin' I would have my peace /

But when I woke up Tom Rushen was shakin' me." In "Green River Blues" Patton sang, "I'm goin' where the Southern cross the Dog"—the junction of the Southern (Yazoo) and the Dog (Mississippi Valley) railroad lines just a few miles south of Dockery Farms; in "Pea Vine Blues" he sang about a lover leaving on a train that ran to and from Dockery: "I think I heard the Pea Vine when it blowed. / I think I heard the Pea Vine when it blowed. / It blow just like my rider getting' on board." "High Water Everywhere (Parts 1 & 2)" is about the Great Flood of 1927 that devastated much of the Mississippi Delta. Patton sang in a loud, rough voice, and many of the lyrics in his recordings are nearly incomprehensible.

Patton also recorded religious songs such as "You Gonna Need Somebody When You Die" (under the pseudonym Elder J. J. Hadley), "Oh Death," and "I Shall Not be Moved." His recordings earned him widespread recognition, but his impact on American music stems primarily from those with whom he played, such as bluesmen Tommy Johnson, Son House, Big Joe Williams, Howlin' Wolf, and Muddy Waters, among others. Bukka White once declared that his ambition in life was "to be a great man—like Charley Patton." Other blues musicians copied his style, and it can be reasonably argued that consciously or unconsciously, every rock and roller has been influenced by his style and music. His influence also extends farther: gospel patriarch Roebuck "Pops" Staples, who also grew up on Dockery Farms, once said that Patton "was one of my great persons that inspired me to play guitar. He was a really great man."

Patton died in Indianola on 28 April 1934, shortly after returning from his final recording session.

James G. Thomas, Jr.
University of Mississippi

Francis Davis, *The History of the Blues* (1995); David Evans, *Big Road Blues: Tradition and Creativity in Folk Blues* (1982); David Evans, *Blues World* (August 1970); Gérard Herzhaft, *Encyclopedia of the Blues* (1997); Giles Oakley, *The Devil's Music* (1977); Robert Palmer, *Deep Blues: A Musical and Cultural History of the Mississippi Delta* (1981); Gayle Dean Wardlow, *Blues Unlimited* (February 1966); Gayle Dean Wardlow and Edward M. Komara, *Chasin' That Devil Music: Searching for the Blues* (1998).

Payton, Walter
(1954–1999) Athlete

Walter Payton, a star in the National Football League (NFL) and first-ballot Pro Football Hall of Fame inductee, is considered one of the greatest football players of all time. His career began in Columbia, Mississippi, where the youngest child of Peter and Alyne Payton was the star running back at John J. Jefferson High School.

Born on 25 July 1954, Walter Jerry Payton did not play organized football until 1968, his sophomore year of high school; he preferred to play drums in the marching band. After the school's lead running back—Walter's brother, Eddie—graduated, Payton joined the football team; on his first play, he ran 65 yards for a touchdown. When Jefferson High School was integrated with Columbia High School in January 1970, Payton continued to dominate. He led the Little Dixie Conference in scoring during his senior year and was named to the all-state team.

Payton followed his brother to Jackson State College (now Jackson State University) in 1971. A four-year starter, he gained 3,563 career yards, averaging 6.1 yards per carry. While there, he earned the nickname Sweetness, a fitting acknowledgment of both his talents on the field and his charisma off it. Payton was named to the National Collegiate Athletic Association Division II-AA all-American team in 1974 and finished fourth in voting for the Heisman Trophy. He earned a bachelor's degree in special education in three and a half years and set nine school records as well as collegiate-level records for career points (464) and points in a single game (46).

The Chicago Bears selected Payton with the fourth overall pick in the 1975 NFL draft. He spent thirteen years with the team and missed only a single game. Payton rushed for 1,390 yards during the 1976 season, the second-highest total in the league. The following year, at age twenty-three, he was named the league's Most Valuable Player, the youngest player to earn that distinction. On 20 November 1977 he gained 275 yards against the Minnesota Vikings to set an NFL single-game rushing record that stood for twenty-three years and that remains one of the highest totals in league history.

Payton was named to the Pro Bowl nine times. When he retired at the end of the 1987 season, he owned the league records for career rushing yards (16,726), rushing attempts (3,838), career combined yards (21,803), rushing touchdowns (110), 1,000-yard seasons (10), and 100-yard games (77). He was inducted into the Pro Football Hall of Fame in 1993.

In 1979 Payton founded Walter Payton Enterprises, a company that went on to own various businesses, including a restaurant, a contractor supply company, and an auto racing team. He and his wife, Connie, also founded the Walter and Connie Payton Foundation and worked tirelessly and often anonymously to better the conditions of underprivileged children in Illinois.

Payton died on 1 November 1999 of complications from cancer. In his honor, the National Football League now recognizes a player's outstanding service to the community with the Walter Payton NFL Man of the Year Award.

Molly Boland Thompson
Vanderbilt University

Nathan Aaseng, *Football's Breakaway Backs* (1980); Donald Hunt, *Great Names in Black College Sports* (1996); Philip Koslow, *Walter Payton* (1995); Randall Liu and Matt Marini, eds., *Official 2004 National Football League Record and Fact Book* (2004); Connie Payton, Jarrett Payton, and Brittney Payton, *Payton* (2005); Walter Payton with Don Yaeger, *Never Die Easy* (2000); Jeff Pearlman, *Sweetness: The Enigmatic Life of Walter Payton* (2011); Mark Sufrin, *Payton* (1988); Mike Towle, *I Remember Walter Payton* (2000).

Peacock, Willie B. Wazir

(1937–2016) Activist

Tallahatchie County native Willie B. Wazir Peacock worked for the Student Nonviolent Coordinating Committee (SNCC) during the early 1960s as Mississippi communities mobilized to demand civil rights, beginning a four-decade career of advocacy for social justice.

Peacock was born in Charleston, Mississippi, on 5 September 1937. His father, a World War II veteran, worked as a sharecropper. In 2001 Peacock explained that his time on the plantation gave him a "chance to see what slavery was probably like."

Peacock received a music scholarship to Rust College in Holly Springs and hoped that higher education would give him skills to improve the lives of black southerners. While at Rust in 1960 Peacock heard of the sit-ins staged by North Carolina A&T College students in Greensboro. He organized a group of students to boycott a segregated Holly Springs theater that relied heavily on the patronage of Rust students. Rather than integrate, the owner closed the theater. After that boycott, the students turned to voter registration. These activities brought Peacock under the surveillance of the Mississippi State Sovereignty Commission, which described him as a "notable racial hate promoter."

In the fall of 1960 SNCC and Peacock began working on voter registration in Ruleville. Peacock's involvement with SNCC continued in the fall of 1961, when he met activist Bob Moses, who was seeking workers to aid voter registration in Tallahatchie County. In the summer of 1962 Peacock continued working with Moses, Amzie Moore, and Frank Smith in Holly Springs. They first met with black civic leaders to encourage the creation of a credit union and then gathered affidavits from those who had attempted to register to vote, sending the documentation to the Civil Rights Division of the US Justice Department.

After Peacock graduated from Rust in 1962, Moses and Moore recruited him to continue organizing. Peacock traveled to Greenwood in the middle of the night, entering the SNCC office shortly after workers had fled a Ku Klux Klan attack on the building. Peacock volunteered to stay, recog-nizing the need to maintain a presence in the community despite intimidation. The workers canvassed rural Leflore County for the Voter Education Project, later expanding to Ruleville, Cleveland, and Indianola. In Ruleville, Peacock met Fannie Lou Hamer the day she volunteered to register to vote, beginning her long career in civil rights activism. Peacock also chaired the food relief committee during the unusually cold winter of 1962–63.

In the fall of 1963 discussion began regarding what would become the Freedom Summer Project. Peacock opposed the inclusion of white student workers, fearing their effects on the creation of an indigenous black leadership in the movement. Peacock, whose family had long been active in the African Methodist Episcopal Church, explained the rift between local, southern-born workers and northern volunteers by noting that "we had spiritual values, most of them did not. . . . They tried to rationalize everything. Because of our different realities, we clashed on many issues."

On 8 June 1964 Peacock, Sam Block, James Jones, and James Black were badly beaten at the Lowndes County Jail after being pulled over for an alleged traffic violation on the way to a SNCC meeting in Atlanta. Their wounds were still visible a week later when they traveled to Oxford, Ohio, for the orientation for summer volunteers, providing a searing illustration of what lay ahead. Holding fast to his opinion on the Summer Project, Peacock spent the summer of 1964 in New York and Madison, Wisconsin, with the SNCC Freedom Singers.

After his close friend, Sammy Younge, was murdered while attempting to enter the white restroom at a Tuskegee gas station, Peacock moved to California in April 1966, working for a program that sought to bring together blacks and Latinos and as an adviser to the Brown Berets. In 1970 he returned to Mississippi to participate in advocacy projects while working at the University of Mississippi Medical Center in Jackson. In 1988 Peacock worked for Jesse Jackson's presidential campaign.

Peacock returned to California the following year, working at a center for developmentally disabled children and adults and continuing his civil rights advocacy. A frequent speaker for the Fannie Lou Hamer National Institute on Citizenship and Democracy in Jackson, Peacock participated in numerous civil rights history programs.

He died on 17 April 2016.

Becca Walton
University of Mississippi

Seth Cagin and Philip Dray, *We Are Not Afraid: The Story of Goodman, Schwerner, and Chaney in the Civil Rights Campaign for Mississippi* (2006); Dustin Cardon, *Jackson Free Press* (27 May 2016); Clayborne Carson, *In Struggle: SNCC and the Black Awakening of the 1960s* (1995); John Dittmer, *Local People: The Struggle for Civil Rights in Mississippi* (1994); James Foreman, *The Making of Black Revolutionaries* (1972); David Levering Lewis and Charles W. Eagles, eds., *The Civil Rights Movement in America: Essays* (1986); Alan Lomax, *Alan Lomax: Selected Writings, 1934–1997,* ed. Ronald D. Cohen (2003); Charles Marsh, *God's Long Summer: Stories of Faith and Civil Rights* (1997); Charles M. Payne, *I've Got the Light of Freedom: The Organizing Tradition and the Mississippi Freedom Struggle* (1995); Joseph A. Sinsheimer, *Journal of Southern History* (May 1989); Howard Zinn, *SNCC: The New Abolitionists* (1965).

Pearl River

Next to the mighty Mississippi, the longest and once most important river in Mississippi is the Pearl, which runs through two-thirds of the state. It rises near Edinburg in Leake County and twists its way 485 miles (190 as the crow flies) through Mississippi to the Gulf of Mexico near the Rigolets. The Pearl drains nearly a fifth of Mississippi's land area, seventy-eight hundred square miles, as well as nine hundred more in southeastern Louisiana. About thirty miles from the Gulf, it forks into the West and East Pearl Rivers, separated by the Honey Island Swamp. The East Pearl marks the boundary between Mississippi and Louisiana below the thirty-first parallel.

American Indians had lived along the Pearl's course for two millennia before Spanish explorers discovered the mouth of the river in 1519. In 1699 Jean-Baptiste Le Moyne, Sieur de Bienville, named the stream La Rivière des Perles, a translation of the Acolapissa Indian name, Taleatcha. In 1732 Louisiana governor Étienne Boucher de Périer directed Lt. Sieur Louis Joseph Guillaume de Régis du Roullet to explore the Pearl River from source to mouth. Régis did so between 18 July and 10 August, recording in detail nearly every one of the watercourse's features. It was a land empty of humans, possibly because of seventeenth-century wars between Choctaw and Chickasaw and possibly because Her-

7080. View of Pearl River, Jackson, Miss.

Pearl River, Jackson, ca. 1916 (Ann Rayburn Paper Americana Collection, Department of Archives and Special Collections, J. D. Williams Library, University of Mississippi [rayburn_ann_28_02_001])

nando de Soto's expedition had spread European disease two centuries earlier.

At a time when water transportation was generally easier than overland travel, the Pearl promised ready access to the interior. However, Régis encountered a huge draft of driftwood choking the lower river in 1732, much as American surveyor Andrew Ellicott did in 1798 while mapping the thirty-first parallel, the boundary between the US Mississippi Territory and Spanish Louisiana.

After the War of 1812, American settlers crowded into the vacant Pearl River Valley and petitioned the government to clear the river for traffic. Area residents then seized control of Mississippi's government from the older Natchez District. Although Mississippi's first territorial capitals were located at Natchez and neighboring Washington, those that followed were on the Pearl—briefly at Columbia and Monticello and finally at Jackson.

Obstructions below the thirty-first parallel were cleared early on, but Natchez residents blocked clearance farther north until about 1830. In December 1835 the *Choctaw* became the first steamboat to ascend the Pearl to Jackson. For the next twenty-five years steamboat traffic thrived on the Pearl, occasionally even above Jackson. The 1840s and 1850s constituted the golden age of steamboats on the Pearl River, with the *Jacques Dupree, Irene, Mad Anthony, Ondine*, and others calling regularly at Pearlington, Logtown, Gainesville, Columbia, Monticello, Georgetown, and up to Jackson. Much of the finished material for the State Capitol, completed in 1842, including copper for the dome, came up from New Orleans on Pearl River steamboats.

By 1856 the Pearl, which had been crystal clear, became threatened environmentally. Planters and rivermen had cut off river bends to increase the water's flow rate and to shorten distances, but this loss of pool increased flooding. In addition, timber clearance on the banks increased silting, erosion, sunken logs, and malarial fever. Nevertheless, the Pearl remained a key transportation highway until the Civil War.

After the war, railroads challenged river transportation. The Illinois Central was first, with its new towns of Osyka, McComb, Crystal Springs, and Hazlehurst. Then, in 1884, the New Orleans and Northeastern (now the Southern) drove up through the Piney Woods. Its whistle stops became the towns of Picayune, Hattiesburg, Laurel, and Meridian, serving the burgeoning longleaf yellow pine industry. Older Pearl River towns shriveled on the vine.

Beginning in 1880 Congress asked the US Army Corps of Engineers to restore navigation on the Pearl River, but after at least three major efforts the Corps gave up, removing its last snag boat, the *Pearl*, in 1922. Much of the flow had already been diverted from the East Pearl to the West Pearl, leading to acrimony between Mississippi and Louisiana. Picayune conservationist Mansfield Downes led an ultimately successful effort to restore the historic flow and save the devastated river.

Today, Mississippi's historic but sullied Pearl River remains important for three reasons. Near its source at Philadelphia, the Mississippi Band of Choctaw operate their profitable Pearl River Casino. Just above Jackson, the Ross Barnett Reservoir furnishes drinking water and recreation for the metropolitan area. And near the river's mouth, including the site of old Gainesville, the Stennis Space Center has served as a key National Aeronautics and Space Administration facility since 1961.

John Hawkins Napier III
Ramer, Alabama

John Hawkins Napier III, *Lower Pearl River's Piney Woods: Its Land and People* (1985), in *Mississippi's Piney Woods: A Human Perspective*, ed. Noel Polk (1986); John Hawkins Napier III, *Gulf Coast Historical Review* (1992).

Pearl River Convention

Delegates from throughout the Mississippi Territory met at the Pearl River Convention to debate whether the territory should enter the Union as one or two states. The assembly took place in October 1816 at the home of John Ford, located near the Pearl River in Marion County. Though Congress ultimately did not act on the convention's resolutions, the gathering is an important event in Mississippi history because it reveals the extent of the sectional rivalry that characterized the territorial period.

Arguments over when and how the Mississippi Territory might achieve statehood had arisen almost immediately after its organization in 1798. Eventually stretching from the Mississippi River in the west to the Chattahoochee in the east and from the Gulf Coast in the south to the Tennessee state line in the north, the territory encompassed an enormous frontier area featuring loosely connected pockets of American settlement. The two most populous settled regions were the Natchez area along the Mississippi River in the west and the area including Mobile and environs in the east. The Natchez area was much more developed at the time of the Mississippi Territory's formation, and it quickly became the dominant political and population center.

Many eastern residents began to feel that the territorial government was neglecting their interests because of the great distance between themselves and the territorial capital at Natchez as well as other inherent differences in economy and lifestyle. In 1803 and again in 1809 the easterners petitioned Congress to divide the territory to create two states. Aware of the economic and political dominance of the Natchez region in the territory's affairs, many western residents favored admission as a single state so that they might maintain their influence. In 1810 and 1811 Natchez resident and territorial delegate to Congress George Poindexter led efforts to admit the Mississippi Territory as a single state.

In the aftermath of the Creek War of 1813–14, however, the situation reversed. The population of the eastern section of the territory began to grow rapidly after the defeated Creek ceded millions of acres in the region to the federal government, opening them to American settlement. Hoping to capitalize on the situation and the potential to more heavily influence any new state of which they were to be a part, many eastern section residents then began to favor admission as one state. Those in the western section feared future declines in their political influence, however, and began to advocate division. In addition, the more wealthy western residents probably feared an increased financial burden if the entire territory were admitted as a single state. Led by territorial delegate William Lattimore, the Mississippi Territory began seriously moving toward statehood in 1815, bringing the matter to a head.

On 29–31 October 1816 representatives from throughout the Mississippi Territory met to discuss division and statehood at the home of Ford, a prominent Methodist minister and government official. Among those in attendance were Creek War hero Sam Dale and territorial judge Harry Toulmin. Though fifteen of the territory's twenty counties were represented, the Pearl River Convention overwhelmingly comprised eastern residents opposed to division. Pointing out what they believed to be the practical, legal, and economic arguments behind their viewpoint, the convention members drafted a memorial to Congress stating their views. They also decided to send Judge Toulmin to Washington, D.C., to request admission of the territory as a single state and instructed him to work with Lattimore.

Lattimore, however, was already working closely with Congress to move the territory toward statehood, viewed Toulmin's presence as unnecessary interference, and virtually ignored him. Finding it impossible to follow the contradictory opinions of all of the territory's citizens, Lattimore requested division. He knew that southern senators would welcome the move because it would mean four new senators from the region instead of two. After much debate, legislators accepted Lattimore's argument, and Pres. James Madison signed the enabling act that granted admission of the western section of the territory as the state of Mississippi on 1 March 1817; the eastern section was organized as the Alabama Territory at the same time. The line of division was designed as a compromise between western and eastern residents, but many people in both sections were angered at what they viewed as an arbitrary boundary. That line still separates the states of Mississippi and Alabama.

The Pearl River Convention remains a landmark event in Mississippi history for its illustration of the complex differences of opinion that shaped Mississippi during the territorial period. The Ford home still stands near the modern community of Sandy Hook, in southern Marion County.

Mike Bunn
Historic Chattahoochee Commission

Clarence Edwin Carter, ed., *The Territorial Papers of the United States*, vols. 5–6 (1938); John Edmond Gonzales, ed., *A Mississippi Reader: Selected Articles from the Journal of Mississippi History* (1980); Richard A. McLemore, ed., *A History of Mississippi* (1973).

Pearl River County

Founded in 1890 from parts of Hancock and Marion Counties, Pearl River County initially had a population of just 2,957, the smallest in the state. This small and sparsely populated county in the Piney Woods grew with the timber industry in South Mississippi.

By 1900 Pearl River County's population had reached 6,697, with whites making up 73 percent. Only two counties had fewer acres of improved farmland. Among farmers, 84 percent of whites and 69 percent of African Americans owned their land. The county had 77 tenant farmers, the lowest number in the state except for the three counties on the Gulf Coast.

The timber industry and related economic activities were far more important than agriculture. For a small county, early Pearl River had a great deal of industry. In fact, by 1900 Pearl River had about 700 industrial employees working at thirty-two establishments, and Picayune, Pearl River County's largest community, had become a railroad center for the South Mississippi timber industry. The Rosa timber mill, a small operation in the nineteenth century, became a major employer when L. O. Crosby Sr. and his colleagues organized the Goodyear Yellow Pine Company in 1916. The mill later expanded to become part of Crosby Forest Products. Pearl River County wood products became popular for construction throughout the country, while the Crosby family expanded into other enterprises and into local leadership.

According to the 1916 religious census, Southern Baptists made up more than two-thirds of all church members in Pearl River County, with almost all other churchgoers attending Methodist or Missionary Baptist congregations.

The county's population grew along with the timber industry, tripling between 1900 and 1930 to 22,411. About three-quarters of the residents were white. Almost 5,000 people lived in Picayune. Pearl River County had twenty-two manufacturing establishments employing 2,254 people, the state's third-largest number of industrial workers. Agriculture remained secondary to timber, and Pearl River was one of only six Mississippi counties where more than 70 percent of all farmers owned their land.

Theodore Bilbo, one of Mississippi's most aggressive advocates of using racial segregation and disfranchisement to protect the privileges of white residents, grew up in the county seat of Poplarville. He died in 1947 while under US Senate investigation for using his influence to finance his new home there. In 1959 Pearl River County became the center of national attention and scrutiny when Mack Charles Parker, a young African American male, was lynched after being accused of rape.

Pearl River County has also been the home of notable writers and storytellers. Novelist James Street grew up in Lumberton and wrote numerous books set in the Piney Woods. In the 1910s S. G. Thigpen Jr. became a Picayune store owner and author, writing stories about rural life in Mississippi collected in books such as *Work and Play in Grandpa's Day*. Born in Picayune in 1943, literary scholar Noel Polk was an important editor and interpreter of the works of Eudora Welty and William Faulkner. He taught at the University of Southern Mississippi and Mississippi State University. His memoir, *Outside the Southern Myth*, recalled his early years in Pearl River County. In addition, television star Gerald McRaney spent much of his childhood in Picayune, and in the 1980s the Pinecote Pavilion, designed by architect E. Fay Jones, opened at the Crosby Arboretum in Picayune.

In 1960 Pearl River County had a population of 22,411, with whites comprising 77 percent of the total. The county continued to rank high in the amount of commercial timberland. About a third of Pearl River's workers were employed in manufacturing, particularly in furniture, timber, and apparel, while about 7 percent worked in agriculture. After two decades of substantial growth, Pearl River's population reached approximately 34,000 in 1980.

Pearl River County, like many counties in southeast Mississippi, has continued to grow, and in 2010 it was predominantly white and had a small but significant Hispanic/Latino minority. Indeed, with a 150 percent increase in size since 1960, the county's population had undergone one of the largest expansions in the state.

Mississippi Encyclopedia Staff
University of Mississippi

Mississippi State Planning Commission, *Progress Report on State Planning in Mississippi* (1938); *Mississippi Statistical Abstract*, Mississippi State University (1952–2010); Charles Sydnor and Claude Bennett, *Mississippi History* (1939); University of Virginia Library, Historical Census Browser website, http://mapserver.lib.virginia.edu; E. Nolan Waller and Dani A. Smith, *Growth Profiles of Mississippi's Counties, 1960–1980* (1985).

Pecans

Mississippi has some of the highest concentrations of wild pecan trees. While cultivated pecans can be found throughout the South, the native varieties grow in a more concentrated area from Alabama to Missouri and through a portion of East Texas and into northwestern Mexico. The trees prefer a warm climate, and while they will grow in open fields, on fence lines, and as far north as Kentucky, the damp, shady areas of the Lower Mississippi River Valley are ideal. Today, if conditions are favorable, Mississippi pecan growers produce between three and four million pounds of pecans per year. National production is usually around three hundred million pounds annually but can vary greatly.

The name *pecan* is derived from *pakan*, a word used by Native Americans, who have been gathering, storing, and eating the nut for thousands of years. They introduced the nut to European explorer Hernando de Soto when he traveled the Lower Mississippi Valley in 1541. European settlers enjoyed the nut, and around 1795 Thomas Jefferson started planting pecan trees at Monticello. In addition, he shared the nuts with George Washington and helped him start the trees at Mount Vernon.

Among the many prominent hickories—shagbarks, pignuts, shellbarks, mockernuts, nutmegs, and blacks—the pecan stands out as a popular edible nut. Pecans (*Carya illinoensis*) are round ovals with four ribs and a thin shell. Reddish-brown in color, they generally measure between 1 and 2.5 inches long. They contain about 70 percent more fat than most other nuts. Like the healthy oil from olives, most of this fat is monounsaturated. When served raw, pecans are a source of vitamin B6.

Pecans are the premier native southern nut, one that European visitors often take home. Southerners as well as those who visit eat pecans raw, roasted, salted, spiced, sugared, and chocolate-coated. The nuts can be cooked in candy, cakes, pies, puddings, breads, buns, and stuffing and stirred into snack mix, salad, and ice cream.

Because of their high fat content, shelled pecans have a short shelf life—as little as two months. They keep for four months in the shell and for years in the freezer. Fresh pecans smell and taste good, but when they spoil, they turn rancid and smell or taste sharp and strong.

Mark F. Sohn
Pikeville College

C. Frank Brockman, *Trees of North America* (1968); Mark F. Sohn, *Mountain Country Cooking: A Gathering of the Best Recipes from the Smokies to the Blue Ridge* (1996); Mark F. Sohn, *Southern Country Cooking* (1992).

Pecan orchard, Mississippi Delta (Photograph by James G. Thomas, Jr.)

Percy, LeRoy
(1860–1929) Politician

LeRoy Percy is the rare Mississippian who may be best known for his tombstone: a bronze statue of a stoic knight in armor stands above Percy's grave in the family cemetery in Greenville. Percy was a lawyer and levee supporter in Washington County, but he is most famous as William Alexander Percy's father and as the best (and perhaps the last) example of the planter paternalist and gentleman in the Mississippi Delta, at least in his son's eyes.

LeRoy Percy was born on 9 November 1860 in Washington County to Nannie Armstrong Percy and William Alexander Percy, a planter and lawyer who went on to serve as a colonel during the Civil War, earning the nickname the Gray Eagle of the Valley. As Speaker of the Mississippi House in 1876, William Alexander Percy was a leader in returning political power to white planters at the end of Reconstruction. Born into a family of land and wealth, LeRoy Percy graduated from the University of the South in Sewanee, Tennessee, in 1879 and earned a law degree from the University of Virginia in 1881. He was admitted to the bar later that year and opened a practice in Greenville. In December 1884 he married Camille Bourges, a native of New Orleans, and they enjoyed a life of travel, dancing, gambling, and hunting. Their first son, William Alexander, was born on 14 May 1885; a second son, LeRoy, was born in 1802 and died in a rifle accident ten years later.

LeRoy Percy supported flood control through building and maintaining levees, made efforts to build new railroads, supported education and civic improvement, and, significantly, encouraged African Americans to remain in the Mis-

LeRoy Percy's home, Greenville, ca. 1912 (Ann Rayburn Paper Americana Collection, Department of Archives and Special Collections, J. D. Williams Library, University of Mississippi [rayburn_ann_24_18_001])

sissippi Delta as inexpensive labor. The owner of tremendous cotton acreage, he saw himself—and his family and supporters saw him—as an old-fashioned paternalist who took care of his workers but demanded that they recognize his control. When one of his farmworkers wanted permission to shop at a store other than the Percy-owned plantation commissary, Percy emphatically rejected the request: allowing the man to shop elsewhere would lessen "control over him, and then it puts notions in the heads of the other negroes." He envisioned himself as a kind father figure and was famous for rejecting the overt racism of the Ku Klux Klan and political figures such as James Vardaman and Theodore Bilbo.

In 1910 the Mississippi legislature elected Percy to fill the US Senate seat vacated by the death of Anselm McLaurin. The 1912 Senate campaign between Percy and Vardaman was particularly brutal and, according to Percy's son, represented the final defeat for the kind of paternalism and good manners he represented. Issues in the campaign challenged the Percy family's self-image as leaders with a sense of noblesse oblige and high character. On a symbolic level, LeRoy Percy sometimes carried himself with a reserve that some voters found too aristocratic. Opponents called him "Prince Percy" and "the dead-game plumed-knight of the Poker-table." More specific charges hurt Percy's pride. One of his supporters faced charges of bribery, though he was found not guilty. Percy also faced allegations that he had kept Italian immigrant workers as debt peons on his Sunnyside Plantation in Chicot County, Arkansas. He denied the charges but had difficulty combating accusations that he was not a man of the people. When some opponents shouted him down during a speech in Pike County, he responded by asking "what kind of cattle they thought these representatives were to be bought and sold on the hoof." Supporters of Vardaman used that somewhat obscure statement to accuse Percy of referring to common people as cattle. Percy lost the election by a wide margin and never again ran for statewide office.

Will Percy wrote a great deal about his father in his autobiography, *Lanterns on the Levee*. The 1912 election was a turning point for the younger Percy, who "became inured to defeat: I have never since expected victory." LeRoy and his cohort cast such a shadow on Will and his generation that he subtitled his book *Recollections of a Planter's Son*, identifying his father but not himself as a planter. Will Percy loved and respected his father but feared he did not live up to all of the standards—the love of hunting, for example, and the comfort with being in charge—he associated with his father. During the Great Flood of 1927, Will, serving as the head of the local Red Cross, wanted to help everyone, including African American farmworkers, leave the region for higher ground. LeRoy, working behind the scenes to support the interests of planters, who feared the loss of their inexpensive farmworkers, left them stranded on the levee.

Camille Percy died in October 1929, and LeRoy Percy died the following Christmas Eve.

Ted Ownby
University of Mississippi

Lewis Baker, *The Percys of Mississippi* (1983); John M. Barry, *Rising Tide: The Great Mississippi Flood of 1927 and How It Changed America* (1997); *Biographical Directory of the United States Congress* (1950); James C. Cobb, *The Most Southern Place on Earth: The Mississippi Delta and the Roots of Regional Identity* (1992); Stephen Cresswell, *Rednecks, Redeemers, and Race: Mississippi after Reconstruction, 1877–1917* (2006); William Alexander Percy, *Lanterns on the Levee: Recollections of a Planter's Son* (1941); Benjamin E. Wise, *William Alexander Percy: The Curious Life of a Mississippi Planter and Sexual Freethinker* (2012); Bertram Wyatt-Brown, *The House of Percy: Honor, Melancholy, and Imagination in a Southern Family* (1994).

Percy, Walker
(1916–1990) Author

In a caustic, funny, and illuminating self-interview published in 1977, novelist Walker Percy commented, "Of all the things I'm fed up with, I think I'm fed up most with hearing about the New South." Although Percy professed exhaustion with the subject, the New South—particularly the Sunbelt South, in which aging plantation manors and gleaming new suburbs coexisted uneasily—remained at the center of his work throughout his career. Of course, Percy was chiefly fed up with tired clichés about the South, New and Old. In his own writing, including five novels and three works of nonfiction, Percy offered a challenging and idiosyncratic perspective on the South, race, religion, language, and the alienation of modern humankind, a perspective informed by his Mississippi Delta adolescence, medical training, fascination with philosophy, and devout Catholicism.

Walker Percy (Bern and Franke Keating Collection, Department of Archives and Special Collections, J. D. Williams Library, University of Mississippi)

Born on 28 May 1916 in Birmingham, Alabama, Percy led a life that was marked by loss. His father, LeRoy Percy (nephew of the US senator from Mississippi by the same name), committed suicide in 1929; his mother, Martha Susan Phinizy Percy, died in a car accident two years after moving with Percy and his brothers to the Mississippi Delta town of Greenville in 1930. These deaths haunted Percy throughout his life: in particular, his struggle to understand his father's suicide is evident in his novels, *The Last Gentleman* and *The Second Coming*. Percy remained in Greenville, home of his lifelong friend and fellow author, Shelby Foote, and of Percy's second cousin, William Alexander Percy, who adopted Walker Percy and his brothers following their mother's death. "Uncle Will" was a prominent Greenville citizen and was perhaps the single most influential figure in Percy's life. A poet, lawyer, and aristocratic planter, Will Percy is most famous for his 1941 memoir, *Lanterns on the Levee: Recollections of a Planter's Son*, a stoic elegy for a doomed Delta lifestyle in which, he believed, agrarian values, a code of stoic honor, benign racial paternalism, and good manners worked together to create a stable social order. Walker Percy's fiction often grappled with his adoptive father's complicated legacy, featuring protagonists who are the sons of once-prominent but fading families adrift in a South where traditional values no longer suffice to explain perplexing new realities.

After completing a bachelor's degree at the University of North Carolina in 1937, Walker Percy entered medical school at Columbia University, graduating in 1941. With a career in psychiatry in mind, he began a residency at Bellevue Hospital but contracted tuberculosis. His long recuperation afforded him the opportunity to pursue in earnest his interests in philosophy and literature. Percy read deeply in the works of novelists such as Thomas Mann and Fyodor Dostoevsky and theologians such as St. Thomas Aquinas and, most important, Søren Kierkegaard, a major influence

on Percy's work. This intellectual exploration inspired Percy to change the course of his life drastically: he elected to give up medicine for a career as a writer. In 1946 Percy married Mary Bernice "Bunt" Townsend, and in 1947 they converted to Catholicism. Percy maintained that his faith was essential to his fiction—and, indeed, to all great fiction: "The intervention of God in history through the Incarnation bestows a weight and value to the individual human narrative which is like money in the bank to the novelist."

In 1948 the Percys moved to Covington, Louisiana, where they reared two daughters. Percy continued to pursue his vocation as a writer, publishing essays on language, religion, philosophy, and literature, many of which are collected in *The Message in the Bottle* (1975) and *Signposts in a Strange Land* (1991). He published his first novel, National Book Award winner *The Moviegoer*, in 1961. The novel's protagonist is a disaffected young New Orleans man who, dissatisfied both with contemporary society and with his family's archaic code of stoic honor, ultimately finds hope in the possibility of Christian grace. *The Last Gentleman* (1966) tells the story of Will Barrett, a southerner taking refuge from the ghosts of the past in New York who finds his return to an unrecognizable South complicated by his comically failed attempts to adhere to his father's paternalist, aristocratic mold and by his gradual recovery of the repressed memory of his father's suicide. *Love in the Ruins* (1971) takes place in the apocalyptic near-flung future of 1983, when America has disintegrated into racial and political chaos and teeters on the brink of ruin. The novel chronicles the misadventures of Dr. Tom More, whose scientific hubris has led him to invent a device he believes will save humankind from itself by healing the Cartesian split, diagnosing and curing metaphysical ills such as depression and paranoia by altering an individual's brain chemistry. *Lancelot* (1977) is the first-person account of a cuckolded husband who murders his wife and a visiting film crew and burns down his home—an antebellum mansion and tourist attraction—and dreams of leading a Third American Revolution to restore the values of the Old South. *The Second Coming* (1980) is a sequel of sorts to *The Last Gentleman* in which Will Barrett, now a middle-aged widower still struggling with the memory of his father and contemplating his own suicide, sees the presence of God and the possibility of redemption in his love for escaped mental patient Allison Huger. Percy brought together his interests in semiotics, psychiatry, philosophy, and popular culture in 1983's comic, complicated *Lost in the Cosmos: The Last Self-Help Book*, an attempt to understand the role of language in the creation of the self. Dr. Tom More returns in Percy's final novel, *The Thanatos Syndrome* (1987), which explores the hollowness and corruption at the heart of scientific attempts to perfect humanity. Tom and his cousin, Lucy, uncover a plot to contaminate their parish's water supply with an isotope that enhances human brainpower but that also suppresses the conscience and turns people from sovereign individuals seeking God into highly suggestible organic machines.

Percy died of cancer at his Covington home on 10 May 1990. Acknowledged as one of the most significant figures in post–World War II southern letters, Percy left behind a unique and challenging body of work that continues to influence contemporary southern writers such as Richard Ford, Josephine Humphreys, and Padgett Powell.

Brannon Costello
Louisiana State University

William Rodney Allen, *Walker Percy: A Southern Wayfarer* (1986); Lewis Baker, *The Percys of Mississippi: Politics and Literature in the New South* (1983); Gary M. Ciuba, *Walker Percy: Books of Revelations* (1991); Edward J. Dupuy, *Autobiography in Walker Percy: Repetition, Recovery, and Redemption* (1996); Jan Nordby Gretlund and Karl-Heinz Westarp, eds., *Walker Percy: Novelist and Philosopher* (1991); Michael Kobre, *Walker Percy's Voices* (2000); Lewis Lawson, *Following Percy: Essays on Walker Percy's Work* (1988); Lewis Lawson and Elzbieta Olesky, eds., *Walker Percy's Feminine Characters* (1995); Farrell O'Gorman, *Southern Literary Journal* (Spring 2002); Patrick Samway, *Walker Percy: A Life* (1997); Jay Tolson, *Pilgrim in the Ruins: A Life of Walker Percy* (1992); Bertram Wyatt-Brown, *The House of Percy: Honor, Melancholy, and Imagination in a Southern Family* (1994).

Percy, William Alexander
(1885–1942) Poet and Autobiographer

William Alexander Percy was born on 15 May 1885 in Greenville, Mississippi, and was named after his grandfather, a planter and lawyer who served as a colonel during the Civil War, earning the nickname the Gray Eagle of the Valley. Will Percy perceived himself as distanced from and overshadowed by his father, LeRoy, a powerful planter, lawyer, and US senator. Percy never felt close to his mother, Camille, and found maternal affection from his young nurse, Nain. The weight of family tradition pressed on Percy, who was marked as different from an early age. During his early education at the Sisters of Mary Convent, Percy accepted Catholicism. His parents withdrew him from the convent when he decided he wanted to be a priest, and he finished his early education with a personal tutor.

Percy attended the University of the South in Sewanee, Tennessee, following a path trod by three generations of earlier Percys. During his time in college, Percy's ten-year-old brother, LeRoy, was accidentally killed by a rifle, which may have led to Percy's disaffection with the Catholic Church. After graduating from Sewanee in 1904, Percy spent a year traveling Europe and Egypt. He then received a law degree from Harvard University in 1908 and returned to Greenville to practice law. Percy composed poetry that was largely ignored in Greenville but won the attention and praise of the Fugitives at Vanderbilt. Percy's first volume of poetry, *Sappho in Levkas and Other Poems* (1915), invokes many themes of classical literature and romantic poetry. The influence of place can be seen in poems such as "To the Mississippi."

Percy was climbing Mount Etna when World War I erupted and in 1916 served on the Commission for Relief in Belgium. He joined the US Army from 1917 to 1919 and trained soldiers in the 92nd Division (the US Army's first African American division), earning the Croix de Guerre in 1918 and rising to the rank of captain. Some of the poems in his collection *In April Once* (1920) reflect his wartime experiences in France.

Percy returned to Greenville to fight battles on the home front against the Ku Klux Klan. Beginning in March 1922, his father began openly campaigning against Klan activists in Greenville. He humiliated Klansmen in several open speeches and letters that led to Klan threats on his life. Will Percy responded by threatening to have KKK Exalted Cyclops Ray Toombs killed. Under the protection of the Percy family, Washington County and Greenville never saw the rise of Klansmen into the seats of local power. Percy's next book of poetry, *Enzio's Kingdom and Other Poems* (1924), contains several "Delta Sketches" that reflect the land conflicted by a pastoral ideal where spring "is too sweet" and by violence "where yet men hate and kill."

If the memory of spring was "too sweet" in the poem "Delta Autumn," the reality of spring became all too nightmarish on 21 April 1927, when the Great Flood broke the Mounds Landing levee and threatened the thirty-two hundred acres of the Percys' Trail Lake plantation. Much of the Delta would not be dry again for months, and people took refuge on the highest ground available—the surviving levee wall and the second story of buildings. LeRoy Percy put Will in charge of the Greenville Relief Committee, where he confronted the task of feeding ten thousand displaced townspeople. White residents were quickly evacuated to Vicksburg, but seventy-five hundred African Americans were concentrated on the seven-mile-long levee to simplify the logistics of delivering food and supplies. Adequate shelter could not be provided, so Percy began to plan for their evacuation. However, his father intervened. He and the other planters feared that their African American laborers would not return to Greenville if they were allowed to leave. Will Percy could not countermand his powerful father, and instead of fleeing with the white citizens to Vicksburg, African Americans were trapped on the levee and forced to work at gunpoint in brutal living conditions. On 31 August Percy resigned his post.

After LeRoy Percy's death in 1929, Will Percy took charge of the family and inherited his father's plantation and business. He became a patron of the arts and paid for various social welfare programs to help African Americans in Greenville, but the schism brought by the flood could never be repaired, nor could Percy, ever resorting to the bonds of paternalism, consider African Americans as his equals.

Shortly after the appearance of *Selected Poems* (1930) Percy adopted his three recently orphaned cousins, LeRoy, Phinizy, and future novelist Walker Percy. At the urging of Alfred Knopf, his publisher, Percy committed many of the events of his life to paper in his autobiography, *Lanterns on the Levee: Recollections of a Planter's Son* (1941). Emphasizing that he was not a planter but a planter's son, *Lanterns* offered a stoic perspective on the decline of upper-class traditions of paternalism, patronage of and respect for the arts, and good manners. *Lanterns* is Percy's only literary effort that has met with critical praise and endured as a masterpiece. After his death on 21 January 1942, Knopf published *The Collected Poems of William Alexander Percy* (1943).

Sean Harrington Wells
Auburn University

Lewis Baker, *The Percys of Mississippi* (1983); Edward J. Dupuy, *Southern Quarterly* (Winter 1991); Jo Gulledge, *Southern Review* (April 1985); Fred Hobson, *Tell about the South: The Southern Rage to Explain* (1983); William F. Holmes, *Mississippi Quarterly: The Journal of Southern Culture* (1973); Walker Percy, "Introduction," *Lanterns on the Levee* by William Alexander Percy (1973); William Armstrong Percy III, in *Carryin' On in the Lesbian and Gay South*, ed. John Howard (1997); Scott Romine, *Southern Quarterly* (Fall 1996); Benjamin E. Wise, *William Alexander Percy: The Curious Life of a Mississippi Planter and Sexual Freethinker* (2012); Bertram Wyatt-Brown, *The House of Percy: Honor, Melancholy, and Imagination in a Southern Family* (1994), *The Literary Percys: Family History, Gender and the Southern Imagination* (1994).

Perkins, John M.

(b. 1930) Religious Leader and Activist

John M. Perkins, a Christian leader in civil rights, community development, and racial reconciliation, was born on 16 June 1930 in New Hebron, in Lawrence County, Mississippi. After the death of his mother when he was seven months old, he was raised by his paternal grandmother in an extended family that supported itself through sharecropping and bootlegging. During his childhood, Perkins spent most of the year in agricultural work, leaving little time for school. His formal education ended when he reached the fifth-grade level, though Perkins read widely later in life. Shortly after his older brother, Clyde, was killed by a New Hebron town marshal in 1946, Perkins left Mississippi for California. There he worked at a foundry and as a United Steel Workers union organizer. He was drafted in 1951 and spent two years on Okinawa. That year he also married Vera Mae Buckley.

Perkins returned to California and remained interested in issues of racial and economic equality. After becoming a Chris-

(Left to right) John Perkins, Douglas Heummer, and Curry Brown, under arrest for demonstrating, February 1970 (Mississippi State Sovereignty Commission Records, Mississippi Department of Archives and History [2-90-0-48-1-1-1])

tian in 1957, he began to integrate his spiritual beliefs with his economic and social concerns. He and his wife returned to Mississippi in 1960 and began to preach a "whole Gospel" that sought both spiritual and economic transformation. He later wrote that he believed God called him back to Mississippi "to identify with my people there, and to help break the cycle of despair—not by encouraging them to leave, but by showing them new life where they were." In 1961 the Perkinses moved from New Hebron to Mendenhall, the Simpson County seat. There, Perkins founded Voice of Calvary Ministries, which eventually encompassed housing development, after-school tutoring and sports programs, medical clinics, family development and training, legal assistance, a farming cooperative, the Genesis One Christian School, and other community-development activities.

Throughout the 1960s Perkins was a leader in the civil rights movement, organizing marches, demonstrations, boycotts of white-owned businesses, and voter registration drives in Simpson County. In late 1970 Perkins was arrested in neighboring Rankin County, where he had gone to contest the earlier arrest and jailing of eighteen minors associated with Perkins's ministry after their van was pulled over. Perkins and two other activists were beaten nearly to death by Mississippi Highway patrolmen and other law enforcement officers at the Brandon Jail.

In 1972 the Perkinses moved Voice of Calvary Ministries to inner-city Jackson, where they continued their tradition of marrying evangelism and community development. In 1982 the Perkinses moved to a Pasadena, California, neighborhood that had the state's highest daytime crime rates and founded the Harambee Christian Family Center (now Harambee Ministries) and later the Harambee Preparatory School. Perkins also founded and organized the Christian Community Development Association, a grassroots network that now encompasses sixty-eight hundred individuals and six hundred churches, ministries, institutions, and businesses in more than one hundred locations across the country, and the John M. and Vera Mae Perkins Foundation for Reconciliation, Justice, and Christian Community Development. The foundation operates the Spencer Perkins Center (named for John and Vera Mae Perkins's son, who died in 1998), which works "to transform lives for Jesus Christ in the crime ridden area of West Jackson, Mississippi."

Perkins is far better known outside Mississippi than he is inside the state. He has for years been a voice from within the evangelical community critical of its disregard of social and racial justice issues. He has also criticized some civil rights activists for their disregard of the message and power of Christian churches. He refers to racism as "satanic" and argues for confronting injustice and working toward reconciliation and forgiveness. Among Perkins's many publications are *He's My Brother* (1994), *Let Justice Roll Down* (1976), and numerous books on Christian social action, including *A Quiet Revolution* (1977), *Beyond Charity: The Call to Christian Community Development* (1993), and *Restoring At-Risk Communities* (1996).

A number of colleges, including Jackson's Belhaven University, have bestowed honorary doctorates on Perkins, and in 2006 he was named distinguished visiting professor at Seattle Pacific University. Two years earlier, Perkins and the university created the John Perkins Center for Reconciliation, Leadership Training, and Community Development, which "helps students engage in discipleship and become leaders in the areas of justice, community development, and reconciliation." As an interdisciplinary research institute, the center works "to better understand structural disparities and develop more effective systemic strategies for alleviating those disparities."

Edward McAllister
Belhaven University

Charles March, *The Beloved Community: How Faith Shapes Social Justice, from the Civil Rights Movement to Today* (2004); John Perkins, *Let Justice Roll Down* (1976); John Perkins Center for Reconciliation, Leadership Training, and Community Development website, https://spu.edu/depts/perkins/about/index.asp; John M. and Vera Mae Perkins Foundation for Reconciliation, Justice, and Christian Community Development website, www.jvmpf.org; Peter Slade, Charles Marsh, and Peter Goodwin Heltzel, eds., *Mobilizing for the Common Good: The Civil Theology of John M. Perkins* (2013); Terry W. Whalin, *Today's Heroes: John Perkins* (1996).

Perry County

Located in the Piney Woods of southeastern Mississippi, Perry County was established in 1820. Named after US Navy commodore Oliver Hazard Perry, its county seat is New August (formerly Augusta). Other notable towns include Beaumont and Richton.

Perry County began with a small population of free people (1,546) and a very small population of slaves (491). Most people worked in agriculture, and just 12 were employed in commerce and manufacturing. The county's population remained virtually the same through 1840, when the census counted 1,435 free people and 454 slaves.

The population increased through the antebellum period, but Perry County never experienced the dramatic growth common in many Mississippi counties. In 1860, 1,868 free people and 738 slaves lived in the county. At 72 percent, Perry County had the eleventh-highest percentage of free persons in the state. In 1857 famous outlaw James Copeland was hanged near Augusta.

As a small county in the Piney Woods, Perry ranked low in most agricultural categories. In 1860 its farms ranked fifty-fifth among Mississippi's sixty counties in total value, and the county ranked in the bottom ten in the state for its livestock, cotton, and corn. It was, however, Mississippi's second-highest producer of rice. Its people remained extremely agricultural, with only four residents working in industry—making leather, boots, and shoes. In 1860 the small county was home to five Baptist churches, four Methodist churches, and two Presbyterian churches.

By 1880 Perry County's population had increased to 3,427, with the 2,357 white residents accounting for 69 percent of the population. Unlike most of Mississippi, Perry County had little experience with sharecropping and tenancy: more than 90 percent of the county's farms were cultivated by their owners. Perry continued to rank near the bottom of Mississippi's counties in farm value and production of cotton and corn, but it again ranked first in rice production.

Between 1880 and 1900 Perry's population mushroomed to 14,682 but remained about two-thirds white. In addition, farm owning rather than tenancy remained the norm. The most dramatic economic change in the late 1800s was the rapid increase in industrial workers. By 1900, Perry ranked near the top of Mississippi counties with 842 industrial workers, most of them in timber.

The creation of Forrest County in 1908 siphoned off some of Perry County's territory and population, and in 1930 it had 8,197 residents. As in previous years, about one-third were African American. Perhaps the most unusual feature of Perry's demography was its sparse population: it had the fewest people per square mile in Mississippi. More a logging than farming county, Perry had a particularly high percentage of wooded land. Landownership rates for farmers remained high—68 percent.

As part of the New Deal, the US government's Division of Subsistence Homesteads attempted to create several farm communities, and the Richton community in Perry County was the only such project ever completed. During World War II, Richton became the site of a camp for prisoners of war. The town is also home to the Mississippi Pecan Festival.

Perry County's population increased to 8,745 in 1960 and was 72 percent white. Perry continued to have a great deal of commercial forestland, so timber and furniture made up the majority of its industrial work. While more than a quarter of the county's workers were employed in furniture, timber, and apparel, 19 percent were employed in agriculture, primarily raising corn, soybeans, and livestock. By 1980 the county's population neared 10,000.

Like most southeastern Mississippi counties, Perry County remained predominantly white and continued to grow through 2010, when it had a population of 12,250.

Mississippi Encyclopedia Staff
University of Mississippi

Mississippi State Planning Commission, *Progress Report on State Planning in Mississippi* (1938); *Mississippi Statistical Abstract*, Mississippi State University (1952–2010); Charles Sydnor and Claude Bennett, *Mississippi History* (1939); University of Virginia Library, Historical Census Browser website, http://mapserver.lib.virginia.edu; E. Nolan Waller and Dani A. Smith, *Growth Profiles of Mississippi's Counties, 1960–1980* (1985).

Pettus, John Jones

(1813–1867) Twentieth and Twenty-Third Governor, 1854, 1859–1863

John Jones Pettus served the shortest term as governor in the state's history—five days beginning with the resignation of Henry Foote on 5 January 1854. Pettus is best known, however, for his second stint in the office, during which he took Mississippi out of the Union in 1861.

John Jones Pettus was born in Wilson County, Tennessee, on 9 October 1813 and moved with his family to Kemper County, Mississippi, as a small boy. By the 1840s he was a wealthy cotton planter, with at least twenty-four slaves and well over one thousand acres of land. A Democrat, Pettus represented Kemper County in the Mississippi House of Representatives from 1846 to 1848 and in the State Senate beginning in 1848. He was named president of the Senate in 1854.

In 1850 Pettus was one of six Democrats and six Whigs whom the Mississippi legislature selected to represent the state at the Nashville Convention, which sought to address sectional disputes, especially involving issues of the expansion of slavery into the West. Pettus decided not to attend, sensing that the convention would likely support compromises he could not endorse. As the sectional crisis worsened during the 1850s, Pettus became identified as a "fire-eater," a term that described the South's strong supporters of secession. His 1859 election as governor by a large majority (34,559 votes for Pettus, 10,308 for his opponent) indicated that secession was becoming more popular with the voters of Mississippi. In his inaugural address, Pettus predicted that the growing sectional animosity would eventually lead to the abolition of slavery and the loss of the South's enormous financial investment in the slave labor system. Condemning John Brown's Raid and the growing Republican Party, he said that secession and the establishment of a southern confederacy would be the South's only way of maintaining slavery, and he called on other slave states to prepare for the possibility of secession.

After the election of Pres. Abraham Lincoln in 1860, South Carolina seceded from the Union and invited other southern states to join in the formation of a southern nation. Under Pettus's leadership, Mississippi followed South Carolina out of the Union on 9 January 1861 and joined the Confederate States of America on 4 February.

Late in the fall of 1860, Pettus instructed Mississippians to start amassing weapons for a likely war. Over the next summer hundreds of militia units were formed throughout the state, and by the fall of the year, after the First Battle of Bull Run, many of those local units were enrolled in the Confederate Army. Pettus won reelection in the fall of 1861 with only token opposition. The following year, in response to the issue of funding, recruiting, and providing supplies for Mississippi's troops, Pettus called for complete commitment: "I recommend that the entire white male population of the State from 16 to 60 years of age, be enrolled in the militia."

To his opponents, Pettus seemed rough in manner and poor at administration, while his supporters considered him a decisive if often combative leader. Like many Mississippians, he suffered personal losses as a consequence of the war—his son, John, died at the Battle of Ball's Bluff in 1861—and frequent displacements from his home. In 1862, during the early stages of the Vicksburg Campaign, Pettus was forced to move the state capital first to Enterprise and then back to Jackson. When his second term expired in October 1863, Pettus urged Mississippi to keep fighting, and in the summer of 1864 he joined the Confederate Army as a private. After Gen. Robert E. Lee's surrender at Appomattox, Pettus refused to surrender and settled in Arkansas, where he continued to resist federal military authorities until his death from pneumonia on 28 January 1867.

David G. Sansing
University of Mississippi

Robert W. Dubay, *John Jones Pettus, Mississippi Fire-Eater: His Life and Times, 1813–1867* (1975); *Mississippi Official and Statistical Register* (1912); Dunbar Rowland, *Encyclopedia of Mississippi History*, vol. 2 (1907).

Phares, David Lewis
(1817–1892) Physician

David Lewis Phares was a prominent physician, educator, scientist, minister, and writer. The son of William Phares and Elizabeth Starnes Phares, he was born on 14 January 1817 in West Feliciana Parish, Louisiana, near the Mississippi state line, and was the youngest child in a large family.

Early on, Phares displayed a passion for intellectual pursuits. By age thirteen he had mastered surveying skills, even inventing a sextant with which accurate angles and measurements could be made. In his teens he began an intense study of solar phenomena, investigating solar spots and eclipses, a pursuit that left him temporarily blind. In 1832 he entered the preparatory department of Louisiana College (later Centenary College) in Jackson, Louisiana, and graduated in 1837 with what was said to be the first bachelor of arts degree ever conferred in the state. In 1836 he married Mary Armstrong Nesmith of Amite County, and the couple went on to rear eight children. Phares also befriended Louisiana College's president, James Shannon, who became Phares's mentor. Both Phares and his mentor, Louisiana College president James Shannon, became followers of the evangelist Alexander Campbell, a founder of the Christian Church (Disciples of Christ) and a leader of the restoration movement. Phares became an influential "Campbellite" minister, organizing churches near his home in Wilkinson County.

Phares declined a faculty position at Louisiana College and other offers to teach and instead pursued a career as a physician, enrolling at the Medical College of Louisiana in New Orleans (now Tulane University). He graduated in 1839 and began practicing medicine in Whitestown (also Whitesville), later known as Newtonia, nine miles southeast of Woodville in Wilkinson County. He practiced there for more than four decades. He also purchased and managed a twelve-hundred-acre plantation.

Despite the burdens of his medical practice, his passion for education was undiminished. In the 1840s Phares became an outspoken proponent of a common school system for Mississippi. During the administration of Gov. A. G. Brown, his proposals influenced the legislature to create a common school system in 1846. Near his home in southern Wilkinson County, he established at his own expense the Newton Female Institute in 1842 and its male counterpart, Newton College, ten years later, serving as its president until 1859. The institutions prospered until the outbreak of the Civil War but closed permanently by 1865.

Although he did not serve in the Confederate Army, Phares cared for many injured and ill soldiers, and his house served as a home for soldiers during their treatment and recovery. During the war, when he could not obtain medications, Phares explored the medicinal properties of local plants and used them in place of traditional drugs. After the war, he published articles detailing new therapeutic indications for native plants such as *Viburnum prunifolium*, *Gelsemium*, and *Ceanothus*. Phares's health had been delicate since his teens, and in 1863 he was thrown from a buggy and sustained painful injuries from which he never fully recovered. In September 1868 he suffered a serious illness, and in 1872–73 his vision again became impaired, leaving him temporarily unable to read or write. By 1875 much of his active medical practice had diminished.

Despite his feeble health and his wife's death on 13 December 1876, Phares continued to address medical, political, and educational issues he considered critical for the welfare of the state. In 1877 Gov. John M. Stone appointed him to serve on the first Mississippi State Board of Health. For that body's first annual report, he prepared at the board's request a "Synopsis of Medical Flora in Mississippi," which detailed more than seven hundred medicinal plants and their therapeutic uses. He also helped the board formulate the state's response to epidemics of yellow fever and smallpox. He served as the Mississippi State Medical Association's vice president in 1880–81 and as its president in 1884–85.

As a leader of the Grange, a prominent farm organization, Phares advocated the establishment of an agricultural and mechanical college. After the legislature approved the creation of the college in 1878, Gov. Stone appointed Phares to the institution's original board of trustees. When the Agricultural and Mechanical College of Mississippi opened in Starkville in 1880, he was appointed to the faculty as chair of horticulture, botany, and animal and vegetable physiology and served as college physician. During the first year of his professorship, he completed a book on one of his favorite subjects, *The Farmer's Book of Grasses and Other Forage Plants, for the Southern United States* (1881), which is considered the first publication by a member of the A&M faculty. In 1887 he published *Japan Clover, Lespedeza Striata, the Best of all Pasturage and Hay Grasses*. Engaging in voluminous correspondence with farmers, he became widely known, writing columns and articles in various medical, agricultural, and veterinary publications.

In 1881 Phares married Laura Blanche Duquercron of Starkville. He retired in 1889 and moved to Madison Station, north of Jackson. He died on 19 September 1892 after suffering a series of strokes.

Lucius M. Lampton
Magnolia, Mississippi

John K. Bettersworth, *People's University: The Centennial History of Mississippi State* (1980); M. F. Harmon, *History of the Christian Churches (Disciples of Christ) in Mississippi* (1929); E. F. Howard, *History of the Mississippi State Medical Association* (1910); John A. Milne, *Journal of Mississippi History* (July 1956); David Lewis Phares Collection, Special Collections, Mitchell Memorial Library, Mississippi State University; Beulah M. Price, *Journal of the Mississippi State Medical Association* (December 1973).

Given the low quality of public education in Mississippi's poorest communities, the Phil Hardin Foundation offers help in areas of the most urgent and desperate need. By not only providing financial backing but also encouraging innovation and creativity, the foundation has helped to bring new solutions to Mississippi's oldest deficiency.

Thomas John Carey
University of Mississippi

Phil Hardin Foundation website, www.philhardin.org.

Phil Hardin Foundation

Founded in 1964, the Phil Hardin Foundation provides grants in support of educational programs in Mississippi. In a state plagued by widespread poverty and one of the worst public school systems in the country, the foundation has funded some of Mississippi's most successful educational initiatives of the past half century. As of 2010 the foundation had distributed nearly forty million dollars in grants and loans.

Phillip B. Hardin (1891–1972) amassed a large fortune by turning a bankrupt bakery in Meridian into the Hardin Bakeries Corporation, the supplier of hamburger buns to McDonald's restaurants in the Mid-South. The process of consolidating older plants in Meridian, Jackson, and Tupelo into one modern production and distribution center in Meridian convinced Hardin of the need to improve the ability of Mississippi's educational system to produce skilled workers. The short-term need to develop trained workers blossomed into a broader vision for the future that championed education as the key to raising the quality of life in the state. When Hardin died with no wife or children, he left the bulk of his estate to the foundation.

The foundation focuses chiefly on early education. A typical program targets a specific community, develops a strategy to prepare local children for kindergarten, and collaborates with other philanthropic organizations, area colleges and universities, the Mississippi Department of Education, and corporations to implement the program. The foundation evaluates the success of the program and promotes the strategies that have proved most effective. In addition to collaborating with state agencies and officials, the foundation works with regional groups such as the Southeastern Council of Foundations and national organizations such as Teach for America. Through the S. A. Rosenbaum Mississippi Teaching Fellows Program at the Earthwatch Institute of Maynard, Massachusetts; the Thomas R. Ward Fellows Program at Harvard University; and the Mount Vernon Ladies' Association of the Nation's George Washington Scholars Program, the foundation allows teachers and administrators to participate in seminars and workshops with national and international experts.

Philips, Martin W.
(1806–1889) Journalist and Industrialist

Described by historian John Hebron Moore as "Mississippi's foremost agricultural authority of the 1840s and 1850s," Martin W. Philips owned a Hinds County plantation, wrote instructional articles about agricultural techniques and equipment, and eventually started his own firm that manufactured agricultural implements. A native of Columbia, S.C., Philips moved to Hinds County in the 1830s to start a plantation with his new wife, Mary. He had a medical degree but did not practice in Mississippi. Philips was one of many Mississippi planters to suffer serious financial losses because of the Panic of 1837, and he resolved both to practice and to publicize agricultural techniques that would reduce expenses and increase productivity. Reflecting on the economic problems of the 1830s, Philips wrote that too many planters used the "common careless mode of planting" that wore out good soil and left planters wanting to move farther and farther west.

Philips wrote numerous articles for journals like *American Agriculturist*, *DeBow's Review*, *Southern Cultivator*, the *Jackson Southron*, and the *Jackson Mississippian*. He wrote from personal experience about cotton gins, cultivators, plows, hoes, and gins, and also commented on seeds and livestock.

Like many planters Philips kept a journal filled with details about agricultural practices. Historian Franklin Riley edited the journal, which ran from 1840 to 1863 and printed it in the *Publications* of the Mississippi Historical Society in 1906. That diary was primarily a record of agricultural decisions Riley made about when and what to plant and how to use his slaves, who numbered between fourteen in 1846 and thirty in the mid-1850s. In January of most years, Riley began his diary with specific plans for acreages of various crops with projected yields for each of those crops and ended it in December with discussions of what went wrong.

In the late 1850s Philips moved from writing about agricultural implements to manufacturing them. He was so impressed by a steel plow invented by Kentuckian Thomas Brinley that he manufactured the plow, along with cotton gins, wagons, and numerous smaller items, in a new firm he called the Southern Implement Company. The company produced goods for the Confederacy until it was destroyed by Union troops in 1863.

After Mary Philips died in 1863, Martin Philips took a series of positions as the head of the State Insane Asylum, the editor of *Southern Farmer*, the head of the new Department of Agriculture at the University of Mississippi, and finally proctor of the university. He died in 1889.

Ted Ownby
University of Mississippi

Franklin L. Riley, Mississippi Historical Society, *Publications* (1909); John Hebron Moore, *The Emergence of the Cotton Kingdom in the Old Southwest: Mississippi, 1770–1860* (1988); Eugene D. Genovese, *Roll, Jordan, Roll: The World the Slaves Made* (1974).

Phillips, Thomas Hal

(1922–2007) Author

Amid the wave of persecution that characterized much of 1950s America, a respected New York publishing house surprisingly published a novel dealing with an explicitly homosexual theme. Perhaps even more surprisingly, the author of the novel was a southerner—a young Mississippian, Thomas Hal Phillips.

Born near Corinth in 1922, Phillips published six novels and several short stories and had a lucrative career as a Hollywood screenwriter, actor, and film consultant. Phillips earned a bachelor's degree from Mississippi State University in 1943 and immediately joined the US Navy. After serving in both North Africa and Europe during World War II, Phillips entered the master's program in creative writing at the University of Alabama. His thesis later became his first published novel, *The Bitterweed Path* (1950).

Like most of Phillips's novels, *The Bitterweed Path* deals with the coming of age of a young, southern man. Darrell Barclay, the son of a poor sharecropper and Klansman, becomes attached to a wealthy plantation owner, Malcolm Pitt, and his son, Roger. Throughout his life Darrell must adjust to the love that he feels for the Pitts and the love that he receives from them. The love between Darrell and Roger is distorted by feelings of brotherhood (a common symbol of homosexual desire for Mississippians of Phillips's generation), while the love between Malcolm and Darrell is also the love between a father and child. All of the main characters, like generations of Mississippi men, choose marriage, and their homosexual desires are represented as commonplace. As a so-called highbrow novel of the time, *The Bitterweed Path* contains no explicit sexual material but explicitly deals with the homoerotic relationships. Phillips handles these relationships with the delicate facility of language for which he received much praise.

Phillips subsequently published four more novels in rapid succession: *The Golden Lie* (1951), *Search for a Hero* (1952), *Kangaroo Hollow* (1954), and *The Loved and Unloved* (1955). *Kangaroo Hollow*, published in Britain but not made available in the United States until 2000, constituted Phillips's only other exploration of explicit homoeroticism. *Search for a Hero*, a subtle and ironic war narrative, was Phillips's most critically successful novel.

Phillips received significant awards and fellowships from the literary community, including Rosenwald, Fulbright, and Guggenheim Fellowships and the O. Henry Prize for his short story, "The Shadow of an Arm." After the early 1950s, however, Phillips retreated from the literary world. He ran two failed gubernatorial campaigns for his brother, served as president of a life insurance company, and served as the first head of the Mississippi Film Commission, a capacity in which he worked on films such as *Ode to Billy Joe*, *The Autobiography of Miss Jane Pittman*, *Walking Tall II*, and *Roll of Thunder, Hear My Cry*. Phillips also worked on many Robert Altman pictures, in particular *Nashville*, for which he wrote and recorded the "Hal Phillip Walker" segments.

Phillips returned to writing novels with 2002's *Red Midnight*, about a young man paroled from prison and living in rural Mississippi after World War II.

Phillips died on 3 April 2007 in Kossuth, Mississippi.

Courtney Chartier
Robert W. Woodruff Library,
Atlanta, Georgia

John Howard, *Men Like That: A Southern Queer History* (1999); James B. Lloyd, ed., *Lives of Mississippi Authors, 1817–1967* (1981); Mississippi Writers and Musicians website, www.mswritersandmusicians.com; University Press of Mississippi website, www.upress.state.ms.us.

Photography

The first photographic images taken in Mississippi were portraits taken using a daguerreotype more than 150 years ago. The process, invented during the 1830s, required silver-coated

P

copper plates developed by harmful mercury vapors. When the Civil War broke out, Americans for the first time saw images of the destructive power of war. This new documentary style became even more popular among photographers when the dry plate method, discovered shortly after the war, replaced the wet collodion method.

One of Mississippi's more renowned photographers, Henry Norman, was working in Henry Gurney's photography studio in Natchez by his early twenties. Norman learned everything he could and opened his own studio in 1877, documenting life in the Natchez area as well as many scenes of the Mississippi River and its travelers.

By 1900 many of Mississippi's larger towns had at least one professional photographer who documented local customs and community events. The majority of photographers made their living taking studio shots, although many also created images during their spare time. With the development of the first personal cameras, photography became a hobby for those who could afford it and in some cases an art form.

Other early photographers who worked in the style of Norman were F. S. McKnight and J. Mack Moore. After capturing images from Guntown, Saltillo, Rienzi, and Ripley, McKnight settled in Aberdeen and maintained a studio for thirty-six years. When he died, Aberdeen's public library received fifteen thousand of his negatives. Moore focused on the Vicksburg riverfront, photographing rallies, reunions, Theodore Roosevelt's 1907 visit, the Vicksburg National Cemetery, and the Great Flood of 1927. His glass negatives are now in Vicksburg's Old Court House Museum.

Under the Farm Security Administration, organized to combat the Great Depression, photographers fanned out across the nation to document America's problems and potential. Eight photographers visited Mississippi, taking twenty thousand images that are now held by the Library of Congress.

As a publicist for the Works Progress Administration, Eudora Welty possessed a flair for photography before she became a writer. She traveled across Mississippi, recording events and conducting interviews. The Mississippi Department of Archives and History holds more than one thousand of her photographs.

After World War II, the possibilities for techniques and styles broadened. Some photographers began manipulating negatives to produce somewhat surreal images, while the advent of color film opened other new avenues. Under a variety of influences, Mississippi's photographers developed a cross-section of styles and images.

By the 1980s and 1990s Mississippi's photographers frequently produced images of dilapidated structures, intimate portraits of common folk, tight focal-length shots of outdated tools, and many others.

William Eggleston, who grew up in Sumner, pioneered color photography as an art form. Eggleston's works were the first color photographs to be included in the Museum of Modern Art in New York and are products of the dye transfer method, during which colored ink is pressed on paper by plates containing the negative image, creating a painterly effect.

Birney Imes III has captured images of honky-tonks and roadhouses along Mississippi's back roads. His interest in juke joints was fueled by his determination to explore the diversity of southern black culture. Imes goes to great lengths to preserve the authentic dimly lit nature within each establishment. Documentary photographers such as William Ferris, Tom Rankin, Maude Schuyler Clay, David Wharton, and Kathleen Robbins have documented the people and places of contemporary Mississippi.

Contemporary Mississippi photographers include Kim Rushing, whose Parchman series provokes thought regarding imprisonment and capital punishment. Eyd Kazery carefully manipulates his negatives to create images of Mississippi that have romantic tendencies but still retain a surreal quality. Wildlife photographers Stephen Kirkpatrick and Joe Mac Hudspeth produce images of animals seemingly oblivious to the human presence.

Mark Brown
Jones County Junior College

Patti Carr Black, *Art in Mississippi, 1720–1980* (1998); John Szarkowski, *Photography until Now* (1989).

Physicians, African American

Following emancipation, Mississippi developed a small but important black medical community. By 1890 the state had thirty-four practicing black physicians (2.1 percent of the total), most of them educated at one of the South's all-black medical schools, which included Flint Medical College in New Orleans and Meharry Medical College in Nashville. Fifty years later, Mississippi had just fifty-five African American physicians. In addition to the hardships that plagued all black Mississippians during the Jim Crow era—segregation, disfranchisement, violence—black physicians in Mississippi faced many of the same obstacles that confronted African American doctors in other parts of the South: exclusion from educational facilities, public hospitals, medical societies, and postgraduate programs; an impoverished clientele; and competition with white doctors for paying patients.

Because Mississippi had no medical school open to African Americans before 1966, aspiring black physicians had to leave the state, and many did not return. To attract more physicians, black and white, to the neediest areas, the Mississippi legislature inaugurated a financial aid program in

1946. Loans were available to Mississippi citizens who completed their premedical education and were accepted at an accredited medical school anywhere in the United States. The state paid the student's tuition and in some cases living expenses, and after graduating, the recipient spent five years practicing in an approved area of Mississippi and the loan was expunged. African Americans were allowed to practice in any area where a black practitioner was needed. Between 1946 and 1953 Mississippi loaned $1.5 million to 420 medical students—including 31 African Americans—to study medicine outside the state, and the program's success inspired twelve other states to establish similar programs.

Once they completed their education, the greatest handicap Mississippi's black physicians faced in attracting patients was the lack of access to hospitals. Many hospitals barred African Americans, and most facilities that admitted black patients usually did so only in segregated basement wards. In addition, hospitals that admitted black patients often did not grant black physicians staff privileges, even if patients requested treatment by their personal physicians. African American physicians therefore had no choice but to turn many of their patients over to white doctors, who could use the hospital facilities and who were usually more than willing to poach the patients—and the fees they paid. As Dr. Albert Dumas of Natchez lamented in 1910, white surgeons "carry the patient to the hospital and often you never see them again."

African American physicians often founded small, private hospitals and clinics, most of which did not meet the American Hospital Association's minimum standards for size, equipment, resources, or even cleanliness. Yet these small clinics met a valuable need for both doctors and patients, especially in rural areas. In some areas of Mississippi, in fact, they were the only hospital facilities for persons of any race for dozens of miles in any direction. As late as 1963, none of Mississippi's public hospitals had black physicians on staff. However, as a result of the US Supreme Court's decision in *Simkins v. Cone* (1963), the Civil Rights Act of 1964, and the creation of Medicare in 1965, most public hospitals accepted both black patients and staff by 1970.

At the vanguard of the movement to desegregate public hospitals were African American medical societies. Excluded from membership in American Medical Association–affiliated societies, black physicians formed separate organizations to share professional information, hold clinics, promote medical advancements, and provide postgraduate training. In 1895 in Atlanta, black physicians formed the National Medical Association, and five years later, thirteen black physicians founded a state affiliate, the Mississippi Medical and Surgical Association. To improve the health of black Mississippians and provide continuing education for its members, the association routinely held clinics as a part of its annual meeting. In 1934, for example, the association met in Yazoo City, with thirty-two of the state's forty-four black physicians in attendance. During free clinics at the Afro-American Hospital,

these doctors performed fifteen operations for members of the local community.

Physicians from remote areas often depended on local and regional medical societies to provide postgraduate education. These meetings also provided badly needed professional companionship, since white physicians frequently ostracized their black counterparts. Recalled Gilbert Mason, secretary of the Gulf Coast Medical, Dental, and Pharmaceutical Association, a black organization that covered Mississippi, Alabama, and Florida, "We saw to it that black practitioners did not work in total isolation." Meetings regularly involved a scientific session, a business session, and a dinner or social gathering. Like public hospitals, American Medical Association–affiliated societies began to drop their racial bars in the late 1960s, ultimately leading many African American medical societies to fold.

Thomas J. Ward Jr.
Spring Hill College

Lucie Robertson Bridgforth, *Medical Education in Mississippi: A History of the School of Medicine* (1984); Douglas L. Connor with John F. Marzalek, *A Black Physician's Story: Bringing Hope in Mississippi* (1985); Gilbert R. Mason with James Patterson Smith, *Beaches, Blood, and Ballots: A Black Doctor's Civil Rights Struggle* (2000); Neil R. McMillen, *Dark Journey: Black Mississippians in the Age of Jim Crow* (1989); D. S. Pankratz and Julia C. Davis, *Journal of Medical Education* (April 1960); Todd Savitt, *Bulletin of the History of Medicine* (Winter 1987); Thomas J. Ward Jr., *Black Physicians in the Jim Crow South* (2003).

Pig Law

On 5 April 1876, in its first session after the end of Mississippi's Reconstruction government, the state legislature revised the state's criminal code. The new law lowered the dollar threshold for what constituted grand larceny, an offense punishable by up to five years in prison, from twenty-five dollars to ten dollars. More drastic still, the law provided that stealing "any hog, pig, shoat, cow, calf, yearling, steer, bull, sheep, lamb, goat or kid, of the value of one dollar or more" would be punished as grand larceny. This provision gave the statute its common name, the Pig Law; made the law notorious; and earned it a prominent place in the mythology of Mississippi backwardness.

The law was blatantly racist in its targeting of cattle and swine theft, because such stealing was stereotypically considered "Negro" behavior, and whites owned the preponderance of cattle and swine. Mississippi legislators sought to protect white property down to the most insignificant monetary value while denying basic civil liberties to blacks.

Yet contrary to the claims of several influential historians, the law had a negligible effect on the size of the state's convict population. In 1947 Millsaps College historian Vernon Lane Wharton argued that the Pig Law caused the prison population to quadruple, that the law made the convict lease system a big business in the state, and that the law's repeal (which he misdated to 1887) immediately resulted in a decline in the prison population and thus led to the demise of convict leasing. Although many southern historians, including Fletcher M. Green, David M. Oshinsky, and C. Vann Woodward, accepted Wharton's claims, they suffered from serious logical and factual errors. First, Wharton based his sweeping conclusions on an extremely short-term correlation derived from mismatched data sources. Because there is always a lag time between a law's passage and its effects in law enforcement, courts, and prisons, it is most implausible that a law passed in 1876 could quadruple the prison population by 1877. Increases in the convict population between 1874 and 1877 resulted primarily from other factors (most likely an 1875 law that legalized convict subleasing). Moreover, to support his hypothesis about a causal relation between this specific law and a rise in convict population, Wharton would have had to provide evidence that any population growth consisted chiefly of persons sentenced for grand larceny, but he did not furnish any crime or sentencing data on the issue. Moreover, data show that the convict population declined by half during the relatively brief period that the Pig Law was in effect—from 1,003 convicts in 1877 to 752 by 1883 to 499 in 1888, when the law was repealed. Finally, contrary to Wharton's argument, Mississippi did not abolish convict leasing until 1907, nineteen years after the Pig Law's repeal.

The evidence, then, points to a narrative that runs directly counter to the one put forth by Wharton: Mississippi's convict population declined while the Pig Law was in effect but climbed steeply after its repeal. The Pig Law has little social historical significance related to its effect on Mississippi's convict population but is more important for cultural historical purposes as a component of the lore concerning Mississippi's retrograde racial and social arrangements.

Matthew J. Mancini
St. Louis University

Matthew J. Mancini, *One Dies, Get Another: Convict Leasing in the American South, 1866–1928* (1996); David M. Oshinsky, *"Worse Than Slavery": Parchman Farm and the Ordeal of Jim Crow Justice* (1996); William Banks Taylor, *Brokered Justice: Race, Politics, and Mississippi Prisons, 1798–1992* (1992); Vernon Lane Wharton, *The Negro in Mississippi, 1865–1890* (1947); C. Vann Woodward, *Origins of the New South, 1877–1913* (1951).

Pigee, Vera Mae
(1924–2007) Activist

Vera Mae Berry was born to sharecropper Wilder Berry and his wife, Lucy Wright Berry, near Glendora in Leflore County, Mississippi, on 2 September 1924. After her father left the family, Lucy Berry raised Vera and her brother, W. C., in Tutwiler, in Tallahatchie County. When Vera was just fourteen, she married Paul Pigee Jr., who was four years older, and their daughter, Mary Jane, was born the day before Vera Pigee's sixteenth birthday. After studying cosmetology in Chicago, she opened Pigee's Beauty Salon in Clarksdale.

Pigee worked with the National Association for the Advancement of Colored People (NAACP) and was the only woman among the early local movement leaders. She helped to charter the group's Coahoma County branch in 1953 before leaving the area to study cosmetology in Chicago. She returned to Clarksdale in 1955 and resumed her activism. She served as secretary of the Coahoma branch of the NAACP for about twenty years. When the NAACP's Coahoma County Youth Council was chartered in 1959, she served as the group's adviser, while her daughter served as president. In December 1961 the two women and a family friend staged a protest that resulted in the desegregation of Clarksdale's bus terminal. Pigee became a surrogate mother to many young activists, feeding them and providing them shelter in her home and salon. She also helped to organize the area's citizenship schools and taught classes to prepare African Americans to register to vote. Because she was self-employed, she had relative economic immunity against retaliation for her organizing efforts in the Delta, although her home suffered a bombing and she was arrested regularly. Pigee exhibited extraordinary bravery, which she credited to the example provided by her mother, who, driven by religious faith, refused to allow segregation to dictate how she was treated. Pigee helped to establish the Council of Federated Organizations but became one of its first critics, clashing with the Student Nonviolent Coordinating Committee workers who continuously berated NAACP officials.

Pigee left Clarksdale in the early 1970s to study sociology and journalism, earning a doctorate from Wayne State University in Detroit. After movement history in Mississippi rendered Pigee and her loyalty to the NAACP invisible, she wrote and published a two-part autobiography, *Struggle of Struggles*, during the 1970s. She continued her activism with the NAACP in Michigan and became an ordained Baptist minister, residing in Detroit until her death on 18 September 2007.

Françoise N. Hamlin
Brown University

Patricia Hill Collins, in *Mothering: Ideology, Experience, and Agency*, ed. Evelyn Nakano Glenn, Grace Chang, and Linda Rennie Forcey (1994); Françoise N. Hamlin, *Crossroads at Clarksdale: The Black Freedom Struggle in the Mississippi Delta after World War II* (2012); Françoise N. Hamlin, in *Mississippi Women, Their Histories, Their Lives*, ed. Martha H. Swain, Elizabeth Anne Payne, Marjorie Julian Spruill, and Susan Ditto (2003); Stanlie M. James, in *Theorizing Black Feminisms: The Visionary Pragmatism of Black Women*, ed. Stanlie M. James and Abena P. A. Busia (1993); National Association for the Advancement of Colored People Papers, Library of Congress, Washington, D.C.; Nancy Naples, *Gender and Society* (September 1992).

Pike County

Located in southern Mississippi, along the Louisiana border, Pike County was one of Mississippi's original counties. Established in 1815, the county was named after explorer and US Army officer Zebulon Pike. Its county seat is Magnolia, and other towns include McComb, Osyka, and Summit.

By 1820 the county's population consisted of 3,444 free people and 994 slaves. Agriculture dominated the economy, though 55 people worked in commerce and industry. Over the next few decades, Pike County's population grew, primarily through an increase in the number of slaves. Pike had 3,777 free people and 2,374 slaves in 1840; those numbers had grown to 6,200 and 4,935, respectively, by 1860. Pike County's farms raised cotton, livestock, and corn, ranking in the middle in all categories. It ranked fourth in rice production and eighth in orchard production. Forty-one men worked in twelve industrial firms, which concentrated on lumber, leather, and saddles. Typical of most Mississippi counties, Pike County had twelve Baptist churches, eleven Methodist churches, and two Presbyterian churches.

The county's population increased dramatically after the Civil War, with 8,572 white residents, 8,112 African American residents, and 4 Native American residents in 1880. Pike remained an agricultural county, with 1,471 farms, 73 percent of them cultivated by their owners. Pike also ranked high in its production of molasses, rice, and potatoes. In contrast, the county ranked relatively low in cotton production. The lumber industry in southern Mississippi became increasingly important in the late 1880s, and in 1881 the first railroad built just for hauling timber began operating in Pike County. As a railroad hub, Pike County (especially McComb) attracted immigrants: most of its nearly 500 foreign-born residents came from Germany, Ireland, England, Sweden, and Scotland.

The population continued to increase, and by 1900 Pike County was home to 27,545 people, roughly half of them African Americans. With McComb as a railroad center, Pike was quickly becoming an industrial center for South Mississippi. In 1900 the county had 1,233 industrial workers, all but 47 of them men. Pike County employers paid the third-highest industrial wages in Mississippi. McComb was home to one of Mississippi's first railroad workers' unions. The census recorded 288 foreign-born residents in Pike County (the eighth most in the state). Most of the immigrants were German and English, with smaller numbers of Irish-, Italian-, and Swedish-born residents. Forty-three percent of African American farmers owned their land, as did 77 percent of white farmers.

In Pike County as in much of Mississippi, Baptists accounted for the largest number of churchgoers in the early twentieth century. According to the 1916 religious census, Missionary Baptists (more than six thousand members) and Southern Baptists (more than four thousand) constituted better than two-thirds of the county's churchgoers. The Methodist Episcopal Church, South was the third-largest group, followed by Catholics, whose seven-hundred-plus members constituted an unusually high number for Mississippi.

The area was also home to a number of educational leaders. Eva Gordon, principal of the African American schools of Pike's county seat, Magnolia, in the 1910s and 1920s, built up schools using the Rosenwald Fund. Gladys Noel Bates, an educator who became a civil rights activist, was born in McComb in 1920. McComb's Vernor Smith Holmes, a member of the Board of Trustees of the Mississippi Institutions of Higher Learning as well as a surgeon, consistently called for responsible and fair education for all state residents. Willie "Rat" McGowen, a successful basketball coach at Alcorn State University, grew up in McComb.

A handful of artists grew up in Pike County, especially in Summit. Painter and art teacher Marie Hull was a founding member and early president of the Mississippi Art Association in the 1910s. Bess Dawson, Halcyone Barnes, and Ruth Holmes made up the Summit Three, a group active in the Mississippi Art Colony in the 1940s. Much later, self-taught artist Loy Allen Bowlin of McComb constructed unique works using sequins and rhinestones to cover his home and car. Musician Bo Diddley (Otha Ellas Bates) was born in McComb in 1946 before moving with his family to Chicago.

By 1930 Pike County had grown to more than 32,000 people, with whites slightly outnumbering African Americans. It was among the state's most densely populated counties. McComb had become a city, with more than 10,000 people, and 1,825 men and women worked in industrial jobs, the fifth-highest total in Mississippi. In 1930 Pike was home to a small but significant number of immigrants from Italy, Palestine and Syria, England, and Sweden as well as to a much larger number of people whose parents had been born outside the United States.

Pike's population growth slowed but continued through the mid-twentieth century. In 1960 Pike County had a population of 35,063, with 56 percent of those residents whites. More than 20 percent of its workers had jobs in industry,

P

primarily furniture and timber, apparel, and food. In addition, Pike County had two functioning oil wells. Just 8 percent of Pike's workers were employed in agriculture, and corn, soybeans, and livestock were their primary concerns.

McComb became a center of civil rights activism, some notable opposition to the civil rights movement, and some significant civil rights era writing. Pike County was home to an active chapter of the National Association for the Advancement of Colored People led by C. C. Bryant, a group of Congress of Racial Equality activists, and a combination of Student Nonviolent Coordinating Committee workers from outside Mississippi and some newly inspired young people in Pike County. Teenaged protesters Brenda Travis, Hollis Watkins, and Joe Martin emerged from school protests, and Robert Moses, James Bevel, Lawrence Guyot, and Marion Barry were among the many activists who went to McComb to support voting rights and other activism. Activists opened Nonviolent High, a freedom school for students who had been kicked out of local schools for protesting segregation. Pike County farmer and activist Herbert Lee was murdered in 1961, and many other activists endured beatings, intimidation, and arrest.

Two powerful Pike County editors, Oliver Emmerich of McComb and Mary Cain of Summit, worked on opposite sides of civil rights issues, with Emmerich criticizing the Citizens' Council and Cain condemning the federal government. Delta editor Hodding Carter's 1965 book, *Why the Heffners Left McComb*, told the story of apparent moderates who had to leave the area.

Pike County's racial profile shifted during the last half of the twentieth century, and by 2010 African Americans accounted for 51 percent of the population. Like many southern Mississippi counties, Pike's population had increased since 1960, growing by 15 percent to a total of 40,404.

Mississippi Encyclopedia Staff
University of Mississippi

Mississippi State Planning Commission, *Progress Report on State Planning in Mississippi* (1938); *Mississippi Statistical Abstract*, Mississippi State University (1952–2010); Charles Sydnor and Claude Bennett, *Mississippi History* (1939); University of Virginia Library, Historical Census Browser website, http://mapserver.lib.virginia.edu; E. Nolan Waller and Dani A. Smith, *Growth Profiles of Mississippi's Counties, 1960–1980* (1985).

Pilgrimage

During the midst of the Great Depression in 1932, entrepreneurial women in the Natchez Garden Club offered the paying public an opportunity to view a selection of the area's antebellum homes over the course of six spring days. Largely owing to effective promotion by organizer Katherine Grafton Miller, the event was a tremendous success. To this day, crowds from across the nation descend on the town "Where the Old South Still Lives." The pilgrimage quickly expanded to several weeks and eventually added an additional period during the fall. The influx of tourist dollars proved a boon to the Natchez economy and inspired a strong local historic preservation movement. By 1940 several communities attempted to duplicate this success, and the Mississippi tourism board promoted a statewide pilgrimage season for several decades in the mid-twentieth century. However, with the notable exception of Holly Springs and Columbus, no other cities had long-term success. Natchez simply possesses a generous concentration of antebellum mansions with architectural grandeur that other locales lack.

The term *pilgrimage* implies a journey to a holy or special place, and advertising for the Natchez Pilgrimage relies heavily on a subtle intermingling of myth and history that invites visitors to step into a specific vision of the southern past. Although earlier territorial governance under the French, English, and Spanish receives nods, the classical antebellum period of the Old South (1830–61) is the focus. Hostesses wearing hoop skirts regale visitors to the homes with family stories and local legends that depict the pre–Civil War plantation era as a golden age of agrarian civilization. Slavery, when addressed at all, is typically characterized as a benign, paternalistic institution.

In addition to the homes, tourists often buy tickets to the Confederate Pageant, which features tableaux of festive antebellum scenes such as Easter egg hunts, fencing lessons, hunting parties, and balls, culminating in a view of soldiers in gray marching off to war. Children participate in the staged production, taking on a succession of roles as the years pass until as young adults they become members of a royal court with a king and queen. Like Mardi Gras, the Natchez Pilgrimage also marks an active social season with a round of private parties for local inhabitants. Both tourist attractions and venues for public history, pilgrimages celebrate an idealized, romantic vision of a lifestyle that only the most elite plantation owners could have experienced.

Leigh McWhite
University of Mississippi

Jack E. Davis, *Race against Time: Culture and Separation in Natchez since 1930* (2001); Michael Fazio, in *Order and Image in the American Small Town*, ed. Michael W. Fazio and Peggy Whitman Prenshaw (1981); David G. Sansing, Sim C. Calhoun, and Carolyn Vance Smith, *Natchez: An Illustrated History* (1992).

Pillars, Eliza Farish

(1892–1970) Nursing Leader

Eliza Farish Pillars was born on 26 April 1892 in Jackson. She attended public schools in Jackson and Utica Junior College before completing her education at the School of Nursing at Meharry Medical College in Nashville, Tennessee. After graduation she worked in several private physicians' offices and owned and operated a small hospital. In 1926 she accepted a position with the Mississippi State Health Department, where she worked with Mary D. Osborne, who was developing a public-health-nurse-led educational program for midwives. Pillars became the state's first black public health nurse.

Pillars educated five hundred granny midwives and held classes for laypeople in a variety of programs, including child hygiene and general health education. She made home visits to the midwives and their patients, organized midwives clubs, conducted well-child clinics, and taught many different types of caregivers how to adapt to the realities of health conditions in rural Mississippi. She played a pivotal role as a health educator and midwife trainer during a crucial period in the state's history. When Pillars began her practice, death rates among mothers and babies in the state were among the highest in the nation, but those numbers fell during her twenty-five-year tenure at the health department, with the infant death rate dropping by more than half. She provided vision, leadership, and critical role modeling to midwives and mothers through the Great Depression and World War II.

Pillars retired in 1950, and the following year the National Association of Colored Graduate Nurses presented her with its Mary Mahoney Award in recognition of her pioneering efforts in public health nursing. She continued to participate in nursing activities and service events until her death on 15 June 1970. A Mississippi organization for black nurses takes its name from this visionary leader.

Linda Sabin
University of Louisiana at Monroe

Public Health Nursing Papers, Mississippi Department of Archives and History; Virginia Henderson International Nursing Library website, www.nursinglibrary.org; Jeannette Waits, presentation on Eliza Farish Pillars, Historical Interest Group of the Mississippi Nurses Association (September 1994).

Pine Forests

Mississippi's pine forests cover over 5.7 million acres from Tennessee to the Gulf of Mexico. These forests provide raw materials for the forest products industry, hunting and fishing opportunities, habitat for endangered species such as the gopher tortoise (*Gopherus polyphemus*) and red-cockaded woodpecker (*Picoides borealis*), and other environmental benefits such as soil stabilization, water purification, and carbon sequestration. As important as these forests are, they account for less than 31 percent of Mississippi's 18.5 million acres of forestland. Hardwood forests and mixed forests of pine and hardwoods comprise the remaining 69 percent of the state's forestland.

Four tree species dominate Mississippi's pine forests: loblolly pine (*Pinus taeda*), shortleaf pine (*Pinus echinata* Mill.), slash pine (*Pinus elliottii* Engelm. var. *elliottii*), and longleaf pine (*Pinus palustris* Mill.). Loblolly pine grows throughout the state except for the Mississippi River bottoms. Because of its abundance and wide range of uses, it is the principal commercial tree species. Shortleaf pine has adapted to a wide variety of conditions and is also found throughout most regions of the state. In natural stands, it is commonly found in association with loblolly pine, with shortleaf dominating the drier sites and ridges and loblolly dominating the moister sites and bottoms. Slash pine naturally occurs in sandy soils typically found in the lower coastal plain; however, it has been widely planted well outside this range. Longleaf pine has the longest needles and largest cones of the southern pines. Longleaf seedlings can remain in a grass stage for many years before initiating height growth. Historically, longleaf and slash provided the major source of naval stores such as turpentine.

These four pine species typically comprise two forest types or associations of forest tree species. The loblolly-shortleaf

Stripping pines for turpentine, near Ellisville, ca. 1921 (Ann Rayburn Paper Americana Collection, Department of Archives and Special Collections, J. D. Williams Library, University of Mississippi [rayburn_ann_25_07_001])

forest type constitutes most of the state's pine forests, accounting for 4.9 million acres. Other tree species such as sweet gum (*Liquidambar styraciflua* L.), oaks (*Quercus spp.*), and hickories (*Carya spp.*) are often present in small amounts. The longleaf-slash forest type accounts for 871,000 acres and is found primarily in the lower coastal plain. Various oaks are often present in small amounts, with loblolly pine, sand pine (*Pinus clausa* V.), bald cypress (*Taxodium distichum* var. *distichum* [L.] Rich.), and pond cypress (*Taxodium distichum* var. *imbricarium* [L.] Nutt.) present on wetter sites.

The composition of Mississippi's pine forest has changed over time. Until the early 1800s Mississippi's forests remained virtually untouched except for limited clearings by homesteaders. After the early 1800s land clearing increased dramatically as public lands were sold at auction. In general, however, the "piney woods" were the least suitable of Mississippi's forested lands for farming. The soils were relatively poor and quickly depleted, and clearings were often abandoned and quickly reverted back to forest. Thus, by the mid-1800s large expanses of Mississippi's pine forests were largely intact. However, in the late 1800s and early 1900s the lumber industry moved into Mississippi, with southern pine its primary target. Southern pine became the leading lumber species produced in the United States, and Mississippi briefly was the nation's leading lumber producer. By the 1930s Mississippi's pine forests were virtually gone. Most of the cutover land was not suitable for farming and consequently was largely abandoned. The forest did not recuperate until changes in tax laws made it profitable to grow timber, advances occurred in forest fire protection and other aspects of forestry, and a variety of other factors came to bear. Perhaps the major contributor was the forest's ability to regenerate itself. Loblolly, shortleaf, and to a lesser extent slash pine readily reestablished themselves throughout their range. Longleaf pine, the most majestic of Mississippi's pines, was not so fortunate. Free-range hogs, wildfires, and the longleaf pine's intolerance to early competition from other trees and shrubs prevented longleaf from reestablishing itself on most of its former range. Loblolly pine has largely replaced it. Sustainable forestry practices developed after the 1930s have been widely adopted, and Mississippi's pine forests are some of the world's most productive. Advances in silviculture (the science of growing trees) have brought another change to Mississippi's pine forests. Until the early 1950s, most pine stands were naturally regenerated. Since that time, the proportion of pine forests that are planted or otherwise artificially regenerated has continuously increased and now tops 40 percent.

Mississippi's pine forests play a major role in the state's economy. In 2010 more than 896 million board feet of pine sawlogs, 5.08 million cords of pine pulpwood, and 51 million board feet of poles and pilings were harvested, accounting for 76 percent of the annual timber harvest from Mississippi forestland. Harvested pines generated more than $403,000 in revenues for Mississippi landowners and provided raw material for the state's pulp mills and sawmills.

With sustainable forestry practices and the natural resilience of the native pines, pine forests have the ability to renew themselves indefinitely. Indeed, in many parts of the state and throughout the South, pine forests have been harvested and regenerated several times since the 1800s.

Ian Munn
Mississippi State University

James E. Fickle, *Mississippi Forests and Forestry* (2001); Ellwood S. Harrar and J. George Harrar, *Guide to Southern Trees* (1946); Andrew J. Hartsell and Jack D. London, *Forest Statistics for Mississippi Counties—1994* (1995); James E. Henderson, *2010 Harvest of Forest Products*, Department of Forestry, Mississippi State University Extension Service website, www.msucares.com; Marc Measells, *2006 Harvest of Forest Products*, Department of Forestry, Mississippi State University Extension Service (February 2007); Society of American Foresters, *Forest Cover Types of North America* (1975); USDA Forest Service, *Silvics of the Forest Trees of the United States* (1965); David N. Wear and John G. Greis, eds., *Southern Forest Resource Assessment* (2002).

Piney Woods

Mississippi's Piney Woods are part of a broad coastal plain stretching from southern Virginia to East Texas. The Mississippi pinelands sit on the Citronelle geological formation, a prairie land of softly rolling hills and originally a dense forest. The Piney Woods lie north of the Gulf Coast and twenty miles or so inland across the Coastal Meadow of sandy soil. The soils of the Piney Woods are a mixture of sand and clay, nurturing the longleaf pines that grew densely on the land but not particularly suitable for farming. The Chickasawhay, Leaf, and Pascagoula Rivers cut through the Piney Woods in its eastern areas, and the Pearl River is a major feature to the west. Along the bottomlands of the rivers, streams,

Turpentine still, State Line, November 1938 (Photograph by Russell Lee, Library of Congress, Washington, D.C. [LC-USF33-011906-M2])

and creeks of South Mississippi were the only large stands of hardwoods in the area, and the soils were more fertile there than in other parts of the Piney Woods.

Native Americans occupied the Piney Woods along the Pearl River as far back as 2000 BC. The Choctaw were the major tribe in the Piney Woods, and they remained in southern and central Mississippi until the federal government removed the majority of the tribe to Indian Territory (now Oklahoma) in the 1830s. French explorers were likely the first Europeans to explore South Mississippi, probably going into the interior in the early 1700s, with French settlers hunting, fishing, trapping, and maintaining subsistence farms along the rivers.

Settlers from southern states had wandered into the Piney Woods even before Mississippi became a state in 1817, and by the antebellum era, Euro-Americans were living in widely scattered spots, raising herds of cattle, sheep, and hogs (known as Piney Woods rooters), all of which lived off the wild grass and reeds that grew as underbrush in the woods. These herder-farmers grew the corn they needed for bread and a few vegetables. Natchez editor J. F. H. Claiborne traveled through the Piney Woods in 1841, praising the hospitality of its residents, their good health, their abundant diet, and their general contentment. With the opening of Indian lands in northern and central Mississippi in the 1830s, the Piney Woods population declined as people sought better farmland to the north.

River life was a key part of the Piney Woods culture, with men earning cash by logging and rafting in winter and spring when the water levels were high, harvesting the timber from open public lands. Until after the Civil War, the Piney Woods were frontier land, with slowly developing public institutions and sparse settlement. Lawlessness often reigned, with legendary groups such as the Copeland Clan notable for robbery, slave stealing, counterfeiting, and livestock rustling in the 1830s and 1840s.

Delegates from Piney Woods counties voted for secession at the Mississippi Secession Convention in January 1861, but the region became famous for hosting one of the most prominent anti-Confederacy movements. The residents of Jones County saw war with the North as a planters' war and wanted no part of it, and one of their own, Newt Knight, and his followers declared the Free State of Jones, with Ellisville as its capital. Operating from hideouts in the swamps around the Leaf River near Ellisville, the raiders conducted guerrilla warfare against Confederate troops. The Confederate Army abandoned the coast in 1862, and lawlessness in general increased. The war hit the subsistence farmers of the Piney Woods hard, with raiding and military confiscation of livestock depleting the key resource for herding families.

The development of the Piney Woods stepped up in the late nineteenth century with the coming of the national timber industry. The industry had depleted the forests of the Great Lakes just as southern public lands were opened for purchase. Northern speculators bought much of that land and soon entered South Mississippi. By the 1870s the Poitevent-Favre mill and the Weston mill were prominent on the Lower Pearl River, providing sawmill jobs for people lured out of the rural areas by the prospect of wages. By 1890 the Poitevent-Favre mill was cutting more than thirty million board feet of timber yearly, operating its own line of steamers and schooners to get timber to market, and employing six hundred men. Southern railroad development also dramatically increased after Reconstruction, providing essential transportation to the timber companies. The New Orleans and Northeastern Railroad crossed South Mississippi in the 1880s, and the Gulf and Ship Railroad connected key Piney Woods towns such as Hattiesburg and Laurel to Jackson. The opening of the Gulfport harbor in 1902 provided new marketing opportunities for the timber industry.

The production of naval stores also became part of southern Mississippi's economic landscape in the late nineteenth century as companies transferred their operations from the Carolinas and South Georgia. Turpentine work brought African Americans into the region, providing an alternative to the sharecropping that had become typical for blacks after the Civil War. Timber and railroad workers produced an enduring musical culture in the area. The Mississippi Blues Trail honors Laurel as one of the state's most important blues centers, and Hattiesburg is acknowledged for its role in the High Hat Chitlin' Circuit. Big Joe Williams's "Piney Woods Blues" is one of many blues songs to come out of the region. Meridian was one of the South's most important railroad towns in the early twentieth century, the nexus of many lines and a meeting place for white and black railroad workers. The town's Jimmie Rodgers knew the Piney Woods well, and his early country songs provide a good entrance to the musical culture of working-class whites there.

The early twentieth century saw a notable increase in the exploitation of the virgin yellow pine forests of South Mississippi. In 1908 US government foresters estimated that more than half of the longleaf pinelands of South Mississippi had been clear-cut and predicted that the pines would be exhausted within another quarter century. The timber industry transformed the Piney Woods, ending the old rural culture, leaving a landscape of stumps, and fostering new communities around the mills and railroad depots. Picayune, for example, had become an important railroad town in the late nineteenth century, but the coming of the Rose Lumber Company mill in the first decade of the new century brought increased prosperity, population, and such institutions as a bank, a newspaper, a real estate company, and churches.

Owners of lumber mills and logging operations became a new leadership elite in the Piney Woods. One of its most famous members was Lucius Olen Crosby, the son of a farmer and former Confederate soldier born in 1869 in Mount Pleasant. After working as a sawyer and a farmer, Crosby became a partner in a sawmill and then a major supplier for International Harvester, and by 1916 he controlled thirty-five mills. He became a primary developer of timber-related activities in South Mississippi and a state-wide leader in economic diversification.

The South Mississippi timber industry peaked in 1911 with 360 million board feet of lumber shipped from the Gulfport harbor. The decline of the industry was already apparent by the late 1920s. Large mills shut down, and once-flourishing river towns such as Pearlington, Logtown, and Gainesville began their decline. The industry had sponsored little reforestation, leaving the area unprepared for the utter depletion of the once-vast longleaf pines that had given the region its character and resources.

In the aftermath of this economic decline, business and agricultural leaders sponsored new initiatives beginning in the 1930s. Garment factories came to towns such as Poplarville and Picayune, and the latter attracted a chemical plant. One of the most important towns of the Piney Woods, Hattiesburg, had never been as dependent on the timber industry alone for economic stability as had other regional towns, and it grew as a railroad hub and home to the state teachers college (now the University of Southern Mississippi) and new industrial plants. Groves of pecans, peaches, and satsuma oranges; truck farms; and occasional dairies soon appeared on the cutover lands left by the timber industry. For a time, Piney Woods promoters saw tung tree orchards as the region's salvation. Tung oil from the tree's nuts was a key preservative in paints and varnishes, and environmental conditions seemed appropriate. The industry thrived until competition from Argentina cut into its success and Hurricane Camille in 1969 destroyed the orchards.

Politics in the Piney Woods reflected the social class, racial, religious, and regional aspects associated with Mississippi politics in general. The area was a center of whitecapping in the late nineteenth century, as hard-pressed white farmers used vigilante tactics to limit opportunities for competing black farmers. The 1959 lynching of Mack Charles Parker in Poplarville for the alleged kidnapping and rape of a white woman was one of the most violent episodes in Mississippi's civil-rights-era history. Resentments against the rich and privileged were just as raw as racial conflicts, with enduring antagonism between the Piney Woods and Delta planters a dominant feature of twentieth-century Mississippi politics. Mill workers and small farmers also often criticized eastern corporations and financial interests that controlled South Mississippi's wealth. The Piney Woods was conservative Christian country from early white settlement, and the dominance of the "dry" Baptists made Prohibition a popular political issue in the Piney Woods, with Delta residents often on the other side of the conflict. Perhaps the most famous political leader from the Piney Woods, Theodore Bilbo, represented all of these political tendencies during his career as a state legislator, governor, and US senator.

Several trends drove post–World War II economic development in the Piney Woods. Reforestation began in earnest and became a new crusade, emphasizing planning for long-term growth. With the indigenous longleaf pines now all but exhausted, timbermen turned to the quick-growing loblollies. Pulpwood and paper products soon became important industries for the region. However, the majority of Piney Woods wealth since the 1940s has come from petroleum. The first well came in during 1930, and today Hattiesburg is a major propane supply link for the Dixie Pipeline, while Lumberton is home to the Hunt Southland Refining Company. Mississippi's poultry industry is concentrated in the central and southern part of the state, with the Piney Woods counties producing between eight million and fifty million chicken broilers in 2001. Poultry-processing plants in Laurel and Collins produce broilers for market in this country and overseas. The space program, too, has provided Piney Woods jobs: more than thirty government agencies and private businesses conduct operations at the John C. Stennis Space Center in Hancock County.

The Piney Woods has produced numerous writers whose stories tell of life in the region. Among the most important was James Street, who wrote seventeen books, thirty-five short stories, and almost two dozen articles for leading national magazines. Born in Lumberton, he wrote about country boys and dogs, preachers, and Piney Woods farmers. Five of his historical novels depict the generational story of the fictional Dabney family from Lebanon, Mississippi. More recently, literary scholar Noel Polk differentiates the Piney Woods from predominant southern symbolism in *Outside the Southern Myth* (1997). The Pine Hills Culture Program, which is part of the University of Southern Mississippi's Center for Oral History and Cultural Heritage, was founded in 1996 and documents historical and contemporary life in the Piney Woods.

Charles Reagan Wilson
University of Mississippi

J. F. H. Claiborne, *Publications of the Mississippi Historical Society* 9 (1906); John Hawkins Napier III, *Lower Pearl River's Piney Woods: Its Land and People* (1985); Nollie W. Hickman, *Mississippi Harvest: Lumbering in the Longleaf Pine Belt* (1962); Noel Polk, *Piney Woods: A Human Perspective* (1986).

Piney Woods Herding

Prior to the development of the cotton gin and the Removal of the Indians from their ancestral lands, more people in Mississippi made their living by raising livestock than by any other means. The agricultural schedules of the US census in 1840, 1850, and 1860 indicate that the same held true throughout the antebellum South. For example, the value of livestock reported in the 1860 census was twice that of the cotton crop and roughly equaled the total value of all crops. Ten years earlier the value of livestock on Alabama and Mississippi farms totaled one-third of the value of all farms—a remarkable figure considering that many range animals likely went unreported. While these figures also included horses, swine, sheep, and goats, cattle raising was of primary importance in Mississippi and the entire Gulf South from the colonial period until the Civil War.

Historian J. F. H. Claiborne recorded one of the earliest descriptions of the vast herds of cattle in 1841 when he returned to Natchez after a lengthy trip through the Piney Woods of the southeastern Mississippi, where he discovered a "valuable trade in cattle." "Thousands of cattle are grazed here for market," he wrote, adding vivid descriptions of grass three feet high, mounted cowboys, and roundups. If Claiborne had referred to cactus and sagebrush rather than pines and canebrakes, parts of his account would read like a script for a movie Western.

Herding in Mississippi was part of a broader cattle frontier that ran from South Carolina through Georgia, Florida, Alabama, and Mississippi to Louisiana. The origins of the post–Civil War Great Plains cattle frontier can be traced back to the colonial South, first in the Carolinas and then through the Gulf South to Texas. To be sure, the longhorns driven up the various trails to the Kansas cow towns trace their genealogical origins to Spanish stock in southwestern Texas, but southern cowboys, both black and white, herded cattle on horseback many decades before the Civil War. By the end of the colonial period, Spanish bloodlines predominated in Mississippi, but settlers introduced cattle from all parts of Europe. The Native Americans indigenous to the southeastern United States, including those in Mississippi, quickly adopted cattle raising, and some of them became famous horse breeders as well.

Most travel accounts written during the colonial and early national periods contain references to the ideal conditions prevailing throughout the Gulf South for the grazing of livestock. It is difficult for even experienced stockmen to accurately estimate the size of herds, particularly when many of them grazed on carpets of grass beneath the pine forests. Nevertheless, anecdotal evidence indicates not only that cattle raising was ubiquitous but also that many of the herds contained hundreds or even thousands of animals. Spanish census data and territorial tax records confirm the existence of a sizable cattle industry. One can assume that such figures are on the conservative side because owners frequently underreport their holdings to minimize tax bills.

According to Spanish officials, the Natchez District had 3,250 cattle in 1784, 4,476 in 1787, 6,966 in 1788, 15,181 in 1792, and 18,302 in 1794. These numbers dwarfed the area's human population: in 1794, for example, the district had more than four times as many cattle as people. In 1788 the Spanish listed 17,351 cattle across the river in the Opelousas region. An 1805 territorial census found 35,041 cattle in Adams, Claiborne, Jefferson, Washington, and Wilkinson Counties. Although most of these animals were in Adams County, large concentrations also resided along the Tombigbee and Chickasawhay rivers north and northwest of Mobile. Vast herds also grazed in southern Alabama and West Florida during the colonial and territorial periods as well as west of the Mississippi River in the Opelousas region. Though many animals belonged to Scots-Irish herders whose existence depended heavily on their cattle and pigs, wealthy planters also maintained considerable herds of livestock, both for their trading value and as sources of food for planter families and slaves.

Primary domestic markets existed in Natchez, New Orleans, Mobile, and Pensacola, and secondary shipping points developed during the nineteenth century along the coast and on the navigable streams. While some markets for fresh beef developed in the cities and at military posts, cattle were generally sold on the hoof or slaughtered for their hides, hooves, horns, or tallow. Prices varied according to the size, quality, and age of the animals as well as prevailing economic conditions, but the value of cattle remained relatively high—commonly between seven and seventeen dollars per head in the late eighteenth and early nineteenth centuries and at times much more.

In the 1980s some historians argued that many of the characteristics considered typical of southern mannerisms can be traced back to the preponderance of the Scots-Irish herders on the southern frontier. While this interpretation caused heated debate, it did bring attention to a facet of life in the antebellum South that previously had received little attention. Regardless of the relative importance of Celtic culture to the southern heritage, there is no doubt about the widespread presence of cattle in Mississippi. Today the Livestock Conservancy is working to protect the rapidly dwindling number of Pineywoods cattle, descendants of those that for three centuries roamed the ranges of South Mississippi.

John D. W. Guice
University of Southern Mississippi

Thomas D. Clark and John D. W. Guice, *The Old Southwest, 1795–1830: Frontiers in Conflict* (1996); John D. W. Guice, *Western Historical Quarterly* (April 1977); Terry G. Jordan, *Trails to Texas: Southern Roots of Western Cattle Ranching* (1981); Livestock Conservancy website, livestockconservancy.org; Grady McWhiney, *Cracker Culture: Celtic Ways in the Old South* (1988).

Piney Woods School

Dr. Laurence C. Jones founded the Piney Woods School in rural Rankin County, about twenty-one miles south of Jackson, in 1909 to educate African American children. More than a hundred years later, Piney Woods has a two-thousand-acre campus with a five-hundred-acre working farm and serves about three hundred students in grades nine through twelve. Virtually all of the school's graduates go on to attend college, including some of the nation's premier institutions.

Born in Missouri and schooled in Iowa, Jones moved to the South after developing a correspondence with Booker T. Washington about the industrial education provided at Tuskegee Institute. After teaching for a year in Jackson, Jones traveled to rural Rankin County, intent on founding an industrial school for the area's African American children. The early days of the school almost immediately became legend. Jones held the first day of lessons on a log underneath a cedar tree, opening the day with the hymn, "Praise God from Whom All Blessings Flow." A symbolic re-creation of the cedar tree and log can be found on the school grounds today.

Over the next twenty years, Jones built the foundation of Piney Woods, beginning with the reappropriation of a rundown sheep shed on land donated to Jones by an African American farmer known as Uncle Ed. Keeping with the principles of Washington's industrial education initiative at Tuskegee, the Piney Woods students learned trades as well as academics. The first building served as both a classroom and a dormitory for students, who came from all over Mississippi. One of only four historically black boarding schools in the United States, Piney Woods today continues the tradition of industrial education. In addition to the working farm, the campus has a printing shop, an automotive shop, and a day care facility. Most students receive financial assistance, primarily in the form of a work-study program. Many of the school's day-to-day services depend on the labor of its students, including groundskeeping, cooking, classroom assistance, and maintenance.

Piney Woods School (Archives and Records Services Division, Mississippi Department of Archives and History [PI ED 1981.0057 Box 11 Folder 63 #1])

Piney Woods exemplifies the industrial-school model and notions of middle-class uplift among African Americans in the South during segregation. Jones received the majority of his initial funding from northern philanthropists, particularly educators he met while in school in Iowa. Other notable contributors included the Maytag family, the Rosenwald and Jeanes Teachers' Funds, Dale Carnegie, and the Kraft family. Like many industrial educators of his era, Jones courted northern white philanthropists by presenting Piney Woods as a way to create constructive and useful African American citizens for the New South.

Piney Woods provided a model for other educators and leaders throughout the world. Jones and his teachers traveled to India, Mexico, China, and other countries in need of rural education programs to teach local educators how to develop schools based on the Piney Woods model. In 1929 the school opened to blind students, offering the only educational opportunity for Mississippi's blind African American community until the state opened a facility in 1950.

While the school has no formal religious affiliation, Jones based the curriculum and philosophy of Piney Woods on strong Christian principles. The motto "Head, Heart, Hands" embodies the tenets of academic, Christian, and industrial education that continue to guide the school today.

Jennifer Nardone
Columbus State Community
College

Beth Day, *The Little Professor of Piney Woods: The Story of Laurence Jones* (1955); Alferdteen Harrison, ed., *Piney Woods School: An Oral History* (1983); Laurence C. Jones, *Piney Woods and Its Story* (1922); Mary A. Marshall, *Chicago Sun-Times* (22 March 1998); Piney Woods School, *The Piney Woods Country Life School* (Pamphlet, 1988); Piney Woods School website, www.pineywoods.org.

Pitchlynn, John
(1764–1835) Choctaw Leader

John Pitchlynn, a trader and interpreter, became one of the most influential European Americans in relations with the Choctaw Nation. Born near Charleston, South Carolina, on 11 June 1764, he was the son of Isaac Pitchlynn and Jemima Hickman Pitchlynn. After arriving in the Choctaw country with his father in 1774, Pitchlynn received no formal education and became fluent in Choctaw. He emerged as an official interpreter at the Hopewell Treaty conference with the Choctaw delegation in January 1786. On 12 August 1797 Benjamin Hawkins, principal agent for the Four Nations, confirmed Pitchlynn's appointment as interpreter and assistant agent to the Choctaw and Chickasaw.

For the next forty years Pitchlynn played a significant role as an adviser and mediator for the Choctaw and the federal government. He served as interpreter at the Nashville Conference in 1792 and at the treaty conferences at Fort Confederation (1802) and Mount Dexter (1805), in which the Choctaw ceded some seven million acres of land to the United States. He became an asset to the Mississippi Territory when he counseled the Choctaw to oppose Tecumseh and convinced them to fight against the Red Stick Creek during the War of 1812. Pitchlynn also served as an adjutant and interpreter during the Pensacola Campaign, and two of his sons, James and John Jr., served with American forces commanded by Andrew Jackson.

Following the War of 1812 Pitchlynn's influence among the Choctaw became more pronounced. He returned as official interpreter at the treaty conference at the Choctaw Trading House near old Fort Confederation in October 1816. Pitchlynn and his son, James, an advocate for Removal, played important roles in the October 1820 Treaty of Doak's Stand when the Choctaw agreed to exchange land in southwestern Mississippi for thirteen million acres in what is now Arkansas and Oklahoma. In September 1824 Pitchlynn accompanied a Choctaw delegation that included the three district chiefs (Pushmataha, Apukshunnubbee, and Mushulatubbee) to Washington, D.C. Despite the deaths of Apukshunnubbee and Pushmataha, the Choctaw signed the Treaty of Washington on 20 January 1825.

Pitchlynn's service to the United States and his support for Removal proved crucial in the years leading to the Treaty of Dancing Rabbit Creek. In November 1826 he assisted John Coffee, Thomas Hinds, and William Clark at a conference with Choctaw commissioners. The Choctaw, including Pitchlynn's son, Peter, rejected a proposal to move to lands west of the Mississippi. Jackson's 1828 election as president, extension of Mississippi state laws over the Choctaw, and passage of the Indian Removal Act in 1830 forced Pitchlynn and the Choctaw to the treaty grounds near Dancing Rabbit Creek in Noxubee County, Mississippi, in mid-September 1830. Deeply divided and desperate, the Choctaw agreed to surrender their last ten million acres in Mississippi by signing the Treaty of Dancing Rabbit Creek on 27 September. Under the treaty and supplementary articles, several individuals received special land reservations, including John Pitchlynn and his sons, Peter, John Jr., Silas, and Thomas, who received 5,120 acres.

John Pitchlynn's influence over the Choctaw and his participation in the market economy of the Lower Mississippi Valley were directly related to his wives and their connection to the Choctaw elite. His first marriage, to the mixed-blood Rhoda Folsom, produced three sons, James, John Jr., and Joseph. Following her death, he married Sophia Folsom, also of mixed blood, and they had eight children: Peter Perkins, Silas, Mary, Rhoda, Thomas, Eliza, Elizabeth, and

Kiziah. Prior to Removal, Peter replaced Mushulatubbee as chief of the Northeastern District in January 1831 and emerged as a prominent Choctaw leader and spokesman.

By 1810 Pitchlynn had moved to Plymouth, on the west bank of the Tombigbee River about five miles north of present-day Columbus. With his investments in livestock, fifty slaves, and two hundred acres of corn and cotton under cultivation, he may have been the wealthiest man in the Choctaw Nation prior to Removal. He became part owner of a stage line that operated between Columbus and Jackson and was a charter member in the Masonic Lodge in Columbus. He provided financial and political support for Cyrus Kingsbury's mission schools at Elliot on the Yalobusha River in 1819 and at Mayhew on Oktibbeha Creek in 1820. He also exposed his family to religious training from visiting Methodist and Presbyterian preachers.

Pitchlynn held great affection for his extended bicultural family and exercised unparalleled influence over the "civilizing" forces that affected his kinsmen and the Choctaw. Deeply conflicted over Removal, he eventually decided to remain in Mississippi and tried to influence his son, Peter, to return. After liquidating most of his assets in anticipation of Removal, John Pitchlynn lived at Waverly, in Clay County, where he died on 20 May 1835, leaving an estate valued at more than thirty-five thousand dollars, mostly in slaves. The other members of his extended family then migrated west.

James P. Pate
University of Mississippi, Tupelo

W. David Baird, *Peter Pitchlynn: Chief of the Choctaws* (1972); James Taylor Carson, *Searching for the Bright Path: The Mississippi Choctaws from Prehistory to Removal* (1999); Clara Sue Kidwell, *Choctaws and Missionaries in Mississippi, 1818–1918* (1995); Don Martini, *Who Was Who among the Southern Indians: A Genealogical Notebook, 1698–1907* (1997).

P

Pitchlynn, Peter Perkins

(1806–1881) Choctaw Leader

Peter Perkins Pitchlynn emerged as an important political and intellectual leader in the Choctaw Nation prior to Removal. Born at Hushookwa, in present-day Noxubee County, on 30 January 1806, he was the son of John Pitchlynn and Sophia Folsom, a mixed-blood Choctaw. Peter Pitchlynn's father, a trader and interpreter, was one of the wealthiest and most influential men in the Choctaw Nation, while his mother provided connections to the Choctaw elite. Peter became immersed in Choctaw culture and as a young boy received the name Ha-tchoc-tuck-nee, "Snapping Turtle."

Prior to 1810 Pitchlynn's family moved to Plymouth Bluff on the west bank of the Tombigbee River, near the junction of Oktibbeha Creek north of present-day Columbus, Mississippi. His father's trading house at the intersection of Indian trails, Gaines Trace, and the Tombigbee became a gathering place for the famous and infamous. As a youth, Peter Pitchlynn encountered prominent Choctaw chiefs and captains as well as such Euro-Americans as Andrew Jackson; George Strother Gaines, factor of the Choctaw Trading House; and Indian agents Silas Dinsmoor and John McKee. Pitchlynn's kinsman and neighbor, Gideon Lincecum, a frontier physician, piqued Pitchlynn's lifelong interest in education and intellectual pursuits.

Pitchlynn's formal education probably started at Charity Hall, a Chickasaw mission school founded in 1820 by Rev. Robert Bell near Cotton Gin Port. Pitchlynn attended Tennessee's Columbia Academy between 1821 and 1823 and enrolled at the University of Nashville from November 1827 through March 1828. He also studied at the Choctaw Academy at Blue Springs, Kentucky, in 1827 and 1828.

On 15 December 1823 Pitchlynn married Rhoda Folsom, his mother's half-sister, in a Christian ceremony performed by Rev. Cyrus Kingsbury, a Presbyterian missionary, that allowed Pitchlynn to demonstrate his opposition to polygamy and support for Christianity. He then launched his political career as a captain in the Choctaw Lighthorse, a mounted police force, with authority to act as judge and jury to exact punishment on law violators, especially whiskey dealers and livestock thieves. His service as secretary for a special national council that drafted the Choctaw Constitution of 1826 exposed him to the nation's political elite.

With his father's support, Pitchlynn joined a small Choctaw landed elite and thrived as a farmer, stockman, and slave owner. He established his home two miles southwest of his father's land and planted corn and cotton and grazed cattle, hogs, and horses on the surrounding open prairie. In 1831 Pitchlynn owned ten slaves and had ninety acres under cultivation.

Increasingly active in tribal affairs, he allied with Mushulatubbee, his uncle, against David Folsom and Greenwood LeFlore. In November 1826 Pitchlynn served as a member of a Choctaw commission that met with John Coffee, Thomas Hinds, and William Clark and rejected a proposal to move to lands west of the Mississippi granted under the 1820 Treaty of Doak's Stand. In 1827 Thomas L. McKenney, commissioner of Indian affairs, made a similar proposal, which led Pitchlynn to join an October 1828 Choctaw-Chickasaw exploring party that made a circuitous trip via St. Louis, the Osage country, and down the Arkansas River but failed to explore the Choctaw lands along the Red River. After returning home in January 1829, Pitchlynn became embroiled in the power struggle over Removal.

With the nation torn by factionalism, the extension of Mississippi laws to cover the Choctaw and the passage of the Indian Removal Act in 1830 forced the Choctaw to attend a conference at Dancing Rabbit Creek near present-day Macon. Pitchlynn, serving as secretary for the Choctaw delegates, played a pivotal role in the deliberations from the opening speeches by John H. Eaton and John Coffee on 18 September 1830. After rejecting the initial proposal, a small group of leaders, including Pitchlynn, grudgingly agreed to Removal. Although most Choctaw opposed Removal, 171 "Mingoes, Chiefs, Captains, and Warriors," including Pitchlynn, signed the Treaty of Dancing Rabbit Creek on 27 September 1830.

Pitchlynn subsequently became a vocal critic of the treaty despite receiving preferential treatment with the other Choctaw elite. Under questionable authority, he replaced Mushulatubbee as district chief and led an emigrant party west in 1831. After selling his land and assets in 1832, he eventually settled on the Mountain Fork River near Eagletown in what is now Oklahoma in 1834. His pro-Union sympathies allowed him to briefly lead the Choctaw Nation during Reconstruction, and he served as a special delegate in Washington, D.C., espousing Choctaw land claims and sovereignty. He died on 17 January 1881.

James P. Pate
University of Mississippi, Tupelo

W. David Baird, *Peter Pitchlynn: Chief of the Choctaws* (1986); Angie Debo, *The Rise and Fall of the Choctaw Republic* (1934); Charles Lanman, *Atlantic Monthly* (April 1870); Clara Sue Kidwell, *Choctaws and Missionaries in Mississippi, 1818–1918* (1995); Richard White, *The Roots of Dependency: Subsistence, Environment, and Social Change among the Choctaws, Pawnees, and Navajos* (1983).

Pittman, Gail Jones

(b. 1951) Artist and Businesswoman

Ceramic artist Gail Jones Pittman was born on 1 May 1951, the second child of Patsy Farmer Jones and Walker William Jones Jr. She lived in Indianola, where her parents operated a construction business, Walker Jones Equipment, until the family moved to Jackson when she was five.

Jones graduated from Murrah High School and earned a bachelor's degree in elementary education from the University of Mississippi. She married John R. Pittman, with whom she had attended high school, and settled in Jackson, where she taught for five years in the public school system before leaving the workforce to raise her two children.

After seeing an Italian ceramic bowl at a local shop, she decided that she wanted to become a potter and in 1979 embarked on a new adventure at her kitchen table. During the early 1980s Pittman sold her creations to friends, at the

Canton flea market, and at the Everyday Gourmet, a Jackson gift store operated by her friend, Carol Daily. By 1986 Pittman's business had outgrown her home, and she purchased a fifteen-hundred-square foot studio space and a commercial kiln and hired three employees. Gail Pittman Designs was born. She soon brought in a business partner, Thomas Maley, and they acquired a seventy-eight-hundred-square-foot studio. By 1992 the business moved to Ridgeland, where she eventually employed more than one hundred people. All of the clay and paint used in her products are made on site at her studio. Pittman's hand-painted dinnerware and accessories are known for their bright, colorful motifs, which include whimsical graphic patterns as well as more traditional designs with flowers and fruit.

Pittman continues to serve as president and CEO of Gail Pittman Designs. From 2005 to 2010 she also held the post of creative director for Southern Living at Home. She has received many awards, including the Ernst and Young 1993 Entrepreneur of the Year. In addition, Pittman is a philanthropist, donating a percentage of the profits from the sale of her Hope and Future collections to help rebuild the Mississippi Gulf Coast following Hurricane Katrina. Since 2002 she has also served on the board of directors of Sanderson Farms, the third-largest US poultry producer and the only member of the Fortune 1000 headquartered in Mississippi.

Linda Arrington

University of Mississippi

S. J. Anderson, *Mississippi Business Journal* (28 April 2008); Gail Pittman Designs website, gailpittman.com; Lynn Lofton, *Mississippi Business Journal* (16 October 2006); Kendra Myers, *Business First* (Spring 2006); Sanderson Farms website, www.sandersonfarms.com.

Pittman, Paul
(1931–1983) Journalist

Paul Howard Pittman, longtime editor and publisher of the *Tylertown Times*, was a prominent journalist, radio station manager, and political commentator during Mississippi's civil rights era. The son of Patrick Howard Pittman and Hattie Dean Pittman, he was born in Tylertown, in South Mississippi, on 13 March 1931 and grew up there, attending public schools. While in high school he worked as sports editor for the *Tylertown Times*, the local weekly newspaper. He attended Copiah-Lincoln Junior College in Wesson for a year before transferring to the University of Mississippi, where he was elected editor of the student newspaper, the *Mississippian*, and earned a bachelor's degree in journalism in 1952.

Pittman served in the US Navy during and after the Korean War. On 17 April 1955 he married Elizabeth Ann MacDonald of Memphis, with whom he went on to have three children. After leaving active military duty in 1957, Pittman purchased his hometown *Tylertown Times* and served for more than a quarter century as its editor-publisher.

Pittman produced what many considered one of the nation's best small-town newspapers. Serving a dairy community he called the Cream Pitcher of Mississippi, the *Times* won the Mississippi Press Association General Excellence Award for weekly newspapers for ten consecutive years. Pittman was frequently asked to cover national political events and interview national political leaders. He enjoyed telling individuals that he was with "the *Times*" and then watching their surprise at learning that he meant the *Tylertown Times*, not the *New York Times*. During the civil rights era his editorials advocated mutual tolerance, and he stressed the need for improvements to public education in the state.

In 1963 he began a weekly syndicated column, "Mississippi Outlook," which ultimately was picked up by more than forty-five newspapers across the state. Beginning in 1978, he also published the monthly *Paul Pittman Newsletter*, sharing his analysis and reflections on various political issues, contests, and leaders. He wrote an insightful essay, "Change in Mississippi and the Media," that was included in *Sense of Place: Mississippi* (1979) and that contained his reflections on the evolution of Mississippi's media during the civil rights period. Pittman also taught journalism classes at the University of Southern Mississippi. In 1969 Pittman established WTYL, Tylertown and Walthall County's first radio station.

Pittman loved both writing about and participating in politics. He was instrumental in organizing Mississippi's Young Democrats and served as the group's president in 1958, becoming an early supporter of John F. Kennedy's presidential campaign. He also served as publicist for Gov. J. P. Coleman's unsuccessful gubernatorial bid in 1963 and worked on William Winter's unsuccessful 1967 gubernatorial campaign.

In 1972 Pittman sought the Democratic nomination for Mississippi's 3rd Congressional District. His bid failed, and the seat was ultimately won by Republican Thad Cochran. Pittman subsequently confined himself to observing and writing about political activities. In this capacity, he often provided Election Night commentaries and other political analyses on Jackson television stations.

On 2 September 1983 Pittman died suddenly at his residence in Tylertown of an apparent heart attack. The Mississippi Press Association Hall of Fame included him among its inaugural group of inductees in 1986, and the following year Walthall County officials renamed the county airport, located three miles northwest of Tylertown, in his memory.

Lucius M. Lampton

Magnolia, Mississippi

Paul Pittman, in *Sense of Place: Mississippi*, ed. Peggy W. Prenshaw and Jesse O. McKee (1979); Paul Howard Pittman Manuscript Collection, Mississippi Department of Archives and History; *Paul Pittman Newsletter*, April 1978–August 1983; Eric Stringfellow, *Jackson Clarion-Ledger* (4 September 1983); *Tylertown Times* (8 September 1983).

Where the Spanish moss grows, Pascagoula, ca. 1907 (Ann Rayburn Paper Americana Collection, Department of Archives and Special Collections, J. D. Williams Library, University of Mississippi [rayburn_ann_36_35_001])

Plants, Native

Mississippi has a diverse native flora of more than 2,700 plant species, including approximately 217 nonvascular plants, 72 ferns and fern allies, 11 conifers, and more than 2,400 flowering plants.

Forests dominate the natural landscape in much of Mississippi and include approximately 200 native tree species. Of these, the pines are among the most familiar and abundant. Virginia pine (*Pinus virginiana*) can be found in northeastern Mississippi. Loblolly (*P. taeda*) and shortleaf pines (*P. echinata*) are common in central Mississippi, while longleaf (*P. palustris*) and slash pines (*P. elliotii*) are more common in the south. Sand pine (*P. clausa)* is found in well-drained, sandy soils near the coast. The spruce pine (*P. glabra*) is relatively shade-tolerant, grows in moist soils, and is often scattered among hardwoods.

The hardwood forests of the northern and central part of the state include many species of oaks and hickories. Common oak species include the white (*Quercus alba*), northern red (*Q. rubra*), post (*Q. stellata*), southern red (*Q. falcata*), cherrybark (*Q. pagoda*), water (*Q. nigra*), and willow oaks (*Q. phellos*). These trees share the canopy with various species of hickory, including mockernut (*Carya alba*), pignut (*C. glabra*), and sand hickories (*C. pallida*), as well as other hardwoods such as the tulip tree (*Liriodendron tulipifera*), red maple (*Acer rubrum*), black gum (*Nyssa sylvatica*), sweet gum (*Liquidambar styraciflua*), and American sycamore (*Platanus occidentalis*). Common understory trees of the deciduous forests include the eastern redbud (*Cercis canadensis*), flowering dogwood (*Cornus florida*), sassafras (*Sassafras albidum*), and common pawpaw (*Asimina triloba*).

Along the coast the southern live oak (*Q. virginiana*) is a dominant feature of the landscape. These evergreen oaks have wide-spreading branches that often sweep close to the ground before curving upward again. Tolerant of salt spray and able to resist strong winds, many of these trees are centuries old, having survived countless storms.

For many people the image of swamps teeming with wildlife is emblematic of native Mississippi. Bald cypress (*Taxodium distichum*) and tupelo gum (*Nyssa aquatica*) dominate the swamps found in flooded areas along major river systems and in the Delta. Their branches are often draped gracefully with Spanish moss (*Tillandsia usneoides*), not a true moss but rather a flowering plant of the pineapple family.

Mississippi has designated the southern magnolia (*Magnolia grandiflora*) as its state flower. This elegant species is, however, only one of six native magnolias, all of which bear attractive flowers. Whereas the southern magnolia is evergreen, the cucumber tree (*M. acuminata*), bigleaf magnolia (*M. macrophylla*), pyramid magnolia (*M. pyramidata*), and umbrella magnolia (*M. tripetala*) are deciduous. The sweetbay magnolia (*M. virginiana*) retains its leaves throughout much of the winter, becoming evergreen toward the south.

Among the state's most unusual natives are its four genera of carnivorous plants, the pitcher plants (*Sarracenia*), sundews (*Drosera*), butterworts (*Pinguicula*), and bladderworts (*Utricularia*). These carnivorous plants typically inhabit wet, acidic environments where nitrogen and other nutrients are in short supply. They obtain supplemental nutrients by capturing and digesting insects or other small organisms. Pitcher plants capture insects in fluid-filled pitchers, each of which is actually a modified leaf. Insects are attracted to nectar secreted at the rim of the pitcher, which is equipped with downward-pointing hairs that make it difficult for the insect to crawl back out. If the insect falls into the fluid at the base of the pitcher, it is decomposed by digestive enzymes. Pitcher plants native to Mississippi include yellow trumpets (*Sarracenia alata*) and the crimson (*S. leucophylla*), parrot (*S. psittacina*), purple (*S. purpurea*), and sweet pitcher plants (*S. rubra*).

Sundews and butterworts trap insects on sticky secretions on their leaves, which release digestive enzymes and absorb nutrients from the prey. Like the pitcher plants, they are found primarily in the Coastal Plain. The dwarf (*Drosera brevifolia*), pink (*D. capillaris*), spoonleaf (*D. intermedia*), roundleaf (*D. rotundifolia*), and Tracy's (*D. tracyi*) sundews are native to Mississippi, as are the yellow (*Pinguicula lutea*), Chapman's (*P. planifolia*), southern (*P. primuliflora*), and small (*P. pumila*) butterworts.

Bladderworts are found in aquatic habitats throughout the state. They are named for the bladderlike suction traps they use to capture and digest small aquatic organisms. The motion of an organism against hairlike projections near the mouth of the trap triggers a change in the shape of the bladder that sucks the animal inside. Species native to Mississippi include the horned (*Utricularia cornuta*), leafy (*U. foliosa*), humped (*U. gibba*), swollen (*U. inflata*), southern (*U. juncea*), piedmont (*U. olivacea*), eastern purple (*U. purpurea*), little floating (*U. radiata*), and zigzag (*U. subulata*) bladderworts.

Mississippi's rarest native plants include four species that are federally listed under the Endangered Species Act of 1973: Price's potato-bean, which is listed as threatened, and the American chaffseed, Louisiana quillwort, and pondberry, which are listed as endangered. Price's potato-bean (*Apios priceana*), also known as traveler's delight, is a scrambling vine associated with rich, calcareous forests in the Black Prairie region. It produces a large, edible tuber that may have been used by Native Americans and early settlers. The American chaffseed (*Schwalbea americana*) is an upright perennial herb with purple to yellow flowers that produce slender seeds with a loose chafflike coat. Partially parasitic, the chaffseed taps into the roots of various other plant species. It is adapted to live in acidic, sandy, or peaty soil in areas that are kept open by fires. The Louisiana quillwort (*Isoetes louisianensis*) is an aquatic fern ally. It lives along streams, where it roots under water in sand or gravel. Pondberry (*Lindera melissifolia*) is a small deciduous shrub that grows along pond margins or seasonally flooded wetlands. The name refers to the bright red fruits that are produced in the fall. In addition to reproducing by seeds, the pondberry frequently reproduces vegetatively, sending up new shoots from underground stolons.

Discovered in 2004, the big-leaf witch-hazel (*Hamamelis ovalis*) apparently exists only in a small area in southern Mississippi. Its large ovate leaves and red flower color distinguish it from the more widely distributed witch-hazel, *H. virginiana*.

Debora L. Mann
Millsaps College

Heather Sullivan
Jackson, Mississippi

S. W. Leonard, *Sida* (2006); Mississippi Department of Wildlife, Fisheries, and Parks website, www.mdwfp.com; *NatureServe Explorer: An Online Encyclopedia of Life*, www.natureserve.org/explorer; US Department of Agriculture, National Plant Data Center website, http://plants .usda.gov; US Department of Agriculture, National Forest Service website, www.fs.fed.us.

Player, Willa B.
(1909–2003) Educator

Born in Jackson, Mississippi, on 9 August 1909, Willa Beatrice Player became the first African American female president of a four-year institution in the nation. Player moved to Akron, Ohio, in 1917 with her family. She attended Ohio Wesleyan College and went on to earn a master's from Oberlin College before being hired to teach Latin and French at Bennett College in Greensboro, North Carolina. While teaching at Bennett, Player continued her studies, earning a doctoral degree in education from Columbia University in 1948. In 1956 she became president of Bennett College.

In 1958, just after the Montgomery Bus Boycott, Player and Bennett College were approached to host Dr. Martin Luther King Jr. in a speaking engagement. Though many institutions in the area were also approached, only Player agreed to host the civil rights leader. King's speech led students at the historically black women's college to form a protest group, the Bennett Belles. Managing a difficult relationship between faculty and the young female activists, Player fully supported her students and their commitment to civil rights. She continued to back the Bennett Belles after they were arrested and jailed, bringing them food and blankets and holding classes at the jail. Player chose not to participate in the protests so that the student activists would have an advocate who was not inside the jail. She also communicated with the students' parents.

She left Bennett College in 1966 and became an administrator with the US Department of Health, Education, and Welfare (later the Department of Health and Human Services). During Richard Nixon's presidency, Player served as the director for the Department of Institutional Development, Bureau of Postsecondary Education in the Office of Education. She retired in 1986 and died on 27 August 2003.

Kathryn McGaw York
University of Mississippi

African American Registry website, www.aaregistry.org; Margaret L. Dwight and George A. Sewell, *Mississippi Black History Makers* (1984); Greensboro Sit-Ins: Launch of a Civil Rights Movement website, www .sitins.com; Darlene Clark Hine, ed., *Black Women in America: An Historical Encyclopedia* (2005); Willa Player, interview by Eugene Pfaff (3 December 1979), Civil Rights Digital Library website, crdl.usg.edu.

P

Pleasant Reed House

Pleasant Reed was born a slave to Charlotte and Benjamin Reed in 1854 on a Perry County plantation owned by John B. Reed. After emancipation, members of the Reed family began to leave Perry County and settle in Biloxi, and in 1869 Pleasant Reed joined them.

On 23 January 1884 Reed married Georgia Anna Harris, a Louisiana native who spoke both English and a French Creole dialect and could read and write. Pleasant Reed worked as a carpenter and made fishnets that the family sold to Gulf Coast fishermen. The couple had five children: Manuel, Victoria, Percy, Theresa, and Paul. In May 1887 Reed purchased land on Elmer Street in Biloxi from Jacob Elmer and began to construct a house on the site. It is one of the first documented houses built and owned outright by a freed slave in Biloxi.

Now known as the Pleasant Reed House, the structure was an altered side-hall, camelback Creole cottage with three rooms running off of the side hall. This design was a well-established regional form that allowed for both cross-ventilation and privacy in a small space. The interior of the house was finished with both vertical bead board and white-washed walls. Reed later added an attached kitchen, a *garçonnière* (a camelback room over the kitchen that served as a boy's bedroom), and a variety of decorative details, including a spindle frieze running across the front porch as well as factory-made furniture and an icebox. Such luxuries indicated the family's increasing financial stability, and by 1908 the Reeds were one of Biloxi's most prosperous African American families.

Georgia Reed died in 1933, while Pleasant Reed died three years later. Their daughter, Therese Reed, lived in the house until the 1970s, by which time it had fallen into disrepair. The Mississippi Gulf Coast Alumnae Chapter of Delta Sigma Theta Sorority took ownership of the house in 1978 and worked to have it restored. In 2000 the sorority donated the house to the Ohr-O'Keefe Museum of Art in Biloxi, which moved the structure from Elmer Street to the museum campus on Beach Boulevard/Highway 90 to increase visibility and access. The Reed House was restored to its ca. 1910 appearance and opened as a museum in May 2003.

On 29 August 2005 Hurricane Katrina destroyed the Pleasant Reed House as well as most of its collection of furniture and interior decorations. However, the extensive archives related to the house, including tax records, contracts, and receipts and bills, were saved and remain in the Ohr-O'Keefe Museum of Art collection. In 2008 the Ohr-O'Keefe Museum of Art completed construction of the Pleasant Reed Interpretive Center, a replica of the house utilized to further the "cultural and educational" importance of the Reed legacy.

Anna Stanfield Harris
Biloxi, Mississippi

The Buildings of Biloxi: An Architectural Survey (2000); John Hopkins and Marsha, *No Two Alike* (2003); Ohr-O'Keefe Museum of Art website, www.georgeohr.org; Beth L. Savage and Carol D. Shull, eds., *African American Historic Places* (1994).

Plummer, Franklin E.
(ca. 1795–1847) Politician

Franklin E. Plummer, a Democratic Party leader in the 1830s, was born in Richmond, Massachusetts, around 1795, the son of Edward Plummer and Esther Raymond Plummer. Earning his passage as a deck hand, Plummer arrived in New Orleans in 1821 or 1822. After a brief stay there and in Pearlington, Mississippi, Plummer settled on land recently ceded to the United States by the Choctaw Indians. He liked to boast that he had delivered the wagonload of logs used to build the first cabin in Jackson, Mississippi.

His connections in the new capital led to his appointment as postmaster at Westville in Copiah County (later Simpson County). Plummer briefly taught school and studied law. He was admitted to the bar in 1825. In 1826 Simpson County elected Plummer to the State House of Representatives, where he served three terms. An effective parliamentarian and orator, Plummer established his credentials as an advocate for the common people by favoring public schools, fair taxation, and internal improvements while opposing the chancery court system and property restrictions for office. His special targets in the House and on the campaign trail were the "swell-heads," the plantation elite from the Mississippi River counties.

Having earned the backing of the settlers of the newly opened territory and the Piney Woods, Plummer won election to the US House of Representatives in 1830 with the campaign slogan, "Plummer for the People, and the People for Plummer." He served two terms in the House. In Washington, Plummer followed an unconventional path in that era of political party formation. He opposed Andrew Jackson's Force Bill against South Carolina and spoke against Martin Van Buren's ambitions to succeed Jackson. But Plummer also tenaciously defended Jackson in his fight with the Bank of the United States. And he continued to articulate a sincere but undeveloped concern for common working men against the wealthy who would deny them their freedom of opportunity.

In 1836 Plummer sought to succeed George Poindexter in the US Senate. Angry that Robert J. Walker had received the Democratic Party's approval, Plummer made a deal with the anti-Jackson Whig forces even though the Democrats incorporated many of his political stances. Whig legislators subsequently betrayed Plummer and supported Poindexter's reelection. Albert Gallatin Brown and other rising politicians proved more effective in representing the developing counties within the Democratic Party and the legislature.

Plummer quickly faded from public view. He relocated to Yalobusha County, practiced law, and became president of a small bank that failed. Plummer died in Jackson on 21 September 1847, according the *Natchez Courier*, "in great destitution."

M. Philip Lucas
Cornell College

Biographical Directory of the United States Congress (1950); J. F. H. Claiborne, *Mississippi as a Province, Territory, and State* (1880); Edwin A. Miles, *Journal of Mississippi History* (January 1952).

Plumpp, Sterling D.
(b. 1940) Poet

Born on 30 January 1940, poet Sterling D. Plumpp grew up on a tenant farm in Clinton, Mississippi. His family moved to Jackson in 1954. As a child, Plumpp tended cotton and corn and anticipated a future in the fields. However, his aunt used her bootlegging money to send Plumpp to Jackson's Holy Ghost High School in Jackson. With the help of a scholarship, he attended St. Benedict's College in Atchison, Kansas, for two years. He began to read James Baldwin's works, which prompted him to experiment with writing. In 1962 Plumpp hitchhiked to Chicago to study psychology at Roosevelt University. Following the example of other Mississippi writers, Plumpp worked in a Chicago post office while writing poetry. He was drafted and served in the US Army from 1964 to 1965. He then returned to Roosevelt University, earning bachelor's and master's degrees in psychology.

In 1969 Plumpp published his first book of poetry, *Portable Soul*, which reflects the upheavals of the time. He followed with more books of poetry as well as prose and essays. Most of his writings are grounded in Mississippi or elsewhere in the South, and he examines the African American experience through psychology, perseverance, and adaptation in a changing world. He is best known for his blues and jazz poetry, as in *Blues: The Story Always Untold* (1989), *Horn Man* (1995), and *Home/Bass: Poems* (2013). His works fuse blues and jazz rhythms with poetic insight, bringing to life the vernacular landscape of African American poetry. Plumpp also edited *Somehow We Survive: An Anthology of South African Writing* (1982), as an antiapartheid gesture. His *Johannesburg and Other Poems* (1993) compares the African American and South African realities.

Plumpp taught English and African American studies at the University of Illinois at Chicago from 1971 until his retirement in December 2001. He has subsequently traveled in South Africa and Mississippi, conducting workshops and teaching part-time. He has also worked as an editor for Third World Press and the Institute for Positive Education, served as poet in residence at Evanston School in Illinois, directed the Young Writer's Workshop for Urban Gateways, and been a visiting professor at Chicago State University. He has tirelessly supported and encouraged aspiring writers.

Plumpp's poems and his prose work, *Black Rituals* (1972), have won three Illinois Arts Council Literary Awards. *The Mojo Hands Call, I Must Go* (1982) received the 1983 Carl Sandburg Literary Award. Plumpp also earned the 1999 Richard Wright Literary Excellence Award. Other notable works by Plumpp include *Half Black, Half Blacker* (1970), *Muslim Men* (1972), *Steps to Break the Circle* (1974), *Clinton* (1976), and *Ornate with Smoke* (1997).

Anna F. Kaplan
Columbia University

Dorothy Abbott, ed., *Mississippi Writers: Reflections of Childhood and Youth* (1988); Poetry Foundation website, www.poetryfoundation.org; History Makers website, www.thehistorymakers.com; Sterling Plumpp Collection, Department of Archives and Special Collections, J. D. Williams Library, University of Mississippi; John Zheng, ed., *Conversations with Sterling Plumpp* (2016).

Poetry

In 1979, in the preface to *An Anthology of Mississippi Writers*, Noel Polk and James Scafidel observed, "It is simply incredible to consider even the sheer number of writers that in one way or another are products of this state, not to say the number of really first-rate ones: Nobel Prize winner William Faulkner; Pulitzer Prize winners Eudora Welty, Hodding Carter, and Tennessee Williams; National Book Award winner Walker Percy; as well as a host of established writers of national and international literary significance—Stark Young, Richard Wright, Elizabeth Spencer, Irwin Russell, and Shelby Foote—and younger writers like Barry Hannah . . . looming large on the literary horizon." An observer of Mississippi's literary landscape in the early twenty-first century would no doubt agree with this assertion made in the latter part of the twentieth. Of course, the later observer would no doubt add a number of names to the list, among them Ellen Douglas, Willie Morris, Ellen Gilchrist, Larry Brown, and John Grisham. But of all these writers, only one,

Irwin Russell, is a poet. The others are noted for their prose fiction, their nonfiction prose, or their plays. And Russell, a nineteenth-century poet who died at the age of twenty-six, left behind fewer than fifty poems. Though Faulkner, Carter, Gilchrist, Wright, Williams, and others published poems, their reputations clearly rest on their successes in other genres. To most of the world's readers, the literature of Mississippi is a literature of prose and drama.

But Mississippi has produced a number of outstanding poets. And while their poems may not have garnered the prestigious prizes ticked off by Polk and Scafidel, the cumulative effect has been impressive.

Russell had at least as much influence on later authors as any other nineteenth-century Mississippi writer. His best-known poem, "Christmas Night in the Quarters," with its use of African American dialect and its depiction of plantation life, was acknowledged by both Thomas Nelson Page and Joel Chandler Harris as a guiding light in their work. Indeed, Russell's poem may be said to have played a part in the continuing tradition of plantation literature and its various offshoots, and his influence, filtered through Page, Harris, and others, resurfaces in a number of later writers.

Another nineteenth-century poet of considerable importance, Eliza Jane Poitevant Nicholson, published under the pseudonym Pearl Rivers, which she adopted from the river that she knew as a youngster. Like Russell, Nicholson did not live a long life (she died in her late forties), although her literary influence cannot be compared to his. However, Nicholson's achievements as a newspaper editor, a traditionally male-dominated profession, point to some of the salient themes in her poetry. In "Hagar," her best-known poem, she provides the biblical outcast with a strong, vibrant, and denunciatory voice. Hagar decries the wrong done to her, and her words speak to the struggles women faced in Nicholson's time.

The twentieth century produced a good many more notable Mississippi poets. Arranging these writers into groups eases the task of grasping their varying achievements and shared affinities. One such grouping would include William Alexander Percy, Hodding Carter Jr., Charles G. Bell, and Brooks Haxton, all of them natives of Greenville except for the Louisiana-born Carter, who moved to the Mississippi town in the 1930s and lived there for the remainder of his life. Percy, a lawyer, played an active role in the affairs of his city, his state, and indeed his country. His best-known literary achievement is undoubtedly *Lanterns on the Levee*, his autobiography, but he also published poetry throughout his life, and *The Collected Poems of William Alexander Percy* appeared in 1943, a year after his death. Although Percy's interest in classical literature can be seen in the title of his first volume, *Sappho in Levkas, and Other Poems*, he turned often to the Delta for subject matter. Carter, an award-winning newspaper editor, also used the Delta and events there as material for his poetry. Some of his poems, such as "Flood Song," use dialect and owe a debt to Russell; other poems draw on the Delta social and political happenings that Carter chronicled in his newspaper.

Both Bell and Haxton have spent their adult years away from Greenville, but it and the Delta figure in their work. Bell devotes a section of his "The Journey Down" to "The Queen City of the Delta" and in other poems writes of "The River" and "The Flood" and "the glimmering swirls of Delta night, our home." Haxton, son of novelist Ellen Douglas (Josephine Ayres Haxton), has taught for many years in New York, and his poems, often long, deal with a wide range of subjects, most notably Mississippi and in particular the civil rights struggles of Greenville in his youth. "Limpopo, Orinoco, or Yazoo," the first poem in *The Sun at Night*, demonstrates Haxton's wide-ranging imagination as well as his use of Delta material. His poems "Justice" and "I Live to See Strom Thurmond Head the Judiciary Committee" explore the tensions of Mississippi in the 1960s.

If Percy can be seen as the patriarch of the Greenville poets, then Margaret Walker Alexander is the matriarch of a lengthy list of poets, many of them still working today. Inspired and encouraged by Langston Hughes, Alexander embarked on a long and distinguished career as a poet while still in her teens. In 1942 Alexander's *For My People* was chosen for the Yale Series of Younger Poets. The title poem begins,

> For my people everywhere singing their slave songs
> repeatedly: their dirges and their ditties and their blues
> and jubilees, praying their prayers nightly to an
> unknown god, bending their knees humbly to an
> unseen power.

Alexander spent the remainder of her career chronicling the African American experience in verse (and in her 1966 novel, *Jubilee*). Poems such as "Jackson, Mississippi," "For Andy Goodman, Michael Schwerner, and James Chaney," and "A Poem for Farish Street" show her continuing engagement with her chosen subject matter. In addition, her work and career as a teacher influenced other African American poets.

While Alexander remains the best-known African American poet with Mississippi connections, a number of others achieved recognition in the second half of the twentieth century, following the injunction that concludes "For My People": "Let a new race of men now rise and take control." Etheridge Knight, Al Young, Sterling Plumpp, and Jerry Ward Jr. are four such men. A quick survey of titles reveals the direction of their work: Knight's "A Poem for Myself (Or Blues for a Mississippi Black Boy)" and "Once on a Night in the Delta: A Report from Hell"; Young's "Pachuta, Mississippi/A Memoir" and "The Blues Don't Change"; Plumpp's "Blues" and "I Hear the Shuffle of the People's Feet"; and Ward's "Don't Be Fourteen (in Mississippi)" and "Jazz to Jackson to John." Nayo-Barbara Watkins and Angela Jackson (another poet born in Greenville) have also heeded Alexander's advice and have earned distinction with their poems about identity (Watkins's "Do You Know Me?" and "Mama's Children"), music (Jackson's "Make/n My Music"), and place (Jackson's "Greenville").

The careers of Hubert Creekmore, Charles Henri Ford, J. Edgar Simmons, and Turner Cassity occurred largely outside Mississippi. All four traveled far from their home state, and those foreign travels played a role in their poetic achievements. Creekmore, a novelist, translator, and editor, wrote most of his poetry in the early part of his career. His best-known book of poems, *The Long Reprieve and Other Poems from New Caledonia*, reflects in its title his experiences during World War II. Ford is remembered for his connections to Gertrude Stein, Paris, and the literary and artistic avant-garde in the early 1930s. After returning to the United States, Ford lived in New York City, where he continued his career as a writer, editor, and translator and developed an interest in the visual arts. He has been hailed as the first surrealist poet produced by the United States. Simmons studied in Paris and traveled throughout the British Isles before teaching at various US colleges and universities. His poems cover such topics as a Mississippi feed and seed store, William Faulkner, and a deranged GI named Osiris. Cassity, born in Jackson, credits his time in the US Army, his stint as a librarian in South Africa, and his love of travel as major influences on his work, an assertion supported by such poems as "Manchuria 1931," "Two Hymns" (with its subsections "The Afrikaners in the Argentine" and "Confederates in Brazil"), and "In Sydney by the Bridge."

Two poets with strong ties to Northeast Mississippi are James Autry and Elmo Howell. Autry's poems, built on the roots of his Benton County past, examine the rituals and everyday events of a largely disappearing rural world. His poems show the rites of a baptism in the country as well as an "All Day Singing with Dinner on the Grounds." "Genealogy" contrasts the ways of life and the interconnections of old families and old times with "new families and new names." Howell, a native of Itawamba County, taught for many years at universities in Alabama and Tennessee. After retirement he produced several travel books about Mississippi that focus on the state's literature and history. Howell's poems also deal with villages and hamlets and with their associated characters, some famous, some not. For example, *Tuesday's Letter* features William Faulkner, Eudora Welty, Nathan Bedford Forrest, and Miss Sudie from Maben, who flew with Lindbergh in 1923.

William Mills, James Whitehead, James Seay, T. R. Hummer, John Freeman, and D. C. Berry came of age after World War II. All are clearly products of the state, although their styles and subject matter vary. Perusing Mills's "Our Fathers at Corinth," Whitehead's "Delta Farmer in a Wet Summer," Seay's "Grabbling in Yocona Bottom," Hummer's "The Rural Carrier Admires Neil Varner's Brand New Convertible," and Freeman's "A Barn in the Morning Light" provides the reader with a thumbnail sketch of Mississippi's social and natural history. Likewise, Berry, another poet with connections to

Greenville, deals with landscape and destiny in his "Dusk between Vicksburg and Rolling Fork" and with nature in such poems as "Bass," "Setter," and "Quail." Berry's first volume of poems, *Saigon Cemetery*, grew out of his stint in Vietnam in the late 1960s.

Two other poets who were born outside the state have developed strong ties to Mississippi. Ohio native Angela Ball has taught at the University of Southern Mississippi since 1979; her poetry ranges over a wide field of topics. In *The Museum of the Revolution* Ball creates fifty-eight "exhibits" that provide a tour of the controversial island nation of Cuba; *Quartet* includes four long poems in the voices of Sylvia Beach, Nora Joyce, Nancy Cunard, and Jean Rhys. Elsewhere in her work, Ball writes about Byron, Shelley, Baudelaire, Rimbaud, and Apollinaire, among others. But she also "studies the habits of rivers," both those far away ("The Seine draped in its heavy jewelry") and those closer to Mississippi ("The Leaf, striated and mysterious / Plied by pairs of beavers.") Born in South Carolina and raised in Kentucky, Aleda Shirley lived in Mississippi for nearly two decades before her death in 2008. Her three volumes of poems contain images from various parts of the world, including the South. Mississippi appears in lines that describe driving "at night along the Gulf Coast, through Bay St. Louis / and Pass Christian and Biloxi." The first poem in *Dark Familiar*, "The Star's Etruscan Argument," set in Neshoba County, "in the hotel of a casino / on an Indian reservation in the deep south," reveals significant changes in her adopted state.

Near the turn of the twenty-first century, two Mississippi poets launched promising careers. Published in 1998, Claude Wilkinson's *Reading the Earth* won the Naomi Long Madgett Poetry Award. The poems explore nature and place and are products of Wilkinson's early years, spent on a farm in DeSoto County. The title of Wilkinson's next volume, *Joy in the Morning*, indicates the continuation of his interest in biblical imagery and religious activity. Wilkinson is also a visual artist whose paintings and drawings have been exhibited widely.

Natasha Trethewey has published four volumes of poetry since 2000. Her third collection, *Native Guard* (2006) won the Pulitzer Prize for Poetry. Trethewey's poems explore in various ways the African American experience in her native Mississippi and in the South. *Domestic Work*, her first volume, offers poems about the Owl Club in North Gulfport in 1950 and the Naola Beauty Academy in New Orleans in 1945. Her second volume, *Bellocq's Ophelia*, chronicles the life of a mixed-race prostitute in New Orleans's infamous Storyville. *Native Guard* includes poems about the Louisiana Native Guards, one of the first black regiments called into service during the Civil War. Other poems in the book depict her family and its history, while "Southern History" and "Southern Gothic" continue her exploration of the past. In 2012 she was named poet laureate both of Mississippi and of the United States.

P

Perhaps the fact that a Mississippi poet rather than a Mississippi novelist is a recent recipient of a Pulitzer Prize indicates that Mississippi poets are finally earning wider recognition and respect. Their accomplishments over the past 150 years should draw more readers. Their poems show the harsh history, the natural beauty, the songs and stories, the blues and the jazz, the voices and faces and places, the bitter defeats and the human triumphs of this always fascinating state.

Michael P. Dean
University of Mississippi

Dorothy Abbott, ed., *Mississippi Writers: An Anthology* (1991).

Pohl, Emma Ody
(1880–1966) Educator

Emma Ody Pohl was a popular physical education teacher at the Mississippi Industrial Institute and College (later Mississippi State College for Women and now Mississippi University for Women) from 1907 to 1955. Pohl became revered, sometimes feared, and ultimately beloved for the Zouave drill and dance teams that she oversaw. The length of her tenure and the intensity and caring of her instruction made Pohl one of the most legendary figures in the history of the W.

Pohl was born on 17 December 1880 in Greenville. In 1907 Henry Lewis Whitfield, president of Mississippi Industrial Institute and College, hired Pohl to create a physical education and recreation program. She immediately became a force of energy and change by developing various dance classes, organizing the school's May Day ceremonies, and reforming the Junior-Freshman Wedding Pageant from a burlesque romp into a serious occasion affirming sisterhood and loyalty to the college. Under Pohl's leadership, physical education courses became mandatory for all students, and the school hired two assistants to fill out the department. When Whitfield left the college in 1920, he singled out Pohl's efforts as the most important factor in the development of a "distinctive college spirit" at the W.

Pohl developed the Zouave routines from French military demonstrations she had studied in Chicago during a summer training program for physical education teachers. Beginning in 1912, Pohl's Zouaves performed annually before the entire school. Pohl's dancers ate a strict diet, endured marathon training sessions, and lived under the critical eye of their indomitable mentor. The hard work paid off in the form of splendid performances that gave the col-

lege a unique identity and its own set of traditions. Dancers played a particularly prominent role in the performances and received the most attention from Pohl, but the entire student body eventually participated in the extravaganzas. The Zouave drills became so popular that they brought alumnae, parents, and relatives to the college from all over the state.

Pohl retired in 1955, and the Zouave performances retired with her. She lived her remaining years at the Alexandria Hotel in Clinton, frequently visiting the alumnae office at Mississippi State College for Women and attending chapter meetings of the school's alumnae association all over the state. She died in Clinton in June 1966. The W has honored Pohl in numerous ways. The Pohl Gymnasium was named in her honor in 1947, in 1964 the Carrier Chapel was dedicated to her, and in 1976 the school erected the seventy-five-thousand-square-foot Emma Ody Pohl Education Assembly Building.

Thomas John Carey
University of Mississippi

Columbus Commercial Dispatch (6 December 2006); Bridget Smith Pieschel and Stephen Robert Pieschel, *Loyal Daughters: One Hundred Years at Mississippi University for Women, 1884–1984* (1984).

Poindexter, George
(1779–1853) Second Governor, 1820–1822

A contemporary historian wrote that the history of George Poindexter's public career is "the history of the Territory and the State of Mississippi, so closely and prominently was he connected with everything that occurred." Poindexter, who was born in Louisa County, Virginia, on 19 April 1779, received an irregular education even by the standards of the time and practiced law in Richmond before migrating to Natchez in 1802 to escape the mounting demands of his creditors. He opened a successful law practice and then launched a long and distinguished political career, serving as a delegate to the territorial assembly, attorney general of the Mississippi Territory, a territorial judge, and a territorial representative to the US Congress, US congressman, and US senator. Poindexter was elected president pro tempore of the US Senate in 1834.

Poindexter arrived in the Mississippi Territory in December 1802. Less than a year later, despite—or perhaps at least in part because of—Poindexter's propensity to gamble and drink, Gov. W. C. C. Claiborne appointed him the territory's attorney general on 19 November 1803. By that time Poindexter had also made a lifelong enemy of Andrew Marschalk, the founder of Mississippi's first newspaper, the *Washington Republican*.

In July 1806 Poindexter represented Adams County in the territory's general assembly. He also served as a captain in the successful march to Natchitoches on 2–14 October 1806 to ward off the encroaching Spaniards. When Col. Aaron Burr, who had been accused of treason, made camp across the Mississippi River from Natchez in January 1807, acting governor Cowles Mead sent a group of men, including Poindexter, to bring Burr into town for questioning. As attorney general, Poindexter concluded that Mississippi Territory authorities had no jurisdiction over the area where Burr had settled and that the charges against Burr therefore had to be dismissed. When the courts overturned Poindexter's ruling, he disassociated himself with any further proceedings in the case.

In February 1807 the territorial legislature elected Poindexter as the Mississippi Territory's delegate to the US Congress. On 7 February he resigned as attorney general and prepared to go to Washington, D.C. He stopped in Richmond, Virginia, in October to appear in court as a witness in Burr's federal trial for treason. As a territorial delegate, Poindexter could not vote in Congress, so during his first term he took part only in matters directly concerning Mississippi Territory. However, he proved more vocal in his second and third terms, speaking out on subjects not pertaining directly to Mississippi. He also laid the groundwork for statehood by forming a committee to oversee the process and proposing the Mississippi River as the divide between the Orleans and Mississippi Territories.

In June 1811, during one of his periodic visits to Mississippi, Poindexter killed a longtime enemy, Abijah Hunt, in a duel, spurring questions about Poindexter's supposedly honorable conduct that plagued him for the remainder of his life. By the end of his third term as the Mississippi delegate in 1813, Poindexter's numerous achievements included stretching the territory's boundary to the Gulf Coast and paving the way for statehood. After refusing a fourth term as delegate, he was appointed a federal district judge for Mississippi, serving from 1813 to 1817.

During Poindexter's tenure as a federal judge, his feud with Marschalk flared up. Marschalk smeared Poindexter's honor in his newspapers, and Poindexter had Marschalk jailed. An 1815 trial found Marschalk guilty of unsubstantiated defamation, and his unsavory writings about Poindexter subsided in fear of a violent physical retaliation.

When delegate William Lattimore obtained permission in Congress for Mississippi to become a state in March 1817, Poindexter left his judgeship to become a congressional representative and delegate to the territory's constitutional convention. Poindexter took charge of creating Mississippi's state constitution, assigning himself to every committee and practically writing it himself. On 15 August 1817 all the delegates to the constitutional convention except two signed the new state constitution and sent it to Washington, D.C., where it was approved. Mississippi became a state on 10 December 1817. Although that first constitution was replaced in 1832, it was one of the highlights of Poindexter's political career.

He later compiled the *Poindexter Code*, the state's first legal compendium. In 1819, while serving in the US Congress, Poindexter was elected as Mississippi's second governor. During Poindexter's administration the state capital was moved from Natchez to Jackson; the judicial system was restructured and a court of chancery was created; the militia was reorganized, enlarged, and strengthened; public assistance for indigent school children was established through the Literary Fund; and the second Choctaw land cession was finalized in 1820 under the Treaty of Doak's Stand.

Approximately two weeks after he was inaugurated, Gov. Poindexter signed a bill emancipating William Johnson, the famous Barber of Natchez. Johnson eventually became Mississippi's most famous and prosperous free black and often lent money to his white friends—including George Poindexter.

In 1822, rather than seeking reelection as governor, Poindexter ran for Congress but was defeated. After that setback, he practiced law in Jackson until his appointment to the US Senate in 1830. During the 1832–33 tariff controversy, Poindexter sided with John C. Calhoun against Pres. Andrew Jackson. In the other great national controversy of that period, Poindexter supported the rechartering of the national bank, a position that again placed him at odds with Jackson, for whom Poindexter had little regard. Some observers have credited Poindexter as the first person to use the term *kitchen cabinet* to describe Jackson's closest advisers.

This opposition to Jackson, who was immensely popular in Mississippi, caused Poindexter's defeat for reappointment to the US Senate in 1835. After living for a short while in Lexington, Kentucky, he returned to establish his law office in Jackson, where he watched his fame dwindle until he was virtually forgotten. In 1840 he ceremoniously gave a portrait of himself to the State of Mississippi. He died on 5 September 1853.

David G. Sansing
University of Mississippi

Anna F. Kaplan
Columbia University

Robert Bailey, *Journal of Mississippi History* (August 1973); *Biographical Directory of the United States Congress* (1950); *Mississippi Official and Statistical Register* (1912); P. L. Rainwater, *Journal of Southern History* (May 1938); Dunbar Rowland, *Encyclopedia of Mississippi History*, vol. 2 (1906); Allene Sugg, "The Senatorial Career of George Poindexter, 1830–1835" (master's thesis, University of Mississippi, 1950); Mack Buckley Swearingen, *The Early Life of George Poindexter: A Story of the First Southwest* (1934).

P

Polk, James K.

No US presidents are natives of Mississippi, but one, James K. Polk, owned substantial property in the state. Polk was born in North Carolina in 1795 and became a lawyer and politician in Tennessee. Though he never lived in Mississippi, from 1835 until his death in June 1849, he was one of the wealthiest owners of land and slaves in the Yalobusha County area. Six years after winning election to the US House of Representatives in 1825, Polk inherited land in in southwestern Tennessee and started a cotton plantation using slave labor. In 1835 he bought 920 acres in Yalobusha County. While living in Washington, D.C., and Tennessee, he and his wife, Sarah, made considerable income from the Mississippi plantation.

When Polk and his partner and brother-in-law, Silas Caldwell, started their Mississippi plantation, they sent twenty slaves—twelve adults and eight children—to start clearing the land. The Polk plantation had thirty-four slaves by 1840 and fifty-six at the time of Polk's death. As a slave owner, Polk aspired to the type of paternalism he associated with benevolence and responsibility. He had an overseer submit monthly reports, worried when slaves escaped or tried to escape, and occasionally stepped in to prevent slaves from being sold away from their family members. However, in at least one case, when Polk declined an offer to sell a slave named Caroline because he preferred "not to separate her from her family relations," he was actually refusing to sell a recently married woman who hoped to move to the neighboring plantation where her new husband lived. Thus, Polk's definition of "family relations" did not match that of the person involved.

Polk's slave-owning career is intriguing because it shows what a public figure found controversial about slavery and what he did not. First, as a political figure, he knew that the buying and selling of slaves was particularly unpopular, so he kept secret the fact that he bought at least nineteen slaves for his Mississippi plantation while serving as president (1845–49). In addition, his will provided that all of his slaves would be freed after he and his wife died. (Sarah Polk lived for more than forty years after her husband's death, by which time slavery had long since been abolished.) While privately planning to free his slaves, Polk much more publicly opposed the abolitionist movement and supported the expansion of the right to own slaves in the American West. He backed the gag order against discussing abolitionist petitions in the US Congress, and during his presidency, the United States went to war against Mexico for Texas, greatly expanding the amount of American territory in which slavery was legal.

Ted Ownby
University of Mississippi

Walter R. Borneman, *Polk: The Man Who Transformed the Presidency and America* (2008); William Dusinberre, *Slavemaster President: The Double Career of James Polk* (2003); John Seigenthaler, *James K. Polk* (2004); Charles Sellers, *James K. Polk, Continentalist, 1843–1846* (1966); Charles Sellers, *James K. Polk, Jacksonian, 1795–1843* (1957).

Polk, Noel
(1943–2012) Literary Scholar

Editor and scholar Noel Polk was born in Picayune, Mississippi, on 23 February 1943. He graduated from Picayune High School in 1961, earned bachelor's and master's degrees from Mississippi College, and then went on to receive a doctorate from the University of South Carolina in 1970. For more than twenty-five years Polk taught English at the University of Southern Mississippi and edited the *Southern Quarterly*. From 2004 to 2008 he taught English at Mississippi State University before retiring and becoming professor emeritus. Polk declared that his proudest accomplishment was working with Aubrey Lucas to create the Mississippi Institute of Arts and Letters, which, in his words, gives "actual cash money to Mississippi writers, musicians, photographers, painters, and sculptors."

Polk became one of the authoritative textual critics of the works of William Faulkner. Working from Faulkner's original and revised typescripts, Polk established the corrected texts of Faulkner's works. Polk figured out the nearly impossible—how Faulkner intended his works to be punctuated, phrased, and worded. Polk also published concordances of Faulkner's novels, wrote several book-length critical studies of Faulkner's prose, and coedited several others.

Faulkner's Requiem for a Nun: A Critical Study (1981) was Polk's earliest volume of Faulkner scholarship. In it, Polk argued that Temple Drake, rather than Nancy Mannigoe, stands at the moral center of the novel, that Mannigoe's infanticide is not morally justified, and that Gavin Stevens crucifies rather than saves Temple. Polk achieved his analysis by closely reading characters' actions, speech, and internal dialogue. Moreover, Polk explicated the chapters pertaining to the mythical and real history of Mississippi.

In 1996 Polk returned to Faulkner criticism with *Children of the Dark House: Text and Context in Faulkner*. This collection compiled ten of Polk's previously published essays, five of which had been presented at the annual Faulkner and Yoknapatawpha Conference at the University of Mississippi. Addressing works from the beginning, middle, and end of Faulkner's career, the collection was thorough, provocative, and firmly grounded in both text and context.

Beyond his Faulkner criticism, Polk published and edited work on a variety of southern authors, including *Eudora Welty: A Bibliography of Her Work* (1994). He also edited or coedited *An Anthology of Mississippi Writers* (1979), *Mississippi's Piney Woods: A Human Perspective* (1986), *Natchez before 1930* (1989), and Robert Penn Warren's *All the King's Men: Restored Edition* (2001). In a 1997 autobiography, *Outside the Southern Myth*, Polk detailed how his Piney Woods upbringing did not conform to any of the southern myths he analyzed in his fiction—neither planter nor sharecropper, not tormented by the past nor given to the telling of stories. In 2008 Polk published *Faulkner and Welty and the Southern Literary Tradition*, a collection of essays from throughout his career.

Polk's scholarship earned him international recognition, though he is perhaps best remembered by the generations of students he mentored over his decades of teaching. He died in Jackson on 21 August 2012.

Ben Gilstrap
University of Mississippi

Mississippi Institute of Arts and Letters website, www.ms-arts-letters.org; Noel Polk, *Outside the Southern Myth* (1997); Stephen M. Ross and Noel Polk, eds., *Reading Faulkner: The Sound and the Fury* (1996); John Ray Skates and Noel Polk, *Turning Points* (1986).

Polk, Ron

(b. 1944) Baseball Coach

Ron Polk led the Mississippi State University baseball team for twenty-nine seasons and coached in the College World Series eight times over his thirty-five-year career. Polk was born on 12 January 1944 in Boston. He graduated from Grand Canyon University in 1965 and received a master's degree from the University of Arizona the following year.

Polk coached at Georgia Southern from 1972 to 1975, leading the team to the College World Series in 1973. After compiling a 155–64 record there, Polk became head coach at Mississippi State University (MSU) in 1976. Prior to his 1997 retirement, Polk led the Bulldogs to the College World Series in 1979, 1981, 1985, 1990, 1997. In addition, MSU won the Southeastern Conference Tournaments in 1979, 1985, 1987, and 1990 and the conference championship in 1979, 1985, 1987, and 1989.

After two years in retirement, Polk returned to coach at the University of Georgia in 2000, and the following year his squad took the Southeastern Conference Championship and played in the College World Series. He then returned to Mississippi State, coaching there from 2002 through 2008. The Bulldogs won the conference tournament in 2005 and finished the 2007 season with a 38–22 record and a trip to the College World Series. Midway through the following season, Polk announced that he would resign at the end of the year. During his two stints at MSU, Polk posted an overall 1,139–590 record.

Polk served as head coach of the USA National Baseball Team in 1991 and 1998. He also held the post of assistant coach on the US teams that won the gold medal at the 1988 Seoul Olympics and the bronze medal at the 1996 Atlanta Olympics.

Polk has authored or coauthored two college-level coaching textbooks, *The Baseball Playbook* and *The Baseball-Softball Playbook*. Since 2009, he has served as a volunteer assistant coach at the University of Alabama at Birmingham.

Polk was named National Coach of the Year in 1973 and 1985 and was inducted into the College Baseball Hall of Fame in 2009. Polk's overall record of 1373–702 as a college baseball head coach places him among the Top 15 all-time in wins.

Ryan Fletcher
University of Mississippi

Mississippi State University Athletics website, www.hailstate.com; *NCAA Baseball Coaching Records*, http://fs.ncaa.org/Docs/stats/baseball_RB/2016/coach.pdf; Ron Polk, *The Baseball Playbook* (1982); Chris Talbott, *USA Today* (29 March 2008).

Pontotoc County

The 1832 Treaty of Pontotoc Creek gave Pontotoc County a permanent place in the history of US-Chickasaw relations. The land around Pontotoc, in northeastern Mississippi, had for generations been one of the centers of Chickasaw life and consequently became a point of contention when white settlers wanted to move into the area. The Treaty of Pontotoc Creek led to at least three major developments: (1) widespread Chickasaw movement out of Mississippi, (2) rapid purchases of northwestern Mississippi public land by speculators, and (3) new migration into the area by whites and their slaves.

Pontotoc County was founded in 1837 and three years later had a small population of 2,898 free people and 1,593 slaves. The county was heavily agricultural, with only 31 people working in manufacturing.

By 1860 Pontotoc had become Mississippi's ninth-largest county, with a population of 14,517 free people and 7,596 slaves. As in many northern Mississippi counties, Pontotoc's residents concentrated on production for home consumption rather than for markets. The county ranked seventh in the state in Irish potatoes, eighth in corn, ninth in livestock, and twenty-first in cotton, the state's leading cash crop. In 1860, 86 people worked in manufacturing, making leather, lumber, saddles, and carriages. That year, Pontotoc had fifty-six churches, among them twenty-five Baptist, sixteen Methodist, seven Cumberland Presbyterian, six Presbyterian, one Episcopal, and one Christian.

The Civil War saw significant fighting in Pontotoc County. Confederate troops moved through in December 1862 as part of Gen. Earl Van Dorn's raid on Union supplies in Holly Springs. In late April 1863 Union colonel Ben Grierson led a destructive raid through Pontotoc County and other parts of northern and central Mississippi, hoping to divert Confederate forces from Gen. Ulysses S. Grant's assault on Vicksburg. Pontotoc native Belle Edmondson, a Confederate supporter, smuggled goods and news through Union lines.

In 1870 sections of Pontotoc County became part of Union County, resulting in a decline in Pontotoc's population to 13,858 by 1880. The county remained agricultural, with more than two thousand farms and only 35 people employed in industry. Sixty percent of the county's farms were cultivated by their owners. Pontotoc ranked highly in the production of wheat and corn but lower in cotton production.

In 1900 Pontotoc's population had rebounded to 18,274, with whites comprising three-quarters of residents. About half of the county's 2,535 white farmers owned their land, more than twice the 21 percent rate for its 833 black farmers. Pontotoc had an unusually high number of white tenant farmers—about 1,200. The county continued to have limited manufacturing activity, with only 55 industrial workers.

Churchgoing in Pontotoc County resembled that in much of northeastern Mississippi, with members primarily in the Southern Baptist Church, Missionary Baptist Church, and the Methodist Episcopal Church, South. The Colored Methodist Episcopal Church and the Presbyterian Church United States had substantially smaller numbers.

Pontotoc's population increased slowly to about 22,000 in 1930. Whites comprised 81 percent of that total. The county remained essentially rural, with only 59 industrial workers. Most of the county's 4,381 farms grew corn, and 63 percent were operated by tenant farmers. Beginning in 1934, Pontotoc received power through the Tennessee Valley Authority, one of the first Mississippi localities to do so.

An intriguing range of creative individuals grew up in Pontotoc County during the twentieth century. Opera singer Ruby Elzy, famous for her performances in *Porgy and Bess*, was born in Pontotoc in 1908. Born in 1922, novelist Borden Deal used his Pontotoc County roots in many of his works, including *Dunbar's Cove*, a novel about the Tennessee Valley Authority. Artist M. B. Mayfield was born in Ecru in 1923. Born in 1939, musician Delaney Bramlett grew up in Pontotoc County. Pontotoc County was also the early home of both

Gladys Smith Presley, the mother of Elvis Presley, and US senator Thad Cochran, born into a family of teachers in 1937.

Pontotoc County's population declined to 17,232 in 1960. While the county still depended more on agriculture than most of the state, with 31 percent of its workers employed raising corn, cotton, soybeans, and livestock, industry had become crucial. In 1960 one-fourth of Pontotoc's workforce had jobs in industry, especially apparel, furniture, and timber. The county began growing again, and the population neared 21,000 in 1980.

In a 1996 case, *Herdahl v. Pontotoc County School District*, judges ruled that the county schools could not hold public prayers over the intercom.

In 2010 Pontotoc's population, like that of many other counties in northern Mississippi, had grown substantially over the previous half century, reaching 29,957. White residents accounted for 80 percent of Pontotoc's population, African Americans for 14 percent, and Hispanics for 6 percent, one of Mississippi's largest Latino communities.

Mississippi Encyclopedia Staff
University of Mississippi

Mississippi State Planning Commission, *Progress Report on State Planning in Mississippi* (1938); *Mississippi Statistical Abstract*, Mississippi State University (1952–2010); Charles Sydnor and Claude Bennett, *Mississippi History* (1939); University of Virginia Library, Historical Census Browser website, http://mapserver.lib.virginia.edu; E. Nolan Waller and Dani A. Smith, *Growth Profiles of Mississippi's Counties, 1960–1980* (1985).

Poor People's Campaign

A mule train beginning in Marks, Mississippi, was one of the more dramatic features of the Poor People's Campaign. In January 1968, with the civil rights movement losing steam, Dr. Martin Luther King Jr. unveiled a new strategy to leaders of the Southern Christian Leadership Conference (SCLC): the Poor People's Campaign would work for the passage of laws to provide jobs and better wages for all people, thus breaking the cycle of poverty.

King and other leaders imagined that the Poor People's Campaign would begin in five major urban areas with rampant inner-city poverty. Poor people from each city would ride in covered wagons pulled by mules to Washington, D.C., and live in a tent city there, disrupting daily life until their demands were met. Marian Wright Edelman convinced Sen. Robert Kennedy to travel through the Mississippi Delta

A sign in Marks, where the mule train portion of the Poor People's March on Washington began (Photograph by James G. Thomas, Jr.)

region as well, and Kennedy suggested to King that the Poor People's Campaign should also include representatives from the Delta. King planned to have the mule train portion of the Poor People's March on Washington begin in Marks and arrive in Washington on 2 May.

On 4 April 1968, just before the march was to start, King was assassinated. After taking a bit of time to regroup, SCLC leaders decided to continue with the plan. In early May Rev. James Bevel and other SCLC activists left Memphis for Marks, where Mayor Howard C. Langford promised to help find housing for the people gathering to begin the march. Residents of Marks secured mules and wagons. Willie Bolden, an SCLC field worker from Marks, served as wagon master, with responsibility for making sure people and animals were taken care of and reached their destination in safety and good health.

On 13 May 1968 the mule train left Marks and headed to Washington, D.C., via Birmingham and Atlanta. Participants encountered myriad challenges, including the daily upkeep and needs of both humans and animals. Marchers frequently encountered low-level harassment, such as passersby honking cars horns to scare the mules, and occasionally faced larger barriers. On 14 June in Douglasville, Georgia, state troopers stopped march participants attempting to use Interstate 20. The marchers persevered, finally reaching Atlanta long after they were already supposed to be in Washington. SCLC leaders then decided to purchase train tickets for both marchers and mules.

The mule train participants did not arrive in Washington until around 25 June 1968, missing the Solidarity Day march to the Washington Monument held on 19 June. Marchers briefly joined other residents of Resurrection City, and residents of Marks were some of the last participants to leave.

Kathryn McGaw York
University of Mississippi

John Dittmer, *Local People: The Struggle for Civil Rights in Mississippi* (1994); Roland Freeman, *The Mule Train: A Journey of Hope Remembered*, ed. David Levine (1998); Michael K. Honey, *Going Down Jericho Road: The Memphis Strike, Martin Luther King's Last Campaign* (2007); Thomas R. Jackson, *From Civil Rights to Human Rights: Martin Luther King, Jr., and the Struggle for Economic Justice* (2007); Hilliard Lackey, *Marks, Martin, and the Mule Train* (1998).

Population Trends

Not surprisingly, Mississippi's population has reflected the major developments in the state's history. Using figures from the US Census is complicated and at times frustrating, because census takers had different questions and standards at different times. Still, statistics show the broad trends of Mississippi life, with dramatic increases in population in periods of agricultural prosperity or when land or new employment became available and declines during times of economic difficulty. Three trends stand out in the state's population centers. First, Hinds County emerged early as a population center and remained one. Second, the other population centers shifted from southwestern Mississippi to northern Mississippi in the mid-1800s, to the Mississippi Delta in the late 1800s, and to the Mississippi Gulf Coast beginning the mid-1900s. Third, the emergence of DeSoto County, just south of Memphis, Tennessee, as the state's third-largest county in 2010 may reflect the beginning of another trend.

Historians estimate that about 19,000 Indians, primarily Choctaw and Chickasaw, lived in Mississippi Territory at the time of the American Revolution. Early in Euro-American settlement, the population counted by US officials—free and enslaved persons but not Indians—was concentrated in the southwestern part of the area that is now Mississippi. The first census, conducted in 1792, found 4,706 whites and African Americans in the Natchez District. In 1817, when Mississippi became a state, almost 47,000 people lived there, 21,440 of them enslaved.

The most dramatic gains in population took place in the 1830s and 1840s. By the mid-1800s the free and slave population had spread across much of the state, Hinds County had emerged as a growing population center, and North Mississippi counties such as Marshall, Monroe, Lowndes, and Tishomingo had large populations. The great majority of the native populations had been forced west.

In the late 1800s and early 1900s African American migration made Delta counties—Washington, Yazoo, and eventually Bolivar and Sunflower—among the state's most populated places. Three significant migrations of African Americans

Year	Official Population	African American Population	Most Populous Counties
1792*	4,706	2,034** (43%)	N/A
1800*	7,667	3,222** (42%)	N/A
1810*	15,630	14,423** (48%)	N/A
1820	75,448	32,814** (43%)	Adams, Wilkinson, Amite
1830	136,621	65,659** (48%)	Adams, Wilkinson, Hinds
1840	375,651	195,211** (52%)	Adams, Hinds, Marshall
1850	606,526	309,878** (51%)	Marshall, Hinds, Monroe
1860	791,305	436,631** (55%)	Hinds, Marshall, Tishomingo
1870	827,922	444,201 (54%)	DeSoto, Lowndes, Hinds
1880	1,131,597	650,291 (57%)	Hinds, Yazoo, Warren
1890	1,289,600	742,559 (58%)	Washington, Hinds, Yazoo
1900	1,551,270	907,360 (58%)	Hinds, Washington, Yazoo
1910	1,797,114	1,009,487 (56%)	Hinds, Washington, Bolivar
1920	1,790,618	935,184 (52%)	Bolivar, Hinds, Washington
1930	2,009,821	1,009,718 (50%)	Hinds, Bolivar, Sunflower
1940	2,183,796	1,074,578 (49%)	Hinds, Washington, Bolivar
1950	2,178,914	986,494 (45%)	Hinds, Harrison, Washington
1960	2,178,141	915,743 (42%)	Hinds, Harrison, Washington
1970	2,216,912	815,770 (37%)	Hinds, Harrison, Jackson
1980	2,520,638	887,206 (35%)	Hinds, Harrison, Jackson
1990	2,573,216	915,858 (36%)	Hinds, Harrison, Jackson
2000	2,844,658	1,041,708 (37%)	Hinds, Harrison, Jackson
2010	2,967,297	1,115,801 (38%)	Hinds, Harrison, DeSoto

* Figures for Natchez District of the Mississippi Territory

** Enslaved

occurred. First, African Americans from Mississippi and other states moved into the Delta counties. Then, in the 1910s, outmigration during the first Great Migration resulted in the state's first net decrease in population. And more dramatically, migration to the northern and western states in the 1940s and 1950s during the Second Great Migration shrank Mississippi's population.

New chances for employment during and after World War II encouraged rapid population growth on the Mississippi Gulf Coast, and Harrison and Jackson Counties have been among the most heavily populated parts of the state since the 1950s. In 2010 an influx of people to northern Mississippi made DeSoto the state's third-most-populous county while most other counties in the rural Mississippi Delta, including Washington, Bolivar, Coahoma, Sunflower, and Humphreys, continued to see significant declines in population. Since the Second Great Migration began, most of these counties have lost more than half of their total population, the combined result of scarce employment opportunities and the gravitation of the younger population to urban areas.

Ted Ownby
University of Mississippi

Nicholas Lemann, *The Promised Land: The Great Migration and How It Changed America* (1991); US Bureau of the Census website, www.census.gov; University of Virginia Library, Historical Census Browser website, http://mapserver.lib.virginia.edu/.

Populist Movement

Support for a new party to represent farmers' interests began to emerge in some Mississippi hill counties in January 1891 as falling cotton prices and rising costs of production meant that many small farmers could not meet the demands of unsympathetic creditors. To help them achieve economic independence, the Southern Farmers' Alliance had proposed an innovative federal subtreasury loan and marketing program, which leaders of the National Alliance endorsed at a December 1890 meeting in Ocala, Florida. The subtreasury plan called for the federal government to store harvested crops in local warehouses, provide farmers with low-interest loans for 80 percent of the market value of the crops, and allow borrowers a reasonable time to redeem loans and sell crops if prices rose. The subtreasury became a controversial issue in state politics and provided fuel for insurgency in the Democratic Party's ranks.

During the 1891 US Senate race, which pitted retired newspaper editor Ethelbert Barksdale, a strong subtreasury supporter, against Sen. James Z. George, an outspoken opponent of the plan, Alliance leader Frank Burkitt traveled from county to county to encourage members to stand united behind Barksdale. Leaders of the Southern Alliance came to the state in the heat of the canvass to boost Barksdale's candidacy. Most of the county Alliances endorsed Barksdale, but the editor of the state's Alliance newspaper and several prominent Alliance lecturers came out for George. The incumbent senator and his supporters aroused fears that militant farm leaders threatened white political solidarity, and he won reelection.

Despite bitterness over the loss, Barksdale opposed the formation of a third party. Burkitt and J. H. Jamison, president of the state Alliance, also defeated a move after the election to convert the farm organization into an agency of the People's Party, known as the Populists. As dissident farm leaders organized the state People's Party in 1892, they branded Burkitt a traitor for not joining them. At the state Democratic convention in April 1892, Burkitt served on the resolutions committee, and the party adopted the Alliance stand on national monetary policy—a bimetallic standard and a full and sufficient supply of money. Party leaders chose Burkitt to serve as one of the state's two Democratic electors at large and as a delegate to the party's national convention. The free and unlimited coinage of silver had become the primary goal of farm leaders by this time, but Burkitt pledged at the convention to support the party's nominee, Grover Cleveland, an advocate of hard-money policies. Several weeks later, however, when Congress failed to pass a silver bill, Burkitt resigned his Democratic electoral post and joined the Populists. His decision injected new life into the third-party movement and gave it the strong leadership needed to challenge the Democratic Party's monopoly in state politics.

In the 1892 general election, the Populists entered candidates in all of the state's congressional districts except the Delta, where a black Republican challenged the Democratic incumbent. As the Democrats rallied to meet the Populist threat, they showed more concern about the 4th District race in North Mississippi between the People's Party's Burkitt and incumbent congressman Hernando de Soto Money. The two men had been political adversaries since 1882, when Money had made disparaging remarks about the Grangers, and some of the white yeomanry had neither forgotten nor forgiven. Prominent Democrats came to the district to denounce the Populists as a threat to white rule and to blame the Republicans for the farmers' woes. Money defeated Burkitt by 2,318 votes, although the latter carried Chickasaw, Choctaw, Pontotoc, and Webster Counties. In the presidential contest, Cleveland received four times as many statewide votes as the Populist candidate, former Union general James B. Weaver, while Pres. Benjamin Harrison, the Republican candidate, trailed even farther behind. The Populists carried only Chickasaw County in the presidential race, but they achieved a measure of success by electing officials in some of the county contests.

The People's Party challenged the Democrats in all of the state's congressional districts in 1894. The Prohibitionists fused with the Populists in some districts, but none of the races generated much interest. Voter turnout fell well below

that in 1892, and the Populists carried only five counties in the north and two in the south. Three of the Populist candidates challenged the results on grounds that the suffrage restrictions in the state's constitution disfranchised illiterate voters, most of whom were black. The House Committee on Elections threw out the challenges, however, and declared that the Democrats were entitled to their seats.

The Populists nominated a full slate of candidates for state offices in 1895, but the gubernatorial contest between Democrat Anselm J. McLaurin and Burkitt attracted the most interest. Burkitt charged that Democrats had been corrupt and inefficient in managing state affairs, but McLaurin put his Populist opponent on the defensive by questioning his endorsement of the national Democratic ticket shortly before his defection to the People's Party. McLaurin had served fourteen months of a vacated term in the US Senate, where he had supported free coinage of silver, an income tax, and other planks in the Populist platform. Rural voters admired and trusted him, and he carried every county except Choctaw. The Democrats easily defeated the Populists in every statewide contest, and only Marion and Choctaw Counties elected Populists to the state legislature. After the election, support for the Populist movement in Mississippi waned.

At the national convention of the People's Party in 1896, the Mississippi delegation opposed a fusion ticket with the Democrats, who earlier had nominated charismatic silver advocate William Jennings Bryan for president and pledged support for the coinage of silver at a ratio of sixteen to one with gold. While the Populists accepted Bryan as their presidential nominee, they rejected the Democrat's vice presidential nominee, Maine industrialist Arthur Sewall, and instead nominated fiery Georgian Tom Watson. The Bryan-Sewall ticket garnered seven times as many votes in Mississippi as the Bryan-Watson slate, which failed to carry a single county. The Populists lost in all of the congressional races and carried only Marion County in the southwestern part of the state.

In 1898 the Populists did not challenge the Democrats in three of Mississippi's congressional districts and offered little opposition in the others. The following year, they nominated Dr. Rufus K. Prewitt of Choctaw County, editor of a Populist newspaper, the *Phagocite*, to oppose Democratic gubernatorial candidate Andrew H. Longino, but Prewitt's candidacy generated little interest, garnering a mere 6,421 votes to Longino's 42,227. Although the Populists in Marion and Franklin elected two legislators, the People's Party never again challenged the Democrats for any statewide office.

Burkitt returned to the Democratic fold in 1900 and voted for Bryan in the presidential election. The Populists entered congressional candidates in two Mississippi districts that year but picked up a total of just eleven hundred votes. A few members of the People's Party met to choose a slate of electors for the presidential elections in 1904 and 1908, but the Populist movement in Mississippi subsequently ceased to exist.

The Populists never had any real chance for success in Mississippi. The Democrats stole the thunder from the Populists and became the party of free silver, and the agricultural economy improved in the late 1890s. The overriding factor, however, was that most of the state's voters simply refused to break the ranks of white political solidarity. After passage of the mandatory statewide primary law in 1902, the Democrats had a virtual monopoly in state politics, and the white man's party did not face another serious political challenge for the next sixty years.

Thomas Neville Boschert
Delta State University

Edward L. Ayers, *The Promise of the New South: Life after Reconstruction* (1992); Bradley G. Bond, *Political Culture in the Nineteenth-Century South: Mississippi, 1830–1900* (1995); Thomas N. Boschert, "A Family Affair: Mississippi Politics, 1882–1932" (PhD dissertation, University of Mississippi, 1995); Lilibel Broadway, "Frank Burkitt: The Man in the Wool Hat" (master's thesis, Mississippi State College, 1948); Stephen Edward Cresswell, *Multiparty Politics in Mississippi, 1877–1902* (2005); James Sharbrough Ferguson, "Agrarianism in Mississippi, 1871–1900" (PhD dissertation, University of North Carolina, 1952); Lawrence Goodwyn, *Democratic Promise: The Populist Moment in America* (1976); William David McCain, "The Populist Party in Mississippi" (master's thesis, University of Mississippi, 1931); May Spencer Ringold, *Journal of Mississippi History* (July 1954).

Populist Party

Beginning in 1892, many of Mississippi's white small farmers rushed to join a new political party. Known as the People's Party or Populist Party, it was part of a nationwide movement that proved strongest among farmers in the southern and western states. In Mississippi, as in many parts of the nation, the Populist Party grew out of the Farmers' Alliance. The party increased in strength as the nation slid into a deep economic depression. Mississippi and other cotton states were particularly hard hit as cotton prices hit near-record lows.

Most of Mississippi's Populist politicians were farmers, with some teachers, physicians, and agrarian editors among the party leaders. The party was strongest in white-majority counties with declining soils where corn was nearly as important as cotton. Many of these counties—Choctaw, Webster, Chickasaw, Winston, and Pontotoc—were located in northeastern Mississippi. In the southwestern corner of the state, Franklin, Amite, and Lawrence Counties also boasted relatively strong support for the Populists.

Economically strapped farmers applauded the Populist platform, which included inflation of the money supply by free coinage of silver, government ownership of railroads, low tariffs, and low taxes. Many Populist leaders also favored prohibition of alcoholic beverages. One favorite proposal of the Populists was the subtreasury system, under which the US government would build warehouses in which farmers could store their crops and wait for a better time to sell. In addition, the government would provide loans to farmers using the stored commodities as collateral.

In January 1894 Mississippi was rocked by the news that twenty-two members of the state legislature had deserted the Democratic Party to form a Populist Party caucus. Yet the Populists proved unable to follow up on this mass defection by winning important elections. Although some 130 Populists were elected to office in Mississippi, most occupied minor positions such as justice of the peace or member of the county board of supervisors. The party's strength in the state peaked with the 1894 election and declined steadily thereafter. Agrarian editor Frank Burkitt garnered only 28 percent of the vote as the People's Party 1895 gubernatorial nominee. Nevertheless, the Populist Party is important for offering a challenge to the Democratic Party in a state where the Democrats typically held all political power.

Stephen Cresswell
West Virginia Wesleyan College

Stephen Cresswell, *Multiparty Politics in Mississippi, 1877–1902* (1995); Albert D. Kirwan, *Revolt of the Rednecks, 1876–1925* (1951); Robert C. McMath Jr., *American Populism: A Social History* (1993).

Port Gibson, Battle of

The Battle of Port Gibson was Union general Ulysses S. Grant's first victory in the campaign that eventually led to the fall of Vicksburg. After failing to capture the strategically important city in late 1862 and early 1863, Grant decided on a new plan. He would march his army down the Louisiana side of the Mississippi River, cross over, and attack the city from the south.

When Union gunboats failed to silence the Confederates' formidable defenses at Grand Gulf, Mississippi, Grant's troops landed farther south at Bruinsburg, where they faced no resistance. By late afternoon on 30 April 1863, twenty-two thousand troops had landed on Mississippi soil. A Union cavalry raid through Mississippi and a feint against the bluffs north of Vicksburg confused Confederate commander John C. Pemberton. Unsure of Grant's intentions, Pemberton did not unite his scattered forces to resist the Union landing.

Grand Gulf's commander, John S. Bowen, saw the danger and quickly notified Pemberton of the need for reinforcements. Bowen then began shifting some of his Grand Gulf troops to Port Gibson to meet Grant's threat. Pemberton also began sending troops from other parts of Mississippi, but these men would not arrive in time and Bowen would be forced to fight greatly outnumbered.

Union and Confederate forces first collided after midnight on 1 May. The vanguard of Union troops ran into Confederate pickets near the A. K. Shaifer House, west of Port Gibson. A brief firefight and an artillery duel ensued. The clash quickly subsided, and both sides prepared for the upcoming battle.

Terrain played a major role at the Battle of Port Gibson. Mazes of ridges and ravines running between tangles of cane and underbrush dominated the landscape. These features provided Bowen with an ideal line of defense. Grant would not be able to take full advantage of his numerical and artillery strengths.

The Battle of Port Gibson took place along two parallel roads that led into the town. During the early phase of the battle, Bowen's sixty-five hundred men held their ground despite being outnumbered, but as Union forces continued to attack the lines, the southern troops withdrew and reformed closer to Port Gibson. Bowen skillfully maneuvered his men against further onslaughts, but the Federals' numerical superiority would eventually take its toll. Grant funneled more men to flank the Southerners while Bowen plugged open gaps in his lines with available men and ordered a counterattack. The attack went well at first, but Union forces were too numerous, and after a full day of fighting, Bowen ordered a retreat. His men gave up Port Gibson and crossed Bayou Pierre to safety. Each side suffered approximately eight hundred casualties.

Grant's bold move to strike south of Vicksburg and subsequent victory at Port Gibson solidified a key beachhead, providing him a secure site where he could gather supplies for his troops as they marched further into Mississippi. Pemberton's failure to mass his troops to stop the Union threat ultimately spelled doom for the Gibraltar of the Confederacy.

Clay Williams
Mississippi Department of
Archives and History

Michael B. Ballard, *Pemberton: A Biography* (1991); Edwin C. Bearss, *The Campaign for Vicksburg*, vol. 2, *Grant Strikes a Fatal Blow* (1986); Ulysses S. Grant, *Personal Memoirs of U. S. Grant*, vol. 1 (1885); Terrence J. Winschel, *Triumph and Defeat: The Vicksburg Campaign* (1999).

Port Gibson and Claiborne County Civil Rights Movement

When Nate Jones returned to Claiborne County after serving in the US Navy during World War II, he had experienced "a little taste of freedom" and was determined to join the National Association for the Advancement of Colored People (NAACP) and register to vote. While still overseas, he urged his wife, Julia, to pay his poll tax. Though she abandoned the attempt after a black friend warned her about possible retaliation, the Joneses saved enough money during the war to purchase a farm near Alcorn College. In the early 1950s the small Claiborne County NAACP branch, founded in the 1940s by Ernest Jones (no relation), began a limited, word-of-mouth recruitment campaign that reached Nate and Julia Jones through a neighboring farmer. They immediately joined and initiated their own quiet recruiting despite the ever-present possibility of violent and economic repercussions. Julia Jones recalled being afraid when her husband picked up their annual membership cards at Collins Barbershop. Every year, she immediately burned the cards.

In the early 1960s state NAACP field secretary Medgar Evers and Student Nonviolent Coordinating Committee activist Bob Moses encouraged Nate Jones's interest in registering to vote, holding two workshops on the subject at the Port Gibson Masonic Temple. Despite implicit white threats and repeated rejections, Jones and a handful of other local NAACP activists returned to the registrar's office again and again. They ultimately shared their experiences with US

Rudy Shields, chief organizer of the Port Gibson movement, 1960s (Mississippi State Sovereignty Commission Records, Mississippi Department of Archives and History [1-112-0-54-1-1-2])

Justice Department lawyers, who filed suit against the Claiborne County registrar as part of a broader 1962 voter registration lawsuit, *U.S. v. Mississippi*.

With Evers's 1963 assassination and the Student Nonviolent Coordinating Committee's 1962 decision to focus on the Mississippi Delta, the movement appeared to bypass Claiborne County. Moreover, J. D. Boyd, president of the historically black Alcorn Agricultural and Mechanical College, aggressively blocked movement involvement by faculty, staff, and students, cutting off an important potential source of support. Despite the difficulties, Nate Jones and others remained determined, and in late 1965, when Medgar Evers's successor as NAACP field secretary, his brother, Charles, initiated high-profile campaigns in nearby communities, they were ready to take a public stand.

Charles Evers began focusing on Southwest Mississippi after a Klan shooting in Natchez. On the verge of being fired after several years of contentious relations with his New York bosses, Evers sought to solidify his personal power and the NAACP's organizational prestige by taking advantage of the newly passed Voting Rights Act, the area's high percentage of voting-age African Americans, and the lack of organizational competition. Evers's success in Port Gibson and nearby communities, along with the accompanying positive national media attention, secured his job.

Evers relied heavily on freelance community organizer Rudy Shields, who came to Mississippi from Chicago and quickly earned a reputation for effectiveness, dedication, and fearlessness. In late 1965 and early 1966, Shields began organizing the Port Gibson movement, working closely with longtime underground NAACP members including Nate Jones as well as activist women and high school students. Together they rejuvenated and expanded the NAACP branch, which quickly grew to seventeen hundred members (more than 40 percent of them blacks over age twenty-one), and spearheaded an extensive campaign that increased the number of registered African American voters from a handful in late 1965 to more than twenty-six hundred (a decisive electoral majority) by May 1966. By early March of that year, with Evers as the featured speaker, weekly mass meetings and marches drew hundreds of enthusiastic participants, and Evers initiated protest marches aimed both at Alcorn College's substandard resources (a result of Mississippi's Jim Crow higher education policies) and at Boyd's heavy-handed, dictatorial policies, which, among other things, isolated the campus from civil rights activism. The Alcorn protests culminated on 4 and 5 April as thousands of African Americans from Claiborne and adjacent Jefferson County gathered near campus. While lawyers battled in court over whether protesters could march on campus, large numbers of lawmen blocked the protesters from entering the college grounds. After two days of peaceful rallies, police officials gave demonstrators one minute to disperse before wading into the crowd with billy clubs and tear gas. Despite considerable

national media attention and years of related legal action, this police riot essentially ended the Alcorn protests.

A few days earlier, on 1 April, the Port Gibson NAACP had initiated a boycott against white merchants after several weeks of unsuccessful negotiations with white business and civic leaders. The black community had issued more than twenty demands, including the immediate desegregation of public accommodations (as mandated by the Civil Rights Act of 1964); the addition of blacks to community boards and juries and hiring of blacks as policemen, sheriff's deputies, and local business and government officials; and the extension of courtesy titles such as *Mr.* and *Mrs.* to African Americans. Though the boycott received widespread support from African Americans, Evers, Shields, and their allies also used peer pressure and coercion to ensure almost 100 percent compliance. After a ten-month standoff, during which time several white merchants went out of business rather than negotiate with African Americans, most merchants agreed to use courtesy titles and hire African American clerks in exchange for an end to the boycott. Those who refused remained targets of an ongoing selective-buying campaign.

By this time, the local movement was looking to the 1967 countywide elections, hoping to translate the overwhelming black population majority into political power. Despite significant white resistance, Claiborne County blacks were more successful than most across the state, electing four blacks to political office, including Geneva Collins as chancery clerk and William Matt Ross to the powerful board of supervisors. By 1975 blacks won twenty-three of thirty-two county elective offices, including a majority on the board of supervisors and every countywide position except sheriff. The Claiborne County movement's political accomplishments reflected Evers's popularity as a political boss as well as Shields's grassroots organizing skill. A generation of skilled local activists mentored by Shields continued organizing after he moved on to other Mississippi communities.

The 1967 boycott settlement and elections brought the mass movement phase of the Claiborne County movement to an end. However, conflicts between African Americans and whites persisted as the former sought to achieve full citizenship rights and the latter clung to inherited power. For example, white officials turned down millions of dollars in federal funding rather than use it to improve public services for African Americans and allow a related annexation that could strengthen black voting power in Port Gibson. Similarly, white leaders turned African Americans away from white churches, removed drugstore seating rather than integrate, and fled the public schools when the US Supreme Court required a single, integrated system. In April 1969 a white police officer with a reputation for racist violence shot and killed an unarmed African American man on his front porch. Blacks reacted by reinstating the boycott against all-white merchants. White merchants, encouraged and supported by the Citizens' Council, responded by filing suit against the NAACP and more than one hundred Claiborne County African Americans, seeking immediate injunctive relief and more than $3.5 million in damages. The case, *Claiborne Hardware, et al., v. NAACP, et al.*, spent thirteen years winding its way through the state and federal court systems. In 1976 the Mississippi Supreme Court awarded the merchants more than $1 million in damages; six years later, the US Supreme Court unanimously reversed the decision, affirming protesters' right to use economic boycotts for political goals.

The Claiborne County movement is best known for the boycott and related litigation and for its association with Charles Evers. It is, however, probably most important for what it reveals about the ways that African Americans challenged entrenched white power—through voter registration, boycotts, aggressive armed self-defense, and the persistent, determined insistence that whites treat them as equals—and the ways whites clung to power and privilege. In many ways, the movement was a struggle over power and was largely the work of long-term local activists like Nate Jones, who, in the words of NAACP president James Dorsey, "fought for those things that are right, those things that are good and those things that are just."

Emilye Crosby
State University of New York
at Geneseo

Emilye Crosby, *A Little Taste of Freedom: The Black Freedom Struggle in Claiborne County, Mississippi* (2005); Regina Devoual, *Southern Exposure* (April–May 1982); John Dittmer, *Local People: The Struggle for Civil Rights in Mississippi* (1994); James Edward Miller, "The Transformation of the Political Process in Claiborne County, Mississippi, 1967–1983" (master's thesis, University of Massachusetts at Amherst, 1987); Frank R. Parker, *Black Votes Count: Political Empowerment in Mississippi after 1965* (1990).

Posey, Carnot

(1818–1863) Confederate General

Carnot Posey, a planter, lawyer, and Confederate brigadier general, was born on 5 August 1818 in Woodville, Wilkinson County. Posey attended college in Jackson, Louisiana, before studying at the University of Virginia Law School in the 1830s. He completed his legal training and returned to Woodville, where he established a law practice and worked as a planter. When the Mexican War broke out in 1846 Posey joined Col. Jefferson Davis's Mississippi Rifles as a first lieutenant; his leadership potential and character were recognized

after he received a wound at the Battle of Buena Vista in February 1847.

After the Mexican War, Posey resumed his law practice. Under Pres. James Buchanan's administration Posey was appointed US district attorney for the southern half of Mississippi, and he served until 1861, when he resigned with Mississippi's secession. Following the formation of the Confederacy, Davis reappointed Posey as district attorney, but he again resigned to support the Confederate war effort.

In late May 1861 Posey officially entered Confederate service in Corinth as colonel of the 16th Mississippi Infantry, where his former militia company, the Wilkinson Rifles, joined nine other Mississippi state militia companies to create a new Confederate regiment. Throughout 1861–62 he served at the head of the 16th Mississippi as part of Thomas J. "Stonewall" Jackson's army during the Shenandoah Valley Campaign as well as the subsequent Peninsula Campaign (Seven Days' Battles). Posey also led the 16th Mississippi under Robert E. Lee's Army of Northern Virginia during the Battles of Second Manassas, Harpers Ferry, and Sharpsburg. His actions in the Sharpsburg Campaign earned him a promotion to brigadier general effective 1 November 1862. Following the Battle of Fredericksburg in December 1862 he received command of a brigade of Mississippians and distinguished himself at the Battles of Chancellorsville and Gettysburg while serving under James Longstreet's 1st Corps and Ambrose P. Hill's 3rd Corps. Following the Confederate defeat at Gettysburg and subsequent retreat into Virginia, Posey suffered a serious wound to the thigh at the Battle of Bristoe Station on 14 October 1863. The wound became infected, and he died on 13 November 1863 in Charlottesville, Virginia.

John Fabian Chappo
American Public University

Edwin B. Coddington, *The Gettysburg Campaign: A Study in Command* (1968); Douglas Southall Freeman, *Lee's Lieutenants* (1943); "Genealogical Notes and Queries," *William and Mary College Quarterly Historical Magazine* (July 1897, July 1934); Stephen W. Sears, *The Landscape Turned Red: The Battle of Antietam* (1983).

Posey, Parker

(b. 1968) Actress

With nearly one hundred film and television roles to her credit, Parker Posey has given life to some of Hollywood's most unconventional characters, ranging from a young woman

P

obsessed with Jacqueline Kennedy Onassis (*The House of Yes*) to an ingénue getting her first taste of "Oscar buzz" (*For Your Consideration*). According to Debra Zimmerman, the executive director of Women Make Movies, "Parker Posey is the quintessential outsider."

Posey was raised far from the grind of show business. Named after 1950s supermodel Suzy Parker, Posey was born two months premature in Baltimore on 8 November 1968 and spent weeks in a hospital incubator. The family moved south when Posey was a child, first to Monroe, Louisiana, and then to Laurel, Mississippi, where her father, Chris, owned a car dealership and her mother, Lynda, was a chef. For an actor defined by the uncanny, in both the roles she chooses and how she approaches her career, Posey's childhood, reported the *New York Times*, was "normal in the extreme."

In fact the future "Queen of the Indies," as *Time* magazine labeled Posey, struggled to find outlets for creative expression in her small-town surroundings. Posey channeled her energy into music, drama, and ballet. She applied to the dance program at the North Carolina School for the Arts but was rejected because the dean thought she would make a better actor. After graduating from high school in Laurel, Posey was accepted into the drama program at the State University of New York at Purchase.

During her senior year she won the role of Tess, a devious teen on the long-running CBS soap opera *As the World Turns*. A supporting part in *Dazed and Confused* (1993) soon followed. Her first lead role was as Mary in the independent film *Party Girl* (1995); subsequent roles in *The House of Yes* (1997) and Christopher Guest's *Waiting for Guffman* (1996) helped cement her status as "the chain-smoking self-parodying star of low-budget" films.

Perhaps Posey drew inspiration for many of her quirky characters from her grandmother, a woman *Biography* magazine described as an "unconventional character" who would wear a "tight, '40s looking skirt and a silk blouse and heels" around her house. According to Posey, her grandmother would "put her feet over her head and play tricks with me. She was very limber. She always painted her nails, and I'd do that, too."

In addition to starring in three more of Guest's mockumentaries (*Best in Show* [2000], *A Mighty Wind* [2003], and *For Your Consideration* [2006]), Posey has appeared on the big screen in *Superman Returns* (2006), *Broken English* (2007), *Ned Rifle* (2014), and two Woody Allen films, *Irrational Man* (2015) and *Café Society* (2016), as well as numerous others. She has also appeared frequently on television, with recurring roles on *Boston Legal*, *The Good Wife*, and *Louie* and guest appearances on *New Girl*, *Inside Amy Schumer*, and *Portlandia*, among many others.

Posey once described herself as having had a "hidden career. Only a small group of people know about [my] films. I'm so on the fringe, I'm on the fringe of the fringe."

Glenn "Pete" Smith Jr.
Mississippi State University

David Carr, *New York Times* (6 May 2007); Michelle Collins, *Bust* (January 2007); Stephen Holden, *New York Times* (17 November 2006); Rebecca Louie, *Daily University Star* (19 November 2002); Alissa Quart, *Film Comment* (November 2002); Michael Schulman, *New York Times* (2 July 2015); Harvey Solomon, *Biography* (January 1999).

Pottery, Folk

Mississippi folk pottery represents a mixture of the two primary American stoneware traditions of the nineteenth century. During the early periods of settlement, potters working in the alkaline-glazing tradition of the Deep South as well as salt-glazing potters from Tennessee and the Ohio Valley came to the state. Pottery-making families such as the Leopards, Loyds, and Mortons moved with the advancing American frontier into Mississippi, where they practiced a cottage industry of stoneware production, providing essential products such as churns, storage jars, bowls, and pitchers for their neighbors. These early potters exploited clays suitable for stoneware, primarily from the eastern Mississippi counties of Winston, Lauderdale, Neshoba, Monroe, and Itawamba. They established lasting "jugtowns" in communities such as Louisville in Winston County, Tremont in Itawamba County, and Lockhart in Lauderdale County.

Most American folk potters used salt to glaze their utilitarian stoneware, a process that requires salt to be thrown into the hot kiln. Early potters such as northern-born Joseph Royal Tanner and Peter Cribbs brought this glaze into northeastern Mississippi long before the Civil War. The resulting gases cause a glass coating to form on the pottery in the kiln. Soon thereafter Tennessee potter William Loyd and family came to the area, also presumably using the salt glaze. The Loyds made stoneware tombstones that can be found the older graveyards of northeastern Mississippi and northwestern Alabama. The family took out a US patent for this tombstone design in 1879 while living in Tremont.

A more distinctly southern style of pottery developed in the Edgefield District of South Carolina, and families from that area such as the Leopards, Presleys, and Rushtons brought their alkaline-glazing tradition into Mississippi. This pottery was dipped into a glaze formula made from clay mixed with either wood ashes or lime. After the ware was fired, this glaze left a shiny green-to-brown finish on the stoneware. These potters also used a type of rectangular kiln known as a groundhog kiln. This style of pottery advanced with the frontier from the Atlantic Ocean to central Texas over two generations. The Leopards were a typical southern pottery-making family, originating in South Carolina before moving to Georgia, then to

Alabama, and finally to Winston County before the Civil War. Some members of the family later moved to Rusk County, Texas. Thad Leopard made pottery in Mississippi well into the twentieth century.

In the latter part of the nineteenth century, an expanding railroad system introduced new types of pottery glazes. The brown Albany slip and white feldspar glaze (also known as Bristol glaze) replaced the salt and alkaline glazes. During this time, potters from Europe and northern states worked in Mississippi. The Scottish McAdams family worked near Meridian. Another group of nonsouthern potters was located in Marshall County.

In Mississippi today, only the Stewart family of Louisville still engages in traditional pottery making. Homer Wade Stewart began making pottery in Winston County in 1888, and his grandson, Frank, and great-grandson, Keith, continue the family tradition. Frank and his family received Mississippi Governor's Award for Excellence in the Arts in 2000.

Joey Brackner
Alabama Center for
Traditional Culture

Joey Brackner, *Alabama Folk Pottery* (2006); James R. Cormany, *The Potteries of Itawamba and Monroe County, Mississippi: Churn Suppliers to the Mid South* (2001); Georgeanna Greer, in *Made By Hand: Mississippi Folk Art*, ed. Patti Carr Black (1980); Mississippi Arts Commission website, www.arts.state.ms.us.

Poverty, Antebellum White

One of the enduring images of the Old South is of the southern poor white. Commentators, writers, and historians have used "poor whites" as caricatures. Southern literature and historiography present powerful and divergent images of poor whites as everything from a dissolute and lazy underclass to the respectable "plain folk" of the Old South. Antebellum Mississippi (as well as the rest of the South) clearly had the latter and no doubt had the former, but these images do very little to help us understand the reality of white poverty at the time.

Antebellum Mississippi had only limited poverty, in part as a consequence of the newness of Euro-American settlement in the area—less than fifty years. As a rural, agrarian state, antebellum Mississippi did not experience significant urbanization, industrialization, and immigration, the prime contributors to poverty in nineteenth-century America. The poor were often mobile and thus invisible to the historical record. Regardless, antebellum Mississippi had no distinct poor white class; rather, individual Mississippians were poor. Their lives were obscure in the extreme but doubtless full of struggle and hardship. According to John Munn, a New Yorker who lived in Mississippi for fifteen years, "It is a remarkable feature of the society in the slave states, that a poor man—that is an object of charity—is seldom or ever seen, the sight of squalid poverty is rarely experienced."

An understanding of poverty and the identification of the poor in the decade before the Civil War can be gleaned from manuscript census returns, tax records, board of police records, and anecdotal fragments from personal journals, letters, newspaper articles, and court records. These documents suggest that poverty was the condition of persisting propertylessness. Land or other forms of personal property were essential for economic and social success, and the absence of property signaled socioeconomic failure. Studies of adult males with stable residences in central Mississippi between 1850 and 1860 suggest that the acquisition of real and personal property was the norm. The small percentage of adult men who failed to acquire property can be considered poor.

A survey of propertyless workers in antebellum Mississippi also reveals the array of low-status jobs that sustained poorer Mississippians. Some scholars suggest that slavery degraded all labor, black and white, but most southerners labored hard and productively throughout their lives. Poorer Mississippians worked as teamsters transporting cotton. Ditchers (mostly Irish immigrants) drained swamps and built levees to open lands to farming. Woodcutters supplied steamships on the Mississippi River. Charcoal burners labored in the Piney Woods. Draymen moved cargo on the wharfs at Natchez. Others worked as shingle makers, raftsmen, herders, hunters, or fishermen. Most poor Mississippians were tenants or farm laborers. Some were squatters on small subsistence farms. While many in antebellum Mississippi held menial jobs and were propertyless at times during their lives, persistence in these conditions was uncommon. All evidence suggests that those who were poor struggled but functioned and participated in the state's economic, political, and social life.

The best suggestion of real poverty in antebellum Mississippi comes from the evidence on paupers—the public dependents who received poor relief from Mississippi counties. For some, age or calamity created a poverty that became destitution. For those who could not sustain themselves, state law obliged county boards of police to serve as the "overseers of the poor." This system of poor relief provided generously for those few people deemed the "deserving poor." Census data from 1850 and 1860 record only 297 individuals receiving some form of public support as paupers. Almost half were elderly, while the rest were orphans, widows, disabled persons, and single women—people who lacked family to take responsibility for them.

Christopher Johnson
Palomar College

Charles C. Bolton, *Poor Whites of the Antebellum South: Tenants and Laborers in Central North Carolina and Northeast Mississippi* (1994); Christopher Johnson, "Poverty and Dependency in Antebellum Mississippi" (PhD dissertation, University of California at Riverside, 1988); Christopher Johnson, *Journal of Mississippi History* (February 1987).

Poverty Rate, Twenty-First Century

Ranking first among the nation's fifty states is usually a matter of much celebration. But not when the issue is poverty. Mississippi has the highest percentage of residents living below the poverty line. Though the state has made important advances in job creation and expansion, improved education, strengthened the quality of the available health care, and accelerated the adoption of information technologies by public and private sector entities, these positive changes have not translated into substantial declines in Mississippi's poverty rate. In 2014 21.5 percent of Mississippians remained poor, a figure that represents more than 623,000 people and is significantly higher than the 14.8 percent recorded for the nation as a whole. And poverty rates are much higher among Mississippi's African American, Latino, and Native American communities than among whites and Asian Americans.

A logical beginning point for the discussion of poverty is to specify the manner in which poverty is measured in the United States. While one could assume that the cost of living in Mississippi would be quite different from that of California or New York, the reality is that the process for determining poverty rates for individuals and households is identical in all forty-eight contiguous states. *Poverty thresholds* represent the amount of "money income" needed to support families whose members are of different ages and of various sizes. Money income includes earnings, unemployment compensation, workers' compensation, social security, Supplemental Security Income, public assistance, veterans' payments, survivor benefits, pension or retirement income, interest, dividends, rents, royalties, income from estates, trusts, educational assistance, alimony, child support, assistance from outside the household, and other miscellaneous sources. It does not include noncash benefits such as food stamps, Medicaid,

and housing assistance. Poverty thresholds are set at three times the cost of a minimally adequate diet. Families whose pretax money income falls below the poverty threshold are considered poor. Poverty thresholds represent key pieces of data employed by the US Census Bureau to estimate poverty levels among a variety of populations (such as the elderly, children under eighteen years old, women, or racial/ethnic minorities). Table 1 illustrates 2012 poverty thresholds for families of various sizes.

Poverty rates can vary significantly when examined by key demographic and geographic factors. Race, age, family structure and composition, educational attainment, and place of residence are important attributes that affect the chances that persons or families will find themselves falling below the poverty line. Table 2 highlights the 2014 poverty rates for demographic groups in Mississippi. As the table illustrates, race clearly plays a role in poverty: African Americans, Hispanics, and Native Americans are more likely to live in poverty. In addition, children, women, and people who lack high school diplomas also have higher poverty rates.

Area of residence also plays a role in the likelihood of poverty. As table 3 shows, poverty rates for Mississippi counties in 2014 ranged from 9.9 percent (DeSoto County) to 47.9 percent (Jefferson County). Poverty rates are higher in the Delta counties and in the Mississippi River counties south of Vicksburg. Rural counties also have higher poverty rates than metropolitan areas.

Given the entrenched nature of poverty in Mississippi, finding the right mix of solutions to reduce the number of people and families in poverty poses a daunting challenge. The numerous strategies for alleviating poverty include investing in education, enhancing workforce skills, improving child care and transportation support, diversifying local economies, and developing regional collaboration among local governments.

Table 1. 2012 Poverty Thresholds by Size of Family and Number of Related Children under Age Eighteen

Size of Family Unit	Related Children under Age 18			
	None	One	Two	Three
Two Persons				
Householder under 65 years	$15,374	$15,825	——	——
Householder 65 years and over	$13,878	$15,765	——	——
Three Persons	$17,959	$18,480	$18,498	——
Four Persons	$23,681	$24,069	$23,283	$23,364

Source: US Census Bureau, *Poverty Thresholds 2012*, http://www.census.gov/hhes/www/poverty/data/threshld/

Table 2. Poverty Rates for Selected Demographic Groups, Mississippi, 2014

Key Characteristics	Poverty Rate
INDIVIDUALS	21.5%
Race	
White	13.4%
African American	34.3%
Asian American	16.2%
Latino	25.9%
Native American	20.4%
Age	
Less than 18	29.0%
18–64	20.3%
65 over	13.2%
Gender	
Male	19.4%
Female	23.5%
Working-age women (ages 18–64)	23.1%
Education	
Less than high school	33.6%
High school graduate	18.7%
Some college	14.4%
Four-year college or more (bachelor's degree or higher)	5.3%
FAMILIES	16.5%
Married Couple	6.7%
With children under age 18	9.7%
Female-headed households (no husband present)	38.9%
With children under age 18	48.0%

Source: US Census Bureau, 2014 American Community Survey

Table 3. Poverty Rates for Mississippi Counties, 2014

Adams County	30.0%
Alcorn County	22.5%
Amite County	26.1%
Attala County	27.1%
Benton County	21.6%
Bolivar County	34.8%
Calhoun County	25.3%
Carroll County	22.1%
Chickasaw County	25.4%
Choctaw County	25.2%
Claiborne County	36.4%
Clarke County	24.1%
Clay County	27.5%
Coahoma County	37.4%
Copiah County	26.7%
Covington County	28.4%
DeSoto County	9.9%
Forrest County	28.5%
Franklin County	18.4%
George County	18.1%
Greene County	16.9%
Grenada County	22.7%
Hancock County	19.8%
Harrison County	20.0%
Hinds County	24.8%
Holmes County	43.9%
Humphreys County	40.5%
Issaquena County	31.6%
Itawamba County	16.9%
Jackson County	15.6%
Jasper County	22.2%
Jefferson County	47.9%
Jefferson Davis County	28.8%
Jones County	23.2%
Kemper County	30.6%
Lafayette County	26.1%
Lamar County	16.1%
Lauderdale County	23.3%
Lawrence County	19.6%
Leake County	27.3%
Lee County	19.2%
Leflore County	41.1%
Lincoln County	25.3%
Lowndes County	25.0%
Madison County	13.1%
Marion County	30.1%
Marshall County	19.4%
Monroe County	21.3%
Montgomery County	27.4%
Neshoba County	22.7%
Newton County	21.8%
Noxubee County	35.1%
Oktibbeha County	33.4%
Panola County	24.6%
Pearl River County	21.9%
Perry County	20.8%
Pike County	27.5%
Pontotoc County	16.2%
Prentiss County	23.4%
Quitman County	38.6%
Rankin County	11.4%

P

Table 3. (continued)	
Scott County	25.2%
Sharkey County	32.2%
Simpson County	24.1%
Smith County	22.7%
Stone County	18.5%
Sunflower County	35.8%
Tallahatchie County	28.5%
Tate County	17.2%
Tippah County	24.9%
Tishomingo County	16.6%
Tunica County	29.6%
Union County	4.0%
Walthall County	24.5%
Warren County	23.2%
Washington County	37.5%
Wayne County	29.5%
Webster County	22.7%
Wilkinson County	28.4%
Winston County	30.3%
Yalobusha County	22.2%
Yazoo County	36.2%

Source: US Census Bureau, 2014 American Community Survey

Lionel J. Beaulieu

Purdue University

Lionel J. Beaulieu, Ferrel Guillory, Sarah Rubin, and Bonnie Teater, *Mississippi: A Sense of Urgency*, Southern Rural Development Center, Mississippi State University (April 2002); Carmen DeNavas-Walt, Bernadette D. Proctor, and Jessica C. Smith, *Income, Poverty, and Health Insurance Coverage in the United States: 2011, Current Population Reports*, www.census.gov; Tracey Farrigan and Timothy Parker, *Amber Waves* website, http://www.ers.usda.gov/amber-waves.aspx (5 December 2012); Leif Jensen, *Rural Realities*, vol. 1, issue 1, Rural Sociological Society website, www.ruralsociology.org; National Poverty Center, "Poverty in the United States: Frequently Asked Questions," University of Michigan, Gerald R. Ford School of Public Policy website, www.npc.umich.edu/poverty/; Talk Poverty website, https://talkpoverty.org/state-year-report/mississippi-2015-report/; US Census Bureau, American Community Survey website, https://www.census.gov/programs-surveys/acs/; US Department of Health and Human Services, *2012 HHS Poverty Guidelines: One Version of the U.S. Federal Poverty Measure*, http://aspe.hhs.gov.

Powell, Susie

(1872–1952) Home Demonstration Leader

A teacher, superintendent, rural school supervisor, civic leader, and Mississippi's first state home demonstration agent, Susie Powell played an instrumental role in improving the standards of living for Mississippi's rural girls and women.

Susan Virginia Powell was born on 3 April 1872 in Batesville, Mississippi, to Sanford Daniel Powell and Susan Virginia Johnson Powell. One of ten children, Powell spent her childhood in Brookhaven. After graduating from high school, she attended Whitworth College in Brookhaven, the University of Mississippi, and the University of Chicago. She then returned to Mississippi and taught in Lawrence and Lincoln Counties. She later served as a superintendent and rural school supervisor for the Mississippi Department of Education. During her tenure as teacher and administrator, she did much to improve the teaching methods, facilities, and grounds of rural schools. She also had a marked influence on early consolidation of schools.

In 1911 the US Department of Agriculture (USDA) invited Powell to organize girls' Tomato Clubs in Mississippi. The Tomato Club movement, which was part of the agricultural extension system, was designed to create an educational organization that would reach rural girls and through them their mothers to improve home conditions. Powell agreed, hoping that girls' club work would improve the rural diet and accord farm women a more important role in family nutrition.

The organization of girls' clubs and their growth in activity and influence in Mississippi was very much a story of rural leadership in action. Powell led the development of the clubs with unfailing enthusiasm and optimism. She was instrumental, for example, in securing the passage of state legislation supporting girls' club work. Since she believed that the girls' club movement and women's organizations marched hand in hand, she called on the Mississippi Federation of Women's Clubs for support. She also sought aid from Mississippi Agricultural and Mechanical College, local merchants, bankers, ministers, boards of supervisors, and school superintendents, pointing out the community value of the movement to anyone who would listen. In 1913 girls' Tomato Clubs became part of the 4-H system.

With the passage of the 1914 Smith-Lever Act establishing the Federal Extension Service, the USDA expanded the girls' club movement to include women's home demonstration work, which sought to reach into the kitchens of farm wives to help them solve problems. Powell was appointed to head the effort in Mississippi. Under her leadership, the club movement spread throughout the state as Powell and her agents attempted to raise the standard of rural life. By the time Powell abruptly resigned in 1924 over an administrative dispute with the director of the Mississippi Agricultural Extension Service, she had led thousands of rural girls and women toward improved standards of living. In a tribute to Powell, a colleague wrote, "She did more for the womanhood of Mississippi than any other one person."

Powell continued to serve Mississippi women as president of the Mississippi Federation of Women's Clubs. During the 1930s she became the state supervisor of the Works Progress Administration's historical project. In 1946 the Mississippi Agricultural Extension honored Powell with a scholarship in her name. She died on 9 July 1952.

Danny B. Moore
Chowan University

Ollie Dean McWhirter, "The Work of Miss Susie V. Powell" (master's thesis, Mississippi State University, 1964); Danny Moore, *Journal of Mississippi History* (Summer 2001); Lee H. Moseley, "History of Mississippi Cooperative Extension Service," Mississippi Cooperative Extension Service Collection, University Archives, Special Collections, Mitchell Memorial Library, Mississippi State University; Susie V. Powell, "Pioneer Club Work," James E. Tanner Papers, University Archives, Special Collections, Mitchell Memorial Library, Mississippi State University.

Powers, Ridgley Ceylon

(1836–1912) Twenty-Ninth Governor, 1871–1874

When Col. Ridgley C. Powers was discharged from the US Army in December 1865, he decided to remain in Mississippi rather than return to his native state of Ohio. He purchased land in Noxubee County near Shuqualak and soon became a successful planter. In 1868 Mississippi's military governor appointed Powers sheriff of Noxubee County.

Powers was born in Trumbull County, Ohio, on 24 December 1836. He graduated from the University of Michigan and studied at Union College in Schenectady, New York. Powers joined the Union Army in 1862 and served with the 125th Ohio Volunteer Infantry. After seeing fighting in Tennessee and in the Atlanta Campaign, he, like many other northerners and midwesterners, settled in the South after the war.

Powers joined Mississippi's newly established Republican Party in 1868 and was elected lieutenant governor alongside James L. Alcorn in 1869. Although most Republican officials were very unpopular during the Reconstruction period, Powers retained the confidence and respect of many Mississippians.

On 30 November 1871 Alcorn resigned to accept a seat in the US Senate, and Powers succeeded him, becoming Mississippi's twenty-ninth governor. Powers favored economic expansion and urged Mississippians to take full advantage of the state's "slumbering resources" through industrial development and agricultural diversification. He especially promoted the increased production of wheat, barley, corn, and other grains to reduce the South's dependence on imported grain. However, a series of bad crops during the early 1870s discouraged Mississippi farmers from experimenting with new crops and left the state with little capital to finance any industrial expansion. Powers was also especially active in supporting the improvement of public schools, arguing that better education would benefit all people and would undercut racial division.

In his first annual message to the legislature in 1872, Gov. Powers reported that a relative tranquillity existed throughout the state and that a "new era of good feeling has sprung up." Mississippi should be recognized, he said, as "an example of reconstruction based upon reconciliation." But that era of good feeling did not last very long, and in 1873 a bitter split within the Republican Party led to the nomination of competing tickets. One faction nominated Adelbert Ames, while the other nominated Alcorn. Powers considered the 1873 governor's election illegal, but the Mississippi Supreme Court validated Ames's election.

When Powers's term expired in 1874, he retired from public life. Shortly after leaving office, Powers married Louisa Born, and he and his family subsequently moved west, first to Prescott, Arizona, and then to Los Angeles, where he was a rancher until his death on 11 November 1912.

David G. Sansing
University of Mississippi

Mississippi Official and Statistical Register (1912); Dunbar Rowland, *Encyclopedia of Mississippi History*, vol. 2 (1907).

Prather, Lenore

(b. 1931) Mississippi Supreme Court Justice

Lenore L. Prather was the first female chief justice of the Mississippi Supreme Court and has been praised as a trailblazer for women in the state. The daughter of Byron Herald Loving, who represented Clay County in the state legislature, and Hattie Hearn Morris Loving, Lenore Loving was born in West Point, Mississippi, on 17 September 1931. She graduated from West Point High School in 1949 and from Mississippi University for Women four years later. Loving earned a law degree from the University of Mississippi in 1955 and practiced privately until 1971, working first with her father and later her husband, Robert Brooks Prather, whom she married in 1957.

In 1965 Prather became the municipal judge of West Point, and in 1971 Gov. John Bell Williams appointed her judge for the 14th Chancery District of Mississippi, which encompasses Lowndes, Clay, Oktibbeha, Noxubee, Webster, and Chickasaw Counties. Prather won election to the court in 1974 and reelection in 1975 and 1982. Later that year, Gov. William Winter appointed her to the state Supreme Court, the first woman to serve as a justice. Prather became presiding justice in 1993 and chief justice in 1998. However, she suffered a stunning defeat in the 2000 judicial election and left the Court. From July 2001 to June 2002 Prather served as interim president of the Mississippi University for Women.

Prather has received numerous honors for her achievements. Mississippi University for Women awarded her its Medal of Excellence in 1990 and its Alumni Achievement Award in 1993. Two years later the University of Mississippi Law School named her Alumna of the Year. Gov. Haley Barbour awarded Prather the Mississippi Medal of Service in 2009, and in 2012 she was inducted into the Law Alumni Hall of Fame at the University of Mississippi's School of Law.

Prather resides in Columbus. She maintains an active speaking schedule, encouraging the continued advancement of women in all spheres of life. In one such speech, Prather asserted, "No matter what direction we travel in our careers we should open the door behind us for the women of the next generation, to ensure that women enrich our society even further in the future."

Becca Walton
University of Mississippi

Mississippi State University, Mitchell Memorial Library, Morris W. H. Collins Speaker Series website, http://lib.msstate.edu/collins/speakers/; Southern Women's Institute, Mississippi University for Women, *Golden Days: Reminiscences of Alumnae, Mississippi State College for Women* (2009).

Premanufactured Buildings

Premanufactured metal building systems came into their own after World War II as a result of increased manufacturing capacity, the need for low-cost and easily portable shelter, increased labor costs, and the invention of the digital computer. The combination of these factors, in Mississippi and elsewhere, helped fuel the development of buildings that are mass-marketed, preengineered, factory-produced, and rapidly installed by an authorized builder, leading to delivery of a durable, finished structure in a relatively short time.

Semicircular premanufactured building, Coldwater (Photograph by David Wharton)

Initially used for utilitarian structures such as industrial and agricultural buildings, metal building systems are now used for a wide range of nonresidential, low-rise building types. Churches, schools, commercial buildings, warehouses, recreational buildings, and community facilities are now routinely constructed using premanufactured building systems.

The primary reason for the wide use of these buildings is economics. Overall construction and maintenance costs are perceived as lower than for competing construction types. The buildings are conceived as off-the-shelf solutions, are designed in a wide range of sizes and with numerous options, and are marketed through local builders with the knowledge to accurately predict prices and construction schedules. Once on-site, they can be erected with simple, commonly available tools by a relatively unskilled workforce.

Vernacular architecture in Mississippi is a product of many of the same forces: a need for economy, making do with materials and resources close at hand, and the desire to modify a structure over time. Though premanufactured buildings are industrially produced, once the pieces arrive at the job site, owners can modify the structures as needs evolve. Many of the premanufactured buildings seen in the Mississippi landscape have been changed, since such low-tech building systems lend themselves to relatively easy modification by nonprofessionals.

Nils Gore
University of Kansas

Building Systems Institute, *Metal Building Systems* (1990).

Prentiss, Seargent S.

(1808–1850) Politician

Seargent Smith Prentiss, a lawyer and politician, was born on 30 September 1808 in Portland, Maine, the third of nine children of Abigail Lewis Prentiss and William Prentiss. Two of his sisters died young, and before he was a year old, Seargent contracted a severe illness and fever that left him an invalid for ten years. He forever had a limp, and in later life he needed a cane. Raised in a strict Congregationalist household, Prentiss attended Bowdoin College, graduating in 1826.

A voracious reader well versed in the classics, Prentiss decided that a practical career lay in the law and that the best opportunities were in the West. He read law in Gorham, Maine; in Cincinnati; and finally with Robert J. Walker in Natchez. Admitted to the bar in June 1829, Prentiss practiced briefly with Felix Huston before relocating to Vicksburg in 1832. Partnering with John Guion and later William C. Smedes, Prentiss had great success. Possessed with natural oratorical gifts, he repeatedly changed jurors' minds.

A great admirer of the ideas and oratory of Daniel Webster and Henry Clay, Prentiss sided with the Whigs in the developing political party conflict of the 1830s. In 1835 Warren County elected Prentiss to the State House of Representatives. While visiting family in Maine, Prentiss halfheartedly competed to represent Mississippi in a special September 1837 session of the US Congress. He did not win, although he and Thomas J. Word won the regular November election. The Democratic incumbents, John F. H. Claiborne and Samuel Gholson, then claimed that their summer victory entitled them to the full two-year term. Permitted to present his claim to Congress, Prentiss made his reputation for oratory a national one. For three days he inspired the Whigs and skewered the Democrats, speaking so effectively that the House narrowly reversed its decision to seat the Democrats and returned the matter to Mississippi for a new election. Prentiss's relentless campaigning then led the Whig ticket to victory in April 1838. His political stands were consistent with the national Whig platform. He favored railroads, other internal improvements, and the national bank while vigorously opposing the repudiation of Mississippi's bonds in the early 1840s. Prentiss ran for the US Senate in January 1840 but suffered a difficult loss to Robert J. Walker. Later that year Prentiss spoke on behalf of William Henry Harrison's presidential campaign at well-attended Whig rallies from Mississippi to Ohio to Maine, efforts he repeated in support of Henry Clay in 1844.

The last decade of his life was largely dedicated to his law practice and land speculation. On 2 March 1842 Prentiss married Mary Jane Williams of Natchez, and the couple had two daughters and two sons. Prentiss gambled and drank excessively, and his real estate speculation proved ill conceived, especially in Vicksburg. After the 1844 presidential campaign Prentiss relocated to New Orleans to practice law, attracting one controversial case after another. Debilitated by cholera and hard drinking and desperate to overcome his debts, Prentiss died on 1 July 1850 at Longwood, outside Natchez.

M. Philip Lucas
Cornell College

Dallas C. Dickey, *Seargent S. Prentiss: Whig Orator of the Old South* (1945); George Lewis Prentiss, ed., A *Memoir of S. S. Prentiss* (1855); Joseph D. Shields, *The Life and Times of Seargent Smith Prentiss* (1883).

Prentiss County

By the time Prentiss County was founded in northeastern Mississippi in 1870, the area had already seen a number of important historical events. Home to the Chickasaw and formed from Tishomingo County land, Prentiss County was the site of the ferry business operated by George Colbert (Tootemastubbe), a powerful Chickasaw leader in the early 1800s. The county was named for lawyer and politician Seargent Smith Prentiss, and the county seat is Booneville.

In June 1864 Union and Confederate troops met near Baldwyn in the Battle of Brice's Cross Roads. There, Union forces attempted to stop Confederate troops led by Gen. Nathan Bedford Forrest from leading attacks on Union supplies and transportation facilities. The battle caused the deaths of more than two thousand Union soldiers and was a victory for Forrest's troops. Citizens of Prentiss County later played important roles in remembering the Civil War, first when locals made the unique decision to rebury Confederate dead in a special cemetery in Booneville and later when women in Baldwyn organized one of Mississippi's first chapters of the United Daughters of the Confederacy in 1894.

Prentiss County began as an agricultural county with an 1880 population of 12,158. About 80 percent of the residents were white. Its farmers practiced mixed agriculture, concentrating on grains, livestock, cotton, and tobacco. Its twenty-four manufacturing firms were small and employed just thirty-eight men.

By 1900 Prentiss County was home to 15,788 people. Industrial growth was substantial, with fifty establishments employing 143 workers. As in much of Mississippi, a substantial difference existed between the landownership rate for white farmers (about 50 percent) and the rate for their African American counterparts (11 percent).

In the early twentieth century, Baptists and Methodists made up more than 90 percent of Prentiss County's church members. In the 1916 religious census, the largest groups of churchgoers belonged to the Methodist Episcopal Church, South; the Southern Baptist Convention; the Colored Methodist Episcopal Church; and the Missionary Baptists.

By 1930 the Prentiss County population had reached 19,265. Like much of northeastern Mississippi, Prentiss County was overwhelmingly white (87 percent). The census counted only two immigrants—one each from Scotland and England. The county had no urban population, and almost two-thirds of the county's 3,713 farms were operated by tenants. Corn and cattle were the most important farm products. Prentiss was one of the early counties to receive power through the Tennessee Valley Authority.

In 1929 the Mississippi State Medical Association inaugurated publication of a journal, *Mississippi Doctor*, in Booneville. In 1948 Northeast Mississippi Junior College was founded in Booneville, and in 1957 it began offering the state's first associate degree in nursing.

Notable natives of Prentiss County include Elijah Pierce and Orma Rinehart "Hack" Smith. Born near Baldwyn in 1892, Pierce became an extraordinary sculptor who used wood to create artworks with religious themes. Smith, born in Booneville in 1904, became a US district judge who oversaw cases involving the integration of Mississippi's schools.

Between 1930 and 1960 Prentiss County's population declined to 17,949, with whites continuing to make up close to 90 percent of county residents. By 1960 more than 30 percent of the workforce was employed in manufacturing, with most women making clothing and men building furniture and harvesting timber. Agriculture accounted for a quarter of the county's workers, who raised corn, soybeans, and livestock. By 1980 the population had risen to 24,025.

In 2010 Prentiss, like most northeastern Mississippi counties, remained predominantly white and growing, with a population of 25,276.

Mississippi Encyclopedia Staff
University of Mississippi

Mississippi State Planning Commission, *Progress Report on State Planning in Mississippi* (1938); *Mississippi Statistical Abstract*, Mississippi State University (1952–2010); Charles Sydnor and Claude Bennett, *Mississippi History* (1939); University of Virginia Library, Historical Census Browser website, http://mapserver.lib.virginia.edu; E. Nolan Waller and Dani A. Smith, *Growth Profiles of Mississippi's Counties, 1960–1980* (1985).

Prentiss Normal and Industrial Institute

African Americans faced limited educational opportunities in Mississippi at the turn of the twentieth century. To challenge those limits, Jonas Edward Johnson and Bertha LaBranche Johnson founded the Prentiss Normal and Industrial Institute in Jefferson Davis County in June 1907. The Johnsons purchased forty acres of land from a white family, and J. E. Johnson became the school's first president, serving until his death in 1953. Bertha succeeded him, remaining at the helm until her death eighteen years later. J. E. Johnson, who graduated as valedictorian from Alcorn Agricultural and Mechanical College, and Bertha Johnson, who studied under Booker T. Washington at the Tuskegee Institute, not only enabled thousands of young black Mississippi men and women to obtain schooling but also helped to build relationships and promote cooperation across racial lines within the local farming community.

The Johnsons' first group of students consisted of forty children from poor local farming families. Many parents paid the tuition with vegetables, chickens, and eggs. In 1909 the Mississippi Department of Education licensed the Prentiss Institute as a private high school. An old plantation house housed the school until the Johnsons raised funds to build an academic building that also served as the girls' rooming house, a boys' dormitory, a boarding hall, two homes for teachers, and a trades building. The institute offered a regular academic curriculum of English, math, and science and in 1917 added courses in agriculture, auto mechanics, blacksmithing, carpentry, and shoe and leather work. The institute was licensed as a private junior college in 1931 and three years later had grown to a campus of 500 acres, 16 buildings,

Prentiss Normal and Industrial Institute graduating class (Archives and Records Services Division, Mississippi Department of Archives and History [PI ED 1982.0044 Box 12 R72 B4 52 Folder 2 #7])

340 students, and 17 teachers. At the time of J. E. Johnson's death the school had more than 700 students, 24 buildings, and 44 faculty members.

In 1955 the Prentiss Institute formed a relationship with the Heifer Project (later renamed Heifer International), a nonprofit organization that promotes sustainable agricultural practices by donating livestock to needy individuals and communities. In June of that year the first shipment of heifers was sent to the Prentiss Institute. When the second batch arrived on Christmas Day, Prentiss administrators asked local white farmers to help distribute the cattle to needy white families in the area, an unprecedented effort to promote goodwill and social justice across racial lines during a tense time in Jim Crow Mississippi.

Because its funding came from private sources, the Prentiss Institute always remained on unsure economic footing. The Supreme Court's 1954 *Brown v. Board of Education* decision declared school segregation unconstitutional, though the State of Mississippi failed to fully enforce the new law until 1969. While the state's public schools slowly integrated, the enrollment at historically black schools dwindled. By 1981 enrollment had dropped to 150 students, and in 1989 the Prentiss Institute closed its doors as an educational facility.

With the help of a preservation grant from the Mississippi Department of Archives and History, alumni subsequently rallied to restore the school's concrete block facility, which had been constructed in 1926 with money provided by the Julius Rosenwald Fund. On 24 February 2013, the building was rededicated, and the following year the Mississippi Heritage Trust awarded the Prentiss Institute Trustee Board a Heritage Award for Restoration. The building now houses an auditorium, classrooms, and a museum, and the board rents space to community organizations, groups, and families.

Cale Nicholson
Little Rock, Arkansas

Natalie Bell, *Mississippi Link* (4 February 2016); Ron Harrist, *Jackson Clarion-Ledger* (31 July 1985); Jaman Matthews, *World Ark* (March–April 2007); Thurl Metzger, *The Road to Development* (1981); Mississippi Heritage Trust website, www.mississippiheritage.com; Charles H. Wilson, *Education for Negroes in Mississippi since 1910* (1974).

Presbyterians

Presbyterians have made up a small but important part of the religious landscape of what is now Mississippi since early in the area's settlement by Euro-Americans. Since the mid-twentieth century, the state's various Presbyterian con-

Presbyterian church, Grenada, ca. 1912 (Ann Rayburn Paper Americana Collection, Department of Archives and Special Collections, J. D. Williams Library, University of Mississippi [rayburn_ann_24_94_001])

gregations have claimed about thirty thousand members. The organizational history of the Presbyterians, especially the relationship between primarily southern and northern or nationwide organizations, has often mirrored broader changes in the state's history.

The Presbyterians who first populated the American South were primarily Scots-Irish immigrants who came through Philadelphia and New York and Appalachia in the late 1700s and early 1800s. Calvinist in theology, optimistic about education and the frontier, and organized into church sessions, presbyteries, synods, and a national general assembly, the Presbyterians grew slowly in early nineteenth-century Mississippi.

In 1800 Presbyterians sent two representatives from North Carolina and Georgia, James Hall and William Montgomery, to tour the Natchez District to consider the possibility of missionary activity. In 1816 Presbyterians met to form their first organization, with Montgomery working with Joseph Bullen, Jacob Rickhow, and James Smylie. Smylie settled in Washington, Mississippi, outside Natchez, working as both a teacher and a minister. The denomination grew relatively slowly, and by 1837 Mississippi was home to three separate presbyteries with twenty-nine ministers and fewer than one thousand members.

The three evangelical denominations—Presbyterians, Baptists, and Methodists—defined in large part by their emphasis on revivalism and their insistence on personal transformation as part of the Christian experience, quickly became the dominant religious force in Mississippi. A defining feature of Presbyterians, their insistence on a formally educated ministry, contributed to their growth at a slower pace than their evangelical colleagues. A major question was whether the individualistic and egalitarian aspects of religious experience or the tendency to emphasize order and hierarchy would emerge from evangelical history. The first Presbyterian to become a leader in Mississippi was Smylie, and his proslavery statements helped cement Presbyterianism's conservative reputation in the state. In the 1830s Smylie rejected abolitionist arguments that slavery was a sin, argued for biblical justification for slavery, and detailed a religious proslavery argument that emphasized the responsibilities of people in charge to care for the bodies and souls of their dependents.

Presbyterians made considerable efforts to establish schools and churches among the American Indian populations first in Mississippi and then in Oklahoma after Removal. The first Presbyterian effort to convert Mississippi Indians started in 1818, when missionary Cyrus Kingsbury accepted Choctaw invitations to set up schools and other concerns at Eliot, on the Yalobusha River, and at Mayhew in Oktibbeha County.

In the late 1830s Presbyterians divided into the "Old School" and "New School." The Old School feared tendencies toward association with multiple denominations in missionary work and a growing liberalism on issues of abolition and other forms of activism. Relying on the notion of the "spirituality of the church" to reject this-worldly activism, the Old School Presbyterians emphasized the centrality of conversion and literal interpretations of the Bible. The division was not explicitly sectional, as New School Presbyterians could be found in Mississippi and other southern states and Old School Presbyterians in the North. Still, the division, intensified by slavery issues, seemed a harbinger of greater sectional conflict.

In 1861 Presbyterians in the South formed the Presbyterian Church United States (PCUS) to differentiate their group from the northern United Presbyterian Church USA (UPCUSA). From the Civil War through the civil rights period, the dominant group within Presbyterianism was the PCUS. Though the PCUS and the UPCUSA may have looked alike to outsiders (as well as many Presbyterians), the two groups had regionally distinct interpretations of church life and the proper responsibilities for Christians in the world. Though the two groups often shared interests, goals, and activities and began exploring the possibility of reunion in the early 1900s, they remained separate denominations until 1983.

The national effort at a reunion of Presbyterian bodies took on great significance in Mississippi because it coincided in large part with the civil rights movement. Presbyterians who feared national union with the UPCUSA criticized the group for being soft on biblical inerrancy, for supporting women in leadership roles, and for pushing for racial desegregation or at least criticizing racial injustice. The relationship between ideas about race, theology, and the potential for a national union of Presbyterian bodies made Mississippi the site of some dramatic organizational tensions between the 1950s and 1980s. Guy Gillespie, a Presbyterian minister and the longtime president of Belhaven College, espoused the conservative view in a mid-1950s sermon, "A Christian View on Segregation." Other Mississippi Presbyterians, however, worked as civil rights activists. Perhaps the most influential Presbyterian in Mississippi was William Winter, the state's governor from 1980 to 1984, who aggressively advocated desegregation and improved education.

A major break came in 1973 when conservatives, almost all of them in the South, broke away from the PCUS to form the Presbyterian Church in America (PCA), in large part out of frustration with the liberal tendencies of those supporting union with the UPCUSA. Sixty of central and southern Mississippi's one hundred Presbyterian congregations withdrew from the PCUS: according to historian R. Milton Winter, "The Synod of Mississippi, one of the smallest in the PCUS, suffered greater loss than any other in the Presbyterian divisions of the 1970s and '80s, with the result that one could no longer speak of a 'solid South' in Presbyterian terms." The conservative PCA quickly became a church of substantial influence in Mississippi. In 2016 the PCA had nearly 120 congregations in Mississippi, many of them historically large and important.

In 1983 the long-discussed union between the PCUS and UPCUSA led to the formation of a new denomination, the Presbyterian Church USA (PCUSA). The PCUSA's Synod of Living Waters includes Mississippi, Alabama, Tennessee, Kentucky, and parts of Arkansas and Missouri. Mississippi is divided into the St. Andrew Presbytery, which includes sixty-four congregations in the northern part of the state, and the Mississippi Presbytery, which covers the southern part of the state. In 2016 Mississippi was also home to fourteen congregations belonging to the Cumberland Presbyterian Church, which was formed in 1810 and is headquartered in Memphis, Tennessee; to twenty-one congregations affiliated with the Evangelical Presbyterian Church, a more conservative denomination founded in 1981; and to a handful of other churches associated with other Presbyterian denominations.

Leadership at Jackson's Belhaven College shifted because of the controversies. The college was founded in 1894 and affiliated for eighty years with the PCUS. In 1972 Belhaven's leaders created a separate board that ran the college with the funding but not direct oversight of the PCUS. Now operating as Belhaven University, the school remains a Christian liberal arts college with close ties to several groups of Presbyterians.

Ted Ownby
University of Mississippi

Joel L. Alvis, *Religion and Race: Southern Presbyterians, 1946–1983* (1994); Association of Religion Data Archives website, www.thearda.com; *Cumberland Presbyterian Church, Yearbook of the General Assembly* (2016); Evangelical Presbyterian Church website, www.epc.org; Walter Brownlow Posey, *The Presbyterian Church in the Old Southwest, 1778–1838* (1952); Presbyterian Church (USA), Synod of Living Waters website, www.synodoflivingwaters.org; Presbyterian Church in America Historical Center website, www.pcahistory.org; Randy Sparks, *On Jordan's Stormy Banks: Evangelicalism in Mississippi, 1773–1876* (1994); Ernest Trice Thompson, *Presbyterians in the South*, 3 vols. (1963–73); R. Milton Winter, *Journal of Presbyterian History* (Spring 2000).

Presley, Elvis

(1935–1977) Musician

In 1953 a young man from Mississippi entered a Memphis recording studio to make a personal record. The office manager asked the youth what type of music he favored. He replied shyly that he liked all kinds. Intrigued, she questioned him about his style. Was it country? Pop? Gospel? He insisted that he adhered to no particular style. She probed again, pushing him to reveal the vocalist he most resembled. The eighteen-year-old delivery truck driver stubbornly yet politely maintained that he did not sound like anyone else. Curious, she placed the young man with the ducktail haircut and sideburns before a microphone. Accompanied only by his own acoustic guitar, he began to sing. His emotional intensity and sensitivity surprised her. When he completed

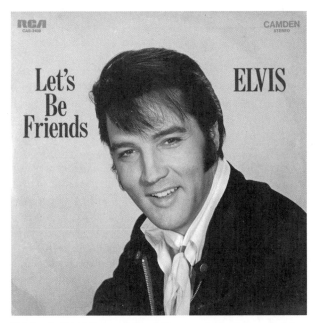

Elvis Presley's *Let's Be Friends* (1970) (Courtesy James G. Thomas, Jr.)

his two songs, Marion Keisker reached the same conclusion as the teenager she had just interrogated: Elvis Presley did not sound like anyone else.

This would not be the last time that Elvis Presley confounded categorization. He was the hip-swiveling "Hillbilly Cat," a complex figure who encompassed within his persona the emotions, aspirations, fears, and particularly the contradictions common to a large segment of his generation. His endeavors challenged many of the cultural norms of his society, conventions that governed such matters as racial segregation, masculinity, sexual expression, middle-class preeminence, teen subordination, and musical tastes. From the moment he stepped onto the national stage in the mid-1950s, the singer excited, exasperated, and enraged countless people. His was a controversial presence that even death failed to diminish. Decades following his demise, historians, music scholars, fans, and casual connoisseurs of popular culture argue over the merits he may or may not have possessed. No consensus regarding his career and significance has been reached. Once likened to a jug of corn liquor at a champagne party, Elvis, uninvited and unsolicited, interjected the intrinsically invisible and interrelated issues of class, race, region, gender, and age into the American mainstream. Bringing to light many of the conflicts and tensions simmering below the seemingly placid post–World War II societal surface, he helped initiate a cultural upheaval that has continued to reverberate well into the new millennium.

Such influence could not have been predicted. Born on 8 January 1935 to anonymity in a two-room East Tupelo shotgun house, Elvis Aron Presley lived as his identical twin died. This factor undoubtedly contributed to a very strong bond forged between Elvis and his mother, Gladys. He was not as close to his father, Vernon, a failed sharecropper. The family was poor and briefly lived near or within Shake Rag, an African American section of the northeastern Mississippi town. The Pentecostal Presleys regularly attended the First Assembly of God Church. Not surprisingly, given his residential and religious surroundings, Elvis developed an attachment to music. He listened to WELO, a local radio station that featured Mississippi Slim, a country performer who served as the first of Presley's many celebrity models. At age ten, Elvis won second prize at the Mississippi-Alabama Fair and Dairy Show for his sentimental rendition—delivered while standing on a chair to reach the microphone—of a song about the death of an aged dog.

After years of struggle against dwindling economic opportunities and eroding status in Mississippi, the Presleys migrated to Memphis in 1948. In the West Tennessee metropolis, young Elvis aspired to overcome his feelings of invisibility and irrelevance. He turned to popular culture to redefine himself. Inspired by movie stars and entertainers, he developed a penchant for flashy clothes, slicked-back hair, and long sideburns. Beale Street beckoned, and Presley frequently ventured down the Main Street of Negro America, absorbing its many sounds and visual manifestations. He often continued his forays into

P

African American culture on Sunday mornings (and Wednesday evenings), visiting Rev. Herbert Brewster's East Trigg Baptist Church. In a seemingly endless quest to establish an identity, Presley also soaked up everything he heard on the radio. Black-appeal stations such as WDIA and eccentric disc jockeys such as WHBQ's Dewey Phillips provided an eclectic assortment of musical styles that would prove formative: rhythm and blues, country, pop, and both black and white gospel.

In 1954 Presley made his first commercial recordings for independent producer Sam Phillips. Along with guitarist Scotty Moore and bassist Bill Black, Presley and Phillips produced five Sun singles in just eighteen months. Exploiting their creation of a working-class and biracial musical synthesis later dubbed rockabilly, Presley, Moore, and Black, newly minted members of the *Louisiana Hayride* radio program, rapidly built a youthful following throughout the South and Southwest.

By the close of 1955 Presley was one of the hottest commodities in country music. Under the tutelage of his flamboyant manager, Col. Tom Parker, Elvis signed an exclusive contract with RCA Victor. In 1956 RCA and Parker, seeking to promote their multifaceted performer in the pop and R&B markets, booked Presley onto several network television programs, including *The Ed Sullivan Show*. Beamed into the living rooms of millions, the singer's popularity skyrocketed. As his fame rose, a national furor mounted over Presley's black-derived and overtly sexual performance style. The criticisms, however, only heightened Presleymania. Following unprecedented record sales, Hollywood called, and Elvis began his stint as a movie idol in *Love Me Tender* (1956). By 1958 he had emerged as the undisputed King of Rock and Roll.

Between 1956 and 1963 Presley dominated popular music. Even a two-year stint in the US Army failed to stifle his popularity. After 1960 he devoted his energy almost exclusively to making motion pictures, averaging three films a year during the ensuing decade. While the results did not bring him critical acclaim, he became one of the highest-paid actors of his era. Yet by the mid-1960s Presley's creativity and influence appeared irreversibly diminished. His films had grown increasingly formulaic, and his music seemed tired and hopelessly tied to inane movie soundtracks. As the sights and sounds that came to dominate the 1960s became younger and more disruptive, Elvis seemed old-fashioned. A highly successful 1968 television special in which he returned to his blues and gospel roots revived his career, and Presley began touring for the first time since the 1950s. To the astonishment of many, Presley recaptured the vitality that had characterized his early stage shows. Assisted by a generational revival that utilized the consumer power of now-middle-aged rock and rollers born during the Great Depression, Elvis returned to pop superstardom. After 1973, however, personal difficulties, including a failed marriage, health problems, and ballooning weight, took their toll. On 16 August 1977 Presley died of heart failure and complications caused by long-term drug abuse.

Elvis Presley, of course, did not invent rock and roll. He did, however, possess the unusual combination of talent, charisma, and luck to become a popular entertainer whose improbable rise to wealth and fame appealed to a large segment of American society. A southern version of the Horatio Alger hero who challenged contemporary boundaries regarding music, taste, race, gender, class, and public behavior, Presley remains a significant key to understanding the postwar world from which he emerged.

Michael T. Bertrand
Tennessee State University

Michael T. Bertrand, *Race, Rock, and Elvis* (2005); Vernon Chadwick, *In Search of Elvis: Music, Race, Art, Religion* (1997); James C. Cobb, *The Most Southern Place on Earth: The Mississippi Delta and the Roots of Regional Identity* (1994); Erika Lee Doss, *Fans, Faith, and Image* (2004); Elaine Dundy, *Elvis and Gladys* (2004); Colin Escott and Martin Hawkins, *Good Rockin' Tonight: Sun Records and the Birth of Rock 'n' Roll* (1992); Peter Guralnick, *Careless Love: The Unmaking of Elvis Presley* (1998); Peter Guralnick, *Last Train to Memphis: The Rise of Elvis Presley* (1995); Jerry Hopkins, *Elvis: The Biography* (2007); George Lipsitz, *Class and Culture in Cold War America: A Rainbow at Midnight* (1981); Bill Malone with Dave Stricklin, *Southern Music, American Music* (2nd rev. ed. 2003); Greil Marcus, *Mystery Train: Images of America in Rock 'n' Roll* (2008); Charles Ponce de Leon, *Fortunate Son: The Life of Elvis Presley* (2006); Joel Williamson, *Elvis Presley, A Southern Life* (2015).

Price, Leontyne
(b. 1927) Opera Singer

Leontyne Price is an American soprano who followed the footsteps of African American singers Elizabeth Taylor Greenfield (1817–76) and Marian Anderson (1897–1993) to break barriers in the classical performing arts. She is widely recognized as one of the leading operatic singers of the twentieth century.

Mary Violet Leontyne Price was born on 10 February 1927 in Laurel, Mississippi. Her interest in music began at an early age, greatly influenced by her mother, Kate Baker Price, who often sang to her, and her father, James Price, who played tuba. Her parents encouraged her to begin piano lessons at age four. She also sang with her mother in the St. Paul's Methodist Church choir in Laurel and later in the school choir at Oak Park High School, where she also played piano at school functions.

Price left Laurel for Wilberforce, Ohio, in 1944 to pursue a music education degree at Wilberforce College (now

Central State University). She received a bachelor's degree in 1948 and went on to enroll at New York's Julliard School of Music. After hearing her sing in a school performance of Verdi's *Falstaff*, composer Virgil Thompson offered her a role in a 1952 production of his opera, *Four Saints in Three Acts*, in which she made her professional opera debut. Price's talent quickly attracted notice, and she began landing leading roles in major operas. Her role as Bess in the 1952–54 touring production of Gershwin's *Porgy and Bess* exposed an international audience to her voice. On this tour, she married the operatic lead baritone, William Warfield, in 1952, though they separated a few years later and divorced in 1973.

In 1955 Price became the first African American to sing an opera role on television, performing Puccini's *Tosca* on NBC. Following several other NBC opera productions, Price performed lead roles at the San Francisco Opera House, the Vienna Staatsoper, and London's Covent Garden. In 1958 she shattered another barrier by becoming the first African American to sing a lead role at Milan's Teatro alla Scala. In 1961 Price made her Metropolitan Opera debut, singing the role of Leonora in Verdi's *Il Trovatore*. Her performance so captivated the audience that she was honored with a staggering forty-two-minute standing ovation. Her success and admiration from fans led the Metropolitan Opera to open its next season with Price singing *Aida*, the role that became her signature. Composer Samuel Barber wrote the opera *Antony and Cleopatra* for Price, and she premiered it at the opening concert at the Metropolitan Opera's new building at Lincoln Center in 1966. Price gave her farewell operatic performance at the Metropolitan Opera in 1985, singing her most famous role, Aida.

Outside of opera, Price premiered Barber's *Hermit Songs*, with the composer playing piano, at the Library of Congress in 1953. During the 1960s she recorded several albums of church hymns and spirituals. Despite the end of her opera career, Price performed art song recitals for the next ten years, often featuring spirituals and songs that were written specifically for her by composers such as Samuel Barber and Ned Rorem. She has also given master classes at universities around the United States. Her last recital took place on 19 November 1997 at the University of North Carolina at Chapel Hill. In October 2001 she briefly came out of retirement to perform at a memorial concert at Carnegie Hall for victims of the 11 September terrorist attacks. In 1990 she authored a children's book, *Aida*.

Price has received many awards and honors, including numerous Grammy Awards for Best Classical Performance, Vocal Soloist; a Grammy Lifetime Achievement Award (1989); the Presidential Medal of Freedom (1964); the Italian Award of Merit (1965); the National Medal of Arts (1985); the Kennedy Center Honors (1980); the Mississippi Institute of Arts and Letters Lifetime Achievement Award (2000), and the National Endowment for the Arts Opera Honors (2008).

Greg Johnson
University of Mississippi

Alan Blyth, *Grove Music Online* website, www.grovemusic.com; Dominique-René De Lerma, in *Encyclopedia of African-American Culture and History*, ed. Cornel West and David Lionel Smith (2006); Hilary Mac Austin, in *Black Women in America*, ed. Darlene Clark Hine (2005).

Price, Zelma Wells
(1898–1974) Political Leader

Zelma Price was a member of the state legislature from Washington County and the first female judge in Mississippi. She was born to Mattie Lou Wells and Walter Wells, a deputy sheriff, in Rishville, Mississippi, in Calhoun County, where she graduated from high school in 1916. Price married and divorced Jimmy Price early in her adult life and raised two daughters while working as a teacher in Tallahatchie County and as a telegraph operator in Memphis. Although she never attended college, she worked her way through law courses while employed by a Greenville law firm and began practicing law there in the 1930s.

She was elected to the Mississippi House of Representatives from Washington County in 1943 and served for ten years. Price chaired the House Temperance Committee, an intriguing position for someone who opposed the state's Prohibition law. In 1948 she proposed a bill that would have mandated a statewide election to outlaw Prohibition, though the measure was never enacted. She claimed that Mississippi laws prohibiting the sale of alcohol yet taxing those sales made the state a "laughing stock," and she believed that a substantial tax on legal alcohol sales could fund a pay raise for schoolteachers.

Price was passionate about her political interests. As a member of the Delta Council, Chamber of Commerce, and lawyers' groups in Washington County, she belonged to the Delta elite. As a member of the House committee on juvenile delinquency, she wrote the bill creating Mississippi's first court system for juveniles accused of breaking the law. After suffering injuries in a car wreck driving to Jackson in 1950, she had hospital employees roll her hospital bed to the floor of the legislature so she could cast her vote to create the state's first medical school.

Price took pleasure in her role as one of the few women in Mississippi politics. Consistently described in newspaper stories as "interesting" and "colorful," Price was a popular speaker at white women's clubs, often lecturing on topics such as "Women in Political Action" and "Strengthening the Foundations of Freedom in the Home."

In 1953 Gov. Hugh White appointed Price to serve as county judge, making her the state's first female to sit on the bench. Her commitment to women in public life inspired

Price not only to call for jury service for women but also to put women on juries in Washington County in the 1950s, years before doing so actually became legal.

A lively individual who loved company and conversation, Price lived in the same Greenville home from 1940 until her death in 1974. With an interest in genealogy, she compiled and in 1959 privately printed a sprawling eight-volume history of her family. Following their mother's example, both of Price's daughters became lawyers.

Ted Ownby
University of Mississippi

Joanne V. Hawks et al., *Journal of Mississippi History* (November 1981); Zelma Wells Price Subject File, Mississippi Department of Archives and History; Zelma W. Price, *Of Whom I Came: From Whence I Came: Wells-Wise, Rish-Wise, and Otherwise* (1959).

Pride, Charley

(b. 1938) Country Musician

Charley Pride Highway, south of Sledge (Photograph by James G. Thomas, Jr.)

Born in Sledge, Mississippi, on 18 March 1938, country singer Charley Frank Pride was one of eleven children born to sharecroppers and cotton pickers. Pride grew up working in the fields near his home and developed two loves, country music and baseball. At age fourteen he bought his first guitar, a Silvertone, from Sears, Roebuck, and Company and taught himself how to play. According to childhood friends, he played both baseball and the six-string every day.

In 1955 Pride traveled to Loew's State Theatre in Memphis for a talent competition. The next day he attended a baseball tryout and landed a job as a pitcher and outfielder in the Negro Leagues. In late 1956 he was drafted by the US Army, and he served through early 1958. He subsequently resumed his baseball career, playing in the Negro Leagues in the late 1950s before moving to Montana and working as a smelter and playing semipro ball in the early 1960s. After unsuccessful tryouts with Major League Baseball's Los Angeles Angels and New York Mets, his baseball career came to an end. Pride married Rozene Cochran in Memphis in December 1957, and they went on to have three children.

While in Montana, Pride had begun a music career, singing the national anthem at baseball games and performing in honky-tonks and nightclubs. He went to Nashville, where a recording session with Jack Clement led to his signing with Chet Atkins, vice president of RCA Records. In 1965 RCA released Pride's first single, "Snakes Crawl at Night." Pride had his first No. 1 single with 1969's "All I Have to Offer You

(Is Me)." In 1971 he released "Kiss an Angel Good Morning," which became his best-selling record and earned a Grammy Award as the year's Best Country Song. That year, he also earned the Country Music Association's Entertainer of the Year and Top Male Vocalist Awards.

Pride's résumé includes thirty-six No. 1 singles and more than seventy million albums sold. He made his first appearance at the *Grand Ole Opry* on 1 January 1967, and as he recalled, "Ernest Tubb brought me on, and I was more nervous than a cat on a hot tin roof." On 1 May 1993 he became the first African American member of the *Grand Ole Opry*. In 2000 he was inducted into the Country Music Hall of Fame, and in 2008 he received a lifetime achievement award from the Mississippi Arts Commission. With his smooth, baritone voice, Pride takes concertgoers back to a time in country music before the flash and glamour of many of today's current singers.

Pride continues to record new music and to tour both in the United States and around the world. A longtime resident of Dallas, Texas, Pride has kept close connections to Mississippi. Two of his hit songs are "Mississippi Cotton Picking Delta Town" and "Roll on Mississippi." In 2003 the State of Mississippi named a thirty-three-mile stretch of Highway 3—from Sledge south to Tutwiler—the Charley Pride Highway, and in 2011 he was honored with a marker on the Mississippi Country Music Trail. In July 2009 he performed at the White House for Pres. Barack Obama and First Lady Michelle Obama. An avid fan of baseball and particularly the Texas Rangers, Pride is a member of the group that bought the team in 2010.

Adam Wilson
University of Mississippi

Paul Kingsbury, ed., *The Encyclopedia of Country Music: The Ultimate Guide to the Music* (1998); Mississippi Country Music Trail website, www.mscountrymusictrail.org; Charley Pride, *Pride: The Charley Pride Story* (1995); Charley Pride website, www.charleypride.com.

Young woman emerging from baptism, Rocky Mount Primitive Baptist Church, Panola City (Photograph by David Wharton)

Primitive Baptists

Primitive Baptists constitute one faction of the Baptist denomination. Sometimes referred to as "Hard-shells" or "Old School" Baptists, the Primitives trace their origins as a distinct religious movement to the first half of the nineteenth century, when debates among Baptists regarding the efficacy of recent practical developments in faith and worship began to erupt into denouncements and divisions. Such developments included the use of instrumental music during worship services, the rise of professionally trained clergy, the institution of Sunday schools, and the decision by many local churches to provide financial support to missionaries. Many Baptists viewed these developments as unwelcome and inappropriate innovations that deviated from the traditional and more simplistic faith and practice of earlier Baptists.

In Mississippi, where Baptists had settled since the late eighteenth century, the divisions between Primitives and "Regular" or "Missionary" Baptists can be traced to the 1820s and 1830s, when the animosity between opponents and supporters of missionary funding began to divide the denomination. Although Baptists are well known for their highly localized governmental structure, early nineteenth-century Baptist churches in Mississippi and elsewhere commonly formed loose local associations. Local churches maintained "fellowship" with others in their association, voting to "disfellowship" a church if a majority of the association's member churches felt that the offending group had deviated from Baptist faith and practice. In 1824 Mississippi's Union, Pearl River, and Mississippi Associations joined together to form the state's first Baptist convention. Even as the convention was forming, debate about developments in faith and worship was creating fissures in the increasingly fragile alliance. Only five years later, the disagreements resulted in the convention's dissolution.

In 1836, as the second statewide Baptist convention was being born, the Buttahatchie Association and several local congregations refused to join on the grounds that they could not fellowship with missionary-supporting churches. In 1838 Buttahatchie withdrew fellowship with several other churches over their support for Sunday schools, and in 1839 the Yazoo Association disbanded as its member churches could not agree on a unified stance either for or against missionary work. The Yazoo Association's antimissionary churches then formed the Primitive Association later that year. The next year saw the founding of the Loocsascoona Primitive Association, which included four churches that had withdrawn their membership from the Yalobusha Association over the missionary issue. Another dissenting church from Yalobusha joined the Primitive Association. In 1841 the Tallahatchie Association disfellowshipped all churches who supported Bible, tract, temperance, or missionary groups or who supported the institution of Sunday schools. By 1846, as the Mississippi Baptist Convention joined the newly created Southern Baptist Convention, the state's Primitive Baptists steadfastly refused to fellowship with the "modernists," choosing instead to retain a loose bond among several associations and independent congregations.

This organizational scheme continued through the first half of the twentieth century. By the 1950s, however, a trend of associational independence was established, as many Primitive Baptist congregations withdrew from their associations and most newer churches formed outside any association. This trend persists. Because of a lack of overarching statewide authority or organization, accurately measuring the number of Primitive Baptists in Mississippi is difficult;

however, as of 2016, the state had roughly three dozen Primitive Baptist churches.

Today's Primitive Baptists maintain the distinctive faith and practice of their forebears. They are composed of independent and fully autonomous local congregations who elect and call their own ministers. These clergy members (known as elders) receive little or no theological training and are expected to maintain full-time secular employment to support themselves and their families. Deacons are the only other recognized church officers. Worship services exclude instrumental music, though a cappella singing of hymns is frequent. Unlike most Baptists in Mississippi, Primitives still use wine during their communion services and practice foot washing as a part of the communion rite. Modern-day Primitive Baptists also retain a prohibition on church-funded missionary efforts, Sunday schools, and special age-oriented church groups. The vast majority of Primitive Baptists prefer the King James Version of the Bible.

Brad Noel
University of Mississippi

Gordon A. Cotton, *Of Primitive Faith and Order: A History of the Mississippi Primitive Baptist Church, 1780–1974* (1974); Primitive Baptist Churches blog, pbchurches.org.

Private Schools since the 1950s

Prior to the US Supreme Court's 1954 *Brown v. Board of Education* decision, Mississippi had only three non-church-run private schools. However, in the wake of the Court's ruling that segregated school systems were unconstitutional, many white opponents of integration started private schools, particularly after passage of the Civil Rights Act of 1964 and after the Court's 1969 decision in *Alexander v. Holmes County* mandated that Mississippi school systems implement desegregation plans by 1970. Since the late 1970s and 1980s, a growing number of private schools have emphasized that their goals have more to do with religion and discipline than with white supremacy.

As early as 1954, while leaders in other parts of the South contemplated shutting down their school systems in response to the *Brown* decision, some Mississippi legislators and educators began discussing the possibility of government support for private schools. But only in the mid-1960s did the state have a private school movement. Following the example provided by several other southern states, the Mississippi legislature in 1964 passed a law creating tuition grants of $185 per student for students to attend nonreligious private schools. Three new private schools opened in that year, and in the 1964–65 school year, more than five hundred students received more than $80,000 in tuition grants. One of the new schools was Citizens' Council School No. 1 in Jackson. The Council made private schools into a crusade, and a 1964 issue of its newsletter featured private schools. At most schools, the grants paid more than 50 percent of the tuition.

Mississippians were quick to charter private schools but not quite so quick to get the schools up and running. The number of actual schools jumped substantially from 121 in 1966 to 236 in 1970, an increase driven in large part by the *Alexander v. Holmes County Board of Education* decision. The fastest growth occurred in the majority-black counties in the Mississippi Delta. In that area as well as in southwestern Mississippi and in the Jackson area, more than one-third of all white students attended private schools by the 1971–72 school year. In 1970, for example, virtually every white student in Canton left public schools for a private academy, while more than 40 percent of Jackson's white students left public schools—some for private schools, others for neighboring white-majority school districts. In other areas, especially those with low African American populations, the private school movement did not take off. In northeastern and southeastern Mississippi, fewer than 10 percent of the white students (and sometimes far less) went to private schools in 1971–72.

Supporters of private schools, as a way to thwart school desegregation, made at least four often overlapping arguments. First, they said public education should be a local and state concern rather than an endeavor controlled by the federal government, and the *Brown* decision undercut parents' right to determine the nature of their children's lives and associates. Second, many argued that integration would lower educational standards because teachers would have to slow down and dilute the curriculum to allow African American children from poor school systems to try to catch up. Third, they said African American children would bring new discipline problems. Finally, some argued integrated schools would ultimately lead to interracial dating and interracial sex.

One of the most striking features of the sudden increase in private school building and attendance in 1970 is that so many of the private institutions used public school equipment and funding. According to historian Michael Fuquay, Mississippi's "academies received books, supplies, sports equipment, organizational resources, facilities, and funds directly from the public school system. In Tunica and Clay counties, private school teachers were kept on the public school payrolls. In Forrest County, private school students were transported on public school buses." Parents and administrators at times moved goods from the public schools to the new private schools; in other cases, public school equipment was auctioned or sold at extraordinarily low prices.

Later in the 1970s, a number of religious groups, most of them Protestant churches, started schools, often for the first time. They tended to use the language of theological conservatism, school discipline, and clear moral and educational standards rather than the language of white supremacy. In the words of historian Joseph Crespino, "Mississippi was in some ways at the forefront of the church school movement in America." Many of those schools emphasize that they practice school prayer and Bible study in ways that public schools cannot.

One of the battles those schools fought involved tax exemption as religious institutions. In May 1969 a group of African Americans in Holmes County filed a lawsuit seeking to prevent private schools that discriminated against African Americans from receiving tax-exempt status. In *Green v. Kennedy* (1970) the US District Court granted the plaintiffs' request. However, organizers and parents at many of the newer schools argued that denying them tax exemptions was unconstitutional. In the early 1980s, at the instigation of Mississippi's Trent Lott and North Carolina's Jesse Helms, the Reagan administration changed federal policy, allowing tax exemptions for far more of the South's private schools.

Many of the state's private schools have more recently sought to include people of diverse backgrounds in their student bodies, and by 2016 14 percent of the fifty-seven thousand students at Mississippi's 257 private schools were nonwhite. The average tuition was just under forty-two hundred dollars per year for elementary schools and just under seven thousand dollars per year for high schools. About 11 percent of the state's students attended private schools, a slight increase since the 1970s. While this figure is close to the national average of 10 percent, the state's history with private schools as an alternative to desegregation means that issues of race and poverty remain central to issues of education in Mississippi.

Ted Ownby
University of Mississippi

Charles C. Bolton, *The Hardest Deal of All: The Battle over School Integration in Mississippi, 1870–1980* (2005); Michael Fuquay, *History of Education Quarterly* (June 2002); Joseph Crespino, *In Search of Another Country: Mississippi and the Conservative Counterrevolution* (2007); Mississippi Association of Independent Schools website, newsite.msais.org; Private School Review website, www.privateschoolreview.com; Charles Westmoreland, "Southern Pharisees: Prayer, Public Life, and Politics in the South" (PhD dissertation, University of Mississippi, 2008).

Prohibition

Efforts to limit or prohibit the sale of alcohol have a long and complex history in Mississippi. It passed its first statewide Prohibition law in 1907 and was the first state to ratify the Eighteenth Amendment, which prohibited the sale of alcohol across the country. In 1966 Mississippi became the last state to repeal its statewide Prohibition law.

Supporters of temperance made occasional efforts to limit the sale of alcohol in the antebellum period, beginning with the Mississippi State Temperance Society in 1833 and the Sons of Temperance and Sisters of Temperance in the late 1840s. Far more organized and aggressive efforts began in the mid-1870s. The first successful effort to limit the sale of alcohol was an 1874 law that required anyone wanting to sell alcohol to obtain a license from a majority of the area's registered voters plus a majority of all women over age fourteen.

New organizations flourished from the 1880s into the 1910s. The Anti-Saloon League and the Woman's Christian Temperance Union (WCTU) became major forces in the state's public and political life, first calling for local option and then pushing for statewide Prohibition. Leaders included Harriet Kells of the WCTU, Baptist minister James H. Gambrell, and Methodist minister Charles B. Galloway. The first major success of the Prohibition movement occurred when the legislature passed a local-option law allowing counties to prohibit the sale of alcohol. By the early twentieth century the sale of alcohol was illegal or seriously limited in a large majority of the state's counties, with the counties along the Mississippi River and the Gulf Coast the primary exceptions. In 1907, after Govs. Andrew Longino and Edmond Noel pressed for statewide Prohibition, the legislature passed a strict bill that went into effect at the end of 1908. It allowed druggists to sell some alcohol for medicinal purposes, allowed people to make and drink homemade wine, and penalized liquor sales with fines and short jail terms. Ten years later, Mississippi became the first state to ratify the Eighteenth Amendment to the US Constitution, which banned the sale of alcohol.

Supporters of Prohibition in Mississippi argued from religious, economic, and racial perspectives. Many religious leaders, especially Baptists and Methodists, emphasized that alcohol led to self-indulgence, violence, and bad company. Most advocates of Prohibition, both male and especially female, said alcohol posed a threat to stable and happy homes. Other supporters of Prohibition believed that limiting excessive drinking would produce better workers and a more stable climate for economic change. Members of both groups argued that Prohibition was necessary to clean up the state's growing towns.

Prohibition and race had a complex relationship in Mississippi. Some white supporters of Prohibition claimed that African American men who drank too much in saloons posed particularly dangerous threats to white women. The rhetoric of Prohibition often referred to the purity of the white home and the dangers of African American infringement into public space. Jackson's Kells, editor of the *Mississippi White Ribbon*, the WCTU journal, condemned "drunken, ignorant black men" while discussing how Prohibition could elevate home life. Partly in response, some African American leaders aggressively supported Prohibition as part of programs to promote uplift and respectability. Some early black and white Prohibitionists worked together, and African American leader J. J. Spellman of Hinds County served as secretary of the first statewide Prohibition convention in 1881. However, in the Delta counties with large African American majorities, political leaders rarely supported Prohibition or aggressive enforcement of it, in part because planters wanted a happy workforce and in part because some members of the Delta elite enjoyed alcohol.

Supporters had great confidence that the new law would eliminate most alcohol sales in the state. The author of the Prohibition bill, C. H. Alexander, took pleasure in his belief that "nowhere has the victory been more marked and complete than in Mississippi, which, through a brave, honest, law-loving, home-loving legislature, drove the legalized traffic from the whole state."

With the state's long history of Prohibition, illegal alcohol became important in much of Mississippi literature and music. The number of blues songs about drinking and drunkenness make clear that alcohol was widely available but also potentially destructive. Richard Wright detailed how African American hotel employees bought illegal alcohol for white hotel customers. William Faulkner, who loved whiskey and made disparaging comments about Prohibition laws and their enforcement, made a bootlegger an important character in *Sanctuary*. The characters in Tennessee Williams's *Cat on a Hot Tin Roof* drink nearly constantly despite the fact that the play is set at a time when the purchase of alcohol was against the law.

In 1966 Mississippi finally did away with its statewide Prohibition. The state's voters had overturned the repeal of Prohibition in 1934 and again in 1952, and the legislature debated repeal again in 1960 and 1964 without changing the law. Despite the fact that alcohol sales were illegal, Mississippi had since 1944 been in the unusual and to some embarrassing position of taxing alcohol at 10 percent of its sales price. Several court challenges had argued that the tax in effect nullified the Prohibition law, and some counties, especially along the Mississippi River and on the Gulf Coast, openly sold alcohol. A combination of forces, including the determination of Gov. Paul B. Johnson, led to the passage of the 1966 law that allowed counties to determine their own alcohol policies and set up a new state agency to tax and license the sale of alcohol.

Today, county governments make and enforce the rules governing alcohol sales. The easiest generalization about contemporary alcohol laws is that they vary widely and have numerous idiosyncrasies, as county governments try to balance the demands of religion, health, education, and business with interests of tourism and personal freedom. Visitors and even residents sometimes find the range of laws hard to understand, and numerous counties have "last chance" establishments that offer alcohol to travelers before they cross into dry counties. While counties debate when to serve alcohol, what sort of establishments can sell it, and what kind of alcohol they can sell, state government policies seem most concerned with the health issues of drunk driving and alcoholism.

Ted Ownby
University of Mississippi

Clayton Sledge Allen, "The Repeal of Prohibition in Mississippi" (master's thesis, University of Mississippi, 1992); Anne Ophelia Bailey, "A Statistical Analysis of the Liquor Referenda in Mississippi, 1934 and 1952" (master's thesis, Mississippi State College, 1953); Stephen Cresswell, *Rednecks, Redeemers, and Race: Mississippi after Reconstruction, 1877–1917* (2006); Miranda Culley, " 'Hooray for Prohibition!': Evangelicals and the Southern Temperance Movement" (master's thesis, University of Mississippi, 2008); William Graham Davis, "Attacking 'The Matchless Evil': Temperance and Prohibition in Mississippi, 1817–1905" (PhD dissertation, Mississippi State University, 1975); Thomas Spight Hines Jr., "Mississippi and the Prohibition Controversy" (master's thesis, University of Mississippi, 1960); Timothy A. Nicholas, " 'The Spirit of an Age': The Prohibition Press of Mississippi, 1876–1890" (PhD dissertation, University of Southern Mississippi, 1996).

Protest Songs

In the mid-1960s several popular musicians wrote protest songs that condemned Mississippi racism and violence as problems that all Americans should recognize and confront. In particular, Bob Dylan, Nina Simone, and Phil Ochs wrote and recorded songs that publicized injustice and sought to inspire change. Some of the songs, particularly Dylan's "Oxford Town," became important as part of the state's image.

None of the three musicians was from Mississippi, but all went to Mississippi in the early 1960s. Dylan helped load trucks with food bound for Mississippi's poor people and visited in 1964. Both he and Simone participated in fundraising concerts, and Dylan sang at the March on Washington. Ochs wrote of his time in the state in "You Should Have Been Down in Mississippi," a song that addressed the complacency of many Americans by reminding them of conditions in the Magnolia State.

"Oxford Town" appeared on Dylan's second album, *The Freewheelin' Bob Dylan* (1963), which also contained the protest songs "Blowin' in the Wind" and "Merchants of War." The fast-paced "Oxford Town" lasts less than two minutes and consists of five rhyming quatrains. A quirky song Dylan described as "a banjo tune I play on the guitar," it raised the issue of racism and violence at the University of Mississippi and the need for national action. Two quatrains deal with

James Meredith, who faced "guns and clubs . . . all because his face was brown." He "Come to the door and he couldn't get in / All because of the color of his skin." The song shifts from Meredith to a narrator's story of fear and uncertainty: "Me and my gal and my gal's son / We got met with a tear gas bomb / Don't even know why we come / Goin' back where we come from." But the song ends with a clear charge to a national audience: "Two men died in the Mississippi moon / Somebody better investigate soon." Dylan has returned to Mississippi themes throughout his career. "Only a Pawn in Their Game" (1964), concerns Medgar Evers's murder, while other Dylan songs refer to Highway 61, levees, Robert Johnson, Bukka White, and other blues legends. "Mississippi" (2001) laments, "Only one thing that we did that was wrong / Stayed in Mississippi a day too long."

Simone, a North Carolina native who became a professional singer in Philadelphia and then New York, wrote "Mississippi Goddam" in response to the 1963 murders of Evers in Jackson and of four girls in a Birmingham, Alabama, church bombing. She performed it at New York's Carnegie Hall in March 1964 and released the live recording later that year on the album *Nina Simone in Concert*. The song provides a fascinating study of the issues involved at that moment in the civil rights movement. Changing rhythms and bouncing from melody to melody, the upbeat piano tune does not sound the way a protest song might be expected to sound. The lyrics address the issue of violence versus nonviolence, the long-standing African American belief in a promised land, the follies of the traditional language of uplift and respectability, the foolishness of critics of the movement who "try to say it's a communist plot," Simone's frustration with religion, and her impatience with people who assumed that desegregation was the movement's only goal: "You don't have to live next to me / Just give me my equality." Growing frustration showed in both by the memorable title and by the powerful challenge near the song's end: "This whole country is full of lies / You're all gonna die and die like flies." The song pays tribute to Mississippi's blues history and intersperses blues lyrics with specific references to the terrors activists were facing: "Hound dog on my trail / School children sitting in jail / Black cat cross my path / I think every day's gonna be my last." And the lyrics twice juxtapose calls for activists to move slowly with the longtime complaints that African Americans worked too slowly. Civil rights workers loved the song and loved Simone for her persistent efforts to raise funds for the movement, to perform for activists, and to keep up the fight even when her actions cost her concerts and record sales.

Ochs, a folksinger, grew up in Texas and New York and spent one week in Mississippi—the week in June 1964 when Andrew Goodman, James Chaney, and Michael Schwerner were murdered in Neshoba County. Ochs avoided the complexities of Dylan's use of multiple perspectives or Simone's quick movement from one topic to another and wrote straightforward melodies with clear lyrics. The chorus of the "Ballad of Oxford (Jimmy Meredith)," repeats, "There was blood, red blood on their hands," and "There was hate, cold hate in their hearts." "Going down to Mississippi" dramatizes activists' fears about traveling among armed opponents. Most memorably, "Here's to the State of Mississippi" offers detailed criticisms of whites who rejected outsiders' criticisms; schools that were "teaching all the children that they don't have to care"; police, judges, and laws that supported white supremacy; and churches where "the fallen face of Jesus is choking in the dust." Ochs went beyond Dylan's suggestion that someone should investigate Mississippi violence, concluding instead, "Mississippi find yourself another country to be part of." In 1971 Ochs decided that the terror he saw in Mississippi was more of a national issue and renamed the song "Here's to the State of Richard Nixon."

These songs and others inspired some protesters and contributed to the image of mid-1960s Mississippi as a terrorist state.

Ted Ownby
University of Mississippi

Joseph Crespino, *In Search of Another Country: Mississippi and the Conservative Counterrevolution* (2007); Bob Dylan website, www.bobdylan.com; Marc Eliot, *Death of a Rebel: A Biography of Phil Ochs* (1978; reprint, 1994); Benjamin Filene, *Romancing the Folk: Public Memory and American Roots Music* (2000); Brian Ward, *Just My Soul Responding: Rhythm and Blues, Black Consciousness, and Race Relations* (1998).

Protohistoric Period

The protohistoric period in southeastern North America is defined by less than a two-hundred-year span from the beginning of European contact in the early sixteenth century to the beginning of European colonization at the end of the seventeenth. This period can be divided into three subperiods: the early protohistoric (1513–43), the middle protohistoric (1543–1682), and the late protohistoric (1682–1700). This period was one of upheaval for American Indian tribal groups across the Southeast as a consequence of European contact through warfare, trade, and disease. Old World diseases such as smallpox, measles, typhus, and influenza may have reduced Indian populations by as much as 80 percent by the end of the protohistoric period.

The main sources of evidence about the protohistoric period are ethnohistoric accounts by Spanish, French, and British explorers, traders, and missionaries as well as archaeological remains. Both lines of evidence about this tumultuous period document patterns of depopulation, migration, and settlement shifts. While the European accounts from the protohistoric period represent the first documentary evidence for the immediate ancestors of many of the historically known Indian tribes of Mississippi, they provide only brief glimpses of native lifeways. The material remains from this period likewise provide limited evidence about lifeways.

As documented in the ethnohistoric accounts, the first subperiod is characterized by the first contact of Indian tribes with Europeans when Hernando de Soto and his conquistadors entered Mississippi in 1540. His chroniclers described town locations, town layouts, and political relationships between towns and villages. According to these accounts, some Indian populations were organized into large territorial chiefdoms led by paramount chiefs residing on top of earthen platform mounds in large walled towns, with lesser tribute-paying chiefs residing in smaller mound and nonmound towns and villages. In contrast, other Indian populations were significantly less centralized and lived in small, dispersed autonomous villages. Population estimates range from the thousands for the large chiefdoms to only a few hundred for the smaller tribes. Most tribal groups shared in a mixed maize-bean-squash horticulture coupled with nut gathering, hunting of riverine-forest-adapted game, and fishing in the area's rivers, streams, and oxbow lakes. The Spanish accounts mention only four town names that correspond to historic tribal groups in Mississippi: Chicasa (Chickasaw), Sacchuma (Chakchiuma), Alibamo (Alabama), and Quizquiz (Tunica).

Although no written accounts exist for the 140-year span of the middle protohistoric period, we know from the late protohistoric accounts that this era witnessed massive regional depopulation, site abandonment, and a continuation of the decentralization that had begun in the early protohistoric period. In 1670 the British colony of Carolina was founded, and trade in human slaves led the Chickasaw to become notorious slave raiders of their enemy tribes for profit. Smaller, less-powerful tribes were victims of the new economic climate fostered by the British and their Indian allies.

The late protohistoric period began with the French exploration of the Mississippi River Valley under the guidance of René-Robert Cavelier, Sieur de La Salle, and his lieutenant, Henri de Tonti. By this time, mound construction had ceased and only the Natchez (southwestern Mississippi) and Taensa (northeastern Louisiana) were recorded as still participating in ceremonies on top of the mounds. In addition to those tribes mentioned in the de Soto chronicles, smaller autonomous tribes enter the record toward the end of the protohistoric period. The French accounts provide brief descriptions for the Muskhogean-speaking Pascagoula, Acolapissa, Houma, and Ibitoupa. Two Siouan-speaking tribes, the Ofo and the Biloxi, are recorded in their dealings with the French. By 1700 the Tunica no longer were located in northwestern Mississippi, where they had encountered de Soto, but instead had moved into the lower Yazoo Basin near other smaller Tunican-speaking tribes, the Koroa, Tiou, and Yazoo.

Using radiocarbon dating and ceramic analysis, archaeological excavations in Mississippi have identified several sixteenth- and seventeenth-century protohistoric Chickasaw sites located just west of the Tombigbee River in the Black Prairie physiographic region of northeastern Mississippi. These sites correspond to the general location of de Soto's first entry point into Mississippi. The protohistoric settlement pattern is distinctive in that settlements are rarely associated with mounds. Rather, they are dispersed on thin upland prairie soils on bluffs overlooking small streams. Most of these sites have no earlier late prehistoric occupation, suggesting a recent population shift to the upland prairie that was part of a political decentralization that began before de Soto.

By contrast, de Soto likely encountered the ancestors of the Choctaw tribe, which still has a major presence in east-central Mississippi and western Alabama. The distinctive decorated combed pottery identifying their settlements does not appear in Mississippi until the early historic period. Archaeologists have identified de Soto's named province of Quizquiz in northwestern Mississippi as ancestral to the Tunica tribe. Protohistoric period sites in this region contain distinctive Tunica ceramic styles. To the south, the chiefly province de Soto's chroniclers called Quigualtam is believed to have been located in the lower Yazoo Basin, perhaps with its paramount town at the Holly Bluff mound center near Vicksburg. Further to the south in the Natchez Bluffs region, the Emerald Mound site, the third-largest earthen mound in North America, appears to represent the paramount center for the protohistoric ancestors of the Natchez. Some scholars have suggested that the protohistoric Natchez may have been part of the Quigualtam chiefdom and participated in the pursuit of de Soto's army down the Mississippi River in 1543.

Shortly after La Salle and Tonti's explorations, the historic period began in Mississippi with the establishment of the French colony of Biloxi in 1699. The historic period is characterized by prolonged and sustained contact between Indian and European populations, resulting in far more detailed descriptions of American Indian lifeways.

Karl Lorenz
Shippensburg University

Raymond Fogelson and William Sturtevant, eds., *Handbook of North American Indians*, vol. 14, *Southeast* (2004); Charles Hudson, *Knights of Spain, Warriors of the Sun: Hernando de Soto and the South's Ancient Chiefdoms* (1997); Bonnie G. McEwan, ed., *Indians of the Greater Southeast: Historical Archaeology and Ethnohistory* (2000).

Public Welfare

Before the Great Depression, public welfare in Mississippi consisted of a collection of disjointed programs. The state provided services for persons with mental illness, mental deficits, and blindness. Support of unemployed and chronically poor persons through direct relief was considered the responsibility of county governments or private charities. The legislature enacted a children's pension law in 1928 that authorized county officials to use a portion of their poor law funds or general treasuries to provide care for dependent and needy children, but several counties chose not to implement this program.

In 1930 Frank Bane, a national authority on welfare, conducted a study of Mississippi's public welfare structure, concluding that while various county and state offices tried to meet the needs of disadvantaged citizens, the lack of coordination resulted in waste and inefficiency. He recommended the creation of a state department of welfare capable of providing direction and supervision related to the distribution of poor relief. Unlike their counterparts in some states, however, officials in Mississippi were slow to see the need for statewide action, likely because substantial authority was vested in county governments rather than because they feared that providing relief for the poor would make them dependent.

The problem of public welfare became more acute as the Great Depression worsened and was further exacerbated in Mississippi by the drought of 1930–31. Many Mississippians lost their homes and farms. When Martin Sennett Conner was inaugurated as governor in 1932, the General Fund of the State Treasury contained $1,326. Conner had to personally pay to feed the patients at the Mississippi State Hospital in Whitfield.

The creation of the Reconstruction Finance Corporation (RFC) in 1932 allowed states to obtain loans for poor relief. Conner applied and was told that Mississippi would receive a loan only if someone knowledgeable in public welfare were brought in to help direct the distribution. Conner turned to Bane for help. Bane, now the executive director of the American Public Welfare Association, recommended an association employee, Aubrey Williams, an Alabama native who became the first director of Mississippi's state-level welfare department.

Williams developed a structure whereby counties could establish local relief offices. He selected each county director and established a program that required citizens to do some useful work in return for relief payments. Williams's tenure lasted just over one month. His successor, George Power, was a banker who had recently served as the clerk for the Mississippi House of Representatives.

While the need for an RFC loan to fund a relief program necessitated the establishment of a state public welfare office, most state leaders believed that the state's public welfare agency would exist only temporarily, since the jobless could return to work as soon as economic circumstances improved. Federal officials also encountered difficulty in securing a commitment from the state to shoulder more of the burden of providing for its unemployed. After the Social Security Act of 1935 required all states to have public welfare plans to continue receiving federal funds, Governor Conner convened the legislature to create a permanent state welfare program. He and state senators clashed over the selection of welfare board members, resulting in a stalemate that dragged on until the state created a temporary welfare department to be administered by a relief board.

Labor and race issues have always influenced Mississippi's public welfare programs. Relief benefits were kept low to ensure that laborers would accept available jobs, no matter how meager the pay. Federal officials noted during the 1930s that planters used their political power to put in place a system under which their tenants did not receive welfare during planting and harvesting periods but returned to the relief rolls at other times of the year. Planters thus evaded responsibility for supporting their tenants, both black and white, when their labor was not needed. Many critics of current welfare policies argue that the practice continues today with the Temporary Assistance for Needy Families program. They contend that many employers have taken advantage of workers whose salaries are subsidized by job training programs and but have provided permanent employment to very few Mississippians.

In addition, from the earliest days of public welfare, federal officials noted that black Mississippians received fewer benefits than did whites. Even skilled African American laborers were more likely to receive unskilled, low-wage relief positions than were white workers. Conversely, Fred Ross, who served as commissioner for the State Department of Public Welfare during the early 1960s, charged that African Americans paid only a small portion of Mississippi's taxes yet received a disproportionate share of welfare benefits.

African Americans long complained of unfair treatment in segregated county welfare offices. Prior to his murder in Neshoba County in 1964, civil rights worker Michael Schwerner attempted to help a young black man with a mild mental impairment who was denied assistance by the Lauderdale County Department of Public Welfare, a predicament that affected many other black citizens in other counties as well. In 1967 members of the Mississippi State Advisory Committee to the US Commission on Civil Rights heard testimony from black citizens about how welfare officials refused to comply with the requirement to provide a reason when denying benefits.

While many practices within the welfare department changed during the next two decades, and more African Americans took on employment and leadership roles, county welfare offices remained plagued by complaints of poor service. Many white Mississippians continued to cling, at least in part, to the belief that African Americans received more than their share of welfare benefits. In addition, critics argued that welfare programs such as Aid to Families with Dependent Children encouraged promiscuity and illegitimacy. These beliefs played a large role in the US Congress's passage of the Personal Responsibility and Work Opportunity Reconciliation Act of 1996, which has led to stricter and supposedly time-limited welfare eligibility.

Control over welfare jobs and funds has also remained an issue in Mississippi. The reorganization of the executive branch of state government during the administration of Gov. Ray Mabus (1988–92) had perhaps the most critical effect on the state's public welfare system. Public welfare had previously been administered by an independent department governed by a board but now became part of a super-bureaucracy, the Department of Human Services. The board was phased out, increasing the governor's authority to hire and fire directors. Critics have contended that the public welfare program now suffers from too much political interference, and public welfare remains a politically charged enterprise. As of 2015 Mississippi ranked last among states in the value of public welfare benefits offered.

Vincent Venturini

Mississippi Valley State University

W. F. Bond, *The First 20 Years of Public Welfare in Mississippi* (1965); James R. W. Lieby, *Frank Bane: Public Administration and Public Welfare* (1965); Howard W. Odum and D. W. Willard, *Systems of Public Welfare* (1925); Fred A. Ross, *Public Welfare in Mississippi: Past and Present* (1965); Fred A. Ross, *Racial Amalgamation Propanda versus Segregation and Racial Cooperation: An Address by Fred A. Ross* (1963); Michael Tanner and Charles Hughes, *The Work versus Welfare Trade-Off: Europe* (2015); Vincent J. Venturini, *Oral Histories with Mississippi Department of Public Welfare Social Workers Who Began Their Careers in the 1960s* (1998); Vincent J. Venturini, *Oral History on Gwendolyn Loper* (2002); *Welfare in Mississippi: A Report of the Mississippi State Advisory Committee to the United States Commission on Civil Rights* (1969).

Puckett, Newbell Niles

(1897–1967) Scholar

Newbell Niles Puckett was a sociologist who wrote the landmark study *Folk Beliefs of the Southern Negro*, one of the earliest inventories of African American belief.

Puckett was born in Columbus, Mississippi, on 8 July 1897. His father, Willis Niles Puckett, was a mason who started a brick factory in the city. Working at the factory brought the younger Puckett into contact with many African Americans, who helped him with his later research. After completing an undergraduate degree at Mississippi College, Puckett continued his education at Yale University, where he received a master's and doctorate in sociology. He began teaching at Western University (now Case Western University) in Cleveland in 1922.

While at Yale, Puckett became interested in incorporating his knowledge of African American culture into his work as a sociologist. He decided to focus his dissertation on the belief systems of African Americans in the South. Puckett returned to Lowndes County several times during the early 1920s to collect data from local residents, gathering religious songs, grave-decorating traditions, voodoo practices, and folk medicine customs. The University of North Carolina Press published his revised dissertation as *Folk Beliefs of the Southern Negro* (1926), which received highly favorable reviews, including praise from culture critic H. L. Mencken and prominent sociologist Charles S. Johnson. Puckett was one of the earliest folklore scholars to utilize photography as part of his documentary work, and the book features several notable images taken by Puckett.

Folk Beliefs has become an important source of data for researchers in many different disciplines, although the theoretical component of the book has fallen out of favor. Puckett and many of his early twentieth-century colleagues advocated the theory of cultural evolution, which contended that cultures evolved from a primitive state to a developed one. Puckett's paternalistic view of African American culture garnered criticism in later decades.

Puckett spent the rest of his career doing fieldwork in a number of areas. He amassed large collections of data on African American surnames, Ohio superstitions and folk beliefs, and religious traditions of African Americans in the South. Puckett did not publish large-scale works using this research during his lifetime; however, support from his estate allowed other scholars to organize and publish his research on surnames and Ohio superstitions after his death on 21 February 1967.

Larry Morrisey

Mississippi Arts Commission

George Kummer, in *Popular Beliefs and Superstitions: A Compendium of American Folklore*, ed. Wayland D. Hand, Anna Casetta, and Sondra B. Thiederman, vol. 3 (1981); Patrick B. Mullen "Race Relations in Folklore Research: The Case of Newbell Niles Puckett," presentation at the 1994 American Folklore Society Meeting; William H. Wiggins Jr., in *Made by Hand: Mississippi Folk Art*, ed. Patti Carr Black (1980).

Pushmataha
(ca. 1764–1824) Choctaw Chief

Pushmataha, a Choctaw warrior and chief, was one of the most influential Native American leaders of the early 1800s. He was born ca. 1764 in what is now Noxubee County. As a young man, he was influenced by white traders, Indian agents, and missionaries. By studying their language, customs, and negotiation techniques, Pushmataha learned to bridge the Choctaw and American cultures and became a strong ally of the Americans. Despite his lifelong efforts to establish coexistence for the Choctaw with whites in Mississippi, most Choctaw were removed from Mississippi to Indian Territory less than a decade after his death. Nonetheless, Pushmataha was instrumental in negotiating permission for some Choctaw to remain in Mississippi after Removal.

Pushmataha's early life is not recorded, although some of his early biographers have said that he was orphaned during wars with other native tribes. In 1805 he was elected chief of one of the three geographical and political districts in the Choctaw Confederacy, the Southern District or Six Towns Division, located along the upper Leaf River and mid-Chickasawhay River watersheds.

Pushmataha was a skilled warrior. Following the Creek Massacre at Fort Mims in Alabama in 1813, Pushmataha organized the Choctaw to fight against the Creek at the Battles of Holy Ground and Horseshoe Bend (Alabama). They also fought with Andrew Jackson's army in the capture of Pensacola, against the British at the Battle of New Orleans in the War of 1812, and in the Seminole Wars. Pushmataha's leadership reportedly earned the respect of Jackson and other white leaders with whom he would later negotiate.

As white settlers continued to push into Mississippi and Congress became impatient to relocate the native peoples to the West, Pushmataha served as one of the key negotiators. He was instrumental in bargaining with Jackson during the talks preceding the Treaty of Doak's Stand. When the Choctaw removed to the West and found white settlers on the land that had been reserved for the Choctaw, Pushmataha traveled to Washington, D.C., to negotiate a resolution. He died there on 24 December 1824 and was buried at the Congressional Cemetery.

Beth A. Stahr
Southeastern Louisiana University

H. B. Cushman, *History of the Choctaw, Chickasaw, and Natchez Indians* (1899); John A. Garraty and Mark Carnes, *American National Biography*, vol. 17 (1999); Clara Sue Kidwell, *Choctaws and Missionaries in Mississippi, 1818–1918* (1995); Anna Lewis, *Chief Pushmataha, American Patriot: The Story of the Choctaws' Struggle for Survival* (1959).

Quilting

A quilt is essentially the combination of three layers of textile—a top, a back, and batting in between—secured by stitches through all three layers. Generations of Mississippi women have made quilts, whether for their family's comfort or to display their domestic skill. The tradition continues today with modern tools and organizations devoted to the promotion and advancement of the art of quilting.

From the late eighteenth century to the 1940s, a quilt was the most common bedcovering among Mississippi families regardless of social, economic, or racial background. Pioneers and plantation families spent time recycling older textiles and clothing—old shirts, blankets, and even feed sacks—into bedcoverings that offered warmth and comfort to those who sheltered under their roofs. Women and girls usually were tasked with the creation and maintenance of such domestic comforts, but many young boys helped to piece patchwork or quilt on communal projects.

Such quilts were primarily utilitarian, but quilts occasionally were much more, displaying exceptional skill or perhaps artistic expression. Family pride and appreciation preserved many exquisite examples of patchwork, appliqué, and embroidery through centuries of Mississippi life and hardships. Textiles are by nature fragile and generally short-lived, but many Mississippi quilts were saved in simple and extraordinary ways from the ravages of the Civil War, the Great Depression, hurricanes, house fires, floods, relocations, and countless other events.

After World War II the increased availability of storebought textiles and the movement of greater numbers of women into careers outside the home reduced the necessity of quilt making. But quilting survived as a pleasant pastime and as an important source of artistic expression and social interaction for women. Around 1976 quilting experienced a national revival as women began to have more leisure time and returned to their quilting roots for purposes of personal creativity and expression.

In the twenty-first century quilting is thriving internationally, as a multi-billion-dollar industry offers fabrics, machines, tools, and publications. Mississippi has numerous local quilting guilds whose members meet regularly to share their love of quilting as well as shops dedicated to supplying quilters' needs. The state also hosts frequent exhibitions of the beautiful and increasingly creative works of art produced by Mississippi quilters.

Quilters from the state have taken top honors at prestigious American quilt shows and have been recognized and honored by institutions such as the Smithsonian Institution at the Festival of American Folk Art. Quilts by Martha Skelton of Vicksburg, Judy Spiers of Foxworth, and Barbara Newman of Brandon are in the collection of the National Quilt Museum in Paducah, Kentucky.

Much of what we know about the history of quilts in Mississippi results from the efforts of the Mississippi Quilt Association (MQA), formed in the early 1990s. Though smaller quilting guilds operated in various communities, the MQA offered expanded educational opportunities and a statewide social network. In addition, the group worked to document the state's quilting history, photographing and collecting provenance and historical data on almost two thousand quilts, some from as early as the 1830s.

The information collected was published in *Mississippi Quilts* (2001), a landmark historical record of the state's quilting culture from the earliest settlement through 1946. In addition to quilt photographs by J. D. Schwalm, the book features photographs by Eudora Welty and quotations from her work as well as photographs of and information on modern Mississippi quilting luminaries.

Today, MQA has about five hundred members in Mississippi and its neighboring states. Each year, the group hosts spring, fall, and June "gatherings" where quilters can attend workshops and learn new techniques, see works of art, and meet others who share their love of quilting.

Pamela D. McRae
Dennis, Mississippi

Mary Elizabeth Johnson, *Mississippi Quilts* (2001); Mississippi Quilt Association website, www.mississippiquilt.org.

Quitman, John Anthony
(1799–1858) Tenth and Sixteenth Governor, 1835–1836, 1850–1851

John Anthony Quitman was born in Rhinebeck, New York, on 1 September 1798. His father, Frederick Quitman, a Lutheran minister, and mother, Anna Quitman, were Dutch immigrants. John Quitman migrated to Natchez in 1821 by way of Ohio and Pennsylvania, where he studied law and taught

John Anthony Quitman (Archives and Records Services Division, Mississippi Department of Archives and History [PI COL 1983.0026 Box 8 Folder 27 #10])

school. In 1824 Quitman began practicing law and married Eliza Turner, the daughter of a wealthy Adams County planter. He eventually became one of Mississippi's largest landowners, with fifteen thousand acres and three hundred slaves. From Monmouth, his Natchez home, Quitman launched a highly successful military and political career. Quitman's first biographer, John F. H. Claiborne, wrote that "a more ambitious man never lived. . . . He was greedy for military fame."

Quitman's first act as a political figure was to help organize a volunteer militia, the Natchez Fencibles, in 1824. After serving briefly in the state legislature, Quitman was elected chancery judge for the State of Mississippi in 1828, an office he held until 1835. In the 1830s Quitman became engaged in national political issues. He opposed Pres. Andrew Jackson on the tariff in 1833 and strongly supported nullification and subsequently secession.

Quitman was elected to the State Senate in 1835. In 1833 Hiram G. Runnels had become the first governor elected under Mississippi's new 1832 constitution. He vacated the office on 20 November 1835, two years after his inauguration, because he considered his term to have expired. However, the legislature had moved the inauguration of the new governor and the opening of the next legislative session from November 1835 to January 1836, meaning that there was no president of the Senate to assume the governorship. For nearly two weeks, Mississippi was without a governor. The secretary of state then called a special session of the Senate to elect a president. The Senate convened on 3 December 1835 and elected Quitman, who became governor and served until

7 January 1836, when Charles Lynch, who had been elected on 2 November 1835, was inaugurated.

In 1846 Quitman was appointed a brigadier general in the US Army and became a national hero during the Mexican War. He was promoted to major general and appointed provisional governor of Mexico during the brief US occupation of that country. His exploits in Mexico made him a contender for the vice presidential nomination in 1848. Instead, Quitman, whose first love was the military, applied for a permanent commission in the Regular Army. After failing to obtain a military appointment, Quitman ran for governor in 1849 and defeated his opponent by ten thousand votes.

While serving as governor, Quitman was invited by the Cuban revolutionary movement to lead its army in a war of independence against Spain. Quitman had long been a supporter of the Cuban insurgency and had gone to Cuba, in violation of America's neutrality laws, to encourage the rebels. Quitman declined the offer, however, because he believed that the South would soon secede from the Union and that a southern confederacy would need his services.

When federal authorities arrested him for violating American neutrality laws, Quitman resigned the governorship in February 1851. The charges were eventually dropped, and Quitman entered the governor's race later that year but subsequently withdrew. In 1855 Quitman was elected to the US House of Representatives, serving until his death on 17 July 1858. Quitman County and the county seat of Clarke County are named in his honor.

David G. Sansing
University of Mississippi

Biographical Directory of the United States Congress (1950); Robert E. May, *John A. Quitman, Old South Crusader* (1985); Richard Aubrey McLemore, ed., *A History of Mississippi* (1973); *Mississippi Official and Statistical Register* (1912); Dunbar Rowland, *Encyclopedia of Mississippi History*, vol. 2 (1907).

Q

Quitman County

Quitman County was established in 1877 from parts of four other Delta counties: Tallahatchie, Tunica, Panola, and Coahoma. The bill to establish Quitman County was introduced by Leopold Marks, a Jewish state legislator, for whom the county seat is named. The county itself was named for Mississippi governor John A. Quitman.

In the 1880 census, Quitman County was home to 815 African Americans and 592 whites. The county had sixty-two farms and plantations with an average size of 417 acres, a figure far higher than the Mississippi average of 156 acres. Quitman County farmers grew cotton and grain and raised livestock. Leopold Marks allowed the Yazoo and Mississippi Valley Railroad to come through his plantation free of charge to encourage growth in the area.

By 1900 Quitman County's population had reached 5,435 and was 77 percent African American. Only 9 percent of the 812 African American farmers owned their land, while about one-third of white farmers did so. Quitman had the fewest industrial workers of any Mississippi county.

The 1916 religious census counted thirty-six hundred Missionary Baptists, a historically African American group, and no more than five hundred members of any of the county's other significant groups, the African Methodist Episcopal Zion Church, the African Methodist Episcopal Church, and the Southern Baptists.

Quitman County's population grew steadily in the early twentieth century. Its 1930 population of 25,304 was 69 percent African American. The county had no urban center and only twenty-seven industrial workers. In Quitman and six other Delta counties, tenants operated more than 90 percent of all farms. Cotton was the dominant crop. In the 1920s and 1930s Quitman County had several of Mississippi's first aerial crop dusting services, which worked for large landowners. Ninety-two percent of Quitman's farms were smaller than fifty acres, far higher than the state average of 72 percent.

Charley Pride, one of the first African American stars of country music, was born in 1938 in the Quitman County community of Sledge. Johnnie Billington, born in Crowder in 1935, performed with numerous blues musicians before returning to the Delta and setting up programs to teach the blues to children. Blues musicians Earl Hooker and Albert "Sunnyland Slim" Luandrew were born in Quitman County and moved north to Chicago.

By 1960, following the Great Migration from the Mississippi Delta, Quitman's population had declined to 21,019 but remained about two-thirds African American. Quitman also had a small population of Chinese immigrants. County farmers produced the sixth-most cotton and soybeans in the state, and almost 60 percent of the county's workers were employed in agriculture. The small but growing industrial workforce concentrated on furniture and timber products. The county had clear educational problems, as Quitman residents trailed all but one other county with just 6.7 median years of education.

During the 1960s Quitman County was a noted site of both rural poverty and organized efforts to fight that poverty. In 1967 activist Marian Wright arranged for Sen. Robert Kennedy to tour Quitman to see the seriousness of poverty in the Delta. Martin Luther King Jr.'s final civil rights initiative, the Poor People's Campaign, in which residents formed a mule train to travel to Washington, D.C., to demand better jobs and wages, began in Marks in 1968.

As in most of the rest of the Delta, Quitman County's population declined over the second half of the twentieth century but remained predominantly African American. According to the 2010 census, Quitman had just 8,223 residents, a decrease of more than 60 percent over the preceding half century.

Mississippi Encyclopedia Staff
University of Mississippi

Mississippi State Planning Commission, *Progress Report on State Planning in Mississippi* (1938); *Mississippi Statistical Abstract*, Mississippi State University (1952–2010); Charles Sydnor and Claude Bennett, *Mississippi History* (1939); University of Virginia Library, Historical Census Browser website, http://mapserver.lib.virginia.edu; E. Nolan Waller and Dani A. Smith, *Growth Profiles of Mississippi's Counties, 1960–1980* (1985).

R

Racism

Numerous ideological and conceptual influences have informed America's historical, cultural, and institutional development. Among the most divisive and polarizing of these influences has been racism, which is the ideological belief that identifies race as the predominant factor determining the physical traits, mental capacities, physiology, and overall potential of humans. Racism further presupposes that historical development, cultural legacy, biological characteristics, and/or other factors make one race necessarily superior or inferior to another.

Such assumptions even contributed to the enslavement of one race by other races and ethnicities. Europeans abducted and forcefully removed Africans to America via the Atlantic slave trade beginning in the sixteenth century. The trade accelerated in the seventeenth and eighteenth centuries and continued into the mid-nineteenth century, even after it became illegal. The first US census, taken in 1790, found a racialized slave community of roughly 1 million, mostly in the southern states. Seventy years later, the nation's slave population topped 4.5 million, about 400,000 of them in Mississippi. The majority of the state's slaves were held in the Natchez District, in the southwest tier of the state along the Mississippi River. Racialized slavery in Mississippi was spawned and rationalized based on the culturally sanctioned belief that dark-skinned people were a deficient species of savages. In colonial America, this belief promoted and facilitated the development of structural, state, and systemic racism, as evidenced by slavery. This institutional racism, in turn, gave rise to a racialized American hierarchy that survived slavery and has endured because of its pervasive and ubiquitous attributes. According to one researcher, American racism has persisted and remains interconnected with "all major social groups, networks, and institutions across the society."

Indeed, after the abolition of American slavery, racism became more pronounced, expansive, and mandated by law, especially in the South. By 1890, the region's state governments began to enact new constitutions with an emphasis on black disenfranchisement and racial segregation, thereby ensuring societal adherence to the practice of separate but unequal facilities as well as to the additional dictates of an emerging southern Jim Crow culture. In Mississippi, white conservative Democrats, alarmed by predictions of a return to carpetbagger days and a second Reconstruction, engineered the convening of a state constitutional convention in 1890. The new Mississippi constitution targeted blacks for implied and race-specific segregation, separation, exclusion, and restrictions. Thus, in the late nineteenth-century South, racism became more than just a matter of culture and choice: it was a matter of law. In an 1896 Louisiana public accommodation case, *Plessy v. Ferguson*, the US Supreme Court ruled that to mandate separate facilities for blacks neither implied inferiority nor violated the Fourteenth Amendment of the US Constitution. The ruling established the legal doctrine of separate but equal while providing judicial protection for states as they enacted laws mandating racial separation. For nearly sixty years this doctrine sanctioned the racial divide and institutional racism in America.

From the Jim Crow era through the civil rights period, popular culture also sanctioned the nation's racial apartheid. At the turn of the century, journalists, academics, and social critics offered commentary on themes of black retrogression, savagery, bestiality, and criminality. Making an equally significant contribution to the gospel of racism were southern politicians such as Mississippi's James Vardaman and Theodore Bilbo, who often resorted to demagoguery in vying for political office. These men emphasized racial stereotypes and used them to stoke white fears and intolerance.

Since the mid-twentieth century, racism has remained one of Mississippi's unresolved societal ills despite the US Supreme Court's repudiation of the separate but equal doctrine in its May 1954 *Brown v. Board of Education* decision. Similarly, the civil rights movement of the 1950s and 1960s failed to end American racism, though it did result in a surge of societal will that enshrined in federal law prohibitions against discrimination in public accommodations, voting, and housing. In addition, the civil rights movement fostered a vision of freedom for blacks that linked social justice and economic democracy. Nevertheless, Mississippi and the rest of the United States maintain vestiges and manifestations of racism.

Dernoral Davis
Jackson State University

Stephen A. Berrey, *The Jim Crow Routine: Everyday Performances of Race, Civil Rights, and Segregation in Mississippi* (2015); George Fredrickson, *The Black Image in the White Mind* (1971); Andrew Hacker, *Two Nations: Black and White, Separate, Hostile, Unequal* (1995); Winthrop D. Jordan, *White over Black: American Attitudes toward the Negro, 1850–1812* (1968); Manning Marable, *Beyond Black and White: Rethinking Race in America* (1995); Neil R. McMillen, *Dark Journey: Black Mississippians in the Age of Jim Crow* (1989); Orlando Patterson, *The Ordeal of Integration: Progress and Resentment in America's "Racial" Crisis* (1997); Ronald Takaki, *Iron Cages: Race and Culture in Nineteenth-Century America* (1979); Cornel

West, *Race Matters* (1993); Joel Williamson, *A Rage for Order: Black-White Relations in the American South since Emancipation* (1986).

Radio

The first federally licensed radio station took to the air in Pennsylvania in 1920, and by 1923 Mississippi was the only state without a radio station. The following year the US Department of Commerce listed four in the state—KFNG in Coldwater, WCBH in Oxford, WDBT in Hattiesburg, and WCBG in Pascagoula. The latter was licensed for a traveling evangelist, and all operated at just ten watts of power—only enough to cover a small town. The radio landscape remained chaotic until Congress passed the Radio Act of 1927; by 1930 much of the programming on radio was provided by the three national networks (CBS, NBC's Red Network, and NBC's Blue Network, which later became ABC). In 1942 Mississippi had just 12 stations, a number that increased rapidly after the end of World War II, reaching 48 in 1952 and 180 in 1960 and topping 250 in 2012.

Radio kept Mississippians informed, providing community calendars, news, farm reports, sports coverage, weather bulletins, and "swap shop of the air" programs. Eudora Welty worked for a year at Jackson's WJDX, writing scripts and newsletters. There and at Hattiesburg's WRBJ (later WPFB), entertainment was provided by staff orchestras, bands, and pianists; talent shows; gospel quartets; serial dramas; and live feeds from churches, hotel ballrooms, and performance venues, including Hattiesburg's Saenger Theater. National performers also appeared on the air during visits to Mississippi, and in 1944 nine-year-old Elvis Presley sang live on Tupelo's WELO, which was broadcasting from the Mississippi-Alabama Fair.

As on national radio, African Americans were seldom heard on the airwaves in Mississippi prior to 1948, when Memphis's WDIA (whose signal reached into Mississippi) became the first station in the nation to feature all-black programming and on-air talent. The most notable exception was the weekday live blues program *King Biscuit Radio Time*, featuring Glendora native Sonny Boy Williamson II (Aleck Miller), which was first broadcast in 1941 over KFFA from Helena, Arkansas. Later fed via Clarksdale's WROX, the show was enjoyed by many Mississippi agricultural workers. In the late 1940s Williamson and Elmore James also hosted a live program in Belzoni that was broadcast via telephone line over Yazoo City's WAZF and Greenville's WJPR. In the mid-1940s a young B. B. King sang with his gospel group over Greenwood's WGRM.

The first African American deejay in the state was apparently Early Wright, who hosted blues and gospel on WROX from 1947 until 1998; other deejays at WROX included a young Ike Turner. Future civil rights activist Charles Evers began broadcasting on Philadelphia's WHOC in the late 1940s, and in 1987 he started Jackson's nonprofit WMPR, which features gospel, blues, and political talk shows. In 1954 Jackson's WOKJ became the first station in the state to institute all-black programming, while Mississippi's first black-owned station was Hattiesburg's WORV, founded in 1969 by Vernon Floyd, Robert Floyd, and Ruben Hughes.

During the civil rights era conservative forces including the Mississippi State Sovereignty Commission and the Citizens' Council used radio to defend white supremacy. African American activists, conversely, had difficulty advertising their goals and brought legal challenges against the stations, a strategy that caused the US Court of Appeals to strip Jackson's WJDX of its Federal Communications Commission license.

Radio continued to expand, and deregulation and changes in programming strategies during the 1980s and 1990s resulted in a relative homogenization of stations, with deejays who chose their own playlists becoming a disappearing breed in Mississippi as in the rest of the nation. Notable players in the contemporary market include national behemoth Clear Channel Communications, which owns multiple stations in larger markets; Jackson-based TeleSouth Communications, which operates the influential Super Talk network; and the Tupelo-based American Family Network. However, many Mississippi stations continue to emphasize local news, sports, and religious events. WCPC in Houston, Mississippi, has broadcast Sacred Harp music every Sunday since 1959.

Notable changes in recent years include the launch in 2008 of two digital stations by Mississippi Public Broadcasting, which was founded in 1983 and broadcasts uniform programming over eight FM stations. In 2000 Gulfport's Rip Daniels, owner of terrestrial station WJZD, launched the American Blues Network, which uploads blues programming via a satellite feed and as of 2011 was being programmed on more than fifty stations nationwide. Noncommercial LPFM (low power FM) stations, encouraged by a 2000 FCC decision, now include Jackson's WLPM and Bay St. Louis's WQRZ, which remained on the air during Hurricane Katrina.

Scott Barretta
Greenwood, Mississippi

Jim O'Neal
Kansas City, Missouri

Bob McRaney Sr., *The History of Radio in Mississippi* (1979); Mississippi Blues Trail website, msbluestrail.org; Brian Ward, *Radio and the Struggle for Civil Rights in the South* (2004).

Railroads

It is no coincidence that the first efforts to build railroads in Mississippi began in the early 1830s, shortly after the signing of treaties that made Choctaw and Chickasaw land available for settlement and investment by US citizens, because nineteenth-century railroad building was closely connected to efforts to profit from Mississippi land. Railroads have played important roles in the state's economy, politics, race relations, migration, music, and literature.

Railroads came to the state as part of the timber industry, and that industry dominated the course of their construction for decades. Many supporters were Whigs who saw connection to a national economy as part of civic improvement. Most antebellum railroads were short tracks that allowed travel from timber areas to waterways, which remained the primary means of moving timber to urban markets until the late 1800s. In 1850 the state had just seventy-five miles of track. Some of the state's first substantial railroads were the Mobile and Ohio and the New Orleans, Jackson, and Great Northern, which also became the first line running north–south through much of the state when it connected New Orleans to Canton in 1858. Both of those lines began in the 1850s in the southern part of the state, connecting timber areas in Clarke, Pike, and Copiah Counties to the Gulf Coast. The Mississippi Central Railroad began in 1853 in Holly Springs, and its north–south line, completed in 1860, connected to the New Orleans, Jackson, and Great Northern to allow travel through the state. The state had 872 miles of railroads on the eve of the Civil War.

Although new, the state's railroads played a major role in Civil War strategy. Significant railroad towns included Corinth (the Mobile and Ohio and the Memphis and Charleston), Meridian (the Mobile and Ohio and the Southern), and

Railroad bridge across Yalobusha River, Grenada, ca. 1912 (Ann Rayburn Paper Americana Collection, Department of Archives and Special Collections, J. D. Williams Library, University of Mississippi [rayburn_ann_24_41_001])

Jackson (the Southern and the New Orleans, Jackson, and Great Northern), all of which experienced significant property damage. William Sherman's forces destroyed twenty-one miles of track around Meridian, and much of the Mississippi Central line as well as railroad bridges, stations, and cars were destroyed or damaged.

Railroad construction and timber became Mississippi's primary industries in the 1870s and 1880s. Whereas only about 120 new miles of track were constructed from 1865 to 1880, track mileage more than doubled from 1880 (1,127 miles) to 1900 (2,788 miles), and by 1910 the state had 4,223 miles of railroads. Many of the lines continued to serve the timber industry, and according to historian James Fickle, Gulf and Ship Island Railroad's "seventy-four-mile section from Hattiesburg to Gulfport averaged one sawmill and one turpentine distillery every three miles" in 1902. About six hundred small, impermanent "dummy lines" were constructed, allowing steam-powered trains to move people and equipment into timber areas and to transport timber out to national markets.

Founded in 1851, the Illinois Central became a major force in Mississippi in the 1870s. It invested in lines owned by Henry McComb, a Delaware businessman who had taken over the Mississippi Central and then the New Orleans, Jackson, and Great Northern. McComb, the founder of the South Mississippi town that took his name, needed considerable funds to improve existing lines and build new ones, especially after merging his two lines to form the New Orleans, St. Louis, and Chicago Railroad. When it turned out that McComb did not have enough money to run his railroads, the lines went into receivership, and the Illinois Central bought them at auction in 1877, creating a network that stretched from New Orleans to Chicago and earning the company its nickname, the Main Line of Mid-America.

The Louisville, New Orleans, and Texas Railroad put together several local lines in the Mississippi Delta and by the 1880s had become central to cotton growing. The Illinois Central's 1892 purchase of the Louisville, New Orleans, and Texas made it by far the state's most powerful company. In 1925 the Illinois Central also acquired the Gulf and Ship Island Railroad.

Along the Gulf Coast, the growing rail lines facilitated the increasingly important activities of the seafood industry and tourism. The New Orleans, Mobile, and Chattanooga allowed tourists easy access to beaches, hotels, and restaurants, while fishing interests used the railroads to find new ways to market their products.

In 1884 the Mississippi legislature established the state railroad commission, and its biennial report quickly became the state's largest, with detailed information about rates, laws, controversies and lawsuits, mileage, new tracks, and accidents. In the 1880s and 1890s, Populists objected to railroad companies' power in the state's economy and government. As supporters of the interests of smaller farmers, Frank Burkitt and other Populist leaders advocated government regulation or even ownership of the railroads.

Railroad work and railroad travel constituted an important part of the opportunities and especially the limitations of life for various Mississippians. European immigrants—first from Ireland and later from Germany, Finland, and other countries—often took jobs as railroad workers, leading to the development of immigrant communities in McComb, Gluckstadt, and Water Valley. However, railroad travel also developed at the same time as racial segregation, and the state's railroad cars became especially important sites where whites made racial distinctions. In 1888 the Mississippi legislature mandated that railroads "shall provide equal but separate accommodations for the white and colored races, by providing two or more passenger cars for each passenger train." The Mississippi Supreme Court upheld the law in an 1889 decision. Mississippi-born reformer Ida B. Wells began her career as an activist by challenging laws that denied her access to the white ladies' car.

In the early 1900s the Illinois Central became the primary way that African Americans left Mississippi for Chicago and other northern cities. Countless blues songs mentioned trains either as reference points—Charley Patton sang of "goin' where the Southern cross the Dog" (the junction of the Yazoo and the Mississippi Valley railroad lines)—or as a way to leave trouble and hope for a better future. For Richard Wright, travel brought both excitement about the potential of starting a new life and nervousness. He recalled that as soon as he got off the train in Chicago, he was "seized by doubt" about his decision to migrate.

A wide range of Mississippians have been involved with the railroads. Postbellum town founder William Harris Hardy and writer William C. Falkner were railroad founders; Mississippi Supreme Court justice Alexander Clayton and Gov. Charles Lynch served as railroad directors or presidents; and McComb civil rights activist C. C. Bryant was a railroad man. Engineer John Luther "Casey" Jones became legendary in 1900 when he gave his life outside of Vaughan, Mississippi, to save the passengers on his train. And Meridian's Jimmie Rodgers, known as the Singing Brakeman, was the state's first country music star, recording numerous songs about the life of a ramblin' man on a train, far from home.

The significance of railroads has declined since the 1920s because of economic changes and the rise of competing forms of transportation. Total mileage has declined from 4,005 in 1940 to 3,691 in 1960 to less than 2,500 in 2010. Today two Amtrak trains run through Mississippi: the *City of New Orleans* runs from New Orleans to Chicago, with stops in McComb, Brookhaven, Hazlehurst, Jackson, Yazoo City, and Greenwood, while the *Crescent* connects New Orleans with New York, stopping along the way in Picayune, Hattiesburg, Laurel, and Meridian.

Ted Ownby
University of Mississippi

James C. Cobb, *The Most Southern Place on Earth: The Mississippi Delta and the Roots of Regional Identity* (1992); James E. Fickle, *Mississippi Forests and Forestry* (2001); Gilbert H. Hoffman, *Dummy Lines through the Longleaf: A History of the Sawmills and Railroads of Southwest Mississippi* (1992); Joseph R. Millichap, *Dixie Limited: Railroads, Culture, and the Southern Renaissance* (2002); John F. Stover, *History of the Illinois Central Railroad* (1975); John F. Stover, *The Railroads of the South, 1865–1900: A Study in Finance and Control* (1955); Mississippi Rails: Mississippi's Railroad History and Heritage website, www.msrailroads.com.

Ralston, Blanche Montgomery

(1892–1958) Civic Leader

Blanche Montgomery Ralston, Delta leader and government official, was born in Durant, Mississippi, to William A. Montgomery and Dona Linder Montgomery, on 3 June 1892. She attended public schools there before entering the Industrial Institute and College at Columbus in 1908 to study music. For three years after leaving college she taught music in Carroll County's schools. In 1913 she married Robert Shaw Ralston and moved to Coahoma County, where her husband was a planter. A gifted speaker with an engaging personality, Blanche Ralston soon rose to prominence in public affairs. In 1922 she began a long association with the Mississippi Federation of Women's Clubs (MFWC) and served as state president 1924–26. She conducted a vigorous "buy more cotton" crusade to stimulate marketing of the state's staple crop. While she was secretary of the Coahoma County Chamber of Commerce, the Clarksdale Cotton Carnival began. From 1924 to 1930 she edited the *Mississippi Woman's Magazine* and the federation's journal, and from 1928 to 1932 she served as state press chair for the Daughters of the American Revolution.

In 1924 Ralston was named to the Board of Trustees of State Universities and Colleges. She served as state legislative chair of the parent-teacher association and was a board member of the Mississippi Conference on Social Welfare. From 1926 to 1932 she was the only woman member of the quasi-public Mississippi State Board of Development. She served as secretary of the Central Committee for the Economic Survey of Mississippi from its creation in 1929–31. That post led to a gubernatorial appointment as one of twenty-five Mississippians directed to make a social and economic survey of the state as a basis for Gov. Martin S. Conner's legislative program.

Ralston was a founding member of the Delta Council in 1935, the year she became one of five (later six) regional supervisors of women's and professional work relief under the Works Progress Administration (WPA). As a close confidant and longtime associate of Ellen S. Woodward in women's organizations and with varied experiences in governmental advisory capacities, Ralston supervised work projects in twelve southeastern states. At the liquidation of most WPA projects in 1942, she became a member of the Woman's Advisory Committee (WAC) of the War Manpower Commission, which met periodically in Washington to determine how best to allocate womanpower in the national defense program without the woman worker's serious neglect of domestic duties, including child care and food services.

With the end of the war, Ralston's association with national programs ended, but she remained vital in the civic programs of her the town of Coahoma and of the county. Following her husband's death, she and her sons operated a plantation. She died in Clarksdale on 20 September 1958 after a year of failing health.

Martha H. Swain
Mississippi State University

Clarksdale Daily Register (22 July 1958); Margaret Hickey Papers, University of Missouri, St. Louis; Ralston Vertical File, Mississippi Department of Archives and History; *American Biography* 66 (1931); Martha H. Swain, *Ellen S. Woodward: New Deal Advocate for Women* (1995).

Ramsay, Claude E.

(1916–1986) Union Leader

Claude Elwood Ramsay, born in Ocean Springs on 18 December 1916, served as president of the Mississippi American Federation of Labor and Congress of Industrial Organizations (AFL-CIO) from 1959 until shortly before his death. Ramsay attended Perkinston Junior College and spent two years in the Civilian Conservation Corps before obtaining a job with the International Paper Company in Moss Point in 1939. After serving in the US Army during World War II, he returned to work at International Paper and became active in United Paperworkers of America Local 203, first as a shop steward and eventually as union president. Ramsay was instrumental in the merger that led to the formation of the Mississippi AFL-CIO in 1958, and he was elected union president the following year.

Motivated by his belief in equality and his understanding that the state's employers used white supremacy to undermine labor solidarity, Ramsay was an often lonely white voice of moderation in Mississippi during the late 1950s and early 1960s. Shortly after the 1962 riots in Oxford triggered by James Meredith's enrollment at the University of Mississippi, Ramsay warned the members of the Pascagoula Metal Trades Council that their participation in acts of racist vio-

lence could jeopardize federal shipbuilding contracts. His opposition to segregation and his eventual embrace of the civil rights movement made him a frequent target of the state's white business and political leaders as well as many rank-and-file trade unionists. Dozens of local unions disaffiliated from the state AFL-CIO to protest Ramsay's efforts to improve race relations, but their departures only strengthened his hand by eliminating his strongest opponents from within the federation. Throughout his tenure he also enjoyed strong backing from the national AFL-CIO and the Democratic Party, which needed white leaders in Mississippi to defend their candidates and programs.

Ramsay had little contact with Mississippi's black-led civil rights movement until the mid-1960s, when he played a key role in organizing an alternative to the all-white state Democratic Party. With other white reformers and leaders of the National Association for the Advancement of Colored People, Ramsay sought to form a biracial Democratic Party that would be loyal to the national party. However, he gained the enmity of some civil rights activists, including members of the Student Nonviolent Coordinating Committee and the Mississippi Freedom Democratic Party, when he attempted to exclude them from the party's leadership. Ramsay, for his part, kept Freedom Democratic Party leaders at a distance, believing that their group was not viable in Mississippi and that their presence in the Democratic Party would alienate white voters. At the same time, Ramsay battled with the Democratic Regulars who fought to maintain an exclusively white party. In the last years of his life, Ramsay led an unsuccessful fight to boost compensation payments for the state's injured workers. He retired from the AFL-CIO on 1 January 1986 and died just sixteen days later.

Kieran W. Taylor
The Citadel

Charles M. Dollar, "Claude Ramsay: A Visionary and Catalyst for Social and Political Change in Mississippi, 1960–1986," http://winterinstitute.org/wp-content/blogs.dir/1/files/2015/12/11–28–2015_Claude-Ramsay_FINAEnd-Noted.pdf; Alan Draper, *Conflict of Interests: Organized Labor and the Civil Rights Movement in the South, 1954–1968* (1994); Bill Minor, *Southern Changes* (1986); Claude Ramsay, interview by Orley B. Caudill, Center for Oral History and Cultural Heritage, University of Southern Mississippi (28, 30 April, 7 May 1981).

R

Rand, Clayton

(1891–1971) Editor and Author

Clayton Rand was the editor of several Mississippi newspapers and author of a range of books, including an autobiographical account of his newspaper work, *Ink on My Hands.* Born in Wisconsin on 25 May 1891, he moved with his family to Bond, Mississippi, in 1899 when his father decided to pursue work in the timber industry. He attended Meridian Male College and Mississippi A&M before earning a law degree from Harvard University. He moved to Neshoba County in 1918 and bought an interest in the local newspaper, the *Neshoba Democrat.* In the 1920s Rand helped start the *DeKalb Independent* and the *Tunica Times,* and in 1925 he sold those newspapers and bought the Dixie Press in Gulfport. He later founded Gulfport's *Mississippi Guide.*

Rand saw himself as a fighting newspaperman, writing editorials critical of local government inaction and corruption, poor health and garbage services, and the Ku Klux Klan of the 1920s. He initially welcomed the New Deal but quickly turned against it. In a 1936 book, *Abracadabra,* he denounced the "New Steal" for undermining people's character by paying them through government programs. Rand wrote a syndicated column, "Crossroads Scribe," in which he offered pithy criticisms of government and modernity from the point of view of what he saw as the high character of small-town Americans.

While he frequently criticized local towns and their leaders, Rand was also a booster. In the 1930s he wrote promotional and tourist publications for Gulfport and other sites on the Gulf Coast. He also began writing short biographical stories of southern leaders as newspaper columns, and in 1940 his press, the Dixie Press, published sixty-five of the sketches in *Men of Spine in Mississippi.* Emphasizing the personal achievements of his subjects, Rand began with explorers in the Spanish, French, and English periods and then concentrated on political leaders, also mentioning some lawyers, frontiersmen, journalists, and a few educators and ministers. Two of the "men of spine," Greenwood LeFlore and Pushmataha, were American Indians. In 1961 Rand expanded his approach to include the entire region in *Sons of the South,* an "inspiring story of a superior breed of stalwarts . . . inscribed to mark the Civil War Centennial" and to "enrich the lives" of its readers. Again, virtually all of the men of note were white southerners, although Booker T. Washington was included. In 1966 Jackson's State Line Productions published a manual for schoolteachers who wished to assign the book in conjunction with a filmstrip designed for classroom use.

Along with his work as editor and columnist, Rand became a popular conservative public speaker from the 1940s through the 1960s. He died on 26 February 1971.

Ted Ownby
University of Mississippi

Charles P. Lowery, in *Lives of Mississippi Authors, 1817–1967,* ed. James B. Lloyd (1981).

Randall, Herbert

(b. 1936) Photographer

Photographer Herbert Eugene Randall took some of the most memorable photographs of the Mississippi civil rights movement. Randall was born on 16 December 1936 to Jane Hunter Randall and Herbert Randall Sr. in the Bronx, New York. After two years at New York City Community College and a brief stint at Hunter College, he left school to pursue a career in photography.

Although Randall studied under renowned photographer Harold Feinstein in the 1950s, his photographic talents were largely self-taught, and he earned a living as a freelance photographer in the late 1950s and early 1960s. In 1962–63 Randall and other African American photographers founded Kamoinge (a Kikuyu word meaning "a group of people working together"), which sought to dispel negative stereotypes by capturing the beauty and strength of New York's black community in the early 1960s.

In April 1964 Randall received the John Hay Whitney Fellowship, which provided funding to pursue a yearlong photography project. Randall felt drawn to the growing civil rights movement in the South, and Julie Prettyman, a good friend and head of the Student Nonviolent Coordinating Committee (SNCC) office in Manhattan, suggested that he go to Mississippi to photograph the Freedom Summer campaign.

During Freedom Summer, Randall joined hundreds of other journalists and photographers—among them Claude Sitton, Karl Fleming, Charles Moore, and Danny Lyon—who risked their lives every day to document the African American struggle for freedom in Mississippi. According to Randall, the greatest challenge faced by Freedom Summer photographers was the constant threat of violence by the state's white segregationists, who had a great deal of contempt for outside media outlets. During Freedom Summer, Randall was stationed in Hattiesburg and nearby Palmer's Crossing. He spent his days following SNCC staff members and summer volunteers as they attempted to register voters and teach in freedom schools. Among the most famous images that Randall captured was the beating of his close friend Rabbi Arthur Lelyveld and of freedom school students and teachers. Randall published hundreds of his Freedom Summer photographs in *Faces of Freedom Summer* (2001). Randall has since donated hundreds of his Freedom Summer photographs to the University of Southern Mississippi's McCain Library and Archives, and many are available through the Civil Rights in Mississippi Digital Archive.

Randall spent the rest of his professional life working with Kamoinge and as a photographer, teacher, and photographic consultant. His images have been displayed at museums throughout the United States. Now retired, Randall resides on the Shinnecock Indian Reservation on Long Island, New York.

William Sturkey
University of North Carolina

Civil Rights in Mississippi Digital Archive website, http://digilib.usm.edu/crmda.php; Charles Payne, *I've Got the Light of Freedom: The Organizing Tradition and the Mississippi Freedom Struggle* (1995); Herbert Randall and Bob Tusa, *Faces of Freedom Summer* (2001).

Rankin, John Elliott
(1882–1960) Politician

Together with politicians such as James Vardaman and Theodore Bilbo, John Rankin belongs to that group of Mississippi demagogues who represented the raw edge of racism in US politics. While other southern congressmen often tried to couch their segregationist ideas in rhetoric about states' rights, Rankin openly expressed his hatred of Jews, blacks, and communists. At the same time, he presented himself as a populist who spoke for the rights of the common man in his fight against the power of Wall Street and big business and in his support for rural electrification.

John Elliott Rankin was born on 29 March 1882 near Bolanda in Itawamba County, Mississippi. After graduation from high school, Rankin enrolled at the University of Mississippi. He graduated from the university's law school in 1910 and was admitted to the bar the same year. Rankin practiced law in West Point and later in Tupelo. From 1911 to 1915 he served as prosecuting attorney of Lee County. Just before World War I ended, Rankin spent twenty-one days at a US Army officers' training camp, subsequently using this brief service to portray himself as an ex-soldier and a defender of war veterans.

Rankin ran unsuccessfully for the US House of Representatives in 1916 and 1918. Shortly after his second campaign, Rankin started a newspaper, the *New Era*. The publication promoted the interests of veterans, advocated strict limits on immigration, and defended segregation and lynching. In one editorial Rankin declared himself a supporter of woman suffrage. Rankin again ran for the US House in 1920, portraying himself as the candidate of change against incumbent Zeke Candler in the Democratic primary. Rankin also pledged to work on behalf of national Jim Crow legislation. The *New Era* was an important instrument in spreading Rankin's populist message. With the support of organized labor, Rankin defeated Candler in the runoff primary.

In Congress, Rankin lived up to his image of an unyielding defender of segregation. He declared that the constitutional rights of blacks were best protected under segregation and that every state in the Union should oppose integration as a way of maintaining racial harmony. In April 1921 Rankin joined other southern congressmen in opposing antilynching legislation introduced by Republican representative Leonidas C. Dyer, calling it "a bill to encourage rape." The Mississippi congressman also held a firm belief in the righteousness of poll tax legislation, considering efforts by the Southern Conference for Human Welfare and northern politicians to repeal the tax a communist-inspired plot to stir up racial trouble in the South.

Although Rankin opposed federal intervention in southern race relations and election laws, he backed the economic recovery programs of Pres. Franklin Roosevelt's New Deal. The Great Depression had hit Mississippi hard, and Rankin was on the front line in the fight for relief programs. With Republican senator George Norris of Nebraska, he coauthored the 1933 bill that created the Tennessee Valley Authority. In 1936 Rankin backed the passage of the Rural Electrification Act, and a year later he threw his support behind the president's controversial court-packing plan. The Mississippi legislator served as chair of the House Committee on World War Veterans' Legislation, and in 1942 he played an important role in passing a bill that doubled the base pay of soldiers. "No man has done more for soldiers than I have," Rankin claimed.

During the more reformist Second New Deal, Rankin started to turn away from the national Democrats and President Roosevelt. Although organized labor had endorsed Rankin in 1920, his concern about unions' growing influence on his party increased after FDR's 1936 victory. During World War II Rankin denounced strikes as sabotage and described the egalitarian policies of the Fair Employment Practices Committee as "illegal and unconstitutional." He particularly targeted the Congress of Industrial Organizations, a labor movement that took a liberal stance on race relations.

As his career progressed, Rankin became more xenophobic and racist. In addition to his bigoted attitude toward blacks, he began to label Jews as dangerous conspirators who tried to subvert Americanism and Christian civilization through communism and international banking. After calling radio commentator Walter Winchell a "slime-mongering kike" during a congressional debate, Rankin was banned from the House floor for a day because of unparliamentary language. As an archenemy of communism, Rankin was one of the leading members of the House Un-American Activities Committee. He considered Hollywood an important base for a Jewish-communist conspiracy to overthrow the US government. His fear of outsiders also made him a strong advocate of strict immigration rules.

During the 1948 presidential election Rankin supported the States' Rights Democratic ticket of Strom Thurmond and Mississippi governor Fielding Wright, a stance that cost Rankin his seat on the Un-American Activities Committee. In 1949 he became chair of the Committee on Veterans' Affairs, a post he occupied until his retirement. In Congress, Rankin remained a strident foe of the Zionist movement, immigrants, organized labor, and the United Nations.

Rankin's reactionary and racist political philosophy did not stand the test of time. In 1952 he lost his congressional seat to the younger and more moderate House member Thomas Abernethy, whose 4th District had been merged with Rankin's 1st after the 1950 census. Rankin returned to Tupelo, where he practiced law and worked in the real estate business until his death on 26 November 1960.

Maarten Zwiers
University of Groningen,
the Netherlands

New York Times (27 November 1960); *Time* (8 October 1951); Kenneth Wayne Vickers, "John Rankin: Democrat and Demagogue" (master's thesis, Mississippi State University, 1993).

Rankin County

Founded 1828, Rankin County is located in central Mississippi and was formed from part of Hinds County. Named for political figure Christopher Rankin, the county is located on Pearl River. Its county seat is Brandon, and other communities and towns include Flowood, Pearl, Richland, Florence, Pelahatchie, and Puckett. Two important Mississippi institutions, the Piney Woods Country Life School and the Mississippi State Hospital at Whitfield, are located in Rankin County. Perhaps just as important is the county's recent shift away from agriculture to become a highly populated suburban area.

In its first census in 1830, the small county had only 1,697 free people and 386 slaves. It grew quickly and by 1840 had 2,780 free people and 1,851 slaves. The population continued to increase, reaching 13,635 in 1860, when 52 percent of residents were enslaved.

The county's farmers practiced mixed agriculture, growing cotton, corn, rice, and potatoes and raising substantial numbers of livestock. The county's thirteen lumber mills, thirteen flour mills, and handful of other enterprises employed a total of 120 men and 1 woman. Of the county's eighteen churches in 1860, eleven were Baptist, six were Methodist, and one was a Christian Church.

The stories of two lawyers help tell the county's history. Brandon attorney Robert Lowry (1829–1910) became a Confederate brigadier general, a state legislator, and ultimately the governor of Mississippi from 1882 to 1890. Samuel Alfred Beadle (1857–1932) was born a slave in Georgia, moved to Rankin County, received legal training, and in 1884 became one of the few African Americans in the state with a law license. Beadle later moved to Jackson to practice law and to write fiction, nonfiction, and poetry.

Rankin County's population increased to 16,752 in 1880 and to almost 21,000 two decades later. The county remained primarily agricultural, and African Americans made up about 60 percent of the population. More than 70 percent of the 1,436 white farmers owned their land, nearly three times the rate for the county's 1,962 black farmers. Industry grew slowly, with forty-four establishments employing eighty-four workers in 1900. In 1909 Laurence C. Jones started the Piney Woods School, an experimental institution near the Simpson County line that continues to educate students more than a century later.

According to the religious census of 1916, three-quarters of Rankin County's church members were Baptists, divided almost evenly between Missionary and Southern Baptists. The other leading group was Methodists, most of them members of the Methodist Episcopal Church, South.

Among the wide range of creative individuals who grew up in Rankin County were musician and instrument maker Otha Turner, born in 1908; blues musician Elmore James, born in 1918 near Richland; and football star Frank "Bruiser" Kinard, born in 1914 in Pelahatchie. All developed their talents outside Rankin County.

In the early twentieth century, Rankin County's population steadied at around 20,000, with African Americans accounting for about 55 percent of that total. By 1930 the county had 973 industrial workers. Despite its location adjacent to Hinds County, with its urban center of Jackson, Rankin had no urban population. Instead, its primary economic activity remained farming, with both tenants and landowners raising cattle, corn, and cotton.

In the 1920s the state moved the Mississippi State Insane Asylum from Jackson to Rankin County and renamed the town where it was located in honor of Rankin native Henry Whitfield, who served as governor from 1924 to 1926.

Between 1930 and 1960 Rankin County's population increased to 34,322, with the number of African American residents declining while the number of whites more than doubled to account for 63 percent of the total. In 1960 nearly a quarter of Rankin's workers were employed in industry, primarily furniture and timber, and more than 1,000 of the county's residents worked in hospitals and health care. The once agricultural county still had farmers, but by 1960 they comprised just 13 percent of Rankin's workforce. The population continued to increase, reaching almost 44,000 in 1970 and topping 69,000 a decade later.

Brandon native Mary Ann Mobley became Miss America in 1959 and went on to a career as a singer and actress. In 1978 Barney McKee, then director of the University Press of Mississippi, and his wife, Gwen McKee, started Brandon's Quail Ridge Press, which initially published Mississippi cookbooks and has since expanded.

Rankin County's 2010 population of 115,327 represented an increase of 312 percent since 1960, the second-highest growth in Mississippi over the period. Overwhelmingly white, the county had an African American population of just under 20 percent of the total and a small but significant Hispanic/Latino minority.

Mississippi Encyclopedia Staff
University of Mississippi

Mississippi State Planning Commission, *Progress Report on State Planning in Mississippi* (1938); *Mississippi Statistical Abstract*, Mississippi State University (1952–2010); Charles Sydnor and Claude Bennett, *Mississippi History* (1939); University of Virginia Library, Historical Census Browser website, http://mapserver.lib.virginia.edu; E. Nolan Waller and Dani A. Smith, *Growth Profiles of Mississippi's Counties, 1960–1980* (1985).

Raspberry, William

(1935–2012) Journalist

Journalist and commentator William Raspberry was born on 12 October 1935 in Okolona, Mississippi. He graduated in 1952 from Okolona College High School, affiliated with an Episcopal Church junior college. Okolona was a deeply segregated town at the time and offered no public schooling to African Americans.

The son of Willie Mae Tucker Raspberry and James Lee Raspberry, both of whom were teachers, William Raspberry was determined to attend college out of state. He graduated from Indiana Central College (now the University of Indianapolis) in 1958 with a major in history and a minor in philosophy. In 1956, while still an undergraduate, he started his journalism career as a reporter at the *Indianapolis Recorder*, an African American weekly. He rose to associate managing editor before being drafted.

From 1960 to 1962 he served as a public information officer in the US Army in Washington, D.C. He then joined the *Washington Post* as a teletype operator and eventually worked for the city desk, first as a reporter and then as an editor. In 1966 he took over the "Potomac Watch" column, specializing in urban affairs. He provided commentary on education, civil rights, crime, and drug abuse. The column originally appeared in the local news section but was moved to the op-ed page in 1979. It was syndicated by the *Washington Post* Writers Group beginning in 1977 and at its peak appeared in more than 225 newspapers. Raspberry retired from the *Washington Post* in 2005. He always wrote clearly, stated the issues immediately, and took a position. He also contributed articles to *Reader's Digest*, *Nation's Cities Weekly*, *America*, *Mother Jones*, and *Conservative Digest*.

Raspberry taught at Howard University from 1971 to 1973 and served as a member of the board of advisers at the Poynter Institute for Media Studies. He worked as a commentator on several Washington, D.C., television stations in the mid-1970s and was a member of the Pulitzer Prize board from 1980 to 1986. He taught as the Knight Professor of the Practice of Journalism and Public Policy Studies at Duke University's DeWitt Wallace Center for Media and Democracy.

Raspberry received a 1994 Pulitzer Prize for commentary, was named Journalist of the Year by the Capitol Press Club in 1965 for his coverage of the Watts riots in Los Angeles, and in 2004 was awarded the Fourth Estate Award by the National Press Club. The National Association of Black Journalists gave Raspberry a Lifetime Achievement Award in 1994. About four dozen of his columns were collected in a book, *Looking Backward at Us* (1991).

In an interview with *Contemporary Authors*, Raspberry said, "I never take into account what a black columnist or black man would say about this issue, what he ought to think about this thing. I write about what makes sense to me about particular issues, and certainly the fact that I'm black has an influence on what I think makes sense about those issues." Raspberry took pride in the fact that he defied easy categorization, writing that he sometimes seemed a conservative for declaring personal responsibility for the solution to problems and other times seemed a liberal for his persistent discussion of problems faced by African Americans. He doubted Afrocentrism, questioned whether racism persisted as much as many African American leaders believed, and announced, "If I could offer a single prescription for the survival of America, and particularly of black America, it would be: restore the family."

In 2003 Raspberry founded Baby Steps, an Okolona-based parent education program designed to help low-income parents of preschoolers prepare their children for school. He died at his Washington, D.C., home on 17 July 2012.

Kathleen Woodruff Wickham
University of Mississippi

Baby Steps website, http://www.takebabysteps.com/; Linda Fibich, *American Journalism Review* (May 1994); Crystal K. Roberts, *Black Collegian*

(October 1999); Gale Reference Team, *Contemporary Authors Online* (2006); Dennis Hevesi, *New York Times* (17 July 2012).

Raymond, Battle of

A sharp engagement fought during the Vicksburg Campaign occurred on 12 May 1863 just outside Raymond. Better intelligence by the Confederates would undoubtedly have forestalled the battle. The opponents consisted of a Confederate brigade under Brig. Gen. John Gregg and portions of the Union's 17th Corps under Maj. Gen. James B. McPherson. After crossing the Mississippi River and winning victories at Grand Gulf and Port Gibson, the Union Army under Maj. Gen. Ulysses S. Grant advanced inland along several routes, with McPherson on the right flank. Grant ordered McPherson to advance to Raymond on 12 May in hopes of capturing the strategic crossroads and commissary stores reported to be there. McPherson had his men moving along the road from Utica by early morning.

John Gregg's brigade had been at Port Hudson, Louisiana, before receiving orders to move to Jackson on 1 May. Gregg had perhaps between twenty-five hundred and three thousand men, and these Tennessee and Texas infantrymen, supported by a Missouri battery, took to the road soon the next day. They marched part of the two hundred miles from Port Hudson before arriving at Jackson by rail on 8 May. Confederate commander John C. Pemberton allowed them to rest briefly before ordering them to Raymond. When Gregg's command entered town on the morning of 11 May, they met citizens anxious about reports that Union troops were advancing from Port Gibson. Gregg expected that cavalry under Col. Wirt Adams would be at Raymond, but only a detached patrol of five men from Adams's command was there, supplemented by a small force of state troops out scouting the approaches to the south. During the night a cavalry detachment discovered the presence of Federal troops nine miles from Raymond, and early the next morning Gregg heard from various couriers that a Union column was advancing via the road from Utica. A cavalry screen shielded the approaching Federal force, and Gregg mistakenly inferred that he faced a "brigade on a marauding expedition." He prepared to attack, unaware that McPherson had two full divisions and more than three times as many men. McPherson's ability to disguise his advance arose in part as a consequence of the difficulties southern cavalry encountered in ascertaining the location, size, and potential movements of Grant's various columns.

If Gregg badly underestimated the size of the approaching force, McPherson for his part did not expect any major resistance near Raymond. Both commanders were operating under false assumptions when musketry opened as the Union advance approached Fourteenmile Creek, two miles southwest of Raymond. Gregg hoped to strike the Union right flank and roll it up, with an eye toward capturing the supposedly smaller, weaker enemy force. Terrain played a role in the engagement, as thick undergrowth and timber, deep ravines, and steep banks along the creek made troop maneuvers difficult. The battle opened around 10:00 in the morning as the two sides clashed near Fourteenmile Creek. Gregg's surprise offensive achieved early success against men from Maj. Gen. John Logan's division. Fighting at close quarters ensued in some areas where the antagonists collided. An Ohio regiment wavered until Logan rode forward to rally them; elsewhere, Confederates drove the isolated 23rd Indiana Regiment back across the creek. Union troops rallied and began to gain the upper hand. Smoke and clouds of dust obscured the field, preventing both Gregg and McPherson from accurately assessing developments. Gregg had intended for units on the left of his line to take up the attack, but he lost contact and could not bring them into concert with the initial assault. McPherson brought up additional troops and extended his line to the right, where the creek bent back to the south. A Tennessee regimental commander in the area finally realized that his men confronted at least an entire Federal division and attempted in vain to apprise Gregg of this revelation.

The disparity in numbers began to tell as Union brigades successively came up and deployed on either side of the Utica road. Gregg belatedly became aware that he had attacked a force several times his own and disengaged. He did so in the afternoon, but not before suffering heavy casualties, particularly in the 3rd Tennessee and 7th Texas Regiments. The Tennesseans counted 187 casualties, while the Texans lost 158 of the 306 men they took into battle. Gregg's survivors retreated through Raymond and encamped, while troops from several Union brigades entered the town and feasted on food originally intended for the Confederates. Looting took place as Union soldiers destroyed fences, raided smokehouses, stole animals, and sacked homes.

Raymond became a hospital for the wounded of both armies. Federal casualty figures show 66 killed, 339 wounded, and 37 missing, while corresponding figures for the Confederates are 73, 252, and 190. Yet in a report written two weeks after the battle, McPherson claimed enemy losses at 103 killed and 720 wounded and captured. Raymond was a brutal soldiers' fight, fought largely on the initiative of individual regimental commanders. Both commanding generals struggled to control the action, partly because they could see little of the battlefield clearly. A cautious McPherson fed in units piecemeal, resulting in uncoordinated assaults that negated his vast numeric superiority. His artillery was relatively ineffective, owing chiefly to the smoke and dust hovering over the battlefield. Gregg for his part attacked without verifying the size of the enemy column and had difficulty managing the battle once it commenced. Throughout much of the battle, he had no idea what regiments on the left of his line were doing.

The battle altered Grant's strategy. Learning of McPherson's encounter near Raymond, Grant abandoned plans to move toward Edwards. He resolved to go immediately to Jackson and deal with the Confederate force under Gen. Joseph E. Johnston before swinging west to contend with southern forces that had come out from the Vicksburg defenses. As a result, his army arrived at Jackson two days later, fought elements of Johnston's command, and captured the capital.

Christopher Losson
St. Joseph, Missouri

Michael B. Ballard, *Vicksburg: The Campaign that Opened the Mississippi* (2004); Edwin Cole Bearss, *The Campaign for Vicksburg*, vol. 2, *Grant Strikes a Fatal Blow* (1986); Warren E. Grabau, *Ninety-Eight Days: A Geographer's View of the Vicksburg Campaign* (2000); *The War of the Rebellion: Official Records of the Union and Confederate Armies*, vol. 24, parts 1 and 3 (1889).

Reagan, Ronald, in Mississippi

Mississippi's political transformation from Democratic to Republican stronghold mirrored closely that of Ronald Reagan. Reagan campaigned for Democrats Franklin D. Roosevelt and Harry S. Truman in the 1930s and 1940s. Between 1876 and 1960 no Republican presidential candidate carried Mississippi. Reagan left the Democratic Party in 1962, the same time that many Mississippians began to abandon their long-held political loyalties. Republican presidential candidates carried the state in 1964, 1972, 1980, and in every election since.

Reagan first visited the state on 16 November 1973, serving as the keynote speaker for the Mississippi Republican Party's annual fund-raiser in Jackson. Reagan criticized the politicization of Watergate and various policies of the Democratic Party. Reagan traveled to Greenville as a guest of Mississippi GOP state chair Clarke Reed on 17 November and later attended a football game between the University of Mississippi and the University of Tennessee.

Reagan returned to Mississippi on 4 August 1976 as part of his challenge to incumbent Gerald R. Ford for the Republican presidential nomination. Ford had visited Mississippi just five days earlier, as both candidates sought the state's thirty uncommitted delegates. Reagan received a more sub-

dued welcome than he had three years earlier. Many Mississippians disapproved of his promise to choose Sen. Richard Schweiker of Pennsylvania, a centrist, as his running mate.

Preparing to run for the presidency in 1980, Reagan returned to Mississippi in 1978, visiting both Jackson and Pearl on 18 October. While in Pearl, Reagan talked about the need to increase America's military strength and the importance of states' rights.

On 2 August 1980, with the presidential election heating up, Reagan arrived at the Neshoba County Fair near Philadelphia, where thirty thousand cheering people greeted him. His speech for the most part offered standard campaign rhetoric, but he generated a national political firestorm when he announced, "I believe in states' rights." Though Reagan had spoken those words for decades and had in fact used them in Mississippi two years earlier, they resonated differently in Neshoba County, where civil rights workers Michael Schwerner, James Chaney, and Andrew Goodman had been murdered during the Freedom Summer just sixteen years earlier. Since the Neshoba visit was the first campaign appearance after the Republican National Convention (though not the official launch of the campaign), the appearance at the fair continues to possess a contested place in Reagan historiography.

Reagan was scheduled to deliver a key address to the National Urban League in New York City just a few days after his Neshoba County appearance. Aides feared that anger over his comments could derail his campaign. With criticism mounting among the national news media, Reagan visited Urban League president Vernon Jordan, who was hospitalized after a recent assassination attempt. He then spoke before the Urban League and visited the South Bronx to criticize Pres. Jimmy Carter's lack of urban reform. After leaving New York, Reagan stopped in Chicago and visited with Rev. Jesse Jackson at the Operation PUSH (People United to Save Humanity) headquarters.

Reagan's damage-control strategy worked, and the Neshoba story soon faded from the national headlines. Subsequent attempts by Carter and others to raise the issue failed. On 20 October Reagan visited the Mississippi Sheriffs' Association Boys and Girls Ranch near Columbus. The Neshoba story did not resurface in the press, and less than two weeks later Reagan won Mississippi by 1 percentage point.

President Reagan visited Mississippi twice. On 20 June 1983 he attended a United Republican Fund dinner in Jackson and praised the leadership of House Minority Whip Trent Lott. On 1 October 1984, while campaigning for reelection, Reagan stopped in Gulfport, where a crowd of forty thousand gathered. When asked whether Mississippi might become a site for the dumping of nuclear waste, Reagan responded that he would never do anything against the will of a state. He continued, "And having been a governor myself of a state, I believe in states' rights." Away from Neshoba, the comment produced no special media attention.

Toby G. Bates
Mississippi State University
at Meridian

Toby Glenn Bates, "The Reagan Rhetoric: History and Memory" (PhD dissertation, University of Mississippi, 2006); Lou Cannon, *Governor Reagan: His Rise to Power* (2003); Joseph Crespino, *In Search of Another Country: Mississippi and the Conservative Counterrevolution* (2007); Jeremy D. Mayer, *Running on Race: Racial Politics in Presidential Campaigns, 1960–2000* (2002); Kenneth O'Reilly, *Nixon's Piano: Presidents and Racial Politics from Washington to Clinton* (1995); Roland Perry, *Hidden Power: The Programming of the President* (1984).

Reconstruction

Reconstruction was particularly divisive in Mississippi. Upper South states such as Tennessee, North Carolina, and Virginia, where former slaves comprised a minority of the population and white citizens had opposed secession until after the Civil War began, had relatively short and mild Reconstruction experiences. In the Deep South, however, where African Americans constituted a majority of the population and white leaders seceded before hostilities erupted, Reconstruction lasted much longer and was much more divisive. Mississippi, the second state to secede, epitomized this group. Reconstruction went through two phases and lasted for eleven years, revealing both the limitless possibilities and depressing realities of postwar America.

In May 1865 Pres. Andrew Johnson's requirements for readmission to the Union seemed simple: Mississippi had to annul its ordinance of secession and abolish slavery. Following Abraham Lincoln's policy, Johnson also requested that southern states consider enfranchising some black males, such as property owners or war veterans. Johnson appointed William L. Sharkey, a Union Whig, as provisional governor to oversee Reconstruction in Mississippi. The state constitutional convention, composed of seventy-one Whigs and eighteen Democrats, proved how unconquered white Mississippians were. Instead of annulling secession, the delegates repealed Mississippi's secession ordinance, implying that they retained the right to secede. Likewise, instead of abolishing slavery, they acknowledged that the institution was destroyed but refused to ratify the Thirteenth Amendment. They never considered black suffrage. Despite the delegates' defiance, Johnson accepted the new state constitution and scheduled state elections for October 1865. National politics influenced Johnson's decision: he wanted to complete Reconstruction before Congress convened in December and challenged his policies.

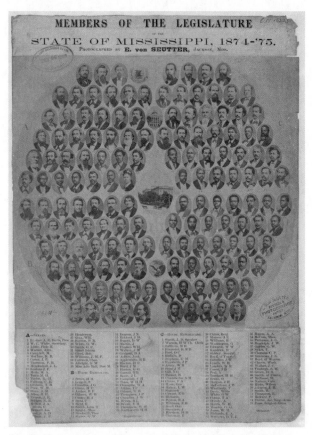

Seventy-five members of the 1874–75 Mississippi State Legislature, including many African American representatives (Photograph by E. Von Seutter, Library of Congress, Washington, D.C. [LC-DIG-ppmsca-12860])

Johnson's leniency emboldened white Mississippians. Col. Samuel Thomas, the assistant commissioner of the Freedmen's Bureau who opened the bureau's office in Vicksburg, noticed white Mississippians' rebellious posture: "Wherever I go—the street, the shop, the house, or the steamboat—I hear the people talk in such a way as to indicate that they are yet unable to conceive of the Negro as possessing any rights at all." White men boasted to Thomas that blacks would "catch hell" after local whites reacquired political control. Whites spread false rumors that former slaves were planning a race war with the aid of the thirteen thousand US soldiers (most of them black) who occupied the state. Mississippi's population was 55 percent African American, and many whites believed that maintaining white supremacy was more important than promoting peace, economic progress, educational reform, or justice. In November 1865 this racism surfaced in Mississippi's Act to Confer Civil Rights on Freedmen, the misleading title of the state's Black Codes. Instead of embracing change, Mississippi legislators passed the first and most extreme postwar racial laws in an attempt to replicate slavery. The codes used vagrancy laws to control African Americans and punished them for any breach of Old South etiquette. Blacks could not be idle, disorderly, or use "insulting" gestures. Blacks could not own guns or preach the Gospel without a special license. Until they turned eighteen, black children were forced to work as "apprentices" for white planters, usually their former masters. Most blatant of all, the state penal codes simply replaced the word *slave* with *freedman*: all the crimes and penalties for slaves remained "in full force" for the emancipated.

The Black Codes not only limited African Americans' political power but also addressed the deeper economic struggle between former masters and freed slaves. Planters wanted to force blacks to work as they had during bondage. The former slaves had different goals: renting or owning land and self-sufficiency and independence from the old ways of plantation agriculture. In short, they wanted physical and economic distance from their terrible past. But whites seldom were willing to sell land to African Americans, even when they had saved up money to buy it. In parts of Mississippi, landowners who refused to sell property to blacks for ten dollars an acre sold it to whites for half that price. Declining land prices and a failing cotton market then threatened white planters' livelihood. Economic recovery stalled because Mississippians depended almost exclusively on agriculture, and the state's transportation system was inadequate and wrecked by war. Planters who had withstood wartime destruction and postwar uncertainties faced spiraling debt. More than 150 planters near Natchez, one of the wealthiest cotton regions in the world, forfeited their land to pay debts or back taxes. Eventually, when neither whites nor blacks could achieve their economic aims, the sharecropping system developed.

Testimony from officials such as Thomas and the Black Codes convinced Congress that Mississippi and other states needed a more thorough approach. Beginning in 1867, Congressional or Radical Reconstruction ensued. In Mississippi this period contained great achievements and embarrassing failures. The state recognized the property rights of married women and established public education. One of the greatest successes was black participation in democracy, both as voters and officeholders. At least 226 black Mississippians held public office during Radical Reconstruction, far more than in Arkansas (46) or Tennessee (20), and among them were the first and only black US senators of this period, Hiram Rhoades Revels and Blanche K. Bruce.

But Radical Reconstruction infuriated southerners committed to white supremacy. As Republicans implemented political equality, terrorist groups used intimidation and violence to reverse progress. The foremost of these organizations was the Ku Klux Klan. Established in 1866, the Klan became a vicious paramilitary organization that promoted planters' interests and the Democratic Party. Klansmen targeted Republicans, "outspoken" blacks, and workers who challenged planter rule. In Monroe County, the Klan killed

Jack Dupree, an African American who led a local Republican group and spoke his mind. Mississippi courts, black churches, and schools became frequent targets of racial violence. In Meridian three black leaders were arrested in 1871 for making "incendiary" speeches. During their trial, Klansmen shot up the courtroom, killing the Republican judge, all three defendants, and African Americans in the audience. The violence sparked a bloodbath in which white rioters murdered dozens of black leaders.

In 1875 these violent tactics ruined democracy in Mississippi. The Democratic Party adopted intimidation, voter fraud, and violence to regain power, a strategy dubbed the First Mississippi Plan. In Vicksburg, white supremacists patrolled the streets with guns and told black voters to stay home on Election Day. In Clinton, Democrats assaulted a Republican barbecue just weeks before the November elections, killing schoolteachers, missionaries, and others in attendance. Former governor James L. Alcorn, a scalawag who had allied with black leaders during his term, rounded up a gang and attacked a meeting held by Coahoma County sheriff John Brown, an African American, slaughtering six blacks and two or three whites and chasing Brown from the area. Alcorn's shift toward violence epitomized white Mississippians' determination to oust Republicans and protect white supremacy at any cost. Gov. Adelbert Ames, a carpetbagger, asked Pres. Ulysses S. Grant for federal troops to quell the insurgents and guarantee a fair election. When the president denied further aid, Ames called out the state militia but then sent them home after Democrats promised to keep the peace on Election Day. They broke their promise. In the absence of the militia, roughnecks scared black voters away from the polls or forced them to vote Democratic. The strategy worked: Democratic candidates committed to white supremacy replaced every Republican incumbent in the 1875 elections. With control of the legislature, the Democrats grabbed the executive branch by impeaching its Republican leaders. Lt. Gov. Alexander K. Davis, an African American, was convicted of bribery, theft, and unconstitutional acts and removed from office. Ames resigned and left Mississippi rather than face the same fate. The federal government refused to address these blatant abuses. In 1876 Rutherford B. Hayes won a contested presidential election by promising to withdraw the last federal troops from the South and ignore the hideous ways that southern Democrats regained power. John Lynch, Mississippi's last Republican congressman, warned that "the war was fought in vain."

Jason Phillips
West Virginia University

Stephen Budiansky, *The Bloody Shirt: Terror after Appomattox* (2008); Eric Foner, *Recostruction: America's Unfinished Revolution, 1863–1877* (1988); William C. Harris, *The Day of the Carpetbagger: Republican*

R

Reconstruction in Mississippi (1979); Peter Kolchin, *A Sphinx on the American Land: The Nineteenth-Century South in Comparative Perspective* (2003); Nicholas Lemann, *Redemption: The Last Battle of the Civil War* (2007).

Patti Carr Black, *Art in Mississippi, 1720–1980* (1998); Patti Carr Black, *The Mississippi Story* (2007); Robert Rector website, www.robertrector art.com.

Rector, Robert
(b. 1946) Artist

Painter and printmaker Robert Rector's major influences are minimalism and expressionism and the tension between the two. His reconciliation of these approaches has produced complex abstractions concerned with the balance between intuition and intellect. Rector was born in Pascagoula and raised in Ocean Springs. He earned his bachelor of fine arts and master of fine arts degrees from Louisiana State University and has lived and worked in Baton Rouge for most of his career. Instead of a focus on literal representation, Rector's color fields, shapes, and textures interact with each other and with the associated shapes of the canvas, frame, and even studio wall angles. Though his work is devoid of narrative intent, the artist says that "as a southerner, the influence of nature is obviously important."

In the tradition of abstract expressionism, Rector's paintings are exquisite statements of color, surface, and gestural form. This dynamic has produced canvases of great surface beauty, such as the painting *Untitled*, from the *Axis* series, which was included in the 2007 *Mississippi Story* exhibition at the Mississippi Museum of Art and is part of the museum's permanent collection. Given its carefully considered combination of geometric structure and spontaneity in paint, *Untitled* is a fine example of Rector's approach. When painting, Rector applies and scrapes layers of color to achieve his textures. Experimenting with impulsive elements and accidents makes his canvases bold exercises in intuitive painting and balances his carefully crafted compositional work. According to Rector, his paintings have "always been about finding a balance, whether it was a balance of spontaneity and order, a balance of philosophy between minimalism and expressionism and balance of color confrontation."

Rector's paintings are held in the corporate collections of Apple, IBM, and Saks Fifth Avenue, among many others, and by the Old State Capitol Museum in Baton Rouge, Louisiana; the University of Texas; Louisiana State University; and the State of Louisiana.

Patti Carr Black
Jackson, Mississippi

Red Shoe (Shulush Homa)
(ca. 1700–1747) Choctaw Chief

Shulush Homa/Shulush Humma, called Red Shoe/Red Shoes/Red Sock, was a Choctaw war chief, possibly with some Chitimacha ancestry, who lived in what is now Jasper County, Mississippi. He was probably from the village of Couëchitto and was of the Imoklata moiety of the Okla Hunnah (Six Peoples) clan. He advocated peace and trade with whites. His opportunistic maneuverings between the French and English provoked a factionalism leading to the catastrophic Choctaw Civil War (1747–50).

Red Shoe left no records, and the only written sources on his life, French and English documents, are sometimes unclear or contradictory. The French made him a medal chief in 1731 for fighting the Chickasaw, who were harboring refugees from the Natchez Rebellion. Hearing rumors that English traders had given smallpox-infected blankets to the Indians, Red Shoe visited English posts in the Chickasaw villages seeking revenge. His real purpose may have been to inspect English goods since French supplies were low. Thereafter he apparently adopted a strategy of trying to obtain English goods for himself or his tribe whenever French supplies dwindled or the French punished his disloyalty by withholding his presents.

From 1732 through early 1734 he fought the Chickasaw with the French. But then, disgusted with French lack of participation and insignificant rewards to the Choctaw, he apparently went to Charleston and Georgia. Hoping for a treaty, he returned with gifts for himself and told the chiefs they would receive presents if they traded with the English. In 1735 he joined Chief Alibamon Mingo in welcoming English traders. The French deprived Red Shoe and Alibamon Mingo of their medals, but in 1736 they joined a French expedition against the Chickasaw. On Red Shoe's advice, Gov. Jean-Baptiste Le Moyne, Sieur de Bienville, attacked Ackia on 22 May, a disastrous decision that ended the campaign. Red Shoe thereupon made a truce with the Chickasaw and returned to Charleston. His efforts there attracted English traders to Choctaw villages, but tribal disagreements arose. Red Shoe began losing followers, especially when French supplies increased. By May 1739 he and a hundred followers returned from a visit to Charleston unhappy after being rebuffed by the English, who were now more interested in preserving their Chickasaw trade. Red Shoe consequently swore allegiance to the French and won reinstatement.

A second Chickasaw campaign failed in 1739–40, but in 1740–42 Red Shoe led devastating attacks on Chickasaw croplands. The tiring Chickasaw obtained Gov. Pierre de Rigaud de Vaudreuil de Cavagnial, Marquis de Vaudreuil's agreement to negotiate; assembled Choctaw chiefs agreed while reprimanding Red Shoe for drunkenness and foul language. The Chickasaw wavered but in January 1745 made peace via Red Shoe. Some Chickasaw raiding continued, however. Amid Choctaw reprisals, Red Shoe led small parties to collect some scalps before the March 1745 presents ceremony. He was welcomed and even treated at the French hospital for wounds and eye trouble. His "repentance" proved fraudulent. With French goods critically scarce again, Red Shoe and some others launched a campaign on 20 July to make peace with the Chickasaw and obtain English goods. Arguments tore apart the Choctaw. In late September two French officers (one in Red Shoe's home village) were accused of rape; at the same time, warriors from Little Wood killed two English traders bound for the Chickasaw. Only four of about fifty villages allegedly remained pro-French by December, and Red Shoe warned the French that all of the regional tribes were making peace.

In late March 1746 some twelve hundred leading Choctaw came to New Orleans, unsuccessfully pleading for French supplies. Red Shoe, perhaps fearing humiliation by other chiefs for disloyalty, stayed away. Word circulated that he was losing ground. Cut off from his French presents and supplies for his followers, he needed English trade, but getting it would require peace with the Chickasaw. He lobbied the chiefs hard but encountered stiff opposition. He also sent his brother, Imataha Pouscouche (the Little King), to negotiate a peace. Through a Chickasaw embassy, English trader James Adair informed Red Shoe that a man had been accused of raping Red Shoe's wife. In July Red Shoe's emissaries threatened to kill several Frenchmen to avenge the two English traders killed in 1745. Choctaw attacked a returning Chickasaw embassy, however, killing two men and a woman. Red Shoe decided to retaliate by killing three Frenchmen, and on 14 August two French traders and the alleged rapist were killed by order of Red Shoe and two allied chiefs.

These deaths apparently satisfied the English, but the French demanded three Choctaw lives. After various negotiations, the French quietly urged other Native American warriors to kill Red Shoe. His support apparently again began to increase, and on 12 November he concluded a peace with the Chickasaw and several prominent English traders. By 11 December he dispatched Imataha Pouscouche with a party to Charleston to negotiate a treaty.

Governor Vaudreuil nevertheless promised large rewards for killing Red Shoe plus two of his Choctaw followers. At Fort Tombigbee on 1 April the chiefs of twenty-three pro-French villages decided to kill Red Shoe. Imataha Pouscouche

concluded a treaty in Charleston on 18 April. Traders started toward the Choctaw while parties hunted for Red Shoe near the fort. On 22 June he and two traders were killed as he was escorting them from the Creek to the Choctaw. The Choctaw sent Red Shoe's head and two English scalps to Vaudreuil, who insisted on two more Choctaw scalps and vowed to destroy Red Shoe's followers. The resulting raids and killings escalated into the civil war that many had feared.

Red Shoe may well have sought to foster Choctaw independence and wealth by imitating the Alabama, who traded with the French and English but refused to fight either one. However laudable his purpose, he gained a reputation for unreliability. Ambitious, magnetic, headstrong, he divided his nation, unintentionally setting it on the road to devastating conflict.

David S. Newhall
Centre College

Frederick J. Dockstrader, *Great North American Indians: Profiles in Life and Leadership* (1977); Patricia Galloway, *Journal of Mississippi History* 44 (1982); Norman J. Heard, *Handbook of the American Frontier: Four Centuries of Indian-White Relationships*, vol. 1, *The Southeastern Woodlands* (1987); Harvey Markovitz, ed., *American Indians*, vol. 3 (1995); Carl Waldman, *Biographical Dictionary of American Indian History to 1900* (2001); Mary Ann Wells, *Native Land: Mississippi, 1540–1798* (1994); Patricia Dillon Woods, *French-Indian Relations on the Southern Frontier* (1980).

Red Tops

Mississippi's most popular dance band during an era when couples and hopeful singles donned their finest clothes for evenings out on the town, Vicksburg's Red Tops played pop songs, blues, and jazz between the 1950s and 1970s. The Red Tops, whose members were African American, first performed at the Sequoia Hill Club in Bovina, east of Vicksburg, on 20 June 1953, but most of the ten original members had played with an earlier Vicksburg band, the Rebops, that had started performing during World War II. The Rebops frequently played on Morrissey's Showboat, a barge moored on DeSoto Island on the Louisiana side of the Mississippi River, where alcohol laws were less strict than in Mississippi.

Under the direction of drummer and manager Walter Osborne, the Red Tops developed a devoted fan base. Most of the group's performances were on weekends, as all of the members had full-time day jobs. Unlike most bands, the Red Tops operated very strictly as a business, with detailed ledgers, annual audits, and bookings often scheduled a year

R

The Red Tops (Red Tops Collection, Department of Archives and Special Collections, J. D. Williams Library, University of Mississippi)

in advance. Their matching red uniforms were tailor-made, members were subject to regular inspections and rules of conduct, and rehearsals were held every Monday evening at the YMCA on Vicksburg's Jackson Street. The group was named after the hit song "Red Top," recorded by Gene Ammons (1947) and King Pleasure (1953). In 1957 the Red Tops released their only studio recording, the single "Swanee River Rock"/"Hello, Is That You?," on Greenville's Sky label. Both songs were written by Leland tunesmith Floyd Huddleston, who also wrote music for Hollywood films, and were recorded at Sam Phillips's Memphis Recording Service.

The Red Tops performed primarily for white audiences at venues including country clubs, restaurants, ballrooms, high schools, and colleges across Mississippi as well as in Louisiana, Arkansas, and Tennessee. They were particularly known for lead singer Rufus McKay's rendition of "Danny Boy" as well as for humorously acting out the themes of songs such as "Baseball Game" and "Drunk." McKay was so convincing in acting out the latter that he was nearly arrested at one show.

Other African American groups in Mississippi that played largely for white dances during this era included the Greenville group led by Winchester "Little Win" Davis, Clarksdale's Top Hatters, Columbus's Rhythm Kings, and the Tupelo group led by George "Bally" Smith.

The Red Tops also performed regularly for African American audiences at the Blue Room in Vicksburg, Stevens Rose Room in Jackson, Ruby's Night Spot in Leland, the Harlem Inn in Winstonville, the Plaza Hotel in Greenwood, and various Elks lodges. They were joined on occasion by blues harmonica great Sonny Boy Williamson II or the Knights, a doo-wop group that included future blues recording artist Terry Evans. Saxophonist and bassist Anderson "Andy" Hardwick, the youngest of the Red Tops, spent many summers touring with various national artists, including Lowell Fulson, B. B. King, Otis Redding, Fats Domino, and James Brown. In the early 1960s Hardwick and McKay left the

Red Tops and formed the Fabulous Corvettes. McKay also recorded a solo single for Jackson's Ace Records.

The Red Tops stopped performing regularly in the mid-1970s but reunited on a number of special occasions. Hardwick continues to perform as a jazz pianist, while McKay moved to Las Vegas and sang with Stanley Morgan's Ink Spots and other groups before returning to Vicksburg in 2000. He died in July 2014.

Scott Barretta
Greenwood, Mississippi

Jim O'Neal
Kansas City, Missouri

Blues Archive, University of Mississippi Libraries, website, http://www.olemiss.edu/depts/general_library/archives/blues/; Sherry Lucas, *Jackson Clarion-Ledger* (21 July 2014); Mississippi Blues Trail website, msbluestrail.org.

Reddix, Jacob L.
(1897–1973) Educator

Jacob Lorenzo Reddix served as president of Jackson State College from its founding in 1940 until 1967. Reddix was born in Vancleave, a small timber town in southern Mississippi, on 2 March 1897 to Nathan Reddix and Frances Chambers Reddix, both of whom were former slaves. According to Jacob Reddix, his enslaved grandmother, Millie Brown, constantly prayed for "freedom for her children and the opportunity for them to learn to read and write." Reddix was educated locally and went to high school in Alabama. Like many African Americans from the Deep South, he then headed north to Illinois, earning a bachelor's degree from Chicago's Lewis Institute in 1927. After working as a schoolteacher and for the US Postal Service, Reddix received a Rosenwald Fellowship to attend graduate school at the University of Chicago.

During Franklin Roosevelt's administration, Reddix worked at the Farm Security Administration, where he specialized in agricultural cooperatives, working on projects throughout the South. In 1940 the State of Mississippi assumed control of Jackson College, an African American school previously run by the American Baptist Home Mission Society, and renamed it the Mississippi Negro Training School. Will Alexander, the Farm Security Administration's director of cooperatives, recommended Reddix to head the school. It became Jackson College for Negro Teachers in 1944 and Jackson State College in 1956 and offered academic programs geared toward training rural and elementary schoolteachers.

At Jackson State, Reddix gained the nickname the Builder for his aggressive pursuit of funds and support for new buildings on campus. When Reddix retired in 1967, English professor Margaret Walker Alexander wrote a sonnet, "Jacob L. Reddix: The Builder." In 1972 the university named its new student union building in his honor.

Reddix at times faced opposition from Jackson State students for his conservatism on issues of both politics and personal behavior. Reddix did not support the civil rights activism that was growing on southern campuses in the early 1960s, and his attempt to stay out of politics earned him occasional criticism as an Uncle Tom. Most dramatically, he refused to allow a large campus protest that activists had planned in response to the jailing of the Tougaloo Nine in 1961, threatening to expel everyone involved. Moreover, some students condemned him for continuing an old college practice of requiring students to attend Sunday afternoon church services and, more broadly, for failing to support student government. Reddix said that he was trying to emphasize education and the training of the character of young Mississippians. He took pride in the school's building programs, the increased size of its student body, and its appropriations from the Mississippi legislature, which grew from $10,000 in 1940–41 to $1,600,000 in 1966–67.

After his retirement, Reddix continued his interest in cooperatives, helping to organize credit unions in Hinds County. Reddix ran unsuccessfully for the Mississippi House of Representatives in 1967. He died in Jackson on 9 May 1973. The University Press of Mississippi published his memoirs, *A Voice Crying in the Wilderness*, the following year.

Ted Ownby
University of Mississippi

John Dittmer, *Local People: The Struggle for Civil Rights in Mississippi* (1995); John A. Peoples Jr., *To Survive and Thrive: The Quest for a True University* (1995); Jacob L. Reddix Subject File, Mississippi Department of Archives and History; Jacob L. Reddix, *A Voice Crying in the Wilderness: The Memoirs of Jacob L. Reddix* (1974); Leila Gaston Rhodes, *Jackson State University: The First Hundred Years, 1877–1977* (1979); Joy Ann Williamson, *Radicalizing the Ivory Tower: Black Colleges and the Black Freedom Struggle in Mississippi* (2008).

Rednecks

According to one popular joke, "You might be a redneck if you've heard a sheep bleat and had romantic thoughts." Another goes, "You might be a redneck if your mother keeps a spit cup on the ironing board." Among the litany of class slurs used to ridicule poor and working-class white southerners, *redneck* ranks as the most popular in modern American English, and the stereotype of the benighted southern redneck, as depicted in such films as *Easy Rider* (1970) and *Pulp Fiction* (1994), remains one of the most pernicious, distinctive, and widespread in American popular culture. For more than a century, this pejorative term has been used to denigrate rural, poor white men of the American South, particularly those who hold conservative, racist, or reactionary views.

The epithet *redneck* emerged as a rural class slur in the Deep South in the last decades of the nineteenth century. Its first known appearance in print came in the 13 August 1891 issue of the *Pontotoc Democrat*, which published the epithet along with several others (*yaller-heels*, *hayseeds*, *gray dillers*) during a hotly contested political campaign for state representative. Two years later, Hubert A. Shands recorded its use in "Some Peculiarities of Speech in Mississippi," his 1893 University of Mississippi doctoral dissertation. "Red-neck," he reported, is "a name applied by the better class of people to the poorer [white] inhabitants of the rural districts." According to most scholars of the American language, *redneck* originally derived from an allusion to sunburn when a pale white complexion was still a significant class marker. One prevailing theory suggests that urban white professionals and large planters coined the slur to denigrate those white farmers, sharecroppers, and agricultural laborers who had sunburned red necks from working in the fields. Other linguists have speculated *redneck* may have originated in black English. According to this theory, African American slaves coined the term *peckerwood*, a folk inversion of *woodpecker*, to ridicule poor whites and that *redneck* may in some way be related to the red head of some species of woodpeckers. Whatever its derivation, early usage of *redneck* suggests that the term ridiculed not only the sweaty, manual labor of farmers and agricultural workers but also their perceived deviation from a pale white complexion.

Redneck did not come into common currency in southern speech until the 1930s, when it was increasingly used to describe racists, bigots, or reactionaries. By the 1960s the term's connotations of racism and bigotry had become firmly cemented, especially for African Americans. At Oxford, Ohio, site of the training sessions for the 1964 Mississippi Freedom Summer, experienced instructors prepared college-age civil rights volunteers for the violence they could expect to encounter from Mississippi segregationists by using a role-playing game, Redneck and Nigger. But in this context, *redneck* lost many of its class and regional connotations, as it came to be applied indiscriminately to any white racist, regardless of class position or birthplace.

During the 1970s *redneck* underwent a dramatic rehabilitation and emerged as a badge of regional class identity. Rural and working-class white southerners refashioned the epithet into a positive term to mean an honest, hardworking, God-fearing blue-collar workingman. As a result, large numbers of white southerners began referring to themselves proudly as rednecks. The 1976 election of Pres. Jimmy Carter—a wealthy but plainspoken Georgia peanut farmer who sometimes described himself and was described by Washington political reporters as "basically a redneck"—also helped to rehabilitate the term's definition. The most famous redneck of the Carter era, however, was the president's brother, Billy Carter, who on occasion hammed it up for photographers in a "Redneck Power" T-shirt with a cold beer in hand and regaled reporters with his down-home anecdotes at his Plains, Georgia, gas station. To identify oneself as a redneck suddenly became fashionable, a national craze that journalist Paul Hemphill termed "redneck chic." Dozens of guidebooks and articles taught redneck wannabes how to act the part convincingly. Female derivatives of this traditionally masculine term also gained popularity, including *redneck girl*, *redneck mother*, and *redneck woman*. Nashville also played a significant role in the reinvention of redneck identity. Beginning in the 1970s the term *redneck* surfaced as a badge of pride in numerous country songs, including David Allen Coe's "Long-Haired Redneck" (1975), Vern Oxford's "Redneck! (The Redneck National Anthem)" (1976), and Jerry Reed's "(I'm Just a) Redneck in a Rock and Roll Bar" (1977), to name only a few.

Although derogatory images of southern rednecks continue to abound in American popular culture, in less than a century the term has also come to represent a positive affirmation of identity for countless white Americans, including many who are not from the South.

Patrick Huber
Missouri University of Science
and Technology

F. N. Boney, *Georgia Review* (Fall 1971); Jim Goad, *The Redneck Manifesto: How Hillbillies, Hicks, and White Trash Became America's Scapegoats* (1997); Patrick Huber, "Rednecks and Woolhats, Hoosiers and Hillbillies: Working-Class Southern Whites, Language, and the Definition of Identity" (master's thesis, University of Missouri-Columbia, 1992); Patrick Huber, *Southern Cultures* (Winter 1995); Albert D. Kirwan, *Revolt of the Rednecks: Mississippi Politics, 1876–1925* (1951); V. S. Naipaul, *A Turn in the South* (1989); John Shelton Reed, *Southern Folk, Plain and Fancy: Native White Social Types* (1986); Raymond S. Rodgers, *Journal of Regional Cultures* (Fall–Winter 1982).

Reed, Jimmy
(1925–1976) Blues Musician

Mathis James Reed was born on 6 September 1925, the youngest of the ten children of Joseph Reed and Virginia Ross, sharecroppers on a Delta plantation near the small hamlet of Dunleith, Mississippi. Jimmy briefly attended public schools but started working in the fields full-time after third grade. A family member gave him his first acoustic guitar when he was ten, and Reed also started playing harmonica.

In the late 1930s the Reed family moved to Shaw, where Jimmy joined a gospel quartet. Although the group was doing well, Reed decided to leave: he later recalled, "I don't know what gave me the idea to get up and want to leave from down there and go somewhere." Reed moved in with a brother in Duncan and continued to work on area plantations. During that time, blues music began to play a more important role in his life. Around noon, he would often slip out of the fields to listen to Sonny Boy Williamson I, Sonny Boy Williamson II, and Robert Jr. Lockwood performing on the *King Biscuit Time* radio show. Reed also met Eddie Taylor, a young guitarist who was trying to make a living by traveling the Mississippi Delta and playing the blues. The two men developed a rocky musical relationship that lasted until Reed's death. Taylor claimed that he taught his friend to play the guitar, frequently declaring, "The Jimmy Reed style is MY style. He don't have no style. And I got the style from Charley Patton and Robert Johnson." According to Reed, however, Taylor "ain't had nothing to with it, no more than just durin' the time when we was down South." In any case, Taylor and Reed often played together after a day of work in the fields until the eighteen-year-old Reed left for Chicago after a falling out with a white overseer.

Reed briefly worked as janitor at the YMCA in Chicago and at the Hefter Coal Company before being drafted into the US Navy in 1943. He was discharged two years later, returned to Mississippi for a short time, and again left for Chicago. While working at menial jobs for different companies, Reed started playing his harmonica and guitar in the blues clubs in the city and around Gary, Indiana. In 1949 Taylor also moved north, and the two boyhood friends performed together in the bars on Chicago's South Side. Four years later, Reed and Taylor began recording for the Vee-Jay label, and in 1955 Reed scored his first hit with "You Don't Have to Go." It marked the beginning of a tumultuous career on the road and in the recording studios.

During the 1950s and early 1960s, Reed was one of the most popular blues artists in the United States. His music appealed to a broad audience and cut across the color line, although at the height of his career Reed played primarily for white audiences. "Ain't That Lovin' You Baby," "Honest I

Do," "Baby, What You Want Me to Do," "Big Boss Man," and "Bright Lights, Big City" all became instant classics. Eleven of Reed's songs appeared on the Billboard Hot 100 pop charts, while more than a dozen appeared on the R&B charts—far more than any other blues musician. His music was popular among British bands such as the Rolling Stones and the Beatles, and Elvis Presley, Ike and Tina Turner, Muddy Waters, Chuck Berry, and other artists covered Reed's music. Reed's songs not only became blues standards but also crossed over into other music styles, such as rock and roll, soul, and country and western.

But like so many other blues singers, most of the profits from his records went not to him but to various record corporations. The strenuous life on the road took a heavy toll on his health, and he suffered from epilepsy and chronic alcoholism. By the late 1960s his popularity had waned considerably. After receiving treatment for his seizures and alcohol abuse, the Big Boss Man tried to make a comeback during the 1970s, but his days as a successful bluesman were over. He died on 29 August 1976 after a show at the Savoy in San Francisco.

Maarten Zwiers
University of Groningen,
the Netherlands

Jim O'Neal, *Living Blues* (May–June 1975); Will Romano, *Big Boss Man: The Life and Music of Jimmy Reed* (2006).

Reed, Julia
(b. 1960) Writer

A native of Greenville, Julia Reed is a well-known journalist, commentator, and humorist. She is a contributing editor for *Elle Décor* and *Garden and Gun* and has written for *Vogue*, *Newsweek*, the *New York Times*, the *Wall Street Journal*, and other publications and has appeared on MSNBC and CNN. While she does not write exclusively about Mississippi or the South, much of her work uses the South either for subject matter or for comparison. The daughter of Greenville's Clarke Reed, "a smiling, silver-haired kingpin of southern Republicanism" and chair of the state's Republican Party in the 1960s, Julia Reed writes from a leftist perspective. She seems particularly drawn to topics that involve food, women's fashion, politics and politicians, stereotypes and people who abuse them, and the interactions of violence, manners, and justice. Reed loves both to hear and to tell entertaining

stories. She has written, "In the Mississippi Delta, where I'm from, entertaining yourself is a high art. There isn't anything else to do."

Reed has published six books, *Queen of the Turtle Derby and Other Southern Phenomena* (2004), a collection of previously published magazine essays; *Ham Biscuits, Hostess Gowns, and Other Southern Specialties: An Entertaining Life (with Recipes)* (2008); *The House on First Street: My New Orleans Story* (2008); *But Mama Always Put Vodka in Her Sangria!: Adventures in Eating, Drinking, and Making Merry* (2013); *One Man's Folly: The Exceptional Houses of Furlow Gatewood* (2014); and *Julia Reed's South: Spirited Entertaining and High Style Fun All Year Long* (2016). Reed has lived in both New York and in New Orleans, and they, along with Greenville, constitute the sources of many of her observations. She seems irked at some academics who have argued for the decline of southern distinctiveness, and she offers in rebuttal stories of the outlandish South—women who earn juries' sympathy and get away with murdering worthless husbands, dinner parties that are so terrible that everyone who attended them tells stories about them for years, and the State of Mississippi's long experiment with taxing alcohol while also prohibiting its sale. Reed amuses readers even when they may not expect it: for example, she began a *New York Times* review of a Miss Manners book by apologizing for not writing thank-you notes after her wedding two years earlier. She was a particularly appealing commentator about events after Hurricane Katrina, offering compassion and some humor. She has also served as a member of the board of the Eudora Welty Foundation.

Ted Ownby
University of Mississippi

Joseph Crespino, *In Search of Another Country: Mississippi and the Conservative Counterrevolution* (2007); HarperCollins Publisher website, www.harpercollins.com; Macmillan Speakers website, http://www.macmillanspeakers.com/juliareed.

Regional Council of Negro Leadership

The Regional Council of Negro Leadership (RCNL) was organized in Mound Bayou in 1951 and worked as a Mississippi civil rights organization into the early 1960s. Its founder, wealthy business leader and physician T. R. M. Howard, conceived the group, organized its first meeting, and remained its most prominent figure throughout its history.

By some combination of necessity and strategic choice, the RCNL, at least originally, seemed a somewhat conservative alternative to other civil rights groups. Howard tended to talk about leadership, personal character, education, and economic empowerment rather than desegregation, and he initially presented the group as an African American version of the powerful and all-white Delta Council. However, the RCNL included a wide range of civil rights leaders active in 1950s Mississippi—Emmett J. Stringer, George Lee, Aaron Henry, Amzie Moore, Jackson journalist Percy Greene, Arenia Mallory of Saints Junior College in Lexington, and J. H. White of Mississippi Vocational College in Itta Bena. Historians David Beito and Linda Royster Beito argue that the "RCNL acted as a kind of advance guard," enabling some people who feared being identified with an activist group to become involved before moving on to the National Association for the Advancement of Colored People (NAACP).

The first RCNL protest took place in 1952, when it boycotted gas stations that did not allow African Americans to use their restrooms. Medgar Evers, who worked for Howard in the insurance business, was involved in the boycott. The group also worked to oppose police brutality against African Americans, investigated specific acts of violence, and staged a number of voter registration drives. In 1953 Howard rejected efforts to equalize rather than segregate schools, an approach the NAACP had already rejected as part of the legal strategy that resulted in the US Supreme Court's 1954 *Brown v. Board of Education* decision. *Time Bomb*, a 1956 pamphlet published by the RCNL, made clear the group's perspective. Author Olive Arnold Adams condemned the killing of Emmett Till, linked it to other violence directed against activists such as George Lee and Gus Courts, criticized the White Citizens' Councils, and concluded that the Till murder could take place in any area where "white supremacy is god. This was the primitive law of plantation life." When the Citizens' Councils exerted economic pressure on African American activists, the RCNL worked with the NAACP to offer financial assistance.

In 1952 the first RCNL convention, held in Mound Bayou and attended by several thousand African Americans, featured an address by US congressman William Dawson of Chicago and music by Mahalia Jackson. Two years later, NAACP lead attorney Thurgood Marshall spoke.

The RCNL's influence began to decline in the late 1950s. In 1956 Howard moved the group's annual conference to Jackson and invited Martin Luther King Jr. and New York congressman Adam Clayton Powell, but neither attended. Howard moved to Chicago the same year, depriving the organization of its founder and most dynamic leader, and first the NAACP and later the Congress of Racial Equality and the Student Nonviolent Coordinating Committee eclipsed the RCNL.

Ted Ownby
University of Mississippi

Olive Arnold Adams, *Time Bomb: Mississippi Exposed and the Full Story of Emmett Till* (1956); David Beito and Linda Royster Beito, *Black Maverick: T. R. M. Howard's Fight for Civil Rights and Economic Power* (2009); John Dittmer, *Local People: The Struggle for Civil Rights in Mississippi* (1995); J. Todd Moye, *Let the People Decide: Black Freedom and White Resistance Movements in Sunflower County, Mississippi, 1945–1986* (2004); Charles M. Payne, *I've Got the Light of Freedom: The Organizing Tradition and the Mississippi Freedom Struggle* (1995).

Religion

A 2000 survey of religious life in America helps identify a few of the most important features of Mississippi religion. Using a variety of methods, the North America Religious Atlas (NARA) did its best to count religious affiliation, and though statistics and religious life do not always mesh easily, the NARA data help outline the major features of church affiliation and introduce some of the differences in different parts of the state. Above all, Mississippi, even more than much of the American South, is a land of evangelical Protestants. Baptists dominate numerically, followed by Methodists and other evangelical groups. Of all the religious groups in Mississippi, largest by far are two groups of Baptists, the Missionary Baptists and the Southern Baptists. Historically, white Baptists, primarily the Southern Baptists, made up 41 percent of all religious adherents. The NARA survey awkwardly gathered several groups into a category it called "Historically African American Protestant," and in Mississippi Missionary Baptists, African Methodist Episcopal, and Christian Methodist Episcopal churches were the primary groups in the category. Historically, African American Protestants made up 34 percent of all religious adherents. United Methodists made up another 10 percent of the state's religious adherents, and combinations of groups called "Other Conservative Christian" (primarily, Churches of Christ, Disciples of Christ, and nondenominational Christian churches) and "Holiness/Wesleyan/Pentecostal" made up 2.5 percent and 3.1 percent. Added together, those groups, all of which fall into categories of evangelical Protestantism, made up more than 90 percent of the state's religious adherents.

In almost all regions of Mississippi, the historically African American Protestants made up a substantial part of religious life. The groups in that category constituted more than a quarter of all religious adherents in all parts of Mississippi except the northeastern corner of the state and seven counties on the Gulf Coast. Those groups make up more than half of all religious adherents in 22 of Mississippi's 82 counties, primarily in the Mississippi Delta. The historically white Baptist groups, primarily the Southern Baptists, are important throughout the state. More than half of all church adherents in northeastern Mississippi and in several counties in south-central Mississippi are part of historically white Baptist groups.

An intriguing statistical comparison shows that while United Methodists make up about 10 percent of all religious adherents, about twice the percentage of Catholics, who make up 4.8 percent, the United Methodists are spread widely throughout the state, present almost everywhere and dominant nowhere, while Mississippi Catholics tend to congregate only in areas with substantial numbers of Catholics. Hancock, Harrison, and Jefferson Counties, the counties along Mississippi's Gulf Coast, were home to the majority of the state's Catholics. In each county, Catholics made up more than 10 percent of all religious adherents, and Hancock County was one of the few counties in the entire South where Catholics made up more than half of all religious adherents. By contrast, in 44 Mississippi counties in 2000, Catholics made up less than 1 percent of all religious adherents.

The other statistical feature distinguishing Mississippi religious life was the relatively small number of people outside these groups. Presbyterians had churches throughout the state but relatively small numbers of members. Jews made up tiny numbers—there were no counties in Mississippi in which Jews made up half of 1 percent of all religious adherents. Muslims, Buddhists, and Hindus appeared in NARA data in even smaller numbers, and most Mississippi counties reported none of those groups. Mormons were small in number, congregating more in areas with larger towns and cities than rural areas.

Religion has played significant, even crucial, roles in almost all of the major issues in Mississippi history. From missionaries to Native Americans to frontier church and school-building, to the growth of African American Christianity and the elaboration of a proslavery argument, religious beliefs and practices were central to many parts of life in colonial and antebellum Mississippi. Beginning in the late 1600s, Catholic missionaries were part of the first permanent European settlers to the area, and both Jesuits and Capuchins faced the challenges of being a minority religion in a struggling colony. Beginning in the early 1800s and operating well into the antebellum period, Christian missionaries tried with varying success to convert Native Americans to Christianity with a combination of education and religious inspiration. Baptists with roots in New England started in the Mississippi Society for Baptist Missions Foreign and Domestic in 1817, and the American Board of Commissioners for Foreign Missions, run by Presbyterians and Congregationalists, began building missionary settlements in Mississippi in the 1820s.

Many of the first attempts to establish permanent churches of different Protestant denominations began in southwestern Mississippi. The first Baptist church began services in 1791 in the area that became Jefferson County, and Methodist circuit riders were leading camp meetings and Presbyterians were starting churches soon after that. All three groups were well established by the 1820s. Episcopalians and the state's first Jewish congregation had roots in antebellum Natchez.

By mid- and late antebellum period, many of those groups had educational institutions, some of them colleges and some of them schools for younger students, especially young women. At the same time, other Protestant groups were challenging their authority, often by calling on some version of a simpler worship style and a rejection of what they saw as worldliness. Primitive Baptists critiqued Regular Baptists for their willingness to form missionary societies, and restorationist groups in the Stone-Campbell tradition came to Mississippi in the later antebellum period, having much of their early success in eastern parts of the state.

The majority of Mississippians in the late antebellum period had at best an uncertain position in the white-run churches. Slaves worked to control their own religious lives and found that they were often welcomed in white-run churches but only in limited ways. Many slaves adapted Christianity to their own purposes, mixing different West African and syncretic worship traditions and often emphasizing the religious goal of liberty. White-run church leaders, many of whom had some reservations about slavery and its impact on southern society in the early 1800s, joined the proslavery movement by the late antebellum period. Mississippi ministers such as Presbyterian James Smylie and Methodist William Winans became leading spokesmen for a form of Christianity that emphasized paternalism, evangelizing the slaves, and social order.

Emancipation brought dramatic changes in church life, with many African Americans interpreting emancipation as part of deliverance from slavery into the Promised Land and leaving the white-run churches in large numbers to establish their own institutions. Missionaries brought church organizations to form Missionary Baptist, African Methodist Episcopal (AME), African Methodist Episcopal, Zion (AME Zion), congregations, and Colored Methodist Episcopal (CME) churches stood out as having southern roots in western Tennessee and northern Mississippi. Many of those churches took on a wide range of roles, with hands in education and political activity. Several colleges for African Americans, including Rust College and Tougaloo College, grew out of new efforts to educate African American teachers and ministers in the late 1800s. White Mississippians likewise used religious language to interpret the consequences of the Civil War, emphasizing that God was testing them with a period of difficulty and holding up Confederate soldiers as exemplars of good behavior.

Two trends in the late 1800s and early 1900s challenged the centrality of Baptists, Methodists, and Presbyterians in Mississippi religion. Immigration brought a wider range of ethnicities to the state, with growing numbers of Catholic immigrants, especially on the Gulf Coast, and smaller increases in Jewish immigrants to the Mississippi Delta. Also significant was the rise of two new Pentecostal denominations, the Church of God in Christ and the Church of Christ

(Holiness). Both grew out of African American Baptist groups seeking the deeper religious experience of sanctification, complete with the potential for healing, speaking in tongues, and other gifts. The Church of God in Christ had its first services in Lexington, where leader Charles Harrison Mason, an Arkansas native, helped lead the group to prominence. Beginning in 1926, COGIC started Saints Industrial and Literary School in Lexington under the long direction of Arenia Mallory, and the denomination has long had headquarters in Memphis. Another former Baptist, Charles P. Jones of Jackson, was a COGIC leader before a split led to the Church of Christ (Holiness) in 1915.

The rise of the Prohibition movement in the late 1800s and early 1900s added some new political dimensions to Mississippi religious life. Several church leaders and church-related groups shifted from calls for sobriety and temperate behavior to demands for laws that prohibited the sale of alcohol. Women's Christian Temperance Union leader Harriet B. Kells, Methodist leader Charles B. Galloway, and Baptist J. H. Gambrell had success demanding local option laws and then statewide Prohibition. Mississippi was the first state to ratify the 18th Amendment to the Constitution, making the sale of alcohol illegal.

Religion has played crucial roles in Mississippi's musical and literary traditions, whether as inspiration or sometimes as the subject of frustration. Churches have long been one of the places Mississippians hear and learn to play music, and spirituals, hymns, and shape-note singing date to the antebellum period. Christian music of many kinds has led to the importance of the Blind Boys of Mississippi, the Blackwood Brothers (both bands with roots in the 1930s), to the inspirational music of Pops Staples and the Staples Singers, to more recent performers such as the Jackson Southernaires, the Mississippi Mass Choir, and Ann Downing. Blues singers long had a pained relationship with organized religion, as some had to choose between sacred and secular music while others felt the blues was the best way to confront the devil. Singers as different as Sam Cooke and Elvis Presley learned musical lessons in church, and often returned to religious traditions as the source of their inspiration. Many of the state's most powerful literary figures brought religious issues to life in memorable ways, from Richard Wright's rejection of his grandmother's religion in *Black Boy* to the characters of William Faulkner and Tennessee Williams who wrestled with Christian demands for self-control, and Anne Moody's critique of calls for religious nonviolence in *Coming of Age in Mississippi*, to Will Campbell's memoirs of farm life, race, and the search for redemption.

For many but far from all people in the civil rights movement, religion was central to the inspiration, language, and organizing strategies for their activism. Many churches were important as meeting sites, and for a few months in 1963, Jackson churches became challenges to desegregation, as integrated groups of visitors attended all-white churches. For activists such as Fannie Lou Hamer, religious life and civil rights activism were part of the same experience, and she used religious language and music throughout her work. Ministers such as Aaron Johnson and R. L. T. Smith balanced their public role as ministers with voting rights and desegregation work, and Belzoni minister George Lee was killed for his public role. Many ministers worked more quietly, and young civil rights activists sometimes grew frustrated when older ministers did not take leadership roles. A number of white activists such as Jackson rabbi Perry Nussbaum, Tougaloo chaplain Ed King, and Christian maverick speaker and writer Will Campbell lived out their religious inspiration through civil rights work, and in 1963 a group of Methodist ministers clarified their opposition to segregation and hatred through the Born of Conviction statement.

White opponents of civil rights called on religion in multiple ways. Some tried to avoid civil rights concerns, saying the role of the church involved spiritual issues and not everyday secular questions. Others developed biblical justifications for racial segregation and encouraged the burning of churches that harbored activists.

Religious changes since the 1960s include the growing importance of religious media, a range of religious efforts at racial reconciliation, and the rise of conservative political groups with strong religious ties. Racial reconciliation efforts through church groups have operated on numerous fronts. Mississippian John Perkins moved Voice of Calvary Ministries to Jackson, with the goals of overcoming poverty and hatred. Mission Mississippi began in Jackson in 1992 with the specific goal of bringing together African American and white Christians. The group's slogan is "Changing Mississippi one relationship at a time." The expansion of church activities to offer services to Latino immigrants and the rise of Spanish-language church groups have been among the visible changes in Mississippi church life. Another has been the growth of groups such as the American Family Association, founded in Tupelo in the 1980s, with interests in fighting what they see as the widespread acceptance of secularism, pornography, abortion, and homosexuality. Mississippi religion continues to evolve in the 21st century, with calls for old-time religion existing at the same time as new religious groups, interests, and forms of worship emerge.

Ted Ownby
University of Mississippi

Charles Marsh, *God's Long Summer: Stories of Faith and Civil Rights* (1997); Donald G. Mathews, *Religion in the Old South* (1977); Michael V. Namorato, *The Catholic Church in Mississippi, 1911–1984: A History* (1998); Mark F. Newman, *Divine Agitators: The Delta Ministry and Civil Rights in Mississippi* (2004); Ted Ownby, in *Religion and Public Life in the South: In the Evangelical Mode*, ed. Charles Reagan Wilson and Mark Silk (2005); Randy J. Sparks, *On Jordan's Stormy Banks: Evangelicalism in Mississippi, 1773–1876* (1994); Randy J. Sparks, *Religion in Mississippi* (2001); Calvin White Jr., *The Rise to Respectability: Race, Religion, and the Church of God in Christ* (2012).

Religion and Slavery

Religion and slavery were mutually supportive pillars that significantly shaped the culture of antebellum Mississippi. From its introduction in the eighteenth century until the maturation of Mississippi's antebellum slave-based society, slavery gained moral sanction from the religious beliefs held by its dominant white inhabitants. In turn, slavery's economic, social, and political significance for Mississippians forced the state's religious leaders and laypersons to structure their teachings and practices to meet the stringent demands of the Old South's peculiar institution. The seamless connection between religion and slavery ultimately helped create separate religious identities for Mississippi's white and African American populations.

Religious beliefs were no impediment to the introduction of slavery in Mississippi. Neither the settlers nor the governments of Catholic colonial powers France and Spain hesitated to import enslaved Africans and African Americans to meet labor needs, and the Protestant-dominated United States followed suit. As a general rule, Mississippi's earliest Catholic, Protestant, and Jewish religious leaders viewed slavery as a civil institution that lay outside their ecclesiastical authority. Christians and Jews who questioned the righteousness of slavery quickly found themselves reminded that the ancient Israelites held slaves and that Jesus Christ never offered any specific opposition to the institution. In fact, proslavery Christians found in the apostle Paul a helpful ally in their attempt to justify slavery. In Ephesians of the New Testament, Paul not only did not condemn slavery but in fact called on slaves to "obey your earthly masters with respect and fear, and with sincerity of heart just as you would obey Christ." Accordingly, Mississippi's religious leaders overwhelmingly focused on limiting the abuse of slaves as fellow children of God rather than challenging the legitimacy of human bondage. Such motivation is clear in the Mississippi Baptist Association's 1819 directive to masters: "Let not avarice nor an animal thirst for riches induce you to oppress your servant lest his groans, his sweat, and his blood ascend up to God as a witness against you."

By the time of the Mississippi cotton boom of the 1830s, turn-of-the-century Southern Baptist and Methodist soul-searching over slavery had long come to an end. In fact, with the emergence of the abolition movement in the 1830s, any Mississippi minister who dared to question slavery's legitimacy faced the very real possibility of losing his ministry and social status and possibly even his life. Mississippi Baptists and Methodists were so united in their support of slavery that they left their national denominational organizations to join regional equivalents when slavery became an irreconcilable issue. As a result of the state's religious unanimity on slavery, Mississippi ministers such as J. B. Thrasher, William Winans, and James Smylie became outspoken, proslavery advocates able to offer sermons with titles such as "Slavery a Divine Institution." Liberty Baptist Church of Amite County was so assured of slavery's righteousness that in 1859 its members elected a "committee to purchase two slaves for the church."

Mississippians' religious attachment to slavery directly influenced how they practiced their faith. Moved by the Second Great Awakening, southern evangelical Christians, the most numerous of the region's religious adherents, actively proselytized among the South's enslaved population. As early as 1815 the Mississippi Baptist Association encouraged ministers to "attend with the members of the African Church as often as they can." Likewise, by the 1830s Mississippi Methodists had established numerous and growing missions among the slaves. A growing African American presence within Mississippi's churches meant that religious services changed to address the racial etiquette slavery required to meet the varied needs of those attending. Segregated seating was the norm, with slaves typically sitting either in rear pews or in second-floor galleries and receiving communion after all whites had been served. Ministers and religious masters adopted specially written catechisms to orally instruct slaves, forbidden from learning to read the Bible, in the tenets of their faith. Ministers, ever watched by the public, often provided two sermons each Sunday, one for whites and another for slaves. Rather than lose access to the slaves, most southern ministers willingly constructed a slave-specific version of the Gospel that emphasized otherworldly salvation in exchange for moral behavior and earthly obedience to whites. Accordingly, sermons for African Americans drew heavily on Paul's admonitions to slaves and from their perspective often amounted to nothing more than "Mind yo mistress. Don't steal der potatoes; don't lie bout nothin' an don' talk back tuh yo boss; ifn yo does yo'll be tied tuh a tree an stripped necked. When dey tell yuh tuh do somethin' run an do hit."

Despite the obvious inequities slaves faced in southern churches, many African Americans converted to Christianity. For example, by 1860 12,684 of Mississippi's 37,976 Methodists were African American. This small but devoted segment of the southern African American population took the faith offered them and made it their own by blending aspects of African traditional religions with the elements of Christianity that had relevance for their lives. The resultant Afro-Christianity gave these believers spiritual relief from the everyday pain of slavery and hope for a better world to come. Most slave Christians also believed that God would ultimately provide them with earthly freedom when the time was right. Identifying themselves with the children of Israel enslaved in Egypt, African American slaves regularly but quietly prophesied about and prayed for the day when God would break the shackles of bondage and set his righteous people free. When that anticipated deliverance arrived, slave Christians stood as a people justified in their faith and served as the greatest testament of their God's power. The Christian core's faithfulness and accuracy in anticipating emancipation thereby attracted ever greater numbers of former slaves to Christianity. Freedom proved the greatest force for conversion among African Americans in Mississippi and the South.

Daniel L. Fountain
Meredith College

Albert E. Casey, *Amite County, Mississippi, 1699–1865*, vol. 1 (1948); John G. Jones, *A Complete History of Methodism as Connected with the Mississippi Conference of the Methodist Episcopal Church, South* (1887); Richard Aubrey McLemore, ed., *A History of Mississippi*, vol. 1 (1973); Randall Miller and Jon Wakelyn, eds., *Catholics in the Old South: Essays on Church and Culture* (1983); Albert J. Raboteau, *Slave Religion: The "Invisible Institution" in the Antebellum South* (rev. ed., 2004); Mitchell Snay, *Gospel of Disunion: Religion and Separatism in the Antebellum South* (1993); Randy Sparks, in *Masters and Slaves in the House of the Lord: Race and Religion in the American South, 1740–1870*, ed. John Boles (1989).

Religion and the Civil Rights Movement

Religion gave many African Americans, among them Fannie Lou Hamer, the inspiration and strength to participate in the civil rights movement, and the movement often organized through the church. Nevertheless, the institutional black church and its leaders generally stood back from the movement, particularly before its enlargement in the early 1960s. In both rural and urban Mississippi, prominent whites made donations to the churches of more amenable African American preachers and gave such clergymen prestige by recognizing them as black community leaders. A few African American ministers, most notably Greenville's H. H. Humes, the president of the 387,000-member General Missionary Baptist State Convention, accepted payment from the Mississippi State Sovereignty Commission as informants. While few black clergymen endorsed Jim Crow, pragmatism made most pastors wary of challenging it. Often dependent on whites for day jobs, ministers were reluctant to risk their incomes and their physical safety as well as that of their churches. Predominantly rural, Mississippi lacked a cadre of urban-based activist clergymen. In more prestigious churches, economically insecure middle-class blacks constrained ministers who might otherwise have supported the movement.

Although small in number, a few clergymen, such as R. L. T. Smith of Jackson, Aaron Johnson of Greenwood, and Tougaloo College chaplain William A. Bender, were active

in the National Association for the Advancement of Colored People (NAACP), which expanded in post–World War II Mississippi. Belzoni minister George W. Lee, a vice president of the Regional Council of Negro Leadership and an NAACP member, was shot and killed in 1955 for encouraging black voter registration.

Most of Mississippi's white clergymen and laypeople favored segregation. The national Episcopalian, Methodist, Southern Presbyterian, and Southern Baptist denominations supported the Supreme Court's 1954 *Brown v. Board of Education* ruling, but their Mississippi branches, except for the Episcopalian Church, refused to follow them. Several prominent Baptist and Presbyterian state leaders condemned their denominational bodies for endorsing *Brown*, and many Protestant churches adopted segregationist resolutions, in some cases claiming biblical justification. Laypeople also organized segregationist pressure groups. Within a year of issuing a January 1963 statement that opposed racial discrimination, all but seven of the twenty-eight young white Methodist signatories had left their pulpits under pressure. Although the Catholic Church was nominally integrated, Bishop Richard O. Gerow, like most other moderate church leaders in Mississippi, remained silent about segregation.

In the early 1960s, activists in the Student Nonviolent Coordinating Committee and the Congress of Racial Equality, many of them black southerners, recruited movement participants through church networks in which women played a major role. Congregants sometimes pressured resistant ministers and members to open their churches to the movement. Bishop Charles F. Golden of the Nashville-Carolina Area in the Methodist Church's all-black Central Jurisdiction directed Mississippi's black Methodist churches to allow civil rights meetings. In 1963 black churches and ministers played a crucial role in protests in Jackson.

African American churches, within and outside the movement, suffered racist attacks across Mississippi, especially during the 1964 Freedom Summer Project. Although the state's leading denominations formed a biracial Committee of Concern that helped rebuild forty-two black churches, white denominations opposed the Delta Ministry, a long-term civil rights project begun by the National Council of Churches in 1964. More black churches became open to the movement, but their ministers remained cautious. However in Greenwood, Rev. William Wallace of the Colored Methodist Episcopal Church, Rev. M. J. Black of the African Methodist Episcopal Church, and Father Nathaniel Machesky, a white Catholic priest, led a mostly successful boycott in the late 1960s. In 1969 black and white religious leaders formed the Mississippi Religious Leadership Conference and called for acceptance of imminent public school desegregation.

Mark Newman
University of Edinburgh

John Dittmer, *Local People: The Struggle for Civil Rights in Mississippi* (1994); Charles Marsh, *God's Long Summer: Stories of Faith and Civil Rights* (1997); Michael V. Namorato, *The Catholic Church in Mississippi, 1911–1984: A History* (1998); Mark Newman, *Divine Agitators: The Delta Ministry and Civil Rights in Mississippi* (2004); Mark Newman, *Journal of Mississippi History* (Spring 1997); Charles M. Payne, *I've Got the Light of Freedom: The Organizing Tradition and the Mississippi Freedom Struggle* (1995); Randy J. Sparks, *Religion in Mississippi* (2001).

Religion and the Civil War

Perhaps the main moral force that propelled Mississippians to secession and brought on the Civil War, religion continued to shape the ways in which all Mississippians interpreted the war once it ensued. Its cadences and beliefs, especially its Protestant evangelical strain, laid the foundation for the Lost Cause mythology even as many believed to the bitter end that Almighty God would deliver white Mississippians and the Confederacy from the scourge of the Union armies.

Current historians and many observers at the time believed that religion had fueled the secessionist impulse among Mississippi's whites by providing a moral justification for slavery, by creating fissures in national denominations that proved to be a prelude to the political separation that came in 1861, and by honing a rhetoric that led many white Mississippians to equate the North with abolitionism and abolitionism with a profound godlessness. Certainly not all religiously minded white Mississippians espoused secession. Baptist minister Thomas Teasdale and Presbyterian cleric James Adair Lyon heaped vitriol on secessionists, but they seemed to be the exception among both religious clergy and laity. The major denominations—Methodists, Baptists, and Presbyterians—if somewhat officially reticent during the secession crisis, endorsed the Confederate States of America shortly after its creation. Both church and state gave formal succor to the war effort through a series of fast days, ritual events steeped in biblical images of public atonement for sins in exchange for heavenly deliverance. African American religious expression followed a different tack, replicating the pattern of the antebellum era in which white ministers' admonitions to obey were presumed to be the antithesis of real religion. African Americans instead blended evangelical beliefs with their earlier traditions and interpreted Christianity from their own perspective as slaves. As the war progressed, African Americans, unlike most of their white Mississippi counterparts, began to see the war as part of a divine plan for emancipation.

Just as the presence of a common religious vocabulary produced different interpretations of the war among blacks and whites, the denominations and the state tended to direct the religious impulse toward different ends. The state government believed that its efforts to secure secession for Mississippi enjoyed divine blessing, but many clergymen and more pious laypeople asserted that secession merely created a purgatory in which southern religious bodies were to rid their region of a range of imperfections. Righteous folk not only lamented worldly amusements such as gambling and horse racing but also noted that slaveholding Mississippians had yet to mold the peculiar institution according to the biblical ideal. Slavery enjoyed biblical support only when it was practiced in a humane fashion and, most important, when it was more of a vehicle for the Christianization of African Americans than for earning profit for slaveholders. Denominations intensified their antebellum calls for legitimizing slave marriages and for new laws to permit teaching slaves to read the Bible. Ministers especially lamented that church attendance lagged during the war, a sure sign that Mississippi might not be godly enough to gain Jehovah's favor.

But the ebb and flow of the war's events and the protean outgrowth of the evangelical religious temper did not point white Mississippians toward defeatism. Although portions of Mississippi fell to the Union as early as 1861 and Union armies marched deep into the state's heartland over the following year, religion produced a strangely consistent response among religious Mississippians. Defeat signaled God's displeasure, but days of repentance, fasting, and prayer promised the return of heavenly favor. Confederate victory, conversely, seemed to show that the Almighty spoke with a southern accent. Even after the fall of Vicksburg and the news of the withdrawal of the Army of Northern Virginia from Gettysburg, white Mississippians of a religious bent seemed to believe that God was testing their faith and would ultimately give them independence.

Even as the marching of armies sometimes disrupted regular worship, the wave of revivals that swept the Confederate Army of Northern Virginia and the Army of Tennessee continually provided proof to white Mississippians that their cause was holy, just, and would prevail. Although the Confederate government did not provide for a chaplaincy when the war erupted, Mississippi churches joined in local, state, and south-wide efforts to send missionaries and Bibles to the troops. Testimony from the war years and later reminiscences indicate that massive conversions occurred in the Rebel armies, especially in the fall of 1863 in the Army of Northern Virginia. Reports came to the home front via army chaplains who rotated back to their congregations and via the religious press.

In Mississippi, revivalism was not confined to the army. Baptists and Methodists in the central and western parts of the state recorded conversion activity and gains in church membership in 1863, perhaps in response to the Union Army's display of the fragility of human life when it wrested

Vicksburg from Confederate control in July. But revivals continued in 1864 and 1865, a sign to the pious of the outpouring of divine grace. Just three months before Robert E. Lee's surrender, a Methodist minister in Columbus reported holding nightly revival meetings that included soldiers stationed in the area. In short, the only common factor in the religious interpretation of the war's direction was that God would determine its outcome.

Revivalism among whites simultaneously constituted a response of formal institutions and private beliefs that grew out of the antebellum culture. From the late 1790s, when portions of Mississippi were still formally Spanish possessions, to 1861, religious people in the region had built up their churches and their denominational structures. Missionary zeal triumphed in most places over a rigid Calvinism; thus, the institutionalized practice of domestic missions before the war and the growth of organizational structures to carry out these benevolent enterprises explain much of the revivalism during the war. But the intense strains of war brought profound experiences to soldiers and civilians alike, and they often turned more deeply to religion, which now offered explanations for victory, defeat, and death in the manner that it had previously sought to explain human prosperity, frailty, and suffering.

In the same manner that antebellum religion served as a foundation for wartime religious expression, the religious dimensions of the war offered a preview of major postwar themes in Mississippi's history. The first of these was the image of the Lost Cause. Forgotten in the years after the war were the cleavages in white society over issues of secession and over slavery itself. According to the Lost Cause mythology, the war was a constitutional and biblical struggle against northern fanatics pursued heroically by righteous and united southerners until the bitter end. The wartime experiences had elevated the feelings of sectional loyalty. Although they might quarrel about the policies of the governments in Jackson and Richmond, those disputes were hardly tantamount to Unionism. Tales of wartime Union atrocities circulated among Mississippians in the same way that rumors of slave and abolitionist conspiracies had circulated in antebellum times. Furthermore, shared religious experiences such as revivalism seemed at once to unify white society and to demonstrate the rectitude of the Mississippians' cause.

Perhaps the keystone in the Lost Cause arch was the symbol of the heroic leader. By all accounts, Lee and Thomas J. "Stonewall" Jackson were Christian heroes, regarded as such on both sides of the Potomac. And Mississippi produced and claimed its share of pious martial leaders. Although a native of Tennessee, Mark Perrin Lowery had fought for the 2nd Mississippi Volunteers in the Mexican War in 1846 and 1847 before entering the Baptist ministry in 1853. Pious and energetic, he volunteered for military service in 1861 and soon rose to the rank of brigadier general, serving at Perryville, Chickamauga, Franklin, and Nashville before resigning his commission in March 1865. After the war, he founded a Baptist institute for young women in Blue Mountain. The presence of flesh-and-blood pious leaders during and after the war confirmed most white Mississippians' belief that they were morally (and martially) superior to their more numerous Yankee foe.

The tocsin of the Lost Cause muted other white voices that focused more on the perception that God's displeasure with the slaveholding Confederacy, including its Mississippi branch, was a bigger cause of defeat than were the numerous and well-armed Union troops. Ministers Samuel Agnew and James Lyon asserted that the failure of Mississippi's white Christians to do more to evangelize their slaves and to treat them with humanity constituted a grievous sin, explaining that God would hold Mississippi's white society accountable in the same way after the war if it did not offer better treatment to the former slaves. Most white Mississippians preferred to blame their troubles on their uppity former slaves, just as they had blamed abolitionism rather than the abuses of slavery for African American unrest before the war. At the same time, white Mississippians concluded that Providence chastened them because it favored them.

Segregation was the second theme with religious overtones initially honed in the maelstrom of war and fully developed over the next thirty years. Slaveholding society brought white owners and masters and their households into extremely close proximity with their African American slaves. Religious structures fostered this proximity, as blacks and whites gathered together to worship in the same churches. Many Baptist and Methodist congregations had both black and white members, and some congregations articulated ideals regarding the equality of all Christians, irrespective of skin color, even if such ideals were poorly reflected in practice. For white Mississippians, the presence of blacks and whites in an ordered and socially hierarchical public worship exercise helped to justify slavery and white Mississippians' claims about its beneficence. For all their glaring imperfections and hypocrisies to modern sensibilities, these prewar religious structures were biracial communities of faith and the only mixed-race associations in Mississippi.

The chaos of the war, the Thirteenth Amendment, the reality of economic dislocation, the material destruction of many of Mississippi's church buildings, and the scattering of white laity and leadership significantly weakened this tense biracial relationship. African Americans, determined to act on their independence and to practice their own Christianity, began to separate from their former congregations and to found their own denominations as early as 1866. The most segregated time in Mississippi, as in the rest of the southern states, became the Sunday morning worship hour, and this transformation occurred before other major features of segregation took shape in law and custom. Just as the sectional cleavage between white evangelicals prior to the Civil War had lent credence to disunion, so the racial segregation of evangelical churches proved a prelude to the horrid opera of postbellum segregation. Although some white evangelicals and evangelical organizations maintained contacts with their African American brethren and attempted to forge formal ties with the nascent African American denominational structures, those efforts died out by 1885. Most white Mississippians interpreted this African American diaspora as proof of black inferiority rather than a bitter fruit of white hypocrisy and cruelty and an understandable desire of independent people to direct their own organizations, especially those as important as the church.

The Civil War intensified rather than transmogrified religious beliefs in Mississippi even as it transformed the racial makeup of its religious denominations. Religiously minded Mississippians continued to believe that God directed the affairs of their lives and held them accountable for their deeds as individuals and, to a great degree, as a people. Black and white Mississippians, however, interpreted the signs of divine favor and disfavor through racial lenses, employing a common textual mythology to argue for radically different ends. Hence, white Mississippians found moral justification and black Mississippians physical liberation as the realities of God's will in the crucible of war.

Edward R. Crowther
Adams State College

John B. Boles, *Masters and Slaves in the House of the Lord: Race and Religion in the American South, 1740–1870* (1988); Edward R. Crowther, *Journal of Mississippi History* (May 1994); Percy Rainwater, *Mississippi: Storm Center of Secession, 1856–1861* (1938); James W. Silver, *Confederate Morale and Church Propaganda* (1957); Randy J. Sparks, *On Jordan's Stormy Banks: Evangelicalism in Mississippi, 1773–1876* (1994); Charles Reagan Wilson, *Baptized in Blood: The Religion of the Lost Cause, 1864–1914* (1983); Stephen E. Woodworth, *While God Is Marching On: The Religious World of Civil War Soldiers* (2001).

Religious Architecture

Mississippi's architectural expressions reflect its religious culture. Evangelicalism, a congregationally oriented faith that has often prized simplicity of approach and rigor of doctrine, has not stressed the importance of originality of design. Concentration of the state's population in rural areas for so long surely shaped religious architectural development, with few large cities providing a concentration of resources for innovative large churches. The predominance of a biracial culture resulted in similarities and differences

The Hebrew Union Temple in Greenville (1906) is an example of Classical Revival architecture [rayburn_ann_24_25_001])

in the religious life of blacks and whites in the state, including in church building. The presence of a diversity of non-evangelical faiths in smaller numbers than the evangelicals resulted in a variety of styles of church building.

The Greek Revival style had an enormous influence on church building in Mississippi, as in the rest of the South. It was a national style, a high-style design, but it cut across denominational and social class lines as Mississippians adapted it to local contexts. The Kingston Methodist Church, a small church near Natchez built in 1856, is a good example of the Greek Revival style, built of brick and then stuccoed to approximate the stone that the Greeks would have used. Worshippers walked through Doric columns that lent a stateliness to their religious experience. By 1860, Methodists in the state had built 454 churches, many of them Greek Revival. The Baptists also grew dramatically in antebellum Mississippi, and their churches were often vernacular adaptations of the Greek Revival style. Mashulaville Baptist Church, built in 1855 in Noxubee County, in eastern Mississippi, is a surviving example. The wood-frame Bethel Presbyterian Church in Lowndes County is an example of a surviving Greek Revival church built in the antebellum era in the prairie region. Pattern books coming from northern architects were well known in antebellum Mississippi and showed local carpenters how to build small-frame Greek Revival churches.

Another popular style was the Gothic Revival. High-church advocates in England's Anglican Church known as the Ecclesiologists promoted a return to medieval church styles, including stained glass windows, images of saints, dim lighting, stone altars, and other features that represented a Victorian Romanticism. Richard Upjohn became a prominent American exponent of Gothic Revival after the success of his Trinity Church in New York City led to a demand for similar design plans adaptable to other places. *Upjohn's Rural Architecture* (1852) enabled builders to construct wooden churches featuring board-and-batten walls,

Rodney's Presbyterian Church (1830) has a Civil War cannonball lodged above the center upper window. (Courtesy Janie Fortenberry)

shingled and pitched roofs, and lancet windows with splayed jambs. A square tower typically contained the belfry and a broach spire. The Episcopal Church, the American branch of the Anglican tradition, became a prime builder of Gothic churches in the nineteenth century. Mississippi had relatively few Episcopalians, but they built fourteen churches in the antebellum era, mostly expressing Gothic design. The Chapel of the Cross, in Madison County, north of Jackson, is a small plantation chapel built as a memorial to John T. Johnstone, a wealthy planter. Completed in 1853, the church was designed by Frank Wills, an Englishman who became the architect for the New York Ecclesiological Society and designed Grace Episcopal Church in Canton. Both of Wills's Mississippi churches embody a pointed style, with Grace Church utilizing arches and pinnacles to achieve the vertical visual reach favored by Gothic designers.

Many rural churches in Mississippi were vernacular or folk buildings, relying on customary ways of construction and building plans that did not reflect formal architectural training. Such high styles as Greek Revival and Gothic Revival have been frequently adapted in country churches. Some folk churches were and are one-story rectangular structures, with gabled roofs and one or two doors. Examples include the Bethany Presbyterian Church, near Centreville in Amite County (1855), and Lebanon Presbyterian Church, near Learned in Hinds County (1854). Both have two doors at the entrance, which tradition suggests were separate entrances for men and women. Other folk churches were two stories, with the second floor used by a fraternal lodge hall: the Shongalo Presbyterian Church in Vaiden (1874) is an example. Finally, vernacular churches have sometimes been built as gable-roofed, rectangular buildings with a single large, high-ceilinged room and a gallery that overlooks the lower level. An example is the Washington United Methodist Church, northeast of Natchez (1828).

Slaves typically sat in church galleries for worship, creating a unique biracial church tradition. With the end of slavery, African Americans withdrew from these churches, seeking spiritual autonomy. They built countless places of worship, favoring the prevailing Gothic Revival style but using a variety of other designs as well. Vicksburg's Bethel African Methodist Episcopal Church, which opened in 1864, was the denomination's first congregation in the state. In 1912 its members constructed a Romanesque Revival building that still stands. The Delta, the area of the state with the highest concentrations of African Americans, is characterized by large numbers of small frame churches, often Missionary Baptist in affiliation. Bell towers are not unusual, towering over the adjacent burial grounds and nearby cotton fields. Each interior typically has a central wooden podium, substantial wooden chairs, and a communion table in front of a railing that separates the seated congregation from the altar. More recent Delta churches are likely to be of brick, with spires atop pitched roofs.

Roman Catholics were not numerous in most areas of nineteenth-century Mississippi, but nine parishes had been established by the time of the Civil War. Annunciation Parish, established in Columbus in 1854, prospered during the cotton boom of the 1850s and even in the early years of the war, encouraging the congregation to begin construction on a Gothic Revival building. The war's devastation prevented the church's completion until 1868, however. Rodney's Sacred Heart Catholic Church, also completed in 1868, is a small building with lovely tall windows and a square tower.

Most of the state's post–Civil War Catholic churches were constructed in a High Gothic style exemplified by Jackson's Cathedral of St. Peter the Apostle, built from 1897 to 1900, and Biloxi's Cathedral of the Nativity of the Blessed Virgin Mary, built in 1901–2. The Gulf Coast was traditionally the center of Mississippi's Catholic population. The center of the state's largest parish, Bay St. Louis's Church of Our Lady of the Gulf, had three thousand communicants in the 1930s. Its members worship in a red-brick Italian Renaissance building that was constructed between 1908 and 1926 and features stained glass windows from Germany. Holy Family, the first African American Roman Catholic Church in Mississippi, was built in Natchez in 1894. The Third Plenary Council of the Church had authorized establishment of separate black parishes in 1885 in hopes of evangelizing African Americans, and Holy Family was one of the first results of the effort. This brick Gothic Revival Church remains in use.

The Civil War resulted in the destruction of many Mississippi churches and halted the construction of new facilities. Postwar political turmoil and economic decline held back church development, and the state escaped the swirl of newer national architectural styles. Congregational stories preserve memories of local church experiences with the war. For example, both Union and Confederate troops sheltered their horses in Holly Springs's First Presbyterian Church, which was under construction when the war began. Rodney's Presbyterian Church, built in 1830, has a cannonball lodged near the center of the building. As the postwar South romanticized the Old South and the Lost Cause,

Greek Revival buildings, including churches, gained new cultural authority in Mississippi and remained popular even after losing favor elsewhere. As the state's towns and cities grew in the late nineteenth and early twentieth centuries, they typically included examples of monumental churches. The "First" Baptists, Methodists, and Presbyterians on town squares were good examples, with Churches of Christ also represented in some towns in northern Mississippi.

Religious architecture in Mississippi has reflected Christian predominance, but Jewish Mississippians, too, have built distinguished places of worship. Jewish settlers arrived in the state early in the nineteenth century, and Jewish cemeteries existed in Biloxi and Natchez as early as 1830. Later generations of Jewish immigrants from Central and Eastern Europe worked as peddlers and shopkeepers, settling in isolated small towns in the Delta and elsewhere. By 1860 at least six Jewish congregations existed in the state, including Gemiluth Chessed in Port Gibson, established in 1859. The congregation's Moorish-Byzantine facade, erected in 1891, is one of the state's most exotic structures. Its architects planned it to resemble synagogues found in Russia, where many of its members had originated. Brookhaven's Temple B'nai Sholom, built in 1896, also uses Moorish touches in windows and on tower panels. Temple B'nai Israel in Natchez (1905) and Hebrew Union Temple in Greenville (1906) are Classical Revival buildings.

The contemporary era has seen the growth of megachurches in Mississippi's urban areas. Jackson's First Baptist Church, founded in 1838, had 8,855 members in 2007, while another of the city's largest churches, Christ United Methodist Church, had 4,946 congregants. Their facilities include abundant classroom space, exercise rooms, kitchen areas to support feeding ministries, and health clinics. The descendants of the small vernacular rural wooden churches are double-wide trailer churches such as the Rising Sun Missionary Baptist Church in West Jackson. Its members began worshiping in 1994 in a private residence and moved their services into a new sacred space in 2001. Few religious symbols mark the outside of the church, and it hardly draws on historic church architectural patterns, but evangelical images meet the worshiper in an interior that reflects the simplicity of an unadorned evangelical church.

Evangelical churches in Mississippi often use their interiors as auditoriums to facilitate the oral dimension of worship. The liturgy is focused on the preacher's sermon, congregational hymn singing, and prayers, and an auditorium design provides for individual seating in curving tiers that rise toward the rear and a large stage with a prominent pulpit, space for the minister to roam while preaching, and seating for a substantial choir. The assembly hall is often surrounded by classrooms where Sunday school students meet and then move easily into worship space.

Charles Reagan Wilson
University of Mississippi

Marilyn J. Chiat, *America's Religious Architecture: Sacred Places for Every Community* (1997); Jean Gordon, *Jackson Clarion-Ledger* (20 May 2007); Sherry Pace, *Historic Churches of Mississippi* (2007); Tom Rankin, *Sacred Space: Photographs from the Mississippi Delta* (1993); Peter W. Williams, *Houses of God: Region, Religion, and Architecture in the United States* (1997).

Religious Right

The Religious Right is a broad coalition of evangelicals that has exercised considerable influence in politics and public policy forums since the mid-1970s. Seeing itself as the antidote to a decadent culture that sought to impose its values through liberal government, this movement represented a new attitude toward politics on the part of conservative Christians, who had often traditionally eschewed political action. It also represented a new constituency for the Republican Party, which historically had not relied on evangelicals as an important part of its base.

A crucial component in the transformation of southern politics, the Religious Right is national, extradenominational, and thrives on grassroots support, though national leaders often attract a great deal of attention. Mississippi contributed significantly to the rise of the Religious Right in part because it possessed the two chief ingredients that nourished this movement: a preponderance of evangelicals and intense resentment toward the liberal movements of the 1960s.

Well before the rise of the Religious Right, evangelicals exerted a great deal of political influence in Mississippi. For example, in 1907, years before the national Prohibition amendment, Mississippi adopted a state-level alcohol ban that remained in place until the 1960s. In 1926 Mississippi passed an antievolution law that was not invalidated by the state Supreme Court until 1970, long after the rest of the country had done away with such measures. In spite of their clear influence on Mississippi law and society, however, evangelicals often disavowed their own influence and discouraged one another from direct political involvement, claiming that politics was not the proper sphere for the church. Evangelical leaders maintained that their most important work was to spread the Gospel; as they faithfully executed this task, they believed, desirable social and political transformations would inevitably ensue—the cumulative effect of salvation wrought one soul at a time.

The social and political upheaval of the 1960s simultaneously transformed many conservative Americans' attitudes toward both the federal government and American culture. Though many Americans regarded that decade's sweeping changes in southern race relations as a long-awaited real-ization of basic democracy, conservatives, including many white southerners and evangelicals, often saw these changes through a dramatically different lens. According to their thinking, the same governmental drive to aggrandize power and to intrude into the personal lives of Americans that had motivated school desegregation and voting rights legislation also produced the high court's 1962 decision rendering public prayer in public schools unconstitutional. The same decadence that had spawned interracial sit-ins and Freedom Rides also flaunted itself in the more permissive morality displayed in the hippie movement, in more explicit material in movies and television, in the lyrics of rock music, in a rising divorce rate, and even in public school textbooks. Believing that a misguided government encouraged an immoral culture, evangelicals needed a new approach to their social and political environment. No longer advocating change through the indirect path of evangelism, religious leaders began in the 1970s to maintain that the "church belong[ed] in politics up to its eyebrows."

Though often perceived as a monolithic bloc of hard-liners, the Religious Right in Mississippi and elsewhere embraces both moderate and extreme elements. Families have found the movement particularly appealing, since the perceived combination of moral license and expanded governmental power appeared to assault their ability to raise children according to their own dictates. With the creation of the Christian Action Commission (organized in part as an answer to the Southern Baptist Convention's Christian Life Commission, which many Mississippi Baptists regarded as too liberal and overly concerned with social issues such as racial equality), Mississippi Baptists endeavored to address rising concerns about public morality by offering programs on the Christian family, pornography, alcohol and drug abuse, and Christian citizenship. Though in its early years the Christian Action Commission claimed it was not a lobbying organization, it did "alert Baptist leaders of pending legislation on pertinent matters." By 1982, when commission director Paul Jones registered as a lobbyist, the agency clearly demonstrated evangelicals' new attitude about the appropriateness of political activity.

An important Religious Right organization, the National Federation for Decency, which became the American Family Association in 1987, has Mississippi origins. Briefly allied with the Moral Majority, the group, under the direction of a Tupelo Methodist minister, Donald E. Wildmon, proved enormously successful at bringing corporate giants such as Sears, Proctor and Gamble, and CBS to adopt sponsorship policies that reflected standards acceptable to conservative Americans. Perhaps even more important, in 1989 Wildmon organized grassroots support for a letter-writing campaign that brought the National Endowment for the Arts to the center of the struggle over issues of decency, public funding, and cultural control.

Highly issue-driven, the Religious Right has consistently opposed abortion rights as one of its highest priorities. Indeed, to many the US Supreme Court's 1973 *Roe v. Wade* decision guaranteeing abortion rights represents the nadir of America's recent immoral trajectory. Nationwide and in Mississippi, the struggle over abortion rights highlights the Religious Right's extradenominational character. The Jackson-based group Capitol Connection and the more radical Christian Action Group, along with representatives of the national Operation Rescue, have worked to increase pro-life activity in the state, to provide free treatment and support for women who decide against abortion, and to pass legislation that might help mitigate the effects of the *Roe* decision. In 1993 these groups worked together with representatives of more than sixty churches to hold demonstrations in Jackson that drew more than two thousand protesters, and their support was essential in the drive to get the Mississippi legislature to pass of a bill requiring parental permission before women under the age of eighteen could receive abortions. Nevertheless, in 2011 the Mississippi electorate voted down the anti-abortion Ballot Initiative 26, or the "Personhood Amendment," which aimed to outlaw abortion by claimed that "personhood" is achieved at conception. The Colorado-based evangelical Christian group Personhood USA sponsored the bill.

In recent years, opposition to homosexuality has been another salient issue for the Religious Right. In Mississippi, this conflict took the shape of organized resistance to the creation of the Metropolitan Community Church in Jackson and, as in many states, the adoption in 2004 of an amendment to the state's constitution banning same-sex marriage. Yet both the campaign against abortion rights and the effort to oppose homosexuality have also vividly and consistently elicited responses from an evangelical contingent that refuses to be aligned with the Religious Right. Furthermore, the large constituent of black evangelicals in Mississippi has also confounded the neat alliance between conservative religion and conservative politics, as many black evangelicals embrace an ideology that merges conservative religious doctrine with a more progressive political philosophy.

In recent developments, in 2016 the Mississippi legislature passed HB 1523, the Protecting Freedom of Conscience from Government Discrimination Act. Authors of the act said it protected the rights of business owners and public officials from providing services to people getting married, or renting or selling them property, or offering child care or medical treatment if doing so would violate religious convictions about same-sex marriage or gender identity. In June 2016 US District Court judge Carlton Reeves ruled that the bill violated the 2015 Supreme Court ruling in *Obergefell v. Hodges* that legalized gay marriage and, more broadly, he stated this ruling overturned efforts by the state legislature to "put its thumb on the scale to favor some religious beliefs over others."

Carolyn Dupont
Eastern Kentucky University

Joseph Crespino, *In Search of Another Country: Mississippi and the Conservative Counterrevolution* (2007); Carolyn Dupont, *Mississippi Praying: Southern White Evangelicals and the Civil Rights Movement, 1945–1975* (2015); Samuel Hill, *Southern Churches in Crisis* (1966); William Martin, *With God on Our Side: The Rise of the Religious Right in America* (1996); Randy Sparks, *Religion in Mississippi* (2001).

Religious Roadside Art

If any one thing comes close to vying with dead dogs and live bait for prevalence on the Mississippi roadside, it is religion—more specifically, religious roadside signs. These signs take many forms—crude portraits of Jesus painted on plywood, elaborate religious displays marking the sites of fatal car crashes, evangelical graffiti on interstate overpasses, marquees in front of almost every church, makeshift re-creations of Golgotha, prefabricated plastic lawn signs featuring the Ten Commandments. Southern evangelical Protestants have claimed their spot on the side of the road, selling salvation through religiously themed signs that mimic and mock commercial signs that market goods and services with significantly shorter shelf lives.

Popular "sentence sermons," as messages on religious roadside signs have come to be known, often adapt well-known commercial slogans: "Wal-Mart Is Not the Only Saving Place," "Forgiven: This Blood's for You," and "Jesus Christ: Like a Rock." Likewise, religious roadside signs frequently mix elements of biblical scripture with common colloquialisms, as in a Waynesboro, Mississippi, sign that read, "Be Ye Fishers of Men. You Catch Them, Jesus Will Clean Them."

Church sign, Waynesboro (Courtesy Joe York)

Other signs pose clever questions such as, "You Think It's Hot Here?," tacitly suggesting that hell is more miserable than a Mississippi summer. Still trickier are questions such as, "If the Rapture Was Today, Would You Be in Church on Sunday?"

In all cases, these signs and their religious reworking of secular slogans are an attempt by evangelical Protestants to adhere to their de facto Eleventh Commandment, the Great Commission. In the last two verses of the book of Matthew, Jesus says to his disciples before ascending to heaven, "Go therefore and teach all nations, baptizing them in the name of the Father and of the Son and of the Holy Ghost, teaching them to observe all things whatsoever I have commanded you; and lo, I am with you always, even to the end of the world."

This mandate, more than any other laid out in the Bible, is the reason why evangelists are evangelists. But in a spiritual climate in which individuals looking for a new place to worship are commonly said to be "church shopping," southern evangelical Protestants looking to make good on their half of the Great Commission have turned evangelism into a form of spiritual advertising and marketing, and the most visible outgrowth of this trend is the religious roadside sign.

Attempting to lure would-be congregants from the pavement to the pew, this reworking of secular slogans and colloquialisms simultaneously attempts to add humor and levity to serious theological concepts and to add spiritual weight to mundane clichés and marketing techniques. This interplay between the vocabulary of this world and that of the perceived world to come is a hallmark of contemporary southern evangelical Protestants, who consciously and cleverly blur the lines between the real and imagined spaces of the sacred and the profane.

Joe York
University of Mississippi

Joe York, *With Signs Following: Photographs from the Southern Religious Roadside* (2007).

Reproductive Rights

Until the twenty-first century, Mississippi had rarely played a major role in national discussions about reproductive rights. But in 2011, 57 percent of Mississippi voters voted against Proposition 26, an initiative that would have defined human life as beginning at conception and therefore made abortion illegal in the state. Even before Proposition 26, Mississippi

A sign opposing Initiative 26 (2011), which would have banned virtually all abortions in the state (Courtesy Ted Ownby)

had the strictest rules about access to abortion and the fewest abortions in the United States.

From 1840 into the 1960s Mississippi had two laws that addressed abortion. One defined giving drugs to a pregnant woman to kill an unborn child as manslaughter. The other prohibited owning, selling, distributing, or advertising drugs "for the prevention of conception, or for causing unlawful abortion."

Until the mid-twentieth century, abortion did not generate much public discussion in the state. Throughout the United States, abortion was illegal but available. The unevenness of its availability according to income or location made abortion dangerous, mysterious, or at least unfair. Historians have shown that abortion increased dramatically across the United States during the Great Depression. Southern midwives had a range of practices, most famously herbal medicines, to terminate pregnancies. In fact, one of the criticisms doctors in the South leveled at midwives was that the informality of their practice encouraged some to perform abortions.

The story of Dewey Dell Bundren in William Faulkner's *As I Lay Dying* (1930) dramatized both the vague knowledge about abortion and some of the difficulties its illegality could cause women. Bundren tells a drugstore employee that she has ten dollars for something for "the female trouble." The drugstore employee extorts both sex and money from her, telling Bundren he could go to jail for helping with an abortion. In the end, however, he gives her a worthless combination of drugs.

In mid-twentieth century Mississippi reproductive rights were inseparable from issues of racial imagery, morality, family definitions, and government policy. For years, white Mississippians had demeaned African Americans for having, as Greenville author David Cohn termed it, "sex without shackles," or notions of permanent responsibility. Cohn wrote in the 1930s that "the average Delta Negro has almost

no criteria by which sexual and domestic relations may be judged." However, in the wake of mass migration from the region, the rise of federal welfare policies, and the civil rights movement, some white Mississippi leaders moved to limit the number of African American children. First, state social security policies encouraged contraception among poor African Americans; later, Mississippi, like many southern states, debated laws that would have required sterilization or imprisonment for unmarried women who had more than one child. In 1958 state representative David Glass proposed an Act to Discourage Immorality of Unmarried Females by Providing for Sterilization of the Unwed Mother. The act did not pass, but its supporters claimed that poor and unmarried African American women were having children to take advantage of national welfare policies. In the early 1970s the Mississippi legislature returned to the topic, dropped sterilization as a potential penalty, and passed a measure that made it a misdemeanor for unmarried women to have multiple children and included jail time among the possible punishments. Such public discussions involved efforts to limit the number of children born to poor women.

In *Griswold v. Connecticut* (1965), the US Supreme Court overturned state laws that prohibited the sale of contraceptives, based on the doctrine that control over one's sexual behavior was part of a constitutional right to privacy. Numerous states, working within suggestions from the American Law Institute, enacted legal changes to allow "therapeutic abortions" that protected the life and health of mothers. In 1966 the Mississippi legislature changed its antebellum laws to allow abortion when two doctors provided written opinions saying that the abortion was necessary to save the mother's life. The new law also allowed abortions for women who had conceived as a result of rape.

In *Roe v. Wade* (1973) the US Supreme Court extended the right-to-privacy argument to questions of abortion, overturning numerous state laws. The Court declared that state governments could not prohibit abortions in the first trimester of a pregnancy, could regulate abortions during the second trimester by requiring that they be performed in certain locations (such as hospitals), and could decide whether abortions were legal in the third trimester as long as exceptions could be made when mothers' lives were threatened.

Since the 1980s Mississippi lawmakers have spent considerable energy debating the ethics, availability, and medical practices of abortion and have passed numerous laws to make abortion more difficult, complicated, and expensive. In the 1980s Mississippi required women under the age of eighteen to obtain consent from both parents before having abortions. In the 1990s the state prohibited so-called partial-birth abortions, instituted one-day waiting periods for all abortions, and required that women seeking abortions receive instruction about alternatives such as adoption and learn about "the probable anatomical and physiological characteristics of unborn children at two-week gestational increments." In 2002 the legislature barred public funding for abortions, and two years later it required doctors to file full reports on all patients who died or needed medical treatment after abortions. A 2007 law required women seeking abortions to see ultrasound images and hear fetal heartbeats. The same year, the legislature passed a speculative law that would prohibit abortions (except in cases of rape or to preserve a woman's life) within ten days after any future US Supreme Court decision overruling *Roe v. Wade*.

Statistics on abortions are difficult to interpret, but they are helpful in comparing differences over time and location. The first recorded legal abortions in the state occurred in 1971, with fewer than 100 that year and in 1972 and 1973. After *Roe v. Wade*, Mississippians obtained 140 abortions in 1974 and 315 the following year. The numbers then began to grow dramatically, with the Mississippi Department of Health recording 6,842 abortions in 1980, 6,448 in 1989, and an all-time high of 7,574 in 1991. The numbers subsequently trended downward, falling to 6,069 in 1994 and 5,653 in 2000 before bottoming out at 4,323 in 2005. Over the next three years, between 6,000 and 6,300 abortions per year were performed. The number has fallen every year since, reaching 4,801 in 2014. According to the US Centers for Disease Control and Prevention, in 2012 Mississippi's abortion rate—that is, the number of abortions per 1,000 women aged fifteen to forty-four—was 3.6, the lowest in the country and far lower than the 13.2 rate for the United States as a whole.

The number of facilities in the state that performed abortions has declined from four in 2005 to two in 2008 to one (in Jackson) in 2013. Though women from all of Mississippi's counties have received abortions, Hinds County and adjacent areas have the highest numbers.

The 2011 debate over Proposition 26, widely called the Personhood Amendment, revealed the state's divisions on the issue of reproductive rights. Observers and pollsters assumed that Mississippi's conservative voting tendencies would enable the measure to pass there even though similar legislation had failed in other states. Church groups and non-church groups used religious language to argue that every individual life has a soul from the moment of conception and used legal and political language to defend the constitutional rights of the unborn. Some said that only clear rules and moral standards would lead to a decline in unwanted pregnancies. Opponents of the proposition included such established groups as the state's medical and nursing associations, Planned Parenthood, and some church leaders as well as new organizations such as Mississippians for Healthy Families and Parents against Mississippi 26. They argued that women should have the right to control their own bodies and that doctors and their patients should be able to make decisions about childbirth without government interference. Many also noted with frustration that Mississippi's high teenage pregnancy rates showed the need for better sex education,

not more laws limiting women's options. These debates have subsequently continued.

Ted Ownby
University of Mississippi

Johnston's Archive website, www.johnstonarchive.net; Rosemary Nossiff, *Before Roe: Abortion Policy in the States* (2001); Leslie J. Reagan, *When Abortion Was a Crime: Women, Medicine, and Law in the United States, 1867–1973* (1997); Mississippi Department of Health, *Mississippi Selected Facts about Teenage Pregnancy* (1995); Mississippi Statistically Automated Health Resource System website, http://mstahrs.msdh.ms.gov /help.html; Rickie Sollinger, *Pregnancy and Power: A Short History of Reproductive Politics in America* (2005); Rickie Sollinger, *Wake Up Little Susie: Single Pregnancy and Race before Roe v. Wade* (2000); Raymond Tatalovich, *The Politics of Abortion in the United States and Canada: A Comparative Study* (1997); US Centers for Disease Control Abortion Surveillance System website, http://www.cdc.gov/Reproductivehealth/Data _Stats/index.htm.

Reptiles

The class Reptilia includes turtles, crocodilians, squamates (lizards and snakes), and the tuatara (found only on islands off the coast of New Zealand). Mississippi has eighty-four species of reptiles, including one crocodilian, twenty-nine turtles, forty-one snakes, and thirteen lizards. The crocodilian is the American alligator, formerly endangered but now so abundant in some areas that it is hunted as a game animal. Five of the turtles (the loggerhead, Kemp's ridley, hawksbill, green, and leatherback sea turtles) are marine species, and they, along with five other turtle species (the

American alligator (*Alligator mississippiensis*) (Photograph by Ginger L. Corbin, courtesy US Fish and Wildlife Service)

black-knobbed, yellow-blotched, and ringed sawbacks; the Alabama redbelly turtle; and the gopher tortoise), are listed as threatened or endangered by state and/or federal wildlife resource agencies. Six of Mississippi's snakes are venomous, including the cottonmouth, the copperhead, the pygmy rattlesnake, the canebrake rattlesnake, the eastern diamondback rattlesnake, and the coral snake. Four species (the eastern indigo, southern hognose, black pine, and rainbow snakes) are considered threatened or endangered in Mississippi. Twelve of the lizard species that occur in Mississippi are native, while the Mediterranean gecko and brown anole are exotic species that have established breeding populations. Only one lizard species, the mimic glass lizard, is listed as endangered in Mississippi.

Robert L. Jones
Mississippi Museum of
Natural Science

Renn Lohoefener and Ronald Altig, *Mississippi Herpetology* (1983); F. Harvey Pough, Robin M. Andrews, John E. Cadle, Martha L. Crump, Alan H. Savitzky, and Kentwood D. Wells, *Herpetology* (1998).

Republic of New Afrika

A black separatist organization, the Republic of New Afrika (RNA), was born in March 1968, when five hundred black nationalists met in Detroit. The RNA's avowed purpose was to culturally and literally separate African Americans from mainstream American culture and to set up a new nation consisting of five states in the South—Alabama, Georgia, Louisiana, Mississippi, and South Carolina.

The 1968 Detroit conference chose outspoken black nationalist Robert Williams to serve as the RNA's provisional president. As head of the Monroe, North Carolina, chapter of the National Association for the Advancement of Colored People, he had advised his constituency to use weapons to defend themselves against racial violence. Williams had fled the United States in 1961 following allegations that he had kidnapped and robbed a white couple. After several years of self-imposed exile in Cuba and China, Williams returned to the United States.

His tenure as RNA president was short. Brothers Richard and Milton Henry took over the group and opted to begin RNA operations in Mississippi. Richard Henry became president of the new nation and changed his name to Imari Abubakari Obadele to symbolize his ancestral affinity with the African diaspora; Milton took the name Gaidi Obadele. As the leaders of the RNA the Obadeles requested that the US government cede the states of Alabama, Georgia, Louisiana, Mississippi, and South Carolina to the organization, along with four hundred billion dollars in reparations. Although Imari Obadele personally delivered his demands in a memorandum to the US State Department, his efforts were never acknowledged. Undaunted, he and the RNA purchased twenty acres of land from Lofton Mason in Bolton, Mississippi, and named the parcel El Malik, in honor of El-Hajj Malik El Shabazz (Malcolm X).

Since the US government refused to acknowledge the RNA's demands, the group began to organize a plebiscite. The RNA anticipated an overwhelming vote in favor of separation and planned to use the vote as leverage in its effort to secure the desired territory. Leaders noted that most African Americans lived in the South and chose to start work in Mississippi because African Americans constituted 40 percent of the state's population. The RNA believed that if its government became functional, African Americans would migrate south from the northern United States and provide a large black vote in support of the proposed plebiscite. If the plebiscite did not succeed, the RNA and its military wing, the Black Legion, anticipated fighting a guerrilla war against the US government until the group garnered international support for its cause.

In Mississippi, the RNA made a number of converts and was growing increasingly popular, but authorities soon began to resist. The City of Jackson and the Federal Bureau of Investigation began surveillance of the organization, culminating in an early morning raid on 18 August 1971 by local and federal authorities on the RNA's main compound. The resulting shootout left one Jackson police officer dead and two federal agents wounded. Eleven members of the RNA were subsequently indicted on charges of murder. Several of the defendants, including Imari Obadele, were convicted on the murder charges and sentenced to life in prison. With their leaders incarcerated, members of the RNA began to campaign for their freedom, banding together with other nationalistic groups.

The RNA's separatist movement was never fully realized, and the government against which members fought quelled their dreams of nationhood.

Saul Dorsey
Jackson State University

Raymond Hall, *Black Separatism in the United States* (1978); Peniel E. Joseph, ed., *The Black Power Movement: Rethinking the Civil Rights–Black Power Era* (2006), *Waiting till the Midnight Hour: A Narrative History of Black Power in America* (2006); Timothy B. Tyson, *Radio Free Dixie: Robert F. Williams and the Roots of Black Power* (2001); William L. Van DeBurg, *Modern Black Nationalism: From Marcus Garvey to Louis Farrakhan* (1997); William L. Van DeBurg, *New Day in Babylon: The Black Power Movement and American Culture, 1965–1975* (1992).

Republicans

The modern-day Republican Party began in Mississippi on 22 March 1956, though the party's history in the state goes back an additional ninety years, to the wake of the Civil War. From 1868 to 1875 Republicans controlled the state government. The 1870 state legislature convened with 110 Republicans, 35 of them black. After ratifying the Fourteenth and Fifteenth Amendments to the US Constitution, legislators moved to fill US Senate seats left vacant by secession. One went to Hiram Rhoades Revels, who became the first African American to serve in the US Senate. Four years later, the legislature appointed the second black senator, Blanche K. Bruce. John R. Lynch became the first black Speaker of the state house and then the first black Mississippi congressman. Over these seven years, black Republicans won election as lieutenant governor, secretary of state, and superintendent of education. The 1874 legislature boasted 64 black Republican members, a black Speaker of the house, and a black president of the senate.

White Democrats could not stomach African American political power and employed both legal and illegal tactics to retake the legislature in the 1875 elections. The first order of business when they assembled in early 1876 was to remove from office the white Republican governor, Adelbert Ames, and two African American Republican officials, Lt. Gov. Alexander K. Davis and superintendent of education T. W. Cordoza. Reconstruction had ended in Mississippi, and the memories would be long-lasting—88 years passed before Mississippi gave its electoral votes to a Republican presidential nominee for president, and 116 years elapsed before a Republican moved back into the Governor's Mansion.

The successor to the party that managed state government during Reconstruction was known as the Black and Tan Republican Party. In 1924 Perry Howard, a Holmes County lawyer and the son of former slaves, assumed control of the party. Howard's nemesis was George Sheldon, a former Nebraska governor who moved to Mississippi in 1909 and organized the Lily-White Republican Party in 1927. These two groups fought for control of the state GOP for the next three decades.

On 22 March 1956 the party held its state convention at the Hinds County Courthouse. The newly formed Young Republicans of Mississippi, headed by Wirt Yerger Jr., joined with the state chapter of Citizens for Eisenhower, headed by E. O. Spencer, to wrest control of the party from the Lily-Whites by electing a majority of the members of the new State Executive Committee, which then chose Yerger as the party chair, a position he held for ten years. Later in 1956, at the Republican National Convention, Yerger and his followers outmaneuvered the aging Black and Tan leadership and took control of the state party apparatus. They then began to build Mississippi's modern Republican Party.

Mississippi's Republicans believed that both national parties took the South for granted—or, more precisely, wrote it off—and sought to reverse that political calculus. They wanted a South involved in the highest reaches of government and sought to reorient the Republican Party away from its northeastern liberalism and toward a conservatism rooted in the South and West. Yerger and his colleagues in other states organized their parties around the single goal of electing Republicans to public office. In Mississippi, they achieved their earliest tastes of success in 1963, when Rubel Phillips, a lifelong Democrat from Alcorn County, was recruited to switch parties and run for governor as a Republican, and 1964, when Barry Goldwater was the GOP's presidential nominee. Phillips surprised even the most optimistic projections by earning almost 40 percent of the vote, and the news was even better in 1964, when Goldwater, one of only six Republican US senators to oppose passage of the 1964 Civil Rights Act, carried Mississippi with more than 87 percent of the total vote. His stunning victory allowed his coattails to help an unknown Republican candidate for Congress in Mississippi's 3rd District, Prentiss Walker, defeat the twenty-two-year Democratic incumbent, Arthur Winstead.

In 1966 Clarke Reed, a member of the State Executive Committee from Greenville, replaced Yerger as the party's chair. In 1972 Republicans Thad Cochran and Trent Lott were elected to the US House of Representatives. Three years later Republican gubernatorial candidate Gil Carmichael came within a few percentage points of defeating Cliff Finch. In Reed's final year as chair, 1976, the Mississippi Republican Party nearly disintegrated over the issue of whether to support Gerald Ford or Ronald Reagan as the party's presidential candidate. Mississippi ultimately surprised the nation by helping Ford secure the nomination, and the state became a battleground in the November election, though Democrat Jimmy Carter took both Mississippi and the presidency. Mississippi's Reagan supporters harbored hard feelings for many years afterward.

In 1978 Cochran moved from the US House to the Senate after the retirement of Mississippi's senior senator, James O. Eastland, defeating Democrat Maurice Dantin and independent Charles Evers. Cochran became Mississippi's first Republican senator since Bruce's departure in 1880. He has won reelection six times, most recently in 2014, and his office and his length of service have enabled him to eclipse the party chair as the state's most important Republican.

For the next twenty years, as senior Mississippi Democrats retired from Congress, Republicans took their places. Lott succeeded Sen. John Stennis in 1988. Roger Wicker succeeded Rep. Jamie Whitten in 1994. Chip Pickering succeeded Rep. Sonny Montgomery in 1996. On 31 December 2007, after Lott's resignation from the Senate, Wicker was named to the seat, and he won a 2008 special election

R

to fill the remainder of Lott's term as well as a full term in 2012.

And in the state elections of 1991, Republicans finally reached the goal for which they had worked since 1963. Vicksburg contractor Kirk Fordice recorded an upset victory over Democrat Ray Mabus to become the first Republican since 1875 to occupy the Governor's Mansion. Fordice was easily reelected in 1995. Though Ronnie Musgrove returned the office to Democratic hands in 2000, Republican Haley Barbour quashed Musgrove's 2003 reelection bid. Republicans have subsequently retained the office, with Barbour winning reelection in 2007 and Phil Bryant succeeding him in 2011. Bryant won reelection in 2015 with an overwhelming two-thirds of the popular vote.

Mississippi appears poised to remain solidly Republican for the foreseeable future. The state has backed the Republican presidential candidate in every election since 1980, and in 2016, both of the state's US senators and 3 of its 4 House members were Republicans. The GOP also held 8 of the state's 11 executive positions, 32 of the 52 seats in the State Senate, and 74 of the 122 seats in the State House of Representatives.

Jere Nash
Jackson, Mississippi

Andy Taggart
Madison, Mississippi

Ballotpedia website, ballotpedia.org; Harry S. Dent, *The Prodigal South Returns to Power* (1978); David J. Ginzl, *Journal of Mississippi History* (1980); Billy B. Hathorn, *Journal of Mississippi History* (1985); Neil R. McMillen, *Journal of Southern History* (May 1982); Jere Nash and Andy Taggart, *Mississippi Politics: The Struggle for Power, 1976–2005* (2006); Martha H. Wilkins, "The Development of the Mississippi Republican Party" (master's thesis, Mississippi College, 1965); Jules Witcover, *Marathon: The Pursuit of the Presidency, 1972–1976* (1977).

Revels, Hiram Rhoades

(1827–1901) Political Leader

On 25 January 1870 Adelbert Ames, the provisional governor of Mississippi, certified that the state legislature had elected Hiram Revels to the US Senate. On 23 February Revels presented his credentials, and two days later he was sworn into office as the first African American US senator. Visitors in the Senate galleries burst into applause, aware that history was being made, but there was opposition. Some white supremacist senators claimed that Revels had not been a citizen for the nine years required to join that body, as African

Hiram Rhoades Revels, ca. 1870 (Library of Congress, Washington, D.C. [LC-USZC4-681])

Americans had only received citizenship with the passage of the 1866 Civil Rights Act. Senator Charles Sumner of Massachusetts rose to refute that logic: "The time has passed for argument. Nothing more need be said. For a long time, it has been clear that colored persons must be Senators." The Senate then voted forty-eight to eight to seat Revels.

Revels arrived in the US Senate by a circuitous route. Born on 27 September 1827 in North Carolina, a slave state, of free parents of African and American Indian descent, he had been apprenticed to his brother, Elias, as a barber. When Elias died suddenly, Hiram found himself in Indiana, being educated at a Quaker seminary, and he became a Methodist minister in 1845. He settled in Baltimore as a church pastor and educator and with the outbreak of war in 1861 became deeply involved in the plight of the freed slaves. At this time he rejected attempts to force him to ride in smoking cars on trains and faced opposition in Missouri for "preaching the gospel to Negroes." Pursuing this mission, he moved to Vicksburg to help organize schools and churches among the former slaves. He also helped organize two regiments of black soldiers for service in the Union Army and served as chaplain to a black regiment.

At the end of the war Revels moved to Natchez, where he continued his Methodist religious and educational work. A contemporary account described him as "a tall, portly man, of light complexion; [with] benevolent features, a pleasant voice, and cultivated manners. He is thoroughly respected by his own people, and by the whites." Perhaps because of these qualities, Revels found it difficult to separate his religious work from politics and was elected to the position of city councilman and then state senator from Adams County in 1865. He described the excitement of political competition during Reconstruction in an 1869 letter: "We have but little money to carry on the canvass, but we are working day and night. Clubs are organized all over the State, and colored men meet in them once and sometimes twice a week, and receive instructions which no Democratic orator can remove from their minds. We are also meeting the enemy on the stump and he inevitably gets the worst of it.

I am working very hard in politics and other matters. We are determined that Mississippi shall be settled on a basis of justice and political and legal equality." Revels served in these positions with so much distinction that the state legislature selected him as the best candidate to represent Mississippi in the US Senate, where he filled out the final year (1870–71) of former Confederate president Jefferson Davis's term. During that time, Revels attempted to avoid friction with white southerners but also supported desegregation of the schools and railroads, spoke on behalf of the federal government's power to guarantee black voting rights in the South, and called on the US Military Academy at West Point to admit an African American cadet, Mississippi native Michael Howard.

When Revels's term ended in 1871 he returned to Mississippi to become president of Alcorn College, Mississippi's first college for black students. Though Gov. Ames dismissed Revels from the position in 1874, he returned to it two years later. His last significant act was to participate in the 1875 political revolt against Mississippi's carpetbag government, which he believed to be corrupt. Rejecting Ames and his associates, Revels converted to the Democratic Party. Continuing at Alcorn until his retirement, he never gave up his church work. He died at a church conference in Aberdeen, Mississippi, on 16 January 1901 and is buried in Holly Springs.

Mary Frances Marx
Southeastern Louisiana University

Eric Foner, *Freedom's Lawmakers: A Directory of Black Officeholders during Reconstruction* (1996); William C. Harris, *The Day of the Carpetbagger: Republican Reconstruction in Mississippi* (1978); National Archives and Records Administration website, http://archives.gov/exhibits/index.html; Julius Thompson, *Hiram Revels, 1827–1901: A Biography* (1973); US Senate, Historical Office website, www.senate.gov/artandhistory/history/minute/First_African_American_Senator.htm.

Rice, Jerry
(b. 1962) Athlete

Widely regarded as the greatest wide receiver and quite possibly the greatest football player ever, Jerry Lee Rice was born in Starkville, Mississippi, on 13 October 1962, the sixth of eight children of Joe Nathan Rice, a bricklayer, and Eddie B. Rice. Rice was raised in Crawford and attended B. L. Moor High School, where he ran track and field and played basketball and football. He accepted a scholarship to play Division I-AA football at Mississippi Valley State College in Itta Bena. In his sophomore year Rice teamed up with quarterback Willie Totten, a connection that became known as the Satellite Express. In 1984, Rice's senior season, he recorded 112 catches for 1,845 yards and 28 touchdowns, earning all-American honors from the Associated Press. He was named Most Valuable Player of the Blue-Gray Game, beating out numerous Division I players for the honor. In his forty-two-game college career, Rice caught 310 passes for 4,856 yards and 51 touchdowns.

While Rice's skills impressed pro scouts, he was not considered particularly fast. Still, in 1985 the San Francisco 49ers of the National Football League (NFL) thought highly enough of Rice to make him the third wide receiver chosen in the first round—the sixteenth pick overall. After some early struggles, Rice was named the league's Rookie of the Year. In 1986 he ranked second in the league in receptions and was named to the Pro Bowl, an honor he repeated every year until 1997, when he suffered a season-ending knee injury in the opening game.

In his third year Rice's 22 touchdown catches set an NFL record, and he led the league in scoring and was named Most Valuable Player. He received the same honor in Super Bowl XXIII, catching 11 passes for 215 yards and a touchdown and helping San Francisco beat the Cincinnati Bengals. In 1992 he broke Steve Largent's record of 100 receiving touchdowns. In 1993 he was named NFL Offensive Player of the Year after catching 98 passes for 1,503 yards and 15 touchdowns. In 1994 Rice broke running back Jim Brown's record of 126 career touchdowns with three scores against the Oakland Raiders. The next year he surpassed Art Monk's record for career receptions with 942 and broke James Lofton's record for career receiving yards with 15,123.

Prior to the 2001 season, after sixteen years in San Francisco, Rice signed with the Oakland Raiders. In 2002, when he was forty years old, he was again voted to the Pro Bowl after catching 92 passes for 1,211 yards and 7 touchdowns. Rice played for Oakland in 2003 and 2004 before being traded to the Seattle Seahawks in October. He then signed with the Denver Broncos but retired at the start of the 2005 season.

Rice played in a total of thirteen Pro Bowls and four Super Bowls. Among the NFL's all-time Top 50 players, Rice holds the league career marks for receptions (1,549), receiving yards (22,895), receiving touchdowns (197), and total touchdowns (207). In 1999 Mississippi Valley State renamed its football stadium in honor of Totten and Rice. Rice was inducted into the College Football Hall of Fame in 2006 and the Pro Football Hall of Fame four years later.

Rice and his wife, Jackie Mitchell Rice, are longtime residents of the San Francisco area, and his 127 Foundation supports numerous charitable organizations, among them Big Brothers and Big Sisters, the March of Dimes, and the Omega Boys Club of San Francisco. In 2005–6 he appeared on television's *Dancing with the Stars*, finishing second.

Stephen Budney
University of Pikeville

Jerry Rice website, www.jerryricefootball.com; *Official 2003 NFL League Record and Fact Book* (2003); Pro Football Reference website, www.pro-football-reference.com; Jerry Rice and Brian Curtis, *Go Long: My Journey Beyond the Game and the Fame* (2007); Jerry Rice and Michael Silver, *Rice* (1996).

Rice Cookery

Mississippi residents have developed a wide variety of ways to prepare rice. Methods range from simply boiling the grain cereal in water to complex composed dishes involving a variety of vegetables, meats, seafood, and seasonings. One common side dish, rice and gravy, is often listed on restaurant "meat-and-three" menus as a vegetable. The gravy is typically brown and derived from roast beef drippings. The practice of combining rice and beans, with or without meat, is also pervasive in the South. In Mississippi, red, black, and white beans are all blended with rice. Cajun-influenced red beans and rice can be found in all regions of the state, as can black beans and rice, a culinary contribution of Spanish-speaking cultures. The red rice of South Carolina and Creole rice of Louisiana are close cousins of what came to be known as Spanish rice, a popular suppertime meal in Mississippi after World War II. It is flavored with tomatoes, green pepper, and onions. "Boxcar" lima beans and butter beans frequently accompany rice in the Magnolia State. Hoppin' John, a type of bean pilaf, is made by cooking black-eyed peas, often in pork-seasoned broth, and mixing them with rice. In many parts of the South, Mississippi included, Hoppin' John is traditionally eaten on New Year's Day for good luck.

In recent years gumbos have become commonplace on Mississippi restaurant menus, and not just on the Coast. These stews are usually served atop a bowl of boiled rice. Mississippians have also readily adopted "dirty rice," another legacy of the South Louisiana Cajun culture. Some cooks, uncomfortable with the name, prefer to call it "rice dressing," but whatever the label, it, too, is a composed rice dish augmented by chopped chicken giblets.

Elementary schools in mid-twentieth century Mississippi regularly served plain boiled rice that children were expected to eat as a side dish with a sprinkling of sugar on top. Rice pudding, moistened with milk and sweetened with sugar, remains a popular dessert.

Mississippi is home to Chinese-style rice cookery as a legacy of the post–Civil War immigrants who were brought to the Delta in experiments to replace freed slaves on the plantations. A number of Chinese immigrants went into the grocery business. The first Chinese grocery in Mississippi likely opened in the 1870s. Chinese restaurants serving fried and steamed rice are found today in virtually every Mississippi community. Food historian John Egerton believed the first one was Greenville's How Joy, which opened in 1968.

The Delta is also home to a significant Lebanese and Syrian population whose ancestors came to the region in the late nineteenth century. Many of these immigrants got their start in business by selling dry goods door to door. A typical style of Lebanese rice cookery practiced in Delta kitchens involves browning broken pieces of vermicelli in butter and then boiling them with rice in water or broth.

Fred Sauceman
East Tennessee State University

Jackson Clarion-Ledger (10 September 2003); John Egerton, *Southern Food: At Home, on the Road, in History* (1987); Mississippi History Now website, http://mshistorynow.mdah.state.ms.us; Doreen Muzzi, *Delta Farm Press* (1 December 2000); Hal White, interview by Fred Sauceman (27 August 2003); Statista website, www.statista.com.

Rice Cultivation

Rice has been a major part of Mississippi agriculture only since the 1940s. It was first grown in Mississippi in the early nineteenth century and first grown in the Delta region around 1909. Planters discontinued production in the Delta, possibly because of the difficulty of working with animal power in the sticky clay soil. Modern rice production in Mississippi began in 1948 when Rex Kimbrell, Malcolm James, and Frank Unkel formed a partnership and planted about 300 acres near Greenville, in Washington County. The state's harvested acreage increased to 5,000 the next year and to 77,000 five years later. The US Department of Agriculture instituted acreage controls following the 1954 crop, and reducing the state's total harvested acres to 52,000 in 1955. Because Mississippi had no long-term history of rice production, federal acreage controls restricted the state's production for the next two decades. Following the elimination of controls in 1973, the amount of harvested acreage increased to 108,000 in 1974 and peaked at 335,000 acres in 1981. In 2013 Mississippi had just 122,641 acres of rice production, the lowest in recent history, though production rebounded to 187,000 acres in 2014 and 144,000 in 2015,

Young rice field, Quitman City (Photograph by David Wharton)

when Mississippi's 259 rice farms produced a crop valued at $132 million and the state ranked fifth in US rice production.

Rice production generally requires high average temperatures during the growing season, a plentiful supply of water, a smooth land surface with less than 1 percent slope to facilitate uniform flooding and drainage, and soil with good water-holding capacity. Rice production in Mississippi has been confined almost entirely to the Yazoo-Mississippi Delta basin, particularly Bolivar, Washington, Coahoma, and Sunflower Counties.

Much of Mississippi's early rice crop was produced by farmers who moved to the Delta from Louisiana, Arkansas, and Texas, but not all of their cultural practices proved adaptable. With the objective of determining the best varieties and cultural practices for the state, the Mississippi State University Delta Branch Experiment Station at Stoneville began a small research program in 1950. In response to efforts by the Delta Council, the Mississippi Rice Growers Association, and the Mississippi Agricultural Experiment Station, the Mississippi legislature in 1958 appropriated funds for a separate rice research project.

When rice production began in Mississippi, the state had no commercial drying, storage, or marketing facilities. Planters thus developed the practice of on-farm drying and storage. Although several commercial rice driers have subsequently been constructed, much of the rice crop is still dried and stored on the farm, providing planters with marketing flexibility. In the early 1970s the Mississippi Rice Growers Association constructed a small rice mill in Cleveland. A few years later both Uncle Ben's and Pacific International Rice Mills established rice mills in Greenville.

Much of the early success of the rice industry in Mississippi resulted from the leadership of the Mississippi Rice Growers Association, which formed in 1954. In 1981 the legislature created the Mississippi Rice Promotion Board, a grower-funded agency that promotes the industry through research, advertisement, promotions, education, and market development.

Joe E. Street
Mississippi State University

Pete Daniel, *Breaking the Land: Transformations of Cotton, Tobacco, and Rice Cultures since 1930* (1986); Rex Kimbrell, *Rice in Mississippi* (1987); Mississippi Rice Promotion Board website, rice.msstate.edu; Statista website, www.statista.com.

Richards, Beah
(1920–2000) Actress

Beulah Elizabeth Richardson was born in Vicksburg, Mississippi, on 12 July 1920. Her father, Wesley R. Richardson, was a Baptist minister; her mother, Beulah Molton Richardson, was a seamstress and an advocate of the Parent-Teacher Association. Richards graduated from Dillard University in New Orleans in 1948 and moved to New York City in 1950 to begin a career as a stage actress. Her first significant role came in 1956 as an eighty-four-year-old grandmother in Louis S. Peterson's Off-Broadway play, *Take a Giant Step*, and she reprised this role in the 1959 film version of the play.

Although frequently cast as a secondary character—a maid, a mother, or a grandmother—and often as a character much older than her actual age, Richards persevered. In 1965 she received a Tony nomination and a Theater World Award for her role in *The Amen Corner*. In 1967 she received Academy Award and Golden Globe nominations for Best Supporting Actress for her performance as the mother of Sidney Poitier's character in *Guess Who's Coming to Dinner*. Her role in *The Great White Hope* earned her a 1970 Image Award from the National Association for the Advancement of Colored People as Best Supporting Actress in a Motion Picture. Her final big-screen performance was as Baby Suggs in the 1998 film *Beloved*, starring Oprah Winfrey, for which Richards was nominated for an Image Award.

After the late 1960s, Richards performed primarily on television, with recurring roles on *ER*, *Designing Women*, *Hearts Afire*, *Beauty and the Beast*, *LA Law*, and numerous other shows. She received a 1998 Emmy Award as Outstanding Guest Performer in a Comedy Series for her appearance on *Frank's Place*; two years later, she was named Outstanding Guest Actress in a Drama Series for her role on *The Practice*. Too ill to attend the 2000 award ceremony in person, Richards received her statuette from actor-director LisaGay Hamilton, who later released a documentary about Richards's life, *Beah: A Black Woman Speaks*.

Richards died in Vicksburg on 14 September 2000. At her request, her ashes were scattered across a Confederate cemetery.

R

In addition to her lengthy acting career, Richards was active in the civil rights movement with others such as Paul Robeson and W. E. B. Du Bois. Because of her ties to black activists and Communist Party leaders, the FBI kept files on Richards from 1951 to 1972. She also wrote plays and poetry, and one of her poems, "Keep Climbing, Girls," was published as an illustrated children's book in 2006.

Teresa Arrington
Blue Mountain College

African American Registry website, www.aaregistry.com; LisaGay Hamilton, director, *Beah: A Black Woman Speaks* (2003); Internet Movie Database website, www.imdb.com; Beah Richards, *Keep Climbing, Girls!* (2006).

Riley, Franklin Lafayette, Jr.
(1868–1929) Historian

Historian and teacher Franklin Lafayette Riley Jr. was born in what was then Lawrence County, Mississippi, on 24 August 1868. His father, Franklin Lafayette Riley, was a successful farmer and merchant in Hebron who married Balsorah I. Weathersby while on furlough from the Confederate Army. Riley earned undergraduate and master's degrees from Clinton's Mississippi College in 1890 and 1891. While in college Riley met Fanny T. Leigh, a student at Clinton's Central Female Institute, and they married on 15 July 1891. They went on to have seven children.

One of numerous southern students welcomed into northern universities during the latter decades of the nineteenth century, Riley gained admittance in 1893 to the graduate program at Johns Hopkins University, where he thrived under the tutelage of Herbert Baxter Adams. Frustrated at the lack of historical resources within his native state, Riley wrote a dissertation on the origins of early American state senates, a topic that reflected Adams's influence. After receiving a doctorate in 1896, Riley returned to Mississippi, serving first as president of Fanny's alma mater, renamed the Hillman College for Young Women, and then accepting a position at the University of Mississippi. History had previously been an afterthought in the university's curriculum, taught by whoever had an opening. Riley became the first historian employed by the university and the first faculty member whose principal responsibility consisted of teaching history.

While he quickly became a key figure in the study of history at the university, perhaps Riley's longest-lasting influence in the state stems from his role in resuscitating its faltering historical society. Attempts to establish a historical society predated the Civil War, but all had become defunct, including the most recent effort, which had begun in 1890 but by 1897 had only nine members. With characteristic energy and optimism, Riley simply announced that the society would meet in January 1897 in Jackson. Skilled at persuasion and conscious of the importance of political regard, he solicited speakers to present papers and invited members of the state legislature to attend. The gathering was a modest success and resulted in more work and responsibility for Riley, who was elected the society's treasurer, a position he held for the next sixteen years.

At that first meeting, Riley assured all dues-paying members that they would receive subscriptions to the society's history journal. At the time of his promise, such a journal did not exist. Riley assumed the responsibility of procuring articles and editing the *Proceedings of the Mississippi Historical Society* for its first fourteen years, a span that saw the publication grow from little more than a record of antiquarian notes to a reputable journal of historical scholarship. Throughout this period, Riley continued to publish works exploring varied aspects of Mississippi's colonial past. Additionally, during this period of nearly frenetic activity, he also authored a textbook of Mississippi state history, with contributions on the Civil War and Reconstruction from former Confederate general Stephen D. Lee and James Wilford Garner. The textbook was immediately adopted throughout the state and went through numerous editions.

Certain that the society could not survive solely on membership dues, Riley persuaded the state legislature to provide modest funding. More important, that body appointed Riley to chair the Mississippi Historical Commission and charged it with surveying the state's historical resources and their well-being. The commission recommended the establishment of a permanent state-funded department of historical records and preservation, and the legislature responded in 1902 with the creation of the Mississippi Department of Archives and History. Encumbered with his teaching position and his essential role in the Historical Society, Riley nevertheless remained a trustee of the department for the next twelve years.

In 1914 Riley broke with the University of Mississippi. While the nature of the breach is not precisely known, his "political interference with University governance" was cited at the time as instrumental in the decision to go their separate ways. The breach could not have been terribly acrimonious, however, as the Law School awarded Riley an honorary degree in 1916. Moreover, the university students dedicated the 1914–15 yearbook to Riley, describing him as one "who never spoke but to inspire," "whose name will never be mentioned by an officer, student or friend of the University . . . without a deep sense of pride and gratitude for what he did for Mississippi."

Riley accepted a position at Washington and Lee College in Lexington, Virginia, and remained there with only brief interruptions for the rest of his life. In 1919 Riley spent a year teaching American history overseas at the American Expeditionary Forces University, in Beaune, France, and he spent the 1925–26 academic year teaching at the University of Southern California. In 1922 he published his last work of history, editing a collective memoir of the professors and students who had known and worked with Robert E. Lee during the former general's postwar tenure as president of Washington and Lee (known at the time as Washington College).

Riley died on 10 November 1929 in Lexington, Virginia.

John Neff
University of Mississippi

American Historical Review (January 1930); John Spencer Barrett, South Atlantic Quarterly (October 1902); Biographical and Historical Memoirs of Mississippi (1891); James B. Lloyd, ed., Lives of Mississippi Authors, 1817–1967 (1981); Albert Nelson Marquis, ed., Who's Who in America (1928); Ole Miss: The Official Yearbook of the University of Mississippi (1915); Howard D. Southwood, Journal of Mississippi History (October 1951); Charles S. Sydnor, Journal of Southern History (May 1937); Roger D. Tate Jr., "Franklin L. Riley: His Career to 1914" (master's thesis, University of Mississippi, 1971).

Rivers, Pearl (Eliza Jane Poitevent Holbrook Nicholson)

(1843–1896) Author and Publisher

Pearl Rivers, the pen name of Eliza Jane Poitevent Holbrook Nicholson, began public life as a poet but achieved prominence by becoming the first woman in the United States to own and publish an important daily newspaper, the New Orleans Picayune. Born in Gainesville, Mississippi, on 11 March 1843 (some sources say 1849), Eliza Jane Poitevent was one of eight children born to William J. Poitevent and Mary A. Russ Poitevent. In 1852 she went to live with an aunt and uncle on the banks of the Hobolochitto River, twenty-five miles away. With no playmates on the estate, Poitevent made friends with the birds and animals that populated the surrounding Piney Woods.

At age fifteen Poitevent went to the Amite Female Seminary in Liberty, Mississippi. When she graduated in July 1859, she had already taken Pearl Rivers as her pseudonym and embarked on a career as a poet. By 1869 she had two poems published in a southern anthology, and more began regularly appearing in the New York Home Journal, the New York Ledger, the New Orleans Times, and the New Orleans Picayune.

While visiting her maternal grandfather, Samuel Potter Russ, in New Orleans, Poitevent met the owner of the Picayune, Col. Alva Morris Holbrook. A short time later Holbrook invited her to join his staff as a literary editor for a salary of twenty-five dollars a week. Despite her family's objections that such work was not proper for a lady of her social standing, Poitevent accepted the position. She became the first woman in New Orleans and one of the first in the South to earn a living working on a newspaper.

In January 1872 Holbrook sold the paper to a group of New Orleans businessmen. The following May, the recently divorced Holbrook, age sixty-four, married the twenty-three-year-old Poitevent at her grandparents' home. When the Picayune began to fail under its new management, Holbrook reinvested, regaining control by 1874. However, he died on 4 January 1876, leaving Eliza Holbrook the Daily Picayune, its eighty thousand dollars in debt, and two hundred thousand dollars in lawsuits against the paper. She could declare bankruptcy and take the one thousand dollars the law allowed her as a widow, or she could attempt to restore the paper. Her family urged her to return to Mississippi, and for more than two months she weighed her options. But when the paper's longtime business manager, Englishman George Nicholson, promised his help, she decided to stay. In March 1876 Eliza announced the change of management and set forth her policies. While the Picayune would remain an independent journal free of political influence, it would seek to reach beyond its limited male readership to become a family paper. In June, Nicholson furthered his support by assuming a quarter interest in the paper.

In 1877, following the death of his first wife, George Nicholson and Eliza Holbrook, nearly thirty years his junior, married. With George overseeing business matters and Eliza in charge of content, the paper became a success, and by 1887 it was debt-free and turning a profit.

During the two decades the Picayune was under her direction, Eliza Nicholson inaugurated many features that became standard. Among the most significant was an expanded Sunday edition intended to appeal to a wide range of readers. In 1879 she introduced New Orleans's first society column, the Society Bee, which reported the week's social events. Other regular Sunday attractions included Woman's World and Work, Lilliput Land (for children), sports coverage, and comics.

The Picayune also regularly featured fashion, household hints, political commentary and cartoons, theater gossip, and reviews of books and art. Both the number of pictures and the amount of advertising increased. Beginning in 1894 the paper featured the "weather prophet"—a cartoon sketch of a dapper frog who would carry an umbrella or a fan to suggest the day's forecast. That year Eliza Nicholson also hired Elizabeth Meriwether Gilmer, who was soon famous as advice columnist Dorothy Dix. Nicholson also used the *Picayune* to campaign for social and governmental reform. The strong stand she took against mistreating animals in editorials and in a section, "Nature's Dumb Nobility," so influenced public opinion that in October 1888 New Orleans residents founded a chapter of the Society for the Prevention of Cruelty to Animals.

In 1873 Pearl Rivers published *Lyrics*, a collection of short poetry. Her next publications—two long dramatic monologues, "Hagar" and "Leah" that appeared in *Cosmopolitan* in 1883 and 1884—differed in tone and outlook from the early work. The change was not surprising: a decade in journalism had made Rivers a shrewd and capable businesswoman who wrote with passion and intensity.

George Nicholson died on 4 February 1896 from complications following an influenza outbreak; eleven days later, his wife, too, succumbed. During their time at the helm, the *New Orleans Picayune* had more than doubled in circulation and had become a newspaper with national importance.

Elizabeth Sarcone

Delta State University

Lamar Whitlow Bridges, *Journalism History* (Winter 1975–76); Thomas Ewing Dabney, *One Hundred Great Years: The Story of the Times-Picayune from Its Founding to 1940* (1944); Elsie S. Farr, *Pearl Rivers* (1951); James Henry Harrison, *Pearl Rivers: Publisher of the Picayune* (1932); Kenneth W. Holditch, *Louisiana Literature* (Spring 1987); Kenneth W. Holditch, in *Mississippi's Piney Woods: A Human Perspective*, ed. Noel Polk (1986); Kenneth W. Holditch, *Southern Quarterly* (Winter 1982).

Roberts, Robin
(b. 1960) Journalist

Robin Roberts, a broadcast journalist famous for her work on ABC News and ESPN, was born on 23 November 1960 in Tuskegee, Alabama, the fourth and youngest child of Lawrence Roberts, one of the famed Tuskegee Airmen during World War II, and Lucimarian Tolliver Roberts. The Roberts family moved to Mississippi when Robin was eight years old, living first in Biloxi and later in Pass Christian. During her senior year at Pass Christian High School, Roberts was an all-state basketball player and was selected by her classmates as Miss Pass Christian High. After graduating as salutatorian in 1979, Roberts enrolled at Southeastern Louisiana University in Hammond, where she starred on the Lady Lions basketball team, finishing in third place on

Robin Roberts, 2010 (Courtesy Heart Truth)

the school's all-time scoring list. She graduated cum laude in 1983 with a bachelor's degree in communications.

After obtaining a job as weekend sports anchor at WDAM-TV in Hattiesburg, she worked her way up the broadcasting ladder, moving to more visible positions at stations in larger markets: in 1984 Biloxi's WLOX-TV hired her as a sportscaster; in 1986 she joined the sports team at WSMV-TV in Nashville, Tennessee; in 1988 she became a sports reporter and anchor at Atlanta's WAGA-TV.

In 1990 Roberts joined cable sports network ESPN, headquartered in Bristol, Connecticut. She remained with the network for the next fifteen years, hosting its flagship program, *SportsCenter*; contributing to *NFL Primetime*; and providing reports and interviews from various sporting events. In addition, Roberts worked as a play-by-play commentator and host of the network's Women's National Basketball Association games and specials and covered the Winter and Summer Olympics. In 1995 she added ABC's *Good Morning America* to her duties, anchoring news reports from the studio and serving as a feature reporter.

In May 2005 Roberts left ESPN and became a coanchor of ABC News's *Good Morning America*, not only hosting the show from New York but covering events around the world, including the devastation Hurricane Katrina caused to the Gulf Coast area where she was raised.

In 2007–8 Roberts underwent surgery, chemotherapy, and radiation treatment for breast cancer, continuing to broadcast during this time. In 2012 she was diagnosed with myelodisplastic syndrome, a bone marrow disease. Her public announcement of her illness resulted in an 1,800 percent spike in the number of registered bone marrow donors. After a leave of absence from broadcasting during which she received a successful bone marrow transplant, Roberts returned to television in early 2013. In December of that year, she publicly acknowledged that she is gay.

Numerous organizations have recognized Roberts's status as a pioneer in women's sports and broadcasting, her role as a survivor of breast cancer and bone marrow disease, and her activism on behalf of gay rights. In 1994 she was inducted as a member of the Women's Institute on Sport and Education Foundation's Hall of Fame. Two years later Southeastern Louisiana University named her its Alumnus of the Year and she endowed a scholarship at the school; in 2011 the school retired her jersey. In July 2008 she received the Inspiration Award from the Women's National Basketball Association. In 2012 she was inducted into the Women's Basketball Hall of Fame and won a Peabody Award for her work on *Good Morning America*. ESPN honored her with its 2013 Arthur Ashe Courage Award, and the following year she received the Walter Cronkite Award for Excellence in Journalism. And in 2015 Equality Forum named her one of its thirty-one Icons of LGBT History Month. The Women's Basketball Coaches Association annually awards the Robin Roberts/WBCA Sports Communications Scholarship Award to a female student-athlete who is studying journalism or communications and is planning to attend graduate school. Roberts has also published four books: *From the Heart: Seven Rules to Live By* (2007); *From the Heart: Eight Rules to Live By* (2008); *My Story, My Song: Mother-Daughter Reflections on Life and Faith* (2012, coauthored with her mother); and *Everybody's Got Something* (2014).

Peggy W. Jeanes
Jackson, Mississippi

Good Morning America website, http://gma.yahoo.com; "Robin Roberts' Biography," http://abcnews.go.com/GMA/robin-roberts-biography/story?id=128237.

Robinson, Cleophus
(1932–1998) Gospel Musician and Minister

Cleophus Robinson left Mississippi as a teenager after working in the cotton fields outside his hometown of Canton. He carried a cardboard box with one pair of pants, a gray coat, and two shirts, and he had two dollars in his pocket. His travels took him first to Chicago, then to Memphis, and in 1957 to St. Louis, where he settled down as a minister and gospel musician. Robinson recorded dozens of albums and made national and international tours, all while working as the minister at the Bethlehem Baptist Church. By the 1970s he had at least two nicknames, the World's Greatest Gospel Singer and the King of Gospel Singers, and by the end of his career, Robinson had recorded at least seventy-five gospel albums.

Born in Canton on 18 March 1932, Robinson made his first recordings in Chicago in 1949. After he moved to Memphis he lived and sometimes sang with an uncle, Rev. L. A. Hamblin. Robinson's first popular single was "Pray for Me." Early in his life Robinson saw the potential of the media, starting a weekly radio program, *Hour of Faith*, in 1959 and a weekly television show that ran from 1964 to 1989. In the 1970s Robinson toured France, Spain, Italy, and Switzerland as well as numerous US locales. He was proud that he made a gospel album at the Missouri State Penitentiary and saw it a part of his mission to perform not only in elite settings such as New York's Carnegie Hall, where he sang with his family and church choir in 1975, but also to all- or mostly black audiences in small towns in the South and Midwest.

Robinson came from a family of singers and raised a singing family. His mother, Lillie, was a gospel singer, and he sang a great deal with his sister, Josephine James. He married Bertha Lou Thomas, a native of Mobile, Alabama, in 1956, and she and some of their six children became musicians as well, with Paul playing drums and Cleophus Jr. becoming a singer and recording artist.

Cleophus Robinson mixed his own gospel compositions with other songs. Seeing himself as part of the tradition exemplified by Mahalia Jackson, Robinson never performed secular music. Like many gospel songwriters he combined the need for individual salvation and the glory, beauty, and kindness of God with the transforming power God gave men and women and the eventual beauty and relief of the afterlife. He sometimes recorded and released his sermons and often recorded gospel songs live, so the give-and-take with an amen-shouting audience was part of the recording. Robinson sometimes used his place as a popular gospel performer to adopt a prophetic stance. As the United States approached its bicentennial in 1976, he took out an advertisement in *Jet* that declared, "For the nation to stand on its feet, it must get back on its knees." He proclaimed July 1976 a month of fasting in which people should eat only one meal a day and concentrate on prayer.

After the death of Cleophus Robinson in 1998, the Greater Bethlehem Baptist, with over five hundred members, called his son Paul Robinson to be its next minister.

Ted Ownby
University of Mississippi

Jason Ankeny, Malaco Records website, www.malaco.com; Greater Bethlehem Baptist Church website, www.greaterbethlehem.com; Anthony Heilbut, *The Gospel Sound: Good News and Bad Times* (25th anniv. ed., 1997).

R

Rodgers, Jimmie

(1897–1933) Country Musician

Jimmie Rodgers, described by many as the Father of Country Music, had two other nicknames during his career: the Singing Brakeman, which referred to his work on trains, and America's Blue Yodeler, which described one of his unique contributions to country music. Publicity photographs also portrayed Rodgers as a guitar-playing cowboy and as a sharply dressed man about town. These images help illustrate the range of Rodgers's musical interests.

James Charles Rodgers was born outside Meridian, Mississippi, on 8 September 1897. Since his father, Aaron Rodgers, worked on the Mobile and Ohio Railroad, Jimmie grew up traveling, especially after his mother, Eliza Rodgers, died when he was only five or six. From age fourteen until he was twenty-eight he worked, sometimes irregularly, as a brakeman or flagman on railroads, traveling through much of the South and Southwest.

Always interested in making music, Rodgers decided to see if he could earn a living from it after he contracted tuberculosis and discovered that railroad work made it hard to breathe. In 1924 Rodgers started singing in vaudeville and medicine shows. In 1927 he first performed on the radio in Asheville, North Carolina, and recorded his first songs in Bristol, Virginia. Although he made records for only six years, Rodgers recorded more than one hundred songs.

His songs were about three minutes long, and almost all featured Rodgers playing the guitar. Some had bands accompanying the singer, while others consisted entirely of Rodgers playing and singing. Part of Rodgers's uniqueness lay in the variety of his music, and part lay in his appealing voice. While most of his records were marketed as country or hillbilly music, he learned a great deal from the styles of Tin Pan Alley, the blues, and jazz, and some of his songs included Hawaiian ukuleles.

Jimmie Rodgers Museum, Meridian (Courtesy Visit Meridian)

Rodgers's most notable innovation was the blue yodel—blues songs in style and sound and lyrics with "yo-de-lay-hee-ho" between verses. He recorded thirteen blue yodels, and all are in the blues AAB format (saying a line twice and then following with a concluding line) and tell of trouble and sometimes violence between men and women. "T for Texas (Blue Yodel No. 1)" begins, "T for Texas, T for Tennessee / T for Texas, T for Tennessee / T for Thelma, that gal that made a wreck out of me." Later Rodgers sings that he is "gonna shoot poor Thelma / Just to see her jump and fall." Yodeling came from various sources—perhaps from cowboy songs or from the songs of travelers in the Swiss Alps—and Rodgers was not the first musician to yodel between verses of his songs, but he made it such a trademark that some people assume that country music always included yodeling.

Rodgers helped write many of his songs, sometimes by reworking older songs and often by writing a tune while another writer supplied the words. Sometimes he modified popular musical styles, but sometimes he was clearly singing about himself, as when he sang, "I had to quit railroading / It didn't agree at all." In "Hobo's Meditation," he asked, "Will there be any freight trains in heaven?" And when he sang "TB Blues" and "My Time Ain't Long," both he and his audience knew he was singing about his own illness.

Three themes dominated Rodgers's songs. One was movement—sometimes leading back home, sometimes not. Second was a sentimental picture of home life. Love and longing for mothers and fathers were common, as in "Daddy and Home" and "Down the Old Road to Home." Finally, he performed numerous songs about love that failed, whether because men or women left, because they cheated, or because they committed crimes and went to jail.

Two features of Mississippi life were especially important for Rodgers in songs such as "Mississippi Moon" and "Mississippi Delta Blues." First, working on trains gave him numerous stories about and insights into traveling people. He empathized with people on the move, in large part because he was one of them. This empathy was especially important during the Great Depression, when so many people had to travel in search of work. "Hobo's Meditation" and other songs portrayed sad men riding the trains from the point of view of a sympathetic narrator. Second, as a Mississippian, Rodgers likely grew up hearing more African American music than most other early country musicians.

In 1933, just six years after his recording career began, Rodgers took a train to New York for what would be his final recording session. He was so weak from tuberculosis that he had to rest on a cot between songs, and he knew death was coming. He died on 26 May, less than thirty-six hours after recording "Years Ago."

Rodgers was extraordinarily popular during his short lifetime and remains popular with generations of music fans. Numerous musicians have remade Rodgers's songs, especially "T for Texas" and "In the Jailhouse Now." He was the first performer inducted into the Country Music Hall of Fame in 1961, and in 1976 the Jimmie Rodgers Memorial Museum opened in his hometown of Meridian.

Ted Ownby
University of Mississippi

William Ivey, *This Is Jimmie Rodgers* (1973), liner notes; Jimmie Rodgers Memorial Museum website, www.jimmierodgers.com; Bill C. Malone, *Country Music U.S.A.* (1985); Bill C. Malone, *Don't Get above Your Raisin': Country Music and the Southern Working Class* (2002); Nolan Porterfield, *Jimmie Rodgers: The Life and Times of America's Blue Yodeler* (1991); Ben Wynne, *In Tune: Charley Patton, Jimmie Rodgers, and the Roots of American Music* (2014).

Rogers, Sulton
(1922–2003) Artist

Sulton Rogers was born on 22 May 1922 near Oxford, Mississippi, and attended school for only a few years. When he was young his father, a carpenter, taught him to carve, making small animals and canes. Rogers married for the first time at age nineteen and went on to father ten children by several different women. He abandoned his family and ultimately settled in Syracuse, New York, in 1952, and found a job working the night shift for Allied Chemical. He began carving again to fill the time.

His carvings are usually a hybrid of animals and people, such as a cat's or bird's head on a neatly dressed woman's body or a dog's head on the body of a man wearing a suit and tie. Most figures measure between twelve and fourteen inches tall and are painted. Rogers found his inspiration in his dreams, in memories of people and animals from his childhood in rural Lafayette County, and in people he met during his travels.

Rogers's witty creations often use satire to ridicule the human condition. His figures—singly or in couples or funeral or wedding scenes—are amusing and disturbing. For example, a pair of legs wearing tidy shoes emerges from a snake's mouth. The faces of his figures are sometimes walleyed or are twisted into grotesque grimaces, with noses and mouths curving toward the back of the head. Sometimes a bystander is two-headed, is visibly injured with blood dripping from an empty eye socket, or has three legs. Snakes emerge from mouths or wrap around breasts or legs. People grin or stick out their tongues.

Rogers also created explicitly sexual scenes and figures, often humorously outrageous. One dog-headed man has his pants down and is aroused as he clutches the third breast of woman with the head of an owl. One woman gives birth to a dog-headed baby and makes an obscene hand gesture while a doctor with devil horns looks on. Rogers's "ghost houses" or "haint houses" depict bodies in open caskets, snakes, and vampires. Often his figures have devil horns or are holding pitchforks. Some do not believe that animals have souls and therefore cannot be "haints," so Rogers's fusion of animal and human creatures has an even more disconcerting effect.

Rogers retired from Allied Chemical in 1984 and moved back to Mississippi, where he created hundreds of carvings and scenes and began to receive recognition as an artist. His work was included in major museum shows, among them *Black Art: Ancestral Legacy: The African Impulse in African-American Art* at the Dallas Museum of Art in 1989 and *Passionate Visions of the American South* at the New Orleans Museum of Art in 1995. His figurative sculptures are found in the permanent collections of the Smithsonian American Art Museum in Washington, D.C.; the University of Mississippi Art Museum; the American Visionary Art Museum in Baltimore; and the Billy R. Allen Folk Art Collection at the African American Museum in Dallas.

Rogers died on 5 April 2003 in Oxford.

Katherine Huntoon
Santa Ana, California

John Foster, *Folk Art Messenger* (2003); Robert V. Rozelle, ed., *Black Art: Ancestral Legacy: The African Impulse in African-American Art* (1989); Wilfrid Wood, *Folk Art Messenger* (1997); Alice Rae Yelen, ed., *Passionate Visions of the American South: Self-Taught Artists from 1940 to the Present* (1995).

Root, Lynn Green
(1954–2001) Painter

Painter Lynn Green Root's signature elements are kinetic lines and bold, assertive colors. Born in Jackson on 18 March 1954, Root was the daughter of artist Myra Hamilton Green, who was also her first teacher. Root received a bachelor's degree from the University of Mississippi, worked on a master of fine arts degree at the University of New Orleans, and completed additional study at Millsaps College and the University of Alabama as well as with noted New York School abstract expressionist Fred Mitchell. Root began exhibiting work at a young age and was first showcased to large audiences as part of the collegiate show at the 1975 Mississippi Arts Festival.

An artist whose personal vision was cast into such a variety of form and media that it is not easily categorized, Root's idiosyncratic technique and content are present in figurative paintings, in portraits, as illustration, and in narrative landscapes. When painting, Root often squirted paint from the tube directly onto the canvas and used sparkles, neon colors, and painted frames. Many have classified her work as neoexpressionistic or neoprimitive, while others have labeled it magical realism. Sensuous, spirited, and spiritual, her work alludes to sources as varied as Byzantine and Renaissance art. It is, in a word, exuberant. Museum curator René Paul Barilleaux described her technique as having an "incredible quality of line. That is her strongest formal element, always strong line work." Gallery curator David Lambert noted, "She creates forms, moods, emotions, portrays action, all through continuous line. . . . Sometimes it is as manic as anything could be; it takes your eye everywhere. You don't know where it stops or starts. Lynn is a standout consistently wonderful artist, based on her linear work. And, by the way, there is color!" Root's *Portrait of Johnny Langston* (1981) exemplifies her lively line work, bold color, unexpected quirkiness, and confidence. The portrait is a frenetic work. The subject's pale face is given depth by brushstrokes of pink, green, and blue shadows. Scratch lines in the paint create the pattern of his pink-and-aqua shirt and tie, adding a sketch-like quality. Set against a dark, marine blue background, the scratches, blotches, and obvious paint layers add an electricity to the leering Langston.

As evidenced by this and other works, Root exulted in the process of creation itself. Alongside her inclusion in *The Mississippi Story*, a 2007 exhibition at the Mississippi Museum of Art, her paintings have been exhibited at the Museum of American Illustration in New York, the Contemporary Arts Center in New Orleans, and elsewhere. She illustrated books for the University Press of Mississippi, and her portrait of dancer and arts enthusiast Thalia Mara hangs in Jackson's city auditorium, Thalia Mara Hall.

Root died on 6 March 2001.

Patti Carr Black
Jackson, Mississippi

Patti Carr Black, *Art in Mississippi, 1720–1980* (1998); Patti Carr Black, *The Lives and Art of Myra Hamilton Green and Lynn Green Root* (2009); Patti Carr Black, *The Mississippi Story* (2007).

Rose, Laura Martin
(1862–1917) Author

Laura Martin Rose served as the historian and president of the Mississippi Division of the United Daughters of the Confederacy (UDC) and wrote a textbook in which she defended the actions of the Ku Klux Klan. Rose also belonged to the Daughters of the Revolution (DAR) and the Mississippi Memorial Literary Association.

Born on 18 September 1862 outside Pulaski, Tennessee, Laura Marcella Martin married fellow Tennessean Solon Edward Franklin Rose, who became a planter in Lowndes County, Mississippi. They had three children. In 1909 Laura Rose published a pamphlet on the Ku Klux Klan, with proceeds from its sale supporting the construction of a Confederate monument at Jefferson Davis's Mississippi home, Beauvoir. In response to the popularity of this pamphlet, Rose wrote a textbook, *The Ku Klux Klan, or Invisible Empire* (1914), which she intended for southern children to read. The UDC endorsed the textbook at its 1913 national convention and advocated its use in southern schools. Rose echoed sentiments expressed by novelist Thomas Dixon and Dunning School scholars, arguing that African Americans, encouraged by carpetbaggers, terrorized law-abiding southern whites during Reconstruction and that the Klan sought to restore order and preserve the purity of the white race. According to Rose, the Klan committed acts of violence only after exhausting all other options. This interpretation constructed African American men as responsible for racial violence during Reconstruction. Rose believed that her work offered southern boys a model for proper behavior—that is, they should commit acts of violence if necessary to preserve justice and defend southern women from the advances of African American men.

In recognition of her efforts to preserve the southern past, Rose succeeded Mildred Rutherford as the historian-general of the UDC in 1916, but her tenure was cut short by her death on 6 May 1917.

J. Vincent Lowery
University of Wisconsin
at Green Bay

Karen Cox, *Dixie's Daughters: The United Daughters of the Confederacy and the Preservation of Confederate Culture* (2003); James B. Lloyd, ed., *Lives of Mississippi Authors, 1817–1967* (1981); Mrs. S. E. F. Rose Subject File, Mississippi Department of Archives and History.

Rosenwald Schools

The Rosenwald rural school building initiative was an important effort to enhance public education for African Americans in the early twentieth-century South. In 1912 Julius Rosenwald, onetime chair of Sears, Roebuck, and Company in Chicago, donated thirty thousand dollars to Tuskegee Institute and authorized Booker T. Washington to use the money to build six small schools in rural Alabama. They opened in 1913 and 1914. Inspired, Rosenwald in 1917 established the Julius Rosenwald Fund, a Chicago-based philanthropic foundation, to finance a major program to construct schoolhouses across the South. By 1928 one of every five rural schools for black students in the region was a Rosenwald School, and they accommodated one-third of the region's rural black schoolchildren and teachers. By the end of the initiative in 1932, Rosenwald had spent $28,408,520 to construct 4,977 schools, 163 shop buildings, and 217 teachers' homes to aid 663,615 students in 883 counties in 15 states. Mississippi's 637 Rosenwald-assisted buildings trailed only North Carolina. Until the late 1960s and early 1970s, the Rosenwald Schools served as the only black primary and secondary educational facilities in many parts of the South.

Rosenwald initially provided grants to specific individuals and to support educational and social service institutions in the South, believing that his philanthropy and others should serve as seed money, encouraging governments and communities to take responsibility for necessary programs and services. He and Rosenwald Fund organizers saw the building program as providing southern states with an incentive to meet their responsibility for respectable public schools for black children, and by 1920 the fund's Southern Office worked to create exemplary rural schools. To receive funds, schools had to meet specific minimum standards for site size and length of school term and have new blackboards and desks for each classroom as well as two sanitary privies. The Rosenwald Fund would increase its grants if county school boards lengthened the black students' school year and provided better teacher pay. Encouraged, county school boards instituted taxes to help finance the schools and incorporated them into the public school system. The Rosenwald Fund also subsidized radios to help students keep abreast of current events, school libraries with books on African American history and culture, and school transportation. Between 1920 and 1928, the fund supported the construction of nearly five hundred schools each year.

The schools ranged from small, one-teacher units to seven-teacher facilities that offered instruction from first grade through high school, often with an emphasis on industrial education. In the program's early years, wooden two-teacher and three-teacher structures commonly appeared. By the mid-1920s, larger brick schools were built. The schools had modern architectural designs with high ceilings and large windows, allowing natural light to pour into classrooms that lacked electricity.

Local support provided the crucial component of the Rosenwald Schools' success. Principals, teachers, ministers, students, and parents gathered to clear land; renovate, clean, and paint the buildings; improve the grounds; and raise and allocate money for other projects. African Americans worked to earn funds to match the Rosenwald grants, raising money at churches and fraternal lodges and donating some of their scarce income from farming, efforts that strengthened local people's commitment. As rural African Americans helped themselves, they became the dynamic force behind the Rosenwald program and the architects of its significance. The schools became community centers, hosting sporting events, public meetings, dramatic performances, and classes on farming techniques, and instilled a work ethic and community values in parents and students.

Even though the Rosenwald program did not solve the South's schooling problems, it confronted the racism behind segregation by compelling southern states to take more interest in education. The schools' cost-efficient designs encouraged officials to escalate vocational education and public school infrastructure for both white and black students. Today, many of the schools have fallen into disrepair and require conservation. In 2002 the National Trust for Historic Preservation placed Rosenwald Schools on its list of endangered sites, and in 2011 it included the schools in its portfolio of National Treasures—nationally significant but threatened historic structures.

Only a few Rosenwald buildings are known to survive in Mississippi: Bay Springs School, Forrest County (1925); Brushy Creek School, Copiah County (ca. 1930); Bynum School, Panola County (1926); Coahoma Agricultural High School (ca. 1930; now Coahoma Community College); Drew School, Sunflower County (1929); Hollandale School, Washington County (1924; only a section survives, and it has been extensively altered); Marks School, Quitman County (1922); Moorhead School-teacher's House, Sunflower County (1932); Nichols Elementary School, Canton, Madison County (1927); Oak Park Principal's Home and Girls' Dormitory, Laurel, Jones County (1928); Pantherburn School, Sharkey County (1927; altered, now serves as a church); Pass Christian (Randolph) School, Pass Christian, Harrison County (1928); Prentiss Institute, Prentiss, Jefferson Davis County (1926); Rose Hill School, Sharkey County (1922; badly deteriorated); Sherman Line School, Amite County (1928); Swiftown School, Leflore County (1921; may not be a Rosenwald School); Walthall County Training (Ginntown) School, Walthall County (1920); John White Schoolteacher's House, Forrest County (1925).

William P. Hustwit
Birmingham Southern University

James D. Anderson, *Black Education in the South, 1860–1935* (1988); James D. Anderson, *History of Education Quarterly* (Winter 1978); Jennifer Baughn, Mississippi History Now website, http://mshistorynow .mdah.state.ms.us; Tom Hanchett, Rosenwald Schools website, www .rosenwaldplans.org; Mary Hoffschwelle, *The Rosenwald Schools of the American South* (2006); Jennifer Nardone, "The Rosenwald School Building Program in Mississippi, 1919–1931" (PhD dissertation, University of Mississippi, 2009); National Trust for Historic Preservation website, www.preservationnation.org; National Trust for Historic Preservation, National Treasures website, https://savingplaces.org/national-treasures #.V119T5ErKM-; Betty Jamerson Reed, *The Brevard Rosenwald School: Black Education and Community Building in a Southern Appalachian Town, 1920–1966* (2004); Jerry Wayne Woods, "The Julius Rosenwald Fund School Building Program: A Saga in the Growth and Development of African-American Education in Selected West Tennessee Communities" (PhD dissertation, University of Mississippi, 1995).

Rowan Oak, Oxford, home of William Faulkner beginning in 1930 (Photograph by James G. Thomas, Jr.)

Rowan Oak

Rowan Oak is the Oxford, Mississippi, home where William Faulkner lived from 1930 until his death in 1962. Today it is a house museum for visitors interested in Faulkner's life.

The property that eventually became Rowan Oak was a US land patent given to a Choctaw, E-Ah-Nah-Yea, in 1832. E-Ah-Nah-Yea deeded the property to a land company in 1836, and Robert Sheegog bought it in December 1844. Sheegog built the house, and his family lived there until 1872, when John M. Bailey purchased it and the grounds. Members of the Bailey family resided there until 1923. Faulkner bought what was known as the Bailey Place in 1930 and renamed it Rowan Oak the following year. The University of Mississippi rented the house from his widow, Estelle Faulkner, after his death. When she died in 1972, the university purchased the house from Jill Faulkner Summers, William and Estelle's daughter.

Sheegog built three buildings still standing at Rowan Oak: the post oak barn, a detached kitchen, and the main house. He also built servants' quarters, which were in ruin by 1910. Evidence suggests that the post oak barn served as a living structure from 1844 until 1848, when the Sheegog family first occupied the main house. The post oak barn originally had two floors, but only the ground floor remains today, with two main stable areas, a corn crib, and a hay loft. The detached kitchen, which consists of two rooms with a central chimney, remained in daily use until 1910, when an indoor kitchen was added to the main house.

The main house is a two-story clapboard house in a modified primitive Greek Revival design, with four Doric columns that support the pediment above the porch. Plans for the house were made by William Turner of Oxford. It was originally L-shaped, with a central entryway flanked on the east by two rooms with two rooms above and on the west by one room with one room above. Above the entryway was a landing leading to the balcony.

Faulkner rebuilt the servants' quarters as a small house, using the two existing chimneys as his guide. A single-story clapboard-sided house with a hallway running down the middle, it has two rooms, a small kitchen, and a bathroom. From 1930 to 1940 the house served as a home for Caroline "Mammy Callie" Barr, a former slave who had helped to raise Faulkner and his brothers as well as his daughter, Jill. From 1940 to 1984 the house was inhabited by Faulkner's groom, Andrew Price; his wife, Chrissy, who served as the Faulkners' housekeeper; and later their son, John. In 1957 Faulkner added a barn to Rowan Oak and stabled his horses there. He took great pride in having constructed the building by himself.

The original landscaping at Rowan Oak consisted of an alley of cedar trees and a concentric circle garden opposite the house. During the Bailey era the landscaping was allowed to expand to include the twenty-nine acres of woods attached to the back of the property. Faulkner maintained the spirit of the Bailey era by allowing self-seeded trees and wild vines to flourish. He also built a brick wall on the east side of the property and designed and maintained a small maze garden made from English tea roses and privet.

The house contains much of the Faulkner family's original furnishings, and both the house and grounds are open to visitors.

William Griffith
Rowan Oak, University
of Mississippi

Jane Isbell Haynes, *William Faulkner, His Lafayette County Heritage: Lands, Houses, and Businesses* (1992); Thomas Hines, *William Faulkner and the Tangible Past: The Architecture of Yoknapatawpha* (1996); Rowan Oak website, www.rowanoak.com.

Rowland, Dunbar
(1864–1937) Archivist and Historian

Dunbar Rowland directed the Mississippi Department of Archives and History from its founding in 1902 until his death. Born in Oakland, in Yalobusha County, Mississippi, on 25 August 1864, Rowland was the youngest of four sons of William Brewer Rowland and Mary Judith Bryan Rowland. Educated at private schools in Memphis and Oakland, Rowland earned an undergraduate degree from Mississippi A&M College (now Mississippi State University) in 1886 and a law degree from the University of Mississippi (1888). Rowland then practiced law, first in Memphis and later in Coffeeville, Mississippi, until 1902.

Though Rowland had no professional historical training, the Board of Trustees of the newly established Mississippi Department of Archives and History (MDAH) selected him in March 1902 to serve as the agency's first director. Rowland spent the bulk of his first decade at the MDAH collecting, organizing, and publishing archival materials. He traveled to England, France, Spain, and Cuba to transcribe documents and acquired material held in private hands closer to home. Mississippi became one of the first states to maintain a government-administered archives: in Massachusetts and other states, private historical societies or individuals held archival materials. The MDAH's design and administration, which Rowland labeled the Mississippi Plan, provided a model for state archives elsewhere in the South. Under Rowland's direction, the MDAH acquired and preserved manuscripts and other materials; maintained a library, museum, and other historic sites; and promoted research and publication, including an annual volume of edited primary and scholarly material. Rowland was also active in the Mississippi Valley Historical Association, serving as its president in 1915–16, as well as in other professional historical organizations.

Rowland's interests covered the state's history from the colonial period through the early twentieth century, although he viewed his work with Confederate records and the Confederate years as his most important. His output as an editor, encyclopedist, and historian was formidable, totaling more than forty volumes. Among his works are a ten-volume edition of the papers of Jefferson Davis (*Jefferson Davis: Constitutionalist*, 1923) as well as multivolume editions of materials from Mississippi's French, British, and territorial periods; the correspondence of W. C. C. Claiborne, governor of the Mississippi Territory from 1801 to 1803; an encyclopedia of the state (1907); and a two-volume history, *Mississippi: The Heart of the South* (1925). He also edited and published an array of statistical and biographical directories containing sketches of the state's judges and legislators and information about the state during the Civil War.

By the standards of his day, Rowland's publications were sound and well-received, although his sympathies, especially with Mississippi's Confederate experience, are apparent. Some of his works, such as the encyclopedia and biographical and statistical registers, remain useful sources of information on early twentieth-century Mississippi. But Rowland shared the racial perspective of most of his white contemporaries, giving little attention to the history of black or female Mississippians. As a whole, Rowland's work on Mississippi promotes a favorable, honorable, and progressive view of the state and its leading men.

Rowland, like other historians, campaigned for the creation of the National Archives in Washington, D.C. When it was established in 1934, however, his hopes of becoming its director were not fulfilled.

In 1906 Rowland married his widowed first cousin, Eron Opha Moore Gregory. She wrote a number of books, among them a two-volume biography of Jefferson Davis's wife, Varina Howell Davis (1927–31), and a history of Andrew Jackson's 1812 campaign in the Mississippi Territory (1926). She administered the MDAH when her husband was away and collaborated with him on a variety of projects, especially after his health began to decline. After her husband's death, she served briefly as acting director of the MDAH.

Rowland died on 1 November 1937 and was buried in Jackson's Cedarlawn Cemetery. On 1 January 1938 William D. McCain succeeded Rowland at the helm of the MDAH. Rowland's work exemplifies the period when southerners embraced and sought to shape broader professional trends in historiography and archival methods, seeing that work as useful in promoting a favorable image of the region's past and present.

Trent Brown
Missouri University of Science and Technology

Ray Allen Billington, *American Historical Review* (April 1973); Patricia Galloway, *American Archivist* (January 2006); Mississippi Department of Archives and History, Dunbar Rowland—Death Subject File; Lisa Speer and Heather Mitchell, *Provenance* 22 (2004).

Ruffin, Susie B.

(1908–1989) Activist

Susie Bolden Ruffin was born on 25 May 1908 and was active in civil rights efforts in Laurel throughout her life. In 1964 she served as an organizing member of both the Student Nonviolent Coordinating Committee (SNCC) and the Mississippi Freedom Democratic Party (MFDP). Traveling with Fannie Lou Hamer and Unita Blackwell, Ruffin worked to energize the MFDP and to register black voters.

Ruffin started the *Freedom Democratic Party Newsletter* and served as its editor from 1965 to 1967. Originally circulated as a SNCC pamphlet to publicize opposition to US involvement in Vietnam, the *Freedom Democratic Party Newsletter* grew into a bimonthly publication of between three and twelve pages that served as the MFDP's main organ. Each newsletter covered a range of issues, including information and tips for voter registration drives; reports on violence and arson; news of organizing meetings for the Deacons of Defense, the Poor People's Corporation, and other groups; and updates on school integration efforts. As editor, Ruffin frequently wrote rousing and pointed calls to action. In July 1965, following the MFDP's failed effort to unseat the white Democratic Party delegates at the Atlantic City Convention, she chided readers to keep the faith: "The Freedom Democratic Party has shaken the foundation of constitutional government in our nation and the white supremacists of Mississippi are afraid they will be left out on a limb that is being hacked from the political tree." Ruffin also championed the efforts of the poor, who took great risks to participate in movement activities, contrasting these black Mississippians to the "middle class urban people" and "Negro businessmen, teachers, and wealthy ministers" who sought change through the National Association for the Advancement of Colored People, which she believed was out of touch with the experience of the majority of the state's African Americans, especially those living in poverty in the Delta. In November 1965 Ruffin accompanied Russ Benedict of the US Department of Agriculture on a tour of impoverished areas in an effort to secure federal aid for the Poor People's Corporation.

The Mississippi State Sovereignty Commission closely monitored Ruffin's activities. In 1965 the commission and others accused the Child Development Group of Mississippi of wrongdoing because of its ties with the MFDP and other movement organizations. A Child Development Group staff member was accused of using a Head Start car to drive Ruffin to speaking engagements in the Delta.

Ruffin died on 12 May 1989. A Laurel, Mississippi, street is named in her honor.

Kathryn McGaw York
University of Mississippi

Chana Kai Lee, *For Freedom's Sake: The Life of Fannie Lou Hamer* (1999); Elizabeth Sutherland Martínez, ed., *Letters from Mississippi* (1965; 2002); Mississippi Freedom Democratic Party newsletter, Department of Archives and Special Collections, J. D. Williams Library, University of Mississippi; Mississippi Department of Archives and History, Sovereignty Commission Online website, www.mdah.ms.gov/arrec/digital_archives/sovcom/.

Runnels, Hiram G.

(1796–1857) Ninth Governor, 1833–1835

In 1831 Hiram Runnels lost the office of governor by the narrowest margin in Mississippi history, 247 votes. Two years later he won the office by the narrowest margin in the state's history, 558 votes. And in 1835 he lost again, by just 426 votes, a defeat attributed at least in part to an emotional outburst he launched against one of his opponents. The excitable and volatile Runnels also fought a duel with a Jackson newspaper editor and struck Gov. Alexander McNutt with a walking cane on a downtown street in Jackson.

Runnels was born on 15 December 1796 in Hancock County, Georgia, and migrated to Mississippi, settling near Monticello in Lawrence County. In 1822, when the legislature appointed him state auditor, Runnels moved to Jackson. He served as auditor until his election to the State Senate from Hinds County in 1830. He sided with Pres. Andrew Jackson during the tariff controversy of 1832, and his close identification with Jackson brought substantial support that enabled Runnels to win the governorship in a May 1833 special election. Although the legislature had authorized the new governor to assume the office immediately, confusion existed about when his term should actually begin, and Runnels did not take office until 20 November 1833, as specified in the new 1832 constitution.

During Runnels's administration the state militia was reorganized and enlarged, and sixteen new counties were created from the lands in North Mississippi that had been ceded by the Choctaw and Chickasaw in 1830 and 1832.

Runnels ran for reelection in 1835 but on 2 November was defeated by Charles Lynch. Eighteen days later—exactly two years after his inauguration—Runnels considered his term to have expired and vacated the office. But the legislature had moved the inauguration of the governor and the opening of the next legislative session to January 1836. With the legislature not in session, there was no president of the Senate to succeed Runnels. Mississippi remained without a governor for thirteen days, until the secretary of state called a special session of the Senate to elect a president who could assume the office of governor. The Senate convened on 3 December and elected John A. Quitman, who served until Lynch's inauguration on 7 January 1836.

Runnels served as president of Jackson's Union Bank from its creation in 1838 until it failed three years later. In July 1840 he not only dueled with a newspaper editor who impugned his banking skills but also attacked McNutt, another Runnels critic. Runnels subsequently moved to Texas, where he remained active in politics and served in the state legislature. While a member of the Texas Senate, Runnels died on 17 December 1857.

David G. Sansing
University of Mississippi

Mississippi Official and Statistical Register (1908, 1912); Dunbar Rowland, *Encyclopedia of Mississippi History*, vol. 2 (1907).

Rural Electrification and Electric Power Associations

Electric power associations are a unique form of electric utility, serving about half of Mississippi's electric meters. Each electric power association is a not-for-profit cooperative owned and governed by the consumers it serves. Consumers become members of the cooperative by paying a membership fee and applying for electric service.

Twenty-six electric power associations provide electricity to more than 1.6 million Mississippians, with service to more than 731,000 electric meters through some 90,800 miles of energized lines. Their combined service territories comprise about 85 percent of the state's land mass. With one exception, all of the electric power associations are distribution cooperatives—that is, they purchase wholesale electricity for distribution to residential, commercial, and industrial members. South Mississippi Electric Power Association, however, is a generation and transmission cooperative, the wholesale power provider for eleven electric power associations serving South Mississippi and the Delta. Fourteen electric power associations serving central and northeastern Mississippi purchase wholesale power from the Tennessee Valley Authority.

Electric power associations grew from grassroots efforts initiated by rural Mississippians—mostly subsistence farmers—in the mid-1930s. At the time, electricity was available to less than 1 percent of Mississippi's farms and only 10 percent nationwide. Farm families labored without electric water pumps, augers, washing machines, lights, or fans. Farmers milked cows before sunrise by the light of kerosene lanterns. The lack of electricity deterred economic growth and escape from a substandard quality of life. With no running water or refrigeration, rural Mississippians suffered high rates of illnesses associated with poor sanitation and bacteria in perishable foods. Investor-owned electric utilities serving cities and towns were unwilling to extend service to sparsely populated rural areas because of the high costs associated with construction and the probability of a low return on investment.

Prospects for rural electrification improved when Pres. Franklin D. Roosevelt became interested in encouraging farmers to form pools to buy power at affordable rates. To that end, he created the Rural Electrification Administration (REA) in 1935 and signed the Rural Electrification Act of 1936. The REA spurred farmers to begin forming not-for-profit electric cooperatives to take advantage of the agency's low-cost loans to finance construction of electrical distribution facilities. The REA also provided technical and managerial guidance to farmers inexperienced in running electric utilities.

Mississippi was an early leader in America's rural electrification. The nation's first rural electric cooperative, the Alcorn County Electric Power Association, was an experimental project established by the Tennessee Valley Authority in Corinth in 1934. The following year Amory's Monroe County Electric Power Association became the first electric cooperative to secure an REA loan and begin operations.

Today's electric power association members include residential developments, shopping centers, industrial parks, hospitals, agricultural enterprises, military bases, and schools. Electric power associations have expanded their services to include economic development efforts, youth programs, electrical safety education, energy management, and community projects. Electric power associations serve an average of only eight consumers per mile of line, compared to the national average of thirty-two for investor-owned utilities and forty-one for municipal-operated systems.

Through membership in the Electric Power Associations of Mississippi, electric power associations share costs and labor associated with emergency power restoration, government relations, employee training, job safety, loss control, economic development, and other services. The organization also produces *Today in Mississippi*, a monthly with the largest circulation of any publication in the state.

Debbie H. Stringer
Electric Power Association
of Mississippi

D. Clayton Brown, *Electricity for Rural America: The Fight for the REA* (1980); Richard Pence, ed., *The Next Greatest Thing* (1984); Winnie Ellis Phillips, *Rural Electrification in Mississippi, 1934–1970* (1985); Amity Shlaes, *The Forgotten Man: A New History of the Great Depression* (2007).

R

Rush, Bobby (Emmit Ellis Jr.)

(b. 1940) Blues Musician

Composer, songwriter, guitarist, and harmonica player Bobby Rush pioneered an original form of blues music he dubbed "folk funk," a blending of classic blues lyrics, modern street talk, and bedroom humor mixed with an insistent, driving blues funk rhythm. *Rolling Stone* magazine named Rush, a tireless businessman, promoter, and entertainer, the King of the Chitlin' Circuit following his 2003 appearance in Martin Scorsese's blues documentary series on PBS.

The son of a preacher, Bobby Rush was born Emmit Ellis Jr. near Homer, Louisiana, on 10 November 1940. He grew up learning music and singing in his father's church in Pine Bluff, Arkansas. In 1953 Rush moved with his older brother to Chicago, where he made a name for himself on the West Side blues scene by blending a comedic lyrical approach influenced by Louis Jordan with the driving rhythms of the "folk-funk" blues sound. In the early 1960s Rush fronted bands that included blues notables Luther Allison and Freddie King. His first single appeared on Kem Records in 1961, followed by tracks such as 1964's "Someday" for Jerry Murray's Jerry-O label. He continued cutting 45s throughout the 1960s on Salem, Palos, Starville, Checker, and ABC.

Rush's first commercial hits came with "Chicken Head" and "Mary Jane," produced in Chicago in 1971 for Galaxy Records. Rush also had success with 1973's "Bow-Legged Woman, Knock-Kneed Man." He rounded out the decade recording singles for Sedgrick, Jewel, Warner Brothers, and London. In 1979 Rush signed a recording contract with Leon Huff and Kenny Gamble's Philadelphia International Records. While there, Rush recorded his first full-length album, *Rush Hour*, which produced the singles "I Wanna Do the Do" and "I Can't Find My Keys."

In the early 1980s Rush, like many of his contemporaries among Chicago's soul artists, moved back South. Settling in Jackson, he signed on to James Bennett's LaJam label, where his music steadily became funkier and his lyrics more bawdy. His tenure with LaJam produced five albums between 1981 and 1985. Rush moved to Waldoxy in the mid-1990s and signed with Urgent! Records, and subsequent albums included 1995's *One Monkey Don't Stop No Show*, 1997's *Lovin' a Big Fat Woman*, and 2000's *Hoochie Man*.

Rush was injured in an April 2001 tour bus crash that killed band member Latisha Brown. Rush recovered and in 2003 partnered with Greg Preston to form the Deep Rush label. Later that year Rush released the *Live at Ground Zero* DVD and CD along with the album *Undercover Lover*. Other recordings for Deep Rush include *Folk Funk* (2004), *Night Fishin'* (2005), *Raw* (2007), *Blind Snake* (2009), and *Show You a Good Time* (2011). His *Down in Louisiana* (2013)

and *Decisions* (2014) received Grammy Award nominations; *Down in Louisiana* also received a Blues Music Award. Rush continues to tour extensively throughout the United States and to play blues and soul festivals around the world, including Mississippi, where he is a frequent and exceptionally popular performer.

Cale Nicholson
Fayetteville, Arkansas

Vladimir Bogdanov, Chris Woodstra, and Stephen Thomas Erlewine, eds., *All Music Guide to the Blues: The Definitive Guide to the Blues* (2003); William Cochrane, Bill Ferris, Peter Lee, and Jim O'Neal, *Living Blues* (January–February 1989); Preston Lauterbach, *Living Blues* (November–December 2003); Robert Pruter, *Living Blues* (January–February 1989); Bobby Rush website, bobbyrushbluesman.com.

Russell, Irwin

(1853–1879) Poet

Irwin Russell was born on 3 June 1853 in Port Gibson, Mississippi. His father, William McNab Russell, was a physician, while his mother, Elizabeth Allen Russell, was an instructor at Port Gibson Female College. Shortly after his birth the family moved to St. Louis, returning to Port Gibson at the outbreak of the Civil War. At the end of hostilities the family moved back to St. Louis, where Russell graduated from the University of St. Louis in 1869. He later returned to Port Gibson and began studying law with Judge Lemuel N. Baldwin.

During the time of his law study, Russell received local attention for the creativity and wit of several poems he published in the *Port Gibson Standard*. For the next decade his Mississippi-based poems were regular features in such national literary magazines as *Scribner's Monthly*, *Appleton's Magazine*, *Century*, and *Puck*, where they appeared under a variety of pseudonyms, including Job Case. His literary popularity was largely based on his ability to write poems in dialect, such as the brogue of working Irishmen and the lilt of the Scots tongue. Most noteworthy were his poems set in the dialect of the recently emancipated Mississippi slaves. Chance encounters with freed slaves on the street, songs in the plantation housing quarters, and simple descriptive dialogue became exotic living language transcribed in the tongue and tense of the speakers. Best known was "Christmas Night in the Quarters," a poetic reenactment of a Christmas celebration Russell overhead on the Jefferies Plantation in Coahoma County. A portion of that extended poem is frequently anthologized as "De Fust Banjo," telling the story of the banjo's creation and stringing the instrument with hair from an opossum's tail. Russell's interpretation of the colloquial language and expressions of the former slaves became his legacy to early African American dialect literature.

During the yellow fever pandemic of 1878 Russell helped his father care for fever-stricken locals when hundreds were ill and scores died. In December 1878 he moved to New York to further his writing career but became ill and homesick within just a few months. After his father died of yellow fever in April 1879, Russell hired on as a coal tender aboard the sea freighter *Knickerbocker*, earning his passage back to New Orleans by August. He was too proud to return to Port Gibson in his penurious condition, so friends assisted him in getting a job as the editor of the All Sorts column at the *New Orleans Times*. On 23 December 1879, wracked by pneumonia and fever, Irwin Russell died in his rented room on Franklin Street, a mere twenty-six years old.

In 1888 friends gathered and published his poems. In 1907 the Mississippi Teachers Association raised funds to have a sculptor create a marble bust of Russell. It was placed in the State Capitol in 1908.

Jeffrey Klingfuss
Jackson, Mississippi

William Malone Baskerville, *Southern Writers: Biographical and Critical Studies*, vol. 1 (1897); Taylor Hagood, Mississippi Writers website, http://mwp.olemiss.edu//dir/russell_irwin/; Carl Holliday, *A History of Southern Literature* (1906); Hollis B. Todd, "An Analysis of the Literary Dialect of Irwin Russell and a Comparison with Spoken Dialect of Certain Native Informants of West Central Mississippi" (PhD dissertation, Louisiana State University, 1965); James Wilson Webb, in *Lives of Mississippi Authors, 1817–1967*, ed. James B. Lloyd (1981).

Russell, Lee Maurice

(1875–1943) Fortieth Governor, 1920–1924

While a student at the University of Mississippi, Lee Russell was a leader in the movement to abolish fraternities. Later, as a member of the state legislature from Lafayette County, he introduced a 1912 bill to prohibit secret and exclusive societies at the public institutions of higher learning. Russell's antifraternity law was enacted and remained in effect for fourteen years. As governor, Russell also served as president of the Board of Trustees of the State Institutions of Higher Learning, and he directed college presidents to follow the letter of the law. The antifraternity law was not very popular and was repealed after Russell left office.

Russell was born in Lafayette County, Mississippi, on 16 November 1875. He graduated from the University of Mis-

sissippi in 1901 and enrolled in the university's law school, completing the course in 1903. While practicing law in Oxford, Russell began a political career, representing Lafayette County in the State House of Representatives from 1908 to 1912 and in the State Senate from 1912 to 1916. Russell was elected lieutenant governor under Theodore G. Bilbo in 1915 and won the governorship four years later.

During his administration Mississippi suffered four consecutive years of agricultural depression and crop failure, primarily as a consequence of sustained drought and the boll weevil. Those conditions created extreme hardships for the state's farmers and a rise in farm tenancy and rural poverty, which in turn prompted a corresponding rise in racial violence. This violence was so widespread that a group of lawyers published a book, *Mississippi and the Mob*, that sought to persuade residents to refrain from mob action. Law enforcement officials were especially urged to arrest and prosecute individuals who participated in lynchings and other assaults on black Mississippians.

In 1921 Russell filed an antitrust suit challenging the business practices of several fire insurance companies. In February 1922 Frances Birkhead, the governor's former secretary, filed a one-hundred-thousand-dollar seduction and breach-of-promise suit against Russell in federal district court. Russell claimed that the fire insurance industry had concocted the suit to "blacken my career" in retaliation for the antitrust action. The jury acquitted Russell after just twenty-five minutes of deliberation.

After leaving office in January 1924, Russell moved to the Gulf Coast and became a real estate agent. He later returned to Jackson, where he practiced law until his death on 16 May 1943.

David G. Sansing
University of Mississippi

Albert D. Kirwan, *The Revolt of the Rednecks: Mississippi Politics, 1876–1925* (1951); *Mississippi Official and Statistical Register* (1920); Lee M. Russell Subject File, Mississippi Department of Archives and History; David G. Sansing, *The University of Mississippi: A Sesquicentennial History* (1999).

R

Rust College

Rust College, a United Methodist Church–supported institution located in Holly Springs and the first historically black college founded in Mississippi, was organized in 1866 through the efforts of former slave Rev. Moses Adams and white clergyman Albert Collier McDonald of the Methodist Episcopal Church, North. Originally started as a church school at Asbury Methodist Church, where Adams was pastor, the school was chartered as Shaw University in 1870, with McDonald serving as its first president. The school took its name from Rev. S. P. Shaw, who contributed ten thousand dollars toward building the institution. During Reconstruction Shaw students served as a base for Republican political support in Marshall County and offered former slaves not only an education but also a community institution from which they could forward the cause of racial equality. Ida B. Wells attended Shaw University during the 1870s and later became a well-known journalist and anti-lynching crusader.

Renamed Rust University in 1890 after Rev. Richard S. Rust, the school trained students to serve as teachers, activists, professionals, and business leaders, and its graduates spread across the United States. After receiving a degree from the school in 1886, Matthew Dogan became a teacher and ultimately the president of Wiley College, a historically black institution in Texas. During the 1890s businessman and entrepreneur Charles Banks briefly attended Rust before opening a bank and an oil factory in Mound Bayou. Perry Howard, an 1899 Rust graduate, became an assistant US attorney general during the administration of Warren G. Harding.

In 1914 the Education Board of the Methodist Episcopal Church renamed the school Rust College. Eighty-two Rust students saw action in World War I. In 1920 Dr. Matthew Davage became the school's first African American president. He was succeeded in 1924 by Lee Marcus McCoy, a 1905 Rust graduate who was instrumental in keeping the college open during the Great Depression. Under the direction of Natalie Doxey, the Rust Singers toured the Midwest to raise funds for the college, and McCoy organized a campus farm and a fruit canning factory to provide additional income. McCoy's self-help projects and promotion of academic excellence brought Rust College through the economic crisis.

In 1957 Earnest A. Smith took on the task of leading Rust College. Smith's administration played a significant role in promoting racial cooperation and ending segregation of public facilities in Marshall County. Though he came under fire from local white political leaders, he did not discourage Rust students from promoting voter registration, and he backed the efforts of civil rights organizations operating in Holly Springs. He opened Rust's doors to Student Nonviolent Coordinating Committee workers and allowed James

Mechanical drawing class, Rust University, ca. 1902 (New York Public Library [Image ID: 1160085])

Meredith, the first African American student to attend the University of Mississippi, to stay at Rust on weekends.

William A. McMillan succeeded Smith in 1967 and oversaw Rust College's accreditation by the Southern Association of Colleges and Universities. McMillan's tenure also witnessed a campus construction boom that included a new gymnasium and mass communication and social science facilities. What McMillan called the school's "upward thrust towards excellence" prepared Rust College for the twenty-first century.

After McMillan's 1993 retirement, Rust graduate David Beckley assumed the presidency. Under Beckley's leadership Rust expanded its academic goals and facilities and maintained its accreditation. A new science building opened in 2008, and Rust College inaugurated the Families First Center, a campus social services agency that works closely with local government agencies to address problems faced by local families. Rust College continues to promote excellence in higher education as one of Mississippi's premier private liberal arts colleges.

Marco Robinson
Rust College

Webster Baker, *History of Rust College, 1866–1924* (1924); Ishmell Edwards, "History of Rust College, 1866–1967" (PhD dissertation, University of Mississippi, 1993); Rust College website, www.rustcollege.edu; Joy A. Williamson, *Radicalizing the Ebony Tower: Black Colleges and the Black Freedom Struggle in Mississippi* (2008).

Rylee, Robert

(1908–1981) Author

Although a native of Tennessee, novelist Robert Rylee is considered a Mississippi writer. He lived in Mississippi for many years, and two of his three novels explore Mississippi and its people.

Rylee was born in Memphis on 17 September 1908 to a family whose members had lived in Tennessee and Mississippi for more than a century. After attending public elementary school in Memphis, he spent his high school years at Phillips Andover Academy, a prestigious Massachusetts preparatory school. Rylee then attended Amherst College, graduating in 1929. The following year Rylee obtained a job as a clerk with the Hardware Dealers Mutual Fire Insurance Company, which sent him first to Mississippi and subsequently to New York, Wisconsin, and Texas, where he settled permanently. While working his way up the company's ranks over the years, Rylee found time to travel in Europe and to write three novels.

Rylee's first novel, *Deep Dark River* (1935), was chosen as a Book-of-the-Month Club Selection. Set in 1930s Mississippi, the novel chronicles the lives of black and white characters on a plantation. Rylee detailed the vicious injustices of the white family operating the plantation and situates Mose Southwick, a black man framed for murder, as the hero. The novel was well received at the time of its publication and tackled progressive subject matter about the psychology of race and power in the South.

Rylee's second novel, *St. George of Weldon* (1937), depicted the life of a middle-class family in the Mississippi Delta. The novel challenged the myth of class binary between the Delta's planters and tenants during this period by focusing on a group that represented an economic middle ground. The book also revealed insights into the sociological conditions in the Delta.

Rylee's final novel, *The Ring and the Cross* (1947), is set in a fictional Texas city and tackles the economic and social conflicts between a US senator and a shipbuilder. The characters in the novel represent the class groups that clashed during this period.

Rylee's novels express his deep understanding of the region and its people, while his writing reveals his view of the novel as a vehicle for interpretation and evaluation of southern life, history, and tradition. He died on 16 October 1981.

Frances Abbott
Digital Public Library of America,
Boston, Massachusetts

L. Moody Simms Jr., *Notes on Mississippi Writers* (Fall 1973).

S

Sail and Shrimp Net Making

Gulf Coast residents have long enjoyed the sight of the local shrimping fleet gliding along in search of bountiful catches, with sails dotting the horizon like white clouds. While the region's shipbuilding tradition has received substantial publicity, less well known are its support industries—specifically, sails and shrimp nets.

As far back as the nineteenth century, sailmakers had made and repaired the canvas sails used on the Biloxi schooner, which served both for leisure and for work. These craftsmen, including the Buckingham family of Biloxi, created the mainsails and multiple jibs and foresails needed to capture the sea breeze. As a workboat, each schooner used at least three sails; as a racing rig, it required six. Consequently, local sailmakers faced a constant demand for sails and repairs.

In the first half of the twentieth century, engine-powered luggers began to change the face of the fleet, and the demand for sails began to decline. However, shrimpers still needed to supply their workboats with nets. Early net makers along the Gulf Coast knitted trawls completely by hand using natural materials such as jute, hemp rope, and linen thread, weaving the rope around a flat wooden paddle and sizing dowel to create a uniform mesh. At the front end the craftsman attached the mesh to a large hemp rope to create the mouth or opening of the trawl. Then he added a length of chain, known as the tickler, which weighted the mouth of the trawl down to the Gulf floor. As the trawl dragged across the bottom, it stirred the sand, provoking the shrimp to jump up and into the trawl. As the trawl moved through the water, the force of the flow caused the shrimp to accumulate at the end of the net, known as the money bag.

Shrimp nets still work in much the same fashion, although synthetic rope has replaced the natural materials used in the past. Many of the makers of this important equipment have also remained much the same, including the Marinovich Trawl Company, the R. F. Ederer Company, and the Glavan Trawl Manufacturing Company, all of which have been in the Biloxi net-making industry for generations. The owners of these companies also became community leaders, serving as benefactors of local churches, charities, and other organiza-tions as well as playing prominent roles in the area's social life as kings of Mardi Gras and in the Blessing of the Fleet. Now run by younger generations of the families, these companies still make trawls for use not only along the Gulf Coast but around the world.

Alice Lachaussee
Spring Hill College

Laura E. Bolton, in *Mississippi Resources and History of the Mississippi Gulf Coast*, vol. 3, ed. Lawrence A. Klein, Mary Landry, and Joe E. Seward (1998); Charles Lawrence Dyer, *Along the Gulf: An Entertaining Story of an Outing among the Beautiful Resorts on the Mississippi Sound* (1894); Val Husley, *Maritime Biloxi* (2000); Shelley Powers, in *Mississippi Resources and History of the Mississippi Gulf Coast*, vol. 3, ed. Lawrence A. Klein, Mary Landry, and Joe E. Seward (1998); Captain Joe Scholtes, *Down South Magazine* (July–August 1969); Chris Snyder, in *Mississippi Resources and History of the Mississippi Gulf Coast*, vol. 3, ed. Lawrence A. Klein, Mary Landry, and Joe E. Seward (1998).

Salter, John R., Jr. (Hunter Gray, Hunter Bear)
(b. 1934) Activist

Civil rights activist John R. Salter Jr., who later changed his name to Hunter Gray, lived and worked in Jackson from 1961 to 1963. A professor at Tougaloo College, author of an important book about the Jackson movement, and an organizer before, during, and after his time in Mississippi, Salter is likely best known for his participation in the 1963 Woolworth's sit-in and as one of the subjects of the most famous photograph of that event.

Salter was born in Chicago on 14 February 1934. His grandfather, Massachusetts native Mack Salter, was a Native American active in the Indian Rights Association and was one of the founders of the National Association for the Advancement of Colored People (NAACP). Salter grew up in Flagstaff, Arizona, where he was troubled from an early age by discrimination against both Native Americans and African Americans. He served in Korea, earned bachelor's and master's degrees in sociology from Arizona State University, and worked with union organizers in the West and Midwest. After teaching for a year in Wisconsin, he and his wife, Eldri, were inspired by the Freedom Rides to move to Jackson, where John Salter took a teaching position at Tougaloo College. He became involved with the civil rights work almost immediately after arriving in Mississippi, accepting an invitation from Colia Liddell to work with the NAACP's youth groups, coming into contact with Medgar Evers and Aaron

Henry, and working with students and others at Tougaloo. In the fall of 1962 he helped organize a boycott of Capitol Street businesses, with activists demanding that stores institute equal hiring practices, use courtesy titles for African American shoppers, and do away with segregated seating and restrooms. Salter was arrested while picketing in December.

On 28 May 1963 a small group of students planned a sit-in to protest the whites-only policy of the lunch counter at Woolworth's on Capitol Street. Salter and other faculty members went to watch, but Salter decided to join in the protest. Jackson police did not arrest the activists but instead allowed a group of white men to harass them, eventually beating some and trying to humiliate them. As participant Ed King wrote, crowd members "seized the closest instruments at hand—plastic, ugly yellow jars of mustard and squirted this all over Salter and the students. Next ketchup, then spray paint, then more lethal weapons of glass ash trays and sugar jars—and soon there was blood mixed in the mustard—and more blood." *Jackson Daily News* photographer Fred Blackwell took a picture of Anne Moody, Joan Trumpauer, and Salter covered in food and surrounded by the angry mob.

Salter worked in Jackson through the summer, took part in the public march after the assassination of Medgar Evers in June 1963, and was the subject of a lawsuit, *City of Jackson v. John R. Salter, Jr.*, that sought to prevent activists from picketing or organizing. In addition to his arrest, Salter faced gunshots and was injured in an automobile wreck that he believed resulted from sabotage. Later in 1963 he and his family moved to North Carolina, where he worked for the Southern Conference Educational Fund. Salter moved to Chicago in 1969 and later to the Northwest, continuing his civil rights activity. In 1979 Salter published *Jackson, Mississippi: An American Chronicle of Struggle and Schism*, a thorough account of his work in Jackson. He later changed his name to Hunter Gray to honor his father's original name. He also goes by the name Hunter Bear as part of his Native American identity.

Ted Ownby
University of Mississippi

Anne Moody, *Coming of Age in Mississippi* (1970); M. J. O'Brien, *We Shall Not Be Moved: The Jackson Woolworth's Sit-In and the Movement It Inspired* (2013); John R. Salter Jr., *Jackson, Mississippi, An American Chronicle of Struggle and Schism* (1987); Veterans of the Civil Rights Movement website, www.crmvet.org.

San Ildefonso, Third Treaty of

The Third Treaty of San Ildefonso, secretly negotiated and signed by French minister Louis Alexandre Berthier and Spanish secretary of state Don Mariano Luis de Urquijo at the Spanish royal residence near San Ildefonso on 1 October 1800, provided for the return of the Louisiana Territory from Spain to France. The Treaty of Aranjuez, on 21 March 1801, and a final agreement of retrocession signed by Carlos IV, king of Spain, on 15 October 1802 completed the transfer. The treaty and events that followed it had significant consequences for Mississippi.

The French effort to recover Louisiana started in 1795 but gained momentum in 1799 with the emergence of Napoleon Bonaparte, who envisioned an American empire anchored by sugar-rich Saint-Domingue (present-day Haiti). In September 1800 Berthier presented Spain with a French ultimatum demanding the transfer of Louisiana, East and West Florida, and ten ships of war. With Spain's fragile control of Louisiana weakened further by the 1795 Treaty of San Lorenzo, in which Spain recognized the western and southern boundaries of the United States as the Mississippi River and the thirty-first parallel, respectively, Carlos IV agreed to give France Louisiana and six ships of war but refused to surrender the Floridas. In exchange, the king received a throne for his son-in-law, the Duke of Parma in Italy.

Pres. Thomas Jefferson's administration heard rumors of the Third Treaty of San Ildefonso and received a copy from Rufus King, American minister to Great Britain, in November 1801. Jefferson directed Robert R. Livingston, American minister to France, to determine the status of Louisiana and offer to buy New Orleans. Although the French minister, Talleyrand, spurned Livingston's initial efforts, a slave insurrection in Saint-Domingue and the specter of war in Europe caused Napoleon to scrap his plans for an American empire. Jefferson pushed the negotiations in Paris and authorized additional military preparations along the Mississippi River after Spanish intendant Juan Ventura Morales suspended the right of deposit at New Orleans in October 1802. James Monroe joined Livingston in Paris on 10 April 1803, and negotiations with the French treasury minister, François Barbé-Marbois, soon concluded with an agreement to transfer Louisiana to the United States for $15,000,000.

The unexpected consequences of the Third Treaty of San Ildefonso allowed the American ministers to acquire not just New Orleans or some territory for a port on the Mississippi, as Jefferson had authorized, but a vast, boundless empire west of the Mississippi. The final cession agreement on 30 April 1803 included a treaty and two financial conventions in which the United States paid France $11,250,000 and settled claims by American citizens against France amounting to $3,750,000. Despite protests from Spain and the Federalists,

S

the US Senate ratified the Louisiana Purchase on 17 October 1803. US commissioners William C. C. Claiborne and James Wilkinson formally accepted the transfer on 20 December, following a similar ceremony on 30 November when the Spanish commissioner officially delivered Louisiana to the French prefect, Pierre Clément Lausset. Claiborne left his position as governor of Mississippi Territory to become governor of the Territory of Orleans and served as governor of Louisiana following its admission to statehood in 1812.

James P. Pate

University of Mississippi, Tupelo

Mary P. Adams, *Journal of Southern History* (May 1955); David B. Gaspar and David Patrick Geggus, eds., *A Turbulent Time: The French Revolution and the Greater Caribbean* (1997); Lawrence S. Kaplan, *Thomas Jefferson: Westward the Course of Empire* (1998); James E. Lewis Jr., *The American Union and the Problem of Neighborhood: The United States and the Collapse of the Spanish Empire, 1783–1829* (1998); Treaty of San Ildefonso, Avalon Project, Yale Law School website, http://avalon.law.yale.edu; Daniel J. Weber, *The Spanish Frontier in North America* (1992).

San Lorenzo, Treaty of (Pinckney's Treaty)

Thomas Pinckney, US special minister to Spain, and Manuel de Godoy y Álvarez de Faria, prime minister of Spain, negotiated and signed the "Treaty of Friendship, Limits, and Navigation between the United States of America and the King of Spain" (known as the Treaty of San Lorenzo or Pinckney's Treaty) at the Royal Monastery of San Lorenzo el Real on 27 October 1795. Godoy endorsed and negotiated this treaty as a consequence of the unknown implications of the 1794 treaty between the United States and Great Britain (Jay's Treaty), a peace treaty between Spain and France, and the aggressive, unbridled western advance by the United States.

Even before Pinckney, the US minister to London, received his appointment as "envoy extraordinary" to Spain, Godoy had expressed a willingness to discuss a permanent Florida boundary and open navigation of the Mississippi River. Spain's inability to foment separatism on the American frontier or to stop American expansion through its southern Indian alliance forced Godoy to make concessions to protect Spain's declining American fortunes. John Jay's 1794 mission to London raised the specter of an Anglo-American alliance that could threaten the fragile Spanish presence in North America. After Godoy deserted the Anglo-Spanish alliance

by signing a secret treaty with France, the Peace of Basel, on 22 July 1795, he needed to reach a peace accord with the United States to protect Spain's possessions. At the same time, Pres. George Washington's administration wanted to maintain peaceful relations with Spain, resolve the southern boundary dispute, and provide western farmers with access to markets via the Mississippi River and the Gulf of Mexico.

With the creation of the Northwest Territory in 1787 and the Southwest Territory in 1790, thousands of new settlers demanded protection from the Ohio and southern Indians and outlets for their tobacco and other products. Under Jay's Treaty, Great Britain agreed to abandon its Great Lakes posts, which contributed to the defeat of the Ohio Indians at the Battle of Fallen Timbers in 1794 and to the Treaty of Greenville in 1795. In Spanish Louisiana, Francisco Luis Héctor, Baron de Carondelet, governor and intendant general, had developed an aggressive defensive strategy, including an alliance with the southern Indians, operating war galleys on the Mississippi and constructing military outposts on the Upper Tombigbee River and on the Chickasaw Bluffs at present-day Memphis, Tennessee. The unsuspecting Carondelet knew nothing about Pinckney's mission or the machinations orchestrated by Godoy, who had received a new title, Prince of Peace, for his efforts in Basel, Switzerland.

Pinckney and Godoy started their negotiations in Madrid shortly after Pinckney's arrival on 28 June 1795. After the Peace of Basel was ratified and war with France formally ended on 7 August 1795, Pinckney proposed treaty articles on 20 August in which he pushed for the American right to free navigation of the Mississippi and a free port near the mouth of the Mississippi. Godoy demurred on a place of deposit and on 18 September demanded a treaty conceding the right of navigation and thirty-first parallel as the boundary with Spanish West Florida. Deciding to make the right of deposit a fundamental condition of a treaty, Pinckney threatened to end the negotiations by demanding his passports on 24 October. Godoy capitulated and agreed to permit US citizens to deposit goods duty-free for three years at New Orleans; he further promised "to continue this permission" or to assign US citizens "an equivalent establishment" on the Mississippi.

Although the US Senate ratified the Treaty of San Lorenzo on 7 March 1796 and Spain did so on 25 April, its full impact and implementation were delayed until May 1799 by the tardy Spanish withdrawal east of the Mississippi and north of the thirty-first parallel. Carondelet did not take steps to abandon his Indian policy, frontier intrigues in Kentucky, or the military posts east of the Mississippi until he received orders in late February 1796 and specific directions to evacuate military posts east of the Mississippi on 22 September 1797. Ironically, Andrew Ellicott's survey of the new boundary line, which took four years to complete, provided more excuses for delays. The garrison at Fort Confederation on the Upper Tombigbee retreated downriver to Fort San Esteban north of Mobile on 17 March 1797, and Spanish forces dismantled and abandoned

Fort San Fernando de las Barrancas (Memphis) three days later. The final Spanish withdrawal from Natchez occurred on 30 March 1798, and Spanish forces surrendered Fort San Esteban on 5 May 1799. Congress formally organized the Mississippi Territory on 7 April 1798 with boundaries from the Mississippi River to the Chattahoochee River and from the thirty-first parallel to the 32°28′ line of north latitude.

James P. Pate
University of Mississippi, Tupelo

Samuel Flagg Bemis, *Pinckney's Treaty: America's Advantage from Europe's Distress, 1783–1800* (1960); Andrew Ellicott, *The Journal of Andrew Ellicott: Late Commissioner on Behalf of the United States . . . for Determining the Boundary between the United States and the Possessions of His Catholic Majesty* (1962); Douglas Hilt, *The Troubled Trinity: Godoy and the Spanish Monarchs* (1987); Abraham P. Nasatir, *Spanish War Vessels on the Mississippi, 1792–1796* (1968); Antonio R. Peña, *Early American Review* (Summer–Fall 2002); David J. Weber, *The Spanish Frontier in North America* (1992).

Sargent, Winthrop
(1753–1820) Territorial Governor

Winthrop Sargent, a Puritan and Federalist from Massachusetts, served as the first governor of the Mississippi Territory. Born into a prominent family on 1 May 1753, he graduated from Harvard in the early 1770s and served on a ship owned by his father prior to the outbreak of the American Revolution. Sargent enlisted in a Massachusetts artillery regiment, serving as an officer and fighting at Boston, Long Island, Brandywine, and Monmouth. Following the conflict, Sargent moved westward and became a surveyor before becoming secretary of the Northwest Territory in 1787.

In 1798 Pres. John Adams appointed Sargent governor of the Mississippi Territory, which was established that year from land ceded by Spain. The Mississippi Territory consisted of the region bounded by the Mississippi River in the west, the Chattahoochee River in the east, the thirty-first parallel in the south, and the point where the Yazoo River emptied into the Mississippi River in the north. The area was plagued by conflicting land claims, disputes with Indians, and the continuing interference of the Spanish. First of all, France, England, Spain, and the state of Georgia had all issued land grants in the region, and the new government had to sort out these disputes. Second, most of the territory was inhabited by various Indian nations who were apprehensive after their ally Spain abandoned them to the ever-expanding United States. Sargent's new government would have to maintain peace between these tribes and land-hungry immigrants. Finally, Spanish officials in West Florida and Louisiana posed a potential threat to the security of the region.

Sargent's tenure had an inauspicious beginning. When he arrived in Natchez, the territorial capital, in August 1799, he was too ill to greet his well-wishers, leading many of them to believe that he had chosen to ignore them. Relations subsequently remained uneasy. Sargent was an aristocratic Federalist, wary of too much public involvement in running the government, and the freedom-loving frontier democrats perceived him as haughty. He favored a strong executive and sought to establish order. The town of Natchez also did not appeal to Sargent's elitist background, and his open distaste for his location did not endear him to the area's residents.

His administration was further hampered by the absence of several important government officials. The legislation creating the territory established a ruling council consisting of a governor, secretary, and three judges who were authorized to write laws. It took months for the necessary quorum of officials to arrive so that the council could produce a code of laws.

Once these laws were written and Sargent began making decisions on a variety of issues such as the selection of militia officers, many citizens immediately opposed his policies. This resulting tone of factionalism persisted throughout the territorial period. The opposing faction, led by Anthony Hutchins, Thomas Green, and Cato West, believed that Sargent's new laws, derisively called Sargent's Code, were too harsh. They also believed that his territorial council was illegal in that it merged the executive, legislative, and judicial powers in too few individuals. Finally, they disagreed with his choices for militia officers. These men were probably looking to gain power for themselves and therefore sought ways to change the structure of the government in their favor.

The new faction soon lobbied the national government for change, sending a delegate to propose that the territory enter the second stage of government, which involved an elected assembly, thereby weakening Sargent's power. Officials passed the necessary legislation, forcing Sargent to conduct elections in which many of his strongest opponents gained office in the newly formed assembly.

Thomas Jefferson's election as president in 1800 sealed Sargent's doom as governor. Sargent traveled to the national capital to defend his administration, but Jefferson, a Democratic Republican, replaced the Federalist Sargent with W. C. C., Claiborne, a Tennessee congressman who had helped draft the legislation regarding Mississippi's territorial government. Sargent retired from public life and lived as a planter until his death in New Orleans on 3 June 1820.

Clay Williams
Mississippi Department of
Archives and History

J. F. H. Claiborne, *Mississippi as a Province, Territory, and State, with Biographical Notices of Eminent Citizens* (1880); Robert V. Haynes, in *A History of Mississippi*, vol. 1 (1973); Robert V. Haynes, *Journal of Mississippi History* (Winter 2002); Dunbar Rowland, *History of Mississippi*, vol. 1 (1925); Dunbar Rowland, *The Mississippi Territorial Archives, 1798–1803, Executive Journals of Governor Winthrop Sargent and Governor William Charles Cole Claiborne* (1905); John Ray Skates, *Mississippi, a Bicentennial History* (1979).

Satterfield, John C.

(1904–1981) Lawyer

John Creighton Satterfield, born in Port Gibson on 25 July 1904, played a pivotal role in Mississippi's fight against desegregation throughout much of the mid-twentieth century. After earning a bachelor's degree from Millsaps College in 1926 and a law degree from the University of Mississippi three years later, Satterfield practiced law in Jackson and Yazoo City. From 1928 to 1932 he served in the Mississippi House of Representatives, helping to pass the laws that built the state's first highways. Recognized as a gifted wordsmith, Satterfield rapidly became one of Mississippi's most talented lawyers and was very successful in both the corporate and public sectors. Through his political and legal connections, Satterfield served as president of the Mississippi Bar (1955–56) and became the only Mississippian to hold the presidency of the American Bar Association (1961–62).

A fierce opponent of the civil rights movement, Satterfield maintained a membership in the Citizens' Council and served on the Mississippi State Sovereignty Commission. He publicly criticized the US Supreme Court's 1954 *Brown v. Board of Education* ruling, which he regarded as judicial tyranny. In 1962, during the crisis over James Meredith's attempt to enroll at the University of Mississippi, Satterfield acted as Gov. Ross Barnett's personal attorney.

When John F. Kennedy proposed groundbreaking legislation to outlaw segregation in public facilities, Mississippi's white leaders unleashed a counteroffensive. In the summer of 1963 Satterfield met with Mississippi's top politicians and business leaders to discuss forming a lobby in Washington, D.C., to fight the legislation. The idea received enthusiastic support. Mississippi segregationists teamed with northern businessmen to create the Coordinating Committee for Fundamental American Freedoms, with the Sovereignty Commission providing money for rent, offices, and personnel. By July 1963 the new lobby had received its first contributions, and Satterfield deposited the money into a special account in the Mississippi State Treasury. Satterfield helped to oversee a wide-reaching financial scheme that filtered hundreds of thousands of dollars into Mississippi's coffers from Wall Street businessmen and southern segregationists who wanted the legislation quashed. The Sovereignty Commission, in turn, used the money to coordinate opposition, publish editorials, distribute pamphlets, and fight the bill in Congress. Satterfield wrote several pamphlets, including *Due Process of Law, or Government by Intimidation?* (1962) to raise funds for the group.

In the wake of Kennedy's assassination, Congress passed the Civil Rights Act of 1964. Angered by the defeat, Satterfield urged the creation of a new national organization that would prove that black southerners were inherently inferior. Satterfield brought in money for the new group, but the violence that accompanied the 1964 Freedom Summer left Mississippi's segregationists with fewer allies, and the plan fizzled. In 1969 Satterfield mounted his last important stand against desegregation, volunteering his services to defend the Holmes County Board of Education in a lawsuit that sought to force the immediate integration of the county's schools. Satterfield's efforts failed. The Supreme Court's landmark decision in *Alexander v. Holmes* finally ended the South's dual public school systems. For his role in the case, *Time* labeled Satterfield "the most prominent segregationist lawyer in the country."

Debilitated by Parkinson's disease, Satterfield committed suicide on 5 May 1981.

William P. Hustwit
Birmingham Southern University

Douglas A. Blackmon, *Wall Street Journal* (11 June 1999); Yasuhiro Katagiri, *The Mississippi State Sovereignty Commission: Civil Rights and States' Rights* (2001); Michael Landon, *The Honor and Dignity of the Profession: A History of the Mississippi State Bar, 1906–1976* (1979); Neil R. McMillen, *The Citizens' Council* (1971); John C. Satterfield, *Blueprint for Total Federal Regimentation: Analysis of the Civil Rights Act of 1963* (1963); John C. Satterfield, *Due Process of Law, or Government by Intimidation?* (1962); John C. Satterfield Papers, Department of Archives and Special Collections, J. D. Williams Library, University of Mississippi.

Sauvole, Jean de

(ca. 1670–1701) French Military Figure

A somewhat mysterious figure in the early history of the northern Gulf Coast, the Jean de Sauvole played a vital role in the founding settlement of what is now Mississippi.

Born in France in the 1670s in the Province of Guyenne, Sauvole (noted in various documents as Sauvol, Sauvolle, Sauvolles, and Souvole, and whose full name is unknown) was serving as an *enseigne de vaisseau* in the French Navy in 1698 when he was selected by Pierre Le Moyne, Sieur d'Iberville, for a strategic mission to protect the Mississippi Valley claims made by René-Robert Cavelier, Sieur de La Salle, in 1682.

The mission, composed mostly of French Canadians and headed by the Le Moyne brothers, Iberville and Bienville, sought to fortify the mouth of the Mississippi. Following the crew's departure from Brest, France, Iberville became impressed with Sauvole's leadership abilities. Sauvole accompanied Iberville on his journeys up the Mississippi River and to Pascagoula Bay in an attempt to plant an establishment at what is now Gautier. When that attempt failed, Sauvole sailed with Iberville to Biloxi Bay, where Sauvole assumed an active role in constructing Fort Maurepas at what is now Ocean Springs.

In May 1699 Iberville commissioned Sauvole as commandant of the new fort, describing him as "a well-behaved young man of ability." When Iberville returned to France, Sauvole took the lead in completing Fort Maurepas's construction. He also concentrated on developing good relations with the native people, in particular the Biloxi, Pascagoula, and Mobile chieftains. In general, Sauvole was very friendly and generous toward the native people, who provided the French forces with much-needed food.

In 1700 Sauvole was heavily engaged in constructing Fort La Boulaye on the Mississippi just below present-day New Orleans, after English traders invaded the lower Mississippi. Bienville was appointed commandant of the new garrison.

Although Sauvole had success with the native people, he had difficulties with his own men. He had no close connections to the French Canadians, although he admired their ability to cope with the wilderness. One point of conflict concerned the addiction many frontiersman had for the "water of life," the hard liquor Sauvole saw as greatly harmful to his forces. He pressed for authority to ban rum and whiskey and replace them with wine and beer, but the effort failed because wine and beer were not easily preserved in the wilderness.

Another problem erupted when Jesuit Paul Du Ru was appointed chaplain of the Fort Maurepas garrison and almost immediately crossed swords with Sauvole. After losing his temper on several occasions, Du Ru was denounced by Sauvole as a malcontent and was reported to the minister of marine.

In December 1701, on his last voyage to Biloxi Bay, Iberville stopped at Pensacola and was informed that Sauvole had died on 22 August of a fever and was buried in the graveyard just outside Fort Maurepas.

Jay Higginbotham
Mobile Municipal Archives

Marcel Giraud, *Histoire de la Louisiane Française*, vol. 1, *Le Regne de Louis XIV* (1953); Jay Higginbotham, *Fort Maurepas: The Birth of Louisiana, 1699–1702* (1998); Jay Higginbotham, *Louisiana Studies* (Summer 1968); Pierre Le Moyne, Sieur d'Iberville, *Iberville's Gulf Journals*, ed. Richebourg Gaillard McWilliams (1981); Richebourg Gaillard McWilliams, *Fleur de Lys and Calumet* (1953); Charles Edwards O'Neil, *Church and State in French Colonial Louisiana: Policy and Politics to 1732* (1968); P. G. Roy, *Bulletin des Recherches Historique* (1908); Jean de Sauvole, *The Journal of Sauvole: Historical Journal of the Establishment of the French in Louisiana*, ed. Jay Higginbotham (1969).

School Consolidation Movement

In the early twentieth century counties across the South closed rural schoolhouses and replaced them with larger consolidated schools. School consolidation centralized educational control by eliminating schools where one teacher supervised all pupils and concentrating authority in the hands of a principal, who supervised multiple teachers and reported to a county school board. The movement swept Mississippi in 1910, and public reaction betrayed the divided mind of the state regarding modernity and traditionalism. While professionals and administrators in towns and cities hailed consolidation as a weapon against ignorance and poverty, some rural Mississippians regarded the movement as a threat to the autonomy of local communities.

School consolidation came to the South as part of a set of educational reforms imported from the North and Midwest. Through groups like the Southern Education Board, industrialists from the region collaborated with northern philanthropists to publicize and fund campaigns for consolidation, compulsory attendance laws, longer school terms, and increased educational expenditures. Because it infused the application of corporate techniques and business efficiency with the noblesse oblige of deceased cotton aristocrats, the educational crusade exemplified the ethos of the New South.

The movement in Mississippi had deep corporate roots. As early as 1871 state superintendent of schools H. R. Pease called for adapting the control structure of railroad companies to the administration of the state's schools. J. C. Hardy, the superintendent of schools in Jackson, renewed Pease's campaign in 1899 and proposed a central body of administrative experts as an alternative to local management by untrained county superintendents. By 1905 the movement had erupted into a full-blown educational reform campaign.

That campaign bore fruit in 1910, when the state legislature authorized counties to build consolidated schools and pass taxes to pay for transportation to the new facilities. Most counties quickly closed old schools and built larger ones. But the arguments that made the virtues of consolidation obvious to county and state officials did not convince all Mississippians so quickly. In small communities, parents worried about the higher taxes the new schools would require, the distance their children would have to travel to attend school,

S

the former rivals with whom their children would now learn and play, and the decreased control parents would have over curriculum and teachers. Consolidation also exacerbated generational tensions about young men and women leaving behind farms for towns and cities.

Though resistance sometimes took drastic and violent forms—arsonists burned some of the new school buildings, and a student fatally shot the principal at East Lincoln High School—reformers ultimately won over public opinion. The implementation of school consolidation conformed to a general pattern of centralization in rural life. Critics may bemoan certain aspects of homogenization, but the positive effects of school consolidation—significant increases in school attendance, drastic decreases in illiteracy, and the general improvement of education in the state—make the movement one of the more successful reform efforts in Mississippi's history.

Thomas John Carey
University of Mississippi

Stephen Edward Cresswell, *Rednecks, Redeemers, and Race: Mississippi after Reconstruction, 1877–1917* (2006); Spencer J. Maxcy, *Peabody Journal of Education* (April 1976); C. Vann Woodward, *Origins of the New South, 1877–1913* (1951).

Scots-Irish

According to the US Census Bureau, by the second decade of the twenty-first century, only about 1.5 percent of Mississippians claim "Scotch-Irish" ancestry, a surprisingly low number in light of the amount of influence this group has had in the state. However, historians have noted that many or most descendants of Irish Presbyterian immigrants designate themselves simply as "Irish." Since Mississippi did not experience a significant influx of Irish from 1845 to the mid-1950s, it is reasonable to assume that most state's descendants of Irish Presbyterians continue to choose that designation. By that reckoning, just over 10 percent of Mississippi's population is of Scots-Irish descent.

Scots-Irish is a slippery term and carries multiple connotations that change with context. An Americanism, it refers to the descendants of people who migrated from Ireland to North America, mainly in the eighteenth century. About a century earlier, the forebears of those migrants had traveled from Scotland to northeastern Ireland, most of them during the Plantation of Ulster. Almost all of the migrants were Presbyterians at the time of their arrival in America, and

although many later became Baptists and Methodists, their Calvinism has left considerable influence wherever they settled, including Mississippi.

The term *Scots-Irish* did not come into frequent use until the mid- to late nineteenth century. The migrants generally described themselves as *Irish*, as did the colonial officials who noted their arrival. *Scots-Irish* later became more common, in part because it indicated descent from the group that had originated in Scotland. Some used the term to express that they were Protestants rather than Catholics of Irish descent.

The Scots-Irish began to arrive in the American colonies (primarily Pennsylvania) in significant numbers in 1718 and almost immediately began to spread across the continent. Some histories claim that by 1760 Scots-Irish settlers were living in the vicinity of Natchez, and within four decades, considerable numbers of Irish- and American-born Scots-Irish had settled the frontier lands of the Old Southwest, arriving from the Carolinas and Kentucky via Tennessee and by following trails from Georgia to Mississippi.

From the start, Scots-Irishmen were leaders in US dealings with the Choctaw. The three men appointed by the United States to negotiate with the Choctaw and the only white signers of the 1816 US-Choctaw treaty were John R. Coffee, John Rhea, and John McKee. Both Rhea and McKee were sons of Scots-Irish immigrants, and despite his Gaelic Irish name, Coffee was very much a part of the Scots-Irish community in the United States. He was Andrew Jackson's business partner and was married to a relative of Jackson's wife: both Jacksons were Scots-Irish. McKee and Coffee also signed the Treaty of Dancing Rabbit Creek with the Choctaw in 1830.

With Jackson's election as president, the Scots-Irish in Mississippi and the United States became unalterably mainstream American. By the twenty-first century, the areas of the United States where the Scots-Irish settled are the areas where the census records the highest percentages of people who declare their ancestry to be American. More than 11 percent of Mississippians described themselves that way, lending credence to the idea that the Scots-Irish really have become the "People with No Name."

Rankin Sherling
Marion Military Institute

D. H. Akenson, *The Irish Diaspora: A Primer* (1996); R. J. Dickson, *Ulster Emigration to Colonial America, 1718–1775* (1966); David Noel Doyle, in *Making the Irish American: History and Heritage of the Irish in the United States*, ed. J. J. Lee and Marion R. Casey (2006); E. R. R. Green, ed., *Essays in Scotch-Irish History* (1969); Patrick Griffin, *The People with No Name: Ireland's Ulster Scots, America's Scots Irish, and the Creation of a British Atlantic World, 1689–1764* (2001); James G. Leyburn, *The Scotch-Irish: A Social History* (1962).

Scott, Abram M.

(1785–1833) Seventh Governor, 1832–1833

Abram Scott was involved in two of the three closest elections for governor in the state's history. In 1831 he defeated Hiram G. Runnels by 247 votes, and two years later he lost to Runnels by 558 votes.

Scott was born in South Carolina in 1785 and migrated to Wilkinson County, Mississippi, as a young man. He became active in politics and was serving as tax collector of Wilkinson County when the War of 1812 began; he served as a lieutenant in the 1st Mississippi Regiment of Volunteers. Scott later represented Wilkinson County in the State Senate prior to winning election as governor.

During Scott's first year in office, the nation was embroiled in a great sectional controversy over the tariff. In 1832 South Carolina, under the leadership of John C. Calhoun, had nullified a tariff passed by the US Congress in 1828 and had threatened to secede. Scott and the Mississippi legislature did not support South Carolina, publicly denouncing the theory that a state could nullify a federal law.

Scott held the governor's office during the transition from the old aristocratic constitution of 1817 to the more democratic constitution of 1832, which created several new state agencies and public offices. Under the new constitution the governor would continue to serve a two-year term but could not serve more than four years in any six-year period. The new constitution also abolished the office of lieutenant governor.

The first legislature under the new constitution convened in January 1833 and authorized a special general election in May to elect the public officials created by that constitution. The legislature authorized the officials chosen in that election to take office immediately, even though the constitution provided that the terms of all public officials would begin in November following their election. During that session the legislature also appropriated ninety-five thousand dollars for a new state capitol and ten thousand dollars for a "suitable house for the governor."

In the May 1833 special election, Runnels defeated Scott. But because of questions about the legality of the special election, Runnels refused to be inaugurated, and Scott remained in office. In June, a cholera epidemic forced a general evacuation of Jackson. Scott, however, refused to leave the capital, contracted the disease, and died on 12 June 1833. Because there was no lieutenant governor, Scott was succeeded by Charles Lynch, the president of the State Senate.

Scott County is named in honor of Mississippi's seventh governor.

David G. Sansing
University of Mississippi

Mississippi Official and Statistical Register (1912); Dunbar Rowland, *Encyclopedia of Mississippi History*, vol. 2 (1907).

Scott, Ed

(1922–2015) Catfish farmer

"If you put your hand and heart to anything you want to do, you can do it." This was Ed Scott's mantra and the key to his success as the first African American entrepreneur and business owner in the Mississippi Delta catfish farming and processing industry. Born on 27 August 1922 in the Delta town of Drew and raised there, Edward Logan Scott Jr. came from a long line of farmers. His father, Ed Scott Sr., had acquired a sizable piece of land in northern Sunflower County prior to the Great Depression and earned a reputation as hardworking and productive. He gained the respect of local white farmers and in 1948 became the state's first African American rice farmer. By the time of his death in the 1950s, the family owned nineteen hundred acres of land.

Ed Scott Jr. capitalized on the family's landholdings, planting and harvesting annual crops of cotton, soybeans, and rice on the rich Delta soil. In the late 1970s Scott noticed a shift in regional farming trends from cotton and soybeans to catfish. Scott remarked, "I'd been row-cropping right along, but I'm one of those versatile kind of farmers. Anything I see anybody else doing, I figure I can do it too. I started digging the ponds with my own equipment." Scott dug eight ponds in 1981 but encountered significant roadblocks in obtaining the funding to stock them, primarily because the Farmers Home Administration's district supervisor refused to aid Scott in acquiring loans. As Scott recalled, "I went to him and asked for a loan to stock them. He said no, and then he turned right around let a white farmer I knew have $5.5 million for catfish."

In response, Scott bypassed the supervisor and directly contacted the agency's state office in Jackson. He received a $150,000 loan, enough to stock the ponds with six hundred thousand fingerlings and nurture them to processing maturity. When white-owned processing plants refused to clean and package his fish, he established Pond Fresh Catfish and the Leflore-Bolivar Catfish Processing Plant.

By 1990 Scott's one-line plant had expanded to two lines, producing two million pounds of catfish annually under the Pond Fresh label. At this time, that output and profit were enough to keep thirty-five employees on regular pay schedules and the company expanding. Scott subsequently began winning government contracts to supply catfish for military camps. In the late 1980s the Scott family also joined with

Robert Bush, a Delta native and aide to Mississippi's first black congressman in the twentieth century, Mike Espy, to open Edna's Gourmet Seafood in Washington, Mississippi.

Scott earned great respect in catfish industry and in southern foodways circles. His story has been highlighted in a Southern Foodways Alliance documentary, *On Flavor*, and in 2001 the Alliance awarded Scott its Keeper of the Flame Award.

He died on 8 October 2015.

Eva Walton Kendrick

Birmingham, Alabama

Julian Rankin, "Pond Fresh: Ed Scott and His Catfish," *Gravy* (Summer 2016); Richard Schweid, *Catfish and the Delta: Confederate Fish Farming in the Mississippi Delta* (1992); Southern Foodways Alliance website, www.southernfoodways.org.

Scott, George "Boomer"
(1944–2013) Athlete

George "Boomer" Scott (Collection of Ted Ownby)

George Charles Scott Jr. was born in Greenville, Mississippi, on 23 March 1944. His father died when he was two. His mother, Magnolia, worked three jobs to support her family, and young George worked in the fields, picking cotton. After graduating from Coleman High School, he signed with the Boston Red Sox on 28 May 1962, receiving a ten-thousand-dollar bonus. Scott turned down college scholarships to play football and basketball because "that $10,000 was all the money in the world." Scott made his Major League Baseball debut with the Red Sox on 12 April 1966. Just five years earlier, the Red Sox had become the last Major League team to integrate, and Scott was among their first African American everyday players. He earned his nickname when fellow rookie Joe Foy saw Scott hit and said, "Man, you really put a boom on that ball." Scott hit 27 home runs during his rookie year, though the Sox finished in ninth place in the American League. The next year, however, Scott and the Red Sox finished in first place and reached the World Series, where Scott went 4 for 11, including a Game 7 triple against Bob Gibson, though the St. Louis Cardinals won. Boomer and his home runs, which he called "taters," took their place in Red Sox history, along with Carl Yastrzemski's American League Triple Crown and Jim Lonborg's dominance on the mound. Known for his glove, "Black Beauty," and for his fielding prowess, Scott earned the first of his eight Gold Glove Awards at first base that season.

After the 1971 season the Red Sox traded Scott, Lonborg, and four others to the Milwaukee Brewers. In 1975 Scott led the American League with 36 home runs and 109 runs batted in. After five seasons in Milwaukee, Scott returned to Boston for the 1977 season, during which he slugged 33 home runs, recorded 95 RBIs, and scored 103 runs. His second stint in Boston lasted until the middle of the 1979 season, when he was traded to Kansas City. The Royals released him two months later, and he finished out the season with the New York Yankees.

Scott played for several more seasons in the Mexican League and then became manager of the Mexico City Tigers. He spent the next two decades managing there and in the Dominican Republic, in Venezuela, and in the North American independent leagues but was never offered a position with a Major League organization. He resented that snub for the rest of his life.

In his fourteen years in the Majors, Scott boomed 271 home runs and drove in 1,051 runs. He amassed 1,992 base hits and a lifetime batting average of .268. He was named to the American League All-Star Team three times and is a member of the Boston Red Sox Hall of Fame and the Mississippi Sports Hall of Fame.

He died in Greenville on 28 July 2013.

Jimmy Robertson

Jackson, Mississippi

Ron Anderson, "George Scott," http://sabr.org/bioproj/person/bc06od6c; Baseball-Reference.com website, www.baseball-reference.com; Gordon Eades, *ESPN.com* (30 July 2013), http://espn.go.com/boston/mlb/story /_/id/9520950/george-boomer-scott-died-feeling-some-resentment; Mississippi Sports Hall of Fame and Museum website, www.msfame.com.

Scott County

Scott County was founded in 1833 and named for Gov. Abram M. Scott. Forest is the county seat, and other communities include Morton, Sebastopol, and Lake. In its first census in 1840, the central Mississippi county had one of the state's smallest populations, with 1,191 free people and 462 slaves.

By 1860 Scott County recorded 5,180 free people and 2,959 slaves. Still relatively small, it ranked in the bottom third of Mississippi counties for agricultural production. The county's five lumber mills employed thirty-one industrial workers. The county also had fourteen churches—eight Baptist, four Methodist, and the state's only two Lutheran churches.

By 1880 Scott County was home to 10,845 people: 6,633 whites, 4,132 African Americans, and 80 Native Americans. Landowners cultivated 61 percent of the county's farms, and few of the county's residents worked in industry.

Scott County's population continued to grow, and by 1900 it had 14,316 residents. A majority of Scott's farmers owned their land, though 68 percent of white farmers did so, compared to just 47 percent of African American farmers. Industrial establishments employed fifty-nine workers, all but two of them male. According to the 1916 religious census, most county residents were Missionary Baptists, Southern Baptists, or members of the Methodist Episcopal Church, South.

By 1930 Scott County's population topped 20,000, with whites accounting for 60 percent of residents. The county's sixteen manufacturing establishments, including some lumber mills, employed more than 900 workers, and Scott's 3,540 farms were run by a combination of tenant farmers (52 percent) and owners (48 percent). Bienville National Forest, established in 1936, provided 178,000 acres of land for fishing, hiking, and camping.

Blues musician Arthur "Big Boy" Crudup was born in Forest in 1905. Crudup became known as the Father of Rock and Roll after three of his songs were recorded by Elvis Presley in the 1950s. Born in Morton in 1968, Angela Boyd moved to California after graduating from high school and pursued a career in R&B music and dance under the name B Angie B, later collaborating with pop star MC Hammer.

Scott County's population grew only slightly in the mid-twentieth century. In 1960 whites made up 62 percent of the residents, and African Americans 38 percent. The county was also home to 46 Native Americans. About 30 percent of the county's workers remained employed in agriculture, primarily raising corn, soybeans, and livestock, and 20 percent worked in manufacturing, especially food products.

Two important figures in Mississippi's political and legal responses to the civil rights movement came from Scott County. Erle Johnston moved to Forest to work for the *Scott County Times*, a newspaper he later purchased. In the early 1960s he served as the public relations director for the Mississippi State Sovereignty Commission, the spying and propaganda organization that sought to discredit civil rights activists. Johnston and his wife, Fay, continued to work at the newspaper, and he served as mayor of Forest in the 1980s. US district judge Sidney Carr Mize, born in Scott County in 1888, ruled in *Meredith v. Fair* (1962) that the University of Mississippi had not discriminated against James Meredith because of issues of race. That decision was soon overturned.

In the 1970s B. C. Rogers Poultry in Morton began hiring Mexican and Mexican American workers for its plant. Those workers did not remain at B. C. Rogers, in part because efforts to organize a union failed, but other employers began to recruit Hispanic workers. Like many counties in central Mississippi, in 2010 Scott County had a small white majority and a significant African American minority and had shown an overall increase in size since 1960. The county's large Hispanic/Latino minority accounted for nearly 11 percent of the 28,315 residents.

Mississippi Encyclopedia Staff
University of Mississippi

Mississippi State Planning Commission, *Progress Report on State Planning in Mississippi* (1938); *Mississippi Statistical Abstract*, Mississippi State University (1952–2010); Charles Sydnor and Claude Bennett, *Mississippi History* (1939); University of Virginia Library, Historical Census Browser website, http://mapserver.lib.virginia.edu; E. Nolan Waller and Dani A. Smith, *Growth Profiles of Mississippi's Counties, 1960–1980* (1985).

S

Sculpture

The most prevalent sculptural forms found in Mississippi are among and around the state's cemeteries, courthouses, and national battlefields. Marble works that commemorate the Civil War can be located in nearly every county or town, especially Vicksburg. However, whether commemorating the Union or the Confederacy, none are known to have been rendered by native Mississippians. In fact, because southerners were hesitant about being involved with federal land, the first monuments erected in Vicksburg National Cemetery following the Civil War honored fallen Union soldiers. All Confederate markers and monuments were erected following World War I. Although no Mississippians were involved, some of the greatest sculptors of the time are represented by works throughout the state.

A second form of sculpture found in all corners of Mississippi is known commonly as folk art. Native Mississippians have produced folk art for generations and continue to do so today, as evidenced by the work of such artists as Bovina's Earl Simmons. These artists often are physically isolated and therefore use any sort of discarded item in the immediate vicinity for artistic purposes.

In 1980 the Mississippi State Historical Museum in Jackson hosted *Made by Hand: Mississippi Folk Art*, an exhibition featuring the works of many leading folk artists, including Luster Willis from the Terry area and George Williams from Amite County. Also featured was musician and sculptor James "Son Ford" Thomas. By far the most mysterious of Mississippi folk artists, Thomas was known for creating sculptures and blues songs inspired by his dreams. Although Thomas's subjects range from animal forms to life-size busts, his red clay skulls with shells for eyes and corn for teeth are his most interesting works.

One of the more celebrated Mississippi sculptors was Richmond Barthé. Born in Bay St. Louis in 1908, Barthé was already exhibiting art in New Orleans by the age of twelve. Barthé eventually studied at the School of the Art Institute of Chicago, where he received two Rosenwald Fellowships that allowed him to go to New York and take part in the Harlem Renaissance. Throughout his career Barthé designed coins and erected bronze monuments, including the nine-foot eagle over the Social Security Building in Washington, D.C., and a statue of Toussaint-Louverture.

Mississippi is also home to many active and prolific contemporary sculptors who work in a variety of media and styles. Sam Gore is renowned for creating clay busts of Christ for church audiences all over Mississippi and beyond. His tenure as a professor in the Mississippi College Art Department has given him far-reaching influence. In addition to working in a number of styles, including Dada, surrealism, and realism based on the figure, William Beckwith of Greenville is also credited with establishing the state's first commercial foundry and has taught at the University of Mississippi. Cleveland's Floyd Shaman, a native of Wyoming, founded the art department of Delta State University in 1970 and creates humorous yet satirical figurative work in laminated wood. Rod Moorehead, originally from California, was raised in Oxford and earned a bachelor's degree from the University of Mississippi. After living in Colorado for several years, Moorehead returned to Oxford and became a noted figurative ceramic sculptor.

Two expatriate artists who have gained national and international fame, Sam Gilliam and William Dunlap, bridge the gap between painting and sculpture. Dunlap often employs found objects associated with life in the South into his real-istic canvases, yielding a product that is both two- and three-dimensional. Dunlap's imagery reflects aspects of life in Mississippi in quite a literal manner, while Gilliam's work is process oriented and nonrepresentational. Gilliam, certainly Mississippi's leading African American artist, has been exhibiting nationally and internationally since the mid-1950s. Although many regard Tupelo native Gilliam as a painter, his enormous soaked and stained canvases are unsupported by any type of frame, creating a draped three-dimensional look. Gilliam also works on multilayered wood constructs with intensely colored hues.

Mark Brown
Jones County Junior College

Romare Bearden and Harry Henderson, *A History of African American Artists: From 1792 to the Present* (1993); Patti Carr Black, *Art in Mississippi, 1720–1980* (1998); William Dunlap website, www.williamdunlap .com; Lauren Rogers Museum of Art, *Handbook of the Collections* (2003); Jane Livingston and John Beardsley, *Black Folk Art in America* (1982).

Sears, Claudius Wistar
(1817–1891) Confederate General

Born in Peru, Massachusetts, on 8 November 1817 to Dr. Thomas Sears and Sophia Sears, Claudius Wistar Sears became a noted educator and soldier. Sears graduated from the US Military Academy at West Point in 1841 and was commissioned into the 8th US Infantry, seeing action against the Seminoles in Florida. After only one year of service, however, Sears resigned on 10 October 1842 to take a teaching position at an Episcopal military school in Mississippi. In 1844 Sears became a mathematics instructor at St. Thomas's Hall in Holly Springs, and the following year he became professor of mathematics and civil engineering at the University of Louisiana (now Tulane University). In New Orleans he met and married Susan Alice Gray. In 1859 Sears moved back to St. Thomas's Hall, ultimately becoming president of the school and commandant of cadets.

Sears remained at Holly Springs during the sectional crisis that led to the Civil War. A staunch Democrat and secessionist, Sears left the classroom for the battlefield. His training and experience at West Point and in the Regular Army was at a premium in early war Mississippi. He entered Confederate service as a private in the 17th Mississippi Infantry but was elected captain of Company G on 5 June 1861. Sears rose through the ranks, becoming colonel of the 46th Mississippi Infantry. He saw action at Port Gibson and surrendered in Vicksburg. Reentering Confederate service after his exchange, Sears became a brigadier general on 1 March 1864 after his brigade commander fell from his horse and died.

Despite frequent illnesses, Sears led his Mississippi brigade through the Atlanta and Tennessee Campaigns. While holding the salient point of the line on the first day at Nashville (15 December 1864), Sears's brigade was overrun in the massive Federal attack. Sears was sitting atop his horse and watching the enemy through his binoculars when a cannonball slammed into his leg, taking it off and killing his horse. Sears recovered and for the remainder of his life wore a wooden leg that squeaked loudly on wooden floors.

After the war, Sears refused to let defeat or his wound stop him from continuing to serve the public. He returned to Mississippi and took a position as professor of mathematics at the newly reopened University of Mississippi. The old general also served as the faculty commander of a military company of students. The board of trustees fired him in 1889, and he lived in Oxford until his death on 15 February 1891.

Timothy B. Smith
University of Tennessee at Martin

Karlem Riess, *Journal of Mississippi History* (April 1949); Claudius Wistar Sears Diaries, Mississippi Department of Archives and History.

Seawright, James
(b. 1936) Artist

Born in Jackson on 22 May 1936, James Lemuel Seawright Jr. is a pioneer of kinetic and electronic sculpture and America's foremost technological artist. A graduate of the University of Mississippi, where he received a bachelor's in English with a minor in physics, Seawright was a member of the art faculty at Princeton University beginning in 1969 and served as director of visual arts at Princeton from 1975 to 2001.

Seawright traces his love of making objects by hand to his boyhood discovery of machine tools at a friend's house in Mississippi. Later, in the US Navy, he worked with additional tools and materials and realized that he could "use modern electronics and controlled technology to apply to sculptures." After moving to New York in 1961 Seawright picked up further technical expertise while an assistant at the Henry Street Playhouse and at the Columbia-Princeton Electronic Music Center. His work at Bell Labs, in conjunction with a year at the Art Students' League, crystallized the direction of his artwork. Writing his own computer programs, Seawright began creating kinetic and interactive sculptures concerned with light and movement. His first art show in New York took place in 1966, and he quickly rose to fame in this abstruse field, showing early works at the Whitney Museum's Sculptors' Annual (1967) and participating in a 1968 Museum of Modern Art exhibition, *The Sixties*. The *New York Times* called his sculptures from this period "the most successful union of contemporary art and contemporary science." Another review of this era described Seawright's art as "combining a million tiny wires, lights, circuits, and quietly-whirring motors all forming the most complex, yet totally pure, sculpture units." By the mid-1970s Seawright moved from analog circuitry to microprocessors, building specialized digital circuits to control interactive sculptures. Many of his sculptures adjust their volume, function, or position to interact with other works or the viewing audience. Alongside his electronic pieces, in the 1970s Seawright experimented with mirror reliefs, as in a large installation created for the Seattle-Tacoma Airport in 1973. Another mirror sculpture, *Hexflector*, is in the Mississippi Museum of Art. Echoing the interactive nature of his electronic pieces, Seawright used complex arrangements of multiple mirror surfaces to reflect complex images based on changing angles of light.

In the 1990s Seawright returned to kinetic computer sculpture. As computer technology advanced, so did the concepts behind his artwork. At this time, the laborious hand-wiring required for his *Houseplants* series of the 1980s was supplanted by more sophisticated and complex computer-based ideas. *Corina*, a work that appeared as part of the Mississippi Museum of Art's *The Mississippi Story* exhibition, is a piece from Seawright's *Constellations* series (2001–5). He describes the series as "meditations on particular constellations, their structure and their history, or rather the history of the lore that has grown up around them." The three-dimensional works are constructed of metal, plastic, and electronic parts. In discussing the future of this original genre, Seawright said, "Nowadays, embedded systems hardware is universally available, and software is the whole ball game. It seems to me that, after a few false starts along the way, digital art has a limitless future—it's no longer the language of a few isolated souls, but a language spoken everywhere."

Seawright received an award from the Solomon R. Guggenheim Museum in 1969 and has won several grants from the National Endowment for the Arts. His work has been collected by the Museum of Modern Art, the Whitney Museum, the Guggenheim Museum, the New Jersey State Museum, and Brandeis University, among others. In 2003 Seawright received a lifetime achievement award from the Mississippi Institute of Arts and Letters, and in 2004 he was given Princeton's Behrman Award for distinguished achievement in the humanities.

Seawright is married to artist and choreographer Mimi Garrard, a Greenwood native.

Patti Carr Black
Jackson, Mississippi

S

Patti Carr Black, *Art in Mississippi, 1720–1980* (1998); Patti Carr Black, *The Mississippi Story* (2007); James Seawright website, www.seawright.net.

Seay, James

(b. 1939) Poet

Poet and documentary filmmaker James Edward Seay III came from a background that made him an unlikely candidate for a future career in literature. Born on 1 January 1939 in Panola County, Seay came from a family that was closer to the earth than to education—lumbermen, farmers, and blacksmiths. Seay became the first member of his family to attend college, earning a bachelor's degree from the University of Mississippi in 1964 and a master's degree from the University of Virginia two years later. At around this time he married noted Virginia author Lee Smith, and they had two sons before divorcing in the early 1980s.

Over his long and celebrated literary career, Seay's poetry has appeared in thirty anthologies, and his essays have been featured in magazines such as *Esquire* and *Antaeus*. Seay has also published four books of poetry—*Let Not Your Heart* (1970), *Water Tables* (1974), *The Light as They Found It* (1990), and *Open Field, Understory* (1997)—and two limited editions of poetry. In 1988 he received the Award in Literature from the American Academy of Arts and Letters. Departing briefly from poetry, Seay teamed with director George Butler in 1990 to write a documentary film, *In the Blood*, about big-game hunting in East Africa.

Seay's poetic vision of the South is directly descended from the viewpoint of such older southern writers as William Faulkner and Eudora Welty. Yet Seay's version of the South is intermingled with the memory of parents and grandparents and with images from today's South. James H. Justus believes that Seay paints a clearer version of the modern southern atmosphere than any other writer of his age: "None of the poets of this generation has done better than James Seay in not only evoking the village culture of the contemporary South but also transforming its commonplaces into objects and events of talismanic significance." Seay's poetry often juxtaposes the epic with the ordinary, as in "The Majorette on the Self-Rising Flour Sign," where the "soldier-girl" in a flour advertisement becomes "this age's superwoman." To avoid giving way to cliché, Seay complicates his "southern" imagery; references to "sweetbreads and wine" and "white whisky in a Clorox jug" are never sweet remembrances of a time past but often are dark in tone and a little unsettling.

Seay taught at the Virginia Military Institute, the University of Alabama, and Vanderbilt University prior to 1974, when he became a lecturer and later professor of English at the University of North Carolina at Chapel Hill. He has also served as director of the school's Creative Writing Program.

Lisa Sloan
University of Mississippi

Julia Bryan, *Endeavors Magazine* website, http://endeavors.unc.edu (Fall 1997); James H. Justus, *The History of Southern Literature*, ed. Louis D. Rubin (1985); David Williamson, University of North Carolina News Services website, http://uncnews.unc.edu (18 February 1997).

Secessionist Movement

The secessionist movement in Mississippi, as in the rest of the South, was rooted in sectional differences over the future of slavery. White Mississippians considered slavery the foundation of their social order and culture and believed that only its survival would preserve their civilization and ensure their prosperity and safety. In the end, the imperative of defending and even promoting the institution distorted whites' religious theology, gender conventions, and nearly all social ethics. When Mississippians spoke of defending slavery, they understood the term broadly to include their slave-based way of life. Thus, the majority of white Mississippians ultimately supported secession to protect slavery and all that it represented in their lives.

Before the 1850s some Mississippians discussed secession as a potential last, desperate measure to protect slavery. As long as the direct threat to the institution remained slight, however, secession was too radical for the vast majority of the state's voters. Support for disunion grew during the controversy surrounding California's admission as a free state and the accompanying Compromise of 1850. Most southerners believed that "free soil" (the nonextension of slavery) posed a threat to the long-term viability and health of slavery, and as support for free soil grew among northern voters, white Mississippians became increasingly anxious and wary.

The most important development in the history of the secessionist movement was the formation and success of the free soil Republican Party. One reason Republicans advocated the nonextension of slavery was to limit planters' political power in the national government, drawing on growing northern resentment of the "Slave Power." Most Republicans were not abolitionists; probably just a minority had real moral misgivings about slavery itself, and many were racists who wanted to exclude all nonwhites from the territories. For a great variety of reasons, then, Republicans were united in their commitment to stop the spread of slavery beyond where it already existed. This program of sectional antagonism presented southerners with a double threat. First was the tangible danger that free soil presented to slavery. Unable to expand, most white southerners believed, slavery would become more and more unstable, ending finally in widespread rebellion as whites were slowly outnumbered by the growing slave population. Southerners would also lose power in the national government as they became an ever-shrinking minority within the country, perhaps ending with a constitutional amendment to abolish slavery. Finally, without fresh land to exploit, the market value of slaves would decline, since they were only as valuable as what they produced. Thus, most white southerners believed free soil to be just as unacceptable as abolition.

Southern whites also resented the Republicans' claim of northern superiority. This "insult" to their "honor" challenged southerners' personal and collective reputations and questioned their equality as good Christians and Americans. As one group of Mississippi voters summarized, "To deny us the right and privilege [of slavery in the territories] would be to deny our equality in the Union, and would be a wrong and degradation to which a high spirited people should not submit." In the words of another Mississippian, "The distinction sought to be made between the South and North cannot be tolerated by honorable men."

Emphasizing these threats to slavery, the insult to southern honor, and the challenge to manhood, the secessionist movement gained strength rapidly after 1856, when Republicans carried a majority of northern states in the presidential contest. Mississippians joined other southerners in denouncing the sectional party, and Magnolia State voters presented a more and more unified front in state and national elections. By 1859 the opposition party received just one-third of the vote in the gubernatorial election. Leaders of the secessionist movement in Mississippi included John Quitman (though he died in 1858) and John Jones Pettus, who was elected governor in 1859. The state's most famous politician, Jefferson Davis, waffled on the question of secession throughout 1859 and 1860.

The presidential campaign of 1860 energized secessionists and gave new urgency to the movement for disunion. The possibility of a Republican victory appalled Mississippians, and a strong majority of voters supported the Southern Democratic candidate, John C. Breckinridge, whose party pledged secession if Abraham Lincoln won. Early elections in several northern states virtually assured a Republican triumph, so Mississippi voters who supported Breckinridge sent a clear message in support of secession.

In the wake of the election, secessionists moved quickly to capitalize on public outrage over Lincoln's victory. While the majority of Mississippi's men expressed support for secession, leaders of the movement took few chances. Vigilance committees, "Minute Men" clubs, and other local organizations held rallies, calling on men to do "their duty as men" and defend the state's honor. Many Unionists were intimidated, some drifted to the secessionist cause, and others just gave up when it became obvious that secession had widespread support. In December the state held an election for delegates to a special convention called by the legislature, and secessionists won a strong majority. The convention passed an ordinance of secession on 9 January 1861, and Mississippi officially withdrew from the Union.

The secessionist movement in Mississippi paralleled that in most Lower South states, although widespread ownership of slaves almost certainly contributed to the state's enthusiastic support for disunion. The Mississippi Declaration of Secession stated, "Our position is thoroughly identified with the institution of slavery—the greatest material interest of the world. Its labor supplies the product which constitutes by far the largest and most important portions of commerce of the earth. These products are peculiar to the climate verging on the tropical regions, and by an imperious law of nature, none but the black race can bear exposure to the tropical sun. These products have become necessities of the world, and a blow at slavery is a blow at commerce and civilization. That blow has been long aimed at the institution, and was at the point of reaching its consummation. There was no choice left us but submission to the mandates of abolition, or a dissolution of the Union, whose principals had been subverted to work out our ruin." Mississippi trailed only South Carolina in the percentage of its residents enslaved, and most estimates suggest that more than half of white households owned slaves. Furthermore, the wild profits made from cotton in the 1850s undoubtedly caused many Mississippians to feel particularly threatened by the Republicans' free soil platform. Because of a combination of factors, then, Mississippi took a leading role in the southern secessionist movement.

Christopher Olsen
Indiana State University

William L. Barney, *The Secessionist Impulse: Alabama and Mississippi in 1860* (1974); Bradley Bond, *Political Culture in the Nineteenth-Century South: Mississippi, 1830–1900* (1995); Christopher Morris, *Becoming Southern: The Evolution of a Way of Life: Warren County and Vicksburg, 1770–1860* (1995); Christopher Olsen, *Political Culture and Secession in Mississippi: Masculinity, Honor, and the Antiparty Tradition, 1830s–1860* (2000); Percy Lee Rainwater, *Mississippi: Storm-Center of Secession, 1856–1861* (1938).

S

Segregation

Segregation touched every aspect of life in Mississippi. Racial discrimination was so prevalent after the demise of Reconstruction that some whites saw no need for Jim Crow legislation. African Americans and whites lived separate lives on almost every level. They were kept apart in private and public hospitals and were prevented from using the same entrances to state-funded health care facilities. Black criminals were not incarcerated in the same prison cells with whites, and the races could not even ride together in taxis.

After 1877 African Americans lost their political rights in Mississippi through intimidation, fraud, and outright murder, and racial segregation became largely a matter of custom. According to historian Neil McMillen, "Mississippi seems to have had fewer Jim Crow laws during the entire segregation period than most southern states." In other words, since African Americans knew their "place," whites did not need legislation to control black behavior. Wherever they turned, black Mississippians faced segregation. More often than not, Jim Crow customs required both separation and exclusion. The state legislature passed laws segregating trains in 1888 and streetcars in 1904. At weddings and funerals, in courtrooms, public facilities, and other places used for social gathering, habit kept the races apart. The code of racial etiquette prohibited any form of interracial activity that might have even remotely implied equality. Nonetheless, blacks were more concerned with having equal access to facilities than they were with integration per se.

In 1890 the Mississippi legislature called a constitutional convention expressly to disfranchise blacks. The Second Mississippi Plan emerged from this meeting, imposing literacy requirements, poll taxes, and laws denying the vote to anyone convicted of bribery, arson, murder, theft, or burglary—crimes for which African Americans were much more likely to be convicted than whites. Following Mississippi's lead, other southern states began to enact laws to deny blacks the franchise. The US Supreme Court's decision in *Williams v. Mississippi* (1898) added to African Americans' political impotence by denying them federal civil rights law protection.

The few blacks who participated in Mississippi's political system during the early Jim Crow years were members of the Republican Party. However, they were still segregated within the party, where their Black and Tan faction often clashed with its Lily-White counterpart. The educational situation was similarly bleak for blacks. Mississippi had the dubious distinction of being the southern state that spent the least on black education. Indeed, great disparities existed in the segregated education provided for black and white children. In 1900, although African American children accounted for 60 percent of the state's school-age population, they received only 19 percent of the state's school funds. Adams County spent $22.23 to educate each white child, but only $2.00 for each black child. And after 1890, biracial education was unconstitutional. However, most African American complaints centered on the inequality inherent in the system as opposed to segregation itself. Blacks deeply resented that their tax dollars were being used disproportionately to fund white education.

African Americans were denied access to private and public recreational facilities. They could not go to skating rinks, tennis courts, bowling alleys, or swimming pools. In fact, not until World War II did Mound Bayou physician Theodore R. M. Howard build the state's first swimming pool for blacks. Likewise, movie theaters often had separate ticket windows for blacks, who had to enter through side or rear doors. Although they paid the same amount as white patrons for their tickets, African Americans also had to sit in the balcony or other segregated portions of the facility.

One of the greatest taboos during the era of segregation was interracial dating and marriage, which was illegal. The state legislature also barred the publication or circulation of printed materials that favored intermarriage, imposing punishments of fines of up to five hundred dollars and jail terms of up to six months. Worse than the legal punishments were the extralegal ones: a black man accused of merely looking at or touching a white woman could suffer mob violence—flogging, lynching, drowning, burning, or being dragged to death behind an automobile.

One way African Americans responded to this repressive system of Jim Crow exclusion and segregation was by developing their own parallel institutions—churches, colleges and universities, Masonic lodges, fraternities and sororities, and professional associations such as the National Negro Business League, the Mississippi Negro Business League, the Negro Bankers Association of Mississippi, the National Association of Colored Women, the Mississippi State Federation of Colored Women's Clubs, the National Medical Association, the National Bar Association, the National Association of Colored Graduate Nurses, and the National Hospital Association.

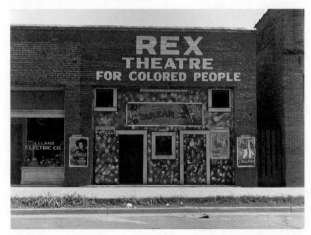

Rex Theatre, Leland, 1937 (Photograph by Dorothea Lange, Library of Congress [LC-USF34-017417-E], Washington, D.C.)

According to historian Darlene Clark Hine, "Without the parallel institutions that the black professional class created, successful challenges to white supremacy would not have been possible. The formation of parallel organizations . . . proved to be far more radical, far more capable of nurturing resistance, than anyone could have anticipated. . . . [S]egregation provided blacks the chance, indeed, the imperative, to develop a range of distinct institutions they controlled." Although blacks looked at segregation with contempt, they had no choice but to live within that system, and creating parallel institutions helped them to do so.

A crack in Mississippi's wall of segregation eventually occurred through its system of higher education. During Reconstruction, some black leaders demanded that African Americans be admitted into the University of Mississippi at Oxford. Whites, however, refused to consider such requests. Although this system of exclusion lasted for nearly a century, James Meredith filed a racial discrimination complaint against the University of Mississippi in 1961, and he enrolled at the university the following year, but only after Pres. John F. Kennedy sent three hundred federal marshals to uphold the Fifth Circuit Court's decision to admit him. Civil rights sit-ins and boycotts also challenged the institution of segregation, often with success. School desegregation took place slowly in the years after the *Brown v. Board of Education* decision, with the rise of all-white private schools negating some of the goals of desegregation. From the late 1800s through the 1960s, Mississippi developed an infamous record as what McMillen has labeled the "heartland of American apartheid."

David H. Jackson Jr.
Florida A&M University

Stephen J. Berrey, *The Jim Crow Routine: Everyday Performances of Race, Civil Rights, and Segregation in Mississippi* (2015); John Hope Franklin, *From Slavery to Freedom: A History of African Americans* (1994); Darlene Clark Hine, *Journal of American History* (March 2003); Darlene Clark Hine, William C. Hine, and Stanley Harrold, *The African-American Odyssey* (2000); David H. Jackson Jr., *A Chief Lieutenant of the Tuskegee Machine: Charles Banks of Mississippi* (2002); Neil R. McMillen, *Dark Journey: Black Mississippians in the Age of Jim Crow* (1989); David M. Oshinsky, *"Worse Than Slavery": Parchman Farm and the Ordeal of Jim Crow Justice* (1996); C. Vann Woodward, *The Strange Career of Jim Crow* (1974).

Semon, Larry
(1889–1928) Actor and Director

Born in Vicksburg, Mississippi, on 16 July 1889, Lawrence "Larry" Semon rose to considerable fame as a silent film actor and director during the 1920s. While today his movies are difficult to find and his name has been virtually erased from American film history, during the early years of cinema he rivaled Charlie Chaplin in comic popularity.

Semon's mother, a vaudeville comedian, and his father, a magician and ventriloquist, trained him in singing, pantomime, and acting, and while still a boy he began performing before audiences. By the time he was a teenager, the family had settled down in Savannah, Georgia, where he attended high school. He had shown an aptitude for drawing, and his father urged him to attend art school. After graduating from high school, Semon moved to New York and found employment drawing cartoons for several newspapers as well as for Vitagraph, a film production company.

Semon grew restless and used his entertainment experience to move into comedy screenwriting and then to become a stunt man, actor, and eventually director. Pleased with Semon's work, Vitagraph allowed him to expand to two-reelers and feature-length films in 1918. An unknown actor, Stan Laurel, joined the Semon comedy team, and Oliver Hardy came onboard a few years later. For several years Semon turned out box office hits, including *The Grocery Clerk* (1920), and he became one of Hollywood's highest-paid entertainers, earning five thousand dollars a week.

His success proved short-lived. An extravagant spender with an egomaniacal personality, Semon often angered his employers, and he and Vitagraph became entangled in court battles over expenditures. In addition, audiences and critics began to lose interest in his comedies, finding his newer films to be less interesting duplicates of his earlier ones. In 1924 Semon had fulfilled his contract for Vitagraph and still held out hope for a return to the public eye. He decided to combat his popular decline with several new films, this time with producer I. E. Chadwick, and several new costars, including Dorothy Dwan, whom he married the following year. While two of his first projects with Chadwick were somewhat successful, *The Wizard of Oz* (1925) was recognized as one of the largest movie failures of the decade. Transforming L. Frank Baum's fantastical story into a forced slapstick comedy routine, the movie found few fans. Following several more failed projects, Semon filed for bankruptcy in 1928. He could find work only by returning to vaudeville. He performed two or three times a day during the first half of 1928 before suffering a nervous and physical breakdown in August. He died unexpectedly of pneumonia on 8 October 1928. The circumstances surrounding his death and his small, closed-casket funeral led to speculation that he faked his demise to escape the country and his personal failures.

Katherine Treppendahl
University of Virginia

Internet Movie Database website, www.imdb.com; Richard M. Roberts, Classic Images website, www.classicimages.com.

Sessions, Cliff

(1931–2005) Journalist

Born in Bolton, Mississippi, on 26 September 1931, to an Episcopal minister and his wife, Clifton Farr Sessions graduated from the University of Southern Mississippi in 1955 and started working at a Hattiesburg radio station. Shortly thereafter, the Jackson office of United Press International hired him as a reporter.

As a white Mississippian, he assumed that many of the people he covered supported the state's official policies about segregation and white supremacy. By giving thorough coverage to violent incidents, the Citizens' Councils, state leaders and their policies, and numerous civil rights protests, Sessions developed an interest in uncovering the ways white supremacists operated and the ways activists were resisting. One controversial 1958 piece described a Citizens' Council contest that encouraged high school students to write and present lectures about race relations and limited government. Sessions called the program "a full scale effort to wipe out any integrationist leanings among the children." One white Mississippi television executive responded with what he considered a damning insult: "Sessions, you're an integrationist. Crawl back under your rock. You've been exposed."

As part of his coverage of the civil rights movement, Sessions developed a friendship with Medgar Evers, the head of Mississippi's chapter of the National Association for the Advancement of Colored People. The relationship was important enough to Sessions and his wife, Shirley, that they violated Jim Crow by inviting Medgar Evers and his wife, Myrlie, to their home for dinner. When Medgar was shot in the driveway of the Evers home in June 1963, Myrlie called Sessions even before she telephoned the police.

Sessions left Mississippi in 1964, working first for United Press International in Washington, D.C., and then helping to found the *National Journal*, which offered straightforward news about federal government agencies. Sessions served as the *Journal*'s editor in 1970 and 1971 and then took a series of communications positions in the US Justice Department; the US Department of Health, Education, and Welfare; and the private sector. Parkinson's disease forced his retirement in 1990, and he and his wife moved to Biloxi, where he died on 24 December 2005.

Ted Ownby
University of Mississippi

Joe Holley, *Washington Post* (29 December 2005); Gene Roberts and Hank Klibanoff, *The Race Beat: The Press, the Civil Rights Struggle, and the Awakening of a Nation* (2007).

Shape-Note Singing

Shape-note singing is a musical tradition and practice of community gatherings singing sacred music using a system of musical notation in which the noteheads are printed in distinct shapes that indicate their scale degree and musical syllable (fa, sol, la, etc.). Shape-note systems used in Mississippi include the "fasola" system, with four shapes, and the "doremi," with seven shapes. Both systems were employed in singing schools: these brief courses in sight-reading and part-singing represented the first American musical institution, improving singing in churches while offering young people a rare chance to socialize with the opposite sex. Denounced by critics as uncouth, the simplified notation, which first appeared in 1801, caught on in rural areas of the South and West and became standard in sacred music publication. Though singers at Natchez churches sang urban music printed in round notes as early as 1820, the settlers in the Chickasaw and Choctaw cessions of the 1830s brought singing schools and shape-note tunebooks, including *Missouri Harmony* (1820) and *Southern Harmony* (1835), into the area.

In 1849 Lazarus J. Jones of Jasper County published *The Southern Minstrel*. Printed in Philadelphia, Pennsylvania, this book contained standard tunes from other southern sources as well as several new compositions and arrangements by Jones and other east-central Mississippians. The book went through a second printing in 1855 but subsequently faded from view. Jesse T. White, a nephew of *Sacred Harp* compiler B. F. White and composer of ten of the songs in that book, was clerk of Winston County in the 1850s before moving to Texas. He may have introduced *The Sacred Harp* to the hill country of central Mississippi.

Evidence indicates that at the close of the Civil War, all-day singings from *The Sacred Harp* occurred in several locations around the state. At least one—in 1866 in Calhoun County—was described as a reunion of soldiers with their families. Such events soon became annual community homecomings and memorials, attracting thousands of attendees. W. A. Beasley of Houston and Henry J. Hawkins of Ellzey were among the leading singers of that period and played a role in the formation of Sacred Harp conventions in Calhoun (1878), Chickasaw (1882), and Webster (1883) Counties. These and other conventions provided a forum where established teachers met to sing together, to examine and certify new teachers, and to demonstrate the accomplishments of their classes. At both annual singings and conventions, leaders were called in turn to stand in the midst of the assembled singers and direct one or more songs. This custom persists today.

As African American literacy increased, black singers established singing schools and conventions. The Alabama-Mississippi Singing Convention (1887), which uses gospel music today, may originally have sung from *The Sacred Harp* or William Walker's *Christian Harmony*. The Pleasant Ridge Colored Musical Convention of Calhoun County (1898) sang from *The Sacred Harp*, as did its sister conventions in Chickasaw and Webster Counties.

Sacred Harp singing in Mississippi, especially in Calhoun, Chickasaw, Webster, and adjoining counties, has long been identified by a unique practice not found elsewhere: the use of seven syllables (doremi) to name the four shaped notes—in effect, disregarding the shapes that help other singers learn the notes. This practice appears to date back to the immediate post–Civil War period. It may derive from the transitional 1854 edition of William Walker's *Southern Harmony*, which offered precisely this alternative to the fasola system for singers who wished to sing the more modern seven syllables with the more conservative repertory of the four-shape books.

After the Civil War, singing schools and shape notes became increasingly identified with the South while declining in popularity in other regions. Many teachers switched from the four-shape system to a seven-shape system to keep pace with new teaching methods. Leading singing masters established "music normal schools" to train teachers. These teachers used books from southern firms such as Ruebush and Kieffer and A. J. Showalter, which began to publish small, cheap collections of music every year or two. These upright songbooks gradually began to supplant the large oblong tunebooks, with their fixed repertoire. Showalter's *Class, Choir, and Congregation* (1888), a transitional book, remained in print well into the twentieth century: a "Class Choir" state convention, chaired by William E. Lane, was organized in Neshoba County in 1956. Mass-market publishers such as J. D. Vaughan (1902), V. O. Stamps (1924), and his partner J. R. Baxter (Stamps-Baxter Music, 1926) served the market by printing one or more books a year in a style known today as shape-note gospel music. The songs, always in major keys and intended to be accompanied on the piano, imitated the popular march and dance music of the postbellum era. While traditional singings, sometimes even unaccompanied, persisted in many areas, other local conventions became little more than quartet concerts. A state singing convention held its first regular session in 1934 in Newton County, with W. D. Rayner presiding. The Blackwood Brothers of Choctaw County emerged from this convention to achieve fame as gospel performers.

During the early twentieth century *The Sacred Harp* held its ground and continued to spread into new territory. The Mississippi State Sacred Harp Singing Convention was founded in 1929 at Houston with W. T. Gwin as its first president. Despite its name, it always included *Christian Harmony* singers and allowed songs from both books. This body gradually began to attract singers from the Delta area, where immigrant hill folk from Webster and Calhoun Counties were holding singings before 1930, and from southeastern Mississippi, where the South Mississippi Convention was organized

in 1947 using the W. M. Cooper revision of *The Sacred Harp*. Black singers established the West Harmony Convention (Grenada County) in 1922 and the Negro Mississippi State Sacred Harp Musical Convention in 1934 (organized by W. A. Wandwick, Frank Payne, and Elmer A. Enochs).

Northeastern Mississippi, where singers used the fasola system popular in Alabama and elsewhere, had little contact with either state convention; the area became a fertile field for Alabama singing teachers such as S. M. Denson, R. A. Canant, and F. M. Frederick. Outside this area, however, Mississippi singers had little contact with their counterparts in Alabama and other states. In 1959 R. A. Stewart of Houston began a weekly half-hour radio program of Sacred Harp singing and announcements that continues to this day. He also attended Alabama singings and established an annual singing in Houston, reestablished in Oxford after his death, where singers from the two states were encouraged to meet.

During the 1960s the Mississippi State Convention reported as many as seventy annual singings, not counting black singings and Northeast Mississippi fasola singings. Since 1970, singings from *The Sacred Harp* and *Christian Harmony* have declined over most of the state. Some conventions have been discontinued, while other three-day conventions have been reduced to two days or even one. The remaining singers, however, travel farther and stay in touch more effectively via the Internet, as Sacred Harp singing has spread beyond the American South. Shape-note gospel singings and conventions have declined as well, and singing schools have become rare except for denominational schools using church hymnals.

David Warren Steel
University of Mississippi

Joe Dan Boyd, *Mississippi Folklore Register* (Fall 1971); Buell E. Cobb Jr., *The Sacred Harp: A Tradition and Its Music* (1978); David Warren Steel, *American Music* (Summer 1988); Paula Tadlock, in *Discourse in Ethnomusicology: Essays in Honor of George List*, ed. John Hasse, Roberta L. Singer, and Ruth M. Stone *(1978)*; Chiquita Walls, *The African American Shape Note and Vocal Music Singing Convention Directory*, special publication of *Mississippi Folklife* (1994); Chiquita Walls, *La-Miss-Ala Shape Note Newsletter* (November–December 1999); John Quincy Wolf, *Mississippi Folklore Register* (Summer 1970); John Quincy Wolf, *Journal of American Folklore* (October–December 1968).

Sharecropping

By 1900 a system of land tenancy and farming known as sharecropping had replaced slavery and yeoman farming as the main form of agriculture in Mississippi and the larger South. The vast majority of black agricultural workers in the

Delta and other plantation areas in the state and region were paid a share of the crop as their wages or paid a smaller share of the crop to their landlords as rent. Those who worked as wage croppers typically received a half share of the crop at the end of the year, with all supplies, tools, and animals provided by the landlord or a furnishing merchant. These supplies were advanced against the worker's share of the crop. Share tenants, including landless white farmers in the nonplantation areas, usually owned mules and tools but still obtained supply advances from landlords and merchants, paying one-third of the crop as rent. Similar to the share-cropper, the share renters pledged their share of the crop in exchange for advances from the landlord or a merchant for supplies. These furnishing merchants charged high interest rates on the advances—from 25 to 65 percent, depending on the risk and on the lenders' unchallenged power to dictate the terms of credit. As a result, the vast majority of share-croppers and tenant farmers ended the year hopelessly in debt to landlords and suppliers, entrapped in an economic box from which there was no easy exit.

This system of sharecropping did not emerge overnight. When the Civil War ended, southern landlords tried to establish a system of labor similar to slavery by promulgating the notorious Black Codes that bound the formerly enslaved to the land as a servile labor force controlled by the planter class, devoid of civil rights, and limited in their mobility as free laborers. This effort ran counter to the wishes of the former slaves as well as of many Radical Republicans, who believed that the plantations should be broken up and distributed to African Americans as family farms. When the federal government refused to endorse the distribution of plantation lands, blacks throughout the South tried to use their labor power to resist being returned to the plantation as agricultural laborers under the close supervision of their former owners. They insisted, often with the help of the Freedmen's Bureau and supportive Republican carpetbaggers, on working as farmers in family units relatively free from close supervision and on paying a share of the crop as rent. They preferred this arrangement over fixed wages paid at the end of the year, which they knew were liable to fraud and beyond their control.

Faced with an army of occupation and a vigilant black population, southern landowners had little choice but to accept the sharecropping arrangement as a temporary solution, often leasing their lands to northern speculators and merchants, who then contracted with African Americans to work the land as sharecroppers. The system also allowed landowners to get their land into production at a time when few had the cash or the credit to pay fixed wages on a weekly or monthly basis. But after the end of Reconstruction, the system left sharecroppers and tenants impoverished and deeply indebted to their suppliers and landlords, with all decisions about farming made by these merchants and landowners.

Part of the reason for this change in the character of sharecropping reflected the high crop yields that depressed prices and pressured landlords to use every means available to control the supply of labor and limit its cost. Landlords and furnishing merchants charged high interest rates not only to offset risks but to increase profits by extracting as much income from the workers as possible. As a result, few black farmers ended the crop year free from debt, and this debt prevented them from moving to find better terms of labor.

Although the larger economic context was important, sharecropping became firmly entrenched principally as a consequence of white landlords' and merchants' success in creating a political economy that enabled them to control the labor power of the formerly enslaved and to eliminate all possibility of political reform of the system. They did so via the law, racial violence, and class politics. In Mississippi and much of the rest of the South, a series of laws and legal interpretations by the courts privileged merchants' and landlords' claims to crops—the crop lien—over claims by farmers; defined sharecroppers as wage hands rather than tenants; limited croppers' ability to contract or move while in debt; and protected creditors' claims for advances to make the crops. These legal mechanisms also disfranchised southern blacks, in cooperation with whites of every class, by imposing impediments to voter registration such as poll taxes, literacy tests, and residency requirements. The Mississippi Constitution of 1890, for example, essentially ended black suffrage in the state, thereby removing all possibility of political reforms that might have addressed the situation. Moreover, these laws complemented Jim Crow social behavior (virulent and violently enforced segregation and lynching) aimed at relegating all blacks to the status of an inferior caste of people without civil or economic rights.

Although sharecropping lasted until the middle of the twentieth century in Mississippi and elsewhere in the South, the Great Depression of the 1930s and the New Deal agriculture relief programs fundamentally undermined the system. New Deal subsidies to southern cotton planters designed to encourage crop reductions and achieve higher crop prices were seldom passed on to sharecroppers. Instead, landlords simply evicted croppers from the land, and the federal subsidy dollars were used to mechanize cotton picking and planting. In addition, minimum wage laws after World War II further motivated the owners of large-scale plantations to abandon what little sharecropping still existed and even to reduce the use of fixed-wage hands. By 1965, a century after the Civil War, few southern farmers or farmhands worked as sharecroppers or share tenants.

Ronald L. F. Davis
California State University
at Northridge

James C. Cobb, *The Most Southern Place on Earth: The Mississippi Delta and the Roots of Regional Identity* (1992); Ronald L. F. Davis, *Good and Faithful Labor: From Slavery to Sharecropping in the Natchez District, 1860–1890* (1982); Gerald David Jaynes, *Branches without Roots: Genesis of the Black Working Class in the American South* (1986); Neil R. McMillen, *Dark Journey: Black Mississippians in the Age of Jim Crow* (1989); Roger L. Ransom and Richard Sutch, *One Kind of Freedom: The Economic Consequences of Emancipation* (1977); Harold D. Woodman, *New South, New Law: The Legal Foundation of Credit and Labor Relations in the Postbellum South* (1995); Gavin Wright, *Old South, New South: Revolutions in the Southern Economy since the Civil War* (1986).

Sharkey, William Lewis

(1797–1873) Twenty-Fifth Governor, 1865

Following the arrest and imprisonment of Gov. Charles Clark in May 1865, Mississippi was for the third time without a chief executive. The state remained under martial law until 13 June, when Pres. Andrew Johnson appointed William Sharkey to serve as provisional governor. Responsibility for restoring order and gaining Mississippi's readmission to the Union fell to Sharkey.

William Lewis Sharkey was born in Tennessee in 1797 and came to Mississippi with his family in 1803. He had a highly successful law practice in Vicksburg, served briefly in the state legislature, and was elected chief justice of the Mississippi High Court of Errors and Appeals, a position he held for eighteen years. After leaving the bench, Sharkey served briefly as the American consul in Cuba and compiled the Mississippi Code of 1857.

Sharkey was a member of the Whig Party and a strong Unionist. He was one of the few Mississippi political leaders who did not support the Confederate States of America, even after the Civil War had begun. His loyalty to the Union earned him the appointment as provisional governor. Pres. Johnson adopted a conciliatory policy toward the southern states and moved quickly to restore them to the Union. He directed Sharkey to call a constitutional convention to declare the ordinance of secession null and void and to abolish slavery. Johnson also directed Sharkey to hold a general election for state officials in October. Addressing the violence of postwar Mississippi, Sharkey ordered Union Leagues disbanded and founded some new local militia units, hoping they would be more effective and more popular than the US military. Sharkey tried to walk a difficult line, supporting plans for Reconstruction while allowing some authority to pre–Civil War officials. Though opposed by the federal government, he encouraged the federal government to relinquish control of the state.

Benjamin Humphreys won the governorship in October 1865, but Sharkey did not yield the office until December. The Mississippi legislature then appointed Sharkey to the US Senate. In addition, the legislature passed a set of laws known as the Black Codes that gave Mississippi's former slaves virtually no civil or constitutional rights.

Because of the Black Codes and because the Mississippi legislature refused to ratify the Thirteenth Amendment abolishing slavery, the US Congress refused to seat Sharkey and the rest of Mississippi's congressional delegation in December 1865. In 1867 Johnson's lenient plan of Reconstruction was replaced by the congressional plan, which imposed certain political restrictions on southern whites but extended the vote to Mississippi's former slaves.

Sharkey did not take an active role in Reconstruction after December 1865. He continued his law practice in Jackson until his death in Washington, D.C., on 30 March 1873. Sharkey County is named in his honor.

David G. Sansing
University of Mississippi

William C. Harris, *Presidential Reconstruction in Mississippi* (1967); *Mississippi Official and Statistical Register* (1912); Dunbar Rowland, *Encyclopedia of Mississippi History*, vol. 2 (1907).

Sharkey County

Sharkey County is likely known most for the origins of the teddy bear and the birth of Muddy Waters. Yet the county has a long history of human settlement dating at least to the Middle Woodland period. An early indicator of settlement is the Little Spanish Fort, a ceremonial site built of earth, six feet high and two thousand feet in diameter. It, along with related Yazoo Basin sites, provides a way to understand a roughly two-thousand-year-old culture.

Part of the Lower Mississippi Delta, the region that became Sharkey County was a river area that in the early to mid-1800s concentrated on cotton, slavery, and relatively little else. Founded in 1876 from parts of Issaquena, Warren, and Washington Counties, Sharkey County began as an area with large numbers of African Americans and a high concentration of cotton on large plantations. In the county's first census in 1880, 4,893 African Americans made up 77 percent of Sharkey's population. The average farm size of 540 acres was among the largest in the state. The 1880 census recorded no manufacturing activity. The county was named for judge and governor William L. Sharkey. Its county seat is Rolling Fork, and communities include Anguilla and Cary.

Like much of the Delta, Sharkey County grew dramatically in the late 1800s. By 1900 the county had 12,178 residents, 88 percent of them African Americans. Sharkey was a rural county dominated by tenancy and sharecropping. Though whites made up a small percentage of the

S

population, more whites than African Americans owned land. Ninety of the county's 222 white farmers (41 percent) owned their land, while only 73 of 1,821 black farmers (4 percent) did so. Agriculture that used tenant farmers and sharecroppers usually produced large numbers of farmers and small farm sizes, and in 1900 the average Sharkey County farm was only fifty-five acres. Industry was growing slowly, with forty-nine firms employing sixty-two workers.

According to the 1916 religious census, 80 percent of Sharkey County church members belonged to Missionary Baptist congregations. Other groups were the African Methodist Episcopal Church; the Methodist Episcopal Church, South; the Southern Baptist Convention; and the Presbyterian Church, U.S.

Bears roamed the much of the wooded areas of the Mississippi Delta, attracting fascination and sport from visiting hunters. In 1902 Pres. Theodore Roosevelt traveled to Sharkey County to hunt bears. Holt Collier, an extraordinary hunter and guide, secured one bear, and some guides tied it to a tree. However, Roosevelt refused to shoot the bear because he considered those circumstances unsportsmanlike, and the incident inspired a political cartoon by Clifford Berryman in the *Washington Post*. Morris Michtom saw this cartoon and designed a toy, "Teddy's Bear." Sharkey County now sponsors an annual festival, the Great Delta Bear Affair.

Bluesman McKinley Morganfield was born in 1913 and grew up in Rolling Fork before moving farther north, first in Mississippi, and then to Chicago. Under the name *Muddy Waters*, he changed the blues world with a new style associated with the electric guitar. Gospel singer Willie Mae Ford Smith was born in Rolling Fork in 1904 and like Muddy Waters traveled widely before and during her musical career. Herman Dennis, a unique artist and minister born in Rolling Fork in 1919, created Margaret's Grocery, an environmental work of art near Vicksburg.

The community of Panther Burn (or perhaps its name) continues to fascinate musicians and authors. Tav Falco has a Memphis-based band called Panther Burns, Mississippi musician Jimmy Phillips wrote a song called "Panther Burn," and experimental jazz band Curlew also has a song titled "Panther Burn." The movie *Blues Brothers 2000* mentions the tiny community. In 2009 Roosevelt Wright Jr. published *The Children of Panther Burn*, a work of historical fiction.

By 1930 Sharkey's population of roughly 14,000 was about 78 percent African American. Sharkey's population was completely rural, with little manufacturing and an economy that concentrated on cotton. Sharkey was one of seven counties in which tenant farmers operated at least 90 percent of the farms, and African Americans comprised almost 90 percent of those tenant farmers.

The Mississippi Delta experienced significant population declines from the 1930s through the 1950s, and by 1960 Sharkey County had just 10,738 residents, 70 percent of them African Americans. The county also had a small Chinese population. Agriculture continued to dominate the economy, with 57 percent of Sharkey's working people involved in farming, primarily growing cotton, wheat, soybeans, and oats. The relatively small numbers who were employed in manufacturing—about 7 percent—worked in textiles. In 1970, Sharkey County's population again fell below 10,000.

The Sharkey County civil rights movement has not attracted great attention from scholars. Issaquena County activist Unita Blackwell filed suit so her son, Jeremiah, could attend integrated schools in Rolling Fork, and the county had a civil rights boycott in 1964.

Like many Mississippi Delta counties, Sharkey's 2010 population was predominantly African American and had declined over the preceding sixty years. Indeed, the county's population had experienced one of the greatest proportional decreases in the state, shrinking by more than 50 percent and making Sharkey the second-smallest county in Mississippi, with only 4,916 people.

Mississippi Encyclopedia Staff
University of Mississippi

Mississippi State Planning Commission, *Progress Report on State Planning in Mississippi* (1938); *Mississippi Statistical Abstract*, Mississippi State University (1952–2010); Charles Sydnor and Claude Bennett, *Mississippi History* (1939); University of Virginia Library, Historical Census Browser website, http://mapserver.lib.virginia.edu; E. Nolan Waller and Dani A. Smith, *Growth Profiles of Mississippi's Counties, 1960–1980* (1985).

Sharp, Jacob Hunter

(1833–1907) Confederate General and Politician

Jacob Hunter Sharp, a lawyer, Confederate general, newspaper publisher, and politician, was born in Pickens County, Alabama, on 6 February 1833. He moved to Lowndes County, Mississippi, as a young child, attending various private schools before enrolling at the University of Alabama in 1850–51. He then read law in Columbus and opened a practice with his brother.

Sharp joined the Confederate Army as a private in the Tombigbee Rangers in 1861 and was later elected captain of the company. His unit was part of Blythe's Mississippi Regiment before becoming Company A of the 44th Mississippi Infantry as part of Gen. J. R. Chalmers's High Pressure Brigade. Sharp was cited for bravery at Shiloh and promoted to colonel shortly thereafter. At his next engagement, the Battle of Munfordville, he again won distinction.

He was placed in temporary command of his brigade at both Chickamauga and Chattanooga after Chalmers was wounded, and Sharp also temporarily commanded the unit at the Battle of Resaca when Gen. William F. Tucker was wounded. Sharp was promoted to the rank of brigadier general in July 1864 for his efforts at the Battle of Atlanta; less than a week later, at the Battle of Ezra Church, he was yet again cited for bravery.

Sharp led his brigade through the campaigns of the Army of Tennessee that followed the fall of Atlanta, taking part in the Battles of Franklin and Nashville. At Franklin, Sharp's troops participated in the fierce fighting at the Locust Grove, capturing three stands of Union colors. Following the destruction of the Confederate Army at Nashville, Sharp and the remnants of his command made their way back to Mississippi. They were ordered to report to Gen. Joseph E. Johnston in North Carolina in the spring of 1865, arriving just in time to be included in Johnston's surrender to Union forces in April.

Sharp returned to Lowndes County after the war and resumed the practice of law. He soon became involved in fighting federal Reconstruction policy and helped organize and lead the Lowndes County chapter of the Ku Klux Klan. In 1879 Sharp became the owner and editor of the *Columbus Independent*, and his success in that capacity later won him the presidency of the Mississippi Press Association.

He was elected to the Mississippi House of Representatives in 1886 and served until 1892, holding the post of Speaker from 1886 to 1888. He again served in the legislature from 1900 to 1902. Sharp died in Columbus on 17 September 1907.

Mike Bunn
Historic Chattahoochee
Commission

Biographical Memoranda in Reference to General Jacob Hunter Sharp, Vertical File, Mississippi Department of Archives and History; Brigadier General Jacob Hunter Sharp, Vertical File, Mississippi Department of Archives and History; Dunbar Rowland, *Military History of Mississippi, 1803–1898* (1908).

Shearer, Cynthia

(b. 1955) Author

Novelist Cynthia Shearer was born in Chicopee, Massachusetts, on 25 June 1955 to Irvine Harrison Shearer, an Air Force officer, and Marjorie Elizabeth Shearer, an English teacher. Within a month the family moved to Alapaha, Georgia, her parents' hometown. Shearer says she was lucky to grow up in a place "where everyone knew everyone else's family tree, and life was simple," even though her father left the family and her mother's liberal views on school integration and the war

in Vietnam created tension with the neighbors. As a teenager, Shearer hung wanted posters for Eldridge Cleaver and Huey Newton on her bedroom walls. She graduated from Valdosta State University in 1977.

Shearer earned a master's degree in English and completed course requirements for a doctorate at the University of Mississippi, where Barry Hannah became her mentor. During the 1990s she published fiction and nonfiction in an unusual range of magazines, from *Ladies' Home Journal* to *Tri-Quarterly* and the *Oxford American*. Many of the stories she developed in Hannah's creative writing workshops became part of her autobiographical first novel, *The Wonder Book of the Air* (1996), winner of the 1997 Mississippi Institute of Arts and Letters Prize for Fiction. In 2000 she was awarded a National Endowment for the Arts fellowship in fiction. From 1994 to 2000 Shearer served as curator at William Faulkner's Rowan Oak.

Since that time, Shearer has taught at the William L. Adams Center for Writing at Texas Christian University, where her husband, Daniel E. Williams, is a professor of English and director of the TCU Press. Her second novel, *The Celestial Jukebox*, set in the Mississippi Delta, was published in 2005. The following year, she won a Pushcart Prize for "The Famous Writers' School: Lessons from Faulkner's House," an essay about her years at Rowan Oak.

Both *The Wonder Book of the Air* and *The Celestial Jukebox* are set in the South during periods of national crisis. Shearer describes the first novel as "a social history of Georgia told through members of my own family." Her central character, Harrison Durrance, grows up in Alapaha during the Great Depression and flies a bomber in World War II; a generation later, his son, a student at the University of Georgia, describes Vietnam as "some fragile lily that our fathers were trampling." With several narrators and a shifting chronology, the book has not escaped comparison to Faulkner's fiction. Although Shearer considers Hannah a stronger influence on her writing, she "borrowed the structure" of her novel from Faulkner's *Go Down, Moses*, "advancing the novel in ten-year increments."

The Celestial Jukebox contrasts the music and art of southern folk culture with the consumerism of Delta casinos as well as the violence of World War II, Vietnam, and 11 September 2001. In this novel, Shearer reflects the contemporary South by depicting the fictitious Delta town of Madagascar as a confluence of twentieth-century immigrants from Africa, Honduras, and China and descendants of slaves and planters. "Ain't no such thing as original Americans," the Celestial Grocery's owner, Angus Chien, tells the African newcomer, Boubacar. Several chapter titles underscore America's diversity by evoking such songs as Son Thomas's "Catfish Blues" and Wanda Jackson's "Fujiyama Mama." Shearer sees the book as "a love letter to all musicians from any epoch or place, regardless of how they might register on Sony's Richter scale." She pays special tribute to Mississippi's African American bluesmen, seeking to "write English

S

words the way these guys could play trance music." Framed by scenes from 1951 and 2001, the novel is even more technically complex than *The Wonder Book of the Air*. Shearer wryly observes that "whenever there seemed to be too many marionettes to manage," she reminded herself not to exceed the number of characters in Don DeLillo's *Underworld*.

Joan Wylie Hall
University of Mississippi

Mississippi Writers and Musicians website, www.mswritersandmusicians.com; Alison Owings, *Hey, Waitress!: The USA from the Other Side of the Tray* (2004); J. C. Robertson, *Southern Literary Review* website, www.southernlitreview.com (7 May 2009); Cynthia Shearer, *Beatrice* (2005); SlushPile.net website, www.slushpile.net.

Shearwater Pottery

The name *Shearwater Pottery* refers to both the product of artistic activities and a place of artistic lifestyle. It is a family-owned art pottery business located in Ocean Springs, Mississippi.

In 1918 Annette McConnell Anderson, the art-educated daughter of a prominent New Orleans lawyer and judge and granddaughter of revered New Orleans public education philanthropist Samuel Jarvis Peters, bought a twenty-four-acre tract of woodland on Biloxi Bay known as the Old Depass Place and renamed it Fairhaven. The site was within walking distance of the cottage that famed Chicago architect Louis Sullivan had built for himself on East Beach. In 1923, Annette; her husband, George Walter Anderson; and their three sons moved from New Orleans to establish a permanent residence in Fairhaven's three 1840s buildings—a main house, a carriage house, and a little cottage.

Within two years the eldest son, Peter, had constructed a groundhog kiln and was firing pottery turned on a kick-wheel that Annette had purchased from George Ohr's estate after the Biloxi potter's death in 1918. Peter consulted Newcomb Pottery's Joseph Fortuné Meyer, who had returned to his native Biloxi and was throwing pottery at his studio on Deer Island, and received inspiration to continue with ceramic pursuits. Peter left Ocean Springs in 1926 to hone his craft under Edmund DeForest Curtis of Conestoga Pottery in Wayne, Pennsylvania, and again in July 1927 for a six-week summer course at the prestigious School of Clay-Working and Ceramics directed by Charles F. Binns at Alfred College in New York.

On 19 January 1928, Peter Anderson opened Shearwater Pottery, taking the name from a waterfowl, and the name

Fairhaven dropped out of use for the Anderson family property. Peter's enterprise benefited from his father's experience as a grain merchant, his mother's studies at Newcomb College, and the participation of his younger brothers, Walter Inglis "Bob" Anderson and James McConnell "Mac" Anderson. Bob studied art at Parsons Institute in New York and graduated from the Pennsylvania Academy of the Fine Arts in 1929. Mac attended Tulane University School of Architecture from 1926 to 1928.

Peter hoped to use on-site sedimentary clay, but the greasy fine-grained beach clay proved unsatisfactory. He briefly tried clay from the Tchoutacabouffa River, north of Biloxi, before switching to clay from the Fish River, a spring-fed tributary of Mobile Bay. Ultimately he settled on using the purple-gray clay found in Lucedale, sixty miles northeast of Ocean Springs in the Pascagoula River Basin.

Shearwater Pottery is produced by turning, jiggering, and casting. Jiggered and cast pieces are decorated with slip and sgrafitto designs or with underglaze painting before they are glazed. Peter's classically shaped pieces were usually glazed without decoration. His first glazes were poetically named blue rain, gray cloud, fall green, and such. His copper red glazes have long since been retired. The palette consisted of six basic glazes of fritted soda and boron, feldspathic lead, and Bristol types in twenty-two varieties, although some of the recipes were lost in Hurricane Katrina.

Early on, Mac Anderson pierced designs in the shoulders of Peter's jars and vases, Bob decorated pieces with art-historically inspired designs, and both produced candlesticks, ashtrays with flora and fauna motifs, lamp bases, bookends, doorstops, paperweights, and tiles for ceramic mold production. As the Great Depression influenced spending habits, Bob and Mac established a fifty-fifty partnership to capitalize on the era's taste for small figurines. In 1931 a second workshop building, the Annex, was constructed, and the pottery showroom was expanded. In the Annex, Bob and Mac produced underglazed castware sculpture pieces that Bob referred to as widgets. The younger Anderson brothers made molds for teapots, various land and sea creatures, and people engaged in a variety of activities. Over the years the Annex has produced an untold number of ceramic pirates, scenes of African American life in the South, literary and folk characters, dancers, athletes, and hunters.

In 1931 Shearwater Pottery figurines gained national recognition in the Contemporary American Ceramics Exhibition in New York, and two of Bob's decorated vessels were exhibited at the Municipal Art Gallery in Jackson. In 1936 a fish vase carved by Mac on pottery thrown and glazed by Peter embarked on a three-year tour of Europe with the Robineaux Exhibition. The following year, three platters carved by Mac, thrown by Peter, and glazed in his rare copper red toured the United States in another Robineaux Exhibition. Within a decade of Shearwater's establishment, its pieces had been on display at Lord and Taylor, Strawbridge, the Society of Arts and Crafts in Boston, Marshall Field and Company in

Chicago, and the Virginia Museum of Fine Art. The Brooks Memorial Art Gallery in Memphis, the Old Capitol Museum in Jackson, and the Lauren Rogers Museum of Art in Laurel began exhibiting Shearwater Pottery in the 1940s and 1950s, expanding the regional and national following for Anderson family artworks.

Throughout the 1930s and 1940s Annette led "plate group" design sessions that created circular arrangements of indigenous flora and fauna for plate production. The matriarch of Shearwater Pottery remained active in the artistic affairs of her family's business until her death in 1964. By that time a third generation of Andersons had been schooled in the ways of their familial art pottery world. Peter Anderson and his wife, Marjorie Patricia Grinstead Anderson, had four children, and they now own and operate Shearwater Pottery. Jimmy succeeded his father as master potter, and Jimmy's son, Peter Wade Anderson, continues the legacy. Marjorie Anderson Ashley succeeded her mother as business manager. Michael revived castware production at the Annex, and Patricia Anderson Findeisen became the pottery's chief decorator. Bob Anderson and his wife, Agnes Hellmuth "Sissy" Grinstead Anderson, had two daughters, Mary Anderson Stebly Pickard and Leif Anderson Philipoff, who became visual and performing artists and authors. Bob's grandson, Christopher Inglis Stebly, is noted for producing Walter Anderson–inspired artworks in a range of media, including pottery. Bob's daughter-in-law, Carolyn, reproduces the linoleum block prints that he had printed as murals on the back side of commercially produced wallpaper and displayed in the pottery showroom. Carolyn later converted this printing production to silkscreen as the original blocks deteriorated. Adele Anderson Lawton, the daughter of Mac Anderson and Sara Lemon Anderson, reproduced Bob's pottery designs and hand-painted blockprint reproductions before developing her own pottery designs. She established Realizations, the blockprint showroom located in Ocean Springs's L&N depot and managed by Linda Kerr, who is the longtime companion of Bob's youngest son.

In 1969 Hurricane Camille blew away the studio and part of the showroom; damage from Hurricane Katrina in 2005 was much more severe and nearly put an end to the family operation. The 1840 "front house" residence where Peter and Pat had raised their family disappeared, as did Mac and Sara's Depression-era rammed-earth house and the more recent homes constructed for Mary and for Michael. The original carriage house, known as the Barn, was demolished. Both Bob's cottage and Sissy's last residence were washed away, while Billy and Carolyn as well as Jimmy and Margaret lost their houses. In all, sixteen of the compound's structures were destroyed. In true Shearwater Pottery spirit, Mary's son, Jason, constructed a new Annex building the following year with materials salvaged from the original one. Pottery production and sales continued at Ocean Springs's Mary C. O'Keefe Cultural Center until 2007, when a new showroom, built with salvaged materials by Marjorie's

son, Patrick, opened to the public. Considering themselves shareholders in an ecological environment of nature and art, the current Anderson generation provides visitors and collectors with what has become a legendary experience.

Susan McClamroch
New Orleans, Louisiana

Patti Carr Black, *Art in Mississippi, 1720–1980* (1998); Christopher Maurer, *Dreaming in Clay on the Coast of Mississippi* (2000); Shearwater Pottery website, www.shearwaterpottery.com; Dod Stewart, *Shearwater Pottery* (2005); Nancy Sweezy, *Raised in Clay: The Southern Pottery Tradition* (1984); Walter Anderson Museum of Art website, www.walteranderson museum.org.

Shields, William Bayard
(1780–1823) Judge

In 1818 William Bayard Shields became the first chief justice of the Mississippi Supreme Court. Born in Maryland to Archibald and Rebecca Shields, Shields studied law in Delaware under Caesar A. Rodney, who later became US attorney general during the presidencies of Thomas Jefferson and James Madison. Shields was admitted to the Delaware bar in April 1803 and shortly thereafter left the state with his mentor, Thomas Rodney, whom Jefferson had appointed to serve as a judge and land commissioner of the Mississippi Territory. Traveling by horse and boat, they arrived in Natchez later that year.

Shields became one of the Mississippi Territory's premier attorneys and a leading public figure in the local Jefferson-Republican Party. He held numerous public posts, including US agent to the Board of Land Commissioners of the Mississippi Territory (1804), aide-de-camp and major of the militia under Mississippi Territorial governor Robert Williams (1805), member of the General Assembly of the Mississippi Territory (1808–9, 1813–14), superintendent of the Bank of Mississippi (1809), attorney general of the Western District of the Mississippi Territory (1809–12), superior court judge of Mississippi (1817), chief justice of the Mississippi Supreme Court (1818), and US district judge for the District of Mississippi (1818–23).

On 5 February 1807 Shields married fifteen-year-old Victoire Benoist, the daughter of Gabriel Benoist, a native of Nantes, France, and Elizabeth Dunbar Benoist, whose father was Robert Dunbar, a local indigo and tobacco farmer. The Shieldses went on to have one daughter and four sons, and in 1812 the family built a plantation home, Rokeby, named after a poem by Sir Walter Scott, in the southwestern corner of Jefferson County. According to the 1820 Census, Rokeby was home to ten whites and forty-one slaves.

On 16 April 1823 Shields suffered a severe stroke at his home, and two days later he took his own life.

John C. Henegan
Jackson, Mississippi

J. F. H. Claiborne, *Mississippi as a Province, Territory, and State* (1880); Frank E. Everett Jr., *Federal Judges in Mississippi, 1818–1968* (1968); W. B. Hamilton, *Anglo-American Law on the Frontier: Thomas Rodney and His Territorial Cases* (1953); W. B. Hamilton, *Thomas Rodney, Revolutionary and Builder of the West* (1953); M. Lewis and W. Clark, *The Definitive Journals of Lewis and Clark*, ed. G. Moulton (2002); Thomas Rodney, *Diary 1804* (1945); Thomas Rodney, *A Journey through the West: Thomas Rodney's 1803 Journal from Delaware to the Mississippi Territory*, ed. D. L. Smith and R. Swick (1997); Dunbar Rowland, *Courts, Judges, and Lawyers of Mississippi* (1935); Dunbar Rowland, *Mississippi, Comprising Sketches of Counties, Towns, Events, Institutions, and Persons* (1907); J. D. Shields, *The Life and Times of Seargent Smith Prentiss* (1884); J. R. Skates, *A History of the Mississippi Supreme Court, 1817–1948* (1973); R. Weems, *Journal of Mississippi History* (1953).

Ship Island during the Civil War

Confederate troops seized Ship Island as soon as Mississippi seceded but realized that they could not hold it without a strong Confederate naval presence in the Gulf. Consequently, the Confederates evacuated Ship Island in September 1861, and a Federal detachment immediately occupied Fort Massachusetts, an unfinished masonry fortification guarding the anchorage north of the island. The strategic importance of Ship Island was obvious: it could serve as a Union staging area for movements against Mobile, New Orleans, or even the Texas coast. In addition, it provided a safe harbor and refitting facilities for the Union's blockading fleet in the Gulf.

During the Civil War, Ship Island served all of these functions as work on Fort Massachusetts continued. Maj. Gen. Benjamin F. Butler used Ship Island as a staging area for his expedition against New Orleans in the spring of 1862. Shortly thereafter, the island became a prison camp for Union soldiers guilty of crimes in New Orleans and civilian detainees. Later in the war, the facility was expanded to accommodate Confederate prisoners of war captured in the Union attempt to take Mobile, and more than forty-two hundred Confederate prisoners were held there by the end of the war. Finally, the Union Navy built machine shops to repair and refit ships from the blockading fleet.

Twenty-seven Union infantry regiments, six batteries of light artillery, and a battalion of cavalry saw service on Ship Island during the Civil War. Union troop strength peaked in April 1862, when more than fifteen thousand men assembled for the final assault on New Orleans. After the city fell, the Union garrison on Ship Island was reduced to one regiment of infantry, the 13th Maine. Three months later, eight companies of this regiment were transferred to the forts below New Orleans, leaving two companies to hold the island by themselves until 12 January 1863, when seven companies from a new regiment of African Americans, the 2nd Louisiana Native Guards, arrived for garrison duty.

The mixture of black and white troops created an explosive atmosphere, and a racial dispute between the men from Maine and the black soldiers from Louisiana broke out within a week. The Union commander of the Department of the Gulf, Nathaniel P. Banks, reacted to the tense situation by ordering the withdrawal of the white soldiers, and the 2nd Regiment of the Louisiana Native Guards remained the primary garrison for the sandy outpost until the end of the war.

Not only was camp life for soldiers on Ship Island boring and uncomfortable, it could be deadly as a result of exposure to foul weather and disease. Plaques mounted at the entrance to Fort Massachusetts bear the names of 153 Confederate prisoners of war who died and were buried on the island. In addition, 232 Union soldiers died and were buried on Ship Island during the Civil War. Over the years, most of the dead washed out to sea, although the remains of a few Union soldiers were disinterred and reburied in the Chalmette National Cemetery outside New Orleans in 1867. Gulfport native Natasha Trethewey honors the African American Union soldiers on the island in her poem, "Elegy for the Native Guards" (2006).

James G. Hollandsworth Jr.
University of Southern Mississippi

James J. Hollandsworth Jr., *The Louisiana Native Guards: The Black Military Experience during the Civil War* (1995); James G. Hollandsworth Jr., *Journal of Mississippi History* (Summer 2000).

Shirley, Aleda
(1955–2008) Poet

For nearly twenty years Aleda Shirley taught at Mississippi universities and public schools while publishing her poetry. Her efforts won awards from the National Endowment for the Arts, the Mississippi Arts Commission, and the Kentucky Arts Council, and she helped establish and promote literary programs.

Aleda Shirley was born in Sumter, South Carolina, on 2 May 1955. Her father, Guy Shirley, served in the military, and the family moved frequently during her childhood, which included stints in Tennessee, Texas, the Philippines, and elsewhere. After graduating from the University of Louisville in 1975, she wrote and taught in Kentucky while pursuing a master of fine arts degree at Indiana University. Over the next fifteen years, she worked to promote education and arts-based programs in Kentucky. With grants from the Kentucky Arts Council and the Kentucky Foundation for Women, her position as poet in the schools served as a national model. In 1988 she received a twenty-thousand-dollar grant from the National Endowment for the Arts. She moved to Mississippi in 1990, settling near Jackson with her husband, architect Michael McBride.

Shirley's first book of poems, *Chinese Architecture* (1986), won the Poetry Society of America's 1987 Norma Faber First Book Award. *Rilke's Children* followed in 1987, and *Silver Ending* won the St. Louis Poetry Society's Stanley Hanks Chapbook competition in 1991. In 1995 she coedited the *Mississippi Writers Directory and Literary Guide* for the University of Mississippi's Center for the Study of Southern Culture, and a year later she published another book of poems, *Long Distance*. Shirley also edited *The Beach Book: A Literary Companion* (1999) and released *Dark Familiar: Poems* (2006). Shirley received a Mississippi Arts Commission grant, served as writer in residence at Millsaps College, taught at the University of Mississippi and in public schools, and helped create and direct All Write!, a Mississippi Arts Commission project designed to help students in literacy programs and correctional facilities obtain high school degrees.

Shirley's poems are noted for their sensory and sensual words and images, evoking taste, sound, and texture. *Dark Familiar*, her most acclaimed collection, also addresses Mississippi and greater American culture. The collection's opener, "The Star's Etruscan Argument" (a title taken from an Emily Dickinson poem) takes place

> in the hotel of a casino
> on an Indian reservation in the deep south,
> a sovereign nation in a county still unable
> to resolve a murder forty years old.

It describes "the sound of waitresses / pushing drinks, the click of disposable lighters / the muscular toll of coins hitting metal tray." Her poems frequently troll the dark overlap of life and death and the rituals, artifacts, visions, and encounters that express this relationship. "The Customary Mysteries" begins,

> When they transferred the site of Hades to the air
> the Stoics brought the dead into closer proximity
> with the living & so for a time the sky
> was full of souls.

Transitioning to the present, the poem ends on the modern-day Mississippi Gulf Coast, where the narrator likens a slip of newspaper floating on air to a "soul ascending," until the scene becomes "littered with planes / pulling banners advertising happy hours & water parks."

After a long battle with cancer, Aleda Shirley died in Jackson on 16 June 2008. A memorial in her honor was held at the Mississippi Museum of Art.

Jamie C. Dakin
University of Mississippi

Odie Lindsey
Nashville, Tennessee

Bowling Green Daily News (24 February 1988); *Glasgow Daily Times* (9 July 2008); Mississippi Writers and Musicians website, www.mswriters andmusicians.com; National Assembly of State Arts Agencies website, http://www.nasaa-arts.org.

Shoo-Fly Decks

In the nineteenth century the Mississippi Gulf Coast developed as a vacation destination for wealthy planters from elsewhere in Mississippi as well as from Louisiana and Alabama. Known as the Queen of the Watering Places, the Gulf Coast became one of the premier areas where vacationers could enjoy a summer getaway. Many people came to believe that the breezes off the Gulf not only were relaxing but also served healthful benefits. Specifically, the salt air was believed to help prevent yellow fever.

One way to take advantage of the climate was on a "shoo-fly." A unique form of Mississippi architecture, the shoo-fly was a gazebo-like structure built around the base of a large tree, preferably oak. The shoo-fly was essentially an octagonal deck that surrounded the trunk of the tree and stood approximately ten feet above the ground. The Gulf Coast shoo-flies varied in size, but many were large enough to accommodate as many as thirty people.

Visitors to a shoo-fly ascended a staircase and enjoyed the breezes and the shade of the tree's branches. In addition, by elevating people and exposing them to the waterfront breeze, the structure provided an escape from the pesky deerflies, mosquitoes, and gnats so prevalent along the Gulf Coast, supposedly leading to the name *shoo-fly*. Some Coast historians, including Murella Powell, now believe that "the name is actually a corruption of the French word chou-fleur. Chou-fleur means cauliflower, an apt description of the white circular structure sitting on a stemlike base."

The shoo-fly was very popular among residents and visitors alike. Images of shoo-flies often served as symbols of the

Shoo-fly deck, Madame Boyle's, Bay St. Louis, ca. 1905 (Photograph by Detroit Publishing Company, Library of Congress, Washington, D.C. [LC-D4-13530])

area, appearing on postcards in the nineteenth and twentieth centuries. The last of the original shoo-flies met their demise in Hurricane Camille in 1969, while most of the replicas became victims of Katrina in 2005. Since Hurricane Katrina, the area has again rebuilt several of these unique structures, promising to preserve the shoo-fly's significance along the Gulf Coast for future generations.

Alice Hull Lachaussee
Spring Hill College

Charles Lawrence Dyer, *Along the Gulf: An Entertaining Story of an Outing among the Beautiful Resorts on the Mississippi Sound* (1894); Val Husley, *Maritime Biloxi* (2000); Murella Powell, *Biloxi Sun Herald* (6 January 2002); Colleen S. Scholtes and L. J. Scholtes, *Biloxi and the Mississippi Gulf Coast* (1985).

Shotgun House

Ubiquitous across the landscape of Louisiana, Mississippi, southern Arkansas, Alabama, and North Florida, the shotgun house was introduced into the American South through the port city of New Orleans from Haiti. The most distinguishing characteristic of the typology is its configuration: one room wide and several rooms deep, with its primary entrance (usually two doors facing a front porch) at the narrow end. It is generally a one-story structure.

There are three variations on the standard type: double shotgun, "camelback" or "humpback" houses, and North Shore houses. The double shotgun house is simply two shotgun houses attached together lengthwise with a central wall. It is generally an urban adaptation designed to make better use of expensive urban lots. The camelback house has a two-story rear addition. The camelback is also an urban adaptation because of crowding. The Louisiana North Shore type, named for its prevalence on the north shore of Lake Pontchartrain, is a shotgun surrounded on three sides by large verandas.

Scholar of vernacular architecture John Michael Vlach has argued that the shotgun house derived originally from Africa. Though some scholars of vernacular architecture question this assertion, his model remains the standard interpretation of the shotgun house. Vlach believes that Haitian slaves, a large portion of whom were Yoruba, brought their indigenous building traditions to Haiti. The houses of this group had room dimensions that closely resembled those of the shotgun houses of Haiti. The Yoruba houses and the *bohio* house type of the Arawak native peoples of Haiti are formally similar. Vlach argues for a cultural connection between the two house types, believing them to be the prototypes for the shotgun house. With the use of French construction techniques, the Yoruba and Arawak house types merged to create the shotgun house. The first shotgun houses in Haiti were rural and were smaller than their later urban counterparts. The urban shotgun houses of Port-au-Prince, called *maison basse*, are essentially the same as many shotgun houses in New Orleans. In the wake of Toussaint-Louverture's rebellion, large numbers of slaves and free blacks migrated from Haiti to New Orleans, introducing the shotgun house to the American South. Thus, the shotgun house is a distinctly African American, creolized house type.

From New Orleans the shotgun house spread throughout the South, at first up the Mississippi River and later throughout much of the Deep South and the rest of the United States. Shotgun houses may be found on Jackson's Farish Street, and recent attempts to improve the neighborhood have concentrated on rebuilding or building new versions of shotgun houses. One of Mississippi's most famous shotgun houses is

Shotgun houses, Canal Street, Natchez (Library of Congress [HABS MS-279-1], Washington, D.C.)

located in Tupelo: it belonged to the parents of Elvis Presley, who was born in the house on 8 January 1935.

Justin Faircloth
University of Virginia

Dell Upton and John Michael Vlach, eds., *Common Places: Readings in American Vernacular Architecture* (1986); John Michael Vlach, *Back of the Big House: The Architecture of Plantation Slavery* (1948).

Shrimp Industry

With twelve large canneries shipping more than fifteen million cans of oysters each year, early twentieth-century Biloxi had the greatest seafood-packing capacity in the world. In 1890, Biloxi's packers processed more than 2,000,000 pounds of oysters and 614,000 pounds of shrimp; a dozen years later, those numbers had risen astronomically, reaching 5,988,788 pounds of oysters and 4,424,000 pounds of shrimp. With more capacity to process than supply, packers outfitted schooners and hired captains and crews of between six and twenty to seine for shrimp in the marshes of Louisiana. In 1915 fishermen organized with the International Longshoremen's Association and presented packers with a contract for wages and working conditions. Because packers controlled the boats and gear, fishermen could stop the supply of shrimp only by interfering with the equipment. Packers complained to the Louisiana Conservation Commission that their shrimpers were being intimidated in Louisiana waters. With Louisiana law enforcement agents ensuring their control of boats, gear, and workers, the packers refused to negotiate, and the union voted to end the strike and return to work under the old wage scale.

Around 1918 shrimp trawls and motorized boats were introduced in Mississippi. Because two men could handle a trawl and individual fishermen could afford powerboats, boat ownership shifted from factories to fishermen as packers got rid of their fleets and purchased shrimp from individual shrimpers. By the end of the 1930s schooners had fallen out of use. Because most fishermen owned their own boats and gear, they were independent of processor influence. With control of their boats and New Deal legislation supporting workers' right to organize, fishermen formed unions. In August 1932 Biloxi shrimpers went on strike. A federal negotiator worked out an agreement under which packers would recognize the union and pay the union's price for shrimp. In a 1955 court case, however, the union was found to be violating antitrust laws, fined, and outlawed, and its officers were sentenced to jail. In 1949 some fishermen began exploring the waters of the Gulf of Mexico for shrimp. Word of their success got out in February 1950, large boats converged on distant fishing grounds, and shrimpers began to build boats for rougher waters and longer voyages. Investing in mechanical processing equipment and freezing technology, packers further increased their capacity and began to import shrimp. Within a few years independent shrimpers found themselves squeezed between the need to earn enough money to pay off debts incurred by investing in new technology and big boats on the one side and declining shrimp prices on the other.

Processors encouraged heavier shrimping efforts to increase the amount of shrimp. Some lent money to shrimpers or advanced ice and fuel against their catches, while others helped to establish Vietnamese immigrants in shrimping beginning in the 1970s. By 1989 about half of Mississippi's shrimpers were Vietnamese. Today, about three-quarters of the state's shrimp harvest is brown shrimp, which are most abundant from June to October, while white and pink shrimp are plentiful in the fall and spring.

Factors affecting shrimpers in the twenty-first century include the influence of environmentalists and regulations requiring the use of turtle excluder devices, natural disasters (Hurricanes Katrina and Rita in 2005), and human-caused disasters (the 2010 Gulf oil spill). Researchers at the Mississippi State University Coastal Research and Extension Center estimate that Katrina and Rita caused more than thirty-five million dollars in damage to the state's commercial fishing fleet and more than one hundred million dollars in damage to Mississippi's 69 seafood-processing plants, 141 seafood dealers, and 5 land-based support facilities. Prior to 2005, the state sold an average of nearly eighteen hundred shrimp licenses each year; subsequently, however, that number has averaged around one thousand. The reduction in the number of shrimpers has generally meant better conditions for those who managed to rebuild their businesses after the hurricanes.

The Deepwater Horizon oil spill resulted in the closing of Gulf fisheries for nearly a year and led to lingering—though largely unfounded—concerns about the safety of Gulf shrimp. Despite its short-term negative effect on Mississippi's shrimp harvest, the closure of the fisheries may prove helpful in the long term, as it allowed shrimp to reproduce unimpeded.

By the second decade of the twenty-first century, the state's commercial shrimp industry generated $57.44 million in income, had a total economic impact of $141.77 million, and created more than three thousand jobs.

E. Paul Durrenberger
Penn State University

E. Paul Durrenberger, *Gulf Coast Soundings: People and Policy in the Mississippi Shrimp Industry* (1996); E. Paul Durrenberger, *Human Organization* (1992, 1994, 1995, 1997); E. Paul Durrenberger, *It's All Politics: South Alabama's Seafood Industry* (1992); E. Paul Durrenberger, *Labor's Heritage* (1994); E. Paul Durrenberger, *Maritime Anthropological Studies*

S

(1988); Christopher L. Dyer and Mark Moberg, *Maritime Anthropological Studies* (1992); Robert Nathan Gregory, "Shrimp Business Bounces Back for Some, Not Others," http://extension.msstate.edu/news/feature-story/2015/shrimp-business-bounces-back-for-some-not-others (27 August 2015); Ed Lallo, "Biloxi's Seafood Industry Is Brown, White, and Pink," http://gulfseafoodnews.com/2014/09/24/biloxis-shrimp-industry/ (24 September 2014); US Department of Commerce, Bureau of Fisheries, *Report of the US Commissioner of Fisheries* (1899–); Hannah Waters, "Breaking Down the Myths and Misconceptions about the Gulf Oil Spill," http://www.smithsonianmag.com/science-nature/clarifying-myths-and-mis conceptions-about-gulf-oil-spill-180951136/?no-ist (17 April 2014).

Sillers, Walter, Jr.

(1888–1966) Political Leader

Walter Sillers Jr. (left) (Archives and Records Services Division, Mississippi Department of Archives and History [PI POL 1983.0020 Box 18 Folder 16 #1])

Walter Sillers Jr., Mississippi Delta planter, attorney, state legislator, and segregationist, was born in Rosedale, Mississippi, in Bolivar County, on 13 April 1888. His parents, Walter Sillers Sr., a former state legislator, and Florence Warfield Sillers, were prominent Delta residents, and by the 1940s, the younger Sillers had become arguably the state's most powerful political figure.

Sillers earned his law degree from the University of Mississippi in 1909 and joined his father's Rosedale law firm. On 22 November 1911 he married Lena Roberts, daughter of state legislator William Beauregard Roberts and his wife, Minnie Poole Roberts.

In 1915 he won the first of his thirteen consecutive terms representing Bolivar County in the Mississippi House of Representatives. During the 1930s and 1940s Sillers, Joseph George, Lawrence Kennedy, and Thomas Bailey were known as the Big Four state legislators, using their positions as chairs of key committees to attempt to control the flow of legislation coming from the Governor's Mansion and causing some famous battles with Gov. Theodore Bilbo. Beginning in 1944, Sillers served as Speaker of the House.

Ever the advocate for Delta planters, Sillers helped found the Delta Council in Cleveland in 1935. He served on it until his death, holding at different times the position of director, committee chair, and officer. As head of the Resolutions Committee, Sillers helped make clear the philosophy of Delta planters: "Federal economy everywhere but in the Delta." Like most members of the Delta Council, Sillers believed in crop subsidies and government loans to planters and federal programs for building and new technology. He also served as counsel to the Bolivar County Board of Supervisors.

After World War II, as the National Democratic Party grew more responsive to the demands of African Americans, Sillers and other key political figures in Mississippi and the other Solid South states of Alabama, Louisiana, and South Carolina chose not to support the national Democratic Party and its candidate, Harry S. Truman, in the 1948 presidential election. Instead, they formed the State's Rights Democratic Party, nicknamed the Dixiecrats, and chose Jackson as its headquarters. The Dixiecrat convention, over which Sillers presided, nominated Strom Thurmond of South Carolina for president and Fielding Wright of Mississippi for vice president. Sillers subsequently remained loyal to the Mississippi Democratic Party but not to the national party, staunchly advocating state's rights and opposing the development of a two-party system in the Magnolia State.

In the 1950s and 1960s Sillers remained an opponent of African American civil rights legislation and worked through the legislature to maintain segregation. He never joined the Citizens' Council but praised its members as "all outstanding, upright white citizens of Mississippi." His tenure as Speaker ended only with his death on 24 September 1966. His body lay in state at the Capitol in Jackson, and he was buried in Rosedale.

Meredith Johnston
University of South Alabama

James C. Cobb, *The Most Southern Place on Earth: The Mississippi Delta and the Roots of Regional Identity* (1992); Pete Daniel, *Lost Revolutions: The South in the 1950s* (2000); Kari Frederickson, *The Dixiecrat Revolt and the End of the Solid South, 1932–1968* (2001); Roger Sharp and Nancy Weatherly Sharp, eds., *American Legislative Leaders in the South, 1911–1994* (1999); Walter Sillers Jr. Papers, Charles W. Capps Jr. Archives and Museum, Delta State University.

Silver, James W.
(1907–1988) Historian

James Wesley Silver, a professor of history at the University of Mississippi from 1936 to 1964, emerged as one of the most critical voices of the state's leadership in the aftermath of the riot surrounding James Meredith's admission to the university in the fall of 1962. His powerful denunciation of the racial status quo and his attack on the politics of conformity eventually led to a self-imposed exile after the publication of his best-selling book, *Mississippi: The Closed Society*.

Born in Rochester, New York, on 28 June 1907, Silver moved with his family to rural North Carolina at the age of twelve. The move had a profound impact on the socially awkward youth. He felt his outsider status keenly in this new place, and the search for acceptance by friends and colleagues became a recurring theme in his life. At age fifteen he enrolled at the University of North Carolina at Chapel Hill, where he received a bachelor's degree. He found a job as a schoolteacher in Tennessee, took education courses at Peabody College, and later entered graduate school at Vanderbilt University, earning a doctorate in history in 1935.

He began teaching at the University of Mississippi in the fall of 1936 and thrived in the low-key, amiable atmosphere of the sleepy southern school. Despite his heavy teaching and administrative load, he enjoyed the collegiality of his fellow faculty members, found time to fish and play cards, and traveled abroad on teaching assignments and fellowships. Nevertheless, Silver in many ways remained an outsider in the hidebound society of rural North Mississippi. Though he and his wife, Margaret McLean "Dutch" Thompson Silver, had the obligatory African American "help"—their housekeeper, Thera—he always seemed somewhat troubled by the relationship and its expected reciprocities. In addition, he possessed a naive ignorance and desire to help, especially in educational matters, that led him to cross the boundaries of race relations in Mississippi. His work with the local African American industrial school, for example, raised eyebrows. By showing even the slightest sympathy for blacks' attempts at self-improvement and development, he appeared to condemn the system that had put them in such a low place. He struck up a friendship of sorts with William Faulkner, who had put southern race issues into such a painful spotlight in his own writings. Silver, in fact, helped arrange the 1955 Peabody Hotel conference in Memphis at which Faulkner gave one of his few public addresses on race in the South.

Silver's evolving views on southern social mores created tensions with the university administration and its political supporters. Known primarily as a scholar of the Old Southwest and the southern home front during the Civil War, he found intriguing comparisons between the Mississippi of the 1850s and that of the 1950s and early 1960s—specifically,

the disturbing atmosphere of political repression and the drowning out of all voices of opposition. In September 1962, when Meredith's attempt to enroll at the University of Mississippi resulted in a riot, Silver was dumbfounded by the lack of leadership at the state level. He made a point of befriending Meredith at the university, ruffling more feathers by lunching with him in the cafeteria and by inviting him to play a round of golf on an Oxford course.

The following November Silver let forth a blistering criticism of Mississippi in his presidential address to the Southern Historical Association. The expanded version of his speech, *The Closed Society*, was released in June 1964—the day after the disappearance of civil rights workers James Chaney, Andrew Goodman, and Michael Schwerner in Philadelphia, Mississippi. In *The Closed Society* Silver argued that at certain points in its history, Mississippi leaders demanded consensus and would not allow dissent and debate, primarily on issues of race; moreover, he accused the state of lacking "the moral resources to reform itself."

The speech prompted state officials to launch an effort to fire Silver from the university despite the fact that he held tenure. In addition, Silver found himself harassed, threatened, and ostracized. Fearing for his family's safety, he chose to leave the University of Mississippi and accept a position at Notre Dame. In 1969 he moved on to the University of South Florida, where he taught until his retirement in 1981. Silver chronicled his story in a 1984 memoir, *Running Scared: Silver in Mississippi*.

Nearly two decades after leaving, Silver returned to Oxford to donate his papers to the university, delivering a well-received speech. He died on 25 July 1988. In September 2011 the university honored Silver by naming a campus pond after him and by holding a symposium on his impact on the school and the state.

J. Matthew Reonas
Baton Rouge, Louisiana

New York Times (26 July 1988); James W. Silver, *Mississippi: The Closed Society* (1964); James W. Silver, *Running Scared: Silver in Mississippi* (1984); James W. Silver Collection, Department of Archives and Special Collections, J. D. Williams Library, University of Mississippi; "UM Tribute Set for Professor James W. Silver," http://news.olemiss.edu/um -tribute-set-for-professor-james-w-silver/ (26 September 2011).

S

Simmons, Earl

(b. 1956) Artist

Earl Wayne Simmons was born in 1956 in Bovina, Mississippi, and has lived there all of his life. As a child, he made toy jukeboxes, trucks, and planes out of cardboard, bottle tops, and jar lids, using a Coca-Cola bottle as a hammer. He also loved drawing and wanted to be an artist, a pursuit that was encouraged by the first-grade teacher at his rural black school. By the time he reached high school, however, Mississippi's schools had integrated, and he was told that he needed no training. He left school in 1971, after his junior year. In 1974 he joined the Job Corps, learning carpentry in Louisville, Kentucky, and made his first jukebox piece. He returned to Bovina planning to build a workshop.

In 1978 he began building Earl's Art Shop, creating a place to live and make toys, art, and furniture. He later added a juke joint, or café, building the tables, booths, and bar and installing a Wurlitzer jukebox loaded with 45s. From his job at Anderson-Tully, a Vicksburg sawmill, Simmons salvaged scrap lumber, nails, and other supplies. During the 1980s, he added the Souvenir Art Store and Art Gallery, a covered entrance, a tin roof, an overhead room, a living room, and a den and expanded the café. Earl's Art Shop became a destination for tourists and a roadside stop for travelers. Nearly all of the building was open to the public, guided by hand-painted signs.

Simmons also made and sold sculptures of jukeboxes; cars, trucks, tractors, airplanes, and riverboats; and roosters, peacocks, and other birds, using wood, chrome strip, reflectors, and many other types of salvaged materials. In addition, he built furniture; created paintings of himself, his family, Dr. Martin Luther King Jr., and John F. Kennedy; and made signs using a stylized western-influenced script. In addition to selling his creations at the Art Shop, Simmons began receiving commissions, including one from the House of Blues nightclub chain, and his works were exhibited and sold at the Southside Gallery in Oxford and the Attic Gallery in Vicksburg. Simmons's works gained further appeal when "serial entrepreneur" Scott Blackwell created the Immaculate Baking Company and commissioned Simmons and other folk artists whose work Blackwell admired to create packaging for the company.

In 1994 the Mississippi Arts Commission awarded Simmons an Artist Fellowship, and he began working on a major addition to the front of the Art Shop. Over the remainder of the decade, he focused primarily on painting, taking as his subject matter such Mississippi pop culture icons as hot tamales, juke joints, and Highway 61 and often riffing on advertising images.

In 2002 fire destroyed all thirty rooms of Simmons's hand-built home, workshop, and art gallery as well as numerous artworks and his stockpile of materials. Simmons rebuilt, but fire again destroyed his home and workshop in 2012. By 2015, he again reconstructed Earl's Art Shop.

Simmons sees his art as a way to "take things that are no good to anybody else and make it worth something." In 2007 Earl's Art Store was the subject of an exhibition at the College of Architecture, Art, and Design at Mississippi State University School of Architecture Jackson Center. His work is in the collection of the Mississippi Museum of Art, and Earl's Art Shop has been featured on Mississippi Educational Television.

Katherine Huntoon
Santa Ana, California

Karekin Goekjian, *Light of the Spirit: Portraits of Southern Outsider Artists* (1998); Lorraine Redd and Jack Davis, *Only in Mississippi: A Guide for the Adventurous Traveler* (1993); Southern Foodways Alliance website, www.southernfoodways.org; Stephen Flinn Young, *Earl's Art Shop: Building Art with Earl Simmons* (1995).

Simmons, J. Edgar, Jr.

(1921–1979) Poet

Joseph Edgar Simmons Jr. was born to Joseph Edgar Simmons Sr. and Dorothy Clark Simmons on 28 May 1921 in Natchez. He grew up in Mississippi before attending Columbia University, where he earned bachelor's (1947) and master's (1948) degrees. After studying at the Sorbonne in Paris, he began teaching English literature at the college level, serving as an instructor at DePauw University, the College of William and Mary, Southern Illinois University, and Mississippi College. From 1967 to 1969 he held the post of director of the Creative Writing Program at the University of Texas at El Paso. He also wrote columns for the *Dublin Irish Press* and the *New Orleans Times-Picayune*.

Simmons's poems frequently appeared in the *Atlantic Monthly*, *New Republic*, *Harper's*, and the *Nation*. Expressing rich experiences through clear and vivid language, his poetry was collected in numerous anthologies, including *Southern Writing in the Sixties: Poetry*, *New Directions*, and *The Honey and the Gall*. He published three volumes of poetry: *Pocahontas and Other Poems* (1957); *Driving to Biloxi* (1967); and *Osiris at the Roller Derby* (1983). The title poem from *Driving to Biloxi* concludes, "knowing these fiery rails will break, anytime now, into green, dusty faced ferns, & shell roads whistling towards the water." Simmons died in Meadville on 26 November 1979. In his memory, family members established a scholarship fund for students with an interest in creative writing and English at Copiah-Lincoln Community College.

Jeffrey Klingfuss
Jackson, Mississippi

Conrad Aiken Collection, Emory University Library; John Crowe Ransom Papers, Vanderbilt University Library; Mississippi Writers and Musicians website, www.mswritersandmusicians.com; Allen Tate Collection, Vanderbilt University Library.

Simmons, William J.

(1916–2007) Editor

Once described as "Dixieland apartheid's number-one organization man," William James Simmons was best known for his leadership as an administrator in the influential Citizens' Council, an organization that fought to keep blacks and whites in separate schools.

Simmons was born in the small town of Utica, Mississippi, on 7 July 1916. His family moved to Jackson when he was eight years old, and his father became one of Jackson's most prominent bankers. Simmons attended Millsaps College before graduating from Mississippi College in 1937. He traveled extensively in Europe and South America and studied at the Institut de Touraine in France prior to World War II. He served in the war with the Royal Engineers of the British Army in the British West Indian Command and with the US State Department in Washington, D.C. Before his involvement with the Citizens' Council, Simmons estab-lished several brief business ventures primarily in the fruit and vegetable brokerage industry. However, he found little financial success in these endeavors.

Simmons lived in New Orleans for nearly a decade before returning to Jackson in 1954, the same year that the US Supreme Court ruled school segregation unconstitutional in *Brown v. Board of Education*. Soon thereafter, Robert "Tut" Patterson organized the first Citizens' Council in the Mississippi Delta town of Indianola, and Simmons joined forces with Patterson in the spring of 1955, when they organized a meeting in the lobby of the King Edward Hotel in downtown Jackson to discuss the expansion of the Council's scope of influence into the capital city. The Council sought to maintain the system of legal segregation, and its motto focused on states' rights: "Dedicated to the maintenance of peace, good order, and domestic tranquility in our community and in our state and to the preservation of our States' Rights." Simmons became a card-carrying member, and he published the first issue of the organization's journal, *Citizens' Council*, in October 1955. Simmons went on to devote himself full time to the council. When the Citizens' Councils of America moved its headquarters to Jackson in 1960, Simmons became the organization's de facto head, serving as the editor and publisher of the *Citizen*, as an administrator for Citizens' Councils of America, and as president of the Citizens' Council Forum. He was also a founder and president of the Council School Foundation, working to enhance the private school movement in Jackson with the establishment of Council schools.

Simmons retired from his duties with the Citizens' Council in 1990. He subsequently ran a bed and breakfast, served as president of the Downtown Jackson Association, and was active in the Jackson Chamber of Commerce and the Sons of Confederate Veterans. He died on 24 November 2007.

Kate Medley
Durham, North Carolina

James Graham Cook, *The Segregationists: A Penetrating Study of the Men and the Organizations Active in the South's Fight against Integration* (1962); *Jackson Clarion-Ledger* (26 November 2007) Neil R. McMillen, *The Citizens' Council: Organized Resistance to the Second Reconstruction, 1954–64* (1994); William J. Simmons, interview by Kate Medley (4 November 2005).

William J. Simmons, 1950s (McCain Library and Archives, University of Southern Mississippi)

Simpson County

Simpson County, founded in 1824, is located in south-central Mississippi and is named for Josiah Simpson, a judge and political figure in early Mississippi. Mendenhall is the

S

county seat, and other communities include Magee, D'Lo, and Braxton. Prior to 1840, slaves constituted less than one-third of the county's population.

A small county on the northern side of the Piney Woods area, antebellum Simpson ranked in the bottom quarter of the state's counties in all forms of agricultural production. Antebellum political leader Franklin Plummer, a lawyer and education supporter by the 1820s, got his start in politics when he was elected to the Mississippi legislature in 1826. By 1860 the county's population included 2,324 slaves and 3,756 free people, and the county had eleven Baptist churches and eight Methodist congregations.

Simpson County's population reached 8,008 by 1880. Nearly 85 percent of its farms were cultivated by their owners, who concentrated more on livestock than on cotton, grains, or other crops. Manufacturing was slow to develop, with only eleven men and two children recorded as working in industry.

At the turn of the twentieth century, Simpson County's population had increased to 12,800, with African Americans accounting for 39 percent of the total. As in many Mississippi counties, African Americans were less likely to own land than whites: while about three-quarters of Simpson's white farmers owned their land, only 43 percent of black farmers did so. Simpson had a small but growing industrial force, with twenty-seven establishments employing seventy-eight workers, all of them male.

More than three-quarters of all churchgoers in early twentieth-century Simpson County were Baptists—primarily members of the Southern Baptist Convention, with substantial numbers of Missionary Baptists as well. Among the remainder, the Methodist Episcopal Church, South, and the Colored Methodist Episcopal Church predominated.

By 1930 Simpson County's population had increased to 20,000, with whites outnumbering African Americans by about two to one. In a dramatic change from the late 1800s, about half of the farms were operated by tenants. The number of industrial workers, most of them in the timber industry, reached 800. From 1918 to the 1950s Magee was home of the Mississippi State Tuberculosis Sanatorium.

Writer Patrick Smith was born in Mendenhall in 1927, and he grew up and spent part of his adult life in Simpson County. Smith's first work, *The River Is Home* (1953), told stories of people living along the Pearl River.

The county's population remained stable through the mid-twentieth century, and as of 1960, Simpson had far more agricultural workers (27 percent of the workforce) than industrial workers (16 percent). Most of the manufacturing growth came in the apparel industry.

In 1961 John Perkins founded the Voice of Calvary Ministries, an ambitious effort to integrate religious life with educational and economic programs. Perkins, who detailed the murder of his brother and other parts of his life in works such as *Let Justice Roll Down* (1976), became a force in the civil rights movement. In the 1970s Dolphus Weary joined

Perkins and others in the ministry, which eventually moved to Jackson.

Like many southern Mississippi counties, Simpson County's 2010 population was predominantly white and had grown since 1960, reaching 27,503. Sixty-three percent of residents were white and 35 percent were African American. The county also had a small Hispanic population and handfuls of Native American and Asian residents.

Mississippi Encyclopedia Staff
University of Mississippi

Mississippi State Planning Commission, *Progress Report on State Planning in Mississippi* (1938); *Mississippi Statistical Abstract*, Mississippi State University (1952–2010); Charles Sydnor and Claude Bennett, *Mississippi History* (1939); University of Virginia Library, Historical Census Browser website, http://mapserver.lib.virginia.edu; E. Nolan Waller and Dani A. Smith, *Growth Profiles of Mississippi's Counties, 1960–1980* (1985).

Sims, Naomi
(1948–2009) Model and Businesswoman

Born in Oxford on 30 March 1948 to John Sims, a porter, and Elizabeth Sims, Naomi Sims went on to become a pioneering African American model and businesswoman. Known as the first black supermodel, she paved the way for such better-known African American models as Tyra Banks and Naomi Campbell.

Sims's parents divorced when she was a baby, and she moved with her mother and sisters to Pittsburgh, Pennsylvania. After her mother became ill, Sims entered the foster care system, and much of her childhood was spent feeling isolated and insecure, in part because she had reached a towering 5'10" by age thirteen. After graduating from high school Sims received a scholarship to attend New York's Fashion Institute of Technology. Though her classmates encouraged her to earn extra money by modeling, every agency turned her down. She then began directly contacting photographers, and the highly regarded Gosta Peterson agreed to photograph her. He shared the shots with his wife, *New York Times* editor Patricia Peterson, who placed Sims on the cover of the paper's 1967 fashion supplement.

Even that was not enough to get Sims a modeling contract: agencies still believed that there was no work for black models. Sims offered model turned agent Wilhelmina Cooper a deal she couldn't refuse: Sims would mail out the *Times* cover herself but list the agency as a contact. If offers came in, Cooper would earn a commission though she had done no work. The strategy worked. Sims first landed a national

AT&T commercial and then became the first African American model to appear on the covers of *Ladies' Home Journal* (1968) and *Life* (1969). By the time she retired in 1973, Sims's photographs had appeared in some of the world's most prestigious magazines, and she had graced the runways for some of the world's most celebrated fashion designers, helping to bring black models into the mainstream. In 1974 designer Halston said, "She was the great ambassador for all black people. She broke down all the social barriers."

Sims then turned to business. As a model, Sims had found a dearth of beauty products for black women, and she set out to fill that void, developing a lightweight wig fiber resembling low-maintenance straightened black hair. The Naomi Sims Collection hit the market in 1976 and sold more than five million dollars worth of wigs during the first year. In 1981 she added a fragrance, Naomi, and four years later she created Naomi Sims Beauty Products, which added a line of skin-care products. She served as the spokesperson for all of her products.

Sims also began writing books about the beauty and health of African American women. She published *All about Health and Beauty for the Black Woman* (1976), *How to Be a Top Model* (1979), *All about Hair Care for the Black Woman* (1982), and *All about Success for the Black Woman* (1982).

In her mid-thirties, however, Sims was diagnosed with bipolar disorder, which crippled her at times and led to several hospitalizations. By 2005, when she was among twenty-five women honored at an Oprah Winfrey "Legends Ball," she had lost control of her business, had suffered financial setbacks, and had completely left the public spotlight.

Sims died of breast cancer on 1 August 2009.

Ronda Racha Penrice
Atlanta, Georgia

John M. Ingham and Lynne B. Feldman, *African-American Business Leaders: A Biographical Dictionary* (1993); *New York Times* (3 August, 22 December 2009); Naomi Sims website, www.naomisims.com; Jesse C. Smith, *Encyclopedia of African American Business* (2006).

Sinclair, Mary Craig
(1882–1961) Writer

The marriage of a Mississippi woman born into wealth and privilege to a major socialist writer led to an intriguing life, as Mary Craig Kimbrough Sinclair chronicled in her 1957 autobiography, *Southern Belle*. Known by her middle name, Craig Kimbrough was born on 12 February 1882 and grew up in Greenwood, where her father, Allan McCaskill Kim-

brough, was a planter, lawyer, and judge, as well as on the Gulf Coast, where the family had a large home, Ashton Hall. At age thirteen, Craig Kimbrough enrolled at Mississippi State College for Women (now Mississippi University for Women) before moving on to study at New York's Gardner School for Young Ladies, from which she graduated in 1900. Lively and well educated, the young Kimbrough aspired to be a writer.

Kimbrough met Upton Sinclair in New York around 1911, when she was looking for help with writing and possibly for a publisher for some of her stories. After she and her mother, Mary Hunter Southworth Kimbrough, attended a reading at which Sinclair discussed his ideas about socialism and healthy food, she approached him to discuss her manuscript about Jefferson Davis's daughter, Winnie. Sinclair's first marriage ended in divorce in 1911, and he and Kimbrough married in Virginia in 1913 and settled in California in the 1920s. Their largely happy marriage succeeded despite her father's doubts about her marrying a divorced man, her dislike of communists and many socialists, and her preference for privacy, which contrasted with her husband's desire to cultivate notoriety as a means of championing justice and changing public opinion.

Craig Sinclair was acquainted with many powerful Mississippi figures, and their friendships made her marriage to a free-thinking socialist even more intriguing. Ashton Hall was just a few doors down the street from Beauvoir, home of the Jefferson Davis family. Craig's first cousin was Mississippi senator John Sharp Williams, and her brother was a friend of segregationist leader Tom Brady. When Brady visited California, he stopped at the Sinclair home and gave the same massive resistance speech he had delivered before numerous other audiences. Upton Sinclair responded that many of the people and groups Brady named as communists "were nothing of the sort."

Southern Belle was Mary Craig Sinclair's only published work. According to literary scholar Peggy Whitman Prenshaw, Sinclair planned the book as a biography of her husband, and the book generally deals with her relationships with family members. Its title announced her southern and specifically upper-class roots, and the book began with two images beloved among wealthy southerners: the natural beauty of life on the Gulf Coast, and the ease and apparent paternalism of life in a wealthy home. Despite offering clear condemnation of the class and racial divisions of the Mississippi of her childhood, Sinclair did not use the book as social criticism but instead concentrated on the narrative of her life, especially with her husband.

Craig and Upton Sinclair often worked closely together—so closely that at times it is unclear which one was the author. Craig helped Upton write parts of his work and may even have written the introduction to *Southern Belle* that is attributed to him; in addition, some scholars have contended that Upton wrote substantial parts of *Southern Belle*. Much of one manuscript volume of the text is in Upton's handwriting, but Craig was extremely frail by the 1950s and consequently dictated to him. It is likely that they collaborated: Craig's letters reveal that she put substantial work into it the book and that she added a number of features that made it particularly her own.

She died on 26 April 1961.

Ted Ownby
University of Mississippi

Anthony Arthur, *Radical Innocent: Upton Sinclair* (2006); Leon Harris, *Upton Sinclair: American Rebel* (1975); Peggy W. Prenshaw, in *Haunted Bodies: Gender and Southern Texts*, ed. Anne Goodwyn Jones and Susan V. Donaldson (1997); Peggy W. Prenshaw, in *Lives of Mississippi Authors, 1817–1967*, ed. James B. Lloyd (1981); Upton Sinclair, *The Autobiography of Upton Sinclair* (1962).

Sisters of Mercy

The Sisters of Mercy, a Roman Catholic community of women dedicated to prayer and service, was founded in Ireland in 1831 by devout, well-educated Catherine McAuley. The Sisters of Mercy first sent teachers and nurses to the United States in 1843. In 1860, urged by Bishop William Elder of Mississippi, the Sisters of Mercy's Baltimore convent sent six nuns to Vicksburg to teach. The order eventually created a network of schools that significantly contributed to the education, health care, and culture of people of diverse races, religions, and backgrounds. The "street sisters" worked with local people to identify and respond to community needs. The Sisters founded twenty-six schools, including institutions for African American and Choctaw students; ran several hospitals and a school of nursing; and spearheaded the training of teachers for children with special needs.

In 1862, during the Civil War bombardment of Vicksburg, the Sisters' school closed and became a hospital. The nuns nursed Confederate soldiers, fleeing with more than one thousand sick and wounded men east to Jackson and north to Oxford before retreating in boxcars to Shelby Springs, Alabama. Sr. Ignatius Sumner's journal of the events vividly describes the nuns' experiences.

After the war, the Sisters returned to Vicksburg and attempted to regain their property, which had been occupied by Union soldiers. Only after an appeal to the US Congress and a direct order from Secretary of War Edwin Stanton was the school released. Within a decade, young Mississippi women joined the Sisters, and schools were founded in Jackson, Meridian, and Pass Christian. More than two hundred Mississippi nuns ultimately served in schools, hospitals, and health and social services throughout the state.

During the 1878 yellow fever epidemic, six Sisters gave their lives serving the ill, and the convent cared for twenty orphans until homes were found. When Edwards, Mississippi, was under quarantine for yellow fever in 1897, Vicksburg nuns volunteered to nurse in the town. During the 1918 influenza outbreak they opened night classes for home caregivers. During the polio epidemics in the 1950s Mercy Hospital in Vicksburg was a regional center for pediatric victims.

The Sisters modeled their institutions across the state on the Vicksburg convent and school, St. Francis Xavier Academy, but developed programs suited to local needs and culture. The girls' schools offered religious instruction that expressed itself in active social development, respect, and celebration of religious, ethnic, and cultural diversity as well as an emphasis on the power and pleasure of the arts, music, and performance. In addition to nursing, the Sisters developed programs to provide prison ministry, home visitation, tutoring, and summer schools for isolated and impoverished rural communities. In turn, graduates organized alumnae associations and for forty years provided funding that enabled the Sisters to earn graduate degrees.

Rising costs and a decline in the number of members led the Sisters to sell Mercy Hospital to a healthcare company in 1991. The order has also reduced members' teaching assignments, though they remain active in the state, motivating, tutoring, and working within the communities most in need of education, health care, and development. Since 2008 the Mississippi Sisters have been part of the South Central Community of the Sisters of Mercy, which includes eighteen states, Guam, and Jamaica. In Mississippi, they have a medical mission in the Delta, provide tutors for the Jackson juvenile detention facility, and run various outreach programs, including one in which retired Sisters work to ease Vietnamese and Hispanic immigrants' transition to America and Mississippi.

Glenda LaGarde
Hinds Community College
at Vicksburg–Warren County

Mary Bernard, *The Story of the Sisters of Mercy in Mississippi, 1860–1930* (1931); Sr. Ignatius Sumner, *Angels of Mercy: A Primary Source by Sr. Ignatius Sumner R.S.M. of the Civil War and Yellow Fever*, ed. Pauline Oakes (1998); Barbara Roberts, *Alabama Heritage* (Winter 1989); Sisters of Mercy: South-Central website, http://www.sistersofmercy.org/south-central/; *St. Francis School: Cradle of the Humanities in Vicksburg, Mississippi, 1860–1990: 35 Oral History Interviews*, Vicksburg Collection, Vicksburg–Warren County Public Library.

Sit-Ins

Sit-ins—nonviolent, direct-action protests intended to desegregate lunch counters, restaurants, and other segregated facilities—were an integral part of the civil rights movement in the 1960s in Mississippi as elsewhere. The movement began on 1 February 1960 when four North Carolina A&T students staged a sit-in at a Woolworth's lunch counter in Greensboro and inspired similar protests across the South as young people mobilized to change their communities. However, such protests tended to be concentrated in urban areas and in border states, and they did not occur with the same frequency in Mississippi as in other southern states. Rural parts of the Deep South were much less affected, and direct action in Mississippi generally tended to favor boycotts and picketing. Still, such efforts by volunteers of the Student Nonviolent Coordinating Committee (SNCC) and local activists in McComb, Jackson, and Greenwood helped to dramatize injustice, garner sympathy, and create a mass movement for racial equality. As an aggressive kind of moral suasion, sit-ins not only elicited violent reactions from hard-core segregationists but also often compelled local governments to capitulate to activists' demands.

On 29 July 1961 Curtis Hayes and Hollis Watkins, two eighteen-year-olds who had been attending SNCC-led workshops in nonviolent direct action in McComb, sat in at the local Woolworth's, the first such action in the area and the catalyst for the nonviolent movement in Pike County. Fifteen-year-old Brenda Travis led five other high-school students in a sit-in in McComb; she was arrested, jailed for thirty-four days, expelled, and sentenced to one year in a reformatory. Direct-action protests slowed in McComb in the face of massive resistance, which included the 25 September murder of Herbert Lee, a farmer and member of the Amite County branch of the National Association for the Advancement of Colored People. Despite the sit-ins, McComb remained as

Greenville Air Force Base sit-in, 31 January 1966 (Mississippi State Sovereignty Commission Records, Mississippi Department of Archives and History [2-44-1-127-7-1-1])

segregated as ever, and the civil rights movement in southwestern Mississippi largely ceased until 1964.

The most famous sit-in in Mississippi occurred on 28 May 1963 when students from Tougaloo College conducted a peaceful demonstration at the Woolworth's in Jackson. Pearlena Lewis, Memphis Norman, and Anne Moody asked for service at the lunch counter. They were joined by Joan Trumpauer, a white student and native Virginian who left Duke University to attend historically black Tougaloo; Lois Chafee, a white professor; John Salter, a young professor of Native American ancestry; fellow students Walter Williams and James Beard; George Raymond, a young activist with the Congress of Racial Equality activist and freedom rider; and A. D. Beittel, the sixty-three-year-old president of Tougaloo. Mercedes Wright, an activist with the National Association for the Advancement of Colored People, and Rev. Ed King, the chaplain at Tougaloo, were also present as observers and supporters of the students, who endured two hours of violent abuse. Counterprotesters, threatened by the "race-mixers" and "outside agitators" in their midst, intimidated and assaulted the students, punching them, kicking them, smearing them with food, and hurling ashtrays and glass figurines. A photograph of the incident, taken by Fred Blackwell of the *Jackson Daily News*, became one of the enduring images of the civil rights movement.

A few days after Pres. Lyndon B. Johnson signed the 1964 Civil Rights Act, Silas McGhee, a high-school senior, conducted a one-man sit-in at the Leflore Theater in Greenwood. His older brother, Jake, went along to watch a movie at the all-white theater and had to fight his way through a mob to get out. Joined by friends, the two brothers began a regular series of sit-ins at the theater. Reprisals included a 16 July kidnapping and beating at a deserted shack, a 25 July shooting incident at the McGhee home, another mob attack on 26 July, and a 15 August shooting incident that left Silas hospitalized with a broken jaw and a .38-caliber slug in his throat. After Silas's recovery, the McGhee brothers continued to frequent the Leflore Theater, which continued to sell them tickets; as a result, whites began to boycott the theater, and the Leflore went out of business. The McGhees subsequently began to patronize the only other white theater in town, the Paramount, which eventually desegregated.

The sit-in idea took other forms, such as "wade-ins" on Gulf Coast beaches and "kneel-ins" at Jackson churches. Opponents of civil rights boycotts participated in what they called "buy-ins" to support white merchants.

Christopher B. Strain
Florida Atlantic University

John Dittmer, *Local People: The Struggle for Civil Rights in Mississippi* (1994); Anne Moody, *Coming of Age in Mississippi* (1968); M. J. O'Brien, *We Shall Not Be Moved: The Jackson Woolworth's Sit-In and the Movement It Inspired* (2013); Charles M. Payne, *I've Got the Light of Freedom: The Organizing Tradition and the Mississippi Freedom Struggle* (1995); John Salter, *Jackson, Mississippi: An American Chronicle of Struggle and Schism* (1979).

S

Six Sisters of the Gulf Coast

During the antebellum period along the Mississippi Gulf Coast, a string of cities along the shoreline welcomed visitors arriving on steamboats, primarily from New Orleans but also from Mobile. Collectively, that line of watering places along the Gulf Coast—Shieldsboro (Bay St. Louis), Pass Christian, Mississippi City, Biloxi, Ocean Springs, and Pascagoula (East and West)—was known as the Six Sisters. Famous for their hotels and salubrious atmospheres, the Six Sisters heavily advertised their attractions locally and in New Orleans to entice tourists to partake of their curative waters and to enjoy their resorts.

In 1790 English general Thomas Shields received title to the area today known as Bay St. Louis after French and Spanish land grants had failed to develop the area. The town of Shieldsboro incorporated on 21 January 1818 and by 1842 included a first-class hotel and numerous boardinghouses for visitors. By 1860 the city had approximately four hundred permanent residents. In 1875 the town changed its name to Bay St. Louis, and three years later the Louisville and Nashville Railroad purchased the New Orleans, Mobile, and Chattanooga Railroad creating a line running all along the Coast, thus ensuring Bay St. Louis's prominence as a watering hole.

Pass Christian's history began when François Carriere received a 1781 Spanish land grant. Upon Carriere's death, his widow, Donna Julia de la Brosse, known as the Widow Asmard, inherited the grant, and when she died in 1799, she deeded 680 acres of land (the area that is now downtown Pass Christian) to Charles Asmard, her former slave. Early in the nineteenth century, New Orleanians began building summer retreats along the four-mile roadway that fronted the Gulf of Mexico, and the town of Pass Christian incorporated in 1848. The area assumed a genteel quality as cotton and sugarcane planters summered there, enjoying saltwater bathing.

To accommodate the increasing numbers of tourists, the Pass Christian Hotel opened in 1836, offering high-style living and social events. The Fourth of July was the liveliest holiday celebrated at the hotel until Gen. Zachary Taylor was honored there in 1848 by a grand ball after his distinguished service in the Mexican War. The next year, Pass Christian established the South's first yacht club, the Southern Regatta Club, and regularly hosted races for the burgeoning numbers of tourists. By the 1850s Pass Christian had undergone an architectural renaissance as wealthy New Orleanians constructed palatial homes along the coast. By 1860 Pass Christian was known as the Queen City of the Mississippi Coast.

In 1837 three entrepreneurs, John J. McCaughan, James McLauren, and Colin McRae, created the Mississippi City Company. They envisioned a port, Mississippi City, serving as the terminus for the proposed Gulf and Ship Island Railroad, which would haul timber to the Gulf Coast for shipment out of Ship Island Harbor. In 1841, as a result of McCaughan's efforts, a new county, named after William Henry Harrison, was created. His campaign to make Mississippi City the county seat resulted in the construction of a log cabin on what is now Courthouse Road. As a Mississippi state senator, McCaughan also urged the state legislature to locate the University of Mississippi in Mississippi City, but the proposal lost by one vote. McCaughan's father-in-law, Dr. William Tegarden, built a grand wharf and hotel, the Gulf View, in 1850. Erecting a private lighthouse to guide steamboats to the Gulf View (known locally as the Barnes Hotel), Tegarden ensured Mississippi City's place as a tourist destination.

Biloxi, founded in 1699 by Pierre Le Moyne, Sieur d'Iberville, for King Louis XIV of France, became part of the Mississippi Territory in 1811 after English and Spanish rule. By 1817, when Mississippi became a state, two of Biloxi's major landowners were the Ladner and Fayard families. On 8 February 1838 the Mississippi legislature granted permission for Biloxi to incorporate as a town, though it did not do so until 1850. Nevertheless, by the 1840s Biloxi hosted tourists in numerous hotels, including the American, the Magnolia, Nixon's, Pradat's, and the Shady Grove. The Biloxi Lighthouse began beckoning tourists in 1848, and they arrived to find fishing, boating, bathing, balls, and billiards.

In the early 1850s George Lynch, a trader-merchant operating a sawmill with Rev. P. P. Bowen on Biloxi Bay near Fort Bayou, rediscovered local iron, sulfur, and magnesium springs that Native Americans had previously used for medicinal purposes. Capitalizing on the believed curative effects of the waters, Bowen constructed marble baths for tourists arriving at what became known as Lynchburg. By 1853 Dr. William G. Austin and the Porter family completed a grand hotel, the Ocean Springs, and the town took that name the following year. It subsequently developed into a resort, and over the following decade, hotels and boardinghouses sprung up to accommodate the numerous visitors who disembarked at the steamboat landing at the foot of Jackson Avenue.

In 1813 a visitor to Pascagoula described the village as always having a sea breeze and situated on a beautiful bay. John J. McRae established a cotton depot by 1819, thus opening the region to economic development. In the 1830s the East Pascagoula House opened for guests who wanted saltwater bathing and fresh seafood. The following year, the West Pascagoula House began hosting visitors. The McRae family eventually came to own both establishments, while John J. McRae operated a steamboat line from New Orleans to Pascagoula. However, by 1852 Pascagoula had lost its status as a watering hole after hurricanes, fire, and an incident involving Americans and Cuban exiles who wanted to launch an attack on Spain after the Mexican-American War. These filibusters, as they were called, congregated on Round Island, attracted national attention, and were killed when they invaded Cuba. Pascagoula subsequently expanded as an industrial area, particularly in shipbuilding.

Deanne Stephens Nuwer
University of Southern Mississippi,
Katrina Research Center

Ray L. Bellande, *Hotels and Tourists Homes of Ocean Springs* (1994); Robert J. Cangelosi Jr. and Liz Ford, in *Maritime Resources and History of the Mississippi Gulf Coast* (1998); Dan Ellis, in *Maritime Resources and History of the Mississippi Gulf Coast* (1998); Murella Hebert Powell, in *Maritime Resources and History of the Mississippi Gulf Coast* (1998); Charles L. Sullivan and Murella Hebert Powell, *The Mississippi Gulf Coast: Portrait of a People* (1985).

Sixteenth Section Lands

Support for public education has long been a standard in the United States. English settlers brought the idea of setting aside land for public education. The Ordinance of 1785, which was authored by Thomas Jefferson, followed the New England colonies' policy of reserving land for school purposes. The unit of measurement utilized for land was a thirty-six-square-mile area, a township. Each township consisted of thirty-six one-mile-square sections containing 640 acres. The ordinance set aside each sixteenth section within that township for the maintenance of public schools.

The Continental Congress's Ordinance of 1787 continued support for public schools. The 1802 agreement that created the state of Georgia provided that when the land area that now includes Alabama and Mississippi achieved statehood, those states would be admitted under the conditions and restrictions set forth in the Ordinance of 1787, and an 1803 act provided that when land south of Tennessee and west of Georgia was sold, the sixteenth section in each township would be set aside for support of public schools, with title vesting in the state as trustee.

It eventually became apparent that some Sixteenth Section Lands had already been sold either by England or the United States. Congress therefore passed another act in 1806 dealing with "lieu lands"—that is, that were provided for the use of schools in to replace lands that had already been conveyed. These lieu lands were later sold, mainly owing to difficulty of managing them: most of the lands were located far from township authorities. The Sixteenth Section Lands were also a subject of dispute after the 1832 Treaty of Pontotoc Creek, under which the United States was to sell the Chickasaw land and give the proceeds to the Chickasaw. The result was that sixteenth sections in the Chickasaw country were sold, and no provisions were made for school lands.

Mississippi became a state in 1817. Instances of neglect and abuse of the land trust started soon thereafter. Section 95 of the 1890 Mississippi Constitution, under which the state still operates, set forth that lands belonging to the state could never be donated to private corporations or individuals, and Section 211 provided that Sixteenth Section Lands could not be sold. The Sixteenth Section Reform Act of 1978, largely accomplished through the efforts of state land commissioner John Ed Ainsworth, established standards for the proper management of Sixteenth Section Lands. Continued efforts by the secretary of state, whose office took up the functions of the state land commissioner, have increased the annual income from those lands from between two and three million dollars per acre to approximately seventy million dollars by 2014. By the second decade of the twenty-first century, the Office of the Secretary of State oversaw the management and leasing of more than 640,000 acres of Sixteenth Section public school trust lands by 106 local school districts.

The Mississippi Supreme Court's decisions in *Talley v. Board of Supervisors of Smith County* (1975) and *Hill v. Thompson* (1989) played a vital role in this effort. The *Hill* case concerned a lease in downtown Forest that had been issued for ninety-nine years for a one-time payment of $7.50. The court held that the Sixteenth Section lease in that case was voidable and that all Sixteenth Section leases must be issued for fair market value.

Today, Sixteenth Section management provides significant financial support for the public schools in Mississippi that have Sixteenth Section lands under their jurisdiction.

Mack Cameron
Flowood, Mississippi

1890 Miss. Const., Art. IV, Sec. 95, Art. VIII, Sec. 211; Richard Clayton and Frank Spencer, eds., *A Special Report on Sixteenth Section Land Management* (9 December 1977); Patricia Galloway, Private Land Claims Research Material, 1984, Mississippi Department of Archives and History; *Hill v. Thompson*, 564 So. 2d 1 (1989); Miss. Code Ann., sec. 29-3-1 et seq.; Mississippi Department of Education website, http://www.mde.k12.ms.us/; Mississippi Secretary of State website, http://www.sos.ms.gov/; David Lamar Powe, "A History of Sixteenth Section Land Laws, Court Decisions, and Management Practices since 1970" (PhD dissertation, University of Southern Mississippi, 1984); *Tally v. Board of Supervisors of Smith County*, 323 So. 2d 547 (1975).

Skelton, Martha
(1919–2008) Quilter

Martha Butcher Skelton stands among the preeminent quilters in Mississippi and indeed in the nation. Born in West Virginia on 22 July 1919 to William Henry Harrison Butcher and Katie Virginia Guthrie Butcher, Martha was reared in Oklahoma and earned bachelor's and master's degrees from the University of Oklahoma in 1939 and 1940. On 26 January

1940 she married Alan Skelton, and they moved to Vicksburg in 1947.

While she was growing up, she spent long evenings doing needlework of all kinds—embroidery, crocheting, knitting, sewing, and quilting—with her mother, five aunts, two grandmothers, and four sisters. She pieced a quilt top in 1934–35 for her hope chest, and over the next seven decades, she produced about two hundred more quilts.

As a wife and mother in Vicksburg during the 1950s and 1960s, Skelton knew no other quilters. But as her children grew older, she found more time to devote to her art, and in 1973 she began teaching quilting in a Vicksburg department store. At around the same time, she also started giving quilting classes for the Cooperative Extension Service, traveling all over Mississippi, and she organized a quilting bee at the Mississippi State Fair. For about a decade beginning in 1992 Skelton worked with the Cultural Crossroads in Port Gibson.

In 1974 the Smithsonian Institution invited Skelton to demonstrate quilting at the Smithsonian American Folklife Festival, held on the Mall in Washington, D.C., for four days in July, establishing her as one of the state's premier heritage crafts practitioners. The Smithsonian invited her again in 1997 as part of its celebration of the folkways of the Mississippi River Delta.

Skelton began entering quilt contests in 1979 and immediately started collecting prizes. In 1987 the American Quilter's awarded *New York Beauty* first place and purchased the quilt for its permanent collection. The quilt was subsequently exhibited at the 1987 Cotton Patchers' Quilt Show, featured in the fall 1987 issue of *The American Quilter*, and published in both the 1991 and 2001 editions of *MAQS Quilts: The Permanent Collection*. Probably the best known of all of Skelton's quilts is *Chips and Whetstones*, which took second place in its category at the 1988 American Quilter's Society show and appeared on the cover of the winter 1989–90 issue of *Quilt Digest*, in the fall 1988 issue of *American Quilter* and again on the magazine's cover in the winter of 1995, and in numerous other magazines and books. In addition, her quilts have been featured in *A Garden of Quilts* (1981), *The Quilt: Beauty in Fabric and Thread* (1997), and *Mastering Quilt Marking* (1999) as well as in magazines and on calendars.

Martha Skelton's lifetime production ranks among the most prolific of contemporary quilters. Skelton frequently exhibited her quilts in Vicksburg, Hattiesburg, and Jackson as well as at other venues across the state and around the world, including the International Quilt Festival in Houston, Texas, and New York's Museum of American Folk Art. Three of her quilts are in the collections of the State Historical Museum at the Old Capitol in Jackson.

Skelton died in Vicksburg on 4 November 2008.

Mary Elizabeth Johnson
Montgomery, Alabama

Mary Elizabeth Johnson, *Martha Skelton: Master Quilter of Mississippi* (2008); *Vicksburg Post* (6 November 2008).

Slaughter-Harvey, Constance
(b. 1946) Attorney and Activist

Born in Jackson on 18 June 1946 and reared in Forest, Constance Slaughter was one of six daughters of Willie L. Slaughter and Olivia Kelly Slaughter, both of whom were educators and civil rights pioneers. Slaughter graduated as valedictorian of at the segregated E. T. Hawkins High School and enrolled in 1963 at Tougaloo College, where she met civil rights leader Medgar Evers. His June 1963 murder, along with the values instilled by her parents and the racial injustices she witnessed, inspired her to join the civil rights movement.

After serving as student body president and graduating from Tougaloo College with a degree in political science, Slaughter attended law school at the University of Mississippi. In 1970, amid death threats and constant prejudice, she became the first African American woman to receive a law degree from the school. She subsequently worked for the Lawyers' Committee for Civil Rights under Law as a staff attorney and represented the families of two students who were killed by highway patrolmen during the Jackson State University massacre. Slaughter-Harvey filed the desegregation lawsuit against the Mississippi State Highway Patrol that resulted in the hiring of African American highway patrolmen.

Slaughter-Harvey became executive director of Southern Legal Rights and later the director of East Mississippi Legal

Constance Slaughter-Harvey (Courtesy University of Mississippi University Communications)

Services, an organization she founded to provide high-quality legal representation for minority and economically disenfranchised people. She joined Mississippi governor William Winter's staff in 1980 as director of human development and later served as assistant secretary of state for elections and public lands under Secretary of State Dick Molpus. Slaughter-Harvey led the effort that resulted in the enactment of mail-in voter registration in 1991 and the movement to permit voter registration at the Department of Motor Vehicles, becoming the first African American and first woman to serve on the Motor Voter National Advisory Board. In 1995 Slaughter-Harvey worked for the Mississippi Democratic Party, coordinating campaigns for all of the party's candidates statewide. She has served as a member of the Board of Trustees of Tougaloo College and was an adjunct professor there from 1970 to 2005. The Constance Slaughter-Harvey Endowed Chair in Political Science was created in her honor; her daughter, Constance Olivia Harvey Burwell, became the fifth generation of the Slaughter family to attend the college. Slaughter-Harvey has formally taught and informally mentored many Mississippi attorneys. Through her work as president of the W. L. and O. K. Slaughter Memorial Foundation, named for her parents, Slaughter-Harvey supervised an after-school tutorial and summer enhancement program for at-risk children and youth.

Slaughter-Harvey has received numerous awards from such organizations as the National Association for the Advancement of Colored People, the Mississippi Women Lawyers, the Mississippi Bar Association, and the American Bar Association. The Black Law Students Association at the University of Mississippi is named in her honor, and in 2001 she received the law school's Public Service Award. Slaughter-Harvey has served as president of the Magnolia Bar Association, was the first African American judge in Mississippi, and was the first African American and woman elected president of the National Association of Election Directors.

Slaughter-Harvey continues to practice law, focusing on promoting and defending the civil rights of all people and protecting the elderly. She is also the founder and president of the Legacy Education and Community Empowerment Foundation, which works to provide youth and student enrichment, mentoring, enhancement services, intergenerational programs, and other educational and empowerment programs in Forest.

Chris Gilmer
Jackson State University

African American Yearbook, 2007–2008 (2008); Clarice Campbell and Oscar Allan Rogers Jr., *Mississippi: The View from Tougaloo* (2nd ed., 2002); Susie Erenrich, *Freedom Is a Constant Struggle: An Anthology of the Mississippi Civil Rights Movement* (1999); Legacy Education and Community Empowerment Foundation website, http://www.leacef.com/home.html; Cora Norman, *Mississippi in Transition: The Role of the Mississippi Humanities Council* (2009); John M. Perkins, *Let Justice Roll Down* (1976); Constance Slaughter-Harvey, interview by George King, *Southern Changes* 1 (1997); Constance Slaughter-Harvey, *University of Mississippi Law Journal* (Fall 2004); Judy H. Tucker and Charline R. McCord, eds., *Growing Up in Mississippi* (2008).

Slave Codes

Like other southern territories and states, Mississippi adopted strict laws to govern the conduct of slaves. Mississippi built on the statutes previously implemented by slaveholding colonies, which codified and promoted white supremacy as they struggled to define the legal status of slaves. Beginning with the creation of the Mississippi Territory in 1798, the Mississippi slave codes became harsher, though some slaves found legal protection through the courts.

The territorial and state legislatures responded to persistent slave resistance and threats of insurrection with more severe codes. Revising an 1805 law that assured that "no cruel or unusual punishment shall be inflicted on any slave within this territory," an 1807 measure stipulated that fugitive slaves "be burned in the hand by the sheriff in open court," and any slave who presented false testimony should receive thirty-nine lashes and have an ear nailed to a pillory for an hour and then cut off. In 1812, on the heels of a slave rebellion in Louisiana, speculation mounted that slaves might use the war with Britain to revolt against their masters, prompting the territorial legislature to place the slave patrols under the supervision of the militia and to streamline the process of trying slaves charged with capital offenses. A three-judge panel would now hear a trial without presentment or indictment, and all participants found guilty in a conspiracy to rebel, murder, or assault a white person would face hanging. Following the 1831 Nat Turner rebellion in Virginia, Mississippi required free blacks to "remove or quit the state," although the 1860 census listed nearly eight hundred free black residents.

After 1814 the territorial legislature moved to limit punishments for various offenses. Thirty-nine lashes became the standard consequence for a slave caught attending a literacy class or engaging in petty theft. Slaves received the same punishment for possessing a firearm or ammunition without a license from the justice of the peace. Assault and battery of a white person carried a penalty of one hundred lashes. The state gave judges full discretion regarding slaves found guilty of "riots, routs, affrays, unlawful assemblies, trespasses, malicious mischief, seditious speeches, or abusive, provoking or insulting language to any person not being a negro or mulatto person." The list of capital offenses included such crimes as arson, rape, grand larceny, and murder. The Mississippi slave code of 1857—the last of the antebellum codes—contained twenty-five offenses that could result in the death penalty. Unlike in noncapital offenses, however, state law mandated that slaves receive legal counsel in capital cases. If found guilty, slaves could appeal to the High Court of Errors and Appeals, which at times overturned convictions. Between 1843 and 1861, the High Court reversed or remanded five out of thirteen convictions of slaves who murdered or attempted to murder white individuals.

While owners and overseers maintained their own regulations and punishments, the state and municipalities issued codes to restrict the mobility of slaves when outside their masters' sight. Slaves throughout Mississippi needed written passes when off their masters' property. Any slave found without a pass went before the local judge and received up to twenty lashes. A slave who tried to purchase or sell anything without the master's permission could receive up to thirty lashes. The gathering together of slaves, particularly for worship, necessitated the presence of at least two reputable white people. Codes prohibited slaves or free blacks from performing the functions of a minister unless the services took place on the master's property. The issue of slaves coming to town on Sundays was a continual problem for the white residents of Woodville, who passed a series of laws in the 1830s and 1840s to try to curtail the mass congregations. Courthouse bells rang at four o'clock in Natchez and nine o'clock in Grenada to clear the towns of slaves on the Sabbath.

The Civil War brought freedom to slaves, but the 1865 legislature passed a series of new laws designed to maintain the subordinate status of black Mississippians. Like slave codes, the new Black Codes restricted the rights and conduct of citizens based on race. The codes prohibited former slaves from renting or leasing land outside of a town and allowed justices of the peace to capture "vagrants" and hire them out. One provision even stipulated that the penal and criminal laws already in effect—that is, the 1857 slave codes—were now "reenacted, and declared to be in full force and effect, against freedmen, free negroes and mulattoes." The Mississippi legislature did not repeal the slave code of 1857 and all the Black Codes until 1870.

Carter Dalton Lyon
St. Mary's Episcopal School,
Memphis, Tennessee

James T. Currie, *Journal of Negro History* (Spring 1980); Eugene D. Genovese, *Roll, Jordan, Roll: The World the Slaves Made* (1972); Winthrop D. Jordan, *White over Black: American Attitudes toward the Negro, 1550–1812* (1968); David J. Libby, *Slavery and Frontier Mississippi, 1720–1835* (2004); Charles S. Sydnor, *Slavery in Mississippi* (1933).

Slave Communities

Slavery undermined all ties between slaves, yet slaves in Mississippi, as elsewhere, formed many communities—communities of work, kinship, struggle, religious fellowship, to name but a few. These communities, in turn, were grounded in neighborhoods. Neighborhoods were a geographic terrain—a place marked by boundaries and a state of mind that mapped an imagined community. The geographic boundaries of neighborhood varied from a single plantation in frontier regions to adjoining farms and plantations in more populous areas, with enslaved men and women extending ties of work, family, resistance, and religion across slaveholders' property lines. The slave population increased sixfold (from 32,814 to 195,211) as planters poured into the state between 1820 and 1840. By then, slaves accounted for more than half the population (52 percent).

The social ingenuity of slaves made work an exercise in community building. Under an exacting system of labor that kept them under the scrutiny of slaveholders from sunup to sundown, slaves managed to forge communities of house servants and field laborers. Coordinating work in the field—opening the ground, planting seeds, and covering them, for example—required plow and hoe gangs to work together on tasks, the pace of their labor, and their bodily movements. Where the sexual division of labor assigned men and women to separate tasks or field gangs, bondpeople formed communities of gender. Women formed bonds of affinity while making or washing clothes. Men honed their sense of manhood in work—for example, hoisting a four-hundred-pound bale onto a wagon—even if there were women on virtually every plantation who picked as much cotton as any man. When gangs left the fields, they often went to work for themselves. In the evenings, on Saturday afternoons, and on Sundays, they performed paid overwork for owners, made handicrafts, tended gardens, and raised surpluses. Some of their earnings went to purchase goods that enlivened sociability—tobacco, whiskey, or clothes for parties or Sunday wear. While labor kept most slaves at home, some worked to create communities beyond the plantation. Unsupervised teamsters carted plantation produce between town and country and camped together at night. Men and women made neighborhood ties doing paid labor on adjoining plantations and mending fences and roads. Slaves worked hard to turn the centripetal effects of labor into a centrifugal force making neighborhoods.

Kinship simultaneously marked enslaved people's most intimate circle of community and engendered larger communities. Owners sold slaves as punishment or to repay debts, bequeathed them at death or on the marriage of planters' children. Yet most slaves probably lived in nuclear families—in a cabin with husband and wife, parents and children. Many lived in extended families—in the same cabin or on the same plantation with family members of three generations (grandparents, parents, children) or bilateral kin (adult siblings, nieces, nephews, cousins). These family ties were sustained by reproductive labor, obligations of solidarity, and subtle practices of recognition and honor. Family members took meals together, worked garden plots, pooled earnings and property, and bequeathed and inherited property. Nurses, midwives, healers, and the women who received their ministrations formed close circles. As slaves took spouses, reared children, and otherwise cultivated bonds of kinship on adjoining places, they multiplied and deepened ties to other families in the neighborhood.

Family ties were undergirded by a range of intimate relations, mediated by neighborhood communities. In the absence of legal recognition of marriage between slaves, men and women were compelled to lend permanence to their bonds by informal modes of recognition. Couples in the early stages of their relationship were said to be "taking up," while slaves distinguished between spouses in terms of "living together" and "marriage," which was reserved for couples united in weddings. Slaves exalted weddings because the ceremonies gave bonds between spouses the imprimatur of owners, fellow slaves, and neighborhoods. Names routinely provided a method of marking family ties. Many families used the surnames of their parents, not of their current owners. Neighbors, in turn, acknowledged family ties by using these surnames for cohabiting and married couples alike. Slaves used terms of kinship such as "Aunt" and "Uncle" as terms of address for people unrelated by direct descent. Thus, slaves relied on neighborhood communities to shore up their most intimate relations and kinship to incorporate newcomers into neighborhoods.

Slaves also formed communities in everyday socializing of all sorts. In off hours, they went visiting in the quarters and on adjoining plantations; from time to time, especially before and after the cotton-picking season, slaves held clandestine dances, balls, weddings, and other "big times." Slaves also assembled for religious purposes, attending church in town or more commonly in the neighborhood. Slaves often convened to hear white missionaries as well as slave preachers and held their own meetings at night. Men and women courted, conspired, displayed finery and other property, and made reputations as cooks, dancers, and fiddlers as well as in verbal arts, singing, preaching, and storytelling. As neighbors told stories of their pasts, their exploits, and their struggles and gossiped about couples, friends, and kinfolk, they gave voice to expectations and the common sense of their neighborhood. Convening in the quarters and the yard, in hollows, ravines, and woods, slaves carved out neighborhood places and sites of neighborhood memory. As they did the work of putting on these affairs, clearing underbrush for a hush arbor or a dance floor, cooking food, playing instruments, keeping lookout, they laid the groundwork for others to reciprocate and to do it all again. Social occasions offered moments when slaves, by word and deed, could consolidate and extend the bonds holding neighborhood communities together.

Slave communities were necessarily communities of struggle. Slaves' status as human property challenged every enduring tie. Increases in burdens of labor obliged work groups to pull together against new demands and exacting discipline. Women banded together in struggles particular to them, and so did men. Women battled slaveholders who exploited them sexually, whereas men were especially prone to run away and often did so together. Men and women contended to keep up kinship ties and for access to adjoining plantations. The pass system, which slaveholders employed to regulate mobility they could not wholly prevent, reflected slaves' success in their campaign to claim a neighborhood terrain. In many neighborhoods, husbands and wives belonging to different owners extracted standing passes to spend three nights together each week. By the same token, slaves forged neighborhoods into a terrain of struggle. Men and women enlisted allies in the neighborhood when running away, stealing, conspiring to lay out, or hiding property. Making neighborhoods a terrain of solidarity also separated insiders from outsiders. Slaves often captured runaways from outside the neighborhood. In the spring of 1861 rebels in southern Adams County along Second Creek recruited men to strike slaveholders in the neighborhood, but some slaves rejected entreaties from recruiters outside their neighborhood. Defining neighborhood as a terrain of solidarity also drew a boundary between communities.

Slaves formed multiple, overlapping, mutually reinforcing communities. They identified with different communities in different ways at different times. Migrants had deep attachments to families in the Upper South yet formed new families in Mississippi. Patterns of work, family obligation, and struggle sorted out communities of women and men. Religious communities transcended boundaries of time and space whenever slaves felt close to God. Neighborhoods were hardly slaves' only community but had pride of place as the everyday nexus of communities. These communities coexisted but by no means did so seamlessly. Conflicting individual interests, conflicting loyalties to multiple communities, and the constraints of neighborhood grounds pulled enslaved men and women in different directions. Yet the communities slaves created, in their multiplicity, flexibility, and durability, gave order to slave society, undercut owners' supposed mastery, and even subverted slavery itself. With emancipation, freedpeople began defining freedom by building on the foundation of communities built in slavery.

Anthony Kaye
Penn State University

John W. Blassingame, *The Slave Community: Plantation Life in the Antebellum South* (rev. ed., 1979); Michael A. Gomez, *Exchanging Our Country Marks: The Transformation of African Identities in the Colonial and*

Antebellum South (1998); Anthony E. Kaye, *Joining Places: Slave Neighborhoods in the Old South* (2007); Lawrence W. Levine, *Black Culture and Black Consciousness: Afro-Americana Folk Thought from Slavery to Freedom* (1977); Walter F. Pitts Jr., *Old Ship of Zion: The Afro-Baptist Ritual in the African Diaspora* (1993); Deborah Gray White, *Ar'n't I a Woman? Female Slaves in the Plantation South* (1985).

Slave Patrols

Mississippi's slave patrol system served as an important mechanism for the white population to control the movement of slaves and prevent insurrections. Groups of four to five white men, consisting of both slaveholders and non-slaveholders, were assigned to patrol an area in their county called a beat. These men, led by a captain of the patrol, walked or rode horses through the beat, looking for slaves out at night without passes from their owners. Patrollers also had the right to enter a slave owner's property and inspect the slave quarters for weapons or illegal assemblies of slaves. Mississippi law authorized patrollers to act as judge and jury, meting out an immediate punishment of up to thirty-nine lashes with a whip. Any fugitive slaves captured by the patrol were supposed to be brought before a justice of the peace for confinement, and the patrol received up to six dollars per captured runaway slave.

The Mississippi slave patrol system originated within the state militia. Local militia commanders assigned the captains of patrols, who were then responsible for assembling the patrols from among the members of the militia. In 1831 Mississippi changed the law to allow towns to form their own systems of slave patrols. Towns faced a different set of circumstances than did rural areas, since slaves often congregated in towns on weekends and thus had the opportunity to collude in their efforts to resist slavery. Two years later, Mississippi decentralized the slave patrol system by shifting control from the state militia to the county police boards, thereby allowing local authorities to modify the patrols to meet local needs.

Although the slave patrol system looked potent on paper, it proved quite ineffective and inefficient. The duty generally offered no reward for patrollers and was considered an onerous and dull task to be avoided in most circumstances. Mississippi law allowed assigned patrollers to send substitutes to fulfill their obligation of service, which required that they patrol once every two weeks—or more often if the police board saw a need. Nearly all patrols operated on weekend nights, when most owners granted slaves free time to visit spouses and neighbors. Since patrols usually operated only twice a month, slaves had numerous opportunities to evade the patrols. A

slave's perception that the patrols operated effectively and with extreme violence was the real power behind the patrols. Former slave testimony often recalled "paddyrollers" as a terrifying presence around plantation areas, harassing slaves traveling at night and disrupting their social gatherings. Other former slaves, however, recalled the patrollers as comically inept and easily foiled. The slave patrol's strength, therefore, rested in its symbolic power to intimidate slaves and control the night. Slave owners had no other institutional mechanism to police their slaves at night.

With the rise in sectional tensions prior to the onset of the Civil War, local authorities increased the size and frequency of slave patrols to quell potential revolts. Some communities also formed extralegal organizations to monitor slave activities. Historians have suggested that the practices used by the slave patrols to intimidate the slave population—which constituted a majority in many areas—led to the development of similar night-riding groups during Reconstruction, including the Ku Klux Klan, although establishing the connections has proven difficult because of a lack of records.

J. Michael Crane
University of Arkansas
at Fort Smith

J. Michael Crane, *Journal of Mississippi History* (Summer 1999); Gladys-Marie Fry, *Night Riders in Black Folk History* (1975); Sally E. Hadden, *Slave Patrols: Law and Violence in Virginia and the Carolinas* (2001); Charles S. Sydnor, *Slavery in Mississippi* (1933).

Slave Revolts

Mississippi experienced only one actual slave revolt, but on several occasions, planters uncovered conspiracies to revolt. The infrequency of slave insurrections in Mississippi, as in the rest of the South, stems from the fact that the likelihood of success was usually limited, making slaves unwilling to take the risk. Indeed, conspiracies seem to have occurred only when instability in the white community suggested to slaves that rebellion might succeed.

Mississippi's only outright rebellion coincided with the Natchez Uprising of 1730, in which Natchez Indians and allied slaves took up arms against French settlers, killing all men. In a subsequent raid on Natchez led by Choctaw allied with the French, African slaves again took up arms, holding off the Choctaw long enough to allow the Natchez to evacuate the town. While in many ways this incident falls outside the mold of slave insurrection and conspiracy, it is instructive because the weakness of French colonizers and the proximity of Natchez allies rendered the chances of success worth the risk of rebellion.

More than forty years later, in the summer of 1776, slaves on the plantation of William Dunbar were discovered plotting insurrection. This incident fits more closely the pattern of slave insurrection conspiracies in Mississippi. As a result of the isolation of Dunbar's plantation, the masters lacked strength in numbers. Dunbar and his fellow planters formed a committee to try the slaves, convicted and hanged the alleged organizers, and then pooled resources to compensate Dunbar for the value of the executed slaves.

In 1814 slaves in the Natchez region were discovered to be conspiring to ally with Creek and French attackers during the War of 1812. This incident also matches the pattern of slave insurrections, as planters generally had grown more harsh in their treatment of slaves following the introduction of cotton. In Natchez, the slaves outnumbered the masters. Another contributing factor was internal division over the war and the rumored threat of an invasion. Slaves likely believed that a divided and outnumbered master class would be overthrown and that invaders and Indian allies would grant freedom. Once again, planters formed a committee to try and punish the organizers.

Another alleged conspiracy was discovered in Livingston, Mississippi, in 1835. Livingston was located in the frontier regions of recently opened lands that formerly had been controlled by Choctaw. Slaves outnumbered masters, and as a result of patterns of slave migration, the slave community was likely stronger and more cohesive than the planter community, which was made up of recent migrants from disparate places of origin. The conspiracy was uncovered at the same time that the outlaw John Murrell hysteria hit the region, although it is unclear how or whether the two events were related. Once again, a committee was formed to try and punish the conspirators. As with other such incidents, the Livingston uprising came after planters introduced harsher working conditions—forcing slaves to simultaneously cultivate cotton and build plantations—and the planters were outnumbered and isolated and had not yet developed a cohesive society.

Mississippi's last known slave conspiracy occurred in 1861, just as the Civil War began, in the Second Creek region near Natchez. Slaves knew that the planters were divided over the issue of war and heard rumors that Union troops would soon invade. When the conspiracy was uncovered, planters again formed a committee and interrogated and punished the conspirators, killing several of them.

Despite the differences between these incidents, several common threads connect them. First, all occurred in areas where the slaves outnumbered the masters. Second, most conspiracies occurred at times when the planters either were isolated or did not present a united front to their slaves. Third, the conspiracies occurred either in isolated frontier regions (Dunbar's plantation and Livingston) or amid widespread rumors of invasion (the British in 1814, Union forces in 1861).

This evidence leads to the reasonable conclusion that for slaves to believe that insurrection had a chance at succeeding, they needed to outnumber masters, needed to know that masters would be unable to call in additional help, and needed an escape route (unsettled lands or with encroaching enemies). Despite the harshness of slavery in Mississippi, slaves did not often organize rebellions because the conditions indicating likely success were rare. Conversely, when those conditions existed, Mississippi's slaves did conspire to revolt.

David J. Libby
University of Texas at San Antonio

Gwendolyn Midlo Hall, *Africans in Colonial Louisiana: The Development of Afro-Creole Culture in the Eighteenth Century* (1992); Winthrop D. Jordan, *Tumult and Silence at Second Creek: An Inquiry into a Civil War Slave Conspiracy* (1993); David J. Libby, *Slavery and Frontier Mississippi, 1720–1835* (2004); Christopher Morris, *Journal of Social History* (Fall 1988).

Slave Trade

In 1820, Mississippi had 33,000 slaves; forty years later, that number had mushroomed to about 437,000, giving the state the country's largest slave population. While new births accounted for much of that increase, the trade in slaves became a crucial part of Mississippians' social and economic life. As historian Charles S. Sydnor wrote, "Few, if any, southern States received as many slaves and exported as few."

Slave sales were painful events. They could be humiliating, since humans were treated as livestock and inspected for their physical features. Being sold also meant the possibility of separation from family and community members as well as the possibility if not likelihood of overwork, illness, and physical punishment.

The US Constitution outlawed the international slave trade nine years before Mississippi became a state, so Mississippians who wanted to buy slaves had to do so from sources inside the United States. The trade in slaves of African birth or ancestry was clearly established in Natchez by the 1700s. In 1810 a notice in a Natchez newspaper advertised "twenty likely Virginia born slaves . . . for sale cheaper than has been sold here in years."

By far the largest and most permanent slave market in the state was located at the Forks of the Road in Natchez. Virginia slave trader Isaac Franklin and his nephew, John Armfield, owned the market at the intersection of two major roads near

S

downtown Natchez. At the height of the trade, their slave pens held between six hundred and eight hundred slaves at one time, and some observers said that Natchez slave traders sold more than a thousand slaves each year.

Vicksburg, Jackson, Aberdeen, Crystal Springs, Woodville, and other towns and cities had smaller and sometimes impermanent slave markets. Some traveling slave traders liked to do their business in or near taverns. Many Mississippi slave dealers were affiliated with large firms with offices in New Orleans; Alexandria, Virginia; and other cities. Slave dealers regularly advertised in Mississippi newspapers.

Traders transported slaves to Mississippi in various ways. Slaves were bound together with chains and forced to walk in groups called coffles. The trip by foot from the East Coast to Mississippi, often down the Natchez Trace from Nashville, could take seven to eight weeks. Other slave traders transported their slaves by water, either from the Ohio River and down the Mississippi, or by ship around Florida, through New Orleans, and up the Mississippi River. Being "sold down the river"—meaning the Mississippi River—was one of the worst threats slave owners in the Upper South and East could make to their slaves.

Many sales and trades of slaves took place in settings smaller than the well-known slave pens of Natchez. Sheriffs frequently sold slaves at courthouses when conducting probate proceedings to dispose of other property belonging to deceased people. Also, many individual slave owners sold slaves to acquaintances. According to historian Steven Deyle, "Despite the tendency of both popular culture and most historians to equate the domestic trade with the interregional trade, the overwhelming majority of enslaved people who were sold never passed through the hands of a professional slave trader nor spent a day in a large New Orleans slave depot. They were sold locally, by one owner to another or by nearby country courts."

From 1833 through 1845, selling slaves was officially illegal in Mississippi. The Constitutional Convention of 1832 prohibited "the introduction of slaves into the state as merchandize, or for sale." Slave traders and buyers consistently broke or ignored the law, so the legislature passed a new law that imposed penalties for bringing slaves into the state for sale. The official reasons for the ban on slave trading were that Mississippi legislators disliked slave traders' reputation for cruelty and dishonesty and feared the growth of huge slave majorities. Many Mississippians, especially in Natchez, also believed that slave traders brought unhealthy chattel. The more specific but usually unstated reason was that elite Mississippians, like many powerful southerners, were frightened by Nat Turner's 1831 uprising in Virginia and wanted to protect the state from slaves who might rebel. Lawmakers required slave owners to demonstrate that slaves to be sold had good character—that is, that they had never participated in a rebellions.

Despite the laws, slave trading continued, and the law expired in 1845, making the slave trade again legal. In fact, in the 1850s a handful of leading slave owners discussed the possibility of reopening the African slave trade.

Slave traders had a dubious reputation among slave owners in Mississippi, in part because traders often moved around but also—and more important—because their role in the process made clear the contradictions involved in seeing human beings as property. Some Mississippi slave owners imagined themselves as kind, paternalistic figures who would never break up slave families, while slave traders routinely broke up families. Some Mississippians blamed all societal problems—illness, family breakup, abuse—on the slave traders and more generally on the slave trade while claiming to practice a more humane form of slavery.

Most slave traders bought slaves in the summer and sold them from winter through early spring, when slave owners were planning or beginning new work. The prices of slaves rose and fell with the price of cotton. Slave prices were low after the Panic of 1837 and were at their highest during the cotton boom of the 1850s. The most expensive slaves—young, healthy males—cost about eighteen hundred dollars in the 1850s, with other slaves costing less.

The slave markets ended with the Civil War and emancipation. Union soldiers, many of them offended by the markets themselves, blocked off Mississippi's slave-trading networks from eastern suppliers early in the Civil War.

Ted Ownby
University of Mississippi

Jim Barnett and H. Clark Burkett, *Journal of Mississippi History* (Fall 2001); Steven Deyle, *Carry Me Back: The Domestic Slave Trade in American Life* (2005); Walter Johnson, *Soul by Soul: Life inside the Antebellum Slave Market* (1999); Winthrop D. Jordan, *Tumult and Silence at Second Creek: An Inquiry into a Civil War Slave Conspiracy* (1993); Thom Rosenblum, *Journal of Mississippi History* (Spring 2005); Charles S. Sydnor, *Slavery in Mississippi* (1933); Michael Tadman, *Speculators and Slaves: Masters, Traders, and Slaves in the Old South* (1989).

Slavery, Arguments for

The proslavery argument refers to the defense of chattel slavery that emerged in the late eighteenth century and became more popular in the nineteenth century. Planters, newspaper editors, ministers, lawyers, politicians, economists, sociologists, and other writers drew from a variety of sources and approaches to justify the existence of slavery. Proslavery writers used religion, politics, racial superiority, political economy, climate, classical and contemporary philosophy, history, and natural and biological sciences to shape their arguments. Proslavery literature came in a variety of forms, including newspaper editorials, books, religious tracts, journal articles, and political speeches.

In the late antebellum era, proslavery ideology emerged in the southern states as a challenge to the growing abolitionist movement in the North. In countering the abolitionist movement, the proslavery argument changed from defending slavery as a necessary evil to depicting it as a positive good. Writers such as James Henry Hammond, Edmund Ruffin, George Fitzhugh, and Mississippian Henry Hughes argued that slavery as a social, economic, and labor system was superior to the free-labor economy found in Europe and the northeastern United States.

Because of its emergence as a slave state in the early antebellum era, Mississippi's political culture aligned with the major proslavery arguments. The state's Hughes and Matthew Estes articulated the major themes of the argument: the biblical defense of slavery, the existence of and need for a permanent laboring class, the inefficiency of free labor, and the superior standard of living experienced southern black slaves. Hughes developed his argument through an elaborate description and definition of sociology in his *Treatise on Sociology* (1854). He argued that slavery (warranteeism) existed in all social organizations and that slaves constituted the southern states' mudsill class. Estes's *Defence of Negro Slavery* (1846) concentrated mostly on the biblical defense of slavery, the history of the slave trade, African slavery, the inferiority of Africans, and the necessity of slavery to maintain white supremacy.

Christopher L. Stacey
Louisiana State University
at Alexandria

Drew Gilpin Faust, *A Sacred Circle: The Dilemma of the Intellectual in the Old South, 1840–1860* (1977); Eugene D. Genovese, *The Political Economy of Slavery: Studies in the Economy and Society of the Slave South* (1967); Eugene D. Genovese, *Roll, Jordan, Roll: The World the Slaves Made* (1972); George Fitzhugh, *Cannibals All! or, Slaves without Masters* (1857); William S. Jenkins, *Pro-Slavery Thought in the Old South* (1935); James Oakes, *The Ruling Race: A History of American Slaveholders* (1982); William K. Scarborough, *Masters of the Big House: Elite Slaveholders of the Mid-Nineteenth-Century South* (2002); Christopher L. Stacey, *Journal of Mississippi History* (September 2001); Larry E. Tise, *Proslavery: A History of the Defense of Slavery in America* (1987); Michael Wayne, *Journal of American History* (December 1990).

Slavery, Colonial

Colonial slavery in Mississippi can be divided into two distinct phases: the French era (ca. 1720–31) and the British-Spanish era (ca. 1770–95). In the intervening decades, no colonial power had a significant presence of slaves in the region.

French colonists first arrived in Natchez for permanent settlement in 1702 but did not attempt to introduce slavery until roughly 1720. The French settled alongside the Natchez Indians in an uneasy truce. French settlers imported slaves from the Senegambia region of West Africa, and the slave population in Natchez reached approximately two hundred. Significant research suggests that most of the slaves were of Bambarra ethnicity and therefore had a great deal of ethnic and linguistic unity, which would serve them well in establishing a slave community. The leadership of the French settlement, by contrast, was poorly organized, and colonists relied heavily on slave labor for their survival. Efforts to produce a tobacco crop failed in the early 1720s, but by mid-decade a regular tobacco crop was under way. The instability of French-Natchez relations, coupled with the poor organization and leadership of the French colony, led to widespread discontent among the slave population. When Natchez leaders resolved in 1729 to rise up and drive out French colonists, slaves cooperated in varying degrees, either standing by or actively supporting the attack. In the ensuing war, the French allied with the nearby Choctaw, while the Natchez allied with the African slaves. The conflict destroyed both the French and Natchez settlements, and French colonial planners abandoned efforts to establish permanent settlements in the Natchez region.

British colonizers arrived in the Natchez region in the late 1760s and came from virtually every one of the thirteen eastern seaboard colonies. Many brought slaves with them, while others stopped along the way in the Caribbean islands or in New Orleans to purchase slaves. In this sense, the settlers of British Natchez saw a tight connection between slavery and the colony's success. Because of the diversity of origins of the slave population, British planters established a more unified front than the slaves. A slave community nonetheless emerged through creolization, or cultural mixing and adaptation to new surroundings. Throughout the 1770s slaves primarily produced lumber and timber products while clearing land for future cultivation. Subsequent staple crops included unsuccessful attempts to produce indigo and tobacco during the 1770s and 1780s. Throughout this era, the planters depended on favorable British and Spanish trade policies to market their products. When the region was transferred to Spain after the American Revolution, the planters continued to rely on mercantilistic Spanish trade policies to access faraway markets for their tobacco and lumber. Spanish trade monopolies for tobacco and British bounties for indigo made these products successful, and when these protections were taken away, the markets dried up. For these reasons, the economics of colonial slavery in Mississippi were extremely unstable.

Mississippi's colonial era ended in 1795 with the transfer of Spanish authority over West Florida to the United States. This change coincided with the introduction of the cotton gin, which transformed the economics of slavery in Mississippi during the territorial and early statehood years.

David J. Libby
University of Texas at San Antonio

Gwendolyn Midlo Hall, *Africans in Colonial Louisiana: The Development of Afro-Creole Culture in the Eighteenth Century* (1992); David J. Libby, *Slavery and Frontier Mississippi, 1720–1835* (2004); Daniel H. Usner, *Indians, Settlers, and Slaves in a Frontier Exchange Economy: The Lower Mississippi Valley before 1783* (1993).

Slavery, Native American

Mississippi was at the height of its Indian slave trade in the last quarter of the seventeenth and first quarter of the eighteenth century, though natives continued to be enslaved in significant numbers afterwards. Slavery also existed in the pre-European contact period, when Native Americans of the Southeast often made captives of their enemies. Typically, adult male captives were ritualistically tortured, while adult females and children were kept as slaves, though they could eventually be assimilated or exchanged to their natal communities. Precontact slaves performed labor in native communities but were neither captured nor kept for economic purposes. Captives were taken for revenge—as compensation for tribe members who had been killed or captured. Slaves were considered nonpersons with no connection to the captor community, a potent reminder of the importance of kinship in these societies. Since southeastern Indians considered people lost to captivity to be dead, released captives/slaves had to go through ceremonies of rebirth to rejoin their natal communities.

The capture of slaves took on new meaning after the arrival of the English on the Atlantic coast of Virginia and South Carolina. The English viewed slaves as commodities to be bought and sold. They acquired captives from Indians in exchange for European goods, such as weapons, metal tools, cookware, textiles, and alcohol. Europeans employed Indian slaves as laborers—farm/plantation workers, domestics, and even artisans. The Virginians and Carolinians kept some of the Indians they purchased but sold most in the Atlantic slave trade, to the Caribbean sugar colonies, and to northern cities such as New York, Boston, and Providence.

The initial raiding for slaves in Mississippi came from Indians to the east who traded with Virginia. The raiders came down the Ohio River into the Mississippi country. In addition, the Westo, an Iroquoian people from New York who migrated to Virginia and established trade relations before moving to the Savannah River, raided the native peoples of the South Atlantic coast. Contemporaries believed that the Westo conducted raids as far west as the Chickasaw in Mississippi. The Westo inaugurated a massive slave trade in the South, particularly after the establishment of the Carolina colony in 1670, but found themselves enslaved and eliminated as a people by the Carolinians and their native slaving allies.

More than one hundred Carolinian traders lived in native villages to spur Indians to raid for slaves, then purchased the captives and transported them to Charles Town (later Charleston), South Carolina. In the east, Carolina's main slaving allies were the Savannah, the Yamasee, and the peoples who coalesced in Alabama and Georgia into the Creek Confederacy. These Indians, sometimes with their English allies, decimated thousands of native peoples in Florida and Georgia. The Creek also attacked Mississippi's Choctaw, who simultaneously were coalescing as a new nation, formed in part to resist the slaving. The main slave raiders in Mississippi, however, were the Chickasaw. From their base in northern Mississippi, the Chickasaw raided across the Mississippi River into Arkansas and down the Mississippi to the Gulf of Mexico. Their slaving created many refugee communities along the Gulf Coast, which the French labeled the Petit Nations. The Chickasaw also conducted slaving in central Mississippi among the Choctaw. All told, between fifteen hundred and twenty-five hundred Choctaw were enslaved, as well as one thousand to three thousand other Indians of the Lower Mississippi Valley and another one thousand to two thousand Arkansas, Taensa, and Tunica, who lived and hunted on both sides of the Mississippi River above Natchez and below the Wabash River.

The French settled permanently in the Lower Mississippi River Valley beginning in 1699 at Mobile and later at New Orleans and at small outposts throughout the South. They tried to end the slaving wars, particularly the Chickasaw (as well as Creek) attacks on the Choctaw, and hoped to unite the Indians against the English. For their part, the English organized massive raids against the Choctaw, especially in 1706 and 1711–12, as a means to reduce French power but mostly to obtain slaves. The French failed to end hostilities between the Chickasaw and Choctaw, largely as a result of the Choctaw refusal to forgive the Chickasaw for their slaving. The French did not oppose the enslavement of Native Americans but rather sought to imitate the English in Carolina and build a plantation society capitalized by the capture and sale of Indian slaves. They generally kept as slaves those brought to them from beyond the Southeast, particularly from the North and West. But they also enslaved Indians in Mississippi. The expansion of French agricultural interests in Mississippi led to warfare with the Natchez over control of the valuable land in the environs of modern-day Natchez. In the Natchez War of 1729–33, the French enslaved many Natchez, most of whom had been captured by the Choctaw. The French sold the Natchez to buyers in the West Indies. Even after the end of the great slaving wars of the Southeast,

French settlers continued to purchase Indian slaves brought to them from the Southwest and the Missouri Country, such as Apache and Sioux.

British enslavement of Native Americans in the Southeast declined significantly after the Yamasee War of 1715, when many southern Indians, including the Chickasaw, killed the Carolina traders. Although the Chickasaw and Creek rarely again went on slaving raids to provide captives for the English, the slaving had created endemic hostilities that continued for at least two generations in Mississippi, pitting Chickasaw against Choctaw and Creek against Choctaw. In other words, the warfare continued, although capturing slaves for sale to the Europeans was no longer the goal. The slaving wars eliminated many Indian peoples from Mississippi and the surrounding region while forcing many refugees to join the Choctaw, Chickasaw, or Creek or move west into Louisiana and Texas.

Alan Gallay
Texas Christian University

Robbie Ethridge, ed., *Mapping the Shatter Zone: The Colonial Indian Slave Trade and Regional Instability* (2009); Alan Gallay, *The Indian Slave Trade: The Rise of the English Empire in the American South, 1670–1717* (2002); Patricia Galloway, *Choctaw Genesis, 1500–1700* (1995).

Slavery and Agriculture

Slavery in Mississippi was inextricably intertwined with agriculture—primarily cotton production. The invention of the cotton gin in the 1790s coincided with the transfer of Mississippi to the United States and the establishment of a territorial government. In the early years of the territorial era, the work patterns associated with cotton production were developed and implemented, and cotton production changed only minimally over the remainder of the antebellum era.

Agricultural slaves in Mississippi were also involved in production of other crops, especially corn and vegetables to provide food supplies for the plantations, but those crops were produced only as the rhythms of cotton production allowed. Planters could make the most money growing cotton and consequently purchased food so that they could focus their slave labor on the most lucrative crop.

Cotton production involved the development of the gang system of labor, which differed from earlier slave regimes. Gangs of slaves worked their way through the fields, plowing, thinning, hoeing, chopping, picking, or whatever else the day's assignment might be. The gang system provided

far less individual autonomy than the task system employed in other regions, under which slaves were assigned a set amount of work that could be completed at a pace defined by the individual. White overseers or slave supervisors watched over the labor gangs to make sure the work proceeded as scheduled. The enforcement of the pace of work—often through public whippings of slaves whose efforts lagged behind the others—introduced a regular element of cruelty to the gang labor system.

Because one of the most significant aspects of cotton production—the removal of the seeds from the lint—is mechanized and must occur after the crop is harvested, nearly year-round labor was involved. In the early years of cotton production, this change resulted in significant acts of resistance against the new machinery, and gin fires seemed to occur regularly at the height of the harvesting and ginning season. From the 1830s onward, however, the cotton gin became normalized as a piece of plantation equipment and was less commonly the target of slave sabotage. By the 1830s the only downtime in the cotton-production cycle was a brief period between the end of harvest and the preparation of fields for the next year's crop.

The success of cotton slavery in Mississippi is best illustrated by its rapid expansion from river towns into the interior of the state. During the mid-1790s the first crops were grown primarily in the Natchez region, but by the 1830s the center of cotton production had moved to the center of the state, and planters flocked with their slaves to lands previously controlled by Choctaw and Chickasaw. Few urban centers developed because the state's greatest opportunities for wealth lay in the countryside.

David J. Libby
University of Texas at San Antonio

David J. Libby, *Slavery and Frontier Mississippi, 1720–1835* (2004); John Hebron Moore, *Agriculture in Antebellum Mississippi* (1958); Adam Rothman, *Slave Country: American Expansion and the Origins of the Deep South* (2005); Charles S. Sydnor, *Slavery in Mississippi* (1933).

Slavery and Settlement

Land and slaves were the foundation of the settlement of Mississippi, the heart of antebellum America's Cotton Kingdom. In 1817, when Mississippi earned statehood, its population of European and African descent was concentrated in the Natchez District, the core of colonial settlement in the eighteenth century, and almost the entire non-Indian population lived in the southern portion of the state. A succession of treaties between the United States and the Choctaw and Chickasaw Indians between 1801 and 1832, culminating in the Treaty of Dancing Rabbit Creek (1830) and the Treaty of Pontotoc (1832), dispossessed Mississippi's indigenous nations of almost all of their lands. As twenty thousand Choctaw and Chickasaw Indians were removed from Mississippi in the 1830s, the federal government surveyed the newly acquired land and converted it to salable real estate, opening millions of acres in central and northern Mississippi to agricultural development. Combined with high cotton prices, the sale of these federal lands generated "flush times" in Mississippi between 1816 and 1819 and again between 1833 and 1837, but the collapse of cotton prices at the end of each boom left many Mississippi landowners struggling with debt. Migration to newly opened areas shifted the center of gravity of Mississippi's population away from the colonial core of settlement. The five southwestern counties comprising the heart of the old Natchez District (Adams, Amite, Franklin, Jefferson, and Wilkinson), harbored more than half the state's non-Indian population in 1820 but accounted for less than 10 percent of the state's population in 1860.

The high cost and sickly reputation of land in Mississippi's fertile floodplain contributed to different patterns of settlement in the western and eastern regions of the state. Large cotton plantations characterized the western counties, where the Mississippi River's alluvial soils attracted wealthy slave owners willing to pay top dollar for the richest cotton-producing lands. The counties of the Natchez District and the Yazoo-Mississippi Delta boasted many of the wealthiest planters and some of the highest proportions of enslaved people (often more than two-thirds) in the United States. In contrast, the eastern counties tended to attract small planters and farmers in search of relatively inexpensive land. These counties were more likely to have white majorities. Enslaved people accounted for less than 30 percent of the population in the southeastern Piney Woods counties of Jackson, Harrison, Greene, and Perry and the hilly northeastern counties of Tishomingo, Itawamba, and Tippah. The plantation-oriented counties of the Upper Tombigbee River Basin (Noxubee, Lowndes, and Monroe) were an important exception to this regional pattern. Most of Mississippi's white households did not have slaves in 1860, and plantation households (conventionally defined as those with twenty or more slaves) constituted a minority of all white households with slaves.

Where did Mississippians come from before the Civil War? According to the 1850 census, more than half of the state's roughly 296,000 white inhabitants came from elsewhere in the United States—most from other southern states. Less than 10,000 had been born in northern states or outside the country. The same census did not enumerate slaves' nativity, but few would have been born in Africa or the Caribbean because of the prohibition on foreign slave importation into the Mississippi Territory enacted by Congress in 1798 and strengthened by the 1808 ban on importing

slaves into the United States. Historian Michael Tadman has estimated that 235,000 slaves were taken to Mississippi from other slave states between 1820 and 1860, some in the company of migrating owners and others ensnared by the interstate slave trade to be sold at venues such as the Forks of the Road market in Natchez. The movement of slaves to Mississippi peaked in the booming 1830s, when more than 100,000 slaves may have entered the state. In every decade except the 1840s, the slave population grew faster than the free population: on the eve of the Civil War, 55 percent of the state's population was enslaved. "We repose on a volcano," warned a Vicksburg newspaper in 1831.

Mississippi's mix of frontier free-for-all and plantation society was highly combustible. One revealing episode occurred in west-central Mississippi in the summer of 1835, when rumors of banditry, slave insurrection, and covert abolitionism rocked Madison County. The panicked response of a local vigilance committee left at least seven white men dead and several others banished. An unknown though certainly larger number of slaves were also executed for their real or imagined participation in the rumored uprising. The panic rippled through the state. In Vicksburg, several gamblers and slaves were hanged after clashing with local citizens. Such proceedings exposed deep fears of social disorder among Mississippi's white elites. They resorted to force when necessary to establish order and protect slavery, but more effective than force in the long run was the emergence of institutions that "civilized" the frontier, including courts, churches, and schools. Historians have often emphasized the rampant materialism that characterized the southern frontier in the first half of the nineteenth century, but Mississippi's history is unfathomable without recognizing that along with all that cotton, the seeds of Mississippi's evangelical religious traditions were sown in camp meetings and revivals and the secret brush arbors of slaves.

Mississippi's ancient landscape underwent a profound ecological transformation in the early nineteenth century. Slaves and small farmers drained swamps, cleared canebrakes, and carved fields out of the forest. The dedication of tremendously fertile lands to cotton catapulted Mississippi into the leading ranks of the world's cotton producers. Its bumper cotton crop for 1859–60 exceeded 1.2 million bales, more than any other state. While the people of Mississippi remained predominantly rural and agricultural, the cotton economy inserted them into the transatlantic Industrial Revolution and made them dependent on the world market, a power beyond their grasp and control.

Adam Rothman
Georgetown University

Thomas D. Clark and John D. W. Guice, *The Old Southwest, 1795–1830: Frontiers in Conflict* (1989); James C. Cobb, *The Most Southern Place on Earth: The Mississippi Delta and the Roots of Regional Identity* (1992);

David J. Libby, *Slavery and Frontier Mississippi, 1720–1835* (2004); John Hebron Moore, *The Emergence of the Cotton Kingdom in the Old Southwest: Mississippi, 1770–1860* (1988); Michael Tadman, *Speculators and Slaves: Masters, Traders, and Slaves in the Old South* (1989).

Slaves, Runaway

Running away served as one of the most pervasive methods of resisting slavery throughout the Americas, although many runaways never gained their freedom. Slaves in Mississippi, as elsewhere in the United States, had few destinations where slavery did not exist.

In the eighteenth century, enslaved Africans and African Americans who ran away faced bleak prospects. Native American nations in Mississippi did not offer havens. Instead, they might reenslave runaways, return them to their owners, or sell them to new owners. Escape via the Mississippi River was dangerous both because of the nature of the river itself and the potential for recapture. Even though Natchez and other towns lacked newspapers to publicize runaways prior to late in the century, owners did post notices at the riverfront to alert travelers. In addition, plantations were isolated, presenting difficulties for those who absconded into the woods. In later periods and other locations runaways bound for free territory might have found temporary solace or rations from slave communities, but those communities could be difficult to locate in eighteenth-century Mississippi.

Most runaways left for short periods and then returned to their owners. Abdul-Rahman Ibrahima took flight from a farm near Natchez in 1788 but found it difficult to survive and reluctantly returned. His experience was shared by most runaways in North America, where escaped slaves had difficulty living on their own as fugitives. Some Brazilian and Caribbean slaves who fled eluded recapture by joining maroon communities (groups of slaves who had run away and lived together in unsettled areas), but such communities existed only rarely in what would become the United States as a result of population densities and well-armed local white authorities.

Slave owners applied inconsistent punishment to these short-term runaways. Ibrahima's owner, Thomas Foster, apparently did not punish him for running away. William Dunbar seems to have expected slaves to run away after being "corrected" with the whip but expressed surprise when they left for reasons other than those related to direct physical attack. When two enslaved women ran away from Dunbar's plantation in 1776, he punished one with twenty-five lashes but offered no reprimand for the other. When two men left his plantation shortly thereafter, Dunbar supposed they had gotten lost in the woods and believed it to be his good fortune when they were returned by a neighbor. By the next year, Dunbar's surprise turned to outrage, and he ordered five hundred lashes for each of two slaves captured after leaving his plantation without permission. For their part, slave owners tended to view flight as an expression of ungratefulness and thoughtless action. Despite Dunbar's confusion about why slaves ran away, they almost always did so when whites infringed on accepted household, farm, or plantation practices.

By the nineteenth century, free territories in the North offered additional incentives to leave the slave South, but the difficulties remained. Along with evading slave catchers and patrols, runaways could not always count on the help or sympathy of others who were enslaved. The fabled Underground Railroad was not available for all, especially residents of Mississippi and other Deep South states, where the journey to free territory meant passing through several other slave states. Slaves certainly worked together to resist white authority, but choosing to flee a plantation or to aid those who did so was primarily an individual decision. As a result of the danger and difficulty, running away was almost always a solitary venture, usually undertaken by young men who did not tell others for fear of damaging the chances of success.

As the Union Army moved through the South during the Civil War, running away became easier but still could result in uncertainty. As a part of Pres. Abraham Lincoln's attempt to prevent the Border South from seceding, he initially ordered commanders in the field to return runaways to their masters unless they were "in rebellion." By the summer of 1862 Congress had passed two Confiscation Acts that allowed Union troops to seize southerners' property, including slaves, who were often referred to as "contrabands." During that summer, former slaves could be employed by the US military. The practice of running away did not end until December 1865, when the ratification of the Thirteenth Amendment formally ended slavery in the United States.

Timothy R. Buckner
Troy University

Terry Alford, *Prince among Slaves: The True Story of an African Prince Sold into Slavery in the American South* (1977); William Freehling, *The South vs. the South: How Anti-Confederate Southerners Shaped the Course of the Civil War* (2002); Peter Kolchin, *American Slavery, 1619–1877* (1993); David J. Libby, *Slavery and Frontier Mississippi, 1720–1835* (2004); Eron Rowland, *Life, Letters, and Papers of William Dunbar of Elgin, Morayshire, Scotland, and Natchez, Mississippi; Pioneer Scientist of the Southern United States; Compiled and Prepared from the Original Documents for the National Society of Colonial Dames in America by Mrs. Dunbar Rowland* (1930).

S

Slaves and Subsistence Economy

Enslaved African Americans working and living on Mississippi's plantations faced conditions of abject poverty. Food rations provided by owners often did not provide enough calories or variety. In most cases, it was cheaper for slave owners to allow the slaves to raise and acquire their own food than to provide full rations. Within this economic context, slaves overcame nutritional deficits by supplementing their diets with food resources they acquired themselves. Their primary methods included tending their own gardens, raising their own livestock, and hunting, fishing, and gathering wild food resources. Slaves practiced these subsistence activities not only to supplement rationed food but also to participate in a trade network with their self-acquired goods and to achieve some autonomy in their lives.

Accounts by former slaves provide some of the most direct evidence regarding the subsistence economy practiced within the slave quarters. Former slaves who were interviewed in the 1930s through the Federal Writers' Project of the Works Progress Administration (WPA) provided rich detail regarding the subsistence economy. Charlie Davenport, a former slave from Natchez, recounted that "almost every slave had his own little garden patch and was allowed to cook out of it." Most of the upkeep in the gardens was carried out on Saturdays and/or Sundays, which were free days on many plantations. Favorite garden items mentioned in the WPA accounts included corn, sweet potatoes, onions, squash, and collard greens. The WPA accounts provide additional information regarding other subsistence practices, including hunting, fishing, and collecting. Favorite game included deer, rabbits, opossums, raccoons, wild turkeys, and rattlesnakes. Davenport also mentioned collecting dewberries and persimmons for wine and gathering black walnuts and storing them under the cabins to dry.

A number of archaeological investigations at antebellum plantations throughout the South have confirmed that slave owners often permitted their slaves to tend gardens and raise livestock within the slave quarters area of plantations and to hunt, fish, and gather wild food resources. Evidence shows that slaves cultivated small garden plots adjacent to their cabins and kept livestock in small pens. A variety of fruits and vegetables were grown in the gardens, including beans, peas, collard greens, corn, squash and pumpkins, onions, okra, potatoes (including sweet potatoes), watermelons, and muskmelons. Poultry were the most common livestock raised by slaves, though many also raised pigs and goats. Archaeological evidence indicates that slaves harvested a wide range of wild species. At Saragossa Plantation near Natchez, bones of wild animals discovered within the slave quarters area indicated that slaves there regularly hunted and fished for wild food, including opossum, deer, turtle, gar, sucker, and catfish.

The WPA slave narratives offer evidence that the food resources grown, raised, hunted, fished, and gathered by the slaves provided a basis on which they entered an informal market economy. Many sold surplus food goods to their masters, to overseers, or at markets and were allowed to keep the proceeds of their sales, which they used to purchase other goods. Former Mississippi slave Pete Franks reported saving ten dollars from selling vegetables grown in his garden, which he used to buy "lots of pretties."

For many slaves, exercising self-sufficiency through subsistence activities was a way to work for their own interests. Tending their gardens, raising their livestock, and fishing, hunting, and gathering wild resources undoubtedly allowed slaves to feel some control in their lives and were likely precious occupations and pastimes.

Michael Tuma
South Pasadena, California

Maria Franklin, "'Out of Site, Out of Mind': The Archeology of an Enslaved Virginian Household, c. 1740–1778" (PhD dissertation, University of California at Berkeley, 1997); Maria Franklin, in *Race and the Archaeology of Identity*, ed. Charles E. Orser Jr. (2001); Barbara Heath and Amber Bennett, *Historical Archaeology* (Summer 2000); Michael W. Tuma, *Mississippi Archaeology* 33 (1998).

Slavic Immigrants

The story of immigrants from the Slavic countries—Russia, Poland, Romania, and Bohemia (now the Czech Republic and Slovakia)—in the South between 1870 and 1900 is one of an uneasy courtship on both sides. In the decades following the Civil War, most southern states saw white immigrant labor as the best way to rebuild their cotton-based economies, either on the plantations or later in the textile mills. To that end, Mississippi's Republican legislature in 1873 established the Department of Agriculture and Immigration, a combination that Louisiana echoed in 1894. Southern rail lines also distributed pamphlets across Europe, seeking to entice settlers to come buy some of the companies' millions of acres of land in Alabama, Mississippi, Arkansas, Texas, and elsewhere. In 1902 the Southeastern Railway Land and Industrial Agents' Association was founded to seek to direct some of the immigrant stream southward. At the same time, however, many southern businessmen, journalists, and politicians expressed a fervent desire to attract only "higher-quality" European immigrants—from Britain if possible, from northwestern Europe if necessary, but not from southeastern Europe. In 1905 the editor of the *Manufacturer's Record* dismissed the Slavs: "The South will have human sewage under no conditions."

Similar xenophobic sentiments were expressed in the industrial centers of the rest of the United States; however, immigrants' own life goals also caused them to bypass the South in favor of the coal, steel, and textile centers of the North and Midwest. Unlike immigrants from some other countries, who came to the United States to escape persecution, to avoid famine, or to buy land and thus intended to stay permanently, Slavs often came with plans to make as much money as possible as quickly as possible so that they could return to their home countries and bolster their status. These immigrants thus generally sought out the higher wages available in the steel mills, factories, coal mines, and woolen mills of the Northeast and Midwest. A few Slavs who were skilled craftsmen or versed in small-business skills became shopkeepers, jewelers, or wireworkers in cities: an 1896 letter in the newspaper *Slovák v Amerike* (Slovak American) told of Jozef Kurncar, a native of Trenčín, in what is now western Slovakia, who had opened a jewelry store in Bay St. Louis.

The 1890 census found just 120 Mississippi residents who had been born in Bohemia, Russia, or Poland, and only Claiborne, Coahoma, and Washington Counties had more than ten people from those countries. A decade later, Mississippi still had a miniscule 504 immigrants from the Slavic countries, with double-digit populations only in Adams, Bolivar, Claiborne, Clay, Coahoma, Harrison, Hinds, Lauderdale, Leflore, Sharkey, Warren, Washington, and Yazoo Counties.

Not surprisingly, given these small numbers, Slavic fraternal organizations had virtually no presence in the state. In fact, the state's sole chapter of the National Slovak Society, located in Perkinston, about twenty miles north of Biloxi, was not founded until March 1955, long after the height of Slavic immigration to the United States.

Robert Zecker
St. Francis Xavier University

June Granatir Alexander, *The Immigrant Church and Community: Pittsburgh's Slovak Catholics and Lutherans, 1880–1915* (1987); Theodore W. Allen, *The Invention of the White Race*, vol. 1, *Racial Oppression and Social Control* (1994); Josef J. Barton, *Peasants and Strangers: Italians, Rumanians, and Slovaks in an American City, 1890–1950* (1975); R. Vladimir Baumgarten and Josef Stefka, *The National Slovak Society, Hundred-Year History, 1890–1990* (1990); Rowland T. Berthoff, *Journal of Southern History* (August 1951); Henry M. Booker, "Efforts of the South to Attract Immigrants, 1860–1900" (PhD dissertation, University of Virginia, 1965); M. Mark Stolarik, *Immigration and Urbanization: The Slovak Experience, 1870–1918* (1989); University of Virginia Library, Historical Census Browser website, http://mapserver.lib.virginia.edu; Mark Wyman, *Round Trip to America: The Immigrants Return to Europe, 1880–1930* (1996); Robert M. Zecker, *American Studies* (Summer 2002).

Slugburgers

In the pantheon of southern food, few dishes are more misunderstood or maligned than the slugburger. Despite its name, this specialty of North Mississippi diners, drugstores, and cafés has a distinguished past, steeped in the history of the South. The practice of stretching meat with cheaper ingredients was widespread in America during the 1920s–30s, but the term *slugburger* is primarily a phenomenon of the Mississippi hill country.

Slugburgers are usually formed into thin patties and cooked so that they are crunchy on the outside but remain soft on the inside. Among the best-known purveyors of slugburgers are the White Trolley Café and Borroum's Drug Store, both in Corinth, the industrial center of the Tennessee River hills. Slugburgers are typically served on buns with yellow ballpark-style mustard, dill pickles, and chopped onions.

Although some mystery and mythology surrounds slugburgers, they never contain even a trace of crawling gastropod. They are a legacy of the Great Depression and the rationing of World War II, when ground beef was a precious commodity and families stretched it as far as it would go by adding bread, cornmeal, or cheaper meats. Today, soybean meal is a common extender. In earlier times, animal fat was the preferred deep-frying medium, but vegetable oils are commonly used now.

The origin of the name is clouded with debate, but the most commonly accepted story is that the burgers sold for a nickel during the Depression, and the word *slug* was a slang term for a five-cent piece. Others theorize that overindulgence will cause a diner to feel as if he or she has been slugged in the stomach. In other parts of the South, bread-extended burgers have been labeled *wish burgers*, since those who eat them often wish for a higher percentage of meat and less bread. In other locales, the sandwiches are simply called *bread burgers*.

The lowly slugburger has been catapulted to tourist attraction status in North Mississippi. Main Street Corinth hosts an annual Slugburger Festival each July on the Alcorn County Courthouse Square, with food vendors and local entertainment. Even though Corinthians try to debunk the garden critter notion, the logo for the annual Slugburger Festival has featured a smiling green snail, complete with teeth and tongue. *The Gourmand's Guide to Dining in and around Corinth* labels the slugburger a "local delicacy" and describes the obligatory squeeze of mustard as a "standard garnish."

Although it is a novelty for tourists and a subject for local jokesters, the slugburger is a lasting reminder of southern resourcefulness during hard times.

Fred Sauceman
East Tennessee State University

S

Southern Foodways Alliance website, "A Hamburger by Any Other Name," http://www.southernfoodways.org/oral-history/a-hamburger-by -any-other-name/; John T. Edge, *Southern Belly: The Ultimate Food Lover's Companion to the South* (2007); Willie Morris and David Rae Morris, *My Mississippi* (2000); Milton Sandy Jr., *The Gourmand's Guide to Dining in and around Corinth* (1992); Regina Smith, manager of the White Trolley Café, interview by Fred Sauceman (11 July 2003).

Smedes, Susan Dabney

(1840–1913) Author

Susan Dabney Smedes, whose book *Memorials of a Southern Planter* offered a romantic depiction of the antebellum South, was born in Raymond, Mississippi, on 10 August 1840, the eighth child of Thomas Smith Gregory Dabney, a planter, and Sophia Hill Dabney. She spent her childhood at Burleigh, the family's four-thousand-acre cotton plantation located ten miles from Raymond. Smedes was educated through a combination of home tutoring and attendance at academies in New Orleans. After a two-year courtship she married Vicksburg minister Lyell Smedes in 1860, but he died just eleven weeks later, and Smedes returned to Burleigh to manage the plantation. During the Civil War the family moved to Alabama and later Georgia, returning to Mississippi only after Union general George Stoneman and his troops occupied Macon in July 1864.

While Burleigh survived the ravages of war, the family's finances did not. Once a prosperous planter with more than five hundred slaves, Thomas Dabney now found himself in debt. To alleviate the family's financial troubles, Smedes established the Bishop Green Training School at Oak Grove. In 1882 Burleigh was sold to pay Dabney's creditors, and the family moved to Baltimore, where Smedes abandoned teaching in favor of work as a newspaper correspondent.

After Thomas Dabney's death in 1885, Smedes wrote *Memorials of a Southern Planter* (1887), a testimony to her father as a benevolent slaveholder. The book, comprised of Smedes's reminiscences and edited family correspondence, romanticized slavery and plantation life in the antebellum South. Describing Dabney as the kind "ruler" of his large "kingdom," Smedes constructed an idealized portrait of contented, "over-indulged" slaves such as "Mammy Harriet" to affirm the "civilizing" effects of bondage and the honor and gentility of the slaveholding South. The book also addressed the effects of war and defeat on the plantation system. It enjoyed widespread success in the South, with many regarding it as a literary refutation of the immoral and corrupt slaveholders depicted in Harriet Beecher Stowe's *Uncle Tom's*

Cabin (1852). Seven editions of the book were published before the turn of the twentieth century. British prime minister William E. Gladstone read the book with "lively interest" and arranged for its publication in London under the title *A Southern Planter* (1890).

Smedes enjoyed her literary success and balanced her writing endeavors with her work as a missionary. In 1887 she became a teacher at the Big Oak School of the Rosebud Agency in the Dakota Territory, remaining there until ill health forced her to resign fourteen months later. She completed a three-year term as a clerk in the surveyor general's office in Montana before moving to Washington, D.C., in 1891, and obtaining a clerkship in the Bureau of Pensions. After traveling throughout England and Europe, she made her home in Sewanee, Tennessee, where she died on 4 July 1913.

Giselle Roberts
La Trobe University,
Melbourne, Australia

Susan Dabney Smedes, *Memorials of a Southern Planter*, ed. Fletcher M. Green (1981).

Smith, Bessie, Death of

The accidental death of Bessie Smith in Mississippi has turned into a myth that has been repeated many times, including several times in print by respected authors. It is true that Smith died after a car accident on Mississippi's Highway 61 near Clarksdale. And her death probably could have been prevented if she had received immediate and adequate medical care. But it is not true that she missed out on that care because she was turned away from a whites-only hospital.

Smith, the Empress of the Blues, was born in Chattanooga, Tennessee, probably on 15 April 1894. She was the most successful and popular blues singer of the 1920s and remains a favorite of blues and jazz fans throughout the world. Smith worked with such prominent musicians as Louis Armstrong and Fletcher Henderson, and she recorded the original versions of such classics as "Back Water Blues," "Gimme a Pigfoot and a Bottle of Beer," "Send Me to the 'Lectric Chair," and "Nobody Knows You When You're Down and Out."

On the morning of 26 September 1937 Smith was past her height of popularity but enjoying a comeback and touring the South as the lead entertainer in a traveling show. She and her boyfriend, Richard Morgan, were traveling from Memphis, Tennessee, to Clarksdale, Mississippi, on Highway 61, with Morgan at the wheel of Smith's Packard automobile. They planned to stop in Clarksdale before heading to Darling for a show. About sixteen miles north of Clarksdale the car struck a truck stopped on the narrow highway and rolled over, severely injuring Smith. The truck driver drove away. Morgan, who was unhurt, flagged down a passing car, which happened to contain a physician, Dr. Hugh Smith, who was going fishing with his friend, Henry Broughton. Hugh Smith later said that Bessie Smith had suffered "severe crushing injuries to her entire right side." She was having trouble breathing, and she probably had abdominal injuries. Hugh Smith and Broughton moved Bessie Smith off the road, and the doctor tended to the singer while Broughton walked to a house to call for an ambulance. But Bessie Smith went into shock while waiting for the ambulance, and the doctor decided to transport her in his car.

As the men moved fishing gear to make room for the injured woman, another car slammed into Hugh Smith's car. The moving car's occupants, a white couple, were not seriously injured but were hysterical. As Dr. Smith examined them, the police arrived, along with the ambulance Broughton had called. Then came a second ambulance, summoned by the truck driver after he drove to Clarksdale. Bessie Smith, accompanied by Morgan, was transported in the first ambulance, while the second vehicle took the white couple to a hospital. Bessie Smith was taken to the G. T. Thomas Afro-American Hospital, where she was pronounced dead at 11:30 in the morning as a consequence of shock, possible internal injuries, and compound bone fractures.

A month after the accident, jazz impresario/critic John Hammond Sr. erroneously wrote in *DownBeat* magazine that the great singer "was refused treatment because of her color and bled to death while waiting for attention." Hammond also got the location wrong, saying that she had been driven to Memphis and turned away from that city's leading hospital. The story was repeated in black newspapers nationwide. Protests from Memphis hospital authorities and the city's mayor motivated *DownBeat* to reinvestigate and do a second story, setting the location right and refuting the racist angle. Hammond admitted thirty-four years later that he had relied on hearsay for the first article but nevertheless restated the incorrect information in his later autobiography. Several other books also repeated the erroneous story. In a 1946 memoir, Chicago jazz musician Mezz Mezzrow, a friend and fan of Bessie Smith's, wrote, "Then one day in 1937 she was in an automobile crash down in Mississippi, the Murder State, and her arm was almost tore out its socket. They brought her to the hospital but it seemed like there wasn't any room for her just then—the people around there didn't care for the color of her skin." That version also became the essence of Edward Albee's 1959 play *The Death of Bessie Smith*. A 1993 nonfiction work by folklorist Alan Lomax, *The Land Where the Blues Began*, repeated the story yet again, raising the number of hospitals that turned Bessie away to three: "In the end she bled to death without medical attention, while her friends pled with the hospital authorities to admit her. And this incident was typical of the Deep South."

Speaking to Chris Albertson for his 1972 biography, *Bessie*, Hugh Smith pointed out that no ambulance driver would have even tried to take a black person to a white hospital—and, at any rate, the black and white hospitals in Clarksdale were less than half a mile from each other. Albertson faulted the truck driver and Dr. Smith (both of whom were white) for not immediately taking the singer to the hospital rather than waiting for ambulances, and it is possible that racism influenced that decision. However, Albertson's book offered a detailed and explicit refutation of the idea that Bessie Smith died because she was turned away from a whites-only hospital. The myth persists because it perfectly and tragically illustrates some harsh realities: (1) hospitals were segregated in the South, and that segregation may have harmed or killed other people, even if it did not cause Bessie Smith's death; (2) prominent entertainers traveling in the South generally were subjected to the same Jim Crow rules as ordinary citizens—no amount of fame could trump skin color.

The G. T. Thomas Hospital at 615 Sunflower Ave. in Clarksdale opened in 1914 and closed about 1940. A few years later, Z. L. Hill bought the building and turned it into the Riverside Hotel, which she operated until her death in 1997. Long one of the only hotels in town that admitted blacks, it housed prominent blues musicians who passed through, including Robert Nighthawk, Sonny Boy Williamson II, and Ike Turner. The hotel remains open, operated by Frank "Rat" Ratliff until his death in 2013. The hotel is still operated by Ratliff's daughter, Zelena, and the room said to be the one in which Smith died is decorated in her memory. It generally is not rented out.

Steve Cheseborough
Portland, Oregon

Chris Albertson, *Bessie* (2003); Steve Cheseborough, *Blues Traveling: The Holy Sites of Delta Blues* (2004); David Evans, *The NPR Curious Listener's Guide to Blues* (2005); Jackie Kay, *Bessie Smith* (1997); Mezz Mezzrow and Bernard Wolfe, *Really the Blues* (1946).

Smith, Frank Ellis
(1918–1997) Politician

Born to hill immigrants in the small Delta town of Sidon, Mississippi, on 21 February 1918, Smith grew up in Greenwood, spending a tremendous amount of time in its public

Frank Ellis Smith (McCain Library and Archives, University of Southern Mississippi)

library. After a black prisoner killed his father, a deputy sheriff, when Smith was eight, he developed into a retiring, intellectual child who escaped the Delta through books. Seeking a reason for his father's murder, Smith came to appreciate that both his father and the prisoner were victims of his society's racism. As a student editor of Mississippi Delta Junior College's *Sunflower Petals*, Smith experimented with liberal ideas on the issue of race. After establishing himself as a freelance writer, Smith graduated from the University of Mississippi in 1941. In the wake of Pearl Harbor, Smith joined the US Army, serving in Europe as a field artillery officer and participating in the Normandy invasion.

When the conflict ended, Smith returned to the Delta and became editor of a new, "liberal" newspaper, the *Greenwood Morning Call*. Smith ran for and was elected to the Mississippi Senate, but the paper's editor fired Smith, and he sought employment with John C. Stennis's campaign for the US Senate. Smith accompanied the victorious senator to Washington as his legislative assistant but returned to Mississippi shortly thereafter to serve his term in the legislature.

Smith won a seat in the US House of Representatives in 1950 despite the opposition of the Delta establishment. He won reelection five times, hiding his liberal racial views at a time when any hint of moderation was political suicide in Mississippi. Despite his private opinions, he opposed civil rights legislation and signed the Southern Manifesto, which denounced the US Supreme Court's 1954 *Brown v. Board of Education* decision. Smith also won over his constituents with his support for the cotton industry, federal flood-control efforts, and other issues popular in the state. He took up tariff reductions because he saw it as a liberal cause acceptable to his cotton-exporting district, and he supported the United Nations in defiance of his constituents' views. He began sponsoring a labeling act to protect cotton interests from synthetic cloth but continued with it as a consumer protection measure.

Smith gradually became more open in his opposition to segregation and strongly supported John F. Kennedy's 1960 presidential campaign. Smith then backed Sam Rayburn's attempt to pack the House Rules Committee to overcome the coalition of Democratic and Republican conservatives that blocked liberal legislation. His "treason" led Mississippi's segregationists to eliminate Smith's district when the state lost a congressional seat after the 1960 census. Smith had to run against ultraconservative Jamie L. Whitten for the seat Whitten had represented since 1941, and Smith lost in the Democratic primary. In 1962 Kennedy appointed Smith to the governing board of the Tennessee Valley Authority, where Smith, a conservationist who favored "wise use" of natural resources, did battle against environmentalists for the next decade. Smith also remained involved in Mississippi politics and worked with civil rights groups such as the Voter Education Project to register black voters.

Smith mounted an unsuccessful 1972 run for Congress before becoming associate director of the Illinois State Board of Higher Education in 1973–74 and a visiting professor at Virginia Tech from 1977 to 1979. In 1980 Gov. William Winter called Smith back to Mississippi to serve as a special assistant. Smith retired from public office in 1983, established a bookstore with his children, and wrote a column for the *Jackson Clarion-Ledger*. He became a fellow of the Southern Regional Council in 1984 and remained active in the Mississippi Historical Society and other organizations. When he died on 2 August 1997, the *Clarion-Ledger* described him as a "visionary" who had earned the state's "gratitude and respect."

Dennis Mitchell
Mississippi State University
at Meridian

Dennis J. Mitchell, *Mississippi Liberal: A Biography of Frank E. Smith* (2001); *New York Times* (6 August 1997); Frank E. Smith, *Congressman from Mississippi* (1964); *Washington Post* (5 August 1997).

Smith, Orma Rinehart "Hack"
(1904–1982) Judge

Orma Rinehart "Hack" Smith served as US district judge for the Northern District of Mississippi from 1968 to 1982, during the time when Mississippi's federal courts were first intensively called on to enforce federal civil rights legislation, including the integration of public schools.

Born in Booneville on 25 September 1904, the third child of Jefferson Davis Smith and Mattie Augusta Eva Lena Rinehart Smith, Smith was educated in the public schools of Corinth, where he lived from the age of two until the end of his life. After graduating from Corinth High School in 1921, Smith enrolled at the University of Mississippi, where he earned a law degree in 1927. His nickname, *Hack*, derived from *Kid Hackensmith*, a play on the name of famous wrestler Georg Hackenschmidt. From college onward, Smith was always known by his nickname.

Smith practiced law in Corinth from 1928 to 1968. His skills and affable personality made him popular with his colleagues, and he served as president of the University of Mississippi Alumni Association in 1961–62, during much of the legal proceedings concerning the James Meredith's admission as the first African American student at the university. Smith was also elected president of the Mississippi Bar in 1965–66.

Pres. Lyndon B. Johnson nominated Smith to the federal bench on 17 July 1968, and he was confirmed by the Senate and commissioned on 25 July. He had been recommended to Johnson by US senator James O. Eastland, a fraternity brother of Smith's at the University of Mississippi. From 1968 to 1980 Smith and Chief Judge William C. Keady of Greenville (who ascended to the federal bench less than four months before Smith) were the only federal district judges serving the Northern District of Mississippi, and they heard and determined the cases that vindicated the civil rights of black Mississippians, making the Northern District of Mississippi a respected southern federal court. Acknowledging the difficult cases that sometimes put Smith at odds with the state's white power structure and his friends, Keady in 1980 described his colleague as "a jurist of courage and dedication to the rule of law, and he has been a United States district judge during a most trying period for federal judges, at least in the southland's history."

Smith assumed federal judge senior status on 16 August 1978 but remained active on the bench until he was disabled by a stroke in May 1981. He died in Corinth on 5 July 1982.

J. Stevenson Ray
Jackson, Mississippi

Federal Judicial Center, History of the Federal Judiciary website, www.fjc.gov/history/home.nsf; Melanie H. Henry, ed., *The Mississippi Bar's Centennial* (2006); Margaret Sage Smith Hoare, interview by J. Stevenson Ray (16, 18 August 2009); Mississippi Bar website, www.msbar.org; Presentation of Portrait of the Honorable Orma R. Smith, 507 F. Supp. LIX (N.D. Miss. 1980); ; H. M. Ray, interview by J. Stevenson Ray (16 August 2009); Orma R. Smith Jr., in *The History of Alcorn County, Mississippi* (1983); Orma R. Smith III, interview by J. Stevenson Ray (11–12 August 2009).

Smith, Hazel Brannon

(1914–1994) Journalist

Described as a flamboyant, headstrong, and sassy amalgam of Auntie Mame, Bella Abzug, and Scarlett O'Hara, Hazel Brannon Smith served for four decades as the editor and publisher of Holmes County's *Durant News* and *Lexington Advertiser*. In 1964 she became the first woman to win the Pulitzer Prize for editorial writing, with the prize committee citing her "steadfast adherence to her editorial duties in the face of great pressure and opposition." Her front page "Through Hazel Eyes" columns and editorials staunchly opposed the Citizens' Council, Mississippi State Sovereignty Commission, and racial violence during the civil rights era of the 1950s and 1960s.

Born on 5 February 1914 near Gadsden, Alabama, Hazel Brannon attended public schools and began her newspaper career with the *Etowah Observer* while still attending Gadsden High School. After graduation, she enrolled at the University of Alabama, serving as an editor of the student newspaper before earning a bachelor's degree in journalism in 1935. The following year, she obtained a three-thousand-dollar loan and purchased the *Durant News*. After paying off the loan in four years, she acquired the *Lexington Advertiser* in 1943. She launched an editorial campaign against bootlegging and gambling in 1945, calling for the sheriff's resignation for failing to enforce the law. In October 1946 she was cited for contempt of court and fined for violating a circuit judge's gag order when she interviewed a trial witness; the Mississippi Supreme Court overturned the contempt conviction in 1947.

Despite skirmishes with local officials, her newspapers prospered, and she participated in the social life of Holmes County, sporting the stylish clothes and hats of a free-spirited southern belle and driving white Cadillac convertibles. She became engaged to a ship purser, Walter Dyer Smith, during a sea cruise in 1949, and they married in Lexington on 21 March 1950. Thereafter, her newspapers listed her as "Hazel Brannon Smith (Mrs. Walter D.)—Editor and Publisher."

In May 1954 Smith reacted to the US Supreme Court's *Brown v. Board of Education* decision declaring segregated schools unconstitutional with a front-page column commenting that the court "may be morally right" even though "we know that it is to the best interest of both races that segregation be maintained in theory and in fact." In July 1954 Smith reported that Holmes County sheriff Richard F. Byrd had shot a twenty-seven-year-old black man, concluding the story, "No charges have yet been filed against Sheriff Byrd in the shooting." A week later, a signed editorial, "The Law Should Be for All," asserted that the sheriff had "violated every concept of justice, decency and right" and called for his resignation. Byrd sued Smith for libel, and in October 1954 the Holmes County Circuit Court awarded the sheriff a ten-thousand-dollar judgment. The Mississippi Supreme Court overturned the libel conviction in November 1955. *Time* magazine's 21 November 1955 edition featured the "good-looking, dark-haired" editor and the libel case in its press section.

Smith's law-and-order editorials on race prompted reprisals. In January 1956 her husband was fired from his position as administrator of the county hospital. Anonymous circulars

S

appeared in Holmes County declaring her an integrationist after her photograph and comments regarding her stance for "equal justice for all, regardless of race" appeared in the November 1957 issue of *Ebony* magazine. In January 1959 prominent businessmen and public officials with connections to the Citizens' Council launched the *Holmes County Herald* in an effort to silence Smith and drive her newspapers out of business. She called the *Herald*'s backers "a kind of Gestapo to determine how people should think and act and pressure them into it."

While the *Herald* siphoned advertising and subscribers from the *Advertiser*, Smith continued to editorialize against racial violence, the Citizens' Council, and the Sovereignty Commission. She called the June 1963 assassination of Medgar Evers a "reprehensible crime against the laws of God and man" and compared the Citizens' Council and Sovereignty Commission to a homegrown version of the Third Reich and "the Gestapo of Hitler's Germany." Smith continued to lose money and piled up substantial debt, mortgaging personal property and borrowing money to publish her newspapers and build a Greek Revival mansion on the outskirts of Lexington. Her husband died in November 1983, and she filed for bankruptcy in 1985, having amassed $250,000 in debt. Banks repossessed her home. The last edition of the *Lexington Advertiser* appeared on 19 September 1985. In declining health and penniless, Smith returned to Gadsden, where relatives cared for her.

Academic and popular accounts of Hazel Brannon Smith often erroneously described her as a conservative Dixiecrat segregationist who underwent a conversion in the mid-1950s to become a liberal champion of civil rights and martyr to the cause of press freedom. Her advocacy of law and order and denunciation of racial violence coexisted with repeated support for "our Southern traditions and racial segregation." She vigorously denied being an "integrationist," writing on 31 October 1957, "I have never, either in print or by spoken word, advocated integration of the races." On 14 January 1965, seven months after winning the Pulitzer Prize, she reminded readers, "We had never advocated school integration at the time of the 1954 high court decision (nor since for that matter)." Hodding Carter of the *Delta Democrat-Times* observed in *First Person Rural*, "The supreme irony is that nowhere outside the Deep South would Hazel Brannon Smith be labeled even a liberal in her racial views. If she must be categorized, then call her a moderate."

Smith died on 14 May 1994.

Arthur J. Kaul
University of Southern Mississippi

Hodding Carter, *First Person Rural* (1963); Dudley Clendinen, *New York Times* (31 March 1986); Lee Freeland, *Jackson Clarion-Ledger* (5 January 1986); Rich Friedman, *Editor and Publisher* (24, 31 October 1964); Fred Grimm, *Chicago Tribune* (26 March 1986); George Harris, *Look* (16 November 1965); Arthur J. Kaul, in *Dictionary of Literary Biography: American Newspaper Publishers, 1950–1990*, ed. Perry J. Ashley (1993); Arthur J. Kaul, in *The Press and Race: Mississippi Journalists Confront the Movement*, ed. David R. Davies (2001); Mark Newman, *Journal of Mississippi History* (February 1992); John A. Whalen, *Maverick among the Magnolias: The Hazel Brannon Smith Story* (2000).

Smith, James Argyle
(1831–1901) Confederate General

James Argyle Smith was born on 1 May 1831 in Maury County, Tennessee. His family relocated to Mississippi, and Smith won an appointment to West Point, graduating forty-fifth in the Class of 1853. His antebellum service in the US Army included stints in Kansas, Missouri, and California; action against the Sioux; and participation in the Mormon expedition under Col. Albert Sidney Johnston. When secession came, Smith resigned his commission on 9 May 1861 and four days later was appointed an infantry lieutenant in the Confederate Army.

Smith initially served on the staff of Maj. Gen. Leonidas Polk, winning promotion to major, and on 15 March 1862 Smith was promoted to lieutenant colonel of the 2nd Tennessee Infantry, which subsequently saw heavy action at Shiloh. Losses there prompted a reorganization that resulted in the unit's consolidation with the 21st Tennessee. The regiment was redesignated the 5th Confederate, and Smith took command, having been promoted to colonel on 21 July 1862.

Smith and his regiment took part in the Kentucky Campaign that summer and fall, fighting at Perryville. Assigned subsequently to a brigade under Lucius Polk in Patrick Cleburne's division, Smith was cited favorably by superiors after he led his regiment at Stone's River (Murfreesboro) and Chickamauga. He won promotion to brigadier general on 1 October 1863 and took charge of a brigade of Texas troops whose commander had been slain at Chickamauga. Smith and his new command distinguished themselves at Missionary Ridge, repelling attacks by Federals under William Tecumseh Sherman. During the retreat Smith was wounded in both thighs, and he did not return to duty until mid-July 1864. At the Battle of Atlanta on 22 July Smith was again wounded and was borne from the field.

Rejoining the army in November 1864 at Tuscumbia, Alabama, Smith took command of a brigade of troops whose division had been disbanded. The brigade was assigned to escort the army's supply train when John Bell Hood invaded Tennessee and therefore did not participate in the Battle of Franklin on 30 November 1864. Smith was later shocked by the horrendous losses suffered at Franklin and noted the lowered morale among survivors. With Cleburne killed at Franklin, Smith took command of the division. After the Battle of

Nashville on 15–16 December, Smith and his men were caught up in the general retreat, which ended at Tupelo.

Smith eventually made his way to North Carolina with remnants of the Army of Tennessee and last saw combat at Bentonville on 19 March 1865. He was paroled at Greensboro on 1 May, returned to Mississippi, and became a farmer. In 1877 he was elected to the first of two terms as state superintendent of public education. Smith died in Jackson on 6 December 1901.

Christopher Losson
St. Joseph, Missouri

Edwin C. Bearss, in *The Confederate General*, ed. William C. Davis (1991); Harold A. Cross, *They Sleep beneath the Mockingbird: Mississippi Burial Sites and Biographies of Confederates Generals* (1994); Charles E. Hooker, *Confederate Military History: Mississippi*, ed. Clement A. Evans (1899); Ezra Warner, *Generals in Gray: Lives of the Confederate Commanders* (1959).

Smith, Patrick D.

(1927–2014) Writer

Writer Patrick Davis Smith was born on 8 October 1927 in Mendenhall, Mississippi, to politician John D. Smith and Nora Eubanks Smith. He earned an associate's degree from Hinds Junior College in 1944 and joined the US Merchant Marine the following year, serving in North Africa and Europe. Upon returning home, he earned a bachelor's degree at the University of Mississippi in 1947 and married Iris Doty, with whom he went on to have two children.

Smith returned to Mendenhall in 1948 and remained there until 1956, owning and operating an automobile dealership and a cattle ranch. Smith served as a correspondent in Korea in 1953 and thereafter continued to contribute to newspapers. He was employed as the director of public relations for the Sperry Rand Corporation, Vickers Division, in Jackson between 1956 and 1958 and then held the post of director of public relations at Hinds Junior College from 1959 to 1962. Smith earned a master's degree from the University of Mississippi in 1959 and moved to Oxford in 1962, spending the next four years as the university's director of public information. Smith then moved to Florida, becoming director of college relations at Brevard Community College until his retirement in 1988.

Smith honed his craft as a writer while employed in other industries but took time to live among the people who would populate his books. His first novel, *The River Is Home* (1953), chronicles the lives of people called "swamp rats" who lived along the Pearl River in Mississippi and Louisiana in the late nineteenth and early twentieth centuries. In his next novel, *The Beginning* (1967), Smith depicts poor white and black communities struggling during the civil rights movement. Smith's focus shifted to Florida after his move there: *Forever Island* (1973) and *Allapattah* (1987) feature the Seminole Indians struggling against development and the encroachment of modernity, while *Angel City* (1978) portrays the virtual slavery suffered by modern-day migrant workers. As part of his research, Smith lived among the Seminoles and in several migrant camps. His 1984 novel, *A Land Remembered*, won the Florida Historical Society's Tebeau Prize as the Most Outstanding Florida Historical Novel. His final novel was *The Seas That Mourn* (2003). Smith also published two nonfiction books, *The Last Ride* (2000), cowritten with and about Glen "Pee Wee" Mercer, a champion bull rider who was paralyzed in a 1995 bull-riding accident, and *In Search of the Russian Bear: An American Writer's Odyssey in the Former Soviet Union* (2001), as well as a collection of short stories, *A White Deer and Other Stories* (2007). *Forever Island, Angel City,* and *A Land Remembered* were nominated for the Pulitzer Prize, and in 1985 Smith was nominated for the Nobel Prize for Literature.

Florida PBS-TV released the 1990 documentary, *Visions of Nature: Patrick Smith's Florida*. In 1995 Smith received the Order of the South from the Southern Academy of Arts, Letters, and Sciences, and in 1999 he was inducted into the Florida Artists' Hall of Fame. In 2002 the Florida Historical Society named Smith the Greatest Living Floridian.

Smith explained that the characters in his novels are "underdogs in life [who] are *real people* although they are basically unknown to the majority of the reading public. I have devoted my writing talent to researching their ways of life and putting this into print in hopes that my novels might in some way improve their status in life."

He died in Florida on 26 January 2014.

Frances Abbott
Digital Public Library of America,
Boston, Massachusetts

Mississippi Writers and Musicians website, www.mswritersandmusicians .com; Patrick D. Smith, *The Beginning* (1967); Patrick D. Smith, *A Land Remembered* (1984); Patrick D. Smith, *The River Is Home* (1953); Patrick D. Smith website, http://patricksmithonline.com/; *Thomson Gale: Contemporary Authors Series*.

Smith, Robert

(b. 1937) Civil Rights Activist and Physician

Born on 20 December 1937 in Terry, Mississippi, Robert Smith was the ninth of Joseph and Wilma Smith's twelve children. The family operated a cattle farm on land purchased by his grandfather during Reconstruction: the farm eventually grew to more than two hundred acres, and the Smiths raised vegetables, pigs, and chickens in addition to cows. Although Robert attended a segregated school and was aware of racism, Joseph Smith shielded his children from segregated businesses and most contact with the local white community. Travel was rare among Mississippi youth at that time, black or white, but as a teenager Smith visited Atlanta and Washington, D.C., and in his role as a national officer in the New Farmers of America even met Pres. Dwight D. Eisenhower.

An excellent student, Smith decided to become a doctor. He earned a bachelor's degree in chemistry from Tougaloo College in 1957 before enrolling at Howard University Medical School. Mississippi had no integrated medical school at the time, and the state operated a program that provided five-thousand-dollar scholarships to African Americans attending medical school outside the state. Smith graduated from Howard in 1961, interned in Chicago, and was preparing to accept a residency in obstetrics and gynecology when the draft board called him back to Mississippi.

At the time, Mississippi had about fifty black doctors—roughly one for every seventeen thousand black citizens, the highest ratio in the country. Fifty-two of Mississippi's eighty-two counties had no practicing black physicians, and many white doctors refused to see black patients unless they could pay in cash. While Mississippi acknowledged its need for more African American doctors, the state refused to train them and had difficulty attracting those trained elsewhere. Aside from the Jim Crow policies that affected all black citizens, the state's African American doctors were barred from most hospitals and found that their roles as community leaders made them targets of white segregationists.

Smith's return to Mississippi coincided with a time of tremendous civil rights activity in the state, and he began what he termed his "real education" and underwent his "great awakening." He began working closely with civil rights movement members, especially Medgar Evers, and treating civil rights workers and students at Tougaloo College, which was considered a radical institution because of its aggressive stance on integration. After Evers's assassination in June 1963, Smith traveled to Atlantic City, New Jersey, to join an integrated protest against the American Medical Association's discriminatory practices. He became known as the "doctor to the movement," an association that won him few friends among the southern white community and earned him a few trips to jail.

Smith frequently treated civil rights workers injured during demonstrations and served as Martin Luther King Jr.'s personal physician during the 1966 March against Fear. Smith also worked closely with the Council of Federated Organizations and founded the Medical Committee for Human Rights to train and supervise the northern doctors who helped care for the hundreds of volunteers who traveled south for Freedom Summer in 1964 and in subsequent years. He worked with the Delta Ministry to improve poor black Mississippians' access to and quality of care. He served as medical director for the Child Development Group of Mississippi, one of the earliest and most successful federally sponsored Head Start Programs, was active in the Mississippi Freedom Democratic Party, and was instrumental in the creation of the Mound Bayou Delta Health Center.

Since its founding in 1963, Smith has headed the Mississippi Family Health Center (now known as Central Mississippi Health Services), which was the state's first multispecialty clinic to provide care regardless of a patient's ability to pay. It now operates three facilities in the Jackson area. He has also worked to educate future doctors through adjunct professorships at Meharry Medical College, Tufts University, Jackson State University, and Brown University. In 2014 the Mississippi Board of Trustees of the State Institutions of Higher Learning honored Smith with its Community Service Award "for his lifetime of service to the state and nation and his commitment to improving the health care profession, strengthening our communities and improving race relations for all citizens of the state of Mississippi." In part as a consequence of Smith's efforts, Mississippi had more than 350 African American doctors by the 2010s.

Danielle Andersen
University of Mississippi

John Dittmer, *The Good Doctors: The Medical Committee for Human Rights and the Struggle for Social Justice in Health Care* (2009); "IHL Press Release: Robert Smith, M.D. Receives Community Service Award, MSU's Professor Named Diversity Educator of the Year" (3 March 2014), Mississippi Public Universities website, www.mississippi.edu/pr/newsstory.asp?ID=1083; "Oral History with Robert Smith, M.D." (2000), Mississippi Oral History Program, University of Southern Mississippi, http://digilib.usm.edu/cdm/compoundobject/collection/coh/id/16683/rec/11; Thomas J. Ward Jr., *Black Physicians in the Jim Crow South* (2003).

Smith, Robert L. T.

(1902–1993) Activist

Among the activists of the modern civil rights era in Mississippi, arguably none was more committed to the movement's causes and objectives than Rev. Robert L. T. Smith. Born on 19 December 1902 in Utica, Hinds County, Smith was the eldest of the five children of James M. Smith and Theresa Schuler Smith. The boy was named in honor of his enslaved maternal grandfather, Robert Shuler. While growing up in rural Hinds County, Smith had both white and black friends. His youthful experiences also included exposure to many instances of inequality, prejudice, bigotry, and racism. Hinds County's vastly underfunded and separate schools for African American children offered classes only through eighth grade, and as Smith recalled, the building was constructed of "ordinary planks" where "he sat on a rough bench during school hours" and attempted to learn using discarded supplies such as crayon stubs from white schools.

These early life experiences profoundly affected Smith, even prompting him to wonder at one point whether he could do anything to change the system. He ultimately answered that question in the affirmative and as an adult committed himself to the struggle for a more just and equitable American society. Smith began by advising poor sharecropping families on how to improve their economic lot, emphasizing increasing their independence by purchasing land (an acre or two if possible) and acquiring farm animals and livestock.

When he was nineteen, Smith became an elementary school teacher, though he possessed only an eighth-grade education. He taught for a year in Copiah County for a salary of twenty-eight dollars per month before moving to Quitman County, where he earned fifty dollars per month. In 1923 he moved to Jackson and secured a position as a mail carrier with the US Postal Service, serving the North State Street area near Millsaps and Belhaven Colleges until his retirement in 1957.

Smith joined the Jackson Branch of the National Association for the Advancement of Colored People (NAACP) in the 1920s and over the next half century was one of its most active and committed members. Prior to the 1950s most of Mississippi's NAACP branches were at best holding operations with irregular and infrequent activities. The Jackson Branch, however, functioned continuously from the 1930s onward, primarily because of the collective efforts of Smith and others who enjoyed relative economic independence from local whites.

As the Mississippi civil rights struggle gained traction in the 1950s, Smith emerged as one of its most energetic and enthusiastic partisans. Smith became an early confidant of and adviser to the NAACP's young Mississippi field secretary, Medgar Evers, and Smith was highly regarded throughout the movement. In 1962 he and Merrill Winston Lindsey became the first twentieth-century African Americans in Mississippi to seek election to the US Congress, though they lost the contests. Over the ensuing quarter century Smith continued his involvement in civil rights actions while pastoring two churches.

Smith served as one of the Mississippi Freedom Democratic Party's alternate delegates to the 1968 Democratic National Convention in Atlantic City, New Jersey. He was a founding board member of Mississippi Action for Progress, a Head Start and antipoverty program, and was one of the original plaintiffs in a lawsuit challenging the broadcast license of Jackson television station WLBT that resulted in the station's transfer to a new ownership group headed by Smith. In 1990 Smith's testimony played an important role in the indictment and subsequent conviction of Byron De La Beckwith for Evers's murder.

Smith died in October 1993.

Dernoral Davis
Jackson State University

John Dittmer, *Local People: The Struggle for Civil Rights in Mississippi* (1995); Erle Johnston, *Mississippi's Defiant Years, 1953–1973* (1990); *Mississippi Action for Progress Newsletter* (April 1984); Ronald Smothers, *New York Times* (19 December 1990).

Smith, Sydney McCain

(1869–1948) Mississippi Supreme Court Justice

Sydney Smith was by far the longest-serving Mississippi Supreme Court justice in history. He was born on 9 April 1869 in Lexington, Mississippi, to Civil War veteran Thomas White Smith and Sarah West Smith, who later had at least five more children.

Sydney Smith attended Lexington public schools and at age nineteen became a bookkeeper at Ingleside, a large plantation on the Yazoo River, where he supervised the loading and unloading of barges and managed the plantation store. In his spare time, he read law books. He was among the first students to enroll at Lexington Normal College when it opened in 1889 and studied there until he transferred to the University of Mississippi in 1891. He graduated in June 1893.

Smith first practiced in Yazoo City with Joseph W. George, a law school classmate and the son of US senator James Z. George. Smith moved home to Lexington in February 1894, practicing law with his brother, Charles W. Smith, for two years, and then with Walter P. Tackett for ten years. On 9 April 1896, he married Mattye Leigh Smith. They remained married until her death in July 1947 and had no children.

Smith was elected to represent Holmes County in the Mississippi House of Representatives in 1899 and won reelection four years later. A founder of the Mississippi Bar Association, Smith gave the opening address at the bar's January 1906 organizational meeting, which was held in the House chamber. He served as the group's secretary-treasurer from 1906 until 1914, when he began a one-year term as the bar's president.

In September 1906 Gov. James K. Vardaman appointed Smith judge of Mississippi's 4th Circuit Court, and on 10 May 1909 Gov. Edmond Noel elevated Smith to the Mississippi Supreme Court. The court was composed of only three judges, with the longest-tenured judge holding the post of chief

S

justice. By 8 August 1912 both of the senior judges had resigned and Smith became chief.

From 1870 to 1916 Mississippi Supreme Court justices were appointed by the governor for nine-year terms. Smith authored an amendment to the state constitution, which voters ratified in 1914, that doubled the size of the court, made the positions elective, and provided for eight-year terms. Smith ran for a seat on the court in 1916, defeating former governor Andrew H. Longino in the Democratic Party primary and thus taking the election in one-party Mississippi. Smith easily won reelection in 1924, 1932, and 1940 before choosing not to seek another term.

Smith wrote roughly eighteen hundred opinions during his nearly forty years as a justice. He authored a 1917 opinion that sustained the constitutional amendment that adopted initiative and referendum procedures as well as a 1922 dissent to the invalidation of those procedures. In 1943, in the middle of World War II, he dissented from the conviction of a man for disloyalty, finding that the state statute was written so broadly that it penalized some valid activities.

The chief justice suffered a heart attack in July 1946 and remained in poor health until his death on 24 July 1948.

Leslie H. Southwick
US Court of Appeals
for the Fifth Circuit

Jackson Daily News (9 June 1916, 1 June 1947); Michael de L. Landon, *The Honor and Dignity of the Profession: A History of the Mississippi Bar Association, 1906–1976* (1979); *Lexington Progress-Advertiser* (1 October 1903, 14 January 1904); John Ray Skates, *A History of the Mississippi Supreme Court, 1817–1948* (1973); Dunbar Rowland, *History of Mississippi: The Heart of the South*, vol. 2 (1925); Dunbar Rowland, ed., *The Official and Statistical Register of the State of Mississippi, 1920–1924* (1923); Sydney Smith Subject File, Mississippi Department of Archives and History; Leslie H. Southwick, *Mississippi College Law Review* (1997).

Smith, Wadada Leo

(b. 1941) Musician

Wadada Leo Smith is a jazz trumpeter and composer who has been an innovator in free, experimental, and avant-garde jazz since the 1960s. His 2012 work, *Ten Freedom Summers*, an ambitious piece about broad themes in the African American experience, was a finalist for the Pulitzer Prize in music.

Smith was born on 18 December 1941 in the Delta town of Leland, where his mother was a cook and caterer (in one interview Smith called her "the best cook, probably, in the history of the South") and his stepfather was a blues musician.

Smith began writing music at age twelve, not long after he began to learn to play the trumpet. He grew up knowing and listening to blues musicians, was the leader of a blues band as a teenager, and played trumpet in his high school band, where "the band director would fix spaces for me to improvise on the football field and in the bleachers. I had arranged 'Fever' for me as a showcase, and the parts were put together communally. When we played those pieces, the whole damn stadium went crazy." The young Smith played for cakewalks in the streets, played "Taps" at funerals, and "played out the ghosts" of former residents when people moved into newly rented homes.

As a young man Smith spent some time playing with blues bands, including Little Milton's band, before joining the army in the mid-1960s. He played in an army band and encountered resistance when he and others improvised too freely. Released from the army in 1967 and newly married, he moved with his wife to Chicago.

There Smith contacted saxophonist-composer Anthony Braxton and became part of the Association for the Advancement of Creative Musicians (AACM), serving as the group's vice president beginning in 1968. According to Smith, "We wanted to be self-sufficient on all levels. From organizing our own performances to recording our own music, interpreting what our music meant, and presenting it in a context that was totally harmonious with the way we thought as a collective people." As an all–African American organization at the height of black cultural nationalism, the AACM was about freedom in many forms. Musicians found encouragement to improvise widely and to experiment with multiple forms of music inside and outside any tradition.

Along with several other AACM musicians, Smith moved to Paris in 1969, following a path blazed by earlier jazz musicians who sought greater artistic and personal freedom in France. Playing in a group that included Braxton, violinist Leroy Jenkins, and drummer Steve McCall, Smith was amazed by the excitement and size of the crowds. Since 1972 Smith has appeared on numerous jazz recordings, primarily as the composer and group leader. Many, such as the 1982 recording *Human Rights*, relate directly to the relationship between artistic and political struggles. In 1998 Smith and Henry Kaiser released *Yo, Miles!*, a reworking of the electric music Miles Davis wrote and performed in the 1970s.

In the 1970s Smith attended Wesleyan University. He has taught at several colleges, including Bard College and the Herb Alpert School of Music at the California Institute of the Arts.

In 2012 he completed a long and ambitious cycle of compositions by recording *Ten Freedom Summers*, influenced by playwright August Wilson's cycle of ten plays about ten decades in African American history. Written between the 1970s and the early 2000s, the nineteen songs have titles that refer to Dred Scott, Emmett Till, Thurgood Marshall, the Freedom Riders, the black church, the New Frontier and Great Society, Medgar Evers, the Little Rock Nine, Malik

Al Shabazz, Fannie Lou Hamer, Martin Luther King Jr., and 11 September 2001. Smith continues to play and lecture throughout the United States and Europe, and in May 2016 he received a Doris Duke Artist Award.

Ted Ownby
University of Mississippi

Daniel Fischlin, Critical Improv website, www.criticalimprov.com; Thom Jurek, AllMusic.com website, www.allmusic.com; George E. Lewis, *A Power Stronger Than Itself: The AACM and American Experimental Music* (2008); Lloyd Peterson, *Music and the Creative Spirit: Innovators in Jazz, Improvisation, and the Avant Garde*; Wadada Leo Smith at the Library of Congress webcast, www.youtube.com/watch?v=YRs_lIsUJco; Wadada Leo Smith website, www.wadadaleosmith.com.

Smith, Willie Mae Ford

(1904–1994) Gospel Singer

Born in Rolling Fork, Mississippi, on 23 June 1904, Mother Willie Mae Ford Smith was one of the most popular and imitated gospel singers in the twentieth century. Her deep contralto and divine onstage splendor influenced such singers as Mahalia Jackson and Brother Joe May.

Willie Mae Ford was the seventh of fourteen children born to devout Baptists Clarence Ford and his wife, Mary. Clarence's job with the railroad took the family first to Memphis and then to St. Louis in 1917. At around this time, Clarence organized four of his daughters—Willie Mae, Mary, Emma, and Geneva—into the Ford Sisters Quartet, a gospel group that performed around the Midwest throughout the early 1920s. An appearance at the 1922 National Baptist Convention in Louisville, Kentucky, ultimately made Willie Mae a sought-after singer when the quartet split a few years later.

Willie Mae Ford married James Peter Smith in 1924, and they had two children while she began a career as solo gospel artist. While on tour in the early 1930s, Smith met Thomas A. Dorsey, beginning a long-lasting professional relationship in which she worked with Dorsey's National Convention of Gospel Choirs and Choruses. From 1936 until the late 1980s, she served as director of the convention's Soloist Bureau, evaluating, coaching, and influencing a who's who of gospel singers: Roberta Martin, Mahalia Jackson, Edna Gallmon Cooke, Martha Bass, Myrtle Scott, the O'Neal Twins, and Brother Joe May. It was May who gave Smith the nickname *Mother.*

With her adopted daughter, Bertha, as her accompanist, Smith toured the Midwest gospel circuit during the 1930s and 1940s. In 1939 Smith joined the Pentecostal Denomination, Church of God Apostolic, a conversion that added fervor and bounce to her singing and performing style. According to Horace Clarence Boyer, Smith's "most notable contribution to gospel . . . was the introduction of the 'song and sermonette' into gospel music whereby a singer delivers a five- or ten-minute sermon, before, during, or after the performance of a song."

Smith recorded beginning in 1950 for a variety of labels, including Nashboro, Savoy, and Spirit Feel, but had only modest success. Her career faded, and she returned to St. Louis, where she lived in a housing project for senior citizens and worked at a local mental health center. An appearance at the 1972 Newport Jazz Festival brought Smith into the national spotlight. She later performed at Radio City Music Hall and was featured in a 1981 gospel documentary, *Say Amen, Somebody,* and in Brian Lanker's *I Dream a World: Portraits of Black Women Who Changed America* (1989). In 1988 she received a National Heritage Award from the National Endowment for the Arts. Smith continued to perform at the Lively Stone Apostolic Church in St. Louis, where she had been an ordained minister since the 1950s, until her death on 2 February 1994.

Mark Coltrain
Central Piedmont
Community College

Horace Clarence Boyer and Lloyd Yearwood, *How Sweet the Sound: The Golden Age of Gospel* (1995); William Thomas Dargan and Kathy White Bullock, *Black Music Research Journal* (Autumn 1989); *New York Times* (3 February 1994).

Smith County

Founded in 1833, Smith County, a small county on the edge of the Piney Woods region in south-central Mississippi, was named for Maj. David Smith, a hero of the American Revolution who later settled in Mississippi. The seat of Smith County is Raleigh, while other communities include Mize and Taylorsville. In the 1840 census, Smith County had three times as many free people (1,542) as slaves (419). By 1860 the population had increased substantially, reaching 5,443 free people and 2,195 slaves.

Antebellum Smith County ranked in the bottom quarter of the state's counties in most forms of agricultural production. However, the county was decidedly agricultural in 1860, with only twenty-five people working in industry—primarily the county's three lumber mills. That year, Smith County had

S

twenty-three churches: ten Baptist, nine Methodist, one Presbyterian, and three Lutheran.

In the 1850s William Harris Hardy founded a school and began practicing law in and around Raleigh. He organized a Confederate military company, the Smith County Defenders, in 1861. He later became an aide to Gen. James Smith before pursuing a postbellum career as a political figure, judge, and the founder of several South Mississippi towns, including Hattiesburg. Confederate general and Mississippi governor Robert Lowry also spent several years practicing law in antebellum Smith County. Raleigh suffered considerable destruction in 1863 when Union forces led by Benjamin Grierson led a raid through northeastern and central Mississippi, destroying transportation facilities and capturing weapons and soldiers.

In the postbellum period, Smith County experienced relatively little population change. In 1880 the county had 8,088 residents, 6,452 of whom were white. Landowners cultivated 88 percent of working farms, so the county had few tenants and sharecroppers. Smith remained low in state rankings in the production of cotton and corn, but its residents ranked in the middle of the state in raising livestock.

By 1900 the county's population had grown to 13,055, with whites accounting for most of the population. Three-quarters of Smith's white farmers and almost half of its black farmers owned their land. Industry was emerging slowly, with just fifty-seven workers in 1900.

According to the religious census of 1916, more than two-thirds of all church members in Smith County belonged to the Southern Baptist Convention. In fact, Smith had the second-highest number of Southern Baptists in the state. Others with substantial memberships included the Methodist Episcopal Church, South, and the Missionary Baptists.

Smith County's population grew slowly in the early 1900s, exceeding 18,000 by 1930. Smith continued to have a large white majority, with whites comprising 81 percent of the population. Smith County had no urban center and few industrial workers. In contrast to late-nineteenth-century trends, by the early 1900s half of the county's 3,277 farms were operated by tenants.

By 1960 the county's population had declined to 14,303 and was 77 percent white. About half of Smith County's working people made their living in agriculture. Smith had a high number of hogs, while its farmers grew substantial amounts of corn, soybeans, and cotton. Almost 20 percent of the county's workers had manufacturing jobs, primarily in the apparel industry. With ten oil wells, Smith County ranked second in oil production. In the twenty-first century Smith County became one of Mississippi's leading producers of poultry.

Prentiss Walker, who in 1964 became the first Republican elected to the US House of Representatives from Mississippi in the twentieth century, was born in Taylorsville. Walker gave up his House seat after only one term and was unable to reclaim it in later elections. Other notable people from Taylorsville include National Football League players Jason Campbell and Eugene Sims.

In 2010 whites made up about three-quarters of Smith County's population, which had increased to 16,182.

Mississippi Encyclopedia Staff
University of Mississippi

Mississippi State Planning Commission, *Progress Report on State Planning in Mississippi* (1938); *Mississippi Statistical Abstract*, Mississippi State University (1952–2010); Charles Sydnor and Claude Bennett, *Mississippi History* (1939); University of Virginia Library, Historical Census Browser website, http://mapserver.lib.virginia.edu; E. Nolan Waller and Dani A. Smith, *Growth Profiles of Mississippi's Counties, 1960–1980* (1985).

Smith Robertson Museum and Cultural Center

The Smith Robertson Museum and Cultural Center documents the history and achievements of African Americans in Mississippi and sponsors workshops and festivals. The museum building, adjacent to the Mississippi State Capitol in Jackson, is the site of the city's first public elementary school for African Americans, built in 1894. In 1903 the school was named for Smith Robertson, Jackson's first African American alderman. The school counts among its graduates writer Richard Wright. The original two-story wooden building burned, and the school was rebuilt in brick in 1909. In 1929 a Jackson architectural firm, Hull and Mulvaney, remodeled the building in the Art Deco style. The school closed its doors in 1971.

Not wanting to lose the historic building, Jessie B. Mosley and Alferdteen Harrison led the community effort that founded the Mississippi Association for the Preservation of Smith Robertson School, which helped establish the museum in 1984 with Mosley as the first director.

Staff and volunteers conduct tours of the permanent exhibitions, which include historical documents and works by artists who are native Mississippians or who work in the state. In addition, the museum offers exhibits on such topics as "Treasures of Africa," the African American lifestyle, historically black colleges and universities. black doctors, and civil rights. The Mississippi African American Folk Art collection features thirty-five quilts donated by the University of Mississippi's Center for the Study of Southern Culture, and the Smith Robertson Room documents the original school's history. Additional exhibits highlight the history of Farish Street, the predominantly African American area of downtown Jackson; Mississippi's slave community; and the Great Migration of African Americans to northern cities between 1915 and 1940. The Hall of Fame honors the state's groundbreaking African American politicians. The museum also hosts traveling and temporary exhibitions focusing on national as well as Mississippi topics and artists.

Anna F. Kaplan
Columbia University

City of Jackson, Mississippi, Smith Robertson Museum website, www.jacksonms.gov/visitors/museums/smithrobertson; Turry Miguel Flucker, *Brown Quarterly* (Winter 1998).

Smylie, James
(1780–1853) Religious Leader

James Smylie was born in 1780 in Richmond County, North Carolina, and attended David Caldwell's Log College, an institution that trained numerous frontier ministers. Smylie moved to Mississippi in 1805 and two years later helped to organize the first Presbyterian church in the Mississippi Territory, located at Pine Ridge, four miles west of Washington in Adams County. The congregation began with twenty-two members, most of them Scottish or, like Smylie, the sons and daughters of Scots. Working with three other ministers, Smylie served the Pine Ridge Church through the 1810s, delivering sermons and administering the sacraments while helping to organize additional Presbyterian churches in Adams and Amite Counties. Smylie also became wealthy, owning more than one thousand acres of land in Amite County and as many as fifty-three slaves.

As a Presbyterian leader in the state's wealthiest area, Smylie held considerable influence in Mississippi's religious circles. A strong supporter of education, Smylie served as a vice president of the Amite and Florida Bible Society, which distributed Bibles to poor people. In 1815 Smylie traveled to Tennessee and convinced Presbyterian leaders to organize the Synod of Mississippi and South Alabama; two decades later, he was involved in the creation of the new Synod of Mississippi.

Smylie is perhaps best known as a vocal defender of slavery. As clerk of the Mississippi Presbytery, Smylie received an 1836 letter from the members of Ohio's Chillicothe Presbytery urging their colleagues in Mississippi to give up the "sin" of slavery. Smylie responded with a letter rejecting the idea that slavery was a sin. Published as a pamphlet, that letter became a popular tract in antebellum southern discussions of slavery. Smylie argued that the Bible did not condemn slavery and asserted instead that the Bible upheld good family order, with wise patriarchal figures in charge of wives, children, and all other dependents, including slaves, as the basis for a kind and just society.

Smylie condemned abolitionists for using the Bible for what he perceived as unbiblical and secular ends. He was one of the Mississippi leaders of the Old School Presbyterians whose views on slavery and abolition led to a split in the Presbyterian Church in 1838. Smylie helped write the document condemning northern Presbyterians as "hostile to at least one of the domestic institutions in the South."

He died on 4 April 1853 in Amite County.

Ted Ownby
University of Mississippi

Donald G. Mathews, *Religion in the Old South* (1977); Walter Brownlow Posey, *The Presbyterian Church in the Old Southwest, 1778–1838* (1952); Randy Sparks, *On Jordan's Stormy Banks: Evangelicalism in Mississippi, 1773–1876* (1994).

Social and Economic History, 1817–1890

During the first seven decades of statehood, Mississippi experienced major social and economic changes. An initial demographic and economic transformation occurred in the two decades after 1817 with the removal of the Choctaw and Chickasaw Indians. Even before statehood, the two tribes faced increasing pressure to cede their substantial landholdings to white settlers looking to establish farms and plantations. These tensions only increased after 1830, when the US Congress passed the Indian Removal Bill, which codified the government's resolve to remove the remaining Indians from the eastern United States to designated areas west of the Mississippi River. Southern Indians such as the Choctaw and Chickasaw faced a clear choice: they could either accept federal assistance and relocate west to lands promised by the federal government, or they could stay in Mississippi and be subject to state laws that destroyed their tribal and personal rights and made them subject to harassment and incursions by white settlers who coveted land. Consequently, in the Treaty of Dancing Rabbit Creek (1830) and the Treaty of Pontotoc (1832), the Choctaw and Chickasaw respectively ceded their remaining tribal lands to the State of Mississippi. Although several thousand Choctaw and a smaller number of Chickasaw stayed in Mississippi after most of the two tribes moved to Indian Territory (now Oklahoma), those who remained in the state faced a difficult life characterized by poverty, few legal protections, and harassment by white Mississippians.

With the Choctaw and Chickasaw removed from their ancient homeland, white settlers flooded into the state, and

S

many of them brought black slaves with them. By 1840 blacks outnumbered whites in the state, and on the eve of the Civil War, Mississippi had 437,404 African American residents. As the population increased, so did the production of cotton. Mississippi became the heart of the Old South's Cotton Kingdom, producing 20 percent of the world's supply of the fiber by 1860. As a result, Mississippi remained an overwhelmingly rural state, and Natchez was the only settlement with a pre–Civil War population that exceeded five thousand. The few towns that developed generally existed to supply the rather limited legal, administrative, and social services required by the surrounding agricultural areas. One of the more notable features of Mississippi's antebellum towns is that they were home to a small population of free blacks, which totaled only 773 in 1860, as well as to small enclaves of residents of various ethnic groups.

Although antebellum Mississippi had significant numbers of cotton plantations worked by African American slaves, the state had three distinct regions prior to the Civil War, each with its own demographic profile and social relations: the plantation districts along the Mississippi River below the Delta and in the valley of the Tombigbee River, where cotton was the primary crop; the white-majority yeoman farming and small slaveholding areas throughout most of northeast and east-central Mississippi, where some farmers produced cotton but most practiced subsistence agriculture; and the livestock-tending and timber region of the southeastern piney woods, where little cotton was produced.

African American slavery existed in all these districts, though the vast majority of slaves worked and lived in the plantation neighborhoods, where their forced labor made possible the "good life" for Mississippi's planter class, especially in Natchez and other places that were home to a number of superplanters. The nature of slavery in Mississippi varied over time and from place to place, as did the conditions of life for the average slave. However, the circumstances of bondage, whatever their harshness, failed to quash the spirit of Mississippi slaves. They creatively resisted slavery in a variety of ways and strove to nurture two important institutions, the family and religion, despite the many obstacles imposed by enslavement.

The Civil War undermined the notion that a slave society represented the best arrangement for maintaining a world in which all white men remained essentially equal. Conscription, draft exemptions for planters, the tax in kind, and Confederate impressment policies heightened class tensions between the "common whites" of Mississippi and wealthier whites. By 1863 halfhearted support of the war effort plagued many parts of the Mississippi home front, and many common whites had come to view the struggle as a rich man's war but a poor man's fight. The war not only revealed class divisions in white society that had festered below the surface for much of the antebellum period but also ravaged the state economically and demographically. In addition to the

massive loss of capital because substantial amounts of the state's wealth had been invested in the ownership of other human beings, fighting on Mississippi soil had left part of the state in ruin. Moreover, not only had thousands of soldiers from the state died in the fighting, but substantial numbers of Mississippi civilians, both black and white, had also been killed.

The disappearance of the state's slave population represented the biggest change to come out of the Civil War. While Abraham Lincoln's Emancipation Proclamation and the Thirteenth Amendment formally eradicated slavery, many black Mississippians helped to force their own emancipation during the war. Some escaped to Union lines when the opportunity arose. Others used the disorder created by the conflict to assert their freedom from bondage. At Davis Bend, the plantation owned by Joseph Davis, brother of Confederate president Jefferson Davis, slaves began to operate the plantation for their own benefit when Davis fled as Yankees approached in 1862. At the end of the war, the freedpeople moved to organize their own communities, with churches, fraternal societies, and a range of other facilities. Among the most important institutions the former slaves sought to create were schools. The desire for an education led black parents to move to the more urban parts of the state and often led plantation workers to make the establishment of a schoolhouse a primary condition of signing labor contracts. This desire for schooling among the freedpeople became perhaps the most important spur for Mississippi's creation of a rudimentary system of public schools in 1870, during the brief time that blacks exercised significant political power during Reconstruction.

White Mississippians did not welcome black emancipation. Indeed, defining the new status of the freedpeople became a vexing question for white Mississippians, who struggled to address that question for at least the next century. Most immediately, black freedom, combined with northern victory and Republican Reconstruction, tended to unite whites after the war, subsuming the class divisions that had arisen briefly during the conflict. With the passage of the Fourteenth and Fifteenth Amendments, which promised equal protection of the laws and suffrage for male former slaves, white Mississippians resolved to regain the upper hand. Fearful of the political power blacks had secured during Reconstruction and certain that blacks wanted not only political and civil rights but also social equality (that is, miscegenation), white Mississippians mounted a campaign of fraud, intimidation, and terror to restore white rule and white supremacy, culminating with the 1875 state elections.

Despite the upheaval and changes of the Civil War and Reconstruction, the legacy of the Old South continued to permeate Mississippi life. The state remained overwhelmingly rural with an agricultural economy still ordered by the production of cotton on plantations. The opening of the Delta lands after the Civil War solidified the state's position as a major cotton supplier. Emancipation, however, transformed the way that cotton was produced. Former slaves dreamed of becoming yeoman farmers, but they had no land and few resources or access to credit to acquire farms. The former planters hoped to maintain their plantations with black labor, but their initial efforts to compel the freedpeople to work in gangs for wages proved unsuccessful. By the late 1860s a compromise had been worked out: sharecropping. White landowners allowed blacks to live on plots of land and provided tools and typically a "furnish" of supplies on which the croppers could live; blacks agreed to provide the landowner with a share of the cotton crop. The arrangement allowed blacks to direct the labor of their families and establish some semblance of agricultural independence—more than under slavery or a wage system of agricultural labor—but many former slaves became trapped in a cycle of permanent debt, in part caused by steadily declining cotton prices after the war but also encouraged by planters who saw the crop lien system associated with sharecropping as a way to entangle nominally free labor in a dependent relationship.

The agricultural economic system fashioned after the Civil War also ensnared many of the state's white yeomen in its trap. Although many of them had focused on subsistence farming before the war, more began to practice commercial cotton farming afterward, lured by the need for cash to pay for debts acquired during four years of war and the increased taxes levied during Reconstruction as well as by the greater possibilities to produce for the market as the state expanded its rail lines. As cotton prices tumbled, many white yeomen who banked their future prosperity on cotton production lost their land and descended into the ranks of tenants and sharecroppers. By 1900, 85 percent of black farmers and more than 35 percent of white agriculturalists did not own the land they worked.

Though cotton remained king in Mississippi after the Civil War, the state experienced some important industrial growth and economic diversification. In large part as a consequence of outside capital and state policies that provided tax breaks and grants of land to developers, Mississippi's system of railroads improved dramatically after the Civil War. In 1860 the state had only 862 miles of track, and much of it was destroyed during the war. By 1900, 2,788 miles of railroad line crisscrossed the state. Industrial development followed the railroad-building boom. Between 1880 and 1900 the value of products manufactured in the state increased by more than 150 percent.

Perhaps the biggest industrial development of the postbellum years was the rapid expansion of the timber industry in the Piney Woods of South Mississippi. By the time of the Civil War, lumbering already represented one of the major economic activities of the Piney Woods, but the improved transportation system developed after the war accelerated development of the industry. During the 1880s speculators (many from outside the state) acquired title to large areas of land, much of it thick with first-growth longleaf yellow pine. For example, one Michigan speculator, Delos Blodgett, acquired 721,000 acres in the Piney Woods region. Within two decades, Mississippi produced enough timber to rank third among US states. The rapidly growing industry attracted new residents to South Mississippi, including a significant number of black migrants searching for work beyond the cotton plantations further north. Many of the workers lived in timber camps, mobile communities that followed the shearing of South Mississippi's pine stands, a process that reached its height between the late 1870s and the early 1930s. At the same time, the timber industry led to the creation of new towns in the southern part of the state. One such settlement founded in the 1880s, Hattiesburg, rapidly grew into a city that served as the capital of Mississippi's lumber landscape.

The timber industry also played a major role in economic growth along the Mississippi Gulf Coast. Gulfport, founded in the 1890s, eventually became the major terminus for exporting pine timber out of South Mississippi. In addition, improved transportation and preservation methods enabled seafood to become a major industry during the 1880s, further boosting the Gulf Coast economy. In 1881 a group of Gulf Coast men started a company that utilized new techniques to can shrimp and oysters caught off the Gulf Coast. Within a few years, Biloxi and then other coastal communities developed seafood plants. The seafood trade, in turn, attracted European immigrants, especially from Yugoslavia.

Charles C. Bolton
University of North Carolina
at Greensboro

Charles C. Bolton, *Poor Whites of the Antebellum South: Tenants and Laborers in Central North Carolina and Northeast Mississippi* (1994); Bradley G. Bond, *Political Culture in the Nineteenth-Century South: Mississippi, 1830–1890* (1995); James E. Fickle, *Mississippi Forests and Forestry* (2001); Winthrop D. Jordan, *Tumult and Silence at Second Creek: An Inquiry into a Civil War Slave Conspiracy* (1993); Anthony Kaye, *Joining Places: Slave Neighborhoods in the Old South* (2009); John Hebron Moore, *The Emergence of the Cotton Kingdom in the Old Southwest: Mississippi, 1770–1860* (1988); John C. Willis, *Forgotten Time: The Yazoo-Mississippi Delta after the Civil War* (2000).

Social and Economic History, 1890–1954

Mississippi's socioeconomic history between 1890 and 1954 presents a dismal record of economic stagnation marked by low per capita income, excessive dependence on one-crop agriculture, underdevelopment of natural and human resources, and overall deficiency of capital investment. Lackluster legislatures and agrarian anti-industrial ideologies have frequently been blamed for the state's failure to advance economically. However, poor farmers and poor legislators are ubiquitous in American life and cannot alone account for Mississippi's history of poverty. Economic growth demanded the multiplier effect that comes from new ideas and circulation of money characteristic of vibrant consumerism, educational opportunities, and urban development. In the Magnolia State, however, crop liens, low commodity prices, and decreasing soil fertility combined with racial constructions of landholding rights to create an agricultural economy in which the majority of farmers, black and white, worked land they did not own and accumulated overwhelming debt for basic necessities. The most ardent industrial proponents favored low-wage mills that added little value to the agricultural and natural resources they processed rather than high-wage, technological development that might undermine traditional economic and racial hierarchies. Over time Mississippi enacted more progressive laws and built modern infrastructure to attract industry, but it did so within the confines of segregation and the economic, educational, and social barriers that prohibited the advancement of approximately half the population.

Mississippi's economic and social development between 1890 and 1920 occurred within the context of national changes that included rapid population growth through immigration, the rise of industrial capitalism, modern urbanization, and mass reform movements that addressed problems ranging from moral reform to economic regulation, from woman suffrage to labor relations. Mississippi's history in this period mimicked national trends in some areas and diverged from the national norm in others. Prohibition of monopolies and trusts, regulation of railroads and utilities, limitations on landholding by foreign investors, and taxation of corporations reflected widespread public concern over the ramifications of emerging industrial capitalism. Such concerns were not limited to Mississippi or the South, nor were they confined to the Democratic Party. First Populists and then Progressives in both parties made similar arguments for reining in timber and oil companies, railroads and meatpackers, and banking and insurance.

The foundations for the middle class traditionally had been grounded in the advancement of small agricultural producers, whose accumulated savings expanded farm production and invested in small-scale manufacturing. Rapid industrialization in the late nineteenth century undermined these historic avenues to family wealth as local manufacturing and retailing firms competed with larger national corporations in the new economy. Worried that men would soon become tenants on land they had previously owned and that well-capitalized investors would strip timber, oil, and mineral resources, leaving devastated lands in their wake, farmers and urban reformers pushed for regulation,

particularly for corporations without state roots. Indeed, Mississippi's laws on landholding and labor attracted positive attention from national Progressive leaders including Robert La Follette.

Corporate claims to the contrary, outside investors found numerous loopholes in the regulatory legislation and eagerly exploited the state's resources by creating multiple individually chartered firms. Delta and Pine Land's British investors farmed thousands of acres of cotton, while the Hines Timber Company of Chicago, among others, harvested yellow pine and hardwoods at a rate that placed Mississippi third in the nation in lumber-producing states between 1904 and 1915. Advances in technology and large stands of easily accessible, old-growth timber encouraged the construction of rail lines and sawmills to meet the national demand for lumber. By 1920, however, most of the old-growth timber was gone, and with it the companies that had profited from the state's forest resources. Citing prohibitive land taxes for their unwillingness to plant new forests, the larger timber companies abandoned Mississippi for investment elsewhere. Sustained profits from Mississippi timber required modern forestry programs and new uses for forest products. Research programs at Mississippi State College (now Mississippi State University) focused on forest development and the science of chemurgy. Some native lumber companies such as the H. Weston Company and Randolph Batson introduced reforestation programs into their business practices. Laurel's Masonite Company developed an innovative process for utilizing forest byproducts to produced pressed board. Although these local firms promised a new day for the future of Mississippi forestry, by the mid-1920s, cutover land and abandoned tracks and equipment signaled the end of the timber boom that had enriched a few, provided low-wage jobs for many, and left the state little better than it had been in 1890.

Mississippi's business leaders entered the 1920s enthusiastically determined to demonstrate the state's modern outlook and investment potential. Tying their efforts to the business progressivism of the postwar South, boosters championed every advance as evidence that the Magnolia State was finally shedding its reputation for one-crop agriculture and anti-industrial laws. The state Chamber of Commerce launched the *Mississippi Builder* in 1923 to publicize good roads, good health, consolidated schools, electric power, and agricultural diversity. Two years later the Mississippi Development Council organized a traveling display accompanied by more than one hundred prominent Mississippians to tour the Midwest and the West under the banner "What about Mississippi?" The intensive, ten-day effort presented a picture of Mississippi that was hard to reconcile with the evidence.

Publicity for the tour and in national periodicals and trade journals touted the state's workforce as 90 percent Anglo-Saxon, playing on nativist fears outside the South and ignoring, with no apparent sense of irony, the population figures that placed whites in the minority. Statistics compiled by Mississippi business leaders claimed the Magnolia State as the nation's healthiest, despite high infant mortality (64.5/1,000 for whites and 78.4/1,000 for blacks), low doctor/patient ratios, and the lingering presence of a number of infectious diseases. Finally, although boll weevil infestations had prompted some farmers to diversify into dairy farming, truck farming, and pecan production, the state remained firmly wedded to cotton.

Nevertheless, boosters could not be dismissed as simply snake oil salesmen. At least for whites, the early twentieth century had produced some improvements in educational opportunities. Mississippi boasted more agricultural high schools than any other state. Every county had at least one high school, and consolidation of public schools was proceeding at a remarkable pace. A new normal school in the Delta and another in South Mississippi promised better-qualified teachers for the future.

Cooperation between the US Public Health Service, the Rockefeller Foundation, and the Mississippi Department of Health under Dr. Felix Underwood resulted in health improvements for many Mississippians. Pellagra- and hookworm-eradication programs enhanced the health of both blacks and whites. The state recorded significant decreases in typhoid fever, smallpox, diphtheria, malaria, and tuberculosis. The state legislature provided funding for new hospitals for psychiatric patients and children with special needs.

Business and legislative leaders worked together to standardize banking practices, improve infrastructure, and assure adequate power. In 1909 Mississippi had 185 miles of paved road that supplemented an extensive rail system. In the 1920s federal support for road construction and a state highway tax funded a modern roadway system that brought new retail and manufacturing opportunities to many small towns. In the 1910s legislators established new banking standards that abolished a corrupt system of state deposits in private banks. Historically, New York firms had underwritten insurance in Mississippi. In 1905 Lamar Life Insurance Company opened offices in Jackson, and four more insurance companies followed over the next fifteen years. In 1925, 60 percent of insurance in Mississippi was underwritten by Mississippi companies. The changes in banking and insurance had positive effects in local settings, with banks and insurance companies boasting of their investments in local creameries, industries, and retail businesses.

Mississippi's experience with power was more complex. In 1920 electrification of cities and towns was provided by local mills or power companies, at a time when the South was experiencing consolidation of large utility companies (Alabama Power and Duke Power) and the establishment of regional power grids. Although Mississippians hailed the 1923 creation of Mississippi Power and Light Company as evidence of the state's progress in the electrical age, a more critical assessment might note the tardiness of that move, even by the standards of the South. In addition, geologists and wildcatters explored the state for oil and gas. In 1926 the

first natural gas field was developed in Monroe County; by the following year a pipeline supplied gas to Amory, Tupelo, and Aberdeen. The first oil field was discovered in 1938 by a Works Progress Administration crew chief in Yazoo County. Twenty years later, Mississippi had 2,500 oil and gas wells in more than 150 fields and produced 125,000 barrels of oil and 750,000 cubic feet of natural gas daily.

Like other agricultural states, Mississippi felt the effects of the economic downturn long before the "official" start of the Great Depression. And like other regions, the effects of natural disaster, such as the Great Flood of 1927, compounded the drop in commodity prices. By 1932 Mississippi was in serious trouble: dependent on an income tax and property tax, the state treasury contained $1,326.17, while the state debt amounted to more than $13,000,000. Foreclosures on farm property placed one-quarter of the land in the state for sale. The response to the economic crisis brought the state into a modern relationship with the federal government and forced Mississippi lawmakers to take responsibility for the public good. The congressional delegation supported the New Deal, which built roads, schools, libraries, and courthouses. The Civilian Conservation Corps replanted cutover and abused land. Rural homes gained access to electricity through the Tennessee Valley Authority and rural electrification programs. At the state level, lawmakers enacted the Balance Agriculture with Industry (BAWI) program to reorganize and modernize the economy and lure industrial investment. A state sales tax, the first in the nation, financed Mississippi's efforts to balance the budget and reconstruct the economy.

By the end of the decade, Mississippi had made real progress in overcoming the effects of the Depression. Federal income tax receipts, a measure of personal income, reached $1,500,000, and corporate tax receipts rose from $356,000 in 1934 to $1,600,000 in 1939. Bank deposits doubled in the same period. Other indicators showed that while progress had been made, recovery was incomplete. Per capita income was $250 in 1929, $117 in 1933, and $207 in 1938—a promising rebound but not a complete victory.

Despite such progress, Mississippi's Great Depression experiences had some consequences—both immediate and long-term—that were more problematic. Agricultural programs embodied in the Agricultural Adjustment Administration and the Soil Conservation Service favored larger planters, who mechanized their farms and reduced the number of tenants and sharecroppers. In the long run, the movement from the land to industrial jobs had positive benefits, but the more immediate effect was less salutary: tenants and sharecropper contracts were not renewed, and impoverished families found themselves with no other options for employment. Furthermore, the BAWI program attracted a number of low-wage, no-benefits industries with unsavory labor histories. As evidence of the state's continued resistance to modernizing trends in work relations, labor unions, national media, and the US Congress pointed to Mississippi's failure to enact protective policies for labor and to its abuse of federal

S

programs intended to train workers for industrial jobs. The rising tide of recovery brought some improvements for everyone, but Mississippi's economy remained at the bottom of national assessments.

The advent of World War II had a positive effect on the Mississippi economy, although the state received less defense spending ($64 million) than any other southern state. Wartime investment went to industries with economies of scale that guaranteed timely production, and Mississippi's recent, small-scale industrialization disqualified state firms for many defense contracts. Nevertheless, the number of manufacturing establishments rose by more than seven hundred between 1939 and 1947. Ingalls Shipyard in Pascagoula, a BAWI industry, produced seventy C-3s, welded-steel ships that were the workhorse of the merchant fleet. Shipyard employment increased from three thousand workers in 1940 to more than twelve thousand at the height of production. In addition to the defense industries, the creation of army and air training bases across the state pumped federal dollars into many communities. The largest bases were Camp Shelby in Hattiesburg and Keesler Field in Biloxi, but small bases were established at Greenville, Columbus, Jackson, Laurel, Greenwood, and Meridian.

The war brought high-wage jobs and full employment as defense industries and military bases employed all excess labor and created boomtowns. With wages ranging from 40 cents per hour to $1.25, per capita income increased from $218 in 1940 to $605 in 1946. Full employment, cash wages, and few consumer goods meant that Mississippians accumulated savings during the 1940s that subsequently provided capital for investing in homes, farms, businesses, and consumer goods. As men of military age volunteered or were drafted into service, Mississippi's farm population shrank from 1,403,142 in 1940 to 1,050,444 in 1945. As farmers mechanized to increase their production for the war effort, the number of tenants and sharecroppers continued to decline. By 1945 returning GIs sought employment in towns and cities, and the tenant shacks that had dotted the countryside began disappearing from the rural landscape.

With the end of the war, Mississippi legislators reinstituted the BAWI program, which had been allowed to lapse in 1940. Between the end of the war and the US Supreme Court's 1954 *Brown v. Board of Education* ruling, Mississippi's economy continued to make impressive gains. Civilian income exceeded $1 billion in 1948 and approached $2 billion a decade later. Nevertheless, agriculture remained the dominant source of income, accounting for $520 million in 1948 and $441 million in 1955. Two important indicators of Mississippi's changing economy can be seen in the total income received for employment in wholesale/retail trade and government service. The trade sector (manufacturing income) accounted for $230 million in 1948 and $341 million in 1955, while income from government employment was $112 million in 1948 and $183 million in 1955. By comparison, trade accounted for $78 million in 1929 and government employment produced $29 million.

Despite its growth, Mississippi continued to lag behind the rest of the region and the nation. Mississippi's average per capita income in 1955 was $946, more than three times the state's average in 1929 yet still at the bottom of the economic ladder: the average per capita income for the Southeast region was $1,291. Economists praised the state's efforts to diversify its economy and readily attributed the growth to the effects of the BAWI programs. However, they also noted that the benefits of industrialization accrued to white workers, while more than half of nonwhite workers remained employed in agriculture. BAWI plants employed almost no black workers in the early 1950s. Between 1890 and 1954, Mississippi's population shifted from majority-black to majority-white, but the dynamics of segregation did not change. With between 42 and 51 percent of the population locked out of economic advancement, the effects of federal and state programs, private investment, and diversification through BAWI were limited.

Connie L. Lester
University of Central Florida

John M. Barry, *Rising Tide: The Great Mississippi Flood of 1927 and How It Changed America* (1997); Eric Charles Clark, "Industrial Development and State Government Policy in Mississippi, 1890–1980" (PhD dissertation, Mississippi State University, 1989); James C. Cobb, *The Most Southern Place on Earth: The Mississippi Delta and the Roots of Regional Identity* (1992); James C. Cobb, *The Selling of the South: The Southern Crusade for Industrial Development* (1982); Pete Daniel, *Breaking the Land: The Transformation of Cotton, Tobacco, and Rice Culture since 1880* (1985); Don H. Doyle, *Faulkner's County: The Historical Roots of Yoknapatawpha* (2001); Ernest J. Hopkins, *Mississippi's BAWI Plan: Balance Agriculture with Industry, an Experiment in Industrial Subsidization* (1944); Sara E. Morris, "'Good Equipment Makes a Good Homemaker Better': Promoters of Domestic Technology in Mississippi, 1930–1940" (master's thesis, Mississippi State University, 2004); Lawrence J. Nelson, *King Cotton's Advocate: Oscar G. Johnston and the New Deal* (1999); Ted Ownby, *American Dreams in Mississippi: Consumers, Poverty, and Culture, 1830–1998* (1999); Jack Edward Prince, "History and Development of the Mississippi Balance Agriculture with Industry Program, 1936–1958" (PhD dissertation, Ohio State University, 1961); Roger D. Tate Jr., "Easing the Burden: The Era of Depression and New Deal in Mississippi" (PhD dissertation, University of Tennessee, 1978).

Soil, Mississippi State: Natchez Silt Loam

In 2003 the Mississippi legislature formally declared that Natchez silt loam was the official state soil. The Professional Soil Classifiers Association of Mississippi, in consultation with Mississippi State University soil scientists, had selected

Location of Natchez Soils in Mississippi (Courtesy Larry Oldham)

Natchez silt loam to represent the soil resources of the state in 1988. Natchez soils exist on 171,559 acres in Mississippi (0.56 percent of the state).

The Natchez soils formed in very deep, wind-blown loess material on strongly sloping to very steep hillsides under a woodland environment and a climate that was warm and humid in the bluff hills that border the Mississippi Delta floodplains. These soils have natural fertility and desirable tilth, but the slopes on which they occur usually limit their use to trees. In areas with less steep slopes, pasture and row crops are grown, and the soil is very productive under good management.

Larry Oldham
Mississippi State University
Extension Service

N. C. Brady and R. R. Weil, *The Nature and Properties of Soils* (2007); Mississippi State University Extension Service website, www.msucares .com; US Department of Agriculture, Natural Resource Conservation Service website, http://soils.usda.gov.

Soils

Soils form via unique combinations of parent materials, climate, biological factors, and topography over time. Mississippi has a wide variety of soils, reflecting the diversity of these factors present in the state. Three general land resource regions

are identified as (1) river floodplain (the Delta); (2) a loess region (a band of soils formed in windblown material that adjoins the Delta); and (3) Coastal Plain (the rest of the state).

As land management, including forest clearing and more recently forest replanting, transitioned from the pre-Columbian to the modern, the soils within a region led to the current predominant activities on the surface. For example, most Mississippi row crop production (cotton, corn, and soybeans) occurs in the relatively flat, deep alluvial soils of the Delta, which are conducive to mechanized farming. Conversely, animal production and forestry dominate on the shallower soils in the hilly sections of East and South Mississippi.

The general land resource areas of the loess and Coastal Plain regions have smaller subunits based on common soils, geology, climate, water resources, and land use. These Major Land Resource Areas are discussed below.

Southern Mississippi Valley Alluvium: The Delta

Soils are naturally diverse in the Delta as a result of their alluvial origin in sediment from areas north of Mississippi. Particle sizes within the sediment decrease as distance from the originating stream increases—that is, soils closer to running water have proportionally more large silt and sand particles than soils further from the stream. Another factor in Delta soil formation is surface water movement over time. Soils formed under standing water have different properties than soils formed under running water.

Soils with a large proportion of clay particles (the smallest basic soil solid) have some unique features. When these soils dry, small round aggregates that look like shotgun buckshot form at the surface; hence, the popular name for Delta clay soils is *buckshot*. Soils with high clay content have very slow water infiltration rates, a property that has led to significant aquaculture and rice production in the region. Mississippi Delta soils originate in sediments left by flooding of the various rivers in the region, which is not a traditional delta fan formed at the mouth of a river. Most Delta soils are farmed, with three-quarters of the cropland to the north and less cropland in the south. Controlling surface water and drainage are major soil-management issues.

Southern Mississippi Valley Uplands: Brown Loam Hills and Thin Loess Areas

When floodwaters receded in what is now the Delta, strong west-to-east winds blew some of the dry sediment left by flooded rivers to the adjacent uplands. The deposited material, called loess, is the parent material of soils formed in the hilly region along the eastern edge of the Delta. The depth of loess decreases from west to east across the state as the distance from the originating flatlands increases. This area, the Brown Loam region or Bluff Hills, has some very deep deposits, as evidenced by the bluffs outside Yazoo

S

City. Natchez silt loam, a soil present on about 170,000 acres in this area, has been designated the Mississippi state soil.

Coastal Plain

Coastal Plain soils in Mississippi are part of an arc along the United States coast from New Jersey to Texas. They are based on unconsolidated fluvial or marine sediments deposited on the edges of ancient seas. These diverse soils are usually best suited to pastures and forests. The northern portion of the Coastal Plain is commonly called the Mississippi Sand Clay Hills. The southern Coastal Plain is the Piney Woods region of the state.

Blackland Prairie

There are two Blackland Prairies, one in northeastern Mississippi in the Tupelo, Aberdeen, and Columbus area, and a smaller area in and near Scott County in south-central Mississippi. Many of the soils are very dark, like midwestern prairies; however, the Mississippi soils form in soft limestone or chalk parent material in humid conditions. Midwestern prairie soils form in glaciated areas predominated by grasslands under drier, less humid conditions.

Gulf Coast Marsh

Zones of marsh along the Gulf of Mexico differ from the rest of the state. The area is almost treeless, has marsh vegetation, and is uninhabited. It is part of the estuarine complex that supports Gulf marine life. Most of the soils of the Gulf Coast Marsh are very poorly drained, and the water table is at or above the surface most of the time. These soils are susceptible to frequent flooding. They formed in alluvial and marine sediments and organic accumulations.

Larry Oldham
Mississippi State University
Extension Service

Stanley W. Buol, ed., *Soils of the Southern States and Puerto Rico* (1972); Douglas Helms, *Agricultural History* (Fall 2000); US Department of Agriculture, *Yearbook of Agriculture: Soil* (1957).

Sold down the River

The central thoroughfare of America's domestic slave trade, the Mississippi River brought slave traders and their cargo southward from the Ohio River to ports along the river's banks in Mississippi. Stops in Vicksburg, Natchez, and other major cities offered antebellum traders markets at which southern plantation owners gathered to negotiate the purchase of black men, women, and children. These purchases met the South's increasing demand for field and house labor, but stories of backbreaking toil, high rates of malaria, and intolerable heat and humidity quickly established the Deep South—and the watery highway that delivered slaves there— as particularly loathsome fates. Thus to be "sold down the river" was to commence a life of crushing circumstances.

Between 1830 and 1860, Virginia sold approximately three hundred thousand slaves farther south to clear land and plant and harvest cotton, rice, and sugar. Slaveholders initially feared this sudden influx of "savage" African Americans, a stereotype recalling owners' practice of banishing their most aggressive slaves to Deep South farms. Nat Turner's 1831 revolt moved Alabama, Mississippi, and Louisiana to ban importing slaves, but bringing slaves south was key to the region's strong agrarian economy: more slaves meant bigger farms, more crops, and increased revenue. Thus a booming cotton trade in the 1850s coaxed all three states to open wide the gates.

Once aboard riverboats, slaves found themselves penned belowdecks, shackled around the ankles or wrists, and roped together at the waist. Traders lessened these measures as the boat approached a harbor. Author William Wells Brown portrayed the steamboat journey as a time of preparation when a young deckhand might blacken old slaves' gray hair or assign haggard slaves younger ages and fictitious work histories. Slaves were made to rehearse their new life stories to bring better prices at auction.

Also adding to the distress of southern transfer was slaves' geographic and symbolic journey away from freedom. Increasing northern resistance to the institution of slavery made escape seem viable, but southern plantations were surrounded by impenetrable forests and deadly swamps, meaning that escape would require a much longer, more perilous journey than simply crossing a border into a free state. The river's terminating port, New Orleans, was home to the largest slave market in the South and represented a type of dead end for slaves imagining escape from the South's "peculiar institution."

Perhaps the most salient feature of relocation was the destruction to slaves' families. The narratives of Frederick Douglass, Harriet Beecher Stowe, and Linda Brent record the trauma of slaves ripped from the bosom of loving relatives at the hands of evil white men. In *The Adventures of Huckleberry Finn*, Mark Twain depicts the forced separation of the Wilks family house slaves as agonizing, reckless, and shocking.

While the Civil War and subsequent dismantling of slavery inform our past, the practice of selling slaves down the river has left a legacy of pain apparent even in our contemporary cultural consciousness. Americans today use the phrase to connote an unexpected betrayal, while projects that "go south" may also bring to mind the deteriorating condition of South-bound slaves.

Leah Preble Holmes
University of Southern Mississippi

William Wells Brown, *Clotel; or, The President's Daughter* (1853); Walter Johnson, *The Chattel Principle: Internal Slave Trades in the Americas* (2005); Joseph P. Reidy, *From Slavery to Agrarian Capitalism in the Cotton Plantation South* (1992); Michael Tadman, *Speculators and Slaves: Masters, Traders, and Slaves in the Old South* (1989).

Somerville, Nellie Nugent
(1863–1952) Feminist Leader

Nellie Nugent Somerville was a reformer active on behalf of women's rights and suffrage and the first woman elected to the Mississippi legislature. Born during the Civil War into a prominent family, she grew up among the prosperous new "leisure class" that emerged in the post-Reconstruction period. Although she never abandoned the role of proper southern lady, she became of necessity an iconoclast, attacking double standards, removing barriers, and breaking ground for women.

Nellie Nugent was born on 25 September 1863 on a plantation near Greenville, Mississippi, in Washington County. Fighting raged in the area, her father was away at war, her grandfather had died from an enemy bullet, and her family home had been burned. When she was only two years old, her mother, Eleanor Smith Nugent, died, leaving Nellie in the care of her father and grandmother, both of whom played profound roles in shaping her character. After serving in the Confederate Army, William Lewis Nugent rose to prominence and wealth as a member of the Mississippi bar and a Methodist philanthropist. Also a devoted Methodist, Myra Smith, Nellie's grandmother, was a pioneer in women's church work during Greenville's early days. Her husband, Abram F. Smith, was the first Washington County representative in the Mississippi legislature and is credited with having given Greenville its name.

Young Nellie exhibited a keen interest in political theory, history, theology, and public affairs, so William Nugent saw to it that his daughter received a sound education, at the time deemed unnecessary for females. She earned a bachelor's degree in 1880 from Martha Washington College in Abingdon, Virginia, finishing first in her class. She later studied law under her father but turned down his offer to join his practice.

Nellie Nugent married Robert Somerville, a Virginia engineer who had moved to Greenville, in 1885, and the couple went on to have four children: Robert N. and Abram D.

Somerville, who became attorneys in Cleveland; Eleanor Somerville Shands, who became a Cleveland community leader; and Lucy Somerville Howorth, who became a distinguished leader in the fields of law, politics, and women's rights.

Nellie Somerville refused to be stymied by the prevailing sentiment in Mississippi that women were not allowed to take part in public life. For a time she found her platform in organizations acceptable for southern ladies: culture and study clubs, church missionary work, and the Woman's Christian Temperance Union. She worked for years to bring about change and to educate women about their rights, proving herself an inspiring leader and organizer and gaining a measure of support from women across the state. When it became apparent that no real reform could be accomplished without the power of the ballot, Somerville began to concentrate her efforts on the issue of woman suffrage, enduring stubborn opposition from Mississippi men. In a barrage of fiery speeches and newspaper articles, she challenged the establishment with a fervor that brought her to the attention of national feminist leaders, who soon came south to garner support for the movement.

When the Mississippi Woman Suffrage Association formed in 1897, Somerville served as its guiding light and prime motivator, and she was chosen the first president. She devoted a significant portion of the remainder of her life to gaining political rights for women. Under her leadership, the state suffrage association and the Greenville Suffrage Club adopted vigorous civic and hygiene programs. She kept her small following hard at work addressing issues such as public health, occupational safety, and protective legislation concerning the welfare of children as well as the ongoing campaign for the vote. Somerville promoted the state's first antituberculosis campaign and procured for Greenville Mississippi's first female community health nurse. In 1915 she was elected vice president of the National American Woman Suffrage Association, becoming the only southern woman on the board.

In 1917, when the United States entered World War I, Somerville interrupted her suffrage work to organize and coordinate home front activities. She chaired the Washington County Woman's Committee, Council of National Defense, while her younger daughter, Lucy, served as treasurer. According to Nellie Somerville, "All [women] can do for our country in this time of peril is less than we want to do. Our ability is limited; our patriotism is unlimited." Her professed patriotism was indeed the keynote in her long campaign for equal rights. "Among thoughtful people," she stated in one of many wartime speeches, "there is a growing belief that American institutions cannot be preserved without the infusion in the body politic of a new moral force, and . . . only the womanhood of the nation can furnish that moral power."

In spite of laboring on many levels, careful never to appear aggressive or offensive, Somerville and her fellow Mississippi suffragists failed to accomplish their ultimate goal: suffrage by state constitutional amendment. Although the Mississippi legislature refused to ratify the Nineteenth Amendment to the US constitution, Somerville proved women's political potential in 1920 by becoming the first female member of the Mississippi House of Representatives. Having achieved the legitimacy she had long sought, she served a four-year term as chair of the Committee on Eleemosynary Institutions, helping to bring about numerous improvements in the state's charitable institutions, child labor laws, and conditions for the blind, deaf, and the mentally ill. She steered to passage the bill that brought about a major reorganization of the state mental hospital, moving the facility from Jackson to Rankin County. She also sponsored legislation that established Delta State Teachers College (now Delta State University). She was active in the Democratic Party and in 1925 served as a delegate to the national convention in New York City.

Although she did not seek a second term in the legislature, Somerville remained involved in politics and was in great demand as a speaker through the state during the 1930s and 1940s. In the late 1940s, she and many other Mississippians became States' Rights Democrats (Dixiecrats). She maintained her involvement in reform efforts, especially where moral issues were involved, through Methodist missionary work and various patriotic and service organizations, receiving numerous awards both before and after her death in Ruleville on 28 July 1952. The Nellie Nugent Somerville Lectures on Government and Public Affairs were inaugurated at Delta State University in 1974, and the Mississippi Woman's Day Annual Woman of the Year Award was renamed for her in 1975. In 1981 the State Department of Archives and History inducted her into the Mississippi Hall of Fame.

Mary T. (Merideth) Bishop
Laurel, Mississippi

Mary Louise Merideth, "The Mississippi Woman's Rights Movement, 1889–1923: The Leadership Role of Nellie Nugent Somerville and Greenville in Suffrage Reform" (master's thesis, Delta State University, 1974); Anne Firor Scott, in *Notable American Women, the Modern Period* (1980); Marjorie Julian Spruill, in *Mississippi Women: Their Histories, Their Lives*, ed. Martha H. Swain, Elizabeth Anne Payne, Marjorie Julian Spruill, and Susan Ditto (2003); Somerville and Howorth Family Papers, 1850–1983, Schlesinger Library on the History of Women, Radcliffe College.

Southern Cross the Dog

Many early blues singers used variations on the phrase "going where the Southern cross the Dog." The expression refers to the place in Moorhead, Mississippi, where the Yazoo and Mississippi Valley rail line intersected with the Southern rail line. Many southerners referred to the Yazoo and Mississippi line as the "Yellow Dog" or simply the "Dog" or "Dawg." The first historical reference to blues lyrics mentions this phrase: when W. C. Handy wrote about first hearing the blues in 1903 at a train station in Tutwiler, he described a man playing guitar and repeating the phrase "Goin' where the Southern cross' the Dog." Handy later popularized the phrase in his "Yellow Dog Blues" (1914). Charley Patton sang the phrase in "Green River Blues" (1929), and Kokomo Arnold used it in "Long and Tall" (1937). Today, the Southern rail line is known as the Columbus and Greenville (C&G) Railway, and the Yazoo and Mississippi rail line has been moved eastward and consolidated by the Illinois Central.

Greg Johnson
University of Mississippi

W. C. Handy, *Father of the Blues* (1941).

Southern Tenant Farmers' Union

The Southern Tenant Farmers' Union (STFU) was founded in 1934 by white activists H. L. Mitchell and Clay East near Tyronza, Arkansas. Influenced by long histories of union and socialist activity in Arkansas, Mitchell and East applied their socialist ideology to the plight of evicted sharecroppers throughout the Mississippi and Arkansas River deltas. Because of the Agricultural Adjustment Act's acreage-reduction component, large plantation owners allowed a percentage of their land to lie fallow while collecting checks from the federal government and evicting sharecroppers en masse, forcing many into roadside tent communities. When a planter and agency official near Tyronza expelled many of his sharecroppers, Mitchell and East met with some of the evicted farmers, both white and black, and formed the STFU. For the better part of a decade, the organization focused on the plight of sharecroppers, staging protests, strikes, and marches and encouraging locals throughout the rural South. Through organizing and direct political action, the STFU hoped to overturn the plantation system of agriculture and in the process remake southern class and race relations into an egalitarian society that drew from both Populism and socialism.

STFU locals initially spread across northeast Arkansas, using residents' experience with grassroots socialism, union organizing, and prophetic religion to gain supporters and organizers. African American organizer E. B. McKinney was drawn to the STFU because of its empowering rhetoric and direct action tactics. A circuit-riding preacher and Garveyite member of the Universal Negro Improvement Association, McKinney experienced the radical Gospel of Jesus that brought many rural African Americans to the STFU.

Union members and organizers faced incarceration and violence wherever they held meetings, particularly in 1935, when white planter resistance to union activity became so focused that many key figures, including Mitchell, fled to Memphis to reorganize the organization's headquarters. Beatings, shootings, maimings, and murders followed many STFU meetings as white planters became more agitated with the interracial union. Despite these obstacles, membership in the STFU rose steadily between 1934 and 1936, and it spread into Missouri, Mississippi, Oklahoma, Texas, and Tennessee. Though the major activities remained in Arkansas, the STFU headquarters in Memphis guaranteed that organizers targeted the Mississippi Delta.

The STFU's presence in Mississippi jumped from negligible to significant when the Delta Cooperative Farm was organized in 1936 in Bolivar County, near Hillhouse. With the help of STFU officials, Christian missionaries, and Socialist Party activists, nearly thirty refugee families in acute physical danger and near starvation were brought to the cooperative for a fresh start. In 1938 a second tract of land in Holmes County was purchased by the same missionaries and activists and christened Providence Cooperative Farm. Each cooperative organized an STFU local, and key officials held meetings at both farms. Through the STFU's efforts, word of the project spread across the Magnolia State. Though STFU locals in Mississippi boasted several thousand members, activities were never as focused as they were in Arkansas.

Beginning in 1937, STFU memberships dwindled and internal divisions prevented the continuation of its success. The STFU sought to increase its visibility by joining the United Cannery, Agricultural, Packing, and Allied Workers of America and became an official member of the Congress of Industrial Organizations. But the STFU withdrew less than two years later as a consequence of bureaucratic red tape, higher dues, disagreements between communists among the cannery workers and socialists in the STFU, and the fact that no one in the umbrella labor federation knew how to deal with a rural union. Throughout the 1940s the STFU was plagued by internal divisions, racial tensions, cash shortages, and a paucity of imagination in an age of increasing mechanization. Key officials and organizers quibbled over how best to run the STFU, and arguments often ended in bruised egos and stagnation.

Misunderstandings between the organizers and the rank and file also damaged working relationships. Disillusioned by what they perceived as discrimination and paternalist attitudes, African American members including McKinney departed. Finally, as the New Deal ended and postwar industry boomed, rural laborers left the land in droves, headed for urban industrial centers. These factors led to the STFU's decrease in influence and effectiveness in the rural South. After World War II the struggling STFU sought recognition in the new labor movement sweeping the country. Renamed the National Farm Labor Union, it officially joined the American Federation of Labor, relocated its headquarters to Washington, D.C., and supported farmworker strikes across the country. Though it remained involved in these disputes, the STFU never again challenged the status quo to the same extent as it had in the Arkansas Delta in the 1930s.

Robert H. Ferguson
Western Carolina University

Mark Fannin, *Labor's Promised Land: Radical Visions of Gender, Race, and Religion in the South* (2003); Donald Grubbs, *Cry from the Cotton: The Southern Tenant Farmers' Union and the New Deal* (1971); Howard Kester, *Revolt among the Sharecroppers* (1997); H. L. Mitchell, *Mean Things Happening in This Land: The Life and Times of H. L. Mitchell, Cofounder of the Southern Tenant Farmers' Union* (1979); Elizabeth Ann Payne, *Southern Cultures* (Summer 1998); Nan Elizabeth Woodruff, *American Congo: The African American Freedom Struggle in the Delta* (2003).

Southwestern Humor

Antebellum southern humor, according to scholar Lucinda MacKethan, was a "literature of resistance" that "debunked notions of class privilege upon which much southern pastoral has been constructed." This brand of comedy, usually a product of newspapers or sporting papers and an exclusively masculine enterprise, flourished between the 1830s and the Civil War in an area that encompassed the frontier regions of the Carolinas, Georgia, Tennessee, Alabama, Louisiana, Mississippi, Arkansas, and Missouri. Its principal practitioners were not professional writers but rather planters, lawyers, judges, newspaper editors, politicians, doctors, and ministers, who often wrote pseudonymously or anonymously and in diverse forms, including tall tales, almanac pieces, mock sermons, autobiographical or pseudoautobiographical sketches, turf reports on horse racing and accounts of other popular outdoor sports, mock yokel letters, and anecdotes about local characters.

While most works of southwestern humor originally appeared in newspapers such as the *New Orleans Picayune*, *St. Louis Reveille*, *La Fayette East Alabamian*, and *Columbia South Carolinian*, many of the better pieces were reprinted (and some were published initially) in the *New York Spirit of the Times*, a national sporting weekly edited by William T. Porter, who encouraged southern correspondents to submit their humorous pieces. The best known among the *Spirit's* many southern correspondents included Johnson Jones Hooper, author of the widely popular *Some Adventures of Simon Suggs* (1845); William Tappan Thompson, the author of *Major Jones's Courtship* (1843); Thomas Bangs Thorpe, who wrote "The Big Bear of Arkansas," the best crafted and most engaging tale in the southwestern humor genre; George Washington Harris, who authored *Sut Lovingood: Yarns Spun by a "Nat'ral Born Durn'd Fool," Warped and Wove for Public Wear* (1867); Henry Clay Lewis, who wrote *Odd Leaves from the Life of a Louisiana "Swamp Doctor"* (1850); Charles F. M. Noland, the most prolific of the southern correspondents to the *Spirit*, who contributing more than 250 separate letters and sporting sketches; and three writers associated with the *St. Louis Reveille*—John S. Robb, Sol Smith, and Joseph M. Field.

Most southwestern humor featured topics appealing to male interests: fights (man versus man and man versus animal), hunts, horse races, camp meetings, courtroom antics, courtship, frolics, pranks and deceptive trickery, militia drills, gambling, and drinking and drunkenness. Its prevalent characteristics involved encounters between conflicting social groups—rural or frontier folk and members of refined, upperclass society. It typically gave extended voice and emphasis to marginalized lower-class characters—the rustic yeoman, hunter, backwoodsman, roarer-braggart, con artist, or rogue. It favored hyperbolic portraiture, emphasizing the extravagant, outlandish, and sometimes even physically grotesque characters and situations, and it showcased lively and colorful vernacular speech.

The first southwestern humorist to collect his newspaper sketches for book publication was Augustus Baldwin Longstreet, who migrated to Mississippi in the late 1840s. His *Georgia Scenes* (1835), consisting of eighteen sketches and using two formal and highly literate narrators named Hall and Baldwin, established the paradigm of the conflict between rural and sophisticated cultures and competing levels of formal and vernacular discourse that later southern humorists applied and modified. Longstreet was at various times a lawyer, a judge, a newspaper editor, a minister, a land speculator, and president of four colleges and universities, including the University of Mississippi from 1849 to 1856.

Longstreet's *Georgia Scenes* inspired another adopted Mississippian, Joseph Beckman Cobb, a planter, politician, and newspaper editor. Cobb, who used the pseudonym *Rambler*, first published some humorous sketches and tales in Mississippi newspapers before collecting some of them for *Mississippi Scenes* (1851), a book he dedicated to Longstreet. Like Longstreet, Cobb employed a genteel narrator and a modification of the frame device with an authorial narrator. Two of the best tales in the collection, "The Legend of Black Creek" and "The Bride of Lick-the-Skillet," are close imitations of Washington Irving's "The Legend of Sleepy Hollow," the story most frequently adapted by southwestern humor writers.

Joseph Glover Baldwin was a native of Virginia's Shenandoah Valley who practiced law both in Alabama and Mississippi. His sketches satirizing the society of the Alabama and Mississippi frontier that he observed firsthand in the financial boom times of the 1830s and 1840s first appeared in the *Southern Literary Messenger* before he revised, collected, and published them as *The Flush Times of Alabama and Mississippi* (1853). Though he did not exploit the vernacular as many of his southwestern humor predecessors had done, Baldwin presented a starkly disparaging view of a fallible and inept legal system of acquisitive and scoundrelly lawyers and disreputable, near-illiterate, and unqualified judges whom he juxtaposed with some distinguished real-life lawyers and politicians.

Three other Mississippians also wrote in the genre of southwestern humor. Alexander Gallatin McNutt, a planter, lawyer, and former Mississippi governor (1838–42), published humorous sketches in Porter's *Spirit* under the pseudonym *The Turkey Runner*. His stories featured the adventures and misadventures of two big-talking, free-spirited backwoodsmen, Jim and Chunkey. In *The Big Bear of Arkansas, and Other Sketches* (1845), Porter praised the Turkey Runner as a "formidable rival" of fellow southwestern humorist Thomas Bangs Thorpe. Writing under the pseudonym *Obe Oilstone*, Phillip B. January, whom Porter called a raconteur of "extraordinary merit," contributed epistolary narratives to the *Spirit*. Employing Uncle Johnny, a rambling and engaging storyteller, January presented an amusingly outlandish account of a drunken man who fights a dog in dog fashion—on all fours—and wins. William C. Hall, a lawyer and resident of Yazoo County writing as *H*, published humorous "Yazoo Sketches" that featured a real-life character, Mike Hooter. These sketches first appeared in the *New Orleans Delta*, and several were subsequently reprinted in the *Spirit*. "How Sally Hooter Got Snake-Bit," Hall's sexually suggestive signature sketch, calls to mind Harris's "Sut Lovingood's Lizards" in demonstrating the naughty and subversive side of southwestern humor.

Overall, the significance of southwestern humor lies in its ongoing legacy for later southern writing, which extends from Mark Twain to William Faulkner, Erskine Caldwell, Flannery O'Connor, Eudora Welty, Harry Crews, Zora Neale Hurston, Ishmael Reed, Cormac McCarthy, Roy Blount Jr., and many others. And among these impressive literary beneficiaries are Faulkner and Welty, arguably Mississippi's two greatest writers.

Ed Piacentino
High Point University

Hennig Cohen and William B. Dillingham, in *Humor of the Old Southwest* (1994); M. Thomas Inge, ed., *The Frontier Humorists: Critical Views* (1975); M. Thomas Inge and Edward J. Piacentino, eds., *Humor of the Old South* (2001); James H. Justus, *Fetching the Old Southwest: Humorous Writing from Longstreet to Twain* (2004); Lucinda MacKethan, *Southern Spaces: An Internet Journal and Scholarly Forum* (March 2004); Gretchen Martin, *The Frontier Roots of American Realism* (2007); Ed Piacentino, in *The Enduring Legacy of Old Southwest Humor*, ed. Ed Piacentino (2006);

Norris W. Yates, *William T. Porter and the Spirit of the Times: A Study of the Big Bear School of Humor* (1957).

Southwick, Leslie Harburd

(b. 1950) Judge

Leslie Harburd Southwick is a judge of the US Court of Appeals for the 5th Circuit. Southwick was born on 10 February 1950 to Dr. Lloyd M. Southwick and Ruth Tarpley Southwick in Edinburg, Texas. He graduated from Rice University in 1972 and from the University of Texas Law School three years later.

After clerking for Judge Charles Clark, later chief judge of the 5th Circuit Court, Southwick practiced law privately in Jackson for twelve years. During that time he became active in Republican politics, including George H. W. Bush's unsuccessful 1970 run for the US Senate and his 1980 and 1988 presidential campaigns, during which Southwick headed efforts in Mississippi. When Bush entered the Oval Office, he appointed Southwick to serve as deputy assistant attorney general, managing the Civil Division of the US Department of Justice, where his responsibilities included defending Pres. Bush's decision to send troops to Kuwait and then Iraq. That experience reignited Southwick's desire to serve in the military, and he obtained an age waiver that enabled him to enlist at age forty-two and receive a commission as a judge advocate general officer in the US Army Reserve.

In 1994, when the Mississippi Court of Appeals was created, Southwick won election as one of the court's first ten judges. The campaign was marked by his high-profile 250-mile walk through the entire congressional district that comprised his judicial district. Southwick won reelection without opposition in 1998 and remained on the court until 31 December 2006, serving as presiding judge for five years and participating in approximately 7,000 opinions, about 850 of which he authored.

In 1997 Southwick transferred from the Army Reserve to the Mississippi Army National Guard. As the second Gulf War loomed Southwick received a transfer into a line combat unit that was deployed to active duty in Iraq in 2005. As a lieutenant colonel, the fifty-four-year-old Southwick served as deputy staff judge advocate and then as the staff judge advocate for the 155th Brigade Combat Team.

Pres. George W. Bush nominated Southwick to the US District Court for the Southern District of Mississippi in 2006, leading him not to seek reelection to the Mississippi Court of Appeals. The nomination was reported out of committee, but the US Senate adjourned without voting on it.

On 9 January 2007 Bush nominated Southwick to the Fifth Circuit Court of Appeals. After a contentious confirmation process during which opponents charged him with racial insensitivity and homophobia based on language from two opinions he had joined but not authored while on the Mississippi Court of Appeals, the US Senate voted fifty-nine to thirty-eight to confirm Southwick on 24 October 2007. He has served on the Fifth Circuit Court of Appeals since his investiture six days later.

Andy Taggart
Madison, Mississippi

Confirmation Hearing on the Nominations of Leslie Southwick . . . May 10, 2007 (2007); Leslie H. Southwick, *The Nominee: A Political and Spiritual Journey* (2013); Leslie H. Southwick, *Presidential Also-Rans and Running Mates, 1788–1996* (2nd ed., 1998).

Soybeans

By 2015 soybeans ranked third among Mississippi's agricultural commodities, trailing only poultry and forestry, with a value of $930 million. That number actually represented a significant decline from 2014, when the state's soybean crop was valued at a record $1.3 billion. In 2015 Mississippi's farmers planted 2.3 million acres of soybeans and harvested more than 100 million bushels.

Soybeans have high nutritional value for humans as well as for livestock. They are a good source of plant protein (with cultivars varying between about 38 and 42 percent) and oil (18 and 22 percent). Most soybeans produced in Mississippi are exported. Soy meal (the by-product of oil crushing) provides a major source of food for livestock, poultry, and catfish, all of which are important industries in Mississippi.

Soybeans became a vital crop in Mississippi and the rest of the mid-South in the late 1940s, when Dr. Edgar Hartwig,

Mature soybeans (Courtesy Scott Bauer)

the Father of Soybeans in the South, came to Mississippi. He was credited with breeding 90 percent of the pest-resistant soybean varieties grown in the region through the mid-1980s. Most of his varieties were designed to be planted in early to mid-June or later and harvested in late October to mid-November.

In the early 1990s soybean varieties that could be planted earlier in the year were introduced. Some soybean varieties were planted in April, an early soybean production system that gradually became the recommended practice. A few varieties are also grown on nonirrigated fields to take advantage of early maturity and avoid late-summer drought stress. Soybean yield has subsequently improved greatly, and soybeans also have been used in double-cropping systems (mostly with wheat) in Mississippi.

Numerous soybean varieties are available on the market each year, making selection a very challenging task for an individual farmer. Like most other row crops, soybeans grown in Mississippi have problems with weeds, diseases, and insects. Some of the most common weeds in Mississippi soybean fields are prickly sida, morning glories, sesbania, and annual grasses. Herbicides are commonly used for soybean weed control.

The Mississippi Soybean Promotion Board is a grower association that focuses on promoting soybean research, production, marketing, and use.

Lingziao Zhang
Agricultural Research Service,
US Department of Agriculture

Mississippi Soybean Promotion Board website, mssoy.org; Mississippi State University, Extension Service website, www.msucares.com.

Spanish Period: Government

The Spanish arrived in Florida in 1539 and concentrated their interest in the peninsula and eastern Florida. They lost Florida to the British in the 1763 Treaty of Paris, but because the British believed that administering the port of New Orleans would be a nightmare, Spain was allowed to keep New Orleans and Louisiana land on the west bank of the Mississippi River. Spain won back Florida in 1783 by supporting the upstart colonies in their successful war of independence. Thus began the second Spanish period of West Florida domination.

More than anything else, Spain was interested in populating West Florida with farmers producing staples needed worldwide—staples that could be shipped through New Orleans. Therefore, they offered current English landholders eighteen months to leave unless they took an oath of allegiance to the king of Spain. They also offered land grants to farmers from nearby southern states and territories. William Dunbar, a planter with a British land grant in the Natchez area, transitioned easily to Spanish rule, offering his language, surveying, and architectural skills to the Spanish.

Spanish land in America, as elsewhere, belonged to the king, who appointed intendants (district administrators) who supposedly controlled grant-making authority in Spanish colonies worldwide. In truth, however, the king's appointed governor in New Orleans controlled all activities in that colony. The first Spanish governor, appointed in 1763, never ventured to New Orleans to take office. He was followed by Don Alexandro O'Reilly (1769–72), Col. Don Louis Unzaga y Aranaga (1772–79), Don Bernardo de Galvez (1779–86), Col. Don Esteban Miro (1786–91), Col. Franco Louis Hector, Baron de Carondelet (1791–96), Brig. Don Manuel Gayoso de Lemos (1796–99), and Col. Don Manuel Juan de Seledo (1799–1803).

Spain claimed that West Florida included the land between the thirty-first and thirty-second parallels, which included Natchez; the United States did not recognize that claim. The boundary dispute created instability in Natchez throughout the period of Spanish rule. Also, increasing numbers of American citizens migrated to Natchez, relegating Spanish officials and settlers to a small minority.

Many of Natchez's planters and farmers nevertheless thrived. Horse racing became a favorite sport, and elegant homes were built. Governor Gayoso, seeking local input and regional peace, created what would be called today a city council of eighteen elected officials, most of them Americans and former British landholders. In 1795 Spain and the United States negotiated the Treaty of San Lorenzo, which allowed the appointment of a joint commission to run the thirty-first parallel. In addition, the treaty guaranteed Americans free use of the Mississippi River and of New Orleans to deposit goods for export and exempted Americans from export duties for three years. In 1798 American and Spanish commissioners ran the thirty-first parallel line, and Natchez became a part of the United States. When Gayoso left Natchez on 29 May 1797 to assume the West Florida governorship in New Orleans, he was applauded and toasted—a good way to end Spanish domination in what was soon to be Mississippi Territory.

Arthur H. DeRosier Jr.
Rocky Mountain College

Francis P. Burns, *Louisiana Historical Quarterly* (1928); William Dunbar, *Life, Letters, and Papers of William Dunbar*, ed. Eron Rowland (1930); Jack D. L. Holmes, *Gayoso, The Life of a Spanish Governor in the Mississippi Valley, 1789–1799* (1965); Lawrence Kinniard, ed., *Annual Report of the American Historical Association for the Year 1945* (1949); Catherine Van

Cortlandt Mathews, *Andrew Ellicott, His Life and Letters* (1908); Daniel H. Usner Jr., *American Indians in the Lower Mississippi Valley: Social and Economic Histories* (2003); Charles A. Weeks, *Paths to a Middle Ground: The Diplomacy of Natchez, Boukfouka, Nogales, and San Fernando de Las Barrancas, 1791–1795* (2005); Arthur Peterson Whitaker, ed., *Documents Relating to the Commercial Policy of Spain in the Floridas with Incidental Reference to Louisiana* (1931).

Speakes, Larry M.
(1939–2014) Press Secretary

Larry M. Speakes is best known as the press secretary for Pres. Ronald Reagan from 1981 to 1987. Speakes was born in Cleveland, Mississippi, on 13 September 1939, although his family lived in the small town of Merigold, about one hundred miles south of Memphis. His father, Harry Earl Speakes, a lifelong resident of Merigold, both worked at the family's grocery store and served as the branch manager of the Cleveland State Bank. Speakes's father worked at the grocery store until nine o'clock in the morning, when he would walk across the street to open the bank. At two o'clock in the afternoon, he would close the bank and go back to work at the grocery store. Speakes's mother, Ethlyn Fincher Speakes, was also a lifelong resident of Merigold. Speakes and several of his friends formed a band, the Cottonchoppers, when he was fourteen, and the group played several venues in western Mississippi and Arkansas. Speakes admits to trying to sound like Elvis, who made a great impression on the group of youngsters. Speakes's love of music continued into the White House, where he occasionally held Elvis trivia contests for the press corps.

During Speakes's senior year in high school, a trip to Washington, D.C., that included a visit to Mississippi senator James O. Eastland's office convinced Speakes that he wanted to enter politics and work in Washington. Speakes then studied journalism at the University of Mississippi, serving as associate editor of the campus newspaper, the *Mississippian*, and working as a stringer for the *Memphis Commercial Appeal*. Speakes left college without graduating to become the editor of a weekly newspaper in Oxford.

Speakes returned to the Delta in 1961 when he was hired to work at the *Bolivar Commercial* in Cleveland. He later worked as the county's deputy civil defense director.

In 1964 he was named editor of the *Bolivar Commercial*, and he left that position to become editor of the weekly *Leland Progress*.

In 1968, just eleven years after his high school visit to Eastland's office, Speakes became the senator's press secretary. Speakes subsequently served as a coordinator for Eastland's

1972 reelection campaign before joining the Nixon administration in 1974 as staff assistant to the president. Speakes later became press secretary to the special counsel to the president. After Nixon's resignation, Speakes became assistant press secretary to Pres. Gerald Ford.

Speakes left political life in 1977 when he became vice president of an international public relations firm, Hill and Knowlton. In 1980 he reentered politics when he joined the communications staff of the Reagan-Bush committee during the 1980 presidential election. When Reagan and his press secretary, James Brady, were shot in 1981, Speakes took over Brady's duties, although Brady retained the title of press secretary for the duration of Reagan's tenure. In 1983 Speakes was named President Reagan's chief spokesperson, and his years in the Reagan White House represented one of the longest stints of any Reagan aide. On behalf of the president, Speakes commented on such notable events as the explosion of the space shuttle *Challenger*, the military invasion of Grenada, the bombing of the US Marine barracks in Lebanon, the hijacking of a TWA plane in Lebanon and holding of forty American hostages, and the Iran-contra scandal, in which the administration traded arms to Iran to secure the release of American hostages.

Speakes left the White House in February 1987 for a public relations position with Merrill Lynch. He left that job the following year and released a book recounting his White House experiences. He later worked in public relations for the US Postal Service, eventually becoming head of advertising for the organization. He retired in 2008 and returned to Mississippi, where he died on 10 January 2014.

Melissa Smith
Mississippi University for Women

American Presidency Project, University of California at Santa Barbara website, www.presidency.ucsb.edu; Ronald Reagan, *The Reagan Diaries*, ed. Douglas Brinkley (2007); Larry Speakes, interview by Jeff Broadwater, John C. Stennis Oral History Project, Congressional and Presidential Research Center, Mississippi State University Library (1991); Larry Speakes, *Speaking Out* (1988).

Spencer, Elizabeth
(b. 1921) Author

Novelist Elizabeth Spencer was born on 19 July 1921, in Carrollton, an old Mississippi town of five hundred people on the eastern edge of the Delta. At an early age, she escaped social and familial strictures by riding her horse to her uncle

Elizabeth Spencer (Bern and Franke Keating Collection, Department of Archives and Special Collections, J. D. Williams Library, University of Mississippi)

Joe McCain's plantation at Teoc, thirteen miles away. This distancing freed her to observe the inhabitants of Carrollton, as she later recounted in her memoir, *Landscapes of the Heart* (1998).

Both sides of Spencer's family settled in Carroll County as early as the 1830s. Her mother's family, the McCains, were big readers, and her mother read to her often from her library, which included Greek and Roman myths, the Arthurian legends, and the Bible. The McCains talked about characters as if they were part of the family. "It was a shame," they might say, "that Fantine (in *Les Miserables*) had to sell all her hair and teeth." Because her brother, James Luther Spencer Jr., was seven years her senior, Spencer kept herself company early on by writing adventure stories. Spencer's father, James Luther Spencer, was a strict Presbyterian who neither encouraged nor supported Elizabeth's writing aspirations. Nevertheless, Spencer attended Belhaven College in Jackson and majored in English, graduating in 1942.

During her senior year, as president of the literary society, Spencer invited Eudora Welty to be the society's guest. It was a short distance for Welty to walk, just across Pinehurst Street, but momentous for Spencer, strengthening her desire to be a writer. In her foreword to *The Stories of Elizabeth Spencer* (1983), Welty describes Spencer's grace and the way her dark blue eyes indicated that she was "a jump ahead of you": "The main thing about her was blazingly clear—this girl was serious. She was indeed already a writer."

Spencer attended graduate school at Vanderbilt University, earning a master's degree in 1943 under Fugitive poet Donald Davidson. Spencer then taught briefly, worked as a reporter, and saved up five hundred dollars, enough to sustain her for a year while she wrote her first novel, *Fire in the Morning* (1948). Before the manuscript was completed, Davidson found her a publisher, and she used the book's meager royalties to hop a freighter to France and travel in Germany and Italy. She taught English and creative writing at the University of Mississippi from 1948–51 and 1952–53. In 1953 she returned to Italy on a Guggenheim fellowship.

Italy provided Spencer with the distance she needed to write *The Voice at the Back Door* (1956), about the night when the Spencers' maid in Carrollton, Laura Henley, showed up at their back door, brutally beaten. Italy also provided the setting for her most famous work, *Light in the Piazza* (1960), and its companion, *Knights and Dragons* (1965). Written in about a month, *Light in the Piazza* became a popular movie and in 2005 a highly acclaimed Broadway musical.

Because Spencer's first three novels are set in Mississippi during the 1940s and 1950s and are concerned with race relations, various critics have deemed her a southern writer. But in subsequent works, beginning with two novellas set in Italy, she broke new ground. In *No Place for an Angel* (1967) she examines the emptiness in the lives of the rich and powerful in such far-flung settings as Washington, D.C., and Key West. In *The Snare* (1972), set in New Orleans, the protagonist, Julia, becomes caught up in the evil underbelly of that city. Conscientious objectors to the Vietnam War who escaped to Canada are the subject of *The Night Travelers* (1991), set in North Carolina and Montreal. Though male characters dominate her early fiction, her female protagonists, such as Nancy in the short story "Ship Island," prove equally compelling when pushing against social, familial, or cultural expectations.

The constant in Spencer's fiction is the captured moment that reveals connection to or alienation from the larger web, be it small town or whole continent. In *The Voice at the Back Door*, it is found in an instant when a white man invites a black man to sit in the front seat of his car. In "The Legacy" it is found when a young girl extracts a promise from her lawyer to keep her ten-thousand-dollar inheritance a secret.

Author of nine novels, five collections of short stories, an exquisite memoir, and a play, Elizabeth Spencer has mastered all these forms. Because she is cosmopolitan, her themes universal, her mind original and versatile, categorizing her is a happy impossibility. She has won numerous awards over her nearly seven-decade career, including the William Faulkner Medal for Literary Excellence, the Mississippi Governor's Award for Achievement in Literature, the Lifetime Achievement Award from the Mississippi Institute of Arts and Letters, the PEN/Malamud Award for Short Fiction, and the Sidney Lanier Award for Southern Fiction. She lives in Chapel Hill, North Carolina.

Marion Barnwell
Jackson, Mississippi

Mississippi Writers and Musicians website, www.mswritersandmusicians .com; Peggy Whitman Prenshaw, ed., *Conversations with Elizabeth Spencer* (1991); Peggy Whitman Prenshaw, *Elizabeth Spencer* (1985); Terry Roberts, *Self and Community in the Fiction of Elizabeth Spencer* (1994); Elizabeth Spencer website, www.elizabethspencerwriter.com.

Split-Ticket Voting

Split-ticket voting occurs when a voter casts his or her ballot for members of different political parties for different offices. It contrasts with straight-ticket voting, in which a citizen votes for the candidates of the same political party for all offices on the ballot in a particular election year.

In virtually all elections from the end of Reconstruction in 1877 to the 1960s, Mississippi, like most of the South, was an entirely one-party state: the Democrats held nearly every elected office and won the state in almost all presidential elections. Political conflicts were settled in the Democratic primary. Mississippi voted for Strom Thurmond's segregationist States' Rights Party in 1948 and an unpledged slate of electors in 1960 but did not support a Republican candidate for president until 1964, when Barry Goldwater, an opponent of the Civil Rights Act of 1964, won the state over Pres. Lyndon Johnson, taking 87 percent of the vote. Mississippi did not elect a Republican US representative until 1964, and Thad Cochran became the first Republican US senator since Reconstruction when he won a three-way race to succeed retiring Democrat James O. Eastland in 1978. In 1991 Kirk Fordice defeated incumbent Ray Mabus to become the first Republican governor since Reconstruction. Split-ticket voting could not become a significant phenomenon in Mississippi until Republicans began to compete seriously in elections.

In recent decades the GOP has become the dominant party in Mississippi, though split-ticket voting remained significant, at least until the second decade of the twenty-first century. After the 2007 elections Republicans held all but one statewide elected executive office, yet the Democratic Party maintained majorities in both houses of the state legislature, and most county and local officials were Democrats. Thus, some Mississippians were engaging in split-ticket voting. Those who did so tended to chose Republicans for higher-level offices and Democrats for lower-level offices. However, Republicans have steadily gained strength down the ballot, and in 2011 the GOP took control of the State House of Representatives for the first time since Reconstruction. The shift toward the Republican Party continued through the 2015 elections.

Split-ticket voting is largely a racial phenomenon in Mississippi. In the state with the most racially polarized electorate in the United States, the vast majority of African American voters have voted Democrat for nearly all offices from president to local officials. When split-ticket voting occurs, it generally involves conservative white voters who support conservative white Democratic candidates for state and especially local positions.

For example, Gene Taylor, a Democrat from southern Mississippi, won a seat in Congress in a 1989 special election and won reelection every two years thereafter, usually by landslide margins of victory, despite the fact that his district was the most Republican congressional district in the state in presidential elections. Taylor compiled a conservative voting record on military, foreign policy, and cultural issues and was one of the few House Democrats to support the impeachment of Pres. Bill Clinton. Taylor's conservative constituents rewarded him for his positions. In 2004 Pres. George W. Bush won the district with 68 percent of the vote in his reelection campaign, while Taylor won reelection with 64 percent. However, Republican Steven Palazzo defeated Taylor in 2011, illustrating the decline in split-ticket voting.

In recent decades split-ticket voting in Mississippi has largely been a case of some conservative white voters' willingness to cast a ballot for conservative white Democratic candidates.

Donald W. Beachler
Ithaca College

Ballotpedia: The Encyclopedia of American Politics website, https:// ballotpedia.org/Main_Page; Donald W. Beachler, *Politics and Policy* (December 2001); V. O. Key, *Southern Politics in State and Nation* (1949); Alexander P. Lamis, *Southern Politics in the 1990s* (1999); Alexander P. Lamis, *The Two-Party South* (2nd ed., 1990).

Sports

Mississippi sports history has featured epic figures such as Archie Manning and Steve McNair, Charlie Conerly and Walter Payton, Margaret Wade and Lusia Harris-Stewart, Sue Gunter and Peggie Gillom-Granderson, Cool Papa Bell and Dizzy Dean. During the first sixty years of the twentieth century, sports were segregated throughout the state. Legal segregation produced three major white postsecondary educational institutions (the University of Mississippi [founded in 1848], Mississippi State University [1878], and the University of Southern Mississippi [1910]) along with three major black institutions (Alcorn State University [1871], Jackson State University [1877], and Mississippi Valley State University [1950]). Sports and the athletes who played them have given each institution a unique history and continuing place among Mississippians. That legacy arguably can be traced to the post–World War II years, when the major sports in general began to see significant growth in fan support and enthusiasm across the country.

Mississippi has never been home to any professional franchise in the major sports of baseball, basketball, or football but has produced numerous players who have starred in those sports. Two early twentieth-century baseball players encapsulate the dual society and the opportunities afforded to individuals based on skin color. James "Cool Papa" Bell was born in Starkville, while Jay Hanna "Dizzy" Dean was a longtime resident of Wiggins. Bell was a star outfielder in the Negro Leagues between 1922 and 1946; Dean was arguably the best pitcher in the Major Leagues during the early 1930s before an arm injury shortened his career. Before Jackie Robinson integrated Major League Baseball in 1947, players from the Majors and the Negro Leagues played against each other in off-season exhibition games, with the black players winning two-thirds of the time. Negro League great Satchel Paige faced off against Dean six times in 1934 and 1935, with Paige winning four of those games. Dean was one of the few white Major Leaguers to publicly admit that many Negro League players had more than enough talent to play in the Majors. Paige, a teammate of Bell's during the early 1930s, summed up Bell's speed: "If Cool Papa had known about colleges or if colleges had known about Cool Papa, Jesse Owens would have looked like he was walking."

Other baseball notables with Mississippi connections include Mississippi State head coach Ron Polk, whose teams won more than eleven hundred games during his twenty-nine seasons in Starkville. During Polk's tenure, Mississippi State produced Major Leaguers Will Clark, Rafael Palmeiro, Bobby Thigpen, and Jeff Brantley. Like Polk, McComb native Willie "Rat" McGowen had a stellar coaching career. In his forty years as head coach at Alcorn State (1968–2009), the Braves won 720 games. Don Kessinger, an all–Southeastern Conference shortstop at the University of Mississippi in the early 1960s, played for three teams during his sixteen Major League seasons. Meridian's Dennis "Oil Can" Boyd attended Jackson State before moving on to a ten-year Major League career.

Mississippians have also had significant roles in the history of women's basketball. McCool native Margaret Wade played at Delta State in the early 1930s. After a long hiatus, the school brought back women's basketball in 1973, and Wade became the coach. Her teams dominated, winning three championships and posting a fifty-one-game winning streak. She is a member of the Naismith Memorial Basketball Hall of Fame, and the trophy awarded to the top collegiate women's player is named in her honor. Walnut Grove's Sue Gunter coached women's basketball (and three other sports) at Stephen F. Austin University from 1965 to 1980. After coaching the US women's team that did not get to compete in the 1980 Olympics because of the US boycott,

Gunter took over the women's program at Louisiana State University, posting a 442–221 record between 1983 and her retirement in 2004. Wade's and Gunter's accomplishments both directly and indirectly created new opportunities for Mississippi's female basketball players. Among the most notable have been Minter City native Lusia Harris-Stewart, who was a dominating player at Delta State from 1975 to 1977 and a member of the silver-medal-winning 1976 US Olympic team; Abbeville sisters Peggie Gillom-Granderson and Jennifer Gillom, who starred at the University of Mississippi in the 1970s and 1980s; and Greenville's LaToya Thomas, who holds all-time scoring record—for both men and women—at Mississippi State and who played in the Women's National Basketball League from 2003 to 2008.

The state's notable men's basketball players include Naismith Memorial Basketball Hall of Famer Bailey Howell, who starred at Mississippi State in the late 1950s before going on to a twelve-year career in the National Basketball Association (NBA). In 1963 the Mississippi State men's basketball team became the state's first white institution to play against an integrated team when it met Loyola University of Chicago in the National Collegiate Athletic Association Tournament. Jeff Malone played at Mississippi State from 1980 to 1983 and for four NBA teams over his thirteen-year career. Jackson State's Purvis Short, a native of Hattiesburg, spent fourteen seasons in the NBA beginning in the late 1970s. Gulfport native Mahmoud Abdul-Rauf (Chris Jackson) was one of the most recognizable figures in American basketball from the late 1980s to the mid-1990s. NBA players who began their basketball careers in the Jackson public school system have included Lindsey Hunter and Monta Ellis (Lanier High School) and Mo Williams (Murrah High School).

Football arguably elicits the most fan support in the state. More than 240 of Mississippi's public high schools and 80 private high schools field teams, and Friday night games are the biggest events in many small towns. Many of these high school players go on to play at the collegiate level, and some have become stars in the National Football League (NFL). Clarksdale's Charlie Conerly played at the University of Mississippi around the time of World War II before spending fourteen years with the New York Giants and leading the team to the 1956 NFL championship. The trophy given to the state's top collegiate player is named in his honor. Drew native Archie Manning is truly legendary in the state, not only for his stints as quarterback at the University of Mississippi (1967–71) and in the NFL (1971–84) but also because two of his sons, Peyton and Eli, have gone on to have exceptional collegiate and professional careers. Archie Manning set numerous records on the field, though perhaps his greatest achievement was his exciting style of play, which brought positive national exposure to the university just a few years after the riot that accompanied James Meredith's integration of the school showed a very different picture.

Jackson State, Mississippi Valley State, and the University of Southern Mississippi have arguably produced the three greatest NFL players at their positions, Columbia's Walter Payton, Crawford's Jerry Rice, and Gulfport's Brett Favre. Running back Walter Payton, a Columbia native who attended Jackson State, was twice named the league's Most Valuable Player and helped the Bears to victory in the 1986 Super Bowl. Wide receiver Jerry Rice of Crawford was relatively obscure while in college at Mississippi Valley State in the early 1980s but won four Super Bowls with the San Francisco 49ers and retired after the 2004 season as the holder of numerous NFL records. Kiln's Brett Favre quarterbacked Southern Mississippi from 1987 to 1991 and finished as the school's career leader in passing yards, completions, and touchdowns before going on to win three NFL MVP awards with the Green Bay Packers, setting many league records over his twenty seasons.

Other notable NFL players from Mississippi include quarterback Steve McNair of Mount Olive, who starred at Alcorn State and for the NFL's Tennessee Titans and Baltimore Ravens; running back Deuce McAllister of Jackson, who played at the University of Mississippi and for the New Orleans Saints; and wide receiver Eric Moulds, a Lucedale native who attended Mississippi State before playing twelve seasons in the NFL, mostly with the Buffalo Bills. On 1 December 2003 Mississippi State hired Sylvester Croom, the first African American head football coach not only at the school but also in the Southeastern Conference.

Outside of team sports, Mississippi offers hunters more than two million acres of wild game habitats within the forty-one state wildlife management areas, twelve National Wildlife Refuges, and six National Forests. Some of the most popular game species include white-tailed deer, eastern wild turkey, and migratory waterfowl as well as small game species such as mourning dove, quail, squirrel, and rabbit. White-tailed deer is the most popular species and can be found in abundant numbers throughout Mississippi, which has the highest deer density per acre in the nation.

Fishing is also one of the most popular outdoor activities in Mississippi. The region's mild climate promotes a year-round growing season for the state's game fish, and the Mississippi Department of Wildlife, Fisheries, and Parks operates twenty-four fishing lakes offering a total of 6,044 acres of picturesque waters. Approximately 175 different species of freshwater fish are found in Mississippi, and the Gulf of Mexico offers saltwater fishing. Species that live in the Mississippi River include catfish, walleye, carp, and gar.

Mississippi has more than 145 golf courses that can test the skill of every level of golfer. Outstanding public courses include the Preserve Golf Club in Ocean Springs, Cranbrake Golf Club in Hattiesburg, Dancing Rabbit Golf Club in Philadelphia, and the Dogwoods at Hugh White State Park in Grenada.

Sports have played a pivotal role in Mississippi's social, economic, and political life, and that impact has arguably been strongest in the area of race relations. Mississippians black and white, young and old, male and female participate in and are fans of sports that were segregated until the 1960s. Since 1992 the State Games of Mississippi have brought together thousands of athletes of all ages and skill levels each June to compete in more than thirty sporting events. The fact that the citizens of Mississippi take for granted integrated sporting events, venues, and teams testifies to the impact sports have had on the state.

Charles Ross
University of Mississippi

Dick Clark and Larry Lester, eds., *The Negro Leagues Book* (1994); Patrick Miller, ed., *The Sporting World of the Modern South* (2002); Jules Tygiel, *Baseball's Great Experiment: Jackie Robinson and His Legacy* (1983).

Staples, Pops, and the Staple Singers
(1914–2000) Blues and Gospel Musician

Noted for his soft singing style and complementary, tremolo-laden guitar, Roebuck "Pops" Staples and his family band, the Staple Singers, changed the pop music landscape by fusing Mississippi blues and gospel with lyrics of uplift and identity. The youngest of fourteen children, Staples was born on a cotton plantation near Kilmichael on 28 December 1914 and raised near Drew. His introduction to music came through the church, and permutations of gospel music remained the dominant force throughout his recording career. He left school in the eighth grade to pick cotton, and local musicians including the legendary Charlie Patton and Robert Johnson soon introduced him to the blues. Staples's early solo guitar work reflected both gospel and blues influences. In addition, he performed spirituals with gospel groups such as the Golden Trumpets and the Four Trumpets.

In 1934 Staples, his wife, Osceola, and their daughter, Cleotha, relocated to Chicago, where he worked in the stockyards as a packer and killer. During World War II he found work in steel mills. During this era, he sang with gospel groups such as the Trumpet Jubilees, though he did not touch a guitar for twelve years. The family grew, and with Osceola Staples working evening shifts, Pops spent time teaching their children to sing. These lessons resulted in the creation of the Staple Singers, which included Pops; daughters Mavis, Cleotha, and Yvonne; and son Pervis.

The group began singing at churches and on gospel radio in Chicago and around the Midwest and recorded for Chicago's Vee-Jay Records from 1956 to 1962. Their first major single, "Uncloudy Day," hit the charts in 1959. During the 1960s the Staple Singers began to fuse their gospel leanings with the message-type folk songs associated with the civil rights movement, resulting in music that resonated with sounds of the church yet was also connected to the popular counterculture and social movements.

The Staple Singers' move to Memphis-based Stax Records in the late 1960s resulted in their most famous recordings. Their gospel and message-oriented songs were partnered with the label's soul and funk aesthetic, resulting in hits such as "Heavy Makes You Happy (Sha-Na-Boom Boom)" and "Respect Yourself." Released in 1972, "I'll Take You There" reached No. 1 on the Billboard Hot 100 and catapulted the band and its mission of black identity and uplift before mainstream audiences. Particular to their sound was the meeting of Pops's gentle singing style with Mavis's raspy soul vocals, and their chart success sustained through a second No. 1, "Let's Do It Again," released on Curtis Mayfield's Custom label in 1975. The band continued to record albums through 1991. Pops and Mavis Staples performed on "The Weight" in Martin Scorsese's 1976 documentary, *The Last Waltz*, and recorded successful solo albums. Pops's *Father Father* marked a return to his Mississippi blues and gospel roots and earned him a 1995 Grammy Award. In 1999 the Staple Singers were inducted into the Rock and Roll Hall of Fame.

Pops Staples died on 19 December 2000.

Charles Williams
Winona, Mississippi

Odie Lindsey
Nashville, Tennessee

Vladimir Bogdanov, Chris Woodstra, Stephen Thomas Erlewine, eds., *All Music Guide to the Blues: The Definitive Guide to the Blues* (2003); National Endowment for the Arts website, http://arts.endow.gov.

Starke, Peter Burwell
(1815–1888) Confederate General

Confederate general Peter Burwell Starke was born in 1815 in Brunswick County, Virginia. He moved to Bolivar County in the early 1840s and became a planter, running unsuccessfully for Congress as a Whig in 1846 but serving several terms in the state legislature in the 1850s. When war erupted, he was a state senator representing Bolivar, Issaquena, and Washington Counties, a post he retained until early 1862. His secessionist sentiments were clearly displayed in February 1860, when he sent resolutions to Virginia requesting that his native state join South Carolina and Mississippi in

convention with an eye to adopting measures necessary for the "protection and perpetuation" of "African Slavery."

Starke was commissioned colonel of the 28th Mississippi Cavalry Regiment on 24 February 1862. His command operated near Vicksburg until it shifted to the upper portion of the Yazoo-Mississippi Delta, where it skirmished with a Federal expedition under Alvin P. Hovey that advanced toward Grenada in late 1862. The following January his regiment combined with two other Mississippi units to form a brigade under Brig. Gen. George Cosby. The troopers participated in a movement into Tennessee led by Maj. Gen. Earl Van Dorn. Cosby's command returned to Mississippi and guarded an approach to Vicksburg via Mechanicsburg. After Vicksburg fell, Starke's cavalry helped screen Joseph E. Johnston's army as it retreated from Jackson. As part of a division under Brig. Gen. William H. Jackson, Starke operated in the vicinity of Clinton in late July, then helped turn back and harassed a Federal column moving toward Canton in mid-October. Starke won praise from his superiors when he sparred regularly with a force under Maj. Gen. William Tecumseh Sherman that cut through the interior of the state to Meridian in February 1864.

Starke served as a brigade commander from December 1863 until he was superseded by the arrival of Brig. Gen. Frank C. Armstrong on 6 April 1864. Returning to his regimental command, he and his men participated in the Atlanta Campaign. They particularly distinguished themselves at New Hope Church on 28 May, when they briefly captured several guns of an Iowa battery. Starke won promotion to brigadier general on 4 November 1864, and his cavalry clashed repeatedly with Federal horsemen during John Bell Hood's ill-fated Tennessee Campaign. Starke's command and others under Nathan Bedford Forrest protected the rear guard of the shattered Army of Tennessee as it retreated following the Battle of Nashville. On 18 February 1865 Forrest selected Starke to lead one of three Mississippi cavalry brigades under Brig. Gen. James R. Chalmers. After organizing his brigade at Columbus, Starke attempted to intercept the Union forces led by Brig. Gen. James H. Wilson that routed Forrest at Selma in early April. Starke signed a parole at Gainesville, Alabama, on 12 May. His older brother, William Edward Starke, was a Confederate division commander killed at Antietam.

After the war Starke served as a member of the board of Mississippi levee commissioners from 1866 to 1872 and was sheriff of Bolivar County for one term. Starke returned to Virginia in 1873, where he lived near his boyhood home in Lawrenceville until his death on 13 July 1888.

Christopher Losson
St. Joseph, Missouri

Edwin C. Bearss, in *The Confederate General*, ed. William C. Harris (1991); Charles E. Hooker, *Confederate Military History: Mississippi*, ed. Clement A. Evans (1899); *New York Times* (24 February 1860).

"Starkville City Jail"

They're bound to get you.
'Cause they got a curfew.
And you go to the Starkville City jail.
—Johnny Cash (1932–2003)

Johnny Cash wrote "Starkville City Jail" after his arrest in the small Mississippi town on 11 May 1965. Cash had played two shows on the campus of Mississippi State University (at the animal husbandry building and the Pi Kappa Alpha fraternity house) the preceding evening, and at about five o'clock in the morning, police arrested him for picking flowers.

Cash played the song during a February 1969 concert at California's San Quentin prison that was recorded and released the following June as an album, *Johnny Cash at San Quentin*. As with much of Cash's music, "Starkville City Jail" evokes an image familiar to his fans—that of the Man in Black, hardened by years of drinking and drug abuse (which likely played a role in the actions leading to his arrest)—and offers a peek into rural life and its struggles.

Listeners not familiar with Cash's past might categorize "Starkville City Jail" as a protest song—a one-man indictment of small-town government rules and restrictions. Indeed, the image of Starkville suggested in Cash's song seems consistent with negative public perceptions of Mississippi. However, Mississippi's recognition of its troubled past and the state's continued attempts to move beyond that past echo Cash's struggles to overcome his drug and alcohol addictions.

Glenn D. "Pete" Smith Jr.
Mississippi State University

Johnny Cash, *Ring of Fire: The Johnny Cash Reader*, ed., Michael Streissguth (2003); Dan Malone, *Reflector* (September 2007).

Starkville Cotton District

Before the term *New Urbanism* was invented, developer Dan Camp was working out its basic concepts in the Cotton District, an upscale to midscale mixed-use neighborhood in Starkville, home to Mississippi State University and a natural market for Camp's innovative mix of shops, townhomes, apartments, and streets.

Termed the "most photographed" area of the university town, the Cotton District takes its name from Starkville history. The area once called Needmore, bounded by Lummus Drive, Holtsinger and Maxwell Streets, and University Drive, was built as tenant housing for workers at the Sanders Cotton Mill in 1926. The mill scaled back operations in the 1950s and shut down completely by 1964. Camp began developing the area in 1969, first building fourplexes on small lots on Lummus Drive and renting them to students and young professionals.

By the turn of the twenty-first century, the development contained more than two hundred duplexes, fourplexes, apartments, townhouses, and cottages in varying architectural styles, ranging from the Charleston-style townhomes on Planters Row to the Seven Sisters, a set of cottages named after women in Camp's family. In addition to Charleston, South Carolina, Camp has cited New Orleans; Alexandria, Virginia; and Vicksburg as inspiration for the classical details in his construction. Design hallmarks of Cotton District buildings include courtyards and fountains reminiscent of New Orleans, wood-post foundations based on an early Mississippi architectural style, and custom millwork, windows, and posts created by Camp's stable of craftsmen, including Camp himself.

New Urbanism is an architectural movement that encourages redevelopment of urban areas through the renovation of older buildings and the creation of mixed-use communities that offer residents easy access to goods and services. Architects founded the Congress for the New Urbanism in 1993, but "Dan Camp was practicing new urbanism for at least twenty years before new urbanism had a name," according to charter member Victor Dover, a Florida architect.

Urban planners have come to consider the combination of livable, affordable, practical, and organic development that the Cotton District exemplifies as a model and are amazed at how Camp has made low-cost housing not only beautiful but profitable. Said Dover, "He's achieved affordable housing, which is the holy grail of city planning in America today, without . . . the government paying part of the bill."

The Cotton District continues to garner national attention, with shows as varied as HGTV's *Dream Builders* and the Turner South Network's *Three-Day Weekend* featuring the area on television. "Everybody said I was the town fool," Camp told the *Mississippi Business Journal* in 2003, "but I knew I needed a better mousetrap."

Julie Whitehead
Brandon, Mississippi

Dan Camp, telephone interview by author (2003); Cotton District website, www.thecottondistrict.net; Victor Dover, "Peer Review: Dan Camp's Cotton District," paper presented at the Congress for the New Urbanism (2003); Victor Dover, telephone interview by author (2003); Wilton J. "Bill" Johnson Jr., *Mississippi Business Journal* (31 July 2000).

S

States' Rights

The US Constitution of 1787 did not enumerate the powers of the states. Article I, Section 8 laid out the powers of the national government in terms of congressional lawmaking authority and said that the national government would be limited to those powers. But some powers granted to the national government were extremely vague, creating the potential for the federal government to expand into areas such as commerce that had previously been the exclusive purview of the states. And since that time, these provisions, combined with Article VI, the National Supremacy Clause, have allowed national government power to expand at the expense of the states.

The Tenth Amendment, ratified as a part of the Bill of Rights in 1791, addressed the issue: "The powers not delegated to the United States by the Constitution, nor prohibited by it to the states, are reserved to the states respectively, or to the people." The phrase to the people remains something of a mystery, but the reserved to the states phraseology has provided the framework for constitutional and political arguments for a large role for states in the federal system. States have laid claim to "police powers"—powers to protect and promote citizens' health, safety, morals, welfare, and convenience. Included within this broad area would be the gamut of domestic governmental activity, with no need to look at a state constitution for authorization—only for explicit prohibitions or limitations.

States' rights advocates are as old as the Constitution. Beginning with Thomas Jefferson and James Madison in the 1790s and continuing through the twenty-first-century governors of western states, constitutional and political arguments have suggested that the national government has exceeded its authority and capacity, intruding into the legitimate domain of the states.

Mississippi has been among the states in which political leaders most frequently and vigorously invoked the doctrine of states' rights. In the 1820s and 1830s Mississippi was a bastion of Jacksonian Democrats, who strongly opposed centralizing tendencies in monetary policy and commercial regulation. Soon thereafter, the issue of slavery became the focus of states' righters. Abraham Lincoln's 1860 election to the presidency was a blow to the states' rights movement and the institution of slavery, and Mississippi quickly followed South Carolina in claiming the ultimate state right: the right to secede from the Union.

The Civil War ended slavery but did not destroy the doctrine of states' rights. Even before Reconstruction ended in 1877, Mississippi political leaders staked a claim to the authority to regulate race relations. In its 1890 Constitution Mississippi concocted devices to firmly establish racial segregation and to disfranchise the black population (then a substantial majority). For several decades in the late nineteenth and early twentieth centuries the US Supreme Court sustained the power of the states to regulate most commercial and social relationships.

The Great Depression and the New Deal marked a shift away from state autonomy and toward an increasingly powerful national government. National responses to the economic crisis of the 1930s and the centralizing forces in marshaling economic as well as military power during World War II marked a significant expansion of national authority. However, until the 1950s, Mississippi and other southern states remained largely unaffected in their quest to preserve racial segregation and deny voting rights to blacks.

Mississippi's power to control race relations did not face serious challenges until the civil rights movement of the 1950s and 1960s. The federal courts, the president, and the US Congress gave new life to the Equal Protection Clause of the Fourteenth Amendment. Led by Gov. Ross Barnett, Mississippi officials defended the "southern way of life," often invoking the doctrine of states' rights by contending that "state sovereignty" trumped the equal protection language of the Fourteenth Amendment.

The states' rights doctrine is not dead, though virtually no one still contends that states have the right to secede from the Union. States outside the South occasionally invoke the doctrine. Oregon's defense of its assisted suicide law and California's defense of its more stringent fuel efficiency requirements represent modern examples of the old but persistent doctrine of states' rights. In Mississippi, conservative responses to the Affordable Care Act and to *Obergefell v. Hodges*, the 2015 Supreme Court decision that overturned state laws against same-sex marriage, have included vehement defenses of states' rights.

Joseph Parker
University of Southern Mississippi

James J. Kilpatrick, *The Sovereign States: Notes of a Citizen of Virginia* (1957); Mississippi State Sovereignty Commission, Message from Mississippi (film, 1960); James F. Zimmerman, Contemporary American Federalism (1992).

Steamboats

As in most of the South, waterways enormously influenced developments in Mississippi. The Mississippi River forms the state's western boundary, while the Gulf of Mexico stretches across the southern border. Elsewhere, rivers such as the Big Black, Pascagoula, Pearl, Tennessee, and Tombigbee and the

The *Natchez* and the *Robert E. Lee* race from New Orleans up the Mississippi River to St. Louis, June 1870 (Charles Reagan Wilson Collection, Center for the Study of Southern Culture, University of Mississippi)

interconnected streams that form the Yazoo River system played important roles in settlement and economic activity.

In 1811 the journey of the steamboat *New Orleans* down the Mississippi presaged the rise of a transportation system that affected the state for more than a century. Although keelboats and flatboats remained viable watercraft throughout the antebellum era, steamboats gradually grew in importance. By 1830 steamboats operated on all the major tributaries of the Mississippi, although the trade on most was dominated by boats of smaller tonnage that ran in the spring and fall. On the Mississippi itself, early steamboats connected New Orleans and Natchez. Antebellum Mississippi River communities such as Commerce, Bolivar, Prentiss, Greenville, and Vicksburg existed in large measure because of the steamboats that landed at their doorsteps. Other nascent towns such as Columbus on the Tombigbee and Yazoo River towns such as Greenwood and Yazoo City (originally Hannan's Bluff) were buoyed by steamboat access. As boats became larger and more numerous, they played a corresponding role in cultural and economic affairs. Steamboats carried away many Choctaw who ceded their lands in northwest Mississippi in 1830 and in turn brought in settlers eager to stake claims to these areas. Steamboats likewise carried large numbers of slaves to their destinations, especially in the fertile wilderness of the Yazoo-Mississippi Delta.

Steamboats transformed the lives of Mississippians, carrying livestock and farm produce from hundreds of individual landings and conveying manufactured goods of every conceivable sort to plantations and towns. The boats offered passengers a conduit to the outside world, served as an information source, and forged community by linking residents along the state's waterways. An enormous variation in size and shape characterized these vessels, from small unadorned workhorses to large, lavishly decorated steamers, but all played roles in the market economy that hinged on river travel.

The nature of southern rivers and the emphasis on carrying freight ultimately led to development of a distinctive design for steamboats on these waters. The typical steamboat was erected on a relatively narrow and shallow flat-bottomed hull. After the mid-1820s most vessels were powered by noisy high-pressure steam engines. Several decks projected above the waterline, with larger steamboats possessing a main deck, a boiler deck, a hurricane, and a texas. Towering above were twin chimneys that carried away the soot and smoke generated by the engine and created a natural draft in the furnace. The vast majority of boats that plied Mississippi's rivers were constructed in Ohio River shipyards at Cincinnati; Jeffersonville, Indiana; Louisville; and Pittsburgh. Steamboat crews varied in size, from perhaps five men for a small boat to several dozen for the larger vessels. Officers were almost invariably native-born white men, while antebellum deck crews included immigrants, slaves, and a few free blacks. The proportion of slaves employed expanded throughout the antebellum era. After the Civil War, African Americans formed a large proportion of cabin and deck crew hands, while other blacks found employment in shipyards and as roustabouts on the levees and wharfs.

The shallow hull contributed to the relatively low life expectancy of a steamboat on Mississippi waters. Snags often resulted in the destruction of boats, although pilots often could maneuver stricken vessels close enough to shore to save both passengers and cargo. One notable exception occurred in late January 1851 above Greenville, when the sidewheeler *John Adams* was broken in half by a snag and sank immediately, killing roughly 123 of the 230 people aboard. Countless other hazards existed, including collisions, sandbars, fire, fog, and storms. Steamboats occasionally struck previously sunken vessels. Boiler explosions could have particularly devastating impacts. In most cases, the valuable machinery was salvaged from steamboat wrecks and transplanted into new vessels.

Mississippi's secession altered life for steamboat owners, captains, and crews. Many steamboats went on the Confederate registry and hauled troops, provisions, and war materiel. Other captains found opportunities doing likewise for the Federals. Both the Union and Confederate governments chartered boats, and wartime demand was so great that many older steamboats found ample work despite their deficiencies. Some were eventually converted into gunboats, rams, or cottonclads. Confederate lieutenant Isaac N. Brown created a naval yard at Yazoo City that produced the formidable ironclad CSS *Arkansas* before being destroyed in May 1862 when a Union flotilla was steaming up the Yazoo. While the war fattened the pockets of some owners, others lost their boats to capture, burning, or deliberate scuttling. Steamboats played a major role in the Vicksburg Campaign and other wartime operations, were instrumental in the thriving (and often illegal) cotton trade, and hauled away thousands of slaves fleeing Mississippi plantations.

Mississippi steamboating reached its zenith in the postwar years. Opulent vessels such as the *J. M. White*, *Natchez*, and *Robert E. Lee* attracted widespread attention and symbolize

S

the grand era of steamboat travel. These boats and dozens of others conveyed thousands of bales of cotton from Mississippi landings and levees to New Orleans. Trade was carried on by individually owned boats apt to move from one river to another, by packets that made regular trips at scheduled intervals, and by lines of two or more steamboats that offered packet service in a particular trade, such as New Orleans to Natchez or Vicksburg to Greenville. Merchants in river towns often used very small steamboats to deliver sundries, plantation supplies, and even ice to customers along the rivers. A few boats were converted to mobile sawmills or cotton gins. The steady encroachment of railroad lines gradually sapped business from the steamboats and led to a slow decline in river commerce.

Only a few steamboats still operated in the 1920s, and the automobile age doomed these holdouts. Despite their demise, the idealized image of steamboats churning along Mississippi rivers exerts a powerful hold on the modern imagination and forms a romantic component of the "moonlight and magnolias" image cultivated by tourism officials.

Christopher Losson
St. Joseph, Missouri

Louis C. Hunter, *Steamboats on the Western Rivers: An Economic and Technological History* (1949); Adam I. Kane, *The Western River Steamboat* (2004); Harry P. Owens, *Steamboats and the Cotton Economy: River Trade in the Yazoo-Mississippi Delta* (1990); Frederick Way Jr., *Way's Packet Directory* (1983, 1994).

Stein Mart

Stein Mart is a chain of discount department stores selling women's, men's, and children's clothing as well as shoes, fragrances, jewelry, bed and bath linens, home accessories, and gifts. The company, which began in Greenville, Mississippi, caters to an upscale clientele by stocking brand-name merchandise and boutique goods and emphasizing customer service and vendor relationships.

In 1908 Russian immigrant Sam Stein opened the Greenville store bearing his name. At his retirement, Stein turned over the business to his son, Jake, who incorporated it in Mississippi in 1968. The company's transition from a local department store began in the late 1970s when Jay Stein succeeded his father, Jake, as chief executive officer. In 1977 Stein Mart opened a store in Memphis and redirected its focus from that of a discount department store to a fashion store.

The company continued to expand, and a third Stein Mart store opened in Nashville in 1980. That year, Jay Stein hired Jack Williams as executive vice president and charged him with helping the chain to grow beyond its regional market. Throughout the early 1980s, Stein Mart continued to grow, opening its first store in Jacksonville, Florida, in 1983 and moving the corporate headquarters there the following year.

By 1992 the company operated forty-five stores, and it incorporated in Florida and became a publicly traded company, listed on the NASDAQ. At the turn of the twenty-first century, the chain had more than two hundred stores in twenty-nine states. In August 2001 Jay Stein retired as chief executive officer; his successor, Williams, became the first head of the company who was not a member of the Stein family, though Jay Stein remained the largest stockholder and chair of the board. In March 2015 Dawn H. Robertson became chief executive officer.

In 2016 the company operated 278 stores in thirty states as well as an Internet store and employed about eleven thousand people.

Carolyn Cooper Howard
University of Mississippi

Mark Basch, *Florida Times-Union* (22 July 2002); David J. Ginzl, *Stein Mart: An American Story of Roots, Family, and Building a Greater Dream* (2014); Don Hogsett, *Home Textiles Today* (10 June 2002); Stein Mart 2015 Annual Report. http://ir.steinmart.com/.

Stennis, John C.
(1901–1995) Politician

John Cornelius Stennis served for more than forty-one years as a US senator from Mississippi. The son of Hampton Howell Stennis and Margaret Cornelia Adams Stennis, he was born on 3 August 1901 on a farm near De Kalb in Kemper County. Stennis earned degrees at Mississippi State University (1923) and the University of Virginia School of Law (1928), where he was elected to Phi Beta Kappa. Stennis won election to the Mississippi House of Representatives in 1928 and served until 1932. He then became a prosecuting attorney from 1932 to 1937 before spending the next decade as a circuit judge.

A Democrat, Stennis won a US Senate seat in a 1947 special election following the death of Theodore G. Bilbo. Pledging to voters that he would "plow a straight furrow right down to the end of the row," Stennis defeated a field of candidates that included sitting US representatives William Colmer and John Rankin. Stennis won reelection in 1952, as he did easily thereafter until 1988, when he chose not to run again. Undefeated in his elections for public office over six decades, Stennis earned a reputation as a man of great personal integrity. In 1954 Stennis was appointed to a bipartisan committee to investigate the conduct of Sen. Joseph McCarthy. When McCarthy attacked the committee, Stennis delivered a forceful speech calling for McCarthy's censure. Stennis respected the authority and institutional prerogatives of the Senate, remarking that he had served "with" rather than "under" eight presidents from Truman to Reagan.

Like most southern Democrats from the 1940s through the 1960s, Stennis opposed antilynching and anti-poll-tax legislation, equal employment legislation, and other civil rights measures, participating in filibusters to keep such measures from receiving votes. In his Senate campaigns, however, Stennis never resorted to strident race-baiting or overt appeals to white supremacy. He signed the 1956 Southern Manifesto condemning the US Supreme Court's *Brown v. Board of Education* decision, supported Barry Goldwater in 1964, opposed the Voting Rights Act of 1965, and deplored Pres. Lyndon Johnson's attention to civil rights—all positions that reflected the wishes of the majority of the state's voters. Stennis did understand, however, that state and national politics had changed by the 1970s and 1980s. In 1982 he voted for the extension of the Voting Rights Act, and in 1986 he supported Mike Espy's successful attempt to become the state's first black member of Congress since John R. Lynch in the late nineteenth century.

Stennis and James O. Eastland represented Mississippi in the Senate for thirty-one years, making them one of the longest-serving pairs in US history. Contrasting in temperament and appearance—Stennis was courtly and polite, while Eastland, longtime chair of the Judiciary Committee, was gruff and raw, especially on the subject of race—the two men held powerful posts as committee chairs and voted together much more often than they disagreed. As head of the Armed Services Committee from 1969 to 1980, Stennis was generally hawkish on defense and supported the modernization of the US Navy's aircraft and nuclear fleet. To honor his long-standing commitment to the nation's military, the Nimitz-class aircraft carrier USS *John C. Stennis* was commissioned in 1995. Just as important to his constituents, Stennis's service on the Appropriations Committee gave him the power to direct federal dollars to Mississippi, with the Tennessee-Tombigbee Waterway, Pascagoula's Ingalls Shipbuilding, and Hancock County's Stennis Space Center benefiting from his Washington clout.

By the 1960s Stennis felt less comfortable with the national Democratic Party than he did with the rising Republican Right. Many Republicans felt comfortable with Stennis as well. In 1973, as the Watergate scandal unfolded, Pres. Richard Nixon proposed that Stennis listen to his White House recordings, compare them with transcripts, and assure special prosecutor Archibald Cox that the transcripts were accurate. The plan failed to attract support. In 1982 Stennis's age became an issue in his reelection campaign against thirty-

four-year-old Republican Haley Barbour, but Stennis and Pres. Ronald Reagan reached an understanding that Reagan would not campaign in Mississippi, and Stennis carried all but two counties. The 100th Congress (1987–89) elected him its president pro tempore. The longest-serving US senator in Mississippi's history, Stennis was succeeded by Republican Trent Lott, elected in 1988.

In 1929 Stennis married Coy Hines of New Albany, a home demonstration agent in Kemper County; "Miss Coy" died in 1983. The couple had two children, John Hampton, born in 1935, and Margaret Jane, born in 1937. Stennis was badly wounded in a robbery attempt outside his Washington home in 1973 but showed remarkable tenacity in his recovery. In the 1980s his health began to decline, and he lost a leg to cancer in 1984. After his retirement, Stennis remained involved in public affairs, returning to Mississippi State University to lecture to political science classes while his health allowed. A Presbyterian, Stennis died in Jackson on 23 April 1995 and is buried in his native Kemper County.

Trent Brown
Missouri University of Science and Technology

Michael S. Downs, *Journal of Mississippi History* (Summer 1993); Joseph A. Fry, *Debating Vietnam: Fulbright, Stennis, and Their Senate Hearings* (2006); Jere Nash and Andy Taggart, *Mississippi Politics: The Struggle for Power, 1976–2006* (2006).

Steptoe, E. W.
(1907–1983) Activist

E. W. Steptoe, born on 14 February 1907, was the founder and head of the National Association for the Advancement of Colored People in Amite County before and during the early years of the civil rights movement. His work helped make the chapter one of the state's largest, with about two hundred members and its own newsletter, the *Informer*, in the mid-1950s.

Along with C. C. Bryant and others, Steptoe assisted Robert Moses when he first brought the Student Nonviolent Coordinating Committee (SNCC) to Mississippi. Like a few other older civil rights workers, Steptoe impressed the younger student activists by keeping weapons for self-defense. A dairy and cotton farmer, Steptoe faced economic pressure and the threat of violence for his activism. A Mississippi State Sovereignty Commission report worried that a "mixed group" had met at his home in 1965. Opponents burned crosses on his yard and threatened his life. Steptoe was a friend of Herbert

Lee, an Amite County man who was killed in 1961 in retaliation for his civil rights activity. Steptoe himself went to jail in Jackson for the charge of protesting without a permit.

Steptoe first attempted to register to vote in Liberty in the early 1950s, and after at least six unsuccessful attempts, he succeeded in 1965. He worked with both SNCC and the Mississippi Freedom Democratic Party in the mid-1960s, serving as one of the party's delegates to the 1964 Democratic National Convention in Atlantic City. In 1967 he was one of the first civil rights activists to run for state representative.

Steptoe died in April 1983.

Ted Ownby
University of Mississippi

John Dittmer, *Local People: The Struggle for Civil Rights in Mississippi* (1995); One Person One Vote website, http://onevotesncc.org/profile/e-w-steptoe/; "Oral History with Eldridge W. Steptoe, Jr." (1995) Mississippi Oral History Program, University of Southern Mississippi, http://digilib.usm.edu/cdm/ref/collection/coh/id/16119; Charles M. Payne, *I've Got the Light of Freedom: The Organizing Tradition and the Mississippi Freedom Struggle* (1997).

Stevens, Stella (Estelle Eggleston)

(b. 1938) Actress

Stella Stevens (born Estelle Caro Eggleston) is an American actress and director born in Yazoo City, Mississippi, on 1 October 1938, the only child of Dovey Estelle Caro Eggleston and Thomas Ellett Eggleston. The family moved to Tennessee when she was four, and she married Herman Stephens in 1954 and gave birth to a son, Andrew, in Memphis on 10 June 1955. The Stevenses divorced a year later, and Stella Stevens moved with her son to California.

Stevens first appeared onscreen with a minor role in 1959's *Say One for Me*, earning a Golden Globe as Most Promising Female Newcomer. In January 1960 she was *Playboy*'s Playmate of the Month. Over the next two decades, she appeared in films with a number of well-known actors, including Bobby Darin (John Cassavetes's 1962 film, *Too Late Blues*), Elvis Presley (1962's *Girls! Girls! Girls!*), Jerry Lee Lewis (1962's *The Nutty Professor*), Dean Martin (Matt Helm's 1966 picture, *The Silencers*), Jason Robards (Sam Peckinpah's 1970 movie, *The Ballad of Cable Hogue*), and Gene Hackman (1972's *The Poseidon Adventure*). Stevens was also featured in an episode of *Bonanza* directed by the esteemed Robert Altman in 1960.

Discovered while performing in a school production of *Bus Stop* at Memphis State College, Stevens first appeared onscreen as "Chorine" in the 1959 film *Say One for Me*. Stevens eventually moved behind the camera, producing and directing the 1979 documentary *The American Heroine* and directing the feature film *The Ranch*, starring her son, Andrew, in 1989. She also continued to act, primarily on television, through 2010, appearing on soap operas such as *Santa Barbara* (1989–90) and *General Hospital* (1996–99) as well as making guest appearances on numerous other shows.

Kathryn Radishofski
Columbia University

Internet Movie Database website, www.imdb.com; David Martindale, *Biography* (June 2001); Stella Stevens website, www.stellastevens.biz.

Still, William Grant

(1895–1978) Composer

William Grant Still, often called the Dean of African American Composers, was born in Woodville on 1 May 1895 and died in Los Angeles on 3 December 1978. Both of his parents were musical, and both had college degrees, though his maternal grandmother had been a slave. His family moved away from Mississippi when he was quite young after the death of his father, although visits to relatives reinforced his connection to his original home. At his mother's urging, Still initially studied medicine at Wilberforce University, but his enduring enthusiasm for music—perhaps a legacy from his father, who had been the local bandmaster—soon won out, and he was traveling to work with ensembles led by W. C. Handy. He later studied at Oberlin, served in World War I, and ultimately moved to New York to pursue his musical career. Still worked as a staff arranger and orchestrator for Handy and others until he was able to shift entirely to composing. He subsequently moved to the West Coast.

Still's best education came from encounters with famous composers. Americanist George Chadwick taught Still for free for some months at the New England Conservatory, and he later benefited from a personal scholarship to work with modernist Edgar Varèse. Still was also strongly influenced by the work of Afro-British composer Samuel Coleridge Taylor and by his immersion in popular music and jazz through his years as arranger and orchestrator.

Still's most famous work was typical of his style. *The Afro-American Symphony*, completed in 1930 and premiered the following year, included a banjo in the orchestra and featured syncopated rhythms that tended to portray blacks with traditional, simple lives. For the same reason, he kept harmonies simple and dissonance tightly in check. Nearly all of his music was similarly programmatic, often with themes of black life in America, and nearly all of it is what scholars call neoromantic, with harmonies that harkened back to the mid-nineteenth century, though they were also imbued with jazz influences.

Still received many honors, including two Guggenheim Fellowships, numerous commissions and prizes, and eight honorary doctorates from institutions that included Howard University, Bates College, the New England Conservatory, and the University of Southern California. Dedicated to encouraging racial harmony and the advancement of African Americans, he was openly troubled that his audiences were almost entirely white. He left a large body of work, including countless arrangements and orchestrations, four ballet scores, nine operas, a dozen symphonies or symphonic poems, many other works for orchestra, and numerous songs.

Chris Goertzen
University of Southern Mississippi

Catherine Parsons Smith, *William Grant Still: A Study in Contradictions* (2000); Judith Anne Still et al., eds., *William Grant Still: A Bio-Bibliography* (1996).

Stockett, Kathryn

(b. 1969) Author

Kathryn "Kitty" Stockett is a fiction writer who was born in Jackson, Mississippi, on 6 February 1969. Stockett graduated from Jackson Preparatory School and the University of Alabama in Tuscaloosa, where she received degrees in creative writing and English.

In 2009 Amy Einhorn Books, a division of Penguin Group (USA), published Stockett's first novel, *The Help*, which reached No. 1 on the *New York Times* best seller list. Set in the early 1960s, the novel uses the voices of three women to expose relationships among African American maids and their white female employers. By interweaving multiple stories, the book addresses issues of class, religion, racial segregation, child care, and employment opportunities for white and black women. An early issue revolves around one character's attempt to pass a law mandating separate bathrooms for African American employees. Above all, the book addresses the difficulties of communication: as the young white woman, Skeeter, tries to break through divisions based on race and class to understand "the help,"

Kathryn Stockett (Courtesy Kem Lee)

one maid, Aibileen, looks for an outlet to express herself, and another maid, Minny, deals with her own outspokenness. Much of the book's drama lies in Skeeter's effort to complete a book, *Help*, of narratives by maids.

While Stockett's book proved extremely popular, she provoked controversy with her use of black vernacular dialogue. Some readers and critics disdained her use of the "black voice" and accused her of creating characters based on real people. In February 2011 Ablene Cooper, who had worked as a maid for Stockett's brother, filed a lawsuit in the Hinds County Circuit Court, claiming that Stockett based Aibileen on Cooper. Stockett denied the charge, and the court dismissed the case in August 2011 because the statute of limitations had expired.

Also in 2011, a film version of *The Help*, directed by Tate Taylor, was released. It received good reviews and was nominated for four Academy Awards, with Octavia Spencer taking home the Oscar for Best Supporting Actress.

Stockett resides in Atlanta.

Neil Linton Knox
University of Mississippi

Amy Einhorn Books/Putnam website, http://us.penguingroup.com; Jerry Mitchell, *Jackson Clarion-Ledger* (17 February 2011); Kathryn Stockett website, www.kathrynstockett.com.

S

Stone, Alfred Holt

(1870–1955) Author

Born in New Orleans on 16 October 1870, Alfred Holt Stone at various times was a planter, lawyer, scholar, legislator, and administrator in the Mississippi government. He served as president of the Mississippi Welfare League, president of the Mississippi Historical Society, founder and editor of the publication of the Staple Cotton Cooperative Association, and a member of the Commission on Interracial Cooperation. He received a law degree from the University of Mississippi and spent much of his early adulthood on Dunleith Plantation in Dunleith.

He is most famous as the author of books and articles that defended plantation life. He argued that as long as planters operated as kindly paternalists, African Americans would find more happiness and security on the plantation than away from it. He wrote positively about slave law in antebellum Mississippi, praised the way slavery and plantation labor brought together whites and African Americans in friendly relations that helped identify the making of a good crop as a mutual concern, and argued that segregation laws minimized conflict and potential violence. *Studies in the American Race Problem* (1908) was one of the most aggressive attempts in the early twentieth century to defend segregation and especially planter control over southern life. In this long work of scholarship, Stone raised and then responded to real or potential northern criticisms of southern racial discrimination. He began with the argument that racial discrimination existed throughout the country and that the demographic dominance of African Americans in parts of the South led to the desire for more aggressive forms of control.

At least two points distinguished Stone from the many other wealthy white southerners who shared his conservative perspective. One was an experiment with a new type of plantation labor in 1899. He rejected sharecropping and rented land to African American workers, refused to give credit or favors through the plantation store, and retained complete control over day-to-day work. Stone was surprised by the failure of this effort, and that surprise inspired his respect for sharecropping as a kindly system of labor control.

More distinctive than his labor experiments was his intellectual curiosity about African American life. Stone collected an extraordinary range and number of materials on the subject, including speeches, newspapers, religious publications, minutes of societies, and scholarly works. The topics varied widely, but he seems to have concentrated on materials involving Africa, slavery and abolitionism, Booker T. Washington, labor, education, and migration. Stone viewed himself as a thoughtful scholar who wanted, as he wrote in his most ambitious book, "to learn what and how the Negro thinks and feels." Stone's most recent biographer describes him as a "scientific racist." Stone's research materials are now located in the Mississippi Department of Archives and History in Jackson and at the University of Mississippi.

From 1932 until his death on 11 May 1955 Stone served as Mississippi's tax commissioner.

Ted Ownby
University of Mississippi

James G. Hollandsworth Jr., *Portrait of a Scientific Racist: Alfred Holt Stone of Mississippi* (2008); Mississippi State Tax Commission, Service Bulletins 1–48; John David Smith, in *The Human Tradition in the New South*, ed. James C. Klotter (2005); Alfred Holt Stone, "The Assessing of Public Utilities by the State Tax Commission: An Informal Discussion" (1935); Alfred Holt Stone, *Studies in the American Race Problem* (1908).

Stone, John

(1936–2008) Poet

Poet, essayist, cardiologist, and lecturer John Henry Stone was born on 7 February 1936 in Jackson to John Stone and Pauline Marler Stone. His father, a production supervisor, died of a heart attack when Stone was a senior at Jackson's Central High School, where he edited the literary magazine. Stone earned a bachelor's degree from Millsaps College in 1958. He married Sarah Lucretia Crymes on 16 August 1954, and the couple went on to have two children, John and James. In 1962 Stone received his medical degree from Washington University in St. Louis. He trained in internal medicine at the University of Rochester and completed a fellowship in

John Stone (Photograph © David G. Spielman)

cardiology at Emory University in Atlanta. From 1964 to 1966 Stone served in the US Public Health Service, attaining the rank of lieutenant commander.

In 1969 Stone joined the faculty at Emory, where he founded one of the first medical school courses in literature and medicine, and he later taught the course at Oxford University. From 1974 to 1985 he worked full time at Atlanta's Grady Memorial Hospital, founding and directing its Emergency Medicine Residency Program. Stone also wrote poetry and essays that explore the common threads between literature and medicine. The author or coeditor of *On Doctoring* and *In the Country of Hearts* as well as several medical textbooks, Stone chronicled the relationship between the poet's sensitivity and the doctor's clinical examination of the human condition.

Beginning with *The Smell of Matches* (1972) and continuing through his final volume, *Music from Apartment 8* (2004), Stone's poetry illustrates the same theme that he brought to the world of medicine: listening to the stories we tell unites us all. In the tradition of poet-physician William Carlos Williams, Stone's witty, insightful, and sensitive lyrics examine the common threads between literature and medicine. Stone sees the duty of the writer to prepare oneself for a "good death" and the poet and the physician as making use of the same materials. Stone wrote that the "words growing all over Mississippi" need the poet to listen to them and give them order. Poetry, he added, is about "what to do in the time remaining, which, it seems to me, is the only important question, whatever stages of growing up one is in." Both Stone's poetry and his prose are about those questions; they offer examples, as he said in his introduction to *On Doctoring*, of "the isolation and alienation that come eventually to us all."

Among his numerous honorary degrees and teaching and writing awards, Stone received the Literature Award from the Mississippi Institute of Arts and Letters in 1986 and again in 1999 and was named Georgia Writer of the Year four times. Stone retired from full-time teaching and lived in Tucker, Georgia, outside Atlanta, until his death from cancer on 6 November 2008. John Stone Hall at Millsaps is now home to the Millsaps Writing Center.

Gary Kerley
Gainesville, Georgia

Dorothy Abbott, ed., *Mississippi Writers: Reflections of Childhood and Youth* (1988); Michael Heffernan, *The Midwest Quarterly* (Winter 1985); Gary Kerley, *New Georgia Encyclopedia* website, www.georgiaencyclopia .org; John Stone and Richard Reynolds, eds., *On Doctoring: Journeys in the Art of Medicine* (1995); J. Walsh, *Speak So I Shall Know Thee: Interviews with Southern Writers* (1990).

Stone, John Marshall

(1830–1900) Thirty-First and Thirty-Third Governor, 1876–1882, 1890–1896

John Marshall Stone, who was inaugurated as governor on three separate occasions and served as governor longer than any other man in Mississippi history, headed the state during some of the most important moments in its history—the end of Reconstruction and the beginning of the disfranchisement of African American voters.

John Marshall Stone was born in Milan, Tennessee, on 30 April 1830. After teaching school in his native state for several years he moved to Eastport, Mississippi, a village near Iuka in Tishomingo County. Before the Civil War, Stone was the station agent for the Mississippi and Ohio Railroad at Iuka. He enlisted in the Confederate Army as a private and eventually rose to the rank of colonel. After the war, he returned to his position with the railroad.

In 1869 Stone, a Democrat, was elected to the Mississippi Senate, serving until 1876. When Gov. Adelbert Ames resigned under great pressure that year, Stone was president pro tempore. Because Lt. Gov. Alexander K. Davis had been impeached and removed from office, Stone was next in the line of succession, assuming the governorship on 29 March. He immediately began to add Democrats to positions in state government, from the Supreme Court and other courts to the board of trustees of the state's universities. As governor, Stone signed numerous laws cutting the size of state government and changing district lines to reduce Republican power. In 1877 Stone did nothing to address the victims of political violence in the Chisholm Massacre.

In the bitter political climate of 1877 the Republican Party did not nominate a candidate for governor. Consequently, Stone was reelected by the astounding margin of 97,729 to 47. The state's Reconstruction constitution, which had been adopted in 1869, lengthened the governor's term to four years and allowed the governor to succeed himself. That provision made Stone's first period of service six years—the two years of Ames's unexpired term and the four-year term to which he was elected in 1877.

In 1889 John Marshall Stone was again elected governor by a vote of 84,929 to 16. During the first year of his second term the state adopted a new constitution. Through a carefully designed set of voting requirements, including a poll tax and a literacy qualification, the 1890 constitution perpetuated or allowed the one-party system, the disfranchisement of African American voters, and racial segregation. Stone supported the constitutional convention and its goals.

In July 1894 secret service agents arrested Stone for counterfeiting US currency. The accusation resulted from the fact that Mississippi had issued a special state warrant that was similar in color, size, shape, and appearance to US currency.

S

The federal agents had acted in haste, and the charges were later dropped, but Stone was infuriated by what he called "a most outrageous proceeding."

The 1890 constitution continued the four-year term but did not allow the governor to succeed himself. The constitution also created several new executive departments whose heads were elected to four-year terms independently of the governor. To allow for a smooth transition from the old to the new constitution, the terms of all public officials were extended for two years. Thus Stone again served as governor for six years (1890–96).

In 1899 Stone was named president of the Mississippi Agricultural and Mechanical College (now Mississippi State University), which had been established during his first administration in 1878. He served only briefly, until his death on 26 March 1900. Stone County is named in his honor.

David G. Sansing
University of Mississippi

William C. Harris, *The Day of the Carpetbagger: Republican Reconstruction in Mississippi* (1979); Albert D. Kirwan, *Revolt of the Rednecks: Mississippi Politics: 1876–1925* (1951); *Mississippi Official and Statistical Register* (1912); Dunbar Rowland, *Encyclopedia of Mississippi History*, vol. 2 (1907).

Stone County

Founded in 1916, Stone County is located in South Mississippi, near the Gulf Coast. In the early twentieth century, Stone County had one of the lowest populations in the state—just 5,704 people in 1930. Whites made up three-quarters of this total, and African Americans made up one quarter. Communities include the county seat, Wiggins, and Perkinston.

Unlike much of the rest of Mississippi, agriculture did not dominate the economy of Stone County, which had the second-lowest percentage of land in farms in the state. As in other areas along or near the Gulf Coast but unlike most counties in Mississippi, tenancy was only a small component of Stone County agriculture. Instead, owners operated 78 percent of the county's 678 farms, more than twice the state average of 30 percent. It was one of the few counties in Mississippi with several canneries, and the timber industry was an important part of the economy.

According to the religious census reports of 1926 and 1936, Baptists and Methodists were the largest religious groups in Stone County, as in much of Mississippi. Uniquely, however, most of the county's church members belonged to churches of the American Baptist Association, a group of Landmark Baptists who had rejected the Southern Baptist Convention.

Baseball Hall of Famer Dizzy Dean spent much of his life after baseball in Wiggins. Actor Anthony Herrera, known for his television work on *As the World Turns*, was born in Wiggins in 1944. Notable persons who studied at Perkinston Junior College include astronaut Fred Haise, labor leader Claude Ramsay, and Gulf Coast restaurateur Mary Mahoney.

By 1960 Stone County's population had increased to 7,013. In addition to a low percentage of people involved in agriculture, Stone had a particularly low population density. A great deal of county land was commercial forestland, and a high percentage of its workers were employed either in timber or food processing.

Like many counties in southeast Mississippi, by 2010 Stone County had a large white majority. The population had topped 17,000 after increasing by more than 10 percent over each of the preceding five decades. Its overall 150 percent increase since 1960 represented one of the largest population expansions in the state.

Mississippi Encyclopedia Staff
University of Mississippi

Mississippi State Planning Commission, *Progress Report on State Planning in Mississippi* (1938); *Mississippi Statistical Abstract*, Mississippi State University (1952–2010); Charles Sydnor and Claude Bennett, *Mississippi History* (1939); University of Virginia Library, Historical Census Browser website, http://mapserver.lib.virginia.edu; E. Nolan Waller and Dani A. Smith, *Growth Profiles of Mississippi's Counties, 1960–1980* (1985).

Street, James

(1903–1954) Author, Journalist, Minister

James Howell Street, an American novelist, journalist, short story writer, essayist, and minister, was born on 15 October 1903 in the sawmill village of Lumberton, Mississippi, to John Camillus Street, a liberal Irish Catholic lawyer, and his uniquely named Scots-Irish Calvinist mother, William Thompson Scott. While Street never considered himself a literary writer, he acquired international recognition for his work in fiction, which relied heavily on his thorough understanding of southern culture and folklore. Street's literary corpus includes seventeen novels and thirty-five short stories. A majority of his novels became best sellers, and *The Biscuit Eater*, *Tap Roots*, and *Good-Bye, My Lady* were later adapted into successful films.

As a teenager, Street accepted journalist positions with newspapers in Laurel and Hattiesburg. In 1923 he married

Lucy Nash O'Briant and decided to follow in his father-in-law's footsteps by becoming a Baptist minister, attending Southwest Baptist Theological Seminary and Howard College. However, Street grew unsatisfied with pastoral work and decided to return to journalism and writing novels.

Street worked as a feature writer for newspapers in Memphis, Nashville, and Atlanta until he was offered a position as a reporter for William Randolph Hearst's *New York American*, where he covered such high-profile national events as the Scottsboro trial and the kidnapping of Charles Lindbergh's son. While working for Hearst, Street published his first book, *Look Away! A Dixie Notebook* (1936), a nonfiction travel narrative. In 1940 he returned to Mississippi and settled his family in Natchez, but five years later they relocated again to Chapel Hill, North Carolina, because Street wanted his two war-veteran sons and daughter to attend the University of North Carolina. Street assisted with the establishment of the University of North Carolina's school of journalism and continued to write fiction. Suffering from glaucoma, Street devised a routine in which he dictated his books for three hours and then turned to editing the day's work. In his spare time, his hobbies included raising cacti and collecting recordings of American ballads, walking sticks, books, and pipes.

During the 1940s and early 1950s Street composed a five-novel historical fiction series regarding the progress of the Dabney family in Lebanon, Mississippi, from the late eighteenth century to the late nineteenth century. The Dabney Pentology—*Oh, Promised Land* (1940), *Tap Roots* (1942), *By Valor and Arms* (1944), *Tomorrow We Reap* (1949), and *Mingo Dabney* (1950)—primarily involved issues of race and honor in the South. Street wrote two semiautobiographical novels classified as works in his "preacher" sequence, *The Gauntlet* (1945) and *The High Calling* (1951). Street believed that his sociological novel, *In My Father's House* (1941), was his best work. Both *The Biscuit Eater* (1939), arguably his most famous work, and *Good-Bye, My Lady* (1954) concerned country boys and dogs. Street also wrote another nonfiction travel narrative, *James Street's South* (1955), and two nonfiction historical pieces, *The Civil War* (1953) and *The Revolutionary War* (1954).

On 28 September 1954 Street died of a heart attack.

Peter J. Morrone
University of Mississippi

James L. Cox, *Mississippi Almanac* (1997); Josephine Frazier, *James Street: A Bio-Bibliography* (1958); Lindsay Roberts, *James Street: A Biography* (1999).

Stringer, Emmett J.
(1919–1995) Activist

Born on 16 September 1919 in Yazoo City, Mississippi, Emmett J. Stringer became a dentist and leader of the National Association for the Advancement of Colored People (NAACP). When he was a child in Mound Bayou, his mother signed him up as an NAACP member. Stringer graduated from Alcorn College in 1941, served in the army, and then graduated from Meharry Medical College in Nashville. Newly credentialed as a dentist, he moved to Columbus, Mississippi, where he and his wife, Flora Ghist Stringer, a teacher, became leaders in the African American community.

Stringer helped organize the NAACP chapter in Columbus in 1953 and encouraged the growth of the organization in the crucial years of the mid-1950s. He was elected the organization's state president in 1953 and had the job of organizing responses to the *Brown v. Board of Education* decision the following year. He and other state NAACP leaders rejected Gov. Hugh White's proposal to equalize funding for African American and white schools and instead agreed to petition school boards to demand desegregation. In 1953 he also sought African American volunteers to apply to the

Emmett J. Stringer, 1950s (Mississippi State Sovereignty Commission Records, Mississippi Department of Archives and History [2-94-0-1-1-1-1])

S

University of Mississippi, a request that helped prompt Medgar Evers to apply to the university's law school.

Stringer's efforts at times brought retaliation. In response to his efforts to desegregate the Columbus schools, white leaders cut off his credit, and the Ku Klux Klan targeted him. Stringer declined to run for a second term at the NAACP's helm but remained active in the organization, working with Evers and other leaders including Aaron Henry and Ruby Hurley on voting drives. Stringer became one of the first African Americans in Lowndes County to register to vote.

In the late 1950s and early 1960s, police officers, sheriffs, and investigators for the Mississippi State Sovereignty Commission consistently looked into Stringer's actions as well as those of his friend, pharmacist James Allen. One secret memo claimed that Stringer had "quieted down," but another investigator claimed, "All officials in Lowndes County have their eyes on Dr. Stringer. They say they would not put anything past Stringer when it came to conniving for integration." Stringer continued his activist work into the late 1960s, serving on the board of the Child Development Group of Mississippi.

Stringer maintained his dental practice until 1992 and died on 6 September 1995.

Ted Ownby

University of Mississippi

Charles C. Bolton, *The Hardest Deal of All: The Battle Over School Segregation in Mississippi, 1870–1980* (2005); Columbus Lowndes Public Library Local History Announcements website, https://lowndeslibar chives.wordpress.com/2012/01/16/dr-emmett-j-stringer/; John Dittmer, *Local People: The Struggle for Civil Rights in Mississippi* (1994); Mississippi Department of Archives and History, Sovereignty Commission Online website, http://mdah.state.ms.us/arrec/digital_archives/sovcom/; Charles M. Payne, *I've Got the Light of Freedom: The Organizing Tradition and the Mississippi Freedom Struggle* (1995).

Stuart, Marty

(b. 1958) Country Musician

A musical prodigy, singer, songwriter, record producer, writer, photographer, raconteur, collector, and archivist, Marty Stuart is among the most versatile figures in modern country music. Born John Martin Stuart in Philadelphia, Mississippi, on 30 September 1958, he was drawn to gospel, bluegrass, and country music almost from infancy. Stuart was already a skillful mandolin and guitar player by the age of twelve, when bluegrass musician Lester Flatt hired him. After the ailing Flatt disbanded his group in 1978, Stuart toured with fiddler Vassar Clements and guitarists Doc and Merle Watson. Stuart next joined Johnny Cash's band, remaining there until he started a solo career in 1985. He also married Cash's daughter, Cindy.

From his boyhood, Stuart had squirreled away country music memorabilia in his room. As his income grew and his contact with his musical heroes intensified, he became a more systematic collector of costumes, instruments, letters, song manuscripts, photos, and related material. He acquired a trove of Hank Williams artifacts so imposing that the Country Music Hall of Fame and Museum borrowed it for an exhibition. Stuart's array, which he labeled Sparkle and Twang, has subsequently been displayed at the Tennessee State Museum and in numerous other venues. Stuart also developed a passion for wearing and collecting the ornately decorated Nudie and Manuel stage costumes long favored by such traditional country acts as Porter Wagoner and Little Jimmy Dickens. The flashy dress and tall "rooster comb" hair became Stuart trademarks.

Stuart released his first album, *Marty, with a Little Help from His Friends*, in 1977. While it did not gain much critical attention, the follow-up collection, *Busy Bee Café* in 1982, did. Critics loved it. Stuart signed with Columbia Records in the mid-1980s but failed to chart any substantial hits there. He had better luck with his next label, MCA, where he scored five Top 10 singles, including "Hillbilly Rock," "Tempted," and "Burn Me Down." His 1991 duet with Travis Tritt, "The Whiskey Ain't Workin'," won a Grammy for Best Country Vocal Collaboration. Stuart has also won several other Grammy Awards.

In 1992 Stuart became a member of the *Grand Ole Opry*. Five years later, after the end of his marriage to Cindy Cash, he married fellow Opry star Connie Smith. Rutledge Hill Press published his annotated book of photographs, *Pilgrims: Sinners, Saints, and Prophets*, in 1999. The next year Stuart produced the soundtrack album for the Matt Damon and Penelope Cruz movie *All the Pretty Horses*. Stuart became increasingly busy as a producer after the turn of the twenty-first century, masterminding records for Billy Bob Thornton, Jerry and Tammy Sullivan, Andy Griffith, Kathy Mattea, and Porter Wagoner, among others. In 2007 he published his second photo book, *Country Music: The Masters*. In recent years he has continued to record, and his Sparkle and Twang exhibition was featured at the Autry National Center of the American West. From 2008 to 2014 Stuart hosted *The Marty Stuart Show*, a television program featuring performances by contemporary and classic country and bluegrass stars. In 2009 Neshoba Country pronounced July 8 Marty Stuart Day, dedicating a road marker in his honor near Philadelphia. In 2010, Stuart was honored with the second marker dedicated on the Mississippi Country Music Trail, which he was instrumental in founding.

Edward Morris

Nashville, Tennessee

Internet Movie Database website, imdb.com; Marty Stuart, *Country Music: The Masters* (2007); Marty Stuart, *Pilgrims: Sinners, Saints, and Prophets* (1999); Marty Stuart website, www.martystuart.net.

Stuart, Thomas C.
(1794–1883) Missionary

Licensed to preach by the South Carolina Presbytery on 19 April 1819, Rev. Thomas C. Stuart, known as Father Stuart, was one of the earliest Presbyterian missionaries in Mississippi. Sent by the Synod of South Carolina in 1820, Stuart established the Monroe Mission and was a missionary among the Chickasaw Indians of northeastern Mississippi. In 1823 Stuart organized the church and by 1830 had a membership of more than one hundred Native Americans, African Americans, and whites. Chickasaw College grew out of a need for an educational institution for the daughters of Presbyterian Church members at Monroe.

The autumn session of the South Carolina and Georgia Synod of 1819 resolved to send a missionary to labor among the "Southern Indians just east of the Mississippi River." In 1819 Stuart set out from Georgia and traveled more than 180 miles before reaching Chickasaw territory. When he first came upon the Creek nation, he "held forth to them that we desired to preach the gospel among them and also establish schools for the education of their children without any cost to them." Stuart recalled that "they listened attentively, but after short consultation they rejected our proposal." Undaunted, Stuart kept pushing west toward Mississippi and arrived in the Chickasaw Nation on the eve of a council to elect a new king, King Ishtohotopah, the last king of the Chickasaw.

On 22 June 1820 the Chickasaw council granted Stuart permission to stay and chose a site for the mission. Stuart, King Ishtohotopah, and several Chickasaw representatives signed a formal agreement, beginning Father Stuart's missionary work among the Chickasaw. In 1821 Stuart and his family reached the site of the future residence of the Monroe Mission in Mississippi. One witness reported that the old Monroe Church "was an interesting sight. It was a diminutive room 16 × 16, built of small poles" and had a "dirt and stick chimney and a large open fireplace, where, in the winter, the worshipers warmed their frost-bitten fingers."

The Monroe Mission originally had eight members. The families built houses, started a farm, founded a school, and preached to the Chickasaw using an interpreter. Monroe Mission was an accessible location at the intersection of the highways of travel for several Native American tradesmen. From the north and south, the Cotton Gin Road passed through Monroe as well as the Natchez Trace, which came from the northeast and went south. In 1827 the Monroe Mission was placed under the American Missionary Board, which supported similar missions to the Cherokee and the Choctaw.

Over the mid- to late 1820s the church grew to twelve times its original size. Distinctions of race and color seemed unimportant in Stuart's missionary model. One acquaintance recalled, "He earned the appreciation of all, regardless of color or condition or creed." Church records showed a racially heterogeneous membership, with twenty-nine whites, sixty-nine African Americans, and twenty-five Indians in the late 1820s. Further, Tishu Miko (Tishomingo), a brave warrior and ruler of the Chickasaw cession where Monroe resided, was a prominent friend of Stuart's and an attendee at the Monroe Mission.

After Chickasaw Removal, Stuart traveled cross-country in 1839 and forded rivers in a wagon with his daughter, Mary Jane Stuart, to visit Chickasaw he knew in the Monroe Mission. During the Civil War, Stuart served as an instructor at Chickasaw Female College and helped carry the college through the tumultuous period of Reconstruction. He died in Tupelo, at the home of his daughter, in 1883.

Otis W. Pickett
Mississippi College

C. W. Grafton, *History of Presbyterianism in Mississippi* (1927); Fred R. Graves, ed., *The Presbyterian Work in Mississippi* (1927); E. T. Winston, *"Father" Stuart and the Monroe Mission* (1927).

Student Nonviolent Coordinating Committee (SNCC)

In the midst of the civil rights sit-ins of 1960, Ella Baker organized a conference for student activists at Shaw University in Raleigh, North Carolina, with money appropriated by the Southern Christian Leadership Conference (SCLC). Out of the Shaw University conference, the Student Nonviolent Coordinating Committee (SNCC, pronounced *Snick*) formed to coordinate the student sit-in movement. The organization elected Marion Barry as its first chair—a position that Chuck McDew, John Lewis, and Stokely Carmichael later occupied. Baker initially served as an adviser to the group, but she encouraged the students to assume leadership of the organization rather than to rely on older activists.

The organization's purpose, as its founding members conceptualized it, was to challenge segregation through nonviolent direct action—a strategy employed by Gandhi in India. Some older civil rights groups, such as the National Association for the Advancement of Colored People (NAACP) and the SCLC, considered that approach too confrontational. SNCC's founders also argued that a localized, participatory model would be more politically effective than the "top-down" approach embraced by other groups. SNCC organizers embraced an egalitarian, antihierarchical approach to grassroots organizing.

Shortly after its formation, SNCC established its national office in Atlanta, in a room rented by the SCLC, and began printing a newsletter, the *Student Voice*. In 1961 the organization redirected its focus away from college campuses and toward the rural communities of the Deep South, targeting southwestern Georgia and western Mississippi. The director of SNCC activities in Mississippi, Bob Moses, immediately began capitalizing on the networks older civil rights workers had already established. SNCC's organizing depended a great deal on the networking of Mississippi natives, especially Amzie Moore, Clyde Kennard, Vernon Dahmer, Medgar Evers, and C. C. Bryant. When organizing Mississippi communities, Moses typically established connections through local NAACP leaders and then cultivated a local leadership among young people and others who were not highly regarded by the older networks. Moses's first trip to Mississippi occurred in the summer of 1960, when he was trying to recruit people for an October conference. He met Moore, to whom Baker sent an introduction. Moore attended the conference and formally invited the organization to come to Mississippi.

Other activists briefly worked in Mississippi when SNCC became involved in the Congress of Racial Equality's Freedom Rides in the summer of 1961. After the first attempt to ride from Washington, D.C., to New Orleans was stopped in Birmingham, Diane Nash and other student organizers in Nashville joined the Riders, who began flooding into Jackson to crowd the jails. By the end of the summer, 328 riders had been arrested in Jackson, and the jails were so crowded that Gov. Ross Barnett sent the Riders to Parchman Prison.

Because of the violence that met the Freedom Riders, the Kennedy administration began urging SNCC organizers to focus on voter registration, which the administration mistakenly believed would generate less violent resistance than the efforts to desegregate public transit. The administration promised organizers federal protection while they worked in Mississippi. SNCC almost split over the shift, with some members believing that registration would not entail enough direct action. Members ultimately decided to work on both fronts, though the two wings quickly merged into one in Mississippi.

During the summer of 1961, at the same time as the Freedom Rides, Bryant invited Moses to begin voter registration work in Pike County, in the southwestern part of the state, where both the Klan and the NAACP were active. Moses believed that SNCC's main task in Mississippi was to develop local, indigenous leadership, and he saw voter registration as way to increase political involvement. While SNCC often operated on a small budget, its work was possible because of the support local residents provided, including food and shelter.

In Pike County, Moses began organizing high school students, who then went house to house to spread word about the movement. In August the first voter registration school was opened. The direct-action wing began holding workshops on nonviolent resistance, and sit-ins began. Two local students who later became SNCC field secretaries, Hollis Watkins and Curtis Hayes, staged the first sit-in of the Pike County nonviolent movement at the local Woolworth's. Students also organized and led a march to the McComb City Hall to protest Brenda Travis's expulsion from school and Herbert Lee's murder.

After hearing about SNCC's activities in Pike County, residents in other counties began requesting that SNCC expand its work into their areas. SNCC field secretaries duplicated Moses's strategies in Hattiesburg, Holly Springs, Canton, Natchez, Ruleville, Drew, Liberty, Clarksdale, Greenwood, and other communities. In 1962 SNCC workers also went to Jackson to campaign on behalf of R. L. Smith, the first African American to run for Congress from Mississippi since Reconstruction. Watkins and Hayes left Pike County for Hattiesburg, where they helped Dahmer start a voter registration drive.

During SNCC's expansion, a number of native Mississippians began working as field secretaries and organizers. By 1963 SNCC had twenty field secretaries in Mississippi, and seventeen—including Lawrence Guyot, June Jordan, Charles McLaurin, Sam Block, and Fannie Lou Hamer—were natives of the state. Many attended SNCC's Highlander Folk School in Monteagle, Tennessee, to learn voter registration techniques and then came home to apply what they learned. Native Mississippians accomplished much of SNCC's work in the state, and many assumed leadership roles in the organization. Watkins and Hamer were elected to SNCC's executive committee and were among the most ardent proponents of SNCC's strategy of developing local, indigenous leadership.

Guyot directed the Freedom Summer Project in 1963 and was elected chair of the Mississippi Freedom Democratic Party (MFDP), which SNCC formed in 1964 to facilitate African American political participation and to challenge the seating of five Mississippi Representatives in the US House. Hamer was elected the MFDP's vice chair, and McLaurin was chosen as part of its delegation to the Democratic National Convention in Atlantic City, New Jersey.

By 1964 most SNCC workers had left the more rural areas for the cities, and after building up local leadership, SNCC began focusing on issues other than community organizing. In 1966 only seventeen SNCC workers remained in Mississippi, and most of them worked in the Jackson area. That same year, SNCC's executive committee voted to expel all white members, and several native Mississippians resigned in protest. In addition, tensions had arisen between SNCC and the MFDP, which felt that SNCC's Atlanta office was not providing enough support to the movement in Mississippi.

While SNCC's official activity in the state steadily decreased after 1963, the local leadership remained politically active, and more than half a century later, many native Mississippians who started out with SNCC continue to work for social justice both within and outside of the state.

Amy Schmidt
Lyon College

Kenneth Andrews, *Freedom Is a Constant Struggle: The Mississippi Civil Rights Movement and Its Legacy* (2004); Clayborne Carson, *In Struggle: SNCC and the Black Awakening of the 1960s* (1981); John Dittmer, *Local People: The Struggle for Civil Rights in Mississippi* (1994); Wesley Hogan, *Many Minds, One Heart: SNCC's Dream for a New America* (2009); Charles M. Payne, *I've Got the Light of Freedom: The Organizing Tradition and the Mississippi Freedom Struggle* (1995); Howard Zinn, *SNCC: The New Abolitionists* (2002).

Sullens, Fred
(1877–1957) Editor

When *Jackson Daily News* editor Fred Sullens died, the *New York Times* remembered him as a columnist not afraid to challenge political leaders or denounce racial equality. Sullens did not consider himself a white supremacist in the vein of "hysterical rabble rousers" such as Mississippi senator Theodore Bilbo but nevertheless supported white supremacy in his front-page editorial column, "The Low Down on Higher Ups," during a career that spanned fifty-two years.

Frederick E. Sullens was born in Missouri on 12 November 1877, the son of a Union soldier, and worked as a reporter at the *St. Louis Post-Dispatch* before moving to Mississippi to write for the state's most widely circulated newspaper, the *Jackson Clarion-Ledger*. Sullens was called a "damn Yankee" when he first arrived in Mississippi, but his segregationist views and his stance against federal intervention soon won him favor among the state's white power structure. Sullens left the *Clarion-Ledger* for the *Daily News*, Mississippi's second-most-popular newspaper, and purchased the paper in 1907. For the next half century, the *Daily News* served as Sullens's editorial mouthpiece, with politicians and federal laws the objects of his contempt. Not a writer to hide behind his pen, Sullens supposedly confronted Mississippi governor Paul

Johnson and broke a walking cane across the governor's back during the 1940s.

Sullens witnessed many changes during his long tenure at the *Daily News*. In the wake of World War II, the nation's increasing support for civil rights for all people was a primary motivation for the creation of the States' Rights Democrats (the Dixiecrats) and the party's nomination of Sen. Strom Thurmond of South Carolina and Gov. Fielding Wright of Mississippi for president and vice president. Sullens realized the futility of the Dixiecrat ticket but remained a staunch supporter of the party's ideals: "Southern Democrats, of course, realize their cause is hopeless, they know the Thurman [*sic*]-Wright ticket . . . cannot possibly win," he wrote. "But they have written a new chapter in the political history of the United States. They have put the nation on notice that we cannot be intimidated." He insisted that the South would "not surrender our most sacred constitutional rights in order to placate a vicious minority that seeks to rupture present racial relations and establish social equity." He lambasted the "damn fool Democrats in other sections" who would "eat, drink, and sleep with negroes."

Not long after the Dixiecrats walked out of the National Democratic Convention, members of the Hederman family, which owned the *Clarion-Ledger*, began secretly acquiring *Daily News* stock in an attempt to take control of the newspaper. Sullens took the case to court and won, but he also went broke because of accrued legal debts. In August 1954 Sullens finally sold the *Daily News* to the Hedermans but remained as editor. "You may think I prostituted myself," he told his flabbergasted *Daily News* staff. "If so, I'm the highest paid he-whore in Mississippi."

The summer of 1954 was rough on Sullens, who was also outraged by the US Supreme Court's *Brown v. Board of Education* decision mandating an end to public school segregation. Sullens believed that the ruling represented the ultimate insult from a Court determined to destroy the southern way of life. "Mississippi will never consent to placing white and Negro children in the same public schools," he wrote in May 1954. "Human blood may stain Southern soil in many places because of this decision, but the dark red stains of that blood will be on the marble steps of the United States Supreme Court building." Sullens continued, "White and Negro children in the same schools will lead to miscegenation. Miscegenation leads to mixed marriages and mixed marriages lead to the mongrelization of the human race."

Sullens persisted in his criticism of the Supreme Court and in declaring that *Brown* would be ignored in Mississippi: "There may be doubts as to what other states intend to do, but the people of Mississippi have always had the intelligence and courage sufficient to manage their own destiny." He predicted, "The white people of the South will evade the Supreme Court decision." Despite his fiery rhetoric, however, he admonished *Daily News* readers who sent letters to the editor to tone down their racial rhetoric: "Please do not send us communication written in the heat

S

of passion." Sullens died on 19 November 1957, more than a decade before school desegregation became widespread in Mississippi.

Susan Weill

Texas State University at

San Marcos

James Loewen and Charles Sallis, eds., *Mississippi: Conflict and Change* (1974); Neil McMillen, *Dark Journey: Black Mississippians in the Age of Jim Crow* (1990); *New York Times* (20 November 1957); Reed Sarratt, *The Ordeal of Desegregation: The First Decade* (1966); *Time* (8 November 1954); Susan Weill, *In a Madhouse's Din: Civil Rights Coverage by Mississippi's Daily Press, 1948–1968* (2002).

Summer, Eugenia
(1923–2016) Artist and Educator

Eugenia Summer is a quiet example of the tremendous influence that art academics have had on art appreciation and understanding in Mississippi. Emily Eugenia Summer was born on 13 June 1923 in Newton and grew up in Yazoo City. She went on to earn a bachelor's degree from Mississippi State College for Women (now Mississippi University for Women [MUW]) and a master's degree from Columbia University before joining the Mississippi State College faculty as an associate professor of art in 1949. She spent summers studying at the Art Institute of Chicago, California College of Arts and Crafts, Seattle University, and Penland School of Crafts in North Carolina.

Summer's first juried show in Mississippi was the Mississippi Art Association's 1947 National Watercolor Exhibition, and her artwork has subsequently been featured at many juried exhibits, including the *Eight Decade* exhibition at Georgia College, selected by Elaine de Kooning.

Summer was one of the earliest and most successful artists in academe working in the modern form. During the 1950s she was drawn to the work of the Precisionists, painting "themes derived from factories, oil fields, industrial shapes, trains, boats in dock, machinery. Even paintings that seem non-objective in the end, almost always start with such things." After the 1960s she became even more experimental, boldly pursuing color juxtapositions and spatial explorations, adding a figurative touch of fantasy. Her themes seem to link the passage of time and the process of change. During the 1970s Summer used plastics as a sculptural medium while continuing to focus on color. Summer's paintings were among the first pieces of nonobjective art acquired by the Mississippi Art Association, which provided the core of the

Mississippi Museum of Art's current collection of her work. Her ink-on-paper work *Barricade*, which appeared the museum's 2007 exhibition, *The Mississippi Story*, was acquired in 1968. It explores color juxtapositions and spatial relationships using industrial allusions. *Barricade* and other works are marked by the sectioning or bordering of space by specific boundary and/or pattern lines and the imprecise filling-in of these sections with different colors.

Summer was named dean of the MUW Division of Fine and Performing Arts in 1982, and she retired from MUW in 1987, receiving emerita status. The Fine Arts Gallery there was named for her in 2002. Three years later, the school awarded her an honorary doctorate "in recognition of her lifelong service to and support of the university." A major influence on the thousands of young women who attended her classes, Summer became one of Mississippi's most exhibited nontraditional artists.

Summer died on 23 April 2016.

Patti Carr Black

Jackson, Mississippi

Patti Carr Black, *Art in Mississippi, 1720–1980* (1998); Patti Carr Black, *The Mississippi Story* (2007); *Jackson Clarion-Ledger* (26 April 2016).

Sumner, Cid Ricketts (Bertha Louise Ricketts)
(1890–1970) Author

Cid Ricketts Sumner became widely known in the mid-twentieth century as a novelist whose works were the basis for several popular films. Born Bertha Louise Ricketts in Brookhaven, Mississippi, on 27 September 1890, she quickly acquired the nickname *Cid* from her parents, Robert Scott Ricketts and Bertha Burnley Ricketts. Homeschooled by her mother and grandmother for much of her early education, she earned a bachelor's degree in 1909 from Millsaps College in Jackson, where her father taught.

Ricketts received a master's degree from Columbia University in 1910, spent another year there doing postgraduate study, and then enrolled as a medical student at Cornell University in 1914. On 20 July 1915 she married one of her professors, James Batcheller Sumner. Cid Sumner dropped out of school and subsequently focused on raising the couple's four children until they were old enough to attend school, when she began writing. After her 1930 divorce, she taught high school English in Jackson and French at Millsaps College. She then moved back north, spending much of the remainder of her life in New York and Massachusetts but frequently visiting family and friends in Mississippi.

Sumner published her first novel, *Ann Singleton*, in 1938 but did not capture the public's attention until her second novel, *Quality* (1946), a propagandist work opposing segregation. The work, which was excerpted in *Ladies' Home Journal* in December 1945, focuses on a young, fair-skinned black woman who moves north, passes for white while attending nursing school, and falls in love with a white doctor. The National Association for the Advancement of Colored People criticized the "Uncle Tom" tone of the book, leading Elia Kazan to work with representatives of the organization when he adapted the novel for film under the title *Pinky* in 1949.

Often referred to as one of Hollywood's first interracial films, *Pinky* starred a white woman, Jeanne Crain, in the title role. Her Academy Award nomination for best actress was one of three the film received. Kazan settled on a melodramatic conclusion for the film, with Pinky leaving behind the doctor and her career and returning to her family and roots as a black woman in the South. As several critics predicted, *Pinky* was highly controversial, and some southern theaters refused to show it, but it became one of the year's top-grossing films.

In 1948 Sumner published *Tammy out of Time*, which became the 1957 film *Tammy and the Bachelor* starring Debbie Reynolds. Its success led to other Tammy novels—*Tammy, Tell Me True* (1959) and *Tammy in Rome* (1965)—as well as two Tammy films starring Sandra Dee: *Tammy, Tell Me True* (1961) and *Tammy and the Doctor* (1963). A short-lived 1965 television series loosely based on Sumner's Tammy was edited into *Tammy and the Millionaire* (1967), starring Debbie Watson.

In addition to *Ann Singleton*, *Quality*, and the Tammy stories, Sumner published eight other novels—*But the Morning Will Come* (1949), *Sudden Glory* (1951), *The Hornbeam Tree* (1953), *Traveler in the Wilderness* (1957), *View from the Hill* (1957), *Christmas Gift* (1959), *Withdraw Thy Foot* (1964), and *Saddle Your Dreams* (1964)—as well as a number of short stories. Sumner also wrote several nonfiction works, mostly based on her travels, including such adventures as floating down the Green and Colorado Rivers, taking freighters, and riding horseback through Europe.

Sumner spent her last years in Duxbury, Massachusetts, where she was beaten to death on 15 October 1970, apparently by her sixteen-year-old grandson, John R. Cutler. Ironically, Sumner's only mystery, *Withdraw Thy Foot*, focused on a brutal murder on the Massachusetts coast with the investigation led by a female schoolteacher.

Verbie Lovorn Prevost
University of Tennessee
at Chattanooga

New York Times (16 October 1970); Richard J. Schrader, ed., *Dictionary of Literary Biography*, vol. 291 (2004); John W. Wilson, *College English* (March 1949).

Sunflower County

Perhaps most famous as the home of Parchman Prison, Fannie Lou Hamer, Archie Manning, and various blues musicians and sites, Sunflower County has played a major role in many of the most dramatic and revealing developments in the history of the Mississippi Delta. Sunflower County was founded in 1844 and named for the Sunflower River. Its county seat is Indianola, and other communities include Drew, Inverness, Moorhead, Parchman, and Ruleville.

In its first census in 1850, the sparsely populated county had a total of 1,162 residents, including 754 slaves and 348 free people. Over the next decade the free population increased somewhat to 1,102, while the slave population increased dramatically to 3,917. Sunflower was very much a plantation county, with its agriculture concentrating on cotton far more than other crops.

In 1871 part of Sunflower County became a section of Leflore County. Early in the postbellum period, it remained a lightly populated county with an African American majority. In 1880 African Americans accounted for 2,867 of Sunflower's 4,661 people. Unlike many areas with African American majorities, most Sunflower County farms were cultivated by their owners rather than by sharecroppers or other tenants. Farmers continued to concentrate on cotton but also grew grains and raised livestock in substantial numbers. The average size of Sunflower County farms was 293 acres, well above the state average.

Sunflower County experienced an extraordinary population increase in the late 1880s and by 1900 was home to 16,000 people, three-quarters of them African American. Only 8 percent of the county's 2,172 black farmers owned their land, and Sunflower had more than 2,000 African American tenant farmers and sharecroppers. As in other Delta counties dominated by tenancy, farms were now small, averaging just forty-five acres, barely half the state average of eighty-three acres. In contrast, 40 percent of Sunflower's 533 white farmers were landowners. Sunflower had a small but growing industrial population, with 57 workers, as well as a burgeoning immigrant population of 96, most of them Germans and Poles.

In 1904 the State of Mississippi established a prison, Parchman Farm, on twenty thousand acres in Sunflower County. Parchman quickly became one of Mississippi's largest plantations and was a penal facility for thousands of male convicts, the large majority of them African Americans, who were put to work in agriculture and prison upkeep. Parchman became legendary for many reasons, including its status as a plantation, its place in blues lyrics and experiences, its policies regarding physical punishment and spousal visitation, and the imprisonment of numerous civil rights activists in the 1960s.

S

In the early twentieth century 7,800 of Sunflower County's 13,000 church members belonged to Missionary Baptist congregations. Likely the most famous Baptist leader from Sunflower County was Rev. C. L. Franklin (father of Aretha Franklin), who became nationally known for his work in Memphis, Buffalo, and Detroit. Three Methodist groups—the African Methodist Episcopal Church; the Methodist Episcopal Church, South; and the Methodist Episcopal Church—had more than 800 members each, as did the Southern Baptists. Sunflower County also had the second-highest number of Disciples of Christ members (287) in Mississippi.

In the early twentieth century Sunflower was a place of dramatic extremes. Its 1930 population of more than 66,000 was the third-highest in Mississippi, and its African American population of 46,646 was the highest in the state. Sunflower trailed only Hinds County in population density. The county's economy continued to focus on agriculture. Sunflower had 12,374 farms (again, the second-most in the state), 94 percent of them run by tenant farmers. Farmers in Sunflower and Bolivar Counties grew the most cotton, and an extraordinary 98 percent of Sunflower's land was farmland, substantially higher than the state average of 66 percent. The county also ranked third in the amount of rice produced and was home to a number of Russian, Italian, and Chinese immigrants.

Scholars know a great deal about Depression-era Sunflower County because of two thorough sociological works, Hortense Powdermaker's *After Freedom: A Cultural Study in the Deep South* and John Dollard's *Caste and Class in a Southern Town*. Both studied everyday life in great detail, with particular emphasis on issues of race and class.

The phrase *Going Where the Southern Cross the Dog* dates to the roots of the music that became known as the blues. It refers to a place in Moorhead where the Yazoo and Mississippi Valley rail line intersected with the Southern line. Perhaps even more revealing about Sunflower County's place in the blues is Dockery Plantation, famous as the home of Charley Patton. Other blues musicians with Sunflower County connections include Patton associate Willie Brown, who worked as a sharecropper on a Sunflower plantation; Little Milton, born on a plantation outside Inverness; and Albert King and B. B. King, both from Indianola, which today is the home of the B. B. King Museum.

As in much of the Delta, Sunflower County's population declined dramatically in the mid-twentieth century. Between 1930 and 1960 Sunflower lost nearly one-third of its residents, and the population fell to 45,750. Three-quarters of those who departed were African Americans. Agriculture remained the primary economic pursuit, with almost half of the county's working people employed in farming. Sunflower County ranked first in cotton production, second in soybeans, third in rice, and fifth in wheat. About 7 percent of the employed people worked in industry, primarily men in textile work, and Sunflower had an unusually high number of people working in hospitals and health care. Sunflower County ranked high among Mississippi counties in the number of residents with less than five years of education.

Sunflower County produced both important civil rights activists and some of their most prominent opponents. At the instigation of founder Robert "Tut" Patterson, Indianola was the home of the first chapter of the Citizens' Council, and Doddsville was the plantation home of Sen. James O. Eastland, a powerful opponent of civil rights efforts. In the 1950s Clinton Battle reinvigorated the county's chapter of the National Association for the Advancement of Colored People. In the 1960s Student Nonviolent Coordinating Committee efforts at voter registration ushered plantation timekeeper Fannie Lou Hamer into her role as an influential spokesperson for the civil rights movement when she was fired after trying to register to vote. Her stirring address to the 1964 Democratic National Convention introduced many people to Sunflower County. In Drew, Mae Bertha Carter worked to integrate public education by sending her children to all-white schools. Charles McLaurin moved to the area in the 1960s as a young activist and has remained a community activist and leader.

Other important figures with roots in Sunflower County include college and professional football star Archie Manning, who grew up in Drew; influential *New York Times* food writer Craig Claiborne; and writer Steve Yarbrough, who has set many of his novels and short stories in the Mississippi Delta.

Like many Mississippi Delta counties, Sunflower County remained predominantly African American in 2010. The county's population of 29,024 represented a decline of more than one-third over the preceding half century.

Mississippi Encyclopedia Staff
University of Mississippi

Mississippi State Planning Commission, *Progress Report on State Planning in Mississippi* (1938); *Mississippi Statistical Abstract*, Mississippi State University (1952–2010); Charles Sydnor and Claude Bennett, *Mississippi History* (1939); University of Virginia Library, Historical Census Browser website, http://mapserver.lib.virginia.edu; E. Nolan Waller and Dani A. Smith, *Growth Profiles of Mississippi's Counties, 1960–1980* (1985).

Sunflower County Civil Rights Movements

The African American people of Sunflower County waged at least three distinct if closely related civil rights movements in the last half of the twentieth century. Each responded to a unique set of concerns, each developed its own indigenous set of leaders, and each strengthened community institutions. The most significant of these movements elevated sharecropper Fannie Lou Hamer to national prominence and brought national attention to Sunflower County.

The first black freedom movement in Sunflower revolved around Dr. Clinton Battle, a gifted physician who resurrected the county's moribund chapter of the National Association for the Advancement of Colored People (NAACP) in 1951 and encouraged more than one hundred blacks in the county seat of Indianola to register to vote for the first time. The NAACP chapter was vibrant enough that it was chosen to host the annual meeting of the Mississippi State Conference of Branches in 1953. However, Battle's organizing was crushed by another advocacy group that originated in Indianola, the Citizens' Council. Using tactics that won the Citizens' Council the nickname of the "white-collar Klan," the group convinced NAACP members to renounce their membership and end their activism. Working in close cooperation with law enforcement authorities, the council drove Battle from the state in 1957, ending this period of community mobilization.

Battle's movement drew support from all classes in the African American community of Indianola and outlying communities, but it was led by members of the black middle class. In comparison, the movement that developed in Ruleville, roughly twenty miles north of Indianola, beginning in 1962 was a poor people's movement. Members of the Student Nonviolent Coordinating Committee (SNCC), including Charles Cobb of Washington, D.C., and Charles McLaurin of Jackson, moved into Ruleville in the summer of 1962 to build support for a voter registration campaign and to help local people develop the leadership skills they would need to solve the problems they faced. Sunflower County blacks worked in an economy based solely on the production of cotton and owned few of the fields. They lived in a black-majority society based on the core concepts of white supremacy and racial segregation and a political order that denied them the right to vote. In other words, the problems facing them were many and complicated, so for the SNCC strategy to bear fruit, it would have to develop sustainable institutions that could succeed only over the long term.

Fortunately for Cobb, McLaurin, and others, William Chapel Missionary Baptist Church was willing to provide them with a home base, and a critical mass of devoted local freedom fighters developed. Chief among them was Hamer, who in short order demonstrated phenomenal abilities to define the systemic obstacles that black Sunflower Countians faced in terms they could all understand, to convince others to join her in dangerous civil rights work, and to embarrass her opponents. Hamer personified SNCC's motto, "Let the People Decide." She began her long and difficult journey as a civil rights worker when she and seventeen others went to Indianola with McLaurin to attempt to register to vote in August 1962. She returned home to Ruleville to learn that the owner of the plantation on which she and her family sharecropped had demanded that she either revoke her application for voter registration or leave the plantation. She left. Before the year ended Hamer had become a SNCC spokesperson,

raising money for the organization on a national speaking and singing tour. In 1963, while returning from a citizenship education workshop in South Carolina, she and several compatriots were jailed in Winona, Mississippi, for violating local segregation statutes. Hamer was severely beaten in jail; she carried the physical and emotional scars for the rest of her life, but she used the experience to rally support for her movement.

In 1964 Hamer's home served as a headquarters for the volunteers in Sunflower County's Freedom Summer project, which received a disproportionate amount of national attention because of Hamer's growing stature and because of its proximity to US senator James O. Eastland's plantation in nearby Doddsville. At the end of the summer Hamer led a group of black Sunflower Countians who had joined the Mississippi Freedom Democratic Party to the Democratic National Convention in Atlantic City, where they attempted to unseat Mississippi's all-white delegation. At the convention Hamer testified in front of a national television audience about the Winona beating and other injustices she had suffered in Sunflower. "All of this is on account of we want to register, to become first-class citizens," she said. The challenge failed, but Hamer and others focused national attention on the problem of voter registration of black southerners. The US Congress passed the Voting Rights Act the following year.

Hamer's movement found it difficult to sustain its momentum after 1965. The steady work of voter registration continued, but so did violence against black activists, and years would pass before African Americans achieved proportionate voting strength in the county and elected their own representatives. Hamer died in 1977 believing that most of her battles had been fought in vain. Arguably the most impossible nut for Hamer and others to crack was the creation of equal educational opportunities for black students. Sunflower County schools never truly desegregated. As soon as a federal court ordered the county's schools to integrate—more than fifteen years after the US Supreme Court's initial *Brown* decision—white families enrolled their children in all-white private academies. Yet local whites dominated local school boards and held the highest administrative positions in schools throughout the county at least into the 1980s.

The Carter family of Drew, in the northern part of Sunflower County, first challenged the so-called freedom of choice plans that kept their district schools segregated by race in 1965. Sharecroppers Matthew and Mae Bertha Carter persevered through economic intimidation, threats, and nighttime drive-by shootings into their home to send ten children through previously all-white Drew schools, seven of whom continued their education at the University of Mississippi. Blacks in Indianola challenged white domination of the nearly all-black school system in 1986, creating the third of Sunflower County's three major civil rights movements. Calling themselves Concerned Citizens, Indianola blacks launched an economic boycott of downtown merchants when the school board hired a white superintendent over an African American candidate whose qualifications were demonstrably superior. Concerned Citizens drew on lessons learned from the two previous Sunflower County movements and forced the Indianola school board to hire the group's preferred candidate, Dr. Robert Merritt. In so doing they realized the three movements' shared goal of self-determination. Blacks in Sunflower County finally won seats at the table where important decisions affecting them were made.

J. Todd Moye
University of North Texas

Chris Myers Asch, *The Senator and the Sharecropper: The Freedom Struggles of James O. Eastland and Fannie Lou Hamer* (2008); Constance Curry, *Silver Rights* (1996); Chana Kai Lee, *For Freedom's Sake: The Life of Fannie Lou Hamer* (2000); Kay Mills, *This Little Light of Mine: The Life of Fannie Lou Hamer* (1993); J. Todd Moye, *Let the People Decide: Black Freedom and White Resistance Movements in Sunflower County, Mississippi, 1945–1986* (2004).

Ken Baldwin, sweet potato vendor, Crystal Springs (Photograph by David Wharton)

Sweet Potatoes

The sweet potato (*Ipomoea batatas*), a member of the morning glory family, is rich in vitamins A, C, and E, folic acid, iron, copper, calcium, fiber, and beta-carotene. It is also low in fat. The sweet potato ranks seventh among the world's top crops, trailing wheat, rice, corn, potato, yam, and cassava. Leading sweet-potato-producing states include North Carolina, Louisiana, Mississippi, California, Alabama, Georgia, and New Jersey. White-fleshed sweet potatoes are common in Central and South America and have begun to appear in those parts of the United States where immigrants from these regions have congregated. Orange-fleshed sweet potatoes are more commonly cultivated and preferred here than in other countries.

Annual sweet potato consumption per person in the United States is usually only five pounds, primarily in pies or other dessert dishes, though sweet potatoes can now be found in such products as yogurt, beverages, noodles, chips, fries, pancake mixes, and other flours. Sweet potatoes have at least 124 medicinal and industrial uses. Researchers have shown that sweet potatoes have antitumor, anti-HIV, anti–muscular dystrophy, antifungal, antibacterial, antihypertensive, and antidiabetic effects. In part, this is because sweet potatoes contain various bioactive components that are physiologically beneficial to human consumers. George Washington Carver produced more than 118 different products from the sweet potato at Tuskegee Institute. The sweet potato is one of the crops selected for NASA's Advanced Life Support Program for potential long-duration lunar/Mars missions.

Freshly harvested sweet potatoes are high in moisture and in the warm temperatures of the South can only be stored for about a week at room temperature. Processing (such as pan-frying, drying, freezing, canning, vacuum-drying, and freeze-drying) not only increases sweet potatoes' shelf life but also increases their palatability. Sweet potato greens are also becoming increasingly popular. White-fleshed sweet potato roots are used as starch and gasohol and are made into pellets for animal rations. Orange-fleshed, high-moisture types of sweet potatoes, such as Beauregard, are erroneously called yams. However, true yams belong to the *Discorea* species, a tropical starchy tuberous root not commercially grown in the United States.

In Mississippi, the Calhoun County town of Vardaman has for decades claimed the title of Sweet Potato Capital of the World. Calhoun County farmers grow the majority of Mississippi's sweet potatoes, followed by four other northern Mississippi counties—Chickasaw, Pontotoc, Yalobusha, and Panola. In 2012 the state's sweet potato farmers planted about 22,500 acres and harvested 394 million pounds valued at approximately seventy-nine million dollars. Since the 1970s Vardaman has been the site of the Sweet Potato Festival, a harvest season event with a festival and banquet, Sweet Potato King and Queen pageant, and multiple contests for the best sweet potato dish, pie, and recipe.

Fatimah Jackson
University of Maryland

Abdullah F. H. Muhammad
Alcorn State University

Lorraine Niba
Virginia Polytechnic Institute
and State University

Franklin W. Martin, Ruth M. Ruberte, and Jose L. Herrera, *The Sweet Potato Cookbook* (1989); Mississippi State University Extension website, http://msucares.com; Sweet Potatoes Mississippi website, www.mssweetpotato.org; Lyniece North Talmadge, *The Sweet Potato Cookbook* (1998); Vardaman Sweet Potato Festival website, http://vardamansweetpotatofestival.org; Jennifer A. Woolfe, *Sweet Potato: An Untapped Food Resource* (1992).

Sydnor, Charles Sackett

(1898–1954) Historian

Southern historian Charles Sackett Sydnor was born on 21 July 1898 in Augusta, Georgia. His father, a prominent Presbyterian minister, modeled the virtues of elite leadership that in time informed the son's scholarly themes. In the course of a tortuous intellectual quest, Sydnor progressed from his peers' neo-Confederate apologetics to more insightful interpretations of the South's social dynamics.

Sydnor graduated from Virginia's Hampden-Sydney College in 1918 and five years later earned a doctorate in history from Johns Hopkins University. He briefly taught at Hampden-Sydney before becoming chair of the University of Mississippi's department of history in 1925. In 1936 he left Oxford for Duke University, where he taught for the next eighteen years. One of his generation's premier historians, he was elected president of the Southern Historical Association in 1939 and appointed Harmsworth Professor of American History at Oxford University in 1950.

Sydnor's Mississippi years proved critical to his intellectual development. His early historical works evidenced a comfortable scholar little inclined to challenge contemporary social values. Sydnor's textbook, *Mississippi History* (1930), was replete with the Negrophobic, anti-Yankee tone typical of southern school literature of the period, and his more substantial *Slavery in Mississippi* (1933) projected a paternalistic image of the peculiar institution. Gov. Theodore Bilbo's 1930 attacks on the University of Mississippi altered Sydnor's perspectives. A fiery leader of the state's downtrodden masses, the governor challenged the school's aristocratic traditions, firing its president and about a quarter of its faculty. Appalled, Sydnor developed a keen sensitivity to the struggles between the South's intransigent elites and the restive underclasses that found voice in the demagogic Bilbo. Influenced by these events, Sydnor produced *Gentleman of the Old Natchez Region: Benjamin L. C. Wailes* (1938), finding in his subject an individual congenial to his own values. Sydnor admired Wailes's promotion of education and cultural uplift in frontier Mississippi as well as his courageous stand for the Union in 1861. Just as Wailes had stood up to "reckless and unprincipled politicians" bent on secession, Sydnor determined to critique the roguish leaders of his own South. No longer confident of academic freedom at the University of Mississippi, he departed for Duke University's more friendly environs.

Sydnor emerged from Mississippi a substantial scholar whose historical writings mirrored his growing concern that modern southern politicians and the system that bred them failed to serve the nation in general and the South in particular. His *Development of Southern Sectionalism, 1819–1848* (1948) decried the qualitative decline of southern leadership from the nationalism of Washington and Jefferson to the unbending sectionalism of John C. Calhoun. Sydnor's historical writings had come to mirror his concerns with modern-day southern politics. Personally alarmed by the states' rights segregationist rhetoric of South Carolina governor Strom Thurmond, Sydnor turned next to an exploration of what he considered the more sagacious political traditions of colonial Virginia. *Gentlemen Freeholders: Political Practices in Washington's Virginia* (1952) was a thinly veiled allegory suggesting that Virginia's cultured, well-educated revolutionary-era elites combined the best of aristocracy and democracy to produce a political climate far superior to the destructive partisanship characteristic of the modern South.

On 26 February 1954 Sydnor spoke before the Mississippi Historical Society meeting in Biloxi. It was his unintended valedictory. Hours later he was struck by a heart attack, and he died on 2 March. Months earlier, Sydnor had written with disdain that the current "fad for displaying Confederate caps and flags" and appealing to "the ancient shibboleths of states' rights, of race, and of Southern tradition" boded ill for his native region. Prepared as remarks before Louisiana State University's Walter Lynwood Fleming Lectures, his words were never uttered. Death had stilled his call for southern moderation.

Fred Arthur Bailey
Abilene Christian University

Fred Arthur Bailey, in *Reading Southern History: Essays on Interpreters and Interpretations*, ed. Glenn Feldman (2001).

S

T

T-House

The one-story T-house is ubiquitous in Mississippi and throughout the South. It is significant as the first widely accepted popular vernacular house type in the region. In its simplest form its plan is that of the letter *T* on its side, with two square rooms, one behind the other, a third square room straddling the others on either the left or the right, with a shed or kitchen space in the rear and a porch on the front. Examples exist from the mid-nineteenth century, but in the Deep South most T-houses were constructed from about 1880 through the early twentieth century, usually to accommodate what W. J. Cash described as the "numerous army" of poor whites moving from the country to southern towns seeking to work in mills or to set up small businesses.

T-houses became widely adopted in the Deep South for a number of reasons: they could be built from readily available, mass-produced lumber, the projecting front room created a porch space and provided privacy from other T-houses in a row, high ceilings and central halls or window alignments kept the house cool during the severe summers, and elevation and lack of cellars helped deal with flooding, moisture problems, and insects and gave cool, dry shelter under the house to dogs and chickens.

Culturally, T-houses were popular because they allowed the new, growing middle class to feel "uptown" and to express individual taste by painting them or embellishing them in Victorian style with mass-produced gingerbread trim or bay windows and because they could easily be expanded. Plan books were available, and the 1908 Sears and Roebuck catalog even offered a T-house.

Architecturally, the T-house is important because it is a hybrid type that has roots in both folk and high-style architecture, featuring cubic rooms that are basic to cabins and dogtrots as well as Georgian mansions. Many T-houses have a central hall as in Georgian style, but this can also be seen as an interpretation of the open passage in a dogtrot. The T-house also draws from popular Gothic Revival styles with its asymmetry (the projecting gable room) and incorporation of decorative wooden flourishes. A lineage for the

T-house can be clearly traced from house plans illustrated in A. J. Davis's 1838 *Rural Residences* and his protégé A. J. Downing's "small bracketed cottage" design to cottages built for mill workers in Graniteville, South Carolina, in 1848 by William Gregg, the father of cotton manufacturing. New South prophet Daniel Augustus Tompkins standardized T-house plans by publishing *Cotton Mill, Commercial Features* (1899), which prescribed specs for mill "operatives' homes" down to the window sills and wainscoting.

Many of these perfectly adapted houses are endangered and are now deteriorating or developing structural problems, but they deserve to be protected and preserved as the first and predominant working-class structures in the region and the house type that has defined the look of many southern towns.

Lisa Howorth
Oxford, Mississippi

Lisa Howorth, "Popular Vernacular: The One-Story T-House in the South" (master's thesis, University of Mississippi, 1984).

Taborian Hospital

In 1926 Perry M. Smith, a Mississippi schoolteacher, was elected chief grand mentor of the Mississippi Jurisdiction of the Knights and Daughters of Tabor, a black fraternal organization with members in a dozen states. When Smith took over the society, its membership was floundering. To revive the chapter, Smith decided to emulate the success of another Mississippi fraternal organization, the Afro-American Sons and Daughters, then in the process of building a hospital in Yazoo City to provide inexpensive health care for the society's members. The thirty-two-bed Afro-American Sons and Daughters Hospital opened in 1928 at a cost of fifty thousand dollars, almost all of which was raised from quarterly taxes of fifty cents per member. Smith first proposed his hospital plan in 1929, but it was rejected by the organization's membership. Undaunted, he continued to press for a society hospital, and in 1938 the membership finally consented to raising one hundred thousand dollars for a facility to be built in Mound Bayou. Funding for the hospital was raised primarily from an assessment on the society's twenty-five thousand members, and on 1 February 1942 the one-story, forty-two-bed Taborian Hospital opened.

Taborian Hospital was a boon to black patients in the Mississippi Delta. Drs. W. L. Smith of Clarksville and Phillip M. George of Mound Bayou served as the facility's codirectors, and Dr. Theodore R. M. Howard was hired as surgeon in chief. Within four years the facility expanded to seventy-six beds, and by 1946 the hospital annually conducted more than twelve hundred operations in its two operating rooms. Members of the Knights and Daughters of Tabor who paid the annual Hospital Emergency Tax of two dollars and the quarterly hospital fee of seventy-five cents were entitled to up to thirty-one days a year of free hospitalization in Taborian's wards, including all their medical and surgical examinations and treatments. Nonmembers were also admitted to the hospital, but at higher costs.

Howard was dismissed from his post as surgeon in chief of the hospital in 1947, and the Board of Directors approached Matthew Walker, a professor of surgery at Meharry Medical College in Nashville, to fill the position. Walker declined the post but proposed a program that benefited both Taborian and Meharry for more than two decades. Walker provided Taborian with surgical residents and interns from Meharry on a rotating basis. This plan alleviated Meharry's problem of finding internships and residencies for its students and Taborian's problem of maintaining a well-trained staff at a price that it could afford. The plan called for Meharry to send two residents to serve four- to six-month stints in Mound Bayou as the hospital's chief surgeon and assistant. These residents were accompanied by Meharry seniors who served two-week shifts as interns. Walker also periodically made the two-hundred-mile trip from Nashville to check on his charges and to perform any especially risky operations.

Differing from any medical training program in the country, the Mound Bayou program was an enormous success between 1947 to 1974. The Meharry contingent hosted daily clinics seven days a week for the people of the Delta and performed a wide rage of minor operations. The residents and interns from Nashville were also responsible for the hospital's obstetrical and gynecological services. In addition to receiving on-the-job training, the Meharry delegation trained locals to work in the hospital as medical technicians. The program was funded by a monthly fee, initially a dollar, from the society's membership. In 1966 the hospital received a federal grant from the US Office of Economic Opportunity to continue the program. In 1967, with the increase of federal funding in hospital care, Taborian Hospital and the Friendship Clinic, a private hospital opened by Dr. Howard following his dismissal from Taborian, were merged into the Mound Bayou Community Hospital. In 1983 the facility closed.

Thomas J. Ward Jr.
Spring Hill College

David T. Beito, *Journal of Southern History* (February 1999); Matthew Walker, *Meharry Medical College Quarterly Digest* (1966); Thomas J. Ward Jr., *Black Physicians in the Jim Crow South* (2003).

Tallahatchie County

Founded in 1833 and named for a Choctaw word roughly meaning "river of rocks," Tallahatchie County is located in the Mississippi Delta. The county has two seats, Charleston and Sumner. Other Tallahatchie communities include Glendora and Tutwiler. In the 1840 census, Tallahatchie was a small but growing plantation county with a population of 1,591 slaves and 1,394 free persons. All of the county's workers were employed in agriculture.

By 1860 the county's population had grown to 5,054 slaves and 2,836 free people. Tallahatchie's commitment to plantation crops showed in its concentration on cotton. It ranked in the upper half of the state's counties in cotton production despite its small population. In 1860, 23 people worked in industry, almost all of them in lumberyards, and the county had ten churches: five Methodist, three Presbyterian, and two Baptist.

In 1877 part of Tallahatchie County became a section of Quitman County. Nonetheless, Tallahatchie County experienced a substantial population increase, with a population of 10,926 in 1880. African Americans made up nearly 62 percent of all residents, and as in many counties with African American majorities, sharecroppers and other tenants, rather than farm owners, did most of the farming. Tallahatchie's farm population concentrated on cotton but also grew corn and potatoes and raised livestock. In 1880 the county had fifteen manufacturing firms, which employed thirty-five men. Residents of Sumner suffered from river flooding from 1882–84, traveling by boat to nearby Webb for supplies.

From 1880 to 1900 Tallahatchie County's population nearly doubled to 19,600, and about two-thirds of the residents were African Americans. Tallahatchie was very much a farming county, and as in much of Mississippi, dramatic differences existed between the percentage of African American farmers who owned their land (192 of 2,262, or 8 percent) and the percentage of white farmers who did so (490 of 1,027, or 48 percent). Tallahatchie County was home to 98 industrial workers, all but one of them male, and 59 immigrants.

In the early twentieth century about half of Tallahatchie County's church members were Baptists—most of them Missionary Baptists. Methodists, especially the Colored Methodist Episcopal Church and the African Methodist Episcopal Zion Church, accounted for more than a third of the county's churchgoers, while substantial numbers of Southern Baptists were also present.

Tallahatchie County played an important role in Mississippi music. At the Tutwiler railroad station, W. C. Handy first encountered the "strangest music I ever heard"—the blues. Sonny Boy Williamson II (Aleck Miller) was born between Tutwiler and Glendora, and old-time country musicians

Narmour and Smith, though not from Tallahatchie County, recorded three songs named after one of the county seats: "Charleston #1," "Charleston #2," and "Charleston #3."

The Tallahatchie County courthouse in Sumner was built in 1903 and destroyed by fire in 1908; its records were destroyed in another fire a year later. The rebuilt Sumner courthouse became a focus of national attention during the 1955 trial and acquittal of Roy Bryant and J. W. Milam for murdering Emmett Till.

Tallahatchie County's population increased substantially in the early twentieth century, topping 35,000 by 1930. African Americans continued to outnumber whites by a ratio of about two to one. Charleston had more than 3,000 residents. Despite the 400 or so industrial workers, Tallahatchie, like most of the Mississippi Delta, remained dominated by agriculture. Tenant farmers operated 88 percent of county farms, and cotton was by far the leading agricultural product. Tallahatchie County native Jamie Whitten, a longtime member of the US Congress, was one of the leading backers of agricultural policies that supported the goals of Delta planters.

Several individuals important to the civil rights movement were natives of Tallahatchie County. Mamie Till-Mobley, mother of Emmett Till, grew up in Webb before moving to Chicago and returned to Tallahatchie for the trial of the men accused of killing her son. Vera Pigee grew up in Tallahatchie County before moving to Coahoma County and becoming an important leader of the National Association for the Advancement of Colored People.

The county's population declined sharply in the mid-twentieth century, and by 1960 Tallahatchie was home to just 24,081 people. African Americans comprised 64 percent of the population, whites accounted for 35 percent, and the remainder were Chinese and Native Americans. Tallahatchie remained an agricultural county, with 61 percent of its workers engaged in farming—the third-highest percentage in the state. Farms concentrated on soybeans and cotton as well as wheat, corn, and livestock. Six percent of the workforce was employed in industry, primarily in making apparel.

Tallahatchie has been the home of some uniquely creative people. Actor Morgan Freeman grew up in Charleston and in 2008 supplied resources and inspiration for his hometown high school to desegregate its senior prom, an event featured in the 2009 film *Prom Night in Mississippi*. Sumner native William Eggleston helped revolutionize both the techniques and subject matter of American photography. Patti Carr Black, longtime director of the Mississippi State Historical Museum and author or editor of numerous books on Mississippi arts and culture, grew up in Sumner. The Tutwiler Quilters emerged in the 1980s as a combination of long traditions of quilting and new efforts to use quilts as a way to support the health and well-being of women in the county.

Like many Delta counties in Mississippi, Tallahatchie County's 2010 population was predominantly African American and had declined over the last half of the twentieth century. Fifty-six percent of the 15,378 residents were African American, 39 percent were white, and about 6 percent were Hispanic/Latino.

Mississippi Encyclopedia Staff
University of Mississippi

Mississippi State Planning Commission, *Progress Report on State Planning in Mississippi* (1938); *Mississippi Statistical Abstract*, Mississippi State University (1952–2010); Charles Sydnor and Claude Bennett, *Mississippi History* (1939); University of Virginia Library, Historical Census Browser website, http://mapserver.lib.virginia.edu; E. Nolan Waller and Dani A. Smith, *Growth Profiles of Mississippi's Counties, 1960–1980* (1985).

Tamales

On 27 November 1936, in a hotel room in San Antonio, Texas, Robert Johnson recorded "They're Red Hot," his homage to hot tamales, a popular food in his native Mississippi. This classic blues song included the lyrics, "Hot tamales and they're red hot / Yes she got 'em for sale" and represents what foodways expert John T. Edge calls a "culinary conundrum." Edge is referring to the ubiquitous presence of the "hot tamale" in the Delta.

Although now a traditional dish in the Delta, as popular as catfish and pork barbecue, the tamale seems to have originated in pre-Columbian Mexico. Mesoamericans used rabbit, boar, and other game animals until Europeans arrived in the New World and beef, goat, and domesticated meats became common ingredients. Then as now, the basic tamale is a cylinder of spiced meat encased in cornmeal, tightly wrapped and steamed inside a cornhusk. Tamales are widely considered a Mexican dish, and in the southwestern states they are a much-anticipated delicacy during the Christmas season.

Historians believe that the tamale first became a staple in the kitchens of Mississippi around the turn of the twentieth century, through local cooks' serendipitous contacts with Mexican Americans, probably farmworkers from Texas who traveled through the Delta during harvesting season.

The tamales' spicy flavors and convenience—they are readily prepared in advance and are extremely portable—recommended them to Delta sharecroppers, who quickly adopted them for quick lunches in the cotton fields. Within a few years of this introduction, tamales had become as popular as hot dogs and were being sold by street vendors throughout the Delta. During the 1930s, Mexican Americans ceased migrating to the Delta in significant numbers, but the tamale remained as their culinary legacy.

The Delta tamale, born of the collision of African American and indigenous Mexican cultures, differs in some ways

Hot tamale cart, Mississippi Delta (Courtesy Amy C. Evans)

from the variety of tamale familiar in Mexico and the American Southwest. Although recipes differ from place to place, most Delta tamales share certain basic characteristics. For example, they use plain cornmeal, while the Mexican tamale is made with the coarser-ground masa harina. Also, they are typically tied with twine, three to a bundle, before they are steamed. Delta tamales are frequently eaten with saltine crackers, which the diner employs to scoop up the savory filling. Finally, though contemporary Delta tamale fillings of pork, beef, or chicken are still flavored with a spicy mixture of chili powder, cumin, and other typical Mexican spices, they are often spicier than their Mexican counterparts.

In 2005 the Southern Foodways Alliance documented a number of sites that together became the Mississippi Delta Hot Tamale Trail. In 2012 Greenville began hosting the annual Delta Hot Tamale Festival.

Cheryl A. Matherly
Southeastern Louisiana University

Steven H. Wilson
Southeastern Louisiana University

John T. Edge, *Southern Belly: The Ultimate Food Lover's Companion to the South* (2000); John T. Edge and Ellen Rolfes, *A Gracious Plenty: Recipes and Recollections from the American South* (2002); Erik Ketcherside, *Texas Journey* (November–December 2003); Jeffrey M. Pilcher, *Que Vivan*

Los Tamales: Food and the Making of Mexican Identity (1998); Southern Foodways Alliance website, "The Tamale Trail at Ten," http://www.southern foodways.org/the-tamale-trail-at-ten/; Jane Stern and Michael Stern, *Gourmet* (December 2002).

Tartt, Donna
(b. 1963) Author

Greenwood native Donna Tartt is best known as the author of the Pulitzer Prize–winning 2013 novel *The Goldfinch*. Born on 23 December 1963 to Don and Taylor Tartt, Donna Tartt was raised in Grenada and educated at the University of Mississippi and Bennington College. A sickly child, she spent her childhood reading and writing and was doted on by a large extended family, as she details in her memoir, "Sleepytown: A Southern Gothic Childhood, with Codeine," published in *Harper's* in 1992. Tartt wrote her first poem at the age of five and published her first sonnet in the *Mississippi Literary Review* at the age of thirteen. In 1981 Tartt enrolled at the University of Mississippi, where her writing for the newspaper captured the interest of Willie Morris, who told her, "I think you're a genius." Although Tartt was seventeen and Morris was in his late forties, they became literary friends, a friendship detailed in Tartt's poignant tribute to Morris in the *Oxford American* after his death in 1999. Morris encouraged her to enroll in Barry Hannah's graduate writing workshop, but Hannah declared that she had already surpassed his graduate students, and the two men encouraged her to transfer to Bennington College in Vermont to further develop her talent. There she forged literary friendships with fellow students Brett Easton Ellis and Jill Eisenstadt and began work on what became her first novel, *The Secret History*. That book and her other novels echo her childhood reading of classic adventure stories such as *The Adventures of Tom Sawyer*, *Huckleberry Finn*, *Peter Pan*, *Treasure Island*, and *The Adventures of Sherlock Holmes* as well as evoke the major themes and questions of the Greek tragedies.

Tartt spent ten years laboring on *The Secret History* (1992), which launched her into literary stardom. She has subsequently maintained that pace, releasing her second novel, *The Little Friend* in 2003 and *The Goldfinch* in 2013. All three novels are haunted by murders, but Tartt describes herself as more interested in the "echoes and repercussions of the act [of murder] through time." In *The Secret History*, classics majors at a northeastern college commit a murder, but the story's real interest lies in the complicity of narrator Richard Papen, his role as an outsider, and the choices he makes once he becomes privy to the secret history.

T

In *The Little Friend* twelve-year-old Harriet tries to solve the mystery of her older brother's disappearance and then avenge his murder. Set in Mississippi, *The Little Friend* meditates on classic themes of good and evil as well as perceptions of truth and reality. While *The Secret History* scrutinized the microscopic community at an elite eastern college, *The Little Friend* widens the lens to explore a variety of ages, classes, and races in the changing Sunbelt South of the 1970s, a time when the cultural, social, and economic norms were undergoing rapid restructuring.

Events in *The Goldfinch*, too, are set in motion by murder—in this case, a terrorist attack at New York City's Metropolitan Museum of Art. After his mother dies in the bombing, thirteen-year-old Theodore Decker embarks on a worldwide odyssey that involves crime, drugs, and ultimately another killing before he finds redemption. The highly acclaimed story spent thirty weeks on the *New York Times* best-seller list and won the 2014 Pulitzer Prize for fiction. Although murder is the central or initiating action of all three novels, they are not mysteries. Instead, Tartt explores how the act has a rippling affect on all those involved.

Anne Evans
Metropolitan State College

Therese Eibeen, *Poets and Writers* (24 August 2007); James Kaplan, *Vanity Fair* (September 1992); *Talk of the Nation*, NPR (5 November 2002); Donna Tartt, *Harper's* (July 1992); Donna Tartt, *Oxford American* (September–October 1999).

Tate County

Situated in the northwestern part of the state, thirty miles south of Memphis, Tate County was organized in 1873 and is named for Col. T. S. Tate, a member of an area family. It was formed from the quickly growing northern Mississippi Delta counties of Tunica, DeSoto, and Marshall. Like many nearby Delta counties in the postbellum period, Tate experienced an agricultural boom. By the time of the 1880 census, it ranked tenth in the state in growing corn, twelfth in cotton, twelfth in the number of mules, and thirteenth in the number of hogs. Because of its successful agricultural production and the presence of a local train station, the county seat, Senatobia, functioned as a shipping point for large quantities of cotton, corn, and other agricultural products. According to the 1880 US Census, Tate County was to home 18,721 residents.

Sharecroppers and tenants cultivated the majority of the Tate County farms, which focused on cotton production. In 1880 owners cultivated about 40 percent of the farms, while sharecroppers and other tenants ran the remainder. Residents had few other employment options, with only nineteen manufacturing firms employing 70 men and 11 women.

By 1900 the population had grown to 20,618, 60 percent of them African American. The county continued to rely heavily on cotton and other agricultural production. Only 4 percent of the county's 2,206 black farmers owned their land, compared to more than a third of the white farmers. Tate's nonagricultural workforce remained small but had grown to 136 employees at sixty-nine establishments.

In the 1916 religious census more than 60 percent of Tate County's 12,000 church members identified as Baptists, including 4,300 Missionary Baptists. Members of the Methodist Episcopal Church, South; Colored Methodist Episcopal Church; and African Methodist Episcopal Church accounted for most of the rest of the county's residents, while Tate County had the state's largest Church of Christ membership (695).

Tate's population declined to 17,671 in 1930, with African Americans continuing to account for 60 percent of residents. The economy remained dependent on agricultural production, primarily cotton. Tenant farmers operated 81 percent of the county's four thousand farms.

Tate County is watered by surrounding rivers and tributary creeks. The Coldwater River runs along the northern and western border, while Senatobia, Arkabutla, Hickahala, Jim Wolf, Bear Trail, and Strayhorn Creeks dot the county's landscape. The abundant water supply contributes to Tate's rich agricultural production but has also made the area susceptible to flooding. In 1942 the US Army Corps of Engineers built Arkabutla Lake to limit flooding in the Delta region. It now provides recreational opportunities for a large population.

Tate County has an intriguing and creative musical history. Coldwater was one of Mississippi's first communities to host a radio station, and numerous well-known Mississippi musicians are associated with Tate. Blues performer Jessie Mae Hemphill was born near the Tate and Panola County line. As a child Otha Turner moved with his family to the Tate County community of Gravel Springs, where he stayed for most of his life, playing instruments he built himself. Country musician O. B. McClinton was born in Senatobia in 1940, and bluesman R. L. Burnside spent much of his childhood in Tate County.

Memphis-born writer Joan Williams had grandparents in Arkabutla, and she used Tate County as the model for parts of her fiction. Historian Dumas Malone, best known for his multivolume biography of Thomas Jefferson, was born in Coldwater. Actor James Earl Jones was born in Arkabutla in 1931 and lived there until the age of five, when his family moved to Michigan. Northwest Community College opened in Senatobia in 1928 and now enrolls more than seven thousand students each year.

Unlike other parts of the Mississippi Delta, Tate did not experience a significant population loss in the second half of the twentieth century, though the county's demographics changed significantly. In 1960 Tate County was home to 18,138 people, 58 percent of them African American. Almost half of Tate's working people were employed in agriculture, with cotton, corn, and soybeans as the primary crops. About 10 percent of the county's workers had jobs in industry, mostly in apparel factories.

Tate County's population grew by nearly 60 percent between 1960 and 2010, reaching 28,996. By 2010 67 percent of Tate's population was white, while 30 percent was African American, and 2 percent was Hispanic/Latino.

Mississippi Encyclopedia Staff
University of Mississippi

City of Senatobia website, www.cityofsenatobia.com; Mississippi State Planning Commission, *Progress Report on State Planning in Mississippi* (1938); *Mississippi Statistical Abstract*, Mississippi State University (1952–2010); Northwest Mississippi Community College website, www.northwestms.edu; Charles Sydnor and Claude Bennett, *Mississippi History* (1939); University of Virginia Library, Historical Census Browser website, http://mapserver.lib.virginia.edu; E. Nolan Waller and Dani A. Smith, *Growth Profiles of Mississippi's Counties, 1960–1980* (1985).

Taulbert, Clifton L.
(b. 1945) Author

Born on 19 February 1945 and raised in Glen Allan, Mississippi, Clifton Taulbert graduated from high school in Greenville in 1963, served in the US Air Force, and went on to earn a bachelor's degree from Oral Roberts University and a graduate degree from the Southwest Graduate School of Banking at Southern Methodist University.

While pursuing his education and banking career, Taulbert began writing a memoir, *Once upon a Time When We Were Colored* (1989), in which he introduced uncles and aunts, godparents, cousins, neighbors, and others who inspired and taught him. Dealing with leisure, religion, work, organizations, and above all family life, the book portrays a community of people who care for and help each other, especially in times of trouble.

Once upon a Time When We Were Colored differs from most African American autobiographies (most obviously Richard Wright's *Black Boy*) in that it has an optimistic tone and considerable nostalgia about the strength of family relationships, church life, and community institutions among African Americans. In addition, Taulbert's book does not concentrate on racism or deprivation. To be sure, the book dramatizes injustices done to African Americans, detailing such painful moments as when Taulbert was turned away from a whites-only circus and was humiliated by a white store clerk. But according to Taulbert, "Even though segregation was a painful reality for us, there were some very good things that happened. Today I enjoy the broader society in which I live and I would never want to return to forced segregation, but I also have a deeply-felt sense that important values were conveyed to me in my colored childhood." The book was made into a 1995 movie.

The volume has attracted some critics who argue that the use of the discredited term *colored* and the overall positive tone do too little to critique a racist system. Taulbert has responded that he wrote to describe the positive features of the people who helped raise him. From memories he described in *Once upon a Time When We Were Colored*, Taulbert developed the concept of the "porch people"—adult neighbors and family members who provided security and good examples to all the children of the neighborhood. He returned to this theme in his first book for children, *Little Cliff and the Porch People* (1999).

His second memoir, *The Last Train North* (1992), describes people's fascination with the possibility of leaving Mississippi. The sound of the train and stories about people who left on the train raised hopes for young people as they dealt with everyday frustrations and wondered about life beyond Mississippi. A high point was his return from St. Louis, where he had moved in 1963, to enjoy the pleasures of home from the perspective of one who had left. The third memoir, *Watching Our Crops Come In* (1997), describes his time in the military and his hopes for the civil rights movement. Again, a trip home to Glen Allan was central to the story, but this time he was observing the changes stimulated by civil rights activism. The latter two books consist more of individual stories and concentrate a bit less on the personalities and moral lessons that dominate Taulbert's first memoir.

Taulbert lives in Tulsa, Oklahoma, and has now written a total of twelve books, including three works for children. He speaks regularly to audiences on education, values, and relationships. His 1997 book, *Eight Habits of the Heart*, uses lessons he learned in Glen Allan that can help people care about and live with each other. The eight habits, all linked to specific moments of his early life in the Mississippi Delta, are Nurturing, Dependability, Responsibility, Friendship, Brotherhood, High Expectations, Courage, and Hope. His work has won an Image Award from the National Association for the Advancement of Colored People and the Mississippi Arts and Letters Award for Nonfiction.

Ted Ownby
University of Mississippi

Mississippi Writers Page website, www.olemiss.edu/mwp; Clifton Taulbert website, www.cliftontaulbert.com.

T

Taxation

Taxation is a method of collecting financial resources from individuals and organizations for government use. For state governments, taxes take on many forms and are collected from different venues. Many states employ taxes on income, retail sales, and real property. In addition to the more common taxes, most states employ special taxes that reflect their unique geography, culture, and economic condition.

Mississippi's tax structure is often classified as regressive, meaning that the people with less ability to pay have a heavier tax burden. Conversely, a progressive tax is one in which individuals with a greater ability to pay contribute a higher percentage of their income in taxes. Compared to most states, Mississippi's tax structure is indeed regressive because it depends heavily on the sales tax and has relatively low property and income taxes, but this approach is fairly similar to that taken by neighboring states.

An example of the regressive nature of Mississippi's tax structure is its taxes on food. Mississippi has the nation's highest state sales tax—7 percent—and the state does not exempt food. Most states with a sales tax do not tax groceries, while other states tax sales of food less than other retail goods. In addition, municipal governments may level additional taxes on food or other items. Revenue received by Mississippi state and local governments from retail sales taxes accounts for close to one-third of the total budget, a percentage higher than most states but in line with neighboring southern states such as Alabama, Louisiana, Arkansas, Georgia, and Tennessee.

Mississippi has a gas tax of 18 cents per gallon; local governments may also add taxes and fees. Again, neighboring states impose similar taxes, ranging from 16 to 21.5 cents per gallon. Mississippi's tax on cigarettes is 68 cents a pack, and Mississippi taxes beer at 43 cents a gallon, a rate that is on the high end when compared to neighboring states.

In the early 1990s the state of Mississippi legalized casino-style gaming. The state taxes the casinos' gross receipts at a rate of about 12 percent.

Property taxes fluctuate greatly within any state as a consequence of local governments' rates. When comparing state rates and exemptions given to homeowners and farmers, Mississippi is near the average among southern states. When compared to all states, Mississippi is below average in property tax rates.

Mississippi has a graduated income tax rate: filers who make five thousand dollars or less per year are taxed at 3 percent; those who make between five thousand and ten thousand dollars per year are taxed at 4 percent; and anyone who makes more than ten thousand dollars per year is taxed at 5 percent. These rates are similar to those of neighboring states with the exception of Tennessee, which does not tax earned income.

James Newman
Southeast Missouri
State University

Federation of Tax Administrators website, www.taxadmin.org; Kevin B. Smith, Alan Greenblatt, and Michele Mariani, *Governing States and Localities* (2007); Stateline website, www.stateline.org.

Taylor, Mildred D.
(b. 1943) Writer

"Racism is offensive. Racism is not polite, and it is full of pain." So says award-winning novelist Mildred Delois Taylor. Racial injustice is a major theme in her literary works for children and young adults. It is what compelled her father, Wilbert Taylor, to move his wife, Deletha Marie Davis Taylor, and their family to Toledo, Ohio, soon after Mildred was born in Jackson on 13 September 1943. Through summers with her relatives and the stories they shared, however, Mildred came to see the South as home. According to Taylor, "Many of the stories told were humorous, some were tragic, but all told of the dignity and survival of a people living in a society that allowed them few rights as citizens and treated them as inferiors." Taylor learned about her great-grandfather, the son of a white plantation owner in Alabama and "an Indian-African woman" during slavery. In the late 1800s Taylor's great-grandfather went to Mississippi, where he bought and settled land that remains in the Taylor family.

The oral history handed down through generations of Taylors became the inspiration for her lifelong work: "I do not know how old I was when the daydreams became more than that, and I decided to write them down, but by the time I entered high school, I was confident that I would one day be a writer." Although Taylor graduated from an integrated high school in Toledo in 1961, she had firsthand experience with segregation from her visits to Mississippi, where she saw signs declaring "whites only." Taylor graduated from the University of Toledo and then spent two years as a Peace Corps volunteer in Ethiopia. Living in Africa had a profound effect on her, and she gained a deeper appreciation for her own personal and family history.

Taylor returned to the United States in 1967 and became a recruiter and instructor with the Peace Corps before enrolling at the University of Colorado's School of Journalism. Just as the Black Power movement took off, Taylor joined the

Black Student Alliance and played an integral role in creating the university's black studies program while earning a master's degree in journalism.

Taylor's first break as a writer came when her *Song of the Trees* won first prize in a contest sponsored by the Council on Interracial Books for Children. At the time, she was working as a copy editor and decided to fiddle with the point of view of a story she had been developing about life during the Great Depression. After several revisions, Taylor used the point of view of eight-year-old Cassie Logan, and the members of the Logan family have recurred throughout her writings.

Her second book, *Roll of Thunder, Hear My Cry*, won the 1977 Newbery Medal, the most prestigious award in children's literature, and was a National Book Award finalist. Set in Mississippi, like all her works, the book is Cassie's coming-of-age tale. The nine-year-old learns about night riders "coming fast along the rain-soaked road like cats eyes in the night" and the indignity of being forced to apologize to a white girl for being on the sidewalk. Taylor's other novels for children include *Let the Circle Be Unbroken* (1981), *The Friendship* (1987), *The Gold Cadillac* (1987), *The Road to Memphis* (1990), *Mississippi Bridge* (1990), *The Well* (1995), and *The Land* (2001). Her writings have received numerous honors, including several Coretta Scott King Awards and an Outstanding Book of the Year citation from the *New York Times*. Mississippi governor Haley Barbour declared 2 April 2004 Mildred D. Taylor Day.

Sally S. Graham
Hot Springs, Arkansas

Mississippi Writers and Musicians website, www.mswritersandmusicians .com; Mississippi Writers Page website, www.olemiss.edu/mwp; Penguin Publishers website, www.penguin.com.

Taylor, Sarah Mary
(1916–2000) Quilter

Born in Anding, Mississippi, just south of Yazoo City, on 12 August 1916, Sarah Mary Taylor grew up in the Mississippi Delta under Jim Crow. The daughter of Pearlie Posey (1894–1984) and niece of Pecolia Warner (1901–83), both of whom were noted Mississippi quilters, Taylor learned by the age of nine how to piece quilts. By 1931 Taylor left home, married, and began making quilts for her own household. Like many African Americans of the era, she also worked at a variety of plantation jobs, including field hand, nanny, cook, and housekeeper.

Taylor often made pieced quilts composed of long strips of colored and printed cloth sewn together to form geometric and abstract designs. However, she is best known for her appliqué quilts, which she made by sewing designs onto the quilt's background fabric. Taylor seems to have decided to make appliqué quilts after folklorist William Ferris interviewed her aunt, Pecolia Warner, for his film, *Four Women Artists* (1978). Wanting to sell her own work, Taylor made a quilt of nine blocks and appliquéd her name, address, and phone number onto each block. A series of appliquéd quilts followed. Some, such as *Taylor's Men Quilt* (1979), *Mermaid Quilt* (1979), and *Purple Hand Quilt* (1985, commissioned for use in the film *The Color Purple*), also included figurative designs. Taylor at times drew the patterns freehand and at other times copied illustrations from magazines, newspapers, catalogs, feed sacks, and even cereal boxes. Sometimes she drew inspiration from three-dimensional forms: a plastic ornament hanging on her bathroom wall inspired the fish design that decorates one of her quilts. Taylor made the pattern for her hand-motif quilts by drawing around her own hand. Taylor used such patterns, rendered in cardboard, over and over again.

Whether Taylor was making strip or appliquéd quilts, she generally preferred bright colors and simple, bold designs, often in multiple patterns. She sewed together strips of different sizes and colors in a seemingly haphazard fashion or cut appliqué designs in different materials and colors and laid them out in a random arrangement that pleased her eye. Neither highly ordered nor symmetrical in design, Taylor's quilts evidence a preference for the irregular and asymmetrical. Such design principles—bold colors, simple designs, multiple patterns, and asymmetry—have been perceived as demonstrating continuities between African and African American textile traditions. For example, appliqué quilts made by African Americans have been associated with the appliqué textiles of the Fon of Benin and of the Ewe, Fanti, and Ashanti of Ghana, where similarly abstracted figurative patterns also appear. Similar motifs have also been related to African American cloth charm traditions. For example, the hand motif that appears in several of Taylor's quilts has been associated with an African American charm known as a *mojo*, meaning "hand" as in "helping hand." However, Taylor rejected the idea that this motif was associated with Haitian voodoo and asserted her Christian faith as a Missionary Baptist.

Taylor's quilts can be found among the holdings of the American Museum of Folk Art, Hampton Institute, the Montgomery Museum of Art, the Philadelphia Museum of Art, and the B. S. Ricks Memorial Library, Yazoo City.

Carol Crown
University of Memphis

Mary Elizabeth Johnson Huff, *Just How I Pictured It in My Mind: Contemporary African American Quilts from the Montgomery Museum of*

T

Art (2006); Liz Lindsey, "Sarah Mary Taylor: Identity in Context" (master's thesis, University of North Carolina at Chapel Hill, 2003); Maude Wahlman, *Signs and Symbols: African Images in African American Quilts* (1993); Maude Wahlman and Ella King Torrey, *Ten Afro-American Quilters* (1983).

Television

Television came relatively late to Mississippi and several other southern states. Following a federal freeze on licensing new stations by the Federal Communications Commission (FCC), television stations came on air in 1953 in Mississippi, Arkansas, and South Carolina. Over the next three years Mississippians built six stations—first WJTV and WLBT in Jackson and WCOC in Meridian and later WCBI in Columbus, WDAM in Hattiesburg, and WTWV in Tupelo. Anticipating WJTV's first broadcast, Pres. Dwight D. Eisenhower's January 1953 inauguration, the station's general manager, John Rossitor, told city leaders and educators that television would "bring the world into your home and accent friendliness among neighbors in this city and state."

While business leaders and other Mississippians expressed great interest in the new medium's potential, local television was quickly confronted by questions regarding the televised representation of racial integration and civil rights struggle. Deeply committed integrationists and African Americans attempted to attract the attention of the national television networks and use local outlets to criticize segregationist myths and practices. Local stations in Mississippi responded to these pressures differently. Some stations included controversial news and public affairs topics and personalities in their regular programming, while other outlets, among them WLBT, chose the road of resistance to integrationist appeals, in alliance with powerful segregationist organizations such as the Citizens' Council and Mississippi State Sovereignty Commission.

During the 1960s WLBT was enmeshed in legal fights stemming from challenges to its segregationist practices. In both 1966 and 1969, the District of Columbia Court of Appeals reversed FCC licensing decisions, inviting public participation in federal hearings and effectively terminating the station's relicensing. In 1980, after years of interim nonprofit management, the station's license was awarded to TV-3, a largely local Jackson group that was 51 percent African American and headed by Aaron Henry. These challenges and court decisions had a wide-ranging impact, encouraging citizen licensing challenges and broadcast reform efforts in local markets across the United States and establishing an important legal precedent regarding the participation of consumers and citizens in federal administrative agency hearings.

Noncommercial television was first broadcast from within Mississippi in 1970. In that year, what evolved into the Mississippi Public Broadcasting network began airing from Jackson's WMAA, owned and operated by the Mississippi Authority for Educational Television, which focused on educational and distance-learning initiatives.

Commercial stations in the state have garnered multiple prestigious George Foster Peabody Awards. This highly competitive national award, recognizing "distinguished achievement and meritorious service by television stations," has been given to WLBT (1976) and to Biloxi's WLOX (1989, 2005).

Since the 1990s television in Mississippi and throughout the United States has been restructured by media conglomeration and consolidation. Small-market stations, often owned and operated independently at their inception, have increasingly become integrated parts of larger broadcast station groups and media corporations. For example, by the second decade of the twenty-first century, Raycom Media owned or operated more than sixty television stations nationwide, including three Mississippi outlets (WLBT, WLOX, and WDAM). Among the state's oldest stations, one exception to this trend is WTVA (formerly WTWV, serving Tupelo–Columbus–West Point), which has been owned and operated by the Spain family since the mid-1950s.

Steven Classen
California State University
at Los Angeles

Steven Classen, *Watching Jim Crow: The Struggles over Mississippi TV, 1955–1969* (2004); Kay Mills, *Changing Channels: The Civil Rights Case That Transformed Television* (2004); George Foster Peabody Awards website, peabodyawards.com.

Tennessee Valley Authority

Congress passed the Tennessee Valley Authority (TVA) Act on 18 May 1933, during the first one hundred days of Pres. Franklin D. Roosevelt's administration. The act chartered a federally owned corporation to improve navigation, flood control, electricity generation, fertilizer manufacturing, and social and economic conditions in the Tennessee River Valley. Although the Tennessee River watershed includes only the northeastern corner of Mississippi, on 7 February 1934 the city of Tupelo became the first municipality to receive TVA power. As the nation's largest producer of electric power, largest user of coal, and the leading investor in nuclear power, the TVA has evolved into an encompassing social, political, and economic institution. It has persisted through a tumultuous and divisive history in the region and in the Magnolia State.

Despite its legacy as one of the most significant New Deal programs, the TVA has been highly controversial from its inception. In performing what Roosevelt called a "great national experiment," the TVA Act developed a system of multipurpose navigation, flood control, and hydroelectric power production. The TVA offered programs encouraging soil conservation, the production and use of fertilizers, and regional economic planning. On the heels of the Great Depression, the TVA was central to the literal and symbolic creation of the Tennessee Valley watershed as a unified region of the South.

Following passage of the TVA Act, public officials and agency representatives eagerly sought to bring TVA power to the state. Mississippi politicians—particularly Sen. Pat Harrison and Rep. John Rankin—were firm TVA supporters, arguing strenuously for the general and equitable distribution of power to the Magnolia State. Debate surrounding the TVA emphasized that Mississippi was devoid of both coal and water power. Hence, the state's industrial growth would depend on equalization of the water-power resources of the South. TVA chair David Lilienthal furiously marketed power in northern Mississippi, promoting the TVA as a source of cheap electricity, grassroots regional democracy, environmental conservation, and peaceful use of energy. Lilienthal created a rural electrification program that Roosevelt copied on a national scale with the creation of the Rural Electrification Administration, which Congress made permanent in 1936. Lilienthal's work attracted Roosevelt to Tupelo, where he told four thousand residents, "What you are doing here is to be copied in every state of the union before we get through."

Hoping to alleviate the socioeconomic woes of the Great Depression, most Mississippians enthusiastically accepted the TVA and its programs. As was true across the South, the depression greatly affected the most important industries in Mississippi—agriculture, forest products, and mining. Dire economic needs, effective public promotion, widespread and affordable distribution of power, and the regional (rather than federal) nature of TVA helped conservative Mississippians reconcile themselves to the "socialistic" characteristics often cited by its critics.

The Alcorn County Electric Power Association (ACEPA) was the first organization the TVA subsumed for the purpose of acquiring and operating distribution systems in Mississippi. ACEPA exemplifies the reciprocal relationships forged between the TVA and regional political and economic entities. Interested citizens organized the ACEPA and other private nonprofit membership corporations, usually on a county basis, to acquire and operate distribution systems. Members who paid the hundred-dollar fee received electricity purchased by their associations from the TVA at wholesale rates. ACEPA was the first organization of this type, chartered under Mississippi law as a nonprofit civic improvement corporation on 17 January 1934. The following June ACEPA entered into a contract with TVA for the purchase of the electrical properties in the county that the TVA had acquired from the Mississippi Power Company.

A 1934 TVA contract extension with the Alabama Power Company provided for the agency to purchase several of the company's municipal power distribution systems in Mississippi. The TVA ultimately provided power for almost one-third of Mississippi's land area, though less than 1 percent of the state was included in the Tennessee River watershed. Sales from the subsidiaries of Alabama Power Company to TVA included the entire generating, transmission, and distribution properties of the Mississippi Power Company in nine counties in northeastern Mississippi for $850,000. This first contract included all of the company's properties in Pontotoc, Lee, Itawamba, Union, Benton, Tippah, Prentiss, Tishomingo, and Alcorn Counties, and the purchase was completed on 1 June 1934. The TVA's power policy was initially developed in northeastern Mississippi. Residents receiving TVA power functioned as an test group for FDR's "great national experiment." Distribution of TVA electricity to the All-America City proved to be the first step in the agency's venture into the power business.

A town of roughly six thousand people in 1934, Tupelo had previously owned its distribution system but purchased power from a private company. TVA service began on 7 February 1934, when the city's franchise with the Mississippi Power Company expired. Mayor J. P. Manney announced that the city had been paying 1.7 cents per kilowatt hour but under the TVA would pay only .7 cents per kilowatt hour. Reductions in domestic rates for the city were estimated at a minimum of 67.7 percent, while commercial rates were 50 percent lower. In the first six months that Tupelo received power from the TVA, the amount of electricity used in the city's homes increased by 83 percent.

In addition to the benefits provided to Tupelo and other towns and cities of the valley, rural electrification greatly benefited Mississippi farmers, generating nearly instantaneous improvements in the regional economy. The TVA also served social and environmental purposes, as administrators worked with farmers to eliminate malaria and improve water quality in the region. Experimental "test farms" helped conserve soil and forest resources, and social programs built mobile libraries and schools.

The TVA's construction of the Pickwick Lock and Dam in the bordering counties of Mississippi (Tishomingo), Tennessee, and Alabama began in 1934 and was completed in 1938. The TVA's 1,611 employees cleared 16,000 acres of land and 382 miles of riverbank, removed and relocated graves, removed five hundred families, and rerouted six miles of road. In addition, excavations conducted by the TVA uncovered thousands of artifacts and more than two hundred sites dating from the Woodland and Mississippian periods of historic occupation.

The TVA's power service area was not formally restricted until 1959, when an amendment confined its authority to Tennessee, the northern third of Mississippi, the northern quarter of Alabama, and about one-tenth of Kentucky. In kilowatt usage and total population served, Mississippi ranks second only to Tennessee as a recipient of TVA power. Following World War II, the agency served primarily as a power distribution company. The TVA remains influential in the region as well as ideologically contentious: cost-cutting conservatives see the agency as a vehicle for disproportionate regional pork-barrel spending, residents seek affordable power, and moderates and liberals view the TVA as beneficial.

Robert Krause
Maryland National Capital Park
and Planning Commission

North Callahan, *TVA: Bridge over Troubled Waters* (1980); Gordon Rufus Clapp, *The TVA: An Approach to the Development of a Region* (1955); Vaughn L. Grisham, "Tupelo, Mississippi: From Settlement to Industrial Community, 1860 to 1970" (PhD dissertation, University of North Carolina at Chapel Hill, 1978); Preston John Hubbard, *Origins of the TVA: The Muscle Shoals Controversy, 1920–1932* (1961); David E. Lilienthal, *TVA: Democracy on the March* (1953).

Tennessee-Tombigbee Archaeology

In 1906 Congress passed the Federal Antiquities Act to preserve historic and prehistoric properties on government lands. Beginning in 1935 the Smithsonian Institution received responsibility for salvaging historic and prehistoric sites threatened by construction of reservoirs and dams along the nation's rivers. In the late 1950s this job was transferred to the National Park Service (NPS). In 1966 Congress required all federal agencies to assess damage their projects might cause the environment; three years later, it added protective regulations for historical and archaeological sites.

In 1968 the US Army Corps of Engineers began to study the potential effects of the proposed Tennessee-Tombigbee Waterway on the environment and the area's archaeological and historical sites. The Mobile District began discussions with the NPS to avoid destruction of important sites and structures. The NPS had little funding but authorized studies by the University of Alabama at the lake above Gainesville, Alabama. The NPS also contracted Mississippi State University to look for sites in areas around Columbus, Mississippi.

From 1970 to 1974 thousands of acres were inspected, and dozens of archaeological sites were found and tested. The most interesting sites received more thorough excavation. During this era the federal government also required agencies to find historical and archaeological sites affected by projects and to determine whether those sites were important enough to warrant inclusion on the National Register of Historic Places.

Dozens of archaeological sites and dozens of buildings lost to the construction of the waterway were excavated by scientists and archaeologists or measured and relocated by historians and architects and engineers. But most of the sites within the waterway project area were identified, evaluated, and preserved. The Corps of Engineers used remote sensing, radiocarbon dating, statistical sampling, and stratigraphic studies and analyzed pollen, soil, and plant and animal remains to discover the environmental and cultural changes that had taken place within the waterway since 10000 BC.

Native American use of the Tombigbee River Valley seems to have followed a cycle over thousands of years. During the Paleo-Indian and Early Archaic periods (10000–6500 BC), most artifacts and the only intact sites were found in northern rock shelters. Environmentalists, geologists, and archaeologists studied a few early artifacts and a handful of very early sites found in the waterway to fill a gap in our knowledge of early prehistory. These sites showed that the earliest Paleo-Indian and Early Archaic peoples in all segments of the waterway were hunters and gatherers who lived in widely spaced small family groups but shared the styles of their chipped stone tools with others across large parts of the Southeast. The widespread hunting patterns of this period must have included vast territories within which all of life's necessities could be found. The entire river valley, from its uplands in the Tennessee hills zone to below where it joins the Black Warrior River, may have served as the hunting territory for only one band of these early Native American families.

During the Middle Archaic period (6500–2500 BC) most large, undisturbed sites were near the boundary of the Tennessee-Tombigbee Hills and Eutaw Hills environmental zones. Larger Native American groups collected seasonally different animals and plants within one section of the river valley and used nearby stone for tools. But with a gradual change to a warmer and drier climate after 4500 BC, the environment in the waterway became like that of today. Increasing ceremonial trade in stone tools with different local styles reveals exchange of raw materials with groups well to both the north and south. This provided families with access to food without having to scatter into small groups at different seasons. In the Black Prairie areas of the waterway, Middle Archaic people continued to live in small and seasonally shifting groups with lifeways similar to other cultures across the Gulf Coastal Plain, but some of the midden mound sites excavated in the central and upper floodplains of the waterway may be the earliest permanent sites in the country.

Between 2000 BC and 200 BC, in the poorly known Late Archaic period and in the following Gulf Formational period, a variety of seeds, nuts, and fruits became more important in the Native Americans' diet. The greatest number of Late Gulf Formational period sites were found in that central part of the waterway where the Eutaw Hills and Black Prairie environmental zones meet and where the greatest number of different plants and animals could be found within a short distance.

There was very little occupation of this portion of the main trunk of the Tombigbee River Valley during the Middle Woodland period (200 BC–AD 600). It is hard to imagine that the causes for near abandonment in this period had much to do with finding food, and economics were not the only reason for Native Americans to act. It is likely that in the Middle Woodland period the kinds of rituals that took place where Native American groups came together put a high value on objects that were difficult to obtain. Perhaps that is why locations farther away from such easy routes for moving goods were favored. Indeed, three of the largest Middle Woodland ritual sites in the southeast lie less than twenty miles from the main Tombigbee River Valley.

Then, in the Late Woodland and Mississippian periods (AD 600–1400), hunting with the bow and arrow became common, and after AD 950 corn and beans from the North and West were introduced to the Tombigbee River Valley, giving a new importance to farming and floodplain wildlife. The largest Native American groups along the Tombigbee River seem to have lived in the Black Prairie zone. But these populations were growing too large even for the productive bottomlands of the Tombigbee River Valley, and they certainly seem to have become so large and dense that traditional family rules and customs no longer regulated social comfort or provided cultural security. Such older customs must have been less and less useful as family groups increasingly relied on the same natural resources. Even cultivated plants only slowly gave more food for more labor.

By AD 1050 Native Americans occupying the broad and fertile floodplains of the Lower Tombigbee and Alabama River Valleys to the south and east, the middle Tennessee River Valley to the north, and the Lower Mississippi River Valley to the west reorganized their societies along theocratic and militaristic patterns reminiscent of those in central Mexico. The Late Woodland peoples of the Black Prairie adopted this more hierarchical way of life that promised more and better crops as well as better protection from conflict with their neighbors and with each other. This new Mississippian way of life may have seemed blessed by the supernatural powers that ran the world. It must only have seemed right that it came with more exciting and gaudy rituals that tied together the rulers of the spiritual world and those who ruled the new society.

Only one major Mississippian site was excavated in the area along the Tombigbee River that would become the waterway, but one of the largest and most elaborate ritual towns of this new Mississippian society existed just a few miles to the east, in the Lower Black Warrior River Valley. During this Mississippian period more use was made of the fish and mollusks and of the easily tilled, well-drained, and rich soils of the Black Prairie river bottoms, and socially distinct Mississippian groups lived in the central and southern portions of the waterway. These groups show differences in their pottery, their houses, and their site planning. In the north, villages were not only fortified but were located on river bluffs up tributary streams.

However, the Latest Woodland cultures had very low populations in the Upper Tombigbee Valley. The social and ritual practices of Mississippian culture seldom occurred in the uplands between the major river valleys, and the Upper Tombigbee may have served as a refuge for Late Woodland people who had less need or desire for a lifestyle in which material and spiritual comfort would come at the cost of individual freedom. Perhaps even in prehistory the more traditional members of a culture felt at home in the hills.

The studies of physical anthropology and analyses of ritual symbols from the Mississippian sites in the project area explain the origin and growth of Mississippian political systems. From those studies archaeologists have determined the possible importance of climatic change for the limits of Mississippian economic and political control. After 1250, crop reductions, malnutrition, and internecine raiding reduced most large Mississippian societies to smaller, more scattered, and less organized groups of Native Americans well before the first Europeans arrived.

Unlike the earlier shifts related to the nature and location of the resources the Native Americans used, conflict seems responsible for the fact that the main Tombigbee River Valley was mostly abandoned as a place to live year round during the three hundred to four hundred years from the end of the Mississippian period to US Removal of the Native Americans beyond the Mississippi in the 1800s. Some of the groups moved to the area around the junction of the Black Warrior and Tombigbee Rivers in the early historic period and finally to the French forts along the Lower Tombigbee and Alabama Rivers. The easy movement of well-organized, hostile tribal groups allied with larger chiefdoms or European colonies apparently made the Tombigbee River Valley unattractive if not dangerous for Native American population concentrations.

Scholarly studies along the Tombigbee River did not end with the opening of the Tennessee-Tombigbee Waterway. As operations of this artery of communication continue, archaeologists and historians monitor the sites and structures that were preserved in the project area, thousands of artifacts still exist in the waterway, and research continues on the drawings, photographs, and artifacts that came from the waterway.

David S. Brose
West Bloomfield, Michigan

Cleveland Museum of Natural History for the US Army Corps of Engineers, Mobile District, *Yesterday's River: The Archaeology of 10,000 Years along the Tennessee-Tombigbee Waterway* (1991); Raymond D. Fogelson, ed., *The Handbook of North American Indians*, vol. 14, *The Southeast* (2004).

Tennessee-Tombigbee Waterway

The Tennessee-Tombigbee Waterway is a connection between these two major river systems in the southern United States that was constructed by the US Army Corps of Engineers between 1971 and 1985. It reduces the costs of shipping from the midlands of the South to ocean ports and makes American industries economically competitive in the world market.

The Tennessee River flows from the Great Smoky Mountains of Tennessee and North Carolina southwest through Tennessee and northern Alabama to northeastern Mississippi, where it meets the rocky hills that separate its drainage from that of the Tombigbee River to the south. At this point the Tennessee turns north to cross the Cumberland plateau of western Tennessee and Kentucky and join the Ohio River about one hundred miles above where it flows into the Mississippi. Since the early 1800s the lower parts of the Tennessee River had been navigable by flatboat and steamboat up to Muscle Shoals, Alabama. For many years the Tennessee River has been a major commercial route for the Mid-South.

The Tombigbee River originates in the red clay hills of northeastern Mississippi as the East Fork and Mackeys Creek, which flow south through low hills and flatlands before joining to form the Tombigbee at Paden, Mississippi. The Black Warrior River joins the Tombigbee at Demopolis, Alabama, and winds south for two hundred miles across the Coastal Plain to join the Alabama River. There it forms a great delta, spilling into Mobile Bay and the Gulf of Mexico. The Tombigbee River was originally navigable by early shallow-draft steamboats from Mobile Bay to Cotton Gin Port, Mississippi. Clearing by the Corps of Engineers opened it as far as Aberdeen, Mississippi, in the early twentieth century, but as recently as 1950 modern barges from the ocean port of Mobile could travel up the Tombigbee only a few miles north of Demopolis.

From Chattanooga, Tennessee, it is eighteen hundred miles to New Orleans via the Tennessee, Ohio, and Mississippi Rivers, and shipping costs were high. The Rivers and Harbor Act of 1946 authorized the Corps of Engineers to plan for a canal between the Tennessee and Tombigbee Rivers that could cut that distance by one thousand miles, saving businesses millions of dollars in just a few years. In

1958 Alabama and Mississippi established the Tennessee-Tombigbee Waterway Development Authority to provide local initiative. After receiving favorable economic reports, Congress accepted the older plans in 1961 but appropriated no funds for another decade.

Building the Tennessee-Tombigbee Waterway proved difficult: the Tennessee River in Pickwick Lake is 414 feet above sea level, while at the junction of the Black Warrior and Tombigbee Rivers the waters at Demopolis Dam are only 73 feet above sea level. The lake and the dam were separated by nearly two hundred narrow, twisting miles of the Tombigbee River, with rapids along Mackeys Creek and thirty-five miles of rugged sandstone and shale hills rising nearly 600 feet above sea level.

The Corps of Engineers' plan called for three types of construction between the Tennessee and the Tombigbee. At the northern end of the waterway, the Nashville District was to cut a channel through the high drainage divide and construct the Bay Springs Lock and Dam. South of this "Divide Section," the Mobile District planned to construct five additional locks, forming a chain of narrow lakes through the "Canal Section." And in the "River Section," which stretched south to the mouth of the Black Warrior River, the Mobile District was to build locks and dams near Aberdeen and Columbus, Mississippi, and near Aliceville and Gainesville, Alabama, creating a series of shallow lakes linked by wider and straighter river segments. The completed Tennessee-Tombigbee Waterway would constitute a level water route about 250 miles long.

Although Pres. Richard Nixon turned the first official spade of earth in May 1971, a number of other hurdles still needed to be overcome. The Corps of Engineers had yet to set long-term construction schedules or complete the required environmental studies. The Corps spent more than a decade conducting those studies, changing construction designs to minimize damage when necessary.

In June 1985 the Corps of Engineers, Mobile District, officially opened the Tennessee-Tombigbee Waterway, the country's first large interdisciplinary cultural resource management program. It served as a model from which other federal and state agencies built programs committed to the protection and preservation of the nation's historic resources.

As planned, the Tennessee-Tombigbee has become the preferred route for transporting large and heavy finished products and raw materials between the Gulf of Mexico and the American heartland. Using the waterway instead of the Mississippi-Ohio River system reduces fuel consumption and lowers shipping costs, with fewer marginal costs, less pollution, and one-tenth the rate of accidents of highways and railroads. Commercial tonnage transported along the waterway has steadily increased, and by the second decade of the twenty-first century, the waterway carried as much as 1.2 billion ton-miles of commerce each year at an annual savings of nearly one hundred million dollars in transportation costs. In addition, the Waterway Development Authority claims that more than five billion dollars worth of industry has sprung up or expanded in the waterway region since its completion. Between 1996 and 2008 the waterway created more than 138,000 jobs nationwide.

New recreational opportunities have also flourished, including world-class fishing, hunting, campgrounds, and natural history. In addition to the 46,000 acres managed by the Corps of Engineers, the Waterway Authority has designated 72,500 acres as high-quality habitat for indigenous and migratory wildlife.

David S. Brose
West Bloomfield, Michigan

Tennessee-Tombigbee Waterway website, www.tenntom.org; US Army Corps of Engineers, Mobile District website, www.sam.usace.army.mil.

Cotton mill machine and operator, Laurel, January 1939 (Photograph by Russell Lee, Library of Congress, Washington, D.C. [LC-USF34-031983-D])

Textile Mills

Compared to southern states such as Georgia and the Carolinas, Mississippi's textile mill history was slow and somewhat erratic. Only a few were built in the antebellum period, and only one of those, the Bankston Mill, had substantial and lasting success. The major period of textile mill building in the state took place from the 1880s through the early 1900s, when inexpensive, nonunion labor of white men and women, especially in eastern and central Mississippi, made the state an attractive place to start new factories that made clothing and other cloth products.

Antebellum efforts to build textile mills in Mississippi were with one exception small, as most people with money to invest concentrated on land and slaves. Two efforts in Adams County accomplished relatively little, but in 1847 James M. Wesson and some associates organized the Mississippi Manufacturing Company, which opened the Bankston Mill in Choctaw County the next year. Wesson had been part of a group that ran a textile mill in Columbus, Georgia. The Bankston Mill had considerable success producing cotton and wool textiles, employing white workers in what became the state's first mill village. According to historian James Hebron Moore, "The little village of Bankston was in every regard a company town. Originally located away from towns and travel routes in order to provide few distractions for the employees and their families, Bankston was Wesson's plantation. He would not permit whiskey to be sold in the vicinity, and he saw to it that the inhabitants of Bankston received religious instruction proper to factory hands." About one hundred employees worked in the mill at its height in the 1850s.

Other textile mills in antebellum Mississippi included the Mississippi Penitentiary, which started a mill first to make clothes for the inmates and later to sell, and mills in Woodville and Jackson. All of the state's larger mills were damaged or destroyed during the Civil War. New textile mills began operation in the late 1860s and 1870s in Corinth, Natchez, Water Valley, and Bay St. Louis and the 1880s in Shuqualak, Natchez, Columbus, and Port Gibson. The largest and most successful new mills were Mississippi Mills in Copiah County and the Stonewall Manufacturing Company in Clarke County.

As the war ended, James Wesson, trying to re-create the success of the Bankston Mill, started a large mill in the new company town of Wesson. One of the two successful textile mills in the late 1800s, the renamed Mississippi Mills became an unusual sight in otherwise rural Copiah County. As historian Narvell Strickland writes, the mills "consisted of four large brick buildings when completed, one of which was five stories high with a seven-story tower, and covered several city blocks. From the beginning they were powered by steam engines and very early illuminated by electricity." Mississippi Mills closed in 1910.

In 1867 three businessmen started the Stonewall Manufacturing Company, named in honor of Stonewall Jackson. The mill became the longest-running establishment of its kind in Mississippi, employing more than five hundred workers in the early 1900s. In 1948 Erwin Mills purchased the Stonewall mill, and in 1962 Burlington Mills bought and expanded it. Stonewall continued to produce clothing until 2002.

Like its counterparts across the South, Mississippi's state government made some efforts to attract textile mills in the late 1800s. Mississippi's "cotton mill crusade" began with an industrial development program that started in 1882 and continued with a small textile school at Mississippi A&M (now Mississippi State University) in 1901. Fourteen mills opened between 1896 and 1906, with new operations in Meridian, West Point, McComb, Kosciusko, Laurel, Moorhead,

Winona, Yazoo City, Tupelo, Starkville, Magnolia, Columbus, and Batesville. Many of these factories established mill villages, with housing, churches, and sports facilities.

In the early twentieth century textile mills came to symbolize southern employers' tendency to pay low wages to industrial workers. The state did not rank high on many national lists of industrial production, but it ranked second, trailing only Tennessee, in making work clothing. In the 1930s, when the Mississippi state government instituted its Balance Agriculture with Industry (BAWI) program, it hoped to attract higher-wage industry, but many of the new factories continued the policies that had attracted investors to the South. According to historian James Cobb, "For the most part the early BAWI plants were low-wage, labor-intensive industries that could capitalize on an abundance of unskilled workers. Four of the plants produced hosiery and a number of them sought an exclusively female work force." Reformers hoped that different types of textile work might improve the nature of such work. Extension worker and social scientist Dorothy Dickins wrote a long 1941 report comparing older textile mills with new garment factories that concentrated on finishing work. Arguing that textile mills in mill villages left people poor, unskilled, and sickly, Dickins was more hopeful that newer garment factories would encourage women to live in the country, take buses or cars to work, and enjoy the benefits of rural life and family connections.

A combination of the Depression and some disasters offered new challenges to textile mill work in the 1930s. Substantial mills closed in Tupelo, McComb, Columbus, and Moorhead; a 1936 tornado in Tupelo killed more than 230 people; and fires damaged several mill communities. Several mills responded to economic difficulties by keeping wages low and sometimes using the "stretchout," which required twelve-hour work days. Above all, they opposed union activity. In 1934 the United Textile Workers of America called for an industry-wide strike, and many but not all textile workers in Mississippi struck in September. Some of the employers, especially at the mills owned by Sanders Industries, fired union leaders and called on local law enforcement to oppose the strikes; in Magnolia, Kosciusko, and Stonewall, the National Guard also was called in.

In number and significance, textile mills have been on the decline in Mississippi since the mid-twentieth century. The Mississippi Department of Employment Security tracks the significance of apparel and other textile products, and using a broad definition, its publications show that apparel and textile manufacturing made up 22 percent of the state's industrial workforce in 1965, 8 percent by 2002, and just over 1 percent in 2012.

Ted Ownby
University of Mississippi

James C. Cobb, *The Selling of the South: The Southern Crusade for Industrial Development, 1936–1990* (2nd ed., 1993); James A. Hodges, *New Deal Labor Policy and the Southern Cotton Textile Industry, 1933–1941* (1986); Mississippi Department of Economic and Community Development, *Textile Mill and Apparel Products in Mississippi* (2003); Mississippi Department of Employment Security website, mdes.ms.gov; John Hebron Moore, *The Emergence of the Cotton Kingdom in the Old Southwest: Mississippi, 1770–1860* (1988); Ted Ownby, in *Mississippi Women: Their Histories, Their Lives*, vol. 2, ed. Elizabeth Payne, Martha Swain, and Marjorie Julian Spruill (2010); Narvell Strickland, "A History of Cotton Mills and the Industrial Revolution," Narvell Strickland website, http://narvell strickland1.tripod.com.

Theater

In the nineteenth century, theater performances in Mississippi, as in the rest of the nation, were a primary source of entertainment. With the advent of rail and steamboats, traveling companies of professional actors and musicians performed in venues generally called opera houses or showboats. *Julius Cahn's Official Theatrical Guide* listed eighteen Mississippi towns on the touring circuit in 1905: Biloxi, Brookhaven, Clarksdale, Columbus, Corinth, Greenwood, Greenville, Grenada, Holly Springs, Jackson, Laurel, Meridian, Natchez, Oxford, Port Gibson, Sardis, Tupelo, and Vicksburg. The opera houses in Corinth and Meridian still stand.

Community Theaters

The introduction of motion pictures in the early twentieth century had a major impact on theater and public entertainment. Live performances by professional touring companies declined, and theater venues were converted into movie houses. Over time, most theater performances at the community level consisted of volunteers who established "little theaters" to present plays and musicals. Some of the earliest in Mississippi include the Meridian Little Theatre (established 1932); Natchez Little Theatre (established 1932); Vicksburg Little Theatre Guild (established 1936), later the Vicksburg Theatre Guild; Biloxi Little Theatre (established 1946); and Bay St. Louis Little Theatre (established 1946). By the 1960s the state had at least sixteen active community theaters. In 1962 the Panola Playhouse in Sardis became the state's first community theater to engage a professional director, with theaters in Corinth, Meridian, Greenville, New Albany, and Vicksburg soon following. In 1965 New Stage, the state's first professional resident theater, was established in Jackson. The Free Southern Theater, established at Tougaloo College in 1964, was Mississippi's first integrated community theater and provided productions free of charge to mostly rural black audiences throughout the state. The theater relocated to New Orleans for funding reasons yet continued to tour Mississippi through the 1970s. While many of these early theaters have not survived, Mississippi had more than forty-five community theaters by the second decade of the twenty-first century.

High School Theaters

Many high school theater programs started as after-school programs where students rehearsed and performed plays for their peers. With increasing interest in adding the arts to the curriculum, theater classes and eventually full theater programs were developed.

In 1963 Dominic J. Cunetto of Mississippi State University founded the first statewide high school drama festival. Ten years later, growing participation led to the festival's division into two regional festivals whose winners advanced to the Mississippi Theatre Association's festival. With the exception of a few years when it was hosted by Delta State University, Mississippi State has continued to host the north regional festival. University of Southern Mississippi faculty member Blaine Quarnstrom founded the south regional festival, which the school has continued to host except for a brief time when southeastern and southwestern festivals took place.

The Mississippi Delta Tennessee Williams Festival in Clarksdale has sponsored an annual high school drama competition since 1993. Student actors perform monologues and scenes from Williams plays and compete for cash awards for their school drama departments.

College/University Theaters

Many Mississippi community colleges and universities house theater departments offering bachelor's, bachelor of fine arts, and master of fine arts degrees. Historical records for productions at institutions of higher learning begin in 1885, when Pauline Orr, head of the Department of English and Elocution at the Industrial Institute and College for the Education of White Girls of the State of Mississippi (now Mississippi University for Women), began holding student performances. A joint production of *As You Like It* by students from the then all-male Millsaps and all-female Belhaven in Jackson created such as fuss about religious schools doing "theatricals" that productions were suspended at Millsaps from 1917 to 1927, when a professor in the English department began producing shows and subsequently founded the Millsaps Players. The University of Mississippi's first theater courses were offered in 1929 as part of the newly established Department of Speech. Theater became a concentration within the department from 1946 until 1980, when the Department of Theatre Arts was founded and the producing arm changed its name from University Theatre to Ole Miss Theatre. In 2004 Ole Miss Theatre launched the Oxford Shakespeare Festival, a repertory theater company that operated until 2013. Mississippi Agricultural and Mechanical College (now Mississippi State University) established a Dramatic Club around 1909. It became the Blackfriars Drama Society in 1959, when Peyton Williams

was the faculty sponsor. In 1963 the Mississippi State University Department of Speech hired Cunetto, who developed the theater program. Mississippi Southern College (now the University of Southern Mississippi) lists productions from 1949. The school's Department of Theatre and Dance provides both undergraduate major and minor degree programs and graduate programs. In 1977 the Department of Theatre established its repertory theater, the Southern Arena Theatre.

Professional Theater, Performing Arts Centers, and Other Notable Theaters

Mississippi has one professional theater, Jackson's New Stage Theatre, which hires Equity actors and stagehands as well as non-Equity actors. Founded and chartered as a nonprofit organization in 1965, New Stage immediately began attracting full houses and the city's first racially integrated audiences. Founding member Jane Reid Petty served as the theater's first managing director, first benefactor, president of the board, fund raiser, playwright, actress, and director. Ivan Rider was the theater's first artistic director. New Stage has subsequently established the Eudora Welty New Play Series, created a professional internship program, and hired an education director to coordinate the internship program, acting classes, day camps for students, and a touring program bringing live drama to schools across Mississippi. In 1978, after the Jackson Little Theatre closed its doors, New Stage acquired the facility.

Mississippi also boasts three major performing arts centers that bring to the region national touring productions, including Broadway shows. The Bologna Performing Arts Center, a multidisciplinary facility at Delta State University in Cleveland, opened in 1995 and houses the 1,178-seat Delta and Pine Land Theatre and the 135-seat Recital Hall. The Gertrude C. Ford Center for the Performing Arts at the University of Mississippi seats 1,250 in the main hall and has become a premier entertainment venue in the Oxford area since it opened in 2003. Since 2006 Mississippi State's Riley Center in Meridian has offered performances, conferences, and educational programs in a restored 1889 grand opera house theater with 950 seats, a 200-seat studio theater, and 30,000 square feet of meeting space.

Other notable programs include the Lynn Meadows Discovery Center's Wings Performing Arts Program in Gulfport and the Vicksburg Theatre Guild's annual production of *Gold in the Hills*. The Discovery Center, an interactive children's museum that opened in 1998 in a refurbished 1915 elementary school, involves 500 children and youth in productions reaching annual audiences of 21,000 on the Mississippi Gulf Coast.

Mississippi Theatre Association

During the 1950s a group formed the Mississippi Little Theatre Association to help foster performances. In 1967 the

T

association's board began the legal process of incorporating as a nonprofit, nonshare corporation. In 1968, before completing bylaws and incorporation, and responding to the urging of past president Robert M. Canon, the association changed its name to the Mississippi Theatre Association and revised its mission to include all types of theater organizations and services. At that time the association began encouraging the retirement of the archaic term *little theater*. The association seeks to foster appreciation of and participation in children's, community, high school, professional, and university theater in Mississippi by sponsoring festivals, workshops, and retreats; communicating with members and the public; acting as an advocate with government agencies, business, and the public; recognizing excellence in performance and production; and sanctioning representatives to regional festivals. The association hosts an annual festival and conference to provide professional development and education through workshops and one-act play competitions for high schools and community theaters. As of 2012, the MTA state convention—held in different locations every year—features the Community Theatre Festival, High School Festival, Theatre for Youth Festival, Ten-Minute Play Festival, College/University Auditions, Playwriting Competition, and Individual Events Festival.

Robert M. Canon
Sardis, Mississippi

Stephen H. Cunetto
Mississippi Theatre Association

William "Peppy" Biddy
Mississippi University for Women

Robert M. Canon, "Community Theatre in Mississippi: Problems and Prospects (master's thesis, University of Mississippi, 1967); Philip C. Lewis, *Trouping: How the Show Came to Town* (1973); Mississippi Theatre Association website, www.mta-online.org; New Stage Theatre website, www.newstage.com; Ellen L. Tripp, "Free Southern Theater: There Is Always a Message" (PhD dissertation, University of North Carolina at Greensboro, 1986).

Thigpen, Grady
(1890–1981) Author

Samuel Grady Thigpen Sr., a prominent Picayune businessman and local chronicler, was born in Lake Como, Mississippi, in Jasper County, to Samuel Forrest Thigpen and Julia Arledge Thigpen. Samuel Thigpen was a farmer, Jasper

County superintendent of education, and publisher of the *Lake Como News*. When Grady, as he was known, was a boy, his grandfather, William Thigpen, recounted stories that he had heard from Revolutionary War veterans. Grady also grew up listening to Confederate veterans reminisce.

Thigpen attended the Lake Como School and Mississippi A&M College (now Mississippi State University) before graduating from Mississippi College in 1912. He then taught school in Poplarville from 1912 to 1917. During the World War I lumber boom he moved to Picayune as a timekeeper for the Goodyear Yellow Pine Company. He married Lorena Tate, the daughter of Col. Monroe David Tate, a prominent local businessman who also served as Pearl River County sheriff and the younger brother of E. E. Tate, the Father of Picayune.

Thigpen founded the Thigpen Hardware Company in Picayune in 1919 and prospered, later extending his interests into land and banking. His *Thigpen Store News* became popular not only for its free advertisements but also for his interspersed articles of local color. In 1947 he began telling his anecdotes about the old days on the Lower Pearl River in a weekly radio broadcast on WRJW. He invited listeners to come to his store to use the "free weight scales" and to drink ice water. He acquired the nicknames *Grandpa Thigpen* and *Grandpa Grady*, possibly bestowing them on himself. In 1961 the *Picayune Item* started printing his yarns, which he later collected and published in five books: *Pearl River: Highway to Glory Land* (1965); *Next Door to Heaven* (1965); *Ninety and One Years* (1965); *A Boy in Rural Mississippi and Other Stories* (1966); and *Work and Play in Grand Day* (1969).

Scholar Noel Polk, who was born and raised in Picayune, wrote that Thigpen's books are not history but rather tell little stories of how people lived in the old days and "how much better things were then." The tales attracted a wide readership and helped waken Pearl River Countians to what Polk called their historyless past.

John Hawkins Napier III
Ramer, Alabama

John H. Napier III, *Lower Pearl River's Piney Woods* (1985); Noel Polk, *Outside the Southern Myth* (1997).

Thomas, James "Son Ford"
(1926–1993) Blues Musician and Sculptor

James "Son Ford" Thomas was born on 14 October 1926 on a farm near Eden in Yazoo County, Mississippi. His life embodied a spectrum of black folklife, including blues music, clay sculpture, and storytelling, all of which are rooted in

Mississippi Delta cultural traditions. Thomas learned to play the guitar by watching his uncle play and then imitating the chords in his own tunes. As a teenager Thomas moved to Leland, where he began playing blues on weekends. He played juke joints and barrelhouses around Leland and Greenville through the 1960s. Beginning in the early 1970s he performed at colleges and universities, including Jackson State University (1971–72), the University of Maine (1972), Tougaloo College (1973), and Yale University (1973–76). He participated in the Smithsonian Festival of American Folklife in Washington, D.C., and in festivals in Norway and Germany. He recorded in the United States, Holland, West Germany, and Italy.

Thomas was also a sculptor, largely teaching himself. As a child he began making clay imitations of animals, patterning his first work after similar figures made by his uncle. He later made clay models of Ford tractors, earning the nickname *Son Ford*. Apart from his uncle, Thomas had no continuing contact with artists who worked with clay. His work was highly personal, and perhaps the most unusual figures in his repertoire were heads and skulls, many of which have openings in their tops and serve as containers or ashtrays. Animals, water, and death were recurring motifs. His clay faces presented images of the black man as poised and proud. Son Thomas's sculpture attracted national attention through a 1981 exhibition, *Black Folk Art in America, 1930–1980*, at the Corcoran Gallery in Washington, D.C. His work also was exhibited in 2015 at New York University's 80 Washington Square East Gallery. Thomas has been featured in several films, including *James "Son Ford" Thomas: Delta Blues Singer* (1970), *Mississippi Delta Blues* (1974), and *Give My Poor Heart Ease: Mississippi Delta Bluesmen* (1975).

Thomas performed until the early 1990s despite health setbacks such as a brain tumor and emphysema. He suffered a stroke and died in Greenville on 26 June 1993.

William Ferris
University of North Carolina
at Chapel Hill

William Ferris, ed., *Afro-American Folk Art and Crafts* (1983); William Ferris, *Blues from the Delta* (1984); William Ferris, *Highway 61 Blues: James "Son" Thomas* (Recording 1983); James "Son Ford" Thomas: The Devil and His Blues Exhibition website, http://steinhardt.nyu.edu/80 wse/gallery/2015/06/jamessonfordthomas?utm_source=redirect&utm _campaign=80wse_gallery-2015–06-jamessonfordthomas.

Thomas, Rufus
(1917–2001) Rhythm and Blues Musician

One of the most colorful personalities in all of American music, Rufus Thomas was also one of the most multifaceted, playing vital roles as a singer, comedian, deejay, emcee, talent and label launcher, soul and funk pioneer, and creator of numerous dance-oriented novelty songs. Professionally active for more than seven decades, Thomas witnessed nearly a century's worth of musical, social, and cultural change from the stage, a rare participant whose career spanned from the last strains of minstrelsy to the commercial crest of hip-hop. Dubbed variously the World's Oldest Teenager, the Crown Prince of Dance, the Funkiest Man Alive, and the Ambassador of Memphis Music, Thomas matched his musical and verbal flamboyance with equally outrageous (and unforgettable) stage attire—one ensemble included hot pants, studded platform boots, and a white cape.

Rufus Thomas Jr., the son of a sharecropper, was born on 26 March 1917 in Cayce, Mississippi, just south of Memphis, where his family moved when he was a year old. By six he had made his public debut hopping around as a frog in a school production, a rather prescient beginning for someone whose recorded legacy ultimately relied on a musical menagerie of dogs, penguins, and chickens. He attended Booker T. Washington High School, where he teamed with history teacher and groundbreaking black deejay Nat D. Williams in a comedy duo as part of the Palace Theater amateur nights that Williams emceed on Beale Street. In 1936 after one semester at Tennessee A&I University, Thomas joined the Rabbit's Foot Minstrels, a popular touring all-black revue that carnival impresario F. S. Wolcott operated from Port Gibson, Mississippi. The fledgling entertainer tap-danced in a duo billed as Rufus and Johnny. Thomas also worked briefly with the Royal American carnival line from Tampa as part of a black revue, *Harlem in Havana*. Marriage sent him back to Memphis, where in 1941 he earned twenty-five cents an hour overseeing the bleach department boilers of a textile factory, a day job he held for the next twenty-two years. In the 1940s he assumed the Palace Theater emcee spot, working with new partner Robert Couch as the comedy duo Rufus and Bones and ushering in such rising stars of the Memphis urban blues scene as B. B. King, Bobby Bland, and Johnny Ace. In 1950 Thomas followed Williams to all-black format WDIA radio, the Mother Station of the Negroes, where on such shows as *Sepia Swing Club* (inherited from King) and *Hoot 'n' Holler* he helped set the stage for the emerging sounds of rock and roll by spinning rhythm and blues records for black and white listeners alike.

Thomas's own brand of rhythm and blues jump-started the fortunes of Memphis's two most important independent labels, Sun and Stax. Though he had made the 1950 single

"I'm So Worried / I'll Be a Good Boy" on the Star Talent label in Dallas, Thomas's 1953 single "Bear Cat," his first record with Sun founder and producer Sam Phillips and an answer song to Big Mama Thornton's "Hound Dog," gave the nascent company its first national hit. Unfortunately, the song was so close a parody that it also resulted in Sun's first copyright infringement lawsuit. Another of Thomas's songs at Sun, "Tiger Man," later became a signature tune for Elvis Presley. In 1960 Thomas provided the commercial spark for a second Memphis label, Satellite (soon rechristened Stax), when he and his daughter, Stax's future Queen of Soul, Carla Thomas, recorded his song "'Cause I Love You," which became the label's first regional success. More significantly, the duet caught the attention of New York's Atlantic Records, which led to a distribution deal through most of the 1960s that established Stax as the South's premier soul label.

At Stax, Thomas became an unlikely star, a middle-aged veteran of southern carnivals and tent shows whose seasoned, prolific résumé pointed simultaneously to the past and to the future, where the tricks of the vaudeville trade served him well in helping define the black urban templates of soul and then funk in the 1960s and 1970s. In such hits as "The Dog" (1963), "Walking the Dog" (1963), "Can Your Monkey Do the Dog" (1964), "Do the Funky Chicken" (1969), and "Do the Funky Penguin" (1971), Thomas tied the latest dance crazes to tight, syncopated groove-oriented song structures combined with imagery, humor, and repartee that took its cue from a century of African American entertainment, folklore, and oral history. The result was popular music that could be profoundly light on its feet, silly yet a spirited and galvanizing force alongside the music of James Brown and others in the foundation of funk. Thomas's most-covered song, "Walking the Dog," was inspired, like a number of his compositions, by a nursery rhyme; he recorded it on a Sunday when, fresh from church, he noticed cars parked in front of the Stax studio. An impromptu session with the MGs followed, yielding the quick classic that the Rolling Stones recorded for their debut album less than a year later. Other highlights from Thomas's weighty Stax catalog include "Sophisticated Sissy" (1967), "Funky Mississippi" (1968), "The Memphis Train" (1968), "(Do the) Push and Pull, Part 1" (1970), and "The Breakdown (Part 1)."

Thomas stayed with Stax through its demise in the mid-1970s and later recorded for a variety of labels, including Chicago blues bellwether Alligator for the 1990 effort *That Woman Is Poison!* Thomas remained musically active on stage as well, performing at the 1996 Summer Olympics in Atlanta and a year later with Prince for a New Daisy Theater show on Beale Street. Thomas also had memorable cameos in several films, notably the 1989 Jim Jarmusch cult favorite *Mystery Train*. Thomas died of heart failure in Memphis on 15 December 2001.

A member of the Blues Hall of Fame and a recipient of a Rhythm and Blues Foundation Pioneer Award, he was honored in 1997 with a lifetime achievement award from songwriting organization ASCAP. Porretta Terme, Italy, which hosts the annual Sweet Soul Music Festival, where Thomas played many times, has named a park in his honor, and Memphis has christened a portion of the Beale Street Historic District where the Palace Theater once stood Rufus Thomas Boulevard. In addition to Carla, Thomas's children include his son, Marvell, a noted Stax keyboardist, arranger, and producer, and his daughter, Vaneese, a New York–based session singer.

William Lee Ellis
Memphis, Tennessee

Rob Bowman, *Soulsville U.S.A.: The Story of Stax Records* (1997); Louis Cantor, *Wheelin' on Beale: How WDIA-Memphis Became the Nation's First All-Black Radio Station and Created the Sound That Changed America* (1992); Colin Escott with Martin Hawkins, *Good Rockin' Tonight: Sun Records and the Birth of Rock 'n' Roll* (1991); Steve Greenberg, *Do the Funky Somethin': The Best of Rufus Thomas* (1996), liner notes; Peter Guralnick, *Lost Highway: Journeys and Arrivals of American Musicians* (1979); Peter Guralnick, *Sweet Soul Music: Rhythm and Blues and the Southern Dream of Freedom* (1986); Dean Rudland, *Rufus Thomas, Funkiest Man Alive: The Stax Funk Sessions, 1967–1975* (2003), liner notes; Robert Santelli, *The Big Book of Blues: A Biographical Encyclopedia* (1993); Rickey Vincent, *Funk: The Music, the People, and the Rhythm of the One* (1996).

Thompson, Cleopatra
(1912–1992) Educator

Cleopatra Davenport Thompson served Mississippi as a talented educator and advocate for civil rights and the advancement of women. Thompson taught at many of the state's schools, including Walthall County Training School, Okolona Industrial School, Rust College, Alcorn State University, Tougaloo College, and Jackson State University, and served as a visiting professor of psychology and education at the University of Liberia in the 1960s.

Cleopatra Davenport was born on 17 February 1912 in Egypt, Mississippi, one of ten children of teacher Alonzo Davenport and Lizzie Blanchard Davenport. She received her early education in local schools before marrying H. McFarland Thompson, a professor of mathematics at Jackson State College and president of the Mississippi Teachers Association.

Thompson graduated from Alcorn State University in 1932 and received a master's degree from Atlanta University in 1936. She later earned a doctorate in education from Cornell University. Her dissertation, completed in June 1960, concerned the effectiveness of the Jackson State education program. Following 306 graduates from 1944 to 1953, she examined how they perceived the effectiveness of their college training in preparing them for professional life as well as how their training prepared them to contribute to the communities in which they taught. Thompson pursued postgraduate studies at the University of Chicago and at Iowa State University.

From 1946 until 1977 Thompson held the position of professor of education at Jackson State. Thompson also served as the director of the Jackson College Extension Center, a program designed to provide two years of college-level classes for Meridian-area elementary and high school teachers that gave Thompson information regarding the condition of schools throughout the state. During Thompson's tenure, Jackson State produced one-third of the principals and half of the teachers at Mississippi's black schools. Thompson became dean of the School of Education in 1973, bolstering curriculum offerings and expanding the school's focus beyond preparing teachers for the state's rural schools. In 1974 Thompson's restructuring and improvement of the School of Education won accreditation from the National Council for Accreditation of Teacher Education, the first division of Jackson State to achieve this milestone.

Thompson served a range of civic organizations, including the YWCA, the National Council of Negro Women, the National Federation of Colored Women's Clubs, and the Girl Scouts. She was also a deacon at Jackson's Farish Street Baptist Church. In 1969 she was a founding member of the Alumni Association of Public Colleges, a political action arm of the alumni associations of Alcorn State, Jackson State, and Mississippi Valley State. Thompson served on the Teacher Education Liaison Committee of the Southern Regional Education Board and as a delegate to the 1960 White House Conference on Children and Youth. She helped organize the 1977 International Women's Year Conference in Jackson, leading a workshop on international affairs. She also worked with the Hinds County Project Head Start and served as director of the Community Welfare and Health Center. She died on 5 May 1992.

Thompson received many honors, and a residence hall at Alcorn State University bears her name. In addition, the Cleopatra D. Thompson Curriculum Center at Jackson State University provides multimedia resources for elementary and secondary educators.

Becca Walton
University of Mississippi

John A. Peoples, *Personalities of the South* (1969); John A. Peoples, *To Survive and Thrive: The Quest for a True University* (1995); Josephine McCann Posey, *Against Great Odds: The History of Alcorn State University* (1994); Lelia G. Rhodes, *Jackson State University: The First Hundred Years, 1877–1977* (1979); Marjorie Julian Spruill, "Awake, Aware, and Deeply Polarized: Mississippi Women and the International Women's Year Conference of 1977," Cora Norman Lecture, Mississippi Humanities Council (2006); Cleopatra D. Thompson, *The History of the Mississippi Teachers Association* (1973).

Thompson, Jacob
(1810–1885) Lawyer and Political Leader

Born in North Carolina on 15 May 1810, Jacob Thompson went on to become a leader in Mississippi education and government and to serve as US secretary of the interior in the 1850s. After graduating from the University of North Carolina at Chapel Hill in 1831 and studying law, Thompson, like many other young men of the time, sought his fortune on the western frontier. He was admitted to the bar in 1834 and began practicing in Pontotoc County the following year. He helped to establish circuit courts in many new counties.

He was elected as a Democrat to the US Congress in November 1838 and a month later married Catharine Ann Jones, the sixteen-year-old daughter of a wealthy Lafayette County planter. Their only child, Caswell Macon Thompson, was born in November 1839, and the family soon moved to the developing town of Panola. There, Thompson added planter to his ongoing roles of lawyer and politician. He won reelection to Congress five times, serving until 1851.

By 1844 Thompson had moved to Oxford, where he became a founding member of St. Peter's Episcopal Church and joined the first board of trustees of the University of Mississippi and served as its president in 1848. He drew on his experience both as a student and tutor at the University of North Carolina in helping to draft the rules and curriculum of the new school, and he laid the foundation for the university's library and later helped persuade the state legislature to create a law school. According to historian Joel Williamson, in the late antebellum period, Thompson "was becoming one of the wealthiest men in northeastern Mississippi," with most of his wealth in land and slaves.

Jacob Thompson (Archives and Records Services Division, Mississippi Department of Archives and History [PI PER T56.5 Box 16 Folder 98 #1])

T

Thompson resigned his role as active trustee when he and Catharine moved to Washington, D.C., where he served as secretary of the interior under Pres. James Buchanan beginning on 6 March 1857 and earning praise from members of both parties. He resigned on 8 January 1861 in anticipation of Mississippi's secession the following day, writing to the president, "It is with extreme regret that I have just learned that additional troops have been ordered to Charleston. . . . Under these circumstances I feel myself bound to resign my commission, as one of your constitutional advisers, into your hands."

During the Civil War, Thompson served as a soldier, one-term state legislator, and head of the controversial Confederate Commission to Canada. He became a target of US government propaganda and was forced to live abroad until 1869, when amnesty allowed him to return to Oxford and he found that his mansion had been used as a Union Army hospital before being looted and burned by US soldiers in August 1864. Thompson realized he could not live happily in Oxford, and he and Catharine moved to Memphis, where he became a businessman who invested time and money in his family, church, and developing the University of the South at Sewanee. He died on 24 March 1885.

Carolyn J. Ross
Oxford, Mississippi

Biographical Directory of the United States Congress (1950); Don H. Doyle, *Faulkner's County: The Historical Roots of Yoknapatawpha* (2001); *A History of St. Peter's Episcopal Church, Proto-Cathedral of Mississippi, Commemorating the One Hundredth Anniversary* (1951); Edward Mayes, *Lucius Q. C. Lamar: His Life, Times, and Speeches, 1825–1893* (1895); Dorothy Zollicoffer Oldham, "Life of Jacob Thompson" (master's thesis, University of Mississippi, 1930); Joel Williamson, *William Faulkner and Southern History* (1993).

Emmett Till, 1955 (Library of Congress, Washington, D.C. [LC-USZ62-111241])

Till, Emmett

(1941–1955)

Emmett Louis Till was born near Chicago on 25 July 1941 and was murdered in the Mississippi Delta on 28 August 1955, making him the best-known young victim of racial violence in American history.

Visiting relatives during the summer before starting eighth grade, Till accompanied his cousins and other black teenagers to Money, in Leflore County, on the evening of 24 August 1955. There he entered a general store and—probably as a prank to impress the locals with his bravado—allegedly whistled at Carolyn Bryant, the twenty-one-year-old wife of the store's owner, who was not present. Till's companions hustled him out of the store and out of Money, but in retaliation for the breach of the Jim Crow etiquette, Carolyn's husband, Roy Bryant, and his halfbrother, J. W. Milam, abducted Till from the home of his great-uncle, Moses "Preacher" Wright, and his wife, Elizabeth Wright. Possibly with the aid of others, Bryant and Milam pistol-whipped Till (whose name they did not bother to learn) and then murdered him near Glendora. The corpse was tied to a cotton gin fan and then dumped into the Tallahatchie River, where it was discovered three days after the sheriff of Leflore County arrested Bryant and Milam on suspicion of murder.

Because the corpse had been recovered in Tallahatchie County, the homicide was presumed to have occurred there, and Bryant and Milam were tried in late September in the county seat of Sumner on two counts of kidnapping and murder. All five of the town's attorneys who were engaged in private practice represented Bryant and Milam pro bono. Even Sheriff H. C. Strider testified for the defense, which claimed that the corpse was not Till's (despite the recovery of a ring bearing the initials of his father). Moses Wright courageously identified each of the defendants in open court ("Thar he") as having abducted Till, whose mother, Mamie Till Bradley, came down from Chicago to testify. On 23 September, the jury of twelve white men deliberated for just over an hour before acquitting Bryant and Milam. The fact that the jury had deliberated that long heartened some observers who discerned progress toward racial justice, though one juror explained, "If we hadn't stopped to drink pop, it wouldn't have taken that long." The trial itself was covered by reporters from the national and even international media, and Michigan Democrat Charles C. Diggs Jr. attended as an observer, to the consternation of locals who had never seen a black congressman.

The exoneration of the defendants was widely condemned in the press outside the South and beyond the United States and added to the shock registered when Bradley had insisted on an open casket at her son's Chicago funeral so that the world could see how his body had been mutilated. The crime—the extremely violent murder of a fourteen-year-old boy accused of doing nothing more than flirting—was more effective than any other incident in highlighting the character of racial inequality in Mississippi in particular and may have quickened the tempo of the civil rights movement. Black activists in the 1960s recalled that Till's fate brought home their own vulnerability and inspired them to combat white supremacy.

The case sharpened the sense of black subjugation and precariousness as had no other and became imprinted in the minds of artists and their audiences. Two major postwar African American novelists, James Baldwin and Toni Morrison, wrote plays based on the Till case (*Blues for Mr. Charlie* and *Dreaming Emmett*, respectively). In addition, the murder has inspired poems, songs, fiction, and documentary films.

Stephen J. Whitfield
Brandeis University

William Bradford Huie, *Wolf Whistle* (1959); *Southern Quarterly* (Summer 2008); Stephen J. Whitfield, *A Death in the Delta: The Story of Emmett Till* (1988).

Till-Mobley, Mamie
(1921–2003) Activist

Mamie Elizabeth Carthan was born on 23 November 1921 in Webb, Mississippi. In January 1924 her mother, Alma Smith Carthan, took her north to the Chicago suburb of Argo, where they reunited with the girl's father, Willy Nash Carthan. In 1940 Mamie Carthan became the fourth black graduate of Argo Community High School and the first to graduate at the top of her class. She went on to work with the Social Security Administration and for the US Air Force.

Carthan married Louis Till on 14 October 1940 and gave birth to her only biological child, Emmett Louis Till, on 25 July 1941. By the following year she had separated from her husband, who was convicted of rape and murder while serving in the US Army in Italy and executed in 1945. She was

(Left to right) Walter Reed, Willie Reed, Mamie Bradley, Michigan congressman Charles Diggs, T. R. M. Howard, and Amanda Bradley at the trial of two white men charged with murdering Emmett Till, 22 September 1955 (Library of Congress, Washington, D.C. [LC-USZ62-135350])

married to Pink Bradley (1951–53) and later Gene Mobley (1957–2000).

On 31 August 1955 Emmett Till's bludgeoned body was found in Mississippi's Tallahatchie River. After her son's body was returned to Chicago, Bradley insisted that the casket be opened. After carefully inspecting the body and confirming that it was her son, she decided to let the world see the results of this lynching by holding an open-casket viewing at Chicago's Roberts Temple Church of God in Christ. So enormous was the outpouring of public sympathy and support that Till's burial had to be delayed for four days: as many as one hundred thousand people came to the church to view the body. Media outlets from around the world covered her son's death, and Bradley authorized the publication of photographs of her son's body in *Jet* magazine and the *Crisis*, the journal of the National Association for the Advancement of Colored People (NAACP).

On 20 September 1955 Bradley traveled to Sumner, Mississippi, to testify in the trial of her son's accused murderers, J. W. Milam and Roy Bryant. Refused a room at the segregated hotel in Sumner and forced to view the trial from the segregated seating reserved for the black press, Bradley nevertheless delivered poignant testimony confirming the identity of the body. Despite her efforts, along with those of several other witnesses who provided damning evidence against the accused, an all-white male jury acquitted the defendants after deliberating for just sixty-seven minutes.

Bradley continued to press for justice, writing letters to Pres. Dwight Eisenhower and speaking under the auspices of the NAACP and various labor unions. Miscommunication and financial disagreements strained her relationship with the NAACP by November 1955, and executive secretary Roy Wilkins dropped her from subsequent speaking engagements.

Bradley dedicated the remainder of her life to helping children and preserving her son's memory. She graduated from the Chicago Teachers College in 1956 and taught in Chicago's

T

public schools until her 1983 retirement. Till-Mobley also earned a master's degree in administration and supervision from Loyola University in Chicago, and in 1973 she founded the Emmett Till Players, a group of student actors devoted to educating the masses about the civil rights movement. Throughout her life Till-Mobley spoke out against acts of injustice across the country, including the 1998 lynching of James Byrd in Jasper, Texas. She died on 6 January 2003, just prior to the release of a book she authored with Christopher Benson, *Death of Innocence: The Story of the Hate Crime That Changed America*. In large part as a result of her efforts, the Federal Bureau of Investigation reopened the Till case in 2004, though no further prosecutions occurred, and in 2005 Congress passed antilynching legislation and called on the Bureau to investigate cold cases from the civil rights era. Today, streets, bridges, highways, schools, placards, statues, and legislation honor her son's memory.

Darryl Mace

Cabrini College

Keith Beauchamp, *The Untold Story of Emmett Till* (film, 2006); Emmett Till Murder website, www.emmetttillmurder.com; Ruth Feldstein, *Motherhood in Black and White: Race and Sex in American Liberalism, 1930–1965* (2000); Clenora Hudson-Weems, *Emmett Till: Sacrificial Lamb of the Civil Rights Movement* (1994); Darryl Mace, "Regional Identities and Racial Messages: The Print Media's Stories of Emmett Till" (PhD dissertation, Temple University, 2007); Christopher Metress, ed., *The Lynching of Emmett Till: A Documentary Narrative* (2002); Stephen J. Whitfield, *A Death in the Delta: The Story of Emmett Till* (1988).

Tinsley Field

Located in Yazoo County, Tinsley Field currently produces both crude oil and natural gas. In 1939 Tinsley Field became the first commercially successful oil field discovered in Mississippi. The giant field classification typically requires the production of 100 million standard forty-two-gallon barrels of crude oil. By the end of 1947 Tinsley had already produced in excess of 100.9 million barrels of oil, thus qualifying for giant field status. Its peak yearly production was in 1942, when it produced more than 28 million barrels of oil.

The accumulation of oil and gas at Tinsley resulted from the arching of geological units over a deep subsurface salt structure. Indications of arching were first discovered by F. F. Mellen, a geologist with the Mississippi State Geological Survey, then headquartered at the University of Mississippi. Mellen had been conducting surface geological mapping in Yazoo County and found indications of arching along streams and other surface exposures of clay beds. On 12 April

1939 the Mississippi State Geological Survey issued a press release with its interpretation of the information gathered in the field. Shortly thereafter, Union Producing completed Mississippi's first commercial oil well, the C. G. Woodruff No. 1 well, at a total depth of 4,560 feet. The well produced from an oil-saturated sand bed that came to be called the Woodruff Sand. The discovery of that oil at Tinsley Field made national news.

By 2007 578 wells had been drilled at Tinsley, with 50 actively producing in the field.

Charles T. Swann

University of Mississippi

T. A. Fitzgerald, in *Giant Oil and Gas Fields of the Decade*, ed. M. T. Halbouty (1980); Kenneth K. Landes, *Petroleum Geology of the United States* (1970); F. F. Mellen and T. E. McCutcheon, *Mississippi State Geological Survey Bulletin 39* (1940); W. H. Moore, *Tinsley Field, 1939–1974: A Commemorative Bulletin* (1974).

Tippah County

Established after the 1832 Chickasaw land cession, Tippah County was created from land that included portions of Benton, Union, Alcorn, and Prentiss Counties. Tippah is located in northeastern Mississippi, on the Tennessee border. The name *Tippah* is said to have come from a Chickasaw word meaning "cut off." The county seat is Ripley.

In the 1840 census, Tippah's population consisted of 7,310 free people (the second-most in the state) and 2,134 slaves. Early residents included farmers, planters, and merchants who settled near waterways throughout the county. Tippah is surrounded by rivers, including the Tallahatchie and Tippah Rivers to the west and south and the West Hatchie and Hatchie Rivers to the east and north. Because of these rivers and nearby limestone, Tippah County's soil was ripe for agricultural development, specifically food crops. This appealed to hill country farmers, who grew fruits and vegetables for home consumption more than cash crops such as cotton. Tippah residents also concentrated more than most Mississippians on raising livestock.

In 1860 the county ranked tenth in the state in the value of its livestock, sixth in sweet potatoes, and fourteenth in corn but only twenty-third in the value of its cotton. The county's 129 industrial workers were employed in a variety of jobs, primarily at Tippah's twenty lumber mills and twenty-one flour mills. The county had grown substantially and had 16,219 free persons and 6,331 slaves. Tippah also had seventy-two churches, including twenty-six Methodist churches, twenty-four Baptist congregations, eight Cumberland Presbyterian houses of worship, seven Union churches, four Christian churches, and three Presbyterian congregations.

After the Civil War, Tippah County's population declined as a consequence of the creation of nearby Benton and Union Counties, which absorbed much of Tippah's population. By 1880 Tippah had just 12,867 residents, 76 percent of them white. As in much of northeastern Mississippi, a substantial majority of farmers owned their land. Most farmers continued to concentrate on grains and tobacco. Tippah residents grew by far the most tobacco in the state.

In 1900 Tippah remained an agricultural economy, with just 71 industrial workers. During this period the majority of white farmers (56 percent) owned their land, though just 20 percent of the 422 African American farmers did so. Between 1880 and 1900 the population grew by a mere 116 people.

In 1873 Gen. Mark Perrin Lowrey established an all-female Southern Baptist institution, Blue Mountain College, in Tippah County. The first faculty members included Lowrey's two daughters, Modena and Margaret. Modena Lowrey Berry, known as *Mother*, became the dominant personality of Blue Mountain and worked for the school for sixty-one years. Blue Mountain College students of note have included Carolyn Bennett Patterson, who went on to become a writer and editor for *National Geographic*, and artist Dusti Bongé.

In 1916 Baptists accounted for more than half of Tippah County's 5,400 church members, with the majority belonging to the Southern Baptist Convention. The Methodist Episcopal Church, South also made up a large portion of Tippah's religious population.

By 1930 Tippah's population had topped 18,000. About 80 percent of the population was white, with African Americans making up 20 percent. Though farm-owning yeomen had dominated agriculture in the nineteenth century, farmers now operated only 41 percent of the farms. Small sawmills employed 114 industrial workers. The county had a tiny population of foreign-born residents—one immigrant born in Russia and one born in Iceland.

Among the notable residents of Tippah County were activist and editor Ida B. Wells, born in 1862, who spent part of her childhood in the area, and members of the well-known Falkner family. Ripley's William Clark Falkner was a novelist, business leader, and military figure whose story was important in the mind of his great-grandson, William Faulkner. Donald Wildmon, the Methodist preacher who started his political activism by protesting sexual and secular content on television and then established the American Family Association in Tupelo, grew up in Tippah County. Ripley native Philip Gibbs was killed in the 1970 Jackson State University shootings. Ripley is also home to the First Monday Trade Day, an event that began in 1893 and continues as a popular spot for buying, selling, and bargaining over a variety of goods.

From 1930 to 1960 the county's population decreased by more than 3,000. Whites accounted for 82 percent of Tippah's

15,000 people in 1960. Farmers, who comprised more than a third of the county's working people, concentrated on corn and hogs, the old standards of a yeoman economy. County farmers raised the second-most corn and third-most hogs in Mississippi as well as soybeans and cotton. Almost a quarter of Tippah's workers were employed in manufacturing, especially in apparel factories.

Like nearly all of the counties in northeastern Mississippi, in 2010 the population in Tippah County was predominantly white, included a small but significant Hispanic/Latino minority, and had grown by almost 50 percent between 1960 and 2010, when it reached 22,232. Whites comprised 80 percent of residents, African Americans 16 percent, and Hispanics/Latinos 4 percent.

Mississippi Encyclopedia Staff
University of Mississippi

Mississippi State Planning Commission, *Progress Report on State Planning in Mississippi* (1938); *Mississippi Statistical Abstract*, Mississippi State University (1952–2010); Charles Sydnor and Claude Bennett, *Mississippi History* (1939); University of Virginia Library, Historical Census Browser website, http://mapserver.lib.virginia.edu; E. Nolan Waller and Dani A. Smith, *Growth Profiles of Mississippi's Counties, 1960–1980* (1985).

Tisdale, Charles
(1926–2007) Journalist

Charles Wesley Tisdale was a civil rights crusader who believed that journalism was a critical part of activism. His motto was to "print the news whether it pinches or comforts." Tisdale also noted, "I think newspapers that provide information are the most essential tool in a democracy. I always wanted to have my say. This is true liberty, when free men speak freely."

Born in Athens, Alabama, on 7 November 1926, Tisdale was the sixth of fifteen children. At age seven he ran away from home and began working at a newspaper, pouring lead into molds in linotype machines. At fourteen he was foreman of a tobacco field in Connecticut and the cofounder of a local chapter of the National Association for the Advancement of Colored People. He later returned to Athens, where he graduated from Trinity High School. In 1950 he received a bachelor's degree from LeMoyne-Owen College in Memphis, Tennessee, working as an advertising and whiskey salesman while in Memphis. He later earned a master's degree in economics from the University of Chicago. An adviser for numerous companies, he found his true profession in reporting for the African American press. His byline appeared in the *Memphis Tri-State Defender*, *Memphis World*, *New York Amsterdam News*, and *Chicago Defender*. He edited the *Memphis Times Herald* and the *Midsouth Times*.

While reporting for the *Tri-State Defender* in 1955 he traveled to Money, Mississippi, to report on the trial of the men accused of murdering fourteen-year-old Emmett Till. Tisdale also covered the 1957 integration of Central High School in Little Rock, Arkansas. After working intermittently selling advertisements for the *Jackson Advocate*, Tisdale purchased the nearly defunct newspaper in 1978 for seventeen thousand dollars. He declared that the paper would "promote civil rights and fight discrimination," a stance that was the complete opposite of that taken by the paper's founding publisher, Percy Greene, a conservative on segregation who took money from the Mississippi State Sovereignty Commission.

Two weeks after he began publishing the *Jackson Advocate*, Tisdale received the first of what became hundreds of death threats. Tisdale and the *Advocate* staff were routinely harassed by racists and local authorities whose policies he challenged, and he and the newspaper were targets of numerous violent attacks, break-ins, and vandalism. On 26 January 1998 Molotov cocktails were thrown through the windows of the *Advocate* offices, and in 2003 men who identified themselves as Ku Klux Klansmen riddled the office with bullets. In addition, the paper faced harassment from the Internal Revenue Service, Federal Bureau of Investigation, and various Mississippi state agencies.

Battling government corruption, prison injustice, and racism, the *Jackson Advocate*, a weekly that cost fifty cents per copy, garnered an impressive national and international readership, with a circulation of twenty thousand. Tisdale also began a weekly radio program, *Views from the Black Side*, on Jackson's WNPR; was a member of the national coordinating committee for the National Alliance against Racist and Political Repression; and helped organize the Eddie J. Carthan Support Project in Los Angeles. His coverage of the Tchula 7 trial, in which the town's former mayor, Eddie Carthan, was accused of capital murder, brought international attention to Tisdale and the *Jackson Advocate*.

The paper's circulation declined to seventeen thousand in 2000 and to little more than 8,000 by 2010. However, the *Advocate* has never missed an issue and maintains a strong online presence.

Tisdale and the *Jackson Advocate* received hundreds of honors for journalism and activism, including the National Black Chamber of Commerce Newspaper of the Year, the Nation of Islam Freedom Fighter Award, the Southern Christian Leadership Conference Journalism Award, City of Jackson Community Service Award, the Mississippi Legislative Black Caucus Award for Excellence, the Southern Christian Leadership Council Journalism Award, and the National Black Chamber of Commerce Newspaper of the Year. The National Alliance of Third World Journalists bestowed the Jose Martí Journalist of Struggle Award on Tisdale and the *Advocate*.

Tisdale died on 7 July 2007 in Jackson; his widow, Alice Tisdale, succeeded him as publisher of the *Advocate*. Within months the Jackson Chapter of the National Association of Black Journalists established the Charles W. Tisdale Scholarship for high school students from Mississippi majoring in journalism. Two years later Jackson's City Council and voters approved the renaming of the Northside Library in his honor. It houses a collection of Tisdale's papers and writings.

Candace J. Semien
Baton Rouge, Louisiana

Herb Boyd, *New York Amsterdam News* (12–18 July 2007); "Human Rights Defender Charles Tisdale," *Front Line: The International Foundation for the Protection of Human Rights Defenders* website, www.frontlinedefenders.org; Benjamin Todd Jealous, *Crisis* (September–October 2007); Freda Darlene Lewis, "The *Jackson Advocate*: The Rise and Eclipse of a Leading Black Newspaper in Mississippi, 1939–1964" (master's thesis, Iowa State University, 1984); Roland McFadden, "A Study of the *Jackson Advocate* Newspaper Reports of Social Change in Mississippi, from 1954 to 1974" (master's thesis, Jackson State University, 1981); C. Leigh McInnis, "Charles Tisdale: Newspaper and Community Man," *ChickenBones: A Journal for Literary and Artistic African-American Themes* website, www.nathanielturner.com; George Sewell and Margaret L. Dwight, *Mississippi Black History Makers* (1984); Jocelyn Y. Stewart, *Los Angeles Times* (14 July 2007); Julius Eric Thompson, *The Black Press in Mississippi, 1865–1985* (1993); Colleen R. White, *The Jackson Advocate, 1938–1995: A Historical Overview* (1996).

Tishomingo County

Founded in 1836, Tishomingo County is located in the northeastern corner of Mississippi, sharing borders with Tennessee and Alabama. Tishomingo sits at the foothills of the Appalachian Mountains and is the site where the Natchez Trace crosses into the state. The highest point in Mississippi, Woodall Mountain, is located in Tishomingo's county seat, Iuka. Geographically, Tishomingo shares more in common with southern parts of Tennessee than with most of the rest of Mississippi. The county is named for a leader of the Chickasaw, the indigenous population that inhabited the area prior to 1832.

In 1840, when the first census was recorded, 6,681 people lived in Tishomingo County. It had the highest percentage of free people of any county in Mississippi—87 percent. During this period, Tishomingo and Itawamba were the only two counties in which slaves comprised less than 20 percent of the population.

In 1860 Tishomingo trailed only Hinds and Marshall Counties in total population, and slaves comprised just 20.6 percent of residents. With an economy based on smaller farms,

Iuka High School, Iuka, seat of Tishomingo County, ca. 1910 (Ann Rayburn Paper Americana Collection, Department of Archives and Special Collections, J. D. Williams Library, University of Mississippi [rayburn_ann_24_75_001])

Tishomingo County produced far more corn, wheat, and tobacco and grew far more livestock than most counties in Mississippi, but it ranked low in the production of cotton. Perhaps the most striking feature of Tishomingo's economy lay in its eighty-seven manufacturing establishments, by far the largest number in Mississippi. Tishomingo's firms employed 477 men and 15 women, also the most in the state. The great majority of those employees worked in the lumber industry. Blacksmithing ranked second, and women found manufacturing employment in the production of cotton cloth. Tishomingo also had a substantial immigrant population of 277, the tenth-highest in Mississippi.

As in much of antebellum Mississippi, Baptists and Methodists dominated the religious landscape of Tishomingo County, which in 1860 was home to fifteen Methodist, eleven Baptist, and three Cumberland Presbyterian churches.

Civil War forces battled twice near Iuka in 1862. Attractive and important to the military because of railroad crossings in Corinth in Alcorn County, Tishomingo witnessed its first combat after the Battle of Shiloh, across the Tennessee border. In the spring of 1862 Federal forces took over the area, though Confederate forces led by Earl Van Dorn experienced some success moving back into the county. Major battles in early October of that year proved disastrous for the Confederacy. Ulysses Grant led more than twenty-three thousand US troops into Tishomingo County and defeated twenty-two thousand Confederate forces, with a total of seven thousand casualties.

Tishomingo County was divided during the Civil War, with both supporters and opponents of the Confederacy. Residents expressed significant Unionist sentiment before the war, and Judge Robert Hill served the county during the Civil War without joining the Confederacy. He called for biracial voting after the war and was appointed a federal judge by Pres. Andrew Johnson. However, Tishomingo also had one of the more active postbellum Ku Klux Klan chapters.

In 1880 Tishomingo's population of 8,774 was 87 percent white. With the state's timber industry migrating to southern Mississippi, Tishomingo witnessed a diminishing industrial workforce, though it continued to have large numbers of farm owners. More than three-quarters of Tishomingo's 1,078 farmers owned their land, and production concentrated mainly on tobacco.

In 1900 Tishomingo County had a population of 10,124 and was 90 percent white. While much of Mississippi shifted to tenancy and sharecropping, about two-thirds of Tishomingo farmers were landowners. As in other areas in which sharecropping and tenancy did not dominate, the average farm size in Tishomingo was far larger than the state average. The area remained largely agricultural, with only 43 industrial workers, all but one of them male. According to the 1916 census of religion, the Methodist Episcopal Church, South was the county's largest church group, followed by the Southern Baptist Convention, the National Baptist Convention, and—relatively rare for Mississippi—the Churches of Christ.

Tishomingo's population rose steadily in the early twentieth century, reaching 16,000 by 1930. Whites continued to comprise a large majority of residents, at 94 percent. Shifts in industrial labor paralleled changes in Tishomingo's agricultural economy. Tishomingo's industrial force increased rapidly, with fifty-eight establishments, including many small sawmills, employing 457 workers. While industrial employment increased, landownership for farmers declined. In a county that had long been a yeoman area rooted in farm ownership, only 46 percent of farms were run by their owners in 1930. All but 4 percent of the county's 1,284 tenant farmers were white.

In 1933 the US Congress established the Tennessee Valley Authority to develop low-cost electricity programs. Tishomingo County was one of the first counties in the state to receive power generated by what became the largest public power provider in the United States. It was also the beneficiary of another New Deal initiative, the Civilian Conservation Corps, which built Tishomingo Park in the mid-1930s.

Between 1930 and 1960 Tishomingo's population declined by about 2,000 to 13,889 people—13,210 whites, 677 African Americans, and 2 Native Americans. About 35 percent of the county's workers had employment in industry, and about 20 percent worked in agriculture. By 1980 the population had exceeded 18,000.

The Tennessee-Tombigbee Waterway opened in 1985 after years of political debate and tensions over the environmental consequences of its construction. The new passage between the two major rivers dramatically increased commercial trafficking in the region and provided employment for nearby residents. Other major industrial development plans for Tishomingo proved less successful. Funding for the Yellow Creek Nuclear Power Plant was canceled in the 1980s, and an effort to build rocket motors for NASA failed in the 1990s.

As in most northeastern Mississippi counties, Tishomingo County was predominantly white in 2010 and had shown an overall increase in size since 1960, growing by about 40 percent to 19,593. The population was 94.5 percent white, 2.6 percent African American, and 2.8 percent Hispanic/Latino.

Mississippi Encyclopedia Staff
University of Mississippi

Mississippi Department of Archives and History, Mississippi Archaeology Trails website, http://trails.mdah.ms.gov; Mississippi State Planning Commission, *Progress R5eport on State Planning in Mississippi* (1938); *Mississippi Statistical Abstract*, Mississippi State University (1952–2010); Charles Sydnor and Claude Bennett, *Mississippi History* (1939); Tennessee-Tombigbee Waterway website, www.tenntom.org; Tennessee Valley Authority website, www.tva.com; University of Virginia Library, Historical Census Browser website, http://mapserver.lib.virginia.edu; E. Nolan Waller and Dani A. Smith, *Growth Profiles of Mississippi's Counties, 1960–1980* (1985).

Tobacco Use

When the first Europeans arrived in what is now Mississippi in the sixteenth century, they found that Native Americans were using tobacco. In fact, they had done so for social, religious, and healing purposes as far back as 3000 BC.

Tobacco became the first major crop the French grew in the Natchez District in the early eighteenth century. Natchez tobacco was sent to New Orleans, then under Spanish control, for curing and shipment to Europe. Mississippi tobacco proved inferior to what was grown in Virginia, but Spanish authorities provided a subsidy for Natchez tobacco until 1790. With the subsidy's demise, however, growing tobacco for export was not viable, and Natchez planters turned to other crops. Tobacco remained a secondary crop in some areas of Mississippi and was generally grown in garden patches for family use.

Agricultural census data from 1840 to 1910 confirm the minor role of tobacco in Mississippi agriculture. In 1880, the year of highest tobacco production, 414,663 pounds of tobacco were grown on 1,471 acres—less than .1 percent of all land in cultivation. By the twentieth century, tobacco had virtually disappeared from the Mississippi landscape, with six acres in production in 1929, only one tobacco farm in 1982, and seven tobacco farms in 2002. In 2012 Mississippi had no tobacco farms.

Early Mississippians smoked tobacco using pipes made from materials at hand, including wood, clay, stone, metal, or corncobs. Plug tobacco became popular in the early nineteenth century when tobacco-chewing Andrew Jackson emerged as a folk hero. The Mexican War (1846–48) brought Mississippi soldiers into contact with cigars. Snuff, another tobacco product, was popular in Europe but was viewed by Mississippi men as too effete, though the state's rural women used it, preferring to dip it into their mouths rather than to sniff it. Mississippi women also smoked corncob pipes and chewed tobacco. By the twentieth century, however, cigarettes became the preferred tobacco product in Mississippi, as in the rest of American culture.

As tobacco use increased, the health hazards of smoking became more and more apparent. Concerns about the health implications of smoking had been raised as early as 1604, when King James I of Great Britain expressed alarm at the danger smoking posed to the lungs. In the United States in the eighteenth and nineteenth centuries, however, opposition focused mainly on the nastiness of chewing, not the health implications of tobacco use.

Prior to the twentieth century, lung cancers were rare, and most physicians never treated them. In 1912 American physician Isaac Adler raised the idea that lung cancer was related to smoking. The post–World War I rise in popularity of cigarettes was accompanied by an explosion in the number of cases of lung cancer. Scientists in both Europe and the United States conducted studies on the effects of cigarette smoking, and in 1964 the US surgeon general issued a report that confirmed the close link between smoking and lung cancer. Scientific knowledge about the harmful effects of tobacco use has continued to develop over the ensuing half century, and studies have proven that cigarette smoking causes not only lung cancer but also heart disease; a variety of other cancers, including those affecting the pancreas, kidney, and cervix; and chronic lung disease. Smoking by pregnant women and new mothers contributes to low birth weight, sudden infant death syndrome, and spontaneous abortions.

Tobacco use in Mississippi has resulted in health problems of almost pandemic proportions. By 2016 Mississippi experienced 5,400 tobacco-related deaths each year and annual tobacco-related health care costs of $1.23 billion. The Medicaid program reported $319.7 million in tobacco-related costs in the state each year.

In 1994 the issue of tobacco-related Medicaid costs led Mississippi's attorney general to initiate a lawsuit against the tobacco industry, seeking compensation for damage the industry had caused in the state. Three years later, Mississippi negotiated a $4 billion settlement with the tobacco industry. The other forty-nine states later reached similar settlements totaling $244 billion.

Tobacco is universally recognized as a consumer product with no utility. No credible resource has claimed that tobacco is of any value to consumers. All scientific evidence confirms the health hazards of tobacco use, yet Mississippians not only continue to use tobacco but do so at much higher rates than residents in other states. Whereas 15.1 percent of US adults smoked in 2015, 23.0 percent of Mississippi adults did so. Even more alarming, whereas 10.8 percent of high school students nationwide were smokers, that number was 15.2 percent in Mississippi.

Walter G. Howell
Clinton, Mississippi

Vicki Betts, *The Citizens Companion* (1998); Allan M. Brant, *The Cigarette Century* (2007); Campaign for Tobacco-Free Kids website, www.tobacco freekids.org; Charles Campbell, Judith Phillips, Denise Keller, and Ben Collins, *Tobacco and Food Taxation: Policy Options for Mississippi* (2007); Jordan Goodman, *Tobacco in History: The Cultures of Dependence* (1993); Richard Kluger, *Ashes to Ashes: America's Hundred-Year Cigarette War, the Public Health, and the Unabashed Triumph of Philip Morris* (1996); Richard A. McLemore, ed., *History of Mississippi*, 2 vols. (1973); R. C. Millen and D. A. Gill, *2004 Mississippi Health Assessment* (2004); US Department of Agriculture, *Census of Agriculture* (1840–2012).

Topp, Mildred Spurrier

(1897–1963) Author and Politician

Mildred Spurrier Topp, a Mississippi legislator and popular memoirist, was born on 5 January 1897 on a farm near Forest City, Illinois, to Lillian White Spurrier and Frank Spurrier, who abandoned his wife before Mildred's birth. With her mother; older sister, Velma; and maternal grandparents, Spurrier moved to Murfreesboro, Tennessee, as a young child. When she was nine, her mother opened the first photography studio in Greenwood, Mississippi. After graduating from Greenwood High School, Spurrier earned a bachelor's degree from the Industrial Institute and College (now Mississippi University for Women) in 1917. That year, she married Robert Graham Topp, a cotton farmer.

From 1918 to 1922 Mildred Topp taught English at Greenwood High. After giving birth to a daughter in 1922 and a son two years later, she became one of the few women serving in the Mississippi legislature, representing Leflore County in the State House of Representatives between 1932 and 1936. She took a special interest in laws relating to marriage, families, and education. During World War II she served on the staff of Greenwood's USO, which provided support services to troops, before becoming a local journalist. At age fifty Topp began to record her early memories of Greenwood. She attended a summer writing workshop at the University of Colorado, where her instructor was Mississippi native Ben Ames Williams, a best-selling novelist. Houghton Mifflin subsequently published Topp's *Smile Please* on Williams's recommendation—he had "laughed for three hours" after reading the manuscript, which included scenes set in her mother's photography studio. In a review for the *New York Herald Tribune*, humorist Emily Kimbrough praised this "lively book" about "a sturdy, independent, courageous child—her mother's own daughter."

Although most reviewers of *Smile Please* and its sequel, *In the Pink*, stressed Topp's comic, sometimes satiric flair, a few noted the presence of cruelty and even tragedy. Lillian Spurrier is not the only struggling single mother in Topp's portrayals of early twentieth-century Greenwood, and the memoirs also feature suffering children, handicapped adults, and lecherous businessmen. An abridgment of the second volume appeared in the December 1950 *Omnibook: Best-Seller Magazine*, a Christmas issue that reprinted cartoons by Charles Addams and a selection from Robert Penn Warren's *World Enough and Time*.

Despite the success of her two volumes, Topp never published another book. Instead, she enrolled in graduate school at the University of Mississippi in Oxford, where she completed a master's thesis on "Chaucer, a Forerunner of the English Renaissance." She emphasized the poet's unique humor, the "truth and vitality" of his work, the concreteness of his details, and his "power to delight and charm the human heart"—qualities that are also apparent in Topp's autobiographical accounts. She died in Greenwood on 15 August 1963.

Joan Wylie Hall
University of Mississippi

Pamela Taylor, *Saturday Review* (11 September 1948); Melanie Topp, "The Life and Writings of Mildred Spurrier Topp" (master's thesis, University of North Carolina at Chapel Hill, 1981); Ovid Vickers, *Neshoba Democrat* (9 May 2007).

Tougaloo College

Tougaloo College was founded in 1869 by the American Missionary Association, a nondenominational Christian organization that sought to provide educational facilities for some of Mississippi's former slaves. The association's agent, Allen P. Huggins, found land north of Jackson, and the school bought the Boddie Plantation, including five hundred acres of land and the house, for $10,500. The Mississippi legislature chartered the school, officially named Tougaloo University, on 13 May 1871. The first normal department was organized the following October, and in 1879 the department graduated its first class of three students. The school's initial board of trustees included Lt. Gov. Ridgley Powers; state legislators H. W. Warren, M. T. Newson, T. W. Stringer, and John R. Lynch; congressmen George McKee and Hiram Rhoades Revels; and representatives of the American Missionary Association.

Frank G. Woodworth served as the school's president from 1887 to 1912. In 1892 the state withdrew funding from the college. Courses for college credit were first offered in 1897, and in 1901 Traverse S. Crawford received the first bachelor's degree awarded by the school.

William T. Holmes succeeded Woodworth as president in 1913 and served until 1933. Holmes campaigned strongly for the school, soliciting money from individuals and organizations. Holmes also shifted the curriculum to focus more on liberal arts than on manual training. In 1916 the school's name was changed to Tougaloo College, and it has subsequently operated under that name except for the 1954–62 period, when it was known as Tougaloo Southern Christian College.

With strong support from Dr. Adam D. Beittel, who served as Tougaloo College's president from 1960 to 1964, students and faculty played a vital role in the civil rights movement, taking part in such actions as the integration of the Jackson public library. Gladys Noel Bates, a Tougaloo alumna, fought for equal pay for Mississippi's African American teachers, and Anne Moody wrote of her years as a student and activist at Tougaloo in *Coming of Age in Mississippi*. Other Tougaloo students and alumni active in the civil rights movement included Joyce Ladner, Lawrence Guyot, and Colia Clark. The school's Woodworth Chapel hosted speeches by Martin Luther King Jr., Medgar Evers, Fannie Lou Hamer, and other civil rights leaders. In 1965, after a year as acting president, George Owens became the college's first African American president, serving until 1984. US congressman Bennie Thompson studied at Tougaloo, as did Walker Turnbull, founder of the Boys Choir of Harlem.

Tougaloo now produces top professionals in a variety of academic fields, including law, medicine, and education. The college has a distinguished art collection, including paintings and sculptures by Jacob Lawrence, David Driskell, Elizabeth Catlett, Hale Woodruff, and other notable artists. In 2002 the college selected its first female president, Dr. Beverly Wade Hogan, and she has overseen the development of the Tougaloo Council for Undergraduate Research, which offers students opportunities to work with faculty mentors on research projects designed to lead to professional opportunities, as well as programs for elementary and high school students in art, leadership, language arts, math, and science and engineering.

Shugana Williams
University of Southern Mississippi

Clarice T. Campbell and Oscar Allan Rogers Jr., *Mississippi: The View from Tougaloo* (1979); Clarice T. Campbell, "The Founding of Tougaloo College" (master's thesis, University of Mississippi, 1967); Tougaloo College website, www.tougaloo.edu.

Tougaloo Nine

In March 1961 the Tougaloo Nine became the first Mississippi students to stage a sit-in against segregation when they staged a demonstration at the main public library in Jackson. Just over a year earlier, on 1 February 1960, students from North Carolina Agricultural and Technical College had launched the sit-in movement with a protest at a Greensboro lunch counter. Students from black colleges across the South followed suit at a variety of public places—lunch counters, libraries, and department stores—that denied service to blacks.

At that time, the city of Jackson had an ordinance that prohibited blacks from using the main library and whites from using the George Washington Carver Library, designated for blacks. Noted civil rights leader Medgar Evers worked with the Tougaloo students preparing and training them for the protest. The nine were prepared to be beaten and to receive threats against their lives or family.

On 27 March 1961 nine members of the Jackson Youth Council of the National Association for the Advancement of Colored People—Meredith Coleman Anding Jr., James Cleo Bradford, Alfred Lee Cook, Geraldine Edwards, Janice Jackson, Joseph Jackson Jr., Albert Earl Lassiter, Evelyn Pierce, and Ethel Sawyer—entered Jackson's main library and began browsing through the card catalog and then sat down to read. When police arrived and asked the students to leave, they refused and were arrested on charges of breach of the peace. Medgar Evers gathered bail for their release, and Jack Harvey Young Sr., a civil rights lawyer, represented the students. They were ultimately convicted, fined one hundred dollars each, and given thirty days in jail, though that part of the sentence was suspended. However, their actions led to the integration of what is now the Jackson Metropolitan Library System, and they have been honored by the college and by the City of Jackson.

Annie Payton
Mississippi Valley State University

Laura Hipp, *Jackson Clarion-Ledger* (13 October 2006); *Jackson Clarion-Ledger* (30 March 1961); *Jackson State Times* (27 March 1961); *The Tougaloo Nine: Retrospection and Present Perception . . . Activism in a Multi-Cultural Society, 27 March 1961–27 March 1991* (anniversary program).

Tourism

More than twenty million leisure and business travelers visit Mississippi each year, drawn to the state by its casino resorts, historic and cultural attractions, and opportunities for outdoor recreation. In 2015 travel and tourism in Mississippi accounted for more than eighty-five thousand direct jobs and more than thirty-two thousand indirect jobs—10.5 percent of all employment in the state—with an annual payroll of approximately $2.79 billion. The tourism industry was the state's fourth-leading private employer. Approximately 22.33 million tourists visited Mississippi. Most domestic visitors came from within Mississippi or from Louisiana, Alabama, Tennessee, Florida, Texas, Georgia, and Arkansas. Mississippi also welcomed visitors from Canada, the United Kingdom, Mexico, Germany, Australia, France, the Netherlands, Japan, Italy, and Norway.

At the forefront of the Mississippi tourism industry is casino gaming. As of 1 February 2016 Mississippi was home to twenty-eight state-licensed casinos, including twelve on the Gulf Coast, nine in the Northern Region (Tunica and Coahoma County), and seven in the Central Region (Greenville, Washington County, Natchez, and Vicksburg). In addition, the Mississippi Band of Choctaw Indians operates three gaming establishments: the Bok Homa Casino near Laurel and the Golden Moon and Silver Star Casinos, both of which are located in the Pearl River Resort in Choctaw. The casinos offer the excitement of slots, blackjack, baccarat, roulette, and poker, as well as a wide range of resort amenities, including stage shows, full-service spas, and fine dining.

Mississippi is a popular destination for history enthusiasts, who are drawn to the state by its antebellum architecture, Civil War battlefields, and civil-rights-era landmarks.

Natchez Hotel, Natchez, ca. 1907 (Ann Rayburn Paper Americana Collection, Department of Archives and Special Collections, J. D. Williams Library, University of Mississippi [rayburn_ann_31_26_001])

Dozens of the state's palatial antebellum mansions are open for tours, with many doubling as bed-and-breakfast inns. Natchez alone is home to more than five hundred antebellum homes, churches, and public buildings. Some of Mississippi's carefully preserved Civil War battlefields host reenactments in which costumed men and women represent Confederate and Union soldiers. Museums, landmarks, and monuments statewide, including those that are part of the Mississippi Freedom Trail, tell the story of the fight for equal rights and of the men and women who influenced the civil rights movement in Mississippi and ultimately nationwide.

Mississippi is home to four national parks and twenty-five state parks, which attract hundreds of thousands of visitors each year. The Natchez National Historical Park includes two antebellum homes: Melrose (1845), the estate of a wealthy cotton planter, and the William Johnson House (1841), the home of a free, African American barber and successful Natchez businessman of the 1840s. The Vicksburg National Military Park, 1,800 acres of rolling hills, monuments, and earthworks, attracts more than 500,000 annual visitors. The Natchez Trace Parkway, a national highway maintained by the National Park Service, stretches diagonally through Mississippi, following a trading path that has existed for more than four hundred years. The Gulf Islands National Seashore extends some 150 miles from Mississippi to Florida. The Mississippi portion of this national park begins on the mainland near Ocean Springs and then stretches into the Mississippi Sound to include the barrier islands of West Ship, East Ship, Horn, and Petit Bois. Protected from development, these natural areas provide habitats for wildlife and are popular for camping, beachcombing, bird watching, and ecotourism. The state parks offer these activities as well as a variety of other recreational opportunities, including water parks, equestrian trails, mountain bike trails, disc golf, and miniature golf. The parks also include four golf courses: Mallard Pointe, the Dogwoods, LeFleur's Bluff, and Quail Hollow. The state also has more than 140 additional golf courses, ranging from simple nine-hole courses to spectacular resort courses created by Tom Fazio, Jack Nicklaus, Arnold Palmer, Davis Love III, Jerry Pate, and other renowned designers.

The state's cultural heritage attracts visitors interested in music, art, and literature. Mississippi is famous as the birthplace of the blues, country music, and Elvis Presley, the King of Rock and Roll. Presley's modest birthplace in Tupelo logs more than sixty thousand visitors each year. Visitors come from around the world to travel along the Mississippi Blues Trail and the Mississippi Country Music Trail, which highlight important sites in the history of those musical genres. In addition, numerous festivals, juke joints, and other venues offer the opportunity to hear current musicians play.

Museums statewide showcase the work of established Mississippi artists, while the next generation of painters, sculptors, and potters thrives in artists' colonies from the northeastern hills to the Gulf Coast. The state's literary heritage is reflected in the masterpieces of William Faulkner,

Willie Morris, Eudora Welty, and Richard Wright and in the best-selling novels of John Grisham, Greg Iles, and Nevada Barr. Visitors are drawn to Mississippi by these famous writers' homes—Faulkner's and Welty's are open for public tours—as well as by the cities and landmarks these writers immortalized in their pages.

On 29 August 2005 Hurricane Katrina slammed into the Mississippi Gulf Coast, causing massive destruction. In the months following the storm, more than half a million volunteers from around the nation poured into the Gulf Coast communities to assist with the rebuilding effort, a phenomenon now known as voluntourism. Many volunteers found themselves entranced by Mississippi's geography, culture, and people and have returned not only to continue helping but also to vacation.

Marlo Kirkpatrick

Madison, Mississippi

Mississippi Development Authority, Tourism Division/Research Unit, "Fiscal Year 2006 Economic Impact for Tourism in Mississippi"; Mississippi Development Authority, Tourism Division/Research Unit, "Fiscal Year Tourism Industry/Economy Projections, 2007" (February 2007); Mississippi Development Authority, Tourism Division/Research Unit, "Fiscal Year 2010 Economic Contribution of Travel and Tourism in Mississippi (February 2011); Marlo Kirkpatrick, *Mississippi Off the Beaten Path* (2007); Mississippi Blues Trail website, msbluestrail.org; Mississippi Country Music Trail website, mscountrymusictrail.org; Visit Mississippi website, www.visitmississippi.org.

Town, A. Hays

(1903–2005) Architect

Although he lived in Mississippi for only thirteen years, architect A. Hays Town had a profound impact on the state's built environment through two very distinct phases of his long and illustrious career. During his first period of influence, when he lived in Mississippi, he helped to introduce modern architecture to the state; during his second period of influence he was instrumental in helping rekindle an interest in Mississippi's vernacular architectural traditions.

Town was born on 17 June 1903 in Crowley, Louisiana, and was educated at Southwestern Louisiana Institute and at Tulane University. He came to Mississippi in 1926 to work as an intern in the office of prominent Jackson-based architect N. W. Overstreet. By the time Town left Jackson in 1939, he and Overstreet had become partners, and with Overstreet's encouragement, Town had designed modern concrete structures across the state. Many of these buildings had been built under the public relief programs of the Great Depression,

and many were schools, including Church Street School in Tupelo, Bailey Junior High School in Jackson, Bowmar Avenue School in Vicksburg, and Columbus High School. This work was widely published nationally and internationally and, as Overstreet had hoped, helped to further Mississippi's reputation as a progressive state and to pave the way for a broader acceptance of modern architecture.

Town's family obligations took him back to Louisiana, where he established what became one of Baton Rouge's largest commercial postwar architectural offices. Despite his great success, Town took increasing interest in the firm's smaller residential commissions, where he could experiment with forms and ideas derived from childhood memories of traditional architecture in southern Louisiana. He also found inspiration in his recollections of his work with the Historic American Buildings Survey, in which he documented Mississippi's early structures. Beginning in the 1960s, Town divested himself of most of his commercial work and much of his staff so that he could focus on exploring the South's diverse vernacular architectural traditions. He developed a unique and flexible architectural vocabulary that was inspired by traditional building materials and methods but that could be effectively applied to contemporary architectural problems.

Town's later, more traditional practice centered on Louisiana but extended into neighboring states. After Overstreet's death, Town renewed his practice in Mississippi, where he designed a number of homes in the suburbs of North Jackson, including the Sturgis House and the Puckett House in Eastover, as well as in other locations around the state, including the Elliott House in Brookhaven and the Lampton House in Columbia. These houses illustrate the stylistic variability and compositional flexibility of Town's later work. He often imagined his buildings to have been built over time as a series of separate projects or subsequent additions, each of which had its own character and form. During this phase of his career, Town designed almost one thousand houses, continuing to work until well into his nineties. He died on 6 January 2005.

Architects and designers from across the Deep South adapted design strategies derived from the final phase of Town's career to a wide range of building types with varying degrees of success. Town's work demonstrated the enduring relevance of vernacular traditions and set a new standard against which work of this type could be judged. His influence continues to echo in ongoing developments in Mississippi and surrounding states.

David Sachs

Kansas State University

David Sachs, *The Life and Work of the Twentieth-Century Architect A. Hays Town* (2003); A. Hays Town, Cyril E. Vetter, and Philip Gould, *The Architectural Style of A. Hays Town* (1985).

Town Building, Antebellum

Mississippi's frontier town-building era spanned the first five decades of the nineteenth century. Following the removal of the Native American population through a series of treaties, white Americans and their black slaves first settled in the southwestern portion of Mississippi, then in the central and eastern counties, and finally in the northern third of the state. Joseph G. Baldwin used his popular and influential 1853 work, *The Flush Times of Alabama and Mississippi*, to emphasize a pattern of speculation and greed as the central dynamic of frontier town creation. Baldwin wrote of Mississippi in the 1830s as a time of "enterprise without honesty," in which "every cross-road and every avocation presented an opening, through which a fortune was seen by the adventurer in near perspective." While Baldwin captured the character of a few colorful individuals, the more lasting and significant theme seems to be one of Mississippians looking to frontier towns to lead the process of transplanting the patterns of the older South to the newer South. Mississippians also looked for towns to establish a legal, political, moral, and social order in the newly settled territory.

The 1830 and 1840 censuses of Mississippi listed only Vicksburg and Natchez as "Cities and Towns." By 1850, however, eighteen Mississippi towns had earned that classification. Many of these towns were quite small—Warrenton (Warren County) had only 178 residents, and Hillsboro (Scott County) had 182. Mississippi frontier towns included both white citizens and black slaves and a small number of free blacks. According to the 1850 census, slaves accounted for 51 percent of the state's total population and 36 percent of the population in towns, though the frontier towns' racial compositions varied widely: the 55 slaves living in Fulton (Itawamba County) comprised 20 percent of the population, while Columbus's 1,222 slaves accounted for 47 percent of residents. Towns were spaces in which whites and blacks shopped, worshipped, tended to legal matters, found entertainment, and gathered in large numbers.

In their newly completed buildings, town folk often found symbols of their conquest of the frontier. On 4 July 1839 a town leader offered a public toast: "Pontotoc—Where the Indians roamed and the panther prowled, now stately churches are seen to rear their lofty spires above the proudest eminence of the loftiest oaks of the forest." Buildings provided frontier Mississippians with the clear evidence that civilization and society were symbolically overcoming and dominating Indians, panthers, oaks, and the frontier itself. The small towns hosted institutions that provided the moorings and stability for the new frontier society. One settler provided an impressive inventory of the Marshall County village of Lamar in 1837: "It contains two dry goods houses, Oak + Dowdy + Such, two groceries, Barnets + Houston + Wilkins, one harness shop, two churches, Methodist + presbyterian, one odd Fellows Lodge, one free Masons Lodge, + one ex-sons of temperance." These merchants, fraternal organizations, and churches reflect a model of social organization and social development far more complicated than Baldwin's picture of a "wholly unorganized" frontier society. As historian Don H. Doyle writes, "The town provided forms of community unknown to those isolated in the countryside."

Far from random or haphazard, the planning, designing, and creation of frontier towns such as Holly Springs grew from a clear desire to create order. According to a South Carolina native who participated in the formation of Holly Springs, "In the center of the town is a large open square about 150 yards by 150 yards, with wide streets crossing at right angles and running out north & south, east & west." Around the square were to be built "the business lots and the storehouses . . . side by side as thick as they stand." Behind these business lots would be a back street on which "the family residences commence and extend in every direction on streets running parallel with the 4 which leave the public square." For town founders, everyone and everything had a proper place: "In the center of the public square stands the Court House which costs 20,000 dollars," while a large public clock "is fixed up in the cupola and has hands on 4 sides so that a man riding into town from any point of the compass can tell the time of day." Towns erected on the Mississippi frontier were a visible construction of the hopes, dreams, and aspirations for ordered lives. For novelist William Faulkner, construction of the county courthouse in fictional Yoknapatawpha served a transformative purpose: "Rising surging like a fixed blast rocket, not even finished yet but already looming, beacon focus and lodestar, already taller than anything else, out of the rapid and fading wilderness."

Bruce Mactavish
Washburn University

Joseph G. Baldwin, *The Flush Times of Alabama and Mississippi: A Series of Sketches* (1853); Don H. Doyle, *Faulkner's County: The Historical Roots of Yoknapatawpha* (2001); John D. W. Guice and Thomas D. Clark, *Frontiers in Conflict: The Old Southwest, 1795–1830* (1986); Bruce Duncan Mactavish, "With Strangers United in Kindred Relation: Education, Religion, and Community in Northern Mississippi, 1836–1890" (PhD dissertation, University of Mississippi, 1993).

T

Training Schools

From roughly 1910 to 1930 county training schools offered elementary education, secondary instruction, and teacher training for African Americans across the South. The training schools emerged out of a reform effort by northern philanthropists, and coalitions of county school boards, local blacks, and northerners typically founded the schools. Despite the widespread success of training schools in developing black high schools and making African American education a component of county school board policies, the movement failed to generate the kind of progress in Mississippi that it fostered in much of the rest of the South.

In 1882 John F. Slater endowed the Slater Fund with one million dollars to educate southern blacks. Until 1910 the fund donated primarily to church schools affiliated with northern philanthropic and missionary efforts. Under the presidency of James H. Dillard, however, the fund shifted its focus from private institutions to public schools that would serve entire counties and become part of existing school systems. The founding of a county school in Newton in 1911 typified the new approach. Newton County officials, a local organization of blacks, and the Slater fund all contributed to the construction of the school and the hiring of teachers, and the new, large, and centrally located facility served students who had previously attended primitive elementary schools scattered throughout the county. A training school like the one in Newton would have begun as essentially a consolidated elementary school; offerings rarely extended beyond the eighth-grade level at the early training schools. The curriculum gradually expanded as pupils grew older and the percentage of students in secondary classes increased. From the beginning, the training schools did their most impressive work in producing teachers for rural elementary programs. In Mississippi, where as late as 1930 more than thirteen hundred teachers at black elementary schools had no secondary education, the fundamentals of teaching that students learned at the training schools proved invaluable.

In most of the South it took approximately twenty years for training schools to mature into high schools, wean themselves off the financial and structural support of the Slater Fund, and become fully funded by county school boards. By 1933, 65 percent of the region's Slater Fund schools offered four years of secondary education, and the overwhelming majority of southern counties had developed public education for blacks beyond the level of the training schools. In Mississippi, however, after twenty-one years of Slater aid, only twenty-two of the fifty-four county training schools offered the full four years of secondary education, and more than half of the state's African Americans lived in counties that did not offer four years of secondary education. In two-thirds of the counties, training schools represented the highest available level of public education. Most alarmingly, only 5 percent of the state's African American population was enrolled in public secondary, far less than the percentages for Texas (24.4), North Carolina (20), Tennessee (16.7), and Louisiana (9.2). Training schools, in short, joined the long list of missed opportunities for educational development in the state.

Thomas John Carey
University of Mississippi

Charles W. Dabney, *Universal Education in the South*, 2 vols. (1936); Edward E. Redclay, *County Training Schools and Public Secondary Education for Negroes in the South* (1935).

Trapping

Aside from foodstuffs, peltry was perhaps one of the earliest and most common mediums of exchange between Native Americans and European colonists. In the lands that became Mississippi, natives bartered all manner of hides to French and English traders for clothing, metal goods, liquor, and other European manufactures. For most of the eighteenth century deerskins were a standard currency in the Lower Mississippi River Valley.

As settlers displaced the native populations and agriculture dominated much of the landscape in the nineteenth century, the hide trade declined in importance. Mississippi never produced as many furs as Louisiana, with its vast southern wetlands, although professional trappers roamed Mississippi, especially along the river systems and in the marshlands of the coast. Small catches of furs were important to farm families, who welcomed the additional income in a cash-poor environment. Part-time trappers sold the hides of raccoons, opossums, mink, and muskrats, among others. Hunters also contributed a significant percentage of the skins, especially from coons and possums, common quarry for hounds. Itinerant buyers bought pelts from people in the countryside, and larger dealers maintained fixed trading houses. By the late 1800s, hunters and trappers might also sell pelts to mail-order firms such as Sears and Roebuck.

Possums made up the bulk of the catch in Mississippi and might have totaled more had not the traditional preparation of the possum as food destroyed the pelt. Folks often singed or scalded the possum and scraped off the hair before cooking. This method saved the fat of the animal for the pot but of course destroyed the fur. In the often-desperate times of the 1930s a possum hide was worth an average of about twenty-six cents. A fat possum on the table might well be worth just as much to a family.

In this context of struggling small-farm life state conservationists began to contemplate the reintroduction of the beaver. Beaver pelts from other parts of the country and Canada were relatively valuable, but beavers were so rare in Mississippi that there was no open trapping season for them, and a late 1930s survey suggested that only about a thousand beavers remained in the state. Biologists saw the beaver as an important addition to the furbearers that trappers could catch. In addition, beavers would create wetlands helpful to other furbearers and to waterfowl. The beaver impoundments could even offer folks a place to fish.

With federal money from the 1937 Pittman-Robertson Act, which placed a tax on sporting equipment and designated the money for conservation, Mississippi created a program to trap and transplant beavers in 1940–41. World events and economic transformation helped the beavers to thrive in the state. Small-farm living declined as people left the countryside for service in World War II and for jobs connected with wartime industry, and the price of beaver pelts never rose high enough to make them truly profitable to trap. The state eventually offered bounties for beavers, which are now classed as nuisance animals with no closed season or bag limit. The federal government employs trappers who remove the more troublesome colonies that destroy too many trees, damage levees, plug culverts, and the like.

The last significant boom in wild fur values in the Southeast occurred in the late 1970s, and interest in trapping has subsequently diminished. While prices have remained depressed, Mississippi's hunters and trappers still take a wide variety of fur animals. Some, primarily coons, are also sold as food. Furbearers such as coons, possums, and muskrats are, in fact, the only truly wild game legally sold for food in Mississippi.

Wiley C. Prewitt Jr.
Yocona, Mississippi

Fannye A. Cook, *Beavers in Mississippi* (1943); Fannye A. Cook, *Fur Resources of Mississippi* (1945); Mattie May Jordan, *Where the Wild Animals Is Plentiful: Diary of an Alabama Fur Trader's Daughter, 1912–1914,* ed. Elisa Moore Baldwin (1999); Daniel H. Usner Jr., *Indians, Settlers, and Slaves in a Frontier Exchange Economy: The Lower Mississippi Valley before 1783* (1992).

Travis, Brenda
(b. 1945) Activist

A teenaged civil rights activist, Brenda Travis dramatized both the demands for change and some of the tensions within the civil rights movement. McComb, Mississippi, was one of the first locations where activists from the National Association for the Advancement of Colored People (NAACP) and those from the Student Nonviolent Coordinating Committee (SNCC) worked together, and members of the two groups sometimes came into conflict over methods and rhetoric. Some SNCC activists, especially Marion Barry, favored direct-action strategies in opposition to racial segregation, while some NAACP activists wanted to continue to work through legal channels and to concentrate most of their efforts on voter registration.

Born in 1945, Brenda Travis was the fourth of seven children of sharecropper L. S. Travis and his wife, Icie Martin Travis. When she was ten, local police burst into the house one night and arrested her thirteen-year-old brother without telling the family what he had allegedly done. The incident occurred around the time of Emmett Till's murder, and when Travis saw pictures of Till's beaten body, "I became enraged and knew that one day I had to take a stand." That day came in August 1961, when the fifteen-year-old girl and two other protesters were arrested for participating in a sit-in at the whites-only section of McComb's Greyhound bus station. She was held in the Pike County Jail for a month, and upon her release she and another classmate who had been arrested, Ike Lewis, were expelled from Burglund High School. On 4 October 1961 more than a hundred Burglund students staged a protest against their classmates' expulsion and the murder of Amite County voting rights activist Herbert

Brenda Travis, 2 June 1962 (Library of Congress, Washington, D.C. [LC-USZ62-135777])

T

Lee on 25 September. SNCC workers joined the students, who congregated on the steps of McComb's City Hall to pray. When the protesters refused to leave, they were arrested and charged with disturbing the peace; all those who were over age eighteen also faced charges of contributing to the delinquency of minors. The SNCC workers were beaten by police while FBI agents took notes, and Travis, who was on probation, received an indeterminate sentence in a juvenile detention center in Oakley. After the march to City Hall, Burglund High's principal asked students to pledge not to participate in demonstrations and demanded that they return to school or be expelled. On 16 October 1961 more than one hundred students arrived at the school to turn in their books. SNCC workers then opened the Nonviolent High of Pike County, where the students took classes until the SNCC workers were tried, convicted, and jailed for several months. Many African Americans in McComb, including a number who were working with the NAACP, were displeased that the SNCC was allowing teenagers to face violence and arrest.

In the summer of 1962, after more than six months at Oakley, Travis was released into the custody of a professor from Talladega College, an African American school in Alabama. Mississippi governor Ross Barnett had agreed to release the girl on condition that the professor take her out of Mississippi within twenty-four hours. He took her back to Talladega, but after he became abusive, Travis fled to Atlanta, where SNCC executive director James Forman and his wife took her in. That fall, Ella Baker helped Travis enroll at the Palmer Memorial Institute, near Sedalia, North Carolina. After a year there, she moved to Connecticut, where she graduated from high school. She returned to Mississippi in 1964 out of "defiance" but felt unsafe and soon left. She worked briefly with Rev. Jesse Jackson in Chicago before settling in California in 1966 and attending business college and becoming involved in community organizations.

In October 2011, during a commemoration of the fiftieth anniversary of the student walkout, the McComb school district awarded honorary diplomas to Travis and other students suspended because of the protests. In 2013 she founded the Brenda Travis Historical Education Foundation to bring youth leadership and community development training opportunities to McComb.

Ted Ownby
University of Mississippi

Raymond Arsenault, *Freedom Riders: 1961 and the Struggle for Racial Justice* (2006); Brenda Travis Historical Education Foundation website, www.brendatravisfoundation.org; Clayborne Carson, *In Struggle: SNCC and the Black Awakening of the 1960s* (1981); John Dittmer, *Local People: The Struggle for Civil Rights in Mississippi* (1994); McComb Legacies website, www.mccomblegacies.org; Charles M. Payne, *I've Got the Light of Freedom: The Organizing Tradition and the Mississippi Freedom Struggle* (1995); Brenda Travis interview (February 2007), http://www.crmvet.org/nars/travisb.htm.

Trees

Novelist Richard Wright drew from his Mississippi childhood in recalling the visual dominance of trees in the American South. Changes in trees marked the seasons. In spring, "from mossy tree to mossy tree—oak, elm, willow, aspen, sycamore, dogwood, cedar, walnut, ash and hickory—bright green leaves jut from a million branches to form an awning that tries to shield and shade the earth." Summer he associated with magnolia trees, which filled "the countryside with sweet scent for long miles." Autumn brought fiery colors: "Red and brown leaves lift and flutter dryly, becoming entangled in the stiff grass and cornstalks." Winter could seem desolate with the leaves gone, but "the forests resound with the bite of steel axes into tall trees as men gather wood for the leaden days of cold." Wright captured the everyday importance of trees to Mississippians and other southerners. Trees have had environmental, economic, and cultural significance for Mississippi and its people.

Long ago, much of Mississippi was part of a great southeastern forest, with dense hardwoods in the Delta, a pine belt to the south, and mixed timber in the northeastern hills. Certain trees grow in certain areas of the state and have become identified with those locations. Delta residents know the sight of bald cypress, with its swollen trunk and woody growths called cypress knees. Slash pine grows best in the wetter areas of South Mississippi, while shortleaf pine appears in the dry, hilly areas of the northern part of the state. William Faulkner opened a 1954 article on Mississippi with the diversity and antiquity of its trees: "In the beginning it was virgin—to the west, along the Big River, the alluvial swamps threaded by black almost motionless bayous and impenetrable with cane and buckvine and cypress and ash and oak and gum; to the east, the hardwood ridges and the prairies where the Appalachian mountains died and buffalo

Two-thousand-year-old cypress tree, Humphreys County, next to Sky Lake Wildlife Management Area (Courtesy Belzoni Humphreys Development Foundation)

grazed; to the south, the pine barrens and the moss-hung live-oaks and the greater swamps less of earth than water and lurking with alligators and water moccasins, where Louisiana in its time would begin."

Trees have provided many resources for Mississippians. The Native Americans made a cedar bark tea to treat whooping cough. Natives and early settlers consumed oak acorns raw or cooked and ground them into a powder for thickening stews. Confederate troops ground and roasted acorns and used them as a coffee substitute. Trees have been essential for wildlife habitat in Mississippi. Quail, wild turkeys, and squirrels eat pine seeds, while cedar cones are a favorite winter food source for birds. Wood ducks, evening grosbeck, and squirrels love cypress seeds. Cottonwood tree sprouts and foliage attract white-tailed deer.

Two types of trees grow in Mississippi: conifers and broadleaves. Conifers are evergreens and have needle-like leaves—pines, red cedar, and bald cypress. Wood of most conifers is softer than that of broadleaves, so that in the lumber business conifers are called *softwoods*. Broadleaf trees such as ashes, maples, hickories, oaks, elms, and gums indeed have broader leaves, and their flowers produce fruit. They are known as *hardwoods*.

Among the most important trees in Mississippi have been pines. Longleaf pine (*Pinus palustris*), also known as hard pine, heart pine, longstraw pine, and southern yellow pine, produces long needles that hang in three dense clusters at the end of branches and droop downward. Longleaf pines grow 80 to 120 feet high and have diameters between 2 and 2.5 feet. These trees provided most of the material for the timber companies that made the industry one of the state's largest employers beginning in the early twentieth century. These ancient trees were cut and replaced by faster-growing pines, but longleaf still provides wood for pulpwood in the Pine Belt. The loblolly pine (*P. taeda*) has become the most frequently planted tree in Mississippi, growing to between 80 and 100 feet tall and routinely measuring 2 feet across, although diameters can occasionally go as high as 4 or 5 feet. Loblollies are planted widely on abandoned or eroded land in North Mississippi to counter extreme runoffs and flooding. Although its wood is not durable, its wood fiber is used in the pulp and paper industry. Pines in general have been at the center of the naval stores industry, providing turpentine, tar, and resin.

The eastern red cedar (*Juniperus virginiana*), also known as the cedar, juniper bush, or savin, is one of the most familiar trees in the state. People see it as a tall tree in old fields, reaching 40 to 50 feet in height, with a trunk diameter between 1 and 2 feet, or as a small shrub along fencerows, with a pyramidal shape and branches near the ground. Historically, it was one of the most frequently used trees in cemeteries. Its wood is moderately heavy, hard, and resistant to shock, making it widely used for cabinets, interior finishes, fence posts, pencils, and furniture. Its oils repel moths, making it appealing as a wood for closets and chests. Folk artists use it for carvings and ornaments. It symbolizes the tree of life for Native American tribes.

Mississippi has many oaks, including post oak, white oak, swamp chestnut oak, southern red oak, cherrybark oak, black oak, shumard oak, blackjack oak, water oak, and scarlet oak. The latter grows on dry, sandy upland soils in northern Mississippi, and people plant it as an ornamental because of its red foliage in autumn. The live oak (*Quercus virginiana*) grows in South Mississippi, mostly along the Gulf Coast and inland as far north as Hinds County. It has long been an icon of the old plantation South, representing a romantic touch because of the tree's beauty. It grows 50 to 60 feet high with a diameter between 3 and 4 feet. The wood is hard, strong, heavy, tough, and close-grained, contributing to its popularity in the early US shipbuilding industry. In 2005 Hurricane Katrina devastated the live oaks along the coast, though numerous artists have created sculptures out of the wood, preserving the presence of the old trees in new creative forms.

Pecan trees (*Carya illinoinensis*) are tall, and wild ones have heavy, brittle, and coarse-grained wood that is used in the furniture industry. Other pecan species are best known for their fruit, a sweet nut that is produced in orchards, with Mississippi a leading grower. Other fruit trees common in the state include peaches and figs. Many urban and suburban Mississippians know trees as ornamentals, with the flowering dogwood, eastern redbud, and various maples prized for their shapes, flowers, and foliage. Other familiar trees in Mississippi include elms, locusts, white ash, river birch, and osage orange.

The southern magnolia (*Magnolia grandiflora*) is particularly associated with Mississippi. It is the official state tree, its bloom is the state flower, and the state's nickname is the Magnolia State. The magnolia can grow 90 feet high and 2 to 3 feet in diameter, with lustrous, thick green leaves. Its flowers are showy—cup shaped and white with purple centers—and have a spicy fragrance. A 1977 *Time* magazine article mentioned "the aphrodisiac-soporific magnolia, more potent by far in midnight bloom than overblown fiction can convey." The article referred to the mythic southern literary symbol of "moonlight and magnolias" to describe a romanticized South, including Mississippi.

Charles Reagan Wilson
University of Mississippi

Claire A. Brown, *Mississippi Trees* (1996); Wilbur H. Duncan and Marion B. Duncan, *Trees of the Southeastern United States* (2000), William Faulkner, *Holiday* (April 1954); John D. Hodges, David L. Evans, and Linda W. Garrett, *Mississippi Trees*, www.mfc.ms.gov; Richard Wright, *Twelve Million Black Voices* (1941).

Trethewey, Natasha
(b. 1966) Poet

Natasha Trethewey, Pulitzer Prize winner and US poet laureate, was born on 26 April 1966 in Gulfport, Mississippi, the daughter of poet Eric Trethewey, who was white, and social worker Gwendolyn Ann Turnbough, an African American. As Trethewey describes in the poem "Miscegenation," their 1965 wedding took place in Ohio because mixed-race marriage was illegal in Mississippi. After her parents divorced, Trethewey moved to Decatur, Georgia, with her mother but returned to Gulfport every summer for long visits with her maternal grandmother. In 1985, when Trethewey was a student and cheerleader at the University of Georgia, her mother was killed by her second husband, whom she had recently divorced, a crisis recorded in several elegies from *Native Guard* (2006). Trethewey graduated from the university and worked for more than a year as a food stamp caseworker before earning a master's degree in English and creative writing at Hollins University in Virginia, where her poetry teachers included her father and her stepmother, Katherine Soniat. In 1995 she graduated from the master of fine arts program at the University of Massachusetts. She holds the Phillis Wheatley Distinguished Chair of Poetry at Emory University in Atlanta, where her husband, historian Brett Gadsden, teaches African American studies.

In her introduction to Trethewey's first book of poetry, *Domestic Work* (2000), former US poet laureate Rita Dove describes the "steely grace" with which Trethewey "tells the hard facts of lives pursued on the margins." "At the Owl Club, North Gulfport, Mississippi, 1950" depicts dockworkers relaxing away from their dangerous jobs; in "Drapery Factory, Gulfport, Mississippi, 1956," Trethewey's grandmother recalls the embarrassment of black women workers when a white male boss inspects their purses at quitting time. "Flounder," "White Lies," and other poems reflect Trethewey's early self-consciousness as a child of mixed racial heritage. She told an interviewer that her grandmother's constant movement, "recreating and remaking herself," corresponded to the idea of "making my own self as poet." Trethewey sought to inscribe the neglected labors of African Americans "into the American literary canon, and into American cultural memory, into public memory."

Trethewey's second and third collections present earlier periods of African American history. Inspired by E. J. Bellocq's photographs of a Storyville prostitute who could pass for white, *Bellocq's Ophelia* (2002) portrays a young woman who leaves Mississippi's cotton fields to work in New Orleans. Recruited by the madam of a brothel, Ophelia eventually escapes her humiliating employment when the fictionalized Bellocq trains her to become a photographer. In March 1912 Ophelia identifies with the "budding" trees and the "throbbing" spring grass as she travels west to a new life. Trethewey adapts many poetic forms in each book, and several pieces in *Bellocq's Ophelia* and *Native Guard* are sonnet variations. Ten poems narrated by a black soldier from Louisiana's Native Guard are linked in a corona sonnet sequence. This centerpiece of Trethewey's third volume memorializes the African American regiment that guarded Confederate prisoners on Ship Island, off Mississippi's Gulf Coast. Insulted by their Yankee leaders and their rebel captives alike, the soldiers have no monument at the island fortress. Trethewey's sonnets remedy the lack, much as the elegies "What Is Evidence?" and "Monument" guard her mother's memory in the same book. *Native Guard* won the 2007 Pulitzer Prize for poetry as well as the Poetry Prize from the Mississippi Institute of Arts and Letters, an honor also bestowed on her two earlier collections.

In 2010 Trethewey published *Beyond Katrina*, which detailed the effects Hurricane Katrina had on the Mississippi Gulf Coast and members of her family. A prose memoir that includes some poetry, the volume concentrates on the story of her brother and his time in jail. Her fourth poetry collection, *Thrall*, was published in 2012. That year Trethewey was also named both Mississippi poet laureate and US poet laureate, and she held the latter position until 2014.

Joan Wylie Hall
University of Mississippi

Jill Petty, *Callaloo* (Spring 1996); Debora Rindge and Anna Leahy, *English Language Notes* (Fall–Winter 2006); Charles Henry Rowell, *Callaloo* (Fall 2004); Deborah Solomon, *New York Times Magazine* (13 May 2007); Natasha Trethewey, *Bellocq's Ophelia* (2002); Natasha Trethewey, *Beyond Katrina: A Meditation on the Mississippi Gulf Coast* (2010); Natasha Trethewey, *Domestic Work* (2000); Natasha Trethewey, *Journal of American History* (September 2004); Natasha Trethewey, *Native Guard* (2006); Natasha Trethewey, *Thrall* (2012); Natasha Trethewey, *Virginia Quarterly Review* (Spring 2005).

Trumpauer, Joan
(b. 1941) Activist

In 1961 Freedom Rider Joan Trumpauer became one of the first white female civil rights activists in Mississippi. She was famously photographed alongside Anne Moody and John Salter during a May 1963 sit-in at the lunch counter at the Woolworth's store on Jackson's Capitol Street.

Trumpauer was born on 14 September 1941 in Washington, D.C., and raised in Arlington, Virginia. Her mother was a staunch segregationist, though her father was more moderate. Raised in the Presbyterian Church, the adolescent

Trumpauer became aware of the contradiction between lessons of social justice inherent in Christianity and the injustice of segregation. Thirteen years old when the Supreme Court handed down the *Brown* decision, Trumpauer organized a group at her church in which the schoolchildren discussed impending integration. While a student at Duke University, Trumpauer attended a meeting at which students from North Carolina Agricultural and Technical College discussed the religious motivations for the sit-in movement. Trumpauer subsequently left Duke because the school did not support student involvement in the movement. She returned to Washington, D.C., and began work in California senator Clair Engle's office. She also became involved with the Nonviolent Action Group, a precursor of the Student Nonviolent Coordinating Committee (SNCC). Trumpauer's Washington apartment served as a clearinghouse for Freedom Riders. In 1961 Trumpauer flew to New Orleans with Stokely Carmichael to continue a Freedom Ride to Jackson, Mississippi. She and other activists were arrested, and she spent two months at Parchman Farm, the Mississippi State Penitentiary. Many in the movement remembered this period in prison as a time when discussions of Gandhian philosophy and the singing of freedom songs solidified the movement and sharpened negotiating skills that activists used in later direct action campaigns.

After her release, Trumpauer became one of the first white students to enroll at Jackson's Tougaloo College. Her time at Tougaloo was initially difficult because her presence was the first interracial experience for many of the students, but she later joined a sorority and made friends, including Mississippian Anne Moody, who became Trumpauer's roommate. On 28 May 1963 the two women were part of a group that staged a peaceful sit-in at the Woolworth's in Jackson. Counterprotesters, threatened by the "race-mixers" and "outside agitators" in their midst, intimidated and assaulted the students, punching them, kicking them, smearing them with food, and hurling ashtrays and glass figurines. Fred Blackwell of the *Jackson Daily News* took a photograph of Moody, Trumpauer, and Tougaloo professor John Salter covered in food and surrounded by angry faces that became one of the enduring images of the civil rights movement. Trumpauer also helped to plan the August 1963 March on Washington.

Trumpauer's actions brought her to the attention of the Mississippi State Sovereignty Commission, which spied on her. Her activism and that of several Tougaloo professors led the commission to recommend that the State of Mississippi revoke the school's accreditation.

Trumpauer graduated from Tougaloo in 1964 and continued her civil rights activities during that year's Freedom Summer. She briefed Michael and Rita Schwerner on being white activists in Mississippi just one day before Michael Schwerner was kidnapped and murdered along with Andrew Goodman and James Chaney. Shortly thereafter, Trumpauer was in a car with Reverend Ed King, his wife, Jeanette, and a Tougaloo professor when their car was threatened by fifteen men on Highway 55 outside Canton. The professor received blows to the head, and the attackers demanded that the group of activists never return to Canton.

Trumpauer believed that her status as a southerner enabled her to better communicate with Mississippi's whites during the 1960s. She felt she was the opposite of the derided "outside agitators" that many white southerners scorned. In a 1963 *Ebony* profile, Trumpauer said, "I'm trying to help America become what it says it is, as a Southerner I'm trying to improve, not destroy, our way of life; I'm a Christian who has read the Declaration of Independence."

Trumpauer subsequently returned to the Washington, D.C., area, where she worked for the Smithsonian Institution and for the US government before becoming a teacher of English as a second language. Now retired, she travels and talks to students about her civil rights activities, often in conjunction with showings of an award-winning 2013 documentary film produced by her son, *An Ordinary Hero: The True Story of Joan Trumpauer Mulholland*. She has established the Joan Trumpauer Mulholland Foundation to help educate youth about the civil rights movement and to empower them to make positive changes in their communities.

Becca Walton
University of Mississippi

Raymond Arsenault, *Freedom Riders: 1961 and the Struggle for Racial Justice* (2006); G. McLeod Bryan, *These Few Also Paid a Price: Southern Whites Who Fought for Civil Rights* (2001); Mississippi Department of Archives and History, Files of the Mississippi State Sovereignty Commission, www.mdah.state.ms.us/arlib/contents/er/sovcom/; Anne Moody, *Coming of Age in Mississippi* (1969); *An Ordinary Hero: The True Story of Joan Trumpauer Mulholland* website, anordinaryhero.com; Joan Sadoff, Robert Sadoff, and Laura J. Lipson, *Standing on My Sisters' Shoulders* (film 2002).

Tucker, Tilghman M.

(1802–1859) Thirteenth Governor, 1842–1844

Tilghman Mayfield Tucker and his first wife, Sarah F. McBee Tucker, were the first residents of the Mississippi Governor's Mansion, and the formal opening of the mansion made his inauguration on 10 January 1842 especially festive. But Tucker was a plain man of simple tastes. He did not enjoy the ceremonial and social trappings of public office, and, to the great disappointment of Jackson residents, the governor and First Lady rarely entertained at the mansion.

Like many of his contemporaries, Tucker migrated to Mississippi from North Carolina, where he was born on 5 February 1802. Initially a blacksmith, Tucker gave up the trade to read law under Judge Daniel W. Wright in Hamilton, Mississippi, the original seat of Monroe County. After his admission to the bar, Tucker opened a law office in Columbus, the seat of recently established Lowndes County.

Tucker, a Democrat, was elected as the county's first representative in the state legislature in 1831, serving in the House of Representatives until 1836, when he was elected to the State Senate. In 1841 the Mississippi Democratic Party was bitterly divided over the issue of whether the state should honor bonds from the Planters Bank and Union Bank, both of which had failed during the Panic of 1833. Some Democrats announced that they would support David Shattuck, the Whig candidate for governor, who favored the redemption of the bonds. When Tucker was offered the Democratic nomination for governor, he at first declined to run but was eventually persuaded to undertake what appeared to be a hopeless campaign. However, Tucker won in a very close election.

The bond issue kept the Democratic Party divided during Tucker's administration, and his term in office was an unhappy time. Political opponents also attacked Tucker after the state treasurer embezzled forty-four thousand dollars and escaped to Canada while under the guard of a local militia. Although he had removed the treasurer from office and ordered his arrest, Tucker was criticized for his slow response to the rumors that something was amiss in the treasurer's office.

After leaving the governor's office, Tucker served one term in the US Congress (1843–45) before retiring from public life and moving to Cottonwood, his plantation home in Louisiana. While visiting his father in Marion County, Alabama, Tucker died on 3 April 1859.

David G. Sansing
University of Mississippi

J. F. H. Claiborne, *Mississippi, as a Province, Territory, and State* (1880); *Biographical Directory of the United States Congress* (1950); *Mississippi Official and Statistical Register* (1912); Dunbar Rowland, *Encyclopedia of Mississippi History*, vol. 2 (1907); David Sansing and Carroll Waller, *A History of the Mississippi Governor's Mansion* (1977).

Tucker, William Feimster

(1827–1881) Confederate General

William Feimster Tucker was born in Iredell County, North Carolina, on 9 May 1827. He graduated from Emory and Henry College in Virginia in 1848 and moved to Houston, Mississippi, where he taught for several years before being elected probate judge of Chickasaw County in 1855. Tucker courted and wed Martha Josephine Shackelford, the daughter of a prominent planter. He studied law, was admitted to the bar, and was a practicing attorney in Okolona when the Civil War began. Tucker was appointed a captain in the Mississippi militia in January 1861 and in May entered Confederate service as a captain in the 11th Mississippi Infantry. He fought with that unit at First Bull Run (Manassas) in Barnard E. Bee's brigade. His company was transferred to the West, where it became part of the 41st Mississippi Infantry, and Tucker was commissioned colonel of the regiment on 8 May 1862.

Tucker and his regiment fought with distinction on a number of battlefields, including Perryville, Kentucky, where Tucker was wounded in the right arm; Stones River (Murfreesboro), Tennessee; Chickamauga, Georgia; and Chattanooga, Tennessee. He won promotion to brigadier general on 1 March 1864 and led a brigade of five Mississippi infantry regiments, including his old command. Tucker was wounded again early in the Atlanta Campaign at Resaca on 14 May 1864, while his brigade was in reserve and he was observing the movements of the enemy. His left arm was severely damaged, probably by an artillery shell fragment, and surgeons amputated a portion of it. With two bad arms, he was forced to retire from active field duty. In April and May 1865 he commanded the District of Southern Mississippi and Eastern Louisiana and negotiated the cessation of hostilities in that region. He was paroled on 15 May 1865.

Tucker returned to Chickasaw County and resumed his law practice. He served in the Mississippi state legislature from 1876 to 1878. On 14 September 1881 Tucker was assassinated at his home by an assailant who fired through an open bedroom window, striking Tucker in the chest and killing him almost immediately. Although several people were questioned in connection with Tucker's murder, no one was ever prosecuted, and the identity of the assassin remains unknown.

Christopher Losson
St. Joseph, Missouri

Harold A. Cross, *They Sleep beneath the Mockingbird: Mississippi Burial Sites and Biographies of Confederate Generals* (1994); John H. Eicher and David J. Eicher, *Civil War High Commands* (2001); Ezra J. Warner, *Generals in Gray: Lives of the Confederate Commanders* (1959); Jack D. Welsh, *Medical Histories of Confederate Generals* (1995).

Tung Trees

On roadsides in South Mississippi, passersby may notice a curious tree, somewhat squat compared to neighboring pines, with large, heart-shaped leaves. Early in spring, the tree will appear draped in brilliant cream and salmon blossoms; some weeks later it will bear ruddy plum-sized nuts. This plant, rarely seen outside a narrow strip along the Gulf Coast, once played a significant role in the economy of the southern part of Mississippi.

Tung trees, named for the Chinese word for "heart," were imported to the United States in 1905 to support the nation's growing industrial need for oils. The reddish tung nuts provided oil well suited for use as a protective coating, solvent, or drying agent in paints and varnishes. Its drying properties made it particularly attractive for industrial purposes, and planters responded to the demand by seeking appropriate land for planting the trees. Because the tree enjoys tropical conditions, experts thought the trees would succeed in California, but they did not. Surprisingly, the trees preferred Mississippi, with its sandy, well-drained soil and gently rolling terrain. Other Gulf States experimented with tung orchards, but Mississippi quickly took the lead in domestic tung oil production. By midcentury some eighty thousand acres in South Mississippi were planted in tung trees, and the state was home to more than half of the 7.5 million tung trees in the United States.

The tung orchards were hubs of activity at harvest time, which generally started as the greenish nuts grew reddish. After changing colors, the nuts dropped to the ground and were usually collected in old feed sacks. The sacks were first hung from the tree's branches to begin the drying process and then hauled to drying barns. Designed specifically for this purpose, the barns sat two to three feet off the ground on concrete supports, allowing air to circulate between the floorboards to accelerate the drying process. Each barn was divided into sections to allow for nuts at varying stages of drying. After sufficient drying, the nuts were loaded onto trucks and taken to one of several presses, such as those at Picayune or Poplarville, where the oil could be extracted.

By the 1960s domestic use of tung oil had fallen, primarily because of competition from cheaper petroleum products. Still, many orchards remained, and planters began to face poor market prices caused by overproduction. In 1969 Hurricane Camille devastated the Mississippi tung industry, destroying more than fifty thousand acres of trees. The industry did not recover, and in 1973 tung oil production in the area ceased completely. A few trees remained, however, lingering along roadsides and fencerows in the most southern part of the state and giving rise to tales of tourists who tried to eat the toxic nuts.

Though Mississippi farmers attempted to revive the tung oil industry in the 1990s, those efforts were abandoned after Hurricane Katrina hit the Gulf Coast in 2005.

Tracie McLemore Salinas
Appalachian State University

Courtney Carter, Lisa House, and Randy Little, *Review of Agricultural Economics* (Autumn–Winter 1998); Lewrene Glaser, *Industrial Uses of Agricultural Materials* (1996); S. E. McGregor, *Insect Pollination of Cultivated Crop Plants* (1976); "Tung Oil," *KnowLA: Encyclopedia of Louisiana* (17 October 2014), http://www.knowla.org/entry/1462/&view=summary.

Tunica County

Tunica County was established in 1840, close to three hundred years after Hernando de Soto traveled through the area. Both the county and county seat (also Tunica) are named for the Tunica Indian word meaning "the people." The county was established with a tiny population of 821, of whom 30 percent were enslaved. By 1860 the free population remained small—just 883 people—though the slave population had increased to 3,483. With slaves making up almost 80 percent of residents, Tunica County had one of the highest percentages of slaves in Mississippi.

Located in the Delta in northwestern Mississippi, the county developed an agricultural economy based on cotton and large-scale slavery. Its agriculture mixed cotton with corn and livestock, and despite its small population the county ranked eighteenth in the state in the value of its agricultural property. In 1860, Tunica had only four churches, all of them Methodist, the fewest in the state, and had no manufacturing establishments or persons employed in manufacturing.

In the postbellum period, large numbers of African Americans moved into the northern Delta. Despite losing part of its territory and population to Tate County in 1873 and Quitman County in 1877, Tunica's 1880 population rose to 8,461, and 85 percent of residents were African American, the third-highest proportion in the state. Sharecroppers and tenants cultivated about three-quarters of the county's farms. As in most counties dominated by tenant labor, Tunica produced far more cotton than corn or livestock. According to the 1880 census, Tunica County remained extraordinarily agricultural, with just one manufacturing firm employing three people.

Tunica County's population almost doubled between 1880 and 1900, reaching 16,479. The vast majority of residents—14,914—were African Americans, and most made their living in agriculture as tenants and sharecroppers. Only 6 percent of the 2,713 black farmers owned their land, while more than a third of white farmers did so. As in other areas dominated by tenancy, farms were small, and the primary crop was cotton. The county had 125 industrial workers and a small but growing immigrant population of 47, most of them from Germany, Ireland, or China.

T

In the early twentieth century, 70 percent of the county's church members belonged to Missionary Baptist groups, while 20 percent worshipped at Colored Methodist Episcopal churches.

By 1930 Tunica County's population had increased to 21,233 and remained overwhelmingly (86 percent) African American. As in much of the Delta, tenant farmers predominated, operating 94 percent of all county farms. Tunica's agriculture concentrated on cotton as well as corn and hogs.

Highway 61, sometimes called the Blues Highway, runs through Tunica County. Blues performer James Cotton, born in 1935, grew up outside of the city of Tunica, and bluesman Son House lived and worked on nearby plantations. Harold "Hardface" Clayton, an African American businessman born in Tunica in 1916, ran a number of small businesses in the city. He found success and fame through his gambling establishments long before the growth of casinos in the region and was celebrated for hosting blues musicians in his cafés and bars.

By 1960 Tunica had experienced a sharp decline in population and employment opportunities that led to severe poverty. The county had just 16,826 residents, 80 percent of them African American. Agricultural workers made up two-thirds of Tunica County's workers, tying Issaquena County for the highest percentage in Mississippi. Cotton continued to lead crop production, with soybeans and wheat increasing in importance. Only 4 percent of Tunica County's workers held jobs in industry.

In the 1960s Tunica contained the state's highest percentage of people with fewer than five years of education and the lowest percentage of people who had completed high school. Tunica County was one of the poorest counties in the United States, and its population continued to decline in the 1970s and 1980s.

Tunica has experienced some economic improvements since the 1990s, though their effects have often been uneven. Casino gambling has provided some benefits for Tunica's communities. In addition, improved roads, new government spending, and a new airport created opportunities for economic growth. Nevertheless, Tunica County's population decreased further between 1960 and 2010, when it had 10,778 residents. As in neighboring DeSoto, Tate, and Panola Counties, the white proportion of Tunica County's population grew during this period, though African Americans remained a substantial majority and a Hispanic/Latino minority emerged. African Americans accounted for 73.5 percent of Tunica County's residents, while 23.7 percent were white, and 2.3 percent were Hispanic/Latino.

Mississippi Encyclopedia Staff
University of Mississippi

Mississippi Blues Trail website, www.msbluestrail.org; Mississippi State Planning Commission, *Progress Report on State Planning in Mississippi* (1938); *Mississippi Statistical Abstract*, Mississippi State University (1952– 2010); Charles Sydnor and Claude Bennett, *Mississippi History* (1939); University of Virginia Library, Historical Census Browser website, http://mapserver.lib.virginia.edu; E. Nolan Waller and Dani A. Smith, *Growth Profiles of Mississippi's Counties, 1960–1980* (1985).

Tunica Indians

The Tunica were a powerful native presence in the Lower Mississippi River Valley during the early historic period. They were one of the most influential and organized tribes in an area that had suffered a catastrophic decline in population from prehistoric levels. The Tunica probably entered the valley from the west.

Tunica ancestors were first encountered in 1541 in northwestern Mississippi and eastern Arkansas by the de Soto entrada. These people, identified as the Quizquiz and perhaps also the Tanico, lived in large villages near the confluence of the Arkansas and Mississippi Rivers. They participated in the Mississippian cultural tradition characterized by dependence on corn agriculture, mound building, complex sociopolitical development, and specific artifactual traits such as shell-tempered pottery.

The Tunica were distinguished from their neighbors, however, in speaking Tunican, a language isolate—that is, a language that is not known to have been related to any other language group. This unique linguistic heritage provides further evidence that the Tunica were recent immigrants to the Lower Mississippi Valley during the late prehistoric period.

Disease and population decline apparently led to a breakdown of social and political structures during the seventeenth century. Refugees from Quizquiz-Tanico migrated to the Lower Yazoo River near its junction with the Mississippi River, where the French, who first identified them as the Tunica (*Tonicas*), found them living with other remnant groups in 1699. They resided at the Haynes Bluff mound site near Vicksburg and perhaps even added to the mounds as late as the eighteenth century. The Tunica, then, like the neighboring Natchez, may have been among the last of the Native American peoples who built mounds.

The Tunica and the French established friendly relations, and during the next several decades the Tunica became important trading partners of the French and reliable allies in their conflicts with the Natchez. In 1706 the Tunica moved yet again, this time to a point on the east bank of the Mississippi River opposite the mouth of the Red River in Louisiana. They lived at several locations near this important riverine junction for the remainder of the eighteenth century. Their most important settlement was the Trudeau site, which was occupied between 1731 and 1764. Trudeau was the provenience of the "Tunica Treasure," an extraordinarily rich collection of grave goods that were found with burials at the site. The wealth and diversity of European artifacts demonstrate the Tunica's success in dealing with the French.

During this period the Tunica had a highly developed entrepreneurial system. They procured and controlled the distribution of resources such as salt and horses that were vital to their neighbors, Indian and European alike. The Tunica also continued to provide important services to the French as guides and military allies.

The Tunica were so closely associated with the French that when the English gained control of the Mississippi Valley after the French and Indian War, the Tunica resorted to an uncharacteristic confrontation and attacked the first English convoy that attempted to ascend the river in 1764. The tribe briefly fled the Mississippi in fear of retribution but then returned and made peace with the English. However, the Native Americans chose to establish themselves as close as possible to the friendly French settlements. This was a time of diminishing economic and political influence for the tribe and of increasing acculturation to European lifeways.

By 1800 the Tunica had moved west of the Mississippi River to Marksville, Louisiana, where some remain today. They intermarried with peoples of other tribes, such as the Biloxi, Ofo, Avoyel, and Choctaw. They suffered a period of economic depression and social repression during the late nineteenth and early twentieth centuries but have since undergone a renaissance after federal recognition as the Tunica-Biloxi Indian Tribe in 1981.

The odyssey of the Tunica is documented in historical records and supported by archaeological evidence. The salient feature reflected in these movements is the preference, at least during the early and middle historic periods, for settlement at major junctions in the riverine system of communication. The selection of such localities enabled the Tunica to continue their entrepreneurial activities along established trade networks. When confronted with an adversarial situation involving either Native American or European antagonists, the typical Tunica response was to move to a new location that minimized the problem but still allowed tribe members to succeed in their role as middlemen between the natives and Europeans in both economic and military ventures.

The Tunica are one of the few Lower Mississippi Valley tribes to survive from prehistory to the present. Their ethnic continuity has resulted primarily from their adaptability to the new world of European influence, an entrepreneurial proclivity that enabled them to play an important role in that new order, and their ability to make successful choices in times of stress.

Jeffrey P. Brain

Peabody Essex Museum,
Salem, Massachusetts

Jeffrey P. Brain, *On the Tunica Trail* (1977); Jeffrey P. Brain, *Tunica Archaeology* (1988); Jeffrey P. Brain, *The Tunica-Biloxi* (1990); Jeffrey P. Brain, *Tunica Treasure* (1979).

Tunica Times

The *Tunica Times* was founded in Austin, Mississippi, in 1878 by P. A. Bobbitt. Little is known about the paper's origins and early years, but it reappeared in 1908 with Otis M. Perrine as publisher. Perrine published the paper from the second floor of the Lowe Building in downtown Tunica.

In the early 1900s, two merchants and planters named Owens acquired the *Tunica Times* through the collection of a debt. A third partner, B. L. Russell, became the paper's manager and editor. The Owens brothers eventually sold their share of the newspaper to Russell, who then partnered with L. C. Cannon. In the summer of 1911 the pair hired editor Frank Barlow, who eventually purchased the paper.

In 1922 Barlow sold the paper to Clayton Rand, who also owned the *Neshoba Democrat*, the *DeKalb Democrat*, the *Dixie Press* in Gulfport, and the *Mississippi Guide*. Rand served as president of the Mississippi Press Association in 1925–26, as a director of the National Editorial Association (now the National Newspaper Association) beginning in 1930, and as the association's president in 1936. He won two national editorial awards and wrote a column, "Crossroads Scribe," that appeared in newspapers across the country.

The Wisconsin-born Rand had moved to Bond, Mississippi, at age seven. He earned bachelor's degrees from Mississippi Agricultural and Mechanical College (now Mississippi State University) in 1911 and from Harvard University in 1913. He also attended Harvard Law School. Rand was a political conservative who campaigned against the New Deal, John F. Kennedy's administration, and the federal government. But he also sought to improve the living standards of the local citizens, backed a consolidated school system, and opposed the Ku Klux Klan. Rand hired Turner Catledge, later the editor of the *New York Times*, as a reporter and editor.

In October 1923 Rand sold the *Tunica Times* to J. B. Snider, who changed the paper's name to the *Tunica Times-Democrat*. Snider employed several editors until 1936, when he sold the paper to Paul E. Phillips. After Phillips's death, his widow, Margaret Phillips, became the editor and publisher. She served two terms as president of the Mississippi Press Women (1960–62 and 1964–66). The paper was known for its conservative stance on civil rights issues.

The Phillips family owned the paper for forty-three years before selling it in 1979 to Joe Lee III, current owner of the

Grenada Daily Star. Lee served as publisher of the *Tunica Times-Democrat* until Brooks Taylor purchased the paper in September 1991. Taylor changed the paper's name back to the *Tunica Times* and relocated it to larger offices. The *Times* is published weekly and reaches newsstands on Thursdays. It has a circulation of about twenty-three hundred and serves Tunica, Robinsonville, and Dundee.

Over the years, the Mississippi Press Association has recognized staff members for numerous accomplishments in reporting, photography, advertising, layout and design, and general excellence. In 2003 the paper received the Mississippi Press Association's inaugural Freedom of Information Award.

Cameron K. Mabry

Atlanta, Georgia

Elizabeth V. Burt, *Women's Press Organizations, 1881–1999* (2000); Clayton Rand Papers, 1918–71, Special Collections, Mitchell Memorial Library, Mississippi State University; Julius E. Thompson, *The Black Press in Mississippi, 1865–1985* (1993).

Tupelo Homesteads

Behind the headquarters buildings of the Natchez Trace Parkway, hidden from view and unannounced by signage, are the remains of the Tupelo Homesteads, one of the most radical economic experiments ever conducted in the United States. Remarkably well preserved and faithful to original design, these three-, four-, and five-room houses are the remnants of a program that sought to have American families demonstrate the way to sustain a certain economic competence in the midst of the Great Depression.

Tupelo Homesteads, August 1935 (Photograph by Arthur Rothstein, Library of Congress, Washington, D.C. [LC-USF33-002053-M1])

Fearing continued underemployment of American wage workers, New Deal planners sought to induce industry to decentralize by moving some of its operations from overcrowded urban centers to more bucolic surroundings. M. L. Wilson and Rexford G. Tugwell proposed the creation of a new American consumer-producer. If families could satisfy most of their nutrition requirements at home, they could sustain themselves and perhaps even prosper by working only part time for wages.

The Division of Subsistence Homesteads (DSH), a short-lived agency within the US Department of Interior, was created by an amendment to the National Industrial Recovery Act. DSH officials authorized funding for twenty-four "industrial" communities designed to combine subsistence agriculture with part-time wage work, on 15 December 1933. Qualified applicants received the opportunity to purchase a homestead financed by the US government. In addition to the Tupelo Homesteads, the DSH approved projects for Hattiesburg, Laurel, Meridian, Richton, and McComb. The Richton project was the only "farm community" ever completed by the DSH. The McComb project, named in honor of First Lady Eleanor Roosevelt, stopped operations after the eviction of its first homesteader. The Laurel project was never started, and the other Mississippi projects faded quickly into the general community.

In Tupelo, the first residents moved into their new homes on 16 November 1934, two days before Pres. Franklin D. Roosevelt, Eleanor Roosevelt, and interior secretary Harold Ickes visited. The First Lady's obvious fascination with the house and equipment became part of the local color, and journalists were amused at the president's discomfiture when he had to send one of his staffers to interrupt his wife's extended conversation with a resident, Mrs. Barron. The president's visit to Tupelo and to the Tupelo Homesteads represented the high-water mark for the project. For various reasons, including a highly localized building boom after a tornado struck in 1936, the community did not meet the DSH's expectations. However, Tupelo was the most successful and most interesting of the DSH's "industrial" communities.

The Tupelo Homesteads were surprisingly well equipped and situated. The community initially consisted of twenty-five houses (nine with three rooms, eight with four rooms, and eight with five rooms) on lots averaging a little over three acres each. Workers wired each house with a single-party phone line, a luxury for the day. Each house received water from a deep well equipped with an electric pump capable of delivering 225 gallons per hour; a pump house enclosed the mechanism. The DSH provided each homestead with fruit trees, berry bushes, farming equipment, fertilizer, seed, a cow, two pigs, and twenty-five chickens as well as a cow stall, chicken run, and hog pen. Each kitchen was equipped with a pressure cooker, a relatively new innovation, and supplies for home canning.

However, none of the homesteaders exercised the option to buy, and the management of the project passed with bewildering rapidity among New Deal agencies, moving from the DSH in the Interior Department to the Resettlement Administration, the Farm Security Administration, and ultimately back to the Department of Interior under the National Park Service.

Although the Tupelo Homesteads did not achieve the objectives envisioned by the planners, it was the most successful of the one hundred or so Depression-era communities built by agencies of the US government. Moreover, the remnants of many other communities have been absorbed into contemporary neighborhoods or have been extensively modified, and most of the communities have simply disappeared. The Tupelo Homesteads remained distinct because they were transferred to the Interior Department for use as the headquarters of the Natchez Trace Parkway.

Today, even though the cleared fields have been overtaken by vegetation and the ordered orchards have disappeared, the houses look very much as they did in the 1930s. In the mid-1950s the Park Service made minor alterations, primarily adding or enclosing porches and installing windows. Though Tennessee's Cumberland Homesteads do so to a lesser degree, the Tupelo Homesteads is the only New Deal community to retain its architectural, structural, and environmental integrity.

Fred C. Smith
Tupelo, Mississippi

Paul W. Conkin, *Tomorrow a New World: The New Deal Community Program* (1959); Donald Holley, *Uncle Sam's Farmers: The New Deal in the Lower Mississippi Valley* (1975); Fred C. Smith, *Journal of Mississippi History* (Summer 2006); Fred C. Smith, *Trouble in Goshen: Plain Folk, Roosevelt, Jesus, and Marx in the Great Depression South* (2014).

Tupelo Miracle

The *Tupelo Miracle* refers to the way this small city, indistinguishable from those that surrounded it in terms of natural resources or landmarks, became one of the most prosperous cities in Mississippi, boasting a per capita income well above the state average and an unemployment rate well below.

Tupelo's success is predicated on a commitment to the belief that the prosperity of an urban center is intimately related to sustaining the economic viability of its surrounding rural areas. Lee County, like many southern counties, largely depended on agriculture throughout the nineteenth century and into the first half of the twentieth century, and Tupelo, the county seat, suffered from the national shift to agricultural mechanization and the subsequent regional shift toward industrialization. Many rural southerners found themselves with no access to jobs.

By the early 1900s the railroad had attracted businesses and made Tupelo a regional manufacturing and cotton trade hub. Tupelo continued to grow, but city leaders recognized that the town's economic well-being depended largely on the surrounding rural county for raw materials and trade. With 80 percent of Lee County's population working in agriculture, primarily in cotton, this arrangement benefited both city and county until the boll weevil infestation of 1916 threatened cotton production and profits. Recognizing the necessity for diversification, city leaders, led by banker Jim High, provided capital that enabled county farmers to purchase dairy cattle. The venture was so successful that in 1927 the Carnation Company opened a condensery and by the end of the 1940s Lee County was Mississippi's largest producer of milk. Tupelo itself prospered as bank deposits tripled between 1916 and 1923, and in 1933 it was chosen as the first town to receive power from the Tennessee Valley Authority.

Diversification was a slow process and was further complicated by the Great Depression and a devastating 1936 tornado. Looking to rebuild and attract new industry, city leaders held to their belief that recovery needed to involve the entire county. In 1945 the *Tupelo Journal*, run by the dynamic and catalytic George McLean, hired the Doane Agricultural Service to develop a plan to alleviate the financial strain on farmers. This resulted in the formation of the rural community development councils (RCDCs), which became the driving force behind the Tupelo model of community development.

McLean hoped the RCDCs would bring together rural residents and townspeople to find solutions to the challenges posed by increasing agricultural mechanization. To get the RCDCs off the ground, rural people had to be convinced to join and business leaders had to be convinced to fund council activities. McLean stressed the economic interdependence of town and county and noted that a large labor force of former farmers would be necessary to attract industry to the area. RCDCs were to receive technical assistance from Doane, the Tennessee Valley Authority, local academics, and experts hired by Tupelo businesspeople, who were asked to commit to financing the groups for three years. Almost all of Tupelo's businesses participated, and forty-one RCDCs stretched across five counties by 1947; fifty-six RCDCs had been created by mid-1950. Although the councils were largely segregated, many black RCDCs worked effectively with city leadership. RCDC success generally equaled success for Tupelo businesses, as higher farm profits and productivity meant more disposable income for goods and services. Despite some economic hardship during the transition, Tupelo emerged in

T

1967 as the first southern city to receive the National Civic League's All-American City designation.

The RCDCs also helped with the transition to industrialization, since workers were already organized and respected by business leaders. This respect, in turn, affected another important component of the Tupelo rebuilding plan, attracting outside industry. City leaders shunned large-scale operations that might hire hundreds of workers and make the region dependent on a single industry and instead courted smaller companies employing fewer than one hundred people each and looked to scatter them throughout the county. This emphasis on small-scale industry led to higher-than-average wages, shorter commutes, and more stability for workers.

In 1986 Lee County still had fifteen RCDCs despite the drastic decline in agriculture, and the county maintained one of Mississippi's highest per capita income levels. In 1987 it was the first city to receive a second All-American City designation. Today, the US Department of Agriculture's Rural Development arm administers rural community development programs. The 2010 census ranked Lee ninth among Mississippi's eighty-two counties in per capita income, far higher than any of the surrounding counties, and in May 2016, Lee County had the state's seventh-lowest unemployment rate.

The Tupelo Model's foundation is a strong bond between the rural and the urban and a recognition that all residents belong to the same economic community. The concept of the Tupelo Miracle honors the community's ability to manifest that belief into real community action.

Danielle Andersen
University of Mississippi

Vaughn Grisham, *Tupelo: The Evolution of a Community* (1999); Mississippi Department of Employment Security website, www.mdes.ms.gov.

Turcotte, William H.
(1917–2000) Wildlife Biologist

William Henry Turcotte first learned to appreciate wildlife while hunting and fishing with his father and older brother in the piney woods of southern Mississippi. Born in Magee, Mississippi, on 24 January 1917, Turcotte ultimately spent more than forty years as a biologist with the Mississippi Game and Fish Commission, conducting research and managing the successful reintroduction of game animals such as white-tailed deer and wild turkey. Known during his long tenure for an interest in nongame species and his commitment to

rational scientific management practices, Turcotte was perhaps the most influential Mississippi wildlife biologist of the twentieth century.

At the age of seven Turcotte moved with his family to Clinton, where he developed an interest in collecting birds and eggs. By his teens he held a scientific permit for his considerable collection of eggs and nests. His interest in birds led to an early association with conservationist Fannye Cook, who often hired him during the 1930s to help with taxidermy work in support of her research interests. Turcotte earned a degree from Mississippi College in 1939 and went to work the next year for the state commission. When World War II intervened, Turcotte joined the US Army Air Corps and became a navigator; he spent nineteen months as a German prisoner of war.

After the war Turcotte returned to some unique opportunities in a changing state. The rural farming population had begun to decline in response to the increasing mechanization of agriculture; at the same time, a system of state refuges set up in the 1930s had begun to provide a surplus of animals for restocking programs that could be funded in part by federal money. With his state on the cusp of a dramatic recovery in large-game animal populations, Turcotte supervised the live trapping and transplanting of deer and turkey to counties where they had been extirpated for generations. Large-game populations continued to expand over much of the state, although the prevailing conditions eventually proved detrimental to small game. By 1979, when Turcotte retired, Mississippi had healthy populations of deer and turkey, with deer alone numbering around half a million.

Turcotte also left a body of scientific work that reflected his concern with wildlife in general and went beyond his career with game species. He spent years collecting the songs of Mississippi birds and frogs and published selections in audiotaped field guides. His lifelong interest in birds culminated in the comprehensive *Birds of Mississippi* (1999), which Turcotte wrote with David L. Watts. Turcotte died on 5 November 2000.

Wiley C. Prewitt Jr.
Yocona, Mississippi

William H. Turcotte, interview by Wiley Prewitt, Mississippi Museum of Natural Science Reference Library.

Turkeys and Turkey Hunting

Both wildlife biologists and hunters consider the resurgence of Mississippi's wild turkey population one of the

Wild turkeys (Photograph by Jeff Vanuga, courtesy US Department of Agriculture)

most dramatic conservation successes of the twentieth century. By the 1930s the state's hunters had nearly extirpated the birds. Restocking, protection, and basic changes in the human way of life made for a spectacular return of the birds, which numbered perhaps four hundred thousand by the late 1980s.

Wild turkeys were important sources of food and raw material for Native Americans. Successful hunters fletched their arrows with the wing and tail feathers and added the body feathers to garments and adornments. Native Americans also made tools from the leg bones and turkey calls from the wing bones, a craft that persists among some modern hunters. Some southeastern tribes associated turkeys with war. Male turkeys perform elaborate mating displays and fight each other for the right to breed. The featherless heads of the tom turkeys sometimes turn bloodred and may have connoted a scalped skull. Some native groups tried to convey the fury and lust of a wild turkey's gobble in their battle cries.

But no amount of raucous breeding could keep pace with the increasing pressures the growing rural population placed on turkeys toward the end of the nineteenth century. By the 1920s turkeys, like white-tailed deer, were found only in Mississippi's most remote areas, such as the remaining uncut bottomland timber in the Delta and the Pascagoula drainage. Turkeys seemed to be creatures of the wilderness, and it appeared that they would eventually go extinct.

Some hunters experimented with restocking efforts, mainly by releasing semiwild turkeys. Sporadic efforts, some under the auspices of the newly formed Mississippi Game and Fish Commission, continued into the 1930s. The use of pen-raised turkeys invariably failed, however, leading biologists to conclude that only wild-trapped birds could survive and reproduce. State wardens and biologists concentrated on capturing and relocating wild turkeys, most of which were caught in pole traps not dissimilar from the structures used by earlier market hunters. The process was slow, however, and not until the mid-1950s, when the cannon-projected net permitted the capture of an entire flock, did trapping and relocation become truly efficient. With better trapping methods and a steady supply of birds from protected public lands, biologists relocated groups of turkeys to as many

suitable areas as possible. The small flocks needed protection from illegal hunting to become established, so many of the releases took place on the holdings of large landowners or among sympathetic communities where poaching could be controlled. At the same time, the rural population was declining, and large areas of the countryside reverted to forest. The constant pressure on turkey populations that had driven them to the point of extinction had eased, and the birds returned almost everywhere, even in areas once believed unsuitable for turkey range.

More turkeys fueled an interest in sport hunting and the material culture it supported. The state's long tradition of hunting male turkeys in the spring breeding season with calls of various types had almost disappeared along with the birds. As turkeys returned, call makers brought back old designs, improved some, and invented others to give hunters a chance for a gobbler. Calls constructed by various twentieth-century Mississippi artisans out of bone, horn, turtle shell, and cedar are among the most valuable and collectible of folk crafts. Turkeys and turkey hunting also helped foster big business in the state, helping to drive the game-call manufacturing of Wilbur Primo and the Mossy Oak camouflage clothing industry of Toxey Haas.

While turkey numbers have declined from their 1980s peak, an era biologist George Hurst described as "our turkey bubble," Mississippi still enjoys a robust population of approximately 240,000 wild turkeys. The spring season lasts more than a month, with a bag of one mature gobbler per day and three per season.

Wiley C. Prewitt Jr.
Yocona, Mississippi

Malcolm Commer Jr., in *Mississippi's Wildlife Monarch, the Wild Turkey*, ed. Malcolm Commer Jr. (1997); Eric Darracq, *Mississippi Outdoors* (July–August 2002); Howard L. Harlan, *Turkey Calls: An Enduring American Folk Art* (1994); Charles Hudson, *The Southeastern Indians* (1976); *Mississippi Outdoor Digest 2008–9*.

Turnbow, Hartman

(1905–1988) Activist

A farmer and the grandson of slaves, Hartman Turnbow was a grassroots civil rights leader in Holmes County. Born in Mileston on 20 March 1905, Turnbow spent most of his life living and working on the farm he inherited from his grandparents. Mileston was a village of black farmers, the majority of whom got the opportunity to buy their own land through a New Deal program in the late 1930s.

During the late fall of 1962 and early spring of 1963, civil rights workers from the Student Nonviolent Coordinating Committee (SNCC) came to Mileston at the request of some of the local farmers. The activists began teaching African American men and women the intricacies of reading and interpreting the Mississippi Constitution in preparation for registering to vote. Turnbow joined this group.

On 9 April 1963 Turnbow and thirteen other Mileston blacks traveled to the county seat of Lexington to register to vote. A phalanx of whites attempted to intimidate the "First Fourteen" and prevent them from registering. As the group stood before the crowd of angry whites, deputy sheriff Andrew Smith slapped his gun holster and called out, "All right now, who will be first?" Turnbow stepped forward and said, "Me, Hartman Turnbow, will be first." He and another black farmer took the test that day, while the other twelve took it the following day. The circuit clerk failed them all, but Turnbow and the rest were proud that they had tried and had not suffered violence or arrest.

Exactly one month later, on 9 May 1963, white night riders fired on Turnbow's home and threw two firebombs into his living room and kitchen. Awakened by the fire, Turnbow ushered his wife and their daughter out of the house. Turnbow grabbed his .22-caliber rifle before going outside. The attackers allowed the two females to pass unharmed but opened fire on Turnbow as he exited his home. Turnbow returned fire and wounded one of the assailants. Then he and his family put out the fire. The next day, the sheriff arrested Turnbow and several SNCC workers, including Bob Moses, for arson. The US Justice Department intervened, and the charges were later dropped. During the Freedom Summer of 1964 Turnbow allowed civil rights workers to stay at his home, which was again fired on by night riders.

Energized by community resolve and a willingness to retaliate when attacked, Turnbow and other Mileston blacks sought support across Holmes County in 1963–64. Turnbow's fiery orations and his willingness to stand up against racist whites inspired many to join the county's civil rights movement. Mileston residents formed an extensive organization that eventually took an important role in the Mississippi Freedom Democratic Party, and Turnbow served as one of the party's delegates to the 1964 Democratic National Convention in Atlantic City, New Jersey. With little education, Turnbow had a propensity for uttering malapropisms and once referred to SNCC as the "Student Violent Uncoordinated Committee." Yet while standing only 5′5″ tall, he had a knack for leadership and served as an inspiration to others.

Turnbow is a classic example of what historians of the Mississippi civil rights movement refer to when they speak of the movement being led by local people. With his roots in the local community and willingness to fight back when attacked, Turnbow and others like him made Holmes County one of the strongest areas of resistance and organization during the civil rights movement.

He died on 19 August 1988.

Jeffery B. Howell
East Georgia State College

John Dittmer, *Local People: The Struggle for Civil Rights in Mississippi* (1995); Jay MacLeod, *Minds Stayed on Freedom: The Civil Rights Struggle in the Rural South*, ed. Youth of the Rural Organizing and Cultural Center (1991); Charles M. Payne, *I've Got the Light of Freedom: The Organizing Tradition and the Mississippi Freedom Struggle* (1995); Sue Lorenzi Sojourner, Civil Rights Movement Veterans website, http://www.crmvet .org/; Studs Terkel, in *American Dreams: Lost and Found* (1980); Hartman Turnbow, interview by Howell Raines, in *My Soul Is Rested* (1977).

Turner, Ike
(1931–2007) Rhythm and Blues Musician

Musician and songwriter Ike Turner was born either Izear Luster Turner Jr. or Ike Wister Turner in Clarksdale, Mississippi, on 5 November 1931. From early in his life, Turner was exposed to the hard realities of life in the Jim Crow South—his father was lynched when Ike was eight, and his family consistently faced severe poverty. Turner became drawn to the Delta's rich blues tradition, first working at a local radio station and then playing guitar and piano behind some of the day's biggest stars. In the late 1940s he formed his own ensemble, Ike Turner's Kings of Rhythm, which specialized in the blend of blues, jazz, and big-band dance music that ultimately became R&B.

Like many African American musicians of the time, Turner's band sought greater opportunity in Memphis, already a premier center for black music. In 1951 the Kings of Rhythm signed with fledgling Sun Records, started by disc jockey Sam Phillips for the express purpose of recording African American blues, gospel, and R&B music. The Kings of Rhythm's first session produced the jumping hit "Rocket 88," written by Turner, which many consider the first rock and roll record. Despite the fact that Turner was both bandleader and composer, the Sun release was credited to the band's vocalist, Jackie Brenston, who soon left Turner's employ to capitalize on his newfound fame. The Kings of Rhythm served as one of Memphis's leading session bands, and Turner played an increasing role in the development of younger talent.

Turner and the band departed for St. Louis in 1955, beginning a multiyear run as successful touring performers. Turner's gift for musical arrangement, his keen ear for talent, and his pioneering style on both piano and guitar helped the Kings of Rhythm gain an avid following throughout the famed Chitlin' Circuit of black venues. In St. Louis, Turner attracted the attention of a young female singer, Anna Mae Bullock. Turner immediately realized the gritty-voiced young woman's potential, married her in 1958, renamed her Tina Turner, and made her a permanent fixture in his band, which became the Ike and Tina Turner Revue.

Ike Turner achieved his greatest success with Tina through both concert appearances and a series of singles that bridged R&B, soul, and funk. Beginning with the smoldering "A Fool in Love" in 1960, which reached No. 2 on the R&B charts, the pair racked up a series of hits over the next fifteen years, with most of the songs composed and produced by Ike. The Turner Revue opened for the Rolling Stones on several occasions and flirted with sounds from the world of rock music, incorporating fuzz-toned guitar, gritty arrangements, and covers of rock material, including a gospel-influenced version of John Fogerty's "Proud Mary" (1971) that became a hit. This infusion of rock sounds helped make Ike and Tina Turner's early 1970s output even more successful than their earlier songs, and the Revue became one of the era's most acclaimed live acts. Tina's intense performances, combined with the proficiency of the Ike-led band, made them a consistent draw, particularly in Europe.

However, as his fame grew, Ike's problems mounted. His penchant for drug use, physical violence, womanizing, and destructive jealousy grew increasingly intense. Tina left Ike in 1976, and they divorced in 1978. She later alleged that he had been violent toward her, charges that he confirmed.

Over the next two decades, Ike Turner experienced a series of personal catastrophes, including a fire that destroyed his Los Angeles recording studio and a number of arrests on drug and weapons charges that culminated in an eighteen-month stint in jail, during which time he and Tina were inducted into the Rock and Roll Hall of Fame.

While in jail Ike Turner kicked his cocaine habit, and he began recording and touring again in the late 1990s. He released a 2001 album, *Here and Now*, that was nominated for Grammy Award. In his autobiography, *Takin' Back My Name*, published the same year, he addressed many of his flaws and failings and claimed to have been married fourteen times. He began using cocaine again in 2004, was diagnosed with emphysema the following year, and died of a cocaine overdose on 12 December 2007.

Charles L. Hughes
Rhodes College

John Collins, *Ike Turner: King of Rhythm* (2003); Jon Pareles, *New York Times* (13 December 2007); Ike Turner with Nigel Cawthorne, *Takin' Back My Name: The Confessions of Ike Turner* (1999).

Turner, Otha
(1907–2003) Musician

Though his music has been featured on recordings, on television, and in documentary and feature films, Otha (or Othar) Turner is perhaps best known for the North Mississippi picnics and performances he hosted. He was born in Rankin County, Mississippi, on 2 June 1907 to Hollis and Betty Turner. His father left soon after his birth, and his mother moved the family to the Gravel Springs area near Senatobia, where she worked as a sharecropper. Except for nine months spent laying railroad ties in Muncie, Indiana, Otha Turner remained in Gravel Springs for the rest of his life.

As a teenager Turner plowed and chopped cotton, watched over younger family members, and learned to play makeshift drums, washtub bass, guitar, and cane fife. His introduction to the fife, which became his signature instrument, occurred at age thirteen, when he witnessed a performance by neighbors. Despite his mother's admonishments against musicianship, Turner practiced the fife incessantly and began to make the instruments himself, a process documented decades later in the film *Gravel Springs Fife and Drum* (1971). As a young man, Turner performed in Tate, Panola, Lafayette, and other North Mississippi counties and formed an ensemble, the Rising Star Fife and Drum Band, featuring a bass drum and one or two snares in support of his fife (and to a secondary degree his singing). An important venue for his and other fife-and-drum bands was the frequent picnics and social gatherings demarcating such holidays as Independence Day and Labor Day. These events set the standard for the annual Labor Day goat roasts or "picnic parties" Turner held on his farm in later decades.

Many folklorists believe the African American fife-and-drum tradition to be a unique offshoot of US military or militia marching-band tradition blended with both African and African American musical styles. Supporting this theory

Photographing Otha Turner marker, Como (Photograph by David Wharton)

is the fact that leading up to the Revolutionary War, though slaves were legally bound to participate in militia training, they were generally restricted to work as parade musicians. Though both white and black versions of fife-and-drum ensembles existed in colonial New England, records indicate that in the South, both during and after the Civil War, they were primarily black outfits. In the Reconstruction-era South, fife-and-drum groups flourished within the black community, performing at parades, holidays, and other social events. The form continued to evolve musically as well, as bands blended military marches with African drum traditions, minstrel tunes of the early nineteenth century, slave songs, and blues.

Alongside Sid Hemphill and other fife players, Turner's Rising Star Fife and Drum Band performances were a noted part of North Mississippi's musical landscape during the middle decades of the twentieth century. Despite the waning of the fife-and-drum tradition, folklorists began to take note in the late 1960s. Both George Mitchell and David Evans recorded Turner in the latter part of the decade, and his songs appeared on several compilations associated with the region. Alan Lomax first came across Turner in the late 1950s, though only because Lomax asked directions to find Mississippi Fred McDowell. Turner later appeared in Lomax's 1978 documentary, *The Land Where Blues Began*. William Ferris documented Turner's fife-making techniques in his book, *Afro-American Folk Art and Crafts*.

As his reputation grew, Turner accepted invitations to perform for larger audiences at events such as the New Orleans Jazz and Heritage Festival and the Chicago Blues Festival, but he did not gain formal recognition for his efforts until the 1990s, when he was well past age eighty. He received the National Heritage Medal from the National Endowment for the Arts in 1992, and his first solo recordings appeared later in the decade. Fans from around the country and even the globe began to attend his annual picnics in Gravel Springs. Perhaps his broadest exposure came via the opening scene of director Martin Scorsese's 2002 film, *Gangs of New York*. As precursor to a battle between two gangs, the director used Turner's version of the fife standard "Shimmie She Wobble" as soundtrack. He also received the Smithsonian Lifetime Achievement Award and the Charley Patton Lifetime Achievement Award from the Mississippi Delta Blues and Heritage Festival. He died on 27 February 2003 and was honored with a marker on the Mississippi Blues Trail in 2009.

Turner's legacy is carried on by young musicians he shepherded, including the North Mississippi Allstars, Slick Ballinger, and family members such as Turner's granddaughter, Shardé Thomas, who is now a heralded fife player and leader of the next generation of the Rising Star Fife and Drum Band.

Odie Lindsey
Nashville, Tennessee

Bill Ellis, *Memphis Commercial Appeal* (27 February 2003); David Evans, William Ferris, and Judy Peiser, *Gravel Springs Fife and Drum* (film, 1971); William Ferris, ed., *Afro-American Folk Art and Craft* (1983).

Turner, Roscoe
(1895–1970) Aviator

One of America's best-known aviators of the early twentieth century, Roscoe Turner, was born on a farm outside of Corinth, Mississippi, on 29 September 1895. Turner had no desire to become a farmer, and at sixteen he quit school and moved to Memphis, where he found a job as an auto mechanic and fell in love with fast cars and motorcycles. Turner enlisted in the US Army in 1917, became a balloon pilot, and soon began taking flying lessons.

After World War I, Turner became a barnstormer. He and his partner, Harry Runser, toured the South in a Curtiss Jenny biplane, performing barrel rolls, wing walking, and parachute jumping. The young aviators often paid their bills by offering sightseeing flights to fairgoers. The partnership dissolved after several years, and Turner then operated the Roscoe Turner Flying Circus until 1925, when he opened a flying school in Florence, Alabama. He purchased a seven-passenger Sikorsky S-29A plane and dreamed of starting an airline. This purchase, along with Turner's flying reputation, caught Hollywood's attention.

Film producer Howard Hughes hired Turner to convert his S-29A into a German Gotha bomber for the World War I epic *Hell's Angels*. Turner's time in Hollywood soon came to an end when a stunt pilot crashed his prized S-29A. The plane was a total loss, but Turner rebounded by piloting a new Lockheed Vega for the air racing circuit in 1929. Moving to Las Vegas, he established the short-lived Nevada Airlines and became a colonel in the Nevada National Guard. The onset of the Great Depression ended his commercial aviation dream, and he returned to speed racing in early 1930.

Always the showman, Turner remarketed himself as the "Colonel," designed himself a military-style uniform, and obtained a sponsorship from the Gilmore Oil Company. The company's mascot was a lion, and Turner purchased a lion cub as a publicity stunt. Named Gilmore, the lion was onboard Turner's new Lockheed Air Express when he gained national attention by setting a May 1930 transcontinental speed record from Los Angeles to New York City.

During the 1930s Turner competed on the speed-racing circuit against noted pilots such as Jimmy Doolittle and Wiley Post. In 1934 Turner piloted a new Boeing 247 airliner in the MacRobertson Air Race from London, England, to Melbourne, Australia. Finishing second, Turner appeared on the cover of *Time* magazine and became an aviation icon. United Airlines soon hired him as a spokesperson, and he traveled the United States, lecturing to large audiences about the benefits of aviation.

With the advent of World War II, Turner moved to Indianapolis and established the Roscoe Turner Aeronautical Corporation to train war pilots. In 1946 Roscoe Turner Airlines began serving the Midwest. In December 1950 Turner sold his interest, and the company's name became Lake Central Airlines. Turner again returned to the lecture circuit and in 1952 received the Distinguished Flying Cross from Congress for his contributions to aviation. In 1961 Corinth renamed its municipal airport in Turner's honor.

Turner died of bone cancer on 23 June 1970. After World War II, he had said, "Aviation is going to control the world economically and militarily whether we like it or not. Airpower is not merely military aviation, it is also civilian aviation and airpower is peace power."

David L. Weatherford
Northwest Florida State College

Carroll V. Glines, *Aviation's Master Showman* (1997); Michael O'Leary, *Air Classics* (2003); National Aviation Hall of Fame website, www.national aviation.org.

Tutor, Glennray
(b. 1950) Artist

The terms *photorealism*, *superrealism*, and *southern pop* have all been used to describe Glennray Tutor's paintings. His precise renderings of everyday objects are infused with an almost fantastic aura of light and color, giving his paintings a sense of wonder. Born in Kennett, Missouri, on 25 August 1950, Tutor earned both bachelor of fine arts and master of fine arts degrees from the University of Mississippi in the mid-1970s. He settled in Oxford and became a full-time painter, working in acrylic, oil, and charcoal and in printmaking.

As if in contemporary dialogue with the still lifes of seventeenth-century Dutch masters, Tutor's work focuses on capturing an arrangement of everyday objects but saturates them with twenty-first-century color. His overall style has been called hyperrealistic, though Tutor's painting technique itself is most closely associated with photorealism: he re-creates, in exact detail, subjects unmarked by brushstroke or abstraction. This precision removes any seam or tip-off to

Tutor's technical process, yet the color clearly skews the work as fantastic. Mississippi writer Barry Hannah compared the final effect to "life after a glaucoma operation. Only [Tutor] could grab the color and the light and the spirit of life out of the stream of the usual."

Small, common emblems of everyday life in the South are the frequent subjects of Tutor's paintings. He is noted for his ability to give new meaning to these familiar sights. Tutor explains, "The subject matter is not something I have to go and find. It is something I experienced by living in the South and always have experienced. These are subjects around me and have an importance to me." His paintings often include household items, such as toys, mason jars filled with pickled vegetables, fireworks, and the like. The composition of the pieces themselves is crucial to the feel of each painting, from the beam of planet-like colored marbles atop black-and-white newspaper comics to the squadron of firecracker airplanes whose nosecone fuses face off in a circle. As part of his process, Tutor takes multiple photographs of his arrangements, then both under- and overexposes a series of prints, allowing him access to the nuances of light and shadow. From these representations he flushes the work with color, overloading the natural hues.

Tutor credits his early love of comic books and book jackets for spurring his interest in visual work. Appropriately, his paintings have appeared as a number of book illustrations, including covers for books by Hannah and Larry Brown and for the University Press of Mississippi. His early paintings evolved from abstractions to idea-laden landscapes of the Mississippi Delta. He won first place in his initial exhibition, the 1975 Mississippi Arts Festival.

Tutor's work has since been featured in solo and group exhibitions in New York, Santa Fe, Nashville, Los Angeles, Jackson, and elsewhere, and is included in collections at Georgia's Morris Museum of Art, the University of Mississippi, and galleries throughout the region. In 2000 Tutor's paintings were included alongside works by Andy Warhol, Roy Lichtenstein, Robert Rauschenberg, Chuck Close, and others as part of the internationally touring *Outward Bound: American Art at the Brink of the Twenty-First Century* exhibition.

Patti Carr Black
Jackson, Mississippi

Odie Lindsey
Nashville, Tennessee

Patti Carr Black, *Art in Mississippi, 1720–1980* (1998); Patti Carr Black, *The Mississippi Story* (2007); Glennray Tutor website, www.glennraytutor.com.

Tutwiler Quilters

In 1983 Sister Anne Brooks, an osteopathic physician and a nun with the Sisters of the Holy Names of Jesus and Mary, started a small medical practice in Tutwiler, Mississippi, in Tallahatchie County. With help from the Catholic Church Extension Society, an organization dedicated to supporting Catholic missionary work in the United States, she established the Tutwiler Clinic to provide health care to this underserved community in one of the poorest counties in the Mississippi Delta where more than a quarter of the population lives below the poverty level.

Sister Maureen Delaney moved to Tutwiler from California in 1987 to help Brooks and to create outreach programs for the clinic. Working to discover the needs and concerns of area residents, Delaney soon began to learn about the African American community's strong quilting tradition. She paid a visit to a local woman, Mary Sue Robertson, who sewed quilt tops by hand in her home. Delaney immediately recognized the wonderful quality of Robertson's creations and believed that they could be sold. Delaney found other women in the community who could finish the pieces into a quilt, and Tutwiler Quilters was born.

Tutwiler Quilters started with women who could sew, women who could quilt, and a few women with little or no experience at all. Skills were tested and skills were taught as new interest arose in a generations-old tradition. At first the quilts were small and the orders few, but the enterprise took off. The group originally worked with scraps of material culled from various sources but now works with new materials, most of them donated by supporters. Eighty percent of the money from each sale goes to the item's creator, while the remainder goes to materials, and their product line, which features geometric designs, not only includes quilts but has expanded to include table runners, placemats, potholders, and handbags.

Not long after Tutwiler Quilters was established, the Tutwiler Community Education Center was opened. The center and the quilting program have grown in tandem, and the group has begun to receive national recognition and exposure. Tutwiler Quilters is a member of the Craftsmen's Guild of Mississippi, which preserves and promotes excellence in traditional craft throughout the state.

Mary Sue Robertson died in 1989, but her spirit and vision have lived on to inspire subsequent generations of quilters. One of her creations hangs in the quilting room at the Tutwiler Community Education Center, serving as a reminder of how a traditional art can serve the heart, the soul, and a community in the Mississippi Delta.

Amy Evans
Houston, Texas

Tutwiler Quilters website, www.tutwilerquilters.org.

Twitty, Conway (Harold Lloyd Jenkins)
(1933–1993) Country Musician

Singer, guitarist, and songwriter Conway Twitty came to be known as "the best friend a song ever had." Born Harold Lloyd Jenkins in Friars Point, Mississippi, on 1 September 1933, he moved with his parents, Floyd Dalton Jenkins and Velma Dunaway Jenkins, to Helena, Arkansas, at the age of ten. There he started his first band, the Phillips County Ramblers. In 1953 he was drafted into the US Army, and while serving in Japan, he formed a country group, the Cimarrons.

After his return to the United States, Jenkins embraced the new rockabilly sound of artists such as Elvis Presley, wrote rock and roll songs, and worked with other artists at Sun Records in Memphis. In 1957 Jenkins changed his name to Conway Twitty, taking his first name from Conway, Arkansas, and his last from Twitty, Texas. In 1958 he wrote and released a single, "It's Only Make Believe," on the MGM label. It went to No. 1 on the pop charts and sold more than a million copies. A string of singles and albums that made the charts followed, but his next gold record did not come until 1960's "Lonely Blue Boy." Between 1958 and the mid-1960s his rock releases sold more than sixteen million copies. He toured in the United States, Canada, and Europe and performed on *American Bandstand* and *The Ed Sullivan Show*. He also appeared in six movies and wrote the scores for three of them: *Platinum High*, *Sex Kittens Go to College*, and *College Confidential*.

In 1965 Twitty returned to his country music roots, relocating to Oklahoma City and forming the Lonely Blue Boys. The group signed with Decca Records before relocating to Nashville in the late 1960s. Twitty had hits in 1968 and 1969 and performed regularly on the *Grand Ole Opry* and other major country shows. Renaming his band the Twitty Birds, he consolidated his place in country music over the ensuing decade. His 1970 hit single, "Hello Darlin'," topped the country charts and crossed over to the pop list, as did many of his recordings. During the decade, nineteen of his solo singles hit No. 1, while nine reached the Top 5. His successful collaboration with Loretta Lynn yielded five chart-topping singles, and they won the Country Music Association's award for best duo from 1971 through 1974. His albums on the MCA label, *Hello Darlin'* and *You've Never Been This Far Before*, sold more than a million copies. During the 1980s Twitty and Lynn notched three Top 10 hits, while twelve of his solo singles reached No. 1 and fourteen others reached the Top 10. Twitty enjoyed less success in the 1990s but fared better than most veteran performers in the onslaught of new country musicians.

Three of Twitty's four children recorded and sang with him as the Twitty Committee. On 4 June 1993 he suffered an abdominal aneurysm while performing in Branson, Missouri, and he died the following day.

Twitty had more No. 1 hits than any other pop music artist and wrote eleven of his chart-topping songs. In 1993 he was elected to the Nashville Songwriters Hall of Fame, and in 1999 he was inducted into the Country Music Hall of Fame. He is also a member of the Rockabilly Hall of Fame, and in 2012 he was honored with a Friars Point marker on the Mississippi Country Music Trail.

Tara Laver
Louisiana State University

Richard Carlin, *Country Music: A Biographical Dictionary* (2003); Barry McCloud, *Definitive Country: The Ultimate Encyclopedia of Country Music and Its Performers* (1995); Mississippi Country Music Trail website, www.mscountrymusictrail.org; Irwin Stambler and Grelun Landon, *Country Music: The Encyclopedia* (1997).

T

U

Ugulayacabé
(?–ca. 1798) Chickasaw Chief

Ugulayacabé emerges in the historical record as an important Chickasaw chief of the late eighteenth century. He was also known by at least two other names or titles: Wolf's Friend and Mooleshawskeko. The name or title *Ugulayacabé* may be a variation of *Okla ayaka abi*, which has been translated "Slayer of Many Nations." By the 1790s outsiders saw him and Piomingo as the two principal chiefs of the Chickasaw. He led a faction of Chickasaw friendly to Spanish interests, whereas Piomingo saw Chickasaw interests better served by close ties with Americans. Ugulayacabé did, however, keep his options open, and in late 1798 he traveled to Philadelphia, Pennsylvania, with other Chickasaw to meet US president John Adams.

Ugulayacabé attended an August 1792 meeting in Nashville between Choctaw and Chickasaw representatives and William Blount, the US governor of the territory south of the Ohio River, but later assured the Spanish governor in Natchez, Manuel Gayoso de Lemos, that the purpose had been simply to observe. The minutes of that meeting suggest that Ugulayacabé was an impressive figure—a "large man, of dignified appearance," wearing a scarlet cloak with silver lace and carrying a large silk umbrella.

By the following year, Ugulayacabé had clearly defined himself as a principal advocate of Spanish interests among the Chickasaw. Gayoso regarded the chief as a person of importance whose "talents and influence" enabled him to counter "the machinations of Piomingo." Gayoso left an account of a fall 1793 congress at the newly created Spanish post of Nogales at the mouth of the Yazoo River. Attended mainly by Choctaw and Chickasaw, the conference sought to create a confederation of Choctaw, Chickasaw, Creek, and Cherokee under Spanish auspices, and Gayoso represented Ugulayacabé as the project's strongest Chickasaw supporter. According to Gayoso, the chief described the proposed confederation as "a hand[,] with the four fingers" representing the four nations and the thumb representing the Spanish nation, which "unit[ed] the power of all."

Ugulayacabé continued to support Spanish interests with regard to the next Spanish project, the creation of a post on the Chickasaw Bluffs where present-day Memphis, Tennessee, is located. By this time the Spanish provided him with an annual stipend and believed that they could do a better job of supplying the Chickasaw with gifts and trade goods than could the Americans. Spanish officials assigned Ugulayacabé responsibility for distributing their gifts, thereby enhancing his status among the Chickasaw.

Ugulayacabé had asked that the goods be delivered to Chickasaw Bluffs, a request the Spanish were happy to accept since it accorded with their desire to establish a post there. To accomplish that goal, other chiefs had to agree. That process required almost two years of diplomacy that culminated with Ugulayacabé persuading enough others to enable construction of a fort and the establishment of a trading post. The Spanish named the post San Fernando de las Barrancas.

In the fall of 1795, however, US and Spanish diplomats in Europe agreed to the Treaty of San Lorenzo, in which Spain accepted the American definition of the southern boundary of the United States. That treaty required the Spanish to give up San Fernando, Nogales, Natchez, and other posts. At a meeting with the Spanish commandant and others at San Fernando in late 1796, Ugulayacabé described himself as a chief of his nation and leader among the warriors from the time of the English and said that he had recognized "the delusory presents of the Americans" and put his trust and that of others in the Spanish. "We could perceive in [the Americans] the cunning of the rattlesnake who caresses the squirrel he intends to devour." He characterized the treaty between Spain and the United States as an act in which "our father has not only abandoned us like the smaller animals to the jaws of tiger and bear" but has encouraged them "to devour us" by driving "us back to their dens and keeping us there."

Ugulayacabé's words reached both Francisco Luis Héctor, Baron de Carondelet, serving as the Spanish governor-general in New Orleans, as well as various American officials, including the secretary of war, who was responsible for Indian affairs. Carondelet tried to reassure Ugulayacabé and the other Chickasaw that they had not been abandoned and that their trade could continue by means of a post on the west bank of the Mississippi River. US general James Wilkinson and the US agent to the Chickasaw, James Robertson, tried to reassure Ugulayacabé and other Chickasaw of benign American intentions. They persuaded him and others to travel in the fall of 1798 to Philadelphia to meet the US president and other officials. In an 1841 interview Malcolm McGee, who had lived among the Chickasaw since the 1780s and served as an interpreter for them, said that Ugulayacabé, suffering from "the gravel" (kidney stones), shot himself shortly after his return.

Charles A. Weeks
Jackson, Mississippi

James R. Atkinson, *Journal of Mississippi History* (Spring 2004); James R. Atkinson, *Splendid Land, Splendid People: The Chickasaw Indians to*

Removal (2004); Charles A. Weeks, *Paths to a Middle Ground: The Diplomacy of Natchez, Boukfouka, Nogales, and San Fernando de las Barrancas, 1791–1795* (2005); Charles A. Weeks, *William and Mary Quarterly* (July 2010).

Underwood, Felix J.
(1882–1959) Physician

Felix Joel Underwood, a physician and the longtime executive officer of the State Board of Health, was the most prominent public health leader in Mississippi during the first half of the twentieth century. The son of Marion Milton Underwood and Amanda Capitola Battle Underwood, he was born on 21 November 1882 in Nettleton, a small railroad town located on the border of Lee and Monroe Counties. At the age of ten he watched helplessly as his mother died of childbirth fever, an experience that played a crucial role in his decision to study medicine. To earn money for medical school, he worked as a clerk in a local drugstore; wrote stories for the local newspaper, the *Nettleton Advance*; and taught in the local schools. In 1904 he married Sarah Beatrice Tapscott, a coworker at the newspaper, and soon thereafter he enrolled at the University of Tennessee in Memphis, receiving his medical degree in 1908.

Underwood returned to his hometown to practice horse-and-buggy medicine for more than twelve years. Early in his career he displayed an interest in both public health and politics. From 1917 to 1920 he served as Monroe County's health officer, and in 1919 he was elected president of the Mississippi State Medical Association.

In January 1921 he began to devote himself exclusively to what he would call "the great and necessary work of protecting life and health in Mississippi" after receiving an appointment to serve as director of the Mississippi State Board of Health's Bureau of Child Hygiene and Welfare. He moved to the state capital, Jackson, where he lived for the rest of his life. Underwood distinguished himself in his new position, and in 1924 he became executive officer and secretary of the State Board of Health, a position he held until his retirement in 1958. He once told his wife, "As a private doctor, I can never care for more than two or three thousand people. As a public health officer, I can care for millions."

Working out of the Board of Health offices at the Old Capitol building, Underwood worked tirelessly to improve public health practices in the state. Opposing local boards of health, he organized a state-centered public health system, imposing uniform services and quality standards across the state. His accomplishments included developing sanitary standards on the shellfish industry, obtaining fluoridated water, registering marriages, organizing training stations for public health workers, initiating postgraduate medical education, inaugurating industrial health and hygiene programs, registering midwives, creating county health units, instituting mental health units, and adopting milk ordinances. He was not afraid to confront subjects often taboo in conservative Mississippi. Asking for "social courage" on the part of physicians, he criticized the "national hush-hush policy concerning syphilis" and encouraged "giving of adequate sex information to younger age groups. The safeguarding of this one growth process can be considered preventive medicine of a high order." He was an early proponent of a "planned parenthood program," calling it "vital" for public health. In 1927 he called the nicotine in tobacco "a deadly poison." He also battled tuberculosis, rabies, malaria, polio, diphtheria, and infant and maternal mortality.

In an era when race dominated all aspects of Mississippi life, Underwood did not overlook the medical problems of African Americans and included them among the recipients of medical education scholarships. He also directed public attention to black morbidity: "With Negroes comprising more than 50 percent of our population, our infant and maternal death rate will continue unreasonably high unless vigorous measures are taken to improve the health of Negro mothers and babies," he said in 1937. He fought indifference to the plight of blacks and argued that poor housing and poverty rather than racial differences caused high levels of disease among African Americans.

In the 1930s Underwood served as a public health adviser to the President's Social Security Committee. Underwood used his national connections when state funding for health dropped during the depression and took advantage of federal New Deal programs to initiate a free immunization program for Mississippi's poor.

After World War II, Underwood stepped up his battle to increase the number of hospitals in the state. In 1946 the legislature set up a Commission on Hospital Care, and Underwood was a force on the commission. With his leadership, Mississippi became the first state to secure Public Health Service approval for a statewide hospital plan. On 9 June 1948 Booneville received the first contract in the nation to build a hospital under the Hill-Burton Act.

From 1945 to 1955 Underwood also battled to relieve state physician deficiencies. As vice chair of the State Medical Education Board, he persuaded the 1946 legislature to establish a program to provide loans for medical students willing to spend two years in rural general practice after they received their degrees. Even more important in solving the postwar physician shortage was the creation of a four-year medical school in Mississippi. He strategized and lobbied relentlessly until the legislature established the University Medical Center in Jackson in 1950.

As president of the State Board of Examiners for Nurses he signed every nurse's license awarded in Mississippi from 1931 to 1958, and as the executive officer of the State Board

U

of Health he signed the license of every Mississippi physician who practiced between 1924 and 1958. He also worked closely with Dr. Henry Boswell to develop and support the Mississippi State Tuberculosis Sanatorium at Magee, which the State Board of Health supervised.

The construction of a new State Board of Health Building represented a fitting climax to Underwood's career. The state legislature named the building in his honor, overlooking the long taboo against naming a public building after a living person. After Underwood's death on 9 January 1959, the state and national press praised him as "the man who saved a million lives."

Lucius M. Lampton

Magnolia, Mississippi

Annual Reports of the Mississippi Board of Health, 1924–60; Karen Evers, *Journal of the Mississippi State Medical Association* (November 1999); Lucius M. Lampton, *Journal of the Mississippi State Medical Association* (September 1999); James Grant Thompson and E. F. Howard, *History of the Mississippi State Medical Association* (2nd ed., 1949); Felix J. Underwood and R. N. Whitfield, *Public Health and Medical Licensure in the State of Mississippi*, 2 vols. (1938, 1950).

Union Bank

After nearly a decade of increasing economic expansion, Mississippi's economy began to fade in the mid-1830s. The worldwide Panic of 1837 contributed to the state's economic collapse. To forestall a downturn, state legislators chartered a quasi-official state bank. Legislators felt certain that although other banks were collapsing, the Union Bank, with the backing of the State of Mississippi, would succeed.

When first proposed, the Union Bank charter passed without substantive opposition. Although the bank would function like other financial institutions chartered in the mid-1830s, the original enabling legislation contained a number of quirky features: only Mississippi property owners could purchase stock, although Mississippians who lacked sufficient cash to buy stock could receive eight-year loans to do so provided they had real estate or slaves to serve as collateral. The sale of stock was supposed to raise $500,000, and the state would raise the remainder of the capital by selling $15,500,000 in bonds.

In 1838 the Union Bank charter returned to the Mississippi legislature for approval. A curious clause in the state's 1832 constitution required that successive legislatures approve bills that extended the financial backing of the state.

Again, the charter passed, though a larger legislative coterie now claimed that creation of the bank constituted an extravagance during an economic depression. After approving the legislation, Gov. Alexander McNutt sought to allay opponents' fears by authorizing a supplement to the charter requiring the state to purchase $5,000,000 in stock, money that was to be raised by the sale of 5 percent state bonds. The supplement effectively altered the relationship of the bank and the state, making the state a stockholder, not merely a backer.

The Union Bank opened in 1838, and its managers, like other bank managers in the 1830s, took great risks and used their position to gain and curry favor. Within two years, the public grew to loathe the bank. At the same time, the legislature became concerned about the continued existence of banks with inadequate specie reserves. In 1840 the legislature demanded that banking houses pay in gold and silver upon demand. Within two years seventeen banks closed for lack of specie, and Gov. McNutt questioned whether his signing of the supplemental charter was constitutional.

McNutt became an early advocate of repudiating state debts incurred in support of the Union Bank. In 1842 recently elected Gov. Tilghman Tucker signed an act authorizing the state not to pay money owed to holders of some $20,500,000 in state bonds. Throughout the 1840s the legislature debated incessantly whether to pay or repudiate state debts. In 1852 Mississippi's High Court of Errors and Appeals ordered the state to pay its debts, but the legislature never appropriated funds to do so.

The saga of the state bonds sold to support the Union Bank continued. In the mid-1990s a group of bondholders, mostly British citizens, sued the state for nonpayment. The Mississippi Supreme Court reversed the earlier court decision.

The debate over the charter of the Union Bank and the state's repudiation of debts to support it led to the development of a strong two-party political system in Mississippi. The faction that favored killing all banks and repudiation became the Democratic Party. It favored nonpayment of the debts because the bank, like all banks, was an institution designed to ensure the wealth of elites and because repayment of the debt would increase the tax liability of ordinary folk. Mississippi's Whig Party, conversely, arose from among those who favored payment of the debt, arguing that that the state had pledged its faith in support of bonds sold to innocent purchasers and that repudiation thus constituted an immoral act that would ruin the credit of the state and its citizens. This two-party system did not survive much beyond 1850, but it suggested that Mississippi could develop a strong multiparty system of politics that revolved around something other than slavery or race.

Bradley G. Bond

Northern Illinois University

Bradley G. Bond, *Political Culture in the Nineteenth-Century South, Mississippi, 1830–1900* (1995); Larry Schweikart, *Banking in the American South from the Age of Jackson to Reconstruction* (1987); Robert Cicero Weems Jr., "The Bank of the State of Mississippi: A Pioneer Bank of the Old Southwest, 1809–1844" (PhD dissertation, Columbia University, 1952).

Union County

Founded in 1870, Union County was formed from sections of Tippah and Pontotoc Counties, with some land added from Lee County in 1874. The county received its name during Reconstruction, after the Union of the United States. Union is located in northeastern Mississippi, a region once populated by the Chickasaw. Ingomar Mound, located five miles south of New Albany, the county seat, was built more than two thousand years ago by early indigenous people and used by the Chickasaw for ceremonial purposes.

Like most counties in northeastern Mississippi, Union relied on an agricultural economy and concentrated on grains far more than cotton in the late nineteenth century. In 1880 Union County farmers grew the fifth-most wheat in the state and thirteenth-most corn but ranked forty-fifth in the production of cotton. Around 60 percent of Union farmers cultivated their own land. Union's population numbered 13,030, the large majority of them white, and included 20 foreign-born residents.

By 1900 Union had grown to 16,522 people. As in much of Mississippi, whites and African Americans had widely divergent rates of landowning. While 46 percent of the county's 2,305 white farmers owned their land, only 14 percent of the 590 black farmers did so, with the rest working as tenants and sharecroppers. Union County had forty-five manufacturing establishments employing ninety-four workers, all but one of them male.

Mirroring other counties in the region, the Baptists dominated religion in Union. According to the religious census of 1916, Missionary Baptists and Southern Baptists were by far the largest groups in the county, followed by the Methodist Episcopal Church, South.

Author William Faulkner was born in New Albany in 1897. He moved with his family to Oxford in 1902, and he based his fictional Yoknapatawpha County on Union, Tippah, Marshall, Panola, and Lafayette Counties. Author Borden Deal also spent part of his youth in Union County. Sam Mosley and Bob Johnson formed the popular Mosley and Johnson blues band in New Albany in 1967 and played together until Johnson's death in 1998.

By 1930 Union County's population had increased to 21,268, with whites outnumbering African Americans by a ratio of about four to one. New Albany had grown to 2,500 people, and the county had 250 industrial workers. In 1948 Morris Futorian, the Father of the Furniture Industry in Mississippi, opened a factory that initially employed 55 people. As in most other areas of northeastern Mississippi, Union County's predominance of family-owned farms had given way to an economy in which 62 percent of farms were run by tenants. Corn and cattle remained the dominant agricultural pursuits.

The county's population declined to just under 19,000 in 1960: 82 percent of those residents were white. About a quarter of Union County's working people held jobs in industry, with men working in furniture and timber and both women and men working in the apparel industry. Agriculture accounted for 28 percent of the workforce, with corn, soybeans, and livestock dominating.

As in most counties in northeastern Mississippi, Union County's 2010 population was predominantly white (81 percent), included a small but significant Hispanic/Latino minority (4.5 percent), and had increased over the preceding half century (to 27,134). The 2010 opening of a large Toyota plant in the community of Blue Springs spurred significant new economic activity.

Mississippi Encyclopedia Staff
University of Mississippi

Judd Hambrick, *Northeast Mississippi Daily Journal* (17 October 2010); Mississippi Blues Trail website, www.msbluestrail.org; Mississippi State Planning Commission, *Progress Report on State Planning in Mississippi* (1938); *Mississippi Statistical Abstract*, Mississippi State University (1952–2010); Charles Sydnor and Claude Bennett, *Mississippi History* (1939); University of Virginia Library, Historical Census Browser website, http://mapserver.lib.virginia.edu; Visit Mississippi website, www.visitmississippi.org; E. Nolan Waller and Dani A. Smith, *Growth Profiles of Mississippi's Counties, 1960–1980* (1985).

Unionists

From the time that Mississippi became a state in 1817 to the mid-1850s, most Mississippi voters, despite a great deal of political posturing, were content within the Union. They lived in a young, frontier state where rich and poor alike wanted nothing catastrophic to alter their chances for prosperity. Local and state concerns usually took precedence over divisive political wranglings in Washington, D.C. Immediately following statehood, Mississippians worked to build up

U

their state's standing in the Union and linked their personal security and their hopes for the future to state and national success. While slavery increasingly became a subject for debate and Mississippians defended it with greater ferocity with each passing decade, the great majority of Mississippi voters saw withdrawal from the Union as an ill-conceived, reckless alternative.

Backed by public opinion, pragmatic politicians comfortably embraced Unionism as a political philosophy beginning in the Jacksonian era. When South Carolina threatened to disrupt the Union during the Nullification Crisis of the early 1830s, many Mississippians were sympathetic, but the state legislature passed resolutions condemning secession. In 1850 the state voted to accept the Compromise of 1850 as a solution to regional conflict, and a year later Henry Stuart Foote, Mississippi's most prominent Unionist voice, defeated Jefferson Davis in the gubernatorial race. During the late 1850s, as the slavery debate reached a fever pitch in Congress, many Mississippians still believed that any differences between the slaveholding states and the federal government should be resolved within the confines of the Union.

Although they sought to distinguish themselves from their political opponents, the basic aims of Mississippi's antebellum Unionists differed little from those of the secessionist fire-eaters of the 1850s. Both groups sought to maintain political and social control in a patriarchal, biracial society. Both groups strongly defended slavery and sought to form working coalitions in a political environment that was often unstable. Doing so required them to embrace or create a primary issue to call their own, one that could both bring together fragmented factions and be easily communicated to the masses. They also had to balance state and local interests with ever-encroaching national concerns. While virtually all white Mississippians were in agreement on the slavery issue, potent arguments could be made concerning slavery's most volatile political by-product—the question of the limits of state and federal authority. Specifically, this question involved defining what course the state should take in the face of increasing federal transgressions. Mississippi Unionists argued for their own brand of states' rights while attempting to paint their opponents as extremists dedicated to promoting shadowy agendas by disrupting the national government.

Like their rivals, Unionists used fear to advance their cause. Radical action, they claimed, would disrupt the state's economy, lead to forced emancipation and bloodshed, and expose the state's residents to various indignities at the point of a bayonet. Because Mississippi was a young state dedicated to its own growth for much of the antebellum period, this argument was effective. The vast majority of Mississippians preferred the status quo as they sought to maintain or better their station.

However, national events in the 1850s finally overwhelmed the Unionist cause. The decade of Dred Scott, *Uncle Tom's Cabin*, and John Brown provided secessionist politicians with enough rhetorical ammunition to convince a majority of Mississippi's population that their security could be better assured outside rather than inside the Union. Still, some resistance to secession persisted even after Abraham Lincoln's election as president lit the fuse that would ignite civil war.

Generally speaking, Unionist sentiment was strongest in extreme northeastern Mississippi and in the southwestern part the state along the Mississippi River around Natchez. The northeastern region had few slaves, and much of the population resented the political authority of the state's slaveholding elite. In contrast, Natchez was home to remnants of the old Whig Party, natural political enemies of the Democrats who promoted secession. Natchez was also home to old-money cotton planters who had personal and economic relationships with northern interests that predated the slavery issue's dominance of national affairs. At the Mississippi Secession Convention of 1861, however, a decidedly vocal prosecession majority quickly drowned out any Unionist sentiment, and on 9 January 1861 the convention voted overwhelmingly to take the state out of the Union.

Ben Wynne
University of North Georgia

Richard Aubrey McLemore, ed., *A History of Mississippi*, 2 vols. (1973); John W. Wood, *Union and Secession in Mississippi* (1863); Ralph A. Wooster, *Journal of Mississippi History* (October 1954).

United Confederate Veterans

The United Confederate Veterans (UCV) was created in June 1889 when representatives of various Confederate veterans' groups met in New Orleans. They selected John B. Gordon to serve as the group's first commanding general. Gordon led the organization until his death in January 1904, when he was succeeded by Mississippian Stephen D. Lee. Unanimously elected commander in chief at the Nashville reunion, Lee told the assembled veterans that he had received "the highest honor that could be conferred upon a living Confederate." Lee remained highly popular and influential until his death in 1908.

The UCV held its first reunion in 1890 in Chattanooga, and the gathering was repeated annually until 1951, when just three aged survivors attended. The organization had a decidedly military structure: local units were called *camps*, each state comprised a *division*, officials at all levels were addressed by military titles, and veterans wore gray uniforms at reunions and other official functions.

The organization grew rapidly through the 1890s, buoyed in part by publicity in the pages of *Confederate Veteran* magazine (1893–1932), which became the UCV's official organ in 1894. Exact membership figures are impossible to ascertain, since the UCV never issued comprehensive statistics, but historian Gaines M. Foster has estimated that between a quarter and a third of all eligible veterans were members in 1903. At the annual reunion in Nashville in 1904, Adj. Gen. William E. Mickle reported that 1,563 camps existed, although some were dormant or had been absorbed, with 102 in Mississippi.

Mississippians exhibited great interest in the UCV. According to Foster, more than 85 percent of Mississippi counties boasted UCV camps. On 2 June 1891 the UCV held its second annual reunion in Jackson, a one-day affair that coincided with the unveiling of the city's imposing Confederate monument. More than five hundred Mississippi veterans attended the twenty-third annual state reunion, held in Greenwood in October 1913. Delegates participated in business meetings and took an "active interest . . . in the cause of dependent comrades" and widows. Greenwood provided a hospitable environment, conveying the veterans around the city in automobiles. Local United Daughters of the Confederacy members hosted an evening reception on the courthouse grounds, and one appreciative veteran confessed that he would "rather come to Greenwood than go to any other place except heaven." On the second day, veterans listened to additional welcoming speeches, heard an invocation by the divisional chaplain, elected officers for the upcoming year, and "swarmed" Mrs. N. V. Noblin after she sang a "charmingly rendered" version of "Dixie."

Veterans were most closely tied to their local camps, bonding based on common wartime experiences, holding local reunions, gathering with family and friends at barbecues and picnics, and receiving honors at public ceremonies including Confederate Memorial Day celebrations and the unveiling of Confederate monuments. The vast majority of UCV members were Democrats and members of mainline Protestant denominations.

The UCV peaked in the early 1900s. Death inexorably reduced its members, and by the time national reunions were held in Jackson in 1937 and Biloxi in 1930, 1946, and 1950, the organization was nearly moribund. Yet at its height, the UCV provided a framework for veterans to share wartime memories; support a host of benevolent causes, including veterans' homes for indigent comrades; and embrace a Lost Cause ideology that idealized the Confederacy and viewed the war as a holy crusade waged on behalf of states' rights.

Christopher Losson
St. Joseph, Missouri

Confederate Veteran (November 1913); Gaines M. Foster, *Ghosts of the Confederacy: Defeat, the Lost Cause, and the Emergence of the New South* (1987); *Minutes of the Fourteenth Annual Meeting and Reunion of the* United Confederate Veterans Held at Nashville, Tennessee on . . . *June 14, 15, 16, 1904* (1904).

United Daughters of the Confederacy

During the Civil War, Mississippians experienced destruction, deprivation, and defeat. The loss of life was compounded by the moral devastation of men who sought to defend their homeland and failed. In the years immediately following the war, many of Mississippi's white women sought to ease this emotional suffering by joining the movement to preserve the memory of Confederate veterans, most specifically through their involvement in ladies' memorial associations. Each 26 April, in towns across the state, these women engaged in a spring ritual of decorating the graves of their fallen heroes with flowers and Confederate flags. Beginning in the 1890s, however, the ways in which women commemorated the Confederacy expanded dramatically.

The Daughters of the Confederacy organized in Mississippi as early as 1893, one year prior to the founding of the general organization. What became the United Daughters of the Confederacy (UDC), which brought together in one body all southern women's Confederate organizations, was founded in Nashville, Tennessee, in 1894. UDC affiliate chapters formed almost immediately in Vicksburg, Meridian, and Baldwyn. On 26 April 1897 members of the three chapters met at the Meridian Public Library to create the UDC's Mississippi Division, making it one of the earliest state branches.

Mississippi women who joined the UDC in the first few decades of its existence continued the tradition of commemorating the Confederacy and its heroes, memorializations that were integral to the regional effort to preserve the values of the Old South that many white southerners believed had made it a superior civilization. Chief among those values was their commitment to the constitutional principle of states' rights. UDC members sought to honor these values as well as those who had fought for them during the Civil War. This commemorative tradition, known to contemporaries and later historians as the Lost Cause, already included decorating graves and monument building and played a vital part in what historian Charles Reagan Wilson has called the South's civil religion. Accordingly, the Daughters regarded both the southern past and the Confederate generation as sacred. Like other UDC members throughout the South, Mississippi's Daughters were also determined to perpetuate what they claimed were Confederate values and the "southern way of life" into the future. They built monuments, founded museums, wrote "true" histories of the war and its aftermath, and

U

monitored textbooks used by children in the public schools. UDC histories rejected any idea that slavery was the cause of the Civil War, celebrated the bravery of Confederates both in battle and on the home front, critiqued Radical Reconstruction as the rule of corrupt northern Republicans and incompetent African Americans, and interpreted the end of Reconstruction as the restoration of legitimate (and all-white) political leadership.

The Mississippi Division grew rapidly, reaching 48 chapters and 1,627 members by 1903 and 65 chapters and 2,347 members two years later. By World War I, the UDC had 124 Mississippi chapters with a membership of almost 4,300. Margaret Kinkhead Thompson, president of Yazoo City's Jefferson Davis Chapter, credited her chapter's success to the fact that its "officers [were] women of unusual executive ability." UDC members in Mississippi, like their sisters across the South, had a strong sense of mission and a quasi-religious zeal: Lizzie George Henderson of Greenwood argued that the organization had grown quickly because God wanted the Daughters to "do great things" for their country.

The organization attracted a variety of women, primarily upper-class, from all regions of the state. Some had experienced the Civil War firsthand, while others grew up in its aftermath, but they were literally daughters of the Confederate generation. Membership required blood descent from "men and women who served honorably in the Army, Navy, or Civil Service of the Confederate States of America, or who gave Material Aid to the Cause" or from former UDC members; however, "No Confederate ancestor who took the Oath of Allegiance before April 9, 1865, shall be eligible to be used for application for membership."

Mississippi's women were drawn to the UDC by a set of common goals—honoring the men and women who had made personal sacrifices for the region; controlling how the Civil War was remembered; and most important, ensuring that future generations of southerners continued to respect their Confederate ancestors.

The Mississippi UDC reached its zenith during World War I. The organization continued to exert influence in the state through its activities in the public school system and through the publication of its newsletter, *Our Heritage*. By the beginning of the twenty-first century, the organization's influence had waned as membership declined to about six hundred. In addition to gathering at an annual statewide convention, many of the state's twenty-eight chapters continued to host services commemorating Confederate Memorial Day.

Karen L. Cox
University of North Carolina
at Charlotte

Karen L. Cox, *Dixie's Daughters: The United Daughters of the Confederacy and the Preservation of Confederate Culture* (2003); Gaines M. Foster, *Ghosts of the Confederacy: Defeat, the Lost Cause, and the Emergence of the New South, 1865–1913* (1987); Caroline E. Janney, *Burying the Dead but Not the Past: Ladies' Memorial Associations and the Lost Cause* (2007); Mississippi Division, United Daughters of the Confederacy website, mississippiudc.homestead.com; Martha H. Swain, Elizabeth Anne Payne, Marjorie Julian Spruill, and Susan Ditto, eds., *Mississippi Women: Their Histories, Their Lives* (2003); United Daughters of the Confederacy website, www.hqudc.org.

United States v. Price

In *United States v. Price* (1966), the US Supreme Court unanimously ruled that the Fourteenth Amendment protects individuals against state action and that the federal government has jurisdiction to prosecute any violations of the amendment. In making this landmark decision, the Court made clear that federal authorities could step in when state and local authorities refused to prosecute individuals who committed civil rights violations.

The case arose after civil rights workers Michael Schwerner, James Chaney, and Andrew Goodman were kidnapped, assaulted, and then murdered by a gang of eighteen men, including deputy sheriff Cecil Ray Price, in Neshoba County, Mississippi, during the summer of 1964. When the State of Mississippi failed to indict the eighteen men, all of whom were members of the Ku Klux Klan, for the murders, US officials brought charges against the men in federal court for violating the victims' due process rights. A district judge dismissed the case on the grounds that the federal government lacked jurisdiction, and the United States appealed to the US Supreme Court.

The Court's opinion, written by Justice Abe Fortas, began by considering the scope of 18 USC sec. 242, which prohibits any individual from willfully depriving any person of any right, privilege, or immunity secured or protected by the Constitution or laws of the United States. The defendants were charged with substantive violations of sec. 242 for depriving Schwerner, Chaney, and Goodman of due process. The district court had ruled that only Price and two other police officers were subject to this charge since the other fifteen defendants were not acting "under color of law."

The US Supreme Court disagreed, holding that "private persons, jointly engaged with state officials in the prohibited action, are acting 'under color' of law for purposes of [sec. 242]. To act 'under color' of law does not require that the accused be an officer of the state. It is enough that he is a willful participant in a joint activity with the State or its agents." State officers had participated in every phase of the action, and the court ruled that anyone who had taken advantage of the state officers' participation had to be held accountable. Thus, all of the private defendants were "indictable as a principle acting under color of law."

The court then addressed the applicability of 18 USC sec. 241, which prohibited two or more people from conspiring to "injure, oppress, threaten, or intimidate any citizen in the free exercise or enjoyment of any right or privilege secured to him by the Constitution or laws of the United States." The district court had dismissed the charge against all eighteen defendants, holding that sec. 241 "did not include rights protected by the Fourteenth Amendment."

The Supreme Court again disagreed, holding that Fourteenth Amendment rights are protected under sec. 241; that as in the analysis of sec. 242, the Fourteenth Amendment protects individuals against state action; and that all eighteen defendants were acting under color of law. Therefore, the indictments against all eighteen defendants for violation of both secs. 242 and 241 were proper. With this decision, the Supreme Court made clear that "the federal government would no longer tolerate the complicity of local and state authorities in the suppression of the constitutional rights of southern blacks."

In 1967, an all-white jury, including a former member of the Klan, convicted seven of the eighteen defendants and sentenced them to between three and ten years in prison. Eight of the defendants were acquitted, and the jury reached no verdict on the remaining three, including Edgar Ray Killen, a preacher suspected of organizing the assault and murder. The film *Mississippi Burning* (1988) offered a fictionalized version of this trial.

Around the turn of the twenty-first century, the State of Mississippi reopened some of the cases involving civil rights violations that it had failed to prosecute four decades earlier. As part of this effort, Killen was convicted in 2005 of manslaughter in the deaths of Schwerner, Chaney, and Goodman and sentenced to three twenty-year terms in prison.

Amanda Brown
University of Mississippi

Howard Ball, *Murder in Mississippi: United States v. Price and the Struggle for Civil Rights* (2004); Douglas O. Linder, *Mississippi Law Journal* 72 (2002–3); *United States v. Price*, 383 U.S. 787 (1966).

Universal Negro Improvement Association (UNIA)

The Universal Negro Improvement Association (UNIA), a black nationalist group founded by Marcus Garvey in 1914, had at least fifty-seven divisions in Mississippi between 1920 and 1940. The state's first known division, located in Forest, received its charter before 1 August 1920. Garvey, a British subject originally from Jamaica, sought to unite all of the dispersed peoples of African ancestry in a "race first" alliance by establishing a black-ruled nation in Africa. To that end, the UNIA promoted political organization, race consciousness, and modernity. An emphasis on social, economic, physical, and political separation from whites made the UNIA different from class- or citizenship-oriented organizations such as the Communist Party and the National Association for the Advancement of Colored People, neither of which was as successful in Mississippi as the UNIA during its heyday in the 1920s, in large part because the UNIA's separatist orientation did not challenge Jim Crow segregation. In Mississippi, UNIA members became devoted to the ideals of self-determination, the liberation of Africa from white imperialists (a goal they called "African redemption"), and the creation of an independent black nation in Africa.

Twenty-three Mississippi counties had at least one UNIA division, but most divisions lay in the Yazoo-Mississippi Delta, where blacks constituted a majority of the population and cotton was cultivated. Bolivar County hosted at least seventeen divisions, the most of any county in the United States. Delta UNIA members were typically middle-aged, male cotton farmers who lived under oppressive conditions of economic dependence, racial violence, and disfranchisement. Other types of black laborers and even some professionals joined the UNIA in towns along the Gulf Coast and the Mississippi River. While many Delta divisions were relatively small, the coastal cities of Biloxi and Gulfport had large memberships, and Natchez, on the Mississippi River, was the biggest division, with at least 133 documented members in 1927. Unaffiliated supporters swelled these numbers for special events and guest speakers.

Ministers dominated the local leadership in at least 20 percent of Mississippi's divisions. Most notable was Adam Newson of Merigold, a town in Bolivar County that was home to four UNIA divisions. Newson organized a 1923 convention attended by more than fifteen hundred people, among them the UNIA high commissioner for Louisiana and Mississippi, Sylvester V. Robertson. The same year, Newson attended a regional convention of UNIA divisions in Pine City, Arkansas, illustrating the Mississippi divisions' links to divisions on the other side of the river. In 1924 Newson represented Mississippi as a delegate to the UNIA's annual convention in Harlem.

Local, regional, and international conventions were essential to the UNIA's goal of promoting race allegiance and unity. In Mississippi as in many places in the United States, UNIA divisions met in churches, sang Christian missionary hymns and UNIA anthems, and listened to readings of Garvey's addresses from the front page of the organization's Harlem-based weekly, *Negro World*. The organization emphasized education (especially Afrocentric education), racial dignity

U

and pride, and self-defense in the face of physical and sexual violence. Women participated in community nursing and service with the UNIA auxiliary Black Cross Nurses. Members showed their loyalty to the organization and to Garvey by providing funds to support numerous causes publicized in the *Negro World*, including the Marcus Garvey Defense Fund, which arose when Garvey was indicted and jailed for mail fraud. In Mound Bayou, 330 citizens signed a petition to the US pardon attorney, and thousands of other black Mississippians from Tutwiler to Gulfport rallied for Garvey's release from federal prison during 1926–27. The UNIA declined abruptly after Garvey's release from prison and deportation from the United States in 1927, but divisions in Tylertown, Sumner, and Natchez remained active well into the 1930s.

Mary G. Rolinson
Georgia State University

Robert A. Hill, ed., *The Marcus Garvey and Universal Negro Improvement Association Papers*, 7 vols. (1983–90); Mary G. Rolinson, *Grassroots Garveyism: The Universal Improvement Association in the Rural South, 1920–1927* (2007); Universal Negro Improvement Association, Records of the Central Division (New York), 1918–1959, Schomburg Center for Research in Black Culture, New York Public Library.

University of Mississippi

In 1839 Mississippi governor Alexander McNutt encouraged the legislature to establish a state university to protect funds set aside for education from being depleted, provide a body of teachers and tutors, and educate Mississippi's sons in their home state. Within two years legislators chose Oxford as the home of the school, and in 1844 the University of Mississippi was chartered. The board of trustees favored a classical curriculum focusing on ancient history, Greek, Latin, literature, philosophy, logic, and rhetoric. The first ten-month session began in 1848 with a president, four professors, and eighty students. Under the daily supervision of the faculty, students began and ended their days with communal prayers, participated in two literary societies, and formed several secret organizations, such as social fraternities and Greek-letter societies. Throughout the antebellum era, the college grew rapidly, adding new courses, professorial positions, and a chemistry lab, an astronomical observatory, and other scientific facilities.

On 2 February 1861 Mississippi seceded from the Union, and after the attack on Fort Sumter the students enlisted to fight for the Confederacy, forcing the university to close its doors. Some students joined the University Greys, a military

Ventress Hall, the second building erected on the campus of the University of Mississippi, at the time it housed the law school, ca. 1920. It currently houses the College of Liberal Arts (Ann Rayburn Paper Americana Collection, Department of Archives and Special Collections, J. D. Williams Library, University of Mississippi [rayburn_ann_26_24_002])

company of students, or the Lamar Rifles, a similar unit for Lafayette County; others returned to their home counties and joined units there. Both the Greys and Rifles became part of the 11th Mississippi Volunteer Infantry Regiment. The student soldiers participated in many of the war's most significant encounters, including Harpers Ferry, the First Battle of Bull Run, and Gettysburg.

With the end of the war, the board of trustees reconvened in July 1865 and appointed new faculty members and a chancellor. During the immediate postwar period, the university temporarily lowered admission standards to avoid rejecting veterans and kept costs down by eliminating tuition, allowing students to board in town, and permitting students to prepare meals in their rooms.

By 1871 the University of Mississippi was a thriving liberal arts college with an elective curriculum, an undergraduate college, a School of Law and Governmental Science, and a College of Agriculture. In 1882 the university began to admit women, though they remained barred from the law school and from living on campus. In 1885 Sarah Isom became the university's first female professor. Ninety years later, the Sarah Isom Center for Women's Studies was named in her honor.

During the Gilded Age student culture incorporated Greek fraternities and athletics, and as enrollment grew, the campus changed, adding such modernizations as a water tower, a sewer system, and electricity. Chancellor Andrew Kincannon worked to counter the university's elitist image through such reforms as the establishment of a student labor fund, a self-help bureau, a student honor system, and a student employment system. During World War II the university contributed to the war effort via the Accelerated Academic Program and offering a training course to military personnel. During this era, sports programs at the University of Mississippi as well as many other universities grew from small recreational programs to large and well-funded spectator sports.

From the end of the war through the 1950s, the university increased enrollment, constructed new buildings, and expanded its medical program. Racial tensions intensified along with the civil rights movement. The university avoided the issue of integration until James Meredith began an effort to enroll in the early 1960s. In spite of massive resistance by the state, the university, and the board of trustees, the US Court of Appeals for the 5th District ordered his admission, and he arrived on campus in September 1962. With Gov. Ross Barnett continuing to insist that Mississippi's schools would not integrate and the legislature attempting to find other ways to bar Meredith, a riot broke out on campus on the night of 30 September, and two people were killed. In response, the Kennedy administration nationalized the Mississippi National Guard and ordered federal troops to campus, and with the protection of federal marshals, Meredith enrolled on 1 October. Despite harassment, Meredith graduated from the University of Mississippi on 18 August 1963 with a major in political science and minors in French and history.

The legacy of this violent opposition to desegregation haunted the image of the university for decades, but beginning in the 1970s, the university also experienced substantial growth and renewed its commitment to academic excellence. Taking advantage of its ties to William Faulkner, the university initiated the annual Faulkner and Yoknapatawpha Conference in 1974. The following year saw the inauguration of the Chancellor's Symposium on Southern History, while the Center for the Study of Southern Culture was created in 1977 and Willie Morris became the school's first writer in residence in 1980.

University leaders, faculty, staff, and students continued to address controversies over issues involving Confederate imagery, especially at sporting events. Since 1983 the university has worked to dissociate itself from the Confederate flag, an effort that has had increasing success. Robert Khayat, who

served as the school's chancellor from 1995 to 2009, set a goal of making the University of Mississippi "a great public university," and to that end, the school has added an honors college and new programs in accountancy, physical acoustics, international studies, and journalism. By the second decade of the twenty-first century, enrollment topped twenty-three thousand.

Mary Clingerman Yaran
Washington, D.C.

Allen Cabaniss, *A History of the University of Mississippi* (1950); Charles W. Eagles, *The Price of Defiance: James Meredith and the Integration of Ole Miss* (2009); David G. Sansing, *Making Haste Slowly: The Troubled History of Higher Education in Mississippi* (1990); David G. Sansing, *The University of Mississippi: A Sesquicentennial History* (1999).

University of Mississippi Gospel Choir

The University of Mississippi Gospel Choir (UMGC) is an African American student-run singing group. Founded in 1974 as the Black Student Union Choir, the choir was one of the first African American student organizations on the historically white campus. In 2001 the choir received a Grammy nomination for its debut album, *Send Up the Praise*. The choir's history and success are a source of pride and encouragement for African American students and alumni. The choir is also a significant symbol of the changes at the university since the violent 1962 riots over desegregation.

In 1974 Otis Sanford, president of the Black Student Union, and his roommate, Jerry Christian, recruited Linda

The University of Mississippi Gospel Choir performs in front of the Lyceum prior to the Christmas tree lighting, 2012 (Photograph by Robert Jordan, courtesy University of Mississippi University Communications)

Redmond, a freshman musician, to help start the Black Student Union Choir. Twelve years after the university's integration, only about three hundred African American undergraduates were enrolled. In this culturally alien and at times hostile environment, the choir provided spiritual and social support for its African American members. The founding of a gospel choir represented a significant moment in the process of integration. By the early 1970s African Americans had started to make their mark on the university's student politics and athletics, but the Black Student Union Choir brought a uniquely African American religious artistic expression to the campus. Rooted in the welcoming tradition of the black church, the choir did not require participants to audition, a practice it continues to this day, and it at times has had more than one hundred members. Performing a selection of contemporary gospel songs, anthems, and spirituals, the students sang at campus concerts as well as at members' home congregations.

In 1991 the choir changed its name to the University of Mississippi Gospel Choir and sought funding as a student organization independent of the Black Student Union. The new name indicated African American students' growing confidence at the university and their continuing desire for integration: the choir wanted not just to be granted a place but to be recognized as a part of the university. In April 1998, accompanied by gospel musicians recruited from Memphis and assisted by Jackson-based Malaco Records, the choir recorded a live concert in the university's Education Auditorium. In 1999 Malaco released the concert on a CD, *Send Up the Praise*, that brought attention from both the gospel world and national media. In 2000 the choir appeared on Black Entertainment Television's *Gospel Explosion*, and in 2001 the CD received a Grammy nomination for Best Gospel Choir or Chorus Album. The morning of the awards ceremony, NBC's *Today Show* ran a piece on the choir, placing the students' achievement against the backdrop of the University of Mississippi's troubled racial history.

The choir's success has raised its profile. In October 2006, forty-four years after James Meredith became the first African American to attend class at the University of Mississippi, UMGC sang at the dedication of the civil rights monument at the heart of the campus. In 2014 the choir celebrated its fortieth anniversary with a concert at the Gertrude C. Ford Center for the Performing Arts on the university campus.

Peter Slade
Ashland University

Peter Slade, *Mississippi Folklife* (Fall 1998); University of Mississippi Gospel Choir website, dos.orgsync.com/org/umgc/home.

University of Mississippi Medical Center

Prior to 1903 the state of Mississippi had no medical school. That year, the University of Mississippi's Oxford campus began offering a two-year certificate program, a common configuration in the first half of the twentieth century. Graduates finished their medical education at four-year schools affiliated with hospitals. At midcentury, however, the state had a desperate need for more hospital beds and physicians. In response, the Mississippi legislature created the University of Mississippi Medical Center in 1950. The center would train health professionals, provide specialized care to Mississippians, and conduct research that would lead to new ways of treating illness. Five years later, the Medical Center—a single T-shaped building that housed the School of Medicine and the two-wing University Hospital—opened on 155 acres of state-owned land in Jackson.

By the second decade of the twenty-first century, the Medical Center had grown into a major complex of five schools and four hospitals. Nursing, which had been a department in the medical school in Oxford, moved to the Medical Center in 1956, and in 1958 it became the state's first baccalaureate program in nursing. The School of Health Related Professions was added in 1971, with the School of Dentistry following in 1973. In 2001 the graduate program became the School of Graduate Studies in the Health Sciences.

The vast majority of the state's health professionals have come from one of the Medical Center's educational programs. In 2012–13 student enrollment—medical students, dental students, nursing students, residents or fellows, health-related-professions students, and graduate students—topped twenty-five hundred. The faculty includes about one thousand full- and part-time members, while the Medical Center employs more than nine thousand people.

The campus now covers 164 acres and includes the Blair E. Batson Hospital for Children (completed in 1997), the Winfred L. Wiser Hospital for Women and Infants (1999), the Wallace Conerly Critical Care Hospital (2001), and the flagship University Hospital (2006). The hospitals have a total of 722 beds and treat approximately twenty-seven thousand patients annually. In addition, more than five hundred thousand outpatient and emergency room visits occur each year. In partnership with Jackson State University and Tougaloo College, the Medical Center bought the nearly abandoned Jackson Mall, one mile west of the Medical Center, and turned it into a thriving center that houses the Medical Center's teaching clinics and cancer institute as well as Mississippi Department of Health clinics and offices.

In 1955 the Medical Center depended solely on state appropriations for its nine-million-dollar budget. By 2016 the overall budget was approximately $1.6 billion, and only

10 percent of that amount came from state appropriations. The Medical Center accounts for 10 percent of the Jackson metro area's economy and 2 percent of the state economy.

Dr. David L. Pankratz, dean of the medical school when it was still in Oxford, oversaw the move to Jackson and the expansion of the curriculum, becoming dean and Medical Center director. He was succeeded by Dr. Robert Marston, who led the Medical Center's peaceful racial integration of its workforce, patient facilities, and student body. Marston was succeeded by Dr. Robert Carter and Dr. Robert E. Blount. The Medical Center has subsequently been headed by a single physician holding the titles of vice chancellor for health affairs and dean of the School of Medicine, the University of Mississippi: Norman C. Nelson (1973–94), Wallace Conerly (1994–2003), Dan Jones (2003–9); James Keeton (2009–15), and LouAnn Woodward (2015–).

The Medical Center has been the site of historic medical advances and home to some of the world's most distinguished scientists. Dr. Arthur C. Guyton was the first chair of the Department of Physiology and Biophysics and authored the *Textbook of Medical Physiology*, originally published in 1956, revised numerous times, and still the most widely used physiology textbook in the world. Guyton also changed the field of physiology with discoveries and scientific observations that gave the world a new understanding of the cardiovascular system. Dr. James D. Hardy, chair of the Department of Surgery from 1955 until 1987, performed the world's first lung transplant at the Medical Center in 1963. In 1964 he performed the world's first heart transplant, placing the heart of a chimpanzee into a human recipient. Other notable achievements at the Medical Center have included the pioneering of deep brain stimulation, innovations and refinements in the treatment of patients with end-stage renal disease and one of the nation's first thirteen artificial kidney units, major contributions to the understanding and treatment of high-risk pregnancies and preeclampsia, the development of interventional radiology for the removal of tumors when conventional surgery is not possible, the development of farm-raised catfish as a model to study the human immune system, and important research on the toxicity of organophosphates. Medical Center scientists have also made significant contributions to the understanding of diseases that disproportionately affect Mississippians (for example, heart disease and hypertension) and have been leaders in national clinical trials of new drugs and treatments. The Medical Center is a partner with Jackson State University and Tougaloo College in the landmark Jackson Heart Study, the largest study ever undertaken of heart disease risk factors in the African American population.

Janis Quinn
University of Mississippi
Medical Center

Lucie Robertson Bridgforth, *Medical Education in Mississippi: A History of the School of Medicine* (1984); Martin L. Dalton, *Annals of Thoracic Surgery* (November 1995); James D. Hardy, in *Jonathan E. Rhoads: Eightieth Birthday Symposium* (1989); Janis Quinn, *This Week at UMC* (22 September 2000); *Neurosurgery News* (July 2001); University of Mississippi Medical Center website, www.umc.edu.

University of Mississippi School of Law

On 27 February 1854 the Mississippi legislature created a "professorship of governmental science and law" at the University of Mississippi. The act was passed at the urging of the Mississippi bar, whose members were concerned about confusion regarding just what laws and legal systems were in force in a state where US law, traditions of Native American law, the civil law systems of both France and Spain, and English common law were all a part of the past and present legal system. In addition, many Mississippi leaders had real concern that young Mississippians who went away to study in law in the northern states might pick up "troubling" ideas about the institution of slavery. At the time, only three US public universities—Maryland, Virginia, and Pennsylvania—had law programs.

On 2 October 1857 the seven members of the first law class at the University of Mississippi assembled in a classroom with Prof. William Forbes Stearns. In spring of that year, the legislature had passed an act granting immediate admission to the state bar to any graduate of the university's law program. For a while, the apprenticeship system, in which one read law in the law office of a member of the bar and then gained bar admission by taking an oral examination administered by a state judge, remained the usual way to gain entrance into the legal profession. However, by 1861 65 of the university's 170 law students had won admission to the bar by earning a bachelor of laws degree.

When the university reopened after the Civil War, Prof. L. Q. C. Lamar taught the law department's students, most of whom were Confederate veterans, from 1866 to 1870. In 1887 Lamar became the first former university law professor appointed to serve on the US Supreme Court. The department closed again from 1874 to 1877 because of a drastic drop in the university's student enrollment caused by Reconstruction. In 1911 what was by then called the School of Law moved into its own campus building, Lamar Hall (now Ventress Hall). Within the next decade, the School of Law's faculty included the dean of law and a law professor as well as a few assistant professors recruited on a part-time basis from among local attorneys, and a few women began to enroll as students. In 1921 the degree program was expanded from two to three years. In 1928 the first volume of the *Mississippi Law Journal* was published.

The law school received accreditation from the American Association of Law Schools in 1922 but lost it in December 1930, partly because Lamar Hall was too small to house the student body and faculty and to accommodate an adequate law library but primarily because Gov. Theodore G. Bilbo had pressured the university's board of trustees to fire Dean Thomas Kimbrough and two other law professors who had opposed the governor politically. The school regained accreditation just two years later after the dean and the professors were rehired and the law school moved into a spacious new building on campus known today as Farley Hall. The number of students and faculty declined again during World War II but rebounded to record levels after veterans returned and enrolled.

During the 1960s the School of Law admitted the first African American students, and in 1967 future Mississippi Supreme Court justice Reuben V. Anderson became the school's first African American graduate. The first African American faculty member, A C Wharton, joined the school on a part-time basis in 1974. And in 1970 Catherine V. Sullivan became the first woman to teach full-time on the faculty. In 1973 the school was renamed the University of Mississippi Law Center, and five years later it moved to a new location next to its former building. It moved to its current location in 2011, when it became the Robert C. Khayat Law Center. Today, the Law Center has some five hundred students and a forty-member faculty and houses the Mississippi Judicial College, the Mississippi Law Research Institute, the National Sea Grant Law Center, the Mississippi-Alabama Sea Grant Legal Program, the Center for Continuing Legal Education, the Business Law Institute, and the National Center for Remote Sensing, Air, and Space Law.

Michael de L. Landon
University of Mississippi

Michael de L. Landon, *The University of Mississippi School of Law: A Sesquicentennial History* (2006); David G. Sansing, *The University of Mississippi: A Sesquicentennial History* (1999).

University of Southern Mississippi

Located in Hattiesburg, the University of Southern Mississippi (USM) is a comprehensive doctoral and research university. It is a nationally recognized institution, offering undergraduate and graduate degree programs in a variety of disciplines and serving approximately sixteen thousand students.

The seeds of USM were sown as early as 1877, when the movement to establish a state teachers college began. After two normal college bills failed to pass the state legislature, T. P. Scott, a member of the Mississippi Teachers Association and head of schools in Brookhaven, launched a publicity campaign. The campaign reached fruition when House Bill 204 was signed into law on 30 March 1910. With that event, Mississippi Normal College became the first state-supported school for teacher training. Forrest County and the city of Hattiesburg issued bonds for $250,000 to build the school on 120 acres of land donated by A. A. Montague, T. E. Ross, and H. A. Camp. The classroom doors opened on 18 September 1912, and the school welcomed a total of 876 students during its inaugural year.

Joseph Anderson Cook served as the school's first president, persevering through a flu epidemic, World War I, and marauding goats on campus. In those first years, the school awarded both two-term certificates and six-term diplomas. The first baccalaureate degree was awarded in 1922 to Biloxi native Kathryn Swetman.

After a change of name to State Teachers College in 1924, a demonstration school was constructed on the campus in 1927 for the training of student teachers. In 1929 the Southern Association of Colleges and Secondary Schools accredited the school for the first time. The school offered extension courses in several counties and built a solid music program.

No longer strictly a teachers college, the school changed its name again in 1940, becoming Mississippi Southern College. It gained nationwide recognition through its Pride of Mississippi Marching Band and its athletic programs. On 27 February 1962 it officially became the University of Southern Mississippi. The first African American students were admitted in 1965. As the twentieth century gave way to the twenty-first, USM consisted of five colleges and offered online classes as an alternative to some traditional classes. USM now sees itself as "a national university for South Mississippi and the Gulf States." Notable centers on its campuses include the Center for International Education, the Polymer Science Institute, and the Center for Oral History and Cultural Heritage.

Among the many notable USM alumni are political figures Evelyn Gandy and Phil Bryant; musician Jimmy Buffett; chef Cat Cora; football stars Brett Favre, Sammy Winder, and Ray Guy; and broadcast journalists Chuck Scarborough and Kathleen Koch.

As early as 1947 USM had a presence on the Gulf Coast through classes organized at the Methodist Campgrounds in Biloxi. As need for the classes grew, they moved to Mary L. Michael Junior High School in 1958 and then to Keesler Air Force Base in 1964. Class offerings were then expanded to include more teaching sites in Harrison and

Jackson Counties, and in 1972 USM Gulf Coast was established on the Long Beach site that had formerly housed Gulf Park College for Women. The university was officially named a dual-campus system in 1998 but the coastal campus offered only junior- and senior-level courses until 2002, when the Mississippi Supreme Court granted permission for freshman- and sophomore-level classes to be held there. In addition to the Long Beach campus and teaching centers on Keesler Air Force Base and at the Stennis Space Center, USM now offers classes at several other coastal locations, including the Gulf Coast Research Laboratory, the J. L. Scott Marine Education Center and Aquarium, and the Hydrographic Science Research Center. In 2013 Rodney D. Bennett became USM's first African American president.

Diane DeCesare Ross
University of Southern Mississippi

Chester M. Morgan, *Dearly Bought, Deeply Treasured: The University of Southern Mississippi, 1912–1987* (1987); University of Southern Mississippi website, www.usm.edu.

Urban Areas

Rural scenes of cotton fields, county fairs, blues music, and country churches and groceries dominate popular and scholarly depictions of life in Mississippi. But the enduring image of the state as equal parts plantation pastoral and impoverished backwater has obscured the importance of cities and towns in the state's history. The small place of cities and towns in Mississippi's self-image and national reputation aside, urban centers have served as sites of some of the greatest dramas in the state's history and have played a crucial role in the development and transmission of political ideologies and economic systems.

Antebellum Natchez typified the peculiar role of the urban environment in Mississippi's identity. Visitors remarked on the beauty of the city's homes and gardens, and the district's residents cultivated an image of agrarian gentility by erecting Greek columns and furnishing their cotton palaces with expensive staircases and ornate woodwork. Behind those pastoral showplaces, however, lurked the dirty work of generating and accumulating capital. On wharves, blacks and immigrants busily loaded and unloaded cotton and goods from steamships; in filthy alleys and dives, laborers laughed, gambled, and fought; and in slave pens, planters, traders, and slaves engaged in high-stakes dramas of accumulation, deception, and survival. The plantation and city thus combined to form what the historian David R. Goldfield has called an "urban hybrid." Cotton dominated every aspect of life in Natchez, but the district's plantations depended on urban institutions such as wharves and slave pens to raise and distribute crops. The most ancient and magnolia-scented of Mississippi's Old South images, in short, derived from crowded streets and filthy docks, not just black soil and river bluffs.

After the Civil War, Mississippi aggressively courted industrialists and investors. An act of the 1892 legislature exempted factories from taxation, and other policies made the state hospitable for railroads, insurance agencies, and utility companies. While the state remained overwhelmingly rural, towns took on added importance as centers of financial power that linked Mississippians to the growing national economy. The infusion of Yankee cash and the ascendancy of a capitalist ethos that made banks, railroads, and utility companies crucial to the state's economy did little to change Mississippi's national reputation as a languid preserve of agrarianism. This was no accident. As historian C. Vann Woodward wrote, southerners reacted to industrialization and urbanization with a "divided mind." To offset the increasing dependency on outside investors, the eroded authority of cotton aristocrats, and the capitulation to Yankee modes of production, champions of the New South dressed their new world in the nostalgic fashions of the plantation past. The more they depended on urban services and the national economy, the harder Mississippians tried to convince themselves and the rest of the country of their uniqueness and independence.

Mississippi's cities in the late nineteenth and early twentieth centuries tended to concentrate more on trade than on manufacturing. Along with Jackson and Natchez, Biloxi, Meridian, and Greenville had periods of significant urban growth. Nonetheless, when rural Mississippians started leaving agriculture in large numbers, they most often headed to Memphis, Chicago, or New Orleans rather than to one of Mississippi's urban areas.

The reliance of urban centers on outside capital ultimately affected social policies within Mississippi. When African Americans in Jackson protested the suppression of their civil rights, government officials such as Gov. Paul B. Johnson, beholden to the Mississippi State Sovereignty Commission and the Citizens Councils, called on white Mississippians to resist federal civil rights legislation. The business elite of Jackson, who owed much of their prosperity to Yankee investors and federal aid, urged compliance with federal policies and worked to combat the kind of lawlessness and violence that would disrupt economic development. Both the Jackson Chamber of Commerce issued an official statement denouncing resistance to the Civil Rights Act of 1964. Business leaders did not abandon their belief in Jim Crow but prioritized economic prosperity over an antiquated racial orthodoxy. Urban development, in short, led an important pillar of the state's power structure to withdraw its support from massive resistance to civil rights.

U

Mississippi's towns and cities thus have had a disproportionate influence on the politics and economy of this overwhelmingly rural state.

Thomas John Carey
University of Mississippi

James C. Cobb, *The Selling of the South: The Southern Crusade for Indus-
trial Development, 1936–1980* (1982); David R. Goldfield, *Cotton Fields
and Skyscrapers: Southern City and Region, 1607–1980* (1982); Matthew D.
Lassiter, *The Silent Majority: Suburban Politics in the Sunbelt South* (2006);
Charles Sallis and John Quincy Adams, in *Southern Businessmen and
Desegregation*, ed. Elizabeth Jacoway and David R. Colburn (1982); C. Vann
Woodward, *Origins of the New South, 1877–1913* (1951).

Several of the young men whom Vaiden mentored, among them Feduccia, Sammy Ray, and Billy Smith-Vaniz, went on to distinguished careers in science. Staples became a writer and immortalized Vaiden in her short story "The Bird Collection."

Vaiden died on 17 June 1975.

Jerome A. Jackson
Florida Gulf Coast University

Beauvais Staples McCaddon, *Virginia Quarterly Review* (Autumn 1993); Merritt Gordon Vaiden, *Oologist* (1940); Merritt Gordon Vaiden, *Wilson Bulletin* (1940); Merritt Gordon Vaiden with J. O. Smith and W. E. Ayres, *Mississippi Agriculture Experiment Station Bulletin* 290 (1931).

Vaiden, Merritt Gordon

(1893–1975) Naturalist

Merritt Gordon Vaiden was born in Jackson, Mississippi, on 31 October 1893 and was educated at the University of Kentucky, Mississippi College, and Bowling Green Business University. He worked for a time in Arkansas, where he met and married Carolyn Joyce, but soon moved to Rosedale, Mississippi, where he worked as a bookkeeper for plantations in the Mississippi Delta. His professional work led him to write of the economics of cotton production in 1931 and 1932, but he is best known for his avocation, studying birds.

Vaiden had a lifelong passion for birds and began collecting them in 1919. His initial collection was destroyed by fire, and he renewed his bird collecting in 1937, preparing scientific study skins and ultimately amassing a personal collection of more than thirty-two hundred birds. In 1943 he taught his wife how to prepare the skins, and she ultimately prepared about two thousand of the specimens. In the late 1960s the collection was donated to the University of Mississippi as a teaching and research collection. Vaiden was a keen observer of nature and carefully recorded his observations, publishing short articles on Mississippi birds in regional and national scientific journals. He regularly corresponded with professional ornithologists, and his observations of Mississippi birds are frequently cited in scientific publications.

On 3 May 1959 Vaiden gathered a number of his friends, especially the young people he considered promising naturalists, and formally organized the Mississippi Delta Naturalists' Club. The group elected Alan Feduccia of Cleveland as president, Edgar Grissom of Cleveland as vice president, and Beauvais Staples of Rosedale as secretary-treasurer. The club began planning a journal to chronicle members' scientific efforts, and the first of the *Mississippi Delta Naturalists' Club Occasional Papers* was issued in July 1960 and included Vaiden's article, "Interesting Mississippi Delta Birds." Each subsequent issue was four pages in length, and most included articles by Vaiden. The journal changed its name to *Mississippi Naturalists' Club: The Mississippi Kite, Occasional Papers*, in October 1962 and continued publishing until September 1967.

Van Dorn, Earl

(1820–1863) Confederate General

Confederate general Earl Van Dorn was born on 17 September 1820 in Port Gibson, Mississippi, the son of Peter Van Dorn and Sophia Caffery Van Dorn. Peter Van Dorn, a prominent attorney and judge, sent Earl and his younger brother to Baltimore to be educated shortly after the death of their mother in 1830. When Judge Van Dorn passed away in early 1837, Earl decided to pursue a career as a professional soldier. He won an appointment to the US Military Academy and graduated fifty-second among the fifty-six cadets in the Class of 1842, amassing 183 demerits along the way. Van Dorn excelled as a horseman at West Point and was commissioned a second lieutenant of infantry. While serving in Alabama he met sixteen-year-old Martha Caroline Godbold, whom he married in late 1843 after a whirlwind courtship.

Van Dorn first saw extensive combat during the Mexican War, where he fought in major battles under both Zachary Taylor and Winfield Scott and was breveted captain and major for gallantry and earned recognition from superior officers. After returning to the United States, Van Dorn served in a number of posts before spending the better part of three years in Pascagoula, where he was assigned as secretary-treasurer to a hospital for disabled veterans. Promoted to captain in the 2nd Cavalry in May 1855, Van Dorn went to Texas, where he fought in several engagements against Comanches. During one battle he was struck by two arrows and seriously wounded. In 1860 he resigned his commission and returned to Mississippi.

Van Dorn entered Confederate ranks as a colonel in March 1861 and returned to Texas to recruit Federal troops into the Confederate Army. While there, he also captured an unarmed steamer, *Star of the West*, near Galveston and negotiated the surrender of several hundred Union troops.

V

He won promotion to brigadier in June 1861 and to major general three months later.

His star seemingly ascendant, Van Dorn was dispatched to the Trans-Mississippi in early 1862 to command Confederate forces led by two squabbling officers, Sterling Price and Benjamin McCullough. Van Dorn's first battle as army commander was an unmitigated disaster. Despite the fact that many of his men were ill and poorly trained, Van Dorn marched them into northwestern Arkansas, where they encountered Union forces under Samuel Curtis near Pea Ridge. Van Dorn was ill and confined to an ambulance for a portion of the time, while poor weather hampered movements and added to the lengthening sick list. In a two-day battle that commenced on 7 March 1862, Van Dorn unwisely split his force and failed to coordinate the movements of his dispersed units. McCullough was killed on the first day, as was his second in command. On the second day, Van Dorn's men, fatigued and hungry, faced another obstacle when their ammunition began to run out. Van Dorn reluctantly retreated, defeated as a consequence of poor reconnaissance and intelligence, an army ill-prepared for the rigors of such a campaign, and his difficulties in managing the battle, which helped secure Missouri for the Union. Ordered to bring his army across the Mississippi River, Van Dorn was excoriated by Arkansans, who charged that he left the state defenseless and vulnerable.

He was soon ordered to command a department, with his main priority the defense of Vicksburg. He acquitted himself well in this endeavor but triggered a furor when he declared martial law in eleven Mississippi counties plus those in Louisiana east of the Mississippi River. Van Dorn did so in part to stem a growing trade in cotton between the lines, but aroused citizens complained vociferously to Richmond that Van Dorn was a tyrant. Confederate authorities instructed Van Dorn to revoke his order, which he did three months after issuing it. The situation did not improve for Van Dorn: an assault on Baton Rouge ended in defeat in mid-August, while a boldly conceived attack on Corinth in early October failed to dislodge defenders under Union general William S. Rosecrans. The Corinth Campaign found Van Dorn repeating many of the same errors he had committed at Pea Ridge: poor intelligence, expecting too much of his troops, and ordering frontal assaults that winnowed his ranks. Stung by criticism after the failure at Corinth, Van Dorn appeared before a court of inquiry in November 1862. Although the court cleared him of the charges, many Mississippians were thoroughly disenchanted with Van Dorn. Authorities in Richmond relieved him of command of his department, perhaps influenced by reports of Van Dorn's reputed propensity for drinking and womanizing.

Van Dorn received a cavalry command and achieved his greatest wartime triumph when he led thirty-five hundred troopers from Grenada to Holly Springs, where he captured and destroyed an immense Union supply depot on 20 December 1862, thwarting Ulysses S. Grant's intended overland drive to Vicksburg. The next year Van Dorn again drove into Tennessee, helping Confederates score a victory at Thompson's Station in early March. These two successful raids suggest that Van Dorn had found his niche as a cavalryman, but Thompson's Station proved to be his last engagement.

On 7 May 1863 he was murdered by Dr. George Peters, who claimed that Van Dorn had "violated the sanctity of [Peters's] home" and engaged in an affair with his wife, Jessie Helen Peters. Others maintained that Peters assassinated the general for political purposes. Whatever Peters's motives, Van Dorn's death ended the life of a general who never lived up to the potential many saw in him at the outset of the war.

Christopher Losson
St. Joseph, Missouri

Arthur B. Carter, *The Tarnished Cavalier: Major General Earl Van Dorn, C.S.A.* (1999); Robert G. Hartje, *Van Dorn: The Life and Times of a Confederate General* (1967); Ezra Warner, *Generals in Gray: Lives of the Confederate Commanders* (1959).

Van Dorn's Raid

In the fall of 1862 Ulysses S. Grant and the Union Army set their sights on Vicksburg. Grant formulated a plan to march his thirty-one men from Grand Junction, Tennessee, south into the interior of Mississippi and approach Vicksburg from the rear. He would supply his army by repairing the Mississippi Central Railroad. He ordered his trusted subordinate, Maj. Gen. William Tecumseh Sherman, to advance simultaneously from Memphis with a column of infantry and rendezvous at Oxford.

The Union Army advanced into Mississippi during the first week of November 1862. Lt. Gen. John C. Pemberton's twenty-four thousand Confederate forces, positioned near Holly Springs, quickly fell back behind the Tallahatchie River. Pemberton considered giving battle at this new position. However, a strong Union contingent under Gen. Alvin Hovey landed near Greenville and advanced inland to threaten the Confederate railroad supply line near Grenada in Pemberton's rear. Although Hovey never seriously damaged the railroad, the movement caused Pemberton to move his forces farther south. By the first week of December, Confederate forces had retreated to the Yalobusha River.

During this period, political intrigue began to surface in the Union high command. One of Grant's subordinates,

Maj. Gen. John A. McClernand, used his political clout to obtain permission to organize an independent army to capture Vicksburg. In the fall of 1862, McClernand recruited and organized new regiments and forwarded them to Memphis. By early December, the majority of McClernand's command had arrived in Memphis, while the ambitious general remained in Illinois eagerly awaiting orders to proceed downriver.

Grant decided to break the stalemate. He ordered Sherman to return to Memphis to take command of the forces assembled there, embark downriver, and capture Vicksburg. In essence, Grant ordered Sherman to take McClernand's army. Throughout Sherman's movement, Grant's army would maintain pressure on Pemberton's forces. On 20 December Sherman's forces departed from Memphis.

Pemberton ordered a counteroffensive. He ordered Gen. Earl Van Dorn to capture the main Union supply depot at Holly Springs. With three brigades numbering roughly thirty-five hundred cavalrymen, Van Dorn's column departed from Grenada on 16 December. Van Dorn's men moved east toward Houston, Mississippi, and arrived at the town around noon on 17 December. Turning his men north, he reached Pontotoc the next day. To deceive the Federals, the Confederate column continued north through New Albany before turning west off the Ripley Road toward Holly Springs. By the evening of 19 December, his column rested between twelve and fifteen miles from Holly Springs.

On 20 December, Union troops were billeted in three major concentrations in Holly Springs. Union infantry occupied the courthouse area and railroad depot in town, while six companies of Union cavalrymen lay encamped near the city limits. The three concentrations were not in ready supporting distance of each other. Col. Robert Murphy, the Union commander at Holly Springs, failed to heed warnings from Grant about enemy activity and, as a result, his five hundred men lay in camp as dawn approached.

A Confederate officer later recalled Van Dorn's plan of attack: "The first or head of the column was to dash into and capture the infantry camped in front of us; the second, following immediately after the first, was to sweep by the encampment, move straight into the town until it reached the street leading north to the fair grounds, then wheel to the right and charge the cavalry camp; the third . . . was to dash through the town, disregarding everything until it struck the infantry occupying the public square." The attack ended in a complete success. Confederate cavalrymen rode roughshod over the infantry camp. The second column sent toward the Union cavalry camp found the soldiers in line for morning inspection. Although startled, the Union cavalrymen managed to mount a brief defense before being overwhelmed and forced to surrender.

The fight had ended by eight o'clock in the morning. Van Dorn's men captured supplies worth $1.5 million, according to estimates by the Confederate commander. Rebels quickly broke open food stores and supplied themselves with new arms. Van Dorn consigned all the remaining stores to fire, and by day's end the Union supply depot lay in ashes.

In the aftermath, Van Dorn's command rode into West Tennessee before returning to Pemberton's army and receiving a hero's welcome. After the destruction of his main supply base, Grant retreated to Tennessee. Sherman landed north of Vicksburg at Chickasaw Bayou and suffered a bloody repulse. Grant's first attempt to capture Vicksburg had ended in failure.

Matt Atkinson
Vicksburg National Military Park

Edwin C. Bearss, *The Vicksburg Campaign*, vol. 1, *Vicksburg Is the Key* (1985); Arthur B. Carter, *The Tarnished Cavalier: Major General Earl Van Dorn, C.S.A.* (1999); Robert G. Hartje, *Van Dorn: The Life and Times of a Confederate General* (1967).

Vardaman, James K.
(1861–1930) Thirty-Sixth Governor, 1904–1908

In 1903, for the first time, the people of Mississippi nominated the candidates for all public offices, from the governor down to the local constable, via a popular primary election. The first governor chosen under this new system was James Kimble Vardaman, an effective campaigner who was known fondly by his followers as the White Chief.

Vardaman, who was born in Jackson County, Texas, on 26 July 1861, was reared in Yalobusha County, Mississippi. After reading law, he was admitted to the bar and began practicing in Winona in 1882. Vardaman also edited the *Winona Advance*. He moved to Greenwood in 1890 to edit the *Greenwood Enterprise*, and in 1896 he founded the *Greenwood Commonwealth*. His first love was politics, however, and beginning in 1890 he represented Leflore County in the State House of Representatives, becoming Speaker in 1894.

After the United States declared war on Spain in 1898, Vardaman enlisted in the army, eventually rising to the rank of colonel. He was stationed in Santiago, Cuba, from August 1898 to May 1899.

Vardaman sought to become the Democratic Party's gubernatorial candidate in 1895 and again in 1899, but party leaders refused to give him the nomination. After those disappointing losses, Vardaman became a supporter of the popular primary law. In Mississippi's first primary election he defeated Frank Critz and Edmond F. Noel, the author of the primary law. Vardaman, who took office on 19 January 1904, was the first governor inaugurated in the New Capitol.

James K. Vardaman at the Democratic National Convention, 1912 (Photograph by Harris and Ewing, Library of Congress, Washington, D.C. [LC-H261-1506])

1930. The town of Vardaman in Calhoun County is named in his honor.

David G. Sansing
University of Mississippi

Biographical Directory of the United States Congress (1950); Stephen Cresswell, *Rednecks, Redeemers, and Race: Mississippi after Reconstruction, 1877–1917* (2006); William F. Holmes, *The White Chief: James Kimble Vardaman* (1970); *Mississippi Official and Statistical Register* (1912); David M. Oshinsky, *"Worse Than Slavery": Parchman Farm and the Ordeal of Jim Crow Justice* (1996); Dunbar Rowland, *Encyclopedia of Mississippi History*, vol. 2 (1907).

As governor, Vardaman advocated government regulation of large corporations. He led the fight against the convict lease system, under which state prisoners were leased to planters and railroad companies as laborers, and he led the effort to make Parchman the state's central prison. He also strongly favored a child labor law. Governor Vardaman is best remembered, however, for his extreme views on race. He did not support public education for African Americans beyond the most basic moral instruction and vocational training because he believed that they should remain in economic servitude and that education was unnecessary for the kind of work they would do. He recommended the closing of black public schools; vetoed state funding for Mississippi Normal Institute, a college for African American teachers; and urged the repeal of the Fourteenth and Fifteenth Amendments, which gave African Americans the right to vote and hold office. Vardaman also supported the efforts to segregate Mississippi's streetcars, and he made numerous remarks supporting the necessity of lynching. He repeatedly mocked Pres. Theodore Roosevelt and the Republican Party for appointing African Americans to jobs in the federal government.

In the third year of his term as governor, Vardaman ran for the US Senate but was defeated by John Sharp Williams. After leaving the governor's office, Vardaman edited a newspaper in Jackson and prepared for another bid for the Senate. He won election in 1912 and as a senator played an instrumental role in the passage of a federal law restricting employment of young children. However, his strong opposition to America's entry into World War I and to Pres. Woodrow Wilson led to his defeat for reelection in 1918. After another unsuccessful bid for the Senate in 1922, Vardaman moved to Alabama where he lived until his death on 25 June

Vaught, John
(1909–2006) Football Coach

John Howard Vaught, head coach at the University of Mississippi during the period of the school's greatest gridiron success, won more football games than any other Mississippi Division 1-A (now Division I Football Bowl Subdivision) coach and led Rebel football to national prominence. Born on 6 May 1909 in Young County, Texas, Vaught was the sixth of eleven children of Rufus Vaught and Sally Harris Vaught. He was class president and valedictorian at Polytechnic High School in Fort Worth and played fullback on the football team. At Texas Christian University he was an honor student and played basketball and football. As a guard on the football team, Vaught was a two-time all–Southwest Conference selection. Texas Christian's 1932 team, which he

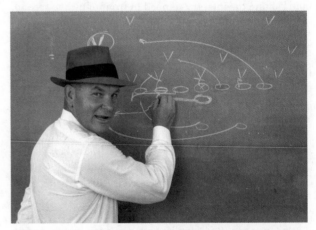

John Vaught (Bern and Franke Keating Collection, Department of Archives and Special Collections, J. D. Williams Library, University of Mississippi)

captained, won the conference championship, and he was named an all-American.

In 1936 Bear Wolf, head coach at the University of North Carolina and Vaught's mentor at Texas Christian, hired him to coach linemen. During World War II Vaught served in the US Navy, attaining the rank of lieutenant commander and coaching football in the navy's Pre-Flight Program, which also produced Bear Bryant, Bud Wilkinson, and several other outstanding college football coaches.

Vaught moved to the University of Mississippi as line coach in 1946. In his first year in Oxford the Rebels won only two games, but head coach Red Drew lauded Vaught's scouting report and game plan for the victory over Arkansas. When Drew left for Alabama in 1947, Vaught was elevated to head coach. His inaugural team won the 1947 Southeastern Conference championship, a first for the university.

Vaught's organizational skills, creativity, discipline, preparation, and recruiting acumen were keys to his success. He hired Tom Swayze as a full-time recruiter and assembled a cadre of talented assistants, retaining most of them throughout his tenure as head coach. Preferring speed and quickness over bulk and brawn, Vaught convinced many of Mississippi's best athletes to play in Oxford. He had strict rules against married players and would not allow them to have cars on campus during football season. A demanding coach and a perfectionist, he stressed the fundamentals of blocking and tackling and installed innovative offensive formations that utilized motion prior to the snap and featured a mobile quarterback sprinting out of the pocket. He also developed outstanding defenses: his 1959 team allowed only three touchdowns all season. On the sidelines Vaught was known for his game-day fedora and his calm demeanor.

In the late 1950s and early 1960s the Rebels were perennially ranked among the Top 10 teams in the country. In 1960 *Time* magazine noted, "Year in and year out, the University of Mississippi plays some of the finest football in the nation." In the fall of 1962, however, the school's reputation suffered tremendously because of state officials' resistance to desegregating the university and the ensuing riots on campus. Despite the disruptions to daily routine and the presence of thousands of federal troops on campus, the Rebels went undefeated and untied (the only perfect season in school history), won the Southeastern Conference championship, defeated Arkansas in the 1963 Sugar Bowl, and were voted national champions by several media organizations. Vaught called that squad his most courageous team.

In 1970, following an upset loss to Southern Mississippi, Vaught entered the hospital with chest pains and missed the rest of the season. In January 1971, following doctor's orders, he retired. At that time he had the second-highest winning percentage among active major-college coaches. After Vaught's successor, Billy Kinard, opened the 1973 campaign by losing two of the first three games, University of Mississippi chancellor Porter L. Fortune fired Kinard and asked Vaught to return. Vaught's first opponent was Southern Mississippi, and the Rebels delivered a 41–0 thrashing. The squad won five of its eight games under Vaught, who retired again but stayed on as athletic director until 1978. The 1973 team included the university's first black football players.

During Vaught's twenty-five seasons, the Rebels compiled a 190–61–12 record, won six Southeastern Conference titles, and brought home a share of three national championships (1959, 1960, 1962). He led the Rebels to eighteen bowl games, including fourteen consecutive appearances, a record at the time. Vaught produced more than two dozen all-Americans and coached many outstanding quarterbacks, including Charlie Conerly and Archie Manning. A Vaught-coached player finished in the top five in the Heisman Trophy balloting four times. And in 1947 and 1962 he was voted Southeastern Conference Coach of the Year. Vaught has been inducted into several halls of fame in Mississippi and Texas, and in 1979 he became a member of the College Football Hall of Fame. In 1982 Hemingway Stadium on the University of Mississippi campus was renamed Vaught-Hemingway Stadium in his honor.

He died on 3 February 2006.

Melvin S. Arrington Jr.
University of Mississippi

Rick Cleveland, *Vaught: The Man and His Legacy* (2000); Francis J. Fitzgerald, ed., *Greatest Moments in Ole Miss Football History* (1999); William W. Sorrels and Charles Cavagnaro, *Ole Miss Rebels: Mississippi Football* (1976); *Time* (28 November 1960); John Vaught, *Rebel Coach: My Football Family* (1971); Larry Wells, ed., *A Century of Heroes* (1993); Larry Wells, *Ole Miss Football* (1980).

Vaux, Calvert
(1824–1895) Architect

An architect, environmental advocate, and landscape designer of national reputation, Calvert Vaux (rhymes with *talks*) enriched Mississippi not only by creating its most renowned antebellum Italianate mansion but also by producing a unique trove of sixteen beautifully drafted drawings used in its construction.

Born to a prosperous English family on 20 December 1824, Vaux was already a competent architect and exceptional draftsman by 1850, when American writer and landscape designer A. J. Downing hired the twenty-six-year-old to apply his skills in the New World. Within ten years Vaux's combined practice of residential design and landscape architecture was flourishing along the Upper East Coast, and he

V

Ammadelle, Oxford, 1975 (Photograph by Jack E. Boucher, Library of Congress, Washington, D.C. [HABS MISS,36-OXFO,1-])

had won fame for his role in designing New York City's Central Park.

In 1857 Vaux published a popular architectural guidebook, *Villas and Cottages*, which probably caught the attention of Thomas Pegues, a North Mississippi cotton and railroad magnate with visions of Italianate domestic splendor in his hometown of Oxford. In 1859 Pegues traveled east and viewed his favorite Vaux design, No. 27, in company with the architect. The superbly drafted house plans were soon on their way to Mississippi, with additional pages arriving in 1860.

Back home, Pegues hired a local builder, William Turner, who was just finishing St. Peter's Episcopal Church, Oxford's Gothic Revival landmark, to realize Vaux's elaborate designs for a two-story, red brick suburban villa. Whether the architect ever visited the house site, a one-hundred-acre estate on North Lamar Avenue, is unknown.

Between 1859 and 1861 Oxford's most imposing private residence took shape. Its sophisticated, asymmetric Italianate facades, combined with Vaux's luxurious interior refinements, must have stirred considerable wonder in this little town of elegant but austere Greek Revival vernacular. In wintertime, hot water pipes maintained an unheard-of coziness in the library and conservatory, while family members and guests could choose between two indoor bathrooms with the novel feature of running water. Built-in closets abounded, and a grand ballroom could be created by opening the massive pocket doors between the double parlors. Pegues's home, Edgecomb, reportedly cost around fifteen thousand dollars, an enormous sum for the time.

Several of Oxford's most prominent families subsequently inhabited Vaux's masterpiece, which was renamed Ammadelle in the early 1900s. The house and grounds now cover a seven-acre parcel, and much of Vaux's landscaping remains intact. William Faulkner may have had Ammadelle in mind when he described the ever-ambitious Thomas Sutpen and his French architect in *Absalom, Absalom!*

A modified version of Vaux's Ammadelle design, Mount Holly, was built circa 1859–61 near Greenville, though not under the architect's supervision. In 2001 the integrity of Vaux and Pegues's vision in Oxford was assured when Dorothy Lee Tatum conveyed a perpetual conservation easement to the state. The house is now a National Historic Landmark.

Vaux continued his distinguished career, designing some of America's most picturesque parks and rural retreats, until his death by accidental drowning on 19 November 1895 in New York.

Bruce Smith
Tupelo, Mississippi

Mary Wallace Crocker, *Historic Architecture in Mississippi* (1973); Thomas S. Hines, *Architectural Digest* (May 2001); Thomas S. Hines, *William Faulkner and the Tangible Past: The Architecture of Yoknapatawpha* (1996); Francis R. Kowsky, *Country, Park, and City: The Architecture and Life of Calvert Vaux* (1998); Mills Lane, *Architecture of the Old South: Mississippi and Alabama* (1989); Mary Carol Miller, *Great Houses of Mississippi* (2004); Calvert Vaux, *Villas and Cottages* (1857).

Veterans, Military

Mississippians have served the United States since the Creek Indian Wars and the War of 1812, when a company of Mississippi volunteers fought with Andrew Jackson at the Battle of New Orleans. Jefferson Davis led the Mississippi Rifles in the Mexican War. An estimated ninety-eight thousand Mississippians served in the Civil War in no fewer than forty-eight infantry regiments and twenty-two cavalry units. The Spanish-American War, the two world wars, Korea, Vietnam, the two Gulf wars, Afghanistan, and Iraq have produced thousands of distinguished Mississippi veterans from all branches of the service.

In 1924 the Mississippi legislature founded the Office of the State Service Commissioner to aid all state residents who had served in the US military forces. In 1948 this group was renamed the State Veterans Affairs Board. Its main claims office is located in Jackson, while officers are also stationed at the US Department of Veterans Affairs hospitals in Jackson, Biloxi, and Memphis, Tennessee, to assist veterans with appeals, casework, and claims paperwork. In addition, the board operates 150-bed State Veterans Nursing Homes in Collins, Jackson, Kosciusko, and Oxford as well as the State Veterans Memorial Cemetery, which opened in April 2011 on eighty-two acres in Newton County donated by Mississippi State University and which is the site of the Persian Gulf War Memorial.

The state has also had other veterans' homes. Beauvoir, Jefferson Davis's home on Biloxi Beach, housed about twenty-five hundred Civil War veterans and their widows between 1902 and 1953; Pres. Franklin D. Roosevelt visited the facility in 1937. Many veterans were interred in the cemetery on the grounds, which is also the location of the Tomb of the Unknown Confederate Soldier. In 1976, the US Naval Home was moved from Philadelphia Naval Yard to the former location of the Gulf Coast Military Academy in Gulfport. Damage from Hurricane Katrina closed the home in 2005, but it was rebuilt and reopened as the Armed Forces Retirement Home in October 2010.

Virtually every community in the state is served by one or more private veterans' organizations, including the American Legion, American Ex-POWs, Blinded Veterans Association, Fleet Reserve Association, Non-Commissioned Officers Association, and the Veterans of Foreign Wars.

Mississippi has numerous military cemeteries, markers, museums, and memorials, many of which originated during or commemorate the Civil War. The battlefield at Vicksburg, for example, contains 18,244 Civil War graves. What are now national cemeteries operated by the US Department of Veterans Affairs in Corinth and Natchez began as Civil War cemeteries, and a third national cemetery for veterans was added in Biloxi in 1934. The Vicksburg National Military Park contains more than 1,300 historical monuments and markers as well as the salvaged USS *Cairo*. In and around Corinth a large segment of the Shiloh National Military Park is preserved as a Civil War memorial. The four-hundred-acre Grand Gulf Military Park near Port Gibson features a museum and the remnants of two Civil War forts. Five miles offshore of Gulfport, Fort Massachusetts, on Ship Island, is a national park. The Mississippi Vietnam Veterans Memorial was established in Ocean Springs in 1996. Similar to the Vietnam Veterans Memorial in Washington, D.C., it contains a remembrance wall honoring those lost in the Vietnam conflict. In addition, counties across the state have erected monuments honoring local men and women who served their country.

Hattiesburg's Camp Shelby, which since 1917 has served as a US Army and National Guard training center, features the Mississippi Armed Forces Museum. Hattiesburg is also home to the African American Military History Museum, which has artifacts and displays relating to nearly two centuries of history, including Mississippian Jesse L. Brown, the first African American naval aviator. Camp Van Dorn, near Centerville, maintains a small museum dedicated to the site's World War II service. Private military museums are also open at the Veterans Memorial Museum in Laurel and the GI Museum in Gautier.

Christopher Eger

Biloxi, Mississippi

Mississippi Veterans Affairs Board website, www.vab.ms.gov; US Department of the Interior, *The National Parks Index, 2001–2003* (2001); US Department of Veterans Affairs, National Cemetery Administration website, www.cem.va.gov/CEM/index.asp.

Vicksburg, Summer 1862

In the summer of 1862 Vicksburg, Mississippi, became the focal point of Union and Confederate efforts in the western theater. Union naval forces converged on Vicksburg from the north and south. Flag officer David Farragut's flotilla captured New Orleans on 25 April and ascended the river to capture Baton Rouge on 9 May and Natchez on 12 May. Simultaneously, a Union fleet under the command of flag officer Charles H. Davis descended the river and captured the Confederate stronghold at Island No. 10 on 8 April and Memphis on 6 June. This series of events made Vicksburg and Port Hudson, Louisiana, the last remaining Confederate strongholds on the Mississippi River.

On 18 May 1862 the vanguard of Union naval forces under Cmdr. S. Phillips Lee arrived outside of Vicksburg as part of Farragut's fleet coming from the south. Lee demanded the surrender of the town and received a curt rebuff from both civil and military authorities. Although indignant over the Confederate response, Lee could only await Farragut's arrival with the rest of the fleet.

Farragut arrived on 21 May, but his forces faced significant obstacles. Vicksburg's natural bluffs were high, all of his vessels were composed of wood, and several of his vessels possessed deep drafts for ocean sailing. If the Mississippi River's water level fell, many of his ships would be trapped. Furthermore, only fourteen hundred troops under Gen. Thomas Williams had accompanied the fleet. Farragut called a council of war and, after much debate, ordered his larger sloops of war to return downriver on 26 May. A small flotilla of six gunboats remained to keep watch at Vicksburg.

Farragut was not gone long. The Navy Department ordered him immediately to return to Vicksburg and attempt to capture the city. Farragut reluctantly reassembled his fleet, including sixteen mortar scows to lob high-trajectory shots into the city. The flotilla arrived at Vicksburg on 25 June.

On 28 June Farragut attacked the Hill City in an attempt to silence the Confederate guns. Thick clouds of smoke from the discharge of cannons blanketed the river and limited both sides' visibility. Union cannoneers found that their guns could not elevate high enough to fire on most of the Confederate battery positions atop the bluffs. The fight, which lasted more than two and a half hours, inflicted little damage on either side. Seven vessels proceeded north past the city and anchored on the opposite side of De Soto Point. On 1 July, Davis arrived with his fleet from Memphis and rendezvoused with Farragut.

At the same time, Gen. Williams pressed fifteen hundred recently freed slaves into service to dig a canal across the peninsula opposite Vicksburg. By July the canal measured eighteen feet wide and thirteen feet deep, but the falling river level and mosquito-related diseases forced the end of the project.

V

To counter the Federal river menace, Confederates had begun construction of an ironclad in 1861 at Memphis. The city's fall necessitated the movement of the vessel to a safer location near Greenwood. Construction slowed to a near standstill until Capt. Isaac N. Brown of the Confederate Navy took command in May 1862. Brown moved the unfinished hull to Yazoo City and within five weeks finished armoring, arming, and equipping the vessel. The CSS *Arkansas* measured 165 feet in length and 35 feet abeam and drew 14 feet. The vessel carried a complement of ten guns and a crew of around 160 officers and men. Its armor consisted of railroad iron fitted to the vertical sides.

On 15 July the *Arkansas* emerged for a fight. Steaming down the Yazoo River, it encountered three boats guarding the entrance to the Mississippi River. The *Arkansas* ran one boat aground and chased the other two vessels toward Vicksburg. Emerging into the main river, the Confederate ironclad confronted the combined Union fleets. Fortunately for Brown, most of the Union vessels did not have adequate steam pressure to make way, and his boat ran the gauntlet to dock at Vicksburg. Farragut twice failed to sink the *Arkansas* at its mooring, but the boat was scuttled in August when its engines failed outside Baton Rouge.

By the end of July the falling water level on the Mississippi forced the Union vessels to retreat from Vicksburg, leaving a portion of the Mississippi River under Confederate control. Despite the US Navy's most energetic efforts, the Confederate forces at Vicksburg remained defiant.

Matt Atkinson
Vicksburg National Military Park

Edwin C. Bearss, *Rebel Victory at Vicksburg* (1963); Isaac N. Brown, in *Battles and Leaders of the Civil War*, vol. 3., ed. C. C. Buell and R. U. Johnson (1884); Tom Z. Parrish, *The Saga of the Confederate Ram Arkansas* (1987).

Vicksburg, Winter 1862–1863

Following a failed attempt to capture Vicksburg employing primarily naval forces in the summer of 1862, Union authorities renewed their efforts over the following winter. Gen. Ulysses S. Grant planned a two-pronged campaign in December, with troops under his command moving overland to threaten Confederates in North Mississippi while William Tecumseh Sherman was to sail down from Memphis with more than thirty thousand men. The plan went awry after Confederate cavalry under Earl Van Dorn burned Grant's supply depot at Holly Springs and Nathan Bedford Forrest wreaked havoc on Grant's supply lines. Grant opted to

Surrender of Vicksburg, 4 July 1863, wood engraving 1894 (Library of Congress, Washington, D.C. [LC-USZ62-90009])

retreat, while Sherman continued downriver and landed troops above the city. Sherman's men were impeded by marshes, swamps, and bayous, but he ordered an assault at Chickasaw Bayou (also known as Chickasaw Bluffs) on 29 December. Confederate defenders rebuffed Sherman's repeated attacks, inflicting more than seventeen hundred casualties while losing roughly two hundred men. Sherman admitted defeat and withdrew to the mouth of the Yazoo River as 1863 arrived. He was superseded by Maj. Gen. John A. McClernand, who proceeded upriver and on 11 January captured Arkansas Post (Fort Hindman), fifty miles up the Arkansas River from its junction with the Mississippi. While McClernand felt that he had eliminated a persistent threat to the Union flank and rear, the fort's capture did not materially weaken the Confederate grip on Vicksburg.

Grant assumed command of three Union corps (a fourth was on detached duty in Tennessee) in late January and began a series of maneuvers designed to capture Vicksburg. Formidable obstacles existed during the rainy winter season, with much of the terrain north and south of the city subject to flooding as water rose in the area's bayous, rivers, streams, and swamps. Grant's troops attempted to construct several canals in vain attempts to bypass Vicksburg's menacing batteries. Troops resumed work on a canal started earlier at De Soto Point, where a horseshoe bend in the Mississippi River formed a peninsula below the city, in hopes of diverting the river through the canal and allowing transports to convey troops to the bluffs below the city. This attempt failed when the river rose in early March, flooding the peninsula and destroying much of the work. When Confederates placed artillery to command the lower end of the canal, the project was abandoned.

Seventy-five miles above Vicksburg, Union soldiers cut another canal from the Mississippi to Lake Providence on the Louisiana side, hoping to gain access to the Red River two hundred miles below the city. It was an ambitious plan, entailing the projected sailing of Union vessels through various bayous and rivers to reach the Red River. If successful, Federal ships might surround and capture Port Hudson, then move north against Vicksburg. The Lake Providence plan ended when engineers were unable to establish a navigable channel along the entire route.

A third effort began in early February, when Union engineers blew the levee at Yazoo Pass, a few miles below Helena, Arkansas, on the west side of the Mississippi. Doing so gave Union gunboats and steamers access to Moon Lake; Yazoo Pass, a small bayou; and the Coldwater River. The Coldwater fed into the Tallahatchie River, which combined with the Yalobusha River to form the Yazoo, which emptied into the Mississippi above Vicksburg. It took weeks to clear the Yazoo Pass of trees felled by Confederates to obstruct passage, but a flotilla eventually entered Yazoo Pass from Moon Lake.

Christopher Losson
St. Joseph, Missouri

Michael B. Ballard, *Vicksburg: The Campaign That Opened the Mississippi* (2004); Edwin C. Bearss, *The Campaign for Vicksburg*, vol. 2, *Grant Strikes a Fatal Blow* (1986); *The War of the Rebellion: Official Records of the Union and Confederate Armies*, vol. 24, pts. 1, 3 (1889).

Vicksburg Citizens' Appeal

The Warren County Freedom Democratic Party, the local branch of the Mississippi Freedom Democratic Party, published the *Vicksburg Citizens' Appeal* from 1964 to 1967 to serve as a voice for African Americans. The front page of the first issue declared, "The paper will print full news of events in the Vicksburg area Negro community—social and club activities, sporting events, and political and civil news. The *Citizens' Appeal* will also keep its readers informed of important events in the struggle for Negro rights, here in Vicksburg and elsewhere in Mississippi." The paper's central message was an end to segregation and racial discrimination.

The first issue of the eight-page tabloid was published on 22 August 1964. Originally a weekly published on Saturdays, by 1965 a second edition appeared each Monday. A one-year subscription cost $3.50, and single issues cost 10 cents. Circulation usually ranged between three hundred and five hundred copies but at times reached three thousand. Ollye Brown Shirley, whose husband, Aaron, was for many years Mississippi's only African American pediatrician, initially served as the paper's editor. She was succeeded on 30 August 1965 by Dilla E. Irwin, who continued as editor until the newspaper ceased in 1967. Constantly in need of financial support, the newspaper received aid not only from local black sources but also from other parts of the country. Advertisements cost about three dollars, and all were bought by black or black-oriented businesses.

Despite its short life, the *Vicksburg Citizens' Appeal* was a significant presence in mid-1960s Mississippi. When many historically white newspapers were ignoring or belittling the civil rights movement and when some African American–run newspapers were counseling slow change, the *Citizens' Appeal* was an activist newspaper.

Margaret Bean
University of Mississippi

Julius Thompson, *The Black Press in Mississippi, 1865–1985* (1993).

Vietnam War

In 1970 Mississippi had a population of 2,217,000. More than 10 percent of those people—an estimated 227,000—served in the Vietnam War, meaning that the conflict personally affected nearly everyone in the state. A total of 637 Mississippians were killed, while 12 are still listed as missing in action. Two men from Mississippi, Ed W. Freeman (1927–2008) and Roy M. Wheat (1947–67), received the Congressional Medal of Honor for their actions in Vietnam. In addition to numerous local monuments honoring area residents who served in the conflict, the Mississippi Vietnam Veterans Memorial in Ocean Springs features a remembrance wall honoring those who gave their lives.

The state also contributed to the war in other ways. Pascagoula's Ingalls Shipbuilding (now Huntington Ingalls Industries) became a major supplier of US Navy vessels that saw action in Vietnam, most notably the USS *Washoe County*. Biloxi's Keesler Air Force Base trained South Vietnamese pilots. Hattiesburg's Camp Shelby provided combat training for members of the 199th Light Infantry Brigade. The Strategic Air Command's 454th Bombardment Wing operated from Columbus Air Force Base. And numerous military personnel who later served in Vietnam spent time at the Meridian Naval Air Station.

Mississippi's most prominent voices in the cacophony of debate and dissension swirling through the Vietnam War era were those of US senators John C. Stennis and James O. Eastland. First elected to the Senate in 1947, Stennis distinguished himself as an informed student of foreign affairs. During the 1960s Stennis served as chair of the Senate Preparedness Investigating Subcommittee, providing him with a platform from which to critique American diplomacy and military policy. After Pres. Lyndon Johnson escalated American military intervention in Vietnam in 1965, the senator took an increasing interest in the administration's management of the conflict. In 1967 Stennis's subcommittee held a series of hearings crafted to highlight policy differences between the Joint Chiefs of Staff and secretary of defense Robert McNamara as well as provide committee members the opportunity to demand a more vigorous use of military power. Frustrated by the administration's adoption of a limited-war paradigm as well as its apparent lack of progress toward victory in the conflict, Stennis decried Johnson's application of graduated military pressure on the ground in South Vietnam and his restrictions on American air power in North Vietnam. During Richard Nixon's administration Stennis frequently voiced approval of the president's war policy, particularly Nixon's intensified bombing strategy and incursions into Cambodia and Laos.

While Stennis often criticized Johnson's prosecution of the Vietnam War, Eastland was generally more supportive. Eastland, who joined the Senate in 1941, was known for his strident anticommunism, race-baiting, and opposition to civil rights reforms, and his interest in foreign policy centered largely on American communism and its purported links to Soviet diplomacy, the civil rights movement, and antiwar protests. The senator chaired the Internal Security Subcommittee and conducted several investigations, including a 1965 examination of anti–Vietnam War "teach-in" protests on college campuses that concluded that communists had infiltrated and exploited the antiwar movement.

Mississippians' opposition to the Vietnam War was intertwined with the civil rights movement, in large part because of the disproportionate number of African Americans serving in the US armed forces. In the mid-1960s blacks comprised 11 percent of the US population yet accounted for almost 14 percent of the military forces in Vietnam and 15 percent of casualties. Some black Mississippians viewed the state's all-white draft boards and military recruiting efforts as racially biased. In Mississippi and elsewhere, whites with wealth or political connections could lessen their chances of serving in Vietnam by joining the National Guard, but African Americans generally lacked that option: at one point the more than 10,000 members of the Mississippi National Guard included only one black.

In addition, civil rights activist Fannie Lou Hamer and others worried that the war would distract from the movement, and the Mississippi Freedom Democratic Party in particular combined its civil rights work with opposition to the war. In March 1965 the party sponsored a prayer meeting against the war at Leflore County's Newton Chapel Church, which was burned to the ground shortly thereafter. The party repeatedly called for an end to the war and argued that blacks should not fight for a country that failed to recognize their rights at home.

When McNamara spoke in Jackson on 24 February 1967, Tougaloo College students and other protesters confronted him, holding signs with slogans such as, "Students can't abide McNamara's genocide!" Over the next two years, students at the University of Mississippi protested the school's required Reserve Officers' Training Corps program, and in 1969 school officials blocked Quaker antiwar activist Earle Reynolds from speaking on campus.

Along with the civil rights movement, the Vietnam War helped to push Mississippians away from the Democratic Party and toward the Republicans. After voting for the Democratic candidate in every presidential election between 1876 and 1960 with the exception of 1948, when the state supported Dixiecrat Strom Thurmond, Mississippi voters backed the presidential candidate with the most hawkish stance on Vietnam in 1964, 1968, and 1972. The state has subsequently become a Republican stronghold, in large part because Ronald Reagan and the party's other candidates have promised to restore US military power in the wake of the country's defeat in Vietnam.

Finally, the war also resulted in the migration of Vietnamese people to Mississippi. By the early 1990s about ten thousand of those displaced by the war had moved to the state, where many of them found work in the seafood industry along the Gulf Coast.

Mark Williams
Charleston Southern University

Christopher Myers Asch, *The Senator and the Sharecropper: The Freedom Struggles of James O. Eastland and Fannie Lou Hamer* (2008); Robert Caro, *The Years of Lyndon Johnson: Master of the Senate* (2002); Joseph A. Fry, *Debating Vietnam: Fulbright, Stennis, and Their Senate Hearings* (2006); David W. Levy, *The Debate over Vietnam* (1991); Mississippi History Now website, http://mshistory.k12.ms.us; Mississippi Legislature, Senate Concurrent Resolution 512, https://legiscan.com/MS/text/SC512/2013/X2 (2 July 2013); US Senate, *Senate Documents*, vol. 2, *Miscellaneous*, 89th Cong., 2nd sess., US Congressional Serial Set No. 12668–2 (1965).

Vietnamese

The Vietnamese presence in Mississippi is a relatively new phenomenon, dating to the late 1970s and early 1980s. Unlike most ethnic groups that settled in the state, the Vietnamese came as refugees from a war-torn country. Many fled in haste by boat with little money and few possessions. The harrowing voyage at sea included pirate raids, storms, and mechanical failures, and while an estimated four hundred thousand Vietnamese refugees reached the United States, an equal number may have died at sea.

According to the 2010 census, Mississippi's 5,387 Vietnamese Americans (0.2 percent of the population) comprised the state's third-largest community of foreign-born residents, trailing only Mexican Americans and German Americans. People of Vietnamese heritage live throughout the state but are concentrated in metropolitan areas and especially in Jackson, Harrison, and Hancock Counties along the coast. More than half of the state's Vietnamese population resides in Harrison County, while Jackson has the second-largest Vietnamese population, and the Hattiesburg area ranks third. Most of Mississippi's Vietnamese people come from families that left Hai Phong in North Vietnam after the communist takeover in 1954. They migrated to Mississippi via South Vietnamese coastal cities such as Vung Tau, Phouc Tinh, Phan Thiet, Rach Gia, and Phu Quoc Island, attracted by Mississippi's warm climate and the opportunities offered by the seafood industry.

A number of religious organizations were instrumental in sponsoring resettled refugees. An overwhelming majority of the Vietnamese who arrived were Catholic, and the Catholic Diocese of Biloxi worked through the Catholic Social Services Migration and Refugee Center to help clients find jobs, receive medical assistance, and learn English. The diocese established a Vietnamese Apostolate, including bringing in a Vietnamese priest, himself a refugee, to serve this new community. More recently, the Church of the Vietnamese Martyrs and the Van Duc Buddhist Temple have been established to serve the community's spiritual needs.

Vietnamese came to Mississippi largely in response to the demands of the seafood industry. In 1977 Richard Gollott of Golden Gulf Coast Packing needed laborers to shuck oysters at his plant. After hearing that Vietnamese were working in New Orleans, he shuttled laborers back and forth for a week before persuading a family to move to Biloxi to work for him full time. Others soon followed. Gollott and many others credit these early Vietnamese workers with resuscitating Mississippi's seafood industry. They did not need strong English skills to work in the plants or on the boats. They labored for long hours, saved money to build and operate their own boats, and moved to neighborhoods such as East Biloxi's Point Cadet and Back Bay, where access to the water was easy and housing was affordable.

Not all coast natives were pleased with the influx of Vietnamese. Their arrival coincided with a stretch of poor shrimping seasons and an already crowded fishing fleet, and the Vietnamese received the brunt of the blame for the economic woes. Most of the problems stemmed from cultural and language differences. Vietnamese fishermen could not read English-language Coast Guard regulations, rigged their boats differently from American fishermen, and trawled north to south (the traditional Vietnamese practice) rather than east to west as locals did, often resulting in tangled nets. Tensions were high for a time, but church and city officials and representatives from both the Vietnamese and native Mississippian communities worked to solve the problems, and the situation gradually improved. Today Vietnamese shrimpers are no longer turned away at the docks. They participate in community events such as the annual Blessing of the Fleet and seafood festivals.

Vietnamese have integrated themselves into the community in other ways—through schools, businesses, and the gaming industry. Vietnamese-owned businesses are common, particularly in East Biloxi, where the Vietnamese population has concentrated. Dockside gambling along the Gulf Coast beginning in the early 1990s created a demand for labor and provided another opportunity for Vietnamese. However, as gaming interests moved into East Biloxi, housing prices rose, causing problems for residents. While some have moved into other business ventures, most Vietnamese have stayed in the seafood industry, usually by acquiring boats.

In August 2005 Hurricane Katrina caused particular problems for members of the coast's Vietnamese community, most of whom lived in low-lying areas that were heavily damaged. In addition, many lost their boats. The language barrier and regulations regarding the distribution of aid complicated recovery and assistance programs. Organizations such as the National Alliance of Vietnamese American Service Agencies, Asian Americans for Change, and Boat People SOS stepped in to provide assistance such as translation services and monetary donations. In 2010, just as the Gulf Coast fishing community was recovering from Katrina, the Deepwater Horizon oil spill in the Gulf dealt the industry another blow. The spill resulted in the closing of Gulf fisheries for nearly a year and led to lingering—though largely unfounded—concerns about the safety of Gulf shrimp. Despite its short-term negative effect on Mississippi's shrimp harvest, the closure of the fisheries may prove helpful in the long term, as it allowed shrimp to reproduce unimpeded. Like others in the industry, Vietnamese who have been able to withstand these setbacks may well find improved economic conditions with decreased competition and stronger fisheries.

Aimée Schmidt
Decatur, Georgia

Harvey Arden, *National Geographic* (September 1981); Robert Nathan Gregory, "Shrimp Business Bounces Back for Some, Not Others," http://extension.msstate.edu/news/feature-story/2015/shrimp-business-bounces-back-for-some-not-others (27 August 2015); Mississippi History Now website, http://mshistorynow.mdah.state.ms.us; Rev. John Noone, *From Vietnam to the Mississippi Gulf Coast* (1981); "The People Within: How the Vietnamese Have Adapted to Life on the Coast" *Biloxi Sun Herald* (Special Issue, 1999); Hannah Waters, "Breaking Down the Myths and Misconceptions about the Gulf Oil Spill," http://www.smithsonianmag.com/science-nature/clarifying-myths-and-misconceptions-about-gulf-oil-spill-180951136/?no-ist (17 April 2014).

V

Viking Range Corporation

The idea for Viking Range Corporation began in 1980 when Greenwood natives Fred E. Carl Jr. and his wife, Margaret Leflore Carl, wanted a professional-quality range for the house they were building but found that those available were too large and not safe for home use. Fred, a fourth-generation builder who studied business, architecture, and city planning at Mississippi State University and Delta State University, began to spend his spare time designing a range for home use, incorporated Viking Range, and had a prototype built in Los Angeles in 1986. Four years later, after working with contract manufacturers in California and Tennessee, Carl began producing ranges in Greenwood and recruited investors to help expand Viking's operation. By the end of the 1990s, Viking was producing cooking and refrigeration products as well as dishwashers in three manufacturing facilities. Viking products are sold in all fifty states and more than eighty countries.

Viking has become the symbol for a gourmet lifestyle and has grown well beyond the kitchen. At its peak, the Viking Hospitality Group comprised Greenwood's Alluvian Hotel, an upscale boutique establishment, and its accompanying spa; Giardina's Restaurant, a Mississippi Delta dining landmark since 1936; the Viking Cooking School, with locations from New York to California; and the Viking Way of Life Culinary Tours. In 2004 *National Geographic Traveler* listed the Alluvian among "56 Hotels We Love," and in 2005 *Forbes* magazine included it as a "destination to visit."

Viking Range made an immense impact on Greenwood, where its corporate headquarters occupy twelve buildings across two entire blocks of historic Cotton Row. In addition to its offices, Viking renovated numerous downtown buildings for retail and housing, and many of them are listed on the National Register of Historic Places. Several of the meticulously restored buildings have received state and national historic preservation awards. Viking won the 2002 Mississippi Heritage Trust Award of Excellence for Outstanding Re-Use of a large property for its restoration of 101 Main Street as the Viking Training Center. In 2003 the Mississippi Heritage Trust recognized the company for saving one of Mississippi's endangered historic places, the Irving Hotel (now the Alluvian). And in 2004 Viking received the National Trust for Historic Preservation's Main Street Business Leadership Award for commercial district revitalization.

Viking is a major employer in Greenwood and has consistently been named by *Mississippi Business Journal* as one of the best places to work in Mississippi. Viking also supports a much larger community, partnering with local colleges to enable Viking employees to earn degrees and making significant financial contributions in and beyond Greenwood.

Viking's founder also enhanced the company's impact through his personal initiatives and contributions. In 2003, for example, Carl donated $2.5 million to endow the Small Town Center at Mississippi State University's College of Architecture. Now named for him, the center provides planning and design assistance to rural Mississippi towns and uses its community projects as teaching tools for architecture students. In 2006 the US Small Business Administration awarded Carl one of eleven American Spirit Awards for his volunteerism and leadership in providing goods and services to areas devastated by Hurricanes Katrina, Rita, and Wilma in 2005.

In December 2012 Viking sold its manufacturing operation and its hospitality subsidiaries, including the cooking schools and the Alluvian Hotel, for $380 million to Middleby Corporation, a maker of commercial cooking equipment in Illinois. Because of the slump in the housing market, Viking's sales had fallen by half from a peak of four hundred million dollars in 2006–7. To increase profits while cutting costs, the new owner laid off 140 of Viking's 700 employees and closed some of the cooking schools. Carl announced his retirement as the company's chair, president, and chief executive officer in January 2013.

Ann J. Abadie
University of Mississippi

Edye Cameron McMillan
Delta State University

Leflore Illustrated (Spring–Summer 2007); *Mississippi Business Journal* (29 December 2012, 4, 31 January 2013); *Monocle: A Briefing on Global Affairs, Business, Culture, and Design* (November 2011); Viking website, www.vikingrange.com; *Wall Street Journal* (1 January 2013).

Voter Education Project

The Voter Education Project (VEP) was an initiative to register African American voters that began in 1962, largely as an effort by Pres. John F. Kennedy and attorney general Robert F. Kennedy to co-opt the nonviolent direct action campaigns of the civil rights movement. In the wake of the 1961 Freedom Rides, the Kennedys hoped to avoid any further outbreaks of white southern violence. The Justice Department, led by Robert Kennedy and Burke Marshall, thought a voter registration campaign aimed at black southerners would both channel civil rights militancy away from more confrontational public demonstrations and invite fewer violent reprisals from white southerners.

The VEP grew out of a series of 1961 meetings between civil rights leaders and Justice Department officials. Between April 1962 and October 1965, the project would disburse funds to help civil rights groups engaged in voter education and registration. It was financed by $870,000 in donations from tax-exempt private foundations, with Stephen Currier, president of the Taconic Foundation, as the principal backer.

In practice, however, the project exacerbated conflict between the civil rights workers and the Kennedy administration. The Student Nonviolent Coordinating Committee (SNCC) took the lead in voter registration efforts but received only a small share of VEP funds. The attorney general preferred to focus on registration in southern cities, but SNCC leader Bob Moses, working as director of voter registration for the Council of Federated Organizations, concentrated on rural counties in Mississippi, especially in the Delta. SNCC officials believed that working in a federally approved project like the VEP would mean federal protection for their volunteers, a notion that Robert Kennedy and Marshall did not actively dispel. However, when whites in McComb and elsewhere responded with violence or economic reprisal against SNCC workers and black voter applicants, the Justice Department moved slowly, citing federalism and the prerogatives of local law enforcement. The Justice Department's reluctance to act angered SNCC volunteers and stymied voter registration efforts, and the VEP ceased funding the council's Mississippi registration efforts in November 1963.

The tensions between the student volunteers and the federal government marked the beginning of SNCC workers' disillusionment with white liberals, a separation that would become a complete split after the 1964 Democratic National Convention in Atlantic City. The VEP strategy also showed how deeply the Kennedys misread the level of violent resistance to any challenge to white supremacy in Mississippi, whether it was civil disobedience or voter registration on the part of African Americans. The VEP established SNCC as the leading voter registration group in the state and thus served as an important precursor to Freedom Summer and the formation of the Mississippi Freedom Democratic Party.

Chris Danielson
Montana Tech of the
University of Montana

Carl M. Brauer, *John F. Kennedy and the Second Reconstruction* (1977); Clayborne Carson, *In Struggle: SNCC and the Black Awakening of the 1960s* (1981); James N. Giglio, *The Presidency of John F. Kennedy* (1991).

Voting and Voting Rights since the Voting Rights Act of 1965

Mississippi was the focus of intense efforts by civil rights activists to register African American voters in the early 1960s, most notably during the violence-filled Freedom Summer of 1964. Despite the work of the Student Nonviolent Coordinating Committee and the Mississippi Freedom Democratic Party, however, fewer than 7 percent of the state's eligible blacks were registered by 1965. Federal intervention to address the problem finally came with the passage of the Voting Rights Act of 1965, which suspended the various disfranchisement clauses passed by the state legislature or contained in the 1890 Mississippi Constitution. Federal registrars arrived in Mississippi just days after the passage of the act and began registering voters. Not all counties received registrars immediately, mainly because the US Justice Department preferred to obtain voluntary compliance from local authorities where it could. Sunflower County, home of Sen. James O. Eastland, did not see registrars until almost a year after the measure's enactment, a delay that indicated how much influence Eastland wielded with the federal government.

By 1967 59 percent of Mississippi's eligible African American voters had registered, a massive increase that still left the state with the lowest rate in the South. The first tangible yields came in the 1967 statewide elections, which saw the victories of twenty-two black candidates for county and local offices, including Robert Clark, who won a seat in the state legislature from Holmes County. All of the victories came in black-majority counties, however, and many more black challengers were defeated.

The state's leading black politician in the late 1960s and early 1970s was Charles Evers, brother of slain civil rights

Federal examiner C. A. Phillips administers voter registration oath to Joe Ella Moore, Magnolia Motel, Prentiss, 25 August 1965 (Moncrief Collection, Archives and Records Services Division, Mississippi Department of Archives and History [339])

leader Medgar Evers and state field secretary for the National Association for the Advancement of Colored People. Evers and his allies conducted voter registration drives in southwestern Mississippi, and he won election as mayor of Fayette in 1969. In 1971 he ran as an independent candidate for governor but was defeated by Democrat William Waller. During this period most black independent candidates, with the exception of those in such Mississippi Freedom Democratic Party strongholds as Holmes County, were defeated, and most successful candidates won nomination as Democrats. The state party, known as the Regulars, dominated the state offices and party leadership, while the mostly black Loyalists won recognition from the national Democratic Party in 1968 and held the national convention seats.

Black political power continued to grow, with 68 percent registration (more than three hundred thousand voters) by 1971. African American candidates began to win control of small municipal governments in the Delta and to take seats in county governments. White incumbents who had opposed the civil rights movement quickly discovered that they could keep their seats by making concessions to African American voters, a practice that split the black vote in many elections and preserved white political power in some black-majority towns and counties.

In the 1970s and 1980s black plaintiffs brought a series of lawsuits challenging vote dilution on the state and local levels. At-large election systems in municipalities kept city councils all white, county gerrymandering prevented or reduced the number of African American county supervisors, and multimember legislative districts prevented the election of additional black state legislators. Federal court rulings, including several by the US Supreme Court, dismantled some of these barriers in the 1970s, and the extension and strengthening of the Voting Rights Act in 1982 effectively eliminated the last of them. These events, combined with Gov. Cliff Finch's 1976 integration of the Democratic Party's Regular and Loyalist wings under a power-sharing scheme, created a significant black political presence in the state. In 1979, seventeen African American candidates won election to the Mississippi legislature, including two members of the State Senate. African American legislators showed their strength in such issues as the passage of the Education Reform Act of 1982, which was pushed through by Clark and supported by every black legislator.

Black political power was not absolute, and white Democrats imposed clear limits to keep white voters from switching to the Republican Party. Gov. William Winter created a political controversy in 1980 when he ended the arrangement to have black and white cochairs of the Democratic Party and instead installed a single white party head. The Jackson city government resisted ward elections until 1985, an action that kept the government completely white even though more than 40 percent of the city's residents were African American.

The last major voting rights barrier was the integration of the state's congressional delegation. In the redistricting following the 1980 census, the 2nd District had a slight majority of black residents. Clark won the Democratic nomination for the seat in 1982 but lost to a white Republican, Webb Franklin, in a race marked by coded racial appeals by Franklin's campaign and a lack of enthusiasm from white Democrats for Clark. After the 1982 race, the federal courts, citing the renewed Voting Rights Act, redrew the district to increase the African American population, but Clark lost again in 1984. Not until 1986 did Clarksdale attorney Mike Espy become the first state's first African American member of Congress in the twentieth century, defeating Franklin. In 1993 Espy became Pres. Bill Clinton's secretary of agriculture, and Bennie Thompson, a black Hinds County supervisor, won the seat. With the political realignment of the white electorate to the Republicans, the Democratic Party has become more dependent then ever on black voters, but the reluctance of white voters to vote for African American candidates means that Mississippi still has yet to elect a black candidate to a statewide office.

In a 2013 case, *Shelby County, Alabama, v. Holder*, the US Supreme Court invalidated the section of the Voting Rights Act that required preclearance from the US attorney general or a three-judge panel of the US District Court for the District of Columbia for institution of new voting practices in Mississippi and other areas with histories of voter discrimination. As a result, beginning with the June 3, 2014, primary election, all Mississippians were required to show a photo ID card before voting.

Chris Danielson
Montana Tech at the University
of Montana

James C. Cobb, *The Most Southern Place on Earth: The Mississippi Delta and the Roots of Regional Identity* (1992); John Dittmer, *Local People: The Struggle for Civil Rights in Mississippi* (1994); Steven F. Lawson, *Black Ballots: Voting Rights in the South, 1944–1969* (1999); Steven F. Lawson, *In Pursuit of Power: Southern Blacks and Electoral Politics, 1965–1982* (1985); Frank Parker, *Black Votes Count: Political Power in Mississippi after 1965* (1990); Abigail Thernstrom, *Whose Votes Count?: Affirmative Action and Minority Voting Rights* (1987); Raymond Wolters, *Right Turn: William Bradford Reynolds, the Reagan Administration, and Black Civil Rights* (1996).

W

Wade, L. Margaret
(1912–1995) Basketball Coach

Born on 30 December 1912 in McCool, Mississippi, Lily Margaret Wade played a pivotal role in the sport of women's basketball as both a player and a coach. Wade played basketball for two years while attending Cleveland High School, from which she graduated in 1929. Wade then spent three years playing for Delta State University, serving as team captain and earning all-conference honors each year and winning the most valuable player award in 1931 and 1932. The school's administration cut the women's basketball program after the 1932 season, however, arguing that the sport was too strenuous for women. Some women protested the decision by burning their athletic uniforms, but Delta State did not restore the program until 1973, when Wade became the coach.

In the intervening forty-one years, Wade had kept busy on the courts. She played semiprofessionally with the Tupelo Red Wings, leading the team to the Southern Championship and serving as the team captain in 1934–35 before a knee injury ended her career. Wade then found a new niche as a coach at Marietta High School (1933–34), Belden High School (1934–35), and Cleveland High School (1935–54), compiling an overall 476–94 record.

Wade headed the women's physical education department at Delta State University from 1959 to 1973, when she brought the school's women's basketball program back to life. She had immediate success, compiling a 16–2 record in her first season and developing the team into a national basketball powerhouse. Prior to her retirement in 1979, Wade's teams won three Association for Intercollegiate Athletics for Women national championships and posted an amazing fifty-one-game winning streak. Wade was the first woman enshrined in the Mississippi Sports Hall of Fame and in the Delta State University Hall of Fame. She was also honored by the Mississippi Coaches Hall of Fame, and in 1984 she was inducted into the Naismith Memorial Basketball Hall of Fame. The Margaret Wade Trophy is now awarded each year to the top women's college basketball player. She died on 16 February 1995. Delta State University dedicated a statue honoring Wade in 2014.

Emily Bowles-Smith
Lawrence University

Naismith Memorial Basketball Hall of Fame website, www.hoophall .com; Ernestine Gichner Miller and Carole A. Oglesby, *Making Her Mark: Firsts and Milestones in Women's Sports* (2002); Margaret Wade Collection, Charles W. Capps Jr. Archives and Museum, Delta State University.

Wages

In 1995 Mississippi's average wage was 77 percent of the average for the United States as a whole. Ten years later that number had fallen to 75 percent. And in 2015 it had dropped even further, to 73 percent, as Mississippi ranked last in the United States with an average weekly wage of $709. Between 1995 and 2005, average annual earnings increased 11 percent in real purchasing power, bringing the average wage up to 152 percent of the poverty threshold for a family of four. Thus, while substantial improvement in real earnings occurred, the rest of the country experienced even greater gains.

Among the industries in which the average wage in Mississippi has historically been higher than that of the country as a whole are forestry and fishing, mining, construction, transportation and warehousing, health care and social assistance, arts and recreation, and accommodation and food. Industries with wages historically at or below 75 percent of the US average included manufacturing, information services, finance and insurance, management of companies, and state and local government.

Mississippi's relatively low average wage has resulted primarily from two factors. First, some large, higher-paying industries, including manufacturing and finance and insurance, paid 75 percent or less of the US average. Second, Mississippi has had a relatively high number of workers in lower-paying industries, including retail trade, accommodation and food services, and state and local government, all of which have paid less than the state average wage.

The sizable wage gaps in manufacturing, information services, finance and insurance, management, educational services, and state and local government indicate the state's generally low level of economic development, which in turn is related to both the skill levels of the population and to the products and processes characterizing economic activities.

In 2006 African Americans with full-time, year-round employment earned 82 percent as much as similarly situated

W

whites across the United States; in Mississippi the ratio was 69 percent. Mississippi also had a higher wage gap by sex, with the state's full-time female workers earning 72 percent as much as men, compared to a national ratio of 77 percent. The wage gaps between women and men and between blacks and whites, however, were less in 2005 than they were in 1989, both in Mississippi and throughout the nation. Some of the decrease in the gender wage gap, however, resulted from stagnation in the real earnings of male high school graduates, a trend that did not hold for female graduates.

Among the state's major demographic groups, black women had the lowest wage rates, with median earnings of $21,046 in 2006. They earned only 69 percent of what African American women earned nationally and only 52 percent of what white men in the state earned. Mississippi's white males, however, had median earnings of $40,260, 88 percent of the figure for their national counterparts, the same ratio as the state's white women. Black males in Mississippi earned 80 percent of the national median for their counterparts and 92 percent of the median for white women in the state. The overall wage gap between women and men in Mississippi ranks the state in the bottom half of the nation. Closing the wage gap between men and women in Mississippi could probably cut the poverty rate in half for women and their families, in both single-parent and two-parent homes.

Part, but not all, of the wage gaps by race and gender can be explained by differences in occupations. A 1996 study showed that occupational differences by race and sex were greater in Mississippi than in the South as a whole and greater in the region than in the entire United States.

Mississippians working to reduce the wage gaps in the state have suggested several strategies. Employers, for example, could encourage women and minorities to pursue non-traditional occupations by providing training opportunities to current employees, instituting broader searches for new employees, and ensuring career advancement paths for all employees. Educational institutions could do more to train all students and to encourage students to consider nontraditional options. Pay equity across job categories would also tend to reduce gender wage gaps by ensuring that the training and skills requirements of different jobs are systematically compared when setting pay rates.

Marianne Hill
Mississippi Board of Trustees
of State Institutions of Higher
Learning

Marianne Hill, *Mississippi Economic Review and Outlook* (February 1996, December 2006); Institute for Women's Policy Research website, www.iwpr.org; Stephanie Jones, ed., *State of Black America* (2007); Laurence Mishel, Jared Bernstein, and Heidi Shierholz, *The State of Working America, 2006–2007,* www.epinet.org; National Urban League website, www.nul.org; Robert Stoker and Michael Rich, *Lessons and Limits: Tax Incentives and Rebuilding the Gulf Coast after Katrina* (August 2006), www.brookings.org; US Bureau of Economic Analysis website, www.bea.gov; US Bureau of the Census website, www.census.gov.

Wailes, Benjamin L. C.
(1797–1862) Scholar

Benjamin Leonard Covington Wailes was born in Columbia County, Georgia, on 1 August 1797, the oldest of nine children of Levin and Eleanor Wailes, who had come to Georgia from Maryland. In 1807 the Wailes family moved to the Mississippi Territory, where young Benjamin received his education at Jefferson College near Washington. He went on to serve as a trustee of the school for forty years, including a stint as president of the board.

Wailes learned the trade of surveying from his father and served as an assistant to the Choctaw agent, taking part in treaty negotiations with the Choctaw. In 1820 Wailes married a distant cousin, Rebecca Susanna Magruder Covington, the daughter of Brig. Gen. Leonard Covington. They made their home near Washington, where he was a cotton planter and served as registrar of the local land office, and they ultimately had ten children, only five of whom survived past the age of four. Wailes served in the state legislature in 1825–26, although he generally avoided politics. He was allied with the Whigs at a time when the Democrats dominated most of Mississippi.

Wailes traveled extensively and became known for his knowledge of the region's geography, geology, and natural history. He began accumulating natural history objects, establishing collections at Jefferson College, the University of Mississippi, and the State Capitol. He also contributed specimens to scientists and museums elsewhere, including the Smithsonian Institution.

In late 1851 Wailes was appointed assistant professor of geology and agriculture at the University of Mississippi. He

Benjamin Wailes (Archives and Records Services Division, Mississippi Department of Archives and History [PI STA W35 Box 20 R72 B4 56 Folder 77 #1])

was to assist Dr. John Millington, professor of geology and agriculture, whom the legislature had charged with conducting an agricultural and geological survey of the state. Millington had barely begun work on the survey when he resigned, and the entire task fell to Wailes, who received the title of state geologist. Wailes traveled seventy-three hundred miles around the state and collected thousands of specimens. By special act of the legislature, the specimens received a room in the State House in Jackson. These efforts culminated in his 1854 *Report on the Agriculture and Geology of Mississippi*. Although it included 356 pages plus appendixes, Wailes was dissatisfied with the effort and declared that it had been "untowardly postponed" and "hurriedly executed." Though he considered his effort just a beginning, the report provided the first lists of Mississippi's plants and animals as well as information on the state's geological and agricultural resources, monthly weather data for Jackson for 1852–53, and an outline of the state's history.

As his understanding of Mississippi grew, Wailes became increasingly interested in the history of the region. In 1858 he was instrumental in founding the Mississippi Historical Society and served as its president. Though the organization existed for little more than a year, under its auspices Wailes accumulated significant historical documents from throughout North America and preserved them. Wailes generously shared his collections with other historians and scientists. He had come to know many of the top scientists of his time and had been of assistance to many of them. British geologist Sir Charles Lyell visited Wailes in Mississippi, and among those who received specimens from him and/or contributed comments for his survey work were Louis Agassiz, John James Audubon, Spencer Fullerton Baird, and John Cassin. Wailes died on 16 November 1862.

The Mississippi Historical Society was reborn in 1898, and today, the highest honor it bestows is the B. L. C. Wailes Award for national distinction in the field of history.

Jerome A. Jackson
Florida Gulf Coast University

Mississippi History Now website, http://mshistorynow.mdah.state.ms.us; Charles S. Sydnor, *A Gentleman of the Old Natchez Region: Benjamin L. C. Wailes* (1938); Charles S. Sydnor, *Journal of Southern History* 1 (1935); Benjamin C. Wailes, *Memoir of Leonard Covington* (1928); Benjamin C. Wailes, *Report on the Agriculture and Geology of Mississippi* (1854).

Waller, William Lowe
(1926–2011) Fifty-Sixth Governor, 1972–1976

In the early 1970s, after the civil rights movement had brought enormous changes to the South, a group of young and progressive southern governors attracted national attention. Among them were Dale Bumpers of Arkansas, Reubin Askew of Florida, Jimmy Carter of Georgia, and William Waller of Mississippi. Waller was elected at a crucial time in the state's history, and his constructive leadership helped chart a new direction for Mississippi.

Waller, who was born in Lafayette County, Mississippi, on 21 October 1926, attended the public schools in the Black Jack community of Panola County and graduated from Oxford High School. After earning his bachelor of arts at Memphis State University and his law degree from the University of Mississippi, Waller established a law practice in Jackson. After serving as an intelligence officer during the Korean War, Waller was elected district attorney for the 7th Judicial District in 1959 and reelected in 1963. His most famous case was the Medgar Evers assassination, in which his vigorous prosecution earned commendations and was often cited as an indication of the changing attitudes of Mississippi's public officials (although two all-white juries deadlocked and refused to convict Byron De La Beckwith at the time).

After an unsuccessful bid for governor in 1967, Waller was elected to the state's highest office four years later. In the Democratic primary, Waller offered himself as a critic of the "Capitol Street Gang"—the lawyers, banks, and corporations that held most of the influence and power in the state. In the general election Waller defeated independent Charles Evers, the brother of Medgar Evers and the first black Mississippian to run for governor.

One of the most important accomplishments of Waller's administration was the removal of tax-collecting responsibilities from the county sheriff's duties. The creation of a separate office to collect taxes, combined with a provision that allowed sheriffs to succeed themselves, improved the quality of law enforcement in Mississippi and professionalized the office of sheriff. Waller also integrated the highway patrol and appointed blacks to boards, commissions, and other state agencies. For the first time in almost a century African Americans participated in affairs of state.

Under the leadership of Mississippi's First Lady, Carroll Overton Waller, the state's historic Governor's Mansion was saved from near collapse. Carroll Waller, who referred to the 130-year-old building as the Home of Our Heritage, presided over the mansion's restoration to its original 1842 design. In 1975, after completion of the three-and-a-half-year restoration, the Governor's Mansion was designated a National Historic Landmark.

W

After leaving office, Waller resumed his law practice in Jackson. He lost elections for US Senate in 1978 and the governorship in 1987. Waller published a memoir, *Straight Ahead*, in 2007 and died on 30 November 2011.

David G. Sansing
University of Mississippi

Jere Nash and Andy Taggart, *Mississippi Politics: The Struggle for Power, 1976–2008* (2nd ed., 2009); *Mississippi Official and Statistical Register* (1972–76); David Sansing and Carroll Waller, *A History of the Mississippi Governor's Mansion* (1977).

Walter Anderson Museum of Art

The Walter Anderson Museum of Art is a private, nonprofit art museum located in downtown Ocean Springs, Mississippi.

Not long after the death of her father, Walter Inglis Anderson, Mary Anderson Stebly Pickard began cataloging the astonishing body of work the Ocean Springs artist had left behind. She and her mother, Agnes Hellmuth Grinstead Anderson, were supported in their efforts to promote recognition for his achievements by family and friends, who formed the Friends of Walter Anderson in 1975. Bitsy Irby, Mary Brister, Betty Scott, Merle Tennyson, Hosford Fontaine, Paul Fugate, and Theo Inman of Jackson, along with Eldon Holmquist and Courtney Blossman of Ocean Springs, determined that the Ocean Spring Community Center should anchor a museum in Anderson's honor. In large part as a consequence of the diligence of Blossman, who served as president of the Friends of Walter Anderson from 1983 until the museum's completion, the Walter Anderson Museum of Art (WAMA) opened in 1991.

The museum building, designed by architect Ed Pickard, features a cruciform plan and is constructed out of redwood painted gray. It is connected to the Ocean Springs Community Center, where wall murals that Anderson painted for the public's education and enjoyment in 1952 have been preserved and are on permanent display. This monumental work depicts the 1699 Mississippi Coast landing of Pierre Le Moyne, Sieur d'Iberville, who established the first capital of the Louisiana Territory at Fort Maurepas in what is now Ocean Springs. Also depicting the region's natural history, the majority of the Community Center's ninety-foot expanses are festooned with the series Anderson called the *Seven Climates* of Ocean Springs. A room from the artist's cottage residence at Shearwater Pottery is installed at the far end of the axial museum structure. In this "Little Room" Anderson painted a four-wall mural depicting his vision of a day on the Gulf Coast, from sunrise to night. With the Little Room's intense scenes based on Psalm 104's praise for the gift of light, and the Community Center's luminescent march through the celestial seasons, the museum is thus flanked by an unmatched set of coup d'oeil interior spaces. In contrast, the gallery spaces provide serene stretches of thirty-foot-tall pickled-pine walls, with vaults and skylights that gaze out on placid patio scenes.

Panels that the Works Progress Administration commissioned Anderson to paint for the Ocean Springs High School auditorium in 1934 are on permanent display in the museum lobby and galleries. Donated to WAMA by the school board in 1989, these massive Aegean-style Art Deco illustrations, *Ocean Springs: Past and Present*, joined a collection of paintings and pottery that the Friends of Walter Anderson began to amass in 1975. Now with more than eight hundred pieces, WAMA's Permanent Collection includes watercolor and oil paintings; drawings in pencil, ink, and crayon; carved linoleum blocks and prints; ceramics; wood sculpture, and furniture—all of which, with the exception of 173 of carved linoleum blocks that were kept in an offsite storage facility that flooded, rode out Hurricane Katrina safely in the museum's vault.

WAMA serves as a center of learning, cultural enrichment, and enjoyment for the many-faceted population of Ocean Springs, the Gulf South Region, and visitors to the area. Originally conceived as a museum dedicated to the work of one artist, the institution's scope has been expanded to collect, preserve, exhibit, and interpret artworks created by Walter Anderson's brothers, Peter and James McConnell Anderson. In 2003 WAMA celebrated the seventy-fifth anniversary of Peter Anderson's pottery enterprise with an exhibition, *Shaping a Legacy: Shearwater Pottery and Its Contemporaries*, and in 2007 James Anderson was the featured artist in the WAMA exhibition *Introspective Mind: The "Mac" Anderson Centennial Exhibition*.

The centennial of Walter Anderson's birth, 2003, was the occasion for two major WAMA exhibitions. The first, *Fortune's Favorite Child: Walter Anderson, 1903–2003*, was coordinated by Christopher Maurer, author of the artist's biography. The second, *The Centennial Exhibition: Walter Anderson, Everything I See Is New and Strange*, was coordinated by Linda Crocker Simmons, curator emeritus at the Corcoran Museum in Washington, D.C. It opened in the Smithsonian Institution's Arts and Industries Building. For this event, WAMA, in conjunction with the University Press of Mississippi, published a comprehensive catalog, *The Art of Walter Anderson*.

Susan McClamroch
Louisiana Landmarks Society

Patti Carr Black, *Art in Mississippi, 1720–1980* (1998); Anne R. King, *Walls of Light: The Murals of Walter Anderson* (1999); Patricia Pinson, ed., *The Art of Walter Anderson* (2003); Walter Anderson Museum of Art website, www.walterandersonmuseum.org.

Walthall, Edward Cary
(1831–1898) Confederate General and Politician

Edward Cary Walthall, a Confederate general and US senator, was born in Richmond, Virginia, on 4 April 1831 to Sally Wilkinson Whitehall and Barrett White Walthall, a merchant who moved his family to Holly Springs, Mississippi, after going bankrupt in 1841. Edward was educated at an Episcopal school, St. Thomas Hall, and spent one year studying law with his brother-in-law, George R. Freeman, in Pontotoc. Walthall was admitted to the bar in 1852 and moved to Coffeeville. In 1856 he was elected district attorney. The same year, he married Sophie Bridges, though she died soon thereafter. He married Mary Lecky Jones in 1859 and adopted her daughter.

After the outbreak of the Civil War Walthall volunteered with the Yalobusha Rifles and was elected first lieutenant. When the Rifles became part of the 15th Mississippi Regiment he was elected lieutenant colonel. Walthall and other members of the command first saw action in eastern Kentucky at Mills Springs on 19 January 1862, where his steady resolve earned him favorable attention despite the fact that the Confederate Army was soundly defeated in the engagement. He won promotion to colonel of the 29th Mississippi Regiment in April 1862 and led it in the Kentucky Campaign, where the unit participated in an assault on a Federal garrison at Munfordville. He was promoted to brigadier general in late November and took command of a brigade of several Mississippi regiments. Although he missed the Battle of Stones River (Murfreesboro) because of illness, he was in command at Chickamauga, where his forces were heavily engaged and acquitted themselves well. During the Battle of Lookout Mountain, his brigade was stationed on the front of the mountain. On 24 November 1863 Union forces launched a massive assault, attempting to capture the summit. Dense fog shrouded the area and made it difficult for Walthall's men to discern enemy movements. After a prolonged resistance, an enormous number of Walthall's men were cut off and captured. With his command reduced to little more than a single regiment, Walthall and his survivors fled down the mountain and made their way across to Missionary Ridge. The next day a wave of Union infantry clambered up Missionary Ridge, breaking the Confederate line in several

places. At a critical juncture Walthall's depleted brigade was ordered to alter its position and check the enemy. Despite receiving a severe wound in the foot, Walthall remained with his troops as they drove the enemy back and held their ground until withdrawing after nightfall.

Walthall's brigade participated in the Atlanta Campaign and fought with distinction at Resaca and Kennesaw Mountain. He was promoted to major general and divisional command on 6 July 1864 and led troops at Peachtree Creek and Ezra Church. During John Bell Hood's ill-fated invasion of Tennessee, Walthall led unsuccessful assaults against Federal forces at Franklin on 30 November 1864, having two horses shot from underneath him. Following the crushing defeat at Nashville the next month, Walthall led eight shrunken brigades that formed the rear guard of the army. This command and cavalry under Nathan Bedford Forrest protected the remnants of Hood's army as they retreated into Mississippi. Walthall and what was left of his division went to North Carolina, where he was paroled on 1 May 1865.

Walthall met L. Q. C. Lamar while traveling home from the war, and that relationship profoundly shaped the remainder of Walthall's life. The two men became close friends, and Lamar served as Walthall's political mentor. For a brief time they practiced law together in Coffeeville. In 1871 Walthall moved to Grenada, where he became a corporate lawyer, representing the Mississippi Central Railroad and the Illinois Central Railroad after it acquired the Mississippi line. He served as a delegate to four Democratic National Conventions between 1868 and 1884 and worked to end Reconstruction in Mississippi. He attended the Democratic-Conservative convention in August 1875 that promised to protect former slaves' civil rights while plotting to restore white supremacy under the auspices of the Democratic Party at the county level. During the ensuing campaign Walthall spoke extensively throughout the state on behalf of the effort to oust Republicans from power. Neither Lamar nor Walthall espoused violence and racial intimidation, and they in fact courted black voters, but they did so primarily to avoid federal intervention in the November state election. Followers were less constrained in many areas, and a combination of fraud and violence resulted in an overwhelming Democratic victory. Walthall did intervene in an Election Day altercation in Grenada sparked by the beating of a black man by an angry white that threatened to flare into a race riot, but intimidated African Americans refused to return to the polls.

Lamar worked assiduously to have the state legislature select Walthall to replace outgoing senator Blanche K. Bruce in 1881, but a deadlock ensued and Walthall withdrew in favor of James Z. George, who embarked on the first of his three terms. When Grover Cleveland selected Lamar to serve as secretary of the interior in 1885, Walthall was chosen to finish out the remaining year of Lamar's term. He was elected by the state legislature to his own term in 1886 and served in the Senate until 1894, when he resigned as a consequence of

W

ill health. However, he regained his seat in March 1895 and continued to represent Mississippi until his death in Washington, D.C., on 21 April 1898.

For all his prominence, Walthall is something of an enigma. No biography exists, in part because no large body of letters has survived in any repository. What can be stated with certainty is that Walthall followed Lamar's lead in pursuing national reconciliation while hoping to limit the federal government's interference in state political affairs.

Christopher Losson
St. Joseph, Missouri

William C. Harris, *The Day of the Carpetbagger: Republican Reconstruction in Mississippi* (1979); Charles Hooker, *Confederate Military History: Mississippi*, ed. Clement A. Evans (1899); Edward Mayes, *Lucius Q. C. Lamar: His Life, Times, and Speeches, 1825–1893* (1896); *Memorial Addresses on the Life and Character of Edward C. Walthall (Late a Senator from Mississippi) Delivered in the Senate and House of Representatives, Fifty-Fifth Congress, Second and Third Sessions* (1899); Dunbar Rowland, *Encyclopedia of Mississippi History: Comprising Sketches of Counties, Towns, Events, Institutions, and Persons* (1907); E. T. Sykes, *Walthall's Brigade: A Cursory Sketch, with Personal Experiences of Walthall's Brigade, Army of Tennessee, C.S.A., 1862–1865* (1905).

Walthall County

Walthall County, located in southern Mississippi, in the longleaf pine belt on the Louisiana border, developed out of sections of Pike and Marion Counties in 1914, making it of one the newest counties in the state. Its name derives from the Confederate general and US senator Edward Cary Walthall. The county seat is Tylertown.

In the 1920 census, Walthall had 13,455 residents, including 7,789 whites and 5,666 African Americans. Walthall depended on agriculture for economic growth, focusing first on cotton and later on cattle. In the first decade of the county's existence, 55 percent of Walthall farmers owned their land.

In 1930 Walthall County's population grew to 13,871, with white residents only slightly outnumbering African Americans. Walthall was very much a rural county, with no urban population and only 80 industrial workers in eight manufacturing establishments. Tenant farmers operated more than half of Walthall's thirty-four-hundred farms. Like many South Mississippi counties, Walthall farmers concentrated first on dairy cattle, then corn, swine, and cotton. Walthall had a very small immigrant population—one person from England, one from France, and two from Greece.

Born in Tylertown in 1931, Paul Pittman became publisher of the *Tylertown Times* in 1957 and continued in that role until his death in 1983. Pittman also helped establish the county's first radio station, WTYL, and took part in Democratic Party politics.

African Americans in Walthall County have a long history of establishing community organizations—initially churches and schools, a chapter of the Universal Negro Improvement Association in the 1920s and 1930s, and an active chapter of the National Association for the Advancement of Colored People that challenged local segregated schools immediately after the US Supreme Court's 1954 *Brown v. Board of Education* decision. C. C. Bryant, an important community activist and civil rights organizer in Pike County in the 1950s and 1960s, was born in Walthall County in 1917.

Two figures important in changing Mississippi education spent significant time in Walthall County. Cleopatra Thompson, a professor at Jackson State from the 1940s through the 1970s, spent part of her early career teaching at the Walthall County Training School. Surgeon Verner Smith Holmes grew up in Walthall County and went on to become a member of the Board of Trustees of the State Institutions of Higher Learning, opposing Gov. Ross Barnett's efforts to prevent the desegregation of the University of Mississippi in 1962.

Walthall County's population remained stable through the 1950s, though the nature of employment shifted. While jobs in agriculture declined, manufacturing employment rose. By 1960 22 percent of all workers in Walthall County held industrial jobs, mostly in the apparel industry, and 35 percent worked in agriculture. In 1960, 13,761 people called Walthall County home.

Like most counties in southern Mississippi, Walthall County's 2010 population was predominantly white and had grown slowly since the 1960s. The county's population of 15,443 was 53.4 percent white and 44.5 percent African Americans.

Mississippi Encyclopedia Staff
University of Mississippi

Mississippi State Planning Commission, *Progress Report on State Planning in Mississippi* (1938); *Mississippi Statistical Abstract*, Mississippi State University (1952–2010); Charles Sydnor and Claude Bennett, *Mississippi History* (1939); University of Virginia Library, Historical Census Browser website, http://mapserver.lib.virginia.edu; E. Nolan Waller and Dani A. Smith, *Growth Profiles of Mississippi's Counties, 1960–1980* (1985); Walthall County Chamber of Commerce website, www.walthallcountychamber.org.

Ward, Jerry W., Jr.
(b. 1943) Writer

A much-respected poet, scholar, and professor, Jerry Washington Ward Jr., the son of Jerry W. Ward Sr. and Mary Theriot Ward, was born in Washington, D.C., on 31 July 1943. When he was six years old, his family moved to Mississippi. Ward attended Our Mother of Sorrows High School in Biloxi and Magnolia High School in Moss Point before enrolling at Tougaloo College after his junior year. He received a bachelor's degree in mathematics from Tougaloo in 1964.

In the spring of 1964 Ward published a set of three poems, "Black Aphrodite," "Five Fingers of French Velvet . . . ," and "Untitled #4," in *Daemon*, a Tougaloo publication. Later that year, "Double Sonnet" was published in *The Tougazette*. In 1966 Ward earned a master's degree from the Illinois Institute of Technology. His career expanded to a more regional audience with the May 1968 publication of "Smoke from a Fire" in *The Word* at the State University of New York at Albany. "Smoke from a Fire" showed T. S. Eliot's influence on Ward's early writings. A revision of the poem appeared as "The Staid Echo" in the *Mississippi Review*. His first national publications were "Ours," printed in 1972 in *Black Creation*; "Generation Gap" and "Heavy Feelings," printed in *Hoo-Doo* in 1973; and "Manhood in a Violent Space," printed in *Black Collegian* in 1983. The publications in *Hoo-Doo* and *Black Collegian* led to Ward's lasting friendships with Ahmos Zu-Bolton and Kalamu ya Salaam. He continued publishing poems in regional journals and became a professor of literature at Tougaloo in 1970.

In the early 1970s Ward's poems began to appear in national publications, and he became associated with BLKARTSOUTH, an outgrowth of New Orleans's Free

Jerry Ward Jr. (Courtesy McNeal Cayette)

Southern Theater, which had been founded in 1964 to nurture and celebrate black theater and to use theater as a tool for social and political reform/activism. Created in 1968, BLKARTSOUTH boasted a number of noted writers and performers from across the South, including Tom Dent, Wendell Narcisse, Kalamu ya Salaam, Lorenzo Thomas, Nayo Barbara Malcolm Watkins, John O'Neal, Chakula Cha Jua (McNeal Cayette), Levi Frazier, Quo Vadis Gex Breaux, Tony Bolden, and Raymond Breaux. In November 1973 Ward met Dent and became involved with the work of the Southern Black Cultural Alliance, a community theater coalition. After earning a doctorate in English at the University of Virginia in 1978, Ward joined the alliance's executive committee, serving until 1983.

Ward was also an early member of the Mississippi Cultural Arts Coalition. Founded in 1982 and directed by Watkins, the coalition was directly responsible for developing the Farish Street Festival, which celebrates the area's history as the center of educational, social, political, religious, and entertainment activities for Jackson's African American community. Ward also worked with jazz bassist John Reese's Black Arts Music Society, a collaboration that inspired Ward's signature poem "Jazz to Jackson to John" (1981). In 1982 Ward became a founding member of the Jackson Writers Workshop, which released a chapbook, *Mississippi Earthworks*. Members also published in the *Jackson Advocate* and national magazines while working to support black theater at Jackson State and Tougaloo and the careers of a new generation of artists.

During the 1990s Ward edited some noted anthologies, including *Redefining American Literary History* (1990), *Black Southern Voices* (1992), and *Trouble the Water: 250 Years of African American Poetry* (1997). In 1993 Ward wrote the introduction to a new edition of Richard Wright's *Black Boy*.

Ward remained the Lawrence Durgin Professor of Literature at Tougaloo College until 2002, serving as chair of the Department of English from 1979 to 1986, as a member of the Mississippi Humanities Council from 1984 to 1988, and on the Mississippi Advisory Committee for the US Commission on Civil Rights from 1987 to 1997. He also cofounded the Richard Wright Circle and the *Richard Wright Newsletter*. In 2003 Ward became a distinguished professor of English and African American world studies at Dillard University. In August 2005 he evacuated New Orleans just prior to Hurricane Katrina, and the following year he published *The Katrina Papers: A Journal of Trauma and Recovery*. In 2011 the Chinese Ministry of Education selected Ward to participate in a four-year teaching program at Central China Normal University as part of the Famous Overseas Professors project. Ward has also coedited *The Richard Wright Encyclopedia* (with Robert Butler, 2008) and *The Cambridge History of African American Literature* (with Maryemma Graham, 2011).

Ward's two most noted poems are "Jazz to Jackson to John" and "Don't Be Fourteen in Mississippi." Both works

W

display Ward's ability to balance and enhance passion with technique, combining vivid imagery with biting wordplay that causes the familiar to ring with a new truth. Ward has received numerous awards, including the Kent Fellowship (1975–77), the Tougaloo College Outstanding Teaching Award (1978–80), the United Negro College Fund's Distinguished Scholar Award (1981–82) and Distinguished Scholar-in-Residence (1987–88), the Public Humanities Scholar Award from the Mississippi Humanities Council (1998), and the Darwin T. Turner Award from African American Literature and Culture Society (2000). In 2001 he was inducted into the International Literary Hall of Fame for Writers of African Descent. He retired from Dillard University in 2012 and now serves on the board of Kansas University's Project on the History of Black Writing.

C. Liegh McInnis
Clinton, Mississippi

Dorothy Abbott, ed., *Mississippi Writers: Reflections of Childhood and Youth: Poetry* (1988); Kansas University Project on the History of Black Writing website, https://hbw.ku.edu/; Rudolph Lewis, *Chicken Bones: A Journal for Literary and Artistic African-American Themes* (April 2006); C. Liegh McInnis, *Prose: Essays and Letters* (2007); Jerry W. Ward, interview by C. Liegh McInnis (18 July 2007).

Ward, Jesmyn
(b. 1977). Author

Born and raised in DeLisle, Mississippi, along the Gulf Coast, Jesmyn Ward has become a leading American writer on issues of race, struggle, and survival. She attended Stanford University and earned a master of fine arts degree from the University of Michigan in 2005, shortly before Hurricane Katrina flooded her family's home. She had a Stegner Fellowship, a writer's residency program at Stanford University, from 2008 to 2010, and taught and wrote as the John and Renée Grisham Writer in Residence at the University of Mississippi the following year. In 2014 she joined the English department at Tulane University. She has published two novels, *Where the Line Bleeds* (2008) and *Salvage the Bones* (2011), and a memoir, *Men We Reaped* (2013).

Where the Line Bleeds follows two teenagers, Joshua and Christopher DeLisle, dealing with difficult realities on the Mississippi Gulf Coast. *Salvage the Bones*, explores the days leading up to Hurricane Katrina and its immediate aftermath from the perspective of pregnant, fifteen-year-old Esch. She struggles to hide her pregnancy from her brothers and father as the family battles poverty, injury, and disaster. Ward focuses on the physical changes her characters undergo and how scars, wounds, and a burgeoning baby bump can reveal hidden internal realities. This emphasis on physical changes extends to the landscape as Katrina engulfs Esch's home. Despite the family's triumphant survival, it comes with heavy losses.

Men We Reaped alternates between Ward's personal and family history and the stories of five male friends and relatives, all of whom died in their early twenties—two in car crashes (including her brother, who was killed by a drunk driver in 2000), one by gunshot, one by suicide, one from a heart attack. Ward described telling the stories in *Men We Reaped* as "the hardest things I've ever done" and said she wrote in part to "understand a bit better why this epidemic happened." More broadly, she says she wrote to make clear that the lives of her brother and her friends matter in an economic, educational, and political system that expects little of young black men except trouble.

Ward received considerable attention when *Salvage the Bones* won the National Book Award as the best work of fiction published in 2011. When a CNN interviewer asked how growing up on the Gulf Coast influenced her work, Ward replied, "I have a love-hate relationship with home. There's so much I love about home, but then there's a lot that I can acknowledge that I dislike about home. And acknowledging that to myself helps me see that place more clearly and to bring readers to that place. I just think these stories are worth being told and these people are worth being written about. I think our stories are universal stories. In the end, it's about us as human beings trying to survive and make the best of what we have right here, right now."

Meghan Holmes
University of Mississippi

Ted Ownby
University of Mississippi

Ed Lavandera, CNN in America website, http://inamerica.blogs.cnn.com; Richard Torres, National Public Radio website, www.npr.org; Jesmyn Ward, "No Mercy in Motion" (3 September 2013), www.guernicamag.com/features/no-mercy-in-motion/.

Ward, Sela
(b. 1956) Actress

Actress Sela Ann Ward, the daughter of Granberry Holland Ward Jr. and Annie Kate Boswell Ward, was born on 11 July 1956 in Meridian. She attended the University of Alabama, where she was a cheerleader and Homecoming queen. After graduating with a degree in art and advertising, Ward worked in advertising in Memphis and in New York City, where she began working as a model and made television commercials. She then moved to Los Angeles to pursue an acting career. Her first big-screen appearance came in *The Man Who Loved Women* (1983). Shortly thereafter, she landed a part in a television series, *Emerald Point N.A.S.* (1983–84). Perhaps best known for her roles in the TV series *Sisters* (1991–95), *Once and Again* (1999–2002), and *CSI: NY* (2010–13), she has also made numerous appearances on other shows and in films, including *Gone Girl* (2014) and *Independence Day: Resurgence* (2016). Ward has received Emmy Awards for her work on *Sisters* and *Once and Again* as well as a CableACE Award for her performance as the title character in a television movie, *Almost Golden: The Jessica Savitch Story* (1995).

Ward has been married to venture capitalist Howard Sherman since 1992, and they have two children. Primarily based in Los Angeles, Ward and her family maintain a farm outside Meridian and visit there several times a year. In 2000 Ward established the Hope Village for Children, a residential home for neglected and abused children in Meridian.

Teresa Arrington
Blue Mountain College

Hope Village for Children website, www.hopevillagems.org; Internet Movie Database website, www.imdb.com; Official Sela Ward Fan Club website, www.selawardtv.com; Jennifer Russell, *Y'all: The Magazine of Southern People* (September–October 2005); Sela Ward, *Guideposts Magazine* (December 2006).

Warner, Pecolia
(1901–1983) Quilter

Born on 9 March 1901 near Bentonia, Mississippi, raised on plantations in the Delta, and educated in Yazoo City, Pecolia Leola Deborah Jackson was taught to sew at the age of seven by her mother, Katherine Brant Jackson, a schoolteacher, who also taught her daughter to cook, clean, wash, and iron. Her first quilt was made from little "strings" of rectangular cloth, sewn into long strips alternately pieced with solid strips to fashion a top quilt. The pattern, which Katherine Jackson called Spider Leg, is the oldest one known for African American quilters. It is similar to African textiles made by sewing woven strips together, and it is the one most often first taught to young children.

Pecolia Jackson married five times and became known as a quilter after her marriage to Sam Warner. She considered her quilt-making skills a gift from God. Inspired by memories of her mother's quilts, by dreams, by pattern books, by household objects, and by farming artifacts, Warner's quilts are in the mainstream of African American textile traditions, which are distinguished from Euro-American textile traditions by organizational strips; bold, contrasting colors; large designs; asymmetrical arrangements; multiple patterns; and improvisation. Warner often commented on the importance of having colors "hit each other right," on how "stripping" a quilt brought out the designs, and how varying parts of a pattern made quilt designs more interesting.

Warner lived in New Orleans, Washington, D.C., and Chicago, working as a domestic servant for white employers. She first received attention as a folk artist in 1977 when folklorist William Ferris featured her in his film, *Four Women Artists*. Her quilts appeared in numerous exhibitions, including *Folk Art and Craft: The Deep South*, a traveling exhibition organized by the Center for Southern Folklore for the Smithsonian Institution. She was a featured artist at folklife festivals in the late 1970s. After suffering a series of small strokes, she died in March 1983.

Maude Southwell Wahlman
University of Missouri at
Kansas City

Patti Carr Black, ed., *Made by Hand: Mississippi Folk Art* (1980); William Ferris, ed., *Afro-American Folk Art and Crafts* (1983); Robert Farris Thompson, *Flash of the Spirit: African and Afro-American Art and Philosophy* (1983); John Michael Vlach, *The Afro-American Tradition in Decorative Arts* (1978); Maude Southwell Wahlman, in *Something to Keep You Warm*, ed. Patti Carr Black (1981); Maude Southwell Wahlman with John Scully, in *Afro-American Folk Art and Crafts*, ed. William Ferris (1983); Maude Southwell Wahlman with Ella King Torrey, *Ten Afro-American Quilters* (1983).

Warren County

Warren County, perhaps best known for the significance of the Siege of Vicksburg during the Civil War, was one of Mississippi's original counties. Located on the bluffs above the Mississippi River in the southwestern part of the state, Warren County lies due west of Jackson. To paraphrase a famous statement by Mississippi writer David Cohn, the Delta starts in Memphis and ends in Vicksburg, the Warren County seat. Before European contact, the area that became Warren County was home to mound-building people with connections up and down the river. The French negotiated with small numbers of Tunica and other Native American groups when establishing a small settlement, Fort St. Pierre, in 1719. They abandoned the fort after the Natchez War in the 1730s.

The county formed in 1809 and was named for Revolutionary War general Joseph Warren. In 1820 Warren County had a population of 1,406 free persons and 1,287 slaves. Like most frontier societies, Warren was overwhelmingly agricultural, with just 37 manufacturing workers. Cattle were important in early Warren County, and cotton was becoming the area's dominant crop. By 1830 Warren County had a population of 7,861, including 4,483 slaves, the state's fourth-highest total.

Vicksburg developed quickly into Mississippi's second-largest community, trailing only Natchez. By 1840 Warren had, by standards of antebellum Mississippi, an urbanizing population. Its total of 15,820 people ranked fourth in the state. About two-thirds of residents were slaves, and Vicksburg had a large slave market. As a river town engaged in considerable commerce, Vicksburg, a popular steamboat stop, had far more people employed in trade (289) than any other Mississippi county, and its 472 manufacturing workers also outnumbered any other county in the state. Free African Americans tended to congregate in Vicksburg and other river towns, and Warren was one of only three counties in Mississippi with more than one hundred free African Americans.

By 1860 Warren County's population had grown to 20,696, including 13,763 slaves. The number of free African Americans had declined to 37. The county's twenty-four manufacturing establishments employed 477 people, including 245 men working on steamboats and others making boots, shoes, and clothing and dealing with lumber and shingles. The county's 1,041 foreign-born residents, many of them Irish and Italian, ranked second-most in the state behind Adams County.

Agriculture thrived in Warren County on the eve of the Civil War, with slaves comprising two-thirds of the population. Warren ranked thirteenth in the state in the production of cotton, first in orchard products, and second in potatoes but near the bottom in corn.

In 1860 Warren County was home to eighteen churches: eight Methodist, six Baptist, two Episcopal, and single Catholic and Presbyterian churches. A Catholic group, the Sisters of Mercy, began a unique educational and religious mission in Vicksburg in 1860. Mississippi's second Jewish congregation started in Vicksburg in 1841. Prominent Mississippians from antebellum Warren County included Jefferson Davis, a planter and West Point–trained military leader who served as a US congressman, head of the War Department, and a US senator before becoming president of the Confederate States of America. Alexander McNutt, Mississippi governor and author of stories about the southwestern frontier, was a Warren County planter. Henry Stuart Foote served Mississippi in the US Senate and as governor.

Vicksburg, sometimes called the Gibraltar of the Confederacy, was crucial to Civil War military strategy. As early as 1861 Abraham Lincoln said, "Vicksburg is the key." Union attempts to take Vicksburg failed in the summer of 1862, in part because of the difficulties of geography, with the city resting high above the river, and in part because of the success of the CSS *Arkansas*, a Confederate ironclad. Late that year, Union general Ulysses S. Grant started planning another, more sustained effort to take Vicksburg that included building a canal so that troops could move beyond the range of Confederate guns; complicated efforts to surround the city; and the gathering of a large force. A series of battles led Grant's troops to the outskirts of Vicksburg, where Confederates led by John C. Pemberton held out from May until 3 July 1863, when they surrendered. Union troops entered the city on Independence Day.

As a consequence of its military importance and of the sacrifices made by so many people, Vicksburg became a symbolic center for memorializing Civil War soldiers. Efforts to honor soldiers began when the federal government created a national cemetery for Union soldiers in Vicksburg in 1865. A broad area known as Soldiers' Rest is the largest Confederate burial ground in Mississippi. In the 1890s women in Vicksburg started one of the first chapters of the United Daughters of the Confederacy, and in 1899 Congress established the Vicksburg National Military Park, with more than 1,300 monuments commemorating specific moments in the Vicksburg Campaign.

Warren County became one of the key areas for contests over the meanings of freedom during and after the war. Vicksburg was home of one of the larger camps for escaped slaves, called *contraband* by Union forces, and Grant's troops included some of the first African American soldiers to fight in Mississippi. During Reconstruction, some whites in Vicksburg formed the Mississippi White Line, which opposed African American voting and office-holding through violence and other intimidation. And Warren County natives Isaiah Montgomery, Joshua Montgomery, and Benjamin Green, all of whom were former slaves from the Davis Bend plantation, became leaders in the all-black settlement at Mound Bayou in the 1880s.

After the Civil War, Warren remained one of Mississippi's largest counties, with a population smaller than only Hinds and Yazoo. While the number of whites in the county increased steadily, the number of African Americans increased dramatically, and in 1880 22,516 of the 31,238 residents (72 percent) were African American. With 1,105 foreign-born people, Warren had by far the state's largest population of immigrants, including more than 400 natives of Ireland and almost 400 Germans as well as smaller but significant numbers of natives of England, Scotland, and France.

Like most of Mississippi, postbellum Warren County remained heavily agricultural. Its farmers ranked twelfth in the state in producing cotton and much lower in most other categories. Yet part of what distinguished the county was its 59 manufacturing establishments, employing 315 men, 17 children, and no women—the third-most industrial workers in the state. In 1880 Warren ranked second in the state in total industrial production, trailing only Copiah County.

By 1900 Warren County had 40,912 residents, three-quarters of them African American. The county's 1,490 industrial workers were the second-most in the state, with the second-highest total industrial wages. Only 72 of those workers were women. The Knights of Labor had some successes organizing Warren County lumber workers in the late 1800s, mounting one major strike in 1887 and playing a role in Vicksburg politics. Nearly 800 foreign-born men and women lived in the county, most of them from Germany and Ireland, with other groups coming from Italy, England, and Sweden. A small but significant group of Syrians and Lebanese lived in Vicksburg. Outside Vicksburg, the county remained heavily agricultural, with more than 4,000 farms. Only 181 of the 3,481 African American farmers owned their land, compared to 313 of the 577 white farmers. Warren had one of the highest numbers of sharecroppers and tenants in the state.

Religious census reports for 1916 and 1926 show the distinctiveness of Warren County. Its largest group were Missionary Baptists, and its second-largest was the Roman Catholic Church. Warren had the third-highest number of Catholics in Mississippi, trailing only the coastal counties of Harrison and Hancock. Other large groups included the Methodist Episcopal Church, South; the African Methodist Episcopal Church; the Southern Baptists; the Episcopalians; and the Presbyterians. Joseph Brunini, born in Vicksburg in 1909, became an important Catholic bishop in Mississippi.

Warren County has produced an impressive array of visual artists. Andrew Bucci, born in Vicksburg in 1923, studied with Mississippi's Marie Hull and achieved renown as a painter. Carver Victor "Hickory Stick Vic" Bobb and quilter Martha Skelton, an Oklahoma native, did their work in Warren County, and in the 1970s self-taught artist Earl Simmons began Earl's Art Shop in Bovina. In the 1980s H. D. Dennis turned his wife's business outside Vicksburg into a singular work of art, *Margaret's Grocery*. William Ferris, a scholar of folk traditions in music, speech, and visual art, grew up outside Vicksburg, and innovative fashion designer Patrick Kelly was born in Vicksburg in 1954.

Numerous innovators in literature, film, and music also have roots in Warren County. Ellen Gilchrist, author of poetry and novels such as *In the Land of Dreamy Dreams*, was born in Vicksburg. One of the early leaders of silent film, actor and director Larry Semon, was born in Vicksburg in 1889. Actress Beah Richards, born in 1926, had a long and impressive career as an actress, while filmmaker Charles Burnett, best known for such unconventional films as *Killer of Sheep*, was born in Vicksburg in 1944. Playwright Mart Crowley, another Vicksburg native, is most famous for his long-running Broadway play, *Boys in the Band*. Chicago blues musicians Willie Dixon and Walter Barnes had roots in Vicksburg, and the Red Tops, led by Walter Osborne, operated from Vicksburg from the 1950s to the 1970s.

By 1930 Warren County had a population of 35,785, including 22,943 urban residents and 12,842 rural residents, making it one of only six Mississippi counties where most of the population did not live on farms. African Americans comprised 58 percent of the population. Warren County's 1,685 industrial workers ranked fifth in the state. Outside Vicksburg, the county remained heavily agricultural, with three-quarters of its 2,604 farms operated by tenants, most of them African American. Compared to most Mississippi counties, Warren had a substantial degree of ethnic diversity, with more than 400 people born outside the United States and more than 1,500 people with parents born abroad. The largest of those groups were Palestinian and Syrian, followed by Italians, Russians, and Czechs.

By the mid-twentieth century, like other counties with urban centers, Warren County experienced a population increase, growing to 42,206 people by 1960. In a significant change from 1930, 53 percent of the residents were white. Warren County ranked in the top 10 counties in Mississippi in per capita income. About 20 percent of the county's workers were employed in manufacturing—furniture and timber, machinery, transportation equipment, and food products. More people (1,200) worked in health care than in agriculture (900).

Warren County's civil rights movement stretches as far back as 1918, when Vicksburg's African Americans established the state's first chapter of the National Association for the Advancement of Colored People. Though that chapter disbanded, Vicksburg was one of the first places where African Americans demanded school desegregation immediately after the US Supreme Court's 1954 *Brown v. Board of Education* decision. In 1964 civil rights activists in the county began publishing the *Vicksburg Citizens' Appeal*, which emphasized news about the African American freedom struggle. Civil rights figures with roots in Vicksburg included Ed King, a chaplain at Tougaloo College and the Mississippi Freedom Democratic Party's candidate for lieutenant governor, and Jackson State University educator Jane McAllister.

The county's population exceeded 50,000 for the first time in 1980, and in 1991 Vicksburg builder Kirk Fordice became Mississippi's first Republican governor since Reconstruction. Tourism, related especially to the Civil War, antebellum homes, and casino gambling, has become an important part of Vicksburg life. Unlike most of the counties along the Mississippi River, the county's 2010 population of 48,733 was predominantly white and had grown significantly during the last half of the twentieth century.

Mississippi Encyclopedia Staff
University of Mississippi

Mississippi State Planning Commission, *Progress Report on State Planning in Mississippi* (1938); *Mississippi Statistical Abstract*, Mississippi State University (1952–2010); Charles Sydnor and Claude Bennett, *Mississippi History* (1939); University of Virginia Library, Historical Census Browser website, http://mapserver.lib.virginia.edu; E. Nolan Waller and Dani A. Smith, *Growth Profiles of Mississippi's Counties, 1960–1980* (1985).

W

Washington County

Washington County was founded in 1827 and named for George Washington. It is located in the Mississippi Delta region, bordering the Mississippi River. Greenville, the county seat, has long been the Delta's largest city, and other communities include Leland, Hollandale, Arcola, and Metcalfe. For much of its history Washington's economic and social life has been intertwined with the history of cotton production.

The area that became Washington County was the site of ancient mound-building people. The Winterville Mounds, located north of Greenville, originally consisted of twenty-three mounds arranged around a single mound more than fifty feet high, though some of the mounds have now been leveled.

Washington County Courthouse, Greenville, seat of Washington County, ca. 1909 (Ann Rayburn Paper Americana Collection, Department of Archives and Special Collections, J. D. Williams Library, University of Mississippi [rayburn_ann_24_81_001])

In the 1830 census Washington County had 792 free persons and 1,184 slaves. By 1840 Washington had 660 free people and 6,627 slaves, establishing its identity as a Delta plantation county with a large slave majority. According to the census, the county had no manufacturing, but its steamboat stop brought people to Greenville and sent cotton to markets. Ten years later the county had even fewer free residents—546 whites and 7 free African Americans—and its slave population had increased to 7,836, giving the county the state's highest percentage of slaves (93.4 percent). Washington County had no public schools and only two churches but had the highest value of farm property and third-highest agricultural production in the state. On the eve of the Civil War, Washington County's population was 15,679, with 14,467 of those residents enslaved.

Washington County mushroomed after the war, with an 1880 population of 25,367. The county had 21,861 African Americans, 3,478 whites, and 28 Chinese. With African Americans comprising 86.2 percent of the population, Washington County continued to have the state's largest African American majority. The county had only 454 farms, among the fewest in the state, but the average farm size of 404 acres was near the top, and its farm property ranked second in total value. Washington County led Mississippi in cotton production. Washington's farmers grew substantial amounts of corn and potatoes and had a large number of mules, but the county ranked low in most other forms of agricultural production. Washington County also began to develop some manufacturing establishments, with nine firms employing 122 men, 3 women, and 62 children. In addition to the Chinese, the county's foreign-born population of 367 consisted largely of natives of Germany and Ireland.

In 1900 Washington County was home to 49,216 people, the second-highest population in Mississippi, with 44,143 African Americans (90 percent), 57 Chinese, and 5,016 whites. Washington's 6,407 tenant farmers and sharecroppers were by far the most in the state. Only 4 percent of the county's 6,525 African American farmers and 38 percent of the 328 white farmers owned their land. Cotton dominated the economy, and as in other areas with high numbers of tenants, the average farm size of less than forty acres was exceptionally low.

Washington County had 578 women and just 14 men working in manufacturing jobs. The county also had a relatively large number of residents born outside the United States, with more than 500 immigrants, including people from Italy, Germany, China, Russia, and Austria. In keeping with its large African American population, Missionary Baptist and African Methodist Episcopal churches dominated, but its ethnic diversity meant that the county also had more Jewish and Catholic residents than did most parts of Mississippi. Two notable institutions began life in Greenville in 1903: the Stein Mart department store chain originated with a store operated by Russian immigrant Sam Stein, and Doe's Eat Place started as a grocery run by Italian immigrant Carmel Signa.

Washington County's population changed relatively little in the early twentieth century, and the county remained one of the most densely populated in the state. Like other Delta counties, it had a substantial African American majority, though the white population increased in the 1910s and 1920s. In 1930 the county's 54,310 residents included 444 who were born outside the United States—primarily in Italy, Palestine, Syria, and Russia. Greenville's population topped 11,000, and Washington County businesses employed almost 1,400 industrial workers, ninth most in the state. Washington County had a cannery, the most cottonseed oil mills in Mississippi, and several of the state's largest hardwood sawmills. Still, Washington remained very much a cotton-growing county and was one of seven Mississippi counties in which more than 90 percent of all farms were operated by tenants.

Washington County was the site of a great deal of experimentation with large-scale agriculture. Leroy Percy and other large planters tried various forms of labor organizing, including importing Italian farmworkers and employing Mexican migrant workers. Leland was home to one of the earliest commercial crop-dusting operations. The Delta Branch Experiment Station was founded at Stoneville to improve cotton production, first by combating the boll weevil. In 1948 agricultural experimentation in Stoneville led to major expansion in rice cultivation in the Delta.

The Delta Council organized in 1935 in Stoneville and sought to improve agriculture, economic development, health, education, and ties to the federal government. It attracted a combination of plantation owners, educators, and business leaders, and it helped set national agricultural policy when it helped form the National Cotton Council.

The Great Mississippi River Flood of 1927 devastated Washington County, with flood conditions lasting four months and causing loss of life, homes, and crops. A levee north of Greenville broke, inundating two million acres in the Delta. City leaders organized a mass evacuation of white women and children to Vicksburg and Memphis, and a relief committee led by William Alexander Percy established a refugee camp that was inhabited largely by African American tenant farmer families. Area white planters, fearful of the loss of labor if an exodus of black farmworkers occurred, barred any opportunities for evacuation. Approximately 7,500 African Americans were stranded in tents on the levee, with men compelled to labor in poor conditions for no pay. Reports of this confinement, squalid conditions, and increasing tensions reached a national audience, and US secretary of commerce Herbert Hoover dispatched an investigative committee to the county. The disaster subsequently became one factor that prompted the growing migration of blacks to northern cities.

In politics, Washington County leaders tended toward the conservatism of plantation owners, but there was room for creativity. For example, Leroy Percy condemned the Ku Klux Klan as supporters of violence and anarchy during a 1922 election, and Clarke Reed helped build Mississippi's modern Republican Party beginning in the late 1960s. Washington County has also had a long history of women in politics. Nellie Nugent Somerville, born in 1863 in Greenville, was the state's leading proponent of woman suffrage, and she became the first woman elected to the state legislature. Her daughter, Lucy Somerville Howorth, became a lawyer and a force in Democratic Party politics in the 1930s and 1940s. Zelma Wells Price served the county for ten years as a legislator and became Mississippi's first female judge.

Washington County has also been home to some of Mississippi's most creative writers and artists. Many of them knew and learned from each other, while others became writers outside existing literary circles. Writers who knew and learned from each other included William Alexander Percy, Shelby Foote, and David Cohn. Percy, author of *Lanterns on the Levee: Recollections of a Planter's Son*, analyzed what he described as the decline of plantation traditions in the early twentieth-century South with the rise of mechanization and mass media, the outmigration of so many people, and the development of popular politics. Foote began his writing career as a novelist before turning his talents to a long narrative of the Civil War. A storekeeper's son with affinities with the planter elite, Cohn offered a unique perspective on African American culture in the Delta with *God Shakes Creation*. Percy protégé Leon Z. Koury, born in 1909 to Syrian immigrants who became Greenville grocers, became a sculptor and painter as well as a leader in the local art scene for three decades. Koury, in turn, mentored Greenville-born sculptor William N. Beckwith.

Outside the Greenville literary circle, Jim Henson became an American children's television and film pioneer with his Muppet characters. Novelist William Alexander Attaway, born in Greenville in 1911, set much of his work, including his best-known novel, *Blood on the Forge*, in the African American migration away from the South. Famous for a series of books about African American small-town life, Glen Allan native Clifton Taulbert, born in 1945, developed the concept of the "porch people"—adults who set community standards high and looked after everyone's children. Authors raised in Greenville include Angela Jackson, who has written poetry, drama, and fiction; poet-translator Brooks Haxton; novelist Beverly Lowry; and essayist Julia Reed. Charles Bell wrote in numerous genres, including a long and creative history of world culture. Artists Valerie Jaudon and P. Sanders McNeal grew up in Greenville, and self-taught artist and musician James "Son Ford" Thomas lived in Leland.

By 1960 Washington County's population had increased to 79,638, the third-highest in Mississippi, and the county had the state's third-highest population density. However, population growth was driven primarily by white movement to Greenville, and African Americans now accounted for just 54 percent of the population. Washington County also had 264 Chinese residents (160 men and 104 women)

W

and 48 Mexicans. Unlike most Delta counties, Washington had an average per capita income that ranked among the highest in the state. About 16 percent of the county's workers were employed in industry—primarily construction, furniture, food production, and textile work. More than 800 residents were employed in hospitals and health care, and 3,100 of the county's women worked in personal service jobs. As in previous decades, Washington ranked high in the state in the production of cotton (fourth), soybeans (fourth), oats (first), and rice (third), and 20 percent of its workers were employed in agriculture.

Two famous moments in the civil rights movement took place in Washington County in 1966. In January some out-of-work farm laborers, in a partnership with the Delta Ministry, took over the buildings of the Greenville Air Base, renamed it Freedom Village, and called on the federal government to address problems of poverty, hunger, and poor education. Late in the year, the phrase Black Power came to prominence in Washington County when Stokely Carmichael (Kwame Ture) and others first began using it during the March against Fear initiated by James Meredith.

Greenville's two major newspapers had unique perspectives on civil rights activities. The *Delta Leader*, under editor H. H. Humes, was a conservative African American newspaper that advocated personal uplift rather than activism. The *Delta Democrat-Times*, edited by Hodding Carter II and Betty Werlein Carter, criticized numerous expressions of white supremacy, from Theodore Bilbo to massive resistance, a stance that provoked threats and condemnation from many members of the area's elite. In 1978 a nonprofit group, Mississippi Action for Community Education, started the Mississippi Delta Blues and Heritage Festival on the site of the Freedom Village protest. Washington County was the home of blues performers Richard Hacksaw Harney, Tyrone Davis, and Eddie Cusic, and the Greenville Chamber of Commerce produced a record of the songs of the mockingbird, Mississippi's state bird.

As in many Delta counties, Washington County's 2010 population remained predominantly African American but had decreased significantly since 1960. With just 51,137 people, Washington had lost 35 percent of its population over the preceding half century.

Mississippi Encyclopedia Staff
University of Mississippi

Mississippi State Planning Commission, *Progress Report on State Planning in Mississippi* (1938); *Mississippi Statistical Abstract*, Mississippi State University (1952–2010); Charles Sydnor and Claude Bennett, *Mississippi History* (1939); University of Virginia Library, Historical Census Browser website, http://mapserver.lib.virginia.edu; E. Nolan Waller and Dani A. Smith, *Growth Profiles of Mississippi's Counties, 1960–1980* (1985).

Waterfowl and Duck and Goose Hunting

With extensive river systems, marshes on the Gulf Coast, and a location in the heart of the flyway, Mississippi has at times been blessed with epic numbers of waterfowl. While Native American groups and early settlers killed waterfowl at any opportunity, the nature of ducks and geese made them generally unavailable to the masses. Passing through in the winter and spring, the birds favored natural lakes, oxbows, backwaters, beaver impoundments, and marshes that were inaccessible to all but the most determined and well prepared hunters. Wetland areas that consistently attracted waterfowl quickly became well known, however, and by 1900 improving shotgun technology and expanding railroad lines made shooting more efficient and eased access for hunters seeking pleasure or profit. Wealthy hunters leased or bought their favored waterfowling spots and sought, with varying degrees of success, to exclude others. Some of the impetus toward organized wildlife conservation and the end of market hunting came from wealthy gunners who wanted to protect their sport. The high cost of waterfowling has been a constant in its history. With a limited number of truly productive areas and wealthy sportsmen competing for shooting rights, duck hunting can be the most expensive type of hunting in the state.

In the Delta, dabbling ducks—widgeons, pintails, teal, and especially mallards—have always been the preferred bag. The most widespread dabbler, the wood duck, is a resident bird that may be encountered along almost any watercourse in the state. Common but not overly abundant, the wood duck was traditionally called the summer duck and suffered greatly from year-round shooting. Historically, hunters waited for ducks in areas of grass or trees naturally flooded by winter rains or rising rivers. Dabblers prefer shallow water with grass seeds and invertebrates or the small mast of trees like water oak or willow oak. Divers prefer larger bodies of water. Both types rest in open, permanent bodies of water. Sandbars also provide resting areas and traditionally made good hunting spots for Canada geese.

Duck hunting has generally been more important than goose hunting in the state, though hunting Canadas on the sandbars along the Mississippi was quite common in the first half of the twentieth century. Changing agricultural practices have recently increased goose populations across the North American continent. Biologists established resident Canada goose populations in Mississippi that have done well enough over the last few decades to warrant their own early season in September. In addition, the snow geese that used to migrate straight through the state to winter along the coast now stop over in the huge fields of winter wheat that start in the Midwest and run down into the Delta. Snow geese have multiplied so prolifically, in part as a result of the easy winters on the wheat fields, that their numbers overtax their Arctic breeding areas, and special seasons for snow geese have been instituted, with quite liberal limits. In addition to the winter wheat, which is relatively new to the Delta, there are vast areas of open water in the form of catfish ponds. Cormorants and pelicans frequent the ponds, much to the dismay of catfish farmers. The addition of the open water has also added greatly to the frequency of diving ducks in the Delta, although few hunters pursue them. The large flood-control reservoirs in the central part of the state have also created new waterfowl habitat. These reservoirs contain large areas of open water and, depending on their level, significant backwater areas.

The folk art of the duck call and hand-carved decoy is well known, and Mississippi certainly has its share of call makers and carvers. What is less known are the decoy factories that once existed on the Gulf Coast. With access to Tupelo gum and ash, wooden decoy manufacturing flourished around Pascagoula from 1920 to 1971.

The state's ongoing agricultural evolution and the efforts to control the hydrology of the Yazoo-Mississippi Delta have affected migrating waterfowl in ways both good and ill, but the flights keep coming. Duck and goose hunting continues to generate sport for hunters and revenue for guides and landowners.

Wiley C. Prewitt Jr.
Yocona, Mississippi

Joe Bosco, *Pascagoula Decoys* (2003); Luther Wayne Capooth, *The Golden Age of Waterfowling* (2001); David Allen Sibley, *The Sibley Guide to Birds* (2000).

Watermelon

Watermelon (*Citrullus lanatus*) is a member of the gourd family. Though technically a vegetable, it is frequently considered a fruit, and it is thought to have originated in the Kalahari Desert, where explorer and missionary David Livingston came across a wild watermelon vine in the 1850s. Archaeologists have found evidence of watermelons from ancient Egypt. Though watermelon had traveled to most reaches of the globe by the seventeenth century, the enslaved Africans brought to the New World are credited with introducing the sweet gourd to the United States.

Possessing both male and female flowers, the watermelon plant requires bees for pollination. The vines thrive in warm soil and typically will not survive a frost. Though watermelon crops abate during times of drought, a severe dearth in rainfall

Watermelon salesman, First Monday, Ripley (Photograph by David Wharton)

will produce an even sweeter fruit. Watermelons flourish in semiarid or humid environments and require a lengthy growing season, making Mississippi's balmy summers and short, mild winters an ideal climate for cultivation. The peak season in Mississippi is June through September, and the state's 2015 watermelon crop was valued at $3.78 million.

All of a watermelon is edible, though the rind is frequently discarded. The melon is most commonly eaten raw but can find its way into a multitude of southern dishes. Some classic favorites include pies, sherbets, salsas, and pickles (rinds). Watermelon seeds were substituted for coffee during the Civil War era. Some southerners spike their watermelons with rum or other liquors. More recent culinary innovations include watermelon stir-fry with chicken and red capers and deep-fried watermelon.

Recent medical research may spark a new demand for pickled watermelon rinds. Apart from containing significant amounts of vitamins A, B6, and C, watermelon rinds also possess beneficial quantities of lycopene, an antioxidant that may aid in the fight against prostate cancer.

Watermelon is most closely associated with the rural South and particularly with African Americans, having found its way into much African American folklore. According to tradition, the year's watermelon crop should always be planted on 1 May by pushing the seed into the soil with one's fingers. In addition, sowing seeds at the head of a grave allows the dead to drink of the gourd's sweet juice. Many folktales involve slaves stealing watermelon.

Watermelon remains culturally pervasive in Mississippi. A guitar fashioned out of a watermelon appears on the cover of B. B. King's *Indianola Mississippi Seeds* album. Every summer Mize and Water Valley host annual watermelon festivals, with a variety of entertainment including contests for seed spitting, watermelon eating, and largest watermelon. On the Fourth of July the annual Watermelon Classic 5K road race takes place in Jackson.

Brooke Butler
New Orleans, Louisiana

W

"2015 State Agriculture Overview: Mississippi," US Department of Agriculture, National Agricultural Statistics Service website, www.nass.usda.gov; John Edgerton, *Southern Food* (1993); Ellen Ficken, *Watermelon* (1984); Felder Rushing and Water Reeves, *The Mississippi Fruit and Vegetable Book* (2002); Joe Gray Taylor, *Eating, Drinking, and Visiting in the South* (1982); Charles Reagan Wilson, in *The Encyclopedia of Southern Culture*, ed. Charles Reagan Wilson and William Ferris (1989); Watermelon.org website, www.watermelon.org.

Waters, Muddy (McKinley Morganfield)

(1913–1983) Blues Musician

Muddy Waters helped chart the course of twentieth-century American music. As a singer, guitarist, songwriter, and bandleader, Waters pioneered black blues music and heavily influenced the development of rock and roll. His career included the Mississippi black string band tradition, acoustic solo Delta blues guitar and vocal styles, the early amplified and electric blues of the urban North, and the blues-rock fusion that influenced countless white British and American rock artists. His bands provided the mold for the Chicago blues sound and launched the careers of many important blues innovators and stylists. Tough, physically powerful, dignified, and regal, he became the archetypal American bluesman.

McKinley Morganfield was born in Jug's Corner in 1913 to poor sharecropper parents who eventually had twelve children. After the death of his mother, Morganfield's grandmother, Della Jones, took him to live at Howard Stovall's plantation near Clarksdale. Jones nicknamed her grandson *Muddy* because of his penchant for playing in the mud. Morganfield began playing harmonica as a child and listened to the recordings of Blind Lemon Jefferson and Blind Blake. He also directly absorbed the string band music of the Son Sims Four, a local group based on the popular Mississippi Sheiks. Taking Muddy Water (he later added the *s*) as his stage name, he eventually joined the Son Sims Four and played juke joints and black social gatherings and occasionally white parties and square dances.

Waters also studied the showmanship skills of Charley Patton, a guitarist and singer who lived on the nearby Dockery Plantation. Although Patton influenced blues music with his slide guitar style, syncopation, and lyrical snapshots of Delta life, the most important direct musical influence on Waters was Son House, a charismatic singer and guitarist who played a heavy, percussive style punctuated with stinging slides and deep, intensely emotional vocals. House's music convinced him to probe deeper into the blues instead of sacred music, but Waters always pointed to the church as a major influence on his singing style. Later in his life, he would say

that many of his younger rock and roll imitators had instrumental skill but lacked the necessary background of the southern black church and its range of emotion.

Waters, who drove a tractor at Stovall, had acquired a solid reputation as a musician among his Delta peers by the time he was first recorded in 1941. Folklorists Alan Lomax and John Work encountered Waters while conducting fieldwork for Fisk University and the Library of Congress. Their recordings of Waters consisted of interviews and music, and although he included songs ("I Be's Troubled," "Country Blues") that he would rework into two of his signature tunes, Waters's solo performances were the rough sounds of Mississippi Delta laborers. He talked about his admiration for Son House, the church music that inspired his blues, and the mundane events that made up his day. Lomax returned to Stovall in July 1942 to record Waters and the Son Sims Four. The Library of Congress issued "I Be's Troubled" and "Country Blues" on a six-sided package in January 1943.

The recording sessions increased Waters's confidence in developing as a professional musician, and he knew that doing so would require leaving Mississippi. The lure of World War II industry jobs in the North and increased farm mechanization in the South caused a surge in the migration of black farm laborers to urban industrial centers. In 1943 Waters moved to Chicago, where he immediately found a job in a paper factory. The blues Waters found in Chicago had been refined for the record-buying public. Swing and big bands dominated the venues for live performances. Waters's first audiences in the city were the house parties of Delta migrants who thought his music spoke to their lives. In these informal sessions, Waters switched to an electric guitar to project his music into the noisy crowds, and in 1946 he recorded eight songs with spare accompaniment for Columbia Records. He recorded thirty-five sides for the Chicago-based Aristocrat label from 1947 to 1949, beginning a relationship with Leonard and Phil Chess that lasted for nearly thirty years.

One of the most formidable bands in blues music included Waters (who had honed his slide guitar technique), Mississippi natives Jimmy Rogers on guitar and Otis Spann on piano, and Louisiana native Marion "Little Walter" Jacobs on harmonica. All of the musicians on the early Chess recordings contributed to the Deep South amplified blues that Waters envisioned, but Little Walter, with a jump blues technique and amplified harmonica blasts that sounded like saxophone solos, particularly proved himself an innovator. One session with this band yielded three Top 10 blues hits—"Louisiana Blues," "Long Distance Call," and "Honey Bee"—and established Waters as a major force in postwar black music.

Although Waters was inspired by the acoustic blues of the Delta, he avoided the rural themes of his field recordings. Loud, electric, raw, aggressive, and sinuous, his new music grafted its unmistakably southern roots onto the gritty street life of Chicago's South Side. It was amplified attitude, and the lyrics boldly proclaimed his new lifestyle. Waters sang proudly and boastfully about power and sex and the deliverance that both could bring from the drudgery of everyday life. Waters exalted masculinity and equated it with independence, confidence, and emotional release. Many of Waters's best-known songs were written by Vicksburg native and Chess staff songwriter Willie Dixon, including "I'm Ready," "Forty Days and Forty Nights," "You Shook Me," "I'm Your Hoochie Coochie Man," "Long Distance Call," and "Got My Mojo Working."

By 1954 nine of Waters's recordings had appeared on the national record charts, including "I Just Want to Make Love to You," which entered at No. 5. But Waters's influence on other musicians threatened to derail his career. Chuck Berry's successful and seminal rock and roll records on the Chess label opened up new musical frontiers for musicians and audiences. When Waters was in danger of becoming a relic, a fascination with America's roots music spread in England, and Waters began traveling abroad to new fans. He also performed at the 1960 Newport Jazz Festival and received an enthusiastic reception. Young whites caught up in the American folk revival began embracing the blues, and Waters found that his audience was changing, even in Chicago. The idolatry that surrounded Waters appeared most visibly in the styles and songs of British rock musicians, including the Rolling Stones, who named themselves after a Waters song.

While Waters's music was rediscovered through reissues of his early landmark recordings, Chess tried to put Waters in experimental situations, including a 1968 psychedelic project, *Electric Mud*. In 1971 *Billboard* bestowed its Trendsetter Award on Waters, and he won his first Grammy Award for *They Call Me Muddy Waters*. Waters left Chess in 1975 and began performing with bands that proclaimed his rock and roll pedigree. Texas rock guitarist Johnny Winter produced Waters's critically acclaimed *Hard Again* in 1977, featuring Waters's trademark Delta blues in rocking arrangements. Waters extended his rock audience with a live performance of a track from *Hard Again*, "Mannish Boy," in Martin Scorsese's 1977 concert film *The Last Waltz*. Winter produced Waters's last album, *I'm Ready*, which reunited Waters with Rogers.

Waters died of a heart attack on 30 April 1983. He was inducted into the Blues Foundation Hall of Fame in 1980 and into the Rock and Roll Hall of Fame in 1987. In 1992 he received a Lifetime Achievement Grammy Award.

Karl Rohr
South Carolina Governor's School
for Science and Mathematics

Willie Dixon with Don Snowden, *I Am the Blues* (1989); Robert Gordon, *Can't Be Satisfied: The Life and Times of Muddy Waters* (2002); Alan Lomax, *Land Where the Blues Began* (1993); Robert Palmer, *Deep Blues: A Musical and Cultural History of the Mississippi Delta* (1981); James Rooney, *Bossmen: Bill Monroe and Muddy Waters* (1971); Sandra Tooze, *Muddy Waters: The Mojo Man* (1997); Muddy Waters, *The Best of Muddy Waters* (CD, 1987); Muddy Waters, *The Complete Plantation Recordings* (CD, 1993), Muddy Waters, *Hard Again* (CD, 1977).

Watkins, Hollis
(b. 1941) Activist

Born near the Lincoln County, Mississippi, town of Summit on 29 July 1941, Hollis Watkins, the youngest of John and Lena Watkins's twelve children, grew up on a farm near the border between Lincoln and Pike Counties. He graduated from the Lincoln County Training School in 1960 and the following year met Bob Moses, who taught him techniques for registering voters.

Watkins participated in the first sit-in in McComb in August 1961, joining Curtis Hayes at Woolworth's. Hayes and Watkins were arrested for breach of the peace and sentenced to thirty days in jail. After his release, Watkins enrolled at Tougaloo College and became an organizer and field secretary for the Student Nonviolent Coordinating Committee (SNCC), working in numerous communities throughout the state. He became one of the first Mississippians to attend SNCC's Highlander Folk School in Monteagle, Tennessee. Watkins then began canvassing neighborhoods and participating in the Pike County nonviolent movement in McComb. There, he was jailed along with Moses, Chuck McDew, and others for marching to protest Brenda Travis's expulsion from Burglund High School and the murder of Herbert Lee. After being released, Watkins left school at Tougaloo, and he and Hayes went to Hattiesburg to start a voter registration campaign.

In Hattiesburg, Watkins worked with Vernon Dahmer, a leader of the National Association for the Advancement of Colored People, and helped establish the Forrest County Voters League. Watkins subsequently left Hattiesburg to establish freedom schools in the Delta. In Greenwood, Watkins taught citizenship classes and was again arrested for disturbing the peace; he was convicted and served part of his sentence at Parchman Prison. In 1965 he was elected to SNCC's executive committee, and he became one of the most ardent supporters of SNCC's strategy of developing indigenous leadership in Mississippi's black communities. Among movement activists, he earned a reputation for being a "song leader" in jail and at mass meetings.

After his work with SNCC, Watkins remained politically active in Mississippi, working to win the redrawing of state legislative district boundaries and helping to develop the Algebra Project in the Delta. He worked with Mississippi Action for Progress and on Jesse Jackson's campaign in the presidential primary of 1988. Watkins founded and serves as president of Southern Echo, which works to develop leaders and empower local residents throughout the South in support of the needs and interests of the African American community. He is also a founder and serves as chair of Veterans of the Mississippi Civil Rights Movement, which seeks to preserve the movement's history. In addition, Watkins serves on the boards of the Highlander Research and Education Center and the Southern Sustainable Agricultural Working Group. In 2011 he received a Fannie Lou Hamer Humanitarian Award from Jackson State University, and in 2015 he received an honorary doctorate from Tougaloo College.

Amy Schmidt
Lyon College

Clayborne Carson, *In Struggle: SNCC and the Black Awakening of the 1960s* (1981); John Dittmer, *Local People: The Struggle for Civil Rights in Mississippi* (1994); Charles M. Payne, *I've Got the Light of Freedom: The Organizing Tradition and the Mississippi Freedom Struggle* (1995); Veterans of the Mississippi Civil Rights Movement website, www.mscivilrightsveterans.com; Howard Zinn, *SNCC: The New Abolitionists* (2002).

Watson, Brad
(b. 1955) Author

Writer Brad Watson was born in Meridian on 24 July 1955 and raised there. He married between his junior and senior years of high school, and after graduation he and his wife moved to Hollywood so that he could try his luck as an actor. He held a variety of non-acting jobs, but he had arrived at the beginning of a screenwriters' strike and a studio shutdown, and after the accidental death of his brother, he and his family, which had grown to include a one-year-old son, returned to Meridian. He ran a bar owned by his father until Watson's lack of business acumen led to the bar's bankruptcy.

Soon thereafter, he enrolled at Meridian Junior College, where he first began writing fiction under the guidance of Niles "Buck" Thomas. After a divorce, Watson earned a bachelor's degree from Mississippi State University in 1978, working closely with Price Caldwell. He subsequently enrolled in the master of fine arts program at the University of Alabama, studying under fellow Mississippian Barry Hannah and graduating in 1985.

Watson worked as a Gulf Coast reporter and then state editor for the *Montgomery Advertiser* and as a copywriter in an ad agency before completing his debut book of short stories, *Last Days of the Dog-Men* (1996). The book features stories linked by the titular animals—as pets, companions, or seeming conduits of the soul. The quaky old poodle in "Bill," for example, serves as stand-in for an elderly woman's incapacitated husband: the dog, like the couple, can only make his "halting, wobbling way" around the house. *Last Days* introduced Watson's lyrical and meditative prose, earning him positive reviews and awards such as the Sue Kaufman Prize for First Fiction from the American Academy of Arts and Letters. His first novel, *The Heaven of Mercury* (2002), was a finalist for the National Book Award and the winner of the Mississippi Institute of Arts and Letters Award for Fiction and the Southern Book Critics Circle Award in Fiction (along with Lee Smith). The novel is set in Mercury, Mississippi, a place inspired by Meridian where the "downtown was pretty lonesome at night, but pleasantly so." Stitching southern influences such as Flannery O'Connor's gothic and William Faulkner's Yoknapatawpha, the novel is built around octogenarian Finus Bates and a lifelong love that he never pursued. Far more than Bates's tale alone, Mercury's "web of acquaintances" illuminates the narrative; various loves and dream lives and even the afterlife sculpt the community's history.

The title story in *Aliens in the Prime of their Lives* (2010) features two Mississippi teenagers, Will and Olivia, in love and in struggle and expecting a child. Bound by "a pair of gold-plated wedding bands" bought at Stuckey's, the two confront larger notions of contentment, reality, and even unreality. Whereas *The Heaven of Mercury* brushes into the afterlife, *Aliens* at times navigates liminal mental states, from the institutionalized to the imaginary to the despairing man whose "troubles had come from attempts to deny the essential hopelessness in his nature." The volume was a finalist for the 2011 PEN/Faulkner Award for Fiction and earned him another Mississippi Institute of Arts and Letters Award for Fiction. He also received a Guggenheim Fellowship in 2011.

Watson's 2016 novel, *Miss Jane*, was inspired by the author's late great-aunt. The title character is shaped by a secret genital birth defect that deprives her of sex, childbearing, and related companionship. Though her intellectual and emotional life at times transcends her condition, her character explores the expectations, implications, and even defiance of what it meant to be a woman in the early twentieth-century South.

Watson taught creative writing at the University of Alabama before spending five years as a Briggs-Copeland Lecturer and director of creative writing at Harvard University. After stints as visiting writer in residence at the University of West Florida, the University of Alabama–Birmingham, the University of Mississippi, and the University of California–Irvine, Watson moved to the University of Wyoming in 2005 to teach creative writing and English in the master of fine arts program.

Mississippi Encyclopedia Staff
University of Mississippi

Susannah Felts, *Chapter 16* (2011), http://chapter16.org/author-in-the-prime-of-his-life/; Lydia Fitzpatrick, *Fiction Writers Review* (24 November 2010), http://fictionwritersreview.com/interview/interesting-characters-an-interview-with-brad-watson/.

Waverley

Waverley (sometimes spelled Waverly) is a mansion and former plantation located between Columbus and West Point, Mississippi, in Clay County. The home was designed by architect Charles Pond and built for Col. George Hampton Young, a lawyer and former member of the Georgia legislature. The property lies off the west bank of the Tombigbee River on land Young purchased in 1835. The following year the family and their 25 slaves arrived at the site. During construction, Col. Young, his wife, Lucy Woodson Watkins Young, and their children lived in a two-story log dogtrot cabin on the property. By the time the building was completed, around 1852, Young had amassed more than two thousand acres of land and owned more than 117 slaves, but Lucy Young had died. The original homestead, which had been moved to accommodate the new residence, became an outdoor kitchen. Young named Waverley after Sir Walter Scott's 1841 novel.

The four-story, eight-thousand-square-foot, H-shaped home is an example of Greek Revival architecture, characterized by symmetry and stately Ionic columns. Waverley is notable for its four interior circular staircases, which connect free-standing cantilevered balconies. Rivaling the staircases is a sixty-five-foot domed foyer topped by an octagonal cupola. The parlor contains a built-in wedding alcove and an ormolu chandelier. The funnel-shaped combination of the foyer and cupola created a kind of suction, pulling hot air to the ceiling so it could escape through the cupola's windows. Transom windows above the bedroom doorways provide cross-ventilation.

In the antebellum period Waverley was a prosperous plantation that was home to orchards, gardens, livestock, and kennels for hunting dogs. The property also contained a cotton gin, a tannery, a brick kiln, an ice house, an artesian well, and a private swimming pool with a bathhouse. In addition, Waverley featured slave cabins, a carriage house, a barn, and a guesthouse as well as woolen, lumber, flour, and grist mills.

The Youngs were staunch secessionists. All six sons fought in the Confederacy, and one lost his life during the war. The plantation's remote location allowed the house to remain virtually untouched by the conflict. Waverley housed many displaced people during the war, including Isabella Buchanan Edmondson, a Confederate scout and spy who fled to the plantation to avoid capture by Union soldiers.

Colonel Young died in 1880, and the mansion remained in the family until 1913, when his last surviving son, Capt. William Young, died. Waverley became vacant for more than fifty years and began to deteriorate, housing squatters as well as a two-hundred-pound beehive in the cupola. Robert and Donna Snow of Philadelphia, Mississippi, purchased the property in 1962 and began a lengthy renovation. Waverley is now a National Historic Landmark and a National Restoration Award winner, and it was added to the National Register of Historic Places in 1973. It remains a private residence but is open for tours.

Linda Arrington
University of Mississippi

Mary Wallace Crocker, *Historic Architecture in Mississippi* (1973); Belle Edmondson, *A Lost Heroine of the Confederacy: The Diaries and Letters of Belle Edmondson*, ed. William Galbraith and Loretta Galbraith (1990); Mary Carol Miller, *Great Houses of Mississippi* (2004).

Wayne County

One of Mississippi's first counties, Wayne County was founded in 1809 and was named for US Army general Anthony Wayne. It is located along the Alabama border in southeastern Mississippi. The Leaf and Chickasawhay Rivers run parallel through the county and provide the area with outdoor recreational activities and an attractive landscape. The county seat is Waynesboro.

In 1820 Wayne County was a fairly small agricultural area with more than twice as many free people (2,258) as slaves (1,065). Wayne County relied very little on manufacturing, employing only 12 workers in commerce and 6 in manufacturing. Unlike some parts of southern Mississippi, Wayne did not attract widespread settlement in the antebellum period. In 1840 the county was home to 1,141 free people and 979 slaves; twenty years later, the population remained small—1,744 free people (including just 7 born outside the United States) and 1,947 slaves.

Despite its small size, Wayne County produced its share of notable residents. Waynesboro's Powhatan Ellis served as a representative, US senator, and Mississippi Supreme Court justice. George Strother Gaines, a planter and trader who helped negotiate the Treaty of Dancing Rabbit Creek with the Choctaw in 1830, spent much of his time in Wayne County, where he owned land and slaves.

W

Antebellum Wayne County ranked near the bottom of Mississippi's counties in the value of its farms and in its livestock, cotton, and corn. The county had twelve Methodist churches, three Baptist congregations, and three Presbyterian houses of worship.

Postbellum Wayne County grew substantially, with 8,741 residents, 57 percent of them white, in 1880. Still largely agricultural, Wayne continued to rank near the bottom of the state's counties in growing both corn and cotton but had reached the middle rank in the production of molasses, rice, and sweet potatoes and in the number of livestock, especially sheep. In 1880 Wayne County ranked third in the production of wool. Wayne continued to attract relatively few foreign-born immigrants but had a small but growing manufacturing sector, with twenty-four firms employing 108 people.

By 1900 Wayne County was home to 12,539 people, 60 percent of them white. Three-quarters of white farmers owned the land they worked, while just under half of African American farmers did so. Wayne's industrial workforce had increased substantially, with 352 men and 6 women employed in manufacturing. The dramatic growth of the timber industry accounted for most of the area's industrial development.

Wayne County's population stayed constant at around 15,000 from 1900 to 1930 and was about two-thirds white. In 1930 Wayne County had 514 industrial workers, many of them employed at a cannery or small sawmills. Despite the development of Eucutta Fields, the first successful oil field in eastern Mississippi, the area continued to rely on agriculture—mainly cattle, swine, and corn. In 1930 far more of Wayne County's farmers (55 percent) owned their farms than the state average (30 percent). Like many southern Mississippi counties, Wayne was sparsely populated, with the sixth-lowest population density in the state.

By 1960 the county's population had increased slightly to 16,258. Wayne's manufacturing industry expanded, providing about 11 percent of the county's workers with jobs, mostly in the furniture and clothing industries. Thirty percent of the residents still worked in agriculture. The major enterprises consisted of corn, livestock, and soybeans, but trees dominated the county's agriculture. In 1960 Wayne County had the most commercial forestland in Mississippi.

Wayne's population jumped to 19,135 people in 1980. As in most southeastern Mississippi counties, Wayne County's 2010 population was predominantly white and had grown significantly since 1960. Among Wayne's 20,747 residents in 2010, 59 percent were white and 39 percent were African American, while the county had small Asian and Hispanic/Latino populations.

Mississippi Encyclopedia Staff
University of Mississippi

Mississippi State Planning Commission, *Progress Report on State Planning in Mississippi* (1938); *Mississippi Statistical Abstract*, Mississippi State University (1952–2010); Charles Sydnor and Claude Bennett, *Mississippi History* (1939); University of Virginia Library, Historical Census Browser website, http://mapserver.lib.virginia.edu; E. Nolan Waller and Dani A. Smith, *Growth Profiles of Mississippi's Counties, 1960–1980* (1985).

Weary, Dolphus
(b. 1946) Religious Leader and Activist

A minister and important voice for racial reconciliation, Dolphus Douglas Weary was born on 7 August 1946 in Sandy Hook, Mississippi, near the Louisiana border. When he was two, his family moved to the Gum Springs community outside D'Lo. In 1951 Weary's father left his mother, Lucille, who subsequently supported her eight children by washing clothes, scrubbing floors, and sharecropping cotton. The family lived in extreme poverty, but through the guidance and discipline of Weary's strong-willed mother and his maternal grandfather, all of Lucille Weary's children were able to rise out of poverty.

Weary graduated at the top of his class from Harper High School. He attended Prentiss Institute and Piney Woods Junior College before leaving for California and becoming one of the first two black students at Los Angeles Baptist College (now Master's College) in the fall of 1967. He vowed never to live in Mississippi again.

Weary received a bachelor's degree in 1969 and went on to earn a master's degree in Christian education from Los Angeles Baptist Theological Seminary, working part time as a basketball coach. During the summers, Weary returned to Mendenhall, Mississippi, to work with John Perkins's Voice of Calvary Ministries, leading vacation Bible school classes and organizing a tutoring program. During these summer breaks, Weary met Rosie Camper, whom he married in the summer of 1970.

Shortly before completing his master's degree, Weary toured Asia with an evangelical basketball team organized by Overseas Crusade. The team's coach urged him to consider Asian missions as a lifetime calling, but Weary felt called by God to return to Mississippi. In 1971 he moved to Mendenhall and joined the Voice of Calvary (subsequently renamed Mendenhall Ministries), becoming executive director after Perkins moved to Jackson. Weary also served as associate pastor of the Mendenhall Bible Church. In 1978 he completed a second master's degree in educational administration and supervision from the University of Southern Mississippi.

In 1990 Weary published an autobiography, *I Ain't Comin' Back*. Weary earned a doctor of ministry degree from Jackson's Reformed Theological Seminary in 1997 and the following year became executive director of Mission Mississippi, a ministry dedicated to promoting racial reconciliation among Christians in Mississippi. He and his wife went on to found the REAL Christian Foundation, which works to enrich the lives of rural Mississippi's children, youth, and families by providing resources, grants, and technical assistance to community-based Christian ministries.

Edward McAllister
Belhaven University

Edward Gilbreath, *Christianity Today* (2000); Wheaton College, Billy Graham Center Archives website, www.wheaton.edu/bgc/archives.

Webster County

Sumner County in central Mississippi was formed in 1874. By 1890 the county was renamed in honor of US secretary of state Daniel Webster, in keeping with neighboring Clay and Calhoun Counties, which also were named for 1830s political heroes. Walthall is the county seat, and other communities include Eupora, Maben, and Mathiston.

In 1880 Sumner County had a population of 9,534. Three-quarters of its residents were white, and just 8 had been born outside the United States. Of the county's 1,410 farmers, 72 percent owned their land, a figure far higher than the Mississippi average of 56 percent. The county's nine industrial establishments employed just 22 people.

In 1900 Webster County was home to 13,619 people, 70 percent of them white. Webster was primarily an agricultural county, with just 100 men and 5 women working in industry. Among the county's farmers, 61 percent of whites owned their land, while only 31 percent of African Americans did so. The turn-of-the century Populist movement had greater success in Webster County than in most of the rest of Mississippi.

According to the 1916 religious census, Southern Baptists accounted for half of Webster County's churchgoers, while Missionary Baptists constituted another substantial group. The county also had a significant number of members of the Methodist Episcopal Church, South. Webster County was home of one of the state's earliest Sacred Harp singing conventions.

Webster County's population declined in the early twentieth century, falling to just over 12,000 people by 1930. Nearly 80 percent of residents were white. Webster had 313 industrial workers, but farming remained the basis of the county's economy. More than half of the 2,429 farms were operated by tenant farmers, who primarily raised cotton and livestock.

State political leader Thomas L. Bailey was born and raised in Webster County before moving to Lauderdale County. He served in the state legislature for more than twenty years before becoming governor in 1944.

Two important Mississippi artists grew up in Webster County. Ethel Wright Mohamed was born near Eupora in 1908. After she and her husband moved to Belzoni, she became an artist, using embroidery to tell stories about Mississippi life. William Dunlap, a painter and sculptor, grew up in Webster County and maintains a studio in Mathiston.

By 1960 the county's population had fallen to 10,580. More than a third of Webster's working people remained employed in agriculture, now mixing cotton and corn with soybeans. About a quarter of the workers had jobs in manufacturing, primarily in the textile and furniture industries.

Like many of its neighboring counties in central Mississippi, Webster County's 2010 population was predominantly white and had remained about the same size since 1960.

Mississippi Encyclopedia Staff
University of Mississippi

Mississippi State Planning Commission, *Progress Report on State Planning in Mississippi* (1938); *Mississippi Statistical Abstract*, Mississippi State University (1952–2010); Charles Sydnor and Claude Bennett, *Mississippi History* (1939); University of Virginia Library, Historical Census Browser website, http://mapserver.lib.virginia.edu; E. Nolan Waller and Dani A. Smith, *Growth Profiles of Mississippi's Counties, 1960–1980* (1985).

Wednesdays in Mississippi

In the spring of 1964 the National Council of Negro Women (NCNW) joined forces with the Young Women's Christian Association, the National Council of Jewish Women, the National Council of Catholic Women, and Church Women United in an effort to foster communication and racial understanding between northern and southern women and among black and white women in the South. These organizations ultimately collaborated to work for racial equality through an interracial, interfaith project, Wednesdays in Mississippi (WIMS). The group mobilized to show support for Mississippi individuals who were engaged in social activism, to encourage additional black and white women to become involved, to facilitate interracial understanding, and to encourage activism in their communities.

The project grew out of a three-day meeting the organizations convened in Atlanta in March 1964 to discuss ways to help women and youth who were being arrested in the South for civil rights activism. Each organization invited local leaders from southern cities that were viewed as having significant racial tensions and where at least one of the

W

sponsoring organizations was firmly established. During the proceedings, Jackson's Clarie Collins Harvey, representing Church Women United and the NCNW, drew attention to the conditions in Mississippi and to the local activists, black and white, who were unaware of each other's activism because of segregation. Harvey argued that a national organization from outside the state would be most effective at initiating efforts to challenge southern segregation. Therefore, Harvey proposed that northern women visit Mississippi during the upcoming Freedom Summer to help build communication between the black and white communities.

The NCNW's president, Dorothy Height, returned to Washington, D.C., and conveyed the meeting's proceedings to colleague Polly Cowan, who suggested recruiting women of various organizations to implement Harvey's proposal. The NCNW agreed to sponsor the program, with participation from all of the organizations present at the March meeting as well as the League of Women Voters and the American Association of University Women. Womanpower Unlimited, which Harvey had founded in May 1961, would serve as one of the project's anchors in Mississippi, providing contacts and resources.

For seven weeks during the summer, teams of six or eight northern black and white women participating in WIMS flew to Jackson on Tuesday, spent Wednesday visiting Freedom Summer projects in different cities, returned to Jackson that night for rallies or meetings, and departed Thursday morning. In 1964 the program included forty-eight women representing a cross-section of women's organizations, religious affiliations, and professions. The project also included a local staff in Mississippi and a national staff in New York.

After the summer visits WIMS women wrote articles for newspapers and organizational newsletters, lectured about their experiences, raised money, and sent supplies to the Mississippi projects, providing much-needed materials for freedom schools and community centers. In addition, participants paved the way for greater communication among local women while connecting the local efforts with the national civil rights agenda. This success led to the decision to continue the WIMS trips the following summer.

In 1965 WIMS took on a more active role. Forty-seven women who participated were charged with assisting in the desegregation of the state in compliance with Title VI of the 1964 Civil Rights Act, which prohibited "discrimination on the basis of race, color, or national origin." Toward this end, their activities included door-to-door canvassing to encourage school integration; meeting with teachers, librarians, and social workers; and working with Head Start programs. WIMS participants and staff also trained teachers for arts education, assisted with the organization of a chapter of Mississippians for Public Education in Philadelphia, and fostered dialogue between black and white educators and professionals.

After the 1965 trips, the NCNW broadened its endeavors to promote similar activism in other southern cities as well as in the North. Wednesdays in Mississippi subsequently became Workshops in Mississippi, an ongoing effort with a focus on economic development for poor blacks and whites.

Tiyi M. Morris
Ohio State University at Newark

Tiyi M. Morris, *Womanpower Unlimited and the Black Freedom Struggle in Mississippi* (2015).

Weidmann's Restaurant

Felix Weidmann came to the United States in 1868 from Zurich, Switzerland, arriving in Mobile, Alabama, aboard an ocean liner on which he served as chef. He and his wife, Clara, a native of Bavaria, settled in Meridian a year later and sold produce in Chimneyville. In 1870 they opened a four-stool café, European House, in the Union Hotel on what was then Hale Street (now 22nd Avenue). The Weidmanns moved the restaurant to the corner of Hale and Front Streets in 1884, expanding to include the thirty-six-room International Hotel. When Felix Weidmann died in 1885, the hotel closed and his son, Phillip, took over the restaurant.

A skilled baseball player and bricklayer, Phillip had an eye for innovation, changing locations and shifting food options. He moved the restaurant to the corner of 24th Avenue and 5th Street and renamed it Taft and Weidmann, maintaining a coffee shop atmosphere. Phillip then launched Weidmann's Delicatessen opposite the Grand Opera on 5th Street. He employed European pastry makers, whose chocolate éclairs became popular afternoon treats for workers on break. Patrons also enjoyed the oyster loaf—a crusty loaf of bread with the insides scooped out, toasted, and filled with fried oysters topped with celery and pickles. Phillip enlarged the business in the early twentieth century, opening an eatery in Hattiesburg to cater to the soldiers stationed at Camp Shelby during World War I as well as a nightclub, the Egyptian Room, and a Chinese restaurant. Weidmann's moved to its present location on 22nd Avenue in 1923.

Phillip died in 1927 and was succeeded by his son, Henry, who developed what have become the restaurant's familiar specialties, including black bottom pie and garlic boiled shrimp. During World War II Henry Weidmann replaced the butter on dining tables with homemade peanut butter; when he tried to return to using butter after the war, customers demanded that the peanut butter remain. Henry also began displaying pictures of famous visitors and local personalities, keeping a special section for photographs of

Meridianites who died in World War II. He brought in a treasure chest filled with candy and small prizes, allowing children to select from the box after finishing their meals. The restaurant's long counter and dining room expanded to include two more dining rooms under Henry's tenure, and by the 1950s the restaurant could seat up to two hundred people. Until Henry's death in 1956, Weidmann's stayed open twenty-four hours a day.

Henry's daughter, Dorothy Weidmann, presided over the restaurant after his death. Weidmann's continued to serve breakfast, lunch, and dinner but no longer stayed open around the clock. The restaurant employed black waiters but like other public establishments throughout the South did not admit African American patrons, and in 1965 the US Justice Department sued Weidmann's and other Meridian restaurants for failing to comply with the Civil Rights Act of 1964. Rather than fight the suit, Weidmann's and twelve other eateries announced that they would integrate. After Mississippi repealed statewide Prohibition in 1966, the restaurant added a bar.

Former Mississippi State University football star Tom "Shorty" McWilliams, whose wife, Gloria Weidmann McWilliams, was the great-granddaughter of Felix Weidmann, bought the restaurant in 1967. McWilliams's celebrity attracted more attention and added to the collection of photographs on the walls. His daughter, Gloria Chancellor, and her husband, Poo, controlled the restaurant from 1989 to 2001, when they sold Weidmann's to a group of local investors. While the building was under renovation in February 2002, Weidmann's new owners sold off much of the restaurant's interior, including kitchenware, waiters' jackets, photographs, menus, and furniture. Nostalgic patrons snapped up peanut butter crocks for forty dollars each.

After being closed for more than a year, the new Weidmann's opened on 31 December 2002 under the management of Nick Apostle, owner of a Jackson restaurant, Nick's. About one hundred photographs from the old main dining room were moved to a new bar upstairs, but the rest of the interior was gutted and the menu was overhauled to feature more upscale entrees and wine selections. In addition, Weidmann's no longer offered lunch. The restaurant failed to attract the following of its predecessor, and in September 2004, Apostle decided to focus on his Jackson establishment and sold the operation to general manager Willie McGehee. Under McGehee, the restaurant became profitable for a time, but by 2009 the economic downturn that had started two years earlier had taken a severe toll. Despite a campaign by the Alliance for Downtown Meridian to save the restaurant, it closed on 17 April 2010.

Just three months later, Weidmann's reopened under the ownership of Charles Frazier, who sought to restore many of the features of the original Weidmann's that had been lost with the renovation, including the peanut butter jars, the photographs, and the treasure chest. He also restored many dishes from the original menu, again began serving lunch, and rehired some employees from the old Weidmann's, creating an atmosphere of familiarity that diners have welcomed.

Carter Dalton Lyon
St. Mary's Episcopal School,
Memphis, Tennessee

Chris Allen Baker, *Meridian Star* (24 February 2002); Jennifer Jacob Brown, *Meridian Star* (2 May 2010); Lindsey Brown, WTOK Television website (2 August 2010), http://www.wtok.com/news; Tametria Conner, WTOK Television website (18 April 2009), http://www.wtok.com/news; "Meridian Cafes to Integrate," *New York Times* (1 May 1965); *Mississippi Business Journal* (5 May 1997, 9 July, 17 December 2001, 2 February 2003); Jack Shank, *Meridian: The Queen with a Past* (1985); Stan Torgerson, WTOK Television website (27 September 2004), http://www.wtok.com/news; Mary Dorothy Weidmann, *The Restaurant, Weidmann's: Since 1870* (1970).

Welfare Reform, 1990s

In August 1996 the federal government replaced Aid to Families with Dependent Children (AFDC) with Temporary Assistance to Needy Families (TANF), ending the sixty-year entitlement of poor families with children to cash assistance. In so doing, Congress and Pres. Bill Clinton followed a path cut by a number of states, including Mississippi, which during the early 1990s had begun to retool their welfare systems into "workfare."

Welfare reform constructed a new social contract between recipients of public assistance and the state. Whereas the AFDC program entitled all families with children and incomes below a state-determined threshold to welfare, TANF mandated that adult recipients work in exchange for receiving assistance. It also set a five-year lifetime limit on family receipt of welfare. Further, reform transformed the structure of the welfare system from a federal-state match grant into a block grant under which states were allowed to reduce spending on welfare by up to 25 percent and granted the option to apply funds to purposes other than supporting low-income families' transitions to work. The amount of each state's annual TANF grant was determined by the state's historical levels of spending on welfare and job training. Because Mississippi had always spent very little, its annual block grant of approximately eighty-six million dollars was significantly below the national median.

The reform process had begun in Mississippi with the 1992 election of Republican governor Kirk Fordice, who had made the issue a central plank of his platform. Most fundamentally, welfare reform in Mississippi was marked by a

W

"get tough" attitude toward recipients, who were expected to make a transition to self-sufficiency with minimal state support. The program emphasized reducing the size of the state welfare caseload and thus state spending on welfare services. The state first consolidated authority over the Department of Human Services, which was responsible for the administration of welfare, under the governor's office. Then, in December 1994, the state implemented a pilot welfare reform program, New Directions, in some counties. New Directions made access to public assistance and support services contingent on a recipient finding a job or participating in state-subsidized "work activities" such as community service. The program imposed the nation's harshest sanctions on recipients who failed to complete work requirements, including loss of the family's entire welfare and food stamps grants. This punitive orientation reflected the administration's belief that adult welfare recipients lacked motivation to work and had become dependent on welfare.

The federal government's 1996 overhaul of the national welfare system reflected Mississippi's approach—mandatory work requirements, sanctions, and time limits. Perhaps the major impact of federal reform in Mississippi was that it led to the implementation of New Directions throughout the state before it was fully prepared to do so. As the state that offered the lowest welfare payments in the nation—a family of three was eligible for a maximum AFDC grant of $120 per month—and that had a workforce development system oriented more toward obtaining federal funds than providing comprehensive services, Mississippi lacked both the fiscal and institutional capacity to support transitions to work. At the same time, however, the federal law subjected state leaders to tough new performance benchmarks, tying federal funds to either supporting TANF recipients' participation in "work activities" or significantly reducing the caseload. Insofar as the costs of providing single mothers with child care and other services needed to sustain employment were effectively prohibitive, Mississippi, like other low-benefit southern states, pursued a strategy of caseload reduction. Between 1996 and 2006 the number of Mississippi families receiving assistance fell from approximately 44,000 to just over 12,000, a decline of roughly 73 percent.

While many state and federal officials point to caseload decline as an unqualified indicator of successful reform, many critical studies argue that Mississippi did not improve its welfare system as much as it severely restricted access to assistance. The program's "work-first" orientation, combined with Governor Fordice's privatization of the delivery system, produced what a Rockefeller Institute report characterized as a system-wide collapse of accountability between 1996 and 1998 accompanied by inadequate service provision and incidents of client abuse. More generally, studies indicate that the caseload decline was achieved through administrative methods designed to deter eligible families from going on welfare and to push others out of the program without providing costly transitional services. One analysis of the status of those who left the program showed that only 18 percent found jobs, while 64 percent returned to TANF within five years. Another study found that only 10 percent of children whose parents left the program were covered by employer-provided health plans, while another 44 percent continued to receive government-funded health insurance.

In sum, Mississippi's high rates of working poverty, illiteracy, and unwed births, combined with its historical aversion to funding work support services, made it one of the most challenging contexts in which to reform welfare. Observers agree that if Mississippi is to develop an effective welfare-to-work system, the state will need to significantly increase its investments in human capital and support services, including child care, job training and placement, education, and transportation. President Clinton envisioned welfare reform as forging a new social contract under which families who "worked hard and played by the rules" would be rewarded with access to a new array of work support services. For a variety of reasons, Mississippi and the federal government have largely failed to fulfill their responsibilities under that contract.

Mark H. Harvey
Florida Atlantic University

David A. Breaux, Christopher M. Duncan, C. Denise Keller, and John C. Morris, *Public Administration Review* (January–February 2002); Center for Law and Social Policy website, www.clasp.org; Jocelyn Guyer, *Health Care after Welfare: An Update of Findings from State Leaver Studies* (2000); Gretchen C. Kirby, L. Jerome Gallagher, LaDonna Pavetti, Milda Saunders, and Tennille Smith, *Income Support and Social Services for Low-Income People in Mississippi* (1 December 1998), Urban Institute website, www.urban.org; Mississippi Department of Human Services, *Monthly Statistical Report: Economic Assistance Programs* (2006); Domenico Parisi, Deborah A. Harris, Steven Michael Grice, Michael Taquino, and Duane A. Gill, *Journal of Poverty* (2005); Domenico Parisi, Diane K. McLaughlin, Steven Michael Grice, and Michael Taquino, *Social Science Quarterly* (2006); Kathleen Pickering, Mark H. Harvey, Gene F. Summers, and David Mushinski, *Welfare Reform in Persistent Rural Poverty: Dreams, Disenchantments, and Diversity* (2006).

Wells-Barnett, Ida B.

(1862–1931) Journalist and Antilynching Activist

A native of Holly Springs, Ida Bell Wells, an African American teacher and pioneer antilynching crusader, developed her gender and race consciousness as she lived and traveled throughout Mississippi as a journalist for the *Free Speech*, a newspaper she co-owned and edited.

From her days as a rural schoolteacher outside of Holly Springs in 1877 to her public exile from Memphis, Tennessee, in 1892 for writing an editorial articulating that white women

Ida B. Wells-Barnett, 1893 (National Portrait Gallery, Smithsonian Institution)

willingly had sexual intercourse with black men, Wells frequently traveled to and resided in areas such as Greenville, Natchez, Mound Bayou, Water Valley, and Vicksburg. During these formative Mississippi years, Wells strengthened political relationships with prominent African American politicians such as Mississippi secretary of state James Hill and Mound Bayou founder Isaiah Montgomery. In addition, in her editorials in the *Free Speech*, she sharpened her political critique of racial injustices and politics. For example, she criticized Montgomery's conciliatory position on restrictions aimed at minimizing black suffrage at the 1890 Mississippi Convention. Furthermore, during these years Wells maximized her father's Masonic fraternal ties to solicit subscriptions for her newspaper.

Born to enslaved parents James and Elizabeth Wells on 16 July 1862, Ida Wells intertwined her parents' memories of slavery and religious convictions, her father's modeling of political activism, and her political relationships to inform a criticism that fueled her demand for racial equity and respectability. As a child, Wells frequently overheard her parents discuss race. The son of a black woman and a white slave owner, native Mississippian Jim Wells witnessed the whipping of his mother, Peggy. He was never beaten or sold. However, his father took him to Holly Springs, away from his mother, to learn carpentry. He earned a reputation of being a solid carpenter, an occupation he would use to bolster his independence from whites after emancipation. On the other hand, a native Virginian and daughter of a part-Indian father and slave mother, Lizzie and her siblings met the auction block several times before arriving in Holly Springs. She repeatedly told her children about the whippings she received as a slave. From stories told by others, Wells vicariously experienced slave women choosing death or sale before succumbing to sexual exploitation. On Sundays her parents permitted only the reading of the Bible.

Therefore, she had read the Bible several times in her youth and adult years. Later in her newspaper columns and anti-lynching publications, she invoked biblical imagery to persuade and gain support from those influenced by Judaism and Christianity. Furthermore, Jim Wells often had Ida read to him and other black men the political news from local papers. Wells recalled later that she heard of the Ku Klux Klan before she knew what it meant. The political agency of her father and the religious convictions of her mother were central to shaping her racial and gender politics, particularly her reactions to a series of life-altering events.

Orphaned at age sixteen by a 1878 yellow fever epidemic, Wells trekked from her grandmother's farm in Tippah County to Holly Springs, against the advice of older relatives, to evaluate the status of her five remaining siblings. When she arrived, she learned that the condition of her mother had worsened after she received poor medical advice from an Irish nurse—the same nurse who had purportedly gone through her father's pockets after he died. Going against the Masons' custodial expectations, Wells became guardian to her siblings. To support the family, she passed a teacher's examination and taught at a rural school outside of Holly Springs. Inheriting a house and three hundred dollars, she took care of her siblings with her twenty-five dollar monthly salary and produce supplied by her students' parents until she moved to Memphis in 1882–83. She later explained that she wrote plainly because her days as a rural teacher taught her that many blacks had limited formal education. Under the name *Iola*, she took pride in her ability to use one-syllable words to help readers understand her editorials.

A railroad incident outside Memphis and the ensuing legal battle launched her career in journalism. In 1884 Wells received a five-hundred-dollar judgment from the Chesapeake and Ohio Railroad, which had refused to honor her first-class ticket. Before three white males forcibly removed her from a racially segregated car reserved for ladies, Wells bit and fought the men, much to the chagrin of white passengers, who applauded the actions of the white males. The company appealed the case in 1887 and won a reversal of the judgment, forcing Wells to pay two hundred dollars in court costs. Yet through her editorials about the railroad case and other issues in the African American community, she gained a loyal following. African American newspaper editor T. Thomas Fortune of the *New York Age* wrote that Wells had "plenty of nerve" and that if she were a man she "would be a humming independent in politics." Fellow African American editor Lucy W. Smith heralded Wells as possessing unmatched talents: "No writer, the male fraternity not excepted, has been more extensively quoted nor struck harder blows at the wrongs and weaknesses of the race."

To hire correspondents and to secure subscriptions for the *Free Speech*, Wells frequently traveled to Mississippi from Tennessee. On one occasion in Vicksburg, Wells forced a prominent pastor to apologize publicly from his pulpit for implying that she and other southern women had

W

questionable virtue. Confronting him in front of other men, she told him that because she had no father or brother to protect her, she needed to safeguard her good name.

In 1892 Wells was in Natchez when she received news of the lynching of three educated black grocery store owners. One of the men lynched was the father of her godchild. The timing of the lynching was crucial. In 1891 Wells had lost a teaching position in Memphis after writing an editorial that criticized the conditions of African American schools and the character of some of her colleagues, leaving her free to pursue her passion for journalism full time. Wells reacted to the Memphis lynching by writing an editorial encouraging migration. Coming of age in Mississippi, Wells heard stories ranging from a voting dispute that precipitated her father's opening of a carpentry shop across the street from his former white employer to black resistance to slavery and unfair politics. Therefore, Wells's response to the Memphis lynching, which is credited for catapulting her onto the national and international spotlight, developed from her reaction to injustices she had seen and experienced in Mississippi.

Wells left Memphis and the South to escape violence from opponents of her editorials, moving to Chicago in 1892. She campaigned energetically against lynching, writing books such as *A Red Record* and *Southern Horrors* to dispute lynching supporters' claims that most African American victims of lynchings had been accused of violence against white women. Her work included long lists of the actual accusations—mostly petty crimes—that lynching victims actually faced. In Chicago she married lawyer and editor Ferdinand Lee Barnett and put much of her reformer's energy into work at settlement houses, support for suffrage, and clubwork.

Wells-Barnett died on 25 March 1931. Among the many memorials to her life is her childhood home in Holly Springs, which now houses a museum of African American history.

LaTonya Thames Taylor
West Chester University

Lee D. Baker, *Ida B. Wells-Barnett and Her Passion for Justice* (1996), http://people.duke.edu/~ldbaker/classes/AAIH/caaih/ibwells/ibwbkgrd .html; Jacquelyn Jones Royster, ed., *Southern Horrors and Other Writings: The Anti-Lynching Campaign of Ida B. Wells, 1892–1900* (1997); Patricia Schechter, *Ida B. Wells-Barnett and American Reform* (2001); Stephanie Shaw, *What a Woman Ought To Be and Do: Black Professional Women during the Jim Crow Era* (1996); Sarah Silkey, *Black Woman Reformer: Ida B. Wells, Lynching, and Transatlantic Activism* (2015); Ida B. Wells, *The Memphis Diary of Ida B. Wells: An Intimate Portrait of the Activist as a Young Woman*, ed. Miriam DeCosta-Willis (1995); Ida B. Wells, *A Red Record: On Lynching* (2002); Ida B. Wells-Barnett, *Crusade for Justice: The Autobiography of Ida B. Wells*, ed. Alfreda M. Duster (1970); Deborah Gray White, *Too Heavy a Load: Black Women in Defense of Themselves, 1894–1994* (1999).

Welty, Eudora
(1909–2001) Author

Eudora Alice Welty was born on 13 April 1909 in Jackson, Mississippi, and lived there for her entire life save for college studies, sojourns of one to six months in New York and San Francisco, and writing residencies at Breadloaf, Yaddo, and Bryn Mawr and Smith Colleges. Her father, Christian Welty, president of the Lamar Life Insurance Company, was a man of progressive ideas who encouraged his employees and family to travel and thereby gain a broader perspective and empathy for others. Eudora's mother, Chestina Andrews Welty, was a teacher from the mountains of West Virginia who taught her daughter and her two younger brothers, Edward and Walter, to love reading.

After attending Jefferson Davis Elementary School across from her home on Congress Street in Jackson, Eudora Welty moved on to Central High School. When she was sixteen, her family moved to the house at 1119 Pinehurst Street, across from Belhaven College, where she lived for the rest of her life. While in high school, she contributed drawings to the *Memphis Commercial Appeal* children's pages, won awards for a drawing and a poem published in *St. Nicholas Magazine*, and contributed graphic designs and satire to her high school yearbooks. *To the Golden Gate and Back Again*, a 1924 souvenir booklet commemorating a Lamar Life Insurance Company rail journey from Memphis to California on which Eudora was her father's guest, includes five humorous drawings by Welty and a concluding spoof addressed to "Mr. Wealty," presumably by the young wordsmith.

Welty graduated from high school in 1925 and enrolled at the Mississippi State College for Women (now Mississippi State University for Women). After two years there, during which time she drew and wrote for school publications, she moved on to the University of Wisconsin at Madison, receiving her degree in English literature in 1929. She spent

Eudora Welty, 1977 (William R. Ferris Collection, Southern Folklife Collection, Wilson Library, University of North Carolina at Chapel Hill)

the following year in Jackson, writing a few pieces for the *Jackson Daily News* but failing to find steady work with publishers or journals. In the fall of 1930, Welty moved to New York City and studied advertising at the Columbia School of Business until the fall of 1931, returning to her family's Pinehurst Street home when her father became ill and died in September.

Welty subsequently worked at numerous writing jobs. She served as the editor of *Lamar Life Radio News*, the society columnist for the *Memphis Commercial Appeal* (1933–35), a researcher for the Mississippi Advertising Commission, and a junior publicity agent for the Works Progress Administration, a position that called for her to travel throughout the state. On those trips, she took numerous photographs of places and people that were later collected and published in *One Time, One Place: Mississippi in the Depression: A Snapshot Album* (1971), *Twenty Photographs* (1980), *In Black and White* (1985), *Photographs* (1989), *Country Churchyards* (2000), and *Eudora Welty as Photographer* (2009). The images illustrate Welty's interest in human dignity. Small exhibitions of her photographs took place in Raleigh and Chapel Hill, North Carolina, at the behest of her Jackson friend Frank Lyell and in New York at Lugene Optics. *Passionate Observer: Eudora Welty among Artists of the Thirties* (2002) places Welty's photographs in the context of local and national painters and photographers, revealing Welty's talents and synchronicities with successful and trained artists.

In 1936 "Death of a Traveling Salesman" became Welty's first published story, appearing in *Manuscript*. This and other stories in little magazines and regional journals led Diarmuid Russell of a newly founded literary agency, Russell and Volkening, to offer to be Welty's literary agent. Others who nurtured Welty's career included Katherine Anne Porter; Albert Erskine, Cleanth Brooks, and Robert Penn Warren, the editors of *Southern Review*; Mary Louise Aswell of *Harper's Bazaar*; and William Maxwell of the *New Yorker*.

Twelve of Welty's forty-one collected stories garnered individual prizes. With humor, irony, compassion, *A Curtain of Green and Other Stories* (1941) and *The Wide Net and Other Stories* (1943) illustrate Mississippi during the Great Depression, using a variety of settings, themes, and conflicts. Her next collection, *The Golden Apples* (1949), is unified by the Natchez Trace setting and the theme of love and separateness. A nine-story composite set in fictional Morgana, Mississippi, and in San Francisco, the volume is Welty's most modernist work and is rightly acclaimed as her finest achievement. *The Bride of the Innisfallen* (1955), Welty's most varied story collection, features stories set in Louisiana, Mississippi, Italy, and Ireland. Some are contemporary, others take place during the Civil War, and others occur in mythic time. In addition, some are ghost stories, some feature modern angst, and some offer memory puzzles. Two stories written in the 1960s that illustrate public and private racial violence and ethics ("Where Is the Voice Coming From?" and "The Demonstrators") are included in

Collected Stories (1980). Among the best known and most frequently anthologized of Welty's stories are "Why I Live at the P.O.," "A Worn Path," and "Petrified Man." "Powerhouse," prompted by a Fats Waller concert in Jackson, is considered one of the finest American jazz stories.

Welty wrote about her youth, education, reading, and family relationships in "Personal and Occasional Pieces" in *The Eye of the Story: Selected Essays and Reviews* (1978); in her memoir, *One Writer's Beginnings* (1984); and in her Pulitzer Prize–winning autobiographical novel, *The Optimist's Daughter* (1972).

Welty published two novellas, both of which were adapted for the stage: *The Robber Bridegroom* (1942, musical drama by Alfred Uhry and Robert Alderman, 1976) and *The Ponder Heart* (1954, stage adaptation by Joseph Fields and Jerome Chodorov, 1956). Although Welty felt most pleased with her talents as a short story writer, her three novels were experimental for their day, and as complex and stylistically challenging as any of their contemporaries: *Delta Wedding* (1946), *Losing Battles* (1970), and *The Optimist's Daughter*. All three novels are set in Mississippi, but their themes—the unremitting power of the past and of complex mysteries of human relationships—are universal.

The majority of Welty's nonfiction is collected in *The Eye of the Story* and *A Writer's Eye: Collected Book Reviews* (1994). She wrote essays on writers Jane Austen, Willa Cather, Anton Chekov, Henry Green, and Katherine Anne Porter and contributed significant critical commentary on Elizabeth Bowen, William Faulkner, E. M. Forster, and Virginia Woolf in book reviews and in occasional speeches and comments. Her essays about the craft of writing are also collected in *On Writing* (2002). *Occasions: Selected Writings* (2009) contains more than sixty previously uncollected pieces from magazines, journals, newsletters, and newspapers.

Welty's talent and importance as a major American writer were recognized both nationally and internationally during her lifetime. In addition to the Pulitzer and short story awards, Welty received a Guggenheim Fellowship, the Howells Medal for Fiction from the American Academy of Arts and Letters, the Gold Medal for Fiction from the National Institute of Arts and Letters, and a Chevalier des Arts et Lettres and a Chevalier de la Légion d'Honneur. Her work has been translated into more than fifteen languages. In 1998 Welty was the first living writer to have her canon published by the Library of America (*Complete Novels* and *Stories, Essays, and Memoir*).

In her home state, Welty edited *Mississippi Women's War Bond News*, contributed a preface for the *Jackson Junior League Cookbook*, wrote letters to the editors of the Jackson newspapers, helped to found and guide the city's New Stage Theatre, campaigned for her choice of political candidates, worked on behalf of the racial integration of Millsaps College, and supported education and arts efforts.

At her death on 23 July 2001, Welty bequeathed the Pinehurst Street house to the State of Mississippi, and the

W

Mississippi Department of Archives and History now operates it as a museum with the assistance of the Eudora Welty Foundation, created in 1999 to "fund educational and research activities and to develop programs that will enhance Eudora Welty's legacy and ensure that her work continues to be recognized as among the greatest in American literature." In addition, the Eudora Welty Society sponsors scholarly panels and awards designed "to foster scholarship and academic community among Welty scholars."

Pearl A. McHaney
Georgia State University

John Bayne, *Eudora Welty Newsletter* (Winter 2002); Eudora Welty Foundation website, eudorawelty.org; Eudora Welty House and Garden website, www.mdah.ms.gov/welty/; Eudora Welty Society website, eudoraweltysociety.org; Michael Kreyling, *Author and Agent: Eudora Welty and Diarmuid Russell* (1991); Suzanne Marrs, *Eudora Welty: A Biography* (2005); Pearl McHaney, *Eudora Welty: The Contemporary Reviews* (2005); Pearl McHaney, *South Atlantic Review* (Spring 1999); Noel Polk, *Eudora Welty: A Bibliography of Her Work* (1994); Peggy Whitman Prenshaw, *Conversations with Eudora Welty* (1984); Peggy Whitman Prenshaw, *More Conversations with Eudora Welty* (1996); Thomas Verich, *Special Collections, 1975–2000: A Silver Anniversary Exhibition* (2001), Department of Archives and Special Collections, J. D. Williams Library, University of Mississippi; Ann Waldron, *Eudora: A Writer's Life* (1998); Eudora Welty Collection, Mississippi Department of Archives and History.

West, Cato

(ca. 1750–1818 or 1819) Territorial Governor

Born about 1750 in Fairfax County, Virginia, Col. Cato Charles West played a major role in politics, serving as acting governor of the Mississippi Territory from 1803 to 1805. He and his wife, Martha Green West, daughter of Thomas Green, reportedly had at least ten children. West spent time in Georgia prior to his arrival in Natchez.

Because of congressional oversight of the Mississippi Territory, national party politics dominated territorial politics in Mississippi. Federalist Winthrop Sargent served as Mississippi's first territorial governor. During Sargent's administration, West served as de facto opposition leader for Mississippi's Republicans. In 1799 West and a "general committee" of the Mississippi Territory petitioned the US Congress to address the "arbitrary" and "oppressive" measures taken by the Sargent government. Congress passed a number of reform measures for the territorial government, with most Republicans supporting West's desire to limit Sargent's power and Federalists generally voting to protect the governor's executive authority. The reforms led Sargent to hold the territory's first legislative elections, and many of those selected for the territorial assembly opposed Sargent. West was among them.

In 1800 West, a slaveholder, petitioned Congress to reverse the ban on the importation of slaves into the Mississippi Territory. The 1795 Treaty of San Lorenzo (Pinckney's Treaty) had resolved boundary issues between Spain and the United States at the thirty-first parallel, leaving the southern portion of modern-day Mississippi under Spanish control. The 1798 act that established the Mississippi Territory prohibited the importation of slaves from foreign "ports or places," posing problems for Mississippi slaveholders who wanted to transport slaves across the border with Spanish territory. In response to West's petition, the US House of Representatives crafted a bill that would have allowed the territory's governor to issue "special licenses" permitting the transportation of slaves across the Spanish border. However, the Senate voted overwhelmingly to kill the bill, denying West's petition.

The election of Pres. Thomas Jefferson shifted political power in the Mississippi Territory away from the Federalists and to the Republicans. Jefferson dismissed Sargent as governor in 1801 and appointed Republican William C. C. Claiborne to the post. The following year Jefferson selected West to serve as secretary of the Mississippi Territory. In the wake of the 1803 Louisiana Purchase, the president temporarily appointed Claiborne to oversee the new territory, and he transferred to New Orleans. West served as acting governor during Claiborne's absence. In the wake of the 1804 legislative elections, however, the Republicans were sharply divided, and the Federalists claimed the speakership of the territorial House, crippling West's ability to confront an aggressive Federalist opposition.

In 1804 Congress organized the Orleans Territory and appointed Claiborne to serve as the territorial governor; legislators then selected North Carolinian Robert Williams as the new governor of the Mississippi Territory. West remained as acting governor until Williams's arrival. Enraged at being passed over for the governorship, West took all the official territorial papers to his private home and refused to surrender them until the territorial legislature threatened to impose punitive fines. Also in 1805, Cowles Mead replaced West as secretary of the Mississippi Territory.

West reemerged in Mississippi politics during the 1817 constitutional convention, in which West represented Jefferson County. He ultimately refused to sign the constitution. He died in 1818 or 1819.

Ryan L. Fletcher
University of Mississippi

J. F. H. Claiborne, *Mississippi, as a Province, Territory, and State with Biographical Notices of Eminent Citizens* (1880); Hazel Kraft Eilers, *Hobbies* (May 1955); Norman E. Gillis, *Early Inhabitants of the Natchez District* (1963); Robert V. Haynes, *A History of Mississippi* (1973); Jefferson County, Mississippi, Probate Records, 1800–1930; *Statutes at Large*, 5th Cong., 2nd sess.

Wetlands

Of Mississippi's original 9.87 million acres of natural wetlands, only about 4.07 million acres remain. Despite this loss of more than 58 percent of its wetlands, Mississippi still has such diverse habitats as marshes, swamps, riverbank pioneer habitats, bottomland hardwood forests, bayheads, coastal flatwoods, and savannahs.

Bottomland hardwood forests, swamps (forested or shrub wetlands), riverine wetlands, and fresh marshes (emergent herbaceous wetlands) account for the majority of Mississippi's wetlands. Estuarine wetlands are the second-most-common wetlands in Mississippi and include tidal and estuarine marshes, freshwater marshes, salt pannes, sea grass beds, mud flats, and cypress–tupelo gum swamps.

Mississippi's main wetland areas include the Gulf Coast, areas in the Lower Central Plain, and the Yazoo-Mississippi River Delta. The coastal area is level to gently sloping and is at sea level on the Gulf of Mexico. These wetlands are dominated by irregularly flooded black needlerush brackish marshes, patches of tidal salt marshes of cordgrasses, and farther inland, freshwater marshes with mixed plant species. In addition, the Gulf Coastal region has pond cypress–coastal evergreen swamps, wet pine flatwoods, and large marshy or boggy areas dominated by carnivorous plants, wax myrtle, and pine.

Inland from the coast, hilly Lower Coastal Plain upland depressions and river edges support tupelo gum and various broadleaf evergreens such as sweet bay magnolia, swamp bay, and titi (swamp cyrilla) in headwater bayheads, swamps, and stream margins. The soils are mostly sandy to loamy and are typically acidic. The shallow clear waters to the north of the extensive barrier islands support submerged beds of sea grasses—underwater meadows of grass-like plants.

The Yazoo-Mississippi River floodplain, known as the Delta, is home to some of the state's major wetlands. It is delineated by the Mississippi River to its west, the Yazoo River to its southeast and south, and the Loess Hills to its east and northeast. The landscape aspect is low and very level (about 75 to 160 feet above mean sea level), and the entire region is dominated by bottomland hardwood forests composed variously of wetland oaks, sugarberry, hickory, pecan, sweet gum, elm, green ash, and red maple.

The Delta area also supports floodplain hardwood swamps, bald cypress–swamp tupelo–buttonball strands and swampy oxbow remnants, buttonball shrub swamps, and willow thickets. Pioneer communities of black and sandbar willows and cottonwood develop on sandy shoals and mudflats in its streams. The soils are alluvial in origin and vary from sandy to clayey and tend to be slightly acidic to alkaline.

Samuel P. Faulkner
Delta State University

M. M. Brinson, *A Hydrogeomorphic Classification of Wetlands* (1993); L. M. Cowardin, V. Carter, F. C. Goulet, and E. T. LaRoe, *Classification of Wetlands and Deepwater Habitats of the United States* (1979); W. J. Mitsch and J. G. Gosselink, *Wetlands* (1986); Public Law 100–4, Federal Clean Water Act of 1987, sec. 404; US Army Corps of Engineers, Environmental Laboratory, *Corps of Engineers Wetland Delineation Manual: Technical Report Y-87-1* (1987).

White, Hugh Lawson

(1881–1965) Forty-Fifth and Fifty-First Governor, 1936–1940, 1952–1956

Hugh Lawson White was perhaps the wealthiest man to hold the office of governor in the state's history, certainly in modern times. An industrialist and lumberman, White was also among the oldest men elected governor. When he was elected to a second term in 1951, White was seventy-one years old and weighed 270 pounds. He often boasted of his voracious appetite.

Born near McComb on 19 August 1881, White was elected mayor of Columbia in 1926 and served until his election as governor in 1935. During the early stages of the Great Depression, White persuaded the Reliance Manufacturing Company to open a plant in Columbia, providing jobs that lessened the

Hugh Lawson White (Archives and Records Services Division, Mississippi Department of Archives and History [PI STA W55.37 Box 20 R72 B4 56 Folder 82 #14])

W

effects of the Depression in the city. In 1935 White campaigned on a pledge to attract new industry to Mississippi and to do for the whole state what he had done for Columbia and Marion County.

During White's first administration the state adopted the Balance Agriculture with Industry (BAWI) program and offered economic incentives to new industries locating in Mississippi. The program encouraged training of workers, building or buying structures for new factories, and allowing local governments to pass bonds to attract new industry. BAWI established the state's first industrial commission. White also initiated the first long-range highway construction program, which increased the number of miles of paved highways in Mississippi from 922 in 1936 to more than 4,000 in 1940. The state highway patrol was organized and the homestead exemption law was also passed.

White served as Mississippi lieutenant governor from 1944 to 1946, becoming governor after Thomas Bailey died in office. He was elected governor in his own right in 1947. During White's administration Mississippi initiated a massive school consolidation program. In November 1953, a month before the US Supreme Court was to hear arguments in the *Brown v. Board of Education* case, White called a special session of the legislature in a belated effort to equalize the state's racially segregated school systems in hopes that the Court would not overturn the "separate but equal" doctrine. After May 1954, when the US Supreme Court declared segregated schools unconstitutional, White attempted unsuccessfully to persuade Mississippi's African American leaders to accept equal but segregated schools rather than pushing for desegregation. For most of the remainder of his term, White focused on preventing or postponing public school integration, and to that end he oversaw the creation of the Mississippi State Sovereignty Commission. The Citizens' Council, a private organization that worked closely with the Sovereignty Commission, was also founded during White's administration.

After leaving the governor's office, White returned to private business. He died on 19 September 1965. The seven-thousand-acre Hugh L. White Game Reserve (also known as the Marion County Wildlife Management Area) and the Hugh White State Park near Grenada are named in his honor.

David G. Sansing
University of Mississippi

Charles C. Bolton, *The Hardest Deal of All: The Battle over School Integration in Mississippi, 1870–1980* (2005); James C. Cobb, *The Selling of the South: The Southern Crusade for Industrial Development, 1936–1990* (1993); *Jackson Clarion-Ledger* (8 September 1851); Richard A. McLemore, *A History of Mississippi*, vol. 2 (1981).

White Flight

The term *white flight* involves residential choice, urban and suburban life, and issues of local government. In Mississippi most forms of white flight are related to schools. The first major movement toward public schools in Mississippi started in 1868, when the state founded an education department and established a school district for each county as well as for each city with a population over five thousand. For the next century, each school district maintained segregated schools. During the Jim Crow period, white schools had better facilities and better funding.

The US Supreme Court's rulings in *Brown v. Board of Education* (1954), *US v. Hinds* (1969), and *Alexander v. Holmes County Board of Education* (1969) forced schools to desegregate. In the late 1960s and early 1970s some white Mississippians (particularly those in districts that had even numbers of white and black students or that had black majorities) decided they did not want their children going to school with black students. White parents removed their children from the public schools across the state but especially did so in the Delta and the Black Belt. At Durant Elementary in Holmes County, for example, 160 of 165 white students failed to show up for class after desegregation in 1965. While many similar examples existed across the state, only a small percentage of all students left Mississippi's public school systems in the 1960s.

Some parents decided to homeschool their children, while others moved their children to private schools. Prior to 1954, the state had only three non-church-run private schools. By 1966, however, the state had 121 private schools, a number that jumped to 236 in 1970. These schools, many of which were propped up by the White Citizens' Councils or local churches, were dubbed white flight schools. In February 1970 all but a few white students left the public schools in Tunica, and most began attending one of three private schools established by local churches. In Indianola, 241 white students left the Indianola Public School District for a private school established by the Baptist and Methodist churches. In 1970 whites in the town of Drew established an academy at the National Guard Armory.

A second type of white flight involved movement to suburbs with separate school systems. As schools integrated, some white families chose to move to school districts with fewer African American students, generally leaving city districts for adjacent county districts. In *Milliken v. Bradley* (1974) the US Supreme Court ruled that states could not force integration across school district lines. In Mississippi, the ruling prompted whites to leave Jackson for suburbs such as Clinton, Brandon, and Madison and to leave Meridian for Lauderdale County. Southaven, Mississippi, founded in 1980 with a population of about sixteen thousand, attracted whites fleeing Memphis, Tennessee, and by the twenty-first century had more than forty thousand people.

White flight led to dramatic changes in the school populations of some towns and small cities in the 1970s and 1980s after federal courts mandated that neighborhood schools be desegregated. For example, in the two years after Laurel desegregated its neighborhood schools in 1976, the city lost more than eight hundred students. While the number of black students in Laurel remained the same, whites dropped from a 53 percent majority to a 25 percent minority. Similarly, more than four thousand white students left Columbus Municipal Schools between the mid-1970s and 1995, and white students went from 43 percent of Hattiesburg students in 1987 to 23 percent after a ruling there. Many of these students moved to Lamar County, where large subdivisions began springing up in Petal and the Oak Grove community.

Census data clearly demonstrate these mass movements. In 1960, prior to any school desegregation, Jackson had roughly 144,000 residents, 64 percent of whom were white. By 1990 Jackson's population had ballooned to 196,637 but was only 44 percent white, meaning an overall decrease of about 6,000 white residents. Over the next decade, Jackson suffered a net loss of a little over 12,000 people, but the city's white population decreased by almost 35,000. By contrast, Clinton, a suburb of Jackson, had 3,500 residents in 1960 but by 1990 had a population of nearly 22,000, and 82 percent of Clintonians were white. In 2010, 79.4 percent of Jackson's 173,514 residents were African American, while 33.9 percent of Clinton's 25,216 residents were African American.

As cities lose people, they lose tax dollars. To recover the revenue lost from white flight, some cities have raised taxes, trimmed municipal budgets, and cut government funding. As city services decline, other residents with the means to do so—often white residents—move away, creating a vicious cycle.

White flight is a national phenomenon, prevalent in many cities throughout the United States, and not all cities in Mississippi have experienced white flight. Tupelo, for example, has experienced constant growth without a major loss in white population.

Caleb Smith
William Carey University

Charles S. Aiken, *The Cotton Plantation South since the Civil War* (1998); Charles C. Bolton, *The Hardest Deal of All: The Battle over School Integration in Mississippi, 1870–1980* (2005); Kevin M. Kruse, *White Flight: Atlanta and the Making of Modern Conservatism* (2005); *Mississippi Statistical Abstract*, Mississippi State University (1981, 2005); J. Todd Moye, *Let the People Decide: Black Freedom and White Resistance Movements in Sunflower County, Mississippi, 1945–1986* (2004); Courtenay Slater and George Hall, *Places, Towns, and Townships* (1993); Stephen Thernstrom and Abigail Thernstrom, *America in Black and White* (1997); US Census Bureau website, www.census.gov; US Department of Commerce, *County and City Data Book, 1977: A Statistical Abstract* (1977).

White Leagues

The White Leagues emerged in the late Reconstruction South with the avowed purpose of overthrowing Republican governments and restoring white supremacy. Considered by both contemporaries and historians as the armed wing of the Democratic Party in the Deep South, they were committed to using violence to reverse the course of Reconstruction by removing Republican leaders from office. They first appeared in Louisiana during the late summer of 1874. In Mississippi, opponents of Radical Reconstruction also formed White Leagues or similar groups known as White Lines.

The earliest harbingers of the White Leagues and White Lines were the White Men's Clubs that formed across Mississippi in 1870. The depression of 1873, which destabilized Republican governance, and the rise of more aggressive black Republican leaders dedicated to obtaining civil rights created a political landscape conducive to the emergence of White Leagues. Conservative white Democrats became more anxious and more determined to stop what they saw as a trend toward "Africanization." The Mississippi White Line first arose in Vicksburg during the August elections of 1874. White dissidents formed a People's or White Man's Party that patrolled the streets, intimidating black voters. The gang forced black sheriff Peter Crosby and his board of supervisors to leave their offices. Planters in the countryside surrounding Vicksburg formed White Leagues to rid their region of "all bad and leading negroes . . . and controlling more strictly our tenants and other hands." Pitched battles between White Liners and Crosby's black supporters resulted in hundreds of black deaths. Gov. Adelbert Ames ultimately requested the assistance of federal troops, who restored Crosby to office in January 1875.

White Leagues could be found throughout Mississippi, though they were especially active in Yazoo, Claiborne, Noxubee, Hinds, and other counties with large numbers of African Americans. Leagues were often filled with young Confederate veterans, and the movement had a strong martial element. Each unit had its own flags, military regalia, and often cannons. Unlike the Ku Klux Klan earlier in Reconstruction, which terrorized African Americans and white Republicans through nocturnal raids, the White Leagues and White Lines operated openly. Editors and their newspapers often played a key role in organizing and leading White Leagues. Such newspapers as the *Pascagoula Star*, *Vicksburg Herald*, and the *Beauregard and Wesson Times* actively supported White League ideas and activities.

The White Leagues targeted Republican leaders for assassination, denied employment to blacks who voted with the Republican Party, and ostracized white Republicans. Armed White Leaguers killed blacks at a Republican rally in Clinton on 4 September 1875. In Kemper County white Republican

W

sheriff W. W. Chisolm and his young son and daughter were essentially lynched by a White League crowd. These actions and others hastened the collapse of Radical Reconstruction. In 1875 Pres. Ulysses S. Grant admitted his weariness of "these annual autumnal outbreaks in the South." A northern public increasingly preoccupied with class conflict, tired from decades of sectional strife, and uncertain about the federal government's role in protecting the black civil rights followed the Grant administration in its retreat from Reconstruction.

Mitchell Snay
Denison University

Eric Foner, *Reconstruction, America's Unfinished Revolution, 1863–1877* (1988); William C. Harris, *The Day of the Carpetbagger: Republican Reconstruction in Mississippi* (1979); Nicholas Lemann, *Redemption: The Last Battle of the Civil War* (2007); H. Oscar Lestage Jr., *Louisiana Historical Quarterly* (July 1935); George C. Rable, *But There Was No Peace: The Role of Violence in the Politics of Reconstruction* (1984); Mitchell Snay, *Fenians, Freedmen, and Southern Whites: Race and Nationality in the Era of Reconstruction* (2007).

White Primary

More than eighty years after the end of slavery, African Americans in Mississippi remained unable to redeem their constitutional promise of equal access to the franchise, in large part as a consequence of the Democratic Party rules that prevented blacks from voting in party primaries. The party argued that as a private organization, it had the right to determine who could participate in intraparty elections. However, in Mississippi and other one-party southern states, the Democratic primary effectively constituted the election, since no viable competitor would appear on the general election ballot. As a result, the party's "white primaries" meant that African American voters had no say in choosing representatives.

Mississippi adopted a primary election system in 1902, replacing the earlier convention/caucus system for choosing party candidates. Although the primary initially was not restricted to white voters, efforts to exclude blacks soon developed. Historian C. Vann Woodward has suggested that the exclusion of African American voters from the Democratic rolls in the South stemmed from attempts to heal divisions between white Democrats and Populists that emerged during the economic hard times of the 1890s: "The only formula powerful enough to accomplish that was the magical formula of white supremacy, applied . . . without any lingering resistance of Northern liberalism, or fear of any further check from a defunct Southern Populism." With its 1890

constitution, Mississippi became the first state to formally adopt provisions denying blacks the ballot, including poll tax and literacy qualifications. Because some African Americans could still qualify to vote, the white primary became the last means of disqualifying them.

Prior to the late 1930s the white primary was largely unnecessary, as almost all of the South's black voters were registered as Republicans. But Pres. Franklin D. Roosevelt's New Deal began to bring African American voters into the Democratic fold, forcing southern party leaders to find ways to exclude blacks from party affairs. While the Fifteenth Amendment prevented African Americans from being denied access to the ballot, southern states enacted legislation recognizing political parties as private organizations, and the parties then contended that they could regulate participation in their internal elections in any way they saw fit.

Beginning in the 1920s, a series of US Supreme Court cases invalidated the white primary. *Nixon v. Herndon* (1924) held unconstitutional a Texas statute explicitly prohibiting African Americans from voting in primaries. *United States v. Classic* (1941) held that Congress had the power to protect the right to vote in primary elections. And in 1944's *Smith v. Allwright*, the Court held that in light of the state's role in regulating elections, discrimination by a political party was equivalent to discrimination by the state.

Although the *Smith* decision explicitly invalidated the white primary, Mississippi and other Deep South states continued to deny African Americans the franchise. Democratic Party officials painted the decision as an issue of states' rights, and the intent to maintain a white primary remained clear: "We still have a few state's rights left, and one of those rights is to have Democratic primaries and say who shall vote in them," Mississippi Democratic Party chair Herbert Holmes told the *Boston Daily Globe* after the *Smith* decision. State and Democratic Party officials required voters to swear allegiance to the party platform, which was openly segregationist; continued to impose poll taxes; and administered literacy tests in ways that were subjective, asking would-be African American registrants questions such as "How many bubbles in a bar of soap?" and then denying applications on the grounds that the questions had been answered incorrectly.

Both the State of Mississippi and the Mississippi Democratic Party continued to prevent most African Americans from voting until the mid-1960s, when the Twenty-Fourth Amendment (1964) banned poll taxes and the Voting Rights Act (1965) banned the use of literacy tests and provided for federal oversight of voter registration in areas where less than 50 percent of the nonwhite population had registered to vote. Whereas only 5 percent of Mississippi's eligible African Americans had registered to vote in 1960, that number topped 70 percent a decade later, and African Americans accounted for 30 percent of the state's total registrants.

Matthew S. Shapanka
Harvard University

Boston Daily Globe (4 April 1944); V. O. Key, *Southern Politics in State and Nation* (1949); Michael Perman, *Struggle for Mastery: Disfranchisement in the South, 1888–1908* (2001); Nancy Weiss, *Farewell to the Party of Lincoln: Black Politics in the Age of FDR* (1983); C. Vann Woodward, *The Strange Career of Jim Crow* (1955).

Whitehead, James

(1936–2003) Author

A poet, novelist, and teacher, James Tillotson Whitehead was born in Missouri and spent most of his life working in the creative writing program at the University of Arkansas. He spent his formative years in Mississippi and in a 1970 interview discussed the childhood suffering he endured growing up as a newcomer to the state, but he also proclaimed, "I'm glad I'm a Mississippian." Writer Barry Hannah and other students from Mississippi who entered the graduate program at Arkansas formed a special bond with Whitehead because of their shared connection to the state.

Born on 13 March 1936 in St. Louis to Dick Bruun Whitehead and Ruth Ann Tillotson Whitehead, James T. Whitehead grew up in Jackson, Mississippi, where he was an all-state lineman at Central High School. He attended Vanderbilt University on a football scholarship before an injury ended his athletic career. Whitehead earned bachelor's (1959) and master's degrees (1960) from Vanderbilt and then returned to Jackson, where he taught at Millsaps College. In 1963 he enrolled in the University of Iowa's Writers' Workshop, completing a master of fine arts degree two years later.

Whitehead then accepted a teaching position at the University of Arkansas, where he and fiction writer William Harrison cofounded the master of fine arts program in creative writing. They were soon joined by Miller Williams, and the program rapidly developed a national reputation for excellence in both fiction and poetry. Among the many outstanding students they mentored are several other highly acclaimed Mississippi writers, including Barry Hannah, Ellen Gilchrist, Margaret McMullan, and Steve Yarbrough.

Whitehead's first published book of poetry, *Domains* (1966), received critical praise and earned him a Bread Loaf Writers' Conference Robert Frost Fellowship in 1967. His next publication was his only novel, *Joiner* (1971), which brought him popular acclaim; critical praise from *Life* magazine, the *New York Times*, and many other sources; and a 1972 Guggenheim Fellowship. In the novel, Sonny Joiner, a former football player who displays Whitehead's passion for the intellectual as well as for sports, politics, philosophy, and antiracism, searches for self-knowledge and self-control in the fictional small town of Bryan, Mississippi, during the civil rights movement.

Whitehead subsequently returned to poetry with three more collections: *Local Men* (1979), *Actual Size* (1985), and *Near at Hand* (1993). Influenced early in his writing career by stream of consciousness and particularly by poet Dylan Thomas, Whitehead consciously sought to move away from such interior writing to a more objective approach and to a focus on narration.

Whitehead's self-declared "aversion to racism" dominated most of his writing. He spoke of himself as a socialist and a "secret Christian" and was a strong supporter of Democratic candidates. He developed a relationship with Jimmy Carter, writing a poem for Carter's return to Georgia after leaving the presidency and subsequently editing the former president's collection of poetry.

Whitehead died of a ruptured aortic aneurysm on 15 August 2003. The English Department at the University of Arkansas honored him with the James T. Whitehead Sonnet or Sestina Prize for undergraduate students.

Verbie Lovorn Prevost
University of Tennessee at
Chattanooga

Marda Burton, *Notes on Mississippi Writers* 6 (1973); John Carr and John Little, eds., *Kite-Flying and Other Irrational Acts: Conversations with Twelve Southern Writers* (1972); *New York Times* (19 August 2003).

Whitfield, Henry Lewis

(1868–1927) Forty-First Governor, 1924–1927

Although Henry Lewis Whitfield served as the state's governor from 1924 to 1928, he is perhaps best known for his career in public education and his many contributions to the development of Mississippi's public school system. While still a student at Mississippi College, Whitfield began his teaching career at age sixteen. Because of his limited financial resources, Whitfield never had the opportunity to attend college for two years in succession, and ten years passed before he earned his bachelor's degree.

Whitfield, who was born in Rankin County on 20 June 1868, served as principal at Westfield and Steen's Creek early in his career. Whitfield aspired to be a lawyer and enrolled in the law department at Millsaps College. However, just before he was about to begin his law practice, he was appointed state superintendent of education by Gov. Anselm McLaurin in 1898. He was subsequently elected superintendent in 1899 and reelected in 1903. As superintendent, Whitfield was

W

Henry Lewis Whitfield at dedication of Mississippi Veterans' Home (Archives and Records Services Division, Mississippi Department of Archives and History [PI STA W55.84 Box 20 R72 B4 56 Folder 85 #3])

a strong advocate of industrial training and agricultural high schools, and he campaigned widely to improve funding and other support for education.

In 1907 Whitfield was appointed president of the Industrial Institute and College (now Mississippi University for Women) at Columbus. The Institute experienced significant growth under his leadership, and in 1920, the same year that Whitfield left the school, its name was changed to Mississippi State College for Women.

In the 1923 governor's race, the first in which women voted, Whitfield narrowly defeated Theodore Bilbo, in large part as a consequence of Whitfield's support among Mississippi's new voters. During his administration Whitfield recommended a broad legislative program that included better mental health care, improving the state's vocational training program, reorganizing and upgrading the entire public school system, expanding economic opportunities for Mississippi's black citizens, and industrial expansion. Whitfield also favored the enactment of a state inheritance tax. Whitfield's effort to attract more industry to Mississippi was a forerunner of the Balance Agriculture with Industry (BAWI) program created in 1936. The Sea Wall Bill, which authorized the construction of a wall to protect the beaches along the Mississippi Sound, was also passed during his administration.

In the winter of 1926 Whitfield became gravely ill, and after a brief treatment in Memphis, he returned to Jackson and conducted affairs of state from his private quarters in the Governor's Mansion until his death on 18 March 1927. After a memorial service at the State Capitol, he was interred in Columbus.

David G. Sansing
University of Mississippi

Bill Baker, *Catch the Vision: The Life of Henry L. Whitfield of Mississippi* (1974); Thomas E. Kelly, *Who's Who in Mississippi* (1914); *Mississippi Official and Statistical Register* (1924–28).

Whitfield, James
(1791–1875) Eighteenth Governor, 1851–1852

James Whitfield became Mississippi's governor under unusual circumstances and served for only about six weeks. Born in Elbert County, Georgia, on 15 December 1791, Whitfield moved to Columbus, in Lowndes County, after the Indian lands were opened for white settlement. He combined his mercantile interests with planting and prospered. He served in the Mississippi House of Representatives from 1842 to 1850 and in the Mississippi State Senate in 1851.

As the 1851 gubernatorial election approached, the Mississippi Supreme Court ruled that "all officers of this state are elected for limited terms, which shall expire at the time of the general election." On 4 November 1851 Henry Stuart Foote faced off against Jefferson Davis in the race for the governorship. In keeping with the court's ruling, incumbent governor John Isaac Guion vacated the office on 4 November. But according to the ruling, the term of the secretary of state, Joseph Bell, had also expired, and the attorney general and others advised him that he could no longer legally act in that capacity. But there was no governor to commission the newly elected secretary of state, and no secretary of state to convene the State Senate to elect a president to assume the office of governor. In addition, no one was authorized to receive and validate the election returns to ascertain who had won the general election. Mississippi remained without a governor for twenty days. Even though he lacked legal authority, Bell continued to act in his official capacity and issued a proclamation convening the State Senate in extraordinary session on 24 November 1851.

The Senate convened and elected Whitfield to serve as its president—on the twenty-first ballot, by one vote. He immediately assumed the office of governor. In addition to performing the routine duties of the office, Whitfield appointed John J. McRae to the US Senate to fill the unexpired term of Davis, who had resigned on 23 September 1851 to run for the governorship. Whitfield left the governor's office on 10 January 1852, when Foote, who had won the November election, was inaugurated.

In 1852 he opened an insurance company and banking house, which remained solvent throughout the Civil War. He returned to the State House of Representatives from 1858 to 1862. In 1870 Whitfield retired from all active business and political affairs, and on 25 June 1875 he died at Snowdoun, his Columbus home.

David G. Sansing
University of Mississippi

Richard Aubrey McLemore, ed., *A History of Mississippi*, vol. 1 (1973); Mississippi Official and Statistical Register (1912); Dunbar Rowland, *Encyclopedia of Mississippi History*, vol. 2 (1907).

Whitfield (Mississippi State Hospital)

Whitfield is the colloquial name for the Mississippi State Hospital, Mississippi's primary public mental institution and hospital, which dates to 1848. The name is derived from the post office and railroad station located at the hospital, which were named for Henry L. Whitfield, a Rankin County native who served as Mississippi's governor from 1924 to 1927 and was in office when the state legislature voted to relocate the Mississippi State Insane Hospital, as it was then known, from Jackson to its current site ten miles to the southeast in Rankin County.

The modern treatment of mental illness in Mississippi dates to antebellum times. Prior to the late eighteenth century the mentally ill, then termed *lunatics* or *idiots*, often were not considered worthy of public concern. They frequently wandered the streets or were kept locked up by families at home, with the violently psychotic sometimes chained to the floors of jails. Early mental institutions developed not to treat the afflicted but rather to confine them away from the general public. By the early nineteenth century physicians such as Philippe Pinel and Benjamin Rush encouraged a more scientific and humane approach that resulted in the creation of benevolent institutions and hospitals for the scientific treatment of the insane. In the early 1840s leaders in the state's medical community, especially Drs. William S. Langley, Edward Pickett, and Thomas J. Catchings, championed the idea of erecting such a hospital in Mississippi. In January 1846 Gov. Albert G. Brown proposed the erection of "an asylum for lunatics" and "a refuge for the insane." Two years later, the legislature appropriated ten thousand dollars and provided a five-acre lot in Jackson. An early superintendent later remarked that Mississippi's asylum was "born in debt" and spent most of its early history "begging and borrowing."

The asylum's commissioners soon purchased a tract of 140 acres of land two miles north of Jackson off the Canton road (the present location of the University of Mississippi Medical Center), and work began on a large central building with two wings on that site in 1848. Assisted by Dorothea L. Dix, a Boston schoolteacher nationally known as a mental health reformer, the commissioners consolidated public support and secured the necessary funding from the legislature. By 1851 the first buildings of the Mississippi State Lunatic Asylum were erected and a cornerstone placed, and the asylum opened its doors to patients in 1855.

The first superintendent, Dr. William Langley, had been among the earliest proponents of the asylum's establishment. By 1856, at the request of the asylum trustees, a few slaves and free persons of color were admitted. In its early years the Jackson asylum survived fires, tornadoes, yellow fever epidemics, and shifting Yazoo clay. The main building, with six marble columns and a classic front crowned with a cupola, had wing after wing added on, sprawling out like a prehistoric bird. For generations, it provided care for thousands of Mississippi's mentally ill.

In 1870 Gov. James Alcorn appointed Dr. William Compton as superintendent. A nationally recognized mental health physician, Compton utilized his great political skill to secure gubernatorial and legislative support. He also embarked on efforts to modernize the medical treatment of the insane and to double the facility's capacity. He requested improved lodging for the "lunatics of color" to equal those provided for the whites while acknowledging, with Alcorn's support, the need for segregation by both race and sex.

Overcrowding continually plagued the institution, and a second hospital, East Mississippi Insane Asylum (now East Mississippi State Hospital), was established in Meridian on 8 March 1882 to help treat the state's mentally ill. In 1890, after considering the possibility of opening an institution in the Delta, the legislature authorized the building of an annex to the Jackson facility for the increasing number of black patients; ten years later, yet another annex was added.

In January 1900 the lunatic asylum changed its name to the Mississippi State Insane Hospital. The institution continued to deteriorate physically as its census swelled to 1,350 beds. Appointed superintendent in 1918, Dr. Charles Mitchell advocated relocating the hospital to create a more modern campus. By 1926 the Jackson hospital reached a census of 2,000 patients, and the grounds totaled more than thirteen hundred acres, which were farmed by the patients. That year, the legislature appropriated $2.5 million for a new hospital to be located on 3,333 acres of state-owned land in Rankin County. The 1926 legislation also dropped *Insane* from the hospital's title, and it became simply Mississippi State Hospital. Because of a significant drop in state income during the Depression and ongoing political squabbles, the hospital did not open at the new site until March 1935 and cost a total of $5 million.

The Whitfield campus was a more isolated environment, based on a modern prototype very different than the interconnected wards and annexes of the old asylum. Highly regarded architect N. W. Overstreet planned the main campus, which covered 350 acres and consisted of more than seventy-five colonial-style red brick buildings with white columns and trim. It had a capacity of thirty-five hundred patients. The original plan included two separate campuses—the western side for African American residents and the eastern side for whites. Whitfield remained segregated racially until the passage of the Civil Rights Act of 1964, when administrator Dr. William L. Jaquith desegregated the campus without incident.

Jaquith, a Vicksburg native who began his service to the hospital in 1947, transformed its approach to mental illness during his three decades of leadership. By 1955 Whitfield had a census of four thousand patients and more than eight hundred employees. However, after legal challenges to the confinement of the mentally ill, the patient population decreased significantly, falling to twenty-six hundred by 1978 and to sixteen hundred by 1983. The legislature considered closing the facility in the early 1980s. As medical professionals have increasingly embraced community-based psychiatric programs, Whitfield has continued to shrink, and several of the buildings that formerly housed patients have closed. As a result of this shift in mental health priorities, in 2016 the hospital contained 405 licensed hospital beds and 379 licensed nursing home beds and provided a variety of community-service programs.

In February 2000 the Mississippi State Hospital Museum opened on the Whitfield campus in Building 23, constructed in 1929 to receive white male residents. The museum offers a concise historical overview of the treatment of mental illness in the state, centering on the critical role played by the Mississippi State Hospital. Original hydrotherapy rooms, needle spray showers, and a fever box are included among the museum's exhibits.

Lucius M. Lampton
Magnolia, Mississippi

Annual Reports of the Board of Trustees and Superintendent of the Mississippi State Lunatic Asylum (1870–77); Whitney E. Barringer, "The Corruption of Promise: The Insane Asylum in Mississippi, 1848–1920" (PhD dissertation, University of Mississippi, 2016); Lucius M. Lampton, *Journal of the Mississippi State Medical Association* (April 2000, January 2003); William D. McCain, *The Story of Jackson* (1953); Mississippi State Hospital website, www.msh.state.ms.us.

Whiting, William H. C.
(1824–1865) Confederate General

Confederate general William Henry Chase Whiting was born on 22 March 1824 in Biloxi, Mississippi, the son of army officer Levi Whiting and Mary A. Whiting of Massachusetts. Educated in the North, he graduated first in the Class of 1845 at West Point, with the highest grades yet attained by a cadet. This achievement earned him assign-

ment to the prestigious Corps of Engineers. In addition to a frontier assignment in Texas, he worked on river and harbor improvements, coastal fortifications, and lighthouses along the California, Gulf, and southeastern coasts. During a two-year posting on the Lower Cape Fear River in North Carolina, he married Katherine Davis Walker of Wilmington on 22 April 1857.

He resigned his commission as a US Army captain on 20 February 1861 to cast his lot with the Confederacy. After serving as Maj. Gen. Joseph E. Johnston's chief of staff during the First Manassas on 21 July 1861 and commanding a division during the Seven Days' Campaign of 1862 in Virginia, he was transferred to command the District of the Cape Fear in November 1862.

Whiting's district included Wilmington, North Carolina, which became the South's most important blockade-running port. To defend the approaches to the port he expanded the existing earthworks of Fort Fisher, which stood at the end of a long sandy peninsula between the Cape Fear River and the Atlantic. Fort Fisher grew into the strongest fort in the Confederacy. Its long-range guns kept Union blockaders well out to sea, enabling blockade-runners to bring vital supplies to the Confederacy nearly until the end of the war.

Whiting's men liked him and good-naturedly nicknamed him Little Billy. Early in the war, he won glowing praise from his superiors, but the praise faded as his increasingly strident criticism of the military and the government was seen as arrogance. He irritated members of Jefferson Davis's administration with constant appeals for more troops and heavy guns to defend Fort Fisher, which he (and many future historians) regarded as one of the most important points in the Confederacy. After requesting a transfer to more active operations, he spent a few disappointing months commanding a division near Petersburg, Virginia, in mid-1864 before returning to Wilmington.

In December 1864 Fort Fisher repelled a massive Union Army and Navy attack. As a stronger assault loomed in January 1865, Lt. Gen. Braxton Bragg, who took over command of the district from Whiting, decided to abandon Wilmington. Fort Fisher was attacked with the largest amphibious operation conducted by the United States until World War II. During the heavy bombardment, Whiting returned to Fort Fisher, telling its commander, "I have come to share your fate. You and your garrison are to be sacrificed." Whiting was wounded while leading a countercharge on 15 January 1865. Taken prisoner after the fort fell, he was held at Fort Columbus in New York Harbor, where he died of dysentery on 10 March.

David A. Norris
Wilmington, North Carolina

C. B. Denson, *An Address Delivered in Raleigh, N.C., on Memorial Day (May 10), 1895, Containing a Memoir of the Late Major-General William Henry Chase Whiting of the Confederate Army* (1895); Chris E. Fonvielle Jr.,

The Wilmington Campaign: Last Rays of Departing Hope (1997); William S. Powell, ed., *Dictionary of North Carolina Biography*, 6 vols. (1979–96); Ezra J. Warner, *Generals in Gray: The Lives of the Confederate Commanders* (1959).

Whitten, Jamie
(1910–1995) Politician

On 5 April 1994 Jamie Whitten announced that he would not seek reelection to the US House of Representatives. "The people of our state have been mighty good to me through the years and it has always been my desire to serve them as well as I possibly could," he said in a statement from his Washington office. "However, the timing seems right and there are other interests I still want to pursue." Whitten had entered Congress in 1941 and held on to his seat for fifty-three years, making him the longest-serving member of the House at the time of his retirement.

Jamie Lloyd Whitten was born on 18 April 1910 in Cascilla, Mississippi. He grew up in a farming family, attended local public schools, and studied literature and law at the University of Mississippi. Before his election to Congress, Whitten briefly served as a school principal, practiced law in Charleston, and was a member of the State House of Representatives in 1931 and 1932. He was elected district attorney of the 17th District in 1933 and occupied that position until 1941. When Mississippi representative Wall Doxey resigned from the US House that year to run for the Senate, Whitten won Doxey's vacated seat and soon became known as an avid supporter of agricultural programs. In 1949 Whitten became the chair of the Agriculture Appropriations Subcommittee, a post he held until 1992.

Like most southern Democrats, Whitten fiercely opposed civil rights and desegregation during the 1950s and 1960s. He believed that the US Supreme Court's 1954 *Brown v. Board of Education* decision would set the United States "on the downhill road to integration and amalgamation and ruin," and he was one of the signers of the 1956 Southern Manifesto, which called the *Brown* decision "a clear abuse of judicial power." Whitten voted against the Civil Rights Act of 1964, the Voting Rights Act of 1965, and an extension of the Voting Rights Act in 1975. However, when the black vote became more powerful after the 1960s, Whitten distanced himself from his segregationist past. "Conditions change," he said in an interview; "You go with conditions as they are, not like what they used to be." With a constituency that was 23 percent African American, he wisely decided that pragmatism would be a surer way to electoral success than race-baiting.

During his career in Congress, Whitten focused primarily on agriculture. His forty-three years on the Agriculture Appropriations Subcommittee earned him the nicknames *Farm Baron* and *Permanent Secretary of Agriculture*. He used his political power to secure subsidies for cotton farmers and agricultural research, and he supported soil conservation and the use of pesticides. In 1966, in response to Rachel Carson's *Silent Spring*, which claimed that the use of insecticides such as DDT would cause ecological disaster, Whitten published *That We May Live*, and he contended that DDT had "produced no known harmful effect to human health when properly used."

In 1979 Whitten was elected chair of the powerful House Appropriations Committee. Although more reform-minded politicians initially opposed his election, Whitten obtained the backing of House Speaker Thomas P. O'Neill, a Massachusetts Democrat. In exchange, Whitten gave his support to a number of liberal programs including food stamps, marking his transition from a staunch conservative to a more mainstream Democrat. In 1976 Whitten voted with his party only 32 percent of the time; eight years later that number was 76 percent. Over the years, he also changed his stance on race issues. According to Aaron Henry, former president of the Mississippi branch of the National Association for the Advancement of Colored People, "Certainly, in his last 12 to 15 years, he got to be pretty strong in his advocacy for equity and justice for all Mississippians."

As a campaigner, Whitten represented the old southern cult of personalism based less on political issues and more on direct contact with the voters. He wielded his political clout to deliver federally funded projects to his home district, such as the Tennessee-Tombigbee Waterway, the Jamie L. Whitten National Center for Physical Acoustics at the University of Mississippi, and subsidies for a NASA plant near Iuka. "My district is part of the nation," went one his catchphrases, "and if you handle a national program and leave out your district, you would not want to go home." However, at the end his career, his power started to wane. A 1992 stroke cost Whitten his positions as committee chairs. Largely ignored during his last two years in Congress, "the Chairman" retired after more than half a century on Capitol Hill.

On 9 September 1995, Whitten died of heart and kidney failure and acute respiratory distress at Baptist Memorial Hospital–North Mississippi in Oxford.

Maarten Zwiers
University of Groningen, the Netherlands

David Binder, *New York Times* (9 September 9 1995); Mac Gordon, *Jackson Clarion-Ledger* (6 April 1994); Anne Millet, *Jamie L. Whitten: Democratic Representative from Mississippi* (1972); Jere Nash and Andy Taggart, *Mississippi Politics: The Struggle for Power, 1976–2008* (2nd ed., 2009); Marty Russell, *Northeast Mississippi Daily Journal* (10 September 1995); Ward Sinclair, *Washington Post* (26 December 1978); J. Y. Smith, *Washington Post* (10 September 1995); Emily Wagster and Butch John, *Jackson Clarion-Ledger* (10 September 1995).

W

Wier, Sadye Hunter

(1905–1995) Teacher and Extension Agent

A home demonstration agent and community leader in and around Starkville, Sadye Hunter Wier was born on 3 December 1905 in McLeod, Mississippi, near Macon, to Samuel J. Hunter and Minnie Lane Hunter, graduates of Memphis's LeMoyne-Owen College who went on to become the founding teachers of the Noxubee Industrial School in Macon. As a young girl, Hunter was an honor student at the school before attending high school at the Mary Holmes College in West Point. She transferred to Nashville's Fisk University and then to Talladega College in Alabama. She became a close friend of the daughter of Talladega's white president, but she also waited tables to make ends meet.

Hunter returned to Macon as a home economics teacher in 1923 but quickly moved to better-paying teaching positions in Okolona, Aberdeen, Shuqualak, Starkville, Senatobia, and Grenada. In 1932 she returned to Starkville to marry Robert Wier, a barber and businessman. Her husband did not want her to work, but she persisted, teaching for eleven years at the segregated Oktibbeha County Training School. She provided instruction in history, English, and music while serving as library director and managing a minstrel troupe that performed in the area on Friday evenings. She also washed towels and did a variety of other tasks for her husband's barbershop.

In March 1943 she left her teaching career to become a "Negro home demonstration agent" with the Mississippi Cooperative Extension Service. She worked with black families in Newton County, Union County, and Winston County until 1954, when she moved to Lowndes County, a change that enabled her to live at home in Starkville and commute to work rather than having to board during the week.

"Miss Sadye" had an enormous impact on her clients, teaching them everything from money management to quilt making. She also became a kind of expert at race relations, getting both white and black leaders to support her efforts. Beginning in 1961 she successfully fought attempts to place her and other black agents under white control.

She retired in 1965 but quickly took on a variety of new duties. For several years she served as coordinator of the federal Neighborhood Youth Corps for twenty-one counties. Working for Prairie Opportunity, she established canneries for poor people in Clay and Noxubee Counties. She was one of the founders of Starkville's Association for Retarded Citizens and served as its first president. She almost single-handedly saved Starkville's Colored Odd Fellows Cemetery from abandonment, and for twelve years she served as a trustee of the Oktibbeha County Library System.

In 1950 Robert and Sadye Wier were instrumental in recruiting black physician Douglas L. Conner to Starkville:

his medical and civil rights activities ultimately left an indelible mark on the community. The Wiers also regularly provided accommodations in their home for visiting blacks whom local hotels would not accept. The Wiers also took in family members in need.

Wier was not a leader in the civil rights movement. A Baptist and a Democrat, she worked within the segregation system to better the lives of black people. When integration came, she simply continued her persistent, nonthreatening pressure on the white power structure. She remained influential until her death in Starkville on 24 August 1995. She was buried in the same cemetery she had helped preserve.

John F. Marszalek
Mississippi State University

John F. Marszalek, in *Mississippi Women, Their Histories, Their Lives*, ed. Martha H. Swain, Elizabeth Anne Payne, Marjorie Julian Spruill, and Susan Ditto (2003); Sadye H. Wier with John F. Marszalek, *A Black Businessman in White Mississippi, 1886–1974* (1977).

Wildmon, Donald

(b. 1938) Religious Leader

Methodist minister Donald Wildmon founded the American Family Association and its predecessor, the National Federation of Decency, as part an increase in conservative religious activism since the 1970s. One of the more cantankerous figures of the Christian Right, Wildmon diverges from other people in the movement in his emphasis on protesting what he sees as sinfulness in the media.

Donald Ellis Wildmon was born on 18 January 1938 in Ripley, Mississippi, where his father worked in the state health department and his mother taught school and Sunday school. Educated at Mississippi State University and Millsaps College, Wildmon attended divinity school at Emory University before returning to Mississippi as a Methodist minister. In the early 1970s he pastored churches in northern Mississippi; developed a telephone ministry; started a small religious press, Five Star Publishers; and wrote several short books of religious advice. With titles such as *Living Thoughts* and *Practical Help for Daily Living*, his books showed little of the anger that fueled his later activism.

In December 1976 Wildmon had what he has described as a life-changing experience: his family sat down to watch television and could not find anything without secularism, violence, or sex. He first organized a one-week boycott of television but quickly moved on to a more aggressive pose he has labeled a "confrontational ministry." Wildmon criticized most churches for ignoring the media's increasing power in daily life and launched a series of boycotts against corporations that sponsored what he sees as the most offensive television shows, movies, and magazines. His 1990 autobiography, *Don Wildmon: The Man the Networks Love to Hate*, described how he came to see television networks as "the unrecognized foe of the Christian faith and its values" because they portray as much sex as possible, mock or ignore Christian religion, and glorify a position he came to characterize as secular humanism.

Wildmon founded the National Federation of Decency as a successor of the Catholic League of Decency, which monitored the content of Hollywood movies from 1934 until the 1960s. In 1988 he renamed his organization the American Family Association. The organization publishes a newsletter that describes the content of offending television shows and encourages people to write to members of Congress, television stations, and corporations to demand changes. Wildmon has led frequent boycotts of corporations that make, advertise, and sell movies, television programs, or magazines that he deems offensive. Wildmon has often used aggressive language in his efforts, referring to the ABC television network as "the prostitute network" and R. J. Reynolds as "the number one 'Porno Pushing Advertiser.'" Wildmon gained some notoriety and had some success protesting *The Last Temptation of Christ*, a 1988 film many Christians condemned for failing to follow the Bible and for suggesting that Jesus was not the son of God but a sinner and tortured soul. Wildmon has consistently argued that the media has become such a powerful social force that it cannot be merely ignored. To react positively, American Family Association started American Family Radio, which combines Christian music with talk shows, but Wildmon has never backed away from fighting forms of media that violate his ideal of Christian family life.

In the 1990s Wildmon grew more interested in opposing the possibility of same-sex marriages. He was one of the leaders of the movement that led to the 2004 passage of an amendment to the Mississippi Constitution that banned the state legislature from the passing any laws recognizing same-sex marriage. Just prior to the US Supreme Court's 2015 decision legalizing same-sex marriage across the United States, Wildmon appeared on American Family radio to express his hope that the Court would not do so.

In March 2010, following an extended hospital stay, Wildmon announced that he was stepping down as chair of the AFA. His son, Tim, succeeded him.

Ted Ownby
University of Mississippi

Ted Ownby, in *Politics and Religion in the White South*, ed. Glenn Feldman (2005); Donald Wildmon with Randall Nulton, *Don Wildmon: The Man the Networks Love to Hate* (1989).

Wilkinson, Claude
(b. 1959) Poet and Artist

Born near Nesbit on 17 December 1959 to Henry Bridgforth Wilkinson and Lula Moncrief Wilkinson, poet and artist Claude Henry Wilkinson was raised on a small farm with his three older sisters, Bernadette, Juliette, and Ernelle. Wilkinson received a bachelor's degree in education from the University of Mississippi in 1981 and a master's degree in English from the University of Memphis nine years later.

Wilkinson's first book, *Reading the Earth* (1998), a collection of forty-four poems, garnered critical praise and won the Naomi Long Madgett Poetry Award. Soon thereafter, he received the 1999 Walter E. Dakin Fellowship in Poetry from the Sewanee Writers' Conference and the 2000 Whiting Writers' Award. In 2000–01 Wilkinson became the first poet to serve as the John and Renée Grisham Visiting Writer in Residence at the University of Mississippi. Wilkinson's second book of poetry, *Joy in the Morning* (2004), also received favorable reviews.

One critic describes Wilkinson's poetry as possessing "nature's delicate details and memory's refining power." Wilkinson opens both *Reading the Earth* and *Joy in the Morning* with epigraphs taken from the Bible, setting the tone for the work that follows. Biblical allusions are numerous in Wilkinson's works, as are images taken from the natural world; references to Jericho, Noah and his ark, and the Book of Revelation are hidden amid images of blackbirds and kookaburras. In "Knell" the speaker quietly confronts God following the illness and death of his mother while taking in the quietness and solitude of a southern night. Wilkinson's vision of the South features Spanish moss and cypress trees and family memories, yet a commanding presence hides behind these seemingly innocuous descriptions. His poetry has appeared in the *Atlanta Review*, *Oxford American*, and *Southern Review* and has been included in several anthologies.

Wilkinson has also published criticism on the work of such writers as Chinua Achebe, Italo Calvino, and John Cheever and taught English courses at a variety of colleges and universities, including Lane College, LeMoyne-Owen College, Christian Brothers University, and Mississippi Valley State University. In addition, he is a highly praised visual artist whose paintings demonstrate the same "quiet intensity and wide-ranging talents" that his poetry possesses.

Lisa Sloan
University of Mississippi

Ethel Brooks, *The Mississippi Writers and Musicians Project of Starkville High School* (May 2001); Deidra Jackson, *Southern Register* (Spring–Summer 2001, Winter 2001); Mississippi Writers and Musicians website, www.mswritersandmusicians.com; Prabook website, prabook.com.

W

Wilkinson County

Located in Mississippi's southwestern corner, on the Louisiana border, Wilkinson County was one of the state's original counties, formed in 1802 and named for Revolutionary War general James Wilkinson, the first governor of the Louisiana Territory. Part of the original Natchez District, the area that became Wilkinson was home to a great deal of early travel and occasional controversy between Americans and Spanish officials. The county seat is Woodville. Other towns include Crosby, Doloroso, Pinckneyville, Rosetta, and Fort Adams. The Homochitto and Buffalo Rivers flow through Wilkinson County, and a portion of the Homochitto National Forest is located there.

In the early 1800s Wilkinson was one of the state's most heavily populated counties, with almost 10,000 people—59 percent of them enslaved—listed on the 1820 census. Ten years later, only Adams County had more residents than Wilkinson's 11,686, and Wilkinson was one of just three counties in which slaves comprised more than two-thirds of the population. Woodville was home to one of Mississippi's slave markets. By 1840 the population had topped 14,000, and more than 76 percent of county residents were slaves.

South Carolina native Abram Scott moved to Wilkinson County as a young man before fighting in the War of 1812 and becoming Mississippi's governor in 1832. Andrew Marschalk, the state's leading newspaper publisher in the early 1800s, worked primarily in Natchez but also established a newspaper in Wilkinson County.

By 1860 Wilkinson's population had grown to almost 16,000, of whom 14,467 (82 percent) were slaves. Like many counties dominated by plantation slavery, Wilkinson produced far more cotton than corn. Wilkinson's twelve manufacturing establishments employed 143 people. Most notable was a large, steam-powered cotton mill that Edward McGehee built in 1850. Eighteen of the county's thirty churches were Methodist institutions.

Born in Kentucky, future Confederate president Jefferson Davis moved with his parents to a plantation home in Wilkinson County. Joseph Davis, Jefferson Davis's nephew, grew up in Woodville, worked as a lawyer in Madison County, and became a Confederate general. Carnot Posey, born in 1818 in Woodville, was a lawyer, planter, and Mexican War figure before serving with the Wilkinson Rifles in the Civil War and rising to the rank of general. William Lindsay Brandon moved from Adams County to Wilkinson in the 1820s and became a planter. He lost a leg early in the war but nevertheless became a brigadier general in 1864. African American troops in the 3rd Regiment Cavalry fought in the Woodville area, which was also the site of a wartime hospital.

Wilkinson's concentration on cotton and its large African American majority continued to define it after the Civil War.

The population grew to almost 18,000 by 1880, with African Americans making up 80 percent of residents. Agriculture in general and cotton in particular continued to dominate the county's economy.

In 1900 Wilkinson County's population was 21,453, with African Americans. Only 9 percent of Wilkinson's 2,072 black farmers were landowners, compared to almost two-thirds of the county's 615 white farmers. Wilkinson was home to about 100 immigrants, mostly Irish, Germans, and Italians, and its forty manufacturing establishments employed 48 workers, all male.

Wilkinson County's population declined steadily in the early twentieth century. By 1930 the county had fewer than 14,000 people, and the share of African Americans had declined to 70 percent. When L. O. Crosby reopened a lumber mill in the county, residents named a community in his honor. The central feature of the economy remained agriculture, with 2,160 farms, 72 percent of them operated by tenants. During World War II large numbers of soldiers trained at the US Army's Camp Van Dorn, located in Wilkinson and Amite Counties. The facility was the site of significant racial tension and violence.

Two notable musicians were born in Woodville and gained fame outside Mississippi. Both William Grant Still, born in 1895, and Lester Young, born in 1909, were the sons of musician parents. Sometimes called the Dean of African American Composers, Still was educated and made most of his music outside the South. Young grew up in New Orleans, became a skilled saxophonist, and moved first to the Midwest and then to New York, where he gained the nickname *Pres*, short for "President of Tenor Saxophonists." Born in Wilkinson County in 1940, Anne Moody wrote a 1968 autobiography, *Coming of Age in Mississippi*, that details her life in and near Centreville as well as her time as a civil rights activist in Jackson.

Between 1930 and 1960 Wilkinson's population remained steady at around 13,000. The county had a growing manufacturing base, primarily in timber, as well as a persistent problem with poverty. In 1960 almost a quarter of the county's working people had manufacturing jobs, particularly in the furniture industry; others found employment related to the county's twenty-three oil wells. More than a quarter of workers were involved in agriculture, producing soybeans, corn, oats, and cotton.

Wilkinson's population declined steadily over the next three decades, shrinking by about 25 percent. In 2010 the county had 9,878 residents, 71 percent of them African American.

Mississippi Encyclopedia Staff
University of Mississippi

Mississippi State Planning Commission, *Progress Report on State Planning in Mississippi* (1938); *Mississippi Statistical Abstract*, Mississippi State University (1952–2010); Charles Sydnor and Claude Bennett, *Mississippi*

History (1939); University of Virginia Library, Historical Census Browser website, http://mapserver.lib.virginia.edu; E. Nolan Waller and Dani A. Smith, *Growth Profiles of Mississippi's Counties, 1960–1980* (1985).

William Carey University

The history of William Carey University, a Baptist institution with campuses in Hattiesburg and Biloxi, reflects intellectual and cultural movements that have drawn Mississippians into a wider world during the twentieth century. In 1906 in the "southern suburbs" of Hattiesburg, W. I. Thames founded South Mississippi College, which burned four years later. Methodist timber baron W. S. F. Tatum then donated the site to Baptists, who wanted to educate women but did not want to admit them to Mississippi College. Opened in September 1911 under Pres. W. W. Rivers, Mississippi Woman's College continued operation in 1912 under the direction of J. L. Johnson Jr., who served as president until his death in 1932. By 1925 Woman's College had gained a three-hundred-thousand-dollar endowment and was accredited by the Southern Association of Colleges and Schools.

Pursuing what its leaders called "the highest type of Southern Womanhood" and "in no sense sectarian," Mississippi Woman's College became one of the South's most noted Christian colleges for women. Faculty had studied at Mississippi, Tulane, Brown, California, Virginia, Cornell, Chicago, and Columbia. At a time when sixteen passenger trains entered Hattiesburg daily and Camp Shelby loomed nearby, campus rules prohibited young male callers, required chaperones for trips to town, and prescribed inspection of student mail by the president and lady principal.

Mississippi Baptists suspended their $10,000 annual subvention during the Depression, when W. E. Holcomb was serving as the school's president. Woman's College accrued a $103,000 deficit, lost its accreditation, and closed in 1940. During World War II campus buildings became housing for officers at Camp Shelby. The college reopened in 1946 under the presidency of Irving E. Rouse, who labored to keep it in operation with fewer resources and only one hundred students. In 1953 Woman's College became coeducational, and in April 1954 the trustees renamed it William Carey College in honor of an English Baptist botanist, linguist, missionary, and social reformer.

On Rouse's retirement in 1956 the board of trustees selected thirty-two-year-old Virginian J. Ralph Noonkester as president. Noonkester led Carey to reaccreditation by the Southern Association of Colleges and Schools in 1958 and directed a building and enrollment boom over the next three decades. In 1965 trustees agreed by one vote to admit African American students. The first African Americans who enrolled, Vermester Jackson and Linda Brown, were honor students from nearby Rowan High School. Desegregation brought angry letters from clergy who wished to separate either church from state or black from white, and someone burned a cross in front of the president's home. Subsequent growth cast a different light on such controversy. In 1968 William Carey College acquired New Orleans's Mather School of Nursing; eight years later, the college purchased the Gulf Coast Military Academy property in Gulfport, and it became William Carey College on the Coast.

James W. Edwards served as William Carey's president from 1989 to 1996, overseeing an expanded program for church vocations students and an increase in faculty. Edwards's successor, Larry Kennedy, who occupied the president's office until 2006, directed extensive renovations and new construction on the Hattiesburg campus, including nursing and education classroom buildings and a sports complex, which bears his name. In 2005 the Gulfport campus in particular suffered damage from Hurricane Katrina, and it was replaced by the William Carey University–Tradition Campus in Biloxi, which opened in August 2009. In 2006, the college's centennial, it began to operate as William Carey University.

The university is divided into the Ralph and Naomi Noonkester School of Arts and Letters, the School of Natural and Behavioral Sciences, the School of Business, the School of Education, the Donald and Frances Winters School of Music and Ministry Studies, the College of Health Sciences, and the College of Osteopathic Medicine, which graduated its inaugural class in 2014. By the second decade of the twenty-first century, William Carey University served more than 4,000 students, including roughly 2,300 undergraduates. The school's motto retains the extended version of William Carey's "deathless sermon" delivered in Nottingham, England, in 1792: "Expect great things from God; attempt great things for God."

Myron C. Noonkester
William Carey University

Mississippi Woman's College, *Annual Register*, 1911–53; J. Ralph Noonkester, unpublished memoir; William Carey College Catalog (1954–2017); William Carey University website, www.wmcarey.edu.

Williams, Ben
(b. 1954) Athlete

In 1971 Robert Jerry "Ben" Williams became one of the first two African Americans to sign a football scholarship at the University of Mississippi. The son of sharecroppers Robert J. Williams and Ernestine Williams, Ben Williams was born on 1 September 1954 in Yazoo City. Williams and his five younger siblings worked the land alongside their parents. A natural athlete, he played baseball and football throughout high school, and during his senior year Williams lettered in football at the recently integrated Yazoo City High School.

After receiving scholarship offers from Mississippi State University, Jackson State, Kansas State, and the University of Mississippi, Williams chose to enroll at the University of Mississippi so he could remain close to home, receive a quality education, and play football in the Southeastern Conference. The fact that he and James Reed would be the only Africans Americans on the team did not influence Williams's decision. Williams excelled both on and off the field. He earned all-American honors in 1975 and was a three-time all-conference selection. Playing defensive end, Williams recorded 377 career tackles, and his 18 quarterback sacks during the 1973 season are a team record. In addition, he graduated in 1976 with a degree in business administration and was the first African American voted Colonel Reb, the highest honor bestowed by the student body on an athlete. Drafted by the Buffalo Bills in the third round of the National Football League draft, Williams played ten seasons for the team and was selected to the 1982 Pro Bowl.

Williams always remained close to his Mississippi roots, working at a Jackson bank during the off-season. After retiring from football in 1986, Williams returned to Jackson and started working in the construction industry. He later founded a commercial construction company, LYNCO, and involved himself in numerous charitable causes. He has been inducted into the Mississippi Hall of Fame and the Ole Miss Hall of Fame, was named to the Buffalo Bills Silver Anniversary team, and has received the University of Mississippi Award of Distinction and the Ralph L. Wilson Leadership Award. He endowed the university's Ben Williams Minority Scholarship Fund in 1992.

Matthew M. Bailey
University of Mississippi

Ben Williams, interview by Matthew M. Bailey (2006); Ben Williams File, Ole Miss Athletic Association.

Williams, Big Joe
(1903–1982) Blues Musician

Joe Lee "Big Joe" Williams was born in the small town of Crawford, Mississippi, in western Lowndes County, on 16 October 1903, the same year W. C. Handy reported waking up at a train station in Tutwiler to what he called the weirdest music he had ever heard. Williams reportedly built

his first guitar at age five, began playing and writing blues in his teens, and joined the Rabbit's Foot Minstrels featuring Ethel Waters in the 1920s. He is most famous for later modifying a series of inexpensive six-string acoustic guitars by rigging them with electric pickups held on by duct tape, drilling three holes in the top of the three-tuning-keys-per-side headstocks he preferred, drilling three more holes in the bridge, and adding strings to the first, second, and fourth strings. He often used a capo on the first or second fret to create his unique tuning.

In the iconic tradition of the itinerant bluesman, Williams traveled any way he could—by bus, train, or car or on foot. He did play big-time gigs—some in later life with Michael Bloomfield, who said that unlike other older bluesmen who held day jobs, Williams "played and traveled, and that was it." He also was known to drink and to fight. He was fond of showing up to play at venues where he was not booked. His career was not resuscitated by the blues revival of the 1960s because he had never quit, whether the times provided an audience or he had to create one for himself.

He began recording with Delmark in 1935. After ten years there he moved to OKeh Records. He also recorded with Bluebird, Prestige, and Vocalion, but some his best work may have been captured on *Tough Times* (Arhoolie, 1960) and on *Going Back to Crawford* (1971), which Williams produced himself and which featured some of his friends, neighbors, and relations.

Williams died in Macon, Mississippi, on 17 December 1982, leaving a legacy of topical songs such as "President Roosevelt," "Army Man in Vietnam," and "Death of Martin Luther King" along with such heavily covered classics as "Baby, Please Don't Go" and "Crawlin' King Snake."

William Mark Franks
University of Mississippi

Big Joe—One More Time (film, 1983); Michael Bloomfield with S. Summerville, *Me and Big Joe* (1980); Vladimir Bogdanov, Chris Woodstra, and Stephen Thomas Erlewine, eds., *All Music Guide to the Blues: The Definitive Guide to the Blues* (2003); Gerard Herzhaft, *Encyclopedia of the Blues* (1997); Paul Oliver, *Aspects of the Blues Tradition* (1970); Paul Oliver, *Blues Fell This Morning: The Meaning of the Blues* (1960).

Williams, Joan
(1928–2004) Writer

Joan Williams's considerable recognition for her five novels and short story collection—National Book Award finalist (1961), John P. Marquand First Novel Award (1961), grant recipient from the National Institute of Arts and Letters

(1962), and a Guggenheim Fellowship (1998)—provides only a glimpse of the rich literary life she led.

Born on 26 September 1928 in Memphis, Tennessee, Williams centered her fiction on Tate County, Mississippi, where her maternal grandmother, Arvenia Moore, and other relatives lived. Williams's parents were not particularly interested in literature, though her mother, Maud Moore Williams (1903–97), read a good deal, and her father, Priestly Howard Williams (1895–1955), a dynamite salesman, made up stories in his head as he drove. Joan Williams later said that this disclosure was as close as her father ever came to telling her he also wanted to be a writer. In Williams's second novel, *Old Powder Man* (1966), her father's larger-than-life character emerged, and it is one of very few novels—and perhaps the only novel—that meticulously re-creates the days of Mississippi's levee camps.

Williams, an only child, attended Miss Hutchison's School for Girls in Memphis and received her bachelor's degree from Bard College. During the summer of 1949, before entering her senior year at Bard and fresh from winning the *Mademoiselle* College Fiction Prize for her short story "Rain Later," Williams met William Faulkner in Oxford. What began as an intense and sustained correspondence between the two eventually led to romantic involvement. Williams was the only writer Faulkner ever mentored, and the art of writing dominated many of their letters. During the four years of their relationship, Williams published one story: a young editor at the *Atlantic Monthly*, Seymour Lawrence, accepted "The Morning and the Evening" in 1952.

In the early 1950s, while working at *Look* magazine in New York, Williams met Ezra Drinker Bowen, a member of the original editorial staff of *Sports Illustrated*. When their romance became serious, Williams ended her relationship with Faulkner in November 1953, though they continued to correspond until his death in 1962. Williams and Bowen married on 6 March 1954 in Memphis.

Ezra Bowen's mother, biographer Catherine Drinker Bowen, recommended Williams for the Bread Loaf Writers' Conference. Bread Loaf was a breakthrough for Williams, who by then had two small sons and a husband who commuted fifty miles from Stamford, Connecticut, to work in New York City. Since parting with Faulkner, Williams had been writing on her own and had taken a creative writing course at Columbia University. On the advice of Nancy Hale, her Bread Loaf adviser, and with suggestions from Berton Roueché, she developed "The Morning and the Evening" into a novel, which was published in 1961 and garnered acclaim and praise.

Williams's marriage to Bowen ended in 1970, and on 28 October of that year, she married John T. Fargason Jr. of Clover Hill Plantation in Coahoma County, whom she had met while he was incarcerated at Parchman Prison for the manslaughter death of his sixteen-year-old stepson, Matthew Carter Stovall, on 12 February 1969. An article Fargason wrote while in prison was republished in the *Memphis Commercial Appeal*, and a friend mailed it to Williams. Like her friendship with Faulkner, their relationship began with a sustained correspondence. Her marriage to Fargason ended in divorce in 1981.

Four books followed *Old Powder Man*: *The Wintering* (1971), a fictionalization of her friendship with Faulkner; *County Woman* (1982); a short story collection, *Pariah and Other Stories* (1983), dedicated to Faulkner's memory; and *Pay the Piper* (1988). Between 1981 and 1995 she also published four short stories and an essay.

When Williams's path again crossed Lawrence's in 1984, his situation had changed substantially. The young *Atlantic* editor who took her short story in 1952 was now a leading publisher of literary authors with his own Houghton Mifflin imprint. Over the next decade, Williams watched and sometimes helped him discover talented authors, continuing and diversifying her literary education. Few writers' lives are intertwined with those of such notable figures as Faulkner, Bowen, and Lawrence, yet Williams is best remembered for her novels and stories. She died on 11 April 2004.

Lisa C. Hickman
Memphis, Tennessee

Lisa C. Hickman, *William Faulkner and Joan Williams: The Romance of Two Writers* (2006); *Memphis Commercial Appeal* (30 October 1971).

Williams, John Alfred
(1925–2015) Author

John Alfred Williams, the author of some twenty-one books of fiction, nonfiction, and poetry, was born in Jackson, Mississippi, on 5 December 1925. An early member of the Black Arts movement, Williams had diverse experiences as an African American living in all regions of the United States. He served in the Pacific as a member of the US Naval Reserve, earned a bachelor's degree from Syracuse University in 1950, and taught at numerous colleges and universities including the City University of New York, the University of California at Santa Barbara, the College of the Virgin Islands, the University of Hawaii, Sarah Lawrence College, Boston University, and Rutgers University, where he served as the Paul Robeson Professor of English from 1979 until his retirement in 1994.

Williams's acute sense of history, time, and place allows his novels to serve as specific documents for the historical researcher as well as a universal contemplation on how historical events and attitudes influence individual lives. His African American characters hail from all social and economic classes and resist the stereotypes that their environments attempt to impose on them.

W

His first novel, *The Angry Ones* (1960), explores the experience of a black professional in an interracial relationship. *Sissie* (1961) relates two siblings' complicated relationship with their strong and forceful mother. Both novels received critical acclaim. *The Man Who Cried I Am* (1967) became a best seller. *Captain Blackman* (1972) was called "among the most important works of fiction of the decade" by the *New York Times Book Review*. The novel articulates the experiences of African American men in the US Army during the Vietnam War and other conflicts. *Sons of Darkness, Sons of Light: A Novel of Some Probability* (1969) investigates racism in the United States during the 1960s, particularly the rippling effect one hate crime has on the entire country. The book reveals the close linkages between people, especially when they strive their hardest to stay separated. Williams explores the little-known history of the African American experience abroad during World War II in *Clifford's Blues*, in which a gay African American jazz musician is imprisoned at Dachau. *Safari West: Poems* (1998) showcases Williams's poetry and illustrates his ability to address the African American experience in verse as well as prose.

Williams also published nonfiction, including works on Martin Luther King Jr., Richard Wright, and Richard Pryor; *Africa: Her History, Lands, and People*, an introduction to the people and politics of Africa in 1962 that emphasizes movements for independence; and a book about traveling in America, *This Is My Country Too* (1963). In addition, Williams edited several important works, beginning with *The Angry Black* (1962) and *Beyond the Angry Black* (1969). In the introduction to the second volume, Williams reflects on how the first book spoke of reason and truth: "What whimsy! . . . In order to nail down truth we must admit that our problems are dead and ugly and gnarled."

Williams died on 3 July 2015.

Anne Evans
St. Mary's Academy, Denver,
Colorado

African American Literature Book Club website, www.aalbc.com; William Grimes, *New York Times* (6 July 2015); Mississippi Writers' Page website, www.olemiss.edu/mwp; Jerry Ward, in *Lives of Mississippi Authors*, ed. James B. Lloyd (1981).

Williams, John Bell

(1918–1983) Fifty-Fifth Governor, 1968–1972

John Bell Williams's political career took an unusual route to the office of governor. Most politicians first run for state or local office and then use those offices to launch a national career. Williams took the opposite approach, serving in the US Congress for more than twenty years prior to his election as Mississippi's governor in 1967.

Williams, who was born in Raymond, Mississippi, on 4 December 1918, graduated from Hinds Junior College and then attended the University of Mississippi. After receiving a degree from the Jackson School of Law, Williams was admitted to the bar and opened a law office in Raymond in 1940. Williams served in the US Army Air Corps as a pilot during World War II but left active service after losing the lower part of his left arm in a 1944 bomber crash. On 12 October of that year, he married Elizabeth Ann Wells, who had also served in the military as a commissioned officer in the Women's Army Corps.

After holding the post of Hinds County prosecuting attorney from 1944 to 1946, Williams won election to the US House of Representatives, becoming the youngest member of Congress in the state's history at age twenty-seven. He remained in Congress until January 1968, championing states' rights and racial segregation. Shortly after the US Supreme Court's 1954 *Brown v. Board of Education* decision, Williams made a dramatic speech on the floor of the House of Representatives during which he criticized the decision on constitutional, educational, and cultural grounds, describing desegregated schools as sites of anarchy. Over the next several years Williams became increasingly alienated from the national Democratic Party. In 1964 he publicly endorsed Republican presidential candidate Barry Goldwater and helped raise funds for his campaign in Mississippi. Goldwater received 87.1 percent of the state's presidential vote.

Because of Williams's support for the Republican candidate and his fund-raising activities, the national Democratic Party expelled him in 1965. Two years later he ran for the governorship as a "Mississippi Democrat." Criticizing his opponents as "ready to surrender to the Great Society" programs of Lyndon Johnson's administration, Williams offered his candidacy as the best way to protect Mississippi from racial desegregation. Williams defeated a large field of candidates, including former governor Ross Barnett and future governors William Waller and William Winter, in the Democratic primaries and cruised to an easy victory over Republican Rubel L. Phillips in the November general election. Williams was inaugurated on 16 January 1968.

Despite Williams's pledges to preserve segregation, the most sweeping integration in Mississippi history occurred during his administration. A federal court did away with the state's dual segregated public school system and replaced it with a unified integrated system in the spring of 1970. Williams did not resist the court order.

Williams left office in 1972 and resumed his law practice in Raymond, continuing it until his death on 25 March 1983. The John Bell Williams Wildlife Management Area in Itawamba and Prentiss Counties is named in his honor.

David G. Sansing
University of Mississippi

Jackson Clarion-Ledger (10 January 2010); *Mississippi Official and Statistical Register* (1949–52, 1968–72); Jere Nash and Andy Taggart, *Mississippi Politics: The Struggle for Power, 1976–2008* (2nd ed., 2009); John Bell Williams Subject File, Mississippi Department of Archives and History.

Williams, John Sharp

(1854–1932) Politician

John Sharp Williams was born on 30 July 1854 in Memphis, Tennessee, the son of Christopher Harris Williams Jr., a lawyer, and Anne Louise Sharp Williams. His paternal grandfather, a Whig, represented Tennessee in the US Congress for ten years, and his great-grandfather's brother, Robert Williams, served as governor of the Mississippi Territory from 1805 to 1809. John Sharp's mother died in 1859, and after his father, a Confederate officer, was killed in the Battle of Shiloh on 6 April 1862, his grandfather, John McNitt Sharp,

John Sharp Williams at the White House, ca. 1920 (Photograph by Underwood and Underwood, Library of Congress, Washington, D.C. [LC-USZ62-96946])

came to Memphis and took John Sharp and his younger brother, Christopher Harris, back to his three-thousand-acre plantation, Cedar Grove, in Yazoo County. John McNitt Sharp, a Confederate officer, died four months later, and John Sharp's step-grandmother assumed responsibility for raising the two boys. Williams received his elementary education in Yazoo City and Memphis, where he joined the Episcopal Church at the age of eleven. After completing his high school work, he graduated from the Kentucky Military Institute in 1870. After briefly enrolling at the University of the South at Sewanee, Tennessee, he spent three years at the University of Virginia, where he was a Phi Beta Kappa scholar. He then studied in Germany and France for two years before returning to the University of Virginia Law School, earning a degree in 1876. He married Elizabeth Dial Webb of Livingston, Alabama, in October 1877, and the following year the young couple moved into the plantation home that his grandfather had built in 1834 and took charge of the Sharp family's plantation. For the next fifteen years he supervised the farming operation at Cedar Grove and practiced law in nearby Yazoo City.

Williams undertook his first political campaign in 1890 but failed to win the Democratic nomination for Congress at the party's district convention; two years later, he tried again and succeeded, going on to defeat a strong Populist opponent in the general election. Williams subsequently won reelection seven times, serving in the US House of Representatives from 1893 to 1909. The young congressman quickly earned respect with his keen intellect, his debating skills, and his sense of parliamentary courtesy and justice. A staunch advocate of a tariff for revenue only and free, unlimited coinage of silver, he opposed imperialistic policies and government ownership of railroads. He never straddled an issue and delighted reporters with his witty remarks and caustic rejoinders to Republican opponents.

His Democratic colleagues elected him minority leader in 1903, 1905, and 1907, and political observers credited him with transforming the party's unruly and undisciplined House membership into a strong, cohesive force. Williams wanted the Democratic Party to adopt progressive policies that would attract independent voters and appeal to businessmen and organized labor in the North and Midwest. He publicized these concepts in his 1904 essays "What Democracy Now Stands For" and "Why Should a Man Vote the Democratic Ticket This Year?" He served as temporary chair of the 1904 Democratic National Convention, and his moderate views on financial and trade policies prevailed in the party's platform. Williams supported Alton Parker for the party's 1904 presidential nomination but supported William Jennings Bryan four years later, though Williams never admired the Great Commoner and opposed his stand on government ownership of railroads. As an influential party leader, Williams emphasized that differences among Democrats should not be magnified and that he thought Bryan was right about most things.

In 1907 Williams faced off against Gov. James K. Vardaman in the contest for the Democratic nomination to

W

represent Mississippi in the US Senate. The race attracted national attention, with William Randolph Hearst and his newspaper chain supporting Vardaman and the *New York Times*, the *Atlanta Constitution*, and other leading newspapers endorsing Williams. *Collier's* magazine sent author and war correspondent Frederick Palmer to cover the only debate between the two candidates. Williams disparaged Vardaman's efforts to exploit racial prejudices and make repeal of the Fifteenth Amendment the primary campaign issue. Believing that it was unwise "for Southern statesmanship to narrow all of its efforts . . . to a futile or dangerous attempt to reinject the race question into the arena of congressional politics," Williams thought "the South ought to take its part in solving the great questions of the day and . . . not occupy itself baying at the moon or in a thing equally useless and much more dangerous." Williams defeated Vardaman by just 648 votes and received congratulatory messages from all sections of the country.

An early booster of Woodrow Wilson for the 1912 Democratic presidential nomination, Williams served on Wilson's executive campaign committee and became one of the president's most faithful supporters in the areas of both foreign policy and economic reform. When controversy arose over the appointment of Louis Brandeis to the Supreme Court, Williams announced that he would vote to confirm Brandeis because a man's views on academic questions should not disqualify him if he were honest and a good lawyer. Williams supported the president's decision to hold Germany to strict accountability for the loss of American lives and property in submarine warfare and accused those who opposed a declaration of war in April 1917 of "grazing on the edge of treason."

Like most white Mississippians and most white southerners, Williams believed in white political supremacy, but he did not exploit the race issue for personal gain. During his senatorial campaign against Vardaman, *Collier's* reported that Williams "shared the feelings of his neighbors on the race question [but] had seen enough of other parts of the world . . . to look at the subject in the proper perspective."

In 1916 Williams was reelected to the Senate without any opposition, but he did not seek a third term in 1922. In March 1923 he returned to his Mississippi plantation to read books, write letters, and enjoy retirement. He made his last formal address at the 12 October 1927 dedication of a bronze monument to Jefferson Davis at the Vicksburg National Military Park. Williams died on 27 September 1932 in the old plantation home of his childhood and was laid to rest in the family cemetery at Cedar Grove. The *New York Times* remembered him as "easy-going, chock-full of common sense, sociable and companionable, [and] utterly remote from the doctrinaire and the prig."

Thomas N. Boschert
Delta State University

Harris Dickson, *An Old Fashioned Senator* (1925); George Coleman Osborn, *John Sharp Williams: Planter-Statesman of the Deep South* (1943); George C. Osborn Collection, Mississippi Department of Archives and History; John Sharp Williams Papers, Department of Archives and Special Collections, J. D. Williams Library, University of Mississippi.

Williams, Tennessee
(1911–1983) Playwright

On 26 March 1911, Edwina Dakin Williams of Columbus, Mississippi, had a baby. At the time of the delivery, Edwina's father, the Rev. Walter Dakin, was conducting services at St. Paul's Episcopal Church. A few days later, Rev. Dakin baptized his grandson, Thomas Lanier Williams III, but the world later came to know him as Tennessee Williams, one of the most significant American playwrights. The details of that birth were indicative of the remarkable life the child grew up to live, including the elements of the southern setting, the involved family connections, and the religious overtones.

Tom's father, Cornelius Coffin Williams, was a traveling salesman who was rarely at home. Williams came from a prominent Knoxville, Tennessee, family, and his background and social standing made him seem the ideal match for Edwina. However, Williams proved a disappointment to both the young bride and to her parents—a heavy drinker and gambler. Edwina and her children—Tom and Rose, who was two years older—consequently continued to live with her parents, first in Columbus and later in the Delta town of Clarksdale, while Cornelius traveled. Something of the psychological strain this arrangement placed on Edwina and her children can be found in *The Glass Menagerie*, a Tennessee Williams play that changed the history of modern drama.

Williams spent only a small percentage of his life in Mississippi, but the state's influence on his character and his work illustrates how much his early childhood shaped his psyche. When he was two, the family moved briefly to Nashville, Tennessee, returning to Mississippi in 1915 when Rev. Dakin became Episcopal rector first in Canton and then in Clarksdale.

Edwina and her parents frequently read to Tom, especially after he was unable to leave the house because of the effects of diphtheria, and he and Rose loved the stories their black nurse, Ossie, told them. Riding around the county with his grandfather as he visited parishioners, the boy heard and absorbed stories of Delta families, experiences that always seemed to him larger than life. He retained an amazing treasury of memories, and his mother later recalled that "he was a little pitcher with big ears." He was impressed by the landscape of the Delta, "so flat," he later wrote, "that the seasons could walk across it abreast." He also described Mississippi as "a deep wide world you can breathe in."

In 1918 Cornelius Williams moved his family to St. Louis, a "cold northern city" where he had taken an office job with the International Shoe Company. Tom and Rose hated their new home. From that point onward, the Mississippi landscape and their childhoods there became and remained precious memories of a lost Eden from which they had fallen or been dragged by their father into "the broken world," to quote one of Tom's favorite lines from poet Hart Crane. The following year, Tom and Rose received another shock when Edwina had a third child, Walter Dakin Williams. Cornelius Williams seems always to have preferred Dakin over Tom, whom Cornelius called "Miss Nancy" because he wrote poetry and was not good at sports.

In 1920 Tom was sent back to Clarksdale for an extended visit while his mother recuperated from an illness. It was probably during this stay that the Delta made its permanent imprint on his imagination as he traveled with his grandfather around the county and listened to Rev. Dakin's stories. By this time Tom was already writing prose and had begun publishing. Rose, however, was beginning to show signs of schizophrenia and was sent to All Saints College in Vicksburg.

After graduating from high school in 1929, Tom entered the University of Missouri at Columbia to study journalism, but in 1932, when he failed the Reserve Officers Training Corps, Cornelius withdrew his financial support and put Tom to work as a clerk at the International Shoe Company. In 1935 he suffered a nervous collapse, and his father allowed him to go to Memphis to stay with his grandparents. While there he wrote a short play, *Cairo! Shanghai! Bombay!*, that was produced by a local amateur group. When he returned to St. Louis, he enrolled at Washington University, where he became involved with an amateur drama group, the Mummers. In 1937 he studied drama at the University of Iowa, receiving a bachelor's degree in English, and at the end of the next year he went to New Orleans for a few months. There he found a new setting for his work, new material, and, as he frequently said, "a freedom I had always needed." He had recently adopted the nom de plume Tennessee Williams, which he continued to use for the rest of his life.

While in New Orleans, Williams wrote poetry, short stories, and short plays and soaked up the ambience of what he called "one of the last frontiers of Bohemia." His next stop was California, and after a few months there he moved to New York to study drama with John Gassner. On Williams's first night in the city, he later recalled, he wrote a short play "about home," *This Property Is Condemned*, which was set in the Mississippi Delta. Late in 1940 the Theatre Guild produced his play *Battle of Angels*, also set in the Mississippi

Delta. Although the play never reached Broadway, it continued to haunt the playwright, and in the 1960s he rewrote it as *Orpheus Descending*.

In 1943 Rose Williams received a prefrontal lobotomy. The influence of this episode is reflected in Tennessee Williams's first major drama, *The Glass Menagerie* (1944), which, though set in St. Louis, is infused with memories of the Mississippi Delta. Amanda Wingfield recalls her early life there, citing real locales and family names as she drifts away from harsh reality into an idyllic reverie about her past.

A tremendous success, *The Glass Menagerie* established Williams as a major playwright. The next year, he settled in the French Quarter of New Orleans with his friend and lover, Pancho Rodríguez y González, to complete a play that had long germinated in his imagination. *A Streetcar Named Desire* was completed and produced on Broadway in 1946, with Elia Kazan directing. Set in New Orleans, the drama, raw and sexually explicit in a innovative way for the American stage, was haunted by the memories of the Mississippi Delta, to which Williams, like his protagonist Blanche DuBois, seemed to cling.

The years between 1945 and 1961 were the richest and most productive of Williams's career. In addition to *The Glass Menagerie* and *A Streetcar Named Desire*, others works written in this period included *The Rose Tattoo* (1951), set on the Mississippi Gulf Coast; *Camino Real* (1953); *Cat on a Hot Tin Roof* (1955), set in the Mississippi Delta; the movie *Baby Doll* (1956), for which Williams wrote the screenplay and briefly visited his native state for the filming; *Orpheus Descending* (1957), also set in the Mississippi Delta; *Garden District* (1958); *Sweet Bird of Youth* (1959), set on the Mississippi Gulf Coast; *Period of Adjustment* (1960); and *The Night of the Iguana* (1961). Several of the plays became successful movies. Even after that fertile period ended, Williams continued to write plays, often at a feverish pace. He ultimately wrote more than seventy plays, two novels, numerous short stories and essays, and an abundance of letters.

For all of his adult life, Williams was something of a vagabond, bouncing between New York, Italy, New Orleans, and Key West as the spirit moved him. Nevertheless, he remained connected to Mississippi, never failing to acknowledge the inspiration and character traits it provided him. He explained that "out of a regret for a South that no longer exists . . . I write of the forces that have destroyed it." That Old South featured "a greater sense of honor, of decency," and represented "a way of life that I am just old enough to remember." In a more jocular but surely no less pertinent vein, he loved to relate the words spoken by one of his ancestors, John Sharp Williams, when he left Congress: "I'd rather be a hound dog and bay at the moon from my Mississippi plantation than remain in the United States Senate."

Williams choked to death in a New York hotel suite on 25 February 1983. According to the coroner's report, drugs and alcohol may have played a role in his death. Today one can

W

visit Tennessee Williams homes in Columbus and Clarksdale as well as in Key West, Florida. Annual festivals in his honor take place in Clarksdale, New Orleans, and Provincetown, Massachusetts.

Kenneth Holditch
New Orleans, Louisiana

Kenneth Holditch and Richard F. Leavitt, *Tennessee Williams and the South* (2002); Esther Jackson, *The Broken World of Tennessee Williams* (1965); Nancy Tischler, *Tennessee Williams: Rebellious Puritan* (1961).

Williams v. Mississippi

In *Williams v. Mississippi* (1898) the US Supreme Court upheld the poll tax, disenfranchisement clauses, literacy tests, and the grandfather clause, all of which were features of the 1890 Mississippi Constitution and statutes. In doing so, the Court added *Williams* to a line of cases including *Plessy v. Ferguson* (1896) that narrowly interpreted the Reconstruction amendments and helped enforce the suppression of African Americans' civil rights in Mississippi and other states.

The case originated when an all-white jury indicted Henry Williams, an African American, for murder in 1896. Williams filed a motion to quash the indictment on the ground that the laws under which the jury was formed were unconstitutional. He argued that the provisions of the Mississippi Constitution and statutes addressing suffrage were nothing more than a scheme on the part of the men who wrote the document to abridge African Americans' voting rights. At issue were provisions regarding residency requirements, poll taxes, literacy tests, the grandfather clause, the requirement that only registered voters could serve on juries, and administrative officers' discretion to determine which citizens were qualified to serve as jurors. Williams argued that this last provision in particular was discriminatorily applied.

The constitutional provisions were not facially discriminatory, but Williams argued that they were discriminatory when applied by the administrative officers. The administrative officers received broad discretion to determine which citizens were qualified to vote and thus to serve as jurors. This was one method, Williams argued, that the state used to abrogate the suffrage rights of African Americans.

The trial court refused to accept Williams's argument and denied his motion to quash the indictment as well as his motion to remove the case out of state court and into federal court. The trial court held that removal could not take place because when racial discrimination was alleged, removal was only justifiable when the discrimination resulted from the constitution or laws of the state, not from their administration. After denying all of Williams's motions, the trial court sentenced him to death by hanging. The Mississippi Supreme Court accepted the case on appeal but affirmed the trial court's decision.

Williams appealed to the US Supreme Court, arguing that the Mississippi Constitution and statutes discriminated against African Americans in violation of the Fourteenth Amendment. The Court's opinion, written by Justice Joseph McKenna, held that the provisions of the Mississippi Constitution and statutes at issue were not unconstitutional and affirmed the judgment against Williams.

The Court refused to interfere with Mississippi's application of its laws because "the constitution of Mississippi and its statutes do not on their face discriminate between the races, and it has not been shown that their actual administration was evil; only that evil was possible under them." This remained true even when the state confessed that its administration of these provisions had been carried out with a discriminatory intent. The court had previously held that states could not use race as an explicit basis for discrimination in civil and political arenas, but in this case, the justices reasoned that as long as the racial oppression was achieved in a facially neutral manner, the Fourteenth Amendment had been satisfied. The court found that merely showing that the provisions of the Mississippi Constitution and statutes might operate as discriminatory against African Americans was not enough; Williams must have presented proof of actual discrimination. Because the provisions were facially nondiscriminatory and could be applied to all individuals, regardless of race, the court found them to be in accordance with the Fourteenth Amendment. The court essentially found that the administrative officers, not the law, were discriminating against African Americans and that no judicial remedy existed for that type of discrimination.

Amanda Brown
University of Mississippi

Wilson R. Huhn, *Hofstra Law Review* (Summer 2006); Ian F. Haney López, *Stanford Law Review* (February 2007); *Williams v. Mississippi*, 170 US 213 (1898).

Williamson, Sonny Boy, II (Aleck Miller)

(1912–1965) Blues Musician

Sonny Boy Williamson II was one of the most influential blues harmonica players, singers, and songwriters of the mid-twentieth century. His history is mysterious, but nothing is more uncertain than Sonny Boy Williamson II's real name. The enigmatic harmonica player has been called Aleck Miller, Alex Miller, Aleck Ford, Alex Ford, and Rice (probably a nickname) Miller, to name a few. He was born to Millie Ford. His father's identity is unclear. He adopted the name Sonny Boy Williamson from another blues harmonica player, John Lee "Sonny Boy" Williamson, from Chicago. Scholars and fans refer to John Lee Williamson as *Sonny Boy Williamson I* and Aleck Miller as *Sonny Boy Williamson II* to reduce confusion, especially since Miller often took credit for Williamson's recordings. To further complicate matters, before finally settling on the name *Sonny Boy Williamson*, Aleck Miller performed as Little Boy Blue, Sonny Boy Miller, Harmonica Blowin' Slim, Willie Miller, and Willie Williamson. We do know that he was born somewhere between Glendora and Tutwiler, though his birthdate is also confusing. Again, sources vary widely, ranging from 1897 to 1912; most sources cite either 1897 or 1899.

At around age five, Aleck Miller began learning to play harmonica. Within a few years he was playing street corners and hopping trains around the South, especially Mississippi, Arkansas, Missouri, and Tennessee. He often performed with blues greats such as Robert Jr. Lockwood, Homesick James, Howlin' Wolf, Elmore James, and Robert Johnson. Though Little Walter is often given credit for amplifying the harmonica, several sources claim that Sonny Boy Williamson II was performing with a microphone and amplifier in the late 1930s. Sonny Boy II also influenced a number of performers through his powerful showmanship and performance tricks, such as playing the harmonica without using his hands.

Williamson landed a steady performing job in 1941 on the *King Biscuit Time* radio show over KFFA in Helena, Arkansas, where he worked with Pinetop Perkins, James "Peck" Curtis, Joe Willie Wilkins, Houston Stackhouse, and others. The radio broadcasts established him as the image of the King Biscuit Flour Company. Though he claimed to have recorded in the 1930s, the earliest verifiable recordings occurred in 1951, when Lillian McMurry tracked him down for her Trumpet Records label in Jackson. Many of his most famous recordings were done for Trumpet, including "Eyesight to the Blind," "Mighty Long Time," "Nine Below Zero," and "She Brought Life Back to the Dead." In 1955 he headed to Chicago, where he recorded more hits for Checker/Chess, including "Fattenin' Frogs for Snakes" and "Don't Start Me Talkin."

In 1963 Williamson toured Europe with the American Folk Blues Festival, wowing audiences with his music and showmanship. While in Europe, he recorded with rock bands the Animals and the Yardbirds. Two years later, he returned to the United States and again performed on *King Biscuit Time* before his death on 25 May 1965 in Helena, Arkansas. He was elected to the Blues Hall of Fame in 1980.

Greg Johnson
University of Mississippi

Sheldon Harris, *Blues Who's Who: A Biographical Dictionary of Blues Singers* (1979); Mississippi Blues Trail website, msbluestrail.org; Marc Ryan, *Trumpet Records: Diamonds on Farish Street* (2004); Jim Trageser, in *Encyclopedia of the Blues*, ed. Edward Komara (2006).

Wilson, Cassandra
(b. 1955) Singer

Born in Jackson on 4 December 1955, singer Cassandra Wilson has developed a style and repertoire that defy conventional descriptions. Sometimes described as a jazz singer because of her lilting, improvised performance style (and because she has recorded on Blue Note, a jazz label), Wilson sings a wide range of songs in her own unique fashion.

Wilson received training as a classical pianist, attended public schools in Jackson, and received her mass communications degree from Jackson State University. She lived briefly in New Orleans before moving to New York to pursue her singing career.

Wilson played in a variety of jazz bands in the mid-1980s and made her first album under her own name in 1986. Since then, she has released an impressive variety of recordings, with nearly twenty albums as of 2015. *DownBeat* magazine named her Most Popular Female Jazz Singer several times in the 1990s, and she won Grammy Awards in 1996 for *New Moon Daughter* and in 2009 for *Loverly*. On 7 January 2010 she received a marker on the Mississippi Blues Trail. And both Millsaps College and the New School have awarded Wilson honorary doctorates. Her 1988 release, *Blue Skies*, consists entirely of versions of jazz standards, and in 1999 she released a salute to Miles Davis, *Traveling Miles*. She has recorded such other jazz standards as "Strange Fruit" and "You Don't Know What Love Is."

Perhaps what characterizes Wilson above all are her unique approach to singing and her willingness to sing a dramatic variety of songs. She has consistently recorded songs created or made famous by Mississippi-born blues performers, among them "Come on in My Kitchen" and "Hellhound on My Trail" by Robert Johnson, Willie Dixon's "I Want to Be Loved," the blues standard "Easy Rider," and "You Gotta Move." One recording included guitar playing by contemporary Mississippi musician Keb' Mo. But Wilson is not constrained by any tradition. She has also recorded "Red River Valley" as well as songs by Van Morrison, Neil Young, Bob Dylan, and Hank Williams. According to Wilson, "Down South, musicians have to be able to play in many different circumstances and in many contexts. They have to play jazz, they have to integrate the blues, and they have to know country. And the lines are kinda blurry sometimes, 'cause that's what everybody wants to hear." Wilson continues to blur lines as one of Mississippi's least predictable musicians.

Ted Ownby
University of Mississippi

John Ephland, *DownBeat* (January 1995); Geoffrey Himes, *Jazz Times* (May 2002); John Leland, *New York Times* (7 March 2002); Cassandra Wilson website, www.cassandrawilson.com.

Winans, William
(1788–1857) Religious Leader

William Winans was not a native Mississippian, but he moved to the territory in 1810 and became one of the most influential ministers at a time when the region's predominant religious culture was emerging.

Born in Chestnut Ridge, Pennsylvania, on 3 November 1788, Winans served as a Methodist minister in Kentucky and Indiana before moving to Mississippi, where he became secretary of the Mississippi Conference in 1813. Winans arrived before statehood, when much of the area was still frontier, and one newspaper described him as having "a rough manner" and "long shaggy hair" and seeming more "like some lawless backwoodsman than the able and devoted minister." He served as a circuit rider, requiring four weeks to make the rounds of the churches in his territory. He participated in camp meetings and revivals that helped Methodists emerge as a leading denomination. In 1823 he estimated that one camp meeting attracted between four thousand and six thousand people, including many slaves. He had little formal education, criticized anyone who called for calm and polite expressions of religion, and was a leading opponent of educational requirements for ministers.

Winans's attitudes toward African Americans to whom he ministered were complex, reflecting the spread of both evangelicalism and proslavery ideology during the antebellum period. He preached to and baptized blacks at separate services and protested 1820s efforts to restrict slaves' right to worship among themselves without white oversight. He wrote admiringly of African Americans' spirituality, viewing their "deep and ardent piety" as representing "the highest attainment to which man can aspire." He continued, "Among the most deeply pious Christians who I have known, have been many black people who, ignorant in other matters . . . were children of God by Faith." At the same time, he was a Mississippi leader of the American Colonization Society, working with some of the state's wealthiest men to transport free blacks to Africa in the 1830s. In the 1840s he was a leading clerical proslavery advocate, referring to abolitionists as "fanatics-lunatics."

Winans supported the formation of the Methodist Episcopal Church, South, after growing numbers of ministers of the Methodist Episcopal Church began to support abolition. He then sought election as one of the first bishops in the Methodist Episcopal Church, South, in 1846, but lost. He subsequently became less active in denominational affairs but remained one of the most prominent antebellum Mississippi ministers. He died on 31 August 1857.

Charles Reagan Wilson
University of Mississippi

Ray Holder, *William Winans, Methodist Leader in Antebellum Mississippi* (1976); Randy J. Sparks, *On Jordan's Stormy Banks: Evangelicalism in Mississippi, 1773–1876* (1994); Randy J. Sparks, *Religion in Mississippi* (2001); William Winans Papers, J. B. Cain Archives, Millsaps College.

Winder, Sammy
(b. 1959) Athlete

Sammy Winder was a star running back for the University of Southern Mississippi before playing for nine seasons in the National Football League for the Denver Broncos. Born in the community of Pocahontas on 15 July 1959, Winder grew up in a large farming family and excelled as a Madison County athlete.

From 1978 to 1981 Winder attended the University of Southern Mississippi, where he played tailback during some of the team's most successful seasons. In 1980 and 1981 the Golden Eagles went to bowl games for the first time since the 1950s. Winder, playing for Coach Bobby Collins on a team quarterbacked by Reggie Collier, led the National Collegiate Athletic Association in touchdowns in 1980. He ended his college career as the second-leading rusher in school history, behind only 1970s star Ben Garry.

Selected by the Denver Broncos in the fifth round of the 1982 National Football League draft, Winder played for the team from 1982 through 1990. In his best year, 1984, he rushed for 1,153 yards and made the Pro Bowl, an honor he also received two years later. He retired with more than 5,400 rushing yards and 48 regular season touchdowns.

Winder was the primary running back for Broncos teams led by quarterback John Elway that went to the Super Bowl in 1987, 1988, and 1990. Winder scored three playoff touchdowns and in 1987 was a key performer in "The Drive," a famous series of plays under late-game pressure that allowed

Denver to defeat the Cleveland Browns and reach the Super Bowl. He was known in Denver for an end zone dance called the Mississippi Mud Walk.

In 1987 Winder founded a Jackson-area business, Winder Construction. As a native of rural Mississippi, Winder said, he "had always been around dirt," so he bought a bulldozer and began clearing land for homes and businesses. He was inducted into the Mississippi Sports Hall of Fame in 1998.

Ted Ownby
University of Mississippi

John W. Cox and Gregg Bennett, *Rock Solid: Southern Miss Football* (2004); Pro Football Reference website, www.pro-football-reference.com; *Rocky Mountain News* (14 January 2006); Total Football Stats website, www.totalfootballstats.com.

Windsor Ruins

Near Port Gibson, off Highway 252 in Claiborne County, stand the ruins of the largest Greek Revival mansion ever built in Mississippi on what was once the twenty-six-hundred-acre Windsor Plantation. Designed by David Schroder, the architect of Rosswood in Lorman, the mansion was erected by slave labor in 1859–60 for farmer Smith Coffee Daniell II (1826–61).

Daniel ordered the seventeen-thousand-square-foot mansion's iron stairs, balustrades (used to join the columns), and Corinthian column capitals from St. Louis and hired New England carpenters to craft the finished woodwork. The project cost $175,000 (equivalent to more than $4,000,000 today) and produced a magnificent classical structure with more than twenty-five rooms, second- and third-level galleries, and twenty-nine forty-five-foot-tall fluted columns supporting a projecting roofline with frieze and molded cornice. The interior featured fireplaces in all the bedrooms, an attic tank supplying running water to all the baths, two parlors, a library, and an above-ground basement replete with a kitchen, a commissary, and a doctor's office. Atop the fourth floor stood a cupola serving as an observatory, from which Confederate troops sent lamp signals across the Mississippi River to their comrades in Louisiana.

Members of the Daniell family saved the house from destruction by allowing Union forces to use it as a hospital following the Battle of Port Gibson (1 May 1863). After the Civil War, Windsor become renowned for grand parties, at least one of which was attended by Mark Twain, who had earlier mistaken the mansion for a college when passing by as a riverboat pilot on the Mississippi.

Windsor Ruins, August 1940 (Photograph by Marion Post Wolcott, Library of Congress, Washington, D.C. [LC-USF34-054814-D])

The mansion burned to the ground on 17 February 1890. The conflagration left only twenty-three of the original columns standing, along with the four iron staircases and sections of the balustrade. Three sets of the iron stairs subsequently disappeared from the site, but the one remaining set and the surviving balustrade now grace Alcorn State University's chapel in nearby Lorman.

Hollywood featured Windsor's haunting columns in the movies *Raintree County* (1957) and *Ghosts of Mississippi* (1996). On 23 November 1971 the Windsor Ruins were added to the National Register of Historic Places. The property remained in the hands of Daniell family descendants until 1974, when it was donated to the State of Mississippi, and the Mississippi Department of Archives and History now administers it. All plans and photographs of the mansion burned in the 1890 fire, meaning that the mansion's appearance was known only from written descriptions until 1991, when a Civil War–era drawing by Union soldier Henry Otis Dwight surfaced. A short distance from the ruins, atop an Indian ceremonial mound, is the Daniell-Freeland family cemetery.

Jim Fraiser
Tupelo, Mississippi

Jim Fraiser, *Mississippi River Country Tales* (2000); National Register of Historic Places Property Report (2 June 1992), http://www.apps.mdah.ms.gov/nom/prop/3600.pdf.

W

Winfrey, Oprah

(b. 1954) Television Producer, Actress, Businessperson

Oprah Winfrey defies easy characterization. She has been a talk show host, an actress, a media mogul, a philanthropist, an author, and many other things. Her success and influence are extraordinary. Oprah Gail Winfrey was born on 29 January 1954 in Kosciusko, Mississippi, to Vernita Lee and Vernon Winfrey, who never married. When Oprah was a baby her mother moved to Milwaukee, Wisconsin, in search of better economic opportunities. Oprah spent her early years in Kosciusko with her maternal grandmother, who taught her to read, enrolled her in kindergarten, and took her to church, where she was introduced to public speaking. When she was six, Winfrey moved to Milwaukee to be with her mother. These were difficult years, because her mother worked long hours as a domestic and came home exhausted to their tiny apartment. In addition, when she was nine years old, Winfrey was raped by a teenage cousin and another family member. A family friend continued the sexual abuse. At fourteen, Winfrey became pregnant, though her son was born prematurely and died. Winfrey ultimately became so rebellious that her mother could not control her, sending the girl to Nashville, Tennessee, to live with her father and his wife.

Winfrey responded favorably to the new environment. She attended East High School, becoming involved in theater, debate, and student council. Winfrey won Nashville's 1971 Miss Fire Prevention contest, which led to an after-school job as a radio news reader. She went on to win Miss Black Tennessee the same year and to compete in the 1972 Miss Black America Pageant. She enrolled at Tennessee State University on a scholarship, and when she was nineteen, the local CBS affiliate named her coanchor, making her the first black woman to hold that position.

In 1976, during her senior year, Winfrey relocated to Baltimore to anchor the evening news for the local ABC affiliate. Soon thereafter she began providing updates for ABC's *Good Morning America*, and later she hosted a morning show, *Baltimore Is Talking*. In 1983 she moved to Chicago to host *AM Chicago*, the lowest-rated talk show in the market, airing opposite the popular *Phil Donahue Show*. Within a month her show equaled Donahue's ratings. After a several months *AM Chicago* was extended to an hour and renamed *The Oprah Winfrey Show*. In 1985, while on a business trip to Chicago, movie producer Quincy Jones saw Winfrey's show, was impressed by her talent, and offered her the role of Sofia in the movie version of Alice Walker's novel, *The Color Purple* (1985), for which she received an Academy Award nomination. She has subsequently appeared in several movies, including *Native Son* (1986), *Beloved* (1998), *Lee Daniels' The Butler* (2013), and *Selma* (2014).

In 1986 Winfrey started Harpo Productions to create videos, films, and television shows. That same year King World Productions syndicated *The Oprah Winfrey Show*, making it the highest-rated show in its time slot in virtually every city. It was seen by an estimated forty-six million viewers per week and aired in 143 countries before she ended the program in 2011. While the show was initially sensationalistic at times, later episodes stressed ways that viewers could improve their lives through a variety of means, including personal growth, access to professional help, reading, and writing. Given her willingness to explore the emotional aspects of life, critics sometimes decried the "Oprahization" of American society. In 1996 Winfrey launched Oprah's Book Club, with featured writers consistently becoming best sellers.

From 1998 to 2011 Winfrey operated a charitable foundation, Oprah's Angel Network. The foundation raised more than eleven million dollars for Hurricane Katrina relief and rebuilt homes all along the Gulf Coast, including in Mississippi. In 2007 she started the Oprah Winfrey Leadership Academy for Girls, a boarding school in South Africa.

Since 2000 she has published the monthly *O: The Oprah Magazine*. In 1998 Winfrey was one of the founders of the Oxygen television network. After that network was sold, she partnered with Discovery Communications, and in 2011 the former Discovery Health Network became the Oprah Winfrey Network, which was available in more than 70 percent of all US households by 2015. Her website, Oprah.com, offers access to magazine articles, television shows, "life-classes," and many other resources.

Winfrey has won dozens of Emmys and has received numerous humanitarian awards and honorary degrees. She received the Presidential Medal of Freedom from Pres. Barack Obama in 2013. The first black billionaire in the United States, she is considered one of the most influential people in America.

Minoa D. Uffelman
Austin Peay University

Helen S. Garson, *Oprah Winfrey: A Biography* (2004); Henry Louis Gates Jr., *Finding Oprah's Roots: Finding Your Own* (2007); Kathryn Lofton, *Journal of Popular Culture* (August 2006); Oprah Winfrey website, www.oprah.com.

Wingate, Henry T.

(b. 1947) Judge

Born on 6 January 1947 in Jackson, Mississippi, Henry Travillion Wingate displayed his leadership potential while at Brinkley Junior-Senior High School, where he was active in school government and athletics as well as in the fight against racial injustice. Wingate integrated the Paramount movie theater and the main branch of the Jackson public library and was the first person of color to purchase a train ticket at the previously all-white train depot. He suffered injuries and was arrested while taking part in a student protest march in downtown Jackson.

Wingate earned a bachelor's degree in philosophy of religion from Grinnell College in 1969 and a degree from Yale Law School three years later. While at Yale, Wingate was a member of the Black Law Students Union and the Trial Advocacy Team, and after his first year, he received a fellowship from the Law Students Civil Rights Research Council to intern with a southern civil rights organization. Wingate became the first fellow to choose an assignment in Mississippi, working with attorney Mel Leventhal, who had been fighting on behalf of civil rights in Jackson since 1965.

After graduation, Wingate worked first for private attorneys and then with Jackson's Community Legal Aid while awaiting the start of his military career as judge advocate with the US Navy Reserve. On active duty from 1973 to 1976, he was the Navy's only African American judge advocate from 1973 to 1975. As a lieutenant with the US Navy Legal Services Office, he served as a criminal trial attorney and senior assistant defense counsel. Judge Wingate began doing criminal defense in 1973 and moved to criminal prosecution from 1974 to 1976. From 1976 to 1980 Wingate served as a special assistant attorney general with the State of Mississippi. He then spent four years as assistant district attorney for the 7th District Circuit Court District (Hinds and Yazoo Counties), the first African American to hold such a full-time position. In February 1984 Wingate became assistant US attorney for the Southern District of Mississippi, prosecuting violations of federal criminal laws, including narcotics offenses, official corruption, white-collar crimes, and violent crimes. In this capacity, he spearheaded Operation Pretense, a corruption investigation that ultimately ensnared fifty-six Mississippi county supervisors.

After Wingate had served for a year in the US attorney's office, Sen. Thad Cochran recommended him to sit on the US District Court for the Southern District of Mississippi. Pres. Ronald Reagan nominated Wingate to the post, and after US Senate confirmation, he was sworn in on 19 October 1985. One of only eight African Americans among Reagan's three hundred judicial appointees, Wingate became the first African American appointed to a life-tenured federal judgeship in Mississippi. In 2003 Wingate became the court's chief judge. He has served on the 5th Circuit Judicial Council and as president of the District Court Judges Association for the 5th Circuit.

Wingate remains active in community affairs, serving on a number of civic boards and as an adjunct professor at the Mississippi College School of Law. He is a prolific public speaker on the subjects of judicial administration, professional development, personal development for youth, racial reconciliation, and the Bible. He created the Court-Watch Program, which educates youth and adults about courts and the law, provides gospel performances for the incarcerated, and offers guidance on taking the Law School Aptitude Test.

Jim Rosenblatt
Mississippi College School of Law

Almanac of the Federal Judiciary (2008); Federal Judicial Center website, www.fjc.gov; Mississippi Senate Concurrent Resolution 595 (2016), https://legiscan.com/MS/text/SC595/id/1363234.

Winston County

Located in central Mississippi, Winston County is named for Col. Louis Winston, a Natchez lawyer. The county seat is Louisville. Winston was founded in 1833 as part of the Treaty of Dancing Rabbit Creek, which forced Choctaw tribes to leave Mississippi for Oklahoma. Winston County is the site of one of Mississippi's most important ancient places, Nanih Waiya, a mound that two well-known Choctaw myths associate with the founding of the tribe. Likely built in the Middle Woodland period sometime between the year 0 and AD 300, the mound gained new importance in the 1800s, when Greenwood LeFlore used it as a site for tribal assemblies. In August 2008 the Mississippi legislature returned Nanih Waiya to the Mississippi Band of Choctaw Indians.

The 1840 census counted 4,650 people living in Winston County, 34 percent of them slaves, a figure well below the state average of 52 percent. The people of Winston County worked mostly in agriculture, producing cotton and corn and raising livestock. Whereas only 2 people worked in industry and commerce in 1840, that number had risen to 50 a decade later.

By 1860, Winston County had 9,811 residents, 43 percent of whom were enslaved. The county's thirty-one churches included fourteen Methodist houses of worship, ten Baptist congregations, six Presbyterian churches, and Mississippi's only Universalist church.

In 1874 a section of Winston County became Choctaw County, but the change did not greatly affect the county's growth. In 1880 Winston was home to 10,087 people, with whites making up 61 percent of the population. Most of the remainder were African American, although the county had a small Native American population. Small farming continued to dominate, with most farmers practicing mixed agriculture and concentrating on corn and other grains, cotton, and livestock. Eighty percent of farmers owned their land. The importance of small farming was evident in county

W

politics, as a high percentage of voters supported Populist candidates over the next two decades.

At the turn of the century, Winston County remained an agricultural and rural county, with no urban center and only 36 industrial workers, all of them male. Winston had the state's fourth-lowest total industrial wages. Among white farmers, 73 percent owned their land, while only 41 percent of African American farmers did so.

Well-known historian Thomas D. Clark was born in Louisville in 1903. During his long tenure at the University of Kentucky, Clark was lauded both for his work as a southern historian and for preserving printed documents. Louisville is also well known for Stewart Pottery, which continues a family lineage of folk potters that dates back to the mid-1800s.

Winston County doubled in size between 1880 and 1930, reaching 21,239 residents, 62 percent of whom were white. The county's businesses employed 840 industrial workers, many of them in sawmills, a creamery, and an ice cream factory. About half of Winston's thirty-four hundred farms were operated by tenants, with corn and cattle the primary products and cotton secondary.

Winston County's population declined by about 2,000 between 1930 and 1960, falling to 19,246. Whites accounted for 56 percent of the residents, African Americans 43 percent, and Native Americans 1 percent. A quarter of Winston's working people now found employment in manufacturing, primarily the furniture and apparel industries.

Like many central Mississippi counties, Winston County was predominantly white in 2010 and had shown little change in size over the last half century, with a population of 19,198. However, African Americans now comprised more than 45 percent of residents.

Mississippi Encyclopedia Staff
University of Mississippi

Mississippi State Planning Commission, *Progress Report on State Planning in Mississippi* (1938); *Mississippi Statistical Abstract*, Mississippi State University (1952–2010); Charles Sydnor and Claude Bennett, *Mississippi History* (1939); University of Virginia Library, Historical Census Browser website, http://mapserver.lib.virginia.edu; E. Nolan Waller and Dani A. Smith, *Growth Profiles of Mississippi's Counties, 1960–1980* (1985).

Winter, William Forrest

(b. 1923) Fifty-Eighth Governor, 1980–1984

For all of William Winter's many contributions to the state of Mississippi, he will be most remembered for the Education Reform Act of 1982, which was passed after Governor

William Winter (Photograph by Joe Ellis, courtesy Jackson Clarion-Ledger)

Winter called a tense and controversial special session of the legislature. With the exception of that measure, which generated intense debate at the time but is now widely considered a model of progressive educational legislation, Winter's administration was marked by an efficiency and a lack of controversy rarely seen in Mississippi politics.

Winter was born in Grenada on 21 February 1923. He earned a bachelor's degree from the University of Mississippi in 1943 and then joined the US Army, serving as an infantryman in the Philippines during World War II. He subsequently enrolled in the University of Mississippi Law School, graduating first in his class in 1949. In 1947, while still in school, Winter was elected to the Mississippi House of Representatives, and he won reelection in 1951 and 1955. In 1950–51 he served as a legislative assistant to US senator John Stennis.

Winter conducted his first statewide campaign in 1959, winning election to the post of tax collector and remaining in office until 1964, when the position was abolished on his recommendation. He was then elected state treasurer. Following an unsuccessful race for governor in 1967, Winter was elected lieutenant governor in 1971. He tried again for the state's highest office in 1975, when the Democratic nomination went to Cliff Finch, and in 1979, when he finally succeeded.

Winter had made education reform a centerpiece of his campaign, and during the first year of his term, he asked the legislature to set up a committee to study the needs of Mississippi's schools. The committee recommended the passage of a compulsory attendance law, increased education funding, the establishment of a lay board of education; and state-supported kindergartens. But the legislature refused to pass the reform measure during its regular 1982 session. In response, the governor, several of his aides, and First

Lady Elise Varner Winter undertook a grassroots campaign designed to drum up public support for reform and increase pressure on the legislature to act. The campaign included more than 450 speeches and public appearances around the state.

In mid-November, Winter called a special session of the legislature to begin on 6 December. The only item on the agenda would be education reform, and the public relations campaign had made sure that Mississippians would be watching. After two weeks of debate, legislators passed the bill. The Education Reform Act of 1982 is considered the most significant educational legislation enacted in Mississippi since the establishment of its public school system in 1870.

Winter left the Governor's Mansion in January 1984 and made one more bid for public office, losing to incumbent Thad Cochran in that year's election for the US Senate. Winter returned to practicing law in Jackson, though he continued his public service through a variety of civic organizations. He has held office in state and national mental health organizations and has served as president of the board of trustees of the Mississippi Department of Archives and History, as a trustee of Belhaven College and Columbia Seminary, and as president of the Mississippi Historical Society and the University of Mississippi Alumni Association. He participated in Pres. Bill Clinton's Initiative on Race and taught for a semester at the University of Mississippi Law School.

The William Winter Professorship of History at the University of Mississippi has been endowed in his honor, and the University of Mississippi's Institute for Racial Reconciliation and the building that houses the Mississippi Department of Archives and History bear his name. While serving as lieutenant governor, William Winter received the Margaret Dixon Freedom of Information Award from the Louisiana-Mississippi Associated Press for his continuing support for the opening of the political process to both the general public and to the press. In 2008 the John F. Kennedy Presidential Library and Museum bestowed its Profile in Courage Award on Winter in recognition of his efforts to advance education and racial reconciliation.

David G. Sansing
University of Mississippi

Charles C. Bolton, ed., *Journal of Mississippi History* (Winter 2008); Andrew P. Mullins Jr., *Building Consensus: A History of the Passage of the Mississippi Education Reform Act, 1982* (1999); Jere Nash and Andy Taggart, *Mississippi Politics: The Struggle for Power, 1976–2008* (2nd ed., 2009); *Mississippi Official and Statistical Register* (1980–84); James G. Thomas, Jr., ed., *Southern Quarterly* (Fall 2016); William Winter Subject File, Mississippi Department of Archives and History; Elise Varner Winter, *Once in a Lifetime: Reflections of a Mississippi First Lady* (2015); William F. Winter and Andrew P. Mullins Jr., *The Measure of Our Days: Writings of William F. Winter* (2006).

Wisdom, John Minor
(1905–1999) Judge

A pioneer in the development of the Republican Party in the South after World War II, John Minor Wisdom was a regional leader in the nomination and election of Pres. Dwight D. Eisenhower. He later selected Wisdom as a judge for the 5th Circuit Court of Appeals, which handled many of the desegregation cases arising from Mississippi and other parts of the South during the 1960s.

Wisdom was born on 17 May 1905 in New Orleans and earned a bachelor's degree from Washington and Lee University and a law degree from Tulane University. He practiced law in New Orleans from 1929 until 1957, when Eisenhower elevated him to the bench.

Judge Wisdom's greatest direct role in Mississippi came in the desegregation crisis at the University of Mississippi. In response to US district judge Sidney Mize's ruling that Meredith had not been denied admission to the university "because of his color or his race," Wisdom wrote that segregation was a product of an "eerie atmosphere of never-never land" and that segregation in higher education in Mississippi was "a plain fact known to everyone." Wisdom subsequently characterized another of Mize's decisions as "a carefully calculated campaign of delay, harassment, and masterly inactivity."

When the legal battle ended, James Meredith had enrolled at the school, and Gov. Ross Barnett faced federal charges of criminal contempt of court for defying orders issued by the 5th Circuit. Barnett's contempt case lingered in the courts for two and a half years. In April 1965 the 5th Circuit ruled four to three that "further prosecution of criminal contempt proceedings [would be] unnecessary."

Judge Wisdom wrote a strong dissent to that ruling, working hard on his final paragraph, a literary classic in legal opinion writing: "There is an unedifying moral to be drawn from this case of *The Man in High Office Who Defied the Nation*: the mills of the law grind slowly—but not inexorably. If they grind slowly enough, they may even come, unaccountably, to a gradual stop, short of the trial and judgment an ordinary citizen expects when accused of criminal contempt. There is just one compensating thought: Hubris is grist for other mills, which grind exceeding small and sure."

Wisdom took senior status in 1977 but never fully retired from the bench. In 1993 he received the Presidential Medal of Freedom from Pres. Bill Clinton. Wisdom died on 15 May 1999.

Jack Bass
College of Charleston

Jack Bass, *Unlikely Heroes* (1981).

W

Witherspoon, Frances
(1886–1973) Activist

In Frances Witherspoon's words, "The essential history of any life is not the record of its long continuity, but of its high significant moments." The "high significant moments" that marked Witherspoon's life were moments of great importance for America's "essential history" as well. Witherspoon was at once a compassionate, kind woman and an ardent, determined supporter of pacifism and woman suffrage.

Born on 8 July 1886 in Meridian, Frances May Witherspoon was the daughter Samuel Andrew Witherspoon, who represented Mississippi in the US House of Representatives from 1911 until his death in 1915, and his wife, Susan May Witherspoon, the Kentucky-born daughter of a Frenchman who had served as a Confederate officer. Fanny May Witherspoon attended public school in Meridian before enrolling at Bryn Mawr College, where she majored in English and Latin, graduating in 1908. College president M. Carey Thomas, a suffragist, provided Witherspoon with a model for activism. Bryn Mawr was also where Witherspoon met Tracy Mygatt, a zealous writer, reader, and activist who became Witherspoon's life partner.

Witherspoon and Mygatt moved to New York City in 1913 and participated in a diverse range of pacifist and suffrage organizations, including the Woman's Peace Party and the Socialist Suffrage Brigade, which they helped to organize. In 1915 Witherspoon helped to found the New York Bureau of Legal Advice, a forerunner of the American Civil Liberties Union, and in 1923, she and Myatt were among the organizers of the War Resisters League. Witherspoon maintained her antiwar activism throughout her life, working with the Women's Committee to Oppose Conscription during World War II and later organizing a campaign against the Vietnam War among Bryn Mawr alumnae.

Witherspoon wrote numerous essays, articles, and pamphlets, including "The Lumberjack and the Constitution," which appeared in *The World Tomorrow* in May 1919; *Who Are the Conscientious Objectors?*, published by the Committee of 100 Friends of Conscientious Objectors in 1919; and *Four Good Reasons*, an argument against a draft for women published by the Committee to Oppose the Conscription of Women in 1943.

Even into her eighties, Witherspoon organized pacifist efforts. She collected signatures for a petition against the war in Vietnam by Bryn Mawr alumnae. During the weeks before her death on 16 December 1973, Witherspoon communicated with newspaper editors and political figures about pacifism, showing that her politics were a lifetime pursuit.

Emily Bowles-Smith
Lawrence University

Frances H. Early, *A World without War: How U.S. Feminists and Pacifists Resisted World War I* (1997); Jean Bethke Elshtain, *Women and War* (1987); Lillian Faderman, *Powerful Brilliant Women* (1998); Nancy Manahan, *Women's Studies Quarterly* (Spring 1982); Lois Scharf and Joan M. Jensen, *Decades of Discontent: The Women's Movement, 1920–1940* (1983); *New York Times* (18 December 1973); Barbara J. Steinson, *American Women's Activism in World War I* (1982).

WLBT-TV and Civil Rights

WLBT-TV in Jackson was the first television station ever to lose its Federal Communications Commission (FCC) license—primarily for its racist defense of segregation. Individual activists and the state chapter of the National Association for the Advancement of Colored People (NAACP) had pressured WLBT for years to allow black Mississippians' response time under the FCC's Fairness Doctrine, which required local stations to offer airtime for opposing views on controversial issues.

WLBT's transgressions were many. In the fall of 1955 Thurgood Marshall, NAACP lawyer and future US Supreme Court justice, appeared on an NBC news program to discuss the implications of the Court's 1954 and 1955 *Brown v. Board of Education* decisions, which declared segregated schools unconstitutional. Marshall had argued the cases before the Court. WLBT interrupted the broadcast and instead aired a slide that read, "Sorry, Cable Trouble from New York." General manager Fred Beard explained that he had broken off the program "because the TV networks were overloading the circuits with Negro propaganda." WLBT's reporters frequently used the terms *nigger* and *nigra* on air, and the station interrupted the evening news, the *Huntley-Brinkley Report*, when the program turned to the civil rights movement. The station routinely voiced opposition to desegregation through news commentaries or by granting airtime to segregation's advocates and ran ads from the Citizens' Councils, a bastion of Deep South massive resistance. Year after year, the station refused African Americans' requests for equal time to respond. WLBT's exclusion of black Mississippians from local television was nearly total during the 1950s, but during the following decade, the civil rights movement's national visibility and influence meant change.

Local black pressure and FCC warnings had two positive effects in 1962–63. When African American minister Robert L. T. Smith ran for Congress against segregationist representative John Bell Williams, WLBT sold Smith thirty minutes of airtime. An even more dramatic exception to the station's routine occurred in May 1963, when Medgar Evers, field secretary of the Mississippi chapter of the NAACP, appeared on air after formally requesting time to respond to

Jackson mayor Allen Thompson's rejection of desegregation. Speaking calmly, and eloquently, Evers declared, "Whether Jackson and the state choose change or not, the years of change are upon us. In the racial picture things will never be as they once were. History has reached a turning point." Three weeks later, Byron De La Beckwith assassinated Evers.

Evers's sense that change was in the air was widely shared. In 1963 national media covered the civil rights movement's protests in Birmingham, Alabama, and the March on Washington. NBC preempted regular programming for a groundbreaking three-hour documentary, *The American Revolution of 1963*, which detailed civil rights activism. When the network coverage turned to white violence against peaceful civil rights protesters at a Jackson lunch counter, WLBT ran "Sorry, Cable Trouble" across its screen. Ironically, it had filmed the incident.

WLBT was in many ways typical of southern stations. The owners and managers of southern network affiliates resented network news programs' sympathetic portrayal of the civil rights movement and presented protesters in a negative light. However, the depth of WLBT's commitment to massive resistance made it extreme. WLBT did not carry network news magazines because they might occasionally cover the civil rights movement, instead running syndicated shows that equated the civil rights movement with communism. WLBT also carried the *Citizens' Council Forum*, a syndicated series of fifteen-minute interviews with segregationists.

The Fairness Doctrine made a station's obligation to serve the local community explicit. About half of WLBT's viewing area was black, making it an excellent test case. Could African Americans force evenhanded treatment under the Fairness Doctrine? WLBT's license had been renewed in 1959 with only perfunctory consideration of local concerns. In 1963 the Office of Communication of the United Church of Christ (UCC) offered help to local activists who sought to challenge WLBT's violations of the Fairness Doctrine. Rev. Everett Parker, who had left behind a career in radio and advertising to attend the University of Chicago's divinity school, headed the church's effort. He met with Aaron Henry, state NAACP president, and A. D. Beittel, president of Tougaloo College. With the threat of violent reprisal hanging over their heads, they gathered local complaints regarding WLBT for a formal petition to the FCC opposing the renewal of WLBT's license.

When WLBT sought to renew its license in 1964, the UCC and local activists submitted their petition. A divided FCC stuck to a narrow bureaucratic interpretation of the Fairness Doctrine, granting WLBT a one-year conditional renewal without holding a hearing. Dissatisfied, the UCC and its Mississippi allies took the case to the Court of Appeals, which ruled against WLBT. The court declared that the FCC had to allow local viewers to make their case against the license renewal because viewers had "standing" based on their interests as consumers.

The hearing did not occur until 1968. WLBT hired as its lawyer Paul Porter, a former chair of the FCC. Acknowledg-

ing some faults, Porter argued that WLBT had mended its ways by hiring a new general manager and allowing black ministers to broadcast devotional services. He insisted that the most egregious accusations were "unsubstantiated." The FCC agreed, awarding a three-year license renewal. The UCC and its local allies again challenged the decision, and in 1971 the court reversed the FCC's license renewal, forcing the sale of the station. These court decisions meant that citizens who had previously been excluded from the process could pressure local stations to deal fairly with their community. The national shift toward a conservative mood, however, meant deregulation in the 1980s and abandonment of this pressure to serve the public interest.

Bryan Hardin Thrift

Johnston Community College

Steven Classen, *Watching Jim Crow: The Struggles over Mississippi TV, 1955–1969* (2004); Myrlie Evers-Williams and Manning Marable, eds., *The Autobiography of Medgar Evers: A Hero's Life and Legacy Revealed through His Writings, Letters, and Speeches* (2005); Fred W. Friendly, *The Good Guys, the Bad Guys, and the First Amendment: Free Speech vs. Fairness in Broadcasting* (1975); Kay Mills, *Changing Channels: The Civil Rights Case That Transformed Television* (2004).

Wolcott, F. S., and His Rabbit's Foot Minstrels

The Rabbit's Foot Minstrels, also known as the Rabbit Foot Minstrels, A Rabbit's Foot Comedy Company, Rabbit Foot Company, or simply the Foots, were established in 1900 by Patrick Henry Chappelle (1869–1911) in Tampa, Florida. The name came from the title of a traveling comedy show, *A Rabbit's Foot*, created by Chappelle; his business partner, R. S. Donaldson; and writer Frank Dumont. Over the next several years, the show rapidly gained widespread recognition, leading the touring company to become known as the Rabbit's Foot Company. Within three years, the troupe had its own specialized railcar. The company featured comedy routines, singers, brass bands, jugglers, wrestlers, and contortionists; the Rabbit's Foot Company even had its own baseball team.

When Chappelle died in 1911, Fred Swift Wolcott (1882–1967) took over. Wolcott, a white man from Michigan, was a bit of a change for the Foots, since Chappelle had prided himself on having "successfully run a Negro show without the help of a single white man." Chappelle had avoided calling the company a minstrel show, but Wolcott embraced the

W

idea in advertising, and the troupe generally became known as F. S. Wolcott's Rabbit's Foot Minstrels.

The company performed extensively throughout the southern United States and in 1918 established its headquarters in Port Gibson, at a building on Carroll and Market Streets that served as the company's main office until 1950. Wolcott purchased the Glen Sade Plantation and declared his occupation as "farmer" when registering for the World War I draft in September 1918.

The Rabbit's Foot Minstrels performed as late as 1959, though audiences had declined rapidly over the preceding decade. Among the performers who got their start with the Rabbit's Foot Minstrels were Gertrude "Ma" Rainey, Ida Cox, Bessie Smith, Butterbeans and Susie, Sleepy John Estes, Brownie McGhee, Big Joe Williams, and Louis Jordan.

Greg Johnson
University of Mississippi

Lynn Abbott and Doug Seroff, *Ragged but Right: Black Traveling Shows, "Coon Songs," and the Dark Pathway to Blues and Jazz* (2007); Paul Oliver, *The Story of the Blues* (1998); Eileen Southern, *Biographical Dictionary of Afro-American and African Musicians* (1982).

Wolfe, Mildred Nungester

(1912–2009) Artist

Mildred Nungester Wolfe was an artist who painted landscapes and townscapes in oil and watercolor as well as portraits of children in oil and pastel. In addition, she pursued printmaking, ceramics, and sculpture and received commissions for stained glass windows, mosaics, murals, and illustrations.

Born on 23 August 1912 in Celina, Ohio, Mildred Nungester moved with her family in 1916 to Alabama, where she was educated. In 1919 she took a correspondence course in art from Columbia University, and in 1928 she began art studies at Athens College. She earned a bachelor's degree at Alabama College, State College for Women in Montevallo, and soon began a career teaching public school, a profession her family considered appropriate. However, she continued to receive art training during the summer, including at the Art Institute of Chicago in 1934. She began exhibiting works in national shows and studying with important American artists such as Will Barnet and George Bridgman.

In 1937 Nungester met Karl Wolfe at the Dixie Art Colony near Montgomery, Alabama. However, their relationship did not blossom until 1943, when they reconnected at the Colorado Springs Fine Arts Center, where she was working on a master's degree. She graduated in 1944 and

Mildred Wolfe, *The Old Canton Road*, 1949, oil on board, 29" × 38" (Collection of Hunter Cole)

moved to Denver and married Wolfe, who was living there while in the army. In 1946 they moved to Jackson, where Karl Wolfe had worked prior to World War II.

The Wolfes eventually established the Wolfe Studio on what were the rural outskirts of Jackson. Karl established himself as a portrait painter, while Mildred produced more varied and independent work while raising their two children. Early in their marriage Mildred and Karl worked out a relationship that protected Mildred's artistic integrity and independence, although they greatly respected each other as artists with individual talents and strengths. During the time Karl taught at Millsaps College in Jackson, Mildred developed an art history course there and taught it for some ten years. Their first studio and most of the artworks it contained were destroyed in a fire in the early 1960s. A new studio with a showroom and work areas was built in 1964 and remains an important outlet for the works of the Wolfe family. Karl Wolfe died in 1984.

The National Portrait Gallery in Washington, D.C., holds Mildred Wolfe's oil portrait of Eudora Welty. In 1994 the Mississippi Museum of Art in Jackson presented a retrospective exhibition of Wolfe's work, and in 2000 the National Museum of Women in the Arts named her Distinguished Mississippi Woman Artist.

Most of Mildred Wolfe's works are American scene painting and regionalism. Her portraiture harkens back to Renoir in its softness and suave color. Wolfe's most innovative works are those in mosaic and printmaking. Her mosaics include ideas drawn from Art Deco and the semiabstract styles of artists such as Gustav Klimt. In lithography, Wolfe used the inherent qualities of the medium and her excellent draftsmanship to create works that convey both the social and human concerns and keen observation that characterize lithographs by artists such as Thomas Hart Benton and Grant Wood. Wolfe's body of work in relief printmaking shows evidence of influence by the modern American woodcut style established by Arthur Wesley Dow and others.

Mildred Wolfe died of congestive heart failure on 11 February 2009, nearly twenty-five years after her husband. Ultimately, her greatest accomplishment was to work with energy, dedication, and high aesthetic and expressive goals in a remarkable variety of media and approaches. She obtained artistic recognition and personal fulfillment in a South where women artists often were not taken seriously and where the lack of public interest and support often made the art profession a difficult pursuit.

Steve Cook
Mississippi College

Mildred Nungester Wolfe, *Mildred Nungester Wolfe*, ed. Elizabeth Wolfe (2005).

Woman Suffrage

During the late nineteenth and early twentieth centuries Mississippi women, like their counterparts across the country, began to work to obtain the right to vote. The groundwork for this activism was laid earlier in the 1800s, as women increasingly chafed against domestic social expectations, championing social issues such as temperance and mission work and receiving encouragement from their churches for such efforts. Though the religious denominations deplored political agitation by women, their involvement in these earlier movements helped prepare many women to take part in a larger national dialogue that encompassed not only the evils of alcohol but also prison reform, child labor laws, the dangers of venereal disease, and eventually women's political rights.

Literary and social clubs began to develop around the state and to encourage members to think about the major issues facing women. During the meetings of Greenville's Hypatia Club, for example, Nellie Nugent Somerville began to speak of the problems women encountered by not having control of their bodies and thus their own fertility.

One of the most important organizations that prepared women for a more vocal role in government was the Woman's Christian Temperance Union, which had 250,000 members nationwide. The organization argued that women needed to vote to protect the family, allowing more conservative women to join the fight for suffrage.

On 5 May 1897 a group of women met in Meridian to form the Mississippi Woman Suffrage Association (MWSA). The organization promoted suffrage via speeches, letters to newspapers and Mississippi congressmen, and participation in local parades and fairs. The first elected officers included president Nellie Nugent Somerville, vice president Belle Kearney, and corresponding secretary Lily Wilkinson Thompson. During its early years the organization suffered from disagreements about the best way to achieve its goals. Several of the members were staunch supporters of states' rights and preferred to have the Mississippi legislature grant women the vote, while others believed that a federal amendment was the only way that Mississippi women would gain suffrage. Moreover, Mississippi's suffragists felt the need to keep themselves at arm's length from their northern counterparts to avoid alienating the state's conservative white male electorate. As a result, the MWSA created most of the publications it distributed, although it also sent copies of a moderate national publication, the *Woman's Journal*, to all members of the state legislature for three months in 1913.

In 1899 Somerville resigned as the MWSA's president for health reasons, and Kearney took over. Since she was often out of the state on lecturing tours, the MWSA did little until 1906, when Kearney returned. For the next decade MWSA members worked to promote their campaign. They argued that it was their duty as mothers to prepare good citizens in the form of their sons and that the ballot was a vital tool for accomplishing this goal. In response to the argument that only men were fit for suffrage as a consequence of their status as workers, the activists demonstrated how many women worked outside the home in schools or in factories. The MWSA largely disapproved of picketing and other techniques used by some suffragists in the North but made its presence known at local fairs by participating in parades and operating booths. In addition, nationally known speakers such as Dr. Anna Howard Shaw visited the state to address both men and women. When some opponents of woman suffrage argued that it would enfranchise thousands of African American women, Mississippi's white suffragists assured the legislature that the same methods used to prevent African American men from voting would also ban African American women.

When the US House of Representatives passed the Nineteenth Amendment in 1918, only Mississippi and South Carolina solidly opposed it. Mississippi was also not among the thirty-six states that ratified the amendment before it went into effect: in fact, Mississippi did not ratify the Nineteenth Amendment until 1984, when it became the last state to do so.

In 1923, just three years after women received the right to vote, Kearney was elected to the State Senate. She continued to work for reform, especially in the areas of Prohibition and public health, publishing *Conqueror or Conquered: The Sex Challenge Answered*, a book that highlighted the widespread effects of venereal disease. Somerville also won a seat in the state legislature and remained a staunch supporter of Prohibition. They and other women who had been active on behalf of suffrage turned their attention to other issues, such as equal pay for equal work, raising the age of consent, prison reform, and child labor.

Stephanie L. McKnight
University of Mississippi

W

Anne Firor Scott, *The Southern Lady: From Pedestal to Politics, 1830–1930* (1970); Martha H. Swain, Elizabeth Anne Payne, Marjorie Julian Spruill, and Susan Ditto, eds., *Mississippi Women: Their Histories, Their Lives* (2003); Lily Thompson Collection, Department of Archives and Special Collections, J. D. Williams Library, University of Mississippi.

Womanpower Unlimited

Founded on 29 May 1961 in Jackson, Mississippi, Womanpower Unlimited was the brainchild of local businesswoman and activist Clarie Collins Harvey. A civil rights organization designed to mobilize and empower women, Womanpower was dedicated to supporting civil and human rights on the local, national, and international levels. Womanpower evolved from a meeting Harvey convened at the Central Methodist Church in response to the arrival and incarceration of the Freedom Riders in Jackson. At their trial, Harvey noticed that many of them were improperly clothed because their belongings had been taken from them when they were detained. As a result, she and Aurelia Young, a professor at Jackson State College (now Jackson State University), sent clothing to the jail. Aware of the growing movement in Mississippi and the fact that these youth, most of whom were not local residents, would need continuing support, Harvey sent a call though local churches to solicit money and other items for the activists.

Womanpower sought to address the immediate needs of the Freedom Riders, yet members' activism was grounded in broadly humanist ideologies of freedom and justice. The group's stated purpose was "to help create the atmosphere, the institutions, and traditions that make freedom and peace possible. We are all women working together for a peaceful world and wholesome community life." During its seven-year existence Womanpower focused on empowering women to engage in social activism, providing moral and material support for civil rights activists, generating resources for civil rights organizations, and improving the conditions of African American life.

In addition to Harvey, who served as Womanpower's chair, vice chair Thelma Sanders and executive secretary A. M. E. Logan were integral to the organization's success. Both had civil rights experience through the National Association for the Advancement of Colored People and other organizations and were economically independent. Sanders owned a women's clothing store, while Logan worked as a traveling sales representative for A. W. Curtis, a distributor of George Washington Carver products. Other Womanpower members included Aura Gary, Dorestine Parker Carey, Jessie Bryant Mosley, Ruth O. Hubert, R. Arline Young, Artisha W. Jordan, and Jane Schutt. Womanpower also had a "chain of friendship"—individuals throughout the country who provided financial assistance.

Womanpower met bimonthly, usually at the Central Methodist Church, the Farish Street Baptist Church, or the Pearl Street African Methodist Episcopal Church. The group provided emotional as well as material support to the Freedom Riders during their incarceration and food, clothing, and housing after their release. After the Freedom Riders left the state, Womanpower turned its attention to voter registration. Womanpower also lent assistance to the Freedom Summer project in 1964 by maintaining freedom houses and supplying lunches for volunteers at the Farish Street Baptist Church. In the fall of 1964, when public school integration began in Jackson, Womanpower members disseminated information and encouraged parents to enroll their children and later provided material and emotional support for the families of children integrating the schools.

Womanpower also engaged in activities that connected members to national and international communities of like-minded women. In 1962 Harvey helped organize the Box Project, in which women in Vermont donated boxes of clothing, food, and household items to needy families in Mississippi. And in 1965, in conjunction with the New York–based Race Relations Committee of the American Ethical Union, Womanpower began a program that sent poor children from the South, most of them black, to summer camps in New England. Womanpower also supported peace activism through an association with Women Strike for Peace.

Womanpower Unlimited disbanded in 1968, with many members joining the newly founded Jackson section of the National Council of Negro Women.

Tiyi M. Morris
Ohio State University at Newark

Raymond Arsenault, *Freedom Riders: 1961 and the Struggle for Racial Justice* (2006); August Meier and Elliot Rudwick, *CORE: A Study of the Civil Rights Movement, 1942–1968* (1973); Tiyi M. Morris, in *Groundwork: Local Black Freedom Struggles in America*, ed. Komozi Woodard and Jeanne Theoharis (2005); Tiyi M. Morris, *Womanpower Unlimited and the Black Freedom Struggle in Mississippi* (2015); James Peck, *Freedom Ride* (1962).

Women for Constitutional Government

Following James Meredith's arrival at the University of Mississippi in 1962, Florence Sillers Ogden, Margaret Preaster, and Edna Whitfield organized Women for Constitutional Government (WCG), which sought to place opposition to the federal government's involvement in the civil rights movement on a platform broader than racial segregation. The organization encouraged white women to understand federal troops on Mississippi soil as one of many examples of an intrusive, left-leaning federal government that subsumed individual rights to liberal social aims.

On 30 October 1962 between fifteen hundred and eighteen hundred white women from Georgia, Alabama, Louisiana, Mississippi, Texas, Florida, Illinois, and Pennsylvania gathered in Jackson, where they heard Ogden, a *Jackson Clarion-Ledger* columnist and daughter of Walter Sillers Sr., the longtime Speaker of the Mississippi House, claim that federal marshals treated white children like criminals and denied their right to assemble and protest. Pres. John F. Kennedy's New Frontier, Ogden continued, promised federal control of families, schools, and religious practices. Every white woman had a responsibility to "preserve the good life for her children—life, liberty, and the pursuit of happiness."

In January 1963 the WCG held its first national meeting in Montgomery, Alabama. Although the group claimed to have nearly one million members, only one thousand women showed up. Delegates from fourteen states were in attendance, including women from Chicago and Peoria, Illinois, though most came from Alabama. Alabama First Lady Lurleen Wallace welcomed the women. Ogden and Mary Cain, a longtime conservative newspaper editor and owner of the *Summit Sun*, provided keynote addresses. The following year, the Mississippi organization urged Gov. Paul Johnson not to enforce the Civil Rights Act of 1964, and the group hesitated to support Barry Goldwater's presidential candidacy, fearing that he would cave in to more moderate demands of the Republican Party.

The organization tried to paint itself as a large conservative umbrella organization but could never really cast aside its racial politics. In addition to support for segregation and states' rights and opposition to federal involvement in civil rights matters, the WCG's platform included opposition to communism, the United Nations, and water fluoridation. In its quest to "preserve the US Constitution," it also called for a repeal of all the constitutional amendments beyond the Bill of Rights. Members worked to elect politicians true to "conservative principles" rather than party politics, to register white voters, and in later years to defeat the Equal Rights Amendment. Local chapters were allowed to develop and pursue their own political strategies.

The WCG urged its members to ignore mainstream media, which had supposedly been infiltrated by liberals, and instead to look to such publications as the *Smoot Report*, the *National Defense Bulletin* (published by the Daughters of the American Revolution), and the *Wall Street Journal*. For twenty years Cain published the WCG's organ, the *Woman Constitutionalist*, which spoke out in support of Phyllis Schlafly, opposed the Equal Rights Amendment, and featured a column Cain wrote as well as excerpts from other conservative periodicals.

Though the WCG eventually spread to forty states and remained active until the mid-1980s, it never achieved the kind of influence for which its founders had hoped. Nevertheless, its actions reveal the importance of women in the rise of the Right in the 1970s and 1980s and demonstrate that movement's links to the politics of white supremacy.

Elizabeth Gillespie McRae
Western Carolina University

Mary Dawson Cain Papers, Mississippi Department of Archives and History Joseph Crespino, *In Search of Another Country: Mississippi and the Conservative Counterrevolution* (2007); Lisa Speer, "Contrary Mary: The Life of Mary Dawson Cain" (PhD dissertation, University of Mississippi, 1998); Elizabeth Gillespie McRae, "Raising Jim Crow: White Women and the Politics of White Supremacy" (PhD dissertation, University of Georgia, 2003); Florence Sillers Ogden Papers, Charles W. Capps Jr. Archives and Museum, Delta State University.

Women's Clubs and Organizations

Other than through church work, Mississippi women did not form organizations until after Reconstruction. Beginning in the late nineteenth century, organizations that had originated in other states began to proliferate in Mississippi as the wives of professional men and middle- to upper-class women enjoyed more leisure time. In addition, the increasing availability of higher education resulted in a growing number of professional women. The need for social services for an increasing urban population led to the creation of groups through which Mississippi women could express a new sense of social usefulness, self-reliance, and initiative.

Moving beyond church missionary societies, Mississippi women joined the Woman's Christian Temperance Union (WCTU) under the leadership of Belle Kearney and Nellie Nugent Somerville. The moral imperatives of the WCTU provided a base from which to crusade for a state-supported college for women, for the establishment of industrial schools and homes for youthful offenders, and for other reforms. More important, WCTU stalwarts formed the Mississippi Woman Suffrage Association in 1897, and this group in turn became the state's chapter of the League of Women Voters. Other women found a venue for civic improvement endeavors through affiliates with the Mississippi Federation of Women's Clubs, organized at Kosciusko in 1898. And many white women became involved in the Daughters of the American Revolution beginning in 1896 and the United Daughters of the Confederacy beginning in 1897.

The National Federation of Business and Professional Women organized clubs in four Mississippi cities in 1924 and soon spread to other locales. Another professional women's group, the Sorosis Club, also came to Mississippi, as did civic clubs such as Altrusa International and the Pilot Club and the

W

PEO, which focused on providing educational opportunities for girls and women. The American Association of University Women formed its first Mississippi branch in 1927. The first Mississippi chapter of Delta Kappa Gamma, an international society for women teachers, organized in 1934. The once-elitist Junior Leagues have been active in the state since 1941 and have now become more open, expanding their focus to encompass a variety of issues affecting women and children.

Fewer organizations have existed for black women, although the Federation of Colored Women's Clubs has been at work in the state since 1903. Beginning in the late twentieth century, such groups as Links, Delta Sigma Theta alumnae, and the National Council of Negro Women have attracted an active membership.

Rural and small-town women, black and white, have been active in Mississippi's home demonstration clubs since as early as 1918. Farm women also work together through affiliates of the Mississippi Farm Bureau, stressing citizenship, safety, and full partnership with men in agricultural pursuits.

As a major tool of social change, federated clubs have been a major impetus for the creation of local libraries, sanitary water and milk supplies, legislation to benefit to women and children, and civic beautification. Mississippi women's interest in their environment and in history resulted in garden clubs that promote memorial plantings, highway beautification, tours of historic homes, and the restoration of historic structures.

As more women have entered the political arena and joined the workforce and previously all-male civic clubs, Mississippi women's organizations have lost membership and voluntarism has declined. Feminist groups such as the National Organization for Women (NOW) have made limited headway in the state. Nonetheless, there is scarcely a Mississippi town where African American and white women do not still join together to launch impressive projects for conviviality, civic improvement, and the advancement of the status of women.

Martha H. Swain
Mississippi State University

Martha H. Swain, in *Sex, Race, and the Role of Women in the South*, ed. Joanne V. Hawks and Sheila Skemp (1983); Marjorie Spruill Wheeler, *New Women of the New South: The Leaders of the Women Suffrage Movement in the Southern States* (1993).

Woodland Period

The Woodland period is an archaeological construct defined by the presence of certain kinds of pottery and earthen mounds. Archaeological sites displaying these characteristics are found throughout the forested portion of eastern North America. In Mississippi, Woodland sites are distributed broadly, in many settings and environments. Based on radiocarbon dating, the period runs from ca. 800 BC to AD 1000.

This long period often is divided into Early (800–200 BC), Middle (200 BC–AD 500), and Late Woodland (AD 500–1000) segments. Within these eras, local phases have been defined for various regions of the state. Among the Early Woodland phases are Tchefuncte in the Mississippi Valley, Alexander and Wheeler in northern and eastern Mississippi, and Bayou La Batre on the Gulf Coast. For Middle Woodland, the respective phases for these three areas are Marksville, Miller I and Miller II, and Porter. Late Woodland phases are Baytown, Miller III, and Weeden Island.

The surfaces of Woodland pottery pieces often display fabric marking (made by a woven fabric, perhaps wrapped around a wooden paddle) or cordmarking (made by twisted strings), with the designs pressed into the surface of the pot before it was fired. Stylized bird and geometric designs, delineated by incised lines and by areas filled with stamped decoration, also were hallmarks of Woodland pottery. Sand and crushed pieces of pottery (grog) were the materials most frequently used to temper the clay to prevent the vessel from cracking during drying and firing.

Conical burial mounds are the most common kind of Woodland mound. They may cover log tombs, as at Pinson Mounds in Tennessee, or mortuary platforms, as at Bynum Mounds in Chickasaw County. Decorated pots from the Mississippi River Valley and axes made of greenstone from central Alabama were found in mounds excavated at Bynum and the nearby Pharr Mounds site. Flat-topped rectangular mounds, with earthen ramps leading up one side, also were built. Mississippi examples include Ingomar Mound 14 in Union County and Nanih Waiya in Winston County. Rectangular mounds appear not to have been used for burial or as substructures for buildings. Some may have been the locations of communal feasting, judging by the animal bones and charred plant remains dumped down their sides.

At a few sites near the Mississippi River, Middle Woodland people built large geometric earthworks, as at Little Spanish Fort, in Sharkey County. The semicircular embankment there is a maximum of six feet high and two thousand feet in diameter. A ditch along the outside was the source of the dirt that composes the earthwork. The wall likely had four gaps in it as part of the original site plan. Despite the name, Little Spanish Fort and places like it probably served not as forts but rather as ceremonial centers.

Woodland peoples lived year-round in small hamlets, villages, or towns. Mounds sometimes were built in association with a hamlet or larger habitation area. Site 22HO654 in Holmes County is an example. It has six conical mounds, each eight to ten feet high, spread across an area of about twenty-two acres. On one edge is a small village, covering slightly more than one acre, that has produced broken pottery dating from the Marksville to Baytown periods. In contrast, some large mound groups appear to have been vacant, lacking evidence of year-round habitation. One such site constructed in Middle Woodland times is Ingomar Mounds, where a rectangular mound and as many as nine conical mounds were built. These uninhabited sites probably served as ceremonial centers for outlying hamlets.

Woodland groups depended for subsistence on hunting wild game, fishing, and gathering nuts, roots, and seeds. In some areas, native plants such as sunflower (*Helianthus annuus* var. *macrocarpa*), lamb's quarter (*Chenopodium berlandieri* var. *Jonesianum*), and marsh elder (*Iva annua* var. *macrocarpa*) were domesticated and became significant sources of food. Another important technological innovation was the introduction of the bow and arrow in Late Woodland times. This occurred by AD 700, based on the appearance of small stone arrow points.

Intergroup conflict became more prevalent in the Late Woodland period, as indicated by human burials with arrow points in the skeletons. Health also declined, with more indicators of anemia, other diseases, and arthritis present on the bones. Living in villages rather than in more scattered settlements helped to protect Late Woodland people from attack by neighboring groups but probably adversely affected their health. As these pressures worked on populations, cultivation of maize became increasingly important. In most parts of the state, this culminated in the sort of full-blown agriculture typical of the succeeding Mississippian archaeological period.

Janet Rafferty

Mississippi State University

David G. Anderson and Robert C. Mainfort Jr., eds., *The Woodland Southeast* (2002); Kenneth H. Carleton, *Mississippi Archaeology* (1999); John L. Cotter and John M. Corbett, *Archeology of the Bynum Mounds, Mississippi* (1951); Edwin H. Jackson, *Midcontinental Journal of Archaeology* (Fall 1998); David T. Morgan, *Mississippi Archaeology* (1988).

Woodpeckers

Nearly four hundred species of birds are known from Mississippi, including nine woodpeckers. These birds are well known for excavating nest and roost cavities in trees and feeding on insects, spiders, other small animals, and at times fruit and seeds. Mississippi's woodpecker diversity reflects its rich forest diversity: pine flatwoods to the south, higher pinelands through the center and east, elements of

Red-cockaded woodpecker (Courtesy Jerome Jackson)

Appalachian mixed forest in the northeast, swamp hardwood forests along the great rivers, and lesser areas of natural savannah and prairie. Such habitat diversity allows woodpeckers to specialize, minimizing competition by exploiting unique resources or similar resources in unique ways. Eight woodpecker species have found conditions suitable for nesting in the state.

The yellow-bellied sapsucker (*Sphyrapicus varius*) is only a winter resident, some arriving from northern breeding areas as early as September and others staying as late as early May. These birds leave behind telltale signs of their searches for food—sapwells, which are rows of tiny holes on tree trunks and limbs. Those that produce a sweet sap are kept open by sapsuckers, who return to them periodically throughout the day to gather the sweet liquid. Horizontal rows of holes are exploratory sapwells. When a sapsucker finds sweet sap, it follows the vessel vertically with new sapwells. Contrary to popular belief, the sapsucker's holes do not kill the tree, although the tree may die. Trees produce sweet sap when mobilizing nutrients to fight off an infection such as a fungal disease. Thus, the presence of numerous vertical sapwells on a tree indicates that the tree is sick. More female sapsuckers than males visit Mississippi. Males stay

W

closer to breeding areas and acclimate to the colder weather, allowing them to return early to claim prime nesting areas.

Red-headed woodpeckers (*Melanerpes erthrocephalus*) and northern flickers (*Colaptes auratus*) nest in the state, but their resident populations are augmented each fall by migrants from farther north. Both of these birds tend to use more open habitats and often go to the ground for food, meaning that northern populations must migrate south when snow blankets the ground. The red-headed woodpecker often sallies out from tree limbs, fence posts, or utility poles to capture flying insects or to seize grasshoppers, crickets, and beetles on the ground. Red-headed woodpeckers also eat fruit in season. The northern flicker (*Colaptes auratus*) feeds extensively on ants and is the least arboreal of Mississippi woodpeckers, sometimes forsaking nests in tree cavities in favor of holes in the ground, thus allowing them to exist in somewhat treeless areas such as the Mississippi Delta.

Red-bellied (*Melanerpes carolinus*), downy (*Picoides pubescens*), hairy (*P. villosus*), red-cockaded (*P. borealis*), pileated (*Dryocopus pileatus*), and ivory-billed woodpeckers (*Campephilus principalis*) are (or were) permanent residents in the state. Most have retained healthy populations throughout the state, although the red-cockaded is endangered and now limited to localized populations in central and southern Mississippi, and the ivory-billed woodpecker may be extinct.

Red-bellied woodpeckers may be Mississippi's most common woodpecker, found in cities and towns as well as in diverse forested areas throughout the state. Red-bellied are generalists among woodpeckers, feeding on a diversity of insects, spiders, small lizards, fruit, and nuts. They also readily come to bird feeders but can be most easily attracted by half an orange impaled on a nail driven into a tree or fence posts. Red-bellieds are easily identified by the black-white barring on their backs.

The downy woodpecker is sparrow-sized and Mississippi's smallest woodpecker. A resident of city yards and forest edges, the downy has the advantage of being able to use small-diameter branches for its nest and roost cavities. One of the downy woodpecker's unique characteristics is that males (with a red patch on the back of the head) feed in different places than females (which have no red on the head). Males generally glean small insects and spiders from the surfaces of tree limbs less than two inches in diameter but also find insects on or in dried weed stems. Females, conversely, usually hunt on larger trunks and limbs. This division of the available habitat is believed to reduce competition between the sexes and thus strengthen the bond between members of a pair.

The hairy woodpecker is a larger look-alike of the downy—white-breasted below and black above, with white lines above and below the eye, a white stripe down the middle of the back, and white outer tail feathers. The smaller downy has a tiny, sharply pointed bill that is shorter than the head and has black spots on its white outer tail feathers. Hairy woodpeckers are much less common than downy and are usually found in mature forests.

The endangered red-cockaded woodpecker is perhaps the most specialized of Mississippi woodpeckers. These birds differ from all other woodpeckers in almost always nesting in the trunk of a living pine. They also characteristically excavate and maintain small holes above and below their cavity entrances, causing a continuous flow of sticky gum that is believed to protect them from climbing rat snakes. Other woodpeckers only occasionally nest in living trees; in Mississippi the red-bellied and red-headed woodpecker and the northern flicker frequently usurp the cavities of red-cockaded woodpeckers for nests or roosts. The average age of a tree housing a red-cockaded woodpecker nest is about one hundred years, because the birds depend on having the heartwood of the tree softened by a fungus that begins to enter the tree through broken branch stubs a decade or two earlier. Because of the fungus, however, foresters harvest the pines at an earlier age, leading to the massive loss of red-cockaded woodpecker habitat. The conversion of forestland to other uses and the restriction of natural fires, which create the open, parklike pine stands the birds prefer, are the main factors that have made this species endangered. Although the red-cockaded woodpecker plays many positive roles within its ecosystem, destroying insect pests and creating nest sites for more than fifty other animals, protection of this species under endangered species laws has created problems for the forest industry.

The pileated woodpecker, with a wingspan of about twenty-eight inches and a length from the tip of its bill to the tip of its tail of about eighteen inches, is the largest woodpecker most Mississippians will see. Early settlers to the region called it Indian hen because it often feeds on the ground on ants and grubs found in rotting logs, is about the size of a small chicken, and was occasionally eaten. Early visitors to the region also sometimes referred to it as the Lord God bird: it was so large that when people saw it, they exclaimed, "Lord God, what a woodpecker!" This designation was also applied to the similar but slightly larger ivory-billed woodpecker. Because of their diet of ants and practice of feeding on the ground and downed timber, pileated woodpeckers have not only survived but seem to have thrived in Mississippi. As planted city trees have grown larger, pileated woodpeckers have moved into city neighborhoods, at times to the dismay of humans, who tend to remove from urban areas the dead trees that pileated woodpeckers use for feeding and nesting. In addition, humans often use natural wood siding on homes: in the absence of suitable nesting sites, the pileated woodpecker sometimes begins to excavate the siding.

The ivory-billed woodpecker is (or was) even larger than the pileated: about thirty inches from wingtip to wingtip and twenty inches long. It is, however, either the rarest bird in America or one of the most recently extinct species. Known only from the southeastern United States and Cuba, the ivory-bill was last documented in Louisiana in 1944. Sightings in Mississippi in the 1980s were never confirmed, nor were widely publicized recent sightings in Arkansas and northwestern Florida. The ivory-billed woodpecker differs from the pileated in subtle respects, most obviously its bill, which appears to be much larger and heavier and is very white, and a shield of white on the folded wings that cross the lower back of a perched bird. The pileated has survived while the ivory-bill was brought to the brink of extinction in part because both Native Americans and early settlers saw the bill of the ivory-bill as having value and hunted the birds extensively. In part their fate was likely also sealed by their dietary preferences. They favored the nearly three-inch-long, half-inch-diameter grubs of very large beetles that were associated with very large trees. As large trees disappeared and forests were cleared or fragmented, the large beetles no doubt declined, and with them the ivory-bill.

Mississippi's William Faulkner wrote of life and culture in "The Big Woods," a name he seems to have bestowed on the region, although the name likely also referred to the bottomland forests of adjacent Arkansas to the west and has been used for a conservation partnership focused on restoring a population of ivory-billed woodpeckers in that state. In his short story "The Bear," Faulkner wrote, "He stood against the big gum tree beside a little bayou whose black still water crept without motion out of a cane-brake, across a small clearing and into the cane again, where, invisible, a bird, the big woodpecker called Lord-to-God by Negroes, clattered at a dead trunk."

Jerome A. Jackson
Florida Gulf Coast University

William Faulkner, *Big Woods: The Hunting Stories* (1955); J. H. Howard, *Memoir of the Missouri Archaeological Society* (1968); Jerome A. Jackson, in *The Birds of North America*, ed. A. Poole and F. Gill (1994); Jerome A. Jackson, *In Search of the Ivory-Billed Woodpecker* (2006); Jerome A. Jackson, with H. R. Ouellet and B. J. S. Jackson, in *The Birds of North America*, ed. A. Poole and F. Gill (2003).

Woodville Republican

In front of an old block building in Woodville stands a historical marker that reads, "*The Republican*, established in 1823 by William A. A. Chisholm, is the oldest newspaper and business institution in continuous operation in Mississippi." Chisholm continued as owner and publisher of the *Woodville Republican* until 1842, when the paper was sold to William A. Norris and Company.

John J. Leatherman followed as editor, with Owen S. Kelley as publisher. Major H. S. Van Eaton succeeded Leatherman, and W. C. Bonney followed Kelley. William J. Keller

served as editor during the beginning of the Civil War and after its close, though no editor's, publisher's, or owner's name appeared during the war. Following the war, John W. Bryant was the publisher and Capt. J. S. McNeily served as editor.

After a brief period in which Republican sheriff Henry W. Noble used his position as editor to advance his party's perspectives, the newspaper returned to the Democratic Party when Col. J. H. Jones, a former Democratic lieutenant governor, became editor in 1876.

In June 1879 Capt. John S. Lewis purchased the paper. Following Lewis's death in 1900, his son, Robert Lewis, took the helm, remaining as editor until his death in 1934. His widow, Helen Latané Lewis, subsequently became editor. After graduating from the University of Mississippi, her son, John S. Lewis, returned home to assist his mother, and in 1938 he became the youngest editor of the state's oldest newspaper.

In 1965 John Lewis was elected president of Mississippi Press Association, a position his father had held in 1907. In 1982 John Lewis became editor emeritus of the *Woodville Republican*, and his son, Andrew Jackson Lewis, became the publisher-editor. The Lewis family continues to operate the paper, as it has for more than 125 years.

In 1924 Robert Lewis wrote of a major change in the production of the paper. "George Washington," the hand-set type machine, was replaced by a linotype machine. The *Woodville Republican* continued to use the hot-type linotype process long after most newspapers had converted to more modern processes. Modernization of production came in 1980, with the purchase of Compugraphic typesetting equipment, and again in 1992, with Macintosh computers. By the second decade of the twenty-first century, the weekly paper had a circulation of approximately twenty-five hundred.

Liz McGraw
Woodville, Mississippi

A Brief History of the Woodville Republican, http://msgw.org/wilkinson/repblcn.htm; Robert Lewis, *Woodville Republican* (19 July 1924); O'Levia Neal Wilson Wiese, *The Woodville Republican: Mississippi's Oldest Existing Newspaper* (2000).

Woodward, Ellen Sullivan
(1887–1971) Politician

Ellen Sullivan Woodward, a Mississippi public official, New Deal relief work administrator, and Social Security Board member, was born on 11 July 1887 in Oxford. Her parents were William Van Amberg Sullivan, an Oxford attorney and

Ellen Sullivan Woodward (Archives and Records Services Division, Mississippi Department of Archives and History [PI STA W66.4 Box 20 R72 B4 56 Folder 89 #3])

later a US congressman and senator, and Belle Murray Sullivan. Ellen Sullivan received her education in Oxford and Washington, D.C., and for one year at Sans Souci, a South Carolina academy.

In 1906 Sullivan married Albert Y. Woodward, an attorney from Louisville, Mississippi. Their only child, a son, was born in 1909. Under the leadership of Woodward and her sister, Belle Sullivan Fair, the town's Fortnightly Club undertook a number of civic improvements that brought such acclaim to Woodward that she was elected to complete his term in the Mississippi House of Representatives after his death in 1925, becoming the second woman to serve in that body. She then joined the Mississippi State Board of Development as director of women's work. She advanced to the office of executive secretary, where her knowledge of social welfare services came to the attention of associates of Harry Hopkins. In August 1933, when Hopkins became the czar of New Deal emergency relief, he named her an assistant administrator and director of the Women's Division of the Federal Emergency Relief Administration. She retained the position when the Works Progress Administration was created in 1935, and the following year she became director of the Division of Women's and Professional Projects, which included the "Four Arts" projects for writers, actors, artists, and musicians.

With the backing of First Lady Eleanor Roosevelt, Woodward developed work programs for women, employing almost five hundred thousand people at the division's peak in February 1936. She was especially careful to see that Mississippi women in need of work relief had the ear of sympathetic supervisors. Woodward's longtime associate in Mississippi public affairs and club work, Blanche Montgomery Ralston, supervised the activities of the Division of Women's and Professional Projects in the southeastern states. More than half the women worked on projects that produced goods, especially food and clothing, or provided community services,

such as libraries, recreation activities, school lunchrooms, and health care, never before available in many communities.

Congressional dissatisfaction with the Works Progress Administration and particularly the white-collar Federal Writers' and Theatre Projects led to the resignations of both Hopkins and Woodward late in 1938. Pres. Franklin D. Roosevelt then named Woodward to serve as one of three members of the Social Security Board; at its demise in 1946 she became a division director within the new Federal Security Agency, where her concerns for social welfare expanded to the international level. Between 1943 and 1947 she was a member of the US delegation to a series of conferences of the United Nations Relief and Rehabilitation Administration. She remained with the Federal Security Agency until December 1953, when her retirement brought to an end nearly two decades of government service in Washington. She died there on 23 September 1971.

Martha H. Swain
Mississippi State University

Martha H. Swain, *Ellen S. Woodward: New Deal Advocate for Women* (1995); Martha H. Swain, *Prologue* (Winter 1983); Susan Ware, *Beyond Suffrage: Women in the New Deal* (1981); Ellen Sullivan Woodward Papers, Mississippi Department of Archives and History.

World War I

Following the demise of Reconstruction in the 1870s, the outside world troubled Mississippi but little for almost half a century. By 1920, however, the war that Woodrow Wilson hoped would end all wars had thrust the state and its people into the maelstrom of modernity. Most directly affected were the 57,740 Mississippians, three-fourths of them draftees, who marched away to make the world safe for democracy in World War I (1914–18, though the United States did not become involved until April 1917). Among them was Henry Jetton Tudury of Bay St. Louis, who became the state's most decorated doughboy and who was among the twenty-five Mississippians who earned Distinguished Service Crosses. Seven natives served as general officers, most notably Fox Conner, who as chief of the General Staff's Operations Section developed battle plans for the American Expeditionary Force. His contributions, which Gen. John J. Pershing considered indispensable to Allied victory, earned Conner a Distinguished Service Medal.

More than any other aspect of the war, the draft engulfed the Magnolia State and its people in the forces of modernization. "This office," Gov. Theodore Bilbo's secretary advised a local draft official, "is confronted with a monumental amount of work. . . . There is hardly a moment that a long distance call has not to be answered or a telegram attended to combined with an immense amount of correspondence from the War Department, inquiries from local boards, individuals, Etc." The Selective Service conducted three registrations, the last and largest of which occurred only two months before the November 1918 armistice. A total of 344,724 Mississippians registered for the draft, but few of the September 1918 pool were inducted. The sheer magnitude of national mobilization demanded a bureaucratic efficiency that overshadowed all else and ironically accentuated social and racial prejudices already deeply embedded in the state's traditional social structure. Bilbo complained to the War Department that "much confusion exists as to just who should be, and who should not be exempted on account of dependents." Perversely, class often trumped race, as white paternalism and planter self-interest converged to shield black tenant labor from federal regulations that fell more heavily on small independent farmers, black and white alike. Poor whites sometimes came to view the Great War as many of their forbears had seen the Civil War: a rich man's war but a poor man's fight.

Despite significant and occasionally violent draft resistance, most Mississippians rallied patriotically to the war effort. Hattiesburg bid for one of sixteen large National Army cantonments built during the war, and when Camp Shelby opened in the fall of 1917, it instantly became the state's largest population center. The following March, Payne Field, an aviation training facility, opened in Clay County, near West Point. Construction of the two installations sparked local economic booms. A decentralized system of councils of national defense coordinated domestic mobilization. From the state council, voluntary campaigns to sell Liberty Bonds, conserve food and fuel, promote patriotism, and harass "slackers" (people who avoided military service) percolated downward through local councils to virtually every crossroads village in the state. In the words of one contemporary, "Men, women, girls, boys, and children eagerly sought work of any kind that helped to 'carry on.'"

Thousands of Mississippians, mostly women, volunteered for Red Cross duty: cheering and entertaining soldiers; collecting clothes, magazines, canned goods, and money for army camps and soldiers' families; sewing and knitting garments for hospital patients and European refugees; adopting French orphans; writing letters and keeping scrapbooks; selling war bonds and savings stamps; and nursing soldiers and civilians. Emma Gene Wensel Venn, one of several Mississippi women who served as Red Cross nurses in Europe, became the state's only known female fatality abroad. She died in Paris in October 1918, and three years later her remains were removed from a French cemetery and reburied with full military honors in her hometown of Natchez. Venn had fallen victim to a worldwide influenza epidemic that killed far more people—perhaps one hundred million—than did the Great War itself.

The war also produced political casualties, including James K. Vardaman, one of only six US senators who voted against the declaration of war. His opposition to the Wilson administration's war policies, including the draft, fractured the forces of political reform in the state, and neither Vardaman nor Mississippi's progressive movement ever fully recovered. In 1918 the senator was defeated for reelection by Byron "Pat" Harrison of Gulfport, and Vardaman's protégé, Theodore Bilbo, despite his support for Wilson and the war, lost his bid for a seat in the US House of Representatives.

The war at first created economic crisis, disrupting the export markets on which the state's two largest revenue producers, cotton and lumber, heavily depended. Eventually, however, both commodities rebounded, and Mississippi shared fully in what turned out to be a national wartime boom. Economic prosperity, coupled with military and domestic mobilization, also spawned labor shortages, aggravated in Mississippi by a steady stream of black migration northward.

The war heightened racial tensions. As a leading black educator later recalled, the black soldier "got the idea in World War I that he was a citizen, fighting for the country just as anyone else." Patriotism at least implied citizenship, and many black Mississippians expected wartime loyalty to yield postwar reward—if not political equality, at least some access to the ballot; if not social access, at least some semblance of the equality premised in segregation. Instead, rising black expectations provoked white fears, especially regarding the anticipated return, as Vardaman put it, of "French-women-ruined negro soldiers." By 1919 racial violence reached levels rarely seen since Reconstruction. Even in the US Army, blacks endured relentless discrimination. Most served in labor battalions, and every aspect of military life was strictly segregated. Black combat veterans were excluded from the Allied victory parade in Paris. A handful of Mississippi's African American veterans lived long enough to receive belated recognition from a changed and chastened society. An assistant adjutant general of the Mississippi National Guard finally delivered Moses Hardy's official discharge papers, along with his Victory and Occupation Medals and two service bars, in 1999, eighty years after he left the army and just after his 106th birthday.

Denied the ballot—and much else—in Mississippi, blacks by 1917 had begun to vote with their feet. As foreign immigration fell from a record 1,200,000 in 1914 to barely 100,000 four years later, desperate northern employers abandoned a long-standing policy of racial exclusion and sent labor agents scurrying south. Thus began what scholars describe as "the largest mass migration in the history of the United States" and possibly "the most momentous internal population movement of the 20th century" anywhere.

Chester M. "Bo" Morgan
University of Southern Mississippi

Biennial Report of the Adjutant General of the State of Mississippi for the Years 1918–1919 to the Governor (1919); James L. McCorkle Jr., *Journal of Mississippi History* (May 1981, May 1983); Charles L. Sullivan, ed., *Journal of Mississippi History* (November 1985); Works Progress Administration, Mississippi Historical Records Survey, Mississippi Department of Archives and History.

World War II

World War II (1941–45) brought economic, social, and cultural changes to Mississippi. From the Civil War to World War II, Mississippi had historical continuity: it was predominantly agricultural, poor, racist, and insulated from the rest of the world, though World War I chipped away at that insulation. Although Mississippi did not eliminate its problems because of World War II, the state did begin to become more closely aligned with the nation as a whole.

From 1941 to 1945 Mississippians' per capita income rose from $313 (44 percent of the national average) to $627 (just over 55 percent). During this period farm mortgages declined from $102 million to $83 million as farmers paid off their debts. Yet at war's end, Mississippi still had the lowest per capita income of any state.

Between 1940 and 1945 Mississippi's farm population declined 26 percent, while the number of farms declined almost 10 percent. During the war years 30 percent of all white tenants and 14 percent of all black tenants left the farms, and most of the exodus occurred among farmers younger than age thirty-five. More than 237,000 Mississippians served in the military. Jobs opened up in the towns. Former sharecroppers could make more money in a week at Ingalls Shipbuilding in Pascagoula than they had made in a year before the war.

Travel within the United States and Europe and Asia reduced Mississippi's provincialism. Not only did Mississippians begin to see the world, but people from other states and countries came to Mississippi for training. Camp Shelby, created during World War I near Hattiesburg, was reactivated and expanded in 1940, and by 1943 the post spread over three hundred thousand acres and was home to as many as seventy-five thousand soldiers. Over the course of the war, hundreds of thousands of soldiers trained there or were inducted into or separated from the service there. In 1940 Biloxi ceded land on which the US Army Air Corps then constructed a basic training and technical training facility, Keesler Field. The installation had a peak military population of sixty-nine thousand, at which time it was the largest air base in the world.

Smaller installations were scattered across Mississippi. Camp Van Dorn was built just outside Centreville to house and train a division. Camp McCain, eight miles south of Grenada, served as many as fifty thousand troops. Foster General Hospital was built in West Jackson and activated on 14 December 1942. Army air fields sprang up across the countryside, with the largest at Greenville, Columbus, Jackson, Laurel, Greenwood, and Meridian and smaller auxiliary bases at Clarksdale, Grenada, Gulfport, Hattiesburg, Madison, and Starkville. Ordnance plants were located near Flora and at Prairie in Monroe County, near Aberdeen. A small naval base was developed at Gulfport. The military also used facilities at the University of Mississippi, Mississippi State College (now Mississippi State University), Mississippi Southern College (now the University of Southern Mississippi), Millsaps College, and Mississippi College.

German prisoners of war captured in North Africa were housed at compounds throughout Mississippi, which had four major prisoner of war camps. Camp Clinton, just outside Jackson, housed about thirty-four hundred prisoners, including the highest-ranking German officers, among them Gen. Hans-Jürgen von Arnim, who had led the Afrika Korps. The other major prisoner of war camps included Camp McCain, which housed seventy-seven hundred prisoners; Camp Shelby, which housed fifty-three hundred prisoners; and Camp Como, in the northern Delta, which at one time held thirty-eight hundred Italian soldiers who had surrendered in North Africa, though they were soon moved out of Mississippi and replaced by a smaller number of Germans. In 1944 the four base camps developed fifteen branch camps, ten of them in the Delta, where prisoners worked in the cotton fields, often in the summer heat. The other five branch camps were in the pinelands, where prisoners worked in forestry.

The war years brought attention to Mississippi's racial problems. On 25 June 1941 Pres. Franklin D. Roosevelt issued an executive order banning discrimination in war industries and addressing grievances. The subsequent national movement to remove racial barriers produced fear and tension in a state long accustomed to segregation and states' rights. Rumors about black veterans planning uprisings back home while white men were away at war led to problems with Mississippi's long allegiance to the Democratic Party. Rumors also surfaced about a 1943 massacre of black soldiers of the 364th Infantry Regiment who were stationed at Camp Van Dorn in Wilkinson County. The rumors persisted until a December 1999 US Army report repudiated the incident. By 1945 not only was the state's agrarianism disappearing, but its politics and racial institutions also were beginning to change.

John Ray Skates
University of Southern Mississippi

Robert F. Couch, *Journal of Mississippi History* (August 1964); Richard Aubrey McLemore, ed., *A History of Mississippi* (1973); Neil McMillen, ed., *Remaking Dixie: The Impact of World War II on the American South*

(1997); Mississippi History Now website, http://mshistorynow.mdah .state.ms.us; Chester M. Morgan, *Journal of Mississippi History* (Winter 1995); Merrill R. Pritchett and William L. Shea, *Journal of Mississippi History* (November 1979); John Ray Skates, *Journal of Mississippi History* (May 1975).

German prisoners of war, Camp Shelby, ca. 1940–45 (Courtesy Armed Forces Museum, Camp Shelby)

World War II Prisoner of War Camps

From 1942 to 1946 more than 440,000 German, Italian, and Japanese prisoners of war were interned in camps in the United States, including about 20,000 German and Italian prisoners who were held in Mississippi. These prisoners had been captured in North Africa, the Mediterranean, and Western Europe. Most were part of field marshal Erwin Rommel's famed Afrika Korps.

Mississippi had four base or main prisoner of war camps: Camp Clinton (Clinton), Camp Como (Como), Camp McCain (Grenada), and Camp Shelby (Hattiesburg). Base camps were typically constructed to hold 3,000 prisoners, with the men segregated by fences into compounds of 1,000 men each. Within the compound, the buildings were arranged into four companies of 250 men each. The company was made up of five barrack buildings of 50 men each, a mess hall, a latrine, and a company administration building. The compound also contained an infirmary, a canteen, a recreation building, a workshop, and an administration building. Most camp buildings were of temporary design, assembled on-site with prefabricated sections.

In March 1943 the War Department announced that prisoners of war would be made available for work in regions suffering from a shortage of labor, but not until the fall of that year did the War Department and other government interests finalize the details for contracting out prisoners. However, concerns about escapes and possible sabotage hindered the use of the prisoners and the construction of new camps. Since base camps were not always located where prisoners were needed, smaller branch camps of between 250 and 1,000 men had to be established in project areas. The War Department constructed these branch camps with less elaborate security features and with simplified housing. Branch camps were erected at eighteen locations in Mississippi between June 1943 and the second half of 1944.

A number of the branch camps were erected on the sites of abandoned Civilian Conservation Corps camps, making use of existing buildings. Others were "tent cities." Barbed wire fences, floodlights, and perhaps a few watchtowers were placed around the perimeters. Most of the branch camps were located in the Mississippi Delta, where the prisoners primarily grew and harvested cotton. In the Piney Woods region, prisoners worked in the lumber and pulpwood industries. The single greatest use of prisoner labor, however, took place at Camp Clinton. Under construction adjacent to the camp was a vast scale model of the Mississippi River Basin covering some two hundred acres. More than 1,500 prisoners helped clear the land, lay the road network and drainage system, and move tons of earth to recontour the terrain. Their work, valued at several million dollars, allowed the US Army Corps of Engineers to proceed with and complete its flood-control project. In the decades after the Basin Model's completion, data collected during tests helped save billions of dollars in property damage.

Camp Clinton was also where the highest-ranking German officers were confined. Thirty-five generals and one admiral were held in a special compound constructed specifically for them. The highest-ranking German general at Clinton was Hans-Jürgen von Arnim, who commanded all Axis forces in North Africa after Rommel's departure. One of the lesser-known but more noteworthy generals was Dietrich von Choltitz, whom Adolf Hitler had ordered to burn Paris rather than let it fall into Allied hands.

Government plans called for the repatriation of German prisoners of war to begin in July 1945. However, because of the ongoing war with Japan and a continued shortage of civilian labor, the prisoners could not be released in the numbers desired. Most of those who were repatriated were officers and noncommissioned officers not required to work, men considered troublesome, the sick and insane, and those who had been particularly cooperative with authorities.

In September 1945, following the Japanese surrender, the War Department announced that there was no longer a need to retain the prisoners of war. However, employers from all over the country, backed by local and state officials, argued that unfilled contracts and unharvested crops would cause great financial loss without sufficient labor to replace the prisoner-workers. Consequently, Pres. Harry S. Truman declared that prisoners would be withdrawn from labor starting in April 1946 and sent home by the end of June.

W

The last twenty or so of Mississippi's prisoner of war camps closed in March and April 1946.

In 2004 Mississippi author Steve Yarbrough published the novel *Prisoners of War*, based on the Mississippi Delta POW camps.

Table 1. WWII POW Camp Location	
Camp Location	**Permanent or Temporary**
Belzoni	Both
Brookhaven	Permanent
Clarksdale	Both
Cleveland	Temporary
Drew	Permanent
Elkas/Lake Washington	Permanent
Greenville	Both
Greenville Army Air Field	Permanent
Greenwood	Permanent
Greenwood Army Air Field	Permanent
Gulfport Naval Training Command	Permanent
Indianola	Both
Leland	Permanent
Merigold	Permanent
Picayune	Permanent
Richton	Permanent
Rosedale	Permanent
Saucier	Permanent

Mike Allard
Mississippi Department of
Archives and History

George G. Lewis and John Mewah, *History of Prisoner of War Utilization by the United States Army: 1776–1945* (1955); Merrill R. Prichett and William L. Shea, *Journal of Mississippi History* (November 1979); Mississippi History Now website, http://mshistorynow.mdah.state.ms.us; Records of the Provost Marshal General's Office, RG 389, Modern Military Branch, National Archives; Waterways Experiment Station Archives, Vicksburg.

WorldCom

WorldCom was at one time the second-largest long-distance telecommunications corporation in the United States, and its roots were in Mississippi. The corporation imploded in scandal, resulting in prison time for its cofounder.

The company began in a Hattiesburg coffee shop in 1983 when businessmen Murray Waldron and William Rector set out a plan to create a telephone service provider that they called Long-Distance Discount Services (LDDS). In 1985 the company named as its chief executive officer Bernard Ebbers, a Canadian-born former basketball star at Mississippi College who was known for serving meals to the homeless at Frank's Famous Biscuits in downtown Jackson and for wearing jeans, cowboy boots, and a turquoise watch to work.

Under Ebbers's leadership, LDDS grew tremendously. The company went public in 1989 through the acquisition of Advantage Companies and over the next decade built itself into a US telecommunications giant through acquisitions and mergers with companies such as Advanced Telecommunications (1992), Resurgens Communications Group and Metromedia Communications (1993), IDB Communications Groups (1994), Williams Telecommunications Group (1995), MFS Communications Group (1996), and, most significantly, CompuServe, Brooks Fiber Properties, and MCI Communications (1998).

After the 1995 acquisition, LDDS became known as WorldCom, and the 1998 merger with MCI Communications was worth forty billion dollars, the largest merger in history to date. In 1999 WorldCom announced an agreement to merge with Sprint, leading WorldCom's stock to peak at sixty-four dollars per share. In its heyday, the company's operations were organized into three divisions: MCI WorldCom, which included US telecommunications; UUNet WorldCom, which provided Internet and technology services; and WorldCom International. At the turn of the twenty-first century, MCI WorldCom was the second-largest long distance company in the United States behind AT&T, was a Wall Street darling, and was poised for continued growth and success.

However, when the US Justice Department forced the abandonment of the proposed merger with Sprint, WorldCom's stock values started to decline. In addition, banks began to pressure Ebbers to cover his margin calls on the WorldCom stock he had used to finance his personal timber and yachting businesses. In 2001 Ebbers received a corporate loan of more than $400 million from the WorldCom board of directors to cover the margin calls in hopes that he would not need to sell substantial company stock. This strategy failed, but the financial confusion surrounding the loans caught the eye of WorldCom internal auditor Cynthia Cooper, a native of Clinton, Mississippi. After discovering a string of accounting irregularities, Cooper and her team began investigating in March 2002, often working at night and in secret to avoid arousing suspicion. Within a few months the internal auditors had uncovered a $3.8 billion accounting fraud, again the largest in US history to that time. On 21 December 2002 *Time* magazine recognized Cooper as one of its three Persons of the Year for her efforts.

In April 2002 John Sidgmore, the former chief executive officer of UUNet Technologies, replaced Ebbers at World-

Com's helm, though Sidgmore was forced out less than a year later. By June 2002, others involved in the three-year fraud scheme—including chief financial officer Scott Sullivan, comptroller David Myers, and director of general accounting Buford Yates—had all been terminated. On 21 July 2002 WorldCom filed for Chapter 11 bankruptcy protection in what was then the largest such filing in US history. After a year of restructuring, WorldCom changed its name to MCI and relocated its corporate headquarters from Clinton, Mississippi, to Ashburn, Virginia, in April 2003. In March 2005 Ebbers was convicted of fraud, conspiracy, and filing false documents with Securities and Exchange Commission regulators. He was sentenced to twenty-five years in prison.

Verizon acquired MCI in a January 2006 deal worth $8.44 billion and is now known as Verizon Enterprise Solutions.

Eva Walton Kendrick
Birmingham, Alabama

Amy Barrett and Peter Elstrom, *Business Week* (14 July 1997); Philip L. Cantelon, *The History of MCI: 1968–1988, the Early Years* (1993); Funding Universe website, www.fundinguniverse.com; Dennis Moberg and Edward Romar, Santa Clara University website, www.scu.edu; Marguerite Reardon, "Verizon Closes Book on MCI Merger" (6 January 2006), http://www.cnet.com/news/verizon-closes-book-on-mci-merger/.

Wright, Early
(1915–1999) Disc Jockey

Known as the Soul Man, Early Wright became Mississippi's first black disc jockey when he started work at Clarksdale's WROX in 1947.

Early Lee Wright was born in Jefferson, Mississippi, on 10 February 1915 and moved to Clarksdale in 1937. His pre-radio jobs included farming, operating a train, running a mechanic shop, and managing a gospel group, the Four Star Quartet.

Wright hosted many well-known musicians on his radio program, including Muddy Waters, B. B. King, Sonny Boy Williamson II, Pinetop Perkins, Robert Nighthawk, and Elvis Presley. In the early 1950s Wright helped introduce a young Ike Turner to radio audiences; Turner went on to host a weekly show on WROX and played live broadcasts with his band, the Kings of Rhythm, and with his wife, Tina Turner. Assuming that listeners knew the music he played, Wright rarely gave the name of the song or artist. He had a very personal delivery, creating a down-home feel to his radio broadcasts. Much of his banter was related to community events, church announcements, and even minor local occurrences: "I want to let you know that some snakes has been seen in the Roundyard neighborhood. The grass has grown up around the sidewalks and snakes has been seen, looking for water. And a man told me the other day, he saw a snake in the street." All of his announcements were unscripted, and he put his personal stamp on advertisements: "At the M&F Grocery and Market, the aisles are so big that two shopping carts can pass each other and never bump into each other." Members of Wright's large audience, which included both black and white listeners, would call into WROX and request blues, soul, gospel, and R&B songs.

Wright's long, distinguished career resulted in the creation of an annual lecture at the University of Mississippi's Center for the Study of Southern Culture in the 1980s and 1990s. Every year, the Sunflower River Blues and Gospel Festival in Clarksdale gives the Early Wright Blues Heritage Award to nonmusicians who have helped "preserve, promote, perpetuate, and document blues in the Mississippi Delta."

Wright retired from broadcasting in 1998 and died of a heart attack on 10 December 1999.

Greg Johnson
University of Mississippi

Kenneth Bays, *Blues Revue* (March 2000); Douglas Martin, *New York Times* (17 December 1999); Panny Mayfield, *Living Blues* (May–June 2000); Andy McWilliams, *Living Blues* (September–October 1988).

Wright, Fielding L.
(1895–1956) Forty-Ninth and Fiftieth Governor, 1946–1952

When the Democratic Party nominated Harry S. Truman and adopted a strong civil rights platform in 1948, southern Democrats organized the States' Rights Democratic Party, popularly known as the Dixiecrats. The party nominated J. Strom Thurmond of South Carolina for president and Gov. Fielding L. Wright of Mississippi for vice president. Thurmond and Wright carried four southern states but failed in their effort to throw the presidential election into the US House of Representatives. The organization of the Dixiecrat Party offered an early indication, however, that white southerners would resist changes in race relations.

Fielding Lewis Wright was born in Rolling Fork, Mississippi, on 16 May 1895 to Frances Foote Clements Wright and Henry James Wright, members of a politically active family. After serving in World War I, Fielding Wright returned to Mississippi vowing that he would never become a "dang

Fielding L. Wright (Archives and Records Services Division, Mississippi Department of Archives and History [PI STA W75.3 Box 20 Folder 72 56 Folder 91 #3])

politician." He played semipro baseball for a time before studying law at the University of Alabama and reading law with an uncle, and he then opened a law office in Rolling Fork. He turned down several opportunities to seek public office but finally ran for and won a seat in the State Senate in 1928. Four years later he was elected to the Mississippi House of Representatives, where he served until 1940. During his second term, he was elected Speaker of the House, and he used that position to strongly support industrial development and highway construction. He tended to identify with Delta planters and South Mississippi oil companies.

In 1943 Wright was elected lieutenant governor. Because Mississippi's lieutenant governor serves as the presiding officer of the State Senate, Wright became one of only two men in the twentieth century to chair both houses of the Mississippi legislature. When Gov. Thomas Lowry Bailey died on 2 November 1946, Wright ascended to the state's top office. Wright then won a full term in the following year's gubernatorial election, parlaying his opposition to civil rights and support for states' rights into a rare first-primary victory over four opponents.

Consistently referring to his supporters as "true Democrats" and "true Jacksonian Democrats," Wright led statewide and regional efforts to oppose Truman's civil rights platform. Speaking at his 1948 gubernatorial inauguration, he threatened to leave the Democratic Party if it continued to support African American rights, and he encouraged others to join him. He became a leader in the movement to form a southern Democratic Party, proposing and then leading the group's first meeting, which took place in Jackson in the spring of 1948. Wright was a prominent figure in the Dixiecrats' July convention in Birmingham, along with

Thurmond, Frank Dixon of Alabama, and Mississippi senators James Eastland and John Stennis and representatives John Bell Williams and William Colmer. Mississippi voters then gave the States' Rights Democrats a large majority in the 1948 presidential election.

Wright's term as governor expired in 1952, when he opened a Jackson law office. He made one last unsuccessful bid for the governorship in 1955 and continued practicing law until his death in Jackson on 4 May 1956.

David G. Sansing
University of Mississippi

Kari Frederickson, *The Dixiecrat Revolt and the End of the Solid South, 1932–1968* (2001); *Jackson Daily News* (8 December 1946); National Governors Association website, www.nga.org; Fielding L. Wright Subject File, Mississippi Department of Archives and History.

Wright, Frank Lloyd, Houses

Frank Lloyd Wright (1867–1959), the American architect famous for his Prairie Style, designed—or at least is credited with designing—four houses in Mississippi. Two of the houses were totally destroyed by hurricanes, while two have been restored.

The first bungalow in Ocean Springs (1890) was designed for Wright's employer and mentor, Louis Sullivan. Sullivan wanted a summer home next door to his friends, Helen and James Charnley, who transferred some of their land to him in exchange for house plans. While there are conflicting accounts regarding who designed both the Sullivan and Charnley properties, the general thought is that Wright, who was a junior architect in the firm of Sullivan and Adler, did the drafting for both Ocean Springs properties.

The Sullivan house was a traditional dogtrot house, with bedrooms on either side of a central living room and a porch across the front, facing Davis Bayou. The stable, demolished in 1942, was a smaller version of the main house. Some renovations throughout the years altered the main structure, but a full restoration in the 1980s brought the bungalow back to its original state. On 30 August 2005, however, Hurricane Katrina destroyed the main house, leaving only a chimney.

The three James Charnley buildings next door (1890) included a main bungalow, a guesthouse, and a stable cottage. The bungalow was similar in plan to Sullivan's, though larger and more detailed. The guesthouse and stable cottage repeated the octagonal detailing found in each corner of the main bungalow. Hurricane Katrina knocked the Charnley bungalow off its foundation, caved in part of the roof, and destroyed the porch and front doors. The Mississippi Department of Archives and History, the Mississippi Department of Marine Resources, the Mississippi Heritage Trust, and the City of Ocean Springs have worked together to restore the house, which the State of Mississippi purchased for $1.4 million in 2011. In 2014 it received the Mississippi Heritage Trust's Heritage Award for Preservation Education and the Trustees Award for Exemplary Restoration of a Mississippi Landmark, and it opened to the public in September 2015.

The J. Willis Hughes Residence, also known as Fountainhead, was built in 1948 and is located in Jackson's Woodland Hills neighborhood. By 1948 Wright's work had evolved into the recognizable modern style for which he was known, and Fountainhead has many Wright hallmarks. The building features concrete walls, a slab floor, and cypress paneling throughout the interior. Its most distinctive feature, aside from its angles and copper roof partially hidden below street level, is the bedroom wing, which ends with a wall of windows looking out onto the fountain that cascades into the wading pool below. After falling into disrepair, the house was entirely restored by Jackson architect Robert Parker Adams, and since 1980 it has been listed on the National Register of Historic Places.

The last Wright-designed house in Mississippi was the Welbie L. Fuller residence in Pass Christian (1951). This large, modern house had many unusual features, such as a post-and-panel structure and exposed asbestos panels for walls and ceilings. It also featured heart pine floors on two of the three floors, copper flashing, and Wright-designed furnishings throughout. On 17 August 1969 Hurricane Camille demolished the structure.

Tracy Carr Seabold
Mississippi Library Commission

"Charnley-Norwood House to Open for Tours" (2 September 2015), http://www.dmr.ms.gov/index.php/news-a-events/recent-news/826-15-59-mms; Michael Martinez and Blair Kamin, *Chicago Tribune* (8 September 2005); Mississippi Heritage Trust website, www.mississippiheritage.com; William Allin Storrer, *The Architecture of Frank Lloyd Wright: A Complete Catalog* (1979); William Allin Storrer, *The Frank Lloyd Wright Companion* (1993).

Wright, Richard
(1908–1960) Author

Author Richard Nathaniel Wright, who was named after both his maternal and paternal grandfathers, was born on 4 September 1908 on Rucker's Plantation in the Cranfield-Roxie

Richard Wright, ca. 1940 (Department of Archives and Special Collections, J. D. Williams Library, University of Mississippi)

area in northeast Adams County, some twenty miles from Natchez. His father, Nathan Wright, was a sharecropper, and his mother, Ella Wilson Wright, was a schoolteacher. It is reasonable to believe that his parentage and his childhood and youth in Mississippi had a strong impact on his personality and on the works he published from the mid-1930s until his death on 28 November 1960 in Paris. His father was a laborer, with hands that worked the earth, dealing stoically with the concrete materials of life; in sharp contrast, his mother was a thinker, a dreamer whose mind explored the realms of abstract ideas and the imagination. Wright, who went on to become one of Mississippi's most famous native sons, combined the best qualities of both parents.

Wright and his younger brother, Leon Alan Wright, experienced displacement and poverty during their earliest years. As Wright explains in dramatic detail in his autobiography, *Black Boy* (1945), his family migrated from Natchez to Memphis in 1913. His father's desertion of the family when Wright was only seven forced his mother to work at low-paying jobs to support her sons. His mother then began having health problems, and he and his brother lived briefly with his maternal grandparents in Jackson before moving to live with an aunt, Maggie Hoskins, in Elaine, Arkansas. Then his uncle, Silas Hoskins, was murdered, and the Wright boys moved first to West Helena, Arkansas, and then back to Jackson. Wright also lived for a year with another uncle and aunt, Clark and Jodie Wilson, in Greenwood before returning to Jackson. The frequent moves resulted in an uneven education. In Memphis, Wright attended Howe Institute (1915–16); in Jackson, he attended the Seventh Day Adventist school (1920–21), spent the fifth through seventh grades at the Jim Hill School, and attended eighth and ninth grade at Smith Robertson Junior High School, graduating in May 1925. He attended Lanier High School for only a few

W

weeks before dropping out to work. Wright moved to Memphis in 1925 and to Chicago in 1927.

Wright was very sensitive to the pain of depending on the kindness of relatives, and his perspectives on life and the dominant themes in his fiction and nonfiction were shaped by the metaphor of hunger he associated with his father: "As the days slid past, the image of my father became associated with my pangs of hunger, and when I felt hunger I thought to him with a deep biological bitterness." The young Wright also resented his Wilson grandmother's strict Seventh Day Adventist beliefs, although he later wrote positively in the unpublished essay "Memories of My Grandmother" about how those beliefs informed his understanding of the folk mind and southern black culture. In his major novels—*Native Son* (1940), *The Outsider* (1953), and *The Long Dream* (1958)—Wright expressed deep suspicion regarding the benefits of religious belief in dealing with the physical, psychological, social, and spiritual problems in southern and American cultures. Wright found solace in his love of reading, which enabled him to discover worlds beyond Mississippi's closed society. Nevertheless, the segregation and racial customs of Mississippi and the South, which promoted what he called the humiliating "ethics of living Jim Crow," made Wright one of the twentieth century's severest critics of human hypocrisy.

As a teenager Wright published a short story, "The Voodoo of Hell's Half-Acre," in the *Southern Register*, a Jackson black newspaper, but his commitment to a life of writing was fueled by his discovery in Memphis of such writers as H. L. Mencken, Theodore Dreiser, and Sherwood Anderson. As a member of the Chicago branch of the communist-sponsored John Reed Club, Wright gained critical notice for the quality of his proletarian poetry in *Left Front*, *Anvil*, *Partisan Review*, and *New Masses*. In the 1930s Wright honed his writing skills through his association with leftist writers when he joined the Communist Party in 1934 and through his work with the Works Progress Administration's Federal Writers' Project. Wright moved to New York in 1937, the year his short story "Fire and Cloud" won first prize in a *Story* magazine contest. This achievement led to the publication of *Uncle Tom's Children* (1938), stories about rural southern life. He married Dhima Rose Meadman in 1939.

His fame as a writer was assured with the appearance of his landmark novel, *Native Son* (1940), and his classic autobiography, *Black Boy* (1945). The year 1941 was good for Wright: he received the prestigious Spingarn Medal from the National Association for the Advancement of Colored People for his distinguished achievements in *Uncle Tom's Children* and *Native Son*, and *12 Million Black Voices*, a text illustrated with Farm Security Administration photographs, marked Wright's foray into writing vernacular history. In addition, having divorced his first wife, he married Ellen Poplar on 12 March 1941, and they went on to have two daughters, Julia and Rachel.

Wright made a public break with the Communist Party in "I Tried to Be a Communist" (1944). He had discovered that the party was a god who failed. However, his exposure to Marxist ideologies broadened his meditations on world affairs and made him an especially keen observer of humanity's condition in the twentieth century. It also subjected him to surveillance and harassment by government agencies in the United States and abroad. But Wright never abandoned the insights he gained as a Mississippian, a southerner, a man equipped by his experiences to be a participant-observer. In this sense Wright may well have created the most expansive international vision of all Mississippi writers.

Literary fame did not satisfy Wright's hunger for freedom and human rights. In 1947 he moved his family to Paris, seeking an atmosphere in which to explore the meaning of being human without the necessity of carrying overmuch racial baggage. Some American critics castigated him for abandoning the United States and his privileged niche as a spokesman for black Americans. Conversely, his exile in France greatly increased his reputation among foreign readers and his opportunities for intellectual exchanges with African and European writers. *The Outsider* (1953), a novel marked by Wright's growing interest in existentialism and his revised thinking about communism and fascism, sought to illuminate how freedom from social responsibilities might serve as a powerful force in art. He discovered in this book and in *Savage Holiday* (1954) and *The Long Dream* (1958) that genuine freedom entails tremendous moral obligations, and he explored issues of law and morality in some detail in his unfinished novel, *A Father's Law* (posthumously published in 2008).

During Wright's thirteen years in exile he created a remarkable body of political writing and travel literature. *Black Power* (1954) was a compelling record of his investigation of the independence movement in the Gold Coast (later Ghana). *The Color Curtain* (1956) was an engaging report on the 1955 Bandung Conference in Indonesia, where Asian and African nations debated their futures in the global order. In *Pagan Spain* (1957), Wright speculated about the peaceful coexistence of Franco's fascism and Roman Catholicism. His collection of lectures, *White Man, Listen!* (1957), was prophetic in its treatment of modernization and the residue of colonialism. Wright also returned to writing poetry, creating approximately 4,000 haiku, 817 of which were published in *Haiku: This Other World* (1998). Other works published after his death were *Eight Men* (1961), *Lawd Today!* (1963), *American Hunger* (1977), and *Rite of Passage* (1994).

Richard Wright, Mississippi's native son, created a body of work that continues to challenge readers. He was a realist, a writer capable of delivering strong critiques of humanity's promise and foibles with wry humor and vivid images. Whether his works deal with the rural South or the urban North or with foreign lands, with the antics and tortured desires of fictional characters or the veiled motives of historical figures, they broadcast Wright's very southern preoccupation with history. Like many southern writers, his writings offer readers an opportunity to "win some redeeming meaning for their having struggled and suffered here beneath the stars."

Jerry W. Ward Jr.
New Orleans, Louisiana

Richard Crossman, ed., *The God That Failed* (1965); Michel Fabre, *The Unfinished Quest of Richard Wright* (1973); Addison Gayle, *Richard Wright: Ordeal of a Native Son* (1980); Yoshinobu Hakutani, *Richard Wright and Racial Discourse* (1996); Abdul R. JanMohamed, *The Death-Bound Subject: Richard Wright's Archaeology of Death* (2005); Hazel Rowley, *Richard Wright: The Life and Times* (2001); Virginia Whatley Smith, ed., *Richard Wright's Travel Writings* (2001); Margaret Walker, *Richard Wright: Daemonic Genius* (1988); Jerry W. Ward Jr. and Robert J. Butler, eds., *The Richard Wright Encyclopedia* (2008); Constance Webb, *Richard Wright: A Biography* (1968).

Wurlitzer

Franz Rudolph Wurlitzer established the Wurlitzer Company in Cincinnati, Ohio, in 1856, selling band instruments to the military. The company rapidly expanded, and within a century manufactured pianos, harps, pipe organs (most famously the Mighty Wurlitzer), jukeboxes, and electronic organs and pianos. Wurlitzer moved its corporate headquarters from Cincinnati to Chicago, and launched additional divisions in North Tonawanda, New York, and DeKalb, Illinois.

When the company began to manufacture electric pianos in the early 1950s, its existing facilities could not accommodate the entire task. When Wurlitzer leaders searched for suitable manufacturing locations, Corinth, Mississippi, caught their eye. The company took advantage of the state's Balance Agriculture with Industry (BAWI) program, which lured businesses by offering incentives to locate in Mississippi. Corinth had other advantages as well, among them abundant natural resources, inexpensive rail rates, and cheap electricity. On 10 May 1956 Wurlitzer celebrated a century of business with the grand opening of its Corinth plant. "Wurlitzer Day" in Corinth featured a parade, speeches by company officials and political leaders, plant tours and an open house, a barbecue, and musical entertainment.

The Corinth plant manufactured component parts for electronic pianos and assembled electronic pianos and organs. Corinth operations later expanded to include factories in Holly Springs and Rienzi, about ten miles south of Corinth, where printed circuit boards were produced.

As technology changed, however, Wurlitzer struggled to keep up, and the Baldwin Piano and Organ Company purchased the company in 1986. The following year production ended in Corinth and all operations were transferred to the Holly Springs factory, which had made piano actions, wooden parts for grandfather clock kits, and wooden cabinets for the pianos made in Corinth. The Holly Springs factory closed in 1989. The Gibson Guitar Corporation purchased Baldwin's assets in 2001 and Wurlitzer's German operations five years later. It continues to make jukeboxes in Germany under the Wurlitzer name.

Kristy White
Corinth, Mississippi

Ed Gaida, *Mechanical Music Digest* (March 1998); "Gibson Acquires Deutsche Wurlitzer," *Music Trades* (2006); Gibson Guitar website, www.gibson.com; Wurlitzer Company, *Wurlitzer World of Music, 1856–1956* (1956).

Wynette, Tammy (Virginia Wynette Pugh)
(1942–1998) Country Musician

Virginia Wynette Pugh was born on 5 May 1942 on a cotton farm in Itawamba County to musician William Hollis Pugh and Mildred Faye Pugh. William Pugh died when his daughter was less than a year old, and his widow left Tammy in the care of her grandparents while working in a defense plant during World War II. In addition to picking cotton, Pugh had music lessons, played her father's instruments, and sang in a trio on a gospel radio show. A month before her high school graduation she married Euple Byrd, and she gave birth to two daughters within three years. Because her husband, a construction worker, was frequently unemployed, she held a variety of jobs, including working as a waitress, a bartender, and a receptionist, before enrolling in cosmetology school in Tupelo. After receiving her beautician's license she moved with her family to Birmingham, Alabama, where her marriage ended around the time of the birth of her third daughter. She spent a year working and traveling back and forth to Nashville in hopes of starting a country music career; unsuccessful, she moved to the city anyway in 1966.

She soon met producer-songwriter Billy Sherrill of Epic Records, who signed her and changed her name to Tammy Wynette. Her first single, "Apartment #9" (1966), received airplay, and her next song, "Your Good Girl's Going to Go Bad" (1967), reached the Top 10. Her third single, "I Don't Want to Play House" (1967) became the first in a string of six straight Wynette releases that topped the country charts: "Take Me to Your World" (1967), "D-I-V-O-R-C-E" (1968), "Stand by Your Man" (1968), "Singing My Song" (1969), and

W

"The Way to Love a Man" (1969). Her next eleven albums also reached No. 1, and within four years, Wynette won two Grammy Awards and three Female Vocalist of the Year awards from the Country Music Association.

After a brief second marriage Wynette married George Jones and had a fourth daughter, Georgette. The extraordinarily popular couple, who divorced in 1975, recorded a series of duets, including "(We're Not) The Jet Set" (1974), "Golden Ring" (1976), and "Two Story House" (1980). In 1978, after another short marriage, Wynette wed her fifth husband, George Richey, who served as her manager for much of the next decade. In 1979 Wynette published her autobiography, *Stand by Your Man*, and two years later ABC broadcast a movie adapted from her book.

Despite her public success, Wynette's life included private difficulties, including abuse, death threats, bankruptcy, and health issues, which included an addiction to painkillers for which she sought treatment at the Betty Ford Clinic in 1986. She nevertheless continued to tour and record, ultimately releasing twenty No. 1 songs and selling more than three million records and earning the title First Lady of Country Music. Wynette's soulful ballads are powerful and raw, with complex lyrics that often have ambivalent meanings. She sang about the difficulties of inequalities within marriage, the heartache of divorce and its effect on children, and the struggles of motherhood.

Wynette died suddenly on 6 April 1998. Her nationally televised funeral was held at the Ryman Auditorium in Nashville, and later in 1998 she was elected to the Country Music Hall of Fame.

Minoa Uffelman
Austin Peay University

Jackie Daly, *Tammy Wynette: A Daughter Recalls Her Mother's Tragic Life and Death* (2000); Kenneth E. Morris, *Popular Music and Society* 16 (1992); Tammy Wynette website, www.tammywynette.com.

Y

Yalobusha County

Located in north-central Mississippi, Yalobusha County was founded in 1833. Named after the Yalobusha River, the county has two seats, Water Valley and Coffeeville. In its first census in 1840, Yalobusha County had a population of 12,248, with 56 percent of residents free and 44 percent enslaved. With 195 people working in industry, the new county had Mississippi's fifth-highest number of manufacturing employees.

By 1860 Yalobusha County's population had topped 16,000, and 56 percent of residents were enslaved. Yalobusha's farms and plantations practiced mixed agriculture, concentrating on corn, livestock, and cotton. Likely because it was a railroad center, Yalobusha attracted a large number of immigrants. In 1860 the county was home to 345 foreign-born free people, the second-highest number in Mississippi. Most were German, English, and Irish.

As in much of Mississippi, Methodists and Baptists dominated religious life in 1860. The county had fifteen Baptist congregations, thirteen Methodist churches, and eight Presbyterian churches.

Coffeeville was the site of Civil War fighting in 1862, when Confederate forces led by William Edwin Baldwin clashed with Union troops under Ulysses S. Grant. After the war, Mississippi military and political leaders Edward Cary Walthall and L. Q. C. Lamar had a law practice for a time in Coffeeville.

The population remained steady in the early postbellum period, and in 1880 African Americans made up a small majority of Yalobusha's 15,649 people. About half of the county's farmers owned their land, and while manufacturing employed only 44 residents, the railroad became crucial to county life. The first labor union in the state, the Brotherhood of Locomotive Engineers, organized in Water Valley in 1869, and famed railroad martyr Casey Jones belonged to a Water Valley union. In the 1870s more than 400 Swedish immigrants lived in Yalobusha County, most of them working for the railroads.

In 1900 Yalobusha County was home to 19,742 people, with African Americans slightly outnumbering whites. The county had a substantial industrial workforce of 420 men and 54 women employed by 57 establishments. As in many parts of Mississippi, most white farmers (just over half) owned their land, while most black farmers (81 percent) worked as tenants and sharecroppers. In the 1930s boosters in Water Valley claimed the town as the Watermelon Capital of the World, and the town hosts an annual Watermelon Festival.

Three writers of note grew up in Yalobusha County in the late 1800s and early 1900s. Historian Dunbar Rowland, born in the small town of Oakland in 1864, became the first director of the Mississippi Department of Archives and History in 1902 and continued in the position until his death in 1937. He wrote and edited numerous works, including a two-volume history of the state published in 1925. Poet and novelist Hubert Creekmore was born in Water Valley in 1907, attended the University of Mississippi in the 1920s, and set much of his work in Mississippi. Journalist Minnie Brewer was born in Water Valley, though her family moved to Clarksdale during her childhood.

Yalobusha's population declined slightly in the early twentieth century, falling to 17,750 by 1930. Whites outnumbered African Americans by about 1,200. Despite the increasing size of Coffeeville, the county retained its agricultural economy with 2,710 farms, two-thirds of them run by tenant farmers.

The county's population declined more dramatically in the mid-twentieth century and by 1960 was just 12,502. Almost a third of the working population had jobs in agriculture, and about 15 percent worked in manufacturing, especially in the apparel industry.

By 2010, Yalobusha County, like many nearby counties in north-central Mississippi, had a predominantly white population and had shown no significant change in size since 1960. An arts community developed in Water Valley, in part as a result of Fat Possum Records, a creative blues studio founded in the 1990s. In 2010 the county had 12,678 residents.

Mississippi Encyclopedia Staff
University of Mississippi

Mississippi State Planning Commission, *Progress Report on State Planning in Mississippi* (1938); *Mississippi Statistical Abstract*, Mississippi State University (1952–2010); Charles Sydnor and Claude Bennett, *Mississippi History* (1939); University of Virginia Library, Historical Census Browser website, http://mapserver.lib.virginia.edu; E. Nolan Waller and Dani A. Smith, *Growth Profiles of Mississippi's Counties, 1960–1980* (1985).

Y

Yarbrough, Steve

(b. 1956) Author

Though he has lived most of his adult life outside Mississippi, Steve Yarbrough and his fiction have deep roots in the Magnolia State. Born in Indianola on 29 August 1956 to John and Earlene Yarbrough, he attended local schools and then enrolled at the University of Mississippi, where he earned a bachelor's degree in 1979 and a master's degree in 1981. He earned a master of fine arts degree from the University of Arkansas in 1984 and taught at Virginia Tech for four years before moving to California State University at Fresno, where he held an endowed professorship in creative writing.

Yarbrough began publishing short stories in such journals such as the *Missouri Review* and *Southern Review* in 1982. He subsequently published three collections of stories, *Family Men* (1990), *Mississippi History* (1994), and *Veneer* (1998). He received a fellowship from the National Endowment for the Arts in 1994, and "The Rest of Her Life" was included in the *Best American Short Stories of 1999*. That year he published *The Oxygen Man*, a novel that earned Yarbrough several significant awards. Alfred A. Knopf published Yarbrough's next novels, *Visible Spirits* (2001) and *Prisoners of War* (2004). He has also published creative nonfiction, reviewed books and music for the *Oxford American* and other periodicals, and written screenplays.

A wide-ranging imagination and a willingness to tackle difficult subjects set Yarbrough apart from many of his peers. Almost all his fiction is set in the Mississippi Delta, and he has written masterfully about the physical and metaphorical changes in the Delta landscape, race and racism, and family members struggling to coexist. Like William Faulkner, he often employs alternating points of view, with two characters, Daze and Ned Rose, in *The Oxygen Man* and upward of ten

Steve Yarbrough (Courtesy Antonina Yarbrough)

in *Visible Spirits*. In *Visible Spirits* and *Prisoners of War* he visits historical periods beyond his own. Yarbrough admits the influence of such popular fiction writers as Graham Greene, who likely provided a model for the taut, suspenseful plots found in Yarbrough's fiction, especially the inexorable movement toward *The Oxygen Man*'s violent crisis. His straightforward prose runs counter to the lush stylings of Faulkner; Yarbrough calls less attention to language and more to characters, each of whom—whether sharecroppers or bankers, men or women, children or parents, blacks or whites—he humanizes with a unique depth.

Yarbrough has published three additional novels: *The End of California* (2006), *Safe from the Neighbors* (2010), and *The Realm of Last Chances* (2013). He won the Richard Wright Award for Literary Excellence in 2010.

In 2009 Yarborough left California to teach in the master of fine arts program at Emerson College. Despite his travels, his fiction may never stray far from the Delta, which Yarbrough claims is "limitless. I could tell any story I wanted and set it there."

Thomas Williams
Morehead State University

Jessica Anya Blau, Nervous Breakdown website, www.thenervousbreakdown.com; Mississippi Writers and Musicians website, www.mswritersandmusicians.com; Thomas Williams, *Arkansas Review* (August 2000); Steve Yarbrough website, www.steveyarbrough.net.

Yardscapes, Vernacular

The yard is a significant aspect of Mississippi's rural culture and history. The term *yardscape* often refers to the domestic compound surrounding the house and containing structures, artifacts, art, and areas for growing plants and trees, doing household chores, socializing, and raising livestock. The yard also sometimes functions as a compound that contains multiple dwellings whose residents are connected by extended kinship networks. Yardscapes are also referred to as *houseyards* or *vernacular yards*: they belong to ordinary people and are not designed by landscape architects.

The yardscape is integrated with other aspects of culture such as economic status, foodways, gender, and ethnicity. Scholars from many disciplines, including archaeology, folklore, cultural geography, and landscape architecture, have studied houseyards or yardscapes. Studies often focus on the ties between past and present layout, the yardscapes' function, and their material culture. Students of contemporary vernacular yardscapes often focus on the traditional gardening and other subsistence activities, social behavior, and folk art displayed in the yard.

In Mississippi, rural small farmers, enslaved people, and tenants used their yards for subsistence purposes. They slept and stored materials in the dwellings, but most of daily life—cooking, washing, gardening, child care, and animal tending—occurred in the domestic outdoor space surrounding the dwellings. Outbuildings such as livestock pens, outhouses, kitchens, storage pits, and smokehouses were found in the yard area, with the most necessary located close to the house and the less desirable, like the outhouse, located on the periphery of the yard. The domestic space around the house contained chickens, pigs, and milk cows and a water source such as a well or a cistern; streams or other bodies of water were often located close by. People hunted and fished and gathered wild berries, nuts, and fruits from nearby woods. The kitchen garden was vital for survival, providing vegetables, fruit, and herbs for most of the year.

One major component of the yardscape both today and in the past is the garden. Native Americans, European Americans, and African Americans have profoundly affected the nature of the garden. Native American crops that are still grown in today's gardens include corn, beans, squash, gourds, and sunflowers. European Americans in Mississippi, mostly Scots-Irish and English, brought many fruits and vegetables grown in Europe, including some that were South American in origin—potatoes, tomatoes, and lima beans. They also imposed a lasting structure on the landscape through the utilitarian division of space in land use. African Americans brought with them many traditions as well as crops such as rice, okra, black-eyed peas, cassava, yams, kidney beans, millet, and sorghum.

Yard layout and use remained similar between the antebellum and postbellum eras, although emancipation and modernization affected material culture and land use. The divisions of social and physical spaces, mass production of goods, mechanization, capitalism, the railroad industry, and the modernization of houses affected postbellum and contemporary houseyards. At the turn of the twentieth century increased access to the market brought more outbuildings, more space, and more tools into the houseyard area. The division of labor according to gender became more visible with the advent of Victorian values: women cooked and tended the gardens and children, while men's chores revolved around the livestock and farming.

World War II modernized farming and household maintenance, bringing many upkeep activities like dishwashing, cooking, and laundry indoors. However, scholars studying how contemporary people use yards in less industrialized areas such the Caribbean and the Deep South have shown that many people, especially the elderly, still engage in yard sweeping, livestock care, child care, and gardening based on traditions passed on through generations. For example, some people still garden by the moon, burn trash, make soap, churn butter, use plants and herbs for healing, and pick their residences according to proximity to kin. Contemporary vernacular landscapes bear the imprint of modernization but still show close ties to the rural nature of Mississippi. Today, studies of yardscapes focus largely on gardening and the display of folk art.

Jennifer Abraham
Louisiana State University

Jennifer Abraham, "Ethnoarchaeology of Rural African-American Houseyards, Natchez Mississippi" (master's thesis, University of Southern Mississippi, 2001); Jennifer Abraham, *Mississippi Folklife* (Summer 1998); Michael Craton, *Searching for the Invisible Man: Slaves and Plantation Life in Jamaica* (1978); Brad M. Duplantis, "An Archaeological Search for Activity Areas: A Case Study of an African-American Yard at Oakley Plantation, West Feliciana Parish, Louisiana" (master's thesis, Louisiana State University, 1999); Jerome S. Handler and Frederick W. Lange, *Plantation Slavery in Barbados: An Archaeological and Historical Investigation* (1978); John M. Vlach, *Back of the Big House: The Architecture of Plantation Slavery* (1993); Richard Westmacott, *African American Gardens and Yards in the Rural South* (1992); Laurie Wilkie, *Southeastern Archaeology Conference Newsletter* (1994).

Yazoo County

Located on the edge of the Mississippi Delta, Yazoo County was established in 1832. Its county seat is Yazoo City, and other towns include Bentonia, Eden, and Satartia. Prior to the county's formal establishment, Yazoo conducted its first census in 1830 and found a population of 6,550, 37 percent of them slaves. Yazoo's population grew to 10,000 in 1840, with 70 percent of that number enslaved. Yazoo County's economy centered on cotton production.

By the late antebellum period, Yazoo County had become an agricultural powerhouse. In 1860 its population of 22,373 was the fifth highest in the state. Yazoo had more enslaved persons (16,716) than all but two other counties, and slaves accounted for three-quarters of the county's total population. In 1860 the economic value of Yazoo farms was the highest of all Mississippi counties, in large part because of its cotton production and the value of its livestock. It ranked ninth in the state in corn production and fourth in sweet potatoes. That year, Yazoo County had a single manufacturing establishment, which employed three men in the leather industry. The religious census of 1860 counted twenty-nine churches in Yazoo County: fifteen Methodist, seven Baptist, three Episcopalian, three Presbyterian, and one Catholic.

Y

The Civil War and Reconstruction had a tremendous impact on Yazoo County. Early in the war, the CSS *Arkansas*, a 165-foot-long ironclad warship, was built in Yazoo City. After Union forces took Jackson in 1863, various Confederate forces regrouped and reorganized in Yazoo City; among those who did so were the African American troops in the 3rd Regiment Cavalry who fought near Yazoo City. Following the war, White Leagues (organizations that used extralegal means, including violence, to oppose Republican politicians) were especially powerful in Yazoo County. Those opposed by the White Leagues included Republican politician Albert Talmon Morgan, who faced condemnation as a carpetbagger. Facing considerable opposition in the early 1870s, he finally fled Mississippi and wrote *Yazoo; or, On the Picket Line of Freedom in the South*.

Like many Delta counties, Yazoo's population grew substantially in the postbellum years, becoming the second-most-populated county in Mississippi, behind only Hinds. In 1880 Yazoo's population had grown to 33,845, including more than 25,000 African Americans. It continued to rank highly in agricultural production, with the highest value of farm property and livestock in Mississippi, the second largest cotton crop, the most mules, the second-most hogs, and the sixth-highest production of corn. Manufacturing was also becoming prominent, with twenty-six establishments employing 129 men, 2 women, and 6 children.

In 1900 Yazoo County's population of 43,948 ranked third in the state. A total of 77 percent of residents were African American, while 23 percent were white. Cotton and tenancy dominated. Yazoo County had the second-most tenant farmers and sharecroppers in the state. Only 6 percent of the 5,291 black farmers owned the land they farmed, compared to 45 percent of the 1,450 white farmers. Yazoo County also had a growing industrial workforce, with 400 employees, almost all male, working at 127 manufacturing establishments. The county had an immigrant population of about 200, mostly Germans and Irish, and Yazoo City had a small but substantial Lebanese and Syrian community. As in much of Mississippi, the largest religious groups were Baptists and Methodists.

In the early twentieth century Yazoo remained a large county, though its population was slowly declining. In 1930 Yazoo was home to 37,262 persons, two-thirds of them African American. Twenty-two establishments, including a number of hardwood sawmills, employed almost 500 industrial workers. As in most of the Delta, Yazoo's farmers emphasized cotton, followed by cattle and corn. Tenants accounted for 84 percent of all farmers.

Several important institutions had their roots in Yazoo County. In the 1920s Julius Zeller, a Yazoo City state senator, brought to the state the idea of junior colleges. Taborian Hospital, one of Mississippi's first hospitals for African Americans, funded by the Knights and Daughters of Tabor, opened in 1928, predating a larger Taborian hospital in Mound Bayou by more than a decade. Yazoo County native Ruby Stutts Lyells, an educational activist and librarian, spent years working to improve libraries for Mississippi's African Americans.

Yazoo's population declined by about 6,000 between 1930 and 1960, leaving the county with about 31,000 residents. African Americans now comprised 59 percent of the population. Yazoo remained a great producer of agricultural goods, and agriculture employed about a third of the county's workers. In 1960 Yazoo farms raised the most livestock in the state, the seventh-most cotton and wheat, and the twelfth-most soybeans. Yazoo County's industrial establishments now specialized in apparel and chemicals rather than timber, and the county had four functioning oil wells. Mississippi's first discovery of oil took place at Tinsley Field outside Yazoo City.

Some noted Mississippians of arts and letters grew up in Yazoo County. In 1844, at the age of twenty, Ethelbert Barksdale began his journalistic career by editing the *Yazoo City Democrat*. Willie Morris detailed life in and around Yazoo City in *North toward Home*, his 1967 memoir, which discussed his love-hate relationship with the city. Morris also wrote about his hometown in *Yazoo*, his 1971 discussion of school desegregation, and in numerous works of fiction and autobiography. Blues singer Skip James grew up on a plantation near Bentonia. Blues musician and sculptor James "Son" Thomas was born near Eden in 1926. Storyteller Jerry Clower was born in South Mississippi and gained fame for his stories after moving to Yazoo City to take a job with the Mississippi Chemical Corporation. Today, Yazoo City has an annual Jerry Clower Festival. Quilter Pecolia Warner learned her art from family members in Bentonia, and her quilting niece, Sarah Mary Taylor, grew up in the Yazoo County community of Anding.

In 1955 Yazoo City's African Americans met powerful opposition when they sought to integrate the city's schools after the US Supreme Court's *Brown v. Board of Education* decision. John Satterfield, an attorney and leader in efforts to use lobbying and the law to oppose desegregation, became a key figure in Coordinating Committee for Fundamental American Freedoms, a conservative group organized in 1963.

Yazoo County has been the home of several important figures in Mississippi political history. Born in 1864, US senator John Sharp Williams grew up on Cedar Grove, a Yazoo County plantation. Two-term governor and Republican political leader Haley Barbour was born in Yazoo City in 1945, and Democratic representative and US secretary of agriculture Mike Espy was born in Yazoo in 1953.

Like most Delta counties in Mississippi, Yazoo County's 2010 population of 28,088 was predominantly African American and had decreased by about 11 percent since 1960. In addition to its large white minority, the county had a small Latino population.

Mississippi Encyclopedia Staff
University of Mississippi

Mississippi State Planning Commission, *Progress Report on State Planning in Mississippi* (1938); *Mississippi Statistical Abstract*, Mississippi State University (1952–2010); Charles Sydnor and Claude Bennett, *Mississippi History* (1939); University of Virginia Library, Historical Census Browser website, http://mapserver.lib.virginia.edu; E. Nolan Waller and Dani A. Smith, *Growth Profiles of Mississippi's Counties, 1960–1980* (1985).

Yazoo Land Frauds

The Yazoo Land Frauds of 1789 and 1795 involved the portion of Georgia west from the Chattahoochee River to the Mississippi River and northward from the thirty-first parallel to what is now the Tennessee state line, forming the present-day states of Alabama and Mississippi.

In 1789 three land companies—the South Carolina Yazoo Company, the Tennessee Yazoo Company, and the Virginia Yazoo Company—organized to buy land in the Yazoo tract. The Georgia legislature agreed to sell about sixteen million acres to the three companies for two hundred thousand dollars in cash to be paid over two years. The companies defaulted, however, and title to the lands reverted to Georgia.

In the mid-1790s, four new and better-financed companies—the Georgia Company, Georgia-Mississippi Company, Tennessee Company, and Upper Mississippi Company—sought to acquire the Yazoo lands. On 7 January 1795 the Georgia legislature approved the sale of thirty-five million acres—two-thirds of the state's lands west of the Chattahoochee—to the four companies for five hundred thousand dollars.

The bill's passage had been accomplished through land company shares and cash gifts to the legislators. Led by US senator James Jackson, the people of Georgia erupted in outrage against the sale. Consequently, the 1796 state legislature, comprised largely of anti-Yazooists, repealed the act on 13 February 1796, voiding any claims or title that arose as a result of the sale and declaring the territory in question the sole property of Georgia. The repeal act provided for refunds to purchasers, but not all purchasers applied, because accepting the money meant abandoning the claim. Further, much of the Yazoo land had been quickly resold, especially to Boston-area investors. Most important for future events, on the same day the repeal act passed, the New England–Mississippi Land Company bought most of the holdings of the Georgia-Mississippi Company—eleven million acres in the southwest section of the Yazoo tract. The New England purchasers maintained their innocence and their ignorance of the dispute surrounding the sale, while the anti-Yazooists argued that there were no innocent purchasers since the repeal act had ordered that the reversal be publicized throughout the country.

Nevertheless, the shareholders pressed their claims, lobbying Congress for compensation between 1803 and 1806. When that effort failed, the shareholders took their case to the US Supreme Court. In *Fletcher v. Peck* (1810), Chief Justice John Marshall, writing for the Court, upheld the Yazooists' position, ruling that Georgia possessed the lands in 1795 and that the sale was valid and binding despite the alleged corruption of the legislature. Further, citing the constitutional prohibition against state laws impairing the obligation of contracts, he declared the repeal act unconstitutional because it had broken the contract between Georgia and the land companies. The decision became a landmark in US constitutional history. It made the Contracts Clause of the Constitution the primary safeguard of private property for the next fifty years and was the first major ruling to overturn a state law for violating the US Constitution. Further, the Yazooists were the first interest group to seek to further their cause through the Supreme Court.

Finally in 1814, in the interest of resolving disputed claims in the Mississippi Territory that impeded its organization as a state and of appeasing New England financial interests harmed by the War of 1812, Congress passed and Pres. James Madison signed an act compensating claimants through the sale of lands in the Mississippi Territory up to five million dollars.

Tara Laver
Louisiana State University

Thomas Dionysus Clark and John D. W. Guice, *The Old Southwest, 1795–1830: Frontiers in Conflict* (1996); C. Peter Magrath, *Yazoo: Law and Politics in the New Republic; The Case of Fletcher v. Peck* (1966).

Yazoo Pass, Battle of

Following an abortive attempt to capture Vicksburg in late 1862, Ulysses S. Grant cast about for alternative methods to reduce the Confederate stronghold. One intriguing possibility involved sending Union troops on transports down a series of waterways into the Yazoo River, which would allow them to land on high ground north of the city. Such an expedition would begin on the east side of the Mississippi River a few miles below Helena, Arkansas. It involved cutting through a levee built by the State of Mississippi in the 1850s to shut off access to the river from Moon Lake. Moon Lake led to Yazoo Pass, a small bayou, which in turn fed into the Coldwater River. The Coldwater flowed into the Tallahatchie River, which combined with the Yalobusha River to form the Yazoo, which empted into the Mississippi above Vicksburg.

Engineering officer Lt. Col. James H. Wilson reported that cutting the levee would allow Union vessels access to the Delta and raise the water level in the region sufficiently for joint army-navy operations. With Grant's approval, Wilson had four hundred men begin cutting the levee in early February 1863. The explosion of a small mine completed the process, and water from the Mississippi rushed through the gap into the old bed. Wilson next supervised the arduous labor of clearing the Yazoo Pass of trees previously felled by Confederates to obstruct the passage, a task that occupied entire regiments for twelve days. On 24 February 1863 a flotilla under Lt. Cmdr. Watson Smith entered Yazoo Pass from Moon Lake. The ironclads *Chillicothe* and *Baron DeKalb* led the way, while five thousand Federal infantry under the command of Brig. Gen. Leonard F. Ross occupied transports. Lighter combat vessels offered additional protection.

Maneuvering through the labyrinthine waters of the Upper Delta proved enormously challenging. The narrow, winding channel of the Coldwater made progress laboriously slow. Overhanging tree limbs battered the boats and sent all sorts of wildlife cascading onto the decks. Army officers, including both Ross and Wilson, chafed at the delay and later berated Smith for not pressing forward more speedily. As the flotilla slowly advanced, many Delta residents along the rivers fled as water inundated their crops and homes; others watched helplessly as Union troops carted off slaves, cotton, corn, and other property. Shots fired at the flotilla invited retaliation as Federal troops alighted from the transports and torched plantation buildings. Some planters began burning cotton to prevent it from falling into enemy hands.

Apprised of the Union expedition, Confederates under Maj. Gen. William W. Loring built a fort of dirt and sand protected by cotton bales on a five-hundred-yard strip between the Tallahatchie and the Yazoo near Greenwood. A line of earthworks protected Fort Pemberton, as did the swampy terrain surrounding the area. Loring had several cannons mounted within the fort, including a thirty-two-pounder that commanded the approach up the Tallahatchie. In addition, Loring ordered that the steamer *Star of the West* be sunk in the channel to impede the Union advance.

The Confederates within Fort Pemberton first made contact with the flotilla on 11 March 1863, when a brief exchange of gunfire between the fort and the *Chillicothe* took place. Union troops disembarked and sniped at the fort's defenders. Wilson supervised the placement of a battery with several cannons obtained from naval vessels but later acknowledged that the distance from Fort Pemberton precluded any reasonable hope of dismounting the enemy guns. Union infantry probed for a land approach, but the flooded ground prevented them from storming the works. As a result, the expedition's success hinged largely on the ironclads. This proved a forlorn hope. The gunboats attacked on both 13 and 16 March, with the *Chillicothe* severely battered on both occasions. It was disabled on the latter day when a Confederate shell sealed its gun ports. Ross recognized the futility of further attempts

and steamed back up the Tallahatchie, where he encountered a relief expedition under Brig. Gen. Isaac F. Quinby. The reinforced command returned to Fort Pemberton, but attacks on 1 and 3 April were similarly repulsed, and Grant ordered the expedition to return. Within a week most of the ships had reached the Mississippi and steamed across to Helena.

While the Yazoo Pass expedition failed to achieve its desired objective, it and the Steele's Bayou expedition in March 1863 demonstrated Grant's willingness to try a variety of expedients to conquer Vicksburg. Both expeditions also laid waste to rich areas within the Delta and brought the war home forcefully to its residents.

Christopher Losson
St. Joseph, Missouri

Michael B. Ballard, *Vicksburg: The Campaign That Opened the Mississippi* (2004); Patricia L. Faust, ed., *Historical Times Illustrated Encyclopedia of the Civil War* (1986); David S. Heidler and Jeanne T. Heidler, eds., *Encyclopedia of the American Civil War: A Political, Social, and Military History* (2000); *Official Records of the Union and Confederate Navies in the War of the Rebellion*, vol. 24 (1911); *War of the Rebellion: The Official Records of the Union and Confederate Armies*, vol. 24 (1889).

Yellow Fever

Yellow fever—also known as hemorrhagic fever, saffron scourge, Yellow Jack, Bronze John, and the "yellow Tyrant of the tropics"—spread destruction and fear throughout Mississippi from colonial times until 1905, when the last epidemic occurred.

A tropical and subtropical acute arbovirus infection, yellow fever initially caused its victim to suffer a sudden onset of fever, usually between 102° and 104°, with bloodshot eyes and chills. Following the initial symptoms, the victim's health appeared to improve as the fever subsided. However, dramatic jaundice often ensued. The victim also experienced nausea, constipation, headache, and muscular pains in the legs and back. In severe cases, passive hemorrhaging and vomiting of semidigested blood ("black vomit") occurred. Damage to the liver, kidneys, and heart could also occur, generally leading to death from renal failure, heart failure, toxemia, or internal infection, if a low white blood cell count left the victim's body unable to fight the disease. Mild infections of yellow fever, however, often were undiagnosed. If a person contracted a mild case, recovery began within a week or two, eventually requiring stringent nursing care to achieve full recovery.

Possibly the earliest reference to yellow fever in Mississippi was when Pierre Le Moyne, Sieur d'Iberville, recorded on 22 August 1701 that Gov. Sauvole had died of the disease along the Mississippi Gulf Coast, two years after permanent French occupation began. Mississippians experienced many epidemics throughout the ensuing years. In 1841 city authorities in Natchez appointed a temporary board of health to combat yellow fever. A particularly virulent epidemic occurred in 1853 with subsequent ones in post–Civil War years. Not until 1877 did the Mississippi legislature organize the State Board of Health. However, it was only as an advisory agency, with no quarantine power or appropriations to sustain it.

During 1878 Mississippians experienced perhaps the worst epidemic of yellow fever, with 16,461 cases and 4,118 deaths. Commerce halted as localities imposed quarantines. By the end of the epidemic, donors across the United States had contributed $522,632.42 for the relief of Mississippians suffering from disease. The strain of the disease that year was particularly virulent, and increased railroad traffic helped spread the disease in spite of quarantine efforts. In 1879, in response to the preceding year's epidemic, Congress created the National Board of Health, and it subsequently proposed Ship Island, a barrier island off of the coast of Mississippi, as a quarantine station for the Gulf of Mexico between New Orleans and Pensacola, Florida.

The exact origin of the disease is unclear, but historians generally believe that yellow fever originated in Africa and was introduced to the Western Hemisphere as a result of colonial contact. The disease is transmitted from person to person by the female *Aedes aegypti* mosquito, a species that has a propensity to breed in manufactured containers such as water casks, calabashes, holds of ships, or cisterns. The mosquito could remain on board maritime vessels for months with a human host who could not escape and comfortable breeding area.

Prior to the mid-nineteenth century, when germ theory became popularized and investigated, the medical profession did not understand how yellow fever was transmitted. In the 1840s and 1850s some doctors believed that the disease spread via human-to-human contact or by contact with bodily secretions from an infected person. Others believed that miasma, or the foul emanations from putrefying animal or vegetable matter, spontaneously generated yellow fever. In 1881 a Cuban doctor, Carlos Finlay, first proposed that yellow fever was transmitted by mosquitos. In 1900, after yellow fever had ravaged US troops during Spanish-American War, surgeon general George Sternberg asked army doctors led by Walter Reed and James Carroll to investigate Finlay's theory, and they isolated the species of mosquito. By 1905 the mosquito vector theory had gained wide acceptance, and when yellow fever appeared that year, Mississippi and other southern states destroyed mosquito breeding grounds, fumigated houses, and screened patients. Mississippi and the rest of the United States have not had a yellow fever epidemic since.

Deanne Stephens Nuwer
University of Southern Mississippi

Robert Berkow, ed., *The Merck Manual of Diagnosis and Therapy* (1977); Jo Ann Carrigan, *The Saffron Scourge: A History of Yellow Fever in Louisiana, 1796–1905* (1994); Henry Rose Carter, *Yellow Fever: An Epidemiological and Historical Study of Its Place of Origin* (1931); Margaret Humphreys, *Yellow Fever and the South* (1992); J. L. Power, *The Epidemic of 1878 in Mississippi: Report of the Yellow Fever Relief Work through J. L. Power, Grand Secretary of Masons and Grand Treasurer of Odd Fellows* (1879).

Yeoman Farmers

Yeoman farmers stood at the center of antebellum southern society, belonging to the ranks neither of elite planters nor of the poor and landless; most important, from the perspective of the farmers themselves, they were free and independent, unlike slaves. In Mississippi, yeoman farming culture predominated in twenty-three counties in the northwest and central parts of the state, all within or on the edges of a topographical region geographers refer to as the Upper Coastal Plain. Situated both physically and agriculturally between the Delta (Mississippi's fertile crescent) to the west and the Blacklands (named for the high concentration of slave laborers there before emancipation as much as for the rich, dark soil) to the south and east, the Upper Coastal Plain is a moderately fertile land of rolling clay hills covered by a thin layer of dark soil and dense hardwood forests.

Those forests, which provided materials for early houses and barns, sources of fish and game, and places for livestock to root or graze, together with the fields in between, which were better suited to growing corn than cotton, befitted the yeomanry, who yearned for independence and self-sufficiency. Yeoman farmers usually owned no more land than they could work by themselves with the aid of extended family members and neighbors. On the eve of the Civil War, farms in Mississippi's yeoman counties averaged less than 225 improved acres. Many yeomen in these counties cultivated fewer than 150 acres, and a great many farmed less than 75. For the yeomanry, avoiding debt, the greatest threat to a family's long-term independence, was both an economic and religious imperative, so the speculation in land and slaves required to compete in the market economy was rare. Instead, yeoman farmers devoted the majority of their efforts to producing food, clothing, and other items used at home.

In 1860 corn production in Mississippi's yeoman counties was at least thirty bushels per capita (ten bushels more than the minimum necessary to achieve self-sufficiency), whereas the average yearly cotton yield in those counties did not exceed thirty bushels per square mile. The cotton that yeomen grew went primarily to the production of home

Y

textiles, with any excess cotton or fabric likely traded locally for basic items such as tools, sewing needles, hats, and shoes that could not be easily made at home or sold for the money to purchase such things. Mississippi's yeomen also cultivated large amounts of peas, sweet potatoes, and other foodstuffs and kept herds of livestock, especially pigs. In 1860 almost every family in Mississippi's hill country owned at least one horse or mule, there were about as many cattle as people, and pigs outnumbered humans by more than two to one.

Not surprisingly, pork and cornbread were mainstays (many travelers said monotonies) of any yeoman family's diet. For yeoman women, who were intimately involved in the daily working of their farmsteads, cooking assumed no special place among the plethora of other daily activities necessary for the family's subsistence. Sewing or mending, gardening, dairying, tending to poultry, and carrying water were just some of the labors in which women and children engaged almost daily, along with spinning, weaving, washing, canning, candle or soap making, and other tasks that occurred less often.

In addition to such tasks as clearing land, planting, and adding to or improving his home and outbuildings, the male head of a yeoman household was responsible for protecting, overseeing the labor of, and disciplining the dependents under his roof. Like almost all white men in the nineteenth-century South, the men of the yeoman class exerted complete patriarchal authority, born of both custom and law, over the property and bodies connected to their households. Within the community, fistfights, cockfights, and outright drunken brawls helped to establish or maintain a man's honor and social standing relative to his peers. Inside the home, domestic violence was encouraged as a way of maintaining order.

The average household on Mississippi's yeoman farmsteads contained 6.0 members, slightly above the statewide average of 5.8 and well above the steadily declining average for northern bourgeois families. A quarter of Mississippi's yeoman households contained at least 8 members, and many included upward of 10. About a quarter of yeoman households included free whites who did not belong to the householder's nuclear family. Most were adult male farm laborers; about a fifth were women (usually unmarried sisters or sisters-in-law or widowed mothers or mothers-in-law of the household head); a slightly smaller percentage were children who belonged to none of the household's adults. All of them contributed their labor to the household economy. In addition, many yeomen purchased, rented, borrowed, or inherited slaves, but slavery was neither the primary source of labor nor a very visible part of the landscape in Mississippi's antebellum hill country.

Despite the size and diversity of their households, most Mississippi yeomen, along with their extended families and any hired hands, slaves, or guests, cooked, ate, drank, worked, played, visited, slept, conceived children, bore, and nursed them in homes consisting of just one or two rooms. More than four-fifths of the two-room houses—and more than a third of all vernacular houses—constructed in the state's yeoman region before 1880 consisted of side-by-side "pens" bisected by an open passageway—the dogtrot house. The state's signature folk architectural type, the dogtrot appealed to yeomen in part for its informality and openness to neighbors and strangers alike. Inside, the typical yeoman home contained a great number of chairs and other furnishings but fewer than three beds. The close proximity of adults and children in the home, amid a landscape virtually overrun with animals, meant that procreation was a natural, observable, and imminently desirable fact of yeoman life.

Beginning in the last twenty years of the nineteenth century, the declining popularity of the once ubiquitous dogtrot signaled the concurrent demise of yeoman farming culture in the state. Although the Civil War had exacted a toll on the lives and livelihoods of Mississippi's yeomanry, the most pronounced shift in this way of life occurred between 1880 and 1910. Demographic factors both contributed to and reveal the end of independent farming life. In those three decades, the number of Mississippians living in cities or towns nearly tripled, while the keeping of livestock, particularly pigs, declined precipitously. As farm animals began to disappear from everyday life, so did appreciation for and visibility of procreation in and around the household. At the same time, family size in the region decreased, families became more nuclear, and houses grew larger and more private. By 1910, 93 percent of the vernacular houses in Mississippi's hill country consisted of three to five rooms, while the average number of household members decreased to around five, and far fewer of those households included extended family or nonrelated individuals.

Susan Ditto
Washington, D.C.

Susan Ditto, "Conjugal Duty: Domestic Culture on the Southern Frontier, 1830–1910" (PhD dissertation, University of Mississippi, 1998); Sam B. Hilliard, *Atlas of Antebellum Southern Agriculture* (1984); Fred Kniffen, in *Common Places: Readings in American Vernacular Architecture*, ed. Dell Upton and John Michael Vlach (1986); Stephanie McCurry, *Masters of Small Worlds: Yeoman Households, Gender Relations, and the Political Culture of the Antebellum South Carolina Low Country* (1995); Ted Ownby, *Subduing Satan: Religion, Recreation, and Manhood in the Rural South, 1865–1920* (1990).

Young, Al
(b. 1939) Writer

Albert James Young was born on 31 May 1939 in Ocean Springs, Mississippi, to Ernest Albert James, a professional musician and autoworker, and Mary Campbell Young. Raised in Mississippi and in Detroit, Al Young attended the University of Michigan at Ann Arbor from 1957 to 1960 and served as coeditor of *Generation*, the campus literary magazine. During this period he began work as a freelance musician. In 1961 he moved to the San Francisco Bay area, where he held a variety of jobs, including folksinger, lab aide, disc jockey, and medical photographer. In 1969 Young graduated from the University of California at Berkeley with a degree in Spanish. From 1969 to 1976 he held the post of Edward B. Jones Lecturer in Creative Writing at Stanford University. Young has subsequently taught at numerous colleges and universities as visiting poet, writer in residence, visiting lecturer, and creative writing professor.

Young's many books include novels, collections of poetry, essays, memoirs, and anthologies. He has received Stanford's Wallace Stegner Fellowship as well as Guggenheim, Fulbright, and National Endowment for the Arts Fellowships; the PEN–Library of Congress Award for Short Fiction; the PEN-USA Award for Nonfiction; two American Book Awards; the Pushcart Prize; and two *New York Times* Notable Book of the Year citations. From 2005 until 2008 Young served as poet laureate of California, and in 2012 he contributed monthly poems about the state to KQED-Radio's *The California Report*.

Young has authored five novels, ten collections of poetry, five memoir-related works of nonfiction, and various screenplays. His first poetry collection, *Dancing: Poems*, appeared in 1969. His first novel, *Snakes*, came a year later and tells the story of a young musician who finds success in Detroit. Through the novel Young explores the meaning of black identity as well as humanity, as his characters comment on racial conditions as well as universal human experience. These themes also emerge as central in Young's next two novels, *Who Is Angelina?* (1975) and *Sitting Pretty* (1976), as well as in his extensive poetic writings.

Young's passions for music and poetry also inform his novels, many of which deal with music as a context for characterization and as metaphor. Young has received critical praise for the rich approach to African American language and poetic ear apparent in the dialogue between characters, particularly in the portrayal of main character Mamie Franklin in *Seduction by Light* (1975). Young's autobiographical writings similarly navigate music and language in the context of his experiences. He has been credited with helping to destroy stereotypes of black Americans and with offering refreshing approaches to the African American experience.

Young's other works of poetry include *Heaven: Collected Poems, 1956–1990* (1992), *The Sound of Dreams Remembered: Poems, 1990–2000* (2001), and *Coastal Nights and Inland Afternoons: Poems, 2001–2006* (2006). His nonfiction works include *Kinds of Blue: Musical Memoirs* (1984) and *Drowning in the Sea of Love: Musical Memoirs* (1995). In 2009 he released an album with musician Dan Robbins, *The Sea, the Sky, and You, and I*. In addition, Young cofounded the literary journals *Yardbird Reader* and *Quilt* with poet-novelist Ishmael Reed.

Young travels extensively, reading, lecturing, and often performing with musicians, and he remains a prolific and powerful contributor to the world of creative writing.

Frances Abbott
Digital Public Library of America,
Boston, Massachusetts

Dorothy Abbott, ed., *Mississippi Writers: Reflections of Childhood and Youth* (1985); Rosalie Murphy, ed., *Contemporary Poets* (1970); Thomson Gale: Contemporary Authors series; Al Young website, www.alyoung.org.

Young, Billie Jean
(b. 1947) Poet, Playwright, Actress

In 1969 Billie Jean Young heard Fannie Lou Hamer give a talk in Tuskegee, Alabama. Ever since, Young has dedicated her talents to continuing the ideals of Hamer through writing, acting, and activism among the rural, often poor women she represented.

Born on 21 July 1947, Young grew up in a sharecropping family in Choctaw County, Alabama. An impressive and energetic student, she became the first African American to graduate from Judson College in Alabama before earning a law degree from Samford University in 1979.

In 1981 she moved to Mississippi, in part to take up the mission of Hamer, who had died four years earlier. Young helped start the Southern Rural Women's Network and the Rural Development Leadership Network, both of which sought to give rural women better access to health care and education and more power over their economic lives. Young served as chair and head of the board of the Rural Development Leadership Network from 1983 to 1996.

Young is best known in Mississippi and beyond for the play *Fannie Lou Hamer: This Little Light*, a one-person play that Young wrote and first performed in 1983 at Tougaloo College. She has subsequently performed the drama with music more than eight hundred times, traveling all over the world to tell the story of Hamer's life. The play includes monologues from her own words and such civil rights anthems as "Ain't Gonna Let No One Turn Me Round," "This Little Light of Mine," and "Precious Lord." Young has also created several other plays, including two about Alabama civil rights martyrs, *JimmyLee* (2009) and *Oh, Mary, Don't You Weep: The Margaret Ann Knott Legacy* (2007).

Young's poems, many of which were published in *Fear Not the Fall* (2003), combine personal stories about life as a rural African American woman with broader stories about the African American diaspora and some overtly political poems about war and government policy. "Mama Rubboard Hands" is a tribute to her mother, and her longest poem, "Five Decades of Living," offers a consideration of what her experiences have taught her.

In the 1990s Young taught at Jackson State University and at the Meridian campus of Mississippi State University. Her work as a unique combination of poet, actress, and activist has earned her many awards, among them a 1984 MacArthur Foundation "Genius Grant." In 1995 she received the Mississippi Governor's Award for Artistic Achievement. She moved back to her hometown of Pennington, Alabama, the following year and now serves as artist in residence and associate professor of fine and performing arts at Judson College.

Ted Ownby

University of Mississippi

New South Books website, www.newsouthbooks.com; Tavis Smiley, "Interview: Billie Jean Young Discusses Fanny [*sic*] Lou Hamer," *The Tavis Smiley Show*; Billie Jean Young, *Fear Not the Fall: Poems and a Two-Act Drama* (2003); Billie Jean Young website, www.billiejeanyoung.org.

Young, Lester
(1909–1959) Jazz Musician

Jazz saxophonist Lester "Prez" Young became a leading swing era instrumentalist and innovator with bandleader Count Basie and in combos of his own during the 1930s. Born in Woodville, Mississippi, on 27 August 1909, Young was the son of Willis H. Young, a schoolteacher and music professor from Thibodaux, Louisiana, and Lizetta Johnson Young, from Woodville, also a schoolteacher and piano teacher. Willis Young left his wife in 1919 and played numerous instruments and led dance and carnival-minstrel bands through the 1920s, taking Les and his brother and sister, Irma and Lee, on the road.

Taught by Willis Young, Les started on drums at age ten, but he and his siblings also learned to dance, and the younger children played and performed in vaudeville. In his early teens Young switched to saxophone and sometimes danced while blowing his horn, becoming a showman from the outset. His rhythmically charged playing on this relatively new jazz instrument showed the influence of the drums he had liked so much as a youngster.

Around 1930 Young moved to Minneapolis, where he played in small dance bands at clubs such as the Nest with trumpeter Le Roy "Snake" Whyte and reedman Eddie Barefield and toured with bands such as the Oklahoma City Blue Devils, whom he joined in 1932. When the Blue Devils broke up in West Virginia the next year, Young and the remaining band members hoboed back to Kansas City, where he joined Joseph "King" Oliver's orchestra. Young starred with these bands as a "get off" man, a hot soloist whose exciting innovations inspired fans and fellow musicians. Young joined New York City bandleader Fletcher Henderson's orchestra in 1934. The other members of the sax section did not like Young's unique tone, which differed from that of their hero, Coleman Hawkins, whom Young had replaced. They ostracized him and refused to help him learn Henderson's arrangements, and Young returned to Minneapolis, playing with Rook Ganz's combo at the city's Cotton Club.

Though usually regarded as a Kansas City musician, Young did not reside in that city until he joined Count Basie at the Reno Club around 1936. Basie had also been a Blue Devil, and he recruited several former band members—including Oran "Hot Lips" Page, Jimmy Rushing, and Walter Page. Basie signed a record contract in 1936, and the band toured midwestern and eastern cities. Young was the premier soloist in an orchestra packed with stars—Rushing, Buck Clayton, Herschel Evans, Harry "Sweets" Edison, and singer Billie Holiday. Young had a profound influence, not only on saxophonists Charlie Parker and Don Byas, trumpeter Miles Davis, and guitarists B. B. King, John Collins, and Barney Kessel but also on Beat writers Jack Kerouac and Allen Ginsberg. Though Young was known as a hot swing stylist, B. B. King and many other musicians credited him with starting the cool school in jazz. He was also highly respected for his stylish dress, including the wide-brimmed porkpie hat that became his trademark, and for using hipster argot or "swing slang" almost exclusively. He earned the nickname *Prez*, for "President of Tenor Saxophonists."

In 1944 Young was drafted into the US Army. Though many white musicians were assigned to band units such as those led by Glenn Miller and Artie Shaw, Young was not; instead, he was sent to basic training at Fort McClellan, Alabama. According to drummer Jerry Potter, who was also stationed at Fort McClellan, Young refused to cut his hair, sleep in a barracks or wear army boots, believing that "he didn't need basic training, because he was never going to fire a gun." Said Young, "I don't want to kill anyone. I want to play and make them happy." Young was subsequently court-martialed for using marijuana, spent a year in detention barracks (an experience that inspired his later composition, "D. B. Blues"), and received a dishonorable discharge in 1945.

His army experience was traumatic and affected his mental state for the rest of his life. Not only did his playing take on a darker tone after the war, but his alcohol consumption dramatically increased. He suffered a nervous breakdown in late 1955, improved and returned to performing, but soon began to decline again. After a short European tour, he returned to New York City on 14 March 1959 and died early the next morning.

Douglas Henry Daniels
University of California
at Santa Barbara

Frank Buchmann-Moller, *You Got to Be Original, Man! The Music of Lester Young* (1990); Douglas Henry Daniels, *Lester Leaps In: The Life and Times of Lester "Pres" Young* (2002); Luc Delannoy, *Pres: The Story of Lester Young* (1993); Tom Vitale, "Lester Young: 'The Prez' Still Rules at 100" (27 August 2009), http://www.npr.org/templates/story/story.php?storyId=112255870.

Young, Stark

(1881–1963) Author and Theater Critic

A teacher, playwright, novelist, painter, and theater critic, Stark Young was born in Como, Mississippi, on 11 October 1881, to Mary Clark Starks Young, who came from a wealthy Virginia planter family, and Alfred Alexander Young, a Civil War veteran and physician. Following the death of his mother when he was eight years old, Young spent the next five years in the care primarily of his maternal aunts and his uncle, Hugh McGehee, who imparted the traditional southern perspective that would shape much of Young's work. Alfred Young remarried in 1895 and moved the family, including Stark and his younger sister, Julia, to Oxford, Mississippi.

Young was educated in private schools before enrolling at the University of Mississippi in 1896. After graduating in 1901, Young, like many early twentieth-century southerners, ventured north for graduate school, completing a master's degree in English at Columbia University in 1902. Under the tutelage of Brander Matthews, Young became acquainted with the methods of literary and theatrical criticism and attended performances by many of the era's leading actors. Over the next fifteen years, Young pursued an academic career, with stints as a professor of English at the University

Stark Young (University of Mississippi University Communications)

of Mississippi, the University of Texas, and Amherst College. While at the University of Mississippi, he published his first volume of poetry, *The Blind Man at the Window* (1906). In Austin, he was a popular instructor and founded the Curtain Club, a little theater organization, as well as the *Texas Review*. After moving to Amherst in 1915 he became a revered teacher and critic, contributing numerous essays to *New Republic*, the *Nation*, and the *Yale Review*.

He studied and wrote in Spain and Italy during 1919, after which his interest in theater and a burgeoning freelance writing career led him to abandon academia for other pursuits. In 1921 he left Amherst and at the invitation of editor Herbert Croly became a drama critic and editorial board member at the *New Republic*. During the 1920s Young published widely not only in the *New Republic* but also in the *New York Times* and *Theatre Arts Magazine*. He lectured on the history of drama at the New School for Social Research and authored a number of plays, including *The Saint* (1925) and *The Colonnade* (1925).

During the late 1920s and early 1930s, Young broadened his interests from drama to fiction, writing four novels set in Mississippi: *Heaven Trees* (1926); *The Torches Flare* (1928); *River House* (1929); and his most famous work, *So Red the Rose* (1934). *So Red the Rose* presents the Civil War saga of the McGehee family, although the war itself is peripheral to the story, which juxtaposes northern industrial society against southern agrarian life. In many regards, *So Red the Rose* is a fictional translation of the ideals expressed in his essay "Not in Memoriam, but in Defense," which appeared in the Agrarian manifesto *I'll Take My Stand* (1930). Young's opening salvo in the essay summarized his basic beliefs concerning southern history. While he agreed that "we can never go back," Young argued that southern civilization contained many "worthwhile things" that ought to be preserved.

Although he disavowed commitment to the political cause of Agrarianism, Young maintained a long correspondence with Donald Davidson and saw himself as an exemplar of the "southern idea." Moreover, his plays and novels reflected a cultural commitment to rural life and a vision of an organic society based on land, family, and tradition.

By 1940 Young had become disenchanted with the New York theater scene. Following Croly's death in 1930, he also became increasingly disillusioned with the direction of the *New Republic*. In 1947 he retired from the magazine, bringing a close to a forty-year career during which he published more than one thousand critical essays. During the 1940s he turned to painting and participated in several exhibitions in New York and Chicago. He suffered a debilitating stroke in 1959 and died in New York on 6 January 1963.

Jay Langdale
Andrew College

Paul Conkin, *The Southern Agrarians* (1988); John Pilkington, *Stark Young* (1985); Stark Young, *Stark Young, a Life in the Arts: Letters, 1900–1962*, ed. John Pilkington (1975).

Young, Thomas Jefferson

(1921–1995) Author

Novelist Thomas Jefferson Young was born on 1 October 1921 in Oma, Mississippi, a hamlet in Lawrence County twelve miles north of Monticello. His parents were Clara Boutwell Young and Thomas Shelby Young.

After graduating from Monticello High School, Young enrolled at Hinds Junior College in Raymond in January 1940, graduating in 1941. While a student at Hinds, Young served as a sports correspondent for the *Jackson Daily News*. He spent two years in the US Army Air Corps, serving as a bomber pilot in England during World War II, before earning his bachelor's degree in journalism at the University of Missouri in June 1946.

Young spent two years working in an editorial and public relations position with the American Association of Oilwell Drilling Contractors in Dallas before moving to New York and submitting a novel in progress for a Eugene F. Saxton Memorial Trust Fellowship, a program established in 1943 to assist talented writers who would otherwise be unable to complete book projects. Young received the Saxton Fellowship in 1951 and moved to New Orleans, where he completed the novel. *A Good Man* was published in 1953, while Young was enrolled in graduate school at Tulane University, but he left before completing a year of study.

A Good Man was a Book-of-the-Month Club selection, and *Reader's Digest* released a condensed version of the novel. It tells the story of how Albert Clayton, a black tenant on the farm of a white man, John Tittle, in the Piney Woods section of Mississippi, strives for self-respect and decency.

Although the *New York Times* said that *A Good Man* was "so good a book that Mr. Young's future career is certain to be followed eagerly," Young drifted into obscurity. Sometime during the 1960s he returned to his hometown of Oma and lived out his life in the house his parents built. He died on 31 March 1995 in Winnsboro, Louisiana.

Peggy W. Jeanes
Jackson, Mississippi

Thomas J. Young Obituary, *Lawrence County Press* (5 April 1995); Jefferson Young File, Bobbs-Merrill MSS., Manuscripts Department, Lilly Library, Indiana University.

Z

Zellner, Bob
(b. 1939) Activist

Born in Alabama on 5 April 1939, John Robert Zellner was the second of James Abraham Zellner and Ruby Hardy Zellner's five sons. James Zellner, an itinerant Methodist preacher and member of the Ku Klux Klan, traveled to Europe during World War II to help support the Jewish resistance to the Nazis. While in Russia, he lived and worked with a group of black gospel singers who were also helping the resistance, and when he returned to the United States, he repudiated his racist beliefs. After graduating from Mobile's Murphy High School in 1957, Bob Zellner attended Huntingdon College in Montgomery, where he took a course in race relations and attended a workshop held by the Student Nonviolent Coordinating Committee (SNCC). Though threatened with expulsion for his involvement with student protests, Zellner graduated in 1961 with a degree in psychology and sociology. After spending the following summer at the Highlander Folk School in Monteagle, Tennessee, Zellner was hired by SNCC to recruit white students for the movement, a position sponsored by a grant from the Southern Conference Education Fund. Until 1962 Zellner was SNCC's only white field secretary.

After working briefly in Atlanta, Zellner went to McComb, Mississippi, with Bob Moses and Chuck McDew for a SNCC planning session. During the visit McComb students organized a march to protest the murder of Herbert Lee and the expulsion of Brenda Travis and Ike Lewis from Burglund High School. The SNCC workers joined the students in front of City Hall to pray, and Zellner, the protest's only white participant, was attacked and severely beaten by several white men while local police watched and FBI agents took notes. The men attempted to drag Zellner away from the other protesters, but Zellner clung to a railing until police finally pulled him off to arrest him, along with the other SNCC workers and 119 students. For several months Zellner, McDew, and Moses ran a freedom school, Nonviolent High of Pike County, for the students who dropped out of Burglund High to protest Travis's expulsion, though the school closed when the three activists were convicted of disturbing the peace and contributing to the delinquency of minors. They were sentenced to four months in jail and fined.

Zellner also participated in SNCC's McComb voter registration campaign and in the Pike County Nonviolent Movement before moving to Leflore County to work with Amzie Moore and the McGhee family on desegregation, voter registration, and the formation of the Leflore County Freedom Democratic Party. After beginning graduate study on race relations and sociology at Brandeis University, Zellner took a leave of absence in 1964 to coordinate SNCC's efforts in Greenwood. During the summer of 1964 he also worked in Neshoba County with Rita Schwerner, investigating the murder of her husband, Michael Schwerner, and two other civil rights workers, James Chaney and Andrew Goodman. Zellner also campaigned for social justice in Alabama, Georgia, and Virginia.

In 1966 SNCC voted to expel white activists from its organization, and although Zellner and his wife, Dorothy Miller Zellner, who also worked for SNCC, appealed, SNCC's central committee rejected their request for reinstatement. The couple subsequently moved to New Orleans to work with the Southern Conference Educational Fund. Zellner earned a doctorate in history from Tulane University in the 1990s and until his retirement taught the history of the civil rights movement at Long Island University. He continues to speak publicly on civil rights and in 2008 published a memoir, *The Wrong Side of Murder Creek: A White Southerner in the Freedom Movement*. He continues his activism and in April 2013 was arrested for protesting North Carolina's voter ID law.

Amy Schmidt
Lyon College

Raymond Arsenault, *Freedom Riders: 1961 and the Struggle for Racial Justice* (2006); Clayborne Carson, *In Struggle: SNCC and the Black Awakening of the 1960s* (1981); John Dittmer, *Local People: The Struggle for Civil Rights in Mississippi* (1994); Moral Heroes website, www.moralheroes.org; Charles M. Payne, *I've Got the Light of Freedom: The Organizing Tradition and the Mississippi Freedom Struggle* (1995); Bob Zellner, *The Wrong Side of Murder Creek: A White Southerner in the Freedom Movement* (2008); Howard Zinn, *SNCC: The New Abolitionists* (2002).

Ziglar, Zig
(1926–2012) Motivational Speaker and Businessperson

Zig Ziglar founded a motivational speaking institution that claims to have reached more than 250 million people. His "Ziglar Way" combines marketing skills, personal improvement strategy, and Christian doctrine, and he shared his approach with a deep, drawling voice and frequent witticisms:

"People often say that motivation doesn't last. Well, neither does bathing. That's why we recommend it daily."

Hilary Hinton Ziglar was born in Coffee County, Alabama, on 6 November 1926 and moved with his family to Yazoo City when he was five. His father died the following year, leaving Ziglar's mother and their twelve children in impoverished circumstances. By age six, Ziglar was selling peanuts on the Yazoo City streets for six cents a bag. He honed this salesmanship through a series of jobs as a young adult and then while serving in the US Navy during World War II. In the 1950s Ziglar took his first motivational speaking engagements; his animated approach and distinguishable southern baritone soon earned him full-time work.

Along with spiritual belief and drawing from the lessons of America's Founding Fathers, Ziglar's success strategies were often packaged in folksiness. Many centered on everyday, domestic situations or humorous anecdotes. On stage, Ziglar referred to his wife as "the Redhead" and utilized sayings such as "grinning so wide you could eat a banana whole." He also employed biographical events to effect, whether noting his "death" at nine days old or his immersion in Christianity after Sister Jessie, an elderly African American woman who was a guest in his home in 1972, witnessed to him. The Ziglar Way continues to stress principles and slogans such as "Will, skill, refill."

After establishing himself in the 1970s, Ziglar wrote nearly thirty books, several of which became *New York Times* best sellers. He appeared on national television and met with former presidents, lawmakers, and celebrities. Ziglar's corporation, Ziglar, now includes family members and former students. The enterprise offers a range of corporate training and consulting services and is operated in part by his son, Tom, and daughters, Julie and Cindy. Among other options, clients can choose whether to include or exclude the religious component of the presentation.

Ziglar met the woman who later became his wife, Jean Abernathy, in Jackson when the two were still teenagers, and they married on 26 November 1946. Though they moved with their family to Dallas, Texas, in the late 1960s, he always maintained his connections to Mississippi: as he noted of Yazoo City in 2011, "My roots in that small Mississippi Delta town run deep, and the things I remember from my time there are still as fresh as yesterday." Ziglar died in Plano, Texas, on 28 November 2012.

Odie Lindsey
Nashville, Tennessee

Darren Grem, *The Blessings of Business: How Corporations Shaped Conservative Christianity* (2016); Teresa Nicholas, *Delta Magazine* (September–October 2011); Jon Vanderlaan, *Plano Star-Courier* (11 September 2010); Zig Ziglar, *Zig: The Autobiography of Zig Ziglar* (2004); William Yardley, *New York Times* (28 November 2012); Ziglar website, www.ziglar.com.

CONTRIBUTORS

Ann J. Abadie
Frances Abbott
Jennifer Abraham
Jane Adams
Charles S. Aiken
Mike Allard
Danielle Andersen
Paul Christopher Anderson
Kenneth T. Andrews
Lee J. Arco
Teresa Arrington
Melvin S. Arrington Jr.
Chris Myers Asch
Joe Atkins
Matt Atkinson
Curtis J. Austin
Brenda Ayres
Fred Arthur Bailey
Matthew M. Bailey
Jack Bales
Michael B. Ballard
Susan R. Barclay
Rene Paul Barilleaux
James F. Barnett Jr.
Marion Barnwell
Scott Barretta
Alan W. Barton
Jack Bass
J. O. Joby Bass
Toby G. Bates
Adria Battaglia
Margaret Donovan Bauer
Donald W. Beachler
Lionel J. Beaulieu
Brandon H. Beck
James M. Beeby

Brian D. Behnken
David T. Beito
Linda Royster Beito
Nancy Bercaw
Michael T. Bertrand
Mary T. (Meredith) Bishop
Patti Carr Black
Michael B. E. Bograd
Jaime Elizabeth Boler
Charles Bolton
Bradley G. Bond
Evelyn Kelsaw Bonner
Jenifer Borum
Thomas Neville Boschert
Emily Bowles-Smith
Sandra Boyd
Deborah Boykin
Joey Brackner
Jeffrey P. Brain
Martha Jane Brazy
William Brescia
Michelle Bright
Samuel Brookes
David S. Brose
Joyce L. Broussard
Amanda Brown
Luther Brown
Mark Brown
Trent Brown
Julian Brunt
Minor Ferris Buchanan
Timothy R. Buckner
Stephen Budney
Mike Bunn
W. Lewis Burke
H. Clark Burkett

Brooke Butler
J. Michael Butler
Gail Buzhardt
Victoria E. Bynum
Richie Caldwell
Mark Camarigg
Rebecca Camarigg
Mack Cameron
Ellie Campbell
Gerri A. Cannon-Smith
Thomas John Carey
James Taylor Carson
George Carter
Daphne R. Chamberlain
Jill R. Chancey
Summer J. Chandler
John Fabian Chappo
Courtney Chartier
Cole Cheek
Steve Cheseborough
Chad Chisholm
Jill Clark
Steven Classen
Rebecca Lauck Cleary
Thomas D. Cockrell
Mary Delorse Coleman
David J. Coles
Mark Coltrain
Edwin L. Combs III
Sarah Taylor Condon
Steve Cook
John M. Coski
Brannon Costello
Karen L. Cox
Robert M. Craig
J. Michael Crane

Stephen Cresswell
Lynda Laswell Crist
James R. Crockett
Emilye Crosby
Betty J. Crouther
Carol Crown
Edward R. Crowther
Jodie Cummings
David Cunningham
Constance Curry
Thomas W. Cutrer
Chad M. Dacus
Jamie C. Dakin
David Daniels
Douglas Henry Daniels
Chris Danielson
Dernoral Davis
Jack E. Davis
Rebecca Miller Davis
Ronald L. F. Davis
Samuel M. Davis
Jacques de Marche
Michael P. Dean
Michelle D. Deardorff
Brian Dempsey
Dawn Dennis
Arthur H. DeRosier Jr.
Tom Dewey II
Robin C. Dietrick
Susan Ditto
Mark K. Dolan
Saul Dorsey
Kevin Dougherty
Alan Draper
John Richard Duke
George H. Dukes Jr.
Nancy McKenzie Dupont
Carolyn Dupont
E. Paul Durrenberger
Thomas Eaton
John T. Edge
Christopher Eger
George B. Ellenberg
Adam C. Evans
Amy Evans
Anne Evans
Camille H. Evans
Robert G. Evans
Walter H. Eversmeyer
Justin Faircloth
Gene C. Fant Jr.
Teresa Parker Farris
Samuel P. Faulkner
Jelani M. Favors
Eric Feldman

Robert H. Ferguson
Abbott L. Ferris
William Ferris
James E. Fickle
Dale L. Flesher
Ryan L. Fletcher
James C. Foley
Daniel L. Fountain
Jessica Foy
Jim Fraiser
William Mark Franks
Deborah Freeland
Mary Leigh Furrh
Jake Fussell
Alan Gallay
LeAnne Gault
Jon L. Gibson
James C. Giesen
Chris Gilmer
Ben Gilstrap
David T. Gleeson
Susan M. Glisson
Karen Glynn
Chris Goertzen
Nils Gore
Maury Gortemiller
Anne R. Gowdy
Sally Graham
Tiff Graham
John M. Grammer
Eleanor M. Green
John J. Green
Josh Green
Kathy Greenberg
Miranda Cully Griffin
Jerry Griffith
William Griffith
Valerie Grim
Marybeth Grimes
John D. W. Guice
Jennie Gunn
John Gunn
Jennifer Gunter
William Mark Habeeb
Taylor Hagood
Joan Wylie Hall
Robert Hamblin
Francoise N. Hamlin
Terry Hanson
David Hargrove
Andy Harper
Anna Stanfield Harris
M. Keith Harris
Tina Harry
Mark H. Harvey

Paul Harvey
Robert Hawkins
John Hayes
Terry Heder
Christopher J. Hedglin
John C. Henegan
Cary W. "Bill" Herndon Jr.
Ernest Herndon
Kevin Herrera
Lisa C. Hickman
Jay Higgenbotham
Sylvia Higginbotham
Matthew Hild
Marianne Hill
S. Homes Hogue
Kenneth Holditch
Richard Holland
James G. Hollandsworth Jr.
Leah Preble Holmes
Gregory S. Hospodor
Davis W. Houck
David Houston
Carolyn Cooper Howard
John Howard
Jeffery B. Howell
Walter G. Howell
Lisa Howorth
Patrick Huber
Berkley Hudson
Harvey Hudspeth
Alan Huffman
Charles L. Hughes
Katherine Huntoon
William P. Hustwit
Alicia Jackson
David H. Jackson Jr.
Fatimah Jackson
Jerome A. Jackson
Mark Allan Jackson
Catherine M. Jannik
Katrina M. Jarding
Peggy W. Jeanes
William L. Jenkins
Landy Carien Johnson
Christopher Johnson
Emilie Johnson
Greg Johnson
Jay K. Johnson
Mary Elizabeth Johnson
Meredith Johnston
Richard Joines
Michelle Jones
Suzanne W. Jones
Robert L. Jones
Andrew W. Kahrl

Anna F. Kaplan
Donald Kartiganer
Yasuhiro Katagiri
Arthur J. Kaul
Anthony Kaye
Edmund D. Keiser
Eva Walton Kendrick
James Kennedy
Gary Kerley
Houssain Kettani
Clara Sue Kidwell
Stephen A. King
James S. Kinsey
Marlo Kirkpatrick
Jeffrey Klingfuss
Neil Linton Knox
Sheldon S. Kohn
Robert Krause
Colby H. Kullman
John A. Kupfer
Royce Kurtz
Patricia Kwachka
Alice Hull Lachaussee
Elizabeth Ladner
P. Huston Ladner
Glenda LaGarde
Lucius M. Lampton
Michael de L. Landon
Jay Langdale
Mary Beth Lasseter
Preston Lauterbach
Tara Laver
Sara Amy Leach
Dayna Bowker Lee
Connie L. Lester
George Lewis
David J. Libby
Ernest M. Limbo
Odie Lindsey
Larry M Logue
Karl G. Lorenz
Mary Lorhrenz
Christopher Losson
J. Vincent Lowery
M. Philip Lucas
Robert E. Luckett Jr.
Karen Saucier Lundy
Linda Arrington Lusk
Newt Lynn
Carter Dalton Lyon
Cameron K. Mabry
Darryl Mace
Bruce Mactavish
Russell M. Magnaghi
Matthew J. Mancini

Debora L. Mann
Adam E. Maroney
Lynn Marshall-Linnemeier
John F. Marszalek
Betsy Martin
Xaris A. Martinez
Mary Frances Marx
Cheryl A. Matherly
Edwin McAllister
Fred Wayne McCaleb
Susan McClamroch
Charline R. McCord
Michael McCoyer
Margaret T. McGehee
Liz McGraw
Pearl A. McHaney
C. Liegh McInnis
Jim McKee
J. Chester McKee
Kathryn McKee
Stephanie L. McKnight
Mac McLaurin
Andrew McMichael
Edye Cameron McMillen
Elizabeth Gillespie McRae
Pamela D. McRae
Leigh McWhite
Ellen B. Meacham
Kate Medley
Jayur Mehta
Kerry Brian Melear
Caroline Millar
Brian Craig Miller
Brian S. Miller
Mark M. Miller
Dennis Mitchell
Jon Moen
Luigi Monge
Danny B. Moore
Chester M. "Bo" Morgan
Mary Jane Morgan
Sammy Landrum Morgan
Mayumi Morishita
Edward Morris
Elli Morris
Sara Morris
Tiyi M. Morris
Larry Morrisey
Minion K. C. Morrison
Tom Mould
J. Todd Moye
Ian Munn
Vanessa Murphree
Michael V. Namorato
John Hawkins Napier III

Jennifer Nardone
Jere Nash
Ron Nassar
LeAnn W. Nealey
Ali Colleen Neff
John Neff
Lawrence J. Nelson
Bruce Nemerov
Caryn E. Neumann
David S. Newhall
James Newman
Mark Newman
Julia Huston Nguyen
Cale Nicholson
Edward Nissan
Brad Noel
Myron C. Noonkester
Dennis S. Nordin
Lisa S. Nored
David A. Norris
Terry Nowell
Deanne Stephens Nuwer
Larry Oldham
Christopher Olsen
Ted Olson
Katherine M. B. Osburn
Karyn Larlee Ott
Ted Ownby
John B. Padgett
Amy Pardo
Joseph Parker
James P. Pate
Bill Patrick
Annie Payton
Evan Peacock
Ronda Racha Penrice
Michael Perman
Emily Wagster Pettus
George Phillips
Jason Phillips
Robert Phillips
Ed Piacentino
Otis W. Pickett
Bridget Smith Pieschel
Craig S. Piper
J. E. Pitts
Noel Polk
Josephine M. Posey
Verbie Lovorn Prevost
Wiley C. Prewitt Jr.
Ernie Price
Nancy Prince
Rene E. Pulliam
Benjamin Purvis
Janis Quinn

Kathryn Radishofski
Janet Rafferty
Lynn Raley
Leslie Campbell Rampey
Maya Rao
Okolo Rashid
Dave Ray
J. Stevenson Ray
Joseph T. Reiff
Rachel B. Reinhard
J. Matthew Reonas
Joe M. Richardson
Catherine Riggs
Giselle Roberts
Jan Humber Robertson
Jimmy Robertson
Edward J. Robinson
Marco Robinson
Stuart Rockoff
Kim Lacy Rogers
Karl Rohr
Mary G. Rolinson
Stephanie R. Rolph
Stephen Rosecan
Joel Nathan Rosen
Jim Rosenblatt
Carolyn J. Ross
Charles Ross
Diane DeCesare Ross
Stephen T. Ross
Adam Rothman
Marty Russell
Linda Sabin
David Sachs
Mikko Saikku
Tracie McLemore Salinas
Crystal R. Sanders
Todd Sanders
David G. Sansing
Elizabeth Sarcone
Fred Sauceman
Phoenix Savage
William Scarborough
Augusta Scattergood
Elizabeth Schroeder Schlabach
Amiee Schmidt
Amy Schmidt
Brad Schultz
Richard Schweid
Tracy Carr Seabold
Natalya Seay
Candace J. Semien
Tony Seybert
Matthew S. Shapanka
Dorothy Shawhan

Sarah Sheffield
Rankin Sherling
Cathy Shropshire
Donald C. Simmons Jr.
John Ray Skates
Sheila L. Skemp
Peter Slade
Jayetta Slawson
Lisa Sloan
Bruce Smith
Caleb Smith
Elise Smith
Fred C. Smith
Glenn D. "Pete" Smith Jr.
James Pat Smith
Jon Smith
Marilyn H. Smith
Melissa Smith
Steven G. Smith
Susan L. Smith
Timothy B. Smith
Trevor Smith
Mitchell Snay
Greg Snowden
Mark F. Sohn
Jennifer Southall
Leslie H. Southwick
Christopher M. Span
Lisa K. Speer
Barton Spencer
Albert Sperath
Seetha Srinivasan
Christopher L. Stacey
Beth A. Stahr
Anthony J. Stanonis
David Warren Steel
Randall J. Stephens
Ricky Stevens
Lee Durham Stone
Christopher B. Strain
Joe E. Street
Debbie H. Stringer
Claire Strom
Angela C. Stuesse
William Sturkey
Jacob Sullins
Heather Sullivan
Martha Swain
Charles T. Swann
Cavett Taff
Andy Taggart
Gregory S. Taylor
Jan Taylor
Kieran W. Taylor
LaTonya Thames Taylor

William Banks Taylor
Roger D. Tate Jr.
James G. Thomas Jr.
Michael Thompson
Molly Boland Thompson
Roseanna Thompson
John Thornell
Bryan Hardin Thrift
Andrew Tillman
Lisa Tolbert
Katherine Treppendahl
Robert C. Tubby
Michael Tuma
Minoa D. Uffelman
Thomas Adams Upchurch
Mona K. Vance
Salli Vargis
William Vaughan
Vincent Venturini
Ovid Vickers
Summer Hill Vinson
Dan Vivian
Daniel C. Vogt
Larry Vonalt
Maude Southwell Wahlman
Paul R. Waibel
Christopher Waldrep
Ryan S. Walters
Becca Walton
Laura R. Walton
Jerry W. Ward Jr.
Thomas J. Ward Jr.
Aaron Watkins
Jay Watson
C. L. Wax
Albert G. Way
David L. Weatherford
David E. Weaver
Clive Webb
Charles A. Weeks
Susan Weill
Julie M. Weise
Sean Harrington Wells
Simon Wendt
Brenda West
Charles Westmoreland
David Wharton
Calvin White Jr.
Kristy White
Malcolm White
Julie Whitehead
Stephen J. Whitfield
Preselfannie L. Whitfield-McDaniels
William Bland Whitley
Thomas A. Wicker

Murray Wickett
Kathleen Woodruff Wickham
Curtis Wilkie
Charles Williams
Clay Williams
Mark Williams
Michael Vinson Williams
Shugana Williams
Thomas Williams
Adam Wilson
Brian Wilson
Charles Reagan Wilson
Christine Wilson
Sacoby M. Wilson
Stephen H. Wilson
John W. Winkle III
Terrence J. Winschel
Hicks Wogan
Spencer D. Wood
Amy Louise Wood
Vivian Wu Wong
Ben Wynne
Mary Clingerman Yaran
Gayle Graham Yates
Joe York
Kathryn McGaw York
Brad W. Young
Mary Jane Zander
Robert Zecker
Lingziao Zhang
Ann Ziker
Gary Phillip Zola
David M. Zuefle
Maarten Zwiers

INDEX

Page numbers in **boldface** indicate main entries. Page numbers in *italics* indicate images and tables.

of Mercy, **1142**; slavery and, 1075;
Vietnamese refugees and, 1289
Cat Island Lighthouse, 734
cattle, 105, 752, 876, **1002–3**
cattle tick, **187**
Cauthen, Jean, 231
Cedar Grover plantation, 1337
Cedar Hill Cemetery (Vicksburg), 188
Cedars Clubs, 721
cedar trees, 126, 1247
Céleron, Pierre-Joseph, de Blainville, 204
cemeteries: Jewish, 1081; twentieth-
century military, 1285. *See also* Deco-
ration Day
cemeteries, Union and Confederate, *188*,
188–89, 236–37; at Beauvoir, 87; in
Booneville, 1033; on Ship Island, 1132;
Soldiers' Rest (Vicksburg), 188, 1302
Center for Oral History and Cultural
Heritage, **189–90**
Center for the Study of Southern Culture,
190–91
Center for the Study of the American
South, 427
Central Methodist Church (Jackson), 1352
Central Mississippi Correctional Facility
(Pearl), 646
Central Mississippi Health Services, 1166
Central Presbyterian Church (Jackson),
964
Central Railroad, 232, 1055
Centreville, 164–65, 1332
ceramic art, and pottery, 44; Anderson,
Walter, *33*, **33–34**, 641, 891, 1130;
Dale, Ron, **313–14**; folk, **1026–27**;
McCarty Pottery, **786**; Pittman, Gail
Jones, **1006–7**; Shearwater Pottery, 33,
641, **1130–31**, 1296; Stewart Pottery,
1346. *See also* sculpture: clay
ceramic art, archaeology and, 38–39, 43;
from Archaic Period, 42; Lower Mississippi Survey, 747; from Mississippian Period, 862; from Woodland
Period, 1354
ceramic art, Ohr, George, 44, 314, **953–54**,
954; *Petticoat Vase*, *953*
cessions of tribal land. *See* Removal;
treaties
chaffseed, American, 1009
Chahta and Chikasa, 214
chain gangs, **281–82**
Chakchiuma Indians, 759
Chalmers, James, **191**, 482
Chamani, Miriam (Mary Robin Adams),
192

Chamberlain, Jeremiah, 950
Chambers, Moreau, 420, 758–59, 862
Chambers, William Pitt, 238
Chambliss, Alvin, 59
Champion Hill, Battle of, **192–93**
chancery courts, 296, 672
Chanche, John Mary Joseph, 186
Chaney, James, 274, 929. *See also* Neshoba
County murders
Chapel of the Cross (Madison County),
1080
Chappelle, Patrick Henry, 1349–50
Charleston, Mississippi, 1213–14
Charleston, South Carolina: earthquake
(1931), 371; shooting (2015), 238
Charles Town slave market, 200
Charnley, James, residence, 1364
Chase, Oscar, 560
Chase, Salmon P., 859
Chase, William Merritt, 247
Chatham, Cliff, 961
Chatmon family, 176–77, **193–94**, 978
Chaze, Elliott, **194–95**, 458
Chekhov, Anton, 365
Chepart, Sieur de, 479–80
Cherry, Bobby, 863–64
Chesapeake and Ohio Railroad, 1317
Chess Records: Dixon, Willie, and, 353;
Edwards, David "Honeyboy" and, 382–
83; Howlin' Wolf (Chester Arthur Bur-
nett) and, 596–97, *597*; Milton, Little
(James Milton Campbell Jr.) and, 823;
Waters, Muddy, and, 1308–9; William-
son, Sonny Boy, II (Aleck Miller) and,
1341
Chew, Chris, 941
Chicago, black Mississippians in, **195**;
civil rights boycotts organized by, 888;
Delta history and, 329; Great Migra-
tion and, 517–18; Highway 61/Blues
Highway and, 571; Illinois Central
Railroad and, 329, 506, 1056
Chicago Defender, 195; in barbershops,
86; Barnes, Walter, and, 76; Great
Migration and, 518; Highway 61/Blues
Highway and, 571; Natchez Rhythm
Club fire coverage by, 913
Chicanos. *See* Mexicans and Mexican
Americans
Chickafalaya, 196
Chickasaw, **196–98**, 921–22; basketry of,
170; Black Belt/Prairie and, 104; chiefs
and leaders of, 264–65, 463–64, 590,
926–27, 1264–65; Choctaw and, 203,
1154–55; Colbert family and, 264–65;

deerskin trade and, 200, **326–27**; environment and, 393; European relations
with, 5–6, 98, 200–201, 203–5, 924–25,
926–27, 1264; marriage, interracial,
and, 202–3; missionaries to, 196–97,
203, 826–27, 1203; Northeastern Hills
and, 942; in Oklahoma, **208–9**, 284,
355; population estimates in 1792,
1019; Removal of (*see under* Removal);
slavery and, 200, 924–25, 1046, **1154–
55**; US relations with, **201–3**, 589–90;
women, 921. *See also* treaties
Chickasaw Bayou, Battle of, **198**, 725–26,
1286
Chickasaw County, 153–54, **199–200**,
1054. *See also* Black Belt/Prairie
Chickasawhay River, 974–75
Chickasaw Manual Labor Academy, 203
Chickasaw War (1732–43), 197, 200–201,
203–5; Ackia, Battle of, **5–6**, 204, 726,
942; French governor and, 98; Red
Shoe in, 1066–67
chicken processing. *See* poultry industry
Child Development Group of Mississippi
(CDGM), **205**; in Canton, 172; Edel-
man, Marian Wright, and, 375–76;
Head Start and, 564–65, 828
child poverty, 280
Children's Crusade, **206**
Children's Defense Fund, 376
children's legal rights, 72
children's literature, 1217; Buffett, Jimmy,
152; Mitchell, Margaree King, **864**;
Parker, Laurie, **972–73**; Taylor, Mil-
dred D., **1218–19**
Chillicothe (ship), 1374
Chinese, **206–7**, 397, 398, 399; in Delta,
206–7, 329; rice cookery traditions
and, 1090
Chinese grocery store (Greenville), *207*
Chinn, C. O., 172, **208**, 348, 762
Chinubbee, 264
Chisholm, William A. A., 1357
Chisholm Massacre, 681, 1199, 1323–24
Chisolm, Reuben Benjamin, 50
Chitlin' Circuit, 76, 823, 1258
Choctaw, **214–15**, 921–24. *See also*
treaties
Choctaw (mansion), 810
Choctaw, antebellum to interwar (1830s–
1930s): Claiborne, John F. H., and,
243; education in, **211**; General Allot-
ment Act of 1887, 210; Leflore, Green-
wood, 328, 728; medicine practiced by,
809; in Oklahoma, **208–9**, 283–84, 355